Texas Rules of Evidence Handbook

2018 Update
Jeff Brown & Reece Rondon

Original Contributors

Thomas Black	Erwin McGee
Newell H. Blakely	M. Michael Sharlot
Kent Caperton	John F. Sutton, Jr.
Steven Goode	Blake Tartt
James J. Hippard, Sr.	James P. Wallace
Murl A. Larkin	Olin Guy Wellborn III
Jeffrey S. Wolfe	

O'Connor's
Houston, Texas

Suggested cite form: Brown & Rondon, *Texas Rules of Evidence Handbook* (2018)

TEXAS RULES OF EVIDENCE HANDBOOK

O'CONNOR'S®

Mailing address:
P.O. Box 3348
Houston, TX 77253-3348

Shipping address:
9364 Wallisville Rd., Ste. 150
Houston, TX 77013

Phone: (713) 335-8200
(800) OCONNOR (626-6667)
Fax: (713) 335-8201

www.oconnors.com

Print date: October 20, 2017
Printed in the United States of America

ISBN 978-1-59839-284-5

WHAT'S NEW

This year's edition of the ***Texas Rules of Evidence Handbook*** has been updated to reflect 2017 legislative changes and case law; see the sections below for summaries of these updates.

LEGISLATIVE CHANGES

Below is a summary of the important changes from the 2017 legislative session affecting the Texas Rules of Evidence.

Determining Foreign Law

In 2017, the Texas Legislature directed the Texas Supreme Court to adopt rules of evidence and procedure limiting the grant of comity to foreign judgments and arbitration awards in certain family-law cases to protect against constitutional and public-policy violations. TEX. GOV'T CODE §22.0041(b). The adopted rules must, among other things, require a party seeking enforcement of a judgment or arbitration award based on foreign law that involves a marriage or a parent-child relationship to provide timely notice to the court and parties, which includes providing the information required by Texas Rule of Evidence 203. TEX. GOV'T CODE §22.0041(c)(1). The rules must be adopted no later than January 1, 2018. H.B. 45, §3, 85th Leg., R.S., eff. Sept. 1, 2017. For the adopted rules, go to the supreme court's website at www.txcourts.gov/supreme. Refer to *Article II: Judicial Notice, infra* p. 148.

Trade Secrets

In 2017, the Texas Legislature significantly amended the Texas Uniform Trade Secrets Act, effective for actions commenced on or after September 1, 2017. H.B. 1995, §§1, 6, 85th Leg., R.S., eff. Sept. 1, 2017. The amendments, among other things, expanded the definition of "trade secret" and created a balancing test for courts to use in considering whether countervailing interests allow the court to exclude a party or its representative from participating in the case or to limit the party's access to the alleged trade secret. *See* TEX. CIV. PRAC. & REM. CODE §§134A.002(6), 134A.006(b). Refer to *Article V: Privileges, infra* p. 467.

Statements Against Interest

In 2017, the Texas Legislature added a subsection to Texas Code of Criminal Procedure article 39.14 that requires the State, if it intends to offer the testimony of a witness to whom the defendant made a statement against the defendant's interest while they were imprisoned in the same correctional facility, to disclose to the defendant any information in the State's possession or control that is relevant to the witness's credibility. TEX. CODE CRIM. PROC. art. 39.14(h-1). This information includes the witness's criminal history, including any plea bargains, any grants or offers of leniency given in exchange for the witness's testimony in the present case, and information on any other cases in which the witness has given similar testimony. *Id.* The subsection applies to prosecutions of offenses committed on or after September 1, 2017. H.B. 34, §14, 85th Leg., R.S., eff. Sept. 1, 2017. Refer to *Article VIII: Hearsay, infra* pp. 934-35.

FEDERAL RULE AMENDMENTS

Since the last edition of the book, the Judicial Conference Committee on Rules of Practice and Procedure has approved—and the U.S. Supreme Court has adopted—amendments to the Federal Rules of Evidence. If Congress does not take contrary action, the amendments will take effect December 1, 2017. For the final version of the amendments, go to www.uscourts.gov/rules-policies.

Federal Rule 803(16)

The amendment to Federal Rule 803(16), the hearsay exception for statements in ancient documents, would change the rule's application from statements in documents that are at least 20 years old to statements in documents that were prepared before January 1, 1998. Refer to *Article VIII: Hearsay, infra* p. 922.

Federal Rule 902

The amendments to Federal Rule 902 would add two new subdivisions to the rule. New Rule 902(13) would allow a party to authenticate records generated by a process or system through certification of a qualified person and without the testimony of a foundation witness. New Rule 902(14) would provide the same self-authentication for data copied from an electronic device, storage medium, or file. Under both rules, the offering party must still comply with the certification requirements of Rule 902(11) or (12) and the notice requirements of Rule 902(11). Refer to *Article IX: Authentication & Identification, infra* p. 964.

CASE-LAW UPDATES

Since the last edition of the book, several significant opinions discussing evidentiary matters have been issued by the Texas Supreme Court and the Texas Court of Criminal Appeals. Some of these opinions include the following:

Rulings on Evidence

In *Petetan v. State*, ___ S.W.3d ___ (Tex. Crim. App. 2017) (No. AP-77,038; 3-8-17), the Texas Court of Criminal Appeals assumed without deciding that the defendant's running objection was broad enough to cover testimony from two witnesses about the defendant's promise to give drugs to one of them. Refer to *Article I: General Provisions, infra* pp. 71-72.

In *Love v. State*, ___ S.W.3d ___ (Tex. Crim. App. 2016) (No. AP-77,024; 12-7-16), the Texas Court of Criminal Appeals restated that in conducting a harmless-error review, the reviewing court takes into account all circumstances apparent from the record and must evaluate the entire record in a neutral manner. Refer to *Article I: General Provisions, infra* pp. 60-61.

In *Balderas v. State*, 517 S.W.3d 756, 781 (Tex. Crim. App. 2016), *cert. denied*, 137 S. Ct. 1207 (2017), the Texas Court of Criminal Appeals restated that the exclusion of evidence may be constitutional error if it "effectively precludes the defendant from presenting a defense." Refer to *Article I: General Provisions, infra* p. 62.

Judicial Notice

In *D Mag. Partners, L.P. v. Rosenthal*, ___ S.W.3d ___ (Tex. 2017) (No. 15-0790; 3-17-17), the Texas Supreme Court held that the court of appeals erred in using Wikipedia as its primary source for a critical issue in the case. The supreme court stated that any court reliance on Wikipedia raises concerns because the content is impermanent and can be edited by anyone, but a bright-line rule on the issue is untenable. *Id.* at ___. Refer to *Article II: Judicial Notice, infra* p. 128.

Presumptions

In *Queeman v. State*, ___ S.W.3d ___ (Tex. Crim. App. 2017) (No. PD-0215-16; 6-14-17), the Texas Court of Criminal Appeals held that the evidence was legally insufficient to support a conviction for criminally negligent homicide; any inference by the jury that the defendant was excessively speeding, which was material because it would support a finding of criminal negligence rather than ordinary negligence, would require impermissible speculation. Refer to *Article III: Presumptions, infra* p. 188.

In *Chavez v. Kan. City S. Ry. Co.*, ___ S.W.3d ___ (Tex. 2017) (No. 15-0717; 5-26-17), the Texas Supreme Court restated that at trial, a presumption operates to establish a fact until the presumption is rebutted. The court also restated that the presumptions and burdens of proof that operate in conventional trials on the merits do not apply to summary-judgment proceedings. *Id.* at ___. Refer to *Article III: Presumptions, infra* p. 168.

In *Villa v. State*, 514 S.W.3d 227, 232 (Tex. Crim. App. 2017), and *Balderas v. State*, 517 S.W.3d 756, 766 (Tex. Crim. App. 2016), *cert. denied*, 137 S. Ct. 1207 (2017), the Texas Court of Criminal Appeals restated that in conducting a sufficiency review, a court must consider the cumulative force of all the evidence. Refer to *Article III: Presumptions, infra* pp. 187-88.

In *Cary v. State*, 507 S.W.3d 750, 757 (Tex. Crim. App. 2016), the Texas Court of Criminal Appeals restated that speculation about the meaning of facts or evidence is never sufficient to uphold a conviction. Refer to *Article III: Presumptions, infra* p. 188.

Relevance

In *In re Nat'l Lloyds Ins.*, ___ S.W.3d ___ (Tex. 2017) (No. 15-0591; 6-9-17) (orig. proceeding), the Texas Supreme Court held that, in response to a challenge of an attorney-fee request, the trial court erred in ordering the production of the opposing party's hourly rates, total amount billed, and total reimbursable expenses. The supreme court held that this information lacked probative value as a comparator for the requesting party's fees and did not make it any more probable that the requesting party's fees were reasonable and necessary. *Id.* at ___. Refer to *Article IV: Relevance & Its Limits, infra* pp. 193, 196.

In *Petetan v. State*, ___ S.W.3d ___ (Tex. Crim. App. 2017) (No. AP-77,038; 3-8-17), the Texas Court of Criminal Appeals held that the defense's opening statement, which insinuated that another person murdered the victim while "high" and "angry," opened the door to rebuttal evidence that the defendant planned to murder the victim and frame this other person for the crime. The court also restated that statements about anticipated acts cannot be excluded under Rule 404(b) and held that even if the defendant's promise to give a witness drugs rose to the level of a bad act that could be excluded under Rule 404(b), the evidence would not be excluded under Rule 403. *Id.* at ___. Rather, the danger of unfair prejudice was not substantially outweighed by the evidence's probative value to show the defendant's plan. *Id.* at ___. Refer to *Article IV: Relevance & Its Limits, infra* pp. 269, 271-72, 285.

Privileges

In *In re Nat'l Lloyds Ins.*, ___ S.W.3d ___ (Tex. 2017) (No. 15-0591; 6-9-17) (orig. proceeding), the Texas Supreme Court held that a request to produce all attorney billing records in a case violated the work-product doctrine because "as a whole, billing records represent the mechanical compilation of information that reveals counsel's legal strategy and thought processes, at least incidentally." Refer to *Article V: Privileges, infra* pp. 426-27.

In *Powell v. Hocker*, 516 S.W.3d 488, 495-97 (Tex. Crim. App. 2017), the Texas Court of Criminal Appeals held that the trial court did not have the authority to order defense counsel to give the defendant copies of materials disclosed under Texas Code of Criminal Procedure article 39.14. Under article 39.14(f), the defendant's attorney can allow the defendant to view this information but cannot allow him to have copies; the statute likewise does not allow for judicial disclosure. Powell, 516 S.W.3d at 497. Refer to *Article V: Privileges, infra* p. 432.

In *Paxton v. City of Dallas*, 509 S.W.3d 247, 262-64 (Tex. 2017), the Texas Supreme Court held that unlike a failure to follow the procedures outlined in Texas Rule of Civil Procedure 193.3(d), missing the statutory deadline in the Public Information Act for requesting a ruling from the Attorney General does not waive the attorney-client privilege. Refer to *Article V: Privileges, infra* p. 543.

In *Bailey v. State*, 507 S.W.3d 740, 747 (Tex. Crim. App. 2016), the Texas Court of Criminal Appeals held that the defendant's express consent to the disclosure of a substantial part of her privileged communications with her attorney, disclosed to establish a reasonable-excuse defense under Texas Penal Code §38.10, was sufficient to implicitly waive the attorney-client privilege for related communications. Refer to *Article V: Privileges, infra* p. 539.

Interpreters

In *Balderas v. State*, 517 S.W.3d 756, 777 (Tex. Crim. App. 2016), cert. denied, 137 S. Ct. 1207 (2017), the Texas Court of Criminal Appeals held that when a trial court appoints an interpreter for a witness, there is no requirement for the record to establish that the witness's English skills are so poor that the defendant would be deprived of effective cross-examination without the interpreter's assistance. The court noted that the use of an interpreter for a material witness who has difficulty communicating in English is something the Confrontation Clause requires rather than prohibits because it allows the defendant to conduct a meaningful cross-examination. *Id.* Refer to *Article VI: Witnesses, infra* p. 574.

Juror Testimony

In *Peña-Rodriguez v. Colorado*, ___ U.S. ___, 137 S. Ct. 855, 869 (2017), the U.S. Supreme Court discussed a new exception to the "no-impeachment rule" in Federal Rule of Evidence 606(b), which generally prohibits juror testimony about any juror's mental processes relating to the verdict. The Court held that the no-impeachment rule must give way under the Sixth Amendment when a juror makes a clear statement indicating he relied on racial stereotypes or racial animus in convicting a criminal defendant. Inquiry into a juror's racial bias may proceed if there is a showing that "one or more jurors made statements exhibiting overt racial bias that cast serious doubt on the fairness and impartiality of the jury's deliberations and resulting verdict." *Id.* at ___, 137 S. Ct. at 869. Refer to *Article VI: Witnesses, infra* pp. 586-87.

Producing Witnesses Statement in Criminal Case

In *Balderas v. State*, 517 S.W.3d 756, 781-82 (Tex. Crim. App. 2016), *cert. denied*, 137 S. Ct. 1207 (2017), the Texas Court of Criminal Appeals held that the exclusion of an audio recording of a witness's statement to police did not violate the *Gaskin* rule because the defendant acknowledged, and the record reflected, that he already had a copy of the statement. Refer to *Article VI: Witnesses, infra* p. 676.

Expert Testimony

In *Bustamante v. Ponte*, ___ S.W.3d ___ (Tex. 2017) (No. 15-0509; 9-29-17), the Texas Supreme Court clarified that an expert testifying on causation must exclude other plausible causes but need not exclude all other potential causes. Refer to *Article VII: Opinions & Expert Testimony, infra* pp. 718-19, 727.

In *Starwood Mgmt., LLC v. Swaim*, ___ S.W.3d ___ (Tex. 2017) (No. 16-0431; 9-29-17) (per curiam), the Texas Supreme Court restated that whether an expert's affidavit is an ipse dixit depends on the inferences required to bridge the gap between the underlying data and the expert's conclusion; if the analytical gap is too great, the testimony is conclusory. Refer to *Article VII: Opinions & Expert Testimony, infra* p. 738.

In *Columbia Valley Healthcare Sys., L.P. v. Zamarripa*, ___ S.W.3d ___ (Tex. 2017) (No. 15-0909; 6-9-17), the Texas Supreme Court restated that an expert in a medical-malpractice case must, to a reasonable degree of medical probability, explain how and why the defendant's negligence caused the plaintiff's injury. The expert's bare statement of a conclusion is insufficient to establish the matter; rather, the expert must explain the basis of the conclusion and link it to the facts of the case. *Id.* at ___. Refer to *Article VII: Opinions & Expert Testimony, infra* p. 718.

In *In re Nat'l Lloyds Ins.*, ___ S.W.3d ___ (Tex. 2017) (No. 15-0591; 6-9-17) (orig. proceeding), the Texas Supreme Court held that because the plaintiffs sought discovery from experts using interrogatories and requests for production, which are not permitted under Texas Rule of Civil Procedure 195.1, the trial court erred in relying on Texas Rule of Civil Procedure 192.3(e) to determine the scope of discovery. The dissent disagreed with the majority's conclusion because (1) the defendant did not object to the method of discovery and (2) the witness could have been considered both a fact witness and an expert witness for discovery purposes. *Id.* at ___ (Johnson, Lehrmann, Boyd, JJ., dissenting). Refer to *Article VII: Opinions & Expert Testimony, infra* pp. 767-68.

In *Rogers v. Zanetti*, 518 S.W.3d 394, 406-07 (Tex. 2017), the Texas Supreme Court restated that an expert witness must provide a basis for the conclusions expressed in the testimony, regardless of whether the conclusion is borrowed from another witness. The court also noted that an expert's familiarity with the facts of a case is not alone a satisfactory basis for the expert's opinion. *Id.* at 409. Refer to *Article VII: Opinions & Expert Testimony, infra* pp. 722, 738.

In *Wolfe v. State*, 509 S.W.3d 325, 337-38 (Tex. Crim. App. 2017), the Texas Court of Criminal Appeals held that physicians with training in pediatric medicine and experience as treating physicians were qualified to testify about the nature and cause of a child's abusive head trauma. The court also held that, under the *Kelly* factors, the experts could testify about the nature of the trauma and the fact that the injuries resulted from intentionally inflicted impact. *Id.* at 336. Refer to *Article VII: Opinions & Expert Testimony, infra* pp. 708-09, 725.

Authentication & Identification

In *Henry v. State*, 509 S.W.3d 915, 918 (Tex. Crim. App. 2016), the Texas Court of Criminal Appeals discussed ways to prove up a prior conviction when a certified copy of the trial court's judgment and sentence or an authenticated copy of the defendant's record is not available. These alternative methods include the defendant's admission or stipulation, testimony by a witness who was present and has personal knowledge of the prior conviction, and documentary proof containing sufficient information to establish the existence of the prior conviction and the defendant's identity. *Id.* Refer to *Article IX: Authentication & Identification, infra* p. 998.

Best-Evidence Rule

In *Henry v. State*, 509 S.W.3d 915, 918 (Tex. Crim. App. 2016), the Texas Court of Criminal Appeals held that, taken together, judgments of conviction, testimony by the defendant and another witness that the defendant had been incarcerated for aggravated assault and aggravated robbery, and another witness's testimony about enhancement offenses were sufficient evidence to link the defendant to the enhancement offenses. The court restated that Texas does not have a "best-evidence" rule requiring a particular method of proving a prior conviction. *Id.* Refer to *Article X: Contents of Writings, Recordings, & Photographs, infra* p. 1034.

CURRENCY

This book provides citations to important opinions that interpret the Texas Rules of Evidence through October 20, 2017. All citations to Texas codes and statutes are current through the 85th Legislature (2017), First Called Session, unless otherwise noted. All citations to the United States Code (U.S.C.) and other state codes and statutes are current through the print date of this edition, unless otherwise noted.

CONVENTIONS

The ***Evidence Handbook*** generally follows traditional law-review style as specified in *The Bluebook: A Uniform System of Citation* (20th ed. 2015). Thus, the term "Supreme Court" refers to the United States Supreme Court, while the term "supreme court" indicates a state tribunal. Following this convention on capitalization, "court of criminal appeals" is also lowercase unless preceded by "Texas." When citation format deviates from Bluebook format, it follows the stylistic conventions of the ***O'Connor's*** series. For example, all case names are printed in bold italic font for ease of reading. Also, Texas codes and statutes do not contain a "Vernon" notation or the year of enactment. All citations to the Advisory Committee's Notes for the Federal Rules of Evidence refer to the initial 1972 proposed rules unless otherwise noted.

This edition of the ***Evidence Handbook*** follows the format of the original edition. The first section of the book contains a reprint of the full text of the current Texas Rules of Evidence. Following the text of the rules is an updated series of articles providing commentary on each article of the Rules of Evidence. These articles reprint each rule and then discuss and analyze it, focusing on recent rule amendments and case law. The commentary also compares the current rules to Texas common law, the former Civil and Criminal Rules, and the Federal Rules of Evidence. The Proposed Rules, as they were drafted and submitted by the State Bar Liaison Committee, are reprinted at the end of the book. The Proposed Rules are provided because they are cited throughout the commentary to emphasize how the promulgated Rules differed from the Proposed Rules, as well as the significance of the amendments to the Rules through the years.

ABOUT THE 2018 AUTHORS

Justice Jeff Brown was appointed to the Supreme Court of Texas in 2013 and won a statewide election in 2014 to keep the seat. He served on the Fourteenth Court of Appeals from 2007 to 2013 and was judge of the 55th District Court from 2001 to 2007. Jeff earned a B.A. in English from the University of Texas (1992) and his law degree from the University of Houston (1995). He then worked as a law clerk for two justices on the Texas Supreme Court, Jack Hightower and Greg Abbott, before practicing as a civil litigator at Baker Botts in Houston. Jeff was named Outstanding Young Lawyer of Texas by the Texas Young Lawyers Association in 2006 and Appellate Judge of the Year by the Texas Association of Civil Trial and Appellate Specialists in 2011. A member of the American Law Institute, Jeff is board-certified in Civil Trial Law. He serves on the boards of the Texas Historical Foundation, the *Houston Law Review*, and the Texas Supreme Court Historical Society. He is also a member of the editorial board of *The Advocate*, the quarterly journal of the State Bar's Litigation Section. A longtime volunteer for the Boy Scouts of America, Jeff received the Outstanding Eagle Scout Award in 2016 from the National Eagle Scout Association. He and his wife, Susannah, a high-school English teacher, have three children.

Reece Rondon, a shareholder at Hall Maines Lugrin, P.C., focuses his practice on trying commercial litigation disputes, including coverage and subrogation litigation involving the London and domestic energy insurance markets. His breadth of practice over the last 20 years gives him a distinctive point of view with which to advise clients and represent them in federal courts, state courts, and arbitration tribunals. Before joining the firm, he served with distinction as a Texas district court judge for nearly nine years, presiding over more than 125 jury trials. In addition, he has been a frequent speaker at continuing legal education conferences on the national, state, and local levels. Reece also taught Trial Advocacy at the University of Houston Law Center for over four years. He graduated from the University of Houston with honors in both accounting and law and served as an editor of the *Houston Law Review* during law school. Reece also serves on various charitable boards of directors including the University of Houston Law Alumni Association and the University of Houston Alumni Association, where he previously served as Chairman. He is a life member of the Houston Livestock Show and Rodeo. Reece is a first-generation American. He and his wife live in Houston with their daughters and son.

THANK YOU

This and previous editions of the *Evidence Handbook* were made possible by the contributions of many people. First, thanks to Professor Newell Blakely, who served as a professor and dean at the University of Houston Law Center. Professor Blakely played a major role in drafting both the original Texas Rules of Civil Evidence and the Texas Rules of Criminal Evidence. He also wrote one of the original articles in the Handbook and provided the inspiration for the creation of the book. He served as Co-Chief Reporter for the State Bar Liaison Committee on Rules of Evidence, which drafted the proposed Texas Rules of Evidence and guided the formulation of the original Civil Rules. He then served on the Advisory Committee to the Subcommittee on the Judiciary that drafted the Criminal Rules in 1984 and was equally influential in the formulation of the Criminal Rules. After the Civil and Criminal Rules were promulgated, he continued to serve on the State Bar's Administration of the Rules of Evidence Committee for many years.

Second, we thank the original authors of the articles in the first edition of the *Evidence Handbook*: Kent Caperton and Erwin McGee ("Background, Scope, & Applicability of the Texas Rules of Evidence"), James P. Wallace ("Article I: General Provisions"), Murl A. Larkin ("Article II: Judicial Notice" and "Article III: Presumptions"), Newell H. Blakely ("Article IV: Relevancy & Its Limits"), Steven Goode and M. Michael Sharlot ("Article V: Privileges"), Thomas Black ("Article VI: Witnesses"), John F. Sutton, Jr. ("Article VII: Opinions & Expert Testimony"), Olin Guy Wellborn III ("Article VIII: Hearsay"), Blake Tartt and Jeffrey S. Wolff ("Article IX: Authentication & Identification"), and James J. Hippard, Sr. ("Article X: Contents of Writings, Recordings, & Photographs"). These authors were all present at the creation of the original Rules and brought unique insight to their endeavors.

Third, we thank the Houston Law Review, which published the first and second editions of the *Evidence Handbook* and has allowed O'Connor's to revise the Handbook and publish the later editions. Special thanks to Edward P. Watt, the Editor in Chief of the first edition of the *Evidence Handbook*, and to David R. Jones, the Editor in Chief of the second edition.

Finally, we thank Cathy Cochran, who served as a judge on the Texas Court of Criminal Appeals from 2001 to 2014, for her tireless work on the first seven editions of the *Evidence Handbook*. Judge Cochran's efforts were invaluable in completing the first edition of the Handbook in 1983, when she served as Editor in Chief of the *Houston Law Review*. She graduated summa cum laude from the University of Houston Law Center in 1984. After graduation, she served as an Assistant District Attorney and an Adjunct Professor in Evidence, Criminal Law, and Criminal Procedure at the University of Houston Law Center. During this time, Judge Cochran was instrumental in the development of the second edition of the *Evidence Handbook*, published in 1993. She updated and revised the original edition, which was solely a primer on the civil rules of evidence, and incorporated a complete analysis of the criminal rules of evidence. In 1998, Judge Cochran again was largely responsible for the update of the *Evidence Handbook*, which addressed another shift in evidentiary law after the unified rules of evidence were promulgated. Our task of editing the *Evidence Handbook* since 1998 would have been impossible without the insight and guidance that Judge Cochran provided. O'Connor's thanks Judge Cochran for her hard work and dedication over the years.

YOUR SUGGESTIONS

We welcome your comments. If you think we should have included (or excluded) something, or if you see anything that needs to be corrected, please let us know. Send your comments to the mailing address or fax number shown on the copyright page, or by e-mail to Kathryn Ritcheske, Managing Legal Editor, at kritcheske@oconnors.com.

CAVEAT

You may disagree with the explanations of the rules and the cases in this book. You should therefore use this book only as a research guide. Read the rules and the cases yourself and make your own evaluation of them.

EDITORIAL & PRODUCTION STAFF

As always, the staff of O'Connor's worked hard to prepare this publication, both in its substance and in its layout. The people who worked on this edition of the *Texas Rules of Evidence Handbook* are listed below.

EXECUTIVE EDITOR
Douglas Rosenzweig, J.D.

MANAGING LEGAL EDITOR
Kathryn A. Ritcheske, J.D.

LEGAL EDITORS
Kristen N. Ellis, J.D.
Jessica Younger Field, J.D.
Jordyn Johnson, J.D.
Jessica Ryan Luna, J.D.
Jamie Milne, J.D.
Sarah Arocha Ostriyznick, J.D.
John R. Passmore, J.D.
Kristen K. Sheils, J.D.

LEGAL EDITORIAL ASSISTANTS
Kristen Anderson
Eun-Jeong Choi, J.D.
Kalina Dalal, J.D.
Leah Rush Easterby, J.D.
Erin Gage, J.D.
Victoria R. Guzman, J.D.
Erwin K. Kristel, J.D.
Brittany Lok
Patrick M. Miller, J.D.
Colin K. Morrison, J.D.
Alejandro Mota, J.D.
Jeannie Nguyen, J.D.
Amanda D. Pesonen, J.D.
Vardan Ramazyan, J.D.
Christian Eric Engelbrecht Ryholt

PRODUCTION MANAGER
Donna E. Vass

PRODUCTION EDITOR
Rachel Kelly

PRODUCTION STAFF
Sara Rhodes Bean
Evan Gabriel Bernard
Nicole E. Hammond
Clare Jensen
Sarah M. Rutledge
Daniel Spence
Emily J. Viehman
Annabelle M. Wilde

PROOFREADER
Sara Rhodes Bean

COPYEDITORS
David W. Schultz, J.D.
Annabelle M. Wilde

HISTORY OF THE TEXAS RULES OF EVIDENCE

The unified Texas Rules of Evidence, adopted in 1998, are a merger of the former Texas Rules of Civil Evidence and Texas Rules of Criminal Evidence, each of which evolved from a set of Proposed Rules drafted in 1982 by the State Bar Liaison Committee on Rules of Evidence. The Texas Supreme Court, under its rulemaking authority from the Texas Legislature, promulgated the original Rules of Civil Evidence on November 23, 1982, effective September 1, 1983. In 1985, the Legislature granted rulemaking authority for criminal proceedings to the Texas Court of Criminal Appeals, and on December 18, 1985, the Texas Rules of Criminal Evidence were promulgated, effective September 1, 1986. In 1995, the State Bar's Administration of the Rules of Evidence Committee began work on the unification of the Civil and Criminal Rules. The unified Texas Rules of Evidence, promulgated by both the supreme court and the court of criminal appeals, became effective March 1, 1998. Anyone interested in further background information about the promulgation of the Civil and Criminal Rules and the merger of those rules in 1998 should consult the first chapter (entitled "Background, Scope, & Applicability of the Texas Rules of Evidence") of the fifth edition of the ***Evidence Handbook***, published in 2003.

In 2015, the Texas Rules of Evidence were restyled. Tex. Sup. Ct. Order, Misc. Docket No. 15-9048 (eff. Apr. 1, 2015). The purpose of the restyling was to keep the Texas Rules as consistent as possible with the Federal Rules of Evidence, which were amended on December 1, 2011, but without making any substantive change in Texas evidence law other than the amendments to Rules 511 and 613. *Id.* §2, ¶¶1, 2. The revisions were designed to make the Rules more easily understood and to make style and terminology consistent throughout, and each revision was intended to be stylistic only. *Id.* §2, ¶1. For more details about the restyling project, see the Texas Supreme Court's order, reprinted on p. 3. For a comparison table identifying numbering changes from the former rules to the restyled ones, see p. 6. This table will be removed after this edition.

TEXAS RULES OF EVIDENCE
PAGE 1

RULES AND COMMENTARY

1982 LIAISON COMMITTEE
PROPOSED TEXAS RULES OF EVIDENCE
PAGE 1075

CASE INDEX
PAGE 1101

TOPIC INDEX
PAGE 1163

TEXAS RULES OF EVIDENCE HANDBOOK

TABLE OF CONTENTS

TABLE OF CONTENTS

IN THE SUPREME COURT OF TEXAS[1]

Misc. Docket No. 15-9048

Final Approval of Amendments to the Texas Rules of Evidence

ORDERED that:

1. By order dated November 19, 2014, in Misc. Docket No. 14-9232, the Supreme Court of Texas approved amendments to the Texas Rules of Evidence and invited public comment. After receiving public comments, the Supreme Court made revisions to the rules. This order incorporates those revisions and contains the final version of the rules. The amendments are effective April 1, 2015.

2. Except for the amendments to Rules 511 and 613, which include substantive amendments, these amendments comprise a general restyling of the Texas Rules of Evidence. They seek to make the rules more easily understood and to make style and terminology consistent throughout. The restyling changes are intended to be stylistic only.

The Restyling Project

Following a lengthy restyling process, the Federal Rules of Evidence were amended effective December 1, 2011. The Texas Rules of Evidence restyling project was initiated with the aim of keeping the Texas Rules as consistent as possible with Federal Rules, but without effecting any substantive change in Texas evidence law.

General Guidelines

Following the lead of the drafters of the restyled Federal Rules, the drafters of the restyled Texas Rules were guided in their drafting, usage, and style by Bryan Garner, Guidelines for Drafting and Editing Court Rules, Administrative Office of the United States Courts (1996) and Bryan Garner, Dictionary of Modern Legal Usage (2d ed. 1995).

Formatting Changes

Many of the changes in the restyled rules result from using format to achieve clearer presentations. The rules are broken down into constituent parts, using progressively indented subparagraphs with headings and substituting vertical for horizontal lists. "Hanging indents" are used throughout. These formatting changes make the structure of the rules graphic and make the restyled rules easier to read and understand even when the words are not changed. Rules 103, 404(b), 606(b), and 612 illustrate the benefits of formatting changes.

Changes to Reduce Inconsistent, Ambiguous, Redundant, Repetitive, or Archaic Words

The restyled rules reduce the use of inconsistent terms that say the same thing in different ways. Because different words are presumed to have different meanings, inconsistent usage can result in confusion. The restyled rules reduce inconsistencies by using the same words to express the same meaning. For example, consistent expression is achieved by not switching between "accused" and "defendant" or between "party opponent" and "opposing party" or between the various formulations of civil and criminal action/case/proceeding.

The restyled rules minimize the use of inherently ambiguous words. For example, the word "shall" can mean "must," "may," or something else, depending on context. The restyled rules replace "shall" with "must," "may," or "should," depending on which one the context and established interpretation make correct in each rule.

The restyled rules minimize the use of redundant "intensifiers." These are expressions that attempt to add emphasis, but instead state the obvious and create negative implications for other rules. The absence of intensifiers in the restyled rules does not change their substantive meaning. See, e.g., Rule 602 (omitting "but need not").

The restyled rules also remove words and concepts that are outdated or redundant.

Rule Numbers

The restyled rules keep the same numbers to minimize the effect on research. Subdivisions have been rearranged within some rules to achieve greater clarity and simplicity.

3. The amendments to Rule 511 align Texas law on waiver of privilege by voluntary disclosure with Federal Rule of Evidence 502.

4. In response to public comments, the Court made the following changes to the version of the restyled rules proposed by Misc. Docket No. 14-9232.

a. The comment to Rule 509 has been revised to add the following sentence to the end of the comment: "Finally, reconciling the provisions of Rule 509 with the parts of Tex. Occ. Code ch. 159 that address a physician-patient privilege applicable to court proceedings is beyond the scope of the restyling project."

b. The comment to Rule 510 has been revised to add the following paragraph: "Tex. Health & Safety Code ch. 611 addresses confidentiality rules for communications between a patient and a mental-health professional and for the professional's treatment records. Many of these provisions apply in contexts other than court proceedings. Reconciling the provisions of Rule 510 with the parts of chapter 611 that address a mental-health-information privilege applicable to court proceedings is beyond the scope of the restyling project."

c. The comment to Rule 613 has been revised. The comment now reads: "The amended rule retains the requirement that a witness be given an opportunity to explain or deny (a) a prior inconsistent statement or (b) the circumstances or a statement showing the witness's bias or interest, but this requirement is not imposed on the examining attorney. A witness may have to wait until redirect examination to explain a prior inconsistent statement or the circumstances or a statement that shows bias. But the impeaching attorney still is not permitted to introduce extrinsic evidence of the witness's prior inconsistent statement or bias unless the witness has first been examined about the statement or bias and has failed to unequivocally admit it. All other changes to the rule are intended to be stylistic only."

d. The Court revised Rule 804(b)(1)(A)(i) to remove redundant language. The change is stylistic only.

e. The Court revised Rule 902(10)(B) to add the following sentence to the text of the rule: "The proponent may use an unsworn declaration made under penalty of perjury in place of an affidavit."

5. The Clerk is directed to:

a. file a copy of this order with the Secretary of State;

b. cause a copy of this order to be mailed to each registered member of the State Bar of Texas by publication in the *Texas Bar Journal*;

c. send a copy of this order to each elected member of the Legislature; and

d. submit a copy of this order for publication in the *Texas Register*.

Dated: March 10, 2015.

1. **Editor's note:** For the corresponding order of the Texas Court of Criminal Appeals, which is identical, see Tex. Ct. Crim. App. Order, Misc. Docket No. 15-001 (eff. Apr. 1, 2015).

IN THE SUPREME COURT OF TEXAS
Misc. Docket No. 98-9043
Final Approval of Revisions to the Texas Rules of Evidence in Civil Cases

ORDERED that:

1. The Texas Rules of Civil Evidence, amended by Order in Misc. Docket No. 97-9184, dated October 20, 1997, 60 TEX. BAR J. 1129 (Dec. 1997), and now changed after public comments, are attached. The format and style of these amended rules are part of the official promulgation.

2. These amended rules take effect March 1, 1998, and apply to all proceedings on or after that date.

3. With the exception of the notes and comments to Rules 509 and 510, the notes and comments appended to these changes are incomplete, are included only for the convenience of the bench and bar, and are not a part of the rules. The notes and comments to Rules 509 and 510 are intended to inform the construction and application of those rules.

4. Pursuant to Section 22.004(c) of the Texas Government Code, Section 611.006(a)(6) of the Texas Health and Safety Code is deemed to be repealed insofar as it conflicts with Rule 510 of the Texas Rules of Evidence.

5. The Clerk is directed to file a copy of this Order with the Secretary of State forthwith, and to cause a copy of this Order to be

mailed to each registered member of the State Bar of Texas by publication in the *Texas Bar Journal*.

SIGNED AND ENTERED this 25th day of February, 1998.

IN THE COURT OF CRIMINAL APPEALS OF TEXAS

Final Approval of Revisions to the Texas Rules of Evidence in Criminal Cases

ORDERED that:

1. The Texas Rules of Criminal Evidence, amended by Order dated October 20, 1997, 60 TEX. BAR J. 1129 (Dec. 1997), and now changed after public comments, are attached. The format and style of these amended rules are part of the official promulgation.

2. These amended rules take effect March 1, 1998, and apply to all proceedings on or after that date.

3. With the exception of the notes and comments to Rules 509 and 510, the notes and comments appended to these changes are incomplete, are included only for the convenience of the bench and bar, and are not a part of the rules. The notes and comments to Rules 509 and 510 are intended to inform the construction and application of those rules.

4. Pursuant to Section 22.004(c) of the Texas Government Code, Section 611.006(a)(6) of the Texas Health and Safety Code is deemed to be repealed insofar as it conflicts with Rule 510 of the Texas Rules of Evidence.

5. The Clerk is directed to file a copy of this Order with the Secretary of State forthwith, and to cause a copy of this Order to be mailed to each registered member of the State Bar of Texas by publication in the *Texas Bar Journal*.

SIGNED AND ENTERED this 25th day of February, 1998.

TEXAS RULES OF EVIDENCE COMPARISON TABLE – FORMER & CURRENT RULES

The table below shows the rearranging of the subdivisions based on the 2015 restyling. This table also indicates by footnote the rules with an official comment.

Former Rule	Current Rule	Former Rule	Current Rule
101(a)	101(a)	201(c)	201(c)(1)
101(b)	101(b)	201(d)	201(c)(2)
101(c)	101(d)*	201(e)	201(e)
101(d)(1)(A)	101(e)(1)	201(f)	201(d)
101(d)(1)(B)	101(e)(2)	201(g)	201(f)
101(d)(1)(C)	101(e)(3)(A)	202	202(a)-(e)
101(d)(1)(D)	101(e)(3)(B)	203	203(a)-(d)
101(d)(1)(E)	101(e)(3)(C)	204	204(a)-(d)
101(d)(1)(F)	101(e)(3)(D)	401	401(a), (b)
101(d)(1)(G)	101(e)(3)(E)	402	402
101(d)(1)(H)	101(e)(3)(F)	403	403
101(d)(2)	101(c)*	404(a)	404(a)(1)
101(d)(3)	101(g)	404(a)(1)(A)	404(a)(2)(A)
New	101(f)	404(a)(1)(B)	404(a)(2)(B)
New	101(h)	404(a)(2)	404(a)(3)(A)-(C)
102	102	404(a)(3)	404(a)(4)
103(a)(1)	103(a)(1)(A), (B), (b)	New	404(a)(5)
103(a)(2)	103(a)(2)	404(b)	404(b)(1), (2)
103(b)	103(c)	405(a)	405(a)(1), (2)
103(c)	103(d)	405(b)	405(b)
103(d)	103(e)	406	406
104(a)	104(a)	407	407*
104(b)	104(b)	408	408(a), (b)*
104(c)	104(c)(1)-(3)	409	409
104(d)	104(d)	410(1)	410(a)(1), (b)(1)
104(e)	104(e)	410(2)	410(a)(2), (b)(2)
105(a)	105(a), (b)(1)	410(3)	410(a)(3), (b)(3)
105(b)	105(b)(2)	410(4)	410(a)(4), (b)(4)
106	106	410, last par.	410(c)
107	107	411	411
201(a)	201(a)	412(a)	412(a)(1)
201(b)	201(b)(1), (2)	412(b)	412(a)(2), (b)

* Restyling includes official comment.

Former Rule	Current Rule	Former Rule	Current Rule
412(c)	412(c)	505(b)	505(b)
412(d)	412(d)	505(c)	505(c)(1)-(3)
New	412(e)	506	506
501(1)	501(a)	507	507(a)-(c)
501(2)	501(b)	508(a)	508(a)(1), (2)
501(3)	501(c)	508(b)	508(b)
501(4)	501(d)	508(c)(1)	508(c)(1)(A), (B)
502	502(a)(1), (2), (b)	508(c)(2)	508(c)(2)(A)-(C)
503(a)(1)	503(a)(1)(A), (B)	508(c)(3)	508(c)(3)(A), (B)
503(a)(2)	503(a)(2)	509(a)(1)	509(a)(1)
503(a)(3)	503(a)(3)	509(a)(2)	509(a)(2)
503(a)(4)	503(a)(4)	509(a)(3)	509(a)(3)(A)-(C)
503(a)(5)	503(a)(5)(A), (B)	509(b)	509(b)(1), (2)
503(b)	503(b)	509(c)(1)	509(c)(1)
503(c)	503(c)(1)-(4)	509(c)(2)	509(c)(2)
503(d)(1)	503(d)(1)	509(c)(3)	Deleted*
503(d)(2)	503(d)(2)	509(d)(1)	509(d)(1), (2)
503(d)(3)	503(d)(3)	509(d)(2)	509(d), last par.
503(d)(4)	503(d)(4)	509(e)(1)	509(e)(1)(A), (B)*
503(d)(5)	503(d)(5)(A)-(C)	509(e)(2)	509(e)(2)
504(a)(1)	504(a)(1)	509(e)(3)	509(e)(3)
504(a)(2)	504(a)(2)	509(e)(4)	509(e)(4)
504(a)(3)	504(a)(3)(A)-(C)	509(e)(5)	509(e)(5)(A), (B)*
504(a)(4)(A)	504(a)(4)(A)	509(e)(6)	509(e)(6)(A)-(C)
504(a)(4)(B)	504(a)(4)(B)(i), (ii)	509(e)(7)	509(e)(7)
504(a)(4)(C)	504(a)(4)(C)(i), (ii)	509(f)(1)	509(f)(1)(A)-(G)*
504(a)(4)(D)	504(a)(4)(D)	509(f)(1)(A)	509(f)(2)(A)
504(a)(4)(E)	504(a)(4)(E)	509(f)(1)(B)	509(f)(2)(B)
504(b)(1)	504(b)(1)*	509(f)(1)(C)	509(f)(2)(C)
504(b)(2)	504(b)(2)	509(f)(2)	509(f)(3)
504(b)(3)	504(b)(3)	509(f)(3)	509(f)(4)
504(b)(4)(A)	504(b)(4)(A)(i), (ii)	510(a)(1)	510(a)(1)
504(b)(4)(B)	504(b)(4)(B)	510(a)(2)	510(a)(2)
505(a)(1)	505(a)(1)	510(a)(3)	510(a)(3)
New	505(a)(2)	510(a)(4)	510(a)(4)(A)-(C)
505(a)(2)	505(a)(3)		

* Restyling includes official comment.

Former Rule	Current Rule	Former Rule	Current Rule
510(b)(1)	510(b)(1)(A)	609(e)	609(e)
510(b)(2)	510(b)(1)(B)	609(f)	609(f)
510(b)(3)	510(b)(2)	610	610
510(b)(4)	Deleted*	611(a)	611(a)(1)-(3)
510(c)(1)	510(c)(1), (2)	611(b)	611(b)
510(c)(2)	510(c), last par.	611(c)	611(c)(1), (2)
510(d)(1)	510(d)(1)(A), (B)	612, first par.	612(a)
510(d)(2)	510(d)(2)	612(1)	612(a)(1)
510(d)(3)	510(d)(3)	612(2)	612(a)(2)
510(d)(4)	510(d)(4)(A)-(C)	612(3)	612(a)(3)
510(d)(5)	510(d)(5)	612, last par.	612(b), (c)
510(d)(6)	510(d)(6)	613(a)	613(a)(1)-(5)*
511, first par.	511(a)*	613(b)	613(b)(1)-(4)*
511(1)	511(a)(1)	613(c)	613(c)
511(2)	511(a)(2)	614, intro. par.	614, intro. par.
New	511(b)*	614(1)	614(a)
512(1)	512(a)	614(2)	614(b)(1), (2)
512(2)	512(b)	614(3)	614(c)
513	513	614(4)	614(d)
601(a)	601(a)	615	615
601(b)	601(b)(1)-(4)*	701	701(a), (b)*
602	602	702	702
603	603	703	703*
604	604	704	704
605	605	705	705*
606(a)	606(a)	706	706
606(b)	606(b)(1)	801(a)	801(a)
606(b)(1)	606(b)(2)(A)	801(b)	801(b)
606(b)(2)	606(b)(2)(B)	801(c)	801(c)(1), (2)
607	607	801(d)	801(d)(1), (2)
608(a)(1), (2)	608(a)	801(e)(1)(A)	801(e)(1)(A)(i), (ii)
608(b)	608(b)	801(e)(1)(B)	801(e)(1)(B)
609(a)	609(a)(1)-(3)	801(e)(1)(C)	801(e)(1)(C)
609(b)	609(b)	801(e)(1)(D)	Deleted*
609(c)	609(c)	801(e)(2)	801(e)(2)*
609(d)	609(d)(1), (2)		

* Restyling includes official comment.

Former Rule	Current Rule	Former Rule	Current Rule
801(e)(3)	801(e)(3)	901(a)	901(a)
802	802	901(b)(1)	901(b)(1)
803(1)	803(1)	901(b)(2)	901(b)(2)
803(2)	803(2)	901(b)(3)	901(b)(3)
803(3)	803(3)	901(b)(4)	901(b)(4)
803(4)	803(4)(A), (B)	901(b)(5)	901(b)(5)
803(5)	803(5)(A)-(C)	901(b)(6)	901(b)(6)
803(6)	803(6)(A)-(E)	901(b)(7)	901(b)(7)(A), (B)
803(7)	803(7)(A)-(C)	901(b)(8)	901(b)(8)(A)-(C)
803(8)	803(8)(A)	901(b)(9)	901(b)(9)
803(8)(A)	803(8)(A)(i)	901(b)(10)	901(b)(10)
803(8)(B)	803(8)(A)(ii)	902(1)	902(1)(A), (B)
803(8)(C)	803(8)(A)(iii)	902(2)	902(2)(A), (B)
803(8), last par.	803(8)(B)	902(3)	902(3)(A)-(C)
803(9)	803(9)	902(4)	902(4)(A), (B)
803(10)	803(10)(A), (B)	902(5)	902(5)
803(11)	803(11)	902(6)	902(6)
803(12)	803(12)(A)-(C)	902(7)	902(7)
803(13)	803(13)	902(8)	902(8)
803(14)	803(14)(A)-(C)	902(9)	902(9)
803(15)	803(15)	902(10)	902(10)
803(16)	803(16)	902(11)	902(11)
803(17)	803(17)	903	903
803(18)	803(18)(A), (B)	1001(a)	1001(a), (b)
803(19)	803(19)	1001(b)	1001(c)
803(20)	803(20)	1001(c)	1001(d)
803(21)	803(21)	1001(d)	1001(e)
803(22)	803(22)(A), (B)	1002	1002
803(23)	803(23)(A), (B)	1003	1003
803(24)	803(24)(A), (B)	1004	1004
804(a)	804(a)	1005	1005
804(b)(1)	804(b)(1)(A), (B)	1006	1006
804(b)(2)	804(b)(2)	1007	1007
804(b)(3)	804(b)(3)	1008	1008(a)-(c)
805	805	1009(a)	1009(a)(1), (2)
806	806	1009(b)	1009(b)

Former Rule	Current Rule
1009(c)	1009(c)(1), (2)
1009(d)	1009(d)
1009(e)	1009(e)
1009(f)	1009(f)
1009(g)	1009(g)

ARTICLE I. GENERAL PROVISIONS

RULE 101. TITLE, SCOPE, & APPLICABILITY OF THE RULES; DEFINITIONS

(a) Title. These rules may be cited as the Texas Rules of Evidence.

(b) Scope. These rules apply to proceedings in Texas courts except as otherwise provided in subdivisions (d)-(f).

(c) Rules on Privilege. The rules on privilege apply to all stages of a case or proceeding.

(d) Exception for Constitutional or Statutory Provisions or Other Rules. Despite these rules, a court must admit or exclude evidence if required to do so by the United States or Texas Constitution, a federal or Texas statute, or a rule prescribed by the United States or Texas Supreme Court or the Texas Court of Criminal Appeals. If possible, a court should resolve by reasonable construction any inconsistency between these rules and applicable constitutional or statutory provisions or other rules.

(e) Exceptions. These rules—except for those on privilege—do not apply to:

(1) the court's determination, under Rule 104(a), on a preliminary question of fact governing admissibility;

(2) grand jury proceedings; and

(3) the following miscellaneous proceedings:

(A) an application for habeas corpus in extradition, rendition, or interstate detainer proceedings;

(B) an inquiry by the court under Code of Criminal Procedure article 46B.004 to determine whether evidence exists that would support a finding that the defendant may be incompetent to stand trial;

(C) bail proceedings other than hearings to deny, revoke, or increase bail;

(D) hearings on justification for pretrial detention not involving bail;

(E) proceedings to issue a search or arrest warrant; and

(F) direct contempt determination proceedings.

(f) Exception for Justice Court Cases. These rules do not apply to justice court cases except as authorized by Texas Rule of Civil Procedure 500.3.

(g) Exception for Military Justice Hearings. The Texas Code of Military Justice, Tex. Gov't Code §§432.001-432.195, governs the admissibility of evidence in hearings held under that Code.

(h) Definitions. In these rules:

(1) "civil case" means a civil action or proceeding;

(2) "criminal case" means a criminal action or proceeding, including an examining trial;

(3) "public office" includes a public agency;

(4) "record" includes a memorandum, report, or data compilation;

(5) a "rule prescribed by the United States or Texas Supreme Court or the Texas Court of Criminal Appeals" means a rule adopted by any of those courts under statutory authority;

(6) "unsworn declaration" means an unsworn declaration made in accordance with Tex. Civ. Prac. & Rem. Code §132.001; and

(7) a reference to any kind of written material or any other medium includes electronically stored information.

Comment to 2015 restyling: The reference to "hierarchical governance" in former Rule 101(c) has been deleted as unnecessary. The textual limitation of former Rule 101(c) to criminal cases has been eliminated. Courts in civil cases must also admit or exclude evidence when required to do so by constitutional or statutory provisions or other rules that take precedence over these rules. Likewise, the title to former Rule 101(d) has been changed to more accurately indicate the purpose and scope of the subdivision.

Comment to 1998 change: "Criminal proceedings" rather than "criminal cases" is used since that was the terminology used in the prior Rules of Criminal Evidence. In subpart (b), the reference to "trials before magistrates" comes from prior Criminal Rule 1101(a). In the prior Criminal Rules, both Rule 101 and Rule 1101 dealt with the same thing—the applicability of the rules. Thus, Rules 101(c) and (d) have been written to incorporate the provisions of former Criminal Rule 1101 and that rule is omitted.

RULE 102. PURPOSE

These rules should be construed so as to administer every proceeding fairly, eliminate unjustifiable expense and delay, and promote the development of evidence law, to the end of ascertaining the truth and securing a just determination.

RULE 103 *(side tab)*

RULE 103. RULINGS ON EVIDENCE

(a) Preserving a Claim of Error. A party may claim error in a ruling to admit or exclude evidence only if the error affects a substantial right of the party and:

(1) if the ruling admits evidence, a party, on the record:

   (A) timely objects or moves to strike; and

   (B) states the specific ground, unless it was apparent from the context; or

(2) if the ruling excludes evidence, a party informs the court of its substance by an offer of proof, unless the substance was apparent from the context.

(b) Not Needing to Renew an Objection. When the court hears a party's objections outside the presence of the jury and rules that evidence is admissible, a party need not renew an objection to preserve a claim of error for appeal.

(c) Court's Statement About the Ruling; Directing an Offer of Proof. The court must allow a party to make an offer of proof outside the jury's presence as soon as practicable—and before the court reads its charge to the jury. The court may make any statement about the character or form of the evidence, the objection made, and the ruling. At a party's request, the court must direct that an offer of proof be made in question-and-answer form. Or the court may do so on its own.

(d) Preventing the Jury from Hearing Inadmissible Evidence. To the extent practicable, the court must conduct a jury trial so that inadmissible evidence is not suggested to the jury by any means.

(e) Taking Notice of Fundamental Error in Criminal Cases. In criminal cases, a court may take notice of a fundamental error affecting a substantial right, even if the claim of error was not properly preserved.

Comment to 1998 change: The exception to the requirement of an offer of proof for matters that were apparent from the context within which questions were asked, found in paragraph (a)(2), is now applicable to civil as well as criminal cases.

RULE 104. PRELIMINARY QUESTIONS

(a) In General. The court must decide any preliminary question about whether a witness is qualified, a privilege exists, or evidence is admissible. In so deciding, the court is not bound by evidence rules, except those on privilege.

(b) Relevance That Depends on a Fact. When the relevance of evidence depends on whether a fact exists, proof must be introduced sufficient to support a finding that the fact does exist. The court may admit the proposed evidence on the condition that the proof be introduced later.

(c) Conducting a Hearing So That the Jury Cannot Hear It. The court must conduct any hearing on a preliminary question so that the jury cannot hear it if:

(1) the hearing involves the admissibility of a confession in a criminal case;

(2) a defendant in a criminal case is a witness and so requests; or

(3) justice so requires.

(d) Cross-Examining a Defendant in a Criminal Case. By testifying outside the jury's hearing on a preliminary question, a defendant in a criminal case does not become subject to cross-examination on other issues in the case.

(e) Evidence Relevant to Weight and Credibility. This rule does not limit a party's right to introduce before the jury evidence that is relevant to the weight or credibility of other evidence.

RULE 105. EVIDENCE THAT IS NOT ADMISSIBLE AGAINST OTHER PARTIES OR FOR OTHER PURPOSES

(a) Limiting Admitted Evidence. If the court admits evidence that is admissible against a party or for a purpose—but not against another party or for another purpose—the court, on request, must restrict the evidence to its proper scope and instruct the jury accordingly.

(b) Preserving a Claim of Error.

(1) *Court Admits the Evidence Without Restriction.* A party may claim error in a ruling to admit evidence that is admissible against a party or for a purpose—but not against another party or for another pur-

pose—only if the party requests the court to restrict the evidence to its proper scope and instruct the jury accordingly.

(2) Court Excludes the Evidence. A party may claim error in a ruling to exclude evidence that is admissible against a party or for a purpose—but not against another party or for another purpose—only if the party limits its offer to the party against whom or the purpose for which the evidence is admissible.

RULE 106. REMAINDER OF OR RELATED WRITINGS OR RECORDED STATEMENTS

If a party introduces all or part of a writing or recorded statement, an adverse party may introduce, at that time, any other part—or any other writing or recorded statement—that in fairness ought to be considered at the same time. "Writing or recorded statement" includes depositions.

RULE 107. RULE OF OPTIONAL COMPLETENESS

If a party introduces part of an act, declaration, conversation, writing, or recorded statement, an adverse party may inquire into any other part on the same subject. An adverse party may also introduce any other act, declaration, conversation, writing, or recorded statement that is necessary to explain or allow the trier of fact to fully understand the part offered by the opponent. "Writing or recorded statement" includes a deposition.

Comment to 1998 change: This rule is the former Criminal Rule 107 except that the example regarding "when a letter is read" has been relocated in the rule so as to more accurately indicate the provision it explains. While this rule appeared only in the prior criminal rules, it is made applicable to civil cases because it accurately reflects the common law rule of optional completeness in civil cases.

ARTICLE II. JUDICIAL NOTICE

RULE 201. JUDICIAL NOTICE OF ADJUDICATIVE FACTS

(a) Scope. This rule governs judicial notice of an adjudicative fact only, not a legislative fact.

(b) Kinds of Facts That May Be Judicially Noticed. The court may judicially notice a fact that is not subject to reasonable dispute because it:

(1) is generally known within the trial court's territorial jurisdiction; or

(2) can be accurately and readily determined from sources whose accuracy cannot reasonably be questioned.

(c) Taking Notice. The court:

(1) may take judicial notice on its own; or

(2) must take judicial notice if a party requests it and the court is supplied with the necessary information.

(d) Timing. The court may take judicial notice at any stage of the proceeding.

(e) Opportunity to Be Heard. On timely request, a party is entitled to be heard on the propriety of taking judicial notice and the nature of the fact to be noticed. If the court takes judicial notice before notifying a party, the party, on request, is still entitled to be heard.

(f) Instructing the Jury. In a civil case, the court must instruct the jury to accept the noticed fact as conclusive. In a criminal case, the court must instruct the jury that it may or may not accept the noticed fact as conclusive.

RULE 202. JUDICIAL NOTICE OF OTHER STATES' LAW

(a) Scope. This rule governs judicial notice of another state's, territory's, or federal jurisdiction's:

- Constitution;
- public statutes;
- rules;
- regulations;
- ordinances;
- court decisions; and
- common law.

(b) Taking Notice. The court:

(1) may take judicial notice on its own; or

(2) must take judicial notice if a party requests it and the court is supplied with the necessary information.

(c) Notice and Opportunity to Be Heard.

(1) *Notice.* The court may require a party requesting judicial notice to notify all other parties of the request so they may respond to it.

(2) *Opportunity to Be Heard.* On timely request, a party is entitled to be heard on

the propriety of taking judicial notice and the nature of the matter to be noticed. If the court takes judicial notice before a party has been notified, the party, on request, is still entitled to be heard.

(d) Timing. The court may take judicial notice at any stage of the proceeding.

(e) Determination and Review. The court—not the jury—must determine the law of another state, territory, or federal jurisdiction. The court's determination must be treated as a ruling on a question of law.

RULE 203. DETERMINING FOREIGN LAW

(a) Raising a Foreign Law Issue. A party who intends to raise an issue about a foreign country's law must:

(1) give reasonable notice by a pleading or other writing; and

(2) at least 30 days before trial, supply all parties a copy of any written materials or sources the party intends to use to prove the foreign law.

(b) Translations. If the materials or sources were originally written in a language other than English, the party intending to rely on them must, at least 30 days before trial, supply all parties both a copy of the foreign language text and an English translation.

(c) Materials the Court May Consider; Notice. In determining foreign law, the court may consider any material or source, whether or not admissible. If the court considers any material or source not submitted by a party, it must give all parties notice and a reasonable opportunity to comment and submit additional materials.

(d) Determination and Review. The court—not the jury—must determine foreign law. The court's determination must be treated as a ruling on a question of law.

RULE 204. JUDICIAL NOTICE OF TEXAS MUNICIPAL & COUNTY ORDINANCES, TEXAS REGISTER CONTENTS, & PUBLISHED AGENCY RULES

(a) Scope. This rule governs judicial notice of Texas municipal and county ordinances, the

contents of the Texas Register, and agency rules published in the Texas Administrative Code.

(b) Taking Notice. The court:

(1) may take judicial notice on its own; or

(2) must take judicial notice if a party requests it and the court is supplied with the necessary information.

(c) Notice and Opportunity to Be Heard.

(1) *Notice.* The court may require a party requesting judicial notice to notify all other parties of the request so they may respond to it.

(2) *Opportunity to Be Heard.* On timely request, a party is entitled to be heard on the propriety of taking judicial notice and the nature of the matter to be noticed. If the court takes judicial notice before a party has been notified, the party, on request, is still entitled to be heard.

(d) Determination and Review. The court—not the jury—must determine municipal and county ordinances, the contents of the Texas Register, and published agency rules. The court's determination must be treated as a ruling on a question of law.

ARTICLE III. PRESUMPTIONS

[No rules adopted at this time.]

ARTICLE IV. RELEVANCE & ITS LIMITS

RULE 401. TEST FOR RELEVANT EVIDENCE

Evidence is relevant if:

(a) it has any tendency to make a fact more or less probable than it would be without the evidence; and

(b) the fact is of consequence in determining the action.

RULE 402. GENERAL ADMISSIBILITY OF RELEVANT EVIDENCE

Relevant evidence is admissible unless any of the following provides otherwise:

- the United States or Texas Constitution;
- a statute;
- these rules; or

- other rules prescribed under statutory authority.

Irrelevant evidence is not admissible.

RULE 403. EXCLUDING RELEVANT EVIDENCE FOR PREJUDICE, CONFUSION, OR OTHER REASONS

The court may exclude relevant evidence if its probative value is substantially outweighed by a danger of one or more of the following: unfair prejudice, confusing the issues, misleading the jury, undue delay, or needlessly presenting cumulative evidence.

RULE 404. CHARACTER EVIDENCE; CRIMES OR OTHER ACTS

(a) Character Evidence.

  (1) *Prohibited Uses.* Evidence of a person's character or character trait is not admissible to prove that on a particular occasion the person acted in accordance with the character or trait.

  (2) *Exceptions for an Accused.*

    (A) In a criminal case, a defendant may offer evidence of the defendant's pertinent trait, and if the evidence is admitted, the prosecutor may offer evidence to rebut it.

    (B) In a civil case, a party accused of conduct involving moral turpitude may offer evidence of the party's pertinent trait, and if the evidence is admitted, the accusing party may offer evidence to rebut it.

  (3) *Exceptions for a Victim.*

    (A) In a criminal case, subject to the limitations in Rule 412, a defendant may offer evidence of a victim's pertinent trait, and if the evidence is admitted, the prosecutor may offer evidence to rebut it.

    (B) In a homicide case, the prosecutor may offer evidence of the victim's trait of peacefulness to rebut evidence that the victim was the first aggressor.

    (C) In a civil case, a party accused of assaultive conduct may offer evidence of the victim's trait of violence to prove self-defense, and if the evidence is admitted, the accusing party may offer evidence of the victim's trait of peacefulness.

  (4) *Exceptions for a Witness.* Evidence of a witness's character may be admitted under Rules 607, 608, and 609.

  (5) *Definition of "Victim."* In this rule, "victim" includes an alleged victim.

(b) Crimes, Wrongs, or Other Acts.

  (1) *Prohibited Uses.* Evidence of a crime, wrong, or other act is not admissible to prove a person's character in order to show that on a particular occasion the person acted in accordance with the character.

  (2) *Permitted Uses; Notice in Criminal Case.* This evidence may be admissible for another purpose, such as proving motive, opportunity, intent, preparation, plan, knowledge, identity, absence of mistake, or lack of accident. On timely request by a defendant in a criminal case, the prosecutor must provide reasonable notice before trial that the prosecution intends to introduce such evidence—other than that arising in the same transaction—in its case-in-chief.

RULE 405. METHODS OF PROVING CHARACTER

(a) By Reputation or Opinion.

  (1) *In General.* When evidence of a person's character or character trait is admissible, it may be proved by testimony about the person's reputation or by testimony in the form of an opinion. On cross-examination of the character witness, inquiry may be made into relevant specific instances of the person's conduct.

  (2) *Accused's Character in a Criminal Case.* In the guilt stage of a criminal case, a witness may testify to the defendant's character or character trait only if, before the day of the offense, the witness was familiar with the defendant's reputation or the facts or information that form the basis of the witness's opinion.

(b) By Specific Instances of Conduct. When a person's character or character trait is an essential element of a charge, claim, or defense, the character or trait may also be proved by relevant specific instances of the person's conduct.

RULE 406. HABIT; ROUTINE PRACTICE

Evidence of a person's habit or an organization's routine practice may be admitted to prove that on a particular occasion the person or organization acted in accordance with the habit or routine practice. The court may admit this evidence regardless of whether it is corroborated or whether there was an eyewitness.

RULE 407. SUBSEQUENT REMEDIAL MEASURES; NOTIFICATION OF DEFECT

(a) **Subsequent Remedial Measures.** When measures are taken that would have made an earlier injury or harm less likely to occur, evidence of the subsequent measures is not admissible to prove:

- negligence;
- culpable conduct;
- a defect in a product or its design; or
- a need for a warning or instruction.

But the court may admit this evidence for another purpose, such as impeachment or—if disputed—proving ownership, control, or the feasibility of precautionary measures.

(b) **Notification of Defect.** A manufacturer's written notification to a purchaser of a defect in one of its products is admissible against the manufacturer to prove the defect.

Comment to 2015 restyling: Rule 407 previously provided that evidence was not excluded if offered for a purpose not explicitly prohibited by the Rule. To improve the language of the Rule, it now provides that the court may admit evidence if offered for a permissible purpose. There is no intent to change the process for admitting evidence covered by the Rule. It remains the case that if offered for an impermissible purpose, it must be excluded, and if offered for a purpose not barred by the Rule, its admissibility remains governed by the general principles of Rules 402, 403, 801, etc.

RULE 408. COMPROMISE OFFERS & NEGOTIATIONS

(a) **Prohibited Uses.** Evidence of the following is not admissible either to prove or disprove the validity or amount of a disputed claim:

(1) furnishing, promising, or offering—or accepting, promising to accept, or offering

to accept—a valuable consideration in compromising or attempting to compromise the claim; and

(2) conduct or statements made during compromise negotiations about the claim.

(b) **Permissible Uses.** The court may admit this evidence for another purpose, such as proving a party's or witness's bias, prejudice, or interest, negating a contention of undue delay, or proving an effort to obstruct a criminal investigation or prosecution.

Comment to 2015 restyling: Rule 408 previously provided that evidence was not excluded if offered for a purpose not explicitly prohibited by the Rule. To improve the language of the Rule, it now provides that the court may admit evidence if offered for a permissible purpose. There is no intent to change the process for admitting evidence covered by the Rule. It remains the case that if offered for an impermissible purpose, it must be excluded, and if offered for a purpose not barred by the Rule, its admissibility remains governed by the general principles of Rules 402, 403, 801, etc.

The reference to "liability" has been deleted on the ground that the deletion makes the Rule flow better and easier to read, and because "liability" is covered by the broader term "validity." Courts have not made substantive decisions on the basis of any distinction between validity and liability. No change in current practice or in the coverage of the Rule is intended.

Finally, the sentence of the Rule referring to evidence "otherwise discoverable" has been deleted as superfluous. The intent of the sentence was to prevent a party from trying to immunize admissible information, such as a pre-existing document, through the pretense of disclosing it during compromise negotiations. But even without the sentence, the Rule cannot be read to protect pre-existing information simply because it was presented to the adversary in compromise negotiations.

RULE 409. OFFERS TO PAY MEDICAL & SIMILAR EXPENSES

Evidence of furnishing, promising to pay, or offering to pay medical, hospital, or similar expenses resulting from an injury is not admissible to prove liability for the injury.

RULE 410. PLEAS, PLEA DISCUSSIONS, & RELATED STATEMENTS

(a) **Prohibited Uses in Civil Cases.** In a civil case, evidence of the following is not admissible against the defendant who made the plea or was a participant in the plea discussions:

(1) a guilty plea that was later withdrawn;

(2) a nolo contendere plea;

(3) a statement made during a proceeding on either of those pleas under Federal Rule of Criminal Procedure 11 or a comparable state procedure; or

(4) a statement made during plea discussions with an attorney for the prosecuting au-

thority if the discussions did not result in a guilty plea or they resulted in a later-withdrawn guilty plea.

(b) Prohibited Uses in Criminal Cases. In a criminal case, evidence of the following is not admissible against the defendant who made the plea or was a participant in the plea discussions:

(1) a guilty plea that was later withdrawn;

(2) a nolo contendere plea that was later withdrawn;

(3) a statement made during a proceeding on either of those pleas under Federal Rule of Criminal Procedure 11 or a comparable state procedure; or

(4) a statement made during plea discussions with an attorney for the prosecuting authority if the discussions did not result in a guilty or nolo contendere plea or they resulted in a later-withdrawn guilty or nolo contendere plea.

(c) Exception. In a civil case, the court may admit a statement described in paragraph (a)(3) or (4) and in a criminal case, the court may admit a statement described in paragraph (b)(3) or (4), when another statement made during the same plea or plea discussions has been introduced and in fairness the statements ought to be considered together.

RULE 411. LIABILITY INSURANCE

Evidence that a person was or was not insured against liability is not admissible to prove whether the person acted negligently or otherwise wrongfully. But the court may admit this evidence for another purpose, such as proving a witness's bias or prejudice or, if disputed, proving agency, ownership, or control.

RULE 412. EVIDENCE OF PREVIOUS SEXUAL CONDUCT IN CRIMINAL CASES

(a) In General. The following evidence is not admissible in a prosecution for sexual assault, aggravated sexual assault, or attempt to commit sexual assault or aggravated sexual assault:

(1) reputation or opinion evidence of a victim's past sexual behavior; or

(2) specific instances of a victim's past sexual behavior.

(b) Exceptions for Specific Instances. Evidence of specific instances of a victim's past sexual behavior is admissible if:

(1) the court admits the evidence in accordance with subdivisions (c) and (d);

(2) the evidence:

(A) is necessary to rebut or explain scientific or medical evidence offered by the prosecutor;

(B) concerns past sexual behavior with the defendant and is offered by the defendant to prove consent;

(C) relates to the victim's motive or bias;

(D) is admissible under Rule 609; or

(E) is constitutionally required to be admitted; and

(3) the probative value of the evidence outweighs the danger of unfair prejudice.

(c) Procedure for Offering Evidence. Before offering any evidence of the victim's past sexual behavior, the defendant must inform the court outside the jury's presence. The court must then conduct an in camera hearing, recorded by a court reporter, and determine whether the proposed evidence is admissible. The defendant may not refer to any evidence ruled inadmissible without first requesting and gaining the court's approval outside the jury's presence.

(d) Record Sealed. The court must preserve the record of the in camera hearing, under seal, as part of the record.

(e) Definition of "Victim." In this rule, "victim" includes an alleged victim.

ARTICLE V. PRIVILEGES

RULE 501. PRIVILEGES IN GENERAL

Unless a Constitution, a statute, or these or other rules prescribed under statutory authority provide otherwise, no person has a privilege to:

(a) refuse to be a witness;

(b) refuse to disclose any matter;

(c) refuse to produce any object or writing; or

(d) prevent another from being a witness, disclosing any matter, or producing any object or writing.

RULE 502

RULE 502. REQUIRED REPORTS PRIVILEGED BY STATUTE

(a) In General. If a law requiring a return or report to be made so provides:

(1) a person, corporation, association, or other organization or entity—whether public or private—that makes the required return or report has a privilege to refuse to disclose it and to prevent any other person from disclosing it; and

(2) a public officer or agency to whom the return or report must be made has a privilege to refuse to disclose it.

(b) Exceptions. This privilege does not apply in an action involving perjury, false statements, fraud in the return or report, or other failure to comply with the law in question.

RULE 503. LAWYER-CLIENT PRIVILEGE

(a) Definitions. In this rule:

(1) A "client" is a person, public officer, or corporation, association, or other organization or entity—whether public or private—that:

(A) is rendered professional legal services by a lawyer; or

(B) consults a lawyer with a view to obtaining professional legal services from the lawyer.

(2) A "client's representative" is:

(A) a person who has authority to obtain professional legal services for the client or to act for the client on the legal advice rendered; or

(B) any other person who, to facilitate the rendition of professional legal services to the client, makes or receives a confidential communication while acting in the scope of employment for the client.

(3) A "lawyer" is a person authorized, or who the client reasonably believes is authorized, to practice law in any state or nation.

(4) A "lawyer's representative" is:

(A) one employed by the lawyer to assist in the rendition of professional legal services; or

(B) an accountant who is reasonably necessary for the lawyer's rendition of professional legal services.

(5) A communication is "confidential" if not intended to be disclosed to third persons other than those:

(A) to whom disclosure is made to further the rendition of professional legal services to the client; or

(B) reasonably necessary to transmit the communication.

(b) Rules of Privilege.

(1) *General Rule.* A client has a privilege to refuse to disclose and to prevent any other person from disclosing confidential communications made to facilitate the rendition of professional legal services to the client:

(A) between the client or the client's representative and the client's lawyer or the lawyer's representative;

(B) between the client's lawyer and the lawyer's representative;

(C) by the client, the client's representative, the client's lawyer, or the lawyer's representative to a lawyer representing another party in a pending action or that lawyer's representative, if the communications concern a matter of common interest in the pending action;

(D) between the client's representatives or between the client and the client's representative; or

(E) among lawyers and their representatives representing the same client.

(2) *Special Rule in a Criminal Case.* In a criminal case, a client has a privilege to prevent a lawyer or lawyer's representative from disclosing any other fact that came to the knowledge of the lawyer or the lawyer's representative by reason of the attorney-client relationship.

(c) Who May Claim. The privilege may be claimed by:

(1) the client;

(2) the client's guardian or conservator;

(3) a deceased client's personal representative; or

(4) the successor, trustee, or similar representative of a corporation, association, or other organization or entity—whether or not in existence.

The person who was the client's lawyer or the lawyer's representative when the communication was made may claim the privilege on the client's behalf—and is presumed to have authority to do so.

(d) Exceptions. This privilege does not apply:

(1) *Furtherance of Crime or Fraud.* If the lawyer's services were sought or obtained to enable or aid anyone to commit or plan to commit what the client knew or reasonably should have known to be a crime or fraud.

(2) *Claimants Through Same Deceased Client.* If the communication is relevant to an issue between parties claiming through the same deceased client.

(3) *Breach of Duty by a Lawyer or Client.* If the communication is relevant to an issue of breach of duty by a lawyer to the client or by a client to the lawyer.

(4) *Document Attested by a Lawyer.* If the communication is relevant to an issue concerning an attested document to which the lawyer is an attesting witness.

(5) *Joint Clients.* If the communication:

(A) is offered in an action between clients who retained or consulted a lawyer in common;

(B) was made by any of the clients to the lawyer; and

(C) is relevant to a matter of common interest between the clients.

Comment to 1998 change: The addition of subsection (a)(2)(B) adopts a subject matter test for the privilege of an entity, in place of the control group test previously used. See *National Tank Co. v. Brotherton*, 851 S.W.2d 193, 197-98 (Tex. 1993).

RULE 504. SPOUSAL PRIVILEGES
(a) Confidential Communication Privilege.

(1) *Definition.* A communication is "confidential" if a person makes it privately to the person's spouse and does not intend its disclosure to any other person.

(2) *General Rule.* A person has a privilege to refuse to disclose and to prevent any other person from disclosing a confidential communication made to the person's spouse while they were married. This privilege survives termination of the marriage.

(3) *Who May Claim.* The privilege may be claimed by:

(A) the communicating spouse;

(B) the guardian of a communicating spouse who is incompetent; or

(C) the personal representative of a communicating spouse who is deceased.

The other spouse may claim the privilege on the communicating spouse's behalf—and is presumed to have authority to do so.

(4) *Exceptions.* This privilege does not apply:

(A) *Furtherance of Crime or Fraud.* If the communication is made—wholly or partially—to enable or aid anyone to commit or plan to commit a crime or fraud.

(B) *Proceeding Between Spouse and Other Spouse or Claimant Through Deceased Spouse.* In a civil proceeding:

(i) brought by or on behalf of one spouse against the other; or

(ii) between a surviving spouse and a person claiming through the deceased spouse.

(C) *Crime Against Family, Spouse, Household Member, or Minor Child.* In a:

(i) proceeding in which a party is accused of conduct that, if proved, is a crime against the person of the other spouse, any member of the household of either spouse, or any minor child; or

(ii) criminal proceeding involving a charge of bigamy under Section 25.01 of the Penal Code.

(D) *Commitment or Similar Proceeding.* In a proceeding to commit either spouse or otherwise to place the spouse or the spouse's property under another's control because of a mental or physical condition.

   (E) *Proceeding to Establish Competence.* In a proceeding brought by or on behalf of either spouse to establish competence.

(b) Privilege Not to Testify in a Criminal Case.

   (1) *General Rule.* In a criminal case, an accused's spouse has a privilege not to be called to testify for the state. But this rule neither prohibits a spouse from testifying voluntarily for the state nor gives a spouse a privilege to refuse to be called to testify for the accused.

   (2) *Failure to Call Spouse.* If other evidence indicates that the accused's spouse could testify to relevant matters, an accused's failure to call the spouse to testify is a proper subject of comment by counsel.

   (3) *Who May Claim.* The privilege not to testify may be claimed by the accused's spouse or the spouse's guardian or representative, but not by the accused.

   (4) *Exceptions.* This privilege does not apply:

     (A) *Certain Criminal Proceedings.* In a criminal proceeding in which a spouse is charged with:

       (i) a crime against the other spouse, any member of the household of either spouse, or any minor child; or

       (ii) bigamy under Section 25.01 of the Penal Code.

     (B) *Matters That Occurred Before the Marriage.* If the spouse is called to testify about matters that occurred before the marriage.

Comment to 2015 restyling: Previously, Rule 504(b)(1) provided that, "A spouse who testifies on behalf of an accused is subject to cross-examination as provided in Rule 611(b)." That sentence was included in the original version of Rule 504 when the Texas Rules of Criminal Evidence were promulgated in 1986 and changed the rule to a testimonial privilege held by the witness spouse. Until then, a spouse was deemed incompetent to testify against his or her defendant spouse, and when a spouse testified on behalf of a defendant spouse, the state was limited to cross-examining the spouse about matters relating to the spouse's direct testimony. The quoted sentence from the original Criminal Rule 504(b) was designed to overturn this limitation and allow the state to cross-examine a testifying spouse in the same manner as any other witness. More than twenty-five years later, it is clear that a spouse who testifies either for or against a defendant spouse may be cross-examined in the same manner as any other witness. Therefore, the continued inclusion in the rule of a provision that refers only to the cross-examination of a spouse who testifies on behalf of the accused is more confusing than helpful. Its deletion is designed to clarify the rule and does not change existing law.

Comment to 1998 change: The rule eliminates the spousal testimonial privilege for prosecutions in which the testifying spouse is the alleged victim of a crime by the accused. This is intended to be consistent with Code of Criminal Procedure art. 38.10, eff. September 1, 1995.

RULE 505. PRIVILEGE FOR COMMUNICATIONS TO A CLERGY MEMBER

(a) Definitions. In this rule:

   (1) A "clergy member" is a minister, priest, rabbi, accredited Christian Science Practitioner, or other similar functionary of a religious organization or someone whom a communicant reasonably believes is a clergy member.

   (2) A "communicant" is a person who consults a clergy member in the clergy member's professional capacity as a spiritual adviser.

   (3) A communication is "confidential" if made privately and not intended for further disclosure except to other persons present to further the purpose of the communication.

(b) General Rule. A communicant has a privilege to refuse to disclose and to prevent any other person from disclosing a confidential communication by the communicant to a clergy member in the clergy member's professional capacity as spiritual adviser.

(c) Who May Claim. The privilege may be claimed by:

   (1) the communicant;

   (2) the communicant's guardian or conservator; or

   (3) a deceased communicant's personal representative.

The clergy member to whom the communication was made may claim the privilege on the communicant's behalf—and is presumed to have authority to do so.

RULE 506. POLITICAL VOTE PRIVILEGE

A person has a privilege to refuse to disclose the person's vote at a political election conducted by secret ballot unless the vote was cast illegally.

RULE 507. TRADE SECRETS PRIVILEGE

(a) **General Rule.** A person has a privilege to refuse to disclose and to prevent other persons from disclosing a trade secret owned by the person, unless the court finds that non-disclosure will tend to conceal fraud or otherwise work injustice.

(b) **Who May Claim.** The privilege may be claimed by the person who owns the trade secret or the person's agent or employee.

(c) **Protective Measure.** If a court orders a person to disclose a trade secret, it must take any protective measure required by the interests of the privilege holder and the parties and to further justice.

RULE 508. INFORMER'S IDENTITY PRIVILEGE

(a) **General Rule.** The United States, a state, or a subdivision of either has a privilege to refuse to disclose a person's identity if:

(1) the person has furnished information to a law enforcement officer or a member of a legislative committee or its staff conducting an investigation of a possible violation of law; and

(2) the information relates to or assists in the investigation.

(b) **Who May Claim.** The privilege may be claimed by an appropriate representative of the public entity to which the informer furnished the information. The court in a criminal case must reject the privilege claim if the state objects.

(c) **Exceptions.**

(1) *Voluntary Disclosure; Informer a Witness.* This privilege does not apply if:

(A) the informer's identity or the informer's interest in the communication's subject matter has been disclosed—by a privilege holder or the informer's own action—to a person who would have cause to resent the communication; or

(B) the informer appears as a witness for the public entity.

(2) *Testimony About the Merits.*

(A) *Criminal Case.* In a criminal case, this privilege does not apply if the court finds a reasonable probability exists that the informer can give testimony necessary to a fair determination of guilt or innocence. If the court so finds and the public entity elects not to disclose the informer's identity:

(i) on the defendant's motion, the court must dismiss the charges to which the testimony would relate; or

(ii) on its own motion, the court may dismiss the charges to which the testimony would relate.

(B) *Certain Civil Cases.* In a civil case in which the public entity is a party, this privilege does not apply if the court finds a reasonable probability exists that the informer can give testimony necessary to a fair determination of a material issue on the merits. If the court so finds and the public entity elects not to disclose the informer's identity, the court may make any order that justice requires.

(C) *Procedures.*

(i) If it appears that an informer may be able to give the testimony required to invoke this exception and the public entity claims the privilege, the court must give the public entity an opportunity to show in camera facts relevant to determining whether this exception is met. The showing should ordinarily be made by affidavits, but the court may take testimony if it finds the matter cannot be satisfactorily resolved by affidavits.

(ii) No counsel or party may attend the in camera showing.

(iii) The court must seal and preserve for appeal evidence submitted under this subparagraph (2)(C). The evidence must not otherwise be revealed without the public entity's consent.

(3) *Legality of Obtaining Evidence.*

(A) *Court May Order Disclosure.* The court may order the public entity to disclose an informer's identity if:

(i) information from an informer is relied on to establish the legality of the means by which evidence was obtained; and

(ii) the court is not satisfied that the information was received from an informer reasonably believed to be reliable or credible.

(B) *Procedures.*

(i) On the public entity's request, the court must order the disclosure be made in camera.

(ii) No counsel or party may attend the in camera disclosure.

(iii) If the informer's identity is disclosed in camera, the court must seal and preserve for appeal the record of the in camera proceeding. The record of the in camera proceeding must not otherwise be revealed without the public entity's consent.

RULE 509. PHYSICIAN-PATIENT PRIVILEGE

(a) **Definitions.** In this rule:

(1) A "patient" is a person who consults or is seen by a physician for medical care.

(2) A "physician" is a person licensed, or who the patient reasonably believes is licensed, to practice medicine in any state or nation.

(3) A communication is "confidential" if not intended to be disclosed to third persons other than those:

(A) present to further the patient's interest in the consultation, examination, or interview;

(B) reasonably necessary to transmit the communication; or

(C) participating in the diagnosis and treatment under the physician's direction, including members of the patient's family.

(b) **Limited Privilege in a Criminal Case.** There is no physician-patient privilege in a criminal case. But a confidential communication is not admissible in a criminal case if made:

(1) to a person involved in the treatment of or examination for alcohol or drug abuse; and

(2) by a person being treated voluntarily or being examined for admission to treatment for alcohol or drug abuse.

(c) **General Rule in a Civil Case.** In a civil case, a patient has a privilege to refuse to disclose and to prevent any other person from disclosing:

(1) a confidential communication between a physician and the patient that relates to or was made in connection with any professional services the physician rendered the patient; and

(2) a record of the patient's identity, diagnosis, evaluation, or treatment created or maintained by a physician.

(d) **Who May Claim in a Civil Case.** The privilege may be claimed by:

(1) the patient; or

(2) the patient's representative on the patient's behalf.

The physician may claim the privilege on the patient's behalf—and is presumed to have authority to do so.

(e) **Exceptions in a Civil Case.** This privilege does not apply:

(1) *Proceeding Against Physician.* If the communication or record is relevant to a claim or defense in:

(A) a proceeding the patient brings against a physician; or

(B) a license revocation proceeding in which the patient is a complaining witness.

(2) *Consent.* If the patient or a person authorized to act on the patient's behalf consents in writing to the release of any privileged information, as provided in subdivision (f).

(3) *Action to Collect.* In an action to collect a claim for medical services rendered to the patient.

(4) *Party Relies on Patient's Condition.* If any party relies on the patient's physical, mental, or emotional condition as a part of the party's claim or defense and the communication or record is relevant to that condition.

(5) *Disciplinary Investigation or Proceeding.* In a disciplinary investigation of or proceeding against a physician under the Medical Practice Act, Tex. Occ. Code §164.001 et seq., or a registered nurse under Tex. Occ. Code §301.451 et seq. But the board conducting the investigation or proceeding must protect the identity of any patient whose medical records are examined unless:

    (A) the patient's records would be subject to disclosure under paragraph (e)(1); or

    (B) the patient has consented in writing to the release of medical records, as provided in subdivision (f).

(6) *Involuntary Civil Commitment or Similar Proceeding.* In a proceeding for involuntary civil commitment or court-ordered treatment, or a probable cause hearing under Tex. Health & Safety Code:

    (A) chapter 462 (Treatment of Persons With Chemical Dependencies);

    (B) title 7, subtitle C (Texas Mental Health Code); or

    (C) title 7, subtitle D (Persons With an Intellectual Disability Act).

(7) *Abuse or Neglect of "Institution" Resident.* In a proceeding regarding the abuse or neglect, or the cause of any abuse or neglect, of a resident of an "institution" as defined in Tex. Health & Safety Code §242.002.

(f) **Consent for Release of Privileged Information.**

    (1) Consent for the release of privileged information must be in writing and signed by:

        (A) the patient;

        (B) a parent or legal guardian if the patient is a minor;

        (C) a legal guardian if the patient has been adjudicated incompetent to manage personal affairs;

        (D) an attorney appointed for the patient under Tex. Health & Safety Code title 7, subtitles C and D;

        (E) an attorney ad litem appointed for the patient under Tex. Estates Code title 3, subtitle C;

        (F) an attorney ad litem or guardian ad litem appointed for a minor under Tex. Fam. Code chapter 107, subchapter B; or

        (G) a personal representative if the patient is deceased.

    (2) The consent must specify:

        (A) the information or medical records covered by the release;

        (B) the reasons or purposes for the release; and

        (C) the person to whom the information is to be released.

    (3) The patient, or other person authorized to consent, may withdraw consent to the release of any information. But a withdrawal of consent does not affect any information disclosed before the patient or authorized person gave written notice of the withdrawal.

    (4) Any person who receives information privileged under this rule may disclose the information only to the extent consistent with the purposes specified in the consent.

Comment to 2015 restyling: The physician-patient privilege in a civil case was first enacted in Texas in 1981 as part of the Medical Practice Act, formerly codified in Tex. Rev. Civ. Stat. art. 4495b. That statute provided that the privilege applied even if a patient had received a physician's services before the statute's enactment. Because more than thirty years have now passed, it is no longer necessary to burden the text of the rule with a statement regarding the privilege's retroactive application. But deleting this statement from the rule's text is not intended as a substantive change in the law.

RULE 509

The former rule's reference to "confidentiality or" and "administrative proceedings" in subdivision (e) [Exceptions in a Civil Case] has been deleted. First, this rule is a privilege rule only. Tex. Occ. Code §159.004 sets forth exceptions to a physician's duty to maintain confidentiality of patient information outside court and administrative proceedings. Second, by their own terms the rules of evidence govern only proceedings in Texas courts. See Rule 101(b). To the extent the rules apply in administrative proceedings, it is because the Administrative Procedure Act mandates their applicability. Tex. Gov't Code §2001.083 provides that "[i]n a contested case, a state agency shall give effect to the rules of privilege recognized by law." Section 2001.091 excludes privileged material from discovery in contested administrative cases.

Statutory references in the former rule that are no longer up-to-date have been revised. Finally, reconciling the provisions of Rule 509 with the parts of Tex. Occ. Code ch. 159 that address a physician-patient privilege applicable to court proceedings is beyond the scope of the restyling project.

Comment to 1998 change: This comment is intended to inform the construction and application of this rule. Prior Criminal Rules of Evidence 509 and 510 are now in subparagraph (b) of this Rule. This rule governs disclosures of patient-physician communications only in judicial or administrative proceedings. Whether a physician may or must disclose such communications in other circumstances is governed by TRCS art. 4495b, §5.08 [now Occ. Code ch. 159]. Former subparagraph (d)(6) of the Civil Evidence Rules, regarding disclosures in a suit affecting the parent-child relationship, is omitted, not because there should be no exception to the privilege in suits affecting the parent-child relationship, but because the exception in such suits is properly considered under subparagraph (e)(4) of the new rule (formerly subparagraph (d)(4)), as construed in *R.K. v. Ramirez*, 887 S.W.2d 836 (Tex. 1994). In determining the proper application of an exception in such suits, the trial court must ensure that the precise need for the information is not outweighed by legitimate privacy interests protected by the privilege. Subparagraph (e) of the new rule does not except from the privilege information relating to a nonparty patient who is or may be a consulting or testifying expert in the suit.

RULE 510. MENTAL HEALTH INFORMATION PRIVILEGE IN CIVIL CASES

(a) Definitions. In this rule:

  (1) A "professional" is a person:

    (A) authorized to practice medicine in any state or nation;

    (B) licensed or certified by the State of Texas in the diagnosis, evaluation, or treatment of any mental or emotional disorder;

    (C) involved in the treatment or examination of drug abusers; or

    (D) who the patient reasonably believes to be a professional under this rule.

  (2) A "patient" is a person who:

    (A) consults or is interviewed by a professional for diagnosis, evaluation, or treatment of any mental or emotional condition or disorder, including alcoholism and drug addiction; or

    (B) is being treated voluntarily or being examined for admission to voluntary treatment for drug abuse.

  (3) A "patient's representative" is:

    (A) any person who has the patient's written consent;

    (B) the parent of a minor patient;

    (C) the guardian of a patient who has been adjudicated incompetent to manage personal affairs; or

    (D) the personal representative of a deceased patient.

  (4) A communication is "confidential" if not intended to be disclosed to third persons other than those:

    (A) present to further the patient's interest in the diagnosis, examination, evaluation, or treatment;

    (B) reasonably necessary to transmit the communication; or

    (C) participating in the diagnosis, examination, evaluation, or treatment under the professional's direction, including members of the patient's family.

(b) General Rule; Disclosure.

  (1) In a civil case, a patient has a privilege to refuse to disclose and to prevent any other person from disclosing:

    (A) a confidential communication between the patient and a professional; and

    (B) a record of the patient's identity, diagnosis, evaluation, or treatment that is created or maintained by a professional.

  (2) In a civil case, any person—other than a patient's representative acting on the patient's behalf—who receives information privileged under this rule may disclose the information only to the extent consistent with the purposes for which it was obtained.

(c) Who May Claim. The privilege may be claimed by:

  (1) the patient; or

  (2) the patient's representative on the patient's behalf.

The professional may claim the privilege on the patient's behalf—and is presumed to have authority to do so.

(d) Exceptions. This privilege does not apply:

(1) *Proceeding Against Professional.* If the communication or record is relevant to a claim or defense in:

(A) a proceeding the patient brings against a professional; or

(B) a license revocation proceeding in which the patient is a complaining witness.

(2) *Written Waiver.* If the patient or a person authorized to act on the patient's behalf waives the privilege in writing.

(3) *Action to Collect.* In an action to collect a claim for mental or emotional health services rendered to the patient.

(4) *Communication Made in Court-Ordered Examination.* To a communication the patient made to a professional during a court-ordered examination relating to the patient's mental or emotional condition or disorder if:

(A) the patient made the communication after being informed that it would not be privileged;

(B) the communication is offered to prove an issue involving the patient's mental or emotional health; and

(C) the court imposes appropriate safeguards against unauthorized disclosure.

(5) *Party Relies on Patient's Condition.* If any party relies on the patient's physical, mental, or emotional condition as a part of the party's claim or defense and the communication or record is relevant to that condition.

(6) *Abuse or Neglect of "Institution" Resident.* In a proceeding regarding the abuse or neglect, or the cause of any abuse or neglect, of a resident of an "institution" as defined in Tex. Health & Safety Code §242.002.

Comment to 2015 restyling: The mental-health-information privilege in civil cases was enacted in Texas in 1979. Tex. Rev. Civ. Stat. art. 5561h (later codified at Tex. Health & Safety Code §611.001 et seq.)

provided that the privilege applied even if the patient had received the professional's services before the statute's enactment. Because more than thirty years have now passed, it is no longer necessary to burden the text of the rule with a statement regarding the privilege's retroactive application. But deleting this statement from the rule's text is not intended as a substantive change in the law.

Tex. Health & Safety Code ch. 611 addresses confidentiality rules for communications between a patient and a mental-health professional and for the professional's treatment records. Many of these provisions apply in contexts other than court proceedings. Reconciling the provisions of Rule 510 with the parts of chapter 611 that address a mental-health-information privilege applicable to court proceedings is beyond the scope of the restyling project.

Comment to 1998 change: This comment is intended to inform the construction and application of this rule. This rule governs disclosures of patient-professional communications only in judicial or administrative proceedings. Whether a professional may or must disclose such communications in other circumstances is governed by Tex. Health & Safety Code §§611.001-611.008. Former subparagraph (d)(6) of the Civil Evidence Rules, regarding disclosures in a suit affecting the parent-child relationship, is omitted, not because there should be no exception to the privilege in suits affecting the parent-child relationship, but because the exception in such suits is properly considered under subparagraph (d)(5), as construed in *R.K. v. Ramirez*, 887 S.W.2d 836 (Tex. 1994). In determining the proper application of an exception in such suits, the trial court must ensure that the precise need for the information is not outweighed by legitimate privacy interests protected by the privilege. Subparagraph (d) does not except from the privilege information relating to a nonparty patient who is or may be a consulting or testifying expert in the suit.

RULE 511. WAIVER BY VOLUNTARY DISCLOSURE

(a) General Rule.

A person upon whom these rules confer a privilege against disclosure waives the privilege if:

(1) the person or a predecessor of the person while holder of the privilege voluntarily discloses or consents to disclosure of any significant part of the privileged matter unless such disclosure itself is privileged; or

(2) the person or a representative of the person calls a person to whom privileged communications have been made to testify as to the person's character or character trait insofar as such communications are relevant to such character or character trait.

(b) Lawyer-Client Privilege and Work Product; Limitations on Waiver.

Notwithstanding paragraph (a), the following provisions apply, in the circumstances set out, to disclosure of a communication or information covered by the lawyer-client privilege or work-product protection.

(1) ***Disclosure Made in a Federal or State Proceeding or to a Federal or State Office or Agency; Scope of a Waiver.*** When the disclosure is made in a federal proceeding or state proceeding of any state or to a federal office or agency or state office or agency of any state and waives the lawyer-client privilege or work-product protection, the waiver extends to an undisclosed communication or information only if:

(A) the waiver is intentional;

(B) the disclosed and undisclosed communications or information concern the same subject matter; and

(C) they ought in fairness to be considered together.

(2) ***Inadvertent Disclosure in State Civil Proceedings.*** When made in a Texas state proceeding, an inadvertent disclosure does not operate as a waiver if the holder followed the procedures of Rule of Civil Procedure 193.3(d).

(3) ***Controlling Effect of a Court Order.*** A disclosure made in litigation pending before a federal court or a state court of any state that has entered an order that the privilege or protection is not waived by disclosure connected with the litigation pending before that court is also not a waiver in a Texas state proceeding.

(4) ***Controlling Effect of a Party Agreement.*** An agreement on the effect of disclosure in a state proceeding of any state is binding only on the parties to the agreement, unless it is incorporated into a court order.

Comment to 2015 restyling: The amendments to Rule 511 are designed to align Texas law with federal law on waiver of privilege by voluntary disclosure. Subsection (a) sets forth the general rule. Subsection (b) incorporates the provisions of Federal Rule of Evidence 502. Like the federal rule, subsection (b) only addresses disclosure of communications or information covered by the lawyer-client privilege or work-product protection. These amendments do not affect the law governing waiver of other privileges or protections.

RULE 512. PRIVILEGED MATTER DISCLOSED UNDER COMPULSION OR WITHOUT OPPORTUNITY TO CLAIM PRIVILEGE

A privilege claim is not defeated by a disclosure that was:

(a) compelled erroneously; or

(b) made without opportunity to claim the privilege.

RULE 513. COMMENT ON OR INFERENCE FROM A PRIVILEGE CLAIM; INSTRUCTION

(a) **Comment or Inference Not Permitted.** Except as permitted in Rule 504(b)(2), neither the court nor counsel may comment on a privilege claim—whether made in the present proceeding or previously—and the fact-finder may not draw an inference from the claim.

(b) **Claiming Privilege Without the Jury's Knowledge.** To the extent practicable, the court must conduct a jury trial so that the making of a privilege claim is not suggested to the jury by any means.

(c) **Claim of Privilege Against Self-Incrimination in a Civil Case.** Subdivisions (a) and (b) do not apply to a party's claim, in the present civil case, of the privilege against self-incrimination.

(d) **Jury Instruction.** When this rule forbids a jury from drawing an inference from a privilege claim, the court must, on request of a party against whom the jury might draw the inference, instruct the jury accordingly.

Comment to 1998 change: Subdivision (d) regarding a party's entitlement to a jury instruction about a claim of privilege is made applicable to civil cases.

ARTICLE VI. WITNESSES

RULE 601. COMPETENCY TO TESTIFY IN GENERAL; "DEAD MAN'S RULE"

(a) **In General.** Every person is competent to be a witness unless these rules provide otherwise. The following witnesses are incompetent:

(1) ***Insane Persons.*** A person who is now insane or was insane at the time of the events about which the person is called to testify.

(2) ***Persons Lacking Sufficient Intellect.*** A child—or any other person—whom the court examines and finds lacks sufficient intellect to testify concerning the matters in issue.

RULE 606

(b) The "Dead Man's Rule."

(1) *Applicability.* The "Dead Man's Rule" applies only in a civil case:

(A) by or against a party in the party's capacity as an executor, administrator, or guardian; or

(B) by or against a decedent's heirs or legal representatives and based in whole or in part on the decedent's oral statement.

(2) *General Rule.* In cases described in subparagraph (b)(1)(A), a party may not testify against another party about an oral statement by the testator, intestate, or ward. In cases described in subparagraph (b)(1)(B), a party may not testify against another party about an oral statement by the decedent.

(3) *Exceptions.* A party may testify against another party about an oral statement by the testator, intestate, ward, or decedent if:

(A) the party's testimony about the statement is corroborated; or

(B) the opposing party calls the party to testify at the trial about the statement.

(4) *Instructions.* If a court excludes evidence under paragraph (b)(2), the court must instruct the jury that the law prohibits a party from testifying about an oral statement by the testator, intestate, ward, or decedent unless the oral statement is corroborated or the opposing party calls the party to testify at the trial about the statement.

Comment to 2015 restyling: The text of the "Dead Man's Rule" has been streamlined to clarify its meaning without making any substantive changes. The text of former Rule 601(b) (as well as its statutory predecessor, Vernon's Ann. Civ. St. art. 3716) prohibits only a "party" from testifying about the dead man's statements. Despite this, the last sentence of former Rule 601(b) requires the court to instruct the jury when the rule "prohibits an interested party or witness" from testifying. Because the rule prohibits only a "party" from testifying, restyled Rule 601(b)(4) references only "a party," and not "an interested party or witness." To be sure, courts have indicated that the rule (or its statutory predecessor) may be applicable to a witness who is not nominally a party and inapplicable to a witness who is only nominally a party. *See, e.g., Chandler v. Welborn,* 156 Tex. 312, 294 S.W.2d 801, 809 (1956); *Ragsdale v. Ragsdale,* 142 Tex. 476, 179 S.W.2d 291, 295 (1944). But these decisions are based on an interpretation of the meaning of "party." Therefore, limiting the court's instruction under restyled Rule 601(b)(4) to "a party" does not change Texas practice. In addition, restyled Rule 601(b) deletes the sentence in former Rule 601(b) that states "[e]xcept for the foregoing, a witness is not precluded from giving evi-

dence ... because the witness is a party to the action..." This sentence is surplusage. Rule 601(b) is a rule of exclusion. If the testimony falls outside the rule of exclusion, its admissibility will be determined by other applicable rules of evidence.

RULE 602. NEED FOR PERSONAL KNOWLEDGE

A witness may testify to a matter only if evidence is introduced sufficient to support a finding that the witness has personal knowledge of the matter. Evidence to prove personal knowledge may consist of the witness's own testimony. This rule does not apply to a witness's expert testimony under Rule 703.

RULE 603. OATH OR AFFIRMATION TO TESTIFY TRUTHFULLY

Before testifying, a witness must give an oath or affirmation to testify truthfully. It must be in a form designed to impress that duty on the witness's conscience.

RULE 604. INTERPRETER

An interpreter must be qualified and must give an oath or affirmation to make a true translation.

RULE 605. JUDGE'S COMPETENCY AS A WITNESS

The presiding judge may not testify as a witness at the trial. A party need not object to preserve the issue.

RULE 606. JUROR'S COMPETENCY AS A WITNESS

(a) At the Trial. A juror may not testify as a witness before the other jurors at the trial. If a juror is called to testify, the court must give a party an opportunity to object outside the jury's presence.

(b) During an Inquiry into the Validity of a Verdict or Indictment.

(1) *Prohibited Testimony or Other Evidence.* During an inquiry into the validity of a verdict or indictment, a juror may not testify about any statement made or incident that occurred during the jury's deliberations; the effect of anything on that juror's or another juror's vote; or any juror's mental processes concerning the verdict or indictment. The court may not receive a juror's affidavit or evidence of a juror's statement on these matters.

(2) *Exceptions.* A juror may testify:

  (A) about whether an outside influence was improperly brought to bear on any juror; or

  (B) to rebut a claim that the juror was not qualified to serve.

RULE 607. WHO MAY IMPEACH A WITNESS

Any party, including the party that called the witness, may attack the witness's credibility.

RULE 608. A WITNESS'S CHARACTER FOR TRUTHFULNESS OR UNTRUTHFULNESS

(a) **Reputation or Opinion Evidence.** A witness's credibility may be attacked or supported by testimony about the witness's reputation for having a character for truthfulness or untruthfulness, or by testimony in the form of an opinion about that character. But evidence of truthful character is admissible only after the witness's character for truthfulness has been attacked.

(b) **Specific Instances of Conduct.** Except for a criminal conviction under Rule 609, a party may not inquire into or offer extrinsic evidence to prove specific instances of the witness's conduct in order to attack or support the witness's character for truthfulness.

RULE 609. IMPEACHMENT BY EVIDENCE OF A CRIMINAL CONVICTION

(a) **In General.** Evidence of a criminal conviction offered to attack a witness's character for truthfulness must be admitted if:

  (1) the crime was a felony or involved moral turpitude, regardless of punishment;

  (2) the probative value of the evidence outweighs its prejudicial effect to a party; and

  (3) it is elicited from the witness or established by public record.

(b) **Limit on Using the Evidence After 10 Years.** This subdivision (b) applies if more than 10 years have passed since the witness's conviction or release from confinement for it, whichever is later. Evidence of the conviction is admissible only if its probative value, supported by specific facts and circumstances, substantially outweighs its prejudicial effect.

(c) **Effect of a Pardon, Annulment, or Certificate of Rehabilitation.** Evidence of a conviction is not admissible if:

  (1) the conviction has been the subject of a pardon, annulment, certificate of rehabilitation, or other equivalent procedure based on a finding that the person has been rehabilitated, and the person has not been convicted of a later crime that was classified as a felony or involved moral turpitude, regardless of punishment;

  (2) probation has been satisfactorily completed for the conviction, and the person has not been convicted of a later crime that was classified as a felony or involved moral turpitude, regardless of punishment; or

  (3) the conviction has been the subject of a pardon, annulment, or other equivalent procedure based on a finding of innocence.

(d) **Juvenile Adjudications.** Evidence of a juvenile adjudication is admissible under this rule only if:

  (1) the witness is a party in a proceeding conducted under title 3 of the Texas Family Code; or

  (2) the United States or Texas Constitution requires that it be admitted.

(e) **Pendency of an Appeal.** A conviction for which an appeal is pending is not admissible under this rule.

(f) **Notice.** Evidence of a witness's conviction is not admissible under this rule if, after receiving from the adverse party a timely written request specifying the witness, the proponent of the conviction fails to provide sufficient written notice of intent to use the conviction. Notice is sufficient if it provides a fair opportunity to contest the use of such evidence.

RULE 610. RELIGIOUS BELIEFS OR OPINIONS

Evidence of a witness's religious beliefs or opinions is not admissible to attack or support the witness's credibility.

Comment to 1998 change: This is prior Rule of Criminal Evidence 615.

RULE 611. MODE & ORDER OF EXAMINING WITNESSES & PRESENTING EVIDENCE

(a) Control by the Court; Purposes. The court should exercise reasonable control over the mode and order of examining witnesses and presenting evidence so as to:

(1) make those procedures effective for determining the truth;

(2) avoid wasting time; and

(3) protect witnesses from harassment or undue embarrassment.

(b) Scope of Cross-Examination. A witness may be cross-examined on any relevant matter, including credibility.

(c) Leading Questions. Leading questions should not be used on direct examination except as necessary to develop the witness's testimony. Ordinarily, the court should allow leading questions:

(1) on cross-examination; and

(2) when a party calls a hostile witness, an adverse party, or a witness identified with an adverse party.

RULE 612. WRITING USED TO REFRESH A WITNESS'S MEMORY

(a) Scope. This rule gives an adverse party certain options when a witness uses a writing to refresh memory:

(1) while testifying;

(2) before testifying, in civil cases, if the court decides that justice requires the party to have those options; or

(3) before testifying, in criminal cases.

(b) Adverse Party's Options; Deleting Unrelated Matter. An adverse party is entitled to have the writing produced at the hearing, to inspect it, to cross-examine the witness about it, and to introduce in evidence any portion that relates to the witness's testimony. If the producing party claims that the writing includes unrelated matter, the court must examine the writing in camera, delete any unrelated portion, and order that the rest be delivered to the adverse party. Any portion deleted over objection must be preserved for the record.

(c) Failure to Produce or Deliver the Writing. If a writing is not produced or is not delivered as ordered, the court may issue any appropriate order. But if the prosecution does not comply in a criminal case, the court must strike the witness's testimony or—if justice so requires—declare a mistrial.

RULE 613. WITNESS'S PRIOR STATEMENT & BIAS OR INTEREST

(a) Witness's Prior Inconsistent Statement.

(1) *Foundation Requirement.* When examining a witness about the witness's prior inconsistent statement—whether oral or written—a party must first tell the witness:

(A) the contents of the statement;

(B) the time and place of the statement; and

(C) the person to whom the witness made the statement.

(2) *Need Not Show Written Statement.* If the witness's prior inconsistent statement is written, a party need not show it to the witness before inquiring about it, but must, upon request, show it to opposing counsel.

(3) *Opportunity to Explain or Deny.* A witness must be given the opportunity to explain or deny the prior inconsistent statement.

(4) *Extrinsic Evidence.* Extrinsic evidence of a witness's prior inconsistent statement is not admissible unless the witness is first examined about the statement and fails to unequivocally admit making the statement.

(5) *Opposing Party's Statement.* This subdivision (a) does not apply to an opposing party's statement under Rule 801(e)(2).

(b) Witness's Bias or Interest.

(1) *Foundation Requirement.* When examining a witness about the witness's bias or interest, a party must first tell the witness the circumstances or statements that tend to show the witness's bias or interest. If examining a witness about a statement—whether oral or written—to prove the witness's bias or interest, a party must tell the witness:

(A) the contents of the statement;

(B) the time and place of the statement; and

(C) the person to whom the statement was made.

(2) *Need Not Show Written Statement.* If a party uses a written statement to prove the witness's bias or interest, a party need not show the statement to the witness before inquiring about it, but must, upon request, show it to opposing counsel.

(3) *Opportunity to Explain or Deny.* A witness must be given the opportunity to explain or deny the circumstances or statements that tend to show the witness's bias or interest. And the witness's proponent may present evidence to rebut the charge of bias or interest.

(4) *Extrinsic Evidence.* Extrinsic evidence of a witness's bias or interest is not admissible unless the witness is first examined about the bias or interest and fails to unequivocally admit it.

(c) **Witness's Prior Consistent Statement.** Unless Rule 801(e)(1)(B) provides otherwise, a witness's prior consistent statement is not admissible if offered solely to enhance the witness's credibility.

Comment to 2015 restyling: The amended rule retains the requirement that a witness be given an opportunity to explain or deny (a) a prior inconsistent statement or (b) the circumstances or a statement showing the witness's bias or interest, but this requirement is not imposed on the examining attorney. A witness may have to wait until redirect examination to explain a prior inconsistent statement or the circumstances or a statement that shows bias. But the impeaching attorney still is not permitted to introduce extrinsic evidence of the witness's prior inconsistent statement or bias unless the witness has first been examined about the statement or bias and has failed to unequivocally admit it. All other changes to the rule are intended to be stylistic only.

RULE 614. EXCLUDING WITNESSES

At a party's request, the court must order witnesses excluded so that they cannot hear other witnesses' testimony. Or the court may do so on its own. But this rule does not authorize excluding:

(a) a party who is a natural person and, in civil cases, that person's spouse;

(b) after being designated as the party's representative by its attorney:

(1) in a civil case, an officer or employee of a party that is not a natural person; or

(2) in a criminal case, a defendant that is not a natural person;

(c) a person whose presence a party shows to be essential to presenting the party's claim or defense; or

(d) the victim in a criminal case, unless the court determines that the victim's testimony would be materially affected by hearing other testimony at the trial.

RULE 615. PRODUCING A WITNESS'S STATEMENT IN CRIMINAL CASES

(a) **Motion to Produce.** After a witness other than the defendant testifies on direct examination, the court, on motion of a party who did not call the witness, must order an attorney for the state or the defendant and the defendant's attorney to produce, for the examination and use of the moving party, any statement of the witness that:

(1) is in their possession;

(2) relates to the subject matter of the witness's testimony; and

(3) has not previously been produced.

(b) **Producing the Entire Statement.** If the entire statement relates to the subject matter of the witness's testimony, the court must order that the statement be delivered to the moving party.

(c) **Producing a Redacted Statement.** If the party who called the witness claims that the statement contains information that does not relate to the subject matter of the witness's testimony, the court must inspect the statement in camera. After excising any unrelated portions, the court must order delivery of the redacted statement to the moving party. If a party objects to an excision, the court must preserve the entire statement with the excised portion indicated, under seal, as part of the record.

(d) **Recess to Examine a Statement.** If the court orders production of a witness's statement, the court, on request, must recess the proceedings to allow the moving party time to examine the statement and prepare for its use.

(e) Sanction for Failure to Produce or Deliver a Statement. If the party who called the witness disobeys an order to produce or deliver a statement, the court must strike the witness's testimony from the record. If an attorney for the state disobeys the order, the court must declare a mistrial if justice so requires.

(f) "Statement" Defined. As used in this rule, a witness's "statement" means:

(1) a written statement that the witness makes and signs, or otherwise adopts or approves;

(2) a substantially verbatim, contemporaneously recorded recital of the witness's oral statement that is contained in any recording or any transcription of a recording; or

(3) the witness's statement to a grand jury, however taken or recorded, or a transcription of such a statement.

Comment to 2016 change: The Michael Morton Act, codified at Texas Code of Criminal Procedure art. 39.14, affords defendants substantial pre-trial discovery, requiring the state, upon request from the defendant, to produce and permit the defendant to inspect and copy various items, including witness statements. In many instances, therefore, art. 39.14 eliminates the need, after the witness testifies on direct examination, for a defendant to request, and the court to order, production of a witness's statement.

But art. 39.14 does not entirely eliminate the need for in-trial discovery of witness statements. Art. 39.14 does not extend equivalent discovery rights to the prosecution, and so prosecutors will still need to use Rule 615 to obtain witness statements of defense witnesses. Moreover, some defendants may fail to exercise their discovery rights under art. 39.14 and so may wish to obtain a witness statement under Rule 615. In addition, the Michael Morton Act applies only to the prosecution of offenses committed after December 31, 2013. Defendants on trial for offenses committed before then have no right to pre-trial discovery of the witness statements of prosecution witnesses.

Consequently, Rule 615(a) has been amended to account for the changed pre-trial discovery regime introduced by the Michael Morton Act. If a party's adversary has already produced a witness's statement—whether through formal discovery under art. 39.14 or through more informal means—Rule 615(a) no longer gives a party the right to obtain, after the witness testifies on direct examination, a court order for production of the witness's statement. But if a party's adversary has not already produced a witness's statement, the party may still use Rule 615(a) to request and obtain a court order requiring production of the witness's statement after the witness finishes testifying on direct examination.

Comment to 1998 change: This is prior Rule of Criminal Evidence 614.

ARTICLE VII. OPINIONS & EXPERT TESTIMONY

RULE 701. OPINION TESTIMONY BY LAY WITNESSES

If a witness is not testifying as an expert, testimony in the form of an opinion is limited to one that is:

(a) rationally based on the witness's perception; and

(b) helpful to clearly understanding the witness's testimony or to determining a fact in issue.

Comment to 2015 restyling: All references to an "inference" have been deleted because this makes the Rule flow better and easier to read, and because any "inference" is covered by the broader term "opinion." Courts have not made substantive decisions on the basis of any distinction between an opinion and an inference. No change in current practice is intended.

RULE 702. TESTIMONY BY EXPERT WITNESSES

A witness who is qualified as an expert by knowledge, skill, experience, training, or education may testify in the form of an opinion or otherwise if the expert's scientific, technical, or other specialized knowledge will help the trier of fact to understand the evidence or to determine a fact in issue.

RULE 703. BASES OF AN EXPERT'S OPINION TESTIMONY

An expert may base an opinion on facts or data in the case that the expert has been made aware of, reviewed, or personally observed. If experts in the particular field would reasonably rely on those kinds of facts or data in forming an opinion on the subject, they need not be admissible for the opinion to be admitted.

Comment to 2015 restyling: All references to an "inference" have been deleted because this makes the Rule flow better and easier to read, and because any "inference" is covered by the broader term "opinion." Courts have not made substantive decisions on the basis of any distinction between an opinion and an inference. No change in current practice is intended.

Comment to 1998 change: The former Civil Rule referred to facts or data "perceived by or reviewed by" the expert. The former Criminal Rule referred to facts or data "perceived by or made known to" the expert. The terminology is now conformed, but no change in meaning is intended.

RULE 704. OPINION ON AN ULTIMATE ISSUE

An opinion is not objectionable just because it embraces an ultimate issue.

RULE 705. DISCLOSING THE UNDERLYING FACTS OR DATA & EXAMINING AN EXPERT ABOUT THEM

(a) Stating an Opinion Without Disclosing the Underlying Facts or Data. Unless the court orders otherwise, an expert may state an opinion—and give the reasons for it—without first testifying to the underlying facts or data. But the expert may be required to disclose those facts or data on cross-examination.

(b) Voir Dire Examination of an Expert About the Underlying Facts or Data. Before an expert states an opinion or discloses the underlying facts or data, an adverse party in a civil case may—or in a criminal case must—be permitted to examine the expert about the underlying facts or data. This examination must take place outside the jury's hearing.

(c) Admissibility of Opinion. An expert's opinion is inadmissible if the underlying facts or data do not provide a sufficient basis for the opinion.

(d) When Otherwise Inadmissible Underlying Facts or Data May Be Disclosed; Instructing the Jury. If the underlying facts or data would otherwise be inadmissible, the proponent of the opinion may not disclose them to the jury if their probative value in helping the jury evaluate the opinion is outweighed by their prejudicial effect. If the court allows the proponent to disclose those facts or data the court must, upon timely request, restrict the evidence to its proper scope and instruct the jury accordingly.

Comment to 2015 restyling: All references to an "inference" have been deleted because this makes the Rule flow better and easier to read, and because any "inference" is covered by the broader term "opinion." Courts have not made substantive decisions on the basis of any distinction between an opinion and an inference. No change in current practice is intended.

Comment to 1998 change: Paragraphs (b), (c), and (d) are based on the former Criminal Rule and are made applicable to civil cases. This rule does not preclude a party in any case from conducting a *voir dire* examination into the qualifications of an expert.

RULE 706. AUDIT IN CIVIL CASES

Notwithstanding any other evidence rule, the court must admit an auditor's verified report prepared under Rule of Civil Procedure 172 and offered by a party. If a party files exceptions to the report, a party may offer evidence supporting the exceptions to contradict the report.

ARTICLE VIII. HEARSAY
RULE 801. DEFINITIONS THAT APPLY TO THIS ARTICLE; EXCLUSIONS FROM HEARSAY

(a) Statement. "Statement" means a person's oral or written verbal expression, or nonver-

bal conduct that a person intended as a substitute for verbal expression.

(b) Declarant. "Declarant" means the person who made the statement.

(c) Matter Asserted. "Matter asserted" means:

(1) any matter a declarant explicitly asserts; and

(2) any matter implied by a statement, if the probative value of the statement as offered flows from the declarant's belief about the matter.

(d) Hearsay. "Hearsay" means a statement that:

(1) the declarant does not make while testifying at the current trial or hearing; and

(2) a party offers in evidence to prove the truth of the matter asserted in the statement.

(e) Statements That Are Not Hearsay. A statement that meets the following conditions is not hearsay:

(1) *A Declarant-Witness's Prior Statement.* The declarant testifies and is subject to cross-examination about a prior statement, and the statement:

(A) is inconsistent with the declarant's testimony and:

(i) when offered in a civil case, was given under penalty of perjury at a trial, hearing, or other proceeding or in a deposition; or

(ii) when offered in a criminal case, was given under penalty of perjury at a trial, hearing, or other proceeding—except a grand jury proceeding—or in a deposition;

(B) is consistent with the declarant's testimony and is offered to rebut an express or implied charge that the declarant recently fabricated it or acted from a recent improper influence or motive in so testifying; or

(C) identifies a person as someone the declarant perceived earlier.

(2) *An Opposing Party's Statement.* The statement is offered against an opposing party and:

(A) was made by the party in an individual or representative capacity;

(B) is one the party manifested that it adopted or believed to be true;

(C) was made by a person whom the party authorized to make a statement on the subject;

(D) was made by the party's agent or employee on a matter within the scope of that relationship and while it existed; or

(E) was made by the party's coconspirator during and in furtherance of the conspiracy.

(3) *A Deponent's Statement.* In a civil case, the statement was made in a deposition taken in the same proceeding. "Same proceeding" is defined in Rule of Civil Procedure 203.6(b). The deponent's unavailability as a witness is not a requirement for admissibility.

Comment to 2015 restyling: Statements falling under the hearsay exclusion provided by Rule 801(e)(2) are no longer referred to as "admissions" in the title to the subdivision. The term "admissions" is confusing because not all statements covered by the exclusion are admissions in the colloquial sense—a statement can be within the exclusion even if it "admitted" nothing and was not against the party's interest when made. The term "admissions" also raises confusion in comparison with the Rule 803(24) exception for declarations against interest. No change in application of the exclusion is intended.

The deletion of former Rule 801(e)(1)(D), which cross-references Code of Criminal Procedure art. 38.071, is not intended as a substantive change. Including this cross-reference made sense when the Texas Rules of Criminal Evidence were first promulgated, but with subsequent changes to the statutory provision, its inclusion is no longer appropriate. The version of article 38.071 that was initially cross-referenced in the Rules of Criminal Evidence required the declarant-victim to be available to testify at the trial. That requirement has since been deleted from the statute, and the statute no longer requires either the availability or testimony of the declarant-victim. Thus, cross-referencing the statute in Rule 801(e)(1), which applies only when the declarant testifies at trial about the prior statement, no longer makes sense. Moreover, article 38.071 is but one of a number of statutes that mandate the admission of certain hearsay statements in particular circumstances. *See, e.g.,* Code of Criminal Procedure art. 38.072; Family Code §§54.031, 104.002, 104.006. These statutory provisions take precedence over the general rule excluding hearsay, see Rules 101(c) and 802, and there is no apparent justification for cross-referencing article 38.071 and not all other such provisions.

RULE 802. THE RULE AGAINST HEARSAY

Hearsay is not admissible unless any of the following provides otherwise:

- a statute;
- these rules; or
- other rules prescribed under statutory authority.

Inadmissible hearsay admitted without objection may not be denied probative value merely because it is hearsay.

RULE 803. EXCEPTIONS TO THE RULE AGAINST HEARSAY— REGARDLESS OF WHETHER THE DECLARANT IS AVAILABLE AS A WITNESS

The following are not excluded by the rule against hearsay, regardless of whether the declarant is available as a witness:

(1) *Present Sense Impression.* A statement describing or explaining an event or condition, made while or immediately after the declarant perceived it.

(2) *Excited Utterance.* A statement relating to a startling event or condition, made while the declarant was under the stress of excitement that it caused.

(3) *Then-Existing Mental, Emotional, or Physical Condition.* A statement of the declarant's then-existing state of mind (such as motive, intent, or plan) or emotional, sensory, or physical condition (such as mental feeling, pain, or bodily health), but not including a statement of memory or belief to prove the fact remembered or believed unless it relates to the validity or terms of the declarant's will.

(4) *Statement Made for Medical Diagnosis or Treatment.* A statement that:

(A) is made for—and is reasonably pertinent to—medical diagnosis or treatment; and

(B) describes medical history; past or present symptoms or sensations; their inception; or their general cause.

(5) *Recorded Recollection.* A record that:

(A) is on a matter the witness once knew about but now cannot recall well enough to testify fully and accurately;

(B) was made or adopted by the witness when the matter was fresh in the witness's memory; and

(C) accurately reflects the witness's knowledge, unless the circumstances of the record's preparation cast doubt on its trustworthiness.

If admitted, the record may be read into evidence but may be received as an exhibit only if offered by an adverse party.

(6) *Records of a Regularly Conducted Activity.* A record of an act, event, condition, opinion, or diagnosis if:

(A) the record was made at or near the time by—or from information transmitted by—someone with knowledge;

(B) the record was kept in the course of a regularly conducted business activity;

(C) making the record was a regular practice of that activity;

(D) all these conditions are shown by the testimony of the custodian or another qualified witness, or by an affidavit or unsworn declaration that complies with Rule 902(10); and

(E) the opponent fails to demonstrate that the source of information or the method or circumstances of preparation indicate a lack of trustworthiness.

"Business" as used in this paragraph includes every kind of regular organized activity whether conducted for profit or not.

(7) *Absence of a Record of a Regularly Conducted Activity.* Evidence that a matter is not included in a record described in paragraph (6) if:

(A) the evidence is admitted to prove that the matter did not occur or exist;

(B) a record was regularly kept for a matter of that kind; and

(C) the opponent fails to show that the possible source of the information or other circumstances indicate a lack of trustworthiness.

(8) *Public Records.* A record or statement of a public office if:

(A) it sets out:

(i) the office's activities;

(ii) a matter observed while under a legal duty to report, but not including, in a criminal case, a matter observed by law-enforcement personnel; or

(iii) in a civil case or against the government in a criminal case, factual findings from a legally authorized investigation; and

(B) the opponent fails to demonstrate that the source of information or other circumstances indicate a lack of trustworthiness.

(9) *Public Records of Vital Statistics.* A record of a birth, death, or marriage, if reported to a public office in accordance with a legal duty.

(10) *Absence of a Public Record.* Testimony—or a certification under Rule 902—that a diligent search failed to disclose a public record or statement if the testimony or certification is admitted to prove that:

(A) the record or statement does not exist; or

(B) a matter did not occur or exist, if a public office regularly kept a record or statement for a matter of that kind.

(11) *Records of Religious Organizations Concerning Personal or Family History.* A statement of birth, legitimacy, ancestry, marriage, divorce, death, relationship by blood or marriage, or similar facts of personal or family history, contained in a regularly kept record of a religious organization.

(12) *Certificates of Marriage, Baptism, and Similar Ceremonies.* A statement of fact contained in a certificate:

(A) made by a person who is authorized by a religious organization or by law to perform the act certified;

(B) attesting that the person performed a marriage or similar ceremony or administered a sacrament; and

(C) purporting to have been issued at the time of the act or within a reasonable time after it.

(13) *Family Records.* A statement of fact about personal or family history contained in a family record, such as a Bible, genealogy, chart, engraving on a ring, inscription on a portrait, or engraving on an urn or burial marker.

(14) *Records of Documents That Affect an Interest in Property.* The record of a document that purports to establish or affect an interest in property if:

(A) the record is admitted to prove the content of the original recorded document, along with its signing and its delivery by each person who purports to have signed it;

(B) the record is kept in a public office; and

(C) a statute authorizes recording documents of that kind in that office.

(15) *Statements in Documents That Affect an Interest in Property.* A statement contained in a document that purports to establish or affect an interest in property if the matter stated was relevant to the document's purpose—unless later dealings with the property are inconsistent with the truth of the statement or the purport of the document.

(16) *Statements in Ancient Documents.* A statement in a document that is at least 20 years old and whose authenticity is established.

(17) *Market Reports and Similar Commercial Publications.* Market quotations, lists, directories, or other compilations that are generally relied on by the public or by persons in particular occupations.

(18) *Statements in Learned Treatises, Periodicals, or Pamphlets.* A statement contained in a treatise, periodical, or pamphlet if:

(A) the statement is called to the attention of an expert witness on cross-examination or relied on by the expert on direct examination; and

(B) the publication is established as a reliable authority by the expert's admission or testimony, by another expert's testimony, or by judicial notice.

If admitted, the statement may be read into evidence but not received as an exhibit.

(19) *Reputation Concerning Personal or Family History.* A reputation among a person's family by blood, adoption, or marriage—or among a person's associates or in the community—concerning the person's birth, adoption, legitimacy, ancestry, marriage, divorce, death, relationship by blood, adoption, or marriage, or similar facts of personal or family history.

(20) *Reputation Concerning Boundaries or General History.* A reputation in a community—arising before the controversy—concerning boundaries of land in the community or customs that affect the land, or concerning general historical events important to that community, state, or nation.

(21) *Reputation Concerning Character.* A reputation among a person's associates or in the community concerning the person's character.

(22) *Judgment of a Previous Conviction.* Evidence of a final judgment of conviction if:

(A) it is offered in a civil case and:

  (i) the judgment was entered after a trial or guilty plea, but not a nolo contendere plea;

  (ii) the conviction was for a felony;

  (iii) the evidence is admitted to prove any fact essential to the judgment; and

  (iv) an appeal of the conviction is not pending; or

(B) it is offered in a criminal case and:

  (i) the judgment was entered after a trial or a guilty or nolo contendere plea;

  (ii) the conviction was for a criminal offense;

  (iii) the evidence is admitted to prove any fact essential to the judgment;

  (iv) when offered by the prosecutor for a purpose other than impeachment, the judgment was against the defendant; and

  (v) an appeal of the conviction is not pending.

(23) *Judgments Involving Personal, Family, or General History or a Boundary.* A judgment that is admitted to prove a matter of personal, family, or general history, or boundaries, if the matter:

(A) was essential to the judgment; and

(B) could be proved by evidence of reputation.

(24) *Statement Against Interest.* A statement that:

(A) a reasonable person in the declarant's position would have made only if the person believed it to be true because, when made, it was so contrary to the declarant's proprietary or pecuniary interest or had so great a tendency to invalidate the declarant's claim against someone else or to expose the declarant to civil or criminal liability or to make the declarant an object of hatred, ridicule, or disgrace; and

(B) is supported by corroborating circumstances that clearly indicate its trustworthiness, if it is offered in a criminal case as one that tends to expose the declarant to criminal liability.

RULE 804. EXCEPTIONS TO THE RULE AGAINST HEARSAY—WHEN THE DECLARANT IS UNAVAILABLE AS A WITNESS

(a) Criteria for Being Unavailable. A declarant is considered to be unavailable as a witness if the declarant:

(1) is exempted from testifying about the subject matter of the declarant's statement because the court rules that a privilege applies;

(2) refuses to testify about the subject matter despite a court order to do so;

(3) testifies to not remembering the subject matter;

(4) cannot be present or testify at the trial or hearing because of death or a then-existing infirmity, physical illness, or mental illness; or

(5) is absent from the trial or hearing and the statement's proponent has not been able, by process or other reasonable means, to procure the declarant's attendance or testimony.

But this subdivision (a) does not apply if the statement's proponent procured or wrongfully caused the declarant's unavailability as a witness in order to prevent the declarant from attending or testifying.

(b) The Exceptions. The following are not excluded by the rule against hearsay if the declarant is unavailable as a witness:

(1) *Former Testimony.* Testimony that:

(A) when offered in a civil case:

(i) was given as a witness at a trial or hearing of the current or a different proceeding or in a deposition in a different proceeding; and

(ii) is now offered against a party and the party—or a person with similar interest—had an opportunity and similar motive to develop the testimony by direct, cross-, or redirect examination.

(B) when offered in a criminal case:

(i) was given as a witness at a trial or hearing of the current or a different proceeding; and

(ii) is now offered against a party who had an opportunity and similar motive to develop it by direct, cross-, or redirect examination; or

(iii) was taken in a deposition under—and is now offered in accordance with—chapter 39 of the Code of Criminal Procedure.

(2) *Statement Under the Belief of Imminent Death.* A statement that the declarant, while believing the declarant's death to be imminent, made about its cause or circumstances.

(3) *Statement of Personal or Family History.* A statement about:

(A) the declarant's own birth, adoption, legitimacy, ancestry, marriage, divorce, relationship by blood, adoption or marriage, or similar facts of personal or family history, even though the declarant had no way of acquiring personal knowledge about that fact; or

(B) another person concerning any of these facts, as well as death, if the declarant was related to the person by blood, adoption, or marriage or was so intimately associated with the person's family that the declarant's information is likely to be accurate.

RULE 805. HEARSAY WITHIN HEARSAY

Hearsay within hearsay is not excluded by the rule against hearsay if each part of the combined statements conforms with an exception to the rule.

RULE 806. ATTACKING & SUPPORTING THE DECLARANT'S CREDIBILITY

When a hearsay statement—or a statement described in Rule 801(e)(2)(C), (D), or (E), or, in a civil case, a statement described in Rule 801(e)(3)—has been admitted in evidence, the declarant's credibility may be attacked, and then supported, by any evidence that would be admissible for those purposes if the declarant had testified as a witness. The court may admit evidence of the declarant's statement or conduct, offered to impeach the declarant, regardless of when it occurred or whether the declarant had an opportunity to explain or deny it. If the party against whom the statement was admitted calls the declarant as a witness, the party may examine the declarant on the statement as if on cross-examination.

ARTICLE IX. AUTHENTICATION & IDENTIFICATION

RULE 901. AUTHENTICATING OR IDENTIFYING EVIDENCE

(a) In General. To satisfy the requirement of authenticating or identifying an item of evidence, the proponent must produce evidence sufficient to support a finding that the item is what the proponent claims it is.

(b) Examples. The following are examples only—not a complete list—of evidence that satisfies the requirement:

(1) *Testimony of a Witness with Knowledge.* Testimony that an item is what it is claimed to be.

(2) *Nonexpert Opinion About Handwriting.* A nonexpert's opinion that handwriting is genuine, based on a familiarity with it that was not acquired for the current litigation.

(3) *Comparison by an Expert Witness or the Trier of Fact.* A comparison by an expert witness or the trier of fact with a specimen that the court has found is genuine.

(4) *Distinctive Characteristics and the Like.* The appearance, contents, substance, internal patterns, or other distinctive characteristics of the item, taken together with all the circumstances.

(5) *Opinion About a Voice.* An opinion identifying a person's voice—whether heard firsthand or through mechanical or electronic transmission or recording—based on hearing the voice at any time under circumstances that connect it with the alleged speaker.

(6) *Evidence About a Telephone Conversation.* For a telephone conversation, evidence that a call was made to the number assigned at the time to:

(A) a particular person, if circumstances, including self-identification, show that the person answering was the one called; or

(B) a particular business, if the call was made to a business and the call related to business reasonably transacted over the telephone.

(7) *Evidence About Public Records.* Evidence that:

(A) a document was recorded or filed in a public office as authorized by law; or

(B) a purported public record or statement is from the office where items of this kind are kept.

(8) *Evidence About Ancient Documents or Data Compilations.* For a document or data compilation, evidence that it:

(A) is in a condition that creates no suspicion about its authenticity;

(B) was in a place where, if authentic, it would likely be; and

(C) is at least 20 years old when offered.

(9) *Evidence About a Process or System.* Evidence describing a process or system and showing that it produces an accurate result.

(10) *Methods Provided by a Statute or Rule.* Any method of authentication or identification allowed by a statute or other rule prescribed under statutory authority.

RULE 902. EVIDENCE THAT IS SELF-AUTHENTICATING

The following items of evidence are self-authenticating; they require no extrinsic evidence of authenticity in order to be admitted:

(1) *Domestic Public Documents That Are Sealed and Signed.* A document that bears:

(A) a seal purporting to be that of the United States; any state, district, commonwealth, territory, or insular possession of the United States; the former Panama Canal Zone; the Trust Territory of the Pacific Islands; a political subdivision of any of these entities; or a department, agency, or officer of any entity named above; and

(B) a signature purporting to be an execution or attestation.

(2) *Domestic Public Documents That Are Not Sealed But Are Signed and Certified.* A document that bears no seal if:

(A) it bears the signature of an officer or employee of an entity named in Rule 902(1)(A); and

(B) another public officer who has a seal and official duties within that same entity certifies under seal—or its equivalent—that the signer has the official capacity and that the signature is genuine.

(3) *Foreign Public Documents.* A document that purports to be signed or attested by a person who is authorized by a foreign country's law to do so.

(A) *In General.* The document must be accompanied by a final certification that certifies the genuineness of the signature and official position of the signer or attester—or of any foreign official whose certificate of genuineness relates to the signature or attestation or is in a chain of certificates of genuineness relating to the signature or attestation. The certification may be made by a secretary of a United States embassy or legation; by a consul general, vice consul, or consular agent of the United States; or by a diplomatic or consular official of the foreign country assigned or accredited to the United States.

(B) *If Parties Have Reasonable Opportunity to Investigate.* If all parties have been given a reasonable opportunity to investigate the document's authenticity and accuracy, the court may, for good cause, either:

(i) order that it be treated as presumptively authentic without final certification; or

(ii) allow it to be evidenced by an attested summary with or without final certification.

(C) *If a Treaty Abolishes or Displaces the Final Certification Requirement.* If the United States and the foreign country in which the official record is located are parties to a treaty or convention that abolishes or displaces the final certification requirement, the record and attestation must be certified under the terms of the treaty or convention.

(4) *Certified Copies of Public Records.* A copy of an official record—or a copy of a document that was recorded or filed in a public office as authorized by law—if the copy is certified as correct by:

(A) the custodian or another person authorized to make the certification; or

(B) a certificate that complies with Rule 902(1), (2), or (3), a statute, or a rule prescribed under statutory authority.

(5) *Official Publications.* A book, pamphlet, or other publication purporting to be issued by a public authority.

(6) *Newspapers and Periodicals.* Printed material purporting to be a newspaper or periodical.

(7) *Trade Inscriptions and the Like.* An inscription, sign, tag, or label purporting to have been affixed in the course of business and indicating origin, ownership, or control.

(8) *Acknowledged Documents.* A document accompanied by a certificate of acknowledgment that is lawfully executed by a notary public or another officer who is authorized to take acknowledgments.

(9) *Commercial Paper and Related Documents.* Commercial paper, a signature on it, and related documents, to the extent allowed by general commercial law.

(10) *Business Records Accompanied by Affidavit.* The original or a copy of a record that meets the requirements of Rule 803(6) or (7), if the record is accompanied by an affidavit that complies with subparagraph (B) of this rule and any other requirements of law, and the record and affidavit are served in accordance with subparagraph (A). For good cause shown, the court may order that a business record be treated as presumptively authentic even if the proponent fails to comply with subparagraph (A).

(A) *Service Requirement.* The proponent of a record must serve the record and the accompanying affidavit on each other party to the case at least 14 days before trial. The record and affidavit may be served by any method permitted by Rule of Civil Procedure 21a.

(B) *Form of Affidavit.* An affidavit is sufficient if it includes the following language, but this form is not exclusive. The proponent may use an unsworn declaration made under penalty of perjury in place of an affidavit.

1. I am the custodian of records [*or* I am an employee or owner] of _____ and am familiar with the manner in which its records are created and maintained by virtue of my duties and responsibilities.

2. Attached are ____ pages of records. These are the original records or exact duplicates of the original records.

3. The records were made at or near the time of each act, event, condition, opinion, or diagnosis set forth. [*or* It is the regular practice of _____ to make this type of record at or near the time of each act, event, condition, opinion, or diagnosis set forth in the record.]

4. The records were made by, or from information transmitted by, persons with knowledge of the matters set forth. [*or* It is the regular practice of _____ for this type of record to be made by, or from information transmitted by, persons with knowledge of the matters set forth in them.]

5. The records were kept in the course of regularly conducted business activity.

[*or* It is the regular practice of _____ to keep this type of record in the course of regularly conducted business activity.]

6. It is the regular practice of the business activity to make the records.

(11) *Presumptions Under a Statute or Rule.* A signature, document, or anything else that a statute or rule prescribed under statutory authority declares to be presumptively or prima facie genuine or authentic.

Comment to 2014 change: At the direction of the Legislature, the requirement that records be filed with the court before trial has been removed. *See* Act of May 17, 2013, 83rd Leg., R.S., ch. 560, §3, 2013 Tex. Gen. Laws 1509, 1510 (SB 679). The word "affidavit" in this rule includes an unsworn declaration made under penalty of perjury. Tex. Civ. Prac. & Rem. Code §132.001. The reference to "any other requirements of law" incorporates the requirements of Sections 18.001 and 18.002 of the Civil Practice and Remedies Code for affidavits offered as prima facie proof of the cost or necessity of services or medical expenses. The form medical expenses affidavit that was added to this rule in 2013 has been removed as unnecessary. It can now be found in Section 18.002(b-1) of the Civil Practice and Remedies Code.

Comment to 2013 change: Rule 902(10)(c) is added to provide a form affidavit for proof of medical expenses. The affidavit is intended to comport with Section 41.0105 of the Civil Practice and Remedies Code, which allows evidence of only those medical expenses that have been paid or will be paid, after any required credits or adjustments. *See Haygood v. Escabedo*, 356 S.W.3d 390 (Tex. 2011). The records attached to the affidavit must also meet the admissibility standard of *Haygood*. 356 S.W.3d at 399-400 ("[O]nly evidence of recoverable medical expenses is admissible at trial.").

RULE 903. SUBSCRIBING WITNESS'S TESTIMONY

A subscribing witness's testimony is necessary to authenticate a writing only if required by the law of the jurisdiction that governs its validity.

ARTICLE X. CONTENTS OF WRITINGS, RECORDINGS, & PHOTOGRAPHS

RULE 1001. DEFINITIONS THAT APPLY TO THIS ARTICLE

In this article:

(a) A "writing" consists of letters, words, numbers, or their equivalent set down in any form.

(b) A "recording" consists of letters, words, numbers, or their equivalent recorded in any manner.

(c) A "photograph" means a photographic image or its equivalent stored in any form.

(d) An "original" of a writing or recording means the writing or recording itself or any counterpart intended to have the same effect by the person who executed or issued it. For electronically stored information, "original" means any printout—or other output readable by sight—if it accurately reflects the information. An "original" of a photograph includes the negative or a print from it.

(e) A "duplicate" means a counterpart produced by a mechanical, photographic, chemical, electronic, or other equivalent process or technique that accurately reproduces the original.

RULE 1002. REQUIREMENT OF THE ORIGINAL

An original writing, recording, or photograph is required in order to prove its content unless these rules or other law provides otherwise.

RULE 1003. ADMISSIBILITY OF DUPLICATES

A duplicate is admissible to the same extent as the original unless a question is raised about the original's authenticity or the circumstances make it unfair to admit the duplicate.

RULE 1004. ADMISSIBILITY OF OTHER EVIDENCE OF CONTENT

An original is not required and other evidence of the content of a writing, recording, or photograph is admissible if:

(a) all the originals are lost or destroyed, unless the proponent lost or destroyed them in bad faith;

(b) an original cannot be obtained by any available judicial process;

(c) an original is not located in Texas;

(d) the party against whom the original would be offered had control of the original; was at that time put on notice, by pleadings or otherwise, that the original would be a subject of proof at the trial or hearing; and fails to produce it at the trial or hearing; or

(e) the writing, recording, or photograph is not closely related to a controlling issue.

RULE 1005. COPIES OF PUBLIC RECORDS TO PROVE CONTENT

The proponent may use a copy to prove the content of an official record—or of a document that was recorded or filed in a public office as authorized by law—if these conditions are met: the record or document is otherwise admissible; and the copy is certified as correct in accordance with Rule 902(4) or is testified to be correct by a witness who has compared it with the original. If no such copy can be obtained by reasonable diligence, then the proponent may use other evidence to prove the content.

RULE 1006. SUMMARIES TO PROVE CONTENT

The proponent may use a summary, chart, or calculation to prove the content of voluminous writings, recordings, or photographs that cannot be conveniently examined in court. The proponent must make the originals or duplicates available for examination or copying, or both, by other parties at a reasonable time and place. And the court may order the proponent to produce them in court.

RULE 1007. TESTIMONY OR STATEMENT OF A PARTY TO PROVE CONTENT

The proponent may prove the content of a writing, recording, or photograph by the testimony, deposition, or written statement of the party against whom the evidence is offered. The proponent need not account for the original.

RULE 1008. FUNCTIONS OF THE COURT & JURY

Ordinarily, the court determines whether the proponent has fulfilled the factual conditions for admitting other evidence of the content of a writing, recording, or photograph under Rule 1004 or 1005. But in a jury trial, the jury determines—in accordance with Rule 104(b)—any issue about whether:

(a) an asserted writing, recording, or photograph ever existed;

(b) another one produced at the trial or hearing is the original; or

(c) other evidence of content accurately reflects the content.

RULE 1009. TRANSLATING A FOREIGN LANGUAGE DOCUMENT

(a) Submitting a Translation. A translation of a foreign language document is admissible if, at least 45 days before trial, the proponent serves on all parties:

(1) the translation and the underlying foreign language document; and

(2) a qualified translator's affidavit or unsworn declaration that sets forth the translator's qualifications and certifies that the translation is accurate.

(b) Objection. When objecting to a translation's accuracy, a party should specifically indicate its inaccuracies and offer an accurate translation. A party must serve the objection on all parties at least 15 days before trial.

(c) Effect of Failing to Object or Submit a Conflicting Translation. If the underlying foreign language document is otherwise admissible, the court must admit—and may not allow a party to attack the accuracy of—a translation submitted under subdivision (a) unless the party has:

(1) submitted a conflicting translation under subdivision (a); or

(2) objected to the translation under subdivision (b).

(d) Effect of Objecting or Submitting a Conflicting Translation. If conflicting translations are submitted under subdivision (a) or an objection is made under subdivision (b), the court must determine whether there is a genuine issue about the accuracy of a material part of the translation. If so, the trier of fact must resolve the issue.

(e) Qualified Translator May Testify. Except for subdivision (c), this rule does not preclude a party from offering the testimony of a qualified translator to translate a foreign language document.

(f) Time Limits. On a party's motion and for good cause, the court may alter this rule's time limits.

(g) Court-Appointed Translator. If necessary, the court may appoint a qualified translator. The reasonable value of the translator's services must be taxed as court costs.

Comment to 1998 change: This is a new rule.

ARTICLE I: GENERAL PROVISIONS

Article I of the Texas Rules of Evidence contains a series of broad provisions that govern all proffers of and objections to evidence. Rule 101 outlines the general scope of the Rules, and Rule 102 provides guidance for trial judges facing evidentiary situations that the Rules do not specifically answer. The rest of the rules in Article I outline the specific mechanisms for offering and excluding evidence at trial, preserving error for appeal, defining the functions of the judge and the jury, and ensuring that the trial record fairly and completely reflects the truth. These rules are the nuts and bolts of making and meeting objections and offering evidence.

The law on objections is not complex or difficult, but the vast majority of appellate issues are rejected because attorneys do not preserve their objections properly or ensure that the trial record supports their arguments. The Rules are designed to uphold the trial judge's rulings on the admission or exclusion of evidence unless a particular error is clearly and specifically pointed out at trial. For the most part, Article I codifies earlier Texas civil and criminal law and follows the federal requirements for objections, offers of proof, preservation of error, remainder evidence, and the division of judge and jury functions.

RULE 101
TITLE, SCOPE, & APPLICABILITY OF THE RULES; DEFINITIONS

(a) Title. These rules may be cited as the Texas Rules of Evidence.

(b) Scope. These rules apply to proceedings in Texas courts except as otherwise provided in subdivisions (d)-(f).

(c) Rules on Privilege. The rules on privilege apply to all stages of a case or proceeding.

(d) Exception for Constitutional or Statutory Provisions or Other Rules. Despite these rules, a court must admit or exclude evidence if required to do so by the United States or Texas Constitution, a federal or Texas statute, or a rule prescribed by the United States or Texas Supreme Court or the Texas Court of Criminal Appeals. If possible, a court should resolve by reasonable construction any inconsistency between these rules and applicable constitutional or statutory provisions or other rules.

(e) Exceptions. These rules—except for those on privilege—do not apply to:

(1) the court's determination, under Rule 104(a), on a preliminary question of fact governing admissibility;

(2) grand jury proceedings; and

(3) the following miscellaneous proceedings:

(A) an application for habeas corpus in extradition, rendition, or interstate detainer proceedings;

(B) an inquiry by the court under Code of Criminal Procedure article 46B.004 to determine whether evidence exists that would support a finding that the defendant may be incompetent to stand trial;

(C) bail proceedings other than hearings to deny, revoke, or increase bail;

(D) hearings on justification for pretrial detention not involving bail;

(E) proceedings to issue a search or arrest warrant; and

(F) direct contempt determination proceedings.

(f) Exception for Justice Court Cases. These rules do not apply to justice court cases except as authorized by Texas Rule of Civil Procedure 500.3.

(g) Exception for Military Justice Hearings. The Texas Code of Military Justice, Tex. Gov't Code §§432.001-432.195, governs the admissibility of evidence in hearings held under that Code.

(h) Definitions. In these rules:

(1) "civil case" means a civil action or proceeding;

(2) "criminal case" means a criminal action or proceeding, including an examining trial;

(3) "public office" includes a public agency;

(4) "record" includes a memorandum, report, or data compilation;

(5) "rule prescribed by the United States or Texas Supreme Court or the Texas Court of Criminal Appeals" means a rule adopted by any of those courts under statutory authority;

(6) "unsworn declaration" means an unsworn declaration made in accordance with Tex. Civ. Prac. & Rem. Code §132.001; and

(7) a reference to any kind of written material or any other medium includes electronically stored information.

Notes and Comments

Comment to 2015 restyling: The reference to "hierarchical governance" in former Rule 101(c) has been deleted as unnecessary. The textual limitation of former Rule 101(c) to criminal cases has been eliminated. Courts in civil cases must also admit or exclude evidence when required to do so by constitutional or statutory provisions or other rules that take precedence over these rules. Likewise, the title to former Rule 101(d) has been changed to more accurately indicate the purpose and scope of the subdivision.

Comment to 1998 change: "Criminal proceedings" rather than "criminal cases" is used since that was the terminology used in the prior Rules of Criminal Evidence. In subpart (b), the reference to "trials before magistrates" comes from prior Criminal Rule 1101(a). In the prior Criminal Rules, both Rule 101 and Rule 1101 dealt with the same thing—the applicability of the rules. Thus, Rules 101(c) and (d) have been written to incorporate the provisions of former Criminal Rule 1101 and that rule is omitted.

COMMENTARY ON RULE 101

The current version of Rule 101 combines the former Civil and Criminal Rules[1] and inserts portions of former Criminal Rule 1101.[2] With one exception concerning the applicability of the Rules of Evidence at suppression hearings, no substantive change was

---

1.   The former Civil and Criminal Rules read:
RULE 101
TITLE AND SCOPE
   (a) Title. These rules shall be known and cited as the Texas Rules of Evidence.
   (b) Scope. Except as otherwise provided by statute, these rules govern civil proceedings in all courts of Texas other than small claims courts.
TEX. R. CIV. EVID. 101, 641-642 S.W.2d (Tex. Cases) xxxvi (1983, amended 1998) (current version at TEX. R. EVID. 101).

RULE 101
TITLE AND SCOPE
   (a) These rules shall be known and cited as the Texas Rules of Criminal Evidence.
   (b) These rules govern criminal proceedings in courts of Texas except where otherwise provided.
   (c) Hierarchical governance shall be in the following order: the Constitution of the United States, those federal statutes which control states under the supremacy clause, the Constitution of Texas, the Code of Criminal Procedure and the Penal Code, civil statutes, these rules, the common law of England. Where possible, inconsistency is to be removed by reasonable construction.
TEX. R. CRIM. EVID. 101, 701-702 S.W.2d (Tex. Cases) xxxii (1986, amended 1998) (current version at TEX. R. EVID. 101).
2.   *See* TEX. R. EVID. 101(e). Former Criminal Rule 1101, outlining the applicability of the Rules, read:
   (a) General Rule. These rules apply in criminal proceedings in all Texas courts and in examining trials before magistrates.
   (b) Rule of privilege. These rules with respect to privileges apply at all stages of all actions, cases, and proceedings.
   (c) Rules inapplicable. The rules (other than with respect to privileges) do not apply in the following situations:
      (1) *Preliminary questions of fact.* The determination of questions of fact preliminary to admissibility of evidence when the issue is to be determined by the court under Rule 104.
      (2) *Grand jury.* Proceedings before grand juries.
      (3) *Miscellaneous proceedings*:
         (A) Application for habeas corpus in extradition, rendition, or interstate detainer proceedings;
         (B) A hearing under Texas Code of Criminal Procedure article 46.02, by the court out of the presence of a jury, to determine whether there is sufficient evidence of incompetency to require a jury determination of the question of incompetency.
         (C) Proceedings regarding bail except hearings to deny, revoke or increase bail;
         (D) A hearing on justification for pretrial detention not involving bail;
         (E) Issuance of search or arrest warrant;
         (F) Direct contempt determination.
   (d) Rules applicable in part. In the following proceedings these rules apply to the extent matters of evidence are not provided for in the statutes which govern procedure therein or in another court rule prescribed pursuant to statutory authority:

intended in the 1998 unification.[3] With the unification of the Rules, the Texas Supreme Court and Court of Criminal Appeals returned to the original concept of one rule outlining the full scope of the Rules' applicability. In 2015, the Rules were restyled.[4]

A. Rule 101(b): Scope

Rule 101(b) and the exceptions in Rule 101(d) through (g) define the scope of the Rules' applicability.[5] Although not mentioned in Rule 101, the Rules do not apply in arbitration proceedings because they are not civil "court" proceedings.[6] Instead, arbi-

---

(1) Sentencing or punishment assessment by the court or the jury;
(2) Probation revocation;
(3) A hearing to proceed to judgment following deferred adjudication of guilt or conditional discharge;
(4) Motions to suppress confessions, or to suppress illegally obtained evidence under Texas Code of Criminal Procedure article 38.23.
(5) Proceedings conducted pursuant to Texas Code of Criminal Procedure Article 11.07.
    (e) Evidence in hearings under the Texas Code of Military Justice, article 5788, shall be governed by that Code.
TEX. R. CRIM. EVID. 1101, 701-702 S.W.2d (Tex. Cases) LXV (1986, amended 1998) (current version at TEX. R. EVID. 101).

3.   *See **Hughes v. State**,* 4 S.W.3d 1, 2 n.1 (Tex. Crim. App. 1999) (scope and application of unified rules are the same as for former separate criminal and civil rules because unified rules are "substantially the same as their predecessors"). The 1998 elimination of former Criminal Rule 1101(d) made the strict Rules of Evidence inapplicable to motions to suppress confessions or illegally obtained evidence. These issues are decided under Rule 104(a) because they are preliminary questions about the admissibility of evidence. Because of this change, Texas law on motions to suppress aligns with federal practice.

4.   Tex. Sup. Ct. Order, Misc. Docket No. 15-9048 (eff. Apr. 1, 2015).

5.   *See* TEX. R. EVID. 101(b). Before the 2015 restyling, Rule 101(b) explicitly stated that the Rules of Evidence applied to examining trials held before magistrates in criminal proceedings. Although restyled Rule 101(b) does not include this language, examining trials are included in the definition of "criminal case" in Rule 101(h)(2); thus, the Rules continue to apply to examining trials. *See* TEX. R. EVID. 101(h)(2) ("criminal case" means a criminal action or proceeding, including an examining trial); *see also* TEX. CODE CRIM. PROC. art. 16.07 ("The same rules of evidence shall apply to and govern a trial before an examining court that apply to and govern a final trial."). The Federal Rules of Evidence, in contrast, do not apply to preliminary examinations, which are the federal counterpart to examining trials. FED. R. EVID. 1101(d)(3); *see* 5 CHRISTOPHER B. MUELLER & LAIRD C. KIRKPATRICK, FEDERAL EVIDENCE §11:5, at 893-918 (3d ed. 2007). There are two rationales for the federal position. First, a preliminary examination in a criminal proceeding ensures that there is probable cause to hold an accused for trial; probable cause is often demonstrated through hearsay evidence. *See* FED. R. CRIM. P. 5.1(e) ("If the magistrate judge finds probable cause to believe an offense has been committed and the defendant committed it, the magistrate judge must promptly require the defendant to appear for further proceedings."); FED. R. EVID. 1101 advisory committee's note, subdiv. (d) ("Hearsay testimony is, however, customarily received in such [preliminary] examinations."). Second, an indictment by a grand jury substitutes for a preliminary examination, and testimony before grand juries has never been subject to evidentiary rules; rules of evidence should not apply to only one method of establishing probable cause. *See* 5 MUELLER & KIRKPATRICK, *supra*, §11:5, at 895-96; *see also* **Perez v. State**, 590 S.W.2d 474, 478 (Tex. Crim. App. [Panel Op.] 1979) (no requirement at examining trial that defendant's witnesses be allowed to testify). "[T]he return of a true bill of indictment independently satisfies the principal purpose and justification of the examining trial—to show that there is probable cause to believe the accused committed the offense charged." *Perez*, 590 S.W.2d at 478. The Advisory Committee on the Federal Rules of Criminal Procedure noted that increasing the procedural and evidentiary requirements for preliminary examinations would only increase the administrative pressure to avoid them entirely and rely only on the grand-jury process. *See* FED. R. CRIM. P. 5.1 advisory committee's note.

6.   *See **Crossmark, Inc. v. Hazar**,* 124 S.W.3d 422, 432 n.10 (Tex. App.—Dallas 2004, pet. denied) (rules of civil procedure and evidence do not apply in arbitration proceedings unless the arbitration agreement provides otherwise); *cf.* **Castleman v. AFC Enters., Inc.**, 995 F. Supp. 649, 653-54 (N.D. Tex. 1997) (federal arbitration proceedings are not governed by formal rules of evidence).

tration proceedings are administrative and are intended as an inexpensive and rapid alternative to traditional litigation.[7]

B. Rule 101(c): Rules on Privilege

Under Rule 101(c), the rules on privilege apply to all stages of a case or proceeding.[8] The same broad scope of privilege rules is also included in the Texas Rules of Civil Procedure.[9] Thus, while the evidentiary rules as a whole do not apply in some types of proceedings or at some stages of a lawsuit, valid evidentiary rules of privilege always apply.[10] The rationale for this broad application is that "the values protected by privileges would be undercut not merely by use of privileged matter at trial, but by forced disclosure itself."[11] Because privileges protect the privacy of relationships or communications, any disclosure in any forum would destroy that purpose. However, in ***United States v. Zolin***, the U.S. Supreme Court stated that Federal Rules 104(a) and 1101(c) would not "categorically" prohibit a trial judge from examining purportedly

RULE 101

---

7.   *See **Prudential Sec. Inc. v. Marshall***, 909 S.W.2d 896, 900 (Tex. 1995) (orig. proceeding) (per curiam). The Texas Arbitration Act does not require that a record be made of the arbitration hearing or that arbitrators state the rationale for their decisions. The Act allows limited judicial review of the arbitration proceeding's structure but virtually no judicial review of the merits. *See* TEX. CIV. PRAC. & REM. CODE §§171.086-171.098; *see also **CVN Grp., Inc. v. Delgado***, 95 S.W.3d 234, 238 (Tex. 2002) (judicial review of arbitration awards "adds expense and delay, thereby diminishing the benefits of arbitration as an efficient, economical system for resolving disputes"). For further discussion of judicial review of arbitration awards, see ***O'Connor's Texas Rules * Civil Trials*** (2017), "Trial court's review of award," ch. 4-C, §9.5, p. 357.

8.   The scope of the Federal Rules of Evidence is similarly broad. *See* FED. R. EVID. 101(a), 1101(c), (d). Texas Rule 101(c) follows earlier Texas and federal common-law doctrine. *See **United States v. Calandra***, 414 U.S. 338, 346 (1974) (dicta; grand jury "may consider incompetent evidence, but it may not itself violate a valid privilege, whether established by the Constitution, statutes, or the common law"). *See generally* 1 ROY R. RAY, TEXAS PRACTICE: TEXAS LAW OF EVIDENCE CIVIL AND CRIMINAL §428, at 412-13, §441, at 429-30 (3d ed. 1980 & Supp. 1991) (citing Texas common law).

9.   *See* TEX. R. CIV. P. 192.3(a) (a party may obtain discovery on any matter that is not privileged and is relevant to the subject matter of the pending action).

10.   *See **Upjohn Co. v. United States***, 449 U.S. 383, 386 (1981) (attorney-client privilege and work-product doctrine apply in IRS enforcement proceedings); ***In re Grand Jury Investigation of Hugle (Hugle v. United States)***, 754 F.2d 863, 864 (9th Cir. 1985) (marital-communications privilege applies in grand-jury proceedings); ***Armour Int'l Co. v. Worldwide Cosmetics, Inc.***, 689 F.2d 134, 135 (7th Cir. 1982) (accountant-client privilege, if valid, would apply to discovery proceedings); ***United States v. Lefkowitz***, 618 F.2d 1313, 1317 n.5 (9th Cir. 1980) (marital privilege applies in proceedings to obtain a search warrant); ***Wearly v. Fed. Trade Comm'n***, 462 F. Supp. 589, 596 (D.N.J. 1978) (trade-secret privilege applies during administrative-agency hearings), *vacated on other grounds*, 616 F.2d 662 (3d Cir. 1980).

The strength of the applicability of privileges was demonstrated in ***Wood v. McCown***, in which the Austin Court of Appeals held that the attorney-client privilege and the work-product doctrine extended to a civil proceeding based on an event litigated in an earlier criminal proceeding. 784 S.W.2d 126, 128-29 (Tex. App.—Austin 1990, orig. proceeding). In this mandamus case, the relator filed a civil assault suit against a man who had been convicted in a criminal proceeding based on that assault. *Id.* at 127. The relator then attempted to require production of the file of the attorney who had represented the assailant in the criminal trial. *Id.* Relying on the criminal rules for the attorney-client privilege, the court held that the attorney-client privilege was a permanent bar to the production of some of the documents. *Id.* at 128. The court then exempted other documents from production by holding that the work-product doctrine extends beyond the conclusion of a criminal case when attorney work product is sought in a later civil case dealing with the same facts. *Id.* at 129. Although the court did not cite former Criminal Rule 1101(b) (now Rule 101(c)), the result for the attorney-client privilege would have been the same under that rule.

11.   5 MUELLER & KIRKPATRICK, *supra* note 5, §11:4, at 887-88.

privileged material in camera to determine whether an exception to the particular privilege applied.[12]

The "rules on privileges" referred to in Rule 101(c) are normally only those that are constitutionally based, created by statute, or specifically mentioned in Article V of the Rules.[13] The work-product doctrine traditionally has not been construed as an evidentiary rule of privilege but simply as a mechanism to protect attorneys from being forced to share the fruits of their labor with their adversaries during lawsuits.[14] Texas Rule of Civil Procedure 192.5 provides a work-product privilege from civil discovery that the Texas Supreme Court, in *Owens-Corning Fiberglas Corp. v. Caldwell*,[15] held "is of continuing duration."[16] However, Rule 192.5 is a court rule "prescribed pursuant to statutory authority" for purposes of Texas Rule of Evidence 501, and thus it is an explicitly recognized evidentiary privilege. The Texas Code of Criminal Procedure contains no such explicit privilege, although article 39.14 governs the defendant's right of discovery and exempts from discovery "the work product of counsel for the State in the case and their investigators and their notes or report."[17] Whether the doctrine would protect a defense attorney's work-product materials at all stages of criminal proceedings under Rule 101(c) is an open question.[18]

---

12. 491 U.S. 554, 565-68 (1989).

13. *See* TEX. R. EVID. 501 (recognizing privileges only as provided by "a Constitution, a statute, or these or other rules prescribed under statutory authority"). For a discussion of the rules on privilege, refer to *Article V: Privileges*, *infra* p. 377.

14. *See* Sherman L. Cohn, *The Work-Product Doctrine: Protection, Not Privilege*, 71 GEO. L.J. 917, 943 (1983) (work-product doctrine is intended to benefit the adversary system, not a particular attorney or client, and thus should not be accorded the status of a privilege). *See generally* **Hickman v. Taylor**, 329 U.S. 495, 511-12 (1947) (explaining the work-product doctrine).

15. 818 S.W.2d 749 (Tex. 1991) (orig. proceeding). In *Owens-Corning*, the supreme court reasoned that it would be inconsistent to protect the client's full and frank communications in perpetuity under former Civil Rule 503 and not protect the attorney's privileged work product, prepared in furtherance of the attorney-client relationship, from disclosure under former Texas Rule of Civil Procedure 166b(3) (now Rule 192.5) once the lawsuit had ended. *Owens-Corning*, 818 S.W.2d at 751.

16. *Id.* at 751-52. Although precedent from other jurisdictions is meager, the supreme court's ruling in *Owens-Corning* accords with the "sounder view" expressed by Wright and Miller and followed in a majority of other jurisdictions. *See* 8 CHARLES A. WRIGHT ET AL., FEDERAL PRACTICE AND PROCEDURE §2024, at 351-54 (2d ed. 1994) (arguing for the "sounder view" in favor of a work-product privilege protecting documents prepared for one case from use in a second case when the cases are closely related in parties or subject matter).

17. TEX. CODE CRIM. PROC. art. 39.14(a). Article 39.14(a) does not define "work product" or its scope for purposes of the exemption. *Cf.* FED. R. CRIM. P. 16(a)(2) ("[T]his rule does not authorize the discovery or inspection of reports, memoranda, or other internal government documents made by an attorney for the government or other government agent in connection with investigating or prosecuting the case."), FED. R. CRIM. P. 16(b)(2) (the rule "does not authorize discovery or inspection of: (A) reports, memoranda, or other documents made by the defendant, or the defendant's attorney or agent, during the case's investigation or defense; or (B) a statement made to the defendant, or the defendant's attorney or agent, by: (i) the defendant; (ii) a government or defense witness; or (iii) a prospective government or defense witness").

18. *See* 1 STEVEN GOODE ET AL., TEXAS PRACTICE SERIES: GUIDE TO THE TEXAS RULES OF EVIDENCE §503.3, at 407-10 (3d ed. 2002).

While the constitutional privilege against self-incrimination, like the privileges contained in Article V, applies in all contexts,[19] evidentiary rules—such as those excluding evidence of subsequent remedial measures,[20] compromise offers,[21] pleas and plea discussions,[22] and a rape victim's prior sexual conduct[23]—are not true rules of privilege and thus are not necessarily applicable at all stages of a case or proceeding.[24]

C. Rule 101(d): Exception for Constitutional or Statutory Provisions or Other Rules

Rule 101(d) discusses the types of laws that control over the Rules of Evidence in both civil and criminal proceedings.[25] Federal constitutional doctrines and federal statutes that preempt state law trump any conflicting evidentiary rules.[26] Similarly, the Texas Constitution and statutes prevail over the Rules of Evidence.[27] Whenever possible, any apparent inconsistency between constitutional provisions or statutes and the Rules of Evidence should be harmonized by reasonable construction.[28]

---

19. *See, e.g.*, **Quinn v. United States**, 349 U.S. 155, 164-65 (1955) (applying the privilege against self-incrimination in a legislative investigation); **McCarthy v. Arndstein**, 266 U.S. 34, 40-41 (1924) (allowing a debtor in bankruptcy proceedings to exercise the privilege against self-incrimination).

20. Tex. R. Evid. 407.

21. Tex. R. Evid. 408.

22. Tex. R. Evid. 410.

23. Tex. R. Evid. 412.

24. *See, e.g.*, **In re Japanese Elec. Prods. Antitrust Litig.**, 723 F.2d 238, 275 (3d Cir. 1983) (Federal Rule 408 does not create a rule of privilege, so judge could consider trustworthiness of underlying agreement between parties in determining the admissibility of a consent decree under former Federal Rule 803(8)(C), now Rule 803(8)(A)(iii)), *rev'd on other grounds sub nom.* **Matsushita Elec. Indus. Co. v. Zenith Radio Corp.**, 475 U.S. 574 (1986); **Oliver v. Comm. for the Re-Election of the President**, 66 F.R.D. 553, 556 (D.D.C. 1975) (settlement negotiations, which would be excludable under Federal Rule 408, are not "privileged" for purposes of pretrial discovery). *But see* 5 Mueller & Kirkpatrick, *supra* note 5, §11:4, at 889 (aim of encouraging plea bargaining would be defeated if Federal Rule 410 were not viewed as a "privilege" under former Rule 1101(c)).

25. Before the 2015 restyling, Rule 101(d) (formerly Rule 101(c)) explicitly applied to the "hierarchical governance" of other statutes and rules only in criminal proceedings; the restyled rule, however, deletes that language and expands the scope to civil proceedings. *See* Tex. R. Evid. 101 cmt. (2015) ("The reference to 'hierarchical governance' … has been deleted as unnecessary. … Courts in civil cases must also admit or exclude evidence when required to do so by constitutional or statutory provisions or other rules that take precedence over these rules.").

26. *See* **Lopez v. State**, 18 S.W.3d 220, 222 (Tex. Crim. App. 2000) (Sixth Amendment Confrontation Clause prevails if it conflicts with Rules of Evidence).

27. *See* **Sells v. State**, 121 S.W.3d 748, 764 (Tex. Crim. App. 2003) ("[W]hile the rules of evidence, *in general*, do not apply to suppression hearings, [Code of Criminal Procedure art. 38.22, §3(a)(5)] has priority over the rules …."); **Fryer v. State**, 68 S.W.3d 628, 631 (Tex. Crim. App. 2002) (statutory provisions govern use of presentence investigation reports, and rules of evidence do not apply to contents of those reports).

28. Tex. R. Evid. 101(d); *see* **Smith v. State**, 5 S.W.3d 673, 677-78 (Tex. Crim. App. 1999) (Code of Criminal Procedure art. 38.36(a), authorizing the admission of extraneous-offense evidence in a murder case to show the parties' relationship, can be harmonized with Rules 403 and 404, limiting the admissibility of extraneous-offense evidence; an evidentiary rule may limit the application of a statutory provision). In **Smith**, the court of criminal appeals stated that before a court holds that a specific statutory or constitutional provision trumps an evidentiary rule, it must first determine whether the two provisions may be applied congruously. *See* **Smith**, 5 S.W.3d at 677; *see also* **Hammer v. State**, 296 S.W.3d 555, 561 (Tex. Crim. App. 2009) ("Generally, the right to present evidence and to cross-examine witnesses under the Sixth Amendment does not conflict with the corresponding rights under state evidentiary rules. Thus, most questions concerning cross-examination may be resolved by looking to the Texas Rules of Evidence. … [C]ompliance with the reasonable construction and application of a rule of evidence will, in most instances, avoid a constitutional question.").

This provision recognizes "the continuing power of the Legislature to prescribe special approaches to evidence in particular civil proceedings" and acknowledges that the Legislature can correct oversights in the Rules.[29] The Texas Supreme Court repealed 37 statutes when it promulgated the Civil Rules, eliminating many conflicts between then-existing statutes and the Rules.[30] Apart from the Texas Family Code, which has several provisions on the admissibility of evidence in civil proceedings relating to delinquent children and children in need of supervision,[31] few other civil statutes take precedence over the Rules of Evidence.[32]

In contrast, a number of criminal evidentiary statutes remained in force when the Texas Court of Criminal Appeals promulgated the Criminal Rules.[33] Under Rule 101(d), these statutes and any newly enacted evidentiary statutes take precedence over the provisions of the Rules of Evidence.

Because the Texas Rules were patterned after the Federal Rules of Evidence, Texas courts may look to federal precedent for guidance in interpreting the scope, content, and applicability of the Rules, especially when addressing questions of first impression.[34]

---

29.   Annotated Supreme Court Transmittal Overlay (Wellborn note on Rule 101), *reprinted in* Record of Senate Interim Study on Rules of Evidence, Transmittal File (available at the Legislative Reference Library, Austin, Texas).

30.   The statute that gives the Texas Supreme Court authority to enact rules of practice and procedure also gives it the power to repeal civil statutes that conflict with its rules. *See* TEX. GOV'T CODE §22.004(a). The Texas Court of Criminal Appeals has the same authority to repeal criminal statutes. *See id.* §22.109(a).

31.   Judges in juvenile court frequently use reliable hearsay reports in making discretionary detention and disposition decisions. *See, e.g.,* TEX. FAM. CODE §54.01(c) (court may consider written reports and testimonial evidence at detention hearings), §54.02(e) (court may consider written reports at hearing to transfer child-supervision case to criminal district court), §54.04(b) (court may consider written reports at disposition hearings), §54.05(e) (court may consider written reports at a hearing to modify disposition). While proceedings in juvenile courts are categorized as civil proceedings, they are quasi-criminal in nature, and thus the Family Code also contains special provisions that restrict the admissibility of certain types of evidence at delinquency hearings. *See id.* §54.03(e) (illegally obtained evidence is not admissible, extrajudicial confessions or accomplice-witness testimony must be corroborated, and extrajudicial confessions are not admissible unless they comply with statutory provisions). The Family Code specifically states that Code of Criminal Procedure chapter 38 and the Rules of Evidence provisions dealing with criminal proceedings apply to all juvenile-adjudication hearings. TEX. FAM. CODE §54.03(d) ("Except as provided by section 54.031, only material, relevant, and competent evidence in accordance with the Texas Rules of Evidence applicable to criminal cases and Chapter 38, Code of Criminal Procedure, may be considered in the adjudication hearing."); *see also **In re A.F.**,* 895 S.W.2d 481, 485 (Tex. App.—Austin 1995, no writ) ("While the legislature explicitly made adjudication hearings subject to the rules of civil evidence, it did not subject to the rules any proceeding which calls for review of the social history report.").

32.   *See* Olin G. Wellborn III, *Article I of the Texas Rules of Evidence and Articles I and XI of the Texas Rules of Criminal Evidence: Applicability of the Rules, Procedural Matters, and Preserving Error,* 18 ST. MARY'S L.J. 1165, 1168 (1987).

33.   *See, e.g.,* TEX. CODE CRIM. PROC. art. 38.07 (allowing conviction based on uncorroborated testimony of victim of sexual offense), art. 38.071 (allowing various procedures for taking out-of-court testimony of child victim of sexual offense), art. 38.072 (allowing hearsay statements made by victim of assault or sexual abuse), art. 38.101 (disallowing communications made by drug abusers to their therapists), art. 38.16 (disallowing all evidence of any overt act not expressly charged in indictment for treason), art. 38.22 (specifying when an accused's statements can be used), art. 38.23 (disallowing illegally obtained evidence), art. 38.27 (allowing evidence of handwriting by comparison), arts. 38.30, 38.31 (allowing testimony of interpreters), art. 38.32 (allowing presumption of death with admission of valid death certificate), art. 38.34(b) (allowing photographic evidence in theft cases).

34.   *See **Reed v. State**,* 811 S.W.2d 582, 586 (Tex. Crim. App. 1991) (Federal Rules guide, but do not bind, state courts construing analogous Texas Rules); ***Bodin v. State**,* 807 S.W.2d 313, 317 (Tex. Crim. App. 1991) (cases inter-

D. Rule 101(e): Exceptions

Rule 101(e) outlines several contexts in which the Rules of Evidence—except the rules on privileges—do not apply.[35] While the Texas provisions exempting certain pretrial criminal proceedings from the Rules may at first seem both internally inconsistent and at odds with the analogous federal provisions, a common thread of logic runs through them. If the hearing is adversarial, Texas law requires the formal evidentiary procedure of a trial on the merits, and the Rules therefore apply. For example, bail hearings[36] are adversarial and may result in lengthy pretrial incarceration. Given the importance of the proceeding to a defendant who could be deprived of liberty, the Texas position is understandable.

1. Rule 101(e)(1): Admissibility determinations. Under Rule 101(e)(1), the Rules do not apply in deciding preliminary questions of fact when the judge is determining issues of admissibility of evidence under Rule 104(a).[37] Strictly speaking, Rule 101(e)(1) is unnecessary because it merely repeats a portion of Rule 104(a),[38] but if Rule 101 had not mentioned preliminary questions of fact, that omission might have created a potential conflict between the two rules. Because trial judges are expected to make admissibility decisions "on the run" during trial, they may consider any reliable material, including inadmissible evidence, that will help them make the right ruling.[39]

When the Civil and Criminal Rules were merged in 1998, former Criminal Rule 1101(d)(4), which provided that the Rules of Evidence applied to motions to suppress confessions or illegally obtained evidence, was not incorporated into Rule 101. Thus, the Rules (except those dealing with privileges) do not apply to suppression hearings.[40]

---

preting Federal Rules should be used for guidance unless Texas rule clearly departs from federal rule); **Montgomery v. State**, 810 S.W.2d 372, 376 n.2 (Tex. Crim. App. 1990) (orig. op.) (when Texas rule duplicates federal rule, federal court's interpretation should receive greater-than-usual deference); **Ortega v. CACH, LLC**, 396 S.W.3d 622, 630 n.4 (Tex. App.—Houston [14th Dist.] 2013, no pet.) ("Because the Texas Rules of Evidence are patterned after the Federal Rules of Evidence, cases interpreting federal rules should be consulted for guidance as to their scope and applicability unless the Texas rule clearly departs from its federal counterpart.").

35.   This section is based on former Criminal Rule 1101(c) and simply moves the provisions dealing with the inapplicability of the Rules of Evidence from the end of the code to the beginning, where the other rules of applicability are found. As with the 2015 restyling changes in Rule 101(d), the restyling deleted the reference to criminal proceedings in the title to more accurately reflect the scope of the rule. *See* TEX. R. EVID. 101 cmt. (2015). Refer to note 25 *supra*.

36.   Refer to notes 63-66 *infra* and accompanying text.

37.   TEX. R. EVID. 101(e)(1); *see* TEX. R. EVID. 104(a); *see, e.g.,* **Alvarado v. State**, 804 S.W.2d 669, 670 (Tex. App.—El Paso 1991) (trial court could consider the Mexican police secretary's explanation of rules for taking of confessions in Mexico as proof of applicable foreign law in determining admissibility of confession under Criminal Rule 104(a)), *aff'd*, 853 S.W.2d 17 (Tex. Crim. App. 1993). For a discussion of Rule 104(a), refer to notes 248-270 *infra* and accompanying text.

38.   *See* Wellborn, *supra* note 32, at 1197; *cf.* 5 MUELLER & KIRKPATRICK, *supra* note 5, §11:5, at 891 (Federal Rule 104(a) encompasses everything in Federal Rule 1101(d) and more).

39.   *See* 5 MUELLER & KIRKPATRICK, *supra* note 5, §11:5, at 891.

40.   **Hall v. State**, 297 S.W.3d 294, 297 (Tex. Crim. App. 2009); **Granados v. State**, 85 S.W.3d 217, 227 (Tex. Crim. App. 2002); *see* TEX. R. EVID. 101(e)(1) (Rules of Evidence, except those on privilege, do not apply to court's determination under Rule 104(a) on preliminary fact question governing admissibility); **Ford v. State**, 305 S.W.3d 530, 534-35 (Tex. Crim. App. 2009) ("A hearing on a pretrial motion to suppress is a specific application of Rule 104(a) …. This rule, based on longstanding common-law principles, explicitly states that a trial judge is not bound by the rules

When deciding at a suppression hearing whether to admit or exclude evidence, a trial judge may (but is not required to) consider otherwise inadmissible evidence—such as hearsay or unauthenticated documents—if the judge considers that information reliable. Strict adherence to the Rules of Evidence is unnecessary in a preliminary hearing under Rule 104(a), but that does not mean that all *procedures* required by the Rules are necessarily inapplicable in such hearings.[41] For example, the rule of witness sequestration set out in Rule 614 (also known as "the Rule") should apply even in hearings to determine the admissibility of evidence because that rule ensures the reliability of evidence.[42]

2. Rule 101(e)(2): Grand-jury proceedings. Under Rule 101(e)(2), the Rules do not apply to grand-jury proceedings.[43] The rationale for exempting grand juries from evi-

---

of evidence in resolving questions of admissibility of evidence, regardless of whether those questions are determined in a pretrial hearing or at some time during trial."); *Broussard v. State*, 68 S.W.3d 197, 211 (Tex. App.—Houston [1st Dist.] 2002, pet. ref'd) (Cohen & Smith, JJ., dissenting) (because suppression motions are not heard by a jury, evidence that might be considered during suppression hearing is not necessarily admissible at trial before the jury). As the *Granados* court noted, "[t]his conclusion is consistent with the United States Supreme Court's interpretation of the Federal Rules of Evidence, which has a counterpart to Rule 104(a) but has never had a counterpart to former Rule 1101(d)(4)." 85 S.W.3d at 227; *see United States v. Raddatz*, 447 U.S. 667, 679 (1980) ("At a suppression hearing, the court may rely on hearsay and other evidence, even though that evidence would not be admissible at trial."); *United States v. Matlock*, 415 U.S. 164, 173-74 (1974) (rules of evidence governing trials do not govern determination of preliminary questions, including Fourth Amendment issues decided at a suppression hearing; reliable hearsay may be considered in deciding the admissibility of evidence). As the U.S. Supreme Court explained in *Matlock*:

> There is, therefore, much to be said for the proposition that in proceedings where the judge himself is considering the admissibility of evidence, the exclusionary rules, aside from rules of privilege, should not be applicable; and the judge should receive the evidence and give it such weight as his judgment and experience counsel.

415 U.S. at 175; *see also United States v. Yousef*, 327 F.3d 56, 145 (2d Cir. 2003) (Federal Rules of Evidence explicitly permit trial judge to consider affidavits at motion-to-suppress hearings); *United States v. Merritt*, 695 F.2d 1263, 1269 (10th Cir. 1982) ("The purpose of the suppression hearing was, of course, to determine preliminarily the admissibility of certain evidence allegedly obtained in violation of the defendant's rights …. In this type of hearing the judge had latitude to receive it, notwithstanding the hearsay rule."). Refer to note 252 *infra* and accompanying text.

41.   *See* 21A CHARLES A. WRIGHT & KENNETH W. GRAHAM, JR., FEDERAL PRACTICE AND PROCEDURE: EVIDENCE §5053.4, at 94 (2d ed. 2005) (rules of admission and exclusion generally do not apply in preliminary hearings, but "the meta-rules that govern the procedure for admission and exclusion continue to apply"); *see, e.g., United States v. Brewer*, 947 F.2d 404, 408 (9th Cir. 1991) ("[T]he *procedure* set forth in [Federal] Rule 615 [exclusion of witnesses] to assist the trier of fact in resolving credibility issues and avoiding contrived testimony applies to an evidentiary proceeding in a motion to suppress evidence.").

42.   *See Brewer*, 947 F.2d at 410 ("We hold that [Federal] Rule 615 is a procedural rule directed at the fairness of the proceedings, and not a rule affecting the type of evidence that can be considered in an evidentiary hearing."); *see also United States v. Warren*, 578 F.2d 1058, 1076 (5th Cir. 1978) (en banc) (trial judge erred in denying defendant's request to exclude government witnesses from suppression hearing). Refer to *Article VI: Witnesses, infra* p. 667.

43.   This rule is in accord with both federal and Texas common law. *See United States v. R. Enters., Inc.*, 498 U.S. 292, 298 (1991) ("This Court has emphasized on numerous occasions that many of the rules and restrictions that apply at a trial do not apply in grand jury proceedings. This is especially true of evidentiary restrictions."); *Costello v. United States*, 350 U.S. 359, 363 (1956) (defendant cannot challenge indictment on the grounds that all evidence before the grand jury was hearsay); *Rummel v. State*, 505 S.W.2d 287, 287 (Tex. Crim. App. 1974) (indictment is valid even if based on "rank hearsay"); *K.W.M. v. State*, 598 S.W.2d 660, 661 (Tex. Civ. App.—Houston [14th Dist.] 1980, no pet.) ("[T]he grand jury is not bound by the rules of evidence in determining whether to return an indictment ….").

dentiary rules is that a grand jury is an ex parte investigative body composed of ordinary citizens who determine probable cause to indict, but not formal guilt or innocence.[44] Historically, grand jurors could always initiate investigations based on "tips, rumors, evidence offered by the prosecutor, or their own personal knowledge."[45] If the grand jury could initiate investigations based on personal knowledge and rumors, it follows that the grand jury should be able to consider the same information in determining whether to indict.[46] Thus, grand jurors may use inadmissible polygraph evidence,[47] illegally obtained evidence,[48] evidence of extraneous offenses,[49] evidence subject to the attorney-client privilege,[50] or even evidence obtained in violation of a person's Fifth Amendment privilege against self-incrimination.[51]

3. Rule 101(e)(3)(A): Habeas corpus in certain proceedings. Under Rule 101(e)(3)(A), applications for habeas corpus in extradition, rendition, or interstate-detainer proceedings are exempt from the Rules. This provision parallels Federal Rule 1101(d)(3), but there are significant differences between the two rules. Under both Federal Rule 1101 and Texas Rule 101, the formal rules of evidence do not apply in extradition or rendition proceedings, but Texas Rule 101(e)(3)(A) also lists interstate-detainer proceedings.[52] These hearings are "essentially administrative"[53] and have traditionally been exempt from formal evidentiary rules.[54] In Texas, the extradition, rendition, and interstate-detention processes are governed by the Code of Criminal Procedure.[55] The Rules do not apply to proceedings held under these statutes because virtually the only question in such hearings is the identity of the person accused in the demanding state, which may be reliably established by hearsay documentation.[56]

---

44. *See R. Enters.*, 498 U.S. at 298 ("The same rules that, in an adversary hearing on the merits, may increase the likelihood of accurate determinations of guilt or innocence do not necessarily advance the mission of a grand jury, whose task is to conduct an *ex parte* investigation to determine whether or not there is probable cause to prosecute a particular defendant.").

45. *United States v. Dionisio*, 410 U.S. 1, 15 (1973).

46. *See United States v. McKenzie*, 678 F.2d 629, 632 (5th Cir. 1982).

47. *United States v. Callahan*, 442 F. Supp. 1213, 1218 (D. Minn. 1978), *rev'd on other grounds sub nom. United States v. Larson*, 596 F.2d 759 (8th Cir. 1979).

48. *See, e.g., United States v. Calandra*, 414 U.S. 338, 354 (1974) (allowing grand jurors to consider evidence obtained through unlawful search and seizure).

49. *United States v. Wilson*, 732 F.2d 404, 409 (5th Cir. 1984).

50. *United States v. Bein*, 728 F.2d 107, 113 (2d Cir. 1984).

51. *United States v. Ocanas*, 628 F.2d 353, 357 (5th Cir. 1980).

52. Tex. R. Evid. 101(e)(3)(A); *see* Fed. R. Evid. 1101(d)(3) (formal rules of evidence do not apply in extradition or rendition proceedings); *see also Messina v. United States*, 728 F.2d 77, 80 (2d Cir. 1984) ("evidentiary rules of criminal litigation are not applicable" in extradition hearings under Federal Rule 1103(d)(3)); *Ex parte Martinez*, 530 S.W.2d 578, 580-82 (Tex. Crim. App. 1975) ("strict common law rules of evidence" do not apply to extradition proceedings).

53. Fed. R. Evid. 1101 advisory committee's note, subdiv. (d).

54. *See, e.g., Collins v. Loisel*, 259 U.S. 309, 317 (1922) (receipt of unsworn statements was approved in extradition hearing); *Bingham v. Bradley*, 241 U.S. 511, 517 (1916) (ex parte affidavits taken without opportunity for cross-examination were admissible in extradition hearing).

55. *See* Tex. Code Crim. Proc. ch. 51.

56. *See Ex parte Martinez*, 530 S.W.2d at 580-82.

4. Rule 101(e)(3)(B): Incompetency determinations. Under Rule 101(e)(3)(B), the trial judge does not need to adhere to the Rules in making a preliminary determination of "whether evidence exists that would support a finding that the defendant may be incompetent to stand trial."[57] There is no federal analogue to this provision. The rationale for this exemption is that resolving the question of a criminal defendant's mental competency to stand trial is essentially a nonadversarial process.[58] Under Code of Criminal Procedure article 46B.005, the trial judge must hold a separate competency hearing if, after an informal inquiry, the judge determines that there is evidence to support a finding of the defendant's incompetency.[59] The evidence may come "from any source."[60] In conducting this informal inquiry, a judge can rely on personal observations of the defendant's behavior or concerns or on suggestions expressed by any court personnel, the defense attorney, the prosecutor, or any other person.[61] The evidentiary exemption under Rule 101 applies only to the trial judge's threshold determination of whether to convene a jury to resolve the issue of a defendant's incompetency; the Rules apply whenever a jury is impaneled to actually resolve the issue.[62]

5. Rule 101(e)(3)(C): Certain bail proceedings. Under Rule 101(e)(3)(C), the Rules apply only to bail hearings that deny, revoke, or increase bail. Most Texas bail hearings are held for those purposes, so the Rules of Evidence effectively apply to all bail hearings except those in which the judge originally sets bail under Code of Criminal Procedure article 17.15[63] or the defendant seeks a bail reduction.[64] The Federal Rules

---

57.   TEX. R. EVID. 101(e)(3)(B); *see* TEX. CODE CRIM. PROC. ch. 46B.

58.   *See **Manning v. State**,* 766 S.W.2d 551, 554-55 (Tex. App.—Dallas 1989), *aff'd*, 773 S.W.2d 568 (Tex. Crim. App. 1989). In ***Manning***, the court held that because of the nonadversarial nature of a competency hearing, a defense attorney could testify about his client's ability to consult with him as long as confidential communications were not revealed. 766 S.W.2d at 558.

59.   TEX. CODE CRIM. PROC. art. 46B.005(a); *see id.* art. 46B.004(c-1) (suggestion of incompetency is threshold requirement for informal inquiry under article 46B.004(c)).

60.   *Id.* art. 46B.004(c); ***Rojas v. State***, 228 S.W.3d 770, 771 (Tex. App.—Amarillo 2007, no pet.); *see* TEX. CODE CRIM. PROC. art. 46B.004(c-1) (suggestion of incompetency "may consist solely of a representation from any credible source that the defendant may be incompetent").

61.   *See* TEX. CODE CRIM. PROC. art. 46B.004(c-1) ("[T]he court is not required to have a bona fide doubt about the competency of the defendant. Evidence suggesting the need for an informal inquiry may be based on observations made in relation to one or more of the factors described by Article 46B.024 or on any other indication that the defendant is incompetent within the meaning of Article 46B.003."); ***McDaniel v. State***, 98 S.W.3d 704, 710 n.19 (Tex. Crim. App. 2003) (trial judge may consider any reliable information in deciding whether defendant's competency is an issue; "the defendant's attorney might orally recite the specific problems he has had in communicating with his client, and the trial judge might consider the defendant's conduct or statements in court. In addition, hearsay letters or reports may be appropriately reliable evidence to consider at this stage").

62.   ***Garcia v. State***, 595 S.W.2d 538, 541 (Tex. Crim. App. [Panel Op.] 1980); *see* TEX. CODE CRIM. PROC. arts. 46B.008, 46B.051; ***Turner v. State***, No. AP-76,580 (Tex. Crim. App. 2017) (no pub.; 3-8-17).

63.   *See* TEX. CODE CRIM. PROC. art. 17.15 (listing factors trial court may consider in setting bail).

64.   *See **Ex parte Allen-Pieroni**,* ___ S.W.3d ___ n.2 (Tex. App.—Waco 2016, no pet.) (No. 10-15-00431-CR; 2-24-16) (rules of evidence do not apply in habeas proceedings to reduce bail); *see, e.g., **Ex parte Parker**,* 26 S.W.3d 711, 713 (Tex. App.—Waco 2000, no pet.) (Davis, C.J., concurring) (because rules of evidence do not apply to bail-reduction hearing, trial court could consider facts derived solely from offense report never formally offered into evidence). *But see **Ex parte Parker**,* 26 S.W.3d at 714-16 (Vance, J., dissenting) (trial court should not have considered information in offense report not offered into evidence by either party).

of Evidence do not apply to any bail hearings.[65] Texas departed from the federal model in this instance largely because of the holding of the court of criminal appeals in *Ex parte Miles* that ex parte affidavits could not be used to justify the denial of bail.[66]

6. Rule 101(e)(3)(D): Pretrial-detention hearings. Under Rule 101(e)(3)(D), the Rules do not apply to pretrial-detention hearings when bail is not an issue. This type of hearing is referred to as a "24-hour," or *Gerstein v. Pugh*,[67] hearing to determine whether there is sufficient probable cause for a pretrial restraint of liberty.[68] While such a hearing is constitutionally required, it does not need to follow formal evidentiary rules.[69] However, when a defendant files a writ of habeas corpus challenging the existence of probable cause to hold him in custody pending indictment, the Rules apply because the hearing is adversarial (i.e., the defendant is entitled to be represented by counsel and the judge's ruling may result in protracted detention).[70]

7. Rule 101(e)(3)(E): Search & arrest warrants. Under Rule 101(e)(3)(E), the Rules do not apply to the process for obtaining search and arrest warrants. This provision conforms with Texas statutory authority[71] and Federal Rule 1101(d)(3).[72] Once again, when probable cause is the issue to be decided, reasonably reliable hearsay evidence will suffice.

8. Rule 101(e)(3)(F): Direct contempt. Under Rule 101(e)(3)(F), as in Federal Rule 1101(b),[73] the Rules do not apply to courts' rulings on direct contempt. Because direct contempt occurs in the presence of the judge, who has personal knowledge of all the

---

65. *See* FED. R. EVID. 1101 advisory committee's note, subdiv. (d) ("Proceedings with respect to release on bail or otherwise do not call for application of the rules of evidence."); *see also* 18 U.S.C. §3142(f)(2) ("The rules concerning admissibility of evidence in criminal trials do not apply to the presentation and consideration of information at the [detention and bail] hearing."); *United States v. Fortna*, 769 F.2d 243, 250 (5th Cir. 1985) (not applying the Rules in a bail hearing); *United States v. Montemayor*, 666 F.2d 235, 237 (5th Cir. 1982) (district judge could take judicial notice of defendant's history, background, and activities as outlined in pending civil proceedings, or of proximity of Brownsville to Mexico, as factors in setting sufficient bail to prevent flight from jurisdiction).

66. 474 S.W.2d 224, 225 (Tex. Crim. App. 1971); *see* Wellborn, *supra* note 32, at 1198.

67. 420 U.S. 103 (1975).

68. *Id.* at 105.

69. *Id.* at 120-22.

70. *See Garcia v. State*, 775 S.W.2d 879, 881 (Tex. App.—San Antonio 1989, no pet.) (while Texas Criminal Rule 1101(c)(3)(D) permits the use of hearsay in probable-cause-detention hearings, hearsay evidence is not sufficient to show probable cause in an adversarial habeas corpus hearing challenging probable cause to hold a defendant for the charged offense). In *Garcia*, the only probable cause offered was the prosecutor's recital of the contents of unsworn police reports. *Id.* at 880. The prosecutor should have called the police officer to testify about the probable cause for the defendant's arrest. *See id.*

71. *See* TEX. CODE CRIM. PROC. arts. 15.03-15.05 (arrest warrant can be issued based on a complaint upon a sworn affidavit), art. 18.01(b) (search warrant can be issued based on a "sworn affidavit setting forth substantial facts establishing probable cause").

72. *See* FED. R. EVID. 1101(d)(3); *see also* FED. R. CRIM. P. 4(a) (arrest warrant can be issued based on affidavits).

73. The federal rule, which is worded differently from the Texas version but has the same effect, provides that the Rules of Evidence apply to contempt proceedings, "except those in which the court may act summarily." FED. R. EVID. 1101(b). Courts may act "summarily" only in instances of direct contempt (i.e., when the contemptuous act is committed in the presence of the judge or magistrate). *See* 5 MUELLER & KIRKPATRICK, *supra* note 5, §11:3, at 883 (court should not act in summary fashion when contempt is directed personally at the judge or when there is a serious question about the mental competency of the person committing the contemptuous act).

pertinent facts,[74] the judge should not have to adhere to the Rules when ruling on what he heard and saw. Conversely, indirect or constructive contempt occurs outside of court and must be determined in a hearing held in accordance with the Rules because testimony is required.[75]

E. Rule 101(f): Exception for Justice Court Cases

The Rules do not apply in small-claims proceedings in justice courts,[76] where informality and a speedy disposition are specified, except as authorized by Texas Rule of Civil Procedure 500.3.[77]

F. Rule 101(g): Exception for Military Justice Hearings

Under Rule 101(g), evidence in hearings conducted under the Texas Code of Military Justice will be governed by that Code, contained in Texas Government Code chapter 432.[78]

G. Rule 101(h): Definitions

Rule 101(h) follows Federal Rule 101(b) and includes definitions of certain terms and phrases incorporated throughout the Rules of Evidence. The Texas definition of "criminal case" includes examining trials.[79] Rule 101(h) also includes a public agency in the definition of "public office,"[80] a memorandum, report, or data compilation in the definition of "record,"[81] and a definition of "unsworn declaration," which means one made under Texas Civil Practice & Remedies Code section 132.001.[82] Finally, the rule explicitly extends all references to "any kind of written material or any other medium" to include electronically stored information.[83]

RULE 102

PURPOSE

These rules should be construed so as to administer every proceeding fairly, eliminate unjustifiable expense and delay, and promote the development of evidence law, to the end of ascertaining the truth and securing a just determination.

---

74. *Ex parte Supercinski*, 561 S.W.2d 482, 483 (Tex. Crim. App. 1977).
75. *See id.* (constructive contempts "relate to acts which require testimony to establish their existence").
76. TEX. R. EVID. 101(f); *see* TEX. R. CIV. P. 500.3(a).
77. *See* TEX. R. CIV. P. 500.3(a); TEX. R. EVID. 101(f).
78. TEX. R. EVID. 101(g); *see* TEX. GOV'T CODE §432.061.
79. TEX. R. EVID. 101(h)(2). Refer to note 5 *supra*.
80. TEX. R. EVID. 101(h)(3).
81. TEX. R. EVID. 101(h)(4).
82. TEX. R. EVID. 101(h)(6); *see* TEX. CIV. PRAC. & REM. CODE §132.001.
83. TEX. R. EVID. 101(h)(7).

COMMENTARY ON RULE 102

Rule 102, which is identical to Federal Rule 102, functions as a guide for construing all the provisions in the Rules of Evidence and codifies preexisting Texas statutory and case law.[84] The rule acts as a governing principle, not as a restatement. It cautions both the trial court and the bar that the Rules should serve the cause of justice and not vice versa: courts must not apply the Rules with wooden formalism at the expense of achieving a just result. Federal Rule 102 also discourages undue attention to technicality.[85]

Although the emphasis on the trial judge's discretion gives judges considerable latitude,[86] this emphasis also burdens judges with enormous responsibilities. Therefore, neither courts nor the bar should interpret Rule 102 as a plenary grant of discretion to trial judges to avoid the Rules' specific mandates or absolute requirements. Rather, trial judges should initially follow the specific "plain language" provisions of the Rules without any reference to Rule 102 whatsoever. However, if the strict application of those provisions becomes so uncertain or inappropriate that it could adversely affect the course of the litigation, then trial judges may properly refer to the principles of Rule

---

84. *See* TEX. CODE CRIM. PROC. art. 1.03 (rules of criminal procedure seek to ensure a fair and impartial trial "with as little delay as is consistent with the ends of justice"); TEX. R. CIV. P. 1 (rules of civil procedure will be given "liberal construction" to ensure just and fair adjudication "with as great expedition and dispatch and at the least expense both to the litigants and to the state as may be practicable"); **Wright v. Traders & Gen. Ins.**, 132 Tex. 172, 178, 123 S.W.2d 314, 317 (1939) ("'[T]he rules of procedure in the courts [concerning evidentiary matters] should be so framed as to secure substantial justice ....'" (quoting **Silliman v. Gano**, 90 Tex. 637, 646, 39 S.W. 559, 561 (1897))).

85. Federal Rule 102 sets out the basic philosophical theme of the Federal Rules and is intended to influence the interpretation of all the other rules. *See* 1 MUELLER & KIRKPATRICK, *supra* note 5, §1:2, at 4; 1 JACK B. WEINSTEIN & MARGARET A. BERGER, WEINSTEIN'S FEDERAL EVIDENCE §102.02[1], at 102-5 to 102-6 (Joseph M. McLaughlin ed., 2d ed. 2008). Although the rule emphasizes fulfillment of its lofty goals, it indicates that a practical construction of the other rules is best calculated to accomplish fairness in administration, elimination of unjustifiable expense and delay, ascertainment of truth, and a just determination. 1 WEINSTEIN & BERGER, *supra*, §102.02[1], at 102-5. Because of these competing policies of idealism and pragmatism, the particular circumstances of each case should be considered to obtain a just result. *See id.* §102.02[3], at 102-8. This individualized approach gives the trial judge considerable discretion in applying Federal Rule 102. Flexibility, therefore, is the overriding principle that judges should use when interpreting and applying a rule's requirements to novel situations. *See* **United States v. Sutton**, 801 F.2d 1346, 1369 (D.C. Cir. 1986) (quoting Federal Rule 102 in crafting a "sensible course" of permitting the prosecution to offer inculpatory statements, then allowing the defense to argue that other portions should be admitted contemporaneously under Federal Rule 106 to remove any possible distortion of prosecution evidence); **United States v. Jackson**, 405 F. Supp. 938, 943 (E.D.N.Y. 1975) (Federal Rule 102 allows the court to interpret the Rules creatively to promote growth and development in the law of evidence in the interests of justice and reliable fact-finding); 1 MUELLER & KIRKPATRICK, *supra* note 5, §1:2, at 4 (no set of rules can be "tailor-made" to deal with all problems); *see also* Andrew E. Taslitz, Daubert's *Guide to the Federal Rules of Evidence: A Not-So-Plain Meaning Jurisprudence*, 32 HARV. J. ON LEGIS. 3, 67-68 (1995) ("**Daubert** reveals a sensitivity to the need for judicial value choices and an awareness of the role of judicial discretion within the broad limits set by text and by whatever other indicators of congressional intent are available. This sensitivity is consistent with the Court's continued adherence to a more flexible, pragmatic approach to reading the Rules that is embodied in portions of other decisions.").

86. *See* **Montgomery v. State**, 810 S.W.2d 372, 380 (Tex. Crim. App. 1990) (orig. op.) (judicial rulings should be affirmed if trial court utilizes the appropriate analysis and does not act in an arbitrary or capricious manner); **Dorsett v. State**, 761 S.W.2d 432, 433 (Tex. App.—Houston [14th Dist.] 1988, pet. ref'd) (Rules 102, 103, and 104 give the trial judge wide discretion in determining admissibility of evidence).

102 in ruling on novel evidentiary issues.[87] Because the Rules cannot cover the full spectrum of possible evidentiary issues, courts must sometimes look beyond the plain language of the Rules.[88] Rule 102 is not, however, a license for judges to reject the explicit requirements of established rules of evidence.

RULE 103
RULINGS ON EVIDENCE

(a) Preserving a Claim of Error. A party may claim error in a ruling to admit or exclude evidence only if the error affects a substantial right of the party and:

(1) if the ruling admits evidence, a party, on the record:

(A) timely objects or moves to strike; and

(B) states the specific ground, unless it was apparent from the context; or

(2) if the ruling excludes evidence, a party informs the court of its substance by an offer of proof, unless the substance was apparent from the context.

(b) Not Needing to Renew an Objection. When the court hears a party's objections outside the presence of the jury and rules that evidence is admissible, a party need not renew an objection to preserve a claim of error for appeal.

(c) Court's Statement About the Ruling; Directing an Offer of Proof. The court must allow a party to make an offer of proof outside the jury's presence as soon as practicable—and before the court reads its charge to the jury. The court may make any statement about the character or form of the evidence, the

---

87. *See* 1 STEPHEN A. SALTZBURG ET AL., FEDERAL RULES OF EVIDENCE MANUAL §102.02[2], at 102-3 to 102-4 (9th ed. 2006) (Federal Rule 102 gives the trial judge authority to fashion evidentiary procedures to deal with situations not specifically covered by the Rules, but the rule "is not … an invitation to Judges to treat other specific Rules as if they were nonexistent"); *see also* **Englund v. State**, 946 S.W.2d 64, 71 (Tex. Crim. App. 1997) (trial court did not abuse its discretion in admitting fax of certified criminal judgment and sentence; purpose and goals of Article X and Rule 102 supported admission, and "the Rules are flexible enough to have allowed for an interpretation leading to the conclusion that the exhibit was admissible under Rules 1005 and 1003 without ignoring or mangling the Rules"); **Bracewell v. Bracewell**, 31 S.W.3d 610, 613 (Tex. App.—Houston [1st Dist.] 1999, pet. denied) (referring to Rule 102 and purpose of Rules as promoting fairness, not gamesmanship, in declining to interpret Rule 105(b) to require proponent of evidence to limit his offer of proof based on a ground his opponent had abandoned); **In re R___ B___**, 741 S.W.2d 525, 527 (Tex. App.—Tyler 1987, no writ) (using Rule 102 as a guide to resolve a possible conflict in the application of Rules 509 and 510). Refer to note 85 *supra* and accompanying text.

88. In using Rule 102 as a guide to addressing novel evidentiary situations, trial judges should articulate their reasoning on the record for the benefit of the parties and reviewing courts. As noted by Jack Weinstein,

> Judges should indicate which factors are significant and which goals paramount in a particular case and why, so that the Bar can adjust to changing nuances in the law in advising their clients and in conducting litigations. This process of accommodation to change will itself promote desirable change while preserving the sound fundamentals of the law of evidence.

1 WEINSTEIN & BERGER, *supra* note 85, §102.05[2], at 102-12 to 102-13.

objection made, and the ruling. At a party's request, the court must direct that an offer of proof be made in question-and-answer form. Or the court may do so on its own.

(d) Preventing the Jury from Hearing Inadmissible Evidence. To the extent practicable, the court must conduct a jury trial so that inadmissible evidence is not suggested to the jury by any means.

(e) Taking Notice of Fundamental Error in Criminal Cases. In criminal cases, a court may take notice of a fundamental error affecting a substantial right, even if the claim of error was not properly preserved.

Notes and Comments

Comment to 1998 change: The exception to the requirement of an offer of proof for matters that were apparent from the context within which questions were asked, found in paragraph (a)(2), is now applicable to civil as well as criminal cases.

COMMENTARY ON RULE 103

Rule 103 codifies the fundamental rules of offering and objecting to evidence. The rule addresses the significance of making objections and offers of proof to preserve potential evidentiary error for appellate review.[89] An offer of proof preserves error for appeal if it is (1) made before the court, opposing counsel, and the court reporter, (2) preserved in the reporter's record, (3) made outside the presence of the jury, and (4) made before the charge is read to the jury.[90] An offer of proof also allows a trial court to reconsider its ruling in light of the evidence presented.[91]

A. Rule 103(a): Preserving a Claim of Error

Rule 103(a), which is identical to Federal Rule 103(a), restates the long-standing common-law rule that a party may claim error on appeal on an evidentiary ruling only if the error affects a "substantial" right of the party.[92] A substantial right is affected

---

89. *See* Frederick C. Moss, *Rethinking Texas Evidence Rule 103*, 56 BAYLOR L. REV. 503, 510 (2004) (title of Rule 103 "insufficiently describes the matters covered by the rule"; title should be "Preservation of Error; Objections; Offers of Proof; Waiver," and rule should be reworded and expanded to provide judges and parties greater assistance with the requirements of preserving evidentiary error).

90. *In re Estate of Miller*, 243 S.W.3d 831, 837 (Tex. App.—Dallas 2008, no pet.); *Fletcher v. Minn. Mining & Mfg. Co.*, 57 S.W.3d 602, 607 (Tex. App.—Houston [1st Dist.] 2001, pet. denied).

91. *In re Estate of Miller*, 243 S.W.3d at 837; *Smith v. Smith*, 143 S.W.3d 206, 211 (Tex. App.—Waco 2004, no pet.).

92. TEX. R. EVID. 103(a); *Walters v. State*, 247 S.W.3d 204, 218 (Tex. Crim. App. 2007); *see Rankin v. Bell*, 85 Tex. 28, 31-32, 19 S.W. 874, 875 (1892); *Carter v. Ferris*, 93 S.W.2d 504, 507-08 (Tex. Civ. App.—Amarillo 1936, writ dism'd).

    The harmless-error doctrine provides that evidentiary errors are prejudicial only if they significantly affect the complaining party's interests. *See, e.g.*, *United States v. Sarmiento-Perez*, 633 F.2d 1092, 1104 (5th Cir. 1981) (admission of coconspirator's confession "constituted reversible error as affecting the substantial rights of the accused"); *Hill v. Rolleri*, 615 F.2d 886, 890 (9th Cir. 1980) (error was harmless because admission of coconspirator's confession did not affect party's substantial right). Otherwise, evidentiary errors cannot be the basis for reversal on

when the error has a "substantial and injurious effect or influence in determining the jury's verdict."[93] If there is no demonstrable prejudice in an evidentiary ruling, then the ruling cannot be a cognizable basis for retrial.[94] The harmless-error doctrine is also codified and amplified in the Texas Rules of Appellate Procedure. Here, the doctrine is defined differently for civil and criminal cases.[95] The initial presumption in civil cases is that both constitutional and nonconstitutional trial errors are harmless, and the complaining party has the burden to show otherwise.[96]

The traditional presumption in Texas criminal cases was that any trial error was harmful to the defendant, and the State had the burden to prove otherwise.[97] That presumption disappeared with the adoption of Texas Rule of Appellate Procedure 44.2(b),

---

appeal even when the complainant made a timely and appropriate objection. *See* 1 MUELLER & KIRKPATRICK, *supra* note 5, §1:20, at 144. Federal Rule 103 "does not purport to change the law with respect to harmless error." FED. R. EVID. 103 advisory committee's note, subdiv. (a). The rule is merely a restatement of previously existing law. *See* 1 MCCORMICK ON EVIDENCE §52, at 266 (Kenneth S. Broun ed., 6th ed. 2006). The same is true under Texas Rule 103(a). *See, e.g.*, *Schaffer v. State*, 777 S.W.2d 111, 115 (Tex. Crim. App. 1989) (introduction of indirect hearsay affected substantial right of defendant under Rule 103(a) and required reversal of conviction); *Jefferson v. State*, 783 S.W.2d 816, 822 (Tex. App.—San Antonio 1990, pet. ref'd) (appellant's statement was inadmissible, and necessary predicate for error had been shown, because both a ruling on the motion to suppress and a timely objection were made and a substantial right was affected).

93. *Kotteakos v. United States*, 328 U.S. 750, 776 (1946); *accord United States v. Dominguez Benitez*, 542 U.S. 74, 81 (2004); *Walters*, 247 S.W.3d at 218.

94. As a practical matter, exceedingly few cases are reversed on appeal for evidentiary errors. *See* Daniel D. Blinka, *Ethics, Evidence, and the Modern Adversary Trial*, 19 GEO. J. LEGAL ETHICS 1, 21 (2006) (citing one commentator's review of 20,000 federal cases decided in two-year span and finding that only 30 cases were reversed for evidentiary error at trial; "fact that appellate courts reverse less than 1% of judgments for evidentiary errors vividly illustrates the suzerainty of the trial court in matters of evidence").

95. For civil cases, Texas Rule of Appellate Procedure 44.1(a) provides:
(a) **Standard for Reversible Error.** No judgment may be reversed on appeal on the ground that the trial court made an error of law unless the court of appeals concludes that the error complained of:
(1) probably caused the rendition of an improper judgment; or
(2) probably prevented the appellant from properly presenting the case to the court of appeals.
See generally Plainsman Trading Co. v. Crews, 898 S.W.2d 786, 790 (Tex. 1995) (discussing harmless-error rule); *Gee v. Liberty Mut. Fire Ins.*, 765 S.W.2d 394, 396 (Tex. 1989) (same).
For criminal cases, Texas Rule of Appellate Procedure 44.2 provides:
(a) **Constitutional Error.** If the appellate record in a criminal case reveals constitutional error that is subject to harmless error review, the court of appeals must reverse a judgment of conviction or punishment unless the court determines beyond a reasonable doubt that the error did not contribute to the conviction or punishment.
(b) **Other Errors.** Any other error, defect, irregularity, or variance that does not affect substantial rights must be disregarded.

96. *See* TEX. R. APP. P. 44.1(a) (no judgment will be reversed unless appellate court determines that error caused rendition of improper judgment); *Lorusso v. Members Mut. Ins.*, 603 S.W.2d 818, 822 (Tex. 1980) (complainant must show that trial in which judgment was rendered against him was "materially unfair"); *City of Galveston v. Hill*, 151 Tex. 139, 145, 246 S.W.2d 860, 863 (1952) (complainants must show that trial court's error resulted in improper judgment); *see, e.g.*, *Christiansen v. Prezelski*, 782 S.W.2d 842, 843-44 (Tex. 1990) (because appellant had not filed complete statement of facts, court of appeals could not determine whether particular evidentiary ruling by trial court was harmful).

97. *See* TEX. R. APP. P. 81(b)(2), 707-708 S.W.2d (Tex. Cases) LXXX (1986) (any error will be grounds for reversal unless it is shown beyond a reasonable doubt that the error did not contribute to conviction or punishment), amended 948-949 S.W.2d (Tex. Cases) CXXVII (1997) (now TEX. R. APP. P. 44.2); *see, e.g.*, *Arnold v. State*, 786 S.W.2d 295, 298 (Tex. Crim. App. 1990) (because State would benefit from the error, State must show beyond a reasonable doubt that error did not contribute to conviction).

which more closely follows Federal Rule of Criminal Procedure 52(a).[98] Both the State and the defendant may explain how the alleged error did or did not have "a substantial and injurious effect or influence in determining the jury's verdict,"[99] but neither party has the formal burden of showing harm or harmlessness under Rule 44.2(b).[100] It is ultimately the reviewing court's responsibility to determine whether nonconstitutional error affected a defendant's substantial rights.[101] Some have argued that any reference to the harmless-error standard in Rule 103 is unnecessary and incorrect because appellate courts should be guided solely by the harmless-error rule in the Texas Rules of Appellate Procedure.[102]

The erroneous admission or exclusion of evidence offered under the Rules of Evidence generally constitutes nonconstitutional error and is reviewed under Rule of Ap-

---

In *Harris v. State*, the Texas Court of Criminal Appeals provided a lengthy analysis of the contours of the Texas harmless-error doctrine in criminal cases under former Texas Rule of Appellate Procedure 81(b)(2). 790 S.W.2d 568, 584-88 (Tex. Crim. App. 1989). The court concluded its discussion of the doctrine by stating the following:

> In summary, a reviewing court in applying the harmless error rule should not focus upon the propriety of the outcome of the trial. Instead, an appellate court should be concerned with the integrity of the process leading to the conviction. Consequently, the court should examine the source of the error, the nature of the error, whether or to what extent it was emphasized by the State, and its probable collateral implications. Further, the court should consider how much weight a juror would probably place upon the error. In addition, the [c]ourt must also determine whether declaring the error harmless would encourage the State to repeat it with impunity.

Id. at 587. The court of criminal appeals later held that some of the *Harris* factors "have no logical bearing" on the constitutional-error analysis conducted under Texas Rule of Appellate Procedure 44.2(a). *Snowden v. State*, 353 S.W.3d 815, 820 (Tex. Crim. App. 2011). The court held that the first and last *Harris* factors—the source of the error and whether declaring the error harmless would encourage the State to repeat it—are not viable under a Rule 44.2(a) analysis and expressly disavowed them. *Snowden*, 353 S.W.3d at 821-22; *see Schmutz v. State*, 440 S.W.3d 29, 39 (Tex. Crim. App. 2014) (factor of whether finding error harmless would encourage State to repeat it is no longer a proper consideration in harm analysis under Rule 44.2(b)). The *Snowden* court concluded that "[t]he remaining *Harris* factors ... remain as viable considerations in deciding whether trial error of a constitutional dimension contributed to the conviction or punishment in many cases. But they are not *exclusive* considerations [for a proper harm analysis] in any particular case ...." *Snowden*, 353 S.W.3d at 822; *see Love v. State*, ___ S.W.3d ___ (Tex. Crim. App. 2016) (No. AP-77,024; 12-7-16) (in determining whether there is a real possibility that error might have contributed to conviction, reviewing court "take[s] into account any and every circumstance apparent in the record that logically informs a determination whether, beyond a reasonable doubt, this particular error contributed to the conviction or punishment"). The reviewing court must "evaluate the entire record in a neutral manner and not 'in the light most favorable to the prosecution.'" *Love*, ___ S.W.3d at ___ (quoting *Harris*, 790 S.W.2d at 586).

98.   *Compare* Tex. R. App. P. 44.2(b) ("Any other error, defect, irregularity, or variance that does not affect substantial rights must be disregarded."), *with* Fed. R. Crim. P. 52(a) ("Any error, defect, irregularity, or variance that does not affect substantial rights must be disregarded.").

99.   *King v. State*, 953 S.W.2d 266, 271 (Tex. Crim. App. 1997).

100.   *Burnett v. State*, 88 S.W.3d 633, 638 (Tex. Crim. App. 2002); *Schutz v. State*, 63 S.W.3d 442, 444 (Tex. Crim. App. 2001); *see Johnson v. State*, 43 S.W.3d 1, 4 (Tex. Crim. App. 2001).

101.   *Burnett*, 88 S.W.3d at 637-38; *see Schutz*, 63 S.W.3d at 444; *Johnson*, 43 S.W.3d at 4. The Texas Supreme Court has acknowledged that the harmless-error standard is a matter of judgment, not a specific test. *Reliance Steel & Aluminum Co. v. Sevcik*, 267 S.W.3d 867, 871 (Tex. 2008). In making a harmless-error determination, the reviewing court must "evaluate the whole case from voir dire to closing argument, considering the 'state of the evidence, the strength and weakness of the case, and the verdict.'" *Id.* (quoting *Std. Fire Ins. v. Reese*, 584 S.W.2d 835, 841 (Tex. 1979)).

102.   *See* Moss, *supra* note 89, at 511-14 (harmless-error standard in Rule 103(a) is "wrong and superfluous"). Nonetheless, a reference to the appellate effect of erroneous rulings in Rule 103(a) is an important reminder that even those evidentiary errors properly brought to the trial judge's attention are not a basis for reversal on appeal unless the errors affected a party's substantial rights.

pellate Procedure 44.2(b).[103] Constitutional violations may occur when evidence offered by the criminal defendant is erroneously excluded and "forms such a vital portion of the case that exclusion effectively precludes the defendant from presenting a defense."[104] The exclusion of evidence might be a constitutional violation if:

> (1) a state evidentiary rule categorically and arbitrarily prohibits the defendant from offering otherwise relevant, reliable evidence vital to his defense; or (2) a trial court's clearly erroneous ruling results in the exclusion of admissible evidence that forms the vital core of a defendant's theory of defense and effectively prevents him from presenting that defense.[105]

The harmless-error doctrine is frequently invoked when a trial court has improperly admitted evidence over an objection and later admits that same evidence through some other witness or questioning and the opponent does not renew the objection.[106] The failure to renew an objection is a type of forfeiture.[107] In Texas, this rule has fre-

---

103. *Walters v. State*, 247 S.W.3d 204, 219 (Tex. Crim. App. 2007); *see Potier v. State*, 68 S.W.3d 657, 666 (Tex. Crim. App. 2002). In *Potier*, the trial court erroneously excluded testimony of rumors that the defendant and a neighbor had heard from people in their neighborhood that the victim intended to kill the defendant on the day of the shooting. 68 S.W.3d at 658, 665-66. The court of criminal appeals concluded the error was not of constitutional dimension. *Id.* at 666.

104. *Walters*, 247 S.W.3d at 219; *Potier*, 68 S.W.3d at 665; *accord Balderas v. State*, 517 S.W.3d 756, 781 (Tex. Crim. App. 2016), *cert. denied*, 137 S. Ct. 1207 (2017); *see Valle v. State*, 109 S.W.3d 500, 507 (Tex. Crim. App. 2003) ("The fact that appellant was not able to present his case in the form he desired does not amount to constitutional error when he was not prevented from presenting the substance of his defense to the jury.").

105. *Walters*, 247 S.W.3d at 219; *accord Williams v. State*, 273 S.W.3d 200, 232 (Tex. Crim. App. 2008); *e.g., Ray v. State*, 178 S.W.3d 833, 835-36 (Tex. Crim. App. 2005) (in drug-possession case, nonconstitutional but reversible error to exclude testimony by defendant's acquaintance that defendant did not possess drugs); *Wiley v. State*, 74 S.W.3d 399, 405 (Tex. Crim. App. 2002) (trial court's ruling that probative value of "alternative perpetrator evidence" was substantially outweighed by danger of unfair prejudice was not a clearly erroneous exclusion of admissible evidence; thus, defendant was not denied Sixth Amendment and due-process rights to present meaningful defense).

106. *See Volkswagen of Am., Inc. v. Ramirez*, 159 S.W.3d 897, 907 (Tex. 2004) ("The general rule is error in the admission of testimony is deemed harmless and is waived if the objecting party subsequently permits the same or similar evidence to be introduced without objection."); *Mancorp, Inc. v. Culpepper*, 802 S.W.2d 226, 230 (Tex. 1990) ("When erroneously admitted evidence is merely cumulative or does not concern a material issue dispositive of the case, the error is harmless."); *Valle*, 109 S.W.3d at 509 ("An error in the admission of evidence is cured where the same evidence comes in elsewhere without objection."); *Leday v. State*, 983 S.W.2d 713, 718 (Tex. Crim. App. 1998) ("[O]verruling an objection to evidence will not result in reversal when other such evidence was received without objection, either before or after the complained-of ruling."); *Jones v. State*, 843 S.W.2d 487, 493 (Tex. Crim. App. 1992) (when defendant testifies to same facts that were proved by State, any error in admitting such facts is harmless), *overruled on other grounds*, *Maxwell v. State*, 48 S.W.3d 196 (Tex. Crim. App. 2001). Although the rule is usually invoked for the improper admission of evidence, it also operates when a trial court improperly excluded evidence that was admitted at a later time. *See Mentis v. Barnard*, 870 S.W.2d 14, 16 (Tex. 1994) (error in exclusion of evidence does not require reversal if excluded evidence is cumulative); *Gee v. Liberty Mut. Fire Ins.*, 765 S.W.2d 394, 396 (Tex. 1989) (no reversible error based on rulings on admissibility of cumulative evidence that is noncontrolling of a material issue).

107. The rationale for requiring the opponent to object every time the matter is raised is that the trial judge will not enforce or repeat earlier rulings unless a party so requests. Furthermore, the party who originally opposed a particular question or piece of evidence may have decided, on further reflection or after the consideration of additional evidence, that the evidence is either neutral or helpful to his cause. Alternatively, he may not want to emphasize harmful evidence by objecting to it again in front of the jury. For these reasons, the parties, not the court, "police" the proof. Refer to note 121 *infra* and accompanying text. A corollary to this type of forfeiture, however, is that the harmful effect of improperly admitted evidence is not affirmatively waived by the introduction of "rebut-

quently been called the doctrine of "curative admissibility,"[108] even though this label is incorrect.[109] Technically, the doctrine of curative admissibility allows one party to offer otherwise inadmissible evidence to counter the unfairly prejudicial use of the same evidence by the opposing party.[110] A closely related waiver doctrine holds that error in the admission of evidence is waived when the objecting party then introduces that same evidence.[111] For example, the U.S. Supreme Court has held that when a party unsuccessfully objects to impeachment evidence and then offers that evidence itself solely "to remove the sting" of the impeachment, the party has forfeited the right to complain about the original ruling on appeal.[112]

Courts are not always precise in distinguishing the concepts of "forfeiture of error" and "waiver of error."[113] A party forfeits error on appeal when the party does not preserve a claim of error in the trial court, such as by not objecting or making an offer of proof; a party waives error when the party intentionally relinquishes a right, such as by expressly stating "no objection" to offered evidence even though it might be inadmissible.[114] A party who offers evidence to which that party had previously objected

---

tal evidence designed to meet, destroy, or explain the improper evidence." **Bush v. State**, 697 S.W.2d 397, 404 (Tex. Crim. App. 1985); **Maynard v. State**, 685 S.W.2d 60, 65 (Tex. Crim. App. 1985); **Howard v. State**, 599 S.W.2d 597, 605 (Tex. Crim. App. 1980) (op. on reh'g). The rule is the same in civil cases. *See Scurlock Oil Co. v. Smithwick*, 724 S.W.2d 1, 4 (Tex. 1986) (party can introduce rebuttal evidence without waiving objection); **State v. Chavers**, 454 S.W.2d 395, 398 (Tex. 1970) (opponent who has objected to the admission of incompetent evidence may "defend himself without waiving his objection" by explaining, rebutting, or demonstrating the untruthfulness of the incompetent evidence). *See generally* 1 JOHN H. WIGMORE, EVIDENCE IN TRIALS AT COMMON LAW §18, at 835-38 (Tillers rev. 1983) (discussing waiver of objection).

108. *See* **Brown v. State**, 757 S.W.2d 739, 741 n.* (Tex. Crim. App. 1988) (doctrine of curative admissibility applies when error accompanying improper admission of evidence is rendered harmless because opponent of the improper evidence offers the same evidence); **In re R.S.C.**, 940 S.W.2d 750, 752 (Tex. App.—El Paso 1997, no writ) (same). *See generally* 1 RAY, *supra* note 8, §27, at 36 (discussing curative admissibility).

109. *See* **Leday**, 983 S.W.2d at 716 (Texas courts have frequently misused the term "curative admissibility"); 1 GOODE ET AL., *supra* note 18, §103.1, at 17-18 (doctrine of curative admissibility is often misidentified).

110. **Leday**, 983 S.W.2d at 716; *see also* 1 WIGMORE, *supra* note 107, §15, at 740-46 (most jurisdictions accept the "Massachusetts rule" of curative admissibility, which permits rebuttal by otherwise inadmissible evidence when the opponent has been allowed to offer inadmissible evidence, but only if the evidence originally submitted by the opponent created significant prejudice that ought to be corrected). *See generally* 1 MUELLER & KIRKPATRICK, *supra* note 5, §1:12, at 65-82 (discussing invited error and "opening the door," but not using the term "curative admissibility").

111. *See* **In re Toyota Motor Sales, U.S.A., Inc.**, 407 S.W.3d 746, 760 (Tex. 2013) ("[W]here ... the party that requested the limine order *itself* introduces the evidence into the record, and then fails to immediately object, ask for a curative or limiting instruction or, alternatively, move for mistrial, the party waives any subsequent alleged error on the point."); *see, e.g.*, **McInnes v. Yamaha Motor Corp., U.S.A.**, 673 S.W.2d 185, 187-88 (Tex. 1984) (plaintiff argued that trial court erred in admitting evidence offered by defendant to prove plaintiff's intoxication; error was waived because plaintiff introduced his own deposition testimony that he drank six beers before motorcycle accident).

112. **Ohler v. United States**, 529 U.S. 753, 755-60 (2000). In **Ohler**, the defense tactic of introducing evidence of the defendant's prior conviction on direct examination forfeited her right to complain on appeal about the trial judge's adverse in limine ruling admitting that evidence. *Id.* at 757-58. *But see* Moss, *supra* note 89, at 559-62 (**Ohler** rule "is an unnecessary and punitive exercise in mechanical jurisprudence"; rule "permits the prosecution to trick the defendant" into eliciting the impeaching conviction on direct examination and allows the State to avoid appellate review of a prior conviction of potentially dubious admissibility).

113. *See* **United States v. Yu-Leung**, 51 F.3d 1116, 1121-22 (2d Cir. 1995).

114. *See* **United States v. Olano**, 507 U.S. 725, 733 (1993) (forfeiture is failure to timely assert a right, and waiver is intentional relinquishment or abandonment of a known right); **Yu-Leung**, 51 F.3d at 1121 ("[F]orfeiture does not

"waives" any error on appeal, while the party who does not object again when previously objected-to evidence is reoffered "forfeits" error on appeal.

A second application of the harmless-error doctrine holds that the trial judge's ruling excluding or admitting evidence will be upheld on any legal theory that applies to the case and is supported by the record, even if the trial judge did not rely on that particular theory.[115] Thus, it is not reversible error to admit or exclude evidence for a wrong reason if there is any valid reason for the ruling.[116]

On occasion, appellate courts will uphold the use and consideration of materials never formally offered into evidence if neither party objected to their use and the parties and the trial court relied on those materials.[117] The materials that the parties considered evidence are deemed admitted on appeal. However, the materials must be contained within the appellate record if the appellate court is to consider them in assessing the sufficiency of the evidence.[118]

---

preclude appellate consideration of a claim in the presence of plain error, whereas waiver necessarily 'extinguishes' the claim altogether."); *Marin v. State*, 851 S.W.2d 275, 279-80 (Tex. Crim. App. 1993) (mere failure to object cannot be waiver; waiver involves a positive relinquishment of a right; forfeiture means a loss of a claim or right unless a party insists on the claim or right by "objection, request, motion, or some other behavior calculated to exercise the right in a manner comprehensible to the system's impartial representative, usually the trial judge"), *overruled on other grounds*, *Cain v. State*, 947 S.W.2d 262 (Tex. Crim. App. 1997); *Amspacher v. State*, 311 S.W.2d 564, 572 (Tex. App.—Waco 2009, no pet.) ("A defendant who fails to preserve error regarding the evidence's admissibility forfeits his complaint on appeal."); *see, e.g.*, *United States v. Weiss*, 930 F.2d 185, 198 (2d Cir. 1991) (defendant who, for tactical reasons, expressly withdrew trial objection to exclusion of documents "waived" his right to claim error on appeal); *Holmes v. State*, 248 S.W.3d 194, 200 (Tex. Crim. App. 2008) (defendant affirmatively waived his right to claim error on appeal when he stated "no objection" to State's offer of crack pipe into evidence); *see also Thomas v. State*, 408 S.W.3d 877, 885 (Tex. Crim. App. 2013) (whether statement of "no objection" will forfeit error that had been preserved earlier depends on context; if record demonstrates that defendant did not intend to abandon claim of error and trial court did not construe statement that way, appellate court should resolve claim on merits); *Saldano v. State*, 70 S.W.3d 873, 887-90 (Tex. Crim. App. 2002) (explaining distinction between "waivable" and "forfeitable" rights as set out in *Marin*; failure to make timely and specific objection during trial forfeits complaints on appeal about admissibility of evidence).

115. *Armendariz v. State*, 123 S.W.3d 401, 404 (Tex. Crim. App. 2003); *Roquemore v. State*, 60 S.W.3d 862, 866 (Tex. Crim. App. 2001); *Prystash v. State*, 3 S.W.3d 522, 527 (Tex. Crim. App. 1999); *see McDuff v. State*, 939 S.W.2d 607, 616 (Tex. Crim. App. 1997) (reviewing court may properly uphold trial court's ruling even when record does not reflect that the specific basis was ever considered by parties or trial court).

116. *See Romero v. State*, 800 S.W.2d 539, 543 (Tex. Crim. App. 1990); *see also* 1 McCormick on Evidence, *supra* note 92, §52, at 263 (normally, trial court's decision to overrule or sustain untenable specific objection will not be overturned if proper ground exists for doing so, even when the proper ground was not advanced at trial); Lynne Liberato & Kent Rutter, *Reasons for Reversal in the Texas Courts of Appeals*, 48 Hous. L. Rev. 993, 1005-06 (2012) (in study of appellate-court opinions issued over a one-year period, courts of appeals almost never reversed based on erroneous admission or exclusion of evidence; even when court of appeals found abuse of discretion, it was almost always harmless error).

117. *See, e.g.*, *Tex. Health Enters., Inc. v. Tex. Dep't of Human Servs.*, 949 S.W.2d 313, 313-14 (Tex. 1997) (per curiam) (in appeal from administrative hearing, reviewing court should have considered record of administrative proceeding because parties and trial court relied on it even though it was not formally offered into evidence); *Leonard v. Burge*, 74 S.W.3d 135, 137 (Tex. App.—Beaumont 2002, pet. denied) (at trial-court hearing, although no testimony was taken and the written sports-arena resolution was not marked as exhibit nor offered into evidence, both parties directed the court's attention to the resolution and its attachments, and trial court took judicial notice of it and reviewed it before ruling; because no objection was made, trial court treated the resolution and its attachment as evidence).

118. *See Vannerson v. Vannerson*, 857 S.W.2d 659, 670-71 (Tex. App.—Houston [1st Dist.] 1993, writ denied) (although inventory was not formally introduced into evidence in divorce proceeding, it was filed in court's papers and

The basic principle inherent in Rule 103 is "party responsibility."[119] Thus, the party complaining on appeal about the trial judge's ruling, regardless of whether the ruling admitted or excluded evidence, "must have done everything necessary to bring the relevant evidentiary rule and its precise and proper application to the trial court's attention."[120] The trial judge does not police the evidence; the judge's role is to rule on the timely and specific objections actually made on the record.[121]

1. Rule 103(a)(1): Objection. Rule 103(a)(1) "promotes finality and economy in litigation by forcing parties to object in the trial court or risk being foreclosed from raising the error on appeal."[122] The rule simply reiterates the common-law doctrine that an appellate court will sustain a claim of error in the admission of evidence only if the objecting party makes a timely complaint that specifically calls the error to the trial court's attention.[123] Texas courts normally require a party to make a timely and specific objection and to obtain an adverse ruling before error is preserved for appellate review.[124] Appellate courts "may *uphold* a trial court's ruling on any legal theory or basis applicable to the case, but usually may not *reverse* a trial court's ruling on any theory or basis that might have been applicable to the case, but was not raised."[125]

---

trial judge could have taken judicial notice of its contents); ***Bryant v. State***, 187 S.W.3d 397, 404 (Tex. Crim. App. 2005) (Johnson, J., concurring) (without some record of a stipulation agreed to by the parties, a reviewing court "could not even say that there was a stipulation, and without a record of the substance of a stipulation, it could not resolve a dispute about the scope of the stipulation, could not determine what was stipulated to, and consequently, could not determine whether the state has sufficiently proven the offense"). In a concurring opinion in ***Bryant***, two judges noted that a written stipulation was contained in the appellate record and thus was sufficient proof of the stipulated facts. 187 S.W.3d at 405 & n.1 (Cochran & Holcomb, JJ., concurring).

119. ***Reyna v. State***, 168 S.W.3d 173, 177 (Tex. Crim. App. 2005); 1 GOODE ET AL., *supra* note 18, §103.2, at 19; *see* ***Martinez v. State***, 91 S.W.3d 331, 335 (Tex. Crim. App. 2002) (Rule 103 and Texas Rule of Appellate Procedure 33.1 are "judge-protecting" rules based on the principle of "party responsibility"); *see also* 1 MCCORMICK ON EVIDENCE, *supra* note 92, §51, at 246 (adversary system requires parties to present evidence at trial).

120. ***Resendez v. State***, 306 S.W.3d 308, 313 (Tex. Crim. App. 2009); *accord* ***Reyna***, 168 S.W.3d at 177; ***Martinez***, 91 S.W.3d at 335-36; 1 GOODE ET AL., *supra* note 18, §103.2, at 20; *see, e.g.*, ***Tristan v. State***, 393 S.W.3d 806, 811 (Tex. App.—Houston [1st Dist.] 2012, no pet.) (defendant did not preserve error about excluded testimony when "[h]e did not identify for the record what the excluded testimony would have been or attempt to draw the court's attention to the reasons the questions were admissible").

121. *See* ***Resendez***, 306 S.W.3d at 313 ("The parties, not the judge, are responsible for the correct application of evidentiary rules ...."); Blinka, *supra* note 94, at 5 (there are no "evidence police," and "it is up to the lawyers to decide which rules to invoke and when"); Moss, *supra* note 89, at 516 n.30 (courts will not enforce their previous evidentiary rulings sua sponte; parties have "the exclusive power to present and resist trial evidence").

122. 1 WEINSTEIN & BERGER, *supra* note 85, §103.02[2], at 103-9. An objection that sparks further inquiry may clarify a situation that might otherwise be obscure to a reviewing court. *See* ***United States v. Indiviglio***, 352 F.2d 276, 279-80 (2d Cir. 1965) (en banc) (Federal Rule 103 allows judge to correct error and prevent future proceedings).

123. *See* TEX. R. EVID. 103(a)(1); *see, e.g.*, ***S. Tex. Elec. Coop. v. Ermis***, 396 S.W.2d 955, 959 (Tex. Civ. App.—Corpus Christi 1965, no writ) (objection made after witness had fully testified on direct, cross-, and re-examination was not timely); ***Withers v. Tyler Cty. Lumber Co.***, 326 S.W.2d 173, 181 (Tex. Civ. App.—Beaumont 1959, writ ref'd n.r.e.) (objections asserted three months after entry of judgment were not timely); *see also* ***Phillips v. State***, 511 S.W.2d 22, 28 (Tex. Crim. App. 1974) (failure to object when evidence is offered precludes review by appellate court); 1 WIGMORE, *supra* note 107, §18, at 814 (failure to invoke rule of evidence results in forfeiture of objection in any later proceeding). Timely and specific objections enable the trial judge to correct evidentiary errors that could be the basis for appellate review. *See, e.g.*, ***United States v. Richardson***, 562 F.2d 476, 478 (7th Cir. 1977) (error complained of could have been easily corrected by objection when evidence was admitted).

124. *See* ***Lopez v. State***, 253 S.W.3d 680, 684 (Tex. Crim. App. 2008).

125. ***Martinez***, 91 S.W.3d at 336.

There are sound practical reasons for this "raise it or forfeit it" rule. First, the offering party's interests are protected by requiring the objecting party to raise complaints about the evidence's admissibility while the offering party has an opportunity to respond to or cure any defects in that offer.[126] Second, it is only fair to the judge to require the objecting party to make complaints known while the court has an opportunity to prevent the erroneous admission of evidence. Third, if a case could be reversed for error that was not raised in a timely or specific manner in the trial court, the losing party would be able to second-guess its unsuccessful tactical or strategic decisions.[127]

Courts have sometimes declined to apply the forfeiture rule when the right to assert a constitutional violation was not recognized at the time of trial.[128] This limited exception to the rule excuses the failure to make a contemporaneous objection only when (1) the claim was so novel that the legal basis of the claim was not reasonably available at the time of trial,[129] or (2) the law was so well settled at the time that an objection would have been futile.[130] In most instances, however, even constitutional errors may be forfeited if a specific and timely objection is not made at trial.[131]

(1) Make objection.

(a) Timeliness required. To preserve an evidentiary error at trial, an objection must be timely.[132] Rule 103(a)(1)(A) follows Texas common law; a timely objection is made at the earliest possible opportunity, as soon as the grounds for the objection become apparent.[133] If the objection is made any later, error is waived.[134] Normally, the objec-

---

126. *See Beall v. Ditmore*, 867 S.W.2d 791, 794 (Tex. App.—El Paso 1993, writ denied); *Young v. State*, 826 S.W.2d 141, 149 (Tex. Crim. App. 1991) (Campbell & McCormick, JJ., dissenting).

127. *See Beall*, 867 S.W.2d at 794; *Young*, 826 S.W.2d at 149.

128. *See Ex parte Bravo*, 702 S.W.2d 189, 190 (Tex. Crim. App. 1982).

129. *See Ex parte Crispen*, 777 S.W.2d 103, 105 (Tex. Crim. App. 1989); *Mathews v. State*, 768 S.W.2d 731, 733 (Tex. Crim. App. 1989); *Chitwood v. State*, 703 S.W.2d 360, 361-62 (Tex. App.—Dallas 1986, pet. ref'd); *Black v. State*, 816 S.W.2d 350, 368 (Tex. Crim. App. 1991) (Campbell, McCormick, Overstreet, Benavides, JJ., concurring); *cf. Reed v. Ross*, 468 U.S. 1, 16 (1984) (establishing federal "novelty" doctrine).

130. *See Chitwood*, 703 S.W.2d at 361-62; *Black*, 816 S.W.2d at 368.

131. *E.g.*, *Saldano v. State*, 70 S.W.3d 873, 889-90 (Tex. Crim. App. 2002) (defendant's failure to object during capital-murder punishment hearing to psychologist's testimony listing 25 different statistical indicators of possible future dangerousness and to psychologist's assertion that minorities were overrepresented in prison forfeited any error in allegedly "racial" testimony, even though State had admitted error); *In re K.A.S.*, 131 S.W.3d 215, 230-31 (Tex. App.—Fort Worth 2004, pet. denied) (parents' constitutional challenge to Family Code statute-of-limitations provision in suit to terminate parental rights was forfeited on appeal when they did not object on this basis at trial); *see also In re B.L.D.*, 113 S.W.3d 340, 355 (Tex. 2003) ("[A] court of appeals must not retreat from our error-preservation standards to review unpreserved charge error in parental rights termination cases.").

132. TEX. R. EVID. 103(a)(1)(A).

133. *See Ethington v. State*, 819 S.W.2d 854, 858 (Tex. Crim. App. 1991) (objection must be made when grounds become apparent); *Montelongo v. State*, 681 S.W.2d 47, 57 (Tex. Crim. App. 1984) (objection must be made at the earliest opportunity); *see, e.g.*, *Schwartz v. Forest Pharm., Inc.*, 127 S.W.3d 118, 123 (Tex. App.—Houston [1st Dist.] 2003, pet. denied) (party did not preserve error when it did not object to admission of testimony "until after he had been asked about several different lawsuits that had been filed on his behalf and after he had given substantial testimony about them"); *Camarillo v. State*, 82 S.W.3d 529, 534 (Tex. App.—Austin 2002, no pet.) (objection to

tion must be made before the evidence is admitted or presented to the jury,[135] but sometimes an objection made after a witness answers the objectionable question will be considered timely. For example, if the witness responds so quickly that the opponent does not have time to object before the answer, a motion to strike that answer may be used.[136] The same is true when the question itself is proper but the answer is not.[137] For example, when a witness responds by reciting unsolicited hearsay or volunteering inadmissible information, a motion to strike is appropriate.[138] A delayed objection and motion to strike would also be permissible when the improper aspects of the evidence are not apparent until cross-examination or when the proponent does not "connect up" evidence that was previously admitted as conditionally relevant.[139] In a bench trial, the timeliness requirement of objections is more relaxed. An objection on appeal is not forfeited as long as it is made "within a reasonable time" after the basis for the objection becomes apparent.[140] In sum, an objection is timely if made when the trial judge has an opportunity to effectively cure the alleged error.[141]

RULE 103

detective's testimony reciting defendant's statement was not timely when made after that topic was complete and State's examination had moved on to other matters).

134. *E.g.*, *Gaytan v. State*, 331 S.W.3d 218, 229 (Tex. App.—Austin 2011, pet. ref'd) (defendant argued that trial court erred by refusing to strike complainant's testimony after she admitted that she did not directly recall being abused; error was waived because defendant did not object or move to strike at that point in complainant's testimony, but waited until she had answered 12 more questions).

135. *Polk v. State*, 729 S.W.2d 749, 753 (Tex. Crim. App. 1987); *see Ethington*, 819 S.W.2d at 858 ("The objection must be timely; that is, the [objecting party] must have objected to the evidence, if possible, before it was actually admitted."); *see, e.g.*, *Gerron v. State*, ___ S.W.3d ___ (Tex. App.—Waco 2016, pet. ref'd) (No. 10-14-00121-CR; 10-26-16) (defendant's hearsay and confrontation objections were preserved when trial court overruled them at hearing outside jury's presence to determine admissibility of testimony; defendant was not required to object every time potentially inadmissible testimony was given before jury). A timely objection enables the judge to insulate the jury from any tainted or improper evidence or, at least, permits the judge to quickly cure whatever impropriety might have occurred. *See Polk*, 729 S.W.2d at 753. It also prevents the proponent of the evidence from being misled into introducing other inadmissible evidence by the opponent's failure to challenge earlier evidence. *See id.* at 754. Finally, the requirement prevents the opponent from "gambling that the answer to a question calling for objectionable matter will be favorable, and then objecting when it proves not to be." *Id.*

136. *See* TEX. R. EVID. 103(a)(1)(A).

137. *See Beall v. Ditmore*, 867 S.W.2d 791, 794 (Tex. App.—El Paso 1993, writ denied). In this case, a proper cross-examination question "effectively opened the door for the well-prepared witness to enter into an oral dissertation regarding each and every conceivable element of compensable damages, and then some." *Id.* When the witness's answer, not counsel's question, is objectionable, the party should not be faulted for not objecting immediately. *See id.*

138. *See, e.g.*, *Heidelberg v. State*, 36 S.W.3d 668, 673-74 (Tex. App.—Houston [14th Dist.] 2001, no pet.) (when witness directly responded to defense counsel's cross-examination question, motion to strike the response would have preserved error if counsel had requested that only inadmissible portion of testimony be stricken; failure to segregate inadmissible from admissible portions of witness's response resulted in forfeiture of error).

139. *See id.* at 673; *see, e.g.*, *Ka-Hugh Enters., Inc. v. Fort Worth Pipe & Supply Co.*, 524 S.W.2d 418, 424 (Tex. Civ. App.—Fort Worth 1975, writ ref'd n.r.e.) (error was not preserved for admission of expert testimony based on a hypothetical question because no motion to strike was made, not because objection was untimely). *See generally* 1 MCCORMICK ON EVIDENCE, *supra* note 92, §58, at 293-94 (majority view is that opponent must move to strike conditionally relevant evidence when failure of condition becomes apparent).

140. *Polk*, 729 S.W.2d at 755.

141. *Beall*, 867 S.W.2d at 795; *see Saldano v. State*, 232 S.W.3d 77, 88 (Tex. Crim. App. 2007).

On the other hand, premature objections, made before the specifically objectionable evidence is actually offered into evidence, do not preserve error unless final evidentiary rulings are made during pretrial hearings.[142] An objection made too early is as improper as one made too late.[143]

(b) Specificity required. To preserve an evidentiary error at trial, an objection must also be specific.[144] A specific objection challenges the admission of evidence if that admission would violate a specific rule of evidence.[145] The Texas Court of Criminal Appeals has noted that there are two rationales for a specific objection: "(1) to inform the trial judge of the basis of the objection and give him the opportunity to rule on it; (2) to give opposing counsel the opportunity to respond to the complaint."[146] Counsel must clearly articulate both the legal and factual grounds for the objection.[147] Additionally,

---

142. *See, e.g.,* ***Tex. Commerce Bank Reagan v. Lebco Constructors, Inc.***, 865 S.W.2d 68, 78 (Tex. App.—Corpus Christi 1993, writ denied) (discussion between judge and attorneys at pretrial hearing was not sufficient to preserve error for rulings to be made later at trial); ***Mo. Pac. R.R. v. Brown***, 862 S.W.2d 636, 638 (Tex. App.—Tyler 1993, writ denied) (although party had objected several times when opponent indicated that it would introduce specific evidence, no error was preserved because party did not object again when evidence was introduced); ***Trailways, Inc. v. Clark***, 794 S.W.2d 479, 488 (Tex. App.—Corpus Christi 1990, writ denied) (objection was premature when made before prejudicial nature of anticipated testimony became apparent); ***Farm Servs., Inc. v. Gonzales***, 756 S.W.2d 747, 750 (Tex. App.—Corpus Christi 1988, writ denied) (objection to expert's testimony before witness was called was both premature and too general to preserve error). Refer to notes 203-206 *infra* and accompanying text.

143. Judge Charles Campbell & William P. Green, *Guidelines for Preserving Error or, How Not to Drop the Ball*, 54 Tex. B.J. 1178, 1180 (1991); *see* ***Johnson v. State***, 977 S.W.2d 725, 728 (Tex. App.—Fort Worth 1998, pet. ref'd) (trial court's statement that it "believed" testimony was admissible, made the day before evidence was offered, did not eliminate need to object when evidence was actually offered).

144. Tex. R. Evid. 103(a)(1)(B).

145. 1 Ray, *supra* note 8, §24, at 31 (3d ed. 1980). However, if the specific objection at trial varies from the specific complaint on appeal, error is not preserved. *See* ***Heidelberg v. State***, 144 S.W.3d 535, 537 (Tex. Crim. App. 2004); ***Montoya v. State***, 744 S.W.2d 15, 33 (Tex. Crim. App. 1987), *overruled on other grounds*, ***Cockrell v. State***, 933 S.W.2d 73 (Tex. Crim. App. 1996); ***Euziere v. State***, 648 S.W.2d 700, 703-04 (Tex. Crim. App. 1983); *see, e.g.,* ***Nelson v. State***, 405 S.W.3d 113, 127-28 (Tex. App.—Houston [1st Dist.] 2013, pet. ref'd) (defendant's motion to suppress preserved error of admissibility of statements; motion specifically asserted arguments and corresponding constitutional grounds); ***Davila v. State***, 930 S.W.2d 641, 650 (Tex. App.—El Paso 1996, pet. ref'd) (objection to nonresponsiveness did not preserve error of inadmissibility of extraneous offenses).

146. ***Resendez v. State***, 306 S.W.3d 308, 312 (Tex. Crim. App. 2009); *accord* ***Martinez v. State***, 91 S.W.3d 331, 336 (Tex. Crim. App. 2002); ***Saldano v. State***, 70 S.W.3d 873, 887 (Tex. Crim. App. 2002).

147. *See, e.g.,* ***Reynolds v. State***, 781 S.W.2d 351, 352-53 (Tex. App.—Houston [1st Dist.] 1989, pet. ref'd) (defendant's objection to "contraband" rather than "cocaine" was specific, timely, and well understood by the prosecutor and the trial court); ***Crider v. Appelt***, 696 S.W.2d 55, 57 (Tex. App.—Austin 1985, no writ) (error was not adequately preserved when grounds for objection were unclear to appellate court, although they were clear to trial judge). A party must be specific in its objection even when the objection itself might reinforce prejudice to the jury. *See, e.g.,* ***Turner v. State***, 719 S.W.2d 190, 194 (Tex. Crim. App. 1986) (objections of "trying to badger the witness" and "bringing the jury into this personally" were not specific and thus legally insufficient).

In articulating how specific an objection must be, Texas courts appear to have moved away from rigid technical formalism and have taken a more realistic approach that hinges on whether the judge and the opponent understand the basis of the complaint. *See* ***Bekendam v. State***, 441 S.W.3d 295, 300 (Tex. Crim. App. 2014) ("The complaining party must let the trial judge know what she wants and why she thinks she is entitled to it, and do so clearly enough for the judge to understand and at a time when the trial court is in a position to do something about it. We are not hyper-technical in examination of whether error was preserved, but the point of error on appeal must comport with the objection made at trial."); ***Pena v. State***, 285 S.W.3d 459, 464 (Tex. Crim. App. 2009) ("Error preservation does not involve a hyper-technical or formalistic use of words or phrases; instead, '[s]traight forward communication in plain English' is sufficient." (quoting ***Lankston***, 827 S.W.2d at 909)); *see, e.g.,* ***Layton v. State***, 280 S.W.3d 235, 240 (Tex. Crim. App. 2009) (in DWI prosecution, defendant's objection to police officer's testimony about de-

if a portion of the evidence in question is admissible and other portions are not, specific objections must be made to the inadmissible portions, or the claim of error is forfeited.[148]

Without more specificity, objections such as "irrelevant," "immaterial," and sometimes even "hearsay" may be insufficient to preserve error for appellate review.[149] The

fendant's prescription-drug use, on the grounds that the State had not shown the accuracy and reliability of the testimony or its relevance to the issue of intoxication by alcohol, was sufficient to put trial court and opposing counsel on notice of the issue and preserved the error for appellate review); *Morales v. State*, 951 S.W.2d 59, 62-63 (Tex. App.—Corpus Christi 1997, no pet.) (defendant's request for *Jackson v. Denno* hearing was sufficient to preserve issue of voluntariness of confession on appeal).

In one Fifth Circuit case, defense counsel's objection—"'[i]t doesn't prove that she had anything to do with altering anything or had knowledge of it'"—was held sufficient to preserve a complaint about evidence of guilt by association with others. *United States v. Polasek*, 162 F.3d 878, 882-84 (5th Cir. 1998). Although the court stated that this objection was not as "eloquent" as possible, it clearly put the prosecutor and trial court on notice that evidence of defendant's friends' convictions showed nothing about the defendant's guilt of the crime charged. *Id.* at 884.

On the other hand, when it is not apparent from the record that the trial judge was aware of the correct legal basis for the objection, the opponent of the evidence does not preserve that particular legal basis for appellate review. *See, e.g.*, *Heidelberg*, 144 S.W.3d at 537 (appellant did not preserve argument that prosecutor commented on defendant's right to post-arrest, pre-*Miranda* silence under Texas Constitution when defense counsel's objections were based on "Fifth Amendment" and did not mention Texas Constitution).

148. *Reyes v. State*, 314 S.W.3d 74, 78 (Tex. App.—San Antonio 2010, no pet.); *see Brown & Root, Inc. v. Haddad*, 142 Tex. 624, 628, 180 S.W.2d 339, 341 (1944) (general objection that does not object to a specific part is properly overruled if any portion of evidence is admissible); *Celotex Corp. v. Tate*, 797 S.W.2d 197, 206 (Tex. App.—Corpus Christi 1990, writ dism'd) ("This rule of specificity is particularly important when evidence may be admissible in part because if a specific objection is made, the trial court can then strike the objectionable portion."); *see, e.g.*, *Whitaker v. State*, 286 S.W.3d 355, 369 (Tex. Crim. App. 2009) (defendant's objections to audiotapes did not preserve error because he did not specifically point out which portions were inadmissible; "[t]he trial court was not obligated to search through these audiotapes and remove 'all of the inadmissible references so that the recorded statements only contained the admissible evidence'"). A trial court does not abuse its discretion in admitting an entire exhibit when the objecting party does not identify the inadmissible portions. *Reyes*, 314 S.W.3d at 78.

149. *See Bridges v. City of Richardson*, 163 Tex. 292, 293, 354 S.W.2d 366, 368 (1962) (objection that evidence is immaterial or irrelevant is insufficient to preserve error); *Euziere*, 648 S.W.2d at 703 (objections based on claims that a question is "global, misleading, repetitive, or immaterial and irrelevant" are insufficient to preserve error); *Breeden v. State*, 438 S.W.2d 105, 108 (Tex. Crim. App. 1969) (statement "[w]e object to this, Your Honor" is insufficient to preserve error); *Town of Flower Mound v. Teague*, 111 S.W.3d 742, 765-66 (Tex. App.—Fort Worth 2003, pet. denied) (general objection to "lack of foundation" that does not specify how foundation is insufficient is not specific enough to preserve error); *Anderson v. State*, 15 S.W.3d 177, 182 (Tex. App.—Texarkana 2000, no pet.) (merely saying "Objection," without stating the specific grounds, is insufficient to preserve error unless the grounds are otherwise made known to trial court); *see, e.g.*, *Gallo v. State*, 239 S.W.3d 757, 768 (Tex. Crim. App. 2007) (defendant's general objection at trial did not preserve argument that trial court improperly denied his motion for mistrial; defendant did not explain which of his constitutional rights were violated when prosecutor cursed during closing argument); *In re C.C.*, 476 S.W.3d 632, 635-36 (Tex. App.—Amarillo 2015, no pet.) (objection in trial court that report was "littered with hearsay," without identifying particular instances, was insufficient to preserve hearsay objection for review; citing specific passages in argument to court of appeals did not transform general objection into proper one); *Tryco Enters., Inc. v. Robinson*, 390 S.W.3d 497, 505 (Tex. App.—Houston [1st Dist.] 2012, pet. dism'd) (general hearsay objection did not preserve error for review; attorney "did not object with specificity, despite the trial court's invitation to him to do so"); *Scherl v. State*, 7 S.W.3d 650, 652 (Tex. App.—Texarkana 1999, pet. ref'd) (objection to Intoxilyzer evidence as "inadmissible under Rule 702, *Daubert*, *Kelly*, and *Hartman*" was effectively a general objection to an improper predicate and was not sufficiently specific). *But see Lankston v. State*, 827 S.W.2d 907, 910 (Tex. Crim. App. 1992) ("Identifying challenged evidence as hearsay or as calling for hearsay should be regarded by courts at all levels as a sufficiently specific objection, except under the most unusual circumstances. Indeed, it is difficult to know how much more specific such an objection could be under most circumstances."); *Baxter v. State*, 66 S.W.3d 494, 498 (Tex. App.—Austin 2001, pet. ref'd) ("hearsay" objection was specific enough to preserve complaint).

last clause of Rule 103(a)(1)(B), however, limits this rule: a general objection suffices when the specific ground for exclusion was or should have been apparent to the judge and opposing counsel.[150] On the other hand, "shotgun" objections—that is, citing many grounds for the objection without any supporting argument—are the equivalent of no objection at all.[151]

(c) Running objections. The judicial and scholarly debate continues about whether running objections will preserve error on appeal.[152] The traditional rationale for the running objection is that when "a party makes a proper objection to the introduction of testimony and is overruled, he is entitled to assume that the judge will make the same ruling as to the other offers of similar testimony, and he is not required to repeat the objection."[153] Texas decisions on the issue are mixed.[154] Some courts have adopted a

---

150. *See* Tex. R. Evid. 103(a)(1)(B) (unless the ground "was apparent from the context"); ***Resendez***, 306 S.W.3d at 313 ("When the correct ground for exclusion was obvious to the judge and opposing counsel, no forfeiture results from a general or imprecise objection."); ***Miller v. State***, 741 S.W.2d 382, 387 (Tex. Crim. App. 1987) ("When the ground for objection or complaint … is obvious to the trial judge and opposing counsel, and there is no suggestion in the record that the parties did not know the basis and nature of the defendant's objection or complaint, a general objection or 'exception' is usually sufficient to preserve the error."); *see, e.g.,* ***Maxson v. State***, 79 S.W.3d 74, 76 (Tex. App.—Texarkana 2002, pet. ref'd) (objection preserved error when defendant had filed motion in limine, State filed response, and context in which objection was raised demonstrated that it was "understood by all involved"); ***Hernandez v. State***, 53 S.W.3d 742, 745-46 (Tex. App.—Houston [1st Dist.] 2001, pet. ref'd) (objection that expert witness did not meet the qualifications of Rule 702 and ***Daubert*** was general, but sufficient in context); ***Veteto v. State***, 8 S.W.3d 805, 810 (Tex. App.—Waco 2000, pet. ref'd) (clear from questions, objections, responses, and trial court's interaction that objections were obvious to trial court); *see also* ***Rivas v. State***, 275 S.W.3d 880, 887 (Tex. Crim. App. 2009) ("Reference to a Rule may save an objection that might otherwise be obscure, but an objection is not defective merely because it does not identify a Rule of Evidence."). Refer to note 173 *infra* and accompanying text.

　　Texas common law included two other exceptions to the requirement of a specific objection. First, general objections were allowed when the evidence was obviously inadmissible for any purpose. ***Fowler v. State***, 171 Tex. Crim. 600, 605, 352 S.W.2d 838, 841 (Tex. Crim. App. 1962); *see* ***Bridges***, 163 Tex. at 293-94, 354 S.W.2d at 368 (when evidence is not relevant to any issue in the case, general objection will preserve error for review). This doctrine seems to have survived under Rule 103's "apparent from the context" language. Second, a party could make a general objection to the entirety of the evidence when a case involved voluminous records. *See, e.g.,* ***Hurtado v. Tex. Employers' Ins.***, 574 S.W.2d 536, 537-39 (Tex. 1978) (examination and segregation of the objection to 280 pages of records was not required). The rationale for this exception was that it would unduly burden a party to search through each page of a voluminous records exhibit to segregate the inadmissible items from the admissible ones.

151. ***Webb v. State***, 899 S.W.2d 814, 818 (Tex. App.—Waco 1995, pet. ref'd); *see, e.g.,* ***Berry v. State***, 813 S.W.2d 636, 639-40 (Tex. App.—Houston [14th Dist.] 1991) (objection citing 25 different federal and Texas constitutional and statutory grounds was the equivalent of no objection at all), *pet. ref'd*, 821 S.W.2d 616 (Tex. Crim. App. 1991). As the court in ***Berry*** noted: "A trial court cannot be forced to sift through dozens of general objections in an effort to determine which complaints, if any, have merit." 813 S.W.2d at 640.

152. *See* 1 Goode et al., *supra* note 18, §103.2, at 26 (most courts allow running objections to preserve error); 1 McCormick on Evidence, *supra* note 92, §52, at 263-64 (same); 1 Mueller & Kirkpatrick, *supra* note 5, §1:10, at 47-49 (running objections should be allowed to preserve error; repetitive objections are distracting and waste time); 21 Wright & Graham, *supra* note 41, §5037.5, at 728-30 (federal courts and some state courts allow continuing or "durable" objections to preserve error).

153. ***Bunnett/Smallwood & Co. v. Helton Oil Co.***, 577 S.W.2d 291, 295 (Tex. Civ. App.—Amarillo 1978, no writ).

154. *Compare* ***Goodman v. State***, 701 S.W.2d 850, 863 (Tex. Crim. App. 1985) (running objection would not "preserve error on a matter referred to by any witness at any time" during trial), ***Mares v. State***, 758 S.W.2d 932, 933 (Tex. App.—El Paso 1988, pet. ref'd) (running objection does not preserve error), *and* ***Killebrew v. State***, 746 S.W.2d 245, 247 (Tex. App.—Texarkana 1987, pet. ref'd) ("In most circumstances a generalized 'running objection' will not preserve error."), *with* ***Sattiewhite v. State***, 786 S.W.2d 271, 283 n.4 (Tex. Crim. App. 1989) (in some situations, run-

case-by-case analysis to determine whether an initial objection covers a later offer of similar evidence based on considerations such as (1) the proximity of the objection to the later testimony, (2) which party has elicited the later testimony, (3) the nature of the later testimony and its similarity to the earlier testimony and its objection, (4) whether the later testimony came from the same witness or a different one, and (5) whether the objecting party sought a running objection.[155] Although a case-by-case appellate analysis to determine whether a single (or even a repeated) objection may be treated as a running objection might appear fair and reasonable, such an approach gives little or no clear guidance to either the parties or the trial judge during the trial itself.[156] Thus, unless a party has explicitly obtained a running objection from the trial court, he should not guess whether to continue to object to the same or similar evidence each time it is mentioned. The party must continue to object to each improper question to ensure preservation of the issue for possible appeal.[157]

The rationale for allowing running objections was summarized by the Texas Court of Criminal Appeals:

> A running objection, in some instances, will actually promote the orderly progression of the trial. When an attorney has an objection to a line of testimony from a witness, it is often disruptive for the trial judge to force him to make the same objection after each question of opposing counsel just so that the attorney can receive the same ruling from the trial judge to preserve error.[158]

The evidentiary problem, however, is the question of when and how far the objection runs. Attorneys should obtain the trial court's explicit permission to lodge a running objection and then specifically outline the nature, grounds, and extent of the objection.[159] Each time a different witness testifies, the objection should be renewed and

---

ning objection is preferable to "redundant and disruptive" objections), *Miranda v. State*, 813 S.W.2d 724, 737 (Tex. App.—San Antonio 1991, pet. ref'd) (court disallowed running objection because of a lack of specificity but implied that a properly phrased running objection is permissible), *and White v. State*, 784 S.W.2d 453, 460 (Tex. App.—Tyler 1989, pet. ref'd) (interpreting *Goodman* as standing for the proposition that a running objection may, depending on facts and circumstances, preserve error for appellate review).

155. *See Correa v. Gen. Motors Corp.*, 948 S.W.2d 515, 518-19 (Tex. App.—Corpus Christi 1997, no writ); *Atkinson Gas Co. v. Albrecht*, 878 S.W.2d 236, 243 (Tex. App.—Corpus Christi 1994, writ denied).

156. *See* Moss, *supra* note 89, at 520 (while such an approach is "perfectly reasonable, if not enlightened, it fails to give trial counsel a bright-line rule").

157. *Lopez v. State*, 253 S.W.3d 680, 684 (Tex. Crim. App. 2008).

158. *Sattiewhite*, 786 S.W.2d at 283 n.4; *see Ethington v. State*, 819 S.W.2d 854, 858-59 (Tex. Crim. App. 1991) (running objections are permissible and favored whenever a continuous stream of objections would be disruptive). Frederick Moss suggests that, as an alternative to an explicit running objection, counsel may ask the trial court if continued objections are necessary. If the trial court states that they are not, counsel may consider this ruling the equivalent of a formal running objection. *See* Moss, *supra* note 89, at 520.

159. *See Sattiewhite*, 786 S.W.2d at 283 n.4 ("[A]n advocate who lodges a running objection should take pains to make sure it does not encompass too broad a reach of subject matter over too broad a time or over different witnesses."); *White*, 784 S.W.2d at 460-61 & n.9 (trial court's permission is "essential to the existence of the running objection"; hearsay objection to one witness's testimony does not carry over to another witness's similar testimony).

thoroughly outlined, unless the trial court has explicitly allowed the objection to extend to testimony by all witnesses on a particular topic.[160]

Further, unless the opponent of the evidence has secured a running objection, he must object not only when improper evidence is first offered but also every time the same evidence is offered; otherwise, the initial objection will be considered forfeited on appeal.[161]

Running objections under Rules 403 and 404(b) are especially inadvisable. The considerations for admitting or excluding evidence under these rules are so complex that neither counsel nor the trial court should ordinarily rely on a blanket running objection.[162]

(2) Obtain ruling on objection. Normally, a party must not only object but also obtain an adverse ruling on its objection before its complaint is preserved for appeal.[163] Attorneys often do not obtain an adverse ruling from the trial court and thus waive any purported error.[164] In criminal proceedings, the proper procedure for a defendant to preserve error under Rule 103 is to (1) object and obtain a ruling, (2) ask for an instruction to disregard if the objection is sustained, and (3) move for a mistrial if an instruc-

---

160. *See In re A.P.*, 42 S.W.3d 248, 261 (Tex. App.—Waco 2001, no pet.) ("[R]unning objections generally apply only to similar testimony by the same witness."), *overruled on other grounds*, *In re A.M.*, 385 S.W.3d 74 (Tex. App.—Waco 2012, pet. denied); *Scaggs v. State*, 18 S.W.3d 277, 292 (Tex. App.—Austin 2000, pet. ref'd) ("A running objection … does not preserve error when another witness testifies to the same matter without objection."); *see, e.g.*, *Petetan v. State*, ___ S.W.3d ___ (Tex. Crim. App. 2017) (No. AP-77,038; 3-8-17) (court of criminal appeals assumed without deciding that defendant's running objection was broad enough to cover testimony from two witnesses about defendant's promise to give drugs to one of them); *Ford v. State*, 919 S.W.2d 107, 113 (Tex. Crim. App. 1996) (court granted running objection to extend to all witnesses testifying to "victim impact" evidence).

161. *See Boyer v. Scruggs*, 806 S.W.2d 941, 946 (Tex. App.—Corpus Christi 1991, no writ); *Posner v. Dall. Cty. Child Welfare Unit*, 784 S.W.2d 585, 587 (Tex. App.—Eastland 1990, writ denied) (per curiam); *Texaco, Inc. v. Pennzoil, Co.*, 729 S.W.2d 768, 842 (Tex. App.—Houston [1st Dist.] 1987, writ ref'd n.r.e.); *see, e.g.*, *Martinez v. State*, 98 S.W.3d 189, 193 (Tex. Crim. App. 2003) (defendant's objections to photos did not preserve error for all other gang-related evidence; defendant should have continued to object, obtained a running objection, or requested a hearing outside jury's presence). Refer to notes 106-107 *supra* and accompanying text.

162. *Cf. United States v. McVeigh*, 153 F.3d 1166, 1200 (10th Cir. 1998) (continuing objections under Federal Rule 403 are generally inappropriate and should be reviewed like pretrial motions in limine; motion in limine will not preserve objection if it is not renewed when the evidence is introduced unless issue is fairly presented to the district court, can be finally decided in a pretrial hearing, and receives a clear ruling from trial judge), *disapproved on other grounds*, *Hooks v. Ward*, 184 F.3d 1206 (10th Cir. 1999).

163. *See Beham v. State*, 476 S.W.3d 724, 733 (Tex. App.—Texarkana 2015, no pet.); *Norman v. State*, 862 S.W.2d 621, 626 (Tex. App.—Tyler 1993, pet. ref'd).

164. *See, e.g.*, *Turner v. State*, 719 S.W.2d 190, 194 (Tex. Crim. App. 1986) ("[A]fter the trial court sustained the objection, the appellant never secured an adverse ruling to his motion for new trial. The appellant should have required the trial court to make a definite ruling on the record."); *Darty v. State*, 709 S.W.2d 652, 654-55 (Tex. Crim. App. 1986) (objection followed by unrecorded bench conference, followed by judge's statement, "All right. Anything else?" was not an adverse ruling and thus did not preserve error); *Tryco Enters., Inc. v. Robinson*, 390 S.W.3d 497, 505 (Tex. App.—Houston [1st Dist.] 2012, pet. dism'd) (hearsay objection was not preserved when defendants' attorney did not "obtain a definitive adverse ruling while the trial court was in a proper position to change its conditional ruling of admissibility and [plaintiff] was in a position to offer other testimony or to subpoena [defendants' former employee] to testify").

tion to disregard is given.[165] No error is preserved if the objecting party has received all the relief that it has requested.[166]

If the trial court refuses to rule, the objecting party may preserve error by objecting to the refusal.[167] A response by the trial court merely qualifying or limiting a line of questioning, however, is not a ruling on the objection and does not preserve error.[168] General remarks by the trial court, such as "Move along, counsel," or "Do not elicit hearsay," are not adverse rulings and do not preserve error.[169]

Under Texas Rule of Appellate Procedure 33.1(a)(2)(A), however, a party may preserve error if the trial court's adverse ruling during trial is either express or implied.[170] While "[a]ppellate courts will generally find that a trial court made an implicit ruling on an objection when the objection was brought to the trial court's attention," they only do so when "the trial court's subsequent action clearly addressed the complaint."[171] However, in reviewing the grant of a summary judgment, appellate courts do not pre-

---

165. ***Brooks v. State***, 642 S.W.2d 791, 798 (Tex. Crim. App. [Panel Op.] 1982); ***Gonzales v. State***, 775 S.W.2d 776, 778 (Tex. App.—San Antonio 1989, pet. ref'd); *see, e.g.*, ***Beham***, 476 S.W.3d at 733 (defendant preserved issue for review when defendant asked witness a question, trial court sustained objection to question, and trial court instructed jury to disregard witness's answer). The standards for preservation of error during voir dire are different from the general standard. *See* ***Samaripas v. State***, 454 S.W.3d 1, 5 (Tex. Crim. App. 2014). If a party asks a proper question of the jury panel, the other party objects, and the trial court sustains the objection, error is preserved. *Id.*

166. *See* ***Trad v. Gen. Crude Oil Co.***, 474 S.W.2d 183, 184 (Tex. 1971) (per curiam); *see, e.g.*, ***Lasker v. State***, 573 S.W.2d 539, 543 (Tex. Crim. App. [Panel Op.] 1978) (trial judge's remarks were not preserved for review because trial court gave all the relief that was requested).

167. Tex. R. App. P. 33.1(a)(2)(B).

168. *See* ***Callahan v. State***, 937 S.W.2d 553, 557 (Tex. App.—Texarkana 1996, no pet.); ***Murillo v. State***, 839 S.W.2d 485, 493 (Tex. App.—El Paso 1992, no pet.).

169. *See, e.g.*, ***Lewis v. State***, 664 S.W.2d 345, 349 (Tex. Crim. App. 1984) (judge's statement, "[i]t is up to the jury to determine," was not an adverse ruling); ***Graham v. State***, 566 S.W.2d 941, 954 (Tex. Crim. App. 1978) (admonition to "confine [your] remarks to the record" was not an adverse ruling); ***Mayberry v. State***, 532 S.W.2d 80, 84 (Tex. Crim. App. 1976) (op. on reh'g) (directive that the "[j]ury will recall the evidence" was not an adverse ruling).

170. Tex. R. App. P. 33.1(a)(2)(A); *e.g.*, ***Gutierrez v. State***, 36 S.W.3d 509, 510-11 (Tex. Crim. App. 2001) (case remanded for court of appeals to determine whether trial court had implicitly ruled on defendant's objection); *see* ***Clarke v. State***, 270 S.W.3d 573, 574 (Tex. Crim. App. 2008) ("[A] claim that the trial court erred in denying a motion for new trial is preserved for appellate review if the nature of the ground allegedly warranting the new trial is raised and litigated, without objection, at some point during the motion-for-new-trial proceedings."); ***Rey v. State***, 897 S.W.2d 333, 336 (Tex. Crim. App. 1995) (court's ruling on a matter does not need to be expressly stated if its actions or other statements unquestionably indicate a ruling). Thus, a party may not need to obtain specific rulings such as "overruled" or "denied" to preserve error. For example, "sit down" could suffice as an adverse ruling.

The problem of implied rulings is more complicated in the context of summary-judgment motions and objections to summary-judgment evidence. See ***O'Connor's Texas Rules * Civil Trials*** (2017), "Secure ruling on objections," ch. 7-B, §10.2, p. 710 (discussing conflict among courts of appeals on whether error is preserved if trial court does not make an express written ruling that overrules the nonmovant's objections).

171. ***State v. Kelley***, 20 S.W.3d 147, 153 n.3 (Tex. App.—Texarkana 2000, no pet.); *see, e.g.*, ***Magnuson v. Mullen***, 65 S.W.3d 815, 829 (Tex. App.—Fort Worth 2002, pet. denied) (because court did not make any ruling, express or implied, on constitutional challenges, nothing was preserved for appeal); ***Wal-Mart Stores, Inc. v. Reece***, 32 S.W.3d 339, 348 (Tex. App.—Waco 2000) (purported error in sidebar remark was not preserved because trial court's response to objection, asking parties to abide by their motions in limine, was too indefinite to constitute even an implicit ruling on the objection), *rev'd on other grounds*, 81 S.W.3d 812 (Tex. 2002).

---

sume that the trial court implicitly granted the movant's evidentiary objections when there is no written ruling or order to that effect.[172]

2. Rule 103(a)(2): Offer of proof. Rule 103(a)(2) restates the common-law requirement that the offering party must include the substance of rejected evidence in the record—that is, make an offer of proof—unless the error or evidence "was apparent from the context" of the questioning.[173] The rule enables the appellate court to determine whether excluding the evidence was error and, if so, whether it was harmful error.[174] It also allows the trial court to reconsider its original ruling once the evidence is presented.[175]

To preserve error in the exclusion of evidence, the proponent must actually offer the evidence or a summary of the evidence[176] and secure an adverse ruling from the

---

172. *See Jones v. Ray Ins. Agency*, 59 S.W.3d 739, 753 (Tex. App.—Corpus Christi 2001), *pet. denied*, 92 S.W.3d 530 (Tex. 2002); *Rogers v. Cont'l Airlines, Inc.*, 41 S.W.3d 196, 200 (Tex. App.—Houston [14th Dist.] 2001, no pet.); *see, e.g.*, *Well Sols., Inc. v. Stafford*, 32 S.W.3d 313, 316-17 (Tex. App.—San Antonio 2000, no pet.) (trial court's ruling on objection to summary-judgment evidence was not implicit in its ruling on the motion for summary judgment; ruling is "implicit if it is unexpressed but capable of being understood from something else").

173. *See* Tex. R. Evid. 103(a)(2); *Echols v. Wells*, 510 S.W.2d 916, 918-19 (Tex. 1974); *Mays v. State*, 285 S.W.3d 884, 889-90 (Tex. Crim. App. 2009); *Garden Ridge, L.P. v. Clear Lake, L.P.*, 504 S.W.3d 428, 438 (Tex. App.—Houston [14th Dist.] 2016, no pet.); *see, e.g.*, *Fields v. State*, 966 S.W.2d 736, 740 (Tex. App.—San Antonio 1998) (error preserved; although attorney could have been clearer in both his foundation questioning and request to call impeaching witness, it was apparent from context what he desired), *rev'd on other grounds*, 1 S.W.3d 687 (Tex. Crim. App. 1999); *Norton v. State*, 771 S.W.2d 160, 166-67 (Tex. App.—Texarkana 1989, pet. ref'd) (counsel's hearsay objection was sufficient to preserve error because hearing was held on hearsay objections before the objection). Refer to note 183 *infra* and accompanying text.

The 1998 unified version of Rule 103(a)(2) made the phrase "or was apparent from the context within which questions were asked," which appeared in the former criminal rule, applicable to civil actions as well. That version of Rule 103(a)(2) was the same as both the original federal rule and the original wording in Civil Rule 103(a)(2). In 1988, the Texas Supreme Court amended the rule to eliminate that phrase. *See Order Adopting and Amending Texas Rules of Civil Evidence*, 733-734 S.W.2d (Tex. Cases) xciv (1987, amended 1998). The unified version of Rule 103(a)(2) thus restored the former civil-law doctrine. *See, e.g.*, *In re Bryce*, 981 S.W.2d 887, 888 (Tex. App.—Houston [1st Dist.] 1998, orig. proceeding) (in civil contempt case, offer of proof was unnecessary when cross-examination of ex-wife's attorney about ex-husband's financial resources made it apparent that ex-husband would have introduced evidence of his inability to make ordered payment); *Life Ins. v. Brister*, 722 S.W.2d 764, 776 (Tex. App.—Fort Worth 1986, no writ) (requiring only that the substance of the evidence was apparent from the context in which questions were asked; court did not require a showing of the expected answer), *overruled on other grounds*, *Sw. Ref. Co. v. Bernal*, 22 S.W.3d 425 (Tex. 2000); *Foster v. Bailey*, 691 S.W.2d 801, 803 (Tex. App.—Houston [1st Dist.] 1985, no writ) (appellant was not required to make a bill of exception under Rule 103 because "[t]he right to cross-examine the sole adverse party on an ultimate disputed issue should not depend upon a showing that the cross-examination will be successful"). The current rule simply states "unless the substance was apparent from the context." *See* Tex. R. Evid. 103(a)(2).

174. *Mays*, 285 S.W.3d at 890; *Garden Ridge*, 504 S.W.3d at 438-39.

175. *Mays*, 285 S.W.3d at 890; *Garden Ridge*, 504 S.W.3d at 438-39.

176. *See Caffe Ribs, Inc. v. State*, 487 S.W.3d 137, 141 (Tex. 2016); *Mays*, 285 S.W.3d at 890-91; *Warner v. State*, 969 S.W.2d 1, 2 (Tex. Crim. App. 1998); *see, e.g.*, *JLG Trucking, LLC v. Garza*, 466 S.W.3d 157, 161 (Tex. 2015) (in personal-injury case, trial court excluded evidence of second accident that occurred three months after accident at issue as alternative cause of plaintiff's injuries; to preserve error after court excluded evidence, defendant submitted offer of proof that included police report on second accident, photos of plaintiff's vehicle after second accident, medical records documenting plaintiff's emergency treatment, and testimony from plaintiff's expert that he had not reviewed those medical records); *Wilson v. State*, 451 S.W.3d 880, 884-85 (Tex. App.—Houston [1st Dist.] 2014, pet. ref'd) (in trial for aggravated sexual assault of a child, trial court excluded defendant's good-character evidence about his moral and safe conduct around young children; issue was properly preserved in offer of proof under Rule 103(a)(2)).

court.[177] A party does not preserve any claim of error arising from the exclusion of evidence unless there is an adequate record of the excluded evidence.[178] The record on appeal must contain sufficient detail to allow the appellate court to determine whether the trial court committed reversible error in rejecting the offered evidence.[179] To adequately preserve error for appeal, the proponent must set forth the rejected evidence in an informal bill of exception[180] or a statement by counsel specifying the substance of the proffered evidence.[181] The proponent must describe the actual content of the testimony, not merely comment on the reasons for the testimony or why it is admissible.[182] However, if the content of the proposed testimony is unquestionably apparent to the trial court and the opposing party, a formal offer of proof is not required.[183] For example, if affidavits or reports containing the witness's proposed testimony are brought

---

177. **Quiroz v. Llamas-Soforo**, 483 S.W.3d 710, 722 (Tex. App.—El Paso 2016, pet. filed 5-25-16); *see* **Basham v. State**, 608 S.W.2d 677, 679 (Tex. Crim. App. 1980) ("To preserve error for review by this Court, the denial of a motion in limine is simply not sufficient. There must be a proper objection to the proffered evidence."); **Bobbora v. Unitrin Ins. Servs.**, 255 S.W.3d 331, 334-35 (Tex. App.—Dallas 2008, no pet.) (even if record contains enough information for reviewing court to conclude that evidence was improperly excluded, offer of proof is necessary to determine whether exclusion was harmful); **Perez v. Lopez**, 74 S.W.3d 60, 66 (Tex. App.—El Paso 2002, no pet.) (same).

178. *See* **In re A.E.A.**, 406 S.W.3d 404, 420 (Tex. App.—Fort Worth 2013, no pet.); **Lewis v. State**, 126 S.W.3d 572, 578-79 (Tex. App.—Texarkana 2004, pet. ref'd); *see, e.g.*, **Balderama v. State**, 421 S.W.3d 247, 250 (Tex. App.—San Antonio 2013, no pet.) (defendant did not properly preserve error when his bill of exception did not summarize excluded evidence or state its relevance); **Mai v. State**, 189 S.W.3d 316, 322 (Tex. App.—Fort Worth 2006, pet. ref'd) (error in excluding evidence is not preserved unless proponent made a sufficient summary of proposed testimony; defendant sufficiently preserved claim for cross-examination of police officer when defense stated his intended question and it was apparent that officer's answer would be "yes"); **Posner v. Dall. Cty. Child Welfare Unit**, 784 S.W.2d 585, 588 (Tex. App.—Eastland 1990, writ denied) (per curiam) (court relied on former Appellate Rule 52(b) and former Civil Rule 103(a)(2) to hold that appellants did not preserve any error because they did not make an offer of proof).

179. *See* **Quiroz**, 483 S.W.3d at 722-23; **Lone Starr Multi-Theatres, Ltd. v. Max Interests, Ltd.**, 365 S.W.3d 688, 703 (Tex. App.—Houston [1st Dist.] 2011, no pet.). However, attaching the excluded material as an appendix to the party's appellate brief does not suffice; the offer of proof must be made in the trial court. *See* **Cherqui v. Westheimer St. Festival Corp.**, 116 S.W.3d 337, 342 & n.2 (Tex. App.—Houston [14th Dist.] 2003, no pet.) (appellate courts will not consider documents attached to appellate brief as an offer of proof).

180. **Wright v. State**, 776 S.W.2d 763, 764-65 (Tex. App.—Corpus Christi 1989, pet. ref'd); *see* **Blackburn v. Brazos Valley Utils., Inc.**, 777 S.W.2d 758, 760 (Tex. App.—Beaumont 1989, writ denied) (under former Civil Rule 103, without a bill of exception, appellate court has no basis to review complaint that trial court erred in excluding evidence).

181. **Watts v. Oliver**, 396 S.W.3d 124, 129 (Tex. App.—Houston [14th Dist.] 2013, no pet.).

182. *See* **Mays v. State**, 285 S.W.3d 884, 891 (Tex. Crim. App. 2009) (a summary, "in the most general and cursory terms, without any of the meat of the actual evidence, will not suffice to preserve error"); **Warner v. State**, 969 S.W.2d 1, 2 (Tex. Crim. App. 1998) ("An offer of proof to be accomplished by counsel's concise statement must include a reasonably specific summary of the evidence offered and must state the relevance of the evidence unless the relevance is apparent, so that the court can determine whether the evidence is relevant and admissible."); *see, e.g.*, **Love v. State**, 861 S.W.2d 899, 900-01 (Tex. Crim. App. 1993) (when counsel merely informed trial judge that he intended to establish a basis for an instruction on the lack of probable cause but did not provide a concise statement of the content of testimony he proposed to elicit from witness, no error was preserved); **Watts**, 396 S.W.3d at 129 (plaintiff's attorney commented generally on expert witness's excluded anticipated testimony and the reasons for it but did not describe its actual content; comments did not preserve exclusion issue for appeal); **Rhoten v. State**, 299 S.W.3d 349, 355-56 (Tex. App.—Texarkana 2009, no pet.) (defendant sought to offer expert- and lay-opinion testimony that she suffered from a mental impairment to negate mens rea but offered no such specific testimony outside the presence or hearing of the jury; summary statement of excluded evidence did not preserve error for review).

183. *See* **Moore v. State**, 275 S.W.3d 633, 635 (Tex. App.—Beaumont 2009, no pet.); **Fox v. State**, 115 S.W.3d 550, 558-59 (Tex. App.—Houston [14th Dist.] 2002, pet. ref'd); **Marathon Corp. v. Pitzner**, 55 S.W.3d 114, 143 (Tex.

to the court's attention but are rejected, those materials may constitute an adequate offer of proof.[184] However, deposition testimony that was neither specifically shown to the trial court in a timely manner nor considered at the time the trial court made its ruling does not constitute an offer of proof.[185]

The rule is not as restrictive on the limitation of cross-examination, however, because the questioner cannot be expected to know the witness's answer.[186] When cross-examination testimony is excluded, it is sufficient to preserve error if the substance of the evidence is apparent from the context in which the proposed questions were asked.[187]

The proponent of the evidence has an absolute right to make a bill of exception or offer of proof.[188] Denial of that right could be reversible error if the excluded evidence is potentially relevant.[189] The remedy for such an error is normally to abate the appeal

---

App.—Corpus Christi 2001), *rev'd on other grounds*, 106 S.W.3d 724 (Tex. 2003). In *Fox*, when the trial court granted the State's motion in limine excluding the defendant's evidence, the judge and the parties repeatedly discussed admissibility of that evidence during trial. 115 S.W.3d at 558. At the end of one of these discussions, the judge stated: "I'm not going to change my ruling on your defenses. You've preserved all this on the record." *Id.* The error was preserved without formal offer of proof because disputed evidence was apparent to all. *Id.* at 559.

184. *See, e.g., Turner v. Peril*, 50 S.W.3d 742, 744-45 (Tex. App.—Dallas 2001, pet. denied) (op. on reh'g) (contents of properly filed affidavits sufficed as offer of proof when they were brought to trial judge's attention, trial judge stated on record that she had read affidavits, and affidavits themselves were contained in appellate record; however, mere filing of affidavits is not a sufficient offer of proof). *But see Wilson ex rel. C.M.W. v. Estate of Williams*, 99 S.W.3d 640, 649-50 & n.12 (Tex. App.—Waco 2003, no pet.) (although a copy of excluded DNA report was contained in appellate record and party had twice unsuccessfully offered it into evidence at trial, she did not make an offer of proof of the report itself at trial; thus, party forfeited complaint on appeal). The conflicting results in *Turner* and *Wilson* may be reconciled because in *Turner*, the record clearly showed that the trial judge actually reviewed the excluded material; in *Wilson*, there was no such explicit showing.

185. *See, e.g., Fletcher v. Minn. Mining & Mfg. Co.*, 57 S.W.3d 602, 608 (Tex. App.—Houston [1st Dist.] 2001, pet. denied) (because substance of expert witness's testimony was not apparent from context at pretrial hearing and would not become apparent until deposition testimony was submitted after trial court lost plenary power, any error in excluding that testimony was forfeited for failure to comply with Rule 103(a)(2)). *But see id.* at 610-11 (Mirabal, J., dissenting) (pretrial motion with exhibits containing excerpts of expert's testimony in earlier trials was sufficient offer of proof to preserve complaint; "[t]he law does not require the offer of proof to show what *specific* facts the examination would reveal; rather, the appellant must clearly inform the trial court of the subject matter about which he wishes to examine the witness").

186. In Texas criminal cases, the offer of proof does not need to show what specific facts the cross-examination would reveal when objecting to the exclusion of evidence that the witness had malice, ill feeling, ill will, bias, or prejudice toward another. *Koehler v. State*, 679 S.W.2d 6, 10 (Tex. Crim. App. 1984). Instead, the cross-examiner must "establish what subject matter he desired to examine the witness about during the cross-examination." *Id.* at 9; *see also Carroll v. State*, 916 S.W.2d 494, 497 (Tex. Crim. App. 1996) ("[T]he defendant should be granted a wide latitude even though he is unable to state what facts he expects to prove through his cross-examination.").

187. *See Foster v. Bailey*, 691 S.W.2d 801, 803 (Tex. App.—Houston [1st Dist.] 1985, no writ) (bill of exception was not required under former Civil Rule 103 because the right to cross-examine an adverse party "should not depend upon a showing that the cross-examination will be successful"). Refer to note 173 *supra* and accompanying text.

188. *Spence v. State*, 758 S.W.2d 597, 599 (Tex. Crim. App. 1988); *Andrade v. State*, 246 S.W.3d 217, 226 (Tex. App.—Houston [14th Dist.] 2007, pet. ref'd). *But see Rivera v. State*, 981 S.W.2d 336, 341 n.4 (Tex. App.—Houston [14th Dist.] 1998, no pet.) (questioning "whether the right to make an informal offer of proof is truly *absolute*" and suggesting several scenarios in which a party does not have such an absolute right).

189. *See M__A__B__ v. State*, 718 S.W.2d 424, 425-26 (Tex. App.—Dallas 1986, no pet.) (not allowing appellant to perfect a bill of exception or offer of proof prevents him from receiving a fair trial); *Ledisco Fin. Servs., Inc. v. Viracola*, 533 S.W.2d 951, 959 (Tex. Civ. App.—Texarkana 1976, no writ) (reversible error to refuse party the right to perfect bill of exception).

to allow a party to develop the appellate record.[190] Nonetheless, when a party has properly made an offer of proof and preserved error in the exclusion of evidence, the party may later waive or forfeit that error.[191]

3. Motions in limine or definitive rulings on admissibility. A party who thinks its opponent may offer prejudicial and arguably inadmissible evidence (or who wants to offer arguably inadmissible evidence) may want to seek an advance ruling on the admissibility of that evidence through a written or oral motion in limine.[192] While a motion in limine is helpful in planning initial trial strategy, a preliminary ruling on a motion in limine generally does not preserve error about the admission or exclusion of evidence.[193] Regardless of whether the motion is granted or denied, a proper trial objection is required to preserve any error for appeal.[194] For example, the supreme court has held that a pretrial sanctions motion, heard and ruled on the day before the trial begins, does not preserve the error in permitting an undesignated witness to testify; rather, the opposing party is required to "object when the testimony or evidence is offered at trial."[195] To preserve error in the exclusion of evidence if a pretrial motion in limine has been granted, a party must do the following: (1) approach the bench during trial and ask for a ruling to admit the evidence, (2) formally offer the evidence outside

---

In *Chance v. Chance*, however, the court held that it was not reversible error to refuse the appellant's request for an offer of proof in question-and-answer form because he was allowed to make a concise statement of what he wanted to ask the witness. 911 S.W.2d 40, 51-52 (Tex. App.—Beaumont 1995, writ denied). Here, the appellant wanted to ask an attorney-witness if she had told another witness not to talk to the appellant's attorney because he represented the opposing side. *Id.* The appellate court found that any error was harmless because the appellant did not show how this line of questioning was relevant or how it affected a substantial right. *Id.* at 52. The court also stated that because the excluded testimony came on cross-examination, the appellant was not required to make an offer of proof of the expected testimony; therefore, the trial court was not required to permit him to do so. *Id.* This latter statement is dubious because the objecting party is entitled to make an offer in question-and-answer form regardless of whether an offer of proof is required.

190. *Andrade*, 246 S.W.3d at 226; *see Spence*, 758 S.W.2d at 599-600.

191. *See, e.g., Duncan v. State*, 140 Tex. Crim. 606, 608-09, 146 S.W.2d 749, 750-51 (1940) (trial court excluded testimony over defendant's proper objection, but error was forfeited when court later permitted defendant to present testimony and he did not do so); *Flores v. State*, 920 S.W.2d 347, 352 (Tex. App.—San Antonio 1996) (when defendants gave trial court the option of accepting their offer of proof in summary form, and did not insist on question-and-answer form, they could not complain on appeal that trial court denied their right to a bill of exception in question-and-answer form), *pet. dism'd, improvidently granted*, 940 S.W.2d 660 (Tex. Crim. App. 1996). Refer to notes 113-114 *supra* and accompanying text.

192. *See Luce v. United States*, 469 U.S. 38, 40 n.2 (1984) ("'*In limine*' has been defined as '[o]n or at the threshold; at the very beginning; preliminarily.' We use the term in a broad sense to refer to any motion, whether made before or during trial, to exclude anticipated prejudicial evidence before the evidence is actually offered.").

193. *See Geuder v. State*, 115 S.W.3d 11, 14-15 (Tex. Crim. App. 2003) ("A trial judge's grant or denial of a motion *in limine* is a preliminary ruling only and normally preserves nothing for … review.").

194. *Pool v. Ford Motor Co.*, 715 S.W.2d 629, 637 (Tex. 1986); *Gonzales v. State*, 685 S.W.2d 47, 50 (Tex. Crim. App. 1985); *Contreras v. State*, 915 S.W.2d 510, 516 (Tex. App.—El Paso 1995, pet. ref'd); *see Luce*, 469 U.S. at 41-42 (ruling on motion in limine is not final because judge may not be aware of all pertinent evidence).

195. *Clark v. Trailways, Inc.*, 774 S.W.2d 644, 647 & n.2 (Tex. 1989); *accord Welsh v. Welsh*, 905 S.W.2d 615, 617-18 (Tex. App.—Houston [14th Dist.] 1995, writ denied). However, in *Owens-Corning Fiberglas Corp. v. Malone*, the court of appeals held that a trial court has the authority to make definitive pretrial evidentiary rulings on proposed exhibits, and that if the court does make pretrial rulings admitting or excluding exhibits, pretrial objections to those exhibits will preserve the issue for appeal. 916 S.W.2d 551, 557 (Tex. App.—Houston [1st Dist.] 1996), *aff'd*, 972 S.W.2d 35 (Tex. 1998).

the presence of the jury, and (3) obtain a ruling on the offer.[196] If the trial judge denies a motion in limine, the opponent must object again when the evidence is offered during trial.[197] Attorneys should always reassert any pretrial evidentiary objections during the trial itself, either in front of the jury or outside the jury's presence.[198] The rationale for the position that a motion in limine does not preserve error is that the judge may reconsider the initial pretrial ruling after hearing new facts.[199] Reconsideration of pretrial rulings that tentatively admit or exclude evidence under Rule 403 is especially likely because the balancing process required by that rule is based heavily on the particular context of the evidence at the time of the final ruling.[200]

The court of criminal appeals distinguished a true motion in limine from a definitive ruling on the admissibility of evidence in *Geuder v. State*.[201] In *Geuder*, the court held that a midtrial objection made outside the presence of the jury on the admissibility of the defendant's prior convictions was not a motion in limine, and that the trial court's ruling on that objection was definitive and preserved error for appellate review.[202]

Trial judges are not required to make definitive pretrial rulings on the admissibility of evidence. Thus, it is counsel's responsibility to ask the trial judge to explicitly clarify whether a pretrial ruling on a motion in limine or motion to exclude is final and definitive.[203] Such a definitive ruling is reviewed based on the facts and circumstances the trial judge knew about at the time of the ruling, not on what later trial evidence or events might reveal, unless those changed facts are specifically brought to the judge's

---

196. *Sw. Country Enters., Inc. v. Lucky Lady Oil Co.*, 991 S.W.2d 490, 493 (Tex. App.—Fort Worth 1999, pet. denied).

197. *See Srite v. Owens-Ill., Inc.*, 870 S.W.2d 556, 565 (Tex. App.—Houston [1st Dist.] 1993), *rev'd in part on other grounds sub nom. Owens-Ill., Inc. v. Estate of Burt*, 897 S.W.2d 765 (Tex. 1995).

198. *See, e.g.*, *Kia Motors Corp. v. Ruiz*, 432 S.W.3d 865, 880 (Tex. 2014) (in products-liability case, after trial court granted defense's motion in limine prohibiting introduction of evidence of other incidents without showing that those incidents were "substantially similar" to the one at issue in case, defense counsel renewed objection to admissibility of evidence during trial outside jury's presence and again when evidence was introduced; trial court overruled objections, and error was preserved).

199. *See Luce*, 469 U.S. at 41-42 (in limine ruling "is subject to change when the case unfolds"; even if nothing unexpected happens during trial, the judge is free to alter a previous in limine ruling); *Reveal v. West*, 764 S.W.2d 8, 11 (Tex. App.—Houston [1st Dist.] 1988, no writ) (trial court may reconsider its pretrial rulings either before or during trial).

200. *See United States v. Griffin*, 818 F.2d 97, 104 (1st Cir. 1987) ("[I]t is too great a handicap to bind a trial judge to a ruling on a subtle evidentiary question, requiring the most delicate balancing, outside a precise factual context.").

201. 115 S.W.3d 11 (Tex. Crim. App. 2003).

202. *Id.* at 15.

203. FED. R. EVID. 103 advisory committee's note to 2000 amendments; *see Greenberg Traurig of N.Y., P.C. v. Moody*, 161 S.W.3d 56, 91 (Tex. App.—Houston [14th Dist.] 2004, no pet.); *see, e.g.*, *Walden v. Ga.-Pac. Corp.*, 126 F.3d 506, 520 (3d Cir. 1997) (although "the district court told plaintiffs' counsel not to reargue every ruling, it did not countermand its clear opening statement that all of its rulings were tentative, and counsel never requested clarification, as he might have done"; alleged evidentiary error was not preserved except for review of "plain error"); *Fletcher v. Minn. Mining & Mfg. Co.*, 57 S.W.3d 602, 608 (Tex. App.—Houston [1st Dist.] 2001, pet. denied) (trial court had expressed only preliminary reluctance to allow party's expert testimony; no definitive ruling was on record).

attention.[204] A judge who makes a definitive pretrial ruling may nonetheless revisit that decision when the evidence is actually offered, especially if other evidence admitted or excluded might affect the rationale for the original ruling.[205] Furthermore, a definitive ruling goes only to the specific evidence for which the ruling was made; it does not apply to any other evidence that might be similar to or associated with the original evidence.[206]

In sum, the trial court's ruling on a motion in limine does not preserve any error for appeal, but a definitive ruling on a motion to exclude evidence made under Rule 103(a)(1) does; thus, attorneys should explicitly designate a motion in limine separately from a motion to exclude evidence or an objection made under Rule 103(a)(1) to avoid any possible confusion.[207]

B. Rule 103(b): Not Needing to Renew an Objection

Rule 103(b) expresses the long-standing Texas rule that a party does not need to repeat in the jury's presence an evidentiary objection that was previously made outside its presence if the evidence has been ruled admissible outside its presence.[208] However, the benefit of an objection made outside the jury's presence is lost if, when the evidence is finally offered in front of the jury, the opponent affirmatively states "no objection."[209] The opponent should either remain silent or state "no new objections" or "I renew my objections" instead of waiving any error by stating "no objection."

---

204. FED. R. EVID. 103 advisory committee's note to 2000 amendments; *see* ***Old Chief v. United States***, 519 U.S. 172, 182 n.6 (1997) ("It is important that a reviewing court evaluate the trial court's decision from its perspective when it had to rule and not indulge in review by hindsight.").

205. *See* FED. R. EVID. 103 advisory committee's note to 2000 amendments.

206. *See, e.g.,* ***Martinez v. State***, 98 S.W.3d 189, 193 (Tex. Crim. App. 2003) (definitive ruling made outside jury's presence on two photographs depicting gang activity did not apply to admission of other gang-related evidence).

207. *See* ***Greenberg Traurig***, 161 S.W.3d at 91.

208. ***Kia Motors Corp. v. Ruiz***, 432 S.W.3d 865, 880 (Tex. 2014); *see* ***Clark v. Trailways, Inc.***, 774 S.W.2d 644, 647 n.2 (Tex. 1989) (dicta; when court hears objections to offered evidence outside jury's presence, litigant does not need to reurge objection in jury's presence to preserve error); ***Peake v. State***, 792 S.W.2d 456, 458-59 (Tex. Crim. App. 1990) (defendant does not need to object at trial to admission of evidence once court has issued adverse ruling on motion to suppress); ***Moraguez v. State***, 701 S.W.2d 902, 904 (Tex. Crim. App. 1986) (same).

Federal Rule 103(b) achieves the same objective as Texas Rule 103(b). The federal rule, however, applies to both admitted and excluded evidence; the Texas rule applies only to evidence that is admitted over objection. *Compare* FED. R. EVID. 103(b) ("Once the court rules definitively on the record—either before or at trial—a party need not renew an objection or offer of proof to preserve a claim of error for appeal."), *with* TEX. R. EVID. 103(b) ("When the court hears a party's objections outside the presence of the jury and rules that evidence is admissible, a party need not renew an objection to preserve a claim of error for appeal."). The federal rule also does not require that the objections first be heard outside the jury's presence. *See* FED. R. EVID. 103(b).

209. *See, e.g.,* ***Gardner v. State***, 306 S.W.3d 274, 293 (Tex. Crim. App. 2009) (any error in admitting murder victim's bloody robe was harmless because defendant affirmatively stated "no objection" when a sample cut from that robe was introduced as a comparison sample to the fibers found in truck defendant had borrowed); ***Holmes v. State***, 248 S.W.3d 194, 200 (Tex. Crim. App. 2008) (defendant affirmatively waived his right to claim error on appeal when he stated "no objection" to State's offer of crack pipe into evidence); ***Dean v. State***, 749 S.W.2d 80, 83 (Tex. Crim. App. 1988) (when counsel stated "no objection" to the admission of fingerprint evidence, he did not preserve the issue for review on appeal). Refer to note 114 *supra* and accompanying text.

Rule 103(b) has also been construed to mean that a "final" definitive ruling during a pretrial hearing on motions to suppress,[210] motions to exclude expert testimony,[211] or motions to require the State to stipulate to certain evidence may carry over to the trial or may form the basis for a conditional appeal in a criminal case.[212]

C. Rule 103(c): Court's Statement About the Ruling; Directing an Offer of Proof

Rule 103(c) follows Federal Rule 103(c) and codifies earlier criminal and civil Texas law[213] with one modification. Texas Rule 103(c) permits counsel to insist on a specific question-and-answer form.[214] The rule is mandatory and gives the offering party and

---

210. *See Thomas v. State*, 408 S.W.3d 877, 881 (Tex. Crim. App. 2013) (adverse ruling on pretrial motion to suppress is ordinarily sufficient to preserve error, and defendant does not need to specifically object to that evidence when offered at trial). *See generally* GEORGE E. DIX & ROBERT O. DAWSON, TEXAS PRACTICE: CRIMINAL PRACTICE AND PROCEDURE §4.179 (2d ed. 2001) (discussing conditions under which the ruling on a motion to suppress evidence preserves error for appellate review).

211. *See, e.g., Huckaby v. A.G. Perry & Son, Inc.*, 20 S.W.3d 194, 205-06 (Tex. App.—Texarkana 2000, pet. denied) (trial court's pretrial or "gatekeeper" ruling on motion to exclude expert testimony was final and definitive ruling on evidence's admissibility; opponent preserved his complaint about admission of that testimony without repeating objection at trial). Not all such pretrial or gatekeeper rulings are final, but this ruling preserves the complaint when the trial court has made it unequivocally clear that the evidence will be admitted at trial. *See id.*; *see also* FED. R. EVID. 103 advisory committee's note to 2000 amendments (amendment "provides that a claim of error with respect to a definitive ruling is preserved for review when the party has otherwise satisfied the objection or offer of proof requirements of [Federal] Rule 103(a)").

212. *See generally* FED. R. EVID. 103 advisory committee's note to 2000 amendments (providing a thorough explanation of the differences between preliminary or tentative pretrial rulings on the admissibility of evidence and definitive rulings that may be made either pretrial or during the trial itself). Under Federal Rule 103, attorneys must ask the court "to clarify whether an *in limine* or other evidentiary ruling is definitive when there is doubt on that point." FED. R. EVID. 103 advisory committee's note to 2000 amendments. For a discussion of error preservation with motions in limine and definitive rulings on admissibility, refer to notes 192-207 *supra* and accompanying text.
    The court of criminal appeals has held that the State cannot refuse a felony DWI defendant's pretrial offer to stipulate to the two jurisdictionally required prior DWI convictions; the defendant may preserve for appeal the trial court's failure to require such a stipulation despite his guilty plea. *E.g., Robles v. State*, 85 S.W.3d 211, 213-14 (Tex. Crim. App. 2002) (pretrial motion to suppress evidence of defendant's prior DWI convictions necessary to prove jurisdiction in felony DWI prosecution preserved error although defendant waived trial and pleaded guilty); *Tamez v. State*, 11 S.W.3d 198, 202 (Tex. Crim. App. 2000) (when "the defendant agrees to stipulate to the two previous DWI convictions ... the proper balance is struck when the State reads the indictment at the beginning of trial, mentioning only the two jurisdictional prior convictions, but is foreclosed from presenting evidence of the convictions during its case-in-chief").

213. *See, e.g., O. v. P.*, 560 S.W.2d 122, 124 (Tex. Civ. App.—Fort Worth 1977, no writ) (commenting on Texas Rule of Civil Procedure 372, now Texas Rule of Appellate Procedure 33.2, which authorizes the court to suggest such corrections to a bill of exception as it deems necessary or to file its own bill to accurately present the court's actual ruling).
    Civil Rule 103(b), now Rule 103(c), was amended in 1988 to begin with a sentence requiring the trial judge to permit a party to make an offer of proof before the jury is charged. *See Order Adopting and Amending Texas Rules of Civil Evidence*, 733-734 S.W.2d (Tex. Cases) XCIV (1987, amended 1998). Parties in a criminal case had always had the absolute right to make an offer of proof, even though it was not explicitly mentioned in the former criminal rule. *See Kipp v. State*, 876 S.W.2d 330, 333 (Tex. Crim. App. 1994) (right to make a bill of exception is absolute); *Tatum v. State*, 798 S.W.2d 569, 571 (Tex. Crim. App. 1990) (right to offer proof under Rule 103 is absolute when evidence is excluded by trial court).

214. *See Kipp*, 876 S.W.2d at 334 (rules "are unequivocal in providing that the trial court shall allow the perfection of a bill in question and answer form at the request of a party"); *see, e.g., Dopico v. State*, 752 S.W.2d 212, 215 (Tex. App.—Houston [1st Dist.] 1988, pet. ref'd) (reversible error in refusing to permit defense counsel to make offer of proof by asking specific questions of witness). The court may also, on its own motion, direct that an offer of proof be made in question-and-answer form. TEX. R. EVID. 103(c).

its opponent an absolute right to decide how the offer of proof will be made. However, any error in refusing to permit a question-and-answer form may be harmless.[215] If the proponent believes that a witness is particularly persuasive, the proponent may opt to call the witness and offer the testimony in question-and-answer form. Conversely, if the witness is not particularly articulate or not presently in the courtroom, the proponent may choose to offer a concise summary of the anticipated testimony.[216] If the proponent wants to offer a summary, the opponent may demand that the prospective witness be questioned to ensure that the advocate is not "puffing up" the proposed testimony. Under the federal rule, the trial judge has discretion to direct the making of an offer in question-and-answer form.[217]

A short, factual recitation of what the testimony would show is sufficient "evidence" to preserve an issue for appeal. Formal proof is not required. Indeed, the Texas Court of Criminal Appeals has indicated that a concise statement is favored whenever practical.[218]

Although the rule certainly applies during a jury trial on the merits, it would also apply during ancillary proceedings (e.g., competency hearings),[219] or during hearings on pretrial motions in criminal actions.[220]

The offer of proof must itself appear in the record; a reference to an off-the-record offer of proof is not sufficient.[221] The proponent of the evidence must explain the factual and legal reasons why the evidence is admissible and cannot offer an entirely new rationale on appeal.[222]

The rule requires that the offer be made "as soon as practicable," allowing the trial judge to postpone the offer until a convenient time, such as during the noon recess or

---

215. *See Andrade v. State*, 246 S.W.3d 217, 226 (Tex. App.—Houston [14th Dist.] 2007, pet. ref'd).

216. *See Tatum*, 798 S.W.2d at 571 (parties are not required to follow one prescribed method for showing what testimony would have been had it been admitted); *Gutierrez v. State*, 764 S.W.2d 796, 798 (Tex. Crim. App. 1989) (defendants are not limited to one method to show what excluded testimony would have been); *Moosavi v. State*, 711 S.W.2d 53, 55-56 (Tex. Crim. App. 1986) (no formal requirements for an offer of proof).

217. *See* FED. R. EVID. 103(c). The Advisory Committee's note states that the application of the rule on a proffer in question-and-answer form was "made discretionary in view of the practical impossibility of formulating a satisfactory rule in mandatory terms." FED. R. EVID. 103 advisory committee's note, subdiv. (b).

218. *See Mays v. State*, 285 S.W.3d 884, 889 (Tex. Crim. App. 2009) ("The offer of proof may consist of a concise statement by counsel, or it may be in question-and-answer form."); *see, e.g., Tatum*, 798 S.W.2d at 572 (concise statement of evidence in support of motion to exclude any mention of prior convictions was sufficient "proof" to preserve issue of admissibility of prior convictions on appeal).

219. *See Kipp*, 876 S.W.2d at 333.

220. *See Spence v. State*, 758 S.W.2d 597, 599 (Tex. Crim. App. 1988).

221. *E.g., Rodriguez v. Hyundai Motor Co.*, 944 S.W.2d 757, 768 (Tex. App.—Corpus Christi 1997) (mere reference to "off-the-record discussion at the bench," without explicit offer of evidence, objection, or court's ruling, preserved nothing for appeal), *rev'd on other grounds*, 995 S.W.2d 661 (Tex. 1999). *But see Glenn v. C&G Elec., Inc.*, 977 S.W.2d 686, 688 (Tex. App.—Fort Worth 1998, pet. denied) (when the parties and trial court treat bench conference as part of jury trial and treat exhibit as if it had been offered and excluded, appellate court will do the same despite lack of formal offer and ruling). If an offer of proof was timely but was not made on the record, the complaining party may file a formal bill of exception in the trial court that sets out the contents of that offer of proof. *See* TEX. R. APP. P. 33.2.

222. *See Driggers v. State*, 940 S.W.2d 699, 710 (Tex. App.—Texarkana 1996, pet. ref'd) (op. on reh'g).

RULE 103

after the jury has left for the day.[223] It is the party's responsibility to pursue that later opportunity to make an offer.[224] The offer must be made before the jury charge is given.[225] This timeliness requirement ensures that the trial court has an opportunity to reconsider and change its ruling based on the content of the proposed testimony and to allow the party to present the evidence to the jury.[226]

The rule reflects the broad grant of discretion inherent in the trial court's powers to insert and clarify its reasons for admitting or rejecting evidence.[227] Indeed, trial judges in criminal proceedings are sometimes required to give findings of fact and conclusions of law.[228] Moreover, the rule's provisions work to crystallize the substance of any contested evidentiary issue so that it will be fully preserved for appellate review.

D. Rule 103(d): Preventing the Jury from Hearing Inadmissible Evidence

Rule 103(d), which is identical to Federal Rule 103(d) and is consistent with earlier Texas law,[229] advises that hearings on the admissibility of evidence should be conducted outside the hearing of the jury.[230] Once a jury has heard inadmissible evidence, removal of the resulting prejudice may be impossible.[231] Inevitably, the trial judge is forced to resort to a curative instruction that focuses the jury's attention on the very evidence the court wants the jury to forget. While an instruction to disregard improper evidence is

---

223. *See* TEX. R. EVID. 103(c).

224. *See, e.g.*, **Callahan v. State**, 937 S.W.2d 553, 557 (Tex. App.—Texarkana 1996, no pet.) (trial judge's ruling to delay making offer of proof does not equal a denial of that right; party who did not pursue right to proffer testimony did not preserve error on appeal); **Emerson v. State**, 756 S.W.2d 364, 368 (Tex. App.—Houston [14th Dist.] 1988, pet. ref'd) (defendant who did not pursue his request to make a bill of exception at a "later time" did not preserve error when excluded testimony was not placed into the record).

225. TEX. R. EVID. 103(c); *e.g.*, **In re A.C.**, 394 S.W.3d 633, 645 (Tex. App.—Houston [1st Dist.] 2012, no pet.) (party waived error when she made offer of proof after charge was read to jury; "[t]he trial court expressly told [her], before the charge was read, to make her offer of proof 'whenever' she wished"); **Sims v. Brackett**, 885 S.W.2d 450, 453 (Tex. App.—Corpus Christi 1994, writ denied) (although appellant did not make formal bill of exception until jury was deliberating, informal bench conference during trial that was recorded by court reporter, in which judge questioned counsel about the substance of witness's testimony, was a sufficient informal offer of proof).

226. *See Fletcher v. Minn. Mining & Mfg. Co.*, 57 S.W.3d 602, 608 (Tex. App.—Houston [1st Dist.] 2001, pet. denied) (by requiring offer of proof to be made before charge is read to jury, trial court can reconsider its ruling in light of the evidence contained in the bill).

227. *See* TEX. R. EVID. 103(c) (court can make any statement about the character or form of the evidence, the objection, and the ruling).

228. *See State v. Cullen*, 195 S.W.3d 696, 699 (Tex. Crim. App. 2006) (trial court is required to make either written or oral findings of fact and conclusions of law when so requested by the losing party at a hearing on a motion to suppress evidence).

229. *See Guest v. Guest*, 235 S.W.2d 710, 714 (Tex. Civ. App.—Fort Worth 1950, writ ref'd n.r.e.) (reversal is proper when arguments contain matters outside admitted testimony, thus furnishing the jury with information that it otherwise would not have and probably affecting the verdict).

230. There are several practical ways to ensure that the jury does not hear evidence that is ruled inadmissible. These include retiring the jury while the parties present the disputed testimony or arguments, retiring the parties and judge to chambers to discuss the disputed testimony or arguments, sidebar conferences outside the jury's earshot, and pre-trial motions in limine. *See* 2 MICHAEL H. GRAHAM, HANDBOOK OF FEDERAL EVIDENCE §103:8, at 139-42 (7th ed. 2012).

231. *See* Joe S. Cecil et al., *Citizen Comprehension of Difficult Issues: Lessons from Civil Jury Trials*, 40 AM. U. L. REV. 727, 771 n.316 (1991) (several empirical studies show that juries have difficulty disregarding inadmissible evidence once they have heard it). Judges, however, are deemed to be able to ignore inadmissible evidence; in bench trials, they often hear evidence that they then exclude and must not consider when making their rulings.

almost always considered legally sufficient to negate any error,[232] its practical efficacy is more doubtful.[233] In some instances, the only true remedy may be to declare a mistrial and start over.[234]

On the other hand, the rule does not require a hearing outside the presence of the jury when there is no reasonable ground for believing that the testimony is inadmissible.[235] Merely objecting to testimony does not, by itself, require such a hearing.

The thrust of the rule is to avoid situations that require post facto curative remedies.[236] By making these remedies unnecessary through discrete nonjury hearings on the admissibility of the evidence, the rule ultimately seeks to ensure both judicial economy and a just and prompt resolution of the evidentiary issue.

E. Rule 103(e): Taking Notice of Fundamental Error in Criminal Cases

Rule 103(e) addresses fundamental error—error so egregious that it is cognizable on appeal even without objection at trial—in criminal cases.[237] It follows Federal Rule

---

232. In criminal cases in which reference has been made to the defendant's inadmissible prior bad acts—evidence that is considered highly prejudicial to the defendant—an instruction to disregard is almost always sufficient to cure the impropriety. *See, e.g.*, **Kemp v. State**, 846 S.W.2d 289, 308 (Tex. Crim. App. 1992) (prosecutor's improper reference to defendant's extraneous convictions was curable by an instruction to disregard); **Moody v. State**, 827 S.W.2d 875, 890 (Tex. Crim. App. 1992) (any potential error in admitting police officer's testimony that he pulled the defendant's "arrest jacket" during his investigation was cured by an instruction to disregard); **Barney v. State**, 698 S.W.2d 114, 124-25 (Tex. Crim. App. 1985) (testimony that victim did not like defendant because defendant "was an ex-con" was cured by an instruction to disregard); **Aliff v. State**, 627 S.W.2d 166, 172 (Tex. Crim. App. 1982) (jury instruction was sufficient to cure error after State's witness testified that he had talked with defendant's probation officer).

233. The Texas Court of Criminal Appeals explained as follows:

> Any error in asking an improper question or in admitting improper testimony may be generally cured or rendered harmless by a withdrawal of such testimony and an instruction to disregard. ... The exception to this general rule occurs where it appears that the question or the evidence or testimony admitted is "clearly calculated to inflame the minds of the jury and is of such character" as to suggest the impossibility of withdrawing the impression produced on their minds.

Livingston v. State, 739 S.W.2d 311, 335 (Tex. Crim. App. 1987) (citations omitted).

234. *See Mathes v. State*, 765 S.W.2d 853, 857 (Tex. App.—Beaumont 1989, pet. ref'd) (declaration of mistrial is necessary when the court believes that it is impossible for jury to follow instructions to disregard evidence).

235. *E.g.*, **Shugars v. State**, 814 S.W.2d 897, 897-98 (Tex. App.—Austin 1991, no pet.) (per curiam) (when defendant repeatedly objected to witness's testimony that events occurred in Travis County, defense counsel could not voir dire the witness outside jury's presence about witness's personal knowledge when there was no suggestion that witness lacked personal knowledge).

236. *Cf.* **United States v. Nace**, 561 F.2d 763, 767 (9th Cir. 1977) (parties should use former Federal Rule 103(c), now Rule 103(d), to discuss highly inflammatory material outside jury's presence to avoid possible mistrials if evidence is later deemed inadmissible).

237. *See* **Robertson v. State**, 397 S.W.3d 774, 776 (Tex. App.—Houston [14th Dist.] 2013, no pet.); **Infante v. State**, 397 S.W.3d 731, 738 (Tex. App.—San Antonio 2013, no pet.); *cf.* **Taylor v. State**, 332 S.W.3d 483, 490 (Tex. Crim. App. 2011) (defining "egregious harm" under Texas Code of Criminal Procedure art. 36.19; "[e]rrors which result in egregious harm are those that affect the very basis of the case, deprive the defendant of a valuable right, vitally affect the defensive theory, or make a case for conviction clearly and significantly more persuasive"); **Almanza v. State**, 686 S.W.2d 157, 171 (Tex. Crim. App. 1985) (op. on reh'g) (predating Texas Rules of Criminal Evidence; if no proper objection is made at trial, defendant must claim fundamental error and will obtain reversal under Texas Code of Criminal Procedure article 36.19 "only if the error is egregious and created such harm that he 'has not had a fair and impartial trial'—in short 'egregious harm'").

103(e) and substitutes "fundamental" error for "plain" error in the federal rule.[238] The comment to the original Criminal Rule 103(d) stated that this provision was intended only to codify prior Texas law.[239] Nonetheless, fundamental error in the admission or exclusion of evidence when opposing counsel has not objected or made an offer of proof is almost nonexistent in current Texas criminal jurisprudence.[240] Generally, a defendant must object even to "incurable" or "unconstitutional" trial errors to preserve review of those errors on appeal.[241] However, a defendant who does not object to evidence at trial might not forfeit the appellate issue if it is based on a novel constitutional right that had not been established at the time of trial.[242]

In *Saldano v. State*, the court of criminal appeals reviewed the two categories of fundamental error for which a timely objection is unnecessary: (1) violations of "rights which are waivable only" and (2) denials of "absolute systemic requirements."[243] "Waiv-

---

238. *See* Fed. R. Evid. 103(e).

239. Tex. R. Crim. Evid. 103(d) cmt., 701-702 S.W.2d (Tex. Cases) xxxiii (1986, amended 1998).

240. *See Hutch v. State*, 922 S.W.2d 166, 171 (Tex. Crim. App. 1996) ("Egregious harm is a difficult standard to prove and such a determination must be done on a case-by-case basis."); *Perry v. State*, 703 S.W.2d 668, 673 (Tex. Crim. App. 1986) ("[N]o procedural principle is more familiar to appellate courts of this Nation than that a constitutional right may be waived or forfeited by the failure to make timely assertion of the right."); *Hernandez v. State*, 508 S.W.3d 752, 756 (Tex. App.—Amarillo 2016, no pet.) (Rule 103(e) is "rarely applied"); *Miller v. State*, 939 S.W.2d 681, 688 (Tex. App.—El Paso 1996, no pet.) (application of "fundamental error" to evidentiary issues "has been extraordinarily frugal"); *see, e.g., Saldano v. State*, 70 S.W.3d 873, 886-87 (Tex. Crim. App. 2002) (purported error in psychologist's testimony during punishment stage of capital-murder trial was not "fundamental error"; thus, defendant forfeited complaint by not objecting at trial); *Moore v. State*, 935 S.W.2d 124, 129-30 (Tex. Crim. App. 1996) (no fundamental error to admit hearsay when defendant did not object at trial). In *Miller*, the court noted that "in our review of case law existing at or near the time of the adoption of Rule 103(d) [now Rule 103(e)], we have been unable to find any decisions holding that the admission of evidence rendered a defendant's trial fundamentally unfair, and therefore, constituted fundamental error so that the defendant's failure to object was excused." 939 S.W.2d at 688.

The Liaison Committee proposed a modified version of former Federal Rule 103(d), now Rule 103(e), for civil cases. Proposed Rule 103(d), titled "Fundamental Error," acknowledged an appellate court's ability to take notice of errors not brought to its attention if those errors were so fundamental and obvious that they might affect a party's substantial rights. *See McCauley v. Consol. Underwriters*, 157 Tex. 475, 477-78, 304 S.W.2d 265, 266 (1957) (appellate court is not required to approve county-court judgment simply because appellant did not raise the question of jurisdiction); *Ramsey v. Dunlop*, 146 Tex. 196, 202, 205 S.W.2d 979, 983 (1947) (appellate court should consider fundamental error when it adversely affects public interest protected by statute or the constitution). Texas Supreme Court pronouncements had so limited the common-law doctrine of fundamental error that the provision was not included in the final version of the Civil Rules. *See Cox v. Johnson*, 638 S.W.2d 867, 868 (Tex. 1982) (fundamental error exists only when court lacks jurisdiction or public interest is directly and adversely affected); *Pirtle v. Gregory*, 629 S.W.2d 919, 920 (Tex. 1982) (same); *see also In re Marriage of Rutland*, 729 S.W.2d 923, 931-32 (Tex. App.—Dallas 1987, writ ref'd n.r.e.) (in child-custody case, mother's failure to raise objection resulted in waiver because public interest was not adversely affected, despite her claim that evidence of her religious beliefs and practices implicated "fundamental" constitutional rights); *In re Marriage of Knighton*, 723 S.W.2d 274, 283 (Tex. App.—Amarillo 1987, no writ) (failure to object to admission of evidence of religious beliefs did not result in waiver on appeal because public interest was directly and adversely affected).

241. *See Wright v. State*, 28 S.W.3d 526, 536 (Tex. Crim. App. 2000); *Cockrell v. State*, 933 S.W.2d 73, 89 (Tex. Crim. App. 1996).

242. *See Mathews v. State*, 768 S.W.2d 731, 733 (Tex. Crim. App. 1989); *see also Rodriguez v. State*, 758 S.W.2d 787, 788 (Tex. Crim. App. 1988) (not objecting to unconstitutional jury charge did not waive the point on appeal). Refer to notes 128-131 *supra* and accompanying text.

243. 70 S.W.3d at 888 (quoting *Marin v. State*, 851 S.W.2d 275, 279 (Tex. Crim. App. 1993), *overruled on other grounds*, *Cain v. State*, 947 S.W.2d 262 (Tex. Crim. App. 1997)). The *Saldano* court acknowledged that these categories are "relatively small." 70 S.W.3d at 888.

able only" rights include the right to the assistance of counsel and the right to a trial by jury.[244] "Absolute systemic" rights include personal jurisdiction, subject-matter jurisdiction, and a penal statute's compliance with the "Separation of Powers" section of the state constitution.[245] None of these fundamental-error categories includes the admission or exclusion of evidence, regardless of how probative or prejudicial that evidence might be. Thus, the court of criminal appeals appears to reject the notion that any category of evidence is so egregiously harmful or so absolutely essential that a defendant can preserve errors in its admission or exclusion for appeal without meeting the requirements of Rule 103.

RULE 104
PRELIMINARY QUESTIONS

(a) In General. The court must decide any preliminary question about whether a witness is qualified, a privilege exists, or evidence is admissible. In so deciding, the court is not bound by evidence rules, except those on privilege.

(b) Relevance That Depends on a Fact. When the relevance of evidence depends on whether a fact exists, proof must be introduced sufficient to support a finding that the fact does exist. The court may admit the proposed evidence on the condition that the proof be introduced later.

---

244. *Saldano*, 70 S.W.3d at 888.

245. *Id.* Other examples of "absolute" requirements include "a constitutional requirement that a district court must conduct its proceedings at the county seat, the constitutional prohibition of ex post facto laws, and certain constitutional restraints on the comments of a judge." *Id.* at 888-89. In *Blue v. State*, four judges stated that former Rule 103(d), now Rule 103(e), was authority to treat some errors as fundamental. 41 S.W.3d 129, 131-33 (Tex. Crim. App. 2000). This plurality held that a trial judge's comments to the jury panel "tainted" the presumption of the defendant's innocence and was fundamental error. *Id.* at 132. One judge concurred in the result because the trial judge's comments violated the defendant's "absolute right" to an impartial judge. *Id.* at 138-39. Another judge concurred without comment. *See id.* at 133. The three dissenters argued that the rule did not apply to nonevidentiary error and that this error was forfeited by the defendant's failure to object to the judge's comments. *See id.* at 142-43. After *Blue*, whether and when a trial judge's comments constitute fundamental error was an unresolved issue. *See Brumit v. State*, 206 S.W.3d 639, 644-45 (Tex. Crim. App. 2006); *Jasper v. State*, 61 S.W.3d 413, 421 (Tex. Crim. App. 2001); *McLean v. State*, 312 S.W.3d 912, 916 (Tex. App.—Houston [1st Dist.] 2010, no pet.). In *Unkart v. State*, however, the court of criminal appeals addressed the significance of *Blue*, concluding that "the *Blue* decision has no precedential value [but] may nevertheless be considered for any persuasive value ..., in the same way as any other opinion that does not command a majority of this Court, such as a concurring opinion." 400 S.W.3d 94, 101 (Tex. Crim. App. 2013); *see also Baez v. State*, 486 S.W.3d 592, 598 & n.7 (Tex. App.—San Antonio 2015, pet. ref'd) (defendant relied on *Blue* to argue that he did not need to object at trial to language in jury-charge instruction because it amounted to "structural" error; court of appeals determined that including instruction was not "structural" error because jury charge properly informed jury of elements of crime and properly instructed what determinations were necessary to vote for conviction), *cert. denied*, 137 S. Ct. 303 (2016). Although the court in *Unkart* left open the possibility that a judicial comment could be fundamental error, such a determination would largely depend on the circumstances of the case. *See, e.g., Unkart*, 400 S.W.3d at 101-02 (judge intended for his comments to benefit defendant, he did not convey any unknown information, he did not tell jurors what he preferred defendant to do, and he gave jurors a logical reason to disregard his personal preference and instructed them to do so; because instruction to disregard judge's comments could have cured residual harm, defendant forfeited error by failing to object); *Proenza v. State*, 471 S.W.3d 35, 53-54 (Tex. App.—Corpus Christi 2015, pet. granted 1-13-16) (in trial for in-

> **(c) Conducting a Hearing So That the Jury Cannot Hear It.** The court must conduct any hearing on a preliminary question so that the jury cannot hear it if:
>
> > (1) the hearing involves the admissibility of a confession in a criminal case;
> >
> > (2) a defendant in a criminal case is a witness and so requests; or
> >
> > (3) justice so requires.
>
> **(d) Cross-Examining a Defendant in a Criminal Case.** By testifying outside the jury's hearing on a preliminary question, a defendant in a criminal case does not become subject to cross-examination on other issues in the case.
>
> **(e) Evidence Relevant to Weight and Credibility.** This rule does not limit a party's right to introduce before the jury evidence that is relevant to the weight or credibility of other evidence.

COMMENTARY ON RULE 104

The primary purpose of Rule 104 is to define the roles of judge and jury in deciding preliminary questions. There is a simple approach to the problem of separating their functions. The jury may decide any preliminary question when the decision reinforces the jury's obligation to find the facts based on admissible evidence. The judge must decide any preliminary question involving counterintuitive legal rules (e.g., exclusionary rules based on external social policies rather than relevance) or requiring the consideration of inadmissible evidence.[246] In short, the jury finds facts, and the judge applies legal principles. Rule 104 is almost identical to Federal Rule 104, with only minor wording differences in Rule 104(c) and (d).[247]

A. Rule 104(a): In General

Rule 104(a) is identical to Federal Rule 104(a). It gives the trial judge broad discretion in determining issues of the competency, capacity, and qualification of witnesses and in ruling on preliminary questions of the general admissibility of evidence.[248] The

---

jury to child, trial court questioned pediatrician about clinic procedure in a way that showed lack of impartiality and conveyed court's opinion of defendant's guilt; court of appeals could not say beyond a reasonable doubt that trial court's error did not contribute to defendant's conviction and thus reversed).

246. *See generally* ***Pierce v. State***, 32 S.W.3d 247, 251-53 (Tex. Crim. App. 2000) (discussing distinction between judge and jury functions in determining the legality of initial seizure of a person). The court explained:

> The decision of a judge is necessary for a defendant to have a fair hearing and a reliable determination of the legality with which evidence was obtained. The jury is given a role to be "a backup protection against erroneous judicial rulings" that have admitted evidence, not to supplant them.

Id. at 253.

247. Refer to notes 290, 296-300 *infra* and accompanying text.

248. *See* Tex. R. Evid. 104(a); ***Bartlett v. State***, 270 S.W.3d 147, 153 n.23 (Tex. Crim. App. 2008); *see, e.g.,* ***Ditto v. Ditto Inv. Co.***, 158 Tex. 104, 107, 309 S.W.2d 219, 221 (1958) (competency); ***Thompson v. State***, 691 S.W.2d 627, 634 (Tex. Crim. App. 1984) (same); ***Holloway v. State***, 613 S.W.2d 497, 501 (Tex. Crim. App. 1981) (expert qualifications); ***Goodyear Tire & Rubber Co. v. Rios***, 143 S.W.3d 107, 115 (Tex. App.—San Antonio 2004, pet. denied)

———————————— ✦ ————————————

admissibility of evidence frequently depends on the existence of a factual condition[249] or involves the application of a specific exclusionary principle under Rule 104(a).[250] Here, the judge may consider public-policy issues in deciding whether to exclude relevant evidence.[251] In using this discretion, the trial judge is not bound by the rules of evidence, except those on privileges.[252] The trial judge may draw on personal experi-

(same); *Mathis v. State*, 930 S.W.2d 203, 205 (Tex. App.—Houston [14th Dist.] 1996, no pet.) (authenticity of document); *State v. Mireles*, 904 S.W.2d 885, 887 (Tex. App.—Corpus Christi 1995, pet. ref'd) (existence of privilege); *Rodriguez v. State*, 896 S.W.2d 203, 205 (Tex. App.—Corpus Christi 1994, no pet.) (existence of conspiracy); *Sw. Bell Tel. Co. v. Sims*, 615 S.W.2d 858, 862 (Tex. Civ. App.—Houston [1st Dist.] 1981, no writ) (qualification).

Rule 104 gives the trial judge exclusive authority to resolve preliminary questions of evidentiary competency. *See* Tex. R. Evid. 104(a). Competency is determined by applying a legal standard; the predominant view is that a jury is not trained to make a reliable and discriminating evaluation that depends on the application of legal doctrines. Thus, Rule 104(a) keeps incompetent evidence from the jury altogether and preserves the effectiveness of exclusionary rules such as the hearsay rule. *See generally* 1 McCormick on Evidence, *supra* note 92, §53; 9 John H. Wigmore, Evidence in Trials at Common Law, §2550 (Chadbourn rev. 1981).

249. For example: Was the child witness mature enough to accurately perceive, remember, and recount the event he is to testify about? Is the witness whose former testimony is now offered "unavailable"? Was a third person present during discussions between an attorney and his client? In deciding these questions, the trial judge acts as the trier of fact under Rule 104(a). *See* Fed. R. Evid. 104 advisory committee's note, subdiv. (a); 1 McCormick on Evidence, *supra* note 92, §53, at 268-71.

250. For example: Was the warrant for searching a house supported by a legally sufficient affidavit? Have the legal requirements that a conspirator's statement be made in the course of an ongoing conspiracy and in furtherance of that conspiracy been met? Was a hearsay statement made "against interest" as that term is defined in Rule 803(24)? Under Federal Rule 104(a), the trial judge is the sole decision-maker on the application and fulfillment of the appropriate legal principles. *See* Fed. R. Evid. 104 advisory committee's note, subdiv. (a); *see also* **Huddleston v. United States**, 485 U.S. 681, 687 & n.5 (1988) (preliminary findings under Federal Rule 104(a) should be determined by the judge); **Bourjaily v. United States**, 483 U.S. 171, 175 (1987) (before admitting coconspirator's statement, trial court must be satisfied that the statement actually falls within the definition of the rule and must resolve all preliminary questions of fact).

251. *See* 2 Weinstein & Berger, *supra* note 85, §402.02[3]-[4], at 402-15 to 402-16.

252. Tex. R. Evid. 104(a); *State v. Petropoulos*, 346 S.W.3d 525, 529 n.1 (Tex. 2011); *Hernandez v. State*, 116 S.W.3d 26, 31 n.11 (Tex. Crim. App. 2003); *see Gilley v. State*, 418 S.W.3d 114, 121 (Tex. Crim. App. 2014) (trial judge is not bound by rules of evidence in determining competency of child witness); *Baldree v. State*, 248 S.W.3d 224, 233 (Tex. App.—Houston [1st Dist.] 2007, pet. ref'd) ("[T]he power to disregard the rules exists, but nothing in the language of [Rule 104(a)] compels the trial [judge] to exercise that power."); *cf. United States v. Matlock*, 415 U.S. 164, 175 (1974) (hearsay statements may be relied on during suppression hearing and should be given such weight as judge's experience and judgment counsel); *United States v. Whitten*, 706 F.2d 1000, 1019 (9th Cir. 1983) (trial judge is not bound by the hearsay rule in making preliminary evidentiary determinations); *United States v. Lee*, 541 F.2d 1145, 1146 (5th Cir. 1976) (Federal Rule 104(a) leaves no doubt that hearsay evidence is admissible in suppression hearing to determine probable cause because judge is empowered to hear any relevant evidence in determining questions of admissibility); Fed. R. Evid. 104 advisory committee's note, subdiv. (a) ("If the question is factual in nature, the judge will of necessity receive evidence pro and con on the issue. [Federal Rule 104(a)] provides that the rules of evidence in general do not apply to this process.").

Under Rule 101(e)(1), formerly Rule 101(d)(1)(A), the formal rules of evidence do not apply to suppression hearings because those hearings involve the determination of preliminary questions of the admissibility of evidence. *Granados v. State*, 85 S.W.3d 217, 227 (Tex. Crim. App. 2002). Refer to notes 37-42 *supra* and accompanying text. Similarly, the protections of the Confrontation Clause do not extend to pretrial suppression hearings. *See Ford v. State*, 305 S.W.3d 530, 534 (Tex. Crim. App. 2009) (Confrontation Clause does not apply to pretrial suppression hearing; suppression hearing involves preliminary issues of admissibility of evidence, not testimony on cross-examination); *Vanmeter v. State*, 165 S.W.3d 68, 74-75 (Tex. App.—Dallas 2005, pet. ref'd) (constitutional right of confrontation is a trial right, not a pretrial one). *But see Curry v. State*, 228 S.W.3d 292, 297-98 (Tex. App.—Waco 2007, pet. ref'd) (because pretrial suppression hearing is critical phase of criminal proceeding, defendant should benefit from protections of Confrontation Clause).

ence, judgment, and legal training,[253] and "may ask questions of the expert witnesses, request more information, ask for additional briefing, or seek clarification concerning the scientific state of the art and reliable sources in the particular field."[254]

The judge is the "gatekeeper" of evidence who ensures that all evidence admitted at trial is relevant, reliable, and admissible under the pertinent legal principles.[255] In this regard, Rule 104 recognizes case law's primary role in constantly reforming our understanding of witness competency, capacity, and qualification. The alternative—codifying a restrictive list of the known categories of, for example, expert qualifications—runs counter to the spirit and purpose of the Rules because it forecloses the possibility of new developments and would make the rule obsolete whenever a new field of expertise or understanding emerged.

The law on privileges is more rigidly defined: a trial court may uphold only those privileges that are constitutionally recognized, adopted by Article V, or enacted by the Legislature. If a valid privilege is properly asserted, the trial court cannot overrule its assertion, even in making the preliminary determination of the admissibility of other evidence. However, the trial judge does have discretion to conduct a hearing to rule on the validity and applicability of the assertion of a privilege in the particular case.[256] Furthermore, the U.S. Supreme Court has held that Federal Rule 104(a) does not prohibit a trial judge from an in camera review of materials when determining whether certain evidence is or is not privileged.[257]

---

253. *See* 1 WEINSTEIN & BERGER, *supra* note 85, §104.11[1][a], at 104-13 (trial judge can rely on experience and legal training to reveal inherent weaknesses of evidence). However, the judge should consider only relevant and reliable materials and testimony when making Rule 104(a) decisions on the admissibility of evidence. *See Johnson v. State*, 803 S.W.2d 272, 284 n.10 (Tex. Crim. App. 1990).

254. *Hernandez*, 116 S.W.3d at 31 n.11.

255. *Ford*, 305 S.W.3d at 535-36. This "gatekeeping" function of the judge has been discussed most thoroughly in the area of determining the admissibility of scientific expertise under Federal Rule 702. *Ford*, 305 S.W.3d at 536 n.22. In *Daubert v. Merrell Dow Pharmaceuticals*, the U.S. Supreme Court articulated a "gatekeeping" function for the trial judge under Federal Rule 104(a) because the judge must "ensure that any and all scientific testimony or evidence admitted is not only relevant, but reliable." 509 U.S. 579, 589 (1993). Texas courts have similarly adopted the gatekeeping role under Texas Rule 104(a). *See E.I. du Pont de Nemours & Co. v. Robinson*, 923 S.W.2d 549, 556 (Tex. 1995) (trial court is responsible, under Rule 104(a), for ensuring that expert testimony meets legal reliability standards); *Hartman v. State*, 946 S.W.2d 60, 62 (Tex. Crim. App. 1997) (trial judge acts as a "gatekeeper" to ensure that scientific testimony is not only relevant but also reliable); *Harnett v. State*, 38 S.W.3d 650, 657 (Tex. App.—Austin 2000, pet. ref'd) (trial court has discretion under Rule 104(a) to determine qualifications of witness to testify as expert or lay witness).

256. *See Kos v. State*, 15 S.W.3d 633, 637 (Tex. App.—Dallas 2000, pet. ref'd) (reviewing court will reverse trial court's determination of a privilege's applicability only when "'the trial court applied an erroneous legal standard, or when no reasonable view of the record could support the trial court's conclusion under the correct law and facts viewed in the light most favorable to its legal conclusion'" (quoting *Carmona v. State*, 947 S.W.2d 661, 664 (Tex. App.—Austin 1997, no pet.))); *see, e.g., Reece v. State*, 772 S.W.2d 198, 202 (Tex. App.—Houston [14th Dist.] 1989, no pet.) (trial court did not abuse its discretion under Rule 104(a) in determining applicability of spousal privilege in pretrial hearing).

257. *United States v. Zolin*, 491 U.S. 554, 568 (1989); *see, e.g., In re John Doe, Inc.*, 13 F.3d 633, 635-37 (2d Cir. 1994) (upholding use of *Zolin* in camera proceeding to determine if crime-fraud exception to attorney-client privilege applied to specific materials sought by government in grand-jury subpoena); *see also In re Carbo Ceramics, Inc.*, 81 S.W.3d 369, 374 (Tex. App.—Houston [14th Dist.] 2002, orig. proceeding) (document submitted by party asserting privilege for in camera review may serve as proof that it was privileged).

Under Texas Rule 104(a), the trial court has great discretion in determining admissibility, and as long as there is sufficient evidence in the record to support the ruling, the appellate courts will uphold that ruling.[258]

Although the rule does not explicitly allocate or specify a burden of proof, the U.S. Supreme Court has held that the proponent must prove by a preponderance of the evidence that the proffered item or testimony is admissible.[259] Texas courts have generally applied the same standard.[260] The major exception to this "preponderance of the evidence" standard is that the proponent of expert testimony in Texas criminal proceedings must demonstrate its reliability by "clear and convincing evidence."[261]

---

258. *See **Baldree v. State**,* 248 S.W.3d 224, 233 (Tex. App.—Houston [1st Dist.] 2007, pet. ref'd) ("The trial court 'must be given wide latitude in its decision to admit or exclude evidence.'" (quoting ***Harris v. State***, 152 S.W.3d 786, 793 (Tex. App.—Houston [1st Dist.] 2004, pet. ref'd))); ***DeLeon v. State***, 985 S.W.2d 117, 119 (Tex. App.—San Antonio 1998, pet. ref'd) (trial court has broad discretion in determining questions of admissibility of evidence; appellate court may not disturb any preliminary finding supported by evidence); ***Boswell v. Brazos Elec. Power Coop., Inc.***, 910 S.W.2d 593, 600 (Tex. App.—Fort Worth 1995, writ denied) (rulings under Rule 104(a) will not be overturned except for abuse of discretion). *But see **Moore v. Polish Power, Inc.**,* 720 S.W.2d 183, 192 (Tex. App.—Dallas 1986, writ ref'd n.r.e.) (trial court erred "as a matter of law" in determining under Rule 104(a) that expert's testimony was inadmissible).

This abuse-of-discretion standard has long been the law in Texas for preliminary rulings. *See, e.g., **Stanley v. S. Pac. Co.**,* 466 S.W.2d 548, 551 (Tex. 1971) (abuse-of-discretion standard applied when reviewing trial court's admission of testimony); ***Werner v. State***, 711 S.W.2d 639, 643 (Tex. Crim. App. 1986) (clear-abuse-of-discretion standard governs trial court's ruling on admissibility of evidence); ***Smith v. State***, 683 S.W.2d 393, 405 (Tex. Crim. App. 1984) (appellate court will not reverse trial court's determination of sufficiency of a predicate absent an abuse of discretion).

However, under the ***Daubert*** "gatekeeping" line of cases reviewing the admissibility of expert testimony, appellate courts have found that a trial court abused its discretion in admitting unreliable expert testimony. *See **Cooper Tire & Rubber Co. v. Mendez**,* 204 S.W.3d 797, 807 (Tex. 2006); ***Robinson***, 923 S.W.2d at 560; *see also **Ford**,* 305 S.W.3d at 536 n.23 ("Obviously, that kind of discretion—basing a preliminary ruling on irrelevant or unreliable evidence—is not what Rule 104(a) contemplates because irrelevant and unreliable evidence is not a sufficient basis to support a preliminary finding—including a finding at a motion to suppress hearing."). The U.S. Supreme Court has also held that the trial court's rulings on the admissibility of expert testimony are reviewed for abuse of discretion. ***Gen. Elec. Co. v. Joiner***, 522 U.S. 136, 143 (1997); *see **United States v. Frazier**,* 387 F.3d 1244, 1259 (11th Cir. 2004) (abuse-of-discretion standard "recognizes the range of possible conclusions the trial judge may reach"); ***Lust v. Merrell Dow Pharm., Inc.***, 89 F.3d 594, 596 (9th Cir. 1996) (rulings under Federal Rule 702 are reviewed for abuse of discretion); ***Pedraza v. Jones***, 71 F.3d 194, 197 (5th Cir. 1995) (court's decision to strike lay or expert testimony is reviewed under abuse-of-discretion standard); ***Benedi v. McNeil P.P.C.***, 66 F.3d 1378, 1384 (4th Cir. 1995) ("***Daubert*** clearly vests the district courts with discretion to determine the admissibility of expert testimony."). *But see **Cook v. Am. S.S. Co.**,* 53 F.3d 733, 738 (6th Cir. 1995) (trial court's fact-finding under Federal Rule 104(a) is reviewed for "clear error," but determination that expert's opinion is properly a subject of specialized knowledge is reviewed de novo, and determination of whether expert's testimony will assist jury is reviewed for abuse of discretion), *and **Borawick v. Shay**,* 68 F.3d 597, 601 (2d Cir. 1995) (adopting "split" test like that in ***Cook***). Refer to *Article VII: Opinions & Expert Testimony, infra* p. 721.

259. *See **Huddleston v. United States**,* 485 U.S. 681, 687 n.5 (1988) (preliminary factual findings are subject to preponderance-of-the-evidence standard); ***Bourjaily v. United States***, 483 U.S. 171, 175 (1987) (Federal Rules "nowhere define the standard of proof the court must observe in resolving [Federal Rule 104(a)] questions" in judicially adopting preponderance-of-the-evidence standard).

260. *See **Vinson v. State**,* 252 S.W.3d 336, 340 n.14 (Tex. Crim. App. 2008); ***Alvarado v. State***, 912 S.W.2d 199, 215 (Tex. Crim. App. 1995); ***Meador v. State***, 812 S.W.2d 330, 333 (Tex. Crim. App. 1991); *see also* 1 McCORMICK ON EVIDENCE, *supra* note 92, §53, at 271-72 (judge requires proponent to present evidence from which a jury could find the existence of the preliminary fact).

261. *See **State v. Medrano**,* 127 S.W.3d 781, 783 (Tex. Crim. App. 2004) (applying clear-and-convincing standard to reliability and admissibility of hypnotically enhanced testimony); ***Hartman v. State***, 946 S.W.2d 60, 63 (Tex. Crim. App. 1997) (applying clear-and-convincing standard to admission of all scientific evidence offered under Rule

Once the evidence is admitted, both sides may produce further evidence, including much of the evidence used to argue the preliminary question of admissibility to the court, in support or rebuttal of that evidence.[262]

If the proponent of otherwise relevant evidence has established the legally required foundational facts, the trial judge cannot exclude that evidence from the jury's consideration under Rule 104(a) simply because the judge does not find it credible or persuasive.[263] The credibility and persuasiveness of evidence are matters for the jury, not the judge.[264]

Rule 104(a) changed earlier Texas criminal law in one very important respect. Before the adoption of the Rules, the judge and jury shared responsibility for determining preliminary questions of fact in several specific areas, including dying declarations,[265] coconspirator statements,[266] and spousal privileges.[267] These peculiarities were much criticized[268] and were abrogated by the adoption of Rule 104.[269] However, when the preliminary question of fact is whether a defendant's confession was voluntary or whether evidence was obtained illegally, the Texas Code of Criminal Procedure mandates that, on request, these questions be resubmitted to the jury.[270] Thus, these par-

---

702); *Kelly v. State*, 824 S.W.2d 568, 573 (Tex. Crim. App. 1992) (adopting clear-and-convincing standard for admission of novel scientific evidence). The Texas position appears to be an anomaly. *See Medrano*, 127 S.W.3d at 791-92 (Cochran, Keller, Holcomb, JJ., concurring) (clear-and-convincing standard for admissibility of expert testimony is not supported by Rule 104(a) or federal precedent; questioning "why we employ an entirely different standard in determining the admissibility of expert evidence than the federal courts do under exactly the same rules of evidence").

262. *See* 1 JACK B. WEINSTEIN & MARGARET A. BERGER, WEINSTEIN'S EVIDENCE ¶104[07], at 104-95 (1995) (with many preliminary questions, "even after the court decides to admit evidence, the parties may still introduce before the jury much of the same evidence that the court has already considered").

263. *Cf. Blake v. Pellegrino*, 329 F.3d 43, 47 (1st Cir. 2003) (jury is "ultimate arbiter of the persuasiveness of the proof").

264. *Cf. Perry v. New Hampshire*, 565 U.S. 228, 245 (2012) ("The fallibility of eyewitness evidence does not, without the taint of improper state conduct, warrant a due process rule requiring a trial court to screen such evidence for reliability before allowing the jury to assess its creditworthiness. ... [T]he jury, not the judge, traditionally determines the reliability of evidence."); *Blake*, 329 F.3d at 48 ("Where, as here, a piece of evidence rests upon a proper foundation, [Federal] Rule 104(a) does not permit a trial judge to usurp the jury's function and exclude the evidence based on the judge's determination that it lacks persuasive force.").

265. *See Berry v. State*, 143 Tex. Crim. 67, 71-72, 157 S.W.2d 650, 653 (1942) (jury determines whether dying declaration is admissible if a conflict exists in the testimony that lays the predicate for a dying declaration).

266. *See Lewis v. State*, 155 Tex. Crim. 544, 551, 237 S.W.2d 293, 297 (1951) (jury could determine whether the accused was a coconspirator).

267. *See Aguilar v. State*, 715 S.W.2d 645, 647 (Tex. Crim. App. 1986) (jury decides whether common-law marriage and spousal privilege exist); *Huffman v. State*, 450 S.W.2d 858, 862 (Tex. Crim. App. 1970) (same), *vacated on other grounds sub nom. Huffman v. Beto*, 408 U.S. 936 (1972).

268. *See* 1 GOODE ET AL., *supra* note 18, §104.1, at 37-38 (Texas peculiarities are "unorthodox"); 1A RAY, *supra* note 8, §975, at 228 (3d ed. 1980) (Texas courts "should revert to the normal common-law practice" in restoring to the trial judge the sole power to determine the sufficiency of predicate for admission of a dying declaration).

269. *See Casillas v. State*, 733 S.W.2d 158, 168 (Tex. Crim. App. 1986) (Rule 104(a) changed Texas law and required that the trial judge alone determine the admissibility of evidence, including coconspirator statements), *appeal dismissed*, 484 U.S. 918 (1987).

270. TEX. CODE CRIM. PROC. art. 38.22, §6 (when a question is raised about the voluntariness of a confession, court must make an independent finding on the issue in the absence of the jury; if it finds that the statement was given voluntarily, the evidence is admissible, although the jury is instructed not to consider the confession unless it deter-

ticular issues are not affected by Rule 104(a) and are subject to (1) a judicial ruling of admissibility by a preponderance of the evidence under Rule 104 and (2) redetermination by the jury beyond a reasonable doubt.

B. Rule 104(b): Relevance that Depends on a Fact

Rule 104(b), which is identical to Federal Rule 104(b), allows the trial court to conditionally admit evidence that is otherwise not relevant without a preliminary fact on counsel's offer to demonstrate its relevance by later proof that such a preliminary fact does exist.[271] The rule also permits the court to admit evidence conditionally when two facts are in question, and the relevance of each fact depends on establishing the other.[272] Procedurally, the trial judge has the discretion to (1) admit the conditionally relevant evidence at once, subject to a motion to strike if the proponent does not offer proof of the connecting fact, (2) defer any ruling until the connecting fact is offered, or (3) reject the conditionally relevant evidence until the proponent has proved the base facts.[273]

Rule 104(b) implicitly grants the court authority to strike a conditionally admitted fact that is not ultimately supported by sufficient evidence of relevance,[274] but it does

---

mines beyond a reasonable doubt that the statement was made voluntarily), art. 38.23(a) (directing jury determination of the legality of all evidence obtained); *see* **Butler v. State**, 872 S.W.2d 227, 236 (Tex. Crim. App. 1994) (before jury instruction on voluntariness of confession is required, some evidence must be presented to jury that raises issue of voluntariness); **Morr v. State**, 631 S.W.2d 517, 518 (Tex. Crim. App. 1982) (if controverted, the lawfulness of a search and seizure should be presented to the jury for determination as a question of fact).

271. *See* Tex. R. Evid. 104(b). The relevance of the proffered evidence depends on the existence of a particular preliminary fact. *See* Fed. R. Evid. 104 advisory committee's note, subdiv. (b). Instances of relevance that depends on a fact (also referred to as conditional relevancy) include the following: (1) a spoken statement relied on as notice to X has no probative value unless it is shown that X heard it, and (2) a letter purportedly from Y has no probative value unless it is shown that Y wrote or authorized it. *Id. See generally* 21A Wright & Graham, *supra* note 41, §5054, at 123-36 (analyzing the concept of conditionally relevant evidence).

272. *See* Cathleen C. Herasimchuk, *The Relevancy Revolution in Criminal Law: A Practical Tour Through the Texas Rules of Criminal Evidence*, 20 St. Mary's L.J. 737, 761 (1989) (describing mutually dependent facts). For example, the prosecutor in a criminal trial may prove that the defendant has previously been convicted of other offenses by offering (1) a certified copy of a prior judgment and sentence and (2) evidence that the person convicted in that case is the same person as the defendant. The prosecutor may offer the certified public record first, as a conditionally relevant fact, and then later offer identification evidence, such as fingerprints, that this defendant is the same person as the one sentenced in the previous case. *See, e.g.,* **Perez v. State**, 21 S.W.3d 628, 630 (Tex. App.—Houston [14th Dist.] 2000, no pet.) (trial court properly admitted certified copies of defendant's prior convictions as conditionally relevant evidence under Rule 104(b) because State later proved defendant was the same person as the one named in the conviction records).

273. *See* **Nguyen v. State**, 21 S.W.3d 609, 611-12 (Tex. App.—Houston [1st Dist.] 2000, pet. ref'd). In **Nguyen**, the court explained:

> [E]vidence that is relevant only upon fulfillment of a condition of fact may be admitted either upon or subject to the introduction of evidence that establishes that fact. Thus, the trial court may (1) admit the conditionally relevant testimony, with the understanding that it may be struck if its relevance is not established by later evidence; or (2) require a showing of relevance before introduction of the conditionally relevant testimony.

Id. at 612.

274. The opposing party must move to strike the conditionally admitted evidence if the proponent does not fulfill the condition by the close of its case. Otherwise, the party forfeits any error in the admission. *See, e.g.,* **Fuller v. State**, 829 S.W.2d 191, 198 (Tex. Crim. App. 1992) (although defendant objected when State offered conditionally relevant evidence of defendant's connection to prison gang, defendant forfeited right to appellate review of State's

not imply that the court may usurp the jury function of determining each fact. Thus, under Rule 104(b), a trial judge has no discretion to exclude a conditionally relevant piece of evidence.[275] Once the proponent of the evidence has produced sufficient admissible[276] evidence to "support a finding" of the fulfillment of the condition, the evidence must be admitted for the jury to decide whether it is relevant.[277] Public policy favors having these issues resolved by the jury because the fact-finder is charged with the duty of weighing the credibility of testimony and assessing the probative value of evidence.[278]

Under both Texas Rule 104(b) and Federal Rule 104(b), "the threshold burden of relevancy is very low: '[t]he preliminary fact can be decided by the judge against the proponent only where the jury could not reasonably find the preliminary fact to exist.'"[279] "Unlike determinations made under Rule 104(a), a rule that employs a 'preponderance of the evidence' standard, the proponent need produce only 'some evidence,' or a 'prima facie' showing, before the trial judge is required to admit the conditionally relevant evidence under Rule 104(b)."[280]

However, the rule may operate differently in Texas criminal proceedings. The court of criminal appeals, in *Harrell v. State*[281] and *George v. State*,[282] declined to follow the

failure to connect up testimony when he did not move to strike evidence at end of State's case); *Rawlins v. State*, 521 S.W.3d 863, ___ (Tex. App.—Houston [1st Dist.] 2017, pet. filed 8-9-17) (although defendant objected when prosecution offered conditionally relevant evidence of his gang affiliation, he did not reurge relevancy objection at end of prosecution's case, move to strike the evidence, or request an instruction to disregard; no error was preserved); *Owens-Corning Fiberglas Corp. v. Keeton*, 922 S.W.2d 658, 661 (Tex. App.—Austin 1996, writ denied) (although defendant objected and requested limiting instruction when plaintiff offered conditionally relevant evidence of defendant's failure to warn about dangers of asbestos, objection and request were not reurged at close of plaintiff's case; no error was preserved).

275. *See* FED. R. EVID. 104 advisory committee's note, subdiv. (b).

276. The trial judge is not bound by the Federal Rules of Evidence in making a determination of admissibility under Federal Rule 104(a). Refer to notes 248-270 *supra* and accompanying text. In making a relevance determination under Federal Rule 104(b), however, a judge may consider only admissible evidence. *See Zenith Radio Corp. v. Matsushita Elec. Indus. Co.*, 505 F. Supp. 1190, 1220 (E.D. Pa. 1980) (although trial judge can consider inadmissible evidence, determination should hinge on admissible evidence).

277. *See* 1 GOODE ET AL., *supra* note 18, §104.2, at 39-41 (explaining importance of conditional relevancy to jury's role as trier of fact).

278. The Advisory Committee's note to Federal Rule 104(b) explains that "[i]f preliminary questions of conditional relevancy were determined solely by the judge, as provided in subdivision (a), the functioning of the jury as a trier of fact would be greatly restricted and in some cases virtually destroyed." FED. R. EVID. 104 advisory committee's note, subdiv. (b); *see also United States v. Barletta*, 652 F.2d 218, 219 (1st Cir. 1981) (criminal defendant's Sixth Amendment right to jury trial might be violated if court denied jury its proper fact-finding role simply because court would make a different finding).

279. *Fischer v. State*, 268 S.W.3d 552, 559 (Tex. Crim. App. 2008) (Cochran & Johnson, JJ., concurring); *see Huddleston v. United States*, 485 U.S. 681, 689-91 (1988) (if there is some evidence, such that a jury could reasonably conclude that defendant committed an extraneous offense, evidence of that offense is conditionally relevant, and, if otherwise admissible, trial judge may not exclude it). *See generally* 21A WRIGHT & GRAHAM, *supra* note 41, §5054.2, at 155-59 (discussing low standard under Federal Rule 104(b)).

280. *Fischer*, 268 S.W.3d at 559; *see* Wellborn, *supra* note 32, at 1189 (Rule 104(b) requires only a "prima facie" showing of the preliminary fact).

281. 884 S.W.2d 154, 159-60 (Tex. Crim. App. 1994).

282. 890 S.W.2d 73, 75-76 (Tex. Crim. App. 1994).

federal standard[283] and held that Texas Rule 104(b) requires the trial court to determine that there is sufficient evidence to support a jury finding beyond a reasonable doubt that the defendant committed the act before the court admits evidence of an extraneous offense.[284] The rationale expressed in *Harrell* for this interpretation of Rule 104(b) was that Texas law has long required judges to instruct jurors not to consider evidence of an extraneous offense unless the jurors believe beyond a reasonable doubt that the defendant committed that offense.[285] The court of criminal appeals perceived a "mirror" connection between the standard of admissibility and the applicable jury instructions.[286] It is not clear from the *Harrell* opinion whether this quantum of proof applies only to extraneous-offense evidence or to all conditionally relevant evidence offered by the State under Rule 104(b). At least one intermediate court has assumed that it applies to all conditionally relevant evidence,[287] but the *Harrell* rationale applies only to those situations in which the jury is explicitly instructed that it should not consider particular types of evidence, such as an extraneous offense or a defendant's confession, unless the State has proved certain predicate facts beyond a reasonable doubt.[288] This heightened burden of proof does not apply in civil cases or, presumably, to conditionally relevant evidence offered by the defendant in criminal proceedings.

The judge applies the law, and the jury decides the facts. The important distinction between Rule 104(a) and Rule 104(b) involves these separate roles of the trial judge and jury in determining the admissibility of evidence. The judge decides preliminary questions of the legal competency of the proffered evidence. The jury resolves questions of the conditional relevance of that evidence.[289] In other words, the jury determines

---

283. *Harrell*, 884 S.W.2d at 160 (recognizing but rejecting standard of proof set out in *Huddleston* for conditionally relevant evidence under Criminal Rule 104(b)); *see Fischer*, 268 S.W.3d at 559.

284. *Harrell*, 884 S.W.2d at 160; *Fischer*, 268 S.W.3d at 559.

285. *Fischer*, 268 S.W.3d at 558 (majority op.); *Harrell*, 884 S.W.2d at 157; *see Tippins v. State*, 530 S.W.2d 110, 111 (Tex. Crim. App. 1975); *Ernster v. State*, 165 Tex. Crim. 422, 423-24, 308 S.W.2d 33, 34-35 (1957); *Nichols v. State*, 138 Tex. Crim. 324, 326, 136 S.W.2d 221, 221-22 (1940). This rationale was called into doubt in the concurring opinion in *Harrell*. 884 S.W.2d at 162-63 (Clinton, J., concurring); *see Fischer*, 268 S.W.3d at 559 n.9 (Cochran & Johnson, JJ., concurring).

286. *Harrell*, 884 S.W.2d at 158-59. *But see Fischer*, 268 S.W.3d at 560 (Cochran & Johnson, JJ., concurring) ("[T]here is nothing in either the rules or logic that requires a 'mirror' connection between the standard of proof for the admissibility of evidence and the standard by which jurors should evaluate that evidence. It is one thing to say that the State must prove the defendant's guilt beyond a reasonable doubt and an entirely different thing to say that the State must establish the relevancy of its evidence beyond a reasonable doubt before the trial judge may admit that evidence for the jury's consideration.").

287. *Gonzales v. State*, 929 S.W.2d 546, 550-51 (Tex. App.—Austin 1996, pet. ref'd).

288. For example, Texas Code of Criminal Procedure article 38.22 requires that whenever a question is raised about whether a defendant's confession was voluntary, the jury must be instructed that unless it believes beyond a reasonable doubt that the statement was voluntarily made, the jury must not consider that statement for any purpose. Tex. Code Crim. Proc. art. 38.22, §6. Under Texas common law, the jury was instructed in the same vein about the use of extraneous offenses. Under Texas Code of Criminal Procedure article 37.07, the same "beyond a reasonable doubt" jury instruction is given on the use of extraneous offenses at the punishment stage of a criminal trial. *Id.* art. 37.07, §3(a)(1).

289. Suppose, for example, that a defendant is charged with possession of cocaine. If a police officer testifies that State's Exhibit 1 is the bag of white powder that he took from the defendant, the trial judge may admit the bag and its contents into evidence even though no witness, such as a chemist, has testified that the white powder is cocaine.

whether the proponent has proved supportive, coordinate facts sufficient to fulfill the condition on which the evidence was admitted, thereby giving the proffered evidence probative value.

Although Rule 104 distinguishes "competency" (which the judge decides under Rule 104(a)) from "relevance" (which the jury decides under Rule 104(b)), the trial judge will address relevance issues in connection with legal determinations. The judge must decide whether offered evidence meets the test of relevance under Rule 401, and, even more important, must perform the balancing of probative value versus prejudicial effect under Rule 403.

C. Rule 104(c): Conducting a Hearing so that the Jury Cannot Hear It

Rule 104(c), which is almost identical to Federal Rule 104(c),[290] serves the same purpose as Texas Rule 103(d) and should be construed in harmony with Rule 103(d) to ensure that prejudicial, inadmissible evidence is not heard by the jury.[291] Rule 104 hearings held outside the presence of the jury are discretionary in civil proceedings, but they are mandatory in two specific circumstances in criminal proceedings. In a criminal case, Rule 104 excludes the jury from hearings held to determine the admissibility of a defendant's confession[292] and hearings in which a defendant wants to testify on a preliminary issue and requests removal of the jury.[293]

Under the Rules of Evidence, as under the common law, the jury's sole function is to determine the facts of the case. Because preliminary hearings on the admissibility of evidence are pure matters of law, the jury does not need to be present for these hearings. The judicial policy of avoiding jury prejudice caused by exposure to inadmissible evidence[294] should dictate that the jury be excused whenever it is reasonable to do so.

The State may "connect it up" later. State's Exhibit 1 is offered as conditionally relevant under Rule 104(b), subject to further proof that the substance is cocaine. Suppose, however, that the defendant argues that the officer's act of seizing the bag and its contents was an unlawful search. That is an issue of legal admissibility under Rule 104(a). To resolve that question, the trial judge both determines the underlying facts (e.g., was there probable cause to stop the defendant, search him, and seize the bag?) and applies the appropriate legal principles in deciding whether to admit the evidence.

290. The Texas rule states that the court, "in a criminal case," must conduct a hearing outside the jury's presence to determine the admissibility of a defendant's confession; the federal rule does not include the phrase. *See* FED. R. EVID. 104(c)(1); TEX. R. EVID. 104(c)(1).

291. *See* TEX. R. EVID. 103(d); *see also* 1 GOODE ET AL., *supra* note 18, §104.3, at 41-42 (keeping such evidence from the jury is the "general purpose" of Rule 104(c)).

292. TEX. R. EVID. 104(c)(1); *see Alvarado v. State*, 912 S.W.2d 199, 211 (Tex. Crim. App. 1995) (due process and Criminal Rule 104(c) require hearing on admissibility of defendant's statement to be held outside jury's presence); *see also* TEX. CODE CRIM. PROC. art. 38.22 (setting conditions that must be fulfilled before a confession may be submitted to a jury); *cf. Jackson v. Denno*, 378 U.S. 368, 395 (1964) ("It is both practical and desirable that … a proper determination of voluntariness be made prior to the admission of [a defendant's] confession to the jury which is adjudicating guilt or innocence.").

293. *See* TEX. R. EVID. 104(c)(2).

294. *See, e.g., Nabors Well Servs., Ltd. v. Romero*, 456 S.W.3d 553, 563 (Tex. 2015) (in automobile-accident cases, trial court may consider relevant evidence of plaintiff's preoccurence, injury-causing conduct, such as nonuse of seat belt, in determining proportionate responsibility; court must first consider evidence outside jury's presence to avoid jury's hearing it before it is deemed relevant). Refer to notes 230-234 *supra* and accompanying text.

The phrase "justice so requires" functions as a catchall provision that grants the trial judge broad discretion in determining when to conduct hearings on preliminary questions outside the jury's presence.[295] For example, if the trial judge has concerns that the proffered evidence might be inadmissible (or even a close call) a hearing outside the presence of the jury is appropriate. Hearings to determine the admissibility of extraneous offenses or the reliability of an expert's opinion should generally be held outside the jury's presence. On the other hand, a preliminary determination can be made in the jury's presence if it is simply a matter of proving up a foundation for the admission of exhibits or the professional qualifications of an expert—if the foundation is insufficient, the exhibit will never be shown to the jury or the expert will never give an opinion to the jury. The jury will not likely be unfairly prejudiced by hearing the preliminary testimony in those situations.

D. Rule 104(d): Cross-Examining a Defendant in a Criminal Case

Rule 104(d) is patterned after Federal Rule 104(d). It is a constitutionally based rule[296] and follows earlier Texas law.[297] The rule is sensible because it would be unfair to force a criminal defendant to give up one constitutional right (e.g., the privilege against self-incrimination) to assert another (e.g., the prohibition against the use of illegally obtained evidence or an involuntary confession).[298] Rule 104(d), however, goes beyond the constitutional requirements and applies to the defendant's testimony taken at any preliminary hearing outside the jury's presence.[299] However, a defendant who testifies before the jury and addresses these same legal issues is subject to cross-examination on any issue relevant to the case.[300]

---

295. *See* TEX. R. EVID. 104(c)(3).

296. *See* ***Simmons v. United States***, 390 U.S. 377, 393-94 (1968) (under the Fifth Amendment, a criminal defendant who testifies on preliminary matters outside the jury's presence is not then subject to cross-examination on other issues related to guilt); ***Cooper v. State***, 769 S.W.2d 301, 303-04 (Tex. App.—Houston [1st Dist.] 1989, pet. ref'd) (same).

297. *See, e.g.*, ***Horne v. State***, 508 S.W.2d 643, 646 (Tex. Crim. App. 1974) (defendant had absolute right to testify at hearing on the motion to suppress on the circumstances surrounding the taking of his confession, with cross-examination limited to the issue of voluntariness of the confession).

298. *See* ***Simmons***, 390 U.S. at 394 ("an undeniable tension is created" when a criminal defendant must surrender one constitutional right to assert another).

299. *See* TEX. R. EVID. 104(d); *see, e.g.*, ***Nelson v. State***, 765 S.W.2d 401, 405-06 (Tex. Crim. App. 1989) (defendant's testimony during preliminary hearing outside the presence of the jury on admissibility of prior convictions for impeachment could not be used by State during punishment phase to prove the existence of those convictions). The corresponding federal rule does not contain language that the defendant's testimony is outside the jury's presence. *See* FED. R. EVID. 104(d).

300. *See* ***Nelson***, 765 S.W.2d at 403; ***Myre v. State***, 545 S.W.2d 820, 825 (Tex. Crim. App. 1977); ***Green v. State***, 670 S.W.2d 332, 333 (Tex. App.—Eastland 1984, no pet.).

In ***Nelson***, the defendant requested a preliminary hearing outside the jury's presence to determine the admissibility of his prior convictions offered to impeach his credibility. 765 S.W.2d at 402. The judge ruled the prior convictions inadmissible because they were too remote to affect his credibility, and the defendant testified during the guilt/innocence stage. *Id.* Then, during the punishment phase, the State called the court reporter to read into evidence the defendant's testimony taken during the preliminary hearing. *Id.* The court noted that testimony taken during a preliminary hearing under Rule 104(d) is not insulated from use as impeachment evidence. *See* ***Nelson***, 765 S.W.2d at 404; *see also* ***Oregon v. Hass***, 420 U.S. 714, 721 (1975) (using statements that would be inadmissible under

E. Rule 104(e): Evidence Relevant to Weight & Credibility

Rule 104(e) emphasizes that Rule 104 was not intended to limit the introduction of probative evidence relevant to the weight or credibility of other testimony.[301] Rule 104(e) is identical to Federal Rule 104(e).

RULE 105
EVIDENCE THAT IS NOT ADMISSIBLE AGAINST OTHER PARTIES OR FOR OTHER PURPOSES

(a) Limiting Admitted Evidence. If the court admits evidence that is admissible against a party or for a purpose—but not against another party or for another purpose—the court, on request, must restrict the evidence to its proper scope and instruct the jury accordingly.

(b) Preserving a Claim of Error.

(1) *Court Admits the Evidence Without Restriction.* A party may claim error in a ruling to admit evidence that is admissible against a party or for a purpose—but not against another party or for another purpose—only if the party requests the court to restrict the evidence to its proper scope and instruct the jury accordingly.

(2) *Court Excludes the Evidence.* A party may claim error in a ruling to exclude evidence that is admissible against a party or for a purpose—but not against another party or for another purpose—only if the party limits its offer to the party against whom or the purpose for which the evidence is admissible.

COMMENTARY ON RULE 105

Rule 105 is modeled after Federal Rule 105 but is considerably more explicit about the operation of waiver rules. Federal Rule 105 is basically identical to Texas Rule 105(a)[302] but does not include a specific waiver provision like the one in Texas Rule 105(b)(1).[303] As a practical matter, however, the two rules are identical in scope and operation. Rule 105, like Rule 103, is predicated on the principle of party responsibility in bringing to the court's attention any matter that is objectionable, inadmissible, or of limited admissibility.[304] Evidentiary objections should be specific about the

---

Miranda to impeach defendant); ***Harris v. New York***, 401 U.S. 222, 226 (1971) (same). However, this testimony was insulated from use as independent substantive evidence, such as proving up a defendant's prior criminal record. *See* *Nelson*, 765 S.W.2d at 404.

301. *See* 1 GOODE ET AL., *supra* note 18, §104.5, at 43 (although a judge may deem a witness competent or qualified, the opposition may still introduce evidence of the witness's lack of credibility); Herasimchuk, *supra* note 272, at 777-78 (once evidence is admitted, either side is free to attack or support the evidence).

302. The federal rule states that the court, "on timely request," must restrict the evidence; the Texas rule just states "on request." *See* FED. R. EVID. 105; TEX. R. EVID. 105(a).

303. Refer to notes 321-322 *infra* and accompanying text.

304. *See* Wellborn, *supra* note 32, at 1192. Refer to notes 119-121 *supra* and accompanying text.

grounds, parts, parties, and purposes. Rule 103(a)(1) deals with the specific grounds and parts of objections, while Rule 105 addresses the objector's responsibility to be specific about parties and purposes.[305]

A. Rule 105(a): Limiting Admitted Evidence

Rule 105(a) allows evidence that is admissible against one party or for one purpose but not against another party or for another purpose.[306] Rule 105 ensures that the evidence may be admitted for its proper or "good" purpose and also gives the opposing party the right to have the jury instructed on this "good" purpose.[307] The trial court must instruct the jury on the evidence's limited purpose when the opposing party so requests.[308] The jury should be told not to consider the evidence "for any other, improper, purpose."[309]

The opposing party has the burden to request a limiting instruction, but Rule 105(a) permits the court to give the instruction sua sponte and also allows the party offering the evidence to request a limiting instruction.[310] Trial judges should be cautious about giving limiting instructions sua sponte; a party might choose, as a matter of trial strategy, not to request a limiting instruction, hoping "'to minimize the jury's recollection of the unfavorable evidence.'"[311] In a bench trial, there is a rebuttable presumption that the trial court considers the evidence only for its proper purpose.[312]

---

305. Wellborn, *supra* note 32, at 1192; *see **Pardue v. State***, 252 S.W.3d 690, 698 (Tex. App.—Texarkana 2008, no pet.); *cf. **United States v. Rhodes***, 62 F.3d 1449, 1453-54 (D.C. Cir. 1995) (burden is clearly on defense counsel to request limiting instruction), *vacated on other grounds*, 517 U.S. 1164 (1996). This provision accurately reflects preexisting Texas law. Refer to note 310 *infra*.

306. The Texas Supreme Court has reiterated that "Rule 105 does not apply when the evidence in question is not admissible against any party for any purpose." ***U-Haul Int'l, Inc. v. Waldrip***, 380 S.W.3d 118, 132 (Tex. 2012); *accord **Kia Motors Corp. v. Ruiz***, 432 S.W.3d 865, 879 (Tex. 2014).

307. *See* TEX. R. EVID. 105(a).

308. *See id.*; ***Kirsch v. State***, 306 S.W.3d 738, 747 (Tex. Crim. App. 2010).

309. ***Kirsch***, 306 S.W.3d at 747; *see, e.g.*, ***Walker v. State***, 300 S.W.3d 836, 851 (Tex. App.—Fort Worth 2009, pet. ref'd) (limiting instruction in jury charge was proper because it specifically instructed jury that impeachment testimony could be used to determine witness's credibility, and "for no other reason"; in-court limiting instruction was improper because it "instructed the jury about what it could consider impeachment testimony for, rather than instructing the jury that it could *only* consider impeachment testimony for one purpose").

310. *See* TEX. R. EVID. 105(a). Under Texas common law, the opponent was required to request the limiting instruction if the trial court did not give it. The trial court, however, was under no obligation to limit the admissibility of evidence. ***Blum Milling Co. v. Moore-Seaver Grain Co.***, 277 S.W. 78, 81 (Tex. Comm'n App. 1925, judgm't adopted). Under Rule 105(a), the trial judge is still not required to give a limiting instruction sua sponte. ***Delgado v. State***, 235 S.W.3d 244, 251 (Tex. Crim. App. 2007); *e.g.*, ***Watson v. State***, 337 S.W.3d 347, 353-54 (Tex. App.—Eastland 2011) (when defendant did not request a limiting instruction, evidence was admissible for all purposes, and trial court did not err in not giving a limiting instruction sua sponte), *aff'd*, 369 S.W.3d 865 (Tex. Crim. App. 2012). For a discussion suggesting that there are occasions in which a trial judge might consider conducting, outside the jury's presence, an inquiry into whether a limiting instruction was inadvertently overlooked, see 1 SALTZBURG ET AL., *supra* note 87, §105.02[3], at 105-3.

311. ***Delgado***, 235 S.W.3d at 250 (quoting ***United States v. Johnson***, 46 F.3d 1166, 1171 (D.C. Cir. 1995)); *see* Blinka, *supra* note 94, at 19 (opponent of evidence will "frequently forego limiting instructions for fear that they will only emphasize the damaging inference").

312. *See **Young v. State***, 994 S.W.2d 387, 389 (Tex. App.—Houston [14th Dist.] 1999, no pet.).

Under Rule 403, the trial court may nonetheless exclude relevant evidence despite the proponent's request to admit it with limiting instructions if the court determines that a limiting instruction would not adequately protect the opposing party's interests.[313] The important considerations in deciding whether to admit the evidence with a limiting instruction under Rule 105(a) or to exclude it under Rule 403 are (1) prejudice to the opposing party, (2) confusion of the issues, and (3) unnecessary time consumption.[314] Therefore, Rules 105 and 403 work together in determining the sufficiency and effectiveness of limiting instructions.[315] This approach follows federal practice.

A party may request that the trial judge (1) affirmatively limit consideration of the evidence to its permissible purpose and (2) instruct the jury on the evidence's impermissible or "forbidden" purpose. Frequently, however, a party may not want to admonish the jury about the forbidden use of the evidence because this instruction may only emphasize the impermissible use of the evidence in the minds of the jurors.[316]

The criminal case of ***Reeves v. State***[317] exemplifies the potential problems with attempting to combine a running objection with limiting instructions. Before any testimony began, the trial judge granted the defendant a running objection to the admission of the victim's testimony about numerous extraneous offenses; the State agreed to a limiting instruction on the use of that testimony.[318] The trial judge denied the defendant's request to repeat the limiting instruction each time that extraneous-offense evidence was admitted during the victim's testimony, but limiting instructions were given before the victim testified and in the written jury instructions.[319] The court of ap-

---

313. *See, e.g.*, **Carter v. District of Columbia**, 795 F.2d 116, 126 (D.C. Cir. 1986) (trial court's limiting instruction that evidence about past complaints against individual police officers was admitted solely for purpose of establishing municipal liability was not sufficient to cure unfair prejudicial effect to individual defendants because less prejudicial evidence could have been introduced).

314. *See, e.g.*, **George v. State**, 959 S.W.2d 378, 380-81 (Tex. App.—Beaumont 1998, pet. ref'd) (trial court in murder trial committed reversible error in admitting deceased child's entire medical record that detailed numerous prior injuries; prosecution offered medical records to show child's condition at time of hospitalization and "complete medical diagnosis"; medical records showed highly prejudicial evidence of extraneous offenses not necessarily committed by defendant).

315. Refer to *Article IV: Relevance & Its Limits, infra* p. 214.

316. *See, e.g.*, **Borunda v. Richmond**, 885 F.2d 1384, 1388 (9th Cir. 1988) ("While it would have been better had the trial court specifically directed the jury not to consider the evidence of acquittals as proof of whether probable cause for arrest existed, Rule 105 does not require all limiting instructions to specifically contain 'forbidden use' language."). Refer to note 311 *supra* and accompanying text.

Texas case law suggests that the party who introduces evidence that would be of only limited admissibility if offered by an opponent cannot then demand a jury instruction limiting its use. Thus, for example, when a defendant impeaches a State's witness with a prior inconsistent statement, prior drug use, or extraneous offenses, the defendant cannot obtain a reversal if the trial court does not give a limiting instruction on the use of this evidence. *See* **Nethery v. State**, 692 S.W.2d 686, 705 (Tex. Crim. App. 1985). However, this waiver doctrine seems unfair when a particular item of evidence has both admissible and inadmissible aspects. The proponent of the evidence should be allowed to limit its offer to the admissible uses and request that the jury be instructed not to consider the evidence for any improper purpose.

317. 99 S.W.3d 657 (Tex. App.—Waco 2003, pet. ref'd).

318. *Id.* at 658.

319. *Id.*

peals held that the trial judge did not err by not recognizing testimony about extraneous offenses and giving a limiting instruction sua sponte at each instance.[320] A trial judge is not required to identify evidence that is offered for a limited purpose; he must give a limiting instruction only if explicitly requested.

B. Rule 105(b): Preserving a Claim of Error

Rule 105(b)(1) expressly states that if the opponent does not request a limiting instruction when evidence is admitted, he may not complain on appeal that the evidence was admissible only for a limited purpose or that the trial court should have instructed the jury on that limited use.[321] This provision is not included in the corresponding federal rule.[322]

Rule 105(b)(2) requires the proponent of evidence originally offered for a limited purpose or against a particular person, but ultimately excluded, to make an express offer of the specific evidence as provided by Rule 103. Failure to make such an offer will preclude appellate review on that point.[323] Thus, if the sponsoring party makes a general offer of the evidence, the sponsoring party cannot complain on appeal that the trial court erred because the evidence should have been admitted for a limited purpose.[324]

---

320. *Id.* at 658-59.

321. Tex. R. Evid. 105(b)(1); ***Pardue v. State***, 252 S.W.3d 690, 698 (Tex. App.—Texarkana 2008, no pet.); *see, e.g.,* ***Horizon/CMS Healthcare Corp. v. Auld***, 34 S.W.3d 887, 906 (Tex. 2000) (because appellant did not request a limiting instruction on admission of survey reports, admission was upheld on appeal because reports were admissible against any party or for any purpose); ***Aluminum Co. of Am. v. Alm***, 785 S.W.2d 137, 139 (Tex. 1990) (because objector did not request a limiting instruction, "admission of the evidence was, for all practical purposes, a general offer"); ***Reliant Energy Servs., Inc. v. Cotton Valley Compression, L.L.C.***, 336 S.W.3d 764, 793-94 (Tex. App.—Houston [1st Dist.] 2011, no pet.) (trial court clearly indicated to parties that it was admitting evidence for limited purpose, but defendant did not request limiting instruction when evidence was admitted or before charge was read to jury; no reversible error in allowing jury to consider evidence for any purpose).

322. *Compare* Fed. R. Evid. 105 (does not include a specific waiver provision), *with* Tex. R. Evid. 105(b)(1) (party who does not request that evidence be limited to its proper scope may not complain on appeal that the evidence was admitted without limitation).

323. Tex. R. Evid. 105(b)(2); *see* ***Wright v. State***, 776 S.W.2d 763, 765 (Tex. App.—Corpus Christi 1989, pet. ref'd) (failure to make a limited offer or to perfect a bill of exception causes evidence to be absent from the record and thus does not preserve error for review); ***Worldwide Anesthesia Assocs., Inc. v. Bryan Anesthesia, Inc.***, 765 S.W.2d 445, 449 (Tex. App.—Houston [14th Dist.] 1988, no writ) ("When evidence is offered for two purposes, and it is admissible for one purpose but not for the other, the exclusion of such evidence is not error where the proponent of the evidence does not limit its offer for the admissible purpose only."); *see, e.g.,* ***Porter v. Nemir***, 900 S.W.2d 376, 382 n.7 (Tex. App.—Austin 1995, no writ) (when party did not limit offer of prior conviction to its permissible purpose as support for expert's opinion, trial court did not err in excluding it); ***State v. Buckner Constr. Co.***, 704 S.W.2d 837, 848 (Tex. App.—Houston [14th Dist.] 1985, writ ref'd n.r.e.) (when opponent objected to the admission of a file that contained inadmissible portions, it became the proponent's burden to separate the inadmissible parts from the admissible and offer only the latter; failure to do so forfeited any complaint that the trial court erred in excluding the entire file).

324. *See, e.g.,* ***Logan v. State***, 71 S.W.3d 865, 869-70 (Tex. App.—Fort Worth 2002, pet. ref'd) (affidavit of nonprosecution might have been admissible to impeach, but trial court did not err in excluding it because it was not offered for that limited purpose). There is no such provision under Federal Rule 105, but this practice parallels Texas common law. *See* ***Blum Milling Co. v. Moore-Seaver Grain Co.***, 277 S.W. 78, 81-82 (Tex. Comm'n App. 1925, judgm't adopted) (failure to request that evidence be limited during trial destroys right to complain on appeal); ***Kaplan v. Goodfried***, 497 S.W.2d 101, 104 (Tex. Civ. App.—Dallas 1973, no writ) (plaintiff who tenders evidence without requesting limitation at trial cannot complain on appeal if trial court does not limit the evidence); ***Fort Worth Hotel***

On the other hand, if a party makes a specific objection that is sustained by the trial court, the proponent of the evidence is not required to limit the offer to "respond" to other valid objections that the opposing party did not make.[325]

C. Timing of Limiting Instructions

Rule 105 does not explicitly address the question of the timing of limiting instructions.[326] In ***Rankin v. State***, the court of criminal appeals addressed the proper timing of the judge's instruction under Rule 105(a) and held that a defendant is entitled to a limiting instruction when the evidence is first admitted, rather than delaying until the submission of the judge's jury instructions.[327] Three judges dissented in ***Rankin***, contending that trial judges should have discretion "to make the call on when to give a

---

Co. v. Waggoman, 126 S.W.2d 578, 585-86 (Tex. Civ. App.—Fort Worth 1939, writ dism'd judgm't cor.) (party cannot argue on appeal that objection to evidence at trial for one reason also serves as a limitation of evidence for another unrelated reason).

325. ***Bracewell v. Bracewell***, 31 S.W.3d 610, 613 (Tex. App.—Houston [1st Dist.] 1999, pet. denied). In ***Bracewell***, the court explained:

> It would make no sense to allow the opponents of evidence to specifically or apparently limit their general objection—thus, abandoning potentially valid grounds of objection—and then require the proponent of the evidence to limit his offer to both the valid specific/apparent objections *and* the valid abandoned objections. If we were to allow this, we would be encouraging parties to make specific grounds of objection at trial and then lie behind the log of rule 105(b) to prevent appellate review. Since the purpose of the rules of evidence is to promote fairness and to ascertain the truth, rather than to promote gamesmanship, we decline to interpret rule 105(b) in a way that requires a proponent of evidence to limit his offer based on a ground that his opponents have already abandoned.

Id.

326. The Dallas Court of Appeals expressed a preference for giving limiting instructions when evidence is admitted but held that the trial judge did not commit reversible error in refusing to instruct the jury at that time. *See* ***Thompson v. State***, 752 S.W.2d 12, 14 (Tex. App.—Dallas 1988), *pet. dism'd, improvidently granted*, 795 S.W.2d 177 (Tex. Crim. App. 1990). The court of criminal appeals granted the appellant's petition for discretionary review on this issue but later determined that it was improvidently granted. Three judges dissented from the dismissal and declared that they "would make the giving of a limiting instruction mandatory, on request, both at the time the evidence is admitted and in the court's charge ...." ***Thompson v. State***, 795 S.W.2d 177, 178 (Tex. Crim. App. 1990) (Miller, Clinton, Teague, JJ., dissenting).

327. 974 S.W.2d 707, 712 (Tex. Crim. App. 1996). The court explained:

> [T]he spirit of the rule and the contemplation of the rule-makers includes two separate notions: First, that limiting instructions actually curb the improper use of evidence and, second, that the rule should act in a way that not only "restrict[s] the evidence to its proper scope", but does so as effectively as possible. Working under these notions, logic demands that the instruction be given at the first opportunity.

Id. (citations omitted); *see also* ***Robbins v. State***, 27 S.W.3d 245, 251 (Tex. App.—Beaumont 2000) (defendant was entitled to contemporaneous limiting instruction, as he requested, when extraneous-offense evidence was first introduced), *aff'd*, 88 S.W.3d 256 (Tex. Crim. App. 2002).

Federal courts have disagreed about whether limiting instructions must be given when the evidence is first offered or whether the trial judge has discretion to wait and include the limiting instruction in the jury instructions. *See, e.g.*, ***United States v. Rivera***, 837 F.2d 906, 913 (10th Cir. 1988) (when evidence of an extraneous offense is offered, trial judge must give a limiting instruction both when the evidence is admitted and in the general charge "to minimize the danger that the jury might use the evidence as proof that the defendant acted in conformity with his past acts on the occasion for which he is being tried"), *vacated on other grounds*, 900 F.2d 1462 (10th Cir. 1990); ***Lubbock Feed Lots, Inc. v. Iowa Beef Processors, Inc.***, 630 F.2d 250, 266 (5th Cir. 1980) (although limiting instructions may be requested and given at the end of a trial, they are "generally more effective at the time the evidence is presented"); ***United States v. Annoreno***, 460 F.2d 1303, 1307-08 (7th Cir. 1972) (limiting instructions may be given when evidence is admitted or in the jury charge).

Rule 105(a) limiting instruction."[328] But the majority's holding is a sensible one. Otherwise, a jury might sit through most of a trial under the mistaken belief that evidence is admissible against all defendants or for all purposes when, in fact, it is not.[329] A corollary to the *Rankin* holding, however, is that if a defendant does not request a limiting instruction when the evidence is first admitted, the trial court has no obligation to limit the evidence later in the jury charge.[330] "Once evidence has been admitted without a limiting instruction, it is part of the general evidence and may be used for all purposes."[331] The opponent must object when the evidence is first offered, or the court will deem any limiting objection to have been forfeited.[332] Thus, attorneys should request limiting instructions at both times, and trial judges should instruct the jury both

328. *Rankin*, 974 S.W.2d at 716 (McCormick, P.J., White & Keller, JJ., dissenting).

329. *Delgado v. State*, 235 S.W.3d 244, 251 (Tex. Crim. App. 2007); *see* 21A WRIGHT & GRAHAM, *supra* note 41, §5066, at 345-46 (jurors will be aware of the proper use of evidence if court gives instructions as each piece of evidence is admitted); *see also* *Gone v. State*, 54 S.W.3d 27, 33-34 (Tex. App.—Texarkana 2001, pet. ref'd) (court could think of no reason why counsel would not request a contemporaneous limiting instruction on extraneous offenses but declined to speculate that there could be no sound strategic reasons for it).

330. *Delgado*, 235 S.W.3d at 251; *see* *Williams v. State*, 273 S.W.3d 200, 230 (Tex. Crim. App. 2008); *Hammock v. State*, 46 S.W.3d 889, 895 (Tex. Crim. App. 2001); *see, e.g.*, *Martin v. State*, 176 S.W.3d 887, 899 (Tex. App.—Fort Worth 2005, no pet.) (when defendant asked for limiting instruction on use of extraneous offense long after he made original objections to testimony, evidence had already been admitted for all purposes; defendant forfeited any error in trial court's failure to give limiting instruction); *Prescott v. State*, 123 S.W.3d 506, 515-16 (Tex. App.—San Antonio 2003, no pet.) (defendant who did not request limiting instruction on use of extraneous offenses "at the moment the evidence [was] admitted" was not entitled to limiting instructions in jury charge); *Baxter v. State*, 66 S.W.3d 494, 502 (Tex. App.—Austin 2001, pet. ref'd) (trial court did not err in refusing to give limiting instruction in jury charge because defendant did not request such instruction when evidence of warrant and affidavit were first admitted; because defendant correctly objected at time of offer that affidavit was inadmissible for any purpose, admission of warrant and affidavit was harmless error); *see also* *Rankin*, 974 S.W.2d at 716 (if defendant does not properly request limiting instruction when evidence is admitted, then evidence is admitted "without limitation").

The court of criminal appeals has held that the rule requiring a limiting instruction on the permissible use of evidence when it is admitted does not extend to a further instruction that the State must prove an extraneous offense beyond a reasonable doubt. *See Delgado*, 235 S.W.3d at 251 (when a party properly requests limiting instruction when evidence is first offered, trial judge does not need to give instruction on burden of proof at that time); *Jackson v. State*, 992 S.W.2d 469, 477 (Tex. Crim. App. 1999) ("Rule 105 addresses parties and purposes; the rule does not address burdens of proof."). However, when the defendant has properly requested a limiting instruction in the jury charge, the trial court must also include an instruction on the State's burden of proof. *Delgado*, 235 S.W.3d at 251; *see Ex parte Varelas*, 45 S.W.3d 627, 631 (Tex. Crim. App. 2001); *Mitchell v. State*, 931 S.W.2d 950, 954 (Tex. Crim. App. 1996); *George v. State*, 890 S.W.2d 73, 76 (Tex. Crim. App. 1994).

331. *Delgado*, 235 S.W.3d at 251; *see Hammock*, 46 S.W.3d at 895; *Rankin*, 974 S.W.2d at 712. An earlier Texas case held that although a trial court could delay giving a limiting instruction until the jury charge, the opponent of the evidence could not wait until that time to request a limiting instruction. *See In re A.F.*, 895 S.W.2d 481, 483-84 (Tex. App.—Austin 1995, no writ); *see also* *McNiel v. State*, 757 S.W.2d 129, 136 (Tex. App.—Houston [1st Dist.] 1988, pet. ref'd) (Criminal Rule 105(a) "provides no support for the contention that error is preserved by a request for a limiting instruction made, not during the presentation of evidence, but as an objection to the court's charge").

332. *See Wesbrook v. State*, 29 S.W.3d 103, 114 n.8 (Tex. Crim. App. 2000) (party opposing evidence has burden of objecting and requesting limiting instruction when evidence is introduced); *Garcia v. State*, 887 S.W.2d 862, 878 (Tex. Crim. App. 1994) (once evidence is received without a proper limiting instruction, it becomes part of the general evidence in the case and may be used as proof to the full extent of its rational persuasive power); *Rodriguez v. State*, 968 S.W.2d 554, 560 (Tex. App.—Houston [14th Dist.] 1998, no pet.) (if party does not request limiting instruction when evidence is offered, judge is not required to put instruction in jury charge); *see, e.g.*, *Cole v. State*, 46 S.W.3d 427, 432 (Tex. App.—Fort Worth 2001, pet. ref'd) (when defendant did not request limiting instruction until trial court read jury charge, any error was forfeited).

when the evidence is offered and in the written jury instructions. The failure to give a limiting instruction when the evidence is introduced is subject to a harmless-error analysis under Texas Rule of Appellate Procedure 44.2(b).[333]

RULE 106
REMAINDER OF OR RELATED WRITINGS OR RECORDED STATEMENTS

If a party introduces all or part of a writing or recorded statement, an adverse party may introduce, at that time, any other part—or any other writing or recorded statement—that in fairness ought to be considered at the same time. "Writing or recorded statement" includes depositions.

COMMENTARY ON RULE 106

Rule 106 is modeled after Federal Rule 106 with minor differences.[334] The rule is based on two practical considerations: (1) the danger that partial evidence may be made misleading when taken out of context and (2) the inadequacy of delayed repair.[335] Rule 106 applies both to portions of a single writing or recorded statement and to separate but related writings or statements that should be considered together.

The rule does not mean that an entire writing or recording is admissible simply because a party has offered a portion of it. The rule permits the admission of only those additional portions necessary to explain the admitted portion or put it in context, to avoid misleading the trier of fact, or to ensure a fair and impartial understanding of

---

333. *Jones v. State*, 944 S.W.2d 642, 653 (Tex. Crim. App. 1996) (interpreting former TEX. R. APP. 81(b)(2), now TEX. R. APP. 44.2(b)); *Jones v. State*, 119 S.W.3d 412, 423-24 (Tex. App.—Fort Worth 2003, no pet.); *see Speer v. State*, 890 S.W.2d 87, 98 (Tex. App.—Houston [1st Dist.] 1994, pet. ref'd) (interpreting former TEX. R. APP. 81(b)(2), now TEX. R. APP. 44.2(b)). Refer to notes 92-121 *supra* and accompanying text.

334. In the federal rule, the opposing party may require the proponent of the evidence to offer the remainder of a writing or related writings. FED. R. EVID. 106. The drafters of former Texas Civil Rule 106 believed it was more appropriate for each party to offer those portions that best supported its own position. The drafters' official "Notes and Comments" to former Civil Rule 106 stated the following:

> Comment. This rule is the federal rule with one modification. Under the federal rule, a party may require his opponent to introduce evidence contrary to the latter's own case. The Committee believes the better practice is to permit the party himself to introduce such evidence contemporaneously with the introduction of the incomplete evidence. This rule does not in any way circumscribe the right of a party to develop fully the matter on cross-examination or as part of his own case. [The amended comment added: *Cf.* TEX. CODE CRIM. PROC. art. 38.24.] Nor does it alter the common law doctrine that the rule of optional completeness, as to writings, oral conversations, or other matters, may take precedence over exclusionary doctrines such as the hearsay or best evidence rule or the firsthand knowledge requirement. [The amended comment added: *See also* TEX. R. EVID. 610(a).]

TEX. R. CIV. EVID. 106 cmt., 641-642 S.W.2d (Tex. Cases) xxxvii (1983, amended 1998); TEX. R. CIV. EVID. 106 cmt., 669-670 S.W.2d (Tex. Cases) xxxi (1984, amended 1998). This comment was deleted in the 1998 unification process. The second sentence of the rule, explicitly applying the rule to depositions, was added in 1984 for clarification. *See In re: Adopted, Amended and Promulgated Rules of Evidence*, 669-670 S.W.2d (Tex. Cases) xxxi (1984, amended 1998). The federal rule does not include similar language. *See* FED. R. EVID. 106.

335. *Jones v. Colley*, 820 S.W.2d 863, 866 (Tex. App.—Texarkana 1991, writ denied).

the admitted portion.[336] Not all portions of a writing or recording that might be relevant to the admitted portion are admissible under the rule; only those that the trial court deems "necessary" and "fair" to put the admitted evidence into context are admissible.[337]

The common-law doctrine of optional completeness applied when a party offered into evidence only the portion of a writing, document, statement, conversation, or transaction that was favorable to its case.[338] Admission of such incomplete evidence often distorted the true impression of the whole and misled the jury.[339] To counteract the harm done by an incomplete presentation, the opposing party could present remainder evidence that (1) was relevant to the subject matter, (2) explained the true meaning of the portion already received, and (3) was nonprejudicial.[340] Because the doctrine was based on the need for clarification, it took precedence over exclusionary rules such as the hearsay and best-evidence rules. Thus, remainder evidence was admissible even if it violated an exclusionary rule.

Even under the doctrine of optional completeness, presentation of a statement out of context under the common law usually prevented the opponent from fully repairing the distortion when the omissions were later supplied.[341] This result occurred because the common-law doctrine required the opponent to introduce the remainder of the evidence during its own case or during cross-examination of the proponent's case.[342] The opponent could not introduce the remainder evidence when the proponent

336. *United States v. Li*, 55 F.3d 325, 329-30 (7th Cir. 1995); *United States v. Soures*, 736 F.2d 87, 91 (3d Cir. 1984); *see United States v. Haddad*, 10 F.3d 1252, 1259 (7th Cir. 1993) ("[T]he trial judge need only admit the remaining portions of the statement which are needed to clarify or explain the portion already received.").

337. *See* Tex. R. Evid. 106; *see, e.g.*, *United States v. Branch*, 91 F.3d 699, 728 (5th Cir. 1996) (although excluded portion of defendant's confession was relevant, court was not persuaded "that it was necessary to qualify, explain, or place into context" other portions of defendant's confession), *overruled on other grounds*, *Castillo v. United States*, 530 U.S. 120 (2000).

338. *See* 1 McCormick on Evidence, *supra* note 92, §56, at 284-85 (party who did not offer the evidence can later offer portions of the evidence that would shed light on the portions already admitted).

339. *Reece v. State* provides an egregious example of distorting the meaning of a document. 772 S.W.2d 198 (Tex. App.—Houston [14th Dist.] 1989, no pet.). In that case, the defendant's confession read: "I want to say that I do believe that I did not kill Mr. Smith cause [sic] I did not do nothing [sic] but hit him three times with my hand." *Id.* at 202. The prosecutor selectively deleted words and offered the words: "I did kill Mr. Smith." *Id.* While this was condemned as a "flagrant abuse of a long accepted trial tactic," the defendant's conviction was upheld because he had the opportunity to offer the rest of the statement under Criminal Rules 106 and 107. *Reece*, 772 S.W.2d at 202-03. Nonetheless, this type of distortion is neither condoned nor permitted by Rules 106 and 107. Their purpose is to permit a party to offer complete, unedited portions of a document, statement, or act and to allow the opponent to offer other complete, unedited portions to put the first into proper perspective.

340. *See Harrington v. State*, 547 S.W.2d 616, 621 (Tex. Crim. App. 1977) (no error in allowing State to offer part of confession when accused possesses and fully utilizes the right to introduce the complete confession); *Holloway v. State*, 148 Tex. Crim. 33, 35, 184 S.W.2d 479, 480 (1944) (no error when State introduces part of a confession and defendant offers the remainder); *Travelers Ins. v. Creyke*, 446 S.W.2d 954, 957 (Tex. Civ. App.—Houston [14th Dist.] 1969, no writ) (opposing party may introduce remainder of incomplete statement if it bears a reasonable relationship to and explains the incomplete statement).

341. *See* 1 McCormick on Evidence, *supra* note 92, §56, at 284.

342. *See id.* §56, at 284-85; 7 John H. Wigmore, Evidence in Trials at Common Law §§2099, 2102, at 617, 629 (Chadbourn rev. 1978).

offered the incomplete evidence because it would be an invasion of the proponent's case-in-chief.[343] The proponent, on the other hand, would not want to introduce the entire statement because it would be producing evidence that was harmful to its own case—evidence that it could not further address on cross-examination because an offering party could not cross-examine its own witnesses under the voucher rule.[344] Consequently, the doctrine allowed the distorted evidence to stand until the remainder evidence was later offered by the adversary.[345] By that time, it might be impossible to overcome the harmful effects of the incomplete evidence. Furthermore, the piecemeal introduction of evidence burdened juries with the difficult task of integrating the evidentiary fragments into a conceptual whole.

Rule 106 avoids the pitfalls of the common-law approach by ensuring that the presentation of a writing or recorded statement accurately reflects its true meaning. Rule 106 does not codify the common-law doctrine of optional completeness.[346] The rule adjusts the time when an opponent can introduce remainder evidence for incomplete writings or recorded statements. Under Rule 106, the opponent can present the remainder when the proponent offers the incomplete evidence.[347] Remainder evidence under the rule includes not only those portions of the writing or recorded statement that the proponent omitted, but also any other document or statement necessary for a proper understanding of the proponent's evidence.[348]

Rules 106 and 107 operate together to admit any type of evidence—acts, declarations, oral conversations, writings, or recorded statements—that should in fairness be

---

343. *See* 1 RAY, *supra* note 8, §33, at 29 (Supp. 1991) (Rule 106 affects the general order of proof).

344. *See* ***Sweeney v. State***, 704 S.W.2d 33, 34 (Tex. Crim. App. 1985) (attorney may impeach his own witness only if the testimony has surprised him and injured his cause); ***Puckett v. State***, 640 S.W.2d 284, 287 (Tex. Crim. App. [Panel Op.] 1982) (State cannot impeach its own witness when no surprise is shown); ***Lewis v. State***, 593 S.W.2d 704, 706 (Tex. Crim. App. [Panel Op.] 1980) (both surprise and injury must be shown). The common-law voucher rule was replaced by Rule 607. *See* ***Hughes v. State***, 4 S.W.3d 1, 5 (Tex. Crim. App. 1999); ***Russeau v. State***, 785 S.W.2d 387, 390 (Tex. Crim. App. 1990). Refer to *Article VI: Witnesses, infra* p. 596.

345. *See* 1 MCCORMICK ON EVIDENCE, *supra* note 92, §56, at 283-85.

346. However, Rule 107 explicitly codifies the common-law doctrine of optional completeness for both civil and criminal proceedings. Texas courts long ago adopted the provisions of former Code of Criminal Procedure article 791 as a part of the civil as well as criminal law of the state. *See* ***Cotton v. Morrison***, 140 S.W. 114, 115 (Tex. Civ. App.—Fort Worth 1911, no writ) (adopting doctrine of optional completeness from the Code of Criminal Procedure; doctrine also applies in civil cases); *see also* ***Travelers Ins. v. Creyke***, 446 S.W.2d 954, 957 (Tex. Civ. App.—Houston [14th Dist.] 1969, no writ) (referring to doctrine of optional completeness as a "general rule" in Texas). Refer to notes 355-372 *infra* and accompanying text.

347. *See* ***Jones v. Colley***, 820 S.W.2d 863, 866 (Tex. App.—Texarkana 1991, writ denied) (Civil Rule 106 is enforced "by allowing the opposing party to contemporaneously introduce any other part of the statement that should be considered with the portion introduced by the proponent"); ***Reece v. State***, 772 S.W.2d 198, 203 (Tex. App.—Houston [14th Dist.] 1989, no pet.) ("Under Rule 106, a party whose opponent introduces part of a writing or recorded statement may *at that time* introduce 'any other part.' Not only may the adverse party immediately offer the remainder, he may interrupt his opponent's case to do so, subject only to [Criminal Rule] 610(a).").

348. *See* TEX. R. EVID. 106; *see, e.g.*, ***Elmore v. State***, 116 S.W.3d 801, 807-08 (Tex. App.—Fort Worth 2003, pet. ref'd) (trial court abused its discretion in excluding letter defendant wrote to police chief in reply to letter from police chief that State had offered into evidence; excluding defendant's letter "gave rise to a strong possibility that the jury could form a false impression" about defendant's intent to commit gambling offense).

considered when a portion has been offered by the opponent. Rule 106 is narrower, applying only to written or recorded statements, and permits the opposing party to offer the remainder at the same time that the proponent offers a portion of a written or recorded statement.[349] With other acts and oral statements, the opponent must wait to offer the remainder evidence, either on cross-examination or in its own case-in-chief.

Both rules operate only to admit evidence, not to exclude it. Thus, the opponent of evidence cannot claim that a portion of a tape recording, letter, or other document is inadmissible under Rule 106 or Rule 107 because other portions have been lost or destroyed.[350] Such incomplete evidence may be excluded under Rule 403 as unfairly prejudicial, but not under the rules of optional completeness.

Rule 106 follows the common-law doctrine by requiring the opponent's evidence to be relevant and nonprejudicial.[351] Similarly, the remainder evidence takes precedence over exclusionary rules. The rule gives the trial judge considerable discretion in ruling on the admissibility of remainder evidence, limiting him only to considerations of "fairness."[352]

Finally, it is important to remember that Rule 106 is a permissive grant, not a requirement.[353] Therefore, the opponent does not need to introduce remainder evidence when the incomplete evidence is presented. The opponent can wait to present the evidence during cross-examination or during the development of its own case.[354] The advantage of Rule 106, however, is that introducing remainder evidence at the same time prevents the jury from receiving a misleading impression that might be difficult to overcome later.

---

349. Tex. R. Evid. 106; *see* **Hill v. State**, 783 S.W.2d 257, 260 (Tex. App.—Texarkana 1989, no pet.). Written or recorded statements include depositions. Tex. R. Evid. 106.

350. *See, e.g.*, **Lomax v. State**, 16 S.W.3d 448, 449-50 (Tex. App.—Waco 2000, no pet.) (court rejected defendant's claim that portions of tape-recorded telephone conversation should be excluded under Rules 106 and 107 because the tape ran out before the telephone conversation ended).

351. Refer to note 340 *supra* and accompanying text.

352. *See* Tex. R. Evid. 106; **Gilmore v. State**, 744 S.W.2d 630, 631 (Tex. App.—Dallas 1987, pet. ref'd). Including a reference to Rule 610 in the official comment to former Civil Rule 106 codified the judge's authority to control the "mode and order of interrogating witnesses and presenting evidence." *See* Wellborn, *supra* note 32, at 1194 (chronicling the development of Rule 106). Thus, the trial judge has considerable discretion in deciding whether the orderly progress of one party's presentation of evidence should be interrupted by the opponent in presenting other evidence that is logically relevant to a more complete understanding of the first party's evidence. *See* 21A Wright & Graham, *supra* note 41, §5077.2, at 500-02 (trial judge must balance damage done both by misleading evidence and by allowing one party to interrupt another).

353. **Gilmore**, 744 S.W.2d at 631.

354. As was explicitly noted in the comment to the former Civil and Criminal Rules: "This rule does not in any way circumscribe the right of a party to develop fully the matter on cross-examination or as part of his own case." Tex. R. Civ. Evid. 106 cmt., 641-642 S.W.2d (Tex. Cases) xxxvii (1983, amended 1998); Tex. R. Crim. Evid. 106 cmt., 701-702 S.W.2d (Tex. Cases) xxxiv (1986, amended 1998).

RULE 107
RULE OF OPTIONAL COMPLETENESS

If a party introduces part of an act, declaration, conversation, writing, or recorded statement, an adverse party may inquire into any other part on the same subject. An adverse party may also introduce any other act, declaration, conversation, writing, or recorded statement that is necessary to explain or allow the trier of fact to fully understand the part offered by the opponent. "Writing or recorded statement" includes a deposition.

Notes and Comments

Comment to 1998 change: This rule is the former Criminal Rule 107 except that the example regarding "when a letter is read" has been relocated in the rule so as to more accurately indicate the provision it explains. While this rule appeared only in the prior criminal rules, it is made applicable to civil cases because it accurately reflects the common law rule of optional completeness in civil cases.

COMMENTARY ON RULE 107

Rule 107 addresses admissibility and permits the introduction of otherwise inadmissible evidence[355] when that evidence is necessary to fully and fairly explain a matter "opened up" by the adverse party.[356] The purpose of Rule 107 is "to reduce the possibility of the jury receiving a false impression from hearing only a part of some act, conversation, or writing."[357] The 1998 unification of the Civil and Criminal Rules ex-

---

355. *Walters v. State*, 247 S.W.3d 204, 217-18 (Tex. Crim. App. 2007); *Credille v. State*, 925 S.W.2d 112, 116 (Tex. App.—Houston [14th Dist.] 1996, pet. ref'd); *see, e.g., Johnson v. State*, 747 S.W.2d 451, 453-54 (Tex. App.—Houston [14th Dist.] 1988, pet. ref'd) (defendant's questioning opened the door to admission of extraneous offenses, although no connection was made between defendant and the extraneous offenses). Former Criminal Rule 107 also allowed the introduction of other types of generally inadmissible evidence. *See, e.g., Jones v. State*, 501 S.W.2d 308, 311 (Tex. Crim. App. 1973) (because the accused partially divulged privileged spousal conversation, State was free to completely explore the previously privileged conversation).

356. *Walters*, 247 S.W.3d at 217-18; *Bezerra v. State*, 485 S.W.3d 133, 142-43 (Tex. App.—Amarillo 2016, pet. ref'd), *cert. denied*, 137 S. Ct. 495 (2016); *see Parr v. State*, 557 S.W.2d 99, 102 (Tex. Crim. App. 1977) ("evidence which is used to fully explain a matter opened up by the other party need not be ordinarily admissible" under the common-law doctrine of optional completeness); *see, e.g., Wright v. State*, 28 S.W.3d 526, 535-36 (Tex. Crim. App. 2000) (when defense attorney asked detective whether witness told detective that murder weapon belonged to witness, State could ask about complete conversation to explain initial statement admitted and to demonstrate that witness had not admitted to participating in the murder himself); *Foster v. State*, 779 S.W.2d 845, 855-58 (Tex. Crim. App. 1989) (admission of entire arrest warrant affidavit offered by State was proper once defendant had impeached arresting officer by pointing out descriptive flaws in the affidavit); *Delapaz v. State*, 297 S.W.3d 824, 827-28 (Tex. App.—Eastland 2009, no pet.) (defendant's statement that he did not want to put victim "through this again" was voluntary; State did not "open the door" to allow questioning of previous sexual assault committed against victim); *Fain v. State*, 986 S.W.2d 666, 682 (Tex. App.—Austin 1998, pet. ref'd) (when defendant first offered evidence of search of his truck to show that hairs found there did not match victim's hair, State could offer evidence of rubber-padded toolbox also found during that search to rebut claim that defendant broke his hand when toolbox lid fell on it).

357. *Walters*, 247 S.W.3d at 218; *e.g., Bezerra*, 485 S.W.3d at 142-43 (in prosecution for indecency with child, testimony by police officer, who watched videotaped interviews with complainants instead of interviewing them himself, "opened up" statements made by complainants; trial court did not abuse its discretion in admitting videotaped

plicitly applied Rule 107 to civil proceedings. Rule 107 has no explicit corollary in the Federal Rules, but it has been expressed and accepted in various federal cases.[358] Rule 107 was based on former Code of Criminal Procedure article 38.24—the last sentence was added only for purposes of clarification.[359] No change in the earlier law was intended by applying the doctrine to depositions.[360]

Rule 107 does not permit the introduction of other similar but inadmissible evidence unless that evidence is truly necessary to explain properly admitted evidence.[361]

interviews); *see Delapaz*, 297 S.W.3d at 827; *see, e.g.*, *Jordy v. State*, 413 S.W.3d 227, 231-32 (Tex. App.—Fort Worth 2013, no pet.) (although witness in DWI case generally cannot correlate defendant's performance on HGN test with conclusion that blood alcohol concentration exceeded legal limit, defendant opened door to this testimony by creating false impression that manual for national field-sobriety test says nothing about correlation between HGN and intoxication; trial court did not abuse its discretion in allowing officer to testify about what the manual says). As explained by the Texas Court of Criminal Appeals in discussing former Code of Criminal Procedure article 38.24:

> The purpose of this provision is to reduce the possibility of the fact finder receiving a false impression from hearing the evidence of only a part of the conversation, writing, act or declaration. The theory behind the rule is that by allowing the jury to hear the rest of the conversation on the same subject the whole picture will be filled out, removing any misleading effect which may have occurred from introduction of only a portion of the conversation. Obviously this purpose is achieved by receipt of the balance of the conversation on the same subject.

Cerda v. State, 557 S.W.2d 954, 957 (Tex. Crim. App. 1977); *see Solano v. State*, 728 S.W.2d 428, 430-31 (Tex. App.—San Antonio 1987, pet. ref'd).

358. *See United States v. Baker*, 432 F.3d 1189, 1222-23 (11th Cir. 2005) (Federal Rule 106 has been extended to apply to oral statements "in light of [Federal] Rule 611(a)'s requirement that the district court exercise 'reasonable control' over witness interrogation and the presentation of evidence to make them effective vehicles 'for the ascertainment of truth'"), *overruled on other grounds*, *Davis v. Washington*, 547 U.S. 813 (2006); *United States v. Bigelow*, 914 F.2d 966, 972 (7th Cir. 1990) (doctrine of optional completeness stems from Federal Rule 106 and applies only to written and recorded materials); *United States v. Castro*, 813 F.2d 571, 575-76 (2d Cir. 1987) (while Federal Rule 106 expressly governs only writings or recorded statements, under Federal Rule 611, a trial judge should protect the parties by exercising a sense of duty to fairness and may require a party offering testimony about a verbal statement to present fairly the "substance or effect" and context of the statement); *see, e.g.*, *United States v. Draiman*, 784 F.2d 248, 258 (7th Cir. 1986) (because defendant had alluded to portions of a hearsay conversation, government could introduce the rest of the hearsay statement).

359. *See Livingston v. State*, 739 S.W.2d 311, 331-32 (Tex. Crim. App. 1987) (no difference in meaning or effect between former Code of Criminal Procedure art. 38.24 and Rule 107).

360. The reference to depositions in Criminal Rule 107 did not broaden the common-law doctrine because depositions were already covered by the doctrine of optional completeness. *See Taylor v. State*, 420 S.W.2d 601, 606-07 (Tex. Crim. App. 1967), *overruled on other grounds*, *Jackson v. State*, 548 S.W.2d 685 (Tex. Crim. App. 1977); *Blum v. State*, 166 Tex. Crim. 541, 549, 317 S.W.2d 931, 936 (1958).

361. TEX. R. EVID. 107; *Walters*, 247 S.W.3d at 218; *see Pena v. State*, 353 S.W.3d 797, 814 (Tex. Crim. App. 2011); *Sauceda v. State*, 129 S.W.3d 116, 123 (Tex. Crim. App. 2004); *see, e.g.*, *Allridge v. State*, 762 S.W.2d 146, 153 (Tex. Crim. App. 1988) (defendant's self-serving hearsay confession was not admissible under Criminal Rule 107 because State had offered a later confession that "did not mislead the jury or leave the jury with only a partial or incomplete version of the facts"); *In re C.C.*, 476 S.W.3d 632, 636-37 (Tex. App.—Amarillo 2015, no pet.) (in case involving termination of parental rights, some portions of DFPS investigative report were admissible to explain children's condition even though those portions may have contained hearsay; portions describing parents' childhoods and criminal histories, mental health, and history of domestic violence were not necessary under Rule 107 and should not have been admitted); *Ziolkowski v. State*, 223 S.W.3d 640, 650 (Tex. App.—Texarkana 2007, pet. ref'd) (no error to exclude defendant's first two post-arrest written statements, which were self-serving under Rule 107; portions of the third statement offered by the State were not on the same subject, and there was no evidence of any false impressions); *Crosby v. Minyard Food Stores, Inc.*, 122 S.W.3d 899, 903 (Tex. App.—Dallas 2003, no pet.) (trial court erred in admitting otherwise inadmissible affidavit when defendant made no attempt to show how testimony of plaintiff's witness could have confused or misled jury about contents of affidavit); *Mendiola v. State*, 61 S.W.3d 541, 545-46 (Tex. App.—San Antonio 2001, no pet.) (fact that defendant's indictment for sexually abusing a different

Nor does the rule allow admission of evidence of unrelated events, acts, or statements merely to show "the whole relationship" between people.[362] "[T]he rule is not invoked by the mere reference to a document, statement, or act";[363] rather, a portion of the matter must be given in evidence before other portions of that evidence are admitted.[364] Also, a party cannot offer an entire recorded interview, a whole diary, or other voluminous material into evidence if the witness responds negatively when questioned about whether that recording, diary, or statement contains certain information.[365] The jury does not need to see the entire recorded interview or diary to prove that the witness's answer, "No, it does not contain that information," is correct. The portion of the material that contradicts the witness's testimony might be admissible to impeach the witness only if the recording or diary does in fact contain that information. Finally, a party cannot introduce parts of the same or a different document or conversation that contain "new" material on a different subject.[366]

The first sentence of Rule 107 is a "remainder" rule. That is, when one party introduces part of some conversation, act, or writing, the opposing party may introduce the rest if it is necessary to explain the already-admitted portion.[367] The second sentence

---

child was dismissed was not admissible under Rule 107 when State offered child's testimony that abuse had occurred but did not offer evidence that defendant had been indicted for that act).

362. *See, e.g.*, *Simpson v. State*, 975 S.W.2d 364, 368-69 (Tex. App.—Waco 1998, no pet.) (in aggravated-assault trial, defendant could not offer evidence of unrelated prior acts of violence against her by victim); *Callaway v. State*, 818 S.W.2d 816, 827 (Tex. App.—Amarillo 1991, pet. ref'd) (once defendant introduced evidence of the discharge of a weapon on a particular date, State could offer evidence to explain that single event).

363. *Walters*, 247 S.W.3d at 218; *accord Pena*, 353 S.W.3d at 814.

364. *Washington v. State*, 856 S.W.2d 184, 186 (Tex. Crim. App. 1993); *see Goldberg v. State*, 95 S.W.3d 345, 386-87 (Tex. App.—Houston [1st Dist.] 2002, pet. ref'd); *see, e.g.*, *Jernigan v. State*, 589 S.W.2d 681, 694-95 (Tex. Crim. App. [Panel Op.] 1979) (when defendant used a deposition to cross-examine a witness, Rule 107 did not permit State to offer entire deposition, but only specific portions relating to the same subject raised during cross-examination); *Moreno v. Tex. Dep't of Transp.*, 440 S.W.3d 889, 893-94 (Tex. App.—El Paso 2013, pet. denied) (trial court did not abuse its discretion in denying admission of disciplinary records under Rule 107 when defendant did not introduce any portion of them; alluding to them during plaintiff's cross-examination was not sufficient to meet rule's requirements); *Araiza v. State*, 929 S.W.2d 552, 555-56 (Tex. App.—San Antonio 1996, pet. ref'd) (although prosecutor questioned witness about whether particular details in his written statement were made at defendant's instruction, prosecutor did not offer any portion of the statement itself; thus, defendant was not entitled to offer the entire written statement under Criminal Rule 107); *Pinkney v. State*, 848 S.W.2d 363, 367 (Tex. App.—Houston [1st Dist.] 1993, no pet.) (merely reading the phrase "I contacted" from an offense report did not invoke Rule 107); *Grunsfeld v. State*, 813 S.W.2d 158, 163 (Tex. App.—Dallas 1991) (mere use of offense report to read an address on cross-examination did not invoke Criminal Rule 107), *aff'd*, 843 S.W.2d 521 (Tex. Crim. App. 1992).

365. *See, e.g.*, *Sauceda*, 129 S.W.3d at 124 (entire videotaped interview of child complainant was not admissible to show that child was never specifically asked about whether defendant used a butcher knife to assault her when defense witness offered to testify that child, during interview with witness, never mentioned that fact); *West v. State*, 121 S.W.3d 95, 103-04 (Tex. App.—Fort Worth 2003, pet. ref'd) (when witness stated that she had not recorded anything about defendant's assault on her in her diary, Rule 107 did not permit opposing party to offer diary into evidence).

366. *See Pena*, 353 S.W.3d at 814; *Sauceda*, 129 S.W.3d at 123; *see, e.g.*, *Edgeworth v. Wilson*, 113 S.W.3d 559, 561 (Tex. App.—Texarkana 2003, no pet.) (when party introduced witness's diagram and testimony explaining it, Rule 107 did not permit opposing party to offer witness's conversation on a different subject).

367. TEX. R. EVID. 107; *see, e.g.*, *Wisdom v. State*, 39 S.W.3d 320, 323 (Tex. App.—Waco 2001, no pet.) (when defendant offered portions of DWI Detection Manual into evidence, State could offer the remainder of the same section because "the jury was entitled to know all of the relevant information regarding the validity of the tests, both as to factors that could invalidate the results as well as the reliability of the tests if done correctly"); *Nunez v. State*,

of the rule permits the introduction of other types of evidence to clarify the opponent's evidence.[368] For example, one party might offer a letter into evidence. Then, under Rule 107, the opponent should be permitted to offer the letter writer's hearsay conversation explaining the letter's contents if that conversation is necessary to avoid giving the jury a false impression of the letter.[369]

Rule 107 does not, however, authorize a party to offer inadmissible evidence to explain inadmissible evidence offered earlier (without objection) by its opponent.[370] That is, a party cannot ignore its obligation to object to inadmissible evidence and then claim that it is entitled, under Rule 107, to offer more inadmissible evidence to explain the opponent's inadmissible evidence. Parties should timely object to inadmissible evidence when it is offered so that it is not heard by the jury.

As noted above, Rule 107 is much broader in scope than Rule 106.[371] It is, however, limited by Rule 403, which permits a trial judge to exclude otherwise relevant evidence if its unfair prejudicial effect or its likelihood of confusing the issues substantially outweighs its probative value.[372]

---

27 S.W.3d 210, 215-16 (Tex. App.—El Paso 2000, no pet.) (State could question defendant about specific circumstances of his acquittal on appeal in prior case when defendant testified that he was "acquitted" of prior forgery).

368. *See* Tex. R. Evid. 107 ("An adverse party may ... introduce any other act, declaration, conversation, writing, or recorded statement that is necessary to explain or allow the trier of fact to fully understand the part offered by the opponent.").

369. *See, e.g.*, *Credille v. State*, 925 S.W.2d 112, 116-17 (Tex. App.—Houston [14th Dist.] 1996, pet. ref'd) (when defendant questioned witness about content of interview that had been videotaped, State could offer videotape itself into evidence); *Solano v. State*, 728 S.W.2d 428, 430-31 (Tex. App.—San Antonio 1987, pet. ref'd) (when defendant cross-examined sheriff about oral statements made by witnesses, State could offer written statements into evidence under Rule 107 because jury could have been misled about the contents of the witnesses' written statements); *see also* *Foster v. State*, 779 S.W.2d 845, 855-58 (Tex. Crim. App. 1989) (State could offer arrest affidavit when defendant had impeached officer with flaws in that affidavit). *But see* *Pratt v. State*, 748 S.W.2d 483, 486-87 (Tex. App.—Houston [1st Dist.] 1988, pet. ref'd) (Rule 107 does not permit introduction of a written affidavit when opponent's questioning relates to conversations about its contents, rather than the precise contents of written document).

370. *See* *Nixon v. State*, 653 S.W.2d 443, 444 (Tex. Crim. App. 1983) (party who does not object to inadmissible character evidence when it is offered cannot then impeach the witness with other inadmissible evidence on rebuttal); *see, e.g.*, *Long v. State*, 10 S.W.3d 389, 399 (Tex. App.—Texarkana 2000, pet. ref'd) (when State offered inadmissible evidence that witness had taken and failed a polygraph test, defendant could not, under Rule 107, ask more questions about the issue; "when a party should have objected to the introduction of inadmissible evidence that was presented, and failed to do so, that party has not been allowed to present additional improper evidence under the guise of rebuttal"). *But see* *Long*, 10 S.W.3d at 406 (Grant, J., dissenting) (under majority's holding, rule of optional completeness would apply only if opposing counsel had objected to inadmissible evidence when it was introduced; opponent may not be aware that proponent will offer only a misleading portion of the evidence, and "[b]y not permitting the defense to inquire regarding the specific questions asked of [polygraph examinee] by the polygraph examiner, the State has benefited unfairly from normally inadmissible, unduly persuasive evidence that was not fully explained").

371. *Hill v. State*, 783 S.W.2d 257, 260 (Tex. App.—Texarkana 1989, no pet.). Refer to note 349 *supra* and accompanying text.

372. *Walters v. State*, 247 S.W.3d 204, 218 (Tex. Crim. App. 2007); *e.g.*, *Ibenyenwa v. State*, 367 S.W.3d 420, 425-26 (Tex. App.—Fort Worth 2012, pet. ref'd) (op. on reh'g) (in sexual-assault case, defendant argued that forensic interviewer improperly coached child complainant in her answers; trial court did not abuse its discretion in allowing State to introduce recording of interview because recording was the only evidence of whether child equivocated during interview and was unlikely to distract jury from issues in case); *see* 1 McCormick on Evidence, *supra* note 92, §56, at 287-88; Wellborn, *supra* note 32, at 1196. Refer to *Article IV: Relevance & Its Limits, infra* p. 209.

ARTICLE II

ARTICLE II: JUDICIAL NOTICE

Judicial notice authorizes the fact-finder, under the trial judge's guidance, to accept certain facts as true without formal proof.[1] The principal purpose of judicial notice is to promote judicial efficiency by saving the time and effort involved in offering unnecessary evidence.[2] In effect, "[j]udicial notice spares the expense of proof."[3] The proponent of a judicially noticed fact does not have to present evidence of that fact.[4] Once judicial notice has been taken, the party against whom the noticed fact operates cannot challenge it.[5] Judicial notice saves considerable time and avoids the "cumbrous process of formal proof,"[6] but it seldom arises in motion practice or at trial.

Article II of the Texas Rules contains four rules. Rule 201 is identical to Federal Rule of Evidence 201; Rule 202 is a revised version of former Texas Rule of Civil Procedure 184a;[7] Rule 203 is a significantly expanded version of Federal Rule of Civil Procedure 44.1, which is substantially the same as Federal Rule of Criminal Procedure 26.1; and Rule 204 has no specific federal analogue. While Article II of the Federal Rules deals only with judicial notice of adjudicative facts, the Texas provisions deal with both adjudicative facts (Rule 201) and law (Rules 202 through 204).

---

1. *See* Graham C. Lilly, An Introduction to the Law of Evidence §7, at 13 (1978); 2 McCormick on Evidence §328, at 428-29 (Kenneth S. Broun ed., 6th ed. 2006); 9 John H. Wigmore, Evidence in Trials at Common Law §2565, at 694 (Chadbourn rev. 1981).
Judicial notice is one of the oldest evidentiary doctrines of the common law. According to James Thayer, judicial notice is traceable to two ancient maxims: *manifesta non indigent probatione* (what is known does not need to be proved) and *non refert quid notum sit judici, si notum non sit in forma judicii* (what is known to a judge does not matter if it is not known in judicial form). James B. Thayer, A Preliminary Treatise on Evidence at the Common Law 277 (Boston, Little, Brown, and Company 1898). Both maxims are mentioned in Bracton's Note Book and cases from the 13th century. *Id.* at 13 n.1, 277 nn.1-2. The former idea, according to Thayer, existed so far back that it may be "coeval with legal procedure itself." *Id.* at 277.

2. *See James v. State*, 546 S.W.2d 306, 310 (Tex. Crim. App. 1977) ("The whole purpose of the rule of judicial notice is one of convenience to save time in the trial by eliminating the need for proof of facts about which there is really no controversy."); *see also Ex parte Turner*, 612 S.W.2d 611, 612 (Tex. Crim. App. 1981) (judicial notice can be a "proper conservation of judicial time and energy").

3. 1 Stephen A. Saltzburg et al., Federal Rules of Evidence Manual §201.02[6], at 201-10 (9th ed. 2006).

4. *See Fender v. St. Louis Sw. Ry. Co.*, 513 S.W.2d 131, 134 (Tex. Civ. App.—Dallas 1974, writ ref'd n.r.e.) (judicial notice eliminates need for taking evidence by usual procedures); *Tex. Sec. Corp. v. Peters*, 463 S.W.2d 263, 265 (Tex. Civ. App.—Fort Worth 1971, no writ) (litigant is not required to prove judicially noticed facts).

5. These challenges are prohibited because "judicial notice implies the absolute truth of the fact known, and, such fact being undisputed, its effect becomes [a] matter of law." *Harper v. Killion*, 162 Tex. 481, 484, 348 S.W.2d 521, 522 (1961) (quoting *Reynolds v. McMan Oil & Gas Co.*, 11 S.W.2d 778, 784 (Tex. Comm'n App. 1928, holding approved)).

6. Charles T. McCormick, Handbook of the Law of Evidence §323, at 687 (1st ed. 1954) [hereinafter McCormick's Handbook I].

7. Rule 184a was added to the Texas Rules of Civil Procedure by an order dated June 16, 1943, and was renumbered as Rule 184 in 1984. A new Rule 184a, "Determination of the Laws of Foreign Countries," was added to the Rules of Civil Procedure in 1984. Both rules were amended in 1988 to conform with Civil Rules of Evidence 202 and 203. Both rules were repealed effective September 1, 1990, because the material was covered by Civil Rules 202 and 203. *Amendments to the Texas Rules of Civil Procedure, Texas Rules of Appellate Procedure, and Texas Rules of Civil Evidence*, 785-786 S.W.2d (Tex. Cases) lx (1990, amended 1998).

RULE 201
JUDICIAL NOTICE OF ADJUDICATIVE FACTS

(a) Scope. This rule governs judicial notice of an adjudicative fact only, not a legislative fact.

(b) Kinds of Facts That May Be Judicially Noticed. The court may judicially notice a fact that is not subject to reasonable dispute because it:

(1) is generally known within the trial court's territorial jurisdiction; or

(2) can be accurately and readily determined from sources whose accuracy cannot reasonably be questioned.

(c) Taking Notice. The court:

(1) may take judicial notice on its own; or

(2) must take judicial notice if a party requests it and the court is supplied with the necessary information.

(d) Timing. The court may take judicial notice at any stage of the proceeding.

(e) Opportunity to Be Heard. On timely request, a party is entitled to be heard on the propriety of taking judicial notice and the nature of the fact to be noticed. If the court takes judicial notice before notifying a party, the party, on request, is still entitled to be heard.

(f) Instructing the Jury. In a civil case, the court must instruct the jury to accept the noticed fact as conclusive. In a criminal case, the court must instruct the jury that it may or may not accept the noticed fact as conclusive.

COMMENTARY ON RULE 201

A. Rule 201(a): Scope of the Rule

Matters that may be judicially noticed are often divided into three categories: adjudicative facts, legislative facts, and law.[8] Different rules apply to each category. Although Texas courts have long used judicial notice in all three categories, they have focused primarily on judicial notice of adjudicative facts.[9] Rule 201 applies only to adjudicative facts and does not extend to legislative facts.[10] Although no rule of evi-

---

8.   *See O'Quinn v. Hall*, 77 S.W.3d 438, 447 (Tex. App.—Corpus Christi 2002, no pet.). The judge's function of determining substantive law, at least for domestic law, has traditionally been described as judicial notice of law. *See* 2 McCormick on Evidence, *supra* note 1, §335, at 458-59.

9.   Under the Texas Rules of Evidence, judicial notice of adjudicative facts is confined to facts that are not subject to reasonable dispute because they are either generally known or verifiably certain. Tex. R. Evid. 201(b). Texas courts generally recognized this limitation before the adoption of the Texas Rules of Evidence. *See Barber v. Intercoast Jobbers & Brokers*, 417 S.W.2d 154, 157 (Tex. 1967) (facts are judicially noticeable if they are "certain and indisputable" or of "verifiable certainty"). Refer to notes 52-114 *infra* and accompanying text.

10.   Tex. R. Evid. 201(a). Federal Rule 201 contains the same express limitation. Fed. R. Evid. 201(a); *see also* 1 Jack B. Weinstein & Margaret A. Berger, Weinstein's Federal Evidence §201.03[2], at 201-12.1 to 201-13,

dence applies to judicial notice of legislative facts, some courts have explicitly relied on these facts to determine the scientific reliability of evidence.[11] Rule 201 does not cover judicial notice of law, but Rules 202 through 204 do.[12]

A fourth category, called "nonadjudicative," "nonevidence," or "legal reasoning" facts, is also not covered by the Rules of Evidence.[13] Courts have taken judicial notice of both legislative facts and "legal reasoning" facts since the promulgation of the Federal and Texas Rules.[14] Because Article II does not regulate these types of facts, there are no specific requirements for notice, hearing, opportunity to rebut, or supporting materials.[15] The parties should, however, have an opportunity to be heard on issues of legislative facts and to rebut the reliability of the court's sources.[16]

1. Adjudicative facts. Adjudicative facts are "those to which the law is applied in the process of adjudication."[17] These facts are specific to the particular case and typically must be established by evidence.[18] They are normally submitted to the trier of fact[19]

---

§201.51[1], at 201-85 to 201-86 (Joseph M. McLaughlin ed., 2d ed. 2008) (discussing distinction between legislative and adjudicative facts). According to the Advisory Committee on the Federal Rules, legislative facts were omitted from Federal Rule 201's scope because of the fundamental differences between adjudicative facts and legislative facts. FED. R. EVID. 201 advisory committee's note, subdiv. (a). Restrictions on judicial notice of legislative facts primarily address the use of extrinsic aids, such as the opinion of a statute's author and legislative floor debates, to interpret legislative enactments. *See Dellmuth v. Muth*, 491 U.S. 223, 230 (1989) (no need to refer to legislative history if Congress's intention is unmistakably clear in statute's language); *Rubin v. United States*, 449 U.S. 424, 430 (1981) (judicial inquiry is complete when statute's terms are unambiguous); *see also* William N. Eskridge, Jr., *The New Textualism*, 37 UCLA L. REV. 621, 623 (1990) (new textualism proposes that legislative history is irrelevant if Supreme Court has determined statute's plain meaning).

The Advisory Committee did not comment on why it made no attempt to cover judicial notice of law, but it did mention that judicial notice of foreign law was expressly covered by rules of federal criminal and civil procedure. FED. R. EVID. 201 advisory committee's note, subdiv. (a); *see* FED. R. CIV. P. 44.1; FED. R. CRIM. P. 26.1.

11. *See Merrell Dow Pharm., Inc. v. Havner*, 953 S.W.2d 706, 724 (Tex. 1997); *E.I. du Pont de Nemours & Co. v. Robinson*, 923 S.W.2d 549, 552-56 (Tex. 1995); *Emerson v. State*, 880 S.W.2d 759, 764-65 (Tex. Crim. App. 1994). Refer to notes 30-33 *infra* and accompanying text.

12. *See* TEX. R. EVID. 202 (laws of other states), TEX. R. EVID. 203 (laws of foreign countries), TEX. R. EVID. 204 (Texas ordinances, contents of Texas Register, and agency rules in Texas Administrative Code).

13. *Cf.* 1 WEINSTEIN & BERGER, *supra* note 10, §201.03[4], at 201-15 to 201-16 (discussing "non-evidence" or "background" facts). The Advisory Committee's note to Federal Rule 201 states that "the regulation of judicial notice of facts by the present rule extends only to adjudicative facts." FED. R. EVID. 201 advisory committee's note, subdiv. (a).

14. 1 STEVEN GOODE ET AL., TEXAS PRACTICE SERIES: GUIDE TO THE TEXAS RULES OF EVIDENCE §201.1, at 58 (3d ed. 2002); *cf.* 1 CHRISTOPHER B. MUELLER & LAIRD C. KIRKPATRICK, FEDERAL EVIDENCE §2:12, at 390-401 (3d ed. 2007) (discussing legislative facts, which are outside the scope of Federal Rule 201).

15. *See* Edmund M. Morgan, *Judicial Notice*, 57 HARV. L. REV. 269, 270-71 (1944).

16. *See* 1 SALTZBURG ET AL., *supra* note 3, §201.02[4], at 201-9 (if facts are "likely to be critical to a decision on the law to be applied to parties, there is every reason to want the parties to be heard on the factual question"); *see also Emerson*, 880 S.W.2d at 771-72 (Clinton & Miller, JJ., dissenting) (by using legislative facts to determine scientific reliability of horizontal gaze nystagmus test without informing parties in advance and permitting parties to debate the propriety of taking judicial notice of such facts, majority abandoned neutrality and sacrificed fairness).

17. *O'Quinn v. Hall*, 77 S.W.3d 438, 447 (Tex. App.—Corpus Christi 2002, no pet.) (quoting *Hill v. Heritage Res., Inc.*, 964 S.W.2d 89, 137 (Tex. App.—El Paso 1997, pet. denied)); Kenneth C. Davis, *Judicial Notice*, 55 COLUM. L. REV. 945, 952 (1955).

18. *Kubosh v. State*, 241 S.W.3d 60, 64 (Tex. Crim. App. 2007).

19. Davis, *supra* note 17, at 952.

and "relate to the parties, their activities, their properties, their businesses."[20] In other words, "'when a court or an agency finds facts concerning the immediate parties, including who did what, where, when, how, and with what motive or intent, the court or agency is performing an adjudicative function, and the facts are called adjudicative facts.'"[21]

2. Legislative facts. Legislative facts are those that "help the tribunal to determine the content of law and policy and to exercise its judgment or discretion in determining what course of action to take."[22] These are "facts" that judges refer to in deciding a law's meaning, scope, and applicability.[23] Although there is always a risk that judges may usurp the jury's role, Justice Oliver Wendell Holmes considered taking judicial notice of legislative facts to be a duty: "As the judge is bound to declare the law, he must know or discover the facts that establish the law."[24]

Legislative facts include, for example, information on the impact of prior and proposed law, used to facilitate lawmaking through judicial decisions; the legislative history of a statute, used to assist in its interpretation; and the basis for the exercise of legislative power, used to enable a court to fulfill its constitutional responsibility.[25] Of course, if a statute is clear and unambiguous on its face, courts cannot take judicial notice of legislative facts to explain its meaning.[26] If a statute is ambiguous, a party may request that the court take judicial notice of pertinent legislative facts to support a par-

---

20. *Id.*

21. *O'Quinn*, 77 S.W.3d at 447 (quoting *Hill*, 964 S.W.2d at 137); FED. R. EVID. 201 advisory committee's note, subdiv. (a) (quoting KENNETH C. DAVIS, 2 Administrative Law Treatise 353 (1958)).

22. Davis, *supra* note 17, at 952. Kenneth Davis explained the rationale for judicial use of legislative facts as follows:

> In the great mass of cases decided by courts and by agencies, the legislative element is either absent, unimportant, or interstitial, because in most cases the applicable law and policy have been previously established. But whenever a tribunal is engaged in the creation of law or of policy, it may need to resort to legislative facts, whether or not those facts have been developed on the record.

Id.; *see also* ***Emerson v. State***, 880 S.W.2d 759, 764-65 (Tex. Crim. App. 1994) (setting out definition of legislative facts and taking judicial notice of scientific articles and treatises outside the record as legislative facts). For a lengthy discussion of the contours of "legislative facts" and a collection of federal cases noticing legislative facts, see 1 MUELLER & KIRKPATRICK, *supra* note 14, §2:12, at 390-401.

23. *See **Kubosh***, 241 S.W.3d at 64 (legislative facts are relevant to overall legal reasoning and the lawmaking process, are not usually proved by evidence, and are not governed by Rule 201).

24. ***Prentis v. Atl. Coast Line Co.***, 211 U.S. 210, 227 (1908).

25. JACK B. WEINSTEIN ET AL., NEW YORK CIVIL PRACTICE ¶4511.01 (1981); *see also* 2 MCCORMICK ON EVIDENCE, *supra* note 1, §331, at 443-44 (legislative facts guide judges in deciding constitutional validity of statutes, interpreting statutes, and extending or restricting common-law rules).

26. *See **Fitzgerald v. Advanced Spine Fixation Sys., Inc.***, 996 S.W.2d 864, 865-66 (Tex. 1999) (when a statute is clear and unambiguous, courts should give the words of the statute their common meaning); ***Boykin v. State***, 818 S.W.2d 782, 785 (Tex. Crim. App. 1991) ("[I]f the meaning of the statutory text ... should have been plain to the legislators who voted on it, we ordinarily give effect to that plain meaning."); ***Ex parte Davis***, 412 S.W.2d 46, 52 (Tex. Crim. App. 1967) (op. on reh'g) ("Where the statute is clear and unambiguous the Legislature must be understood to mean what it has expressed, and it is not for the courts to add or subtract from such a statute."), *overruled on other grounds*, ***Ex parte Hill***, 528 S.W.2d 125 (Tex. Crim. App. 1975).

ticular construction. The requesting party must provide the court with the appropriate information and materials.[27]

Judicial notice of legislative facts is not confined to materials developed by or for legislatures. Courts, especially the Supreme Court, will frequently reach out to social-science information or statistical data, historical treatises, and even literature for material that supports particular social values and provides the basis for its constitutional analysis.[28] A judge should never inform the jury that he has taken judicial notice of a legislative fact, and the jury never receives an instruction on that judicial notice.[29]

Because Rule 201 covers only judicial notice of adjudicative facts, judicial notice of legislative facts is ordinarily limited only by the court's own sense of propriety.[30] For example, in *Emerson v. State*, the court of criminal appeals treated the question of the

---

27. Such materials would include information on (1) the Legislature's purpose in enacting the statute, (2) the particular circumstances under which it was enacted, (3) any applicable legislative history, (4) any former statutes dealing with the same subject or common-law precedent, (5) the consequences of a particular construction, (6) any administrative construction of the statute, and (7) the effect of the caption, preamble, and any emergency provisions. TEX. GOV'T CODE §311.023.

28. Although a large number of decisions involve judicial consideration of societal, economic, sociological, or historical matters outside the record, few cases recognize that relying on these materials is a form of judicial notice. *See, e.g.*, *Lawrence v. Texas*, 539 U.S. 558, 576-77 (2003) (Court examined historical basis for laws against homosexual conduct and relied, in part, on perceived evolution of social mores and on international tribunals to support the decision to decriminalize homosexual conduct); *United States v. Leon*, 468 U.S. 897, 906-08 (1984) (Court cited and relied on cases discussing the Fourth Amendment's rule excluding evidence obtained through unlawful search and seizure; that rule created good-faith requirement for prosecutors introducing evidence collected under search warrant); *Roe v. Wade*, 410 U.S. 113, 129-32 (1973) (Court relied on medical treatises and scientific studies as partial explanation for creating constitutionally protected right to abortion in certain circumstances); *Turner v. United States*, 396 U.S. 398, 407-08 (1970) (Court cited statutory inference to conclude that jury was "wholly justified in accepting the legislative judgment" that possession of heroin is equivalent to possession of imported heroin because heroin is not produced in the United States). Judicial notice of legislative facts is particularly prevalent in Supreme Court death-penalty jurisprudence. *See, e.g.*, *Roper v. Simmons*, 543 U.S. 551, 573-74 (2005) (Court relied on the American Psychiatric Association's prohibition on diagnosing juveniles with antisocial personality disorder to support decision that juvenile offenders cannot be sentenced to death); *Atkins v. Virginia*, 536 U.S. 304, 313-16 (2002) (Court relied on historical and state legislative data to find national consensus that mentally retarded offenders should be exempt from death penalty); *Ford v. Wainwright*, 477 U.S. 399, 407-10 (1986) (Court relied on common-law principles, religious postulates, and state statutes to conclude that execution of insane individuals is unconstitutional); *Gregg v. Georgia*, 428 U.S. 153, 169 (1976) (Court relied on historical treatises, legislative enactments, statistical studies, and law-review articles to determine that death penalty is not always "cruel and unusual" punishment); *see also* *Kansas v. Marsh*, 548 U.S. 163, 189-90 (2006) (Scalia, J., concurring) (in a decision upholding the constitutionality of Kansas's death-penalty statute, Justice Scalia discussed and criticized social studies that "bemoan the alleged prevalence of wrongful death sentences" and cited cases in which DNA testing confirmed an executed defendant's guilt).

29. *See, e.g.*, *O'Connell v. State*, 17 S.W.3d 746, 748-49 (Tex. App.—Austin 2000, no pet.) (reversible error when trial court told jury it had taken judicial notice of scientific reliability of a field sobriety test and instructed jury that it could take judicial notice of reliability as well).

30. *See In re Sigmar*, 270 S.W.3d 289, 301-02 (Tex. App.—Waco 2008, orig. proceeding) (legislative facts are not governed by Rule 201); Warren F. Schwartz, *A Suggestion for the Demise of Judicial Notice of "Judicial Facts,"* 45 TEX. L. REV. 1212, 1212 (1967) (legislative facts "can better be explored by the judge free of the limitations imposed by the rules of evidence"); *cf.* FED. R. EVID. 201 advisory committee's note, subdiv. (a) (this view of legislative facts "renders inappropriate any limitation in the form of indisputability, any formal requirements of notice other than those already inherent in affording opportunity to hear and be heard and exchanging briefs, and any requirement of formal findings at any level"). The problem with judicial reliance on extrinsic materials is that these materials frequently have not been thoroughly examined by the parties.

reliability of the horizontal gaze nystagmus test—a scientific test of sobriety—as a legislative fact; the court freely used scientific articles outside the record, which were not provided by the parties, to support its conclusion.[31] The court did not discuss the notoriety or indisputability of the scientific articles it relied on, nor did it follow any of the other restrictions of Rule 201. According to Kenneth Davis, "judge-made law would stop growing if judges, in thinking about questions of law and policy, were forbidden to take into account the facts they believe, as distinguished from facts which are 'clearly … within the domain of the indisputable.'"[32] On the other hand, an argument could be made that the reliability of a particular scientific test is a question of fact that should be governed by Rule 201, not a question of law or policy.[33]

Courts do not, however, always carefully distinguish judicial notice of legislative facts from judicial notice of adjudicative facts.[34] The lack of a bright-line distinction

---

31. 880 S.W.2d 759, 764-65 (Tex. Crim. App. 1994).

32. Kenneth C. Davis, *A System of Judicial Notice Based on Fairness and Convenience*, in PERSPECTIVES OF LAW 69, 82 (Roscoe Pound et al. eds., 1964); *accord* FED. R. EVID. 201 advisory committee's note, subdiv. (a).

33. *See Hernandez v. State*, 116 S.W.3d 26, 31-32 (Tex. Crim. App. 2003) (party cannot request judicial notice of scientific treatises on appeal when those materials were not brought to trial court's attention; "judicial notice on appeal cannot serve as the sole source of support for a bare trial record concerning scientific reliability"); *Forte v. State*, 935 S.W.2d 172, 177 n.4 (Tex. App.—Fort Worth 1996, pet. ref'd) (court of appeals refused to take judicial notice of a "considerable body of scientific literature" on eyewitness identification because literature was not "capable of ready determination by resort to sources whose accuracy cannot be reasonably questioned"). The court of criminal appeals has clarified that the rule in *Hernandez* is limited to scientific evidence and has refused to extend it to testimony based on experience. *Morris v. State*, 361 S.W.3d 649, 655 n.28 (Tex. Crim. App. 2011). The court explained:

> In general, judges are not scientists and lack expertise to assess the reliability of scientific principles on their own. [T]he experience-based testimony at issue in the present case involved a topic with which courts are familiar: behaviors engaged in by criminals. Courts are far better qualified to assess the reliability of this type of evidence than scientific evidence.

Id.

34. In one case, the El Paso Court of Appeals held that the trial court did not err in declining to take judicial notice of the "fact" that a witness in Mexico could not be subpoenaed to a Texas court. *Rodriguez v. State*, 90 S.W.3d 340, 359-60 (Tex. App.—El Paso 2001, pet. ref'd). The appellate court's conclusion was correct because the requesting party relied only on the opposing attorney's statement that "a witness in a foreign country could not be subpoenaed through the normal subpoena process." *Id.* Statements made by a witness, party, or attorney are not, by themselves, a sufficiently indisputable source of information for purposes of judicial notice. However, the *Rodriguez* appellate court held that the ability to subpoena a witness from Mexico was a legislative fact about the content of law and policy. *Id.* at 360; *see also In re Sigmar*, 270 S.W.3d at 302 (following *Rodriguez*, court concluded that facts about another country's compliance with Hague Convention on the Civil Aspects of International Child Abduction were legislative facts subject to judicial notice by trial or appellate court). Normally, the term "legislative fact" refers to the information, policies, and societal facts on which statutory or judicial law is based. *See Rodriguez*, 90 S.W.3d at 360. The question of whether a specific person can be subpoenaed from a particular foreign state or country is usually an issue of law (whether there is a governing statute, treaty, or legal process in place) or possibly an issue of fact (there is a statute, treaty, or legal process, but for specific factual reasons it cannot be used or is inapplicable or ineffective in this situation). *See id.* In either case, a judge could take judicial notice of this law or fact under Rules 201-203 if supplied with sufficient information from indisputable sources. *See Rodriguez*, 90 S.W.3d at 359.

In *Gaston v. State*, the court of appeals stated that it would take judicial notice of "legislative facts" about the Dallas County district clerk's administrative practices of numbering criminal cases as they are filed. 63 S.W.3d 893, 900 (Tex. App.—Dallas 2001, no pet.). The administrative procedures of a governmental office may be subject to judicial notice as an adjudicative fact, but they do not support the basis or purpose of either statutory or judicial law.

between legislative and adjudicative facts is problematic because judges must instruct juries on judicial notice of adjudicative facts but should not instruct them on judicial notice of legislative facts.[35]

3. Law. The concept of judicial notice has traditionally included a judge's informal investigation when determining applicable law.[36] "Law" includes not only the law of the forum[37] but also the law of sister states[38] and foreign countries.[39] Because the judge may take judicial notice of the law of sister states and foreign countries, it is axiomatic that the judge may also take judicial notice of federal law.[40] No rules restrict the judge's investigation into and conclusions about the content or applicability of foreign law—he may reject the propositions offered by any or all parties and may choose either to consult the sources presented by the parties or to make an independent search for persuasive data.[41]

The trial judge "determines" the law of the forum; however, when foreign law is involved, determination of that law has generally been considered a question of fact subject to formal pleading and proof requirements.[42] Regardless of the type of law to be determined, Rule 201(b)'s requirement of general knowledge or accurate and ready determination does not apply. Rule 202 covers judicial notice of the law of other American jurisdictions,[43] while Rule 203 regulates judicial notice of the content of the law of foreign countries.[44]

4. Nonadjudicative facts. Another category of knowledge that is not subject to the limitations of judicial notice under Rule 201 is what the Federal Advisory Committee

RULE 201

---

35. *See Watts v. State*, 99 S.W.3d 604, 612 n.28 (Tex. Crim. App. 2003). The court of criminal appeals noted that: [t]rial courts may not instruct juries that the judge has taken judicial notice of legislative facts. Such facts have relevance to legal reasoning, the admissibility of other evidence, and the lawmaking process. Legislative facts may provide the rationale for a legal ruling, but they are not an appropriate topic for a judicial notice instruction to the jury. *Id.* Refer to note 29 *supra* and accompanying text.

36. *See* 2 McCORMICK ON EVIDENCE, *supra* note 1, §335, at 458.

37. *See id.* §335, at 459-60.

38. *See id.* §335, at 460-62.

39. *Cf.* RESTATEMENT (THIRD) OF FOREIGN RELATIONS LAW OF UNITED STATES §113 (1987) (determination or interpretation of international law is appropriate for judicial notice without pleading or proof). State practice on judicial notice of foreign law is not unified. *See* 2 McCORMICK ON EVIDENCE, *supra* note 1, §335, at 464.

40. *See, e.g.*, *Daugherty v. S. Pac. Transp. Co.*, 772 S.W.2d 81, 83 (Tex. 1989) (trial court should have taken judicial notice of OSHA regulations even though party did not properly plead them); *Lawson-Avila Constr., Inc. v. Stoutamire*, 791 S.W.2d 584, 590 n.1 (Tex. App.—San Antonio 1990, writ denied) (trial court took judicial notice of OSHA regulations); *Sw. Bell Tel., L.P. v. Chappell*, No. 02-12-00071-CV (Tex. App.—Fort Worth 2013, no pet.) (memo op.; 1-24-13) (footnote 7; court of appeals took judicial notice of federal tax law setting time limit to claim refund).

41. *See* TEX. R. EVID. 203(c); *Watts v. State*, 99 S.W.3d 604, 610 (Tex. Crim. App. 2003); Morgan, *supra* note 15, at 270.

42. 2 McCORMICK ON EVIDENCE, *supra* note 1, §335, at 458. Refer to notes 219-220 *infra* and accompanying text.

43. Refer to notes 199-216 *infra* and accompanying text.

44. Refer to notes 217-238 *infra* and accompanying text.

calls "nonadjudicative facts"[45] or "nonevidence facts."[46] These terms refer to the basic, general knowledge that the average fact-finder has about mankind, human affairs, and our environment—knowledge that must be used without formal notice in drawing inferences, evaluating evidence, judging the credibility of witnesses, and interpreting what is seen and heard from the witness stand.[47] These subjects are common-reasoning facts "imputed to judges and juries as part of their necessary mental outfit"[48] that cannot possibly be introduced into evidence and, because of their multiplicity and fundamental nature, are not appropriate subjects for formalized judicial notice.[49] Texas courts have long recognized this notion.[50] Common knowledge would include such facts as "that there are twelve inches in a foot, that the sun rises in the morning, or even that a person drinking alcoholic beverages will become intoxicated."[51] The legal system does not require the judge or jury to come to court with a *tabula rasa*—a mind devoid of all basic, common knowledge or background facts.

45. FED. R. EVID. 201 advisory committee's note, subdiv. (a); *see United States v. Amado-Núñez*, 357 F.3d 119, 121-22 (1st Cir. 2004) (although "background" or "evaluative" facts may be important in a given case, the parties do not have an advantage over the fact-finder in gaining access to evidence about them).

46. FED. R. EVID. 201 advisory committee's note, subdiv. (a).

47. Charles McCormick refers to this information as "the residual data the jury members bring along with them as rational human beings." 2 McCORMICK ON EVIDENCE, *supra* note 1, §329, at 438. Other authority states that this information is based on the general experience that the fact-finder possesses "in common with the generality of mankind." R.T.K., Annotation, *Propriety of Instructions on Matters of Common Knowledge*, 144 A.L.R. 932, 932-33 (1943); *see also Kroger Grocery & Baking Co. v. Woods*, 167 S.W.2d 869, 871 (Ark. 1943) (jurors are not expected to ignore matters of common knowledge or their own observation and experience). *See generally* A. Leo Levin & Robert J. Levy, *Persuading the Jury with Facts Not in Evidence: The Fiction-Science Spectrum*, 105 U. PA. L. REV. 139, 139-45 (1956) (discussing the competing forces of common sense, knowledge, fairness, and admissibility in the content and presentation of evidence). In *City of Houston v. Federal Aviation Administration*, the Fifth Circuit rejected a challenge to FAA regulations that "no rational basis connects the FAA's goals—to protect Dulles and to preserve the short-haul status of National—to the means it has adopted." 679 F.2d 1184, 1191 (5th Cir. 1982). The court noted that "[h]aving traveled through these two airports, we may take judicial notice of their problems of under- and over-use." *Id.*

48. THAYER, *supra* note 1, at 280.

49. FED. R. EVID. 201 advisory committee's note, subdiv. (a); *see* 1 WEINSTEIN & BERGER, *supra* note 10, §201.03[4], at 201-15 to 201-16.

50. *See, e.g., El Chico Corp. v. Poole*, 732 S.W.2d 306, 311 (Tex. 1987) ("[W]e know by common knowledge that alcohol distorts perception, slows reaction, and impairs motor skills, while operation of an automobile requires clear perception, quick reaction, and adept motor skills. Our everyday use and reliance on the automobile is unquestionable [as] is the tragic relationship between intoxicated drivers and fatal or injury-producing accidents."); *Mo. Pac. R.R. v. Kimbrell*, 160 Tex. 542, 546-47, 334 S.W.2d 283, 286-87 (1960) (common knowledge includes current interest rates and the earning power of money); *Diaz v. State*, 660 S.W.2d 93, 94 (Tex. Crim. App. 1983) ("It is common knowledge that from time to time inmates of the Texas Department of Corrections are released on parole."); *Cardona v. State*, 134 S.W.3d 854, 859 (Tex. App.—Amarillo 2004, pet. ref'd) ("formula for or ingredients of methamphetamine and amphetamine or the process by which either is made" is not common knowledge); *Serrano v. State*, 123 S.W.3d 53, 62 (Tex. App.—Austin 2003, pet. ref'd) ("It is common knowledge that fruits, vegetables, and other items are sold and transported in tied-off plastic bags which are also used for storing items."); *Arrick v. State*, 107 S.W.3d 710, 715 (Tex. App.—Austin 2003, pet. ref'd) ("It is a matter of common knowledge that criminals who commit bloody crimes commonly attempt to hide evidence of the crime by cleaning the scene.").

51. *Brune v. Brown Forman Corp.*, 758 S.W.2d 827, 830-31 (Tex. App.—Corpus Christi 1988, writ denied).

B. Rule 201(b): Kinds of Facts that May Be Judicially Noticed

Adjudicative facts that are relevant to the ultimate issues in a judicial proceeding, but are not themselves the subject of any controversy, may be subject to judicial notice.[52] They may be judicially noticed under Rule 201—and thus not subject to formal proof—only if they are "not subject to reasonable dispute."[53] A potential problem under Rule 201 is determining the scope of "reasonable dispute."[54]

Facts that are "somewhat" disputable are frequently disputed by the opposing party. As a result, attorneys spend more time and effort presenting arguments about the degree of disputability of the fact offered for judicial notice than they would offering evidentiary proof of that fact. To avoid this problem, both the federal and Texas drafters chose the more stringent test of permitting judicial notice only of facts that are "not subject to reasonable dispute."[55] As a practical matter, judicial notice should not be used—by the judge or by the party proffering the evidence—if there is any question about the level of disagreement.

---

52. ***Kubosh v. State***, 241 S.W.3d 60, 64 (Tex. Crim. App. 2007); ***Watts v. State***, 99 S.W.3d 604, 610 (Tex. Crim. App. 2003).

53. Tex. R. Evid. 201(b); *see* ***Kubosh***, 241 S.W.3d at 64; ***Watts***, 99 S.W.3d at 610.

54. *See* Tex. R. Evid. 201(b). Long before the Federal Rules took effect, the leading evidence scholars were divided on the issue of whether judicial notice of adjudicative facts should be confined to substantially indisputable facts or could include facts that are unlikely to be disputed. Edmund Morgan and Charles McCormick argued that judicial notice should be confined to indisputable facts, while John Wigmore, James Thayer, and Kenneth Davis contended that judicial notice should also extend to facts that are unlikely to be disputed. *Compare* McCormick's Handbook I, *supra* note 6, §330, at 710-11 (taking issue with Wigmore-Thayer view of judicial notice and arguing that "the weight of reason and the prevailing authority" dictate that judicial notice be confined to indisputable facts), *and* John T. McNaughton, *Judicial Notice—Excerpts Relating to the Morgan-Wigmore Controversy*, 14 Vand. L. Rev. 779, 779 (1961) (Morgan's view restricts judicial notice to "patently indisputable" matters), *with* Davis, *supra* note 32, at 76-78 (propounding Wigmore-Thayer view and arguing that trial judges should entertain evidence that contradicts judicially noticed facts), *and* McNaughton, *supra*, at 805 (Wigmore-Thayer view allows courts to judicially notice matters that are "somewhat disputable but unlikely to be disputed"). Both sides presented cogent arguments and contended that the weight of existing case law supported their views. *See* McNaughton, *supra*, at 796 n.3. In providing that "[a] judicially noticed fact must be one not subject to reasonable dispute," the Federal Rules followed the Morgan-McCormick view requiring substantial indisputability. *See* Fed. R. Evid. 201(b). The Advisory Committee's note to the federal rule stated that this more stringent standard was based on "the theory that these considerations call for dispensing with traditional methods of proof only in clear cases." Fed. R. Evid. 201 advisory committee's note, subdiv. (b).

55. Fed. R. Evid. 201(b); Tex. R. Evid. 201(b). Several old cases set forth a more rigorous third standard, permitting judicial notice only of those facts that were certain and indisputable. *See* ***Utah Constr. Co. v. Berg***, 205 P.2d 367, 370 (Ariz. 1949); ***Varcoe v. Lee***, 181 P. 223, 227 (Cal. 1919). Most modern decisions and the Federal Rules reject this standard because any rule of absolute indisputability would seriously restrict the scope of judicial notice and place an unwarranted burden on the trial judge. *See* Edward J. Imwinkelried, *Impoverishing the Trier of Fact: Excluding the Proponent's Expert Testimony Due to the Opponent's Inability to Afford Rebuttal Evidence*, 40 Conn. L. Rev. 317, 347-48 (2007) ("No matter how many successful experiments have been conducted to validate a theory, another experiment is always conceivable. As long as there is another potential experiment, there is a possibility of falsification. Requiring that a fact be certainly verifiable to be judicially noticeable would set the bar impossibly high."); Christopher Onstott, *Judicial Notice and the Law's "Scientific" Search for Truth*, 40 Akron L. Rev. 465, 482 (2007) ("A standard that only recognizes facts that are 'indisputable,' 'certain,' or 'not reasonably question[able],' is inherently inconsistent with a knowledge from a method deriving its value from the continued questioning of a working hypothesis."). Some common-law Texas decisions appeared to follow this rigorous standard, stating that adjudicative facts must be "certain and indisputable" to be noticed. *See, e.g.*, ***Harper v. Killion***, 162 Tex. 481, 485,

Both Texas Rule 201(b) and Federal Rule 201(b) permit judicial notice of two kinds of facts and state that both kinds must not be "subject to reasonable dispute."[56] The two categories are facts that are generally known (also called "notorious" facts) and facts that are verifiably certain.[57] "[I]f the fact is one that a reasonable person would not know from memory but would know where to find it, [the fact] falls within subdivision (2),"[58] rather than subdivision (1). Under either category, the party requesting judicial notice must identify a single, discrete adjudicative fact that the party wants the court to judicially notice.[59] The requesting party should also give the trial judge sufficient notice of the request and draft a jury instruction for the judge.[60]

1. Rule 201(b)(1): Notorious facts. Under early common law, a fact could be judicially noticed as a "notorious" fact (that is, a fact that is publicly or generally known) if it was within the common knowledge of all persons of ordinary understanding and intelligence.[61] Under Federal Rule 201(b), this extremely broad category was wisely restricted to general knowledge "within the trial court's territorial jurisdiction," a standard now commonly accepted as a sufficient basis for judicial notice.[62] Texas Rule

348 S.W.2d 521, 523 (1961) ("[A] district court sitting in Cherokee County can judicially notice the certain and indisputable fact of common knowledge that the entire city of Jacksonville is located within such county ...."); **Johnson v. Cooper**, 379 S.W.2d 396, 399 (Tex. Civ. App.—Fort Worth 1964, no writ) (trade meaning of "square" was not "certain and indisputable"). When these cases are analyzed, however, it becomes clear that the courts were actually applying the same standard adopted by the federal rule. Texas Rule 201(b) follows this standard and uses substantially the same fact categories that were used under earlier case law.

56.   FED. R. EVID. 201(b); TEX. R. EVID. 201(b); *see, e.g.*, **Derichsweiler v. State**, 301 S.W.3d 803, 812 (Tex. App.—Fort Worth 2009) (trial court's finding of fact that "it is within the realm of general knowledge of a police officer that parking lots are locations where break ins and thefts occur" was not supported by the record and was not the type of fact subject to judicial notice), *rev'd on other grounds*, 348 S.W.3d 906 (Tex. Crim. App. 2011). As indicated, this "not subject to reasonable dispute" standard is essentially the "substantially indisputable" standard favored by Morgan and McCormick. Refer to note 54 *supra*.

57.   **Tranter v. Duemling**, 129 S.W.3d 257, 262 (Tex. App.—El Paso 2004, no pet.); *see* **Freedom Commc'ns, Inc. v. Coronado**, 372 S.W.3d 621, 623 (Tex. 2012) (per curiam).

58.   21 CHARLES A. WRIGHT & KENNETH W. GRAHAM, FEDERAL PRACTICE AND PROCEDURE §5105, at 489 (1977).

59.   *See, e.g.*, **United States v. Mitchell**, 365 F.3d 215, 252 (3d Cir. 2004) (trial court erroneously took judicial notice of a scientific conclusion, not a discrete adjudicative fact); **Longtin v. Country One Stop, Inc.**, 129 S.W.3d 632, 635-36 (Tex. App.—Dallas 2003, pet. denied) (when party asked trial court to take judicial notice of temporary-injunction proceeding, but did not identify any particular adjudicative fact for trial court to consider, trial court did not err in declining to take judicial notice of evidence and testimony offered at that hearing). As the court in **Mitchell** noted, "[m]atters like 'February 7, 1977 was a Monday' (a fact) are suitable for judicial notice, while propositions like 'daily exercise reduces the likelihood of heart disease' (a scientific conclusion) are not." 365 F.3d at 252 n.30.

60.   Refer to note 168 *infra* and accompanying text.

61.   *See, e.g.*, **Roden v. Conn. Co.**, 155 A. 721, 723 (Conn. 1931) (judicially noticed facts must be "generally accepted by mankind as true"); **In re Buszta's Estate**, 186 N.Y.S.2d 192, 193 (Sur. Ct. 1959) (judicial notice is proper only for facts that are "universally known and recognized").

62.   *See* FED. R. EVID. 201(b)(1); **Stessman v. Am. Black Hawk Broad. Co.**, 416 N.W.2d 685, 686 (Iowa 1987); 2 MCCORMICK ON EVIDENCE, *supra* note 1, §329, at 434-35; *see, e.g.*, **Henry v. Butts**, 591 So. 2d 849, 851-52 (Ala. 1991) (upholding trial court's decision not to take judicial notice of the fact that there are 5,280 feet in a mile; courts may, but are not required to, take judicial notice of matters of common knowledge); **Akers v. Baldwin**, 736 S.W.2d 294, 305-06 (Ky. 1987) (court took judicial notice of the fact that, in many instances, the owner of a mineral estate can and does cause severe damage to the surface estate while mining); **State v. Armendariz**, 449 N.W.2d 555, 558 (Neb. 1989) (court may take judicial notice that substances such as cocaine may be easily and quickly disposed of by flushing them down a drain), *overruled on other grounds*, **State v. Johnson**, 589 N.W.2d 108 (Neb. 1999).

201(b)(1) uses the same language.[63] Judicial notice of notorious facts tracks the particular community's current standards and sources of knowledge—what is indisputable can change with time and location.

Texas courts have long recognized that notorious facts can be subject to judicial notice.[64] The decisions have differed, however, in the language used to define such facts. One test asked whether the facts to be noticed were "of common, everyday knowledge in the jurisdiction, which everyone of average intelligence and knowledge can be presumed to know, and are not disputable ...."[65] Other cases merely asked whether the fact was "well-known by all reasonably intelligent people in the community ...."[66] The language in the second group of cases is consistent with the language of Rule 201(b)(1). Indeed, some post-Rules decisions rely explicitly on early case law in stating that geographic facts of common knowledge within the district are suitable for judicial notice under Rule 201.[67]

Several Texas decisions restrict the category of notorious facts. For example, courts have held that a trial judge cannot take judicial notice based on his personal knowledge of an ordinary fact because personal knowledge is not equivalent to common knowledge by persons in the community.[68] Courts have also held that judicial notice may not be taken of facts that are commonly known by only a specially informed class of persons.[69]

---

63. TEX. R. EVID. 201(b)(1).

64. *See, e.g.*, **Jenkins v. State**, 912 S.W.2d 793, 819 (Tex. Crim. App. 1995) (op. on reh'g) (trial court could have taken judicial notice of general availability of drugs in prison); **Sudderth v. Grosshans**, 581 S.W.2d 215, 217 (Tex. Civ. App.—Austin 1979, no writ) (taking judicial notice that San Angelo is in Tom Green County).

65. **City of Garland v. Louton**, 683 S.W.2d 725, 726 (Tex. App.—Dallas 1984), *rev'd on other grounds*, 691 S.W.2d 603 (Tex. 1985); *see* **Harper v. Killion**, 162 Tex. 481, 483, 348 S.W.2d 521, 522 (1961) (some facts may be judicially noticed because of their "public notoriety and indisputable existence").

66. **Harper v. Killion**, 345 S.W.2d 309, 311 (Tex. Civ. App.—Texarkana 1961), *aff'd*, 162 Tex. 481, 348 S.W.2d 521 (1961); *see* **Eagle Trucking Co. v. Tex. Bitulithic Co.**, 612 S.W.2d 503, 506 (Tex. 1981) ("Well known and easily ascertainable facts may be judicially noticed."); **Barber v. Intercoast Jobbers & Brokers**, 417 S.W.2d 154, 158 (Tex. 1967) (courts often judicially notice well-known geographical facts); *see, e.g.,* **Fender v. St. Louis Sw. Ry. Co.**, 513 S.W.2d 131, 135 (Tex. Civ. App.—Dallas 1974, writ ref'd n.r.e.) (foreign court proceedings do not meet "common knowledge" test); **Alexander v. Firemen's Ins.**, 317 S.W.2d 752, 755 (Tex. Civ. App.—Waco 1958, no writ) (court may take judicial notice of scientific facts and principles that "are generally recognized and ought to be known by men of ordinary understanding and intelligence"; court refused to take judicial notice that a sonic boom is an "explosion" without sufficient scientific evidence to support the proposition).

67. *See, e.g.,* **Apostolic Church v. Am. Honda Motor Co.**, 833 S.W.2d 553, 555-56 (Tex. App.—Tyler 1992, writ denied) (party who requested judicial notice did not need to offer any additional information to support trial court's finding that certain cities and highways were located within the same county as the court; "[h]ighway nomenclature and designations within the trial court's jurisdiction are matters of common knowledge and proper subjects for judicial notice"); **Bella v. State**, 792 S.W.2d 542, 544-45 (Tex. App.—El Paso 1990, no pet.) (evidence of a building located at 6210 Montana, two blocks from the intersection of Wieland and Airport in El Paso County, Texas, was a sufficient basis for a jury to conclude from common knowledge that the site was within El Paso city limits).

68. **Eagle Trucking**, 612 S.W.2d at 506; **Guyton v. Monteau**, 332 S.W.3d 687, 692-93 (Tex. App.—Houston [14th Dist.] 2011, no pet.); *see* **Ex parte Rains**, 555 S.W.2d 478, 481 (Tex. Crim. App. 1977) (judge's personal knowledge of matters not in the record is not proper for judicial notice); 1 ROY R. RAY, TEXAS PRACTICE: TEXAS LAW OF EVIDENCE CIVIL AND CRIMINAL §152, at 195 (3d ed. 1980) (judicial notice and the judge's personal knowledge are not "coextensive"); Olin G. Wellborn III, *Judicial Notice Under Article II of the Texas Rules of Evidence*, 19 ST. MARY'S L.J. 1, 14 (1987) ("[A] matter does not qualify as 'generally known' merely because the individual judge knows it."); *see,*

2. Rule 201(b)(2): Verifiable facts. Texas Rule 201(b)(2) and Federal Rule 201(b)(2) follow a well-established modern doctrine by allowing courts to take judicial notice of facts that "can be accurately and readily determined from sources whose accuracy cannot reasonably be questioned."[70] Texas case law also used this standard before the adoption of the Rules.[71] In *Eagle Trucking Co. v. Texas Bitulithic Co.*, the court noted that the proper test for judicial notice is "verifiable certainty" based on a "source for the ascertainment of [the] fact from which a judge could refresh his memory or inform his conscience in any manner in which that judge deems trustworthy."[72] Thus, adoption of the federal language into Texas Rule 201(b)(2) did not change Texas law on the appropriate standard for taking judicial notice.

The category of verifiably certain facts, however, may be more liberal under Texas Rule 201(b)(2) than it was under the common law. Earlier Texas decisions indicated that courts could not take judicial notice of substantially indisputable facts merely because those facts could be ascertained by reference to dictionaries, encyclopedias, or other

e.g., *Wilson v. State*, 677 S.W.2d 518, 524 (Tex. Crim. App. 1984) (trial judge could not take judicial notice of "Nunc Pro Tunc Order" purportedly signed by another judge; personal knowledge, based on hearsay, of what another judge might have done is not a proper basis for judicial notice); *1.70 Acres v. State*, 935 S.W.2d 480, 489 (Tex. App.—Beaumont 1996, no writ) (trial judge could not take judicial notice of a ten-minute time span to drive an alleged distance of 9.2 miles because personal knowledge is not judicial knowledge); *Havins v. First Nat'l Bank*, 919 S.W.2d 177, 184 (Tex. App.—Amarillo 1996, no writ) (trial judge could not take judicial notice that in Cottle County, Texas, cattle are normally sold through livestock-auction commission merchants); *Stowe v. State*, 745 S.W.2d 568, 570 (Tex. App.—Houston [1st Dist.] 1988, no pet.) (judge could not take judicial notice of juror statements he overheard after trial).

69.   Wellborn, *supra* note 68, at 14; *see, e.g.*, *Haden Co. v. Mixers, Inc.*, 667 S.W.2d 316, 317 (Tex. App.—Dallas 1984, no writ) (abbreviation that was customary in the construction trade was not a proper subject for judicial notice because it was not generally known); *Johnson v. Cooper*, 379 S.W.2d 396, 399 (Tex. Civ. App.—Fort Worth 1964, no writ) (party had to provide competent evidence of the term "square" even though the specific meaning of the term is well known to persons in the roofing trade); *State v. Ark. Fuel Oil Co.*, 268 S.W.2d 311, 320 (Tex. Civ. App.—Austin 1954) (court declined to take judicial notice that increase in gas prices was due solely to economic forces because this conclusion was based on information that persons of average knowledge and intelligence did not have), *rev'd on other grounds*, 154 Tex. 573, 280 S.W.2d 723 (1955). However, specialized facts known only by persons who are interested in that specialty may be judicially noticeable under the "verifiably certain" category of facts. Refer to notes 70-114 *infra* and accompanying text.

In one interesting post-Rules decision, the El Paso Court of Appeals took judicial notice of the notorious facts "of recent courthouse shootings in Tarrant and Dallas Counties, and of the more recent bombing of the federal courthouse in Oklahoma City." *Gibson v. State*, 921 S.W.2d 747, 755 (Tex. App.—El Paso 1996, pet. denied). While the Oklahoma City bombing might have qualified as a "notorious" fact throughout the United States in the latter half of 1996, it is considerably more questionable whether every reasonably well-informed person within the jurisdiction of the El Paso Court of Appeals would have been aware of the specific courthouse shootings in Tarrant and Dallas Counties to which the court referred.

70.   FED. R. EVID. 201(b)(2); TEX. R. EVID. 201(b)(2); *see* Edmund M. Morgan, *Foreword* to MODEL CODE OF EVID. 66 (1942) (explaining that Rule 801 of the Model Code of Evidence, which allows judicial notice of verifiably certain facts, simply restates settled common-law doctrine); 2 MCCORMICK ON EVIDENCE, *supra* note 1, §330, at 438-43 (discussing judicial notice of facts capable of certain verification); 9 WIGMORE, *supra* note 1, §2571, at 731 (citing statutes that expressly permit judicial notice through verifiable sources and stating that such facts fall within the scope of judicial notice); *see also* Onstott, *supra* note 55, at 474 (noting the confusion in case law and treatises about who performs the "reasonable question[ing]" function—the judge, scientific and technical experts, or both).

71.   *See Harper v. Killion*, 162 Tex. 481, 483-84, 348 S.W.2d 521, 522 (1961) (court may take judicial notice of a fact that is readily verifiable); *Fender*, 513 S.W.2d at 135 ("The theory of judicial notice is that the fact to be noticed is so notorious or its existence so easily ascertainable that proof will not be required.").

72.   612 S.W.2d at 506.

publications.[73] Post-Rules decisions, however, liberalize such holdings. For example, in **Bender v. State**, the court held that under Rule 201 an appellate court could, "by resort to obtainable, accurate reference materials,"[74] take judicial notice of the fact that "the 2100 block of West Loop South, is located in Houston, Texas and that an 'MBank' building is located at that address."[75] Although the court did not specify what reference materials might be used, items such as maps or current telephone directories would presumably be acceptable if that material demonstrated the indisputability of the fact.[76] Under Rule 201, information found in dictionaries is considered easily accessible.[77] Texas and federal courts have also been increasingly willing to take judicial notice of facts from government websites and some commercial websites as verifiably certain.[78]

Texas courts may take judicial notice of a wide variety of verifiably certain facts,[79] such as a county's population,[80] the court's own records or practices,[81] the contents of

73. *See, e.g.*, **Johnson**, 379 S.W.2d at 399 (trial court could not judicially notice trade meaning of "square," even though definition might have been found in dictionary).

74. 739 S.W.2d 409, 413 (Tex. App.—Houston [14th Dist.] 1987), *pet. ref'd*, 761 S.W.2d 378 (Tex. Crim. App. 1988).

75. *Id.* This result appears to be consistent with Federal Rule 201. *See, e.g.*, **United States v. Perez**, 776 F.2d 797, 801-02 (9th Cir. 1985) (court took judicial notice of minimum distance between Rota and Guam, which includes travel through international water or airspace), *overruled on other grounds*, **United States v. Cabaccang**, 332 F.3d 622 (9th Cir. 2003); **United States v. Hughes**, 542 F.2d 246, 248 n.1 (5th Cir. 1976) (district court could have taken judicial notice that certain streets and intersections were located on a federal enclave).

76. *See, e.g.*, **Tranter v. Duemling**, 129 S.W.3d 257, 262-63 (Tex. App.—El Paso 2004, no pet.) (page from telephone directory did not "show that [defendant's] address was capable of accurate and ready determination while [plaintiff] was attempting to locate her" for service of process; page from directory showed, "at most, what her listed address was at some undefined point in time" and thus was insufficient to support request for judicial notice).

77. *See, e.g.*, **Drake v. Holstead**, 757 S.W.2d 909, 911 (Tex. App.—Beaumont 1988, no writ) (court accepted number of feet in a mile as specified in dictionary). It may, however, be inappropriate to take judicial notice of just one of the dictionary definitions of a word that has various meanings. *See* **Alaniz v. Hoyt**, 105 S.W.3d 330, 351 n.6 (Tex. App.—Corpus Christi 2003, no pet.) (in defamation action in which usage of a word with multiple definitions is in controversy, word's definition is subject to reasonable dispute and judicial notice is improper).

78. Refer to notes 105-111 *infra* and accompanying text.

79. *See, e.g.*, **Univ. of Hous. v. Barth**, 403 S.W.3d 851, 856 (Tex. 2013) (per curiam) (court reversed Whistleblower Act case and dismissed for lack of subject-matter jurisdiction after taking judicial notice of Board of Regents' policies, which "support the conclusion that the chancellor provides the authoritative act that makes the internal policies in the [university's System Administrative Memorandum] effective"; because memorandum was approved by chancellor and not enacted by Board of Regents, it was not a "law" under the Whistleblower Act); **Concord Oil Co. v. Pennzoil Expl. & Prod. Co.**, 966 S.W.2d 451, 459 (Tex. 1998) (court had previously taken judicial notice of prevailing royalty rates in private oil and gas leases during time period when deed was executed); **In re Baker**, 404 S.W.3d 575, 578 (Tex. App.—Houston [1st Dist.] 2010, orig. proceeding) (court took notice of candidate in Democratic primary election); **Wagner & Brown v. E.W. Moran Drilling Co.**, 702 S.W.2d 760, 773 (Tex. App.—Fort Worth 1986, no writ) (court could take judicial notice of the discount rate on 90-day commercial paper in effect at federal reserve bank as stated in Federal Reserve Bulletin). Facts that are "typically" true are not verifiably certain and thus are not subject to judicial notice. *E.g.*, **Grimes v. State**, 135 S.W.3d 803, 820-21 (Tex. App.—Houston [1st Dist.] 2004, no pet.) (newspaper article stating that a police-department recommendation that officer be terminated "typically" leads to dismissal from the department was not evidence of a well-known or "easily ascertainable" fact).

80. *See, e.g.*, **Graff v. Whittle**, 947 S.W.2d 629, 635 (Tex. App.—Texarkana 1997, writ denied) (appellate court took judicial notice that county's population was less than 50,000).

81. *See, e.g.*, **Holloway v. State**, 666 S.W.2d 104, 108-09 (Tex. Crim. App. 1984) (instrument containing terms and conditions of probation was part of court records and thus a proper subject for judicial notice); **Harris v. Borne**,

RULE 201

handbooks, safety codes, or treatises,[82] local geographical facts and landmarks,[83] information about schools and governmental entities,[84] and dates and holidays.[85]

Courts take judicial notice of the scientific principles underlying various evidentiary tests (e.g., radar, blood and breath tests for intoxication, fingerprinting, and ballistics),[86] which saves time because courts do not have to take lengthy testimony on these basic scientific principles.[87] "Trial courts are not required to re-invent the scientific wheel in every trial. However, some trial court must actually examine and assess the reliability of the particular scientific wheel before other courts may ride along behind."[88]

933 S.W.2d 535, 537 (Tex. App.—Houston [1st Dist.] 1995, order) (per curiam) (appellate court could take judicial notice of its clerks' practice in exchanging wrongly delivered papers between the 1st and 14th Courts of Appeals).

82. *See, e.g.*, ***Heritage on the San Gabriel Homeowners Ass'n v. Tex. Comm'n on Envtl. Quality***, 393 S.W.3d 417, 433 n.9 (Tex. App.—Austin 2012, pet. denied) (court of appeals took judicial notice of regulatory guidelines for municipal drainage plan); ***Jones v. City of Stephenville***, 896 S.W.2d 574, 576 (Tex. App.—Eastland 1995, no writ) (court could take judicial notice of contents of city employee handbook); ***Hernandez v. Hous. Lighting & Power Co.***, 795 S.W.2d 775, 776-77 (Tex. App.—Houston [14th Dist.] 1990, no writ) (trial court could take judicial notice of the National Electric Safety Code).

83. *See **In re J.M.H.***, 414 S.W.3d 860, 863 (Tex. App.—Houston [1st Dist.] 2013, no pet.) (courts have taken judicial notice of locations of cities and counties, as well as boundaries and distances); *see, e.g.*, ***Eagle Trucking Co. v. Tex. Bitulithic Co.***, 612 S.W.2d 503, 506 (Tex. 1981) (court could not take judicial notice of the fact that accident "along FM Road 2001" occurred outside of a business or residence district as defined by statute; "[t]here is no source for the ascertainment of this fact from which a judge could refresh his memory or inform his conscience in any manner in which that judge deems trustworthy"); ***Issac v. State***, 982 S.W.2d 96, 99-100 (Tex. App.—Houston [1st Dist.] 1998) (when portion of Houston map was introduced into evidence, court could take judicial notice that the place where defendant was stopped was in Harris County), *aff'd*, 989 S.W.2d 754 (Tex. Crim. App. 1999); ***Williams v. State***, 924 S.W.2d 189, 191-92 (Tex. App.—Eastland 1996, pet. ref'd) (appellate court could take judicial notice that offense occurring at Ron's Place in Sweetwater, Texas, was in Nolan County).

84. *See, e.g.*, ***Lovelady v. State***, 65 S.W.2d 810, 813-14 (Tex. App.—Beaumont 2002, no pet.) (trial court could have taken judicial notice of fact that Willis High School is "real property" owned, rented, or leased by or to that school or school board); ***Trujillo v. State***, 809 S.W.2d 593, 595 (Tex. App.—San Antonio 1991, no pet.) (trial court could take judicial notice that Edgewood High School is accredited by state education agency).

85. *See, e.g.*, ***Higginbotham v. Gen. Life & Acc. Ins.***, 796 S.W.2d 695, 696 (Tex. 1990) ("The trial court could properly take judicial notice that 12:01 p.m. on March 18, 1986 was an early afternoon on a Tuesday that was not a statutory holiday."); ***Sanders v. Constr. Equity, Inc.***, 42 S.W.2d 364, 367 (Tex. App.—Beaumont 2001, pet. denied) (court took judicial notice of state holiday when courthouse was closed); ***Donaldson v. State***, No. 02-15-00206-CR (Tex. App.—Fort Worth 2016, pet. ref'd) (memo op.; 9-29-16) (footnote 5; court took judicial notice of date of Easter in 2011).

86. *See* 1 PAUL C. GIANNELLI & EDWARD J. IMWINKELRIED, JR., SCIENTIFIC EVIDENCE §1.02, at 4-5 (4th ed. 2007); 2 MCCORMICK ON EVIDENCE, *supra* note 1, §330, at 439; Imwinkelried, *supra* note 55, at 348-39; *see, e.g.*, ***United States v. Mitchell***, 365 F.3d 215, 251-54 (3d Cir. 2004) (in prosecution involving use of fingerprint evidence, district court took judicial notice that "human friction ridges are unique and permanent throughout the area of the friction ridge skin, including small friction ridge areas, and that ... human friction skin arrangements are unique and permanent"; harmless error for court to take judicial notice of scientific conclusion—not a discrete adjudicative fact—that was hotly disputed during ***Daubert*** hearing); ***Holmes v. State***, 135 S.W.3d 178, 194-95 (Tex. App.—Waco 2004, no pet.) (court took judicial notice of scientific validity and reliability of blood-spatter analysis because it is not a novel scientific technique that needs to be subjected to extensive proof).

87. *See* Onstott, *supra* note 55, at 486 ("To efficiently use science and technical knowledge in the courtroom, judicial notice must be an available tool, or many proceedings will become bogged down by lengthy proofs of scientific principles.").

88. ***Hernandez v. State***, 116 S.W.3d 26, 29 (Tex. Crim. App. 2003); *see also* Onstott, *supra* note 55, at 486-87 (if courts cannot properly evaluate scientific principles, a net loss of public trust may result, even if the application of judicial notice to science results in more efficient trials and more correctly decided cases).

On the other hand, a judge may not take judicial notice of adjudicative facts that are open to reasonable dispute,[89] even if the judge is convinced of a particular conclusion's correctness.[90] Judicial notice depends on whether the general community or authoritative sources accept the fact as true, not on whether the judge personally believes it is true.

Under Texas Rule 201(b)(2), a court may take judicial notice of its own records concerning the same subject matter and substantially the same parties.[91] That is, a court may always judicially notice the existence of its own records, when those records were created, and the fact that they are contained within the court's official file.[92] Furthermore, if judicial notice of a court's own records is proper, it makes no difference whether notice is taken by the same judge or his successor.[93]

89.   *See, e.g.,* ***In re J.L.***, 163 S.W.3d 79, 83-84 (Tex. 2005) (court of appeals erred in taking judicial notice of expert testimony given in a related criminal proceeding; cause of child's rib fractures was disputed and should not have been judicially noticed); ***In re J.M.H.***, 414 S.W.3d 860, 863 (Tex. App.—Houston [1st Dist.] 2013, no pet.) (State asked court of appeals to take judicial notice of fact that person worked in law library at Texas Department of Criminal Justice facility and that all employees of law library had been verbally designated as agents for service; court refused because State provided no source confirming this information); ***Vargas v. Tex. Dep't of Crim. Justice***, No. 03-12-00119-CV (Tex. App.—Austin 2012, pet. denied) (memo óp.; 11-30-12) (footnote 4; plaintiff asked court of appeals to take judicial notice of disputed issues, including "fact" that trial court's findings proved plaintiff's case, and court noted that "[n]one of the 'facts' that [plaintiff] requests us to take judicial notice of are adjudicative facts under rule 201").

90.   *See, e.g.,* ***Hardy v. Johns-Manville Sales Corp.***, 681 F.2d 334, 347-48 (5th Cir. 1982) (court should not have taken judicial notice that asbestos causes cancer with regard to an asbestos-related product-liability action because that proposition was inextricably linked to disputed issues); *see also* ***Prestige Homes, Inc. v. Legouffe***, 658 P.2d 850, 853-54 (Colo. 1983) (court of appeals erred in taking judicial notice of a disputed medical issue based on medical treatises that contradicted expert's trial testimony). Refer to note 68 *supra* and accompanying text.

91.   ***Fletcher v. State***, 214 S.W.3d 5, 7 (Tex. Crim. App. 2007); ***Turner v. State***, 733 S.W.2d 218, 223 (Tex. Crim. App. 1987); ***Resendez v. State***, 256 S.W.3d 315, 323 (Tex. App.—Houston [14th Dist.] 2007), *rev'd on other grounds*, 306 S.W.3d 308 (Tex. Crim. App. 2009); ***Douglas v. Am. Title Co.***, 196 S.W.3d 876, 878 n.1 (Tex. App.—Houston [1st Dist.] 2006, no pet.); *see* ***Gardner v. Martin***, 162 Tex. 156, 158, 345 S.W.2d 274, 276 (1961); ***Hudson v. Aceves***, 516 S.W.3d 529, 536 n.5 (Tex. App.—Corpus Christi 2016, n.p.h.); *see, e.g.,* ***In re Britt***, ___ S.W.3d ___ (Tex. App.—Texarkana 2016, orig. proceeding) (No. 06-16-00074-CV; 11-29-16) (at default-judgment hearing, trial court took judicial notice of its file including return of service on defendant); ***Staten v. State***, 328 S.W.3d 901, 903 & n.1 (Tex. App.—Beaumont 2010, no pet.) (in community-supervision-revocation case, State's motion to revoke alleged that defendant committed aggravated assault after being placed on community supervision; appellate court took judicial notice of its own record in case affirming defendant's aggravated-assault conviction); ***Tello v. Bank One, N.A.***, 218 S.W.3d 109, 113 n.4 (Tex. App.—Houston [14th Dist.] 2007, no pet.) (appellate court took judicial notice of pertinent pleadings included in record for appeal from original summary judgment); ***In re Shell E&P, Inc.***, 179 S.W.3d 125, 130 (Tex. App.—San Antonio 2005, orig. proceeding) (trial judge could take judicial notice of his own order from related case); *see also* ***United States v. Montemayor***, 666 F.2d 235, 237 (5th Cir. 1982) (when determining appropriate amount of bail for a criminal defendant, district court could take judicial notice of allegations and information revealed during civil proceedings before the court).

92.   *See* ***In re C.S.***, 208 S.W.3d 77, 81 (Tex. App.—Fort Worth 2006, pet. denied) (court can take judicial notice of file to show that documents are part of court's files, that they were filed on a certain date, and that they were before the court at time of trial or hearing); ***Fuller v. State***, 30 S.W.3d 441, 445 (Tex. App.—Texarkana 2000, pet. ref'd) (same); *see, e.g.,* ***Musgrave v. Brookhaven Lake Prop. Owners Ass'n***, 990 S.W.2d 386, 402 (Tex. App.—Texarkana 1999, pet. denied) (trial court could take judicial notice of its case file when awarding attorney fees).

93.   *E.g.,* ***Holloway v. State***, 666 S.W.2d 104, 108-09 (Tex. Crim. App. 1984) (visiting judge could take judicial notice of an instrument containing the terms and conditions of probation during a hearing on a motion to revoke probation because probationary conditions were easily verifiable from reliable sources); *see* ***McCowan v. State***, 739 S.W.2d 652, 656 (Tex. App.—Beaumont 1987, pet. ref'd) ("If the matter of which notice was taken was within the proper scope of judicial notice, it would make no difference that a different judge presided at each proceeding.").

RULE 201

Texas courts have generally held that a trial judge may not take judicial notice of the accuracy or truth of allegations in the court's records; judicial notice is limited to the existence and content of those records.[94] This issue has arisen, for example, in the context of property inventories in divorce cases that were filed with the court clerk but never formally admitted into evidence.[95] A document such as a property inventory prepared by a party may be open to factual dispute; thus, the court should not take judicial notice of the truth of its contents.[96]

A court may take judicial notice of the records of another court in another case if the party requesting such notice provides adequate proof of the indisputability of those records.[97] However, a court may not take judicial notice of a witness's testimony based on the trial judge's own memory of the testimony.[98] Nor may a judge take judicial notice of the actions of the court's staff.[99]

---

94. ***Kenny v. Portfolio Recovery Assocs., LLC***, 464 S.W.3d 29, 34 (Tex. App.—Houston [1st Dist.] 2015, no pet.); ***In re K.F.***, 402 S.W.3d 497, 505 (Tex. App.—Houston [14th Dist.] 2013, pet. denied); ***In re C.S.***, 208 S.W.3d at 81; *see **Tex. Dep't of Pub. Safety v. Claudio***, 133 S.W.3d 630, 633 (Tex. App.—Corpus Christi 2002, no pet.) (trial court's judicial notice of contents of pleadings in its file does not constitute proof of allegations in those pleadings); *see also **In re Doe***, 501 S.W.3d 313, 335-36 (Tex. App.—Houston [14th Dist.] 2016, n.p.h.) (Frost, C.J., concurring) (court of appeals' presumption that trial court took judicial notice of its own files does not extend to adjudicative facts; taking judicial notice cannot "be used as a means to add to the trial evidence considered by the trial court in a bench trial"). Refer to note 92 *supra* and accompanying text. Federal courts have generally held that a court may not take judicial notice of the truth of factual findings made in a different case. *See **Wyatt v. Terhune***, 315 F.3d 1108, 1114 & n.5 (9th Cir. 2003), *overruled on other grounds*, ***Albino v. Baca***, 747 F.3d 1162 (9th Cir. 2014).

95. *See, e.g.*, ***Vannerson v. Vannerson***, 857 S.W.2d 659, 670-71 (Tex. App.—Houston [1st Dist.] 1993, writ denied) (when trial court's conclusions of law referred to inventory not admitted into evidence, inventory could be considered as evidence because trial judge could have taken judicial notice of it). An alternative explanation of the holding in ***Vannerson*** is that when both parties treat an exhibit as if it had been formally admitted into evidence, neither party can complain on appeal that the fact-finder relied on that exhibit. *See **Tex. Dep't of Pub. Safety v. Latimer***, 939 S.W.2d 240, 243 (Tex. App.—Austin 1997, no writ) ("A number of cases have held that evidence that is treated by the trial court and the parties as if it had been admitted is, for all practical purposes, admitted.").

96. *Cf. **In re Shifflet***, 462 S.W.3d 528, 539 (Tex. App.—Houston [1st Dist.] 2015, orig. proceeding) (factual findings in temporary order about mother's possession of children was not a proper subject of judicial notice); ***In re Striegler***, 915 S.W.2d 629, 647 (Tex. App.—Amarillo 1996, writ denied) (Reynolds, C.J., dissenting) (reasonableness of attorney fees is a question of fact that may be disputed and thus is not subject to judicial notice).

97. ***WorldPeace v. Comm'n for Lawyer Discipline***, 183 S.W.3d 451, 459 (Tex. App.—Houston [14th Dist.] 2005, pet. denied); ***Krishnan v. Ramirez***, 42 S.W.3d 205, 222-23 (Tex. App.—Corpus Christi 2001, pet. denied); *e.g.*, ***Freedom Commc'ns, Inc. v. Coronado***, 372 S.W.3d 621, 623-24 (Tex. 2012) (per curiam) (supreme court took judicial notice of trial judge's plea agreement to federal racketeering charges from district court for Southern District of Texas; judicial notice was necessary to determine whether judge's order was void, which would preclude appellate jurisdiction by court of appeals and supreme court); *see **San Pedro Impulsora de Inmuebles Especiales, S.A. de C.V. v. Villarreal***, 330 S.W.3d 27, 43 n.12 (Tex. App.—Corpus Christi 2010, no pet.) ("A court may take judicial notice of the records in another court when it is provided with copies of those records."); *see, e.g.*, ***MCI Sales & Serv., Inc. v. Hinton***, 329 S.W.3d 475, 497 n.21 (Tex. 2010) (Texas Supreme Court took judicial notice of amicus brief filed before U.S. Supreme Court); ***Stephens v. LNV Corp.***, 488 S.W.3d 366, 372-73 (Tex. App.—El Paso 2015, no pet.) (court of appeals took judicial notice of file-stamped copy of federal complaint attached as appendix to appellant's brief; appellee did not object to document); ***Bhalli v. Methodist Hosp.***, 896 S.W.2d 207, 210 (Tex. App.—Houston [1st Dist.] 1995, writ denied) (appellant who did not provide either trial or appellate court with proof of records of former proceeding before a different court could not obtain judicial notice of "fact" that opposing party's claims were collaterally estopped); ***Elwell v. State***, 872 S.W.2d 797, 799 (Tex. App.—Dallas 1994, no pet.) (appellant who attached a copy of an earlier judgment to his pleading but did not offer that judgment into evidence or ask trial judge to take judicial notice of it could not obtain judicial notice of that judgment from appeals court or rely on it for his plea of double jeopardy); *cf. **Colonial Leasing Co. v. Logistics Control Grp. Int'l***, 762 F.2d 454, 459 (5th Cir. 1985) (federal

While judicial proceedings may be subject to judicial notice in proper circumstances, statements or events that occur in the presence of a judge but outside a judicial proceeding are not subject to judicial notice.[100] Before the adoption of the Rules, Texas law provided that a trial judge who presided over a criminal trial and later presided over a hearing to revoke probation for the same offense could take judicial notice at the second hearing of the evidence admitted at the previous trial.[101] An argument could be made that this doctrine did not survive the adoption of Rule 201 because it relied on matters within a particular judge's personal knowledge that were neither "notorious" nor capable of accurate and ready determination by referring to indisputably accurate sources.[102] Even if the doctrine permitting a judge to take judicial notice of the evi-

---

district judge in Texas could take judicial notice of an Oregon state-court judgment because those records constituted "a source whose accuracy cannot reasonably be questioned").

Some cases have held that one court cannot take notice of records from a different court. *Wilson v. State*, 677 S.W.2d 518, 523 (Tex. Crim. App. 1984); *Resendez v. State*, 256 S.W.3d 315, 323 (Tex. App.—Houston [14th Dist.] 2007), *rev'd on other grounds*, 306 S.W.3d 308 (Tex. Crim. App. 2009); *Penix v. State*, 748 S.W.2d 629, 630-31 (Tex. App.—Fort Worth 1988, no pet.). This principle follows earlier Texas law. *See Culver v. Pickens*, 142 Tex. 87, 93, 176 S.W.2d 167, 171 (1943) (court cannot judicially notice records of another court). However, precluding judicial notice of the existence of specific recorded proceedings in other courts has been criticized as illogical. *See* 2 MC-CORMICK ON EVIDENCE, *supra* note 1, §330, at 442 (judicial notice of another court's matters of record is usually denied "even though it would appear manifest that these public documents are logically subject to judicial notice as readily verifiable facts"). Indeed, it might seem anomalous that dictionary entries carry more weight as easily verifiable facts in legal proceedings than do official judicial entries in sister courts. Refer to note 77 *supra* and accompanying text.

98. *Davis v. State*, 293 S.W.3d 794, 797 (Tex. App.—Waco 2009, no pet.); *see In re E.W.*, 494 S.W.3d 287, 296-97 (Tex. App.—Texarkana 2015, no pet.) (improper for trial judge to take judicial notice of testimony from prior hearing or trial; for prior testimony to be considered in later proceeding, transcript must be authenticated and admitted into evidence); *Guyton v. Monteau*, 332 S.W.3d 687, 693 (Tex. App.—Houston [14th Dist.] 2011, no pet.) (same); *see, e.g.*, *Garza v. State*, 996 S.W.2d 276, 279-80 (Tex. App.—Dallas 1999, pet. ref'd) (trial court could not take judicial notice of testimony given in codefendant's separate trial to determine admissibility of coconspirator's statements in present case).

99. *See, e.g.*, *O'Quinn v. Hall*, 77 S.W.3d 438, 447 (Tex. App.—Corpus Christi 2002, no pet.) (trial court could not take judicial notice of the "information" provided by the court's staff about whether a party's attorney had been given notice of a particular order).

100. *See Ex parte Rains*, 555 S.W.2d 478, 481 (Tex. Crim. App. 1977) (judge's personal knowledge of matters not contained in official judicial records is not a proper subject for judicial notice); *Stowe v. State*, 745 S.W.2d 568, 570 (Tex. App.—Houston [1st Dist.] 1988, no pet.) (statements made outside a judicial proceeding "may be subject to varying interpretations" and are not the type of adjudicative facts covered by Rule 201). In *Hogan v. State*, the trial court refused to take judicial notice of the defendant's asserted fact that he was arrested without a warrant, which he based on written discovery responses by an "unknown person" outside the judicial proceeding. 954 S.W.2d 875, 876-77 (Tex. App.—Houston [14th Dist.] 1997, pet. ref'd). The judge took judicial notice of the State's "agreement" to produce copies of any arrest warrant but did not extrapolate from the existence of that agreement that the defendant was arrested without a warrant; the defendant simply presented a copy of the written discovery motion, which had an unidentified handwritten notation of "none known" under the discovery request for a copy of the arrest warrant. *Id.* The court of appeals agreed with the trial court that these discovery responses were not subject to judicial notice because they were not the kind of adjudicative facts covered by Rule 201. *Hogan*, 954 S.W.2d at 877.

101. *Barrientez v. State*, 500 S.W.2d 474, 475 (Tex. Crim. App. 1973). *But see id.* at 477 (Onion, P.J., dissenting) (common law traditionally indicated that courts could take judicial notice of orders but not testimony from a previous trial).

102. *See McCowan v. State*, 739 S.W.2d 652, 655 (Tex. App.—Beaumont 1987, pet. ref'd) (expressing "grave doubts" that the *Barrientez* rule survived enactment of Rule 201(b)).

dence from a previous trial applied to a later probation-revocation hearing, it would not apply when different judges presided over the two hearings.[103] However, one post-Rules case has held that a trial judge could take judicial notice of the defendant's prior conviction when the judge presided over both cases.[104]

Courts are sometimes reluctant to take judicial notice of facts found on websites, as many courts treat information derived from the Internet as inherently unreliable because of potential hearsay problems and difficulties in authenticating the evidence.[105] This skepticism appears to be based on the courts' perception that information from the Internet is especially vulnerable to unauthorized manipulation and adulteration,[106] making it difficult to declare such information as coming from a source "whose accuracy cannot reasonably be questioned."[107] But an increasing number of courts have begun to examine the type of website and its particular content before deciding whether to take judicial notice of a fact found on the site. For example, both federal and Texas courts are more amenable to taking judicial notice of facts found on official websites of government agencies, courts, and similar entities,[108] but they will still look carefully at the characteristics of the particular website and information before doing so.[109] Courts today also seem less resistant to taking judicial notice of facts from private and

---

103. ***Harris v. State***, 738 S.W.2d 207, 219 n.10 (Tex. Crim. App. 1986).

104. ***Miller v. State***, 21 S.W.3d 327, 330 (Tex. App.—Tyler 1999, pet. ref'd).

105. *See **United States v. Jackson***, 208 F.3d 633, 637 (7th Cir. 2000) (any information from the Internet is "adequate for almost nothing" (quoting ***St. Clair v. Johnny's Oyster & Shrimp, Inc.***, 76 F. Supp. 2d 773, 775 (S.D. Tex. 1999))); ***Monotype Imaging, Inc. v. Bitstream, Inc.***, 376 F. Supp. 2d 877, 885 n.6 (N.D. Ill. 2005) ("[P]rintouts from websites should be closely scrutinized for reliability."); ***St. Clair v. Johnny's Oyster & Shrimp, Inc.***, 76 F. Supp. 2d 773, 775 (S.D. Tex. 1999) (material taken from the Internet is "voodoo information"). Refer to *Article IX: Authentication & Identification, infra* p. 973.

106. *See **D Mag. Partners, L.P. v. Rosenthal***, ___ S.W.3d ___ (Tex. 2017) (No. 15-0790; 3-17-17) ("[a]ny court reliance on Wikipedia may understandably raise concerns" because content is impermanent and can be edited by anyone at any time, but "a bright-line rule is untenable"; CA erred in using Wikipedia as its primary source for a critical issue in case); *see, e.g., **Flores v. State***, No. 14-06-00813-CR (Tex. App.—Houston [14th Dist.] 2008, no pet.) (memo op.; 10-23-08) (footnote 3; court declined to take notice of Wikipedia page because Wikipedia pages can be edited anonymously by anyone). *But see **In re Marriage of Rivers***, No. 10-16-00031-CV (Tex. App.—Waco 2016, no pet.) (memo op.; 11-2-16) (footnote 4; court cited Wikipedia page in taking judicial notice that Houston is county seat of Harris County).

107. *See* TEX. R. EVID. 201(b)(2).

108. *See **In re Doe***, 501 S.W.3d 313, 321 & n.11 (Tex. App.—Houston [14th Dist.] 2016, n.p.h.); *see, e.g., **Gent v. CUNA Mut. Ins. Soc'y***, 611 F.3d 79, 84 n.5 (1st Cir. 2010) (court took judicial notice of facts about bacterium found on website of Centers for Disease Control and Prevention as "not subject to reasonable dispute"); ***Oliphant Fin. L.L.C. v. Hill***, 310 S.W.3d 76, 76 n.2 (Tex. App.—El Paso 2010, pet. denied) (court of appeals took judicial notice of trial court's procedures as set out in trial court's website); ***Payan v. State***, 199 S.W.3d 380, 383 n.4 (Tex. App.—Houston [1st Dist.] 2006, pet. ref'd) (court took judicial notice of city's incorporated status based on State Library and Archives Commission's website, which listed city as incorporated); ***Hayden v. State***, 155 S.W.3d 640, 647 (Tex. App.—Eastland 2005, pet. ref'd) (court took judicial notice of time of sunset on certain date as listed on website of U.S. Naval Observatory); ***Ex parte Molina***, No. 04-17-00012-CR (Tex. App.—San Antonio 2017, pet. ref'd) (memo op.; 4-19-17) (court took judicial notice of who was Oklahoma's lieutenant governor as listed on official Oklahoma website).

109. *See, e.g., **Ex parte Alakayi***, 102 S.W.3d 426, 436-37 (Tex. App.—Houston [14th Dist.] 2003, pet. ref'd) (court refused to take judicial notice of victim's age based on printout from official Texas sex-offender website because that fact is supplied by offender and not verified by anyone else).

commercial websites when individual examination shows that they are reliable.[110] Of course, once a court determines that information from a website is not subject to reasonable dispute, taking judicial notice may become mandatory under Texas Rule 201(c)(2) or Federal Rule 201(c)(2) if the rule's other requirements are met.[111]

Texas courts have held that judges must exercise their authority to take judicial notice and that every reasonable doubt should be resolved against taking judicial notice.[112] This holding is consistent with the cautious approach urged by the Advisory Committee in its note to Federal Rule 201(b).[113] When a court improperly takes judicial notice, that evidence may be legally insufficient to support a jury verdict.[114]

C. Rule 201(c): Taking Judicial Notice

Rule 201(c) reflects existing practice, is simple and workable, and avoids troublesome distinctions in many situations.[115] Most importantly, both Federal Rule 201 and Texas Rule 201 address all adjudicative facts that are subject to judicial notice, whether mandatory or discretionary. The drafters decided not to follow a system like California's, which separates adjudicative facts that must be judicially noticed from those that may be judicially noticed.[116]

Texas Rule 201(c)(1), which authorizes a court to take judicial notice regardless of whether a party requested it,[117] did not change preexisting Texas law.[118] Appellate

---

110. *See, e.g.,* ***O'Toole v. Northrup Grumman Corp.***, 499 F.3d 1218, 1224-25 (10th Cir. 2007) (trial court erred in refusing to take judicial notice of defendant-corporation's postings of its retirement-fund earnings on its own website). *But see* ***Victaulic Co. v. Tieman***, 499 F.3d 227, 236 (3d Cir. 2007) (district court improperly took judicial notice of company website; anyone can buy webpage, so court cannot assume without further authentication that company owns webpage just because company's trade name appears in URL).

111. *See* FED. R. EVID. 201(c)(2); TEX. R. EVID. 201(c)(2); *see, e.g.,* ***Denius v. Dunlap***, 330 F.3d 919, 926 (7th Cir. 2003) (district court abused its discretion in determining that it was unnecessary to take judicial notice of data from National Personnel Records Center because information from website would have corroborated plaintiff's testimony about his medical records; "fact that [website] maintains medical records of military personnel is appropriate for judicial notice because it is not subject to reasonable dispute"). Refer to notes 120-133 *infra* and accompanying text.

112. *See* ***Johnson v. Cooper***, 379 S.W.2d 396, 399 (Tex. Civ. App.—Fort Worth 1964, no writ); ***State v. Ark. Fuel Oil Co.***, 268 S.W.2d 311, 320 (Tex. Civ. App.—Austin 1954), *rev'd on other grounds*, 154 Tex. 573, 280 S.W.2d 723 (1955).

113. *See* FED. R. EVID. 201 advisory committee's note, subdiv. (b) ("With respect to judicial notice of adjudicative facts, the tradition has been one of caution in requiring that the matter be beyond reasonable controversy. This tradition of circumspection appears to be soundly based, and no reason to depart from it is apparent.").

114. *See* ***Kenny v. Portfolio Recovery Assocs., LLC***, 464 S.W.3d 29, 34 (Tex. App.—Houston [1st Dist.] 2015, no pet.) (evidence that is the subject of improper judicial notice constitutes no evidence); ***Guyton v. Monteau***, 332 S.W.3d 687, 693 (Tex. App.—Houston [14th Dist.] 2011, no pet.) (same).

115. *See* FED. R. EVID. 201 advisory committee's note, subdivs. (c), (d). The original Federal Rules 201(c) and 201(d) were restyled as Rules 201(c)(1) and 201(c)(2) in 2011. The substance of the rules has not changed. FED. R. EVID. 201 advisory committee's note to 2011 amendments.

116. *See* CAL. EVID. CODE §§451, 452.

117. TEX. R. EVID. 201(c)(1); *see* ***Apostolic Church v. Am. Honda Motor Co.***, 833 S.W.2d 553, 556 (Tex. App.—Tyler 1992, writ denied) ("In matters involving geographical knowledge, it is not necessary that a formal request for judicial notice be made by the party. It is, therefore, not required that the court formally announce that [it] was taking judicial notice of such fact.").

118. *See, e.g.,* ***Harper v. Killion***, 162 Tex. 481, 485, 348 S.W.2d 521, 523 (1961) (trial court could judicially notice that Jacksonville is located in Cherokee County even though party did not request it); ***Vahlsing, Inc. v. Mo. Pac.***

courts, in upholding a trial court's judgment, sometimes "presume" that the trial court took judicial notice of various facts on its own initiative even though it was not asked to do so and did not announce that it had done so.[119]

Rule 201(c)(2) changed earlier Texas practice[120] by making judicial notice mandatory if (1) judicial notice is properly requested by a party, (2) the court is supplied with the appropriate information,[121] and (3) the fact is of a kind that may properly be noticed.[122] The practical significance of the change is that a trial judge's refusal to take judicial notice when asked to do so and supplied with the necessary information may lead to an appellate reversal under Rule 201; the refusal would have been discretionary under the common law.[123]

R.R., 563 S.W.2d 669, 674 (Tex. Civ. App.—Corpus Christi 1978, no writ) (trial court was presumed to have judicially noticed the necessity of third party to plaintiff's cause of action under a promissory note even though party did not request it); *Tex. Sec. Corp. v. Peters*, 463 S.W.2d 263, 264 (Tex. Civ. App.—Fort Worth 1971, no writ) (trial court was presumed to have judicially noticed the date filed and contents of pleadings even though party did not request it); *Buckaloo Trucking Co. v. Johnson*, 409 S.W.2d 911, 913 (Tex. Civ. App.—Corpus Christi 1966, no writ) (trial court was presumed to have judicially noticed the fact that an accident occurred within Nueces County, Texas, even though party did not request it).

119. *See Rogers v. RREF II CB Acquisitions, LLC*, ___ S.W.3d ___ (Tex. App.—Corpus Christi 2016, no pet.) (No. 13-15-00321-CV; 11-17-16) (trial court does not need to announce it is taking judicial notice); *Sierad v. Barnett*, 164 S.W.3d 471, 481 (Tex. App.—Dallas 2005, no pet.) (same); *see, e.g.*, *Marble Slab Creamery Inc. v. Wesic, Inc.*, 823 S.W.2d 436, 439 (Tex. App.—Houston [14th Dist.] 1992, no writ) (court of appeals could presume that trial court took judicial notice of record on its own initiative and without announcing that it had done so). *But see In re C.L.*, 304 S.W.3d 512, 515-16 (Tex. App.—Waco 2009, no pet.) (when court takes judicial notice on its own initiative, "it must at some point notify the parties that it has done so and give them an opportunity to challenge that decision"; appellate court held that trial court did not take judicial notice because party did not request it and trial court did not announce that it was doing so). For a discussion of the interplay between Rule 201(c)(1) and Rule 201(e), which gives parties the opportunity to challenge the court's decision to take judicial notice, refer to notes 158-164 *infra* and accompanying text.

120. *See* 1 RAY, *supra* note 68, §153, at 197-98 (line between facts that *may* be noticed and those that *must* be noticed is "difficult to draw"; distinction between mandatory and discretionary judicial notice is "not sufficiently recognized … to make it practical to treat the two groups separately").

121. TEX. R. EVID. 201(c)(2); *Freedom Commc'ns, Inc. v. Coronado*, 372 S.W.3d 621, 623 (Tex. 2012) (per curiam); *Office of Pub. Util. Counsel v. Pub. Util. Comm'n of Tex.*, 878 S.W.2d 598, 600 (Tex. 1994). Neither a trial court nor an appellate court is required to take judicial notice of an adjudicative fact if the requesting party does not provide sufficient information, usually an "indisputable source" document. *See, e.g.*, *Singleton v. State*, 91 S.W.3d 342, 350 (Tex. App.—Texarkana 2002, no pet.) (trial court did not err in refusing to take judicial notice of NHTS Administrative Guidelines to demonstrate that officer was not certified to perform standardized field sobriety tests because requesting party did not provide court with a copy of those guidelines).

122. *Hernandez v. Hous. Lighting & Power Co.*, 795 S.W.2d 775, 776-77 (Tex. App.—Houston [14th Dist.] 1990, no writ); *see Office of Pub. Util. Counsel*, 878 S.W.2d at 600.

123. For example, in *Drake v. Holstead*, the Beaumont Court of Appeals held that trial judges may be required to take judicial notice of mathematical calculations if they are supplied with the necessary mathematical computations. 757 S.W.2d 909, 911 (Tex. App.—Beaumont 1988, no writ). In *Drake*, a negligence case arising from a car accident, the trial court erred in refusing to take judicial notice of rates of speed after the plaintiff supplied the court with a typewritten sheet of mathematical computations and the defendant did not object to the accuracy of the computations. *Id.* at 911 & n.2. The court of appeals held that the trial judge's error was harmless because no issues of statutory negligence were submitted to the jury, and the trial court's failure to take judicial notice of the speed calculations thus did not cause an improper judgment in the case. *Id.* at 911. The court of appeals noted that mandatory judicial notice applies to scientific facts and principles that "ought to be known by men of ordinary understanding and intelligence." *Id.* at 910. The court cited 21 WRIGHT & GRAHAM, *supra* note 58, §5105, at 232 (Supp. 1987), for the proposition that "[a] fact is generally known even though it has to be processed with commonly

Rule 201(c)(2) does not specify when a party must request that the court take judicial notice. Presumably, a request must be timely; otherwise, the party who would have benefited from judicial notice cannot complain on appeal that the trial court abused its discretion.[124] Under pre-Rules decisions, Texas appellate courts were reluctant to take judicial notice of adjudicative facts for the first time on appeal.[125] Although that same concern is expressed in some post-Rules cases,[126] appellate courts frequently take judicial notice of adjudicative facts presented for the first time on appeal.[127] The judi-

---

possessed mental skills." *Drake*, 757 S.W.2d at 910. The plaintiff's computations, however, might not have been considered simple; in fact, they were not entirely accurate. *See id.* at 911 n.2.

On the other hand, a trial judge cannot be faulted for not taking judicial notice of mathematical computations if he is not given the necessary information to support judicial notice of those computations. *See, e.g., Davenport v. State*, 807 S.W.2d 635, 638 (Tex. App.—Houston [14th Dist.] 1991, no pet.) (although trial court could have taken judicial notice of time-distance mathematical calculations that defense attorney wanted to use during closing argument, it was not error to sustain opponent's objection to their use when attorney did not give the court any means of verifying the accuracy of his calculations).

124. Wright and Graham comment that:

[t]he failure to make a timely request does not mean that judicial notice cannot be taken; it simply means that notice is not mandatory. The trial court can, as a matter of discretion, take judicial notice on the basis of an untimely request, so long as the opponent is given an opportunity to be heard on the question.

21 WRIGHT & GRAHAM, *supra* note 58, §5107, at 510. A trial court could abuse its discretion by taking untimely notice. *Colonial Leasing Co. v. Logistics Control Group Int'l* provides a clear example of why timely notice should be required. 762 F.2d 454 (5th Cir. 1985). Colonial Leasing, the alleged creditor, sued its debtor and a third party, alleging a fraudulent transfer of assets. *Id.* at 457. The trial court excluded evidence of an Oregon state-court judgment rendered for Colonial against the debtor. *Id.* The transferee, Logistics, then declined to present evidence and correctly argued that Colonial had not established a creditor status and thus had not presented a prima facie case. *Id.* However, after the trial, the plaintiff requested that the judge take judicial notice of the Oregon judgment. *Id.* The trial judge did so and rendered judgment for Colonial. *Id.* The court of appeals reversed and remanded, reasoning that while the trial court could have taken judicial notice of the judgment during trial, the fact that it did not do so reasonably led Logistics to believe that it did not need to present evidence on that critical fact during the trial. *Id.* at 460-61.

125. *See Sparkman v. Maxwell*, 519 S.W.2d 852, 855 (Tex. 1975) (appellate courts are "reluctant" to take judicial notice when the trial court was not asked to do so, but appellate courts may do so under "circumstances where necessary to avoid an unjust judgment"); *see, e.g., Cont'l Oil Co. v. Simpson*, 604 S.W.2d 530, 535 (Tex. Civ. App.—Amarillo 1980, writ ref'd n.r.e.) (because the entire content of a document is a proper and necessary source for trial court to notice in determining the document's legal effect, appellate court took notice of a document's entire content on appeal even though the record was silent about the attention given to the document by trial court).

126. *See Watkins v. State*, 245 S.W.3d 444, 456 (Tex. Crim. App. 2008) ("[T]he question of whether an appellate court should take judicial notice of an adjudicative fact when the underlying data or materials in support of that notice are presented for the first time in that court should be a matter of the appellate court's discretion, never mandatory."). In *Duderstadt Surveyors Supply, Inc. v. Alamo Express, Inc.*, the plaintiff-shipper sued Alamo Express, the carrier of its COD products, for accepting a fraudulent cashier's check in payment for delivery. 686 S.W.2d 351, 352-53 (Tex. App.—San Antonio 1985, writ ref'd n.r.e.). The trial court found that Alamo did not breach its duty to the shipper and rendered judgment for Alamo. *Id.* at 353. While the case was pending in the appeals court, Duderstadt filed a motion to take judicial notice of a Railroad Commission tariff. *Id.* The court of appeals declined to do so because the tariff was never presented to the trial judge. *Id.* at 354. The court of appeals refused to reverse the trial court's judgment based on materials, whether evidentiary or subject to judicial notice, that were never presented to the trial court. *Id.*

127. *Trapnell v. John Hogan Interests, Inc.*, 809 S.W.2d 606, 608 (Tex. App.—Corpus Christi 1991, writ denied); *see Watkins*, 245 S.W.3d at 456 (judicial notice on appeal should be taken when necessary to avoid an unjust judgment); *Emerson v. State*, 880 S.W.2d 759, 765 (Tex. Crim. App. 1994) (judicial notice of both adjudicative and legislative facts can be taken on appeal); *In re Estate of Hemsley*, 460 S.W.3d 629, 638-39 (Tex. App.—El Paso 2014, pet. denied) (appellate courts generally take judicial notice of facts outside record only to determine jurisdiction

cial debate about whether judicial notice may or should be taken at the appellate level when the trial court was not expressly asked to take judicial notice may be resolved by dividing appellate judicial notice into two categories: (1) notice that upholds the lower court and (2) notice that undermines the lower court. If judicial notice of a fact supports the fact-finder's ruling or verdict, judicial notice may properly be taken for the first time on appeal.[128] If judicial notice would reverse the judgment or ruling of the fact-finder, such notice should not normally be taken for the first time on appeal if judicial notice was not timely requested in the lower court.[129]

Rule 201(c)(2) also does not define the "necessary information" that the requesting party must furnish. Presumably, no extrinsic information is required for judicial notice of generally known or "notorious" facts because all the parties and the judge are well aware of the facts.[130] For verifiable facts, the requesting party should produce both the source containing the fact to be noticed (e.g., the published map showing that 900 Westheimer Road is in the city of Houston), and any additional information the party needs to demonstrate to the judge or the opposing party that the source is one "whose accuracy cannot reasonably be questioned." For example, a statement on the frontispiece of a book of maps that the book was compiled by the City of Houston within the previous year based on information supplied by its corps of engineers would dem-

and resolve ancillary matters; courts are reluctant to take judicial notice of matters that go to merits of dispute); ***Dutton v. Dutton***, 18 S.W.3d 849, 856 (Tex. App.—Eastland 2000, pet. denied) (court of appeals can take judicial notice even if trial court was not asked to do so and did not announce it had done so); *see, e.g.,* ***MCI Sales & Serv., Inc. v. Hinton***, 329 S.W.3d 475, 484 n.7 (Tex. 2010) (supreme court took judicial notice of study on desirability of seat belts in intercity buses, but study was not relevant to preemption issue in case); ***W. Hills Harbor Owners Ass'n v. Baker***, ___ S.W.3d ___ (Tex. App.—El Paso 2017, no pet.) (No. 08-15-00060-CV; 3-22-17) (court of appeals took judicial notice of homeowners association's amended bylaws after appellant included certified copies from county clerk's office in appendix; appellee did not object to request for judicial notice); ***Stephens v. LNV Corp.***, 488 S.W.3d 366, 372-73 (Tex. App.—El Paso 2015, no pet.) (court of appeals took judicial notice of file-stamped copy of federal complaint attached as appendix to appellant's brief; appellee did not object to document); *see also* ***Nubine v. State***, 721 S.W.2d 430, 434 (Tex. App.—Houston [1st Dist.] 1986, pet. ref'd) (appellate court is not confined solely to the trial record for "evidence" of the laws of a sister state).

128. *See, e.g.,* ***Trujillo v. State***, 809 S.W.2d 593, 595-96 (Tex. App.—San Antonio 1991, no pet.) (teacher could testify that her school district was accredited by the Texas Education Agency because court could have rejected any inadmissible testimony and instead taken judicial notice of accreditation at any stage of the proceeding, a fact easily ascertainable from a state agency); ***Ex parte Preston***, 801 S.W.2d 604, 605 (Tex. App.—Houston [1st Dist.] 1990) (appellate court took judicial notice of the record of a previous prosecution while affirming trial court's decision), *rev'd on other grounds*, 833 S.W.2d 515 (Tex. Crim. App. 1992); ***City of Mesquite v. Moore***, 800 S.W.2d 617, 619 (Tex. App.—Dallas 1990, no writ) (appellate court took judicial notice of census figures to support trial court's finding that the city of Mesquite had a population greater than 10,000 and was thus subject to a former statute requiring overtime pay for excess hours).

129. *See, e.g.,* ***Hadley v. State***, 735 S.W.2d 522, 530 (Tex. App.—Amarillo 1987, pet. ref'd) (appellate court refused to take judicial notice of Oklahoma law because notice was never requested of the trial court and proof of Oklahoma law was never offered). *But see* ***Martinez v. City of San Antonio***, 768 S.W.2d 911, 914-15 (Tex. App.—San Antonio 1989, no writ) (appellate court took judicial notice of local ordinance and maintenance agreement in reversing lower court to avoid "an injustice").

130. *See* 1 MUELLER & KIRKPATRICK, *supra* note 14, §2:6, at 365 (for judicial notice of generally known facts, "it usually suffices to bring the fact to the court's attention, and no supporting sources are needed"); *see, e.g.,* ***Harper v. Killion***, 162 Tex. 481, 485, 348 S.W.2d 521, 523 (1961) ("[A] district court sitting in Cherokee County can judicially notice the certain and indisputable fact of common knowledge that the entire city of Jacksonville is located in such county ....").

onstrate that the source is one "whose accuracy cannot reasonably be questioned."[131] If the source is routinely used and relied on by those individuals who work in a particular profession, the information the source contains generally is sufficiently accurate for judicial notice. Although one Texas court held that a trial judge erred in refusing to take judicial notice when a witness testified that she telephoned an indisputable source and was informed of the verifiable fact,[132] the party seeking judicial notice generally must supply the court with *written* material demonstrating the indisputability of the fact. It is not sufficient that a witness, whose credibility could be disputed, merely testifies that he consulted an indisputable source. A record based on a party's self-reported information is not a source "whose accuracy cannot reasonably be questioned."[133]

Like a court's rulings on preliminary questions of fact under Rule 104(a), the Rules of Evidence do not apply to the information or evidence the court uses in determining whether judicial notice is proper.[134] The judge may consider any reliable materials, regardless of whether they would be admissible as evidence.[135] The materials that support the court's action in taking judicial notice do not need to be formally offered into evidence or presented in admissible form.[136] On the other hand, if a party wants to complain on appeal about the propriety of taking or refusing to take judicial notice of an adjudicative fact, that party must ensure that the court reporter marks the documents as exhibits and must request a record that includes that exhibit.[137] Similarly, if the requesting party does not provide the necessary information, the court may properly refuse to take judicial notice.[138]

RULE 201

---

131. *See Gov't of the Canal Zone v. Burjan*, 596 F.2d 690, 694 (5th Cir. 1979) ("[O]fficial government maps have long been held proper subjects of judicial notice."); *see, e.g.*, *Williams v. Chew*, 19 S.W.2d 68, 69 (Tex. Civ. App.—Galveston 1929, no writ) (court could take judicial notice of surveys and grants of land on which Houston is located).

132. *Magee v. Ulery*, 993 S.W.2d 332, 338-39 (Tex. App.—Houston [14th Dist.] 1999, no pet.) (in medical-malpractice case, trial court should have taken judicial notice that nondefendant physician was 84 and a general practitioner when witness testified that she had called Texas Board of Medical Examiners and was given this information).

133. *See Ex parte Alakayi*, 102 S.W.3d 426, 436-37 (Tex. App.—Houston [14th Dist.] 2003, pet. ref'd). In *Alakayi*, the appellant asked the appellate court to take judicial notice of the victim's age at the time of the offense based on a printout of his online "Sex Offender Registration Report," downloaded from the Texas Department of Public Safety's website. *Id.* at 436. The court of appeals declined to do so because the registration record was based solely on the offender's self-reported information, which could reasonably be questioned. *Id.* at 437.

134. *See* 1 MUELLER & KIRKPATRICK, *supra* note 14, §2:5, at 364. Refer to *Article I: General Provisions, supra* p. 86.

135. *See* 1 MUELLER & KIRKPATRICK, *supra* note 14, §2:5, at 364.

136. *See, e.g.*, *In re A.L.J.*, 929 S.W.2d 467, 472 (Tex. App.—Tyler 1996, writ denied) (party did not need to formally introduce into evidence pleadings and decree from earlier divorce proceeding before court could take judicial notice of their existence and contents). This policy follows pre-Rules Texas law. *See Cont'l Oil Co. v. Simpson*, 604 S.W.2d 530, 535 (Tex. Civ. App.—Amarillo 1980, writ ref'd n.r.e.) ("[T]he source from which a fact is judicially noticed is not evidence to establish the fact and is not subject to the rules of evidence.").

137. *See Kaman v. State*, 923 S.W.2d 129, 131-32 (Tex. App.—Houston [1st Dist.] 1996, no pet.).

138. *E.g.*, *Robinson v. State*, 783 S.W.2d 648, 653 (Tex. App.—Dallas 1989) (appellate court refused to take judicial notice of Merck Index, even though defendant requested notice under mandatory provision of Rule 201(d), because he did not supply the necessary information), *aff'd*, 841 S.W.2d 392 (Tex. Crim. App. 1992).

Finally, a judge is never required to take judicial notice of a legislative fact[139] because Rule 201 covers only adjudicative facts.[140]

D. Rule 201(d): Timing

Under Rule 201(d), a court may take judicial notice "at any stage of the proceeding."[141] The Advisory Committee characterized the federal counterpart to this rule as in accordance with the accepted view.[142] Charles McCormick stated that it is an "axiom" that appellate courts may take judicial notice to the same extent as trial courts.[143] Texas courts are fully in accordance with this view,[144] holding, for example, that courts may take judicial notice in a summary-judgment proceeding[145] or in the appellate court.[146] Texas courts emphasize that an appellate court may take judicial no-

---

139. *See* TEX. R. EVID. 201(a). Refer to notes 8-35 *supra* and accompanying text for a discussion of the distinction between adjudicative and legislative facts.

140. *See Aguirre v. State*, 948 S.W.2d 377, 380 (Tex. App.—Houston [14th Dist.] 1997, pet. ref'd) (judicial notice is always discretionary for legislative facts). In *Aguirre*, the trial court declined to take judicial notice of a state law, the DWI implied-consent statute in Texas Transportation Code §724.019. 948 S.W.2d at 380. Texas courts are required to take judicial notice of the existence and contents of Texas state law. The *Aguirre* court apparently confused legislative facts with legislative enactments. *See id.* The trial judge should have taken judicial notice of the existence and contents of the implied-consent statute. Even so, the trial judge certainly had the discretion to refuse to admit a copy of it into evidence because that law was irrelevant to the issues at hand. Refer to notes 22-35 *supra* and accompanying text.

141. TEX. R. EVID. 201(d); *see Bob Smith Bail Bonds, Sur. v. State*, 963 S.W.2d 555, 556 (Tex. App.—Fort Worth 1998, no pet.) (trial court may take judicial notice of its own file at any time and "is presumed to have done so with or without a request from a party").

142. FED. R. EVID. 201 advisory committee's note, subdiv. (f). The original Federal Rule 201(f) was restyled as Rule 201(d) in 2011. The substance of the rule has not changed. FED. R. EVID. 201 advisory committee's note to 2011 amendments.

143. 2 MCCORMICK ON EVIDENCE, *supra* note 1, §333, at 454. As expressed by another commentator:

> The taking of judicial notice of a fact outside the record is part of the inherent power and function of every court, whether a trial or appellate tribunal. Whether an appellate court will take judicial notice of a fact on appeal which was not noticed by the trial court, or called to that court's attention, rests largely in the discretion of the appellate court.

George R. Currie, *Appellate Courts Use of Facts Outside the Record by Resort to Judicial Notice and Independent Investigation*, 1960 WIS. L. REV. 39, 39; *see also* 1 DAVID W. LOUISELL & CHRISTOPHER B. MUELLER, FEDERAL EVIDENCE §59, at 482-83 (1977) (court must "take judicial notice of an adjudicative fact if the necessary information has been supplied, but only if a request is timely made … at an appropriate time during trial"). For examples of such appellate-court cases, see *Oberwetter v. Hilliard*, 639 F.3d 545, 552 & n.4 (D.C. Cir. 2011) (taking judicial notice of Jefferson Memorial's salient features in deciding that memorial was not a public forum), *United States v. Akinrosotu*, 637 F.3d 165, 168 (2d Cir. 2011) (taking judicial notice of Bureau of Prisons' official website for limited purpose of obtaining projected date of defendant's release from prison to determine ripeness of defendant's question on appeal), and *Duluth News-Tribune v. Mesabi Publ'g Co.*, 84 F.3d 1093, 1096 n.2 (8th Cir. 1996) (taking judicial notice of plaintiff's registration of the trademark "Duluth News-Tribune"). While an appellate court may take judicial notice, it is only required to do so if a requesting party made a timely request to the trial court or if the trial court committed "plain error." 1 LOUISELL & MUELLER, *supra*, §59, at 482-83.

144. *See Langdale v. Villamil*, 813 S.W.2d 187, 189-90 (Tex. App.—Houston [14th Dist.] 1991, no writ).

145. *See Fender v. St. Louis Sw. Ry. Co.*, 513 S.W.2d 131, 134-35 (Tex. Civ. App.—Dallas 1974, writ ref'd n.r.e.) (trial court can take judicial notice of the law of foreign jurisdictions during a summary-judgment proceeding).

146. *See, e.g.*, *Routier v. State*, 273 S.W.3d 241, 244 n.2 (Tex. Crim. App. 2008) (taking judicial notice of appellate record in ruling on capital-murder defendant's motion for postconviction DNA testing). Refer to notes 127-129 *supra* and accompanying text.

tice of a proper fact even if the trial court did not receive a request from a party or formally announce that it had taken judicial notice.[147]

The question arises whether an appellate court should take judicial notice of a fact that was not noticed by the trial court in a criminal case. Both Texas[148] and federal[149] appellate courts have done so. The main concern is the constitutionality of directing the jury to find any adjudicative fact against a criminal defendant. The issue is addressed by the permissive language in Texas and Federal Rule 201(f).[150]

E. Rule 201(e): Opportunity to Be Heard

The U.S. Supreme Court has suggested that due process may be violated when a court takes judicial notice of a fact and the party against whom the fact operates is not given an opportunity to challenge it.[151] The Advisory Committee on the Federal Rules echoed this sentiment when it noted that such an opportunity was required by "[b]asic considerations of procedural fairness."[152] Accordingly, both Federal Rule 201(e) and Texas Rule 201(e) give parties the right to be heard on both the appropriateness of taking judicial notice and the nature of the facts to be noticed.[153]

---

147. ***Harper v. Killion***, 162 Tex. 481, 485, 348 S.W.2d 521, 523 (1961); ***McCulloch v. State***, 740 S.W.2d 74, 75 (Tex. App.—Fort Worth 1987, pet. ref'd); *see, e.g.*, ***Gonzales v. State***, 723 S.W.2d 746, 751-52 (Tex. Crim. App. 1987) (defendant's indictment was sufficient, even though there was no predicate laid in the trial court, to establish that San Antonio had a home-rule charter on file, a fact that may be judicially noticed); ***City of Garland v. Louton***, 683 S.W.2d 725, 726 (Tex. App.—Dallas 1984) (appellate court could take judicial notice of the fact that the city of Garland held a municipal election even though evidence of election was not presented to the trial court), *rev'd on other grounds*, 691 S.W.2d 603 (Tex. 1985). Refer to notes 124-129 *supra* and accompanying text.

148. *See, e.g.*, ***McCulloch***, 740 S.W.2d at 75-76 (taking judicial notice of the explosive nature of gasoline); ***Lewis v. State***, 674 S.W.2d 423, 426 (Tex. App.—Dallas 1984, pet. ref'd) (taking judicial notice that one location was within several blocks of another); ***Siroky v. State***, 653 S.W.2d 476, 480 (Tex. App.—Tyler 1983, pet. ref'd) (taking judicial notice that over four ounces of marijuana is a "usable amount"); ***Ex parte Molina***, No. 04-17-00012-CR (Tex. App.—San Antonio 2017, pet. ref'd) (memo op.; 4-19-17) (taking judicial notice of who was lieutenant governor of Oklahoma, assuming trial court had not done so).

149. In ***United States v. Mauro***, 501 F.2d 45, 49 (2d Cir. 1974), and ***Ross v. United States***, 374 F.2d 97, 103 (8th Cir. 1967), the appellate courts took judicial notice of notorious facts that were neither noticed nor proved at the trial level. Neither court considered remand for the jury's consideration of such facts essential for a fair trial. ***Mauro***, 501 F.2d at 49; ***Ross***, 374 F.2d at 103. *But see* ***United States v. Judge***, 846 F.2d 274, 276-77 (5th Cir. 1988) (case remanded to trial court for limited purpose of allowing the government an opportunity to present to trial judge DEA materials supporting a conclusion that car inventory was conducted using "standard procedure"). In ***Judge***, the appellate court refused to take judicial notice of portions of a DEA manual submitted by the government because (1) the materials might arguably be subject to reasonable dispute in the present fact scenario, (2) the government submitted only select portions of the manual, and (3) the defendant did not have an adequate opportunity to challenge the applicability and administration of provisions. 846 F.2d at 276-77. The remand in ***Judge*** was a fair and reasonably expeditious method of dealing with questions of judicial notice of adjudicative facts raised on appeal from a trial judge's ruling. The remand procedure would not, however, be applicable to jury fact-finding. *See* Hobart Taylor, Jr., Comment, *Evidence—Judicial Notice by Appellate Courts of Facts and Foreign Law Not Brought to the Attention of the Trial Court*, 42 MICH. L. REV. 509, 512-13 (1943) (appellate courts are much more likely to take judicial notice of facts to uphold a trial-court verdict than to reverse that verdict).

150. *See* FED. R. EVID. 201(f); TEX. R. EVID. 201(f). Refer to notes 175-198 *infra* and accompanying text.

151. *See* ***Garner v. Louisiana***, 368 U.S. 157, 173 (1961); ***Ohio Bell Tel. Co. v. Pub. Utils. Comm'n***, 301 U.S. 292, 302-03 (1937).

152. FED. R. EVID. 201 advisory committee's note, subdiv. (e).

153. FED. R. EVID. 201(e); TEX. R. EVID. 201(e). Texas Rule 201(e) applies in both bench and jury trials. *See* ***In re C.L.***, 304 S.W.3d 512, 516 (Tex. App.—Waco 2009, no pet.).

To understand the proper context of Texas Rule 201(e), the rule must be considered with Rules 201(b) and 201(f). As indicated, Rule 201(b) provides that a court can take judicial notice only of facts that are not subject to reasonable dispute. Rule 201(f) mandates that the jury in civil cases be instructed "to accept the noticed fact as conclusive"[154] and "contemplates [that] there is to be no evidence before the jury in disproof [of the fact]."[155] The opportunity to be heard under Rule 201(e) is thus limited to challenges made directly to the judge. Other states, having adopted positions different from those found in Texas and Federal Rules 201(b) and 201(f), hold differently on the Rule 201(e) question. Those jurisdictions give the party against whom a noticed fact operates the right to present rebuttal evidence for jury consideration.[156] This position would, at least in theory, apply to Texas Rule 201(f) in criminal cases because the jury in a criminal case is never required to accept as conclusive those facts that are judicially noticed by the judge.[157] As a practical matter, however, a court should not take judicial notice of any fact that is subject to contrary proof.

Rule 201(e) also interacts with Rule 201(c)(1), which permits a court to take judicial notice on its own initiative.[158] In such cases, and because the court does not need to announce that it has taken judicial notice,[159] the parties might not receive any indication that a court has taken judicial notice until after the fact.[160] Some commentators point out that "judicial notice without notification may deprive the adversely affected party of the right to trial by jury as well, since it will miss its opportunity to request a hearing at which rebutting information may be introduced."[161] The final sentence of subdivision (e) addresses this situation by allowing a party who received no notice of

---

154. TEX. R. EVID. 201(f).

155. FED. R. EVID. 201 advisory committee's note, subdiv. (g). The original Federal Rule 201(g) was restyled as Rule 201(f) in 2011. The substance of the rule has not changed. FED. R. EVID. 201 advisory committee's note to 2011 amendments.

156. *See State v. Zayas*, 490 A.2d 68, 70-71 (Conn. 1985) (even if a judicially noticed fact is not open to argument, the "better practice is to give the parties an opportunity to be heard before judicial notice is taken"); *Stewart v. Davis*, 571 So. 2d 926, 928-29 (Miss. 1990) (opposing counsel could present rebuttal evidence to the jury even though reasonable minds would not differ on the matter); *see also* Arthur J. Keefe et al., *Sense and Nonsense About Judicial Notice*, 2 STAN. L. REV. 664, 668 (1950) (if the opponent of a judicially noticed fact is permitted to dispute the matter, "[s]hould not the proponent then also have the right to offer evidence disputing the opponent, and if the court permits this, what happens to the doctrine of judicial notice?"). If both parties are permitted to argue the matter before judicial notice is taken, neither should complain. *See Skinner v. HCC Credit Co. of Arlington*, 498 S.W.2d 708, 711 (Tex. Civ. App.—Fort Worth 1973, no writ).

157. *See* TEX. R. EVID. 201(f).

158. *See* TEX. R. EVID. 201(c)(1). Refer to notes 115-140 *supra* and accompanying text.

159. Refer to note 119 *supra* and accompanying text.

160. *See* TEX. R. EVID. 201(e). *But see* 1 JACK B. WEINSTEIN ET AL., WEINSTEIN'S EVIDENCE ¶201[05], at 201-51 to 201-52 (1995) (court has an obligation to notify parties before taking judicial notice when such notice would not otherwise be clear).

161. WEINSTEIN ET AL., *supra* note 160, ¶201[05], at 201-53 to 201-54. One commentator has noted:
   An elementary sense of fairness might indicate that a judge before making a final ruling that judicial notice will be taken should notify the parties of his intention to do so and afford them an opportunity to present information which might bear upon the propriety of noticing the fact, or upon the truth of the matter to be noticed.

the court's action to request a hearing even after the court takes judicial notice.[162] The rule does not provide any specific information on the form, timing, or procedures for the hearing, nor does it indicate how the trial court should notify the parties that it has taken judicial notice. However, the Advisory Committee's note to the federal rule calls attention to the provision in the Administrative Procedure Act for a hearing on a timely request.[163] If a party does not object to the trial court's procedure in taking judicial notice and does not seek an opportunity to be heard, it may waive its complaint on the propriety of such notice.[164]

Very few Texas cases address the procedural aspects of taking judicial notice of adjudicative facts, although several cases suggest that the parties will present information and data for the judge to use in his rulings on judicial notice.[165] As a practical matter, this presentation should take place before the pretrial conference.[166]

F. Rule 201(f): Instructing the Jury

1. Civil cases. The first sentence of Rule 201(f) states the rule for instructing the jury in a civil case on judicial notice.[167] This rule completes the process started by Rule 201(b), which states that judicially noticed facts must not be subject to reasonable dispute, and continued by Rule 201(e), which gives parties a right to be heard on the pro-

2 McCORMICK ON EVIDENCE, *supra* note 1, §333, at 452; *see also **Emerson v. State**,* 880 S.W.2d 759, 771-72 (Tex. Crim. App. 1994) (Clinton & Miller, JJ., dissenting) (court should not have taken judicial notice of certain legislative facts without permitting defendant an opportunity to debate the propriety of that action; doing so is "distortion of the adversarial system").

162. TEX. R. EVID. 201(e).

163. FED. R. EVID. 201 advisory committee's note, subdiv. (e) (citing 5 U.S.C. §556(e)).

164. *See, e.g., **MacMillan Bloedel Ltd. v. Flintkote Co.**,* 760 F.2d 580, 587 (5th Cir. 1985) (rejecting appellant's request for an opportunity to be heard on the taking of judicial notice because appellant did not properly challenge district court's action); *In re Martin*, 881 S.W.2d 531, 533 (Tex. App.—Texarkana 1994, writ denied) (when party did not object to trial judge's discussion with physician before trial about facts relevant to the case, did not request a hearing, and did not show he was harmed by judge's use of information gained from the discussion, party waived any error related to that discussion; appeals court noted that trial judge's action was more in the nature of a factual determination rather than an act of judicial notice under Rule 201).

165. *See **Harper v. Killion**,* 162 Tex. 481, 484, 348 S.W.2d 521, 522-23 (1961) (maps are proper sources to support facts to be judicially noticed); *see, e.g., **Eagle Trucking Co. v. Tex. Bitulithic Co.**,* 612 S.W.2d 503, 506 (Tex. 1981) (trial court could not take judicial notice of whether a road was inside or outside a business or residence district without any source to support the conclusion). An appellate court may refuse to take judicial notice of a fact, regardless of whether the trial court did, if the opponent was not given an opportunity to be heard on the propriety of taking judicial notice or the nature of the fact noticed. *See* TEX. R. EVID. 201(e); ***Nat'l Cty. Mut. Fire Ins. v. Hood**,* 693 S.W.2d 638, 639 (Tex. App.—Houston [14th Dist.] 1985, no writ). See ***O'Connor's Texas Rules * Civil Trials*** (2017), "Motion for Judicial Notice," ch. 5-M, p. 465.

166. See ***O'Connor's Texas Rules**,* "Pretrial Conference," ch. 5-A, p. 373. Roy Ray suggested that fairness to the parties ordinarily requires the judge to notify the parties of the intention to notice a given fact and to give them an opportunity to informally present data indicating that the matter is not a proper subject for judicial notice. 1 RAY, *supra* note 68, §152, at 195. Texas courts seem to give this suggestion considerable weight. *See, e.g., **Skinner v. HCC Credit Co. of Arlington**,* 498 S.W.2d 708, 711 (Tex. Civ. App.—Fort Worth 1973, no writ). The *Skinner* court noted that an aggrieved party who was aware before trial that in all probability a question subject to judicial notice might be presented but took no action cannot complain. *Id.* Conversely, the trial court has the right to take judicial notice of a matter if it is a proper subject for such notice even without advance notice that the litigant will challenge proof of the matter. *Id.*

167. TEX. R. EVID. 201(f).

priety of the court's taking of judicial notice. After the parties in a civil case have had an opportunity to contest the taking of judicial notice and the judge has determined that judicial notice is proper, the jury must be instructed to accept the noticed fact as true.[168] Thus, once the court takes judicial notice of a fact in a civil case, no evidence will be admitted to rebut it. This rule is simply the corollary to the requirement in Rule 201(b) that noticed facts must not be subject to reasonable dispute.[169]

The Advisory Committee's note to Federal Rule 201 suggests three reasons for adopting the conclusive-fact standard in civil cases: "the undesirable effects of the opposite rule in limiting the rebutting party, though not his opponent, to admissible evidence, in defeating the reasons for judicial notice, and in affecting the substantive law to an extent and in ways largely unforeseeable."[170]

The first reason refers to the practice of permitting the party against whom the judicially noticed fact operates to rebut that fact only with admissible evidence, while permitting the party who sought judicial notice to present any material the trial judge finds acceptable.[171] Rule 201(e) resolves this objection by permitting both parties to argue the propriety of taking judicial notice.

The second reason—that the other standard defeats the purpose of judicial notice—is not explained but probably refers to the argument that permitting parties

---

168. *Id.* The party requesting judicial notice should prepare a jury instruction for the judge.

169. *See* 1 WEINSTEIN & BERGER, *supra* note 10, §201.33[1], at 201-79. Whether the party against whom a judicially noticed fact operates is precluded from challenging the truth of that fact depends on whether judicial notice in the jurisdiction involved is limited to substantially indisputable facts or also includes facts that are merely unlikely to be controverted. If judicial notice is limited to indisputable matters, "it must follow that no evidence to the contrary is admissible." Morgan, *supra* note 15, at 279. If, however, judicial notice is more relaxed and is viewed as a time-saving device to eliminate the necessity of formal proof in instances in which dispute is unlikely, the noticed fact should be subject to rebuttal evidence that the opponent offers. *See* THAYER, *supra* note 1, at 308-09 (judicial notice should be no more than prima facie recognition of the matter, thus leaving it open to controversy). Refer to note 54 *supra*.

In one post-Rules decision, ***First National Bank of Amarillo v. Jarnigan***, the Amarillo Court of Appeals stated that a trial court may not instruct a jury that it has taken judicial notice of a series of particularized "findings of fact" if doing so would constitute "unnecessary and impermissible comments on the weight of the evidence." 794 S.W.2d 54, 62 (Tex. App.—Amarillo 1990, writ denied). In that case, the concept of judicial notice seems to have been misapplied because the 13 findings of fact submitted to the jury as conclusive were neither matters of common knowledge nor readily ascertainable. Instead, they were factual and legal conclusions based on specific evidence. For example, the court took judicial notice of the following "adjudicative facts": "The mechanic's and materialmen's lien contract, original mechanic's and materialmen's lien note and the renewal note and deed of trust constitute a single transaction [and] the First National Bank of Amarillo is not a holder in due course of the renewal note and deed of trust dated April 6, 1983." *Id.* at 59-60. The court of appeals' assumption that "the trial court was authorized to take judicial notice of these 13 facts" was improper; the appellate court was then forced to hold that the jury should not have been instructed that the trial court had taken judicial notice of these findings. *Id.* at 61-62. Under Rule 201(f), a judge must instruct the jury when he has properly taken judicial notice of an adjudicative fact. TEX. R. EVID. 201(f). The real question the court of appeals should have considered was whether a judge may submit factual and legal conclusions about which reasonable minds might differ to a jury under the rubric of judicial notice. Thus, while the result in *Jarnigan* was correct, both the premise and the reasoning were faulty.

170. FED. R. EVID. 201 advisory committee's note, subdiv. (g). The original Federal Rule 201(g) was restyled as Rule 201(f) in 2011. The substance of the rule has not changed. FED. R. EVID. 201 advisory committee's note to 2011 amendments.

171. *See* Keefe et al., *supra* note 156, at 668.

to rebut judicially noticed facts with formally introduced evidence offsets the time-saving purpose of the rule.[172]

The third reason for rejecting the alternate standard—that substantive law might be affected—is similarly unexplained. This justification possibly refers to the argument that while the fact-finder would determine all debatable adjudicative facts, disputable but uncontroverted facts are conclusive in civil cases once they are noticed.[173] Beyond these reasons, the Advisory Committee points to the "soundly based" tradition of caution requiring that judicially noticed matters be beyond reasonable controversy.[174]

2. Criminal cases. The second sentence of Rule 201(f) states the rule for instructing the jury in a criminal case on judicial notice, which is different from the rule in civil cases.[175] In the 1972 version of Federal Rule 201(f), judges were required to instruct juries in both civil and criminal proceedings to accept as conclusive any judicially noticed fact.[176] The Advisory Committee proceeded on the theory that the right to a jury trial did not extend to matters beyond reasonable dispute; therefore, the instruction that a noticed fact was conclusively established did not violate that right.[177] Before the rule became law, the House Committee on the Judiciary amended it to distinguish between civil and criminal proceedings, stating that the Committee viewed a mandatory jury instruction to accept judicially noticed facts in criminal cases as contrary to the spirit of the right to a jury trial under the Sixth Amendment.[178] The House Committee did not cite support for its view, and no conclusive authority existed.[179] Nevertheless, the rule precludes an instruction in criminal cases that a judicially noticed fact is conclusive.[180]

RULE 201

172. *See* William B. Nichols, Comment, *Judicial Notice and Presumptions Under the Proposed Federal Rules of Evidence*, 16 WAYNE L. REV. 135, 140 (1969).

173. *See* FED. R. EVID. 201(f); TEX. R. EVID. 201(f).

174. *See* FED. R. EVID. 201 advisory committee's note, subdiv. (b).

175. *See* TEX. R. EVID. 201(f).

176. *See* FED. R. EVID. 201(g) (1972 proposed final draft), 56 F.R.D. 183, 201 (1973).

177. *Id.* at 207; *see also* David L. Hefflinger, *Proposed Rule Broadens Scope of Judicial Notice*, 53 NEB. L. REV. 333, 337-38 (1974) (judicial notice is proper in a criminal case only if defendant has been given an opportunity to rebut the presumed fact and if jurors are instructed that the noticed fact is not binding on them).

178. H.R. REP. No. 93-650, at 6 (1974), *reprinted in* 1974 U.S.C.C.A.N. 7075, 7080.

179. *Compare* **United States v. Alvarado**, 519 F.2d 1133, 1135 (5th Cir. 1975) (judicial notice of facts that are plainly true does not abridge Sixth Amendment rights), *and* **Gold v. United States**, 378 F.2d 588, 592 (9th Cir. 1967) (defendant in criminal case has constitutional right to trial by jury, but jury does not have discretion "to decide that the earth is flat"), *with* **State v. Lawrence**, 234 P.2d 600, 603 (Utah 1951) (conclusive instruction invaded the province of the jury in a criminal case).

180. *See* FED. R. EVID. 201(f); H.R. REP. No. 93-650, *supra* note 178, at 6, *reprinted in* 1974 U.S.C.C.A.N. 7075, 7080; *see, e.g.*, **United States v. Mentz**, 840 F.2d 315, 322-23 (6th Cir. 1988) (defendant's conviction for bank robbery was reversed because trial judge gave jury a mandatory instruction that banks are insured by the FDIC). The *Mentz* court recognized that a "trial court commits constitutional error when it takes judicial notice of facts constituting an essential element of the crime charged, but fails to instruct the jury according to Rule 201(g) [now Rule 201(f)]." 840 F.2d at 322. For an example of a proper jury instruction under the federal rule, see **United States v. Deckard**, in which the court stated the following:

> When the Court declares it will take judicial notice of some fact or event, you may accept the Court's declaration as evidence, and regard as proved the fact or event which has been judicially noticed, but you are not required to do so since you are the sole judge of the facts.

816 F.2d 426, 428 (8th Cir. 1987).

Some federal courts have suggested that an appellate court may never take judicial notice of an adjudicative fact on appeal in a criminal case because doing so would deny the defendant the constitutional right to a jury determination of every element of the charged offense.[181] But judicial notice by appellate courts should be considered on a case-by-case basis. An appellate court should not take judicial notice to prove a factual element of the offense for which no proof was ever offered at trial;[182] judicial notice may be taken, however, of common, ordinary inferences that may be deduced from facts proved.[183] Allowing an appellate court to take judicial notice of the factual meaning or interpretation of evidence to sustain a jury's verdict supports the general notion of jury integrity in a criminal trial.[184]

Texas Rule 201(f) follows the federal rule's permissive provision.[185] Thus, Rule 201(f) treats judicial notice in a criminal case like a presumption; it eliminates the need for formal proof but does not prevent the other party from contesting the existence of the fact.[186] Thomas Black considers any complaints about the provision to be "more theoretical than real for it is unlikely that a conscientious jury will find contrary to facts 'not

181. In **United States v. Jones**, the Sixth Circuit refused to take judicial notice that South Central Bell Telephone Company was a carrier engaged in the transmission of interstate communications. 580 F.2d 219, 223-24 (6th Cir. 1978). The defendant had been convicted of illegally intercepting telephone conversations by tapping a telephone furnished by the South Central Bell Telephone Company. *Id.* at 221. However, no witness explicitly testified that South Central Bell was a "person engaged in providing or operating ... facilities for the transmission of interstate or foreign communications," as the penal statute is worded. *See* 18 U.S.C. §2510(1); *Jones*, 580 F.2d at 222-23. After the jury returned a guilty verdict, the defendant asked for and received a directed verdict from the judge because the government failed to offer proof on this statutory element. *Jones*, 580 F.2d at 221. The court of appeals affirmed the acquittal, reasoning that the congressional intent manifested in former Federal Rule 201(g), now Rule 201(f), which gives the jury in a criminal case authority to disregard a judicially noticed fact, requires that facts not noticed and made the subject of an instruction at trial level may not be noticed on appeal. *Jones*, 580 F.2d at 224. This decision has been characterized as extreme and incorrect because every member of the jury undoubtedly knew that Bell Telephone and all the regional telephone companies are common carriers. 1 GOODE ET AL., *supra* note 14, §201.9, at 80-81; 2 MICHAEL H. GRAHAM, HANDBOOK OF FEDERAL EVIDENCE §201:7, at 322-23 & n.15 (7th ed. 2012); 1 WEINSTEIN & BERGER, *supra* note 10, §201.32[3][c], at 201-78.2 to 201-79.

182. *See Gov't of the Canal Zone v. Burjan*, 596 F.2d 690, 694 (5th Cir. 1979) (Sixth Circuit read Federal Rule 201(g), now Rule 201(f), to preclude taking judicial notice of "an element of the crime" by an appellate court in criminal proceedings); William M. Carter, Jr., *"Trust Me, I'm a Judge": Why Binding Judicial Notice of Jurisdictional Facts Violates the Right to Jury Trial*, 68 Mo. L. REV. 649, 654-58 (2003) (if federal government's special jurisdiction over the physical location of the offense is an element of the offense, trial judge should not take judicial notice that this element is satisfied without extrinsic evidence admitted before jury of that jurisdictional fact).

183. For example, if a witness in a DWI trial testifies that a suspect was stopped while driving on Westheimer Road in Houston, an appellate court could take judicial notice that Westheimer Road is a "public place" for purposes of the DWI statute. This example is more akin to the "legal reasoning" process that is always susceptible to judicial notice but is not covered by rules of evidence. Refer to notes 13-16 *supra* and accompanying text. Conversely, if the witness merely testifies that a suspect was stopped while driving in Houston, an appellate court could not take judicial notice that the suspect was driving in a public place because not all roads are public places.

184. *See* Wellborn, *supra* note 68, at 25-26. Saltzburg and Redden have commented that if a criminal defendant does not raise an issue at trial, then the appellate court that considers the issue on its merits may resolve it by taking judicial notice. STEPHEN A. SALTZBURG & KENNETH R. REDDEN, FEDERAL RULES OF EVIDENCE MANUAL 61 (4th ed. 1986). They further comment that "[b]y failing to offer proof at trial, the defendant has placed himself in a position from which it is difficult to complain successfully about the binding nature of appellate notice." *Id.*

185. *See* TEX. R. EVID. 201(f); *see also* Thomas Black, *The Texas Rules of Evidence—A Proposed Codification*, 31 Sw. L.J. 969, 974 (1977) (provision is probably required by the Sixth Amendment).

186. **United States v. Bello**, 194 F.3d 18, 24 (1st Cir. 1999).

subject to reasonable dispute,'" as would be required by Rule 201(b).[187] Nonetheless, under the notion of jury nullification, American juries in criminal cases are always entitled to return a "not guilty" verdict that may be illogical or unreasonable.[188] However, judges cannot instruct juries that they can do so.[189]

Texas Rule 201(f) and Federal Rule 201(f)—by requiring the court to instruct a jury that it may, but need not, accept a judicially noticed fact as true—seem to come close to a "jury nullification" instruction.[190] However, this permissive language should be used only in instructions on judicial notice of adjudicative facts and should not be used in instructions on judicial notice of legislative facts or the law that applies in the case.[191] Thus, when a judge instructs a jury on the applicable law, the instructions should be given in mandatory terms. For example, under Texas statutory law, a firearm is a deadly weapon per se.[192] If a trial judge took judicial notice that a particular gun introduced into evidence was a "firearm," a Texas jury, passing on the question of a defendant's use of a deadly weapon in a given case, would be instructed that a firearm is a deadly weapon. The jury would not be instructed that they could, but were not required to, accept as conclusive that a firearm is a deadly weapon. The jury would, however, be free

---

187. Black, *supra* note 185, at 974.

188. *See Horning v. Dist. of Columbia*, 254 U.S. 135, 138 (1920) ("[T]he jury has the power to bring in a verdict in the teeth of both law and facts."); *United States v. Moylan*, 417 F.2d 1002, 1006 (4th Cir. 1969) ("We recognize ... the undisputed power of the jury to acquit, even if its verdict is contrary to the law as given by the judge and contrary to the evidence."); *United States v. Spock*, 416 F.2d 165, 182 (1st Cir. 1969) ("[T]he jury, as the conscience of the community, must be permitted to look at more than logic."). *See generally* Alan W. Scheflin, *Jury Nullification: The Right to Say No*, 45 S. CAL. L. REV. 168 (1972) (discussing jury's right to decide questions of law and fact).

189. *See United States v. Dougherty*, 473 F.2d 1113, 1133-36 (D.C. Cir. 1972); *see also* 1 LOUISELL & MUELLER, *supra* note 143, §60, at 502 n.8 (instruction on the right of jury nullification is improper).

190. *See United States v. Piggie*, 622 F.2d 486, 489-90 (10th Cir. 1980); *see also* Carter, *supra* note 182, at 654-58 (trial judges should not take judicial notice of jurisdictional facts that are elements of an offense). In *Bello*, the First Circuit approved the following jury instruction under former Federal Rule of Evidence 201(g), now Rule 201(f), when the trial court took judicial notice of the fact that a prison in Puerto Rico was within the territorial jurisdiction of the United States:

> Even though no evidence has been introduced about it in your presence, I believe that the fact that the Metropolitan Detention Center is within a land reserved for the use of the United States and under its exclusive jurisdiction ... is of such common knowledge and can be so accurately and readily determined from the Metropolitan Detention Center officials that it cannot reasonably be disputed. You may, therefore, reasonably treat this fact as proven even though no evidence has been presented on this point before you. As with any fact presented in the case, however, the final decision whether or not to accept it is for you to make and you are not required to agree with me.

194 F.3d at 25.

191. *E.g.*, *O'Connell v. State*, 17 S.W.3d 746, 749 (Tex. App.—Austin 2000, no pet.) (reversible error to take judicial notice, in front of jury, of reliability of HGN test and to instruct jury that HGN test "is a reliable indicator of intoxication"; scientific reliability of certain evidence may be a legislative fact, but not an adjudicative fact; jury should not be told of judicial notice of legislative facts). In *United States v. Gould*, the court held that the trial court did not err in a case involving a conspiracy to import cocaine by giving the following jury instruction: "If you find the substance was cocaine hydrochloride, you are instructed that cocaine hydrochloride is a schedule II controlled substance under the laws of the United States." 536 F.2d 216, 218 (8th Cir. 1976). The court held that this was a "legislative" fact not capable of a jury determination and that to rule otherwise "would be preposterous, thus permitting juries to make conflicting findings on what constitutes controlled substances under federal law." *Id.* at 221.

192. TEX. PENAL CODE §1.07(a)(17)(A).

under Rule 201(f) jury instructions to reject the court's judicial notice that the particular gun introduced into evidence was, in fact, a firearm.

Although a criminal defendant is entitled to a permissive instruction on judicial notice, some federal courts have held that the right may be waived by the failure to assert it.[193] In ***Van Hoang v. State***, however, the defendant's conviction was reversed when the trial court did not submit a jury instruction on a judicially noticed fact.[194] The State offered evidence to the judge, outside the presence of the jury, of the undisputed fact that the statute of limitations had been tolled, and the judge then took judicial notice of that fact.[195] The defendant did not request an opportunity to be heard, nor did he object to the court's taking judicial notice.[196] Nonetheless, because the State bears the burden of proving that an indictment is returned within the limitations period, the ***Van Hoang*** court ruled that the trial court erred in not submitting a jury instruction on this issue.[197] Judge Mansfield, in dissent, asserted that the defendant was not entitled to a Rule 201(g) (now Rule 201(f)) instruction on the judicially noticed facts because he did not object and "there was no dispute or question as to their validity to be presented to the jury."[198] Under the rule, however, the defendant in a criminal case is always entitled to a permissive instruction on judicially noticed facts, even when there is no factual dispute over the accuracy or verifiability of the adjudicative fact that has been judicially noticed. Attorneys in criminal cases should always ask the trial judge to take judicial notice of adjudicative facts under Rule 201 in front of the jury, not outside its presence. Similarly, the trial judge should, when requested, always give a permissive instruction on judicially noticed facts to the jury in a criminal case.

RULE 202
JUDICIAL NOTICE OF OTHER STATES' LAW

(a) Scope. This rule governs judicial notice of another state's, territory's, or federal jurisdiction's:

- Constitution;
- public statutes;

---

193. *See, e.g.*, ***United States v. DeJohn***, 638 F.2d 1048, 1055 (7th Cir. 1981) (based in part on defense counsel's acknowledgements in closing arguments, court rejected defendant's contention that court's judicial notice of Illinois law governing liability on checks was error); ***Piggie***, 622 F.2d at 488 (no error for trial court to take judicial notice of the fact that Leavenworth penitentiary is U.S. territory because defendant did not ask trial court for instruction under Federal Rule 201(g), now Rule 201(f)); *see also* 21 WRIGHT & GRAHAM, *supra* note 58, §5111, at 535 (1977), §5111, at 271 (Supp. 1998) (judge's failure to give instruction is not reversible error if parties do not request an instruction).

194. 939 S.W.2d 593, 597 (Tex. Crim. App. 1996).

195. The State demonstrated both that the current indictment itself alleged that it was a reindictment of a pending case and that the original indictment had been returned well within the applicable limitations period. *Id.* at 607 (Mansfield, J., dissenting).

196. *Id.*

197. *Id.* at 597 (majority op.).

198. *Id.* at 607 (Mansfield, J., dissenting).

- rules;
- regulations;
- ordinances;
- court decisions; and
- common law.

(b) Taking Notice. The court:

(1) may take judicial notice on its own; or

(2) must take judicial notice if a party requests it and the court is supplied with the necessary information.

(c) Notice and Opportunity to Be Heard.

(1) *Notice.* The court may require a party requesting judicial notice to notify all other parties of the request so they may respond to it.

(2) *Opportunity to Be Heard.* On timely request, a party is entitled to be heard on the propriety of taking judicial notice and the nature of the matter to be noticed. If the court takes judicial notice before a party has been notified, the party, on request, is still entitled to be heard.

(d) Timing. The court may take judicial notice at any stage of the proceeding.

(e) Determination and Review. The court—not the jury—must determine the law of another state, territory, or federal jurisdiction. The court's determination must be treated as a ruling on a question of law.

COMMENTARY ON RULE 202

Under Rule 202, a Texas court may, on its own motion, or must, on a party's motion,[199] take judicial notice of the constitutions, public statutes, rules, regulations, ordinances, court decisions, and common law of any other U.S. state, territory, or jurisdiction.[200] Judicial notice of the laws of sister states is mandatory on request in

---

199. In practice, motions under Rule 202 rarely take place. Judges can easily find the laws of sister states online; thus, a formal request by an attorney for judicial notice is unnecessary.

200. TEX. R. EVID. 202(a). The Federal Rules of Evidence contain no provision covering judicial notice of law. The Federal Rules Advisory Committee felt that matters of law traditionally requiring pleading and proof were more appropriately left to the Rules of Civil and Criminal Procedure. *See* FED. R. EVID. 201 advisory committee's note, subdiv. (a).

Under early common law, judicial notice of state law stopped at the border. *See Perkins v. Perkins*, 237 S.W.2d 659, 661 (Tex. Civ. App.—Amarillo 1951, no writ) (Texas court could not take judicial notice of statutory laws of another state); *Lawrence v. Pa. Cas. Co.*, 175 S.W.2d 972, 973 (Tex. Civ. App.—San Antonio 1943, no writ) (court of appeals could not take judicial notice of Missouri statutes). Until the adoption of former Texas Rule of Civil Procedure 184a, Texas courts could not take judicial notice of the laws of sister states in civil cases. A.J. Thomas, Jr., *Proof of Foreign Law in Texas*, 25 Sw. L.J. 554, 555 (1971). Refer to note 7 *supra* for a discussion of Texas Rule of Civil Procedure 184a. The original version of Civil Rule of Evidence 202 adopted former Rule of Civil Procedure 184a with the addition of the words "rules, regulations, and ordinances" in the first sentence. *See Re: New Rules of Evidence*, 641-642 S.W.2d (Tex. Cases) xxxviii (1983, amended 1998). The rule was amended in 1984 and 1988 to its current version. *See Order Adopting and Amending Texas Rules of Civil Evidence*, 733-734 S.W.2d (Tex. Cases) lxxxvi (1987, amended 1998) (authorized court to take judicial notice on its own motion and provided that consti-

both civil and criminal proceedings.[201] If a party does not ask the court to take judicial notice of the law of another jurisdiction under Rule 202 and the court does not choose to take judicial notice on its own, the pertinent law in that jurisdiction is presumed to be the same as in Texas.[202] Similarly, if a party does not provide adequate proof of the content of the sister state's law, courts will apply the same presumption.[203]

---

tutions are subject to judicial notice); *In re: Adopted, Amended and Promulgated Rules of Evidence*, 669-670 S.W.2d (Tex. Cases) xxxi (1984, amended 1998) (added requirement for opponent to be heard, authorized judicial notice at any stage of the proceeding, and added a specific standard of review). The added language in Rule 202(a) authorizes courts to take judicial notice of the rules, regulations, and ordinances of other states, whereas these matters were previously subject to proof only by competent evidence. *See* 2 McCORMICK ON EVIDENCE, *supra* note 1, §335, at 460. Constitutions of sister states were always suitable subjects for judicial notice as part of their statutory laws, so Rule 202 merely clarifies the earlier law.

201. *See* Tex. R. Evid. 202(b)(2); *see, e.g.*, **Huff Energy Fund, L.P. v. Longview Energy Co.**, 482 S.W.3d 184, 190 n.3 (Tex. App.—San Antonio 2015) (defendants filed unopposed motion to take judicial notice of Delaware law), *aff'd*, ___ S.W.3d ___ (Tex. 2017) (No. 15-0968; 6-9-17). Before the promulgation of the Rules of Criminal Evidence, Texas courts followed the common-law position in criminal cases that the court could take judicial notice of the laws of the United States but not the laws of another state because Rule 184a did not apply in criminal proceedings. *See* **Plaster v. State**, 567 S.W.2d 500, 502 (Tex. Crim. App. [Panel Op.] 1978). Instead, the laws of other states were presumed to be the same as those of Texas without competent proof to the contrary. **Acosta v. State**, 650 S.W.2d 827, 836-37 (Tex. Crim. App. 1983) (Clinton & McCormick, JJ., concurring); *see, e.g.*, **Green v. State**, 165 Tex. Crim. 46, 47, 303 S.W.2d 392, 393 (1957) (because there was no showing of the applicable California law on juvenile offenders, court had to assume that California law was the same as Texas law). Under the Rules of Criminal Evidence, judicial notice of out-of-state statutes, rules, and regulations was always discretionary. *See* Tex. R. Crim. Evid. 202, 701-702 S.W.2d (Tex. Cases) xxxv (1986, amended 1998) (current version at Tex. R. Evid. 202). The first sentence of the rule read: "A court upon its own motion *may*, or upon the motion of a party *may*, take judicial notice of the constitutions, public statutes, rules, regulations, ordinances, court decisions, and common law of every other state, territory, or jurisdiction of the United States." *Id.* (emphasis added).

202. **Vince Poscente Int'l, Inc. v. Compass Bank**, 460 S.W.3d 211, 219 (Tex. App.—Dallas 2015, no pet.); *see* **Collins v. Tex Mall, L.P.**, 297 S.W.3d 409, 414 (Tex. App.—Fort Worth 2009, no pet.); *see, e.g.*, **Continuum Health Servs., LLC v. Cross**, No. 05-11-01520-CV (Tex. App.—Dallas 2012, no pet.) (memo op.; 11-19-12) (footnote 4; in reviewing arbitration agreement governed by Delaware law, court of appeals presumed that Delaware law was identical to Texas law when neither party argued otherwise).

203. **Ward v. Hawkins**, 418 S.W.3d 815, 820 (Tex. App.—Dallas 2013, no pet.); *e.g.*, **Pittsburgh Corning Corp. v. Walters**, 1 S.W.3d 759, 769-70 (Tex. App.—Corpus Christi 1999, pet. denied) (court did not have to take judicial notice of California law when party merely referred to it without offering its content or any written documentation); *see* Tex. R. Evid. 202(b)(2); Wellborn, *supra* note 68, at 27; *see, e.g.*, **Ibarra v. State**, 961 S.W.2d 415, 417 (Tex. App.—Houston [1st Dist.] 1997, no pet.) (in case ordering extradition to Alabama, no evidence was offered about Alabama law; "unless shown to the contrary, it is presumed that the law of the demanding state is the same as that of the asylum state"); **Graco Robotics, Inc. v. Oaklawn Bank**, 914 S.W.2d 633, 645 (Tex. App.—Texarkana 1995, writ dism'd) (bank did not offer proof that a lien satisfies a judgment under Michigan law; Texas procedural law controlled). *But see* **Coca-Cola Co. v. Harmar Bottling Co.**, 218 S.W.3d 671, 685 (Tex. 2006) (although no proof was shown that antitrust statutes of Arkansas, Louisiana, and Oklahoma were inconsistent with that of Texas, no presumption arose that law of sister states was same as that of Texas). In **Harmar**, the court would not presume that the antitrust laws of the other states were identical to that of Texas because the purpose of the Texas Free Enterprise and Antitrust Act was "'to maintain and promote economic competition in trade and commerce occurring wholly or partly *within the State of Texas* and to provide the benefits of that competition to consumers *in the state.*'" 218 S.W.3d at 685 (quoting Tex. Bus. & Com. Code §15.04). Four justices dissented, stating the Rule 202 presumption should have applied because the defendant—by not proving that Texas law conflicts with the laws of Arkansas, Louisiana, and Oklahoma—waived any claim that the laws of the sister states were not the same as Texas. **Harmar**, 218 S.W.3d at 695-96 (Brister, Jefferson, O'Neill, Medina, JJ., dissenting). The dissent argued that the majority's ruling requires trial courts to analyze choice-of-law issues in every case because appellate courts may not look for conflicts in statutes between sister states and will simply presume the laws are different. *Id.* at 696.

Rule 202 carries forward the rule from former Rule of Civil Procedure 184a that the laws of other states are presumed to be the same as those of Texas without competent proof to the contrary.

While a court must take judicial notice of federal regulations or a sister state's laws if sufficient information is supplied, "the determination of compliance with these requirements is within the discretion of the trial court."[204] Rule 202(b) does not define the "necessary information" a party must supply for the court to take judicial notice under the rule. When possible, a party should supply the court with deposition testimony or an affidavit from a practicing attorney in the sister state to prove that the documentary evidence, such as a copy of the pertinent statute or case law, is still controlling law in that jurisdiction.[205]

If a party is requesting that the court take judicial notice under Rule 202, the court may require the party to notify all other parties of the request.[206] A party who makes a timely request must be heard on the propriety of taking judicial notice and the nature of the matter to be noticed.[207] If the court takes judicial notice before a party is notified, the party must still be heard if a request is made.[208]

Like Rule 201, Rule 202 allows the court to take judicial notice "at any stage of the proceeding."[209] Thus, an appellate court is not limited to the trial court's record on the laws of other states.[210]

Because judicial notice of law falls within the general category of "determining the law," which is "a function for judges, not juries,"[211] a trial judge should notice the con-

---

204. ***Daugherty v. S. Pac. Transp. Co.***, 772 S.W.2d 81, 83 (Tex. 1989); *see, e.g.*, ***Holden v. Capri Lighting, Inc.***, 960 S.W.2d 831, 833 (Tex. App.—Amarillo 1997, no pet.) (when the only information presented to trial court on the content of pertinent California law was an incomplete copy of a single 20-year-old case, trial court was not required to take judicial notice of sister state's law and could presume that California law was identical to Texas law); ***Knops v. Knops***, 763 S.W.2d 864, 867 (Tex. App.—San Antonio 1988, no writ) (trial court was not required to act on a "broad, general request" for judicial notice that did not specify which laws the party relied on or give the court sufficient information to properly comply); ***Ewing v. Ewing***, 739 S.W.2d 470, 472 (Tex. App.—Corpus Christi 1987, no writ) (trial court did not err in refusing to take judicial notice of the laws of California because requesting party did not "set forth with some particularity the law that is to be relied upon"); *see also* ***River Oaks Place Council of Co-Owners v. Daly***, 172 S.W.3d 314, 320 (Tex. App.—Corpus Christi 2005, no pet.) (trial court erred in refusing to take judicial notice of federal regulation because there was no indication in the record that the party offering the evidence did not comply with requirements of Rule 202).

205. *See, e.g.*, ***Holden***, 960 S.W.2d at 833 (when the only information presented to the trial court in support of judicial notice of a specific California legal doctrine was an incomplete copy of a single 20-year-old case, and party did not provide additional information that case was still controlling authority, trial court did not abuse its discretion in applying Texas law).

206. TEX. R. EVID. 202(c)(1). Rule 201 does not have a similar notice provision for the requesting party.

207. TEX. R. EVID. 202(c)(2).

208. *Id.* Rule 202(c)(2) is identical to the hearing provision in Rule 201. *See* TEX. R. EVID. 201(e). Refer to notes 151-166 *supra* and accompanying text.

209. TEX. R. EVID. 202(d); *see* TEX. R. EVID. 201(d). Refer to notes 141-150 *supra* and accompanying text.

210. *See* TEX. R. EVID. 202(d); ***Nubine v. State***, 721 S.W.2d 430, 434 (Tex. App.—Houston [1st Dist.] 1986, pet. ref'd); *see, e.g.*, ***Hill v. State***, 392 S.W.3d 850, 857 & n.4 (Tex. App.—Amarillo 2013, pet. ref'd) (in trial for assault against family member, appellate court took judicial notice under Rule 202 of Oklahoma domestic-abuse statute, which was not in appellate record); ***Jones v. State***, 758 S.W.2d 356, 356 (Tex. App.—Houston [14th Dist.] 1988, pet. ref'd) (appellate court could take judicial notice of Maryland law on the use of commitment papers in establishing proof of defendant's conviction); ***Ex parte Molina***, No. 04-17-00012-CR (Tex. App.—San Antonio 2017, pet. ref'd) (memo op.; 4-19-17) (appellate court took judicial notice of Oklahoma constitutional provision and case law authorizing lieutenant governor to act in capacity of governor when sitting governor is absent from state).

211. ***Watts v. State***, 99 S.W.2d 604, 611 & n.23 (Tex. Crim. App. 2003) (quoting 1 CHRISTOPHER B. MUELLER & LAIRD C. KIRKPATRICK, FEDERAL EVIDENCE §59, at 294 (2d ed. 1994)); *see* TEX. R. EVID. 202(e).

RULE 202

tent, scope, and applicability of sister-state law outside the presence of the jury.[212] The jury is not instructed on the trial court's determination of sister-state law; it is simply instructed on the law applicable to the case.[213] The trial court's determination of law—whether the law of the forum state, of a sister state, or of a foreign nation—is then reviewed as a question of law.[214]

Rule 202 deals only with the existence and content of a sister state's law. It does not address the issue of whether to apply the law of another jurisdiction to a particular Texas proceeding. As one court has noted, "the rule does not mandate the application of the law requested to be noticed; rather, it is contemplated by the rule that the request merely presents the question of which state's law will apply, a question of law."[215] If the state laws differ on a particular issue, the court will use traditional choice-of-law tests to determine which state's law applies.[216]

RULE 203
DETERMINING FOREIGN LAW

(a) Raising a Foreign Law Issue. A party who intends to raise an issue about a foreign country's law must:

    (1) give reasonable notice by a pleading or other writing; and

    (2) at least 30 days before trial, supply all parties a copy of any written materials or sources the party intends to use to prove the foreign law.

(b) Translations. If the materials or sources were originally written in a language other than English, the party intending to rely on them must, at least 30 days before trial, supply all parties both a copy of the foreign language text and an English translation.

(c) Materials the Court May Consider; Notice. In determining foreign law, the court may consider any material or source, whether or not admissible. If the court considers any material or source not submitted by a party, it must give all parties notice and a reasonable opportunity to comment and submit additional materials.

---

212. *Cf. Watts*, 99 S.W.3d at 610-11 (discussing judicial notice of Texas law by Texas courts).

213. *See, e.g., id.* at 613 (trial judge erred by commenting on weight of evidence; judge "did not judicially notice an adjudicative fact, but rather directly addressed the jury on the specific application of law to facts in a different judicial decision").

214. *See* Tex. R. Evid. 202(e), 203(d). Refer to notes 237-238 *infra* and accompanying text.

215. *Bartley v. Budget Rent-A-Car Corp.*, 919 S.W.2d 747, 754 (Tex. App.—Amarillo 1996, writ denied); *see also Huff Energy Fund, L.P. v. Longview Energy Co.*, 482 S.W.3d 184, 190 n.3 (Tex. App.—San Antonio 2015) (parties agreed at oral argument that Delaware law applied to substantive issues), *aff'd*, ___ S.W.3d ___ (Tex. 2017) (No. 15-0968; 6-9-17).

216. *See Coca-Cola Co. v. Harmar Bottling Co.*, 218 S.W.3d 671, 684-85 (Tex. 2006); *Bartley*, 919 S.W.2d at 754.

> **(d) Determination and Review.** The court—not the jury—must determine foreign law. The court's determination must be treated as a ruling on a question of law.

COMMENTARY ON RULE 203

Rule 203 is not a true rule of judicial notice.[217] It has been characterized as a "hybrid rule by which the presentation of the foreign law to the court resembles the presentment of evidence but which ultimately is decided as a question of law."[218] Although Rule 203 does not expressly refer to the process as "judicial notice," and treating the determination of foreign law as a question of law is not consistent with the traditional view of judicial notice as being limited to adjudicative facts, the placement of this rule in Article II of the Texas Rules of Evidence indicates that the process is a type of judicial notice rather than merely a relaxation of the rules of evidence.[219] When the only evidence presented to the court is the uncontroverted opinion of an expert on foreign law, the court will evaluate the evidence as it would a question of fact—that is, the court will generally accept the opinion as true if it is reasonable and consistent with the text of the law.[220] Courts can be quite liberal in their acceptance of source materials sup-

---

217. *See PennWell Corp. v. Ken Assocs., Inc.*, 123 S.W.3d 756, 760-61 (Tex. App.—Houston [14th Dist.] 2003, pet. denied) (procedure under Rule 203 is "not considered a judicial notice procedure because that term refers only to adjudicative facts and not to matters of law"); *Reading & Bates Constr. Co. v. Baker Energy Res. Corp.*, 976 S.W.2d 702, 707 (Tex. App.—Houston [1st Dist.] 1998, pet. denied) ("Although [Rule 203] is contained within the article designated, 'Judicial Notice,' the rule itself does not refer to judicial notice. It sets forth the procedural mechanism for raising an issue concerning the law of a foreign country, for giving notice to other parties, and for furnishing materials concerning the foreign law.").

218. *Long Distance Int'l, Inc. v. Telefonos de Mex., S.A. de C.V.*, 49 S.W.3d 347, 351 (Tex. 2001); *accord Cal Dive Offshore Contractors Inc. v. Bryant*, 478 S.W.3d 914, 920-21 (Tex. App.—Houston [14th Dist.] 2015, no pet.); *see also Gardner v. Best W. Int'l, Inc.*, 929 S.W.2d 474, 483 (Tex. App.—Texarkana 1996, writ denied) (questions of foreign law are mixed questions of law and fact); *CPS Int'l, Inc. v. Dresser Indus., Inc.*, 911 S.W.2d 18, 22 (Tex. App.—El Paso 1995, writ denied) (determination of foreign law is question of law for court; issue is whether trial court reached proper legal conclusion about content of foreign law).

219. Before the adoption of Rule 203, Texas Revised Civil Statutes article 3718 provided for the receipt in evidence of printed statute books of foreign jurisdictions. Act approved May 13, 1871, 1st Leg., R.S., An Act to Regulate Proceedings in the District Courts: Evidence, §92, 1846 Tex. Gen. Laws 388, *reprinted in* 2 H.P.N. GAMMEL, THE LAWS OF TEXAS 1822-1897, at 1694 (Austin, Gammel Book Co. 1898) (former Texas Revised Civil Statutes art. 3718 deemed repealed as to civil proceedings effective 1983 and as to criminal proceedings effective 1986).

The statute was narrowly interpreted to apply only to proof of statutes of foreign countries. *See, e.g., Martin v. Payne*, 11 Tex. 292, 294 (1854) (unofficial publication could not be received as evidence of Tennessee law). The content of foreign law was otherwise regarded as a question of fact subject to strict rules of pleading and proof. *Franklin v. Smalldridge*, 616 S.W.2d 655, 657 (Tex. Civ. App.—Corpus Christi 1981, no writ). Rule 104(a), by granting trial courts broad discretion in determining the admissibility of evidence, eliminated article 3718's strict proof requirements for foreign law. Refer to *Article I: General Provisions*, *supra* p. 86. And Rule 203 significantly increased the efficiency of the process for requesting judicial notice of the law of foreign countries. *See San Benito Bank & Trust Co. v. Rio Grande Music Co.*, 686 S.W.2d 635, 639 n.1 (Tex. App.—Corpus Christi 1984, writ ref'd n.r.e.); R. Doak Bishop, *International Litigation in Texas: Texas Rules of Evidence and Recent Changes in the Texas Rules of Civil Procedure*, 36 BAYLOR L. REV. 131, 146-47 (1984).

220. *See, e.g., AG Volkswagen v. Valdez*, 897 S.W.2d 458, 461-62 (Tex. App.—Corpus Christi 1995, orig. proceeding) (based on affidavit and other evidence presented by party, trial judge properly determined that German law prohibits the disclosure of VW's current corporate telephone book), *mand. granted*, 909 S.W.2d 900 (Tex. 1995).

porting the content of foreign law if the opposing party does not provide sufficient materials to counter the proponent's evidence.[221]

The procedure for invoking the law of a foreign country in federal courts is covered in Federal Rule of Civil Procedure 44.1 and Federal Rule of Criminal Procedure 26.1.[222] Texas Rule 203 adopts the substantive provisions of these rules and includes procedural additions dealing with notice and the opportunity to be heard.[223]

The federal counterparts to Texas Rule 203 were added in 1966 to furnish a uniform and effective procedure for raising and determining the law of a foreign country.[224] The first sentence of the federal rule, concerning notice, is designed to avoid unfair surprise.[225] The second sentence—which permits consideration of any relevant material, including testimony, regardless of whether it is otherwise admissible—recognizes that the ordinary rules of evidence are often time consuming, inefficient, expensive, and generally not relevant to the problem of determining foreign law.[226] The second sentence also allows the court to conduct its own research and to consider any relevant material regardless of whether it would be admissible as evidence because the court may have at its disposal better foreign-law materials than those presented by counsel.[227] The final sentence makes the determination of an issue of foreign law equivalent to a ruling on a question of law, so any appellate review will not be narrowly confined.[228]

The provisions in Rule 203 that are not in the counterpart federal rules are designed to ensure adequate notice of intent to prove foreign law and to give an adverse party an adequate opportunity to rebut the materials or sources submitted to or considered

221. *See, e.g.*, **PennWell Corp.**, 123 S.W.3d at 760-61 (court upheld "judicial notice" of copy of Illinois case referring indirectly to attorney fees under Japanese law, excerpts presented by both parties from treatise titled *Doing Business in Japan*, and opponent's submission of pages from *Martindale-Hubbell International Law Digest*; "[i]n determining the foreign law, the trial court can consider any material or source, whether or not admissible under the rules of evidence, including affidavits, testimony, briefs, and treatises").

222. *See* FED. R. CIV. P. 44.1; FED. R. CRIM. P. 26.1. The Federal Rules of Evidence contain no provision covering judicial notice of law. Refer to note 200 *supra*.

223. *See* TEX. R. EVID. 203(c). Refer to notes 229-234 *infra* and accompanying text. In 2017, the Texas Legislature directed the Texas Supreme Court to adopt rules of evidence and procedure limiting the grant of comity to foreign judgments and arbitration awards in certain family-law cases to protect against constitutional and public-policy violations. TEX. GOV'T CODE §22.0041(b). The adopted rules must, among other things, require a party seeking enforcement of a judgment or arbitration award based on foreign law that involves a marriage or a parent-child relationship to provide timely notice to the court and parties, which includes providing the information required by Texas Rule of Evidence 203. TEX. GOV'T CODE §22.0041(c)(1). The rules must be adopted no later than January 1, 2018. H.B. 45, §3, 85th Leg., R.S., eff. Sept. 1, 2017. For the adopted rules, go to the supreme court's website at www.txcourts.gov/supreme.

224. FED. R. CIV. P. 44.1 advisory committee's note.

225. *Id.*; *see* TEX. R. EVID. 203(a)(1).

226. FED. R. CIV. P. 44.1 advisory committee's note; *see* TEX. R. EVID. 203(c).

227. FED. R. CIV. P. 44.1 advisory committee's note.

228. *Id.*; *see* TEX. R. EVID. 203(d); *see also* **Richmark Corp. v. Timber Falling Consultants**, 959 F.2d 1468, 1473 (9th Cir. 1992) (questions of foreign law are reviewed de novo); **United States v. First Nat'l Bank**, 699 F.2d 341, 344 (7th Cir. 1983) (determination of foreign law is a question of law freely reviewable on appeal).

by the court.[229] The notice provisions in Rule 203 are more detailed than those in Rule 202, reflecting the additional problems often presented in proving the law of foreign countries.[230] The rule states that a party who intends to raise an issue about the law of a foreign country must give reasonable notice in the pleadings or other written documents[231] and, at least 30 days before trial, furnish the parties with the written material or sources that he intends to use as proof of the foreign law.[232] If the materials were originally written in a foreign language, the party intending to rely on them must, at least 30 days before trial, furnish all parties with both a copy of the foreign-language text and an English translation.[233] The court must also give all parties notice and a reasonable opportunity to comment or to provide additional materials if the court considers any materials or sources not submitted by a party.[234] The procedures in Rule 203 must be strictly followed for the court to determine foreign law.[235]

Rules 201(c), 202(b), and 204(b) all authorize the court to act on its own motion as well as that of a party. Rule 203 is less clear about whether a court can inquire into the law of a foreign country without a party's request, but nothing in the language of the rule explicitly prohibits that inquiry. Furthermore, the Federal Advisory Committee's notes to Federal Rule of Civil Procedure 44.1 include this statement: "There is no requirement that the court give formal notice to the parties of its intention to … raise

---

229. *See* TEX. R. EVID. 203(a)-(c). The Fourteenth Court of Appeals has held that if a party does not provide adequate proof of the content of a foreign law, the court will presume that the law of the foreign jurisdiction is identical to Texas law. *PennWell Corp. v. Ken Assocs., Inc.*, 123 S.W.3d 756, 761 (Tex. App.—Houston [14th Dist.] 2003, pet. denied). This presumption has operated under Rule 202, which deals with judicial notice of the law of other states. *See Pittsburgh Corning Corp. v. Walters*, 1 S.W.3d 759, 769 (Tex. App.—Corpus Christi 1999, pet. denied). Refer to notes 202-203 *supra* and accompanying text.

230. *See Lawrenson v. Glob. Marine, Inc.*, 869 S.W.2d 519, 525 (Tex. App.—Texarkana 1993, writ denied).

231. TEX. R. EVID. 203(a)(1); *see Cal Dive Offshore Contractors Inc. v. Bryant*, 478 S.W.3d 914, 920 (Tex. App.—Houston [14th Dist.] 2015, no pet.).

232. TEX. R. EVID. 203(a)(2); *Phillips v. United Heritage Corp.*, 319 S.W.3d 156, 164 (Tex. App.—Waco 2010, no pet.); *Lawrenson*, 869 S.W.2d at 525. In *Cal Dive*, the appellee was seeking to apply foreign law and had timely raised the issue with the trial court; thus, the court of appeals held that the appellant's response was timely even though it was filed less than 30 days before trial when the record did not indicate the trial court had set a deadline for the response. 478 S.W.3d at 921. The appellee argued that the appellant's submission improperly included materials outside the scope of the appellee's original submission; however, because the appellee did not properly preserve this argument for review, the court of appeals considered the appellant's arguments based on foreign law. *Id.*

233. TEX. R. EVID. 203(b). Rule 1009 (Translating a Foreign Language Document) requires that the translation of foreign-language documents, along with the translator's affidavit or unsworn declaration, be served on all parties at least 45 days before trial. TEX. R. EVID. 1009(a). Thus, any foreign law or other materials that must be translated from a foreign language should be submitted within the time frame and according to the procedures outlined in Rule 1009 if a party wants to dispense with the need for live testimony of the translation of foreign-language documents. *See* TEX. R. EVID. 1009(a), (e). Refer to *Article X: Contents of Writings, Recordings, & Photographs, infra* p. 1070.

234. TEX. R. EVID. 203(c); *Cal Dive*, 478 S.W.3d at 921 n.3. In determining foreign law, the trial court may consider any material—regardless of whether it is submitted by a party or is admissible—including affidavits, testimony, briefs, and treatises. *Cal Dive*, 478 S.W.3d at 921.

235. *E.g.*, *Pet. Workers Union of the Rep. of Mex. v. Gomez*, 503 S.W.3d 9, 22 (Tex. App.—Houston [14th Dist.] 2016, no pet.) (court overruled appellant's argument that agreement was illegal under Mexican law and thus unenforceable; appellant did not mention Rule 203 or assert that it had fulfilled any of rule's requirements when it presented declaration from Mexican Attorney General that was untimely under rule).

RULE 203

and determine independently an issue [regarding the determination of foreign law] not raised by them."[236] As long as all parties have an adequate opportunity to be heard on the issue, courts should not interpret Rule 203 to preclude trial judges from making a determination of foreign law on their own motion.

Like judicial notice of sister-state law under Rule 202, determination of foreign law is a question for the court, not the jury.[237] The determination of foreign law is reviewed as a question of law.[238]

RULE 204
JUDICIAL NOTICE OF TEXAS MUNICIPAL & COUNTY ORDINANCES, TEXAS REGISTER CONTENTS, & PUBLISHED AGENCY RULES

(a) Scope. This rule governs judicial notice of Texas municipal and county ordinances, the contents of the Texas Register, and agency rules published in the Texas Administrative Code.

(b) Taking Notice. The court:

(1) may take judicial notice on its own; or

(2) must take judicial notice if a party requests it and the court is supplied with the necessary information.

(c) Notice and Opportunity to Be Heard.

(1) *Notice.* The court may require a party requesting judicial notice to notify all other parties of the request so they may respond to it.

(2) *Opportunity to Be Heard.* On timely request, a party is entitled to be heard on the propriety of taking judicial notice and the nature of the matter to be noticed. If the court takes judicial notice before a party has been notified, the party, on request, is still entitled to be heard.

(d) Determination and Review. The court—not the jury—must determine municipal and county ordinances, the contents of the Texas Register, and published agency rules. The court's determination must be treated as a ruling on a question of law.

COMMENTARY ON RULE 204

Rule 204 governs judicial notice of Texas municipal and county ordinances, the contents of the Texas Register, and the agency rules published in the Texas Administra-

---

236. FED. R. CIV. P. 44.1 advisory committee's note; *see also* TEX. R. EVID. 203(c) ("If the court considers any material or source not submitted by a party, it must give all parties notice and a reasonable opportunity to comment and submit additional materials.").

237. TEX. R. EVID. 203(d); *see* TEX. R. EVID. 202(e). Refer to notes 211-214 *supra* and accompanying text.

238. TEX. R. EVID. 203(d).

tive Code.[239] By its own terms, the rule applies only to Texas ordinances, rules, and regulations. Federal rules and regulations were traditionally subject to judicial notice under Texas common law.[240] The Federal Register Act states that "[t]he contents of the Federal Register shall be judicially noticed,"[241] and some commentators suggest that the federal act should bind state courts under the Supremacy Clause.[242] However, Texas Rule 202, which covers judicial notice of the law of sister states, has been broadly written and covers federal rules and regulations—the laws, ordinances, rules, regulations, judicial decisions, and common law of all U.S. jurisdictions are subject to judicial notice in Texas courts.[243] These matters need not be pleaded before they are subject to judicial notice.[244]

As with Rules 201 through 203, Rule 204 gives the trial court the discretion to take judicial notice on its own motion and requires the court to do so on the request of a party who complies with the requisite procedure.[245] If a party provides the appropri-

---

239. TEX. R. EVID. 204(a). Rule 204 was added to the Texas Rules of Civil Evidence in 1984 and was included in the original promulgation of the Texas Rules of Criminal Evidence in 1986. *See Order Adopting Texas Rules of Criminal Evidence*, 701-702 S.W.2d (Tex. Cases) xxxvi (1985, effective Sept. 1, 1986, amended 1998); *In re: Adopted, Amended and Promulgated Rules of Evidence*, 669-670 S.W.2d (Tex. Cases) xxxii (1984, amended 1998). At common law, the contents of ordinances and administrative rules and regulations were not subject to judicial notice because they were considered "in the nature of a special act or law." *See Howeth v. State*, 645 S.W.2d 787, 788 (Tex. Crim. App. 1983). Thus, they had to be proved up, usually by means of a certified copy from the custodian of the record. *See id.* ("The municipal court, of course, may take judicial notice of the ordinances of its municipality. However, if the conviction is appealed to a county court at law, and heard de novo, as here, it is incumbent upon the State to prove the ordinance or its terms."); *Green v. State*, 594 S.W.2d 72, 74 (Tex. Crim. App. 1980) ("The courts of this State cannot take judicial notice of the existence of city ordinances or their terms, and where they enter into a transaction and are relied on, proof of them is essential."). In 1981, the Administrative Procedure and Texas Register Act was amended to provide for judicial notice of the contents of the Texas Register and the Texas Administrative Code. Act approved April 30, 1981, 67th Leg., R.S., ch. 76, §1, 1981 Tex. Gen. Laws 168 (former Texas Revised Civil Statutes art. 6252-13a, §4(c), repealed 1993, now codified at TEX. GOV'T CODE §2002.022(a)); Act approved June 15, 1977, 65th Leg., R.S., ch. 678, 1977 Tex. Gen. Laws 1703, *amended by* Act approved April 30, 1981, 67th Leg., R.S., ch. 76, §3, 1981 Tex. Gen. Laws 169 (former Texas Revised Civil Statutes art. 6252-13b, §4, repealed 1993, now codified at TEX. GOV'T CODE §2002.054). Local ordinances were not covered by the Act and thus not subject to judicial notice. A municipal court could, however, take judicial notice of an ordinance of its own municipality. *Howeth*, 645 S.W.2d at 788.

240. *See Tippett v. Hart*, 497 S.W.2d 606, 613 (Tex. Civ. App.—Amarillo 1973), *writ ref'd n.r.e.*, 501 S.W.2d 874 (Tex. 1973); *Dall. Gen. Drivers, Warehousemen & Helpers v. Jax Beer Co.*, 276 S.W.2d 384, 390 (Tex. Civ. App.—Dallas 1955, no writ).

241. 44 U.S.C. §1507.

242. *See* 2 McCORMICK ON EVIDENCE, *supra* note 1, §335, at 460 n.8.

243. TEX. R. EVID. 202(a); *see, e.g.*, *River Oaks Place Council of Co-Owners v. Daly*, 172 S.W.3d 314, 320 (Tex. App.—Corpus Christi 2005, no pet.) (trial court should have taken judicial notice of Code of Federal Regulations section). Refer to notes 199-216 *supra* and accompanying text.

244. *Daugherty v. S. Pac. Transp. Co.*, 772 S.W.2d 81, 83-84 (Tex. 1989).

245. TEX. R. EVID. 204(b); *see Volosen v. State*, 227 S.W.3d 77, 81 (Tex. Crim. App. 2007). Under former Civil Rule 204, a judge could take judicial notice without being asked to do so by either party; under former Criminal Rule 204, counsel had to request that the court take judicial notice of an ordinance. *See* TEX. R. CIV. EVID. 204, 733-734 S.W.2d (Tex. Cases) lxxxvii (1987, amended 1998) (current version at TEX. R. EVID. 204) ("A court *upon its own motion* may, or upon the motion of a party shall, take judicial notice of the ordinances of municipalities and counties of Texas, of the contents of the Texas Register, and of the codified rules of the agencies published in the Administrative Code.") (emphasis added); TEX. R. CRIM. EVID. 204, 701-702 S.W.2d (Tex. Cases) xxxvi (1986, amended 1998) (current version at TEX. R. EVID. 204) ("Judicial notice may be taken of the ordinances of municipalities and counties of Texas, of the contents of the Texas Register, and of the codified rules of the agencies published in the Ad-

ate materials to demonstrate the existence and contents of a specific ordinance, no judge should have the discretion to refuse to recognize that law. If the requesting party does not provide the trial court with the appropriate documentation, neither the trial court nor the appellate court is required to take judicial notice of the ordinance.[246] On the other hand, the court can still decide to take judicial notice of the ordinance.[247] Some appellate courts have held that a trial court has a mandatory duty, even in the absence of a request by a party, to judicially notice administrative agency regulations published in the Texas Register and Texas Administrative Code.[248] This mandatory duty is imposed not by Rule 204, however, but by sections 2002.022(a) and 2002.054(1) of the Texas Government Code.[249] Unlike local laws and ordinances, "agency regulations are like statutes or the decisions of a higher court to which a lower court owes obedience under the doctrine of stare decisis."[250]

Like Rule 202, Rule 204(b) does not define the "necessary information" a party must supply for the court to take judicial notice under the rule.[251] Because municipal and county ordinances are difficult to research and verify, attorneys should provide the trial court with a certified copy of the applicable ordinance and ensure that this copy is included in the court's record.[252] Without a complete record, the appellate court may be unable to determine precisely which law was at issue and may refuse to accept a bare record recital that the trial court took judicial notice of a particular ordinance.[253]

---

ministrative Code."); *see, e.g.,* ***Martin v. State***, 731 S.W.2d 630, 631 (Tex. App.—Houston [1st Dist.] 1987, pet. ref'd) (in a criminal case, court correctly refused to take judicial notice of municipal ordinance because State did not request judicial notice or offer ordinance into evidence; only evidence was police officer's testimony that speed-limit signs were posted). The 1998 unification of the Civil and Criminal Rules adopted the wording of the former civil rule for both civil and criminal cases. Rule 204(b) retains the discretionary provision of the former civil rule. *See* Tex. R. Evid. 204(b)(1).

246. *See* ***Lone Star Gas Co. v. EFP Corp.***, 63 S.W.3d 463, 467 (Tex. App.—Waco 2000), *rev'd on other grounds*, 92 S.W.3d 417 (Tex. 2001).

247. *See* Tex. R. Evid. 204(b)(1); *see, e.g.,* ***Thompson v. State***, 44 S.W.3d 171, 175 (Tex. App.—Houston [14th Dist.] 2001, no pet.) (reviewing court assumed that trial court took judicial notice of ordinance without physical documentation because trial court "indicated its familiarity with the specific provisions of the ordinance when it articulated its reasons" for denying defendant's motion).

248. ***In re Doe***, 501 S.W.3d 313, 319 n.7 (Tex. App.—Houston [14th Dist.] 2016, n.p.h.); ***Eckmann v. Des Rosiers***, 940 S.W.2d 394, 399 (Tex. App.—Austin 1997, no writ).

249. Tex. Gov't Code §2002.022(a) ("The contents of the Texas Register are to be judicially noticed ...."), §2002.054(1) ("State agency rules published in the administrative code, as approved by the secretary of state and as amended by documents later filed with the office of the secretary ... are to be judicially noticed ....").

250. ***Eckmann***, 940 S.W.2d at 399.

251. Refer to notes 203-205 *supra* and accompanying text.

252. *See* ***City of Hous. v. Sw. Concrete Constr., Inc.***, 835 S.W.2d 728, 733 n.5 (Tex. App.—Houston [14th Dist.] 1992, writ denied) ("To be part of the record before an appellate court, municipal ordinances must be submitted in verified form."); ***Metro Fuels, Inc. v. City of Austin***, 827 S.W.2d 531, 532 (Tex. App.—Austin 1992, no writ) ("To enable an appellate court to review a municipal or county ordinance, parties must both comply with the provisions of Rule 204 and make the ordinance part of the trial-court record.").

253. *See* ***Metro Fuels***, 827 S.W.2d at 532 ("parties must both comply with the provisions of Rule 204 and make the ordinance part of the trial-court record" if the appellate court is to review the propriety of judicial notice of a municipal or county ordinance).

Rule 204 contains the same provisions dealing with notice and opportunity to be heard as does Rule 202.[254] Rule 204 does not, however, contain the language found in both Rules 201(d) and 202(d) that allows courts to take judicial notice at any stage of the proceeding.[255] Although the language of Rule 204 is seemingly broad enough to permit an appellate court to take judicial notice of ordinances, the failure to include the same phrase found in Rules 201(d) and 202(d) could be construed as an intended bar to such action. Thus, it might be argued that appellate courts should not take judicial notice of ordinances that were not noticed in the trial court.[256] Most Texas cases, however, have held that an appellate court, as well as a trial court, may take judicial notice under Rule 204.[257]

Like judicial notice of sister-state law under Rule 202 and determination of foreign law under Rule 203, judicial notice under Rule 204 is a question for the court, not the jury.[258] Judicial notice under Rule 204 is reviewed as a question of law.[259]

---

254. *See* Tex. R. Evid. 204(c). Refer to notes 206-208 *supra* and accompanying text.

255. Refer to notes 141-150, 209-210 *supra* and accompanying text.

256. *See **Hollingsworth v. King**,* 810 S.W.2d 772, 774 (Tex. App.—Amarillo 1991) (Civil Rule 204, unlike Civil Rules 201 and 202, does not address the question of whether an appellate court may take judicial notice for the first time on appeal; appellate court refused to decide the issue because it was not presented with sufficient information to take judicial notice), *writ denied,* 816 S.W.2d 340 (Tex. 1991).

257. *E.g., **In re Doe**,* 501 S.W.3d 313, 319 n.7 (Tex. App.—Houston [14th Dist.] 2016, n.p.h.); ***Eckmann v. Des Rosiers**,* 940 S.W.2d 394, 399 (Tex. App.—Austin 1997, no writ); ***Int'l Ass'n of Firefighters Local 624 v. City of San Antonio**,* 822 S.W.2d 122, 127 (Tex. App.—San Antonio 1991, writ denied); *see, e.g., **Heritage on the San Gabriel Homeowners Ass'n v. Tex. Comm'n on Envtl. Quality**,* 393 S.W.3d 417, 433 n.9 (Tex. App.—Austin 2012, pet. denied) (court of appeals took judicial notice of regulatory guidelines for municipal drainage plan); ***City of Paris v. Abbott**,* 360 S.W.3d 567, 573 n.6 (Tex. App.—Texarkana 2011, pet. denied) (court of appeals took judicial notice of ordinances of City of Paris, Texas); *see also **Sparkman v. Maxwell**,* 519 S.W.2d 852, 855 (Tex. 1975) ("[A]n appellate court is naturally reluctant to take judicial notice of matters such as municipal charters and regulations promulgated by state agencies when the trial court was not requested to do so and was not given an opportunity to examine the necessary source material. This does not mean that we would refuse to take judicial notice under similar circumstances where necessary to avoid an unjust judgment.").

258. Tex. R. Evid. 204(d); *see* Tex. R. Evid. 202(e), 203(d). Refer to notes 211-214, 237-238 *supra* and accompanying text.

259. Tex. R. Evid. 204(d).

ARTICLE III: PRESUMPTIONS[1]

I. INTRODUCTION

A presumption is a procedural device that requires the court, once it finds the existence of a certain fact or group of facts (usually called the "basic facts"),[2] to assume the existence of another fact (usually called the "presumed fact").[3] The presumption continues unless a party rebuts the presumed fact by sufficient evidence, causing the presumption to disappear.[4] Sometimes called "the slipperiest member of the family of legal terms,"[5] presumptions have generated much debate.[6]

Following a vast outpouring of scholarly articles[7] and extensive judicial treatment, Mason Ladd concluded that "[d]espite the extensive commentary that has been devoted to the subject of presumptions, there is still no agreement on how their use should be

---

1. Neither the Texas Supreme Court nor the Texas Court of Criminal Appeals has promulgated rules governing civil or criminal presumptions. This article focuses on current Texas law and compares it with the federal approach, which was rejected in Texas.

2. *See* Edmund M. Morgan, *Foreword* to MODEL CODE OF EVID. 52-54 (1942).

3. *See id.* A "true" presumption makes the assumption mandatory. If the fact-finder has discretion to make the assumption from the proven facts, the presumption is a mere inference. In other words, a presumption is compulsory and remains so until a party adequately rebuts the presumed fact. Commenting on a presumption's general effect on the relationship between a basic fact, A, and an assumed fact, B, Edmund Morgan observed:

> Thayer, Wigmore, the American Law Institute, and commentators generally have argued, and many courts have agreed, that the term "presumption" should be used only to mean that when A is established in an action, the existence of B must be assumed unless and until a specified condition is fulfilled. All courts agree that "presumption" is properly used in this situation, but there is wide disagreement as to the terms of the condition.

EDMUND M. MORGAN, BASIC PROBLEMS OF EVIDENCE 32 (1962); *see also State v. Corby*, 145 A.2d 289, 293 (N.J. 1958) (contrasting the compulsory nature of presumptions with the permissive nature of inferences); *Turpin v. State*, 606 S.W.2d 907, 911 n.3 (Tex. Crim. App. 1980) ("Most courts use presumptions to designate an assumption which must be drawn by the trier of the facts from a given fact or group of facts.").

4. *Temple Indep. Sch. Dist. v. English*, 896 S.W.2d 167, 169 (Tex. 1995); *Vibbert v. PAR, Inc.*, 224 S.W.3d 317, 321 (Tex. App.—El Paso 2006, no pet.); *see* 1 JACK B. WEINSTEIN & MARGARET A. BERGER, WEINSTEIN'S FEDERAL EVIDENCE §301App.100[2][a], at 301App-13 to 301App-15 (Joseph M. McLaughlin ed., 2d ed. 2008) (discussing the "bursting bubble" theory, which asserts that a presumption disappears when contradictory evidence is introduced).

5. 2 MCCORMICK ON EVIDENCE §342, at 495 (Kenneth S. Broun ed., 6th ed. 2006).

6. Over a hundred years ago, James Thayer made the following observations:

> [T]he numberless propositions figuring in our cases under the name of presumptions, are quite too heterogeneous and non-comparable in kind, and quite too loosely conceived of and expressed, to be used or reasoned about without much circumspection. … Some are maxims, others mere inferences of reason, others rules of pleading, others are variously applied. … Among things so incongruous as these and so beset with ambiguity there is abundant opportunity for him to stumble and fall who does not pick his way and walk with caution.

JAMES B. THAYER, A PRELIMINARY TREATISE ON EVIDENCE AT THE COMMON LAW 351-52 (1898). Nearly 50 years later, John McKelvey remarked:

> No term has been more frequently or more variously defined. We read of presumptions of law, and presumptions of fact, mixed presumptions, accumulative, violent, mild, conclusive, conflicting, strong, and weak presumptions, until the whole subject seems an entanglement of definition and explanation, which leaves the mind in a hopeless state of bewilderment.

JOHN J. MCKELVEY, HANDBOOK OF THE LAW OF EVIDENCE §53, at 114-15 (5th ed. 1944) (footnote omitted).

7. Edmund Morgan wrote six articles on this subject between 1931 and 1946, and Charles McCormick wrote three between 1928 and 1943. For a listing of the principal articles in this area, see 1 ROY R. RAY, TEXAS PRACTICE: TEXAS LAW OF EVIDENCE CIVIL AND CRIMINAL §50, at 69 n.16 (3d ed. 1980).

governed."[8] This complexity and confusion are understandable. The rules that make up the confusing field of presumptions have vastly varying importance, serve widely divergent purposes, and may shape rules of decision. However, these rules all describe the relationship between an admitted or proved fact or group of facts and another fact that is sought to be proved.[9]

A. Purposes of Presumptions

Scholars and courts have cited numerous reasons for creating presumptions. Courts inconsistently assign the basic purposes of presumptions. Scholars, not court opinions, produce most of the analysis in this area.[10] In general order of importance, these purposes include the following:

(1) To permit a jury instruction on the relationship between certain facts;[11]

(2) To promote convenience or to bring out the real issues in dispute;[12]

(3) To save the court's time by favoring probable findings of fact;[13]

(4) To correct an imbalance resulting from one party's greater access to proof of the presumed fact;[14]

---

8.   Mason Ladd, *Presumptions in Civil Actions*, 1977 ARIZ. ST. L.J. 275, 275 (footnote omitted). The confusion about presumptions and their effect was exacerbated by the Supreme Court's adoption of presumptions and burden-shifting frameworks in discrimination lawsuits. *See* **Fisher v. Vassar Coll.**, 114 F.3d 1332, 1336-37 (2d Cir. 1997) (en banc) (discrimination is presumed if plaintiff submits minimal elements of prima facie case, but employer rebuts presumption if it gives nondiscriminatory reasons for its conduct). *See generally* Ronald J. Allen & Craig Callen, *Teaching "Bloody Instructions": Civil Presumptions and the Lessons of Isomorphism*, 21 QUINN. L. REV. 933, 947-59 (2003) (noting confusion in lower federal courts caused by Supreme Court's reliance on presumption devices to implement employment-discrimination laws). Refer to note 30 *infra* and accompanying text.

9.   *See* Ronald J. Allen, *Presumptions in Civil Actions Reconsidered*, 66 IOWA L. REV. 843, 845 (1981) (presumptions have been used to instruct the jury about the relationship between facts).

10.   *See* Edward W. Cleary, *Presuming and Pleading: An Essay on Juristic Immaturity*, 12 STAN. L. REV. 5, 11 (1959) (court opinions "rarely contain any satisfying disclosure of the ratio decidendi").

11.   Allen, *supra* note 9, at 845; *see also* A. Leo Levin, *Pennsylvania and the Uniform Rules of Evidence: Presumptions and Dead Man Statutes*, 103 U. PA. L. REV. 1, 14 (1954) (describing a presumption that allows a jury to infer that suicide was not the cause of death in an accidental-death case). This type of presumption frequently develops from judicial experience, even though the relationship between the basic fact and the presumed fact may be tenuous at best. *See* Allen, *supra* note 9, at 855.

12.   **O'Dea v. Amodeo**, 170 A. 486, 487 (Conn. 1934). An illustration of this type of presumption is that an insured is presumed to have performed all the conditions of his policy. *Id.*

13.   *See* 2 MCCORMICK ON EVIDENCE, *supra* note 5, §343, at 500-01 (courts create presumptions as a time-saving device); *see also* **Greer v. United States**, 245 U.S. 559, 561 (1918) ("A presumption upon a matter of fact, when it is not merely a disguise for some other principle, means that common experience shows the fact to be so generally true that courts may notice the truth."). An example of this type of presumption is that once a condition has been shown to exist, it is presumed to continue to exist. *See* **Buckley v. Heckler**, 739 F.2d 1047, 1049 (5th Cir. 1984).

14.   2 MCCORMICK ON EVIDENCE, *supra* note 5, §343, at 500 (citing as an example the presumption that when goods are transported between two or more carriers, any damage to goods occurred on the last carrier's line). In **Hunsucker v. Omega Industries**, the court expressed the rationale for this type of presumption as follows:

> The presumption [that an operator of a motor vehicle is the agent or employee of its owner acting within the scope of employment] grows out of the fact that not infrequently the evidence necessary to establish the character of the mission in which the servant was engaged is exclusively within the possession of the defendant. The effect of the rule is to "smoke out" the defendant and compel him to disclose the true facts within his knowledge. ... A defendant should not be able to "hide behind

(5) To avoid the factual indeterminacy of an impasse;[15]

(6) To serve a social or economic policy favoring a contention by giving that contention the benefit of the presumptions;[16] and

(7) To provide a shorthand description of the initial assignment of the burdens of persuasion and production on an issue.[17]

B. Attributes & Effects of Presumptions

When a presumed fact has been adequately rebutted, courts agree that the basic fact remains as evidence for the trier of fact to consider.[18] Beyond this basic principle, the treatment of presumptions depends on why they have been used in a particular case. The following unresolved questions about the attributes and effects of presumptions have provoked confusion and inconsistency:

(1) Should the term "presumption" encompass both permissive and mandatory assumptions of fact, and should the term include both conclusive and rebuttable presumptions?[19]

---

the log" simply because the accident victim is unable to identify the driver, especially where, as here, it is relatively easy for the owner to rebut the presumption.
659 S.W.2d 692, 695 (Tex. App.—Dallas 1983, no writ) (citations omitted).

15. 2 McCORMICK ON EVIDENCE, *supra* note 5, §343, at 500 (providing as an example a presumption about survivorship for people who die in a common disaster, which avoids the impasse that would be caused by the factual indeterminacy of which person died first); *see also* Allen, *supra* note 9, at 846-47 (courts create these kinds of presumptions for reasons independent of any concept implicit in the general nature of presumptions).

16. For example, the presumption of ownership from possession tends to stabilize estates. *See* 2 McCORMICK ON EVIDENCE, *supra* note 5, §343, at 500. Similarly, the presumption of bailee negligence ensures that those with superior access to proof come forward with their evidence. *See O'Dea*, 170 A. at 487-88 (when one party has peculiar knowledge of circumstances, that party has the burden of proving those circumstances); *Buchanan v. Byrd*, 519 S.W.2d 841, 843 (Tex. 1975) (person in possession of article is more likely to know what has occurred and thus is better able to explain).

17. In this category is the so-called "presumption of innocence," which assumes that any person's conduct on a given occasion was lawful if there are no facts to the contrary. *See* 2 McCORMICK ON EVIDENCE, *supra* note 5, §346, at 525 ("The 'presumption of innocence' is not a presumption at all, but simply another way of stating the rule that the prosecution has the burden of proving the guilt of the accused beyond a reasonable doubt."); *see also Carr v. State*, 4 So. 2d 887, 888 (Miss. 1941) (presumption of innocence compels the State to maintain the burden of proving guilt).

18. *Gen. Motors Corp. v. Saenz ex rel. Saenz*, 873 S.W.2d 353, 359 (Tex. 1993); *see Southland Life Ins. v. Greenwade*, 138 Tex. 450, 456, 159 S.W.2d 854, 857 (1942) ("We agree with [defendant's] contention that a presumption, as such, is not evidence and that it vanished as such in view of the opposing evidence; but we do not agree that the evidentiary facts upon which it was established, could no longer be considered by the trier of the facts."); *Sellers v. Foster*, 199 S.W.3d 385, 392 (Tex. App.—Fort Worth 2006, no pet.) (rebuttal of presumption creates fact issue for trial court to resolve); *D&M Vacuum Serv., Inc. v. Zavala Cty. Appr. Dist.*, 812 S.W.2d 435, 437 (Tex. App.—San Antonio 1991, no writ) ("Even though the *presumption* vanishes, we hold that the *evidence* ... continues to exist and have probative value."); *see, e.g., Texaco, Inc. v. Phan*, 137 S.W.3d 763, 767 (Tex. App.—Houston [1st Dist.] 2004, no pet.) (presumption of party's receipt of default judgment through proper mailing of document was established; rebuttal of presumption by evidence denying receipt presented fact issue for fact-finder to resolve).

19. *See* 2 McCORMICK ON EVIDENCE, *supra* note 5, §342, at 496-98 (courts continue to use the term "presumption" loosely to designate both technical presumptions and permissible inferences); 9 JOHN H. WIGMORE, EVIDENCE IN TRIALS AT COMMON LAW §2491 (Chadbourn rev. 1981) (distinguishing between presumptions of law, which force the jury to reach a certain conclusion if there is no contrary evidence, and presumptions of fact, which are not really presumptions because they have no legal significance), §2492 (discussing conclusive presumptions, which effectively operate when the demonstration of a basic fact makes a presumed fact's existence immaterial); 21B CHARLES A.

ARTICLE III

(2) May a presumption be based on a fact that is itself established by a presumption?[20]

(3) Which presumptions merely shift the burden of production to the party against whom they operate?[21]

(4) When the presumption operates only to shift the burden of production, what quality of proof is necessary to rebut the presumption?[22]

(5) Which presumptions shift the burden of persuasion to the party against whom they operate?[23]

WRIGHT & KENNETH W. GRAHAM, JR., FEDERAL PRACTICE & PROCEDURE §5124, at 488-505 (2d ed. 2005) (defining presumptions and distinguishing them from inferences and assumptions of fact); W.E. Shipley, Annotation, *Modern Status of the Rules Against Basing an Inference upon an Inference or a Presumption upon a Presumption*, 5 A.L.R.3d 100, 104-05 (1966) [hereinafter Shipley, *Modern Status of the Rules*] (discussing presumptions of law and of fact, or mandatory presumptions and inferences); *see also* Bruce L. Ackerman, *The Conclusive Presumption Shuffle*, 125 U. PA. L. REV. 761, 762-63 (1977) (advocating procedural restraints in conclusive-presumption cases); Irving A. Gordon & Marvin A. Tenenbaum, *Conclusive Presumption Analysis: The Principle of Individual Opportunity*, 71 NW. U. L. REV. 579, 582-83 (1976) (proposing a narrowing of existing conclusive-presumption doctrine). Note that California Evidence Code §§600 and 601 define presumptions as mandatory and as either conclusive or rebuttable.

20.   *See* **E. Tex. Theatres, Inc. v. Rutledge**, 453 S.W.2d 466, 469 (Tex. 1970) (presumptions of fact may not rest on a basic fact that is itself presumed); Shipley, *Modern Status of the Rules*, *supra* note 19, at 131 (generally, a presumption cannot be based on another presumption). Refer to notes 223-239 *infra* and accompanying text.

21.   Historically, there have been few attempts to decide which presumptions affect only the burden of production. *See, e.g.*, CAL. EVID. CODE §603 (burden-of-production presumption is a presumption that furthers no public policy other than facilitating the litigation); *O'Dea*, 170 A. at 487-89 (examining the different types of presumptions, including burden-of-production presumptions). However, the issue of burden-of-persuasion presumptions versus production-shifting presumptions received considerably more attention from the Supreme Court in civil-rights and discrimination cases. *See generally* **Tex. Dep't of Cmty. Affairs v. Burdine**, 450 U.S. 248, 252-56 (1981) (discussing burden-of-production presumptions in Title VII cases). Refer to note 30 *infra* and accompanying text.

22.   There are at least five views on the quality of evidence required to rebut this type of presumption. *See* Morgan, *supra* note 2, at 55-57, 60-62; *see also* 2 MCCORMICK ON EVIDENCE, *supra* note 5, §345, at 522 (there must be a rational connection between a basic fact and a presumed fact); 9 WIGMORE, *supra* note 19, §2493d, at 319 ("as probable as not" should be enough to rebut a presumption); Allen, *supra* note 9, at 861-62 (trial judges should have the power to determine whether a party satisfied the burden of production); W.E. Shipley, Annotation, *Effect of Presumption as Evidence or upon Burden of Proof Where Controverting Evidence Is Introduced*, 5 A.L.R.3d 19, 66-69 (1966) (describing the quality of proof required to rebut a similar presumption in different jurisdictions).

23.   In this connection, note the long-standing dispute between Edmund Morgan, who favored a rule that all presumptions shift the burden of persuasion, and James Thayer, who espoused the "bursting bubble" theory, in which the presumption disappears when a party presents evidence sufficient to rebut the presumed fact. *See* THAYER, *supra* note 6, at 336-43 (discussing bursting-bubble theory); 1 WEINSTEIN & BERGER, *supra* note 4, §301App.100[2][b], at 301App.-15 (Morgan preferred burden-shifting for presumptions); 9 WIGMORE, *supra* note 19, §2493c, at 314-20 (Thayer preferred bursting-bubble theory); Edmund M. Morgan, *Instructing the Jury upon Presumptions and Burden of Proof*, 47 HARV. L. REV. 59, 82 (1933) (criticizing Thayer's bursting-bubble theory as not giving enough effect to the presumption); *see also* Lara Lenzotti Kapalla, Note, *Some Assembly Required: Why States Should Not Adopt the ALI's System of Presumptive Alimony Awards in Its Current Form*, 2004 MICH. ST. L. REV. 207, 217-18 (2004) (Morgan's view was adopted by the Uniform Rules of Evidence and is followed by states with presumption rules patterned after the Uniform Rules). California defines presumptions that shift the burden of persuasion as presumptions established for the following reason:

> [T]o implement some public policy other than to facilitate the determination of the particular action in which the presumption is applied, such as the policy in favor of establishment of a parent and child relationship, the validity of marriage, the stability of titles to property, or the security of those who entrust themselves or their property to the administration of others.

CAL. EVID. CODE §605.

(6) Should the presumption itself have an evidentiary effect?[24]

(7) How should courts handle conflicting presumptions?[25]

(8) What is the propriety and content of jury instructions on presumptions?[26]

II. FEDERAL RULE 301 & CONGRESSIONAL HISTORY

Common-law presumptions present much confusion. One possible solution is for legislators and rulemakers to identify problem areas and remedy them with clearly written legislation or rules. The California Law Revision Commission made such an attempt when it drafted the California Evidence Code,[27] and this approach was followed by the Advisory Committee on the Federal Rules in its 1969 preliminary draft.[28] As finally enacted, however, the substantive provisions on presumptions were condensed into Federal Rule 301.[29]

Under Federal Rule 301, a presumption shifts the burden of production to the opposing party, who must submit sufficient evidence for the fact-finder to act on a contested issue.[30] The amount of evidence needed to either trigger or defeat a presumption will vary depending on the substantive legal issue and the presumption's purpose

---

24. *See Mullins v. Ritchie Grocer Co.*, 35 S.W.2d 1010, 1012-13 (Ark. 1931) (op. on reh'g) (presumptions of law created by statute have no probative weight and disappear when contrary evidence is introduced; presumptions of fact require proof and must be weighed against contrary evidence by the fact-finder); ***Gen. Motors Corp. v. Saenz ex rel. Saenz***, 873 S.W.2d 353, 359 (Tex. 1993) ("Once ... evidence contradicting the presumption has been offered, the presumption disappears and 'is not to be weighed or treated as evidence.' The evidence on the issue is then evaluated as it would be in any other case. The presumption has no effect on the burden of persuasion." (quoting ***Combined Am. Ins. v. Blanton***, 163 Tex. 225, 227, 353 S.W.2d 847, 849 (1962))); ***McMullen v. Warren Motor Co.***, 25 P.2d 99, 101 (Wash. 1933) (presumption that driver of vehicle is driving for vehicle's owner is not evidence of the fact, and it disappears when opposing party presents evidence rebutting the presumption); Alfred L. Gausewitz, *Presumptions in a One-Rule World*, 5 VAND. L. REV. 324, 333-34 (1952) (presumptions, as rules of law, cannot be evidence); James P. McBaine, *Presumptions, Are They Evidence?*, 26 CALIF. L. REV. 519, 549-51 (1938) (same).

25. This question results from the dispute about whether a specific presumption's purposes determine its weight or whether all presumptions are of equal weight. *Compare* 2 MCCORMICK ON EVIDENCE, *supra* note 5, §344, at 512 (the weightier presumption prevails), *with* 9 WIGMORE, *supra* note 19, §2493, at 308-09 (presumptions either are or are not present and cannot conflict), *and* Allen, *supra* note 9, at 855-59 (arguing against the weighing of presumptions).

26. This is a corollary of the dispute about whether the judge or the jury should decide that a party has adequately rebutted a presumption. Responses range from not mentioning the presumption to the jury at all to requiring intricate instructions. *See **Alpine Forwarding Co. v. Pa. R.R.***, 60 F.2d 734, 736-37 (2d Cir. 1932) (presumption should not be mentioned to jury); MORGAN, *supra* note 3, at 39-43 (giving detailed rules of presumptions and jury charges).

27. Sections 600-607 deal with presumptions generally. Sections 620-624 deal with conclusive presumptions. Sections 630-647 define specific presumptions that affect only the burden of production. Sections 660-670 define specific presumptions that affect the burden of proof.

28. *See* FED. R. EVID. 3-01 to 3-03 (1969 preliminary draft), 46 F.R.D. 161, 207-19 (1969). Proposed Rule 3-03, which covered presumptions in civil cases, had 11 subsections. *See id.* at 212-14.

29. *See* FED. R. EVID. 301. Federal Rule 302 provides that courts must apply the state law on presumptions when state law supplies the rule of decision.

30. *See, e.g.*, ***Tex. Dep't of Cmty. Affairs v. Burdine***, 450 U.S. 248, 253-55 (1981) (in a Title VII case, once an employee makes out a prima facie case against an employer, the burden of production shifts to the employer); ***McDonnell Douglas Corp. v. Green***, 411 U.S. 792, 802-03 (1973) (same); *see also* ***St. Mary's Honor Ctr. v. Hicks***, 509 U.S. 502, 521 (1993) ("[T]he ***McDonnell Douglas*** presumption is a *procedural* device, designed only to establish an order of proof and production."); ***Reeves v. Gen. Foods Corp.***, 682 F.2d 515, 521-22 (5th Cir. 1982) (after the presumption has disappeared, evidence sufficient to produce a presumption of prima facie discrimination under Title VII may not merit an inference of intentional discrimination).

or weight.[31] This rule resolves only a few of the questions listed above.[32] The problem with Federal Rule 301 is that it operates to shift the burden of production for all presumptions but does not allow for shifting the burden of persuasion, regardless of a presumption's purpose or relative weight.

The history of Federal Rule 301 illustrates the dilemma of attempting to treat all presumptions as equally important. The Advisory Committee's version of the rule, prescribed by the Supreme Court, was essentially the opposite of the final version because all presumptions would have shifted the burden of *persuasion*.[33] The Advisory Committee recognized that the same considerations dictating a plaintiff's prima facie case and a defendant's affirmative defenses—fairness, policy, and probability—also underlie the creation of presumptions.[34] Nonetheless, the Advisory Committee rejected the bursting-bubble theory, in which a presumption vanishes when any rebuttal evidence is introduced, in favor of a rule allowing presumptions to shift the ultimate burden of persuasion.[35]

The House Committee on the Judiciary considered the Supreme Court's version of Federal Rule 301 and proposed a modified version. This proposed modified version provided that presumptions (1) shifted only the burden of production[36] and (2) remained sufficient evidence of the presumed fact to be considered by the trier of fact even when the opposing party offered contradictory evidence.[37] The House of Representatives passed this version.[38] The House Committee's version represented a compromise between the bursting-bubble theory (which gave presumptions too little force) and the Advisory Committee's version on shifting the burden of proof (which gave presumptions too much force).[39] Thus, under the House Committee's intermediate position, a presumption does not automatically vanish when contradicting evidence is introduced, but neither does it change the burden of persuasion.[40] Instead, a presumption under the House Committee's version of Federal Rule 301 was merely "deemed sufficient evidence of the fact presumed, to be considered by the jury or other finder of fact."[41]

---

31. *See* 1 WEINSTEIN & BERGER, *supra* note 4, §301.02[3], at 301-13 to 301-16.

32. Refer to notes 19-26 *supra* and accompanying text.

33. The proposed rule read as follows: "In all cases not otherwise provided for by Act of Congress or by these rules a presumption imposes on the party against whom it is directed the burden of proving that the non-existence of the presumed fact is more probable than its existence." FED. R. EVID. 301 (1972 proposed final draft), 56 F.R.D. 183, 208 (1973).

34. FED. R. EVID. 301 advisory committee's note (citations omitted).

35. *See id.* Refer to note 23 *supra*.

36. H.R. REP. NO. 93-650, at 7 (1974), *reprinted in* 1974 U.S.C.C.A.N. 7075, 7080-81.

37. *Id.* Commentators have characterized the House's action as a "blunder." 1 WEINSTEIN & BERGER, *supra* note 4, §301App.01[3], at 301App.-6.

38. *See* Pub. L. No. 93-595, 88 Stat. 1926 (1975) (passing the House version).

39. *See* H.R. REP. NO. 93-650, *supra* note 36, at 7, *reprinted in* 1974 U.S.C.C.A.N. 7075, 7080-81 (the Committee took an intermediary position between the burden-of-proof and bursting-bubble positions).

40. *Id.*

41. *Id.*

The Senate Committee on the Judiciary accepted without comment the House Committee's modification to the Supreme Court rule about the effect of presumptions on the burden of persuasion but considered the provision that gave presumptions evidentiary effect "ill-advised."[42] According to the Senate Committee, a court should use a presumption as a way of dealing with evidence and not as evidence itself; requiring a jury to consider a presumption as evidence only causes confusion.[43]

The Conference Committee accepted the Senate Committee's amendment, which deleted the presumption-as-evidence clause.[44] The Conference Committee also left intact the House Committee's production-shifting framework.[45] Congress enacted Federal Rule 301 in this form.[46]

As enacted, Federal Rule 301 seems to be an adaptation of the bursting-bubble approach toward presumptions.[47] The rule certainly rejects both the burden-of-persuasion-shifting and presumption-as-evidence approaches. There is still debate over how, if at all, courts should instruct juries about presumptions.[48] The Senate Report states that "it would be inappropriate under this rule to instruct the jury that the inference they are to draw is conclusive."[49] This statement leaves unanswered the question

---

42. S. REP. NO. 93-1277, at 9-10 (1974), *reprinted in* 1974 U.S.C.C.A.N. 7051, 7056. The Senate Committee quoted Charles McCormick's criticism of the presumption-as-evidence rule:

> Another solution, formerly more popular than now, is to instruct the jury that the presumption is "evidence," to be weighed and considered with the testimony in the case. This avoids the danger that the jury may infer that the presumption is conclusive, but it probably means little to the jury, and certainly runs counter to accepted theories of the nature of evidence.

Id. (citing MCCORMICK ON EVIDENCE §345, at 825 (Edward W. Cleary ed., 2d ed. 1972)).

43. S. REP. NO. 93-1277, *supra* note 42, at 9-10, *reprinted in* 1974 U.S.C.C.A.N. 7051, 7056 (citing CAL. EVID. CODE §600). California had a rule, set out in *Smellie v. Southern Pacific Co.*, 299 P. 529, 549-51 (Cal. 1931), that was much like the rule in the House Amendment. Justice Traynor sharply criticized the California rule in *Speck v. Sarver*, 128 P.2d 16, 21 (Cal. 1942) (Traynor & Edmonds, JJ., dissenting) (rule of law cannot be weighed against facts). The second sentence of California Evidence Code §600(a) states that "[a] presumption is not evidence." The sentence was added "to repudiate specifically" the rule in *Smellie*. 7 Cal. Law Revision Comm'n Rep. (1965), p. 1084 (comment to CAL. EVID. CODE §600).

44. *See* H.R. CONF. REP. NO. 93-1597, at 5-6 (1974), *reprinted in* 1974 U.S.C.C.A.N. 7098, 7099; David W. Louisell, *Construing Rule 301: Instructing the Jury on Presumptions in Civil Actions and Proceedings*, 63 VA. L. REV. 281, 284-85 (1977).

45. *See* H.R. CONF. REP. NO. 93-1597, *supra* note 44, at 5-6, *reprinted in* 1974 U.S.C.C.A.N. 7098, 7099; Louisell, *supra* note 44, at 284-85.

46. Pub. L. No. 93-595, 88 Stat. 1926 (1975).

47. *See Lupyan v. Corinthian Colls. Inc.*, 761 F.3d 314, 320 (3d Cir. 2014).

48. *See* 2 MICHAEL H. GRAHAM, HANDBOOK OF FEDERAL EVIDENCE §§301:12-301:13, at 387-96 (7th ed. 2012). Most commentators urge that, for practical reasons, courts should not mention presumptions to the jury because such instructions confuse rather than clarify. *See id.* §301:13, at 392 (the term "presumption" should not be mentioned to jury); Edmund M. Morgan, *Further Observations on Presumptions*, 16 S. CAL. L. REV. 245, 264 (1943) (confusion is likely "if anything is said to a jury about presumptions"). *But see* 2 MCCORMICK ON EVIDENCE, *supra* note 5, §344, at 515 n.43 (the term presumption should be used "so that the jury may appreciate the legal recognition of a slant of policy or probability as the reason for placing on the party this particular burden"); Louisell, *supra* note 44, at 312-18 (jury should be instructed on the use of presumptions). For examples of pattern jury instructions on inferences and presumptions under Federal Rule 301, see 4 LEONARD B. SAND ET AL., MODERN FEDERAL JURY INSTRUCTIONS ¶¶75.01, 75.02 (2008).

49. S. REP. NO. 93-1277, *supra* note 42, at 9-10, *reprinted in* 1974 U.S.C.C.A.N. 7051, 7056.

of what courts should tell the jury. The legislative commentary does not clear up these ambiguities:

> If the adverse party offers no evidence contradicting the presumed fact, the court will instruct the jury that if it finds the basic facts, it may presume the existence of the presumed fact. If the adverse party does offer evidence contradicting the presumed fact, the court cannot instruct the jury that it may presume the existence of the presumed fact from proof of the basic facts. The court may, however, instruct the jury that it may infer the existence of the presumed fact from proof of the basic facts.[50]

The Conference Report states that if no party rebuts the presumed fact or the basic facts giving rise to the presumed fact, the court must instruct the jury that it "may" presume the existence of the presumed fact; neither the language of Rule 301 nor the Conference Report provides any criteria for the jury to decide whether it should do so.[51] Further, the average juror will probably not be helped by the slight distinction between the words "presume" and "infer." Because the court can instruct the jury that it may infer the presumed fact from proof of the basic fact even in the face of conflicting evidence, the approach under Federal Rule 301 might resemble the bursting-bubble approach more than its drafters intended.[52]

III. PRESUMPTIONS IN TEXAS CIVIL PROCEEDINGS

The original Texas Rules of Civil and Criminal Evidence did not include any rule covering presumptions. The Liaison Committee explained this decision in a comment to its proposed civil rules by emphasizing that the limited scope of Federal Rule 301 made it inconsistent with Texas law on presumptions.[53] This observation can be illus-

---

50. H.R. CONF. REP. NO. 93-1597, *supra* note 44, at 5-6, *reprinted in* 1974 U.S.C.C.A.N. 7098, 7099. *See generally* Ronald J. Allen, *Presumptions, Inferences and Burden of Proof in Federal Civil Actions—An Anatomy of Unnecessary Ambiguity and a Proposal for Reform*, 76 Nw. U. L. REV. 892, 893 (1982) (Federal Rule 301 did not clarify ambiguities about the proper role of presumptions).

51. *See* H.R. CONF. REP. NO. 93-1597, *supra* note 44, at 5-6, *reprinted in* 1974 U.S.C.C.A.N. 7098, 7099; *see also* 21B WRIGHT & GRAHAM, *supra* note 19, §5127, at 576-77 (jury instructions should explain (1) what facts the jury may presume or infer and the basic facts it must find to do so, (2) what public policy authorizes the presumption, and (3) that the jury is not bound to presume or infer the presumed fact).

52. *See* Louisell, *supra* note 44, at 312-21 (Federal Rule 301 should be construed broadly to permit jury instructions that "impart to the jury [a sense] of the force in logic or policy that called the presumption into existence in the first place"; continuing with the form of the instruction depends on the state of the evidence at the close of proof). In Louisell's view, an "inference" instruction would be appropriate if two conditions were met:

> First, the facts established by the evidence or supported by sufficient evidence to enable the jury to find their existence … must themselves be a sufficient basis in logic and reason to support a finding of the presumed fact. Second, the adversary's proof of the nonexistence of the presumed fact must not be so strong as to require a finding of its nonexistence as a matter of law.

Id. at 311.

53. *See* TEX. R. EVID. 301 cmt. (1982 Liaison Committee proposal), *reprinted infra* p. 1078. Specifically, the Liaison Committee commented:

> Rule 301 of the Federal Rules of Evidence dealing with presumptions in civil cases has not been included. It deals with a very limited aspect of the overall subject of presumptions and may be in-

trated by comparing the operation of Federal Rule 301 with the operation of presumptions in Texas civil cases.[54] Under the federal approach, presumptions operate to shift only the burden of production.[55] Under Texas law, on the other hand, presumptions can shift either the burden of persuasion or the burden of production.

A. Presumptions that Shift the Burden of Persuasion

Some presumptions in Texas shift the burden of persuasion—proof of the basic fact raises the presumed fact and shifts the burden to disprove the presumed fact, sometimes even by a heightened standard of proof, to the opposing party. These presumptions effectively create an affirmative defense. Most of the burden-of-persuasion presumptions are based on strong public-policy grounds, and some are also supported by the "access-to-evidence" rationale.

1. Legitimacy presumption. A child born to lawfully married parents is presumed to be legitimate.[56] This presumption places the burden of persuasion on the party asserting illegitimacy.[57] Texas's legitimacy presumption is codified in its Family Code.[58] The weight of the policy considerations underlying the legitimacy presumption, "one of the strongest known to our law,"[59] has even induced one legislature to require the party asserting illegitimacy to prove it beyond a reasonable doubt.[60] Texas's legitimacy presumption requires proof of illegitimacy only by a preponderance of the evidence.[61]

---

consistent with Texas law in several respects. It was therefore considered advisable to leave this matter to the courts for further definition and development.
Id.

54. Refer to notes 117-132 *infra* and accompanying text.

55. Refer to notes 27-52 *supra* and accompanying text.

56. *Joplin v. Meadows*, 623 S.W.2d 442, 443 (Tex. App.—Texarkana 1981, no writ).

57. *See* 1 RAY, *supra* note 7, §90, at 128 & n.33; Ann Lents, Comment, *Presumptions in Texas: A Study in Irrational Jury Control*, 52 TEX. L. REV. 1329, 1350 (1974); *see also* ***Pinkard v. Pinkard***, 252 S.W. 265, 266 (Tex. Civ. App.—Beaumont 1923, no writ) (prenuptial conception does not weaken the presumption of legitimacy).

58. *See* TEX. FAM. CODE §160.204(a)(1) ("A man is presumed to be the father of a child if ... he is married to the mother of the child and the child is born during the marriage ...."), §160.204(b) (procedure for rebutting presumption); ***Gomez v. Gomez***, 327 S.W.3d 189, 191 (Tex. App.—San Antonio 2010, no pet.) (presumption of paternity exists if man is married to child's mother and child is born during the marriage; presumption legally establishes father-child relationship). For further discussion of the creation and rebuttal of the paternity presumption under the Family Code, see ***O'Connor's Texas Family Law Handbook*** (2017), "Father by presumed paternity," ch. 1-B, §4.1, p. 28.

59. ***In re Marriage of Collins***, 870 S.W.2d 682, 685 (Tex. App.—Amarillo 1994, writ denied); ***Joplin***, 623 S.W.2d at 443; ***Pinkard***, 252 S.W. at 268.

60. *See* ME. R. EVID. 302.

61. *See* TEX. FAM. CODE §160.204(b) & cmt., §160.601 cmt. *See generally* ***In re J.W.T.***, 872 S.W.2d 189, 193-94 (Tex. 1994) (tracing historical development and modernization of legitimacy presumption). The Texas Family Code required proof of illegitimacy by clear and convincing evidence before DNA testing made this heightened standard of proof unnecessary. *See* TEX. FAM. CODE §160.110(a) (clear and convincing evidence is required to rebut paternity presumption) (repealed eff. June 14, 2001). Until 1983, "Texas statutory law prohibited a presumed father, one who was married to and living with his wife at the time the child was born, from denying paternity, unless he could establish non-access to the wife, or impotence." ***Amanda v. Montgomery***, 877 S.W.2d 482, 486 (Tex. App.—Houston [1st Dist.] 1994, no writ).

A person challenging a child's legitimacy may rebut the Texas presumption only with genetic-test results.[62]

2. Marriage-validity & community-property presumptions. The performance of a ceremonial marriage creates a presumption that the marriage is valid.[63] The court also presumes that any earlier marriage terminates upon entering the ceremonial marriage at issue.[64] Like the legitimacy presumption, the marriage-validity presumption is among the strongest recognized by law[65] and places the burden of persuasion on the party challenging the validity of the marriage.[66] Specifically, the challenging party must prove that death, divorce, or annulment has not occurred in the earlier marriage.[67] The rebuttal evidence must negate death, divorce, and annulment only in the jurisdictions where those events could reasonably have occurred.[68]

All property possessed by either party during or on dissolution of marriage is presumed to be community property,[69] and the party challenging the presumption must trace and demonstrate by clear and convincing evidence that the property is separate.[70]

---

62. TEX. FAM. CODE §160.631(b). In most cases, a suit to adjudicate parentage must be brought no later than the child's fourth birthday. *Id.* §160.607(a). The limitations period does not apply if the court determines that the child's mother and presumed father did not live together or engage in sexual intercourse during the probable time of conception or the presumed father did not bring a suit to adjudicate parentage within the limitations period because he mistakenly believed he was the child's biological father based on misrepresentations to that effect. *Id.* §160.607(b); *see, e.g., Gomez*, 327 S.W.3d at 191 (when presumed father was listed as child's father on child's birth certificate, in school records, and on tax returns, there was insufficient evidence to prove exception to limitations period).

63. TEX. FAM. CODE §1.101; *see also* ***Tex. Employers' Ins. v. Elder***, 155 Tex. 27, 32, 282 S.W.2d 371, 374-75 (1955) (presumption of the validity of a marriage and of the parties' competency extends to common-law marriages).

64. *See* TEX. FAM. CODE §1.102; ***Estate of Claveria v. Claveria***, 615 S.W.2d 164, 165 & n.2 (Tex. 1981); ***Jordan v. Jordan***, 938 S.W.2d 177, 179 (Tex. App.—Houston [1st Dist.] 1997, no writ); ***Snyder v. Schill***, 388 S.W.2d 208, 210 (Tex. Civ. App.—Houston 1964, writ ref'd n.r.e.); *see also* Robert A. Allen, Comment, *Presumption of the Validity of a Second Marriage*, 20 BAYLOR L. REV. 206, 208-11 (1968) (discussing the presumptions of death, divorce, and annulment). For further discussion of the marriage-validity presumption, see *O'Connor's Texas Family Law Handbook* (2017), "Most recent marriage presumed valid," ch. 3-C, §3.2.1, p. 288.

65. ***Mpiliris v. Hellenic Lines, Ltd.***, 323 F. Supp. 865, 880-81 (S.D. Tex. 1969), *aff'd*, 440 F.2d 1163 (5th Cir. 1971); ***Elder***, 155 Tex. at 30, 282 S.W.2d at 373; ***Wood v. Paulus***, 524 S.W.2d 749, 758 (Tex. Civ. App.—Corpus Christi 1975, writ ref'd n.r.e.); ***Dixon v. Dixon***, 348 S.W.2d 210, 213 (Tex. Civ. App.—Austin 1961, no writ); ***Watson v. Todd***, 322 S.W.2d 422, 424 (Tex. Civ. App.—Fort Worth 1959, no writ).

66. See *O'Connor's Fam. Law Handbook*, "Rebutting presumption," ch. 3-C, §3.2.2, p. 288.

67. *See* ***Claveria***, 615 S.W.2d at 165 (presumption of current marriage's validity stands until a previous marriage's validity is established); ***Elder***, 155 Tex. at 31, 282 S.W.2d at 374 (party challenging the validity of the current marriage must prove that the previous marriage had not ended).

68. *See* ***Davis v. Davis***, 521 S.W.2d 603, 605 (Tex. 1975) (presumption that previous marriage was terminated can be rebutted on a showing that divorce did not occur in jurisdictions where the spouse might have reasonably obtained a divorce); ***Rodriguez v. Avalos***, 567 S.W.2d 85, 87 (Tex. Civ. App.—El Paso 1978, no writ) (only necessary to look at jurisdictions where the termination could reasonably have occurred in order to rebut the presumption that it actually did occur in that jurisdiction); ***Caruso v. Lucius***, 448 S.W.2d 711, 715 (Tex. Civ. App.—Austin 1969, writ ref'd n.r.e.) (to rebut the presumption that the previous marriage was terminated, only evidence from jurisdictions where a divorce or annulment might reasonably have taken place needs to be shown). Earlier cases effectively held that the challenging party had to negate every possible means of terminating the earlier marriage. *See* ***Simpson v. Simpson***, 380 S.W.2d 855, 858 (Tex. Civ. App.—Dallas 1964, writ ref'd n.r.e.); ***Cas. Underwriters v. Flores***, 125 S.W.2d 371, 375 (Tex. Civ. App.—Galveston 1939, writ dism'd judgm't cor.).

69. TEX. FAM. CODE §3.003(a); ***Pearson v. Fillingim***, 332 S.W.3d 361, 363 (Tex. 2011); ***Warriner v. Warriner***, 394 S.W.3d 240, 247 (Tex. App.—El Paso 2012, no pet.); *see also* ***Newberry v. Newberry***, 351 S.W.3d 552, 559 (Tex.

3. Undue-influence presumption in fiduciary context. When there is a fiduciary relationship between two parties and the fiduciary obtains an advantage as a result of the relationship, a presumption arises that the fiduciary gained the advantage by undue influence or unfairness.[71] This presumption shifts the burden of persuasion to the fiduciary to disprove undue influence.[72] The policy behind this presumption is to hold those in positions of trust accountable and to protect the security of those who entrust themselves or their property to the administration of others.[73] To some extent, the presumption is also based on access to information because the party relying on the relationship is not in the best position to provide specific information about the fiduciary's activities.[74]

4. Negligence presumption in common-carrier context. When a shipper shows that it delivered property to a common carrier in good condition and that the common carrier later delivered the property in damaged condition, or failed or refused to return the goods on demand, a presumption arises that the carrier's negligence caused the property damage or loss.[75] This presumption places the burden of persuasion on the carrier to show either that it was not negligent or that the cause of the damage or loss

App.—El Paso 2011, no pet.) (community-property presumption applies to liabilities as well as assets). See *O'Connor's Fam. Law Handbook*, "Community-property presumption," ch. 2-A, §3.2, p. 97.

70. TEX. FAM. CODE §3.003(b); *Pearson*, 332 S.W.3d at 363; *Warriner*, 394 S.W.3d at 247; *see also Monroe v. Monroe*, 358 S.W.3d 711, 718 (Tex. App.—San Antonio 2011, pet. denied) (testimony of spouse challenging community-property presumption does not need to be corroborated to meet clear-and-convincing standard, but it may not meet that standard if it is contradicted); *Pace v. Pace*, 160 S.W.3d 706, 714 (Tex. App.—Dallas 2005, pet. denied) (same). See *O'Connor's Fam. Law Handbook*, "Rebutting community-property presumption," ch. 2-A, §3.3, p. 97.

71. Texas Pattern Jury Charges—Business, Consumer, Insurance & Employment (2016), PJC 104.2 cmt.; *see Keck, Mahin & Cate v. Nat'l Union Fire Ins.*, 20 S.W.3d 692, 699 (Tex. 2000) (presumption of unfairness or invalidity arises for contracts between attorneys and clients negotiated during attorney-client relationship); *Cooper v. Lee*, 75 Tex. 114, 120-21, 12 S.W. 483, 486 (1889) (approving jury charge that incorporated a presumption against validity of deal between attorney and client); *Gen. Dynamics v. Torres*, 915 S.W.2d 45, 49 (Tex. App.—El Paso 1995, writ denied) (presumption that interested transactions between corporate fiduciaries and their corporations are unfair on part of the officer or director and fraudulent on the corporation).

72. Texas Pattern Jury Charges—Business, Consumer, Insurance & Employment (2016), PJC 104.2 cmt.; *see Archer v. Griffith*, 390 S.W.2d 735, 739 (Tex. 1964) (attorney who bargains with his client must show transaction was fair); *Cooper*, 75 Tex. at 120-21, 12 S.W. at 486 (same); *Brazosport Bank v. Oak Park Townhouses*, 889 S.W.2d 676, 684 (Tex. App.—Houston [14th Dist.] 1994, writ denied) (when there is a fiduciary relationship, fiduciary must show that he acted fairly and informed the beneficiary of all material facts relating to the challenged transaction). In *Moore v. Texas Bank & Trust Co.*, the court of civil appeals determined the following: "We hold that the fiduciary has the burden of persuasion on the issue of whether the transaction was ultimately fair and equitable." 576 S.W.2d 691, 695 (Tex. Civ. App.—Eastland 1979), *rev'd on other grounds*, 595 S.W.2d 502 (Tex. 1980). In holding that the presumption was not rebutted by the facts of the case, the Texas Supreme Court agreed with the lower court that equity gives the fiduciary "the burden of showing the fairness of the transactions." *Tex. Bank & Tr. Co. v. Moore*, 595 S.W.2d 502, 509 (Tex. 1980).

73. *See Cooper*, 75 Tex. at 120-21, 12 S.W. at 486 (presumption is designed to protect against "dangerous influences arising from the confidential relation of the parties"); *Bell v. Ramirez*, 299 S.W. 655, 658 (Tex. Civ. App.—Austin 1927, writ ref'd) (presumption is based on the "highest considerations of public policy").

74. *See* Lents, *supra* note 57, at 1360 (presumption of invalidity stems from the fiduciary's superior access to information); Basil Stapleton, *The Presumption of Undue Influence*, 17 U. NEW BRUNSWICK L.J. 46, 59 (1967) (presumption is used because of the subtlety of the influence in confidential relationships).

75. *See Travelers Ins. v. Delta Air Lines, Inc.*, 498 S.W.2d 443, 445 (Tex. Civ. App.—Texarkana 1973, no writ); *Strickland Transp. Co. v. Int'l Aerial Mapping Co.*, 423 S.W.2d 676, 677 (Tex. Civ. App.—San Antonio 1968, no writ);

relieves the carrier of liability.[76] Factors supporting this presumption include the balance of probability, the carrier's readier access to evidence of its own care and the cause of the damage or loss, and the carrier's statutory duty to provide safe and speedy transportation.[77]

5. Course-of-employment presumption. When a party demonstrates that a person performed work for another, courts presume that there was an employment relationship and that the employee was acting within the course and scope of the employment.[78] This presumption places the burden of persuasion on the presumed employer[79] because the employer will normally have greater access to the relevant information.[80]

6. Presumption of sanity. When a person's mental capacity or sanity is challenged in a civil proceeding, there is a presumption that the person is sane.[81] This presump-

---

Mo. Pac. R.R. v. Whittenburg & Alston, 380 S.W.2d 733, 734 (Tex. Civ. App.—San Antonio 1964, no writ); *Tex. & Pac. Ry. Co. v. Empacadora de Ciudad Juarez,* 309 S.W.2d 926, 931 (Tex. Civ. App.—El Paso 1957, writ ref'd n.r.e.).

76. *Ryan & Co. v. Mo., K. & T. Ry. Co.,* 65 Tex. 13, 19 (1885); *see Mo. Pac. R.R. v. Elmore & Stahl,* 377 U.S. 134, 137 (1964); *see, e.g., Texarkana & Fort Smith Ry. v. Brass,* 260 S.W. 828, 834 (Tex. Comm'n App. 1924, judgm't adopted) (defendant had burden of proof to show that the goods were not destroyed by his negligence); *Whittenburg & Alston,* 380 S.W.2d at 734 (when shipper shows that the goods were delivered to carrier in good condition, carrier has the burden of establishing that he did not cause the damage).

The exemptions from liability include an act of God, the action of a public enemy, an act of the shipper himself, public authority, or the inherent vice or nature of the goods shipped. *Elmore & Stahl,* 377 U.S. at 137; *see Davis v. Sullivan & Opry,* 258 S.W. 157, 159 (Tex. Comm'n App. 1924, judgm't adopted) (excluding public authority); *Port Terminal R.R. v. Rohm & Haas Co.,* 371 S.W.2d 403, 404 (Tex. Civ. App.—Houston 1963, no writ) (same). Although earlier cases were in conflict, there is no "fire and theft" exception to the general presumption. *Cf. Mayhar v. Triana,* 701 S.W.2d 325, 326-27 (Tex. App.—Eastland 1985, writ ref'd) (presumption of negligence by bailee applies in bailment cases, including those involving fire and theft losses of bailed items).

77. *See* Tex. Transp. Code §7.002 (statutory duty); *Davis,* 258 S.W. at 161 (same; interpreting former Tex. Rev. Civ. Stat. art. 731). Public policy influenced the early common-law rule that included consideration for the inequality of the parties, the compulsion under which the shipper is placed, and the obligation of the carrier to the public. *Hous. & T.C. R.R. v. Burke,* 55 Tex. 323, 333 (1881). The carrier is also in a better position to know "'[a]ll the facts and circumstances upon which [it] may rely to relieve [it] of [its] duty. ... In consequence, the law casts upon [it] the burden of the loss which [it] cannot explain or, explaining, bring within the exceptional case in which [it] is relieved from liability.'" *Elmore & Stahl,* 377 U.S. at 143-44 (quoting *Schnell v. The Vallescura,* 293 U.S. 296, 304 (1934)).

78. *See Empire Gas & Fuel Co. v. Muegge,* 135 Tex. 520, 527-28, 143 S.W.2d 763, 767 (1940) (presumption that employee was working within the course of his employment); *Broaddus v. Long,* 135 Tex. 353, 356, 138 S.W.2d 1057, 1058 (1940) (presumption of both an employment relationship and that the actions occurred in the course of employment); *Taylor, Bastrop & Hous. Ry. Co. v. Warner,* 88 Tex. 642, 648, 32 S.W. 868, 870 (1895); *Brentwood Fin. Corp. v. Lamprecht,* 736 S.W.2d 836, 845 (Tex. App.—San Antonio 1987, writ ref'd n.r.e.).

79. *See Ochoa v. Winerich Motor Sales Co.,* 127 Tex. 542, 548, 94 S.W.2d 416, 418 (1936) (presumed employer must show that no employee-employer relationship existed); *Taylor, Bastrop & Hous. Ry.,* 88 Tex. at 648, 32 S.W. at 870 ("[I]t devolves upon him who claims such exemption [from liability] to make proof of the terms of the contract, showing that the relation of master and servant did not exist."); *Cont'l Moss-Gordin, Inc. v. Martinez,* 480 S.W.2d 800, 803 (Tex. Civ. App.—San Antonio 1972, no writ) (presumed employer must show that employment relationship does not exist); *Tex. Co. v. Freer,* 151 S.W.2d 907, 910 (Tex. Civ. App.—Waco 1941, writ dism'd judgm't cor.) (same); *Buckley v. Gulf Ref. Co.,* 123 S.W.2d 970, 972 (Tex. Civ. App.—Amarillo 1938, writ dism'd judgm't cor.) (same). This presumption differs from the one that says the operator of a vehicle is the owner's agent and is acting within the scope of his employment at the time of an accident. The latter presumption shifts only the burden of production. *See* 1 Ray, *supra* note 7, §97, at 144-45; Lents, *supra* note 57, at 1375-76.

80. *See* Lents, *supra* note 57, at 1375-76 (party without access to evidence should not be forced to produce evidence like the party with access to evidence).

81. *See Handel v. Long Trs.,* 757 S.W.2d 848, 854 (Tex. App.—Texarkana 1988, no writ) (per curiam); *Arnold v. Arnold,* 657 S.W.2d 506, 507 (Tex. App.—Corpus Christi 1983, no writ); *Fuller v. Middleton,* 453 S.W.2d 372, 376 (Tex. Civ. App.—Fort Worth 1970, writ ref'd n.r.e.); *Hall v. Hall,* 352 S.W.2d 765, 767 (Tex. Civ. App.—Houston

tion places the burden of proof on the party asserting lack of mental capacity or sanity,[82] which saves the court's time by recognizing that most persons are capable of managing their own affairs.[83] To some extent, the presumption also serves the policy of protecting parties by ensuring that courts fully consider claims relating to parties' sanity.[84]

7. Other common-law presumptions. Texas has several common-law presumptions that shift the burden of persuasion. For example, the presumption that a transfer of property between family members is a gift has been held rebuttable only by "certain, definite, reliable, and convincing" evidence.[85] In addition, there is a strong common-law presumption against suicide, which places the burden of persuasion and the burden of going forward with the evidence on the party asserting suicide in life-insurance-policy cases.[86]

8. Other statutory presumptions. Texas has several statutory presumptions that shift the burden of persuasion.[87] For example, the presumption of death after an unexplained absence of seven years[88] places the burden of persuasion to rebut the presump-

---

1962, no writ); *Fulcher v. Young*, 189 S.W.2d 28, 32 (Tex. Civ. App.—Austin 1945, writ ref'd w.o.m.); *Kern v. Smith*, 164 S.W.2d 193, 195 (Tex. Civ. App.—Texarkana 1942, writ ref'd w.o.m.); *Redmon v. Leach*, 130 S.W.2d 873, 877 (Tex. Civ. App.—Dallas 1939, writ dism'd judgm't cor.). In probate proceedings involving a will that is not self-proved, however, the proponent of the will must prove that the testator was of sound mind. *See* Tex. Est. Code §256.152(a)(2)(B).

82.   *Handel*, 757 S.W.2d at 854; *Hall*, 352 S.W.2d at 767; *Fulcher*, 189 S.W.2d at 32; *Kern*, 164 S.W.2d at 195.

83.   *See In re Estate of Weeks*, 103 A.2d 43, 48 (N.J. Super. Ct. App. Div. 1954).

84.   Lents, *supra* note 57, at 1354.

85.   *Hall v. Barrett*, 126 S.W.2d 1045, 1048 (Tex. Civ. App.—Fort Worth 1939, no writ); *see Kyles v. Kyles*, 832 S.W.2d 194, 197 (Tex. App.—Beaumont 1992, no writ) (to rebut presumption of a gift, evidence must be clear and convincing).

86.   *See Prudential Ins. v. Krayer*, 366 S.W.2d 779, 780 (Tex. 1963) (presumption against suicide is a "true presumption"); *Reserve Life Ins. v. Estate of Shacklett*, 412 S.W.2d 920, 922 (Tex. Civ. App.—Tyler 1967, writ ref'd n.r.e.) (strong presumption against suicide exists). *But see Hopfer v. Commercial Ins.*, 606 S.W.2d 354, 356 (Tex. Civ. App.—Eastland 1980, writ ref'd n.r.e.) (presumption against suicide only places on the opposing party the burden of producing evidence "from which the jury could reasonably find that deceased committed suicide"; once this burden is met, the presumption is not to be treated as evidence).

87.   There are some statutory presumptions that may shift the burden of persuasion, although the Texas Supreme Court has not explicitly held that they do. For example, the Civil Practice & Remedies Code contains a rebuttable presumption in products-liability actions related to design defects, which appears to shift the burden of persuasion. *See* Tex. Civ. Prac. & Rem. Code §82.008 (rebuttable presumption that manufacturer is not liable for injuries caused by design defects if product complies with certain federal safety standards); *see also Wright v. Ford Motor Co.*, 508 F.3d 263, 273-74 & n.9 (5th Cir. 2007) (discussing difference between presumptions that shift burden of production and those that shift burden of persuasion and suggesting language of §82.008 may indicate that presumption shifts burden of persuasion; not "clear or obvious" that trial court erred in treating presumption as shifting burden of persuasion). The presumption applies only if the safety standard governs the product risk that allegedly caused the harm. Tex. Civ. Prac. & Rem. Code §82.008(a); *see Kia Motors Corp. v. Ruiz*, 432 S.W.3d 865, 873-74 (Tex. 2014).

88.   Tex. Civ. Prac. & Rem. Code §133.001; *see S. Pac. Transp. Co. v. State*, 380 S.W.2d 123, 125 (Tex. Civ. App.—Houston 1964, writ ref'd) (without evidence to show the actual time of death, death of an absent person cannot be inferred to have taken place at any particular time during the seven-year period); *Borden v. Hall*, 255 S.W.2d 920, 927 (Tex. Civ. App.—Beaumont 1951, writ ref'd n.r.e.) (no need to show that a person has been searched for and not found before presumption of death applies).

ARTICLE III

tion on the party against whom it operates.[89] The Family Code places the burden of persuasion on the party seeking to rebut the presumption that property possessed by either spouse during or on the dissolution of marriage is community property.[90] The Family Code also contains a strong presumption favoring parents as the managing conservators of their children.[91]

B. Presumptions that Shift the Burden of Production

Not all presumptions in Texas civil proceedings affect the burden of persuasion. Some operate like those in Federal Rule 301[92] and merely place the burden of production on the party against whom they operate; that party must produce evidence justifying a finding that the presumed fact does not exist.[93] This is the classic bursting-bubble theory of presumptions.[94] Such presumptions may be created by statute, contract, or judicial decision.[95] For example, the mailing of a properly addressed and

89. *See Kan. City Life Ins. v. Fisher*, 83 S.W.2d 1063, 1065 (Tex. Civ. App.—Amarillo 1935, writ dism'd); *see, e.g.*, *Mut. Life Ins. v. Burgess*, 174 S.W.2d 324, 325 (Tex. Civ. App.—Fort Worth 1943, writ ref'd) (defendant introduced testimony of four witnesses that was sufficient to rebut presumption of death).

90. Refer to notes 69-70 *supra* and accompanying text.

91. TEX. FAM. CODE §153.131; *In re R.R.*, 209 S.W.3d 112, 116 (Tex. 2006) (per curiam); *Lewelling v. Lewelling*, 796 S.W.2d 164, 167 (Tex. 1990); *e.g.*, *Danet v. Bhan*, 436 S.W.3d 793, 797 & n.1 (Tex. 2014) (per curiam) (child's foster-care providers rebutted presumption with evidence of mother's specific acts and omissions, as required by jury charge; evidence of mother's drug use, criminal record, failure to provide stable home, abandonment of child, and inconsistent communication with child supported jury finding that her appointment as conservator would substantially impair child's physical health or emotional development). See *O'Connor's Texas Family Law Handbook* (2017), "Nonparent seeking SMC or JMC against parent," ch. 4-E, §15.4.1, p. 500.

92. Refer to notes 27-52 *supra* and accompanying text.

93. *See Chavez v. Kan. City S. Ry. Co.*, 520 S.W.3d 898, 899 (Tex. 2017) (at trial, presumption operates to establish fact until rebutted); *First Nat'l Bank v. Thomas*, 402 S.W.2d 890, 893 (Tex. 1965) (presumption vanishes when opponent produces evidence sufficient to justify a finding against the presumed fact); 1 RAY, *supra* note 7, §53, at 76-77 (both Federal Rules of Evidence and the established Texas rule state that the party opposed to the presumption need only produce evidence sufficient to justify nonexistence of the presumed fact); *see, e.g.*, *Associated Indem. Corp. v. CAT Contracting, Inc.*, 964 S.W.2d 276, 283 n.5 (Tex. 1998) (particular indemnity provision concerning surety's sworn account shifted only the burden of production to demonstrate good faith, not the burden of persuasion); *In re Estate of Glover*, 744 S.W.2d 197, 200 (Tex. App.—Amarillo 1987) (presumption that the deceased destroyed her will could not stand in the face of contrary evidence), *writ denied*, 744 S.W.2d 939 (Tex. 1988). The presumptions and burdens of proof that operate in conventional trials on the merits do not apply to summary-judgment proceedings. *Chavez*, 520 S.W.3d at 900; *Mo.-Kan.-Tex. R.R. v. City of Dallas*, 623 S.W.2d 296, 298 (Tex. 1981).

94. In *General Motors Corp. v. Saenz ex rel. Saenz*, the Texas Supreme Court set out the operation of the Texas bursting-bubble theory of presumptions:

> The presumption [that a user would have read and heeded adequate product warnings or instructions] is subject to the same rules governing presumptions generally. Its effect is to shift the burden of producing evidence to the party against whom it operates. Once that burden is discharged and evidence contradicting the presumption has been offered, the presumption disappears and "is not to be weighed or treated as evidence." The evidence on the issue is then evaluated as it would be in any other case. The presumption has no effect on the burden of persuasion. The facts upon which the presumption was based remain in evidence, of course, and will support any inferences that may be reasonably drawn from them.

873 S.W.2d 353, 359 (Tex. 1993) (citations omitted). Refer to notes 23-24 *supra* and accompanying text.

95. For example, Texas Alcoholic Beverage Code §101.32 states that possession of more than one quart of liquor or more than 24 twelve-ounce bottles of beer is prima facie evidence of possession with intent to sell. The use of the phrase "prima facie evidence" denotes a statutory presumption that shifts the burden of production, but not the burden of persuasion. Once the opposing party produces some evidence that he possessed the liquor for a pur-

ARTICLE III

stamped letter will support the finding that the addressee received the letter.[96] While a party may rebut the presumption by introducing proof of nonreceipt, the unrebutted presumption has the force of a rule of law.[97] A presumption that merely shifts the burden of production is not evidence, and it vanishes whenever a party introduces opposing evidence.[98] The basic facts giving rise to the presumption, however, remain as evidence for the trier of fact to consider.[99]

---

pose other than selling it, the statutory presumption disappears, and the case proceeds solely on the basis of evidence, including the fact of the alcohol possession. *Cf. Tomhave v. Oaks Psychiatric Hosp.*, 82 S.W.3d 381, 386 (Tex. App.—Austin 2002, pet. denied) (discussing rebuttable presumption under TEX. HEALTH & SAFETY CODE §161.134 that plaintiff in retaliatory-employment-termination suit was fired for making report of violation of law; "[e]ven if the presumption is rebutted, the facts surrounding the timing of suspension and termination remain for the finder of fact's consideration"), *disapproved on other grounds*, *Binur v. Jacobo*, 135 S.W.3d 646 (Tex. 2004); *Gold v. City of Coll. Station*, 40 S.W.3d 637, 645 (Tex. App.—Houston [1st Dist.] 2001, pet. granted, judgm't vacated w.r.m.) (discussing rebuttable presumption under Whistleblower Act, TEX. GOV'T CODE §554.004(a); "[o]nce sufficient evidence is produced to support a finding of the non-existence of the presumed fact, the case then proceeds as if no presumption ever existed").

In construing contracts, courts will enforce explicit or implicit rebuttable presumptions to which the parties have agreed. *See Am. Realty Tr., Inc. v. JDN Real Estate-McKinney, L.P.*, 74 S.W.3d 527, 531 (Tex. App.—Dallas 2002, pet. denied) ("A broad arbitration clause, purporting to cover all claims, disputes, and other matters relating to the contract or its breach, creates a presumption of arbitrability.").

Similarly, courts have created presumptions that shift the burden of production. *See Light v. State*, 15 S.W.3d 104, 107 (Tex. Crim. App. 2000) (presumption of regularity is a judicial construct that requires a reviewing court, "absent evidence of impropriety," to indulge every presumption in favor of the regularity of the trial court's judgment).

96. *See Thomas v. Ray*, 889 S.W.2d 237, 238 (Tex. 1994) ("When a letter, properly addressed and postage prepaid, is mailed, there exists a presumption that the notice was duly received by the addressee."); *Hardman v. State*, 614 S.W.2d 123, 128 (Tex. Crim. App. [Panel Op.] 1981) ("When a letter or other mail matter is properly addressed and mailed with postage prepaid, there is a rebuttable presumption of fact that it was received by the addressee as soon as it could have been transmitted to him in the ordinary course of the mails."); *see, e.g.*, *McMillin v. State Farm Lloyds*, 180 S.W.3d 183, 206 (Tex. App.—Austin 2005, pet. denied) (without evidence of proper address or postage, defendant was not entitled to any presumption that plaintiffs received insurance check).

97. *Thomas*, 889 S.W.2d at 238; *see Cliff v. Huggins*, 724 S.W.2d 778, 780 (Tex. 1987) (unrebutted presumption that notice of a trial was received if properly sent has force of a rule of law); *Gonzalez v. Stevenson*, 791 S.W.2d 250, 252 (Tex. App.—Corpus Christi 1990, no writ) (executing a certificate of service under Texas Rule of Civil Procedure 21a raises the presumption that service was proper and, without evidence to the contrary, is prima facie evidence of service); *Krchnak v. Fulton*, 759 S.W.2d 524, 528 (Tex. App.—Amarillo 1988, writ denied) (once the production of a certificate of service under Texas Rule of Civil Procedure 21a has created a presumption that notice was served, it has the force of law unless contrary evidence is shown), *disapproved on other grounds*, *Carpenter v. Cimarron Hydrocarbons Corp.*, 98 S.W.3d 682 (Tex. 2002); *see, e.g.*, *Khalilnia v. Fed. Home Loan Mortg. Corp.*, No. 01-12-00573-CV (Tex. App.—Houston [1st Dist.] 2013, pet. denied) (memo op.; 3-21-13) (properly addressed and stamped first-class mailer that was unreturned raised rebuttable presumption that letter was received; because addressee presented no evidence to rebut presumption, there was no fact issue about delivery).

98. *See Saenz*, 873 S.W.2d at 359 (when evidence contradicting presumption is offered, presumption disappears and is not treated as evidence); *Cliff*, 724 S.W.2d at 780 (a presumption is not evidence; once evidence is shown that a letter was not received, the presumption disappears); *Empire Gas & Fuel Co. v. Muegge*, 135 Tex. 520, 528, 143 S.W.2d 763, 767 (1940) ("It is settled in this state, and by weight of authority elsewhere, that such presumption is not evidence but rather a rule of procedure or an 'administrative assumption' which 'vanishes' or is 'put to flight' when positive evidence to the contrary is introduced."); *Tyler Car & Truck Ctr. v. Empire Fire & Marine Ins.*, 2 S.W.3d 482, 485 (Tex. App.—Tyler 1999, pet. denied) (name on car title certificate raises only "'an administrative presumption' of ownership … 'which vanishes when positive evidence to the contrary is introduced'" (quoting *Minter v. Joplin*, 535 S.W.2d 737, 739 (Tex. Civ. App.—Amarillo 1976, no writ))); *Langdale v. Villamil*, 813 S.W.2d 187, 191 (Tex. App.—Houston [14th Dist.] 1991, no writ) (presumption cannot be maintained when rebutted by evidence).

99. Refer to note 18 *supra* and accompanying text.

ARTICLE III

Presumptions shifting the burden of production in a civil case neither require nor permit any instruction on the existence or role of presumptions.[100] If a party does not introduce any evidence to rebut the basic fact, the court should instruct the jury to find the presumed fact, either conditionally or absolutely.[101] Conversely, if a party introduces rebuttal evidence, the presumption disappears and the jury should receive no special instruction on the use of the evidence.[102] The presumption will have no practical effect on the case when the party against whom the presumption operates already has both the burdens of production and persuasion.[103] Also, when the presumption disappears and the remaining evidence gives rise to opposing inferences of fact (each of which is equally reasonable) without indicating that one fact is more probable than the other, neither fact can be inferred.[104] In that instance, the party with the burden of proof loses on the issue.

Two or more presumptions may apply to a single situation and conflict such that "the presumed fact of one presumption is inconsistent with the presumed fact of another presumption."[105] If two or more presumptions conflict, courts will apply the presumption that is more logical and based on more important policy considerations.[106] Although no Texas case has so held, Rule 302(b) of the Uniform Rules of Evidence states, with regard to inconsistent presumptions, that "[i]f considerations of policy are of equal weight neither presumption applies."[107]

C. Irrebuttable Presumptions

Some Texas statutory presumptions are conclusive or irrebuttable; that is, they operate as a complete bar to action.[108] Once a party proves the basic facts giving rise to

---

100. *See **Kroger Tex. Ltd. P'ship v. Suberu**,* 113 S.W.3d 588, 605 (Tex. App.—Dallas 2003) ("Including a presumption in a jury charge which has been rebutted by controverting facts is an improper comment on the weight of the evidence."), *rev'd on other grounds*, 216 S.W.3d 788 (Tex. 2006).

101. *See **United Founders Life Ins. v. Carey**,* 347 S.W.2d 295, 307-08 (Tex. Civ. App.—Austin 1961), *rev'd on other grounds*, 363 S.W.2d 236 (Tex. 1962).

102. *See **Southland Life Ins. v. Greenwade**,* 138 Tex. 450, 456-57, 159 S.W.2d 854, 858 (1942) (basic facts retain their evidentiary power after the presumption has been rebutted); ***Pete v. Stevens***, 582 S.W.2d 892, 895 (Tex. Civ. App.—San Antonio 1979, writ ref'd n.r.e.) (after a presumption vanishes, the facts that gave rise to the presumption remain as evidence).

103. *See **McGuire v. Brown**,* 580 S.W.2d 425, 431 (Tex. Civ. App.—Austin 1979, writ ref'd n.r.e.); 1 RAY, *supra* note 7, §57, at 92.

104. *$9,050 v. State*, 874 S.W.2d 158, 162 (Tex. App.—Houston [14th Dist.] 1994, writ denied).

105. UNIF. R. EVID. 301(2) (1999).

106. For example, an issue may arise about whether two people are married. Proof of their ceremonial marriage raises a presumption that they are legally married. *See* TEX. FAM. CODE §1.101 (every marriage entered into in Texas is presumed valid). Proof of one spouse's earlier common-law marriage also raises a presumption of that marriage's legality. *See id.* When evidence is introduced to show both of these basic facts—a person's common-law marriage, followed by a ceremonial marriage to someone else—"the most recent marriage is presumed to be valid as against each marriage that precedes the most recent marriage until one who asserts the validity of a prior marriage proves the validity of the prior marriage." TEX. FAM. CODE §1.102. Refer to notes 63-70 *supra* and accompanying text.

107. UNIF. R. EVID. 302(b) (1999).

108. For a discussion of the constitutionality of irrebuttable statutory presumptions, focusing on federal and Virginia law, see James J. Duane, *The Constitutionality of Irrebuttable Presumptions*, 19 REGENT U. L. REV. 149 (2006-2007).

the presumption, the proposition is proved and cannot be rebutted by any other evidence.[109] Irrebuttable or conclusive presumptions are not really presumptions at all, but rather rules of substantive law.[110] For example, if no renewal or extension of a recorded lien is made within four years after its maturity date, there is a conclusive presumption that the lien has been paid.[111] Similarly, a Local Government Code provision sets out a conclusive presumption that a municipal annexation ordinance has been adopted with the consent of all appropriate persons if the ordinance has not been challenged within two years after its enactment.[112]

Irrebuttable presumptions can also be judicially created. For example, the Texas Supreme Court has held that if an attorney works on a case, there is an irrebuttable presumption that the attorney gains confidential information about the case.[113] When the attorney moves to a new firm, a second irrebuttable presumption arises that the attorney will share the confidential information with members of the new firm.[114] If a legal assistant or other nonattorney employee works on a case, there is an irrebuttable presumption that the nonattorney gains confidential information about the case.[115] But

---

109. *See In re Am. Home Prods. Corp.*, 985 S.W.2d 68, 74-75 (Tex. 1998) (in attorney-disqualification proceeding, there is a conclusive presumption that a lawyer or legal assistant who worked on a particular case shared in the client's confidences and secrets).

110. *See* 2 GRAHAM, *supra* note 48, §301:9, at 383. Refer to notes 136-138 *infra* and accompanying text.

111. *See* TEX. CIV. PRAC. & REM. CODE §16.035(d) (at the end of the four-year limitations period, real-property lien and power of sale to enforce it become void), §16.036(d) (maturity date stated in original instrument or in recorded renewal and extension is conclusive evidence of maturity date of obligation); *Cadle Co. v. Butler*, 951 S.W.2d 901, 909 (Tex. App.—Corpus Christi 1997, no pet.) (a bona fide third person is entitled to the statutory presumption that the debt was paid and that the lien became void and ceased to exist).

112. TEX. LOC. GOV'T CODE §43.901.

113. *In re Guar. Ins. Servs., Inc.*, 343 S.W.3d 130, 134 (Tex. 2011) (per curiam); *In re Columbia Valley Healthcare Sys., L.P.*, 320 S.W.3d 819, 824 (Tex. 2010); *see Phoenix Founders, Inc. v. Marshall*, 887 S.W.2d 831, 833 (Tex. 1994); *NCNB Tex. Nat'l Bank v. Coker*, 765 S.W.2d 398, 400 (Tex. 1989) (orig. proceeding). Even if an attorney at a firm does not work on a particular case, there is an irrebuttable presumption that the attorney gains confidential information about the case—that is, confidences are imputed from one attorney to another. *See In re Mitcham*, 133 S.W.3d 274, 276 (Tex. 2004); *Nat'l Med. Enters., Inc. v. Godbey*, 924 S.W.2d 123, 131 (Tex. 1996). See *O'Connor's Texas Rules * Civil Trials* (2017), "Rule 1.09 – attorney conflict of interest," ch. 1-H, §8.2.1(1), p. 71.

114. *In re Guar. Ins. Servs.*, 343 S.W.3d at 134; *In re Columbia Valley Healthcare*, 320 S.W.3d at 824; *Phoenix Founders*, 887 S.W.2d at 834. The Fifth Circuit, however, has held that if there is a presumption that knowledge of confidential information has been imputed from one attorney to another, that presumption can be rebutted for an attorney moving to a new firm. *See In re ProEducation Int'l, Inc.*, 587 F.3d 296, 300-01 (5th Cir. 2009); *see also* TEX. DISCIPLINARY R. PROF'L CONDUCT 1.09 cmt. (if "lawyers cease to be members of the same firm as the lawyer [disqualified under Rule 1.09(a)] without personally coming within its restrictions, they thereafter may undertake representation against the lawyer's former client unless prevented from doing so by some other [disciplinary rule of professional conduct]"). If the attorney, while at the former firm, did not participate in the representation of or receive any confidential information about a client of another attorney at the firm, the attorney can represent a party opposing that client when the attorney joins a new firm. *See In re ProEducation Int'l*, 587 F.3d at 301-03. The Fifth Circuit noted that the Texas Supreme Court has not addressed how the imputed-knowledge issue in Texas Disciplinary Rule of Professional Conduct 1.09 applies to the "migrating attorney scenario." *See In re ProEducation Int'l*, 587 F.3d at 300 & n.3.

115. *In re Guar. Ins. Servs.*, 343 S.W.3d at 134; *In re Columbia Valley Healthcare*, 320 S.W.3d at 824; *In re Mitcham*, 133 S.W.3d at 276; *In re Am. Home Prods. Corp.*, 985 S.W.2d 68, 74 (Tex. 1998).

when the nonattorney moves to a new firm, a *rebuttable* presumption arises that the nonattorney will share the information with members of the new firm.[116]

IV. CONTRAST BETWEEN FEDERAL RULE 301 & PRESUMPTIONS IN TEXAS CIVIL PROCEEDINGS

All presumptions under Federal Rule 301 shift only the burden of production, regardless of the strength of the policy considerations underlying the presumptions.[117] The rule expressly provides that the burden of persuasion does not shift, but remains throughout the trial on the party who originally had it.[118] In contrast, several Texas civil presumptions clearly operate to shift the burden of persuasion, while others are only sometimes held to do so.[119] Thus, adoption of the federal rule in Texas would have significantly altered the effect of certain Texas presumptions.

---

116. *In re Guar. Ins. Servs.*, 343 S.W.3d at 134; *In re Mitcham*, 133 S.W.3d at 276; *see* **In re Columbia Valley Healthcare**, 320 S.W.3d at 824; **Phoenix Founders**, 887 S.W.2d at 834-35. This presumption may be rebutted by a showing that:

> (1) the assistant was instructed not to perform work on any matter on which she worked during her prior employment, or regarding which the assistant has information related to her former employer's representation, and (2) the firm took "other reasonable steps to ensure that the [assistant] does not work in connection with matters on which the [assistant] worked during the prior employment, absent client consent."

In re Columbia Valley Healthcare, 320 S.W.3d at 824 (quoting *In re Am. Home Prods.*, 985 S.W.2d at 75). Thus, to avoid disqualification, the new firm must use effective screening measures. *See In re Columbia Valley Healthcare*, 320 S.W.3d at 824. The supreme court held that "the other reasonable measures must include, at a minimum, formal, institutionalized screening measures that render the possibility of the nonlawyer having contact with the file less likely"; an informal warning, even if repeated, is not sufficient. *Id.* at 826; *see In re Guar. Ins. Servs.*, 343 S.W.3d at 134. The ultimate effectiveness of the screening measures is not determinative. *In re Guar. Ins. Servs.*, 343 S.W.3d at 135. If the nonattorney actually worked on the matter at the employer's directive, the presumption is still rebuttable if the employer reasonably should not have known about the conflict of interest. *E.g., id.* (firm was not disqualified, even though assistant actually worked on matter, because firm had effective screening measures, had no reason to know of conflict, and ordered assistant to stop working on matter once conflict was known). The presumption is conclusive, however, if (1) information relating to the party's earlier representation was in fact disclosed to the employer, (2) the employer's screening is or would be ineffective, (3) the employer necessarily will need the nonattorney employee to work on the current matter, or (4) the employee actually performed work, including clerical work, on the current matter at the employer's directive and the employer reasonably should have known about the conflict of interest. *In re Columbia Valley Healthcare*, 320 S.W.3d at 828; *see In re Guar. Ins. Servs.*, 343 S.W.3d at 135.

Whether the standards and presumptions that apply to former nonattorney employees of opposing counsel also apply to former nonattorney employees of the opposing party depends on the following criteria: (1) whether the nonattorney employee was hired specifically for litigation purposes and (2) whether the employee reported directly to the opposing party's attorneys. *See In re RSR Corp.*, 475 S.W.3d 775, 782 (Tex. 2015) (orig. proceeding). In determining whether to apply these standards and presumptions, a court will look not only to the employee's former job title but also to her former duties. *See id.* at 780-81. If the employee performed the same duties that a full-time legal assistant of a law firm or a party's legal department would, then the same standards and presumptions applicable to nonattorney employees of opposing counsel would apply; however, if the duties are not the same, then the employee is likely to be considered merely a fact witness, and the standards and presumptions would not apply. *See id.* For further discussion of these presumptions, see **O'Connor's Texas Rules**, "Rule 5.03 – work performed by nonattorney employee," ch. 1-H, §8.2.1(2), p. 73.

117. *See* Fed. R. Evid. 301.

118. *Id.*

119. Refer to notes 56-91 *supra* and accompanying text.

An example may help to illustrate the difference in how "strong" presumptions operate under Federal Rule 301 and Texas law. Suppose both jurisdictions recognize a strong public policy supporting children's legitimacy. Consequently, both have created a presumption that a child born to lawfully married parents is legitimate. In a particular paternity suit, the mother testifies that when she gave birth to her daughter Susan, she was married to the defendant. The defendant then testifies that Susan is not his daughter.

Under Federal Rule 301, the presumption merely shifts the burden of production to the defendant, who must offer evidence to rebut that presumption. At best, a federal judge could instruct the jury that it "may infer" that Susan is legitimate from the fact that her mother was married to the defendant when Susan was born. The plaintiff, however, must still prove by a preponderance of the evidence that Susan is legitimate. Even though the federal presumption expresses a strong public policy, it carries very little weight.

In Texas, however, a strong public-policy presumption shifts the burden of persuasion to the opposing party. In the above example, once the legitimacy presumption is invoked by proof of the basic fact of marriage, the defendant would be required to rebut the presumption that Susan is legitimate by a preponderance of the evidence.[120] While the federal rule treats all presumptions equally by according them relatively little weight,[121] the Texas method allows the Legislature and courts to establish and maintain presumptions of different weight and effect and to vary the degree of evidence necessary to rebut those presumptions in accordance with their underlying public policies.[122]

Moreover, Federal Rule 301 presents an anomaly—a result of the functional similarities between presumptions and affirmative defenses—that could have unforeseen effects on the substantive law of any jurisdiction that adopts it. The judicial power to allocate burdens of persuasion for various issues presented in civil trials is well established[123] and has been exercised in response to a variety of factors,[124] a number of which are identical to those underlying the creation of presumptions.[125] In this respect, presumptions and affirmative defenses often represent opposite sides of the same

---

120. *See* TEX. FAM. CODE §160.204(b) & cmt., §160.601 cmt. Refer to notes 61-62 *supra* and accompanying text.

121. *See* 2 McCORMICK ON EVIDENCE, *supra* note 5, §344, at 518-19. Refer to notes 27-52 *supra* and accompanying text. Federal courts have been willing to find that certain federal statutes create presumptions stronger than those in Rule 301. 2 McCORMICK ON EVIDENCE, *supra* note 5, §344, at 518-19.

122. Refer to note 53 *supra* and accompanying text.

123. *See* Cleary, *supra* note 10, at 11 (policy, fairness, and probability are issues the court should consider in allocating the burden of persuasion); Fleming James, Jr., *Burdens of Proof*, 47 VA. L. REV. 51, 52 (1961) (through the allocation of the burden of persuasion, the court helps members of the jury who may be confused). *Cf.* FLEMING JAMES, JR., ET AL., CIVIL PROCEDURE §7.15, at 342 (4th ed. 1992) (judge, not jury, allocates burden of production on each issue).

124. For a list of factors affecting the allocation of burdens of proof, see JAMES ET AL., *supra* note 123, §7.16, at 343-45, and 2 McCORMICK ON EVIDENCE, *supra* note 5, §337, at 473-77.

125. Refer to notes 11-17 *supra* and accompanying text.

coin because they rely on the same policies and frequently produce the same practical results. For example, a presumption that there is sufficient consideration to support a written contract may shift the burden of persuasion to the party claiming failure of consideration.[126] Conversely, failure of consideration in a written contract may be held as an affirmative defense on which the defendant has the burden of persuasion.[127] Similarly, to say "that there is a 'presumption of legitimacy that allocates or shifts the burden of persuasion' to the defendant and that there is an 'affirmative defense of illegitimacy' that requires the defendant to prove the fact is to make functionally identical statements."[128]

On the other hand, Federal Rule 301 may give greater effect than Texas courts traditionally have to presumptions that affect only the burden of production.[129] If a federal judge tells a jury that it "may infer" the existence of the presumed fact from evidence of the basic facts, even when the opponent has offered evidence rebutting the presumed fact, this instruction (singling out specific evidence for emphasis) makes the federal presumption slightly stronger.[130] A Texas court will not give an instruction on a production-shifting presumption once rebuttal evidence is introduced.[131]

The drafters of the Texas Rules of Civil Evidence rejected the federal approach to presumptions because of (1) the difficulties and confusion encountered in federal courts with cases decided under the rule, (2) the collateral consequences of leveling all presumptions to the same burden-of-production common denominator, and (3) the federal rule's possible deviation from the true bursting-bubble theory of presumptions with a "may infer" jury instruction.[132] They decided not to adopt any rules for presumptions in Texas civil cases, leaving the issue to the Legislature and courts.

V. PRESUMPTIONS IN CRIMINAL PROCEEDINGS

As originally drafted, the Federal Rules included Rule 303, Presumptions in Criminal Cases.[133] Although there was no opposition to its substantive provisions, the House

---

126. See **City of San Antonio v. Lane**, 32 Tex. 405, 416 (1869); **Dyer v. Metallic Bldg. Co.**, 410 S.W.2d 56, 59 (Tex. Civ. App.—Tyler 1966, no writ).

127. See **Loe v. Murphy**, 611 S.W.2d 449, 451 (Tex. Civ. App.—Dallas 1980, writ ref'd n.r.e.); **Green v. Enen**, 270 S.W. 929, 931 (Tex. Civ. App.—San Antonio 1925, writ dism'd).

128. Allen, *supra* note 9, at 850 (a presumption that allocates the burden of persuasion is simply an alternative label for an affirmative defense).

129. Refer to notes 92-107 *supra* and accompanying text.

130. For a discussion of different instructions that federal judges could give juries about presumptions, *see* 2 McCormick on Evidence, *supra* note 5, §344, at 512-14.

131. See **Hailes v. Gentry**, 520 S.W.2d 555, 559 (Tex. Civ. App.—El Paso 1975, no writ); *see also* 1 Ray, *supra* note 7, §57 (instructions about presumptions tend to mislead and confuse the jury).

132. Refer to notes 51-52 *supra* and accompanying text.

133. Fed. R. Evid. 303 (1972 proposed final draft), 56 F.R.D. 183, 212 (1973), read as follows:
   (a) Scope. Except as otherwise provided by Act of Congress, in criminal cases, presumptions against an accused, recognized at common law or created by statute, including statutory provisions that certain facts are prima facie evidence of other facts or of guilt, are governed by this rule.
   (b) Submission to jury. The judge is not authorized to direct the jury to find a presumed fact against the accused. When the presumed fact establishes guilt or is an element of the offense or negatives a

of Representatives eliminated Federal Rule 303 because the House expected that a revised federal criminal code would deal with the topic of presumptions in criminal cases.[134] Unfortunately, Congress has not addressed presumptions in revisions to the criminal code, and judicial decisions alone have determined presumptions' scope and applicability in criminal proceedings. This failure has resulted in the piecemeal, ad hoc development of principles for using evidentiary presumptions in federal criminal proceedings.[135]

A. Nature of Presumption or Inference

1. Conclusive presumptions. A conclusive or irrebuttable presumption "relieves the State of its burden of persuasion by removing the presumed element from the case entirely if the State proves the predicate facts."[136] Irrebuttable presumptions are really substantive rules of law in which the law deems that proof of fact X proves fact Y.[137] An irrebuttable presumption that is part of the substantive law will not violate a defendant's due-process rights if the presumption is rationally related to a legitimate governmental interest in the context of the particular case, and the government does not use the presumption to prove a disputed element of its case.[138] For example, in the Drug Abuse Prevention and Control Act there is an implicit irrebuttable presumption that all narcotics sales within 1,000 feet of school property have an especially detrimental effect on children that justifies increasing the penalty for drug sales in those locations.[139] Because there is a rational connection between the basic fact (drug sales

---

defense, the judge may submit the question of guilt or of the existence of the presumed fact to the jury, if, but only if, a reasonable juror on the evidence as a whole, including the evidence of the basic facts, could find guilt or the presumed fact beyond a reasonable doubt. When the presumed fact has a lesser effect, its existence may be submitted to the jury if the basic facts are supported by substantial evidence, or are otherwise established, unless the evidence as a whole negatives the existence of the presumed fact.

(c) **Instructing the jury.** Whenever the existence of a presumed fact against the accused is submitted to the jury, the judge shall give an instruction that the law declares that the jury may regard the basic facts as sufficient evidence of the presumed fact but does not require it to do so. In addition, if the presumed fact establishes guilt or is an element of the offense or negatives a defense, the judge shall instruct the jury that its existence must, on all the evidence, be proved beyond a reasonable doubt.

By its own terms, Federal Rule 303 would have applied only to presumptions directed against the defendant in a criminal case. Those presumptions directed against the government would have fallen under Federal Rule 301. *See* 1 WEINSTEIN & BERGER, *supra* note 4, §303.03, at 303-9.

134. *See* 1 WEINSTEIN & BERGER, *supra* note 4, §303App.01[3], at 303App.-4 (House eliminated Rule 303 because it expected to deal with the matter in different legislation).

135. *See* 2 McCORMICK ON EVIDENCE, *supra* note 5, §347, at 530-36 (explaining how U.S. Supreme Court developed the rules on mandatory and conclusive presumptions).

136. *Francis v. Franklin*, 471 U.S. 307, 317 (1985); *see Neder v. United States*, 527 U.S. 1, 10 (1999) (a conclusive presumption directs the jury to presume an ultimate element of the offense based on certain predicate facts: "[l]ike an omission, a conclusive presumption deters the jury from considering any evidence other than that related to the predicate facts"); *see also Brown v. State*, 122 S.W.3d 794, 799 (Tex. Crim. App. 2003) (discussing *Francis* and mandatory presumptions in context of improper judicial comments to jury).

137. *See Sandstrom v. Montana*, 442 U.S. 510, 517 (1979) (irrebuttable presumption is a mandatory directive from the court to find the presumed fact once a party convinces the trier of fact that the basic facts exist).

138. *See generally* Duane, *supra* note 108. Refer to notes 153-154 *infra* and accompanying text.

139. *See* 21 U.S.C. §860(a).

made in close proximity to a school) and the presumed fact (a detrimental effect on the health and safety of schoolchildren), and because the statute penalizes for the basic fact and not the presumed fact, the statute does not violate due-process standards.[140] A statute that triggered an increased penalty whenever a particular drug sale had a detrimental effect on children and instructed courts and juries to presume this detrimental effect if the sale occurred within 1,000 feet of a school would contain an irrebuttable evidentiary presumption in violation of *Sandstrom v. Montana*.[141]

2. Mandatory rebuttable presumptions. A mandatory rebuttable presumption requires the jury, if it is convinced that the basic facts trigger the presumption, to find the elemental fact unless the defendant offers evidence rebutting the presumed connection between the two facts.[142] Mandatory rebuttable presumptions fall into two subcategories: those that shift the burden of production and those that shift the burden of persuasion.[143] The first type requires that the defendant come forward with "some" evidence, but the entire burden of persuasion remains on the government.[144] The second type requires that the jury find the elemental or presumed fact unless the defendant proves the contrary by "some quantum of proof," thus shifting the burden of persuasion on that element to the defendant.[145] Mandatory presumptions that relieve the government of the burden of persuasion on an element of the offense are unconstitutional because they violate the defendant's due-process rights.[146]

3. Permissive inferences. A permissive inference (or permissive presumption) is a conclusion that the law permits the jury to draw if it finds a given set of facts (as opposed to a mandatory presumption, which is a conclusion that the law directs the jury to draw once it finds basic facts).[147] Such an inference violates the Due Process Clause "only if the suggested conclusion is not one that reason and common sense justify in light of the proven facts before the jury."[148]

---

140. *See, e.g.*, **United States v. Crew**, 916 F.2d 980, 983 (5th Cir. 1990) (upholding an irrebuttable presumption that selling narcotics in the vicinity of an elementary school endangers schoolchildren because it is rationally related to the government's legitimate goal of protecting schoolchildren); **United States v. Nieves**, 608 F. Supp. 1147, 1149 (S.D.N.Y. 1985) (allowing an irrebuttable presumption that narcotics sales within 1,000 feet of a school have a detrimental effect on schoolchildren). Refer to notes 162-165 *infra* and accompanying text.

141. *See Sandstrom*, 442 U.S. at 524 (State must prove every element of offense beyond a reasonable doubt; presumption cannot shift burden of persuasion on an essential element).

142. *See Cty. Ct. of Ulster Cty., N.Y. v. Allen*, 442 U.S. 140, 157 (1979).

143. *Id.* at 157 n.16.

144. *See id.*

145. *Sandstrom*, 442 U.S. at 517.

146. *Francis v. Franklin*, 471 U.S. 307, 314 (1985); *see Sandstrom*, 442 U.S. at 524. Refer to note 161 *infra* and accompanying text. The *Francis* Court did not address the constitutionality of a mandatory presumption that shifts only the burden of production to the defendant. 471 U.S. at 314 n.3.

147. *Francis*, 471 U.S. at 314; *Allen*, 442 U.S. at 157; *United States v. Burns*, 597 F.2d 939, 943 n.7 (5th Cir. 1979); *see Pigee v. Israel*, 670 F.2d 690, 693 (7th Cir. 1982); **Willis v. State**, 790 S.W.2d 307, 310 (Tex. Crim. App. 1990); *see also United States v. Thomas*, 728 F.2d 313, 320-21 & n.3 (6th Cir. 1984) (inference of intent is allowed, but presumption of intent is not). The Supreme Court generally uses the terms "permissive inference" and "permissive presumption" as synonyms. *See Allen*, 442 U.S. at 157; *see also* BLACK'S LAW DICTIONARY 1377 (10th ed. 2014) (permissive presumption is "[a]lso termed *permissive inference*").

148. *Francis*, 471 U.S. at 314-15; *see Allen*, 442 U.S. at 157. Refer to notes 162-163 *infra* and accompanying text.

B. Constitutional Concerns

The constitutional validity of any presumption used in a criminal proceeding raises a due-process issue involving an evidentiary presumption's effect on the burden of proof for each element of the offense. "[T]he Due Process Clause protects the accused against conviction except upon proof beyond a reasonable doubt of every fact necessary to constitute the crime with which he is charged."[149] On the other hand, it is constitutionally permissible to give a criminal defendant the burden of proof for an affirmative defense (e.g., insanity[150] or self-defense[151]). One conceptual difficulty, then, is separating affirmative defenses—which constitutionally shift the burden of production or persuasion to a defendant—from evidentiary presumptions.[152]

Due process is violated if a presumption shifts to a criminal defendant the burden of persuasion about a critical fact or an element of the offense.[153] Therefore, courts cannot instruct a jury to use any evidentiary presumption that would relieve the government of its burden of persuasion beyond a reasonable doubt on every essential element of the offense.[154]

A trio of Supreme Court cases has created a three-step analysis to decide whether a specific presumption or inference violates due process.[155] First, the court must determine the nature of the presumption or inference.[156] Second, the court must analyze jury instructions as a whole to determine whether they create a mandatory presumption, which shifts the burden of persuasion to the defendant, or merely a permissive inference.[157] Jury instructions beginning with "You may, but are not required to, infer …" create a permissive inference and are constitutionally acceptable.[158] Jury instruc-

---

149. *In re Winship*, 397 U.S. 358, 364 (1970).

150. *Leland v. Oregon*, 343 U.S. 790, 799 (1952).

151. *Martin v. Ohio*, 480 U.S. 228, 236 (1987).

152. *See Patterson v. New York*, 432 U.S. 197, 210 (1977) (Due Process Clause limits extent to which state legislatures can constitutionally reallocate burdens of proof on some elements of crimes by labeling those elements affirmative defenses).

153. *See Francis*, 471 U.S. at 313; *Mullaney v. Wilbur*, 421 U.S. 684, 701-02 (1975).

154. *Francis*, 471 U.S. at 313; *see Sandstrom v. Montana*, 442 U.S. 510, 524 (1979); *Cty. Ct. of Ulster Cty., N.Y. v. Allen*, 442 U.S. 140, 156 (1979).

155. *See Francis*, 471 U.S. at 313-25; *Sandstrom*, 442 U.S. at 514-19; *Allen*, 442 U.S. at 157-63; *see also Ward v. State*, 72 S.W.3d 413, 419-20 (Tex. App.—Fort Worth 2002, no pet.) (discussing constitutional distinction between mandatory presumptions and permissive inferences).

156. *Sandstrom*, 442 U.S. at 514. Refer to notes 136-148 *supra* and accompanying text.

157. The focus is on how a reasonable juror would have understood the instructions. *See Francis*, 471 U.S. at 315-16; *Sandstrom*, 442 U.S. at 514. The court examines any ambiguity in a particular phrase by referring to the entire charge to determine whether a reasonable juror might conclude that any burden had shifted to the defendant. *See Francis*, 471 U.S. at 315.

158. *See, e.g.*, *United States v. Graham*, 858 F.2d 986, 992 (5th Cir. 1988) (the sentence "'[t]he jury may draw the inference'" is a constitutionally permissible instruction); *United States v. Thomas*, 728 F.2d 313, 320 & n.3 (6th Cir. 1984) (court upheld the following: "You may consider it reasonable to draw the inference and find that the person intends the natural and probable consequences of acts knowingly done, or knowingly omitted. … [I]t's entirely up to you to decide what facts you find from the evidence."). The court in *United States v. Gaines* upheld a charge that stated the following:

tions beginning with "The law presumes …" generally create a mandatory presumption, either rebuttable or conclusive, and are unconstitutional.[159] As a practical rule, the jury instructions should never even imply that the defendant has any duty to rebut the presumption or the basic facts. Third, the jury instructions must leave the jury free to accept or reject the elemental fact and must impose no evidentiary burden on the criminal defendant.[160] Any mandatory presumption in a criminal case that deals with an elemental fact is unconstitutional because it would relieve the government of its constitutionally required burden of proving every element of an offense beyond a reasonable doubt.[161]

A separate due-process issue that courts must confront when using presumptions in criminal proceedings concerns the logical "fit" between the basic facts and the presumed fact. Not all permissive presumptions or inferences will automatically be constitutional. Under the Due Process Clause, there must be a "rational connection" between the basic facts proved and the ultimate fact presumed. The latter must be "more likely than not to flow from" the former.[162] A permissive inference violates the Due Process Clause unless it is justified by reason, experience, and common sense in light of the particular facts proved.[163] Thus, a presumption in criminal proceedings must satisfy a conclusion that "it can at least be said with substantial assurance that the presumed fact is more likely than not to flow from the proved fact on which it is made to depend"[164] as supported in the record, as well as a conclusion that the presumption is valid in most cases.[165]

[W]henever the fact appears beyond a reasonable doubt from the evidence in the case that the defendant signed his income tax return, the jury may draw the inference and find that the defendant had knowledge of the contents of the return. Whether or not the jury draws such an inference is left entirely to the jury.

690 F.2d 849, 853 (11th Cir. 1982).

159. *E.g.*, *Sandstrom*, 442 U.S. at 515, 524 (instruction that stated "'[t]he law presumes that a person intends the ordinary consequences of his voluntary acts'" was unconstitutional); *see, e.g.*, *Carella v. California*, 491 U.S. 263, 265-66 (1989) (instruction that stated "a person 'shall be presumed to have embezzled' a vehicle if it is not returned within five days of the expiration of the rental agreement; and second, that 'intent to commit theft by fraud is presumed' from failure to return rented property within 20 days of demand" was unconstitutional); *Francis*, 471 U.S. at 315-16, 325 (instruction that stated "'[t]he acts of a person of sound mind and discretion are presumed to be the product of a person's will, but the presumption may be rebutted'" and "'[a] person of sound mind and discretion is presumed to intend the natural and probable consequences of his acts, but the presumption may be rebutted'" was unconstitutional).

160. *See Allen*, 442 U.S. at 160-62 (allowing a permissive presumption or inference).

161. *See Carella*, 491 U.S. at 265-66; *Garrett v. State*, 220 S.W.3d 926, 930 (Tex. Crim. App. 2007).

162. *Allen*, 442 U.S. at 165; *Leary v. United States*, 395 U.S. 6, 36 (1969); *see Tot v. United States*, 319 U.S. 463, 467-68 (1943) (there must be a rational connection, and the basic fact should tend to be evidence of the presumed fact). *See generally* 21B WRIGHT & GRAHAM, *supra* note 19, §5148 (discussing historical evolution of "rational connection" test).

163. *Francis*, 471 U.S. at 314-15; *United States v. Washington*, 819 F.2d 221, 225 (9th Cir. 1987) (quoting *Francis*).

164. *Leary*, 395 U.S. at 36.

165. *See Allen*, 442 U.S. at 159-60.

C. Operation of Presumptions in Criminal Proceedings

The operation of presumptions in criminal cases is even more complicated than it is in civil proceedings because no single definition is generally recognized.[166] In fact, the most well-known criminal presumption, the "presumption of innocence," is not actually a presumption.[167] All true presumptions depend on proof of a basic fact from which other inferences or conclusions must or might flow.[168] Because no basic facts need to be proved for the presumption of innocence to apply, a more accurate term for this doctrine is the "assumption of innocence"; the court merely assumes that every person's conduct on a given occasion is lawful until the State has offered proof to the contrary.[169]

As in civil cases, presumptions in criminal proceedings result either from statutes[170] or from common-law judicial decisions.[171] The presumed fact may be an element of the crime or defense, or it may be some intermediate fact.[172] While the basic definition and classification of presumptions may be similar in civil and criminal proceedings, a criminal defendant's constitutional right to a jury determination of every essential fact of the offense ensures that their operation is dissimilar.[173]

Presumptions may operate for either the criminal defendant or the government,[174] but the consequences are different. The government's failure to sufficiently rebut a pre-

---

166. *See* FED. R. EVID. 303 advisory committee's note (1972 proposed final draft), 56 F.R.D. 183, 213 (1973); 2 MCCORMICK ON EVIDENCE, *supra* note 5, §346, at 525. Refer to notes 133-135 *supra* and accompanying text.

167. *See* 2 MCCORMICK ON EVIDENCE, *supra* note 5, §346, at 525.

168. Refer to notes 1-6 *supra* and accompanying text.

169. *See* **Griffith v. State**, 976 S.W.2d 241, 246-47 (Tex. App.—Amarillo 1998, pet. ref'd) ("The presumption of innocence is not a true presumption because the defendant is not required to come forward with proof of innocence once evidence of guilt is introduced so as to avoid a directed verdict of guilty."); 2 MCCORMICK ON EVIDENCE, *supra* note 5, §342, at 499 ("assumption of innocence" is better phrase because it "describes our assumption that, in the absence of contrary facts, it is to be assumed that any person's conduct upon a given occasion was lawful"); 9 WIGMORE, *supra* note 19, §2511, at 530-31 ("presumption of innocence" is a misnomer).

170. *See, e.g.*, 15 U.S.C. §54(a) (conclusive presumption that meat and meat food products duly inspected, marked, and labeled according to federal regulations are not injurious to health); 16 U.S.C. §1538(c)(2) (presumption that importing fish or wildlife into the United States does not violate any conservation laws if the fish or wildlife is not on the endangered-species list, if the taking or exportation of the fish or wildlife does not violate the Endangered Species Convention, and if the importation of the fish or wildlife does not occur in the course of a commercial activity); 18 U.S.C. §545 (proof of defendant's possession of unlawfully imported goods, unless explained to jury's satisfaction, is sufficient evidence to authorize conviction for smuggling goods into the United States), *id.* §892(b) (listing factors that, when found in connection with the extension of credit, provide "prima facie evidence that the extension of credit was extortionate").

171. *See, e.g.*, **Barnes v. United States**, 412 U.S. 837, 843 (1973) (presumption that a person in possession of recently stolen property knew the property had been stolen is a common-law inference "deeply rooted in our law"); **United States v. Green**, 680 F.2d 520, 524 (7th Cir. 1982) (common-law presumptions that a person's death occurs where the body is found and that life continues until it is proved otherwise).

172. *See, e.g.*, **Hagner v. United States**, 285 U.S. 427, 430 (1932) (in fraud case, indictment alleged proper address and postage on letter, raising presumption of receipt); **Green**, 680 F.2d at 524 (in prosecution for kidnapping for purpose of committing murder, court properly applied presumptions that life continues until it is proved otherwise and that death occurs where the body is found).

173. Refer to notes 149-165 *supra* and accompanying text.

174. *See* 9A FEDERAL PROCEDURE LAWYER'S EDITION §22:1389 (Thomas R. Trenker et al. eds., 1993) (listing federal statutory presumptions favorable to an accused), §22:1390 (listing presumptions unfavorable to an accused).

ARTICLE III

sumption against it may result in a directed verdict for the defendant.[175] However, the defendant's failure to rebut a presumption will never result in a directed verdict against him because he is entitled to a jury determination of every essential element or fact of the offense.[176]

The government has used presumptions in federal criminal cases to overcome two separate problems. First, presumptions authorize shortcuts in proof and lessen the government's evidentiary burden by placing pressure on the defendant, the person with the most knowledge, to come forward with an explanation in certain situations.[177] Second, presumptions make undesirable activities amenable to federal jurisdiction by presuming that items such as drugs, guns, and automobiles circulate in interstate or foreign commerce.[178] Thus, activities normally subject only to local and state penal sanctions are, through the use of various jurisdictional presumptions, subject to federal prosecution.[179]

D. Burden-of-Production Presumptions & Evidentiary Presumptions

Texas criminal courts have frequently used the same label and analysis to describe two distinct types of presumptions. First, there is the burden-of-production presumption, which shifts to the defendant the burden of producing some evidence to raise a disputed issue. Then there is the evidentiary presumption, which is a means of inferring an ultimate fact from the proof of a basic fact.

1. Burden-of-production presumptions. An example of a burden-of-production presumption is the operation of a motion to suppress. A defendant who seeks to suppress evidence because of an illegal arrest has the initial burden to produce evidence rebutting the presumption of proper police conduct.[180] The defendant meets this burden by offering evidence that the police seized him without a warrant and that he has standing to contest the search or seizure.[181] Once the defendant offers some evidence of a

---

175. ***Sandstrom v. Montana***, 442 U.S. 510, 516 n.5 (1979).

176. *See* 21B WRIGHT & GRAHAM, *supra* note 19, §5142, at 711.

177. 1 WEINSTEIN & BERGER, *supra* note 4, §303.04[1], at 303-10; *see* ***United States v. Gainey***, 380 U.S. 63, 65 (1965) ("The legislative record shows that Congress enacted these provisions [26 U.S.C. §5601(b), permitting conviction for illegal distillation on proof of defendant's presence at a still] because of the 'practical impossibility of proving … actual participation in the illegal activities except by inference, drawn from [the defendant's] presence when the illegal acts were committed ….'"); *see also* 21B WRIGHT & GRAHAM, *supra* note 19, §5142.1, at 732 (some Prohibition-era commentators described presumptions as "first aid to the District Attorney").

178. *See* 1 WEINSTEIN & BERGER, *supra* note 4, §303.04[1], at 303-11 (Congress can use the power to tax or the commerce power to make certain activities amenable to federal jurisdiction).

179. *See, e.g.*, ***Leary v. United States***, 395 U.S. 6, 30 (1969) (defendant was prosecuted for failure to pay a marijuana tax and for importing marijuana). *But see* ***United States v. Lopez***, 514 U.S. 549, 561 (1995) (Gun-Free School Zones Act of 1990, which made it a federal crime to knowingly possess a firearm in a school zone, exceeded Congress's authority under the Commerce Clause in part because it was "a criminal statute that by its terms has nothing to do with 'commerce'"; Court found factually unsupportable the congressional presumption that bringing firearms to school had a substantial effect on commerce).

180. ***Amador v. State***, 221 S.W.3d 666, 672 (Tex. Crim. App. 2007); ***Handy v. State***, 189 S.W.3d 296, 298-99 (Tex. Crim. App. 2006).

181. ***Handy***, 189 S.W.3d at 298-99; *see* ***Amador***, 221 S.W.3d at 672.

warrantless search or seizure, the burden shifts to the State to produce evidence of a valid warrant or to prove the reasonableness of the search or seizure under one of the recognized exceptions to the warrant requirement.[182] The State has the ultimate burden of proving the reasonableness of the search or seizure once the defendant raises a disputed issue.

The burden of persuasion can be shifted to a criminal defendant on some issues, though never on the ultimate issue of guilt or innocence of a specified crime.[183] In Texas, for example, the defendant must be competent to stand trial, and he is required to prove present incompetency by a preponderance of the evidence.[184] In the punishment phase of a trial for aggravated kidnapping, to reduce the punishment from a first-degree to a second-degree offense, the defendant has the burden of proving that he voluntarily released the victim in a safe place.[185]

2. Evidentiary presumptions. Evidentiary presumptions in Texas criminal proceedings operate quite differently from those in Texas civil cases. First, unlike in civil cases, jurors in criminal cases receive specific instructions on the scope and effect of certain specified presumptions.[186] Second, Texas Penal Code section 2.05(a) narrowly circumscribes the use of presumptions that favor the State in criminal proceedings. Subsection (a) turns all trial-level presumptions into permissive inferences.[187] Under section 2.05(a), no presumption arises in the case unless the State proves the facts that give rise to the presumption beyond a reasonable doubt.[188] If there is sufficient evidence of the basic facts to give rise to the presumption, the court must submit the issue of the presumed fact's existence to the jury unless the judge believes that "the evidence as a whole

---

182. ***Taylor v. State***, 945 S.W.2d 295, 298 (Tex. App.—Houston [1st Dist.] 1997, pet. ref'd); *see **Amador***, 221 S.W.3d at 672-73.

183. Refer to notes 155-161 *supra* and accompanying text.

184. Tex. Code Crim. Proc. art. 46B.003(b); *see **Morris v. State***, 301 S.W.3d 281, 285 (Tex. Crim. App. 2009); ***Penry v. State***, 903 S.W.2d 715, 729 (Tex. Crim. App. 1995).

185. Tex. Penal Code §20.04(c), (d).

186. *See generally* Luther Hugh Soules, III, *Presumptions in Criminal Cases*, 20 Baylor L. Rev. 277, 285-93 (1968) (discussing the instructions for permissive presumptions and their impact on juries). In civil cases, jurors never receive instructions on the role and effect of presumptions. Refer to note 100 *supra* and accompanying text.

187. *See **Garrett v. State***, 220 S.W.3d 926, 931 (Tex. Crim. App. 2007); ***Willis v. State***, 790 S.W.2d 307, 310 (Tex. Crim. App. 1990); ***Tottenham v. State***, 285 S.W.3d 19, 31 (Tex. App.—Houston [1st Dist.] 2009, pet. ref'd); ***Scott v. State***, 253 S.W.3d 736, 744 (Tex. App.—Amarillo 2007, pet. ref'd). The ***Willis*** decision discussed the impact of permissive presumptions as follows:

> [T]he permissive presumption allows, but does not require, the trier of fact to infer the elemental fact or ultimate fact from the predicate evidentiary fact or facts. It places no burden on the accused to refute or disprove the elemental fact once the predicate facts have been established. Since it does not relieve the State's burden of proving guilt beyond a reasonable doubt, a permissive presumption is generally deemed constitutional if the reviewing court determines that a rational trier of fact could make the connection permitted by the presumption.

790 S.W.2d at 310.

188. ***Wilson v. State***, 658 S.W.2d 615, 617-18 (Tex. Crim. App. 1983); *see **Scott***, 253 S.W.3d at 744; *see also **Bellamy v. State***, 742 S.W.2d 677, 681 n.5 (Tex. Crim. App. 1987) (§2.05(2)(A) [now §2.05(a)(2)(A)] requires a jury charge that instructs the jury to find the predicate fact beyond a reasonable doubt).

ARTICLE III

clearly precludes a finding beyond a reasonable doubt of the presumed fact."[189] Even then, the judge must instruct the jury that it may not use the presumption for any purpose if it has a reasonable doubt about the existence of the basic facts[190] and that it is not bound to use the presumption even if it finds those basic facts beyond a reasonable doubt.[191]

Section 2.05(b) deals with statutory presumptions that favor the defendant. Subsection (b) provides that if the defendant offers evidence of the basic facts that give rise to a presumption, the jury must be instructed on that presumption unless "the evidence as a whole clearly precludes a finding beyond a reasonable doubt of the presumed fact."[192] When a presumption favoring the defendant is submitted to the jury, the court must instruct the jury that the presumption applies unless the State proves beyond a reasonable doubt that the basic facts giving rise to the presumption do not exist.[193] If the State does not meet this burden, the jury must find that the presumed fact exists.[194] Furthermore, if the jury has a reasonable doubt as to whether the presumed fact exists, the presumption applies and the jury must consider the presumed fact to exist.[195]

Thus, with presumptions that favor the defendant, the burden is exactly the opposite of the burden when presumptions favor the State: a presumption does not apply in favor of the State unless the State proves the basic facts beyond a reasonable doubt, but a presumption does apply in favor of the defendant unless the State disproves the basic facts beyond a reasonable doubt.

Juries in Texas criminal proceedings receive instructions about the effect of presumptions only when the presumption has a statutory basis in the Penal Code or another penal provision.[196] Thus, while Texas courts have recognized and used various presumptions in analyzing the sufficiency of evidence,[197] courts may not instruct ju-

---

189. TEX. PENAL CODE §2.05(a)(1).

190. *Id.* §2.05(a)(2)(D); *see **Eckman v. State***, 600 S.W.2d 937, 939 (Tex. Crim. App. 1980) (jury instructions were inadequate because they did not specifically inform the jury that it could not consider the presumption for any purpose if it had a reasonable doubt about any basic fact).

191. TEX. PENAL CODE §2.05(a)(2)(B); ***Easdon v. State***, 552 S.W.2d 153, 154-55 (Tex. Crim. App. 1977); *see also **Bellamy***, 742 S.W.2d at 684 (instruction that does not adequately alert the jury that it is free to reject the presumption is constitutionally defective); ***Coberly v. State***, 640 S.W.2d 428, 429-30 (Tex. App.—Fort Worth 1982) (lack of limiting instructions making a presumption irrebuttable requires reversal), *pet. ref'd*, 644 S.W.2d 734 (Tex. Crim. App. 1983).

Even a charge stating that "the jury may presume," without explicit language explaining that it is not required to presume, is usually not sufficient. *See **Alexander v. State***, 757 S.W.2d 95, 98-100 (Tex. App.—Dallas 1988, pet. ref'd) (jury instructions must make clear that a reasonable juror may ignore the presumption).

192. TEX. PENAL CODE §2.05(b)(1).

193. *Id.* §2.05(b)(2)(A).

194. *Id.* §2.05(b)(2)(B).

195. *Id.* §2.05(b)(2)(D).

196. *Id.* §2.05. Sections 2.05(a) and (b) both begin by stating that they apply only when "this code or another penal law establishes a presumption." *Id.*; *see **LaPoint v. State***, 750 S.W.2d 180, 192 (Tex. Crim. App. 1988) (op. on reh'g) (improper to give jury instruction under §2.05 when the penal statute does not expressly authorize the presumption).

197. This analysis may occur either on appeal or in the trial court during a motion for instructed verdict or motion for new trial by a defendant. ***LaPoint***, 750 S.W.2d at 182 (orig. op.).

rors on these judicially created presumptions.[198] To do so would be an impermissible comment on the weight of the evidence.[199] Some of these judicially crafted presumptions include the following: the intent to kill may be inferred from the use of a deadly weapon;[200] a person's recent, unexplained possession of recently stolen property gives rise to an inference of guilt in a theft case;[201] the presumption of an intent to commit theft arises from the unpermitted nighttime entry into a home or building;[202] the presumption that the law in another state is the same as that in Texas, without contrary proof;[203] the presumption that public officers have performed their duties in a regular and lawful manner and have not exceeded their lawful authority;[204] and the presumption that persons intend the natural and probable consequences of their acts.[205] While jurors may not receive instructions on these judicially crafted presumptions, attorneys may nonetheless suggest to the jury that it may make commonsense inferences from the evidence.[206]

The statutory presumptions favoring the State about which a Texas jury may receive instructions under section 2.05(a) include the following: the presumption that a dealer in secondhand property who knowingly or recklessly fails to keep adequate records knew that stolen property in his possession was stolen when he paid $25 or more for it;[207] the presumption that a person intends to avoid payment for services if he leaves

---

198. *See id.* at 192 (op. on reh'g). In ***Brown v. State***, the court of criminal appeals discussed the distinction between statutory trial-level presumptions and judicial presumptions by which the sufficiency of evidence is measured. 122 S.W.3d 794, 799-800 (Tex. Crim. App. 2003). These judicial presumptions are legal devices used to review the evidence and determine its legal sufficiency. *See id.* at 800. "[G]iving an instruction to the jury on these judicial evidentiary sufficiency review rules improperly picks out one specific, though entirely logical, inference that could flow from the base facts from all other plausible inferences ...." *Id.*

199. ***Brown***, 122 S.W.3d at 800; ***LaPoint***, 750 S.W.2d at 182-83 (orig. op.); *see also* ***Peterson v. State***, 942 S.W.2d 206, 207-08 (Tex. App.—Texarkana 1997, pet. ref'd) (reviewing Texas decisions holding that instructing the jury on nonstatutory inferences is a forbidden comment on the weight of the evidence).

200. ***Godsey v. State***, 719 S.W.2d 578, 580 (Tex. Crim. App. 1986). The presumption of an intent to kill may be rebutted by evidence of an accident. *See* ***Foster v. State***, 639 S.W.2d 691, 694-95 (Tex. Crim. App. 1982).

201. ***Hardesty v. State***, 656 S.W.2d 73, 76 (Tex. Crim. App. 1983); *see also* ***Sweeny v. State***, 925 S.W.2d 268, 270-71 (Tex. App.—Corpus Christi 1996, no pet.) (inference is not conclusive and merely states conditions under which reviewing courts may regard the evidence as sufficient to support a finding of guilt).

202. ***Mauldin v. State***, 628 S.W.2d 793, 795 (Tex. Crim. App. [Panel Op.] 1982); *see also* ***Aguilar v. State***, 682 S.W.2d 556, 558 (Tex. Crim. App. 1985) (the presumption is "an appellate vehicle employed to review the sufficiency of the evidence, not a trial vehicle used to prove an element of the State's case"); ***Wilkerson v. State***, 927 S.W.2d 112, 115 (Tex. App.—Houston [1st Dist.] 1996, no pet.) ("This presumption is actually a permissive inference utilized by appellate courts.").

203. ***Smith v. State***, 683 S.W.2d 393, 406 (Tex. Crim. App. 1984). Refer to *Article II: Judicial Notice, supra* p. 143.

204. ***Sheffield v. State***, 165 Tex. Crim. 354, 362, 307 S.W.2d 100, 105 (1957) (op. on reh'g).

205. ***Duhon v. State***, 136 Tex. Crim. 404, 408, 125 S.W.2d 550, 552 (1939) (op. on reh'g).

206. *See* ***Brown v. State***, 122 S.W.3d 794, 803 (Tex. Crim. App. 2003) (although judge may not give jury instruction that "intent or knowledge may be inferred by acts done or words spoken," both defense and prosecution may argue that commonsense proposition to jury); *see, e.g.,* ***Albiar v. State***, 739 S.W.2d 360, 362-63 (Tex. Crim. App. 1987) (prosecutor could comment during closing argument on defendant's failure to call a competent and material witness; "failure to produce available evidence justifies an inference that it would be unfavorable to the defendant"); ***Mauldin***, 628 S.W.2d at 795 (prosecutor could argue that common sense dictated that someone who was alone in a locked building that had been broken into had intent to steal).

207. TEX. PENAL CODE §31.03(c)(3); *see* ***Willis v. State***, 790 S.W.2d 307, 308-12 (Tex. Crim. App. 1990) (using §2.05 in conjunction with Penal Code §31.03); ***McNiel v. State***, 757 S.W.2d 129, 133-34 (Tex. App.—Houston [1st Dist.]

without paying for services in circumstances in which payment is ordinarily made immediately after the service is rendered;[208] the presumption that a person intends to avoid payment for services if he does not make payment under a service agreement within ten days after receiving notice demanding return;[209] the presumption of recklessness and danger, under the deadly-conduct statute, if a person knowingly points a firearm at or in the direction of another;[210] a presumption that the assailant knew that the person assaulted was a public servant if the person was wearing a distinctive uniform or badge;[211] a presumption that a person who possesses six or more pornographic images of children intended to promote the material;[212] a presumption, in certain specified circumstances, that a person who pays by bad check intends to steal property;[213] and a presumption of intent to commit an offense when a public servant does not make public disclosure of certain property interests.[214] Of course, the State does not need to rely on a statutory presumption to prove the criminal offense to which the presumption applies.[215] And even if a prosecutor does prove up the basic facts from which the presumption flows, he does not need to request a jury instruction on the statutory presumption. He may simply argue that the facts logically lead to the conclusion of guilt.

Whenever the jury is instructed that it may presume a certain fact from other basic facts, the trial judge must also include a section 2.05 instruction.[216] The failure to include section 2.05(a) instructions to the jury is, however, subject to a harmless-error analysis.[217]

1988, pet. ref'd) (Penal Code §31.03(c)(3) must be presented in conjunction with §2.05); *see also* **Naranjo v. State**, 217 S.W.3d 560, 564-65 (Tex. App.—San Antonio 2006, no pet.) (Penal Code §31.03(c)(6)(B) must be presented in conjunction with §2.05).

208. TEX. PENAL CODE §31.04(b)(1).

209. *Id.* §31.04(b)(2).

210. *Id.* §22.05(c); *see* **Bartlett v. State**, 270 S.W.3d 147, 151 (Tex. Crim. App. 2008); *see, e.g.*, **Webber v. State**, 29 S.W.3d 226, 230-31 (Tex. App.—Houston [14th Dist.] 2000, pet. ref'd) (trial court committed statutory and constitutional harmless error in failing to instruct jury on effect of presumption under §22.05 when it charged jury that "'[r]ecklessness and danger are presumed if the actor knowingly pointed a firearm ....'"; this charge created a mandatory presumption).

211. TEX. PENAL CODE §22.02(c); *see* **Garrett v. State**, 220 S.W.3d 926, 930-31 (Tex. Crim. App. 2007).

212. TEX. PENAL CODE §43.26(f).

213. *Id.* §31.06(f).

214. TEX. GOV'T CODE §§553.002, 553.003(b).

215. *See, e.g.*, **State v. Larue**, 28 S.W.3d 549, 552 (Tex. Crim. App. 2000) (arresting officer had probable cause to believe defendants were committing theft of service by holding rental car beyond due date even though officer did not have probable cause to believe in existence of basic facts that give rise to statutory presumption of theft of service; failure to meet presumption does not mean the offense itself is not or cannot be proved).

216. *See, e.g.*, **Ramirez-Memije v. State**, 466 S.W.3d 894, 896-97 (Tex. App.—Houston [14th Dist.] 2015, no pet.) (trial court erred by not giving Penal Code §2.05(a)(2) instructions when court instructed jury it could presume defendant had intent to harm or defraud another if defendant possessed identifying information of three or more other persons); **Anderson v. State**, 11 S.W.3d 369, 373-74 (Tex. App.—Houston [1st Dist.] 2000, pet. ref'd) (trial court erred by refusing to give Penal Code §2.05(2) [now §2.05(a)(2)] jury instruction when court had instructed jury that it could presume defendant knew that the person assaulted was a public servant if that person was wearing a distinctive uniform or badge indicating the person's employment as a public servant).

217. *See* **Garrett v. State**, 220 S.W.3d 926, 931-32 (Tex. Crim. App. 2007); *see, e.g.*, **Ramirez-Memije**, 466 S.W.3d at 897-98 (defendant did not object to jury charge or request instruction under Penal Code §2.05(a)(2), but court

ARTICLE III

If the court adequately incorporates section 2.05(a) into the jury's instructions, a Texas criminal presumption is considered permissive and generally satisfies the preliminary due-process requirement.[218] The statutory presumption is unconstitutional if, under the facts of a given case, a rational trier of fact could not find a natural connection between the basic facts and the ultimate fact presumed or could not find that the ultimate fact was more likely than not to flow from the basic facts proved.[219]

Texas common law has traditionally authorized a separate jury charge on statutory criminal presumptions,[220] and section 2.05 provides a relatively simple instructional guide to the jury for using permissive presumptions. This methodology seems preferable to the present federal procedure, which relies on judicially crafted instructions that too frequently misstate the nature and consequences of a presumption in criminal proceedings.[221]

Neither the Texas Legislature nor the judiciary has created a simple method for applying presumptions and instructing juries on how to use them. Most Texas criminal cases involving the use of statutory presumptions are reversed on appeal because either the presumption itself is deemed unconstitutional or its application in the particular case was faulty.[222]

---

found egregious harm because presumed fact was primary contested issue at trial and evidence of presumed fact was not overwhelming); *State v. Lewis*, 151 S.W.3d 213, 223-24 (Tex. App.—Tyler 2004, pet. ref'd) (defendant did not object to failure to include §2.05 instruction about statutory presumption that a person committing aggravated assault is presumed to have known the person assaulted was a public servant if that person was wearing a distinctive uniform or badge indicating the person's employment as a public servant; defendant did not show "egregious" harm in charge even though element of defendant's knowledge of complainants' status as public servants was disputed); *cf. Carella v. California*, 491 U.S. 263, 266 (1989) (mandatory-presumption error under *Sandstrom v. Montana*, 442 U.S. 510 (1979), "is subject to the harmless-error rule").

218. *See Willis v. State*, 790 S.W.2d 307, 310 (Tex. Crim. App. 1990); *Ramirez-Memije*, 466 S.W.3d at 897; *see also* TEX. PENAL CODE §2.05 practice commentary (Vernon 1974) (presumptions in Penal Code "satisfy this due process requirement and the purpose of this section is to specify the procedural consequences of a presumption to satisfy other constitutional strictures"). Refer to notes 155-161 *supra* and accompanying text.

219. *See Bellamy v. State*, 742 S.W.2d 677, 682-83 (Tex. Crim. App. 1987) (constitutionality of permissive presumption will depend on "strength of the invited inference as supported *in the record as a whole*, not simply on the strength of the inference arising from the bare predicate fact"); *McNiel v. State*, 757 S.W.2d 129, 134 (Tex. App.—Houston [1st Dist.] 1988, pet. ref'd) ("A permissive presumption is constitutional unless, under the facts of the given case, there is no rational way the trier of fact could make the connection permitted by the inference."); *Coit v. State*, 728 S.W.2d 105, 107 (Tex. App.—Austin 1987) ("In any criminal statutory presumption, there must be a rational connection between the fact giving rise to the presumption and the ultimate fact presumed; that is, the presumed fact must, more likely than not, flow from the proved fact."), *rev'd on other grounds*, 808 S.W.2d 473 (Tex. Crim. App. 1991). Refer to notes 162-165 *supra* and accompanying text.

220. *See* TEX. PENAL CODE §2.05 practice commentary (Vernon 1974) (§2.05 continues prior Texas law practice).

221. *See* 21B WRIGHT & GRAHAM, *supra* note 19, §5147, at 812 (unfortunate that rejected Federal Rule 303 did not offer more guidance on the proper mode of instructing jury on presumptions). Refer to notes 133-135 *supra* and accompanying text.

222. *See, e.g., Green v. State*, 893 S.W.2d 536, 537-39 (Tex. Crim. App. 1995) (reversing conviction for criminal mischief on basis of unconstitutional presumption); *Bellamy*, 742 S.W.2d at 683-86 (reversing conviction because of unconstitutional instruction on mandatory presumption); *Davis v. State*, 658 S.W.2d 572, 580 (Tex. Crim. App. 1983) (reversing conviction on basis of unconstitutionally applied presumption); *Gersh v. State*, 714 S.W.2d 80, 81-82 (Tex. App.—Dallas 1986) (reversing conviction because of unconstitutional application of statutory presumption),

VI. STACKING INFERENCES & PRESUMPTIONS

Courts and practitioners frequently confuse the distinction between a presumption and an inference. A presumption is a logical conclusion that *will* flow from certain basic facts; an inference is a logical conclusion that *may* flow from certain basic facts.[223] Courts sometimes compound the confusion by stating the "rule" that fact-finders may not "stack" an inference on an inference or a presumption on a presumption in assessing the sufficiency of circumstantial evidence. There is no such rule of evidence—the doctrine simply guards against the use of remote, unwarranted, and tenuous inferences.

Inference stacking, or "basing an inference upon an inference," occurs when a fact-finder draws an inference from circumstantial evidence and then, solely from that initial inference, draws another inference.[224] The origin of the "rule" against basing an inference on an inference or a presumption on a presumption is obscure, but the doctrine was a part of Texas evidence law by the early 1900s.[225] Despite criticism from evidence

pet. ref'd, 738 S.W.2d 287 (Tex. Crim. App. 1987); **Gonzales v. State**, 676 S.W.2d 437, 439 (Tex. App.—Houston [1st Dist.] 1984) (reversing conviction on basis of unconstitutional instruction on presumption), *pet. ref'd*, 689 S.W.2d 231 (Tex. Crim. App. 1985).

223. In **Marshall Field Stores, Inc. v. Gardiner**, the court set out its understanding of the term "inference":
> In the law of evidence, a truth or proposition drawn from another which is supposed or admitted to be true. A process of reasoning by which a fact or proposition sought to be established is deduced as a logical consequence from other facts, or a state of facts, already proved ....

859 S.W.2d 391, 400 (Tex. App.—Houston [1st Dist.] 1993, writ dism'd) (op. on reh'g) (quoting BLACK'S LAW DICTIONARY 700 (5th ed. 1979)). As the court noted, "[f]or a jury to infer a fact, it must be able to deduce the fact as a logical consequence from other proven facts." *Id.* Refer to notes 155-161 *supra* and accompanying text.

224. An inference can be drawn only from some piece of direct evidence, not from facts established by another inference (i.e., an inference based on an inference). **Ice Bros. v. Bannowsky**, 840 S.W.2d 57, 61 (Tex. App.—El Paso 1992, no writ); *see* **Tex. Sling Co. v. Emanuel**, 431 S.W.2d 538, 540-41 (Tex. 1968). For example, evidence that X mailed the check for his monthly phone bill in a properly stamped, addressed envelope on Monday will support an inference that the phone company received the check by Friday. Similarly, evidence that X normally writes the checks for his monthly bills on Monday will support an inference that he wrote his phone-bill check on Monday. However, evidence that X normally writes the checks for his monthly bills on Monday will not, by itself, support the inference that the phone company received the check by Friday. This is an inference based on an inference. It is too long and too tenuous a chain of logic, unsupported by evidence of the intermediate but essential fact—X, in accordance with his normal routine, wrote and properly mailed the phone-bill check on Monday.
> In **Fort Worth Belt Railway v. Jones**, Chief Justice Brown set out the general rule:
> > A presumption of fact cannot rest upon a fact presumed. The fact relied upon to support the presumption must be proved. 'No inference of fact should be drawn from premises which are uncertain. Facts upon which an inference may legitimately rest must be established by direct evidence, as if they were the facts in issue. One presumption can not be based upon another presumption.'

106 Tex. 345, 350, 166 S.W. 1130, 1132 (1914); *see also* **Entex v. Gonzalez**, 94 S.W.3d 1, 8 (Tex. App.—Houston [14th Dist.] 2002, pet. denied) ("[F]acts from which an *inference* may properly be drawn must be established by direct evidence, not by other *inferences*."). Although a chain of inferences cannot be built solely on one underlying circumstantial fact or legal presumption, several conclusions may be drawn from the same set of facts. An inference based in part on another inference and in part on facts is a "parallel inference" and, if reasonable, it may be made by a fact-finder and upheld by a reviewing court. *See* **Travelers Ins. v. Warrick**, 172 F.2d 516, 519 (5th Cir. 1949) ("A jury is not proscribed from drawing multiple inferences in a case with multiple facts and circumstances in evidence. It may draw as many separate inferences as there are separate facts or circumstances. It may not, however, treat a fact inferred as a fact established that, in turn, can serve as the basis for a further inference and thereby spin out a chain of inferences into the realm of pure conjecture.").

225. *See* **Maddox v. State**, 76 Tex. Crim. 217, 222-23, 173 S.W. 1026, 1028 (1915). In **Maddox**, the defendant wanted to show that he was temporarily insane at the time of the murder because the victim had given him whiskey laced

ARTICLE III

scholars,[226] this rule is frequently quoted in Texas civil and criminal cases.[227] However, the Texas Court of Criminal Appeals has rejected an outright rule against inference stacking.[228] Using the legal-sufficiency test set out in *Jackson v. Virginia*,[229] the court of criminal appeals held that juries may draw multiple inferences "as long as each inference is supported by the evidence presented at trial."[230]

In a civil or criminal case based on circumstantial evidence, every fact need not point directly and independently to the element to be proved; the cumulative force of all the

---

with cocaine. The defendant offered to show that the victim was a habitual cocaine user, but the trial court excluded this evidence. The court of criminal appeals questioned: "[F]or what purpose? That the jury might first presume as to the quantity of cocaine probably in the whiskey, and from this presumption the jury then presume that such a quantity would probably produce temporary insanity." *Id.* at 222, 173 S.W. at 1028. The court then quoted an early evidence textbook:

> The requirement that the logical inference styled a presumption of fact should be a strong, natural and immediate one brings as a corollary the rule that no inference can be based upon a fact the existence of which itself rests upon a prior inference. In other words, there can be no presumption upon a presumption.

Id. The court also concluded that "[t]his rule has always prevailed in this court; such presumption sometimes being referred to as too remote." *Id.* at 222-23, 173 S.W. at 1028. Thus, the court held that the trial court properly excluded the evidence because its relevance depended on stacking one weak presumption on another. *See id.*

226. *See* 1A JOHN H. WIGMORE, EVIDENCE IN TRIALS AT COMMON LAW §41, at 1112 (Tillers rev. 1983). Wigmore denounced the strict bar of the "inference stacking" rule as meaningless sophistry:

> Today most students of the problem of inference recognize that *any* single vision about the world or conclusion of fact rests on a *multitude* of inferences, premises, and beliefs, on a large complex of assumptions, and on a body of implicit or explicit principles by which the human organism perceives, organizes, structures, and understands experience; thus it is generally conceded that it is meaningless to denounce multistaged or cascaded inferences.

Id.

227. *See, e.g., Marathon Corp. v. Pitzner*, 106 S.W.3d 724, 728 (Tex. 2003) ("[A]n inference stacked only on other inferences is not legally sufficient evidence."); *Schlumberger Well Surveying Corp. v. Nortex Oil & Gas Corp.*, 435 S.W.2d 854, 858 (Tex. 1968) ("[A] vital fact may not be established by piling inference upon inference ...."); *Tex. & N.O. R.R. v. Grace*, 144 Tex. 71, 76, 188 S.W.2d 378, 381 (1945) ("It is elementary that inferences can be drawn only from facts and not from other inferences. That rule has special application in a case, like this, where a very doubtful inference is sought to be drawn from another one equally doubtful."); *Williamson v. State*, 156 Tex. Crim. 520, 522, 244 S.W.2d 202, 204 (1951) (conviction for keeping a brothel was reversed for insufficient evidence; "[o]ne of the cardinal principles touching the sufficiency of circumstantial evidence is that an inference based upon an inference will not suffice"); *Hart v. State*, 152 Tex. Crim. 537, 539, 215 S.W.2d 883, 884 (1948) (conviction for possessing whiskey for the purpose of sale in a dry area was reversed; "[t]hat appellant's conduct was highly suspicious there can be no question, but the facts must rise higher than creating a strong suspicion of guilt, and presumptions upon presumptions can not take the place of evidentiary facts").

228. *Hooper v. State*, 214 S.W.3d 9, 15 (Tex. Crim. App. 2007).

229. 443 U.S. 307, 319 (1979) ("[T]he relevant question is whether, after viewing the evidence in the light most favorable to the prosecution, *any* rational trier of fact could have found the essential elements of the crime beyond a reasonable doubt."); *see also Brooks v. State*, 323 S.W.3d 893, 895 (Tex. Crim. App. 2010) ("[T]he *Jackson v. Virginia* legal-sufficiency standard is the only standard that a reviewing court should apply in determining whether the evidence is sufficient to support each element of a criminal offense that the State is required to prove beyond a reasonable doubt.").

230. *Hooper*, 214 S.W.3d at 15; *accord Tate v. State*, 500 S.W.3d 410, 413 (Tex. Crim. App. 2016); *see Villa v. State*, 514 S.W.3d 227, 232 (Tex. Crim. App. 2017); *see, e.g., Lewis v. State*, No. AP-77,045 (Tex. Crim. App. 2017) (no pub.; 4-26-17) (jury's inference that murder defendant intended to cause victim's death was reasonable and supported by defendant's own testimony, by testimony of others about defendant's actions on night of murder, and by testimony of firearms analyst, which tended to disprove defendant's testimony that gun "went off").

ARTICLE III

circumstances may suffice.[231] However, when conducting a legal-sufficiency review, a vital fact or element may not be established *solely* by stacking an inference on other inferences without a solid foundation of fact.[232] A chain of inferences without the reinforcement of factual evidence can be stretched only so far before it snaps.[233]

However, the rule does not forbid inference stacking if each level is a reasonable deduction from the base facts proved.[234] The true nature of the rule against stacking inferences is correctly stated as merely "a shorthand rendition of the rule which requires that verdicts be based upon more than surmise and guesswork."[235] Thus, circumstantial evidence may be used to prove any material fact, as long as the evidence is more than mere suspicion.[236] However, a material fact may "not be proved by unreasonable inferences from other facts and circumstances or by piling inference upon inference."[237] The rule merely avoids using remote or implausible inferences and lengthy se-

---

231. *See Villa*, 514 S.W.3d at 232 ("The court conducting a sufficiency review must not engage in a 'divide and conquer' strategy but must consider the cumulative force of all the evidence."); *Balderas v. State*, 517 S.W.3d 756, 766 (Tex. Crim. App. 2016) ("Each fact need not point directly and independently to a defendant's guilt, as long as the cumulative force of all the incriminating circumstances is sufficient to support the conviction."), *cert. denied*, 137 S. Ct. 1207 (2017); *Hooper*, 214 S.W.3d at 16-17 ("[C]ourts of appeals should adhere to the *Jackson* standard and determine whether the necessary inferences are reasonable based upon the combined and cumulative force of all the evidence when viewed in the light most favorable to the verdict."); *Felker v. Petrolon, Inc.*, 929 S.W.2d 460, 464 (Tex. App.—Houston [1st Dist.] 1996, writ denied) ("In reviewing circumstantial evidence, we must look at the *totality* of the known circumstances rather than reviewing each piece of evidence in isolation.").

232. *See Cary v. State*, 507 S.W.3d 750, 757 (Tex. Crim. App. 2016) (speculation about meaning of facts or evidence is never sufficient to uphold conviction); *Tate*, 500 S.W.3d at 413 (jury is not allowed to draw conclusions based on speculation); *Ramsey v. State*, 473 S.W.3d 805, 809 (Tex. Crim. App. 2015) (inferences based on mere speculation are insufficient to support conviction); *Hooper*, 214 S.W.3d at 15 (juries may not come to conclusions based on "mere speculation or factually unsupported inferences"); *Bradford v. Vento*, 997 S.W.2d 713, 728 (Tex. App.—Corpus Christi 1999) ("vital facts" may not be proved by unreasonable inferences), *rev'd in part on other grounds*, 48 S.W.3d 749 (Tex. 2001).

233. *Bradford*, 997 S.W.2d at 728; *e.g.*, *San Antonio Credit Union v. O'Connor*, 115 S.W.3d 82, 92 (Tex. App.—San Antonio 2003, pet. denied) (single evidentiary fact that credit union and property owner froze builder's account could not support ultimate inference that credit union and property owner intended, at that moment, to defame and inflict emotional distress on builder).

234. *Hooper*, 214 S.W.3d at 15.

235. *Phoenix Ref. Co. v. Powell*, 251 S.W.2d 892, 902 (Tex. Civ. App.—San Antonio 1952, writ ref'd n.r.e.); *see Briones v. Levine's Dep't Store, Inc.*, 446 S.W.2d 7, 10 (Tex. 1969) ("[T]he law does not permit the pyramiding of one assumption upon another because an ultimate fact thus arrived at is too conjectural and speculative to support a judgment."); *Halliburton Co. v. Sanchez*, 996 S.W.2d 216, 219 (Tex. App.—San Antonio 1999, pet. denied) ("The inferences which the jury drew amounted to impermissible inference stacking. In other words, each inference raised by the evidence would ultimately be premised on another inference. At best, the circumstantial evidence presented amounted to a mere suspicion that Halliburton acted intentionally.").

236. *KPH Consol., Inc. v. Romero*, 102 S.W.3d 135, 145 (Tex. App.—Houston [14th Dist.] 2003), *aff'd*, 166 S.W.3d 212 (Tex. 2005); *see Suarez v. City of Tex. City*, 465 S.W.3d 623, 634 (Tex. 2015); *Hooper*, 214 S.W.3d at 16.

237. *Romero*, 102 S.W.3d at 145; *accord Bradford*, 997 S.W.2d at 728; *see Tate*, 500 S.W.3d at 413 ("Unlike a reasonable inference, speculation is insufficiently based on the evidence to support a finding beyond a reasonable doubt."); *see, e.g.*, *Queeman v. State*, 520 S.W.3d 616, 625 (Tex. Crim. App. 2017) (in trial for criminally negligent homicide, evidence was legally insufficient to support conviction; any inference by jury that defendant was excessively speeding, which was material because it would support finding of criminal negligence rather than ordinary negligence, would require impermissible speculation). A related concept is the "equal-inference rule," under which a fact-finder "may not reasonably infer an ultimate fact from 'meager circumstantial evidence which could give rise to any number of inferences, none more probable than another.'" *Hancock v. Variyam*, 400 S.W.3d 59, 70-71 (Tex.

ries of inferences based on meager facts.[238] Linking remote or implausible inferences is different from collecting discrete circumstantial facts that, as a whole, point toward a logical conclusion.[239]

VII. CONCLUSION

Three possible approaches to codification of the law of presumptions appear much more desirable than adoption of the piecemeal, oversimplified, and possibly disruptive provisions of Federal Rule 301. First, the legislature could leave the issue to the courts to handle in their traditional, common-law fashion. The drafters of the Texas Rules of Evidence adopted this course.[240] Second, the legislature could draft a detailed and comprehensive statute that recognizes specific presumptions and categorizes them according to whether they affect the burden of persuasion. Such a solution was adopted in the California Evidence Code.[241] The Texas Legislature also took this course when it adopted Penal Code section 2.05 to deal with presumptions in criminal proceedings. Thus, while the Texas Rules of Evidence do not contain any mention of evidentiary presumptions, the Texas Penal Code fully addresses the topic for criminal cases. Third, the legislature could adopt a detailed coverage of the civil presumptions that should shift only the burden of production. The situations covered by the stronger presumptions could be regulated with specific statutes that would prescribe rules of decision, thus eliminating presumptions in these areas. This third solution has been applied at least once in Texas[242] and has been recommended by the National Conference of Commissioners on Uniform State Laws for the presumption of death following five years' disappearance.[243] Such a course appears preferable because weaker presumptions

---

2013) (quoting ***Hammerly Oaks, Inc. v. Edwards***, 958 S.W.2d 387, 392 (Tex. 1997)); *see, e.g.*, ***Suarez***, 465 S.W.3d at 634-35 (in premises-liability case involving drowning deaths, evidence of generic warning signs that were not re-placed after Hurricane Ike and of city's designating and then eliminating a designated swimming area did not prove city's knowledge of perilous conditions at that location beyond mere knowledge of risks inherently associated with swimming in open water; "[a]n inference is not reasonable if it is susceptible to multiple, equally probable inferences, requiring the factfinder to guess in order to reach a conclusion").

238. *See generally* Shipley, *Modern Status of the Rules*, *supra* note 19 (discussing rules for presumptions in se-lected cases).

239. *See* ***Galloway v. United States***, 319 U.S. 372, 395 (1943) (discussing evidentiary standards for directed ver-dict in civil cases; "[w]hatever may be the general formulation, the essential requirement is that mere speculation be not allowed to do duty for probative facts, after making due allowance for all reasonably possible inferences favor-ing the party whose case is attacked"); ***Hooper***, 214 S.W.3d at 16-17 (language of "inference stacking" is not im-proper, just unnecessarily confusing; "courts of appeals should ... determine whether the necessary inferences are reasonable based upon the combined and cumulative force of all the evidence when viewed in the light most favor-able to the verdict").

240. Refer to note 53 *supra* and accompanying text.

241. Refer to note 27 *supra* and accompanying text.

242. *See* TEX. EST. CODE ch. 121 (discussing survival presumptions). For a history of this statute, see Roy R. Ray, *Three New Rules of Evidence*, 5 Sw. L.J. 381, 387-92 (1951). The article indicates that the statute was adopted in-stead of evidentiary presumptions promulgated by the Texas Supreme Court.

243. The Uniform Probate Code establishes a presumption of death after a five-year continuous absence with-out a satisfactory explanation. UNIF. PROB. CODE §1-107(5), 8 U.L.A. 30 (1998).

would be governed by a single rule, and stronger presumptions—which shift the burden of persuasion—would be recast as rules of decision that do not use the confusing term "presumption."[244]

---

244. For somewhat similar recommendations, see Allen, *supra* note 9, at 860. For a collection of several proposals in this area, see 9 WIGMORE, *supra* note 19, §§2493a-2493g, at 309-37.

ARTICLE III

ARTICLE IV: RELEVANCE & ITS LIMITS

RULE 401
TEST FOR RELEVANT EVIDENCE

Evidence is relevant if:

    (a) it has any tendency to make a fact more or less probable than it would be without the evidence; and

    (b) the fact is of consequence in determining the action.

RULE 402
GENERAL ADMISSIBILITY OF RELEVANT EVIDENCE

Relevant evidence is admissible unless any of the following provides otherwise:

- the United States or Texas Constitution;
- a statute;
- these rules; or
- other rules prescribed under statutory authority.

Irrelevant evidence is not admissible.

COMMENTARY ON RULES 401 & 402

The purpose of litigation is to resolve disputes by determining critical facts and applying the law to those facts. Courts should receive evidence that will help resolve those critical facts and reject evidence that will not.[1] Rule 402 recognizes that axiom, stating that irrelevant evidence is inadmissible and that all relevant evidence, with exceptions, is admissible. Rule 401 defines relevance for purposes of admission or exclusion under Rule 402, the operative rule of Article IV.

Rule 401 is identical to Federal Rule 401.[2] The minor language differences between Texas Rule 402 and Federal Rule 402 merely reflect the distinctions in hierarchical governance between the two sets of rules.[3]

---

1. JAMES B. THAYER, A PRELIMINARY TREATISE ON EVIDENCE AT THE COMMON LAW 264-65 (1898); *see* MCCORMICK ON EVIDENCE §184, at 540 (Edward W. Cleary ed., 3d ed. 1984) (courts should permit parties to present all evidence that bears on the issue to be decided); 1 JOHN H. WIGMORE, A TREATISE ON THE ANGLO-AMERICAN SYSTEM OF EVIDENCE IN TRIALS AT COMMON LAW §§9-10, at 289-95 (3d ed. 1940) (court should receive all evidence rationally calculated to persuade the fact-finder unless precluded by law).

2. Cases construing the Federal Rules should be considered when interpreting a Texas rule unless the Texas rule clearly deviates from the federal rule. *Bodin v. State*, 807 S.W.2d 313, 317 (Tex. Crim. App. 1991); *see Campbell v. State*, 718 S.W.2d 712, 716-17 (Tex. Crim. App. 1986) (in adopting Texas Criminal Rule of Evidence 801, the intent was to adopt not only the wording of Federal Rule 801 but also its interpretation); *Rodda v. State*, 745 S.W.2d 415, 418 (Tex. App.—Houston [14th Dist.] 1988, pet. ref'd) (because federal and Texas rules on relevance are identical, courts' opinions interpreting the rules should be in harmony).

3. Federal Rule 402 refers to the U.S. Constitution, a federal statute, the other Federal Rules of Evidence, and rules prescribed by the U.S. Supreme Court. Refer to note 83 *infra*.

A. Relevance Requirements of Rule 401

Evidence must satisfy two requirements to be relevant under Rule 401. First, the offered evidence must be relevant—that is, the evidence must make the existence of a fact "more or less probable than it would be without the evidence."[4] Second, the proposition to be proved must be material.[5] That is, the evidence must support a proposition that is a fact of consequence in determining the action.[6] If either element—relevance or materiality—is lacking, the evidence fails the test of Rule 401. So, "an offered item of evidence may be excluded as 'irrelevant' for either of these two quite distinct reasons: because it is not probative of the proposition at which it is directed, or because that proposition is not provable in the case."[7]

There are four possible permutations under Rule 401:

(1) The offered evidence tends to prove the proposition for which it is offered, and that proposition is provable in the case. No objection under Rule 401 is valid. The evidence meets Rule 401's definition of "relevant evidence" because both elements (relevance and materiality) are present.[8]

The 1998 unification of the Texas Civil and Criminal Rules of Evidence modified the language of both versions of Rule 402 slightly, but no substantive difference was intended. The 1998 wording of Rule 402 eliminated the phrase "by the Supreme Court" in the former Civil Rule 402. *See Texas Rules of Evidence*, 960 S.W.2d (Tex. Cases) xxxvii (1998); *Re: New Rules of Evidence*, 641-642 S.W.2d (Tex. Cases) xxxix (1983, amended 1998). Now, both the court of criminal appeals and the supreme court have authority to promulgate evidentiary rules under statutory authority. *See* Tex. Const. art. V, §31; Tex. Gov't Code §22.109.

4. Tex. R. Evid. 401(a); *Hedrick v. State*, 473 S.W.3d 824, 829 (Tex. App.—Houston [14th Dist.] 2015, no pet.); *see, e.g., Perez v. State*, 830 S.W.2d 684, 687-88 (Tex. App.—Corpus Christi 1992, no pet.) (identities of gang members not involved in case were irrelevant to any material issue); *CNA Ins. v. Scheffey*, 828 S.W.2d 785, 787-88 (Tex. App.—Texarkana 1992, writ denied) (trial court erred in excluding evidence of events before the complained-of incident because evidence was relevant to an analysis of the cause of plaintiff's damages); *Blackburn v. State*, 820 S.W.2d 824, 825-26 (Tex. App.—Waco 1991, pet. ref'd) (photograph seized from defendant's residence of an unidentified woman inhaling what appeared to be cocaine was irrelevant to any fact of consequence in a trial for possession of an amphetamine; even if the photograph were relevant, its probative value would be substantially outweighed by the danger of unfair prejudice).

5. *See, e.g., Blackburn*, 820 S.W.2d at 825-26 (photograph seized at defendant's residence, depicting a woman with a white substance, was not material to the issue of defendant's guilt on drug-possession charge for amphetamines); *Trans-State Pavers, Inc. v. Haynes*, 808 S.W.2d 727, 732-33 (Tex. App.—Beaumont 1991, writ denied) (evidence of plaintiff's alcohol consumption was material to issues of causation and contributory negligence in suit against highway-construction company for damages resulting from one-car accident); *Dion v. Ford Motor Co.*, 804 S.W.2d 302, 310 (Tex. App.—Eastland 1991, writ denied) (when plaintiffs offered evidence to establish defendant's breach of post-sale duty and the court found no such duty, evidence was not material and thus not relevant to any issue in the trial).

6. *See* Tex. R. Evid. 401(b); *Hedrick*, 473 S.W.3d at 829; McCormick on Evidence, *supra* note 1, §185, at 541.

7. George F. James, *Relevancy, Probability and the Law*, 29 Calif. L. Rev. 689, 690-91 (1941). Texas attorneys should object that evidence is "immaterial" only when the proposition for which the evidence is offered is not a provable proposition in the case. Likewise, attorneys should object that evidence is "irrelevant" only when the offered evidence does not tend to prove the proposition for which it is offered. In practice, however, the two objections are often conflated into an objection to irrelevant evidence.

8. *See, e.g., McHenry v. State*, 823 S.W.2d 667, 672-73 (Tex. App.—Dallas 1991) (expert evidence on cocaine distribution and its impact on property crime was relevant to the issue of punishment in case for conspiracy to possess more than 400 grams of cocaine; evidence showed attempted possession of drugs beyond amount for personal use), *vacated on other grounds*, 829 S.W.2d 803 (Tex. Crim. App. 1992); *Willmann v. State*, 720 S.W.2d 543, 547

(2) The offered evidence does not tend to prove the proposition for which it is offered, although that proposition is provable in the case. The proposition is material, but there is a valid objection that the evidence is irrelevant. The evidence does not meet Rule 401's definition of "relevant evidence" because the first element (relevance) is missing.[9]

(3) The offered evidence tends to prove the proposition for which it is offered, but that proposition is not provable in the case. Although the evidence is relevant to the proposition, the proposition is immaterial.[10] An objection that the evidence is immaterial is valid. The evidence does not meet Rule 401's definition of "relevant evidence" because the second element (materiality) is missing.[11]

(4) The offered evidence does not tend to prove the proposition for which it is offered, and that proposition is not provable in the case. Objections that the evidence is immaterial and irrelevant are both valid. The evidence does not meet Rule 401's definition of "relevant evidence" because both elements (relevance and materiality) are missing.

B. Rule 401(a): Relevance

Rule 401(a) requires that, to be relevant, evidence have some tendency to make the existence of a material fact "more or less probable than it would be without the evidence."[12] Evidence must be relevant to legal issues and facts raised in the particular case.[13] The appropriate practical test for relevance is whether "a reasonable person, with some experience in the real world," would believe that a particular piece of evidence is

---

(Tex. App.—San Antonio 1986, pet. ref'd) (evidence that defendant removed furniture from and planned to rent victim's house within a week and a half after victim's death was material and relevant because it went to defendant's motive for murder).

9.   *See, e.g.*, ***Pondexter v. State***, 942 S.W.2d 577, 583-84 (Tex. Crim. App. 1996) (evidence of defendant's purported gang affiliations and activities was not relevant in capital-murder case; evidence was introduced as an attempt to show defendant's bad character).

10.   *See* ***Henley v. State***, 493 S.W.3d 77, 83-84 (Tex. Crim. App. 2016).

11.   *See, e.g.*, ***Murchison v. State***, 93 S.W.3d 239, 250-51 (Tex. App.—Houston [14th Dist.] 2002, pet. ref'd) (in securities-fraud case, expert testimony that company owners could not foresee a decrease in bond value and thus would not know they would be unable to repay debts was not material to issue of whether they intentionally failed to disclose facts to investors).

12.   TEX. R. EVID. 401(a); ***Petetan v. State***, ___ S.W.3d ___ (Tex. Crim. App. 2017) (No. AP-77,038; 3-8-17); ***Henley***, 493 S.W.3d at 84; *e.g.*, ***In re Nat'l Lloyds Ins.***, ___ S.W.3d ___ (Tex. 2017) (No. 15-0591; 6-9-17) (orig. proceeding) (in response to challenge of attorney-fee request, trial court erred in ordering production of opposing party's hourly rates, total amount billed, and total reimbursable expenses; this information lacked probative value as comparator for requesting party's fees and did not make it any more probable that requesting party's fees were reasonable and necessary); *see, e.g.*, ***Thomas v. State***, 916 S.W.2d 540, 543 (Tex. App.—Waco 1995, no pet.) (in expunction case, harmful error to exclude evidence that petitioner's daughter fabricated allegations of sexual abuse, which was clearly relevant; "for evidence to be relevant, it must have probative value that tends to make a particular proposition more or less likely; and that proposition must be of some consequence at trial").

13.   Thus, evidence that demonstrates the underlying purpose of a law or statute may not be relevant in a particular case. *See, e.g.*, ***Roise v. State***, 7 S.W.3d 225, 237-38 (Tex. App.—Austin 1999, pet. ref'd) (expert's testimony that child pornography harms children and society was not relevant in proving defendant committed offense of possession of child pornography).

helpful in determining the truth or falsity of any material fact.[14] Thus, a particular trial judge does not personally need to find a logical connection between the evidence offered and the fact in issue to determine that the evidence is relevant, as long as rational jurors could reasonably find such a connection.[15] For the evidence to be relevant, "[t]here must be some logical connection, either directly or by inference, between the fact offered and the fact to be proved...."[16]

Therefore, in determining relevance, the court looks to the purpose for offering the evidence—the material fact to be proved—and whether there is a direct or logical connection between the offered evidence and the proposition to be proved.[17] If there is any reasonable logical nexus, the evidence will pass the Rule 401 relevance test.[18]

---

14. ***Montgomery v. State***, 810 S.W.2d 372, 376 (Tex. Crim. App. 1990) (orig. op.); ***Hernandez v. State***, 327 S.W.3d 200, 206 (Tex. App.—San Antonio 2010, pet. ref'd); *accord* Cathleen C. Herasimchuk, *The Relevancy Revolution in Criminal Law: A Practical Tour Through the Texas Rules of Criminal Evidence*, 20 ST. MARY'S L.J. 737, 743-44 (1989); *see, e.g.*, ***Martinez v. State***, 327 S.W.3d 727, 736-37 (Tex. Crim. App. 2010) (witness's testimony that defendant threatened her unborn child after she testified against him at his capital-murder trial was relevant to jury's determination of defendant's future dangerousness, which was an issue in the punishment stage).

15. *See Montgomery*, 810 S.W.2d at 382; *cf. United States v. 478.34 Acres of Land, Tract No. 400*, 578 F.2d 156, 160 (6th Cir. 1978) (discussing relevance under Federal Rule 104(b)).

16. ***Pittman v. Baladez***, 158 Tex. 372, 381, 312 S.W.2d 210, 216 (1958); *accord* ***Rhey v. Redic***, 408 S.W.3d 440, 460 (Tex. App.—El Paso 2013, no pet.); ***Clark v. Randalls Food***, 317 S.W.3d 351, 357 (Tex. App.—Houston [1st Dist.] 2010, pet. denied).

17. ***Layton v. State***, 280 S.W.3d 235, 240 (Tex. Crim. App. 2009); *Rhey*, 408 S.W.3d at 460; ***Republic Waste Servs., Ltd. v. Martinez***, 335 S.W.3d 401, 406 (Tex. App.—Houston [1st Dist.] 2011, no pet.); *see Henley*, 493 S.W.3d at 83-84; *cf. **Richards v. Hertz Corp.***, 953 N.Y.S.2d 654, 656-57 (N.Y. App. Div. 2012) (defendant sought information from plaintiff's Facebook account to rebut personal-injury claims; trial court was ordered to conduct in camera inspection of account to determine relevance of material while protecting plaintiff's privacy).

In *Henley*, an assault case, the defendant claimed he was justified in assaulting his ex-wife because he acted in defense of a third person. 493 S.W.3d at 81-82. He called his ex-wife to testify, outside the jury's hearing, and also offered his own testimony, to prove that his ex-wife was an unfit parent and their sons were in danger of being harmed by her new husband and his former stepson. *Id.* at 81-84. The trial judge excluded this evidence as irrelevant to the defense. *Id.* at 88. Because there was no evidence that the defendant needed to make a split-second decision to save his sons from immediate harm, which is required for a theory of defense of a third person, the Texas Court of Criminal Appeals held that the exclusion was not an abuse of discretion. *Id.* at 92-93. That is, the offered evidence was irrelevant because it did not tend to make the likelihood that the boys were in immediate danger any more or less probable. *Id.* at 92. Even if the evidence had been relevant, the court of criminal appeals further held that the trial judge had authority under Rule 403 to exclude it. *Id.* at 93. Refer to notes 111-159 *infra* and accompanying text.

18. ***Reed v. State***, 59 S.W.3d 278, 281 (Tex. App.—Fort Worth 2001, pet. ref'd); ***Moreno v. State***, 944 S.W.2d 685, 691 (Tex. App.—Houston [14th Dist.] 1997), *aff'd*, 22 S.W.3d 482 (Tex. Crim. App. 1999); ***Fletcher v. State***, 852 S.W.2d 271, 276-77 (Tex. App.—Dallas 1993, pet. ref'd); *e.g.*, *Ex parte Twine*, 111 S.W.3d 664, 666-67 (Tex. App.—Fort Worth 2003, pet. ref'd) (reversible error to exclude record excerpt from different trial in which prosecutor had asked another defendant a similar question about her post-arrest silence when excerpt was offered to show that prosecutor was aware of the danger of commenting on post-arrest silence and thus acted recklessly in causing mistrial).

Attorneys should always attempt to establish an explicit connection or nexus between the offered evidence and the material fact. Without an explicit connection, the evidence will not pass the relevance test. *See, e.g.*, ***Willingham v. State***, 897 S.W.2d 351, 358 (Tex. Crim. App. 1995) (defense could not impeach State's witness with alleged motive to curry favor with the State because there was no evidence of link between asserted motive and witness's testimony); *In re C.P.*, 998 S.W.2d 703, 711-12 (Tex. App.—Waco 1999, no pet.) (State did not show relevance of juvenile's unauthorized use of motor vehicle to "joyride" throughout state, which occurred after the charged offense of unauthorized use of her father's car); ***Duncan v. State***, 899 S.W.2d 279, 280-81 (Tex. App.—Houston [14th Dist.] 1995, pet. ref'd) (defense could not cross-examine State's witness about his deferred adjudication on an unrelated charge because there was no evidence that this mere status exposed him to pressure from the prosecution to testify favorably for the State).

1. General principle of relevance. Direct evidence rarely presents relevance problems.[19] No one would question that a witness's testimony "A shot B" tended to show that A was the person who shot B. This testimony is direct evidence of a material proposition and is always relevant. The chain of inferences is very short—if the jury believes the witness, the proposition is true. Similarly, a reasonable person seeking to determine the intent of a testator would want to examine the will itself. The question of relevance arises primarily when fact X, in the form of either testimonial or real evidence, is offered as circumstantial proof of fact Y. When the prosecution offers a witness's testimony that A was running from the scene where B was shot or seeks to introduce a pistol bearing A's fingerprints that was found at the scene, the relevance of the evidence depends on whether a reasonable person might infer from the evidence that A shot B.[20] Thus, the probative value of circumstantial evidence depends on the chain of inferences between the evidence and the material proposition.[21]

Relevance is not an inherent characteristic of an item of evidence.[22] Rather, it describes the relationship between the evidence and the proposition to be proved.[23] No purely legal test determines whether evidence tends to prove or disprove a proposi-

---

19.   Some Texas courts and commentators suggest that the term "relevant" refers only to circumstantial evidence instead of to the probative value of both direct and circumstantial evidence. *See* **Grp. Hosp. Servs., Inc. v. Daniel**, 704 S.W.2d 870, 879-80 (Tex. App.—Corpus Christi 1985, no writ) ("'Material' should refer to proof, whether direct or circumstantial, of a pleaded element of the case or other provable matters such as impeachment or background information helpful to the trier of fact. 'Relevant' in turn should refer only to proof by circumstantial evidence ...."); McCORMICK ON EVIDENCE, *supra* note 1, §185, at 543-46 (describing the relevance of circumstantial evidence); Hulen D. Wendorf, *The 1984 Texas Rules of Evidence Amendments*, 37 BAYLOR L. REV. 81, 88 (1985) (describing the amendments and noting the dichotomy between direct and circumstantial evidence). But Rule 401 makes no distinction—the term "relevant" refers to both direct and circumstantial evidence.

20.   *See* McCORMICK ON EVIDENCE, *supra* note 1, §185, at 544; *see also* **E-Z Mart Stores, Inc. v. Havner**, 832 S.W.2d 368, 375 (Tex. App.—Texarkana 1992) (Grant, J., dissenting) (discussing the reasonableness of inferences required by circumstantial evidence), *writ denied*, 846 S.W.2d 286 (Tex. 1993).

21.   *See* **In re Lipsky**, 460 S.W.3d 579, 588-89 (Tex. 2015) (orig. proceeding) ("Circumstantial evidence can, of course, be vague, indefinite, or inconclusive, but it is not so by definition. Rather, it is simply indirect evidence that creates an inference to establish a central fact. It is admissible unless the connection between the fact and the inference is too weak to be of help in deciding the case."); *see, e.g.*, **Rivera v. State**, 130 S.W.3d 454, 460 (Tex. App.—Corpus Christi 2004, no pet.) (evidence that child-abuse victim's mother had declined to press charges after reporting an act of sexual misconduct by a male relative when she was 16 lacked probative value when offered to establish that mother was "a troubled young woman who was capable of hurting her own child"). Circumstantial evidence that tends to prove an elemental fact or that is a link in the chain of proof of an elemental fact is relevant even if a verdict could not be supported on that fact alone. *See, e.g.*, **Moyer v. State**, 948 S.W.2d 525, 530-31 (Tex. App.—Fort Worth 1997, pet. ref'd) (magazines depicting nude women were admissible as circumstantial evidence of defendant's intent to kidnap and sexually abuse victim); **Darby v. State**, 922 S.W.2d 614, 620 (Tex. App.—Fort Worth 1996, pet. ref'd) (evidence of sexually explicit magazine found in defendant's closet was admissible as circumstantial evidence of defendant's intent to commit indecency with a child).

22.   *Henley*, 493 S.W.3d at 84.

23.   *Id.*; FED. R. EVID. 401 advisory committee's note; James, *supra* note 7, at 690; *see* **Lone Star Gas Co. v. State**, 137 Tex. 279, 313-14, 153 S.W.2d 681, 699-700 (1941) (evidence of conditions and events occurring before and after a disputed administrative order is admissible if it tends to prove or disprove the validity of the order), *leave denied sub nom.* **Ex parte Texas**, 315 U.S. 8 (1942); *see, e.g.*, **Wirtz v. Orr**, 575 S.W.2d 66, 71 (Tex. Civ. App.—Texarkana 1978, writ dism'd) (tax return was admissible because it tended to disprove defendant's claim that he was entitled to equity gains).

tion;[24] rather, the test is one of "logic and common sense."[25] There must be a direct or logical connection between the offered evidence and the fact to be proved;[26] the evidence must have "rational probative value"[27] and must "naturally and logically" tend to establish a fact;[28] or the trier of fact must be able to reasonably infer the connection.[29]

Relevance is a yes-or-no binary proposition—either it is present or it is not.[30] Evidence is relevant if it alters the probabilities involved to any degree.[31] An item of evidence may be more or less probative, not more or less relevant. Evidence with weak probative value may not be excluded as irrelevant, but its probative value may be substantially outweighed by one or more of the Rule 403 counterfactors.[32]

---

24. *Miller v. State*, 36 S.W.3d 503, 507 (Tex. Crim. App. 2001); *see Pound v. Popular Dry Goods Co.*, 139 S.W.2d 341, 343 (Tex. Civ. App.—El Paso 1940, no writ); James, *supra* note 7, at 693-94.

25. *Miller*, 36 S.W.3d at 507; James, *supra* note 7, at 694; *see* FED. R. EVID. 401 advisory committee's note (relevance depends on principles of "experience or science"); THAYER, *supra* note 1, at 265 (in determining relevance, law refers to logic and general experience).

26. *Pittman v. Baladez*, 158 Tex. 372, 381, 312 S.W.2d 210, 216 (1958); *Clark v. Randalls Food*, 317 S.W.3d 351, 357 (Tex. App.—Houston [1st Dist.] 2010, pet. denied); *Pope v. State*, 161 S.W.3d 114, 123 (Tex. App.—Fort Worth 2004), *aff'd*, 207 S.W.3d 352 (Tex. Crim. App. 2006); *see, e.g.*, *JLG Trucking, LLC v. Garza*, 466 S.W.3d 157, 162-63 (Tex. 2015) (in personal-injury case, trial court improperly excluded evidence of second accident that occurred three months after accident at issue as alternative cause of plaintiff's injuries; evidence was relevant because there was a direct connection between evidence and fact to be proved); *In re Nat'l Lloyds Ins.*, 449 S.W.3d 486, 488-89 (Tex. 2014) (orig. proceeding) (per curiam) (in case involving alleged underpayment of insurance claims, trial court abused its discretion by issuing overbroad discovery order compelling production of claim files for storm-damaged properties of unrelated third parties involving same adjusting firm that handled plaintiff's claim; information was not reasonably calculated to lead to discovery of relevant evidence); *Goff v. State*, 931 S.W.2d 537, 553 (Tex. Crim. App. 1996) (trial court properly excluded evidence of murder victim's prior convictions, work ethic, and drug use because defendant showed no relevance between that evidence and the charged crime).

27. *E.g.*, *Pound*, 139 S.W.2d at 343 (evidence that plaintiff's suit against manufacturer and distributor of product was dismissed was not relevant to show retailer's liability for injuries; however, admission was not reversible error).

28. *Id.*

29. *See Lange Cable Tool Drilling Co. v. Barnett Pet. Corp.*, 142 S.W.2d 833, 835 (Tex. Civ. App.—Galveston 1940, no writ); *Dudley v. Strain*, 130 S.W. 778, 782 (Tex. Civ. App.—Austin 1910, no writ).

30. *Cf.* Richard D. Friedman, *Irrelevance, Minimal Relevance, and Meta-Relevance*, 34 HOUS. L. REV. 55, 65 (1997) (discussing relevance under Federal Rule 401).

31. *See Brown v. State*, 757 S.W.2d 739, 740 (Tex. Crim. App. 1988) ("[A]ny item of evidence that alters the probability of a consequential fact is relevant because to alter the probabilities of a fact there must be a subjective relationship between the proffered evidence and the ultimate fact."); *see, e.g.*, *Davis v. State*, 329 S.W.3d 798, 820-21 (Tex. Crim. App. 2010) (in sentencing stage of trial for capital murder of 15-year-old girl, trial court did not err in admitting audio recording of defendant telling misogynistic jokes while he was incarcerated; evidence was relevant to defendant's future dangerousness); *Republic Waste Servs., Ltd. v. Martinez*, 335 S.W.3d 401, 408 (Tex. App.—Houston [1st Dist.] 2011, no pet.) (evidence of decedent's illegal immigration status was relevant to issue of his potential earning capacity; "it has a tendency to make the existence of the fact that [decedent] would have continued to earn $33,000 per year in the United States for the remainder of his working lifetime less probable and to make the fact that he would have earned his wages in El Salvador more probable"). This viewpoint follows Texas common law. *See Waldrop v. State*, 138 Tex. Crim. 166, 168, 133 S.W.2d 969, 970 (1939) (evidence that "conduces to the proof of a pertinent hypothesis" is relevant (quoting 1 E.T. BRANCH, BRANCH'S ANNOTATED PENAL CODE OF THE STATE OF TEXAS §97 (1916))).

32. Refer to notes 111-159 *infra* and accompanying text.

The offered item of evidence may be relevant without establishing a prima facie case.[33] Charles McCormick states the distinction between relevancy and sufficiency:

> The test of relevancy, which is to be applied by the trial judge in determining whether a particular item or group of items of evidence is to be admitted is a different and less stringent one than the standard used at a later stage in deciding whether all the evidence of the party on an issue is sufficient to permit the issue to go to the jury. A brick is not a wall.[34]

To be relevant, evidence must provide only "a small nudge toward proving or disproving some fact of consequence"; it does not need to make that fact more likely than not.[35] Furthermore, the proposition at issue does not even need to be the most likely inference from the evidence.[36]

Moreover, the proposition to be proved may be made more or less likely by evidence only remotely connected to it. Thus, if fact A tends to prove fact B, which in turn tends to prove material proposition C, fact A is relevant to proposition C.[37] Neither Federal Rule 401 nor Texas Rule 401 has changed the traditional concept of logical relevance. If the evidence is immaterial, it cannot be relevant under Rule 401 and will be excluded under Rule 402.[38] If the evidence has no tendency to prove the material proposition, it will also be excluded under Rule 402. But if the evidence tends to prove the material proposition, it will be admitted under Rule 402 unless there is another basis for exclusion in the Rules.[39]

---

33. McCormick's Handbook of the Law of Evidence §185, at 435-38 (Edward W. Cleary et al. eds., 2d ed. 1972) [hereinafter McCormick's Handbook II].

34. *Id.* §185, at 436; *see* **Transp. Ins. v. Moriel**, 879 S.W.2d 10, 24-25 (Tex. 1994). *See generally* Friedman, *supra* note 30, at 57-63 (examining the minimalist definition of relevancy). The Texas common law also used this approach. *See* **West v. First Baptist Church**, 123 Tex. 388, 402, 71 S.W.2d 1090, 1097 (1934) (mere evidence of suspicious circumstances will not, in and of itself, support an inference of bad faith; in conjunction with other evidence, it could form a part of the necessary proof); **Int'l & Great N. R.R. v. Jackson**, 47 Tex. Civ. App. 26, 31, 103 S.W. 709, 710 (Austin 1907, no writ) (weight of the evidence does not affect its admissibility).

35. **Stewart v. State**, 129 S.W.3d 93, 96 (Tex. Crim. App. 2004); **Montgomery v. State**, 810 S.W.2d 372, 376 (Tex. Crim. App. 1990) (orig. op.); **Henderson v. State**, 906 S.W.2d 589, 594 (Tex. App.—El Paso 1995, pet. ref'd); *accord* **Mendiola v. State**, 21 S.W.3d 282, 284 (Tex. Crim. App. 2000); **Castillo v. State**, 939 S.W.2d 754, 758 (Tex. App.—Houston [14th Dist.] 1997, pet. ref'd); *e.g.*, **Simpson v. State**, 181 S.W.3d 743, 749 (Tex. App.—Tyler 2005, pet. ref'd) (excerpt from letter to defendant's girlfriend that defendant wrote while in jail "could have been read to mean that Appellant pleaded not guilty and was not guilty, or that he pleaded not guilty, but was guilty of the charged offense. Either reading could provide the jury with a 'small nudge' towards determining whether Appellant committed the charged offense, a fact of consequence."); *see* 22 Charles A. Wright & Kenneth W. Graham, Jr., Federal Practice and Procedure §5165, at 49 (1978) (evidence is relevant "if it has the slightest bit of probative worth").

36. McCormick on Evidence, *supra* note 1, §185, at 542-43; *see* **Menchaca v. State**, 901 S.W.2d 640, 648 (Tex. App.—El Paso 1995, pet. ref'd) (only one theory of relevance is needed to admit evidence, regardless of whether that theory is first shown to be "true or even likely").

37. *See, e.g.*, **Lange Cable Tool Drilling Co. v. Barnett Pet. Corp.**, 142 S.W.2d 833, 835 (Tex. Civ. App.—Galveston 1940, no writ) (evidence that a party agreed to drill the plug out of a well could support the inference that the party was an independent contractor; evidence was admissible because it supported an inferential chain).

38. *See* Tex. R. Evid. 401(b). Refer to notes 60-82 *infra* and accompanying text.

39. *See, e.g.*, **Nabors Well Servs., Ltd. v. Romero**, 456 S.W.3d 553, 563 (Tex. 2015) (in automobile-accident cases, trial court may consider relevant evidence of plaintiff's preoccurrence, injury-causing conduct, such as nonuse of

2. Relevance of specific types of evidence. Evidence bearing on credibility—whether it impeaches, corroborates, or rehabilitates the witness—is always relevant, although not always admissible.[40] For example, a witness may testify to fact B, which tends to prove material proposition C. Impeachment evidence can make the witness less worthy of belief and thus can make proposition C less likely.[41] Rehabilitation or corroboration evidence can make the witness more believable and thus make proposition C more likely.[42]

Similarly, evidence proving an expert's qualifications is always relevant.[43] Because proof of an expert's qualifications makes the expert more believable, an expert's opinion about a material proposition (or some evidence ultimately leading to a material proposition) carries greater weight with the trier of fact and thus makes the material proposition more likely.

General background evidence is relevant.[44] The trier of fact is in a better position to evaluate evidence and determine facts for deciding a material proposition after learning the background. Such background evidence thus tends to make the material proposition more or less likely. However, the Texas Court of Criminal Appeals has cautioned attorneys about offering background evidence:

---

seat belt, in determining proportionate responsibility; relevant seat-belt evidence is subject to objection and exclusion under Rule 403). Refer to notes 93-96, 100 *infra* and accompanying text.

40.   *See, e.g., Castillo*, 939 S.W.2d at 758-59 (witnesses' motives are never regarded as immaterial or collateral, but questioning police officer about making "marginal arrests knowing he would collect more overtime pay for each additional arrest he made" was too attenuated and thus was properly excluded under Rule 403); *Villanueva v. State*, 768 S.W.2d 900, 902 (Tex. App.—San Antonio 1989, pet. ref'd) (evidence demonstrating that defendant had knowledge of real-estate business was admissible to impeach claims that he did not); *see also Richards v. Hertz Corp.*, 953 N.Y.S.2d 654, 656-57 (N.Y. App. Div. 2012) (in personal-injury case, plaintiff claimed her injuries impaired her ability to play sports; court ordered disclosure of photographs on plaintiff's Facebook page depicting her participating in sporting activities after the accident).

41.   *See, e.g., Cruz v. State*, 122 S.W.3d 309, 313 (Tex. App.—Houston [1st Dist.] 2003, no pet.) (reversible error to exclude evidence that codefendant, identified by victim as one of the robbers, had an alibi when offered to impeach accuracy of victim's testimony identifying codefendant and to create question of whether victim could accurately identify any of the robbers).

42.   *See, e.g., Amunson v. State*, 928 S.W.2d 601, 604-05 (Tex. App.—San Antonio 1996, pet. ref'd) (trial court erred in excluding defendant's offer of child murder victim's school records that showed victim's father had been reported to Department of Human Services for alleged child abuse and that child had bruises on his arms; evidence was relevant because it tended to corroborate defendant's testimony that he believed the victim was afraid of his father).

43.   Refer to *Article VII: Opinions & Expert Testimony*, *infra* p. 705.

44.   *See Schuessler v. State*, 719 S.W.2d 320, 329 (Tex. Crim. App. 1986) (op. on reh'g) (circumstances of the offense and life experiences of criminal defendant may aid jury in considering whether defendant was insane when he committed the offense); *Jackson v. Creditwatch, Inc.*, 84 S.W.3d 397, 404-05 (Tex. App.—Fort Worth 2002) (evidence of acts occurring outside statute of limitations may be relevant contextual background evidence of purportedly tortious acts occurring within statute of limitations), *rev'd in part on other grounds*, 157 S.W.3d 814 (Tex. 2005); *Callaway v. State*, 818 S.W.2d 816, 826 (Tex. App.—Amarillo 1991, pet. ref'd) ("[B]ackground evidence is relevant … because it furnishes the context for a realistic comprehension and evaluation of evidence of the offense by the factfinder."); *see, e.g., Kimes v. State*, 740 S.W.2d 903, 907 (Tex. App.—Corpus Christi 1987, pet. ref'd) (in capital-murder trial, witness's testimony about codefendant's unsuccessful attempts to purchase a gun from witness was admissible because it provided background information and illuminated circumstances leading up to victim's murder); *Majid v. State*, 713 S.W.2d 405, 412-13 (Tex. App.—El Paso 1986, pet. ref'd) (general background information on the "family context out of which the crime arose" was relevant).

Typically, so-called "background" evidence is admissible, not because it has particularly compelling probative value with respect to the elements of the alleged offense, but simply because it provides the jury with perspective, so that the jury is equipped to evaluate, in proper context, *other* evidence that more directly relates to elemental facts. But it is not necessary to go into elaborate detail in setting the evidentiary scene, and there is a danger inherent in doing so. Because the relevance of "background" evidence is marginal to begin with, the introduction of too much incriminating detail may, whenever the evidence has some objectionable quality not related to its marginal relevance, prove far more prejudicial than probative.[45]

Evidence of conduct that shows a "consciousness of guilt" or acceptance of responsibility is relevant because such evidence tends to prove that a person committed a particular act.[46] "A consciousness of guilt is perhaps one of the strongest kinds of evidence of guilt."[47] Thus, evidence of attempting to conceal or destroy incriminating evidence,[48] fleeing the scene of a crime or evading arrest,[49] tampering with a witness,[50]

---

45. *Langham v. State*, 305 S.W.3d 568, 580 (Tex. Crim. App. 2010).

46. 2 ROY R. RAY, TEXAS PRACTICE: TEXAS LAW OF EVIDENCE CIVIL AND CRIMINAL §1538, at 242 (3d ed. 1980); *see Bartlett v. State*, 270 S.W.3d 147, 153 & n.20 (Tex. Crim. App. 2008) (defendant's refusal to take a breath test is relevant to show consciousness of guilt in DWI prosecution); *see, e.g., Torres v. State*, 794 S.W.2d 596, 598 (Tex. App.—Austin 1990, no pet.) (evidence of threatening phone calls from jail was admissible to show consciousness of guilt).

Circumstantial evidence of innocence may also be relevant under Rule 401. For example, in *Renfro v. State*, the court of appeals held that a defendant charged with indecency with a child should have been permitted to offer exculpatory evidence—instances of indecent exposure committed by a man matching the defendant's description—to prove that he had been misidentified as the perpetrator on two similar contemporaneous occasions. 822 S.W.2d 757, 758 (Tex. App.—Houston [14th Dist.] 1992, pet. ref'd); *see also Daggett v. State*, 187 S.W.3d 444, 452 n.18 (Tex. Crim. App. 2005) ("'[T]he doctrine of chances' might be equally applicable to prove the commission of the charged offense *or* the fabrication of the [complainant's] testimony."); *Fox v. State*, 115 S.W.3d 550, 561 (Tex. App.—Houston [14th Dist.] 2002, pet. ref'd) ("A defendant may also use the doctrine of chances defensively if the series of unusual events, alone or with other evidence, tends to negate the defendant's guilt of the crime charged."). For a discussion of the doctrine of chances, refer to notes 512-537 *infra* and accompanying text. Evidence of such misidentification tends to make it more probable that another person, not the defendant, committed the crime charged. *Renfro*, 822 S.W.2d at 759; *see Holt v. United States*, 342 F.2d 163, 165 (5th Cir. 1965) ("[W]here the identity of a defendant is an important issue in a prosecution for a crime, evidence showing that another person similar in appearance to the defendant was committing similar crimes at about the same time, and that one person had mistakenly identified the defendant as such criminal is admissible."); *see, e.g., Jackson v. State*, 551 S.W.2d 351, 352-53 (Tex. Crim. App. 1977) (trial court improperly excluded evidence that complainant in another criminal proceeding had erroneously identified defendant as the perpetrator and then later identified another person who had also confessed to the charged offense); *Kesterson v. State*, 997 S.W.2d 290, 294-95 (Tex. App.—Dallas 1999, no pet.) (defendant should have been allowed to offer evidence of child complainant's prior statement accusing another male relative of molesting her to prove that this man, not defendant, committed charged sexual offense); *see also Contreras v. State*, 915 S.W.2d 510, 518-19 (Tex. App.—El Paso 1995, pet. ref'd) (acknowledging common-law doctrine of admissibility of third-party-guilt evidence, but noting that it was superseded by the Rules; defendant's proffered evidence of a police investigation of another person, without more, does not tend to show that third person's guilt).

47. *Hedrick v. State*, 473 S.W.3d 824, 831 (Tex. App.—Houston [14th Dist.] 2015, no pet.); 2 RAY, *supra* note 46, §1538, at 242.

48. *See Schuessler*, 719 S.W.2d at 329 (op. on reh'g) (concealment of evidence could show that, contrary to his claim, defendant was not insane when he committed the offense); *Johnson v. State*, 583 S.W.2d 399, 409 (Tex. Crim. App. [Panel Op.] 1979) (any attempt to fabricate evidence is admissible against the accused); *see, e.g., Brown v. State*,

RULES 401-402

using a false name,[51] or other similar conduct is relevant as circumstantial evidence of guilt.[52]

Evidence of a person's motive to perform a certain act is relevant to prove that the person performed that act. From proof of the motive, the fact-finder is entitled to draw the inference of the act's commission.[53] On the other hand, opinion testimony that is conclusory or speculative is not relevant under Rule 401 "because it does not tend to make the existence of material facts more probable or less probable."[54]

---

657 S.W.2d 117, 119 (Tex. Crim. App. 1983) (evidence that defendant had a gun and threatened to kill complaining witness's family was admissible to show an effort to suppress evidence); *Martin v. State*, 151 S.W.3d 236, 244-45 & n.6 (Tex. App.—Texarkana 2004, pet. ref'd) (evidence that defendant burned murder victim's truck on the night of the murder was "powerful evidence" of his consciousness of guilt; defendant's course of action in which he "fled the scene of the shooting, burned the truck where the shooting occurred, disposed of the murder weapon, changed into clean clothes, and tried to avoid police for a couple of days" was consistent only with a consciousness of guilt).

49. *See Bigby v. State*, 892 S.W.2d 864, 883 (Tex. Crim. App. 1994) (evidence of flight or escape is admissible as a relevant circumstance from which an inference of guilt may be drawn if it appears that the flight has some legal relevance to the charged offense; to exclude such evidence, defendant must affirmatively show that the flight is directly connected to some other transaction and that it was not connected with the charged offense); *Cantrell v. State*, 731 S.W.2d 84, 92 (Tex. Crim. App. 1987) ("Flight is a circumstance from which guilt may be inferred. Consequently, evidence of flight is admissible even though it may show the commission of other crimes. Such evidence is also relevant to show efforts made to locate or apprehend a defendant, his pursuit and capture, [and] circumstances of his arrest including his resistance."); *see, e.g., Cardenas v. State*, 971 S.W.2d 645, 649 (Tex. App.—Dallas 1998, pet. ref'd) (defendant denied involvement in shooting, but admitted that he fled the scene; "[s]uch evidence of flight shows consciousness of guilt").

50. *See, e.g., Wilson v. State*, 7 S.W.3d 136, 140-41 (Tex. Crim. App. 1999) (defendant asked witness about witness's father and new baby; comments "reasonably could have been interpreted as a veiled attempt to influence [witness's] testimony" and were evidence of consciousness of guilt); *Rodriguez v. State*, 577 S.W.2d 491, 492-93 (Tex. Crim. App. [Panel Op.] 1979) (murder defendant "confronted one of the State's key witnesses, who was also the brother of the deceased, outside a bar at night. He told that witness to drop the charges against him. These are hardly the actions of an innocent accused. This evidence is every bit as probative of guilt, as would be flight by the accused."); *Wingate v. State*, 365 S.W.2d 169, 170 (Tex. Crim. App. 1963) (evidence that defendant offered police officers a bribe was admissible to show consciousness of guilt).

51. *See, e.g., Edwards v. State*, 156 Tex. Crim. 146, 149, 239 S.W.2d 618, 620 (1951) (evidence that murder defendant checked into hotel under an assumed name three hours after murder was probative of guilt).

52. *See, e.g., Hedrick*, 473 S.W.3d at 831 (evidence that defendant told witness her family "could be put" where murder victim's remains were if she said anything about defendant's showing her the remains was relevant as indicating consciousness of guilt); *Ross v. State*, 154 S.W.3d 804, 812 (Tex. App.—Houston [14th Dist.] 2004, pet. ref'd) (police-videotaped interviews with defendant containing false and inconsistent statements were admissible to show consciousness of guilt); *Couchman v. State*, 3 S.W.3d 155, 163-64 (Tex. App.—Fort Worth 1999, pet. ref'd) (inconsistent explanations by defendant were admissible to show consciousness of guilt); *see also Marles v. State*, 919 S.W.2d 669, 671 (Tex. App.—San Antonio 1996, pet. ref'd) (debating, without deciding, the relevance of evidence that defendant defecated in his pants when arrested; "[m]any nonverbal actions of a defendant at the time of arrest are relevant and admissible").

53. *See, e.g., Brimage v. State*, 918 S.W.2d 466, 505 (Tex. Crim. App. 1996) (op. on reh'g) (evidence of pornographic magazines and other sexual paraphernalia was relevant to show defendant's motive to commit kidnapping that was part of charged capital murder); *Saxer v. State*, 115 S.W.3d 765, 774-75 (Tex. App.—Beaumont 2003, pet. ref'd) (witness's testimony that he and victim split an amount of marijuana with defendant that they gave defendant to cover a debt they owed him, that witness and victim owed defendant money for drugs purchased from defendant, and that victim was afraid of defendant because she had helped defendant's wife move out of apartment was relevant to show defendant's motive to kill).

54. *Whirlpool Corp. v. Camacho*, 298 S.W.3d 631, 637 (Tex. 2009); *accord Gen. Motors Corp. v. Iracheta*, 161 S.W.3d 462, 470-71 (Tex. 2005); *Coastal Transp. Co. v. Crown Cent. Pet. Corp.*, 136 S.W.3d 227, 232 (Tex. 2004). Such "incompetent" evidence cannot support a jury verdict, even when the opponent does not make a timely objection. *See Iracheta*, 161 S.W.3d at 471; *Coastal Transp.*, 136 S.W.3d at 232.

3. **Conditional relevance.** On occasion, fact A is relevant to prove material proposition C only if fact B exists. The Advisory Committee on the Federal Rules considered the situation in which a party relies on a spoken statement to prove notice.[55] The relevance of such a statement is conditioned on evidence that the person sought to be charged with notice heard the statement.[56] Rule 401, together with Rule 104(b), allows the admission of conditionally relevant evidence.[57] Texas courts have long held that a court may admit evidence before the proponent establishes its relevance as long as (1) the proponent gives the court some sort of assurance that the other necessary evidence will be offered later or (2) the pleadings show that the tendered evidence will probably become relevant.[58] On the other hand, it is not error to exclude evidence when the conditional fact has not already been proved.[59]

C. Rule 401(b): Materiality

Rule 401(b) requires that the proposition for which the evidence is offered be "of consequence in determining the action"[60] (that is, provable or controlling), which depends mainly on the pleadings and the substantive law.[61] For example, a plaintiff who brings suit on a negligent-entrustment theory must plead that (1) the owner or the person having the right of control over a vehicle entrusted the vehicle to another person, (2) the other person was an unlicensed, incompetent, or reckless driver, (3) at the time of the entrustment, the owner knew or should have known that the other person was an unlicensed, incompetent, or reckless driver, (4) the driver was negligent on the occasion in question, and (5) the driver's negligence was the proximate cause of the accident.[62] These elements would constitute the material facts or issues in the lawsuit

---

55. FED. R. EVID. 401 advisory committee's note.

56. *Id.*

57. Refer to *Article I: General Provisions, supra* p. 91.

58. *See, e.g., **Thomas v. Atlanta Lumber Co.**,* 360 S.W.2d 445, 447-48 (Tex. Civ. App.—Texarkana 1962, no writ) (bill of sale was properly excluded because it did not go to the issue of what lumber had been transferred and no showing was made that it might later become relevant to another issue); ***Thompson v. State***, 319 S.W.2d 368, 370-71 (Tex. Civ. App.—Waco 1958, no writ) (price that condemnee paid for condemned property was not admissible because the purchase was not recent, value of the property had changed since the date of purchase, and there was no showing that defendant purchased the property in a free-market sale).

59. *See, e.g., **Houghton v. Port Terminal R.R.**,* 999 S.W.2d 39, 50-51 (Tex. App.—Houston [14th Dist.] 1999, no pet.) (engine-inspection reports that noted poor braking and flat spots on brakes were properly excluded because plaintiff did not offer evidence that any defect in brakes caused rough coupling that led to plaintiff's seat becoming dislodged).

60. TEX. R. EVID. 401(b); *In re Nat'l Lloyds Ins.*, ___ S.W.3d ___ (Tex. 2017) (No. 15-0591; 6-9-17) (orig. proceeding); *see Henley v. State*, 493 S.W.3d 77, 84 (Tex. Crim. App. 2016) ("A 'fact of consequence' includes either an elemental fact or an evidentiary fact from which an elemental fact can be inferred.").

61. *See **Henderson v. State**,* 906 S.W.2d 589, 597 (Tex. App.—El Paso 1995, pet. ref'd) ("The theories of the prosecution and the defensive theories determine the 'material' issues in each individual case."); ***San Antonio Traction Co. v. Higdon***, 58 Tex. Civ. App. 83, 87, 123 S.W. 732, 734 (San Antonio 1909, writ ref'd) (test of relevancy depends on the issues of fact and law raised by the pleadings, not the issues submitted to the jury); *cf. **John Hancock Mut. Life Ins. v. Dutton***, 585 F.2d 1289, 1294 (5th Cir. 1978) (under Federal Rule 401, "[d]etermining whether a fact is 'of consequence to the determination of the action' requires an examination of the applicable substantive law").

62. *See **Goodyear Tire & Rubber Co. v. Mayes**,* 236 S.W.3d 754, 758 (Tex. 2007) (per curiam).

if, after the defendant's denial, the pleadings rested there. If the plaintiff offers evidence at trial showing a principal-agent relationship between the defendant and the driver, the court should reject the evidence as immaterial. A principal-agent relationship is not material under the pleadings and substantive law.

As the substantive law develops and changes, so will the facts considered material to a particular type of lawsuit.[63] For example, Texas courts have expanded the scope of evidence deemed material to punitive damages in civil suits and in the punishment stage of a criminal trial.[64] The Texas Supreme Court held that a civil defendant's ability to pay a damages award bears directly on the issue of proper punishment and deterrence and is a material fact when the substantive law permits assessment of punitive damages.[65] Evidence of a civil defendant's net worth was traditionally neither discoverable nor admissible,[66] but the judicially created change in substantive law affected the definition of material facts.[67] Similarly, traditional Texas law in criminal cases had not recognized the materiality of the impact of a specific crime on the crime victim in determining the proper punishment for a defendant.[68] More recently, however,

---

63. Determining what facts are material to a lawsuit can depend on public-policy concerns as well as statutory elements. *See Sallings v. State*, 789 S.W.2d 408, 415 (Tex. App.—Dallas 1990, pet. ref'd). In *Sallings*, an aggravated-sexual-assault case, the 81-year-old complainant used the pseudonym "Jane Doe" to protect her privacy during the indictment and at trial. *Id.* at 412. Because the defendant received adequate notice of the complainant's name and complaints, the court found her name irrelevant and immaterial to the case. *Id.* at 415. Unfortunately, the court of appeals perpetuated the confusion between the two distinct concepts of relevance and materiality when it stated that the complainant's "true name was irrelevant in that it was not of consequence to the action." *Id.* More accurately, her name was immaterial; testimony about her name would have been more probative (or relevant) if her real name had been a material fact in the pleadings. But the proposition was not a matter in issue and thus was not provable in the case. The second element of Rule 401 was missing. *See* TEX. R. EVID. 401(b). Refer to note 11 *supra* and accompanying text.

64. In *Mendiola v. State*, the court of criminal appeals explained why the issue of legal "relevancy" is not entirely helpful in deciding the admissibility of evidence at the punishment stage of a criminal trial. 21 S.W.3d 282, 284-85 (Tex. Crim. App. 2000). Under current Texas statutes, punishment evidence is "'*a function of policy rather than relevancy*'" because there are no discrete factual questions to be resolved. *Id.* at 285 (quoting *Miller-El v. State*, 782 S.W.2d 892, 895 (Tex. Crim. App. 1990)). Rather, it is a "normative" process of deciding what punishment, out of a continuum of possibilities, is most appropriate. *See Mendiola*, 21 S.W.3d at 285.
 For guidance in deciding what types of specific evidence are admissible at the punishment stage as helpful to the jury, courts have looked to the legislative policies about punishment in Texas Penal Code §1.02. Section 1.02 sets out the objective of the Penal Code, including ensuring the public safety through the rehabilitation of those convicted and proscribing penalties proportionate to the seriousness of the offense. *See Rogers v. State*, 991 S.W.2d 263, 265-66 (Tex. Crim. App. 1999); *Najar v. State*, 74 S.W.3d 82, 87 (Tex. App.—Waco 2002, pet. dism'd).

65. *See Lunsford v. Morris*, 746 S.W.2d 471, 472-73 (Tex. 1988) (orig. proceeding), *disapproved on other grounds*, *Walker v. Packer*, 827 S.W.2d 833 (Tex. 1992).

66. *See Young v. Kuhn*, 71 Tex. 645, 652, 9 S.W. 860, 862 (1888); *Murphy v. Waldrip*, 692 S.W.2d 584, 588 (Tex. App.—Fort Worth 1985, writ ref'd n.r.e.).

67. *See Lunsford*, 746 S.W.2d at 473 ("In a suit in which exemplary damages may be recovered, we hold the defendant's net worth is 'relevant' and therefore discoverable ....").

68. *See, e.g.*, *Fowler v. State*, 171 Tex. Crim. 600, 605, 352 S.W.2d 838, 840-41 (1962) (reversible error to admit doctor's testimony about debilitating injuries suffered in car accident because this evidence did not resolve any issue in the case and probably resulted in a heavier penalty for defendant).

courts have noted that a crime victim's degree of injury is material in guiding the jury's assessment of a sentence if the fact-finder can rationally attribute moral culpability[69] for that injury to the defendant.[70]

Legislative enactments may state that a certain type of evidence is or is not relevant to prove a particular proposition. For example, Texas Code of Criminal Procedure chapter 38 makes evidence of other crimes, wrongs, or acts committed by the defendant against a child complainant admissible to prove the defendant's state of mind or his prior or subsequent relationship to the complainant in certain criminal prosecutions.[71] Similarly, crimes or bad acts such as gang membership may be considered as relevant evidence at the punishment stage of a criminal trial.[72]

The Model Code of Evidence and the common law use the term "material" broadly in determining the relevance of evidence.[73] The drafters of the Federal Rules rejected the word "material" as "ambiguous" and "loosely used."[74] Instead, Federal Rule 401

---

69. However, "evidence that draws comparisons between the victim and other members of society based on the victim's worth or morality should usually be excluded under Rule 403." *Hayden v. State*, 296 S.W.3d 549, 552 (Tex. Crim. App. 2009). Refer to notes 111-159 *infra* and accompanying text.

70. *See Hayden*, 296 S.W.3d at 552; *see, e.g.*, *Miller-El v. State*, 782 S.W.2d 892, 896-97 (Tex. Crim. App. 1990) (evidence of victim's paraplegia and its consequences was fully admissible during punishment stage to help jury assess appropriate penalty); *Ortiz v. State*, 825 S.W.2d 537, 541-42 (Tex. App.—El Paso 1992, no pet.) (evidence of long-term effects of aggravated sexual assault on victim was admissible during punishment stage); *Hunter v. State*, 799 S.W.2d 356, 360 (Tex. App.—Houston [14th Dist.] 1990, no pet.) (evidence of defendant's HIV infection was admissible during punishment stage of sexual-assault trial to show defendant's moral culpability); *Killebrew v. State*, 746 S.W.2d 245, 247-48 (Tex. App.—Texarkana 1987, pet. ref'd) (evidence of aggravated-assault victim's lingering fears was admissible during punishment stage to help jury assess appropriate penalty); *see also Cantu v. State*, 738 S.W.2d 249, 254 (Tex. Crim. App. 1987) (evidence of the severity of robbery victim's gunshot wounds was admissible to show the continuing nature of the crime); *Boone v. State*, 60 S.W.3d 231, 238 (Tex. App.—Houston [14th Dist.] 2001, pet. ref'd) ("Whether victim impact testimony is deemed relevant depends on whether the testimony has some bearing on the defendant's personal responsibility and moral guilt. If the defendant should have anticipated the particular effect on the victim or the victim's family (in other words: if the impact was foreseeable) then the evidence is relevant."); *Mathis v. State*, 67 S.W.3d 918, 930-31 (Tex. Crim. App. 2002) (Cochran, Womack, Hervey, Holcomb, JJ., concurring) (distinguishing "victim impact" evidence about the emotional consequences on the crime victim or his relatives from "victim impact" evidence about the physical consequences of defendant's actions toward the crime victim). This same evidence, however, is immaterial at the guilt stage of the criminal proceeding. *See, e.g.*, *Brown v. State*, 757 S.W.2d 739, 740-41 (Tex. Crim. App. 1988) (evidence of complainant's emotional trauma after her rape was immaterial because the only disputed issue in the case was rapist's identity).

71. TEX. CODE CRIM. PROC. art. 38.37, §1(b); *accord Sanders v. State*, 255 S.W.3d 754, 758 (Tex. App.—Fort Worth 2008, pet. ref'd); *see Dixon v. State*, 201 S.W.3d 731, 734 (Tex. Crim. App. 2006); *McCulloch v. State*, 39 S.W.3d 678, 679-80 (Tex. App.—Beaumont 2001, pet. ref'd). Refer to notes 1118-1125 *infra* and accompanying text.

72. *See* TEX. CODE CRIM. PROC. art. 37.07, §3(a)(1); *see also Woodward v. State*, 170 S.W.3d 726, 729-30 (Tex. App.—Waco 2005, pet. ref'd) (evidence of "White Pride" tattoo was relevant and admissible under Rule 403 at punishment stage to show that shootings were racially motivated and to rebut defendant's claim that he did not intend to kill anyone). Refer to note 298 *infra*. Under Rule 404(b), gang affiliation may also be relevant and admissible at either stage of trial to prove something besides conforming conduct, such as motive. *See Vasquez v. State*, 67 S.W.3d 229, 239 (Tex. Crim. App. 2002); *Rawlins v. State*, 521 S.W.3d 863, ___ (Tex. App.—Houston [1st Dist.] 2017, pet. filed 8-9-17); *Tibbs v. State*, 125 S.W.3d 84, 89 (Tex. App.—Houston [14th Dist.] 2003, pet. ref'd). Refer to notes 538-542 *infra* and accompanying text.

73. *See* MODEL CODE OF EVID. R. 104 (1942) (defining a material matter as anything provable in an action); *see also* 1 WIGMORE, *supra* note 1, §10, at 293-95 (describing the general rule that all facts having "rational probative value" are admissible absent a specific rule to the contrary).

74. FED. R. EVID. 401 advisory committee's note.

discusses facts "of consequence" to encompass the materiality requirement. While the original Texas Rule 401 explicitly distinguished between the concepts of materiality and probative value,[75] the rule was amended in 1984 to conform to Federal Rule 401.[76] In requiring that the proposition to be proved by the evidence must be a provable or controlling matter (i.e., material),[77] Rule 401 codified Texas common law.[78]

Rule 401's definition of relevant evidence does not require that the fact to be proved be in dispute.[79] In fact, the Advisory Committee on the Federal Rules noted that evidence may be admissible under Federal Rule 401 even when it is not offered to prove a

---

75. Texas Rule 401 as originally promulgated read as follows:

TEST OF RELEVANCY

(a) "Materiality" inquires whether there is any rational relationship or pertinence of the proffered evidence to any provable or controlling fact issue in dispute.

(b) "Relevancy" inquires whether the proffered evidence has probative value tending to establish the presence or absence, truth or falsity, of a fact.

(c) TEST: Is it material? If not, exclude. If yes, and only in that event, is it relevant? If not, exclude. If yes, admit.

Re: New Rules of Evidence, 641-642 S.W.2d (Tex. Cases) xxxix (1983, amended 1998). The Texas State Bar Liaison Committee on the Federal Rules of Evidence had originally recommended the wording of Federal Rule 401. *See* Tex. R. Evid. 401 (1982 Liaison Committee proposal), *reprinted infra* p. 1078. However, as it reviewed the proposed rules, the Supreme Court of Texas was persuaded to change the proposed rule by a letter from Houston attorney Tom Edwards. *See Transcript of Deliberations*, State Bar of Tex., Comm. on the Admin. of Rules of Evidence in Civil Cases (1984) (available in the Legislative Reference Library, Austin, Texas). Edwards's point was that "materiality" and "relevancy" are not synonymous and required separate definitions if the bench and bar were to ever escape the persistent confusion of the terms. Letter from Tom Edwards to Erwin McGee (Feb. 12, 1982), *reprinted in* Texas Senate Interim Study on Rules of Evidence File, pt. II, Post Adoption Correspondence 49 (available in the Legislative Reference Library, Austin, Texas). After making his arguments, Edwards proposed a test to differentiate between materiality and relevancy, which the Texas Supreme Court adopted virtually verbatim as Rule 401. *See* Letter from Tom Edwards to Erwin McGee (Feb. 12, 1982), *supra*, at 50-51.

76. *See In re: Adopted, Amended and Promulgated Rules of Evidence*, 669-670 S.W.2d (Tex. Cases) xxxiii (1984, amended 1998); *Transcript of Deliberations*, *supra* note 75. Rule 401 is identical to Federal Rule 401. Refer to note 2 *supra* and accompanying text.

77. *See* **Grp. Hosp. Servs., Inc. v. Daniel**, 704 S.W.2d 870, 879 (Tex. App.—Corpus Christi 1985, no writ) ("'Material' should refer to proof, whether direct or circumstantial, of a pleaded element of the case or other provable matters such as impeachment or background information helpful to the trier of fact.").

78. Texas has traditionally required that, to be admissible, the evidence offered must tend to prove or disprove "the issues being litigated," "some issue in the case," or "a material fact in issue." *See* **Stewart v. Control Data Corp.**, 580 S.W.2d 879, 882 (Tex. Civ. App.—Texarkana 1979, no writ) ("Ordinarily, acts of persons who are not parties to the lawsuit and which are unrelated to the issues being litigated are irrelevant and are not admissible in evidence."); **Wirtz v. Orr**, 575 S.W.2d 66, 71 (Tex. Civ. App.—Texarkana 1978, writ dism'd) ("Any competent evidence not privileged is admissible if it logically tends to prove or disprove a material fact in issue."); **Herfurth v. City of Dall.**, 410 S.W.2d 453, 456 (Tex. Civ. App.—Dallas 1966, writ ref'd n.r.e.) ("[E]vidence which does not tend to prove or disprove some issue in the case, and is therefore immaterial and irrelevant, is inadmissible."). Post-Rules cases have used the same or similar language in addressing the materiality requirement. *See* **King v. State**, 17 S.W.3d 7, 20 (Tex. App.—Houston [14th Dist.] 2000, pet. ref'd) ("Evidence that would have had no influence over any consequential fact for the jury's resolution is not relevant."); **Webb v. State**, 991 S.W.2d 408, 418 (Tex. App.—Houston [14th Dist.] 1999, pet. ref'd) (to be relevant, evidence "must have influence over a consequential fact"); **CPS Int'l, Inc. v. Harris & Westmoreland**, 784 S.W.2d 538, 544 (Tex. App.—Texarkana 1990, no writ) (describing relevant and material evidence as "any material fact involved in the issue or the question being tried"); *see, e.g.,* **Sallings v. State**, 789 S.W.2d 408, 416 (Tex. App.—Dallas 1990, pet. ref'd) (evidence that police officer was "out to get" defendant's family was irrelevant to "any material issue" in the case and inadmissible).

79. Texas common law had been unclear on this issue, and cases frequently suggested that evidence must be relevant to a contested issue. **Johnson v. State**, 698 S.W.2d 154, 160 (Tex. Crim. App. 1985); **Stone v. State**, 574 S.W.2d

disputed fact.[80] If a court decides to reject evidence on a particular fact already resolved for purposes of the lawsuit by judicial notice, stipulation, or failure of the opponent to deny the fact by sworn pleading, it should reject such evidence as "unfairly prejudicial," a "waste of time,"[81] or "cumulative" under Federal Rule 403 rather than rejecting it as immaterial under Rule 401.[82]

85, 89 (Tex. Crim. App. [Panel Op.] 1978); *see Lanham v. State*, 474 S.W.2d 197, 199 (Tex. Crim. App. 1971) (photographs must be legally relevant to the solution of a disputed issue of fact).

Even after the adoption of the Rules of Evidence, Texas courts have occasionally stated that relevance is determined by whether a consequential fact is disputed. In *Brown v. State*, the court of criminal appeals held that a rape victim's testimony about the long-term emotional effects of rape was inadmissible during the guilt-innocence stage of the trial because the defendant did not contest the fact that the victim was raped. 757 S.W.2d 739, 740-41 (Tex. Crim. App. 1988). Evidence of the victim's emotional difficulty after the rape, the majority reasoned, would not alter the probability that the rape occurred because that consequential fact was not disputed. *Id.* at 740. The concurrence, however, asserted that evidence of the victim's emotional and psychological state after the rape tended to make the victim's version of the rape more probable. *See id.* at 743 (McCormick, Onion, Davis, JJ., concurring).

80. The Advisory Committee states the following about Federal Rule 401:

The fact to which the evidence is directed need not be in dispute. While situations will arise which call for the exclusion of evidence offered to prove a point conceded by the opponent, the ruling should be made on the basis of such considerations as waste of time and undue prejudice (see Rule 403), rather than under any general requirement that evidence is admissible only if directed to matters in dispute. Evidence which is essentially background in nature can scarcely be said to involve disputed matter, yet it is universally offered and admitted as an aid to understanding. Charts, photographs, views of real estate, murder weapons, and many other items of evidence fall in this category. A rule limiting admissibility to evidence directed to a controversial point would invite the exclusion of this helpful evidence, or at least the raising of endless questions over its admission.

FED. R. EVID. 401 advisory committee's note. Some commentators note that requiring a fact to be "disputed" before it is material might lead courts to conclude that a litigant could bar the introduction of prejudicial but probative evidence by offering to stipulate to the fact that the evidence is offered to prove. *E.g.*, 22 WRIGHT & GRAHAM, *supra* note 35, §5164, at 44 (1978) (prosecutors offer proof of prior convictions of marijuana possession to prove that defendant knew the appearance of marijuana; requiring the fact to be in dispute would allow defendant to stipulate to knowledge of the appearance of marijuana to bar evidence of prior convictions); *see United States v. Grassi*, 602 F.2d 1192, 1197 (5th Cir. 1979) ("A piece of evidence can have probative value even in the event of an offer to stipulate to the issue on which the evidence is offered. A cold stipulation can deprive a party 'of the legitimate moral force of his evidence' … and can never fully substitute for tangible, physical evidence or the testimony of witnesses." (quoting 9 JOHN H. WIGMORE, A TREATISE ON THE ANGLO-AMERICAN SYSTEM OF EVIDENCE IN TRIALS AT COMMON LAW §2591, at 589 (3d ed. 1940))), *vacated on other grounds*, 448 U.S. 902 (1980).

The U.S. Supreme Court has held that although the prosecution generally does not need to agree to a stipulation of evidence, a defendant can sometimes prevent the prosecution from offering evidence of a fact by stipulating to that fact. *See Old Chief v. United States*, 519 U.S. 172, 191-92 (1997). For example, when a defendant is charged with the crime of being a felon in possession of a firearm, he can stipulate to the fact of his prior felony conviction and thus prevent the prosecution from offering any evidence on that element. *See id.* The Court explained that the name and nature of the defendant's prior conviction was relevant under Federal Rule 401 but excluded under Rule 403 because the risk that the jury would use that evidence for its impermissible purpose—evidence of criminal propensity—substantially outweighed its evidentiary value offered for the permissible purpose of proving the defendant's status as a felon. *Old Chief*, 519 U.S. at 178-81. *But see id.* at 193-94 (O'Connor, Rehnquist, Scalia, Thomas, JJ., dissenting) (disputing that the "prejudice" resulting from evidentiary use of the name and nature of a prior conviction is "unfair"). Texas courts have followed the *Old Chief* reasoning and result. Refer to notes 486-487 *infra* and accompanying text.

81. Refer to notes 166-167 *infra* and accompanying text.

82. In *Castro v. Sebesta*, a driver stipulated at trial that his gross negligence had proximately caused an automobile collision. 808 S.W.2d 189, 191 (Tex. App.—Houston [1st Dist.] 1991, no writ). The trial court excluded as irrelevant photographs of the accident scene and testimony that the defendant regularly smoked marijuana while driving. *Id.* at 192-94. The court of appeals, however, noted that the testimony was relevant to the determination of puni-

D. Rule 402: General Rule of Admissibility

After generally admitting all relevant evidence, Rule 402 categorizes exceptions to the general rule.[83] A variety of underlying policies justify these limitations.[84] A court may exclude relevant evidence because its admission (1) would contravene the U.S. Constitution (e.g., the privilege against self-incrimination),[85] (2) would contravene the Texas Constitution (e.g., the privilege against self-incrimination),[86] (3) would violate federal statutes (e.g., the results of certain electronic surveillance as set out in the Omnibus

---

tive damages and held that it was admissible to show the context of the defendant's actions on the night of the accident. *Id.* at 194. The court also concluded that the photographs of the accident scene were relevant to the issue of punitive damages. *See id.* at 193. The court then applied the appropriate Rule 403 analysis, noting that Rule 403 permits exclusion of relevant evidence only when its probative value is substantially outweighed by its unfair prejudice. *Castro*, 808 S.W.2d at 193. The court held that the photographs of the accident scene, which were taken at a distance and showed no blood or gore, were not unfairly prejudicial and were thus admissible. *Id.*

83. Rule 402 follows the federal rule, with only those changes necessary to adapt the rule to Texas. Refer to note 3 *supra* and accompanying text. The federal rule is derived from the Uniform Rules of Evidence and the Model Code of Evidence and is consistent with the common law. *See **Stuart v. Noble Ditch Co.**,* 76 P. 255, 257 (Idaho 1904) (if the pleadings raise an issue, evidence that tends to illuminate that issue is admissible); ***Neosho Valley Inv. Co. v. Hannum**,* 66 P. 631, 633 (Kan. 1901) (for evidence to be admissible, it must tend to prove or disprove a matter in controversy); ***Stroh v. Hinchman**,* 37 Mich. 490, 497 (1877) (if evidence has "some legitimate tendency to establish or disprove the fact in controversy," it is admissible); FED. R. EVID. 402 advisory committee's note (acknowledging the Uniform Rules); UNIF. R. EVID. 7 (1953), *superseded by* UNIF. R. EVID. 402 (1974) (stating that "[a]ll relevant evidence is admissible, except as otherwise provided by statute or by these rules or by other rules applicable in the courts of this State"); MODEL CODE OF EVID. R. 9 (1942) (stating that "except as otherwise provided in these Rules, … all relevant evidence is admissible").

84. Jack Weinstein and Margaret Berger explain these policies as follows:

> These policies [of excluding relevant evidence] find their expression in two classes of exclusionary rules that have very different objectives.
>
> One class—termed "auxiliary rules of probative force" by Wigmore—excludes certain types of evidence although relevant in the hopes of "improving the quality of proof and strengthening the probability of ascertaining the truth."
>
> The second class of rules limits admissibility in order to implement some extrinsic policy which the law considers more important than ascertaining the truth in a particular law suit.

1 JACK B. WEINSTEIN & MARGARET A. BERGER, WEINSTEIN'S EVIDENCE ¶402[01], at 402-11 (1995) (citations omitted).

85. U.S. CONST. amend. V; *see **Malloy v. Hogan**,* 378 U.S. 1, 8 (1964) (Fourteenth Amendment prohibits state infringement of the privilege against self-incrimination just as Fifth Amendment prevents the federal government from denying the privilege, thus elevating the constitutional principle above the State's need to admit relevant evidence); *see also **Maness v. Meyers**,* 419 U.S. 449, 465-66 (1975) (attorney cannot be held in contempt for counseling witness to assert Fifth Amendment privilege against self-incrimination and refuse to produce relevant evidence).

While the admission of all relevant evidence advances the truth-seeking mission of a trial, the exclusion of some types of relevant evidence is based on other important goals of the justice system "which the law considers more important than ascertaining the truth in a particular law suit." 1 WEINSTEIN & BERGER, *supra* note 84, ¶402[01], at 402-11. As Weinstein and Berger explain:

> Trials in our judicial system are intended to do more than merely determine what happened. Adjudication is a practical enterprise serving a variety of functions. Among the goals—in addition to truth finding—which the rules of procedure and evidence in this country have sought to satisfy are terminating disputes, economizing resources, inspiring confidence, supporting independent social politics, permitting ease in prediction and application, adding to the efficiency of the entire legal system, and tranquilizing disputants.

Id. ¶402[01], at 402-07.

86. TEX. CONST. art. I, §10; *see **Heitman v. State**,* 815 S.W.2d 681, 690 (Tex. Crim. App. 1991) (Texas Constitution may afford greater protection than U.S. Constitution).

Crime Control and Safe Streets Act),[87] (4) is prohibited by Texas statutes[88] (e.g., the Texas exclusionary rule set out in Texas Code of Criminal Procedure article 38.23),[89] (5) is prohibited by "these rules," meaning the Rules of Evidence (e.g., Rule 802, excluding hearsay),[90] or (6) is prohibited by other rules prescribed under statutory authority[91] (e.g., the Texas Rules of Civil Procedure).[92] Rule 402 did not change Texas law in this respect. Texas courts have always been bound by Texas and federal constitutional law, legislation, and rules prescribed pursuant to statutory authority. Texas courts must also be aware that relevant evidence could be excluded by specific provisions in the Texas Rules of Evidence.

Under Rule 402, relevant evidence is generally admissible[93] and should not be excluded without "very good cause."[94] Rules or principles that exclude relevant evidence must be supported by solid policy reasons.[95] Even improperly obtained evidence that

---

87. *See* 18 U.S.C. §2515 (excluding certain wire or oral communications intercepted by law-enforcement authority or other individuals).

88. The Texas Rules of Evidence supersede preexisting, inconsistent statutes and rules. *See* TEX. GOV'T CODE §22.004(c). When the supreme court adopts a rule, "all conflicting laws … governing practice and procedure in civil actions" are repealed. *Id.* When the court adopts new rules, it must file a list of those articles and sections of the general law that are repealed or modified in any way by the new rules. *Id.* That list has the same weight as a court decision. *Id.* Legislation enacted after the adoption of the rules supersedes those rules. *See, e.g.*, ***Few v. Charter Oak Fire Ins.***, 463 S.W.2d 424, 425-26 (Tex. 1971) (statute allowing a spouse to sue without joining the other spouse as plaintiff took precedence over a previously promulgated rule of civil procedure requiring the joinder of the other spouse); ***Harper v. Am. Motors Corp.***, 672 S.W.2d 44, 44-45 (Tex. App.—Houston [14th Dist.] 1984, no writ) (statute took precedence over time limitations in previously promulgated rule of civil procedure); ***Purolator Armored, Inc. v. R.R. Comm'n***, 662 S.W.2d 700, 702 n.4 (Tex. App.—Austin 1983, no writ) (later-enacted statute governing administrative procedure superseded the Texas Rules of Civil Procedure). The court of criminal appeals has similar rulemaking power for criminal cases. *See* TEX. GOV'T CODE §22.109.

89. This statute reads in part as follows:
> No evidence obtained by an officer or other person in violation of any provisions of the Constitution or laws of the State of Texas, or of the Constitution or laws of the United States of America, shall be admitted in evidence against the accused on the trial of any criminal case.

TEX. CODE CRIM. PROC. art. 38.23(a). The statute includes an exception for evidence obtained by a law-enforcement officer acting in objective good-faith reliance on a warrant based on probable cause. *Id.* art. 38.23(b); ***McClintock v. State***, ___ S.W.3d ___ (Tex. Crim. App. 2017) (No. PD-1641-15; 3-22-17).

90. *See* ***Schaffer v. State***, 777 S.W.2d 111, 114-15 (Tex. Crim. App. 1989) (while an officer's testimony about an accident will almost always be relevant, testimony containing hearsay elements should nevertheless be excluded); ***Edwards v. State***, 807 S.W.2d 338, 340 (Tex. App.—Houston [14th Dist.] 1991, pet. ref'd) (even if relevant, an individual's hearsay statements are inadmissible); *cf.* ***Decker v. Hatfield***, 798 S.W.2d 637, 639 (Tex. App.—Eastland 1990, writ dism'd) (in child-custody case, child's statement to expert that "he wanted to live with his mother" could have been excluded under Civil Rule 403 if its probative value had been substantially outweighed by the danger of unfair prejudice).

91. *See* TEX. R. EVID. 402.

92. *See, e.g.*, TEX. R. CIV. P. 215.2(b)(4) & 215.3 (court can prohibit a party who abuses discovery from introducing certain evidence in a civil trial).

93. ***Henley v. State***, 493 S.W.3d 77, 83 (Tex. Crim. App. 2016); ***Bartlett v. State***, 270 S.W.3d 147, 153 n.20 (Tex. Crim. App. 2008); ***Moses v. State***, 105 S.W.3d 622, 626 (Tex. Crim. App. 2003).

94. ***LSR Joint Venture No. 2 v. Callewart***, 837 S.W.2d 693, 698 (Tex. App.—Dallas 1992, writ denied).

95. ***Farr v. Wright***, 833 S.W.2d 597, 599 (Tex. App.—Corpus Christi 1992, writ denied).

is relevant to a material fact is admissible unless one of the Rules' explicit exclusionary provisions prohibits its admission.[96]

The trial court has broad discretion in determining the relevance and materiality of evidence under Rule 401, and its ruling will not be disturbed unless there is an abuse of discretion resulting in substantial prejudice to the rights of a party.[97] Only if an appellate court

> can say with confidence that by no reasonable perception of common experience can it be concluded that proffered evidence has a tendency to make the existence of a fact of consequence more or less probable than it would otherwise be, then it can be said the trial court abused its discretion to admit that evidence.[98]

Together, Rules 401 and 402 codified the common law in Texas.[99] The rules clarified the common law and expressed it concisely for uniform application in all civil and criminal proceedings. Rule 401 has, however, greatly affected the practical orientation of the Texas judicial system by favoring a broad definition of materiality and a liberal application of relevance. Rules 401 and 402 work with Rule 403 to provide the trial judge a simple guiding principle favoring the admissibility of evidence.[100]

---

96. *See, e.g.,* ***Barham v. Turner Constr. Co.***, 803 S.W.2d 731, 740 (Tex. App.—Dallas 1990, writ denied) (even if photographs were obtained by fraud, by misrepresentation, or in violation of disciplinary rules, they were admissible under Civil Rule 402 to impeach plaintiff); ***State v. Taylor***, 721 S.W.2d 541, 551-52 (Tex. App.—Tyler 1986, writ ref'd n.r.e.) (in condemnation proceeding, real-estate broker's property appraisal was relevant and admissible under Civil Rule 402 even though broker was not licensed by the State and thus was in violation of penal statute); ***Sims v. Cosden Oil & Chem. Co.***, 663 S.W.2d 70, 73-74 (Tex. App.—Eastland 1983, writ ref'd n.r.e.) (although defendant's expert may have improperly acquired mechanical information about the accuracy of an oil-flow meter, his testimony was relevant and material as a defense to plaintiff's claim that defendant overcharged for oil because plaintiff did not show that any of Civil Rule 403's exclusionary bases applied). *See generally* 8 JOHN H. WIGMORE, EVIDENCE IN TRIALS AT COMMON LAW §2183, at 6-7 (McNaughton rev. 1961) (generally, the illegality of the procurement of evidence is incidental to the conduct of the trial and will not be a focus of the litigation).

97. *See* ***Henley***, 493 S.W.3d at 83 (trial court's decision on relevance will not be disturbed on appeal unless it is "clearly wrong"); ***Nat. Gas Pipeline Co. of Am. v. Pool***, 30 S.W.3d 618, 632 (Tex. App.—Amarillo 2000) (appellate judge should not disturb trial court's ruling on relevance if the ruling is reasonable, even if other inferences are available from the evidence based on common experience), *rev'd on other grounds*, 124 S.W.3d 188 (Tex. 2003); ***Amis v. State***, 910 S.W.2d 511, 518 (Tex. App.—Tyler 1995, pet. ref'd) (in determining the relevance and admissibility of evidence, "[t]he mere fact that a trial judge may decide a matter within his discretionary authority in a different manner than an appellate judge in a similar circumstance does not demonstrate that an abuse of discretion has occurred" (quoting ***Montgomery v. State***, 810 S.W.2d 372, 380 (Tex. Crim. App. 1990) (orig. op.))); ***Rathmell v. Morrison***, 732 S.W.2d 6, 19 (Tex. App.—Houston [14th Dist.] 1987, no writ) (Civil Rules 401, 402, and 403 grant the trial court wide discretion in determining admissibility). This grant of discretion follows earlier Texas civil and criminal practice. *See, e.g.,* ***Johnson v. State***, 698 S.W.2d 154, 160 (Tex. Crim. App. 1985); ***Williams v. State***, 535 S.W.2d 637, 639-40 (Tex. Crim. App. 1976).

98. ***Montgomery v. State***, 810 S.W.2d 372, 391 (Tex. Crim. App. 1991) (op. on reh'g). Alternatively, if it is clear that what the trial judge perceived as "common experience" is only "common prejudice" that is not supported by logic or reason, the trial court has abused its discretion under Rules 401 and 402. ***Montgomery***, 810 S.W.2d at 391 (op. on reh'g).

99. ***Sims***, 663 S.W.2d at 74; *see* ***Plante v. State***, 692 S.W.2d 487, 491 & n.6 (Tex. Crim. App. 1985) (Texas common-law definition of relevance is no different from Rule 401).

100. *See* ***Montgomery***, 810 S.W.2d at 375 (orig. op.) ("The new rules favor the admission of all logically relevant evidence for the jury's consideration."); *see also* ***Henley***, 493 S.W.3d at 83 (even though Rules favor admission of all logically relevant evidence for jury's consideration, trial judge still makes threshold decision on relevance).

> ## RULE 403
> ### EXCLUDING RELEVANT EVIDENCE FOR PREJUDICE, CONFUSION, OR OTHER REASONS
>
> The court may exclude relevant evidence if its probative value is substantially outweighed by a danger of one or more of the following: unfair prejudice, confusing the issues, misleading the jury, undue delay, or needlessly presenting cumulative evidence.

COMMENTARY ON RULE 403

After Rule 401 defines relevant evidence and Rule 402 states generally that relevant evidence is admissible, Rule 403 excludes relevant evidence if its probative value is "substantially outweighed" by its prejudicial effect. The question is whether the value of the evidence is worth its costs. Under Rule 403, it is presumed that the probative value of relevant evidence exceeds any danger of unfair prejudice, confusing the issues, or other counterfactors.[101] Thus, the rule excludes evidence only when there is a "clear disparity between the degree of prejudice of the offered evidence and its probative value."[102] The probative value of legally relevant evidence outweighs the counterfactors listed in Rule 403 and other social-policy concerns.[103] Legally relevant evidence, then, has a plus

---

101. *See Hammer v. State*, 296 S.W.3d 555, 568 (Tex. Crim. App. 2009); *Shuffield v. State*, 189 S.W.3d 782, 787 (Tex. Crim. App. 2006); *Moses v. State*, 105 S.W.3d 622, 626 (Tex. Crim. App. 2003).

At common law, most courts used a balancing test to determine the admissibility of relevant evidence that had negative effects. *See* McCormick's Handbook II, *supra* note 33, §185, at 439-40 (listing prejudicing the jury, distracting the jury, unduly consuming time, and unfair surprise as factors that might require the exclusion of relevant evidence); 6 John H. Wigmore, Evidence in Trials at Common Law §1864, at 642-44 (Chadbourn rev. 1976) (providing that confusion of issues and undue prejudice are grounds for exclusion of otherwise relevant evidence). Before the adoption of Rule 403, Texas did not have a clear or consistent approach to this issue. Some Texas courts suggested that the mere existence of a negative effect was enough to exclude relevant evidence. *See, e.g., Mo., Kan. & Tex. Ry. Co. of Tex. v. Bailey*, 53 Tex. Civ. App. 295, 304-05, 115 S.W. 601, 607-08 (Dallas 1908, writ ref'd) (in employee's suit for damages resulting from personal injuries, court excluded impeachment evidence designed to show that plaintiff's medical expert had previously misdiagnosed an injury to a third party because it would have unduly prolonged trial and confused the real issues). Others suggested that trial courts should admit relevant evidence even if such evidence may have negative effects. *See, e.g., Davis v. Davis*, 521 S.W.2d 603, 607-08 (Tex. 1975) (rejecting Lord Mansfield's Rule that neither husband nor wife may testify after marriage that they had no sexual relations and that their supposed offspring is illegitimate; "[r]ules that exclude evidence bearing directly on the truth to be determined ought not to survive without very good cause"); *Howell v. Burch*, 616 S.W.2d 685, 688 (Tex. Civ. App.—Texarkana 1981, writ ref'd n.r.e.) (in suit by daughter against mother and other parties for conversion and to set aside an allegedly forged deed, court rejected mother's assertion that documents from mother and father's divorce proceedings and father's probate file should have been excluded as prejudicial; evidence contradicted mother's substantive allegations and tended to show that father never knew of deed and conveyance). The court of criminal appeals held that relevant evidence was admissible only when its probative value outweighed any negative effect such as prejudice or distraction. *See Morgan v. State*, 692 S.W.2d 877, 879 (Tex. Crim. App. 1985); *Williams v. State*, 662 S.W.2d 344, 346 (Tex. Crim. App. 1983); *Albrecht v. State*, 486 S.W.2d 97, 99 (Tex. Crim. App. 1972); *see also Charter Med. Corp. v. Miller*, 605 S.W.2d 943, 953-54 (Tex. Civ. App.—Dallas 1980, writ ref'd n.r.e.) (civil case, using same balancing test; "we do consider whether its probative effect would be outweighed by the probability of its introducing undue prejudice and leading away from the main issues in this case").

102. *Conner v. State*, 67 S.W.3d 192, 202 (Tex. Crim. App. 2001); *Joiner v. State*, 825 S.W.2d 701, 708 (Tex. Crim. App. 1992).

103. *See* 1 Steven Goode et al., Texas Practice: Guide to the Texas Rules of Evidence: Civil and Criminal §401.4, at 98 (2d ed. 1993).

value beyond the bare minimum of probative value.[104] "Because Rule 403 permits the exclusion of admittedly probative evidence, it is a remedy that should be used sparingly ...."[105]

Rule 403 rulings depend on the evidentiary content of a particular trial, taking into account "the ebb and flow of trial testimony, the unique circumstances and facts, and the specific contested issues."[106] Legal precedents, though they help courts determine what factors to consider in the balance, do not help dictate the proper weight that should be given to the particular factors in another case.[107] For this reason, reviewing courts are highly deferential to a trial judge's individualized, discretionary rulings under Rule 403.[108]

Under Rule 403, the court may exercise discretion in excluding evidence only when the probative value of the evidence is *substantially* outweighed (not merely outweighed) by one or more of the specific counterfactors listed in the rule.[109] This change in the relative balance between probative value and specific counterfactors has shifted Texas evidentiary law dramatically from its common-law heritage.[110]

---

104. MCCORMICK ON EVIDENCE, *supra* note 1, §185, at 548.

105. *Hammer*, 296 S.W.3d at 568; *see In re D.O.*, 338 S.W.3d 29, 37 (Tex. App.—Eastland 2011, no pet.); *In re C.J.F.*, 134 S.W.3d 343, 356 (Tex. App.—Amarillo 2003, pet. denied); *see also State v. Mechler*, 153 S.W.3d 435, 443-44 (Tex. Crim. App. 2005) (Cochran, Meyers, Price, Johnson, JJ., concurring) ("All Rule 403 rulings are subject to three general considerations: 1) the trial judge should exercise his power to exclude evidence under Rule 403 sparingly; 2) the trial judge's discretion under Rule 403 is not an invitation to rule reflexively or without careful reasoning; 3) the trial judge may not exclude evidence merely because he disbelieves the testimony."). In *Hammer*, Judge Cochran emphasized the limited use of Rule 403, "especially in 'he said, she said' sexual-molestation cases that must be resolved solely on the basis of the testimony of the complainant and the defendant." 296 S.W.3d at 568. The Rules of Evidence have a special balancing test for the use of evidence of previous sexual conduct in criminal cases. Unlike Rule 403, which allows evidence to be excluded if its probative value is substantially outweighed by the danger of unfair prejudice, Rule 412(b)(3) excludes evidence of an alleged victim's past sexual behavior unless its probative value outweighs the danger of unfair prejudice. Refer to notes 1044-1046, 1094-1095 *infra* and accompanying text.

106. *Mechler*, 153 S.W.3d at 443 (Cochran, Meyers, Price, Johnson, JJ., concurring); *see Winegarner v. State*, 235 S.W.3d 787, 791 (Tex. Crim. App. 2007) ("The rule gives the trial court considerable latitude to assess the courtroom dynamics, to judge the tone and tenor of the witness' testimony and its impact upon the jury, and to conduct the necessary balancing."); *Costilla v. Crown Equip. Corp.*, 148 S.W.3d 736, 740 (Tex. App.—Dallas 2004, no pet.) (Rule 403 determinations often depend on facts of the particular case).

107. *Mechler*, 153 S.W.3d at 443.

108. *Id.*; *see Winegarner*, 235 S.W.3d at 791 (Rule 403 "allows different trial judges to reach different conclusions in different trials on substantially similar facts without abuse of discretion"); Lynne Liberato & Kent Rutter, *Reasons for Reversal in the Texas Courts of Appeals*, 48 HOUS. L. REV. 993, 1005-06 (2012) (courts of appeals are reluctant to find abuse of discretion based on erroneous admission or exclusion of evidence); *cf. Caldarera v. E. Airlines, Inc.*, 705 F.2d 778, 782 (5th Cir. 1983) (trial court's balance of factors under Federal Rule 403 "is not subject to scrutiny by an appellate Bureau of Weights and Standards that balances the factors gram for gram").

109. *See* TEX. R. EVID. 403; *Ex parte Lane*, 303 S.W.3d 702, 709 (Tex. Crim. App. 2009).

110. *See Gilbert v. State*, 808 S.W.2d 467, 471 (Tex. Crim. App. 1991); *Crank v. State*, 761 S.W.2d 328, 342 n.5 (Tex. Crim. App. 1988); *see also* Herasimchuk, *supra* note 14, at 785 (asserting that "[i]f probative value and the countervailing factor are in 'rough parity,' the evidence may not be excluded"). *But see* 1 GOODE ET AL., *supra* note 103, §403.1, at 127 (suggesting that "no dramatic change in Texas law was intended by the adoption of this rule"). Refer to note 101 *supra*.

A. Analysis of Rule 403

Texas Rule 403 is essentially the same as its federal counterpart.[111] Rule 403 embodies a number of evidentiary and Texas common-law principles. Analyzing the rule's words and phrases helps explain how the rule works and how it relates to earlier Texas law.[112]

1. "The court may exclude relevant evidence …" The trial court has the discretion to admit or exclude evidence under Rule 403, even if it is relevant.[113] If evidence is irrelevant as determined by Rule 401,[114] Rule 402 excludes it absolutely. Thus, the trial court has no discretion to admit any irrelevant evidence and does not need to consider the Rule 403 factors for that evidence. The discretion to exclude relevant evidence is conditioned, however, on the fulfillment of the clause beginning with "if."[115]

2. "[I]f its probative value …" Both the Texas and federal rules state that the trial court must weigh the probative value of the evidence against the listed negative effects. Relevance and probative value, however, are not identical concepts. Rule 401 defines relevance in terms of the required minimum relationship between the evidence offered and the proposition to be proved. Probative value, then, refers to the strength of that relationship.[116] The inference from the evidence to the proposition may be strong (high probative value) or weak (low probative value).

3. "[I]s substantially outweighed by …" The trial court may exercise the discretion authorized by the rule only when the "probative value [of the evidence in question] is

---

111. Federal Rule 403 includes the phrase "wasting time" as a consideration that might support exclusion of relevant evidence, but Texas Rule 403 does not. Refer to notes 166-167 *infra* and accompanying text.

112. This format for discussing Rule 403 follows the structure outlined in Andrew K. Dolan, *Rule 403: The Prejudice Rule in Evidence*, 49 S. Cal. L. Rev. 220, 230-44 (1976).

113. *See Powell v. State*, 189 S.W.3d 285, 289 (Tex. Crim. App. 2006) ("We have emphasized that the trial judge, not the appellate judge, is in the best position to assess the extent of the prejudice caused a party by a piece of evidence. [I]f judicial self-restraint is ever desirable, it is when a Rule 403 analysis of a trial court is reviewed by an appellate tribunal." (quoting *United States v. Cruz*, 326 F.3d 392, 396 (3d Cir. 2003))); *State v. Mechler*, 153 S.W.3d 435, 439 (Tex. Crim. App. 2005) ("When an objection on [Rule] 403 grounds is raised at trial, we review the judge's ruling for an abuse of discretion."); *Montgomery v. State*, 810 S.W.2d 372, 378 (Tex. Crim. App. 1990) (orig. op.) ("Courts and commentators universally recognize that with the enactment of Federal Rule 403 there was a conscientious decision to give the trial court a considerable freedom in evaluating proffered evidence's probative value in relation to its prejudicial effect."); *cf. United States v. Long*, 574 F.2d 761, 767 (3d Cir. 1978) (trial court has great discretion in making Federal Rule 403 determinations; appellate court reversal of trial judge's balancing under Federal Rule 403 must be based on highly subjective reasons that are not always readily definable or recognizable).

114. Refer to notes 4-59 *supra* and accompanying text.

115. *Montgomery*, 810 S.W.2d at 378 (orig. op.); *see CNA Ins. v. Scheffey*, 828 S.W.2d 785, 789-90 (Tex. App.—Texarkana 1992, writ denied) (trial court has discretion to keep out relevant evidence under Rule 403 but must first apply Rule 403 balancing test). Even if the probative value of the evidence is outweighed by countervailing factors, the court may consider other matters in exercising its discretion and still admit the evidence. Dolan, *supra* note 112, at 231-32 & n.43.

116. *See Casey v. State*, 215 S.W.3d 870, 879 (Tex. Crim. App. 2007) (probative value is "the inherent probative force of an item of evidence—that is, how strongly it serves to make more or less probable the existence of a fact of consequence to the litigation—coupled with the proponent's need for that item of evidence"); *Gigliobianco v. State*, 210 S.W.3d 637, 641 (Tex. Crim. App. 2006) (same); *see also* Dolan, *supra* note 112, at 233-35 (analyzing probative value in terms of relevance and logical distance).

substantially outweighed by" one of the listed factors.[117] This balancing test rejects the suggestion of some Texas courts that even a slight negative side effect is enough to exclude relevant evidence.[118] Instead, the rule follows the position of the Texas Supreme Court that courts should not exclude relevant evidence without "very good cause."[119]

4. "[T]he danger of ... unfair prejudice ..." This factor is the first in a series of factors that may lead to the exclusion of relevant evidence. In Federal Rule 403, the phrase "unfair prejudice" refers not to evidence's potentially adverse or detrimental effect but to "an undue tendency to suggest decision on an improper basis, commonly, though not necessarily, an emotional one."[120]

---

117. *See* TEX. R. EVID. 403 (emphasis added); *see, e.g.*, **JBS Carriers, Inc. v. Washington**, 513 S.W.3d 703, 713-15 (Tex. App.—San Antonio 2017, pet. filed 4-27-17) (in personal-injury negligence suit arising from car collision with 18-wheeler, trial court did not abuse its discretion in excluding testimony from physician who had never examined or even met decedent that decedent was schizophrenic drug addict; probative value of this evidence was substantially outweighed by danger of unfair prejudice); **Commerce & Indus. Ins. v. Ferguson-Stewart**, 339 S.W.3d 744, 747 & n.2 (Tex. App.—Houston [1st Dist.] 2011, no pet.) ("[a]ny connection between [decedent's] use of prescription pain medication and his worker's compensation claim rests on speculation"; trial court did not err in excluding evidence under Rule 403 because danger of unfair prejudice substantially outweighed evidence's probative value); **Davis v. State**, 786 S.W.2d 77, 79 (Tex. App.—Beaumont 1990, pet. ref'd) (while there was some danger that witness's testimony about penitentiary time cuts might disclose the effect of parole laws to jury, court could not determine that probative worth "was substantially outweighed by its potential for unfair prejudice"); **Dinkins v. State**, 760 S.W.2d 374, 377 (Tex. App.—Fort Worth 1988, pet. ref'd) (trial court properly excluded testimony of murder victim's character for provoking another into anger because such evidence was not pertinent; even if the testimony was pertinent, its probative value was substantially outweighed by the danger of unfair prejudice, confusion of issues, or misleading the jury).

A trial court has great discretion in determining the appropriate balance between evidence's probative value and the Rule 403 counterfactors. *See* **Montgomery**, 810 S.W.2d at 379 (orig. op.); *see, e.g.*, **Webb v. State**, 760 S.W.2d 263, 276 (Tex. Crim. App. 1988) (court of criminal appeals would not "second guess" the trial court's determination that a tape recording "was not needlessly cumulative or more prejudicial than probative"); **First Sw. Lloyds Ins. v. MacDowell**, 769 S.W.2d 954, 958 (Tex. App.—Texarkana 1989, writ denied) (refusing to eliminate trial court's discretion in excluding facially admissible evidence). In **Perez v. Baker Packers**, the court rejected the plaintiff's complaint that the trial court had improperly admitted a doctor's testimony that he suspected the plaintiff's wound was self-inflicted. 694 S.W.2d 138, 140-41 (Tex. App.—Houston [14th Dist.] 1985, writ ref'd n.r.e.). The **Perez** court noted that Civil Rule 403 requires the trial judge to use a balancing test weighing probative value against prejudicial effect but declined to hold that the trial court's balancing of factors was incorrect. *Id.*

In federal courts, the trial judge's admission or exclusion of evidence under Rule 403 will be upheld on appeal unless there was a clear abuse of discretion. *See* **United States v. Maggitt**, 784 F.2d 590, 597 (5th Cir. 1986). Texas courts use the same or similar language. *See, e.g.*, **Babineaux v. State**, 777 S.W.2d 724, 731 (Tex. App.—Beaumont 1989) (no abuse of discretion when the trial judge excluded evidence and used "reasonable, judicial discretion in making his rulings as to admissibility"), *pet. dism'd, improvidently granted*, 803 S.W.2d 301 (Tex. Crim. App. 1990).

118. *See* **Rodda v. State**, 745 S.W.2d 415, 417-18 (Tex. App.—Houston [14th Dist.] 1988, pet. ref'd) (court may exclude relevant evidence only when its probative value is substantially outweighed by negative factors); 1 GOODE ET AL., *supra* note 103, §401.6, at 106 (same). Refer to note 101 *supra*.

119. *See* **Davis v. Davis**, 521 S.W.2d 603, 607 (Tex. 1975); **Ford Motor Co. v. Pool**, 688 S.W.2d 879, 882-83 (Tex. App.—Texarkana 1985), *rev'd in part on other grounds*, 715 S.W.2d 629 (Tex. 1986); *see also* **Shuffield v. State**, 189 S.W.3d 782, 787 (Tex. Crim. App. 2006) ("Rule 403 favors the admission of relevant evidence and carries a presumption that relevant evidence will be more probative than prejudicial.").

120. FED. R. EVID. 403 advisory committee's note; *accord* **Casey**, 215 S.W.3d at 879; **Gigliobianco**, 210 S.W.3d at 641; *see* **Old Chief v. United States**, 519 U.S. 172, 180 (1997) (defining "unfair prejudice" in the context of criminal cases as "the capacity of some concededly relevant evidence to lure the factfinder into declaring guilt on a ground different from proof specific to the offense charged"); **United States v. Jamil**, 707 F.2d 638, 644-45 (2d Cir. 1983) (showing of prejudice does not constitute a showing of unfair prejudice); *see, e.g.*, **United States v. Mills**, 704 F.2d 1553, 1559-60 (11th Cir. 1983) (while evidence of gang membership, history, and activities "may have been damag-

Unfair prejudice does not arise solely because evidence injures a party's case.[121] Virtually all evidence that a party offers will be prejudicial to its opponent's case; only evidence that unfairly prejudices the other party may be excluded under Rule 403.[122] If

---

ing" to imprisoned defendant accused of murdering a fellow inmate, it was not unfairly prejudicial); *cf.* ***Wheeler v. State***, 67 S.W.3d 879, 889-90 (Tex. Crim. App. 2002) (Keller, P.J., concurring) (unfair prejudice is kind of prejudice that suggests improper basis for decision; rule admitting evidence can significantly affect Rule 403 analysis). As was stated in ***United States v. Figueroa***:

> All evidence introduced against a defendant, if material to an issue in the case, tends to prove guilt, but is not necessarily prejudicial in any sense that matters to the rules of evidence. Evidence is prejudicial only when it tends to have some adverse effect upon a defendant beyond tending to prove the fact or issue that justified its admission into evidence. The prejudicial effect may be created by the tendency of the evidence to prove some adverse fact not properly in issue or unfairly to excite emotions against the defendant. ... When material evidence has an additional prejudicial effect, Rule 403 requires the trial court to make a conscientious assessment of whether the probative value of the evidence on a disputed issue in the case is substantially outweighed by the prejudicial tendency of the evidence to have some other adverse effect upon the defendant.

618 F.2d 934, 943 (2d Cir. 1980) (citations omitted). Andrew Dolan classifies "unfair" prejudicial evidence into three categories: evidence that (1) "seeks to affect irrationally the jurors' perception of a party ... because of some intrinsic characteristic of the individual litigant," (2) "involves damaging the position of a party because of the party's association with certain groups," and (3) may "excite the jury's rage or its lust for revenge in the hope that the jury will 'take it out' on whomever is most convenient, *i.e.*, the defendant." Dolan, *supra* note 112, at 238-39.

121. ***Casey***, 215 S.W.3d at 883; ***Cohn v. State***, 849 S.W.2d 817, 820 (Tex. Crim. App. 1993). Under the common law, Texas courts sometimes used the word "prejudicial" to refer to evidence that was merely disadvantageous or derogatory to a party. *See, e.g.*, ***Fid. Union Cas. Co. v. Koonce***, 51 S.W.2d 777, 780 (Tex. Civ. App.—Amarillo 1932, no writ) ("'Prejudicial' has been defined as disadvantageous, harmful, hurtful, injurious. The word may mean merely derogatory, or it may mean actually or naturally and probably bringing about a wrong result. When considered as meaning disadvantageous or derogatory, all testimony introduced by a litigant in his behalf ... is prejudicial to the case made by his adversary, and is intended so to be and is rightfully produced."). But substantial authority rejects this broad definition as a ground for excluding evidence and properly applies the term to emotional, irrational, or other similarly improper decisional grounds. *See* ***Montgomery***, 810 S.W.2d at 378 (orig. op.) (only "unfair" prejudice is sufficient to exclude relevant evidence); ***Soto v. State***, 156 S.W.3d 131, 136 (Tex. App.—Fort Worth 2005, pet. ref'd) ("Evidence is unfairly prejudicial if it inflames and prejudices the jury to the point that it creates an undue tendency to suggest a verdict on an improper basis, such as an emotional basis."); *see, e.g.*, ***Campbell v. State***, 118 S.W.3d 788, 797-98 (Tex. App.—Houston [14th Dist.] 2003, pet. denied) (in annual recommitment hearing, court rejected insanity acquittee's claim of unfair prejudice from admission of evidence of gruesome criminal offenses that led to his commitment; jury responded objectively to special issues and was not "inflamed" by the evidence). *But see* ***Sallings v. State***, 789 S.W.2d 408, 415 (Tex. App.—Dallas 1990, pet. ref'd) (in prosecution for sexual assault, court applied Rule 403 to exclude evidence on privacy grounds; prejudicial potential of violating victim's privacy outweighed probative value of her true name).

122. ***Casey***, 215 S.W.3d at 883; ***Montgomery***, 810 S.W.2d at 378 (orig. op.); *see* ***Davis v. State***, 329 S.W.3d 798, 806 (Tex. Crim. App. 2010) ("All testimony and physical evidence are likely [to] be prejudicial to one party or the other. It is only when there exists a clear disparity between the degree of prejudice of the offered evidence and its probative value that Rule 403 is applicable."); ***Martinez v. State***, 327 S.W.3d 727, 737 (Tex. Crim. App. 2010) ("Rule 403 does not require exclusion of evidence simply because it creates prejudice; the prejudice must be 'unfair.'"); ***State v. Mechler***, 153 S.W.3d 435, 440 (Tex. Crim. App. 2005) ("Rule 403 does not exclude all prejudicial evidence. It focuses only on the danger of 'unfair' prejudice. 'Unfair prejudice' refers only to relevant evidence's tendency to tempt the jury into finding guilt on grounds apart from proof of the offense charged."); *see, e.g.*, ***TXI Transp. Co. v. Hughes***, 306 S.W.3d 230, 245 (Tex. 2010) (evidence of decedent's illegal immigration status was improperly admitted because it was unduly prejudicial under Rule 403); ***Pawlak v. State***, 420 S.W.3d 807, 810-11 (Tex. Crim. App. 2013) (in sexual-assault case, admission of extraneous-offense evidence of pornographic images found on defendant's computer was unfairly prejudicial; possession of pornography was not at issue at trial, and photos did not show that assault or attempted assault was more likely to have occurred); ***Buxton v. State***, ___ S.W.3d ___ (Tex. App.—Houston [1st Dist.] 2017, n.p.h.) (No. 01-15-00857-CR; 7-6-17) (op. on reh'g) (in prosecution for continuous sexual abuse of child, evidence that defendant sexually abused another child was clearly prejudicial but not unfairly prejudicial; child witness's testimony discussed actions that were no more severe than allegations in present case, and defendant did not

the offered item of evidence gives rise to both exculpatory and inculpatory inferences, it will rarely be deemed unfairly prejudicial.[123]

The Advisory Committee's note to Federal Rule 403 suggests two variables that may affect whether evidence should be excluded on the basis of unfair prejudice: (1) the probable effectiveness of a limiting instruction to the jury and (2) the availability of other means of proof.[124] The note to Federal Rule 105, which deals with limited admissibility and is functionally equivalent to Texas Rule 105(a),[125] explicitly refers to Rule 403 in its discussion of limiting instructions.[126] According to the note, a trial court should consider Rule 403 when dealing with the possibility of prejudice if evidence is admitted only for limited purposes.[127] On the other hand, the trial court has the discretion to exclude the entirety of a specific evidentiary offer under Rule 403 based on its overall unfair prejudicial effect, even when a party could have offered an unobjectionable portion of the evidence.[128]

Texas courts have set out a more elaborate balancing test under Rule 403 for determining whether the danger of unfair prejudice substantially outweighs the evidence's probative value in the context of the admission of extraneous offenses. Here, the Texas Court of Criminal Appeals has suggested that the trial court

> must balance (1) the inherent probative force of the proffered item of evidence along with (2) the proponent's need for that evidence against (3) any tendency of the evidence to suggest decision on an improper basis, (4) any ten-

---

specify facts about child's testimony that he thought made it unfairly prejudicial); ***Fields v. State***, 515 S.W.3d 47, 56-57 (Tex. App.—San Antonio 2016, no pet.) (crime-scene video was not unfairly prejudicial when it did nothing more than show gruesomeness of murder); ***Republic Waste Servs., Ltd. v. Martinez***, 335 S.W.3d 401, 409-10 (Tex. App.—Houston [1st Dist.] 2011, no pet.) (evidence of decedent's illegal immigration status was properly excluded; "[u]ndeniably, the issue of immigration is a highly charged area of political debate. As a result, a trial court is prudent to weigh carefully evidence revealing a [party's] illegal immigrant status against the probative value of such evidence").

123. *See, e.g.*, ***Blakeney v. State***, 911 S.W.2d 508, 516 (Tex. App.—Austin 1995, no pet.) (in case for aggravated sexual assault of a child, no abuse of discretion to admit defendant's statements to police that child had once grabbed his penis, was being "forward," and was at fault for sexual contact; "the evidence may be either advantageous or prejudicial to the State and appellant, depending on the inferences drawn therefrom").

124. FED. R. EVID. 403 advisory committee's note; *see* ***Huynh v. R. Warehousing & Port Servs., Inc.***, 973 S.W.2d 375, 378 (Tex. App.—Tyler 1998, no pet.) (when evidence "has [a] clear prejudicial effect on one issue, a limiting instruction to focus the jury's attention only on another issue may not be effective. Under such circumstances, a jury cannot be expected to parse out the ways in which the evidence can be considered and the ways it cannot.").

125. Refer to *Article I: General Provisions, supra* p. 97.

126. *See* FED. R. EVID. 105 advisory committee's note ("A close relationship exists between this rule and Rule 403 which requires exclusion when 'probative value is substantially outweighed by the danger of unfair prejudice, confusion of the issues, or misleading the jury.' The present rule recognizes the practice of admitting evidence for a limited purpose and instructing the jury accordingly. The availability and effectiveness of this practice must be taken into consideration in reaching a decision whether to exclude for unfair prejudice under Rule 403.").

127. *Id.*

128. *See, e.g.*, ***Olson v. Bayland Publ'g, Inc.***, 781 S.W.2d 659, 665 (Tex. App.—Houston [1st Dist.] 1989, writ denied) (trial court properly excluded lengthy letter from attorney containing a legal opinion about the validity of the contract that formed the basis of the lawsuit when plaintiff could have edited the letter to exclude the objectionable portions), *overruled on other grounds*, ***Sage St. Assocs. v. Northdale Constr. Co.***, 863 S.W.2d 438 (Tex. 1993).

dency of the evidence to confuse or distract the jury from the main issues, (5) any tendency of the evidence to be given undue weight by a jury that has not been equipped to evaluate the probative force of the evidence, and (6) the likelihood that presentation of the evidence will consume an inordinate amount of time or repeat evidence already admitted.[129]

One Texas commentator has suggested that the opponent of the offered evidence must show by specific proof or argument how the evidentiary item is unfairly prejudicial.[130] Texas courts have stated that while Rule 403 does not assign a formal burden of proof to either the proponent or the opponent of the evidence, "the court should

---

129. *Casey v. State*, 215 S.W.3d 870, 880 (Tex. Crim. App. 2007); *see Henley v. State*, 493 S.W.3d 77, 93 (Tex. Crim. App. 2016); *Gigliobianco v. State*, 210 S.W.3d 637, 641-42 (Tex. Crim. App. 2006); *see, e.g.*, *Rodriguez v. State*, 203 S.W.3d 837, 843-44 (Tex. Crim. App. 2006) (at punishment stage of prosecution for facilitating a prison escape, trial court did not err in admitting evidence of post-escape crimes committed by escapees); *Powell v. State*, 189 S.W.3d 285, 287-89 (Tex. Crim. App. 2006) (trial court did not abuse its discretion in admitting evidence that defendant, who was stopped for traffic violation, was a parolee and thus had motive to throw gun out of driver's door when his defense at trial was that he was not the driver of the car; other jurisdictions had held such evidence "to be probative of why a defendant would take extra steps to hide his criminal activity"); *Barlow v. State*, 175 S.W.3d 839, 844 (Tex. App.—Texarkana 2005, pet. ref'd) (trial court did not abuse its discretion in excluding evidence that four of State's witnesses were affiliated with a gang, as that fact was highly prejudicial but not relevant to show any bias of witnesses); *Soto v. State*, 156 S.W.3d 131, 136 (Tex. App.—Fort Worth 2005, pet. ref'd) (in trial for attempted murder of a child, evidence of defendant's prior assaults against child victim and mother was admissible to show motive and intent even when there was no direct evidence that child had been struck on this occasion); *Hudson v. State*, 112 S.W.3d 794, 804 (Tex. App.—Houston [14th Dist.] 2003, pet. ref'd) (in trial for aggravated assault, extraneous-offense evidence that defendant used knife in previous assault of victim was not unfairly prejudicial); *Peters v. State*, 93 S.W.3d 347, 351-52 (Tex. App.—Houston [14th Dist.] 2002, pet. ref'd) (in trial for possession of cocaine, evidence that defendant possessed a shotgun was improperly admitted under Rule 403 because gun possession was not a contested issue); *Alexander v. State*, 88 S.W.3d 772, 777-78 (Tex. App.—Corpus Christi 2002, pet. ref'd) (admission of evidence that .357 Magnum was found in residence where defendant was arrested three weeks after murder occurred was error because no evidence tied defendant to .357 Magnum, and the murder weapon was left at scene; no probative value but danger of unfair prejudice was high).

The *Gigliobianco* court explained that the six listed factors "may well blend together in practice." 210 S.W.3d at 642. The court further clarified that by this extended formulation of the Rule 403 balancing test—which previously included, but was not limited to, four factors—"we do no more than refine and build upon our previous analysis, and bring it in line with the plain text of Rule 403." *Id.* at 642 n.8. For a discussion of the balancing test under those four factors, see *State v. Mechler*, 153 S.W.3d 435, 440-41 (Tex. Crim. App. 2005), *Wyatt v. State*, 23 S.W.3d 18, 26 (Tex. Crim. App. 2000), and *Montgomery v. State*, 810 S.W.2d 372, 392-93 (Tex. Crim. App. 1991) (op. on reh'g).

The same type of Rule 403 balancing test may apply in civil cases when evidence of prior bad acts or wrongs is offered. *Compare McLellan v. Benson*, 877 S.W.2d 454, 458-59 (Tex. App.—Houston [1st Dist.] 1994, no writ) (applying four-factor *Montgomery* balancing test in civil case; trial court did not abuse discretion in admitting evidence of prior sexual offense to show intent), *and Hudetts v. McDaniel*, No. 07-96-0353-CV (Tex. App.—Amarillo 1997, no pet.) (no pub.; 11-18-97) (applying four-factor *Montgomery* balancing test in civil case; trial court did not abuse its discretion in admitting evidence that plaintiff owned the marijuana that her son possessed, offered to impeach plaintiff's testimony that she did not know her son smoked marijuana), *with Schlueter v. Schlueter*, 929 S.W.2d 94, 98 (Tex. App.—Austin 1996) (declining to adopt four-factor *Montgomery* balancing test for civil cases; trial court did not abuse its discretion in admitting evidence of prior fraudulent behavior to show motive and intent), *rev'd in part on other grounds*, 975 S.W.2d 584 (Tex. 1998).

130. HULEN D. WENDORF ET AL., TEXAS RULES OF EVIDENCE MANUAL IV-16 to IV-17 (5th ed. 2000); *see Boone v. State*, 60 S.W.3d 231, 239 (Tex. App.—Houston [14th Dist.] 2001, pet. ref'd); *see, e.g.*, *Amis v. State*, 87 S.W.3d 582, 587 (Tex. App.—San Antonio 2002, pet. ref'd) (defendant who beat victim to death did not explain how danger of unfair prejudice substantially outweighed probative value of evidence that he had displayed a knife to a friend approximately four months before murder and said he was going to use it to "get" victim).

ask the proponent to explain the probative value of the evidence, then question the opponent as to the nature and degree of the prejudice."[131] Although it is helpful, the trial judge is not required to articulate the Rule 403 balancing test on the record.[132] The court may deem that mere assertions of the evidence's prejudicial effect are insufficient to preserve any potential error; attorneys should make specific arguments or offers of proof about why the evidence is prejudicial.[133]

Courts should generally admit evidence that is highly damaging to a party if the evidence is particularly probative or is the only evidence available on the material fact.[134] If a particular item of evidence is critical to the party's case, its probative value is enhanced.[135] Thus, Texas courts frequently state that "'the greater the State's need to resort to extraneous offenses to prove up some material issue in the case, the higher

---

131. ***Massey v. State***, 826 S.W.2d 655, 659 (Tex. App.—Waco 1992, no pet.); *see Montgomery*, 810 S.W.2d at 389 (op. on reh'g).

132. *See* ***Belcher v. State***, 474 S.W.3d 840, 848 (Tex. App.—Tyler 2015, no pet.) (Rule 403 does not require that balancing test be performed on record); ***Maldonado v. State***, 452 S.W.3d 898, 905-06 (Tex. App.—Texarkana 2014, no pet.) ("[w]hile a trial court must conduct the balancing test when a Rule 403 objection is lodged, there appears to be no requirement that the court formally conduct the test on the record"; following precedent of Second Court of Appeals based on transfer of case); ***Williams v. State***, 82 S.W.3d 557, 562 (Tex. App.—San Antonio 2002, pet. ref'd) (trial judge is not required to articulate Rule 403 balancing test during formal hearing); ***Hitt v. State***, 53 S.W.3d 697, 706 (Tex. App.—Austin 2001, pet. ref'd) (trial judge is assumed to have conducted the balancing test and determined the admissibility of the evidence); ***Mechler***, 153 S.W.3d at 444 n.8 (Cochran, Meyers, Price, Johnson, JJ., concurring) ("Although a trial judge is not required to articulate his Rule 403 analysis on the record, it is most helpful to reviewing courts. 'Rulings that provide more than bare conclusions and indicate the nature of the danger of the underlying considerations are more satisfying and more likely to survive review.'" (quoting 1 CHRISTOPHER B. MUELLER & LAIRD C. KIRKPATRICK, FEDERAL EVIDENCE §93, at 481 (2d ed. 1994))). In criminal cases, a trial judge's articulation of the balancing test on the record can help appellate judges determine whether the trial judge considered any constitutional implications of excluding evidence that could aid the defendant's case. *See, e.g.,* ***Hammer v. State***, 296 S.W.3d 555, 568-69 (Tex. Crim. App. 2009) (in suit for indecency with a child, although trial judge may have used correct balancing test, nothing in the record indicated that she considered constitutional issues when she excluded all of defendant's evidence offered to demonstrate complainant's motive to testify against defendant; allowing cross-examination of complainant would not have been unfair prejudice).

133. ***Torres v. State***, 794 S.W.2d 596, 600 n.4 (Tex. App.—Austin 1990, no pet.); *see, e.g.,* ***Webb v. State***, 760 S.W.2d 263, 276 (Tex. Crim. App. 1988) (declining to find the contents of a tape recording "especially inflammatory" when the appellant did not specify how the admission of the tape recording was prejudicial).

134. For example, in ***Gonzales v. State***, the court admitted evidence that showed that the defendant kept $67,218 in a safe-deposit box. 761 S.W.2d 809, 814-15 (Tex. App.—Austin 1988, pet. ref'd). The court held that the evidence was probative of his intent to deliver more than 400 grams of cocaine, even though no direct evidence showed that the defendant derived this money from the illegal sale of narcotics. *Id.* The court reasoned as follows:

> Given the nature of the issue in question—[defendant's] subjective intent—and the fact that it could only be proved by circumstantial evidence in this case, we believe the probative value of the evidence was not substantially outweighed by the danger of unfair prejudice or the other adverse factors mentioned in [Criminal] Rule 403.

Id. at 815; *see also* ***Doe v. Mobile Video Tapes, Inc.***, 43 S.W.3d 40, 57 (Tex. App.—Corpus Christi 2001, no pet.) (in suit for defamation and invasion of privacy, admission of reporter packages, scripts, and rundowns of television news segments was not barred by Rule 403 when complete videotapes were not available and parties were able to present testimony of captions that purportedly accompanied videos).

135. *See* ***Manning v. State***, 114 S.W.3d 922, 928 (Tex. Crim. App. 2003) ("If the issue is disputed and the proponent has no other evidence to prove the fact, then the proponent's need for the evidence is great, and that weighs in favor of admitting the evidence."); ***Willis v. State***, 932 S.W.2d 690, 697 (Tex. App.—Houston [14th Dist.] 1996, no pet.) (the greater the need for the evidence to prove a material issue, the higher the probative value).

will be the probative value of that offense in relation to its potential for prejudice.'"[136] A party's offer to stipulate to certain facts may so decrease the probative value of the evidence offered to prove those facts that the risk of unfair prejudice would outweigh the probative value.[137] The danger of unfair prejudice is diminished when the trial judge, not a jury, is the trier of fact.[138]

5. "[C]onfusing the issues, misleading the jury ..." Both Texas Rule 403 and Federal Rule 403 list confusing the issues and misleading the jury as alternative, though possibly overlapping, factors to balance against relevance. Texas Rule 403 does not substantially change Texas common-law practice, which excluded evidence tending to divert or lead the jury away from the issue of a case,[139] confuse the issues,[140] or mislead the jury.[141]

Commentators have provided useful analysis of these factors for excluding relevant evidence. According to Charles McCormick, one factor that the trial court must consider is "the probability that the proof and the answering evidence that it provokes may create a side issue that will unduly distract the jury from the main issues."[142] His con-

---

136. *Crank v. State*, 761 S.W.2d 328, 344 (Tex. Crim. App. 1988) (quoting *Morgan v. State*, 692 S.W.2d 877, 880 n.3 (Tex. Crim. App. 1985)); *accord Willis*, 932 S.W.2d at 697.

137. Refer to note 80 *supra*.

138. *E.g.*, *Ex parte Twine*, 111 S.W.3d 664, 668 (Tex. App.—Fort Worth 2003, pet. ref'd) (in habeas corpus hearing, trial court abused its discretion under Rule 403 by excluding excerpt of record from another trial in which prosecutor had asked similar question of different defendant to determine whether same prosecutor intentionally or recklessly provoked defendant into requesting mistrial).

In a bench trial, the party offering the evidence first asks the judge to decide the evidence's admissibility. If the judge admits the evidence, he then evaluates it as the fact-finder. If the judge excludes the evidence, he will have already heard it. But because of their training, judges are deemed to be able to ignore inadmissible evidence when making their rulings.

139. *See Charter Med. Corp. v. Miller*, 605 S.W.2d 943, 953-54 (Tex. Civ. App.—Dallas 1980, writ ref'd n.r.e.).

140. *See Giles v. Kretzmeier*, 239 S.W.2d 706, 715 (Tex. Civ. App.—Waco 1951, writ ref'd n.r.e.); *Mo., Kan. & Tex. Ry. Co. of Tex. v. Bailey*, 53 Tex. Civ. App. 295, 304-05, 115 S.W. 601, 607-08 (Dallas 1908, writ ref'd).

141. *See Giles*, 239 S.W.2d at 715.

142. McCORMICK'S HANDBOOK II, *supra* note 33, §185, at 439; *see Casey v. State*, 215 S.W.3d 870, 880 (Tex. Crim. App. 2007); *Gigliobianco v. State*, 210 S.W.3d 637, 641 (Tex. Crim. App. 2006); *see, e.g.*, *Ex parte Wheeler*, 203 S.W.3d 317, 324-25 (Tex. Crim. App. 2006) (trial court correctly declared a mistrial in manslaughter case arising from auto accident when prosecutor asked defense's accident-reconstruction expert, "Are you aware that her [the defendant's] insurance carrier found her at fault?"; question had very little probative value but was "extremely prejudicial, likely to confuse and mislead the jury, and [would] lead to time-consuming collateral litigation"); *State v. Villegas*, 506 S.W.3d 717, 739-40 (Tex. App.—El Paso 2016, pet. granted 6-7-17) (trial court did not abuse its discretion in excluding recording of defendant using phrase "actual innocence," offered as admission of guilt; providing proper context for statement would expend time and resources and would likely involve explaining habeas corpus proceedings and their standards, which would "risk exposing the jury to the highly prejudicial fact that [defendant] was previously found guilty and incarcerated for the same crime"); *Wilson v. State*, 179 S.W.3d 240, 254-55 (Tex. App.—Texarkana 2005, no pet.) (error, but harmless, to admit evidence that murder defendant gave prescription pain medication to his mistress and used those drugs to control and manipulate her; probative value was minimal, evidence was unnecessary to prove elements of murder, and risk of unfair prejudice was substantial); *Martin v. State*, 176 S.W.3d 887, 896-97 (Tex. App.—Fort Worth 2005, no pet.) (when defendant was charged with sexual assault and indecency with a child, including oral sex and touching child's breasts, trial court erred under Rule 403 in admitting evidence that he penetrated child's sexual organ with his penis; uncharged act was "more heinous" than charged act, and evidence that "she was crying and shaking during the rape had the potential to impress the jury in some irrational but nevertheless indelible way").

RULE 403

cern about side issues and their effect on the main issues fits within the "confusion of the issues" factor.[143] Undue distraction of the jury also relates to the concern of misleading the jury.[144] Undue confusion, along with unfair prejudice, are the factors that Wigmore lists as grounds for exclusion.[145] However, Wigmore's construction of undue confusion covers both confusing the issues and misleading the jury under Texas Rule 403.[146] Ray seems to combine both factors in his statement that courts may reject relevant evidence because of the "danger of leading the jury away from the main issues."[147] In his discussion of Federal Rule 403, Dolan draws a useful distinction between confusing the issues and misleading the jury.[148] He explains that confusing the issues relates to evidence that could produce a rational but incorrect result.[149] Evidence

---

143. *See, e.g.*, **Silcott v. Oglesby**, 721 S.W.2d 290, 294 (Tex. 1986) (under Civil Rule 403, trial court properly excluded evidence in child-abduction case that child was plaintiff's adopted son to avoid "injecting confusing collateral issues into the proceedings"); **Mumphrey v. State**, 155 S.W.3d 651, 664-65 (Tex. App.—Texarkana 2005, pet. ref'd) (trial court did not abuse its discretion in preventing defendant from cross-examining assault victim about her prior assaults of defendant because those incidents raised confusing collateral issues); **New Braunfels Factory Outlet Ctr., Inc. v. IHOP Realty Corp.**, 872 S.W.2d 303, 311-12 (Tex. App.—Austin 1994, no writ) (trial court properly excluded evidence of prior similar acts showing fraud because its admission would have resulted in a "trial within a trial," confusing the issues in present lawsuit); **Rodriguez v. Univ'l Fastenings Corp.**, 777 S.W.2d 513, 517-18 (Tex. App.—Corpus Christi 1989, no writ) (in an action to recover for a worker's death, trial court properly excluded witness's deposition about a possible sham minority-business enterprise in a government-funded project because issues of whether minority-business requirements were met would only serve "the purpose of confusing and potentially prejudicing the jury"); **Ybarra v. State**, 768 S.W.2d 491, 494-95 (Tex. App.—Houston [1st Dist.] 1989, no pet.) (in trial for delivery of controlled substance, defendant could not offer evidence that he was a police informant; evidence was tangential to the central issue of whether he participated in the offense).

144. *See* **Casey**, 215 S.W.3d at 880; **Gigliobianco**, 210 S.W.3d at 641; *see, e.g.*, **Buxton v. State**, ___ S.W.3d ___ (Tex. App.—Houston [1st Dist.] 2017, n.p.h.) (No. 01-15-00857-CR; 7-6-17) (op. on reh'g) (in prosecution for continuous sexual abuse of child, testimony of other child whom defendant had sexually abused did not have a tendency to distract jury or to be given undue weight; evidence was not confusing or technical, and child witness testified after complainant, which helped prevent confusion of issues or misleading of jury).

145. 6 WIGMORE, *supra* note 101, §1864, at 642-44.

146. Wigmore defines "undue confusion" as "diverting [the jury's] attention from the real issue and fixing it upon a trivial or minor matter, or by making the controversy so intricate that the disentanglement of it becomes difficult." *Id.* §1864, at 643.

147. 2 RAY, *supra* note 46, §1481, at 168.

148. Dolan, *supra* note 112, at 240-42.

149. *Id.* at 241; *see* **Smith v. State**, 959 S.W.2d 1, 13 (Tex. App.—Waco 1997, pet. ref'd) ("Confusion of the issues occurs where introduction of the contested evidence raises 'the probability that the proof and the answering evidence that it provokes may create a side issue that will unduly distract the jury from the main issues.'" (quoting 1 GOODE ET AL., *supra* note 103, §403.2, at 134)). In **Frank v. State**, the court held that the trial judge did not err at the punishment stage in excluding the defendant's evidence that he had already been sentenced in federal court to 30 years in prison for basically the same offense, as this evidence would only mislead the jury and confuse the issues. 992 S.W.2d 756, 757-58 (Tex. App.—Houston [1st Dist.] 1999, pet. ref'd). The defendant wanted to argue that he had already been severely punished for this conduct in federal court, so little further punishment was needed, but he was appealing his federal sentence. *Id.* at 757. If he offered proof of the federal sentence, the State should have been entitled to show that the sentence was on appeal, and the defendant would have wanted to reply that the appeal would probably be rejected. *Id.* at 757-58. None of this evidence or argument would be directed at the issue of what state-court punishment this defendant deserved for his offense, and it was likely to distract and mislead the jury from their proper duties. *Id.* at 758.

that misleads the jury, on the other hand, is seductively persuasive or causes the jury to give the evidence too much weight.[150]

6. "[U]ndue delay ..." Both Texas Rule 403 and Federal Rule 403 list undue delay as a factor to be weighed against probative value. McCormick lists "the likelihood that the evidence offered and the counter proof will consume an undue amount of time" as a factor that may outweigh the probative value of the evidence.[151] Four factors that courts should consider in deciding whether to admit such evidence are the following: (1) how difficult it will be to establish the evidentiary fact, (2) how the offered fact will fit in with other facts already in evidence, (3) how this fact will affect major issues, and (4) whether the evidence is merely cumulative.[152] Evidence should be excluded if the costs, in terms of delay, outweigh the benefits.[153]

7. "[O]r needlessly presenting cumulative evidence." The Texas and federal versions of Rule 403 recognize that courts may exclude evidence to avoid the needless presentation of cumulative evidence. In discussing the federal rule, Weinstein and Berger explain that judges must have discretion to exclude evidence under this factor so they can conduct trials efficiently.[154] Texas courts also recognize cumulativeness as a factor that may allow the exclusion of relevant evidence.[155] Any evidence of the same kind and directed to the same point as other admitted evidence is cumulative,[156] but the rule operates to allow the exclusion only of "needlessly" cumulative evidence.[157] Needlessly cumulative evidence has no effect other than to consume time; if the jury is to be persuaded to adopt a party's position on an issue, it will be persuaded by the evidence

---

150. Dolan, *supra* note 112, at 241-42; *see* **Casey v. State**, 215 S.W.3d 870, 880 (Tex. Crim. App. 2007); **Gigliobianco v. State**, 210 S.W.3d 637, 641 (Tex. Crim. App. 2006). "Junk science," for example, is often excluded because it misleads the jury.

151. McCORMICK'S HANDBOOK II, *supra* note 33, §185, at 439-40.

152. *See* James, *supra* note 7, at 702.

153. **Ahlschlager v. Remington Arms Co.**, 750 S.W.2d 832, 836 (Tex. App.—Houston [14th Dist.] 1988, writ denied); McCORMICK ON EVIDENCE, *supra* note 1, §185, at 544.

154. 1 WEINSTEIN & BERGER, *supra* note 84, ¶403[06], at 403-82 to 403-86.

155. *See* **R.R. Comm'n v. Shell Oil Co.**, 369 S.W.2d 363, 373 (Tex. Civ. App.—Austin 1963), *aff'd*, 380 S.W.2d 556 (Tex. 1964); *see also* **B.B.M.M., Ltd. v. Tex. Commerce Bank-Chem.**, 777 S.W.2d 193, 197 (Tex. App.—Houston [14th Dist.] 1989, no writ) (trial court had merely excluded cumulative evidence and had not prevented appellant from presenting its case).

156. *E.g.*, **Linthicum v. Richardson**, 245 S.W. 713, 715 (Tex. Civ. App.—Beaumont 1922, no writ) (newly discovered evidence, of a kind not given at trial, was not cumulative). However, courts rarely exclude evidence based on cumulativeness. The Texas Court of Criminal Appeals has held that videos and still photographs are "not entirely cumulative of each other" because of the panoramic view the video offers. **Ripkowski v. State**, 61 S.W.3d 378, 392 (Tex. Crim. App. 2001); *see, e.g.*, **Fields v. State**, 515 S.W.3d 47, 56 (Tex. App.—San Antonio 2016, no pet.) (video offered panoramic view depicting dimensions, size, and close proximity of crime scene not shown in photos).

157. *See* TEX. R. EVID. 403. Wright & Graham state that

> [a] court could not refuse, on the grounds of undue consumption of time, to hear the testimony of a fifth eyewitness to an assault with a baseball bat. But if the parties are professional baseball players, as in the celebrated Marichal-Roseboro case, surely not everyone in the ball park is entitled to a seat in the witness box.

22 WRIGHT & GRAHAM, *supra* note 35, §5213, at 260.

already presented. On the other hand, a party has a right to prove its case in the most persuasive way possible, which may mean offering evidence from several different witnesses, different documents, or a variety of testimonial and real or illustrative evidence to prove one specific material fact.[158] In deciding whether the exclusion of cumulative testimony is harmless error, the decisive factor is how important the excluded testimony is to the offering party's case, not merely whether the excluded testimony is the same as or substantially similar to evidence that has been admitted.[159]

B. Exclusivity of Rule 403 Counterfactors

The five factors listed in Rule 403 are the only factors to be balanced against probative value. In rules that have nonexclusive lists, such as Rules 404(b), 407(a), 408(b), and 411, the drafters carefully set up the listed factors as examples. For instance, Rule 404(b) states that evidence "may be admissible for another purpose, such as proving motive, opportunity, intent, preparation, plan, knowledge, identity, absence of mistake, or lack of accident."[160] In Rule 403, the absence of "such as" or a similar phrase indicates that the listed factors are the only factors to be considered.[161]

C. Counterfactors Not Included in the Rule 403 List

1. Unfair surprise. Unfair surprise is not included as a counterfactor in either Texas Rule 403 or Federal Rule 403.[162] In explaining the decision to omit unfair surprise from the federal rule, the Advisory Committee observed that the rule follows Wigmore's view of the common law rather than McCormick's position that unfair surprise is a ground for exclusion.[163] The Committee suggested that for justified claims of unfair surprise, the "granting of a continuance is a more appropriate remedy than exclusion of the evidence."[164]

While this remedy may be proper if the surprise evidence has high probative value, Weinstein and Berger explain that "if a continuance is required because of surprise, and the evidence is insignificant, the delay caused by the necessary continuance may jus-

---

158. *See, e.g.*, ***Alvarado v. State***, 912 S.W.2d 199, 212-13 (Tex. Crim. App. 1995) (cumulative effect of evidence "may heighten rather than reduce its probative force"; admission of six crime-scene photographs was not "needlessly" cumulative).

159. *See* ***Sims v. Brackett***, 885 S.W.2d 450, 454 (Tex. App.—Corpus Christi 1994, writ denied).

160. TEX. R. EVID. 404(b)(2).

161. *See* TEX. R. EVID. 403 (evidence can be excluded if "probative value is substantially outweighed by a danger of one or more" factors listed in rule). Texas courts have not always recognized the exclusivity of Rule 403's specific counterfactors and have excluded evidence on the basis of "other disadvantages such as harassment, embarrassment, confusion of issues, undue delay and the witness['s] well-being." ***Munoz v. State***, 763 S.W.2d 30, 33 (Tex. App.—Corpus Christi 1988, pet. ref'd).

162. In adopting the Texas Uniform Commercial Code, the Texas Legislature stated that unfair surprise may be a ground for the exclusion of specific evidence. The Code states that "[e]vidence of a relevant usage of trade offered by one party is not admissible unless that party has given the other party notice that the court finds sufficient to prevent unfair surprise to the other party." TEX. BUS. & COM. CODE §1.303(g).

163. FED. R. EVID. 403 advisory committee's note.

164. *Id.*

tify exclusion."[165] Because a continuance may not always be a satisfactory remedy, unfair surprise probably should have been included in Rule 403 as a ground for exclusion.

2. Wasting time. Federal Rule 403 includes wasting time as a counterfactor.[166] Texas Rule 403 does not, but the omission does not limit the coverage of the Texas rule. The general concern of consumption of time is still covered by the factors of undue delay and needless presentation of cumulative evidence.[167]

D. Relation of Rule 403 to Other Rules

Rule 403 works with the other rules in Article IV. Both the Texas and federal versions of Rule 404(b) recognize that evidence of other wrongs or acts are inadmissible to prove character but "may be admissible for another purpose."[168] The drafters of the federal rule indicate that Rule 403 has a role in determining the admissibility of that evidence.[169] In addition, Texas Rule 406 provides that evidence of habit or routine practice may be admitted to prove conforming conduct.[170] The analysis under Texas Rule 403 would then come into play, allowing exclusion of the evidence under proper circumstances.[171]

Under Rule 407, evidence of subsequent remedial measures is inadmissible to prove negligence (despite being relevant) but is admissible if offered for another purpose.[172] On the issue of when such evidence would be admissible, the drafters of Federal Rule 407 suggest that "the factors of undue prejudice, confusion of issues, misleading the jury, and waste of time remain for consideration under Rule 403."[173]

Rules 408, 409, and 411 are similar to Rule 407. Rule 408 provides that evidence of compromise and offers to compromise is not admissible to prove or disprove the validity or amount of a disputed claim (despite being relevant) but may be admissible when offered for another purpose.[174] Rule 409 makes evidence of payment of medical and similar expenses inadmissible to prove liability, but such evidence may be admis-

---

165. 1 WEINSTEIN & BERGER, *supra* note 84, ¶403[06], at 403-89.

166. *See* FED. R. EVID. 403.

167. *See* 2 DAVID W. LOUISELL & CHRISTOPHER B. MUELLER, FEDERAL EVIDENCE §128, at 68-69 (1985).

168. FED. R. EVID. 404(b)(2); TEX. R. EVID. 404(b)(2). Refer to notes 445-577 *infra* and accompanying text.

169. *See* FED. R. EVID. 404 advisory committee's note, subdiv. (b) (under Federal Rule 404(b), courts must determine "whether the danger of undue prejudice outweighs the probative value of the evidence in view of the availability of other means of proof and other facts appropriate for making decisions of this kind under Rule 403"); S. REP. No. 93-1277, at 24-25 (1974), *reprinted in* 1974 U.S.C.C.A.N. 7051, 7071 (excluding evidence allowed under Federal Rule 404(b) on the basis of Federal Rule 403); *cf.* **Montgomery v. State**, 810 S.W.2d 372, 377 (Tex. Crim. App. 1990) (orig. op.) (Texas Rule 404(b) "is simply a specific codification for a general balancing determination under Rule 403"). Refer to notes 578-585 *infra* and accompanying text.

170. TEX. R. EVID. 406. Refer to notes 617-668 *infra* and accompanying text.

171. *See, e.g.*, **Durbin v. Dal-Briar Corp.**, 871 S.W.2d 263, 268-70 (Tex. App.—El Paso 1994, writ denied) (in wrongful-termination case, evidence of other similar terminations was admissible under Texas Rule 406 and 403), *overruled on other grounds*, **Golden Eagle Archery, Inc. v. Jackson**, 24 S.W.3d 362 (Tex. 2000). For a discussion of the exclusion of habit evidence, refer to notes 662-666 *infra* and accompanying text.

172. TEX. R. EVID. 407(a). Refer to notes 669-721 *infra* and accompanying text.

173. FED. R. EVID. 407 advisory committee's note.

174. TEX. R. EVID. 408. Refer to notes 722-859 *infra* and accompanying text.

sible for other purposes.[175] And under Rule 411, evidence of liability insurance is inadmissible on the issue of whether a person acted negligently or otherwise wrongfully but may be admitted "for another purpose, such as proving a witness's bias or prejudice or, if disputed, proving agency, ownership, or control."[176] Rule 403 supplements Rules 408, 409, and 411 when these rules explicitly or implicitly admit evidence.

In essence, Rule 403 preserves Texas common law. In particular, the rule favors the admissibility of relevant evidence but gives the trial court discretion to exclude relevant evidence if the evidence's probative value is substantially outweighed by certain negative factors. Although earlier Texas law allowed exclusion of evidence when a negative factor outweighed the probative value of the evidence to any degree,[177] Rule 403 allows evidence to be excluded only if its probative value is substantially outweighed by a negative factor.[178]

RULES 401-403
SPECIAL APPLICATIONS

COMMENTARY

A. Relation of Rules 401-403 to Similar Happenings & Transactions

The general principles of relevance declared in Rules 401 through 403 do not specifically provide for evidence of similar events and transactions. Courts in Texas and elsewhere have traditionally admitted such evidence for a variety of purposes.[179] For example, a party may establish the value of litigated property by providing evidence of the price paid for similar property in other transactions.[180] On the other hand, Texas courts exclude the fact that the plaintiff has made similar claims in other suits when the defendant offers such evidence to prove that the plaintiff is litigation-minded and is pressing an invalid claim.[181]

---

175. *See* TEX. R. EVID. 409. Refer to notes 860-886 *infra* and accompanying text.

176. TEX. R. EVID. 411. Refer to notes 969-1010 *infra* and accompanying text.

177. Refer to note 101 *supra*.

178. Refer to notes 117-119 *supra* and accompanying text.

179. *See* 22 WRIGHT & GRAHAM, *supra* note 35, §5170, at 113-16. Some commentators have noted the logical difficulty of admitting evidence of similar happenings when the jury must infer a generalized proposition from proof of a series of specific incidents but has no way of knowing whether the probabilities of such happenings may be attributed to chance or to the general theory that the evidence is being offered to prove. *Id.* §5170, at 115. Nonetheless, such evidence is generally admitted if it has any tendency to prove a consequential fact unless the opponent shows that a negative factor substantially outweighs the evidence's probative value. *See* 2 RAY, *supra* note 46, §1521, at 200-01; 22 WRIGHT & GRAHAM, *supra* note 35, §5170, at 116-17; *see also* 2 JOHN H. WIGMORE, EVIDENCE IN TRIALS AT COMMON LAW, §333, at 2378 (Chadbourn rev. 1979) (discussing when other transfers of property may be admitted to show intent to defraud the transferor's creditors).

180. *See City of Abilene v. Blackburn*, 447 S.W.2d 474, 476 (Tex. Civ. App.—Eastland 1969, writ ref'd n.r.e.) (trial court has discretion to decide whether sales are similar enough for admission). Refer to notes 203-213 *infra* and accompanying text.

181. *See Bonham v. Baldeschwiler*, 533 S.W.2d 144, 148 (Tex. Civ. App.—Corpus Christi 1976, writ ref'd n.r.e.) (generally an error to admit evidence of prior claims unless the evidence constitutes a statement against interest). Refer to notes 214-218 *infra* and accompanying text.

Evidence of similar happenings or transactions almost always makes some aspect of the litigated transaction or event more or less probable. Thus, the evidence is relevant under Rule 401 and admissible under Rule 402. Evidence of similar events could be excluded under Rule 403 if the evidence's probative value is substantially outweighed by one of the negative factors listed in the rule.[182] Evidence of similar events or transactions is admissible to show the atmosphere surrounding the litigated events.[183] For the evidence to be admissible under Rules 401 through 403, the degree of similarity between the two events or transactions does not need to be high.[184]

1. Similar contracts between parties. Evidence of similar contracts between two parties may be relevant as circumstantial proof of a contracting party's interpretation, conduct, or intent for the present contract.[185] The following has been the general rule in Texas for the admissibility of evidence of similar transactions between the parties to a suit:

> "Evidence as to prior transactions between the parties is admissible where it tends to illustrate the transaction in question, or to show the existence of a claimed relation between them, or where the question of intent or knowledge is material, or where it is offered to explain a party's conduct in other transactions shown by the adverse party."[186]

The Texas Uniform Commercial Code also allows evidence of a course of dealing between the parties to explain or supplement the terms of an agreement.[187] The only limitation is that the other contracts or agreements to be proved must not be too remote in time.[188] These principles also apply under Rules 401 through 403.

---

182. *See, e.g.*, ***New Braunfels Factory Outlet Ctr., Inc. v. IHOP Realty Corp.***, 872 S.W.2d 303, 311-12 (Tex. App.—Austin 1994, no writ) (trial court did not abuse discretion in excluding defendant's evidence of plaintiff's previous attempt to enforce a restrictive covenant in a similar situation because the evidence would have required a "trial within trial" and would have permitted plaintiff to call witnesses to prove justification for its actions in that situation).

183. *See **Pena v. Neal, Inc.***, 901 S.W.2d 663, 671 (Tex. App.—San Antonio 1995, writ denied) (evidence of similar conduct over a period of time is admissible to show conformity with habit and course of dealing between parties); *see, e.g.*, ***Soto v. El Paso Nat. Gas Co.***, 942 S.W.2d 671, 677 (Tex. App.—El Paso 1997, writ denied) (evidence of prior sexual-harassment incidents, although not actionable because they were barred by statute of limitations, were relevant to show "hostile work environment").

184. *See **Sears, Roebuck & Co. v. Menegay***, 907 S.W.2d 72, 74 (Tex. App.—Fort Worth 1995, no writ) ("requisite degree of similarity is plainly not very high" before evidence of prior similar accidents may be admissible); *see, e.g.*, ***Fredericksburg Indus., Inc. v. Franklin Int'l, Inc.***, 911 S.W.2d 518, 522-23 (Tex. App.—San Antonio 1995, writ denied) (in action by furniture maker against glue manufacturer claiming that laminating glue did not hold, plaintiff's evidence of glue problems with other manufacturers was sufficiently similar and should have been admitted).

185. McCORMICK'S HANDBOOK II, *supra* note 33, §198, at 469; *see, e.g.*, ***Adams v. Petrade Int'l, Inc.***, 754 S.W.2d 696, 711 (Tex. App.—Houston [1st Dist.] 1988, writ denied) (allowing evidence of earlier partnership arrangements between the parties to show the parties' general understanding, intent, and course of conduct in the litigated transaction).

186. ***Utils. Nat. Gas Corp. v. Hill***, 239 S.W.2d 431, 435 (Tex. Civ. App.—Dallas 1951, writ ref'd n.r.e.) (quoting 17 Tex. Jur. *Evidence—Civil Cases* §130, at 378 (1932)); *see **PGP Gas Prods., Inc. v. Reserve Equip., Inc.***, 667 S.W.2d 604, 607 (Tex. App.—Austin 1984, writ ref'd n.r.e.).

187. *See* TEX. BUS. & COM. CODE §1.303(d).

188. *See **Carter v. Converse***, 550 S.W.2d 322, 332 (Tex. Civ. App.—Tyler 1977, writ ref'd n.r.e.) (allowing evidence of events "within reasonable proximity" to a crucial date).

2. Similar contracts with others. While Texas courts have been generous in admitting evidence of other contracts between the parties, evidence of contracts between a party and a third person or between two nonparties was generally excluded under the common law.[189] This policy, known as the doctrine of irrelevance of *res inter alios acta*,[190] rests on the assumption that a particular contract made with one person does not tend to show the making of a similar contract with another.[191] Commentators have criticized *res inter alios acta* and its underlying assumption as unnecessarily excluding relevant evidence.[192] Perhaps to address this concern, courts have made an exception to *res inter alios acta* by admitting evidence of contracts with others for the limited purposes of showing a plan or scheme and proving a party's intent.[193] Although Texas courts have not been consistent in deciding the issue of agent authority, they have generally allowed evidence of prior transactions between an alleged agent and third persons to establish the alleged agent's authority to act for the principal in the litigated transaction.[194]

---

189. *See Esteve Cotton Co. v. Hancock*, 539 S.W.2d 145, 159 (Tex. Civ. App.—Amarillo 1976, writ ref'd n.r.e.).

190. *See Magnet Cove Barium Corp. v. Brown*, 419 S.W.2d 697, 698 (Tex. Civ. App.—Waco 1967, writ ref'd n.r.e.) (the doctrine, as applied by Texas courts, had no categorical rules for admissibility); BLACK'S LAW DICTIONARY 1503 (10th ed. 2014) (term is Latin for "a thing done between others").

191. In *Linthicum v. Richardson*, the court held that evidence of an essentially identical transaction between the defendant and the plaintiff's brother was inadmissible. 245 S.W. 713, 715-16 (Tex. Civ. App.—Beaumont 1922, no writ). The court said that the jury might have been induced to believe, from the fact that the defendant had made such an agreement with one person, that he had made a similar one with the plaintiff. *Id.* at 716.

192. *See* McCORMICK ON EVIDENCE, *supra* note 1, §198, at 583-84 (contracts with third parties may demonstrate a party's usual practices and could be probative for the disputed contract); 2 RAY, *supra* note 46, §1523, at 214-15 & n.78 (decision to admit evidence of third-party contracts should be based on probative value); 2 WIGMORE, *supra* note 179, §377, at 307, 310-14 & n.5 (courts have been overcautious in excluding such evidence). McCormick, for example, maintains that contracts with others may show a course of business conduct that is highly probative of the terms of the litigated agreement. McCORMICK'S HANDBOOK II, *supra* note 33, §198, at 470.

193. *See Carousel's Creamery, L.L.C. v. Marble Slab Creamery, Inc.*, 134 S.W.3d 385, 396 (Tex. App.—Houston [1st Dist.] 2004, pet. dism'd) (exception to *res inter alios acta* doctrine permits admission of prior acts or transactions with other people to show party's intent, when material, if those people are so connected with transaction at issue that they may all be parts of system, scheme, or plan); *Underwriters Life Ins. v. Cobb*, 746 S.W.2d 810, 815 (Tex. App.—Corpus Christi 1988, no writ) (same); *see, e.g., Magnet Cove Barium Corp.*, 419 S.W.2d at 698-99 (deeds with third persons were admissible to show mutual mistake in the omission of an item from a litigated deed); *Wilson Fin. Co. v. State*, 342 S.W.2d 117, 123 (Tex. Civ. App.—Austin 1960, writ ref'd n.r.e.) (admitting transactions with others to show a scheme to evade usury laws).

194. *See Int'l & Great N. Ry. Co. v. Ragsdale*, 67 Tex. 24, 26, 2 S.W. 515, 516 (1886) ("[i]t seems to be well settled that an agency may be established by showing that the alleged principal had habitually ratified the acts of the alleged agent in similar transactions" with third persons); *see, e.g., Osage Oil & Gas Co. v. Caulk*, 243 S.W. 551, 554 (Tex. Civ. App.—Amarillo 1922, writ dism'd) (evidence from witness that defendant's agent had made a contract with witness similar to the contract made with plaintiff, offered to show agent's authority to make contracts for defendant, was clearly admissible under *Ragsdale*); *Tex. Land & Loan Co. v. Watson*, 3 Tex. Civ. App. 233, 241, 22 S.W. 873, 875 (Galveston 1893, no writ) (admitting evidence that lawyer was agent for lender on other occasions involving third persons to show agency on the litigated occasion). *But see Davis v. Commercial Std. Ins.*, 194 S.W.2d 599, 606 (Tex. Civ. App.—Dallas 1946, writ ref'd n.r.e.) (excluding evidence that doctor was agent of insurer on other occasions involving third parties to show agency on the litigated occasion and citing the general principle excluding *res inter alios acta*).

Rule 403 mandates a less restrictive test for excluding relevant evidence than the common law required.[195] Thus, one Texas court has used Rule 403 to abolish the principle of *res inter alios acta* as a general exclusionary policy.[196] Other Texas courts, however, have shown little inclination to do so or even to analyze the doctrine under Rules 401 through 403.[197] One Texas court of appeals used Rule 403 and the doctrine of *res inter alios acta* to hold that it was error to admit expert testimony on the "profile" of a sexual harasser in a sexual-harassment suit brought by an employee against her former employer.[198] The court held that such profile evidence was not relevant under Rule 401.[199] Even if it were relevant, this evidence was inadmissible under Rule 403 because "the dangers of the profile testimony substantially outweigh its probative value."[200] Finally, such profile testimony was inadmissible character evidence under Rule 404.[201] The court noted that, for the doctrine of *res inter alios acta*, the most "useful" rule is that "evidence of a similar event can only be admissible when a party to the lawsuit (or

---

195. ***Mo. Pac. R.R. v. Roberts***, 849 S.W.2d 367, 369 n.1 (Tex. App.—Eastland 1993, writ denied). Refer to note 101 *supra*.

196. *See **Mo. Pac. R.R.***, 849 S.W.2d at 369 (there is no longer a *res inter alios acta* doctrine in Texas independent from Texas Civil Rules of Evidence 401, 402, 403, and 404(b)). Under this approach, evidence of similar contracts with others is logically relevant, complies with the requirements of Rule 401, and is admissible under Rule 402. *See* 1 GOODE ET AL., *supra* note 103, §401.4, at 121-26 (3d ed. 2002 & Supp. 2004). The court would then consider the evidence in light of the Rule 403 counterfactors. Refer to notes 111-159 *supra* and accompanying text.

197. *See, e.g.,* ***Tex. Cookie Co. v. Hendricks & Peralta, Inc.***, 747 S.W.2d 873, 881 (Tex. App.—Corpus Christi 1988, writ denied) (citing and applying the traditional doctrine of *res inter alios acta* without reference to Rules of Evidence); ***Klorer v. Block***, 717 S.W.2d 754, 763 (Tex. App.—San Antonio 1986, writ ref'd n.r.e.) (evidence failed the relevance test of Civil Rule 401 because of the application of the *res inter alios acta* doctrine); ***State v. Buckner Constr. Co.***, 704 S.W.2d 837, 848 (Tex. App.—Houston [14th Dist.] 1985, writ ref'd n.r.e.) (applying the *res inter alios acta* doctrine without reference to the Rules). In ***City of Houston v. Leach***, the court rejected the argument that the *res inter alios acta* doctrine barred evidence of expert testimony in a whistleblower suit about the witness's opinion and observations of employees' fears about reporting wrongdoing. 819 S.W.2d 185, 190-91 (Tex. App.—Houston [14th Dist.] 1991, no writ). In doing so, the court noted an exception to the general doctrine:

> "when the intent with which an act is done is material, other similar acts of the party whose conduct is drawn in question may be shown, provided they are so connected with the transaction under consideration in point of time that they may all be regarded as parts of a system, scheme, or plan."

Id. at 191 (quoting ***Tex. Cookie Co.***, 747 S.W.2d at 881).

198. ***Bushell v. Dean***, 781 S.W.2d 652, 655-56 (Tex. App.—Austin 1989), *rev'd on other grounds*, 803 S.W.2d 711 (Tex. 1991).

199. ***Bushell***, 781 S.W.2d at 656. "Profile" evidence seeks to demonstrate that people of a particular class share certain characteristics, outlines the particular characteristics, and then asks the fact-finder to infer that a person is a member of that class because he has some of the characteristics that typify the class. *See id.* at 655.

200. *Id.* at 656. The court noted the following:

> The probative value of the profile testimony is low because it contains no facts about [the defendant-employer] or about the relationship between [the defendant and employee]. The danger of prejudice, confusion, or misleading the jury is high because the profile testimony was presented as expert opinion and because evidence of other, similar situations is highly persuasive by its nature.

Id.

201. *Id.* The court stated that "[c]haracter evidence in this context depends upon the following logic: (1) sexual harassers have particular personality traits; (2) the defendant possesses these traits; (3) therefore, the defendant probably did harass the victim." *Id.* This logic is precisely the type that Rule 404 prohibits. Refer to notes 298-327 *infra* and accompanying text.

his agent, servant, etc.) participated in the similar event."[202] As a general proposition, this court's statement goes too far in establishing an absolute bar to evidence of similar events. However, the underlying logic is valid under the Rules of Evidence: if the offered transactions or conduct between nonlitigants has little probative value when compared to any substantial negative dangers of unfair prejudice, confusing the issues, and misleading the jury, the judge could exclude the evidence under Rule 403.

3. Similar sales. A party may seek to establish the value of litigated property by introducing as evidence the price paid for similar property.[203] Landowners frequently offer this type of evidence in condemnation suits when they are claiming that the amount of money offered for the condemned land is insufficient.[204] Owners of personal property also offer this type of evidence when seeking damages for injury to the property.[205] Texas courts have traditionally admitted such value evidence,[206] subject to a number of limitations:

(1) The other property must be so similar in character and so similarly situated to the property in question as to afford a fair basis for comparison.[207]

(2) The sale of the other property must not be too remote in time or place.[208]

---

202. **Bushell**, 781 S.W.2d at 656 n.4. The Texas Supreme Court reversed the decision in **Bushell** because the employer did not properly preserve his trial objection. **Bushell v. Dean**, 803 S.W.2d 711, 712 (Tex. 1991).

203. *See, e.g.*, **City of Abilene v. Blackburn**, 447 S.W.2d 474, 476 (Tex. Civ. App.—Eastland 1969, writ ref'd n.r.e.) (in eminent-domain proceeding, owner introduced evidence of comparable sales to prove value of condemned land and depreciated value of remaining land). Value is "nothing more than the nature or quality of [property] as measured by the money that others show themselves willing to [pay for] it." 2 WIGMORE, *supra* note 179, §463, at 503; *see* **City of Pearland v. Alexander**, 483 S.W.2d 244, 247 (Tex. 1972) (market value is the price that property will bring when offered for sale to a person desiring but under no pressure to buy); *see also* **Austin Nat'l Bank v. Capital Lodge No. 23**, 558 S.W.2d 947, 950 (Tex. Civ. App.—Austin 1977, no writ) ("The word 'value' means market value when used without qualification. Both terms are used interchangeably and both are synonymous with actual value and salable value. The word 'value' implies sales value as opposed to intrinsic value or value to a particular person.").

204. *See* **Blackburn**, 447 S.W.2d at 476; *see also* **United States v. 33.90 Acres of Land, More or Less, Situated in Bexar Cty.**, 709 F.2d 1012, 1013-14 (5th Cir. 1983) (condemning authority complained that the judge should have admitted further evidence of comparable sales to prove the value of remaining property; no abuse of discretion in excluding evidence).

205. *See, e.g.*, **Pac. Express Co. v. Lothrop**, 20 Tex. Civ. App. 339, 341, 49 S.W. 898, 899 (Dallas 1899, no writ) (admitting evidence of the sales of similar hogs near the date of the event to show damages to the hog in question).

206. *See* **Blackburn**, 447 S.W.2d at 476.

207. *Id.*; *see* **Austin Nat'l Bank**, 558 S.W.2d at 950 ("[T]he best evidences of value are recent comparable sales in the area."); *see, e.g.*, **State v. Taylor**, 721 S.W.2d 541, 550-51 (Tex. App.—Tyler 1986, writ ref'd n.r.e.) (error, but harmless, to admit details of property sales that were not "reasonably similar"); **Sw. Bell Tel. Co. v. Ramsey**, 542 S.W.2d 466, 476 (Tex. Civ. App.—Tyler 1976, writ ref'd n.r.e.) (admitting evidence of sales of "similar," "comparable," or "like" property); *see also* **City of Odessa v. Meek**, 695 S.W.2d 775, 776 (Tex. App.—El Paso 1985, no writ) (prices paid for improved lots cannot be used to establish the value of unimproved lots because of lack of similarity). The trial court has discretion to decide whether other sales are sufficiently similar. *See* **Austin Nat'l Bank**, 558 S.W.2d at 950; **Sw. Bell**, 542 S.W.2d at 476.

208. *See* **Blackburn**, 447 S.W.2d at 476; *see, e.g.*, **Holiday Inns, Inc. v. State**, 931 S.W.2d 614, 623-24 (Tex. App.—Amarillo 1996, writ denied) (evidence of sale of property more than seven years after taking was not admissible to prove market value of remainder); **Taylor**, 721 S.W.2d at 550 (evidence of similar sales within three years was admissible). The trial court has discretion to decide whether other sales are not too remote. *See* **Austin Nat'l Bank**, 558 S.W.2d at 950; **Sw. Bell**, 542 S.W.2d at 476.

(3) The other sales must have been voluntary, arm's-length transactions.[209] Prices obtained at forced or distress sales are inadmissible.[210] Proof of sales to an entity with power of eminent domain is also inadmissible because such sales are not free and voluntary.[211]

(4) Unaccepted offers and unexercised options are not consummated sales and thus are inadmissible to show the sale price of property.[212]

Evidence of similar sales is admissible under the Rules, as it was under the common law.[213]

4. Similar claims. Texas courts have excluded evidence of claims similar to the litigated claim used to prove that the plaintiff is claims-minded or a chronic litigant.[214]

---

209. *See 33.90 Acres of Land*, 709 F.2d at 1014 (acknowledging the willingness of buyer and seller); ***Bradfield v. State***, 524 S.W.2d 438, 440 (Tex. Civ. App.—Austin 1975, writ ref'd n.r.e.) (other sales must be free and open, not compulsory).

210. *See Wendlandt v. Wendlandt*, 596 S.W.2d 323, 325 (Tex. Civ. App.—Houston [1st Dist.] 1980, no writ); ***Bradfield***, 524 S.W.2d at 439-40.

211. ***Gomez Leon v. State***, 426 S.W.2d 562, 565 (Tex. 1968); *see, e.g.*, ***Blackburn***, 447 S.W.2d at 477-78 (court erred by admitting evidence of prior sale of similar land to city with eminent-domain power even though sale was voluntary and seller set price paid). Commentators have criticized this per se position and have submitted as a "better reasoned view" the position that such evidence may be allowed at the judge's discretion if the price paid is not "too far out of line" and neither party is "compelled to agree on a price." McCORMICK ON EVIDENCE, *supra* note 1, §199, at 586 & n.11. Some earlier Texas cases did not absolutely exclude evidence of other sales to a condemning authority. *See, e.g.*, ***City of Gladewater v. Dillard***, 312 S.W.2d 530, 531-32 (Tex. Civ. App.—Texarkana 1958, no writ) (upholding trial court's decision to admit evidence of price paid by city for similar right-of-way property when record did not indicate a forced sale); ***Marsh v. State***, 276 S.W.2d 852, 854 (Tex. Civ. App.—San Antonio 1955, no writ) (court would not presume that sales to the county were not voluntary). The Fifth Circuit admits evidence of other sales to a condemning authority "when it is certain that those sales *truly* represent the market value of the land in question. That necessarily means that the party ... must show that the sales were uninfluenced by the buyer's possession of the eminent domain power. The burden is a heavy one." ***Transwestern Pipeline Co. v. O'Brien***, 418 F.2d 15, 19 (5th Cir. 1969). *But see* ***United States v. 5.00 Acres of Land, More or Less, Situate in Orange Cty.***, 507 F. Supp. 589, 596 (E.D. Tex. 1981) (condemnation commission holds that power of eminent domain and economic duress go to the weight, not the admissibility, of evidence), *rev'd on other grounds sub nom.* ***United States v. 8.41 Acres of Land, More or Less, Situated in Orange Cty.***, 680 F.2d 388 (5th Cir. 1982).

212. *See, e.g.*, ***Hanks v. Gulf, Colo. & Santa Fe Ry. Co.***, 159 Tex. 311, 314-17, 320 S.W.2d 333, 335-37 (1959) (unaccepted offer was inadmissible); ***Niemann v. State***, 471 S.W.2d 124, 131 (Tex. Civ. App.—San Antonio 1971) (option to purchase property was inadmissible), *rev'd on other grounds*, 479 S.W.2d 907 (Tex. 1972).

213. *See Keeton v. State*, 803 S.W.2d 304, 306 (Tex. Crim. App. 1991) (jury may infer value from the opinions of witnesses acquainted with actual sales of like property); ***Finch v. Finch***, 825 S.W.2d 218, 223 (Tex. App.—Houston [1st Dist.] 1992, no writ) (sales of property that are near in time and involve property similar in location, character, and improvements may be received into evidence to establish value).

214. *See Bonham v. Baldeschwiler*, 533 S.W.2d 144, 148 (Tex. Civ. App.—Corpus Christi 1976, writ ref'd n.r.e.); *see, e.g.*, ***St. Paul Fire & Marine Ins. v. Murphree***, 347 S.W.2d 817, 819 (Tex. Civ. App.—Amarillo 1961) (excluding evidence of other claims, payments, and settlements), *aff'd*, 163 Tex. 534, 357 S.W.2d 744 (1962); ***L.B. Price Mercantile Co. v. Moore***, 263 S.W. 657, 658 (Tex. Civ. App.—Beaumont 1924) (excluding evidence of other litigation by plaintiff and her family offered to show that they were chronic litigants), *writ dism'd sub nom.* ***National Compress Co. v. Hamlin***, 114 Tex. 375, 269 S.W. 1024 (1925).

    Courts in other jurisdictions have not excluded such evidence. *See, e.g.*, ***Gastineau v. Fleet Mortg. Corp.***, 137 F.3d 490, 495-96 (7th Cir. 1998) (admitting evidence that wrongful-termination plaintiff had filed similar prior lawsuits; relevant to show plaintiff's modus operandi because other claims were close in time and similar in nature and to explain why defendant kept diary of events in this case); ***Mintz v. Premier Cab Ass'n***, 127 F.2d 744, 744-45 (D.C. Cir. 1942) (allowing evidence of prior claims against a beauty parlor and another cab company on cross-examination of plaintiff; jury should decide whether plaintiff was unlucky or "claims-minded").

This exclusionary policy is based on the theory that such evidence might unfairly prejudice the jury against the plaintiff.[215] Evidence of similar claims has been allowed, however, as statements of an opposing party to show inconsistent statements and to rebut allegations of causation.[216] Evidence of a prior false claim is admissible to show that the present claim is false, but the proponent of the evidence must prove that the prior claim is false, not just that it was made.[217] Similarly, Texas courts have admitted an insurance company's denial of other claims near the time of its denial of the plaintiff's claim on the same basis to show the insurer's general business practice of refusing claims.[218]

5. Other fraud or misconduct. The Texas Rules generally exclude evidence of a person's character offered to prove that he acted in conformity with his character on a particular occasion.[219] This doctrine has a corollary principle that a party cannot prove an opponent's prior acts to show bad character in an attempt to prove the opponent's fraud or misconduct on the occasion in question.[220] But relevant evidence of prior misconduct is admissible to prove some material fact other than character, such as "motive, opportunity, intent, preparation, plan, knowledge, identity, absence of mistake, or lack of accident."[221] Thus, evidence of prior misconduct that is part of a plan, scheme, system, or design may be admissible to show that the act in question was also part of the plan, scheme, system, or design.[222] The evidence of prior misconduct may

---

215. *Murphree*, 347 S.W.2d at 819.

216. *E.g.*, *Middleton v. Palmer*, 601 S.W.2d 759, 762-63 (Tex. Civ. App.—Dallas 1980, writ ref'd n.r.e.) (allowing evidence that plaintiff was in two accidents within three months and filed two suits, "each asserting that she suffered neck and back injuries as a result of each accident," to show inconsistent statements by plaintiff). For a discussion of statements of an opposing party under Rule 801(e)(2), refer to *Article VIII: Hearsay, infra* p. 845.

217. *See, e.g.*, *Brinkley v. Liberty Mut. Ins.*, 331 S.W.2d 423, 425-26 (Tex. Civ. App.—Texarkana 1959, no writ) (in workers' compensation case, trial court improperly admitted evidence of prior claims, settlements, and payments as tending to show that plaintiff exaggerated disability in the present case); *San Antonio Traction Co. v. Cox*, 184 S.W. 722, 724 (Tex. Civ. App.—San Antonio 1916, no writ) (excluding evidence of 17 other claims for like injuries filed by plaintiff's relatives without a showing of conspiracy to defraud a streetcar company when plaintiff sought damages for injuries received in exiting street car).

In *Thomas v. State*, the trial court refused to permit the defendant, charged with aggravated rape of his ten-year-old stepdaughter, to cross-examine the complainant about two previous alleged incidents of rape and attempted rape by strangers. 669 S.W.2d 420, 421-22 (Tex. App.—Houston [1st Dist.] 1984, pet. ref'd). The court of appeals held that this refusal amounted to a violation of the defendant's constitutional right to cross-examine his accusers because the testimony showed that at least one of the prior accusations was false. *Id.* at 423. Though this evidence might indicate emotional or psychological trauma rather than a lack of trustworthiness, the trial court should have admitted it for the jury's consideration of the complainant's credibility. *Id.*

218. *Underwriters Life Ins. v. Cobb*, 746 S.W.2d 810, 815 (Tex. App.—Corpus Christi 1988, no writ); *see, e.g.*, *Lawyers Sur. Corp. v. Royal Chevrolet, Inc.*, 847 S.W.2d 624, 628-29 & n.9 (Tex. App.—Texarkana 1993, writ denied) (evidence of other lawsuits and judgments against surety was admissible to prove "a pattern of knowing failure to act in good faith in claims denials").

219. TEX. R. EVID. 404(a)(1). Refer to notes 322-328 *infra* and accompanying text.

220. *See* TEX. R. EVID. 404(b)(1); MCCORMICK'S HANDBOOK II, *supra* note 33, §197, at 468.

221. TEX. R. EVID. 404(b)(2). The common law also allowed evidence of similar incidents occurring at or about the same time to prove intent. *See Posey v. Hanson*, 196 S.W. 731, 733 (Tex. Civ. App.—Austin 1917, no writ).

222. *See Plante v. State*, 692 S.W.2d 487, 492 (Tex. Crim. App. 1985); *Miller v. State*, 677 S.W.2d 737, 741-42 (Tex. App.—Corpus Christi 1984, no pet.); *see, e.g.*, *Sturges v. Wal-Mart Stores, Inc.*, 39 S.W.3d 608, 613-14 (Tex. App.—Beaumont 2001) ("other acts" evidence of prior lawsuits against retailer for interfering with contractual re-

also be admissible to prove some mental element—such as knowledge, intent, or motive—at issue in later litigation.[223] For example, in a wrongful-termination case, the El Paso Court of Appeals held that the trial court abused its discretion in excluding evidence of other similar terminations.[224] The court noted that evidence of prior similar events had been admitted in many Texas cases and that the doctrine of *res inter alios acta* does not bar evidence offered to show a party's intent.[225] On the other hand, evidence of unrelated later acts of misconduct may be excluded under Rule 403.[226]

In a civil assault case, like a criminal assault prosecution, the defendant can assert self-defense. In such a case, the plaintiff can offer evidence of other acts of misconduct that tends to rebut the self-defense claim. In an assault case involving a claimed self-defense shooting, the court of appeals held that the trial court did not abuse its discretion in allowing the victim to offer evidence of two prior shootings by the defendant in which the defendant claimed self-defense.[227] Here, the defendant's intent to assault was the primary disputed issue, and the fact that he had previously shot two people during altercations was some indication of his "philosophy" that in a fight "he preferred

---

lationships was admissible to support land purchasers' exemplary-damages claim in tortious-interference lawsuit; defendant had argued to jury that retailer's conduct was "one isolated event"; evidence of other acts was relevant to defendant's course of conduct, the frequency of similar wrongs, the character of conduct involved, and degree of retailer's culpability), *rev'd on other grounds*, 52 S.W.3d 711 (Tex. 2001); ***Payne v. Hartford Fire Ins.***, 409 S.W.2d 591, 594-95 (Tex. Civ. App.—Beaumont 1966, writ ref'd n.r.e.) (evidence of prior fires set by plaintiff was admissible to show that the fire in question was set by plaintiff as part of a "plan, scheme, system, or design" to defraud insurers).

223. *See, e.g.*, ***Day v. Stone***, 59 Tex. 612, 614-15 (1883) (in action to recover land conveyed in fraud of creditors, reversible error to exclude evidence of similar conveyance as tending to show motive); ***Schlueter v. Schlueter***, 929 S.W.2d 94, 97-98 (Tex. App.—Austin 1996) (in divorce case, evidence that husband's father had aided another son to commit fraud during that son's divorce proceeding was admissible to show father's intent to assist his children by fair or foul means during their divorces), *rev'd in part on other grounds*, 975 S.W.2d 584 (Tex. 1998); ***Goree v. Uvalde Nat'l Bank***, 218 S.W. 620, 624 (Tex. Civ. App.—San Antonio 1920, writ dism'd) (evidence of other fraud was not admissible to show intent, scienter, or motive because the prior acts had "no similarity" to the litigated transaction and were "wholly disconnected"); ***Posey***, 196 S.W. at 733 (evidence that defendant defrauded witness in a similar transaction was admissible to show intent). Subsequent good acts have also been admitted to show intent. *Cf.* ***Ansell v. Green Acres Contracting Co.***, 347 F.3d 515, 523-24 (3d Cir. 2003) (in employment-discrimination case, subsequent good act by employer was admissible to show nondiscriminatory intent under Federal Rule 404(b)).

224. ***Durbin v. Dal-Briar Corp.***, 871 S.W.2d 263, 268-69 (Tex. App.—El Paso 1994, writ denied), *overruled on other grounds*, ***Golden Eagle Archery, Inc. v. Jackson***, 24 S.W.3d 362 (Tex. 2000).

225. ***Durbin***, 871 S.W.2d at 268. In ***Durbin***, the testimony was offered as circumstantial evidence of an essential element of the plaintiff's claim: a causal connection between his workers' compensation claim and his termination. *Id.* at 269. As such, it was relevant and was not unfairly prejudicial, misleading, or confusing under Rule 403. *Id.* at 270.

226. *See, e.g.*, ***Mackey v. U.P. Enters., Inc.***, No. 12-99-00355-CV (Tex. App.—Tyler 2005, no pet.) (memo op.; 7-29-05) (trial court did not abuse its discretion in excluding evidence of acts of sexual harassment occurring after plaintiff had been discharged); *cf.* ***Ansell***, 347 F.3d at 525-26 (in employment-discrimination case, employee did not show any prejudice from admission of employer's subsequent good act, so probative value was not substantially outweighed by unfair prejudice under Federal Rule 403); ***Wyvill v. United Cos. Life Ins.***, 212 F.3d 296, 302-03 (5th Cir. 2000) (trial court erred in admitting plaintiffs' anecdotal evidence of age discrimination involving employees who were not similarly situated; evidence lacked probative value and substantially prejudiced defendant); ***Coletti v. Cudd Pressure Control***, 165 F.3d 767, 777 (10th Cir. 1999) (trial court did not abuse its discretion in excluding evidence offered to show retaliatory discharge when the events occurred after plaintiff was discharged).

227. *See* ***Rogers v. Peeler***, 146 S.W.3d 765, 777-78 (Tex. App.—Texarkana 2004, no pet.).

to shoot someone before taking a blow."[228] The court of appeals then applied various factors developed in criminal cases to analyze the prejudicial effect of this evidence under Rule 403 and decided that its probative value was not substantially outweighed by the danger of unfair prejudice.[229]

Texas courts have not formulated a precise, consistent test in civil cases that defines how similar or how close other acts must be to be admissible in the later litigation. One court has required "precisely similar" acts,[230] and others require only that the acts must be "similar."[231] Some courts have specified that the acts must be "closely connected in time" with the litigated event[232] or occur "about the same time."[233] Still other courts have held that the other acts must be so closely connected in time with the transaction at issue that they may all be regarded as parts of a system, scheme or plan.[234] Other decisions have followed the general Rule 403 balancing test used in criminal cases when addressing the admissibility of extraneous misconduct in civil cases.[235] Generally, evidence of other fraud or misconduct should be admitted when it shows a "reasonable approximation in purport, time and circumstance" to the litigated event.[236] Rule 403 requires such a liberal standard unless the probative value of the evidence is substantially outweighed by its negative effect.[237]

In criminal proceedings, there is a concern that a jury might misuse evidence of prior misconduct to convict a defendant of the present crime based on evidence of other crimes that may indicate the defendant's propensity toward criminality.[238] Under Rule

---

228. *Id.* at 774.

229. *Id.* at 775-77.

230. *Goree v. Uvalde Nat'l Bank*, 218 S.W. 620, 624 (Tex. Civ. App.—San Antonio 1920, writ dism'd).

231. *Day v. Stone*, 59 Tex. 612, 614 (1883); *Posey v. Hanson*, 196 S.W. 731, 733 (Tex. Civ. App.—Austin 1917, no writ).

232. *Day*, 59 Tex. at 614.

233. *Posey*, 196 S.W. at 733.

234. *See Oakwood Mobile Homes, Inc. v. Cabler*, 73 S.W.3d 363, 375 (Tex. App.—El Paso 2002, pet. denied); *Tex. Osage Coop. Royalty Pool, Inc. v. Cruze*, 191 S.W.2d 47, 51-52 (Tex. Civ. App.—Austin 1945, no writ); *see, e.g.*, *Serv. Corp. Int'l v. Guerra*, 348 S.W.3d 221, 236 (Tex. 2011) (in fraud case brought by decedent's family after cemetery moved decedent's body without family's permission because burial plot had been sold to someone else, trial court erred in admitting evidence of other lawsuits allegedly involving sales of plots that already belonged to someone else; "[t]he events occurred at different cemeteries and there was no evidence that any of the same employees were involved or that they occurred under similar circumstances. The events also occurred more than a year apart. There is no evidence that the events were part of a system, scheme, or plan."). Whether the proponent of the evidence needs to prove a scheme or plan is unclear.

235. *See, e.g.*, *Olivarez v. Doe*, 164 S.W.3d 427, 433-34 (Tex. App.—Tyler 2004, pet. denied) (evidence of relative's prior acts of sexual misconduct with different child victims was admissible in suit for damages for sexual misconduct; "overall similarity of the misconduct" favored admission of relevant evidence).

236. McCORMICK'S HANDBOOK II, *supra* note 33, §197, at 468; *see United States v. Franklin*, 452 F.2d 926, 929 n.1 (8th Cir. 1971).

237. *See* TEX. R. EVID. 403. For a discussion of the Rule 403 counterfactors, refer to notes 111-159 *supra* and accompanying text.

238. *See Michelson v. United States*, 335 U.S. 469, 475-76 (1948). Justice Jackson noted the following:

> The State may not show defendant's prior trouble with the law, specific criminal acts, or ill name among his neighbors, even though such facts might logically be persuasive that he is by propensity a probable perpetrator of the crime. The inquiry is not rejected because character is irrelevant; on the

404(b), however, evidence of extraneous misconduct that is logically relevant to some material issue other than bad character is ordinarily admissible; such evidence should be excluded only if its probative value is substantially outweighed by one of the five counterfactors listed in Rule 403.[239]

6. Other accidents & injuries. Texas courts have traditionally admitted evidence of similar accidents or injuries for several purposes. First, the evidence is admissible to show that a condition or operation is dangerous.[240] Second, the evidence is admissible to prove that the defendant knew or should have known about an allegedly dangerous condition.[241] Third, the evidence is admissible to show causation.[242] Fourth, the evidence is admissible to rebut the defendant's claim of impossibility.[243] Finally, evidence of safety history (the absence of similar accidents and injuries) is admissible to prove lack of negligence in manufacturing and selling an item or in maintaining premises.[244]

---

contrary, it is said to weigh too much with the jury and to so overpersuade them as to prejudge one with a bad general record and deny him a fair opportunity to defend against a particular charge. The overriding policy of excluding such evidence, despite its admitted probative value, is the practical experience that its disallowance tends to prevent confusion of issues, unfair surprise and undue prejudice.

Id. (footnotes omitted).

239. *See id.*; ***Crank v. State***, 761 S.W.2d 328, 342 n.5 (Tex. Crim. App. 1988) ("Rule 403 shifts the focus ... to *admit relevant evidence* unless the probative value of that relevant evidence is *substantially* outweighed by the danger of unfair prejudice to a defendant."). Refer to notes 111-159 *supra* and accompanying text.

240. *See, e.g.*, ***Mo.-Kan.-Tex. R.R. v. May***, 600 S.W.2d 755, 756 (Tex. 1980) (evidence of prior accidents was admissible to show that railroad crossing was extrahazardous); ***Fredericksburg Indus., Inc. v. Franklin Int'l, Inc.***, 911 S.W.2d 518, 522-23 (Tex. App.—San Antonio 1995, writ denied) (evidence of other accidents involving same product under "reasonably similar circumstances" was admissible to demonstrate product's dangerous character); ***Henry v. Mrs. Baird's Bakeries***, 475 S.W.2d 288, 293-94 (Tex. Civ. App.—Fort Worth 1971, writ ref'd n.r.e.) (evidence of similar fall was admissible to show that defendant allowed an area on its sidewalk to remain slippery); ***Team v. Tex. & Pac. Ry. Co.***, 199 S.W.2d 274, 276-77 (Tex. Civ. App.—Fort Worth 1947, writ ref'd n.r.e.) (evidence that other locomotives had emitted sparks was admissible to show defendant's negligence).

241. *See, e.g.*, ***Uniroyal Goodrich Tire Co. v. Martinez***, 977 S.W.2d 328, 340-41 (Tex. 1998) (evidence of 34 other lawsuits against tire maker about similar accident involving same tire design was admissible in products-liability action to show defect in product); ***N. Am. Van Lines, Inc. v. Emmons***, 50 S.W.3d 103, 125 (Tex. App.—Beaumont 2001, pet. denied) (evidence of prior accidents was probative of whether moving company was or should have been aware that it needed to exercise care to ensure that its agents were not using unqualified, unlicensed drivers or falsifying records); ***Sears, Roebuck & Co. v. Kunze***, 996 S.W.2d 416, 426 (Tex. App.—Beaumont 1999, pet. denied) (evidence of nearly 90 other accidents involving radial-arm saw made by defendant was admissible on issues of notice and conscious indifference in personal-injury case); ***Hyundai Motor Co. v. Alvarado***, 989 S.W.2d 32, 40 (Tex. App.—San Antonio 1998, pet. granted, judgm't vacated w.r.m.) (evidence of other accidents involving seat-belt failure in defendant's cars was admissible in products-liability action to show defect in product); ***Firestone Tire & Rubber Co. v. Battle***, 745 S.W.2d 909, 912 (Tex. App.—Houston [1st Dist.] 1988, writ denied) (evidence of prior tire explosion was admissible to show that defendant knew about the dangerous condition of "spin break"); ***May v. Mo.-Kan.-Tex. R.R.***, 583 S.W.2d 694, 697-98 (Tex. Civ. App.—Waco 1979) (evidence of prior accidents was admissible to determine whether railroad knew or should have known about unusually dangerous crossing conditions), *writ ref'd n.r.e.*, 600 S.W.2d 755 (Tex. 1980).

242. *See, e.g.*, ***Weaver v. Benson***, 152 Tex. 50, 54-56, 254 S.W.2d 95, 97-98 (1952) (evidence of blasting damage to a nearby building was admissible to show that defendant's blasting caused injuries to plaintiff's building).

243. *See, e.g.*, ***Tex. & N.O. R.R. v. Glass***, 107 S.W.2d 924, 926 (Tex. Civ. App.—Waco 1937, writ dism'd) (when defendant claimed that its oil-burning locomotives would not emit sparks large enough to cause a fire, plaintiff was allowed to rebut with evidence that other oil-burning locomotives had caused fires on other occasions).

244. *See, e.g.*, ***Bonner v. Mercantile Nat'l Bank***, 203 S.W.2d 780, 782 (Tex. Civ. App.—Waco 1947, writ ref'd n.r.e.) (allowing defendant to show a lack of other accidents on stairs); ***Pound v. Popular Dry Goods Co.***, 139 S.W.2d 341,

Before the evidence can be admitted, the proponent must show that the conditions surrounding the earlier accident or injury were reasonably similar, the conditions of the two accidents or injuries were connected in a special way, or the earlier accident or injury was attributable to the same conditions that caused the later accident or injury.[245] Evidence of other accidents and injuries is admissible whenever it is probative of a material fact and its probative value is not substantially outweighed by the Rule 403 counterfactors.[246]

In *Nissan Motor Co. v. Armstrong*,[247] the Texas Supreme Court analyzed the admissibility of evidence of other similar accidents admitted to show that a product is unreasonably dangerous. The supreme court stated that such evidence may be admitted if (1) the other incidents occurred under reasonably similar (though not necessarily identical) conditions,[248] (2) evidence of other incidents does not cause unfair prejudice,

---

344-45 (Tex. Civ. App.—El Paso 1940, no writ) (in personal-injury suit arising from alleged defect of safety latch on washing machine, evidence of the lack of similar injuries was admissible to show that defendant's failure to inspect machine before delivery was not negligent).

245. *See Columbia Med. Ctr. Subsidiary, L.P. v. Meier*, 198 S.W.3d 408, 411-12 (Tex. App.—Dallas 2006, pet. denied); *Huckaby v. A.G. Perry & Son, Inc.*, 20 S.W.3d 194, 202 (Tex. App.—Texarkana 2000, pet. denied). Before the Rules of Evidence were promulgated, the Texas Supreme Court articulated and reiterated a liberal and flexible test for the admissibility of evidence of other accidents: such events must have occurred under "reasonably similar but not necessarily identical circumstances" to those at the time of the litigated event. *Mo.-Kan.-Tex. R.R.*, 600 S.W.2d at 756; *Mo. Pac. R.R. v. Cooper*, 563 S.W.2d 233, 236 (Tex. 1978). The Rules continued this flexible approach. *See, e.g.*, *John Deere Co. v. May*, 773 S.W.2d 369, 372-73 (Tex. App.—Waco 1989, writ denied) (admitting evidence of other incidents involving John Deere tractors that shifted into gear after being left in neutral because the other incidents occurred under "reasonably similar" circumstances).

246. *See* 1 GOODE ET AL., *supra* note 103, §401.6, at 137-40 (3d ed. 2002 & Supp. 2007) (listing various theories of relevance that might permit admission of evidence of other accidents); *see, e.g.*, *City of Fort Worth v. Holland*, 748 S.W.2d 112, 113 (Tex. App.—Fort Worth 1988, writ denied) (evidence of other water-main breaks in plaintiff's neighborhood was relevant to his cause of action for damage to his residence caused by broken water main because the evidence was probative of whether the city was negligent in constructing, maintaining, and repairing the water main). Similarity enhances probative value in the Rule 403 balancing test, and dissimilarity increases the likelihood that the evidence's probative value will be substantially outweighed by one or more of the Rule 403 counterfactors.

247. 145 S.W.3d 131 (Tex. 2004).

248. *Id.* at 138; *cf. U-Haul Int'l, Inc. v. Waldrip*, 380 S.W.3d 118, 133-34 (Tex. 2012) (in negligence case against trucking company, trial court erred in admitting expert testimony about safety investigations that was offered to show "pattern of indifference" by defendant; investigations did not address issues similar to those presented in case). The degree of similarity required depends on the particular issue that the evidence is offered to prove. *Nissan Motor*, 145 S.W.3d at 138. In a recent products-liability case against a vehicle manufacturer, the Court held that a spreadsheet produced by the plaintiffs summarizing several hundred paid warranty claims was improperly admitted. *Kia Motors Corp. v. Ruiz*, 432 S.W.3d 865, 882-83 (Tex. 2014). The defendant argued that the claims summarized on the spreadsheet were not sufficiently similar to the underlying case and should not have been admitted as evidence. *Id.* at 881. The alleged design defect involved the design of particular clock-spring connectors in the air-bag system of their vehicle, which caused a short circuit. *See id.* at 881-82. Although the Court held that the warranty claims reflecting a problem with one of those connectors were sufficiently similar to the design defect in this case, the plaintiffs argued they were relying on the spreadsheet evidence to prove that the defendant had notice of the defect, not to prove the defect itself. *Id.* The plaintiffs further argued that the spreadsheet was admissible for all purposes because the defendant did not request a limiting instruction. *Id.* at 882; *see* TEX. R. EVID. 105(a). The Court rejected this argument, noting that "[t]he reasonable-similarity requirement does not disappear simply because other incidents are being offered to show notice rather than negligence"; thus, the spreadsheet should not have been admitted for any purpose. *Kia Motors*, 432 S.W.3d at 882-83. Because the evidence was inadmissible for any purpose, the defendant did not waive error by failing to request a limiting instruction. *Id.* at 883. Refer to *Article I: General Provisions*, *supra* p. 97.

confusion of the issues, or delay,[249] and (3) the relevance (and probative value) of such evidence is closely related to the specific purpose for which it is offered.[250] The supreme court then reviewed various lower-court holdings on the admission of such evidence and admonished trial courts to "carefully consider the bounds of similarity, prejudice, confusion, and sequence before admitting evidence of other accidents involving a product."[251] Implicit in *Nissan*'s discussion is that the proponent of the evidence must establish the occurrence of the other accident.[252]

B. Relation of Rules 401-403 to Scientific Evidence

The general principles of relevance declared in Rules 401 through 403 do not specifically provide for the admissibility of scientific evidence.[253] Scientific evidence, like all other evidence, must meet the test of relevance as defined in Rule 401.[254] For non-scientific evidence, judges can use experience and logic to decide whether evidence tends to prove the proposition for which it is offered. But judges often lack the expertise to determine the relevance of scientific evidence.

Scientific evidence is not logically relevant unless both the scientific principle involved and the technique applying the principle are valid, and the technique was properly applied on the occasion in question.[255] Courts have used two major tests for determining the admissibility of scientific evidence.[256] The first test, expressed in *Frye v. United States*, requires that a scientific principle be generally accepted in its field.[257] The second test is based on Rules 401 and 702 and focuses on a "gatekeeping" role for the judge based on the reliability and relevance of proffered scientific expertise.[258] The sec-

---

249. *Nissan Motor*, 145 S.W.3d at 138. The evidence should not be allowed if its presentation is unduly prolonged and threatens to distract the jury's attention from the litigated incident. *Id.*

250. *Id.* at 138-39. Proof of similar accidents would be relevant to show that a product was unreasonably dangerous, a warning should have been given, a safer design was available, or (in determining punitive damages) a manufacturer was consciously indifferent about accidents. *Id.*

251. *Id.* at 139.

252. *E.g.*, *McKee v. McNeir*, 151 S.W.3d 268, 270 (Tex. App.—Amarillo 2004, no pet.) (when the only evidence of the prior incidents was allegations contained in other lawsuit pleadings and orders, proponent did not show that trial court erred in excluding such evidence).

253. For a more thorough discussion of the admissibility of expert testimony, refer to *Article VII: Opinions & Expert Testimony*, *infra* p. 700.

254. Refer to notes 4-59 *supra* and accompanying text.

255. Paul C. Giannelli, *The Admissibility of Novel Scientific Evidence: Frye v. United States, A Half-Century Later*, 80 COLUM. L. REV. 1197, 1200-01 (1980).

256. *Id.* at 1203.

257. 293 F. 1013, 1014 (D.C. Cir. 1923); *see* Giannelli, *supra* note 255, at 1205. The *Frye* court reasoned:
Just when a scientific principle or discovery crosses the line between the experimental and demonstrable stages is difficult to define. Somewhere in this twilight zone the evidential force of the principle must be recognized, and while courts will go a long way in admitting expert testimony deduced from a well-recognized scientific principle or discovery, the thing from which the deduction is made must be sufficiently established to have gained general acceptance in the particular field in which it belongs.
293 F. at 1014. Refer to *Article VII: Opinions & Expert Testimony*, *infra* p. 722.

258. *See* *Daubert v. Merrell Dow Pharm., Inc.*, 509 U.S. 579, 589 (1993).

ond test is now used by Texas courts, federal courts, and an increasing number of other state courts.[259]

A trial judge's gatekeeping obligation under the Rules of Evidence is to ensure that the expert witness's testimony rests on a reliable foundation and is relevant to the task at hand.[260] Thus, in determining whether an expert's testimony should be admitted for the fact-finder, the trial judge has the responsibility under Rules 702 and 403 to determine if the offered testimony is sufficiently reliable and relevant to help the jury reach accurate results. If the trial court is persuaded that the evidence is both reliable and relevant, the evidence is admissible under Rule 402 unless its probative value is substantially outweighed by the Rule 403 counterfactors.[261] The Rule 403 test does not require a specific formula for determining the strength of the offered evidence's probative value; instead, courts must determine probative value with the help of science.[262] In a Rule 104 hearing outside the jury's presence, the judge should exclude untested or invalid scientific or professional theories and methodologies and allow the jury to consider only those that are tested and valid.[263] Unreliable expertise or "junk science" does not assist the jury in understanding the evidence or determining a fact of consequence. Such evidence is likely to confuse the issues and mislead the jury and should be excluded under Rule 403.

The opponent of relevant expert testimony must show that the probative value of the evidence is substantially outweighed by the Rule 403 counterfactors.[264] The trial judge's decision to admit or exclude expert testimony is reviewed by appellate courts for abuse of discretion,[265] as long as the rationale for the ruling is clear. Thus, the trial

---

259. McCORMICK HANDBOOK II, *supra* note 33, §203, at 490 n.33; *see* Cathleen C. Herasimchuk, *A Practical Guide to the Admissibility of Novel Expert Evidence in Criminal Trials Under Federal Rule 702*, 22 ST. MARY'S L.J. 181, 184-99 (1990) (discussing the inconsistent rulings on expert testimony and the ongoing debate between the *Frye* test and McCormick's relevancy approach); Edward J. Imwinkelried, *Judge Versus Jury: Who Should Decide Questions of Preliminary Facts Conditioning the Admissibility of Scientific Evidence?*, 25 WM. & MARY L. REV. 577, 578 (1984) (recognizing that by 1984, 15 states and two federal circuits had explicitly rejected or questioned the precedential value of the *Frye* test under codified rules of evidence). For a detailed discussion of the tests for the reliability and relevance of expert testimony, refer to *Article VII: Opinions & Expert Testimony, infra* p. 721.

260. *See Kumho Tire Co. v. Carmichael*, 526 U.S. 137, 141 (1999); *Daubert*, 509 U.S. at 597.

261. *Kelly v. State*, 824 S.W.2d 568, 572-73 (Tex. Crim. App. 1992). Refer to notes 111-159 *supra* and accompanying text.

262. In stating his relevancy test, McCormick recognizes the possibility of excluding scientific evidence for reasons of the sort included in Rule 403. He states that "[a]ny relevant conclusions which are supported by a qualified expert witness should be received unless there are other reasons for exclusion. Particularly, probative value may be overborne by the familiar dangers of prejudicing or misleading the jury, and undue consumption of time." McCORMICK'S HANDBOOK II, *supra* note 33, §203, at 491. For a helpful analysis of the dangers of scientific evidence and problems in the balancing process of Rule 403, see Giannelli, *supra* note 255, at 1237-39.

263. *See* Judge Harvey Brown, *Procedural Issues Under Daubert*, 36 HOUS. L. REV. 1133, 1159 (1999) (trial court "enjoys wide latitude in its determination of whether expert testimony is admissible"); Judge Harvey Brown, *Eight Gates for Expert Witnesses*, 36 HOUS. L. REV. 743, 812 (1999) (trial court must evaluate data that expert offers to support bottom-line opinions and determine if data supports expert's testimony as reliable).

264. *See Buls v. Fuselier*, 55 S.W.3d 204, 208 (Tex. App.—Texarkana 2001, no pet.). Refer to notes 111-159 *supra* and accompanying text.

265. *See K-Mart Corp. v. Honeycutt*, 24 S.W.3d 357, 360 (Tex. 2000) (per curiam); *Gammill v. Jack Williams Chevrolet, Inc.*, 972 S.W.2d 713, 718-19 (Tex. 1998).

judge should articulate on the record the factors that the court has considered in admitting or excluding expert evidence. A note in **Montgomery v. State** hints that courts may remand cases for further explanation when the record is not clear.[266] While the trial judge has discretion in *how* he conducts a hearing on the admissibility of expert testimony, he has no discretion in *whether* to conduct a hearing. Federal courts have noted that while trial judges have great discretion in how they evaluate the expert's qualifications and methodology, they must perform a gatekeeping function and make that analysis clear to a reviewing court.[267] Before an appellate court can determine whether the trial court acted within its discretion in performing its required analysis of the reliability and relevance of expert testimony, there must be "a sufficiently developed record in order to allow a determination of whether the district court properly applied the relevant law."[268] Without specific findings, discussion, analysis, or comments on the record, it may be impossible for the appellate court to determine whether the trial court "carefully and meticulously" reviewed the proposed expert testimony or simply made an "off-the-cuff" decision to admit it.[269]

C. Relation of Rules 401-403 to Real & Demonstrative Evidence

The concept of relevance expressed in Rules 401 through 403 applies not only to testimonial evidence but also to the use of tangible objects in the courtroom. Physical evidence may be subdivided into two broad categories: "real" and "demonstrative." Real evidence is an object that is intimately connected to the lawsuit (e.g., the murder weapon).[270] Demonstrative or illustrative evidence is not independently relevant to the lawsuit; rather, it is an object that replicates or is similar to the "real thing" when the real object is not available. Illustrative evidence includes models, maps, diagrams, charts, photographs, and drawings. Such evidence is offered to help explain or summarize a witness's testimony[271] or to put events and conditions into a better perspective.[272]

---

266. 810 S.W.2d 372, 393 n.4 (Tex. Crim. App. 1991) (op. on reh'g). The court explained:

> Appellate review of the trial court's balancing under Rule 403 would be facilitated by on-the-record articulation of the considerations that governed the trial court's decision. [W]e note that the Fifth Circuit has required the federal district courts, upon request, to make the record reflect those considerations, on pain of remand.

Id.

267. *See, e.g.,* **Goebel v. Denver & Rio Grande W. R.R.**, 215 F.3d 1083, 1087-88 (10th Cir. 2000) (reversing judgment for FELA plaintiff who had alleged that diesel exhaust caused brain injury and remanding for new trial when trial judge did not make any **Daubert** reliability findings on the record related to expert testimony about diesel exhaust causing brain injury).

268. **United States v. Nichols**, 169 F.3d 1255, 1262 (10th Cir. 1999); *see* **United States v. Velarde**, 214 F.3d 1204, 1209 (10th Cir. 2000) ("[T]he court must, on the record, make *some* kind of reliability determination."); **United States v. Lee**, 25 F.3d 997, 999 (11th Cir. 1994) (encouraging district courts "to make specific fact findings concerning their application of Rule 702 and **Daubert**").

269. **Goebel**, 215 F.3d at 1088.

270. *See* 22 WRIGHT & GRAHAM, *supra* note 35, §5173, at 127-33 (1978), at 165-68 (Supp. 2005) (discussing uses and admissibility of "real proof").

271. *See* **Speier v. Webster Coll.**, 616 S.W.2d 617, 618 (Tex. 1981) (charts and diagrams that summarize or emphasize "testimony of witnesses are, within the discretion of the trial court, admissible into evidence" assuming that the testimony summarized is admissible and already before the jury).

Tangible objects make particularly potent evidence because they provide the jury with a firsthand impression and immediacy that oral testimony can rarely match.[273] Not only does demonstrative evidence have a much stronger immediate impact than oral testimony, but it also has a continued effect on the jury because it may remain in the courtroom throughout the trial and may be taken to the jury room during deliberations if it has been admitted as substantive evidence.[274] Such evidence is frequently objected to as being unfairly prejudicial under Rule 403 because it can elicit strong emotional reactions from the jury, the danger of which may outweigh the object's probative value.[275]

Demonstrative evidence, such as photographs, slides, motion pictures, and videotapes that are fair and accurate depictions, is generally admissible if verbal testimony about the contents of the demonstrative evidence is admissible.[276] But Rule 403 may

---

272. *See* McCORMICK ON EVIDENCE, *supra* note 1, §212, at 668 (listing items frequently offered to provide clarification and help the trier of fact); 22 WRIGHT & GRAHAM, *supra* note 35, §5174, at 133-37 (discussing the use of illustrative objects).

273. *See* McCORMICK ON EVIDENCE, *supra* note 1, §212, at 664 (such evidence "appeals directly to the senses of the trier of fact"); Melvin Belli, *Demonstrative Evidence: Seeing Is Believing*, TRIAL, July 1980, at 70, 71 (such evidence gives trier of fact a precise image that verbal description cannot match).

274. *See* TEX. R. CIV. P. 281 (on request, trial judge must send any exhibit properly admitted into evidence to the jury room; sole exception is depositions, which may never be taken into jury room); ***Baugh v. Cuprum S.A. de C.V.***, 730 F.3d 701, 710 (7th Cir. 2013) (trial court abused its discretion in allowing item to go into jury room during deliberations after item had been treated as demonstrative exhibit and not as substantive evidence during trial); McCORMICK ON EVIDENCE, *supra* note 1, §217, at 681-83 (discussing use of exhibits in the jury room); 2 RAY, *supra* note 46, §1468, at 158-60 (jurors may experiment with exhibits that are properly admitted into evidence). Weinstein and Berger state the following:

> Real proof often has enormous apparent probative force because the lay trier may lose sight of the fact that its connection to a party may depend upon the credibility of an authenticating witness. Particularly since such proof is often taken into the jury room it continues to "speak" long after the witnesses have departed. Even the most unbelievable statements tend to take on an air of verity when they are connected to a tangible object.

5 WEINSTEIN & BERGER, *supra* note 84, ¶901(a)[01], at 901-23 to 901-24. If demonstrative evidence is not admitted as substantive evidence, it cannot be taken into the jury room. ***Baugh***, 730 F.3d at 708.

275. *See* McCORMICK ON EVIDENCE, *supra* note 1, §212, at 664. In one Texas case, an anti-abortion group, sued by the State for violations of the Deceptive Trade Practices Act, attempted to introduce a videotape and slides showing a graphic depiction of abortion procedures. ***Mother & Unborn Baby Care of N. Tex., Inc. v. State***, 749 S.W.2d 533, 544 (Tex. App.—Fort Worth 1988, writ denied). The trial court excluded this evidence on the basis that the films "would turn the trial into a debate on abortion issues, thus leading the jury away from the issues properly before the court[,]" because this evidence "would *give an unnecessary dramatic effect or would unduly emphasize some issues at the expense of others.*" *Id.* (quoting 29 AM. JUR. 2d *Evidence* §769, at 838 (1967)); *cf.* ***Pittsburgh Corning Corp. v. Walters***, 1 S.W.3d 759, 771-73 (Tex. App.—Corpus Christi 1999, pet. denied) (admission of "death-bed videotape" of deceased in wrongful-death case, made four days before he died, was not unfairly prejudicial because deceased's condition at or near time of his death was necessary part of spouse's action).

On the other hand, in ***Mayhew v. Dealey***, the court upheld the admission of an audio recording of the defendant and the deceased, taped three years before the deceased's death, offered in a wrongful-death suit to show the defendant's "volatile temper and his abusive treatment" of the deceased. 143 S.W.3d 356, 370 (Tex. App.—Dallas 2004, pet. denied). This recording demonstrated how the defendant verbally abused the deceased and allowed the jury to decide for itself whether the witnesses' descriptions of the defendant's behavior were accurate. *Id.*

276. *See* ***Gallo v. State***, 239 S.W.3d 757, 762 (Tex. Crim. App. 2007); ***Williams v. State***, 958 S.W.2d 186, 195 (Tex. Crim. App. 1997).

limit the admissibility of relevant demonstrative or illustrative evidence.[277] Once such items are found to be relevant under Rule 401, trial courts should determine their possible unfair prejudicial effect under Rule 403 by considering such factors as "the number of exhibits offered, their gruesomeness, their detail, their size, whether they are in color or black-and-white, whether they are close up, whether the body depicted is clothed or naked, the availability of other means of proof, and other circumstances unique to the individual case."[278]

Several cases have held that the admission of photographs—particularly those of autopsies and crime victims—should be analyzed more rigorously under Rule 403.[279] In *Prible v. State*,[280] the court of criminal appeals held that the admission of numerous post-autopsy photographs of three young children's lungs and tracheas was error

---

277. ***Long v. State***, 823 S.W.2d 259, 271-72 & n.18 (Tex. Crim. App. 1991); *see, e.g.*, ***Jones v. State***, 944 S.W.2d 642, 652-53 (Tex. Crim. App. 1996) (in punishment stage of capital-murder trial, photographs of gang members, including defendant, were admissible under Rule 403 to demonstrate defendant's character); ***Sonnier v. State***, 913 S.W.2d 511, 519 (Tex. Crim. App. 1995) (in punishment stage of capital-murder trial, although murder-scene photographs were gruesome and disagreeable to look at, "they depict nothing more than the reality of the brutal crime committed ... when the power of the visible evidence emanates from nothing more than what the defendant has himself done we cannot hold that the trial court has abused its discretion merely because it admitted the evidence"); ***Alvarado v. State***, 912 S.W.2d 199, 212 (Tex. Crim. App. 1995) (in guilt stage of capital-murder trial, probative value of crime-scene photographs outweighed danger of unfair prejudice); ***Russell v. State***, 113 S.W.3d 530, 545 (Tex. App.—Fort Worth 2003, pet. ref'd) (in guilt stage of capital-murder trial, photographs of crime scene from extraneous-offense murder and of deceased victim were unfairly prejudicial under Rule 403; heinous nature of extraneous-offense murder and emotionally charged testimony of surviving victim from that incident could not be "filed away in some compartment of the mind and considered only for a limited purpose").

278. ***Davis v. State***, 313 S.W.3d 317, 331 (Tex. Crim. App. 2010); *accord* ***Williams v. State***, 301 S.W.3d 675, 690 (Tex. Crim. App. 2009); ***Long***, 823 S.W.2d at 272; *see, e.g.*, ***Young v. State***, 283 S.W.3d 854, 874-75 (Tex. Crim. App. 2009) (autopsy identification photograph of murder victim, which was not enhanced or particularly gruesome, was admissible; medical examiner's office used it to connect victim with case number, so photograph was not cumulative of other autopsy photographs); ***Shuffield v. State***, 189 S.W.3d 782, 786-88 (Tex. Crim. App. 2006) (crime-scene and autopsy photographs showing shotgun-blast damage to capital-murder victim's head were admissible); ***Hayes v. State***, 85 S.W.3d 809, 816 (Tex. Crim. App. 2002) (post-autopsy photographs of capital-murder victim were not barred by Rule 403 because alterations during autopsy did not make evidence significantly more gruesome); ***Salazar v. State***, 38 S.W.3d 141, 151-53 (Tex. Crim. App. 2001) (autopsy photographs showing internal organs after removal from victim's body were not unfairly prejudicial because there was no danger that jury would attribute removal of organs to defendant's conduct); ***Reese v. State***, 33 S.W.3d 238, 242-43 (Tex. Crim. App. 2000) (trial court abused its discretion during punishment stage of capital-murder trial by admitting photograph of murder victim in her coffin with her unborn child lying next to her; photograph, showing the "tiny, innocent, and vulnerable" unborn child, had "an emotional impact that suggests that the jury's decision be made on an emotional basis and not on the basis of the other relevant evidence introduced at trial"); ***Dawkins v. State***, ___ S.W.3d ___ (Tex. App.—El Paso 2016, no pet.) (No. 08-13-00012-CR; 10-14-16) (trial court did not err in admitting autopsy photographs when defendant challenged medical examiner's credentials, character, diligence, and truthfulness; photographs verified that autopsy had taken place and allowed jury to decide whether medical examiner's findings were trustworthy); ***Reyes v. State***, 491 S.W.3d 36, 49-50 (Tex. App.—Houston [14th Dist.] 2016, no pet.) (autopsy photographs, though gruesome, were highly probative to show extent of murder victim's injuries and to prove she was alive when defendant committed aggravated sexual assault); ***Hill v. State***, 392 S.W.3d 850, 856 (Tex. App.—Amarillo 2013, pet. ref'd) (photographs of assault victim's injuries and of locations where assaults took place were properly admitted under Rule 403; photographs were not gruesome or cumulative, and victim was clothed in all photographs).

279. The court of criminal appeals has held that autopsy photographs are generally admissible unless they show mutilation of the victim caused by the autopsy. ***Davis***, 313 S.W.3d at 331; ***Williams***, 301 S.W.3d at 690; ***Santellan v. State***, 939 S.W.2d 155, 172 (Tex. Crim. App. 1997).

280. 175 S.W.3d 724 (Tex. Crim. App. 2005).

under Rule 403 when the capital-murder defendant was charged only with causing the deaths of the children's parents.[281] Although the cause of the children's deaths by smoke inhalation was of some probative value to show the full context of the charged crime and to corroborate the testimony of a State's witness, introducing the post-autopsy photographs of the children was unfairly prejudicial and threatened to confuse the disputed issues.[282] Similarly, in **Erazo v. State**, the court of criminal appeals held that it was error to admit a photograph of a fetus removed from the murder victim's womb during the autopsy.[283] The court distinguished between the admissibility of crime-scene photographs, which depict the direct results of a defendant's actions, and other photographs, such as those taken after an autopsy, which demonstrate the collateral results of a crime or illustrate steps in the investigatory process.[284] The court noted that such photographs are not necessarily admissible merely to show the fact of death, but because they may help explain "something more" that is relevant to the case.[285] In **Resendiz v. State**, that same rationale upheld the exclusion of crime-scene photographs of extraneous-offense murders offered by the defendant to show that he was insane at the time of all of his killings because those crimes were so gruesome.[286] Under Rule 403, if the use of a photograph is genuinely helpful and "relevant, legitimate, and logical to the testimony that accompanies it," the trial judge may exclude it only if its prejudicial aspects substantially outweigh the helpful aspects.[287]

---

281. *Id.* at 736; *see also* **Potter v. State**, 74 S.W.3d 105, 113-15 (Tex. App.—Waco 2002, no pet.) (prejudicial effect of morgue photograph of second shooting victim, for whose murder the defendant was not on trial, substantially outweighed any probative value of photo, but error was harmless). Autopsy photographs showing internal organs that have been removed to portray the extent of the injury to the organs themselves may be highly probative to explain the manner of death if the cause of that person's death is an important issue at trial. *See Salazar*, 38 S.W.3d at 151-53.

282. *Prible*, 175 S.W.3d at 736; *cf. Santellan*, 939 S.W.2d at 173 (changes made by autopsy of capital-murder victim are of minor significance if the disturbing nature of the photograph is primarily due to defendant's conduct); *Sosa v. State*, 230 S.W.3d 192, 196 (Tex. App.—Houston [14th Dist.] 2005, pet. ref'd) (upholding admission of gruesome autopsy photographs of murder victims at punishment stage that depicted "the wounds inflicted by appellant and are no more gruesome than the facts of the offense itself"); *Williams v. State*, 176 S.W.3d 476, 481-82 (Tex. App.—Houston [1st Dist.] 2004, no pet.) (autopsy photographs showing nature of wounds inflicted were admissible during punishment stage as "helpful to the court in devising an appropriate sentence because appellant had repeatedly changed her story about the complainant's death and had denied that she intended to stab the complainant"); *Hall v. State*, 137 S.W.3d 847, 854-55 (Tex. App.—Houston [1st Dist.] 2004, pet. ref'd) (although autopsy photographs depicting murder victim's brain and skull were graphic, they depicted internal damage caused by defendant's shooting and were not unfairly prejudicial or unduly time-consuming).

283. 144 S.W.3d 487, 488 (Tex. Crim. App. 2004); *see also Fields v. State*, 515 S.W.3d 47, 57 (Tex. App.—San Antonio 2016, no pet.) (in capital-murder case in which defendant was on trial for murder of woman and unborn child, autopsy photograph of unborn child was relevant and admissible; court distinguished *Erazo* on facts of case).

284. *See Erazo*, 144 S.W.3d at 493.

285. *Id.* Photographs that were frequently excluded under the common law, such as "booking photographs," could be admissible under Rules 401 through 403 if they help resolve a material issue. *See, e.g.*, **Hajjar v. State**, 176 S.W.3d 554, 560 (Tex. App.—Houston [1st Dist.] 2004, pet. ref'd) ("booking photo" of defendant taken shortly after arrest for assault that showed no visible injuries was admissible because photo tended to rebut a defensive theory that he had acted in self-defense).

286. 112 S.W.3d 541, 545-46 (Tex. Crim. App. 2003).

287. *Erazo*, 144 S.W.3d at 491-92; *see, e.g.*, **Maldonado v. State**, 452 S.W.3d 898, 902 (Tex. App.—Texarkana 2014, no pet.) (in punishment phase of trial for injury to child by omission, photographs depicting nature and extent of

To establish the relevance of any real or demonstrative evidence, the proponent of the evidence must first authenticate it.[288] With real evidence, the proponent must make a sufficient showing that the offered item is the object connected to the lawsuit and that the item is in substantially the same condition that it was in at the time of the event in question.[289] With demonstrative evidence, the proponent must merely establish that the evidence is fair and accurate and that it helps the witness demonstrate or illustrate his testimony.[290]

Trial courts have great discretion in admitting illustrative evidence,[291] but such evidence is admitted solely to help a witness explain his testimony. It "has no probative

---

child's injuries at time of death were helpful to jury in assessing defendant's moral blameworthiness and were thus relevant despite her guilty plea; Rule 403 factors weighed in favor of admission).

288. For a more complete explanation of the authentication of real and demonstrative evidence, refer to *Article IX: Authentication & Identification, infra* p. 961.

289. *See* ***Imperial Cas. & Indem. Co. v. Terry***, 451 S.W.2d 303, 307 (Tex. Civ. App.—Tyler 1970, no writ).

290. *See, e.g.*, ***Vollbaum v. State***, 833 S.W.2d 652, 657 (Tex. App.—Waco 1992, pet. ref'd) (upholding the introduction of a Styrofoam model of a woman's head during medical examiner's testimony because it was offered as a summary of witness's testimony and could assist the jury in understanding that testimony); ***Shaw v. State***, 730 S.W.2d 826, 828 (Tex. App.—Houston [14th Dist.] 1987, pet. ref'd) (admitting a videotape because witness testified that she had viewed the tape and found it to be accurate); ***Sinko v. City of San Antonio***, 702 S.W.2d 201, 204-05 (Tex. App.—San Antonio 1985, writ ref'd n.r.e.) (excluding a videotape that "did not purport to be a reenactment of the accident or to accurately portray the scene of the accident"); *see also* McCORMICK ON EVIDENCE, *supra* note 1, §213, at 669-70 (stating that "illustrative objects will be identified by the witness as substantially correct representations and will be formally introduced as part of the witness' testimony").

In ***Miskis v. State***, the appellate court's opinion set forth a considerably more elaborate foundation requirement for the admission of demonstrative evidence. 756 S.W.2d 350, 352 (Tex. App.—Houston [14th Dist.] 1988, pet. ref'd). The ***Miskis*** court held that an object that is not an exact replica of the original may be admissible if (1) the original item is unavailable, (2) the original would be admissible if available, (3) "it is relevant *and* material to an issue in controversy," (4) its probative value outweighs its inflammatory effect, and (5) a limiting instruction is offered that the evidence merely demonstrates or illustrates the object used in the offense. *Id.* The court went on to state, however, that "the substitute object should have no inflammatory attributes. Further, when it is not an exact replica and differs in its distinguishing characteristics, 'the probative value of the non-exact weapon or instrumentality will be very slight.'" *Id.* (quoting ***Simmons v. State***, 622 S.W.2d 111, 114 (Tex. Crim. App. 1981)). The court did not consider that Rule 403 admits all relevant evidence unless its probative value is *substantially* outweighed by unfair prejudice. It also did not consider that evidence may be material even when offered on a fact that is not in dispute. *See* ***Bradford v. State***, 608 S.W.2d 918, 920-21 (Tex. Crim. App. 1980) (overruling earlier cases holding that bloody clothing needed to lead to solution of some disputed issue before it was admissible); *see also* ***Valdez v. State***, 776 S.W.2d 162, 169 (Tex. Crim. App. 1989) (real evidence does not need to prove disputed issue; murder victim's bloody shirt was admissible because it "gave a descriptive insight into the location and the nature of the wounds"). Nor did the ***Miskis*** court cite any precedent or express any logical rationale for the requirement that demonstrative evidence is admissible only if real evidence is "unavailable." A wrecked car might be available, but if a reasonably accurate drawing of it would help a witness explain his testimony, the drawing should not be excluded merely because the proponent could have produced the car itself. *See* ***Onwukwe v. State***, 186 S.W.3d 81, 84 (Tex. App.—Houston [1st Dist.] 2005, no pet.) (nonexact replica of a relevant object may be admissible even without showing that the original is unavailable; no "unavailability" foundation requirement for the admission of demonstrative evidence).

On the other hand, in ***Orrick v. State***, the court of appeals (ostensibly following ***Miskis***) concluded that the trial court abused its discretion in admitting as demonstrative evidence a full, unopened bottle of vodka clearly labeled as such, to demonstrate the size and shape of "an old whiskey bottle" filled with water that the DWI defendant testified he carried in his car. 36 S.W.3d 622, 626 (Tex. App.—Fort Worth 2000, no pet.). The size and shape of defendant's water bottle was not in dispute, the use of a full vodka bottle was clearly prejudicial in a DWI trial, and the defendant denied that the exhibit looked like his own bottle. *Id.* The error was deemed harmless. *Id.* at 627.

291. ***Petty v. Ideco, Div. of Dresser Indus., Inc.***, 761 F.2d 1146, 1150-51 (5th Cir. 1985); *see* ***Univ. of Tex. v. Hinton***, 822 S.W.2d 197, 202-03 (Tex. App.—Austin 1991, no writ) (trial court has great discretion in determining the

force beyond that which is lent to it by the credibility of the witness whose testimony it is used to explain."[292] Thus, for example, a mere summary chart of other evidence and testimony is not itself probative of any fact and is inadmissible as evidence.[293]

In-court demonstrations may be admissible if they are conducted under conditions substantially similar to those they are intended to replicate.[294] Similarly, evidence of out-of-court experiments may be admissible under the same type of analysis as evidence of similar events and illustrative evidence. For evidence of an out-of-court experiment to be admissible, the conditions at the time of the experiment must be substantially similar to those at the time of the litigated event, and evidence of the experiment must assist the jury in determining a fact in issue.[295] When the conditions are dissimilar, the trial judge has discretion in deciding whether those differences are minor or can be adequately explained to the fact-finder.[296] An out-of-court "jury view"

admissibility of out-of-court experiments; even though accident involved a plastic grate, trial court did not abuse its discretion in admitting a videotape showing a plywood cutout falling and striking a dummy when the differences were explained to the jury).

292. *Carson v. Polley*, 689 F.2d 562, 579 (5th Cir. 1982) (admission of a knife taken into the jury room as "similar" to the one said to be in plaintiff's possession was prejudicial error when judge failed to clarify that the knife was admitted only for demonstrative purposes).

293. *See, e.g., Wheatfall v. State*, 882 S.W.2d 829, 839 (Tex. Crim. App. 1994) (admission of prosecutor's summary of other evidence was "clearly error"); *Markey v. State*, 996 S.W.2d 226, 231 (Tex. App.—Houston [14th Dist.] 1999, no pet.) (chart that prosecutor prepared as officer recounted defendant's symptoms of intoxication had no probative value, and thus was not relevant to DWI charge; chart was simply reiteration of evidence and did not itself constitute proof of intoxication). *But see N. Am. Van Lines, Inc. v. Emmons*, 50 S.W.3d 103, 130 (Tex. App.—Beaumont 2001, pet. denied) ("Video animation and other demonstrative evidence that 'summarize, or perhaps emphasize, testimony are admissible if the underlying testimony has been admitted into evidence, or is subsequently admitted into evidence.'" (quoting *Uniroyal Goodrich Tire Co. v. Martinez*, 977 S.W.2d 328, 342 (Tex. 1998))); *Barnes v. State*, 797 S.W.2d 353, 357 (Tex. App.—Tyler 1990, no pet.) (dicta; if the evidence summarized by charts is admissible, "admission of summary charts into evidence, and their use before the jury, is within the discretion of the trial court"). For a discussion of the proper use of summaries, refer to *Article X: Contents of Writings, Recordings, & Photographs, infra* p. 1060.

294. *See, e.g., Wright v. State*, 178 S.W.3d 905, 919-20 (Tex. App.—Houston [14th Dist.] 2005, pet. ref'd) (probative value of prosecutor's in-court demonstration showing theory of how defendant allegedly murdered her husband by stabbing him in his bed while he was tied to bedposts was not substantially outweighed by the dangers of unfair prejudice, confusion of issues, or misleading jury; all parts of the demonstration were supported by and consistent with testimony based on personal observations and deductions from facts in evidence, and conditions were substantially similar to the actual event); *Moore v. State*, 154 S.W.3d 703, 708-09 (Tex. App.—Fort Worth 2004, pet. ref'd) (upholding detective's use of doll during testimony to demonstrate how defendant used similar doll during police interview to show how he had shaken child in the past; upholding use of doll during State's cross-examination of defendant to show jury how he had handled child when he became frustrated and angry with her); *see also Runnels v. State*, 193 S.W.3d 105, 107-08 (Tex. App.—Houston [1st Dist.] 2006, no pet.) (upholding use of in-court demonstration with mannequin dressed in victim's clothing; although dummy was significantly smaller than victim and, on appeal, defendant argued that this fact undermined his self-defense theory and thus was unfairly prejudicial under Rule 403, this argument was not made in trial court).

295. *See Kainer v. Walker*, 377 S.W.2d 613, 616 (Tex. 1964); *see also Alice Leasing Corp. v. Castillo*, 53 S.W.3d 433, 446 (Tex. App.—San Antonio 2001, pet. denied) (trial court did not err in admitting videotape of simulated accident used by testifying expert to explain basis of his opinion).

296. *See, e.g., Hinton*, 822 S.W.2d at 202-03 (admission of experiment was within trial court's discretion because videotape of experiment was sufficiently similar to actual event and there was no likelihood of jury confusion).

demonstration may be permissible if certain conditions are met and its implementation and effect is not unfairly prejudicial.[297]

RULE 404
CHARACTER EVIDENCE; CRIMES OR OTHER ACTS

(a) Character Evidence.

(1) *Prohibited Uses.* Evidence of a person's character or character trait is not admissible to prove that on a particular occasion the person acted in accordance with the character or trait.

(2) *Exceptions for an Accused.*

(A) In a criminal case, a defendant may offer evidence of the defendant's pertinent trait, and if the evidence is admitted, the prosecutor may offer evidence to rebut it.

(B) In a civil case, a party accused of conduct involving moral turpitude may offer evidence of the party's pertinent trait, and if the evidence is admitted, the accusing party may offer evidence to rebut it.

(3) *Exceptions for a Victim.*

(A) In a criminal case, subject to the limitations in Rule 412, a defendant may offer evidence of a victim's pertinent trait, and if the evidence is admitted, the prosecutor may offer evidence to rebut it.

(B) In a homicide case, the prosecutor may offer evidence of the victim's trait of peacefulness to rebut evidence that the victim was the first aggressor.

(C) In a civil case, a party accused of assaultive conduct may offer evidence of the victim's trait of violence to prove self-defense, and if the evidence is admitted, the accusing party may offer evidence of the victim's trait of peacefulness.

(4) *Exceptions for a Witness.* Evidence of a witness's character may be admitted under Rules 607, 608, and 609.

(5) *Definition of "Victim."* In this rule, "victim" includes an alleged victim.

---

297. *See Mauricio v. State*, 153 S.W.3d 389, 393 (Tex. Crim. App. 2005). In *Mauricio*, the court of criminal appeals explained:

A trial court, in exercising its discretion to grant or deny a request for a jury view, must consider the totality of the circumstances of the case, including, but not limited to, the timing of the request for the jury view, the difficulty and expense of arranging it, the importance of the information to be gained by it, the extent to which that information has been or could be secured from more convenient sources (*e.g.*, photographs, videotapes, maps, or diagrams), and the extent to which the place or object to be viewed may have changed in appearance since the controversy began.

Id.

(b) Crimes, Wrongs, or Other Acts.

(1) *Prohibited Uses.* Evidence of a crime, wrong, or other act is not admissible to prove a person's character in order to show that on a particular occasion the person acted in accordance with the character.

(2) *Permitted Uses; Notice in Criminal Case.* This evidence may be admissible for another purpose, such as proving motive, opportunity, intent, preparation, plan, knowledge, identity, absence of mistake, or lack of accident. On timely request by a defendant in a criminal case, the prosecutor must provide reasonable notice before trial that the prosecution intends to introduce such evidence—other than that arising in the same transaction—in its case-in-chief.

RULE 405
METHODS OF PROVING CHARACTER

(a) By Reputation or Opinion.

(1) *In General.* When evidence of a person's character or character trait is admissible, it may be proved by testimony about the person's reputation or by testimony in the form of an opinion. On cross-examination of the character witness, inquiry may be made into relevant specific instances of the person's conduct.

(2) *Accused's Character in a Criminal Case.* In the guilt stage of a criminal case, a witness may testify to the defendant's character or character trait only if, before the day of the offense, the witness was familiar with the defendant's reputation or the facts or information that form the basis of the witness's opinion.

(b) By Specific Instances of Conduct. When a person's character or character trait is an essential element of a charge, claim, or defense, the character or trait may also be proved by relevant specific instances of the person's conduct.

COMMENTARY ON RULES 404 & 405

Rule 404 addresses the admissibility of character evidence.[298] If evidence of character is admissible under Rule 404 or otherwise, Rule 405 specifies the circumstances

---

298. No substantive change was intended to Rule 404(a) or 404(b) for either civil or criminal proceedings in the unification of the Rules. The rule was reworded slightly to make the language gender-neutral. Former Criminal Rule 404(c), which regulated the admissibility of character evidence during the punishment stage of a criminal trial, was eliminated as unnecessary. Former Criminal Rule 404(c) read:

> **(c) Character Relevant to Punishment.** In the penalty phase, evidence may be offered by an accused or by the prosecution as to the prior criminal record of the accused. Other evidence of his character may be offered by an accused or by the prosecution. Nothing herein shall limit provisions of Article 37.071, Code of Criminal Procedure.

TEX. R. CRIM. EVID. 404(c), 701-702 S.W.2d (Tex. Cases) xxxvii (1986, repealed 1998). The procedures and evidentiary considerations for the punishment stage are outlined in the Texas Code of Criminal Procedure. *See* TEX. CODE CRIM. PROC. art. 37.07, §3(a)(1) ("[E]vidence may be offered by the state and the defendant as to any matter the court

in which each of the three methods of proving character—reputation, opinion, and specific instances of conduct—are allowed.[299] The definition of "character" as the term is used in Rules 404 and 405, which derives from Federal Rules 404 and 405,[300] is a generalized personality trait or a propensity to behave in a certain manner.[301] For example, a person may have a propensity to conduct himself in a peaceable manner and is thus said to have a good "character" for peacefulness. Rule 404(a) states that character evidence is generally not admissible to prove conforming conduct[302] and then lists three exceptions:

(1) the character of either the defendant in a criminal trial or a party in a civil case accused of conduct involving moral turpitude.[303] In both instances, the person accused has the option of offering evidence of a pertinent character trait.[304] If he does so, the prosecution or opposing party may offer rebuttal character evidence.[305]

---

deems relevant to sentencing, including but not limited to the prior criminal record of the defendant, his general reputation, his character, an opinion regarding his character, the circumstances of the offense for which he is being tried, and, notwithstanding Rules 404 and 405, Texas Rules of Evidence, any other evidence of an extraneous crime or bad act that is shown beyond a reasonable doubt by evidence to have been committed by the defendant or for which he could be held criminally responsible, regardless of whether he has previously been charged with or finally convicted of the crime or act."), art. 37.071, §2(a)(1) ("[E]vidence may be presented by the state and the defendant or the defendant's counsel as to any matter that the court deems relevant to sentence, including evidence of the defendant's background or character or the circumstances of the offense that mitigates against the imposition of the death penalty.").

299. The only substantive change resulting from the unification of Civil Rule 405 and Criminal Rule 405 was to limit the criminal rule's requirement that all character witnesses be substantially familiar with the defendant's character before the offense; this provision now applies only to character evidence offered at the guilt stage. Former Criminal Rule 405(a) read in pertinent part:

> **(a) Reputation or Opinion.** In all cases in which evidence of character or trait of character of a person is admissible, proof may be made by testimony as to reputation or by testimony in the form of an opinion. Provided however that to be qualified to testify concerning the character or trait of character of an accused, a witness must have been familiar with the reputation, or with the underlying facts or information upon which the opinion is based, prior to the day of the offense.

TEX. R. CRIM. EVID. 405(a), 789-790 S.W.2d (Tex. Cases) XXXII (1990, amended 1998) (current version at TEX. R. EVID. 405(a)). Thus, under the current version of Rule 405, character witnesses who testify during the punishment stage of a criminal trial do not need to have heard of the defendant's reputation or formed an opinion about his character before the commission of the offense. Refer to notes 341-354 *infra* and accompanying text.

300. *See* FED. R. EVID. 404 & 405 advisory committee's notes; 2 WEINSTEIN & BERGER, *supra* note 84, ¶404[01], at 404-17 n.4.

301. *See* ***Reid v. State***, 964 S.W.2d 723, 734 (Tex. App.—Amarillo 1998, pet. ref'd) (defining character as "'a generalized description of a person's disposition, or of the disposition in respect to a general trait such as honesty, temperance, or peacefulness'" (quoting MCCORMICK ON EVIDENCE §195 (John W. Strong et al. eds., 4th ed. 1992))).

This usage does not change the common law or earlier Texas law. *See* ***Landa v. Obert***, 5 Tex. Civ. App. 620, 624, 25 S.W. 342, 344 (San Antonio 1893, writ ref'd) ("When character, from the very nature of the proceedings, is in issue, it is the general character as to some particular trait involved in the matter charged against such party, and this can only be evidenced by general reputation, and not by evidence of general bad conduct."); MCCORMICK'S HANDBOOK II, *supra* note 33, §188, at 444 (defining character as disposition and tendencies); 1 WIGMORE, *supra* note 1, §52, at 446 (defining character as a personal trait).

302. *See* TEX. R. EVID. 404(a)(1).

303. *See* TEX. R. EVID. 404(a)(2).

304. *Id.*

305. *Id.*

RULES 404-405

(2) the character of the victim in a criminal case or the alleged victim of assaultive conduct in a civil case.[306] In both instances, the person accused has the option of initiating evidence of the victim's character, and the prosecution or opposing party may offer rebuttal character evidence.[307] Additionally, when a homicide defendant asserts that the victim was the first aggressor, the prosecution may initiate evidence of the victim's character.[308]

(3) the character of a witness, but only as permitted under Rules 607, 608, and 609.[309]

Rule 404(b) prohibits the use of evidence of other crimes, wrongs, or acts to prove character or to show conforming conduct but allows evidence of other crimes, wrongs, or acts as circumstantial evidence to show motive, opportunity, intent, or other similar purposes. Rule 404 makes no explicit reference to evidence of character when character is an ultimate issue rather than offered as proof of conforming conduct. Because Rule 404 does not exclude evidence of character when character is an ultimate issue, such evidence is admissible to the extent required or allowed by Rules 401 through 403.

Rule 404 is the first of several Article IV provisions that outline specific applications of the Rule 403 balancing test.[310] The same problems of unfair prejudice, confusing the issues, and misleading the jury have arisen in so many instances with character evidence, evidence of subsequent remedial measures or notification of defect,[311] offers to compromise,[312] payment of medical expenses,[313] plea discussions,[314] and liability insurance[315] that the drafters of the Federal and Texas Rules enacted specific rules to balance probative value and prejudicial effect. The structure of these rules is the same throughout. The rules begin with a statement that evidence is excluded when offered for a specific prohibited purpose. For example, when character evidence is offered to prove conforming conduct on the occasion in question, the evidence is probative of the particular purpose, but the prejudicial effect of the evidence substantially outweighs its probative value. However, when the evidence is offered for some other purpose—any other purpose[316]—it may be admissible under Rules 401 through 403, which deal with general relevance.

---

306. *See* Tex. R. Evid. 404(a)(3). A "victim" includes an alleged victim. Tex. R. Evid. 404(a)(5).

307. *See* Tex. R. Evid. 404(a)(3)(A), (a)(3)(C).

308. *See* Tex. R. Evid. 404(a)(3)(B).

309. *See* Tex. R. Evid. 404(a)(4). Refer to *Article VI: Witnesses, infra* p. 596.

310. *See* **Montgomery v. State**, 810 S.W.2d 372, 377 (Tex. Crim. App. 1990) (orig. op.) ("Rule 404(b) is simply a specific codification for a general balancing determination under Rule 403.").

311. Tex. R. Evid. 407. Refer to notes 669-721 *infra* and accompanying text.

312. Tex. R. Evid. 408. Refer to notes 722-859 *infra* and accompanying text.

313. Tex. R. Evid. 409. Refer to notes 860-886 *infra* and accompanying text.

314. Tex. R. Evid. 410. Refer to notes 887-968 *infra* and accompanying text.

315. Tex. R. Evid. 411. Refer to notes 969-1010 *infra* and accompanying text.

316. As frequently stated by Texas courts, evidence of other crimes, wrongs, or acts may be admitted if such evidence has relevance apart from the tendency to prove the character of the accused. *See* Edward J. Imwinkelried, *An Evidentiary Paradox: Defending the Character Evidence Prohibition by Upholding a Non-Character Theory of*

Rule 404 is considered the most complex and frequently litigated evidentiary rule in criminal proceedings.[317] According to one commentator, the improper admission of extraneous offenses is the single largest cause for appellate reversals in criminal cases.[318] Because extraneous-offense evidence can have a devastating impact, the offering party must clearly explain to the trial judge why the evidence is being offered, and the opposing party must clearly explain its opposition. The trial court should precisely articulate the factors considered in the decision to admit or exclude that evidence.[319]

The rule prohibits only evidence that is offered to prove a person's character, from which the trier of fact is then asked to infer conduct in accordance with that character trait on the occasion in question.[320] Evidence that is not offered to demonstrate character is not prohibited under Rule 404, and its admissibility is subject only to the general relevance analysis under Rules 401 through 403.[321]

Logical Relevance, the Doctrine of Chances, 40 U. RICH. L. REV. 419, 429-30 (2006). Imwinkelried states that the question under Rule 404(b)

> is whether the item of evidence is relevant not only on a forbidden character theory but also on a legitimate non-character theory. ... The issue is not an either-or problem; rather, the issue is both-and. Does the item also possess relevance on a legitimate non-character theory? If it does, the typical solution is to admit the evidence but to give the jury a limiting instruction under Rule 105.

Imwinkelried, *supra*, at 429-30.

317. 22 WRIGHT & GRAHAM, *supra* note 35, §5239, at 427 (no question of evidence is more frequently litigated in appellate courts than the admissibility of evidence of other crimes, wrongs, or acts); Imwinkelried, *supra* note 316, at 433 ("On the criminal side, Rule 404(b) is the most litigated provision in the Federal Rules of Evidence. It generates more published opinions than any other provision of the Rules. In many states, errors admitting this species of evidence are the most common cause for reversal on appeal."). A review of cases shows that considerably more criminal appellate cases have addressed the contours of Rule 404 than any other single rule.

318. EDWARD J. IMWINKELRIED, UNCHARGED MISCONDUCT §1:04, at 18 (1996) ("Federal Rule of Evidence 404(b) has generated more reported decisions than any other Rule"). The same is true under Texas Rule of Evidence 404(b).

319. *See* ***United States v. Zabaneh***, 837 F.2d 1249, 1264-66 (5th Cir. 1988) (trial judge must articulate his rationale for the admission or exclusion of evidence of extrinsic offenses; "in the absence of an on-the-record articulation of a trial court's ***Beechum*** probative value/prejudice findings at the time of a party's request we must remand unless the factors upon which the probative value/prejudice evaluation was made were readily apparent from the record and there was no substantial uncertainty about the correctness of the ruling"); *see, e.g.,* ***United States v. Hudson***, 843 F.2d 1062, 1066-67 (7th Cir. 1988) (reversing conviction when trial judge did not engage in careful, on-the-record balancing of relevant factors; some evidence of other crimes should not have been admitted); ***United States v. Rivera***, 837 F.2d 906, 911-12 (10th Cir. 1988) (reversing defendant's conviction on the grounds of the improper admission of extraneous offenses; government did not articulate its Federal Rule 404(b) analysis, and trial judge did not identify the specific purpose for which the evidence was admitted), *vacated on other grounds*, 900 F.2d 1462 (10th Cir. 1990); *see also* ***United States v. Beasley***, 809 F.2d 1273, 1279 (7th Cir. 1987) ("The district judge must both identify the exception that applies to the evidence in question and evaluate whether the evidence, although relevant and within the exception, is sufficiently probative to make tolerable the risk that jurors will act on the basis of emotion or an inference via the blackening of the defendant's character."); 1 STEPHEN A. SALTZBURG ET AL., FEDERAL RULES OF EVIDENCE MANUAL 379-80 (7th ed. 1998) (***Rivera*** "stands as a lesson for lawyers and Judges about the need for specific articulation of not-for-character purposes under Rule 404(b)").

320. The 2015 restyling of Rule 404(a) changed the phrase "in conformity" to "in accordance." *See* TEX. R. EVID. 404(a)(1). No substantive change was intended. *See* Tex. Sup. Ct. Order, Misc. Docket No. 15-9048, §2 (eff. Apr. 1, 2015).

321. For example, in ***Reid v. State***, the State offered evidence that the defendant exhibited conduct consistent with a medical diagnosis of Munchausen's Syndrome by Proxy (MSBP). 964 S.W.2d 723, 733 (Tex. App.—Amarillo 1998, pet. ref'd). MSBP is a mental disease that induces persons to create or cause symptoms of illness in children to attract attention and sympathy to themselves. *See id.* at 728-29. The evidence was not offered to prove character

A. Rule 404(a): Character Evidence

1. Rule 404(a)(1): Prohibited uses. Evidence of character offered to prove conduct in accordance with that character is logically relevant. The trier of fact may infer a particular character trait from evidence of prior specific acts exhibiting that character trait, evidence of others' opinions of whether a person has a particular character trait, or evidence of that person's reputation in the community for the trait. For example, if a person has a reputation for violence, such a reputation alters the probability that he is a violent person. Likewise, his nature as a violent person alters the probability that he acted violently on a particular occasion. Thus, evidence of his character for violence is circumstantial or indirect evidence that he acted in conformity with that violent manner on the specific occasion. Assuming that his violent conduct on the occasion in question is material, evidence of his violent character is relevant under Rule 401 and admissible under Rule 402.

Despite the logical relevance of character evidence offered to prove conforming conduct, the common law and earlier Texas law generally rejected such evidence.[322] Rule 404(a) codified earlier Texas law.[323] Rule 404(a)(1) provides that "[e]vidence of a person's character or character trait is not admissible to prove that on a particular occasion the person acted in accordance with the character or trait."[324] This type of evidence tends to inject into a trial a "dangerous baggage of prejudice, distraction from the issues, time consumption, and hazard of surprise."[325] The use of character evidence is especially problematic in criminal proceedings because a jury might convict a defendant for being a "bad person" rather than for having committed a specific bad act.[326]

conformity but to show the medical basis of the defendant's condition that itself related directly to the murder charge. *Id.* at 733. Thus, Rule 404 did not apply because the evidence was offered to establish a medical diagnosis.

322. *See* McCORMICK'S HANDBOOK II, *supra* note 33, §188, at 445; 1 WIGMORE, *supra* note 1, §§55-68a, at 449-91; *see, e.g.*, **Bell v. State**, 433 S.W.2d 443, 444 (Tex. Crim. App. 1968) (excluding evidence of defendant's prior prison history in assault case); **Argonaut Sw. Ins. v. Pollan**, 424 S.W.2d 38, 39-40 (Tex. Civ. App.—Amarillo 1968, no writ) (excluding evidence of reputation for truth and veracity offered to prove the validity of injury in a workers' compensation suit).

323. *See* **Lovelace v. Sabine Consol., Inc.**, 733 S.W.2d 648, 654 (Tex. App.—Houston [14th Dist.] 1987, writ denied) (Rule 404(a) prohibits evidence of a person's character to prove that he acted "in conformity therewith on a particular occasion"); *see, e.g.*, **Kirby v. State**, 208 S.W.3d 568, 572-73 (Tex. App.—Austin 2006, no pet.) (State was improperly allowed to offer testimony that defendant had been victim of sexual abuse and, therefore, it was more likely that she had committed the present offense; this was propensity evidence and barred by Rule 404(a)).

324. TEX. R. EVID. 404(a)(1). Texas Rule 404(a)(1) is identical to Federal Rule 404(a)(1).

325. McCORMICK'S HANDBOOK II, *supra* note 33, §188, at 445.

326. As one appellate judge noted: "Our law makes some allowance for the possibility of reform, and does not yet say 'once a moonshiner, always a moonshiner.'" **Baker v. United States**, 227 F.2d 376, 378-79 (5th Cir. 1955) (Rives, J., concurring). The rationale for exclusion was best expressed by U.S. Supreme Court Justice Jackson, who stated that evidence of the defendant's bad character is inadmissible, but not because it is irrelevant:

> [O]n the contrary, it is said to weigh too much with the jury and so to over persuade them as to prejudice one with a bad general record and deny him a fair opportunity to defend against a particular charge. The overriding policy of excluding such evidence, despite its admitted probative value, is the practical experience that its disallowance tends to prevent confusion of the issues, unfair surprise, and undue prejudice.

Michelson v. United States, 335 U.S. 469, 475-76 (1948); *see* **Crank v. State**, 761 S.W.2d 328, 341 (Tex. Crim. App. 1988); **Albrecht v. State**, 486 S.W.2d 97, 100 (Tex. Crim. App. 1972); *see also* **Galvez v. State**, 962 S.W.2d 203, 205-07

That is, the trier of fact, whether consciously or not, may be tempted to penalize the defendant for past misdeeds and is likely to overvalue the evidence of prior misconduct.[327] The drafters of the Federal and Texas Rules recognized that character evidence should not always be excluded.[328] Texas Rule 404(a), following the federal rule, lists exceptions to the general exclusion of character evidence.

2. Rules 404(a)(2)(A) & 405(a): Exception for accused in criminal case. Rule 404(a)(2)(A) allows a criminal defendant to offer evidence of the defendant's pertinent character trait. This exception acknowledges the importance of ensuring that criminal defendants can present the most complete defense.[329] The rule is also based on the logic that when a defendant offers character evidence that might prejudice the jury in his favor, the unfair prejudice against the prosecution is not significant.[330] Thus, a criminal defendant may "put his character in issue"[331] by offering evidence of his general good character for a specific pertinent character trait.[332] The rule limits such evidence to

---

(Tex. App.—Austin 1998, pet. ref'd) ("[e]vidence of bad character may distract the jury from considering whether the accused is guilty of the crime charged and tempt it to convict an individual for general bad behavior"; reversing conviction because State introduced evidence that defendant was a gang member, purportedly to identify him as the robber; such use constitutes pure "bad character" evidence and is prohibited under the rule).

327. *See* Imwinkelried, *supra* note 316, at 429 ("It is the concurrence of the probative dangers of misdecision and overvaluation which accounts for the general rule excluding character evidence. Although the evidence is logically relevant, reliance on a character theory poses these two significant risks.").

328. *See* FED. R. EVID. 404 advisory committee's note, subdiv. (a). The Advisory Committee explained the exceptions as follows:

> In most jurisdictions today, the circumstantial use of character is rejected but with important exceptions: (1) an accused may introduce pertinent evidence of good character (often misleadingly described as "putting his character in issue"), in which event the prosecution may rebut with evidence of bad character; (2) an accused may introduce pertinent evidence of the character of the victim, as in support of a claim of self-defense to a charge of homicide or consent in a case of rape, and the prosecution may introduce similar evidence in rebuttal of the character evidence, or, in a homicide case, to rebut a claim that deceased was the first aggressor, however proved; and (3) the character of a witness may be gone into as bearing on his credibility. This pattern is incorporated in the rule. While its basis lies more in history and experience than in logic as underlying justification can fairly be found in terms of the relative presence and absence of prejudice in the various situations.

Id. (citations omitted).

329. *See* H. Richard Uviller, *Evidence of Character to Prove Conduct: Illusion, Illogic, and Injustice in the Courtroom*, 130 U. PA. L. REV. 845, 855 (1982) (asserting that "somewhere, somehow the rule was relaxed to allow the criminal defendant with so much at stake and so little available in the way of conventional proof to have special dispensation to tell the fact-finder just what sort of person he really is").

330. MCCORMICK ON EVIDENCE, *supra* note 1, §191, at 566.

331. The Advisory Committee's note to Federal Rule 404 points out that this phrase, often used by attorneys, is somewhat misleading because a criminal defendant does not put his whole character in issue under former Rule 404(a)(1), now Rule 404(a)(2)(A). *See* FED. R. EVID. 404 advisory committee's note, subdiv. (a); FED. R. EVID. 404 advisory committee's note to 2011 amendments. He may offer only evidence of a specific and relevant character trait. FED. R. EVID. 404 advisory committee's note, subdiv. (a). Presenting character witnesses to testify to a pertinent character trait of the defendant does not make the defendant's character an element or operative fact in the case. This action simply opens the door to circumstantial proof of an essential element through character evidence.

332. The character trait offered must be relevant to the crime charged. *See Spector v. State*, 746 S.W.2d 946, 950 (Tex. App.—Austin 1988, pet. ref'd) (pertinent trait "relates to a trait involved in the offense charged or a defense raised"); *see, e.g.*, *Wilson v. State*, 451 S.W.3d 880, 885-86 (Tex. App.—Houston [1st Dist.] 2014, pet. ref'd) (in trial for aggravated sexual assault of a child, trial court erred in excluding defendant's good-character evidence about his moral and safe conduct around young children); *Stitt v. State*, 102 S.W.3d 845, 849 (Tex. App.—Texarkana 2003,

proof of a true trait of character such as violence, honesty, morality, or sobriety; there is no character trait of "murderer," "pedophile," or "drug user."[333] This evidence is offered as indirect proof that the character trait is inconsistent with the offense charged and thus makes it more probable that the defendant did not commit the crime. Rule 404(a)(2)(A) is consistent with earlier law[334] and operates in the same way as Federal Rule 404(a)(2)(A). Prohibiting a defendant from offering evidence of a pertinent character trait is normally reversible error.[335]

Under Rule 404(a)(2)(A), the prosecution cannot offer evidence of a defendant's character as part of its case-in-chief.[336] Once the defendant offers character evidence,

pet. ref'd) (character trait of truthfulness was not pertinent when defendant was charged with interference with public duties); ***Holt v. State***, 912 S.W.2d 294, 301-02 (Tex. App.—San Antonio 1995, pet. ref'd) (trial court properly excluded character evidence that defendant was a "good parent" as irrelevant in sexual-assault case); ***Mowbray v. State***, 788 S.W.2d 658, 668 (Tex. App.—Corpus Christi 1990, pet. ref'd) (testimony describing the defendant as a "warm and caring person" did not relate to any element of the charged offense of murder or any defense raised); ***Wiggins v. State***, 778 S.W.2d 877, 893 (Tex. App.—Dallas 1989, pet. ref'd) (excluding evidence of defendant's honesty because it was not a relevant character trait in trial for aggravated sexual assault). Honesty is a pertinent character trait in a theft prosecution, but not in a murder case. Peacefulness is a pertinent trait in a murder prosecution, but not in a theft case. Both traits, however, are pertinent in a robbery trial. *See, e.g.*, ***Cockrell v. State***, 131 Tex. Crim. 3, 6, 95 S.W.2d 408, 409 (1936) (reversing robbery conviction because trial court excluded defendant's evidence of good character for honesty). A defendant's character for being "law-abiding" is general enough to be relevant to virtually any criminal case. *See* McCORMICK ON EVIDENCE, *supra* note 1, §191, at 566-67; *see, e.g.*, ***Canto-Deport v. State***, 751 S.W.2d 698, 700 (Tex. App.—Houston [1st Dist.] 1988, pet. ref'd) (in price-tag-switching case, trial court should have allowed testimony on defendant's reputation for "honesty and fair dealing" because offense involved moral turpitude and defendant's reputation was at issue; exclusion was harmless error because court admitted testimony that defendant was a "law-abiding citizen").

333. *See* ***Valdez v. State***, 2 S.W.3d 518, 520 (Tex. App.—Houston [14th Dist.] 1999, pet. ref'd) (being a "non-pedophile" is not a character trait); *see, e.g.*, ***Hernandez v. State***, No. 05-13-00202-CR (Tex. App.—Dallas 2014, no pet.) (memo op.; 1-7-14) (question asking whether defendant "was the 'kind of person' who would molest children" was properly excluded). *But see* ***Brazelton v. State***, 947 S.W.2d 644, 650 (Tex. App.—Fort Worth 1997, no pet.) (evidence that defendant did not use or sell drugs was a pertinent character trait). In ***Valdez***, the court defined "character" as "'the complex of accustomed mental and moral characteristics and habitual ethical traits marking a person, group or nation … a composite of good moral qualities typically of moral excellence and firmness ….'" 2 S.W.3d at 520 n.1 (quoting WEBSTER'S NEW INTERNATIONAL DICTIONARY (3d ed. 1961)).

334. 2 RAY, *supra* note 46, §1492, at 169 n.11. In ***Michelson v. United States***, Justice Jackson explained the traditional common-law position: "[The defendant] may introduce affirmative testimony that the general estimate of his character is so favorable that the jury may infer that he would not be likely to commit the offense charged." 335 U.S. 469, 476 (1948).

335. *See, e.g.*, ***Turner v. State***, 413 S.W.3d 442, 453 (Tex. App.—Fort Worth 2012, no pet.) (reversible error in murder case to exclude character evidence from longtime friend that he had never known defendant to be violent or aggressive); ***Brazelton***, 947 S.W.2d at 650 (trial court erred in excluding character evidence that defendant did not use or sell drugs, which was essential to her defense that the only reason she possessed the marijuana was because she reasonably believed that possession was immediately necessary to avoid imminent harm); ***Waddell v. State***, 873 S.W.2d 130, 137-39 (Tex. App.—Beaumont 1994, pet. ref'd) (reversible error to exclude defendant's evidence of good character and habits, which tended to rebut prosecution's case).

336. *See, e.g.*, ***Roberts v. State***, 866 S.W.2d 773, 775-76 (Tex. App.—Houston [1st Dist.] 1993, pet. ref'd) (character question was harmless error when question was only asked, not answered; generally reversible error "for the State to put the reputation of the accused in issue when he himself has not done so"); ***Richardson v. State***, 860 S.W.2d 214, 216-17 (Tex. App.—Fort Worth 1993, no pet.) (trial court erred in admitting State's character evidence that defendant was "possessive" and "jealous" when defendant had not first put his character in issue, but error was harmless because other evidence of those traits was properly admitted); *see also* ***Brokenberry v. State***, 788 S.W.2d 103, 105 (Tex. App.—Houston [14th Dist.] 1990, pet. ref'd) (State's reference to defendant's failure to call a character

however, the State can cross-examine the testifying witness about the defendant's character and can offer evidence to rebut the character evidence offered by the defendant.[337] The Rules contain specific procedures for proving or rebutting character evidence and for cross-examining character witnesses.

(1) Proving character. The common law established three main modes of proving character:[338] (1) establishing the subject's reputation in the community[339] through the testimony of a witness familiar with the person's reputation, (2) eliciting the personal opinion of a witness with adequate background to form an opinion of the subject's character, and (3) proving the conduct of the subject on other occasions through testimony of a witness with firsthand knowledge of the conduct.[340] These methods of proving character continue under the Texas and Federal Rules, but the circumstances of each case determine which mode or modes are permitted. Consider a case in which a defendant is charged with embezzling funds from a bank. Rule 404(a)(2) permits the defendant to offer evidence of his good character for honesty or law-abiding conduct, and Rule 405(a) provides that the defendant may call a witness to testify to the defendant's good reputation for those character traits.

(a) Reputation or opinion evidence. Rule 405(a)(1) permits a criminal defendant to offer reputation evidence of his good character.[341] Reputation testimony is admissible based on the theory that the aggregate judgment of the community is more reliable than the personal opinion of a witness, who might be prejudiced by his own relationship with the defendant.[342] The trustworthiness of reputation testimony stems from the fact that a person is observed on a daily basis by fellow members of the community, that these observations are discussed, and that eventually a synthesis of these discussions leads

---

witness was the functional equivalent of improperly injecting defendant's character into the case); *cf. United States v. Gilliland*, 586 F.2d 1384, 1389 (10th Cir. 1978) (government may not turn defendant's eyewitness into a character witness on cross-examination by asking him what kind of man defendant was and then using those questions to "bootstrap" defendant's prior convictions into evidence as impeachment).

337. *See* TEX. R. EVID. 404(a)(2)(A), 405(a)(1).

338. *See* McCORMICK'S HANDBOOK II, *supra* note 33, §186, at 443; 1 WIGMORE, *supra* note 1, §52, at 447; *see also Hedicke v. State*, 779 S.W.2d 837, 839 (Tex. Crim. App. 1989) (discussing the three modes of proving character).

339. Under early common law, the term "community" meant a person's residential community. Texas courts, like those of most other jurisdictions, have expanded the meaning of that term to include any social or professional group in which the person is likely to have a settled reputation. *See O'Bryan v. State*, 591 S.W.2d 464, 476 (Tex. Crim. App. 1979) ("community" includes the business circle).

340. McCORMICK'S HANDBOOK II, *supra* note 33, §186, at 443; 1 WIGMORE, *supra* note 1, §52, at 441-48.

341. *See* TEX. R. EVID. 405(a)(1); *Lancaster v. State*, 754 S.W.2d 493, 495 (Tex. App.—Dallas 1988, pet. ref'd). This allowance of reputation evidence accords with common law and earlier Texas law. *See* McCORMICK'S HANDBOOK II, *supra* note 33, §186, at 443; 1 WIGMORE, *supra* note 1, §52, at 446-48; *see, e.g., Tarwater v. Donley Cty. State Bank*, 277 S.W. 176, 178-79 (Tex. Civ. App.—Amarillo 1925, no writ) (admitting general reputation evidence, but not opinion evidence, to prove character in a suit for conversion of a bank account); *Negociacion Agricola y Ganadera de San Enrique v. Love*, 220 S.W. 224, 229-30 (Tex. Civ. App.—Amarillo 1920, no writ) (admitting reputation evidence, but not opinion evidence, to prove honesty in an employment-commissions suit).

342. *See* Mason Ladd, *Techniques and Theory of Character Testimony*, 24 IOWA L. REV. 498, 513 (1939).

to a community conclusion about that person's character.[343] Such reputation testimony may be less trustworthy in today's urban society.[344]

Reputation testimony should be based on a witness's discussions with others about the defendant or on discussions the witness has heard about the defendant's reputation, and should not be based exclusively on the witness's personal knowledge.[345] For example, discussions with other police officers are sufficient to qualify a police officer as a reputation witness, but his testimony may not be grounded solely on his knowledge of specific acts that the defendant has committed.[346]

Texas Rule 405(a)(1) allows evidence of opinion as well as reputation whenever character evidence is admissible.[347] Thus, a defendant who was charged with embez-

---

343. *See Hernandez v. State*, 800 S.W.2d 523, 524 (Tex. Crim. App. 1990); *Moore v. State*, 663 S.W.2d 497, 500 (Tex. App.—Dallas 1983, no pet.).

344. *See* Ladd, *supra* note 342, at 514-15.

345. *Turner v. State*, 805 S.W.2d 423, 429 (Tex. Crim. App. 1991); *Ferrell v. State*, 968 S.W.2d 471, 474 (Tex. App.—Fort Worth 1998, pet. ref'd); *House v. State*, 909 S.W.2d 214, 218 (Tex. App.—Houston [14th Dist.] 1995), *aff'd*, 947 S.W.2d 251 (Tex. Crim. App. 1997); *see, e.g.*, *Manning v. State*, 126 S.W.3d 552, 555-56 (Tex. App.—Texarkana 2003, no pet.) (trial court abused its discretion in permitting witness to testify at punishment stage to defendant's reputation for being peaceable and law-abiding because witness's testimony was based only on two urine-analysis reports and a personal observation, and there was no evidence that witness had discussed defendant with anyone).

346. *See Wagner v. State*, 687 S.W.2d 303, 313-14 (Tex. Crim. App. 1984) (op. on reh'g); *House*, 909 S.W.2d at 218. Once the defendant has put his character in issue, the prosecution may rebut with witnesses who may testify to the reputation of the accused. Familiarity with specific acts is not familiarity with reputation. *Hernandez*, 800 S.W.2d at 524. As the court of criminal appeals explained in *Hernandez*:

> The trustworthiness of reputation testimony stems from the fact that a person is observed in his day to day activities by other members of his community and that these observations are discussed. Over a period [of] time there is a synthesis of these observations and discussions which results in a conclusion as to the individual's reputation. When reputation is based solely on specific acts, this synthesis is lost, as well as its reliability.

Id. (quoting *Wagner*, 687 S.W.2d at 313); *see also Lopez v. State*, 860 S.W.2d 938, 944-46 (Tex. App.—San Antonio 1993, no pet.) (reversible error to permit detective to testify to defendant's reputation based solely on information obtained from a confidential informant about a single, specific occurrence). A reputation witness's testimony can, however, be based on both community reputation and personal experience. *See, e.g.*, *Cooks v. State*, 844 S.W.2d 697, 736-37 (Tex. Crim. App. 1992) (court overruled defendant's objection to reputation testimony that was based on defendant's general reputation in the community as well as the witness's knowledge of specific instances).

347. TEX. R. EVID. 405(a)(1); 2 RAY, *supra* note 46, §1432, at 24 (Supp. 1991); *see Hunt v. State*, 779 S.W.2d 926, 928 (Tex. App.—Corpus Christi 1989, pet. ref'd) (accused may offer both reputation and opinion evidence of his good character, and character witnesses may be cross-examined about relevant specific conduct); *Lancaster v. State*, 754 S.W.2d 493, 495 (Tex. App.—Dallas 1988, pet. ref'd) (same); *Thomas v. State*, 669 S.W.2d 420, 423 (Tex. App.—Houston [1st Dist.] 1984, pet. ref'd) (defendant is allowed to introduce evidence of a specific good character trait to show that it is improbable that he committed the offense when that trait is involved in the offense). Federal Rule 405(a) is substantively identical to Texas Rule 405(a)(1). *See* FED. R. EVID. 405(a).

This admissibility of opinion evidence to prove character departs from common-law practice and earlier Texas law. *See* MCCORMICK'S HANDBOOK II, *supra* note 33, §186, at 443; 1 WIGMORE, *supra* note 1, §52, at 447; *see, e.g.*, *Jackson v. State*, 628 S.W.2d 446, 450 (Tex. Crim. App. [Panel Op.] 1982) (disallowing witness's testimony of defendant's bad character because witness's opinion was not based on discussions with others); *Courtney v. State*, 735 S.W.2d 949, 953 (Tex. App.—Beaumont 1987, pet. ref'd) (under Texas common law, character traits could not be proved by evidence of personal opinion or specific acts); *Morgan v. City of Humble*, 598 S.W.2d 364, 365 (Tex. Civ. App.—Houston [14th Dist.] 1980, no writ) (excluding opinion evidence that a night club was a site for prostitution because testimony about reputation cannot merely reflect the personal opinion of the witness). Commentators criticized the traditional disallowance of opinion as a misapplication of the opinion rule (i.e., the principle that laymen's opinions are generally inadmissible). 2 RAY, *supra* note 46, §1432, at 105; *see* 7 JOHN H. WIGMORE, EVIDENCE

zling funds from a bank could call a neighbor or another witness with an adequate background to give his personal opinion that the defendant is an honest and law-abiding person. Rule 405(a)(1) also permits expert opinion on a pertinent character trait.[348]

Under Rule 405(a)(2), when a character witness testifies during the guilt stage of a criminal trial, the witness must have been familiar with the reputation, or with the underlying facts or information on which the opinion is based, before the day of the offense to qualify to testify about the character or trait of character of an accused.[349] This provision was probably prompted by the frequency with which prosecutors called police officers to testify to a criminal defendant's bad reputation.[350] Similarly, crime victims, frequently the victims of uncharged offenses, were called during the guilt stage to testify to a defendant's bad reputation if the defendant's character for law-abiding conduct was in issue.[351] While this provision was probably instituted to deal with prosecution witnesses, it could raise potential constitutional issues by barring crucial opinion or reputation testimony about a defendant's good character from a witness who

---

IN TRIALS AT COMMON LAW, §§1980-1986, at 142-72 (Chadbourn rev. 1978) (discussing the opinion rule as applied to character testimony). Texas Rule 405(a) and Federal Rule 405(a) eliminate this criticized restriction.

348. *See, e.g.*, ***Townsend v. State***, 776 S.W.2d 316, 317-18 (Tex. App.—Houston [1st Dist.] 1989, pet. ref'd) (in trial for indecency with a child, psychiatrist could testify that defendant's psychological profile was not typical of individuals who commit sexual crimes; expert's character opinion opened the door to testimony by two other victims that defendant had, during the course of seven years, sexually molested them as well); *cf.* ***United States v. Hill***, 655 F.2d 512, 516-17 (3d Cir. 1981) (error to exclude psychologist's testimony in support of an entrapment defense that defendant was unusually susceptible to government inducements).

349. TEX. R. EVID. 405(a)(2). Federal Rule 405 does not contain a similar provision. Texas Rule 405(a)(2) changed earlier Texas law and departed from the original text of Criminal Rule 405(a). Refer to note 299 *supra*. Texas common law made no distinction between a character witness who gained familiarity with a defendant's reputation after the commission of the offense but before trial and a witness who knew the defendant's reputation before the date of the offense. *See, e.g.*, ***Chamberlain v. State***, 453 S.W.2d 490, 494 (Tex. Crim. App. 1970) (police officers who did not know defendant before the offense date were nonetheless qualified); ***Ross v. State***, 763 S.W.2d 897, 904 (Tex. App.—Dallas 1988, pet. ref'd) (trial court erred because there was no showing that witness, who did not know defendant at the time of the offense, was substantially familiar with defendant's reputation before the offense; error was harmless). Witnesses were qualified to testify once they had discussed the defendant's reputation with others—such as police officers or fellow victims—without any knowledge of the defendant before the date of the offense or of his reputation in his own residential, social, or professional community. *See* ***Fearance v. State***, 771 S.W.2d 486, 512 (Tex. Crim. App. 1988); ***Lindley v. State***, 736 S.W.2d 267, 276-77 (Tex. App.—Fort Worth 1987, pet. ref'd, untimely filed).

350. *See, e.g.*, ***Hernandez***, 800 S.W.2d at 524-25 (reversing defendant's murder conviction when testimony by deputy constable and justice of the peace about defendant's bad reputation for being a peaceful and law-abiding citizen was based solely on conversations with others about specific complaints against the defendant; neither witness discussed defendant's reputation with community members); ***Fearance***, 771 S.W.2d at 512 (prison guard's testimony about defendant's reputation for being peaceful and law-abiding was properly admitted because it was based on discussions with other guards). The ***Hernandez*** court noted that Criminal Rule 405 plainly requires that the witness "must have been substantially familiar with that reputation and this familiarity must have existed prior to the date of the offense." 800 S.W.2d at 525.

While calling a law-enforcement official to testify to a criminal defendant's bad character may carry an implicit message to the jury that the defendant has had previous difficulties with the law, that fact alone will not make his testimony objectionable. *See, e.g.*, ***Rougeau v. State***, 738 S.W.2d 651, 667-68 (Tex. Crim. App. 1987) (assistant warden could testify about capital-murder defendant's bad reputation).

351. *See* ***Jackson***, 628 S.W.2d at 450.

gained familiarity with the defendant only after the commission of the offense.[352] The restriction in this provision does not apply to punishment hearings.[353] Thus, both defense and prosecution witnesses can testify to their opinions or knowledge of the defendant's reputation acquired after the offense to prove his character in mitigation or aggravation of the sentence. This testimony cannot, however, be based on the offense for which the defendant is on trial.[354]

(b) Specific instances of conduct. When a defendant calls a witness to testify to his character, he may not, on direct examination, elicit testimony from the witness about specific instances of his conduct to prove his character.[355] Thus, a witness may not testify, for example, that the defendant has gone to church every Sunday for the last year to prove that the defendant is a good person and not an embezzler. Similarly, the witness may not testify that the defendant did not steal money from the bank on Monday, on July 17th, or during the year 2015. Evidence of prior specific instances of conduct is not admissible on direct examination, even for the limited purpose of showing the basis for the witness's opinion.[356] Evidence of specific instances of conduct is disallowed on direct examination under Rule 405(a) because, while it is "the most convinc-

---

352. For example, a psychologist might have examined the defendant after the defendant's arrest, but before the trial and formed an expert medical opinion about his character for "deliberate" or "intentional" violence. The defendant's constitutional right to present his defense on a critical issue outweighs society's interests in conflicting procedural and evidentiary rules. *See **Rock v. Arkansas**,* 483 U.S. 44, 56 (1987) ("In applying its evidentiary rules a State must evaluate whether the interests served by a rule justify the limitation imposed on the defendant's constitutional right to testify."); ***Chambers v. Mississippi**,* 410 U.S. 284, 302 (1973) ("[T]he hearsay rule may not be applied mechanistically to defeat the ends of justice."); *see also* 1 GOODE ET AL., *supra* note 103, §405.2.3, at 209-10 & n.46 (the limitation raises constitutional issues if the proffered evidence is critical and reliable).

353. *See, e.g., **Sims v. State**,* 273 S.W.3d 291, 296 (Tex. Crim. App. 2008) (during punishment stage of trial for aggravated assault with a deadly weapon, police officer could give his opinion on defendant's character for truthfulness, based on a single encounter at the time of the offense).

354. *See **Davis v. State**,* 831 S.W.2d 839, 844 (Tex. App.—Dallas 1992, pet. ref'd). The common law recognized this restriction. ***Rodriquez v. State**,* 509 S.W.2d 319, 321 (Tex. Crim. App. 1974).

355. *See **Valdez v. State**,* 2 S.W.3d 518, 519 (Tex. App.—Houston [14th Dist.] 1999, pet. ref'd) (when evidence of accused's character or character trait is admissible, proof may be made through reputation or opinion testimony, but specific instances of conduct are inadmissible to show circumstantially that accused did or did not commit offense); *see, e.g., **Turner v. State**,* 413 S.W.3d 442, 453 n.6 (Tex. App.—Fort Worth 2012, no pet.) ("have you known" questions were broad enough to elicit witness's opinion and knowledge of defendant's reputation without including specific instances of conduct); ***Garcia v. State**,* 819 S.W.2d 667, 668 (Tex. App.—Corpus Christi 1991, no pet.) (defendant was precluded from introducing specific incidents to support his claim of good character). This restriction in Rule 405 follows earlier Texas law. *See **Schmidt v. State**,* 449 S.W.2d 39, 40 (Tex. Crim. App. 1969) (while the defendant may offer reputation evidence of his law-abiding character, he may not testify that he has never been in trouble); ***Robinson v. Lovell**,* 238 S.W.2d 294, 299 (Tex. Civ. App.—Galveston 1951, writ ref'd n.r.e.) ("Character may not be shown by specific instances of misconduct."). When the defendant's character is an ultimate issue, however, Rule 405(b) permits proof of character by specific instances of conduct. Refer to notes 609-616 *infra* and accompanying text.

356. *See, e.g., **Biagas v. State**,* 177 S.W.3d 161, 175 (Tex. App.—Houston [1st Dist.] 2005, pet. ref'd) (defendant charged with theft could offer testimony from his former employer about his character traits of "honesty" and "trustworthiness," but because defendant did not sort out admissible opinion or reputation testimony from inadmissible testimony about prior specific instances that demonstrated these traits, trial court did not err in excluding witness's testimony).

ing" of the three modes of proving character, it also "possesses the greatest capacity to arouse prejudice, to confuse, to surprise, and to consume time."[357]

(2) Cross-examination of defendant's character witnesses. Once the defendant puts his character in issue by introducing the reputation or opinion testimony of character witnesses, the State may then cross-examine the character witnesses.[358] During this cross-examination, Rule 405(a) allows inquiry into specific instances of the defendant's conduct,[359] subject to two limitations.[360] First, the examiner must have a factual basis for the incidents inquired into.[361] Second, these specific instances must be relevant to and inconsistent with the character trait at issue.[362] Suppose that the defendant in the

---

357. FED. R. EVID. 405 advisory committee's note. Mason Ladd explained the collateral consequences:
> If the law were to permit proof of the bad acts of each witness, to allow those to be counteracted by showing the good deeds which each had done, then to endeavor to solve the truth of the existence of the good or bad deeds, and finally to permit the results to be considered as they disclose the character of the witness which in turn may have a bearing upon the truth of testimony as to other facts in the actual controversy in the litigation, all trials would become burdened with confusion and be endlessly prolonged. Furthermore, if the details of the past life of all witnesses were to be generally opened to investigation it would make the task of being a witness an unpopular one.

Ladd, *supra* note 342, at 508-09.

358. *See, e.g.*, *Harrison v. State*, 241 S.W.3d 23, 27-28 (Tex. Crim. App. 2007) (State could cross-examine defense witness with evidence of defendant's prior assault convictions after witness stated that defendant was a "good" and "sweet" boy; "[a]lthough [defendant] did not intentionally elicit [witness's] character testimony, the nonrespo[n]siveness of [witness's] statement does not change the fact that it was character evidence offered by a defense witness"); *Burke v. State*, 371 S.W.3d 252, 261 (Tex. App.—Houston [1st Dist.] 2011, pet. dism'd, untimely filed) (in prosecution for aggravated sexual assault of a child, State could cross-examine defendant's mother about allegation of defendant's sexual abuse of another child after she testified that defendant was a "good boy" and stated "I know my son's heart, and I know he didn't do this"); *Hernandez v. State*, 351 S.W.3d 156, 161 (Tex. App.—Texarkana 2011, pet. ref'd) (State could cross-examine defendant's girlfriend with "did you know" questions after she was asked on direct examination what kind of person defendant was and she responded that he was "really nice" to her and her children and was a "good guy").

359. TEX. R. EVID. 405(a)(1); *see Wheeler v. State*, 67 S.W.3d 879, 886 n.16 (Tex. Crim. App. 2002) ("On cross-examination, the State may test the character witness' familiarity with the defendant's character or demonstrate that the witness has a low standard for what he considers good character by inquiring into prior specific instances of conduct that are inconsistent with the particular character trait ...."); *Bratcher v. State*, 771 S.W.2d 175, 186-87 (Tex. App.—San Antonio 1989, no pet.) (allowing "were you aware" questions about prior specific acts by the defendant on the cross-examination of an opinion witness); *Turner v. State*, 762 S.W.2d 705, 706 (Tex. App.—Houston [14th Dist.] 1988, pet. ref'd) (reputation witness may be cross-examined about specific instances of conduct that have not resulted in a final conviction); *Lancaster v. State*, 754 S.W.2d 493, 494-95 (Tex. App.—Dallas 1988, pet. ref'd) (character witnesses may be questioned about specific instances of conduct); *see, e.g.*, *Blevins v. State*, 884 S.W.2d 219, 228-29 (Tex. App.—Beaumont 1994, no pet.) (when defendant attempted to portray himself as a peaceful and law-abiding person who had never been armed with a deadly weapon, State was entitled to cross-examine him about a prior shooting incident).

360. *See generally Wilson v. State*, 71 S.W.3d 346, 350-51 (Tex. Crim. App. 2002) (discussing methods of and limitations on cross-examination of character witnesses).

361. *Lancaster*, 754 S.W.2d at 496; *see Quiroz v. State*, 764 S.W.2d 395, 399 (Tex. App.—Fort Worth 1989, pet. ref'd) (foundation for inquiring into specific instances of conduct must be laid outside the jury's presence unless already admitted into evidence).

362. *See Livingston v. State*, 589 S.W.2d 395, 402 (Tex. Crim. App. 1979) (when a witness testifies to defendant's broad conduct to imply that he has a good general character, witness's credibility may be impeached by inquiring into specific instances of defendant's conduct that are inconsistent with good character); *Quiroz*, 764 S.W.2d at 399 (character witnesses may be cross-examined about specific acts if they are relevant to the character trait at issue).

Attorneys should carefully construct their questions to a character witness, and the witness should be cautioned about the legally acceptable responses. For example, in a prosecution for aggravated sexual assault, the de-

above embezzlement hypothetical had called a witness who testified to the defendant's good character for honesty—a pertinent character trait in an embezzlement trial. Suppose also that it is well known that the defendant had twice been convicted of murder.[363] The State could not then cross-examine the defendant's character witness about the murders when the witness testified to the character trait of "honesty," not "peacefulness." The State also cannot "push" a defense witness into "endorsing the character of the defendant" and then cross-examine the witness about prior specific instances of the defendant's bad conduct.[364]

To rebut the positive character evidence relating to the defendant's honesty, the State could also question the defendant's character witness about the defendant's reputation for being a law-abiding person. In doing so, the State is actually offering its own character evidence to rebut the defendant's character evidence, even though the evidence is coming from the defendant's witness and is on a slightly different character trait. Although the language of Rule 404(a)(2)(A) is ambiguous about whether such a rebuttal is permitted, commentators suggest that a broad interpretation of the rule should allow the State to rebut with any character evidence that tends to defeat the inference that the defendant is attempting to place before the jury.[365]

Although the witness may be cross-examined about prior specific instances of the defendant's conduct that are inconsistent with the particular character trait, the State may not go further and offer extrinsic evidence of those incidents.[366] The purpose of the cross-examination is to demonstrate that (1) the character witness is not really familiar with the defendant's character because he was unaware of this prior incident or (2) the character witness, who is familiar with this incident and nonetheless asserts that the defendant has a good character for this trait, has a very low threshold for "good"

---

fendant called his mother to give her opinion about his truthfulness. *Wiggins v. State*, 778 S.W.2d 877, 887 (Tex. App.—Dallas 1989, pet. ref'd). The witness, perhaps misunderstanding the question, stated that the defendant was an honest person. *See id.* Honesty and truthfulness, though related, are not interchangeable character traits and raise different cross-examination possibilities. *See id.* at 889 ("honesty" is a broader term than "truthfulness"; an honest person will always be truthful, but a truthful person may not always be honest). The State contended that once the witness testified to the defendant's honesty, she could be cross-examined with "have you heard" questions about whether the defendant stole money at college parties, pleaded guilty to stealing shoes several years earlier, burglarized a car, and committed several other theft-related acts. *Id.* at 887-88. The court of appeals disagreed and held that the character testimony was inadmissible because honesty is not a pertinent character trait in a prosecution for aggravated sexual assault. *Id.* at 893. The State should have objected to the improper testimony and should not have used it to offer further improper evidence. *Id.*

363. However, Rule 405 does not require that a defendant have been convicted of a crime before the character witness may be cross-examined about it. *See Turner*, 762 S.W.2d at 706; *Lancaster*, 754 S.W.2d at 495-96.

364. *See* 1 CHRISTOPHER B. MUELLER & LAIRD C. KIRKPATRICK, FEDERAL EVIDENCE §102, at 563-66 (2d ed. Supp. 2003).

365. 22 WRIGHT & GRAHAM, *supra* note 35, §5236, at 396.

366. *See Wheeler v. State*, 67 S.W.3d 879, 886 n.16 (Tex. Crim. App. 2002); *Villarreal v. State*, 504 S.W.3d 494, 523 (Tex. App.—Corpus Christi 2016, pet. ref'd); *see, e.g., Matthews v. State*, 979 S.W.2d 720, 722 (Tex. App.—Eastland 1998, no pet.) (error, though harmless, to permit extrinsic proof of specific acts about which State had properly cross-examined defendant's character witness).

character.[367] The purpose is not to prove the defendant's character—that may be accomplished only through reputation or opinion evidence—but to impeach the character witness's testimony.[368]

Texas evidentiary tradition had allowed, in the cross-examination of a character witness, questions that begin with the phrase "have you heard" because this type of question properly tests the witness's credibility. This same tradition had disallowed more direct questions that begin with a phrase such as "did you know."[369] The drafters of the federal rule decided that the difference between such questions has "slight if

---

367. *Wheeler*, 67 S.W.3d at 886 n.16; *see* **Wilson v. State**, 71 S.W.3d 346, 350 (Tex. Crim. App. 2002) ("A witness who testifies to a defendant's good character may be cross-examined to test the witness's awareness of relevant 'specific instances of conduct.'" (quoting **Drone v. State**, 906 S.W.2d 608, 616 (Tex. App.—Austin 1995, pet. ref'd)).

368. *See* **Harrison v. State**, 241 S.W.3d 23, 25 (Tex. Crim. App. 2007); **Brown v. State**, 477 S.W.2d 617, 620 (Tex. Crim. App. 1972); **Villarreal**, 504 S.W.3d at 523; *see, e.g.*, **Juarez v. State**, No. 05-12-00125-CR (Tex. App.—Dallas 2013, pet. ref'd) (no pub.; 7-31-13) (when defense witnesses testified that defendant was a "good person" who would not have committed burglary without the bad influence of others, State could cross-examine them about defendant's prior thefts as juvenile).

369. *See* **Republic Nat'l Life Ins. v. Heyward**, 568 S.W.2d 879, 885 (Tex. Civ. App.—Eastland 1978, writ ref'd n.r.e.) (disallowing "did you know" questions but approving of "have you heard" questions in cross-examining a general reputation witness). The rationale for this rule was discussed in **Brown v. State**:

> The rationale behind the rule is that reputation is an opinion based on hearsay. The reputation witness states his opinion based on that which he has heard from others concerning the defendant. In order to test this opinion, the prosecution is allowed to determine whether the witness has *heard* (not whether he *knows*) of acts or reports which would be inconsistent with a good reputation. The theory is that if the witness is truly familiar with the reputation of the defendant, he will have also heard of adverse reports which are circulating in the community. This is consistent with the nature of reputation evidence, that is, an opinion based on hearsay. Reputation does not concern that which a person *is*, but rather, that which he is thought to be. Thus, a question regarding an act of misconduct which, by its very nature, is likely to be a part of the person's reputation in the community, is appropriate as a means of testing the weight or credibility of the witness' opinion.

477 S.W.2d at 620. In **Rutledge v. State**, a pre-Rules decision, the Texas Court of Criminal Appeals held that a witness who testified to his opinion of the defendant's character could not be cross-examined with "have you heard" questions. 749 S.W.2d 50, 53 (Tex. Crim. App. 1988). During the punishment stage of this aggravated-kidnapping prosecution, the defendant called an acquaintance to testify to "what type of man" the defendant appeared to be. *Id.* at 51. The unartfully phrased question seemed closer to a request for opinion rather than reputation testimony, but the witness responded that the defendant was "impeccable" and then proceeded to explain that "he'd never drink, he didn't curse, and he was just a nice person to be with." *Id.* On cross-examination, the prosecutor asked the witness if he had heard about two prior sexual assaults of children involving the defendant. *Id.* at 52. The court of criminal appeals held that the State's method of cross-examination was reversible error. *Id.* at 54. The court insisted that it was not indulging in hair-splitting semantics or requiring "magic words" in distinguishing between opinion and reputation witnesses. *Id.* Nonetheless, commentators justly criticized the court's reasoning and result. 1 GOODE ET AL., *supra* note 103, §405.2.4, at 217; *see also* **Harrison**, 241 S.W.3d at 26 (**Rutledge** and other similar cases were decided before Rules of Evidence were adopted and do not "address the proper use of rebuttal character evidence under Rule 405(a)"). Other courts were more flexible in their approach. *See, e.g.*, **Rodriguez v. State**, 919 S.W.2d 136, 141 (Tex. App.—San Antonio 1995, no pet.) (phrasing of reputation question by State to its witnesses asking their opinions about defendant's character in the community for being peaceful and law-abiding was not impermissible, but court should have permitted defendant to test qualifications of character witnesses); **Bratcher v. State**, 771 S.W.2d 175, 185-87 (Tex. App.—San Antonio 1989, no pet.) (allowing "were you aware" questions on the cross-examination of defense witness who testified to his opinion of defendant's character); **Lancaster v. State**, 754 S.W.2d 493, 495 (Tex. App.—Dallas 1988, pet. ref'd) (allowing "have you heard" and "do you know" questions to determine the scope of witness's knowledge of defendant's character and reputation).

any practical significance,"[370] and the Texas drafters agreed.[371] The court of criminal appeals explained that

> the better practice is to follow the traditional method of impeaching opinion witnesses with "did you know" questions and reputation witnesses with "have you heard" questions. Since the reputation witness purportedly bases his or her testimony on hearsay in the community, his knowledge of the defendant's reputation in the community can best be impeached by questions of whether he has heard about specific instances of conduct inconsistent with that reputation. Conversely, the witness who testifies to the defendant's character on the basis of personal knowledge is most effectively challenged by "did you know" questions regarding conduct inconsistent with the traits to which he has offered his opinion and not about rumors affecting the subject's character.[372]

Cross-examination under Rule 405(a)(1) does not discriminate between character witnesses testifying to reputation and those testifying to opinion; "did you know" questions can be asked of both.[373] The language of the rule is broad enough to embrace "have you heard" questions during cross-examination of the opinion witness as well as cross-examination of the reputation witness because this type of question is a form of "inquiry" into relevant specific instances of conduct. This broad permission to ask either type of question of both reputation and opinion witnesses prevents reversals based on a counsel's failure to comply with the overly meticulous phrasing requirements of earlier Texas law.[374]

(3) Rebuttal character evidence. Once the criminal defendant has offered evidence of his good character, the State may offer rebuttal evidence under Rule 404(a)(2)(A).[375] The character trait about which the rebuttal evidence is offered must be similar to the one the defendant has put in issue. In the embezzlement hypothetical above, the State

---

370. FED. R. EVID. 405 advisory committee's note.

371. *See, e.g., Quiroz v. State*, 764 S.W.2d 395, 398 (Tex. App.—Fort Worth 1989, pet. ref'd) (both "did you know" and "have you heard" questions are proper cross-examination questions under Rule 405(a)); *Lancaster*, 754 S.W.2d at 495 (same).

372. *Wilson*, 71 S.W.3d at 350 n.4 (citations omitted); *see also Thomas v. State*, 759 S.W.2d 449, 452 (Tex. App.—Houston [14th Dist.] 1988, pet. ref'd) (counsel could ask "have you heard" questions only to affect the weight of a reputation witness's testimony; opinion witnesses could be asked "do you know" questions only to test the basis for their opinions).

373. *See Murphy v. State*, 4 S.W.3d 926, 932 (Tex. App.—Waco 1999, pet. ref'd) ("Texas Rule of Evidence 405(a) does not draw a distinction between 'reputation' witnesses and 'opinion' witnesses, nor does the rule itself limit cross-examination of character witnesses to any particular form."). The reputation witness arguably has held himself out to have heard and not to have known. If he responds that he does not know, the cross-examiner must accept his answer.

374. Refer to note 369 *supra* and accompanying text.

375. Federal Rule 404(a)(2)(A) also allows for rebuttal of the character evidence offered by the defendant. *See* FED. R. EVID. 404(a)(2)(A).

could call witnesses to attest to the defendant's bad character for honesty or law-abiding conduct but could not offer evidence of bad character for drug use.[376]

The rebuttal may take the form of reputation or opinion testimony under Rule 405(a).[377] Rule 405 does not, however, permit proof of specific instances of the defendant's conduct on rebuttal in such circumstances.[378] The State's rebuttal witnesses who give reputation or opinion testimony are subject to the same type of cross-examination under Rule 405(a) as the defendant's character witnesses.[379]

3. Rules 404(a)(2)(B) & 405(a)(1): Exception for party accused of conduct involving moral turpitude in a civil case. Rule 404(a)(2)(B) provides that "[i]n a civil case, a party accused of conduct involving moral turpitude may offer evidence of the party's pertinent trait, and if the evidence is admitted, the accusing party may offer evidence to rebut it."[380] Federal Rule 404(a), however, explicitly limits the use of character evidence to criminal cases.[381]

---

376. *Cf. United States v. Reed*, 700 F.2d 638, 645 (11th Cir. 1983) (State could not rebut defendant's character witnesses by cross-examining defendant on his marijuana use).

377. *Harrison v. State*, 241 S.W.3d 23, 25 (Tex. Crim. App. 2007).

378. *E.g., Matthews v. State*, 979 S.W.2d 720, 722 (Tex. App.—Eastland 1998, no pet.) (error, but harmless, for State to offer evidence of defendant's extraneous act of hitting fellow high-school student with chair as rebuttal to defendant's character witnesses; "[a]lthough appellant's character for violence would have been admissible rebuttal, proof of the specific incident involving an assault on a classmate was not admissible"). Refer to notes 355-357 *supra* and accompanying text.

379. Refer to notes 358-374 *supra* and accompanying text.

380. Tex. R. Evid. 404(a)(2)(B). The standards for proving character under Rule 405(a)(1) and for rebutting character evidence under Rule 404(a)(2)(B) in civil cases are applicable in the same manner as in criminal cases. Refer to notes 338-348, 355-379 *supra* and accompanying text. Rule 404(a)(2)(B) follows pre-Rules Texas law for criminal cases. *See Lucas v. State*, 378 S.W.2d 340, 342 (Tex. Crim. App. 1964) (evidence of defendant's reputation for veracity is not admissible unless defendant testifies and his veracity is in issue); *Day v. State*, 117 Tex. Crim. 173, 175, 34 S.W.2d 871, 872-73 (1931) (evidence of defendant's reputation for being law-abiding is not admissible unless defendant puts his reputation in issue). Texas courts also consistently followed this exception in civil cases. *See, e.g., Waggoman v. Fort Worth Well Mach. & Supply Co.*, 124 Tex. 325, 327, 76 S.W.2d 1005, 1006 (1934) (involving a charge of embezzling); *Grant v. Pendley*, 39 S.W.2d 596, 599 (Tex. Comm'n App. 1931, holding approved) (allegation of fraud in a real-estate-conveyance dispute is not per se the charge of a crime involving moral turpitude); *Wells v. Lewis*, 108 S.W.2d 926, 928 (Tex. Civ. App.—Texarkana 1937, writ dism'd) (involving an accusation of false swearing and the subornation of false swearing, both felonies).

McCormick noted that several states allow character evidence in civil cases, in recognition of the "serious consequences to the party's standing, reputation, and relationships which such a charge, even in a civil action, may bring." McCormick's Handbook II, *supra* note 33, §192, at 460; *see, e.g., Cont'l Nat'l Bank v. First Nat'l Bank*, 68 S.W. 497, 499 (Tenn. 1902) (allowing evidence of good character in fraudulent-loan case). *See generally* Charles C. Marvel, Annotation, *Admissibility of Evidence of Character or Reputation of Party in Civil Action for Assault on Issues Other Than Impeachment*, 91 A.L.R.3d 718, 725-58 (1979) (listing and discussing categories in which various states admit character evidence in civil actions).

381. *See* Fed. R. Evid. 404(a)(2). In 2006, the rule was amended "to clarify that in a civil case evidence of a person's character is never admissible to prove that the person acted in conformity with the character trait." Fed. R. Evid. 404(a)(1) advisory committee's note to 2006 amendments. The Advisory Committee noted:

In criminal cases, the so-called "mercy rule" permits a criminal defendant to introduce evidence of pertinent character traits of the defendant and the victim. But that is because the accused, whose liberty is at stake, may need "a counterweight against the strong investigative and prosecutorial resources of the government." ... Those concerns do not apply to parties in civil cases.

Id. The committee believed that "[t]he circumstantial use of character evidence is fraught with peril in *any* case, because it could lead to a trial of personality and could cause the jury to decide the case on improper grounds." Fed.

Rule 404(a)(2)(B) is limited to conduct involving moral turpitude and thus has a much more restricted application than Rule 404(a)(2)(A), which applies to criminal proceedings.[382] The conduct does not need to amount to the commission of a crime.[383] All the reasons supporting admissibility when the accusation is one of a "crime" involving moral turpitude also support admissibility when the "conduct" involves moral turpitude, even without an element that makes such conduct criminal. "Moral turpitude" is not defined by rule or statute in Texas,[384] but Rule 609 carries forward the earlier Texas common-law application of convictions for "moral turpitude" that can be used to impeach a testifying witness.[385] The term clearly includes conduct that involves dishonesty or crimen falsi[386] and offenses against public decency, such as prostitution.[387]

4. Rules 404(a)(3)(A), (a)(3)(B) & 405(a)(1): Exception for the character of the victim in a criminal case. Rule 404(a)(3) provides for the admission of pertinent character traits of crime victims.[388] Texas common law allowed a homicide defendant to show the alleged victim's character for violence to support the defendant's claim of self-defense.[389] Rule 404(a)(3) carries forward the earlier law and expands the scope of

R. EVID. 404(a), Advisory Committee on Evidence Rules, Minutes of the Meeting of October 18, 2002, www.uscourts .gov/rules-policies/archives/meeting-minutes/advisory-committee-rules-evidence-october-2002.

382. Refer to notes 329-379 *supra* and accompanying text.

383. In *State Bar v. Evans*, a disciplinary proceeding was brought against an attorney alleged to have violated Disciplinary Rule 1-102(A)(3): "A lawyer shall not engage in conduct involving moral turpitude." 774 S.W.2d 656, 657-58 (Tex. 1989). Violation of the Code of Professional Responsibility is not a crime, but because the allegations against the attorney included conduct involving moral turpitude, he was allowed to offer evidence of pertinent character traits, including honesty and integrity. *See id.* Once he did, however, the State Bar was entitled to offer rebuttal testimony. *Id.* at 658. The common law required that the conduct be criminal. *See Grant*, 39 S.W.2d at 599 (character evidence should be admitted only "where the nature of the action directly involves the character of a party, where a witness has been impeached, or where a party by his pleading or evidence charges his adversary with the commission of a crime involving moral turpitude").

384. *See In re G.M.P.*, 909 S.W.2d 198, 207-08 (Tex. App.—Houston [14th Dist.] 1995, no writ) (Rule 405 does not define what conduct constitutes "moral turpitude" for purposes of character testimony, but court assumed that common-law definition was carried forward under the rule and held that sexual assault of a child is conduct involving moral turpitude).

385. Refer to *Article VI: Witnesses, infra* p. 615.

386. "Crimen falsi" is a crime in the nature of perjury or any other offense that involves some element of dishonesty or false statement. BLACK'S LAW DICTIONARY 454 (10th ed. 2014); *see Compton v. Jay*, 389 S.W.2d 639, 642 (Tex. 1965) (moral turpitude "includes more than crimes of perjury, forgery and the like").

387. *See Holgin v. State*, 480 S.W.2d 405, 408 (Tex. Crim. App. 1972).

388. The rule also covers pertinent character traits of the alleged victims of assaultive conduct in civil cases. *See* TEX. R. EVID. 404(a)(3)(C). Refer to notes 426-442 *infra* and accompanying text. Under Rule 404, a "victim" includes an alleged victim. TEX. R. EVID. 404(a)(5).

389. *See Dempsey v. State*, 159 Tex. Crim. 602, 605-06, 266 S.W.2d 875, 877-78 (1954) (evidence of deceased's character becomes admissible when his character tends to explain his aggression); *see, e.g., Thompson v. State*, 659 S.W.2d 649, 653-54 (Tex. Crim. App. 1983) (evidence of deceased's reputation for violence or prior specific acts of violence are admissible to explain deceased's conduct; deceased's prior convictions for unlawfully carrying a weapon did not support defendant's claimed belief that deadly force was necessary for self-defense); *Lewis v. State*, 463 S.W.2d 186,

coverage.[390] The rule is no longer limited to cases involving homicide;[391] it encompasses attempted murder[392] and assault and may even be extended to nonassaultive offenses.[393] But the general rule of Rule 404(a)(3) is not without its limitations; "specific acts are admissible only to the extent that they are relevant for a purpose other than character conformity."[394] Character evidence offered under Rule 404(a)(3) is also explicitly limited by Rule 412, which deals with evidence of an alleged victim's previous sexual conduct offered in sexual-assault prosecutions.[395]

Before a defendant can introduce extraneous-misconduct evidence to support the defendant's claim of self-defense under Rule 404(a)(3), "there must be some evidence of a violent or aggressive act by the [victim] that tends to raise the issue of self-defense and that the specific act may explain."[396] The victim's extraneous act will be admissible to support a claim of self-defense if: "1) some ambiguous or uncertain evidence of a

---

188 (Tex. Crim. App. 1971) (evidence of deceased's violent character, though unknown to appellant at the time of the stabbing, was admissible to show that deceased was the first aggressor). In ***Beecham v. State***, the court of criminal appeals expressed the Texas common-law rule:

> The general reputation of the deceased as a violent and dangerous character and specific acts of violence or misconduct of the deceased which show his violent character are admissible in a homicide case where there is evidence of some act of aggression by the deceased which gives rise to a claim of self-defense on the part of the defendant.

580 S.W.2d 588, 590 (Tex. Crim. App. [Panel Op.] 1979).

390. *See **Mozon v. State***, 991 S.W.2d 841, 845 (Tex. Crim. App. 1999); ***Tate v. State***, 981 S.W.2d 189, 192 & n.5 (Tex. Crim. App. 1998); *see also **In re A.A.B.***, 110 S.W.3d 553, 561 (Tex. App.—Waco 2003, no pet.) (Rule 405(b) permits introduction of prior specific instances of conduct when actor's character "'is an essential element of a charge, claim or defense,'" but a victim's character is not an essential element of self-defense (quoting Tex. R. Evid. 405(b))); ***Davis v. State***, 104 S.W.3d 177, 181-82 (Tex. App.—Waco 2003, no pet.) (child's character is not an essential element when defendant seeks to justify his conduct as necessary to discipline child); ***Hernandez v. State***, 774 S.W.2d 319, 327 (Tex. App.—Dallas 1989, pet. ref'd) (discussing codification of Criminal Rule 404(a)(2), now Rule 404(a)(3)); *cf.* MCCORMICK ON EVIDENCE, *supra* note 1, §193, at 571-72 (discussing Federal Rule 404(a)(2), now Rule 404(a)(2)(B), (a)(2)(C)).

391. *See* TEX. R. EVID. 404(a)(3)(A), (a)(3)(B). A murder victim's character evidence is included in the evidence that the Code of Criminal Procedure allows either the State or the defendant to offer in murder prosecutions. *See* TEX. CODE CRIM. PROC. art. 38.36(a) ("In all prosecutions for murder, the state or the defendant shall be permitted to offer testimony as to all relevant facts and circumstances surrounding the killing and the previous relationship existing between the accused and the deceased, together with all relevant facts and circumstances going to show the condition of the mind of the accused at the time of the offense.").

392. *Cf.* ***Kolar v. State***, 705 S.W.2d 794, 798 (Tex. App.—Houston [1st Dist.] 1986, no pet.) (evidence of intended murder victim's character for violence would have been admissible if the proper predicate—evidence of some act of aggression by intended victim—had been laid).

393. *See* Uviller, *supra* note 329, at 856 (defendant accused of bribing a public official might be able to show the official's character for greed or abuse of power to support his defense of extortion by the official); *cf.* 22 WRIGHT & GRAHAM, *supra* note 35, §5237, at 399 (drafters of the Federal Rules chose to abandon the limits of the common-law rules in drafting Rule 404). Because the drafters of the Texas criminal rule must have been aware of the language used in the corresponding civil rule, which applies only to assaultive conduct, it is a logical inference that the rule was intended to apply to more than assaultive offenses.

394. ***Torres v. State***, 71 S.W.3d 758, 760 (Tex. Crim. App. 2002); *accord **Smith v. State***, 355 S.W.3d 138, 150 (Tex. App.—Houston [1st Dist.] 2011, pet. ref'd); *see* TEX. R. EVID. 404(b). Refer to notes 445-577 *infra* and accompanying text.

395. *See* TEX. R. EVID. 404(a)(3)(A). Refer to notes 1011-1095 *infra* and accompanying text. Federal Rule 404(a)(2) contains the same limitation. *See* FED. R. EVID. 404(a)(2)(B).

396. ***Torres***, 71 S.W.3d at 761.

violent or aggressive act by the victim ... exist[s] that tends to show the victim was the first aggressor; and 2) the proffered evidence ... tend[s] to dispel the ambiguity or explain the victim's conduct."[397] If the victim's alleged conduct is unambiguous and needs no explanation, extraneous-misconduct evidence "admitted in conjunction with [the] unambiguous act would have no relevance apart from its tendency to prove the victim's character conformity, and thus would be inadmissible."[398]

Rule 404(a)(3)(B) further provides that in homicide cases, the State may offer evidence of the victim's good character for peacefulness or nonviolence, even if the defendant has not attacked the victim's character for peacefulness, when the defendant offers evidence that the victim was the first aggressor.[399] The prosecution is allowed to initiate the introduction of character evidence in these cases because the deceased cannot testify to his own character.[400] Once the prosecution offers reputation or opinion evidence of the victim's character for nonviolence, the defendant can cross-examine the witness about prior specific instances of violence by the victim.[401]

A defendant charged with an assaultive offense can offer evidence of the victim's character under two separate theories—"communicated character" and "uncommunicated character."[402] Once the defendant offers evidence of the victim's bad character, the prosecution may rebut this evidence with reputation or opinion evidence of the victim's good character.[403] The State may not, however, elicit testimony of the victim's bad character through cross-examination of the defense witnesses or through its own

---

397. **Reyna v. State**, 99 S.W.3d 344, 347 (Tex. App.—Fort Worth 2003, pet. ref'd); *see* **Torres**, 71 S.W.3d at 762.

398. **Reyna**, 99 S.W.3d at 347; *see* TEX. R. EVID. 404(b)(1); *see, e.g.*, **Smith**, 355 S.W.3d at 151 (defendant testified that victim pulled a knife and attempted to stab him first, "both unambiguous acts of aggression and violence that need no explanation"; trial court did not err in excluding evidence of victim's prior acts of violence); **James v. State**, 335 S.W.3d 719, 728 (Tex. App.—Fort Worth 2011, no pet.) (in domestic-assault case, defendant testified that he acted in self-defense because victim attacked him first; because victim's conduct was unambiguous, defendant could not offer evidence of previous incidents in which she attacked him); **London v. State**, 325 S.W.3d 197, 206 (Tex. App.—Dallas 2008, pet. ref'd) (victim's act of shooting at defendant was "an unambiguous act of aggression and violence"; evidence of victim's gang affiliation would do no more than show character conformity and was properly excluded).

399. *See* TEX. R. EVID. 404(a)(3)(B); **Hill v. State**, 748 S.W.2d 314, 316 (Tex. App.—Houston [1st Dist.] 1988, pet. ref'd). The federal rule contains the same provision. *See* FED. R. EVID. 404(a)(2)(C).

400. *See* MCCORMICK ON EVIDENCE, *supra* note 1, §193, at 572-73.

401. *See* TEX. R. EVID. 405(a)(1); *see, e.g.*, **Hill**, 748 S.W.2d at 315-16 (defendant could cross-examine witness about deceased's prior murder conviction but not about deceased's burglary conviction because there was no evidence that the burglary involved acts of violence). For a discussion of proving character through reputation or opinion testimony and of cross-examination of character witnesses, refer to notes 338-348, 355-374 *supra* and accompanying text.

402. **Ex parte Miller**, 330 S.W.3d 610, 618-19 (Tex. Crim. App. 2009); *see* **Mozon v. State**, 991 S.W.2d 841, 845 (Tex. Crim. App. 1999) (discussing two theories for admitting victim's character for violence); **Tate v. State**, 981 S.W.2d 189, 192-93 (Tex. Crim. App. 1998) (discussing historical rationale for admitting evidence of victim's character); **Fry v. State**, 915 S.W.2d 554, 560-61 (Tex. App.—Houston [14th Dist.] 1995, no pet.) (same).

403. **Armstrong v. State**, 718 S.W.2d 686, 695 (Tex. Crim. App. 1985); *see* TEX. R. EVID. 404(a)(3)(A), 405(a)(1). For a discussion of rebuttal character evidence, refer to notes 375-379 *supra* and accompanying text.

Under the corresponding federal rule, the prosecution can also rebut evidence offered by the defendant of the victim's character with evidence of the defendant's same character trait. *See* FED. R. EVID. 404(a)(2)(B)(ii). Thus, if the defendant in a federal murder trial offers evidence of the victim's bad character for violence, then the prosecution may rebut that evidence with evidence that the *defendant* has a bad character for violence.

witnesses and then argue that it is entitled to rebut that testimony.[404] Similarly, the defendant may not convert an eyewitness into a character witness by his own cross-examination.[405]

(1) Communicated character. Under the "communicated character" theory, the defendant may offer testimony of the victim's reputation, opinion, or specific instances of conduct to show the "reasonableness of defendant's claim of apprehension of danger" from the victim.[406] Thus, the defendant will have a valid claim of self-defense if he reasonably believed he was in danger of imminent attack by the victim. The defendant must have either been aware of the victim's reputation for violence or formed an opinion of the victim's character for violence.[407] This theory does not invoke the Rule 404(a)(3) exception because Rule 404 prohibits character evidence only when offered to prove conduct in conformity.[408] The defendant is not attempting to prove that the victim was a violent person or the first aggressor. Rather, the defendant is "proving his own self-defensive state of mind and the reasonableness of that state of mind."[409] This use of character evidence is frequently termed "communicated character"[410] because "the defendant is aware of the victim's violent tendencies and perceives a danger posed by the victim, regardless of whether the danger is real or not."[411] The defendant may offer evidence of either the victim's reputation in the community or the defendant's knowledge of prior specific acts of violence.[412] Rule 403 limits the admissibility of "communicated character" evidence; the trial court has great discretion in determin-

---

404. *Hatley v. State*, 533 S.W.2d 27, 29 (Tex. Crim. App. 1976).

405. *See, e.g.*, ***Rivera v. State***, 82 S.W.3d 64, 67-68 (Tex. App.—San Antonio 2002, pet. ref'd) (defense questioning of eyewitness about victim's prior violent act was not permissible when witness testified about events at scene of crime, not as a character witness; witness's statement that victim was "crazy funny" was not evidence of victim's peaceable character and did not convert fact witness into character witness).

406. *Ex parte Miller*, 330 S.W.3d at 618; ***Dempsey v. State***, 159 Tex. Crim. 602, 605, 266 S.W.2d 875, 877 (1954); *see Torres v. State*, 71 S.W.3d 758, 760 & n.4 (Tex. Crim. App. 2002) (evidence of victim's prior specific violent acts may be admitted to show the reasonableness of defendant's fear if he was aware of those specific acts).

407. *See Dempsey*, 159 Tex. Crim. at 605-07, 266 S.W.2d at 877-78; *see, e.g.*, ***Hayes v. State***, 124 S.W.3d 781, 785-86 (Tex. App.—Houston [1st Dist.] 2003) (evidence of victim's prior assault with a wrench was admissible to show reasonableness of defendant's fear because defendant personally knew of that incident, but evidence of prior assault with a gun was not admissible under this theory because defendant had no knowledge of it), *aff'd*, 161 S.W.3d 507 (Tex. Crim. App. 2005); *see also* ***Gonzales v. State***, 2 S.W.3d 600, 605-06 (Tex. App.—Texarkana 1999, pet. ref'd) (fact that aggravated-assault victim had been convicted of murdering a woman by stabbing her 20 times and proof of another aggravated assault would have been admissible to show that defendant reasonably feared for his own safety if there had been evidence he had known these facts; because there was no such evidence, not error to exclude).

408. *Ex parte Miller*, 330 S.W.3d at 618-19.

409. *Id.* at 619; *see, e.g.*, ***Espinoza v. State***, 951 S.W.2d 100, 102 (Tex. App.—Corpus Christi 1997, pet. ref'd) (reversible error to exclude defendant's offer of evidence to show victim's reputation for violence when defendant testified that he was aware of victim's violent nature).

410. 2 RAY, *supra* note 46, §1493, at 179.

411. *Ex parte Miller*, 330 S.W.3d at 618; *see, e.g.*, ***Mozon v. State***, 991 S.W.2d 841, 845 (Tex. Crim. App. 1999) (when defendant's claim rested on a perceived danger from victim, defendant could present evidence of victim's violent character to show her reasonable belief that force was immediately necessary to protect herself from victim's perceived threat).

412. *See Espinoza*, 951 S.W.2d at 102.

ing whether the evidence's probative value is substantially outweighed by unfair prejudice.[413] For example, the prior instances may be so remote or of such low probative value in showing threatening conduct by the victim, while highly prejudicial in showing deplorable morals or a bad character for law-abidingness, that the court may exclude this evidence under Rule 403.

(2) Uncommunicated character. Under the "uncommunicated character" theory, the defendant may offer reputation or opinion testimony of the victim's violent character to demonstrate that the victim was the first aggressor.[414] This use of character evidence is termed "uncommunicated character" because it does not matter whether the defendant was aware of the victim's violent character.[415] When character evidence is offered under this theory, one witness testifies that the victim made an aggressive move against the defendant, and another witness testifies about the victim's character for violence.[416] This violent character makes it more likely that the victim conformed to his character by acting violently on the occasion in question; this increased likelihood of violent behavior raises the probability that the defendant was in actual danger. Here, however, the defendant must first offer evidence of an actual act of aggression by the victim at the time of the offense.[417]

Evidence that the victim was the first aggressor is relevant only if self-defense is a complete defense to the crime charged. For example, a victim's character for violence or aggression is not pertinent when the defendant is charged with aggravated robbery.[418] Such a defense, that the victim was the first aggressor, is no defense to robbery[419]—stealing another's property by force or threat of force. If the defendant had been charged with aggravated assault, the victim's character for violence might have been relevant.[420] In one case, the Fourteenth Court of Appeals held that if the State

---

413. *See Mozon*, 991 S.W.2d at 846. Refer to notes 111-159 *supra* and accompanying text.

414. *Ex parte Miller*, 330 S.W.3d at 619.

415. *Id.*

416. *Id.* In *Carrasquillo v. State*, the defendant argued that he should have been allowed to offer testimony about the victim's prior homosexual experiences to illustrate the victim's violent character and aggression. 742 S.W.2d 104, 110 (Tex. App.—Fort Worth 1987, no pet.). The court of appeals noted that this argument was "weak at the least," but the court held that even if homosexual acts are indicative of aggression, the exclusion of that evidence was harmless. *Id.*; *see also Peck v. State*, 923 S.W.2d 839, 842-43 (Tex. App.—Tyler 1996, no pet.) (defendant was properly prohibited from offering testimony of victim's reputation as a "troublemaker" because "[a] reputation for being a troublemaker is not a violent or aggressive act by itself"); *Reich-Bacot v. State*, 914 S.W.2d 666, 669 (Tex. App.—Texarkana 1996) (evidence that victim frequently carried a gun was properly excluded because it was within trial court's discretion to consider surrounding circumstances and determine that this was not evidence of his aggressive character), *vacated on other grounds*, 936 S.W.2d 961 (Tex. Crim. App. 1996).

417. *Currie v. State*, 692 S.W.2d 95, 97-98 (Tex. Crim. App. 1985) (act of aggression could include "drawing a gun or knife or reaching for a pocket where one is usually carried"); *Dinkins v. State*, 760 S.W.2d 374, 377 (Tex. App.—Fort Worth 1988, pet. ref'd) (same).

418. *See Patterson v. State*, 783 S.W.2d 268, 272-73 (Tex. App.—Houston [14th Dist.] 1989, pet. ref'd).

419. *See id.*

420. *Id.* at 272.

has conceded or stipulated that the victim was the first aggressor, his character trait for violence is no longer relevant, and thus, the defendant may not offer such evidence under Rule 404(a)(3).[421]

The testimony about the victim's character for violence must be reputation or opinion testimony under Rule 405(a)(1);[422] "the defendant may *not* offer evidence of the victim's prior specific acts of violence to prove the victim's violent character."[423]

Courts have held that Rule 404(a)(3) applies only to the actual victim of the crime, not to someone else who might be acting in concert with the victim.[424] This doctrine probably should not be applied to the use of "communicated character" evidence because that theory involves the defendant's state of mind, not the actual danger posed by the victim or someone acting in concert with him.[425]

5. Rule 404(a)(3)(C) & 405(a)(1): Exception for violent character of assault victim on self-defense issue in a civil case. Rule 404(a)(3)(C) provides that "[i]n a civil case, a party accused of assaultive conduct may offer evidence of the victim's trait of violence

---

421. *See, e.g.,* **Ceasar v. State**, 939 S.W.2d 778, 780 (Tex. App.—Houston [14th Dist.] 1997, pet. ref'd) (because evidence was clear that victim drew his gun first and pointed it at defendant, there was "no evidence of an act which [needed] to be explained by reputation").

422. For a discussion of proving character through reputation or opinion testimony, refer to notes 338-348, 355-357 *supra* and accompanying text.

423. *Ex parte Miller*, 330 S.W.3d 610, 619 (Tex. Crim. App. 2009); *see* Tex. R. Evid. 404(b)(1). Rule 405 prohibits evidence of prior specific instances of violent acts offered to prove conduct in conformity with general character under Rule 404. *See, e.g.,* **Carson v. State**, 986 S.W.2d 24, 27-28 (Tex. App.—San Antonio 1998) (although defendant could introduce evidence of victim's violent or aggressive nature to show that victim was the first aggressor, defendant could not offer evidence of specific instances of victim's violent behavior), *rev'd on other grounds*, 6 S.W.3d 536 (Tex. Crim. App. 1999); **Evans v. State**, 876 S.W.2d 459, 463-64 (Tex. App.—Texarkana 1994, no pet.) (defendant could not offer evidence of prior specific instances of the deceased's condut to prove his character; only opinion and reputation testimony is admissible under Criminal Rule 404(a)(2), now Rule 404(a)(3)(A)). Texas common law was broader and permitted such proof. *See* **Dempsey v. State**, 159 Tex. Crim. 602, 605, 266 S.W.2d 875, 877-78 (1954); *see, e.g.,* **Gonzales v. State**, 838 S.W.2d 848, 859 (Tex. App.—Houston [1st Dist.] 1992) (reversible error when defendant was prevented from offering evidence of prior specific instances to show deceased's character for violence), *pet. dism'd, improvidently granted*, 864 S.W.2d 522 (Tex. Crim. App. 1993).
    Evidence of the victim's prior specific acts of violence are admissible under Rule 404(b), however, when offered to show the victim's specific intent, malice, hostility, or motive in the particular case. *See* Tex. R. Evid. 404(b)(2); *see, e.g.,* **Torres v. State**, 71 S.W.3d 758, 761-62 (Tex. Crim. App. 2002) (defendant could offer evidence that days before the murder, victim had climbed through his ex-girlfriend's aunt's window and threatened the aunt and her children; evidence was relevant to show that victim had a specific motive or intent to be the first aggressor when he climbed through his ex-girlfriend's bathroom window the morning of the murder). The court of criminal appeals reexamined the **Torres** case and concluded that because the defendant had laid a sufficient foundation that the victim was the first aggressor, it was error to exclude the evidence of the earlier confrontation. **Torres v. State**, 117 S.W.3d 891, 896-97 (Tex. Crim. App. 2003); *see also* **Tate v. State**, 981 S.W.2d 189, 193 (Tex. Crim. App. 1998) (evidence of victim's prior specific acts may shed light on his intent or motive in the confrontation); **Davis v. State**, 104 S.W.3d 177, 181-82 (Tex. App.—Waco 2003, no pet.) (defendant, charged with injury to his son, could offer evidence of his son's school disciplinary referrals to establish defendant's state of mind in disciplining his son to support his defense that he reasonably believed force was necessary to discipline the child). For a discussion of Rule 404(b), refer to notes 445-577 *infra* and accompanying text.

424. *See, e.g.,* **Hernandez v. State**, 774 S.W.2d 319, 327-28 (Tex. App.—Dallas 1989, pet. ref'd) (defendant could not introduce evidence of the victim's uncle's violent character to show defendant's state of mind).

425. *See* 1 Goode et al., *supra* note 103, §404.4, at 196-97 & n.19 (3d ed. 2002 & Supp. 2007); *see also* **Mozon v. State**, 991 S.W.2d 841, 845-46 (Tex. Crim. App. 1999) (victim's acts of violence against third persons would be relevant though subject to exclusion under Rule 403).

to prove self-defense, and if the evidence is admitted, the accusing party may offer evidence of the victim's trait of peacefulness."[426] As noted above, there is a threshold requirement in criminal cases for the admissibility of evidence of the alleged victim's violent character or other violent acts—this evidence is admissible only when "there is evidence of some act of aggression by the [victim] which gives rise to a claim of self-defense on the part of the defendant."[427] Although no such explicit requirement has been articulated for civil assault cases, the criminal evidentiary doctrine could serve as a useful corollary to the general principles of relevance announced in Rules 401 through 403.

Except for the burden of proof, the law of self-defense in Texas is the same in civil and criminal cases.[428] Since the adoption of the Texas Penal Code, Texas courts have looked to the Penal Code for the law of self-defense in civil assault cases.[429] Thus, precedent established in criminal cases should be persuasive in civil assault cases for both "communicated" and "uncommunicated" character. The Penal Code specifies that "a person is justified in using force against another when and to the degree the actor reasonably believes the force is immediately necessary to protect the actor against the other's use or attempted use of unlawful force."[430] The Texas Court of Criminal Appeals has interpreted this provision to allow the plea of self-defense in two situations: (1) when the defendant was in actual danger from the alleged victim's violent behavior and (2) when the defendant was, from his own perspective, in apparent danger from the alleged victim's behavior.[431] In both situations, especially the second, the defendant's belief about the alleged victim's conduct and the ensuing or apparent danger to the defendant must have been reasonable.[432] Another requirement for both theories of self-defense is that the degree of force used by the defendant to counter the real or apparent danger from the victim must have been reasonable.[433]

---

426. TEX. R. EVID. 404(a)(3)(C). The definition of "victim" in Rule 404 includes an alleged victim. TEX. R. EVID. 404(a)(5). Federal Rules 404(a)(2)(B) and 404(a)(2)(C) apply only in criminal cases. Refer to note 381 *supra* and accompanying text.

427. *Beecham v. State*, 580 S.W.2d 588, 590 (Tex. Crim. App. [Panel Op.] 1979); *see also Brown v. State*, 632 S.W.2d 191, 193 (Tex. App.—Waco 1982, no pet.) (such evidence is admissible in a homicide case). Refer to notes 388-425 *supra* and accompanying text.

428. *Gibbins v. Berlin*, 162 S.W.3d 335, 340 (Tex. App.—Fort Worth 2005, no pet.); *Rogers v. Peeler*, 146 S.W.3d 765, 769 (Tex. App.—Texarkana 2004, no pet.).

429. *See Gibbins*, 162 S.W.3d at 340; *Rogers*, 146 S.W.3d at 769; *Forbes v. Lanzl*, 9 S.W.3d 895, 901 (Tex. App.—Austin 2000, pet. denied).

430. TEX. PENAL CODE §9.31(a). Penal Code §9.31(a) includes factors that give rise to a presumption that the defendant reasonably believed that force was immediately necessary. *See id.*

431. *See Semaire v. State*, 612 S.W.2d 528, 530 (Tex. Crim. App. 1980) (a person is justified in using force when he has a reasonable apprehension that force is required to protect himself); *see, e.g., Bennett v. State*, 726 S.W.2d 32, 38 (Tex. Crim. App. 1986) (jury could reject defendant's self-defense claim only if it believed victim acted lawfully and if defendant, at the moment he acted, also reasonably believed victim acted lawfully).

432. *See, e.g., Valentine v. State*, 587 S.W.2d 399, 400-01 (Tex. Crim. App. [Panel Op.] 1979) (trial court correctly instructed the jury that the defendant is only required to reasonably believe that the deceased was using or intended to use deadly force). This interpretation of the reasonableness requirement follows pre-Penal Code law. *See Jones v. State*, 544 S.W.2d 139, 142 (Tex. Crim. App. 1976).

433. *See Jones*, 544 S.W.2d at 142.

If this interpretation of the Penal Code also applies to self-defense pleas in civil assault cases,[434] Rule 404(a)(3)(C) appears to apply primarily, if not exclusively, to situations of actual danger to the defendant from the plaintiff's violent behavior. Rule 404(a)(3)(C) admits evidence of the plaintiff's character, by means of reputation or opinion testimony,[435] to prove conforming conduct. Rule 404(b) explicitly forbids a witness from testifying on direct examination to specific instances of conduct to prove the plaintiff's violent character if the aim is to show conforming violent conduct, and Rule 405 implicitly includes the same prohibition.[436] If the defendant in the civil assault suit has offered evidence of the plaintiff's character under the defendant's plea of self-defense, Rules 404(a)(3)(C) and 405(a)(1) allow the plaintiff to rebut this evidence by offering reputation or opinion testimony on the plaintiff's character for peacefulness.[437] In cross-examining the defendant's witness who is testifying to the plaintiff's character for violence, or in cross-examining the plaintiff's witness called to rebut this testimony, the cross-examining party can ask about specific instances of conduct under Rule 405(a) using "have you heard" or "did you know" questions.[438]

When the issue is the reasonableness of the defendant's belief about the actual or apparent danger to himself, Rule 404(a)(3)(C) does not apply—the defendant is trying to prove his own belief and reasonableness, not to use evidence of the plaintiff's character to prove the plaintiff's conforming conduct. In this situation, the general principles of relevance expressed in Rules 401 through 403 govern.[439] These principles suggest that when the defendant's belief or the reasonableness of that belief is in issue, the defendant must have known at the time of the litigated event of the plaintiff's violent character, or of previous acts by the plaintiff indicating a violent character, before evidence of such character or acts would be admissible.[440] Under the general principles of relevance expressed in Rules 401 through 403, the defendant's belief or the reason-

---

434. *Cf.* WILLIAM L. PROSSER, HANDBOOK OF THE LAW OF TORTS §19, at 108-12 (4th ed. 1971) (the elements of self-defense are (1) real danger to defendant or his reasonable belief that danger existed and (2) reasonable degree of force).

435. For a discussion of proving character through reputation or opinion testimony in criminal cases, refer to notes 338-348 *supra* and accompanying text. The standards for proving character in civil cases are applicable in the same manner as those in criminal cases.

436. Refer to notes 355-357 *supra* and accompanying text.

437. For a discussion of rebuttal character evidence in criminal cases, refer to notes 375-379 *supra* and accompanying text. The standards for rebuttal character evidence in civil cases are applicable in the same manner as those in criminal cases.

438. Refer to notes 369-374 *supra* and accompanying text.

439. Refer to notes 406-413 *supra* and accompanying text.

440. As the Texas Supreme Court explained:
> [t]here being direct proof before the court as to the battery [of plaintiff by defendant], it is not perceived that the court erred in refusing to admit evidence of the character of the plaintiff, and especially so, as it appears from the evidence that the plaintiff was unknown to the defendant, and [the defendant] could not, therefore, have been influenced in his conduct by anything other than what occurred at the time of the battery ....

McCormick v. Schtrenck, 59 Tex. Civ. App. 139, 143, 130 S.W. 720, 721 (Austin 1910, no writ) (quoting **Shook v. Peters**, 59 Tex. 393, 396 (1883)). The general common law also followed this position. *See* PROSSER, *supra* note 434,

ableness of that belief may be proved by evidence of the plaintiff's reputation, opinion of the plaintiff's character, or specific instances of the plaintiff's conduct. Rules 404 and 405 do not apply in this situation. Those rules address evidence of character to show conforming conduct (provable by reputation or opinion) and character as an ultimate issue (provable by reputation, opinion, or specific instances of conduct); they do not address evidence of reputation, opinion, or specific acts as circumstantial evidence to prove issues other than character.

In civil assault cases, as in criminal assault prosecutions, evidence of prior specific instances of the plaintiff's aggression may be admissible under Rule 404(b) for a specific noncharacter purpose, such as to prove the plaintiff's intent, motive, or state of mind.[441] When the plaintiff's conduct is offered to show the *defendant's* state of mind, as under the "communicated character" theory of character evidence, Rule 404(b) does not apply.[442]

6. Rule 404(a)(4): Exception for character of a witness. Rule 404(a)(4), the third exception to the general prohibition of Rule 404(a), provides that "[e]vidence of a witness's character may be admitted under Rules 607, 608, and 609."[443] Rules 607, 608, and 609 deal with the general problem of impeaching and rehabilitating witnesses with character evidence. These rules contain their own provisions governing the general admissibility and modes of proof of such character evidence.[444]

B. Rule 404(b): Evidence of Other Crimes, Wrongs, or Acts to Show "Other Purposes"

Rule 404(a) generally prohibits the use of character evidence to prove conforming conduct, except as provided by Rules 404(a)(2) through 404(a)(4).[445] Rule 404(b)(1) elaborates on the general exclusionary principle of Rule 404(a) by specifying that evidence of other crimes, wrongs, or acts committed by a person is not admissible to "show

---

§19, at 109 (evidence of defendant's "state of mind and nerves, and the threats, *past conduct*, and *reputation* of his assailant *which may have induced it*, is important and admissible on the issue of what was reasonable") (emphasis added).

When a defendant pleaded self-defense and sought to prove his reasonable belief that the victim's conduct endangered him, earlier Texas law admitted evidence of the victim's reputation or of specific instances of the victim's conduct, but not evidence of opinion about the victim's conduct, if the defendant knew of such reputation or prior conduct at the time of the assault. *See Lowe v. State*, 612 S.W.2d 579, 580-81 (Tex. Crim. App. 1981); *Beecham v. State*, 580 S.W.2d 588, 590 (Tex. Crim. App. [Panel Op.] 1979); *Lewis v. State*, 463 S.W.2d 186, 188 (Tex. Crim. App. 1971); *Dempsey v. State*, 159 Tex. Crim. 602, 605, 266 S.W.2d 875, 877 (1954). The Rules imply that opinion evidence is also admissible on this point if the defendant was aware of the opinion at the time of the litigated event. *See* Tex. R. Evid. 404(a)(3), 405(a)(1), (b).

441. *E.g., Rogers v. Peeler*, 146 S.W.3d 765, 773-75 (Tex. App.—Texarkana 2004, no pet.) (applying criminal-law standards in civil case; defendant's prior acts of aggression were admissible to show his intent and motive when he claimed self-defense). Refer to notes 445-577 *infra* and accompanying text.

442. Refer to notes 406-413 *supra* and accompanying text.

443. Tex. R. Evid. 404(a)(4); *see Hammer v. State*, 296 S.W.3d 555, 563 (Tex. Crim. App. 2009).

444. Refer to *Article VI: Witnesses, infra* p. 596.

445. Refer to notes 322-444 *supra* and accompanying text.

that on a particular occasion the person acted in accordance with the character."[446] The evidence offered under the rule may be either prior or subsequent crimes, wrongs, or acts.[447] Rule 404(b)(2) qualifies the general prohibition by allowing evidence of other crimes, wrongs, or acts for "another purpose."[448] The other purposes include, but are not limited to,[449] mental states such as motive, intent, and knowledge, as well as elements such as opportunity, preparation, plan, identity, absence of mistake, and lack of accident.[450] The proponent of the evidence "must be able to explain to the trial court, and to the opponent, the logical and legal rationales that support its admission on a basis other than 'bad character' or propensity purpose."[451] Rule 404(b) embodies the traditional Texas rule.[452]

---

446. Tex. R. Evid. 404(b)(1). The 2015 restyling of Rule 404(b) changed the phrase "in conformity" to "in accordance." *See* Tex. R. Evid. 404(b)(1). No substantive change was intended. *See* Tex. Sup. Ct. Order, Misc. Docket No. 15-9048, §2 (eff. Apr. 1, 2015).

447. *See, e.g.*, **Mason v. State**, 99 S.W.3d 652, 656 (Tex. App.—Eastland 2003, pet. ref'd) (admitting evidence of extraneous 2001 drug transaction as circumstantial evidence of defendant's knowing possession of cocaine in 1999); **Powell v. State**, 5 S.W.3d 369, 383 (Tex. App.—Texarkana 1999, pet. ref'd) (evidence that defendant traveled on same highway with multiple bags of cocaine only a few weeks after charged offense was admissible to show defendant intended to deliver the cocaine involved in charged offense); *cf.* **United States v. Peterson**, 244 F.3d 385, 392-93 (5th Cir. 2001) (evidence of later misconduct may be admissible to demonstrate earlier intent; sequence of events may affect possible inferences but does not necessarily preclude admission of evidence of later events).

448. Tex. R. Evid. 404(b)(2); *see* **Rankin v. State**, 974 S.W.2d 707, 709 (Tex. Crim. App. 1996). In **Rankin**, the court stated: "if evidence (1) is introduced for a purpose other than character conformity, (2) has relevance to a 'fact of consequence' in the case and (3) remains free of any other constitutional or statutory prohibitions, it is admissible." 974 S.W.2d at 709. If the opposing party objects, the proponent must explain precisely how the proffered evidence is probative of a fact of consequence. *See id.*

449. The other purposes listed in Rule 404(b)(2) are not mutually exclusive or collectively exhaustive. **De La Paz v. State**, 279 S.W.3d 336, 343 (Tex. Crim. App. 2009); **Montgomery v. State**, 810 S.W.2d 372, 377 (Tex. Crim. App. 1990) (orig. op.); **Sandoval v. State**, 409 S.W.3d 259, 297 (Tex. App.—Austin 2013, no pet.); *see* **Banda v. State**, 768 S.W.2d 294, 296 (Tex. Crim. App. 1989) (catalogue of "other purposes" is not exhaustive, and "[w]hether or not it neatly fits one of these categories, an extraneous transaction will be admissible so long as it logically tends to make the existence of some fact of consequence more or less probable"); **Hedrick v. State**, 473 S.W.3d 824, 830 (Tex. App.—Houston [14th Dist.] 2015, no pet.) ("Texas courts recognize 'consciousness of guilt' as an exception to rule 404(b)'s general prohibition against evidence of extraneous offenses. Acts that are designed to reduce the likelihood of prosecution, conviction, or incarceration for the offense on trial are admissible under rule 404(b) as showing 'consciousness of guilt.'").

450. Tex. R. Evid. 404(b)(2); *see* **Devoe v. State**, 354 S.W.3d 457, 469 (Tex. Crim. App. 2011); **Williams v. State**, 301 S.W.3d 675, 687 (Tex. Crim. App. 2009); **Moses v. State**, 105 S.W.3d 622, 626 (Tex. Crim. App. 2003).

451. *De La Paz*, 279 S.W.3d at 343.

452. The prohibition in Rule 404(b)(1) was formerly expressed as a general admonition in criminal cases that "[t]he accused is entitled to be tried on the accusation made in the state's pleading and he should not be tried for some collateral crime nor for being a criminal generally." **Crank v. State**, 761 S.W.2d 328, 341 (Tex. Crim. App. 1988); *see also* **Albrecht v. State**, 486 S.W.2d 97, 100 (Tex. Crim. App. 1972) (although evidence of the defendant's prior criminal conduct is inherently prejudicial, it can be legally relevant). Evidence showing the commission of an uncharged crime was usually excluded, even if it had probative value, because it tended to confuse the issues and forced the defendant to defend himself against charges for which he had not been given prior notice. *Albrecht*, 486 S.W.2d at 100. However, the general prohibition against the admissibility of extraneous offenses was virtually swallowed up by specific common-law exceptions. *See id.* at 100-01 (listing six specific purposes for which evidence of extraneous offenses was admissible under the common law—to prove res gestae, identity, scienter, malice or state of mind, or motive, or to refute a defensive theory). This "laundry list" of specific exceptions led Texas courts to force given sets of facts into rigid categories without sufficiently analyzing whether the evidence was relevant for that particular purpose. *See* **De La Paz**, 279 S.W.3d at 343; **Williams v. State**, 662 S.W.2d 344, 346 (Tex. Crim. App. 1983).

Texas civil cases follow the analysis established for criminal cases: instances of prior misconduct are inadmissible to prove character but are admissible for some other relevant purpose.[453] The traditional Texas civil rule had been that proof of similar acts at or about the same time was admissible as tending to explain the motive for the act under investigation when it was necessary to decide, for example, whether the act was done with intent to defraud or with other evil intent.[454] Rule 404(b) follows this analysis because the other fraudulent acts would be offered as circumstantial evidence of a fraudulent intent on the litigated occasion, not to prove bad character.

On its face, Rule 404(b)(2) permits the use of other crimes by both the defense and the prosecution in a criminal case.[455] Some commentators call this "reverse 404(b)

Shortly before the adoption of the Criminal Rules, the court of criminal appeals in **Williams** adopted a much broader statement of admissibility. 662 S.W.2d at 346. The court noted that extraneous transactions constituting offenses committed by the accused may be admissible on a showing by the prosecution that (1) the transaction is relevant to a material issue in the case and (2) the relevance value of the evidence outweighs its inflammatory or prejudicial potential. *Id.* Because a propensity to commit crimes is not a material fact in either criminal or civil cases, the **Williams** test adequately expresses the "other purposes" test of Rule 404(b). Rule 403, however, changed the focus of the inquiry from determining whether the "relevancy value of the evidence outweighs its inflammatory or prejudicial potential" of the **Williams** test to determining whether the evidence's "probative value is *substantially* outweighed" by the rule's counterfactors. **Crank**, 761 S.W.2d at 342 n.5. Refer to notes 111-159 *supra* and accompanying text.

The court of criminal appeals later expressed the **Albrecht** exceptions in somewhat different terms. In **Santellan v. State**, the court stated that the proponent of extraneous acts must persuade the court that the evidence
"tends to establish some elemental fact, such as identity or intent; that it tends to establish some evidentiary fact, such as motive, opportunity or preparation, leading inferentially to an elemental fact; or that it rebuts a defensive theory by showing, e.g. absence of mistake or accident. ... [or] that it is relevant upon a logical inference not anticipated by the rulemakers."
939 S.W.2d 155, 168-69 (Tex. Crim. App. 1997) (quoting **Montgomery v. State**, 810 S.W.2d 372, 387-88 (Tex. Crim. App. 1991) (op. on reh'g)).

453. *See, e.g.*, **Burton v. Kirby**, 775 S.W.2d 834, 837 (Tex. App.—Austin 1989, no writ) (evidence of defendant's prior use of excessive force was not admissible to prove excessive force on the occasion in question); **Lovelace v. Sabine Consol., Inc.**, 733 S.W.2d 648, 654 (Tex. App.—Houston [14th Dist.] 1987, writ denied) (evidence of defendant's negligence on one occasion was not admissible to prove negligence on the occasion in question); **Amoco Chems. Corp. v. Stafford**, 663 S.W.2d 147, 148-49 (Tex. App.—Houston [1st Dist.] 1983, no writ) (prior DWI convictions were inadmissible to prove that defendant was intoxicated on the occasion in question). However, evidence of other crimes, wrongs, or acts is admissible to show a plan or scheme. See **Johnson v. J. Hiram Moore, Ltd.**, 763 S.W.2d 496, 500 (Tex. App.—Austin 1988, writ denied); *see, e.g.*, **Aztec Life Ins. v. Dellana**, 667 S.W.2d 911, 915 (Tex. App.—Austin 1984, no writ) (insurance company's previous consistent denial of claims was admissible to show a plan or scheme); *cf.* **Vance v. Union Planters Corp.**, 209 F.3d 438, 445-46 (5th Cir. 2000) (evidence that bank had prior adverse verdict in pay-discrimination case was admissible in Title VII trial to rebut bank's defense that it chose not to hire plaintiff because of administrative concerns). Such evidence may also be admissible to prove character and culpability for purposes of punitive damages. *See, e.g.*, **Castro v. Sebesta**, 808 S.W.2d 189, 194 (Tex. App.—Houston [1st Dist.] 1991, no writ) (evidence that defendant in personal-injury lawsuit regularly smoked marijuana while driving a car should have been admitted under Rule 404(b) to show his actual level of culpability when jury was responsible for determining punitive damages).

454. **Posey v. Hanson**, 196 S.W. 731, 733 (Tex. Civ. App.—Austin 1917, no writ); *see also* **Bach v. Hudson**, 596 S.W.2d 673, 677 (Tex. Civ. App.—Corpus Christi 1980, no writ) (mental capacity); **Tex. Farm Bureau Mut. Ins. v. Baker**, 596 S.W.2d 639, 643 (Tex. Civ. App.—Tyler 1980, writ ref'd n.r.e.) (intent); **Payne v. Hartford Fire Ins.**, 409 S.W.2d 591, 594 (Tex. Civ. App.—Beaumont 1966, writ ref'd n.r.e.) (plan, scheme, system, or design); **Bridges v. Bridges**, 404 S.W.2d 48, 51-52 (Tex. Civ. App.—Beaumont 1966, no writ) (knowledge).

455. *See* **Torres v. State**, 71 S.W.3d 758, 760-62 (Tex. Crim. App. 2002); *cf.* **United States v. Vaglica**, 720 F.2d 388, 393-94 (5th Cir. 1983) (evidence is not barred under Federal Rule 404(b) when offered on behalf of criminal defendant).

evidence."[456] Typically, the defense seeks to offer evidence of crimes or acts by a third person to prove that the third person, not the defendant, committed the charged offense.[457] In other situations, the defense may offer evidence of a third person's prior acts to show that person's intent or motive for the present act.[458] Although the standard of admissibility should not be as high for defensive uses of Rule 404(b),[459] few trial judges admit such evidence, and these decisions are usually upheld on appeal.[460]

A defendant's opening statement may directly raise a defensive theory, including identity, intent, motive, knowledge, or opportunity to commit the charged offense.[461] If so, the State can then offer extraneous-offense evidence under Rule 404(b)(2) to rebut that theory.[462] At least one court has held that a defendant may rebut anticipated

---

456. 1 MUELLER & KIRKPATRICK, *supra* note 364, §115, at 684; *see Torres*, 71 S.W.3d at 761 n.5.

457. *See Wiley v. State*, 74 S.W.3d 399, 406 (Tex. Crim. App. 2002) (defendant who offers evidence of alleged alternative perpetrator must show that this evidence, on its own or in combination with other evidence, is sufficient to establish nexus between crime charged and alleged alternative perpetrator); *see, e.g., Dickson v. State*, 246 S.W.3d 733, 740-41 (Tex. App.—Houston [14th Dist.] 2007, pet. ref'd) (in prosecution for aggravated robbery, trial court did not err in excluding defendant's offered alternative-perpetrator evidence because it showed nothing other than robberies occurring around the same time; no nexus between crime charged and alleged alternative perpetrator); *Alonzo v. State*, 67 S.W.3d 346, 361 (Tex. App.—Waco 2001) (defendant had a constitutional right to present alternative-perpetrator evidence via police videotape despite hearsay rules), *pet. dism'd, improvidently granted*, 158 S.W.3d 515 (Tex. Crim. App. 2005); *cf. United States v. Stevens*, 935 F.2d 1380, 1404 (3d Cir. 1991) (defendant may offer similar other-crimes evidence that, alone or with other evidence, tends to negate his guilt). *See generally* Claudia G. Catalano, *Admissibility of Evidence of Commission of Similar Crime by One Other Than Accused*, 22 A.L.R.5th 1 (1994 & Supp. 2006).

458. *See Torres*, 71 S.W.3d at 760-61. The defendant in *Torres* also offered evidence of the victim's violent character under Rule 404(a)(2), now Rule 404(a)(3). Refer to note 423 *supra*.

459. *Cf. United States v. Aboumoussallem*, 726 F.2d 906, 911 (2d Cir. 1984) (discussing Federal Rule 404(b); "the standard of admissibility when a criminal defendant offers similar acts evidence as a shield need not be as restrictive as when a prosecutor uses such evidence as a sword").

460. *Cf. United States v. Walton*, 217 F.3d 443, 449-50 (7th Cir. 2000) (in ATM-theft case, evidence of similar unsolved ATM theft occurring four months before charged offense was properly excluded under Federal Rule 404(b) because evidence did not prove or disprove defendants' involvement in the charged offense); *United States v. Dakins*, 872 F.2d 1061, 1063 (D.C. Cir. 1989) (evidence of police officer's other acts, offered to show likelihood of entrapment, was inadmissible as it might prejudice the jury against the police and divert attention from defendant's own guilt or innocence; evidence was properly excluded under Federal Rules 403, 404(b), and 608(b)); *United States v. Wright*, 783 F.2d 1091, 1100 (D.C. Cir. 1986) (evidence that defendant threatened a third person with a gun, offered to show duress of codefendant, was properly excluded under Federal Rule 404(b)).

461. *See De La Paz v. State*, 279 S.W.3d 336, 344-45 (Tex. Crim. App. 2009); *Bass v. State*, 270 S.W.3d 557, 563 (Tex. Crim. App. 2008); *Powell v. State*, 63 S.W.3d 435, 438-39 (Tex. Crim. App. 2001); *Leassear v. State*, 465 S.W.3d 293, 303 (Tex. App.—Houston [14th Dist.] 2015, no pet.); *see, e.g., Sharper v. State*, 485 S.W.3d 612, 621 (Tex. App.—Texarkana 2016, no pet.) (defendant put identity in issue during opening statement by arguing that earlier suspect in case was the more likely perpetrator, and then continued this theory in cross-examination of State's witnesses over police investigation of this other suspect); *Knight v. State*, 457 S.W.3d 192, 202-03 (Tex. App.—El Paso 2015, pet. ref'd) (in opening statement in prosecution for possession of controlled substance, defendant argued that State could not prove she intentionally and knowingly possessed hydrocodone and also asserted mistake as defense to her receipt of drug). The defensive theory is sometimes presented more broadly than the nonconformity purposes listed in Rule 404(b)(2), such as a "fabrication" defense. *See Bass*, 270 S.W.3d at 563 & n.8; *Banks v. State*, 494 S.W.3d 883, 892-93 (Tex. App.—Houston [14th Dist.] 2016, pet. ref'd); *Tucker v. State*, 456 S.W.3d 194, 205-06 (Tex. App.—San Antonio 2014, pet. ref'd).

462. *See De La Paz*, 279 S.W.3d at 346-47; *Bass*, 270 S.W.3d at 563; *Powell*, 63 S.W.3d at 439-40; *see, e.g., Petetan v. State*, ___ S.W.3d ___ (Tex. Crim. App. 2017) (No. AP-77,038; 3-8-17) (in opening statement, defense insinuated that another person murdered victim while "high" and "angry"; statement opened the door to rebuttal evidence offered to prove that defendant planned to murder victim and frame this other person for crime); *Dabney v. State*,

extraneous-offense evidence based on reasonable reliance on the State's opening statement.[463]

Rule 404(b) is substantively identical to Federal Rule 404(b),[464] except for a distinction in the notice provision.[465] The Advisory Committee on the Federal Rules noted that the admissibility of evidence for purposes other than to show character conformity should not be absolute, but rather discretionary and based on balancing the probative value of the evidence against its prejudicial impact and the availability of other means of proof.[466] This "balancing" under Rule 404(b) implies the use of the Rule 403 balancing test, which is the same in federal and Texas courts.[467]

Introducing evidence for a purpose other than character conformity is not sufficient to make that evidence admissible.[468] The evidence's admissibility also depends on its relevance to a fact of consequence in the case; the phrase "fact of consequence" includes an elemental fact (such as identity or intent) or an evidentiary fact (such as motive) from which an elemental fact can be inferred.[469] An evidentiary fact that is uncon-

---

492 S.W.3d 309, 317 (Tex. Crim. App. 2016) (opening statement asserting that defendant did not know there was a methamphetamine lab on his property opened the door for rebuttal evidence that police had previously found such a lab on his property); **Hedrick v. State**, 473 S.W.3d 824, 832-33 (Tex. App.—Houston [14th Dist.] 2015, no pet.) (during opening statement, defense introduced theory that witness went to police only because she was upset that defendant had moved on from their relationship; trial court did not abuse discretion in admitting rebuttal evidence that defendant ransacked witness's apartment just before she went to police).

463. *E.g.*, **Lopez v. State**, 288 S.W.3d 148, 171-72 (Tex. App.—Corpus Christi 2009, pet. ref'd) ("Under **Powell** and its progeny, we find it difficult to discern why [defendant] could not rely on [State's] opening statement as to what evidence the State intended to present, and rebut this anticipated prosecutorial evidence during the State's case-in-chief as opposed to waiting until his case-in-chief.").

464. As noted by Mueller & Kirkpatrick:

> Proof of specific acts of violence by the victim toward the defendant is often admissible to show hostility, plan, intent to inflict harm, and similar matters. Here the argument is not so much that the acts show character, hence conduct in conformity with character, but rather that the acts shed direct light on more particular aspects of the victim's outlook or state of mind toward the defendant, and the proof is admissible under FRE 404(b).

1 MUELLER & KIRKPATRICK, *supra* note 364, §103, at 569-70 (2d ed.1994).

465. Refer to note 588 *infra* and accompanying text.

466. *See* FED. R. EVID. 404 advisory committee's note, subdiv. (b). After examining the approach of the Federal Rules to this balancing, Weinstein and Berger concluded that once evidence satisfies the relevance requirements of Rule 402, Rule 404(b) requires the court to assess the probative worth of the evidence and to weigh it against the factors specified in Rule 403. 2 WEINSTEIN & BERGER, *supra* note 84, ¶404[08], at 404-49; *see also* **United States v. Beechum**, 582 F.2d 898, 911 (5th Cir. 1978) (en banc) (applying a two-step test to determine admissibility of evidence under Federal Rule 404(b): (1) determine whether the evidence is relevant, and (2) determine whether the probative value is not substantially outweighed by prejudice).

467. *See* **United States v. Myers**, 589 F.3d 117, 124 (4th Cir. 2009); **Montgomery v. State**, 810 S.W.2d 372, 377 (Tex. Crim. App. 1990) (orig. op.); **Crank v. State**, 761 S.W.2d 328, 342 & n.5 (Tex. Crim. App. 1988).

468. **Rankin v. State**, 974 S.W.2d 707, 709 (Tex. Crim. App. 1996); *see* **Leassear v. State**, 465 S.W.3d 293, 303 (Tex. App.—Houston [14th Dist.] 2015, no pet.).

469. *See* **Henley v. State**, 493 S.W.3d 77, 84 (Tex. Crim. App. 2016); **Rankin**, 974 S.W.2d at 709-10. For example, intent to speed is not an element in the offense of speeding. *See* TEX. TRANSP. CODE §§545.351, 545.352. Thus, other acts of misconduct offered to show a driver's intent or offered to show motive, from which one could infer intent, would not be admissible in a hearing involving a speeding ticket.

nected to any elemental fact is not a fact of consequence for purposes of either Rule 401 or Rule 404(b).[470]

Under either the Federal or Texas Rules, the "true test" of the admissibility of extraneous offenses involves a two-part balancing test:

(1) Is the extraneous-misconduct evidence relevant to a fact of consequence in the case apart from its tendency to prove conduct in conformity with character?[471]

(2) Is the probative value of the evidence strong enough that it is not substantially outweighed by unfair prejudice?[472]

If the answer is "yes" to both, then the evidence is admitted. If the answer is "no" to either, then the evidence is excluded.[473] The first question refers to Rule 404(b), and the second refers to the Rule 403 balancing test.[474] The proponent of the evidence must be prepared to demonstrate why the answer to both questions is "Yes," and the opponent must object under *both* rules to preserve and address the second question. If the opponent does not object under Rule 403, neither the trial court nor the appellate court will consider the prejudicial effect of the extraneous offense.[475]

The extraneous conduct does not need to constitute the commission of a criminal offense or result in any official sanction.[476] A federal court may admit evidence of an

---

470. In *Rankin*, the court of criminal appeals noted the following:

> A court that articulates the relevancy of evidence to an evidentiary fact but does not, in any way, draw the inference to an elemental fact has not completed the necessary relevancy inquiry because it has not shown how the evidence makes a "fact of consequence" in the case more or less likely.

974 S.W.2d at 710.

471. *See* FED. R. EVID. 404(b); TEX. R. EVID. 404(b); *United States v. Phaknikone*, 605 F.3d 1099, 1107 (11th Cir. 2010); *Torres v. State*, 71 S.W.3d 758, 760 (Tex. Crim. App. 2002). As part of the relevance analysis under Federal Rule 404(b), "there must be sufficient proof so that a jury could find that the defendant committed the extrinsic act." *Phaknikone*, 605 F.3d at 1107.

472. Refer to notes 111-159 *supra* and accompanying text.

473. *United States v. Beechum*, 582 F.2d 898, 911 (5th Cir. 1978) (en banc); *Montgomery v. State*, 810 S.W.2d 372, 387-88 (Tex. Crim. App. 1991) (op. on reh'g); *see Williams v. State*, 662 S.W.2d 344, 346 (Tex. Crim. App. 1983); *Hartsfield v. State*, 305 S.W.3d 859, 871 (Tex. App.—Texarkana 2010, pet. ref'd).

474. These rules work in tandem, regardless of other statutes that might appear to implicitly permit the admission of extraneous acts under other standards without regard to Rules 404(b) and 403. For example, in *Smith v. State*, the court of criminal appeals held that Texas Code of Criminal Procedure article 38.36(a), which permits both the State and defendant to offer "'all relevant facts and circumstances surrounding the killing and the previous relationship existing between the accused and the deceased'" in a homicide case, does not abrogate the application of Rules 404(b) and 403 to that evidence. 5 S.W.3d 673, 676-77 (Tex. Crim. App. 1999) (quoting TEX. CODE CRIM. PROC. art. 38.36(a)). Article 38.36(a) is a statute defining relevant evidence in a homicide case; it does not mandate the introduction of that evidence if it would be prohibited by other evidentiary rules. *See Smith*, 5 S.W.3d at 678-79. Refer to notes 578-585 *infra* and accompanying text.

475. *See Montgomery*, 810 S.W.2d at 388 (op. on reh'g); *Lum v. State*, 903 S.W.2d 365, 371 (Tex. App.—Texarkana 1995, pet. ref'd).

476. *See Brandley v. State*, 691 S.W.2d 699, 706 (Tex. Crim. App. 1985) ("The established rule in this area applies to extraneous transactions which include but are not limited to acts which are offenses."); *In re V.V.*, 349 S.W.3d 548, 557 n.3 (Tex. App.—Houston [1st Dist.] 2010, pet. denied) (Rule 404(b) does not require final conviction as predicate to admission of extraneous-offense evidence if that evidence is otherwise relevant and admissible); *Shugart v. State*, 796 S.W.2d 288, 293 (Tex. App.—Beaumont 1990, pet. ref'd) (extraneous offense is "any act of misconduct, whether resulting in prosecution or not"). The court of criminal appeals has held that Rule 404(b) excludes

extraneous act even if the defendant has been acquitted of that offense.[477] In addressing the burden of proof necessary to make an extraneous act admissible under Federal Rule 404(b), the U.S. Supreme Court held that the trial judge addresses the admissibility of an extraneous offense under Rule 104(a) by a preponderance of the evidence and that the issue of whether the defendant committed the uncharged offense is a question of conditional relevancy under Rule 104(b).[478] Thus, evidence of the extraneous conduct "should be admitted if there is sufficient evidence to support a finding by the jury that the defendant committed the similar act."[479]

The Texas Court of Criminal Appeals, however, explicitly rejected the federal standard and declared that the burden of proof for the admission of extraneous offenses in Texas is proof beyond a reasonable doubt.[480] Accordingly, when the trial court is deciding whether to admit extraneous-offense evidence, it must make an initial determination under Rule 104(b) that "a jury could find beyond a reasonable doubt that the defendant committed the extraneous offense."[481] This distinction between the federal

---

only evidence of bad conduct; it does not address the admissibility of evidence of bad thoughts such as statements by the defendant of his desire to kidnap or kill a person. *Moreno v. State*, 858 S.W.2d 453, 463-64 (Tex. Crim. App. 1993); *see Petetan v. State*, ___ S.W.3d ___ (Tex. Crim. App. 2017) (No. AP-77,038; 3-8-17) (statements about anticipated acts are "mere inchoate thoughts that are not excludable under Rule 404(b)"). But evidence of contemplated bad acts, like evidence of actual misconduct, may be excluded under Rule 403 as unfairly prejudicial. *See Moreno*, 858 S.W.2d at 464; *see, e.g., Petetan*, ___ S.W.3d at ___ (evidence of defendant's promise to give witness drugs had some tendency to show that defendant was a drug dealer, but danger of unfair prejudice was not substantially outweighed by evidence's probative value; State needed this evidence to show full context of murder, including defendant's plan, and to substantiate underlying offense of retaliation).

477. *See, e.g., Dowling v. United States*, 493 U.S. 342, 349-50 (1990) (government was not collaterally estopped from offering evidence of a residential burglary on the issue of identity because the burden of proof for conviction is higher than for the admissibility of evidence).

478. *Huddleston v. United States*, 485 U.S. 681, 689-90 (1988).

479. *Id.* at 685.

480. *George v. State*, 890 S.W.2d 73, 76 (Tex. Crim. App. 1994); *Harrell v. State*, 884 S.W.2d 154, 159-60 (Tex. Crim. App. 1994); *see Huizar v. State*, 12 S.W.3d 479, 484 (Tex. Crim. App. 2000) (op. on reh'g) (TEX. CODE CRIM. PROC. art. 37.07, §3(a), requires reasonable-doubt standard for evidence of extraneous acts at punishment stage); *Higginbotham v. State*, 356 S.W.3d 584, 591 (Tex. App.—Texarkana 2011, pet. ref'd) ("Although neither TEX. PENAL CODE ANN. §31.03(c)(1) nor TEX. R. EVID. 404(b) explicitly provide that extraneous evidence at the guilt/innocence phase must be proven beyond a reasonable doubt, it is well-established that such a requirement is implied."). Earlier Texas law had been unclear on the required burden of proof. *See Phillips v. State*, 659 S.W.2d 415, 418 (Tex. Crim. App. 1983) ("[S]uch evidence should not be admitted unless the commission of the other crime is clearly proved and the accused is shown to be the perpetrator."); *Owens v. State*, 450 S.W.2d 324, 326-27 (Tex. Crim. App. 1969) (jury charge included "beyond a reasonable doubt" burden of proof for jury to consider uncharged offenses); *see, e.g., Tex. Farm Bureau Mut. Ins. v. Baker*, 596 S.W.2d 639, 643 (Tex. Civ. App.—Tyler 1980, writ ref'd n.r.e.) (evidence of previous fire was inadmissible when the alleged commission of that fire was never proved).

481. *Fischer v. State*, 268 S.W.3d 552, 558 (Tex. Crim. App. 2008); *Harrell*, 884 S.W.2d at 160. *But see Fischer*, 268 S.W.3d at 561 (Cochran & Johnson, JJ., concurring) (*Harrell* "ignored both the plain language of [Rule 104(b)] and its purpose"); *Ex parte Varelas*, 45 S.W.3d 627, 639-41 (Tex. Crim. App. 2001) (Womack, Keller, Keasler, JJ., dissenting) (*George* and *Harrell* were decided incorrectly under Rules of Evidence, and *George* should be overruled). Refer to *Article I: General Provisions, supra* p. 91. In *Fischer v. State*, the court of criminal appeals clarified that "*Harrell* was meant only to clarify the standard that a trial court applies" in admitting evidence at the initial Rule 104(b) proffer; "*Harrell* did not decide that a trial court's ruling on an initial proffer is dispositive of the admissibility issue regardless of what evidence is presented afterwards during the trial." *Fischer*, 268 S.W.3d at 557.

and Texas rules implies that evidence of an extraneous offense for which the defendant has been acquitted is prohibited under Texas law.[482]

Regardless of the particular burden-of-proof standard, both Texas and federal courts require the prosecution to show that it was the defendant himself who did the extraneous act.[483] Guilt by association or proximity is not sufficient.[484] If extraneous-offense evidence is improperly admitted, an instruction to disregard may be a proper legal remedy.[485]

A party can offer to stipulate to an element of the offense or cause of action, usually a jurisdictional element, which may eliminate the opponent's need to offer inherently prejudicial evidence of an extraneous offense.[486] The trial court should allow these stipulations; failure to do so is reversible error.[487]

---

482. This prohibition follows Texas common-law precedent. *See* ***Dedrick v. State***, 623 S.W.2d 332, 336 (Tex. Crim. App. [Panel Op.] 1981); ***Stuart v. State***, 561 S.W.2d 181, 182 (Tex. Crim. App. 1978).

483. *See* ***Phillips***, 659 S.W.2d at 418; *see, e.g.*, ***United States v. Veltmann***, 6 F.3d 1483, 1499 (11th Cir. 1993) (in arson case, codefendant's statements to insurance investigator were not admissible because government did not demonstrate that either codefendant set the earlier fires); ***Harris v. State***, 790 S.W.2d 568, 583-84 (Tex. Crim. App. 1989) (testimony about an earlier car theft was inadmissible because State was unable to prove clearly that the accused was the perpetrator in the extraneous act; testimony about a robbery on the same day as the primary offense was inadmissible without a showing that the two offenses were one continuous episode), *overruled on other grounds*, ***Snowden v. State***, 353 S.W.3d 815 (Tex. Crim. App. 2011).

484. *See, e.g.*, ***United States v. Parada-Talamantes***, 32 F.3d 168, 169-70 (5th Cir. 1994) (evidence that codefendant had purchased van in which marijuana was hidden from defendant's brother was reversible error; no "guilt by association" theory); ***Veltmann***, 6 F.3d at 1499 (reversible error to admit certain evidence of earlier fires in arson case when they were not similar and the genesis of those fires was unknown; only parallel between the two earlier fires and present one was that they occurred on property owned by codefendants; evidence did not meet threshold relevance requirement under Federal Rule 404(b)); ***United States v. Gilan***, 967 F.2d 776, 780-81 (2d Cir. 1992) (although there were striking similarities between two shoe thefts, nothing linked defendant to first one, and it was thus irrelevant in proving his theft in charged offense; there must be some link between defendant and uncharged act to be relevant under Federal Rule 404(b)).

485. *See, e.g.*, ***Gamboa v. State***, 296 S.W.3d 574, 581 (Tex. Crim. App. 2009) (court overruled defendant's point of error regarding extraneous-offense testimony from State's witness; "[a]ssuming that the testimony was improper, the trial judge quickly instructed the jury to disregard the statement and the question. Nothing in the record suggests that the jury was unable to follow the instruction."). The practical effect or remedial value of such an instruction, however, is debatable. For a discussion of preserving error after the jury has heard inadmissible evidence, see *O'Connor's Texas Rules * Civil Trials* (2017), "When jury hears inadmissible evidence," ch. 8-D, §6.7, p. 806.

486. *See* ***Tamez v. State***, 11 S.W.3d 198, 202 (Tex. Crim. App. 2000) ("[A] defendant's stipulation to a previous conviction should suffice when it carries the same evidentiary value as the judgments of prior convictions, yet substantially lessens the likelihood that the jury will improperly focus on the previous conviction or the defendant's 'bad character.' Such improper focus by the jury not only violates the unfair prejudice rationale of Rule 403, it violates the basic policy of Rule 404(b).").

487. *See, e.g.*, ***Old Chief v. United States***, 519 U.S. 172, 174 (1997) (in prosecution of felon in possession of firearm, error to permit government to introduce record of judgment of underlying felony when defendant offered to stipulate to prior felony conviction; trial court abused its discretion in rejecting offer when the nature of the prior offense raised risk of a verdict tainted by improper considerations); ***Robles v. State***, 85 S.W.3d 211, 213-14 (Tex. Crim. App. 2002) (error to refuse defendant's offer to stipulate and to admit evidence of two of his four prior DWI convictions, even though evidence was offered only to prove jurisdiction over felony DWI); ***Smith v. State***, 12 S.W.3d 149, 152 (Tex. App.—El Paso 2000, pet. ref'd) (error to allow State to read indictment with allegations of six prior DWI convictions when defendant offered to stipulate to the two jurisdictional DWI enhancement convictions). Refer to note 80 *supra* and accompanying text. Situations in which the prosecution should agree to a stipulation are limited: "[I]f ... there were a justification for receiving evidence of the nature of prior acts on some issue other than

As discussed earlier, the list of exceptions in Rule 404(b)(2) is illustrative, not exhaustive.[488] Evidence is not automatically admissible because it fits one of the exceptions. The categories are often not clear or distinct, and more than one theory may apply to a single act. The list of exceptions in Rule 404(b)(2) nonetheless provides a useful framework for permissible uses of extraneous-offense evidence.

1. Identity. Evidence of extraneous offenses is frequently offered to prove the identity of the offender.[489] The theory of relevance is usually that of modus operandi, in which the pattern and characteristics of the crimes are so distinctively similar that they constitute a "signature."[490] In this context, the similarity of the offenses and the distinctiveness of the common characteristics are crucial.[491] As the court of criminal appeals has explained:

[defendant's] status [as a felon] (*i.e.*, to prove 'motive, opportunity, intent, preparation, plan, knowledge, identity, or absence of mistake or accident'), [Federal] Rule 404(b) guarantees the opportunity to seek its admission." ***Old Chief***, 519 U.S. at 190 (quoting FED. R. EVID. 404(b)).

488. Refer to note 449 *supra* and accompanying text.

489. See ***Castillo v. State***, 739 S.W.2d 280, 289 (Tex. Crim. App. 1987); ***Linder v. State***, 828 S.W.2d 290, 297 (Tex. App.—Houston [1st Dist.] 1992, pet. ref'd) (evidence of extraneous offense admitted to establish defendant's identity "must reveal certain distinguishing features in common with the charged offense"); ***Bevers v. State***, 811 S.W.2d 657, 661 (Tex. App.—Fort Worth 1991, pet. ref'd) (one purpose of allowing evidence of extraneous offenses is to prove defendant's identity by showing that "certain distinguishing features are shared between the extraneous offense and the present offense"). Although such evidence is almost always offered by the prosecution, defendants may use the exception as well. See, e.g., ***Cole v. State***, 735 S.W.2d 686, 688-89 (Tex. App.—Amarillo 1987) (to impeach rape victim's identification and present theory of mistaken identity, defendant offered evidence that crime fit the modus operandi of a different assailant), *rev'd on other grounds*, 839 S.W.2d 798 (Tex. Crim. App. 1990). The court of appeals in ***Cole*** held that the trial court did not abuse its discretion in excluding the evidence because the probative value was tenuous and weak. 735 S.W.2d at 691.

490. ***Segundo v. State***, 270 S.W.3d 79, 88 (Tex. Crim. App. 2008); see ***Page v. State***, 213 S.W.3d 332, 336 (Tex. Crim. App. 2006); ***Leassear v. State***, 465 S.W.3d 293, 303 (Tex. App.—Houston [14th Dist.] 2015, no pet.); see, e.g., ***Beets v. State***, 767 S.W.2d 711, 740-41 (Tex. Crim. App. 1988) (op. on reh'g) (noting the defendant's "signature" use of the same weapon, the same motive, the same time of day, and the same means of disposing of bodies in two different murders); ***Mason v. State***, 416 S.W.3d 720, 740-41 (Tex. App.—Houston [14th Dist.] 2013, pet. ref'd) (similarity of specific characteristics of robberies, proximity of locations, and time interval between them showed that danger of unfair prejudice did not substantially outweigh probative value of extraneous offenses in proving defendant's identity as perpetrator); ***Phat Van Bui v. State***, 68 S.W.3d 830, 838 (Tex. App.—Houston [1st Dist.] 2002, no pet.) (proximity in time and place of each robbery, the common mode in which they were committed, and the circumstances surrounding the offenses were sufficiently similar to justify admission of the extraneous-offense evidence); ***Faison v. State***, 59 S.W.3d 230, 242 (Tex. App.—Tyler 2001, pet. ref'd) (upholding admission of evidence of three extraneous aggravated sexual assaults in prosecution for aggravated sexual assault when extraneous offenses bore striking similarities to charged assault: all four assaults occurred in apartment complexes in same general area; each victim was approximately the same age; defendant gained access to victims' apartments through either a sliding glass door or window; each assault occurred in early morning hours; and defendant threatened to cut each victim, robbed or threatened to rob each victim, talked to each victim, and covered or attempted to cover each victim's face with a pillowcase or pillow); ***Avila v. State***, 18 S.W.3d 736, 741 (Tex. App.—San Antonio 2000, no pet.) (although there were similarities between extraneous rape and charged offense, the similarities were "'more in the nature of the similarities common to the type of crime itself, [rape], rather than similarities peculiar to both offenses'" (quoting ***Ford v. State***, 484 S.W.2d 727, 730 (Tex. Crim. App. 1972))).

Federal cases also require a "signature" similarity to prove identity. See, e.g., ***United States v. Phaknikone***, 605 F.3d 1099, 1108-09 (11th Cir. 2010) (in bank-robbery case, trial court erred in admitting evidence from defendant's MySpace account, offered as modus operandi evidence to prove that defendant "robbed the banks 'like a gangster'"; although photograph of tattooed defendant holding a handgun sideways while in a car with a child "may portray a 'gangster-type personality,' the photograph does not evidence the modus operandi of a bank robber who commits his crimes with a signature trait" and was evidence of bad character that should have been excluded under

No rigid rules dictate what constitutes sufficient similarities; rather, the common characteristics may be proximity in time and place, mode of commission of the crimes, the person's dress, or any other elements which mark both crimes as having been committed by the same person. But if the similarities are "generic," *i.e.*, typical to this type of crime, they will not constitute a "signature" crime.[492]

Evidence of extraneous conduct offered to prove identity does not need to be the repeated commission of one or more similar offenses. There may be other distinctive

Federal Rule 404(b)); *United States v. Clemons*, 32 F.3d 1504, 1508-09 (11th Cir. 1994) (three prior carjackings by defendant during three weeks before charged carjacking were sufficiently similar in nature and style; "[w]hen extrinsic offense evidence is introduced to prove identity, the likeness of the offenses is the crucial consideration. The physical similarity must be such that it marks the offense as the handiwork of the accused"); *United States v. Tai*, 994 F.2d 1204, 1209-10 (7th Cir. 1993) (defendant's threats toward persons other than victim were admissible to show defendant's identity and intent); *United States v. Sanchez*, 988 F.2d 1384, 1393-94 (5th Cir. 1993) (defendant's later heroin transaction—which took place in front of same house, in which heroin was also in pink balloons, and in which defendant was using same distinctive VW with same license plates—was admissible to show identity and rebut misidentification defense); *United States v. Carrillo*, 981 F.2d 772, 775 (5th Cir. 1993) (in trial for selling heroin to undercover officer, evidence of defendant's other heroin sales in the vicinity were not so unusual or so similar to constitute proof of identity under Federal Rule 404(b)).

491. *See Taylor v. State*, 920 S.W.2d 319, 322 (Tex. Crim. App. 1996) ("When an extraneous offense is offered to prove identity, the common characteristics or the device used in each offense must be so unusual and distinctive as to be like a 'signature.'"); *Russell v. State*, 665 S.W.2d 771, 778 (Tex. Crim. App. 1983) (extraneous-offense evidence is admissible in the State's case-in-chief to show identity if the extraneous offense has sufficient common characteristics to show that it was the handiwork of the accused "and [if] the State's case is entirely circumstantial on the issue of identity"); *Mayfield v. State*, 803 S.W.2d 859, 867 (Tex. App.—Corpus Christi 1991, no pet.) ("For the purposes of showing identity, the test is whether there is some sufficiently *distinguishing* characteristic common to both the extraneous offense and the offense for which the defendant is charged such that both offenses can be earmarked as the accused's handiwork."); *see, e.g., Ransom v. State*, 503 S.W.2d 810, 812 (Tex. Crim. App. 1974) (admitting evidence of extraneous offenses when both offenses were robberies committed three days apart and defendant was identified as the perpetrator of both); *Chaparro v. State*, 505 S.W.3d 111, 118 (Tex. App.—Amarillo 2016, no pet.) (when identity was contested in trial for aggravated robbery, State could introduce "signature" evidence of other robberies that occurred around the same time in the same area; evidence established modus operandi including use of gloves, distinctive Halloween masks, shotgun, and large knife); *Clarke v. State*, 785 S.W.2d 860, 865-66 (Tex. App.—Fort Worth 1990) (evidence of extraneous offenses was admissible when both offenses involved sexual assaults committed in basically the same manner), *aff'd*, 811 S.W.2d 99 (Tex. Crim. App. 1991); *see also Leassear*, 465 S.W.3d at 304 (extraneous offense and charged offense can be different offenses, as long as similarities between them are such that evidence is relevant).

492. *Segundo*, 270 S.W.3d at 88. The Corpus Christi Court of Appeals has held that the defendant's extraneous residential burglary was not particularly distinctive—taking place during the day, in a rural area rather than an urban neighborhood, parking close to the homes of elderly individuals, stealing televisions and jewelry—and would not justify admission of the uncharged misconduct. *See Pena v. State*, 867 S.W.2d 97, 99 (Tex. App.—Corpus Christi 1993, pet. ref'd). However, the defendant used the same car, which belonged to his wife, for both burglaries. *Id.* Because that was unique and a "signature" characteristic, the extraneous-offense evidence was admissible. *Id.*; *see also Collins v. State*, 548 S.W.2d 368, 376 (Tex. Crim. App. 1976) (sustaining the admission of four prior robberies that were closely related in time to the present offense, involved small businesses in the same city, and involved one assailant brandishing a pistol, as did the present offense); *Ford v. State*, 484 S.W.2d 727, 730 (Tex. Crim. App. 1972) (extraneous offense was inadmissible because it occurred two months before the present offense, involved three more assailants than the present offense, and was carried out differently from the present offense); *Baize v. State*, 790 S.W.2d 63, 64-65 (Tex. App.—Houston [1st Dist.] 1990, pet. ref'd) (evidence of an extraneous offense was admissible at trial because crimes occurred within 1.3 miles of each other, were separated by only six hours, and involved three young Hispanic males, one black male, and a gun); *Clarke*, 785 S.W.2d at 865-66 (sustaining the admission of prior sexual assault that, like present offense, involved use of knife and duct taping victim's eyes, hands, and ankles and was committed by white assailant in same city).

characteristics about the Rule 404(b) evidence that identifies the defendant as the person who committed the charged offense.[493] Thus, any evidence—regardless of whether it shows the commission of some other offense—that tends to show a distinctive modus operandi or signature may be admissible to establish identity.

Evidence of modus operandi or a signature does not alone justify admission of an extraneous offense—identity must be a disputed issue in the case.[494] If the defendant admits that he is the person involved but claims that no offense occurred, identity is not disputed.[495] On the other hand, once a defendant raises an alibi defense, identity is in dispute.[496] Identity might even be raised by a defendant's opening statement if that opening statement directly raises that defense.[497] Identity might become a disputed issue in the State's case-in-chief when the State's identifying witness is impeached during cross-examination about (1) a material detail of the identification, (2) the conditions surrounding the charged offense and the witness's identification of the defendant in that situation, or (3) an earlier misidentification of the defendant.[498] Even if identity is disputed, the extraneous-offense evidence may be excluded if it does not tend to show that

---

493. *See **Segundo**,* 270 S.W.3d at 88; ***Leassear**,* 465 S.W.3d at 303-04; *see, e.g.,* ***Page v. State**,* 125 S.W.3d 640, 649-50 (Tex. App.—Houston [1st Dist.] 2003, pet. ref'd) (evidence that the defendant "carried a black handgun" was admissible under Rule 404(b) because it tended to establish defendant's identity as the robber who had carried a similar black handgun during the offense); *cf.* ***Tai**,* 994 F.2d at 1209-10 (evidence of defendant's actual control over participant in attack was admissible under Federal Rule 404(b) to show connection to extortion offense).

494. *See **Lane v. State**,* 933 S.W.2d 504, 519 (Tex. Crim. App. 1996) (identity may become a disputed issue by cross-examining State's witnesses or disputing accuracy of defendant's confession); *see, e.g.,* ***Dickey v. State**,* 646 S.W.2d 232, 234 (Tex. Crim. App. 1983) (after defendant asserted alibi, State could offer extraneous-offense rape in which both victims were female Texas A&M students, both victims were near their residences, rapist wore sunglasses, and rapist used a sharp object); ***Wysner v. State**,* 763 S.W.2d 790, 792-93 (Tex. App.—Dallas 1987, pet. ref'd) (finding insufficient distinctive characteristics between extraneous thefts and the charged robbery to make them relevant to the issue of identity, particularly because robbery victim "consistently" testified that the defendant was the person who robbed him).

495. *See, e.g.,* ***Owens v. State**,* 827 S.W.2d 911, 916 (Tex. Crim. App. 1992) (error to admit evidence of defendant's prior sexual conduct with his elder daughter at age 11 in prosecution for sexual assault of younger daughter at age 11 even though defendant testified and denied that event occurred and implied that he was a victim of "frame-up" by daughters who lied); ***Cooper v. State**,* 901 S.W.2d 757, 761 (Tex. App.—Beaumont 1995) (evidence of anal intercourse with mother of minor victim, even if a signature, was inadmissible when identity was not disputed), *pet. dism'd, improvidently granted,* 933 S.W.2d 495 (Tex. Crim. App. 1996); ***Wells v. State**,* 730 S.W.2d 782, 786 (Tex. App.—Dallas 1987) (despite remarkable similarities between the charged and a later offense, evidence of the later offense was not admissible to prove defendant's identity when complainant had met defendant on seven or eight occasions, had identified him in lineup, and never wavered in identification), *pet. ref'd,* 810 S.W.2d 179 (Tex. Crim. App. 1990).

496. ***Booker v. State**,* 103 S.W.3d 521, 530 (Tex. App.—Fort Worth 2003, pet. ref'd) ("when appellant's witnesses raised the defense of alibi, it is clear that identity becomes a disputed issue," but evidence of extraneous aggravated kidnapping and aggravated sexual assault of another woman was unfairly prejudicial and therefore inadmissible under Rule 403 to prove identity); *see, e.g.,* ***Regan v. State**,* 7 S.W.3d 813, 817 (Tex. App.—Houston [14th Dist.] 1999, pet. ref'd) (evidence of two prior offenses was admissible to show defendant's modus operandi when he relied on alibi defense).

497. Refer to notes 461-463 *supra* and accompanying text.

498. ***Siqueiros v. State**,* 685 S.W.2d 68, 71 (Tex. Crim. App. 1985); *see, e.g.,* ***Page v. State**,* 137 S.W.3d 75, 78-79 (Tex. Crim. App. 2004) (extraneous-offense evidence was admissible because defendant's cross-examination of victim about weight of her assailant sufficiently challenged her identification of him and rose to level of impeachment; impeachment does not need to be "particularly damaging or effective" to place identity in issue); ***Price v. State**,* 351 S.W.3d 148, 151-52 (Tex. App.—Fort Worth 2011, pet. ref'd) (in aggravated-robbery case, evidence of extraneous

this defendant committed both the charged and uncharged acts.[499] The trial court has "considerable latitude" in determining whether identity is disputed in the case.[500]

Probative value decreases with the passage of time between the extraneous offense and the charged offense. The factor of remoteness of the extraneous offense is important not in itself, but only as it affects the relevance and probative value of the offered evidence.[501] Because Rule 404(b) (unlike Rule 609(b)) does not contain an express time limitation, remoteness does not make an extraneous offense per se inadmissible.[502] The circumstances of the case determine whether uncharged misconduct should be excluded on the basis of remoteness.[503]

2. Intent. Extraneous-offense evidence is commonly offered to prove intent when intent cannot be easily inferred from the conduct itself.[504] Proving intent through evi-

---

acts could be offered to show identity when defense counsel cross-examined witness with questions that "obviously emphasized the issue of identity" and repeatedly asked witness whether he could clearly see defendant's face during robbery).

499. *See, e.g.*, *Johnston v. State*, 145 S.W.3d 215, 221-22 (Tex. Crim. App. 2004) (photographs of healing injuries of child victim's sister, who had also been assaulted by both defendant and victim's mother, were not admissible to prove that defendant, not victim's mother, had burned victim with a cigarette; no proof that defendant, rather than victim's mother, had caused injuries to victim's sister); *Russell v. State*, 113 S.W.3d 530, 541 (Tex. App.—Fort Worth 2003, pet. ref'd) (evidence of defendant's association with another person during commission of later murder did not make his identity as participant in charged murder with that same person more probable).

500. *Segundo v. State*, 270 S.W.3d 79, 86 (Tex. Crim. App. 2008).

501. *See Gaytan v. State*, 331 S.W.3d 218, 226-27 (Tex. App.—Austin 2011, pet. ref'd) ("[R]emoteness is but one aspect of an offense's probativeness. It is therefore an element of the factorial analysis that courts should conduct in deciding whether to exclude evidence under Rule 403 ....").

502. *See Gaytan*, 331 S.W.3d at 226; *Newton v. State*, 301 S.W.3d 315, 318 (Tex. App.—Waco 2009, pet. ref'd); *Hernandez v. State*, 203 S.W.3d 477, 480 (Tex. App.—Waco 2006, pet. ref'd); *see, e.g.*, *Stringer v. State*, 845 S.W.2d 400, 402 (Tex. App.—Houston [1st Dist.] 1992, pet. ref'd) (extraneous-offense evidence of two rapes occurring five years earlier at same apartment complex with same modus operandi was not too remote because defendant was released from prison just 66 days before charged rape); *Linder v. State*, 828 S.W.2d 290, 296-97 (Tex. App.—Houston [1st Dist.] 1992, pet. ref'd) (seven years between extraneous and charged offenses was not so remote as to automatically exclude evidence); *Clarke v. State*, 785 S.W.2d 860, 865-66 (Tex. App.—Fort Worth 1990) (when State's case of identity was circumstantial, it was proper to use extraneous offense in which identity evidence was also circumstantial; "common element may be the mode of commission of the crimes, or the mode of dress of the perpetrator, or any other element which marks both crimes as having been committed by the same person"; 11-month interval was not too remote), *aff'd*, 811 S.W.2d 99 (Tex. Crim. App. 1991); *cf. Ansell v. Green Acres Contracting Co.*, 347 F.3d 515, 525 (3d Cir. 2003) ("no bright line rule for determining when evidence is too remote to be relevant" under Federal Rule 404(b)). Refer to *Article VI: Witnesses, infra* p. 624.

503. *See Gaytan*, 331 S.W.3d at 226-27; *see, e.g.*, *Lane v. State*, 933 S.W.2d 504, 519 (Tex. Crim. App. 1996) (evidence of extraneous-offense murder that had occurred ten years earlier in a different state was admissible; mode of committing the offenses and surrounding circumstances were so similar that the evidence was sufficiently probative of defendant's identity); *Bachhofer v. State*, 633 S.W.2d 869, 872 & n.2 (Tex. Crim. App. 1982) ("Under all the circumstances of this case, we conclude that the remoteness of time of this particular offense, coupled with no evidence of other intervening similar offenses, and no final conviction for the extraneous offense, are such as to render the extraneous Oklahoma offense inadmissible. ... While the reversal of this cause is bottomed on the remoteness of the extraneous offense, the opinion should not be taken to imply that the extraneous offense would have otherwise been admissible."); *James v. State*, 554 S.W.2d 680, 683 (Tex. Crim. App. 1977) ("Under all the circumstances of this case, we conclude that remoteness of time of this particular extraneous offense, with no evidence of other intervening similar offenses sufficient to show a continuing course of conduct, together with the other facts and circumstances, were such as to render the evidence of the rape in Florida two years and nine months prior to the instant offense, when appellant was less than 13 years old, to be inadmissible ....").

504. *See, e.g.*, *Plante v. State*, 692 S.W.2d 487, 492-93 (Tex. Crim. App. 1985) (evidence of numerous prior instances of defendant's failure to pay for goods received was admissible to prove his intent to steal); *Corley v. State*,

dence of extraneous offenses does not require the degree of similarity between the extraneous and charged offense that is required when proving identity.[505] That the extraneous offense "derives from the defendant's indulging himself in the same state of mind in the perpetration of both the extrinsic and charged offenses" is sufficient.[506] The court may exclude the extraneous-offense evidence, however, if it finds that there is not a sufficient nexus between the extraneous-offense events and the litigated one.[507]

If intent is obvious from the conduct (e.g., the intent to kill is easily inferred from pointing a gun and shooting someone in the heart), or if the defendant admits intent but raises some other defense, the extraneous-offense evidence is not admissible.[508] Once a defendant claims that he lacked intent to commit the charged act, however, intent can no longer be inferred from the other uncontested evidence, and extraneous acts to prove culpable intent are relevant.[509] When a crime requires both intentional or

---

987 S.W.2d 615, 619 (Tex. App.—Austin 1999, no pet.) (extraneous conduct was admissible when neighbor intervened to prevent defendant from completing sexual assault such that defendant's intent could not be inferred from acts alone and defendant attempted to rebut inference of intent by arguing his conduct was a "drunken misdemeanor"); *Payton v. State*, 830 S.W.2d 722, 730 (Tex. App.—Houston [14th Dist.] 1992, no pet.) (defendant's previous sale of cocaine was admissible to show that defendant possessed narcotics with intent to deliver); *see also Parks v. State*, 746 S.W.2d 738, 740 (Tex. Crim. App. 1987) (difficult to prove intent to defraud in a forgery prosecution so that "as a practical matter, evidence of extraneous offenses is nearly always admissible").

Some Texas cases have held that extraneous offenses are relevant to show intent only if intent or guilty knowledge cannot be inferred from the act itself. *See Castillo v. State*, 910 S.W.2d 124, 128 (Tex. App.—El Paso 1995, pet. ref'd, untimely filed). This statement may be too broad. Instead, the extraneous offense is relevant if it makes a defendant's criminal intent more likely than would be assumed without it. *Prieto v. State*, 879 S.W.2d 295, 298 (Tex. App.—Houston [14th Dist.] 1994, pet. ref'd). Or, as another court of appeals expressed, "[e]xtraneous evidence offered to prove intent is not relevant if the State's direct evidence clearly establishes the intent element and that evidence is not contradicted by appellant nor undermined by appellant's cross-examination of the State's witnesses." *Hernandez*, 203 S.W.3d at 479.

505. *Plante*, 692 S.W.2d at 492-93; *Smith v. State*, 420 S.W.3d 207, 221 (Tex. App.—Houston [1st Dist.] 2013, pet. ref'd); *Johnson v. State*, 932 S.W.2d 296, 302 (Tex. App.—Austin 1996, pet. ref'd); *see* 2 WIGMORE, *supra* note 179, §302, at 241.

506. *United States v. Beechum*, 582 F.2d 898, 911 (5th Cir. 1978) (en banc); *see also Dabney v. State*, 816 S.W.2d 525, 528-29 (Tex. App.—Houston [1st Dist.] 1991, pet. ref'd) (in prosecution for theft of real estate, evidence of 150 property transactions was admissible under the doctrine of chances to prove that defendant never intended to make mortgage payments).

507. *See, e.g., First Sw. Lloyds Ins. v. MacDowell*, 769 S.W.2d 954, 956-57 (Tex. App.—Texarkana 1989, writ denied) (evidence of fire at plaintiff's rental property nine months earlier was not admissible because it did not "conclusively" establish any wrongdoing in the earlier fire); *Tex. Farm Bureau Mut. Ins. v. Baker*, 596 S.W.2d 639, 643 (Tex. Civ. App.—Tyler 1980, writ ref'd n.r.e.) (excluding evidence of a previous fire that was remote in time to the charged offense and was a single, isolated event). In each of these cases, only one prior event, a suspicious fire, could be offered as proof that the present fire was arson. It is in the multiplicity of prior events that Wigmore's doctrine of chances operates. Thus, had there been two, three, or four prior suspicious fires, the evidence probably would have been admissible even without evidence showing wrongdoing in connection with the earlier fires.

508. *See, e.g., Montgomery v. State*, 810 S.W.2d 372, 396-97 (Tex. Crim. App. 1991) (op. on reh'g) (when defendant claimed that he had not committed acts of sexual indecency, State could not offer evidence of extraneous lewd conduct to prove his specific intent to arouse or gratify his sexual desire because defendant was disputing not the intent but the conduct itself); *Hargraves v. State*, 738 S.W.2d 743, 748 (Tex. App.—Dallas 1987, pet. ref'd) (intent was obvious from the circumstances surrounding the aggravated sexual assault; error to admit an extraneous offense). *But see Wiggins v. State*, 778 S.W.2d 877, 881-85 (Tex. App.—Dallas 1989, pet. ref'd) (extraneous offense offered to show lack of consent was admissible, even though defendant denied the act of intercourse).

509. *Ludwig v. State*, 969 S.W.2d 22, 30 (Tex. App.—Fort Worth 1998, pet. ref'd); *see Bradshaw v. State*, 65 S.W.3d 232, 236 (Tex. App.—Waco 2001, no pet.) ("When a defendant claims his act was free from criminal intent, extraneous offenses are relevant to prove guilty intent."); *see, e.g., Martin v. State*, 173 S.W.3d 463, 466-68 (Tex. Crim.

knowing conduct plus a specific intent (e.g., possession of drugs with intent to distribute), evidence of uncharged misconduct is necessarily relevant and is likely to be admissible in the prosecution's case-in-chief.[510] A person's intent may also be a disputed issue in civil cases, and extraneous crimes, wrongs, or other acts may be admissible under Rule 404(b) in those instances.[511]

What theory of relevance justifies using extraneous-offense evidence to prove intent? The more frequently a defendant commits the same seemingly culpable conduct under similar circumstances, the more objectively improbable it is that he was merely in the wrong place at the wrong time.[512] Random chance cannot explain such coincidences.[513] As John Wigmore notes, the relevance of the extraneous conduct derives purely from

> the point of view of the doctrine of chances—the instinctive recognition of that logical process which eliminates the element of innocent intent by multiplying instances of the same result until it is perceived that this element cannot explain them all. Without formulating any accurate test, and without attempting by numerous instances to secure absolute certainty of inference, the

---

App. 2005) (when defendant testified that sexual encounter was consensual, evidence of his modus operandi of falsely claiming to be a deputy sheriff "as a ruse" to gain trust of victim was admissible under either doctrine of chances or Rule 404(b)); ***Morgan v. State***, 692 S.W.2d 877, 881-82 (Tex. Crim. App. 1985) (in prosecution for indecency with a child, evidence that defendant had previously touched the genitals of complainant and other children was admissible to rebut defendant's claim that touching in this case was accidental); ***Hudson v. State***, 112 S.W.3d 794, 803 (Tex. App.—Houston [14th Dist.] 2003, pet. ref'd) (when defendant claimed he was suffering from a "delusion" when he assaulted his wife and burned her, evidence of his prior assaults of her with a knife was relevant to show his intent to assault); ***Robison v. State***, 35 S.W.3d 257, 263 (Tex. App.—Texarkana 2000, pet. ref'd) (in prosecution for indecency with a child, extraneous-offense evidence of defendant's previous sexual abuse of his daughter was admissible to rebut defensive theory that his improper touching of the child was accidental).

510. *See United States v. Gruttadauro*, 818 F.2d 1323, 1327-28 & n.5 (7th Cir. 1987) (in general-intent crimes, intent is only a "formal" element and not an "essential element" of the crime, so that the mental state can be inferred from the surrounding circumstances; defendant was found guilty of willfully receiving money; "willfulness" is not a specific intent, so extraneous offense is not automatically relevant; error, but harmless, to admit it); *see also **United States v. Brown***, 34 F.3d 569, 573 (7th Cir. 1994) (even though defendant was willing to stipulate to intent, evidence of prior drug crimes was admissible because he made a general denial of all charges in pleading not guilty); ***United States v. Stubbs***, 944 F.2d 828, 836 (11th Cir. 1991) ("'[E]vidence of prior drug dealings is highly probative of intent to distribute a controlled substance, as well as involvement in a conspiracy.'" (quoting ***United States v. Hitsman***, 604 F.2d 443, 448 (5th Cir. 1979))).

511. *See, e.g.*, *Schlueter v. Schlueter*, 929 S.W.2d 94, 97-98 (Tex. App.—Austin 1996) (in divorce case, evidence that husband's father had helped another son commit fraud during that son's divorce proceeding was admissible to show father's intent to assist his children by fair or foul means during their divorces), *rev'd in part on other grounds*, 975 S.W.2d 584 (Tex. 1998); ***Porter v. Nemir***, 900 S.W.2d 376, 381-82 (Tex. App.—Austin 1995, no writ) (evidence of extraneous sexual-assault offense, which did not bear any significant similarity to conduct alleged in negligence lawsuit, was inadmissible to prove intent); ***McLellan v. Benson***, 877 S.W.2d 454, 457-58 (Tex. App.—Houston [1st Dist.] 1994, no writ) (in civil lawsuit for sexual assault, earlier rape was admissible to prove intent and lack of consent); ***City of Hous. v. Leach***, 819 S.W.2d 185, 192 (Tex. App.—Houston [14th Dist.] 1991, no writ) (in "whistleblower" suit, testimony from a prior lawsuit was admissible to prove retaliatory intent).

512. *See* Imwinkelried, *supra* note 316, at 437 ("[T]he proponent offers the evidence to establish the objective improbability of so many accidents befalling the defendant or the defendant becoming innocently enmeshed in suspicious circumstances so frequently. The proponent must establish that, together with the uncharged incident, the charged incident would represent an extraordinary coincidence.").

513. *See id.* at 456-57.

mind applies this rough and instinctive process of reasoning, namely, that an unusual and abnormal element might perhaps be present in one instance, but the oftener similar instances occur with similar results, the less likely is the abnormal element likely to be the true explanation of them.[514]

What Wigmore calls the "doctrine of chances" is the theory of relevance in admitting proof of extraneous offenses to prove the actus reus, or criminal act. The doctrine of chances does not require any inference about a defendant's general character for truthfulness.[515] The most famous case applying the doctrine is commonly known as the "brides in the bath" case.[516] In that case, Mr. Smith's new bride was found drowned in her bath.[517] Mr. Smith had recently purchased a large life-insurance policy on his new wife.[518] Everyone felt sorry about the tragic accident until it was discovered that Mr. Smith had been married twice before and that both of the other brides were well-insured and had also drowned in the bathtub.[519] Although no evidence was offered to prove that Mr. Smith had drowned the two other women, evidence of these incidents was admissible to prove that Mr. Smith murdered the third Mrs. Smith.[520]

The Texas case of **Jones v. State**[521] also relied on the doctrine of chances. In that case, a nurse was charged with injury to a child, caused by injecting a baby with a massive overdose of Heparin.[522] The prosecution offered evidence that the infant mortality rate during the defendant's hospital shifts was higher than usual.[523] The defendant objected that this evidence did not clearly prove any extraneous offense or show that the defendant was the perpetrator, but rather the evidence "did nothing more than assign a statistical association between appellant and the increased mortality rate and CPR events."[524] The court of appeals held that the evidence was properly admitted to prove that a criminal act had occurred—that the deceased baby was not accidentally or mistakenly injected with Heparin.[525]

---

514. 2 WIGMORE, *supra* note 179, §302, at 241.

515. *De La Paz v. State*, 279 S.W.3d 336, 348 (Tex. Crim. App. 2009).

516. *Rex v. Smith*, 11 Crim. App. 229 (1915) (Eng.).

517. *Id.* at 229.

518. *Id.*

519. *Id.*

520. *Id.* at 237; *see also* **State v. Lanier**, 598 S.E.2d 596, 602-03 (N.C. App. 2004) (when defendant claimed that her husband's death was an accident caused by eating "turkey medication, rat poison, and other toxic substances found around the farm," prosecution could offer evidence that a previous husband had drowned; even though the cause of death was dissimilar, the two men's "deaths shared sufficiently similar characteristics to provide some evidence that [the murder victim's] death was not accidental").

521. 751 S.W.2d 682 (Tex. App.—San Antonio 1988, no pet.).

522. *Id.* at 683.

523. *See id.* at 684-85.

524. *Id.* at 685.

525. *Id.* at 686; *see also* **United States v. Woods**, 484 F.2d 127, 133 (4th Cir. 1973) (government could offer evidence that nine children in defendant's custody over a 25-year period had experienced 20 cyanotic episodes once defendant asserted accidental-suffocation defense to a charge of infanticide when a baby died of cyanosis).

In **Fox v. State**,[526] the Fourteenth Court of Appeals explicitly relied on **Rex v. Smith** and the doctrine of chances to show the implausibility of an event. In that case of aggravated sexual assault of a child, the defense wanted to offer evidence of the defendant's alleged extraneous conduct of repeatedly sexually molesting his own daughter and two stepdaughters.[527] The complainant, one of the defendant's stepdaughters, slept in the same bunk bed as the other two girls.[528] Each child said that the defendant repeatedly molested them while the other two girls slept soundly.[529] None of the girls ever woke up during the molestation of the other two.[530] The State objected to this "reverse 404(b) evidence,"[531] but the court of appeals held that it was reversible error to prevent the defense from offering evidence that tended to show the improbability of the charged molestation through proof of its similarity to precisely the same allegations of abuse, occurring at the same time and in the same way, made by the defendant's two other children.[532] The defensive theory was that the defendant's wife, who wanted a divorce, had "planted" the story of sexual abuse in the mind of each of her daughters, who then each made the same "outcry" to law enforcement on the same day.[533]

Wigmore's doctrine of chances is now a well-accepted nonpropensity theory of relevance for the admission of evidence of uncharged misconduct under appropriate circumstances.[534] The doctrine is used most frequently in criminal cases to prove culpable intent, but it may also be used to prove the actus reus or, in drug prosecutions, to show that a person "knowingly" possessed drugs.[535] The doctrine may also be invoked by the plaintiff in a civil-rights lawsuit to show that the defendant's other discriminatory acts against persons situated similarly to the plaintiff are unlikely to be random.[536] Because the distinction between character and noncharacter theories of rel-

---

526. 115 S.W.3d 550 (Tex. App.—Houston [14th Dist.] 2002, pet. ref'd).

527. *Id.* at 558.

528. *Id.* at 556.

529. *Id.* at 556-57.

530. *Id.*

531. *See* **Torres v. State**, 71 S.W.3d 758, 761 n.5 (Tex. Crim. App. 2002) (discussing concept of "reverse 404(b) evidence" offered by defendant to prove that another person committed the charged offense). Refer to notes 455-460 *supra* and accompanying text.

532. *See* **Fox v. State**, 115 S.W.3d 550, 561 (Tex. App.—Houston [14th Dist.] 2002, pet. ref'd) ("Under the doctrine of chances, evidence of the allegations of [each child] is material because it is addressed to proof of a fact of consequence—appellant's defensive theory that the allegations of these girls were false and were planted by Ms. Fox.").

533. *Id.*

534. *See* Imwinkelried, *supra* note 316, at 422 (doctrine of chances "has become a mainstay of child abuse and drug prosecutions").

535. *See id.* at 423 (in drug prosecutions, courts may admit evidence of the defendant's involvement in prior drug trafficking to show mens rea when he claims that he was "'merely present' at or an 'innocent bystander' to a drug transaction"); *see, e.g.,* **United States v. Tyndale**, 56 M.J. 209, 213-14 (C.A.A.F. 2001) (when defendant claimed that he unknowingly ingested methamphetamine, government could offer evidence under the doctrine of chances that he had previously used that drug under similar circumstances).

536. *See* Imwinkelried, *supra* note 316, at 423 ("[E]vidence of a defendant's other discriminatory acts serves as the backbone of the plaintiff's case in many civil rights actions."); Lisa Marshall, Note, *The Character of Discrimination Law: The Incompatibility of Rule 404 and Employment Discrimination Suits*, 114 YALE L.J. 1063, 1080-82

evance is thin, the opponent should seek and obtain appropriately worded limiting instructions, both when the uncharged misconduct evidence is admitted under the doctrine of chances and in the final written instructions to the jury.[537]

3. Motive. Extraneous-offense evidence is traditionally offered to prove a person's motive. While proof of motive is not a required element in criminal cases, it is always relevant and admissible to prove that the defendant committed the offense.[538] While intent (or knowledge, recklessness, or negligence) is the legal element that accompanies the proscribed conduct, motive is an intermediate material fact (an evidentiary fact) that is usually offered to prove an elemental fact such as identity.[539] Sometimes the extraneous act is the cause for the offense—for example, when a robber with an outstanding arrest warrant is stopped by a police officer and then shoots the officer, his motive

---

(2005) (in discrimination lawsuits, courts frequently allow plaintiffs to show employer's propensity to discriminate by offering statistical evidence of the "'degree of disparity between the expected and actual ... composition [indicating the workers' race, sex, age, or other protected trait] necessary to support an inference of discrimination'"; however, this type of evidence runs afoul of the ban on character evidence under Rule 404 (quoting ***Berger v. Iron Workers Reinforced Rodmen Local 201***, 843 F.2d 1395, 1412 (D.C. Cir. 1988))).

537. *See **Daggett v. State***, 187 S.W.3d 444, 452-53 (Tex. Crim. App. 2005); Imwinkelried, *supra* note 316, at 457-59. The trial court's limiting instruction

> ought to highlight the difference between legitimate doctrine of chances reasoning and forbidden character reasoning. In particular, the instruction should condemn the latter in no uncertain terms. Given the difficulty that the jury may have understanding the distinction, the judge can repeat the instruction, giving it once when the evidence is admitted and again in the final jury charge. For his or her part, in closing argument the opponent should dwell on the instruction to ensure that the jury both understands the distinction and appreciates its obligation to follow the instruction.

Imwinkelried, *supra* note 316, at 457-59 (footnotes omitted).

538. ***Crane v. State***, 786 S.W.2d 338, 349-50 (Tex. Crim. App. 1990); *see **Turner v. State***, 715 S.W.2d 847, 852 (Tex. App.—Houston [14th Dist.] 1986, pet. ref'd) (evidence of an extraneous offense is admissible in proving motive to commit the primary offense); *see, e.g., **Biera v. State***, 391 S.W.3d 204, 212-13 (Tex. App.—Amarillo 2012, pet. ref'd) (evidence of defendant's drug use was admissible to show motive for robbery); ***Williamson v. State***, 356 S.W.3d 1, 22-23 (Tex. App.—Houston [1st Dist.] 2010, pet. ref'd) (in case of medical child abuse by parent, or Munchausen syndrome by proxy, evidence that child victim's siblings had also been subject to medical child abuse was admissible because it "assisted the jury in understanding what motivated a mother to harm her own child in such a pervasive and insidious manner"); ***Stern v. State***, 922 S.W.2d 282, 287 (Tex. App.—Fort Worth 1996, pet. ref'd) (trial court did not abuse its discretion by admitting gang-intelligence officer's testimony describing the malice that existed between two gangs to show defendant's motive for murder; "[m]otive is not an essential element of a criminal offense, but the prosecution is always entitled to offer evidence of motive to commit the charged offense because it is relevant when it fairly tends to raise an inference that the accused had a motive to commit the crime alleged"); *cf.* ***United States v. Madden***, 38 F.3d 747, 751-52 (4th Cir. 1994) (reversing bank-robbery conviction because government introduced "highly imprecise" evidence of drug usage without corresponding evidence of financial need; "[j]ust as a need to buy a pocket radio would not be admitted to establish motive to commit a bank robbery, so too we do not believe that evidence of occasional drug use should be admitted; financial need is the key element to establish motive").

539. For example, evidence showing motive to commit murder is relevant and admissible to prove that the defendant committed the murder. *See **Guevara v. State***, 152 S.W.3d 45, 50 (Tex. Crim. App. 2004). Sometimes evidence of a series of seemingly unrelated acts and circumstances may collectively show motive. *See, e.g., **Lopez v. State***, 200 S.W.3d 246, 251-52 (Tex. App.—Houston [14th Dist.] 2006, pet. ref'd) (in prosecution for injury to a child, evidence of defendant's sexual relationship with his wife before, during, and after her pregnancy to show a deterioration of their physical relationship, his indifference to whether his wife kept the child, and an argument between them about their baby was admissible as evidence of defendant's motive to kill his daughter). Refer to notes 468-470 *supra* and accompanying text.

for the shooting is to escape arrest.[540] At other times, a single motive produces both the uncharged conduct and the charged offense.[541] Rule 404(b) also permits parties to offer evidence of a person's motive for acts such as making false allegations against a defendant.[542]

4. Knowledge or opportunity. Extraneous-offense evidence may be offered to circumstantially prove that the defendant had the knowledge or opportunity to commit the charged act. Opportunity is often established by proving that the defendant had access to the crime scene, was present at the scene, or possessed special skills that were used in the commission of the crime.[543] As with other evidence offered under Rule 404(b)(2),

---

540. *See, e.g.*, *Vasquez v. State*, 67 S.W.3d 229, 239-40 (Tex. Crim. App. 2002) (evidence of defendant's affiliation with "the Mexican Mafia" was admissible to show motive for gang-related crime); *Ladd v. State*, 3 S.W.3d 547, 568 (Tex. Crim. App. 1999) (evidence that defendant smoked cocaine on night of victim's murder was admissible to prove defendant's motive was to kill victim to obtain his property and exchange it for cocaine); *Knox v. State*, 934 S.W.2d 678, 682-83 (Tex. Crim. App. 1996) (evidence of defendant's drug use was admissible to prove his motive in robbing pharmacy); *Valdez v. State*, 776 S.W.2d 162, 168 (Tex. Crim. App. 1989) (evidence of appellant's parole and his knowledge of outstanding arrest warrants was admissible to prove the appellant's motive in shooting a police officer); *Barefoot v. State*, 596 S.W.2d 875, 886-87 (Tex. Crim. App. 1980) (evidence that appellant was charged with the sexual penetration of a minor, kidnapping, and escape from jail was admissible to show appellant's motive to kill a police officer); *Williams v. State*, 974 S.W.2d 324, 331 (Tex. App.—San Antonio 1998, pet. ref'd) (evidence of defendant's gang membership was admissible to show that defendant's motive for robbing pawnshop was to obtain weapons to attack or defend against attacks by rival gangs).
    This logic is sometimes carried to extremes. In *Dunn v. State*, a trial for aggravated robbery and kidnapping, the appellate court upheld the admission of the shirt the defendant was wearing when he was arrested. 979 S.W.2d 403, 409 (Tex. App.—Amarillo 1998, pet. ref'd). The shirt had "Oklahoma Corrections" written on it. *Id.* This shirt implicitly identified the defendant as a prison escapee and was admissible to show the defendant's motive for the crimes because he was "a desperate man on the run, without a job, and in need of cash." *Id.* Logically, however, the shirt demonstrates the defendant's motive only if one first draws the forbidden character inference that the defendant was a desperate man on the run and thus was more likely to commit a criminal offense than people who are not prison escapees.

541. *See, e.g.*, *Simpson v. State*, 975 S.W.2d 364, 366-67 (Tex. App.—Waco 1998, no pet.) (evidence that victim's ex-girlfriend had kicked in his door and refused to leave his apartment and that police had been called to escort her away was admissible to show "she had a reason for and a purpose in attacking" victim); *Jones v. State*, 716 S.W.2d 142, 161 (Tex. App.—Austin 1986, pet. ref'd) (in murder trial of nurse, prosecution offered evidence of deaths of other children to demonstrate defendant's motive that she wanted hospital to establish a special pediatric-care unit and that she wanted to demonstrate her capabilities as a nurse); *see also Bisby v. State*, 907 S.W.2d 949, 959 (Tex. App.—Fort Worth 1995, pet. ref'd) (evidence of prior acts committed by defendant against victim and defendant's participation in threatening telephone calls showed defendant's ill will or hostility toward victim and thus his motive to commit charged offense); *Bevers v. State*, 811 S.W.2d 657, 661-62 (Tex. App.—Fort Worth 1991, pet. ref'd) (trial court properly admitted evidence of prior rape conviction in later rape prosecution involving the same victim to prove defendant's motive; during prior rape, defendant had told victim that if she contacted the police, he would return and punish her).

542. *Hammer v. State*, 296 S.W.3d 555, 563 (Tex. Crim. App. 2009); *see, e.g.*, *Kelly v. State*, 321 S.W.3d 583, 593 (Tex. App.—Houston [14th Dist.] 2010, no pet.) (evidence of sexual abuse by foster father was relevant to show foster father's motive in coaching foster children to make false allegations of sexual abuse against defendant).

543. *See, e.g.*, *United States v. Hamilton*, 992 F.2d 1126, 1130-31 (10th Cir. 1993) (testimony that defendant burglarized witness's house and stole his .38 revolver was admissible to prove defendant had access to working firearm when he testified that he was using a carved wooden replica, not a real gun, during aggravated robbery); *United States v. DeJohn*, 638 F.2d 1048, 1051-52 (7th Cir. 1981) (testimony of YMCA security guard and city police officer revealing that defendant had obtained checks from a mailbox at YMCA on other occasions was "highly probative of the defendant's opportunity to gain access to the mailboxes and obtain the checks that he cashed" with forged endorsements); *United States v. Barrett*, 539 F.2d 244, 248 (1st Cir. 1976) (evidence was admissible to show familiarity with sophisticated means of neutralizing burglar alarms).

knowledge or opportunity must be a disputed issue before evidence of an extraneous offense is admissible to prove it,[544] and the chain of logic from proof of the uncharged misconduct to knowledge or opportunity in the charged offense must be reasonably direct.[545]

Proof of a person's knowledge of the risk of harm when recklessness is an element of a civil or criminal charge may be established by evidence of prior occasions in which the person recognized or should have recognized the same or a similar risk.[546] Similarly, evidence of a defendant's prior drug possession and drug use may be admissible to show the likelihood that he knew a bag in his possession contained drugs.[547]

In ***Williams v. State***, the defendant was charged with arson. 948 S.W.2d 954, 956 (Tex. App.—Waco 1997, pet. ref'd). When firefighters arrived at the fire, all of the doors and windows of the building were locked, indicating that the fire might have started accidentally. *Id.* at 959. The State offered evidence linking the defendant to two prior burglaries of the burned building, in which the thief had entered the business through a skylight, to demonstrate that the defendant had the knowledge and opportunity to set the fire in the locked building. *Id.* at 958-59.

544. *See **Arnott v. State***, 498 S.W.2d 166, 176-77 (Tex. Crim. App. 1973) (extraneous-offense evidence that tends to show knowledge should be admitted only when State relies on circumstantial evidence or defendant denies knowledge); *cf. **United States v. Corona***, 34 F.3d 876, 881 (9th Cir. 1994) (defendant's possession of a list of drug customers 11 months after his arrest for drug possession was relevant to show knowledge when defendant claimed ignorance about charged act); ***United States v. Simpson***, 992 F.2d 1224, 1228-29 (D.C. Cir. 1993) (plain error to allow government to use prior arrest for possession of Dilaudid to impeach defendant's cross-examination answer that he did not know how Dilaudid is commonly packaged; defense was that he was "framed," not that he didn't know he possessed a drug); ***United States v. Alessi***, 638 F.2d 466, 477 (2d Cir. 1980) ("We have instructed that normally evidence of a defendant's prior conviction introduced to show knowledge or intent should not be admitted until the conclusion of the defendant's case, since by that time the court is in a better position to determine whether knowledge or intent is truly a disputed issue and whether the probative value of the evidence outweighs the risk of unfair prejudice.").

545. In ***Nolen v. State***, a trial for possession of amphetamine, the State offered evidence of an extraneous-offense burglary. 872 S.W.2d 807, 812 (Tex. App.—Fort Worth 1994), *pet. ref'd*, 897 S.W.2d 789 (Tex. Crim. App. 1995). The State maintained that the defendant had stolen not only a chain saw, stereo speakers, VCRs, and a television set, but also glassware of a type commonly used in the manufacture of illegal drugs. *Id.* The State argued that the fact that he took otherwise ordinary glassware "makes it highly unlikely that [defendant] coincidentally selected these items by random chance" and, thus, "a strong inference is raised that [defendant] had knowledge of the contraband amphetamine and its production." *Id.* The court of appeals concluded that the prior burglary offense was not relevant to prove the defendant knew the substance being manufactured in another person's bathroom was amphetamine without a showing that the defendant had experience with amphetamine itself. *Id.* at 812-13.

546. *See, e.g.*, ***Prescott v. State***, 123 S.W.3d 506, 514-15 (Tex. App.—San Antonio 2003, no pet.) (in defendant's trial for recklessly causing injury to her child—who drowned in apartment complex's hot tub—by failing to adequately supervise the child, evidence that defendant had previously allowed the four-year-old victim and her sister to wander unsupervised around the apartment complex was admissible to show defendant was aware of the risk that her children "could get out of the apartment and the resulting dangers they faced").

547. *See, e.g.*, ***Carter v. State***, 145 S.W.3d 702, 708 (Tex. App.—Dallas 2004, pet. ref'd) (evidence that cocaine was seized from a house where defendant was arrested, but not in the room where defendant was arrested, was not admissible to show defendant's knowledge or intent to deliver drugs two weeks earlier; defense was misidentification, not that he sold drugs but did not know it was cocaine or that he did not intend to sell drugs); ***Mason v. State***, 99 S.W.3d 652, 655-56 (Tex. App.—Eastland 2003, pet. ref'd) (evidence of drug sale in 2001 was admissible to show knowing possession of drugs in 1999); ***Perry v. State***, 933 S.W.2d 249, 254 (Tex. App.—Corpus Christi 1996, pet. ref'd) (evidence that defendant had prior conviction for possession of cocaine was not admissible to prove he possessed cocaine on present occasion; defendant did not dispute that he knew what cocaine looked like); ***Kemp v. State***, 861 S.W.2d 44, 46 (Tex. App.—Houston [14th Dist.] 1993, pet. ref'd) (prior convictions for cocaine offenses were admissible to prove defendant knowingly possessed cocaine in charged offense when he had testified that he was unaware that there was cocaine in the bedroom); ***Marable v. State***, 840 S.W.2d 88, 94-95 (Tex. App.—Texarkana 1992, pet. ref'd) (extraneous offense that defendant had previously brought a sack of marijuana to the jail was admissible to prove that he was growing marijuana and that he knew the nature of the substance).

Evidence of knowledge or opportunity may be introduced by the prosecution to rebut a defensive claim.[548] In a trial for sexual assault of a child, for example, the defense might be that the defendant lacked an opportunity to commit the offense because there were other children or adults present whenever the defendant was with the complainant. In such a case, the State may offer evidence that the defendant had, on previous occasions, committed the same offense despite the presence of others.[549]

5. Preparation, plan, scheme, or design. Extraneous-offense evidence may be used to prove that the charged offense is part of a larger plan, scheme, or conspiracy. The common-plan exception includes crimes committed in preparation for the charged offense.[550] The court of criminal appeals has given the following example:

> [I]f the defendant steals a car on Monday, buys a machine gun on Tuesday, pastes together a robbery note on Wednesday, parks illegally in front of the Wells Fargo building on Thursday while casing out the bank, and then robs the bank on Friday using the machine gun and driving off in the stolen car, all of the extraneous offenses are relevant to prove each step of the defendant's ultimate plan to rob the bank.[551]

---

548. *See* ***Powell v. State***, 63 S.W.3d 435, 438-39 (Tex. Crim. App. 2001) (extraneous-offense evidence is admissible to rebut defensive theory of "lack of opportunity," which may be raised in opening statement or on cross-examination); *see, e.g.*, ***Richardson v. State***, 328 S.W.3d 61, 71-72 (Tex. App.—Fort Worth 2010, pet. ref'd) (per curiam) (in trial for fraudulent use or possession of identifying information, State could offer extraneous-offense evidence of defendant's "dumpster diving" for identifying information to rebut defensive theory that defendant had no knowledge of the identifying information found in his car and that the information was in his car by mistake); *cf.* ***Espinosa v. State***, 328 S.W.3d 32, 43 (Tex. App.—Corpus Christi 2010, pet. ref'd) (State could offer evidence of defendant's pretrial supervision in an unrelated case and that he had been found competent to stand trial in that case to show motive for his acts and rebut his affirmative defense of insanity).

549. *See, e.g.*, ***Wheeler v. State***, 67 S.W.3d 879, 887-88 (Tex. Crim. App. 2002) (when defensive theory was that defendant was never alone with child victim, evidence of extraneous offense involving another child victim "with family members in the immediate vicinity" was admissible to rebut claim of lack of opportunity and impossibility); ***Powell***, 63 S.W.3d at 438 (evidence of extraneous offenses with other children was admissible when defendant claimed that he lacked opportunity to commit offense because many children were always in the same room); ***Abshire v. State***, 62 S.W.3d 857, 860 (Tex. App.—Texarkana 2001, pet. ref'd) (in trial for sexual assault of a child, extraneous-offense evidence was admissible when defense was lack of opportunity and defendant's family members testified that they never saw defendant do anything unusual with child complainant).

550. *See* Russell J. Davis, Annotation, *Admissibility, Under Rule 404(b) of the Federal Rules of Evidence, of Evidence of Other Crimes, Wrongs, or Acts Similar to Offense Charged to Show Preparation or Plan*, 47 A.L.R. Fed. 781, 784 (1980 & Supp. 2006) (evidence of a continuing scheme or plan "does not necessarily amount to an element of the charged offense which must be proved … but its existence is strong circumstantial evidence pointing forward to the doing of the charged offense, and it may also lead to proof of an actual element of the offense, such as intent or absence of mistake"); *see, e.g.*, ***Petetan v. State***, ___ S.W.3d ___ (Tex. Crim. App. 2017) (No. AP-77,038; 3-8-17) (even if defendant's promise to give witness drugs rose to level of bad act that could be excluded under Rule 404(b), it was relevant to show defendant's plan to set up murder and frame witness for it).

551. ***Daggett v. State***, 187 S.W.3d 444, 451 (Tex. Crim. App. 2005); *cf.* ***United States v. Cepulonis***, 530 F.2d 238, 246 (1st Cir. 1976) (testimony that bank robbers shot at a police officer and a passing motorist and evidence of a shotgun not used in the robbery were properly admitted under Federal Rule 404(b) to show that defendants' plan was to distract police by firing at civilians); ***United States v. Carroll***, 510 F.2d 507, 509 (2d Cir. 1975) (other crimes committed to determine if conspirators were capable of handling mail-truck robbery were admissible under Federal Rule 404(b) in prosecution for attempted robbery of the mail truck).

A plan may also be shown by escalating events, such as a case in which an initial touch leads to pinching that leads to fondling that leads to an outright proposition for sexual favors. Each step along the way may be viewed as the deliberate execution of an ongoing conscious plan to achieve the final goal of sexual gratification. *See* ***Bryson***

Separate and distinct offenses that are independent crimes do not necessarily constitute a plan or scheme despite their proximity in time and place. They may be mere repetition of the same offense offered to show "he has done it before, and he is doing it again," which is pure propensity evidence prohibited by Rule 404(b)(1).[552] If the proponent of extraneous-offense evidence "is unable to articulate exactly how an extraneous act tends to prove a step toward an ultimate goal or overarching plan," the evidence is inadmissible under the plan exception of Rule 404(b).[553]

6. Absence of mistake or lack of accident. A defendant can raise the defense that the conduct at issue in the case was a mistake or an accident. In those cases, the State (or the plaintiff in a civil case) may rebut the defense with evidence of an extraneous offense to show that the conduct was not accidental or unintentional.[554] Evidence of extraneous offenses is thus admissible to rebut defensive theories raised during either direct examination or cross-examination.[555]

---

v. State, 820 S.W.2d 197, 199 (Tex. App.—Corpus Christi 1991, no pet.); *see, e.g.*, *Lazcano v. State*, 836 S.W.2d 654, 660 (Tex. App.—El Paso 1992, pet. ref'd) (in murder case, State could not offer one other extraneous offense of attempted rape committed in a similar manner to demonstrate a scheme or plan; "[w]ithout some indication that the acts constituted the necessary steps in the completion of a formed design, we expressly decline to hold that the occurrence of a single comparable act constitutes a common scheme or plan"); *Mares v. State*, 758 S.W.2d 932, 937 (Tex. App.—El Paso 1988, pet. ref'd) (when it was apparent that defendant exploited his authority as the teacher of elementary-school girls to obtain sexual gratification from his students, extraneous offenses were admissible as proof of a common criminal scheme to use students' requests for tutorial assistance to become progressively more intimate with them).

552. *See United States v. Krezdorn*, 639 F.2d 1327, 1331 (5th Cir. 1981); *Daggett*, 187 S.W.3d at 451-52. In *Krezdorn*, the defendant was charged with forging the immigration inspector's signature. 639 F.2d at 1328-29. The government introduced evidence of 32 extraneous-offense forgeries under the theory that these demonstrated that Krezdorn had a scheme to forge entry cards permitting the entry of illegal aliens. *Id.* at 1330. But these forgeries did not show the existence of any larger goal of which the charged forgeries were some aspect. *Id.* at 1331. They were simply a large number of forgeries in a short period of time. *See id.*; *see also United States v. Fountain*, 2 F.3d 656, 667-68 (6th Cir. 1993) (court erred in admitting testimony by defendant's ex-girlfriend about selling crack out of pill bottles and using firearms while dealing drugs on other occasions; "Rule 404(b) ... allows the admission of other acts evidence in order to prove 'plan' if the purpose is to establish the doing of a criminal act as a step toward completing a larger criminal plan. The gateway requirement is that proof of a larger criminal plan is material."); *United States v. Tai*, 994 F.2d 1204, 1211 (7th Cir. 1993) ("The plan exception to Rule 404(b) applies when the evidence helps explain how the charged offense unfolded or developed, not where the evidence merely indicates that the defendant committed the same crime on other occasions."); *Allstate Tex. Lloyds v. Potter*, 30 S.W.3d 658, 660-62 (Tex. App.—Texarkana 2000, no pet.) (evidence of prior fires at insured's property might be admissible to illustrate "a continuing design, system, or scheme ... to commit insurance fraud," but trial court properly excluded such evidence because insurer produced "no evidence that any of those fires were the result of wrongdoing except the fire which is the basis of this suit").

553. *Daggett*, 187 S.W.3d at 452.

554. *See Johnston v. State*, 145 S.W.3d 215, 222 & n.23 (Tex. Crim. App. 2004) (evidence of an extraneous act might be admissible to demonstrate that an injury was the result of an intentional act, not an accident or mistake, even though there is no independent evidence that defendant is the person who committed that act or that the extraneous act was committed in a strikingly similar manner). For example, in *Hernandez v. State*, evidence that the defendant hit the 17-month-old victim in the stomach two weeks before the charged incident was admissible to disprove defendant's theory of accident—that he improperly performed a Heimlich maneuver to dislodge a piece of food in the child's throat. 914 S.W.2d 226, 232-33 (Tex. App.—Waco 1996, no pet.). This evidence negated the innocent-mistake defense and proved intent to injure the child. *Id.* at 233; *see also Logan v. State*, 840 S.W.2d 490, 497 (Tex. App.—Tyler 1992, pet. ref'd) (when felony-murder defendant vigorously contended that the fire in which victim died was an accident, not arson, State was entitled to offer evidence showing defendant's role in helping to burn a relative's mobile home, also for insurance proceeds); *Burton v. State*, 762 S.W.2d 724, 726-27 (Tex. App.—

7. Implicit exceptions under Rule 404(b)(2). The list of exceptions in Rule 404(b)(2) does not include all of those recognized under the common law or now used by Texas or federal courts. While Rule 404(b) does not prohibit the use of uncharged misconduct for reasons other than those set out in the rule, it does require that any use of the evidence be governed by the rule's standards. That is, the use of the evidence cannot involve an inference of bad character or propensity, and the evidence must satisfy the Rule 403 balancing test.[556] Evidence of an extraneous offense may be admissible whenever the defendant raises an affirmative defense or raises a defensive issue that negates one of the elements of the offense.[557] However, the extraneous-offense evidence must rebut a defense that is raised by the defendant, not by the State in its questioning of the defendant or other witnesses.[558]

The term "res gestae" (literally translated as "things done") has been the source of considerable confusion in the law. The phrase has long been used in Texas and other states as a catchall, justifying the admission of virtually any uncharged-misconduct evidence offered to show the context or circumstances surrounding an offense or an arrest.[559] The court of criminal appeals has clarified and narrowed this very broad doctrine of background evidence. Res gestae evidence may be of two types: (1) "'same transaction' contextual evidence" or (2) contextual evidence offered to correct a false impression.[560]

Houston [1st Dist.] 1988, no pet.) (in prosecution of defendant for attempted murder of his wife, evidence of numerous prior assaults and threats directed toward wife and children was admissible to not only explain defendant's behavior but also rebut his assertion that the shooting was accidental).

555. *See **Williams v. State***, 301 S.W.3d 675, 687 (Tex. Crim. App. 2009); ***Daggett***, 187 S.W.3d at 453-54; ***Ransom v. State***, 920 S.W.2d 288, 301 (Tex. Crim. App. 1996) (op. on reh'g).

556. Refer to notes 111-159 *supra* and accompanying text.

557. ***Casey v. State***, 215 S.W.3d 870, 879 (Tex. Crim. App. 2007); ***Johnston***, 145 S.W.3d at 219; *see **De La Paz v. State***, 279 S.W.3d 336, 343 (Tex. Crim. App. 2009); ***Martin v. State***, 173 S.W.3d 463, 466 (Tex. Crim. App. 2005); *see, e.g.,* ***Mendiola v. State***, 995 S.W.2d 175, 180 (Tex. App.—San Antonio 1999) (in trial for indecency with a child, evidence of extraneous sexual acts with children after defendant's prostate surgery was admissible to rebut defense that defendant did not have physical capability or drive to commit charged offense because of operation), *rev'd on other grounds*, 21 S.W.3d 282 (Tex. Crim. App. 2000); ***Pleasant v. State***, 755 S.W.2d 204, 205-06 (Tex. App.—Houston [14th Dist.] 1988, no pet.) (extraneous offenses were admissible to rebut the testimony of an alibi witness); ***Yarbough v. State***, 753 S.W.2d 489, 490 (Tex. App.—Beaumont 1988, no pet.) (extraneous offenses were admissible to rebut claim of self-defense).

In ***Garrett v. State***, the court held that evidence that complainant did not want the defendant in her home because of his drug use was admissible under Rule 404(b) to show that she did not consent to have sex with the defendant. 998 S.W.2d 307, 316 (Tex. App.—Texarkana 1999, pet. ref'd). The evidence was not offered to show that the defendant was a drug user and was using drugs at the time of the offense, which would have been an impermissible "bad character" use under Rule 404(b), but to rebut the defense of consensual sex. *See id.*

558. *See, e.g.,* ***Roberts v. State***, 29 S.W.3d 596, 601-02 (Tex. App.—Houston [1st Dist.] 2000, pet. ref'd) (defense did not "open the door" to rebuttal with an extraneous offense when State cross-examined defense witness).

559. *See **Mayes v. State***, 816 S.W.2d 79, 86-87 (Tex. Crim. App. 1991). Courts have continued to use the phrase "res gestae." *See **Wesbrook v. State***, 29 S.W.3d 103, 115 (Tex. Crim. App. 2000).

560. *See **Hayden v. State***, 296 S.W.3d 549, 554 (Tex. Crim. App. 2009) (false impression); ***Daggett***, 187 S.W.3d at 452 (same); ***Mayes***, 816 S.W.2d at 86-87 (same transaction).

Common-law formulations of "res gestae" also mentioned "background contextual evidence" as a permissible rationale for admitting evidence of uncharged misconduct. *See **Albrecht v. State***, 486 S.W.2d 97, 100 (Tex. Crim. App. 1972). The court of criminal appeals questioned this rationale in ***Mayes***, noting that "background evi-

(1) "Same transaction" contextual evidence. "Same transaction" contextual evidence refers to those events and circumstances that are intertwined, inseparable parts of an event—parts that, if viewed in isolation, would make no sense at all.[561] This type of evidence is admissible "simply because in narrating the one it is impracticable to avoid describing the other ...."[562] Only if the facts and circumstances of the instant offense would make little or no sense without also bringing in the same-transaction contextual evidence should the same-transaction contextual evidence be admitted.[563] The prejudicial nature of same-transaction contextual evidence rarely makes the evidence inad-

---

dence often comes in only because no one objects to it." 816 S.W.2d at 87. The court ultimately held that "character evidence offered on the rationale that it is 'background' evidence helpful to a jury, but apparently in conflict with the proscription of Rule 404(b), is not admissible as one of the alternative purposes" under the rule. *Id.* at 88. The probative value of evidence offered simply to put the events into a general context is substantially outweighed by the danger of unfair prejudice that the jury will misuse that evidence for the forbidden purpose of showing conduct in conformity with bad character. *See, e.g.,* ***Blakeney v. State***, 911 S.W.2d 508, 514-15 (Tex. App.—Austin 1995, no pet.) (error to admit evidence of defendant's sexual preference, which was only background contextual evidence and "could only serve to send to the jury the message that all homosexual men are also molesters of little boys").

561. *See* ***Devoe v. State***, 354 S.W.3d 457, 469 (Tex. Crim. App. 2011) ("[U]nder Rule 404(b), same-transaction contextual evidence is admissible only when the offense would make little or no sense without also bringing in that evidence ...."); ***Wesbrook***, 29 S.W.3d at 115 (same-transaction contextual evidence is admissible to show the context for a crime "under the reasoning that events do not occur in a vacuum, and the jury has a right to hear what occurred immediately prior to and subsequent to the commission of that act so that it may realistically evaluate the evidence"); ***Mayes***, 816 S.W.2d at 86 n.4 ("Same transaction contextual evidence is deemed admissible as a so-called exception to the propensity rule where 'several crimes are intermixed, or blended with one another, or connected so that they form an indivisible criminal transaction, and full proof by testimony, whether direct or circumstantial, of any one of them cannot be given without showing the others.'" (quoting ***Nichols v. State***, 97 Tex. Crim. 174, 176, 260 S.W. 1050, 1051 (1924))). Sometimes "same transaction" contextual evidence is extraneous-offense evidence. For example, in ***Miller v. State***, an aggravated-assault trial, the court admitted evidence of an earlier incident at a park in which the defendant's companion allegedly fired a pistol toward the victim's car as the defendant stood nearby. 2 S.W.3d 475, 480-81 (Tex. App.—Tyler 1999, no pet.). The evidence made it more probable than not that the defendant pointed that same pistol at the victim in a second incident at a highway intersection because the confrontation at the park occurred shortly before the second incident, the defendant was standing near the shooter in the first incident, and the defendant asked another companion to load the pistol as they followed the victim's vehicle. *Id.* at 479. Regardless of whether this evidence is categorized as "same transaction" or "extraneous transaction" evidence, it was relevant to show that the defendant, not a companion, actually fired the shot at the intersection and that he had a motive for doing so. *See id.* at 481.

562. 2 WIGMORE, *supra* note 179, §365, at 364.

563. ***Devoe***, 354 S.W.3d at 469; *e.g.,* ***Rogers v. State***, 853 S.W.2d 29, 33-34 (Tex. Crim. App. 1993) (defendant's possession and use of marijuana at time of arrest were not admissible as "same transaction contextual evidence" in trial for burglary and possession of amphetamine); ***Parks v. State***, 463 S.W.3d 166, 171-72 (Tex. App.—Houston [14th Dist.] 2015, no pet.) (in case involving serious bodily injury to child, testimony of teacher and police investigator about child's head injuries was necessary as same-transaction contextual evidence for jury to understand how investigation of injuries came about); *see, e.g.,* ***Nelson v. State***, 864 S.W.2d 496, 498-99 (Tex. Crim. App. 1993) (in capital-murder trial, surviving victim could testify that defendant stabbed and raped her as well as the deceased, because both crimes occurred during the same criminal episode; "[t]he facts and circumstances of the charged offense would make little or no sense without also admitting the same transaction contextual evidence as it related to the second victim"); ***Lockhart v. State***, 847 S.W.2d 568, 571 (Tex. Crim. App. 1992) (evidence that defendant attempted to make drug purchase and drove car with stolen license plates was relevant to capital murder; extraneous offenses indivisibly connected to charged offense and necessary to State's case may be admissible to explain context); ***Swarb v. State***, 125 S.W.3d 672, 681-82 (Tex. App.—Houston [1st Dist.] 2003, pet. dism'd) (evidence of arrest warrant for extraneous drug offense committed in different county was admissible to show why officers were searching for defendant, why they were at jail when they came across defendant's truck, and how they found drugs in truck).

missible as long as the evidence fairly sets the stage for the jury's understanding of the whole criminal transaction.[564]

Not all events and circumstances that surround the charged offense or arrest are automatically admissible as part of the same transaction. The uncharged misconduct must be "part and parcel" of the charged crime, not two distinct and separate offenses merely committed at the same time.[565] The evidence must be independently relevant to a material issue in the lawsuit.[566] For example, in a burglary trial, the fact that the defendant had a hypodermic needle in his pocket when he was arrested inside the building is not independently relevant to any material fact in the case and is inadmissible.[567] On the other hand, when a person is arrested for possession of a large quantity of drugs, evidence that he had a rifle in his car with the drugs may be admissible to show that the defendant was protecting the drugs.[568] Evidence of a "crime spree" either immedi-

---

564. *Smith v. State*, 949 S.W.2d 333, 337 (Tex. App.—Tyler 1996, pet. ref'd).

565. *See Maynard v. State*, 685 S.W.2d 60, 66 (Tex. Crim. App. 1985) ("It is well settled that where one offense or transaction is one continuous episode, or another offense or transaction is a part of the case on trial, or blended or closely interwoven therewith, proof of all the facts is proper."); *see, e.g., Prible v. State*, 175 S.W.3d 724, 731-32 (Tex. Crim. App. 2005) (evidence in capital-murder trial that three children died of smoke inhalation as a "collateral consequence" when defendant set fire to destroy evidence that he had killed their mother was admissible as "same transaction contextual evidence"); *Santellan v. State*, 939 S.W.2d 155, 167-68 (Tex. Crim. App. 1997) (evidence that defendant had sexually abused murder victim's corpse gave "valuable insight into appellant's motive, plan, and intent in perpetrating the crime. This information was crucial to the State's argument that appellant had the specific intent necessary for attempted kidnapping, and, therefore, for capital murder."); *Camacho v. State*, 864 S.W.2d 524, 532 (Tex. Crim. App. 1993) (in capital-murder case, evidence of kidnapping and double murder of deceased homeowner's wife and son was "'[s]ame transaction contextual evidence' [that] imparts to the trier of fact information essential to understanding the context and circumstances of events which, although legally separate offenses, are blended or interwoven. As such, it is admissible, not for the purpose of showing character conformity, but to illuminate the nature of the crime alleged.").

566. *See, e.g., Harris v. State*, 790 S.W.2d 568, 584 (Tex. Crim. App. 1989) (extraneous robbery that occurred after the charged murder and robbery was "a separate and independent offense committed for pure profit and could not aid the jury in understanding the factual context of appellant's other violent, nonsensical conduct"; admission of extraneous offense was harmless error), *overruled on other grounds*, *Snowden v. State*, 353 S.W.3d 815 (Tex. Crim. App. 2011); *Carter v. State*, 145 S.W.3d 702, 707-08 (Tex. App.—Dallas 2004, pet. ref'd) (admission of evidence that cocaine was seized from house where defendant was arrested was not "same transaction contextual evidence" of cocaine sale two weeks earlier; "the jury's understanding of the charged offense would not have been impaired or clouded had the State described appellant's later arrest without including the evidence that cocaine was found in the house when appellant was arrested").

567. *Couret v. State*, 792 S.W.2d 106, 107-08 (Tex. Crim. App. 1990); *see also Wyle v. State*, 777 S.W.2d 709, 715-16 (Tex. Crim. App. 1989) (trial court erroneously allowed a portion of defendant's confession in which he admitted possession of a .357 Magnum and marijuana; although defendant possessed this weapon at least 24 hours before the time of the capital murder, he did not use it in commission of the offense, and his possession of marijuana "did not in any way facilitate [his] escape from law enforcement or place the alleged capital murder in its immediate context"); *Cunningham v. State*, 500 S.W.2d 820, 824 (Tex. Crim. App. 1973) (evidence that defendant had a shotgun in his possession shortly after a robbery in which the robbers used pistols, not shotguns, was inadmissible); *Hernandez v. State*, 484 S.W.2d 754, 755 n.2 (Tex. Crim. App. 1972) (rejecting evidence that defendant had a stolen television set when he was arrested for possession of narcotics).

568. *See, e.g., Maddox v. State*, 682 S.W.2d 563, 565 (Tex. Crim. App. 1985) (evidence of assault rifle on floorboard beneath seat when defendant was arrested for narcotics transaction was shown to be directly connected to and inseparable from defendant's arrest); *Hargrove v. State*, 211 S.W.3d 379, 388-89 (Tex. App.—San Antonio 2006, pet. ref'd) (evidence that police found 11 firearms in house when defendant was arrested for possession of controlled substance was admissible as affirmative link between defendant and his knowing possession of drugs because it raised an inference that he used the firearms to protect the drugs); *Sandoval v. State*, 946 S.W.2d 472, 477-78 (Tex.

ately before or after the commission of the charged offense may also be relevant to show a number of material facts—including intent, common scheme, or plan—and to demonstrate the context of the charged offense.[569]

This "contextual" exception to the bar on evidence of uncharged misconduct is generally based on statutory authority in murder prosecutions. Code of Criminal Procedure article 38.36 permits either the State or the defendant to offer evidence of all relevant facts surrounding the killing itself, including the relationship between the victim and the defendant and the defendant's state of mind.[570] This provision operates independently of Rule 404(b) and may be more broadly construed than the rule.[571] The court of criminal appeals has harmonized Rule 404(b) and article 38.36(a), holding that the statute does not abrogate the trial court's duty to exclude evidence of extraneous offenses offered solely to show that the defendant acted in conformity with a character trait exemplified by prior bad acts.[572] While Rule 404(b) limits the admissibility of specific acts used to show only the defendant's character, it does not block the admission of all relationship evidence.[573] Thus, the purposes set out in article 38.36 provide

---

App.—Corpus Christi 1997, pet. ref'd) (error to admit evidence of pistol, clips, and ammunition found in closet of house where defendant was arrested for possession of cocaine when there were no evidentiary links of ownership or possession between defendant and gun); *Menefee v. State*, 928 S.W.2d 274, 277 (Tex. App.—Tyler 1996, no pet.) (presence of pistol at defendant's business was probative of whether defendant, charged with possession of controlled substance with intent to deliver, was conducting a drug business); *Hawkins v. State*, 871 S.W.2d 539, 541 (Tex. App.—Fort Worth 1994, no pet.) (evidence of defendant's pistol and bullet found in a box in bathroom near cocaine was relevant to issue of defendant's control and knowledge that cocaine was in bathroom). The dissent in *Hargrove* argued that the probative value of the firearms was minimal—they were found in the master bedroom, while the drugs were found in the utility room—but the risk of unfair prejudice was high because "the presence of the weapons throughout the trial only helped to inflame the juror's minds and encourage speculation and conjecture as to their use." 211 S.W.3d at 390-91 (Simmons, J., dissenting).

569. *See, e.g., Lawton v. State*, 913 S.W.2d 542, 552-53 (Tex. Crim. App. 1995) (testimony by numerous witnesses that defendant and his accomplices burglarized various vehicles the night before the capital murder, in furtherance of a planned conspiracy, was admissible; defendant's role in conspiracy was to act as an armed guard, ready to kill anyone who jeopardized the planned endeavor); *Smith v. State*, 898 S.W.2d 838, 842 (Tex. Crim. App. 1995) (evidence of robbery immediately before murder showed defendant's intent and motive to kill victim because he needed victim's truck to escape from foiled robbery); *Smith*, 949 S.W.2d at 337 (no error in admitting evidence that defendant, charged with escape, stole a pickup truck to effectuate escape from prison).

570. Article 38.36(a) reads:
> In all prosecutions for murder, the state or the defendant shall be permitted to offer testimony as to all relevant facts and circumstances surrounding the killing and the previous relationship existing between the accused and the deceased, together with all relevant facts and circumstances going to show the condition of the mind of the accused at the time of the offense.

571. *See Jackson v. State*, 160 S.W.3d 568, 574 (Tex. Crim. App. 2005) (defendant might be able to offer evidence of his prior mental illness under art. 38.36(a), but "the trial judge has discretion to determine whether evidence of mental illness may be presented to negate the element of *mens rea*, or whether the evidence should be excluded on special grounds" under Rule 403); *see, e.g., Dickey v. State*, 979 S.W.2d 825, 828 (Tex. App.—Houston [14th Dist.] 1998) (description of a previous fight between victim and defendant was admissible to help explain the relationship between them and to show defendant's state of mind at time of killing, *rev'd on other grounds*, 22 S.W.3d 490 (Tex. Crim. App. 1999).

572. *See Smith v. State*, 5 S.W.3d 673, 678 (Tex. Crim. App. 1999); *see also Ex parte Varelas*, 45 S.W.3d 627, 632 n.5 (Tex. Crim. App. 2001) (Rule 404(b) and art. 38.36(a) can be applied congruously).

573. *E.g., Garcia v. State*, 201 S.W.3d 695, 703-04 (Tex. Crim. App. 2006) (evidence that defendant pushed his wife, the murder victim, out of the car, drove away, and left her on the side of the road without her purse or cell phone

relevant bases for which extraneous-offense evidence might be offered, but that article does not "trump" Rule 404(a)(1), the general ban against "bad character" evidence offered to prove conforming conduct.[574]

(2) Contextual evidence to correct false impression. Extraneous-offense evidence may be admissible to correct a false impression left by the opposing party.[575] This evidence is not admitted as substantive evidence of the charged offense, however, but only as evidence that the defendant created the misrepresentation.[576] Even if the opposing party opens the door to rebuttal evidence, the trial court may still exclude it under Rule 403.[577]

C. Rule 403 Balancing Test & Extraneous Offenses

A party objecting to the admission of uncharged misconduct should always object under both Rule 404(b) (the extraneous offense is not admissible) and Rule 403 (the risks raised by one of the counterfactors under that rule substantially outweigh the probative value of the evidence). An objection under Rule 404(b) applies only to whether the evidence fits the exception outlined in that rule; it does not raise any issue of the unfair prejudicial effect, likelihood of misleading the jury, or confusing the issues.[578]

---

was admissible because it was offered to show both the stormy relationship between them and the fact that they had separated and were getting divorced and because it inferentially showed defendant's intent and motive for murder; probative value of evidence was not substantially outweighed by danger of unfair prejudice); *see, e.g.,* **Rogers v. State**, 183 S.W.3d 853, 862-63 (Tex. App.—Tyler 2005, no pet.) (two unsigned, undated affidavits purportedly drafted by murder victim were admissible under art. 38.36(a) to show murder victim's ongoing relationship with defendant and why victim was afraid for her life and for her children's lives; evidence was not barred under Rule 403 because it showed defendant's intent to murder and rebutted his defense that victim's shooting was an accident); **Hernandez v. State**, 171 S.W.3d 347, 359-61 (Tex. App.—Houston [14th Dist.] 2005, pet. ref'd) (evidence of defendant's prior drug transactions with the capital-murder victim was relevant under art. 38.36(a) and admissible under Rule 403 because it showed "the basis for his relationship with [victim] and his familiarity with [victim's] routine, his residence, and his possessions, to reveal the basis for appellant's plan to rob [victim]. It also was relevant to whether appellant intended to kill [victim] because [victim] knew and could identify him.").

574. **Smith**, 5 S.W.3d at 678-79.

575. **Hayden v. State**, 296 S.W.3d 549, 554 (Tex. Crim. App. 2009); **Daggett v. State**, 187 S.W.3d 444, 452 (Tex. Crim. App. 2005); *see* **Williams v. State**, 301 S.W.3d 675, 687 (Tex. Crim. App. 2009); **Renteria v. State**, 206 S.W.3d 689, 697-98 (Tex. Crim. App. 2006); *see, e.g.,* **Dana v. State**, 420 S.W.3d 158, 166-67 (Tex. App.—Beaumont 2012, pet. ref'd) (when defense witness's testimony on direct examination left impression that defendant could have taken only prescription drugs, prosecution could cross-examine witness about her using methamphetamines with defendant); **Houston v. State**, 208 S.W.3d 585, 591 (Tex. App.—Austin 2006, no pet.) (in trial for delivery of cocaine, defense counsel cross-examined arresting officer and "elicited evidence that [defendant] dressed shabbily, drove an old car, and did not make a lot of money in the drug business"; this testimony left false impression and opened door to testimony about another drug sale arranged by defendant).

576. **Daggett**, 187 S.W.3d at 452. On request, the judge must give a limiting instruction informing the jury that this evidence is admissible only to gauge the defendant's credibility and not as proof of guilt of the charged offense. *Id.* at 452-53.

577. **Hayden**, 296 S.W.3d at 554.

578. *See* **Montgomery v. State**, 810 S.W.2d 372, 388-89 (Tex. Crim. App. 1991) (op. on reh'g); **Butler v. State**, 936 S.W.2d 453, 458 (Tex. App.—Houston [14th Dist.] 1996, pet. ref'd); *see also* **Johnson v. State**, 932 S.W.2d 296, 301 (Tex. App.—Austin 1996, pet. ref'd) ("Two objections, rather than one, may now be necessary to preserve error in the admission of extraneous offenses: one objection on the basis of Rule 404(b) and, if that is overruled, another objection on the basis of Rule 403.").

The Rule 403 balancing test for evidence of extraneous offenses is somewhat more elaborate than for other evidence. The factors that the trial judge should consider in this balancing process include:

(1) the inherent probative value of the evidence;

(2) the similarity of the extraneous conduct to the charged offense;

(3) the strength of the evidence of the extraneous offense;

(4) the nature of the extraneous conduct and its potential for impressing the jury in irrational but indelible ways;

(5) the trial time necessary to develop the evidence, considering whether the jury's attention will be diverted from the charged offense; and

(6) the State's "need" for the evidence, including:

(a) the availability of other evidence that tends to accomplish the same purpose;

(b) the strength of that other evidence; and

(c) whether the purpose served by the admission of the extraneous conduct relates to a disputed issue.[579]

The admission or exclusion of extraneous-offense evidence under Rules 404(b) and 403 is within the trial court's discretion.[580] A ruling will be affirmed by the appellate court if the trial court conducted the required balancing analysis, unless the appellate court determines, after affording due deference to the trial court's decision, that the evidence is substantially more prejudicial than probative.[581]

The party against whom the evidence is offered is entitled to an instruction limiting the jury's consideration of the extraneous-offense evidence to the specific material

579. *See Santellan v. State*, 939 S.W.2d 155, 169 (Tex. Crim. App. 1997); *Montgomery*, 810 S.W.2d at 389-90 (op. on reh'g); *see, e.g., Beham v. State*, 476 S.W.3d 724, 737-38 (Tex. App.—Texarkana 2015, no pet.) (in aggravated-robbery case, trial court abused discretion in admitting extraneous-offense evidence of "contact with law enforcement" when record established those charges were dismissed and there was no evidence that would show defendant committed those acts; evidence that defendant was previously arrested for a similar violent crime, without more, made that evidence unfairly prejudicial); *Williams v. State*, 27 S.W.3d 599, 602-03 (Tex. App.—Waco 2000, pet. ref'd) (evidence of another inmate's sexual misconduct was irrelevant; even if it had been relevant, its prejudicial effect substantially outweighed any probative value); *Phelps v. State*, 5 S.W.3d 788, 795-96 (Tex. App.—San Antonio 1999, pet. ref'd) (in trial for aggravated sexual assault of a child, court upheld admission of testimony by defendant's ex-wife about his conduct toward her and her children when defense expert testified that victim's mother programmed victim's testimony and defendant was not aggressive and not at fault; ex-wife testified to similar events, which substantiated testimony by victim and her mother); *Broussard v. State*, 999 S.W.2d 477, 482 (Tex. App.—Houston [14th Dist.] 1999, pet. ref'd) (evidence in public-lewdness trial that defendant masturbated with another man immediately before charged offense helped establish his intent to be sexually gratified and his recklessness in engaging in conduct regardless of the presence of others).

580. *See Owens v. State*, 827 S.W.2d 911, 917 (Tex. Crim. App. 1992); *Pleasant v. State*, 755 S.W.2d 204, 206 (Tex. App.—Houston [14th Dist.] 1988, no pet.); *Rodda v. State*, 745 S.W.2d 415, 418 (Tex. App.—Houston [14th Dist.] 1988, pet. ref'd); *Cole v. State*, 735 S.W.2d 686, 690 (Tex. App.—Amarillo 1987), *rev'd on other grounds*, 839 S.W.2d 798 (Tex. Crim. App. 1990).

581. *See Montgomery*, 810 S.W.2d at 391-92 (op. on reh'g) (trial court's ruling will not be reversed if the ruling is "within the zone of reasonable disagreement").

issue or issues for which it is offered.[582] If requested, this limiting instruction should be given both at the time the evidence is first admitted and again when the judge gives the final written jury charge.[583] No such instruction is required, however, when the extraneous offense is offered to directly prove one of the main issues of the charged offense[584] or to show the context of the offense.[585]

D. Rule 404(b)(2): Notice Requirement in Criminal Cases

In criminal cases, Rule 404(b)(2) requires the State to give the defendant reasonable pretrial notice, if requested, of the State's intent to use extraneous-offense evidence in its case-in-chief.[586] The notice provision is intended to prevent the defendant from being surprised at trial by testimony about uncharged offenses and to aid him in preparing his defense.[587] While the provision has some strategic value, the practical effect has been to shift the prosecutor's strategy to reserving extraneous-offense evidence until the rebuttal case, when notice is not required.[588] The notice requirement does not apply to same-transaction contextual evidence.[589]

---

582. *See Taylor v. State*, 920 S.W.2d 319, 323 (Tex. Crim. App. 1996) (limiting instruction may set out several material issues, such as motive, intent, identity, and rebuttal of defensive theory if extraneous offense was probative of each such issue); *Abdnor v. State*, 871 S.W.2d 726, 738 (Tex. Crim. App. 1994) (reversible error for trial judge to refuse defendant's request for a limiting instruction on the use of an extraneous offense), *disapproved on other grounds*, *Warner v. State*, 245 S.W.3d 458 (Tex. Crim. App. 2008); *Reed v. State*, 751 S.W.2d 607, 612-13 (Tex. App.—Dallas 1988, no pet.) (instruction limiting jury's consideration of extraneous offenses to the issue of the accused's identity may lessen the inherent prejudicial effect of such evidence). Refer to *Article I: General Provisions*, *supra* p. 97.

583. *See Rankin v. State*, 953 S.W.2d 740, 742 (Tex. Crim. App. 1996) (Meyers, J., concurring).

584. *Johnson v. State*, 509 S.W.2d 639, 640 & n.3 (Tex. Crim. App. 1974); *Harper v. State*, 930 S.W.2d 625, 630 (Tex. App.—Houston [1st Dist.] 1996, no pet.).

585. *See Devoe v. State*, 354 S.W.3d 457, 471 (Tex. Crim. App. 2011); *Castaldo v. State*, 78 S.W.3d 345, 352 (Tex. Crim. App. 2002); *Wesbrook v. State*, 29 S.W.3d 103, 114-15 (Tex. Crim. App. 2000); *Camacho v. State*, 864 S.W.2d 524, 535 (Tex. Crim. App. 1993).

586. Tex. R. Evid. 404(b)(2); *McDonald v. State*, 179 S.W.3d 571, 577 (Tex. Crim. App. 2005). This provision of Rule 404(b) changed earlier Texas law, which did not require any such notice. *See Milton v. State*, 599 S.W.2d 824, 827 (Tex. Crim. App. 1980) (defendant is not entitled to notice before extraneous offense is introduced as evidence). If the State provides notice voluntarily, it must provide complete information. *Agbogwe v. State*, 414 S.W.3d 820, 836 (Tex. App.—Houston [1st Dist.] 2013, no pet.); *Blackmon v. State*, 80 S.W.3d 103, 108 (Tex. App.—Texarkana 2002, pet. ref'd).

587. *See Worthy v. State*, 312 S.W.3d 34, 38-39 (Tex. Crim. App. 2010) (notice rules for evidence of uncharged misconduct guard against surprise and promote early resolution of admissibility issue); *Hayden v. State*, 66 S.W.3d 269, 272 (Tex. Crim. App. 2001) ("[T]he purpose of Rule 404(b) notice is to prevent surprise ...."); *Owens v. State*, 119 S.W.3d 439, 443-44 (Tex. App.—Tyler 2003, no pet.) (purpose of notice requirement "is to avoid unfair surprise and trial by ambush"; no showing that State "laid behind the log" to ambush or surprise defendant when State gave notice as soon as it learned about extraneous offense).

588. *See Dabney v. State*, 492 S.W.3d 309, 317 (Tex. Crim. App. 2016) ("While Rule 404(b) requires the State to provide notice of other crimes, wrongs, or acts it plans to introduce in its case-in-chief, there is an exception to this requirement when the defense opens the door to such evidence by presenting a defensive theory that the State may rebut using extraneous-offense evidence. To hold otherwise would impose upon the State the impossible task of anticipating, prior to the beginning of trial, any and all potential defenses that a defendant may raise."). Under Federal Rule 404(b)(2), no specific form of notice is mandated, but reasonable notice is required regardless of whether the prosecution intends to offer evidence of extraneous offenses in its case-in-chief, for impeachment, or during rebuttal. *See* Fed. R. Evid. 404(b)(2); Fed. R. Evid. 404 advisory committee's note to 1991 amendments.

589. Tex. R. Evid. 404(b)(2); *McDonald*, 179 S.W.3d at 577; *see Harper*, 930 S.W.2d at 630; *see also Hayden v. State*, 13 S.W.3d 69, 75 (Tex. App.—Texarkana 2000) (State could not evade notice requirements of rule by incor-

The court of criminal appeals has stated that there are two ways to request notice under Rule 404(b).[590] First, a defendant can file a discovery motion requesting notice; if such a motion is filed, the defendant must obtain the trial court's ruling on that motion before trial.[591] Second, a defendant can file a separate document entitled "Request for Notice of Intent to Offer Extraneous Offenses."[592] The second method may be easier because the trial court does not need to rule on such a specific request for notice before the State must comply.[593]

Although the State's notice does not need to be elaborate, a prosecutor's open-file policy does not, by itself, satisfy Rule 404(b)'s notice requirement.[594] Because the provision does not define how much advance notice is "reasonable," courts determine

---

rectly claiming that extraneous-offense evidence was really same-transaction contextual evidence because none of these incidents were necessary to jury's understanding of the indicted offense), *rev'd on other grounds*, 66 S.W.3d 269 (Tex. Crim. App. 2001).

There is a statutory notice requirement for unadjudicated-offense evidence offered during the punishment stage of a criminal proceeding. *See* TEX. CODE CRIM. PROC. art. 37.07, §3(g). This section reads as follows:

> On timely request of the defendant, notice of intent to introduce evidence under this article shall be given in the same manner required by Rule 404(b), Texas Rules of Evidence. If the attorney representing the state intends to introduce an extraneous crime or bad act that has not resulted in a final conviction in a court of record or a probated or suspended sentence, notice of that intent is reasonable only if the notice includes the date on which and the county in which the alleged crime or bad act occurred and the name of the alleged victim of the crime or bad act. The requirement under this subsection that the attorney representing the state give notice applies only if the defendant makes a timely request to the attorney representing the state for the notice.

Id. Refer to notes 599-603 *infra* and accompanying text.

590. *See Espinosa v. State*, 853 S.W.2d 36, 38-39 (Tex. Crim. App. 1993).

591. *Id.* at 39; *see, e.g.*, *Simpson v. State*, 991 S.W.2d 798, 801 (Tex. Crim. App. 1998) (defendant's request for notice of extraneous offenses contained within a "motion" was not self-executing request for notice; when defendant did not obtain ruling on motion, notice requirement was not triggered); *Harmon v. State*, 889 S.W.2d 521, 524 (Tex. App.—Houston [14th Dist.] 1994, pet. ref'd) (when defendant included request for notice of extraneous offenses in his discovery motion, he was required to obtain ruling on that motion before State was required to give notice of its intent to use extraneous offenses).

592. *Espinosa*, 853 S.W.2d at 38 n.3.

593. *See id.* at 38.

594. *See Buchanan v. State*, 911 S.W.2d 11, 15 (Tex. Crim. App. 1995). In explaining its holding, the court stated the following:

> We cannot conclude that the mere opening of its file containing an offense report detailing extraneous evidence satisfies the requirement of giving notice "of intent to introduce" such evidence. The mere presence of an offense report indicating the State's awareness of the existence of such evidence does not indicate an "intent to introduce" such evidence in its case in chief.

Id.; *see also Ortiz v. State*, 4 S.W.3d 851, 853-54 (Tex. App.—Eastland 1999, pet. ref'd) (filing defendant's penitentiary packet with Rule 902(10) business-records affidavit in clerk's file and giving notice to defendant of that filing is sufficient notice of intent; there is no purpose in filing a self-authenticated document under Rule 902(10) except to give opposing party notice that proponent will introduce such self-authenticated evidence); *Roman v. State*, 986 S.W.2d 64, 66-68 (Tex. App.—Austin 1999, pet. ref'd) (general written notice of State's intent to offer extraneous offense attached to police report elaborating on that evidence is sufficient notice of its intent); *Cole v. State*, 987 S.W.2d 893, 896-97 (Tex. App.—Fort Worth 1998, pet. ref'd) (as long as defendant has actual knowledge of information that State had in its possession about extraneous offense, notice is sufficient); *Woodard v. State*, 931 S.W.2d 747, 749 (Tex. App.—Waco 1996, no pet.) (notice sufficient when State gives defendant copies of his penitentiary packet and tells him that everything in those documents is subject to introduction).

whether notice is reasonable based on the facts and circumstances of each case.[595] Texas courts have given various interpretations of that term.[596]

The court of criminal appeals has held that the notice requirements of Rule 404(b) may, in an appropriate case, be satisfied by giving the defense statements by the State's witnesses detailing the extraneous offenses the State seeks to offer.[597] While acknowledging that the "better practice" is to explicitly inform the defense in writing of the State's intent to offer specific extraneous-offense evidence, the court held that delivery of witness statements may constitute an implicit statement: "These are the extraneous offenses that we intend to offer in the case-in-chief."[598]

Under Texas Code of Criminal Procedure article 37.07, the State must also give the defense reasonable notice of its intent to offer extraneous-offense evidence during its case-in-chief at the punishment stage of a criminal trial.[599] Like Rule 404(b), article 37.07, §3(g) does not define "reasonable notice." Courts must determine whether notice is reasonable based on the facts and circumstances of each case.[600] The article 37.07 notice requirement does not apply to the State's rebuttal evidence during the punishment stage.[601] Further, the court of criminal appeals has held that this requirement applies only to extraneous-offense evidence, not to same-transaction contextual evi-

---

595. *Francis v. State*, 445 S.W.3d 307, 318 (Tex. App.—Houston [1st Dist.] 2013), *aff'd*, 428 S.W.3d 850 (Tex. Crim. App. 2014).

596. *See, e.g.*, *Neuman v. State*, 951 S.W.2d 538, 539-40 (Tex. App.—Austin 1997, no pet.) (one day's notice before testimony on extraneous offense was insufficient); *Hernandez v. State*, 914 S.W.2d 226, 234 (Tex. App.—Waco 1996, no pet.) (no reasonable notice given when defendant requested notice ten months before trial and State gave notice three days before trial); *Self v. State*, 860 S.W.2d 261, 264 (Tex. App.—Fort Worth 1993, pet. ref'd) (reasonable notice given when defendant requested notice 19 days before trial and State gave notice 11 days before trial and again 5 days before trial).

597. *Hayden v. State*, 66 S.W.3d 269, 272 (Tex. Crim. App. 2001).

598. *Id.* at 272-73.

599. *See* TEX. CODE CRIM. PROC. art. 37.07, §3(g) ("On timely request of the defendant, notice of intent to introduce evidence under this article shall be given in the same manner required by Rule 404(b) ...."); *see, e.g.*, *Roethel v. State*, 80 S.W.3d 276, 280-83 (Tex. App.—Austin 2002, no pet.) (notice of intent to introduce evidence of extraneous offenses was unreasonable because it provided insufficient notice of the date of the extraneous offense as required by art. 37.07; evidence was inadmissible as a matter of law, but error was harmless). Some courts have held that substantial compliance with the statute is sufficient, as long as there was no unfair surprise to the defendant. *See Andrews v. State*, 429 S.W.3d 849, 860-61 (Tex. App.—Texarkana 2014, pet. ref'd); *Nance v. State*, 946 S.W.2d 490, 492-93 (Tex. App.—Fort Worth 1997, pet. ref'd); *see, e.g.*, *Hohn v. State*, 951 S.W.2d 535, 537 (Tex. App.—Beaumont 1997, pet. ref'd) (giving range of three months in which extraneous offenses took place, rather than specific dates, substantially complied with statute). Error in admitting evidence with insufficient notice under article 37.07, §3(g) is nonconstitutional error. *Apolinar v. State*, 106 S.W.3d 407, 414 (Tex. App.—Houston [1st Dist.] 2003), *aff'd*, 155 S.W.3d 184 (Tex. Crim. App. 2005). For a discussion of nonconstitutional error, refer to *Article I: General Provisions*, *supra* p. 61.

600. *Francis*, 445 S.W.3d at 318; *Sebalt v. State*, 28 S.W.3d 819, 822 (Tex. App.—Corpus Christi 2000, no pet.); *Patton v. State*, 25 S.W.3d 387, 392 (Tex. App.—Austin 2000, pet. ref'd).

601. *E.g.*, *Jaubert v. State*, 74 S.W.3d 1, 3-4 (Tex. Crim. App. 2002) (defendant was not entitled to notice of State's intent to use extraneous bad-acts evidence introduced during cross-examination and rebuttal testimony in punishment stage of murder trial after defendant had pleaded guilty); *see Washington v. State*, 943 S.W.2d 501, 506 (Tex. App.—Fort Worth 1997, pet. ref'd).

dence.[602] "[P]retrial notice must be given under Article 37.07, §3(g), only when pretrial notice is required under Rule 404(b)."[603]

The State's failure to give sufficient notice of its intent to offer extraneous-offense evidence when the defendant has requested such notice is subject to a harmless-error analysis under Texas Rule of Appellate Procedure 44.2(b).[604]

E. Noncharacter Uses of Reputation & Opinion Evidence

Rule 404(b)(2) concerns the use of evidence of other wrongs or acts for purposes other than to prove character. Reputation and opinion evidence may be used to prove character under Rule 404(a).[605] This evidence is also admissible for noncharacter purposes. Reputation may be an ultimate issue, as it is in a defamation case—evidence of damage to the plaintiff's reputation may be admissible to either prove or mitigate the extent of the damage.[606] Reputation and opinion evidence may also be offered to circumstantially prove a noncharacter issue.[607] Expert witnesses, for example, are called to give their opinions on numerous technical or specialized subjects unrelated to character.

Rules 404 and 405 do not apply to the admissibility of reputation or opinion evidence when offered for purposes other than to prove character. Courts must look instead to other rules, such as the general principles of relevance and admissibility contained in Rules 401 through 403 or the rules on lay and expert opinions, contained in Rules 701 through 705.[608]

F. Rule 405(b): Character as an Ultimate Issue

Character may be an ultimate issue—an essential element of a charge, claim, or defense.[609] For example, in a negligent-entrustment case, the plaintiff must show that

---

602. *See **Worthy v. State**,* 312 S.W.3d 34, 38-39 (Tex. Crim. App. 2010). Refer to note 589 *supra* and accompanying text.

603. *Worthy,* 312 S.W.3d at 37.

604. *See **McDonald v. State**,* 179 S.W.3d 571, 578 (Tex. Crim. App. 2005); ***Webb v. State**,* 36 S.W.3d 164, 181 (Tex. App.—Houston [14th Dist.] 2000, pet. ref'd).

605. *See* Tex. R. Evid. 404(a)(2)-(a)(4), 405(a)(1). Refer to notes 322-444 *supra* and accompanying text.

606. *See* Tex. R. Evid. 405(b); *see, e.g.,* Prosser, *supra* note 434, §111, at 737, 739, §116, at 801 (discussing the tort of defamation as that which tends to "injure" reputation). Refer to notes 609-616 *infra* and accompanying text.

607. *See, e.g.,* ***Carbo v. United States**,* 314 F.2d 718, 740-41 (9th Cir. 1963) (in federal extortion case, evidence of defendant's underworld reputation as a "strong-arm" man was offered not to show conformity with character but rather because prosecution's case was based on a theory of extortion by fear of violence; defendant intended to intimidate victims, and codefendants were aware of this reputation when they asked him to participate in extortion conspiracy).

608. Refer to *Article VII: Opinions & Expert Testimony, infra* p. 683.

609. *See* Fed. R. Evid. 404 advisory committee's note, subdiv. (a); McCormick's Handbook II, *supra* note 33, §186, at 442; 1 Wigmore, *supra* note 1, §§55-69, at 449-91; *see also* Black's Law Dictionary 960 (10th ed. 2014) (defining "ultimate issue" as "[a] not-yet-decided point that is sufficient either in itself or in connection with other points to resolve the entire case").

the driver is a characteristically reckless or incompetent driver.[610] That character trait is an element of the plaintiff's claim.[611]

If character is an ultimate issue, it must be proved. In this instance, Rule 404 is not pertinent because it deals only with proof of character as circumstantial evidence to show conduct in conformity with that character on a particular occasion.[612] Permission to prove character as an ultimate issue comes from the principle of Rule 402 to admit all relevant evidence as defined in Rule 401.

The common law[613] and earlier Texas law[614] allowed all three methods of proving such character: reputation, opinion, and specific instances of conduct. The Texas Rules, following the Federal Rules, codified this practice. Rule 405(a) allows proof of character by reputation or opinion whenever evidence of character is admissible.[615] Rule 405(b) permits proof of character by specific instances of the subject's conduct when the subject's character is an ultimate issue.[616]

RULE 406

HABIT; ROUTINE PRACTICE

Evidence of a person's habit or an organization's routine practice may be admitted to prove that on a particular occasion the person or organization acted in accordance with the habit or routine practice. The court may admit this evidence regardless of whether it is corroborated or whether there was an eyewitness.

COMMENTARY ON RULE 406
A. Admissibility of Habit & Routine Practice to Show Conforming Conduct

Unlike most of the relevance rules following Rule 403, Rule 406 is a rule of admission rather than exclusion. Rule 406 covers evidence of a person's habit or of an orga-

---

610. *See Hines v. Nelson*, 547 S.W.2d 378, 385-86 (Tex. Civ. App.—Tyler 1977, no writ) (owner must know or should know that the driver is reckless or incompetent).

611. For an interesting discussion suggesting that evidence showing that the user of a product is "irresponsible or lax in judgment" is admissible to demonstrate a character trait that constitutes an essential element of defense in a products-liability case, see *Magro v. Ragsdale Bros.*, 721 S.W.2d 832, 837 (Tex. 1986) (Gonzalez, J., concurring in part and dissenting in part) (analogizing to negligent-entrustment cases; "the user's character for irresponsibility or lax judgment is precisely the fact on which the manufacturer's defense hinges; it is an essential element of the defense"). This suggestion seems incorrect, however, because the product user's character trait for irresponsible use of products is not in issue. The user's misuse of the product on a particular occasion is the essential element. Thus, the evidence offered in this case is precisely the "propensity" use barred by Rule 404.

612. *See* FED. R. EVID. 404 advisory committee's note, subdiv. (a); 2 WEINSTEIN & BERGER, *supra* note 84, ¶404[01], at 404-18.

613. McCORMICK's HANDBOOK II, *supra* note 33, §186, at 443; 1 WIGMORE, *supra* note 1, §§70-81, at 491-511.

614. *See* 2 RAY, *supra* note 46, §1501, at 187; *see, e.g., Moore v. Davis*, 27 S.W.2d 153, 157 (Tex. Comm'n App. 1930, judgm't adopted) (in libel case, evidence of specific acts was admissible to show that plaintiff was unfit to become a judge); *Brook v. Morriss, Morriss & Boatwright*, 212 S.W.2d 257, 259 (Tex. Civ. App.—Austin 1948, no writ) (in legal-fee controversy in which reputation was an element for valuing legal services, evidence of attorneys' good reputation was admissible).

615. Refer to notes 322-444 *supra* and accompanying text.

616. TEX. R. EVID. 405(b). The rule is identical to Federal Rule 405(b).

nization's routine practice, explicitly making this evidence admissible. Specifically, the rule declares this evidence admissible to prove that the conduct of a person or organization conformed with the person's habit or the organization's routine practice on a particular occasion. Thus, Rule 406 is the reverse of Rule 404, which prohibits the use of character evidence to prove conforming conduct. Rule 406 derives from Federal Rule 406 and is identical to it.

The policy underlying the distinction between character evidence and habit is that "the uniformity of one's response to habit is far greater than the consistency with which one's conduct conforms to character or disposition."[617] Thus, habit evidence is more probative and less prejudicial than character evidence.[618]

1. Defining habit & distinguishing character. Habit and character are "close akin" but still distinguishable.[619] While character refers to personal disposition, such as honesty or aggressiveness,[620] habit describes "one's regular response to a repeated specific situation," a "regular practice of meeting a particular kind of situation with a specific type of conduct," or "uniformity" or "semi-automatic" behavior.[621] Because Rule 406

---

617. *See* McCormick's Handbook II, *supra* note 33, §195, at 463.

618. The common law, at least in civil cases, had generally been hostile to evidence of character to prove conforming conduct. Refer to notes 322-328 *supra* and accompanying text. However, it had been more receptive to evidence of habit or routine practice to prove such conduct. *See* McCormick's Handbook II, *supra* note 33, §195, at 462-65; 2 Ray, *supra* note 46, §1511, at 194-95; 1 Wigmore, *supra* note 1, §92, at 519-20; *see, e.g.,* **Dearing v. Nutter**, 402 S.W.2d 889, 889 (Tex. 1966) (per curiam) (evidence of habit was admissible to prove that a route was traveled); **Deuberry v. Tex. Pac. Indem. Co.**, 478 S.W.2d 606, 608 (Tex. Civ. App.—Fort. Worth 1972, writ ref'd n.r.e.) (evidence of habitual intemperance was admissible to show intoxication). Thus, Rule 406 follows the common-law approach to evidence of habit or routine practice. The only major difference is that the rule rejected the "eyewitness exception" found in the common law. Refer to notes 640-647 *infra* and accompanying text.

619. McCormick's Handbook II, *supra* note 33, §195, at 462.

620. *Id.*

621. *Id.* §195, at 462-63; *see* **Ortiz v. Glusman**, 334 S.W.3d 812, 816 (Tex. App.—El Paso 2011, pet. denied); **Haggar Clothing Co. v. Hernandez**, 164 S.W.3d 407, 424 (Tex. App.—Corpus Christi 2003) (memo op.), *rev'd on other grounds*, 164 S.W.3d 386 (Tex. 2005). In one unusual case, the court of appeals held that it was reversible constitutional error to exclude the assault defendant's evidence that the complainant, his wife, had a "habit" of reacting aggressively during their arguments. **Dietz v. State**, 123 S.W.3d 528, 532-33 (Tex. App.—San Antonio 2003, pet. ref'd). There was no evidence of precisely how frequently the couple argued during their 12-year marriage or what percentage of the time the complainant reacted "aggressively," and there was no showing that she routinely reacted with a specific response. *See id.* at 531-33. The defendant merely stated that she was "aggressive" and "violent," and would "throw things" at him and "hit" him. *Id.* at 531. This is not the type of habitual reaction to a specific stimulus that is usually covered by Rule 406, but rather more like evidence of the complainant's aggressive character. This testimony may have been admissible, however, as "communicated character" to establish the reasonableness of the defendant's fear of his wife's physical violence during their verbal arguments. Refer to notes 406-413 *supra* and accompanying text.

Habit has, on occasion, been used to introduce extraneous offenses in child-abuse cases, as when a child sexual-assault victim testifies that he has been molested by the defendant on "numerous" occasions over a lengthy period of time. *See, e.g.,* **Waddell v. State**, 873 S.W.2d 130, 132, 138 (Tex. App.—Beaumont 1994, pet. ref'd) (victim's statement that defendant had sexually molested him "many times" during five-year period was admissible as habit evidence). Without some foundation demonstrating a regular and frequent response by the defendant when he encounters the victim in a particular situation, this conduct is propensity evidence barred under Rule 404, not habit evidence admissible under Rule 406. In both **Waddell**, 873 S.W.2d at 138, and **Miller v. State**, 882 S.W.2d 936, 938 (Tex. App.—Beaumont 1994, no pet.), the Beaumont Court of Appeals appeared to mischaracterize propensity evidence as habit. In neither case was there any showing of regularity of response to a specific stimulus. For an unusual case in which the appellate court held that evidence of other incidents of improper touching of female em-

includes no definition of "habit," the nonexclusive, alternative definitions above seem appropriate.[622] The Advisory Committee's note to the federal rule appears to refer to two distinct types of habit. The first, sometimes called the "psychological theory,"[623] focuses on the semiautomatic nature of a habit, a Pavlovian response to stimuli. The second, sometimes called the "probability theory,"[624] focuses on the person's regular, though conscious, response to a specific situation (e.g., driving within the speed limit or stopping for a red light).

To constitute a "habit," the person's response must be the same one directed at the same specific stimulus.[625] Several different responses that could all be characterized as "negligent" or "wrongful" do not qualify as a habit.[626]

Evidence of character and of habit are also distinguishable from an evidentiary standpoint. It is easier to describe with particularity a person's specific actions that constitute a habit than it is to explain the particularized basis of a character trait. Evidence of habit is also more probative as circumstantial evidence of conduct on the particular occasion and is less likely to create unfair prejudice in the jury's eyes.[627] The term "habit" is typically applied only to the behavior of a person.[628] The equivalent term used when dealing with an organization is "routine practice" or "custom."[629] Trial courts have considerable discretion in deciding whether the proffered evidence reaches the level of a true habit or routine practice.[630]

---

ployees was admissible as "habit" evidence in a suit for assault and intentional infliction of emotional distress, see *Stokes v. Puckett*, 972 S.W.2d 921, 926-27 (Tex. App.—Beaumont 1998, pet. denied). Although it might be possible to have a "habit" of groping female employees, there was no evidence in this case of the frequency, duration, or number of employees that the defendant allegedly touched. This appears to be Rule 404(b)(1) character evidence that was mischaracterized as Rule 406 habit evidence.

622. The drafters of the federal rule approved of McCormick's definitions of "habit." *See* FED. R. EVID. 406 advisory committee's note.

623. *See* 23 WRIGHT & GRAHAM, *supra* note 35, §5273, at 24-25 (1980).

624. *Id.* §5273, at 25-26. *See generally* Thomas M. Mengler, *The Theory of Discretion in the Federal Rules of Evidence*, 74 IOWA L. REV. 413, 417 (1989) (describing the probability theory).

625. *Ortiz*, 334 S.W.3d at 816.

626. *See, e.g.*, *Jones v. S. Pac. R.R.*, 962 F.2d 447, 449-50 (5th Cir. 1992) (nine different safety violations did not show "habit" of negligence); *Waldon v. City of Longview*, 855 S.W.2d 875, 879-80 (Tex. App.—Tyler 1993, no writ) (three car accidents in six years do not prove a "habit" of careless driving).

627. *See* Mengler, *supra* note 624, at 417 (reliability of evidence of habit is based on a habit's mechanical, automatic nature); *see also* Harriet R. Galvin, *Shielding Rape Victims in the State and Federal Courts: A Proposal for the Second Decade*, 70 MINN. L. REV. 763, 832-33 (1986) (the reason "courts are more receptive to habit evidence than they are to character evidence is that the former ... does not give rise to jury prejudice").

628. 1 GOODE ET AL., *supra* note 103, §406.2, at 224.

629. *See* FED. R. EVID. 406 advisory committee's note; *see, e.g.*, *Hot Shot Messenger Serv., Inc. v. State*, 798 S.W.2d 413, 415 (Tex. App.—Austin 1990, writ denied) (per curiam) (proper mailing may be proved by evidence of customary mailing routine); *Mediacomp, Inc. v. Capital Cities Commc'n, Inc.*, 698 S.W.2d 207, 212 (Tex. App.—Houston [1st Dist.] 1985, no writ) (introduction of a standard industry contract was relevant evidence of custom and practices and circumstantial evidence of the intent of the parties); *Cooper v. Hall*, 489 S.W.2d 409, 415 (Tex. Civ. App.—Amarillo 1972, writ ref'd n.r.e.) (proper mailing may be proved by evidence of the "customary mailing routine" of an attorney's office). *See generally* 1 WIGMORE, *supra* note 1, §92, at 519-20 (discussing "habit" or "custom"). Refer to notes 637-639 *infra* and accompanying text.

630. *See, e.g.*, *United States v. Quattrone*, 441 F.3d 153, 191-92 & n.40 (2d Cir. 2006) (trial court correctly held that defendant's evidence of sending responsive e-mails on other occasions did not reach the level of habit under

RULE 406

2. Examples of admissible habit & routine-practice evidence. Texas courts have often admitted evidence of habit to show conforming conduct.[631] For example, a party's testimony about the route he habitually drives is admissible to show that he followed that route on the occasion in question.[632] Testimony that a deceased pedestrian "was seen on other occasions to look down at the sidewalk while walking, shuffled along and went kinda slow" is admissible to show that the decedent was not being observant when he was struck by a car.[633] Similarly, an insured vehicle owner's practice of letting another person use his car is admissible to show the existence and scope of the owner's permission on the litigated occasion.[634] Evidence that a convenience-store manager regularly provided a known alcoholic with alcoholic beverages may be admissible in a wrongful-death case to show the relationship and course of dealing between the parties.[635] Testimony that a deceased wife never opened the door to strangers is admissible in a murder-burglary prosecution.[636]

In the same vein, an organization's routine practice has generally been admissible in Texas to show conforming conduct. For example, the customary mailing routine of a sender's business is admissible to prove that the sender properly addressed, stamped, and mailed a particular letter.[637] Frequently, proof of a regular business routine is the only evidence a business can produce to show that it performed a specific act on a specific occasion. For example, a secretary is not likely to remember whether a particular letter was mailed on a specific date.[638] For this reason, courts accept evidence of a business's routine more readily than evidence of a person's habit.[639]

3. Eyewitness exception in negligence cases. Rule 406 departs from past Texas practice in its rejection of the "eyewitness" exception. Before the promulgation of the Rules,

---

Federal Rule 406 because that "email was not a reflexive response to a repeated, specific situation"); **United States v. Angwin**, 271 F.3d 786, 798-800 (9th Cir. 2001) (defendant's conduct during military training showing that he prudently took the least confrontational course of action was not "sufficiently reflexive and specific to constitute habit evidence"; "a district court's ruling on whether proffered evidence qualifies as habit evidence … is highly fact-specific"), *overruled on other grounds*, **United States v. Lopez**, 484 F.3d 1186 (9th Cir. 2007).

631. That liberal interpretation follows earlier Texas law. 1 Goode et al., *supra* note 103, §406.2, at 223. Federal courts have also liberally admitted evidence of habit and have interpreted Federal Rule 406 with flexibility. *See id.* §406.2, at 222; Mengler, *supra* note 624, at 424-25. The rule has been infrequently litigated in federal courts. Thomas Mengler notes that between 1975 and 1989, only 24 reported cases discussed whether evidence of a person's behavior qualified as a habit under Federal Rule 406. Mengler, *supra* note 624, at 421 & n.54. This trend does not appear to have changed since 1989.

632. **Dearing v. Nutter**, 402 S.W.2d 889, 889 (Tex. 1966).

633. **Morsch v. Metzger**, 520 S.W.2d 564, 570 (Tex. Civ. App.—Corpus Christi 1975, writ ref'd n.r.e.).

634. **Allstate Ins. v. Smith**, 471 S.W.2d 620, 624-25 (Tex. Civ. App.—El Paso 1971, no writ).

635. **Pena v. Neal, Inc.**, 901 S.W.2d 663, 671-72 (Tex. App.—San Antonio 1995, writ denied).

636. **Anderson v. State**, 15 S.W.3d 177, 182-83 (Tex. App.—Texarkana 2000, no pet.).

637. **Hot Shot Messenger Serv., Inc. v. State**, 798 S.W.2d 413, 415 (Tex. App.—Austin 1990, writ denied) (per curiam); **Cooper v. Hall**, 489 S.W.2d 409, 415 (Tex. Civ. App.—Amarillo 1972, writ ref'd n.r.e.).

638. *See* 23 Wright & Graham, *supra* note 35, §5274, at 45 (1980).

639. *See* McCormick on Evidence, *supra* note 1, §195, at 576 (even jurisdictions reluctant to accept evidence of personal habits are willing to allow evidence of a custom of a regular business activity); 23 Wright & Graham, *supra* note 35, §5274, at 45 (1980) (traditionally, courts are more liberal in admitting evidence of business routine than personal habit because the need for such evidence is greater and the costs are less).

Texas courts had held that habit evidence was inadmissible to establish negligence, contributory negligence, or lack of care, unless the act at issue was not witnessed.[640] The courts maintained this position even when the sole eyewitness was an employee of the opponent of the party offering habit testimony.[641] When, however, a party sought to prove an issue other than care or negligence (e.g., a route traveled), Texas courts admitted habit evidence despite the testimony of eyewitnesses.[642]

The drafters of Federal Rule 406 rejected the eyewitness exception,[643] presumably on three grounds: (1) the exception is irrational;[644] (2) if habit evidence is prejudicial, it is equally prejudicial when there are no eyewitnesses;[645] and (3) evidence of habit is highly probative.[646] The Texas drafters agreed; thus, both Federal Rule 406 and Texas Rule 406 provide that evidence of habit is admissible to prove conforming conduct "regardless of … whether there was an eyewitness."[647]

4. Means & sufficiency of proof. Rule 406 does not specify how habit may be proved or what constitutes sufficient proof of habit.[648] On the question of sufficiency, at least, the drafters of the federal rule concluded that "precise standards … cannot be formulated."[649] One of the factors that should be considered is the particularity of the conduct in question. For example, negligent driving is a character trait, while stopping for

---

640. *See Mo.-Kan.-Tex. R.R. v. McFerrin*, 156 Tex. 69, 86, 291 S.W.2d 931, 942 (1956) (when no eyewitnesses observe an accident, the weight of authority is that habit evidence is admissible); *see, e.g., Dearing v. Nutter*, 402 S.W.2d 889, 889 (Tex. 1966) (admitting evidence to prove that defendant was following a habitual route at the time of the accident and distinguishing the admission from the inadmissible use of habit evidence to prove care or negligence when there is an eyewitness); *Morsch v. Metzger*, 520 S.W.2d 564, 570 (Tex. Civ. App.—Corpus Christi 1975, writ ref'd n.r.e.) (because plaintiff was not an eyewitness to the events before the accident, habit evidence was admissible to show decedent's contributory negligence); *Sanchez v. Billings*, 481 S.W.2d 911, 914 (Tex. Civ. App.—Houston [14th Dist.] 1972, writ ref'd n.r.e.) (excluding evidence of defendant's past driving habits because an eyewitness observed the accident); *Hudson v. Hightower*, 394 S.W.2d 46, 50 (Tex. Civ. App.—Austin 1965, writ ref'd n.r.e.) (defendant's testimony that he always drove slowly through the intersection where the collision occurred was inadmissible because an eyewitness saw the collision).

641. *See McFerrin*, 156 Tex. at 86-88, 291 S.W.2d at 942-44.

642. *See Dearing*, 402 S.W.2d at 889.

643. FED. R. EVID. 406 advisory committee's note.

644. *See Cereste v. N.Y., New Haven & Hartford R.R.*, 231 F.2d 50, 53 (2d Cir. 1956) (eyewitness exception "lacks reason").

645. *See id.*

646. *See id.* at 53-54 (quoting at length from CHARLES MCCORMICK, HANDBOOK OF THE LAW OF EVIDENCE §162, at 340-41 (1st ed. 1954)).

647. FED. R. EVID. 406; TEX. R. EVID. 406.

648. The drafters of the federal rule had originally included the following paragraph as subdivision (b) of Rule 406, as in Uniform Rule of Evidence 406(b): "Habit or routine practice may be proved by testimony in the form of an opinion or by specific instances of conduct sufficient in number to warrant a finding that the habit existed or that the practice was routine." FED. R. EVID. 406(b) (1972 proposed final draft), 56 F.R.D. 183, 223 (1973); UNIF. R. EVID. 406(b) (1974). Congress deleted subdivision (b) because "[t]he method of proof of habit and routine practice should be left to the courts to deal with on a case-by-case basis. [Deleting subdivision (b) must not] be construed as sanctioning a general authorization of opinion evidence in this area." H.R. REP. No. 93-650, at 5 (1974), *reprinted in* 1974 U.S.C.C.A.N. 7075, 7079.

649. FED. R. EVID. 406 advisory committee's note.

RULE 406

the stop sign at the intersection of Elm and Main is very particularized conduct.[650] Another factor courts should consider in determining whether a habit has been established is the frequency of the response. A court is less likely to find that a person has a habit of stopping at a particular stop sign, for instance, if he has stopped there only two known times than if he had done so 30 known times.[651] Two instances of conduct do not make a habit.[652]

The regularity of the conduct is important in establishing a habit.[653] A court may distinguish a situation in which the person in the above example passes the intersection once a week and has stopped every time during the past month from a situation in which he passes the intersection once a day and has stopped four times during the same month.[654]

If a witness is sufficiently familiar with the habit or routine practice offered as evidence, Texas courts permit the witness to testify in summary fashion by describing the habit or practice as the witness has observed it.[655] A court need not reject an attempt

---

650. *See United States v. Angwin*, 271 F.3d 786, 799-800 (9th Cir. 2001), *overruled on other grounds*, *United States v. Lopez*, 484 F.3d 1186 (9th Cir. 2007).

651. *See, e.g.*, *Simplex v. Diversified Energy Sys.*, 847 F.2d 1290, 1294 (7th Cir. 1988) (rejecting evidence of numerous other contracts involving Simplex, offered to establish the routine practice of late deliveries and defective performance, because the offering party did not establish sufficient similarity of specific conduct or frequency of uniform response); *Perrin v. Anderson*, 784 F.2d 1040, 1045-46 (10th Cir. 1986) (five instances are normally insufficient to demonstrate habit, but sufficient when offered to show that shooting victim had a habit of reacting violently to police officers and when no evidence was offered to show any peaceful reactions); *United States v. Pinto*, 755 F.2d 150, 152 (10th Cir. 1985) (four instances in which defendant entered the premises uninvited in an eight-year period were insufficient to establish the habit of wandering into others' houses while intoxicated); *United States v. Holman*, 680 F.2d 1340, 1350-51 (11th Cir. 1982) (one incident is insufficient to establish habit); *Reyes v. Mo. Pac. R.R.*, 589 F.2d 791, 795 (5th Cir. 1979) (four public-intoxication convictions during more than a three-year period were insufficient to establish habit); *Felix v. Gonzalez*, 87 S.W.3d 574, 579-80 (Tex. App.—San Antonio 2002, pet. denied) (four traffic accidents in 17 years did not constitute evidence of a habit; error to admit evidence of most recent prior accident on this basis); *Waldon v. City of Longview*, 855 S.W.2d 875, 879-80 (Tex. App.—Tyler 1993, no writ) (evidence that police officer had had three low-speed accidents under apparently low-risk conditions in six years did not establish a habit).

652. *See Ortiz v. Glusman*, 334 S.W.3d 812, 816 (Tex. App.—El Paso 2011, pet. denied); *see, e.g.*, *McClure v. Landis*, 959 S.W.2d 679, 681 (Tex. App.—Austin 1997, pet. denied) (two instances of plaintiff's failure to respond in discovery matters did not establish evidence of "habit"); *Johnson v. City of Hous.*, 928 S.W.2d 251, 254 (Tex. App.—Houston [14th Dist.] 1996, no writ) (testimony showing one other claimed act of retaliation did not meet the test of frequency and regularity to establish a "routine practice" under Civil Rule 406); *Pacesetter Corp. v. Barrickman*, 885 S.W.2d 256, 263 (Tex. App.—Tyler 1994, no writ) (in wrongful-discharge suit, two other instances of employer's handling of workers' compensation claims were not admissible as habit evidence).

653. *See, e.g.*, *Miller v. State*, 882 S.W.2d 936, 938 (Tex. App.—Beaumont 1994, no pet.) (witness's testimony that defendant "likes to shoot his gun every day and that this was a frequent act" was admissible as evidence of habit under Rule 406).

654. *See G.M. Brod & Co. v. U.S. Home Corp.*, 759 F.2d 1526, 1533 (11th Cir. 1985) (adequacy of sampling and uniformity of response are controlling considerations in determining whether a pattern of conduct constitutes habit); *see, e.g.*, *United States v. West*, 22 F.3d 586, 592 (5th Cir. 1994) (when FDIC dealt with thousands of debtors, a few instances of FDIC allegedly permitting "straw purchaser" transactions were insufficient to establish routine practice).

655. *See, e.g.*, *Bellefonte Underwriters Ins. v. Brown*, 663 S.W.2d 562, 581 (Tex. App.—Houston [14th Dist.] 1983) (insured could offer evidence of an insurance policy on another unheated building with a wet sprinkler system to impeach defendant, who testified that he would never have knowingly issued a policy for such a building), *rev'd in*

to prove the existence of a habit by showing a series of specific instances, but the court should exercise its discretion to ensure that the instances are frequent enough to show habit and that testimony about the instances does not consume too much time.[656]

Courts in some jurisdictions allow testimony about an organization's routine practice only if such testimony is corroborated.[657] The drafters of Federal Rule 406, believing that corroboration goes to the weight of habit evidence rather than to its admissibility, specifically rejected the corroboration requirement.[658] Texas courts have never required the proponent to corroborate evidence of an organization's routine practice.[659] Rule 406 continues this practice by specifying that evidence of habit or routine practice is admissible "regardless of whether it is corroborated."[660] Once again, however, the proponent of the evidence must show sufficient frequency and regularity of the same response before the proffered evidence demonstrates a routine practice under the rule.[661]

B. Excluding Habit Evidence Under Rule 403

Rule 406 presumes that habit evidence is admissible to prove conforming conduct. The trial court may exclude this evidence under Rule 403, however, if its probative value is substantially outweighed by any of the rule's counterfactors.[662]

Texas courts have often confronted the risk of the prejudicial effect of habit evidence in automobile-collision cases. Specifically, courts have faced the issue when one

part on other grounds, 704 S.W.2d 742 (Tex. 1986); *Wendlandt v. Sommers Drug Stores Co.*, 551 S.W.2d 488, 490 (Tex. Civ. App.—Austin 1977, no writ) (evidence of lessee's general procedure for mailing rental checks to lessor was admissible to establish that a particular check was mailed); *Cooper v. Hall*, 489 S.W.2d 409, 415 (Tex. Civ. App.—Amarillo 1972, writ ref'd n.r.e.) (when a fact issue has been raised by the testimonial denial of the receipt of a letter, opponent may offer evidence of its customary mailing practices); *Smith v. F.W. Heitman Co.*, 44 Tex. Civ. App. 358, 362-63, 98 S.W. 1074, 1076-77 (Galveston 1906, writ ref'd) (testimony about ordinary custom in mailing letters is sufficient to uphold jury's inference that a letter was properly mailed).

656. *See* Tex. R. Evid. 403 (court can exclude relevant evidence if its probative value is substantially outweighed by the possibility of unfair prejudice, undue delay, or other factors); McCormick's Handbook II, *supra* note 33, §195, at 465 (proof of habit by specific instances is subject to the court's discretion to require that the instances are not too many or too few in number); *see, e.g.*, *Whittington v. Dep't of Pub. Safety*, 342 S.W.2d 374, 375 (Tex. Civ. App.—Fort Worth 1961, writ ref'd n.r.e.) (nine notices of conviction for traffic violations, including seven within one year, were admissible to support a judgment suspending the driver's license of a habitual traffic violator).

657. Fed. R. Evid. 406 advisory committee's note.

658. *Id.*

659. *See Wendlandt*, 551 S.W.2d at 490 (courts have recognized the impracticality of requiring direct proof of mailing and have allowed circumstantial evidence for this purpose); *Cooper*, 489 S.W.2d at 415 (attorney's testimony about the mailing of a letter to defendant is sufficient to support the court's finding that the letter was properly mailed); *Smith*, 44 Tex. Civ. App. at 362-63, 98 S.W. at 1076-77 (president's testimony about the company's custom in mailing letters is sufficient evidence to uphold a jury inference that letter was mailed).

660. Tex. R. Evid. 406.

661. *See, e.g.*, *Oakwood Mobile Homes, Inc. v. Cabler*, 73 S.W.3d 363, 375-76 (Tex. App.—El Paso 2002, pet. denied) (trial court erred in admitting evidence from one other dissatisfied mobile-home buyer of poor workmanship and repair services; not sufficient to show "routine" business practice).

662. *See generally* Mengler, *supra* note 624, at 441-46 (analyzing the trial court's discretionary balancing under Rule 403 in the context of habit evidence). Refer to notes 111-159 *supra* and accompanying text.

RULE 406

party has sought to introduce evidence of the opponent's prior drunk driving to show that the opponent was driving while intoxicated at the time of the collision.[663] Under the common law, Texas courts maintained that evidence of an intemperate habit was admissible only to corroborate independent evidence of the opponent's intoxication at the time of the collision.[664] If other such independent evidence was admitted, the evidence must have established a habit, not just "particular or isolated instances."[665]

Under the plain terms of Rule 406, evidence of an intemperate habit to prove conforming conduct is admissible, as long as a habit is clearly established. If the trial court finds, however, that the probative value of the evidence is substantially outweighed by the danger of unfair prejudice, the trial court may, in its discretion, exclude the evidence under Rule 403. This operation of the rules seems to have modified Texas practice in that intemperate-habit evidence is no longer relegated to the role of corroborating other evidence. Rather, the more flexible balancing test of Rule 403 governs the admission of such evidence. Further, the trial court has discretion under Rules 403 and 611(a) to limit the amount and type of evidence a party may offer to show habit or business custom.[666]

C. Habit Evidence Admissible for Other Purposes

Although Rule 406 declares that evidence of habit or routine practice is admissible to prove conforming conduct, it does not mention whether this evidence is admissible for other purposes. For instance, is habit evidence admissible either to prove prescriptive possession or as a substitute for present recollection?[667] Texas courts have admitted habit or routine-practice evidence on issues other than conforming conduct. For example, a bank's routine practice of inserting a certain clause in a deed of trust was held admissible to show an absence of mutual mistake between lender and borrower.[668]

---

663. *See* **Compton v. Jay**, 389 S.W.2d 639, 642-43 (Tex. 1965) (history of drunkenness can be shown by evidence of general reputation but not by evidence of specific instances); **R.T. Herrin Pet. Transp. Co. v. Proctor**, 161 Tex. 222, 234, 338 S.W.2d 422, 431 (1960) (testimony of past drunkenness is admissible only if evidence shows that the driver was intoxicated at the time of the accident).

664. *See, e.g.*, **Compton**, 389 S.W.2d at 642 (two prior instances of drunk driving did not constitute a habit, and that evidence of the prior specific instances was inadmissible); **Proctor**, 161 Tex. at 234, 338 S.W.2d at 431 (absence of viable independent evidence indicating that a driver was drunk at the time of a collision prohibited the court from admitting evidence of prior drunken driving to prove negligence, even though prior DWI charge was admissible for a limited purpose on the issue of contribution the deceased "might have made (to his mother's support)").

665. *See* **Compton**, 389 S.W.2d at 642-43 (approving of McCormick's definition of a habit as a "regular response to a repeated specific situation"; two instances of drunken driving are insufficient to constitute a habit).

666. *See, e.g.*, **Perrin v. Anderson**, 784 F.2d 1040, 1045-46 (10th Cir. 1986) (trial court properly permitted only four out of eight witnesses to offer relevant habit evidence of shooting victim's habit of behaving aggressively toward police). Refer to *Article VI: Witnesses, infra* p. 636.

667. *See* 2 WIGMORE, *supra* note 179, §378, at 399 (habit evidence is admissible to show prescriptive possession); 1 WIGMORE, *supra* note 1, §98, at 533 (habit evidence is admissible as a substitute for present recollection).

668. **Walker v. Citizens Nat'l Bank**, 212 S.W.2d 203, 209-10 (Tex. Civ. App.—Waco 1948, writ ref'd n.r.e.).

RULE 407
SUBSEQUENT REMEDIAL MEASURES; NOTIFICATION OF DEFECT

(a) Subsequent Remedial Measures. When measures are taken that would have made an earlier injury or harm less likely to occur, evidence of the subsequent measures is not admissible to prove:

- negligence;
- culpable conduct;
- a defect in a product or its design; or
- a need for a warning or instruction.

But the court may admit this evidence for another purpose, such as impeachment or—if disputed—proving ownership, control, or the feasibility of precautionary measures.

(b) Notification of Defect. A manufacturer's written notification to a purchaser of a defect in one of its products is admissible against the manufacturer to prove the defect.

Notes and Comments

Comment to 2015 restyling: Rule 407 previously provided that evidence was not excluded if offered for a purpose not explicitly prohibited by the Rule. To improve the language of the Rule, it now provides that the court may admit evidence if offered for a permissible purpose. There is no intent to change the process for admitting evidence covered by the Rule. It remains the case that if offered for an impermissible purpose, it must be excluded, and if offered for a purpose not barred by the Rule, its admissibility remains governed by the general principles of Rules 402, 403, 801, etc.

COMMENTARY ON RULE 407

A. Rule 407(a): Subsequent Remedial Measures

1. When evidence of subsequent remedial measures is inadmissible. After an event that causes an injury or other harm, the person who is either in control of the place where the event occurred or responsible for the instrumentality that supposedly caused the event may take measures that, if they had been taken before the event, would have made the event less likely to occur.[669] The injured party would benefit from using evidence of subsequent remedial measures as an implicit admission of fault for the event by the defendant. Even though such evidence may have more than one explanation, it is none-

---

669. *See* ***Penley v. State***, 2 S.W.3d 534, 540 (Tex. App.—Texarkana 1999, pet. ref'd) ("Subsequent remedial measures can take many forms: repairs, installation of safety devices, changes in policy, design changes, providing or modifying warnings, or the firing of an employee.").

theless logically relevant because it tends to show the defendant's consciousness of fault, contradicting the defendant's position at trial.[670]

Texas courts have long held that evidence of subsequent remedial measures, although logically relevant, is inadmissible to prove liability.[671] That is, if someone made repairs after an accident, evidence of those repairs would not be admissible against him to prove that he was negligent at or before the time of the accident.[672] The prevalent reason for this policy is that admitting such evidence would discourage safety measures.[673] Accordingly, courts have traditionally allowed what amounts to a privilege for evidence of subsequent remedial measures when offered to prove negligence or other culpable conduct.[674] While the modern trend is to support the exclusion of evidence of subsequent remedial measures by considering such evidence to be privileged, the result is not a "privilege" for purposes of the Texas or Federal Rules. Thus, Texas Rules 501 through 513 on privileges apply neither to evidence of subsequent remedial measures nor to the types of evidence excluded by Rules 408 through 411, which derive from a similar philosophy of privilege.[675]

---

670. *See* McCORMICK'S HANDBOOK II, *supra* note 33, §275, at 666 (such evidence might indicate the defendant's acknowledgment that the measures should have been taken before the injury).

671. *See* 2 WIGMORE, *supra* note 179, §283, at 151 (evidence of subsequent repairs should be excluded because "the supposed inference from the act is not the plain and most probable one"—a belief by the defendant that the condition is capable of causing injury); *see, e.g.,* **Tex. Trunk Ry. v. Ayres**, 83 Tex. 268, 270-71, 18 S.W. 684, 685 (1892) (trial court erred in admitting evidence of subsequent repair to prove liability).

672. Rule 407(a) applies to all post-accident remedial improvements by the defendant, regardless of where they are made. *See, e.g.,* **Brookshire Bros. v. Lewis**, 911 S.W.2d 791, 796 (Tex. App.—Tyler 1995, writ denied) (plaintiff argued that evidence of subsequent remedial repairs made at new grocery store was admissible because ban on that evidence applies only to repairs made at the site of the litigated event, not to those made at other premises; court rejected this argument).

673. FED. R. EVID. 407 advisory committee's note; McCORMICK'S HANDBOOK II, *supra* note 33, §275, at 666; *see* **Penley**, 2 S.W.3d at 540 (the two reasons for excluding such evidence of remedial repairs are that the rule encourages safety precautions and that it excludes unreliable evidence); **Brookshire Bros.**, 911 S.W.2d at 796 ("[C]ourts hope to avoid discouraging the implementation of safety measures after accidents which make the need for such measures clear."); *cf.* **Kaczmarek v. Allied Chem. Corp.**, 836 F.2d 1055, 1060 (7th Cir. 1987) (admitting evidence of a pre-accident decision to adopt a safety measure, but excluding evidence of the post-accident implementation of safety measures).

This prevailing view, however, has not been without critics. For example, Clarence Morris responded to the argument that admitting evidence of subsequent remedial measures would discourage defendants from making repairs or changes:

> That any general practice of postponing repairs results from receiving proof of them seems doubtful. Many claims are in the mill for a long time. A defendant's interest is seldom well served by running risks of more claims to gain a slight strategic advantage on one pending. Most claimants who could use such evidence against the defendant could probably get their cases before a jury without it …. Furthermore many defendants are insured and have little financial interest in the outcome of a particular claim.

Clarence Morris, *Admissions and the Negligence Issue*, 29 TEX. L. REV. 407, 424-25 (1951). Others have argued that no valid empirical evidence supports the proposition that business decision-makers would willingly forego safety measures merely because a court might use that change in some future lawsuit. 23 WRIGHT & GRAHAM, *supra* note 35, §5282, at 93 & n.36 (1980); *see also* 1 GOODE ET AL., *supra* note 103, §407.1, at 234 (most defendants are not familiar with the rule, and most who are familiar with the rule do not want to risk additional injuries).

674. *See* McCORMICK'S HANDBOOK II, *supra* note 33, §275, at 666-67 (courts will exclude such evidence when offered to prove fault); 2 WIGMORE, *supra* note 179, §283, at 158 ("almost all" courts will exclude such evidence).

675. For a discussion of privileges, refer to *Article V: Privileges, infra* p. 377.

Influential codifications of evidence rules (e.g., the Uniform Rules and the Federal Rules) have followed this view.[676] Texas Rule 407 is somewhat broader than the traditional common-law doctrine because it bars the admissibility of any remedial measures taken after any event and has been applied outside the typical negligence and products-liability fields.[677] Thus, under Rule 407(a), evidence of a defendant's subsequent remedial measures is not admissible to prove negligence, other culpable conduct, a defect in a product or its design, or a need for a warning or instruction.[678]

---

676. *See* FED. R. EVID. 407; UNIF. R. EVID. 407 (1974). However, when Maine first adopted a version of the Uniform and Federal Rules, it rejected the common-law position and specified that evidence of subsequent remedial measures is admissible to prove negligence or culpability. ME. R. EVID. 407(a) (former rule); *see* Richard H. Field, *The Maine Rules of Evidence: What They Are and How They Got That Way*, 27 ME. L. REV. 203, 217-19 (1975) ("enlightened self-interest would cause defendants to make repairs despite the possibility of evidence about them being received on the issue of fault"; Rule 403 would allow the exclusion of evidence of subsequent remedial measures in certain circumstances); Comment, *The Repair Rule: Maine Rule of Evidence 407(a) and the Admissibility of Subsequent Remedial Measures in Proving Negligence*, 27 ME. L. REV. 225, 244-45 (1975) ("The probity of repairs on important issues of negligence such as risk, duty, and defect will no longer be unnecessarily sacrificed to social policy. ... Because a choice between relevant evidence and promotion of public safety is unnecessary, Rule 407(a) presents an excellent alternative to the subsequent repair rule.").

In proposing rules of evidence to the Texas Supreme Court, the Texas State Bar Liaison Committee drafted a rule also admitting evidence of subsequent remedial measures, which was identical to the Maine rule and skeptical of the public-policy rationale. *See* TEX. R. EVID. 407(a) (1982 Liaison Committee Proposal), *reprinted infra* p. 1079. The Texas Supreme Court, however, chose to follow tradition and promulgated Civil Rule 407(a), which followed the then-existing federal and uniform rules in excluding evidence of subsequent remedial measures and did not change Texas law. *Compare* TEX. R. CIV. EVID. 407(a), 641-642 S.W.2d (Tex. Cases) XL (1983, amended 1998) (current version at TEX. R. EVID. 407(a)) (barring evidence of subsequent remedial measures to show negligence or culpable conduct except in strict products-liability cases), *with* FED. R. EVID. 407 (barring evidence of subsequent remedial measures to prove negligence, culpable conduct, defect in product or product's design, or a need for warning or instruction), *and* UNIF. R. EVID. 407 (1974) (barring evidence of remedial measures to prove negligence or culpable conduct). Rule 407(a) is identical to Federal Rule 407.

677. *Cf. Noble v. McClatchy Newspapers*, 533 F.2d 1081, 1090 (9th Cir. 1975) (applying Federal Rule 407 to an antitrust case), *vacated on other grounds*, 433 U.S. 904 (1977); *Vander Missen v. Kellogg-Citizens Nat'l Bank*, 481 F. Supp. 742, 746 (E.D. Wis. 1979) (barring evidence that defendant took steps to prevent future acts of discrimination).

678. TEX. R. EVID. 407(a). Rule 407(a), however, does not exclude evidence of a third party's subsequent remedial measures when offered to demonstrate that the third party's negligence may have caused the occurrence in question. *Beavers v. Northrop Worldwide Aircraft Servs., Inc.*, 821 S.W.2d 669, 676-77 (Tex. App.—Amarillo 1991, writ denied); *see, e.g., Huckaby v. A.G. Perry & Son, Inc.*, 20 S.W.3d 194, 207 (Tex. App.—Texarkana 2000, pet. denied) (evidence of subsequent remedial measures taken by Department of Public Safety to improve highway conditions was not barred by Rule 407 because DPS was not a defendant in lawsuit; thus, "the purpose of the rule was not implicated"). *But see Brookshire Bros.*, 911 S.W.2d at 797 (plaintiff could not offer evidence of subsequent remedial measures taken by defendant-grocery store's landlord when plaintiff was not attempting to show landlord's negligence); *Burnett v. Rutledge*, 284 S.W.2d 944, 949 (Tex. Civ. App.—Amarillo 1955, writ ref'd n.r.e.) (evidence of third party's subsequent remedial measures was inadmissible when offered to show that defendant was negligent). In *Northrop*, the widow and children of an army officer who died in a helicopter crash alleged that Northrop had negligently maintained the helicopter. 821 S.W.2d at 672. The trial court permitted Northrop to offer evidence of the army's post-accident remedial measures—changes in its maintenance and contemplated changes to the helicopter's design—to demonstrate that the army's actions, not Northrop's, caused the crash. *Id.* at 676. The Amarillo Court of Appeals upheld the admission of this evidence because the policy behind Rule 407 is not served by excluding remedial measures taken by a nonparty; in these circumstances, the "party making the repair is not penalized by the admission of the evidence." *Id.* Federal decisions generally uphold the admission of evidence of a third party's subsequent remedial measures. *See Pau v. Yosemite Park & Curry Co.*, 928 F.2d 880, 888 (9th Cir. 1991) (upholding admission of evidence that the U.S. Park Service, a nonparty, erected a warning sign after the accident oc-

When Texas Rule 407 was originally promulgated, neither the Federal Rules nor the Uniform Rules contained any explicit provision for admitting evidence of subsequent remedial measures in products-liability (or strict-liability) cases. In 1974, the California Supreme Court decided *Ault v. International Harvester Co.*, a products-liability case in which the plaintiff wanted to establish the product's defectiveness by showing that the defendant had, after the accident in question, changed the materials for making the product.[679] In an influential opinion, with one justice dissenting, the California court decided that the evidence was admissible under a provision of the California Evidence Code that was very similar to Federal Rule 407.[680]

The federal courts in the Eighth and Tenth Circuits, favoring *Ault*, decided that Federal Rule 407 did not apply in products-liability cases resting on the theory of strict liability; in such cases, evidence of subsequent remedial measures would be admissible on the issue of liability.[681] Similarly, Texas Civil Rule 407(a) resolved the issue in favor of admissibility: "Nothing in this rule shall preclude admissibility [of evidence of subsequent remedial measures] in products liability cases based on strict liability."[682] Most

---

curred); *Grenada Steel Indus., Inc. v. Ala. Oxygen Co.*, 695 F.2d 883, 889 (5th Cir. 1983) (Federal Rule 407 did not bar the admission of evidence of subsequent repairs made by third-party manufacturer, but evidence was inadmissible under Federal Rule 403).

679. 528 P.2d 1148, 1150 (Cal. 1974).

680. *See id.* The *Ault* court gave several reasons for its decision. First, negligence or culpability is not an element of an action based on strict liability against a manufacturer. *Id.* Second, the policy underlying the general exclusion of evidence of subsequent remedial measures does not properly apply in the field of products liability because it would merely shield a mass producer of goods from liability. *Id.* at 1151-52. Third, the economic self-interest of manufacturers will compel them to make repairs regardless of the rules of evidence. *Id.* at 1152 n.4. Finally, in products liability, policy focuses not on the conduct of the manufacturer but on the nature of the product. *Id.* at 1152. The Texas Supreme Court similarly focused on this last rationale in holding that evidence of subsequent remedial measures was admissible in a strict-liability context. *Melody Home Mfg. Co. v. Barnes*, 741 S.W.2d 349, 355 n.8 (Tex. 1987). Specifically, the *Melody Home* court noted that "[i]n strict liability cases, the focus is on the product and not on the conduct of the producer. By contrast, the inquiry in a breach of warranty case concerns the performance of the service provider." *Id.*; *see also O'Neal v. Sherck Equip. Co.*, 751 S.W.2d 559, 561 (Tex. App.—Texarkana 1988, no writ) ("Negligence evaluates the conduct of the products supplier while strict tort liability focuses on the condition of the product.").

681. *See Bizzle v. McKesson Corp.*, 961 F.2d 719, 721 (8th Cir. 1992); *Huffman v. Caterpillar Tractor Co.*, 908 F.2d 1470, 1480-81 (10th Cir. 1990); *Meller v. Heil Co.*, 745 F.2d 1297, 1300 (10th Cir. 1984); *Unterburger v. Snow Co.*, 630 F.2d 599, 603 (8th Cir. 1980); *Farner v. Paccar, Inc.*, 562 F.2d 518, 528 (8th Cir. 1977); *Robbins v. Farmers Union Grain Terminal Ass'n*, 552 F.2d 788, 793 (8th Cir. 1977).

682. Tex. R. Civ. Evid. 407(a), 641-642 S.W.2d (Tex. Cases) xl (1983, amended 1998) (current version at Tex. R. Evid. 407(a)). By adopting that part of the rule, the Texas Supreme Court announced that it was following the position of the California Supreme Court in *Ault*, the view of the Eighth Circuit, the decisions of a number of other jurisdictions, and the recommendation of commentators that evidence of subsequent remedial measures was admissible on the issue of liability in products-liability cases. *See Caterpillar Tractor Co. v. Beck*, 624 P.2d 790, 794 (Alaska 1981); *Roberts v. May*, 583 P.2d 305, 309 (Colo. App. 1978); *Sutkowski v. Univ'l Marion Corp.*, 281 N.E.2d 749, 753 (Ill. App. Ct. 1972); *Ginnis v. Mapes Hotel Corp.*, 470 P.2d 135, 140 (Nev. 1970); *Caprara v. Chrysler Corp.*, 417 N.E.2d 545, 551 (N.Y. 1981); *Chart v. Gen. Motors Corp.*, 258 N.W.2d 680, 683 (Wis. 1977); 2 Louisell & Mueller, *supra* note 167, §166, at 421-23; Don L. Davis, *Evidence of Post-Accident Failures, Modifications and Design Changes in Products Liability Litigation*, 6 St. Mary's L.J. 792, 798 (1974-75); C. Andrew Fuller & A. Leroy Toliver, Comment, *Exclusion of Evidence of Subsequent Repairs in Drug Products Liability Actions—An Unnecessary Resurrection of an Obsolete Rule*, 31 Mercer L. Rev. 801, 807-08 (1980); Note, *Products Liability and Evidence of Subsequent Repairs*, 1972 Duke L.J. 837, 845-50; *see, e.g., Uniroyal Goodrich Tire Co. v. Martinez*, 977 S.W.2d 328, 341 (Tex. 1998) (trial court properly admitted evidence that defendant had redesigned its radial tires after the acci-

of the federal circuit courts, however, agreeing with the dissent in *Ault*, held that Federal Rule 407 does apply in products-liability cases and that evidence of subsequent remedial measures is thus inadmissible to prove liability because manufacturing a defective product is "culpable conduct," and the same policy of encouraging safety measures applies in both negligence and strict-liability cases.[683] In 1997, Federal Rule 407 was amended to clarify that the rule does indeed bar evidence of subsequent repairs in a products-liability case.[684] In 2003, the Texas Legislature, as a part of its tort-reform package, explicitly ordered the Texas Supreme Court to amend Rule 407(a) to conform to the 1997 amendments to Federal Rule 407.[685] Thus, Rule 407(a) applies to both products-liability cases and negligence cases.[686]

For evidence of subsequent remedial measures to be inadmissible, the measures must have been taken after the injury or harm to the plaintiff occurred.[687] Thus, if a manufacturer makes remedial changes to its product or notification procedures after the product has been put into the stream of commerce but before the accident giving rise to the lawsuit, evidence of those measures is not barred by the rule.[688]

---

dent at issue, incorporating the type of "bead" that plaintiff claimed was more likely to prevent explosions like the one in this case; "Rule 407(a) simply does not apply in products liability cases based on strict liability.").

683. *See Prentiss & Carlisle Co. v. Koehring-Waterous Div. of Timberjack, Inc.*, 972 F.2d 6, 10 (1st Cir. 1992); *Kelly v. Crown Equip. Co.*, 970 F.2d 1273, 1275-76 (3d Cir. 1992); *Gauthier v. AMF, Inc.*, 788 F.2d 634, 636-37 (9th Cir. 1986), *amended*, 805 F.2d 337 (9th Cir. 1986); *Grenada Steel*, 695 F.2d at 886-89; *Cann v. Ford Motor Co.*, 658 F.2d 54, 59-60 (2d Cir. 1981); *Oberst v. Int'l Harvester Co.*, 640 F.2d 863, 866-67 (7th Cir. 1980); *Werner v. Upjohn Co.*, 628 F.2d 848, 857 (4th Cir. 1980).

684. *See* FED. R. EVID. 407.

685. *See* Act of June 2, 2003, 78th Leg., R.S., ch. 204, §5.03, 2003 Tex. Gen. Laws 847, 862 ("As soon as practicable after the effective date of this Act, the supreme court shall amend Rule 407(a), Texas Rules of Evidence, to conform that rule to Rule 407, Federal Rule of Evidence.").

686. The rule recognizes that, under either a negligence or products-liability theory, a manufacturer's incentive to take remedial measures is greatly diminished if evidence of subsequent remedial measures is admissible to prove liability. *Cf. Gauthier*, 788 F.2d at 637 (rationale for exclusion of evidence—to encourage remedial measures—is the same under either theory); *Flaminio v. Honda Motor Co.*, 733 F.2d 463, 469 (7th Cir. 1984) (under either strict-liability or negligence theory, incentive to take subsequent remedial measures is reduced if those measures may be used against defendant). In *Flaminio*, Judge Posner explained:

> One might think it not only immoral but reckless for an injurer, having been alerted by the accident to the existence of danger, not to take steps to correct the danger. But accidents are low-probability events. The probability of another accident may be much smaller than the probability that the victim of the accident that has already occurred will sue the injurer and, if permitted, will make devastating use at trial of any measures that the injurer may have taken since the accident to reduce the danger.

733 F.2d at 469.

687. *See* TEX. R. EVID. 407(a). Before the 2015 restyling of the Texas Rules, Rule 407(a) had specified an "event" that caused injury or harm to the plaintiff as the point after which evidence of remedial measures would be excluded. The restyling deleted the word "event," but no substantive change was intended. *See* Tex. Sup. Ct. Order, Misc. Docket No. 15-9048, §2 (eff. Apr. 1, 2015). The current wording of the rule maintains the same "timing" as the previous rule. *See* TEX. R. EVID. 407(a) (subsequent remedial measures are inadmissible "[w]hen measures are taken that would have made an earlier injury or harm less likely to occur").

688. For example, suppose a consumer buys a rifle in 2012. That rifle explodes in the purchaser's hands in June 2014. If the rifle manufacturer made remedial changes to the design of the rifle in 2013, evidence of those changes would be admissible because they occurred before the explosion that injured the consumer, although the changes were made after the consumer had purchased the rifle. Only those repairs made after the rifle explosion would be inadmissible under Rule 407(a).

While the most frequently cited rationale for excluding evidence of remedial repairs is the logically dubious one of public policy,[689] a better argument for excluding such evidence would rely on the Rule 403 counterfactors.[690] Although remedial acts are probative of a defendant's knowledge of hazards after the accident and thus relevant to show the foreseeability of harm to others, the relevant time frame for foreseeability of harm is at or before the time of the litigated accident. Thus, evidence of subsequent repairs is likely to confuse the issues and mislead the jury into considering that if the defendant recognized the risk after the accident, he should have foreseen it before the event.[691] This phenomenon is sometimes called "hindsight bias," which Rule 407 attempts to mitigate in certain cases.[692]

2. When evidence of subsequent remedial measures is admissible. While the common law in Texas excluded evidence of subsequent remedial measures to prove negligence or other culpability, it admitted such evidence for other purposes.[693] This "back door" has opened rather widely, as the ingenuity of attorneys in suggesting other purposes has made substantial inroads on the general rule of exclusion.[694] Some of the "other purposes" for which evidence of subsequent remedial measures has been admitted include showing ownership or control,[695] showing condition at the time of the accident,[696] rebutting testimony that a product could not be improved,[697] and rebutting tes-

---

689. Refer to note 673 *supra* and accompanying text.

690. Refer to notes 111-159 *supra* and accompanying text.

691. *See* 1 SALTZBURG ET AL., *supra* note 319, at 571-72.

692. *See generally* Kimberly Eberwine, Note, *Hindsight Bias and the Subsequent Remedial Measures Rule: Fixing the Feasibility Exception*, 55 CASE W. RES. L. REV. 633, 636-37 (2005) (discussing the psychological theory of hindsight bias; "[h]indsight bias is the tendency to regard events that have already occurred as having always been inevitable. As a general rule, finding out that an outcome has already occurred increases that outcome's perceived *ex ante* likelihood. People tend to believe that this perceived inevitability was apparent in foresight as well as with hindsight, and generally remember their own outcome predictions as being more accurate than they actually were.").

693. *See Hous. Lighting & Power Co. v. Taber*, 221 S.W.2d 339, 344 (Tex. Civ. App.—Galveston 1949, writ ref'd n.r.e.) (evidence of subsequent repairs is admissible to show control and possession).

694. McCORMICK's HANDBOOK II, *supra* note 33, §275, at 667.

695. *See* TEX. R. EVID. 407(a); *see, e.g., Tyson Foods, Inc. v. Guzman*, 116 S.W.3d 233, 237-42 (Tex. App.—Tyler 2003, no pet.) (because Tyson did not stipulate to all aspects of its control over "the manner and means by which the third party contractors accomplish the objective of the contract," plaintiff could introduce evidence of subsequent remedial measures requiring workers to wear reflective vests to increase their visibility to driver/forklift operators); *Exxon Corp. v. Roberts*, 724 S.W.2d 863, 869 (Tex. App.—Texarkana 1986, writ ref'd n.r.e.) (when an oil company's defense was that it was not responsible for the tool-lifting procedure that caused the accident, wrongful-death plaintiffs were entitled to prove control by showing that defendant had changed its method of moving tools); *Taber*, 221 S.W.2d at 344 (admitting evidence of defendant's replacement of old wires to show control and ownership of the wires).

696. *See, e.g., Rash v. Ross*, 371 S.W.2d 109, 114 (Tex. Civ. App.—San Antonio 1963, writ ref'd n.r.e.) (photograph of an accident scene showing post-accident safety changes was admissible to show the condition of the location at the time of injury), *disapproved on other grounds*, *Southern Pac. Co. v. Castro*, 493 S.W.2d 491 (Tex. 1973).

697. *See, e.g., Bristol-Myers Co. v. Gonzales*, 548 S.W.2d 416, 430 (Tex. Civ. App.—Corpus Christi 1976) (evidence of changes in a warning was admissible to rebut testimony that manufacturer's knowledge about the product had not changed), *rev'd on other grounds*, 561 S.W.2d 801 (Tex. 1978).

timony that a different design was not feasible or practical.[698] Given the number and breadth of exceptions to the general rule, the rule against the admission of subsequent repairs has rarely resulted in the exclusion of evidence.[699]

The second sentence of Rule 407(a) continues the traditional approach. The rule allows evidence of subsequent remedial measures for impeachment and for issues other than negligence only if such matters are disputed.[700] This limitation maintains the general exclusionary policy of the rule.[701] As the drafters of Federal Rule 407 explained, "[t]he requirement that the other purpose be controverted calls for automatic exclusion unless a genuine issue be present and allows the opposing party to lay the groundwork for exclusion by making an admission."[702]

When interpreting Rule 407(a), courts face the same problem of determining when an issue is disputed that is inherent in Rule 404(b).[703] Although federal courts interpreting Federal Rule 407 have not reached any consensus,[704] the purposes of the general rule of exclusion would not be served unless the admission of evidence of remedial actions were conditioned on actual, active dispute, rather than mere silence on the issue.[705] Because a witness's credibility is inherently controversial, the rule has no explicit requirement that there be controversy before evidence of subsequent remedial measures is admissible to impeach a witness. On the other hand, the general rule would

---

698. *See* TEX. R. EVID. 407(a); *see, e.g.*, **Hous. Lighting & Power Co. v. Brooks**, 319 S.W.2d 427, 436 (Tex. Civ. App.—Houston 1958) (evidence that electrical current was rerouted a few days after the accident was admissible to rebut defendant's claim that such change was impractical), *rev'd on other grounds*, 161 Tex. 32, 336 S.W.2d 603 (1960).

699. 1 GOODE ET AL., *supra* note 103, §407.2, at 237; 2 LOUISELL & MUELLER, *supra* note 167, §165, at 389; MCCORMICK ON EVIDENCE, *supra* note 1, §275, at 816-17; 23 WRIGHT & GRAHAM, *supra* note 35, §5282, at 90 (1980).

700. *See* TEX. R. EVID. 407(a) (subsequent remedial measures can be admitted to prove ownership, control, or feasibility of precautionary measures if those matters are disputed); *see, e.g.*, **Hathcock v. Hankook Tire Am. Corp.**, 330 S.W.3d 733, 742-43 (Tex. App.—Texarkana 2010, no pet.) (plaintiff could not introduce evidence of tire manufacturer's subsequent remedial measure of nylon cap ply because manufacturer did not controvert the feasibility of the feature); **Brookshire Bros. v. Lewis**, 911 S.W.2d 791, 796-97 (Tex. App.—Tyler 1995, writ denied) (trial court should not have admitted evidence of remedial measures taken after accident in question, offered by plaintiff to show feasibility of those measures; court of appeals found no evidence that defendant contested the feasibility of remedial measures). The language of this sentence from the rule was simplified in the 2015 restyling and now states that the court can admit evidence if offered for a permissible purpose; however, no substantive change was intended. *See* TEX. R. EVID. 407 cmt. ("There is no intent to change the process for admitting evidence covered by the Rule. It remains the case that if offered for an impermissible purpose, it must be excluded, and if offered for a purpose not barred by the Rule, its admissibility remains governed by the general principles of Rules 402, 403, 801, etc.").

701. MCCORMICK'S HANDBOOK II, *supra* note 33, §275, at 668.

702. FED. R. EVID. 407 advisory committee's note.

703. Refer to notes 445-577 *supra* and accompanying text.

704. *See, e.g.*, **Fish v. Ga.-Pac. Corp.**, 779 F.2d 836, 839-40 (2d Cir. 1985) (when defendant stated that it was willing to admit the feasibility of providing a warning, feasibility was not controverted and evidence submitted under Federal Rule 407 would not be admitted); **Meller v. Heil Co.**, 745 F.2d 1297, 1300 n.7 (10th Cir. 1984) (feasibility of alternative design is "deemed" controverted in a products-liability case unless defendant makes an "unequivocal admission of feasibility").

705. 1 GOODE ET AL., *supra* note 103, §407.2, at 239-40; *see* **Eoff v. Hal & Charlie Peterson Found.**, 811 S.W.2d 187, 196 (Tex. App.—San Antonio 1991, no writ) (evidence of subsequent remedial measures purportedly offered to show ownership of an emergency room was properly excluded because ownership was not in dispute); **Russell v. Dunn Equip., Inc.**, 712 S.W.2d 542, 546-47 (Tex. App.—Houston [14th Dist.] 1986, writ ref'd n.r.e.) (evidence that plaintiff's brakes could have been repaired was properly excluded because the issue was not controverted).

be defeated if evidence of a remedial measure were admissible to impeach a witness who made even the slightest claim that the product, premises, or procedure was safe.[706] Commentators agree that evidence of subsequent remedial measures should be admissible to impeach only when it contradicts facts testified to by the adversary's witness.[707]

The other purposes specified in Rule 407(a)—impeachment, ownership, control, and feasibility of precautionary measures—are merely examples and not an exhaustive list.[708] Further, the probative value of the evidence offered for these other purposes may vary according to the purpose for which it is offered, the degree to which that purpose is disputed, and the inherent probative value of the offered evidence.[709] If evidence of subsequent remedial measures is admissible for one purpose (e.g., to show control) but not for another (e.g., to show negligence), the party against whom such evidence is being offered should request a limiting instruction under Rule 105(a).[710]

B. Rule 407(b): Notification of Defect—"Recall Letters" Admissible

Federal law requires manufacturers of motor vehicles or component parts to notify owners, purchasers, and dealers of defects that impair safety.[711] Such notifications, popularly known as "recall letters,"[712] are logically relevant evidence, especially in strict-liability cases in which the plaintiff must prove that a product was defective when it left the manufacturer's control.[713] While some courts have excluded these letters under the common-law doctrine that bars evidence of subsequent remedial measures,[714] the prevalent view admits them to show the existence of a defect in a product when it left the manufacturer's control, as long as the plaintiff has produced independent evidence

---

706. *See Flaminio v. Honda Motor Co.*, 733 F.2d 463, 468 (7th Cir. 1984) ("Although any evidence of subsequent remedial measures might be thought to contradict and so in a sense impeach a defendant's testimony that he was using due care at the time of the accident, if this counted as 'impeachment' the exception would swallow the rule."); *see, e.g., Hathcock v. Hankook Tire Am. Corp.*, 330 S.W.3d 733, 743-44 (Tex. App.—Texarkana 2010, no pet.) (plaintiff did not attempt to impeach defense expert on issue of testing nylon cap ply in tires and did not raise issue with trial court; trial court did not err in sustaining defendant's Rule 407 objection and excluding evidence of the subsequent remedial measure).

707. 1 GOODE ET AL., *supra* note 103, §407.2, at 240.

708. *See* TEX. R. EVID. 407(a). Refer to notes 160-161 *supra* and accompanying text.

709. *Cf. Fish*, 779 F.2d at 839-40 (applying Federal Rule 403 to exclude evidence that was also inadmissible under Rule 407); *Stallworth v. Ill. Cent. Gulf R.R.*, 690 F.2d 858, 868-69 (11th Cir. 1982) (excluding evidence under Federal Rule 407 because the danger of unfair prejudice or confusing the jury outweighed its probative value); FED. R. EVID. 407 advisory committee's note to 1997 amendments (factors in Rule 403 must be considered after determining that the evidence is admissible under Rule 407). Refer to notes 111-159 *supra* and accompanying text.

710. *See Exxon Corp. v. Roberts*, 724 S.W.2d 863, 869 (Tex. App.—Texarkana 1986, writ ref'd n.r.e.) (opponent must ask for an instruction limiting the consideration of evidence admitted under Rule 407 to relevant issues); *see, e.g., Fed. Pac. Elec. Co. v. Woodend*, 735 S.W.2d 887, 892 (Tex. App.—Fort Worth 1987, no writ) (trial court correctly instructed the jury, both when the evidence was admitted and in the charge to the jury, that evidence of remedial repairs was not admissible to prove defendant's negligence). Refer to *Article I: General Provisions*, *supra* p. 97.

711. *See* 49 U.S.C. §30118(b)(2)(A).

712. *See Carey v. Gen. Motors Corp.*, 387 N.E.2d 583, 587-88 (Mass. 1979).

713. *See id.* Refer to notes 679-686 *supra* and accompanying text.

714. *See, e.g., Vockie v. Gen. Motors Corp.*, 66 F.R.D. 57, 61 (E.D. Pa. 1975) (recall letters are mandated by statute), *aff'd*, 523 F.2d 1052 (3d Cir. 1975) (table case).

of the product's defectiveness at the time of the injury.[715] While such letters issued by a manufacturer would be hearsay if offered against a retail seller, they are statements of an opposing party when offered against the manufacturer and thus do not violate the hearsay rule.[716]

Texas Rule 407(b), which has no counterpart in either the Federal Rules or the Uniform Rules, applies to "written notification[s]" such as letters and newspaper notices. The rule applies only to notifications issued by manufacturers, not to notifications from other parties in the chain of distribution.[717] Further, the notifications are admissible only against manufacturers, not against other parties (such as retail sellers) who might be codefendants.[718] The notifications must have been sent to purchasers, not to dealers or others (unless they are also purchasers).[719] The notifications can be admitted in both negligence and strict-liability cases,[720] but they are admissible only to prove the existence of the defect, not to prove causation or other issues.[721]

RULE 408

COMPROMISE OFFERS & NEGOTIATIONS

(a) Prohibited Uses. Evidence of the following is not admissible either to prove or disprove the validity or amount of a disputed claim:

(1) furnishing, promising, or offering—or accepting, promising to accept, or offering to accept—a valuable consideration in compromising or attempting to compromise the claim; and

---

715. *See Carey*, 387 N.E.2d at 588 (recall letter is admissible against manufacturer if plaintiff has proved that the defect addressed by the recall existed in his vehicle at time of accident; citing cases from the Fifth Circuit, the Eighth Circuit, Arkansas, Florida, New Jersey, New York, and Oklahoma); John S. Herbrand, Annotation, *Products Liability: Admissibility, Against Manufacturer, of Product Recall Letter*, 84 A.L.R.3d 1220, 1227-29 (1978 & Supp. 2006) (recall letters warning purchasers of possible defects are "relevant to the issue of whether the defects existed when the vehicles left the hands" of manufacturer).

716. *See* TEX. R. EVID. 801(e)(2); *see, e.g.*, *Wright v. Gen. Motors Corp.*, 717 S.W.2d 153, 155 (Tex. App.—Houston [1st Dist.] 1986, no writ) (op. on reh'g) (plaintiff could introduce a recall letter into evidence against manufacturer as proof of an existing defect); *cf. Higgins v. Gen. Motors Corp.*, 465 S.W.2d 898, 900 (Ark. 1971) (contents of manufacturing recall letters were hearsay and not proper evidence against the automobile retailer). Refer to *Article VIII: Hearsay*, *infra* p. 845.

717. *See* TEX. R. EVID. 407(b).

718. *See id.*; *see also* TEX. R. EVID. 105(a) (allowing limiting instructions when evidence is admissible against one party but not against another).

719. *See* TEX. R. EVID. 407(b). *See generally* TEX. BUS. & COM. CODE §1.201(b)(29) (defining "purchase"), §1.201(b)(30) (defining "purchaser").

720. *See* Herbrand, *supra* note 715, at 1227-29.

721. *See* TEX. R. EVID. 407(b); Field, *supra* note 676, at 219. A recall letter is admissible as evidence of a defect, but "the converse is not true: evidence that a manufacturer did *not* recall a product or evidence that the product at issue fell outside the recall is no evidence that the product is not defective." *Alza Corp. v. Thompson*, No. 13-07-00090-CV (Tex. App.—Corpus Christi 2010, no pet.) (memo op.; 4-1-10).

Even when the evidence is admissible under Rule 407(b), the trial court may give limiting instructions under Rule 105(a) or exclude the evidence under another rule, such as Rule 403 or 801. *See* TEX. R. EVID. 407 cmt. Refer to notes 111-159 *supra* and accompanying text, *Article I: General Provisions*, *supra* p. 97, and *Article VIII: Hearsay*, *infra* p. 816.

(2) conduct or statements made during compromise negotiations about the claim.

(b) Permissible Uses. The court may admit this evidence for another purpose, such as proving a party's or witness's bias, prejudice, or interest, negating a contention of undue delay, or proving an effort to obstruct a criminal investigation or prosecution.

Notes and Comments

Comment to 2015 restyling: Rule 408 previously provided that evidence was not excluded if offered for a purpose not explicitly prohibited by the Rule. To improve the language of the Rule, it now provides that the court may admit evidence if offered for a permissible purpose. There is no intent to change the process for admitting evidence covered by the Rule. It remains the case that if offered for an impermissible purpose, it must be excluded, and if offered for a purpose not barred by the Rule, its admissibility remains governed by the general principles of Rules 402, 403, 801, etc.

The reference to "liability" has been deleted on the ground that the deletion makes the Rule flow better and easier to read, and because "liability" is covered by the broader term "validity." Courts have not made substantive decisions on the basis of any distinction between validity and liability. No change in current practice or in the coverage of the Rule is intended.

Finally, the sentence of the Rule referring to evidence "otherwise discoverable" has been deleted as superfluous. The intent of the sentence was to prevent a party from trying to immunize admissible information, such as a pre-existing document, through the pretense of disclosing it during compromise negotiations. But even without the sentence, the Rule cannot be read to protect pre-existing information simply because it was presented to the adversary in compromise negotiations.

COMMENTARY ON RULE 408

Rule 408 excludes offers to compromise when offered as evidence of the validity or amount of a disputed claim.[722] The party contending that the evidence is barred by Rule 408 must prove that the evidence is (1) part of settlement negotiations, (2) offered to

---

722. *See* TEX. R. EVID. 408(a). Texas courts had uniformly recognized this rule. *See **Masco Int'l, Inc. v. Stokley**,* 567 S.W.2d 598, 603 (Tex. Civ. App.—Eastland 1978, writ ref'd n.r.e.) (acknowledgments of liability in an offer to compromise are inadmissible); ***Allen v. Avery***, 537 S.W.2d 789, 791 (Tex. Civ. App.—Texarkana 1976, no writ) (compromise settlements are inadmissible, but unequivocal demands and statements of damages are admissible); ***Hamilton v. Hannus***, 185 S.W. 938, 941 (Tex. Civ. App.—Fort Worth 1916, no writ) (op. on reh'g) (offers to compromise are inadmissible). The general common-law rule also excluded offers to compromise when offered for those purposes. *See* 2 WEINSTEIN & BERGER, *supra* note 84, ¶408[01], at 408-10.

Before the 2015 restyling of the Texas Rules, Rule 408 said that offers to compromise were inadmissible when offered to prove "liability for or invalidity of the claim or its amount." *See* Tex. Sup. Ct. Order, Misc. Docket No. 15-9048 (eff. Apr. 1, 2015). The reference to "liability" was deleted because "liability" is covered by "validity" and courts had not made a substantive distinction between the two words. TEX. R. EVID. 408 cmt. No change in the

prove or disprove the validity of the claim or the amount of damages, and (3) not offered for some other purpose.[723] Rule 408 does not distinguish between actual offers to compromise and other statements or conduct occurring during compromise negotiations; rather, Rule 408 mandates that all such statements and conduct are inadmissible on the issue of the validity or amount of a disputed claim.[724] Similarly, Rule 408 does not distinguish between accepted and unaccepted offers to compromise; the same principles apply to both.[725] Finally, Rule 408 gives a nonexclusive list of other purposes—those besides the validity or amount of a disputed claim—for which evidence of compromises is admissible.[726]

The Texas rule used to be almost identical to Federal Rule 408, but in 2006, the federal rule was amended in several important respects.[727] First, the 2006 amendments clarify that in criminal cases, Federal Rule 408 does not bar the use of statements or conduct during compromise negotiations with a government regulatory, investigatory, or enforcement agency about a civil dispute.[728] The trial judge does have discretion to exclude such statements under Rule 403.[729] This amendment does not appear to conflict with the interpretation of Texas Rule 408.[730] Second, the amendments bar the use of settlement-negotiation statements when offered to impeach a witness with a prior inconsistent statement or through contradiction.[731] Although no cases have directly addressed the issue, Texas Rule 408 appears to permit the use of settlement statements

scope of the rule was intended. *Id.* The change follows the 2011 restyling of Federal Rule 408 and was made for the same reason. *See* FED. R. EVID. 408 advisory committee's note to 2011 amendments.

723. *See* TEX. R. EVID. 408; *Vinson Minerals, Ltd. v. XTO Energy, Inc.*, 335 S.W.3d 344, 352 (Tex. App.—Fort Worth 2010, pet. denied); *TCA Bldg. Co. v. Nw. Res. Co.*, 922 S.W.2d 629, 636 (Tex. App.—Waco 1996, writ denied); *Haney v. Purcell Co.*, 796 S.W.2d 782, 789-90 (Tex. App.—Houston [1st Dist.] 1990, writ denied). The trial court has considerable discretion in determining whether evidence should be excluded as evidence of a settlement offer or is being offered for some other purposes permitted under Rule 408. *See TCA Bldg. Co.*, 922 S.W.2d at 636.

724. Earlier Texas law held that independent admissions of fact made during compromise negotiations were admissible as admissions of a party-opponent unless they were hypothetical or expressly qualified as "without prejudice" or inseparably intertwined with an offer. Rule 408 simplified the process, thus avoiding extensive interpretation of the provision by Texas courts. Refer to notes 794-802 *infra* and accompanying text. After the 2015 restyling of the Texas Rules, admissions of a party-opponent are referred to as statements of an opposing party. Refer to *Article VIII: Hearsay, infra* p. 845.

725. Pre-Rules Texas law was unsettled and inconsistent on this point, and Rule 408 avoids the controversy. Refer to notes 776-793 *infra* and accompanying text.

726. The common law in Texas and elsewhere admitted evidence of compromise offers for other purposes such as to explain delay, to show that other evidence is material, and to impeach witnesses for bias or prejudice. Refer to notes 803-854 *infra* and accompanying text.

727. Federal Rule 408 was restyled in 2011. The substance of the rule was not changed. FED. R. EVID. 408 advisory committee's note to 2011 amendments. Refer to note 722 *supra*.

728. *See United States v. Roti*, 484 F.3d 934, 936 (7th Cir. 2007) ("Note that the new [Federal] Rule 408(a)(2), by creating a partial exception for criminal cases, shows that the rest of the rule applies to both civil and criminal litigation."); FED. R. EVID. 408 advisory committee's note to 2006 amendments ("Where an individual makes a statement in the presence of government agents, its subsequent admission in a criminal case should not be unexpected.").

729. *See* FED. R. EVID. 408 advisory committee's note to 2006 amendments.

730. Refer to notes 752-753 *infra* and accompanying text.

731. *See* FED. R. EVID. 408 advisory committee's note to 2006 amendments ("Such broad impeachment would tend to swallow the exclusionary rule and would impair the public policy of promoting settlements.").

for impeachment.[732] Third, "[t]he amendment makes clear that [Federal] Rule 408 excludes compromise evidence even when a party seeks to admit its own settlement offer or statements made in settlement negotiations."[733]

A. Theories for Excluding Offers to Compromise

Two theories have been proposed to support the exclusion of offers to compromise as admissions about the validity of a claim: relevancy and privilege.[734] The relevancy theory, attributed primarily to Wigmore,[735] has been expressed as follows:

> The true reason for excluding an offer of compromise is that it does not ordinarily proceed from and imply a specific belief that the adversary's claim is well-founded, but rather a belief that the further prosecution of that claim, whether well founded or not, would in any event cause such annoyance as is preferably avoided by the payment of the sum offered. In short, the offer implies merely a desire for peace, not a concession of wrong done.[736]

Evidence of an offer to compromise is considered unreliable on the issue of a claim's validity because it does not necessarily represent a party's actual position on the merits of a claim but instead may be the amount a party is willing to give or take to avoid the expense and annoyance of litigation.[737]

Courts in many jurisdictions, including Texas, have used the relevancy theory to exclude offers to compromise as evidence of a claim's validity.[738] But the theory has been harshly criticized by commentators,[739] who insist that an offer to compromise is probative on the issue of a claim's validity because a defendant's desire to avoid litigation may be coextensive with its belief that the plaintiff's claims are valid.[740] Thus, an offer to compromise cannot be excluded merely on the grounds that it is irrelevant.[741] Some Texas cases have supported this contention as well.[742]

---

732. Refer to notes 829-832 *infra* and accompanying text.

733. Fed. R. Evid. 408 advisory committee's note to 2006 amendments. The rule's protections cannot be unilaterally waived "because the Rule, by definition, protects both parties from having the fact of negotiation disclosed to the jury." *Id.* Furthermore, such statements would usually be offered through the testimony of attorneys who were present during settlement negotiations, thus leading to the risk and increased costs of attorney disqualification. *Id.*

734. McCormick's Handbook II, *supra* note 33, §274, at 663; 2 Weinstein & Berger, *supra* note 84, ¶408[02], at 408-19 to 408-24; George M. Bell, *Admissions Arising Out of Compromise—Are They Irrelevant?*, 31 Tex. L. Rev. 239, 240-41 (1953).

735. *See* Bell, *supra* note 734, at 241.

736. 4 John H. Wigmore, Evidence in Trials at Common Law §1061, at 36 (Chadbourn rev. 1972).

737. *Avary v. Bank of Am.*, 72 S.W.3d 779, 798 (Tex. App.—Dallas 2002, pet. denied); *see Sullivan v. Mo., Kan. & Tex. Ry. Co. of Tex.*, 110 Tex. 360, 362, 220 S.W. 769, 770 (1920); *State Farm Mut. Auto. Ins. v. Wilborn*, 835 S.W.2d 260, 261 (Tex. App.—Houston [14th Dist.] 1992, orig. proceeding); *Krenek v. S. Tex. Elec. Coop., Inc.*, 502 S.W.2d 605, 609 (Tex. Civ. App.—Corpus Christi 1973, no writ).

738. *See* 4 Wigmore, *supra* note 736, §1062, at 48.

739. *See id.* §1061, at 36 n.4 (quoting extensively from authorities that criticize relevancy theory).

740. *See* Bell, *supra* note 734, at 242-43.

741. *See* 1A Ray, *supra* note 46, §1142, at 287-89; Bell, *supra* note 734, at 240 n.1; Charles T. McCormick, *The Scope of Privilege in the Law of Evidence*, 16 Tex. L. Rev. 447, 457-58 (1938); *see also* 2 Weinstein & Berger, *supra*

The second theory for excluding evidence of offers to compromise, which has been used in many Texas cases, is the privilege theory.[743] This theory is based on the social policy of encouraging settlements and discouraging litigation.[744]

Basing the rule on a privilege theory generally allows only a party involved in the compromise to object to its admission,[745] even though other litigants could object under Rule 403.[746] Thus, Rule 408 does not bar the admission of evidence of settlement negotiations or statements made during those negotiations when offered "to establish the existence of a promise or agreement made by a non-party to the settled lawsuit."[747] Even more significantly, a party can waive the privilege[748] by failing to object to the submission of the offer[749] or by introducing its own testimony about the offer.[750] The 2006 amendments to Federal Rule 408 reject the privilege theory as a basis for the rule by prohibiting any party to the settlement negotiations from unilaterally offering its own settlement offer or statements.[751]

B. Rule 408(a): Prohibited Use of Compromise Offers

Texas Rule 408 is broader than the common-law position because it excludes not only settlement agreements and the discussions made during settlement negotiations but also evidence of the conduct of any of the participants during settlement negotiations.[752] The rule does not apply to criminal plea negotiations by a defendant,

---

note 84, ¶408[02], at 408-21 (no doubt that offer to compromise, "taken alone or in connection with other evidence in the case, might suggest to a reasonable man that the offeror believed that the adversary's claim had substantial merit").

742. *See, e.g.,* **Lloyds Am. v. Poe**, 69 S.W.2d 160, 162 (Tex. Civ. App.—El Paso 1934, writ dism'd) ("[I]t is said the letter was an offer of compromise and conditional offer to settle ... and therefore has no probative force as an admission. Offers to compromise cannot be admitted in evidence over objection, but they are not without probative force when admitted.").

743. *See* 1A RAY, *supra* note 46, §1142, at 288-89.

744. *Id.*; 2 WEINSTEIN & BERGER, *supra* note 84, ¶408[02], at 408-21 to 408-22; Bell, *supra* note 734, at 252; *see* **Vinson Minerals, Ltd. v. XTO Energy, Inc.**, 335 S.W.3d 344, 353 (Tex. App.—Fort Worth 2010, pet. denied) ("The purpose of rule 408 is to encourage settlement."); **State Farm Mut. Auto. Ins. v. Wilborn**, 835 S.W.2d 260, 261 (Tex. App.—Houston [14th Dist.] 1992, orig. proceeding) (Rule 408 excludes offers to compromise or settle "to allow a party to buy his peace and encourage settlement of claims outside of the courthouse").

745. *See* McCORMICK'S HANDBOOK II, *supra* note 33, §274, at 663; Bell, *supra* note 734, at 252.

746. *See* 2 WEINSTEIN & BERGER, *supra* note 84, ¶408[02], at 408-23. Refer to notes 111-159 *supra* and accompanying text.

747. **MG Bldg. Materials, Ltd. v. Moses Lopez Custom Homes, Inc.**, 179 S.W.3d 51, 61 (Tex. App.—San Antonio 2005, pet. denied).

748. *See* Bell, *supra* note 734, at 252.

749. **United States v. Baskes**, 649 F.2d 471, 480 n.8 (7th Cir. 1980); *see also* **Int'l & Great N. Ry. Co. v. Ragsdale**, 67 Tex. 24, 27-28, 2 S.W. 515, 517 (1886) (offer to compromise cannot be admitted into evidence when objected to).

750. *See* **United States v. Meadows**, 598 F.2d 984, 989 (5th Cir. 1979) (testimony solicited by defense counsel on cross-examination is not barred by Federal Rule 408; interpreting former version of rule).

751. *See* FED. R. EVID. 408 advisory committee's note to 2006 amendments. Refer to note 733 *supra* and accompanying text.

752. *See* TEX. R. EVID. 408(a); **Rural Dev., Inc. v. Stone**, 700 S.W.2d 661, 668 (Tex. App.—Corpus Christi 1985, writ ref'd n.r.e.), *disapproved on other grounds*, **Sterner v. Marathon Oil Co.**, 767 S.W.2d 686 (Tex. 1989). For permissible uses under the rule, refer to notes 803-854 *infra* and accompanying text.

however, because they do not concern "the validity or invalidity of a claim or its amount."[753]

Generally, any evidence about an offer to compromise is inadmissible to prove or disprove the validity or amount of a disputed claim. That is, evidence of an offer to compromise, whether the offer was accepted or not, and evidence of any conduct or statements made during compromise negotiations are inadmissible to prove or disprove the validity or amount of a disputed claim.[754]

1. Definition of offer to compromise. The precise definition of an offer to compromise is not clear. In Texas, courts seem to require two elements: a preexisting dispute and a proposal of concession to avoid litigation.[755]

(1) Preexisting dispute. Both Texas Rule 408 and Federal Rule 408 require a preexisting dispute before evidence is excluded as an offer to compromise.[756] When both par-

---

753. *E.g.*, *Smith v. State*, 898 S.W.2d 838, 843-44 (Tex. Crim. App. 1995) (Criminal Rule 408 "is applicable in criminal cases because of its presence in the Criminal Rules of Evidence, but we do not agree that it applies to criminal plea negotiations"; evidence of defendant's refusal of State's pretrial plea offer of life sentence in capital-murder trial, offered by defendant as mitigating evidence during punishment phase, was properly excluded under Rule 403 instead); *accord* **L.M.W. v. State**, 891 S.W.2d 754, 764 (Tex. App.—Fort Worth 1994, pet. ref'd) (expressing doubt that Criminal Rule 408 should apply in criminal proceedings at all because "the primary policy justification for [Criminal] Rule 408's exclusion in the civil context does not apply to criminal prosecutions"); *see also* **Prystash v. State**, 3 S.W.3d 522, 527-28 (Tex. Crim. App. 1999) (discussing and applying **Smith**; trial court properly excluded evidence that prosecution had previously made plea offer of 55 years in capital-murder case). *But cf.* **United States v. Verdoorn**, 528 F.2d 103, 107 (8th Cir. 1976) (plea offers are inadmissible under Federal Rule of Evidence 408).

Although plea bargaining is essential to the administration of justice, evidence of plea offers should be excluded under Rule 403, as the court of criminal appeals has stated, not under Rule 408. *See* **Smith**, 898 S.W.2d at 843-44 & n.6. The latter rule, on its face, does not apply to criminal plea bargaining. The fact and terms of a plea offer made to a defendant by the prosecution may have nothing to do with the prosecution's assessment of the strength of its case or the appropriate punishment for the defendant. *See id.* at 843. The terms of a plea offer, and the reasoning for making it, may be influenced by county resources, the court's docket, the interests or welfare of the alleged victims or witnesses, and internal policies in the prosecutor's office. *Id.* at 843-44. Because evidence of an offered plea is only minimally probative to the merits of the issue of guilt or punishment, and that evidence raises the risk of unfair prejudice and the likelihood of confusion of the issues or misleading the jury, trial courts have great discretion to exclude it under Rule 403. Rule 408 could operate in criminal proceedings only if the evidence of settlement negotiations were offered to show civil liability. Statements made during criminal plea negotiations would be excluded under Rule 410(b)(4) if offered against the person who made the statements. Refer to notes 892, 952-964 *infra* and accompanying text.

754. *See* TEX. R. EVID. 408(a) (evidence of "furnishing, promising, or offering" consideration to compromise or attempt to compromise a claim, "accepting, promising to accept, or offering to accept" such consideration, or conduct or statements made during compromise negotiations is inadmissible to prove or disprove validity or amount of disputed claim).

755. **Hundere v. Tracy & Cook**, 494 S.W.2d 257, 260-61 (Tex. Civ. App.—San Antonio 1973, writ ref'd n.r.e.); *see, e.g.*, **Tex. Imps. v. Allday**, 649 S.W.2d 730, 736-37 (Tex. App.—Tyler 1983, writ ref'd n.r.e.) (test of "whether the evidence amounts to an offer of compromise ... seems to be as to whether or not something is given up by one of the parties for the sake of avoiding litigation (buying peace) where some concession is made by one or both of the parties"; check tendered as payment for some but not all of the cattle referenced in a contract of sale was an unconditional tender for conforming goods and not an offer to compromise).

756. *See* FED. R. EVID. 408(a) (evidence of offer to compromise is not admissible "to prove or disprove the validity or amount of a disputed claim"); TEX. R. EVID. 408(a) (same); *see, e.g.*, **Kan. City S. Ry. Co. v. Carter**, 778 S.W.2d 911, 913-14 (Tex. App.—Texarkana 1989, writ denied) (Civil Rule 408 did not bar evidence that defendant acknowledged liability and reimbursed the company for losses because trial judge could conclude that the claim was not disputed). The rules preserve the common-law requirement of a preexisting dispute. *See* **Allstate Ins. v. Winnemore**, 413 F.2d 858, 863 n.10 (5th Cir. 1969) ("The law wishes to encourage settlement over litigation. Obviously, this policy

ties agree on the validity and amount of a claim, there is no dispute; an offer to pay less than the admitted amount is clearly admissible.[757] The difficulty appears primarily with the timing of an offer in relation to instituting proceedings to collect a claim.

In confronting the problem of timing, one Texas court held that an offer is admissible when, before the plaintiff made the offer, there had been no indication that the defendant denied liability or that the parties disagreed on the amount of the claim, even if the plaintiff threatened to file suit at the same time that he made the offer.[758] In addition, an offer is admissible if the record shows no formal preexisting dispute.[759] Texas courts have generally recognized a preexisting dispute if the offer was made after some legal action had been taken or threatened,[760] such as a threat to bring suit on a claim,[761] the delivery of a claim to an attorney for legal action,[762] or the filing of a suit with the court.[763] Rule 408 did not change Texas law in this area.[764] Federal courts take a similar approach in interpreting and applying Federal Rule 408. They have admitted con-

---

argument cannot be invoked unless a controversy is pending between the parties."); *see, e.g.*, **Reese v. McVittie**, 200 P.2d 390, 392-93 (Colo. 1948) (in suit to recover for services rendered as a real-estate broker, defendant's offer to pay plaintiff a certain amount was admissible on the issue of liability because it was not a dispute over liability between the parties at the time of the offer); **Nehring v. Smith**, 49 N.W.2d 831, 835 (Iowa 1951) (in suit for the death of an auto passenger, offer to settle made by defendant before suit was instituted was admissible as an admission of liability); **Ogden v. George F. Alger Co.**, 91 N.W.2d 288, 290 (Mich. 1958) (policy of encouraging compromise of claims does not exclude offers made before the controversy arose; because both parties agreed that there was no controversy at the time of offer, offer was admissible).

757. *See* FED. R. EVID. 408 advisory committee's note ("The policy considerations which underlie the rule do not come into play when the effort is to induce a creditor to settle an admittedly due amount for a lesser sum."); Mc-CORMICK'S HANDBOOK II, *supra* note 33, §274, at 663 (offer to pay an admitted sum is not privileged); 2 WEINSTEIN & BERGER, *supra* note 84, ¶408[01], at 408-12 to 408-13 (distinguishing between cases in which liability is admitted but amount of damages is unresolved—offer to compromise is inadmissible—and cases in which both liability and damages are admitted—offer to compromise is admissible); *see, e.g.*, **Tag Res., Inc. v. Pet. Well Servs., Inc.**, 791 S.W.2d 600, 606 (Tex. App.—Beaumont 1990, no writ) (when defendant orally agreed to a liquidated, undisputed amount owed by him to plaintiff, and he later confirmed the agreement in writing and made payments under the oral and written agreement, Civil Rule 408 did not bar use of that agreement as summary-judgment evidence).

758. **Tex. & Pac. Ry. Co. v. Spann**, 173 S.W. 600, 601 (Tex. Civ. App.—Texarkana 1915, writ ref'd).

759. *See* **Smith v. Smith**, 460 S.W.2d 204, 205-06 (Tex. Civ. App.—Dallas 1970, no writ); **Sawyer v. Willis**, 310 S.W.2d 398, 399 (Tex. Civ. App.—San Antonio 1958, no writ).

760. *See, e.g.*, **Hundere**, 494 S.W.2d at 260-61 (dispute existed when attorney told his client that he would accept $3,500 in attorney fees; the two had previously argued about the proper fee amount, with attorney claiming he was owed $7,500 to $10,000, and client had discharged attorney over the disagreements); **Ditto v. Piper**, 244 S.W.2d 547, 550 (Tex. Civ. App.—Fort Worth 1951, writ ref'd n.r.e.) (dispute existed when father offered consideration to his daughter to sign a deed to give him title to land because of their "strained relationship").

761. *See, e.g.*, **Merchants' Cotton Oil Co. v. Acme Gin Co.**, 284 S.W. 680, 682 (Tex. Civ. App.—Eastland 1926, no writ) (before a telegram offering a compromise was sent, plaintiff's agent called defendant's witness and threatened to bring suit if agent was not paid a commission).

762. *See, e.g.*, **Hamilton v. Hannus**, 185 S.W. 938, 940 (Tex. Civ. App.—Fort Worth 1916, no writ) (op. on reh'g) (proposed settlement of a promissory note was inadmissible because it was made after a demand for payment and delivery to an attorney for legal action).

763. *See* **Hundere**, 494 S.W.2d at 260-61.

764. *See, e.g.*, **Payne v. Edmonson**, 712 S.W.2d 793, 797-98 (Tex. App.—Houston [1st Dist.] 1986, writ ref'd n.r.e.) (Civil Rule 408 did not exclude evidence of settlement discussions that occurred before any dispute arose between parties; evidence of further negotiations immediately before filing of lawsuit was barred by rule because there was a disputed claim).

versations held during informal investigations,[765] communications made before litigation was threatened,[766] and offers of just compensation made before eminent-domain proceedings were instituted[767] because these circumstances did not meet the rule's requirement of a preexisting dispute.

(2) Proposal of concession. The second element traditionally required in Texas for an offer to compromise to be excluded is that the offer must not be a mere statement of an amount legally due but must be an offer of a lesser amount as a concession to avoid litigation.[768] Texas courts have focused on the "intrinsic character of the transaction"[769] and the "entire context" of the offer, rather than considering the wording of the offer in isolation.[770] Rule 408 did not change Texas law in these respects.[771]

In discussing Federal Rule 408, Weinstein and Berger suggest that courts should not define the term "compromise" too narrowly because the policy underlying Rule 408 demands broad exclusionary power.[772] To help ensure proper interpretation of the term, Texas appellate courts give the trial judge almost exclusive power to determine whether a statement offered as evidence was an offer to compromise or an admission of the validity of a claim.[773] The judge, not the parties, makes the legal determination of whether

---

765. *United States v. Meadows*, 598 F.2d 984, 989 (5th Cir. 1979).

766. *Big O Tire Dealers, Inc. v. Goodyear Tire & Rubber Co.*, 561 F.2d 1365, 1372-73 (10th Cir. 1977).

767. *United States v. 320.0 Acres of Land, More or Less in the Cty. of Monroe*, 605 F.2d 762, 822-25 (5th Cir. 1979).

768. *See Sullivan v. Mo., Kan. & Tex. Ry. Co. of Tex.*, 110 Tex. 360, 361-62, 220 S.W. 769, 770 (1920); *Certain Underwriters at Lloyd's London v. Chi. Bridge & Iron Co.*, 406 S.W.3d 326, 339-40 (Tex. App.—Beaumont 2013, pet. denied); *Tatum v. Progressive Polymers, Inc.*, 881 S.W.2d 835, 837 (Tex. App.—Tyler 1994, no writ).

769. *See Hamilton v. Hannus*, 185 S.W. 938, 941 (Tex. Civ. App.—Fort Worth 1916, no writ) (op. on reh'g).

770. *See, e.g., Sullivan*, 110 Tex. at 361, 220 S.W. at 770 (letter from plaintiff to defendant presenting a claim of $500 for personal-injury damages, stating that the sum was "offered as a compromise," and suggesting that defendant pay that amount to avoid litigation, was inadmissible; letter as a whole demonstrated unmistakable intent to compromise). On the other hand, a telegram from a defendant to a plaintiff threatening to institute bankruptcy proceedings unless the plaintiff accepted a specified sum in settlement of the plaintiff's claim, with no evidence of prior negotiations, was not an offer to compromise and was admissible. *Ginsberg v. Selbest Dress, Inc.*, 238 S.W.2d 621, 622-23 (Tex. Civ. App.—Dallas 1951, writ ref'd n.r.e.). The court held that telegram was "an ultimatum rather than an overture for peaceful settlement of the controversy; an arbitrary effort to secure relief on defendant's own terms." *Id.* at 623; *see also Mercedes-Benz of N. Am., Inc. v. Dickenson*, 720 S.W.2d 844, 857 (Tex. App.—Fort Worth 1986, no writ) (letter threatening to seek indemnification was an ultimatum and not a compromise offer).

771. *See* TEX. R. EVID. 408(a)(1); *see, e.g., Mieth v. Ranchquest, Inc.*, 177 S.W.3d 296, 304-05 (Tex. App.—Houston [1st Dist.] 2005, no pet.) (op. on reh'g) (when party's written offer to purchase property stated specifically that it was not a settlement offer and "did not ask appellants to compromise their claim in any way," admission was not barred under Rule 408); *Stergiou v. Gen. Metal Fabricating Corp.*, 123 S.W.3d 1, 5 (Tex. App.—Houston [1st Dist.] 2003, pet. denied) (trial court improperly excluded letters of intent under Rule 408; letters did not mention a compromise or settlement, ask plaintiff to drop any claims or relinquish any rights, suggest any concessions, or seek to impose any conditions); *GTE Mobilnet v. Telecell Cellular, Inc.*, 955 S.W.2d 286, 298-99 (Tex. App.—Houston [1st Dist.] 1997, writ denied) (op. on reh'g) (letter detailing alternative agency-commission plan was not an offer to settle any claim because it did not propose any concessions or seek to impose any conditions; recipient accepted alternate plan with the explicit proviso that it would continue with its lawsuit).

772. 2 WEINSTEIN & BERGER, *supra* note 84, ¶408[01], at 408-14.

773. *See Duval Cty. Ranch Co. v. Alamo Lumber Co.*, 663 S.W.2d 627, 634 (Tex. App.—Amarillo 1983, writ ref'd n.r.e.); *Allen v. Avery*, 537 S.W.2d 789, 791 (Tex. Civ. App.—Texarkana 1976, no writ); *Ditto v. Piper*, 244 S.W.2d 547, 550 (Tex. Civ. App.—Fort Worth 1951, writ ref'd n.r.e.); *Merchants' Cotton Oil Co. v. Acme Gin Co.*, 284 S.W. 680, 682 (Tex. Civ. App.—Eastland 1926, no writ).

certain evidence is a settlement offer under Rule 408.[774] A party's subjective belief that a letter is a "settlement offer" is not determinative.[775]

2. Accepted offers. To be excluded under Rule 408, evidence of an accepted offer to compromise (such as a third-party settlement agreement[776]) must meet the same requirement as any other offer to compromise: the objecting party must be a party to the compromise and a litigant in the case.[777] Any party, however, can raise objections under Rule 403.[778] Courts applying the common-law rule were not consistent on whether to exclude evidence of third-party settlement agreements.[779] Such agreements were usually held inadmissible as evidence of an admission of liability,[780] but many courts (apparently following the relevancy theory)[781] would not exclude a third-party settlement unless it was based on an intent to avoid litigation rather than an intent to admit liability.[782] Texas courts often required that a specific disclaimer of liability be written into the settlement agreement,[783] or at least required a finding that the settlement was made for the purpose of compromise and was therefore not a true admission.[784]

---

774. *See Certain Underwriters at Lloyd's London v. Chi. Bridge & Iron Co.*, 406 S.W.3d 326, 340 (Tex. App.—Beaumont 2013, pet. denied); *TCA Bldg. Co. v. Nw. Res. Co.*, 922 S.W.2d 629, 636 (Tex. App.—Waco 1996, writ denied); *Tatum v. Progressive Polymers, Inc.*, 881 S.W.2d 835, 836-37 (Tex. App.—Tyler 1994, no writ). Some early Texas decisions suggested that submission of the issue to a jury would be permissible, or at least not prejudicial error. *See, e.g., Merchants' Cotton*, 284 S.W. at 682-83 (dicta; question of whether a certain telegram was an offer to compromise could properly be submitted to jury); *Sanford v. John Finnigan Co.*, 169 S.W. 624, 626 (Tex. Civ. App.—San Antonio 1914, writ ref'd) (although it was court's duty to decide whether the letter in question was an offer to compromise, submission to the jury for such determination was not harmful error); *cf. Nehring v. Smith*, 49 N.W.2d 831, 836 (Iowa 1951) ("Where it is doubtful whether a statement of a litigant is an admission of liability or an offer of compromise it is proper to submit the question to the jury."). *But cf. Paster v. Pa. R.R.*, 43 F.2d 908, 911 (2d Cir. 1930) (evidence of settlement must be excluded and, if admitted erroneously, "no instruction to the jury would cure the damage, and ... the only relief would be a mistrial"). According to Weinstein and Berger, allowing the jury to determine what constitutes a settlement offer would violate the policy underlying the rule: "If it is remembered that [Federal] Rule 408 is based upon extrinsic policy—i.e., it provides, in effect, a privilege—it becomes apparent that the proper practice is for the trial court to decide such questions." 2 WEINSTEIN & BERGER, *supra* note 84, ¶408[01], at 408-14; *see also* TEX. R. EVID. 104(a) (court must decide preliminary questions, including existence of privileges).

775. *GTE Mobilnet*, 955 S.W.2d at 299.

776. In a third-party settlement agreement, the defendant settles with a party injured in the same transaction, or a plaintiff settles with one of several defendants.

777. 2 WEINSTEIN & BERGER, *supra* note 84, ¶408[02], at 408-23.

778. *See* TEX. R. EVID. 403. Refer to notes 111-159 *supra* and accompanying text.

779. *See* FED. R. EVID. 408 advisory committee's note; 2 WEINSTEIN & BERGER, *supra* note 84, ¶408[04], at 408-30 to 408-34. Refer to notes 794-798 *infra* and accompanying text.

780. 4 WIGMORE, *supra* note 736, §1061, at 47-48. *See generally* W.R. Habeeb, Annotation, *Admissibility of Evidence that Defendant in Negligence Action Has Paid Third Persons on Claims Arising from the Same Transaction or Incident as Plaintiff's Claim*, 20 A.L.R.2d 304 (1951).

781. Refer to notes 734-742 *supra* and accompanying text.

782. In *Colburn v. Groton*, the New Hampshire Supreme Court stated that

> [p]ayment, or an offer of payment, may be made to a plaintiff, or to another person having a claim so far like the plaintiff's that the defendant's admission of liability would be applicable to both. ... An offer of payment, whether accepted or rejected, is evidence when the party making it understood it to be, and made it as, an admission of his liability. It is not evidence when he made it for the purpose of averting litigation ....

28 A. 95, 98 (N.H. 1889); *see* Habeeb, *supra* note 780, at 307.

783. *See, e.g., McGuire v. Commercial Union Ins.*, 431 S.W.2d 347, 352 (Tex. 1968) (settlement of a prior wrongful-death action by insured's widow without insurance company's consent was not admissible on the issue of liability

On the other hand, courts following the privilege rationale[785] have not focused so much on explicit disclaimers or the mental state of the person initiating the offer to compromise; nonetheless, they have excluded such agreements because admitting them would contravene the policy of encouraging settlement of suits.[786] In one such case, the appellate court rejected the trial court's explanation that the third-party settlement was admissible because "such a substantial payment ... would not have been made ... merely to buy peace."[787]

Rule 408 is broader in its exclusionary scope than the common-law rule and avoids the controversy over the distinction between factual admissions and offers to compromise.[788] The rule eliminates the traditional requirement that the offer to compromise explicitly state that the party denies liability.[789]

3. Repudiated settlements. By its plain terms, Rule 408 refers to all offers to compromise, whether accepted or not.[790] As the Advisory Committee on the Federal Rules noted: "While [Federal Rule 408] is ordinarily phrased in terms of offers of compro-

---

in a separate claim against the insurance company when "it was made in settlement of disputed claims and expressly disclaims any liability"); *Skyline Cab Co. v. Bradley*, 325 S.W.2d 176, 181 (Tex. Civ. App.—Houston 1959, writ ref'd n.r.e.) (compromise settlement between plaintiff and third party was not admissible when "the party offering the settlement does not admit liability"); *see also Otwell v. Scott*, 425 S.W.2d 9, 13-14 (Tex. Civ. App.—Texarkana 1968, no writ) (proof of settlement by defendant with one party involved in a multi-car accident was not admissible because defendant may admit liability to that party and deny liability to plaintiff).

784. *See, e.g.*, *Conn. Gen. Ins. v. Reese*, 348 S.W.2d 549, 551 (Tex. Civ. App.—Waco 1961, writ ref'd n.r.e.) (plaintiff's settlement agreement of a prior workers' compensation suit arising out of the same accident was inadmissible to show the extent of plaintiff's injury because it was not an admission but was made for the purpose of compromise).

785. Refer to notes 743-746 *supra* and accompanying text.

786. *See, e.g.*, *De Lude v. Rimek*, 115 N.E.2d 561, 565 (Ill. App. Ct. 1953) (plaintiff's settlement with third party in exchange for a covenant not to sue was inadmissible because "it would tend to discourage settlement of this type of litigation when two or more defendants are involved").

787. *Hawthorne v. Eckerson Co.*, 77 F.2d 844, 847 (2d Cir. 1935). The court based its reversal on the underlying policy of the privilege:

> Settlements have always been looked on with favor, and courts have deemed it against public policy
> to subject a person who has compromised a claim to the hazard of having a settlement proved in a
> subsequent lawsuit by another person asserting a cause of action arising out of the same transaction.

Id. Federal courts have followed this approach in applying Federal Rule 408, and some Texas courts have also used this rationale to exclude accepted offers. *See Scaramuzzo v. Glenmore Distilleries Co.*, 501 F. Supp. 727, 733 (N.D. Ill. 1980) ("It would be logically inconsistent to uphold the vitality of Federal Rule 408, while at the same time holding that a settlement offer could be used against the offeror in related cases."); *Gen. Motors Corp. v. Simmons*, 558 S.W.2d 855, 857 (Tex. 1977) ("[S]ettlement agreements between the plaintiff and a co-defendant should be excluded from the jury. A contrary rule would frustrate the policy favoring the settlement of lawsuits."); *see, e.g.*, *Saf-Gard Prods., Inc. v. Serv. Parts, Inc.*, 491 F. Supp. 996, 1008-09 (D. Ariz. 1980) (citing Federal Rule 408 as authority for excluding third-party licensing agreements compromising claims of patent-rights infringement made in a similar earlier suit); *Henry v. Felici*, 758 S.W.2d 836, 841-43 (Tex. App.—Corpus Christi 1988, writ denied) (settlement agreements between plaintiff and third-party defendant should have been excluded; defendant-doctors in medical-malpractice action improperly questioned plaintiffs about the existence of the settlement agreement with third-party defendant-hospital; error was harmless because the jury was not told of the terms or amount of settlement).

788. Refer to notes 794-802 *infra* and accompanying text.

789. *See* FED. R. EVID. 408 advisory committee's note.

790. *See* TEX. R. EVID. 408(a)(1).

mise, it is apparent that a similar attitude must be taken with respect to completed compromises when offered against a party thereto."[791] Texas Rule 408 thus overruled Texas cases that allowed completed compromises into evidence and approved cases holding that both unaccepted and accepted offers to compromise were privileged on the issues of the validity or amount of a disputed claim.[792] By prohibiting parties from introducing evidence of rejected settlement offers to prove or dispute the validity of a claim, Rule 408 is broader than the traditional common-law rule.[793]

4. Conduct and statements during compromise negotiations. Under Rule 408, evidence of any conduct or statements made during compromise negotiations is inadmissible unless offered to prove some issue other than the validity or amount of a disputed claim.[794] This general exclusion marked a major change in Texas law—under the common law, admissions made in furtherance of compromise were excluded, but admissions of independent facts were not.[795] Admissions of independent facts were admis-

---

791. FED. R. EVID. 408 advisory committee's note; *see* 2 WEINSTEIN & BERGER, *supra* note 84, ¶408[04], at 408-28.

792. *See, e.g.*, ***Int'l & Great N. Ry. Co. v. Ragsdale***, 67 Tex. 24, 27-28, 2 S.W. 515, 516-17 (1886) (in negligence action to recover damages from a fire, error to admit evidence of a compromise between an agent and the injured party that was repudiated by the agent; repudiated compromise came under the general rule excluding offers to compromise); ***Bedner v. Fed. Underwriters Exch.***, 133 S.W.2d 214, 217 (Tex. Civ. App.—Eastland 1939, writ dism'd judgm't cor.) (evidence of payments in a workers' compensation suit made as advances on a compromise settlement of claim, offered as evidence of weekly wages of a deceased employee, was inadmissible because "[b]eing part of a compromise, the checks did not constitute an admission"); *see also* Bell, *supra* note 734, at 259 (traditional common-law interpretation of privilege is too narrow; "[t]he privilege is granted in order to get disputes settled; if the acceptance of an offer does not result in a settlement of the dispute, the privilege should remain"); *cf.* ***Ershig Sheet Metal, Inc. v. Gen. Ins.***, 383 P.2d 291, 294 (Wash. 1963) (for purposes of exclusion, accepted offers should not be distinguished from repudiated offers). *But see* ***Tag Res., Inc. v. Pet. Well Servs., Inc.***, 791 S.W.2d 600, 606 (Tex. App.—Beaumont 1990, no writ) (dicta; Civil Rule 408 does not apply to completed agreements for compromise and does not bar admission of a compromise agreement when plaintiff sues to enforce that agreement).

793. *See* ***Reese v. McVittie***, 200 P.2d 390, 392 (Colo. 1948) (dicta; "when such an offer is made and accepted, it becomes an independent contract [and] evidence thereof may be introduced for the purpose of establishing an admission of liability of the person making the offer ... if he who proposes it thereafter repudiates"); ***Farnum v. Colbert***, 293 A.2d 279, 282 (D.C. 1972) ("[W]hen an offer of compromise is accepted and thus becomes a settlement agreement, and is later repudiated, this policy consideration no longer dictates exclusion of the agreement as evidence."); MCCORMICK'S HANDBOOK II, *supra* note 33, §274, at 666 ("The shield of the privilege does not extend to the protection of those who repudiate the agreements the making of which the privilege is designed to encourage."); L.C. Warden, Annotation, *Admissibility of Evidence of Unperformed Compromise Agreement*, 26 A.L.R.2d 858, 860, 865 (1952) ("[I]n view of the meeting of the minds and the completion of a contract which itself could be sued on, there is no justification for excluding such evidence.").

A Texas case decided shortly before the adoption of the Rules took a middle path. It held that "each case must be analyzed on its merits and though the agreement may be tentatively accepted by both parties, the mere acceptance of the offer should not change the admissibility problem." ***In re J___ T___ H___***, 630 S.W.2d 473, 476 (Tex. App.—San Antonio 1982, no writ). The court went on to favor the exclusion of compromise agreements, even if repudiated. Thus, on the facts of the paternity suit before it, the court excluded an "agreed compromise settlement" in which the respondent agreed that he was the father of the petitioner's child; the petitioner repudiated the agreement and sought to introduce it into evidence against the respondent as an admission. *Id.* at 475-76.

794. TEX. R. EVID. 408(a)(2), (b).

795. *See* ***Spiritas v. Robinowitz***, 544 S.W.2d 710, 722 (Tex. Civ. App.—Dallas 1976, writ ref'd n.r.e.) ("To the extent that any statements constitute an admission of liability, they are admissible even though made in the context of settlement negotiations."); ***Charter Oak Fire Ins. v. Adams***, 488 S.W.2d 548, 550 (Tex. Civ. App.—Dallas 1972, writ ref'd n.r.e.) ("[A]n independent admission of liability is admissible in evidence, even though coupled with an offer of compromise."); ***Shaw v. Mass. Bonding & Ins.***, 373 S.W.2d 553, 557 (Tex. Civ. App.—Dallas 1963, no writ) ("[T]he law is plain that if a statement forming a part of or connected with an offer of a compromise is an admis-

sible unless they were stated hypothetically, expressly stated to be without prejudice, or so interwoven with the compromise offer as to be inseparable from it.[796] Admissions of fact that are "so tied up with the offer that they cannot be separated so as to disclose clearly what the offeror had in mind, that is, whether he is stating his belief as to a fact, or whether he is merely making a concession for the sake of negotiation,"[797] were also excluded from evidence under the common law.[798]

One problem with these distinctions was the difficulty in applying them,[799] which increased the possibility of contradictory or unfair results.[800] Another problem arose because the application of the common-law rule stifled free communication, thus

---

sion of an independent fact pertinent to the question in issue, evidence of such statement is admissible."); *Sanford v. John Finnigan Co.*, 169 S.W. 624, 626 (Tex. Civ. App.—San Antonio 1914, writ ref'd) ("It is the rule that when any fact stated in an offer of compromise can be separated from the offer and still convey the idea in the writer's mind, it is admissible in evidence."); *see, e.g.*, *Smith v. Smith*, 620 S.W.2d 619, 624 (Tex. Civ. App.—Dallas 1981, no writ) (in a dispute over property awarded in divorce case, husband's statement during negotiations about his lack of interest in the property was not an offer to let wife have the property and thus was admissible as an admission). In *Cooper v. Brown*, the Third Circuit noted that

> [w]hile facts assumed to be true for the purpose of compromise are ordinarily not competent as admissions against interest, a distinct admission of a fact will not be summarily excluded simply because it was made in connection with an effort to compromise. It is the offer to do something in furtherance of compromise which is deemed not to be admissible.

126 F.2d 874, 878 (3d Cir. 1942).

796. *Leija v. Am. Auto. Ins.*, 242 S.W.2d 814, 815 (Tex. Civ. App.—San Antonio 1951, writ dism'd); MᶜCORMICK'S HANDBOOK II, *supra* note 33, §274, at 663-64; *see, e.g.*, *In re J___ T___ H___*, 630 S.W.2d at 478 ("The statement [in the settlement agreement] was not an admission of an independent fact but a conditional, tentative or hypothetical statement which indicated that it was made in confidence that a compromise would be effected. ... Since this agreement specifically stated that appellee would admit to paternity only 'as a compromise,' this agreement was not in the nature of an admission by appellee, it being made without prejudice."). An express condition or disclaimer accompanying an admission of fact made the admission of fact inadmissible under the common law. *See Hamilton v. Hannus*, 185 S.W. 938, 940 (Tex. Civ. App.—Fort Worth 1916, no writ) (op. on reh'g); *Sanford*, 169 S.W. at 626; *see, e.g.*, *In re Evansville TV, Inc.*, 286 F.2d 65, 70 (7th Cir. 1961) (statements made in negotiations were inadmissible because the discussion was prefaced with the condition that the contents would not be used as evidence). Texas law has never required an express provision that offers to compromise be made "without prejudice." *See Ragsdale*, 67 Tex. at 27, 2 S.W. at 517 ("If the object of the party in making the offer was to buy his peace (which is impliedly manifested by a mere proposition to pay a sum in settlement), it is deemed to have been made without prejudice, and will be excluded.").

797. 1A RAY, *supra* note 46, §1142, at 290-91.

798. *See Merchants' Cotton Oil Co. v. Acme Gin Co.*, 284 S.W. 680, 682 (Tex. Civ. App.—Eastland 1926, no writ) (independent admission is not admissible when it is so coupled with the offer that they are inseparable); *see, e.g.*, *Home Ins. v. Balt. Whs. Co.*, 93 U.S. 527, 548 (1876) (letter sent by warehouse company president was an inadmissible offer to compromise; court below correctly refused to admit any portion of the letter because it contained no statement that could be separated from the offer to reveal an "idea ... in the writer's mind"); *Sanford*, 169 S.W. at 626 (in "letter in question there was no connection whatever between the last sentence [containing the offer to compromise] and the other portions of it"; those portions were admissible).

799. MᶜCORMICK'S HANDBOOK II, *supra* note 33, §274, at 664.

800. 2 WEINSTEIN & BERGER, *supra* note 84, ¶408[03], at 408-25. For example, in two different cases, Texas courts confronted the issue of whether documents prepared strictly for negotiations would be considered independent factual admissions. In one case, the court held that such documents were admissible because it was not apparent from the face of the documents that they were made in furtherance of the compromise and because they appeared to contain a mere "recitation of facts." *Leija*, 242 S.W.2d at 815. The court seemed to require an express statement of "without prejudice" on the face of the documents themselves. *See id.* Another Texas court, however, excluded similar documents under the rationale that they "are a part of and entwined in this negotiation and settlement process and as such are not admissible as an admission against interest." *Lapsley v. State*, 405 S.W.2d 406, 411 (Tex. Civ. App.—Texarkana 1966, writ ref'd n.r.e.).

thwarting the policy of encouraging compromises.[801] To avoid these problems, both Texas Rule 408 and Federal Rule 408 make all statements made during compromise negotiations inadmissible unless offered to prove some issue other than the validity or amount of a disputed claim.[802]

C. Rule 408(b): Permissible Use of Compromise Offers for Other Purposes

Offers to compromise are inadmissible under Rule 408 to prove or disprove the validity or amount of a disputed claim, but they are admissible for other purposes.[803] The rationale is that the value of this evidence outweighs the policy of fostering compromises.[804] However, the breadth of the phrase "for another purpose" requires courts to determine how far the exception extends. Commentators and appellate courts warn that to ensure that the underlying policy of privilege is not undermined, trial courts must exercise great caution in admitting evidence of offers to compromise for other purposes.[805] Courts should weigh the probative value of the evidence against the potential for discouraging future settlements before allowing it into evidence.[806] A lim-

---

801. *See* McCormick's Handbook II, *supra* note 33, §274, at 664; *see also* **Connor v. Mich. Wis. Pipe Line Co.**, 113 N.W.2d 121, 123-25 (Wis. 1962) (although public policy supports excluding independent fact admissions made during compromise negotiations, precedent requires them to be admitted); Bell, *supra* note 734, at 257 ("[T]o ask parties to negotiate away their difference under conditions which compel them to state their positions in hypothetical or conditional form is so unrealistic that it borders on the farcical. Infusing reserve and dissimulation, uneasiness, suspicion, and fear into negotiations vitiates any policy of encouragement."); John E. Tracy, *Evidence— Admissibility of Statements of Fact Made During Negotiation for Compromise*, 34 Mich. L. Rev. 524, 529 (1936) ("Full and frank disclosure by each party to the controversy of the position taken by him and the facts on which he relies to sustain his position or to justify a recession therefrom must be expected if the end desired is to be achieved. It should be assumed that the law has written over the door of every such conference room the words 'without prejudice.'").

802. The Advisory Committee expressly rejected the common-law rule: "An inevitable effect is to inhibit freedom of communication with respect to compromise, even among lawyers. Another effect is the generation of controversy over whether a given statement falls within or without the protected area. These considerations account for the expansion of the rule …." Fed. R. Evid. 408 advisory committee's note; *see also* **Ramada Dev. Co. v. Rauch**, 644 F.2d 1097, 1106-07 (5th Cir. 1981) (exclusion of a report prepared for negotiations proceeding was objected to because it was not prepared with the understanding that it could not be used in evidence; Rule 408 "does not indicate that there must be a pre-trial understanding or agreement between the parties regarding the nature of the report").

803. *See* Tex. R. Evid. 408(b). The language of this sentence from the rule was simplified in the 2015 restyling and now states that the court can admit evidence if offered for a permissible purpose; however, no substantive change was intended. *See* Tex. R. Evid. 408 cmt. ("There is no intent to change the process for admitting evidence covered by the Rule. It remains the case that if offered for an impermissible purpose, it must be excluded, and if offered for a purpose not barred by the Rule, its admissibility remains governed by the general principles of Rules 402, 403, 801, etc."). The change follows the 2011 restyling of Federal Rule 408 and was made for the same reason. *See* Fed. R. Evid. 408 advisory committee's note to 2011 amendments.

804. *See* 2 Weinstein & Berger, *supra* note 84, ¶408[05], at 408-35 to 408-42.

805. *See* **Rauch**, 644 F.2d at 1107 ("[T]his provision, surely, was not intended to completely undercut the policy behind the rule."); 2 Weinstein & Berger, *supra* note 84, ¶408[05], at 408-37 (courts should ensure that "an indiscriminate and mechanical application of this 'exception' to Federal Rule 408 does not result in undermining the rule's public policy objective").

806. *See, e.g.*, **Rauch**, 644 F.2d at 1107 (upholding trial court's decision to exclude a report connected with settlement negotiations because other means of proof were available); **John McShain, Inc. v. Cessna Aircraft Co.**, 563 F.2d 632, 634-35 (3d Cir. 1977) (upholding trial court's decision to allow evidence of a compromise agreement used to show the impartiality of a testifying expert witness); **Reichenbach v. Smith**, 528 F.2d 1072, 1075 (5th Cir. 1976) (upholding trial court's decision to exclude testimony relating to a trial-time settlement; trial court might have concluded that the testimony would have been superfluous and prejudicial).

iting instruction to the jury under Rule 105(a), for instance, would help reduce the danger that the jury will misapply the evidence.[807] The other purposes specified in Rule 408(b) are merely examples and not an exhaustive list.[808]

1. Other material facts in issue. Rule 408 allows the admission of compromise offers and agreements to prove consequential material facts other than the validity or amount of a disputed claim.[809] A party will not avoid the rule simply by claiming that the evidence is offered for other purposes; the court will examine the evidence to determine whether the evidence could be used to prove or disprove the validity of the claim or the amount of damages.[810] Federal courts admit evidence of compromises under Rule 408 when a material proposition besides the validity or amount of a disputed claim is at issue[811] or when information in settlement agreements is essential for determining whether a legal prerequisite of a lawsuit has been met.[812] This exception also encompasses compromise negotiations admitted to show notice or knowledge,[813] or agency, control, or ownership in a vicarious-liability case.[814] Compromise negotiations

---

807. *See* McCormick's Handbook II, *supra* note 33, §274, at 664 (any available limiting instructions should be considered). Refer to *Article I: General Provisions*, *supra* p. 97.

808. Refer to notes 160-161 *supra* and accompanying text.

809. 2 Weinstein & Berger, *supra* note 84, ¶408[05], at 408-35.

810. *See, e.g.*, ***Barrett v. U.S. Brass Corp.***, 864 S.W.2d 606, 634 (Tex. App.—Houston [1st Dist.] 1993) (defendant argued that settlement letters were "relevant on mental anguish damages, unconscionability, causes of action [and] rebuttal evidence," but the court held that all of these issues would "directly defeat [defendant's] alleged liability and the amount of damages claimed"), *rev'd in part on other grounds sub nom.* ***Amstadt v. U.S. Brass Corp.***, 919 S.W.2d 644 (Tex. 1996).

811. *See, e.g.*, ***United States v. Hauert***, 40 F.3d 197, 200 (7th Cir. 1994) (evidence of negotiations with IRS was admissible to show defendant's awareness of the pertinent law); ***Freidus v. First Nat'l Bank of Council Bluffs***, 928 F.2d 793, 795 (8th Cir. 1991) (settlement documents were admissible to impeach testimony that bank never gave reasons for its foreclosure actions); ***Urico v. Parnell Oil Co.***, 708 F.2d 852, 854-55 (1st Cir. 1983) (evidence of settlement negotiations was admissible to excuse plaintiff's failure to mitigate damages); ***In re Gen. Motors Corp. Engine Interchange Litig.***, 594 F.2d 1106, 1124 & n.20 (7th Cir. 1979) (trial court should have admitted evidence of the conduct of negotiations to evaluate the fairness of the settlement because such admission is consistent with the policy underlying Federal Rule 408); ***Overseas Motors, Inc. v. Imp. Motors Ltd.***, 375 F. Supp. 499, 537-38 (E.D. Mich. 1974) (rejecting plaintiff's contention that settlement negotiations were admissible to show conspiracy to restrain trade because plaintiff made no prima facie showing of conspiracy), *aff'd*, 519 F.2d 119 (6th Cir. 1975); *see also* Bell, *supra* note 734, at 258 (supporting the use of evidence of compromise negotiations in a suit on a binding contract of compromise).

812. *See, e.g.*, ***Crouse-Hinds Co. v. InterNorth, Inc.***, 518 F. Supp. 413, 415 (N.D.N.Y. 1980) (as a result of the unique nature of antitrust suits, which require determination of the future effect of a merger on competition, not determination of liability of parties, consent decrees issued in prior antitrust actions come under this exception to Federal Rule 408), *rev'd in part on other grounds*, 634 F.2d 690 (2d Cir. 1980); ***Taylor v. Union Carbide Corp.***, 93 F.R.D. 1, 7 (S.D. W. Va. 1980) (in class-certification action, documents of prior settlement agreements were "laden with information germane not only to the adequacy of the named parties as representatives of the class, but also as to competency of counsel"); ***B&B Inv. Club v. Kleinert's, Inc.***, 472 F. Supp. 787, 791 (E.D. Pa. 1979) (affidavit establishing prior settlement between plaintiff and defendant was admissible to show, as required by Pennsylvania law, defendant's success in the prior suit before indemnification was allowed against codefendant).

813. *See, e.g.*, ***United States v. Gilbert***, 668 F.2d 94, 97 (2d Cir. 1981) (evidence of a civil consent decree given in a prior SEC suit was admissible under the exception to Federal Rule 408 to show knowledge of reporting requirements); *see also* ***Huntley v. Snider***, 86 F.2d 539, 540 (1st Cir. 1936) (trustee could show a compromise with bankrupt man's wife to prove bankrupt man's knowledge of assets).

814. 2 Weinstein & Berger, *supra* note 84, ¶408[04], at 408-34.

are also admissible to show the materiality of other evidence.[815] One case held that evidence of a settlement offer was admissible to show that the opposing party did not suffer any damages from the defendant's conduct, even though that is not "another purpose" expressly mentioned in Rule 408.[816]

However, courts should not allow the use of such evidence under Rule 408 without considering the potential prejudicial effect of the disclosure, the policy of encouraging settlements, and the availability of other evidence tending to prove the same issue.[817] In some instances, the trial court may sever two causes of action if the evidence in one would be barred by Rule 408 and the evidence in the other would be essential to the claim.[818] The trial court retains the discretion to exclude settlement-negotiation evidence that might be admissible under Rule 408 when its probative value is substantially outweighed by any of the Rule 403 counterfactors.[819]

2. Undue delay. Rule 408 expressly allows evidence of compromise negotiations to explain or excuse undue delay.[820] Texas courts have applied this doctrine to support the finding of a waiver of the right to object when the other party did not give notice of a

---

815. *See, e.g.*, ***Portland Sav. & Loan Ass'n v. Bernstein***, 716 S.W.2d 532, 537 (Tex. App.—Corpus Christi 1985, writ ref'd n.r.e.) (allowing introduction of compromise negotiations to show that certain misrepresentations were made in those negotiations; Civil Rule 408 did not apply because the evidence related to a claim of misrepresentation instead of liability), *overruled on other grounds*, ***Dawson-Austin v. Austin***, 968 S.W.2d 319 (Tex. 1998); *see also* ***Tarrant Cty. v. English***, 989 S.W.2d 368, 377-78 (Tex. App.—Fort Worth 1998, pet. denied) (county's settlement letter was admissible in suit brought by former landowner to recover for contamination with diesel fuel from county's asphalt trucks when offered to show plaintiff's state of mind). The common law also allowed the admission of compromise-negotiation evidence for this purpose. *See, e.g.*, ***Battles v. Adams***, 415 S.W.2d 479, 483 (Tex. Civ. App.—Austin 1967, writ ref'd n.r.e.) (testimony about a settlement is admissible to show the effect of a boundary agreement in a real-property dispute).

816. ***TCA Bldg. Co. v. Nw. Res. Co.***, 922 S.W.2d 629, 636-37 (Tex. App.—Waco 1996, writ denied).

817. *See, e.g.*, ***Ramada Dev. Co. v. Rauch***, 644 F.2d 1097, 1107 & n.9 (5th Cir. 1981) (approving the exclusion of a report containing compromise negotiations when other proof was available).

818. *See, e.g.*, ***In re State Farm Mut. Auto. Ins.***, 395 S.W.3d 229, 234 (Tex. App.—El Paso 2012, orig. proceeding) (when plaintiff brought both uninsured-motorist and bad-faith claims against insurer, proper solution was to sever actions because evidence of settlement offer would not be admissible in uninsured-motorist claim, but would be admissible to establish essential elements of bad-faith claim); ***In re Am. Nat'l Cty. Mut. Ins.***, 384 S.W.3d 429, 434-35 (Tex. App.—Austin 2012, orig. proceeding) (same); ***U.S. Fire Ins. v. Millard***, 847 S.W.2d 668, 672-73 (Tex. App.—Houston [1st Dist.] 1993, orig. proceeding) (same).

819. *See* Tex. R. Evid. 408 cmt.; *see, e.g.*, ***Allison v. Fire Ins. Exch.***, 98 S.W.3d 227, 259-60 (Tex. App.—Austin 2002, pet. granted, judgm't vacated w.r.m.) (although trial court could have admitted evidence of homeowner's demands at mediation to counter her contention that insurer unduly delayed in paying her claims, it did not abuse its discretion by excluding the evidence "because of the danger of unfair prejudice and because of the general rule that settlement discussions are confidential"). Refer to notes 111-159 *supra* and accompanying text.

820. *See* Tex. R. Evid. 408(b); *see, e.g.*, ***Auto. Ins. v. Davila***, 805 S.W.2d 897, 910 (Tex. App.—Corpus Christi 1991, writ denied) (Rule 408 "provides an exception when the evidence is offered for another purpose, such as negating a contention of undue delay. When the settlement evidence is immaterial to the main trial issue, refusing to admit the settlement evidence is not reversible error"; plaintiff's contention that defendant "drug its feet" on her insurance claim did not open the door under Rule 408 for defendant to introduce settlement letters from its attorney to plaintiff because that evidence was immaterial to the main trial issue and because the delay about which the plaintiff complained occurred before defendant's denial of her claim and the beginning of compromise negotiations), *disapproved on other grounds*, ***Hines v. Hash***, 843 S.W.2d 464 (Tex. 1992); *cf.* ***Iberian Tankers Co. v. Gates Constr. Corp.***, 388 F. Supp. 1190, 1192 (S.D.N.Y. 1975) (evidence of negotiations toward a settlement was admissible under Federal Rule 408 to show delay and loss of interest to plaintiff). This evidence was also admissible at common law. McCormick's Handbook II, *supra* note 33, §274, at 664.

claim within the required time[821] or did not give proof of loss.[822] A Texas court has also admitted evidence of compromise negotiations to excuse failure to file a claim within the time required.[823] These holdings are consistent with the exception as stated in Rule 408.

3. Impeachment. Compromise offers and acceptances made between a party and a witness, as well as statements and conduct during compromise negotiations, are admissible under Rule 408 to impeach a party or witness by showing the party's or witness's bias, prejudice, or interest.[824] A party's right to offer evidence of compromise negotiations, however, is usually limited to proof that negotiations or an agreement took place; statements or conduct during these negotiations cannot be used to show the general malice of a party or witness.[825]

The danger that the jury will use the evidence substantively has caused commentators to caution against indiscriminate admission of compromise evidence for impeachment purposes,[826] and some courts have refused to admit it.[827] The Advisory Commit-

---

821. *E.g.*, **Graham v. San Antonio Mach. & Supply Corp.**, 418 S.W.2d 303, 310-11 (Tex. Civ. App.—San Antonio 1967, writ ref'd n.r.e.) (allowing evidence of compromise negotiations in a construction-contract suit to prove that a waiver of a condition precedent occurred).

822. *E.g.*, **U.S. Fid. & Guar. Co. v. Bimco Iron & Metal Corp.**, 464 S.W.2d 353, 357 (Tex. 1971) (admitting evidence of attempts by insurer to settle a claim after the time permitted for filing proofs of loss to show that insurer waived notification-of-loss requirement); **Alamo Cas. Co. v. Trafton**, 231 S.W.2d 474, 476 (Tex. Civ. App.—San Antonio 1950, writ dism'd) (allowing introduction of settlement negotiations to prove that insurer had waived notification-of-loss requirement).

823. **Travelers Ins. v. Barrett**, 366 S.W.2d 692, 694 (Tex. Civ. App.—El Paso 1963, no writ).

824. TEX. R. EVID. 408(b); *see* **Kan. City S. Ry. Co. v. Carter**, 778 S.W.2d 911, 913 (Tex. App.—Texarkana 1989, writ denied) (Rule 408 permits evidence of offers to compromise to prove bias, prejudice, or interest of a witness or party to show a motive for the testimony offered); *cf.* **John McShain, Inc. v. Cessna Aircraft Co.**, 563 F.2d 632, 634-35 (3d Cir. 1977) (allowing cross-examination as to a compromise; "[t]he fact that a sister corporation of [expert's] employer had been released from liability in exchange for [expert's] testimony cast doubt upon [expert's] impartiality"); **Reichenbach v. Smith**, 528 F.2d 1072, 1075-76 (5th Cir. 1976) (although trial court did not abuse its discretion in excluding evidence of a compromise, "[t]he existence of a settlement agreement goes directly to the issue of credibility and usually the better approach is that codified in [Federal] Rule 408"). Refer to *Article VI: Witnesses, infra* p. 660.

Impeachment was also allowed under common law, under the theory that the jury's need to evaluate the credibility of witnesses outweighs the policy of encouraging compromise and that rules of evidence should not unduly hinder the right of cross-examination. *See* **Hyde v. Marks**, 138 S.W.2d 619, 623 (Tex. Civ. App.—Fort Worth 1940, writ dism'd judgm't cor.) (evidence of compromises and offers to compromise are admissible in some situations because "a party on cross-examination may develop any fact or circumstance which tends to show interest, prejudice or bias of a witness"); *see also* **E.R. Squibb & Sons, Inc. v. Heflin**, 579 S.W.2d 19, 21 (Tex. Civ. App.—Beaumont 1979, writ ref'd n.r.e.) (codefendant's interest in plaintiff's recovery is a proper subject of cross-examination to show bias or prejudice but did not apply to this case because settlement with codefendant was only discussed, not accepted); **Tex. & Pac. Ry. Co. v. Spann**, 173 S.W. 600, 601 (Tex. Civ. App.—Texarkana 1915, writ ref'd) (letter in question, asking for settlement, was not admissible to impeach the party because it was written by party's attorney).

Federal Rule 408(b) allows for impeachment by showing only a witness's bias or prejudice; interest is not included, and neither is a party's bias or prejudice. *See* FED. R. EVID. 408(b). Refer to notes 833-838 *infra* and accompanying text.

825. *See* **Rural Dev., Inc. v. Stone**, 700 S.W.2d 661, 668 (Tex. App.—Corpus Christi 1985, writ ref'd n.r.e.) (evidence of whether the parties liked or disliked one another may be a proper subject for jury consideration, but the "evidence must come from some other source than conduct and statements at a meeting to attempt a settlement"), *disapproved on other grounds*, **Sterner v. Marathon Oil Co.**, 767 S.W.2d 686 (Tex. 1989).

826. *See* 2 WEINSTEIN & BERGER, *supra* note 84, ¶408[05], at 408-41 (although evidence is normally admissible for a witness's credibility, a trial judge should avoid "unnecessarily undercutting the basic exclusionary rule").

tee's note to Federal Rule 408 does not mention this issue, however, and both Texas Rule 403 and Federal Rule 403 allow the trial court to exclude relevant evidence only if its probative value is *"substantially* outweighed" by unfair prejudice or another negative factor.[828]

The language of Rule 408(a) seems to also allow impeachment of a witness by showing prior inconsistent statements made in compromise negotiations.[829] Commentators take strong positions for[830] and against[831] this sort of impeachment, but admitting such evidence to impeach seems to be the better view. No Texas cases have directly addressed the issue. In one Texas case, the situation presented itself, but the court sidestepped the issue by declaring that it was not properly raised.[832]

---

827. *See, e.g., **Paster v. Pa. R.R.**,* 43 F.2d 908, 911 (2d Cir. 1930) (allowing such evidence is "especially apt to deflect the minds of a jury from the issues"); ***Fenberg v. Rosenthal**,* 109 N.E.2d 402, 405 (Ill. App. Ct. 1952) ("[I]t is a practical impossibility to eradicate from the jury's minds the consideration that where there has been a payment there must have been liability.").

828. Fed. R. Evid. 403 (emphasis added); Tex. R. Evid. 403 (emphasis added). Refer to notes 111-159 *supra* and accompanying text.

829. *See, e.g., **Mo. Pac. Transp. Co. v. Norwood**,* 90 S.W.2d 480, 480-81 (Ark. 1936) (witnesses' statements about a settlement of claims against defendant were "admissible as tending to contradict their testimony" in a later trial). The phrase "such as" in Rule 408(b) implies that the list of other purposes is not exclusive. *See* Tex. R. Evid. 408(b). Federal Rule 408, however, bars this use of prior inconsistent statements for impeachment purposes. *See* Fed. R. Evid. 408(a). Refer to notes 731-732 *supra* and accompanying text. Impeachment by prior inconsistent statements is generally governed by Rule 613(a). Refer to *Article VI: Witnesses, infra* p. 652.

830. *See* 23 Wright & Graham, *supra* note 35, §5314, at 286-87 (1980). Wright and Graham note the following:

> A party who is impeached at trial by an inconsistent statement made during settlement negotiations, in the absence of some mistake, must have been lying at one time or the other. It is difficult to see why the law would care to encourage falsehood in either venue. The purpose of Rule 408 is to foster "complete candor" between the parties, not to protect false representations. … In this situation, it would seem that the injunction in Rule 102 to interpret the rules so as to foster the values of "fairness" and "truth" should lead courts to conclude that prior inconsistent statements in the course of settlement negotiations should be admitted to impeach a party who testifies.

Id.

831. Michael Graham has stated that

> [a] question arises concerning whether evidence of conduct or statements … is admissible as inconsistent conduct and statements for purposes of impeachment. … Rule 408 … states that evidence need not be excluded when it is offered for a purpose other than to prove liability for or invalidity of the claim or its amount. Negating this argument to some extent is the fact that impeachment is not specifically included as illustrative of such other purposes in Rule 408 ….

Michael H. Graham, Evidence: Text, Rules, Illustrations and Problems ch. XI, §B, 460 (1983); *see also* Jon R. Waltz & J. Patrick Huston, *The Rules of Evidence in Settlement,* 5 Litigation 11, 16 (1978) (stating that "[w]e agree with the conclusion of other commentators that courts should almost never admit a party's bargaining statements as discrediting prior inconsistent statements"). One commentator asserted that

> [i]f the privilege theory is unequivocally adopted, then statements made during compromise will become an attractive means for impeaching a witness who is a party to the action. The statement would be offered … to show a prior inconsistent statement. … In order to preserve and maintain the privilege, such a method of impeachment probably should not be allowed.

Bell, *supra* note 734, at 258.

832. *See **Ochs v. Martinez**,* 789 S.W.2d 949, 959 & n.6 (Tex. App.—San Antonio 1990, writ denied). In this suit to modify a child-custody agreement, the mother attempted to use the father's statements, made in settlement negotiations, to impeach his testimony. *Id.* at 959. The father had stated that he would let the mother retain custody of their older daughter if he could have custody of their younger daughter, but at trial, the father said that he had never

4. Interest of a party or witness. Texas Rule 408(b), unlike Federal Rule 408(b), includes the "interest" of a party or a witness as "another purpose" for which evidence of compromises is admissible.[833] The federal rule does not mention "interest," and it mentions "witness" but not "party."[834]

This additional language in the Texas rule was intended to continue the judicial policy favoring the disclosure of Mary Carter agreements—settlements between a defendant and a plaintiff in which the plaintiff agrees to share with the settling defendant the proceeds of any recovery the plaintiff receives from the settlor's codefendants.[835] This type of arrangement creates a conflict of interest among defendants, and the settling defendant often gives testimony that is damaging to the codefendants.[836] By adopt-

---

considered "giving up" their older daughter. *Id.* The court held that the evidence did not show bias or prejudice on the father's part but declined to address the question of whether it should have been admitted as a prior inconsistent statement. *Id.* at 959-60 & n.6.

833. TEX. R. EVID. 408(b). The interest of a party does not include generalized malice or dislike of one party by another. *See* **Rural Dev., Inc. v. Stone**, 700 S.W.2d 661, 668 (Tex. App.—Corpus Christi 1985, writ ref'd n.r.e.) (evidence of whether parties liked or disliked one another may be a proper subject for jury consideration, but the "evidence must come from some other source than conduct and statements at a meeting to attempt a settlement"), *disapproved on other grounds*, **Sterner v. Marathon Oil Co.** 767 S.W.2d 686 (Tex. 1989).

834. FED. R. EVID. 408(b).

835. *See* **Gen. Motors Corp. v. Simmons**, 558 S.W.2d 855, 857-58 (Tex. 1977) ("Agreements with a settling defendant who remains a party at the trial and retains a financial stake in the plaintiffs' recovery have been called 'Mary Carter' agreements ...."); *see, e.g.,* **City of Hous. v. Sam P. Wallace & Co.**, 585 S.W.2d 669, 673-74 (Tex. 1979) (treating as a Mary Carter agreement a settlement between a coplaintiff and defendant when coplaintiff remained a party but undermined the other coplaintiff's case). *See generally* Robin Renee Green, Comment, *Mary Carter Agreements: The Unsolved Evidentiary Problems in Texas*, 40 BAYLOR L. REV. 449, 452-64 (1988) (discussing Texas's struggle in developing evidentiary standards when Mary Carter agreements are involved).

836. *See* David L. Nigh, Note, General Motors Corp. v. Simmons: *Admissibility of Mary Carter Agreements and Indemnity Among Joint Tortfeasors*, 19 S. TEX. L.J. 473, 476 (1978) (noting how settling parties use each other's testimony in cross-examination to present a stronger case to the jury). Because of the possibility of deception, Texas courts allowed evidence of such agreements not only to impeach the settling party for bias or prejudice but also to show directly and substantively the true interests and alignment of the parties. *See* **Scurlock Oil Co. v. Smithwick**, 724 S.W.2d 1, 4 (Tex. 1986) (Mary Carter agreements are admissible to show bias or prejudice of witness); *see, e.g.,* **Sam P. Wallace & Co.**, 585 S.W.2d at 674 ("The Mary Carter agreements and the misalignment of the plaintiffs in this case both possess a more basic vice. Both of them are false and misleading portrayals to the jury of the real interests of the parties and witnesses."); **Simmons**, 558 S.W.2d at 858 (when a witness who "was the real party at interest took the witness stand under the semblance of being a disinterested witness to testify against the opposing party, his connection with the [calling party] was not exempt from cross-examination"); **Mi-Jack Prods., Inc. v. Braneff**, 827 S.W.2d 493, 499 (Tex. App.—Houston [1st Dist.] 1992, no writ) (evidence of Mary Carter agreement was admissible under Civil Rule 408 to show settling defendant's true alignment in the case, even when nonsettling defendant could not demonstrate bias of any testifying witness); **Martinez v. RV Tool, Inc.**, 737 S.W.2d 17, 18 (Tex. App.—El Paso 1987) (compromise settlement that was not a true Mary Carter agreement was inadmissible for impeachment purposes because the jury already had evidence of the witness's bias and interest), *writ denied*, 747 S.W.2d 379 (Tex. 1988).
    Moreover, Texas courts have held that the jury should be able to learn not just the fact that an agreement has been made but also the details of the agreement, including the financial interests of the parties. *See, e.g.,* **Simmons**, 558 S.W.2d at 857 (trial court improperly excluded evidence that settling defendant would be entitled to 50% of each dollar received by plaintiff up to $200,000). On the other hand, the jury could not learn of the existence of an agreement or its terms if the settling defendant did nothing to help the plaintiff. *See* **Clayton v. Volkswagenwerk, A.G.**, 606 S.W.2d 15, 17-19 (Tex. Civ. App.—Houston [1st Dist.] 1980, writ ref'd n.r.e.) ("Clearly, a party is not entitled to introduce otherwise inadmissible, prejudicial evidence just to discredit testimony that he alone offered."). Further, if no showing is made that the particular witness has any interest in the outcome of the present lawsuit, he may not be impeached with the existence or terms of a settlement agreement. *See, e.g.,* **Smithwick**, 724 S.W.2d at 4

ing Texas Rule 408, the Texas Supreme Court explicitly recognized that Rule 408 does not exclude evidence of compromises, including Mary Carter agreements, to show the interest of a witness or party.[837] However, in 1992, the Texas Supreme Court held that Mary Carter agreements are void as contrary to public policy.[838]

5. Explaining prior statements. A party may also use evidence of a compromise to explain prior statements that contradict present testimony.[839] Courts have used this exception to admit evidence showing that the compromise offer induced the prior inconsistent statement[840] and to explain the motive behind that prior inconsistent statement.[841] This use is consistent with Rule 408. Of course, if one party "opens the door" or volunteers evidence of settlement negotiations, he cannot then complain when the other party explains that agreement;[842] such conduct operates as a waiver.

6. "Bad-faith" claims. Courts addressing "bad-faith" claims brought by an insured against its insurance company have struggled with the issue of admitting evidence of an insurer's offer to compromise to show that the insurer made a good-faith effort to settle a claim.[843] Such evidence of an offer to settle is irrelevant and risks unfair prejudice when offered to show the insurer's liability under the policy. But this same evidence is essential to the insurer's defense against a bad-faith claim.[844] When offered by the insurer to show good faith, the evidence is not being offered to prove underlying liability. Thus, Rule 408 does not bar the admissibility of evidence of compromise efforts when offered to defeat a distinct legal cause of action alleging an insurer's bad faith.[845] Conversely, a plaintiff may offer such evidence to show that an insurer exercised bad faith in its refusal to settle a claim in a reasonable manner.[846]

(defendant's former employee could not be impeached with Mary Carter settlement agreement between defendant oil company and plaintiff in wrongful-death case when no showing was made that the witness had any interest in the outcome of the present litigation).

837. *See Smithwick*, 724 S.W.2d at 4 (Mary Carter agreements are admissible to show bias or prejudice of a witness); *Barras v. Monsanto Co.*, 831 S.W.2d 859, 864 (Tex. App.—Houston [14th Dist.] 1992, writ denied) ("when a settling defendant retains a financial stake in the plaintiff's recovery," the agreement may be admitted into evidence); *see, e.g., Mi-Jack Prods.*, 827 S.W.2d at 494-95 (trial court committed reversible error when it excluded evidence of agreement between plaintiff and codefendants in which codefendants obtained an interest in plaintiff's recovery).

838. *Elbaor v. Smith*, 845 S.W.2d 240, 250 (Tex. 1992).

839. *See* McCORMICK'S HANDBOOK II, *supra* note 33, §274, at 664.

840. *See Fieve v. Emmeck*, 78 N.W.2d 343, 349 (Minn. 1956) (evidence may be properly admitted to explain the circumstances that triggered the inconsistent statements); *see, e.g., Malatt v. United Transit Co.*, 207 A.2d 39, 41 (R.I. 1965) (using evidence of a compromise offer to show that the statement signed by the party was prepared by the opposing party's adjuster).

841. *See Hayes v. Coleman*, 61 N.W.2d 634, 639 (Mich. 1953).

842. *See, e.g., Evans v. Covington*, 795 S.W.2d 806, 809 (Tex. App.—Texarkana 1990, no writ) (when one party elicited testimony of settlement negotiations from an adverse witness, he could not then complain about the admission of letters outlining offers of settlement).

843. *Avary v. Bank of Am.*, 72 S.W.3d 779, 798-99 (Tex. App.—Dallas 2002, pet. denied).

844. *Id.* at 798.

845. *Id.* at 799.

846. *See, e.g., Athey v. Farmers Ins. Exch.*, 234 F.3d 357, 361-62 (8th Cir. 2000) (in bad-faith lawsuit by motorist against his insurer, Rule 408 did not bar evidence that defendant "refused to offer any amount" unless motorist

7. Proving an effort to obstruct justice. Finally, Rule 408(b) includes in its list of permissible uses "proving an effort to obstruct a criminal investigation or prosecution."[847] Efforts to "buy off" a witness are illegal[848] and are not subject to any of the public-policy considerations discussed above.[849] Instead, such efforts are admissible to show "consciousness of guilt."[850]

While the application of this final provision is clear in a criminal prosecution, how does it apply to civil trials? If an "effort to obstruct a criminal investigation or prosecution" is a material proposition in a civil case (i.e., an element of a claim or defense), the application is obvious: Rule 408 presents no obstacle to admissibility. The most frequent application is in a litigated transaction giving rise to both criminal and civil liability. For example, suppose the injured party, P, is a potential civil plaintiff and a potential prosecuting witness in a criminal case. D, the potential defendant in both the civil and criminal cases, offers a consideration to P, calling for at least the withdrawal of the criminal complaint. At the civil trial, P offers as an admission of liability D's offer, and D objects that it is an inadmissible offer to compromise. McCormick states that

> [a]n offer by the accused to pay money to "buy off" the prosecuting witness and stifle prosecution, though sometimes mistakenly theorized as an offer of compromise and held inadmissible, is not within the policy of encouraging compromises, and hence is not usually regarded as privileged. Indeed, we have seen that it is classed as an implied admission and received in evidence as such.[851]

Excluding the evidence under such circumstances is an abuse of the privilege rationale discussed by McCormick. Accordingly, Rule 408 does not hinder admissibility. For example, in ***L.M.W. v. State***,[852] a prosecution for injury to a child, the court of appeals held that the defendant should have been allowed to introduce evidence of a divorce-court settlement offer to show that her ex-husband, a State's witness, was biased against her and had attempted to bribe or influence another witness.[853] As the court noted, the

---

"agreed to abandon his bad faith claim"; court concluded that this condition was itself evidence of bad faith, thus Rule 408 did not require exclusion because evidence was offered for "another purpose").

847. TEX. R. EVID. 408(b).

848. *See* TEX. PENAL CODE §36.05(a).

849. FED. R. EVID. 408 advisory committee's note; *see* McCORMICK'S HANDBOOK II, *supra* note 33, §274, at 665.

850. *See, e.g.,* **United States v. Peed**, 714 F.2d 7, 9-10 (4th Cir. 1983) (secretly recorded conversation in which defendant offered to return valuable dolls to the owner in exchange for dropping a criminal investigation was not an effort to resolve a civil claim, but rather an attempt to avoid criminal prosecution, and thus was not barred by Federal Rule 408).

851. McCORMICK'S HANDBOOK II, *supra* note 33, §274, at 665.

852. 891 S.W.2d 754, 763-64 (Tex. App.—Fort Worth 1994, pet. ref'd).

853. *Id.* The court noted that

> [e]vidence that [the ex-husband] was attempting to use the criminal justice system for his own personal ends, or may have been retaliating against appellant for failing to comply with his divorce wishes, was probative of his bias against appellant, as well as probative of evidence that the charges could have been fabricated.

Id.

policy behind Rule 408 is to encourage civil settlements; it is not to be used as a shield to exclude probative evidence in criminal prosecutions.[854]

D. Rule 408 & Otherwise Discoverable Evidence

Before the 2015 restyling, the third sentence of Rule 408 provided that "evidence otherwise discoverable" was not excluded from evidence by Rule 408 "merely because it is presented in the course of compromise negotiations." This provision was intended to preserve the right of discovery[855] and to prevent parties from intentionally making evidence inadmissible by offering it in compromise negotiations.[856] The sentence was deleted as surplusage in the restyling.[857] As the comment to the restyling explains, "even without the sentence, the Rule cannot be read to protect pre-existing information simply because it was presented to the adversary in compromise negotiations."[858] Thus, internal memoranda and in-house statements made in the course of preparing for settlement discussions are covered by Rule 408, but in-house materials that are otherwise discoverable and admissible are not protected by the rule merely because they are produced as a part of settlement discussions.[859]

RULE 409

OFFERS TO PAY MEDICAL & SIMILAR EXPENSES

Evidence of furnishing, promising to pay, or offering to pay medical, hospital, or similar expenses resulting from an injury is not admissible to prove liability for the injury.

COMMENTARY ON RULE 409

A. Common Law & Texas Background

The common law excluded from evidence the payment of medical expenses as proof of liability for an injury.[860] The basis for this exclusion is not irrelevance; a logical in-

---

854. *Id.* at 764.

855. 2 WEINSTEIN & BERGER, *supra* note 84, ¶408[01], at 408-18 to 408-19.

856. S. REP. NO. 93-1277, *supra* note 169, at 10, *reprinted in* 1974 U.S.C.C.A.N. 7051, 7057; *see* TEX. R. EVID. 408 cmt.; *cf. In re Special Nov. 1975 Grand Jury*, 433 F. Supp. 1094, 1096-97 (N.D. Ill. 1977) (documents containing personal records of trust officers, ordered for a grand-jury investigation, did not fall under the protection of Federal Rule 408 because they were otherwise discoverable under Federal Rule 1101(d)(2); legislative history of Federal Rule 408 states that a person should not be able to immunize admissible documents).

857. TEX. R. EVID. 408 cmt.

858. *Id.*

859. *Cf. Ramada Dev. Co. v. Rauch*, 644 F.2d 1097, 1107 (5th Cir. 1981) (report drafted specifically for use in negotiation proceedings was properly excluded under Federal Rule 408; exception for otherwise discoverable evidence "does not cover the present case where the document, or statement, would not have existed but for the negotiations"); 2 MUELLER & KIRKPATRICK, *supra* note 364, §135, at 18 (internal settlement memoranda and statements are protected by the rule; "organizational parties can hardly conduct settlement talks without undertaking internal reviews and discussions, and FRE 408 can hardly achieve its intended purpose in this setting if its coverage is limited to statements actually made or forwarded to the other side").

860. McCORMICK ON EVIDENCE, *supra* note 1, §275, at 818. *See generally* Karl H. Larsen, Annotation, *Admissibility of Evidence Showing Payment, or Offer or Promise of Payment, of Medical, Hospital, and Similar Expenses of*

———————————— ✯ ————————————

ference from the payment is consciousness of fault for having caused or allowed the injury leading to the expenses. Rather, the law does not want to discourage humanitarian gestures or contractual arrangements, such as insurance, that help an injured party before a court has determined legal liability.[861] This policy of excluding evidence of payment as proof of liability thus closely resembles the rules that exclude evidence of subsequent remedial measures[862] and offers to compromise.[863] In effect, these rules create an evidentiary privilege for all such conduct. Before the enactment of the Rules of Evidence, this point had been controlled by Texas statutes[864] with essentially the same effect as the common-law doctrine.[865] Rule 409, which is identical to Federal Rule 409, essentially continued the policy of the common law[866] and of the previously applicable Texas statutes.[867]

B. Scope of Rule 409

1. Type of conduct covered. Rule 409 applies to "evidence of furnishing, promising to pay, or offering to pay medical … expenses."[868] This scope is broader than that of the previously applicable Texas statutes, which focused on evidence of the payment itself and did not mention offers or promises.[869]

Injured Party by Opposing Party, 65 A.L.R.3d 932, 940-63 (1975) (discussing the rule's application and scope in several jurisdictions).

861. *See* FED. R. EVID. 409 advisory committee's note (quoting W.R. Habeeb, Annotation, *Admissibility of Evidence to Show Payment, or Offer or Promise of Payment of Medical, Hospital, and Similar Expenses of an Injured Party by the Opposing Party*, 20 A.L.R.2d 291, 293 (1951)); McCORMICK ON EVIDENCE, *supra* note 1, §274, at 811.

862. *See* TEX. R. EVID. 407. Refer to notes 669-721 *supra* and accompanying text.

863. *See* TEX. R. EVID. 408. Refer to notes 722-859 *supra* and accompanying text.

864. Act approved June 16, 1977, 65th Leg., R.S., ch. 817, §9.02, 1977 Tex. Gen. Laws 2039 (former Texas Revised Civil Statutes art. 4590i, §9.02, deemed repealed as to civil proceedings effective 1983 and as to criminal proceedings effective 1986); Act of May 28, 1975, 64th Leg., R.S., ch. 364, §3, 1975 Tex. Gen. Laws 962 (former Texas Revised Civil Statutes art. 3737g deemed repealed as to civil proceedings effective 1983 and as to criminal proceedings effective 1986); Act of May 27, 1969, 61st Leg., R.S., ch. 511, §1, 1969 Tex. Gen. Laws 1639 (former Texas Revised Civil Statutes art. 3737f deemed repealed as to civil proceedings effective 1983 and as to criminal proceedings effective 1986).

865. *See* ***Robertson Tank Lines, Inc. v. Watson***, 491 S.W.2d 706, 708-09 (Tex. Civ. App.—Beaumont 1973, writ ref'd n.r.e.) (evidence of settlement is not admissible to show liability but is admissible to show bias and prejudice of witness).

866. *See* FED. R. EVID. 409 advisory committee's note; 23 WRIGHT & GRAHAM, *supra* note 35, §5322, at 298-300 (1980).

867. When the Texas Supreme Court promulgated the Texas Rules of Civil Evidence, it directed the repeal of the statutes that had previously controlled the exclusion of evidence of payment of medical expenses as proof of liability in civil cases. *See* 641-642 S.W.2d (Tex. Cases) LXVIII (1983, amended 1998).

868. TEX. R. EVID. 409.

869. Act approved June 16, 1977, 65th Leg., R.S., ch. 817, §9.02, 1977 Tex. Gen. Laws 2039 (former Texas Revised Civil Statutes art. 4590i, §9.02, deemed repealed as to civil proceedings effective 1983 and as to criminal proceedings effective 1986) (excluding evidence of advance payments); Act of May 28, 1975, 64th Leg., R.S., ch. 364, §3, 1975 Tex. Gen. Laws 962 (former Texas Revised Civil Statutes art. 3737g deemed repealed as to civil proceedings effective 1983 and as to criminal proceedings effective 1986) (excluding evidence "of or concerning" advance payments); Act of May 27, 1969, 61st Leg., R.S., ch. 511, §1, 1969 Tex. Gen. Laws 1639 (former Texas Revised Civil Statutes art. 3737f deemed repealed as to civil proceedings effective 1983 and as to criminal proceedings effective 1986) (excluding evidence that "informs the jury that the property damage claim or medical expense has been paid or settled").

Rule 409 does not exclude incidental statements or conduct accompanying payment, or such behavior accompanying offers or promises to pay. The Advisory Committee on the Federal Rules explained the reason for this limitation:

> Contrary to [Federal] Rule 408, dealing with offers of compromise, the present rule does not extend to conduct or statements not a part of the act of furnishing or offering or promising to pay. This difference in treatment arises from fundamental differences in nature. Communication is essential if compromises are to be effected, and consequently broad protection of statements is needed. This is not so in cases of payments or offers or promises to pay medical expenses, where factual statements may be expected to be incidental in nature.[870]

For example, after an automobile collision, one driver approaches the other and, seeing that the other driver is hurt, says, "The accident was all my fault. Here's a hundred dollars to help out with your doctor bills." On the issue of liability, Rule 409 excludes the second sentence as an offer to pay medical expenses, but the rule does not exclude the first sentence, which is admissible as an opposing party's statement under Rule 801(e)(2).[871]

While generalized statements of remorse are not barred by Rule 409, they frequently have such low probative value and are so ambiguous that they are unfairly prejudicial. Thus, they may be excluded under Rule 403. For example, if the driver in the above hypothetical ran up and said, "Oh, I'm so sorry that you're hurt," the statement is not an offer to pay medical expenses or a compromise of a disputed claim and is also not very probative of fault. It is the type of statement that could easily be made by any Good Samaritan or bystander to an accident. When offered to show consciousness of guilt or fault, it might reasonably be excluded under Rule 403.[872]

2. Type of expenses covered. Rule 409 applies to "medical, hospital, or similar expenses."[873] Arguably, the word "similar" refers only to expenses for injury to the human body or expenses for human bodily care.[874] On the other hand, the same policy that supports exclusion of evidence of payments for bodily injury also supports excluding evidence of payment for property damage and lost wages.[875] The phrase "similar expenses" could be interpreted broadly because one of the formerly applicable Texas

---

870. Fed. R. Evid. 409 advisory committee's note.

871. *See* Tex. R. Evid. 801(e)(2). In **Port Neches Independent School District v. Soignier**, the court held that a letter acknowledging coverage of workers' compensation insurance was not barred by Civil Rule 409 when the disputed issue was whether the worker was within the scope of employment at the time of the injury because the letter admitted coverage and thus was a party admission. 702 S.W.2d 756, 757 (Tex. App.—Beaumont 1986, writ ref'd n.r.e.). Refer to *Article VIII: Hearsay, infra* p. 845.

872. *See* 1 Saltzburg et al., *supra* note 319, at 626-27.

873. Tex. R. Evid. 409.

874. *See* 2 Louisell & Mueller, *supra* note 167, §178, at 492.

875. *See id.* The version of Rule 409 (or its enacted equivalent) in some states explicitly includes payments for property damages in its scope. *See, e.g.,* Ind. R. Evid. 409; N.J. R. Evid. 409; Or. Rev. Stat. §40.195; 42 Pa. Cons. Stat. §6141(b), (c).

statutes excluded evidence not only of payment of medical expenses but also of a wide range of other expenses including lost wages, incidentals, and property damage or destruction.[876]

3. Evidence of payment admissible for other purposes. Rule 409 excludes evidence of payment to prove liability for an injury. Unlike Rule 407, dealing with subsequent remedial measures, and Rule 408, dealing with offers to compromise, Rule 409 contains no provision implying that evidence excluded when offered to prove fault is admissible to impeach or to prove other issues such as agency, ownership, or control. This situation in Federal Rule 409 led at least one commentator to propose that evidence of payment should not be admissible to show narrow, specific elements essential to a finding of liability, such as ownership or agency.[877]

In Texas, under one of the formerly applicable statutes, evidence of payment for damage to a nonparty witness's automobile, damaged in the same collision that injured the plaintiff, was held admissible to impeach the witness for bias, interest, or prejudice.[878] The court admitted the evidence for impeachment even though the statute explicitly said that "no evidence is admissible which informs the jury that the property damage claim or medical expense has been paid or settled."[879] This precedent, although not controlling, supports the view that Rule 409 should not exclude evidence of payment when offered for impeachment. Such evidence is clearly relevant under Rule 401 because the bias, interest, or prejudice of a witness is relevant, and Rule 402 declares relevant evidence admissible unless excluded by constitution, statute, or judicially promulgated rule. Similarly, the common law admitted evidence of payment to prove issues such as agency or ownership.[880] Although no Texas precedent deals with the matter, the arguments discussing impeachment also strongly suggest that Rule 409 should not exclude evidence of payment if offered for such purposes.

Nothing in Rule 409 prohibits the party who has made payments from offering evidence of the payments to seek a reduction in the amount of the final judgment rendered.[881] To structure the law otherwise would unjustly allow the plaintiff a double recovery.[882] The common law forbids such double payment.[883] Additionally, the for-

---

876. *See* Act of May 28, 1975, 64th Leg., R.S., ch. 364, §§1-3, 1975 Tex. Gen. Laws 962 (former Texas Revised Civil Statutes art. 3737g deemed repealed as to civil proceedings effective 1983 and as to criminal proceedings effective 1986).

877. *See* 2 LOUISELL & MUELLER, *supra* note 167, §179, at 493.

878. *See* **Robertson Tank Lines, Inc. v. Watson**, 491 S.W.2d 706, 708-09 (Tex. Civ. App.—Beaumont 1973, writ ref'd n.r.e.).

879. *See id.* at 708.

880. *See* Larsen, *supra* note 860, at 951-53.

881. *See* 2 LOUISELL & MUELLER, *supra* note 167, §179, at 492-93.

882. *Cf.* **Walsh v. Bos. Sand & Gravel Co.**, 175 F. Supp. 411, 414 (D. Mass. 1959) (crediting amounts previously awarded to "avoid double payment").

883. *See, e.g.*, **Spielman v. N.Y., New Haven & Hartford R.R.**, 147 F. Supp. 451, 453 (E.D.N.Y. 1956) (deducting railroad's payment of plaintiff's medical expenses from the amount of judgment later awarded); **Lundy v. Calmar S.S. Corp.**, 96 F. Supp. 19, 22 (S.D.N.Y. 1951) (ordering a similar deduction).

merly applicable Texas statutes admitted evidence of advance payments after judgment and allowed a reduction of the judgment by the amount of the advance payments.[884]

If evidence is admissible for one purpose but not for another, or against one party but not another, Rule 105(a) permits a limiting instruction to explain to the jury why the evidence is being admitted and how the jury may use it.[885] Rule 403 allows the trial court to exclude evidence admissible under Rule 409 if undue prejudice or another listed negative factor substantially outweighs its probative value.[886]

RULE 410
PLEAS, PLEA DISCUSSIONS, & RELATED STATEMENTS

(a) Prohibited Uses in Civil Cases. In a civil case, evidence of the following is not admissible against the defendant who made the plea or was a participant in the plea discussions:

(1) a guilty plea that was later withdrawn;

(2) a nolo contendere plea;

(3) a statement made during a proceeding on either of those pleas under Federal Rule of Criminal Procedure 11 or a comparable state procedure; or

(4) a statement made during plea discussions with an attorney for the prosecuting authority if the discussions did not result in a guilty plea or they resulted in a later-withdrawn guilty plea.

(b) Prohibited Uses in Criminal Cases. In a criminal case, evidence of the following is not admissible against the defendant who made the plea or was a participant in the plea discussions:

(1) a guilty plea that was later withdrawn;

(2) a nolo contendere plea that was later withdrawn;

(3) a statement made during a proceeding on either of those pleas under Federal Rule of Criminal Procedure 11 or a comparable state procedure; or

(4) a statement made during plea discussions with an attorney for the prosecuting authority if the discussions did not result in a guilty or nolo contendere plea or they resulted in a later-withdrawn guilty or nolo contendere plea.

---

884. Act approved June 16, 1977, 65th Leg., R.S., ch. 817, §9.03, 1977 Tex. Gen. Laws 2039 (former Texas Revised Civil Statutes art. 4590i, §9.03, deemed repealed as to civil proceedings effective 1983 and as to criminal proceedings effective 1986); Act of May 28, 1975, 64th Leg., R.S., ch. 364, §4, 1975 Tex. Gen. Laws 962 (former Texas Revised Civil Statutes art. 3737g deemed repealed as to civil proceedings effective 1983 and as to criminal proceedings effective 1986).

885. Refer to *Article I: General Provisions*, *supra* p. 97.

886. Refer to notes 111-159 *supra* and accompanying text.

> **(c) Exception.** In a civil case, the court may admit a statement described in paragraph (a)(3) or (4) and in a criminal case, the court may admit a statement described in paragraph (b)(3) or (4), when another statement made during the same plea or plea discussions has been introduced and in fairness the statements ought to be considered together.

COMMENTARY ON RULE 410

Rule 410 is designed to encourage the plea-bargaining process without which our criminal-justice system would be even more overwhelmed than it is.[887] To further this goal, it is essential that discussions made during plea negotiations be protected from later disclosure because "[m]eaningful dialogue between the parties would ... be impossible if either party had to assume the risk that plea offers would be admissible in evidence."[888] Thus, the same policy concerns that exclude statements made during civil settlement or compromise discussions under Rule 408 operate to exclude statements made in the criminal plea-bargaining context under Rule 410.[889]

Rule 410 has several important limitations. The most important is that the rule envisions plea bargains conducted by or under the direct authority of prosecuting attorneys.[890] Statements to law-enforcement officials such as police investigators or FBI agents do not qualify.[891] Second, the general exclusion mandated by Rule 410 affects

---

887. *See* Donald J. Newman, *Reshape the Deal*, TRIAL, May-June 1973, at 11; *see also* **Blackledge v. Allison**, 431 U.S. 63, 71 (1977) ("Whatever might be the situation in an ideal world, the fact is that the guilty plea and the often concomitant plea bargain are important components of this country's criminal justice system."); **Santobello v. New York**, 404 U.S. 257, 260 (1971) ("If every criminal charge were subjected to a full-scale trial, the States and the Federal Government would need to multiply by many times the number of judges and court facilities."); **Perkins v. Third Ct. of Appeals**, 738 S.W.2d 276, 282 (Tex. Crim. App. 1987) (up to 90% of felony convictions in state courts are the result of plea bargains); McCORMICK ON EVIDENCE, *supra* note 1, §274, at 814 (stating that "[e]ffective criminal law administration in many localities would hardly be possible if a large proportion of the charges were not disposed of by compromise"). *See generally* TEX. CODE CRIM. PROC. art. 26.13 (outlining the requisites of a negotiated guilty plea).
   The plea-bargain process itself requires that (1) an offer be made or promised, (2) by an agent of the State who has authority to make such promises or offers, (3) to promise a recommendation of sentence or other concession, (4) subject to the trial judge's approval. *Wayne v. State*, 756 S.W.2d 724, 728 (Tex. Crim. App. 1988).
888. **United States v. Verdoorn**, 528 F.2d 103, 107 (8th Cir. 1976).
889. *See* Annotation, *When Is Statement of Accused Made in Connection with Plea Bargain Negotiations so as to Render Statement Inadmissible Under Rule 11(e)(6) of the Federal Rules of Criminal Procedure*, 60 A.L.R. FED. 854, 856 (1982). Refer to notes 734-751 *supra* and accompanying text.
890. *See* TEX. R. EVID. 410(a)(4), (b)(4); *cf.* **United States v. Serna**, 799 F.2d 842, 848-49 (2d Cir. 1986) (Federal Criminal Rule 11(e)(6), now Rule 11(f), requires the participation but not the actual presence of a prosecuting attorney; Rule covered statements made to a DEA agent who was acting under a prosecutor's authority); **United States v. Rosenthal**, 793 F.2d 1214, 1239 (11th Cir. 1986) (statements made to a DEA agent could not be excluded under Federal Criminal Rule 11(e)(6), now Rule 11(f), because the statements were not made to the prosecutor himself), *modified on other grounds*, 801 F.2d 378 (11th Cir. 1986). *See generally* **Wayne**, 756 S.W.2d at 729 (noting common-law precedent, which held that negotiations between a police officer and a defendant could qualify as "plea" negotiations). Refer to notes 952-964 *infra* and accompanying text.
891. *See* **Rachlin v. United States**, 723 F.2d 1373, 1376 (8th Cir. 1983) (Federal Rule 410 is limited to negotiations between a defendant or his attorney and an attorney for the government or "'where the law enforcement official is acting with express authority from a government attorney'" (quoting **United States v. Grant**, 622 F.2d 308, 313 (8th Cir. 1980))); **United States v. Bernal**, 719 F.2d 1475, 1478 (9th Cir. 1983) (Rule 410 does not require the exclusion of

---

only the admissibility of certain pleas or statements when used against the defendant who made the plea or participated in the plea discussions in question.[892] Thus, for example, Rule 410 does not bar the use of a witness's plea or plea-discussion statement to impeach that witness in a civil or criminal trial as long as the witness is not a named party or the criminal defendant.[893] Third, Rule 410 does not bar evidence of the fact of conviction. Thus, a written judgment of conviction may be offered to impeach a testifying witness under Rule 609.[894] It may also be used to establish the fact of conviction for enhancement purposes in criminal cases.[895] Indeed, the fact of conviction may be an essential element in another lawsuit and would be admissible for that purpose.[896] Fourth, the rule covers only those statements made to obtain a concession from the government. It does not cover gratuitous remarks made without an intent to negotiate a plea.[897] Fifth, the defendant may affirmatively waive the protections offered by Rule 410.[898]

---

a defendant's incriminating statement to a law-enforcement officer because the officer is not a prosecutor); 2 WEINSTEIN & BERGER, *supra* note 84, ¶410[08], at 410-55 to 410-61 (statements made during informal pre-charging sessions with law-enforcement investigating personnel are generally not excluded under Federal Rule 410). *But see* 23 WRIGHT & GRAHAM, *supra* note 35, §5347, at 382-89 (1980) (rule should not be confined solely to plea negotiations with the actual prosecuting authority but should be extended to those with apparent authority to bargain as well).

892. TEX. R. EVID. 410(a), (b). Rule 410 does not itself bar evidence of plea bargaining or plea discussions when offered by the defendant. *See Jenkins v. State*, 493 S.W.3d 583, 607 (Tex. Crim. App. 2016) ("We note that Rule 410 is silent on the admissibility of plea negotiations when that evidence is presented for, rather than against, a defendant."); *Moss v. State*, 860 S.W.2d 194, 196 (Tex. App.—Texarkana 1993, no pet.) ("Rule 410 excludes certain evidence obtained during plea discussions only when offered *against* the defendant."). In *Moss*, the court of appeals held that while the defendant's attempt to introduce evidence that the State had offered him a 25-year sentence in return for his guilty plea was not barred by Rule 410, it was prohibited under Rule 408. 860 S.W.2d at 196. The court of criminal appeals, however, has held that Rule 408 does not apply to the criminal plea-bargain context. *Smith v. State*, 898 S.W.2d 838, 843 (Tex. Crim. App. 1995). Instead, such plea offers are excludable under Rule 403 as being unfairly prejudicial and likely to mislead the jury. *Id.*; *see Jenkins*, 493 S.W.3d at 608 ("[E]vidence of a capital defendant's own plea offer is even less probative and poses an even greater danger of misleading the jury than does evidence of a State's plea offer because the defendant potentially benefits, by offering to plead guilty in exchange for a sentence other than death. Without additional evidence of [defendant's] and his attorneys' motivations, the jury could only speculate as to the mitigating value, if any, of [defendant's] plea offer evidence."). For a discussion of the Rule 403 counterfactors, refer to notes 111-159 *supra* and accompanying text.

893. *See United States v. Roth*, 736 F.2d 1222, 1226 (8th Cir. 1984) (evidence of codefendant's guilty plea is admissible to show testifying witness's acknowledgment of participation in the offense or to reflect on his credibility); *United States v. Mathis*, 550 F.2d 180, 182 (4th Cir. 1976) (use of a guilty plea to impeach testifying witness who is not a defendant in the case is proper at trial).

894. *See* 1 GOODE ET AL., *supra* note 103, §410.1, at 274-75. For a discussion of Rule 609, refer to *Article VI: Witnesses, infra* p. 615.

895. *See* TEX. PENAL CODE §12.42.

896. *See, e.g.*, *Turton v. State Bar*, 775 S.W.2d 712, 715 (Tex. App.—San Antonio 1989, writ denied) (in disciplinary action against attorney based entirely on his criminal conviction for aggravated assault, State Bar could use the judgment of conviction to seek a mandatory suspension despite the fact that defendant had pleaded nolo contendere to the criminal charge; order of probation, not plea, constituted grounds for disbarment).

897. *See, e.g.*, *Wayne v. State*, 756 S.W.2d 724, 733-34 (Tex. Crim. App. 1988) (defendant's discussion while in police custody was not part of the plea-negotiation process); *Henson v. State*, 794 S.W.2d 385, 399 (Tex. App.—Dallas 1990, pet. ref'd) (Kinkeade, J., dissenting) (defendant's letter to friend about plea negotiations should have been held admissible by court of appeals as statement made without intent to negotiate a plea); *cf. United States v. Cunningham*, 723 F.2d 217, 227-28 (2d Cir. 1983) (interview that was merely an attempt by defendant to convince government of his innocence was not a plea negotiation); *United States v. Ceballos*, 706 F.2d 1198, 1203 (11th Cir.

Rule 410 also governs the exclusion in later civil litigation of plea discussions made during a criminal case.[899] A single event may give rise to both criminal and civil liability. For example, an automobile driven by an intoxicated driver may collide with another vehicle. The State may prosecute the drunk driver for driving while intoxicated, and the driver or owner of the other vehicle may sue the drunk driver to recover for damage to the vehicle or injuries to its occupants.[900] During the criminal proceeding, the defendant (the drunk driver) may make statements that the plaintiff would like to use against the defendant in the civil case. These statements may include a guilty plea accepted by the court and used as the basis for a conviction, a guilty plea offered by the defendant but refused by the court or withdrawn by the defendant, a nolo contendere plea, statements made to officials during plea-bargain negotiations, or other incidental statements made during the criminal process. The plaintiff may want to use these statements either as substantive admissions of guilt in the civil trial or to impeach the defendant. The question is whether, to what extent, and for what purpose these pleas and statements are admissible in the civil trial.

A. Common Law & Earlier Texas Law

The classic common-law position is that pleas and statements submitted in one proceeding are inadmissible in another proceeding.[901] This stance rests on several grounds: (1) a pleading in one case is irrelevant in another case, (2) pleadings are fictitious, conventional, hypothetical allegations, (3) a pleading is not a statement of a party but of his attorney, and (4) criminal and civil cases have different parties and issues.[902] However, as commentators have noted, (1) pleadings in one case are logically probative of issues in a related case, (2) modern pleadings reject the fictions and rigidities of the past and reflect a party's real position, (3) attorneys, as agents of their clients, have author-

---

1983) (letter was admissible when no plea negotiations were underway). *See generally* William J. Cox, Recent Case, *Withdrawal of Negotiated Guilty Pleas: Quid Pro Quo from Defendants*, 5 Sw. U. L. Rev. 214, 214-19 (1973) (discussing cases involving withdrawal of guilty pleas).

898. In *United States v. Mezzanatto*, the defendant, as he entered into plea negotiations, agreed to waive the protections offered by Federal Rule 410 to the extent that any statements he made during the discussions could be used to impeach his testimony if the case went to trial. 513 U.S. 196, 198 (1995). Plea negotiations broke down, and the defendant testified at trial that he was not involved in methamphetamine trafficking and denied knowing that the package he had delivered to the undercover officer contained methamphetamine. *Id.* at 199. The Supreme Court held that the prosecutor was then entitled to cross-examine him with the prior inconsistent statements he had made during the unsuccessful plea discussion because the defendant had affirmatively waived the protections offered by Rule 410. *See id.* at 210-11.

899. *See* Tex. R. Evid. 410(a).

900. For an example other than a traffic accident, see *White v. State*, 329 S.W.2d 446 (Tex. Civ. App.—Dallas 1959, writ ref'd n.r.e.) (bootlegging conviction was admissible in a later automobile-forfeiture case).

901. 1A Ray, *supra* note 46, §1145, at 294; 4 Wigmore, *supra* note 736, §1066, at 74.

902. *See* 1A Ray, *supra* note 46, §1145, at 294; 4 Wigmore, *supra* note 736, §1066, at 74; Millard M. Bush, Jr., *Criminal Convictions as Evidence in Civil Proceedings*, 29 Miss. L.J. 276, 276 (1958); Thomas H. Davis IV, Comment, *Criminal Judgments as Evidence in Civil Cases*, 11 Sw. L.J. 230, 231 (1957); Comment, *Judgments and Pleas in Prior Criminal Prosecutions as Evidence in Civil Actions*, 1962 Duke L.J. 97, 97-98 [hereinafter *Judgments and Pleas*]; W.E. Shipley, Annotation, *Conviction or Acquittal as Evidence of the Facts on Which It Was Based in Civil Action*, 18 A.L.R.2d 1287, 1289 (1951).

ity to bind them, and (4) although the issues and parties may not be identical in criminal and civil cases, the higher standard of proof in criminal cases affords the defendant substantial protection.[903]

As a result, the strict position of the common law has been eroded, and most jurisdictions now admit pleas and statements made in criminal cases as evidentiary admissions or for the purpose of impeachment in later civil or criminal cases.[904] The modern trend is to find pleas and statements made in criminal cases relevant in later litigation because a person usually does not plead guilty and subject himself to a fine or jail unless he believes that he was somehow in the wrong.[905] Under current views, the probative value of this evidence is high even though a guilty plea or a similar statement may rest not on an acknowledgment of fault but on ignorance, mistake, or a desire to avoid the expense and vexation of litigation.[906]

On the other hand, policy reasons have caused courts and legislatures to restrict the modern trend of admitting pleas and statements made by a criminal defendant into evidence in a later proceeding. First, the law supports compromise and generally excludes offers to compromise to prove or disprove the validity of a claim.[907] Second, the criminal-justice system cannot manage the plenary litigation of every dispute. It must rely on negotiations and plea bargaining and must tolerate frank discussions among the prosecution, the court, and the defense.[908] As the Eighth Circuit explained, "[m]eaningful dialogue between the parties would … be impossible if either party had to assume the risk that plea offers would be admissible in evidence."[909] Therefore, most jurisdictions impose limits on the admissibility of pleas and statements originating in criminal cases.[910]

Texas courts follow the modern trend that guilty pleas accepted by the court and not withdrawn are admissible as an opposing party's statement[911] in a later civil[912] or

---

903. *See* 1A RAY, *supra* note 46, §1145, at 294; 4 WIGMORE, *supra* note 736, §1066, at 75-76; Bush, *supra* note 902, at 279; Davis, *supra* note 902, at 231-32; *Judgments and Pleas, supra* note 902, at 98.

904. *See* MCCORMICK ON EVIDENCE, *supra* note 1, §265, at 783-84; Shipley, *supra* note 902, at 1299; *see, e.g.*, **United States v. Walker**, 871 F.2d 1298, 1303 (6th Cir. 1989) (witness's guilty plea and plea agreement were admissible in later proceeding as evidence of his credibility); *cf.* **United States v. Benson**, 640 F.2d 136, 138 (8th Cir. 1981) (applying FED. R. CRIM. P. 11(e)(6), now Rule 11(f); guilty plea accepted by the court and not withdrawn is admissible in other proceedings). Statements and pleas in one case are judicial admissions in that case and, until withdrawn, are conclusive against the declarant. *See* MCCORMICK ON EVIDENCE, *supra* note 1, §265, at 783-84; 1A RAY, *supra* note 46, §1146, at 297-99; 4 WIGMORE, *supra* note 736, §1064, at 67.

905. *See* 2 WEINSTEIN & BERGER, *supra* note 84, ¶410[01], at 410-25.

906. *Id.*

907. *See* FED. R. EVID. 408; TEX. R. EVID. 408. Refer to notes 722-859 *supra* and accompanying text.

908. *See* **United States v. Arroyo-Angulo**, 580 F.2d 1137, 1148 (2d Cir. 1978) (plea bargains are necessary to dispose of the bulk of cases in the criminal system).

909. **United States v. Verdoorn**, 528 F.2d 103, 107 (8th Cir. 1976).

910. *Cf.* Shipley, *supra* note 902, at 1289 (many courts exclude evidence of a previous conviction or acquittal offered in a later civil action).

911. For a discussion of an opposing party's statement in an individual or representative capacity under Rule 801(e)(2)(A), refer to *Article VIII: Hearsay, infra* p. 849.

912. *See, e.g.*, **Lillie Sales, Inc. v. Rieger**, 437 S.W.2d 872, 874 (Tex. Civ. App.—Texarkana 1969, writ ref'd n.r.e.) (plea of nolo contendere to traffic violation was admissible in later negligence suit).

criminal[913] proceeding. To be admissible, however, the plea must have been valid. A forfeiture of a bond or payment of a fine or a plea not entered by the defendant or his attorney is not conclusive on the issue of liability in the civil case,[914] and Texas practice has been to instruct the jury accordingly.[915] To a great extent, pleas in criminal cases and their effects are controlled in Texas by statute, particularly the Code of Criminal Procedure. The Code authorizes defendants to enter pleas, including guilty and nolo contendere pleas.[916] For a nolo contendere plea, "the legal effect ... shall be the same as that of a plea of guilty, except that such plea may not be used against the defendant as an admission in any civil suit based upon or growing out of the act upon which the criminal prosecution is based."[917] The Code contains detailed provisions governing guilty and nolo contendere pleas, including requirements that the court admonish the defendant about the range of punishment attached to the offense, that the plea be free and voluntary, and that the defendant be mentally competent to enter the plea.[918]

---

913. *See, e.g.*, **Rodriguez v. State**, 130 Tex. Crim. 438, 440, 94 S.W.2d 476, 477 (1936) (guilty plea to a burglary charge was admissible in a later prosecution when the first indictment was held defective; former guilty plea is an admission of guilt made in the course of a judicial proceeding); **Wallace v. State**, 707 S.W.2d 928, 934 (Tex. App.—Texarkana 1986) (defendant's admission of guilt at a previous trial was admissible as evidence in later criminal proceedings when the first information was held defective), *aff'd*, 782 S.W.2d 854 (Tex. Crim. App. 1989); *see also* 1A RAY, *supra* note 46, §1145, at 87 (Supp. 1991) (guilty plea that is not withdrawn is admissible against the defendant in any later proceeding).

914. *See* **Lucas v. Burrows**, 499 S.W.2d 212, 214 (Tex. Civ. App.—Beaumont 1973, no writ) (guilty plea must be validly entered to be an admission); **Barrios v. Davis**, 415 S.W.2d 714, 716 (Tex. Civ. App.—Houston 1967, no writ) (a plea is inadmissible if entered by defendant's spouse); **Johnson v. Woods**, 315 S.W.2d 75, 77 (Tex. Civ. App.—Dallas 1958, writ ref'd n.r.e.) (plea must be entered by defendant or his attorney); **Mooneyhan v. Benedict**, 284 S.W.2d 741, 742 (Tex. Civ. App.—Austin 1955, writ ref'd n.r.e.) (mailing a fine does not constitute a guilty plea; trial court correctly refused to admit such evidence); **Sherwood v. Murray**, 233 S.W.2d 879, 882-83 (Tex. Civ. App.—El Paso 1950, no writ) (traffic bond could have been forfeited for reasons other than admitting guilt, such as absence from the city, urgency of business, or following the path of least resistance; evidence of the forfeiture was inadmissible for any purpose).

915. *See* **Sumner v. Kinney**, 136 S.W. 1192, 1195 (Tex. Civ. App.—San Antonio 1911, no writ) (guilty plea is admissible, but is not conclusive evidence); *cf.* **McCormick v. Tex. Commerce Bank**, 751 S.W.2d 887, 889-90 (Tex. App.—Houston [14th Dist.] 1988, writ denied) (evidence of a criminal conviction after a jury trial in which defendant pleaded not guilty was both admissible and conclusive on the identical issue to be litigated in a later civil proceeding).

916. *See* TEX. CODE CRIM. PROC. art. 27.02(3), (5).

917. *Id.* art. 27.02(5). A plea of "no contest" is the same as "nolo contendere." **Odom v. State**, 962 S.W.2d 117, 119 (Tex. App.—Houston [1st Dist.] 1997, pet. ref'd) (the phrase "nolo contendere" is Latin translated as "I will not contest it"; by pleading "no contest," a defendant merely pleads the English translation of the Latin phrase).

918. TEX. CODE CRIM. PROC. art. 26.13(a)(1), (b). Before the adoption of the Criminal Rules, the Code provided for the consequences of a defendant's withdrawal of his guilty or nolo contendere plea:

> Should the court reject any such [plea-bargaining] agreement, the defendant shall be permitted to withdraw his plea of guilty or nolo contendere, and neither the fact that the defendant had entered a plea of guilty or nolo contendere nor any statements made by him at the hearing on the plea of guilty or nolo contendere may be used against the defendant on the issue of guilt or punishment in any subsequent criminal proceeding ....

Act of May 27, 1985, 69th Leg., R.S., ch. 685, §8(a), 1986 TEX. GEN. LAWS 194 (current version as amended at TEX. CODE CRIM. PROC. art. 26.13(a)(2)). Everything after the clause that ends with "shall be permitted to withdraw his plea of guilty or nolo contendere" was eliminated from the above-quoted code provision when the Criminal Rules became effective because Rule 410 effectively carries forward that earlier law. *See* TEX. CODE CRIM. PROC. art. 26.13(a)(2). Neither Texas statutes nor case law answered the question whether withdrawn pleas and statements made

B. Basic Structure of Rule 410

Rule 410 declares that certain types of pleas and statements are "not admissible against the defendant who made the plea or was a participant in the plea discussions."[919] The only exception in Rule 410 is essentially a rule of optional completeness, allowing the admission of a generally excluded statement if a connected statement from the same context has been introduced.[920] Thus, unless the exception stated in Rule 410(c) applies, the types of pleas and statements mentioned in Rule 410 are excluded in later criminal or civil cases, whether offered as substantive evidence or as impeaching evidence against the defendant who was a participant in the plea negotiations.[921]

As noted above, the policy behind Rule 410 is the strong protection of plea bargaining, plea discussion, and plea negotiations in criminal cases.[922] This policy is so strong that if a defendant admits liability by pleading guilty, withdraws his plea, and then defends a civil suit in which he denies liability, the plaintiff may not use the withdrawn plea, even to show the most blatant prevarication. To the objection that this process allows the defendant to lie with impunity, perhaps to the detriment of a civil plaintiff, the drafters of Rule 410 would say that (1) plea bargaining is essential to the functioning of the criminal-justice system;[923] (2) the law fosters compromise and generally excludes offers to compromise;[924] and (3) Rule 410 does not exclude evidence of convictions, which is admitted by Rules 609 and 803(22).[925]

There is one major difference between Federal Rule 410 and Texas Rule 410. In a later perjury trial, the federal rule would allow admission of statements made by the defendant during plea negotiations or hearings that are conducted in the presence of his counsel, on the record, and under oath,[926] but the Texas rule does not.[927]

---

at plea hearings were admissible as admissions or as impeaching evidence in civil suits. Likewise, earlier Texas law did not deal with the admissibility of extrajudicial statements made by the defendant to representatives of the prosecuting authority during plea negotiations. The adoption of Rule 410, however, filled this void.

919. TEX. R. EVID. 410(a), (b). Rule 410(a) addresses the admissibility of pleas and statements in civil cases, and Rule 410(b) addresses it in criminal cases.

920. *See* TEX. R. EVID. 410(c).

921. *See generally* 2 LOUISELL & MUELLER, *supra* note 167, §184 (emphasizing legislative history); 2 WEINSTEIN & BERGER, *supra* note 84, ¶410[01], at 410-26 to 410-30 (same).

922. *See* FED. R. EVID. 410 advisory committee's note.

923. *See id.*

924. *See* TEX. R. EVID. 408; FED. R. EVID. 408 advisory committee's note. Refer to notes 722-859 *supra* and accompanying text.

925. Refer to *Article VI: Witnesses, infra* p. 615, and *Article VIII: Hearsay, infra* p. 928.

926. *See* FED. R. EVID. 410(b)(2). This provision was intended to ensure that the defendant who perpetrates a fraud on the court by lying under oath on the record in connection with his plea may be prosecuted. *See* 2 LOUISELL & MUELLER, *supra* note 167, §188, at 570-71; 23 WRIGHT & GRAHAM, *supra* note 35, §5349, at 409-13 (1980).

927. *See Bowie v. State*, 135 S.W.3d 55, 65 (Tex. Crim. App. 2004) (Texas Rule 410, unlike Federal Rule 410, does not include any exception for perjury prosecutions). The Texas drafters may have believed that the policy favoring plea bargaining is so strong that even perjury should not break the protection of Criminal Rule 410. *See Bowie*, 135 S.W.3d at 65 ("The reasons for this omission [of an exception for perjury prosecutions in Rule 410] are not clear. Regardless of this Court's opinion of the policy issues involved, we cannot read into the rule an exception for per-

---

★

C. Contours of Rule 410

1. Rule 410(a)(1) & (b)(1): Withdrawn guilty pleas. The first type of evidence to which Rule 410 applies is withdrawn guilty pleas. Historically, courts have permitted criminal defendants to withdraw a previously entered guilty plea if that plea was "unfairly obtained or given through ignorance, fear or inadvertence."[928] The rationale for protecting those withdrawn pleas is that a jury undoubtedly would be greatly influenced by knowing that at some point the defendant was willing to admit he had committed the crime, even though the plea might have been unfairly or incorrectly entered. This is a classic example of unfair prejudice substantially outweighing probative value under Rule 403. A contrary position would nullify the right of withdrawal and place the defendant "in a dilemma utterly inconsistent with the determination of the court awarding him a trial."[929]

Before Rule 410 was promulgated, the Code of Criminal Procedure excluded evidence of withdrawn guilty pleas in criminal cases only if the defendant had withdrawn the plea because the court rejected a plea-bargain agreement.[930] Rule 410 excludes evidence of withdrawn guilty pleas regardless of the reason for the withdrawal and regardless of the context in which the plea was offered. As noted above, the exclusion of evidence by Rule 410 also applies to statements sought to be used for impeachment purposes.

Rule 410 does not apply to guilty pleas that have not been withdrawn by the defendant.[931] Such pleas are obviously relevant evidence of liability or guilt under Rule 401, admissible under Rule 402 as relevant evidence, likely not excluded under Rule 403, and not hearsay under Rule 801(e)(2) when offered against the people who made them. Therefore, under the Texas Rules, as under the Texas common law, guilty pleas that are not withdrawn are admissible as an opposing party's statement to prove liability in a civil case or guilt in a criminal case.[932]

2. Rule 410(a)(2) & (b)(2): Nolo contendere pleas. The second type of evidence to which Rule 410 applies is a nolo contendere plea. A nolo contendere plea is essentially the same as a guilty plea but is inadmissible to prove fault in a civil case.[933] The Texas

---

jury prosecutions."); 1 SALTZBURG ET AL., *supra* note 319, at 633 (Federal Rule 410 should protect these statements because "[d]uring the plea bargaining process defendants do whatever must be done to secure the benefits of the plea, including saying what the Court wants to hear").

928. *Kercheval v. United States*, 274 U.S. 220, 224 (1927).

929. *Id.*

930. Refer to note 918 *supra*.

931. *See, e.g.*, *Dennis v. State*, 925 S.W.2d 32, 41-42 (Tex. App.—Tyler 1995, pet. ref'd) (trial court did not err in allowing State to impeach defendant with statements he had made during federal plea proceeding; although defendant argued that he had not yet been sentenced in federal court and therefore could have withdrawn his guilty plea, there was no evidence that he had withdrawn it).

932. For a discussion of an opposing party's statement under Rule 801(e)(2), refer to *Article VIII: Hearsay*, *infra* p. 845.

933. *Lynch v. Port of Hous. Auth.*, 671 S.W.2d 954, 959 (Tex. App.—Houston [14th Dist.] 1984, writ ref'd n.r.e.); *see* TEX. CODE CRIM. PROC. art. 27.02(5); FED. R. EVID. 410 advisory committee's note.

criminal statute authorizing nolo contendere pleas specifically excludes them "as an admission" in a civil case.[934] This phrase implies that, under the Code of Criminal Procedure, these pleas would be admissible to impeach the criminal defendant who was a party or witness in a civil case. Rule 410 changes this implication. In circumstances in which Rule 410 excludes pleas, it excludes them as both substantive and impeaching evidence.

Rule 410(a)(2), the rule for civil cases, applies to all nolo contendere pleas, whether or not they are withdrawn.[935] Rule 410(b)(2), the rule for criminal cases, protects only those nolo contendere pleas that are later withdrawn.[936] Thus, a consummated nolo contendere plea may be used against the defendant in later criminal proceedings but not in civil proceedings. This distinction in admissibility serves the original purpose underlying the creation of nolo contendere pleas. Before Rule 410 was promulgated, Texas Code of Criminal Procedure article 26.13(a)(2) authorized the withdrawal of nolo contendere pleas and mandated the exclusion of the withdrawn plea as evidence on the issue of guilt or punishment in later criminal proceeding, but the exclusion applied only to pleas that were withdrawn because the court refused to accept a plea-bargain agreement.[937] Rule 410(b)(2) has no such restrictions; it excludes evidence of a withdrawn nolo contendere plea regardless of why it was withdrawn or the context in which it was offered.

The Code of Criminal Procedure contains a special provision that in misdemeanor cases arising out of a traffic violation for which the maximum punishment is a fine, the payment of the fine without entering a plea in open court serves as the equivalent of entering a nolo contendere plea.[938] This rule encourages the person who does not want to contest a traffic ticket simply to mail the payment of the fine without this act being used against him in any later civil litigation under Rule 410.[939] On the other hand, if

---

934. *See* Tex. Code Crim. Proc. art. 27.02(5).

935. Tex. R. Evid. 410(a)(2); *see* 1A Ray, *supra* note 46, §1145, at 85-86 (Supp. 1991) (although the civil rule does not explicitly exclude withdrawn nolo contendere pleas, it would be illogical to admit withdrawn pleas while excluding consummated pleas); *see also* **In re Commitment of Young**, 410 S.W.3d 542, 552 (Tex. App.—Beaumont 2013, no pet.) (in proceeding to commit respondent as sexually violent predator, State could ask in requests for admissions whether respondent had been charged, convicted, and sentenced based on prior crimes; requests for admissions did not ask whether respondent pleaded nolo contendere and were thus admissible).

936. Tex. R. Evid. 410(b)(2).

937. Refer to note 918 *supra*.

938. Tex. Code Crim. Proc. art. 27.14(c).

939. Even when the defendant goes to court and pays the traffic ticket, the payment of the fine cannot be used against him in later civil litigation if he does not personally plead guilty to the judge. *See, e.g.,* **Cox v. Bohman**, 683 S.W.2d 757, 758 (Tex. App.—Corpus Christi 1984, writ ref'd n.r.e.) (when defendant testified that he did not plead guilty in open court but merely paid the traffic-ticket fine to the clerk, evidence that defendant received and paid a traffic ticket should have been excluded in a later personal-injury suit). However, the payment of the fine could have been used against the defendant in a later criminal trial because former Criminal Rule 410 did not bar the use of consummated nolo contendere pleas.

RULE 410

the defendant appears in open court and pleads guilty to the traffic offense, this plea is admissible against him as an admission in a later civil or criminal suit.[940]

3. Rule 410(a)(3) & (b)(3): Statements made at plea hearings. Federal Rule of Criminal Procedure 11, which deals with guilty or nolo contendere pleas, requires a hearing at which (1) the judge advises the defendant of certain matters and determines that the plea is voluntary, (2) the plea agreement, if any, is disclosed, and (3) if an agreement is disclosed, the judge informs the defendant whether the court will accept or reject the plea.[941] The Texas Code of Criminal Procedure requires similar proceedings before the entry of a guilty or nolo contendere plea.[942] Rule 410 excludes statements about a withdrawn guilty or nolo contendere plea made at these hearings or proceedings when the statements are offered against the defendant who made the statements or participated in the discussions.[943] Again, the policy is to promote frank discussions among the defendant, the prosecutor, and the court. Rule 410(b)(3) is narrower than Rule 410(a)(3) because it applies only to the defendant's statements made in hearings connected to guilty or nolo contendere pleas that are later withdrawn.[944]

The exclusion of any statements made in connection with the plea discussions is an essential corollary to protecting the plea itself. It would hardly serve the purpose of promoting plea bargaining if the court excluded the formal plea itself but admitted all of the statements, concessions, and discussions surrounding its formation.

In one unusual case, the court of criminal appeals held that a trial court's "timely pass for plea" proceeding was analogous to Federal Rule 11, and Rule 410(3) (now Rule 410(b)(3)) thus barred the admission of the defendant's sworn testimony taken during the punishment stage of that trial court's proceedings when the defendant was later allowed to withdraw his guilty plea.[945] Under the trial court's unique system, a defendant could enter an open guilty plea, both the defense and State would present punishment evidence, the trial court would then announce its proposed sentence, and the defendant could then either withdraw or reaffirm his guilty plea.[946] If the defendant opted to with-

---

940. *See Cox*, 683 S.W.2d at 758 (evidence of a guilty plea to a traffic offense is not admissible in a civil suit for damages unless the plea was made in open court); ***Lillie Sales, Inc. v. Rieger***, 437 S.W.2d 872, 874 (Tex. Civ. App.—Texarkana 1969, writ ref'd n.r.e.) (accused's guilty plea to a traffic violation is admissible against him in a later civil suit in which he is charged with negligence).

941. *See* FED. R. CRIM. P. 11(a)-(c).

942. *See* TEX. CODE CRIM. PROC. art. 26.13. Texas law requires the judge to inform the defendant of matters such as (1) the range of punishment attached to the offense, (2) the fact that any recommendation of the prosecutor is not binding on the court, but that if the court decides not to follow that recommendation the defendant may withdraw his plea, (3) the limited right to appeal when a defendant enters a guilty or nolo contendere plea, and (4) possible collateral consequences if the defendant is not a U.S. citizen. *Id.* art. 26.13(a)(1)-(a)(4). Further, the plea must appear to be a voluntary one entered by a mentally competent person. *Id.* art. 26.13(b).

943. *See* TEX. R. EVID. 410(a)(3), (b)(3).

944. *Compare* TEX. R. EVID. 410(a)(2) (rule in civil cases; "a nolo contendere plea"), *with* TEX. R. EVID. 410(b)(2) (rule in criminal cases; "a nolo contendere plea that was later withdrawn").

945. ***Bowie v. State***, 135 S.W.3d 55, 62-65 (Tex. Crim. App. 2004).

946. *Id.* at 62-63.

draw his guilty plea, then his earlier sworn testimony was protected from any future use against him under Rule 410(3) (now Rule 410(b)(3)).[947] This methodology of plea bargaining with the judge, however, puts the trial judge very far forward in the plea-bargaining process and finds no support in federal or Texas statutes.[948] It might, in some instances, violate a defendant's right to due process and fundamental fairness.[949]

In neither civil nor criminal cases does Rule 410 exclude the defendant's statements made at a hearing connected with a guilty plea that is not withdrawn.[950] Because the guilty plea itself is admissible in a civil or criminal trial as an admission of a party-opponent, incidental statements (which probably have less of an impact than the plea itself) should also be admissible unless they are merely cumulative.[951]

4. Rule 410(a)(4) & (b)(4): Statements made in plea discussions. The last type of evidence to which Rule 410 applies is any "statement made during plea discussions with an attorney for the prosecuting authority."[952] The policy behind this provision is to facilitate frank discussions between the defendant and the prosecutor so that the criminal case may be resolved without trial.

Texas originally adopted Rule 410 with the intent of narrowly interpreting the phrase "with an attorney for the prosecuting authority." The provision thus does not apply to purported plea offers or other statements to anyone other than attorneys for

---

947. *Id.* at 63-65.

948. *See id.* at 72 (Cochran, Keasler, Hervey, JJ., dissenting) ("timely pass for plea" procedure exacts a "heavy expense of excluding the State from the plea bargaining process; putting the trial judge very far forward in that process; and wholly insulating a defendant's public, sworn testimony during the punishment stage from any future consequences if he declines the trial judge's proffered sentence and withdraws his plea").

949. *See* **State v. McDonald**, 662 S.W.2d 5, 9 (Tex. Crim. App. 1983) ("[j]udicial involvement in plea negotiations runs afoul of due process and fundamental fairness"; trial judge's "practice of issuing proposed assessments of punishment" violated Texas Constitution).

950. *See* Tex. R. Evid. 410(a)(1), (b)(1).

951. *See* Tex. R. Evid. 403 (allowing trial court to exclude relevant evidence if its probative value is substantially outweighed by, among other things, needless presentation of cumulative evidence).

952. Tex. R. Evid. 410(a)(4), (b)(4). Until the adoption of this rule, Texas had no statutory or common-law mandate on the admissibility of such evidence in any kind of proceeding. The original version of Federal Rule 410 generally excluded plea-bargain offers from evidence. *See* Fed. R. Evid. 410 (1972 proposed final draft), 56 F.R.D. 183, 228 (1973). Some federal courts interpreted this rule broadly and considered exclusion of statements made by defendants to individuals who had no authority to negotiate pleas if the defendants reasonably expected that the other persons had that authority. *See* **United States v. Robertson**, 582 F.2d 1356, 1366 (5th Cir. 1978) (trial court's initial inquiry must focus on defendant's perception of alleged plea-bargain discussion); *see, e.g.*, **United States v. Herman**, 544 F.2d 791, 798-99 (5th Cir. 1977) (defendant's statements to postal inspectors in an effort to reach a plea agreement were inadmissible, even though postal inspectors have no authority to make plea agreements, because defendant may have reasonably believed that postal inspectors had that authority). Other federal courts interpreted the same version of the rule narrowly, deciding that the rule protected only statements made in formal plea negotiations with a U.S. Attorney or someone with express authority from a U.S. Attorney. *See* **United States v. Grant**, 622 F.2d 308, 312-13 (8th Cir. 1980) (protection of the rule normally requires formal plea negotiations, except in circumstances in which the law-enforcement official is acting with express authority). The conflict was resolved in favor of the narrower construction with the 1980 amendment of Federal Rule 410. *See* Act of July 31, 1979, Pub. L. No. 96-42, §1(1), 93 Stat. 326; Fed. R. Crim. P. 11 advisory committee's note to 1979 amendment. Federal Rule 410 now refers only to "plea discussions with an attorney for the prosecuting authority." Fed. R. Evid. 410(a)(4).

the prosecuting authority, regardless of what the defendant believed when he made the statement.[953]

Another difficulty with the scope of this provision is the meaning of the phrase "statement made during plea discussions." The federal courts interpret the phrase as follows: First, Federal Rule 410 protects statements made by a person to seek concessions for himself, but it does not exclude statements made on behalf of others.[954] Second, to be excludable under this provision of Federal Rule 410, the defendant's statement must have been offered to receive a concession from the government.[955] Gratuitous remarks made with no attempt to negotiate a plea are admissible as confessions.[956] Third, statements made by a person cooperating with law-enforcement officials before charges have been contemplated or filed are not statements connected with plea discussions.[957] Fourth, statements made after a plea bargain has been struck are not protected by Federal Rule 410.[958] Fifth, grand-jury testimony given by an accused as a result of a plea agreement is not excluded under Federal Rule 410.[959] Sixth, a de-

---

953. 1 GOODE et al., *supra* note 103, §410.3 at 282; *see **Cantu v. State***, 993 S.W.2d 712, 722 (Tex. App.—San Antonio 1999, pet. ref'd) ("Plea offers or other statements to anyone other than an attorney for the prosecution are not covered by Rule 410, and are admissible, even if offered 'against' the defendant."); *cf. **Pichon v. State***, 756 S.W.2d 16, 21 (Tex. App.—Houston [14th Dist.] 1988, pet. ref'd) (voluntary statements made to polygraph operator were not barred by Criminal Rule 408; rejecting defendant's argument that because prosecutor had promised to dismiss indictment if defendant passed lie-detector test, such statements were made in furtherance of a negotiated settlement). *But see **Monreal v. State***, 947 S.W.2d 559, 567 n.4 (Tex. Crim. App. 1997) (Baird, J., concurring in part and dissenting in part) (defendant's plea discussions with his attorney are protected under Criminal Rule 410 because the accused exhibited an actual subjective expectation to negotiate a plea at the time of the discussion and his expectation was reasonable given the totality of the objective circumstances). In **Monreal**, the State's plea offer and defendant's rejection of it were put into the record by the defense attorney, ostensibly to protect herself from a later claim of ineffective assistance of counsel. 947 S.W.2d at 565-67 & n.3 (Baird, J., concurring in part and dissenting in part). Under any other circumstances, these plea discussions would have been protected by the attorney-client privilege under Rule 503. Refer to *Article V: Privileges, infra* p. 390.

954. *See, e.g.*, ***United States v. Brooks***, 670 F.2d 625, 628 (5th Cir. 1982) (defendant who inculpated himself to "save his girlfriend," but not in contemplation of plea negotiations for himself, was not protected by rule); ***United States v. Doe***, 655 F.2d 920, 925 (9th Cir. 1980) (defendant who attempted to exculpate another by inculpating himself was simply "making the best of a bad situation" and was not engaged in plea negotiations).

955. *See **United States v. Levy***, 578 F.2d 896, 901 (2d Cir. 1978) (Federal Rule 410 does not exclude defendant's admission unless defendant makes the admission with the hope that prosecutor will reduce his punishment); ***Herman***, 544 F.2d at 797 ("Statements are inadmissible if made at any point during a discussion in which defendant seeks to obtain concessions from the government in return for a plea.").

956. *See, e.g.*, ***United States v. Karr***, 742 F.2d 493, 496 (9th Cir. 1984) (when defendant never offered to plead guilty and never inquired into agents' authority to bargain, incriminatory statements were not excluded by Rule 410; any subjective belief that defendant may have had about agents' authority to bargain was unreasonable); *cf. **United States v. Watson***, 591 F.2d 1058, 1061 (5th Cir. 1979) (defendant showed no intention of pleading guilty).

957. *Cf. **United States v. Arroyo-Angulo***, 580 F.2d 1137, 1147-49 (2d Cir. 1978) (construing similar language in Federal Rule of Criminal Procedure 11(e)(6), now Rule 11(f)).

958. *See **Hutto v. Ross***, 429 U.S. 28, 30 (1976) (confession made after plea bargain, when plea bargain did not require a confession, is not per se inadmissible); ***United States v. Perry***, 643 F.2d 38, 52 (2d Cir. 1981) (statements made after negotiating plea bargain that were not efforts to secure further concessions are admissible).

959. *See, e.g.*, ***United States v. Stirling***, 571 F.2d 708, 730-32 (2d Cir. 1978) (even if Federal Rule 410 were generously interpreted, testimony was not excludable when not given in an attempt to obtain concessions in exchange for a plea).

fendant who breaches a plea bargain loses the protection of the rule.[960] Seventh, Federal Rule 410 applies to offers to initiate plea-bargaining.[961] Texas courts should look to the federal courts for further interpretations of Texas Rule 410 when the need arises.

Rule 410(b)(4), the rule in criminal cases, applies only to those statements made during plea discussions that do not result in a guilty or nolo contendere plea or resulted in a later-withdrawn plea. If the defendant pleads guilty or nolo contendere and never withdraws the plea, Rule 410 does not exclude statements made at plea discussions leading to the plea.[962] As noted above, the guilty plea itself is admissible in such circumstances, so there is no practical need to exclude incidental statements. But if the defendant withdraws a guilty or nolo contendere plea or pleads not guilty, statements made at the plea discussion fall within the Rule 410 exclusion, assuming the defendant was engaged in actual plea discussions with an authorized person. This interpretation follows from the general policy underlying Rule 410 of protecting the process of plea bargaining.

Rule 410(a)(4), the rule in civil cases, applies to statements made during plea discussions that did not result in a guilty plea or resulted in a later-withdrawn guilty plea.[963] Later-withdrawn nolo contendere pleas are not excluded under the rule.[964]

D. Rule 410(c): Principle of Optional Completeness

Rule 410(c), the only exception to the rule, is a principle of optional completeness. If a statement made during a plea hearing or during plea discussions has been introduced, typically by the defendant who made the statement, the defendant may not object to the admission of a related statement from the same context that "in fairness ... ought to be considered" with the first statement.[965] For example, if the defendant tes-

---

960. *See, e.g.*, **Perry**, 643 F.2d at 52 (when defendant violated his plea agreement by refusing to plead guilty, statements he made after plea agreement had been negotiated were admissible); **Stirling**, 571 F.2d at 731 (defendant's grand-jury testimony, made after plea negotiations, was admissible because he later refused to plead guilty under the plea agreement).

961. *See* FED. R. EVID. 410(a)(4). Federal Rule 410 conforms to Federal Rule of Criminal Procedure 11(e)(6) (now Rule 11(f)), which was amended in 1979 to clarify that the rule covers even attempts to open plea bargaining. *See* FED. R. CRIM. P. 11 advisory committee's note to 1979 amendments, subdiv. (e)(6); FED. R. EVID. 410 advisory committee's note to 1979 amendments.

962. TEX. R. EVID. 410(b)(4); *see* **Dennis v. State**, 925 S.W.2d 32, 41 (Tex. App.—Tyler 1995, pet. ref'd) (statements defendant made during entry of federal plea were admissible in later state criminal trial to impeach his testimony when defendant did not demonstrate that he had withdrawn his federal plea).

963. TEX. R. EVID. 410(a)(4).

964. *See id.*

965. *See* TEX. R. EVID. 410(c); FED. R. EVID. 410(b)(1). The analogous federal rule also contains a perjury exception permitting the evidentiary use of pleas or plea discussions in a later perjury or false-statement proceeding if the plea-related statement was made by the defendant during plea negotiations or hearings that were conducted in the presence of his counsel, on the record, and under oath. FED. R. EVID. 410(b)(2). Refer to notes 926-927 *supra* and accompanying text. This exception is exceedingly narrow because it refers only to those statements made directly before the bench. Nonetheless, the integrity of the judicial process requires that flagrant deceit and untruthfulness committed in open court not be protected. The drafters of the Texas rule went the other way, perhaps concerned that defendants who enter a guilty plea are willing to say whatever they believe the court and prosecutor want to hear to obtain the benefit of the bargain.

tifies on direct examination that the State offered him a plea on a reduced charge but that he refused the plea bargain because he was innocent, the opposition may then introduce a counteroffer by the defendant.[966] No limiting instruction is necessary because the first statement, once it is admitted without objection, is admissible for all purposes.[967] The exception applies to statements made under Rule 410(a)(3), (a)(4), (b)(3), or (b)(4).[968]

RULE 411

LIABILITY INSURANCE

Evidence that a person was or was not insured against liability is not admissible to prove whether the person acted negligently or otherwise wrongfully. But the court may admit this evidence for another purpose, such as proving a witness's bias or prejudice or, if disputed, proving agency, ownership, or control.

COMMENTARY ON RULE 411

A. Insurance Offered on Fault Issue

The first sentence of Rule 411 excludes evidence of the presence or absence of liability insurance when that evidence is offered on the issue of negligence or other wrongful conduct.[969] The exclusion expressed in the first sentence applies whether the evidence is offered by the plaintiff or the defendant.[970] The sentence is identical to the

---

966. *United States v. Doran*, 564 F.2d 1176, 1177 (5th Cir. 1977); *see* *State v. Linden*, 664 P.2d 673, 682 (Ariz. Ct. App. 1983) (when defendant injects plea-bargain discussions into his own testimony, he cannot object when prosecution examines him about the circumstances of those discussions).

    The Texas Court of Criminal Appeals has held that when a defendant testifies on direct examination that he pleaded guilty in previous cases "because [he] was guilty," the State may then cross-examine the defendant to ask if he did not plead guilty in the current case because he is not guilty, and the jury may consider that the lack of a guilty plea in the current case was the result of a failed plea negotiation. *Bowley v. State*, 310 S.W.3d 431, 435 (Tex. Crim. App. 2010). Further, if the defendant relies on statements made during plea negotiations, any error in the State's use of that information will likely be harmless. *See, e.g.*, *Whitaker v. State*, 286 S.W.3d 355, 364 (Tex. Crim. App. 2009) (because defense "opened the door" to evidence of plea negotiations by using it during direct examination and relied heavily on plea negotiations to support mitigation case, State's use of the evidence was harmless error).

967. *See Bowley*, 310 S.W.3d at 435-36. *But see Doran*, 564 F.2d at 1177 (trial judge cautioned jury not to consider the guilty plea when determining guilt or innocence). For a discussion of limiting instructions under Rule 105(a), refer to *Article I: General Provisions*, *supra* p. 97.

968. Tex. R. Evid. 410(c).

969. Tex. R. Evid. 411; *see Jilani ex rel. Jilani v. Jilani*, 747 S.W.2d 504, 507-08 (Tex. App.—Amarillo 1988) (courts may not consider the probable existence of insurance when determining liability), *rev'd on other grounds*, 767 S.W.2d 671 (Tex. 1988); *see, e.g.*, *Brownsville Pediatric Ass'n v. Reyes*, 68 S.W.3d 184, 193 (Tex. App.—Corpus Christi 2002, no pet.) (economist's general reference to insurance, in context of insurance company issuing an annuity, was not the type of evidence that could be excluded under Rule 411).

970. *See* Tex. R. Evid. 411. The Advisory Committee on the Federal Rules of Evidence stated that "[t]he rule is drafted in broad terms so as to include contributory negligence or other fault of a plaintiff as well as fault of a defendant." Fed. R. Evid. 411 advisory committee's note.

first sentence of Federal Rule 411. The rule is also in accord with the common law[971] and earlier Texas law.[972]

Practitioners may question whether evidence of liability insurance meets the requirement of logical relevance expressed in Rules 401 and 402.[973] If a plaintiff offers evidence that the defendant has liability insurance, the proposition underlying the plaintiff's argument of logical relevance is that a person with liability insurance is more likely to be at fault on a particular occasion than someone without it. If a defendant offers evidence that he himself has liability insurance, his argument of logical relevance implies that a person who has insurance is a generally prudent person and thus is more likely to have acted prudently on the present occasion. On the other hand, if he did not have liability insurance, his argument about relevance might be that a person without liability insurance is more apt to be cautious on a particular occasion than someone with insurance who can better afford a "devil may care" attitude. The Advisory Committee on the Federal Rules virtually rejected these propositions, maintaining that "[a]t best the inference of fault from the fact of insurance coverage is a tenuous one, as is its converse."[974]

Even if the logical relevance of liability insurance offered on the issue of fault were conceded, policy considerations dictate the exclusion of this evidence. Rule 404, which excludes character evidence when offered to show conforming conduct, applies in this

971. *See* McCORMICK ON EVIDENCE, *supra* note 1, §201, at 593; 2 WIGMORE, *supra* note 179, §282a, at 148; Annotation, *Admissibility of Evidence and Propriety and Effect of Questions, Statements, Comments, Etc., Tending to Show that Defendant in a Personal-Injury or Death Action Carries Liability Insurance*, 56 A.L.R. 1418, 1418-19 (1928) [hereinafter *Admissibility of Evidence*]; *see, e.g.*, **Janse v. Haywood**, 259 N.W. 347, 348 (Mich. 1935) (prejudicial error to intentionally inject into the jury's deliberations the subject of insurance, which was reflected in its verdict).

972. *See* **St. Louis Sw. Ry. v. Gregory**, 387 S.W.2d 27, 33 (Tex. 1965) (statements about insurance should not be made, but not every mention requires setting aside jury's verdict if jury instruction is adequate to eliminate the harmful effect); **Dennis v. Hulse**, 362 S.W.2d 308, 309 (Tex. 1962) (appellate court is not authorized to reverse a judgment when the record discloses an erroneous mention of insurance, unless appealing party shows that the error caused an improper judgment); **Myers v. Thomas**, 143 Tex. 502, 507, 186 S.W.2d 811, 813 (1945) (testimony about insurance is irrelevant to the issue of negligence and is prejudicial because it confuses and misleads the jury); **Finck Cigar Co. v. Campbell**, 134 Tex. 250, 254, 133 S.W.2d 759, 761 (1939) (error to inform jury that defendant is protected by indemnity insurance); *see, e.g.*, **Ford v. Carpenter**, 147 Tex. 447, 450, 216 S.W.2d 558, 559 (1949) (reversible error for defendant's counsel to refer to plaintiff's insurance); **Tex. Textile Mills v. Gregory**, 142 Tex. 308, 313, 177 S.W.2d 938, 940 (1944) (no reversible error when a defense witness suddenly and inadvertently disclosed, without fault by plaintiff's counsel, that defendants were insured); **Moncada v. Snyder**, 137 Tex. 112, 118, 152 S.W.2d 1077, 1080 (1941) (although not referencing an insurance company, counsel's reference to "some power behind the defense" was improper); **Page v. Thomas**, 123 Tex. 368, 372, 71 S.W.2d 234, 236 (1934) (reversible error to permit cross-examination eliciting testimony that suggested an insurance company would be financially liable for jury's verdict against defendant).

973. *See* **Brown v. Walter**, 62 F.2d 798, 800 (2d Cir. 1933) (Vermont and New York courts are hostile to insurance references because the relevance of such evidence depends on the flimsy argument that a person with insurance is more likely to be careless); **Sutton v. Bell**, 77 A. 42, 43 (N.J. 1910) (information about insurance should be excluded because it confuses the issues, not because it lacks any relevance); FED. R. EVID. 411 advisory committee's note ("[T]he inference of fault from the fact of insurance coverage is a tenuous one."); McCORMICK ON EVIDENCE, *supra* note 1, §201, at 593 (relevance of evidence of insurance coverage is "doubtful"); 2 RAY, *supra* note 46, §1539, at 246 (it "may be conceded that the fact of insurance is not relevant as tending to show negligence").

974. FED. R. EVID. 411 advisory committee's note.

RULE 411

context.[975] The logic suggested by the plaintiff is that because the defendant has liability insurance, he is a careless driver and was therefore negligent on the occasion in question. The logic suggested by the defendant is either that because he has no liability insurance, he is a careful person and was therefore careful on the occasion in question or that he has liability insurance, prudent people carry insurance, and therefore he was prudent on the occasion in question. Character evidence that would be excluded by Rule 404(a)(1) is a link in all three chains of logic.[976]

The Advisory Committee on the Federal Rules, after expressing doubt about the logical relevance of insurance, stated that "[m]ore important, no doubt, has been the feeling that knowledge of the presence or absence of liability insurance would induce juries to decide cases on improper grounds."[977] Excluding evidence of liability insurance is a specific application of the philosophy of Rule 403, which excludes logically relevant evidence when counterfactors substantially outweigh its probative value.[978] In promulgating Rule 411, the Supreme Court of Texas expressly excluded evidence of liability insurance on the issue of fault. It decided that one or more of the counterfactors in Rule 403 substantially outweigh the probative value of liability insurance offered to show fault.[979]

---

975. *See* Tex. R. Evid. 404(a)(1) ("Evidence of a person's character or character trait is not admissible to prove that on a particular occasion the person acted in accordance with the character or trait.").

976. Refer to notes 322-327 *supra* and accompanying text.

977. Fed. R. Evid. 411 advisory committee's note; *cf. Barrington v. Duncan*, 140 Tex. 510, 516, 169 S.W.2d 462, 465 (1943) (Texas courts have taken judicial notice that juries are more apt to find against insured individuals, and for larger amounts, than against uninsured).

978. Refer to notes 111-159 *supra* and accompanying text. Not all critics agree with the Advisory Committee's conclusion about the unfairness of the prejudice engendered by this evidence. *See* Leon Green, *Blindfolding the Jury*, 33 Tex. L. Rev. 157, 162-63 (1954). Green argues the following:

> On the issue of damages the ability to pay is a highly significant fact, as it is in all affairs of life. Even in the support of churches, local, state and national governments, and other institutions, ability to pay is of the greatest importance. Lawyers, doctors, engineers and others who render professional services take into account the economic status of a client, patient or other patron. If an adequate recovery for the plaintiff in a personal injury case would wipe the defendant out financially, can it be said that this fact is not relevant? Why should an insurance carrier get the benefit of the jury's thinking the defendant is unable to pay at all or to pay full damages? Why should a plaintiff in such a case be denied his full remedy if the insured has paid for protection against his negligence[?]

Id. Of course, in this situation, the plaintiff is not offering evidence of insurance to prove liability, but to prove damages once liability is established.

979. Unfair prejudice (i.e., an undue tendency to influence the jury's decision) is the pertinent factor. *See In re Essex Ins.*, 450 S.W.3d 524, 527 n.4 (Tex. 2014) (orig. proceeding) (per curiam) ("Texas law has long recognized the prejudice that results from the admission of evidence of liability insurance that covers an insured defendant."). Texas courts have suggested that a jury might find against a party with insurance coverage and award larger damages against an insured believing that not he, but the insurance company, will have to bear the full burden. *See Barrington*, 140 Tex. at 516, 169 S.W.2d at 465; *Kuntz v. Spence*, 67 S.W.2d 254, 256 (Tex. Comm'n App. 1934, holding approved); *Carter v. Walker*, 165 S.W. 483, 486-87 (Tex. Civ. App.—San Antonio 1913, writ dism'd) (op. on reh'g). Conversely, the jury might reject or reduce a proper award because the party himself would have to bear the burden rather than an insurance company, thus upholding his "plea of poverty." *See Rojas v. Vuocolo*, 142 Tex. 152, 157, 177 S.W.2d 962, 964 (1944); *see also* Green, *supra* note 978, at 162-63 (disputing the premise that defendant's ability to pay, including consideration of his insurance coverage, is irrelevant to a jury's deliberations on liability and damages). Refer to notes 120-138 *supra* and accompanying text.

RULE 411

Rule 411 also applies in criminal cases. In *Ex parte Wheeler*, the prosecutor asked the defendant's accident-reconstruction expert if he was aware that the defendant's insurance company had found her at fault for hitting and killing a pedestrian.[980] The court of appeals held that this question was barred by Rule 411 and was proper grounds for a mistrial.[981] Questioning the defense expert's knowledge of the results of an insurance investigation informed the jury that the defendant had insurance coverage and that "others had independently determined that appellant had acted negligently or recklessly."[982] On further review, the court of criminal appeals held that the prosecutor did not violate Rule 411 because the question did not go to the fact of insurance offered to show liability (the fact that the defendant was covered by insurance had already been mentioned during the trial), but rather to the decision of the defendant's insurance carrier to concede liability or "fault."[983] Thus, Rule 411 did not bar the prosecutor's question, but the question "was far more prejudicial (and more misleading) than any mere mention of the existence of insurance as proof of Ms. Wheeler's negligence or fault" because it asserted the result of an insurance investigation and the conclusion that the defendant's "own agent, her insurance carrier, had conceded her 'fault.' Thus, the question was outside Rule 411, but even more prejudicial than the questioning that is prohibited by that rule."[984] The court of criminal appeals concluded that the trial court had properly granted a mistrial because the question was barred by Rule 403.[985]

B. Insurance Offered on Issues Other than Fault

As was the policy at common law[986] and under earlier Texas law, the second sentences of both Texas Rule 411 and Federal Rule 411 limit the exclusion of their respec-

---

980. 146 S.W.3d 238, 243 (Tex. App.—Fort Worth 2004), *rev'd*, 203 S.W.3d 317 (Tex. Crim. App. 2006).

981. *Ex parte Wheeler*, 146 S.W.3d at 249.

982. *Id.* at 253.

983. *Ex parte Wheeler*, 203 S.W.3d 317, 329-30 (Tex. Crim. App. 2006).

984. *Id.*

985. *See id.* at 324-25. In *Mitchell v. State*, the Waco Court of Appeals admitted evidence of insurance coverage and held that, based on the particular facts of the case, the probative value of a determination of liability by an insurance-claims representative was not substantially outweighed by the danger of unfair prejudice under Rule 403. 377 S.W.3d 21, 28-29 (Tex. App.—Waco 2011, pet. dism'd). The court noted that the State asked the claims representative whether she had determined liability, unlike the questioning in *Ex parte Wheeler* of a witness unassociated with the insurance company's investigation. *Mitchell*, 377 S.W.3d at 26.

986. *See Pickett v. Kolb*, 237 N.E.2d 105, 108 (Ind. 1968) (trial court may not exclude otherwise competent evidence merely because it reveals that an insurance carrier is involved); *Dempsey v. Goldstein Bros. Amusement Co.*, 121 N.E. 429, 429-30 (Mass. 1919) (information revealing insurance is admissible to show witness's bias); *Scholte v. Brabec*, 224 N.W. 259, 260 (Minn. 1929) (same); *O'Donnell v. Bachelor*, 240 A.2d 484, 487 (Pa. 1968) (revealing insurance is necessary at times). *See generally Admissibility of Evidence*, *supra* note 971, at 1439-48 (discussing exceptions to show bias); Bernard R. Rapoport, Note, 26 CORNELL L.Q. 137 (1940) (unusual for a trial not to include "an opportunity legitimately to inform the jury ... that the defendant is insured"). Evidence of insurance can be offered as proof of agency. *See, e.g., Cherry v. Stockton*, 406 P.2d 358, 360 (N.M. 1965) (insurance provision of lease should have been admitted as evidence of disputed employer-employee relationship); *Biggins v. Wagner*, 245 N.W. 385, 387 (S.D. 1932) (insurance policy was properly admitted into evidence to determine whether a truck-driver/owner was an independent contractor). Evidence of insurance can be offered as proof of ownership. *See Barnett v. Butler*, 112 So. 2d 907, 909 (Fla. Dist. Ct. App. 1959). Evidence of insurance can also be offered as proof of management. *See, e.g., Pinckard v. Dunnavant*, 206 So. 2d 340, 342-43 (Ala. 1968) (when a paramount issue was whether defendant

RULE 411

tive first sentences by not excluding evidence of liability insurance on issues other than fault.[987] This explicit limitation on the rule's exclusion may be unnecessary. The evidence must still be relevant under Rule 401 in order to be admitted under Rule 402. Because Rule 411 deals specifically with insurance, however, the second sentence clarifies the issue and avoids possible misconstruction.[988]

The other purposes listed in Rule 411 are illustrative and not exclusive.[989] Uses in Texas include evidence of liability insurance (1) to prove agency,[990] ownership,[991] or control,[992] (2) to explain delay,[993] and (3) to impeach.[994]

---

was responsible for maintenance of the premises where injury occurred, evidence of liability insurance was admissible because court instructed jury to consider the fact of the insurance solely in connection with the maintenance issue); *Perkins v. Rice*, 72 N.E. 323, 324 (Mass. 1904) (evidence of liability insurance covering an elevator where an injury occurred was admissible to show evidence of management and control of the elevator).

987. *See* FED. R. EVID. 411 ("But the court may admit this evidence for another purpose, such as proving a witness's bias or prejudice or proving agency, ownership, or control."); TEX. R. EVID. 411 ("But the court may admit this evidence for another purpose, such as proving a witness's bias or prejudice or, if disputed, proving agency, ownership, or control.").

988. The Advisory Committee's note to the federal rule states that "[t]he second sentence points out the limits of the rule, using well established illustrations." FED. R. EVID. 411 advisory committee's note.

989. Refer to notes 160-161 *supra* and accompanying text.

990. *See, e.g.*, *Conner v. Angelina Cty. Lumber Co.*, 146 S.W.2d 1093, 1095 (Tex. Civ. App.—Beaumont 1940, no writ) (letters between defendant and its insurance company discussing coverage of independent contractor's employees under defendant's insurance policy were admissible on the issue of whether negligent truck driver was defendant's employee).

991. *See, e.g.*, *Meuth v. Hartgrove*, 811 S.W.2d 626, 628-29 (Tex. App.—Austin 1990, writ denied) (when defendant-subcontractor denied ownership of subcontractor company, insurance certificates issued to "Wayne Meuth d/b/a Production Enterprises" were admitted to prove ownership; notation of policy limits on the certificate was properly excluded because it did not explain any portion of the document to prove ownership or control and was prejudicial on the issue of damages); *Jacobini v. Hall*, 719 S.W.2d 396, 401 (Tex. App.—Fort Worth 1986, writ ref'd n.r.e.) (evidence of defendant's purchase of insurance after an accident was admissible to prove ownership of the vehicle in a negligent-entrustment lawsuit); *Harper v. Highway Motor Freight Lines*, 89 S.W.2d 448, 451 (Tex. Civ. App.—Dallas 1935, writ dism'd) (when ownership of a truck was disputed, evidence of insurance was material and relevant to prove ownership).

992. *See, e.g.*, *St. Joseph Hosp. v. Wolff*, 999 S.W.2d 579, 595 (Tex. App.—Austin 1999) (evidence that hospital provided doctor with medical-malpractice insurance was admissible to prove hospital's right to control doctor; because trial court specifically instructed jury on evidence's limited admissibility, it was not excludable under Rule 403), *rev'd on other grounds*, 94 S.W.3d 513 (Tex. 2002); *Thornhill v. Ronnie's I-45 Truck Stop, Inc.*, 944 S.W.2d 780, 793-94 (Tex. App.—Beaumont 1997, writ dism'd) (references to insurance in loan agreement were admissible to show that party was exercising control over premises); *Davis v. Stallones*, 750 S.W.2d 235, 237-38 (Tex. App.—Houston [1st Dist.] 1987, no writ) (when defense expert in wrongful-death trial repeatedly made references to "missing" and "unavailable" wreckage, he raised the issue of control over wreckage; evidence that wreckage was controlled by insurance underwriters was admissible).

993. *See, e.g.*, *W. Tex. State Bank v. Tri-Serv. Drilling Co.*, 339 S.W.2d 249, 254-55 (Tex. Civ. App.—Eastland 1960, writ ref'd n.r.e.) (reference to insurance was admissible to explain plaintiff's delay in taking action to recover funds from defendant).

994. *See Aguilera v. Reynolds Well Serv., Inc.*, 234 S.W.2d 282, 285 (Tex. Civ. App.—San Antonio 1950, writ ref'd) ("We are unwilling to hold that an agent of an insurance company which is a real party at interest may take the stand as an apparently disinterested witness, give testimony damaging to the opposing party, and then be exempt from cross-examination designed to show his connection to the company."); *see, e.g.*, *Gothard v. Marr*, 581 S.W.2d 276, 281 (Tex. Civ. App.—Waco 1979, no writ) (allowing introduction of plaintiff's proofs of loss, over plaintiff's objections, on the ground that defendants tendered the instruments for the limited purpose of impeaching plaintiff; introduction of the instruments "met the test of being 'clearly relevant and with substantial probative value on (a) disputed issue in the case'" (quoting *Kainer v. Walker*, 377 S.W.2d 613, 617 (Tex. 1964), *overruled on other grounds*, *Burk Royalty Co. v. Walls*, 616 S.W.2d 911 (Tex. 1981))); *Polk Cty. Motor Co. v. Wright*, 523 S.W.2d 432, 434-35

Contrary to the federal rule, Texas Rule 411 requires that the other issues for which liability insurance is offered be in dispute, unless the issue is an allegation of bias or prejudice.[995] This requirement parallels the comparable provision of Rule 407 on subsequent remedial measures.[996] Loopholes may be created, and legitimate use may too easily cause illegitimate spillover, despite limiting instructions.[997] A dispute over the legitimate issue is required, as indicated by earlier Texas case law.[998] The Texas rule leaves the word "disputed" to a case-by-case determination rather than providing a definition. The drafters' intent may have been to require that a "genuine issue be present,"[999] regardless of how or when it arose.

C. Scope of Rule 411

The language of Rule 411, that evidence of liability insurance is "not admissible," could be read narrowly to refer only to formal offers of evidence at the evidence-taking stage of a trial. Under this reading, the rule would not cover instances in which counsel suggests liability-insurance coverage or lack thereof in voir dire, opening statements or closing arguments, sidebar remarks reaching the jury, or other instances when the suggestion reaches the jury. Certainly, all of these communications contravene the philosophy and purpose of Rule 411. Indeed, they were all prohibited by the common law[1000] and earlier Texas law.[1001] These holdings have been borrowed by the Texas courts as case law or by a broad reading of "not admissible" in Rule 411.[1002]

(Tex. Civ. App.—Houston [1st Dist.] 1975, no writ) (plaintiff was entitled to question an independent physical-damage estimator, employed by defendant's insurance company, to show interest, bias, or motive); *S. Tex. Nat. Gas Gathering Co. v. Guerra*, 469 S.W.2d 899, 914 (Tex. Civ. App.—Corpus Christi 1971, writ ref'd n.r.e.) (investigator employed by defendant's insurance company could be questioned for the "purpose of revealing every relation tending to show … bias … even though such examination may have disclosed that the defendant … was protected by insurance"); *Griggs Furniture Co. v. Bufkin*, 348 S.W.2d 867, 869-70 (Tex. Civ. App.—Amarillo 1961, writ ref'd n.r.e.) (proof of loss was admissible for impeachment purposes). *But cf. Eoff v. Hal & Charlie Peterson Found.*, 811 S.W.2d 187, 197 (Tex. App.—San Antonio 1991, no writ) (rejecting plaintiff's contention that evidence of hospital's liability insurance was admissible after witness testified that hospital was a charitable institution; "[t]he fact that a hospital is a non-profit charitable institution has nothing whatsoever to do with its liability for damages"); *Mendoza v. Varon*, 563 S.W.2d 646, 649 (Tex. Civ. App.—Dallas 1978, writ ref'd n.r.e.) (mere fact that both witness and defendant were insured by the same company was an insufficiently impeachable interest in the outcome of the litigation to outweigh its prejudicial impact).

995. *Compare* Tex. R. Evid. 411 (adding "if disputed" before "proving agency, ownership, or control"), *with* Fed. R. Evid. 411 (omitting the phrase).

996. *See* Tex. R. Evid. 407(a) ("But the court may admit this evidence for another purpose, such as impeachment or—if disputed—proving ownership, control, or the feasibility of precautionary measures."). Refer to notes 703-707 *supra* and accompanying text.

997. *See, e.g.*, *Kenneth H. Hughes Interests, Inc. v. Westrup*, 879 S.W.2d 229, 238 (Tex. App.—Houston [1st Dist.] 1994, writ denied) (incident report, which stated that the accident was reported to defendant's insurance company, was projected on a screen for the jury by plaintiff's counsel; harmless error).

998. *See, e.g.*, *Tex. Co. v. Betterton*, 126 Tex. 359, 361-62, 88 S.W.2d 1039, 1039-40 (1936) (evidence of defendant's insurance was inadmissible on cross-examination because the evidence was immaterial); *Conner v. Angelina Cty. Lumber Co.*, 146 S.W.2d 1093, 1095 (Tex. Civ. App.—Beaumont 1940, no writ) (evidence of insurance was admissible because agency was a contested issue).

999. *Cf.* Fed. R. Evid. 407 advisory committee's note (evidence of subsequent repairs is automatically excluded unless the evidence goes to prove a controverted issue).

1000. *See Tom Reed Gold Mines Co. v. Morrison*, 224 P. 822, 824-25 (Ariz. 1924) (reversible error to refer to existence of insurance during voir dire); *Martin v. Lilly*, 121 N.E. 443, 445 (Ind. 1919) (same); *Loughlin v. Brassil*, 78

Rule 411 does not prohibit all mentions of insurance to the jury. For example, good-faith inquiry of veniremembers about any possible connection with an insurance company to discover possible bias or prejudice is allowed, as long as the inquiry does not convey to the jury the impression that a party is insured.[1003] Other examples include: proof of insurance coverage introduced collaterally because it is inseparably appended to an admissible statement;[1004] an admission of negligence by a party, if a reference to insurance is an "integral part" of the admission;[1005] and instances when the opposing party has "opened the door."[1006]

N.E. 854, 857 (N.Y. 1907) (reversible error to refer to existence of insurance during summation); **Yoast v. Sims**, 253 P. 504, 505-06 (Okla. 1927) (same); **Adams v. Cline Ice Cream Co.**, 131 S.E. 867, 867-68 (W. Va. 1926) (reversible error to refer to existence of insurance during voir dire).

1001. *See, e.g.*, **St. Louis Sw. Ry. v. Gregory**, 387 S.W.2d 27, 33 (Tex. 1965) (although it was error for defense counsel to state during voir dire that there was "no insurance here," it was not so highly prejudicial to plaintiff's case as to be incurable by an instruction); **Shoppers World v. Villarreal**, 518 S.W.2d 913, 920-21 (Tex. Civ. App.—Corpus Christi 1975, writ ref'd n.r.e.) (mentioning liability insurance during jury examination is reversible error when it is reasonably calculated to cause a miscarriage of justice and results in the rendition of an improper judgment); **A.J. Miller Trucking Co. v. Wood**, 474 S.W.2d 763, 766 (Tex. Civ. App.—Tyler 1971, writ ref'd n.r.e.) (mention of insurance during voir dire is grounds for a new trial); **Johnson v. Reed**, 464 S.W.2d 689, 691-92 (Tex. Civ. App.—Dallas 1971, writ ref'd n.r.e.) (preventing the mention of insurance during voir dire is not reversible error).

1002. *See, e.g.*, **AccuBanc Mortg. Corp. v. Drummonds**, 938 S.W.2d 135, 152 (Tex. App.—Fort Worth 1996, writ denied) (plaintiff's jury argument referring to indemnification of defendant "was designed to induce the jury to render judgment against [defendant] and for as large an amount as possible—the very things Civil Rule 411 is meant to protect against"; harmless error). Although these communications are generally prohibited under Rule 411, the mere mention of insurance is not necessarily grounds for reversal. **Babcock v. Nw. Mem'l Hosp.**, 767 S.W.2d 705, 708 (Tex. 1989) (op. on reh'g); *see* **Nguyen v. Myers**, 442 S.W.3d 434, 440 (Tex. App.—Dallas 2013, no pet.) (mere mention of insurance in jury argument does not automatically result in reversal; complaining party must prove that the evidence of insurance was harmful); **Isern v. Watson**, 942 S.W.2d 186, 198-99 (Tex. App.—Beaumont 1997, pet. denied) (same).

1003. *See, e.g.*, **Cavnar v. Quality Control Parking, Inc.**, 678 S.W.2d 548, 556 (Tex. App.—Houston [14th Dist.] 1984) (no error existed when questioning did not create a reasonable inference that defendant was insured), *rev'd in part on other grounds*, 696 S.W.2d 549 (Tex. 1985); **Kollmorgan v. Scott**, 447 S.W.2d 236, 238 (Tex. Civ. App.—Houston [14th Dist.] 1969, no writ) (no error because there was no inference that defendant was insured); **S. Austin Drive-In Theater v. Thomison**, 421 S.W.2d 933, 941 (Tex. Civ. App.—Austin 1967, writ ref'd n.r.e.) (without a clear inference that defendant carried liability insurance, no error occurred).

1004. *See, e.g.*, **Taylor v. Owen**, 290 S.W.2d 771, 774 (Tex. Civ. App.—San Antonio 1956, writ ref'd n.r.e.) (plaintiff could introduce defendant's statement that defendant admitted traveling 60 mph, an excessive rate of speed, even though the fact that defendant was insured might be introduced collaterally); **McDonald v. Alamo Motor Lines**, 222 S.W.2d 1013, 1013-14 (Tex. Civ. App.—San Antonio 1949, no writ) (several letters from plaintiff to his insurance company could be admitted for impeachment, even though a reference to insurance would then be introduced collaterally).

1005. *See, e.g.*, **Young v. Carter**, 173 S.E.2d 259, 261 (Ga. Ct. App. 1970) (defendant's admission "that it was his fault—that his insurance company would take care of it for her" was admissible and therefore properly mentioned in the plaintiff's opening statement); **Herschensohn v. Weisman**, 119 A. 705, 705 (N.H. 1923) (defendant's statement, after being warned to be careful or he could kill somebody: "Don't worry, I carry insurance for that," was admissible); **Reid v. Owens**, 93 P.2d 680, 684 (Utah 1939) (testimony of liability insurance is admissible when the testimony is part of an admission of liability or responsibility).

1006. *See* **Tex. Textile Mills v. Gregory**, 142 Tex. 308, 313, 177 S.W.2d 938, 940 (1944); **Finck Cigar Co. v. Campbell**, 134 Tex. 250, 254, 133 S.W.2d 759, 761 (1939); **Tex. Coca-Cola Bottling Co. v. Lovejoy**, 138 Tex. 254, 257 (Tex. Civ. App.—Eastland 1940, writ ref'd); **Jacobini v. Hall**, 719 S.W.2d 396, 401 (Tex. App.—Fort Worth 1986, writ ref'd n.r.e.); **Burrous v. Knotts**, 482 S.W.2d 358, 363 (Tex. Civ. App.—Tyler 1972, no writ); **Sprague v. Hubert**, 77 S.W.2d 738, 740 (Tex. Civ. App.—El Paso 1934, no writ); *see, e.g.*, **Roosth & Genecov Prod. Co. v. White**, 281 S.W.2d 333, 338 (Tex. Civ. App.—Texarkana 1955, writ ref'd n.r.e.) (exhibit containing references to defendant's insurance coverage could be used because defendant himself introduced the exhibit).

In some instances, the existence and amount of insurance coverage may be part of an essential claim, such as in a suit for bad-faith insurance settlement. In those instances, obviously, reference to and evidence of insurance is necessary. Because the evidence is not being offered to show negligence or wrongful conduct, Rule 411 does not apply. However, a plaintiff might combine a claim for personal injury with a bad-faith claim against the original defendant's insurer. In that case, a trial judge should sever the two claims so that evidence of insurance will not be admitted at the trial on the original tortfeasor's liability but will be admitted at a later trial on the bad-faith claims.[1007]

D. Remedies for Improper Reference to Insurance

If an improper reference to insurance is made, the reference will be struck on request, and the jury will, on request, be instructed to disregard the reference.[1008] The court will not grant a mistrial if the complaining party intentionally or inadvertently elicited or injected the reference to insurance. The court will generally grant a mistrial, however, if the noncomplaining party intentionally elicited or injected the reference to insurance.[1009] If the noncomplaining party inadvertently elicited or injected the refer-

---

When the defendant's witness mentions insurance on cross-examination by the plaintiff, the defendant cannot complain about the statement. *See Tex. Co. v. Betterton*, 126 Tex. 359, 361-62, 88 S.W.2d 1039, 1039-40 (1936) (even though defendant impeached witness with a signed statement that witness had made to his insurance company, on redirect plaintiff could not ask who wrote the statement because authorship was neither disputed nor material); *see also Chapin v. Hunt*, 521 S.W.2d 123, 126 (Tex. Civ. App.—Beaumont 1975, writ dism'd) (unresponsive statement by witness is not reversible error unless it is shown that the statement led to an improper judgment); *Bishop v. Carter*, 408 S.W.2d 520, 521 (Tex. Civ. App.—Waco 1966, writ ref'd n.r.e.) (unresponsive answer by the complaining party is not reversible error). *But see Tex. Power & Light Co. v. Stone*, 84 S.W.2d 738, 742-43 (Tex. Civ. App.—Eastland 1935, writ ref'd) (reversible error occurred when, on cross-examination by plaintiff, defense witness informed the jury that an insurance company had asked him to examine plaintiff; answer was responsive to the question).

1007. *See, e.g., In re Reynolds*, 369 S.W.3d 638, 655-56 (Tex. App.—Tyler 2012, orig. proceeding) (severance of claims was proper when plaintiff brought personal-injury claim against motorist and uninsured-motorist claim against insurance company because evidence of motorist's insurance was inadmissible to support personal-injury claim but necessary to establish uninsured-motorist claim); *F.A. Richard & Assocs. v. Millard*, 856 S.W.2d 765, 766-67 (Tex. App.—Houston [1st Dist.] 1993, orig. proceeding) (trial judge has no discretion to deny severance when personal-injury claims are combined with bad-faith claim against that alleged tortfeasor's insurance company because "[s]uch a simultaneous trial would require detailed and extensive evidence of insurance, prejudicing [negligence defendant's] defense and violating his substantial right to have his liability decided without any mention of insurance. ... Conversely, to exclude evidence of insurance and settlement negotiations would prejudice [plaintiff's] substantial right to develop her bad-faith case against [insurer and independent adjuster]."); *see also In re Foremost Ins.*, 966 S.W.2d 770, 772 (Tex. App.—Corpus Christi 1998, orig. proceeding) (abatement of bad-faith claims must accompany severance when severance is required because bad-faith claim requires extensive evidence of insurance and settlement offers in violation of Rules 408 and 411).

1008. *See St. Louis Sw. Ry. v. Gregory*, 387 S.W.2d 27, 33 (Tex. 1965); *Dennis v. Hulse*, 362 S.W.2d 308, 309 (Tex. 1962); *Univ. of Tex. v. Hinton*, 822 S.W.2d 197, 201 (Tex. App.—Austin 1991, no writ); *see, e.g., Dall. Ry. & Terminal Co. v. Flowers*, 284 S.W.2d 160, 163 (Tex. Civ. App.—Waco 1955, writ ref'd n.r.e.) (refusing to grant a new trial because "counsel could have asked for a jury instruction to disregard" references to insurance); *see also Shell Oil Co. v. Reinhart*, 371 S.W.2d 722, 727-28 (Tex. Civ. App.—El Paso 1963) (granting a mistrial despite a jury instruction to disregard a reference to insurance because the court's instruction was incapable of curing the error), *writ ref'd n.r.e.*, 375 S.W.2d 717 (Tex. 1964); *Carter v. Walker*, 165 S.W. 483, 486-87 (Tex. Civ. App.—San Antonio 1913, writ dism'd) (op. on reh'g) (granting a new trial for incurable harm).

1009. There is a general presumption that an intentional reference to insurance prejudices the insured party. *See Betterton*, 126 Tex. at 362, 88 S.W.2d at 1040; *Hinton*, 822 S.W.2d at 201; *see, e.g., Kuntz v. Spence*, 67 S.W.2d 254, 256 (Tex. Comm'n App. 1934, holding approved) (court took judicial notice that juries are more likely to find against

ence, the court must determine on a case-by-case basis whether the reference will or did prevent a fair verdict.[1010]

RULE 412
EVIDENCE OF PREVIOUS SEXUAL CONDUCT
IN CRIMINAL CASES

(a) In General. The following evidence is not admissible in a prosecution for sexual assault, aggravated sexual assault, or attempt to commit sexual assault or aggravated sexual assault:

(1) reputation or opinion evidence of a victim's past sexual behavior; or

(2) specific instances of a victim's past sexual behavior.

(b) Exceptions for Specific Instances. Evidence of specific instances of a victim's past sexual behavior is admissible if:

(1) the court admits the evidence in accordance with subdivisions (c) and (d);

(2) the evidence:

(A) is necessary to rebut or explain scientific or medical evidence offered by the prosecutor;

(B) concerns past sexual behavior with the defendant and is offered by the defendant to prove consent;

(C) relates to the victim's motive or bias;

(D) is admissible under Rule 609; or

(E) is constitutionally required to be admitted; and

(3) the probative value of the evidence outweighs the danger of unfair prejudice.

(c) Procedure for Offering Evidence. Before offering any evidence of the victim's past sexual behavior, the defendant must inform the court outside the jury's presence. The court must then conduct an in camera hearing, recorded by

---

insured party and award larger damages if they know insurance company, rather than insured party, will bear burden of loss); ***Rhoden v. Booth***, 344 S.W.2d 481, 486-87 (Tex. Civ. App.—Dallas 1961, writ ref'd n.r.e.) (incurable error to allow intentional references to defendant's insurance coverage; error could be brought for the first time on a motion for new trial).

1010. *See **United Cab Co. v. Mason***, 775 S.W.2d 783, 786 (Tex. App.—Houston [1st Dist.] 1989, writ denied) (injection of insurance into a trial, even if always error, is not reversible per se); ***Roosth & Genecov***, 281 S.W.2d at 338 (court must determine from the facts and circumstances contained in the record as a whole whether a question was reasonably calculated to cause and probably did cause rendition of an improper judgment; key issue is generally whether the improper evidence or reference actually caused rendition of an improper judgment).

a court reporter, and determine whether the proposed evidence is admissible. The defendant may not refer to any evidence ruled inadmissible without first requesting and gaining the court's approval outside the jury's presence.

(d) Record Sealed. The court must preserve the record of the in camera hearing, under seal, as part of the record.

(e) Definition of "Victim." In this rule, "victim" includes an alleged victim.

COMMENTARY ON RULE 412

Rule 412 represents an evidentiary codification of the Texas "rape shield" law,[1011] which was originally promulgated in 1975 as part of the Penal Code.[1012] In enacting its rape-shield law, Texas followed Federal Rule 412[1013] and virtually all other states in

---

1011. *See generally* James A. Vaught & Margaret Henning, *Admissibility of a Rape Victim's Prior Sexual Conduct in Texas: A Contemporary Review and Analysis*, 23 ST. MARY'S L.J. 893 (1992) (reviewing and analyzing former Texas Criminal Rule 412, Federal Rule 412, and the Texas Penal Code); Sarah Weddington, *Rape Law in Texas: H.B. 284 and the Road to Reform*, 4 AM. J. CRIM. L. 1 (1975-76) (discussing the genesis of the Texas statute); Andrew J. Cloutier, Texas Development, *The Texas Rape-Shield Law: Texas Rule of Evidence 412*, 14 AM. J. CRIM. L. 281 (1987) (discussing changes from former Texas Penal Code §22.065 to former Texas Criminal Rule 412).

1012. Act of May 8, 1975, 64th Leg., R.S., ch. 203, §3, 1975 Tex. Gen. Laws 476, 477-78, *amended by* Act of May 29, 1983, 68th Leg., R.S., ch. 977, §4, 1983 Tex. Gen. Laws 5311, 5315-16 (former Texas Penal Code §22.065 deemed repealed as to criminal proceedings effective 1986). That statute read as follows:

EVIDENCE OF PREVIOUS SEXUAL CONDUCT

(a) Evidence of specific instances of the victim's sexual conduct, opinion evidence of the victim's sexual conduct, and reputation evidence of the victim's sexual conduct may be admitted under Sections 22.011 and 22.021 of this code only if, and only to the extent that, the judge finds that the evidence is material to a fact at issue in the case and that its inflammatory or prejudicial nature does not outweigh its probative value.

(b) If the defendant proposes to ask any question concerning specific instances, opinion evidence, or reputation evidence of the victim's sexual conduct, either by direct examination or cross-examination of any witness, the defendant must inform the court out of the hearing of the jury prior to asking any such question. After this notice, the court shall conduct an in camera hearing, recorded by the court reporter, to determine whether the proposed evidence is admissible under Subsection (a) of this section. The court shall determine what evidence is admissible and shall accordingly limit the questioning. The defendant shall not go outside these limits nor refer to any evidence ruled inadmissible in camera without prior approval of the court without the presence of the jury.

(c) The court shall seal the record of the in camera hearing required in Subsection (b) of this section for delivery to the appellate court in the event of an appeal.

(d) This section does not limit the right of the state or the accused to impeach credibility by showing prior felony convictions nor the right of the accused to produce evidence of promiscuous sexual conduct of a child 14 years old or older as a defense to sexual assault, aggravated sexual assault, or indecency with a child. If evidence of a previous felony conviction involving sexual conduct or evidence of promiscuous sexual conduct is admitted, the court shall instruct the jury as to the purpose of the evidence and as to its limited use.

Id.

1013. *See* FED. R. EVID. 412. Unlike the Texas rule, the federal rule applies to both civil and criminal proceedings. *See* FED. R. EVID. 412. For a discussion of the rationale and scope of the federal provision, see 23 WRIGHT & GRAHAM, *supra* note 35, §5382, at 492 (1980). The federal rule was revised in 1994 to alleviate some of the confusion caused by the original rule and to expand its protection. FED. R. EVID. 412 advisory committee's note to 1994 amendments; *see* 23 WRIGHT & GRAHAM, *supra* note 35, §5382.1, at 240-46 (Supp. 2005).

protecting the privacy of complainants when they testify at trial.[1014] The rule represented a departure from early Texas law, which permitted a criminal defendant to offer evidence of his alleged victim's promiscuous conduct to prove that she consented to the act of intercourse.[1015]

The nearly universal implementation of rape-shield laws was influenced by the concern that the vast majority of sexual assaults suffered by women went unreported partly because complainants feared that they themselves would be placed on trial by the defense.[1016] This fear was justified—courts typically held that once a defendant claimed consent, he could delve into the alleged victim's sexual behavior.[1017] Evidence of an alleged rape victim's prior sexual behavior is frequently of very low probative value,[1018] but it carries enormously unfair prejudicial baggage.[1019]

Rule 412, like its predecessor statute,[1020] represents an explicit public-policy decision to eliminate trial practices that frustrated society's interest in the prosecution of sex crimes.[1021]

1014. See *Doe v. United States*, 666 F.2d 43, 48 & n.9 (4th Cir. 1981) (45 states had enacted some type of rape-shield law). *See generally* J. Alexander Tanford & Anthony J. Bocchino, *Rape Victim Shield Laws and the Sixth Amendment*, 128 U. PA. L. REV. 544 (1980) (analyzing rape-shield statutes in 46 American jurisdictions). Currently, all 50 states and the District of Columbia have rape-shield laws. *See* Allison Menkes, Note, *Rape and Sexual Assault*, 7 GEO. J. GENDER & L. 847, 848 (2006).

1015. See *Mitchell v. State*, 544 S.W.2d 927, 928 (Tex. Crim. App. 1977) (when the issue of consent is raised, rape victim's reputation as a "common prostitute" is admissible); *Burton v. State*, 471 S.W.2d 817, 821 (Tex. Crim. App. 1971) (specific acts of unchastity between rape victim and others are admissible when defendant asserts a consent defense). The rule also represents a reversal of the traditional common-law view, expressed by Lord Hale, that rape is "an accusation easily to be made and hard to be proved, and harder to be defended by the party accused, though ever so innocent." 1 M. HALE, THE HISTORY OF THE PLEAS OF THE CROWN 635 (1778).

1016. See *Williams v. State*, 690 S.W.2d 656, 658 (Tex. App.—Dallas 1985), *rev'd on other grounds*, 719 S.W.2d 573 (Tex. Crim. App. 1986); Vivian Berger, *Man's Trial, Woman's Tribulation: Rape Cases in the Courtroom*, 77 COLUM. L. REV. 1, 5, 12-15 (1977); Abraham P. Ordover, *Admissibility of Patterns of Similar Sexual Conduct: The Unlamented Death of Character for Chastity*, 63 CORNELL L. REV. 90, 93 n.7 (1977).

1017. See, e.g., *Roper v. State*, 375 S.W.2d 454, 455-56 (Tex. Crim. App. 1964) (defendant could be prevented from questioning a rape victim about her use of birth-control devices because he had not raised issue of consent); *see also* Edwinna Gayle Johnson, Note, 27 BAYLOR L. REV. 362 (1975) (discussing former Texas Penal Code §21.13 and the judge's in camera balancing test to determine admissibility of a victim's past sexual conduct).

1018. As noted by the Texas Court of Criminal Appeals, evidence of prior prostitution is
> irrelevant to the issue of whether the victim consented to sexual intercourse with the appellant. To rule otherwise would be to agree with the appellant's implied suggestion that a prostitute cannot be raped. This is as ridiculous as assuming that a philanthropist cannot be robbed because he has a past history of instances where he gave away money and property to people he did not know.

Holloway v. State, 751 S.W.2d 866, 871 (Tex. Crim. App. 1988).

1019. See *United States v. Kasto*, 584 F.2d 268, 271-72 (8th Cir. 1978) (rape victim's unchastity is ordinarily not probative of her consent to intercourse with defendant but is highly prejudicial).

1020. Refer to note 1012 *supra*.

1021. *Kesterson v. State*, 959 S.W.2d 247, 248 (Tex. App.—Dallas 1997, order); *see Estes v. State*, 487 S.W.3d 737, 753 (Tex. App.—Fort Worth 2016, pet. granted 9-14-16) ("Rule 412 is designed to limit abusive, embarrassing, and irrelevant inquiries into a complainant's private life and to encourage victims of sexual assault to report those crimes."); *Cuyler v. State*, 841 S.W.2d 933, 936 (Tex. App.—Austin 1992, no pet.) ("Before the statute was enacted, sexual assault victims often found themselves subjected to abusive, embarrassing, and irrelevant inquiries into their private lives, with the result that many sexual assault victims chose not to report the attack rather than face such questioning."), *disapproved on other grounds*, *Halstead v. State*, 891 S.W.2d 11 (Tex. App.—Austin 1994, no pet.).

A. Rule 412 & Changes to Earlier Texas Law

The original Texas rape-shield law was little more than a procedural device, similar to a motion in limine.[1022] Its purpose was to ensure that evidence of the complainant's previous sexual conduct did not come before the jury until the trial judge had heard the evidence outside the jury's presence and had ruled that its inflammatory or prejudicial nature did not outweigh its probative value.[1023] It had little substantive effect, however, because it explicitly permitted the use of reputation and opinion evidence as well as proof of prior specific conduct.

The adoption of Rule 412 changed the former Texas rape-shield law in numerous respects. First, under the former Penal Code provision, any limitation on offering evidence of the alleged victim's previous sexual conduct was confined to cases of sexual assault and aggravated sexual assault.[1024] Rule 412 explicitly extends the limitation on admissibility of the victim's[1025] prior sexual conduct to include attempts to commit sexual assault or aggravated sexual assault as well as the completed offenses.[1026] However, the rule does not specifically exclude such evidence when the defendant is charged with indecency with a child,[1027] even though the original Rule 412(e)—which has been eliminated—allowed the admission of evidence of "promiscuous" sexual conduct of a child 14 or older.[1028]

1022. *Ex parte Rose*, 704 S.W.2d 751, 760 (Tex. Crim. App. 1984) (Clinton, J., concurring).

1023. Refer to note 1012 *supra*.

1024. It was not always so applied, however. *See Johnson v. State*, 633 S.W.2d 888, 890 (Tex. Crim. App. 1982) (trial court, which had applied former Texas Penal Code §21.13 to an attempted-rape prosecution, was not constrained by the procedures of §21.13).

1025. The rule's definition of "victim" includes an alleged victim. TEX. R. EVID. 412(e). The term "complainant" is used interchangeably with "victim" throughout this discussion.

1026. *See* TEX. R. EVID. 412(a). The analogous federal rule applies in all criminal and civil cases involving sexual misconduct, regardless of whether either the alleged victim or the accused person is a party to the litigation. FED. R. EVID. 412 advisory committee's note to 1994 amendments; *see* FED. R. EVID. 412(a). For a criticism of expanding the rule to apply to civil cases, see 23 WRIGHT & GRAHAM, *supra* note 35, §5382.1, at 240-46, §5383.1, at 248-51 (Supp. 2005). In Texas, evidence of a person's prior sexual conduct would normally be inadmissible in a civil case under Rule 404(a)(1).

1027. *See Reyna v. State*, 168 S.W.3d 173, 176 (Tex. Crim. App. 2005) (Rule 412 does not on its face apply to case of indecency with child); *see, e.g.*, *Gonzalez v. State*, No. 12-11-00205-CR (Tex. App.—Tyler 2012, pet. ref'd) (memo op.; 9-28-12) (trial court abused discretion by excluding evidence of child complainant's sexual history under Rule 412 because the rule does not apply to cases involving indecency with a child).

1028. In 2006, Rule 412 was amended to eliminate the former "promiscuity" defense in Rule 412(e). *See* 209 S.W.3d (Tex. Cases) XXIII (2007) (setting out amendments to Texas Rules of Evidence, effective Jan. 1, 2007). Former Texas Penal Code §22.011(d)(1) had provided that it was an absolute defense to prosecution for sexual assault of a child if, at the time of the offense, the child was 14 years of age or older and had engaged in promiscuous sexual conduct before the time of the offense. Act approved June 19, 1983, 68th Leg., R.S., ch. 977, §3, 1983 Tex. Gen. Laws 5312 (former Texas Penal Code §22.011(d)(1), deemed repealed effective 1994). *See generally* Maryanne Lyons, Comment, *Adolescents in Jeopardy: An Analysis of Texas' Promiscuity Defense for Sexual Assault*, 29 HOUS. L. REV. 583 (1992) (addressing former Texas Penal Code §22.011 and discussing the historical development of statutory rape provisions). Because the Penal Code had specifically permitted this promiscuity defense, Rule 412 could not operate to prohibit the admission of evidence to support that defense. However, the promiscuity defense was repealed in the 1994 Penal Code, and former Rule 412(e) was specifically disapproved by the Texas Legislature. Act approved June 19, 1993, 73rd Leg., R.S., ch. 900, §1.01, 1993 Tex. Gen. Laws 3705. Thus, former Rule 412(e) would only permit the defense to offer evidence of promiscuous sexual conduct of a child of 14 years or older if the offense itself had occurred before September 1, 1994, when the Penal Code defense was eliminated. *See May v. State*, 919 S.W.2d

RULE 412

A second major change from earlier law is that reputation and opinion evidence of a victim's past sexual behavior is never admissible under Rule 412, even though it was under the former provision.[1029] This provision turns the traditionally preferred mode of proving character upside down. As noted in relation to Rules 404 and 405, character (when provable at all) must be proved through opinion or reputation testimony, not through prior specific instances of conduct.[1030] In Rule 412, the opposite occurs: opinion and reputation testimony is never admissible,[1031] and evidence of specific conduct might be admissible under limited conditions.[1032] The rationale is that the evidence is never admissible to prove the complainant's character,[1033] rather to prove only very specific, enumerated factual defenses. Further, the ban on opinion and reputation testimony demonstrates the commonly held belief that evidence of specific conduct is generally more probative and reliable than opinion or reputation evidence.[1034]

A third change from earlier Texas law is that Rule 412 limits the permissible purposes of evidence of prior sexual conduct to those few that are specifically enumerated in sections 412(b)(2)(A)-(b)(2)(E). Under former Texas Penal Code section 22.065, the only statutory requirement for the proffered evidence's purpose was the law's general restriction that the evidence be "material to a fact at issue."[1035] As a practical matter, consent had been the primary rationale for admitting evidence of prior sexual conduct by the complainant.[1036] Rule 412(b)(2)(A)-(b)(2)(D) restricts the permissible purposes to four specific categories recognized under the common law: (1) rebuttal or explana-

---

422, 423 n.1 (Tex. Crim. App. 1996) (promiscuity defense applied to promiscuous acts and sexual offenses committed before the effective date of its repeal, September 1, 1994). Further, even before repeal of the statutory defense, the subsection did not apply to the offense of aggravated sexual assault. *Johnson v. State*, 800 S.W.2d 563, 567 (Tex. App.—Houston [14th Dist.] 1990, pet. ref'd).

1029. *See Mitchell v. State*, 544 S.W.2d 927, 927-28 (Tex. Crim. App. 1977) (when consent is an issue, complainant's reputation for chastity is relevant); *see, e.g.*, *Campbell v. State*, 147 Tex. Crim. 192, 197, 179 S.W.2d 547, 549-50 (1944) (general reputation of rape complainant as a "common prostitute" was admissible to show consent as well as to impeach credibility).

1030. Refer to notes 298-444 *supra* and accompanying text.

1031. *See* Tex. R. Evid. 412(a)(1). While the rule states that opinion and reputation testimony is never admissible, such a rule might bend if constitutionally required in a specific case. Refer to note 1041 *infra* and accompanying text.

1032. *See* Tex. R. Evid. 412(b).

1033. *See Doe v. United States*, 666 F.2d 43, 47 (4th Cir. 1981) (constitutional justification for excluding opinion and reputation evidence under Federal Rule 412 is that such testimony is not a relevant indicator of general credibility or of the likelihood of consent on the specific occasion).

1034. *See* 23 Wright & Graham, *supra* note 35, §5385, at 550 (1980).

1035. Refer to note 1012 *supra*.

1036. *See Allen v. State*, 700 S.W.2d 924, 929 (Tex. Crim. App. 1985) (rape victim's prior sexual conduct was admissible to rebut the victim's testimony, to establish conduct indicative of prostitution, and to show felonies and misdemeanors involving moral turpitude); *see, e.g.*, *Williams v. State*, 690 S.W.2d 656, 658 (Tex. App.—Dallas 1985) (evidence of 17-year-old complainant's prior dating activity and the facts that she had a baby and had bragged about giving a man a venereal disease were not probative of consent; evidence of prior sexual conduct was only marginally relevant to the issue of consent), *rev'd on other grounds*, 719 S.W.2d 573 (Tex. Crim. App. 1986).

tion of scientific or medical evidence,[1037] (2) proof of the victim's consent,[1038] (3) proof of the victim's bias or motive,[1039] and (4) prior convictions to impeach.[1040] In addition to these specific exceptions, a general caveat remains in Rule 412(b)(2)(E), which states that evidence of sexual behavior is admissible when it "is constitutionally required to be admitted."[1041] Technically, this subsection is unnecessary because all of the Rules are subject to preemption by constitutional considerations.[1042] While no Texas cases addressed this issue under the former Penal Code statute, Rule 412(b)(2)(E) reminds the bench and bar that there may be factual circumstances that do not fit neatly into the first four categories but that still require admission of evidence of prior sexual conduct. It also preserves the rule from a facial constitutional attack.[1043]

A fourth change from earlier law is that Rule 412 reverses the normal balance of probative value versus unfair prejudicial effect. Under the former Penal Code provision, a trial judge had discretion to admit evidence of specific instances of the victim's prior sexual conduct if "its inflammatory or prejudicial nature does not outweigh its probative value."[1044] In contrast, Rule 412(b)(3) states that such evidence is not admissible unless "the probative value of the evidence outweighs the danger of unfair prejudice."[1045] This change of wording tips the scales in favor of excluding the evidence and protecting the complainant's privacy.[1046]

1037. *See, e.g.*, **Bader v. State**, 57 Tex. Crim. 293, 294-95, 122 S.W. 555, 556 (1909) (evidence of prior specific acts was admissible to rebut complainant's testimony that she was a virgin before the rape and to explain physician's testimony about the physical condition of the vagina). Refer to notes 1059-1063 *infra* and accompanying text.

1038. **Mitchell v. State**, 544 S.W.2d 927, 928 (Tex. Crim. App. 1977); **Roper v. State**, 375 S.W.2d 454, 456 (Tex. Crim. App. 1964); **Campbell v. State**, 147 Tex. Crim. 192, 197, 179 S.W.2d 547, 549-50 (1944). Refer to notes 1064-1067 *infra* and accompanying text.

1039. *See, e.g.*, **Shoemaker v. State**, 58 Tex. Crim. 518, 521-22, 126 S.W. 887, 888-89 (1910) (evidence of prior sexual conduct that shows motive was admissible "as affecting the credibility of the witness, and to be considered by the jury as a circumstance going to show that the defendant had never had intercourse with her"). Refer to notes 1068-1078 *infra* and accompanying text.

1040. Refer to notes 1079-1081 *infra* and accompanying text. For a discussion of Rule 609, refer to *Article VI: Witnesses, infra* p. 615.

1041. *See* **Rock v. Arkansas**, 483 U.S. 44, 55-56 (1987) (evidentiary rulings must not arbitrarily deny a defendant his ability to defend himself); **Davis v. Alaska**, 415 U.S. 308, 319-20 (1974) (state's interest in protecting juveniles must be balanced with defendant's right to cross-examination); **Chambers v. Mississippi**, 410 U.S. 284, 302 (1973) (applying rules mechanistically may violate constitutional rights that directly affect the ascertainment of guilt); **Whitmore v. State**, 570 S.W.2d 889, 898 (Tex. Crim. App. 1976) (when there is a conflict, a valid procedural rule of law must yield to a superior constitutional right). Refer to notes 1082-1084 *infra* and accompanying text.

1042. *See* Tex. R. Evid. 101(d), 402.

1043. *See* **Allen v. State**, 700 S.W.2d 924, 932 (Tex. Crim. App. 1985) (former Penal Code §21.13 did not violate Sixth Amendment right of confrontation).

1044. *See, e.g., id.* at 928-29 (whether the complainant was a virgin was immaterial to any issue but that "even if the court finds the evidence is material to an issue in the case, its inflammatory or prejudicial nature must not outweigh its probative value"). Refer to note 1012 *supra*.

1045. Tex. R. Evid. 412(b)(3).

1046. *See* **Alford v. State**, 495 S.W.3d 63, 67 (Tex. App.—Houston [14th Dist.] 2016, pet. ref'd) (Rule 403 balancing test weighs in favor of admissibility, while Rule 412(b)(3) weighs against admissibility); **Todd v. State**, 242 S.W.3d 126, 129 (Tex. App.—Texarkana 2007, pet. ref'd) (general principle favoring admission of evidence "does not apply to [a] victim's past sexual behavior during a trial for sexual assault or aggravated sexual assault"; Rule 412 creates "an extremely high hurdle ... which the accused's proposed evidence must clear" before the trial court may admit it).

RULE 412

B. Scope of Rule 412

By its explicit terms, Rule 412 applies only when a defendant is charged with sexual assault, aggravated sexual assault, or an attempt to commit either of those offenses.[1047] However, the public-policy concerns behind the rape-shield rule should limit the admissibility of evidence of a complainant's past sexual behavior whenever any part of the charged conduct involves an alleged sexual assault.[1048] Thus, the court of criminal appeals relied on Rule 412 in a capital-murder case in which the underlying felony offense was alleged as either aggravated sexual assault or kidnapping.[1049] The rule should logically apply to prosecutions for indecency with a child as well. Although the rule itself applies only in criminal proceedings, evidence of a sexual-assault plaintiff's prior sexual conduct might well be excluded in a civil proceeding under Rule 403, based on the same public-policy rationale and analysis that underlie Rule 412.[1050]

1. Past sexual behavior. Rule 412 excludes reputation or opinion evidence of a victim's past sexual behavior.[1051] Unless one of the exceptions in Rule 412(b) applies, evidence of specific instances of a victim's past sexual behavior is also prohibited.[1052] The rule speaks of "past" sexual behavior without further elaboration on whether that term applies solely to sexual conduct occurring before the charged offense or includes conduct occurring after the charged offense but before the date of trial. However, the spirit and policy of the rule apply as much to a complainant's sexual behavior after the date of the charged offense as to sexual behavior before it. The issue should be analyzed in terms of whether the probative value of the evidence outweighs its prejudicial effect rather than whether it occurred before or after the charged offense.[1053]

1047. Tex. R. Evid. 412(a).

1048. *See* Fed. R. Evid. 412 advisory committee's note to 1994 amendments. In extending the federal rule to all criminal proceedings, the Advisory Committee's note stated the following:

> The strong social policy of protecting a victim's privacy and encouraging victims to come forward to report criminal acts is not confined to cases that involve a charge of sexual assault. The need to protect the victim is equally great when a defendant is charged with kidnapping, and evidence is offered, either to prove motive or as background, that the defendant sexually assaulted the victim.

Id., subdiv. (a).

1049. *Boyle v. State*, 820 S.W.2d 122, 145-46 (Tex. Crim. App. 1989) (op. on reh'g).

1050. Federal Rule 412 was amended in 1994 to apply to all criminal proceedings involving alleged sexual misconduct, not just to sexual-assault offenses, and to all civil proceedings as well. *See* Act of Sept. 13, 1994, Pub. L. No. 103-322, Title IV, §40141(b), 108 Stat. 1919. Refer to note 1013 *supra*.

1051. Tex. R. Evid. 412(a)(1); *Alford*, 495 S.W.3d at 66.

1052. Tex. R. Evid. 412(a)(2), (b). Refer to notes 1059-1088 *infra* and accompanying text.

1053. The Austin Court of Appeals took this approach in *Cuyler v. State*, concluding that "the point of reference of Rule 412 is the date of trial, and that 'past sexual behavior' means sexual behavior that occurs before trial." 841 S.W.2d 933, 936 (Tex. App.—Austin 1992, no pet.), *disapproved on other grounds*, *Halstead v. State*, 891 S.W.2d 11 (Tex. App.—Austin 1994, no pet.) (per curiam). The *Cuyler* court held that Criminal Rule 412 governed the admission of all evidence of the complaining witness's extraneous sexual behavior including sexual behavior that occurred after the alleged offense. *Id.* at 936 & n.3. *But see Rankin v. State*, 821 S.W.2d 230, 233 (Tex. App.—Houston [14th Dist.] 1991, no pet.) (excluding, under exceptions to Rule 412, defense evidence of complainant's sexual conduct to explain medical testimony because it occurred after the date of the alleged offense; implying that rule applies only to complainant's sexual behavior before the alleged offense); *Chew v. State*, 804 S.W.2d 633, 641 n.2 (Tex. App.—San Antonio 1991, pet. ref'd) (Peeples, J., dissenting) (Rule 412 "by its express terms does not apply to evidence of subsequent sexual conduct in an aggravated kidnapping case").

The rule does not define the term "sexual behavior," but it logically should include "all activities that involve actual physical conduct, i.e. sexual intercourse and sexual contact," or activities that imply sexual intercourse or sexual contact.[1054] The rule does not, however, cover tangential nonsexual conduct that might have sexual overtones.[1055] Further, the rule covers only evidence of the past sexual behavior of the complainant; evidence of other people's past sexual behavior is excluded.[1056]

Texas courts have generally been reluctant to find evidence of prior sexual conduct to be material, much less sufficiently probative to outweigh the danger of unfair prejudicial effect.[1057] To be material, the evidence must fall within one of the five specifically enumerated sections of Rule 412(b)(2); to be admissible, the probative value of that evidence must outweigh the danger of unfair prejudice under Rule 412(b)(3).[1058]

2. Exceptions. Rule 412(b)(2) lists five specific exceptions to the general prohibition on evidence of specific instances of a victim's past sexual conduct: (1) rebuttal or explanation of scientific or medical evidence, (2) proof of the victim's consent, (3) proof of the victim's bias or motive, (4) impeachment with prior convictions, and (5) constitutionally required evidence.

(1) Rule 412(b)(2)(A): Rebuttal or explanation of scientific or medical evidence. Rule 412(b)(2)(A) permits the admission of evidence that is necessary to rebut or explain scientific or medical evidence offered by the prosecution.[1059] Originally known as the "Scottsboro rebuttal" from the famous 1930s rape trial,[1060] this exception permits the defendant to offer evidence that another person was the source of semen or the cause of the complainant's injuries.[1061] Under the language of the rule, the proffered evidence must be not only relevant but also "necessary" to explain or rebut the State's medical evidence.[1062] Thus, if the defendant admits that he had sexual intercourse with the com-

---

1054. *See* FED. R. EVID. 412 advisory committee's note to 1994 amendments, subdiv. (a).

1055. *See, e.g.,* ***Thomas v. State***, 137 S.W.3d 792, 795-96 (Tex. App.—Waco 2004, no pet.) (memo op.) (evidence that child complainant sent a boy a picture of herself in a swimsuit over the Internet is not within the meaning of "sexual behavior" under Rule 412; trial court erred in excluding evidence under that rule, and because the evidence was probative of complainant's possible motive for bringing charges against defendant, exclusion was error, although harmless).

1056. *See* TEX. R. EVID. 412(a); *see, e.g.,* ***Pierson v. State***, 398 S.W.3d 406, 414 n.6 (Tex. App.—Texarkana 2013) (Rule 412 did not apply to evidence of alleged false accusation involving sexual behavior of defendant's daughter, who was not the complainant), *aff'd*, 426 S.W.3d 763 (Tex. Crim. App. 2014).

1057. *See* ***Boyle v. State***, 820 S.W.2d 122, 148 (Tex. Crim. App. 1989) (op. on reh'g).

1058. *Id.*; ***Woods v. State***, 301 S.W.3d 327, 334 (Tex. App.—Houston [14th Dist.] 2009, no pet.); ***Delapaz v. State***, 297 S.W.3d 824, 827 (Tex. App.—Eastland 2009, no pet.); ***Hood v. State***, 944 S.W.2d 743, 745-46 (Tex. App.—Amarillo 1997, no pet.).

1059. TEX. R. EVID. 412(b)(2)(A).

1060. 23 WRIGHT & GRAHAM, *supra* note 35, §5388, at 590-91 (1980).

1061. *See* ***Allen v. State***, 700 S.W.2d 924, 929 n.4 (Tex. Crim. App. 1985); *see, e.g.,* ***Arnold v. State***, 679 S.W.2d 156, 159 (Tex. App.—Dallas 1984, pet. ref'd) (evidence of other sexual intercourse by complainant five or six days before the charged offense was not admissible to rebut evidence of vaginal tearing when an expert testified that such tears would heal within 36 hours).

1062. *See, e.g.,* ***LaPointe v. State***, 196 S.W.3d 831, 836 (Tex. App.—Austin 2006) (evidence that complainant had previously gone to the emergency room with bruises all over her body and had told medical personnel "that she had recently been diagnosed with a bipolar disorder, had been intoxicated on a daily basis for several weeks, and did

plainant but contends that it was consensual, evidence that the defendant was not the source of the semen or the cause of the injury is no longer necessary to his defense. Now the underlying purpose of the offered evidence is the improper one of showing the complainant's character. However, if the State relies on medical testimony that a young complainant's hymen was torn, had "well-healed tears," or was stretched, with the obvious implication that it was the defendant who caused these injuries, the defense must be allowed to rebut that scientific evidence with evidence that those injuries may have been caused by her prior sexual encounters, whether consensual or not.[1063]

(2) Rule 412(b)(2)(B): Victim's consent. The most frequently invoked exception is Rule 412(b)(2)(B), which admits evidence offered by the defendant of the complainant's past sexual conduct with the defendant to show that she consented to the sexual conduct.[1064] The rationale for this exception is that "[t]he probative value of the evidence flows not from an inference regarding the complainant's character, but rests instead on the nature of the specific relationship between the complainant and the defendant."[1065] The rule does not specify any time limits, but the courts have great discretion to exclude evidence of isolated or remote sexual contacts between the defen-

---

not remember recent events," and that her injuries might be related to a "sexual advance," did not show that she consented to the charged sexual assault, nor did it rebut any medical evidence offered by the State), *aff'd*, 225 S.W.3d 513 (Tex. Crim. App. 2007); *Kennedy v. State*, 184 S.W.3d 309, 313-16 (Tex. App.—Texarkana 2005, pet. ref'd) (trial court did not abuse its discretion in excluding child complainant's purported statement to friend that she had sex with "thirty-three guys," offered to explain evidence of scars on her hymen when complainant denied having made this statement; trial court also excluded friend's testimony, offered to explain medical evidence, that complainant told her that defendant had caught her with a boy as the boy was "pulling up his pants"; even if true, conduct was too vague and speculative to constitute alternative explanation for medical evidence).

1063. *See, e.g.*, *Miles v. State*, 61 S.W.3d 682, 686-87 (Tex. App.—Houston [1st Dist.] 2001, pet. ref'd) (trial court abused its discretion in prohibiting cross-examination of child sexual-abuse victim about sexual conduct with third person offered to explain hymenal tear); *Hood*, 944 S.W.2d at 746-47 (when State offered nurse's testimony that child complainant had two "well-healed tears" in hymen to prove that defendant penetrated her and defendant denied conduct, he should have been allowed to offer evidence that child had told nurse she had previously had sexual intercourse with someone other than defendant); *Reynolds v. State*, 890 S.W.2d 156, 157 (Tex. App.—Texarkana 1994, no pet.) (defendant should have been permitted to offer evidence that child complainant had had sex with three other men over a lengthy period of time to explain the State's medical evidence, which stated that "'[t]he vaginal introitus appears to be slightly stretched'"); *see also Alford v. State*, 495 S.W.3d 63, 66-67 (Tex. App.—Houston [14th Dist.] 2016, pet. ref'd) (trial court did not abuse discretion in excluding complainant's testimony about whether she was sexually active during time of alleged sexual abuse by defendant; even if testimony could be considered evidence of specific instances of sexual conduct, it did not explain how or when complainant sustained hymen tear and did not rebut specific charge). *But see Marx v. State*, 953 S.W.2d 321, 337 (Tex. App.—Austin 1997) (State offered medical evidence that child complainant's hymen had been broken, but because doctor testified that he could not tell when child had been penetrated, his testimony did not tend to corroborate child's identification of defendant as the assailant; therefore, defense testimony that child had been previously abused by an uncle was immaterial because it was not necessary to explain or rebut State's medical evidence), *aff'd*, 987 S.W.2d 577 (Tex. Crim. App. 1999).

1064. *See* TEX. R. EVID. 412(b)(2)(B). If the complainant was younger than 17 at the time of the sexual conduct that is the subject of the case, the defense cannot raise the issue of consent. *See Estes v. State*, 487 S.W.3d 737, 752 n.16 (Tex. App.—Fort Worth 2016, pet. granted 9-14-16).

1065. 1 GOODE ET AL., *supra* note 103, §412.2, at 300; *see Boyle v. State*, 820 S.W.2d 122, 149 (Tex. Crim. App. 1989) (op. on reh'g); *see, e.g.*, *Gotcher v. State*, 435 S.W.3d 367, 374-76 (Tex. App.—Texarkana 2014, no pet.) (error, though harmless, to exclude witness's testimony about observing prior sexual contact between complainant and defendant; although testimony was critical to defensive theory of consent, and its probative value outweighed prejudicial effect, court concluded that jury did not believe other defense testimony and that excluded testimony had little or no effect on jury's decision).

dant and complainant under the balancing test of Rule 412(b)(3).[1066] Although evidence of sexual conduct with the defendant is admissible under this section, evidence of prior acts with others is not.[1067]

(3) Rule 412(b)(2)(C): Victim's bias or motive. Rule 412(b)(2)(C) permits the defendant to introduce evidence of the complainant's past sexual conduct to the extent that this evidence shows bias or motive.[1068] In one controversial case, **Chew v. State**,[1069] the defendant's conviction for aggravated kidnapping[1070] resulting from a "gang rape" was reversed because the trial court refused to admit evidence that the complainant was a "nymphomaniac" who had multiple sexual encounters with various men approximately eight months after the alleged kidnapping.[1071] The defendant contended that the complainant had consented to the group sexual contacts and that she had a motive to fabricate her testimony "to hide her sexual affliction from the public as well as from her jealous husband ...."[1072] Without referring to or relying on Rule 412, the court held that the exclusion of this impeachment evidence violated the defendant's constitutional right of meaningful confrontation and cross-examination.[1073] The court's reach appears too broad and, as the dissent points out, would seemingly permit inquiry into any extraneous sexual conduct whenever the defendant asserts that the complainant has a motive to hide the "true" fact that she initiated or consented to the conduct.[1074] It is precisely this type of character assassination that Rule 412 was intended to prevent. Instead, the exception permits impeachment for bias or motive when other evidence independently demonstrates the existence of the motive or bias.[1075] For example, the independently proven fact that the complainant had an ongoing sexual relationship with a person who suspected that she had sexual intercourse with the defendant might explain the complainant's motive to accuse the defendant of rape.[1076] On the other

---

1066. Refer to notes 1094-1095 *infra* and accompanying text.

1067. *Boyle*, 820 S.W.2d at 149; *see, e.g.*, *Leger v. State*, 774 S.W.2d 99, 101 (Tex. App.—Beaumont 1989, pet. ref'd) (excluding evidence that complainant had worked as a topless dancer, had been paid for sex by others in the past, and had lived with another man outside of marriage).

1068. Tex. R. Evid. 412(b)(2)(C); *see* **Hammer v. State**, 296 S.W.3d 555, 567 (Tex. Crim. App. 2009); *see, e.g.*, **Johnson v. State**, 490 S.W.3d 895, 912-13 (Tex. Crim. App. 2016) (trial court erred in not allowing defense to ask complainant whether he was in counseling because his parents found out about his long-standing sexual abuse of his sister; defense counsel argued complainant had motive to fabricate allegations against defendant to "get attention" because he was in "bad trouble" with his parents).

1069. 804 S.W.2d 633 (Tex. App.—San Antonio 1991, pet. ref'd).

1070. *See id.* at 633 (defendant was charged with kidnapping with intent to commit sexual assault).

1071. *Id.* at 634.

1072. *Id.* at 638.

1073. *Id.* at 637.

1074. *Id.* at 645 (Peeples, J., dissenting).

1075. *See, e.g.*, **Hale v. State**, 140 S.W.3d 381, 395-96 (Tex. App.—Fort Worth 2004, pet. ref'd) (when defendant did not offer any independent evidence that child complainant or his stepbrother was biased or motivated to lie about alleged sexual assault, trial court did not abuse its discretion in excluding that testimony under Rule 412(b)(2)(C)).

1076. *See, e.g.*, **Olden v. Kentucky**, 488 U.S. 227, 231-32 (1988) (trial court improperly excluded evidence that alleged rape victim may have lied about her conduct with the defendant to protect her relationship with her boyfriend). *But see* **Stephens v. State**, 978 S.W.2d 728, 734-35 (Tex. App.—Austin 1998, pet. ref'd) (trial court properly excluded

hand, in ***Wofford v. State***, the Dallas Court of Appeals held that third-party witnesses could not testify that the complainant had a history of exchanging sex for drugs in an effort to show that the complainant had a motive to bring rape charges to retaliate for the defendant's refusal to buy her more cocaine.[1077] The court held that "[t]he proffered promiscuity testimony had no relation to her bringing 'rape' charges."[1078] If the complainant's motive was retaliation, the evidence proffered must be that of prior retaliation, not prior sexual conduct.

(4) Rule 412(b)(2)(D): Impeachment with prior convictions. Rule 412(b)(2)(D) permits evidence of sexual conduct resulting in a criminal conviction if it is admissible for impeachment purposes under Rule 609.[1079] For example, the complainant's prior prostitution conviction can be used for general credibility impeachment purposes. However, the trial court may exclude such impeachment evidence if its probative value is outweighed by the danger of unfair prejudice.[1080] Further, only criminal *convictions* for sexual conduct, not prior unadjudicated instances of sexual conduct, are admissible to impeach the complainant. Evidence of prior specific instances of sexual conduct is forbidden under Rule 608(b).[1081]

(5) Rule 412(b)(2)(E): Constitutionally required evidence. Rule 412(b)(2)(E) permits the defendant to introduce evidence of the complainant's past sexual behavior if it "is constitutionally required to be admitted."[1082] Because all of the Rules are subject to constitutional requirements, this exception is a reminder that the previously enumerated exceptions are not necessarily exclusive and ensures that the rule is not overturned as facially invalid.[1083] Despite its apparent breadth, few post-Rules Texas cases have dis-

---

evidence that teenage rape complainant was pregnant when she had sexual intercourse with defendant because defense "did not demonstrate a definite and logical link between the complainant's past sexual conduct and the alleged motive and bias under Rule 412(b)(2)(C)"; admission of this evidence "would contravene the intent of Rule 412 and subject the victim to ridicule, embarrassment, and humiliation").

1077. 903 S.W.2d 796, 800 (Tex. App.—Dallas 1995, pet. ref'd).

1078. *Id.*; *see also* ***Arriola v. State***, 969 S.W.2d 42, 43 (Tex. App.—Beaumont 1998, pet. ref'd) (defendant was attempting to establish victim's character, not specific bias or motive, in arguing that prior instances of sexual conduct were admissible to show that complainant would "seek revenge as part of her overall pattern and character" to lie; evidence was inadmissible).

1079. TEX. R. EVID. 412(b)(2)(D). Rule 609 permits impeachment with a final conviction of a felony or a crime involving moral turpitude if the probative value of the conviction outweighs its prejudicial effect. TEX. R. EVID. 609(a). Refer to *Article VI: Witnesses*, *infra* p. 615.

1080. *See* TEX. R. EVID. 412(b)(3), 609(a)(2).

1081. *See, e.g.*, ***Wofford***, 903 S.W.2d at 799-800 (testimony that sexual-assault complainant had allegedly traded sex for drugs on specific occasions with specific people, offered to impeach her denial of that conduct, was barred under Criminal Rule 608(b); "[a] party may not inquire into, nor prove by extrinsic evidence, specific instances of a witness's misconduct to attack a witness's credibility"). In ***Wofford***, the court concluded that the complainant's denial, on cross-examination by the defense, that she had exchanged sex for drugs, also did not "open the door" to this impeachment evidence. *Id.* at 800. A party cannot open the door for himself to walk through. Refer to *Article VI: Witnesses*, *infra* p. 608.

1082. TEX. R. EVID. 412(b)(2)(E).

1083. 1 GOODE ET AL., *supra* note 103, §412.2, at 301-02; *see, e.g.*, ***Allen v. State***, 700 S.W.2d 924, 932 (Tex. Crim. App. 1985) (rejecting defendant's claim that a prior rape-shield statute was unconstitutional on its face and as applied).

cussed the admission of evidence of the complainant's past sexual behavior under this exception.[1084]

There are no other bases for admitting evidence of the complainant's prior sexual conduct under Rule 412.[1085] However, the rule does not logically apply to evidence of the complainant's prior accusations against others for committing the charged act. For example, in **Kesterson v. State**, the court of appeals held that the defendant was constitutionally entitled to cross-examine the State's psychologist with the fact that during the child complainant's interview with that expert, she had accused another male relative of sexually abusing her.[1086] The court assumed that Rule 412 applied to evidence of this accusation that another person, not the defendant, had molested her, and held that the exclusion of the evidence violated the defendant's constitutional right of cross-examination.[1087] But it is doubtful whether Rule 412 applies in this situation because the rule bars evidence only of the complainant's "past sexual behavior." It does not bar evidence of the complainant's past statements about the sexual behavior that is the subject of the prosecution. Rule 412 would, however, bar evidence that a child complainant had also been molested by another person on a different occasion, unless the defendant can "establish that the prior acts clearly occurred and that the acts so closely resembled those of the present case that they could explain the victim's knowledge about the sexual matters in question."[1088]

1084. *See, e.g.*, **Johnson v. State**, 490 S.W.3d 895, 910-11 (Tex. Crim. App. 2016) (trial court should have allowed defendant to cross-examine complainant about complainant's sexual abuse of his sister as evidence of complainant's bias or motive to accuse defendant; restriction on cross-examination violated Confrontation Clause when record did not indicate that trial court excluded this evidence because court was concerned about harassment, prejudice, confusion of issues, witness safety, or repetitive questions); **Estes v. State**, 487 S.W.3d 737, 753-54 (Tex. App.—Fort Worth 2016, pet. granted 9-14-16) (trial court properly excluded evidence of complainant's sexual history and did not violate defendant's right of confrontation; defendant did not show that complainant's sexual history so closely resembled acts in question that it could be an alternative source of complainant's sexual knowledge); **Wheeler v. State**, 79 S.W.3d 78, 85-88 (Tex. App.—Beaumont 2002, no pet.) (trial court properly excluded evidence that complainant had told her mother shortly before trial that an older stepbrother had sexually abused her before the defendant had but had told child-victim advocate that no one else had ever touched her or molested her; this evidence was attempt at general impeachment and not constitutionally required); **Kesterson v. State**, 997 S.W.2d 290, 295-96 (Tex. App.—Dallas 1999, no pet.) (defendant was constitutionally entitled to cross-examine State's psychologist on fact that five-year-old complainant, who had a borderline IQ, had told psychologist that a different man had molested her); **Chew v. State**, 804 S.W.2d 633, 638 (Tex. App.—San Antonio 1991, pet. ref'd) (defendant was constitutionally entitled to present evidence of complainant's alleged nymphomania and extraneous sexual conduct with others after the charged kidnapping and sexual assault).

1085. *See, e.g.*, **Draheim v. State**, 916 S.W.2d 593, 599 (Tex. App.—San Antonio 1996, pet. ref'd) (defendant was not entitled to offer evidence of other sexual offenses committed against child complainant by other perpetrators because Rule 412 does not apply to a complainant's nonconsensual sexual behavior and because the evidence was inadmissible under other rules of evidence).

1086. 997 S.W.2d at 295-96.

1087. *Id.*

1088. **Matz v. State**, 989 S.W.2d 419, 422-23 (Tex. App.—Fort Worth 1999), *rev'd on other grounds*, 14 S.W.3d 746 (Tex. Crim. App. 2000); *see* **Estes**, 487 S.W.3d at 753-54. In **Matz**, the court of appeals noted that "[a] number of states have held that the United States Constitution compels the admission of evidence to show an alternative basis for a child victim's knowledge of sexual matters." 989 S.W.2d at 422. In this case, the defense offered evidence, outside the presence of the jury, that the complainant said Adam, the 12-year-old son of her father's fiancée, also sexually abused her, but her vague descriptions of this abuse were not at all similar to the conduct she stated the defendant performed. *Id.* at 422-23. Thus, the evidence of Adam's conduct would not have explained her familiarity with

RULE 412

C. Procedural Requirements

Rule 412 sets forth specific procedural requirements that the defendant must meet before he is entitled to introduce evidence of the complainant's past sexual behavior under Rule 412(b). First, the defendant must inform the court, outside the jury's presence, that he intends to offer such evidence.[1089] Failure to give such notice may result in the exclusion of the proffered evidence.[1090] Second, the trial court will conduct an in camera hearing, recorded by a court reporter, to decide whether the evidence is admissible under the Rule 412(b) exceptions.[1091] The court shall decide what, if any, evidence is admissible and inform the parties of its ruling and the limits of the permissible questioning. The defendant may not go beyond those stated limits without prior approval from the judge outside the presence of the jury.[1092] Third, under Rule 412(d), the trial court will seal the record of the in camera hearing for delivery to the appellate court if the defendant is convicted and appeals.[1093] Fourth, the trial court must balance the probative value of the evidence against the risk of unfair prejudice to the State and, more importantly, to the complainant, the person for whose benefit the rule was

---

sexual matters and was properly barred by Rule 412. *Id.* at 423; *see also* **Hale v. State**, 140 S.W.3d 381, 395-97 (Tex. App.—Fort Worth 2004, pet. ref'd) (defendant did not establish that the alleged prior sexual acts between child complainant and his stepbrother clearly occurred or that those acts so closely resembled the acts alleged against defendant that they could explain the complainant's knowledge about the sexual matters in question; trial court did not abuse its discretion in excluding evidence).

1089. TEX. R. EVID. 412(c).

1090. *See* **Golden v. State**, 762 S.W.2d 630, 632 (Tex. App.—Texarkana 1988, pet. ref'd) (notice of intent to offer testimony about past sexual conduct is a threshold requirement); *see, e.g.,* **Marx v. State**, 953 S.W.2d 321, 337 (Tex. App.—Austin 1997) (when defendant did not request in camera hearing and did not inform court of his intention to inquire into prior sexual encounter, his complaint about its exclusion was waived on appeal), *aff'd*, 987 S.W.2d 577 (Tex. Crim. App. 1999); **Wofford v. State**, 903 S.W.2d 796, 798-99 (Tex. App.—Dallas 1995, pet. ref'd) (trial court erred in allowing defendant to offer evidence about complainant's sexual history in open court, but error harmed complainant, not defendant).

1091. TEX. R. EVID. 412(c). The rule does not specify whether the defendant or his attorney is entitled to be present during this in camera hearing. The court of criminal appeals has held that because a Rule 412 hearing is adversarial, all parties are entitled to be present, and the prosecutor and defense counsel are entitled to question witnesses and present evidence. **LaPointe v. State**, 225 S.W.3d 513, 523-24 (Tex. Crim. App. 2007). *But see* **Miles v. State**, 61 S.W.3d 682, 685 (Tex. App.—Houston [1st Dist.] 2001, pet. ref'd) (court noted that trial court held hearing outside the presence of both prosecutor and defense counsel).

1092. TEX. R. EVID. 412(c).

1093. *See* TEX. R. EVID. 412(d); **Estes**, 487 S.W.3d at 752 n.15. Texas courts of appeals disagree about whether the defendant is entitled to review the sealed record from a Rule 412 in camera hearing to determine what complaints to raise on appeal. *Compare* **Ukwuachu v. State**, 494 S.W.3d 733, 734 (Tex. App.—Waco 2016, order) (per curiam) (court granted defendant's motion to unseal court records for his appellate counsel for limited purpose of determining meritorious issues on appeal; attorney could review record multiple times as necessary in clerk's office but could not make copies), *and* **Robisheaux v. State**, 509 S.W.3d 448, 450 (Tex. App.—Austin 2015, order) (per curiam) (court granted defendant's motion to unseal court record only for his attorneys for purpose of preparing appeal), *with* **Kesterson v. State**, 959 S.W.2d 247, 248 (Tex. App.—Dallas 1997, order) (if court "were now to unseal the record of the in camera hearing for appellant's use, we would be making public the very information subsections (c) and (d) of [Criminal Rule] 412 are intended to keep private. Such action would defeat the purpose of the rule from the standpoint of the complainant."). Federal Rule 412 requires that the motions, the related materials, and the record of the hearing remain sealed unless the court orders otherwise. FED. R. EVID. 412(c)(2). However, without access to the in camera testimony, the defendant may be caught in an appellate "catch-22." He cannot complain on appeal about the exclusion of evidence if he does not know what that evidence is.

RULE 412

drafted.[1094] Unlike the general Rule 403 balance that tips toward admissibility, under Rule 412, the defendant must show that the probative value of the evidence outweighs its unfairly prejudicial effect.[1095]

NOTE ON FEDERAL RULES 413-415

Congress enacted Federal Rules of Evidence 413 through 415 as part of the Violent Crime Control and Law Enforcement Act of 1994.[1096] Rules 413 and 414 permit the government to introduce evidence of a defendant's prior sexual misconduct to be "considered on any matter to which it is relevant" in sexual-assault or child-molestation cases.[1097] Federal Rule 413 deals with the admission of evidence in any sexual-assault prosecution, while Rule 414 deals solely with child-molestation prosecutions. Federal Rule 415 makes Rules 413 and 414 applicable to civil actions. Although Rule 404 generally prohibits evidence of a defendant's prior bad acts offered to prove conduct in conformity with a character trait or the propensity to commit a crime, these rules permit the introduction of evidence of prior sexual misconduct to prove that the defendant has a propensity to commit acts of sexual misconduct and is therefore more likely to have committed the charged offense.[1098]

Under Federal Rule 413 or 414, the prosecutor must show that (1) the defendant is accused of an offense involving sexual assault or child molestation, (2) the offered evidence relates to the accused's commission of another sexual assault or child molestation, and (3) the evidence is relevant.[1099] The same predicate applies to evidence offered in a civil proceeding under Federal Rule 415.[1100] The prior acts do not need to have re-

---

1094. *See, e.g.*, *Allen v. State*, 700 S.W.2d 924, 929-30 (Tex. Crim. App. 1985) (even if evidence that complainant was not a virgin were relevant and material to an issue, its inflammatory or prejudicial nature certainly outweighed its probative value); *Marx*, 953 S.W.2d at 337 (trial court "felt that the unfair prejudice suffered by [complainant] if forced to testify concerning the prior incident outweighed the probative value of the testimony").

1095. *Compare* Tex. R. Evid. 403 ("The court may exclude relevant evidence if its probative value is substantially outweighed by a danger of one or more of the following: unfair prejudice, confusing the issues, misleading the jury, undue delay, or needlessly presenting cumulative evidence."), *with* Tex. R. Evid. 412(b)(3) ("Evidence of specific instances of a victim's past sexual behavior is admissible if ... the probative value of the evidence outweighs the danger of unfair prejudice.").

1096. Pub. L. No. 103-322, 108 Stat. 1796 (1994). For a history of the legislative enactment process, see 23 Wright & Graham, *supra* note 35, §5411 (Supp. 2008).

1097. Fed. R. Evid. 413, 414.

1098. *See* *United States v. Tyndall*, 263 F.3d 848, 850 (8th Cir. 2001) ("Although Federal Rule of Evidence 404(b) generally excludes the admission of evidence of other crimes to show the propensity to commit a particular crime, Congress excepted sexual assault cases from this rule when it enacted Federal Rule of Evidence 413."); *United States v. Meacham*, 115 F.3d 1488, 1491 (10th Cir. 1997) (Rule 414 supersedes the general restrictions of Rule 404(b) in child-molestation cases).

1099. Fed. R. Evid. 413(a), 414(a); *United States v. Guardia*, 135 F.3d 1326, 1328 (10th Cir. 1998). Propensity evidence is, by its very nature, relevant in a criminal prosecution. "A defendant with a propensity to commit acts similar to the charged crime is more likely to have committed the charged crime than another. Evidence of such a propensity is therefore relevant." *Guardia*, 135 F.3d at 1328.

1100. Fed. R. Evid. 415(a); *see, e.g.*, *Johnson v. Elk Lake Sch. Dist.*, 283 F.3d 138, 151 (3d Cir. 2002) (applying Rule 415 but upholding trial court's decision to exclude propensity evidence in student's lawsuit against counselor, school district, and administrators for counselor's sexual misconduct); *Doe v. Glanzer*, 232 F.3d 1258, 1268 (9th Cir. 2000) (applying Rule 415 to civil action by minor plaintiff against her grandfather for committing acts of sexual

RULE 412

sulted in a conviction before they may be admitted under these three rules.[1101] The extraneous acts offered under the rules may have occurred either before or after the charged offense.[1102] The standard for admitting such evidence is that set out in *Huddleston v. United States*[1103]—whether the jury could believe, by a preponderance of the evidence, that the misconduct occurred.[1104] The rules also require the proponent of the "other-acts" evidence to give the opponent timely notice of its intent to offer such evidence, and failure to give such notice may result in exclusion of the evidence.[1105]

These rules have not found favor with most federal courts or commentators because they contravene the traditional ban on the use of bad-character evidence to prove conduct in conformity with that character trait.[1106] According to the Rules Committee Support Office of the Administrative Office of the United States Courts, 100 individuals

---

molestation on her); *Frank v. Cty. of Hudson*, 924 F. Supp. 620, 625-26 (D.N.J. 1996) (applying Rule 415; evidence of prior similar assaultive behavior was admissible and relevant, but its "probative value stacks up weakly against [its] large potential for unfair prejudice," so evidence would fail Rule 403 balancing test).

1101. *See United States v. Guidry*, 456 F.3d 493, 502 (5th Cir. 2006) (Rule 413 "provides no basis for limiting admissibility of evidence of the act of doing or perpetrating other sexual offenses only to those acts proven by conviction"); *Meacham*, 115 F.3d at 1493 ("Evidence of offenses for which the defendant has not previously been prosecuted or convicted will be admissible, as well as evidence of prior convictions."). The legislative history of Rules 413-415 indicates that Congress intended to allow admission not only of prior convictions for sexual offenses, but also of uncharged conduct. *See* 140 CONG. REC. 23,603 (1994) (Statement of Rep. Molinari) ("The practical effect of the new rules is to put evidence of uncharged offenses in sexual assault and child molestation cases on the same footing as other types of relevant evidence that are not subject to a special exclusionary rule."). Some state cases have admitted evidence of acts of sexual misconduct for which the defendant has been acquitted, though refusing to inform the jury of the prior acquittal may be error. *See, e.g.*, *Hess v. State*, 20 P.3d 1121, 1128-29 (Alaska 2001) (upholding admission of evidence of defendant's prior sexual assault, but "it was error not to inform the jury of [defendant's] acquittal"); *People v. Mullens*, 14 Cal. Rptr. 3d 534, 549-50 (Cal. Ct. App. 2004) (error to exclude evidence that defendant had been acquitted of other sexual-molestation charges that were admitted to show his propensity for such acts).

1102. *See United States v. Sioux*, 362 F.3d 1241, 1245 (9th Cir. 2004) (language and logic of the rules apply to post-offense as well as pre-offense conduct: there is "little doubt that the plain language of the rule permits admission of subsequent acts evidence to the same extent it permits the introduction of evidence tending to demonstrate prior acts of sexual misconduct").

1103. 485 U.S. 681, 690 (1988).

1104. *Id.*; *Guidry*, 456 F.3d at 503 n.5; *United States v. Enjady*, 134 F.3d 1427, 1433 (10th Cir. 1998).

1105. *See* FED. R. EVID. 413(b), 414(b), 415(b).

1106. *See* Aviva Orenstein, *Deviance, Due Process, and the False Promise of Federal Rule of Evidence 403*, 90 CORNELL L. REV. 1487, 1492 (2005) ("Many judges, lawyers, and law professors have expressed serious and well-founded reservations about Rules 413 and 414."); Paul R. Rice, *The Evidence Project: Proposed Revisions to the Federal Rules of Evidence*, 171 F.R.D. 330, 346 (1997) ("The new character evidence rules, Current Rules 413-15, are without precedent. They were enacted over the express disapproval of the Federal Rules of Evidence Advisory Committee, without empirical evidence of the enhanced reliability of this type of character evidence over other similar character evidence for which no specific rules have been enacted, and without demonstrated need in light of existing rules and practices."). *See generally* Judicial Conference of the United States, Report of the Judicial Conference on the Admission of Character Evidence in Certain Sexual Misconduct Cases, 159 F.R.D. 51 (1995) (setting out a strongly negative response to Rules 413-415 as enacted and urging Congress to reject the changes or, at a minimum, consider an alternative draft that would clarify ambiguities and eliminate possible constitutional infirmities in the Rules); *Perspectives on Proposed Federal Rules of Evidence 413-415; American Bar Association Criminal Justice Section Report to the House of Delegates*, 22 FORDHAM URB. L.J. 343 (1994-1995) [hereinafter ABA Report] (publishing report written by Myrna S. Raeder in support of the American Bar Association House of Delegates resolution reading, "Resolved, that the American Bar Association opposes the substance of Rules 413, 414, and 415 of the Federal Rules of Evidence concerning the admission of evidence in sexual assault and child molestation cases, as enacted by the Violent Crime Control and Law Enforcement Act of 1994, Pub. L. No. 103-322, 108 Stat. 1796 (1994)").

and organizations opposed the rules during the public-comment period, while only ten supported them.[1107] "Opponents included 11 lawyers, 56 evidence professors, 19 judges, and 12 organizations, among others."[1108] These commentators noted that "existing caselaw in state and federal courts generously interprets Rule 404(b) to permit evidence of the defendant's prior bad acts in sex crimes cases so long as any nexus exists to a purpose other than propensity."[1109]

One congressional Representative set out the rationale for these rules:

> The past conduct of a person with a history of rape or child molestation provides evidence that he or she has the combination of aggressive and sexual impulses that motivates the commission of such crimes and lacks the inhibitions against acting on these impulses. A charge of rape or child molestation has greater plausibility against such a person.[1110]

The policy problem posed by Federal Rules 413 through 415 is whether character evidence relating to the trait for sexual misconduct really is more predictive of future conduct than character evidence relating to other types of crimes, such as theft or murder.[1111] If it is not, then these rules cannot logically be justified as an appropriate departure from the traditional policy of Rule 404(b).[1112]

The primary argument against these rules is that they impinge on the constitutional doctrine of the presumption of innocence by forcing the accused to defend not only against the charged offense but also against any and all prior allegations of sexual misconduct.[1113] Further, Federal Rules 413 through 415 may "become the first volley

---

1107. ABA Report, *supra* note 1106, at 345.

1108. *Id.*

1109. *Id.* at 348.

1110. 140 CONG. REC. H7,817 (Apr. 19, 1994) (statement of Rep. Molinari).

1111. ABA Report, *supra* note 1106, at 350-51 ("[I]f propensity is allowed for sex crimes, how is this to be distinguished from using propensity in other cases, except for the outrage which is understandably directed at the commission of sexual crimes? While sexual offenses are often hard to prove, so are drug conspiracies and other categories of crimes.").

1112. The logic underlying Rules 413 through 415 relies on three related arguments: (1) because women and children are sometimes perceived as less credible than other witnesses, the rules address this "credibility gap" and affirm the accuser's credibility by allowing evidence that others have been subjected to the same treatment, (2) because sex offenders are especially likely to be recidivists, prior acts of misconduct are highly probative of the likelihood that the defendant committed the charged crime, and (3) because predatory sexual propensities and aggressiveness are "unique," the probative value of prior sexual misconduct is high. Orenstein, *supra* note 1106, at 1498-99. The rules also have a practical justification. *See id.* at 1500 ("Rape and child molestation are notoriously hard to prove because the crimes often occur in secret, under circumstances with no witnesses and little physical evidence …."). Finally, there is some historical support in the law of evidence supporting these rules: the common-law doctrine of "lustful disposition" was an acknowledged exception to the bar against propensity evidence now codified in Federal Rule 404. *Id.* at 1502.

1113. *See* Mark A. Sheft, *Federal Rule of Evidence 413: A Dangerous New Frontier*, 33 AM. CRIM. L. REV. 57, 82 (1995) ("Rule 413 erodes the presumption of innocence in violation of the Fifth Amendment's Due Process Clause."); Margaret C. Livnah, Comment, *Branding the Sexual Predator: Constitutional Ramifications of Federal Rules of Evidence 413 Through 415*, 44 CLEV. ST. L. REV. 169, 181 (1996) ("The risk of due process violation is increased by the potential that a jury will be prejudiced by explicit reference to prior bad sexual acts.").

RULE 412

in a larger attempt to reject the ban against character evidence."[1114] Finally, opponents of the rules note that there is very little empirical evidence to support the arguments in favor of their adoption.[1115]

Nonetheless, federal courts have generally upheld the admission of evidence offered under these rules as long as the trial judge conscientiously balanced its probative value against the risks of unfair prejudice, misleading the jury, and confusing the issues under Federal Rule 403.[1116] The application of Rule 403 has allowed federal courts to uphold the constitutionality of these rules.[1117]

Although Texas has not adopted Rules 413 through 415, the Texas Legislature enacted Code of Criminal Procedure article 38.37, which is analogous to Federal Rule 414. Article 38.37, section 1, allows for the admission of prior acts of misconduct (e.g., sexual molestation and assaultive acts) against the same child complainant when offered on a "relevant" matter, including the defendant's or complainant's state of mind

---

1114. ABA Report, *supra* note 1106, at 351.

1115. *See id.* at 349-50 (there is scant empirical evidence supporting a conclusion that recidivism rate for sex offenders is higher than for other categories of crimes; "[r]ules permitting propensity evidence are particularly inadvisable in light of developing scientific evidence which has consistently demonstrated the high percentage of mistaken identifications in cases where the assailant's identity is at issue"); James Joseph Duane, *The New Federal Rules of Evidence on Prior Acts of Accused Sex Offenders: A Poorly Drafted Version of a Very Bad Idea*, 157 F.R.D. 95, 125-26 (1994) (rules are largely unnecessary, carry serious and potentially constitutional dangers, and rest on "dubious and unsupported assumptions about recidivism and other variables, most of which assumptions are called into serious question by the best available data").

1116. *See Martinez v. Cui*, 608 F.3d 54, 60-61 (1st Cir. 2010) ("[D]istrict courts must apply Rule 403 with awareness that Rule 415 reflects a congressional judgment to remove the propensity bar to admissibility of certain evidence. That awareness includes the fact that the Rule 403 analysis also applies."); *United States v. Benais*, 460 F.3d 1059, 1063 (8th Cir. 2006) ("We have stated that evidence found admissible under Rule 413 or its close analog, Rule 414 ('Evidence of Similar Crimes in Child Molestation Cases'), may still be subject to exclusion under Rule 403 if its probative value is substantially outweighed by the danger of unfair prejudice."); *Seeley v. Chase*, 443 F.3d 1290, 1294-95 (10th Cir. 2006) (courts must apply Rule 403 to evidence offered under Rule 413 or Rule 414); *United States v. LeMay*, 260 F.3d 1018, 1026-27 (9th Cir. 2001) (applying Rule 403 to evidence offered under Rule 414); *see, e.g., United States v. Lewis*, 796 F.3d 543, 547-48 (5th Cir. 2015) (evidence offered under Rule 413 is still subject to Rule 403 analysis; high probative value of evidence that defendant had committed other sexual assaults against minors was not substantially outweighed by danger of unfair prejudice).

1117. *See LeMay*, 260 F.3d at 1027 ("We therefore conclude that as long as the protections of Rule 403 remain in place so that district judges retain the authority to exclude potentially devastating evidence, Rule 414 is constitutional."); *United States v. Mound*, 149 F.3d 799, 800-01 (8th Cir. 1998) (Rule 413 passes constitutional muster if Rule 403 protections remain in place); *United States v. Enjady*, 134 F.3d 1427, 1432-33 (10th Cir. 1998) ("[W]ithout the safeguards embodied in Rule 403 we would hold [Rule 413] unconstitutional."). Circuit courts disagree on how a district court should conduct the Rule 403 balancing test for evidence offered under Rule 414. *Compare United States v. Kelly*, 510 F.3d 433, 437 (4th Cir. 2007) ("In applying the Rule 403 balancing test to prior offenses admissible under Rule 414, a district court should consider a number of factors, including (i) the similarity between the previous offense and the charged crime, (ii) the temporal proximity between the two crimes, (iii) the frequency of the prior acts, (iv) the presence or absence of any intervening acts, and (v) the reliability of the evidence of the past offense."), *and LeMay*, 260 F.3d at 1027-28 (articulating same factors), *with United States v. Majeroni*, 784 F.3d 72, 76 (1st Cir. 2015) ("In exercising their broad discretion under Rule 403, trial judges have a feel for the evidence and the courtroom that is difficult to replicate on the pages of a transcript, so our deference to judgment calls of this type is great. In challenges to inherently prejudicial Rule 414 evidence, we are also mindful that Rule 403 only guards against unfair prejudice. Finally, we employ no heightened or special test for evaluating the admission of Rule 414 evidence under Rule 403.").

or the relationship between the two.[1118] Article 38.37, section 2, allows for the admission of evidence of separate offenses—not against the same complainant—for a more restricted list of prior acts of misconduct (e.g., online solicitation of a minor, possession or promotion of child pornography) when offered on a "relevant" matter, including the defendant's character and acts performed in conformity with that character.[1119] Article 38.37, section 3, contains a notice provision similar to those in Federal Rules 413 through 415.[1120]

Article 38.37 "trumps" Rules 404 and 405,[1121] but it does not trump Rule 403.[1122] Texas courts, like federal courts, have held that the statute allowing admission of extraneous acts of misconduct for any relevant purpose, including bad character, is constitutional because Rule 403 is a brake on the admission of unfairly prejudicial or misleading evidence.[1123]

1118. *See* Tex. Code Crim. Proc. art. 38.37, §1(b).

1119. Tex. Code Crim. Proc. art. 38.37, §2; *see Fisk v. State*, 510 S.W.3d 165, 172 (Tex. App.—San Antonio 2016, no pet.); *Alvarez v. State*, 491 S.W.3d 362, 367 (Tex. App.—Houston [1st Dist.] 2016, pet. ref'd). Article 38.37, §2, became effective September 1, 2013. Acts 2013, 83rd Leg., R.S., ch. 387, §3, eff. Sept. 1, 2013. The statute applies to the admissibility of evidence in any criminal proceeding commenced on or after September 1, 2013. *Id.* §2; *see Bezerra v. State*, 485 S.W.3d 133, 138-39 (Tex. App.—Amarillo 2016, pet. ref'd) (interpreting "criminal proceeding" to mean any proceeding of criminal prosecution, including trial), *cert. denied*, 137 S. Ct. 495 (2016); *Belcher v. State*, 474 S.W.3d 840, 849 (Tex. App.—Tyler 2015, no pet.) (same); *Fahrni v. State*, 473 S.W.3d 486, 494-96 (Tex. App.—Texarkana 2015, pet. ref'd) (interpreting "criminal proceeding" to mean trial or one of the phases of trial).

1120. *See* Tex. Code Crim. Proc. art. 38.37, §3 (State must notify defendant of intent to use evidence under §1 or 2 at least 30 days before trial); Fed. R. Evid. 413(b) (notice must be given at least 15 days before trial, unless court grants extension for good cause), Fed. R. Evid. 414(b) (same), Fed. R. Evid. 415(b) (same).

1121. Tex. Code Crim. Proc. art. 38.37, §§1(b), 2(b); *see Carmichael v. State*, 505 S.W.3d 95, 102 (Tex. App.—San Antonio 2016, pet. ref'd) (article 38.37 creates exception to Rule 404(b) for certain cases, including continuous sexual abuse of child); *Alvarez*, 491 S.W.3d at 367 (special circumstances of sexual assault of child outweigh usual concerns about extraneous-offense evidence); *Hinds v. State*, 970 S.W.2d 33, 35 (Tex. App.—Dallas 1998, no pet.) ("By enacting article 38.37, the legislature in effect determined that, in certain sexual abuse cases, evidence of 'other crimes, wrongs, or acts' committed by the accused against the child victim *are* relevant and admissible under rule 402.").

1122. *See Fisk*, 510 S.W.3d at 172 (evidence admissible under art. 38.37 is still subject to exclusion under Rule 403); *Bezerra*, 485 S.W.3d at 140 (evidence admissible under art. 38.37, §2, is still subject to Rule 403); *Belcher*, 474 S.W.3d at 847 (before evidence is admitted under art. 38.37, trial court must still conduct Rule 403 balancing test on proper objection or request); *Bradshaw v. State*, 466 S.W.3d 875, 880-81 (Tex. App.—Texarkana 2015, pet. ref'd) (although art. 38.37 "specifically provides that Rules 404 and 405 ... do not render inadmissible evidence of certain separate offenses described therein, it makes no such exception for Rule 403").

1123. *See Buxton v. State*, ___ S.W.3d ___ (Tex. App.—Houston [1st Dist.] 2017, n.p.h.) (No. 01-15-00857-CR; 7-6-17) (op. on reh'g) (article 38.37, §2(b), does not lessen presumption of innocence or State's burden of proof and thus does not violate due process); *Harris v. State*, 475 S.W.3d 395, 402 (Tex. App.—Houston [14th Dist.] 2015, pet. ref'd) (article 38.37 has sufficient procedural safeguards that it does not violate defendant's due-process rights; before evidence is admitted, trial court must conduct hearing outside jury's presence to determine if the evidence will be adequate to support jury finding that defendant committed the separate offense beyond a reasonable doubt, defense counsel can cross-examine any witness, and State must give notice of its intent to use this evidence at least 30 days before trial); *Jenkins v. State*, 993 S.W.2d 133, 136 (Tex. App.—Tyler 1999, pet. ref'd) (article 38.37 does not violate a defendant's due-process rights because (1) other acts of misconduct offered under the statute may explain the charged act, (2) special circumstances surrounding the sexual assault of a child outweigh normal concerns associated with this evidence, and (3) fairness is preserved by a defendant's right to cross-examination); *see also* Tex. Code Crim. Proc. art. 38.37, §2-a (before evidence offered under art. 38.37 can be introduced, trial judge must determine that evidence likely to be admitted at trial will be adequate to support jury finding that defendant committed the separate offense beyond a reasonable doubt and must conduct hearing outside jury's presence for that purpose).

Article 38.37 is both broader and more limited than Federal Rules 413 through 415. It is broader because under section 1, for example, it allows for the admission of prior acts of assaultive misconduct when a defendant is charged with a crime involving physical abuse, as well as instances of sexual misconduct when a defendant is charged with a crime involving sexual molestation, human trafficking, or compelling prostitution.[1124] It is narrower than the corresponding federal rules because it applies only when the defendant is charged with a crime against a person younger than 17 years old.[1125] It does not apply when the defendant is charged with a sexual offense against an adult, nor does it apply in civil proceedings. Thus, article 38.37 is more targeted than the corresponding federal rules. It furthers the public policy concerns expressed by Congress in enacting Federal Rules 413 through 415 without unduly trampling on the defendant's rights or starting down the slippery slope of entirely abrogating the Rule 404 ban on propensity evidence.

1124. *See* TEX. CODE CRIM. PROC. art. 38.37, §1.
1125. *See id.* §§1(a), 2(a).

RULE 412

ARTICLE V: PRIVILEGES

Unlike almost all other rules of evidence, rules of privilege suppress relevant and sometimes vital evidence. They acknowledge that other societal values such as privacy,[1] the desire to encourage effective medical care[2] or legal counsel,[3] and governmental efficiency[4] sometimes take precedence over the goal of discovering the truth in legal proceedings.[5] Underlying most privileges is the belief that, in some contexts, unrestricted communication without any fear of disclosure furthers important public interests.[6] However, because "privileges contravene the fundamental principle that 'the public ... has a right to every man's evidence,'"[7] courts should recognize them only when parties make a convincing showing that society strongly values the protected interest and that a rule of privilege is necessary to foster that interest.[8] Federal courts are cautious about recognizing new evidentiary privileges under Federal Rule 501,[9] and Article V of the Texas Rules of Evidence reflects this approach.[10]

---

1. Refer to notes 69-73, 362-365, 626-629 *infra* and accompanying text.

2. *See Trammel v. United States*, 445 U.S. 40, 51 (1980) (physician's disclosure of patient's statements would impair diagnosis and treatment because it would inhibit patient from speaking freely to physician).

3. *See Wood v. McCown*, 784 S.W.2d 126, 128 n.2 (Tex. App.—Austin 1990, orig. proceeding) (attorney-client privilege attempts to "foster communication by creating a private zone in which clients and lawyers are permitted to talk outside the scrutiny of others rather than risk impairment of the attorney-client relationship").

4. Refer to notes 51-54 *infra* and accompanying text.

5. *See Developments in the Law—Privileged Communications*, 98 HARV. L. REV. 1450, 1454 (1985) (discussing the traditional theories of privileges). The desire to promote interests other than accuracy in adjudication also explains why evidence of subsequent remedial measures, compromise and offers to compromise, payment of medical and similar expenses, pleas and plea discussions, and related statements is not admissible. *See* TEX. R. EVID. 407-410. Refer to *Article IV: Relevance & Its Limits, supra* p. 305.

6. *See* 8 JOHN H. WIGMORE, EVIDENCE IN TRIALS AT COMMON LAW §2285, at 527 (McNaughton rev. 1961) (one of the necessary conditions for establishing a privilege is that "[t]he *injury* that would inure to the relation by the disclosure of the communications must be *greater than the benefit* thereby gained for the correct disposal of litigation").

7. *Trammel*, 445 U.S. at 50 (quoting *United States v. Bryan*, 339 U.S. 323, 331 (1950)).

8. *See* 8 WIGMORE, *supra* note 6, §2285, at 527; *see also* *United States v. Nixon*, 418 U.S. 683, 710 (1974) (privileges "are not lightly created nor expansively construed, for they are in derogation of the search for truth").

9. *See Nixon*, 418 U.S. at 710 n.18 ("Because of the key role of the testimony of witnesses in the judicial process, courts have historically been cautious about privileges."); *see, e.g.*, *Univ. of Pa. v. EEOC*, 493 U.S. 182, 189 (1990) (declining to recognize privilege under Federal Rule 501 for peer-review materials contained in tenure files).

10. *See* Donald B. McFall & Caroline B. Little, *Privileges Under Texas Law: A Dying Breed?*, 31 S. TEX. L. REV. 471, 507 (1990) (in Texas, "there is a perception both by the courts and by lawmakers that privileges should be strictly confined within the narrowest possible limits consistent with their applicability"); *cf.* Thomas G. Krattenmaker, *Testimonial Privileges in Federal Courts: An Alternative to the Proposed Federal Rules of Evidence*, 62 GEO. L.J. 61, 85 (1973) ("Perhaps the majority of evidence experts share the Advisory Committee's apparent perspective that testimonial privileges are mere bothersome exclusionary rules, born of competing professional jealousies, that impede the accuracy of fact finding and serve no other important societal goals."). When adopted, the Rules neither created new privileges nor expanded any previously existing privileges. *See* Linda L. Addison, *Evidence*, 40 Sw. L.J. 459, 467 (1986) (Article V of the Rules of Evidence does not create any new privileges).

As part of the changes considered for the 1998 unification of the Civil and Criminal Rules, the Supreme Court Advisory Committee rejected a proposal by a majority of the members of the Administration of the Rules of Evidence Committee that had approved the adoption of a "self-critical analysis" privilege. *See* Mark K. Sales, *The 1998 Texas Rules of Evidence: Changes Made and Changes Rejected*, STATE BAR OF TEXAS PDP 13-16 (1998). The general rule of privilege for proposed Rule 514 (Self-Critical Analysis Privilege) read as follows:

(b) **General Rule of Privilege.** An organization has the privilege to refuse to disclose and to prevent any other person from disclosing information resulting from a self-critical analysis if (1) the self-critical analysis was

---

RULE 501
PRIVILEGES IN GENERAL

Unless a Constitution, a statute, or these or other rules prescribed under statutory authority provide otherwise, no person has a privilege to:

(a) refuse to be a witness;

(b) refuse to disclose any matter;

(c) refuse to produce any object or writing; or

(d) prevent another from being a witness, disclosing any matter, or producing any object or writing.

COMMENTARY ON RULE 501

Rule 501 provides that only those privileges codified in Article V or otherwise provided by constitution, statute, the Rules of Evidence, or other rules prescribed under statutory authority[11] will be recognized.[12] The Rules make no attempt to codify any

---

undertaken by the organization claiming the privilege, (2) there is a strong public interest in preserving the internal free-flow of the type of information sought, (3) the information is of the type whose internal flow would be curtailed if discovery was allowed, and (4) the self-critical analysis was prepared with the expectation that it would be kept confidential and it has in fact been kept confidential.

Id. at Appendix B. The Fifth Circuit declined to recognize such a "self-critical analysis" or "self-evaluative" privilege. *In re Kaiser Aluminum & Chem. Co.*, 214 F.3d 586, 593 & n.20 (5th Cir. 2000) (federal courts have uniformly refused to apply a self-evaluation privilege when documents have been sought by a governmental agency); *see also Freiermuth v. PPG Indus., Inc.*, 218 F.R.D. 694, 696-98 (N.D. Ala. 2003) (federal circuit courts that have addressed the question have refused to recognize a "self-critical analysis" privilege; collecting district court cases that are split on the issue and declining to recognize a self-critical-analysis privilege in the employment context). The rationale for such a privilege is to avoid a chilling effect on a company's desire to engage in candid self-appraisal that would presumably lead to beneficial operational changes when appropriate. Some courts have recognized such a privilege to encourage employers to undertake candid self-evaluations of their performance in the equal-employment-opportunity context. *See Reid v. Lockheed Martin Aeronautics Co.*, 199 F.R.D. 379, 385 (N.D. Ga. 2001). On the other hand, some courts note that employers routinely use company personnel to ensure compliance with numerous federal and state regulations and that the failure to engage in open, critical self-evaluation might be considered irresponsible by corporate shareholders. Thus, "[c]loaking self-evaluative materials in privilege would be contrary to this climate of corporate *glasnost.*" *Freiermuth*, 218 F.R.D. at 698.

11.   TEX. R. EVID. 501.

12.   *See Great Nat'l Life Ins. v. Davidson*, 708 S.W.2d 476, 478 (Tex. App.—Dallas 1986) (trial court improperly permitted the assertion of an unrecognized privilege; general rule in Texas "is that no person has a privilege to refuse to disclose any matter. The only privileges recognized are those enumerated in the rules of evidence or specifically granted by statute."), *rev'd on other grounds*, 737 S.W.2d 312 (Tex. 1987); *see, e.g.*, *Port v. Heard*, 764 F.2d 423, 428-33 (5th Cir. 1985) (declining to find any constitutionally based parent-child or "family" privilege in Texas courts under the right of privacy, equal protection, or First Amendment freedom of religion; parent-child relationship, rooted in "bonds of blood," is less susceptible to dissolution than the marriage bond and thus less in need of judicial protection); *In re Jobe Concrete Prods., Inc.*, 101 S.W.3d 122, 128 (Tex. App.—El Paso 2002, orig. proceeding) (declining to find an evidentiary privilege in federal regulations about confidentiality of research involving "human research subjects").

Although not specifically denominated as an evidentiary privilege, the work-product doctrine, whose contours in civil proceedings are set out in Texas Rule of Civil Procedure 192.5, is a common-law quasi-privilege that has been carried forward under the Rules of Evidence. Thus, Rule 501 does not trump the work-product doctrine in either civil or criminal cases. *See Oyster Creek Fin. Corp. v. Richwood Invs. II, Inc.*, 957 S.W.2d 640, 645-46 (Tex. App.—Amarillo 1997, pet. denied) (although not specifically provided for in the Rules of Evidence, work-product is an exception to the rule that no person has a right to refuse to produce any object or writing that has been prop-

constitutionally based privilege, such as the privilege against self-incrimination.[13] Since the adoption of the Rules, litigants have attempted, with varying degrees of success, to create new, constitutionally based privileges in Texas.[14] Although most of the statutes creating privileges were repealed, to the extent that they applied to proceedings governed by the Rules, a few statutory privileges survived the adoption of the Rules and thus remain in effect.[15] The Legislature, supreme court, and court of criminal appeals are free to create additional privileges. For example, the Legislature created a statutory privilege protecting both the identity of "tipsters" who report crimes to a crime-stoppers organization and the content of their communications.[16] However, the court of criminal appeals has held that these confidentiality provisions cannot deny a criminal defendant access to information that has a reasonable probability of affecting the outcome of a criminal trial.[17] Thus, federal due-process rights may trump this privilege statute under certain circumstances.[18]

erly subpoenaed). *See generally* 3 ROY W. MCDONALD & ELAINE A. GRAFTON CARLSON, TEXAS CIVIL PRACTICE §12.24 (2d ed. 2000) (discussing origin, scope, duration, and waiver of work-product doctrine). Refer to notes 280-326 *infra* and accompanying text.

13. U.S. CONST. amend. V; TEX. CONST. art. I, §10.

14. *Compare **Dall. Morning News Co. v. Garcia**,* 822 S.W.2d 675, 678 (Tex. App.—San Antonio 1991, orig. proceeding) (finding a qualified journalist's privilege under the First Amendment of the U.S. Constitution and Article I, §8, of the Texas Constitution), *and **Channel Two TV Co. v. Dickerson**,* 725 S.W.2d 470, 471-72 (Tex. App.—Houston [1st Dist.] 1987, no writ) (same), *with **Port**,* 764 F.2d at 428-33 (refusing to adopt a constitutionally based parent-child or "family" privilege), *and **Portland Sav. & Loan Ass'n v. Bernstein**,* 716 S.W.2d 532, 540 (Tex. App.—Corpus Christi 1985, writ ref'd n.r.e.) (refusing to find a privilege for communications with trial court), *overruled on other grounds, **Dawson-Austin v. Austin**,* 968 S.W.2d 319 (Tex. 1998).

15. *See* TEX. FIN. CODE §§31.301-31.308 (stating confidentiality requirements for disclosures to banking commissioner and employees of the Texas Department of Banking or a financial institution); TEX. HEALTH & SAFETY CODE §161.032(a) (records and proceedings of a medical committee are confidential and not subject to court subpoena), §242.049(e) (information collected for evaluation of care in nursing facilities is not subject to discovery or subpoena and is inadmissible); *see also **Barnes v. Whittington**,* 751 S.W.2d 493, 496 (Tex. 1988) (orig. proceeding) (the privilege under TEX. HEALTH & SAFETY CODE §161.032 "extends only to information generated by the hospital committee in its investigation or review process"); ***Hobson v. Moore**,* 734 S.W.2d 340, 340-41 (Tex. 1987) (orig. proceeding) (recognizing the privilege in civil actions of law-enforcement agencies for records of ongoing criminal investigations under former TEX. REV. CIV. STAT. art. 6252-17a, §3(8), now TEX. GOV'T CODE §552.108); ***Stewart v. McCain**,* 575 S.W.2d 509, 511-12 (Tex. 1978) (orig. proceeding) (interpreting former TEX. REV. CIV. STAT. art. 342-210, now TEX. FIN. CODE §31.301, as establishing an absolute privilege against the disclosure of a state bank's financial condition by the State Banking Department); ***Tex. Nat'l Bank v. Lewis**,* 793 S.W.2d 83, 86 (Tex. App.—Corpus Christi 1990, orig. proceeding [leave denied]) (discussing former TEX. REV. CIV. STAT. art. 342-705, now TEX. FIN. CODE §59.006, and noting that the "balancing of interests under an ambiguous statute to achieve the necessary discovery while protecting the privacy addressed by the statute is a proper exercise of the trial court's discretion"); ***McAllen State Bank v. Salinas**,* 738 S.W.2d 381, 385 (Tex. App.—Corpus Christi 1987, no writ) (privilege applies only to those banking records that are "obtained" by the Texas Banking Department and related to the financial condition of a state bank); ***Valley Int'l Props., Inc. v. Los Campeones, Inc.**,* 568 S.W.2d 680, 688-89 (Tex. Civ. App.—Corpus Christi 1978, writ ref'd n.r.e.) (books and records of savings-and-loan associations are privileged under former TEX. REV. CIV. STAT. art. 852a, §3.07, now TEX. R. EVID. 501).

16. *See* TEX. GOV'T CODE §414.008(a).

17. ***Thomas v. State**,* 837 S.W.2d 106, 113-14 (Tex. Crim. App. 1992).

18. *Id.* This same crime-stoppers privilege has also been held unconstitutional in a civil lawsuit when a tipster reported that the plaintiff, a high-school student, had drugs or alcohol in the trunk of his car on school property. ***In re Hinterlong**,* 109 S.W.3d 611, 632-33 (Tex. App.—Fort Worth 2003, orig. proceeding [mand. denied]). As a consequence of the tip, the student was expelled and placed in an alternative school despite the strong suggestion that he had been "set up" by vengeful fellow students. *Id.* at 618-19. A municipal-court jury acquitted the student of pos-

The Texas Legislature has also created a statutory journalist's privilege.[19] Texas Civil Practice & Remedies Code chapter 22, subchapter C, gives journalists extremely broad protection to decline to divulge confidential and nonconfidential information in civil trials; Texas Code of Criminal Procedure articles 38.11 and 38.111 provide equivalent protection in criminal proceedings.[20] These provisions prohibit any judicial, legislative, administrative, or other body with subpoena power from compelling a journalist[21] to testify, produce, or disclose in any official proceeding[22] "any confidential or nonconfi-

---

sessing alcohol on school property, and he then sued the school district and the anonymous tipster. *Id.* at 619. The school refused to provide the name of the tipster, citing the statutory privilege, but the court of appeals relied on *Thomas* and granted the student's writ of mandamus, finding that the crime-stopper's privilege was unconstitutional as applied in the particular case because it violated the state's open-courts provision. *In re Hinterlong*, 109 S.W.3d at 630-33.

19. *See* Tex. Civ. Prac. & Rem. Code §§22.021-22.027; Tex. Code Crim. Proc. arts. 38.11, 38.111. See *O'Connor's Texas Rules * Civil Trials* (2017), "Certain information in journalist's possession," ch. 6-B, §2.27, p. 543; "Journalist's privilege," ch. 6-B, §3.18, p. 556.

20. The bill analysis to the legislation creating the privilege stated that:
> [W]histleblowers are hesitant to come forward to discuss matters of public concern ... because of fear of retribution. As the law stands, a journalist can make no assurance that a whistleblower's identity or the information the whistleblower provides will be kept confidential without the journalist risking going to jail. Without the promise of confidentiality, information may not be provided to reporters, and the public will suffer from the resulting lack of information, the continued "behind the scenes" malfeasance, and the inability to shine light on corruption that impacts society at large.

Senate Comm. on Jurisprudence, Bill Analysis, Tex. H.B. 670, 81st Leg., R.S. (2009). Legal commentators have noted, however, that there is no empirical data to show that investigative reporting has suffered over the past three decades because of the lack of a journalist's privilege, or that journalists have been served with an unprecedented number of subpoenas. *See* Randall D. Eliason, *Leakers, Bloggers, and Fourth Estate Inmates: The Misguided Pursuit of a Reporter's Privilege*, 24 Cardozo Arts & Ent. L.J. 385, 415-21 (2006) (collecting statistics and anecdotal incidents to conclude that "despite a few recent high-profile cases and the protestations of large and well-funded media organizations, cases in which a reporter is compelled to testify and reveal confidential sources are still extremely rare."). If a journalist's article results in civil litigation or a criminal investigation, the parties may discover the source's identity and information through means other than by subpoenaing the journalist who first broadcast the information. For example, details in the journalist's story may make it possible for others to deduce the source's identity and go directly to that person. Conversely, a "whistleblower" who wants to remain anonymous can simply make an anonymous phone call to the journalist or mail an anonymous package.

21. A "journalist" is defined as a person who "gathers, compiles, prepares, collects, photographs, records, writes, edits, reports, investigates, processes, or publishes news or information that is disseminated by a news medium or communication service provider" for a substantial portion of his livelihood or for substantial financial gain. Tex. Civ. Prac. & Rem. Code §22.021(2); Tex. Code Crim. Proc. art. 38.11, §1(2). "News medium" generally means a newspaper, magazine, periodical, television or radio station, Internet company or provider, or other entity that disseminates news or information to the public through print, television, radio, or other photographic, mechanical, or electronic means. Tex. Civ. Prac. & Rem. Code §22.021(3); Tex. Code Crim. Proc. art. 38.11, §1(3). "Communication service provider" means a person or entity (e.g., a telecommunications carrier, an information-service provider, an interactive-computer-service provider, an information content provider) that electronically transmits information chosen by a customer. Tex. Civ. Prac. & Rem. Code §22.021(1); Tex. Code Crim. Proc. art. 38.11, §1(1); *see also* 47 U.S.C. §153(24) (defining "information service"), *id.* §153(51) (defining "telecommunications carrier"), *id.* §230(f)(2) (defining "interactive computer service"), *id.* §230(f)(3) (defining "information content provider").

22. An "official proceeding" is defined as "any type of administrative, executive, legislative, or judicial proceeding that may be conducted before a public servant, including a proceeding under Rule 202, Texas Rules of Civil Procedure." Tex. Civ. Prac. & Rem. Code §22.021(4). The term "public servant" includes government officers, employees, or agents, jurors, arbitrators, and attorneys or notaries public who are performing a governmental function. *Id.* §22.021(5). A person can be a public servant even if the person has not yet qualified for office or assumed the person's duties. *Id.* The term also includes a person performing a governmental function under a claim of right without out legal qualification. *Id.* §22.021(5)(E).

dential information, document, or item obtained or prepared while acting as a journalist" or to reveal the source of any such information.[23] Further, a parent company, subsidiary, division, or affiliate of a news medium or communication-service provider has the same protection as a journalist regarding the disclosure of information or the sources of that information.[24] All information obtained or prepared by the journalist, regardless of its confidentiality, is subject to protection.[25] Publication or dissemination of privileged information by a news medium or communication-service provider does not waive the journalist's privilege.[26]

The privilege, however, is qualified and may be pierced when the information is crucial in a lawsuit. Specifically, a court may compel a journalist, a journalist's employer, or an independent contractor for a journalist to testify, produce, or disclose any information, document, or item or the source of any such information if, after notice and a hearing, there is a clear and specific showing that (1) all reasonable efforts have been made to get the information from alternative sources, (2) the subpoena is not overbroad, unreasonable, or oppressive and, when appropriate, is limited to the verification of published information and the circumstances related to the accuracy of that published information, (3) reasonable and timely notice was given of the demand for the information, (4) the interest of the subpoenaing party outweighs the public interest in gathering and disseminating the news, (5) the subpoena is not being used to get nonessential or speculative information, and (6) the information is relevant and material to the official proceeding for which the information is sought and is essential to maintaining the claim or defense of the person seeking the information.[27]

23. Tex. Civ. Prac. & Rem. Code §22.023(a); *see* Tex. Code Crim. Proc. art. 38.11, §3(a).
24. Tex. Civ. Prac. & Rem. Code §22.023(b); Tex. Code Crim. Proc. art. 38.11, §3(b).
25. *See* Tex. Civ. Prac. & Rem. Code §22.023(a)(1); Tex. Code Crim. Proc. art. 38.11, §3(a)(1).
26. Tex. Civ. Prac. & Rem. Code §22.026; *see* Tex. Code Crim. Proc. art. 38.11, §7.
27. Tex. Civ. Prac. & Rem. Code §22.024. In criminal proceedings, the specific showing that must be made to compel a journalist to testify, disclose information, or produce information depends on whether the information is (1) unpublished or from nonconfidential sources or (2) from confidential sources. A court may compel a journalist to testify or disclose any unpublished information, document, or item, or the nonconfidential source of the information, document, or item, if the person seeking the information makes a clear and specific showing that it has exhausted all reasonable efforts to obtain the information from alternative sources. Tex. Code Crim. Proc. art. 38.11, §5(a)(1). The person seeking the information must also show that the unpublished information, document, or item is (1) relevant and material to the administration of the proceeding and essential to the maintenance of a claim or defense of the person seeking the information or (2) central to the investigation or prosecution of a criminal case and there are reasonable grounds to believe that a crime has occurred. *Id.* §5(a)(2). These reasonable grounds must be "based on something other than the assertion of the person requesting the subpoena." *Id.* §5(a)(2)(B). When hearing a motion to compel a journalist to testify about or to disclose or produce any unpublished information, document, or item, a court should also consider whether (1) the subpoena is overbroad, unreasonable, or oppressive, (2) reasonable and timely notice was given of the demand for the information, (3) the interest of the subpoenaing party outweighs the public interest in gathering and disseminating the news, and (4) the subpoena is being used to get nonessential or speculative information. *Id.* §5(b).

A court may compel a journalist to testify about or disclose the confidential source of any information, document, or item if there is a clear and specific showing that all reasonable efforts have been made to get the confidential source from alternative sources and (1) the journalist observed the source committing a felony criminal offense, (2) the source confessed or admitted to committing a felony criminal offense, or (3) there is probable cause the source participated in a felony criminal offense. *Id.* §4(a)(1)-(a)(3). A criminal court may also compel a journalist to testify

Proposed Article V of the Federal Rules served as a model for the Texas privilege rules. As originally approved by the U.S. Supreme Court, Article V contained thirteen rules, nine of which defined separate privileges.[28] However, when Article V was submitted to Congress, there was great controversy over the rules on testimonial privileges.[29] Ultimately, Congress did not codify any nonconstitutional privileges and left the problem to the courts to resolve on a case-by-case basis.[30]

Texas Rule 501 ensures that the lower courts will not create new common-law privileges, allow witness exemptions, or permit the nondisclosure or nonproduction of evidence without express authorization from the state's highest courts or the Legislature.[31] Rule 501 reasserts the basic principle that the public is entitled to every person's testimony unless there is such a strong countervailing public policy that the exclusion of particular evidence is allowed under a specific constitutional provision, a legislatively enacted statute, or a court rule adopted under statutory authority.[32] For example, the court of criminal appeals has held that under former Criminal Rule 501(3), now Rule 501(d), a criminal defendant could not assert that a witness's testimony should be excluded because the defendant had not been allowed to appear and object at a hearing

---

about or disclose the confidential source of any information, document, or item if disclosure of the source is reasonably necessary to stop or prevent substantial bodily harm or death. *Id.* §4(a)(4). If the alleged criminal offense is "the act of communicating, receiving, or possessing the information, document, or item," however, the procedures in article 38.11, §5, for unpublished information and nonconfidential sources govern. *Id.* §4(b). If the journalist's information was obtained in violation of the grand-jury oath given to a juror or a witness, the journalist may be compelled to testify if the person seeking the information "makes a clear and specific showing that the subpoenaing party has exhausted reasonable efforts" to obtain the information from alternative sources. *Id.* §4(c). The court may conduct an in camera hearing but may not order the journalist to reveal the confidential source until the court has ruled on the motion to compel. *Id.*

28. *See Rules of Evidence for United States Courts and Magistrates* (1972 proposed final draft), 56 F.R.D. 183, 230-61 (1973) [hereinafter *Proposed Rules*] (listing the proposed federal rules of evidence for privileges). The nine nonconstitutional privileges were required reports, political votes, trade secrets, state secrets and other official information, identities of informers, and communications between attorneys and clients, psychotherapists and patients, husbands and wives, and clergy members and communicants. *See id.* at 230-58.

29. For a discussion of the political problems and undercurrents surrounding proposed Article V of the Federal Rules, see 2 JACK B. WEINSTEIN & MARGARET A. BERGER, WEINSTEIN'S EVIDENCE ¶501[01], at 501-14 to 501-20 (1995) (discussing conflict between federal and state laws of privilege); 23 CHARLES A. WRIGHT & KENNETH W. GRAHAM, FEDERAL PRACTICE AND PROCEDURE §5421, at 652-56 (1980) (discussing the controversy over the proposed privilege rules); Irving Younger, *Federal Rules of Evidence: Defining and Refining the Goals of Codification*, 12 HOFSTRA L. REV. 255, 276 (1984) (suggesting that the very reason Congress passed Rule 501 was to avoid political turmoil).

30. *See* FED. R. EVID. 501. The last sentence of the rule incorporates the "*Erie* doctrine." Thus, if state law governs a civil claim or defense, or an element of a civil claim or defense, that state's privilege rules apply. *See, e.g.,* **Somer v. Johnson**, 704 F.2d 1473, 1478-79 (11th Cir. 1983) (recognizing a state privilege protecting internal hospital reviews and personnel files in a medical-malpractice diversity action); **Samuelson v. Susen**, 576 F.2d 546, 551 (3d Cir. 1978) (Pennsylvania federal court properly applied Ohio privilege rules because Ohio had the more significant relationship to the dispute, and thus a Pennsylvania state court would have applied Ohio law); *see also* **R.R. Salvage v. Japan Freight Consol. (U.S.A.) Inc.**, 97 F.R.D. 37, 40 (E.D.N.Y. 1983) (in diversity action, Federal Rule 501 did not require courts to follow the state "work product" rule because Federal Rule 501 looks to state law for traditional evidentiary privileges but not to rules that provide immunity from discovery); Olin G. Wellborn III, *The Federal Rules of Evidence and the Application of State Law in the Federal Courts*, 55 TEX. L. REV. 371, 446 (1977) (because legislative history of Federal Rule 501 is unclear, the judiciary must resolve the choice-of-law question created by Congress's ambiguous reference to "State law").

31. *See* TEX. R. EVID. 501(a)-(c).

32. *See* TEX. R. EVID. 501.

in which the State offered, and a judge granted, transactional immunity to the witness in return for truthful testimony at the defendant's trial.[33]

Confidentiality of information is not the same as an evidentiary privilege. "Statutory provisions providing for duties of confidentiality do not automatically imply the creation of evidentiary privileges binding on courts."[34] Unless the applicable law clearly expresses that specific information should also be protected from disclosure in judicial proceedings, material that is required to be kept "confidential" may be discoverable and admissible in civil or criminal trials.[35]

A. Procedural Concerns in Asserting & Proving a Privilege

A party invoking an evidentiary privilege under Article V has the burden to prove that the particular privilege is recognized, properly applies to the situation, and protects the specific testimony or documents sought by the opponent.[36] If the party asserting a privilege makes a prima facie showing that the privilege applies and submits the specific documents to the trial court, the court must conduct an in camera review of the material to assess the validity of the asserted privilege when such review is critical in evaluating the privilege claim.[37] The prima facie showing is minimal—only the "'minimum quantum of evidence necessary to support a rational inference'" that the privilege applies.[38] Sometimes the documents themselves may suffice to constitute a prima facie showing of the privilege,[39] although usually such materials are accompanied by a sworn affidavit or oral testimony in open court about the purpose for and circumstances under which the documents were created.[40] The opponent may also sub-

---

33. **Goff v. State**, 931 S.W.2d 537, 549 & n.10 (Tex. Crim. App. 1996). Specifically, the rule provides that a person—without express authorization from the Constitution, a statute, the Rules of Evidence, or other rules—cannot prevent someone from being a witness, disclosing a matter, or producing an object or writing. Tex. R. Evid. 501(d).

34. **Pearson v. Miller**, 211 F.3d 57, 68 (3d Cir. 2000); see **Sonnino v. Univ. of Kan. Hosp. Auth.**, 220 F.R.D. 633, 642 (D. Kan. 2004) ("It is well settled that a concern for protecting confidentiality does not equate to privilege, and that information and documents are not shielded from discovery on the sole basis that they are confidential.").

35. For example, the statutory accountant-client privilege in Texas Occupations Code §901.457 generally does not prevent disclosure of information under a court order. See Tex. Occ. Code §901.457(b)(3); see, e.g., **In re Patel**, 218 S.W.3d 911, 919-20 & n.6 (Tex. App.—Corpus Christi 2007, orig. proceeding) (court assumed without deciding that accountant-client evidentiary privilege exists in Texas and noted that statutory privileges do not automatically imply creation of corresponding evidentiary privilege). For a discussion of the statutory accountant-client privilege, refer to note 147 infra.

36. See **In re E.I. DuPont de Nemours & Co.**, 136 S.W.3d 218, 223 (Tex. 2004) (orig. proceeding) (per curiam); **Jordan v. Fourth Ct. of Appeals**, 701 S.W.2d 644, 648-49 (Tex. 1985) (orig. proceeding); see also **United States v. Nixon**, 418 U.S. 683, 709-10 (1974) (burden of proving existence and applicability of an evidentiary privilege is a heavy one, because privileges are neither "lightly created nor expansively construed"). See **O'Connor's Texas Rules * Civil Trials** (2017), "Asserting privileges," ch. 6-A, §18.2, p. 510. There is no presumption that documents are privileged. **In re E.I. DuPont**, 136 S.W.3d at 225.

37. **In re E.I. DuPont**, 136 S.W.3d at 223; **In re ExxonMobil Corp.**, 97 S.W.3d 353, 357 (Tex. App.—Houston [14th Dist.] 2003, orig. proceeding).

38. **In re E.I. DuPont**, 136 S.W.3d at 223 (quoting **Tex. Tech Univ. Health Scis. Ctr. v. Apodaca**, 876 S.W.2d 402, 407 (Tex. App.—El Paso 1994, writ denied)).

39. **In re E.I. DuPont**, 136 S.W.3d at 223.

40. See **In re E.I. DuPont**, 136 S.W.3d at 223-24; **In re USA Waste Mgmt. Res., L.L.C.**, 387 S.W.3d 92, 96 (Tex. App.—Houston [14th Dist.] 2012, orig. proceeding [mand. denied]); see, e.g., **In re Buspirone Antitrust Litig.**, 211

mit materials or testimony rebutting the privilege claim.[41] When there is conflicting evidence on the factual issues underlying a claim of privilege, the trial court's determination is deferentially reviewed for abuse of discretion.[42] But if the facts are undisputed, the trial court abuses its discretion if it does not follow the controlling law on privilege claims or on the proper procedure for determining whether specific documents are privileged.[43]

For a thorough discussion of the intersection between the civil discovery rules and (1) the assertion of privileges and their proof, (2) in camera review, and (3) appellate review, practitioners should consult both *In re E.I. DuPont de Nemours & Co.*[44] and *In re Monsanto Co.*[45]

B. Privileges & Conflict of Laws

When a communication at issue in a lawsuit is made in one state and the lawsuit is pending in a different state, a court must answer the question of which jurisdiction's law applies to a particular privilege. In *Ford Motor Co. v. Leggat*, the supreme court addressed this conflict-of-laws question in the context of the attorney-client privilege.[46] The court adopted the approach of the Restatement (Second) of Conflict of Laws, which directs a court to identify the state with the most significant relationship to a communication when determining which law of privilege should apply.[47] While noting that it might reach a different result for other privileges, the supreme court held that,

---

F.R.D. 249, 253-55 (S.D.N.Y. 2002) (declaration by corporation's Vice-President of Scientific Operations, explaining circumstances under which documents were created and their purposes, supported claim that documents were protected by attorney-client privilege); *In re Valero Energy Corp.*, 973 S.W.3d 453, 457-58 (Tex. App.—Houston [14th Dist.] 1998, orig. proceeding) (op. on reh'g) (affidavits attached to party's confidential memorandum, explaining nature of documents listed on privilege log, were sufficient to establish prima facie case for application of attorney-client privilege).

41. *In re E.I. DuPont*, 136 S.W.3d at 226 n.4.

42. *In re ExxonMobil Corp.*, 97 S.W.3d at 363.

43. *See In re E.I. DuPont*, 136 S.W.3d at 223 (abuse of discretion if trial court does not clearly analyze or apply the law correctly in ordering the disclosure of privileged information); *In re ExxonMobil Corp.*, 97 S.W.3d at 359 (abuse of discretion to order production of privileged document).

44. 136 S.W.3d 218 (Tex. 2004) (orig. proceeding) (per curiam).

45. 998 S.W.2d 917 (Tex. App.—Waco 1999, orig. proceeding).

46. 904 S.W.2d 643, 645-48 (Tex. 1995) (orig. proceeding).

47. Restatement (Second) of Conflict of Laws §139 (1988) reads:
   (1) Evidence that is not privileged under the local law of the state which has the most significant relationship with the communication will be admitted, even though it would be privileged under the local law of the forum, unless the admission of such evidence would be contrary to the strong public policy of the forum.
   (2) Evidence that is privileged under the local law of the state which has the most significant relationship with the communication but which is not privileged under the local law of the forum will be admitted unless there is some special reason why the forum policy favoring admission should not be given effect.
As the supreme court noted:
   The *Restatement* favors admission of the evidence unless "some special reason" not to admit it exists, and identifies four factors to consider when determining admissibility: number and nature of contacts of the forum with the parties or transaction, materiality of the evidence, kind of privilege, and

in addressing conflict-of-laws questions about the attorney-client privilege, the law of the state with the most significant relationship to the communication governs which state's privilege applies.[48] In *Gonzalez v. State*, the court of criminal appeals relied on Restatement section 139 in holding that the admissibility of a Texas murder defendant's confession to a California clergyman should be governed by California's clergy-penitent privilege because that state had the most significant relationship to the communication itself.[49] Thus, conflict-of-laws issues about privileges should generally be resolved under the "most significant relationship to the communication" analysis. The party seeking to apply another forum's privilege law has the burden to prove both the substance of that law and its applicability to the case.[50]

RULE 502

REQUIRED REPORTS PRIVILEGED BY STATUTE

(a) In General. If a law requiring a return or report to be made so provides:

(1) a person, corporation, association, or other organization or entity—whether public or private—that makes the required return or report has a privilege to refuse to disclose it and to prevent any other person from disclosing it; and

---

fairness to the parties. It goes on to explain that "the forum will be more inclined to give effect to a foreign privilege that is well established and recognized in many states," and if the privilege "was probably relied upon by the parties."
Leggat, 904 S.W.2d at 647 (citations omitted).

48. *Leggat*, 904 S.W.2d at 647. In *Leggat*, the supreme court concluded that Michigan, the state where the communication took place, had the most significant relationship to that communication; thus, Michigan's attorney-client privilege, which incorporated the "subject matter test" for corporate communications, applied and precluded the discovery of internal reports prepared by or at the request of Ford's general counsel and shared with select employees. *Id.* at 647-48.

49. 45 S.W.3d 101, 103-07 (Tex. Crim. App. 2001). In *Gonzalez v. State*, the defendant and his girlfriend traveled from California to Texas. 21 S.W.3d 595, 596 (Tex. App.—Houston [1st Dist.] 2000), *aff'd*, 45 S.W.3d 101 (Tex. Crim. App. 2001). They met the victim at a bar in Houston and he invited them to stay with him. *Gonzalez*, 21 S.W.3d at 596. They murdered him and then returned to California. *Id.* Later, the defendant confessed this murder to his pastor during a counseling session in California. *Id.* at 597. At trial, the defendant claimed that his statement was protected by the Texas clergy-communicant privilege under Rule 505, although it would not be protected by the analogous California privilege. *See Gonzalez*, 21 S.W.3d at 597. The court of criminal appeals applied §139 of the Restatement (Second) of Conflict of Laws and held that California was the state with the most significant relationship to the communication. *Gonzalez*, 45 S.W.3d at 106. Thus, the defendant's statement was properly admitted. *See id.* at 107.

In an earlier criminal case, the Dallas Court of Appeals held that, although New Mexico was the state with the most significant relationship to the communications at issue because they were made there, and New Mexico recognizes a physician-patient privilege in criminal proceedings, there was no "special reason" why the Texas policy favoring admission of such statements should not apply. *Kos v. State*, 15 S.W.3d 633, 637 (Tex. App.—Dallas 2000, pet. ref'd). Therefore, the trial court did not err in admitting the defendant's statements to his New Mexico doctor in that state because (1) the defendant lived in Texas for more than ten years and allegedly molested Texas children, (2) the defendant's communications were highly relevant to the case because he admitted molestations to doctor, (3) Texas has specifically disavowed the physician-patient privilege in criminal cases, and (4) disallowing the privilege was fair because it was not clear that the defendant made these statements in reliance on the privilege. *Id.* at 637-38.

50. *See In re Avantel, S.A.*, 343 F.3d 311, 321-22 (5th Cir. 2003).

(2) a public officer or agency to whom the return or report must be made has a privilege to refuse to disclose it.

(b) Exceptions. This privilege does not apply in an action involving perjury, false statements, fraud in the return or report, or other failure to comply with the law in question.

COMMENTARY ON RULE 502

To enhance the government's ability to gather data cheaply and efficiently, numerous federal, state, and local statutes and regulations require citizens to report information to the government.[51] Many of these laws give the reporting party a privilege against disclosure of the information[52] and prohibit disclosure by the recipient.[53] The rationale for these confidentiality provisions is that without such guarantees, citizens may be less likely to voluntarily furnish potentially self-damaging information needed by the government.[54] The cost of excluding this information from court proceedings is outweighed by the public benefit of gathering the information by self-reporting.

Reference to a particular statutory or regulatory nondisclosure provision determines whether a party may successfully assert the privilege because nondisclosure provisions are not uniform.[55] Some statutes provide an absolute ban against disclosure in court,[56] while others permit disclosure for certain purposes.[57] Rule 502 continues the

---

51. Texas statutes require various persons and entities to make reports to the government. *See, e.g.*, TEX. TAX CODE §24.32(a) (any person who "owns or manages and controls as a fiduciary any rolling stock used in the operation of a railroad shall file a property information report"); TEX. WATER CODE §26.034(b) (every person who intends to build or change the efficiency of a treatment-works plant must file the plans with the Water Commission before construction).

52. *See* 2 WEINSTEIN & BERGER, *supra* note 29, ¶502[02], at 502-4 to 502-5; 8 WIGMORE, *supra* note 6, §2377, at 781; 23 WRIGHT & GRAHAM, *supra* note 29, §5437, at 894-95; *see, e.g.*, TEX. TAX CODE §22.27 (information that property owner provides to appraisal office is confidential); *see also* 1 ROY R. RAY, TEXAS PRACTICE: TEXAS LAW OF EVIDENCE CIVIL AND CRIMINAL §445, at 437-39 (3d ed. 1980 & Supp. 1991) (state government encourages full and truthful disclosure by individuals and organizations by assuring that the information will be kept secret; this principle justifies numerous statutory privileges).

53. *See generally* A.W. Gans, Annotation, *Constitutionality, Construction, and Effect of Statute or Regulation Relating Specifically to Divulgence of Information Acquired by Public Officers or Employees*, 165 A.L.R. 1302 (1946) (discussing various statutes prohibiting disclosure of information given to public officials); David E. Joyce, Note, *Raiding the Confessional—The Use of Income Tax Returns in Nontax Criminal Investigations*, 48 FORDHAM L. REV. 1251, 1252-53 & n.11 (1980) (listing state statutes restricting disclosure of information contained in tax returns).

54. *In re Grand Jury Impaneled Jan. 21, 1975*, 541 F.2d 373, 380 (3d Cir. 1976); Comment, *The Required Report Privileges*, 56 NW. U. L. REV. 283, 286 (1961). Another justification for the nondisclosure requirement is that it serves a "housekeeping" function by, for example, preventing public officers from being burdened by frequent demands for documents. *The Required Report Privileges, supra*, at 286. In addition, the privilege against self-incrimination may sometimes require nondisclosure. *See Proposed Rules, supra* note 28, at 235 (FED. R. EVID. 502 advisory committee's note). *But see Balt. City Dep't of Soc. Servs. v. Bouknight*, 493 U.S. 549, 555-56 (1990) (privilege against self-incrimination would not permit a mother to avoid the requirement to produce the child in compliance with court order pursuant to regulation); *California v. Byers*, 402 U.S. 424, 433-34 (1971) (compliance with the statutory requirement that drivers of cars involved in traffic accidents must stop and provide their names and addresses did not violate the privilege against self-incrimination).

55. *See The Required Report Privileges, supra* note 54, at 285.

56. *See, e.g.*, TEX. TRANSP. CODE §601.005 (no party in a civil suit may refer to or offer as evidence of negligence or due care any actions taken or findings made by the Department of Public Safety).

latter approach. Rather than stating one rigid rule of privilege, it simply provides that a person (or organization or entity) who makes a required report may prevent its disclosure if the law requiring the report to be made so provides.[58] Similarly, the public officer or agency to whom the report must be made may refuse to disclose it if the law requiring the report so provides.[59] The party asserting a privilege has the burden of proving that the privilege protects a certain report and applies to a given situation.[60] Rule 502 is not mere surplusage, however, for it compels Texas courts to honor similar privilege provisions from other jurisdictions.[61] Because this privilege does not have a constitutional dimension, courts may pierce it when necessary to uphold fundamental principles of due process.[62]

Rule 502 includes one exception to the privilege. A person may not invoke the privilege in "an action involving perjury, false statements, fraud in the return or report, or other failure to comply with the law in question."[63] Thus, a party cannot hide behind the required-reports privilege when he has, by his own actions, violated the public policy behind those reports—full, honest, and complete disclosure.

---

57. *See, e.g.*, Tex. Tax Code §171.210(b) (financial information that must be filed with state comptroller can be disclosed in proceedings to which the state is a party).

58. Tex. R. Evid. 502(a)(1) (person, corporation, association, or other organization or entity, whether public or private, is covered by the privilege). The rule protects such reports only if the law requires the report to be made and also specifically makes the report privileged. *See* Tex. R. Evid. 502(a); *see, e.g.*, **Star-Telegram, Inc. v. Schattman**, 784 S.W.2d 109, 111 (Tex. App.—Fort Worth 1990, orig. proceeding [leave denied]) (because EEOC guidelines did not require reports on sexual-harassment claims, they were not privileged; handwritten notes by attorney who was advising newspaper in connection with the investigation of sexual-harassment claims were discoverable).

59. Tex. R. Evid. 502(a)(2).

60. **Davidson v. Great Nat'l Life Ins.**, 737 S.W.2d 312, 314 (Tex. 1987); **Peeples v. Honorable Fourth Sup. Jud. Dist.**, 701 S.W.2d 635, 637 (Tex. 1985) (orig. proceeding).

61. *See* **Ford Motor Co. v. Leggat**, 904 S.W.2d 643, 646 n.4 (Tex. 1995) (orig. proceeding) (Texas courts will honor statutory reporting privileges of foreign jurisdictions under Civil Rule 502); **Davidson**, 737 S.W.2d at 314 (Civil Rule 502 requires Texas courts to honor a foreign jurisdiction's privilege if that jurisdiction requires that certain information not be reported); **AG Volkswagen v. Valdez**, 897 S.W.2d 458, 462 (Tex. App.—Corpus Christi 1995, orig. proceeding) ("[T]he Rule 502 privilege not to reveal certain required reports which are protected by statute may encompass a foreign law privilege, if foreign law required such report to be made in the first place."), *mand. granted*, 909 S.W.2d 900 (Tex. 1995). Even without Rule 502, Texas courts would have to honor statutory privileges created by the Legislature. *See* Tex. R. Evid. 501. By extending the privilege to any report required to be made by law, however, Rule 502 ensures the recognition of the required-report privileges enacted by sister states. *See* Tex. R. Evid. 502(a). Privileges created by federal law would, of course, have to be honored under the Supremacy Clause, regardless of Rule 502. In practice, the rule is rarely invoked or litigated.

62. *See* **Tex. Dep't of Corr. v. Dalehite**, 623 S.W.2d 420, 423 (Tex. Crim. App. 1981) ("[T]he invocation of a privilege, statutory or otherwise, will not prevent the disclosure of information when confronted with the fundamental principles of due process of law in the fair administration of justice.").

63. Tex. R. Evid. 502(b); *see* Peter Sugar & Richard P. Zipser, Comment, *Federal Rules of Evidence and the Law of Privileges*, 15 Wayne L. Rev. 1287, 1304 (1969) (conferring privilege in cases involving failure to comply with the law "would defeat the more efficient administration of the agency that the legislature was attempting to create by enacting the protective provision"); *see also* 2 Weinstein & Berger, *supra* note 29, ¶502[02], at 502-6 to 502-7 (there is no privilege when a report contains false information because the submission of a fraudulent report frustrates the rationale behind the privilege); 24 Wright & Graham, *supra* note 29, §5461, at 33-34 (a party should not be able to invoke a privilege whose policy he frustrates by his own actions).

RULE 503
LAWYER-CLIENT PRIVILEGE

(a) Definitions. In this rule:

(1) A "client" is a person, public officer, or corporation, association, or other organization or entity—whether public or private—that:

(A) is rendered professional legal services by a lawyer; or

(B) consults a lawyer with a view to obtaining professional legal services from the lawyer.

(2) A "client's representative" is:

(A) a person who has authority to obtain professional legal services for the client or to act for the client on the legal advice rendered; or

(B) any other person who, to facilitate the rendition of professional legal services to the client, makes or receives a confidential communication while acting in the scope of employment for the client.

(3) A "lawyer" is a person authorized, or who the client reasonably believes is authorized, to practice law in any state or nation.

(4) A "lawyer's representative" is:

(A) one employed by the lawyer to assist in the rendition of professional legal services; or

(B) an accountant who is reasonably necessary for the lawyer's rendition of professional legal services.

(5) A communication is "confidential" if not intended to be disclosed to third persons other than those:

(A) to whom disclosure is made to further the rendition of professional legal services to the client; or

(B) reasonably necessary to transmit the communication.

(b) Rules of Privilege.

(1) *General Rule.* A client has a privilege to refuse to disclose and to prevent any other person from disclosing confidential communications made to facilitate the rendition of professional legal services to the client:

(A) between the client or the client's representative and the client's lawyer or the lawyer's representative;

(B) between the client's lawyer and the lawyer's representative;

(C) by the client, the client's representative, the client's lawyer, or the lawyer's representative to a lawyer representing another party in a pending action or that lawyer's representative, if the communications concern a matter of common interest in the pending action;

(D) between the client's representatives or between the client and the client's representative; or

(E) among lawyers and their representatives representing the same client.

(2) *Special Rule in a Criminal Case.* In a criminal case, a client has a privilege to prevent a lawyer or lawyer's representative from disclosing any other fact that came to the knowledge of the lawyer or the lawyer's representative by reason of the attorney-client relationship.

(c) Who May Claim. The privilege may be claimed by:

(1) the client;

(2) the client's guardian or conservator;

(3) a deceased client's personal representative; or

(4) the successor, trustee, or similar representative of a corporation, association, or other organization or entity—whether or not in existence.

The person who was the client's lawyer or the lawyer's representative when the communication was made may claim the privilege on the client's behalf—and is presumed to have authority to do so.

(d) Exceptions. This privilege does not apply:

(1) *Furtherance of Crime or Fraud.* If the lawyer's services were sought or obtained to enable or aid anyone to commit or plan to commit what the client knew or reasonably should have known to be a crime or fraud.

(2) *Claimants Through Same Deceased Client.* If the communication is relevant to an issue between parties claiming through the same deceased client.

(3) *Breach of Duty by a Lawyer or Client.* If the communication is relevant to an issue of breach of duty by a lawyer to the client or by a client to the lawyer.

(4) *Document Attested by a Lawyer.* If the communication is relevant to an issue concerning an attested document to which the lawyer is an attesting witness.

(5) *Joint Clients.* If the communication:

(A) is offered in an action between clients who retained or consulted a lawyer in common;

(B) was made by any of the clients to the lawyer; and

(C) is relevant to a matter of common interest between the clients.

Notes and Comments

Comment to 1998 change: The addition of subsection (a)(2)(B) adopts a subject matter test for the privilege of an entity, in place of the control group test previously used. See *National Tank Co. v. Brotherton*, 851 S.W.2d 193, 197-198 (Tex. 1993).

COMMENTARY ON RULE 503

The attorney-client privilege can be traced at least as far back as the reign of Elizabeth I[64]—perhaps even earlier.[65] Over time, the rationale for the privilege has changed. During the Elizabethan era, the privilege was premised on a consideration for the oath and honor of the attorney.[66] Thus, the privilege belonged to the attorney, "permitting him to keep the secrets confided in him by his client and thus preserve his honor."[67] In the eighteenth century, however, an instrumental justification for the privilege emerged.[68] Focusing on the need for attorneys to be fully apprised of the facts in order to provide effective representation, this justification held that the attorney-client privilege was vital for encouraging clients to tell all.[69] This view continues to provide the primary justification for the attorney-client privilege:

> [T]he purpose of the attorney-client privilege is to promote the unrestrained communication and contact between an attorney and client in all matters in which the attorney's professional advice or services are sought, without fear that these confidential communications will be disclosed by the attorney, voluntarily or involuntarily, in any legal proceeding.[70]

---

64.   8 WIGMORE, *supra* note 6, §2290, at 542; *see* **Paxton v. City of Dallas**, 509 S.W.3d 247, 261 (Tex. 2017).

65.   McCORMICK ON EVIDENCE §87, at 204 (Edward W. Cleary ed., 3d ed. 1984) [hereinafter McCORMICK ON EVIDENCE I]; *see* **United States v. Jicarilla Apache Nation**, 564 U.S. 162, 165 (2011) ("The attorney-client privilege ranks among the oldest and most established evidentiary privileges known to our law."); **Upjohn Co. v. United States**, 449 U.S. 383, 389 (1981) (attorney-client privilege is the oldest privilege for confidential communications in common law); **Paxton**, 509 S.W.3d at 259 (same). For a revisionist view of the origins of the attorney-client privilege, see Geoffrey C. Hazard, Jr., *An Historical Perspective on the Attorney-Client Privilege*, 66 CALIF. L. REV. 1061, 1069-91 (1978).

66.   McCORMICK ON EVIDENCE I, *supra* note 65, §87, at 204; 2 WEINSTEIN & BERGER, *supra* note 29, ¶503[02], at 503-15; 8 WIGMORE, *supra* note 6, §2290, at 543.

67.   **In re Colton**, 201 F. Supp. 13, 15 (S.D.N.Y. 1961), *aff'd sub nom.*, **Colton v. United States**, 306 F.2d 633 (2d Cir. 1962). Today, the client is the privilege holder. *See* TEX. R. EVID. 503(c). Refer to notes 226-233 *infra* and accompanying text.

68.   McCORMICK ON EVIDENCE I, *supra* note 65, §87, at 204; 8 WIGMORE, *supra* note 6, §2290, at 543.

69.   McCORMICK ON EVIDENCE I, *supra* note 65, §87, at 204-05; 8 WIGMORE, *supra* note 6, §2290, at 543. Some still contend, however, that the attorney-client privilege is justified by privacy concerns. *See* 2 DAVID W. LOUISELL & CHRISTOPHER B. MUELLER, FEDERAL EVIDENCE §208, at 731-32 (rev. ed. 1985) (Wigmore "underestimates" the principled bases of the attorney-client privilege; the privilege is significant in the developing law of privacy); Thomas G. Krattenmaker, *Interpersonal Testimonial Privileges Under the Federal Rules of Evidence: A Suggested Approach*, 64 GEO. L.J. 613, 647-57 (1976) (discussing the right to privacy as a rationale for the attorney-client privilege).

70.   **West v. Solito**, 563 S.W.2d 240, 245 (Tex. 1978) (orig. proceeding); *see* **Paxton**, 509 S.W.3d at 250 ("The attorney-client privilege reflects a foundational tenet in the law: ensuring the free flow of information between attorney and client ultimately serves the broader societal interest of effective administration of justice."); **Austin v.**

The extent to which the privilege promotes "unrestrained communication" and whether its benefits outweigh the costs to justice of nondisclosure are matters of speculation.[71] Consequently, courts have limited the privilege by creating exceptions[72] and strictly construing its terms.[73]

The attorney-client privilege is an evidentiary privilege that protects against compelled disclosure of confidential communications in judicial and administrative proceedings.[74] Third-party communications to the attorney fall outside the scope of the privilege, except for those made by the client's representatives.[75] When the privilege applies, however, it is absolute.[76] It covers the "complete" communication between the attorney and the client.[77] Once it is established that a written or oral communication contains privileged information, the privilege extends to the entire conversation or

State, 934 S.W.2d 672, 673 (Tex. Crim. App. 1996) (purpose of the privilege is to promote communication by protecting against the fear that confidences will be revealed).

The same rationale underlies the attorney-client privilege in the federal system. *See Upjohn Co.*, 449 U.S. at 389; **United States v. BDO Seidman, LLP**, 492 F.3d 806, 815 (7th Cir. 2007); **Wachtel v. Health Net, Inc.**, 482 F.3d 225, 231 (3d Cir. 2007). However, federal courts increasingly limit the privilege to those communications that they determine would not have occurred without the existence of a privilege. *See Fisher v. United States*, 425 U.S. 391, 403 (1976) (privilege protects only those disclosures necessary to obtain informed legal advice); **Wachtel**, 482 F.3d at 231 (when purpose of attorney-client privilege ends, so does protection of privilege); **United States v. Oloyede**, 982 F.2d 133, 141 (4th Cir. 1992) (attorney-client privilege should be "strictly confined within the narrowest possible limits consistent with the logic of its principle" (quoting *In re Grand Jury Proceedings*, 727 F.2d 1352, 1355 (4th Cir. 1984))); **Athridge v. Aetna Cas. & Sur. Co.**, 184 F.R.D. 200, 209 (D.D.C. 1998) (District of Columbia Circuit strictly construes attorney-client privilege; "'strict-construction cases reason that a lawyer's communications can be privileged only derivatively—if disclosure of the lawyers' communications would reveal the content of the client's communication to the lawyer'" (quoting EDNA SELAN EPSTEIN, THE ATTORNEY-CLIENT PRIVILEGE AND THE WORK-PRODUCT DOCTRINE 41 (1997))). *But see Rhone-Poulenc Rorer Inc. v. Home Indem. Co.*, 32 F.3d 851, 862 (3d Cir. 1994) (privilege serves justice and is worthy of maximum protection).

71. *See* 8 WIGMORE, *supra* note 6, §2291, at 552-54; *see also* 2 WEINSTEIN & BERGER, *supra* note 29, ¶503[02], at 503-17 (assumption that the benefits to justice of the attorney-client privilege outweigh any costs is unverifiable).

72. Refer to notes 234-279 *infra* and accompanying text.

73. *See Austin*, 934 S.W.2d at 673 ("[B]ecause the attorney-client privilege is an exclusionary rule of evidence, the privilege has been limited both by statutory exception and strict construction to situations which encourage full disclosure."); **Duval Cty. Ranch Co. v. Alamo Lumber Co.**, 663 S.W.2d 627, 634 (Tex. App.—Amarillo 1983, writ ref'd n.r.e.) ("The policy of the [Texas] Supreme Court has been to restrict application of the rule of privilege of communications between attorney and client, because it tends to prevent full disclosure of truth.").

74. The Texas Rules of Civil Procedure place privileged matter outside the scope of discovery. "If the matter sought to be discovered is privileged ... it is not subject to discovery. [I]t is clear that the intent is to encompass all privileges known to Texas law, one of the most common being that of the attorney-client privilege." *West*, 563 S.W.2d at 243-44. Texas Rule of Civil Procedure 192.3 defines the scope of permissible discovery. Walter Jordan asserts that the privilege may properly be invoked in response to requests for admissions pursuant to former Texas Rule of Civil Procedure 169 (now Rule 198). 2 WALTER E. JORDAN, MODERN TEXAS DISCOVERY §10.02 (1974); *see also* 6 WILLIAM V. DORSANEO III, TEXAS LITIGATION GUIDE §90.06[2][c] (2011) (outlining and discussing the scope of privileged communications between attorneys and clients).

75. *See* TEX. R. EVID. 503(b)(1). Refer to notes 204-205 *infra* and accompanying text.

76. *See Wood v. McCown*, 784 S.W.2d 126, 128 (Tex. App.—Austin 1990, orig. proceeding) (attorney-client privilege "is permanent unless waived"); *cf.* Act of May 25, 1967, 60th Leg., R.S., ch. 435, §1, 1967 Tex. Gen. Laws 1005 (former Texas Revised Civil Statutes art. 3715a deemed repealed as to civil proceedings effective 1983 and as to criminal proceedings effective 1986) (allowing for breach of the clergyman-penitent privilege when necessary for the proper administration of justice).

77. *See Marathon Oil Co. v. Moyé*, 893 S.W.2d 585, 589 (Tex. App.—Dallas 1994, orig. proceeding [leave denied]).

document, not simply to the specific portions relating to legal advice.[78] Thus, a court may not require a party to redact the "legal advice" portions of an attorney-client communication and produce the remainder of the document.[79]

The Texas Disciplinary Rules of Professional Conduct protect against voluntary disclosure of a client's confidential communications to his attorney. With limited exceptions, Rule 1.05 prohibits an attorney from knowingly revealing "confidential information" about the representation of a client.[80] This protection is broader than the attorney-client privilege—a client's "confidential information" includes not only matters that the attorney-client privilege protects, but also "unprivileged client information" that the attorney acquires by representing the client.[81]

Rule 503 essentially codified the common-law doctrine.[82] It left the law of attorney-client privilege in Texas largely unchanged, making only some relatively minor changes

---

78. *See In re Park Cities Bank*, 409 S.W.3d 859, 868 (Tex. App.—Tyler 2013, orig. proceeding) (privilege attaches to complete communication between attorney and client, including both legal advice and factual information; subject matter of information communicated is irrelevant to whether privilege applies); *Pittsburgh Corning Corp. v. Caldwell*, 861 S.W.2d 423, 425 (Tex. App.—Houston [14th Dist.] 1993, orig. proceeding) (privilege extends to entire document). In *Caldwell*, the court reasoned that "[i]f we were to hold that all or part of a document containing privileged information should be disclosed because it also included facts pertinent to the lawsuit, the purpose of the attorney-client and work-product privileges would be annihilated. The ultimate effect of such a holding would be that clients would be reluctant to give their attorneys any factual information for fear that it would be subject to discovery." 861 S.W.2d at 425.

79. *Caldwell*, 861 S.W.2d at 425.

80. Tex. Disciplinary R. Prof'l Conduct 1.05(b); *see Duncan v. Bd. of Disciplinary Appeals*, 898 S.W.2d 759, 761 (Tex. 1995) ("A lawyer has a solemn obligation not to reveal privileged and other confidential client information, except as permitted or required in certain limited circumstances as provided in the [disciplinary] rules."); *see also Perez v. Kirk & Carrigan*, 822 S.W.2d 261, 265 (Tex. App.—Corpus Christi 1991, writ denied) ("[B]ecause of the openness and candor within this relationship, certain communications between attorney and client are privileged from disclosure in either civil or criminal proceedings ....").

81. Tex. Disciplinary R. Prof'l Conduct 1.05(a). This duty of confidentiality, however, is not absolute. Even without the client's consent, an attorney may reveal the client's intention to commit a crime or fraudulent act and the information necessary to prevent the crime or fraudulent act. *See* Tex. Disciplinary R. Prof'l Conduct 1.05(c)(7). The attorney may also reveal a client's confidences and secrets when necessary to establish or collect his fee or to defend himself against accusations of wrongdoing. Tex. Disciplinary R. Prof'l Conduct 1.05(c)(5). In certain instances, the disciplinary rules, other law, or a court order may require the attorney to divulge confidences or secrets. For example, Disciplinary Rule 1.05(c)(8) requires an attorney to reveal a client's confidences if necessary to rectify the consequences of his client's criminal or fraudulent acts when the attorney's services have been used in the commission of those acts. Under Disciplinary Rule 1.05(e), an attorney "shall" reveal confidential information that clearly establishes that a client is likely to commit a crime or fraudulent act likely to result in death or serious bodily injury, at least to the extent that revelation reasonably appears necessary to prevent the client from committing that act. Further, Disciplinary Rule 3.03(b) may require a lawyer to reveal privileged information when necessary to correct an earlier offer of material false evidence, and Disciplinary Rule 4.01(b) requires the attorney to reveal privileged information when necessary to avoid becoming a party to a criminal act or to prevent knowingly assisting the client in perpetrating a fraudulent act.

82. *See DeWitt & Rearick, Inc. v. Ferguson*, 699 S.W.2d 692, 693 (Tex. App.—El Paso 1985, orig. proceeding [leave denied]) (citing Steven Goode & M. Michael Sharlot, *Article V: Privileges*, 20 Hous. L. Rev. 273, 282 (1983 Tex. R. Evid. Handbook)). Texas Rule 503 is derived from Uniform Rule of Evidence 502 (1974), which is in turn derived from proposed Federal Rule 503. *See Proposed Rules, supra* note 28, at 235-36.

Before the adoption of the Texas Rules of Civil Evidence, statutory recognition of the attorney-client privilege was found in former Code of Criminal Procedure article 38.10. That statute read: "[A]n attorney at law shall not disclose a communication made to him by his client during the existence of that relationship, nor disclose any other fact which came to the knowledge of such attorney by reason of such relationship." Act of May 27, 1965, 59th

and closing some gaps. Although the general statement of the privilege is broad in scope, many communications passing between attorney and client may not, in fact, be privileged.[83] Even though a statement may appear to meet all the requisites of a privileged communication, it may fall within one of the exceptions to the privilege.[84] Furthermore, the precise contours of the terms used in defining the privilege—"client," "representative of the client," "confidential," and "communication"—are not always clear.

A. Rule 503(a): Definitions

1. Rule 503(a)(1) & (a)(2): Client & client's representative. A client is a natural person, or any kind of entity, who "is rendered professional legal services by a lawyer."[85] Governmental units,[86] corporations, unincorporated associations, and trustees may all be clients.[87] The attorney-client relationship may be expressly created by contract, but it may also be implied by the actions of the parties.[88] In addition, even if the person or

---

Leg., R.S., ch. 722, §1, art. 38.10, vol. 2, 1965 Tex. Gen. Laws 317, 467, *amended by* Act of May 25, 1983, 68th Leg., R.S., ch. 310, §1, art. 38.10, 1983 Tex. Gen. Laws 1643, 1643-44 (former TEX. CODE CRIM. PROC. art. 38.10 deemed repealed as to criminal proceedings effective 1986). Despite its codification as a rule of criminal procedure, courts also applied it to civil cases. *See, e.g.,* **Miller v. Pierce**, 361 S.W.2d 623, 625 (Tex. Civ. App.—Eastland 1962, no writ); **Cochran v. Cochran**, 333 S.W.2d 635, 641 (Tex. Civ. App.—Houston 1960, writ ref'd n.r.e.); **Williams v. Williams**, 108 S.W.2d 297, 299 (Tex. Civ. App.—Amarillo 1937, no writ).

83. *See* TEX. R. EVID. 503(a)(5) (defining "confidential" in context of attorney-client privilege); **Borden, Inc. v. Valdez**, 773 S.W.2d 718, 720-21 (Tex. App.—Corpus Christi 1989, orig. proceeding) (privilege does not apply to terms or purpose of attorney's employment); *see, e.g.,* **Ledisco Fin. Servs., Inc. v. Viracola**, 533 S.W.2d 951, 959 (Tex. Civ. App.—Texarkana 1976, no writ) (client's statement to attorney was not privileged because it was made in presence of third person). Refer to notes 156-189 *infra* and accompanying text.

84. Refer to notes 234-279 *infra* and accompanying text.

85. TEX. R. EVID. 503(a)(1)(A).

86. *See* **United States v. Jicarilla Apache Nation**, 564 U.S. 162, 170 (2011) ("Unless applicable law provides otherwise, the Government may invoke the attorney-client privilege in civil litigation to protect confidential communications between Government officials and Government attorneys."); **Markowski v. City of Marlin**, 940 S.W.2d 720, 726 (Tex. App.—Waco 1997, writ denied) ("[A] governmental body has as much right as an individual to consult with its attorney without risking the disclosure of important confidential information."); *see also* TEX. GOV'T CODE §551.071 (governmental body may consult privately with its attorney about pending or contemplated litigation, settlement offers, or matters in which the duty of the attorney to the governmental body under the Rules of Professional Conduct clearly conflicts with the Open Meetings Act of chapter 551).

87. *See* TEX. R. EVID. 503(a)(1) (definition of "client" includes people as well as public and private organizations). "[T]he trustee who retains an attorney to advise him or her in administering the trust is the real client, not the trust beneficiaries." **Huie v. DeShazo**, 922 S.W.2d 920, 925 (Tex. 1996) (orig. proceeding). In *Huie*, the supreme court disapproved of **Burton v. Cravey**, 759 S.W.2d 160, 162 (Tex. App.—Houston [1st Dist.] 1988, no writ), which had suggested that the right of condominium owners to inspect the condominium-association books trumped the privilege for confidential attorney-client communications that might have been contained in the records of the association's attorney. *Huie*, 922 S.W.2d at 924. As the supreme court explained, the mere fact that a person owes a legal duty to another does not make them joint clients of an attorney nor does that relationship give the other person the right to discover the first person's confidential communications with the attorney. *See id.* at 924-25.

88. **In re DISH Network, LLC**, ___ S.W.3d ___ (Tex. App.—El Paso 2017, orig. proceeding) (No. 08-16-00300-CV; 6-30-17); **Kennedy v. Gulf Coast Cancer & Diagnostic Ctr. at Se., Inc.**, 326 S.W.3d 352, 357 (Tex. App.—Houston [1st Dist.] 2010, no pet.). The determination of whether an attorney-client relationship can be implied is based on objective standards of what the parties said and did, not on their subjective expectations. *In re DISH Network*, ___ S.W.3d at ___; *Kennedy*, 326 S.W.3d at 357-58. In **State v. DeAngelis**, the Assistant City Attorney had once represented the police department, but by the time of the telephone call sought to be protected, she had been relieved of those duties and reassigned. *See* **State v. DeAngelis**, 116 S.W.3d 396, 400-01 (Tex. App.—El Paso 2003,

entity does not actually become the attorney's client, the privilege attaches to communications made while consulting the attorney with a view to obtaining legal services.[89] Payment of a fee is not required.[90] However, statements made by a person who knows that an attorney represents someone else involved in a controversy are not privileged.[91] Regardless of whether the attorney and client enter into an employment relationship, the attorney must be consulting in his capacity as an attorney.[92] Thus, if the attorney

---

no pet.). Because she had been threatened with the loss of her job and law license and with criminal prosecution, she agreed to call the defendant and give him false information about an investigation to see if he relayed that information to the media. *Id.* at 401-02. During that telephone conversation, the defendant made statements that were inconsistent with statements he later made to a grand jury. *Id.* at 402. He was indicted for aggravated perjury and sought to suppress the tape-recorded telephone conversation as a confidential attorney-client communication. *Id.* The attorney testified that the defendant had never asked her to represent him personally and that she had never done so, yet she had referred to him, on many occasions, as her "client" in discussions with another attorney. *Id.* at 402 & n.7. The defendant, who had a personal relationship with the attorney, had written notes to her stating that he knew his communications to her were protected by the attorney-client relationship. *Id.* at 402. Thus, even though the attorney was not in fact acting as an attorney for the City at the time of the telephone call, and the attorney and the defendant did not have a personal attorney-client relationship—indeed, city policy prohibited individual representation—the court of appeals held that the trial court did not abuse its discretion in finding that the conversation was protected by the attorney-client privilege. *Id.* at 406; *see, e.g.*, **State v. Martinez**, 116 S.W.3d 385, 394-95 (Tex. App.—El Paso 2003, no pet.) (city attorney's individual representation, in violation of city policy, did not defeat attorney-client privilege).

89.   TEX. R. EVID. 503(a)(1)(B); **Mixon v. State**, 224 S.W.3d 206, 212 (Tex. Crim. App. 2007); *see, e.g.*, **Hart v. Gossum**, 995 S.W.2d 958, 962 (Tex. App.—Fort Worth 1999, no pet.) (attorney-client privilege covered redacted portions of letter that attorney sent to facilitate rendition of legal services even though attorney had not yet been retained); *see also* McFall & Little, *supra* note 10, at 474 (attorney-client privilege is defined by the purpose of the relationship, not any financial arrangements). However, communications made after the attorney has declined employment remain unprivileged. **McGrede v. Rembert Nat'l Bank**, 147 S.W.2d 580, 584 (Tex. Civ. App.—Texarkana 1941, writ dism'd judgm't cor.).

In **United States v. Munoz**, the court held that the defendant had not offered sufficient evidence to demonstrate an attorney-client relationship with a corporate attorney even though the defendant, the company's sales agent, had referred the attorney to the company based on his prior relationship with that attorney, had furnished information to the attorney about the company, and allegedly believed that the company attorney was his attorney as well. 233 F.3d 1117, 1128 (9th Cir. 2000). The Ninth Circuit relied on evidence that the attorney addressed all of his correspondence to the company without copying the defendant, that the defendant did not consult with the attorney for personal legal advice, and that only the company signed a retainer agreement and paid the attorney's fees. *Id.* Here, the defendant's purported subjective belief was not supported by objective facts that would lead a reasonable person to believe that the defendant and the attorney had a personal attorney-client relationship. *See id.*

90.   2 LOUISELL & MUELLER, *supra* note 69, §209, at 740-41. This is the common-law rule. *See* McCORMICK ON EVIDENCE I, *supra* note 65, §88, at 209 (payment or agreement to pay fee is not essential); 1 RAY, *supra* note 52, §423, at 406 (3d ed. 1980) (payment of fee not controlling; attorney may give services gratuitously); *see also* **In re Grand Jury Proceedings (In re Pavlick)**, 680 F.2d 1026, 1031 n.1 (5th Cir. 1982) (Politz, Tate, Williams, JJ., dissenting) (if payment of a fee were required, "a person would be compelled to retain the first attorney consulted in order to preserve the privilege").

91.   *See, e.g.*, **Boring & Tunneling Co. of Am., Inc. v. Salazar**, 782 S.W.2d 284, 289 (Tex. App.—Houston [1st Dist.] 1989, orig. proceeding) (trial court could not reasonably conclude that a truck driver was seeking legal advice when attorney introduced himself to truck driver as the attorney of the company investigating an accident between truck driver and plaintiff).

92.   *See* **In re Tex. Farmers Ins. Exch.**, 990 S.W.2d 337, 340 (Tex. App.—Texarkana 1999, orig. proceeding) (privilege does not apply if attorney acted in any other capacity), *mand. denied*, 12 S.W.3d 807 (Tex. 2000); *see e.g.*, **Harlandale Indep. Sch. Dist. v. Cornyn**, 25 S.W.3d 328, 332-35 (Tex. App.—Austin 2000, pet. denied) (although attorney-client privilege does not apply to communications between client and attorney if attorney is employed in a nonlegal capacity, attorney who conducted a factual investigation before preparing report on potential legal liability was retained to provide legal, not merely investigative, assistance; attorney's report was privileged).

is acting as an accountant,[93] bail bondsman,[94] friend,[95] parent,[96] or in some other capacity,[97] the privilege does not apply. The attorney-client relationship must exist at the time of the communication.[98]

The attorney-client privilege protects the confidential communications of a client's representative, defined in Rule 503(a)(2), as well as all those of the client.[99] When the client is an individual, there is little difficulty in determining who is the client's representative.[100] Organizations, however, speak only through agents. If the communications of all of an organization's agents are brought within the privilege, too much information may be kept from the trier of fact. On the other hand, organizations need the protection of the privilege so that they may receive effective legal counsel. In their efforts to resolve this problem, both commentators[101] and courts[102] have focused on how to define the representative of a corporate client.

93.   *See Clayton v. Canida*, 223 S.W.2d 264, 266 (Tex. Civ. App.—Texarkana 1949, no writ); *see also In re Grand Jury Investigation*, 842 F.2d 1223, 1224-25 (11th Cir. 1987) (preparation of a tax return is generally not legal advice and thus not protected by attorney-client privilege); *United States v. Lawless*, 709 F.2d 485, 488 (7th Cir. 1983) (information transmitted to an attorney for preparation of a tax return is not protected by attorney-client privilege); *Huie v. DeShazo*, 922 S.W.2d 920, 927 (Tex. 1996) (orig. proceeding) (federal cases have held that the privilege does not apply when an attorney is employed to prepare tax returns because the attorney is primarily performing accounting, not legal services). *But see Colton v. United States*, 306 F.2d 633, 637 (2d Cir. 1962) (communications relating to preparation of tax returns and tax advice are within attorney-client privilege).

94.   *See Cathey v. State*, 467 S.W.2d 472, 473-74 (Tex. Crim. App. 1971) (defendant's invocation of the privilege was overruled on the grounds that attorney had been acting as a bondsman, not as an attorney, and that the testimony elicited did not concern a confidential communication).

95.   *See Modern Woodmen v. Watkins*, 132 F.2d 352, 354 (5th Cir. 1942) (federal attorney-client privilege does not protect matters discussed with an attorney "merely as a personal friend").

96.   *See, e.g., In re Kinoy*, 326 F. Supp. 400, 403-05 (S.D.N.Y. 1970) (attorney was not immune from appearance before a grand jury that sought to learn the whereabouts of the attorney's daughter, whom the grand jury wanted to question).

97.   *See, e.g., Pondrum v. Gray*, 298 S.W. 409, 412 (Tex. Comm'n App. 1927, holding approved) (requiring attorney to testify about execution of a deed because attorney was acting as conveyancer and not legal adviser), *modified on other grounds*, 1 S.W.2d 278 (Tex. Comm'n App. 1928, holding approved); *In re Tex. Farmers Ins. Exch.*, 990 S.W.2d at 341 (attorney-client privilege did not apply to sworn statements by plaintiffs gathered while attorney was acting as an investigator before claim was denied and lawsuit was filed); *Childress v. Tate*, 148 S.W. 843, 844 (Tex. Civ. App.—Fort Worth 1912, writ ref'd) (rejecting attorney-client privilege when attorney was acting as a scrivener).

98.   *See United States v. Wilson*, 798 F.2d 509, 513 (1st Cir. 1986).

99.   *See* Tex. R. Evid. 503(a)(2), (b)(1).

100. *See Rosebud v. State*, 50 Tex. Crim. 475, 476-77, 98 S.W. 858, 859 (1906) (communications between an attorney and friends of the attorney's client cannot be admitted into evidence).

101. *See* 2 Weinstein & Berger, *supra* note 29, ¶503(b)[04], at 503-59 to 503-93 (tracing the development of the attorney-client privilege in the corporate arena); David Simon, *The Attorney-Client Privilege as Applied to Corporations*, 65 Yale L.J. 953, 956-69 (1956) (reviewing the policies and origins of allowing corporations privileges in discovery); Glen Weissenberger, *Toward Precision in the Application of the Attorney-Client Privilege for Corporations*, 65 Iowa L. Rev. 899, 921-22 (1980) (employees who may have authority to initiate contact with an attorney may not have the authority to act on behalf of the corporation based on that advice); Michael W. Tankersley, Note, *The Corporate Attorney-Client Privilege: Culpable Employees, Attorney Ethics, and the Joint Defense Doctrine*, 58 Tex. L. Rev. 809, 835-43 (1980) (proposing criteria for granting the corporate client an attorney-client privilege).

102. *See Upjohn Co. v. United States*, 449 U.S. 383, 393-95 (1981) (attorney-client privilege can protect communications by employees at all levels of the corporation); *In re Grand Jury Investigation*, 599 F.2d 1224, 1233-37 (3d Cir. 1979) (the position of the individual in the corporate hierarchy determines the extent to which any disclosure made by that individual to an attorney is entitled to privilege); *Diversified Indus., Inc. v. Meredith*, 572 F.2d 596,

Two basic approaches emerged in the literature and published opinions—the subject-matter test[103] and the control-group test.[104] Briefly stated, the subject-matter test protects a communication made by an employee at the direction of a corporate superior for the purpose of securing legal advice.[105] The subject matter of the communication must be within the scope of the employee's duties and must not be disseminated beyond those persons who need to know its contents.[106] The control-group test, which has been rejected both in Texas and under federal common law,[107] treated the status of the communicating employee as dispositive.[108] The privilege applied only if

608-11 (8th Cir. 1978) (en banc) (discussing the development of the competing tests used by the federal courts to determine the extent of the attorney-client privilege in the corporate context); *Harper & Row Publ'rs, Inc. v. Decker*, 423 F.2d 487, 490-92 (7th Cir. 1970) (employee's communications are privileged if that employee acted with the authority of the corporation and acted in the course of employment), *aff'd by an equally divided court*, 400 U.S. 348 (1971).

103. *See Decker*, 423 F.2d at 491-92 (formulating the subject-matter test); *see also Diversified Indus.*, 572 F.2d at 609-11 (applying the subject-matter test because it achieves the objectives of the attorney-client privilege).

104. *City of Phila. v. Westinghouse Elec. Corp.*, 210 F. Supp. 483, 485 (E.D. Pa. 1962) (originating the control-group test), *mand. denied sub nom. General Elec. Co. v. Kirkpatrick*, 312 F.2d 742 (3d Cir. 1962). *See generally Nat'l Tank Co. v. Brotherton*, 851 S.W.2d 193, 198 (Tex. 1993) (orig. proceeding) (setting out and distinguishing the subject-matter and control-group tests); Bryson P. Burnham, *The Attorney-Client Privilege in the Corporate Arena*, 24 Bus. Law. 901, 906-08 (1969) (discussing the "control group" theory in regard to corporate clients); Michael L. Waldman, *Beyond Upjohn: The Attorney-Client Privilege in the Corporate Context*, 28 Wm. & Mary L. Rev. 473, 506-10 (1987) (federal courts should adopt a control-group test "modified by an unlimited representational privilege" to determine which attorney-corporate client communications are protected); Note, *Attorney-Client Privilege for Corporate Clients: The Control Group Test*, 84 Harv. L. Rev. 424, 429-35 (1970) [hereinafter *Corporate Clients*] (comparing the control-group test and the *Harper & Row Publishers, Inc. v. Decker* test).

105. *See In re USA Waste Mgmt. Res., L.L.C.*, 387 S.W.3d 92, 96 (Tex. App.—Houston [14th Dist.] 2012, orig. proceeding [mand. denied]); *In re Monsanto Co.*, 998 S.W.2d 917, 931 (Tex. App.—Waco 1999, orig. proceeding). Under the subject-matter test, a corporate employee's statement is deemed to be that of the corporate client if "the employee makes the communication at the direction of his superiors in the corporation and where the subject matter upon which the attorney's advice is sought by the corporation and dealt with in the communication is the performance by the employee of the duties of his employment." *Decker*, 423 F.2d at 491-92; *accord Brotherton*, 851 S.W.2d at 198. Thus, statements made by lower-level employees to the corporation's attorney at the behest of corporate management are protected. *See Upjohn Co.*, 449 U.S. at 394-95.

106. *Diversified Indus.*, 572 F.2d at 609; *see In re USA Waste Mgmt.*, 387 S.W.3d at 96; *In re Monsanto Co.*, 998 S.W.2d at 931.

107. *See Upjohn Co.*, 449 U.S. at 396-97. When the original Civil Rules were promulgated in 1983, the Texas Supreme Court opted for the control-group-test language. Tex. R. Civ. Evid. 503(a)(2), 641-642 S.W.2d (Tex. Cases) xlii (1983, amended 1998) ("A representative of the client is one having authority to obtain professional legal services, or to act on advice rendered pursuant thereto, on behalf of the client."). The court of criminal appeals followed suit when it promulgated the Criminal Rules of Evidence in 1986. Tex. R. Crim. Evid. 503(a)(2), 701-702 S.W.2d (Tex. Cases) xli (1986, amended 1998) ("A representative of the client is one having authority to obtain professional legal services, or to act on advice rendered pursuant thereto, on behalf of the client."). The test was rejected when the unified Rules were promulgated in 1998. *See In re Segner*, 441 S.W.3d 409, 412 (Tex. App.—Dallas 2013, orig. proceeding) ("[T]he 'control group' test no longer applies under Rule 503 of the Texas Rules of Evidence."). *But see In re Tex. Health Res.*, 472 S.W.3d 895, 902 (Tex. App.—Dallas 2015, orig. proceeding) ("Subpart A of [Rule] 503(a)(2) adopts what is known as the 'control group' test for determining who falls within the coverage of the privilege afforded to communications with client representatives, while subpart B adopts the 'subject matter' test."). Refer to notes 112-121 *infra* and accompanying text.

108. *See Brotherton*, 851 S.W.2d at 197. As the supreme court noted, the control-group test "reflects the distinction between the corporate entity and the individual employee and is based on the premise that only an employee who controls the actions of the corporation can personify the corporation." *Id.* Under this test, even those communications made by lower-level employees who speak at the urging of and with the "blessing" of upper-level corporate management are not privileged. *Id.* at 198.

the employee was empowered to control or take a substantial part in a decision about any action the corporation may take based on the legal advice rendered (or was an authorized member of a group that has decision-making authority).[109]

The claimed benefit of the subject-matter test—that it allows low- and mid-level employees to communicate necessary information—was considered to be largely illusory. If corporate counsel were to be completely frank with low- and mid-level employees, the attorney would inform them that the information they give is privileged only if the corporation wants it to be privileged. That is, the corporation is the client; the privilege is for the corporation's benefit and does not protect its employees.[110] Thus, a properly informed employee is not likely to be forthcoming with facts that implicate him in wrongdoing.[111]

The language of the control-group test, however, was criticized as impairing a corporation's right to effective legal counsel. Under the original Rule 503, the ability of counsel and upper-level management to seek out crucial information from lower-level employees, who were most aware of pertinent events and were responsible for making critical operational decisions and inquiries on a daily basis, was substantially impaired because those communications were not privileged.[112] Furthermore, the lower-level employees' ability to obtain legal advice in order to make informed decisions about day-to-day operations was hindered because neither their request nor the attorney's advice to them was protected.[113] Thus, as a part of the 1998 unification of the Civil and Crimi-

---

109. *See Ford Motor Co. v. Leggat*, 904 S.W.2d 643, 646 (Tex. 1995) (orig. proceeding); *Osborne v. Johnson*, 954 S.W.2d 180, 184 (Tex. App.—Waco 1997, orig. proceeding [mand. denied]); *Cigna Corp. v. Spears*, 838 S.W.2d 561, 565 (Tex. App.—San Antonio 1992, orig. proceeding); *see, e.g.*, *Tex. Dep't of MHMR v. Davis*, 775 S.W.2d 467, 473 (Tex. App.—Austin 1989, orig. proceeding [leave denied]) (refusing to extend attorney-client privilege to department of mental health when none of the investigators of drowning at state school were "persons entitled to engage in confidential communication, or were persons whose participation was needed in order to facilitate rendition of any legal services"); *see also City of Phila.*, 210 F. Supp. at 485 (whether attorney-client privilege applies to employee's communication is determined by employee's actual authority).

110. *See In re Grand Jury Investigation*, 599 F.2d 1224, 1236 (3d Cir. 1979). Even those within the control group may lose the ability to decide whether to waive the privilege. *See In re O.P.M. Leasing Servs., Inc.*, 670 F.2d 383, 385-86 (2d Cir. 1982) (trustee in bankruptcy, not former corporate officers, has the right to waive the privilege on behalf of the corporation); *Citibank v. Andros*, 666 F.2d 1192, 1195 (8th Cir. 1981) (power to waive the privilege passes with other corporate property to trustee).

111. On the other hand, an employee who has not engaged in wrongdoing will likely follow his superiors' instructions and speak with the attorney. The employer, in turn, will have sufficient incentive to request the information obtained from the employee in the attorney's interview and will use that information to correct inefficiencies and comply with governmental and industry regulations. *See In re Grand Jury Investigation*, 599 F.2d at 1236. Furthermore, the attorney-client privilege is frequently inapplicable because corporate communications lack the requisite confidentiality or involve nonlegal purposes. *See* 2 LOUISELL & MUELLER, *supra* note 69, §211, at 806-11.

112. *See Valero Transmission, L.P. v. Dowd*, 960 S.W.2d 642, 646 (Tex. 1997) (Owen & Hecht, JJ., dissenting from overruling of motion for leave to file petition for writ of mandamus) ("[N]either the lawyer nor members of upper management can seek out this information and maintain the attorney-client privilege.").

113. *See id.* ("[A] communication between the lawyer and the employee who has possession of the facts that the lawyer needs to know to render legal advice is not privileged."). Justice Owen noted the deficiencies of the control-group test and recommended that Rule 503 be amended to incorporate the subject-matter test. *Id.* Justice Owen stated that

[a] large corporation ... must have the means of obtaining meaningful legal advice without waiving its privileges. A hypothetical example illustrates the inadequacy of the current definition of who is a

nal Rules, the supreme court proposed an amended definition of "representative of a client" under Rule 503(a)(2) that incorporated a broad subject-matter test.[114]

"representative of the client." Rule 503 now says that a "representative of the client" is one who has authority to obtain legal services or to act on that legal advice. Suppose a corporation seeks legal advice about some aspect of its operations to determine if it is in compliance with its contracts or perhaps with governmental regulations. And assume that its lawyer cannot adequately advise the client without knowing all the facts about this aspect of the company's operations. It is extremely naive to think that the "upper echelon" of management ... in a large organization will possess the kind of detailed, nitty-gritty facts that are often necessary to such an analysis. The knowledge of operational or middle management personnel is essential.

Id. (citations omitted).

114. *Approval of Revisions to the Texas Rules of Civil and Criminal Evidence*, 954-55 S.W.2d (Tex. Cases) XLII-XLIII (1998); *see In re Monsanto Co.*, 998 S.W.2d 917, 922 (Tex. App.—Waco 1999, orig. proceeding). In the "Statement Regarding Attorney-Client Privilege" that accompanied the proposed Texas Rules of Evidence, Justices Spector and Baker noted the expansion of the definition of a client's representative to incorporate the subject-matter test and invited public comment. 954-955 S.W.2d (Tex. Cases) XXX-XXXI (1998). The two justices also noted that several years earlier the State Bar Administration of the Rules of Evidence Committee had proposed that Rule 503(a)(2) be amended to incorporate a "modified subject matter test" based on *Diversified Industries, Inc. v. Meredith*, 572 F.2d 596 (8th Cir. 1978) (en banc). 954-955 S.W.2d (Tex. Cases) XXX (1998). Under the State Bar's proposal, a representative of a client would have included

an agent or employee of the entity who has been requested by such partner, officer, director, or such superior employee to communicate with a lawyer on a subject matter within the scope of the employee's or agent's duties in connection with securing legal advice by the entity. The term "agent" as used in this Rule does not include an independent contractor.

Id. (setting out proposed Rule 503(a)(2)(B)). This proposal would have enlarged the corporate-client representative to include lower-level employees who were specifically asked to communicate with an attorney by appropriate upper-level management. The privilege would have protected only those communications on a subject matter within the scope of the lower-level employee's job duties. The communication would have had to have been made for the purpose of securing legal advice for the entity. Under this proposal, independent contractors do not qualify as a representative of the client.

The Supreme Court Advisory Committee, in a close vote, rejected this proposal and recommended that the Texas Supreme Court make no change in the control-group test. *Id.* The supreme court then requested further guidance on this issue from the Administration of the Rules of Evidence Committee. *Id.* Through an ad hoc subcommittee, a different "subject matter test" for representatives of a corporate client was proposed, which provided that a "representative of the client" includes

(a) a member of the control group as defined by current Rule 503(a)(2) and/or

(b) other employees or agents of the client or organization if:

(1) the communication between the employee or agent and the lawyer was made for the purpose of securing legal advice or legal services;

(2) the employee or agent making the communication was expressly or implicitly authorized to do so by the client or a member of its control group so that the client could secure legal advice or legal services;

(3) the subject matter of the communication was expressly authorized by the client or a member of its control group or was within the scope of the employee's or agent's duties with the organization; and

(4) the privilege is not waived by a dissemination of the privileged communication beyond those persons who, because of the organization's structure, need to know its contents.

954-955 S.W.2d (Tex. Cases) XXX-XXXI (1998). This proposal was certainly longer than the first and was broader in some respects while narrower in others.

First, this proposal seems to include independent contractors if they were acting as agents of the client. Second, the requirement that the legal advice or legal services must be secured on behalf of the entity is deleted in the second proposal. Third, the requirement that a member of the control group specifically request the subordinate to communicate with the attorney is eliminated. Fourth, the subject matter of the communication includes both matters within the scope of the employee or agent's job duties and any other matter that was explicitly requested by the control group. Fifth, the privilege may be waived by disclosing the contents of the communication to other employ-

Rule 503(a)(2) is the broadest possible construction of the subject-matter test.[115] The rule includes as a "client's representative" any person who has authority to obtain legal services for the client or to act on the client's behalf based on the legal advice given[116] or who is acting in the "scope of employment" for the client.[117] Under Rule 503(a)(2)(B), the privilege covers not only the lower-level employee or agent who *makes* a confidential communication but also one who *receives* a confidential communication, as long as the communication "facilitate[s] the rendition of professional legal services to the client."[118] The definition does not require that the communication be made at the request of any member of the control group.[119] It does not require that the communication relate to the subject matter of the employee's job. It does not require that the communication be made to an attorney or his representative if the communication was made to effectuate legal representation for the entity. Thus, for example, if a shipyard's corporate attorney asks a lower-level dock superintendent to investigate a legally questionable situation involving bribes to customs officials, and the superintendent then makes and receives confidential communications from the lowest-level company stevedores, day laborers, and dockyard accountants about the bribes, all of these people and all of these conversations would be protected by the attorney-client privilege as long as the superintendent was making the inquiry to effectuate legal representation for the shipyard company.[120] Of course, a former employee has no control over a corporation's assertion of a privilege and can neither invoke it nor waive it against the corporation's wishes.[121]

---

ees and agents within the client entity. That is, if the attorney, any member of the control group, or any lower-level employee disclosed the contents of the communication to anyone who did not "need to know its contents," then the privilege would be pierced.

The Texas Supreme Court rejected both of those suggested revisions and instead proposed its own, much broader, amendment to Rule 503(a)(2). *See* 954-955 S.W.2d (Tex. Cases) XLII-XLIII (1998).

115. Abandoning the control-group test brought the Texas rule more in line with federal common law. In ***Upjohn Co. v. United States***, the U.S. Supreme Court rejected the control-group test for purposes of federal common law, although it did not expressly adopt the subject-matter test. *See **Upjohn Co. v. United States***, 449 U.S. 383, 396-97 (1981).

116. TEX. R. EVID. 503(a)(2)(A); *see, e.g.*, ***In re Segner***, 441 S.W.3d 409, 412 (Tex. App.—Dallas 2013, orig. proceeding) (independent contractor was client's representative under Rule 503(a)(2), even though he was not client's employee, when he was given authority to obtain and act on legal advice on client's behalf).

117. TEX. R. EVID. 503(a)(2)(B). *See generally* Craig W. Saunders, Comment, *Texas Rule of Evidence 503: Defining "Scope of Employment" for Corporations*, 30 ST. MARY'S L.J. 863 (1999) (discussing 1998 changes in attorney-client rule for corporate employees and examining when communications are made relating to employee's "scope of employment"). Presumably, this definition includes independent contractors such as accountants, subcontractors, temporary personnel, and other agents if they make or receive confidential communications while acting within the scope of their employment for the client.

118. TEX. R. EVID. 503(a)(2)(B); *see, e.g.*, ***In re Monsanto Co.***, 998 S.W.2d at 931 (although corporate documents had "many persons" listed as recipients of communications, documents were privileged because all recipients were corporate employees or attorneys).

119. *See* TEX. R. EVID. 503(a)(2). *But see **In re Monsanto Co.***, 998 S.W.2d at 931 ("The expanded 'subject matter' test deems an employee's communication privileged if it is made at the direction of his superiors ….").

120. *See* TEX. R. EVID. 503(a)(2)(B), 503(b)(1)(A), (b)(1)(D).

121. *E.g.*, ***In re Mktg. Inv'rs Corp.***, 80 S.W.3d 44, 49 (Tex. App.—Dallas 1998, orig. proceeding) (terminated employee who took corporate documents with him could not claim any privilege or waive any privilege for their possession).

Information protected from disclosure by the attorney-client privilege may still have to be revealed, and information not covered by the privilege may nevertheless be shielded. The privilege shields only the communication between the attorney and the client or the client's representative, not the factual information conveyed. Thus, although both the attorney and the client may refuse to state what they said to each other, the client must reveal what he knows in response to discovery requests.[122] Factual information cannot be insulated from discovery simply by relating it to counsel.[123]

On the other hand, information conveyed to counsel by corporate employees may not be obtained from the attorney if it is considered work product.[124] Thus, communications to counsel receive substantial protection when they relate to potential litigation, even if they are unprivileged.

In *Commodity Futures Trading Commission v. Weintraub*, the U.S. Supreme Court held that when a corporate client holds the attorney-client privilege, the management of the corporation has the exclusive power to waive the attorney-client privilege.[125] The corporation's officers and directors exercise this power of waiver, which must be consistent with their fiduciary duty to the corporation.[126] Even under the subject-matter test for deciding who is a representative of the client, an employee who is not an officer or director of the corporation may not waive the privilege,[127] and unauthorized disclosures do not act as a waiver against the corporate client. When control of the corporation passes to new management, the authority to assert the privilege passes as well.[128] On the other hand, when a company is dissolved and its assets and liabilities are assigned to another entity, there is no continuing attorney-client relationship to protect.[129]

One question that Rule 503 leaves unanswered is whether a corporation may properly claim the attorney-client privilege in a shareholder derivative action.[130] In theory, because the plaintiff brings the suit on behalf of the corporation, the corporation should not object to the plaintiff's requests for disclosure. In practice, however, the cor-

---

122. Corporations must respond to discovery requests by designating individuals with the necessary knowledge to answer interrogatories. *See* TEX. R. CIV. P. 197. The rules may also require corporations to produce documents and other tangible items, even if the corporation is not a party to the action. *See* TEX. R. CIV. P. 205.3. Nevertheless, the dispersion of relevant knowledge among numerous employees and former employees may make it difficult to unearth. *See* James A. Gardner, *A Personal Privilege for Communications of Corporate Clients—Paradox or Public Policy?*, 40 U. DET. L.J. 299, 344 (1963).

123. *Huie v. DeShazo*, 922 S.W.2d 920, 923 (Tex. 1996) (orig. proceeding).

124. Refer to notes 280-326 *infra* and accompanying text.

125. 471 U.S. 343, 348 (1985).

126. *Id.* at 348-49; *see also In re Mktg. Inv'rs Corp.*, 80 S.W.3d at 50 (former officers and directors have no control over assertion of corporation's privilege).

127. *Cf. Menton v. Lattimore*, 667 S.W.2d 335, 341 (Tex. App.—Fort Worth 1984, orig. proceeding) (discussing work-product privilege under former Texas Rule of Civil Procedure 186a).

128. *In re Cap Rock Elec. Coop., Inc.*, 35 S.W.3d 222, 227 (Tex. App.—Texarkana 2000, orig. proceeding).

129. *See id.* at 229.

130. Similar problems arise when the action against the corporation is based directly on the stockholder's alleged right. *See Garner v. Wolfinbarger*, 430 F.2d 1093, 1097 & n.11 (5th Cir. 1970).

poration typically controls those who committed acts that generated the litigation. Thus, the plaintiff-shareholder and the corporation are often antagonistic toward each other. Several federal courts have considered this issue. For instance, ***Garner v. Wolfinbarger***, the leading case in this area, stresses the importance of weighing management's need to confer confidentially with counsel against the consequences of allowing management to cloak its actions in a veil of secrecy.[131] Thus, when a plaintiff-stockholder charged a corporation with acting against stockholder interests, the Fifth Circuit held that the stockholder must receive an opportunity to show good cause why the corporation's claim of privilege should be rejected.[132] The flexible ***Garner*** position has found support in other federal courts[133] and with commentators[134] and is certainly consistent with the policies underlying Rule 503.

2. Rule 503(a)(3) & (a)(4): Lawyer & lawyer's representative. Rule 503(a)(3) defines "lawyer" as a person licensed to practice law in any state or nation.[135] The attorney does not need to be a member of the bar of the jurisdiction where his counsel is sought.[136] In addition, a client's confidential communications to a person he reasonably believes[137] to be an attorney fall within the privilege.[138]

The privilege extends to confidential communications made to an attorney's representative—that is, someone employed by the attorney to assist in the rendition of legal services.[139] Thus, communications made to office personnel such as law clerks and secretaries fall within the privilege because they, like interpreters,[140] may be "persons

---

131. *Id.* at 1101.

132. *Id.* at 1103-04. The court listed nine factors for the lower court to consider on remand in deciding whether the plaintiffs satisfied the good-cause requirement. *Id.* at 1104.

133. *See **Ohio-Sealy Mattress Mfg. Co. v. Kaplan***, 90 F.R.D. 21, 31-32 (N.D. Ill. 1980); ***Cohen v. Uniroyal, Inc.***, 80 F.R.D. 480, 483-84 (E.D. Pa. 1978). *But see **Shirvani v. Capital Investing Corp.***, 112 F.R.D. 389, 390 (D. Conn. 1986) (good-cause exception is "ill-defined in origin" and "troublesome in application").

134. *See, e.g.*, 2 LOUISELL & MUELLER, *supra* note 69, §212, at 815-21 (discussing ***Garner***). *But see* Steven A. Saltzburg, *Corporate Attorney-Client Privilege in Shareholder and Similar Cases:* Garner Revisited, 12 HOFSTRA L. REV. 817, 839-841 (1984) (criticizing ***Garner*** and suggesting an alternative); H. Richard Dallas, Note, *The Attorney-Client Privilege and the Corporation in Shareholder Litigation*, 50 S. CAL. L. REV. 303, 321-24 (1977) (***Garner*** inadequately protects legitimate corporate interests).

135. TEX. R. EVID. 503(a)(3); *see also* 8 WIGMORE, *supra* note 6, §2300, at 580-81 (averring that "[t]here is no ground for encouraging the relation of client and legal adviser except when the adviser is one who has been formally admitted to the office of attorney or counselor as duly qualified to give legal advice").

136. *See Proposed Rules*, *supra* note 28, at 238 (FED. R. EVID. 503 advisory committee's note).

137. ***Strong v. State***, 773 S.W.2d 543, 549 (Tex. Crim. App. 1989).

138. *See* TEX. R. EVID. 503(a)(3); 1 RAY, *supra* note 52, §423, at 133 (Supp. 1991).

139. TEX. R. EVID. 503(a)(4)(A). *But see **United States v. Pipkins***, 528 F.2d 559, 563 (5th Cir. 1976) (nothing in the policy of privileges suggests that attorneys may simply place accountants, investigators, or others on the payroll, maintain them in their offices, and invest all communications between them and clients with a privilege that would not follow if such persons were "operating under their own steam").

140. *E.g.*, ***United States v. Salamanca***, 244 F. Supp. 2d 1023, 1025-26 (D.S.D. 2003) (trial court disqualified interpreter as a proposed expert witness for government because trial court had appointed interpreter to assist defendant's attorney in communicating with defendant, interpreter had been privy to and translated confidential communications between attorney and client, and interpreter was "a necessary component of" defendant's communication with his attorney and therefore was attorney's agent; disqualification served to "preserve the integrity of the judicial process, promote fundamental fairness, and prevent any possible conflict of interest").

who are the media of communication."[141] In addition, if an attorney employs an expert to assist in communicating with the client or in planning and executing litigation, the privilege shields confidential communications with the expert.[142] For example, if an attorney retains a psychiatrist for advice about a client's mental state, communications made to and by the psychiatrist are privileged.[143] The attorney-client privilege also applies to experts retained solely as consultants. However, when an expert is hired with the expectation that he will testify at trial, neither the attorney nor the expert intends for the communications to remain confidential. Therefore, knowledge that the expert gains from such communications is unprivileged.[144] Texas Rule 503 specifically includes in the definition of "lawyer's representative" the clause "an accountant who is reasonably necessary for the lawyer's rendition of professional legal services."[145] Presumably, the purpose of this change was to eliminate the requirement that an accountant be employed by the attorney for the attorney-client privilege to apply. Courts should consider any expert employed at the attorney's request to be "employed by the lawyer," even

---

141. *See* ***Morton v. Smith***, 44 S.W. 683, 684 (Tex. Civ. App. 1898, no writ); *cf.* ***Burnett v. State***, 642 S.W.2d 765, 768-69 (Tex. Crim. App. 1982) (tape recording of "pre-hypnotic" interview was protected by attorney-client privilege because hypnotist was acting as the means of communication between attorney and client).

142. *See* ***Burnett***, 642 S.W.2d at 769; *see also Proposed Rules, supra* note 28, at 238 (Fed. R. Evid. 503 advisory committee's note).

143. *See* ***Burnett***, 642 S.W.2d at 769 n.12; 2 Louisell & Mueller, *supra* note 69, §209, at 751; *see, e.g.*, ***In re Houseman***, 66 S.W.3d 368, 371 (Tex. App.—Beaumont 2001, orig. proceeding) (communications by subject of guardianship proceeding to psychiatrist were privileged because psychiatrist, who was retained by subject's previous attorney to assess her mental and testamentary capacity, was acting as attorney's representative by assisting in rendition of professional legal advice); *see also* ***United States v. Alvarez***, 519 F.2d 1036, 1045-46 (3d Cir. 1975) (attorney-client privilege extends to psychiatrist consulted for professional advice about client); ***City & Cty. of S.F. v. Super. Ct.***, 231 P.2d 26, 31 (Cal. 1951) (attorney-client privilege extends to attorney's agents, including physician who examines client and reports client's medical condition to attorney). Communications to other kinds of experts acting in a similar capacity would also be privileged.

144. In ***Rogers v. State***, 598 S.W.2d 258, 261 (Tex. Crim. App. 1980), and ***Granviel v. State***, 552 S.W.2d 107, 114-16 (Tex. Crim. App. 1976), the court rejected the accused's claim that the attorney-client privilege barred testimony by his examining psychiatrist because the expert had been appointed by the trial court as the court's disinterested expert. The Code of Criminal Procedure provides that when the accused's competency to stand trial is in question or an insanity defense is raised, the court may appoint such disinterested experts to examine the accused, report to the court, and testify about their findings. Tex. Code Crim. Proc. art. 46B.021(a) (competency), art. 46C.101(a) (insanity defense). In addition, the court may force an attorney to disclose documents used to prepare the expert in advance of trial. Texas Rule 612 extends the common-law rule that an adverse party can inspect and use a writing used to refresh a witness's memory while testifying. Rule 612 provides that if a witness uses a writing to refresh his memory either before or while testifying, the court has discretion to require production of the document for such inspection and use. *See* Tex. R. Evid. 612(a), (b). Courts have held that Federal Rule 612, which is analogous to the Texas rule, takes precedence over claims of attorney-client privilege or work-product protection. *See* ***Wheeling-Pittsburgh Steel Corp. v. Underwriters Labs., Inc.***, 81 F.R.D. 8, 10-11 (N.D. Ill. 1978). Further, the rights afforded to the adverse party under Federal Rule 612 have been held to apply to documents shown to the witness in preparation for deposition testimony as well as trial testimony. *See* ***James Julian, Inc. v. Raytheon Co.***, 93 F.R.D. 138, 144-46 (D. Del. 1982). Thus, an attorney's disclosure of documents to a future witness may result in waiver of the protections afforded by the attorney-client privilege or the work-product doctrine. Refer to notes 309-312 *infra* and accompanying text.

145. Tex. R. Evid. 503(a)(4)(B). This language was not in the version of the rules proposed by the State Bar Liaison Committee on the Rules of Evidence. *See* Tex. R. Evid. 503(a)(4) (1982 Liaison Committee proposal), *reprinted infra* p. 1081. Nor can such language be found in any other codified versions of the attorney-client privilege. *See, e.g.*, Cal. Evid. Code §§950, 954; Model Code of Evid. R. 210 (1942); 2 Weinstein & Berger, *supra* note 29, ¶503[03].

if the client pays the expert's fee directly. Otherwise, the applicability of the privilege would hinge on the formalism of whether the expert is paid directly by the client or indirectly by the client as reimbursement to the attorney for expenses.

The attorney-client privilege applies only to confidential communications made between the expert and the attorney or his representative that facilitates the rendition of professional legal services to the client.[146] Thus, the privilege does not protect information communicated to an accountant for the purpose of obtaining accounting services simply because an attorney later consults with the accountant; that privilege protects only those communications among attorney, accountant, and client that relate to legal services.[147]

While the Texas Rules of Civil Procedure protect a party during discovery from having to divulge information communicated to a consulting expert,[148] this immunity applies only to discovery. The Rules of Procedure are not evidentiary rules.[149] Thus, without the attorney-client privilege, a party would be free to call an opponent's consulting expert at trial and ask about communications between the expert and the attorney or client.[150] The attorney-client privilege also provides greater protection than the discov-

---

146. *See* Tex. R. Evid. 503(b). If the attorney is merely acting as the client's business adviser, investigator, or friend, their communications are not protected by the privilege. Refer to notes 92-97 *supra* and accompanying text. However, if the attorney was retained to give legal advice, his factual investigation or business advice, which is a necessary part of the rendition of legal advice, is protected. *See, e.g.,* **Harlandale Indep. Sch. Dist. v. Cornyn**, 25 S.W.3d 328, 333-35 (Tex. App.—Austin 2000, pet. denied) (when attorney was retained to provide legal advice to school district based on her independent investigation, her entire report, including factual findings of investigation, was privileged).

147. *See, e.g.,* **Parker v. Carnahan**, 772 S.W.2d 151, 157-58 (Tex. App.—Texarkana 1989, writ denied) (when evidence showed that attorneys had no control over an accountant's work, attorney-client privilege did not apply even though attorneys had hired accountant for client's benefit). The Texas Occupations Code contains a separate accountant-client privilege that generally protects information disclosed by a client to a licensed accountant or to a partner, member, officer, shareholder, or employee of the accountant or the accountant's firm in connection with accounting services. *See* Tex. Occ. Code §901.457(a). The statute does, however, provide exceptions to the privilege to make accountant-client information discoverable in certain circumstances. *See id.* §901.457(b). See **O'Connor's Texas Rules * Civil Trials** (2017), "Certain accountant-client communications," ch. 6-B, §2.15, p. 537. Federal law does not recognize an accountant-client privilege. **United States v. Arthur Young & Co.**, 465 U.S. 805, 817 (1984).

148. Tex. R. Civ. P. 192.3(e).

149. *See* **State v. Biggers**, 360 S.W.2d 516, 517-18 (Tex. 1962) (per curiam); **City of Hous. v. Autrey**, 351 S.W.2d 948, 949-50 (Tex. Civ. App.—Waco 1961, writ ref'd n.r.e.). *But see* **Gass v. Baggerly**, 332 S.W.2d 426, 430 (Tex. Civ. App.—Dallas 1960, no writ) (driver's statement to his insurance company, inadvertently disclosed to the plaintiff's attorney, was properly excluded). The better justification for the **Gass** decision is that the attorney-client privilege protects the statement and that inadvertent disclosure does not waive the privilege. Refer to notes 912-933 *infra* and accompanying text. A similar confusion between the evidentiary privilege and the rules of discovery occurred in **Hiebert v. Weiss**, 622 S.W.2d 150, 151-52 (Tex. App.—Fort Worth 1981, writ ref'd n.r.e.), in which the court held that a statement made by the defendant to an investigator for his insurance company was not admissible at trial because the document was not discoverable.

150. Of course, it may be difficult to discover the identity of an opponent's consulting expert because the Texas Supreme Court has shielded such information from discovery. **Werner v. Miller**, 579 S.W.2d 455, 456 (Tex. 1979). Even when the identity of the expert was discovered by other means, the long-standing common-law rule that a party "vouched" for his witnesses and could cross-examine them only if their testimony caused surprise or injury to the party's case discouraged the calling of an opponent's consultants. *See* 1 Ray, *supra* note 52, §631, at 561-62 (3d ed. 1980). Under Rule 607 (party calling witness may attack witness's credibility) and Rule 611(c) (party may ask leading questions on cross-examination and when party calls hostile witness, adverse party, or witness identified with

ery rules do. The privilege shields communications between an expert retained by counsel to assist in the rendition of legal services and a client who is not a party to the litigation.[151] Further, the privilege continues even after litigation ceases and the attorney-client relationship ends.[152]

Also among those considered a representative of the attorney is an insurance company's investigator who takes a statement from an insured to assist the insurance company's attorney in defending a possible claim against the insured.[153] However, the privilege does not apply to an insured's communication to its liability insurer about an incident that may give rise to legal liability covered by the insurance policy.[154]

If an attorney simply directs or asks the client's employees to conduct an investigation, these investigators are not necessarily the representatives of the attorney or the client for purposes of the privilege rule.[155] As a practical matter, an attorney who wants

---

adverse party), however, a party may be more willing to cross-examine an opponent's consulting expert. For a discussion of Rule 607, refer to *Article VI: Witnesses, infra* p. 596. For a discussion of Rule 611, refer to *Article VI: Witnesses, infra* p. 636.

151. *See Metroflight, Inc. v. Argonaut Ins.*, 403 F. Supp. 1195, 1197-98 (N.D. Tex. 1975).

152. Refer to note 232 *infra* and accompanying text.

153. In *Metroflight*, Metroflight sued its insurers when they claimed that certain exclusions in Metroflight's policy were applicable. 403 F. Supp. at 1196. The defendant sought to discover the substance of communications between Shaffer, the insurance agent who secured Metroflight's coverage with the defendant, and the agent of Floyd West Co., which insured Shaffer and was obligated to defend him against a charge of negligence, error, or omission. *Id.* Neither Shaffer nor Floyd West Co. was a party to the suit. *Id.* at 1197. Thus, if the case had been brought in state court, the provision of Texas Rule of Civil Procedure 192.5 (exempting from discovery communications made in anticipation of litigation or for trial between or among a party or his agents, representatives, or employees) could not have been invoked. The attorney-client privilege would have to protect such communications. Similarly, under the Federal Rules of Civil Procedure, courts could bar disclosure only if the communications were privileged. *See* FED. R. CIV. P. 26(b)(1). Because *Metroflight* was a diversity case, state privilege law controlled this discovery issue. *See* FED. R. EVID. 501. The court, therefore, had to determine whether communications between an insured and his insurance company were privileged in Texas. *See Metroflight*, 403 F. Supp. at 1196. While noting that case law was not decisive on this issue, the court concluded that Texas provides a "limited privilege" for communications between an insured and his insurer as an "outgrowth of the privilege protecting communications between a lawyer and his client." *Id.* at 1196-97. The court reasoned that the privilege covers communications between the insured and the insurance company's attorney when the latter is preparing a defense to an actual or anticipated claim. *Id.* at 1197. Thus, extending the privilege to communications between the insured and the insurer, through a nonattorney investigator, is a small step and is consistent with the policy of encouraging full disclosure. *Id.* at 1197-98; *see also Hiebert*, 622 S.W.2d at 151-52 (upholding exclusion of communications between the insured and an investigator for the insurance company, but mistakenly relying on the provisions of discovery rules). However, the privilege protects only the communications intended to assist an attorney in the defense of a possible claim against the insured. *Metroflight*, 403 F. Supp. at 1197. In reaching its conclusion on the status of Texas law on this point, the federal court cited *Dobbins v. Gardner*, 377 S.W.2d 665 (Tex. Civ. App.—Houston 1964, writ ref'd n.r.e.), *Gass v. Baggerly*, 332 S.W.2d 426 (Tex. Civ. App.—Dallas 1960, no writ), *Lantex Constr. Co. v. Lejsal*, 315 S.W.2d 177 (Tex. Civ. App.—Waco 1958, writ ref'd n.r.e.), and *Hurley v. McMillan*, 268 S.W.2d 229 (Tex. Civ. App.—Galveston 1954, writ ref'd n.r.e.). *Metroflight*, 403 F. Supp. at 1196-97.

154. *E.g.*, *In re Ford Motor Co.*, 988 S.W.2d 714, 719 (Tex. 1998) (orig. proceeding) (insurer's claim file and engineer's report were not privileged).

155. *E.g.*, *Tex. Dep't of MHMR v. Davis*, 775 S.W.2d 467, 473 (Tex. App.—Austin 1989, orig. proceeding [leave denied]) (when the department's attorney instructed school to investigate the drowning of student, and department did not prove that investigating employees of the school were client representatives, taped statements of witnesses and investigative report were not privileged); *Brown & Root U.S.A., Inc. v. Moore*, 731 S.W.2d 137, 139-40 (Tex. App.—Houston [14th Dist.] 1987, no writ) (attorney-client privilege did not apply to investigation of claims representative because investigator was under direct control of company and not of attorney); *see also Sterling Drilling*

to maintain the attorney-client privilege when using investigators should retain the investigator for the purpose of this specific investigation as a part of providing legal services to the specific client.

3. Rule 503(a)(5): Confidential communication. Not all information that a client communicates to an attorney to facilitate the rendition of legal services is protected from disclosure. The attorney-client privilege extends only to communications made confidentially. However, it has been held that "the subject matter of a completed attorney-client communication is immaterial when deciding if the privilege applies."[156] In determining whether the privilege protects a particular oral or written communication, courts focus on whether (1) the client intended, by this specific communication, to obtain legal advice, (2) the communication was intended to be confidential, and (3) the communication was made by the attorney, the client, or the representative of either, in relation to the legal advice sought by the client.[157] Only confidential communications made in furtherance of professional legal services are protected.[158] Once this predicate has been met, the privilege protects any disclosure of the specific subject matter of the communication.

On the other hand, a person "cannot cloak a material fact with the privilege merely by communicating it to an attorney."[159] For example, a witness or party can be asked if he stole money from the bank, but he cannot be asked if he told his attorney that he

---

Co. v. Spector, 761 S.W.2d 74, 76 (Tex. App.—San Antonio 1988, orig. proceeding) (statements taken by attorney hired by workers' compensation carrier were not privileged because no evidence could show that attorney worked for the drilling company that asserted the privilege).

156. *Marathon Oil Co. v. Moyé*, 893 S.W.2d 585, 591 (Tex. App.—Dallas 1994, orig. proceeding [leave denied]). *But see Austin v. State*, 934 S.W.2d 672, 676 (Tex. Crim. App. 1996) (Maloney, J., concurring) ("To state that the subject matter of a communication is irrelevant in determining whether a communication is privileged under Rule 503(b) would make the privilege available to any type of confidential communication between an attorney and his client."). Judge Maloney's concern is undercut by the general requirement that a party asserting the privilege must show that the confidential communication was made to further the rendition of legal advice. The proponent must offer some evidence of the general topic discussed, but need not divulge the precise subject matter or details of the discussion.

157. *See* TEX. R. EVID. 503(a)(5).

158. *See* TEX. R. EVID. 503(a)(5)(A); *see, e.g.*, *Swearingen v. State*, 101 S.W.3d 89, 100-01 (Tex. Crim. App. 2003) (trial court properly denied motion to suppress letter written by defendant because no evidence was given that letter was intended to be confidential attorney-client communication; the letter claimed to be from a third party with information exonerating defendant and was seized from defendant's attorney's office); *In re Tex. Health Res.*, 472 S.W.3d 895, 904 (Tex. App.—Dallas 2015, orig. proceeding) (notes about employers' liability claim, between a lawyer and representatives of entity, were a confidential communication under Rule 503 when they showed on their face that they documented discussion of issues related to defense of claim).

159. *Huie v. DeShazo*, 922 S.W.2d 920, 923 (Tex. 1996) (orig. proceeding); *see Upjohn Co. v. United States*, 449 U.S. 383, 395-96 (1981); *Nat'l Tank Co. v. Brotherton*, 851 S.W.2d 193, 199 (Tex. 1993) (orig. proceeding). In *Huie*, the court set out the following hypothetical to distinguish between privileged communications and nonprivileged facts:

> Assume that a trustee who has misappropriated money from a trust confidentially reveals this fact to his or her attorney for the purpose of obtaining legal advice. The trustee, when asked at trial whether he or she misappropriated money, cannot claim the attorney-client privilege. The act of misappropriation is a material fact of which the trustee has knowledge independently of the communication. The trustee must therefore disclose the fact (assuming no other privilege applies), even though the trustee confidentially conveyed the fact to the attorney. However, because the attorney's only knowl-

stole money from the bank, and the attorney cannot be asked if his client told him he had stolen money from the bank. The facts, and the client's knowledge of these facts, are not privileged, but the content of the confidential communications between attorney and client are privileged.[160]

If an attorney-client communication is confidential, the privilege extends to the complete communication, including the otherwise nonprivileged factual information contained within that communication as well as the legal advice or request for advice.[161]

(1) Confidentiality. Rule 503 defines confidentiality in terms of intent. A communication is confidential if it is not intended to be disclosed to persons other than those who facilitate the rendition of legal services.[162] The party invoking the privilege must prove that the communication was "'(1) intended to remain confidential *and* (2) under the circumstances was *reasonably* expected and understood to be confidential.'"[163]

By focusing on intent, the rule resolves a possible conflict among Texas cases about the effect of the inadvertent disclosure of an otherwise privileged communication. For

---

edge of the misappropriation is through the confidential communication, the attorney cannot be called on to reveal this information.
922 S.W.2d at 923.

In *In re Learjet, Inc.*, the defendant aircraft manufacturer made a videotape composed of various statements of its employees, who had previously been designated as expert witnesses, to use in mediation with the plaintiff. 59 S.W.3d 842, 844 (Tex. App.—Texarkana 2001, orig. proceeding). When the mediation failed, the plaintiff obtained copies of the tape through judicially compelled discovery. *Id.* The defendant sought mandamus, arguing that the videotape was protected by the attorney-client privilege because it was prepared to "'facilitate the rendition of legal services, specifically for use as materials in mediation.'" *Id.* The court of appeals held that, although materials prepared for mediation are confidential, the witnesses' statements themselves were discoverable independent of the mediation process because they were factual statements made by prospective witnesses. *Id.* at 845-46. Further, the tape contained no confidential communications or statements about trial strategy or legal analysis. *Id.*

160. For example, a computer database created by an attorney is not protected by the attorney-client privilege if it contains facts, as opposed to confidential communications, conveyed by a client; it may, of course, be protected as attorney work product. *See* *In re Bloomfield Mfg. Co.*, 977 S.W.2d 389, 392 (Tex. App.—San Antonio 1998, orig. proceeding) ("For an instrument to be protected by the attorney-client privilege, it needs to constitute a communication between an attorney and client and owe its existence to an effort to transmit information from one to the other."); *see also* *Freiermuth v. PPG Indus., Inc.*, 218 F.R.D. 694, 699-700 (N.D. Ala. 2003) (privilege does not protect the disclosure of underlying facts by those who communicated with an attorney; "[w]hile a memorandum analyzing the legal risk of the proposed reduction in force would be privileged, ... the facts provided to counsel which support a business decision to engage in a workforce reduction are not protected"); *Smith v. Texaco, Inc.*, 186 F.R.D. 354, 357 (E.D. Tex. 1999) (data table listing employee information was not privileged, though interpretive material, graphs, and analysis were privileged; "[m]erely reorganizing material at the direction of counsel does not invoke the privilege").

161. *In re Valero Energy Corp.*, 973 S.W.2d 453, 457 (Tex. App.—Houston [14th Dist.] 1998, orig. proceeding) (op. on reh'g); *see* *Huie*, 922 S.W.2d at 923. Neither courts nor counsel are required to redact a phrase of legal advice or a sentence of confidential communication within a single document. Courts have even held that otherwise discoverable documents attached to a confidential communication may be privileged. *See* *In re Monsanto Co.*, 998 S.W.2d 917, 931 n.19 (Tex. App.—Waco 1999, orig. proceeding).

162. Tex. R. Evid. 503(a)(5)(A); *see, e.g.*, *Tex. Dep't of MHMR v. Davis*, 775 S.W.2d 467, 473 (Tex. App.—Austin 1989, orig. proceeding [leave denied]) (attorney-client privilege did not protect the investigation of a drowning because the record did not establish that the investigation was conducted with the intent and belief that communications would be confidential).

163. *Bogle v. McClure*, 332 F.3d 1347, 1358 (11th Cir. 2003) (quoting *United States v. Bell*, 776 F.2d 965, 971 (11th Cir. 1985)).

example, while some pre-Rules cases indicated that the communications overheard by an eavesdropper were not privileged,[164] others stated that an inadvertent disclosure did not defeat the privilege.[165] The rule adopted the latter approach, reflecting the belief that, given modern electronic-eavesdropping techniques, a client should not be penalized for failing to ensure absolute secrecy.[166] Still, the privilege requires an intent that the communications be made confidentially, and the failure of a client to take reasonable precautions to ensure confidentiality may bear on intent.[167] Therefore, communi-

---

164. In **Clark v. State**, the court upheld the trial court's decision to admit the testimony of a telephone operator who had eavesdropped on a conversation between the defendant and his attorney. 159 Tex. Crim. 187, 193, 261 S.W.2d 339, 343 (1953). The court's initial opinion justified the lower court's action on the ground that the communication was not confidential because it had been overheard. *Id.* at 191-93, 261 S.W.2d at 342-43. On rehearing, however, the court relied primarily on the notion that the communication was not privileged because the defendant was seeking advice as to the commission of a crime in the future. *Id.* at 199-200, 261 S.W.2d at 347. Although it did not repudiate its earlier reasoning, the court limited its applicability to "comparable fact situations." *Id.* at 198-99, 261 S.W.2d at 346. Also, in **Patella v. State**, the court stated in dicta that a third person who overhears an otherwise privileged communication may testify to its contents but that the attorney to whom the communication was made may not. 106 Tex. Crim. 652, 654, 294 S.W. 571, 572 (1927). A possible explanation for this distinction may derive from the attorney's obligation to keep confidential even those communications that are not privileged. Refer to notes 80-81 *supra* and accompanying text. Thus, had the attorney volunteered the testimony in **Patella**, he would have violated his professional obligations.

165. See **Gass v. Baggerly**, 332 S.W.2d 426, 430 (Tex. Civ. App.—Dallas 1960, no writ); **Lantex Constr. Co. v. Lejsal**, 315 S.W.2d 177, 183 (Tex. Civ. App.—Waco 1958, writ ref'd n.r.e.); *cf.* **Gross v. State**, 61 Tex. Crim. 176, 182, 135 S.W. 373, 376-77 (1911) (inadvertent disclosure of a letter between spouses does not abrogate the marital-communications privilege); **Eloise Bauer & Assocs., Inc. v. Elec. Realty Assocs., Inc.**, 621 S.W.2d 200, 204 (Tex. Civ. App.—Texarkana 1981, writ ref'd n.r.e.) (document was not privileged when disclosure was deliberate). These cases differ from those cited in note 164 *supra* on the ground that the former involve inadvertent disclosure of documentary communications and the latter involve conversations. See **Clark**, 159 Tex. Crim. at 193, 261 S.W.2d at 343. *But see* **Harris v. State**, 72 Tex. Crim. 117, 121, 161 S.W. 125, 128 (1913) (letters inadvertently disclosed stand in the same category as overheard conversations). Whatever the merits of such a distinction, the issue of inadvertent disclosure is better dealt with as a problem of waiver. Refer to notes 882-933 *infra* and accompanying text.

166. See 2 LOUISELL & MUELLER, *supra* note 69, §209, at 751; 2 WEINSTEIN & BERGER, *supra* note 29, ¶503(b)[02], at 503-51 to 503-52. *But see* 8 WIGMORE, *supra* note 6, §2326, at 633-34 (because the means of preserving secrecy of a communication are largely in the client's hands, the privilege should not protect inadvertent disclosures). *See generally* James M. Grippando, *Attorney-Client Privilege: Implied Waiver Through Inadvertent Disclosure of Documents*, 39 U. MIAMI L. REV. 511, 526-27 (1985) (suggesting procedures for attorneys to minimize inadvertent disclosure of privileged documents).

167. *E.g.*, **Cameron Cty. v. Hinojosa**, 760 S.W.2d 742, 745-46 (Tex. App.—Corpus Christi 1988, orig. proceeding [leave denied]) (routine transmission of apparently privileged documents to the county personnel office, the auditor's office, and the county judge's office was evidence of the lack of intent of confidentiality). Unless the intent to disclose is apparent, courts should regard the communication as confidential. See *Proposed Rules, supra* note 28, at 238 (FED. R. EVID. 503 advisory committee's note, subdiv. (a)(4)). *But see* **Jordan v. Fourth Ct. of Appeals**, 701 S.W.2d 644, 649 (Tex. 1985) (orig. proceeding) (privilege is waived when documents are disclosed to the grand jury; "[i]f the matter for which a privilege is sought has been disclosed to a third party, thus raising the question of waiver of the privilege, the party asserting the privilege has the burden of proving that no waiver occurred"). Courts outside Texas have considered whether e-mails between a client and her attorney retain their confidentiality when sent using equipment belonging to the client's employer. *Compare* **Scott v. Beth Israel Med. Ctr. Inc.**, 847 N.Y.S.2d 436, 439-40 (N.Y. Sup. Ct. 2007) (e-mails sent between client and attorney using equipment and server belonging to client's employer were not privileged because employer's policy on computer use and e-mail monitoring stated that employees had no personal privacy rights using employer's equipment; "the effect of an employer e-mail policy, such as that of [employer], is to have the employer looking over your shoulder each time you send an e-mail"), *with* **Stengart v. Loving Care Agency, Inc.**, 990 A.2d 650, 663-64 (N.J. 2010) (e-mails sent between client and attorney using client's personal e-mail account were privileged, even though they were sent using laptop belonging to client's em-

cations knowingly made in the presence of third parties,[168] divulged by the client to other persons,[169] or made for the purpose of being disclosed to others[170] are not considered confidential.[171] Routine, fact-oriented investigations into accidents, even though litigation is likely, are also not considered privileged communications.[172] On the other hand, the privilege may still apply when documents are simultaneously distributed to the attorney and selected members of the client corporation if such conduct is necessary to keep those members appraised of what the attorney is being told.[173]

---

ployer; because employer's policy on computer use did not address use of personal e-mail accounts and did not warn employees that personal e-mails could be forensically retrieved, client had reasonable expectation that her messages would remain confidential).

    Federal Rule of Evidence 502 protects against waiver of the attorney-client privilege and work-product protection when an inadvertent disclosure is made in a federal proceeding or to a federal office or agency if the privilege holder (1) took reasonable steps to prevent disclosure and (2) promptly took reasonable steps to rectify the error. FED. R. EVID. 502(b). Refer to note 333 *infra* and accompanying text. For a detailed discussion of the application and effect of Federal Rule 502, see *O'Connor's Federal Rules * Civil Trials* (2017), "Disclosure of privileged or protected information – attorney-related privileges," ch. 6-A, §9.3.2, p. 488. Texas Rule 511(b)(2) incorporates a similar standard to the one in Federal Rule 502 for inadvertent disclosure of information covered by the attorney-client privilege or work-product protection. *See* TEX. R. EVID. 511 cmt. Refer to notes 935-942 *infra* and accompanying text.

    168. *See, e.g., Johnson v. State*, 76 Tex. Crim. 346, 346-47, 174 S.W. 1047, 1048 (1915) (third party could testify about statements made by appellant to his attorney during a visit to the murder scene because the statements were unprivileged remarks made to all persons present at the scene); *Lewis v. State*, 709 S.W.2d 734, 736 (Tex. App.—San Antonio 1986, pet. ref'd, untimely filed) (statement made by rape victim's sister to attorney ad litem was not privileged when it was made in the presence of the victim and a caseworker, both of whom had interests adverse to the declarant at the time the statement was made); *Ledisco Fin. Servs., Inc. v. Viracola*, 533 S.W.2d 951, 959 (Tex. Civ. App.—Texarkana 1976, no writ) (appellant waived attorney-client privilege because a third person was present when appellant made the statement to his attorney); *Coe v. Widener*, 122 S.W.2d 258, 259 (Tex. Civ. App.—Dallas 1938, no writ) (trial court did not err in admitting statements appellant had made to her attorney because opposing party was present at the time); *Smith v. Guerre*, 159 S.W. 417, 419 (Tex. Civ. App.—Amarillo 1913, no writ) (attorney-client privilege did not apply when the communication was made in the presence of all parties to the suit).

    169. *See Hodges, Grant & Kaufmann v. U.S. Gov't*, 768 F.2d 719, 721 (5th Cir. 1985); *see, e.g., Roberts v. State*, 795 S.W.2d 842, 844-45 (Tex. App.—Beaumont 1990, no pet.) (trial court properly admitted defendant's letter to aggravated-kidnapping victim telling her that he had instructed his attorney to collect evidence of her bigamy and that he would give the evidence to the district attorney if victim did not get district attorney to drop charges against him; letter was evidence of witness tampering and was not a confidential communication under Criminal Rule 503); *see also Hayes v. Pennock*, 192 S.W.2d 169, 174 (Tex. Civ. App.—Beaumont 1945, writ ref'd n.r.e.) (attorney-client privilege was waived when circumstances showed that client did not want communication to be secret). *See generally* 1 RAY, *supra* note 52, §425, at 408 (courts look at the circumstances in which communication was made in determining whether information communicated was confidential and thus entitled to the privilege).

    170. *See, e.g., Clayton v. Canida*, 223 S.W.2d 264, 266 (Tex. Civ. App.—Texarkana 1949, no writ) (client's income information, disclosed to attorney for purposes of forwarding the information to the IRS, was going to become a public record and was not privileged); *League v. Galveston City Co.*, 192 S.W. 350, 353 (Tex. Civ. App.—Galveston 1917, writ ref'd) (statements made by client to answer his opponent's interrogatories were meant to be disclosed to others and were not privileged).

    171. *See Landers v. State*, 256 S.W.3d 295, 309 (Tex. Crim. App. 2008) ("If the information conveyed to the attorney is also made known to others or is discovered by a third person through independent means, it is not confidential.").

    172. *E.g., Tex. Dep't of MHMR v. Davis*, 775 S.W.2d 467, 474 (Tex. App.—Austin 1989, orig. proceeding [leave denied]) (privilege did not cover the routine investigation into a drowning death because nothing in record established that interviews were intended to be confidential or that interviewees were advised that the information furnished would be held in confidence).

    173. *In re Buspirone Antitrust Litig.*, 211 F.R.D. 249, 252-53 (S.D.N.Y. 2002) (documents prepared for "simultaneous review" of a given problem or practice by legal and nonlegal personnel may not be privileged, but when a

Not all conversations between the attorney and his client are privileged; only those communications intended to be kept confidential when they were made are protected.[174] Thus, an attorney cannot claim the privilege simply to avoid a deposition on his representation merely because some matters may be privileged.[175] Further, the court of criminal appeals has held that an attorney informing a client of a trial date is not a "confidential" communication because the attorney is acting as a "mere conduit" from the trial court passing on a routine message.[176] These communications do not involve the subject matter of the client's legal problems.[177]

Communications made in the presence of or disclosed to third parties are confidential as long as these disclosures further the rendition of legal services to the client.[178] Rule 503(a)(5) reaches third persons such as spouses, parents, business associates, and joint clients.[179] In addition, the rule specifically provides that when a third person, such as an interpreter, facilitates communication between attorney and client, that person's presence does not breach confidentiality.[180]

(2) Communication. Rule 503 does not define the term "communication"—all exchanges qualify as communications, regardless of whether they are spoken or written.[181] Thus, documents prepared to facilitate the rendition of legal services are com-

---

document is being provided to corporate personnel "for the purpose of informing them that legal advice has been sought or obtained, that act is not inconsistent with the underlying communication being for the 'purpose' of obtaining legal advice").

174. In *In re Avila*, the Texas Supreme Court was asked to decide whether the attorney-client privilege protects a party from having to disclose that her attorney referred her to a physician for treatment. The court denied the petition for writ of mandamus, but Justice Hecht wrote a dissent to that denial. *In re Avila*, 22 S.W.3d 349, 349 (Tex. 2000) (Hecht, J., dissenting from denial of petition for writ of mandamus). Justice Hecht reasoned that the communication must have been intended to be confidential because both plaintiff and defendant claimed that disclosure of that referral would "hurt" plaintiff's position in the case. *Id.* at 350. Normally, however, the intent at the time of the communication, not the negative effect on a party's current litigation position, determines whether the communication was made in confidence. *See, e.g.*, *Harvey v. State*, 97 S.W.3d 162, 168 (Tex. App.—Houston [14th Dist.] 2002, pet. ref'd) (although former attorney's testimony about whether defendant had provided him with some evidence to substantiate her civil claims against third party concerned a communication between attorney and client, it did not disclose any confidences; "[t]he privilege protects *what* the client has disclosed in confidence, not *the fact* that an attorney has requested such disclosure").

175. *Borden, Inc. v. Valdez*, 773 S.W.2d 718, 720 (Tex. App.—Corpus Christi 1989, orig. proceeding) ("The attorney-client privilege was never intended to foreclose any opportunity to depose an attorney, but rather only precludes those questions which may somehow invade upon the attorney-client confidences.").

176. *Austin v. State*, 934 S.W.2d 672, 674-75 (Tex. Crim. App. 1996) (attorney has a duty to inform the client of the trial date, and "[t]he communication of a trial date is a matter collateral to the attorney-client relationship … [which] does not involve the subject matter of the client's legal problems").

177. *Id.* at 675; *see, e.g.*, *Solomon v. State*, 999 S.W.2d 35, 39 (Tex. App.—Houston [14th Dist.] 1999, no pet.) (former attorney could testify that he sent notice of trial hearings to defendant).

178. Tex. R. Evid. 503(a)(5)(A).

179. *See Proposed Rules, supra* note 28, at 238 (Fed. R. Evid. 503 advisory committee's note). For a discussion of joint clients, refer to notes 277-279 *infra* and accompanying text.

180. Tex. R. Evid. 503(a)(5)(B); *see Proposed Rules, supra* note 28, at 238 (Fed. R. Evid. 503 advisory committee's note, subdiv. (a)(4)). Rule 503(a)(4) covers the presence of employees. Refer to notes 139-145 *supra* and accompanying text.

181. 1 Ray, *supra* note 52, §424, at 407. *But see id.* §424, at 135 (Supp. 1991) (privilege does not include attorney's testimony as to his observations of client's nonassertive, nonverbal conduct). Courts routinely reject attempts to

munications. For example, letters in an attorney's correspondence file to and from a liability insurer about the progress and defense of personal-injury claims are privileged communications even when there is no lawsuit in progress.[182] However, documents that predate the attorney-client relationship are not privileged. Similarly, a client cannot protect a document simply by giving it to the attorney.[183]

Communications may include conduct such as facial expressions or gestures as well as words. For example, showing an attorney a hidden scar is a communication and, if intended to be confidential, is privileged.[184] On the other hand, an attorney cannot invoke the privilege to avoid, for example, testifying to his observation of a scar readily apparent to others because the observation involves no confidential information.[185] Between these extremes lies the problem of whether the attorney's opinion about the client's mental state is privileged. Texas courts have held that it is privileged, but only when based on observations from privileged transactions and conferences.[186] Nothing in Rule 503 indicates that such holdings should be overruled. However, the court of criminal appeals has upheld a lower-court ruling that an attorney can testify to an opinion based on observations and conversations that any person could have made and that were not directly related to the attorney-client relationship.[187] Items such as an individual's handwriting, documents, or photographs, which can be observed by anyone, are generally

---

invoke the attorney-client privilege when the substance of the testimony does not involve a communication between attorney and client. *See, e.g.,* **Brasfield v. State**, 600 S.W.2d 288, 295-96 (Tex. Crim. App. 1980) (permitting an attorney who had represented the defendant in an unrelated matter to testify that he happened on the defendant in the vicinity of the crime approximately one hour before it occurred), *overruled on other grounds,* **Janecka v. State**, 739 S.W.2d 813 (Tex. Crim. App. 1987); *see also* **Jackson v. State**, 624 S.W.2d 306, 309 (Tex. App.—Dallas 1981, no pet.) (former attorney could testify that he dictated an affidavit of nonprosecution later signed by the rape complainant).

182. *Wiley v. Williams*, 769 S.W.2d 715, 716-17 (Tex. App.—Austin 1989, orig. proceeding [leave denied]).

183. McCormick on Evidence I, *supra* note 65, §89, at 213-214; *see* Burnett v. State, 642 S.W.2d 765, 769-70 (Tex. Crim. App. 1982); *see, e.g.,* **Methodist Home v. Marshall**, 830 S.W.2d 220, 224 (Tex. App.—Dallas 1992, orig. proceeding) (correspondence between adoption agency and third parties did not become privileged when agency officials forwarded correspondence to their attorney); *cf.* **Fisher v. United States**, 425 U.S. 391, 403-04 (1976) ("[P]re-existing documents which could have been obtained by court process from the client when he was in possession may also be obtained from the attorney by similar process following transfer by the client in order to obtain more informed legal advice.").

184. McCormick on Evidence I, *supra* note 65, §89, at 213.

185. *Cf. Brasfield*, 600 S.W.2d at 295-96 (attorney who had represented the defendant in an unrelated matter could testify that he saw defendant in the vicinity of the crime because the attorney had disclosed no confidential attorney-client communications).

186. *Pollard v. El Paso Nat'l Bank*, 343 S.W.2d 909, 912-13 (Tex. Civ. App.—El Paso 1961, writ ref'd n.r.e.); **Gulf Prod. Co. v. Colquitt**, 25 S.W.2d 989, 994 (Tex. Civ. App.—El Paso 1930), *aff'd as modified,* 52 S.W.2d 235 (Tex. Comm'n App. 1932, judgm't adopted). *But cf.* **United States v. Kendrick**, 331 F.2d 110, 113-14 (4th Cir. 1964) (attorney-client privilege protects only confidential communications and not attorney's observations of "[the client's] complexion, his demeanor, his bearing, his sobriety and his dress").

187. *See Manning v. State*, 766 S.W.2d 551, 556-58 (Tex. App.—Dallas 1989) (defendant's former attorney could give his opinion on defendant's competency to stand trial; opinion was based on personal observations and conversations that do not intrude on confidential communications), *aff'd,* 773 S.W.2d 568 (Tex. Crim. App. 1989).

not privileged.[188] In sum, "attorneys may testify regarding information they possess about a client as long as no communication is revealed."[189]

4. Confidentiality of client's identity. Another problem not explicitly addressed by Rule 503 is whether the attorney-client privilege covers facts such as the client's identity, the scope or object of the attorney's employment, or fee arrangements. The privilege does not ordinarily shield such matters from disclosure.[190] However, courts have carved out a limited exception to this rule—such facts are privileged if they "tend to implicate the client in the commission of a crime, or to show an admission on his part subjecting him to a civil liability."[191] One Fifth Circuit case held that a client's identity and fee arrangements may be protected from disclosure when the confidential purpose for which the client sought legal advice is "inextricably intertwined" with his identity and fee arrangements.[192] Only in rare situations, however, will this exception legitimately apply.[193]

Cases invoking this exception fall into three categories.[194] In the first category, the client retains the attorney to make anonymous restitution of taxes or property.[195] In cases involving tax repayment, courts have held that the client's identity is privileged.[196] Commentators have strongly criticized the tax decisions on the ground that the attorney is purveying anonymity, not rendering professional services.[197]

---

188. *See, e.g., In re Grand Jury Proceedings (85 Misc. 140)*, 791 F.2d 663, 665 (8th Cir. 1986) (information from an attorney about the authenticity of a former client's signatures and photographs was not privileged); *United States v. Pipkins*, 528 F.2d 559, 563 & n.2 (5th Cir. 1976) (client's handwriting samples given to attorney were not privileged).

189. *E.g., Austin v. State*, 934 S.W.2d 672, 673 (Tex. Crim. App. 1996) (in bail-jumping prosecution, defense attorney could testify that he had told defendant of trial date in underlying case); *see, e.g., Brasfield*, 600 S.W.2d at 295 (former attorney's testimony about client's location on a particular afternoon did not violate attorney-client privilege); *Russell v. State*, 598 S.W.2d 238, 252-53 (Tex. Crim. App. 1980) (former attorney's testimony that he did not forge client's name on document did not violate attorney-client privilege); *Church v. State*, 552 S.W.2d 138, 142 (Tex. Crim. App. 1977) (attorney's testimony that he was present during a police lineup did not violate attorney-client privilege); *Jackson v. State*, 624 S.W.2d 306, 309 (Tex. App.—Dallas 1981, no pet.) (former attorney's testimony that he prepared affidavits of nonprosecution did not violate attorney-client privilege).

190. *See Allstate Tex. Lloyds v. Johnson*, 784 S.W.2d 100, 105 (Tex. App.—Waco 1989, orig. proceeding) (terms and conditions of an attorney's employment or purposes for which a client retains an attorney do not fall within the attorney-client privilege and are subject to discovery); *Jim Walter Homes, Inc. v. Foster*, 593 S.W.2d 749, 752 (Tex. Civ. App.—Eastland 1979, no writ) (attorney-client privilege does not protect the attorney-client fee arrangement); *cf. Tornay v. United States*, 840 F.2d 1424, 1428-29 (9th Cir. 1988) (amount, date, and form of payments to an attorney are not protected by the attorney-client privilege).

191. *Jim Walter Homes*, 593 S.W.2d at 752 (quoting 97 C.J.S. *Witnesses* §283(f) (1957)).

192. *In re Grand Jury Subpoena*, 926 F.2d 1423, 1431-32 (5th Cir. 1991) ("In such circumstances, we protect the anonymous client's identity not because it may incriminate the client but because disclosure would allow the Government to obtain information given to the attorney as part of a confidential communication.").

193. As Charles McCormick observed, a "prevailing flavor of chicanery and sharp practice" pervades most attempts to assert the privilege in this context. MᴄCᴏʀᴍɪᴄᴋ ᴏɴ Eᴠɪᴅᴇɴᴄᴇ I, *supra* note 65, §90, at 216.

194. 2 Lᴏᴜɪsᴇʟʟ & Mᴜᴇʟʟᴇʀ, *supra* note 69, §210, at 780-85.

195. *Id.* §210, at 777.

196. *See Tillotson v. Boughner*, 350 F.2d 663, 665-66 (7th Cir. 1965); *Baird v. Koerner*, 279 F.2d 623, 633-35 (9th Cir. 1960).

197. 2 Lᴏᴜɪsᴇʟʟ & Mᴜᴇʟʟᴇʀ, *supra* note 69, §210, at 780-81; MᴄCᴏʀᴍɪᴄᴋ ᴏɴ Eᴠɪᴅᴇɴᴄᴇ, §90, at 186-87 n.68 (Edward W. Cleary ed., 2d ed. 1981) [hereinafter MᴄCᴏʀᴍɪᴄᴋ ᴏɴ Eᴠɪᴅᴇɴᴄᴇ II]; *see also In re Grand Jury Subpoena*, 204

In the second category, the client wants to remain anonymous, and the attorney is hired so the client can reveal information about wrongs committed by third persons. Several courts have held that the attorney can refuse to divulge the client's identity in such circumstances.[198]

In the third and most controversial category, an unidentified client retains an attorney to represent another individual charged with criminal activity.[199] Some courts have held that the attorney-client privilege applies when disclosure would tend to implicate the unidentified client in the commission of past crimes.[200] However, when a prima facie showing reveals that an unidentified client retained the attorney to assist the unidentified client in continuing criminal or fraudulent activity, the privilege does not apply.[201] Some decisions indicate that courts will take a restrictive view of when attorneys may protect a client's identity.[202]

F.3d 516, 522 n.5 (4th Cir. 2000) (a client cannot protect his identity by having his attorney make a disclosure for him; "[a]n individual cannot purchase anonymity by hiring a lawyer to deliver his money or his messages"); *cf.* **Hughes v. Meade**, 453 S.W.2d 538, 540-42 (Ky. 1970) (client's identity is not privileged when the attorney is hired to return apparently stolen property to the police department because the delivery was not the rendition of a legal service).

198. *See, e.g.*, **Ex parte Enzor**, 117 So. 2d 361, 365-66 (Ala. 1960) (attorney did not have to divulge the name of a client who had contacted the attorney for legal advice about a bribe offered to the client to miscount votes); **In re Kozlov**, 398 A.2d 882, 883-86 (N.J. 1979) (attorney-client privilege applied when a client told an attorney, on condition of anonymity, that a juror in a recent criminal case had bragged that the juror had "gotten even" with the defendant, a former police chief, for the arrest and prosecution of a member of the juror's family); **In re Kaplan**, 168 N.E.2d 660, 660-62 (N.Y. 1960) (attorney, who was confidentially retained, did not have to divulge the name of a client who had given information to the attorney to hand over to an investigatory body).

199. 2 LOUISELL & MUELLER, *supra* note 69, §210, at 782.

200. *See, e.g.*, **In re Grand Jury Proceedings (United States v. Lawson)**, 600 F.2d 215, 218-19 (9th Cir. 1979) (names of appellant's clients and fee arrangements involving other conspirators were privileged because disclosure to the grand jury would implicate the clients in a past conspiracy); **In re Grand Jury Proceedings (United States v. Jones)**, 517 F.2d 666, 674-75 (5th Cir. 1975) (names of unidentified persons who possibly arranged bonds and legal fees on behalf of known clients were privileged when disclosure would supply additional incriminating information about persons suspected of income-tax offenses).

201. *See* **United States v. Hodge & Zweig**, 548 F.2d 1347, 1352-55 (9th Cir. 1977) (identity of client paying legal fees is not privileged when legal representation is secured in furtherance of intended, present, or continuing illegality, regardless of counsel's awareness of the improper arrangement).

202. *See* **In re Grand Jury Investigation**, 723 F.2d 447, 453 (6th Cir. 1983) ("[I]t is the link between the client and the communication, rather than the link between the client and the possibility of potential criminal prosecution, which serves to bring the client's identity within the protective ambit of the attorney-client privilege."); **In re Grand Jury Proceedings (In re Pavlick)**, 680 F.2d 1026, 1027-29 (5th Cir. 1982) (adopting the holding in **Hodge** and compelling an attorney to disclose the identity of a person who furnished bond and fees for defendant). *But see* **In re Grand Jury Subpoena**, 926 F.2d 1423, 1431-32 (5th Cir. 1991) (when a party retains an attorney to represent both himself and another, the attorney-client privilege protects the client's identity when it is inextricably intertwined with confidential communications). *See generally* **In re Grand Jury Subpoenas (United States v. Anderson)**, 906 F.2d 1485, 1488-93 (10th Cir. 1990) (discussing the "last link" doctrine, the legal-advice exception, and the confidential-communications exception); Steven Goode, *Identity, Fees, and the Attorney-Client Privilege*, 59 GEO. WASH. L. REV. 307, 311-12 (1991) (discussing the attorney-client privilege as it relates to client identity and fee arrangements and arguing that the attorney-client privilege should protect the client's identity when the client's status as a client is the information sought); Stephen A. Saltzburg, *Communications Falling Within the Attorney-Client Privilege*, 66 IOWA L. REV. 811, 820-24 (1981) (discussing the applicability of the attorney-client privilege to protect the client's identity from disclosure).

B. Rule 503(b): Rules of Privilege

1. Rule 503(b)(1): General rule. Rule 503(b)(1) states the basic elements of the attorney-client privilege. A client is privileged from disclosing, and may prevent others from disclosing, communications made in confidence for the purpose of obtaining legal services.[203] Additionally, as Rule 503(b)(1)(A) through (b)(1)(E) makes clear, communications by the attorney to the client are also privileged,[204] as are communications among various combinations of attorney, attorney's representative, client, and client's representative.[205]

Rule 503(b)(1)(C) is somewhat more complicated. It covers situations in which two or more clients sharing some common interest[206] retain separate counsel, and the cli-

---

203. TEX. R. EVID. 503(b)(1); *see In re Ford Motor Co.*, 988 S.W.2d 714, 718 (Tex. 1998); *Huie v. DeShazo*, 922 S.W.2d 920, 922 (Tex. 1996); *In re Hicks*, 252 S.W.3d 790, 794 (Tex. App.—Houston [14th Dist.] 2008, orig. proceeding).

204. *In re XL Specialty Ins.*, 373 S.W.3d 46, 49 (Tex. 2012); *see Austin v. State*, 934 S.W.2d 672, 673 (Tex. Crim. App. 1996) (statements and advice of attorney are just as protected as client communications); *Head v. State*, 299 S.W.3d 414, 445 (Tex. App.—Houston [14th Dist.] 2009, pet. ref'd) (same); *Cantrell v. Johnson*, 785 S.W.2d 185, 189 (Tex. App.—Waco 1990, orig. proceeding) (confidential communication "is clearly a two-way street once the attorney/client relationship has arisen"). These rule provisions codify Texas common law. *See Harrell v. Atl. Ref. Co.*, 339 S.W.2d 548, 554 (Tex. Civ. App.—Waco 1960, writ ref'd n.r.e.) (title opinion furnished by attorney to client is a privileged communication).

205. *In re XL Specialty Ins.*, 373 S.W.3d at 49-50. *See generally* D.E. Ytreberg, Annotation, *Attorney-Client Privilege as Affected by Communications Between Several Attorneys*, 9 A.L.R.3d 1420 (1966) (discussing the extent of the attorney-client privilege). Rule 503(b) is an exception to the general rule that voluntary disclosure to a third party waives the privilege. *In re XL Specialty Ins.*, 373 S.W.3d at 50; *see* TEX. R. EVID. 511(a)(1). For a discussion of waiver under Rule 511, refer to notes 876-942 *infra* and accompanying text.

206. The rule does not require complete alignment of interest; "some" common interest is sufficient. *See Strong v. State*, 773 S.W.2d 543, 549 (Tex. Crim. App. 1989) (quoting the Advisory Committee's note to proposed Federal Rule 503 in suggesting that "the positions of the parties need not be compatible in all respects"). Furthermore, parties who share an actual common interest can invoke the rule even when they are formally aligned against each other. *See, e.g.*, *Ryals v. Canales*, 767 S.W.2d 226, 228-29 (Tex. App.—Dallas 1989, orig. proceeding) (even though parties were nominally adverse, their interests "most likely coincided" on an issue; defendant could assert privilege).

In *Strong*, the murder defendant wrote a letter to his codefendant's attorney asking him to stop urging the codefendant, an accomplice, to cooperate with the prosecution. 773 S.W.2d at 546. Nonetheless, the codefendant testified against the defendant. *Id.* The court of criminal appeals upheld admission of the defendant's letter over his assertion of an attorney-client privilege because the defendant did not demonstrate that he and his accomplice had a common interest. *Id.* at 552. The accomplice obviously would not benefit from a joint defense because she received a much lighter sentence in return for her testimony against the defendant. *See id.* Thus, because the letter benefited only the defendant, the court held that "[u]nilaterally asserting a joint defense based on a common interest does not give rise to the lawyer-client privilege." *Id.* But see 1 STEVEN GOODE ET AL., TEXAS PRACTICE: A GUIDE TO THE TEXAS RULES OF EVIDENCE: CIVIL AND CRIMINAL §503.2, at 320 (2d ed. 1993) (argument in *Strong* that only the defendant would benefit from the exclusion of the letter "misses the point," and "[t]he relevant focus must be on the nature of the relationship between the accomplice and defendant at the time the communication was made"). Rule 503 should not protect the relationship between individual parties or criminal defendants; it should protect the relationship between a client and his own attorney. Thus, if the defendant's *attorney* had written the letter in *Strong*, the claim of privilege might have had more merit. No public policy justifies protecting a party's unilateral attempt to create a joint defense through another person's attorney. *See Gov't of V.I. v. Joseph*, 685 F.2d 857, 862 (3d Cir. 1982) (when one defendant's interests are consistently antagonistic to those of another defendant, self-incriminating statements made by the former that exonerate the latter are not privileged; privilege does not apply "where the defendant did not intend confidentiality and made his statements wholly divorced from an attorney-client relationship").

In *Strong*, the court suggested a two-pronged analysis in defining the term "common interest" in Rule 503(b). First, a court should examine the purpose of the communication to determine whether the party made it both in

ents and attorneys then pool information or design a joint defense;[207] the communication, however, must be made in the context of a pending action involving the other party.[208] The Texas Supreme Court has concluded that the privilege under Rule 503(b)(1)(C) is most accurately termed the "allied litigant privilege."[209] The allied-litigant privilege "protects communications made between a client, or the client's lawyer, to another party's lawyer, not to the other party itself."[210] The privilege would also apply when the communications involve the attorney's representative.[211] Thus, the rule does not cover statements made between two civil parties or two criminal defendants when they are communicating without the assistance of their attorneys or their attorneys' representatives. Similarly, the parties waive the privilege if one discloses the communication to anyone outside the "allied litigant" team.[212]

---

confidence and for the purpose of seeking or rendering legal services. 773 S.W.2d at 551. Second, a court should determine the commonality of the interest to which the communication relates. *Id.* at 552. Under this analysis, the privilege would not cover any communication that does not relate to the joint interests of the parties.

207. Courts of appeals have generally applied Rule 503(b)(1)(C) to joint-defense situations. *In re XL Specialty Ins.*, 373 S.W.3d at 51 & n.6. The drafters of proposed Federal Rule 503 stated that because various clients may have conflicting as well as common interests, a client can reveal his own statements made at a joint conference even if the others object. Thus, courts should absolutely bar disclosure only when all the clients agree to nondisclosure. *Proposed Rules, supra* note 28, at 239.

208. *In re XL Specialty Ins.*, 373 S.W.3d at 51-52. Proposed Federal Rule 503 was broader than the Texas rule because it did not have a pending-action requirement. *See Proposed Rules, supra* note 28, at 236 (proposed federal rule required only that communication relate to matter of common interest); *see also In re Teleglobe Commc'ns Corp.*, 493 F.3d 345, 363-66 (3d Cir. 2007) (discussing the modern "community of interest" privilege in a complex corporate setting).

209. *In re XL Specialty Ins.*, 373 S.W.3d at 52. The supreme court discussed the different terms that courts have used to refer to the privilege in Rule 503(b)(1)(C), including the joint-client privilege, joint-defense privilege, and common-interest privilege. *See id.* at 50-51. These privileges, however, are distinct doctrines that serve different purposes; only the allied-litigant privilege serves the purposes intended by Rule 503(b)(1)(C). *Id.* at 50-52. The joint-client doctrine applies when the same attorney represents multiple clients simultaneously in the same case; however, Rule 503(b)(1)(C) requires that the parties have separate attorneys. *See id.* The joint-defense doctrine applies when separately represented parties communicate for the purpose of forming a common defense strategy; however, Rule 503(b)(1)(C) applies to any parties in a pending action, not just defendants. *Id.* at 51-52. The common-interest doctrine, which is broader than the joint-defense doctrine, applies to separately represented persons regardless of whether they are involved in litigation; however, Rule 503(b)(1)(C) has a pending-action requirement. *Id.* For these reasons, the supreme court concluded that "Rule 503(b)(1)(C)'s privilege is more appropriately termed an 'allied litigant privilege.'" *Id.* at 52; *see also Nester v. Textron, Inc.*, No. A-13-CA-920-LY (W.D. Tex. 2015) (no pub.; 3-9-15) (in products-liability case, plaintiffs argued that allied-litigant doctrine precluded application of attorney-client privilege when attorney represented both defendants; although allied-litigant doctrine would arguably not have applied in this case because the communications sought predated the litigation, district court found argument moot because *XL Specialty* does not change Texas law that one attorney can simultaneously represent two clients on the same matter). For a discussion of the joint-client privilege and an exception to the privilege in suits between joint clients, refer to notes 277-279 *infra* and accompanying text.

210. *In re XL Specialty Ins.*, 373 S.W.3d at 52-53.

211. *See* TEX. R. EVID. 503(b)(1)(C) (client has privilege to protect communications "by the client, the client's representative, the client's lawyer, or the lawyer's representative to a lawyer representing another party in a pending action or that lawyer's representative, if the communications concern a matter of common interest in the pending action"); *see, e.g.*, *United States v. McPartlin*, 595 F.2d 1321, 1336 (7th Cir. 1979) (defendant's statements, made while devising a plan to discredit a prosecution witness, were privileged because the statements were made in confidence to an investigator for codefendant's attorney). Refer to note 205 *supra* and accompanying text.

212. *See In re XL Specialty Ins.*, 373 S.W.3d at 50; *cf. United States v. Melvin*, 650 F.2d 641, 646 (5th Cir. 1981) (there is no common-law attorney-client privilege when a party shares information with one who has not joined the defense team and for whom there is no reasonable expectation of confidentiality).

2. Rule 503(b)(2): Special rule in a criminal case. Rule 503(b)(2), a special rule for criminal cases, protects from disclosure any "fact that came to the knowledge of the lawyer or the lawyer's representative by reason of the attorney-client relationship."[213] Although the language of Rule 503(b)(2) appears to be broad enough to apply to matters that were neither communications nor intended to be held confidential, it has never been interpreted that way.[214] In *Manning v. State*, the Dallas Court of Appeals held that this section did not protect facts an attorney learned through personal observations that were not the subject of confidential communications between attorney and client.[215] Thus, a defendant's attorney could testify to his opinion about his client's competency because "[a]ny person could have observed [the defendant's] demeanor and could have conversed with him; the happenstance that the observer was his attorney does not mean that the observation arose 'by reason of the attorney-client relationship.'"[216] The court of criminal appeals adopted the result and reasoning of *Manning* as its own,[217] and later suggested that the provision may have been intended to provide greater privilege protection to criminal defendants.[218]

In *Mixon v. State*, the court held that when a person consults an attorney with the intent of hiring him professionally, any information acquired by the attorney in interviews or preliminary discussions is privileged and cannot be disclosed, even when he ultimately does not represent the person.[219] The State argued that Rule 503(b)(2) uses the phrase "attorney-client relationship" as a special requirement in criminal cases, thus

---

213. TEX. R. EVID. 503(b)(2); *Bailey v. State*, 507 S.W.3d 740, 745 (Tex. Crim. App. 2016); *see, e.g.*, *Porter v. State*, 513 S.W.2d 695, 701-02 (Tex. App.—Houston [1st Dist.] 2017, pet. ref'd) (Rule 503(b)(2) did not shield from disclosure attorney's testimony about his unlawful acts of tampering with evidence at murder scene; actions were not in furtherance of or by reason of attorney-client relationship). This provision carries forward the language from former Code of Criminal Procedure article 773, which courts had occasionally interpreted as protecting more than "communications" between the attorney and client. *See, e.g.*, *Downing v. State*, 61 Tex. Crim. 519, 525, 136 S.W. 471, 474 (1911) (attorney's knowledge of location of deed of trust was privileged in perjury prosecution); *Holden v. State*, 44 Tex. Crim. 382, 383-84, 71 S.W. 600, 601 (1903) (payment of $10 to an attorney for his fee was privileged in theft trial).

214. *See, e.g.*, *Russell v. State*, 598 S.W.2d 238, 252-53 (Tex. Crim. App. 1980) (attorney-client privilege was not violated when attorney testified that he appeared in court with defendant, signed a stipulation of evidence as defendant's attorney, and did not forge defendant's name on that document); *Church v. State*, 552 S.W.2d 138, 141-42 (Tex. Crim. App. 1977) (attorney-client privilege was not violated when attorney testified about his presence and activities at a lineup because no confidential communications were revealed); *Lopez v. State*, 651 S.W.2d 830, 838 (Tex. App.—San Antonio 1983, pet. ref'd) (rejecting claim of attorney-client privilege and allowing former attorney's testimony that defendant was present at the crime scene, even though defendant argued that attorney could only identify him because attorney had previously represented him); *Jackson v. State*, 624 S.W.2d 306, 309 (Tex. App.—Dallas 1981, no pet.) (privilege was not violated when attorney testified that he prepared an affidavit of non-prosecution signed by complainant because no client communication was revealed).

215. 766 S.W.2d 551, 558 (Tex. App.—Dallas 1989), *aff'd*, 773 S.W.2d 568 (Tex. Crim. App. 1989); *see, e.g.*, *Kay v. State*, 340 S.W.3d 470, 475 (Tex. App.—Texarkana 2011, no pet.) (defense attorney's personal observations while in the courtroom were not facts he became aware of solely because of the attorney-client relationship; "anyone present in the courtroom that day was able to observe 'how and under what circumstances [defendant] left the courthouse.'").

216. *Manning*, 766 S.W.2d at 558.

217. *Manning v. State*, 773 S.W.2d 568, 569 (Tex. Crim. App. 1989).

218. *Mixon v. State*, 224 S.W.3d 206, 209 (Tex. Crim. App. 2007).

219. *Id.* at 212. Refer to note 89 *supra* and accompanying text.

"restricting the availability of the privilege only to the cases where the lawyer has already agreed to represent the client."[220] The court rejected this argument, noting that the phrase does not appear anywhere in the rule except for that section, not even in Rule 503(b)(1), which outlines the general rule of privilege.[221] The court observed:

> [I]f we were to follow the State's interpretation—viewing the phrase as a special restriction on the availability of the privilege in criminal cases—we would have to conclude that the rule was intended to provide lesser protection to persons accused of criminal offenses than those seeking a lawyer's help in non-criminal matters. But if anything, the use of the words 'any other fact' in Rule 503(b)(2), the '[s]pecial rule of privilege in criminal cases,' indicates the intent to provide greater, not lesser, protection to the criminally accused.[222]

Sometimes an attorney may be required to turn over to law enforcement inculpatory evidence obtained from his client. In **Sanford v. State**, the prosecution attempted to introduce into evidence the fact that the defendant's attorney had told law-enforcement officers where they could find the defendant's car, which was used in an aggravated kidnapping.[223] In a case of first impression in Texas, the El Paso Court of Appeals followed other jurisdictions in concluding that the prosecution could not introduce the fact that the defendant's attorney was the source of that information.[224] The court stated that "[b]y allowing the State to recover the evidence, the public interest is served, and by refusing the State an opportunity to disclose the source of the evidence, the attorney-client privilege is preserved."[225]

C. Rule 503(c): Who May Claim

Rule 503(c) makes clear that the client, not the attorney, holds the privilege.[226] Thus, the client has the burden of establishing the existence of the privilege.[227] Either the cli-

---

220. **Mixon**, 224 S.W.3d at 209.

221. Id.

222. Id.

223. 21 S.W.3d 337, 341 (Tex. App.—El Paso 2000, no pet.).

224. Id. at 344. Other states that require attorneys to release physical evidence in their possession to the authorities also prevent the government from disclosing that the evidence came from the defendant's attorney. **Henderson v. State**, 962 S.W.2d 544, 556 (Tex. Crim. App. 1997); see, e.g., **Hitch v. Pima Cty. Super. Ct.**, 708 P.2d 72, 79 (Ariz. 1985) (defendant's attorney should release physical evidence to State under assumption that prosecutor may not mention to jury the fact that the evidence came from defendant or his attorney); **People v. Meredith**, 631 P.2d 46, 54 n.8 (Cal. 1981) (when offering evidence at trial, a prosecutor should do so in a manner that avoids revealing the original source of the information); **State ex rel. Sowers v. Olwell**, 394 P.2d 681, 685 (Wash. 1964) (State should take "extreme precautions" not to reveal the source of physical evidence being admitted in front of a jury).

225. **Sanford**, 21 S.W.3d at 344.

226. See **In re XL Specialty Ins.**, 373 S.W.3d 46, 49 (Tex. 2012); **West v. Solito**, 563 S.W.2d 240, 244 n.2 (Tex. 1978) (orig. proceeding); **Cameron v. State**, 241 S.W.3d 15, 19 (Tex. Crim. App. 2007); see, e.g., **Cole v. Gabriel**, 822 S.W.2d 296, 296 (Tex. App.—Fort Worth 1991, orig. proceeding) (attorney did not have standing in his individual capacity to bring a mandamus action in support of his client's privilege; he must bring such an action on behalf of his client, not on his own behalf). The same is true under federal common law. **United States v. Doe**, 429 F.3d 450, 452 (3d Cir. 2005); **In re Sarrio, S.A.**, 119 F.3d 143, 147 (2d Cir. 1997).

227. **Austin v. State**, 934 S.W.2d 672, 674 (Tex. Crim. App. 1996); **Head v. State**, 299 S.W.3d 414, 445 (Tex. App.—Houston [14th Dist.] 2009, pet. ref'd).

ent or his representative can invoke or waive the privilege.[228] The attorney can invoke the privilege on the client's behalf[229] and normally is required to do so by the Disciplinary Rules of Professional Conduct.[230] No other person may do so, including another attorney who does not represent the client.[231] The privilege continues even after the attorney-client relationship terminates[232] or the client dies.[233]

D. Rule 503(d): Exceptions

Even if a communication meets all the requirements of the attorney-client privilege, courts will not shield it from disclosure if it falls within one of the exceptions to the privilege. Rule 503 recognizes five exceptions to the attorney-client privilege, all traditionally observed at common law. Generally, trial courts may not carve out new exceptions to the privilege,[234] but in one case, the Fourteenth Court of Appeals announced an implicit "litigant" exception to the attorney-client privilege when fundamental fairness so requires.[235]

---

228. *See* Tex. R. Evid. 503(c); *West*, 563 S.W.2d at 244 n.2; *Bailey v. State*, 507 S.W.3d 740, 745 (Tex. Crim. App. 2016).

229. Tex. R. Evid. 503(c); *see In re XL Specialty Ins.*, 373 S.W.3d at 49; *Ex parte Lipscomb*, 111 Tex. 409, 415, 239 S.W. 1101, 1103 (1922); *Cameron*, 241 S.W.3d at 19; *Peterson v. Martin*, 69 S.W.2d 484, 485-86 (Tex. Civ. App.—Texarkana 1934, writ dism'd); *see also Fisher v. United States*, 425 U.S. 391, 402-05 (1976) (interpreting Texas law to allow an attorney to assert attorney-client privilege when the client would be able to assert it); 2 Jordan, *supra* note 74, §10.12, at 98 (same). Federal cases are in accord. *See In re Sarrio*, 119 F.3d at 147; *Haines v. Liggett Grp. Inc.*, 975 F.2d 81, 90 (3d Cir. 1992).

230. *See* Tex. Disciplinary R. Prof'l Conduct 1.05 (attorney shall not knowingly reveal confidential information, privileged or unprivileged, except in specified situations); *Duncan v. Bd. of Disciplinary Appeals*, 898 S.W.2d 759, 761 (Tex. 1995) ("A lawyer has a solemn obligation not to reveal privileged and other confidential client information, except as permitted or required in certain limited circumstances as provided in the [disciplinary] rules.").

231. *See Smith v. State*, 770 S.W.2d 70, 71 (Tex. App.—Texarkana 1989, no pet.) (prosecutor may not claim attorney-client privilege on behalf of deceased victim).

232. *Bearden v. Boone*, 693 S.W.2d 25, 27-28 (Tex. App.—Amarillo 1985, orig. proceeding). The original version of Civil Rule 503(d) stated that "[t]he prohibitions of this section continue to apply to confidential communications or records concerning any client irrespective of when the client received the services of an attorney." 641-642 S.W.2d (Tex. Cases) XLIII (1983, amended 1998). This section was deleted in 1984. *See* 669-670 S.W.2d (Tex. Cases) XXXIII (1984, amended 1998). Neither proposed Federal Rule 503 nor Uniform Rule 502 contains explicit statements about the duration of the privilege. Both provide that the privilege may be claimed by, among others, the personal representative of a deceased client and the attorney at the time of the communication. Therefore, both contemplate that the privilege will continue beyond the termination of the attorney-client relationship. *See* Unif. R. Evid. 502(c) (1974); *Proposed Rules*, *supra* note 28, at 236. Texas common law took this position. *See Md. Am. Gen. Ins. v. Blackmon*, 639 S.W.2d 455, 458 (Tex. 1982) (orig. proceeding); *Foster v. Buchele*, 213 S.W.2d 738, 743 (Tex. Civ. App.—Fort Worth 1948, writ ref'd n.r.e.); 1 Ray, *supra* note 52, §428, at 412-13.

233. *See* Tex. R. Evid. 503(c)(3) (privilege may be claimed by the personal representative of a deceased client); *see also Swidler & Berlin v. United States*, 524 U.S. 399, 410 (1998) (under federal common law, the attorney-client privilege survives the client's death).

234. *See, e.g.*, *Tex. Utils. Elec. Co. v. Marshall*, 739 S.W.2d 665, 667 (Tex. App.—Dallas 1987, orig. proceeding) (trial court could not create a "public interest" exception to the attorney-client privilege that would have required majority owners of a nuclear plant to disclose presumptively privileged documents to minority owners).

235. *Westheimer v. Tennant*, 831 S.W.2d 880, 883-84 (Tex. App.—Houston [14th Dist.] 1992, orig. proceeding). In *Westheimer*, the plaintiff filed a professional-malpractice suit against his accountants who had advised him to invest in an "Art Master" tax shelter, which the IRS later declared a fraudulent investment. *Id.* at 881. The defendants attempted to depose an attorney whom they believed had advised the plaintiff to invest in the Art Master program before the plaintiff consulted with the accountants, but the plaintiff asserted the attorney-client privilege to prevent discovery of any such advice. *Id.* at 882. When the trial court upheld the plaintiff's claim of privilege, the

1. Rule 503(d)(1): Furtherance of crime or fraud. Rule 503(d)(1) provides that the attorney-client privilege does not apply if a person knowingly seeks or obtains the attorney's services to further criminal or fraudulent activity. The party seeking discovery of otherwise privileged information has the burden of proving the exception.[236] The crime-fraud exception applies to both the attorney-client privilege under Rule 503 and the work-product doctrine under Texas Rule of Civil Procedure 192.5.[237] Texas cases have long recognized that communications intended to aid the commission of a crime[238] or fraud[239] do not fall within the privilege's rationale of furthering legitimate objectives and are not protected. Thus, communications about past acts of crime or fraud are protected, while communications about an intended future or continuing crime or fraud are not.[240]

Proof of an intended future or continuing crime by the client is, by itself, insufficient to pierce the privilege. There must also be evidence that the attorney's services were sought or obtained to enable, further, or aid in the commission of the intended crime or fraud.[241] Thus, the fact that an attorney has learned that the client intends to com-

---

accountants petitioned for a writ of mandamus to compel discovery. *Id.* The court of appeals noted that while there is no express "litigant" or "offensive/defensive" exception to the privilege, "[p]rinciples of fundamental fairness aimed at preventing a litigant from offensively hiding behind a privilege, in order to hamstring an opponent, do not need specific statutory wording to make them legally effective." *Id.* at 883-84. The court held that a litigant cannot use an evidentiary privilege offensively to shield relevant facts that bear on the merits of the lawsuit when that litigant is seeking affirmative relief in court. *Id.* at 884. Thus, the court of appeals effectively created a litigant exception to the attorney-client privilege similar to that expressed in Texas Rules of Evidence 509(e)(4) and 510(d)(5).

236. *In re USA Waste Mgmt. Res., L.L.C.*, 387 S.W.3d 92, 98 (Tex. App.—Houston [14th Dist.] 2012, orig. proceeding [mand. denied]); *In re Small*, 346 S.W.3d 657, 666 (Tex. App.—El Paso 2009, orig. proceeding); *see Warrantech Corp. v. Comput. Adapters Servs., Inc.*, 134 S.W.3d 516, 527 (Tex. App.—Fort Worth 2004, no pet.).

237. *Woodruff v. State*, 330 S.W.3d 709, 728 (Tex. App.—Texarkana 2010, pet. ref'd); *Freeman v. Bianchi*, 820 S.W.2d 853, 861 (Tex. App.—Houston [1st Dist.] 1991, orig. proceeding), *leave granted, mand. denied*, *Granada Corp. v. First Ct. of Appeals*, 844 S.W.2d 223 (Tex. 1992).

238. *See Helton v. State*, 670 S.W.2d 644, 645-46 (Tex. Crim. App. 1984); *Clark v. State*, 159 Tex. Crim. 187, 199-200, 261 S.W.2d 339, 347 (1953); *Ott v. State*, 87 Tex. Crim. 382, 385-86, 222 S.W. 261, 262-63 (1920); *Everett v. State*, 30 Tex. Ct. App. 682, 685-86, 18 S.W. 674, 675 (1892), *overruled on other grounds*, *Melton v. State*, 47 Tex. Crim. 451, 83 S.W. 822 (1904); *Orman v. State*, 22 Tex. Ct. App. 604, 615-17, 3 S.W. 468, 471-72 (1886); *see also Wesbrook v. State*, 29 S.W.3d 103, 125 (Tex. Crim. App. 2000) (Keller & McCormick, JJ., concurring) ("Statements that constitute a present crime or propose a future crime are uniquely outside the attorney-client relationship because there is no right to the assistance of counsel in committing a new crime. These types of statements are not covered by the attorney-client privilege, and the ethical rules do not require attorneys to keep such information confidential.").

239. *See Hyman v. Grant*, 102 Tex. 50, 54, 112 S.W. 1042, 1044 (1908); *Williams v. Williams*, 108 S.W.2d 297, 299-300 (Tex. Civ. App.—Amarillo 1937, no writ); *Stone v. Stitt*, 56 Tex. Civ. App. 465, 466, 121 S.W. 187, 188 (Fort Worth 1909, no writ); *Taylor v. Evans*, 29 S.W. 172, 173-74 (Tex. Civ. App. 1894, no writ). *See generally* J.F. Rydstrom, Annotation, *Applicability of Attorney-Client Privilege to Communications with Respect to Contemplated Tortious Acts*, 2 A.L.R.3d 861, 863-67 (1965) (discussing the applicability of the attorney-client privilege to contemplated tortious, as opposed to criminal, acts).

240. *See In re Small*, 346 S.W.3d at 666 (crime-fraud exception applies only if the party asserting the exception establishes a prima facie case of fraud and some relationship between that prima facie case and the allegedly privileged document); *Warrantech Corp.*, 134 S.W.3d at 527 (same); *In re AEP Tex. Cent. Co.*, 128 S.W.3d 687, 692-93 (Tex. App.—San Antonio 2003, orig. proceeding) ("mere allegations" of fraud are insufficient; alleged fraud "must have occurred at or during the time the [allegedly privileged] document was prepared and in order to perpetrate the fraud"; no evidence that party hired attorney to commit or plan to commit fraud).

241. *Henderson v. State*, 962 S.W.2d 544, 552 (Tex. Crim. App. 1997); *In re USA Waste Mgmt.*, 387 S.W.3d at 98; *Woodruff*, 330 S.W.3d at 728; *see Volcanic Gardens Mgmt. Co. v. Paxson*, 847 S.W.2d 343, 348 (Tex. App.—El Paso

mit a future crime or fraud does not raise the crime-fraud exception to the privilege.[242] In *Henderson v. State*, the court of criminal appeals also suggested that

> [a] client who informs his attorney that he … intends to commit a future crime—but does not convey the information for the purpose of securing the attorney's services in furtherance of his plan—has arguably made a communication that is not for the purpose of facilitating the rendition of professional legal services. Hence, while such communications would fall outside the crime-fraud exception, they would also fall outside the definition of the privilege itself so that the privilege would present no bar to disclosure.[243]

The court noted a potentially irreconcilable conflict between the attorney-client privilege and the ethical rules that permit, or sometimes require, an attorney to disclose privileged information when necessary to prevent the client from committing a criminal or fraudulent act.[244] The ethical rules permit or require disclosure regardless of whether the client intended to use the attorney's services to further or aid in the commission of the crime or fraud. When the ethical and privilege rules conflict, the privilege must yield to some extent in deference to the stronger public policy of protecting and preserving the life and physical safety of others.[245] In *Henderson*, the court held that a proper balance of interests in the case of an attorney who learns from his client the location of a kidnapping victim is that "the attorney must disclose the victim's location to enable law-enforcement authorities to terminate the kidnapping, but the client's communication to the attorney or the fact that the attorney conveyed the infor-

---

1993, orig. proceeding) ("[U]nder the crime/fraud exception to the lawyer-client privilege, 'fraud' would include the commission and/or attempted commission of fraud on the court or on a third person, as well as common law fraud and criminal fraud. The crime/fraud exception comes into play when a prospective client seeks the assistance of an attorney in order to make a false statement or statements of material fact or law to a third person or the court for personal advantage."); *see, e.g.*, *In re Tex. Health Res.*, 472 S.W.3d 895, 906 (Tex. App.—Dallas 2015, orig. proceeding) (with no evidence that entity was falsifying facts related to employee's employment or that there was an attempt to make a false statement of law to the court, crime-fraud exception did not authorize disclosure of otherwise privileged notes).

242. *See, e.g.*, *Henderson*, 962 S.W.2d at 553 (in trial for kidnapping and capital murder of baby, there was no evidence to support conclusion that defendant, the victim's babysitter, made maps leading to baby's grave site and gave them to her attorneys for the purpose of seeking their aid in committing any crime); *see also* *In re Richard Roe, Inc.*, 68 F.3d 38, 40 (2d Cir. 1995) (crime-fraud exception requires that the communication be made in furtherance of criminal or fraudulent activity, not merely "related" to it); *Purcell v. Dist. Att'y for Suffolk Dist.*, 676 N.E.2d 436, 439-40 (Mass. 1997) (no evidence that client discussed arson with attorney and prepared to commit it, so no connection between attorney-client communication and the crime). *But see* *X Corp. v. Doe*, 805 F. Supp. 1298, 1307 (E.D. Va. 1992) (under federal common law, communication is covered by crime-fraud exception to attorney-client privilege if it "reflect[s] an ongoing or future unlawful or illegal scheme or activity"), *aff'd sub nom.* *Under Seal v. Under Seal*, 17 F.3d 1435 (4th Cir. 1994) (table case).

243. 962 S.W.2d at 555.

244. *Id.*; *see* TEX. DISCIPLINARY R. PROF'L CONDUCT 1.05(e); *see also* *Sanford v. State*, 21 S.W.3d 337, 344 (Tex. App.—El Paso 2000, no pet.) (trial court erred in admitting evidence that law-enforcement officers recovered the victim's vehicle after speaking to defendant's attorney; when ethical obligations require attorney to divulge or turn over inculpatory evidence to law enforcement, State may not reveal that defense counsel was source of the evidence). Refer to notes 223-225 *supra* and accompanying text.

245. *Henderson*, 962 S.W.2d at 556.

mation to law-enforcement personnel cannot be admitted into evidence at trial."[246] However, a third party, such as a law-enforcement official, may compel the attorney to disclose the privileged information "only if needed to prevent or terminate a crime or fraud that is likely to result in death or serious bodily injury."[247] A third party who seeks to compel disclosure of the privileged information must show only a "reasonable possibility" of a future or continuing crime that is likely to result in death or serious bodily injury.[248]

Whether the exception applies depends on the client's knowledge, not the attorney's.[249] If the client knows or reasonably should know that his proposed act or objective is criminal or fraudulent, the communication is not privileged.[250] If, however, the client seeks advice about a contemplated act when doubtful or ignorant of its illegal nature, is told of its illegality, and decides not to act, the communication is privileged.[251] The exception does not apply when a client seeks advice about crimes or frauds already committed, but the privilege does not protect communications relating to past crimes when the communication is made in furtherance of a continuing criminal conspiracy.[252]

In **Huie v. DeShazo**, the supreme court held that the exception did not apply when the beneficiary of a trust was suing the trustee for alleged fraud in not disclosing communications between the trustee and his attorney.[253] In that case, the beneficiary did not claim that the alleged breaches of trust were separate crimes or frauds within the Rule 503(d)(1) exception.[254] Because the court held that a trustee's invocation of the

---

246. *Id.*

247. *Id.*

248. *Id.* at 557.

249. *See* **Clark v. United States**, 289 U.S. 1, 15 (1933) (if a client consults an attorney for advice about the commission of a fraud, the attorney-client privilege does not apply; this exception does not depend on the motives of the attorney and client because the privilege is lost if only the client is guilty); **United States v. Ballard**, 779 F.2d 287, 292-93 (5th Cir. 1986) (applicability of attorney-client privilege does not turn on the attorney's complicity in the intended fraud or crime).

250. TEX. R. EVID. 503(d)(1).

251. **Williams v. Williams**, 108 S.W.2d 297, 299-300 (Tex. Civ. App.—Amarillo 1937, no writ). The requirement that the client must have known or reasonably should have known that a proposed action would be illegal serves to protect clients who are misinformed by an attorney that the action would be legal. *See Proposed Rules, supra* note 28, at 239 (FED. R. EVID. 503 advisory committee's note, subdiv. (d)(1)).

252. *See* **United States v. Harrelson**, 754 F.2d 1153, 1167 (5th Cir. 1985); **United States v. Hodge & Zweig**, 548 F.2d 1347, 1354 (9th Cir. 1977).

253. 922 S.W.2d 920, 926 (Tex. 1996); *see also* **Avary v. Bank of Am.**, 72 S.W.3d 779, 802 (Tex. App.—Dallas 2002, pet. denied) (following *Huie*; attorney-client privilege protects confidential communications between a fiduciary and his attorney, although fiduciary has legal duty to disclose all material facts and provide a full accounting to his beneficiary). Federal cases, however, may recognize a fiduciary exception to the common-law attorney-client privilege. In **United States v. Jicarilla Apache Nation**, the U.S. Supreme Court assumed the existence of the fiduciary exception because neither party disputed it. 564 U.S. 162, 170-71 & n.3 (2011). However, the Court held that the fiduciary exception did not apply to the government's administration of the Indian tribe's trusts. *Id.* at 187.

254. *Huie*, 922 S.W.2d at 926.

attorney-client privilege did not violate his duty of full disclosure to the beneficiary, the exception to the privilege did not apply.[255]

To defeat the privilege under the crime-fraud exception, the opponent must first demonstrate a sufficiently serious violation and make a prima facie showing of the elements of a fraud or crime that was ongoing or about to be committed when the communication was made.[256] Second, the court must find a valid relationship between the confidential communication and the crime or fraud.[257]

Federal prosecutors have asserted the crime-fraud exception to defeat the attorney-client privilege in corporate criminal investigations.[258] Most federal courts require prosecutors to make only a minimal threshold showing, often ex parte, either demonstrating that an in camera review of privileged documents is appropriate or establishing a prima facie case that the exception applies.[259] The court is not required to consider rebuttal evidence from the corporation before deciding to review the purportedly privileged information in camera.[260] But the corporation can submit additional materials for the trial court to review before the court makes its ultimate ruling under Rule 104(a) on whether the privilege bars the discoverability or admissibility of the purportedly privileged materials.[261]

2. Rule 503(d)(2): Claimants through same deceased client. Ordinarily, the attorney-client privilege survives the client's death and may be claimed by his personal representative.[262] However, when different parties both claim the privilege through a deceased client, Rule 503(d)(2) provides an exception to the privilege.[263] For example,

---

255. *Id.*

256. *Freeman v. Bianchi*, 820 S.W.2d 853, 861 (Tex. App.—Houston [1st Dist.] 1991, orig. proceeding), *leave granted, mand. denied*, *Granada Corp. v. First Ct. of Appeals*, 844 S.W.2d 223 (Tex. 1992).

257. *Freeman*, 820 S.W.2d at 861; *see In re Sealed Case*, 676 F.2d 793, 812-16 (D.C. Cir. 1982); *see, e.g.*, *In re Monsanto Co.*, 998 S.W.2d 917, 934 (Tex. App.—Waco 1999, orig. proceeding) (opponent did not establish crime-fraud exception when no evidence was presented to show that corporation obtained legal services to commit fraud and no relationship was established between the documents sought and the claimed fraud).

258. *See* American College of Trial Lawyers, *The Erosion of the Attorney-Client Privilege and Work Product Doctrine in Federal Criminal Investigations*, 41 Duq. L. Rev. 307, 310 & n.9 (2003); David J. Fried, *Too High a Price for Truth: The Exception to the Attorney-Client Privilege for Contemplated Crimes and Frauds*, 64 N.C. L. Rev. 443, 470 (1986).

259. Courts derive this requirement from the Supreme Court's opinion in *United States v. Zolin*, 491 U.S. 554, 556-57 (1989). In *Zolin*, the Court held that a court may review privileged documents in camera to decide whether the crime-fraud exception applies. 491 U.S. at 574. Thus, the crime-fraud exception may be applied to overcome privilege based entirely on the contents of the privileged documents themselves.

260. *See id.* at 573-74; *In re Grand Jury Subpoena 92-1(SJ)*, 31 F.3d 826, 830 (9th Cir. 1994).

261. *Cf. Haines v. Liggett Grp. Inc.*, 975 F.2d 81, 97 (3d Cir. 1992) (importance of attorney-client privilege and "fundamental concepts of due process require that the party defending the privilege be given the opportunity to be heard, by evidence and argument, at the hearing seeking an exception to the privilege" under Federal Rule 104(a)).

262. Tex. R. Evid. 503(c)(3).

263. Before the 2015 restyling of the Texas Rules, Rule 503(d)(2) specifically stated that the exception applied regardless of whether the claims were by inter vivos transactions or by testate or intestate succession. That portion of the rule was deleted in the restyling; however, no substantive change was intended. *See* Tex. Sup. Ct. Order, Misc. Docket No. 15-9048, §2 (eff. Apr. 1, 2015).

a decedent's heir might seek to invalidate a will, claiming undue influence. Because such a case turns on the issue of who steps into the decedent's shoes, the question of which disputant is entitled to claim the privilege will not be resolved until the end of the litigation. Given the choice of allowing both sides or neither to assert the privilege, Rule 503(d)(2) opts for the latter,[264] adhering to earlier Texas case law[265] and the weight of authority elsewhere.[266] The exception does not apply when a party makes a claim adverse to both the client and those claiming under him.[267]

3. Rule 503(d)(3): Breach of duty by a lawyer or client. Rule 503(d)(3) codifies the well-established exception for controversies between attorney and client.[268] Thus, when a client attacks his attorney's performance, or an attorney sues a client to recover his fee, the privilege is inapplicable, but only to the extent the otherwise confidential communications are relevant and necessary to the parties' dispute.[269] Courts justify this exception on notions of fairness[270] and waiver,[271] as well as the "practical necessity that if effective legal service is to be encouraged the privilege must not stand in the way of

---

264. *See, e.g.,* ***In re Tex. A&M-Corpus Christi Found.***, 84 S.W.3d 358, 361 (Tex. App.—Corpus Christi 2002, orig. proceeding) (discovery material about contributor's mental capacity was relevant and unprivileged under Rule 503(d)(2) in lawsuit between university foundation and deceased's estate because both were claiming through the same deceased client).

265. *See* ***Krumb v. Porter***, 152 S.W.2d 495, 497 (Tex. Civ. App.—San Antonio 1941, writ ref'd); ***Pierce v. Farrar***, 60 Tex. Civ. App. 12, 14, 126 S.W. 932, 933 (Dallas 1910, no writ); 1 RAY, *supra* note 52, §425. The Texas cases justify the exception by stating that testators intend such communications to be confidential only until death. ***Hayes v. Pennock***, 192 S.W.2d 169, 174 (Tex. Civ. App.—Beaumont 1945, writ ref'd n.r.e.); ***Pierce***, 60 Tex. Civ. App. at 14-15, 126 S.W. at 933; *cf. **Suddarth v. Poor***, 546 S.W.2d 138, 141 (Tex. Civ. App.—Tyler 1977, writ ref'd n.r.e.) (communications about a client's will are privileged before testator's death).

266. *See* McCORMICK ON EVIDENCE I, *supra* note 65, §94, at 227-28.

267. *See* TEX. R. EVID. 503(d)(2).

268. *See* ***West v. Solito***, 563 S.W.2d 240, 245 n.3 (Tex. 1978) (orig. proceeding) (when a client challenges an attorney's professional conduct, client waives the privilege as far as necessary for attorney to defend his character); ***Smith v. Guerre***, 159 S.W. 417, 419-20 (Tex. Civ. App.—Amarillo 1913, no writ) (attorney may reveal privileged attorney-client communications to protect himself when the client charges that the attorney has been unfaithful to the client's interests).

269. *See* TEX. R. EVID. 503(d)(3); ***In re Harris***, 491 S.W.3d 332, 335 (Tex. Crim. App. 2016); ***In re Medina***, 475 S.W.3d 291, 302 (Tex. Crim. App. 2015); ***Judwin Props., Inc. v. Griggs & Harrison, P.C.***, 981 S.W.2d 868, 870 (Tex. App.—Houston [1st Dist.] 1998), *pet. denied*, 11 S.W.3d 188 (Tex. 2000). At issue in ***Judwin Properties*** was whether a law firm committed legal malpractice by negligently disclosing a former client's confidential information in the firm's suit to collect its fee. A divided court of appeals held that because Rule 503(d)(3) permits disclosure of otherwise confidential communications, to the extent they are relevant, in a suit to recover fees, the law firm was entitled to summary judgment because it "conclusively disproved the duty element of [the former client's] claim." ***Judwin Props.***, 981 S.W.2d at 870. In rejecting a petition for discretionary review, the supreme court specifically disapproved of this language. ***Judwin Props., Inc. v. Griggs & Harrison, P.C.***, 11 S.W.3d 188, 188-89 (Tex. 2000). Justice O'Connor, dissenting in the court of appeals, correctly noted that Rule 503(d)(3) permits disclosure "only so far as necessary to assert his claim." ***Judwin Props.***, 981 S.W.2d at 871 (O'Connor, J., dissenting). A dispute between an attorney and a former client does not remove the privilege for all confidential communications. *Cf.* TEX. DISCIPLINARY R. PROF'L CONDUCT 1.05(c)(5) ("A lawyer may reveal confidential information [t]o the extent reasonably necessary to enforce a claim or establish a defense on behalf of the lawyer in a controversy between the lawyer and the client.").

270. *See* ***Smith***, 159 S.W. at 419-20.

271. *See* ***In re Harris***, 491 S.W.3d at 335; ***In re Medina***, 475 S.W.3d at 302; ***West***, 563 S.W.2d at 245; 1 RAY, *supra* note 52, §430, at 414.

the lawyer's just enforcement of his rights to be paid a fee and to protect his reputation."[272]

4. Rule 503(d)(4): Documents attested by a lawyer. When an attorney acts as an attesting witness to a document, he is not rendering professional legal services.[273] Consequently, Rule 503(d)(4) exempts communications about the document from the attorney-client privilege.[274] The attorney must testify, just as any other attesting witness, on matters of the document's validity, such as the client's intent or competence.[275] Thus, an attorney should be hesitant to act as an attesting witness to a client's document.[276]

5. Rule 503(d)(5): Joint clients. When two or more clients jointly consult an attorney on a matter of common interest, their communication will be privileged in a dispute between one or more of them and a third party.[277] In an action between the joint clients, however, Rule 503(d)(5) provides that statements made by any of the clients to the lawyer that are relevant to a matter of common interest between the clients are not privileged.[278] Parties are not "joint clients" for purposes of the exception simply because one party is the fiduciary of another's interest.[279]

---

272. McCORMICK ON EVIDENCE I, *supra* note 65, §91, at 221.

273. *Id.* §88, at 209-10.

274. Because the attorney-client privilege applies only to communications made for the purpose of facilitating the rendition of professional legal services, the exception may be redundant. *See* TEX. R. EVID. 503(b). The Advisory Committee chose to rely on a waiver theory to justify this exception to the proposed federal rule. *Proposed Rules*, *supra* note 28, at 240 (FED. R. EVID. 503 advisory committee's note, subdiv. (d)(4)).

275. *See In re Estate of Hardwick*, 278 S.W.2d 258, 262 (Tex. Civ. App.—Amarillo 1954, writ ref'd n.r.e.) (one ground for allowing an attorney to testify about the validity of a will is that the attorney drafted the will). Although no Texas cases directly address the existence of such an exception, many other jurisdictions recognize it. *See generally* E. S. Stephens, Annotation, *Privilege as to Communications to Attorney in Connection with Drawing of Will*, 66 A.L.R.2d 1302 (1959) (listing cases discussing the attorney-client privilege in the drawing of a will or the advisability of the drawing of a will).

276. 2 WEINSTEIN & BERGER, *supra* note 29, ¶503(d)(4)[01], at 503-125.

277. *See In re XL Specialty Ins.*, 373 S.W.3d 46, 50 (Tex. 2012); McCORMICK ON EVIDENCE I, *supra* note 65, §91, at 219.

278. TEX. R. EVID. 503(d)(5); *see Marathon Oil Co. v. Moyé*, 893 S.W.2d 585, 591 (Tex. App.—Dallas 1994, orig. proceeding [leave denied]) ("The attorney-client privilege does not apply to a communication relevant to a matter of common interest between or among two or more clients if the communication was made by any of the clients to a lawyer retained or consulted in common, when offered in an action between or among any of the clients."). Clients who have a common interest but employ separate counsel can claim the privilege for their own statements in a later dispute between those clients. *See* TEX. R. EVID. 503(b)(1)(C). Refer to notes 206-212 *supra* and accompanying text.

     Rule 503(d)(5) codifies Texas common law. *See Minor v. Bishop*, 180 S.W. 909, 910 (Tex. Civ. App.—Texarkana 1915, no writ); 1 RAY, *supra* note 52, §425, at 408-10 (3d ed. 1980). This exception covers not only situations when two or more parties with identical interests consult the same attorney, but also when two or more parties with potentially divergent interests consult the same attorney. Thus, when an insurance company retains an attorney to represent both the company and the insured pursuant to a liability policy, confidential statements made by each are privileged as to third parties. Should a dispute arise between the insurance company and the insured, however, this exception would not apply. *See* McCORMICK ON EVIDENCE I, *supra* note 65, §91, at 219-20. Nevertheless, the attorney would still have an obligation to preserve client confidences; thus, even though a court may compel disclosure of this nonprivileged matter, the attorney cannot voluntarily disclose the confidences of the insured to the insurance company. *See Emp'rs Cas. Co. v. Tilley*, 496 S.W.2d 552, 559 (Tex. 1973); A.B.A. Nat'l Conference of Lawyers & Liab. Insurers, *Guiding Principles*, 20 FED'N INS. COUNS. Q. 93, 97-98 (1970); Lawrence L. Germer &

E. Work-Product Doctrine

The scope of the attorney-client privilege is often confused with that of the work-product doctrine and the attorney's professional obligation to maintain confidences and secrets.[280] While the attorney-client privilege belongs to and protects the client,[281] the work-product doctrine belongs to and protects the attorney.[282] Premised on the belief that attorneys should not be compelled to disclose the fruits of their labor to their adversaries,[283] the common-law doctrine shielded from discovery all "specific documents, reports, communications, memoranda, mental impressions, conclusions, opinions, or legal theories, prepared and assembled [by an attorney] in actual anticipation

Cecil W. Tebbs, *Conduct of Defense Attorney and Insurance Company in Defending an Insured Where a Coverage Question Is Involved*, 13 S. Tex. L.J. 223, 242 (1972); *cf.* ***Brennan's, Inc. v. Brennan's Rests., Inc.***, 590 F.2d 168, 171-72 (5th Cir. 1979) (disqualifying an attorney who represented joint clients from representing one against the other in a later dispute because of the obligation to preserve client confidences, even if communications were not privileged).

279. *See, e.g.*, ***Huie v. DeShazo***, 922 S.W.2d 920, 924-25 (Tex. 1996) (Rule 503 contains no exception applicable to fiduciaries and their attorney-client communications; beneficiary of trust could not pierce trustee's confidential communications to his attorney about the trust); ***Kennedy v. Gulf Coast Cancer & Diagnostic Ctr. at Se., Inc.***, 326 S.W.3d 352, 358 (Tex. App.—Houston [1st Dist.] 2010, no pet.) (former corporate counsel claimed that he asked law firm to prepare memo with the intent that it benefit not only the corporate client but also its officers; trial court did not abuse its discretion in holding that joint-client exception did not apply when there was no evidence of dual representation); ***In re Valero Energy Corp.***, 973 S.W.2d 453, 458 (Tex. App.—Houston [14th Dist.] 1998, orig. proceeding) (op. on reh'g) (although joint venturers owed fiduciary duty to one another, they were not joint clients for purposes of rule; in-house attorney was acting solely for his own employer's benefit, even though he rendered some undefined legal services to joint venture and joint venturer paid for some portion of legal expenses; trial court erred in ordering production of privileged documents to joint venturer).

280. *See* ***Pope v. State***, 207 S.W.3d 352, 357 (Tex. Crim. App. 2006). *See generally* Fred A. Simpson, *Has the Fog Cleared? Attorney Work Product and the Attorney-Client Privilege: Texas's Complete Transition into Full Protection of Attorney Work in the Corporate Context*, 32 St. Mary's L.J. 197, 222-55 (2001) (discussing development and operation of work-product doctrine in Texas). For further discussion of the work-product doctrine, see ***O'Connor's Texas Rules * Civil Trials*** (2017), "Work-product privilege," ch. 6-B, §3.3, p. 544.

281. *Pope*, 207 S.W.3d at 357. Refer to notes 226-233 *supra* and accompanying text.

282. *Pope*, 207 S.W.3d at 357; *see* ***United States v. Nobles***, 422 U.S. 225, 238 (1975) ("At its core, the work-product doctrine shelters the mental processes of the attorney, providing a privileged area within which [the attorney] can analyze and prepare his client's case.").

283. *Pope*, 207 S.W.3d at 358; *see* ***Occidental Chem. Corp. v. Banales***, 907 S.W.2d 488, 490 (Tex. 1995) (orig. proceeding) (per curiam) ("The attorney work-product privilege protects two related but different concepts. First, the privilege protects the attorney's thought process, which includes strategy decisions and issue formulation, and notes or writings evincing those mental processes. Second, the privilege protects the mechanical compilation of information to the extent such compilation reveals the attorney's thought processes."); ***Owens-Corning Fiberglas Corp. v. Caldwell***, 818 S.W.2d 749, 750 (Tex. 1991) (orig. proceeding) ("The primary purpose of the work product rule is to shelter the mental processes, conclusions, and legal theories of the attorney, providing a privileged area within which the lawyer can analyze and prepare his or her case."); *Moyé*, 893 S.W.2d at 589 (work-product exemption "extends not only to documents the attorney generates, but also to memoranda, reports, notes or summaries of interviews, etc. prepared by other persons for an attorney's use"); *see also* 2 Jordan, *supra* note 74, §10.01 (work-product doctrine characterizes "the essential notion that the attorney is entitled to reasonable privacy in the performance of his professional work"); 2 Louisell & Mueller, *supra* note 69, §211, at 792 (highlighting Supreme Court's view that the work-product doctrine "provides an additional barrier" to discoverability of documents). *See generally* ***Hickman v. Taylor***, 329 U.S. 495, 511-12 (1947) (general policy against invading the privacy of an attorney's course of preparation is so essential to an orderly working of the system of legal procedure that the one who invades that privacy must establish adequate reasons to justify production).

of litigation or for trial."[284] Materials prepared by the attorney's agent were also protected.[285]

The rationale for the work-product doctrine is that attorneys must be free to investigate and assemble information about a potential or pending lawsuit without undue interference from their opponents.[286] As the U.S. Supreme Court has stated:

> Proper preparation of a client's case demands that [the attorney] assemble information, sift what he considers to be the relevant from the irrelevant facts, prepare his legal theories and plan his strategy without undue and needless interference. That is the historical and the necessary way in which lawyers act within the framework of our system of jurisprudence to promote justice and to protect their clients' interests. This work is reflected, of course, in interviews, statements, memoranda, correspondence, briefs, mental impressions, personal beliefs, and countless other tangible and intangible ways—aptly though roughly termed ... as the 'work product of the lawyer.' Were such materials open to opposing counsel on mere demand, much of what is now put down in writing would remain unwritten. An attorney's thoughts, heretofore inviolate, would not be his own. Inefficiency, unfairness and sharp practices

---

284. *Nat'l Tank Co. v. Brotherton*, 851 S.W.2d 193, 200 (Tex. 1993) (orig. proceeding); *accord* **Huie**, 922 S.W.2d at 927; *see* ***DeWitt & Rearick, Inc. v. Ferguson***, 699 S.W.2d 692, 694 (Tex. App.—El Paso 1985, orig. proceeding [leave denied]); *see also* **In re Bexar Cty. Crim. Dist. Attorney's Office**, 224 S.W.3d 182, 186 (Tex. 2007) (orig. proceeding) (work-product doctrine protects attorney's selection and ordering of documents); ***Nat'l Union Fire Ins. v. Valdez***, 863 S.W.2d 458, 460 (Tex. 1993) (orig. proceeding) (attorney's litigation file goes to the heart of the work-product exemption because the organization of the file, as well as the actual inclusion or omission of documents, necessarily reveals the attorney's thought processes). *See generally* Helen A. Cassidy & Edward L. Rice, *Privileges and Discovery: Part One—The Expanding Scope of Discovery*, 52 Tex. B.J. 462 (1989) (analyzing how an attorney can secure protection of privileges in light of important policy justifications favoring disclosure); James B. Sales, *Pretrial Discovery in Texas Under the Amended Rules: Analysis and Commentary*, 27 S. Tex. L. Rev. 305 (1985) (examining the status of pretrial discovery under the amended rules and decisions interpreting those rules); Daniel F. Knox, Comment, *Texas Work Product Protection: Time for a Change*, 15 Hous. L. Rev. 112 (1977) (discussing the balance of protecting attorney work product against discovery and the stated purpose of the Texas Rules of Civil Procedure to achieve equity in litigation).

285. *See Brotherton*, 851 S.W.2d at 202-03 & n.12 (neither federal nor Texas work-product doctrine distinguishes between an investigation conducted by a party and one conducted by the party's representative); ***Toyota Motor Sales, U.S.A., Inc. v. Heard***, 774 S.W.2d 316, 317-18 (Tex. App.—Houston [14th Dist.] 1989, orig. proceeding [leave denied]) (per curiam) (attorney work-product privilege protects not only work product of attorney but also certain materials prepared by attorney's agents in anticipation of litigation); *see, e.g.*, ***Humphreys v. Caldwell***, 888 S.W.2d 469, 471 (Tex. 1994) (orig. proceeding) (per curiam) (trial court abused its discretion in ordering production of entire claims file that included memos and correspondence prepared by attorney or attorney's agents); ***Marshall v. Hall***, 943 S.W.2d 180, 183 (Tex. App.—Houston [1st Dist.] 1997, orig. proceeding) (summaries and interview notes prepared by attorney's employee were protected by work-product privilege). The opinions of nonwitness expert consultants and information obtained by investigators were also protected. *See, e.g.*, ***Bearden v. Boone***, 693 S.W.2d 25, 27-28 (Tex. App.—Amarillo 1985, orig. proceeding) (both attorney-client privilege and work-product doctrine protected from disclosure information gathered for attorney by private investigator). *See generally* James B. Sales, *Pre-Trial Discovery in Texas*, 31 Sw. L.J. 1017 (1977) (exploring the parameters and limitations of discovery procedure under the amended rules). For a discussion of the applicability of the attorney-client privilege to communications involving the attorney's representative, refer to notes 135-155 *supra* and accompanying text.

286. *See Pope*, 207 S.W.3d at 357-58 (purpose of work-product doctrine "is to stimulate the production of information for trials, and it rewards an attorney's creative efforts by giving his work product a qualified privilege from being shared with others").

would inevitably develop in the giving of legal advice and in the preparation of cases for trial. The effect on the legal profession would be demoralizing. And the interests of the clients and the cause of justice would be poorly served.[287]

Until 1999,[288] the term "work product" was not expressly defined in either the Federal or Texas Rules of Civil Procedure.[289] However, both Texas and federal courts had recognized that the work-product doctrine protects two distinct types of material: (1) factual information collected by the attorney—labeled "ordinary" or "noncore" work product—which could be discoverable on a showing of substantial need and undue hardship, and (2) the attorney's mental impressions, conclusions, opinions, or legal theories—labeled "opinion" or "core" work product—which, if discoverable at all, could only be obtained on a much higher showing of necessity.[290] Traditionally, the work-product doctrine has played a less important role in Texas than in many other jurisdictions because of the separate discovery privilege under Texas law that protected communications between a party's representatives;[291] however, "[t]here appears to have been more reliance on the work product privilege since 1986, when the scope of the party communication privilege was narrowed."[292] The adoption of Texas Rule of Civil Procedure 192.5 formally established the privilege for core work product by prohibiting discovery of the attorney's "mental impressions, opinions, conclusions, or legal theories."[293] Rule 192.5 is a court rule "prescribed under statutory authority" for purposes of Texas Rule of Evidence 501 and thus is an explicitly recognized evidentiary privilege.[294]

---

287. *Hickman*, 329 U.S. at 511.

288. As of January 1, 1999, the Rules of Civil Procedure were amended to define "work product" and provide relevant exceptions to the doctrine. *See* TEX. R. CIV. P. 192.5; *Final Approval of Revisions to the Texas Rules of Civil Procedure*, 977-978 S.W.2d (Tex. Cases) XLVIII (1999). Rule of Civil Procedure 192.5 combines the work-product doctrine and the party-communications privilege that were previously found in Rule of Civil Procedure 166b. TEX. R. CIV. P. 192 cmt. 8.

289. *See Brotherton*, 851 S.W.2d at 201.

290. *See In re Nat'l Lloyds Ins.*, ___ S.W.3d ___ (Tex. 2017) (No. 15-0591; 6-9-17) (orig. proceeding) (Texas approach); *Occidental Chem. Corp. v. Banales*, 907 S.W.2d 488, 490 (Tex. 1995) (orig. proceeding) (per curiam) (same); *Brotherton*, 851 S.W.2d at 201-02 (development of work-product doctrine under federal law); *see, e.g., Goode v. Shoukfeh*, 943 S.W.2d 441, 448-49 (Tex. 1997) (attorney's notes made during trial were core work product); *Nat'l Union Fire Ins. v. Valdez*, 863 S.W.2d 458, 460 (Tex. 1993) (orig. proceeding) (party was not required to produce attorney's entire litigation file; organization of file was core work product); *Garcia v. Peeples*, 734 S.W.2d 343, 348 (Tex. 1987) (orig. proceeding) (indexes, notes, and memos prepared by attorney were core work product).

291. *Brotherton*, 851 S.W.2d at 201; *see* TEX. R. CIV. P. 192.5(a), (b); *see also* Alex Wilson Albright, *The Texas Discovery Privileges: A Fool's Game?*, 70 TEX. L. REV. 781, 831 (1992) (party-communications privilege provides protection for ordinary attorney work product).

292. *Brotherton*, 851 S.W.2d at 201 (federal and Texas courts have applied the work-product doctrine only to materials prepared in anticipation of litigation).

293. TEX. R. CIV. P. 192.5(b)(1); *see In re Bexar Cty. Crim. Dist. Attorney's Office*, 224 S.W.3d 182, 186 (Tex. 2007). The Texas Supreme Court has held that a request to produce all attorney billing records in a case violated the work-product doctrine because "as a whole, billing records represent the mechanical compilation of information that reveals counsel's legal strategy and thought processes, at least incidentally." *In re Nat'l Lloyds Ins.*, ___ S.W.3d at ___. Specifically, billing records reveal attorneys' strategic deployment of client resources, which issues were addressed by more experienced lawyers, attorneys' subject-matter expertise, and information on hiring of consultants. *Id.* at

In **Owens-Corning Fiberglas Corp. v. Caldwell**, the Texas Supreme Court held that "the work product privilege in Texas is of continuing duration."[295] The supreme court reasoned that it would be inconsistent to protect the client's full and frank communications in perpetuity under Texas Rule of Civil Evidence 503 but permit discovery of the attorney's protected work product done under that same attorney-client relationship once the particular lawsuit had ended.[296] As a practical consideration, the supreme court noted that some parties, such as manufacturers like Owens-Corning, civil-rights organizations, and environmental groups, may be repeat litigants.[297] These parties and their attorneys should be allowed to develop an overall legal strategy for a broad spectrum of individual cases without concern that, once a lawsuit is completed, all of the material that the attorney has assembled and the strategy he has developed for the client will be subject to discovery in the future or in other pending litigation.[298]

The work-product doctrine also covers information gathered or acquired in "anticipation of litigation,"[299] which is ambiguously defined as "after there is good cause

___. The dissent, however, argued that the requested documents were "limited, specific, and unquestionably relevant to an issue in this case" and that the order to redact privileged information before producing documents was sufficient to protect the privileged information. *Id.* at ___ (Johnson, Lehrmann, Boyd, JJ., dissenting).

Although Rule 192.5 is a civil rule, it has also been applied in criminal cases. *See* **Woodruff v. State**, 330 S.W.3d 709, 729 (Tex. App.—Texarkana 2010, pet. ref'd) ("[T]he distinction between core work product and other work product applies in criminal cases."); *see also* **Pope v. State**, 207 S.W.3d 352, 365 (Tex. Crim. App. 2006) ("Juries are always entitled to draw reasonable inferences from known, unprivileged facts, even though those inferences may have the effect of indirectly disclosing an attorney's (or his agent's) mental impressions. What the work-product doctrine protects is the production of material—documents, e-mails, letters, disclosure of conversations, and so forth—and statements that set out an attorney's litigation strategy or opinions concerning the result of his investigation or that of his agents. It does not prevent the factfinder from making reasonable inferences from known facts.").

294. *See* Tex. R. Evid. 501.

295. 818 S.W.2d 749, 751-52 (Tex. 1991) (orig. proceeding); *accord* **Occidental Chem.**, 907 S.W.2d at 490; *see* **In re Bexar Cty. Crim. Dist. Attorney's Office**, 224 S.W.3d at 186 ("The privilege continues indefinitely beyond the litigation for which the materials were originally prepared.").

296. **Owens-Corning**, 818 S.W.2d at 751. The Texas Supreme Court's ruling in **Owens-Corning** is in accord with the "sounder view" expressed by Wright and Miller and followed in a majority of other jurisdictions. *See* 8 Charles A. Wright & Arthur R. Miller, Federal Practice and Procedure §2024, at 350-51 (2d ed. 1994) (lower courts generally recognize the "sounder view" in favor of a work-product doctrine that protects documents prepared for one case in a second case when cases are closely related in parties or subject matter).

297. **Owens-Corning**, 818 S.W.2d at 751.

298. *Id.* Even before the decision in **Owens-Corning**, one Texas appeals court held that the attorney work-product protection did not terminate at the end of a criminal case when that information was sought in a later civil trial. **Wood v. McCown**, 784 S.W.2d 126, 129 (Tex. App.—Austin 1990, orig. proceeding). The court based its holding on the potential "chilling effect" on an attorney who is recording his mental impressions, factual investigation, and legal research in a criminal case if he knows that this information will be subject to discovery after the conclusion of his client's criminal case. *Id.* The court concluded that "[t]he reasons justifying the criminal work product doctrine also dictate that the completion of the criminal case should not necessarily abort the work product exemption, and therefore, we are unwilling to carve out an exception to the current criminal work product doctrine in the absence of precedent." *Id.*

299. Tex. R. Civ. P. 192.5(a); *see* **In re Bexar Cty. Crim. Dist. Attorney's Office**, 224 S.W.3d at 186 ("The work product privilege is broader than the attorney-client privilege because it includes all communications made in preparation for trial, including an attorney's interviews with parties and non-party witnesses."); *see, e.g.*, **Huie v. DeShazo**, 922 S.W.2d 920, 927 (Tex. 1996) (rejecting contention that work-product doctrine did not apply in the trustee-attorney relationship before the trust beneficiary filed suit against trustee; while it might be improper for a trustee to pay attorney from trust fund for work done in anticipation of lawsuit by beneficiary, "any such impropriety would not abrogate the work-product privilege"); *see also* **Tex. Dep't of MHMR v. Davis**, 775 S.W.2d 467, 471 (Tex.

to believe a suit will be filed."[300] The party resisting discovery has the burden to prove that evidence was acquired or developed in anticipation of litigation.[301] In ***National Tank Co. v. Brotherton***,[302] the supreme court adopted a two-prong test to determine whether a particular document has been prepared in anticipation of litigation and is thus protected by the work-product doctrine. A document is prepared in anticipation of litigation if (1) a reasonable person would conclude from the totality of the circumstances that there was a substantial chance that litigation would ensue and (2) the party claiming the privilege had a good-faith belief that there was a substantial chance that litigation would ensue and prepared the document primarily for such litigation.[303] The first part of the test is objective; the second part is subjective.[304]

App.—Austin 1989, orig. proceeding [leave denied]) (determination of when litigation is reasonably anticipated is a matter of legal judgment made by the court based on the totality of the circumstances). *See generally* Cassidy & Rice, *supra* note 284, at 462-65 (discussing "anticipation of litigation" standard).

Certain information, however, is discoverable even if it was collected or prepared in anticipation of litigation: (1) witness information discoverable under Texas Rule of Civil Procedure 192.3, (2) trial exhibits required to be disclosed under Texas Rule of Civil Procedure 166 or 190.4, (3) the name, address, and phone number of any potential party or potential fact witness, (4) photographs and other electronic evidence that contain images of underlying facts or that a party intends to introduce into evidence, and (5) any work product created under circumstances within an exception to the attorney-client privilege in Texas Rule of Evidence 503(d). Tex. R. Civ. P. 192.5(c).

300. ***Stringer v. Eleventh Ct. of Appeals***, 720 S.W.2d 801, 802 (Tex. 1986) (orig. proceeding) (per curiam), *disapproved on other grounds*, ***Nat'l Tank Co. v. Brotherton***, 851 S.W.2d 193 (Tex. 1993); *see* ***Boring & Tunneling Co. of Am., Inc. v. Salazar***, 782 S.W.2d 284, 286-87 (Tex. App.—Houston [1st Dist.] 1989, orig. proceeding).

301. ***Turbodyne Corp. v. Heard***, 720 S.W.2d 802, 804 (Tex. 1986) (orig. proceeding) (per curiam).

302. 851 S.W.2d 193 (Tex. 1993) (orig. proceeding).

303. *Id.* at 203-04. In ***Brotherton***, the court modified the rule originally set out in ***Flores v. Fourth Ct. of Appeals***, 777 S.W.2d 38, 41 (Tex. 1989) (orig. proceeding), which stated that "'[c]onsideration should be given to outward manifestations which indicate litigation is *imminent*.'" ***Brotherton***, 851 S.W.2d at 203 (quoting ***Flores***). The supreme court decided that requiring litigation to be "imminent" impaired the policy goals of the witness-statement and party-communication privileges. ***Brotherton***, 851 S.W.2d at 203. Accordingly, the ***Brotherton*** court included not only situations in which litigation is imminent, but also circumstances in which there is substantial chance of litigation. *Id.* at 204.

In a case decided under Rule 192.5, the San Antonio Court of Appeals held that once the defendant-corporation learned that the prospective plaintiff had hired an attorney, litigation was anticipated and the investigative report, witness statements, photographs, and surveillance video made by the defendant's investigator after that time were privileged work product. ***In re Weeks Marine, Inc.***, 31 S.W.3d 389, 391 (Tex. App.—San Antonio 2000, orig. proceeding) (per curiam) ("Upon learning that an employee complaining of a work-related injury has hired an attorney, a reasonable defendant would believe a substantial chance of litigation existed."); *see also* ***In re AEP Tex. Cent. Co.***, 128 S.W.3d 687, 691-92 (Tex. App.—San Antonio 2003, orig. proceeding) (work-product doctrine protected attorneys' memorandum analyzing potential claims arising from dispute even though memorandum was prepared before lawsuit was filed).

304. ***Brotherton***, 851 S.W.2d at 203-04. The ***Brotherton*** decision noted that under the first prong, the trial court must examine the totality of circumstances to determine whether a particular investigation is conducted in anticipation of litigation. *Id.* at 204. It is not sufficient that an accident occurred, but if it is a serious accident and other circumstances indicate a substantial chance that litigation would ensue, the prong of the test is satisfied. *Id.* The prospective plaintiff does not need to have engaged in some action indicating an intent to sue. "Common sense dictates that a party may reasonably anticipate suit being filed, and conduct an investigation to prepare for the expected litigation, before the plaintiff manifests an intent to sue." *Id.*

The second prong requires that the investigation actually be conducted for the purpose of preparing for litigation. *Id.* An investigation that is merely a routine practice of the party, without regard for the possibility of litigation, does not suffice. *See id.* at 206. However, if the court determines that the party routinely investigates this type of event primarily to prepare for potential litigation, then the investigation will satisfy the second prong of the ***Brotherton*** test. *See id.* There is no bright-line ordinary-course-of-business exception. *Id.*; *see also* ***In re Tex. Farmers Ins. Exch.***, 990 S.W.2d 337, 342 (Tex. App.—Texarkana 1999, orig. proceeding) (following and applying ***Brother-***

Both the Texas and Federal Rules of Civil Procedure provide for disclosure of some materials prepared or collected by an attorney in anticipation of litigation on a showing of "substantial need,"[305] but neither set of rules permits disclosure of the attorney's mental impressions, opinions, or trial strategy.[306] While the work-product doctrine pro-

---

ton; litigation was not "anticipated" until insurance company had conducted its investigation, decided not to pay claim, and sent denial letter to insured), *mand. denied*, 12 S.W.3d 807 (Tex. 2000); *Oyster Creek Fin. Corp. v. Richwood Invs. II, Inc.*, 957 S.W.2d 640, 646-48 (Tex. App.—Amarillo 1997, pet. denied) (following and applying *Brotherton*; attorney's calculation of principal and interest to help his client collect note under threat of private foreclosure did not constitute attorney work product); *Valero Transmission, L.P. v. Dowd*, 960 S.W.2d 642, 644-49 (Tex. 1997) (Owen & Hecht, JJ., dissenting from overruling of motion for leave to file petition for writ of mandamus) (discussing and applying the two-pronged *Brotherton* test for determining whether an inquiry was conducted "in anticipation of litigation"; noting that the "party-communication privilege should not depend on whether the investigating party foresaw who the actual plaintiff would be. It should be enough that litigation over the situation was anticipated").

In federal courts, materials created in the ordinary course of business, to comply with regulatory requirements, or for nonlitigation reasons are not prepared in anticipation of litigation. *Martin v. Bally's Park Place Hotel & Casino*, 983 F.2d 1252, 1260 (3d Cir. 1993); FED. R. CIV. P. 26 advisory committee's note to 1970 amendments, subdiv. (b)(3); *see, e.g.*, *Freiermuth v. PPG Indus., Inc.*, 218 F.R.D. 694, 700-01 (N.D. Ala. 2003) (company's "Reduction in Force Worksheet"—prepared in the regular and ordinary course of business to ensure compliance with company policy—was not protected by work-product doctrine); *see also* *In re Grand Jury Subpoenas Dated Mar. 19, 2002 & Aug. 2, 2002 (Mercator Corp. v. United States)*, 318 F.3d 379, 384-85 (2d Cir. 2003) ("[T]he work product doctrine does not extend to documents in an attorney's possession that were prepared by a third party in the ordinary course of business and that would have been created in essentially similar form irrespective of any litigation anticipated by counsel."). The Second Circuit has addressed a "selection and compilation" exception to the third-party-document rule if an attorney has so specifically selected and compiled certain documents in anticipation of litigation that production of this sifted material would necessarily reveal the attorney's developing litigation strategy. *See* *In re Grand Jury Subpoenas*, 318 F.3d at 385-86 (accepting "selection and compilation" exception but narrowly confining it and requiring the party invoking the exception to show "'a real, rather than speculative, concern' that counsel's thought processes 'in relation to pending or anticipated litigation' will be exposed through disclosure of the compiled documents" (quoting *Gould, Inc. v. Mitsui Mining & Smelting Co.*, 825 F.2d 676, 680 (2d Cir. 1987))).

305. *See* FED. R. CIV. P. 26(b)(3)(A)(ii) (permitting discovery of materials prepared in anticipation of litigation only if the party seeking discovery "shows that it has substantial need for the materials to prepare its case and cannot, without undue hardship, obtain their substantial equivalent by other means"); TEX. R. CIV. P. 192.5(b)(2) (work product, other than core work product, is discoverable "only upon a showing that the party seeking discovery has substantial need of the materials in the preparation of the party's case and that the party is unable without undue hardship to obtain the substantial equivalent of the material by other means"); *In re Bexar Cty. Crim. Dist. Attorney's Office*, 224 S.W.3d 182, 188 (Tex. 2007) (orig. proceeding) ("Substantial need is not merely substantial desire."); *see, e.g.*, *State v. Lowry*, 802 S.W.2d 669, 673 (Tex. 1991) (orig. proceeding) (defendant made sufficient showing of substantial need when State collected information during investigation that led to lawsuit and could provide evidence for defense); *Dillard Dep't Stores, Inc. v. Sanderson*, 928 S.W.2d 319, 321-22 (Tex. App.—Beaumont 1996, orig. proceeding [leave denied]) (issues of witness credibility and failing memory were sufficient to show substantial need). The Texarkana Court of Appeals has extended the undue-hardship requirement to criminal cases. *Woodruff v. State*, 330 S.W.3d 709, 729 (Tex. App.—Texarkana 2010, pet. ref'd).

In *Hickman v. Taylor*, the U.S. Supreme Court set out a two-part test for exemption of information from work-product protection. 329 U.S. 495, 511 (1947). First, the factual information must be "hidden in an attorney's file," and second, the facts sought to be discovered must be "essential to the preparation of one's case." *Id.*; *see also* *Marshall v. Hall*, 943 S.W.2d 180, 183 (Tex. App.—Houston [1st Dist.] 1997, orig. proceeding) (party seeking discovery of attorney work product had not proved either part of the *Hickman* test); *Enos v. Baker*, 751 S.W.2d 946, 950 (Tex. App.—Houston [14th Dist.] 1988, orig. proceeding) (work-product doctrine is not absolute, but it applied when wife sought all of her estranged husband's law-firm files during divorce proceeding in an effort to assess the value of their community property).

306. *See* FED. R. CIV. P. 26(b)(3)(B) ("If the court orders discovery of [attorney work product], it must protect against disclosure of the mental impressions, conclusions, opinions, or legal theories of a party's attorney or other representative concerning the litigation."); TEX. R. CIV. P. 192.5(b)(1) (exempting the work product of an attorney

tects the communications of parties, attorneys, and their agents,[307] the underlying factual information is not protected, regardless of whether it is contained within that communication.[308]

The use of experts, both before and during trial, may affect the scope of work-product protection in some cases. Federal rules do not typically permit discovery of materials relating to consulting experts who are not intended to be trial witnesses.[309] The same is true under the Texas Rules of Civil Procedure.[310] Consulting experts cannot be deposed about the strategies, ideas, concerns, or evidence they obtain from the attorney who hired them.[311] Once an expert is designated as a testifying expert, however, the opposition can depose the expert; in most jurisdictions, work-product protection for materials given to the expert has essentially been waived.[312]

Sometimes, an attorney decides not to use the testimony of an expert who was designated as a testifying expert but who ultimately developed opinions that are detrimen-

---

as a general proposition), Tex. R. Civ. P. 192.5(b)(4) (if court orders discovery of noncore work product, court must protect against disclosure of attorney's mental impressions, opinions, conclusions, or legal theories that are not otherwise discoverable); *see also* **Owens-Corning Fiberglas Corp. v. Caldwell**, 818 S.W.2d 749, 751 (Tex. 1991) (orig. proceeding) (former Rule 166b(3)(e), now Rule 192.5(b)(2), contains a "substantial need" exception for the discoverability of party communications and witness statements, but not for true work product; Texas Rules of Civil Procedure and case law indicate "the high degree of protection to be afforded the mental processes of an attorney"); **Gen. Motors Corp. v. Gayle**, 924 S.W.2d 222, 229 (Tex. App.—Houston [14th Dist.] 1996, orig. proceeding) ("In Texas, the work product privilege contains no exception for substantial need ...."), *mand. granted*, 951 S.W.2d 469 (Tex. 1997).

307. When an attorney's agent interviews witnesses, makes factual summaries of the interviews, and organizes those facts into a strategic overview for the attorney, the agent's summary and interview notes may be protected by the work-product doctrine. *See* **Marshall**, 943 S.W.2d at 183.

308. **Pope v. State**, 207 S.W.3d 352, 358 (Tex. Crim. App. 2006); *see* **Axelson, Inc. v. McIlhany**, 798 S.W.2d 550, 554 n.8 (Tex. 1990) (orig. proceeding) (work-product doctrine "protects only the mental impressions, opinions, and conclusions of the lawyer and not the facts"); *see, e.g.*, **Leede Oil & Gas, Inc. v. McCorkle**, 789 S.W.2d 686, 687 (Tex. App.—Houston [1st Dist.] 1990, orig. proceeding) (attorney's notes that were mere "neutral recitals of facts" and contained no commentary by attorney were not covered by work-product doctrine); *see also* **Hickman**, 329 U.S. at 511 ("Where relevant and non-privileged facts remain hidden in an attorney's file and where production of those facts is essential to the preparation of one's case, discovery may properly be had."). For example, in **City of Denison v. Grisham**, the court held that descriptions of potential witnesses and statements that would reveal whether the plaintiff had spoken to potential witnesses were not work product and hence discoverable. 716 S.W.2d 121, 123-24 (Tex. App.—Dallas 1986, orig. proceeding). The Fourteenth Court of Appeals later stated that not all facts contained within attorney-client documents are exempt from the protection of the work-product doctrine. *See* **Pittsburgh Corning Corp. v. Caldwell**, 861 S.W.2d 423, 426 (Tex. App.—Houston [14th Dist.] 1993, orig. proceeding). When the protected documents are related to the party's trial strategy and defense, the facts contained within those documents are not a "neutral recitation of facts" that would be subject to discovery. *Id.*

309. Fed. R. Civ. P. 26(b)(4)(D). Consulting experts frequently need access to confidential information and other attorney work product to provide useful guidance or advice. Thus, discovery about consulting experts would essentially be discovery of attorney work product. *See* **Durflinger v. Artiles**, 727 F.2d 888, 891 (10th Cir. 1984) (preventing discovery about consulting experts advances fairness concerns; otherwise, opposing parties would have unreasonable access to their opponent's trial preparations); **House v. Combined Ins.**, 168 F.R.D. 236, 245 (N.D. Iowa 1996) ("[A] consulted-but-never-designated expert might properly be considered to fall under the work product doctrine that protects matters prepared in anticipation of litigation.").

310. Tex. R. Civ. P. 192.3(e); *see* **In re City of Georgetown**, 53 S.W.3d 328, 334 (Tex. 2001) (orig. proceeding); **Castellanos v. Littlejohn**, 945 S.W.2d 236, 239 (Tex. App.—San Antonio 1997, orig. proceeding [leave denied]).

311. *See* Tex. R. Civ. P. 192.3(e).

312. *See* Tex. R. Civ. P. 192.3(e)(3), (e)(4).

tal or unhelpful to the client's case. The opposing party might then want to depose the expert or present his testimony at trial. This creates a "Red Rover" issue, with the attorney who first hired the expert seeking to exclude the testimony and the opposing party seeking to use the expert for its own purposes at trial.[313] Courts should consider (1) whether the designating party can "dedesignate" the expert by declaring that the party will not use the expert as a trial witness and (2) what consequence, if any, this dedesignation should have at trial.[314] Federal courts have taken various positions on the Red Rover issue, relying on fairness concerns, potential prejudice, and other fact-based tests.[315] Texas courts have permitted a party to dedesignate a testifying witness under some circumstances; by downgrading the witness's status to that of consulting expert, the party protects any confidential work product in the expert's possession.[316] To maximize work-product protection, an attorney should not designate an expert as a witness until the attorney is thoroughly familiar with the expert's opinion on the relevant issues. Alternatively, if time constraints force the attorney to designate a person as a testifying expert before the expert's opinion is fully developed, the attorney should limit or avoid sharing confidential materials or strategies with the expert.

The nature and extent of the work-product doctrine in Texas criminal cases is considerably less developed.[317] Discovery in Texas criminal proceedings is largely a one-

---

313. *See Pope*, 207 S.W.3d at 361 & n.29; Edward J. Imwinkelried, *The Applicability of the Attorney-Client Privilege to Non-Testifying Experts: Reestablishing the Boundaries Between the Attorney-Client Privilege and the Work Product Protection*, 68 WASH. U. L.Q. 19, 37-38 (1990). *See generally* Stephen D. Easton, *"Red Rover, Red Rover, Send that Expert Right Over": Clearing the Way for Parties to Introduce the Testimony of Their Opponents' Expert Witnesses*, 55 SMU L. REV. 1427 (2002) (comprehensive and generalized discussion of Red Rover issues).

314. *Pope*, 207 S.W.3d at 361.

315. *Compare Koch Ref. Co. v. Jennifer L. Boudreaux MV*, 85 F.3d 1178, 1181 (5th Cir. 1996) ("[N]o one would seriously contend that a court should permit a consultant to serve as one party's expert where it is undisputed that the consultant was previously retained as an expert by the adverse party in the same litigation and had received confidential information from the adverse party pursuant to the earlier retention."), *and Durflinger v. Artiles*, 727 F.2d 888, 891 (10th Cir. 1984) (opposing party may not call dedesignated witness unless under exceptional circumstances, even though expert had formed opinions and given report), *with Peterson v. Willie*, 81 F.3d 1033, 1037-38 (11th Cir. 1996) (discretion of district court to decide when designated testifying expert should be permitted to testify for opposing party, although that party should not be allowed to establish that witness was originally retained by the other party). *See O'Connor's Federal Rules * Civil Trials* (2017), "Testifying expert + dedesignation = consulting expert," ch. 6-D, §3.1.3, p. 586. The Fifth Circuit discussed this issue in terms of witness disqualification, using a two-part balancing test: first, was it objectively reasonable for the first party who claims to have retained the expert to conclude that a confidential relationship existed; and second, was any confidential or privileged information disclosed by the first party to the expert? *Koch Ref.*, 85 F.3d at 1181.

316. *See In re Doctors' Hosp. of Laredo, L.P.*, 2 S.W.3d 504, 506 (Tex. App.—San Antonio 1999, orig. proceeding); *see, e.g.*, *Tom L. Scott, Inc. v. McIlhany*, 798 S.W.2d 556, 559-60 (Tex. 1990) (orig. proceeding) (dedesignation was improper when parties bargained for "rights" to experts during settlement negotiations and sought to exclude expert testimony by making discovery provisions "a sword to be used to thwart justice or to defeat the salutary objects" of discovery); *Castellanos v. Littlejohn*, 945 S.W.2d 236, 240 (Tex. App.—San Antonio 1997, orig. proceeding [leave denied]) (party could dedesignate expert witness when uncontroverted direct evidence established that he was designated as a testifying expert only through clerical error). Even without the type of misconduct present in *Tom L. Scott, Inc.*, one Texas court has disallowed the dedesignation of a witness. *Harnischfeger Corp. v. Stone*, 814 S.W.2d 263, 265 (Tex. App.—Houston [14th Dist.] 1991, orig. proceeding). The court reasoned that the witness had already been designated as a testifying expert, and therefore any opinions or information held by the expert were no longer privileged. *Id.*

317. *Pope*, 207 S.W.3d at 360.

way street: the State has little pretrial right to discover materials, witnesses, expert reports, or evaluations from the defense.[318] Texas Code of Criminal Procedure article 39.14 controls the defense's discovery rights. The defense is allowed to inspect, electronically duplicate, and copy various materials—including offense reports and any designated documents, papers, written or recorded statements by the defendant or a witness, books, letters, or objects not otherwise privileged—if the defense timely requests the materials.[319] Work product "of counsel for the state in the case and their investigators and their notes or report" are specifically exempt from pretrial discovery under the statute.[320] Similarly, the work product of a defense attorney or the attorney's agent is not normally subject to discovery by the State.[321] However, article 39.14(b) allows limited reciprocal discovery of the opposing side's potential expert witnesses.[322]

In *In re George*,[323] the supreme court addressed how the work-product rule in Rule 192.5 affects a successor counsel's access to the work-product materials of a predecessor. After the supreme court had disqualified two law firms, the successor counsel wanted to obtain the former counsels' work product.[324] The supreme court majority stated that "[t]he purposes underlying the initial disqualification will often require

---

318. *See id.*

319. TEX. CODE CRIM. PROC. art. 39.14(a); *see also id.* art. 39.15(c) (material that constitutes child pornography cannot be copied or reproduced if State makes material reasonably available to defendant). Article 39.14(a) includes police offense reports as material that is specifically discoverable; before the 2013 amendments to article 39.14, police offense reports were included as part of the nondiscoverable work product. *See* **Quinones v. State**, 592 S.W.2d 933, 940 (Tex. Crim. App. 1980); **Brem v. State**, 571 S.W.2d 314, 322 (Tex. Crim. App. 1978). Scientific-testing results and prosecution files and papers—which, before the amendments, were also included as part of the nondiscoverable work product—would still seem to fall within that category. *See* TEX. CODE CRIM. PROC. art. 39.14(a); **Quinones**, 592 S.W.2d at 940; **Brem**, 571 S.W.2d at 321-22.
　Although various materials can be disclosed to the defendant, a defendant, his attorney, or an agent of the attorney generally cannot disclose the materials or the information contained within them to a third party unless (1) the court orders disclosure on a showing of good cause or (2) the materials have already been publicly disclosed. *See* TEX. CODE CRIM. PROC. art. 39.14(e); **Powell v. Hocker**, 516 S.W.3d 488, 496-97 (Tex. Crim. App. 2017). Further, the defendant's attorney can allow the defendant, a witness, or a prospective witness to view the information provided under article 39.14 but cannot allow that person to have copies. TEX. CODE CRIM. PROC. art. 39.14(f); *e.g.*, **Powell**, 516 S.W.3d at 495-97 (trial court did not have authority to order defense counsel to give defendant copies of materials disclosed under article 39.14; article 39.14(f) does not allow for judicial disclosure). Parties can agree, however, to discovery requirements that are equal to or greater than those allowed under article 39.14. TEX. CODE CRIM. PROC. art. 39.14(n).

320. TEX. CODE CRIM. PROC. art. 39.14(a); *see, e.g.*, **In re State ex rel. Skurka**, 512 S.W.3d 444, 455 (Tex. App.—Corpus Christi 2016, orig. proceeding) (trial court's order directing State to identify which of the more than 1,000 recorded jail telephone calls it intended to use would not force State to reveal its thought processes on importance of recordings or any strategic conclusions).

321. *See, e.g.*, **Washington v. State**, 856 S.W.2d 184, 190 (Tex. Crim. App. 1993) (taped interview between witness and investigator for defense was protected work product, and privilege not waived by questioning witness at trial about conversation).

322. *See* TEX. CODE CRIM. PROC. art. 39.14(b) (on party's timely request, opposing party must disclose name and address of each person that may be used at trial to present evidence under Rules 702, 703, and 705). Even with such limited criminal discovery provisions, the court of criminal appeals has already addressed the "Red Rover" issue of designated testifying experts who are ultimately not called by the attorney who retained them. *See* **Pope**, 207 S.W.3d at 361-62. Refer to notes 313-316 *supra* and accompanying text.

323. 28 S.W.3d 511 (Tex. 2000) (orig. proceeding).

324. *Id.* at 512-13.

a partial or total restriction on the successor counsel's access to the disqualified counsel's work product."[325] The court then announced a rebuttable presumption that a former, disqualified counsel's work product contains confidential information that the successor attorney is not entitled to receive.[326]

F. Waiver in Corporate Criminal Investigations

In 1999, the Justice Department issued a document known as the "Holder Memo," which established guidelines for investigating corporations and filing criminal charges against them.[327] The Holder Memo instructed prosecutors to consider whether a corporation agreed to waive its attorney-client privilege and work-product protection as a factor in deciding whether to indict the corporation.[328] The Holder Memo was superseded by the "Thompson Memo," issued in 2003.[329] Like the Holder Memo, the Thompson Memo expressly listed willingness to waive attorney-client privilege and work-product protection as one factor in evaluating a corporation's degree of cooperation with a criminal investigation.[330] The degree and authenticity of a corporation's cooperation affected the likelihood of indictment and the applicable range of punishment under the Organizational Sentencing Guidelines, which the U.S. Sentencing Commission promulgated in 1991.[331]

The emphasis on authentic cooperation as demonstrated by, among other things, the waiver of the attorney-client privilege and work-product protection raises several crucial issues for corporations and corporate counsel. First, a company must undertake self-policing, internal audits, and early investigation by counsel with an understanding that the corporation may feel pressured to waive its privileges if it hopes to

---

325. *Id.* at 515.

326. *Id.* at 518.

327. Memorandum from Eric H. Holder, Jr., Deputy Attorney Gen., on Bringing Criminal Charges Against Corporations (June 16, 1999), www.justice.gov/sites/default/files/criminal-fraud/legacy/2010/04/11/charging-corps .PDF.

328. *Id.* §§II(A)(4), VI.

329. Memorandum from Larry D. Thompson, Deputy Attorney Gen., on Principles of Federal Prosecution of Business Organizations (Jan. 20, 2003) (on file with Department of Justice).

330. *Id.* §§II(A)(4), VI.

331. Chapter 8 of the U.S. Sentencing Guidelines was added in 1991 to provide guidelines dealing specifically with corporations. Commentary added to the chapter in 2004 clarified that, under some circumstances, waiver of attorney-client privilege and work-product protection would be required for a reduction in culpability score. *See* U.S. SENTENCING GUIDELINES MANUAL §8C2.5 cmt. n.12 (2004). A November 2006 amendment deleted this commentary. U.S. SENTENCING GUIDELINES MANUAL app. C, amend. 695 (2011). As one commentator has noted, however, formal revision of the Sentencing Guidelines

> does not alone make a pronounced difference. When it comes to assessing credit for assisting an ongoing investigation at sentencing, corporate cooperation is only as valuable as prosecutors say it is. Prosecutors are unlikely to agree that a corporation that has retained its privilege is cooperative in other respects, and a corporation will have an uphill battle arguing to a court that it has helped the government more than prosecutors are letting on.

Lisa Kern Griffin, *Compelled Cooperation and the New Corporate Criminal Procedure*, 82 N.Y.U. L. REV. 311, 348 (2007).

survive a federal criminal investigation without indictment.[332] Second, a few courts recognize a limitation on the scope of the waiver once it is made, although most courts have declined to adopt a "selective waiver" rule.[333] This treatment of waiver becomes

---

332. In 2015, the Justice Department issued a memo that, although not directly addressing waiver of attorney-client privilege or work-product protection, focused on the importance of corporations holding individuals accountable for illegal activity. Memorandum from Sally Quillian Yates, Deputy Attorney Gen., on Individual Accountability for Corporate Wrongdoing (Sept. 9, 2015), www.justice.gov/dag/file/769036/download. The memo explained:

> Companies cannot pick and choose what facts to disclose. That is, to be eligible for any credit for co-operation, the company must identify all individuals involved in or responsible for the misconduct at issue, regardless of their position, status or seniority, and provide to the Department all facts relating to that misconduct. If a company seeking cooperation credit declines to learn of such facts or to provide the Department with complete factual information about individual wrongdoers, its cooperation will not be considered a mitigating factor ....

Id.

333. *See Pac. Pictures Corp. v. U.S. Dist. Ct. for the Cent. Dist. of Cal.*, 679 F.3d 1121, 1127-28 (9th Cir. 2012). *Compare* **In re Qwest Commc'ns Int'l Inc.**, 450 F.3d 1179, 1192 (10th Cir. 2006) (court declined to adopt a rule of "selective waiver" allowing production of privileged materials to certain government agencies without waiving the privilege for other litigants seeking those same corporate documents), *In re Columbia/HCA Healthcare Corp. Billing Practices Litig.*, 293 F.3d 289, 302-03 (6th Cir. 2002) (voluntary waiver is a general waiver, without exception), *United States v. Mass. Inst. of Tech.*, 129 F.3d 681, 686 (1st Cir. 1997) (same), *Genentech, Inc. v. U.S. Int'l Trade Comm'n*, 122 F.3d 1409, 1417 (Fed. Cir. 1997) (rejecting concept of limited waivers), *Westinghouse Elec. Corp. v. Republic of the Phil.*, 951 F.2d 1414, 1425 (3d Cir. 1991) (rejecting rule of selective waiver), *In re Martin Marietta Corp.*, 856 F.2d 619, 623-26 (4th Cir. 1988) (rejecting selective waiver of attorney-client privilege but allowing selective waiver of opinion work product), *and Permian Corp. v. United States*, 665 F.2d 1214, 1219-20 (D.C. Cir. 1981) (waiver of privilege with respect to government is waiver of privilege with respect to everyone), *with In re Steinhardt Partners, L.P.*, 9 F.3d 230, 236 (2d Cir. 1993) (rules relating to privilege in matters of governmental investigation must be crafted on a case-by-case basis), *and Diversified Indus., Inc. v. Meredith*, 572 F.2d 596, 611 (8th Cir. 1978) (en banc) (waiver for purposes of SEC investigation was effective only as to government; corporation retained its privileges as to other parties). *See generally* Nolan Mitchell, Note, *Preserving the Privilege: Codification of Selective Waiver and the Limits of Federal Power over State Courts*, 86 B.U. L. Rev. 691 (2006) (discussing the different approaches to the selective-waiver doctrine taken by federal courts). The Northern District of Texas considered the stance taken by the Eighth Circuit in *Diversified Industries* and rejected it based on "an overwhelming amount of authority" refuting the Eighth Circuit's argument. *SEC v. Brady*, 238 F.R.D. 429, 440 (N.D. Tex. 2006). The court referred to the limited waiver created by the Eighth Circuit as the "selective waiver doctrine," and explained, "the Fifth Circuit has yet to adopt the selective waiver doctrine. Moreover, this court is persuaded by the reasoning of the great weight of authority which has declined to adopt the selective waiver doctrine." *Id.*

The adoption of Federal Rule of Evidence 502 left largely untouched the problem of selective waiver. *See* Statement of Cong. Intent Regarding Rule 502 of the Fed. Rules of Evidence, 110 Cong. Rec. H7818-H7819, subdiv. (d) (daily ed., Sept. 8, 2008), www.congress.gov/crec/2008/09/08/CREC-2008-09-08.pdf. (Federal Rule 502(d) "does not provide a basis for a court to enable parties to agree to a selective waiver of the privilege, such as to a federal agency conducting an investigation, while preserving the privilege as against other parties seeking the information"). The rule does, however, contain several important provisions that give some protection to litigants who intentionally or inadvertently disclose privileged communications and information. First, when a disclosure is made in a federal proceeding or to a federal office or agency and that disclosure causes a waiver of the attorney-client privilege or work-product protection, the waiver does not cover any undisclosed communications or information unless (1) the waiver was intentional, (2) the disclosed and undisclosed communications or information relate to the same subject matter, and (3) the disclosed and undisclosed communications or information should in fairness be considered together. *See* Fed. R. Evid. 502(a). Thus, a party who has selectively disclosed information to a federal agency may argue that the disclosure does not waive the privilege or protection for undisclosed, but similar, communications and information. Second, when a disclosure is made in a federal proceeding or to a federal office or agency, the disclosure does not operate as a waiver in either federal or state proceedings if (1) the disclosure was inadvertent, (2) the holder of the privilege or protection took reasonable steps to prevent disclosure, and (3) the holder promptly took reasonable steps to rectify the error. Fed. R. Evid. 502(b). Refer to note 167 *supra* and accompanying text. Subsection (b) of the rule thus provides a "claw-back" provision to reclaim the privilege for an inadvertent disclosure. Inadvertent disclosure, which requires a finding that a party mistakenly disclosed information it had intended to keep

particularly important in any later civil litigation based on the same conduct that initially subjected the corporation to a criminal investigation. Third, joint-defense agreements may also be affected because they are based on an extension of the attorney-client privilege.[334] Finally, counsel should be aware that waiver of attorney-client privilege can become an inadvertent waiver of an individual employee's Fifth Amendment privilege against self-incrimination if the employee has cooperated with an internal investigation and later becomes a target of the federal investigation.[335]

Responding to criticism from business groups and defense counsel, the Justice Department in 2006 issued the "McNulty Memo," a newer version of its policy entitled "Principles of Federal Prosecution of Business Organizations."[336] The McNulty Memo acknowledges the purpose and history behind the attorney-client privilege and work-product protection, but maintains that waiver of these protections expedites investigations and indicates the degree to which a company is genuinely cooperating with the government.[337] The memo establishes a four-part test that prosecutors must meet to show a legitimate need for privileged communications and requires prosecutors to get written approval from the deputy attorney general before requesting the waiver.[338] The prosecutor must also identify the scope of the waiver sought. If a corporation declines to waive its privileges to protect information that is not "purely factual", the prosecutor must not consider this fact against the corporation in deciding whether to indict.[339] However, the prosecutor may consider the corporation's decision to waive privilege as a positive factor indicating genuine cooperation.[340]

---

secret, is separate from selective waiver. ***Dellwood Farms, Inc. v. Cargill, Inc.***, 128 F.3d 1122, 1126 (7th Cir. 1997). Finally, when the disclosure is made in a state-court proceeding and would not be considered a waiver (1) in that proceeding or (2) under Rule 502 if the disclosure had been made in a federal proceeding, the disclosure (whether selective or otherwise) will not be considered a waiver in a federal proceeding. *See* FED. R. EVID. 502(c). For further discussion of the applications of Federal Rule 502, see ***O'Connor's Federal Rules * Civil Trials*** (2017), "Disclosure of privileged or protected information – attorney-related privileges," ch. 6-A, §9.3.2, p. 488.

334. The "joint-defense privilege" is not an independent privilege, but rather an extension of the attorney-client privilege. It provides for limited waiver when a party shares privileged information with a colitigant. *See **In re Teleglobe Commc'ns Corp.***, 493 F.3d 345, 362-63 (3d Cir. 2007); ***Waller v. Fin. Corp. of Am.***, 828 F.2d 579, 583 n.7 (9th Cir. 1987). Just as prosecutors would like corporations to waive their attorney-client privilege and work-product protection, they also have an interest in discouraging joint-defense agreements because those agreements allow for the exchange of otherwise privileged information without waiver.

335. *See generally* Michael L. Seigel, *Corporate America Fights Back: The Battle Over Waiver of the Attorney-Client Privilege*, 49 B.C. L. REV. 1 (2008) (analyzing the McNulty Memo and suggesting amendments to better protect rights of individual employees).

336. Memorandum from Paul J. McNulty, Deputy Attorney Gen., on Principles of Federal Prosecution of Business Organizations (Dec. 12, 2006), www.justice.gov/sites/default/files/dag/legacy/2007/07/05/mcnulty_memo.pdf.

337. *Id.* §VII(B)(2).

338. *Id.*

339. *Id.* The earlier Justice Department memos had also been interpreted as influential in persuading corporations to renege on their contractual promises to pay the legal defense fees for their corporate directors and officers. At least one federal court has held that dismissal of the criminal charges against the corporate officers is an appropriate remedy for the corporation's refusal to fulfill its contractual obligation to pay its officers' legal fees as a result of governmental coercion. *See **United States v. Stein***, 495 F. Supp. 2d 390, 422 (S.D.N.Y. 2007).

340. Memorandum from Paul J. McNulty, *supra* note 336, at §VII(B)(2).

The McNulty Memo was modified again by the Filip Revisions (named after Deputy Attorney General Mark Filip) on August 28, 2008. The Filip Revisions made clear that

> [e]ligibility for cooperation credit is not predicated upon the waiver of attorney-client privilege or work product protection. Instead, the sort of co-operation that is most valuable to resolving allegations of misconduct by a corporation and its officers, directors, employees, or agents is disclosure of the relevant *facts* concerning such misconduct.[341]

The Filip Revisions emphasized that a waiver can be requested only for privileged factual information, not for core attorney work product such as legal advice or an attorney's mental impressions and legal theories.[342] Nonetheless, a corporation that turns over privileged information to the government faces a significant risk that the privilege will be considered at least partially waived in later litigation with third parties.[343] This risk continues even with the waiver limitations in Federal Rule 502.[344]

RULE 504
SPOUSAL PRIVILEGES

(a) Confidential Communication Privilege.

    (1) *Definition.* A communication is "confidential" if a person makes it privately to the person's spouse and does not intend its disclosure to any other person.

    (2) *General Rule.* A person has a privilege to refuse to disclose and to prevent any other person from disclosing a confidential communication made to the person's spouse while they were married. This privilege survives termination of the marriage.

---

341. UNITED STATES ATTORNEYS' MANUAL §9-28.720, www.justice.gov/usam/usam-9-28000-principles-federal-prosecution-business-organizations.

342. *See id.* §9-28.720(b) ("A corporation need not disclose, and prosecutors may not request, the disclosure of such attorney work product as a condition for the corporation's eligibility to receive cooperation credit.").

343. *See, e.g., **SEC v. Roberts**,* 254 F.R.D. 371, 378 (N.D. Cal. 2008) (when corporation's attorneys made presentations to the board of directors and government investigators about instances of stock-option backdating, trial court held that work-product protection was waived for that information). *Roberts* was decided August 22, 2008, less than a week before the Filip Revisions were published.

344. Refer to note 333 *supra* and accompanying text. Federal Rule 502 does protect a party who has inadvertently disclosed communications or information in litigation with a government agency or office against use of the communications or information in a later action with nonparties. *See* FED. R. EVID. 502(d) (court can order that attorney-client privilege or work-product protection is not waived by disclosure connected to litigation before the court; order is enforceable against nonparties in any federal or state proceeding); FED. R. EVID. 502, Explanatory Note to 2008 amendments, subdiv. (d) ("[T]he utility of a confidentiality order in reducing discovery costs is substantially diminished if it provides no protection outside the particular litigation in which the order is entered."). It may also limit the scope of intentional waiver. *See* FED. R. EVID. 502(a).

(3) *Who May Claim.* The privilege may be claimed by:

(A) the communicating spouse;

(B) the guardian of a communicating spouse who is incompetent; or

(C) the personal representative of a communicating spouse who is deceased.

The other spouse may claim the privilege on the communicating spouse's behalf—and is presumed to have authority to do so.

(4) *Exceptions.* This privilege does not apply:

(A) *Furtherance of Crime or Fraud.* If the communication is made—wholly or partially—to enable or aid anyone to commit or plan to commit a crime or fraud.

(B) *Proceeding Between Spouse and Other Spouse or Claimant Through Deceased Spouse.* In a civil proceeding:

(i) brought by or on behalf of one spouse against the other; or

(ii) between a surviving spouse and a person claiming through the deceased spouse.

(C) *Crime Against Family, Spouse, Household Member, or Minor Child.* In a:

(i) proceeding in which a party is accused of conduct that, if proved, is a crime against the person of the other spouse, any member of the household of either spouse, or any minor child; or

(ii) criminal proceeding involving a charge of bigamy under Section 25.01 of the Penal Code.

(D) *Commitment or Similar Proceeding.* In a proceeding to commit either spouse or otherwise to place the spouse or the spouse's property under another's control because of a mental or physical condition.

(E) *Proceeding to Establish Competence.* In a proceeding brought by or on behalf of either spouse to establish competence.

(b) Privilege Not to Testify in Criminal Case.

(1) *General Rule.* In a criminal case, an accused's spouse has a privilege not to be called to testify for the state. But this rule neither prohibits a spouse from testifying voluntarily for the state nor gives a spouse a privilege to refuse to be called to testify for the accused.

(2) *Failure to Call Spouse.* If other evidence indicates that the accused's spouse could testify to relevant matters, an accused's failure to call the spouse to testify is a proper subject of comment by counsel.

(3) *Who May Claim.* The privilege not to testify may be claimed by the accused's spouse or the spouse's guardian or representative, but not by the accused.

(4) *Exceptions.* This privilege does not apply:

(A) *Certain Criminal Proceedings.* In a criminal proceeding in which a spouse is charged with:

(i) a crime against the other spouse, any member of the household of either spouse, or any minor child; or

(ii) bigamy under Section 25.01 of the Penal Code.

(B) *Matters That Occurred Before the Marriage.* If the spouse is called to testify about matters that occurred before the marriage.

Notes and Comments

Comment to 2015 restyling: Previously, Rule 504(b)(1) provided that, "A spouse who testifies on behalf of an accused is subject to cross-examination as provided in Rule 611(b)." That sentence was included in the original version of Rule 504 when the Texas Rules of Criminal Evidence were promulgated in 1986 and changed the rule to a testimonial privilege held by the witness spouse. Until then, a spouse was deemed incompetent to testify against his or her defendant spouse, and when a spouse testified on behalf of a defendant spouse, the state was limited to cross-examining the spouse about matters relating to the spouse's direct testimony. The quoted sentence from the original Criminal Rule 504(b) was designed to overturn this limitation and allow the state to cross-examine a testifying spouse in the same manner as any other witness. More than twenty-five years later, it is clear that a spouse who testifies either for or against a defendant spouse may be cross-examined in the same manner as any other witness. Therefore, the continued inclusion in the rule of a provision that refers only to the cross-examination of a spouse who testifies on behalf of the accused is more confusing than helpful. Its deletion is designed to clarify the rule and does not change existing law.

Comment to 1998 change: The rule eliminates the spousal testimonial privilege for prosecutions in which the testifying spouse is the alleged victim of a crime by the accused. This is intended to be consistent with Code of Criminal Procedure article 38.10, effective September 1, 1995.

COMMENTARY ON RULE 504

A. Overview of the Two Distinct Spousal Privileges

There are two distinct privileges associated with the marital relationship. The first is a privilege for confidential marital communications. Rule 504 codifies this doctrine;[345] however, in civil cases, the exceptions to the rule of confidentiality are so large that the rule has little significance.[346]

The second is a testimonial privilege, which permits one spouse to refuse to testify against the other in a criminal case.[347] It flows from the common-law doctrine of spousal incompetency or spousal disqualification, which held as a matter of law that one spouse could not testify against the other.[348] By stating that the witness spouse (and not the defendant spouse) holds the privilege, Rule 504(b) dramatically changed Texas criminal common law. A defendant cannot use a sham marriage to prevent a potential witness from testifying.[349] The rationale for the change is that when one spouse willingly testifies against the other, "there is probably little in the way of marital harmony for the privilege to preserve."[350]

Charles Alan Wright outlined the distinction between the two privileges as follows:

> The rule against adverse spousal testimony depends on a marital relation at the time the testimony is offered, and it is immaterial whether the persons were

---

345. *See* Tex. R. Evid. 504(a). Common law may not have recognized the privilege for marital communications simply because spousal disqualification served the same purpose. *See Fasken v. Fasken*, 113 Tex. 464, 468-72, 260 S.W. 701, 702-04 (1924). *See generally* 8 Wigmore, *supra* note 6, §2333, at 644-45 (tracing the historical development of the marital privilege). Because a spouse could not testify at all, inquiry into the privileged nature of particular marital communications was unlikely.

346. The Liaison Committee recommended that the privilege for confidential marital communications in civil cases be omitted entirely from the Rules. *See* Tex. R. Evid. 504 (1982 Liaison Committee proposal), *reprinted infra* p. 1082. Other states have enacted evidence codes that do not include a marital-communications privilege for civil cases. *See* Ark. R. Evid. 504; Okla. Stat. Ann. tit. 12, §12-2504. Article 3715 previously articulated the privilege for marital communications in Texas civil proceedings: "The husband or wife of a party to a suit or proceeding, or who is interested in the issue to be tried, shall not be incompetent to testify therein, except as to confidential communications between such husband and wife." Tex. Rev. Civ. Stat. art. 3715 (former Texas Revised Civil Statutes art. 3715 deemed repealed as to civil proceedings effective 1983 and as to criminal proceedings effective 1986) [now Tex. R. Evid. 504]. Under the statutory privilege, an unwilling witness could not be compelled to disclose such confidential communications, nor could a willing witness make such disclosures over proper invocation of the privilege. However, "eavesdroppers" could testify to confidential communications, and third parties could testify to the contents of documents that they had surreptitiously read. 1 Ray, *supra* note 52, §438, at 428. Permitting eavesdropper testimony is more properly understood not as permitting disclosure of confidential communications but as a failure to maintain confidentiality, thus removing the communication from the scope of the privilege. 8 Wigmore, *supra* note 6, §2326, at 633, §2339, at 667. The wording of Rule 504(a) emphasizes the intention of the holder, thus preserving the confidentiality of communications overheard by eavesdroppers, as long as the parties take reasonable precautions not to be overheard. *See* 1 Ray, *supra* note 52, §438, at 156 (Supp. 1991). Refer to notes 393-401 *infra* and accompanying text.

347. Tex. R. Evid. 504(b).

348. *See Fasken*, 113 Tex. at 468, 260 S.W. at 702.

349. *See Lutwak v. United States*, 344 U.S. 604, 614 (1953) (one ostensible spouse is competent to testify against the other when the marriage is part of a scheme to defraud). This change accords with modern federal common law. *See Trammel v. United States*, 445 U.S. 40, 51-53 (1980).

350. *Trammel*, 445 U.S. at 52.

married at the time about which the witness is asked to testify. The confidential communications privilege, however, applies only to communications between the persons while they are married, but it survives death or divorce. Second, the former rule applies only to defendant and his spouse, while the confidential communications privilege applies to any witness. Third, the rule against adverse spousal testimony applies to all testimony of any kind, while the confidential communications privilege reaches only those communications made in confidence and intended to be confidential.[351]

B. Definition of "Spouse" for Purposes of Rule 504

Rule 504 applies only to the testimony and confidential communications of a "spouse." The scope of protection includes the parties to a valid, ceremonial marriage,[352] at least until a final divorce decree terminates the marriage.[353] Because the marital status at the time of trial determines who can claim the testimonial privilege under Rule 504(b), the testimonial privilege continues during the pendency of the divorce proceedings, and the State cannot compel the nondefendant spouse to testify.[354] The privilege also protects common-law marriages, but courts carefully scrutinize their existence in these situations.[355]

---

351. 2 CHARLES A. WRIGHT, FEDERAL PRACTICE AND PROCEDURE §406, at 438 (1982) (citations omitted).

352. See *O'Connor's Texas Family Law Handbook* (2017), "Ceremonial Marriage," ch. 1-A, §2, p. 5. If the marriage has been annulled, it is void ab initio, and Rule 504 would offer no privilege. *Bruni v. State*, 669 S.W.2d 829, 835 (Tex. App.—Austin 1984, no pet.). Similarly, if the putative spouse was previously married and that marriage has not been terminated, the later marriage to the accused is invalid and the marital-communications privilege does not apply. *Phillips v. State*, 701 S.W.2d 875, 893-94 (Tex. Crim. App. 1985). Hallowed privacy rights belong only to those who are married in the eyes of the law, not to those who merely believe they are married. *See id.*; *Riley v. State*, 849 S.W.2d 901, 902-03 (Tex. App.—Austin 1993, pet. ref'd). In *Riley*, the State produced uncontroverted evidence that the defendant had a previous, undissolved common-law marriage to another woman, which would have precluded the defendant's current wife from claiming the spousal testimonial privilege. 849 S.W.2d at 902. However, the Family Code contained a statute of limitations disallowing proof of any informal marriage outside the prescribed time period. *Id.* (discussing former TEX. FAM. CODE §1.91(b), now TEX. FAM. CODE §2.401). Because the limitations period for proving the validity of the previous marriage had expired, the State could not rely on proof of the previous marriage to defeat the witness's claim of spousal privilege. *Riley*, 849 S.W.2d at 903.

353. Whether the parties are divorced is relevant only to the nondefendant spouse's privilege not to be called as a witness (testimonial privilege). TEX. R. EVID. 504(b)(1). The privilege for confidential communications survives a divorce. TEX. R. EVID. 504(a)(2).

354. *See Freeman v. State*, 786 S.W.2d 56, 58 (Tex. App.—Houston [1st Dist.] 1990, no pet.); *Babineaux v. State*, 777 S.W.2d 724, 732 (Tex. App.—Beaumont 1989), *pet. dism'd, improvidently granted*, 803 S.W.2d 301 (Tex. Crim. App. 1990).

355. *See Tompkins v. State*, 774 S.W.2d 195, 208 (Tex. Crim. App. 1987), *aff'd by an equally divided court*, 490 U.S. 754 (1989); *see, e.g.*, *Bodde v. State*, 568 S.W.2d 344, 352 (Tex. Crim. App. 1978) (refusing to find a common-law marriage without proof of a specific agreement of marriage on both sides).
   In *Colburn v. State*, the court of criminal appeals held that the trial court could reasonably infer that the capital-murder defendant and his common-law wife merely intended to marry sometime in the future and did not consider themselves actually married until they filed a written declaration of informal marriage under former Texas Family Code §1.94(d) (now TEX. FAM. CODE §2.404). 966 S.W.2d 511, 514-15 (Tex. Crim. App. 1998). This Family Code section states that a properly recorded declaration of informal marriage constitutes prima facie proof of the informal marriage, but that presumption may be overcome by evidence to the contrary. *Id.* at 514. Thus, the court of criminal appeals concluded that the marital privilege did not preclude the wife from testifying about communications made before that declaration was filed. *Id.* at 515.

To establish a common-law marriage in Texas, the person invoking the privilege must prove that (1) the parties agreed to be married, (2) the parties live together as spouses, and (3) the parties represent to others that they are married.[356] Although these elements may occur at different times, there is no common-law marriage in Texas until all of these prerequisites are met.[357] The rule does not grant any privilege to putative spouses—those who believe themselves to be married but, because of some encumbrance, are not legally married.[358] Further, it is not sufficient that the parties agree to marry sometime in the future.[359] The privilege also does not protect couples who merely live together and have intimate relations.[360] The witness's testimony to the existence of a common-law marriage is insufficient to invoke the privilege—direct or circumstantial evidence must support each of the three prongs of a common-law marriage, and the proponent of the privilege must prove the existence of the marriage by a preponderance of the evidence.[361]

---

356. Tex. Fam. Code §2.401(a)(2); *Colburn*, 966 S.W.2d at 514; *Tompkins*, 774 S.W.2d at 208. See *O'Connor's Fam. Law Handbook*, "Statutory elements," ch. 1-A, §3.2.1, p. 13.

357. *Flores v. Flores*, 847 S.W.2d 648, 650 (Tex. App.—Waco 1993, writ denied) (per curiam); *see Winfield v. Renfro*, 821 S.W.2d 640, 645 (Tex. App.—Houston [1st Dist.] 1991, writ denied).

358. *See Weaver v. State*, 855 S.W.2d 116, 120-21 (Tex. App.—Houston [14th Dist.] 1993, no pet.) ("The rule does not say 'putative spouse,' 'significant other,' or 'girlfriend.' … Absent proof of a ceremonial or common law marriage recognized as a legal marriage by the law of this state, we hold that the privilege not to testify against one's spouse does not extend to putative marriages."). See *O'Connor's Fam. Law Handbook*, "Putative Marriage," ch. 1-A, §4, p. 17.

359. *Aguilar v. State*, 715 S.W.2d 645, 648 (Tex. Crim. App. 1986); *see, e.g.*, *Jasper v. State*, 61 S.W.3d 413, 419-20 (Tex. Crim. App. 2001) (when testimony conflicted on whether potential witness claimed to be capital-murder defendant's girlfriend, "soon-to-be-wife," or common-law spouse, trial court did not err in concluding that defendant did not establish existence of informal marriage).

360. *E.g.*, *Tompkins*, 774 S.W.2d at 209 (no protection for illicit relationship or "secret" common-law marriage because there was no evidence that the parties held themselves out to the general public as married); *see Welch v. State*, 908 S.W.2d 258, 265 (Tex. App.—El Paso 1995, no pet.) ("mere cohabitation" is insufficient to establish common-law marriage). See *O'Connor's Fam. Law Handbook*, "Meretricious Relationship," ch. 1-A, §5, p. 19.

361. *Tompkins*, 774 S.W.2d at 208-09; *see* Tex. Fam. Code §2.401(a)(2) (methods of proving informal marriage); *Quinonez-Saa v. State*, 860 S.W.2d 704, 709-10 (Tex. App.—Houston [1st Dist.] 1993, pet. ref'd) ("The existence of a common-law marriage is a fact question, with the burden of proof on the party seeking to establish the existence of the marriage."); *see, e.g.*, *Bodde v. State*, 568 S.W.2d 344, 352 (Tex. Crim. App. 1978) (no direct or circumstantial evidence of an agreement to become husband and wife); *see also Hightower v. State*, 629 S.W.2d 920, 924 (Tex. Crim. App. [Panel Op.] 1981) (alleged common-law wife's testimony was admissible to rebut claim of common-law marriage). See *O'Connor's Fam. Law Handbook*, "Informal marriage," ch. 3-A, §3.2.2, p. 216.

When the evidence is "inconsistent," "inconclusive," or "conflicting," the trial court does not abuse its discretion in ruling that there was no common-law marriage and thus no marital privileges. *See Anderson v. State*, 880 S.W.2d 35, 37 (Tex. App.—Tyler 1994, pet. ref'd); *see, e.g.*, *Freeman v. State*, 230 S.W.3d 392, 402-03 (Tex. App.—Eastland 2007, pet. ref'd) (because of conflicting evidence about whether defendant and his wife represented to others that they were married before their ceremonial marriage, trial court did not abuse its discretion in finding that there was no common-law marriage; witness referred to defendant as her boyfriend, indicated that they were living together, and wrote "not applicable" on apartment lease when asked for spouse's information); *McDuffie v. State*, 854 S.W.2d 195, 212-13 (Tex. App.—Beaumont 1993, pet. ref'd) (because of conflicting testimony "ranging from an absolute agreement to *be* married, to an agreement to *get* married, to no representation of marriage at all," trial court did not abuse its discretion in finding that there was no common-law marriage).

Under earlier law, when a disputed fact issue arose about whether there was a common-law marriage, the trial judge submitted the issue to the jury. *See Brooks v. State*, 686 S.W.2d 952, 954 (Tex. Crim. App. 1985); *see also Bodde*, 568 S.W.2d at 352 (criticizing the submission of the issue of the existence of a common-law marriage to the jury, but acknowledging precedent). Only if the jury determined that a common-law marriage did not exist could

C. Rule 504(a): Marital-Communications Privilege

1. Justifications for the privilege. The privilege for confidential marital communications has traditionally been justified with the argument that without the privilege, spouses would be less likely to confide in one another, thus eroding the strength and significance of the institution of marriage.[362] This justification may be called the instrumental rationale. It can be distinguished from a second, and possibly more persuasive, justification based on "a feeling of indelicacy and want of decorum in prying into the secrets" of a married couple.[363]

The opposition to the first and more commonly offered rationale challenges the assumption that the marital-communications privilege has any effect on marital conduct, much less a significant one. The Advisory Committee on the Federal Rules explained its recommended elimination[364] of the privilege in these terms:

---

they then consider the witness's testimony. *Huffman v. State*, 450 S.W.2d 858, 862 (Tex. Crim. App. 1970), *vacated on other grounds sub nom. Huffman v. Beto*, 408 U.S. 936 (1972). Rule 104(a), which requires the trial judge to make all preliminary determinations on the admissibility of evidence, including the existence of a privilege, superseded this procedure. *See McDuffie*, 854 S.W.2d at 212 (under Criminal Rule 104(a), the trial court determines preliminary questions of the existence of a privilege); *Reece v. State*, 772 S.W.2d 198, 201 n.3 (Tex. App.—Houston [14th Dist.] 1989, no pet.) (declining to decide whether Criminal Rule 104(a) precludes the accused from submitting the issue of the existence of common-law marriage to the jury); *see also* 1 GOODE ET AL., *supra* note 206, §504.2, at 365 ("it would seem clear" that Rule 104(a) abolishes the requirement that the jury resolve the issue of the existence of a common-law marriage; use of Rule 104(a) "will avoid the difficult problem of exposing the jury to presumptively reliable evidence and then telling them to ignore it on the basis of a finding unrelated to the trust worthiness of the testimony").

362. *See Trammel v. United States*, 445 U.S. 40, 44 (1980) ("The modern justification for this privilege against adverse spousal testimony is its perceived role in fostering the harmony and sanctity of the marriage relationship."). The Victorians were the first to give statutory expression to the privilege for confidential marital communications. *See* Evidence Amendment Act, 1853, 16 & 17 Vict., ch. 83, §3 (Eng.). The privilege has also been defended in the modern era: "A marriage without the right of complete privacy of communication would necessarily be an imperfect union. Utter freedom of marital communication from all government supervision, constraint, control or observation, save only when the communications are for an illegal purpose, is a psychological necessity for the perfect fulfillment of marriage." David W. Louisell, *Confidentiality, Conformity and Confusion: Privileges in Federal Court Today*, 31 TUL. L. REV. 101, 113 (1956). Texas Rule 504(a)(4)(A) embodies Louisell's view that communications made "for an illegal purpose" should not be protected by the privilege. Louisell, *supra*, at 113.

363. MCCORMICK ON EVIDENCE I, *supra* note 65, §86, at 202. One commentator has suggested that the marital-communications privilege may have a constitutional basis and thus could not be abolished. Mark Reutlinger, *Policy, Privacy, and Prerogatives: A Critical Examination of the Proposed Federal Rules of Evidence as They Affect Marital Privilege*, 61 CALIF. L. REV. 1353, 1356 n.9 (1973) (*Griswold v. Connecticut*, 381 U.S. 479 (1965), implies that the marital-communication privilege is constitutionally protected). Even Thomas Krattenmaker, a passionate defender of privileges, concedes that this claim is without merit. Krattenmaker, *supra* note 10, at 96-98; *see also United States v. Lefkowitz*, 618 F.2d 1313, 1319 (9th Cir. 1980) (rejecting the argument that marital privileges are constitutionally protected); *LaRoche v. Wainwright*, 599 F.2d 722, 726 (5th Cir. 1979) (refusing to extend the constitutionally protected right of privacy to cover evidentiary privileges protecting marital relationships). *But cf. In re Agosto*, 553 F. Supp. 1298, 1325-26 (D. Nev. 1983) (a child has a privilege not to reveal confidential communications with his parents and not to be compelled to testify against his parents because of "a constitutionally protectable interest of the family in American society").

364. *See Proposed Rules*, *supra* note 28, at 233 (FED. R. EVID. 501 advisory committee's note). Although the privilege provisions of the proposed Federal Rules were not adopted, the federal common law of privileges still exists, subject to development "in the light of reason and experience." *See Trammel*, 445 U.S. at 45 n.5 (privilege for marital communications, previously recognized by the U.S. Supreme Court in *Wolfle v. United States*, 291 U.S. 7 (1934), and *Blau v. United States*, 340 U.S. 332 (1951), remains in force).

Nor can it be assumed that marital conduct will be affected by a privilege for confidential communications of whose existence the parties in all likelihood are unaware. The other communication privileges, by way of contrast, have as one party a professional person who can be expected to inform the other of the existence of the privilege.[365]

The limited protection afforded by the marital-communications privilege further weakens the instrumental rationale. The privilege is available only in connection with litigation. Rule 504(a)(4) also creates enormous exceptions to the privilege in civil cases because the privilege does not apply in any civil proceeding between the two spouses.[366] Further, it does not apply in either civil or criminal proceedings when the statement was made to aid in the commission of a crime or fraud[367] or when one spouse is accused of a crime against the other, any minor child, or any member of either spouse's household.[368] The exceptions to the privilege apply when society has a legitimate interest in seeking disclosure of the communication because of its demonstrated relevance to the resolution of litigation.

The privilege for confidential communications to attorneys is a rule-based expression of an independently existing obligation imposed and enforced by the professional body of which the attorney is a member.[369] But there is no similar institution for disciplining spouses or former spouses who betray a confidence.

As to the second rationale, the offensiveness of inquiring into marital communications, similar concerns are raised when discussing the confidences of unmarried couples, siblings, parents, or children, yet no evidentiary privilege protects those relationships.[370] Perhaps more importantly, the subject matter of the communications

---

365. *Proposed Rules, supra* note 28, at 246 (FED. R. EVID. 505 advisory committee's note, subdiv. (a)). The Advisory Committee supported its position by invoking the oft-cited Robert M. Hutchins and Donald Slesinger article, *Some Observations on the Law of Evidence: Family Relations*, 13 MINN. L. REV. 675 (1929), as authority. Hutchins and Slesinger used the then-current psychological and sociological views of marriage to support their extremely skeptical view of both the privilege and the marital disqualification. They wrote:

> [V]ery few people ever get into court, and practically no one outside the legal profession knows anything about the rules regarding privileged communications between spouses. As far as the writers are aware ... marital harmony among lawyers who know about privileged communications is not vastly superior to that of other professional groups.

Hutchins & Slesinger, *supra*, at 682 (footnote omitted). *But see* Reutlinger, *supra* note 363, at 1371-78 (spouse's lack of awareness of the privilege is not sufficient reason to abolish it). Another early and excellent challenge to the privilege is Frederick E. Hines, *Privileged Testimony of Husband and Wife in California*, 19 CALIF. L. REV. 390, 410-14 (1931) (spousal privilege should be abolished because of its doubtful benefits and the confusion surrounding its application).

366. TEX. R. EVID. 504(a)(4)(B).

367. TEX. R. EVID. 504(a)(4)(A).

368. TEX. R. EVID. 504(a)(4)(C)(i). It also does not apply in a trial for bigamy. TEX. R. EVID. 504(a)(4)(C)(ii).

369. *See* TEX. DISCIPLINARY R. PROF'L CONDUCT 1.05; MODEL CODE OF PROF'L RESPONSIBILITY DR 4-101, EC 4-1 (1983).

370. *See* **Port v. Heard**, 764 F.2d 423, 428-33 (5th Cir. 1985) (Texas does not have a parent-child privilege, and the U.S. Constitution does not require the recognition of one); **In re Grand Jury Subpoena of Santarelli**, 740 F.2d 816, 817 (11th Cir. 1984) (per curiam) (there is no privilege under Federal Rule 501 to refuse to testify against one's parent); **United States v. Penn**, 647 F.2d 876, 885 (9th Cir. 1980) (en banc) ("There is no judicially or legislatively

at issue in most of the reported cases seems far removed from any notion of intimacy.[371] Indeed, the litigation most likely to involve disclosure of true marital intimacies is that of divorce, and the privilege does not apply in divorce proceedings.[372]

In most litigation other than cases of divorce or nonsupport, the presumed reluctance of the witness spouse to testify against the other reinforces our society's respect for marital privacy. But in civil cases, a witness spouse cannot assert a testimonial privilege.[373] Therefore, only the marital-communications privilege prevents the coercion of marital intimacies from an unwilling spouse to the injury of the other.[374] This argument is unconvincing. The privilege protects communications made after a marriage has ended and prevents former spouses from testifying even if they are willing to do so.[375] Most significantly, a major justification of the privilege is the fear that coerced communications would involve personal intimacies that deserve protection.[376] How-

recognized general 'family' privilege ...."); *see also* David A. Schlueter, *The Parent-Child Privilege: A Response to Calls for Adoption*, 19 ST. MARY'S L.J. 35, 36-37 (1987) (judicial and legislative recognition of the family privilege is inappropriate). *But see In re Agosto*, 553 F. Supp. 1298, 1325-26 (D. Nev. 1983) (finding a privilege for communications from parent to child, as well as for familial witnesses, without regard to confidentiality); *People v. Harrell*, 450 N.Y.S.2d 501, 505 (N.Y. App. Div. 1982) (communications between a parent and child are generally not privileged, but communications between a child and his mother after the child was arrested could be shielded if the police did not give the parent and child privacy or warn them that the statements might not be privileged), *aff'd*, 449 N.E.2d 1263 (1983); *In re Application of A&M*, 403 N.Y.S.2d 375, 380 (N.Y. App. Div. 1978) ("[T]he interest of society in protecting and nurturing the parent-child relationship is of such overwhelming significance that the State's interest in fact-finding must give way."); *People v. Fitzgerald*, 422 N.Y.S.2d 309, 311-12 (Westchester Cty. Ct. 1979) (parent-child privilege is grounded in the right to privacy found in the Constitutions of the United States and New York); Krattenmaker, *supra* note 10, at 94 (lending support for the extension of privileges to such relationships and even to communications between roommates).

371. *See* 1 RAY, *supra* note 52, §433-41, at 421-30.

372. *See* TEX. FAM. CODE §6.704; TEX. R. EVID. 504(a)(4)(B)(i). Texas Family Code §6.704(a) provides that "[i]n a suit for dissolution of a marriage, the husband and wife are competent witnesses for and against each other." This language, in a previous statute, was interpreted as eliminating the privilege. *Fasken v. Fasken*, 113 Tex. 464, 470-72, 260 S.W. 701, 703-04 (1924).

373. *See* TEX. R. EVID. 504(b). Refer to notes 443-482 *infra* and accompanying text.

374. However, former Texas Revised Civil Statutes article 3715 demonstrated that a reluctance to injure a present or former spouse is not enough to excuse a witness from testifying. For example, by definition, the privilege did not excuse a witness from testifying to a nonconfidential communication even when such testimony would be injurious to the spouse or former spouse who is a party. *See* TEX. REV. CIV. STAT. art. 3715 (former Texas Revised Civil Statutes art. 3715 deemed repealed as to civil proceedings effective 1983 and as to criminal proceedings effective 1986) [now TEX. R. EVID. 504]. Nor, presumably, did it permit a witness to refuse to describe the spouse's conduct if the spouse did not intend that conduct as a communication. *See* 8 WIGMORE, *supra* note 6, §2337, at 657-58 (supporting the view of the husband-wife privilege as limited to explicit communications or acts intended as a substitute for such communications); *see, e.g.*, *Lanham v. Lanham*, 62 Tex. Civ. App. 431, 433-35, 146 S.W. 635, 637 (Texarkana 1910, no writ) (wife's description of her husband's behavior toward her did not involve a confidential communication); *see also Butler v. State*, 645 S.W.2d 820, 824 (Tex. Crim. App. 1983) (interpreting former TEX. CODE CRIM. PROC. art. 38.11, now TEX. R. EVID. 504, as not excluding testimony about noncommunicative events). Thus, in theory at least, a husband could be required to testify in a tort action that he observed his wife fall asleep at the wheel of their car, even though the wife's confidential declaration to him that she fell asleep would be privileged.

375. TEX. R. EVID. 504(a)(2); *see, e.g.*, *Wiggins v. Tiller*, 230 S.W. 253, 254 (Tex. Civ. App.—San Antonio 1921, no writ) (man's statements to his ex-wife about the ownership of a vehicle were privileged, even though they were divorced at the time of trial and the ex-wife was a willing witness).

376. *See, e.g.*, *Gross v. State*, 61 Tex. Crim. 176, 181-82, 135 S.W. 373, 376 (1911) (letter to defendant's wife, which might have revealed defendant's consciousness of his guilt of the charge of incest with his daughter, was inadmissible).

ever, that concern does not seem to apply in most litigation. Certainly this premise appears irrelevant to matters such as a letter revealing that the couple's business was unprofitable[377] or a husband's alleged statement surrendering all claims to the family car.[378]

It is perhaps because personal intimacies are so unlikely to be involved in conversations relating to property and business that courts have often created exceptions to the privilege for such conversations.[379] Texas courts have held that conversations between spouses dealing with business or property were admissible based on the theory that such conversations were not "confidential," at least when they concerned a fraud on third persons[380] or on the would-be witness spouse.[381] Indeed, there seems to be an exception whenever disclosure of the communication is necessary to vindicate the interests of one spouse wronged by another.[382] Despite the arguably unconvincing justifications for the marital-communications privilege, Texas law codified the privilege for marital communications long ago,[383] and Rule 504 contains a modified version of the privilege.

2. Rule 504(a)(1)-(a)(3): Outline of the marital-communications privilege.

(1) Rule 504(a)(1): Definition of confidential communication. The marital-communications privilege protects only those statements that were intended to be made privately to the speaker's spouse and not intended to be disclosed to any other person.[384] A marital communication is considered confidential under the rule if (1) there

---

377. ***Mitchell v. Mitchell***, 80 Tex. 101, 116, 15 S.W. 705, 709-10 (1891).

378. *Wiggins*, 230 S.W. at 254.

379. *See, e.g.*, ***Earthman's, Inc. v. Earthman***, 526 S.W.2d 192, 205-06 (Tex. Civ. App.—Houston [1st Dist.] 1975, no writ) (wife's testimony about business dealings was admissible despite the marital privilege). *See generally* J.E. Macy, Annotation, *Conversations Between Husband and Wife Relating to Property or Business as Within Rule Excluding Private Communications Between Them*, 4 A.L.R.2d 835, 837-861 (1949) (discussing exclusion of certain private communications).

380. *See* ***Eddy v. Bosley***, 34 Tex. Civ. App. 116, 121-22, 78 S.W. 565, 568 (Austin 1903, no writ). An interesting modern examination of this issue by another jurisdiction can be found in ***Federated Department Stores, Inc. v. Esser***, 409 N.Y.S.2d 353, 354-56 (N.Y. Sup. Ct. 1978). In ***Federated Department Stores***, the court held that the privilege protected a wife's refusal to tell a judgment creditor where her judgment-debtor husband was or how much financial support he provided to her. 409 N.Y.S.2d at 355-56. The court viewed these communications as not falling within either the exception for "ordinary business communications" or that for "fraud." *Id.*

381. *See* ***First Bank v. Hill***, 151 S.W. 652, 654 (Tex. Civ. App.—Texarkana 1912, writ dism'd).

382. In ***King v. Sassaman***, a woman sued her ex-husband for slander on the basis of his assertion that she must have contracted her venereal disease from someone else. 64 S.W. 937, 937 (Tex. Civ. App. 1901, no writ). The court held that the woman could testify that her ex-husband was the source of the disease despite the obvious sensitivity and confidentiality of the subject matter. *Id.* The ***King*** case might also represent a tacit refusal to apply the privilege to conduct that was not intended as a communication.

383. *See* Tex. Rev. Civ. Stat. art. 3715 (former Texas Revised Civil Statutes art. 3715 deemed repealed as to civil proceedings effective 1983 and as to criminal proceedings effective 1986) [now Tex. R. Evid. 504]; Act of May 27, 1965, 59th Leg., R.S., ch. 722, §1, 1965 Tex. Gen. Laws 317, 467, *amended by* Act of May 23, 1985, 69th Leg., R.S., ch. 791, §2, 1985 Tex. Gen. Laws 2703 (former Code of Criminal Procedure art. 38.11 deemed repealed as to criminal proceedings effective 1986).

384. Tex. R. Evid. 504(a)(1); *e.g.*, ***Cooper v. Cochran***, 288 S.W.3d 522, 539 (Tex. App.—Dallas 2009, no pet.) (privilege did not apply when ex-wife stated that conversations she testified about took place in front of a third party; presence of third party does not need to be corroborated); ***Gibbons v. State***, 794 S.W.2d 887, 892 (Tex. App.—Tyler

is physical privacy between the spouses, and (2) the speaker intended to maintain secrecy of the communication.[385] However, "marital communications are presumptively confidential";[386] thus, once the party asserting the privilege establishes the existence of a private communication with the spouse, the opposing party must produce evidence to overcome that presumption.[387] The following factors may be considered in determining whether the presumption of confidentiality has been rebutted: (1) the nature of the communication or the circumstances suggesting that the speaker did not intend the statement to be confidential,[388] (2) the substance of the communication,[389] (3) whether the communication was revealed to a third person before litigation developed,[390] and (4) whether the speaker expressed an intent to divulge the substance of the communication in the future.[391] Rule 504(a)(1)'s definition of the privilege, which includes the language "does not intend [the statement's] disclosure to any other person,"[392] protects the communication from disclosure by eavesdroppers.

(2) Rule 504(a)(2): Rule of privilege. Rule 504(a)(1)'s position on eavesdroppers is reinforced by the language of Rule 504(a)(2), which authorizes the privilege holder or his representative[393] to invoke the privilege "to prevent any other person from disclosing."[394] Rule 504(a)(2) may permit invocation of the privilege to prevent disclosure by an eavesdropper when the communicating spouse takes ordinary precautions

---

1990, no pet.) (refusing to protect a taped telephone conversation in which a wife discussed her fears and concerns about her defendant spouse's drug dealing with a friend because it was not a confidential communication); *see Fasken v. Fasken*, 113 Tex. 464, 469, 260 S.W. 701, 702 (1924) ("Communications between husband and wife made in the presence and hearing of third parties have never been considered confidential, or within the rule excluding such communications.").

385. *See* Tex. R. Evid. 504(a)(1); *United States v. McCollum*, 58 M.J. 323, 336 (C.A.A.F. 2003).

386. *Blau v. United States*, 340 U.S. 332, 333 (1951).

387. *See id.*

388. *See Wolfle v. United States*, 291 U.S. 7, 14 (1934) ("[W]herever a communication, because of its nature or the circumstances under which it was made, was obviously not intended to be confidential it is not a privileged communication.").

389. *See, e.g., Blau*, 340 U.S. at 333-34 (statement between spouses that could put them at risk for being jailed for contempt of court was likely intended to be confidential).

390. *See Fasken v. Fasken*, 113 Tex. 464, 469, 260 S.W. 701, 702 (1924) (communication made in third party's presence is not privileged); *Wiggins v. Tiller*, 230 S.W. 253, 254 (Tex. Civ. App.—San Antonio 1921, no writ) (same); Joseph W. McKnight, *Family Law: Husband and Wife*, 36 Sw. L.J. 97, 101 (1982) (spouse may testify "to communications made between the spouses during marriage if a third person was present during the conversation, because those statements are not privileged statements"); *see, e.g., Bear v. State*, 612 S.W.2d 931, 931-32 (Tex. Crim. App. [Panel Op.] 1981) (wife could testify about defendant's confession when confession was made in the presence of defendant's mother); *Gibbons v. State*, 794 S.W.2d 887, 892 (Tex. App.—Tyler 1990, no pet.) (admitting evidence of phone calls between wife and third parties did not violate marital-communications privilege).

391. *See, e.g., Zimmerman v. State*, 750 S.W.2d 194, 201 (Tex. Crim. App. 1988) (husband did not intend that letter to his wife remain confidential because letter explicitly stated: "'Don't hide this letter because the lawyers and doctors are going to know it all. I'm going to tell them everything.'").

392. Tex. R. Evid. 504(a)(1).

393. Refer to note 409 *infra*.

394. The language of Rule 504(a)(2) derives largely from California Evidence Code §980. The purpose of that provision was to alter California law to permit assertion of the privilege and prevent an eavesdropper's testimony. Cal. Evid. Code §980 cmt.

against being overheard.[395] Similarly, unilateral acts of disclosure by one spouse do not destroy the privileged status of a particular confidential communication.[396]

Using the rationale of the "eavesdropper doctrine," some Texas[397] and federal[398] courts have excluded from the privilege letters that contain privileged communications and have been stolen or independently discovered by third persons;[399] however, letters that the receiving spouse has intentionally delivered to a third party are privileged.[400] Under Rule 504, such letters are inadmissible regardless of how the third party obtained them if, when they were written, the writer intended them to be confidential[401] and took reasonable measures to ensure their confidentiality.

Rule 504(a)(2) codifies Texas common law on the duration of the marital-communications privilege: it remains in effect after the marriage ends[402] or the com-

---

395. *See Proposed Rules*, *supra* note 28, at 236-38 (FED. R. EVID. 503(a)(4) & advisory committee's note) (for purposes of attorney-client privilege, communication is confidential if there is no intent to disclose it to third persons; rule adopts policy of protecting privilege against eavesdropping); *cf.* **State v. Fischer**, 270 N.W.2d 345, 353-54 (N.D. 1978) (eavesdropping does not constitute illegal search unless communicating parties have a reasonable expectation of privacy). *But see* MCCORMICK ON EVIDENCE I, *supra* note 65, §82, at 196 (weight of authority supports the view that the testimony of third parties about a communication between a husband and wife is admissible whether the third person accidentally overheard the communication or deliberately eavesdropped). Earlier Texas law had been contradictory on whether an eavesdropper could testify to spousal communications. *Compare* **Hampton v. State**, 78 Tex. Crim. 639, 644, 183 S.W. 887, 890 (1916) (visitor who overheard an argument between a husband and wife could testify about the statements made), *with* **McDaniel v. State**, 46 Tex. Crim. 560, 561, 81 S.W. 301, 301 (1904) (testimony of a sheriff's daughter who overheard conversations between defendant and his wife should have been excluded), *aff'd*, 48 Tex. Crim. 342, 87 S.W. 1044 (1905). For a discussion of eavesdropping in the context of the attorney-client privilege, refer to notes 164-167 *supra* and accompanying text.

396. *See, e.g.*, **Walker v. State**, 64 Tex. Crim. 70, 72-73, 141 S.W. 243, 244 (1911) (refusing to admit a letter that wife received in confidence and then turned over to officials).

397. *See* **Zimmerman v. State**, 750 S.W.2d 194, 198-201 (Tex. Crim. App. 1988) (adopting the doctrine that "'where a written confidential communication between husband and wife falls into the hands of a third party inadvertently and without the consent or connivance of the addressee spouse, the third party should be permitted to testify as to the communication'" (quoting **State v. Myers**, 640 P.2d 1245, 1248 (Kan. 1982))); *see, e.g.*, **Harris v. State**, 72 Tex. Crim. 117, 121, 161 S.W. 125, 128 (1913) (if it had been shown that letters were obtained by wife's mother without knowledge or connivance of either husband or wife and that letters had been lost or destroyed, mother could have testified to their contents; "[l]etters stand in the same category as third persons overhearing conversations between the husband and wife").

398. *See, e.g.*, **Dickerson v. United States**, 65 F.2d 824, 827 (D.C. Cir. 1933) (letter containing privileged communications between husband and wife lost privileged status when it came into prosecution's hands through a third party).

399. *See generally* 1 RAY, *supra* note 52, §438, at 427-28 (3d ed. 1980) (the privilege protects a letter voluntarily delivered by the addressee but does not cover a letter that comes into possession of a third party without consent of the addressee); Caroll J. Miller, Annotation, *Applicability of Marital Privilege to Written Communications Between Spouses Inadvertently Obtained by Third Person*, 32 A.L.R.4th 1177, 1180-87 (1984) (collecting cases that examined whether the privilege prevents the third party from disclosing the contents of the communication).

400. *See, e.g.*, **Walker**, 64 Tex. Crim. at 72-73, 141 S.W. at 244 (letter that defendant wrote to his "alleged former wife," who gave the letter to her father to bring to Texas and deliver to authorities "for the purpose of being used as evidence against defendant" was inadmissible).

401. *See* TEX. R. EVID. 504(a)(1), (a)(2); *see, e.g.*, **Zimmerman**, 750 S.W.2d at 201 (husband intended no confidentiality in letter to his wife because letter contained sentence that said: "'Don't hide this letter because the lawyers and doctors are going to know it all. I'm going to tell them everything.'").

402. *See* TEX. R. EVID. 504(a)(2); **Freeman v. State**, 786 S.W.2d 56, 58 (Tex. App.—Houston [1st Dist.] 1990, no pet.). Some federal and out-of-state decisions have held that the trial court may look to the nature and quality of the marital relationship in determining whether the privilege should apply. If a couple is permanently separated,

municating spouse dies.[403] The spouse must, of course, make the confidential communication during the marriage.[404]

"Communication" is not defined in the rule, but the common-law definition generally limited the privilege to express communications.[405] Communications that are threats directed toward the spouse are not protected, as they are assumed not to be intended as "confidential" communications.[406] Of course, the privilege does not protect testimony about the spouse's acts, only words spoken by the spouse or assertive conduct that is intended to be a substitute for words.[407]

(3) Rule 504(a)(3): Who may claim the privilege. Traditionally, either spouse could claim the privilege.[408] Rule 504(a)(3), however, settles this issue by adopting Wigmore's

---

though not formally divorced, the marital-communications privilege may not apply because society's need to secure evidence in search of the truth outweighs the interest in protecting the confidentiality of the relationship. *See United States v. Singleton*, 260 F.3d 1295, 1300 (11th Cir. 2001) ("We agree with the other circuits which have determined that the [marital] privilege is not available when the parties are permanently separated; that is, living separately with no reasonable expectation of reconciliation."); *United States v. Jackson*, 939 F.2d 625, 627 (8th Cir. 1991) (privilege does not protect information communicated after couple has permanently separated); *United States v. Roberson*, 859 F.2d 1376, 1380-81 (9th Cir. 1988) (trial court has responsibility to balance specific facts of a marriage in ruling whether the marriage is "defunct"). In deciding whether a marriage is still viable, courts may look to the particular circumstances, including the absence of present cohabitation, the brevity of original cohabitation, or the fact that one spouse has a child by another person. *See United States v. Cameron*, 556 F.2d 752, 756 (5th Cir. 1977) (policy reasons for marital-communications privilege did not apply in a particular case when the marriage was "moribund"). These cases reflect the federal courts' general hostility toward privileges, which are in derogation of the search for truth.

403. *Lanham v. Lanham*, 105 Tex. 91, 93, 145 S.W. 336, 338 (1912); *Wiggins v. Tiller*, 230 S.W. 253, 254 (Tex. Civ. App.—San Antonio 1921, no writ); *see* Tex. R. Evid. 504(a)(2), (a)(3)(C).

404. Tex. R. Evid. 504(a)(2).

405. *See, e.g., Sterling v. State*, 814 S.W.2d 261, 261-62 (Tex. App.—Austin 1991, pet. ref'd) (per curiam) (wife could testify about her husband's abusive conduct because marital-communication privilege applies only to utterances and not to acts); *Freeman*, 786 S.W.2d at 58-59 (refusing to protect ex-wife's testimony that defendant habitually carried a handgun). Refer to note 407 *infra* and accompanying text.

406. *Weaver v. State*, 855 S.W.2d 116, 121 (Tex. App.—Houston [14th Dist.] 1993, no pet.). The court stated that "the communications appellant made to [his putative spouse] in the form of threats were clearly not intended to be kept private, and would not fall within the purview of the rule." *Id.* The court also held that the spouse's testimony about what happened, as opposed to what the defendant might have told her about what he had done, was not privileged information. *Id.* Finally, because the defendant signed two confessions admitting the details of the capital murder, any privilege that might have existed for any confidential communications to his putative spouse was waived when he informed third parties of the contents of those communications. *Id.* This final holding in *Weaver* is suspect because the marital-communications privilege is not waived when the speaking spouse simply tells a third person about the underlying events. Unless the speaking spouse tells a third person that he related the underlying events to the listening spouse, a disclosure of the underlying events themselves does not waive the privilege. The communication itself, not the underlying facts, is privileged. *See State v. Mireles*, 904 S.W.2d 885, 890 (Tex. App.—Corpus Christi 1995, pet. ref'd) (privilege was not waived when defendant discussed the same subject with a third party).

407. *See Mireles*, 904 S.W.2d at 890 ("[T]he confidential communication privilege applies to utterances and not acts ...."); *Weaver*, 855 S.W.2d at 121 (confidential-communications privilege does not prohibit a spouse's testimony about the other spouse's conduct); *cf. Pereira v. United States*, 347 U.S. 1, 6 (1954) ("The privilege, generally, extends only to utterances, and not to acts."); *United States v. Koehler*, 790 F.2d 1256, 1258 (5th Cir. 1986) (testimony about a spouse's "violent acts" is not protected under the confidential-communications privilege).

408. *See Developments in the Law—Privileged Communications*, 98 Harv. L. Rev. 1563, 1571 (1985).

view that the privilege belongs only to the communicating spouse.[409] This position treats the receiving spouse as a joint holder if, for example, that spouse's silence could be seen as an admission.[410] The Wigmore position has been described as an artificial distinction because a statement by the receiving spouse about a privileged communication could be admitted into evidence against the communicating spouse.[411] However, Rule 504(a)(3) specifies that the receiving spouse is presumed to have authority to invoke the privilege on behalf of the holder.[412] Thus, there is rarely a question about whether one spouse or both holds the privilege.[413] Nevertheless, a privilege holder can refuse to permit disclosure of a privileged communication even when that disclosure is sought on behalf of the privilege holder's present or former spouse.[414]

3. Rule 504(a)(4): Exceptions to the marital-communications privilege.

(1) Rule 504(a)(4)(A): Furtherance of crime or fraud. The language of Rule 504(a)(4)(A), applicable in both civil and criminal cases, parallels that of the crime-fraud exception to the attorney-client privilege.[415] Before the Rules, no Texas court explicitly adopted an exception to the spousal privilege for communications in furtherance of a crime.[416] The common law, however, supported an exception covering communications in furtherance of a fraud.[417] Rule 504(a)(4)(A) adopted this exception; thus, under the Texas rule, a spouse's statement unsuccessfully soliciting the other

---

409. *See* TEX. R. EVID. 504(a)(3)(A); 8 WIGMORE, *supra* note 6, §2340(1), at 670-71. The privilege may be invoked by the communicating spouse or someone authorized to act for that person. *See* TEX. R. EVID. 504(a)(3)(A) (communicating spouse), TEX. R. EVID. 504(a)(3)(B) (guardian of incompetent spouse), TEX. R. EVID. 504(a)(3)(C) (personal representative of deceased spouse).

410. 8 WIGMORE, *supra* note 6, §2338(6), at 667, §2340(1), at 670-71.

411. 2 LOUISELL & MUELLER, *supra* note 69, §219, at 893-94. This view does not seem to acknowledge the protection given to the receiving spouse whose silence constitutes an admission. *See* MCCORMICK ON EVIDENCE I, *supra* note 65, §83, at 198 (receiving spouse would be privileged if the State were trying to prove that the silence was an adoption of the statement).

412. TEX. R. EVID. 504(a)(3).

413. *Cf.* CAL. EVID. CODE §980 (making both spouses privilege holders by referring to a communication made "between him and the other spouse").

414. *See* TEX. R. EVID. 504(a)(2).

415. *See* TEX. R. EVID. 503(d)(1), 504(a)(4)(A). Refer to notes 236-261 *supra* and accompanying text.

416. This fact is not surprising given the existence of the spousal disqualification. *See* **Fasken v. Fasken**, 113 Tex. 464, 468, 260 S.W. 701, 702 (1924) (at common law, husband and wife were not allowed to testify for or against each other). *But cf.* **Goforth v. State**, 100 Tex. Crim. 442, 445-46, 273 S.W. 845, 846-47 (1925) (communications of spouse were admissible against defendant spouse because court could view the communications as coconspirator's declarations). Refer to note 353 *supra* and accompanying text. When the crime results in the death of the victim spouse, so that she could have testified if she had survived, the victim spouse's disclosure of presumptively confidential communications has been held admissible if they are otherwise competent as nonhearsay or within an exception to the hearsay rule. **Robbins v. State**, 82 Tex. Crim. 650, 653, 200 S.W. 525, 526 (1918); *see also* **Butler v. State**, 645 S.W.2d 820, 824 (Tex. Crim. App. 1983) (spousal testimony would be admissible if it related to the res gestae of the offense).

417. *See* **Eddy v. Bosley**, 34 Tex. Civ. App. 116, 122, 78 S.W. 565, 568 (Austin 1903, no writ) ("It is not believed that it is the spirit of the law to regard a communication of the husband to the wife of the existence of a right of third parties which he is attempting to convey to her, and which, if accomplished, would operate as a fraud upon such parties, as privileged, on the ground that such communication is confidential.").

spouse to assist the speaker in committing a crime or fraud would not be privileged.[418] Federal case law is generally in accord, but it largely confines the exception to those instances in which the spouses are acting as joint participants in a contemplated or ongoing crime or fraud.[419] Under the federal privilege, communications made before both spouses became involved in the criminal activity would normally be privileged.[420]

(2) Rule 504(a)(4)(B): Proceedings between spouse and other spouse or claimant through deceased spouse. Rule 504(a)(4)(B), which applies only in civil proceedings, contains two exceptions. The first eliminates the privilege in litigation "brought by or on behalf of one spouse against the other."[421] This exception is a broader expression of a principle that Texas law already recognized. For example, the privilege was already inapplicable in proceedings for divorce,[422] for the enforcement of support obligations,[423] or for the abuse or neglect of a child.[424] Because the Texas Supreme Court did not re-

---

418. *See* Tex. R. Evid. 504(a)(4)(A). The rationale may be that if such an exception is justified for the attorney-client privilege, there should be an exception for a privilege with a far weaker rationale.

419. *See United States v. Ramirez*, 145 F.3d 345, 355 (5th Cir. 1998) (although wife was not indicted for crime, "where both spouses are substantial participants in a patently illegal activity, even the most expansive marital privilege should not bar testimony"); *United States v. Malekzadeh*, 855 F.2d 1492, 1496 (11th Cir. 1988) (federal common-law marital privilege does not protect spousal communications made in furtherance of conspiracy); *United States v. Parker*, 834 F.2d 408, 411 (4th Cir. 1987) (no spousal testimonial or marital-communications privilege when the communication is related to ongoing or future criminal activity in which both spouses are involved).

420. *See United States v. Montgomery*, 384 F.3d 1050, 1059-60 (9th Cir. 2004) (communications made before a spouse becomes a joint participant in the crime are privileged); 2 Christopher B. Mueller & Laird C. Kirkpatrick, Federal Evidence §207 (2d ed. 1994) (exception does not apply to "communications made before both spouses have become involved in the criminal activity"); *see, e.g.*, *United States v. Estes*, 793 F.2d 465, 466 (2d Cir. 1986) (marital-communications privilege protected statements made to spouse before she became an accessory after the fact, but not those made after); *see also United States v. Westmoreland*, 312 F.3d 302, 308 (7th Cir. 2002) ("'The more carefully reasoned decisions distinguish between the initial disclosure, as to which the listening spouse is *not* a joint participant, and the later activities by which the second spouse may join the criminal enterprise.'" (quoting 3 Weinstein & Berger, *supra* note 29, §505.11[2][c] (2d ed. 2002))). *But see Parker*, 834 F.2d at 413 & n.9 (marital-communications privilege does not apply to "statements made in the course of successfully formulating and commencing joint participation in criminal activity").

421. Tex. R. Evid. 504(a)(4)(B)(i); *see, e.g.*, *Earthman's, Inc. v. Earthman*, 526 S.W.2d 192, 206 (Tex. Civ. App.—Houston [1st Dist.] 1975, no writ) (testimony about discussions between spouses was admissible in lawsuit between them, "insofar as relevant to the existing controversy").

422. Act of June 2, 1969, 61st Leg., R.S., ch. 888, §1, 1969 Tex. Gen. Laws 2707, 2725 (former Tex. Fam. Code §3.62, repealed 1997) [now Tex. Fam. Code §6.704].

423. *See* Tex. Fam. Code §231.108(c).

424. *Id.* §261.202; *see also* Tex. Health & Safety Code §260A.010 (in proceedings involving the abuse, neglect, or exploitation of residents of nursing facilities and similar institutions, "evidence may not be excluded on the ground of privileged communication except in the case of a communication between an attorney and client"). Texas Health & Safety Code §260A.010 is a specific exception to the physician-patient and mental-health-information privileges for abuse or neglect. *See* Tex. R. Evid. 509(e)(7) & 510(d)(6) (providing exceptions to physician-patient and mental-health-information privileges in abuse and neglect cases). Refer to notes 693-694, 867-870 *infra* and accompanying text.

The failure to provide a similar exception to Rule 504 might have been unintentional, or it could indicate the supreme court's decision not to permit the exception for marital communications. Regardless of the reason for the omission, to read Rule 504 as permitting the invocation of the privilege in abuse-and-neglect proceedings would be inconsistent with a statute that was in force when the Rules of Evidence were promulgated. *See Few v. Charter Oak Fire Ins.*, 463 S.W.2d 424, 425 (Tex. 1971) (when a rule of the court conflicts with a statutory enactment, the rule must yield); *Mo., Kan. & Tex. Ry. Co. of Tex. v. Beasley*, 106 Tex. 160, 170, 155 S.W. 183, 187 (1913) (court-made rules and legislative statutes must harmonize and not contradict). Refer to note 15 *supra* and accompanying

peal these statutes when promulgating the Civil Rules, their provisions continue to apply under the Rules. In addition, case law suggests that a court must recognize an exception whenever disclosure is necessary to correct wrongs done by one spouse to the other.[425]

The second exception in Rule 504(a)(4)(B) negates the privilege in proceedings between a surviving spouse and a party claiming through the deceased spouse.[426] The same principle of seeking to vindicate the interests of the deceased, expressed under the attorney-client privilege with respect to claimants through a deceased client,[427] seems applicable here. In such litigation, Rule 601(b) might make the surviving spouse incompetent to testify to a communication from the deceased.[428]

(3) Rule 504(a)(4)(C): Crime against family, spouse, household member, or minor child. Under Rule 504(a)(4)(C), a spouse can be compelled to testify to confidential communications made by the other spouse in a proceeding in which the other spouse is accused of conduct that constitutes any crime against the person of the spouse, any member of the household of either spouse, or any minor child.[429] The exception also

---

text. When the Rules were promulgated, article 4442c, §16(d), of the Texas Revised Civil Statutes governed the applicability of privileges in abuse-and-neglect proceedings involving nursing-home residents. Former article 4442c, §16(d), was not repealed under Texas Government Code §22.004 when the Rules were promulgated; rather, it was recodified at Texas Health & Safety Code §242.129. In 2011, the Texas Legislature repealed the subchapter of the Texas Health & Safety Code that contained §242.129. Acts 2011, 82nd Leg., 1st C.S., ch. 7, §1.05(m), eff. Sept. 28, 2011. However, the Legislature enacted a new chapter to address reports of abuse, neglect, or exploitation. *See* TEX. HEALTH & SAFETY CODE ch. 260A; Acts 2011, 82nd Leg., 1st C.S., ch. 7, §1.05(c), eff. Sept. 28, 2011. Section 260A.010 is substantively identical to former §242.129, except that it also refers to the exploitation of residents of nursing facilities. *See* TEX. HEALTH & SAFETY CODE §260A.010. The statute defines "exploitation" as "the illegal or improper act or process of a caregiver, family member, or other individual who has an ongoing relationship with the resident using the resources of a resident for monetary or personal benefit, profit, or gain without the informed consent of the resident." *Id.* §260A.001(4).

425. *See, e.g.*, *First Bank v. Hill*, 151 S.W. 652, 654 (Tex. Civ. App.—Texarkana 1912, writ dism'd) (wife could testify to communications about the illegal disposal of her property by her husband); *King v. Sassaman*, 64 S.W. 937, 937 (Tex. Civ. App. 1901, no writ) (wife could testify in slander suit against her husband). *See generally* 8 WIGMORE, *supra* note 6, §2338(1)-(3), at 665-66 (discussing the exceptions to the spousal privilege).

426. TEX. R. EVID. 504(a)(4)(B)(ii).

427. TEX. R. EVID. 503(d)(2). Refer to notes 262-267 *supra* and accompanying text.

428. *See* TEX. R. EVID. 601(b)(1) & (b)(2) (discussing the incompetence of certain witnesses in actions involving executors, administrators, or guardians). Refer to *Article VI: Witnesses, infra* p. 563.

429. TEX. R. EVID. 504(a)(4)(C)(i). Under the 1998 version of Rule 504(a)(4)(C), the State could compel the disclosure of confidential communications made between the spouses when the defendant spouse was charged with a crime "against the person" of the other spouse, any minor child, or any member of the household of either spouse. This provision marked a major change in Texas law because under the former statute, a spouse could never testify to confidential communications, even in cases of child abuse by the other spouse. *See* Act of May 27, 1965, 59th Leg., R.S., ch. 722, §1, 1965 Tex. Gen. Laws 317, 467, *amended by* Act of May 23, 1985, 69th Leg., R.S., ch. 791, §2, 1985 Tex. Gen. Laws 2703 (former Code of Criminal Procedure art. 38.11 deemed repealed as to criminal proceedings effective 1986); *see, e.g.*, *Niles v. State*, 104 Tex. Crim. 447, 450, 284 S.W. 568, 569 (1926) (lower court erred in allowing the prosecution to bring out intraspousal communications); *Norwood v. State*, 80 Tex. Crim. 552, 564, 192 S.W. 248, 254 (1917) (op. on reh'g) (defendant's wife could not be made to answer cross-examination questions that would reveal conversations between her and her husband).

applies in a criminal proceeding when the other spouse is charged with the offense of bigamy.[430]

Rule 504(a)(4)(C) significantly limits invocation of the marital-communications privilege in domestic-violence situations.[431] The witness spouse can be forced to divulge confidential communications made by the defendant spouse (or to testify against a defendant spouse)[432] whenever that spouse is accused of a crime against the witness spouse, a minor child, or a member of the household.[433] Society has an even stronger interest in protecting children than it does in preserving marital privacy.[434] Perhaps for that reason, Rule 504 covers all minor children.[435] Thus, the child does not need to be the offspring of either spouse; an offense "against the person" of a neighbor's child, a foster child, a child in day care, or even a complete stranger provides sufficient justification for piercing the marital-communications privilege.[436] It also covers any "mem-

---

430. TEX. R. EVID. 504(a)(4)(C)(ii). This provision was added in response to the Legislature's addition of a bigamy exception to Texas Code of Criminal Procedure article 38.10. *See* TEX. CODE CRIM. PROC. art. 38.10(2).

431. The rationale for this exception is that "'it would be unconscionable to permit a privilege grounded on promoting communications of trust and love between marriage partners to prevent a properly outraged spouse with knowledge from testifying against the perpetrator of such a crime.'" *United States v. Martinez*, 44 F. Supp. 2d 835, 837 (W.D. Tex. 1999) (quoting *United States v. Bahe*, 128 F.3d 1440, 1446 (10th Cir. 1997)). The *Martinez* court held that the marital-communications privilege did not apply in a child-abuse prosecution. 44 F. Supp. 2d at 837.

432. *See* TEX. R. EVID. 504(b)(4)(A)(i). Refer to notes 476-478 *infra* and accompanying text.

433. *See* TEX. R. EVID. 504(a)(4)(C)(i).

434. *See* 25 WRIGHT & GRAHAM, *supra* note 29, §5593, at 761-62 (1989) (adding that "[a] contrary rule would make children a target population").

435. TEX. R. EVID. 504(a)(4)(C)(i). The term "minor" is not defined in the rule. The former statute had limited its definition to minor children under 16. Former article 38.11, after setting forth the general testimonial privilege, read as follows:

> However, a wife or husband may voluntarily testify against each other in any case for an offense involving any grade of assault or violence committed by one against the other or against any child of either under 16 years of age, in any case where either is charged with incest of a child of either, in any case where either is charged with bigamy, in any case where either is charged with interference with child custody, in any case where either is charged with nonsupport of his or her spouse or minor child, or in any case where either is charged with an offense under Section 22.041, Penal Code.

Act of May 27, 1965, 59th Leg., R.S., ch. 722, §1, 1965 Tex. Gen. Laws 317, 467, *amended by* Act of May 23, 1985, 69th Leg., R.S., ch. 791, §2, 1985 Tex. Gen. Laws 2703 (former Code of Criminal Procedure art. 38.11 deemed repealed as to criminal proceedings effective 1986). Thus, the change in Rule 504 presumably is intended to refer to the criminal offense for which the defendant is charged. For example, the code provision criminalizing sexual assault defines a "child" as one younger than 17, TEX. PENAL CODE §22.011(c)(1), while the provision criminalizing injury to a child defines a "child" as one "14 years of age or younger," *id.* §22.04(c)(1).

436. *See* TEX. R. EVID. 504(a)(4)(C)(i); *Ludwig v. State*, 931 S.W.2d 239, 243-44 (Tex. Crim. App. 1996). In *Ludwig*, the court of criminal appeals examined the legislative history of the amendment to former Criminal Rule 504(1)(d)(2): "This amendment changed 'a minor child' to 'any minor child,' and struck the prepositional phrase 'of either spouse' that followed immediately thereafter." *Ludwig*, 931 S.W.2d at 243. The court concluded that the legislative intent was "that the exception should apply to 'any minor child,' without qualification." *Id.*; *see also Huddleston v. State*, 997 S.W.2d 319, 320-21 (Tex. App.—Houston [1st Dist.] 1999, no pet.) (no spousal privilege prevented wife from testifying against defendant spouse in trial for aggravated sexual assault of child even though neither was a parent of the child victim; rule is intended to protect all minor children); 1 GOODE ET AL., *supra* note 206, §504.8, at 392 (breadth of the exception reflects perception of two social phenomena: public concern about perceived increase of sexual and physical assaults against children and increased frequency with which children are placed in foster or day care).

ber of the household" of either spouse.[437] Under the rule, the defendant's spouse is a compellable witness whenever the defendant is charged with an assaultive crime against anyone who lives with either spouse, including minor children, parents, aunts, uncles, adult children, and adults in foster care.[438]

(4) Rule 504(a)(4)(D) & (a)(4)(E): Proceedings to commit or to establish the competence of a spouse. The exceptions to the spousal privilege for commitment[439] and competency[440] proceedings are consistent with both the rationale for the privilege and the decision to provide for similar exceptions to the physician-patient privilege.[441] The reason for these provisions has been explained:

> Commitment and competency proceedings are undertaken for the benefit of the subject person. Frequently, much or all of the evidence bearing on a spouse's competency or lack of competency will consist of communications to the other spouse. It would be undesirable to permit either spouse to invoke a privilege to prevent the presentation of this vital information inasmuch as these proceedings are of such vital importance both to society and to the spouse who is the subject of the proceedings.[442]

D. Rule 504(b): Spousal Testimonial Privilege in Criminal Cases

1. Rule 504(b)(1): Rule of privilege. Rule 504(b) sets out an additional spousal privilege that is applicable only in criminal proceedings.[443] It permits one spouse to refuse to be called as a witness by the State against the other spouse.[444] The privilege applies at all stages of a criminal proceeding, including before the grand jury[445] and in ancil-

---

437. Tex. R. Evid. 504(a)(4)(C)(i). Like the term "minor," the phrase "member of the household" is not defined within the evidentiary rule. That term is defined by the Family Code for purposes of a protective order. "'Household' means a unit composed of persons living together in the same dwelling, without regard to whether they are related to each other." Tex. Fam. Code §71.005. "'Member of a household' includes a person who previously lived in a household." *Id.* §71.006. Because Rule 504 is intended to exclude domestic-violence offenses from the protection of the spousal privileges, courts should use this Family Code definition for purposes of Rule 504. *See* 1 Goode et al., *supra* note 206, §504.8, at 392-93; *see, e.g.,* ***Riley v. State***, 849 S.W.2d 901, 903 (Tex. App.—Austin 1993, pet. ref'd) (applying Family Code definition of "member of a household" in determining that murder defendant's wife could not invoke testimonial privilege when unrelated victim had been living in their home at time of murder).

438. *See* 1 Goode et al., *supra* note 206, §504.8, at 392 (impetus for the "member of the household" language was a concern for violence committed against elderly persons and young children).

439. *See* Tex. R. Evid. 504(a)(4)(D). Under Rule 504(a)(4)(D), the spousal privilege does not apply in a commitment proceeding or a proceeding to put the spouse or the spouse's property under someone else's control because of the spouse's mental or physical condition. *Id.*

440. *See* Tex. R. Evid. 504(a)(4)(E).

441. *See* Tex. R. Evid. 509(e)(6). Refer to notes 687-692 *infra* and accompanying text.

442. Cal. Evid. Code §982 cmt. California Evidence Code §§982 and 983 were the sources of Texas Civil Rule 504(a)(4)(D).

443. *See* ***Marshall v. Ryder Sys., Inc.***, 928 S.W.2d 190, 195 (Tex. App.—Houston [14th Dist.] 1996, writ denied) ("Only in criminal cases is there a broad, general privilege protecting a person from being a witness against his or her spouse.").

444. Tex. R. Evid. 504(b)(1).

445. *See* ***In re Grand Jury Proceedings***, 640 F. Supp. 988, 989-90 (E.D. Mich. 1986).

lary hearings,[446] and belongs entirely to the testifying spouse, not to the defendant.[447] The defendant's spouse is always competent to testify and is not prohibited from testifying voluntarily for the State.[448] This privilege does not apply to extrajudicial statements[449] and thus is not violated when a third person testifies against the defendant spouse and discusses statements made outside the courtroom by the witness spouse.[450] Hearsay rules may nonetheless bar this kind of testimony.[451]

The testimonial privilege applies only during the marriage itself.[452] Once a divorce terminates a marital relationship, a court may compel a former spouse to testify against the other; confidential communications made during the marriage, however, remain privileged.[453]

Rule 504(b)(1) does not provide "a spouse a privilege to refuse to be called to testify for the accused"; thus, a defendant spouse can compel the other spouse's testimony.[454] The rule formerly provided that "[a] spouse who testifies on behalf of an accused is subject to cross-examination as provided in Rule 611(b)."[455] The sentence

---

446. *See, e.g.*, **Solis v. State**, 673 S.W.2d 270, 275-76 (Tex. App.—Corpus Christi 1984) (privilege applies at a probation-revocation hearing as does the exception for spousal abuse; wife was competent to testify against her abusive husband because her testimony was voluntarily given), *aff'd*, 718 S.W.2d 282 (Tex. Crim. App. 1986).

447. Refer to note 472 *infra* and accompanying text.

448. *See* Tex. R. Evid. 504(b)(1). The former statutory provision prohibited the State from calling the spouse of the accused as a witness except in certain situations. Act approved June 18, 1965, 59th Leg., ch. 722, 1965 Tex. Gen. Laws 317, *amended by* Act approved June 15, 1985, 69th Leg., ch. 791, §2, 1985 Tex. Gen. Laws 2703 (former Code of Criminal Procedure art. 38.11 deemed repealed as to criminal proceedings effective 1986); *see, e.g.*, **Burns v. State**, 556 S.W.2d 270, 281-82 (Tex. Crim. App. 1977) (spouse was incompetent to testify against her husband's codefendant); **Carabajal v. State**, 477 S.W.2d 640, 641 (Tex. Crim. App. 1972) (spouse was incompetent to testify in punishment stage). The defendant could not waive this disqualification and did not need to object to preserve the error. **Johnigan v. State**, 482 S.W.2d 209, 210-11 (Tex. Crim. App. 1972); *see* **Stewart v. State**, 587 S.W.2d 148, 154 (Tex. Crim. App. [Panel Op.] 1979).

449. *Cf.* **United States v. Chapman**, 866 F.2d 1326, 1333 (11th Cir. 1989) (extrajudicial statements by a spouse cannot be excluded under spousal privilege).

450. *See, e.g.*, **Poole v. State**, 910 S.W.2d 93, 95 & n.6 (Tex. App.—Eastland 1995, no pet.) (police officer's testimony that defendant's wife said defendant had "thrown the cocaine out the back door" did not violate the husband-wife privilege, which merely protects the accused's spouse from being called as a witness at trial by the State); **Wolf v. State**, 674 S.W.2d 831, 842 (Tex. App.—Corpus Christi 1984, pet. ref'd) (trial court properly allowed third party to testify about extrajudicial statements made by defendant's husband in furtherance of a conspiracy; husband-wife privilege is not violated when husband and wife are coconspirators and there is independent evidence establishing a joint act of the parties); *cf.* **United States v. Archer**, 733 F.2d 354, 358-59 (5th Cir. 1984) (in bank-embezzlement trial, FBI agent could testify to statements that defendant's wife had made to him; statements made in confidence to a third person before trial would not threaten present marital harmony).

451. *See, e.g.*, **Poole**, 910 S.W.2d at 95-96 (police officer's testimony about statement made by defendant's wife was inadmissible hearsay; trial court committed reversible error in admitting the testimony).

452. *See* **Freeman v. State**, 786 S.W.2d 56, 58 (Tex. App.—Houston [1st Dist.] 1990, no pet.) (once divorced, a spouse is no longer disqualified from testifying).

453. *Id.* at 58-59.

454. Tex. R. Evid. 504(b)(1).

455. Tex. R. Evid. 504 cmt. (2015); *see* **Blackwell v. State**, 818 S.W.2d 134, 137 (Tex. App.—Waco 1991, pet. ref'd) (spouse is subject to cross-examination as allowed under former Rule 610(b)). Under earlier law, an accused's spouse could always testify on the accused's behalf. *See* **Ferrell v. State**, 429 S.W.2d 901, 902 (Tex. Crim. App. 1968); **Watts v. State**, 87 Tex. Crim. 442, 443, 222 S.W. 558, 558 (1920). When the accused spouse called the other spouse to testify, the State could cross-examine only on those matters covered or directly related to matters covered on direct

was included in the original version of Criminal Rule 504, which changed the rule to a privilege held by the witness spouse.[456] Before the rule was promulgated, a spouse was deemed incompetent to testify against a defendant spouse, "and when a spouse testified on behalf of a defendant spouse, the state was limited to cross-examining the spouse about matters relating to the spouse's direct testimony."[457] The sentence from the criminal rule eliminated that limitation to allow the State to cross-examine the testifying spouse as it would any other witness.[458] However, the inclusion of that provision referring only to a spouse testifying on behalf of the accused was confusing because "[m]ore than twenty-five years later, it is clear that a spouse who testifies either for or against a defendant spouse may be cross-examined in the same manner as any other witness."[459]

2. Rule 504(b)(2): Failure to call spouse as witness. Rule 504(b)(2) permits the State to comment on a defendant's failure to call his spouse as a witness when the evidence indicates that the spouse could testify to relevant matters.[460] Contrast this provision with Rule 513(a), which prohibits any adverse comment on or inference from the exercise of other privileges.[461] However, because the rationale supporting the privilege is the preservation of marital harmony and commenting on the exercise of the privilege does not damage that harmony, allowing such comments is both logical[462] and consistent with earlier Texas law.[463]

---

examination. **Mitchell v. State**, 517 S.W.2d 282, 287 (Tex. Crim. App. 1974); **Smith v. State**, 141 Tex. Crim. 577, 582, 150 S.W.2d 388, 390 (1941); **Firo v. State**, 654 S.W.2d 503, 507 (Tex. App.—Corpus Christi 1983), aff'd, 657 S.W.2d 141 (Tex. Crim. App. 1983).

456. Tex. R. Evid. 504 cmt. (2015); see Tex. R. Crim. Evid. 504(2)(a), 701-702 S.W.2d (Tex. Cases) XLIII (1986, amended 1998).

457. Tex. R. Evid. 504 cmt. (2015).

458. Id.; see Tex. R. Evid. 611(b). Refer to Article VI: Witnesses, infra p. 639.

459. Tex. R. Evid. 504 cmt. (2015). The deletion of the sentence is intended to clarify Rule 504(b)(1) and does not change existing law. Id.

Although the State may cross-examine the witness exactly as any other witness, confidential communications remain privileged unless an exception under 504(a)(4) applies or the witness voluntarily discloses the confidential communications. See Tex. R. Evid. 504(a)(4), 511(a)(1). On the other hand, the context of the hearing defines the relevant issues on which the State may cross-examine the spouse. For example, in a pretrial suppression hearing, the State cannot cross-examine a defendant's spouse on matters that are irrelevant to the issues to be determined at the pretrial hearing, even if they are relevant to the prosecution of the offense. See, e.g., **Johnson v. State**, 803 S.W.2d 272, 284-85 (Tex. Crim. App. 1990) (improper for State to cross-examine defendant's wife about the purchase of blue jeans for defendant because such questioning was irrelevant to whether she voluntarily consented to a police search of her home, but the error was harmless).

460. See **Babineaux v. State**, 777 S.W.2d 724, 731-32 (Tex. App.—Beaumont 1989) (under Rule 504(2)(a), prosecutor's argument that defendant's wife was not called as a witness was permissible), pet. dism'd, improvidently granted, 803 S.W.2d 301 (Tex. Crim. App. 1990).

461. See Tex. R. Evid. 513(a) (except as permitted under Rule 504(b)(2), no adverse comment or inference may be drawn from a witness's invocation of a valid privilege). Refer to notes 970-972 infra and accompanying text.

462. See generally 1 Goode et al., supra note 206, §504.7, at 387-88 (such a comment is proper and permissible when the failure to call a particular witness who had knowledge of relevant facts is normally considered an admission by conduct).

463. See **Boles v. State**, 598 S.W.2d 274, 280 (Tex. Crim. App. [Panel Op.] 1980) (prosecutor's jury argument, which called attention to the absence of defendant's husband as a defense witness, was proper); **Fisher v. State**, 511 S.W.2d

While the State can comment on the defendant's failure to call a spouse as a witness, it should not call the witness spouse to the stand and force her to invoke the testimonial privilege in front of the jury.[464] The rationale for this recommendation is that there would be too strong an inference that the spouse would testify against the defendant: "The spouse's invocation of privilege in front of the jury, without more, almost necessarily compels the jury to draw an inference adverse to the defendant."[465] Thus, the prosecution should first call the spouse to the stand outside the presence of the jury to determine whether the witness will invoke the testimonial privilege.[466] However, the State can attempt to demonstrate that it is not practicable to allow the witness spouse to invoke the privilege outside the presence of the jury.[467]

Suppose, however, that the defendant spouse wants to compel the witness spouse's exculpatory testimony and the witness spouse wants to claim the testimonial privilege. Rule 504(b)(1) provides only "a privilege not to be called to testify for the state."[468] Thus, no privilege allows a spouse to refuse to testify when called as a witness by the defendant spouse.[469] The defendant spouse, unlike the State, can compel the unwilling spouse's testimony unless the witness spouse claims a valid privilege against self-

---

506, 507-08 (Tex. Crim. App. 1974) (prosecutor's argument may include an inference that defendant's wife was not called as a defense witness because her testimony would have been damaging to the defense); *Stallings v. State*, 476 S.W.2d 679, 681-82 (Tex. Crim. App. 1972) (prosecution's argument to the jury may comment on the failure of defendant to produce defendant's spouse as a witness); *Veracruz v. State*, 713 S.W.2d 745, 749 (Tex. App.—Houston [1st Dist.] 1986, pet. ref'd) (prosecutor may imply that the testimony of a defendant's absent spouse would have been material and damaging).

464. *Johnson*, 803 S.W.2d at 283. In *Benitez v. State*, the State called the defendant's spouse as a witness, and she later invoked her testimonial privilege outside the presence of the jury. 5 S.W.3d 915, 918 (Tex. App.—Amarillo 1999, pet. ref'd). The court of appeals discussed the reasoning and result in *Johnson* and stated that:

> Error arises when the spouse is called as a witness by the State when it has reason to believe that the privilege will most likely be invoked and the jury perceives that the spouse invoked the privilege. We caution ... that, to the extent practicable, the proceeding should be conducted in a manner which facilitates the making of the claim without the knowledge of the jury. Yet, it is not automatic error if the jury divines what occurred. Rather, it is the jury's perception of the situation, coupled with the knowledge by the prosecutor that the claim would likely be invoked, which creates the error.

Benitez, 5 S.W.3d at 919. The court concluded that there was no error in this particular case because the spouse did not, in fact, invoke the privilege within the presence of the jury, and there was no showing that the prosecutor knew that she would decline to testify. *Id.* at 920. Indeed, she had testified during a pretrial hearing. *Id.*

465. *Johnson*, 803 S.W.2d at 282.

466. *See United States v. Chapman*, 866 F.2d 1326, 1333 (11th Cir. 1989) (generally improper to permit witness to claim the testimonial privilege in the presence of the jury when witness's intention not to testify is known in advance); *Labbe v. Berman*, 621 F.2d 26, 28 (1st Cir. 1980) (although trial court incorrectly ruled that defendant's wife was required to claim testimonial privilege on the witness stand, its ruling was not a denial of due process); *San Fratello v. United States*, 340 F.2d 560, 566-67 (5th Cir. 1965) (government may not call a spouse to testify to force her to claim testimonial privilege in front of the jury); 2 Weinstein & Berger, *supra* note 29, ¶505[02], at 505-16 (prosecution must ascertain, outside the presence of the jury, if the accused's spouse will assert the privilege).

467. *E.g.*, *Johnson*, 803 S.W.2d at 283 (suggesting that State may be able to show that it is not practicable for the spouse to invoke the privilege outside the presence of the jury, but finding unpersuasive State's argument that spouse's assertion of the privilege in front of the jury would help the jury understand why her prior testimony was being read).

468. Tex. R. Evid. 504(b)(1).

469. *Id.* Refer to notes 454-459 *supra* and accompanying text.

incrimination.[470] If the witness spouse invoked that privilege, the State presumably could not make any comment on the defendant's failure to call the witness spouse to testify because other evidence would indicate that the witness spouse could not testify to relevant matters.[471]

3. Rule 504(b)(3): Who may claim. Rule 504(b)(3) clarifies that the witness spouse, not the defendant spouse, controls the exercise of the privilege.[472] Only the witness or the witness's guardian or representative can claim it.[473] The witness spouse can also waive the privilege. For example, if both a defendant and his spouse are charged with crimes, the spouse might agree to a plea bargain requiring that she testify fully and truthfully at the defendant spouse's trial.[474]

4. Rule 504(b)(4): Exceptions. Texas recognizes only two exceptions to the spousal testimonial privilege in criminal cases. The privilege of a person's spouse to refuse to be called as a witness does not apply (1) in certain criminal proceedings and (2) to matters occurring before the marriage.[475]

(1) Rule 504(b)(4)(A): Certain criminal proceedings. As with the marital-communications privilege, there is no privilege to refuse to testify against the defendant spouse when the defendant is charged with a crime against the other spouse, any mem-

---

470. *See Johnson*, 803 S.W.2d at 282 n.6. The court explained:
> To allow the defendant's spouse to refuse to give exculpatory testimony when called by the defense would be inconsistent with the right of a criminal defendant to compulsory process for obtaining favorable witnesses. However, the accused spouse may properly assert the privilege for confidential marital communications.

Id. (citations omitted).

471. *See Wolf v. State*, 674 S.W.2d 831, 842 (Tex. App.—Corpus Christi 1984, pet. ref'd) (raising the issue, but declining to decide whether State may properly comment on defendant's failure to call as a witness a spouse who is "unavailable" because of pending criminal charges).

472. Tex. R. Evid. 504(b)(3); *see Janecka v. State*, 937 S.W.2d 456, 472 (Tex. Crim. App. 1996) (absolute disqualification of one spouse from testifying against another under former statute was superseded by Criminal Rule 504, and "[u]nder Rule 504 only the spouse called to testify may assert the privilege"); *Anderson v. State*, 880 S.W.2d 35, 37 (Tex. App.—Tyler 1994, pet. ref'd) (testimonial privilege under Criminal Rule 504 permits spouse to testify voluntarily for State even over objection of defendant spouse).

473. Tex. R. Evid. 504(b)(3).

474. *See, e.g., United States v. Bad Wound*, 203 F.3d 1072, 1075 (8th Cir. 2000) (defendant's wife waived testimonial privilege when she signed plea agreement containing provision that she would provide "complete and truthful testimony" in future criminal proceedings).

475. While Rule 504(a)(4)(A) may pierce the privilege for marital communications when the person makes the communication to facilitate the commission or planning of a fraud or crime, Rule 504(b) is silent on whether a spouse is a compellable witness when the spouses jointly participate in a crime for which only one spouse is on trial. Federal cases, decided under common-law principles, generally hold there is no joint-participant exception. *See United States v. Ramos-Oseguera*, 120 F.3d 1028, 1042 (9th Cir. 1997) (no joint-participant exception to spousal testimonial privilege), *overruled on other grounds*, *United States v. Nordby*, 225 F.3d 1053 (9th Cir. 2000); *In re Grand Jury Subpoena United States*, 755 F.2d 1022, 1025 (2d Cir. 1985) (same), *vacated on other grounds sub nom. United States v. Koecher*, 475 U.S. 133 (1986); *In re Grand Jury (Malfitano)*, 633 F.2d 276, 279-80 (3d Cir. 1980) (same). *But see United States v. Clark*, 712 F.2d 299, 301 (7th Cir. 1983) (upholding the exception). Because the Texas drafters specifically created an exception for the marital-communications privilege in the context of furtherance of crimes or fraud and did not draft a similar exception for the testimonial privilege, it would seem that they intended no such exception. *See* 1 GOODE ET AL., *supra* note 206, §504.8, at 396. Refer to notes 415-420 *supra* and accompanying text.

ber of either spouse's household, or any minor child,[476] or when the defendant is charged with bigamy.[477] Unlike Rule 504(a)(4)(C)(i)'s exception to the marital-communications privilege, the wording of the Rule 504(b)(4)(A)(i) exception does not limit it to offenses committed "against the person" of the protected class.[478]

(2) Rule 504(b)(4)(B): Matters that occurred before the marriage. Under Rule 504(b)(4)(B), there is no testimonial privilege "[i]f the spouse is called to testify about matters that occurred before the marriage."[479] Thus, the State may compel the spouse to testify against the defendant whenever that testimony relates to events that occurred before the marriage.[480] This exception prevents the defendant from silencing a potential witness by a sham marriage.[481] While the State can compel the spouse to testify, the marital-communications privilege still protects any confidential communications made after the date of the marriage.[482]

---

476. TEX. R. EVID. 504(b)(4)(A)(i). Until the 1998 unification of the Rules, the defendant's spouse could assert the privilege not to testify even when the spouse was the victim of the crime. *See, e.g.*, **Fuentes v. State**, 775 S.W.2d 64, 65-66 (Tex. App.—Houston [1st Dist.] 1989, no pet.) (trial court erred in compelling a wife to testify against her husband when husband was accused of abusing his wife). The Texas Legislature corrected this anomaly in 1995 by passing Texas Code of Criminal Procedure article 38.10, which requires the defendant's spouse to testify against the defendant, if called to do so, when that spouse is the alleged victim of the charged offense. *See* TEX. CODE CRIM. PROC. art. 38.10(1). The rationale for the former provision was that the victim spouse was "in the best position to decide whether or not to invoke the privilege." 1 GOODE ET AL., *supra* note 206, §504.8, at 390. As a practical matter, the issue arises almost exclusively in cases of spousal assault. Some commentators have suggested that the victim of the crime is in the best position to know whether marital harmony will be threatened either by her testimony against the abuser or by the punishment of the abuser. *Id.* Other commentators have noted that the law should not protect this type of marital "peace." *See* 8 WIGMORE, *supra* note 6, §2239, at 243 ("[I]f there were, conceivably, any such peace, would it be a peace such as the law could desire to protect? Could it be any other peace than that which the tyrant secures for himself by oppression?").

477. TEX. R. EVID. 504(b)(4)(A)(ii); *see* **Hernandez v. State**, 205 S.W.3d 555, 558-59 (Tex. App.—Amarillo 2006, pet. ref'd) (interpreting the privilege's "charged with a crime against" language and rejecting defendant's argument that the privilege did not apply because he was not charged with a crime that requires, as an element of the offense, proof that it was committed against a member of one of the groups specified in the privilege; "[a]s the exception uses the same 'charged with a crime against' language in reference to the testifying spouse as it does in reference to a minor, we conclude that the exception was intended to abrogate the privilege whenever a minor is the alleged victim of the crime charged"). Refer to the discussion of Rule 504(a)(4)(C), notes 429-438 *supra* and accompanying text.

478. In theory, then, the witness spouse could be compelled to testify against the defendant spouse when he is charged with a property offense committed against any member of the protected class, although she could not testify to confidential marital communications. Presumably, however, a witness spouse who has filed charges against the defendant spouse for a property crime would be a willing witness. As for property crimes committed against a minor child or a member of either spouse's household, it does not appear that these groups deserve or need greater protection than other property-crime victims. The rationale for the exception to the privilege is based on the physical and sexual vulnerability of children and the elderly, not on their special economic vulnerability. There seems to be little public policy to support such an unlimited exception, and it is likely that the omission of the "against the person" language in this provision was a drafting oversight.

479. TEX. R. EVID. 504(b)(4)(B); **Walker v. State**, 406 S.W.3d 590, 598 (Tex. App.—Eastland 2013, pet. ref'd).

480. *See, e.g.*, **Welch v. State**, 908 S.W.2d 258, 264-65 (Tex. App.—El Paso 1995, no pet.) (when defendant and spouse were not ceremonially married at the time of the offense and defendant did not prove that all elements of common-law marriage were established at time of offense, wife was a compellable witness against defendant).

481. *See, e.g.*, **United States v. Apodaca**, 522 F.2d 568, 571 (10th Cir. 1975) (appellant could not invoke spousal privilege because evidence demonstrated that the marriage was fraudulent).

482. Refer to notes 384-442 *supra* and accompanying text.

RULE 505

PRIVILEGE FOR COMMUNICATIONS TO A CLERGY MEMBER

(a) Definitions. In this rule:

(1) A "clergy member" is a minister, priest, rabbi, accredited Christian Science Practitioner, or other similar functionary of a religious organization or someone whom a communicant reasonably believes is a clergy member.

(2) A "communicant" is a person who consults a clergy member in the clergy member's professional capacity as a spiritual adviser.

(3) A communication is "confidential" if made privately and not intended for further disclosure except to other persons present to further the purpose of the communication.

(b) General Rule. A communicant has a privilege to refuse to disclose and to prevent any other person from disclosing a confidential communication by the communicant to a clergy member in the clergy member's professional capacity as spiritual adviser.

(c) Who May Claim. The privilege may be claimed by:

(1) the communicant;

(2) the communicant's guardian or conservator; or

(3) a deceased communicant's personal representative.

The clergy member to whom the communication was made may claim the privilege on the communicant's behalf—and is presumed to have authority to do so.

COMMENTARY ON RULE 505

Rule 505 provides a privilege for confidential communications made to clergy members in their capacity as spiritual advisers. Commentators have offered various rationales for such a privilege,[483] including the demands of religious liberty,[484] the need for individuals to be able to disclose "flawed acts or thoughts" to a spiritual counselor,[485] and the desire to avoid confrontations with clergy who refuse to divulge communica-

---

483. *See generally* Michael J. Callahan, *Historical Inquiry into the Priest-Penitent Privilege*, 36 JURIST 328 (1976) (examining theological and constitutional implications of the privilege, as well as its value in providing a break with English law); Seward Reese, *Confidential Communications to the Clergy*, 24 OHIO ST. L.J. 55 (1963) (discussing rationales such as the generally accepted detestability of the violation of confidence, the strict standards of conduct imposed on the clergy for maintaining the inviolability of confidential communications, and the psychological and therapeutic value of penitential communications).

484. *See Mullen v. United States*, 263 F.2d 275, 280 (D.C. Cir. 1958) (Fahy & Edgerton, JJ., concurring). Even Jeremy Bentham, no friend of evidentiary privileges, supported a clergy-communicant privilege on the ground that permitting such communications to be revealed would inhibit the exercise of religious freedom. *See* 4 JEREMY BENTHAM, RATIONALE OF JUDICIAL EVIDENCE, SPECIALLY APPLIED TO ENGLISH PRACTICE 586-92 (1827).

485. *Trammel v. United States*, 445 U.S. 40, 51 (1980).

tions they feel ethically obligated to keep confidential.[486] Whatever its justification, all 50 states and the District of Columbia have adopted statutes or rules protecting some form of the privilege.[487]

The Texas Legislature first recognized a clergy-communicant privilege in 1967. This statutory privilege was qualified, however, and disclosure could be compelled when the administration of justice required it.[488] Rule 505, based on the proposed federal rule,[489] broadened the scope of the statutory privilege by removing this qualification.[490]

Under Rule 505, confidential communications are privileged if made to a member of the clergy or an individual whom the communicant[491] reasonably believed was a member of the clergy.[492] A clergy member is a "minister, priest, rabbi, accredited Christian Science Practitioner, or other similar functionary of a religious organization."[493] Rule 505 is designed to encompass those persons regularly engaged in activities like those performed by the clergy of the major religious denominations but exclude at least

---

486. *See* Roy R. Ray, *Annual Survey of Texas Law: Evidence*, 22 Sw. L.J. 167, 173 (1968). One commentator chronicles a highly publicized Delaware alienation-of-affection suit in which a subpoenaed Episcopal rector flatly refused to testify about conversations he had with one of the parties, even though Delaware had no clergy-communicant privilege at the time. Reese, *supra* note 483, at 55. Before a contempt ruling was made, the Delaware Legislature enacted the privilege. *Id.*

487. *See* Norman Abrams, *Addressing the Tension Between the Clergy-Communicant Privilege and the Duty to Report Child Abuse in State Statutes*, 44 B.C. L. Rev. 1127, 1133-34 & nn.29-36 (2003); R. Michael Cassidy, *Sharing Sacred Secrets: Is It (Past) Time for a Dangerous Person Exception to the Clergy-Penitent Privilege?*, 44 Wm. & Mary L. Rev. 1627, 1639 & nn.60-65 (2003). At least in Texas practice, however, the privilege is rarely invoked or litigated.

488. Former article 3715a read as follows:

CLERGYMAN-PENITENT PRIVILEGE

No ordained minister, priest, rabbi or duly accredited Christian Science practitioner of an established church or religious organization shall be required to testify in any action, suit, or proceeding, concerning any information which may have been confidentially communicated to him in his professional capacity under such circumstances that to disclose the information would violate a sacred or moral trust, when the giving of such testimony is objected to by the communicant; provided, however, that the presiding judge in any trial may compel such disclosure if in his opinion the same is necessary to a proper administration of justice.

Act approved June 12, 1967, 60th Leg., ch. 435, §1, 1967 Tex. Gen. Laws 1005 (former Texas Revised Civil Statutes art. 3715a deemed repealed as to civil proceedings effective 1983 and as to criminal proceedings effective 1986).

489. *Proposed Rules*, *supra* note 28, at 247. Before the gender-neutral language was added in 1998, the Texas rule was identical to Uniform Rule of Evidence 505 (1974), which modified proposed Federal Rule 506 by adding "accredited Christian Science Practitioner" to the definition of clergyman and by rewording section (c). For cases applying and interpreting the federal common-law privilege, see Russell G. Donaldson, Annotation, *Communications to Clergyman as Privileged in Federal Proceedings*, 118 A.L.R. Fed. 449, 453-54 (1994).

490. This change did not significantly affect Texas practice because no cases had been reported under the statutory privilege. Roy Ray made a similar assertion when the statutory privilege was initially enacted, stating that a de facto privilege already existed in Texas. Ray, *supra* note 486, at 173.

491. A communicant is someone who consults a clergy member in his professional capacity as a spiritual adviser. Tex. R. Evid. 505(a)(2).

492. Tex. R. Evid. 505(a)(1), (b); **Nicholson v. Wittig**, 832 S.W.2d 681, 684-85 (Tex. App.—Houston [1st Dist.] 1992, orig. proceeding).

493. Tex. R. Evid. 505(a)(1); *cf.* **In re Grand Jury Investigation**, 918 F.2d 374, 380 (3d Cir. 1990) (discussing proposed Federal Rule 506); **Eckmann v. Bd. of Educ.**, 106 F.R.D. 70, 72-73 (E.D. Mo. 1985) (Catholic nun acting as plaintiff's spiritual adviser could invoke privilege under both Missouri and federal law).

some self-denominated "ministers."[494] Definitional problems under the rule arise infrequently.[495]

In **Simpson v. Tennant**, the Fourteenth Court of Appeals held that the privilege protects the name of the communicant as well as the entire content of the confidential communication.[496] In this case, a three-year-old child was paralyzed when a set of monkey bars collapsed on her in the church playground.[497] Her parents sued both the church and the church conference. The church's minister, during his deposition, indicated that he had some information about who had set up the monkey bars, but he then invoked the clergyman's privilege.[498] Although there was no evidence that the communicant had, in making his confession, specifically told his minister not to divulge his identity, the court stated that the minister could claim the privilege on behalf of the communicant.[499] In holding that the scope of the privilege encompasses the identity of the communicant, the court relied on Wigmore's four criteria for determining when a communications privilege is justified:

> (1) The communications must originate in a *confidence* that they will not be disclosed; (2) This element of *confidentiality must be essential* to the full and satisfactory maintenance of the relation between the parties; (3) The relation must be one which in the opinion of the community ought to be sedulously *fostered*; and (4) The injury that would inure to the relation by the disclosure of the communications must be *greater than the benefit* thereby gained for the correct disposal of litigation.[500]

The court stated that by adopting Rule 505, the Texas Supreme Court had made it unnecessary to justify the clergy member's privilege on a case-by-case basis, though Wigmore's criteria are useful in examining the scope of even established privileges.[501] In concluding that the communicant would have understood when he made his con-

---

494. *See Proposed Rules*, *supra* note 28, at 247-48 (FED. R. EVID. 506 advisory committee's note, subdiv. (a)).

495. *See generally* Erwin S. Barbre, Annotation, *Who is "Clergyman" or the Like Entitled to Assert Privilege Attaching to Communications to Clergymen or Spiritual Advisors*, 49 A.L.R.3d 1205, 1207-09 (1973) (statutes are not uniform in their descriptions of individuals to whom the communications may be made, and final determinations tend to depend on facts of the individual case). Such problems rarely arise in connection with the solemnization of marriages. *Proposed Rules*, *supra* note 28, at 248 (FED. R. EVID. 506 advisory committee's note, subdiv. (a)); *cf.* TEX. FAM. CODE §2.202 (defining persons authorized to conduct marriage ceremonies). Unlike attorneys, physicians, and psychotherapists, clergy members are generally not licensed. Thus, licensing and certification requirements could not be used as a definitional reference point. *See Proposed Rules*, *supra* note 28, at 248 (FED. R. EVID. 506 advisory committee's note, subdiv. (a)).

496. *See* **Simpson v. Tennant**, 871 S.W.2d 301, 302-03 (Tex. App.—Houston [14th Dist.] 1994, orig. proceeding) (rejecting relators' contention that "the privilege protects only the divulgence of the *substance* of the confidential communications made to a clergyman, not the *identity* of the communicant").

497. *Id.* at 302.

498. *Id.*

499. *Id.* at 305-06; *see* TEX. R. EVID. 505(c).

500. **Simpson**, 871 S.W.2d at 306 (quoting 8 WIGMORE, *supra* note 6, §2285 at 527); *accord* **In re Grand Jury Investigation**, 918 F.2d 374, 383-84 (3d Cir. 1990).

501. **Simpson**, 871 S.W.2d at 306.

fession that his identity would not be revealed, the court noted that people take for granted the fact that they have the right to talk to their ministers in complete confidence and that "it is essential that the person seeking moral and spiritual guidance feels assured from the outset that whatever he may say will be forever kept confidential."[502] The court was not persuaded by the analogy to the attorney-client privilege, in which the client's identity is usually not privileged.[503] First, a person seeking advice from an attorney does not usually expect that his identity will be protected from disclosure.[504] Second, people do not talk with a minister to obtain representation in a public forum, as they do with attorneys, but rather to seek spiritual absolution as an end in itself.[505] Third, in this case revealing the communicant's name would reveal the content of his privileged communication.[506] Finally, the court noted that the clergy-communicant privilege in Texas is broader in scope than many other states' analogous privileges and contains no express exceptions to its coverage.[507]

Communications do not need to be penitential to qualify for the privilege's protection.[508] As long as the person makes the communication in confidence[509] to a person acting in a professional capacity as a spiritual adviser, the rule shields it from dis-

---

502. *Id.* at 306-07.

503. *Id.* at 309.

504. *Id.* The court noted that a legal client "typically approaches an attorney in anticipation of judicial proceedings where it is highly likely that his identity will be discoverable at some point in the litigation process." *Id.*

505. *Id.*

506. *Id.* at 309-10. The court of appeals held that, from the known facts, the trial court could have inferred that the communicant was either directly or indirectly implicated in the events leading up to the playground accident. *Id.* at 309.

507. *Id.* at 310.

508. *Easley v. State*, 837 S.W.2d 854, 856 (Tex. App.—Austin 1992, no pet.). Some states, with a narrower privilege than Texas has, limit the privilege to penitential communications. *See id.*; *see, e.g.*, CAL. EVID. CODE §1032 ("As used in this article, 'penitential communication' means a communication made in confidence, in the presence of no third person so far as the penitent is aware, to a member of the clergy who, in the course of the discipline or practice of the clergy member's church, denomination, or organization, is authorized or accustomed to hear those communications and, under the discipline or tenets of his or her church, denomination, or organization, has a duty to keep those communications secret."); KAN. STAT. ANN. §60-429(a)(5) ("'penitential communication' means any communication between a penitent and a regular or duly ordained minister of religion which the penitent intends shall be kept secret and confidential and which pertains to advice or assistance in determining or discharging the penitent's moral obligations, or to obtaining God's mercy or forgiveness for past culpable conduct"). In *Gonzalez v. State*, the court held that the defendant's confession to a California pastor in California was governed by California law on penitential communications because California had the most significant relationship to the communication. 45 S.W.3d 101, 106 (Tex. Crim. App. 2001). The communication was thus not privileged in the Texas trial because the pastor had warned the defendant in advance that he did not intend to keep it confidential. *Id.* Normally, the law of the jurisdiction in which the communication took place has the most significant relationship to the communication and controls whether a particular privilege applies. Refer to notes 46-50 *supra* and accompanying text.

509. *See* TEX. R. EVID. 505(a)(3) ("A communication is 'confidential' if made privately and not intended for further disclosure except to other persons present to further the purpose of the communication."); *cf. United States v. Webb*, 615 F.2d 828, 828 (9th Cir. 1980) (confession to minister in security officer's presence destroyed confidentiality necessary to invoke privilege under federal law); *United States v. Wells*, 446 F.2d 2, 4 (2d Cir. 1971) (letter from defendant to priest was not privileged under federal law because there was no indication it was intended to be confidential). The definition of "confidential" in Rule 505(a)(3) is broad enough to cover situations such as joint consultations with a minister by spouses. This is analogous to group therapy.

closure.[510] Thus, the privilege covers marital counseling and advice on other spiritual or moral matters.[511] The definition of "confidential" logically covers both individual counseling and "group therapy" situations.[512] However, when the meeting is not about the "state of the speaker's soul" but rather is a "disciplinary intervention" with fellow clergy members, the communications are not intended to be confidential and thus are not protected.[513] For communications to be protected, clergy members must be acting in their professional capacity as a spiritual adviser, not in an administrative capacity.[514]

The communicant, his guardian or conservator, or his personal representative (if he is deceased) may claim the privilege.[515] In addition, the clergy member may claim it on behalf of the communicant.[516]

In another case, **Nicholson v. Wittig**, the First Court of Appeals held that confidential communications to a clergy member may be protected under the rule even when made in front of other persons who are not directly involved in the counseling relationship.[517] The court also held that the clergy-communicant privilege focuses on

---

510. TEX. R. EVID. 505(b); *see also* **Snyder v. State**, 68 S.W.3d 671, 674-76 (Tex. App.—El Paso 2000, pet. ref'd) (defendant's statements to police sergeant, who was also youth director at defendant's church, were not privileged under rule; officer was not acting as clergy member when he interviewed defendant at police station, and defendant offered no evidence that he reasonably believed sergeant was acting as clergy member during interview).

511. *See Proposed Rules, supra* note 28, at 248 (FED. R. EVID. 506 advisory committee's note, subdiv. (b)). Matters of political or legal concern do not fall within the privilege. *Proposed Rules, supra* note 28, at 248 (FED. R. EVID. 506 advisory committee's note, subdiv. (b)); *see, e.g.,* **United States v. Dube**, 820 F.2d 886, 889-90 (7th Cir. 1987) (privilege did not apply to defendant's conversations with minister about income-tax law). *See generally* Annotation, *Matters to Which the Privilege Covering Communications to Clergyman or Spiritual Adviser Extends*, 71 A.L.R.3d 794, 804-35 (1976) (thoroughly developing the nature and scope of the clergyman's privilege).

512. *See* **In re Grand Jury Investigation**, 918 F.2d 374, 384 (3d Cir. 1990) (clergy-communicant privilege should be expansively applied to cover family-counseling sessions with multiple parties unrelated by blood or marriage if the presence of each person was essential to and in furtherance of the communications to the parties).

513. **Kos v. State**, 15 S.W.3d 633, 639-40 (Tex. App.—Dallas 2000, pet. ref'd). In *Kos*, the Dallas Court of Appeals upheld the trial court's ruling that Rule 505 did not apply to communications between the defendant-priest charged with sexual assault of child and a fellow priest who called a meeting to confront the defendant about the abuse allegations. *Id.* The statements "were not made in an effort to obtain some sort of spiritual advice or guidance." *Id.* at 640. Because the communications were not motivated by any religious or spiritual considerations, Rule 505 did not apply. *Kos*, 15 S.W.3d at 640.

514. *Id.* at 639 n.4.

515. TEX. R. EVID. 505(c); *see* **Nicholson v. Wittig**, 832 S.W.2d 681, 685 (Tex. App.—Houston [1st Dist.] 1992, orig. proceeding) (communicator has right to prevent disclosure by clergyman).

516. TEX. R. EVID. 505(c); *cf.* **In re Grand Jury Investigation**, 918 F.2d at 385 n.15 (clergy can invoke privilege on communicant's behalf); **Eckmann v. Bd. of Educ.**, 106 F.R.D. 70, 72-73 (E.D. Mo. 1985) (Catholic nun acting as plaintiff's spiritual adviser could invoke privilege on plaintiff's behalf). Before the Rules, the communicant was required to invoke the privilege. Act approved June 12, 1967, 60th Leg., ch. 435, §1, 1967 Tex. Gen. Laws 1005 (former Texas Revised Civil Statutes art. 3715a deemed repealed as to civil proceedings effective 1983 and as to criminal proceedings effective 1986). Now, the clergy member is presumed to have the authority to invoke the privilege on the communicant's behalf. TEX. R. EVID. 505(c).

517. *See* **Nicholson**, 832 S.W.2d at 685. The plaintiff in this wrongful-death case alleged that the defendants (doctors and hospital) had negligently delayed in treating her deceased husband's ruptured abdominal aneurysm. *Id.* at 682. The defendants wanted to take the deposition of the hospital chaplain who had met with the plaintiff when her husband was admitted to the emergency room. *See id.* at 683. The court of appeals upheld the trial court's refusal to permit the chaplain's deposition on what the plaintiff had told him about the deceased's care and treatment because that communication was within the scope of Rule 505. **Nicholson**, 832 S.W.2d at 688. The defendants argued that the conversation was not confidential because it took place in a hospital waiting room where a doctor

the societal importance of the counseling opportunity rather than the content of the specific communication.[518] Thus, a clergy member cannot divulge those portions of a conversation that he unilaterally deems were made outside his capacity as a spiritual adviser. Nor does the rule require that the communicant be the person who seeks out the clergy member for spiritual advice.[519]

Although written in absolute terms,[520] the privilege may be pierced in two specific situations. First, the Family Code provides that in proceedings involving child abuse or neglect, the court will recognize no claims of privilege except attorney-client privilege.[521] The Texas Attorney General declared that the Family Code provision takes precedence over the general evidentiary privilege[522] and requires the clergy member to not only testify about communications of child abuse or neglect but also report any suspected abuse to authorities.[523] Second, under Rule 511, when a person calls a clergy member to testify as a character witness, that person waives any privilege for confidential communications that are pertinent to the character trait to which the clergy member testifies.[524]

RULE 506

POLITICAL VOTE PRIVILEGE

A person has a privilege to refuse to disclose the person's vote at a political election conducted by secret ballot unless the vote was cast illegally.

---

and nurses were intermittently present. *Id.* at 685. The court noted, however, that hospital settings rarely provide complete privacy, and common experience shows that clergy members normally provide assistance and comfort to family members in public waiting rooms while hospital personnel periodically bring news of the patient's condition. *Id.* Under such circumstances, it seems appropriate that the privilege applies despite the lack of complete privacy. *But see id.* at 691 (O'Connor, J., dissenting) (proper solution to the lack of privacy is to temporarily suspend conversation when a doctor or a nurse is present, and plaintiff's communication to the chaplain was merely a discussion of her husband's medical condition and treatment, not information that she intended to be confidential).

518. *Id.* at 686-87. *But see id.* at 690 (O'Connor, J., dissenting) (because there was no showing that plaintiff's statements were motivated by spiritual considerations, privilege did not apply: "[t]he mere fact that a communication was made to a minister is not enough to invoke the privilege").

519. *Id.* at 687. The court rejected the defendant's argument that because the hospital summoned the chaplain to provide comfort and counsel to the patient's wife, no privilege attached to her communications with him. *Id.*

520. *See id.* at 686 (Rule 505 contains no exceptions, unlike the attorney-client privilege and the privileges protecting communications between patients and their physicians or mental-health professionals).

521. TEX. FAM. CODE §261.202 ("In a proceeding regarding the abuse or neglect of a child, evidence may not be excluded on the ground of privileged communication except in the case of communications between an attorney and client."); *see* **Bordman v. State**, 56 S.W.3d 63, 67-68 (Tex. App.—Houston [14th Dist.] 2001, pet. ref'd) (§261.202 creates a statutory exception to the clergy-communication privilege in child-abuse cases).

522. Tex. Att'y Gen. Op. No. JM-342 (1985).

523. *Id.*; *see also* TEX. HEALTH & SAFETY CODE §260A.010 (report that a resident of a nursing facility has been abused, neglected, or exploited cannot be excluded on grounds of privilege, except for attorney-client privilege); TEX. HUM. RES. CODE §48.051(b) & (c) (any person with knowledge of suspected or known abuse or neglect of an elderly person or a person with a disability must report that information, regardless of any privilege). *See generally* David T. Fenton, *Texas' Clergyman-Penitent Privilege and the Duty to Report Suspected Child Abuse*, 38 BAYLOR L. REV. 231, 238-48 (1986) (discussing Tex. Att'y Gen. Op. No. JM-342 (1985) and arguing that the opinion is correct, but on different grounds). Refer to notes 693-694 *infra* and accompanying text.

524. TEX. R. EVID. 511(a)(2). Refer to note 934 *infra* and accompanying text.

COMMENTARY ON RULE 506

Secrecy in voting is essential to a democracy's vitality because it allows voters to freely exercise their right to vote.[525] Rule 506 recognizes the importance of the secret ballot by protecting voters from having to disclose how they voted.[526] "[C]ertain 'public interests [exist, however,] which outweigh the individual's right to have his ballot kept secret.'"[527] Therefore, Rule 506 grants no privilege to an individual whose vote was cast illegally.[528]

RULE 507
TRADE SECRETS PRIVILEGE

(a) General Rule. A person has a privilege to refuse to disclose and to prevent other persons from disclosing a trade secret owned by the person, unless the court finds that nondisclosure will tend to conceal fraud or otherwise work injustice.

(b) Who May Claim. The privilege may be claimed by the person who owns the trade secret or the person's agent or employee.

(c) Protective Measure. If a court orders a person to disclose a trade secret, it must take any protective measure required by the interests of the privilege holder and the parties and to further justice.

COMMENTARY ON RULE 507

The right to protect trade secrets from unnecessary disclosure fosters technological innovation and advances in business practices.[529] Because the demands of litigation sometimes outweigh the need for secrecy, courts seek to balance these competing

---

525. *See **United States v. Exec. Comm. of Democratic Party**,* 254 F. Supp. 543, 546 (N.D. Ala. 1966) ("The secrecy of the ballot is one of the fundamental civil liberties upon which a democracy must rely most heavily in order for it to survive."); Charles B. Nutting, *Freedom of Silence: Constitutional Protection Against Governmental Intrusions in Political Affairs,* 47 MICH. L. REV. 181, 191-95 (1948) (secrecy helps ensure honest elections, free from various forms of corrupt influence).

526. TEX. R. EVID. 506. The rule is rarely invoked in practice.

527. ***Oliphint v. Christy**,* 157 Tex. 1, 9, 299 S.W.2d 933, 939 (1957) (quoting ***Sewell v. Chambers**,* 209 S.W.2d 363, 367 (Tex. Civ. App.—Fort Worth 1948, no writ)).

528. *See **Simmons v. Jones**,* 838 S.W.2d 298, 300 (Tex. App.—El Paso 1992, no writ) ("[L]egal voters may not be compelled to disclose how they voted, but … it does not follow that illegal voters enjoy the same privilege."). This rule codifies earlier Texas law. *See* TEX. ELEC. CODE §221.009(a) (providing for compelled disclosure of candidates for whom fraudulent or illegal ballots were cast). In ***Oliphint**,* the court noted that "the privilege of nondisclosure belongs only to the legal voter and the individual who votes illegally cannot be considered a 'voter' for any purpose." 157 Tex. at 9, 299 S.W.2d at 939. The illegal voter may still be in a position to assert his privilege against self-incrimination. *Id.* It is the act of voting illegally that is incriminating. Thus, once a witness admits to having voted illegally, he may be forced to disclose for whom he cast his ballot. *Id.*

529. *See* 2 WEINSTEIN & BERGER, *supra* note 29, ¶508[02], at 508-5; 8 WIGMORE, *supra* note 6, §2212(3), at 155. *See generally* McFall & Little, *supra* note 10, at 481-82 (discussing the purpose and limitations of the trade-secret privilege).

interests.[530] The result, both in Texas[531] and elsewhere,[532] is a qualified trade-secret privilege.[533] Rule 507 continues this tradition, protecting trade secrets from disclosure "unless the court finds that nondisclosure will tend to conceal fraud or otherwise work injustice."[534] Traditionally, the privilege has been "sparingly permitted" and cannot prevail "against [the] demand for the truth in a court of justice."[535]

Although the rule does not define trade secrets, the term has been interpreted to include information that gives its owner an improved competitive position and whose value is substantially enhanced by secrecy.[536] Texas civil courts frequently refer to the

---

530. *See Fed. Open Mkt. Comm. v. Merrill*, 443 U.S. 340, 362 (1979) (courts weigh claim to privacy against need for disclosure). As noted by the Texas Supreme Court: "Our trade secret privilege seeks to accommodate two competing interests. First, it recognizes that trade secrets are an important property interest, worthy of protection. Second, it recognizes the importance we place on fair adjudication of lawsuits." *In re Cont'l Gen. Tire, Inc.*, 979 S.W.2d 609, 612 (Tex. 1998); *accord In re Leviton Mfg. Co.*, 1 S.W.3d 898, 902 (Tex. App.—Waco 1999, orig. proceeding).

　　In *In re Continental General Tire*, the products-liability plaintiff who claimed to have been injured by a failed tire requested the tire company's chemical formula for a rubber compound used in manufacturing the tires. 979 S.W.2d at 610. The court held that Rule 507 required the plaintiff to show much more than mere relevance; it "clearly contemplates a heightened burden for obtaining trade secret information." *In re Cont'l Gen. Tire*, 979 S.W.2d at 613-14. The court rejected the defendant's argument that a protective order can never protect trade secrets because of the risk of disclosure, but also stated that a party's willingness to produce some trade-secret material under a protective order does not waive Rule 507 protection for other such information. *Id.* at 614.

531. *See In re Bridgestone/Firestone, Inc.*, 106 S.W.3d 730, 732 (Tex. 2003) (court determines whether information is necessary for fair adjudication by weighing requesting party's need for information against potential harm to resisting party); *In re Cont'l Gen. Tire*, 979 S.W.2d at 613 (same); *Garcia v. Peeples*, 734 S.W.2d 343, 346-48 (Tex. 1987) (orig. proceeding) (Texas discovery rules are tailored to prevent public dissemination of trade secrets and promote the importance of protective orders to safeguard such secrets, but those interests must be balanced against the need for full discovery and shared information); *Automatic Drilling Machs., Inc. v. Miller*, 515 S.W.2d 256, 259 (Tex. 1974) (court should weigh the need for the discovery of trade secrets and confidential information against the desirability of preserving the secrecy of the material in question). *See generally* Fred Hagans, *Confidentiality Agreements and Orders: When Should Discoverable Materials Be Kept Secret?*, 31 S. Tex. L. Rev. 455, 459-60 (1990) (discussing the use of protective orders to prevent discovery and dissemination of trade secrets).

532. *See Goodyear Tire & Rubber Co. v. Cooey*, 359 So. 2d 1200, 1202 (Fla. Dist. Ct. App. 1978) (facts of each case govern a court's decision to compel disclosure of trade secrets); *Harrington Mfg. Co. v. Powell Mfg. Co.*, 216 S.E.2d 379, 381 (N.C. Ct. App. 1975) ("[P]rotective orders may be issued to prevent disclosure of trade secrets for good cause shown ...."); *Loveall v. Am. Honda Motor Co.*, 694 S.W.2d 937, 939 (Tenn. 1985) (courts may choose to protect trade secrets for good cause shown).

533. This conflict usually arises during pretrial discovery. *See* Tex. R. Civ. P. 192.4 (court should protect a party during the discovery process from undue burden, unnecessary expense, or harassment); *Automatic Drilling Machs.*, 515 S.W.2d at 259 (witness may be required to disclose a trade secret if the information sought is material and is unavailable from another source); *see, e.g., Jampole v. Touchy*, 673 S.W.2d 569, 574 (Tex. 1984) (while a "valid proprietary interest" may justify denying discovery to a direct competitor, plaintiff was not such a person, and a protective order could safeguard its proprietary interest), *disapproved on other grounds*, *Walker v. Packer*, 827 S.W.2d 833 (Tex. 1992). However, the conflict occasionally emerges at trial. 2 LOUISELL & MUELLER, *supra* note 69, §222, at 923; *cf. Segal Lock & Hardware Co. v. Fed. Trade Comm'n*, 143 F.2d 935, 937 (2d Cir. 1944) (conflict over the privilege not to reveal a trade secret arose during hearings held before a trial examiner).

534. Tex. R. Evid. 507(a).

535. *Lehnhard v. Moore*, 401 S.W.2d 232, 235 (Tex. 1966) (orig. proceeding) (quoting 8 WIGMORE *supra* note 6, §§2212, 2286); *accord Chapa v. Garcia*, 848 S.W.2d 667, 670-71 (Tex. 1992) (orig. proceeding) (Doggett, J., concurring). The privilege arises more often in discovery than during trial. See *O'Connor's Texas Rules * Civil Trials* (2017), "Certain trade secrets," ch. 6-B, §2.24, p. 542.

536. *See* 3 MICHAEL H. GRAHAM, HANDBOOK OF FEDERAL EVIDENCE §508:1, at 1238 (7th ed. 2012) (discussing and defining "trade secret").

definition of trade secrets set forth in the Restatement of Torts[537] or in the Restatement (Third) of Unfair Competition.[538] The Texas Uniform Trade Secrets Act[539] defines the term "trade secret" as "information, including business, scientific, technical, economic, or engineering information, and any formula, design, prototype, pattern, plan, compilation, program device, program, code, device, method, technique, process, procedure, financial data, or list of actual or potential customers or suppliers" that (1) the owner of the trade secret has taken reasonable measures to keep secret and (2) derives actual or potential independent economic value from its secrecy (i.e., it is not generally known or ascertainable through proper means by another person who can obtain economic value from the information's disclosure or use).[540] The information can be considered a trade secret whether it is tangible or not and regardless of whether or how it is stored, compiled, or memorialized physically, electronically, graphically, photographically, or in writing.[541] In criminal cases, the Penal Code defines a trade secret as "the whole or any part of any scientific or technical information, design, process, procedure, formula, or improvement that has value and that the owner has taken measures to prevent from becoming available to persons other than those selected by the owner to have access for limited purposes."[542] Limited disclosure to others who have also pledged their secrecy does not destroy the trade secret's status.[543]

---

537. *See Comput. Assocs. Int'l, Inc. v. Altai, Inc.*, 918 S.W.2d 453, 455 (Tex. 1996); *Luccous v. J.C. Kinley Co.*, 376 S.W.2d 336, 338 (Tex. 1964); *Hyde Corp. v. Huffines*, 158 Tex. 566, 586, 314 S.W.2d 763, 776 (1958) (op. on reh'g). The Restatement of Torts provides the following definition:

> A trade secret may consist of any formula, pattern, device or compilation of information which is used in one's business, and which gives him an opportunity to obtain an advantage over competitors who do not know or use it. It may be a formula for a chemical compound, a process of manufacturing, treating or preserving materials, a pattern for a machine or other device, or a list of customers …. A trade secret is a process or device for continuous use in the operation of the business. Generally it relates to the production of goods, as, for example, a machine or formula for the production of an article.

RESTATEMENT OF TORTS §757, cmt. b (1939).

538. *See In re Bass*, 113 S.W.3d 735, 739-40 (Tex. 2003) (original 1939 RESTATEMENT OF TORTS §757 was omitted from the RESTATEMENT (SECOND) OF TORTS, but incorporated into the RESTATEMENT (THIRD) OF UNFAIR COMPETITION); *In re XTO Res. I, L.P.*, 248 S.W.3d 898, 901 (Tex. App.—Fort Worth 2008, orig. proceeding) (citing *Bass* and listing six Restatement factors).

539. TEX. CIV. PRAC. & REM. CODE ch. 134A. The Act is intended to provide a uniform framework for actions involving trade-secret misappropriation. *See* Senate Cmte. on State Affairs, Bill Analysis, Tex. S.B. 953, 83rd Leg., R.S. (2013). For a complete discussion of trade-secret misappropriation, see *O'Connor's Texas Causes of Action* (2017), "Trade-Secret Misappropriation," ch. 28, p. 1001.

540. TEX. CIV. PRAC. & REM. CODE §134A.002(6). Section 134A.002(6) was amended in 2017, and the amendments are effective for actions commenced on or after September 1, 2017. H.B. 1995, §§1, 6, 85th Leg., R.S., eff. Sept. 1, 2017. Actions commenced before that date are governed by the former law in effect at that time. *Id.* §6. Although the Act addresses misappropriation of trade secrets, the definition is consistent with the Restatements' definition and should be instructive in cases involving Rule 507.

541. TEX. CIV. PRAC. & REM. CODE §134A.002(6).

542. TEX. PENAL CODE §31.05(a)(4).

543. *Schalk v. State*, 767 S.W.2d 441, 446 (Tex. App.—Dallas 1988), *aff'd*, 823 S.W.2d 633 (Tex. Crim. App. 1991).

The owner of the trade secret, his agent, or his employee may claim the privilege.[544] Of course, the proponent of the privilege must prove that a particular item, formula, or process is a "trade secret" before the privilege applies.[545] A conclusory statement that an item is a trade secret will not invoke the protection of the rule.[546]

Once the party resisting disclosure makes a prima facie showing that a particular item is a trade secret, or if the requesting party concedes that the item is a trade secret,[547] the burden shifts to the requesting party to show that the information is both material and necessary to that party's case.[548] The requesting party must make this showing for each category of trade-secret information sought.[549]

---

544. TEX. R. EVID. 507(b).

545. *In re Cont'l Gen. Tire, Inc.*, 979 S.W.2d 609, 613 (Tex. 1998); *In re Rockafellow*, ___ S.W.3d ___ (Tex. App.—Amarillo 2013, orig. proceeding) (No. 07-12-0372-CV; 4-30-13); *In re Goodyear Tire & Rubber Co.*, 392 S.W.3d 687, 693 (Tex. App.—Dallas 2010, orig. proceeding). In *In re Bass*, the supreme court stated that the six-factor test in the RESTATEMENT OF TORTS §757, cmt. b (1939) sets out relevant, but not dispositive, factors for determining the existence of a trade secret. 113 S.W.3d 735, 739 (Tex. 2003). Those factors are the following: (1) the extent to which the information is known outside of his business, (2) the extent to which it is known by employees and others involved in his business, (3) the extent of the measures taken by him to guard the secrecy of the information, (4) the value of the information to him and to his competitors, (5) the amount of effort or money expended by him in developing the information, and (6) the ease or difficulty with which the information could be properly acquired or duplicated by others. *In re Union Pac. R.R.*, 294 S.W.3d 589, 592 (Tex. 2009) (per curiam); *In re Bass*, 113 S.W.3d at 739; *In re XTO Res. I, L.P.*, 248 S.W.3d 898, 901 (Tex. App.—Fort Worth 2008, orig. proceeding); *see also Chapa v. Garcia*, 848 S.W.2d 667, 668 (Tex. 1992) (orig. proceeding) (parties cannot shield discoverable documents from discovery by placing them in a file with trade secrets). The supreme court also quoted the RESTATEMENT (THIRD) OF UNFAIR COMPETITION §39, cmt. d (1995), which states the following:

> It is not possible to state precise criteria for determining the existence of a trade secret. The status of information claimed as a trade secret must be ascertained through a comparative evaluation of all the relevant factors, including the value, secrecy, and definiteness of the information as well as the nature of the defendant's misconduct.

In re Bass, 113 S.W.3d at 739. Thus, the party claiming a trade secret is not required to satisfy all six of these factors, and other circumstances may also be relevant in deciding the trade-secret issue. *Id.* at 740; *In re PrairieSmarts LLC*, 421 S.W.3d 296, 304 (Tex. App.—Fort Worth 2014, orig. proceeding); *see In re Rockafellow*, ___ S.W.3d at ___.

546. *See In re Lowe's Cos.*, 134 S.W.3d 876, 879 (Tex. App.—Houston [14th Dist.] 2004, orig. proceeding) (a party's or expert's conclusory opinion that "information is a trade secret or is not used industry-wide, or a party's mere desire to avoid disclosing information to others" does not establish existence of a trade secret); *Humphreys v. Caldwell*, 881 S.W.2d 940, 946 (Tex. App.—Corpus Christi 1994, orig. proceeding) (party must show "expectation of privacy beyond merely conclusory allegations that ... such information [is] private and [to be kept] confidential"), *mand. granted*, 888 S.W.2d 469 (Tex. 1994).

547. *In re Valero Refining-Tex., LP*, 415 S.W.3d 567, 570 (Tex. App.—Houston [1st Dist.] 2013, orig. proceeding); *see In re Cont'l Gen. Tire*, 979 S.W.2d at 615.

548. *See In re Cont'l Gen. Tire*, 979 S.W.2d at 613; *In re PrairieSmarts*, 421 S.W.3d at 305; *In re Valero Refining*, 415 S.W.3d at 570; *see, e.g.*, *In re Cont'l Tire N. Am., Inc.*, 74 S.W.3d 884, 885-86 (Tex. App.—Eastland 2002, orig. proceeding) (plaintiff had not established that she was entitled to discover trade secrets merely by making allegation that the information is "reasonably calculated" to lead to admissible evidence).

In deciding whether the information is both "material" and "necessary" to the requesting party's case, the supreme court has stated that the requesting party must first show that a claim or defense exists to which the information would be material. *In re Bass*, 113 S.W.3d at 743. Next, the requesting party must show that the information is actually "necessary" to a fair adjudication of its claims; the mere possibility of unfairness is not enough to warrant disclosure. *In re Union Pac. R.R.*, 294 S.W.3d at 592; *In re Bridgestone/Firestone, Inc.*, 106 S.W.3d 730, 732-33 (Tex. 2003); *In re PrairieSmarts*, 421 S.W.3d at 305; *In re Valero Refining*, 415 S.W.3d at 570; *see John Paul Mitchell Sys. v. Randalls Food Mkts., Inc.*, 17 S.W.3d 721, 739 (Tex. App.—Austin 2000, pet. denied) (party requesting access to trade secrets "must describe with particularity how the protected information is required to reach conclusions in the case"; "information must be necessary, not merely useful"); *In re Leviton Mfg. Co.*, 1 S.W.3d 898, 902-03

If the court determines that disclosure is necessary, the rule directs the court to take protective measures "required by the interests of the privilege holder and the parties and to further justice."[550] Examples of such protective measures include taking testimony in camera,[551] sealing the testimony,[552] ordering those involved in the litigation not to make further disclosure without court approval,[553] limiting access to the trade-secret information to only the attorneys and their experts,[554] and issuing nondisclosure orders with terms agreed to by the parties.[555] By judicious use of various protective devices,[556] a court can satisfy the litigant's need for information necessary to develop its case while protecting the owner of the trade secret from harm caused by unnecessary disclosure.[557]

(Tex. App.—Waco 1999, orig. proceeding) ("showing of relevance alone is not adequate"; party seeking trade-secret information did not carry burden of showing that "the information was necessary to a fair adjudication of the claim"); *see also In re Bridgestone/Firestone*, 106 S.W.3d at 736 (O'Neill & Schneider, JJ., concurring) ("[T]rade secret information is generally discoverable when not allowing discovery would significantly impair a party's ability to establish or rebut a material element of a claim or defense. A party's ability is significantly impaired when the information is unavailable from any other source and no adequate alternative means of proof exist. Discovery is also necessary when the party seeking trade secret information could not knowledgeably cross-examine opposing witnesses without it, or when the party's experts would be unable to formulate opinions supported by an adequate factual foundation. On the other hand, information that is merely cumulative is not necessary for a fair adjudication.").

549. *In re PrairieSmarts*, 421 S.W.3d at 305; *In re Goodyear*, 392 S.W.3d at 696.

550. Tex. R. Evid. 507(c); *see In re Cont'l Gen. Tire*, 979 S.W.2d at 613; *In re Valero Refining*, 415 S.W.3d at 571. To determine whether disclosure is necessary and, if so, what protective measures should be taken, the court usually must review the item in camera. *See, e.g., In re M-I L.L.C.*, 505 S.W.3d 569, 579 (Tex. 2016) (orig. proceeding) (trial court abused discretion in ordering disclosure of affidavit that allegedly contained trade secrets without first reviewing it in camera).

551. Tex. Civ. Prac. & Rem. Code §134A.006(a); *see John T. Lloyd Labs., Inc. v. Lloyd Bros. Pharmacists*, 131 F.2d 703, 707 (6th Cir. 1942).

552. Tex. Civ. Prac. & Rem. Code §134A.006(a); *see Am. Dirigold Corp. v. Dirigold Metals Corp.*, 104 F.2d 863, 865 (6th Cir. 1939).

553. Tex. Civ. Prac. & Rem. Code §134A.006(a); *see Paul v. Sinnott*, 217 F. Supp. 84, 86 (W.D. Pa. 1963).

554. Tex. Civ. Prac. & Rem. Code §134A.006(a); *see In re Cont'l Gen. Tire*, 979 S.W.2d at 613 & n.3. An order that restricts those who can view the trade secrets, by itself, has generally been held to be insufficient to ensure the order will not violate the trade-secret privilege. *See In re Union Pac. R.R.*, 294 S.W.3d 589, 593 (Tex. 2009); *In re Waste Mgmt.*, 392 S.W.3d 861, 869 (Tex. App.—Texarkana 2013, orig. proceeding).

555. *See In re Cont'l Gen. Tire*, 979 S.W.2d at 613 & n.3.

556. *See* Tex. Civ. Prac. & Rem. Code §134A.006(a) (presumption in favor of granting protective order to preserve secrecy of trade secrets in misappropriation cases). *See generally* C.T. Foster, Annotation, *In Camera Trial or Hearing and Other Procedures to Safeguard Trade Secret or the Like Against Undue Disclosure in Course of Civil Action Involving Such Secret*, 62 A.L.R.2d 509, 516-32 (1958) (methods are available for the court to safeguard trade secrets against undue disclosure in the course of litigation, including permitting off-the-record disclosure to the court, omitting details from the record, omitting details of the secret from the published opinion, and sealing or impounding in camera evidence).

557. *See In re Cont'l Gen. Tire*, 979 S.W.2d at 614-15 (rejecting "all or nothing" approach of either not allowing any discovery of trade secrets or requiring full disclosure under Rule 507, but concluding that plaintiff had not carried its burden of demonstrating that the trade-secret information was necessary for a fair trial). In misappropriation cases, there is a presumption in favor of allowing a party to participate and assist counsel with the party's case. Tex. Civ. Prac. & Rem. Code §134A.006(b). The statute creates a balancing test for courts to use in considering whether countervailing interests overcome that presumption and allow the court to exclude a party or its representative or limit the party's access to the alleged trade secret. *See id.* The factors the court can consider are the following: (1) the value of the alleged trade secret, (2) the competitive harm the owner would suffer if the alleged trade secret were disseminated to the other party, (3) whether the owner is alleging that the alleged trade secret is already in the other party's possession, (4) whether a party's representative acts as a competitive decision-maker, (5) the im-

RULE 508
INFORMER'S IDENTITY PRIVILEGE

(a) General Rule. The United States, a state, or a subdivision of either has a privilege to refuse to disclose a person's identity if:

(1) the person has furnished information to a law enforcement officer or a member of a legislative committee or its staff conducting an investigation of a possible violation of law; and

(2) the information relates to or assists in the investigation.

(b) Who May Claim. The privilege may be claimed by an appropriate representative of the public entity to which the informer furnished the information. The court in a criminal case must reject the privilege claim if the state objects.

(c) Exceptions.

(1) *Voluntary Disclosure; Informer a Witness.* This privilege does not apply if:

(A) the informer's identity or the informer's interest in the communication's subject matter has been disclosed—by a privilege holder or the informer's own action—to a person who would have cause to resent the communication; or

(B) the informer appears as a witness for the public entity.

(2) *Testimony About the Merits.*

(A) *Criminal Case.* In a criminal case, this privilege does not apply if the court finds a reasonable probability exists that the informer can give testimony necessary to a fair determination of guilt or innocence. If the court so finds and the public entity elects not to disclose the informer's identity:

(i) on the defendant's motion, the court must dismiss the charges to which the testimony would relate; or

(ii) on its own motion, the court may dismiss the charges to which the testimony would relate.

(B) *Certain Civil Cases.* In a civil case in which the public entity is a party, this privilege does not apply if the court finds a reasonable probability exists that the informer can give testimony necessary to a fair determination of a material issue on the merits. If the court so finds and the public entity elects not to disclose the informer's identity, the court may make any order that justice requires.

---

pairment to a party's defense if its access to the alleged trade secret were limited, (6) whether a party or its representative possesses specialized expertise that would not be available to a party's outside expert, and (7) the stage of the action. *Id.* Section 134A.006(b) is effective for actions commenced on or after September 1, 2017. H.B. 1995, §§5, 6, 85th Leg., R.S., eff. Sept. 1, 2017.

(C) *Procedures.*

(i) If it appears that an informer may be able to give the testimony required to invoke this exception and the public entity claims the privilege, the court must give the public entity an opportunity to show in camera facts relevant to determining whether this exception is met. The showing should ordinarily be made by affidavits, but the court may take testimony if it finds the matter cannot be satisfactorily resolved by affidavits.

(ii) No counsel or party may attend the in camera showing.

(iii) The court must seal and preserve for appeal evidence submitted under this subparagraph (2)(C). The evidence must not otherwise be revealed without the public entity's consent.

(3) *Legality of Obtaining Evidence.*

(A) *Court May Order Disclosure.* The court may order the public entity to disclose an informer's identity if:

(i) information from an informer is relied on to establish the legality of the means by which evidence was obtained; and

(ii) the court is not satisfied that the information was received from an informer reasonably believed to be reliable or credible.

(B) *Procedures.*

(i) On the public entity's request, the court must order the disclosure be made in camera.

(ii) No counsel or party may attend the in camera disclosure.

(iii) If the informer's identity is disclosed in camera, the court must seal and preserve for appeal the record of the in camera proceeding. The record of the in camera proceeding must not otherwise be revealed without the public entity's consent.

COMMENTARY ON RULE 508

A. Rule 508(a) & (b): The Informer's Privilege

The use of informers is a common law-enforcement technique. Without the promise of anonymity, however, both the ordinary citizen and the paid informer are less likely to communicate their knowledge of the commission of crimes to law-enforcement officials for fear of retaliation.[558] Recognizing the role of informers in effective law en-

---

558. ***Dole v. Local 1942, Int'l Bhd. of Elec. Workers***, 870 F.2d 368, 372 (7th Cir. 1989); *see **United States v. Herrero***, 893 F.2d 1512, 1525 (7th Cir. 1990).

forcement,[559] Texas Rule 508 provides a qualified privilege against the compelled disclosure of an informer's identity.[560] Questions about the application of this privilege most frequently arise in the criminal arena,[561] but the issue does appear in a civil context.[562] For example, in one Texas Supreme Court decision, the privilege was invoked by the State in an investigation under the Texas Free Enterprise and Antitrust Act.[563] While the consequences of disclosure are generally not as drastic in civil cases as in criminal cases, in which government informers are sometimes murdered, "the likelihood of ostracism, employer retaliation or malicious prosecution suits"[564] may be sufficient to deter an informer unprotected by anonymity.

---

559. *See State v. Lowry*, 802 S.W.2d 669, 673 n.8 (Tex. 1991) (orig. proceeding) ("By protecting the anonymity of consumers who report illegal activity, the privilege encourages people to assist law enforcement officials ....").

560. *See* Tex. R. Evid. 508(a). Rule 508 is a composite of proposed Federal Rule 510 (1972 proposed final draft), 56 F.R.D. 183, 255-56 (1973), and Uniform Rule of Evidence 509 (1974). The language of proposed Federal Rule 510 draws heavily on the leading case of *Roviaro v. United States*, 353 U.S. 53 (1957). Fear of physical reprisal is not required to trigger the privilege. *In re United States*, 565 F.2d 19, 22 (2d Cir. 1977). Courts recognize that retaliation may also take the form of economic duress, blacklisting, or social ostracism. *See id.*

561. 2 LOUISELL & MUELLER, *supra* note 69, §235, at 1073. All but one of the Texas cases that recognized this privilege under the common law were criminal cases. The Texas Court of Criminal Appeals consistently held that an entity does not need to disclose the identity of an informer unless the informer participated in the offense, was present at the time of the offense or the arrest, or was otherwise shown to be a material witness to the transaction or to whether the defendant knowingly committed the act charged. *Rodriguez v. State*, 614 S.W.2d 448, 449 (Tex. Crim. App. [Panel Op.] 1981); *Hardeman v. State*, 552 S.W.2d 433, 439 (Tex. Crim. App. 1977).

562. *See Hobson v. Moore*, 734 S.W.2d 340, 341 (Tex. 1987) (orig. proceeding) (recognizing the informer's privilege in civil litigation); *Hous. Chronicle Publ'g Co. v. City of Hous.*, 531 S.W.2d 177, 187 (Tex. App.—Houston [14th Dist.] 1975) (Open Records Act, now known as the Public Information Act, does not provide a right of access to statements by informers), *writ ref'd n.r.e.*, 536 S.W.2d 559 (Tex. 1976); *cf. Holman v. Cayce*, 873 F.2d 944, 946 (6th Cir. 1989) (informer's privilege applies in civil cases). In federal civil cases, the privilege is most often invoked in actions under the Fair Labor Standards Act of 1938, 29 U.S.C. §201 et seq. *See In re Perez*, 749 F.3d 849, 855-56 (9th Cir. 2014); *Brock v. On Shore Quality Control Specialists, Inc.*, 811 F.2d 282, 283 (5th Cir. 1987). The informer's privilege is also invoked in both public and private antitrust actions. *See, e.g., Westinghouse Elec. Corp. v. City of Burlington*, 351 F.2d 762, 769 (D.C. Cir. 1965) (recognizing the privilege in a private antitrust action); *United States v. Grinnell Corp.*, 30 F.R.D. 358, 362 (D.R.I. 1962) (upholding the privilege in a public antitrust action); *Lowry*, 802 S.W.2d at 673 (asserting the privilege in a state-court antitrust action). The privilege has been invoked in many other types of actions. *See, e.g., Dole*, 870 F.2d at 372 (invoking the privilege in an action protesting a labor-union election); *In re United States*, 565 F.2d at 22-24 (asserting the privilege in an action for civil-rights violations); *Timken Roller Bearing Co. v. United States*, 38 F.R.D. 57, 65-66 (N.D. Ohio 1964) (invoking the privilege in an action for a tax refund); *Bocchicchio v. Curtis Publ'g Co.*, 203 F. Supp. 403, 406-07 (E.D. Pa. 1962) (invoking the privilege in an action for libel). *See generally* Thomas J. Oliver, Annotation, *Application, in Federal Civil Action, of Governmental Privilege of Nondisclosure of Identity of Informer*, 8 A.L.R. FED. 6, 20 (1971) ("[I]t is well established that the qualified privilege against disclosure of the identities and statements of government informers is generally applicable in civil proceedings ...."). The privilege might also be invoked in quasi-criminal proceedings, such as actions under Texas Code of Criminal Procedure chapter 59 for forfeiture.

563. *Lowry*, 802 S.W.2d at 670-71. In this case, the Attorney General sought to protect, under Civil Rule 508, a portion of citizen-complaint letters about insurance practices unless the authors' consent was obtained because the letters identified the authors. *Lowry*, 802 S.W.2d at 673. However, the State did not present affidavits or testimony as a factual basis for the claim that these citizens provided information to law-enforcement officers assisting them in the investigation of a possible violation of the law. *Id.* Because the content of the letters might provide that evidence, the court of appeals ordered the trial court to conduct an in camera review to make this initial determination. *Id.* at 673-74.

564. 2 WEINSTEIN & BERGER, *supra* note 29, ¶510[02], at 510-18.

Rule 508(a) provides that the federal government, a state government, or a subdivision of either may refuse to divulge the identity[565] of a person who furnishes information to a law-enforcement officer or a member of a legislative committee or its staff conducting an investigation of a possible violation of a law when the furnished information relates to or assists in the investigation.[566] This privilege is one of right; thus, the government does not need to make any threshold showing of concern for reprisal, retaliation, or other future consequence in the particular case.

Under Rule 508(b), an appropriate representative of the public entity to which the informer provided the information may claim the privilege in a civil case.[567] The entity, not the individual informer, controls the privilege.[568] In criminal proceedings, however, the entity that originally received the information (e.g., a police department) cannot claim the privilege if the attorney for the State objects.[569]

B. Rule 508(c): Exceptions

The informer's privilege is not absolute. Rule 508(c) requires the court to balance the public's interest in protecting the flow of information to law-enforcement officials against parties' right to prepare their cases adequately.[570] Even if a court requires the disclosure of the informer's identity, the government is under no general obligation to produce the informer at trial.[571] The rule requires only the informer's identity, not his presence. There are three exceptions to the general rule of privilege.

1. Voluntary disclosure. Under Rule 508(c)(1), there is no privilege when (1) the informer's identity or his interest in the communication's subject matter has been volun-

---

565. Only the informer's identity is privileged. The contents of the communication are privileged only to the extent that disclosure would reveal the informer's identity. *See Proposed Rules, supra* note 28, at 257 (Fed. R. Evid. 510 advisory committee's note, subdiv. (a)); *cf. Roviaro*, 353 U.S. at 60 (informer's privilege is limited to disclosures of communications that tend to identify the informer); *Michelson v. Daly*, 590 F. Supp. 261, 266 (N.D.N.Y. 1984) (ordering disclosure of all information furnished by the informer except information that tended to disclose his identity).

566. Tex. R. Evid. 508(a).

567. Tex. R. Evid. 508(b); *see, e.g.,* **Sanders v. State**, 102 S.W.3d 134, 135 (Tex. App.—Amarillo 2002, pet. ref'd) (police officer was a proper "representative of the public entity to which the information was furnished" for purposes of invoking informer's privilege under Rule 508(b)). In a purely private action, effective implementation of the privilege demands that others be considered appropriate representatives. *See Proposed Rules, supra* note 28, at 257 (Fed. R. Evid. 510 advisory committee's note, subdiv. (b)); *see, e.g.,* **Bocchicchio**, 203 F. Supp. at 406-07 (in libel action, police officer who had transmitted information to article's authors was permitted to claim privilege protecting identity of his source of information).

568. *See Roviaro*, 353 U.S. at 59 (although called the informer's privilege, it is government's privilege to withhold informer's identity from disclosure); **Simmons v. City of Racine**, 37 F.3d 325, 328 (7th Cir. 1994) (same); *see, e.g.,* **Brock v. On Shore Quality Control Specialists, Inc.**, 811 F.2d 282, 283 (5th Cir. 1987) (Secretary of Labor may assert the informer's privilege to protect the names of individuals who provided information to the department).

569. Tex. R. Evid. 508(b).

570. In striking this balance, the court should consider various factors, such as the relevance of the informer's information to issues in the case, the significance of the information, the seriousness of the litigation, and other relevant factors. *See* **Westinghouse Elec. Corp. v. City of Burlington**, 351 F.2d 762, 771 (D.C. Cir. 1965).

571. **Ashorn v. State**, 802 S.W.2d 888, 893-94 (Tex. App.—Fort Worth 1991, no pet.); *cf.* **United States v. Turbide**, 558 F.2d 1053, 1060 (2d Cir. 1977) (even if *Roviaro* test is met, government has no burden to produce the informer); **Velarde-Villarreal v. United States**, 354 F.2d 9, 11-12 (9th Cir. 1965) (judge should not use government's inability to produce informer as rationale to dismiss charges even if informer is important in preparation of a defense).

tarily divulged to "a person who would have cause to resent the communication"[572] or (2) the informer appears as a witness for the public entity that has a right to claim the privilege.[573] Disclosure to another law-enforcement agency or other qualified public entity, however, does not destroy the privilege.[574]

2. Testimony about the merits. Under Rule 508(c)(2), a court may require the disclosure of an informer's identity when it reasonably appears that he can give testimony necessary, in a criminal case, to a fair determination of the defendant's guilt or innocence[575] or, in a civil case in which the public entity is a party, to "a fair determination of a material issue on the merits."[576] With most evidentiary privileges, the party who asserts the privilege must prove its existence, scope, and applicability. Here, however, the opponent of the privilege must establish the need for disclosure.[577] The privilege will not yield to a "fishing expedition."[578] Thus, the defendant cannot merely speculate that the informer may help his defense.[579] The defendant must bring evidence supporting that argument[580] but needs to make only a "plausible" showing that the informer could give testimony necessary to a fair determination of guilt or innocence.[581]

---

572. Tex. R. Evid. 508(c)(1)(A); *Roviaro*, 353 U.S. at 60. Either the privilege holder can voluntarily disclose the information or the informer's own action can cause the voluntary disclosure. Tex. R. Evid. 508(c)(1)(A).

573. Tex. R. Evid. 508(c)(1)(B); *see Smith v. State*, 392 S.W.3d 190, 198 (Tex. App.—San Antonio 2012, pet. ref'd); *State v. Sustaita*, 186 S.W.3d 1, 2-3 (Tex. App.—Houston [1st Dist.] 2004, no pet.). If the public entity calls the informer as a witness, the entity cannot claim the privilege to shield the witness's status as an informer, as that status greatly affects his credibility. *See Proposed Rules, supra* note 28, at 257 (Fed. R. Evid. 510 advisory committee's note, subdiv. (c)).

574. *See Proposed Rules, supra* note 28, at 257 (Fed. R. Evid. 510 advisory committee's note, subdiv. (c)).

575. Tex. R. Evid. 508(c)(2)(A); *see Roviaro*, 353 U.S. at 60-61 ("Where the disclosure of an informer's identity, or of the contents of his communication, is relevant and helpful to the defense of an accused, or is essential to a fair determination of a cause, the privilege must give way."); *Dole v. Local 1942, Int'l Bhd. of Elec. Workers*, 870 F.2d 368, 372 (7th Cir. 1989) ("[T]he privilege is qualified; it yields when the identification of the informant or of a communication is essential to a balanced measure of the issues and the fair administration of justice."); *Anderson v. State*, 817 S.W.2d 69, 71-72 (Tex. Crim. App. 1991) ("[Criminal] Rule 508(c)(2) ... requires only that there be a reasonable probability that the informant can give testimony 'necessary to a fair determination of the issues of guilt, innocence.' [A] defendant is only required to make a plausible showing that the informer could give testimony necessary to a fair determination of guilt.").

576. Tex. R. Evid. 508(c)(2)(B).

577. *Dole*, 870 F.2d at 373; *Bodin v. State*, 807 S.W.2d 313, 318 (Tex. Crim. App. 1991); *Haggerty v. State*, 429 S.W.3d 1, 8 (Tex. App.—Houston [14th Dist.] 2013, pet. ref'd); *Thomas v. State*, 417 S.W.3d 89, 91 (Tex. App.—Amarillo 2013, no pet.).

578. *Dole*, 870 F.2d at 373; *see Pickel v. United States*, 746 F.2d 176, 181 (3d Cir. 1984).

579. *Bodin*, 807 S.W.2d at 318; *Haggerty*, 429 S.W.3d at 8; *Thomas*, 417 S.W.3d at 91.

580. *See Bailey v. State*, 804 S.W.2d 226, 230 (Tex. App.—Amarillo 1991, no pet.) (person seeking to overcome a privilege must make a "substantial preliminary showing"). In *Bailey*, the court reasoned the following:

> If the mere allegation of the informant's identity was necessary to determine whether the informant might be able to give the requisite testimony was sufficient, without a preliminary showing that the informant could reasonably be expected to give such testimony, then the identity of the informant would necessarily have to be disclosed in every case.

Id.; see also Smith v. State, 781 S.W.2d 418, 421 (Tex. App.—Houston [1st Dist.] 1989, no pet.) (no in camera hearing is necessary when the accused does not present evidence on motion to reveal the name of an informer).

581. *Bodin*, 807 S.W.2d at 318; *Haggerty*, 429 S.W.3d at 8; *e.g.*, *Anderson v. State*, 817 S.W.2d 69, 72 (Tex. Crim. App. 1991) (defendant in a drug-delivery prosecution made a plausible showing of need for an informer's identity when police officer testified that informer was present when drug delivery was made); *Hernandez v. State*, 956 S.W.2d 699, 702 (Tex. App.—Texarkana 1997, no pet.) (defendant had not produced any evidence to demonstrate that in-

If the defendant does not establish the importance of the informer's testimony, the court does not need to balance the competing interests or conduct an in camera hearing.[582]

Rule 508(c)(2) does not define what type of testimony is material to trigger the disclosure of the informer's identity. The U.S. Supreme Court first announced the applicable standard for criminal cases in *Roviaro v. United States*,[583] outlining several relevant factors for determining whether to disclose an informer's identity.[584] Texas courts have traditionally outlined *Roviaro*'s general balancing analysis as a more precise three-pronged test requiring disclosure if the informer (1) participates in the offense, (2) is present at the time of the offense or arrest, or (3) is a material witness to the transaction or to the defendant's knowing commission of the charged act.[585]

Under earlier Texas law, the informer had to match one of these three categories before a court could compel disclosure.[586] The court of criminal appeals has noted that the wording of Rule 508(c)(2) is broader than that under *Roviaro* or Texas prece-

---

former's testimony would be relevant to defendant's guilt or innocence; "[c]onjecture or speculation is not enough to require the disclosure of the informant; evidence, from any source, is required"); *Murray v. State*, 864 S.W.2d 111, 118 (Tex. App.—Texarkana 1993, pet. ref'd) (trial court properly declined to hold an in camera hearing or to order disclosure of informer's identity when defendant's evidence showed that informer's testimony would have related only to those events that occurred before the offense).

This low evidentiary threshold seems appropriate to trigger either disclosure or an in camera inspection because the party seeking disclosure will rarely know the possible substance of the informer's testimony. *See Hernandez*, 956 S.W.2d at 702 ("The burden is set low so that even if the defendant does not know the nature of the informer's testimony, the defendant may have an opportunity to demonstrate to the court how the informant's testimony may be relevant.").

Merely filing a pro forma pretrial motion to discover the informer's name is not sufficient. *See Bodin*, 807 S.W.2d at 318; *Menefee v. State*, 928 S.W.2d 274, 279 (Tex. App.—Tyler 1996, no pet.); *Brokenberry v. State*, 853 S.W.2d 145, 148 (Tex. App.—Houston [14th Dist.] 1993, pet. ref'd). However, the facts in a sworn affidavit attached to such a motion may be enough to require either disclosure or an in camera hearing. *See Rodriguez v. State*, 870 S.W.2d 597, 600 (Tex. App.—Houston [1st Dist.] 1993, no pet.).

582. *See United States v. Kerris*, 748 F.2d 610, 614 (11th Cir. 1984); *Haggerty*, 429 S.W.3d at 8; *see, e.g., Long v. State*, 137 S.W.3d 726, 733 (Tex. App.—Waco 2004, pet. ref'd) (defendant was not entitled to in camera hearing to determine whether informer could give testimony necessary to a fair determination of defendant's guilt or innocence when informer supplied only information police used to obtain search warrant instead of information that was relied on to convict defendant). Refer to notes 596-599 *infra* and accompanying text.

583. 353 U.S. 53 (1957).

584. Whether the privilege must yield in a particular situation depends on the type of lawsuit and the significance of the informer's testimony under the particular circumstances. As the Supreme Court stated in *Roviaro*:

> We believe that no fixed rule with respect to disclosure is justifiable. The problem is one that calls for balancing the public interest in protecting the flow of information against the individual's right to prepare his defense. Whether a proper balance renders nondisclosure erroneous must depend on the particular circumstances of each case, taking into consideration the crime charged, the possible defenses, the possible significance of the informer's testimony, and other relevant factors.

Id. at 62.

585. *See Bodin*, 807 S.W.2d at 317 (informer's privilege under both the Texas and Federal Rules is based on *Roviaro*); *see also Warford v. Childers*, 642 S.W.2d 63, 66-67 (Tex. App.—Amarillo 1982, no writ) ("It is apparent that the general rule is a recognition of the fact that most informants relay rumor, gossip and street talk of no evidentiary value and the exceptions are designed for the rare case where the informant can give eyewitness testimony about the alleged crime or arrest.").

586. *Bernard v. State*, 566 S.W.2d 575, 577 (Tex. Crim. App. [Panel Op.] 1978).

dent,[587] though the court did not suggest how much broader. In one post-Rules case, a court of appeals, without citing to Rule 508, decided that the State had to disclose the informer's identity when he may have served as the interpreter between the defendant and an undercover police officer.[588] Further, if the informer, though not an actual eyewitness to the offense, was present both before and after the commission of the crime and could presumably identify the person who committed the offense, disclosure of his identity is necessary to a fair determination of the case.[589] If the defendant asserts an entrapment defense, an informer who was present at or a participant in the criminal transaction may be important to a fair determination of that defense.[590] On the other hand, the State does not need to disclose the informer's identity when his testimony is material only to an admissible extraneous offense and not to the charged offense.[591]

Generally, when the informer is a mere "tipster" who conveys information but is not himself a party or witness to the crime, no disclosure is required.[592] Similarly, if the in-

---

587. *Bodin*, 807 S.W.2d at 317-18. In *Bodin*, the court of criminal appeals held that the trial court erred in refusing to conduct a hearing to determine whether the informer's identity should have been disclosed even though the defendant knew a "James," knew where to locate him, and believed that he was the informer. *Id.* at 318. The court concluded that the defendant was entitled to verification of this fact, so that if "James" were the informer, the defendant could pursue an entrapment defense. *Id.*

In *Bridges v. State*, a drug-possession case, the facts were very similar to those in *Bodin*. 909 S.W.2d 151, 158 (Tex. App.—Houston [14th Dist.] 1995, no pet.). However, the appellate court held that the informer's name did not need to be disclosed because the defendant in *Bridges* did not claim an entrapment defense and did not assert that the informer left the drugs at defendant's home. *Id.*

In *Washington v. State*, the court held that the informer's identity did not need to be disclosed when he actively participated in the drug transactions that led to the development of probable cause and the issuance of a search warrant but was not present when the search warrant was executed and the defendant was arrested for possession of drugs. 902 S.W.2d 649, 656-57 (Tex. App.—Houston [14th Dist.] 1995, pet. ref'd). The defendant claimed that he had an alibi at the time of these "controlled buys" and thus the informer had mistaken his identity. *Id.* at 656. However, the charged offense was not the "controlled buys" that the informer had made, but rather the possession of drugs that the police found when they executed the search warrant. *Id.*

588. *Crawford v. State*, 772 S.W.2d 493, 496 (Tex. App.—Houston [14th Dist.] 1989, no pet.) (informer was a material witness to the "transaction" because he was present at and material to preliminary negotiations even though he was not present when the actual offense was committed).

589. *See, e.g., Edmond v. State*, 911 S.W.2d 487, 488 (Tex. App.—Texarkana 1995, no pet.) (reversible error not to disclose the informer's identity when evidence showed that he was in the car when drug deal was made and "he saw the person immediately before and immediately after the transaction, turning his head momentarily so as not to see the actual transaction, as instructed"; his testimony would have been material to prove the identity of the person selling cocaine); *Loving v. State*, 882 S.W.2d 42, 45-46 (Tex. App.—Houston [1st Dist.] 1994, no pet.) (reversible error when trial court determined that disclosure of informer's identity was unnecessary without support of in camera evidence to support finding when evidence showed he was present at the scene of the offense and observed a quantity of drugs immediately before police arrested defendant and seized drugs; trial court's unsupported assertion that "the informant's potential testimony would not significantly aid the defendant" was insufficient).

590. *E.g., Sanchez v. State*, 98 S.W.3d 349, 356 (Tex. App.—Houston [1st Dist.] 2003, pet. ref'd) (when informer witnessed drug transaction and was the only person "who could possibly corroborate" defendant's entrapment defense, trial court erred in overruling motion to disclose).

591. *Martinez v. State*, 782 S.W.2d 262, 263 (Tex. App.—Houston [14th Dist.] 1989, no pet.).

592. *United States v. Bourbon*, 819 F.2d 856, 860 (8th Cir. 1987); *see, e.g., United States v. Hemmer*, 729 F.2d 10, 15 (1st Cir. 1984) (when informer gave hearsay statement and had no personal knowledge of bank-robbery events, no disclosure was required).

In *Appling v. State*, the defendant claimed that he was entitled to the identity of the informer who had tipped off the police that two men were selling a large quantity of liquor out of a pickup truck. 904 S.W.2d 912, 919 (Tex. App.—Corpus Christi 1995, pet. ref'd). The police investigated, detained the defendant, and charged him with theft

former's only information is the name of an eyewitness, the defendant is not entitled to the informer's name unless he has tried and failed to obtain the eyewitness's name from other sources.[593] On the other hand, if the informer is not an eyewitness but provides crucial information to police, such as the hidden location of what the informer says is the murder weapon, the defendant is entitled to a hearing to determine whether this person's testimony is "necessary to a fair determination of guilt or innocence."[594] Although there is no bright-line rule on when an informer's testimony may be necessary for a fair determination of guilt or innocence, the court of criminal appeals has held that the informer's testimony must "significantly" aid the defendant.[595]

If the party seeking disclosure establishes the need for that disclosure, and the public entity invokes the privilege, the judge must provide the entity an in camera opportunity to demonstrate facts pertinent to whether the informer can testify.[596] Although this demonstration is usually done by affidavit, the judge may order that oral testimony be taken.[597] The evidence presented must be sealed and preserved for appeal.[598] No counsel or parties may attend the in camera showing.[599] In a civil proceeding, if the judge finds that there is a reasonable probability that the informer can testify, and the public entity still declines to disclose his identity, the judge can make any order that jus-

---

of several cases of liquor. *Id.* at 915. The court held that the informer could not testify to any material fact concerning the charged offense and that his testimony on whether the defendant was selling liquor out of his pickup truck was irrelevant. *Id.* at 920. Thus, the trial court did not err in declining to conduct an in camera hearing or to require the disclosure of the informer's identity. *Id.*

593. *See, e.g., **Quinonez-Saa v. State**,* 860 S.W.2d 704, 709 (Tex. App.—Houston [1st Dist.] 1993, pet. ref'd) (evidence at pretrial hearing showed there was a third-party eyewitness to the killing, but defendant did not demonstrate that informer's identity had to be disclosed because defendant "did not show that he could not find out the identity of the eyewitness through other means, such as by directly asking the State or its witnesses for the identity of any eyewitness").

594. *See, e.g., **Heard v. State**,* 995 S.W.2d 317, 319-21 (Tex. App.—Corpus Christi 1999, pet. ref'd) (trial court erred in refusing in camera hearing to determine whether informer who told investigator where murder weapon was hidden when this person's knowledge would indicate he was present during disposal of weapon and might be able to impeach State's eyewitness to murder).

595. ***Bodin v. State**,* 807 S.W.2d 313, 318 (Tex. Crim. App. 1991); *see **Williams v. State**,* 62 S.W.3d 800, 802 (Tex. App.—San Antonio 2001, no pet.); *see, e.g., **Jackson v. State**,* 495 S.W.3d 398, 415 (Tex. App.—Houston [14th Dist.] 2016, pet. ref'd) (no ineffective assistance of counsel in not filing motion for disclosure of informants' identities under Rule 508(c)(2); informants provided only background information that was later corroborated, and defendant's claim that one informant was an eyewitness was unsubstantiated), *cert. filed,* ___ S. Ct. ___ (2016) (No. 17-5088; 12-19-16).

596. Tex. R. Evid. 508(c)(2)(C)(i). Either the public entity or the defendant may request an in camera hearing under Rule 508(c)(2). *See **Bodin**,* 807 S.W.2d at 319. In camera proceedings are necessary to protect the informer's identity until a decision has been reached on whether it should be disclosed. *See **Heard**,* 995 S.W.2d at 320. On the other hand, a trial judge's denial of the defendant's request for the informer's identity may be reversible error if the defendant makes a "plausible" showing of the importance of the informer's testimony and the court does not conduct an in camera hearing. *See id.* at 320-21 (trial court erred in ordering hearing in open court that "precluded any meaningful verification of the investigator's testimony" on informer's role and how his testimony might be crucial).

597. Tex. R. Evid. 508(c)(2)(C)(i).

598. Tex. R. Evid. 508(c)(2)(C)(iii). The evidence cannot otherwise be revealed without the public entity's consent. *Id.; see **Southwell v. State**,* 80 S.W.2d 647, 649 (Tex. App.—Houston [1st Dist.] 2002, no pet.) ("Unsealing the record of the in camera hearings would expose informants to detection and defeat the public policy behind the rule.").

599. Tex. R. Evid. 508(c)(2)(C)(ii).

tice requires, including dismissal of the action.[600] In a criminal case, the court must, on the defendant's request, dismiss the charges to which the informer's testimony relates,[601] or the court may dismiss the charges on its own motion.[602] Failure to follow this procedure may result in reversible error.[603]

3. Legality of obtaining evidence. Under Rule 508(c)(3), when an informer's information is relevant to the legality of the means by which evidence was obtained, the court may require disclosure of the informer's identity if it is not satisfied that the informer is reliable or credible.[604]

---

600. *See* Tex. R. Evid. 508(c)(2)(B). In practice, judges rarely issue orders under Texas Rule 508(c)(2). The Advisory Committee's note to proposed Federal Rule 510 does not specify the types of orders a judge might consider. *Proposed Rules*, *supra* note 28, at 258 (Fed. R. Evid. 510 advisory committee's note, subdiv. (c)(2)). The Advisory Committee does, however, refer to its note to proposed Federal Rule 509 (state secrets and other official information), which mentions dismissal of the action and striking testimony as possible judicial actions. *Id.* The state-secrets privilege is a common-law privilege that permits exclusion of evidence when disclosure would jeopardize national security. *See* **Gen. Dynamics Corp. v. United States**, 563 U.S. 478, 484 (2011); **United States v. Reynolds**, 345 U.S. 1, 10 (1953); **El-Masri v. United States**, 479 F.3d 296, 302 (4th Cir. 2007). See **O'Connor's Federal Rules * Civil Trials** (2017), "State-secrets privilege," ch. 6-B, §3.10.2, p. 537. Some courts have imposed issue-preclusive sanctions in cases involving claims of the state-secrets privilege. *See, e.g.*, **Smith v. Schlesinger**, 513 F.2d 462, 467 & n.10 (D.C. Cir. 1975) (imposing "preclusion" sanctions on the government for the willful refusal to comply with a discovery order calling for an in camera inspection of an investigation file). More recently, however, some courts have deferred significantly to claims of state-secrets privilege. *See, e.g.*, **Al-Haramain Islamic Found., Inc. v. Bush**, 507 F.3d 1190, 1202-04 (9th Cir. 2007) (in suit against President for monitoring telephone conversations through secret National Security Agency program, in camera review led court to uphold district court's determination that government had met its burden for state-secrets privilege); **El-Masri**, 479 F.3d at 311 (dismissing suit against former CIA director for alleged kidnapping, illegal detention, abusive interrogation, and "extraordinary rendition" to Afghanistan, resulting in extended imprisonment and torture; facts central to litigation were protected by state-secrets privilege); **Terkel v. AT&T Corp.**, 441 F. Supp. 2d 899, 917 (N.D. Ill. 2006) (state-secrets privilege prohibited disclosure of whether telephone company provided phone records to federal government); *see also* **Arar v. Ashcroft**, 414 F. Supp. 2d 250, 287 (E.D.N.Y. 2006) (in suit for wrongful detention and "extraordinary rendition" to Syria, state-secrets issue was moot because court granted motions to dismiss the statutory and constitutional claims), *aff'd*, 585 F.3d 559 (2d Cir. 2009) (en banc). The Advisory Committee's note to proposed Federal Rule 509 also states that when the privilege is successfully claimed by the government in litigation to which it is not a party, the evidence simply becomes unavailable. *Proposed Rules*, *supra* note 28, at 254 (Fed. R. Evid. 509 advisory committee's note, subdiv. (e)). For more recent discussions of the state-secrets privilege, see **Gen. Dynamics Corp.**, 563 U.S. at 492 (discussing the privilege in the context of contract law; "[c]ourts should be ... hesitant to declare a Government contract unenforceable because of state secrets. ... Our decision today clarifies the consequences of [using the state-secrets privilege] only where it precludes a valid defense in Government-contracting disputes, and only where both sides have enough evidence to survive summary judgment but too many of the relevant facts remain obscured by the ... privilege to enable a reliable judgment."), Amanda Frost, *The State Secrets Privilege and Separation of Powers*, 75 Fordham L. Rev. 1931 (2007) (arguing that the judiciary should not forgo exercise of jurisdiction unless it is satisfied that Congress will take over executive oversight), and Jared Perkins, Note, *The State Secrets Privilege and the Abdication of Oversight*, 21 BYU J. Pub. L. 235 (2007) (analyzing how the modern application of state-secrets privilege poses problems to the separation-of-powers doctrine and to effective oversight of the executive branch).

601. Tex. R. Evid. 508(c)(2)(A)(i).

602. Tex. R. Evid. 508(c)(2)(A)(ii).

603. *E.g.*, **Lary v. State**, 15 S.W.3d 581, 585 (Tex. App.—Amarillo 2000, pet. ref'd) (because identity was a central issue in drug prosecution, trial court committed reversible error in not following procedure required by Rule 508 and not requiring disclosure of informer's identity). A trial court's decision about the disclosure of the informer's identity under this exception may be reviewed only for abuse of discretion. **Haggerty v. State**, 429 S.W.3d 1, 8 (Tex. App.—Houston [14th Dist.] 2013, pet. ref'd); **Thomas v. State**, 417 S.W.3d 89, 91-92 (Tex. App.—Amarillo 2013, no pet.).

604. Tex. R. Evid. 508(c)(3)(A); *see* **Blake v. State**, 125 S.W.3d 717, 728 (Tex. App.—Houston [1st Dist.] 2003, no pet.) ("Rule 508(c)(3) is written in discretionary terms. Only if the trial court judge is not satisfied that the informa-

Disclosure is usually not required at a motion-to-suppress hearing when the issue is the legal sufficiency of probable cause; unless the judge believes that the affiant or police officer is not credible or has acted improperly in relying on the informer or his information, the State will usually not need to disclose the informer's identity before the trial on the merits.[605] The issue is the reasonableness of the police officer's reliance on the informer's information, not the quality of that information to establish probable cause.[606]

A trial court may conduct an in camera hearing in proper circumstances regardless of whether it is requested by the State or public entity.[607] If disclosure of the informer's identity is to be made, the court must, on the public entity's request, order that the disclosure be made in camera.[608] But no counsel or parties may attend the in camera

---

tion was received from an informer reasonably believed to be reliable or credible may he require the identity of the informer to be disclosed."); *Ashorn v. State*, 802 S.W.2d 888, 892 (Tex. App.—Fort Worth 1991, no pet.) (when nothing in the record indicates that officer doubted informer's credibility and reliability, State is not required to disclose informer's identity); *see, e.g., Jones v. State*, 338 S.W.3d 725, 740-41 (Tex. App.—Houston [1st Dist.] 2011) (op. on reh'g) (trial court did not err in refusing to require disclosure of confidential informant's identity because another credible informant provided the same information; failure of affidavit to establish first informant's reliability or credibility did not affect legality of search warrant issued based on informants' information), *aff'd*, 364 S.W.3d 854 (Tex. Crim. App. 2012); *Hall v. State*, 778 S.W.2d 473, 474 (Tex. App.—Houston [14th Dist.] 1988, pet. ref'd) (trial judge did not abuse his discretion in finding that "he was satisfied the information upon which the search warrant was based was received from an informer reasonably believed to be reliable or credible"). *See generally* Jerry Schlichter, Note, *The Outwardly Sufficient Search Warrant Affidavit: What If It's False*, 19 UCLA L. Rev. 96, 123-39 (1971) (discussing circumstances under which disclosure of informer's identity is proper). Although this rule is used primarily in criminal cases, illegally obtained evidence may be suppressed in some civil cases. *See* McCormick on Evidence I, *supra* note 65, §167, at 458-59; Hans W. Baade, *Illegally Obtained Evidence in Criminal and Civil Cases: A Comparative Study of a Classic Mismatch II*, 52 Tex. L. Rev. 621, 648 (1974).

    The informer's reliability or credibility may occasionally be relevant to the merits of a case. For example, in *Hampton v. Hanrahan*, Black Panther Party members based their civil-rights claim, in part, on the fact that defendant's informer provided unreliable information in the affidavit supporting the issuance of a warrant. 600 F.2d 600, 635-38 (7th Cir. 1979), *rev'd in part on other grounds*, 446 U.S. 754 (1980). The Seventh Circuit held that the defendant, who was a police officer, had to disclose his informer's identity. *Hampton*, 600 F.2d at 639. When the informer's reliability or credibility goes to the merits rather than to a suppression issue or to the officer's reasonable reliance, Rule 508(c)(2) controls. *See* Tex. R. Evid. 508(c)(2)(A), (c)(2)(B). Refer to notes 594-595 *supra* and accompanying text.

    605. *See McCray v. Illinois*, 386 U.S. 300, 305 (1967) (when the issue is probable cause, disclosure of informer's identity is not required); *United States v. Payden*, 613 F. Supp. 800, 822 (S.D.N.Y. 1985) (witness list containing informer's identity does not need to be produced until he testifies). Earlier Texas law mandated no disclosure requirement when the informer merely provided information that was the basis for an arrest or a search. Unless the defendant could show that the informer fell into one of the three *Roviaro* categories, disclosure was not required at a motion-to-suppress hearing. *See Lancaster v. State*, 734 S.W.2d 161, 166-67 (Tex. App.—Fort Worth 1987, pet. ref'd) (if the defendant does not satisfy one of the three *Roviaro* categories, the court has no basis to determine whether the informer's identity is crucial to the defense).

    606. *See Shedden v. State*, 268 S.W.3d 717, 734 (Tex. App.—Corpus Christi 2008, pet. ref'd); *Blake*, 125 S.W.3d at 728. The informer may frequently be motivated more by the hope of collecting a reward, getting revenge, or avoiding a lengthy jail sentence for his own misconduct than by a public-spirited effort to prevent crime. Nonetheless, the issue in a motion-to-suppress hearing generally is whether the police officers acted reasonably in relying on the information supplied by a particular informer, not whether the informer is reliable.

    607. *Hackleman v. State*, 919 S.W.2d 440, 450 (Tex. App.—Austin 1996, pet. ref'd, untimely filed); *see also Hall*, 778 S.W.2d at 474 (defendant does not have the right to demand an in camera hearing under Criminal Rule 508(c)(3)).

    608. Tex. R. Evid. 508(c)(3)(B)(i).

disclosure.[609] If the trial court grants the disclosure request, it must seal and preserve for appeal the record from the in camera hearing.[610] The record cannot otherwise be revealed without the public entity's consent.[611]

A trial court's decision about the disclosure of the informer's identity under this exception may be reviewed only for abuse of discretion.[612] Whenever there is conflicting testimony on whether the information was received from an informer and, if so, whether the informer is reasonably believed to be reliable, the trial court is the exclusive judge of the credibility of the witnesses and the weight of their testimony.[613]

RULE 509
PHYSICIAN-PATIENT PRIVILEGE

(a) Definitions. In this rule:

    (1) A "patient" is a person who consults or is seen by a physician for medical care.

    (2) A "physician" is a person licensed, or who the patient reasonably believes is licensed, to practice medicine in any state or nation.

    (3) A communication is "confidential" if not intended to be disclosed to third persons other than those:

        (A) present to further the patient's interest in the consultation, examination, or interview;

        (B) reasonably necessary to transmit the communication; or

        (C) participating in the diagnosis and treatment under the physician's direction, including members of the patient's family.

(b) Limited Privilege in a Criminal Case. There is no physician-patient privilege in a criminal case. But a confidential communication is not admissible in a criminal case if made:

    (1) to a person involved in the treatment of or examination for alcohol or drug abuse; and

    (2) by a person being treated voluntarily or being examined for admission to treatment for alcohol or drug abuse.

---

609. Tex. R. Evid. 508(c)(3)(B)(ii).

610. Tex. R. Evid. 508(c)(3)(B)(iii).

611. *Id.*

612. ***Shedden v. State***, 268 S.W.3d 717, 731 (Tex. App.—Corpus Christi 2008, pet. ref'd); *see **Hall**,* 778 S.W.2d at 474.

613. ***Hall***, 778 S.W.2d at 474.

(c) General Rule in a Civil Case. In a civil case, a patient has a privilege to refuse to disclose and to prevent any other person from disclosing:

(1) a confidential communication between a physician and the patient that relates to or was made in connection with any professional services the physician rendered the patient; and

(2) a record of the patient's identity, diagnosis, evaluation, or treatment created or maintained by a physician.

(d) Who May Claim in a Civil Case. The privilege may be claimed by:

(1) the patient; or

(2) the patient's representative on the patient's behalf.

The physician may claim the privilege on the patient's behalf—and is presumed to have authority to do so.

(e) Exceptions in a Civil Case. This privilege does not apply:

(1) *Proceeding Against Physician.* If the communication or record is relevant to a claim or defense in:

(A) a proceeding the patient brings against a physician; or

(B) a license revocation proceeding in which the patient is a complaining witness.

(2) *Consent.* If the patient or a person authorized to act on the patient's behalf consents in writing to the release of any privileged information, as provided in subdivision (f).

(3) *Action to Collect.* In an action to collect a claim for medical services rendered to the patient.

(4) *Party Relies on Patient's Condition.* If any party relies on the patient's physical, mental, or emotional condition as a part of the party's claim or defense and the communication or record is relevant to that condition.

(5) *Disciplinary Investigation or Proceeding.* In a disciplinary investigation of or proceeding against a physician under the Medical Practice Act, Tex. Occ. Code §164.001 et seq., or a registered nurse under Tex. Occ. Code §301.451 et seq. But the board conducting the investigation or proceeding must protect the identity of any patient whose medical records are examined unless:

(A) the patient's records would be subject to disclosure under paragraph (e)(1); or

(B) the patient has consented in writing to the release of medical records, as provided in subdivision (f).

(6) *Involuntary Civil Commitment or Similar Proceeding.* In a proceeding for involuntary civil commitment or court-ordered treatment, or a probable cause hearing under Tex. Health & Safety Code:

> **(A)** chapter 462 (Treatment of Persons With Chemical Dependencies);

> **(B)** title 7, subtitle C (Texas Mental Health Code); or

> **(C)** title 7, subtitle D (Persons With an Intellectual Disability Act).

(7) *Abuse or Neglect of "Institution" Resident.* In a proceeding regarding the abuse or neglect, or the cause of any abuse or neglect, of a resident of an "institution" as defined in Tex. Health & Safety Code §242.002.

(f) Consent for Release of Privileged Information.

> **(1)** Consent for the release of privileged information must be in writing and signed by:

>> **(A)** the patient;

>> **(B)** a parent or legal guardian if the patient is a minor;

>> **(C)** a legal guardian if the patient has been adjudicated incompetent to manage personal affairs;

>> **(D)** an attorney appointed for the patient under Tex. Health & Safety Code title 7, subtitles C and D;

>> **(E)** an attorney ad litem appointed for the patient under Tex. Estates Code title 3, subtitle C;

>> **(F)** an attorney ad litem or guardian ad litem appointed for a minor under Tex. Fam. Code chapter 107, subchapter B; or

>> **(G)** a personal representative if the patient is deceased.

> **(2)** The consent must specify:

>> **(A)** the information or medical records covered by the release;

>> **(B)** the reasons or purposes for the release; and

>> **(C)** the person to whom the information is to be released.

> **(3)** The patient, or other person authorized to consent, may withdraw consent to the release of any information. But a withdrawal of consent does not affect any information disclosed before the patient or authorized person gave written notice of the withdrawal.

> **(4)** Any person who receives information privileged under this rule may disclose the information only to the extent consistent with the purposes specified in the consent.

Notes and Comments

Comment to 2015 restyling: The physician-patient privilege in a civil case was first enacted in Texas in 1981 as part of the Medical Practice Act, formerly codified in Tex. Rev. Civ. Stat. art. 4495b. That statute provided that the privilege applied even if a patient had received a physician's services before the statute's enactment. Because more than thirty years have now passed, it is no longer necessary to burden the text of the rule with a statement regarding the privilege's retroactive application. But deleting this statement from the rule's text is not intended as a substantive change in the law.

The former rule's reference to "confidentiality or" and "administrative proceedings" in subdivision (e) [Exceptions in a Civil Case] has been deleted. First, this rule is a privilege rule only. Tex. Occ. Code §159.004 sets forth exceptions to a physician's duty to maintain confidentiality of patient information outside court and administrative proceedings. Second, by their own terms the rules of evidence govern only proceedings in Texas courts. See Rule 101(b). To the extent the rules apply in administrative proceedings, it is because the Administrative Procedure Act mandates their applicability. Tex. Gov't Code §2001.083 provides that "[i]n a contested case, a state agency shall give effect to the rules of privilege recognized by law." Section 2001.091 excludes privileged material from discovery in contested administrative cases.

Statutory references in the former rule that are no longer up-to-date have been revised. Finally, reconciling the provisions of Rule 509 with the parts of Tex. Occ. Code ch. 159 that address a physician-patient privilege applicable to court proceedings is beyond the scope of the restyling project.

Comment to 1998 change: This comment is intended to inform the construction and application of this rule. Prior Criminal Rules of Evidence 509 and 510 are now in subparagraph (b) of this Rule. This rule governs disclosures of patient-physician communications only in judicial or administrative proceedings. Whether a physician may or must disclose such communications in other circumstances is governed by Tex. Rev. Civ. Stat. Ann. art. 4495b, §5.08 [now Tex. Occ. Code ch. 159]. Former subparagraph (d)(6) of the Civil Evidence Rules, regarding disclosures in a suit affecting the parent-child relationship, is omitted, not because there should be no exception to the privilege in suits affecting the parent-child relationship, but because the exception in such suits is properly considered under subparagraph (e)(4) of the new rule (formerly subparagraph (d)(4)), as construed in *R.K. v. Ramirez*, 887 S.W.2d 836 (Tex. 1994). In determining the proper application of an exception in such suits, the trial court must ensure that the precise need for the information is not outweighed by legitimate privacy interests protected by the privilege. Subparagraph (e) of the new rule does not except from the privilege information relating to a non-party patient who is or may be a consulting or testifying expert in the suit.

COMMENTARY ON RULE 509

The Texas physician-patient rule, codified in Rule 509, is based on two public-policy rationales: (1) to encourage the full and complete communication necessary for effective medical diagnosis and treatment, and (2) to prevent the unnecessary disclosure of highly personal information.[614] Because there are so many exceptions to the rule, the second rationale, addressing privacy concerns, is directed primarily at preventing needless disclosures.

Common law did not embrace a privilege for physician-patient communications.[615] In 1828, New York passed the first statute protecting physician-patient communications.[616] Eventually, most states enacted statutory physician-patient privileges.[617] Texas civil[618] and criminal[619] courts, however, consistently refused to create a common-law physician-patient privilege. For many years, the Texas Legislature also resisted the nationwide trend.[620] This resistance finally crumbled during a 1981 special session of the

---

614. *In re Collins*, 286 S.W.3d 911, 916 (Tex. 2009) (orig. proceeding); *R.K. v. Ramirez*, 887 S.W.2d 836, 840 (Tex. 1994) (orig. proceeding). In discussing the privacy rationale, the court quoted McCormick: "'[T]he privacy of the physician-patient relationship should not be subject to casual breach by every litigant in single-minded pursuit of the last scrap of evidence which may marginally contribute to victory in litigation.'" *R.K.*, 887 S.W.2d at 840 (quoting McCORMICK ON EVIDENCE §105, at 149 (John W. Strong et al. eds., 4th ed. 1992)).

615. *See R.K.*, 887 S.W.2d at 839-40 ("Neither the physician-patient privilege nor the mental health privilege existed at common law. However, every state has adopted one or both of these privileges in some form."); *State v. Hardy*, 963 S.W.2d 516, 524-25 (Tex. Crim. App. 1997) ("The physician-patient privilege did not exist at common law but is purely a statutory innovation. The drafters of the Federal Rules of Evidence dropped the physician-patient privilege from their proposed list, but most states protect the privilege in some form.").

616. 8 WIGMORE, *supra* note 6, §2380, at 818-20.

617. *See* Kenneth S. Broun, *The Medical Privilege in the Federal Courts—Should It Matter Whether Your Ego or Your Elbow Hurts?*, 38 LOY. L.A. L. REV. 657, 682 & n.160 (2004); Ralph Ruebner & Leslie Ann Reis, *Hippocrates to HIPAA: A Foundation for a Federal Physician-Patient Privilege*, 77 TEMP. L. REV. 505, 563-64 & n.439 (2004).

618. *See Biggers v. State*, 358 S.W.2d 188, 191 (Tex. Civ. App.—Dallas 1962) (rule of privileged communications does not extend to professionals), *writ ref'd n.r.e.*, 360 S.W.2d 516 (Tex. 1962); *Caddo Grocery & Ice v. Carpenter*, 285 S.W.2d 470, 474 (Tex. Civ. App.—Austin 1955, no writ) (doctrine of privileged communications does not extend to physician and patient); *see also Hood v. Phillips*, 554 S.W.2d 160, 167 (Tex. 1977) (medical records not protected by the hospital-records privilege are discoverable).

619. *See Ex parte Watson*, 606 S.W.2d 902, 904 (Tex. Crim. App. 1980) (there is no common-law privilege between doctor and patient); *Granviel v. State*, 552 S.W.2d 107, 116 (Tex. Crim. App. 1976) (there is no common-law confidential relationship between physicians and patients); *Dodd v. State*, 83 Tex. Crim. 160, 165, 201 S.W. 1014, 1015 (1918) ("[C]ommunications between physician and patient in the absence of statute are not privileged.").

620. In 1969, the Legislature enacted a privilege for the records and proceedings of medical committees. Act of May 31, 1969, 61st Leg., R.S., ch. 568, §1, 1969 Tex. Gen. Laws 1719-20 (current version at TEX. HEALTH & SAFETY CODE §161.032); *see* TEX. OCC. CODE §160.007(a) (general rule of privilege for medical peer-review committee); *Romero v. KPH Consol., Inc.*, 166 S.W.3d 212, 216 (Tex. 2005) ("[W]ith certain exceptions, the proceedings and records of a peer review committee are confidential and communications to it are privileged from disclosure."); *In re Univ. of Tex. Health Ctr.*, 33 S.W.3d 822, 827 (Tex. 2000) (per curiam) (under former Texas Revised Civil Statutes art. 4495b, §5.06(j) [now codified at TEX. OCC. CODE §160.007(e)-(g)], medical peer-review records are not subject to subpoena or discovery and are not admissible as evidence without written waiver of privilege unless disclosure is required or authorized by law); *Terrell State Hosp. v. Ashworth*, 794 S.W.2d 937, 939 (Tex. App.—Dallas 1990,

67th Legislature, when a physician-patient privilege was enacted as part of the Medical Practice Act.[621]

---

orig. proceeding [leave denied]) (under §161.032, records of a hospital committee's investigation, review, or deliberative proceeding are privileged and immune from discovery); *see also* Tex. Health & Safety Code §161.031(a) (defining "medical committee"). *See generally* Gail N. Friend et al., *The New Rules of Show and Tell: Identifying and Protecting the Peer Review and Medical Committee Privileges*, 49 Baylor L. Rev. 607 (1997) (discussing the history and implementation of peer-review and medical-committee privileges). There are, however, certain exceptions. For example, if a medical peer-review committee takes action that could negatively affect a physician's privileges in a health-care entity, a copy of the committee's recommendation and final decision must be provided to the physician. Tex. Occ. Code §160.007(d); *see, e.g.*, *In re Christus Santa Rosa Health Sys.*, 492 S.W.3d 276, 282-83 (Tex. 2016) (orig. proceeding) (exception under §160.007(d) applies only to committee's recommendation and final decision, which means committee completed its review rather than just convened a meeting; trial court abused discretion in ordering disclosure of peer-review committee's records without first conducting in camera hearing to determine whether privilege applied and, if so, whether §160.007(d) exception applied).

The medical-committee privilege is designed to facilitate thorough self-review and investigation of medical practices. *Texarkana Mem'l Hosp., Inc. v. Jones*, 551 S.W.2d 33, 35 (Tex. 1977). It protects only committee records, providing no shield from disclosure for records kept for individual patients. *E.g.*, *Hood*, 554 S.W.2d at 167 (doctor's patient records were not covered under the statute); *Texarkana Mem'l Hosp.*, 551 S.W.2d at 35 (same). The mere fact that a document was reviewed and considered by a medical-review committee does not automatically transform that document into a committee record. *Barnes v. Whittington*, 751 S.W.2d 493, 496 (Tex. 1988). The names of committee members are not privileged. These members may also be deposed and questioned about their knowledge of pertinent facts that did not arise from information prepared by or for a medical-review committee. *Santa Rosa Med. Ctr. v. Spears*, 709 S.W.2d 720, 724 (Tex. App.—San Antonio 1986, orig. proceeding) (per curiam).

Similar to documents considered by a medical committee, a document is not privileged simply because it passed through a peer-review committee. *In re Mem'l Hermann Hosp. Sys.*, 464 S.W.3d 686, 699 (Tex. 2015) (orig. proceeding); *In re Living Ctrs. of Tex., Inc.*, 175 S.W.3d 253, 257 (Tex. 2005) (orig. proceeding). Records made in the regular course of business of a hospital or medical organization are also not protected under either the peer-review or the medical-committee privilege; however, the fact that those records were reviewed by the committee is protected. *In re Mem'l Hermann Hosp. Sys.*, 464 S.W.3d at 699-700 & n.31; *see* Tex. Health & Safety Code §161.032(f); *In re Living Ctrs. of Tex., Inc.*, 175 S.W.3d at 257. For further discussion of the peer-review and medical-committee privileges, see *O'Connor's Texas Rules * Civil Trials* (2017), "Peer-review & medical-committee privileges," ch. 6-B, §3.13, p. 551.

621. Tex. Rev. Civ. Stat. art. 4495b, §5.08 [now codified at Tex. Occ. Code ch. 159]. The 1998 comment to Rule 509 states that it governs disclosure of such communications only in judicial or administrative proceedings. Tex. R. Evid. 509 cmt. (1998). The 2015 restyling of the Texas Rules deleted the reference to "administrative proceedings" in Rule 509(e) (exceptions in a civil case), but no substantive change was intended. *See* Tex. Sup. Ct. Order, Misc. Docket No. 15-9048, §2 (eff. Apr. 1, 2015). The comment to the restyling explained that the Rules of Evidence only govern proceedings in Texas courts and that "[t]o the extent the rules apply in administrative proceedings, it is because the Administrative Procedure Act mandates their applicability." Tex. R. Evid. 509 cmt. (2015). Texas Occupations Code §159.003 contains some exceptions similar to Rule 509(e) that apply to the privilege of confidentiality in court or administrative proceedings. *See* Tex. Occ. Code §159.003; *see also* Tex. R. Evid. 509 cmt. (2015) (reconciling Rule 509 with parts of Texas Occupations Code ch. 159 that address physician-patient privilege in court proceedings was beyond scope of restyling project). The statute, however, is broader because it applies to both civil and criminal proceedings. *See* Tex. Occ. Code §159.003. In addition to exceptions related to criminal proceedings, Texas Occupations Code §159.003 differs from Rule 509(e) by allowing disclosure if the information is relevant to a proceeding brought under Texas Occupations Code §159.009 (unauthorized release of confidential information), to satisfy a request for the billing or medical records of a deceased or incompetent person under Texas Civil Practice & Remedies Code §74.051(e), or under court order. Tex. Occ. Code §159.003(a)(9), (a)(11), (a)(12). Texas Occupations Code §159.004 also addresses exceptions to a physician's duty to maintain confidentiality of patient information, but those exceptions apply outside court and administrative proceedings. *See* Tex. Occ. Code §159.004; Tex. R. Evid. 509 cmt. (2015). For a discussion of Rule 509(e), refer to notes 655-699 *infra* and accompanying text.

Former Texas Revised Civil Statutes article 4495b, §5.08, had been repealed only to the extent that it related to proceedings governed by the Texas Rules of Evidence. Thus, the statute remained applicable when (1) it delineated those situations other than court or administrative proceedings in which the physician may or must disclose confidential information, Tex. Rev. Civ. Stat. art. 4495b, §5.08(c), (h) (repealed 1999) [now codified at Tex. Occ. Code §§159.002(c), 159.004], (2) it granted the patient access to his medical records, Tex. Rev. Civ. Stat. art. 4495b,

Rule 509 retains the basic language of the Medical Practice Act and largely follows the language of the statutory psychotherapist-patient privilege.[622] Rule 509(b) states that the physician-patient privilege cannot be invoked in any criminal proceeding.[623]

Although the Texas rule retains the statutory privilege in civil cases, its exceptions lessen the rule's significance.[624] A 1988 amendment to the patient-litigant exception in

§5.08(k) [now codified at Tex. Occ. Code §159.006], or (3) it provided a cause of action for injunctive relief and damages for violations of its provisions, Tex. Rev. Civ. Stat. art. 4495b, §5.08(*l*) (repealed 1999) [now codified at Tex. Occ. Code §159.009]. The supreme court and court of criminal appeals did not repeal any of these provisions when promulgating the Texas Rules of Civil or Criminal Evidence.

622. Tex. Health & Safety Code §§611.001-611.008. The psychotherapist-patient privilege is now embodied in Rule 510, but it applies only to civil proceedings. *See* Tex. R. Evid. 510(b)(1).

623. Tex. R. Evid. 509(b). This position follows long-standing Texas common law. *See Rougeau v. State*, 738 S.W.2d 651, 664 (Tex. Crim. App. 1987) ("Our research has yet to reveal a single case where this Court has ever held that there is a physician-patient privilege in a criminal case."). Rule 509(b) does, however, carry forward the limited drug- and alcohol-treatment privilege. Refer to notes 637-650 *infra* and accompanying text.

While the original 1981 legislation adopting a physician-patient privilege allowed the assertion of the privilege in criminal cases, the Legislature amended that statute in 1983 to eliminate the privilege whenever the patient was a victim, defendant, or witness in a criminal case. *See* Act of May 27, 1983, 68th Leg., R.S., ch. 511, §2, 1983 Tex. Gen. Laws 2970, 2973. Thus, Texas law permitted the assertion of a physician-patient privilege in criminal proceedings only between 1981 and 1983. *See, e.g., Abdnor v. State*, 756 S.W.2d 815, 821 (Tex. App.—Dallas 1988) (improper admission of physician-patient communications at first trial was harmless error because statute was amended before retrial to permit admission of that evidence), *rev'd on other grounds*, 808 S.W.2d 476 (Tex. Crim. App. 1991); *Harper v. State*, 686 S.W.2d 738, 740-41 (Tex. App.—Austin 1985, no pet.) (per curiam) (although blood-test results were subject to a statutory privilege when test was taken, evidence of test was admitted at trial on the day the amendment that excluded evidence in criminal proceedings from the privilege took effect; test results were admissible).

624. Physician-patient privileges have had many exceptions, largely because of the lack of a persuasive rationale for the privilege. *See* 2 Weinstein & Berger, *supra* note 29, ¶504[01], at 504-9 to 504-10. Instrumental justification for the privilege must rest on its marginal effect on individuals' decisions to seek medical help. Confidentiality outside the courthouse is, of course, imposed on physicians by federal law and their own professional ethics. *See* Clinton Dewitt, Privileged Communications Between Physician and Patient 22-23 (1958); *see also* 45 C.F.R. pts. 160 & 164 (recognizing the important public and private interests in protecting medical records from wholesale public disclosure and defining the circumstances under which patients' medical records may be disclosed by health plans, health-care clearinghouses, and most health-care providers). Refer to notes 626-629 *infra* and accompanying text. The Hippocratic Oath, for example, provides in part: "Whatsoever things I see or hear concerning the life of men, in my attendance on the sick or even apart therefrom which ought not to be noised abroad, I will keep silence thereon, counting such things to be as sacred secrets." Dewitt, *supra*, at 22-23.

As Charles McCormick bluntly put it: "More than a century of experience with the statutes has demonstrated that the privilege in the main operates not as the shield of privacy but as the protector of fraud." McCormick on Evidence II, *supra* note 197, §105, at 228; *see also* 8 Wigmore, *supra* note 6, §2380a, at 831-32 (discussing the privilege's policy justifications); Zechariah Chafee, Jr., *Privileged Communications: Is Justice Served or Obstructed by Closing the Doctor's Mouth on the Witness Stand?*, 52 Yale L.J. 607, 609-17 (1943) (same); Ronan E. Degnan, *The Law of Federal Evidence Reform*, 76 Harv. L. Rev. 275, 300 (1962) (arguing that the physician-patient privilege "operates primarily as an instrument of fraud"); Edmund M. Morgan, *Suggested Remedy for Obstructions to Expert Testimony by Rules of Evidence*, 10 U. Chi. L. Rev. 285, 290-91 (1943) (no reason to justify the continued existence of the privilege). *But see Trammel v. United States*, 445 U.S. 40, 51 (1980) ("[B]arriers to full disclosure would impair diagnosis and treatment"). The drafters of the Federal Rules agreed, dropping the physician-patient privilege while opting to protect psychotherapist-patient communications. *Proposed Rules, supra* note 28, at 240-42 (Fed. R. Evid. 504); *see Jaffee v. Redmond*, 518 U.S. 1, 15-17 (1996) (recognizing a "psychotherapist privilege" under Federal Rule 501); *In re Sealed Case (Med. Records)*, 381 F.3d 1205, 1213-14 (D.C. Cir. 2004) (same). This decision was consistent with the federal common law, which did not and still does not recognize a physician-patient privilege. *See Whalen v. Roe*, 429 U.S. 589, 602 n.28 (1977); *see, e.g., Patterson v. Caterpillar, Inc.*, 70 F.3d 503, 506 (7th Cir. 1995) (admitting testimony of treating physician because federal law does not recognize physician-patient privilege); *United States v. Bercier*, 848 F.2d 917, 920 (8th Cir. 1988) (admitting statements that the defendant made to the treating physician because federal courts do not recognize the physician-patient privilege in criminal proceed-

former Rule 509(d)(4)[625] (now Rule 509(e)(4)) eviscerated what little confidentiality remained. Thus, the privilege rarely results in the exclusion of relevant evidence.

Litigants and nonparty witnesses may nevertheless have limited protection from the disclosure of private medical records and information under the Health Insurance Portability and Accountability Act of 1996 (HIPAA).[626] Under HIPAA, disclosure of "individually identifiable health information" by entities covered by the statute is a federal offense.[627] As a general rule, state law contrary to any provision of HIPAA is preempted.[628] Therefore, state statutes, discovery rules, and rules of evidence pertaining to health records and information covered by HIPAA must be reconciled with HIPAA to be given effect.[629]

A. Rule 509(a): Definitions

For the purposes of the physician-patient privilege, a patient is "a person who consults or is seen by a physician for medical care."[630] A physician is "a person licensed,

ings); *United States v. Meagher*, 531 F.2d 752, 753 (5th Cir. 1976) (admitting letters from a criminal defendant to his psychiatrist because no psychiatrist-patient privilege exists under federal law). Refer to notes 712-713 *infra* and accompanying text. Such communications may still be protected as an aspect of the right of privacy under the Ninth Amendment. *See Miofsky v. Super. Ct.*, 703 F.2d 332, 335 (9th Cir. 1983) (federal district court has jurisdiction under 42 U.S.C. §1983 to consider a tort defendant's claim that a state-court order permitting discovery of his communications to psychiatrists would violate his constitutional rights).

625. 733-734 S.W.2d (Tex. Cases) LXXXVII (1987, amended 1998). Former Rule 509(d)(4) had originally read as follows:

in any litigation or administrative proceeding, if relevant, brought by the patient or someone on his behalf if the patient is attempting to recover monetary damages for any physical or mental condition including death of the patient. Any information is discoverable in any court or administrative proceeding in this state if the court or administrative body has jurisdiction over the subject matter, pursuant to rules of procedure specified for the matters;

641-642 S.W.2d (Tex. Cases) XLVII (1983, amended 1998).

626. *See* Health Insurance Portability and Accountability Act of 1996, Pub. L. No. 104-191, 110 Stat. 1936; 45 C.F.R. pt. 160, §§164.102-164.106, 164.500-164.534. HIPAA authorized the U.S. Department of Health and Human Services (HHS) to issue safeguards protecting the confidentiality and security of health information. 42 U.S.C. §§1320d-1, 1320d-2(d); *see* 45 C.F.R. pt. 160, §§164.102-164.106, 164.500-164.534 (regulations enacting HIPAA referred to as the "Privacy Rule"). In general, protected health information cannot be disclosed unless it falls within a specific exception. *See* 45 C.F.R. §164.502(a). Several exceptions to the general rule permit disclosure without authorization from the individual. *Id.* §164.512. Private medical information can be disclosed under a court order as long as the disclosure precisely follows the order's scope. *Id.* §164.512(e)(1)(i). This information can also be disclosed under a discovery request or "other lawful process." *Id.* §164.512(e)(1)(ii). However, the disclosing party must follow many procedural safeguards designed to give the patient maximum privacy protection. *See id.* §164.512(e)(1).

627. 42 U.S.C. §§1320d-5, 1320d-6; *see id.* §1320d(6) (defining "individually identifiable health information").

628. 45 C.F.R. §160.203; *see* Beverly Cohen, *Reconciling the HIPAA Privacy Rule with State Laws Regulating Ex Parte Interviews of Plaintiffs' Treating Physicians: A Guide to Performing HIPAA Preemption Analysis*, 43 Hous. L. Rev. 1091, 1105 (2006). Cohen points out that state legal provisions are rarely contrary to HIPAA because the exceptions and provisions incorporated in HIPAA allow state laws to be reconciled with HIPAA requirements. Cohen, *supra*, at 1139-41.

629. *See Abbott v. Tex. Dep't of MHMR*, 212 S.W.3d 648, 662-63 (Tex. App.—Austin 2006, no pet.) (giving effect to both HIPAA and the Texas Public Information Act); *see also* 45 C.F.R. §164.512(a) (allowing disclosures required by law).

630. Tex. R. Evid. 509(a)(1); *see, e.g.*, *Tarrant Cty. Hosp. Dist. v. Hughes*, 734 S.W.2d 675, 677 (Tex. App.—Fort Worth 1987, orig. proceeding) (because nothing in the record demonstrated that blood donors were ever seen by a doctor or received medical care, the donors were not "patients" for purposes of Rule 509 and thus the donors' identities were discoverable); *see also* *Gulf Coast Reg'l Blood Ctr. v. Houston*, 745 S.W.2d 557, 560 (Tex. App.—Fort

or who the patient reasonably believes is licensed, to practice medicine in any state or nation."[631] The rule's definition of "physician" does not include full-time dentists,[632] optometrists, or other similar practitioners.[633] Whether a communication is confidential is determined in much the same way as under the attorney-client privilege.[634] Al-

---

Worth 1988, orig. proceeding) (in a wrongful-death suit based on an HIV-tainted blood transfusion, trial court properly permitted limited discovery of identity and location of donors, but documents were to be sealed and kept with the court). The method employed in *Gulf Coast* provides a careful balance between the parties' right to discover relevant and essential evidence and the privacy rights the privilege was designed to protect. *See Gulf Coast*, 745 S.W.2d at 560.

The physician-patient relationship is voluntary and contractual, created by an express or implied agreement. *Garay v. Cty. of Bexar*, 810 S.W.2d 760, 764 (Tex. App.—San Antonio 1991, writ denied). Physicians may also agree in advance to the creation of a physician-patient relationship in which the physician may not refuse to treat a hospital's clients. *Lection v. Dyll*, 65 S.W.3d 696, 704 (Tex. App.—Dallas 2001, pet. denied) (op. on reh'g); *see Hand v. Tavera*, 864 S.W.2d 678, 680 (Tex. App.—San Antonio 1993, no writ).

631. Tex. R. Evid. 509(a)(2). The original Rule 509 did not specify whether the physician must be licensed in Texas or whether licensure in another jurisdiction would suffice. 641-642 S.W.2d (Tex. Cases) xlvi (1983, amended 1998). A 1984 supreme court amendment to the rule, stating that the physician does not need to be licensed to practice medicine in Texas for the privilege to apply, resolved this ambiguity. *See* 669-670 S.W.2d (Tex. Cases) xxxiii (1984, amended 1998).

The definition of "physician" in the original version of Civil Rule 509 did not include a person who is not licensed to practice medicine but whom the patient reasonably believes to be licensed. 641-642 S.W.2d (Tex. Cases) xlvi (1983, amended 1998). This differed from provisions on the attorney-client privilege and the psychotherapist-patient privilege. *See* Tex. R. Evid. 503(a)(3), 510(a)(1)(D). The 1984 amendment to the rule repaired this deficiency as well. *See* 669-670 S.W.2d (Tex. Cases) xxxiii (1984, amended 1998).

632. *See* Tex. Occ. Code §151.052(a)(1); *Buchanan v. Mayfield*, 925 S.W.2d 135, 138 (Tex. App.—Waco 1996, orig. proceeding) (Medical Practice Act is the statutory scheme that governs the licensing of physicians in Texas, and dentists who confine their practice strictly to dentistry are specifically excluded from application of that Act). In *Buchanan*, a patient sued her dentist for negligence, claiming that due to his assistant's negligence, she drank out of a prior patient's "spit cup." 925 S.W.2d at 136. The trial court denied her motion to compel discovery of prior patient's identity, based on the dentist's assertion of the physician-patient privilege, but the court of appeals granted mandamus relief to make the identity of the prior patient discoverable because the dentist did not have a valid privilege to assert. *Id.* at 138-39. The dentist argued that even if he was not a "physician" under the rule, he performed "physician-like" procedures and had his own statutory duty to preserve confidential information under the Dental Practice Act. *Id.* at 138. The court noted that while the Dental Practice Act requires dentists to keep their records confidential, the plaintiff was not seeking to discover the prior patient's dental records; she merely wanted to discover that patient's identity and take her deposition. *Id.* Indeed, it is hard to imagine that, even if the physician-patient privilege applied in this context, it would protect the patient's name. A person making a dentist appointment rarely, if ever, intends to keep his name confidential. Thus, this information, like the client's name under the attorney-client privilege, should normally not be privileged.

633. The scope of "practicing medicine" is found in the Medical Practice Act. Tex. Occ. Code §151.002(a)(13). Among those who are not deemed by the Medical Practice Act to be practicing medicine, and who therefore do not fall within the privilege, are dentists, optometrists, chiropractors, registered nurses or licensed vocational nurses, podiatrists, psychologists, and physical therapists. *Id.* §151.052(a)(1)-(a)(7). While it seems unlikely that one would need to communicate highly confidential and private matters to a podiatrist to receive adequate medical treatment, the Texas Legislature enacted a statutory podiatrist-patient privilege in 1995. Tex. Rev. Civ. Stat. art. 4575d (repealed 1999) [now codified at Tex. Occ. Code §202.401 et seq.]. One Texas court has held that Rule 509 does apply to chiropractors. *In re Dolezal*, 970 S.W.2d 650, 652 n.3 (Tex. App.—Corpus Christi 1998, orig. proceeding). In *In re Dolezal*, the court stated that:

> We are aware that as a chiropractor, Dolezal is not, technically, a physician. He is, however, a doctor of chiropractic. For purposes of maintaining the confidentiality of a patient's records, we cannot conceive of any rational basis upon which to distinguish between a doctor of medicine or osteopathy and a doctor of chiropractic.

Id.

634. The definition of confidential communication found in Rule 509(a)(3) is an addition to the statutory formulation and is derived from proposed Federal Rule 504. *Proposed Rules, supra* note 28, at 240-41. Of course, if

lowances are made for those persons who are present to further the interest of the patient, who are reasonably necessary for the transmission of the communication, or who are participating in the patient's treatment under the physician's direction.[635] Thus, the presence of or disclosure to persons such as nurses, medical students, secretaries, translators, and family members does not destroy confidentiality.[636]

B. Rule 509(b): Limited Privilege in a Criminal Case

There is no physician-patient privilege in a criminal case.[637] The need for accurate and complete evidence in a criminal case is more important than the privacy interests fostered by these privileges. Only in one small area, substance abuse, is the need for re-

---

the patient is specifically told that a particular conversation is not privileged, it will not be protected under the rule because it was never intended to be kept confidential. *See, e.g.*, ***Dudley v. State***, 730 S.W.2d 51, 54 (Tex. App.—Houston [14th Dist.] 1987, no writ) (when physician told an involuntarily committed patient that a particular communication was not confidential, communication was not covered by Rule 509 or 510 and was admissible).

635. TEX. R. EVID. 509(a)(3).

636. *See* TEX. R. EVID. 509(a)(3)(C).

637. TEX. R. EVID. 509(b); *see* ***State v. Hardy***, 963 S.W.2d 516, 523 (Tex. Crim. App. 1997). In ***Hardy***, the DWI defendant argued that a grand-jury subpoena for the hospital records showing his blood-test results after an accident should be suppressed based both on a physician-patient privilege and privacy rights under the Fourth Amendment. 963 S.W.2d at 518. The trial court granted the motion to suppress, but the court of appeals reversed that decision; that reversal was upheld by the court of criminal appeals. *Id.* The defendant had argued that although the enactment of Criminal Rule 509 had abrogated §5.08(g)(8) of the Texas Medical Practice Act in 1986, the passage of the Emergency Health Care Act in Texas Health & Safety Code chapter 773 restored the privilege. ***Hardy***, 963 S.W.2d at 518. That Act, however, "does not apply to physicians, nurses, or other health care practitioners unless they 'staff[ ] an emergency medical services vehicle regularly.'" *Id.* at 523 (quoting former TEX. HEALTH & SAFETY CODE §773.004(a)(5), now §773.004(a)(4)). The court of criminal appeals reasoned that such a narrow provision cannot be construed as any legislative intent to overturn Criminal Rule 509's applicability to the physician-patient relationship as a general proposition. ***Hardy***, 963 S.W.2d at 523. The court noted that the Legislature had had numerous opportunities since 1986 to overturn Criminal Rule 509 but had declined to do so. *Id.* Thus, the court concluded that Criminal Rule 509 prohibits the assertion of a physician-patient privilege in Texas criminal proceedings. *Id.*; *see* ***Peto v. State***, 51 S.W.3d 326, 327-28 (Tex. App.—Houston [1st Dist.] 2001, pet. ref'd) (collecting cases holding that there is no physician-patient or psychiatrist-patient privilege in Texas criminal law). The court also found that, in the context of blood-alcohol-test results taken from persons involved in a traffic accident, the patient-defendant has no reasonable expectation of privacy for those medical records under the Fourth Amendment. ***Hardy***, 963 S.W.2d at 527; *see, e.g.*, ***Ramos v. State***, 124 S.W.3d 326, 336-38 (Tex. App.—Fort Worth 2003, pet. ref'd) (defendant did not have a constitutional or statutory expectation of privacy for medical records created by private hospital containing blood-alcohol-test results that were later submitted to police under subpoena); ***Clark v. State***, 933 S.W.2d 332, 333 (Tex. App.—Corpus Christi 1996, no pet.) (no seizure involved when defendant's records were subpoenaed by the grand jury because his blood sample was drawn and tested for medical purposes at the request of the attending physician; because physician-patient privilege in criminal cases had been repealed, blood-test results were no longer protected). In ***Thurman v. State***, the court rejected the defendant's contention that he had a physician-patient privilege, reasoning that

> [n]ow that article 4495b, section 5.08 has been repealed in criminal cases, rule 509 shows that society does not consider this expectation reasonable in criminal cases. We conclude that [***State v. Comeaux***, 818 S.W.2d 46 (Tex. Crim. App. 1991),] does not control this case because no matter how reasonable appellant's subjective expectation of privacy may have been, it is one that society has rejected. The policy choice has been made by the Court of Criminal Appeals: Society can afford the physician-patient privilege in certain civil cases in order to protect personal privacy, but the need to protect the public from crime requires disclosure of the same information in criminal cases.

861 S.W.2d 96, 99-100 (Tex. App.—Houston [1st Dist.] 1993, no pet.).

Although there is no physician-patient privilege in criminal cases, physicians still have a duty of confidentiality enforced by statute, subject to certain listed exceptions. ***Richardson v. State***, 865 S.W.2d 944, 953 n.7 (Tex. Crim. App. 1993); *see* TEX. OCC. CODE ch. 159. Refer to note 624 *supra*.

habilitative therapy thought to outweigh the general interest in full disclosure of relevant information.[638] Rule 509(b) is closely patterned after Texas Code of Criminal Procedure article 38.101, which provides that

> [a] communication to any person involved in the treatment or examination of drug abusers by a person being treated voluntarily or being examined for admission to voluntary treatment for drug abuse is not admissible. However, information derived from the treatment or examination of drug abusers may be used for statistical and research purposes if the names of the patients are not revealed.[639]

The rule differs from the statute in two ways. First, the statute applies only to individuals receiving treatment for drug abuse, while the rule also covers individuals being treated for alcohol abuse.[640] This expansion is beneficial because medical treatment for alcoholism is frequently a term of pretrial release or probation for criminal offenses. It hardly makes sense for a court to require substance-abuse treatment and then in a later criminal proceeding permit the State to use the confidential communications that the patient made during treatment.

Second, the statute protects statements made in connection with examinations for admission to voluntary treatment programs for substance abuse but does not address involuntary commitment. The rule's elimination of the word "voluntary" in the phrase "being examined for admission to treatment"[641] means that the privilege does not depend on the voluntary/involuntary status of the communicant when being examined for admission to treatment for alcohol or drug abuse.[642] This expansion is appropriate considering the frequency with which criminal courts order substance-abuse treatment for offenders. However, the rule does not completely dispense with the voluntariness component: the privilege extends to statements made "by a person being treated voluntarily … for alcohol or drug abuse."[643]

One issue left unresolved by Rule 509(b) is whether the privilege applies to communications made by probationers to probation officers. Is a probation officer a person "involved in the treatment of or examination for alcohol or drug abuse"?[644] There is some tangential involvement because the probation officer usually makes a recommen-

---

638. *See* Tex. R. Evid. 509(b).

639. Tex. Code Crim. Proc. art. 38.101.

640. *See* Tex. R. Evid. 509(b).

641. Tex. R. Evid. 509(b)(2).

642. *See* **In re G.K.H.**, 623 S.W.2d 447, 448 (Tex. App.—Texarkana 1981, no writ) (in pre-Rules decision, statutory privilege was not applicable when treatment was not voluntary). The analogous provision for civil proceedings still requires that the examination for treatment be voluntary before the privilege applies. Tex. R. Evid. 510(a)(2)(B).

643. Tex. R. Evid. 509(b)(2); *see, e.g.*, **Absalon v. State**, 460 S.W.3d 158, 162-63 (Tex. Crim. App. 2015) (statements made by defendant during substance-abuse treatment that was part of his plea bargain were not protected by Rule 509(b), now Rule 509(b)(2); "us[ing] substance-abuse treatment as a bargaining chip to avoid a criminal trial" did not make defendant's participation in treatment voluntary).

644. *See* Tex. R. Evid. 509(b)(1).

dation to the trial court about a particular offender's need for substance-abuse treatment. Thus, while the probation officer's main duties do not include substance-abuse screening, such screening is an indirect part of the officer's duties. Therefore, the rationale for including this privilege in criminal proceedings probably should cover any confidential communications to the probation officer.

The rule covers all persons to whom such communications are made and requires no inquiry into whether they are licensed or a "professional," unlike some of the analogous civil provisions.[645] Under Rule 509(b), even confidences made to a janitor or orderly are covered if a party shows that the janitor or orderly was involved in the treatment or examination of substance-abuse patients. Similarly, statements made during group- or family-therapy sessions would be covered by the rule if the sessions were intended to be confidential.[646]

Because any communication covered by the rule is not admissible, either the State or the defendant may object to the offer of such evidence.[647] The privilege applies to any person undergoing treatment for drug or alcohol abuse and thus covers a witness as well as a defendant. Because such communications are not admissible, they are not discoverable by the defendant in a pretrial setting.[648]

---

645. *See Johnson v. State*, 926 S.W.2d 334, 337 (Tex. App.—Fort Worth 1996) (because Rule 510, now Rule 509, does not define the "person" who receives the communication, nonprofessionals involved in the rehabilitation process are subject to the rule), *vacated on other grounds*, 938 S.W.2d 65 (Tex. Crim. App. 1997); *cf.* Tex. R. Evid. 510(b)(1)(A) ("In a civil case, a patient has a privilege to refuse to disclose and to prevent any other person from disclosing … a confidential communication between the patient and a professional …."). Refer to notes 738-780 *infra* and accompanying text.

646. *See, e.g., Johnson*, 926 S.W.2d at 337 (statements defendant made about sexual abuse of stepdaughter during joint counseling sessions for drug abuse with counselor, defendant, and defendant's wife would have been inadmissible during State's case-in-chief). In *Johnson*, the court held that the defendant's counsel had opened the door to admission of the drug counselor's testimony that the defendant's wife had confronted him during one joint session about sexually abusing her daughter when he argued, during his opening statement, that she had never mentioned any alleged sexual abuse of her daughter until he left her four years later. *Id.* at 337-38. However, the counselor went further and testified that the defendant had admitted the abuse during that same session. *Id.* at 338-39. This elaboration was held to be reversible error. *Id.* at 339.
    This case is another example of upholding a privilege when the rationale for the privilege does not apply. The privilege for drug-abuse counseling is intended to protect communications relating to the person's drug or alcohol problems. It was never intended to provide a shield for confessions of wholly unrelated crimes, particularly of child sexual abuse. Indeed, as the dissent in *Johnson* contended, the only privilege that is recognized in the context of reporting and communicating child sexual abuse is the attorney-client privilege. *Id.* at 341 (Barron, J., dissenting in part, concurring in part) (citing former Tex. Fam. Code §34.04, now Tex. Fam. Code §261.202).
    For a more reasoned analysis, see *Tatum v. State*, 919 S.W.2d 910, 913 (Tex. App.—Fort Worth 1996, no pet.), in which the court held that former Criminal Rule 510 did not protect a sexual-assault defendant's statements to his therapist because the defendant sought counseling as a sex offender and not for alcohol abuse.

647. Rule 509(b) does not prohibit *disclosure* of the information, only the *admission* into evidence of the confidential communication. *See Johnson v. State*, 977 S.W.2d 725, 727 n.3 (Tex. App.—Fort Worth 1998, pet. ref'd).

648. *See* Tex. Code Crim. Proc. art. 39.14(a); *cf. Poe v. State*, 630 S.W.2d 885, 888 (Tex. App.—Fort Worth 1982, pet. ref'd) (State's failure to disclose inadmissible hearsay information was not a cause for reversal). For a discussion of a defendant's discovery rights under Texas Code of Criminal Procedure art. 39.14, refer to notes 317-322 *supra* and accompanying text.

The rule also does not define the word "communication," but verbal, nonverbal, and written communications would all presumably be covered by the rule.[649] Other issues might arise, however, because the rule does not define "communication." Suppose a person undergoing voluntary treatment for cocaine addiction tells his therapist that he murdered his wife. Is that communication inadmissible in a murder prosecution? The communication is made within the literal terms of the patient-therapist relationship, but it is certainly outside the rationale for the privilege because it does not further any societal interest in the rehabilitation of substance abusers.

Finally, unlike the analogous civil provisions, Rule 509(b) contains no exceptions to the general rule of inadmissibility. The perceived importance of drug- and alcohol-abuse counseling is so great that the protection offered by the rule cannot be pierced under any circumstances in a criminal proceeding. That same communication might be admissible in a civil lawsuit that arises from the criminal proceeding if it falls within one of the exceptions under Rule 510(d).[650]

C. Rule 509(c) & (d): General Rule of Privilege in Civil Proceedings & Who May Claim Privilege

In a civil case, the privilege protects confidential communications between a physician and a patient that relates to or was made in connection with professional services rendered by the doctor to the patient.[651] In addition, records created or maintained by the physician about the patient's identity, diagnosis, evaluation, or treatment are privileged.[652] The privilege continues even after the physician-patient relationship terminates. The patient, his representative, or the physician acting on behalf of the patient may claim the privilege.[653] A hospital, however, may not have standing to assert the privilege on behalf of nonparty patients.[654]

D. Rule 509(e) & (f): Exceptions & Consent

1. Rule 509(e)(1), (e)(3) & (e)(5): Physician-patient disputes & disciplinary actions.
Rules 509(e)(1) and 509(e)(3) provide exceptions to the physician-patient privilege when

---

649. *Johnson*, 926 S.W.2d at 337.

650. Refer to notes 802-875 *infra* and accompanying text.

651. Tex. R. Evid. 509(c)(1). The patient can refuse to disclose a communication and can prevent any other person from disclosing the communication. Tex. R. Evid. 509(c).

652. Tex. R. Evid. 509(c)(2); *see, e.g.*, *In re Columbia Valley Reg'l Med. Ctr.*, 41 S.W.3d 797, 801-02 (Tex. App.—Corpus Christi 2001, orig. proceeding) (redaction of privileged portions of nonparty medical records would not defeat privilege; information about nurse's charting customs related to patient's treatment and thus was privileged).

653. Tex. R. Evid. 509(d); *see Bristol-Myers Squibb Co. v. Hancock*, 921 S.W.2d 917, 920 (Tex. App.—Houston [14th Dist.] 1996, orig. proceeding) (privilege may be claimed by the patient or his representative, but may be claimed by the physician only on behalf of the patient).

The original version of what is now Rule 509(d)(1) did not include the patient's representative as one who could assert the privilege. *See* 641-642 S.W.2d (Tex. Cases) xlvi (1983, amended 1998). The supreme court rectified this oversight in its 1984 amendments to the rule. *See* 669-670 S.W.2d (Tex. Cases) xxxiv (1984, amended 1998).

654. *See, e.g., In re Fort Worth Children's Hosp.*, 100 S.W.3d 582, 588-89 & n.4 (Tex. App.—Fort Worth 2003, orig. proceeding) (under Rule 509, physician-patient privilege can be asserted only by the patient, the patient's representative, or the physician on behalf of the patient; hospital contended that the physicians whose conduct was in issue were not hospital employees but independent contractors).

disputes arise between doctors and patients. In those instances in which the patient either brings an action against the physician[655] or is the complaining witness in a license-revocation proceeding,[656] Rule 509(e)(1) allows the disclosure of physician-patient communications if they are relevant to a claim or defense.[657] Under Rule 509(e)(3), the privilege does not apply in suits to collect a claim for medical services provided to the patient.[658]

Rule 509(e)(5) allows the disclosure of physician-patient communications in disciplinary actions conducted under the Medical Practice Act,[659] even though the patient's identity must be protected unless the patient is the complaining witness under Rule 509(e)(1) or consents to the disclosure under Rule 509(f).[660]

2. Rule 509(e)(4): Party relies on patient's condition. Rule 509(e)(4) provides for the disclosure of communications and records relevant to the patient's physical, mental, or emotional condition in any proceeding in which a party relies on the condition for a claim or defense.[661] The original version of Rule 509(e)(4) provided an exception for

---

655. TEX. R. EVID. 509(e)(1)(A); *In re Collins*, 286 S.W.3d 911, 916 (Tex. 2009) (orig. proceeding); *see McGowan v. O'Neill*, 750 S.W.2d 884, 886 (Tex. App.—Houston [14th Dist.] 1988, orig. proceeding) ("By initiating a malpractice suit, [the] relator created an exception to the rule of confidentiality as to those physicians she named as defendants, thereby enabling them to disclose certain information without fear of violating the physician-patient privilege.").

656. TEX. R. EVID. 509(e)(1)(B).

657. TEX. R. EVID. 509(e)(1).

658. TEX. R. EVID. 509(e)(3). Unlike the exceptions under Rule 509(e)(1), (e)(4), (e)(6), and (e)(7), the exceptions under Rule 509(e)(3) and (e)(5) do not explicitly require that the otherwise privileged information be relevant. However, normal standards of relevance and materiality apply in all proceedings under the Rules of Evidence. *See* TEX. R. EVID. 401. Information that is covered by any of the exceptions in Rule 509(e) should be divulged only when it is relevant and only to the extent that it is relevant. *See* TEX. R. EVID. 401; *R.K. v. Ramirez*, 887 S.W.2d 836, 843 (Tex. 1994) (orig. proceeding).

659. TEX. OCC. CODE ch. 164.

660. TEX. R. EVID. 509(e)(5). Refer to notes 695-699 *infra* and accompanying text. The exception in Rule 509(e)(5) also applies in disciplinary actions against a registered nurse under Texas Occupations Code §§301.451-301.471. The corresponding exception in the Texas Occupations Code protects patients whose medical records are examined, as well as patients whose billing records are examined. TEX. OCC. CODE §159.003(a)(5).

661. TEX. R. EVID. 509(e)(4); *see R.K.*, 887 S.W.2d at 843 (party-litigant exception to medical and mental-health privileges applies when (1) the records sought to be discovered are relevant to the condition at issue and (2) the condition is relied on as part of a party's claim or defense, meaning that the condition itself is a fact that carries some legal significance).
    Former Civil Rules 509(d)(6) and 510(d)(6), which set out exceptions to the physician-patient and mental-health-information privileges "when the disclosure is relevant in any suit affecting the parent-child relationship," were omitted from the unified Rules of Evidence as unnecessary and overbroad. See the former provisions in Texas Rule of Civil Evidence 509(d)(6), 641-642 S.W.2d (Tex. Cases) XLVI-XLVII (1983, amended 1998) ("Exceptions to confidentiality or privilege in court or administrative proceedings exist … when the disclosure is relevant in any suit affecting the parent-child relationship."), and 510(d)(6), 641-642 S.W.2d (Tex. Cases) XLIX-L (1983, amended 1998) ("Exceptions to the privilege in court proceedings exist … when the disclosure is relevant in any suit affecting the parent-child relationship."). Under the literal wording of the provisions, the medical and mental-health records of *any* witness, including expert witnesses, as well as any party or other person affected by the lawsuit, were subject to disclosure during discovery. *See Smith v. Gayle*, 834 S.W.2d 105, 107 (Tex. App.—Houston [1st Dist.] 1992, orig. proceeding) (former Civil Rule 510(d)(6) exception to mental-health-information privilege applies to both parties and nonparties alike); *Cheatham v. Rogers*, 824 S.W.2d 231, 234 (Tex. App.—Tyler 1992, orig. proceeding) (under literal reading of former Civil Rule 510(d)(6), exception applied to court-appointed mental-health counselor; thus, party in child-custody proceeding could require disclosure of that testifying expert's personal mental-health records).

otherwise privileged communications when the plaintiff (the patient or someone acting on the patient's behalf) sought damages for any mental or physical condition relating to the patient.[662] This exception prevented the plaintiff's "offensive" use of the privilege.[663] For example, if the plaintiff-patient sued for personal injuries arising from an accident and placed his mental or physical condition in issue, he could not conceal evidence of that condition that might weaken or defeat his claim by asserting a privilege as to records, reports, or communications relating to that condition.[664] By placing his medical condition in the public forum and invoking the courts' jurisdiction to recover for that condition, the patient affirmatively waives any privacy interest in those records.

Suppose, however, that the defendant, rather than the plaintiff, affirmatively relies on his medical condition as a defense to the plaintiff's action. Should the rule be any different? The original version of Rule 509(e)(4) retained the privileged status of reports, records, and communications in this instance. Thus, when an injured pedestrian sued a driver, claiming that the defendant caused the accident because he was intoxi-

---

The intent of the exception was to allow for disclosure of a party's prior communications to a professional if either party in a child-custody suit raised the issue of the other party's fitness to have custody of or access to the children because of a mental or emotional condition. *See, e.g.*, **Gillespie v. Gillespie**, 644 S.W.2d 449, 450-51 (Tex. 1982) (in custody proceeding, admission of hospital records containing references to mother's alcoholism was not reversible error; mother's own admissions corroborated records, and other witnesses testified she was intoxicated while caring for child and drove while intoxicated with child in car). The argument against the exception was its negative impact on the basic rationale of the privilege that would encourage troubled families, or parents as individuals, to turn to a professional for counseling to deal with family problems in the hope of preserving the family unit and providing a stable environment for children. With the exception in place, however, parents might have been unwilling to fully disclose their problems to therapists and faced the realistic threat of compelled disclosure in proceedings for the custody of and access to their children. In one extraordinary case under Rule 510(d)(6), the exception was interpreted to require production of the mental-health records of a nonparty—a court-appointed counselor in the underlying child-custody suit. **Cheatham**, 824 S.W.2d at 232. That situation led to the demise of this exception and the institution of other safeguards in these types of cases. *See* Tex. R. Evid. 509 cmt. (1998) (former Rule 509(d)(6) "is omitted, not because there should be no exception to the privilege in suits affecting the parent-child relationship, but because the exception in such suits is properly considered under subparagraph (e)(4) .... In determining the proper application of an exception in such suits, the trial court must ensure that the precise need for the information is not outweighed by legitimate privacy interests protected by the privilege."), Tex. R. Evid. 510 cmt. (1998) (same; Rule 510(d)(5) encompasses former Rule 510(d)(6)); *see also* Tex. Fam. Code §6.705 (confidentiality protections for communications of parents seeking counseling).

662. 641-642 S.W.2d (Tex. Cases) XLVII (1983, amended 1998). The corresponding provision in the Texas Occupations Code still includes monetary damages. *See* Tex. Occ. Code §159.003(a)(4).

663. *See* **R.K.**, 887 S.W.2d at 840-41 (reviewing history of the physician-patient privilege and its "offensive use" exception in Texas). The court noted that the 1984 and 1988 amendments to both the physician-patient and mental-health-information privileges "eliminated the distinction between living and deceased patients, deleted the requirement that the patient be the party who puts his condition in issue, and replaced the word 'element' of a claim or defense with the word 'part' of a claim or defense." *Id.* at 841.

664. **Scheffey v. Chambers**, 790 S.W.2d 879, 881 (Tex. App.—Houston [14th Dist.] 1990, orig. proceeding) (exception to privilege depends on the "offensive" use of privilege). In **Ginsberg v. Fifth Court of Appeals**, the Texas Supreme Court recognized that "'[a] plaintiff cannot use one hand to seek affirmative relief in court and with the other lower an iron curtain of silence against otherwise pertinent and proper questions which may have a bearing upon his right to maintain his action.'" 686 S.W.2d 105, 108 (Tex. 1985) (orig. proceeding) (quoting **Pavlinko v. Yale-New Haven Hosp.**, 470 A.2d 246, 251 (Conn. 1984)); *see also* **Republic Ins. v. Davis**, 856 S.W.2d 158, 163 (Tex. 1993) (orig. proceeding) (offensive-use waiver of a privilege "should not lightly be found"; listing factors to guide trial courts in determining whether a waiver has occurred).

cated, the defendant could simultaneously deny intoxication and prevent the plaintiff from obtaining the hospital medical records showing he had a .24 blood alcohol level at the time of the accident. Because the defendant in such a case should not be allowed to use the privilege as an "offensive" weapon any more than a plaintiff should, the Texas Supreme Court amended what is now Rule 509(e)(4) in 1988[665] to provide that the privilege does not apply if any party relies on the patient's condition as a part of the party's claim or defense.[666]

In *R.K. v. Ramirez*,[667] the supreme court reviewed the effect of the 1988 amendments to the "patient-litigant"[668] exception to Rules 509 and 510. In this case, R.K., the physician-defendant, was sued for malpractice in the delivery of the plaintiffs' twins.[669] The plaintiffs, as a part of their amended complaint, alleged that R.K.'s prior medical and emotional problems affected his ability to care for the patient-plaintiff, and they sought discovery of R.K.'s medical and mental-health records.[670] R.K. sought mandamus to protect his records from disclosure, arguing that (1) the supreme court intended its 1988 amendments merely to codify the offensive-use doctrine that exceptions to the privileges apply only when a patient-party brings his own medical or mental health into issue as part of his claim or defense, (2) the language of the rule means that the patient's condition must be an element of the claim or defense, and (3) the patient-litigant exception to these privileges violates a patient's rights under both the Texas and federal constitutions.[671] The supreme court disagreed with each of his contentions.

The court noted that the intermediate courts of appeals were split on the issue of whether the 1988 amendments were intended only to codify the offensive-use doctrine.[672] The supreme court then rejected R.K.'s contentions and held that the patient-

---

665. 733-734 S.W.2d (Tex. Cases) LXXXVII (1987) (amendments to rule effective Jan. 1, 1988).

666. TEX. R. EVID. 509(e)(4). This exception is the most commonly invoked application of the rule.

667. 887 S.W.2d 836 (Tex. 1994) (orig. proceeding).

668. For convenience, the exception continues to be called the "patient-litigant" exception, even though the patient no longer needs to be a party to the lawsuit for the exception to apply. The exception does not permit a party to discover the identities or medical records of nonparties who are neither witnesses nor claimants in the present lawsuit. *See, e.g., In re Xeller*, 6 S.W.3d 618, 625 (Tex. App.—Houston [14th Dist.] 1999, orig. proceeding) (workers' compensation claimant could not discover medical reports of thousands of nonparty claimants and their workers' compensation medical-evaluation forms that were privileged under Medical Practices Act and constitutional right to privacy; Rule 509(e)(4) did not apply); *In re Anderson*, 973 S.W.2d 410, 411-12 (Tex. App.—Eastland 1998, orig. proceeding) (patient who sued doctor for technician's alleged sexual assault was not entitled to discover identity of other nonparty patients who had complained about doctor, his clinic, or technician; identity of patients is protected under Rule 509(b)(2)); *In re Dolezal*, 970 S.W.2d 650, 652-53 (Tex. App.—Corpus Christi 1998, orig. proceeding) (in personal-injury case, defendant's discovery request for names and billing records of all of chiropractor's patients who were represented by plaintiff's attorney's law firm was improperly granted; material was privileged under Rule 509).

669. *R.K.*, 887 S.W.2d at 838-39.

670. *Id.* at 839.

671. *Id.* at 841.

672. *Id.* Some intermediate courts held that the 1988 amendments to Civil Rules 509 and 510 aimed merely to codify the offensive-use doctrine. *See, e.g., K.P. v. Packer*, 826 S.W.2d 664, 666-67 (Tex. App.—Dallas 1992, orig. proceeding); *Scheffey v. Chambers*, 790 S.W.2d 879, 881 (Tex. App.—Houston [14th Dist.] 1990, orig. proceeding).

litigant exception in Rules 509 and 510 is distinct from and unrelated to the offensive-use doctrine.[673] The supreme court explained that, under the current Rule 509(e)(4) patient-litigant exception, the privilege terminates

> whenever any party relies upon the condition of the patient as a part of the party's claim or defense, even though the patient has not personally placed the condition at issue, and even though the patient is not a party to the litigation. Thus on their face, the 1988 amendments abrogate much of the control that patients once exercised over the release of privileged information.[674]

Thus, the exception applies whenever a patient's medical or mental condition relates "in a significant way" to a party's claim or defense.[675] This is true regardless of whether the patient is a party to the suit. On the other hand, the exception limits disclosure to those matters that are relevant and "reasonably related to the injuries or damages asserted."[676] The condition itself must be a fact of legal significance in the particular lawsuit.[677] For example, if the defendant-doctor in a medical-malpractice suit asserts that treatment of the plaintiff did not fall below the applicable standard of care because the doctor had successfully performed the same treatment on many other pa-

---

Other courts of appeals concluded that such a narrow interpretation of the 1988 amendments ignores the clear language of the rules, giving insufficient effect to the wording of the exception. *See, e.g.,* **Gustafson v. Chambers**, 871 S.W.2d 938, 944-45 (Tex. App.—Houston [1st Dist.] 1994, orig. proceeding); **S.A.B. v. Schattman**, 838 S.W.2d 290, 294-95 (Tex. App.—Fort Worth 1992, orig. proceeding) (op. on reh'g).

The decision in **Scheffey v. Chambers** particularly exemplifies why such a narrow construction was inappropriate. In **Scheffey**, the patient sued his physician for negligently performing back surgery while mentally and physically impaired by cocaine use. 790 S.W.2d at 880. The defendant later entered a California hospital for treatment of his cocaine addiction, and the plaintiff sought discovery of those hospital records. *See id.* When the trial court ordered production of the hospital records without an in camera inspection, the defendant sought and obtained a writ of mandamus from the court of appeals. *Id.* The court of appeals granted relief on the basis that Dr. Scheffey did not bring the litigation and thus was not using the privilege offensively. *Id.* at 881. In that case, the Fourteenth Court of Appeals held that the plaintiff could not rely on either Civil Rule 509(d)(4) (now Rule 509(e)(4)) or 510(d)(5) to discover the defendant's medical records even though they might relate to his defensive claim. **Scheffey**, 790 S.W.2d at 881. The dissent correctly noted, however, that the plaintiff/defendant distinction was no longer tenable under Civil Rule 509(d)(4) or 510(d)(5). By precluding the discovery of those medical records, the defendant could assert with impunity that he was not under the influence of cocaine while treating patients, that his cocaine use did not affect his care of the plaintiff, and even that he had not been at the hospital during an immediate post-use period. *Id.* at 882 (Ellis, J., dissenting).

673. **R.K.**, 887 S.W.2d at 841.

674. *Id.* at 842; *see* **In re Collins**, 286 S.W.3d 911, 916 (Tex. 2009) (orig. proceeding).

675. **R.K.**, 887 S.W.2d at 842; *see, e.g.,* **Rios v. Tex. Dep't of MHMR**, 58 S.W.3d 167, 169 (Tex. App.—San Antonio 2001, no pet.) (defendant in personal-injury suit could depose physician whom plaintiff consulted for second opinion); **M.A.W. v. Hall**, 921 S.W.2d 911, 915 (Tex. App.—Houston [14th Dist.] 1996, orig. proceeding) (in medical-malpractice case, medical records concerning physician's substance abuse were part of negligence claim and were admissible under exception to privilege). Confidential communications and records should be subject to discovery only when the condition is "central" to a claim or defense, not when the patient's condition is merely an evidentiary or intermediate issue of fact, such as for purposes of impeachment. **R.K.**, 887 S.W.2d at 842.

676. Tex. R. Civ. P. 194.2(j); *see also* **McGowan v. O'Neill**, 750 S.W.2d 884, 886 (Tex. App.—Houston [14th Dist.] 1988, orig. proceeding) (when a patient's physical or mental condition is at issue, privileged matters are discoverable if relevant; trial court's order compelling plaintiff to completely waive physician-patient privilege was overly broad).

677. **R.K.**, 887 S.W.2d at 843; *see, e.g.,* **In re Turney**, ___ S.W.3d ___ (Tex. App.—Houston [14th Dist.] 2017, orig. proceeding) (No. 14-16-00999-CV; 6-15-17) (in suit arising from death after single-vehicle collision at racetrack,

tients, that treatment and the condition of those other patients may carry legal significance as part of the defense.[678] But even when a trial court finds that this first requirement is satisfied, only those records and communications that are actually necessary to provide relevant evidence about the alleged condition should be disclosed.[679]

Some portions of a particular medical record may be discoverable and admissible while other portions are not.[680] Information or communications that are contained in medical records but are not relevant to the claim or defense remain privileged under the rule.[681] Medical records relevant to neither a claim nor a defense but only to the impeachment of a testifying party are probably not discoverable because impeachment evidence does not relate directly to a claim or defense.[682]

Courts have debated whether ex parte conversations with a patient's current or former treating physician or other health-care provider violate either Rule 509 or other medical-privacy provisions. The Texas Supreme Court has held that a broad medical authorization waiving the physician-patient privilege for *all* matters, including matters

---

patient-litigant exception applied to medical records related to decedent's alleged heart condition; jury determination of existence of condition and whether it caused collision would have legal significance in case). In **R.K.**, the court stated that

> [t]his approach is consistent with the language of the patient-litigant exception, ... because a party cannot truly be said to "rely" upon a patient's condition, as a legal matter, unless some consequence flows from the existence or non-existence of the condition. As a general rule, a mental condition will be a "part" of a claim or defense if the pleadings indicate that the jury must make a factual determination concerning the condition itself.

Id. However, as Justice Enoch pointed out in his dissent, relying solely on the face of pleadings may result in applying the exception too broadly. *See id.* at 845 (Enoch, J., dissenting). While the plaintiff's pleading did, on its face, allege that R.K.'s physical or mental condition caused his negligence, the legal consequence stems from *whether* R.K. was negligent in his failure to determine that Mrs. Ramirez was carrying twins, not *why* R.K. was negligent. *Id.* If a party can gain access to another's medical or mental treatment records merely by adding a claim about that person's medical or mental state, then there is very little left to these privileges.

678. *See In re Whiteley*, 79 S.W.3d 729, 733 (Tex. App.—Corpus Christi 2002, orig. proceeding).

679. **R.K.**, 887 S.W.2d at 843; *see In re Collins*, 286 S.W.3d at 916 ("In light of the potentially sensitive nature of information that may have been disclosed within the patient/physician relationship, we have stressed that trial courts bear a 'heavy responsibility ... to prevent any disclosure that is broader than necessary.'" (quoting **R.K.**, 887 S.W.2d at 844)); **Groves v. Gabriel**, 874 S.W.2d 660, 661 (Tex. 1994) (per curiam) ("[A] trial court's order compelling release of medical records should be restrictively drawn so as to maintain the privilege with respect to records or communications not relevant to the underlying suit."); *see, e.g.*, **In re Turney**, ___ S.W.3d at ___ (trial court abused discretion by permitting production of decedent's medical records without first reviewing them in camera to determine which were relevant to alleged condition and by not limiting production to those records and redacting irrelevant information).

680. *See* **Midkiff v. Shaver**, 788 S.W.2d 399, 402-03 (Tex. App.—Amarillo 1990, orig. proceeding) (when plaintiffs do not place their general mental condition in issue, discovery should be limited to medical records related to medical attention sought for the symptoms of plaintiffs' mental anguish).

681. *See* **Mutter v. Wood**, 744 S.W.2d 600, 601 (Tex. 1988) (under the rule, a party is entitled to a protective order to safeguard privileged communications and records not relevant to the underlying suit); *see, e.g.*, **Smith v. Gayle**, 834 S.W.2d 105, 107 (Tex. App.—Houston [1st Dist.] 1992, orig. proceeding) (affirming trial court's ruling that nonparty's medical records were not relevant to any issue in the modification of a child-custody suit); **Batson v. Rainey**, 762 S.W.2d 717, 721 (Tex. App.—Houston [1st Dist.] 1988, no writ) (per. curiam) (discovery order that limited disclosure to records of a particular doctor relating to alcohol and drug use was appropriate when plaintiff sued his employer for wrongful termination based on a negligently performed blood test).

682. *See, e.g.*, **Munoz v. State**, 763 S.W.2d 30, 32-33 (Tex. App.—Corpus Christi 1988, pet. ref'd) (upholding trial court's decision to disallow any cross-examination of witness about her "psychiatric history").

that are not relevant to the physical or mental condition at issue in the lawsuit, is improper.[683] But that decision says nothing about the proper scope of the waiver. Some Texas appellate courts have held that the patient-litigant exception under Rule 509(e)(4) results in an automatic waiver of confidentiality of relevant communications, which would allow the opposing party to have a private interview with the patient's treating physician.[684] Other courts have held that such ex parte conversations are improper.[685] Because any state law contrary to HIPAA is preempted, however, any such communications might be illegal unless authorized by written consent of the patient, specific court order, or other lawful procedure.[686]

3. Rule 509(e)(6) & (e)(7): Compelling need for evidence. Rule 509 also provides exceptions to the physician-patient privilege when there is a compelling need for the evidence. Rule 509(e)(6) provides that there is no privilege when the information is relevant to an involuntary civil commitment or hospitalization proceeding.[687] Because psychiatrists are also physicians, there is a question about when the Rule 509(e)(6) exception applies as opposed to the more restrictive analogous Rule 510(d)(4) exception to the psychotherapist-patient privilege.[688] The answer must turn on why the patient

---

683. *Mutter*, 744 S.W.2d at 601.

684. *See* **Durst v. Hill Country Mem'l Hosp.**, 70 S.W.3d 233, 237-38 (Tex. App.—San Antonio 2001, no pet.) (neither the Occupations Code nor Rule 509 explicitly addresses whether ex parte communications are proper when an exception to physician-patient privilege applies; plaintiffs did not show they were harmed by ex parte communications and did not identify any privileged communications that were improperly disclosed); *see, e.g.*, **Rios v. Tex. Dep't of MHMR**, 58 S.W.3d 167, 169-70 (Tex. App.—San Antonio 2001, no pet.) (upholding admission of doctor's testimony although one of his depositions was taken ex parte when plaintiffs were not represented by counsel; declining to establish a new rule of privilege and finding that plaintiff, who had signed authorization for release of medical records, pointed to no confidential, privileged medical information that was elicited ex parte); **Hogue v. Kroger Store No. 107**, 875 S.W.2d 477, 480-81 (Tex. App.—Houston [1st Dist.] 1994, writ denied) (op. on reh'g) (because plaintiff-patient waived physician-patient privilege for matters relevant to lawsuit, plaintiff-patient met with physician only once for medical care in connection with injury allegedly sustained as result of fall in store, and there was no indication that plaintiff's doctor communicated any privileged information to defendant's counsel, the private interview between defendant's counsel and doctor was not improper).

685. *See* **James v. Kloos**, 75 S.W.3d 153, 158-60 (Tex. App.—Fort Worth 2002, no pet.) (noting that federal courts construing Texas law have found ex parte conversations improper; assuming without deciding that trial court erred in admitting treating doctor's testimony after he had ex parte conversation with defendant's attorney); **Travelers Ins. v. Woodard**, 461 S.W.2d 493, 496 (Tex. Civ. App.—Tyler 1970, writ ref'd n.r.e.) (nothing in the rules requires a party to give his adversary access to files of his doctors and of other witnesses and allow him to interrogate them outside of party's presence); *see also* **Perkins v. United States**, 877 F. Supp. 330, 333-34 (E.D. Tex. 1995) (privately contacting a physician could expose the physician to civil liability or professional sanctions; "[i]n a personal injury suit a defense lawyer may not contact *ex parte* a plaintiff's non-party treating physician without the plaintiff's authorization"; rejecting **Hogue**); **Horner v. Rowan Cos.**, 153 F.R.D. 597, 601 (S.D. Tex. 1994) (when treating physician is interviewed ex parte by defense counsel, there are no safeguards against disclosure of irrelevant matters that may be personally damaging to the patient, and the potential for breaches in confidentiality can have a chilling effect on the underlying relationship; thus, defendant is limited to formal methods of discovery unless plaintiff expressly consents to ex parte communication).

686. Refer to notes 626-629 *supra* and accompanying text.

687. *See* Tex. R. Evid. 509(e)(6). The exception covers proceedings for involuntary commitment or court-ordered treatment or probable-cause hearings for people with a mental illness or intellectual disability under Texas Health & Safety Code title 7, subtitles C and D, and for chemical dependency under Texas Health & Safety Code chapter 462. *See* Tex. R. Evid. 509(e)(6).

688. The converse is also true. All physicians are "professionals" within the terms of Rule 510(a)(1)(A). For example, in **In re R___ B___**, the patient was involuntarily committed to Rusk State Hospital. 741 S.W.2d 525, 526

sought the physician's services. Rule 509 defines a patient as one who sees a physician to receive medical care.[689] Rule 510 defines a patient as one who seeks treatment of a mental or emotional condition or disorder.[690] Thus, if a patient consults any type of physician, including a psychiatrist, about a mental or emotional problem, Rule 510 should govern. Although distinguishing between medical care and treatment for mental or emotional problems will not always be easy,[691] it is the only sensible way of reconciling the otherwise contradictory mandates of Rules 509 and 510.[692]

Moreover, society's concern for accurate determinations in proceedings to determine appropriate residential patient care is sufficiently strong to justify the Rule 509(e)(7) exception for evidence relevant to the abuse or neglect of a resident of an institution.[693] This exception applies both to litigation brought by public entities and to private lawsuits based on the abuse or neglect of a resident.[694]

(Tex. App.—Tyler 1987, no writ). The patient claimed that the trial court erred in admitting expert medical testimony and disclosing communications between himself and physicians relating to the diagnosis, evaluation, and treatment of his mental illness. *Id.* The court of appeals noted the conflict between what are now Rules 509(e)(6) and 510(d)(4). *In re R___ B___*, 741 S.W.2d at 527. Rule 509(e)(6) states that there is no physician-patient privilege in a proceeding for involuntary civil commitment. *In re R___ B___*, 741 S.W.2d at 527. With regard to Rule 510(d)(4), the court stated that the privilege does exist unless the court makes a finding, supported by clear and convincing evidence, that the patient had previously been informed that any communications made in the course of a court-ordered examination would not be privileged. *In re R___ B___*, 741 S.W.2d at 527. The court concluded that "in circumstances where a 'patient' is examined, consulted, interviewed or treated by a medical doctor, regardless of his specialty, pursuant to a court order, the exception expressed in Rule 510(d)(4) is applicable." *Id.* Because the patient met the initial burden of showing the confidential relationship under Rules 509 and 510, the burden shifted to the State to demonstrate that the strict requirements of Rule 510(d)(4) had been met. *In re R___ B___*, 741 S.W.2d at 528. The State did not satisfy that burden. *Id.*; *cf. Dial v. State*, 658 S.W.2d 823, 825-26 (Tex. App.—Austin 1983, no writ) (applying the exception to communications between patient and person licensed to practice medicine under the Medical Practice Act rather than applying the exception to privilege for communications between patient and professional in the Medical Health Code). Refer to notes 811-838 *infra* and accompanying text.

689. Tex. R. Evid. 509(a)(1).

690. Tex. R. Evid. 510(a)(2)(A).

691. For example, a patient may go to a physician for treatment of what the patient believes to be a medical problem, but which turns out to be of psychosomatic origin. A Texas Attorney General opinion reconciled the predecessors to Rules 509 and 510 by stating that the physician-patient statute (Tex. Rev. Civ. Stat. art. 4495b, §5.08) took precedence over the psychotherapist-patient statute (Tex. Rev. Civ. Stat. art. 5561h) because it was enacted more recently. *See* Tex. Att'y Gen. Op. No. MW-569 (1982).

692. *See* Tex. Att'y Gen. Op. No. MW-569 (1982).

693. *See* Tex. R. Evid. 509(e)(7). This exception is designed to protect residents of convalescent and nursing facilities and related institutions, as defined in Texas Health & Safety Code §242.002. Tex. R. Evid. 509(e)(7); *see* Tex. Health & Safety Code §260A.001(5) ("facility" means institution as defined by §242.002, assisted-living facility as defined by §247.002, and prescribed pediatric extended-care center as defined by §248A.001). Texas Health & Safety Code §260A.002 requires anyone having cause to believe that an institution resident's physical or mental health or welfare has been or may be adversely affected by abuse, neglect, or exploitation to report that information to the Department of Aging and Disability Services or any local or state enforcement agency. Tex. Health & Safety Code §260A.002; *see also id.* §260A.002(a-1) (reports made under §260A.002, other than those related to a prescribed pediatric extended-care center, must be investigated by the Department of Family and Protective Services). In proceedings on the abuse, neglect, or exploitation of a resident or the cause of any such abuse, neglect, or exploitation, evidence may not be excluded because it involves a privileged communication unless it is privileged as an attorney-client communication. *Id.* §260A.010.

694. *See* Tex. R. Evid. 509(e)(7); *In re Arriola*, 159 S.W.3d 670, 675 (Tex. App.—Corpus Christi 2004, orig. proceeding). In *In re Arriola*, the plaintiffs brought suit against a nursing home and others alleging that Ms. Ar-

4. Rule 509(e)(2) & (f): Consent to release information. Rule 509(e)(2) provides an exception for instances in which a patient or his agent consents in writing to the release of information protected by the physician-patient privilege.[695] The consent must conform to the requirements set forth in Rule 509(f).[696] Even when a patient consents to disclosure, the information can be disclosed "only to the extent consistent with the purposes specified in the consent."[697] The patient, or another person authorized to consent, always has the right to withdraw consent to release information in the future, but that withdrawal does not affect the waiver of privileged material already released.[698] The patient's voluntary disclosure as provided in Rule 511 may also waive the privilege.[699]

---

riola had been sexually assaulted by a fellow resident. 159 S.W.3d at 672-73. The plaintiffs alleged that the nursing home was aware that the assailant had previously molested staff members and other residents, and they sought medical and psychiatric records of other residents, including those of the alleged assailant. *Id.* at 673. The trial court denied discovery of those records, but the court of appeals conditionally granted a writ of mandamus and ordered production of the materials. *Id.* at 672-73. The court of appeals first rejected the nursing home's contention that the abuse-and-neglect exceptions of Rules 509 and 510 apply "only to proceedings brought by appropriate law enforcement agencies" and held that the exceptions contained no such limitations. *In re Arriola*, 159 S.W.3d at 675. Instead, they apply in "any proceeding" for abuse or neglect. *Id.* Second, the court rejected the contention that other state statutes and administrative rules prohibited discovery because these confidentiality statutes provided for disclosure when required by law or by court order. *Id.* at 675-76. The court of appeals stated that Rules 509 and 510, with their abuse-and-neglect exceptions to the privilege, are the "law" that required release of the information. *In re Arriola*, 159 S.W.3d at 677. Third, the court of appeals distinguished its holding in *In re Diversicare General Partner, Inc.*, 41 S.W.3d 788, 793 (Tex. App.—Corpus Christi 2001, orig. proceeding), in which the court had held that the trial court did not have authority to disclose certain medical information about a nursing-home resident, because none of the parties in that case had raised or relied on the rules of evidence. *In re Arriola*, 159 S.W.3d at 677.

695. Tex. R. Evid. 509(e)(2); *In re Collins*, 286 S.W.3d 911, 916 (Tex. 2009) (orig. proceeding). Information protected by the physician-patient privilege may be released without written consent from the patient or his representative, however, under Texas Occupations Code §159.002(f). This statute allows this disclosure if the disclosure or release is (1) related to a judicial proceeding in which the patient is a party and (2) requested under a subpoena issued under the Texas Rules of Civil Procedure, the Texas Code of Criminal Procedure, or Texas Civil Practice & Remedies Code chapter 121 (Acknowledgments & Proofs of Written Instruments). Tex. Occ. Code §159.002(f). Section 159.002(f) does not limit a physician's authority to claim the privilege on a patient's behalf. Tex. Occ. Code §159.002(g).

696. Tex. R. Evid. 509(e)(2); *see* Tex. R. Evid. 509(f). The consent must specify (1) the information or records being released, (2) why the information is being released, and (3) the person to whom the information is being released. Tex. R. Evid. 509(f)(2). The consent must be in writing and signed by the patient or a representative of the patient (e.g., parent, attorney ad litem). *See* Tex. R. Evid. 509(f)(1).

697. Tex. R. Evid. 509(f)(4); *In re Christus Health Se. Tex.*, 167 S.W.3d 596, 601 (Tex. App.—Beaumont 2005, orig. proceeding) (per curiam); *see, e.g., Alpha Life Ins. v. Gayle*, 796 S.W.2d 834, 836 (Tex. App.—Houston [14th Dist.] 1990, orig. proceeding) (patient's authorization for physician to release information to insurance company did not authorize insurance company to release that information in a different lawsuit in which patient was not a party).

698. *See* Tex. R. Evid. 509(f)(3).

699. Tex. R. Evid. 511(a)(1). Refer to notes 882-933 *infra* and accompanying text.

RULE 510
MENTAL HEALTH INFORMATION PRIVILEGE IN CIVIL CASES

(a) Definitions. In this rule:

(1) A "professional" is a person:

(A) authorized to practice medicine in any state or nation;

(B) licensed or certified by the State of Texas in the diagnosis, evaluation, or treatment of any mental or emotional disorder;

(C) involved in the treatment or examination of drug abusers; or

(D) who the patient reasonably believes to be a professional under this rule.

(2) A "patient" is a person who:

(A) consults or is interviewed by a professional for diagnosis, evaluation, or treatment of any mental or emotional condition or disorder, including alcoholism and drug addiction; or

(B) is being treated voluntarily or being examined for admission to voluntary treatment for drug abuse.

(3) A "patient's representative" is:

(A) any person who has the patient's written consent;

(B) the parent of a minor patient;

(C) the guardian of a patient who has been adjudicated incompetent to manage personal affairs; or

(D) the personal representative of a deceased patient.

(4) A communication is "confidential" if not intended to be disclosed to third persons other than those:

(A) present to further the patient's interest in the diagnosis, examination, evaluation, or treatment;

(B) reasonably necessary to transmit the communication; or

(C) participating in the diagnosis, examination, evaluation, or treatment under the professional's direction, including members of the patient's family.

(b) General Rule; Disclosure.

(1) In a civil case, a patient has a privilege to refuse to disclose and to prevent any other person from disclosing:

(A) a confidential communication between the patient and a professional; and

(B) a record of the patient's identity, diagnosis, evaluation, or treatment that is created or maintained by a professional.

(2) In a civil case, any person—other than a patient's representative acting on the patient's behalf—who receives information privileged under this rule may disclose the information only to the extent consistent with the purposes for which it was obtained.

(c) Who May Claim. The privilege may be claimed by:

(1) the patient; or

(2) the patient's representative on the patient's behalf.

The professional may claim the privilege on the patient's behalf—and is presumed to have authority to do so.

(d) Exceptions. This privilege does not apply:

(1) *Proceeding Against Professional.* If the communication or record is relevant to a claim or defense in:

(A) a proceeding the patient brings against a professional; or

(B) a license revocation proceeding in which the patient is a complaining witness.

(2) *Written Waiver.* If the patient or a person authorized to act on the patient's behalf waives the privilege in writing.

(3) *Action to Collect.* In an action to collect a claim for mental or emotional health services rendered to the patient.

(4) *Communication Made in Court-Ordered Examination.* To a communication the patient made to a professional during a court-ordered examination relating to the patient's mental or emotional condition or disorder if:

(A) the patient made the communication after being informed that it would not be privileged;

(B) the communication is offered to prove an issue involving the patient's mental or emotional health; and

(C) the court imposes appropriate safeguards against unauthorized disclosure.

(5) *Party Relies on Patient's Condition.* If any party relies on the patient's physical, mental, or emotional condition as a part of the party's claim or defense and the communication or record is relevant to that condition.

(6) *Abuse or Neglect of "Institution" Resident.* In a proceeding regarding the abuse or neglect, or the cause of any abuse or neglect, of a resident of an "institution" as defined in Tex. Health & Safety Code §242.002.

Notes and Comments

Comment to 2015 restyling: The mental-health-information privilege in civil cases was enacted in Texas in 1979. Tex. Rev. Civ. Stat. art. 5561h (later codified at Tex. Health & Safety Code §611.001 et seq.) provided that the privilege applied even if the patient had received the professional's services before the statute's enactment. Because more than thirty years have now passed, it is no longer necessary to burden the text of the rule with a statement regarding the privilege's retroactive application. But deleting this statement from the rule's text is not intended as a substantive change in the law.

Tex. Health & Safety Code ch. 611 addresses confidentiality rules for communications between a patient and a mental-health professional and for the professional's treatment records. Many of these provisions apply in contexts other than court proceedings. Reconciling the provisions of Rule 510 with the parts of chapter 611 that address a mental-health-information privilege applicable to court proceedings is beyond the scope of the restyling project.

Comment to 1998 change: This comment is intended to inform the construction and application of this rule. This rule governs disclosures of patient-professional communications only in judicial or administrative proceedings. Whether a professional may or must disclose such communications in other circumstances is governed by Tex. Health & Safety Code §§611.001-611.008. Former subparagraph (d)(6) of the Civil Evidence Rules, regarding disclosures in a suit affecting the parent-child relationship, is omitted, not because there should be no exception to the privilege in suits affecting the parent-child relationship, but because the exception in such suits is properly considered under subparagraph (d)(5), as construed in *R.K. v. Ramirez*, 887 S.W.2d 836 (Tex. 1994). In determining the proper application of an exception in such suits, the trial court must ensure that the precise need for the information is not outweighed by legitimate privacy interests protected by the privilege. Subparagraph (d) does not except from the privilege information relating to a nonparty patient who is or may be a consulting or testifying expert in the suit.

COMMENTARY ON RULE 510

A. Derivation & Rationale

Rule 510, which applies only in civil cases,[700] draws largely from two Texas statutes: the mental-health-information privilege adopted in 1979[701] and the slightly older privi-

---

700. The rule is rarely invoked in discovery or during trial.

701. Act of May 9, 1979, 66th Leg., R.S., ch. 239, 1979 Tex. Gen. Laws 512 (former Texas Revised Civil Statutes art. 5561h deemed repealed as to civil proceedings effective 1983 and as to criminal proceedings effective 1986) [now codified at Tex. Health & Safety Code ch. 611]. The 1998 comment to Rule 510 states that it governs disclosure of such communications only in judicial or administrative proceedings. Tex. R. Evid. 510 cmt. (1998). The 2015 restyling of the Texas Rules deleted the reference to "administrative proceedings" in Rule 510(d) (exceptions), but no

lege for communications by individuals being treated for drug abuse.[702] There is no general privilege in criminal proceedings for either physician-patient communications[703] or mental-health information; the information must be protected by a specific privilege, such as the attorney-client privilege[704] or one created by statute.[705]

The privilege for communications about the treatment of mental and emotional conditions derives from the privilege for communications between patients and physicians. The privilege for physicians, which originated with an 1828 New York stat-

---

substantive change was intended. *See* Tex. Sup. Ct. Order, Misc. Docket No. 15-9048, §2 (eff. Apr. 1, 2015). Texas Health & Safety Code chapter 611 addresses confidentiality rules for communications between a patient and a mental-health professional and for the professional's records, and many of these provisions apply outside court proceedings. *See* Tex. R. Evid. 510 cmt. (2015). Texas Health & Safety Code §611.006 addresses authorized disclosure of confidential mental-health information in judicial or administrative proceedings and contains some exceptions that are substantially similar to those in Rule 510(d). *See* Tex. Health & Safety Code §611.006; *see also* Tex. R. Evid. 510 cmt. (2015) (reconciling Rule 510 with parts of Texas Health & Safety Code ch. 611 that address mental-health-information privilege in court proceedings was beyond scope of restyling project). The statute, however, is broader because it applies to both civil and criminal proceedings. *See* Tex. Health & Safety Code §611.006(a)(7) (disclosure authorized in "any criminal proceeding, as otherwise provided by law"). The statute also differs from Rule 510(d) by authorizing disclosure in a judicial proceeding affecting the parent-child relationship, a judicial proceeding relating to a will (if the patient's physical or mental condition is relevant to the will's execution), or under an order or a subpoena issued by a court or an agency. *See id.* §611.006(a)(6), (a)(9), (a)(11). Finally, the statute includes an exception—not present in Rule 510(d)—that is substantially similar to Rule 509(e)(6), which applies to the physician-patient privilege. *See* Tex. Health & Safety Code §611.006(a)(10) (authorizing disclosure when information is relevant to certain involuntary-commitment or hospitalization proceedings). Refer to notes 687-692 *supra* and accompanying text. For a discussion of Rule 510(d), refer to notes 802-875 *infra* and accompanying text.

The Texas Health & Safety Code controls matters such as access to the records of a patient-client for such purposes as financial or management audits, program evaluations, or research, Tex. Health & Safety Code §611.004(a)(3), the payment of fees for service, *id.* §611.004(a)(6), and treatment, *id.* §611.004(a)(7). Furthermore, the statute provides for injunctive relief and damages for violation of its provisions. *Id.* §611.005.

702. Tex. Code Crim. Proc. art. 38.101. This article, which was adopted in 1971, provides:

A communication to any person involved in the treatment or examination of drug abusers by a person being treated voluntarily or being examined for admission to voluntary treatment for drug abuse is not admissible. However, information derived from the treatment or examination of drug abusers may be used for statistical and research purposes if the names of the patients are not revealed.

Id. Rule 510 incorporates this provision in its definition of "professional." Tex. R. Evid. 510(a)(1)(C). This provision may be unnecessary because the definition of "patient" in Rule 510(a)(2) refers to the diagnosis, evaluation, and treatment of alcoholism and drug addiction. Tex. R. Evid. 510(a)(2)(A). A similar reference is found in the Texas Health & Safety Code. *See* Tex. Health & Safety Code §611.001(1) ("'Patient' means a person who consults or is interviewed by a professional for diagnosis, evaluation, or treatment of any mental or emotional condition or disorder, including alcoholism or drug addiction."). Although this language covers individuals receiving treatment for drug and alcohol abuse as sources of the communications, it does not seem to include nonprofessional recipients of the communication within its protection, as appears to have been intended by article 38.101 and Rule 509(b). *See* Tex. R. Evid. 510(b)(1)(A). Refer to notes 645-646 *supra* and accompanying text.

703. Rule 509(b) provides a limited privilege that protects from disclosure in criminal cases certain communications by individuals receiving treatment for alcohol or drug abuse. Tex. R. Evid. 509(b). Refer to notes 637-650 *supra* and accompanying text.

704. *See, e.g.,* **Ballew v. State**, 640 S.W.2d 237, 240 (Tex. Crim. App. [Panel Op.] 1980) (defendant's attorney-client privilege extended to protect disclosures made to psychiatrist hired by attorney to aid in preparation of insanity defense).

705. *See* Tex. Code Crim. Proc. art. 46B.007 (defendant's statements during a court-ordered competency examination may not be used as evidence against him in any criminal proceeding other than at a trial on his incompetency or a proceeding in which he first introduces such statements).

ute,[706] traditionally includes a privilege for psychiatrists because they possess medical training.[707] The growth of clinical psychology led to the perception that a privilege predicated on medical qualifications, rather than on the psychotherapeutic relationship, is both over-inclusive and inadequate.[708]

Texas, unlike most other states, did not create a medical privilege first and then a privilege for psychotherapy. Instead, the Legislature first adopted a privilege for mental-health information[709] and two years later created a privilege for physicians.[710]

The perceived absence of credible rationales for a physician-patient privilege led to its rejection by the Advisory Committee on the Federal Rules.[711] However, the committee distinguished the psychotherapist-patient relationship and proposed a privilege to protect it.[712] One justification given for this privilege was that

> "[a]mong physicians, the psychiatrist has a special need to maintain confidentiality. His capacity to help his patients is completely dependent upon their willingness and ability to talk freely. This makes it difficult if not impossible for him to function without being able to assure his patients of confidentiality and, indeed, privileged communication. Where there may be exceptions to this general rule ..., there is wide agreement that confidentiality is a sine qua non for successful psychiatric treatment. The relationship may well be likened to that of the priest-penitent or the lawyer-client. Psychiatrists not only explore the very depths of their patients' conscious, but their unconscious feelings and attitudes as well. Therapeutic effectiveness necessitates going beyond a patient's awareness and, in order to do this, it must be possible to communicate freely. A threat to secrecy blocks successful treatment."[713]

---

706. 8 Wigmore, *supra* note 6, §2380, at 819 n.4.

707. *See* Ralph Slovenko, *Psychiatry and a Second Look at the Medical Privilege*, 6 Wayne L. Rev. 175, 184 (1960) (coverage and narrow construction of the physician-patient privilege is inadequate to the needs of the psychiatrist-patient relationship); *see also* Chafee, *supra* note 624, at 611 (privilege applies to any licensed physician).

708. David W. Louisell, *The Psychologist in Today's Legal World: Part II*, 41 Minn. L. Rev. 731, 735-39 (1957). Louisell makes it clear that in some states a privilege for psychologists was adopted before, or in the absence of, one for physicians, with the potential anomalous problem of leaving unprotected communications made in the course of psychotherapy conducted by a psychiatrist. *Id.* at 741.

709. Act of May 9, 1979, 66th Leg., R.S., ch. 239, 1979 Tex. Gen. Laws 512, *repealed by* Act of Apr. 29, 1991, 72nd Leg., R.S., ch. 76, §19, 1991 Tex. Gen. Laws 515, 647-48.

710. Act of July 28, 1981, 67th Leg., 1st C.S., ch. 1, §5.08, 1983 Tex. Gen. Laws 1, 31 (repealed 1983 (civil rules), 1986 (criminal rules)).

711. Refer to note 624 *supra*.

712. *Proposed Rules*, *supra* note 28, at 242 (Fed. R. Evid. 504 advisory committee's note). The federal courts have been influenced by proposed Rule 504 even though no rules on privilege were adopted by Congress. *See, e.g.*, **United States v. Meagher**, 531 F.2d 752, 753 (5th Cir. 1976) (even under proposed Federal Rule 504, a defendant could not avail himself of the privilege); **Robinson v. Magovern**, 83 F.R.D. 79, 91 (W.D. Pa. 1979) (proposed Federal Rule 504 is evidence of the special relationship between a patient and his psychotherapist); **Flora v. Hamilton**, 81 F.R.D. 576, 578 (M.D.N.C. 1978) (proposed Federal Rule 504 should be looked to for guidance).

713. *Proposed Rules*, *supra* note 28, at 242 (Fed. R. Evid. 504 advisory committee's note) (quoting Report No. 45, Group for the Advancement of Psychiatry 92 (1960)).

The U.S. Supreme Court later held that a psychotherapist-patient privilege applies in federal court, while a physician-patient privilege does not. In ***Jaffee v. Redmond***, the Court distinguished between the two distinct types of treatment and stated that

> [t]reatment by a physician for physical ailments can often proceed success-fully on the basis of a physical examination, objective information supplied by the patient, and the results of diagnostic tests. Effective psychotherapy, by contrast, depends upon an atmosphere of confidence and trust in which the patient is willing to make a frank and complete disclosure of facts, emotions, memories, and fears. Because of the sensitive nature of the problems for which individuals consult psychotherapists, disclosure of confidential communica-tions made during counseling sessions may cause embarrassment or disgrace. For this reason, the mere possibility of disclosure may impede development of the confidential relationship necessary for successful treatment.[714]

Thus, one rationale for the privilege is similar to the one underlying the attorney-client privilege. By this rationale, without the privilege, persons in need of treatment would be less likely to seek it; if they did seek treatment, they would be less likely to reveal what is necessary for an optimal therapeutic relationship.[715] These undesirable

---

714. 518 U.S. 1, 10 (1996). In ***Jaffee***, the patient was a former police officer who responded to a "fight in progress." *Id.* at 4. At the scene, the officer shot and killed a man armed with a butcher knife. *Id.* The deceased man's estate sued the officer for civil-rights violations and wrongful death. *Id.* at 5. As a result of the shooting, the police officer had participated in about 50 counseling sessions with a clinical social worker, and the plaintiff sought to discover the notes the counselor took during those sessions for cross-examination purposes. *Id.*

The Supreme Court held that the privilege served both the privacy interests of the psychotherapist-patient relationship and the public interest of "facilitating the provision of appropriate treatment for individuals suffering the effects of a mental or emotional problem." *Id.* at 11. Further, the Court reasoned, because all 50 states and the District of Columbia had enacted some type of psychotherapist-patient privilege, denial of that privilege in federal courts would frustrate the very purposes of the state provisions that had been enacted to protect those confidential communications. *Id.* at 12-13.

Since ***Jaffee***, courts have been divided on the proper balance between the psychotherapist-patient privilege and a defendant's Sixth Amendment right of confrontation. *Compare* ***Bassine v. Hill***, 450 F. Supp. 2d 1182, 1185-86 (D. Or. 2006) (habeas petitioner's rights of confrontation, cross-examination, and due process outweighed psycho-therapist-patient privilege; distinguishing ***Jaffee*** as a civil case), *and* ***United States v. Mazzola***, 217 F.R.D. 84, 88-90 & n.9 (D. Mass. 2003) (evidentiary and social benefit of allowing defense counsel access to medical records of an important government witness under Sixth Amendment right to cross-examine outweighed witness's privacy inter-est), *with* ***Kinder v. White***, 609 F. App'x 126, 131 (4th Cir. 2015) (district court erred in balancing psychotherapist-patient privilege against defendant's right of confrontation; "now that the psychotherapist privilege has been rec-ognized, it would be both counterproductive and unnecessary for a court to weigh the opponent's evidentiary need for disclosure any time the privilege is invoked"), *and* ***Johnson v. Norris***, 537 F.3d 840, 845-47 (8th Cir. 2008) (ha-beas petitioner's confrontation and due-process rights were not violated when trial court denied access to witness's psychiatric records; Supreme Court has not "establish[ed] a specific legal rule that answers whether a State's psychotherapist-patient privilege must yield to an accused's desire to use confidential information in defense of a criminal case").

715. David W. Louisell & Kent Sinclair, Jr., *Foreword: Reflections on the Law of Privileged Communications—The Psychotherapist-Patient Privilege in Perspective*, 59 CALIF. L. REV. 30, 52 (1971); *see also* Slovenko, *supra* note 707, at 184-94 (articulating the reasons that support maintaining confidentiality of psychotherapeutic services). For a discussion of the similar rationale for the attorney-client privilege, refer to notes 69-73 *supra* and accompanying text.

results would occur either because the prospective patient knows there is no privilege or because the therapist, knowing the law, tells the patient of the danger of future compelled disclosure.

One argument against this rationale is also frequently made against the general physician-patient privilege: no evidence can support claims that the absence of the privilege affects the willingness of patients to seek, or of physicians to provide, health care.[716] Of course, the utilitarian rationale for a privilege is intuitively more persuasive in the context of psychotherapy than it is in the context of orthopedic surgery or an eye examination.[717] As expressed by one of the staunchest advocates for privileges: "Psychiatric communications are uniquely sensitive, and successful treatment requires a degree of self-revelation by the patient which can only be accomplished in an atmosphere of inviolate privacy."[718]

Yet even in the context of psychotherapy, Justice Tobriner, on behalf of the California Supreme Court—hardly a judge or bench unsympathetic to legal innovation—wrote:

> Although petitioner has submitted affidavits of psychotherapists who concur in his assertion that total confidentiality is essential to the practice of their profession, we cannot blind ourselves to the fact that the practice of psychotherapy has grown, indeed flourished, in an environment of a non-absolute privilege. No state ... recognizes as broad a privilege as petitioner claims is constitutionally compelled. Whether psychotherapy's development has progressed only because patients are ignorant of the existing legal environment can only be a matter for speculation; psychotherapists certainly have been aware of the limitations of their recognized privilege for some time.[719]

---

716. *See* McCormick on Evidence II, *supra* note 197, §105, at 225 (rejecting the idea that a patient will not communicate with his doctor if there is a risk of courtroom disclosure); 8 Wigmore, *supra* note 6, §2380a, at 829 (disbelieving that people would be reluctant to seek treatment if there were no privilege); Chafee, *supra* note 624, at 609 (one unsatisfactory reason for the privilege is the fear that a patient will not seek help if his confidences are not protected); Morgan, *supra* note 624, at 290-91 (assumption that people will avoid medical help or not fully confide in the therapist without the privilege is unreasonable). Refer to note 624 *supra*.

717. The legitimacy of such a distinction has been suggested by David Louisell, a devoted supporter of privileges. Louisell, *supra* note 708, at 740-41.

718. Stephen A. Saltzburg, *Privileges and Professionals: Lawyers and Psychiatrists*, 66 Va. L. Rev. 597, 620 (1980). Despite this absolutist language, Saltzburg acknowledges that some exceptions are necessary. *Id.* at 622-23. The argument made by Saltzburg and the Advisory Committee in favor of the privilege is predicated on the model of psychotherapy drawn from the teachings of Sigmund Freud. *See* Ralph Slovenko, Psychotherapy, Confidentiality and Privileged Communication 40-42 (1966) (attributing the development of psychotherapy to Freud and recognizing the importance of confidentiality to a successful therapeutic relationship). Group therapy, however, is perceived to be effective despite the therapist's inability to guarantee confidentiality. *See* John G. Fleming & Bruce Maximov, *The Patient or His Victim: The Therapist's Dilemma*, 62 Calif. L. Rev. 1025, 1041-43 (1974).

719. *In re Lifschutz*, 467 P.2d 557, 564 (Cal. 1970) (footnote omitted). Justice Scalia, in his dissenting opinion in *Jaffee*, which was joined by Chief Justice Rehnquist, expressed a similar skepticism that the lack of a psychotherapist-patient privilege would inhibit disclosure of information to a mental-health provider. 518 U.S. at 22-24 (Scalia & Rehnquist, JJ., dissenting).

Furthermore, empirical studies question whether patients seeking psychiatric assistance would refrain from telling their therapist the truth if they thought that the therapist might someday divulge their communications.[720] Nonetheless, both the U.S. Supreme Court and the Texas Supreme Court have held that the privilege is justified by a policy of encouraging communication between patients and psychotherapists.[721] The balance struck by the supreme court and Rule 510 is to recognize that the privilege is subject to exceptions[722] that, although significant, leave a substantial zone of privacy guaranteed against judicially compelled intrusion.

---

720. Daniel W. Shuman & Myron S. Weiner, *The Privilege Study: An Empirical Examination of the Psychotherapist-Patient Privilege*, 60 N.C. L. Rev. 893, 895 (1982). The Shuman and Weiner study used four questionnaires designed for different groups—patients in therapy, laypeople not in therapy, judges, and therapists. *Id.* at 896. It also used data from a health-insurance company about the incidence of claims for psychotherapy before and after the privilege was enacted. *Id.* Finally, the authors interviewed a number of the judges who received questionnaires. *Id.* at 922. The study concluded that "[w]ithholding information from therapists is common but ... it probably has little relationship to fear of disclosure, and would therefore probably not be greatly enhanced by a statutory privilege. The basic reason why patients withhold items is because they fear the judgment of their therapists." *Id.* at 926. Shuman and Weiner also concluded that when the therapist threatens to disclose or actually discloses, patients communicate violent urges less frequently and sometimes terminate the treatment relationship. *Id.* Although patients value the confidentiality of their treatment sessions, they rely on the therapist's ethics rather than on a statutory privilege. *See id.* Whether such reliance is well-founded has been sharply questioned:

> In the jurisdictions without a medical privilege law, the patient is protected only by the weakly worded ethical canons of the medical profession, the Hippocratic Oath, and basic professional integrity. The degree of protection afforded ... is necessarily scanty; the moral and legal sanctions for unauthorized disclosure are weak and ineffective.

Louisell & Sinclair, *supra* note 715, at 32-33 (footnotes omitted).

It is true that when a patient was told to assume the absence of any privilege, the expressed willingness to disclose information dropped markedly among the laypersons not in therapy. Shuman & Weiner, *supra*, at 926. Although the "disclosure rate" dropped from 76% to 53%, the predicted reluctance by these nonpatients was more likely to involve criminal acts than the most private sexual thoughts and acts. *Id.* at 920, 926. This decline in a willingness to disclose is consistent with other studies. *See, e.g.*, Toni P. Wise, Note, *Where the Public Peril Begins: A Survey of Psychotherapists to Determine the Effects of* Tarasoff, 31 Stan. L. Rev. 165, 177 n.67 (1978) (survey results indicate that an absence of assured confidentiality makes a patient more reluctant to disclose or discuss the more violent aspects of his life); Comment, *Functional Overlap Between the Lawyer and Other Professionals: Its Implications for the Privileged Communications Doctrine*, 71 Yale L.J. 1226, 1255 (1962) (survey shows more reluctance to fully disclose information when there is no professional privilege). Nevertheless, it is crucial to recognize that the choice is not between assuring patients and potential patients of an absolute privilege and advising them that there is no privilege. Such a dramatic control may produce significantly different predicted disclosure rates. Rather, if the patient is to be advised, it must be of the possibility of disclosure. The privilege in Texas has exceptions, and no legal scholar has been found who advocates an absolutist position in this regard. The possible application of these exceptions to the patients' confidences is both unpredictable and, except for litigants under Rule 510(d)(5), beyond the control of the patient; it thus seems unlikely that some decline in the disclosure rate can be avoided.

721. *See Jaffee*, 518 U.S. at 10 ("Effective psychotherapy ... depends upon an atmosphere of confidence and trust in which the patient is willing to make a frank and complete disclosure of facts, emotions, memories, and fears."); *R.K. v. Ramirez*, 887 S.W.2d 836, 840 (Tex. 1994) (orig. proceeding) (basis for privilege is to encourage full communication necessary for effective treatment and to prevent unnecessary disclosure of highly personal information); *Ginsberg v. Fifth Ct. of Appeals*, 686 S.W.2d 105, 107 (Tex. 1985) (orig. proceeding) ("The justification for this privilege lies in the policy of encouraging the full communication necessary for effective treatment of a patient by a psychotherapist.").

722. *See, e.g.*, *Coates v. Whittington*, 758 S.W.2d 749, 752 (Tex. 1988) (orig. proceeding) (prohibiting the discovery of plaintiff's psychiatric records because defendant did not establish a nexus to plaintiff's claim that would defeat the privilege); *Ginsberg*, 686 S.W.2d at 107 (permitting the admission of patient's mental-health record because patient was using the privilege as an offensive weapon). Refer to notes 802-875 *infra* and accompanying text.

B. Rule 510(b): General Rule of Privilege

1. Rule 510(b)(1)(A): Confidential communication between patient & professional.

The basic proposition of the rule is that confidential communications[723] "between the patient and a professional" are protected by the privilege.[724] Rule 510 would seem to make privileged any communication between patient and professional without regard to the substance of the communication. Such an interpretation arises from the definition of a patient: a patient generally is a person who consults a professional[725] for evaluation or treatment of "any mental or emotional condition or disorder."[726] Because the phrase "mental or emotional condition or disorder" identifies the purpose of the consultation rather than the substance of the communication, a party could claim the privilege for communications unrelated to the provision of mental-health care. But this reading is contrary to the purpose and spirit of the rule. Further, it is arguably inconsistent with Rule 510(a)(4), which defines a "confidential" communication by reference to the patient's interest in "the diagnosis, examination, evaluation, or treatment."[727] Because

---

723. The application of privileges raises the question of what constitutes a "communication." Wigmore was a strong advocate of the view that only express communications, as distinguished from acts that are not clearly intended as a means of communication, should be privileged. *See* 8 WIGMORE, *supra* note 6, §2307, at 591-95 (attorney-client privilege), §2337, at 657-58 (marital privilege). Wigmore recognized, however, that physicians obtain much of the information needed for diagnosis and treatment by their own observations, rather than from the patient's narrative. *Id.* §2384, at 844-45. To the extent that the observation is made possible by the patient's deliberate submission, the data obtained should be privileged. *Id.* §2384, at 845. Psychiatry and psychology would seem to share this characteristic because persons suspected of mental disorders are commonly committed for observation. *See* TEX. HEALTH & SAFETY CODE ch. 573 (governing the emergency detention of a person for mental-health services and evaluation). The process of diagnosing and treating mental and emotional distress is likely to involve inferences drawn by the therapist about the patient's subconscious. *See* Saltzburg, *supra* note 718, at 620 (patients undergoing psychotherapy are often unaware of the magnitude of their own problems). By hypothesis, patients are frequently unaware of what they reveal through their behavior or even their verbal responses, as with techniques such as word association or the thematic-apperception test. *See* SLOVENKO, *supra* note 718, at 186 (certain techniques encourage a patient to verbalize his every thought so that the therapist can evaluate the unedited and unadulterated information). As long as the patient fits the definition in Rule 510(a)(2), "communication" should be broadly interpreted. *See C.V. v. State*, 616 S.W.2d 441, 442-43 (Tex. Civ. App.—Houston [14th Dist.] 1981, no writ) (psychiatrist's "observations" are privileged).

724. TEX. R. EVID. 510(b)(1)(A). The patient can refuse to disclose a communication and can prevent any other person from disclosing it. TEX. R. EVID. 510(b)(1).

725. Refer to notes 738-780 *infra* and accompanying text.

726. TEX. R. EVID. 510(a)(2)(A). Refer to notes 781-782 *infra* and accompanying text. There may be an issue about whether the person who wants to claim the privilege was "seeking" professional services for diagnosis or treatment. In *Mosby v. State*, the defendant, who was convicted of sexual abuse of his stepdaughter, complained that a psychologist should not have been permitted to testify that the defendant admitted during therapy sessions that he had committed the charged offense. 703 S.W.2d 714, 715 (Tex. App.—Corpus Christi 1985, no pet.). Originally, the court of appeals agreed and reversed the conviction. Chief Justice Nye dissented and argued that the defendant's statements to the psychologist were not protected by the privilege because he did not "seek" treatment for any mental disorder. *Id.* at 718 (Nye, C.J., dissenting). Rather, he and his wife visited the psychologist for family counseling because the defendant feared that he would never see his stepdaughter again if he refused. *Id.* at 718-19. Chief Justice Nye suggested that because the defendant did not envision his visit with the psychologist as being one of a patient seeking treatment, he was not entitled to claim a privilege under Rule 510. *Mosby*, 703 S.W.2d at 719. This reading of the word "seeking" would appear to be extraordinarily narrow. On rehearing, the appellate court upheld the conviction because the psychiatrist-patient privilege statute, though in effect at the time the defendant made his admissions, had been amended by the time of trial to provide an exception to the privilege in criminal proceedings. *Id.* at 720-21.

727. TEX. R. EVID. 510(a)(4)(A). Refer to notes 786-798 *infra* and accompanying text.

a statement unrelated to the patient's interest in such care is clearly outside the definition of "confidential," confidentiality should be recognized only when the communication relates to the provision of such care.[728]

The privilege applies regardless of when the professional's services were received. Confidentiality attaches and continues even if the professional therapeutic relationship has ended, or the patient has died.[729]

2. Rule 510(b)(1)(B): Records. Rule 510 also protects "a record of the patient's identity, diagnosis, evaluation, or treatment that is created or maintained by a professional."[730] The identities of both former and current patients are protected.[731] This protection is broader than that normally provided under the attorney-client privilege,[732] thus emphasizing the importance of confidentiality of information relating to mental-health care.[733]

3. Rule 510(b)(2): Restriction on disclosure. Rule 510(b)(2) reiterates the general rule that information privileged under Rule 510 may be disclosed "only to the extent consistent with the purposes for which it was obtained."[734] This provision makes it clear that the rule extends to all recipients of any information derived from confidential communications except representatives of the patient acting on the patient's behalf.[735] Persons who might obtain confidential information include those who provide or assist in the provision of psychotherapy, those participating in group therapy,[736] and those who gain access to such information through one of the exceptions in Rule 510(d).[737]

C. Rule 510(a): Definitions

1. Rule 510(a)(1): Professional. Given the general rule of the mental-health-information privilege, one crucial question is the definition of a "professional." The definition in Rule 510(a)(1) includes four groups.

---

728. If the professional is consulted for other types of medical care, the physician-patient privilege may be available. *See* Tex. R. Evid. 509. Refer to notes 688-692 *supra* and accompanying text.

729. *See* Tex. R. Evid. 510(a)(3)(D) & (c)(2) (defining "patient's representative" as a personal representative of a deceased patient and permitting that person to claim the privilege on the patient's behalf); *cf.* **Swidler & Berlin v. United States**, 524 U.S. 399, 410 (1998) (under federal common law, attorney-client privilege survives client's death).

730. Tex. R. Evid. 510(b)(1)(B).

731. *See* Tex. Health & Safety Code §611.002 (records of patient's identity are confidential and generally may not be disclosed). In **Ex parte Abell**, the Texas Supreme Court took this position in interpreting §2(b) of former article 5561h, which was retained in Rule 510(b)(1)(B). *See* **Ex parte Abell**, 613 S.W.2d 255, 262-63 (Tex. 1981) (orig. proceeding). **Ex parte Abell** was a 5-4 decision with a vigorous and well-argued dissent. *Id.* at 263-69 (Spears, Campbell, Ray, Wallace, JJ., dissenting).

732. *See* **In re Grand Jury Subpoena**, 926 F.2d 1423, 1431 (5th Cir. 1991) ("As a general rule, client identity [is] not protected as privileged" unless disclosure would itself reveal a confidential communication).

733. Fleming & Maximov, *supra* note 718, at 1050-51.

734. Tex. R. Evid. 510(b)(2).

735. *Id.*

736. Refer to notes 794-798 *infra* and accompanying text.

737. For a discussion of the exceptions to Rule 510, refer to notes 802-875 *infra* and accompanying text.

(1) Rule 510(a)(1)(A): Authorized to practice medicine in any state or nation. The first group defined as "professionals" are persons "authorized to practice medicine in any state or nation."[738] This definition derives from former article 5561h,[739] which had been interpreted by an exhaustive commentary as arguably including not only doctors of medicine and osteopathy, but also of dentistry, chiropractic, and all other healing arts.[740] However, the 1981 enactment of the Medical Practice Act[741] points strongly to a less inclusive view. The Act provides for the regulation of the practice of medicine in Texas and specifically excludes practitioners of other healing arts from its application.[742] Moreover, the Medical Practice Act, which defines "physician" as "a person licensed to practice medicine," includes the physician-patient privilege, now embodied in Rule 509.[743] It is reasonable to treat "authorized" in the mental-health-information privilege as equivalent to "licensed" in the physician-patient privilege. This view is consistent with the principle of narrow construction of privileges.[744] A patient might address confidential communications about a mental or emotional condition to a podiatrist, but this communication should not be privileged. Both the content of the communication and the identity of the listener must be shown to relate to the legitimate purpose of providing psychotherapeutic care.

(2) Rule 510(a)(1)(B): Licensed or certified by the State of Texas in the diagnosis, evaluation, or treatment of any mental or emotional disorder. The second group included in the definition of "professional" are persons "licensed or certified by the State of Texas in the diagnosis, evaluation, or treatment of any mental or emotional disorder."[745] This provision brings communications made to psychologists[746] within the

---

738. Tex. R. Evid. 510(a)(1)(A).

739. Act of May 9, 1979, 66th Leg., R.S., ch. 239, §1(a), 1979 Tex. Gen. Laws 512, 512 (former Texas Revised Civil Statutes art. 5561h deemed repealed as to civil proceedings effective 1983 and as to criminal proceedings effective 1986) [now codified at Tex. Health & Safety Code §611.001(2)(A)].

740. *See* Barry K. Green, Comment, *The Psychotherapist-Patient Privilege in Texas*, 18 Hous. L. Rev. 137, 146-48 (1980) (a broad interpretation of "authorized to practice medicine" would include optometry, podiatry, dentistry, and chiropractic medicine).

741. Act of July 28, 1981, 67th Leg., 1st C.S., ch. 1, 1983 Tex. Gen. Laws 1 (repealed 1999) [now codified at Tex. Occ. Code tit. 3, subtit. B].

742. *See* Tex. Occ. Code §151.052(a) (the Act does not apply to dentists, optometrists, chiropractors, nurses, podiatrists, psychologists, or physical therapists).

743. *See id.* §§151.002(a)(12), 159.002(a).

744. *See* **Tex. Dep't of MHMR v. Davis**, 775 S.W.2d 467, 473 (Tex. App.—Austin 1989, orig. proceeding [leave denied]) (attorney-client privilege "tends to prevent full disclosure of the truth [and therefore] is narrowly construed"); **Wade v. Abdnor**, 635 S.W.2d 937, 938 (Tex. App.—Dallas 1982, writ dism'd) (psychotherapist-patient privilege is narrowly construed because "it is a deviation from common law ... and because of the limitation it places on disclosure in judicial proceedings"); *cf.* **Lehnhard v. Moore**, 401 S.W.2d 232, 235 (Tex. 1966) (orig. proceeding) (testimonial privilege should be "sparingly permitted" and cannot be created by a nondisclosure agreement).

745. Tex. R. Evid. 510(a)(1)(B).

746. A person engages in the practice of psychology when he provides or offers to provide psychological services in the context of a professional relationship. Tex. Occ. Code §501.003(b); *see also id.* §501.003(a)(1) (defining "practice of psychology"). The advice will generally be considered the practice of psychology when (1) the person represents that he is licensed under Texas Occupations Code chapter 501 and that the advice is psychological in nature, and (2) the advice is offered in the context of a professional relationship focused primarily on the delivery of health-care services for mental, emotional, or behavioral health. *See id.* §501.003(c).

scope of the privilege's protection.[747] Persons employed as psychologists by any regionally accredited institution of higher education, if they provide their services exclusively for such employers, are exempt from the licensing and certifying requirements.[748] Rule 510 technically excludes communications to such psychologists, given the explicit requirement that they be licensed or certified.[749]

This exclusion is unlikely to cause problems because the patient would probably be able to claim that he "reasonably believed" the psychologist to be licensed or certified, which brings the therapist within another definition of "professional."[750] Further, an unlicensed or uncertified psychologist is often "participating in the diagnosis, examination, evaluation, or treatment under [a] professional's direction,"[751] and the directing professional is probably a licensed psychiatrist.[752]

In addition to psychologists, two other groups might claim inclusion within this portion of the privilege's definition of "professional." One group is licensed professional counselors. According to this profession's authorizing legislation,[753] counseling is defined as "assisting a client through a therapeutic relationship, using a combination of mental health and human development principles, methods, and techniques, including the use of psychotherapy, to achieve the mental, emotional, physical, social, moral, educational, spiritual, or career-related development and adjustment of the client throughout the client's life."[754]

---

747. Rule 510's statutory predecessor also protected these communications. *See Ex parte Abell*, 613 S.W.2d 255, 262 (Tex. 1981) (orig. proceeding) (under former TEX. REV. CIV. STAT. art. 5561h, §1(a), now TEX. HEALTH & SAFETY CODE §611.001(2)(B), a professional is one who is licensed by the state to evaluate, diagnose, or treat mental disorders).

748. TEX. OCC. CODE §501.004(a)(1). Employees of governmental agencies are also exempt if they perform their duties "within the confines of the agency" and do not represent that they are psychologists. *Id.* §501.004(a)(6).

749. *See State v. Gotfrey*, 598 P.2d 1325, 1327-28 (Utah 1979) (communications to an unlicensed clinical psychologist employed at a mental-health clinic are unprotected); Pamela Heffernan, Comment, *The Scope of the Psychologist-Patient Testimonial Privilege in Utah*, 1980 UTAH L. REV. 385, 385 (commenting on *Gotfrey* and contending that the privilege protects only licensed psychologists).

750. TEX. R. EVID. 510(a)(1)(D). Refer to notes 777-780 *infra* and accompanying text. If this interpretation is correct, an unlicensed psychologist is arguably obliged to advise patients that their communications are not privileged. A failure to do so, thus knowingly permitting the patient to act with a mistaken perception of the relationship, should constitute a breach of professional ethics. *Cf. Gotfrey*, 598 P.2d at 1330 (Stewart & Maughan, JJ., dissenting) (the purpose of the Utah Psychologist's Licensing Act was to assure the public that those holding themselves out as psychologists were adequately trained and qualified to engage in psychology). The Texas State Board of Examiners of Psychologists requires licensed psychologists to "inform their patients or clients about confidentiality and foreseeable limitations on confidentiality created by existing and reasonably foreseeable circumstances prior to the commencement of services ...." 22 TEX. ADMIN. CODE §465.12(b). Psychologists who do not comply with the Board's rules and orders may be subject to a Board-initiated complaint and disciplinary action. *Id.* §461.15; *see id.* §470.24.

751. *See* TEX. R. EVID. 510(a)(4)(C). Refer to notes 786-798 *infra* and accompanying text.

752. *See* TEX. R. EVID. 510(a)(1)(B). *But cf. Gotfrey*, 598 P.2d at 1328 (statutory privilege at issue did not extend to communications made to an unlicensed psychologist acting as an agent of a professional psychologist). Refer to note 746 *supra* and accompanying text.

753. TEX. OCC. CODE ch. 503.

754. *Id.* §503.003(b)(3).

The question is whether these services are within "the diagnosis, evaluation, or treatment of any mental or emotional disorder."[755] It has been suggested that Rule 510(a)(1)(B) should be read as referring to in-depth psychotherapy for which psychiatrists and psychologists are trained and should not include career guidance, life-adjustment seminars, or similar activities that are arguably included within the term "counseling."[756] The definition of "counseling" in the Licensed Professional Counselor's Act mentions psychotherapy,[757] but it is readily distinguishable from the definition of the "practice of psychology," which includes the application of psychological principles to "preventing, predicting, treating, remediating, or eliminating ... symptomatic, maladaptive, or undesired behavior; ... emotional, interpersonal, learning, substance use, neuropsychological, cognitive, or behavioral disorders or disabilities, including those that accompany medical problems; or ... mental illness ...."[758]

The difference in professional training required for membership in these groups strongly supports this proposed distinction between psychologists and other counselors. In order to take the required examination, an applicant for certification as a psychologist must have, among other credentials, a "doctoral degree in psychology from a regionally accredited educational institution."[759] In contrast, an applicant for a license to practice counseling must only possess a master's or doctorate degree in counseling or a related field, complete a graduate degree at a regionally accredited institution of higher learning, and complete at least 48 graduate semester hours.[760] This type of training would not appear to be as rigorous as that which the Legislature had in mind in enacting former Texas Revised Civil Statutes article 5561h, or the supreme court in promulgating Rule 510. Indeed, the Legislature and the court designed the privilege to

---

755. *See* TEX. R. EVID. 510(a)(1)(B).

756. An excellent discussion of this distinction can be found in ***Allred v. State***. 554 P.2d 411 (Alaska 1976). In ***Allred***, the court recognized a common-law psychotherapist-patient privilege but split on whether the privilege covered communications by a murder defendant to a psychiatric social worker. Four of the five justices believed that there was no applicable statutory privilege, but that a psychotherapist-patient privilege should be recognized as a matter of common law. *See id.* at 416-18. Two justices thought that this privilege should not cover a psychiatric social worker because a social worker's services do not amount to psychiatric treatment. *See id.* at 418-21 & n.25. Two other justices thought that the privilege did extend to the communications because the social worker was acting on behalf of a psychiatrist and this was understood by the defendant. *See id.* at 425-26 (Rabinowitz & Dimond, JJ., concurring). The chief justice believed that the communications were protected from disclosure by a statutory privilege. *See id.* at 422-24 (Boochever, C.J., concurring). An interesting contrast is provided by ***In re Pittsburgh Action Against Rape***. 428 A.2d 126 (Pa. 1981). In that case, a rape defendant sought access to the records of communications made by his alleged victim to the personnel of a rape-crisis center. *Id.* at 129. The center resisted and requested creation of a privilege for such communications. *Id.* at 129-30. The court, over one impassioned dissent, declined to do so, relying in large measure on the defendant's Sixth Amendment right of confrontation. *Id.* at 131-33. The reasoning and result in ***In re Pittsburgh Action Against Rape*** was inferentially overruled by the enactment of a statutory privilege prohibiting the disclosure of confidential communications between a sexual-assault victim and a counselor. *See* 42 PA. CONS. STAT. §5945.1(b); ***Commonwealth v. Wilson***, 602 A.2d 1290, 1292-93 (Pa. 1992).

757. TEX. OCC. CODE §503.003(b)(3).

758. *Id.* §501.003(a)(1)(A)(i). Refer to notes 745-749 *supra* and accompanying text.

759. TEX. OCC. CODE §501.255(a)(1)(A).

760. *Id.* §503.302(a)(2), (a)(3); *see* 22 TEX. ADMIN. CODE §681.82.

encourage patients to seek the care of those trained to provide psychotherapeutic services and to enhance the effectiveness of those services.

Moreover, if licensed professional counselors are professionals under Rule 510,[761] similar claims might be expressed on behalf of "licensed social workers," a second group that has statutory certification procedures.[762] The statutory definition of the "practice of social work" includes "the professional use of self to restore or enhance social [or] psychosocial ... functioning" of individuals, families, or groups.[763] Academic credentials for certification involve only an advanced degree in social work without any requirement of training in the provision of psychotherapy.[764] The functions and academic preparation of both licensed professional counselors and certified social workers are too loosely related to psychotherapy to permit the extension of the privilege, with the possible exception of activities they perform under the direction of a "professional."[765]

Thus, perhaps a large proportion, if not the vast majority, of mental-health-care communications are unprivileged because a nonprofessional provides treatment.[766] Moreover, these unprivileged communications will normally be made by patients from lower socioeconomic levels who cannot afford access to professionals.[767] Nevertheless,

---

761. Such claims have been made on behalf of licensed professional counselors because their rules provide that communications with them are confidential "under the provisions of the Texas Health and Safety Code, Chapter 611 and other state or federal statutes or rules where such statutes or rules apply to a licensee's practice." 22 TEX. ADMIN. CODE §681.45(a). The Board of Examiners of Professional Counselors, however, cannot create a privilege. *See* TEX. R. EVID. 501 (privileges are provided by a constitution, by statute, or by rules prescribed under statutory authority). The Board requires licensed professional counselors to inform clients in writing about the limits on confidentiality before services are provided. 22 TEX. ADMIN. CODE §681.41(e)(4).

762. *See* TEX. OCC. CODE ch. 505. Arguably, the Texas Legislature intended the privilege to extend to licensed social workers. The Texas Occupations Code specifies that certification can be denied or revoked when the license holder discloses a "confidential communication transmitted to the license holder by a client ... unless revealing the communication is required by law." *Id.* §505.451(9). It seems incorrect, however, to read this provision as a directive to treat licensed social workers as professionals under Rule 510 because §505.451(9) could have referred to the confidentiality provisions of Texas Health & Safety Code §§611.001-611.008. On the contrary, §505.451(9) probably recognizes that the mental-health-information privilege does not apply; otherwise, this provision would be redundant. The equivalent provision for disciplining psychologists—who are clearly within the scope of Texas Health & Safety Code §611.001(2) (and Rule 510)—contains no reference to required confidentiality. *See* TEX. OCC. CODE §501.401.

763. TEX. OCC. CODE §505.0025(a).

764. *See id.* §505.353.

765. *See* TEX. R. EVID. 510(a)(4)(C) (privilege extends to persons who "participat[e] in the diagnosis, examination, evaluation, or treatment" of the patient if their participation is under a professional's direction). Refer to notes 786-798 *infra* and accompanying text. The privilege would also apply if the patient acted under a reasonable mistake about the counselor's status. TEX. R. EVID. 510(a)(1)(D); *cf.* TEX. R. EVID. 505(a)(1) (protecting confidential communications made in the course of marital and similar counseling performed by a person believed to be a member of the clergy). Refer to notes 777-780 *infra* and accompanying text.

766. *See* Mary K. Stroube, Comment, *The Psychotherapist-Patient Privilege: Are Some Patients More Privileged than Others?*, 10 PAC. L.J. 801, 803-04 (1979) (most mental-health patients are not treated by a psychologist or a psychiatrist, but by a nurse, a social worker, or some other type of mental-health professional).

767. *See* Stroube, *supra* note 766, at 804 (patients seeking mental-health care are disproportionately lower-income). The definition of "patient" in the rule includes the requirement that the consultation be with a "professional." TEX. R. EVID. 510(a)(2)(A). Refer to notes 781-782 *infra* and accompanying text. Thus, a person seeking care in the situation under discussion would not be a patient for purposes of the privilege unless he reasonably

the rule's rationale necessarily dictates this lack of protection for communications made to nonprofessionals. Furthermore, it is consistent with the rule's language and with the principle of narrow construction of statutes that create privileges contrary to the common law.[768] If the Legislature and supreme court had wanted to extend the privilege to include communications to certified social workers,[769] licensed professional counselors, and similar groups,[770] it would have been simple to do so unambiguously, as has been done in other states.[771] On the other hand, the U.S. Supreme Court held that a licensed clinical social worker is covered by the privilege in federal courts, largely because "[t]heir clients often include the poor and those of modest means who could not afford the assistance of a psychiatrist or psychologist, ... but whose counseling sessions serve the same public goals."[772]

(3) Rule 510(a)(1)(C): Involved in the treatment or examination of drug abusers. The third group included in the definition of "professional" consists of persons "involved in the treatment or examination of drug abusers."[773] This extremely general definition

believed he was speaking to a professional or the nonprofessional was working under a professional's direction. *See* Tex. R. Evid. 510(a)(1)(D), (a)(4)(C). Refer to notes 777-780, 786-798 *infra* and accompanying text.

768. *See Fitzgerald v. A.L. Burbank & Co.*, 451 F.2d 670, 682 (2d Cir. 1971) (refusing to construe a New York privilege statute to extend to a psychiatric social worker because the statute was in derogation of the common law). An additional reason for this narrow interpretation lies in the overinclusive definition of "professional" found in Texas Rule 510(a)(1)(D).

769. *See generally* Richard Delgado, Comment, *Underprivileged Communications: Extension of the Psychotherapist-Patient Privilege to Patients of Psychiatric Social Workers*, 61 Calif. L. Rev. 1050 (1973) (communications with psychiatric social workers should be privileged).

770. Licensed social psychotherapists were granted recognition as professionals by the Social Psychotherapist Regulation Act, 64th Leg., R.S., ch. 714, §2(4), 1975 Tex. Gen. Laws 2286, 2286. That Act expired on September 1, 1981, by virtue of the Texas Sunset Act, former Texas Revised Civil Statutes article 5429k, now Texas Government Code ch. 325. During its existence, the Texas State Board of Examiners in Social Psychotherapy imposed confidentiality requirements on its licensees. State Bd. of Exam'rs in Soc. Psychotherapy, Rules on Licensing Soc. Psychotherapists 407.02.00, 1 Tex. Reg. 1188 (1976). One commentator argued that social psychotherapists were professionals within the meaning of former Texas Revised Civil Statutes article 5561h (now Texas Health & Safety Code §611.002). Green, *supra* note 740, at 155-56. This position is questionable for the same considerations (described function and training) discussed in the text in connection with social workers and licensed professional counselors. Refer to notes 753-765 *supra* and accompanying text.

771. *See, e.g.*, Cal. Evid. Code §1010 (including psychiatrists, psychologists, clinical social workers, school psychologists, and marriage and family therapists within the term "psychotherapist"); 740 Ill. Comp. Stat. 110/2 (therapist "means a psychiatrist, physician, psychologist, social worker, or nurse providing mental health or developmental disabilities services").

772. *Jaffee v. Redmond*, 518 U.S. 1, 16 (1996); *see also Oleszko v. State Comp. Ins. Fund*, 243 F.3d 1154, 1157 (9th Cir. 2001) (privilege extended to communications with unlicensed Employee Assistance Program counselors; "EAP personnel are trained as counselors, are held out as counselors in the workplace, and, like psychotherapists, their job is to extract personal and often painful information from employees in order to determine how best to assist them"); *United States v. Schwensow*, 151 F.3d 650, 657 (7th Cir. 1998) (privilege did not apply to communications with volunteer Alcoholics Anonymous phone operators; operators "did not identify themselves as therapists or counselors, nor did they confer with [defendant] in a fashion that resembled a psychotherapy session"); *Jane Student 1 v. Williams*, 206 F.R.D. 306, 310 (S.D. Ala. 2002) (federal psychotherapist-patient privilege applied to communication made to licensed professional counselors but not to unlicensed ones). *But see Jaffee*, 518 U.S. at 28-30 (Scalia & Rehnquist, JJ., dissenting) (there are significant differences between a licensed psychiatrist or psychologist and a licensed clinical social worker, who may have no training in psychotherapy and who interviews people for many reasons); *United States v. Durham*, 93 F. Supp. 3d 1291, 1295 (W.D. Okla. 2015) (declining to extend privilege to unlicensed psychotherapist).

773. Tex. R. Evid. 510(a)(1)(C).

derives from Texas Code of Criminal Procedure article 38.101,[774] which has been commented on by only a few courts since its enactment in 1971.[775] Unlike other "professionals," this broadly defined group includes unlicensed and uncertified persons (even people such as orderlies and volunteers) if courts see them as "involved in the treatment ... of drug abusers." Technically, communications from any type of patient to such nonprofessionals could be seen as privileged. The breadth of this category can be limited if this group of professionals is restricted, for privilege purposes, to persons receiving communications from a patient who "is being treated voluntarily or being examined for admission to voluntary treatment for drug abuse."[776] This restriction preserves the parallel structure found in article 38.101, even though the limitation of that group of professionals to that group of patients is not a specific part of the structure of Rule 510.

(4) Rule 510(a)(1)(D): Who the patient reasonably believes to be a professional. The final category of "professional" is "a person ... who the patient reasonably believes to be a professional under this rule."[777] This provision differs from proposed Federal Rule 504, which would have permitted a patient's reasonable but mistaken belief to invoke the privilege only when the mistake related to a physician's status; the patient's reasonable but mistaken belief did not extend to any other "professional" who provided psychotherapeutic assistance.[778] The rationale for the rule's narrow construction was that too many persons purported to render psychotherapeutic aid to apply the privilege to all psychologists; the privilege applied only to those who were licensed.[779] Moreover,

---

774. *See* TEX. CODE CRIM. PROC. art. 38.101 (communication between a person who is being voluntarily treated or examined for admission to voluntary treatment for drug abuse and any person involved in the examination or treatment of that person is inadmissible).

775. *See* ***Lovorn v. State***, 536 S.W.2d 356, 356 n.1 (Tex. Crim. App. 1976) (if the defendant had objected in a timely manner, the witnesses' testimony might have been inadmissible under art. 38.101); ***Cunningham v. State***, 488 S.W.2d 117, 121 n.5 (Tex. Crim. App. 1972) (art. 38.101 does not prevent a probation officer from testifying to a parole violation because the parolee "was on probation for robbery and was not being treated by or examined for admission for treatment for drug abuse by the probation officer"); ***In re G.K.H.***, 623 S.W.2d 447, 448 (Tex. App.—Texarkana 1981, no writ) (art. 38.101 is inapplicable when the juvenile receiving drug treatment and counseling did not submit voluntarily, but was instead ordered to do so).

776. TEX. R. EVID. 510(a)(2)(B).

777. TEX. R. EVID. 510(a)(1)(D).

778. Proposed Federal Rule of Evidence 504(a)(2) stated the following:
   A "psychotherapist" is (A) a person authorized to practice medicine in any state or nation, or reasonably believed by the patient so to be, while engaged in the diagnosis or treatment of a mental or emotional condition, including drug addiction, or (B) a person licensed or certified as a psychologist under the laws of any state or nation, while similarly engaged.
Proposed Rules, supra note 28, at 240.
   The Texas rule allows the privilege to be invoked whenever the patient reasonably believes that the person with whom he is communicating is *any* professional listed in Rule 510, whereas under the proposed federal rule, only if the patient reasonably believed that the person with whom he was communicating was licensed to practice medicine (i.e., someone with an M.D.), would the privilege apply.

779. *Proposed Rules, supra* note 28, at 243 (FED. R. EVID. 504 advisory committee's note); *see also* CAL. EVID. CODE §1010 (definition of "psychotherapist" includes licensed psychologists, licensed clinical social workers, school psychologists authorized by the state, licensed marriage and family therapists, and any person "authorized to practice medicine ... who devotes, or is reasonably believed by the patient to devote, a substantial portion of his or her time

the all-inclusive nature of Rule 510(a)(1)(D) is an additional reason for narrowly construing the nonmedical "professional" defined in Rule 510(a)(1)(B).[780] However, given that the applicability of the privilege is a question for the judge, courts should construe the "reasonableness" of the patient's belief narrowly.

2. Rule 510(a)(2): Patient. The definition of "patient" in Rule 510(a)(2) is straightforward. The rule defines two basic categories. The first category is any person who "consults or is interviewed by a professional for diagnosis, evaluation, or treatment of any mental or emotional condition or disorder, including alcoholism and drug addiction."[781] This category derives directly from former Texas Revised Civil Statutes article 5561h. It overlaps with the second category, which derives from Texas Code of Criminal Procedure article 38.101 and includes any person who "is being treated voluntarily or being examined for admission to voluntary treatment for drug abuse."[782]

3. Rule 510(a)(3): Patient's representative. Rule 510(a)(3) defines a "patient's representative" as a person who has the patient's written consent, a parent of a minor patient, a guardian of an incompetent patient, or the personal representative of a deceased patient.[783] This last category leads to an inference that the privilege, which presumably attaches to any qualifying communication whenever made,[784] does not end when the patient dies.[785] Such an inference is consistent with the rationale for the privilege.

4. Rule 510(a)(4): Confidential communication. Rule 510(a)(4) defines a "confidential" communication as one not intended to be disclosed to third persons other than those present to further the patient's interest in the diagnosis, examination, evaluation, or treatment, those reasonably necessary to transmit the communication, and those participating in the diagnosis, examination, evaluation, or treatment under the professional's direction.[786] Although only communications between the patient and a profes-

---

to the practice of psychiatry"). The language of Texas Rule of Evidence 510(a)(1)(D) is drawn from former Texas Revised Civil Statutes article 5561h, §1(a). Act of May 9, 1979, 66th Leg., R.S., ch. 239, §1(a), 1979 Tex. Gen. Laws 512, 512-13 (former Texas Revised Civil Statutes art. 5561h deemed repealed as to civil proceedings effective 1983 and as to criminal proceedings effective 1986) [now codified at TEX. HEALTH & SAFETY CODE §611.001(2)(C)].

780. *See, e.g., In re Pittsburgh Action Against Rape*, 428 A.2d 126, 131-33 (Pa. 1981) (alleged rapist had the right to discover communications between his alleged victim and her rape-crisis counselor).

781. TEX. R. EVID. 510(a)(2)(A); *see, e.g., Gillespie v. Gillespie*, 631 S.W.2d 592, 593 (Tex. App.—Beaumont 1982) (privilege was invoked for communications made during treatment for alcoholism), *rev'd on other grounds*, 644 S.W.2d 449 (Tex. 1982).

782. TEX. R. EVID. 510(a)(2)(B); *see also In re G.K.H.*, 623 S.W.2d 447, 448 (Tex. App.—Texarkana 1981, no writ) (article 38.101, the source of Rule 510(a)(2)(B), was not available to a patient ordered to a drug-abuse center by a court because the patient was not there voluntarily).

783. TEX. R. EVID. 510(a)(3).

784. *See Ex parte Abell*, 613 S.W.2d 255, 259 (Tex. 1981) (orig. proceeding) (privilege applies to communications made before effective date of the statute). *But see Ex parte Watson*, 606 S.W.2d 902, 904-05 (Tex. Crim. App. 1980) (former article 5561h did not apply to communications and records made and admitted into evidence in a hearing held before the statute's effective date). Any communication or record privileged under former article 5561h should be entitled to similar treatment under Rule 510. Application of the *Ex parte Abell* rationale, should such a situation arise, indicates that an item generated in reliance on confidentiality is privileged.

785. Refer to note 729 *supra* and accompanying text.

786. TEX. R. EVID. 510(a)(4). This rule derives its language from proposed Federal Rule 504. *Proposed Rules, supra* note 28, at 241; *see* HULEN D. WENDORF ET AL., TEXAS RULES OF EVIDENCE MANUAL V-103 (5th ed. 2000) (Texas

sional are privileged,[787] other persons who do not fit in either of these groups can nevertheless participate in or receive the communication without causing it to lose its privileged character. First, nurses, orderlies, and secretaries, although they are not professionals, may become privy to a patient's communications[788] because they "participat[e] in the diagnosis, examination, evaluation, or treatment under the professional's direction"[789] or because they "further the patient's interest in the diagnosis, examination, evaluation, or treatment."[790]

Explicitly included among those who may be "participating ... under the professional's direction" are members of the patient's family.[791] This specific inclusion may mean only that disclosure in their presence, as with other necessary agents, does not destroy the privilege. But several commentators suggest that the courts should interpret the proposed federal provision, from which the relevant language of Rule 510 derives, so that the communications of family members made in furtherance of the diagnosis or treatment of another family member are also deemed confidential.[792] This reading is broad, but it is justified by the presumed special needs of effective psychotherapy.[793]

---

rule emulates the proposed federal rule). By stressing the intent of the patient during the communication, this paragraph protects the communication against disclosure by eavesdroppers.

787. *See* Tex. R. Evid. 510(b)(1)(A).

788. The need to include the professional's agents in the privilege has long been recognized in the context of the attorney-client privilege. Refer to notes 139-155 *supra* and accompanying text.

789. Tex. R. Evid. 510(a)(4)(C). In *In re G.K.H.*, the court held that the "parent coordinator" at a drug-abuse center was not a "professional" within the meaning of former Texas Revised Civil Statutes article 5561h, §1(a). 623 S.W.2d 447, 448 (Tex. App.—Texarkana 1981, no writ). Thus, a juvenile patient at the center could not invoke the privilege to preclude the parent-coordinator from testifying to a conversation in which the juvenile admitted an act of delinquency. *Id.* at 447-48. The court stressed that the conversation was "not in connection with any treatment or counseling, but was merely a casual conversation." *Id.* at 448. The question of whether the witness was working under the direction of a "professional" was not addressed, perhaps because that language was not found in former article 5561h.

790. Tex. R. Evid. 510(a)(4)(A).

791. Tex. R. Evid. 510(a)(4)(C).

792. 2 Weinstein & Berger, *supra* note 29, ¶504[05], at 504-25 (because effective treatment requires family participation, communications of family members should be protected).

793. *See id.* In *Grosslight v. Superior Ct.*, the court was required to rule on whether the California psychotherapist privilege, currently covered by California Evidence Code §§1010-1027, applied to communications made by family members to the hospital staff on behalf of the patient. 140 Cal. Rptr. 278, 280 (Cal. Ct. App. 1977). The court acknowledged that the family members were not within the definition of "patient," but nonetheless held their communications to be absolutely privileged. *Id.* at 280-81. The court reasoned that the privilege must be liberally construed to avoid its erosion and that it would be threatened unless family members were ensured confidentiality for their efforts to aid the patient's treatment. *Id.* at 281. This case suggests that family members are in some sense viewed as speaking for the patient.

An analogy may be drawn between the idea that a family's communications to a professional might be privileged and the operation of Rule 803(4), the hearsay exception for statements made for medical diagnosis or treatment. A feature of this exception is that, unlike virtually every other common exception to the hearsay rule, the declarant's statement does not need to relate to his own medical condition. *See* 4 Weinstein & Berger, *supra* note 29, ¶803(4)[01], at 803-152 to 803-153 (statements about someone else's physical condition, made to facilitate diagnosis or treatment, are admissible under Tex. R. Evid. 803(4)). A need to permit such statements to be offered for their truth is evident when the patient is comatose or a young child. Moreover, the declarant's presumed motivation for obtaining medical aid for the patient provides a guarantee of reliability similar to when the declarant is

The special status for communications by a patient's family members is distinguishable from their status as participants in family therapy. The language of the rule indicates that group-therapy situations were intended to be covered by the privilege.[794] Each patient in a group-therapy setting holds the privilege for his own communications with the professional. The more difficult problem involves the patient's obligations for communications made by other patients in the group. Although efforts are sometimes made to impress on each participant his role and responsibility as a "therapeutic agent" for the others,[795] a participating patient is obviously not within the definition of "professional." If a patient wants to waive the privilege, must the other patients agree to the waiver? This issue is not free from doubt.[796] However, the decision of one participant to waive the privilege should not keep other participants from effectively invoking the privilege.[797] Such invocation might well be predicated on the command of Rule 510(b)(2) that "[i]n a civil case, any person—other than a patient's representative acting on the patient's behalf—who receives information privileged under this rule may disclose the information only to the extent consistent with the purposes for which it was obtained."[798] This invocation is suggested even though the provision was probably intended to cover those who receive such information by virtue of exceptions to the privilege rather than as participants in the therapeutic process.

D. Rule 510(c): Who May Claim Privilege

The patient or his representative, if acting on the patient's behalf, holds the privilege.[799] This view is consistent with the modern view of privileges; under the common law the professional held the privilege in recognition of the honor of the profession.[800] The professional may also claim the privilege under Rule 510(c), but only on behalf of the patient.[801]

---

the patient. *See id.* ¶803(4)[01], at 803-152 (a patient is motivated to tell the truth when his treatment depends on what he discloses). Refer to *Article VIII: Hearsay, infra* p. 891.

794. *See* TEX. R. EVID. 510(a)(4)(C) (communications not intended to be disclosed to third persons other than those "participating in the ... treatment" are confidential); 2 LOUISELL & MUELLER, *supra* note 69, §216, at 857 (privilege should apply to group therapy).

795. Fleming & Maximov, *supra* note 718, at 1042 n.72.

796. *See* Green, *supra* note 740, at 162 (some courts hold that a patient in group therapy must have the others acquiesce to waiver of the privilege, while other courts hold that it is up to each individual).

797. *See* George A. Huber & Loren H. Roth, *Preserving the Confidentiality of Medical Record Information Regarding Nonpatients*, 66 VA. L. REV. 583, 585-91 (1980) (discussing the problem that no privilege protects personal information revealed during therapy that includes the relatives, friends, and associates of the patient).

798. TEX. R. EVID. 510(b)(2). Refer to notes 734-737 *supra* and accompanying text.

799. TEX. R. EVID. 510(c).

800. *See generally* 8 WIGMORE, *supra* note 6, §2290, at 542-45 (discussing the history of the privilege of confidentiality). Refer to notes 66-67 *supra* and accompanying text.

801. TEX. R. EVID. 510(c); *cf. Haw. Psychiatric Soc'y v. Ariyoshi*, 481 F. Supp. 1028, 1037 (D. Haw. 1979) (psychiatrists had standing to raise both their own privacy rights and those of their patients to challenge a law authorizing the issuance of warrants to inspect, copy, and maintain health-care records of Medicaid recipients). In *Ex parte Abell*, former patients of a psychologist brought a malpractice action against him, alleging that he took sexual advantage of them. 613 S.W.2d 255, 256 (Tex. 1981) (orig. proceeding). The defendant successfully resisted a demand for the names of other patients with whom he may have had sexual contact by invoking the privilege of confidentiality on behalf of those other unnamed patients. *Id.* at 263.

E. Rule 510(d): Exceptions—Specific Provisions

1. Rule 510(d)(1) & (d)(3): Actions involving breach of duty by the professional or the patient. The first class of litigation under this exception assumes that the patient is either the plaintiff or the complaining witness, as in a license-revocation proceeding.[802] The second involves efforts by the professional to collect for services.[803] Recognition of an exception for both types derives from similar long-standing exceptions to the attorney-client privilege.[804]

The first exception, Rule 510(d)(1), applies only when "the communication or record is relevant to a claim or defense."[805] A medical professional cannot automatically reveal a patient's confidential communications merely because that patient has complained about the professional's conduct. Those communications may be revealed only if they are relevant to a claim or defense. The second exception, Rule 510(d)(3), contains no similar limitation in the exception for claims for payment of professional services.[806] An explicit limitation is unnecessary; the normal rules of relevance[807] preclude any breach of confidentiality beyond the fact and frequency of the patient's treatment.

It is reasonable to assume that Rule 510(d)(1) covers only communications or records relating to a patient who is a party or complaining witness and does not apply to communications or records of other patients, even if the disclosure would be relevant to the claim of the plaintiff or the State or to a claim or defense. Commentators urge this reading because the exception is best viewed as a form of implicit waiver.[808]

Under the rule, the professional is presumed to have the authority to claim the privilege on behalf of the patient. TEX. R. EVID. 510(c). A reasonable reading of this language requires that when the professional makes the claim of privilege for the patient, the proponent of the evidence has the burden of producing evidence to rebut the inference of an authorized claim. Under Rule 104(a), a judge (rather than the jury) decides whether the facts necessary to the inference or its rebuttal have been satisfactorily established. Refer to *Article I: General Provisions, supra* p. 86.

802. *See* TEX. R. EVID. 510(d)(1).

803. *See* TEX. R. EVID. 510(d)(3).

804. *See* TEX. R. EVID. 503(d)(3). Refer to notes 268-272 *supra* and accompanying text.

805. TEX. R. EVID. 510(d)(1).

806. *See* TEX. R. EVID. 510(d)(3).

807. *See* TEX. R. EVID. 401-403.

808. *See* 2 LOUISELL & MUELLER, *supra* note 69, §215, at 845-46 (if a patient puts his own condition at issue, he waives the privilege of confidentiality). In *In re Pebsworth*, the court upheld a grand-jury subpoena issued pursuant to an investigation of possible medical-insurance fraud by a provider of psychotherapy. 705 F.2d 261, 263 (7th Cir. 1983). The court found that even under the assumption that there is a privilege, the patients waived the privilege through their authorization of disclosure for purposes of payment by the insurers. *Id.* The result in *Hawaii Psychiatric Society v. Ariyoshi* is distinguishable from the *Pebsworth* decision because it involved both a greater degree of disclosure and Fourth Amendment concerns associated with the use of administrative warrants. *Haw. Psychiatric Soc'y v. Ariyoshi*, 481 F. Supp. 1028, 1046-50 (D. Haw. 1979) (discussing Fourth Amendment problems involved with administrative searches and noting that these searches require extensive reading and copying of confidential medical files). Such investigations, to the extent that they do not involve judicial or administrative proceedings, may find authorization in Texas Health & Safety Code §611.004(a)(3) (management and financial audits) and §611.004(a)(6) ("governmental agencies involved in paying or collecting fees").

Given the importance of the privilege to nonparticipating patients, it is improper to assume or infer any waiver on their part.

2. Rule 510(d)(2): Written waiver. Either the patient or a person authorized to act on his behalf can waive the privilege in writing.[809] This provision addresses the situation in which a patient wants to release personal confidential records[810] that are within the control of a professional. A written waiver does not affect the interpretation of acts alleged to constitute an implied waiver or acts of the patient triggering another specific exception.

3. Rule 510(d)(4): Communication made in court-ordered examination. Under Rule 510(d)(4), the mental-health-information privilege does not apply to communications made "during a court-ordered examination relating to the patient's mental or emotional condition or disorder."[811] However, such communications are unprivileged only if the examiner first warns the patient that they are.[812] This exception derives from former Texas Revised Civil Statutes article 5561h,[813] which was probably designed to foreclose claims of privilege for communications made during court-directed examinations of criminal defendants to determine either their competency to stand trial[814] or their sanity at the time of the offense.[815] These issues are beyond the scope of the rules.[816]

---

809. TEX. R. EVID. 510(d)(2). Because the privilege holder likely has a greater probability of mental distress, questions may arise about whether the waiver is made with adequate understanding. The patient's personal written waiver should be effective unless a court has determined the patient is incompetent. It should be noted that a "guardian," within the meaning of Rule 510(a)(3)(C), could waive the privilege for an incompetent person.

810. *See* TEX. R. EVID. 510(b)(1)(B).

811. TEX. R. EVID. 510(d)(4).

812. TEX. R. EVID. 510(d)(4)(A); *see, e.g.,* **Subia v. Tex. Dep't of Human Servs.**, 750 S.W.2d 827, 830 (Tex. App.—El Paso 1988, no writ) (trial court erred in permitting psychologist to testify after court-ordered examination of defendant; neither trial court nor psychologist informed defendant that communications made during examination would not be privileged); **Dudley v. State**, 730 S.W.2d 51, 54 (Tex. App.—Houston [14th Dist.] 1987, no writ) (psychologist could testify about communications made by defendant after psychologist warned defendant that the communications were not confidential). Similar constructions had been given to Rule 510(d)(4)'s predecessor. *See* Act approved May 17, 1979, 66th Leg., R.S., ch. 239, 1979 Tex. Gen. Laws 512 (former Texas Revised Civil Statutes art. 5561h deemed repealed as to civil proceedings effective 1983 and as to criminal proceedings effective 1986) [now codified at TEX. HEALTH & SAFETY CODE ch. 611] (allowing an exception to the privilege when a patient was informed that communications were not privileged); **C.V. v. State**, 616 S.W.2d 441, 443 (Tex. Civ. App.—Houston [14th Dist.] 1981, no writ) (same); **Jones v. State**, 610 S.W.2d 535, 536-37 (Tex. Civ. App.—Houston [1st Dist.] 1980, writ ref'd n.r.e.) (same); **Salas v. State**, 592 S.W.2d 653, 656-57 (Tex. Civ. App.—Austin 1979, no writ) (same).

813. Act approved May 17, 1979, 66th Leg., R.S., ch. 239, 1979 Tex. Gen. Laws 512 (former Texas Revised Civil Statutes art. 5561h deemed repealed as to civil proceedings effective 1983 and as to criminal proceedings effective 1986) [now codified at TEX. HEALTH & SAFETY CODE ch. 611].

814. *See* TEX. CODE CRIM. PROC. art. 46B.021 (mental-health experts may be appointed to examine defendant and testify about his competency to stand trial).

815. *See id.* art. 46C.101 (mental-health experts may be appointed to examine defendant and testify about his sanity at the time of the offense).

816. *See* **Estelle v. Smith**, 451 U.S. 454, 465 (1981) (Fifth Amendment applies to disclosures made to psychiatrist at court-ordered examination, but no privilege issue arises when disclosures are used for neutral purpose of determining competency to stand trial); *see also* Green, *supra* note 740, at 164-67 (discussing privilege issues arising in court proceedings, including right to refuse the exam, right to counsel, and right to be warned of exam's purpose);

This provision, however, creates an apparent conflict between its terms and the terms of other possible exceptions. For example, with court-ordered examinations controlled by Rule 510(d)(4), the examiner must warn the patient about the lack of confidentiality; there was no such warning requirement, however, under former Rule 510(d)(6)'s exception for suits affecting the parent-child relationship.[817]

The apparent conflict between the two provisions was discussed in ***Subia v. Texas Department of Human Services***,[818] a proceeding to terminate the parent-child relationship. The court resolved the issue by holding that the provision relating to court-ordered examinations took precedence over the exception for parent-child suits because Rule 510(d)(4) covers all court-ordered examinations, while former Rule 510(d)(6) pertained to situations in which mental-health information might be available without resorting to a court-ordered examination.[819] Thus, an examiner must warn the patient of nonconfidentiality any time a mental-health examination or treatment is conducted under a court order. Otherwise, the confidential communications will not be discoverable or admissible even if another exception applies. Although this result is consistent with the language of the exceptions under Rule 510, it does not follow the rationale for the exceptions. The rules have already made clear, for example, that the privilege must yield to the stronger societal value of the best interests of the child. It is peculiar that when the court orders a psychological evaluation of the parent, the parent's privacy interest trumps the best interests of the child if the parent is not properly warned about nonconfidentiality. The warnings required under Rule 510(d)(4) derive from the criminal context, in which the court orders competency or insanity evaluations. Thus, these warnings protect not only the patient's privacy interest, but also the privilege against self-incrimination in criminal proceedings.

The Rule 510(d)(4) exception applies to civil-commitment proceedings, the context in which appellate courts most frequently address the mental-health-information privilege.[820] The statutory physician-patient privilege, adopted two years after article 5561h, also includes an exception for disclosures relevant to "an involuntary civil com-

---

*cf. **Mena v. State**,* 633 S.W.2d 564, 565 (Tex. App.—Houston [14th Dist.] 1982, no pet.) (no Fifth Amendment issue arises in psychiatric examination directed under TEX. FAM. CODE §54.02 to determine whether juvenile should be certified for trial as an adult).

817. The 1998 unified Rules omitted former Civil Rule 510(d)(6) because the exception is considered under Rule 510(d)(5). TEX. R. EVID. 510 cmt. (1998). Refer to notes 839-866 *infra* and accompanying text. For a discussion of former Rule 510(d)(6), refer to note 661 *supra*.

818. 750 S.W.2d 827 (Tex. App.—El Paso 1988, no writ).

819. *Id.* at 830-31 (warning requirement of Rule 510(d)(4) applies even in the context of suits involving a parent-child relationship). Even though the broad exception for suits affecting the parent-child relationship has been eliminated, the same situation outlined in *Subia* could occur in a conflict between Rules 510(d)(4) and 510(d)(5).

820. *See **In re R___ B___**,* 741 S.W.2d 525, 528 (Tex. App.—Tyler 1987, no writ) (medical exams and interviews conducted under commitment proceedings establish relationships under which Rule 509 and 510 privileges can arise); *see, e.g.,* **C.V. v. State**, 616 S.W.2d 441, 442 (Tex. Civ. App.—Houston [14th Dist.] 1981, no writ) (examination under an application for temporary hospitalization).

mitment" or hospitalization proceeding.[821] The exception to the statutory privilege, however, neither requires that the communication occur during a court-directed examination nor demands that the examiner first advise the patient of the nonprivileged nature of the communication.[822]

The Rules continue the distinction in the treatment of the physician-patient and mental-health-information privileges.[823] Under Rule 509, a physician arguably could disclose communications relevant to civil-commitment proceedings without complying with the prerequisites required of professionals under Rule 510. The removal of these obstacles to obtaining the physician's testimony presumably aids the courts and professionals in providing the patient with needed security and care. The physician most likely to have such information, however, is a psychiatrist within the Rule 510(a) definition of "professional."[824] Psychiatrists are thus unable to disclose communications relevant to civil-commitment proceedings except under the more stringent circumstances of a court-ordered examination and a prior warning to the patient about the absence of any privilege. The courts should determine the controlling provision, Rule 509(e)(6) or 510(d)(4), by considering the patient's reason for consulting the professional: if for mental or emotional concerns, the physician who is not a psychiatrist is bound by Rule 510; if for physical medical problems, the psychiatrist's obligations should be considered under Rule 509.[825]

The requirement of a prior warning is not burdensome and has been held to be satisfied when a nonprofessional employee of the hospital's admissions office advised the patient of the nonprivileged nature of any later communications.[826] Nor is it necessary

821. Tex. Rev. Civ. Stat. art. 4495b, §5.08(g)(7) [now codified at Tex. Occ. Code §159.003(a)(7)].

822. *See* Tex. Occ. Code §159.003(a)(7) ("An exception to the privilege of confidentiality in a court or administrative proceeding exists ... in an involuntary civil commitment proceeding, proceeding for court-ordered treatment, or probable cause hearing ....").

823. *Compare* Tex. R. Evid. 509(e)(6) (no physician-patient privilege in involuntary-civil-commitment proceeding or proceeding for court-ordered treatment), *with* Tex. R. Evid. 510(d)(4)(A) & (d)(4)(B) (privilege does not apply to communication made by patient to professional if communication is made after patient is advised that communication is not privileged and if communication is offered to prove issues involving patient's emotional or mental health).

824. Refer to notes 738-780 *supra* and accompanying text.

825. *See In re R___ B___*, 741 S.W.2d at 527-28 (examining distinct applications of Rule 509 covering physicians and medical care and Rule 510 covering professionals and emotional or mental care). It is noteworthy that the Attorney General had a different resolution for this anomaly arising under the predecessor statutes, articles 5561h and 4495b. *See* Tex. Att'y Gen. Op. No. MW-569 (1982). His position was that physicians were subject to the less-restrictive terms of article 4495b, enacted later. *Id.* The Attorney General decided that this lesser standard for disclosure applies to nonphysicians supervised by physicians and to any records maintained by a physician without regard to who created them. *Id.*; *see also Dial v. State*, 658 S.W.2d 823, 825-26 (Tex. App.—Austin 1983, no writ) (art. 4495b [now codified at Tex. Occ. Code tit. 3, subtit. B-C] does not modify former art. 5561h, but provides an exception to confidentiality for physicians in the context of involuntary commitment or hospitalization proceedings). This analysis pertains only to disclosure in judicial and administrative proceedings, leaving the professional with the ability to make disclosures in other circumstances to avoid injury to the patient or others. Refer to notes 687-694 *supra* and accompanying text.

826. *See Jones v. State*, 613 S.W.2d 570, 571-72 (Tex. Civ. App.—Austin 1981, no writ).

that the order committing the patient to a hospital use the specific statutory language if it otherwise clearly authorizes an examination of the patient's mental condition or emotional disorder.[827]

The exception is self-limiting in that a communication is not privileged only if it "is offered to prove an issue involving the patient's mental or emotional health."[828] The clause does not explain how communications could be irrelevant to the patient's mental or emotional health and yet privileged, especially when the privilege extends only to communications involving mental-health information.[829]

Finally, the rule directs courts to impose "appropriate safeguards against unauthorized disclosure."[830] Inclusion of this proviso reflects that these authorized disclosures are the result of a court order, unlike those addressed by other exceptions that do not contain a similar provision. These exceptions do not cover situations when the professional believes that disclosure is necessary in the interest of the patient or of some third person. Texas Health & Safety Code section 611.002 addresses these questions and controls disclosure in proceedings other than civil judicial or administrative proceedings. Proposed Federal Rule 504(d)(1) would have created a specific exemption for communications relevant to the question of hospitalization for mental illness that the professional determined necessary for the patient.[831] Although Rule 509(e)(6) provides an exception for disclosure by physicians related to certain court proceedings,[832] mental-health professionals have no similar authority under Rule 510. The Texas Health & Safety Code authorizes disclosure by mental-health professionals "to medical or law enforcement personnel if the professional determines that there is a probability of imminent physical injury by the patient to the patient or others or there is a probability of immediate mental or emotional injury to the patient."[833] Such disclosures are permitted by the statute, but not required.[834] Thus, Health & Safety Code section

---

827. *See Brown v. State*, 612 S.W.2d 83, 84-85 (Tex. Civ. App.—Austin 1981, no writ).

828. Tex. R. Evid. 510(d)(4)(B).

829. If the content of the communication does not relate to the patient's mental health, it should not have privileged status even without a warning of its nonprivileged status. In view of Rule 501, Rule 510 is the only apparent source for creating a privilege for these communications. The definition of "confidential" in Rule 510(a)(4) apparently precludes a claim of privilege in the case of court-ordered observation and communications because it is difficult to claim that information obtained from this involuntary relationship was "not intended to be disclosed to third persons." *See* Tex. R. Evid. 510(a)(4).

830. Tex. R. Evid. 510(d)(4)(C). However, the rule, like the statute before it, does not specify when the need for such safeguards arises or what they should be. *See Brown*, 612 S.W.2d at 85 (court need not supply safeguards for all future hazards involving some aspect of disclosure).

831. *See Proposed Rules, supra* note 28, at 241.

832. Refer to notes 687-694 *supra* and accompanying text.

833. Tex. Health & Safety Code §611.004(a)(2).

834. *Thapar v. Zezulka*, 994 S.W.2d 635, 639 (Tex. 1999); *see* Tex. Health & Safety Code §611.004(a)(2). Thus, the professional may freely advise a peace officer of his client/patient's need for a preliminary examination, which allows a 48-hour detention period on consent of the facility administrator. *See* Tex. Health & Safety Code §573.021(b). During that period, there may be unprivileged observation and examination to support an extension of the commitment if appropriate. *See id.* §573.022(a)(3)(C); Tex. R. Evid. 510(d)(4). It is highly unlikely that a professional psychiatrist, qualified under Texas Health & Safety Code §573.022 to present a magistrate with a written

611.004(a)(2) raises the issue of disclosure to protect third persons. ***Tarasoff v. Regents of the University of California***[835] made this issue famous. ***Tarasoff*** held that, under California law, liability attached to a psychotherapist for a failure to warn a third party of the danger posed to her by the therapist's patient.[836] Under Texas law, however, the section 611.004(a)(2) exception permits disclosure only to "medical or law enforcement personnel," who presumably then have the responsibility to warn the third person.[837] Thus, there is no "dangerous patient" exception to the mental-health-information privilege under Rule 510.[838]

4. Rule 510(d)(5): Party relies on patient's condition. Rule 510(d)(5) provides an exception to the mental-health-information privilege when "any party relies on the patient's physical, mental, or emotional condition as a part of the party's claim or defense and the communication or record is relevant to that condition."[839] As with the correlative exception to Rule 509,[840] the exception for piercing the mental-health privilege whenever the patient's condition is relevant to any party's claim or defense severely limits the privilege. When the supreme court first adopted the Civil Rules, this exception applied only to communications and records relevant to a proceeding in which the pa-

---

statement of the detained person's need for emergency detention, would not have the authority to do so in light of psychiatrist-patient confidentiality, as authorized by Texas Health & Safety Code §§611.001-611.005. However, magistrates do not fall within the Texas Health & Safety Code §611.004(a)(2) exception for "law enforcement personnel" because it seems that this term refers to "peace officers" as defined by Texas Code of Criminal Procedure article 2.12. The argument against disclosure to a magistrate assumes that the psychiatrist acts in his capacity as a professional and not as a physician. Without an applicable exception, Rule 510 and Texas Health & Safety Code §611.002 forbid disclosure by a professional.

835. 551 P.2d 334 (Cal. 1976).

836. *Id.* at 353. *See generally* Fleming & Maximov, *supra* note 718, at 1026-30 (discussing a therapist's duty to protect third parties).

837. *See **Boren v. Texoma Med. Ctr., Inc.**,* 258 S.W.3d 224, 228 (Tex. App.—Dallas 2008, no pet.) ("On numerous occasions, the Texas Supreme Court has declined to create or recognize a duty from a healthcare provider to a third party non-patient arising out of the healthcare provider's treatment of a patient."); Marilyn Hammond, *Predictions of Dangerousness in Texas: Psychotherapists' Conflicting Duties, Their Potential Liability, and Possible Solutions,* 12 St. Mary's L.J. 141, 154 (1980) (unclear whether disclosure to potential victims is precluded); *see, e.g.,* ***Thapar***, 994 S.W.2d at 639 (disclosure of threat by therapist to one of victim's family members would have violated confidentiality statute because "no exception in the statute provides for the disclosure to third parties threatened by the patient"). *See generally* Green, *supra* note 740, at 167-68 (discussing medical and law-enforcement personnel's responsibility to warn).

838. Federal courts differ in their interpretation of the dangerous-patient exception. *See, e.g.,* ***United States v. Ghane***, 673 F.3d 771, 785-86 (8th Cir. 2012) (refusing to adopt dangerous-patient exception to psychotherapist-patient privilege); ***United States v. Auster***, 517 F.3d 312, 320-21 (5th Cir. 2008) (declining to rule on dangerous-patient exception); ***United States v. Chase***, 340 F.3d 978, 984-85 (9th Cir. 2003) (en banc) (discussing dangerous-patient exception to psychotherapist-patient confidentiality laws and holding that psychotherapist properly disclosed patient's threats to authorities although the exception to confidentiality did not abrogate federal privilege against testimony about content of those threats in criminal prosecution); ***United States v. Hayes***, 227 F.3d 578, 583-86 (6th Cir. 2000) (discussing policy and purposes of mental-health-information privilege and concluding that there is no dangerous-patient exception to the federal psychotherapist-patient privilege); ***United States v. Glass***, 133 F.3d 1356, 1360 (10th Cir. 1998) (disclosure of threat could be compelled only if "the threat was serious when it was uttered and … its disclosure was the only means of averting harm to the [intended victim] when the disclosure was made").

839. Tex. R. Evid. 510(d)(5). Refer to note 817 *supra.*

840. *See* Tex. R. Evid. 509(e)(4). Refer to notes 661-686 *supra* and accompanying text.

tient was suing for damages for his mental condition.[841] The original exception recognized the inequity of permitting a party to claim, for example, that the defendant's acts caused emotional or mental harm while precluding the defendant from learning from the plaintiff's psychotherapist about the plaintiff's mental health before the defendant's alleged wrongful acts.[842] The instrumental argument for the privilege is weakened when the patient controls the decision to put a mental condition in issue.[843] Further, the privacy rationale is weak in this situation. When the plaintiff publicly discloses a mental condition to make a case for damages, further intrusion into the plaintiff's privacy by the disclosure of earlier communications on this subject seems relatively insignificant. For these reasons, many of the strongest supporters of the privilege accept the need for a "litigant" exception.[844] Recognizing that the privacy rationale applies when the patient is a defendant and makes a mental condition part of a defensive claim, the Texas Supreme Court expanded the exception in 1984.[845]

Rule 510(d)(5), like Rule 509(e)(4), does not depend on the patient's party-litigant status.[846] The court will pierce the privilege whenever the patient's medical condition

---

841. Rule 510(d)(5) originally read as follows: "in any litigation or administrative proceeding, if relevant, brought by the patient/client or someone on his behalf if the patient/client is attempting to recover monetary damages for any mental condition." 641-642 S.W.2d (Tex. Cases) L (1983, amended 1998).

842. *Cf. In re Lifschutz*, 467 P.2d 557, 568-69 (Cal. 1970) (patient should not be allowed to "establish a claim while simultaneously foreclosing inquiry into relevant matters").

843. However, Judge Hufstedler, in *Caesar v. Mountanos*, wrote the following:
> There is nothing voluntary about the injury suffered. The injured patient "controls" the "intrusion" only in the sense that he can give up redress instead of seeking legal relief for the injury. If he seeks redress ..., relinquishment of his constitutionally protected zone of privacy is in no sense voluntary; Section 1016 [of the California Evidence Code] compels him to choose between his privacy and his right to seek legal redress. That Hobson's choice is not a waiver ....

542 F.2d 1064, 1074 (9th Cir. 1976) (Hufstedler, J., concurring in part and dissenting in part).

844. *E.g.*, Saltzburg, *supra* note 718, at 622-25 (favoring the litigant exception). *See generally* Ellen E. McDonnell, *Certainty Thwarted: Broad Waiver Versus Narrow Waiver of the Psychotherapist-Patient Privilege After Jaffee v. Redmond*, 52 HASTINGS L.J. 1369 (2001) (discussing division among federal district courts on waiver of privilege where patient claims emotional damages).

845. 669-670 S.W.2d (Tex. Cases) XXXVI (1984, amended 1998); *see* 733-734 S.W.2d (Tex. Cases) LXXXVIII (1987) (amendments to rule effective Jan. 1, 1988). Thus, the present exception would apparently be available in a case such as *Prink v. Rockefeller Center, Inc.*, 398 N.E.2d 517 (N.Y. 1979). In *Prink*, the deceased patient's wife brought a wrongful-death action based on negligence in the maintenance of a window from which the deceased fell while allegedly trying to open it. *Id.* at 522. The plaintiff acknowledged that her husband had been under a psychiatrist's care. *Id.* at 519-20. The New York Court of Appeals held that the likelihood of suicide allowed the court to treat the plaintiff's initiation of the action as a waiver of the privilege. *Id.* at 522. Under the original Texas Rule of Evidence 510(d)(5), therefore, the exception might not have applied because the suit did not seek recovery for any mental condition.

846. Refer to notes 661-679 *supra* and accompanying text. However, in *K.P. v. Packer*, the Dallas Court of Appeals rejected a broad reading of Rule 510(d)(5) and held that the exception encompasses only offensive, not defensive, use of the mental-health-information privilege. 826 S.W.2d 664, 667 (Tex. App.—Dallas 1992, orig. proceeding). In this case, a mother had sued a child-care center, individually and as her son's next friend, for injuries her son sustained from another child's alleged sexual act on him. *Id.* at 665. The defendant had sought the mother's mental-health records, alleging that her psychological problems, not the incident at the center, were the primary cause of the child's emotional damage. *Id.* The trial court ordered production of the records, even after the mother nonsuited her individual claims. *Id.* The court of appeals acknowledged that under a literal reading of the exception under Rule 510(d)(5), the patient does not need to be a party at all, as long as the patient's condition is relevant to a party's claim or defense. *K.P.*, 826 S.W.2d at 666. However, it reasoned that the policy underlying the exception ap-

is relevant to any party's claim or defense.[847] However, the exception does not permit the discovery of privileged material for impeachment purposes. Although the exception may not be used as a "fishing expedition" into otherwise privileged material, the Texas Supreme Court, in *Ginsberg v. Fifth Court of Appeals*,[848] has taken a very expansive view of the right to discover relevant medical and psychiatric records. In *Ginsberg*, the supreme court upheld the trial court's order requiring the production of the patient's mental-health records in a trespass-to-try-title suit.[849] The plaintiff claimed that the defendant had tricked her into signing a deed in 1972.[850] The defendant asserted that the statute of limitations barred the plaintiff's claim, but the plaintiff stated in her deposition that she could not remember when she signed the deed and did not know of the transfer until 1981.[851] However, her psychiatrist's records noted that the plaintiff had told him, during the course of therapy, that she sold the building in question in 1972.[852] The supreme court, even before the exception under Rule 510(d)(5) was revised, held that the plaintiff was attempting to use the mental-health-information privilege as an offensive weapon against the defendant.[853] Thus, the records were outside the intended scope of the evidentiary privilege.[854] The *Ginsberg* reasoning and result are in line with the rationale for the privilege. The defendant had an arguably valid claim that the statute of limitations barred the suit, and the evidence sought was of great probative value to that defense. Also, what would appear to be idle conversation—"the

---

plies only to an offensive use of the privilege when the patient seeks affirmative relief. *Id.* at 667. Thus, once the mother abandoned her individual claim for relief, her assertion of the mental-health-information privilege was not an offensive use of the privilege and her mental-health records remained exempt from discovery. *Id.* at 668.

847. Tex. R. Evid. 510(d)(5); *see R.K. v. Ramirez*, 887 S.W.2d 836, 843 (Tex. 1994) (orig. proceeding) ("As a general rule, a mental condition will be 'part' of a claim or defense if the pleadings indicate that the jury must make a factual determination concerning the condition itself."); *see also Coates v. Whittington*, 758 S.W.2d 749, 753 (Tex. 1988) (orig. proceeding) (routine allegation of mental anguish or emotional distress does not place party's mental condition in controversy); *In re Whipple*, 373 S.W.3d 119, 124 (Tex. App.—San Antonio 2012, orig. proceeding) (same). Whether the patient's condition is part of a party's claim or defense is determined from the face of the pleadings. *R.K.*, 887 S.W.2d at 843 n.7; *see also Easter v. McDonald*, 903 S.W.2d 887, 891 n.1 (Tex. App.—Waco 1995, orig. proceeding [leave denied]) (following *R.K.*, but expressing concern that "because the determination is made on the basis of pleadings and anyone can plead anything at any time, the exception will eventually swallow the privilege").

848. 686 S.W.2d 105 (Tex. 1985) (orig. proceeding).

849. *Id.* at 108.

850. *Id.* at 106.

851. *Id.*

852. *Id.*

853. *Id.* at 107; *see also Hyundai Motor Co. v. Chandler*, 882 S.W.2d 606, 619-20 (Tex. App.—Corpus Christi 1994, writ denied) (following *Ginsberg* and holding that because plaintiff sought affirmative relief against car company, defendant was entitled to introduce testimony of plaintiff's counselor about sessions in which plaintiff discussed cause of car collision). The dissent in *Chandler* argued that for the exception under Civil Rule 510(d)(5) to apply, the affirmative relief that the party is seeking must have some relationship to the counseling or treatment sought or received by the patient. 882 S.W.2d at 621 (Dorsey, J., dissenting). Otherwise, any plaintiff who seeks affirmative relief risks opening his mental-health records and confidential communications to public purview even when the lawsuit is unrelated to the treatment. *Id.* Indeed, Justice Dorsey appears to have the better argument. The exception is expressly intended to apply only when the party, either plaintiff or defendant, is relying on the physical, mental, or emotional condition as a part of that party's claim or defense.

854. *Ginsberg v. Fifth Ct. of Appeals*, 686 S.W.2d 105, 107 (Tex. 1985) (orig. proceeding).

building was sold while we were in Padre Island"[855]—between a patient and therapist is not, on its face at least, the type of confidential communication in which a patient would have a particularly great privacy interest. Furthermore, the material sought was arguably not covered by Rule 510(d)(5) because the record was not relevant to the patient's physical, mental, or emotional condition as required under the exception.[856]

In ***Kentucky Fried Chicken National Management Co. v. Tennant***,[857] a Houston court of appeals recognized that the right to discover potentially relevant evidence may give a party an expansive right to pierce the mental-health-information privilege under Rule 510, but such pretrial orders do not necessarily mean that the otherwise privileged material is admissible at trial under the Rule 403 balancing test.[858] In this case, the plaintiffs alleged that food poisoning caused by the defendant's products required medical treatment by antibiotics.[859] The antibiotics, in turn, caused the plaintiffs (a mother and daughter) to fear for their health and that of the daughter's unborn child.[860] The defendant discovered that the daughter had a history of psychiatric care and sought production of related medical records, claiming that preexisting problems, not purported food poisoning, caused her mental anguish.[861] The plaintiff argued that the defendant had not established that the plaintiff's mental condition was genuinely in controversy or that there was good cause for discovery of the records, and the trial court refused the requested production.[862] The court of appeals disagreed, holding that Rule 510(d)(5) placed the burden on the plaintiff to plead and prove why her records were not relevant for purposes of pretrial discovery.[863] Legitimate privacy interests and the relevance of the material to the claim or defense seem well balanced in this case.

Finally, in ***R.K. v. Ramirez***,[864] the Texas Supreme Court reviewed the 1988 amendments to the party-litigant exception under both Rules 509 and 510 and clarified the purpose and scope of these exceptions.[865] The court held that

---

855. *Id.* at 106.

856. *See* 1 GOODE ET AL., *supra* note 206, §510.4.4, at 463-64 (the exception requires both a party's reliance on the patient's condition and relevance of the material sought to that condition before the Rule 510(d)(5) exception applies).

857. 782 S.W.2d 318 (Tex. App.—Houston [1st Dist.] 1989, orig. proceeding).

858. *See id.* at 320-21 (requiring application of Civil Rule 403 despite the applicability of Civil Rule 510).

859. *Id.* at 319.

860. *Id.*

861. *Id.*

862. *Id.* at 319-20. The court of appeals stated that it appeared that the trial court's order denying discovery was based on the assumption that ***Coates v. Whittington***, 758 S.W.2d 749 (Tex. 1988) (orig. proceeding), prohibited the discovery of the plaintiff's psychiatric records. *Tennant*, 782 S.W.2d at 321. In *Coates*, the party seeking discovery had not shown any nexus between the plaintiff's psychiatric history and her claim. 758 S.W.2d at 752. In ***Tennant***, however, the defendant made a prima facie showing of relevance, and thus the burden shifted to the plaintiff to plead and prove that the records were not relevant. *Tennant*, 782 S.W.2d at 321.

863. *See Tennant*, 782 S.W.2d at 320-21 (plaintiffs should have attempted to demonstrate that records were irrelevant by producing them for the court's inspection in camera).

864. 887 S.W.2d 836 (Tex. 1994) (orig. proceeding).

865. Refer to notes 661-686 *supra* and accompanying text.

the exceptions to the medical and mental health privileges apply when (1) the records sought to be discovered are relevant to the condition at issue, and (2) the condition is relied upon as a part of a party's claim or defense, meaning that the condition itself is a fact that carries some legal significance. Both parts of the test must be met before the exception will apply.[866]

5. Rule 510(d)(6): Abuse or neglect of "institution" resident. The final exception to the privilege is for communications relevant to proceedings involving the abuse or neglect of residents of nursing facilities and similar institutions.[867] This provision, also added to the physician-patient privilege,[868] originally derived from a 1977 amendment of the law controlling the licensing of convalescent and nursing facilities.[869] It applies both to proceedings brought by state officials and to private-party litigation.[870]

F. Rule 510(d): Exceptions—Scope of Disclosure

If the opponent of a privilege establishes that an exception applies, Rule 510(d) does not facially limit the records or communications subject to disclosure except by the concept of relevance. In the context of the claim-or-defense exception, this balancing of interests is an area of special sensitivity to judges[871] and commentators.[872] As explained

---

866. *R.K.*, 887 S.W.2d at 843; *see, e.g.*, *M.A.W. v. Hall*, 921 S.W.2d 911, 915 (Tex. App.—Houston [14th Dist.] 1996, orig. proceeding) (in medical-malpractice case, medical records concerning physician's substance abuse were part of negligence claim and were admissible under exception to privilege); *Easter v. McDonald*, 903 S.W.2d 887, 890-91 (Tex. App.—Waco 1995, orig. proceeding [leave denied]) (psychotherapist records concerning treatment of stepfather were part of plaintiff-father's claim against psychotherapist for negligently diagnosing stepfather and were admissible under exception to privilege). The court in *R.K.* also concluded that even when the exception does apply, the patient is entitled to an in camera inspection of the pertinent documents to "assure that the proper balancing of interests ... occurs before production is ordered." 887 S.W.2d at 843; *see also* *Groves v. Gabriel*, 874 S.W.2d 660, 661 (Tex. 1994) (per curiam) (when plaintiff alleged severe emotional damage, including "post-traumatic stress disorder," she placed her mental and emotional condition in issue and triggered the Rule 510(d)(5) exception; however, trial court's order compelling discovery of medical records "should be restrictively drawn so as to maintain the privilege with respect to records or communications not relevant to the underlying suit").

867. *See* Tex. R. Evid. 510(d)(6).

868. Tex. R. Evid. 509(e)(7).

869. Act approved July 22, 1977, 65th Leg., 1st C.S., ch. 2, §9, 1977 Tex. Gen. Laws 54 (former Texas Revised Civil Statutes art. 4442c, §16(d), repealed 1989). Section 16(d) stated that in such proceedings, "evidence may not be excluded on the ground of privileged communication except in the case of communications between an attorney and client." *Id.* Subsection (d)(7) resolved a potential conflict between Rule 510's general prohibition on disclosure and the Legislature's judgment as expressed in §16(d) and reiterated in its 1981 amendment of §16, which did not alter §16(d). Former article 4442c, §16(d), was recodified at Texas Health & Safety Code §242.129. In 2011, the Texas Legislature repealed the subchapter of the Texas Health & Safety Code that contained §242.129 and enacted a new chapter to address reports of abuse, neglect, or exploitation involving residents of nursing facilities. Refer to note 424 *supra* and accompanying text.

870. *See* *In re Arriola*, 159 S.W.3d 670, 675 (Tex. App.—Corpus Christi 2004, orig. proceeding). Refer to notes 693-694 *supra* and accompanying text (discussing abuse-and-neglect exception to physician-patient privilege).

871. *See* *Caesar v. Mountanos*, 542 F.2d 1064, 1074-75 (9th Cir. 1976) (Hufstedler, J., concurring in part and dissenting in part) (relevant confidential communications should be restricted to the fact of treatment, the time and length of treatment, the cost of treatment, and the ultimate diagnosis, unless the party seeking disclosure can establish a compelling need for production); *In re Lifschutz*, 467 P.2d 557, 567 (Cal. 1970) (courts use protective measures beyond the relevance standard to protect confidential information that may be embarrassing).

872. *See, e.g.*, Louisell & Sinclair, *supra* note 715, at 41-46 (relevancy requirement should adequately protect patients' rights, but it must be delicately administered).

by one judge, the relevance standard creates a "Hobson's choice"[873] between forego-ing recovery and surrendering confidential information.[874] Other states address this problem by giving trial judges discretion in balancing the probative value of the mate-rial sought against the importance of the therapist-patient relationship.[875]

RULE 511
WAIVER BY VOLUNTARY DISCLOSURE

(a) General Rule.

A person upon whom these rules confer a privilege against disclosure waives the privilege if:

(1) the person or a predecessor of the person while holder of the privilege voluntarily discloses or consents to disclosure of any significant part of the privileged matter unless such disclosure itself is privileged; or

(2) the person or a representative of the person calls a person to whom privileged communications have been made to testify as to the person's character or character trait insofar as such communications are relevant to such character or character trait.

(b) Lawyer-Client Privilege and Work Product; Limitations on Waiver.

Notwithstanding paragraph (a), the following provisions apply, in the cir-cumstances set out, to disclosure of a communication or information covered by the lawyer-client privilege or work-product protection.

---

873. *Caesar*, 542 F.2d at 1074 (Hufstedler, J., concurring in part and dissenting in part).

874. *Id.* at 1073-75 (Hufstedler, J., concurring in part and dissenting in part).

875. *See, e.g.*, 740 ILL. COMP. STAT. 110/10(a)(1) (Mental Health and Developmental Disabilities Confidentiality Act). The Act's litigant exception reads as follows:

> Records and communications may be disclosed … if and only to the extent the court … finds, after in camera examination of testimony or other evidence, that it is relevant, probative, not unduly preju-dicial or inflammatory, and otherwise clearly admissible; that other satisfactory evidence is demon-strably unsatisfactory as evidence of the facts sought to be established by such evidence; and that dis-closure is more important to the interests of substantial justice than protection from injury to the therapist-recipient relationship or to the recipient or other whom disclosure is likely to harm. [Ex-cept as to the insanity defense,] no record or communication between a therapist and a recipient shall be deemed relevant for purposes of this subsection, except the fact of treatment, the cost of services and the ultimate diagnosis unless the party seeking disclosure … clearly establishes … a compelling need for its production.

Id. The paragraph contains an additional limitation on the exception's operation in divorce cases and in any action in which pain and suffering is an element of the claim by providing that mental condition shall not be deemed in-troduced by a mere claim of pain and suffering. *Id.* Only if the patient offers testimony about the record or com-munications is the privilege to be deemed waived even to the limited extent provided for by that paragraph. *Id.*; *see also* MASS. GEN. LAWS ch. 233, §20B(e) (in child-custody cases, judge must balance welfare of child against relation-ship between patient and psychotherapist to determine whether disclosure is required).

In *R.K. v. Ramirez*, the Texas Supreme Court held that the trial court must apply this type of balancing in determining precisely what privileged materials must be produced under the claim-or-defense exceptions set out in Rules 509(e)(4) and 510(d)(5). 887 S.W.2d 836, 843 (Tex. 1994) (orig. proceeding).

---

(1) *Disclosure Made in a Federal or State Proceeding or to a Federal or State Office or Agency; Scope of a Waiver.* When the disclosure is made in a federal proceeding or state proceeding of any state or to a federal office or agency or state office or agency of any state and waives the lawyer-client privilege or work-product protection, the waiver extends to an undisclosed communication or information only if:

    (A) the waiver is intentional;

    (B) the disclosed and undisclosed communications or information concern the same subject matter; and

    (C) they ought in fairness to be considered together.

(2) *Inadvertent Disclosure in State Civil Proceedings.* When made in a Texas state proceeding, an inadvertent disclosure does not operate as a waiver if the holder followed the procedures of Rule of Civil Procedure 193.3(d).

(3) *Controlling Effect of a Court Order.* A disclosure made in litigation pending before a federal court or a state court of any state that has entered an order that the privilege or protection is not waived by disclosure connected with the litigation pending before that court is also not a waiver in a Texas state proceeding.

(4) *Controlling Effect of a Party Agreement.* An agreement on the effect of disclosure in a state proceeding of any state is binding only on the parties to the agreement, unless it is incorporated into a court order.

Notes and Comments

Comment to 2015 restyling: The amendments to Rule 511 are designed to align Texas law with federal law on waiver of privilege by voluntary disclosure. Subsection (a) sets forth the general rule. Subsection (b) incorporates the provisions of Federal Rule of Evidence 502. Like the federal rule, subsection (b) only addresses disclosure of communications or information covered by the lawyer-client privilege or work-product protection. These amendments do not affect the law governing waiver of other privileges or protections.

COMMENTARY ON RULE 511

Rule 511 expresses the principle that all privileges are subject to waiver.[876] This provision, together with Rules 512 and 513, applies to all privileges provided in Article V. Specific privileges may address waiver in terms that impose requirements in addition to those found in Rule 511.[877] Properly understood, those provisions apply in narrow

---

876. *See* 8 WIGMORE, *supra* note 6, §§2327, 2388. The author notes that a "privilege implies option. A privilege without a waiver becomes a vain use of words, and means no more nor less than an absolute rule of exclusion, a thing of a very different type." *Id.* §2242, at 256.

877. *See* TEX. R. EVID. 508(c)(1), 509(e)(2), 509(f), 510(d)(2). For example, under Rule 508(c)(1), the conduct of either the informer or the privilege holder can waive the privilege. But the rule requires that disclosure of the in-

circumstances and are not inconsistent with the operation of Rule 511. For example, the physician-patient privilege contains elaborate directions for waiver, using the term "consent" instead.[878] That provision, requiring the patient's written consent, deals with a patient who wants to release confidential records that are under the physician's control. In such situations, the specific directions of the physician-patient privilege should be observed. Observing these directions, however, may not prevent a patient from waiving the privilege through voluntary disclosure under Rule 511, even if written consent was not given.[879] Similarly, Rule 511 does not hinder the operation of exceptions to the privileges that can be conceptualized as involving a waiver because their effect turns on the holder's decision to pursue a certain course of action.[880]

The general rule of waiver is expressly stated in Rule 511(a), and Rule 511(b) sets out exceptions and limitations on waiver for disclosure of a communication or information covered by the attorney-client privilege or work-product protection.[881]

---

former's identity or his interest in the subject matter of his communication has been made "to a person who would have cause to resent the communication." TEX. R. EVID. 508(c)(1)(A). This specific additional requirement should control over the general language of Rule 511.

878. *See* TEX. R. EVID. 509(e)(2), 509(f). Refer to notes 695-699 *supra* and accompanying text. The provision for waiving the mental-health-information privilege is not as elaborate but also requires that the waiver be in writing. *See* TEX. R. EVID. 510(d)(2). Refer to notes 809-810 *supra* and accompanying text.

879. This problem results from drawing the language of the privileges largely from the Uniform Rules of Evidence and in part from existing Texas statutory provisions. Most of the privileges do not refer to waiver because, as part of the Uniform Rules, they were structured with an eye to the existence of the general provisions represented in the Texas Rules by Rules 511-513. However, both the physician-patient and mental-health-information privileges were based on state statutes that were designed to be self-contained. Unlike Texas Rule 511, proposed Federal Rule 511 expressly applied to disclosures of "any significant part of the matter or communication." *Proposed Rules, supra* note 28, at 258. The phrase "or communication" was added to the federal version to clarify the extension of the general-waiver concept to privileges involving facts, such as the identity of an informer under Rule 508, as well as to communications. *See* 2 WEINSTEIN & BERGER, *supra* note 29, ¶511[01], at 511-3. However, the Texas rule is taken from Uniform Rule of Evidence 510 (1974), and nothing indicates that the absence of "or communication" reflected an intent to limit the scope of the rule.

880. *See* TEX. R. EVID. 503(d)(3) (decision by a client to sue the attorney for breach of duty), TEX. R. EVID. 508(c)(1)(B) (decision to offer the informer as a witness for the government), TEX. R. EVID. 509(e)(1)(A) (decision by a patient to sue the physician for malpractice). In *West v. Solito*, the defendants, former attorneys of the plaintiff, sought to depose other former attorneys about services the proposed deponents rendered to the plaintiff in connection with a release previously granted to defendants. 563 S.W.2d 240, 243 (Tex. 1978) (orig. proceeding). This release allegedly absolved the defendants of liability for conduct underlying the current breach-of-duty litigation. *Id.* at 242-43. The plaintiff invoked her privilege for the proposed depositions, but the trial judge directed full cooperation, reserving for trial the question of whether matters thus disclosed were privileged. *Id.* at 243. The plaintiff sought a writ of mandamus to compel the trial judge to amend the order. *Id.* The defendants claimed that the plaintiff had waived any such privilege because her suit was an implied attack on the proposed deponents' services to her for the release and because her suit put the information in issue, honoring the privilege would be unfair. *Id.* at 244. The court did not answer these questions because the trial judge had not had an opportunity to pass on them. However, it spoke of these issues in terms of "waiver." *Id.* Under Rule 503(d)(3), the action against the defendants would permit their disclosure of any privileged communications relevant to the alleged breach of duty as an exception to the privilege. Whether the plaintiff's actions constituted an implied waiver of her privilege is unclear. Because the plaintiff apparently did not disclose any "significant part of the privileged matter," it seems that there was no waiver.

881. TEX. R. EVID. 511 cmt. Refer to notes 935-942 *infra* and accompanying text.

A. Rule 511(a): General Rule

1. Rule 511(a)(1): Waiver by disclosure. The party who asserts a privilege has the burden of showing its existence, scope, and applicability in the particular situation.[882] In *Peeples v. Honorable Fourth Supreme Judicial District*,[883] the Texas Supreme Court articulated a four-step process when a party asserts an attorney-client privilege for purposes of civil discovery. The process should apply whenever a person asserts any privilege under Article V or any other statute during the discovery process. The party must (1) specifically plead the particular privilege claimed, (2) request an in camera inspection of all the materials, (3) segregate all privileged from unprivileged materials, and (4) produce the requested material to the court.[884] Failure to follow these four steps generally results in a waiver of the privilege.[885] In *Jordan v. Fourth Court of Appeals*, the Texas Supreme Court announced that "[i]f the matter for which a privilege is sought has been disclosed to a third party, thus raising the question of waiver of the privilege, the party asserting the privilege has the burden of proving that no waiver has occurred."[886] Thus, in civil cases, once the party against whom the privilege is asserted produces some facts showing waiver, the burden shifts to the party asserting the privilege to prove there was no waiver under Rule 511.

This burden-shifting does not operate in precisely the same way in criminal proceedings. In *Carmona v. State*,[887] the court of criminal appeals held that once a party

---

882. *See* TEX. R. CIV. P. 193.4(a) (party making an objection or asserting a privilege must present any evidence necessary to support the objection or privilege); *In re Christus Santa Rosa Health Sys.*, 492 S.W.3d 276, 279 (Tex. 2016) (orig. proceeding) (party seeking to avoid discovery has burden to plead and prove existence of privilege); *In re E.I. DuPont de Nemours & Co.*, 136 S.W.3d 218, 227 (Tex. 2004) (orig. proceeding) (per curiam) (party asserting a privilege from discovery must produce evidence supporting the applicability of the privilege); *cf. United States v. Harrelson*, 754 F.2d 1153, 1167 (5th Cir. 1985) (no privilege when defendant did not produce evidence that he retained an attorney in connection with his case on trial or that the attorney was acting as an attorney during the conversations).

883. 701 S.W.2d 635 (Tex. 1985).

884. *See id.* at 637; *In re Crestcare Nursing & Rehab. Ctr.*, 222 S.W.3d 68, 73 (Tex. App.—Tyler 2006, orig. proceeding) (merely listing a specific privilege in a privilege log is insufficient to meet burden of production for asserting privilege). Because the assertion of a privilege runs counter to the general truth-seeking interest of a trial, this burden is sensible. *See Trammel v. United States*, 445 U.S. 40, 50 (1980) (testimonial exclusionary rules and privileges are contrary to the principle that the public has a right to every party's evidence).

885. *Peeples*, 701 S.W.2d at 637; *see, e.g., Freeman v. Bianchi*, 820 S.W.2d 853, 858-59 (Tex. App.—Houston [1st Dist.] 1991, orig. proceeding) (documents not segregated and produced to the court were not exempt from discovery or admissibility on the basis of the privilege because defendants did not follow the necessary procedural steps to preserve their claim of privilege), *leave granted, mand. denied*, *Granada Corp. v. First Ct. of Appeals*, 844 S.W.2d 223 (Tex. 1992); *Fina Oil & Chem. Co. v. Salinas*, 750 S.W.2d 32, 34 (Tex. App.—Corpus Christi 1988, orig. proceeding) (failure to comply with *Peeples* procedure constituted a waiver of the asserted privileges).

886. 701 S.W.2d 644, 649 (Tex. 1985) (orig. proceeding); *see also Osborne v. Johnson*, 954 S.W.2d 180, 189 (Tex. App.—Waco 1997, orig. proceeding [mand. denied]) (when evidence showed that internal investigative reports had been disclosed "to some extent" to other employees who were not within control group, this was sufficient evidence to support trial court's finding of waiver); *Aetna Cas. & Sur. Co. v. Blackmon*, 810 S.W.2d 438, 440 (Tex. App.—Corpus Christi 1991, orig. proceeding) (party asserting the privilege must prove that no waiver has occurred).

887. 941 S.W.2d 949 (Tex. Crim. App. 1997). In this case, the defendant was charged with aggravated sexual assault of a child. *Id.* at 950. The defendant testified at trial and denied committing any offense. *Id.* The State then announced that it intended to call a polygraph examiner in rebuttal to testify from some of his notes about various

has asserted a specific privilege and produced sufficient evidence to demonstrate the existence, scope, and applicability of that valid privilege, the burden shifts to the party seeking to benefit from a waiver to produce some evidence that supports a finding of waiver.[888] A showing that the privileged material or communication has been disclosed to a third party is evidence of a waiver, but that disclosure does not establish a "presumptive" or "automatic" waiver.[889] Rather, it is from the "totality of the circumstances and reasonable inferences" that the trial court, acting under Rule 104(a), determines whether there has been a waiver of the privilege.[890]

Only the holder of the privilege can waive it.[891] For example, in the context of the attorney-client privilege, only a disclosure by the client waives the privilege. Disclosure by the attorney does not waive the privilege unless he has been authorized by the client to disclose the privileged material or communication.[892] Likewise, a former employee of a corporation cannot waive the company's attorney-client privilege after he

---

incriminatory statements made by the defendant during a pretest polygraph interview. *Id.* The evidence showed that the defense counsel had hired the polygraph examiner who conducted the examination and concluded that the defendant "passed" the test based on the specific questions that the defendant was asked. *Id.* The polygraph examiner then wrote a report that contained the "favorable" test results but omitted the incriminatory pretest statements. *Id.* at 950-51. The examiner did, however, tell the defense attorney about those incriminatory statements. *Id.* at 951. The prosecutor then testified that the defense attorney sent him that polygraph report, as well as two others for different defendants, to persuade him to give some consideration to those "favorable" polygraph tests in deciding whether to present the cases to the grand jury. *Id.* At trial, the defendant claimed that the polygraph report and the examiner's written notes were privileged attorney-client communications. *Id.* at 952. The trial court held that the privilege had been waived by disclosing the report to the prosecutor. *See id.*

The court of criminal appeals disavowed the Eastland Court of Appeals' opinion in *Fuller v. State*, 835 S.W.2d 768 (Tex. App.—Eastland 1992, pet. ref'd), to the extent that it had held that "'the party asserting the privilege has the burden of disproving the waiver.'" *Carmona*, 941 S.W.2d at 954 (quoting *Fuller*, 835 S.W.2d at 769). The court of criminal appeals held that the court of appeals erred "to the extent it found a waiver based solely on evidence that [the polygraph examiner's] written report was disclosed by appellant's lawyer to the prosecution and the police." *Carmona*, 941 S.W.2d at 955.

On remand, the court of appeals found that the trial court had sufficient evidence before it to find that the defendant had consented to his attorney's disclosure of the polygraph report to the prosecution, especially because there was no testimony that the defendant did not authorize his attorney to disclose the privileged material. *Carmona v. State*, 947 S.W.2d 661, 664 (Tex. App.—Austin 1997, no pet.).

888. *See Bailey v. State*, 507 S.W.3d 740, 746 (Tex. Crim. App. 2016); *Carmona*, 941 S.W.2d at 953-54.

889. *Bailey*, 507 S.W.3d at 746; *Carmona*, 941 S.W.2d at 953. In *Carmona*, the court of criminal appeals stated that the approach taken by Justice Gonzalez in his concurring and dissenting opinion in *Jordan* was consistent with the way the court has treated issues of waiver in criminal cases. *Carmona*, 941 S.W.2d at 954.

890. *See Bailey*, 507 S.W.3d at 746; *Carmona*, 941 S.W.2d at 954; *see also Sanford v. State*, 21 S.W.3d 337, 343 (Tex. App.—El Paso 2000, no pet.) (following *Carmona* and finding no waiver of the privilege merely because defense attorney disclosed confidential communications to police while defendant was nearby; State did not carry its burden to show waiver).

891. *In re Ford Motor Co.*, 211 S.W.3d 295, 301 (Tex. 2006) (per curiam); *Bailey*, 507 S.W.3d at 745.

892. *See Carmona*, 941 S.W.2d at 953 ("[T]he power to waive the attorney-client privilege belongs to the client, or his attorney or agent both acting with the client's authority."); *In re Hicks*, 252 S.W.3d 790, 794 (Tex. App.—Houston [14th Dist.] 2008, orig. proceeding) ("The [attorney-client] privilege may be waived through voluntary disclosure or consent to disclosure under Texas Rule of Evidence 511."); *Carmona*, 947 S.W.2d at 663 ("Disclosure by the attorney does not waive the privilege absent the client's consent.").

is terminated.[893] Furthermore, a person does not waive his attorney-client privilege merely by assigning his legal claims to another person.[894]

A waiver occurs only if the privilege holder discloses a "significant part" of the privileged matter.[895] Disclosure of a summary description of a privileged document, for example, does not amount to waiver of the privilege.[896]

Rule 511(a)(1) poses no difficulty if there is an express waiver of a privilege; when the waiver is implied from the conduct of the holder[897] or his representatives, however, the issue is not as clear-cut.[898] Throughout the late 1980s and into the 1990s, Texas courts had found an implied waiver to the assertion of evidentiary privileges.[899] Given the inclusionary slant of the Rules as a whole, the expansion of pretrial discovery rights in civil cases, and the U.S. Supreme Court's general disfavor of exclusionary rules, this trend was hardly surprising. Nonetheless, the amorphous nature of the implied-waiver doctrine created great uncertainty for the judicial system and its participants.[900]

One traditional definition of waiver—the *Zerbst* standard—requires the party claiming waiver to demonstrate "an intentional relinquishment or abandonment of a known right or privilege."[901] This language may require a showing that the holder made

---

893. *See, e.g.,* ***In re Mktg. Inv'rs Corp.***, 80 S.W.3d 44, 50 (Tex. App.—Dallas 1998, orig. proceeding) (employee's right to assert attorney-client privilege terminated on his departure from company; current management was solely responsible for asserting or waiving privilege).

894. *See, e.g.,* ***In re Cooper***, 47 S.W.3d 206, 207-09 (Tex. App.—Beaumont 2001, orig. proceeding) (personal-injury suit defendant who had assigned his *Stowers* claim to plaintiff did not implicitly waive any right that defendant had to assert attorney-client privilege).

895. Tex. R. Evid. 511(a)(1); *e.g.,* ***In re Monsanto Co.***, 998 S.W.2d 917, 925-26 (Tex. App.—Waco 1999, orig. proceeding) (defendant's oral description of privileged document that was offered to explain when party anticipated litigation was not a disclosure of a "significant part" of privileged document and did not waive work-product protection).

896. ***In re Monsanto Co.***, 998 S.W.2d at 925-26.

897. More than one person can hold a privilege. The most common situation occurs when joint clients hold a privilege. Rule 503(d)(5) explicitly creates an exception for the use of such communications in a later action between or among the clients. Refer to notes 277-279 *supra* and accompanying text.

When clients have a common interest in an action, a privilege extends to communications made in the course of joint consultation. *See* Tex. R. Evid. 503(b)(1). Because the attorney is the representative of each client, each client should be required to waive the privilege. This view is consistent with the basic rationale of protecting the professional's communications because revealing them may result in the disclosure of the client's communications.

Wigmore advocates a rule that presumably governs actions with third parties. 8 Wigmore, *supra* note 6, §2328, at 639. He states that "[t]he waiver should be joint for joint statements, and neither could waive for the disclosure of the other's statements; yet neither should be able to obstruct the other in the disclosure of the latter's own statements." *Id.* Presumably, this view should also apply to communications made in the course of marital, family, or group counseling by a mental-health professional. Refer to notes 794-798 *supra* and accompanying text.

898. *See generally* Note, *Developments in the Law—Privileged Communications*, 98 Harv. L. Rev. 1629, 1629-65 (1985) (discussing issues of implied waiver).

899. *See, e.g.,* ***Freeman v. Bianchi***, 820 S.W.2d 853, 861 (Tex. App.—Houston [1st Dist.] 1991, orig. proceeding) (privilege was waived when documents were voluntarily submitted to opposing party), *leave granted, mand. denied,* ***Granada Corp. v. First Ct. of Appeals***, 844 S.W.2d 223 (Tex. 1992); ***Eloise Bauer & Assocs., Inc. v. Elec. Realty Assocs., Inc.***, 621 S.W.2d 200, 204 (Tex. Civ. App.—Texarkana 1981, writ ref'd n.r.e.) (party waived attorney-client privilege by unintentionally producing exhibit during pretrial discovery).

900. *See* Richard L. Marcus, *The Perils of Privilege: Waiver and the Litigator*, 84 Mich. L. Rev. 1605, 1609-16 (1986) (implied waiver from inadvertent disclosures increases litigation costs and delay).

901. ***Johnson v. Zerbst***, 304 U.S. 458, 464 (1938).

a conscious choice to waive the privilege.[902] However, this language emerged from and has generally been applied in criminal cases involving the alleged waiver of a defendant's constitutionally protected right. The U.S. Supreme Court has never suggested that this extremely high standard of subjective waiver is required or appropriate in civil cases[903] or for evidentiary privileges that are not constitutionally based. In *Schneckloth v. Bustamonte*, the Supreme Court held that this high standard does not apply to the Fourth Amendment right to refuse consent to a police search.[904] Rather than drawing a line between criminal and civil cases, the Court based its distinction on whether the Constitution guaranteed the allegedly waived right "in order to preserve a fair trial."[905] "Fair," in this context, appears to mean "accurate" because the Court has stressed that Fourth Amendment rights are unrelated to the ascertainment of truth. Instead, they are guaranteed to protect very different values—"values reflecting the concern of our society for the right of each individual to be let alone."[906] Although *Bustamonte* was a criminal case involving a constitutional right, the privilege at issue did not promote the ascertainment of truth. The Court thus applied a lower standard of "waiver"—an uncoerced surrender of a right—than that applied in *Zerbst*.

Most, if not all, of the privileges found in Article V have no explicit constitutional foundation. Thus, one premise of the *Zerbst* standard does not apply. Second, and more importantly, privileges impede rather than aid the ascertainment of truth. Therefore, the reasoning of *Bustamonte* on Fourth Amendment rights fully applies to the standards for waiver of evidentiary privileges and strongly points to the application of a far less stringent standard than "an intentional relinquishment ... of a known right or privilege."[907] Thus, in *Granada Corp. v. First Court of Appeals*,[908] the supreme court held that there was a distinction between an "inadvertent" disclosure of privileged material,

---

902. George E. Dix, *Waiver in Criminal Procedure: A Brief for More Careful Analysis*, 55 TEX. L. REV. 193, 205 (1977) (waiver should be defined as a conscious choice).

903. *Schneckloth v. Bustamonte*, 412 U.S. 218, 235-36 (1973).

904. *Id.* at 248-49.

905. *Id.* at 237.

906. *Id.* at 242 (quoting *Tehan v. United States ex rel. Shott*, 382 U.S. 406, 416 (1966)); *see* Dix, *supra* note 902, at 202 (the *Bustamonte* court held that Fourth Amendment rights have nothing to do with determining truth but instead they involve the right to be free from unreasonable searches).

907. *Johnson v. Zerbst*, 304 U.S. 458, 464 (1938); *see* 8 WIGMORE, *supra* note 6, §2327, at 636 (a "privileged person would seldom be found to [have] waive[d], if his intention not to abandon could alone control the situation"). This position was not the same as the one expressed by the court of criminal appeals in *Cruz v. State*. 586 S.W.2d 861 (Tex. Crim. App. 1979). In *Cruz*, the murder defendant had confessed to his attorney, who wrote a statement for the defendant and gave it to the police. *Id.* at 863. The defendant, on advice of counsel but allegedly without receiving *Miranda* warnings or having read the confession, then signed it. *Id.* The statement was inadmissible as a privileged attorney-client communication. *Id.* at 865. The privilege had not been waived because the prosecution did not show the defendant's intention to waive or a sufficient awareness of the significance of his conduct. *Id.*; *see Burnett v. State*, 642 S.W.2d 765, 770 (Tex. Crim. App. 1982). *But cf. Johnson v. State*, 95 Tex. Crim. 483, 487, 255 S.W. 416, 417 (1923) (finding a waiver of the marital-communications privilege in failure of apparently unrepresented defendant to object to the offer of letters written by defendant to his wife).

908. 844 S.W.2d 223, 226 (Tex. 1992) (inadvertent disclosure does not necessarily result in waiver of the privilege, but it is some indication that privilege holder either may not have intended to preserve the privilege or has not taken reasonable measures to protect it).

which may constitute waiver,[909] and an "involuntary" disclosure, which does not constitute waiver.[910] The result in **Granada**—finding a waiver when forfeiture of the privilege was not subjectively intended—is based on the rationale that "the essential function of the privilege is to protect a confidence which, once revealed by any means, leaves the privilege with no legitimate function to perform."[911]

However, in 1999, the Rules of Civil Procedure were amended to overrule **Granada** and provide that inadvertent disclosure does not waive the privilege if the producing party asserts the privilege within ten days of actually discovering its inadvertent production of privileged material.[912] The party claiming the privilege bears the burden, at least in civil cases, of proving that the disclosure was inadvertent and thus involuntary.[913]

To establish waiver, a party must show that the disclosure of the privileged fact or communication was voluntary, but a conscious decision to waive the pertinent privilege does not need to be shown.[914] Further, voluntary disclosure must be made by either

---

909. *Id.* (setting out relevant factors—precautionary measures, extent of disclosure, delay in rectifying error, and scope of discovery—in determining whether inadvertent disclosure has resulted in waiver). In **Granada**, the supreme court held that "a party seeking to preserve a privilege after disclosure must do more than show inadvertence; rather, the producing party has the burden of justifying preservation of the privilege by showing that the circumstances demonstrate the involuntariness of the disclosure." *Id.* at 227; *see also* **M.A.W. v. Hall**, 921 S.W.2d 911, 916 (Tex. App.—Houston [14th Dist.] 1996, orig. proceeding) ("Inadvertent production occurs when a party permits disclosure of a document due to inattention.").

910. *See Granada*, 844 S.W.2d at 226; *see also* **M.A.W.**, 921 S.W.2d at 916 ("Involuntary disclosure occurs 'if efforts reasonably calculated to prevent the disclosure were unavailing.'" (quoting *Granada*, 844 S.W.2d at 226)).

911. 1 McCormick on Evidence §93, at 371-72 (5th ed. 1999).

912. *See* Tex. R. Civ. P. 193.3(d); **In re Living Ctrs. of Tex., Inc.**, 175 S.W.3d 253, 260 (Tex. 2005) (orig. proceeding); *see also* **In re Ford Motor Co.**, 211 S.W.3d 295, 301 (Tex. 2006) (orig. proceeding) (per curiam) ("Under Texas law, discovery privileges are waived by *voluntary* disclosure by the *holder* of the privilege. Mistaken document production by a court employee in violation of a court-signed protective order cannot constitute a party's voluntary waiver of confidentiality."). Refer to note 939 *infra* and accompanying text.

Under Rule 193.3(d), the focus is on the intent to waive the privilege, not the intent to produce the material or information. Tex. R. Civ. P. 193.3(d) & cmt. 4; *e.g.*, **In re AEP Tex. Cent. Co.**, 128 S.W.3d 687, 693-94 (Tex. App.—San Antonio 2003, orig. proceeding) (party who did not have actual knowledge of the inadvertent production of memorandum until months later did not waive claim of privilege). Even when a party does not diligently screen documents before producing them, the claim of privilege is not waived, but the party must amend the original response and assert the applicable privilege within ten days after first becoming aware of the mistake. **In re AEP Tex.**, 128 S.W.3d at 693; *see also* **Warrantech Corp. v. Comput. Adapters Servs., Inc.**, 134 S.W.3d 516, 524-25 (Tex. App.—Fort Worth 2004, no pet.) (repair company did not waive its attorney-client privilege by inadvertent disclosure of privileged letter three years before trial when trial court could reasonably have determined that party only discovered during trial that it had been inadvertently produced). The Beaumont Court of Appeals examined the phrase "party who produces" in Rule 193.3(d) and concluded that the drafters did not intend to confine the rule's application solely to people or entities named as parties to the lawsuit. **In re Certain Underwriters at Lloyd's London**, 294 S.W.3d 891, 903 (Tex. App.—Beaumont 2009, orig. proceeding) (per curiam). The court reasoned that "a person may be a party who produces information related to a lawsuit without necessarily also being a party to the suit, as nonparties can be subpoenaed to require their cooperation in a civil suit." *Id.*

913. *Granada*, 844 S.W.2d at 226; **M.A.W.**, 921 S.W.2d at 916.

914. *See* **Jordan v. Fourth Ct. of Appeals**, 701 S.W.2d 644, 649 (Tex. 1985) (orig. proceeding); **Bendele v. Tri-Cty. Farmer's Co-op**, 635 S.W.2d 459, 464 (Tex. App.—San Antonio 1982), *vacated in part on other grounds*, 641 S.W.2d 208 (Tex. 1982); **Eloise Bauer & Assocs., Inc. v. Elec. Realty Assocs., Inc.**, 621 S.W.2d 200, 204 (Tex. Civ. App.—Texarkana 1981, writ ref'd n.r.e.). This disclosure is distinguishable from a showing of a conscious decision to speak

the privilege holder or his agent acting within the scope of the agent's authority.[915] Thus, if an eavesdropper or a person who obtains a document without the voluntary act of the holder or his agent makes the disclosure, no waiver should be found.[916] But if the holder chooses to disclose—certainly if he does so by testifying—the court will not permit him to claim a privilege when questioned on the same subject matter.[917] This re-

---

despite knowing that the communication will not be privileged. *See* Tex. R. Evid. 510(d)(4). Refer to notes 811-838 *supra* and accompanying text. Mere disclosure does not automatically establish waiver. Refer to notes 887-890 *supra* and accompanying text.

915. For example, the client holds the attorney-client privilege, but the attorney can claim the privilege on the client's behalf and is presumed to have the authority to do so. *See* Tex. R. Evid. 503(b), (c). The attorney's testimony at trial about communications with the client has been given as a reason for denying a privilege claim for questions on cross-examination. *See, e.g.,* **Mills v. Browning**, 59 S.W.2d 219, 221 (Tex. Civ. App.—Fort Worth 1933, no writ) (allowing an attorney's voluntary prior testimony revealing client communications); **Conyer v. Burckhalter**, 275 S.W. 606, 613 (Tex. Civ. App.—Dallas 1925) (attorney who voluntarily testified for client was subject to cross-examination), *rev'd on other grounds*, 9 S.W.2d 1029 (Tex. Comm'n App. 1928, judgm't adopted). Holding the client-party responsible for the offer of such testimony appears reasonable because the decision to call witnesses is within the scope of an attorney's authority. However, both **Mills** and **Conyer** involved cross-examination about fee arrangements, which is traditionally viewed as outside the scope of privilege. *See* **Borden, Inc. v. Valdez**, 773 S.W.2d 718, 720-21 (Tex. App.—Corpus Christi 1989, orig. proceeding).

916. *See* **Gass v. Baggerly**, 332 S.W.2d 426, 430 (Tex. Civ. App.—Dallas 1960, no writ) (privilege afforded to the communication between a party's agents is not waived by inadvertent disclosure to the opponent). Some case law suggests a contrary result in criminal cases. *See, e.g.,* **Clark v. State**, 159 Tex. Crim. 187, 191-93, 261 S.W.2d 339, 342-43 (1953) (testimony of telephone operator about conversation between defendant and his attorney, which operator heard by eavesdropping, was not protected by attorney-client privilege). However, the cases often involve a failure to create the privilege because the communication was made in the presence of an unnecessary third party. *See, e.g.,* **Bear v. State**, 612 S.W.2d 931, 932 (Tex. Crim. App. [Panel Op.] 1981) (husband's statements to his ex-wife were not privileged because they were made in the presence of a third party); **Stallings v. State**, 476 S.W.2d 679, 681 (Tex. Crim. App. 1972) (defendant's wife's statements to third parties were not privileged). Refer to notes 164-180 *supra* and accompanying text. Similarly excluded from waiver are documents that reach the possession of third persons without the holder's consent. *See, e.g.,* **Hilton v. State**, 149 Tex. Crim. 22, 24, 191 S.W.2d 875, 876 (1945) (wife's letters to her husband were privileged and could not be admitted to impeach her testimony); **Gross v. State**, 61 Tex. Crim. 176, 181-82, 135 S.W. 373, 376 (1911) (third party could not testify about the contents of a privileged letter from a husband to his wife). *But see* **Harris v. State**, 72 Tex. Crim. 117, 121, 161 S.W. 125, 128 (1913) (third party could testify about the contents of a wife's letter from her husband if the letter were lost or destroyed). Analogous to this situation is the problem of unauthorized disclosure because of a willful or negligent act of the holder's agent. Because privileges are intended to protect confidential communications from both inadvertent and deliberate disclosure, disclosure because of a breach of duty or error by the holder's attorney, for example, is not a waiver. *See* **Mendenhall v. Barber-Greene Co.**, 531 F. Supp. 951, 955 (N.D. Ill. 1982) (counsel's negligence is not enough to waive the privilege because inadvertent disclosure is the antithesis of waiver); *see also* **Gray v. Bicknell**, 86 F.3d 1472, 1484 (8th Cir. 1996) (adopting a five-part test to determine whether the attorney-client privilege is jeopardized by the unintentional release of privileged documents); **Alldread v. City of Granada**, 988 F.2d 1425, 1433-34 (5th Cir. 1993) (adopting a similar five-factor test); **Koch Foods of Ala. LLC v. Gen. Elec. Capital Corp.**, 531 F. Supp. 2d 1318, 1325 (M.D. Ala. 2008) (favoring totality-of-the-circumstances approach rather than per se waiver rule), *aff'd*, 303 F. App'x 841 (11th Cir. 2008). Failure to correct an inadvertent disclosure at the earliest opportunity, however, can imply waiver. *See* **In re Sealed Case**, 877 F.2d 976, 980 (D.C. Cir. 1989) (allowing the privilege only in situations where all precautions against disclosure were taken); *see, e.g.,* **In re Grand Jury Investigation of Ocean Transp.**, 604 F.2d 672, 675 (D.C. Cir. 1979) (privilege was destroyed after the government used inadvertently released documents for several years and counsel had been notified of the release). *But see* Note, *The Attorney-Client Privilege After Attorney Disclosure*, 78 Mich. L. Rev. 927, 934-45 (1980) (criticizing **Ocean Transp.** and advocating a client-consent predicate).

917. *See* **United States v. Jones**, 696 F.2d 1069, 1072 (4th Cir. 1982) ("Any voluntary disclosure by the client to a third party waives the privilege not only as to the specific communication disclosed, but often as to all other communications relating to the same subject matter."); **West v. Solito**, 563 S.W.2d 240, 245 (Tex. 1978) (orig. proceeding) (offering privileged testimony as evidence destroys the privilege); **Aetna Cas. & Sur. Co. v. Blackmon**, 810 S.W.2d 438, 440 (Tex. App.—Corpus Christi 1991, orig. proceeding) (if a party designates an individual as an expert wit-

sult follows from basic notions of fair play. Courts and commentators commonly describe this result in terms of a refusal to permit the holder to use the shield of the privilege as a sword through selective disclosure.[918] There is no right to pick and choose portions of a privilege. Once a person decides to disclose a portion of otherwise privileged material, the privilege disappears, "not because of voluntariness or involuntariness, but because the need for confidentiality served by the privilege is inconsistent with such disclosure."[919] Further, disclosure of some privileged material can result in an implied waiver of other similar or connected material.[920] It does not, however, automatically result in a blanket waiver of all privileged material.[921]

---

ness, the party waives any privilege for the information the expert relied on for his testimony but does not waive it for all documents in the expert's possession); *see, e.g., Jordan*, 701 S.W.2d at 649 (party waived the privilege by voluntary disclosure of information to grand jury); *Rodriguez v. State*, 130 Tex. Crim. 438, 443-44, 94 S.W.2d 476, 479-80 (1936) (attorney could testify when defendant waived attorney-client privilege by testifying about attorney's advice); *Spearman v. State*, 68 Tex. Crim. 449, 455-56, 152 S.W. 915, 918-19 (1913) (defendant could not claim marital privilege after calling his ex-wife to testify); *see also Indus. Clearinghouse, Inc. v. Browning Mfg.*, 953 F.2d 1004, 1007 (5th Cir. 1992) (complaint in attorney-malpractice action revealed no client communications and thus did not waive attorney-client privilege; mere institution of suit against attorney is not sufficient to waive privilege as to third parties in separate action involving same subject matter as attorney-malpractice action).

918. *See Bailey v. State*, 469 S.W.3d 762, 774 (Tex. App.—Houston [1st Dist.] 2015) ("[A]fter a partial disclosure is used as a sword to gain litigation advantage, the privilege cannot then be used to shield the remainder of the privileged communication."), *aff'd*, 507 S.W.3d 740 (Tex. Crim. App. 2016); *Langham v. Gray*, 227 S.W. 741, 743 (Tex. Civ. App.—Beaumont 1920, no writ) (the privilege is a shield that cannot be converted into an offensive weapon). As stated by Wigmore:

> There is always also the objective consideration that when his conduct touches a certain point of disclosure, fairness requires that his privilege shall cease whether he intended that result or not. He cannot be allowed, after disclosing as much as he pleases, to withhold the remainder. He may elect to withhold or to disclose, but after a certain point his election must remain final.

8 WIGMORE, *supra* note 6, §2327, at 636; *see Bailey*, 469 S.W.3d at 775 ("The touchstone of … implied waiver is that some litigation conduct requires, in fairness, that the remainder of the privileged communication be divulged."); *cf.* TEX. R. EVID. 106 (rule of optional completeness allows a party to introduce any portion of a writing or statement that in fairness ought to be considered at the same time).

Numerous Texas cases have held that a party may "open the door" to otherwise privileged information by introducing evidence in the protected area. *See, e.g., Wilkens v. State*, 847 S.W.2d 547, 550-51 (Tex. Crim. App. 1992) (State could introduce testimony from examining psychiatrists to rebut appellant's presentation of an insanity plea; defendant waived his Fifth Amendment privilege when he introduced examination evidence to prove his insanity defense); *Draper v. State*, 596 S.W.2d 855, 857 (Tex. Crim. App. [Panel Op.] 1980) (having opened the door by relating some facts of a transaction, a defendant should not be permitted to assert Fifth Amendment privilege to prevent disclosure of additional relevant facts); *Johnson v. State*, 926 S.W.2d 334, 338 (Tex. App.—Fort Worth 1996) (defendant waived drug-abuse-counselor privilege to the extent that he had testified in contradiction to protected communications, but rebuttal evidence should have been limited to the precise contradictory point), *vacated on other grounds*, 938 S.W.2d 65 (Tex. Crim. App. 1997).

919. *In re John Doe Corp.*, 675 F.2d 482, 489 (2d Cir. 1982); *see, e.g., In re W.E.C.*, 110 S.W.3d 231, 248 (Tex. App.—Fort Worth 2003, no pet.) (when appellant revealed majority of information about her problems with drug and alcohol abuse to caseworkers, therapists, and friends, she waived any mental-health-information privilege about her communications to drug-treatment counselor); *Carmona v. State*, 947 S.W.2d 661, 664 (Tex. App.—Austin 1997, no pet.) (polygraph examiner's written report and pretest interview "were essentially one communication," and disclosure of one operated as a waiver of the other).

920. *Marathon Oil Co. v. Moyé*, 893 S.W.2d 585, 590 (Tex. App.—Dallas 1994, orig. proceeding [leave denied]); *see, e.g., Bailey v. State*, 507 S.W.3d 740, 747 (Tex. Crim. App. 2016) (defendant's express consent to disclosure of substantial part of her privileged communications with her attorney, disclosed to establish reasonable-excuse defense under Texas Penal Code §38.10, was sufficient to implicitly waive privilege for related communications); *Berger v. Lang*, 976 S.W.2d 833, 837 (Tex. App.—Houston [1st Dist.] 1998, pet. denied) (defendant-attorney waived any privilege for confidential deliberations and findings of State Bar Grievance Committee about conduct giving

In ***Republic Insurance Co. v. Davis***,[922] the supreme court discussed the "offensive use" waiver of a privilege and concluded that because privileges represent society's desire to protect certain professional and private relationships, an offensive-use waiver "should not lightly be found."[923] Such a waiver requires a trial judge to find that (1) the party asserting the privilege must be seeking affirmative relief, (2) the privileged information must be outcome-determinative evidence, and (3) disclosure of the privileged material must be the only way that the other party can obtain the evidence.[924]

These are, of course, examples of implied waiver. An implied waiver may also be found in a failure to object to the introduction of the matter claimed to be privileged,[925] or by voluntary disclosure at some earlier time.[926] Sharing information with

---

rise to current lawsuit when he testified that client had filed grievance against him and asserted that client's accusations were untrue, which falsely suggested that outcome of grievance was favorable); ***Terrell State Hosp. v. Ashworth***, 794 S.W.2d 937, 940-41 (Tex. App.—Dallas 1990, orig. proceeding [leave denied]) (hospital waived privilege for psychological autopsy when hospital superintendent's response to inquiry on behalf of suicide victim's mother was based on and disclosed a "significant part" of the autopsy); *see also **Nguyen v. Excel Corp.***, 197 F.3d 200, 207 nn.18-19 (5th Cir. 1999) (corporation waived attorney-client privilege by permitting its employees to testify about portions of attorney-client communications). After the promulgation of Rule 511(b), voluntary disclosure of privileged material can result in "subject-matter waiver" for communications or information covered by the attorney-client privilege or work-product protection if certain requirements are met. Refer to notes 937-938 *infra* and accompanying text.

921. *Moyé*, 893 S.W.2d at 590; *see, e.g.*, ***In re Bexar Cty. Crim. Dist. Attorney's Office***, 224 S.W.3d 182, 189 (Tex. 2007) (orig. proceeding) (district attorney's production of prosecution file did not require production of personnel "so that their mental processes and related case preparation may be further probed"); ***In re Carbo Ceramics, Inc.***, 81 S.W.3d 369, 377 (Tex. App.—Houston [14th Dist.] 2002, orig. proceeding) (production of one letter waived attorney-client privilege for that letter but was "not an automatic blanket waiver of the privilege for all other documents withheld on the basis of attorney-client privilege"); ***Nat'l Union Fire Ins. v. Hoffman***, 746 S.W.2d 305, 310-11 (Tex. App.—Dallas 1988, orig. proceeding) (attorney's letter to client waived attorney-client privilege for that letter but did not waive privilege for "all communications, knowledge and opinions" of underlying matter).

922. 856 S.W.2d 158 (Tex. 1993).

923. *Id.* at 163.

924. *Id.*; ***Bailey***, 507 S.W.3d at 746; *see, e.g.*, ***In re M-I L.L.C.***, 505 S.W.3d 569, 579 (Tex. 2016) (orig. proceeding) (no offensive-use waiver of trade-secrets privilege when privilege holder conceded that its trade secrets were discoverable and simply wanted to prevent disclosure to alleged competitive decision-maker during temporary-injunction hearing); ***Tex. Dep't of Pub. Safety Officers Ass'n v. Denton***, 897 S.W.2d 757, 761-64 (Tex. 1995) (plaintiff's invocation of Fifth Amendment privilege for matters directly related to his claim constituted "offensive use" under ***Republic Ins.***, but court remanded to determine whether dismissal of his claim was appropriate remedy); ***Nat'l Union Fire Ins. v. Valdez***, 863 S.W.2d 458, 461-62 (Tex. 1993) (orig. proceeding) (because insurance company was not seeking affirmative relief, no offensive-use waiver of its work-product protection occurred); ***In re Houseman***, 66 S.W.3d 368, 372-73 (Tex. App.—Beaumont 2001, orig. proceeding) (attorney-client privilege for testimony by psychiatrist retained by attorney was not waived by "offensive use" when neither client nor her attorney sought affirmative relief in guardianship proceeding brought by client's relative).

925. *See, e.g.*, ***Briddle v. State***, 742 S.W.2d 379, 391 (Tex. Crim. App. 1987) (marital-communications privilege was waived when defendant did not object to the interrogation of his ex-wife), *overruled on other grounds*, ***Cockrell v. State***, 933 S.W.2d 73 (Tex. Crim. App. 1996); ***Johnson v. State***, 95 Tex. Crim. 483, 487, 255 S.W. 416, 417 (1923) (defendant's failure to object to the use of letters he wrote to his wife waived his privilege); ***Allen v. State***, 761 S.W.2d 384, 387 (Tex. App.—Houston [14th Dist.] 1988, pet. ref'd) (defendant's failure to object to the admission and reading of a letter she had written to her ex-husband was a waiver of her privilege).

926. *See **Freeman v. Bianchi***, 820 S.W.2d 853, 861 (Tex. App.—Houston [1st Dist.] 1991, orig. proceeding) (in civil proceedings, "voluntary" disclosures are not limited to those made knowingly and intentionally, and the court looks "to whether the disclosure was made involuntarily or was compelled erroneously"), *leave granted, mand. denied*, ***Granada Corp. v. First Ct. of Appeals***, 844 S.W.2d 223 (Tex. 1992); ***Gulf Oil Corp. v. Fuller***, 695 S.W.2d 769, 773 (Tex. App.—El Paso 1985, orig. proceeding) ("[T]he test of waiver is not whether the disclosure was intentional or

others is not only evidence of waiver; it is also pertinent in showing that no confidential communication was intended in the first place.[927] This last point raises the sometimes-difficult question of whether the waiver of a privilege in one proceeding for one party constitutes a waiver in all other proceedings as to all other parties.[928] Selective waiver as to a particular party cannot be permitted—a party cannot withdraw a waiver at one of several proceedings involving a particular adversary.[929] Any other position threatens significant inequity and is a tactically aggressive use of the privilege. Yet situations arise in which a holder waives this privilege for one person or entity and then seeks to invoke the privilege against another party in a different context. In fact, the holder sometimes seeks to limit the scope of a waiver by explicit agreement with the party to whom the disclosure is voluntarily made.[930] In such situations, the inequity argument against partial waiver is much weaker even though any disclosure is inconsistent with the confidential relationship.

Suppose that a person announces the intention to disclose privileged material but has not yet done so. At least one federal court has held that in that instance no waiver has occurred until the privileged material has actually been disclosed.[931]

---

inadvertent, but whether the disclosure was voluntary or was consented to or whether the disclosure was compelled erroneously or was made without opportunity to claim the privilege."); *see, e.g., Axelson, Inc. v. McIlhany*, 798 S.W.2d 550, 553-54 (Tex. 1990) (orig. proceeding) (any attorney-client privilege surrounding a company's internal investigation of bribes and kickbacks was waived when evidence indicated that investigation had been disclosed to the FBI, IRS, and Wall Street Journal); *Eloise Bauer & Assocs., Inc. v. Elec. Realty Assocs., Inc.*, 621 S.W.2d 200, 204 (Tex. Civ. App.—Texarkana 1981, writ ref'd n.r.e.) (voluntary pretrial production of privileged document for copying by opponent waived attorney-client privilege); *Dobbins v. Gardner*, 377 S.W.2d 665, 668 (Tex. Civ. App.—Houston 1964, writ ref'd n.r.e.) (defendant-physician implied waiver when he sent a privileged description of his treatment of plaintiff to a fellow physician); *Lucas v. Wright*, 370 S.W.2d 924, 927 (Tex. Civ. App.—Beaumont 1963, orig. proceeding) (defendant's testimony at preliminary hearing waived the privilege despite his later statements that he had not intended to waive the privilege); *Hurley v. McMillan*, 268 S.W.2d 229, 233 (Tex. Civ. App.—Galveston 1954, writ ref'd n.r.e.) (plaintiff waived privilege by responding to questions about the privileged information instead of claiming the privilege).

927. *See, e.g., Strong v. State*, 773 S.W.2d 543, 552 n.11 (Tex. Crim. App. 1989) (murder defendant who sent a copy of a letter to a third party must not have intended confidentiality, and thus disclosure waived any privilege); *Cameron Cty. v. Hinojosa*, 760 S.W.2d 742, 746 (Tex. App.—Corpus Christi 1988, orig. proceeding [leave denied]) (letters seeking legal advice routinely sent to other, nonlegal county offices showed no intent to maintain confidentiality or, alternatively, that any privilege was waived by disclosure to third parties).

928. In *Axelson, Inc. v. McIlhany*, the court of appeals held that any confidentiality of an oil-well operator's internal investigation into kickbacks was waived by a lawsuit against one of its suppliers and disclosure to various law-enforcement agencies and a newspaper. 755 S.W.2d 170, 178 (Tex. App.—Amarillo 1988, orig. proceeding). The supreme court conditionally granted mandamus and held that an in camera inspection must take place to review the information for relevance. *Axelson*, 798 S.W.2d at 551, 553.

929. *See Lucas*, 370 S.W.2d at 927 (waiver once made is made for all times and all purposes). Federal Rule of Evidence 502 generally does not allow the parties to agree to a selective waiver. Refer to note 333 *supra* and accompanying text. Presumably, Texas Rule of Evidence 511(b), which incorporates the provisions of Federal Rule 502, also does not permit selective waiver. *See In re Fisher & Paykel Appliances, Inc.*, 420 S.W.3d 842, 851 (Tex. App.—Dallas 2014, orig. proceeding) ("[T]he weight of authority does not favor recognition in Texas of a doctrine of selective waiver of privilege ...."). Refer to note 935 *infra*.

930. *See Ryals v. Canales*, 767 S.W.2d 226, 228 (Tex. App.—Dallas 1989, orig. proceeding) (no implied waiver occurs if a party demonstrates that materials are protected by the joint-defense doctrine of the attorney-client privilege). For agreements to limit waiver for disclosure of communications covered by the attorney-client privilege or work-product protection, refer to notes 941-942 *infra* and accompanying text.

931. *See Tennenbaum v. Deloitte & Touche*, 77 F.3d 337, 341 (9th Cir. 1996).

Finally, Rule 511(a)(1) provides that voluntary disclosure does not waive a privilege if the disclosure is itself privileged.[932] For example, a patient under the mental-health-information privilege may reveal communications with his therapist to his wife in confidence without the privilege being waived.[933]

2. Rule 511(a)(2): Testimony of character witness. Rule 511(a)(2) is a simple fairness doctrine. When a party calls a clergy member, doctor, or other person who possesses privileged information as a character witness, the witness cannot claim a privilege on cross-examination when questioned about knowledge of prior conduct inconsistent with the party's good character.[934]

B. Rule 511(b): Lawyer-Client Privilege & Work Product; Limitations on Waiver.

Rule 511(b) sets out exceptions and limitations on waiver for disclosure of a communication or information covered by the attorney-client privilege or work-product protection.[935] The rule does not affect the law governing waiver of other privileges or protections.[936]

1. Rule 511(b)(1): Disclosure made in a federal or state proceeding or to a federal or state office or agency; scope of a waiver. If a party discloses a communication or information covered by the attorney-client privilege or work-product protection in a federal or state proceeding or to a federal or state office or agency, the disclosure can result in a "subject-matter waiver"—that is, waiver of privilege for both disclosed and undisclosed information.[937] Subject-matter waiver of the attorney-client privilege or work-product protection occurs only when (1) the waiver is intentional, (2) the disclosed and undisclosed privileged information concern the same subject matter, and (3) the disclosed and undisclosed privileged information should in fairness be considered together.[938]

---

932. Tex. R. Evid. 511(a)(1).

933. This provision is distinguishable from, but consistent with, the usual principle that the disclosure of a privileged communication to an agent or representative of the client or professional to assist in obtaining or providing services for which the communication was originally made is itself privileged. *See Burnett v. State*, 642 S.W.2d 765, 769-70 (Tex. Crim. App. 1982) (extending the attorney-client privilege to a hypnotist whom attorney hired to refresh defendant's memory). Various privileges for communications to professionals address this issue. *See, e.g.*, Tex. R. Evid. 503(a)(5) (lawyer), Tex. R. Evid. 505(a)(3) (clergy), Tex. R. Evid. 509(a)(3) (physician), Tex. R. Evid. 510(a)(4) (mental-health professional).

934. *See* Tex. R. Evid. 511(a)(2).

935. Tex. R. Evid. 511 cmt.; *see Paxton v. City of Dallas*, 509 S.W.3d 247, 263 (Tex. 2017) (Rule 511(b) affords attorney-client privilege additional protection against waiver). Rule 511(b) was designed to align Texas law with federal law on waiver of privilege by voluntary disclosure and incorporates the provisions of Federal Rule 502. Tex. R. Evid. 511 cmt. For a discussion of Federal Rule 502, refer to note 333 *supra*. Thus, Texas courts may look to federal cases for guidance in interpreting Rule 511(b). For a discussion of Federal Rule 502, see *O'Connor's Federal Rules * Civil Trials* (2017), "Disclosure of privileged or protected information – attorney-related privileges," ch. 6-A, §9.3.2, p. 488.

936. Tex. R. Evid. 511 cmt.

937. *See* Tex. R. Evid. 511(b)(1).

938. *Id.*; *see* Fed. R. Evid. 502(a). The rule does not define "same subject matter" or expand on considerations of "fairness."

2. Rule 511(b)(2): Inadvertent disclosure in state civil proceedings. The inadvertent disclosure of a communication or information covered by the attorney-client privilege or work-product protection in a state civil proceeding does not automatically waive the claim of privilege if the privilege holder followed the procedures of Texas Rule of Civil Procedure 193.3(d).[939]

3. Rule 511(b)(3) & (b)(4): Controlling effect of a court order or party agreement. A federal or state court order providing that a communication or information covered by the attorney-client privilege or work-product protection is not waived by a disclosure connected to the litigation pending before that court is also not a waiver of the privilege or protection in a Texas state proceeding.[940] Similarly, the parties can enter into an agreement to limit the effect of waiver by disclosure between them in any state proceeding.[941] The agreement applies only to communications or information covered by the attorney-client privilege or work-product protection and is binding only on the parties to the agreement unless it is incorporated into a court order.[942]

RULE 512
PRIVILEGED MATTER DISCLOSED UNDER COMPULSION OR WITHOUT OPPORTUNITY TO CLAIM PRIVILEGE

A privilege claim is not defeated by a disclosure that was:

(a) compelled erroneously; or

(b) made without opportunity to claim the privilege.

COMMENTARY ON RULE 512

Texas Rule 512 deals with two basic situations.[943] In the first, disclosure that was erroneously compelled,[944] the rule's position reflects the common-law view that such a

---

939. TEX. R. EVID. 511(b)(2); *see* TEX. R. CIV. P. 193.3(d). Under Rule 193.3(d), the privilege holder must serve on the other parties an amended withholding statement that (1) identifies the information produced, (2) identifies the privilege asserted for that information, and (3) requests that all copies of the privileged information be returned. TEX. R. CIV. P. 193.3(d). Generally, the privilege holder must amend the withholding statement within ten days of discovering the accidental production. *Id.* For further discussion of Rule 193.3(d), see *O'Connor's Texas Rules * Civil Trials* (2017), "Use snap-back provision," ch. 6-A, §18.2.4, p. 512.

In *Paxton v. City of Dallas*, the Texas Supreme Court held that unlike a failure to follow the procedures outlined in Texas Rule of Civil Procedure 193.3(d), missing the statutory deadline in the Public Information Act for requesting a ruling from the Attorney General does not waive the attorney-client privilege. 509 S.W.3d at 262-64; *see* TEX. GOV'T CODE §§552.301(a), (b), 552.302. The court reasoned that Rule 193.3(d) contemplates inadvertent but actual disclosure followed by conduct that is inconsistent with claiming the privilege. *Paxton*, 509 S.W.3d at 263. In this case, however, there was no disclosure and the party made efforts to maintain the confidentiality of the information. *Id.* at 263-64. The court concluded that the attorney-client privilege was a "compelling reason" to rebut the presumption of disclosure in the Public Information Act despite the untimely request for an Attorney General decision. *Id.* at 250.

940. TEX. R. EVID. 511(b)(3); *see* TEX. R. EVID. 511(b)(1).

941. *See* TEX. R. EVID. 511(b)(4).

942. TEX. R. EVID. 511(b)(4) & cmt.; *see* TEX. R. EVID. 511(b)(1).

943. The rule is derived from Uniform Rule of Evidence 511 (1974).

944. TEX. R. EVID. 512(a).

mistake does not result in waiver of the privilege.[945] However, in the second, disclosure without opportunity for objection by the holder,[946] the rule arguably represents a departure from the common-law view that inadvertent, unintentional, or innocent disclosure of privileged information resulted in waiver of the privilege under certain circumstances.[947]

There is an apparent internal contradiction in the idea that a disclosure of a privileged matter through a judge's erroneous direction should still be treated as privileged in a civil proceeding.[948] The holder's privacy interest cannot be vindicated after disclosure has been made either through judicial error or without the holder having had an opportunity to object.[949] Nor would the instrumental justification for privileges likely be threatened if the judicial error were the subject of admonishment by the appellate court and society had the advantage of this presumptively reliable and relevant evidence. Similarly, when the disclosure occurs through a deliberate or negligent act by an agent or an eavesdropper, courts might admonish the privilege holder[950] to be more careful in the future, leaving him only such relief as could be obtained through civil litigation against the disclosing party.

---

945. 8 WIGMORE, *supra* note 6, §2270, at 413-19. Although the cited section refers to an erroneous denial of the privilege against self-incrimination, it has been asserted that "the principle is equally sound when applied to other privileges." *Proposed Rules*, *supra* note 28, at 260 (FED. R. EVID. 512 advisory committee's note).

In *Anderson v. State*, the defendant's sentencing for theft by receipt was reversed when the trial court erroneously compelled the defendant to be sworn in and to testify after he had made a spontaneous, unsworn, in-court statement during the punishment stage. 871 S.W.2d 900, 905-06 (Tex. App.—Houston [1st Dist.] 1994, no pet.). The defendant had invoked his privilege against self-incrimination, and this outburst did not constitute a waiver of his Fifth Amendment privilege. *Id.*

946. TEX. R. EVID. 512(b).

947. *See* McCORMICK ON EVIDENCE I, *supra* note 65, §74, at 175-76, §82, at 197. One such circumstance involves bystander cases, in which inadvertent communication to third parties such as eavesdroppers destroyed the privilege. *E.g., Clark v. State*, 159 Tex. Crim. 187, 191-93, 261 S.W.2d 339, 342-43 (1953) (telephone operator who eavesdropped on conversation between attorney and client in violation of company rules could testify to contents of otherwise privileged conversation). Presumably, the justification for this approach was that if the parties to a communication intended for it to be kept confidential, they could take measures to protect its confidentiality. *See id.* at 192, 261 S.W.2d at 342. Refer to notes 956-965 *infra* and accompanying text. On rehearing, the court also observed that the conversation involved the disposal of the murder weapon and thus was not privileged under the attorney-client privilege. *See Clark*, 159 Tex. Crim. at 199-200, 261 S.W.2d at 347.

948. In applying the privileges of Article V, no constitutional mandate can compare to the Fifth Amendment's commandment that "[n]o person ... shall be compelled in any criminal case to be a witness against himself." U.S. CONST. amend. V. Without such an imperative, the Rules arguably allow courts to treat erroneously compelled disclosure as a windfall in the search for truth.

949. In the trial underlying the mandamus proceeding of *West v. Solito*, the trial court had ordered an attorney to cooperate fully in giving a deposition, over his former client's objection. 563 S.W.2d 240, 243 (Tex. 1978) (orig. proceeding). Claims of privilege were left for resolution at trial. *Id.* Holding this order to be in error, the supreme court noted that "[a] motion in limine or objection to the testimony at the time it is offered as evidence is totally inadequate to preserve the privilege, for once the matter has been disclosed, it cannot be retracted or otherwise protected." *Id.* at 245.

950. When the party "injured" by the erroneous denial of a privilege is not the holder, there is even less reason for making the error a basis for reversal. *See* 8 WIGMORE, *supra* note 6, §2196, at 112-13, §2321, at 629, §2340, at 672-73. Nevertheless, in *Bell v. State*, the court reversed a murder conviction because the trial judge permitted the State to offer, over objection, a confidential marital communication impeaching the testimony of the witness's husband, a key defense witness. 88 Tex. Crim. 64, 67-68, 224 S.W. 1108, 1109 (1920). The court was arguably correct in view-

Nevertheless, this view is not traditionally taken. Instead, as indicated by Rule 512(a), the erroneously compelled disclosure of a privileged matter can be the basis for mandamus[951] or an appeal and reversal.[952] If disclosure is erroneously coerced from the privilege holder—or a representative of a nonparty privilege holder, so that appeal is then unavailable—Rule 512 at least ensures that the disclosure will not defeat a future claim of privilege for the matter thus disclosed.[953] Thus, a disclosure improperly compelled during discovery proceedings is not a waiver of the privilege.[954] Nor will improperly compelled disclosure in one proceeding act as a waiver to the proper assertion of that privilege in a different setting.[955]

Rule 512(b) continues the protection of the privilege when disclosure is "made without opportunity to claim the privilege."[956] The most common situation in which a person might invoke this provision is when disclosure is made by an eavesdropper or by a

---

ing the communication as within the privilege, but the court did not give its reasoning for its decision to reverse. *See id.* at 68, 224 S.W. at 1109. Rule 512 itself does not speak to the question of whether reversal in such a situation is correct. *See* TEX. R. EVID. 512. Rather, it provides that if a court erroneously compelled testimony to a privileged communication, such disclosure does not preclude the holder from enjoying the privilege. TEX. R. EVID. 512(a).

951. *See **Mem'l Hosp.-The Woodlands v. McCown**,* 927 S.W.2d 1, 12 (Tex. 1996) (erroneous order requiring production of privileged documents leaves party claiming privilege no adequate remedy by appeal; mandamus granted); *see, e.g., **Riverside Hosp., Inc. v. Garza**,* 894 S.W.2d 850, 856-57 (Tex. App.—Corpus Christi 1995, orig. proceeding) (privileged hospital peer-review-committee records that had been disclosed under a court order in a separate lawsuit remained privileged in present case; no waiver under Rule 511 because prior order released documents only to parties in that case for use in that litigation), *overruled on other grounds,* ***Mem'l Hosp.-The Woodlands v. McCown**,* 927 S.W.2d 1 (Tex. 1996).

952. In ***Ex parte Lipscomb**,* the witness, an attorney, refused to testify in a case in which a former client was a party despite the trial court's rejection of the claim of privilege. 111 Tex. 409, 413, 239 S.W. 1101, 1102 (1922). The court held him in contempt and committed him to the sheriff's custody. *Id.* at 412, 239 S.W. at 1101. The supreme court rejected the attorney's writ of habeas corpus on the ground that he had no right to refuse to testify under these circumstances; the privilege belonged to the client, who was a party and thus had a complete remedy by appeal from any erroneous ruling. *Id.* at 418, 239 S.W. at 1105. Under Rule 512, there is no need, other than the privacy interest, to risk jail to protect the privileged matter because erroneously compelled disclosure can be remedied on appeal. *See* TEX. R. EVID. 512.

953. The court of criminal appeals implicitly endorsed this position in ***Burnett v. State**.* 642 S.W.2d 765 (Tex. Crim. App. 1982). In ***Burnett**,* the murder defendant's attorneys hired a hypnotist to discuss the facts of the case with the defendant. *Id.* at 767. The majority found that the hypnotist was an agent of counsel and that the defendant's taped communications made before the hypnotic trance were privileged. *Id.* at 769. The grand jury had compelled the hypnotist to provide the tape in his possession, and the trial court admitted the tape over the defendant's objection based on the attorney-client privilege. *Id.* at 768. Although the court of criminal appeals did not directly address the question, its analysis necessarily assumed that the erroneously compelled disclosure did not preclude the claim of privilege. *Id.* at 770. Indeed, the majority seemed to hold that even a later disclosure by counsel of another tape of the same conversation (to an investigator for transcription and testing) did not constitute a waiver. *Id.* & n.15. Apparently, the majority was of the view that even if the client authorized disclosure to the investigator, the court should not imply waiver because the disclosure was a necessary response to the original improperly compelled disclosure. The implication is that the disclosure to the investigator was in some sense compelled. *Id.* at 770-71 & n.15.

954. *See, e.g., **Ginsberg v. Johnson**,* 673 S.W.2d 942, 943 (Tex. App.—Dallas 1984, orig. proceeding) (medical records produced under an improper discovery order remained privileged despite the fact that they had been in the other party's possession for nearly a year), *mand. granted sub nom. **Ginsberg v. Fifth Ct. of Appeals**,* 686 S.W.2d 105 (Tex. 1985).

955. *See* TEX. R. EVID. 512(a).

956. TEX. R. EVID. 512(b).

person who has obtained a privileged document without the holder's voluntary act.[957] The communications privileges in Article V represent a strong desire to protect the holder from losing the privilege through such disclosures.[958] Rule 512(b) is fully consistent with this view and with Texas case law on the subject.[959] The provision is equally applicable when the privilege holder voluntarily entrusts the witness with the confidence, but the witness discloses the confidence when the holder has no opportunity to object because, for example, he is not present at the proceeding. If the intention of the holder controls, implied waiver should not be found when there was no opportunity for objection.[960] Similarly, a valid privilege is not waived if the holder did not have an opportunity to object to disclosure because he did not know that he had a privilege or did not know that he could refuse to disclose confidential communications.[961]

The party claiming lack of waiver must produce evidence showing that the disclosure was made without opportunity to claim the privilege. In **Jordan v. Fourth Court of Appeals**, the Texas Supreme Court held that because "[t]he record ... is completely silent as to the circumstances surrounding the disclosure of the [privileged] documents to the Bexar County grand jury,"[962] it would not find that the disclosure occurred without an opportunity to claim the privilege. Justice Gonzalez, in dissent, argued that the burden to prove waiver should remain with the opponent of the privilege, not shift to the holder of the privilege.[963] He also noted several public-policy considerations that

---

957. *See, e.g.*, **Santa Rosa Med. Ctr. v. Spears**, 709 S.W.2d 720, 723 (Tex. App.—San Antonio 1986, orig. proceeding) (when an investigative-news reporter apparently stole privileged hospital-committee minutes and excerpts were then broadcast on the evening news, no waiver was made because disclosure occurred without the hospital's having an opportunity to claim the privilege).

958. *See* Tex. R. Evid. 503(a)(5), 504(a)(1), 505(a)(3), 509(a)(3), 510(a)(4).

959. *See, e.g.*, **Gross v. State**, 61 Tex. Crim. 176, 181-82, 135 S.W. 373, 376 (1911) (third party could not testify to the contents of a husband's letter to his wife); **Gass v. Baggerly**, 332 S.W.2d 426, 430 (Tex. Civ. App.—Dallas 1960, no writ) (inadvertent disclosure to opponent did not waive privilege).

960. *See* Tex. R. Evid. 503(a)(5), 504(a)(1), 505(a)(3), 509(a)(3) & 510(a)(4) (all focusing on the intention of the disclosing party).

961. *See* Tex. R. Evid. 512(b); **Reyes v. State**, 845 S.W.2d 328, 332-33 (Tex. App.—El Paso 1992, no pet.). In **Reyes**, the defendant had called a witness at his first trial who incriminated himself and exculpated the defendant. 845 S.W.2d at 332. At the second trial, that witness invoked his Fifth Amendment privilege against self-incrimination, and the defendant then offered the witness's former testimony under Criminal Rule 804(b)(1). *See* **Reyes**, 845 S.W.2d at 332-33. The evidence in a bill of exceptions showed that the witness had not informed his own attorney, before testifying at the first trial, that he had been subpoenaed to testify, and thus his attorney never had the opportunity to counsel him about his Fifth Amendment right. *See id.* The attorney also testified that he would have counseled his client to claim the privilege. *Id.* The trial judge found that the witness's waiver of his Fifth Amendment privilege at the first trial was made without opportunity to claim the privilege, and he therefore excluded the prior trial testimony. *Id.* This analysis would be correct if the witness had been the defendant on trial or if the witness's testimony from the first trial was ever offered against the witness himself. *Id.* at 333 n.5. However, because the witness still had a valid privilege to invoke—it had not been waived because he testified without an informed opportunity to invoke the privilege—he was "unavailable" for purposes of Rule 804(a), and his former testimony could be introduced by the defendant under Rule 804(b)(1). **Reyes**, 845 S.W.2d at 333.

962. 701 S.W.2d 644, 649 (Tex. 1985) (orig. proceeding).

963. *Id.* at 651 (Gonzalez, J., concurring in part and dissenting in part). The court of criminal appeals explicitly approved of and adopted Justice Gonzalez's position in **Carmona v. State**, 941 S.W.2d 949, 953 (Tex. Crim. App. 1997).

are contrary to implied waiver.[964] No matter which party carries the burden of showing waiver or nonwaiver, courts should engage in a careful analysis of the public-policy and privacy interests at stake when deciding whether there is an implied waiver of a privilege. Just as the *Zerbst* standard of intentional relinquishment of a known right creates too high a standard for waiver,[965] courts should be wary of being too quick to find an implied waiver behind every inadvertent or improper disclosure.

RULE 513
COMMENT ON OR INFERENCE FROM A PRIVILEGE CLAIM; INSTRUCTION

(a) Comment or Inference Not Permitted. Except as permitted in Rule 504(b)(2), neither the court nor counsel may comment on a privilege claim—whether made in the present proceeding or previously—and the factfinder may not draw an inference from the claim.

(b) Claiming Privilege Without the Jury's Knowledge. To the extent practicable, the court must conduct a jury trial so that the making of a privilege claim is not suggested to the jury by any means.

(c) Claim of Privilege Against Self-Incrimination in a Civil Case. Subdivisions (a) and (b) do not apply to a party's claim, in the present civil case, of the privilege against self-incrimination.

(d) Jury Instruction. When this rule forbids a jury from drawing an inference from a privilege claim, the court must, on request of a party against whom the jury might draw the inference, instruct the jury accordingly.

Notes and Comments

Comment to 1998 change: Subdivision (d) regarding a party's entitlement to a jury instruction about a claim of privilege is made applicable to civil cases.

COMMENTARY ON RULE 513

Rule 513, along with Rule 512, enhances the value of the privilege to the holder. Rules 513(a), 513(b), and 513(d)[966] resolve issues posed by the invocation of a privi-

---

964. Justice Gonzalez argued the following:
> The public policy of vigorous prosecution of those that violate the law should be a factor against a finding of waiver. By holding that the statutory privilege has been waived because of cooperation with the Grand Jury, the court discourages full disclosure by those with knowledge of relevant facts. Persons or institutions will be reluctant to fully provide information because of potential civil liability. In turn, this potential reduction in information will hinder law enforcement officials in bringing future wrongdoers to justice.

Jordan, 701 S.W.2d at 651.

965. Refer to notes 901-906 *supra* and accompanying text.

966. Rule 513 is taken from the language of Uniform Rule of Evidence 512 (1974). When the Civil Rules were first proposed, Rule 513 included a section (c) that was substantively identical to current Rule 513(d). *See* TEX. R. EVID. 513 (1982 Liaison Committee proposal), *reprinted infra* p. 1086; *Federal Rules-Proposed Texas Code Overlay:*

lege in such a way as to ensure minimal injury to the holder. The clash of competing values is particularly vivid in Rule 513(a).

The application of Rule 513 differs in two important respects in civil and criminal proceedings. First, as noted in the discussion of Rule 504(b)(2), the State may comment on a criminal defendant's failure to call his spouse when other evidence shows that the spouse can testify to relevant matters.[967] Because no spousal testimonial privilege can be claimed in civil proceedings, this exception does not apply in civil cases. Second, Rule 513(c) allows a party in a civil case to comment on the other party's invocation of the Fifth Amendment privilege against self-incrimination.[968] Furthermore, the rule allows a party to call the opposing party, knowing that the opposing party will invoke the privilege against self-incrimination in front of the jury. This situation is not permitted in a criminal proceeding, in which a defendant's privilege against self-incrimination is never subject to adverse comment or inference.[969]

Part IV, 45 Tex. B.J. 1049, 1051 (1982). It is not known why the supreme court omitted this provision, but the omission had little or no practical effect. Although the deliberate omission implied that a party in a civil suit had no right to such an instruction, a trial judge, in the exercise of discretion, may give such an instruction. Gregory N. Woods, *Invocation of Fifth Amendment Privilege Against Self-Incrimination as Evidence in a Texas Civil Trial*, 52 Tex. B.J. 994, 998 (1989). As a result of the 1998 unification of the Civil and Criminal Rules, the right to a jury instruction is now explicit in Rule 513(d). The trial court can minimize the need for any jury instruction by observing Rule 513(b) and ensuring that a claim of privilege is made outside the presence of the jury whenever feasible.

967. *See Babineaux v. State*, 777 S.W.2d 724, 732 (Tex. App.—Beaumont 1989) (prosecutor could comment on defendant's failure to call his wife as witness), *pet. dism'd, improvidently granted*, 803 S.W.2d 301 (Tex. Crim. App. 1990). Refer to notes 460-471 *supra* and accompanying text.

968. Tex. R. Evid. 513(c). Refer to notes 981-998 *infra* and accompanying text.

969. *See Griffin v. California*, 380 U.S. 609, 614 (1965); *Cruz v. State*, 225 S.W.3d 546, 548 (Tex. Crim. App. 2007). The Texas Court of Criminal Appeals has held that a defendant's pre-arrest, pre-*Miranda* silence, however, is not protected by the Fifth Amendment privilege against self-incrimination and may be subject to adverse comment regardless of whether the defendant testifies. *Salinas v. State*, 369 S.W.3d 176, 179 (Tex. Crim. App. 2012), *aff'd*, ___ U.S. ___, 133 S. Ct. 2174 (2013) (plurality op.). The court reasoned that this silence is admissible evidence because the defendant's interaction with police officers is not compelled under those circumstances. *Id.* In affirming the Texas Court of Criminal Appeals, the U.S. Supreme Court issued a 5-4 decision with two justices concurring in the judgment that the defendant's Fifth Amendment claim failed. The plurality opinion reasoned that a defendant must expressly invoke his Fifth Amendment privilege against self-incrimination and "normally does not invoke the privilege by remaining silent." *Salinas v. Texas*, ___ U.S. ___, 133 S. Ct. 2174, 2181 (2013) (plurality op.). A witness's failure to invoke the privilege must be excused, however, when "governmental coercion makes his forfeiture of the privilege involuntary." *Id.* at ___, 133 S. Ct. at 2180. In this case, the defendant was not deprived of his right to voluntarily invoke the Fifth Amendment because his interview with the police was voluntary; "he agreed to accompany the officers to the station and 'was free to leave at any time during the interview.'" *Id.* The express-invocation requirement puts the government on notice when a witness intends to rely on the privilege and gives the court a record of the witness's reasons for refusing to answer. *Id.* at ___, 133 S. Ct. at 2179. Silence, if it is not in response to *Miranda* warnings or does not follow a defendant's expressed intention to invoke his "right to remain silent," does not put police on notice that the defendant is relying on his Fifth Amendment privilege. *See id.* at ___, 133 S. Ct. at 2182.

Justice Thomas concurred in the judgment but did not join the plurality opinion because he believed the Court did not need to reach the express-invocation question: "in my view, [defendant's Fifth Amendment] claim would fail even if he had invoked the privilege because the prosecutor's comments regarding his precustodial silence did not compel him to give self-incriminating testimony." *Id.* at ___, 133 S. Ct. at 2184 (Thomas & Scalia, JJ., concurring). The dissent disagreed with the plurality that the defendant needed to expressly invoke his privilege against self-incrimination; in the dissenters' view, the circumstances of the interview—that it took place at a police station, in the context of a criminal investigation in which the defendant was a suspect, and that the defendant was

A. Rule 513(a): Comment or Inference Not Permitted

A person who invokes a privilege suppresses evidence that is peculiarly within his control. For a nonprivileged matter, suppression constitutes an admission by conduct, which permits an inference that the testimony or exhibit would have been unfavorable to that party if it had been produced.[970] For a privileged matter, however, Rule 513(a) assumes that such a comment places an undue burden on the valid invocation of a privilege. Thus, the rule permits the suppression of this class of evidence without any cost to the holder.[971] The no-inference provision appears largely consistent with the weight of authority.[972]

---

not represented by counsel—"give rise to a reasonable inference that [defendant's] silence derived from an exercise of his Fifth Amendment rights." *Id.* at ___, 133 S. Ct. at 2189 (Breyer, Ginsburg, Sotomayor, Kagan, JJ., dissenting).

970. McCORMICK ON EVIDENCE I, *supra* note 65, §347, at 991-92.

971. *See* TEX. R. EVID. 513(a) ("Except as permitted in Rule 504(b)(2), neither the court nor counsel may comment on a privilege claim—whether made in the present proceeding or previously—and the factfinder may not draw an inference from the claim."); *Romero v. KPH Consol., Inc.*, 166 S.W.3d 212, 215 (Tex. 2005) ("[T]he Rules of Evidence prohibit drawing any inference from a claim of privilege in a civil case ...."). If a third-party witness invokes the privilege, it is normally improper to draw an inference against either party. In *Rodriguez v. State*, the court of criminal appeals outlined the rationale for prohibiting comment on a witness's assertion of the privilege against self-incrimination:

> The reason for the rule is that, in refusing to answer a question on the ground that the answer would tend to incriminate him, the witness is exercising a constitutional right personal to himself, the exercise of which would neither help nor harm a third person. If no inference of guilt can be indulged against the person who declines to testify, none could be drawn as to the guilt or innocence of a defendant on trial.

513 S.W.2d 594, 595-96 (Tex. Crim. App. 1974); *see also Ellis v. State*, 683 S.W.2d 379, 382-83 (Tex. Crim. App. 1984) (when a witness other than the accused declines to testify on self-incrimination grounds, that refusal may not be the basis of any inference by the jury favorable to either prosecutor or accused).

The rule requiring that no inference attach to a claim of privilege by a witness occasionally leads to some extraordinary results. For example, in *Vargas v. State*, the defendant was convicted of delivery of cocaine. 781 S.W.2d 356, 357 (Tex. App.—Houston [1st Dist.] 1989), *rev'd on other grounds*, 838 S.W.2d 552 (Tex. Crim. App. 1992). He sought a new trial on the ground that the arresting officers had perjured themselves at his original trial. *Id.* at 360. At the hearing on his motion for new trial, two officers who were under investigation by the police department at that time and were later fired invoked their Fifth Amendment privilege against self-incrimination. *Id.* at 361. The court upheld the denial of a new trial because no affirmative evidence showed that the officers perjured themselves in this particular defendant's trial. *Id.* Because the trial court could not draw any inference from the officers' invocation of their privilege against self-incrimination, the defendant did not prove that their original testimony was perjured. *Id.* The dissent argued that when Criminal Rule 513 clashes with a defendant's constitutionally protected right to a fair trial, the evidentiary rule must yield. *Id.* at 364-65 (O'Connor, J., dissenting). Indeed, that is the normal result. *See, e.g., Rock v. Arkansas*, 483 U.S. 44, 62 (1987) (state evidentiary rule prohibiting all hypnotically refreshed testimony violated defendant's constitutional right to testify); *Chambers v. Mississippi*, 410 U.S. 284, 298 (1973) (state evidentiary "voucher rule" must yield to defendant's constitutional right to present his defense).

972. *See* McCORMICK ON EVIDENCE I, *supra* note 65, §74.1, at 177 (cases are in dispute); 8 WIGMORE, *supra* note 6, §§2243, 2322 (acknowledging the tradition, but arguing that an adverse inference should be permitted). Before the Rules of Evidence were adopted, however, the court of criminal appeals held in *Stewart v. State* that it was not reversible error for the trial judge to instruct the jury, over the defendant's objection, that "[t]he State may not call the wife of a Defendant to testify against the Defendant" regardless of waiver. 587 S.W.2d 148, 153 (Tex. Crim. App. [Panel Op.] 1979). This comment by the judge, although accurate and not a comment on the weight of the evidence, seemed to call the jury's attention to the defendant's failure to call the spouse as a witness for himself. *See id.* at 153-54. *Stewart*, however, involved a special problem because defense counsel arguably misled the jury into thinking that control of the decision to call the wife had passed to the prosecutor. Thus, the instruction was apparently a means of correcting the "manufactured" witness problem. *See id.* at 154. Moreover, this view is consistent with the rule that a legally accurate instruction on a defendant's Fifth Amendment privilege cannot be prevented by the defendant on the grounds that it is "like waving a red flag in front of the jury." *Lakeside v. Oregon*, 435 U.S. 333, 335

B. Rule 513(b): Claiming a Privilege Without the Jury's Knowledge

Rule 513(b) represents a similar effort to shield parties from injury from the adverse inference that jurors probably draw after witnessing a successful claim of privilege.[973] Again, the rationale is predicated on the zealous protection of an accused's privilege not to testify.[974] Extension of this position to Article V privileges is consistent with their structure.[975] It is reasonable to anticipate that in most instances, the parties know whether the opposing party will rely on the privilege.[976] Thus, the parties can implement Texas Rule 513(b) by using motions in limine.[977] On the other hand, Texas cases have held that if a witness does not have the right to invoke a privilege, he may be called to the stand and required to make the invalid assertion of privilege before the jury.[978] Similarly, if a party cannot reasonably anticipate that a witness will invoke a privilege,[979] or if a witness selectively invokes a privilege, courts may find that having the witness assert the privilege in the jury's presence does not violate Rule 513.[980]

(1978). Nevertheless, such a comment on privileges other than that against self-incrimination seems barred by Rule 513(a), which prohibits both comment and inference separately. *See* TEX. R. EVID. 513(a).

973. 8 WIGMORE, *supra* note 6, §2272, at 426.

974. *See Proposed Rules*, *supra* note 28, at 261 (FED. R. EVID. 601 advisory committee's note). When the privilege against self-incrimination is invoked by a nonparty, the normal rule in criminal cases is that the invocation should be outside the presence of the jury. *See* **Mendoza v. State**, 552 S.W.2d 444, 450 (Tex. Crim. App. 1977). This rule is predicated on the idea that such a refusal to testify, without more, cannot be the basis for any legitimate inference by the jury because neither party controls the witness's invocation and neither has the opportunity to cross-examine the witness about any matter thus inferred. 8 WIGMORE, *supra* note 6, §2272(b), at 437. The rule presupposes that it is known that the witness will properly invoke the privilege for all or almost all questions. *See, e.g.*, **Chambliss v. State**, 633 S.W.2d 678, 683-84 (Tex. App.—El Paso 1982) (witness did not have to testify when he indicated on voir dire that he would invoke the Fifth Amendment), *aff'd*, 647 S.W.2d 257 (Tex. Crim. App. 1983); *cf.* **Bowles v. United States**, 439 F.2d 536, 541 (D.C. Cir. 1970) (en banc) (upholding a district court's refusal to compel a witness to testify when the court ascertained, outside the presence of the jury, that the witness intended to claim the privilege against self-incrimination).

975. *See* TEX. R. EVID. 503(a)(5), 504(a)(1), 505(a)(3), 509(a)(3), 510(a)(4).

976. **In re L.S.**, 748 S.W.2d 571, 575 (Tex. App.—Amarillo 1988, no writ).

977. *Id.*; 7 DORSANEO, *supra* note 74, at §114.14[2] (2009); *see* Linda L. Addison, *Keeping Claims of Privileges from the Jury*, 52 TEX. B.J. 414, 414 (1989) (motions in limine can effectively implement the mandate of Rule 513(b)).

978. In **Coffey v. State**, for example, the court of criminal appeals held that the State could call to the witness stand a witness previously granted use immunity for her testimony and allow the jury to see her invoke the Fifth Amendment. 796 S.W.2d 175, 179 (Tex. Crim. App. 1990). Because she had been granted immunity, she had no valid basis for refusing to testify. *Id.*; *see, e.g.*, **McDuffie v. State**, 854 S.W.2d 195, 217 (Tex. App.—Beaumont 1993, pet. ref'd) (witness whom trial court found was not defendant's common-law wife had no marital privilege to invoke, thus, once she was offered immunity, State could call her as a witness, require her to invoke invalid privilege before the jury, and, under Criminal Rule 504(b)(2), comment on her refusal to testify). *But see* **Washburn v. State**, 164 Tex. Crim. 448, 450-51, 299 S.W.2d 706, 706-07 (1956) (jury may not hear a witness invoke the privilege against self-incrimination when immunity has been offered to the witness but not granted by the trial court).

979. *See, e.g.*, **Benitez v. State**, 5 S.W.3d 915, 919-20 (Tex. App.—Amarillo 1999, pet. ref'd) (because State apparently did not know spouse would invoke testimonial privilege, no error in calling her to witness stand; defense attorney immediately approached bench, jury was excused, wife was informed of her testimonial privilege, and she invoked it outside presence of jury).

980. *See, e.g.*, **United States v. Kaplan**, 832 F.2d 676, 684 (1st Cir. 1987) (witness invoked the privilege selectively on cross-examination); *cf.* **Johnson v. State**, 803 S.W.2d 272, 283 (Tex. Crim. App. 1990) (State may demonstrate the necessity of allowing a spouse to invoke the privilege in the presence of the jury).

C. Rule 513(c): Claim of Privilege Against Self-Incrimination in a Civil Case

Rule 513(c) has no counterpart in the proposed Federal Rules or the Uniform Rules of Evidence.[981] The supreme court apparently added the provision in order to adopt the view of *McInnis v. State*[982] on the treatment of the invocation of the privilege against self-incrimination in civil cases. The intention of Rule 513(c) is to provide that, notwithstanding Rule 513(b), a party may require the opposing party to invoke any privilege against self-incrimination before the trier of fact.[983] Moreover, although *McInnis* does not discuss this point, the rule permits comment and inference, despite Rule 513(a), about such invocation in that proceeding.[984] Rule 513(c) does not authorize similar treatment of a nonparty-witness's invocation of the privilege.

It seems anomalous to single out the only privilege with a clear constitutional basis for adverse treatment. However, this differential treatment merely reflects the difference in the function of the privilege against self-incrimination. It is possible that the difference in treatment reflects the different jurisprudential stature of these privileges. The privileges protected by Rule 513(a) and (b) are products of statute and common law. Their desirability and scope are functions of judgments by authorities relatively responsive to the popular will. Permitting explicit or implicit comment or inference might weaken the hypothesized desirable effects of the nonconstitutional communication privileges. In theory, at least, a person is less likely to create a confidential relationship or impart a confidential communication knowing that the rule allows indi-

---

981. Refer to note 966 *supra.* The text of proposed Federal Rule 513(c) is identical to the position quoted there. *Proposed Rules, supra* note 28, at 260.

982. 618 S.W.2d 389 (Tex. Civ. App.—Beaumont 1981, writ ref'd n.r.e.). *McInnis* was a disbarment proceeding in which the defendant was questioned about then-unresolved criminal matters. *Id.* at 391-92. Nonetheless, because disbarment is a civil matter, it was held proper to call him as a witness and to force him to invoke his privilege before the jury. *Id.* at 392; *see also Ex parte Butler*, 522 S.W.2d 196, 197-98 (Tex. 1975) (orig. proceeding) (proper to call opposing party as witness in civil contempt proceeding; party can still invoke privilege against self-incrimination).

983. In a civil case, there is no equivalent to the criminal accused's privilege not to testify. *See Murray v. Tex. Dep't of Family & Prot. Servs.*, 294 S.W.3d 360, 366 (Tex. App.—Austin 2009, no pet.) ("[U]nlike in criminal proceedings, in civil proceedings there is no right to make a blanket assertion of the privilege and refuse to answer any questions. Instead, the privilege must be asserted on a question-by-question basis."); *McInnis*, 618 S.W.2d at 392 (in disbarment action, a civil proceeding, Fifth Amendment does not preclude attorney from being called as a witness; once he becomes a witness, he retains the right and privilege against self-incrimination); Woods, *supra* note 966, at 996 (party can inform the jury of the opposing party's claim of privilege).

984. *See Tex. Dep't of Pub. Safety Officers Ass'n v. Denton*, 897 S.W.2d 757, 760 (Tex. 1995); *Matbon, Inc. v. Gries*, 288 S.W.2d 471, 489 (Tex. App.—Eastland 2009, no pet.); *Blake v. Dorado*, 211 S.W.3d 429, 433 (Tex. App.—El Paso 2006, no pet.). Rule 513(c)'s limitation on inference from and permitted comment on a party's invocation of the privilege in the same proceeding reflects the significant complexities posed in determining the appropriate inference to be drawn from an earlier invocation. Perhaps reasons for the previous invocation would reduce or eliminate the probative value of any inference to be drawn therefrom. *Cf. Grunewald v. United States*, 353 U.S. 391, 421 (1957) (defendant's testimony at trial was not subject to impeachment because of his invocation of the privilege before a grand jury). *But cf. Fletcher v. Weir*, 455 U.S. 603, 606-07 (1982) (defendant's silence after his arrest but before receiving his *Miranda* warnings could be used to impeach his trial testimony if it were found to be inconsistent); *Jenkins v. Anderson*, 447 U.S. 231, 238 (1980) (defendant's exculpatory testimony at trial could be impeached with his failure to offer a similar explanation before surrendering himself two weeks after the homicide). *See generally* 8 WIGMORE, *supra* note 6, §2273, at 445-52 (discussing the practical effect of claiming privilege).

rect "disclosure." It is easy to imagine questions asked in such a manner that the invocation of a privilege gives rise to an inference that invades the privacy interest supposedly protected by that privilege. In contrast, the privilege against self-incrimination and the extraordinary expansion of its reach are imposed by the U.S. Constitution as interpreted by the U.S. Supreme Court.[985] A person satisfies the privilege against self-incrimination, which is not a "communication" privilege, if there is no danger that the answer demanded will directly or indirectly "furnish a link in a chain of evidence" connecting the witness with a prosecutable crime.[986] Thus, a witness may have to answer if granted "use plus derivative use" immunity.[987] There is no similar basis for compelling disclosure of privileged communications.

Thus, in a civil case, if a party asserts his Fifth Amendment privilege to refuse to testify in response to probative evidence, that assertion is a proper subject for comment.[988] Rule 513(c) expresses the prevailing position in the United States.[989]

Although the provision does not specify who is a party for purposes of Rule 513(c), Rule 801(e)(2) provides a useful outline of statements that qualify as nonhearsay statements of an opposing party.[990] Some federal cases expand the class of persons whose invocation of a Fifth Amendment privilege is the subject of adverse comment to in-

---

985. *See Murphy v. Waterfront Comm'n*, 378 U.S. 52, 79 (1964) (State cannot, without a grant of immunity, compel testimony that may incriminate a witness under laws of another jurisdiction); *Malloy v. Hogan*, 378 U.S. 1, 10-11 (1964) (Fourteenth Amendment prohibits a state from infringing on the privilege against self-incrimination during an investigatory proceeding).

986. *See Malloy*, 378 U.S. at 13.

987. *See Kastigar v. United States*, 406 U.S. 441, 462 (1972); John P. Venzke, Comment, *Texas Immunity Law: A Survey and a Proposal*, 10 Hous. L. Rev. 1120, 1121-24 (1973).

988. *Baxter v. Palmigiano*, 425 U.S. 308, 318 (1976); *Ikeda v. Curtis*, 261 P.2d 684, 690 (Wash. 1953). Few Texas civil cases address Rule 513. In *Smith v. Smith*, the plaintiff-mother sued her ex-husband and others for interference with child custody. 720 S.W.2d 586, 590 (Tex. App.—Houston [1st Dist.] 1986, no writ). On appeal, the defendants claimed that the jury should not have been read portions of pretrial depositions in which the defendants invoked their privilege against self-incrimination. *Id.* at 594. The court rejected this argument, stating the following:

> Since the present case was a civil proceeding, any of the appellants, including those with pending criminal charges, could have been called to testify …. For the parties who were called or could have been called to testify, Tex. R. Evid. 513(c) permits the asking of questions that would necessitate the assertion of the privilege against self-incrimination before the jury.

Id. (citation omitted); *see also Tex. Capital Sec., Inc. v. Sandefer*, 58 S.W.3d 760, 773 (Tex. App.—Houston [1st Dist.] 2001, pet. denied) (jury was entitled to draw negative inference from witness's invocation of privilege against self-incrimination and refusal to answer deposition question). The *Smith* court also noted that the defendants waived any argument about the reading of the depositions by not filing a pretrial motion in limine or a motion for protective order. 720 S.W.2d at 594.

989. *See Baxter*, 425 U.S. at 318. *Baxter* involved a prison disciplinary proceeding during which the inmate invoked his Fifth Amendment privilege, and the hearing board drew an adverse inference. *Id.* at 312-13. In upholding this practice, the majority stressed that a decision adverse to the inmate had to rest on substantial evidence apart from the inference. *Id.* at 317-18. This restricted use of the inference did not unduly burden the inmate's exercise of the privilege. In reliance on this limitation, it has been held that if a civil defendant properly invokes the privilege to justify his refusal to answer averments in the plaintiff's complaint, he is not to be deemed to have admitted them pursuant to Federal Rule of Civil Procedure 8(d), thus justifying an adverse final judgment. *Nat'l Acceptance Co. v. Bathalter*, 705 F.2d 924, 932 (7th Cir. 1983).

990. *See* Tex. R. Evid. 801(e)(2) (outlining the categories of persons who may make admissions on behalf of others). Refer to *Article VIII: Hearsay, infra* p. 845.

clude nonparty witnesses bearing a special relationship to either the party[991] or the litigated facts.[992] The El Paso Court of Appeals, in a case of first impression in Texas, has held that the fact-finder may draw an adverse inference from evidence that a party's agent has exercised the Fifth Amendment privilege, at least when the questions "substantially relate to a party's claim or defense."[993]

When a plaintiff in a civil case invokes the privilege against self-incrimination, the trial court can prohibit the plaintiff from introducing evidence on the subject.[994] Although the exercise of the privilege against self-incrimination generally should not be penalized, that rule "does not prohibit a trial court from taking acts to ensure that the civil proceeding remains fair."[995] While the fact-finder may draw reasonable inferences from a party's assertion of the privilege against self-incrimination,[996] "the claim of privilege is not a substitute for relevant evidence."[997] By themselves, inferences are "mere suspicion" and cannot be considered as evidence.[998]

D. Rule 513(d): Jury Instruction

Rule 513(d) specifically permits any party to request an instruction to the jury that it may not draw any adverse inference from a valid invocation of privilege.[999] That is,

---

991. See *Rosebud Sioux Tribe v. A. & P. Steel, Inc.*, 733 F.2d 509, 521-22 (8th Cir. 1984) (allowing an adverse inference from a nonparty-witness's invocation of privilege against self-incrimination when the nonparty has a special relationship with a party).

992. See, e.g., *Cerro Gordo Charity v. Fireman's Fund Am. Life Ins.*, 819 F.2d 1471, 1481-82 (8th Cir. 1987) (defendant-insurer could call the former director of a charity to the witness stand to invoke the privilege before the jury because of the witness's relationship to the litigation rather than a technical relationship to the plaintiff); *RAD Servs., Inc. v. Aetna Cas. & Sur. Co.*, 808 F.2d 271, 275 (3d Cir. 1986) (defendant-insurer could introduce depositions of former employees of a company seeking to recover costs for disposing of hazardous waste when testimony reflected the invocations of Fifth Amendment privileges; questions testing the extent of the privilege neither intended adverse inferences nor took unfair advantage).

993. *Wil-Roye Inv. Co. II v. Wash. Mut. Bank*, 142 S.W.3d 393, 407 (Tex. App.—El Paso 2004, no pet.). In this case, two witnesses for the plaintiffs acted as plaintiffs' agents. The plaintiffs introduced significant portions of the witnesses' deposition testimony but argued that the opposing party could not introduce evidence that the plaintiffs had asserted their Fifth Amendment privilege against self-incrimination. *Id.* at 403. Relying on federal precedent, the court of appeals stated that the plaintiffs "would have obtained an unfair advantage had they been able to present favorable portions of [witness's] deposition testimony while precluding cross-examination." *Id.* at 407. The court discussed an analogy between admissions by a party's agent, admissible under Rule 801(e)(2), and the invocation of the privilege against self-incrimination by that agent in concluding that the relationship between the plaintiffs and the witnesses was such that the fact-finder could draw an adverse inference under Rule 513(c). *Id.* at 404-05.

994. *Tex. Dep't of Pub. Safety Officers Ass'n v. Denton*, 897 S.W.2d 757, 760 (Tex. 1995).

995. *Id.*

996. See TEX. R. EVID. 513(c). Refer to note 984 *supra* and accompanying text.

997. *United States v. Rylander*, 460 U.S. 752, 761 (1983); *Webb v. Maldonado*, 331 S.W.3d 879, 883 (Tex. App.—Dallas 2011, pet. denied).

998. *Mathon, Inc. v. Gries*, 288 S.W.3d 471, 489-90 (Tex. App.—Eastland 2009, no pet.); *Blake v. Dorado*, 211 S.W.3d 429, 434 (Tex. App.—El Paso 2006, no pet.); see *Webb*, 331 S.W.3d at 883; *see also Lozano v. Lozano*, 52 S.W.3d 141, 149 (Tex. 2001) (per curiam) (Phillips, C.J., concurring in part and dissenting in part) ("Circumstantial evidence may be used to establish any material fact, but it must transcend mere suspicion.").

999. During the 1998 unification of the Civil and Criminal Rules, Rule 513(d), which had always applied in criminal cases, was made expressly applicable to civil proceedings as well. This was not a change in the law; trial judges in both civil and criminal cases have always had authority to instruct a jury that it may not draw any adverse inference from a valid claim of privilege.

as long as Rule 513 "forbids a jury from drawing an inference from a privilege claim," a party can request a "no adverse inference" instruction.[1000] The right to an instruction applies regardless of who has invoked a privilege; thus, a criminal defendant is entitled to such an instruction when a codefendant invokes a privilege against self-incrimination.[1001] It would also apply when the defendant requests an instruction about a State's witness who has validly invoked a privilege.

The instruction on a defendant's right to invoke the privilege against self-incrimination is constitutionally based.[1002] Because a defendant can invoke that privilege at either or both of the guilt/innocence and punishment phases of a criminal trial, a trial judge must instruct the jury not to draw any adverse inference from the invocation of the privilege during any and all phases of the trial in which the defendant exercises the privilege not to testify.[1003] This instruction must be given whenever the defendant requests it.[1004] If the defendant does not request a "no adverse inference" jury instruction, the trial court does not err by not giving the instruction.[1005]

1000. *See* Tex. R. Evid. 513(d).

1001. *See* ***Torres v. State***, 137 S.W.3d 191, 197-98 (Tex. App.—Houston [1st Dist.] 2004, no pet.).

1002. *See* ***Lakeside v. Oregon***, 435 U.S. 333, 341-42 (1978) (even when a defendant does not request an instruction on the right not to testify, it is not error to give an instruction that no inference of guilt arises from the silence of the accused).

1003. *See* ***Beathard v. State***, 767 S.W.2d 423, 432 (Tex. Crim. App. 1989); *see, e.g.*, ***White v. State***, 779 S.W.2d 809, 828 (Tex. Crim. App. 1989) (although trial court erred when it did not give "no adverse inference" instruction during punishment phase of capital-murder trial, error was harmless); ***De La Paz v. State***, 901 S.W.2d 571, 578 (Tex. App.—El Paso 1995, pet. ref'd) (reversible error in refusing defendant's request for a "no adverse inference" instruction during punishment stage of trial; similar instruction given during guilt/innocence portion of trial did not carry over to second stage).

1004. Tex. R. Evid. 513(d); ***Carter v. Kentucky***, 450 U.S. 288, 300 (1981); ***Duke v. State***, 365 S.W.3d 722, 726 (Tex. App.—Texarkana 2012, pet. ref'd); ***Michaelwicz v. State***, 186 S.W.3d 601, 623 (Tex. App.—Austin 2006, pet. ref'd). The jury may be instructed not to consider the defendant's "failure" to testify even when the defendant objects to such an instruction. *See Carter*, 450 U.S. at 301; *Lakeside*, 435 U.S. at 341-42.

1005. ***Duke***, 365 S.W.3d at 727; ***Michaelwicz***, 186 S.W.3d at 624.

ARTICLE VI: WITNESSES

RULE 601
COMPETENCY TO TESTIFY IN GENERAL; "DEAD MAN'S RULE"

(a) In General. Every person is competent to be a witness unless these rules provide otherwise. The following witnesses are incompetent:

(1) *Insane Persons.* A person who is now insane or was insane at the time of the events about which the person is called to testify.

(2) *Persons Lacking Sufficient Intellect.* A child—or any other person—whom the court examines and finds lacks sufficient intellect to testify concerning the matters in issue.

(b) The "Dead Man's Rule."

(1) *Applicability.* The "Dead Man's Rule" applies only in a civil case:

(A) by or against a party in the party's capacity as an executor, administrator, or guardian; or

(B) by or against a decedent's heirs or legal representatives and based in whole or in part on the decedent's oral statement.

(2) *General Rule.* In cases described in subparagraph (b)(1)(A), a party may not testify against another party about an oral statement by the testator, intestate, or ward. In cases described in subparagraph (b)(1)(B), a party may not testify against another party about an oral statement by the decedent.

(3) *Exceptions.* A party may testify against another party about an oral statement by the testator, intestate, ward, or decedent if:

(A) the party's testimony about the statement is corroborated; or

(B) the opposing party calls the party to testify at the trial about the statement.

(4) *Instructions.* If a court excludes evidence under paragraph (b)(2), the court must instruct the jury that the law prohibits a party from testifying about an oral statement by the testator, intestate, ward, or decedent unless the oral statement is corroborated or the opposing party calls the party to testify at the trial about the statement.

Notes and Comments

Comment to 2015 restyling: The text of the "Dead Man's Rule" has been streamlined to clarify its meaning without making any substantive changes. The text of former Rule 601(b) (as well as its statutory predecessor, Vernon's Ann. Civ. St. art. 3716) prohibits only a "party" from testifying about the dead man's statements. Despite this, the last sentence of former Rule 601(b) requires the court to instruct the jury when the rule "prohibits an interested party or witness" from testifying. Because the rule prohibits only a "party" from testifying, restyled Rule 601(b)(4) references only "a party," and not "an interested party or witness." To be sure, courts have indicated that the rule (or its statutory predecessor) may be applicable to a witness who is not nominally a party and inapplicable to a witness who is only nominally a party. *See, e.g., Chandler v. Welborn*, 156 Tex. 312, 294 S.W.2d 801, 809 (1956); *Ragsdale v. Ragsdale*, 142 Tex. 476, 179 S.W.2d 291, 295 (1944). But these decisions are based on an interpretation of the meaning of "party." Therefore, limiting the court's instruction under restyled Rule 601(b)(4) to "a party" does not change Texas practice. In addition, restyled Rule 601(b) deletes the sentence in former Rule 601(b) that states "[e]xcept for the foregoing, a witness is not precluded from giving evidence ... because the witness is a party to the action..." This sentence is surplusage. Rule 601(b) is a rule of exclusion. If the testimony falls outside the rule of exclusion, its admissibility will be determined by other applicable rules of evidence.

COMMENTARY ON RULE 601

A. Rule 601(a): In General

Early Texas law imposed many limitations on the competency of witnesses.[1] Most of these restrictions were eliminated before the adoption of the Rules[2] because they acted as a serious impediment to ascertaining the truth.[3] The rigid rules forbidding certain witnesses from testifying were abolished because it was believed that factors such as the witness's interest, prior convictions, and lack of religious fervor should go to the weight of the witness's testimony, not its admissibility.[4] A few vestiges of the old rules

---

1. An extreme example provided that "[a]ll negroes and indians ... shall be incapable of being a witness in any case whatever, except for or against each other." Act approved May 13, 1846, 1st Leg., §65, 1846 Tex. Gen. Laws 363, 379 (repealed 1871), *reprinted in* 2 H.P.N. GAMMEL, THE LAWS OF TEXAS 1822-1897, at 1669, 1685 (Austin, Gammel Book Co. 1898). Refer to note 2 *infra*.

2. The Texas rule authorizing race as a ground for incompetency was superseded by the Act approved May 19, 1871, 12th Leg., R.S., ch. 104, §1, 1871 Tex. Gen. Laws 108, *reprinted in* 6 H.P.N. GAMMEL, THE LAWS OF TEXAS 1822-1897, at 1010 (Austin, Gammel Book Co. 1898) (former Texas Revised Civil Statutes art. 3714 deemed repealed as to civil proceedings effective 1983 and as to criminal proceedings effective 1986), which also eliminated party-interest as grounds for incompetency. Eventually, spousal relationship, religion, and prior convictions were also eliminated as grounds for incompetency. *See* TEX. REV. CIV. STAT. art. 3715 (former Texas Revised Civil Statutes art. 3715 deemed repealed as to civil proceedings effective 1983 and as to criminal proceedings effective 1986) [now codified at TEX. R. EVID. 504] (husband and wife are not incompetent); Act of March 4, 1925, 39th Leg., R.S., ch. 28, §1, 1925 Tex. Gen. Laws 146 (repealed 1985) (religious beliefs or prior convictions are not proper grounds for disqualification). *See generally* McCORMICK ON EVIDENCE §§61, 63, 64, 66, at 155-62 (Edward. W. Cleary ed., 3d ed. 1984) (discussing early common-law rules of witness incompetency such as interested parties, spouses, race, religion, and prior conviction).

3. *See* McCORMICK ON EVIDENCE, *supra* note 2, §71, at 168.

4. *See* 1 ROY R. RAY, TEXAS PRACTICE: TEXAS LAW OF EVIDENCE CIVIL AND CRIMINAL §277, at 303 (3d ed. 1980) (mental incapacity should be abolished as a ground for witness disqualification because the question is more properly one of credibility for the jury to decide); 2 JOHN H. WIGMORE, EVIDENCE IN TRIALS AT COMMON LAW §501, at 709 (Chadbourn rev. 1979) (jury should be allowed to hear testimony of mentally incompetent witnesses).

remain, including the infamous Dead Man's Rule[5] and the provisions of Rule 601 that detail mental incompetency due to insanity or lack of sufficient intellect.[6]

At least two alternatives were available to the Texas State Bar Liaison Committee on Rules of Evidence (the "Liaison Committee") when they codified the common law on mental incompetency. The first is represented by the Federal Rules, which do not expressly disqualify witnesses on the grounds of mental incompetency.[7] Instead, the Federal Rules trust in the good sense of lawyers and jurors. After all, very few lawyers would call as a witness someone who is incapable of testifying. Should a lawyer put such a witness on the stand, the jury can most certainly discern that the witness is incompetent. Moreover, allowing the judge to disqualify such witnesses is arguably inappropriate because nothing in a judge's background or training makes him better able than a lawyer or a juror to determine mental incompetency.

The second alternative, embodied in the Texas Code of Criminal Procedure and Texas common law, requires witnesses suspected of mental incompetency to prove their qualifications to the trial judge before testifying.[8] Judges, however, are not always correct in their determinations; thus, time and expense are wasted by an appeal and new trial.[9]

Initially, the Liaison Committee approved the first alternative and thereby proposed to adopt the applicable Federal Rules without change.[10] However, the Committee ultimately proposed a rule that required a preliminary trial-court determination of a witness's mental competency in some situations.[11]

Rule 601(a) creates a general presumption that all witnesses are competent to testify.[12] A competent witness possesses all of the following attributes:

(1) the capability to perceive intelligently the events in question,

---

5.   Act approved May 19, 1871, 12th Leg., R.S., ch. 104, §2, 1871 Tex. Gen. Laws 108, *reprinted in* 6 H.P.N. GAMMEL, THE LAWS OF TEXAS 1822-1897, at 1010 (Austin, Gammel Book Co. 1898) (former Texas Revised Civil Statutes art. 3716 deemed repealed as to civil proceedings effective 1983 and as to criminal proceedings effective 1986). Refer to notes 47-85 *infra* and accompanying text.

6.   TEX. R. EVID. 601(a).

7.   *See* FED. R. EVID. 601.

8.   *See* Code of Criminal Procedure, 59th Leg., R.S., ch. 722, art. 38.09, vol. 2, 1965 Tex. Gen. Laws 317, 467 (former Code of Criminal Procedure art. 38.09 deemed repealed as to criminal proceedings effective 1986) (court has power to determine competency); **Ditto v. Ditto Inv. Co.**, 158 Tex. 104, 107, 309 S.W.2d 219, 221 (1958) (Norvell, J., concurring) (judge determines competency).

9.   For example, in **Callicott v. Callicott**, the trial court was reversed when the judge ruled, without an examination or observation, that an eight-year-old boy was incompetent simply because of his age. 364 S.W.2d 455, 458 (Tex. Civ. App.—Houston 1963, writ ref'd n.r.e.).

10.   Texas Senate Interim Study on Rules of Evidence File, pt. IV at 77-101 (Jan. 8-9, 1982) [hereinafter Interim Study IV].

11.   *See* TEX. R. EVID. 601(a)(1) (1982 Liaison Committee proposal), *reprinted infra* p. 1086; Interim Study IV, *supra* note 10, at 15-27 (Mar. 19-20, 1982).

12.   **Baldit v. State**, 522 S.W.3d 753, ___ (Tex. App.—Houston [1st Dist.] 2017, no pet.); **Hogan v. State**, 440 S.W.3d 211, 213 (Tex. App.—Houston [14th Dist.] 2013, pet. ref'd); **Reyna v. State**, 797 S.W.2d 189, 191 (Tex. App.—Corpus Christi 1990, no pet.).

(2) the ability to recollect the events in question at the time of trial, and

(3) the ability to narrate adequately his recollection of those events.[13]

Special note is made of insane persons and witnesses (including children) who may not have sufficient intellect to testify about the matters at issue only because they are more likely to lack one or more of the three attributes of general witness competency.[14] A party who claims that a prospective witness is incompetent to testify has the burden of proving by a preponderance of the evidence that the person is, in fact, deficient in one or more of the witness capacities.[15]

Except for insanity and lack of sufficient intellect, all other witness disabilities affect the weight of the testimony, not the competency of the witness.[16] For example, the fact that a witness is a drug user will affect his credibility but not his competency.[17] On the other hand, the potential witness may be rendered so inebriated by the consumption of alcohol or drugs, either at the time of the event or the time of testifying, that

---

13. *See Watson v. State*, 596 S.W.2d 867, 870-71 (Tex. Crim. App. [Panel Op.] 1980); *Baldit*, 522 S.W.3d at ___; *In re Commitment of Edwards*, 443 S.W.3d 520, 528 (Tex. App.—Beaumont 2014, pet. denied); *Escamilla v. State*, 334 S.W.3d 263, 266 (Tex. App.—San Antonio 2010, pet. ref'd); *Davis v. State*, 268 S.W.3d 683, 699 (Tex. App.—Fort Worth 2008, pet. ref'd); *see also* HULEN D. WENDORF ET AL., TEXAS RULES OF EVIDENCE MANUAL VI-2 (5th ed. 2000) (witness competency is divided into four elements: "(1) the capacity of the witness to perceive by any of the senses; (2) the capacity of the witness to remember; (3) the capacity of the witness to communicate; and (4) the truthfulness or veracity of the witness").
The third element, the ability to recount accurately, "involves on the one hand, both an ability to understand the questions asked and to frame intelligent answers and, on the other hand, a moral responsibility to tell the truth." *Watson*, 596 S.W.2d at 870; *see Torres v. State*, 33 S.W.3d 252, 255 (Tex. Crim. App. 2000); *Baldit*, 522 S.W.3d at ___; *Escamilla*, 334 S.W.3d at 266; *Davis*, 268 S.W.3d at 699. The second and third elements are often merged and considered together. *Watson*, 596 S.W.2d at 870. While the witness's truthfulness or credibility is essential in determining the weight of the testimony, the judge should never declare a witness incompetent to testify under Rule 601 because he disbelieves the content of the witness's testimony. *See Robinson v. State*, 368 S.W.3d 588, 604 (Tex. App.—Austin 2012, pet. ref'd) ("Any inconsistencies or inabilities to recall certain facts do not render [the witness] incompetent to testify, but go to the credibility of her testimony—an issue for the jury."); *Escamilla*, 334 S.W.3d at 266 ("Confusing and inconsistent responses from a child are not reasons to determine she is incompetent to testify; rather, they speak to the credibility of her testimony. The trial court's role is to make the initial determination of competency, not to assess the credibility or weight to be given the testimony."). Even a liar may take the witness stand if he understands, as a general proposition, the moral obligation to give truthful testimony and swears to do so.
14. *See* TEX. R. EVID. 601(a). The disqualifying factor under the rule is lack of sufficient intellect rather than age. Children are presumed competent to testify unless the court finds they lack sufficient intellect. Refer to notes 33-46 *infra* and accompanying text.
15. *See In re Commitment of Edwards*, 443 S.W.3d at 528; *In re R.M.T.*, 352 S.W.3d 12, 25 (Tex. App.—Texarkana 2011, no pet.); *see, e.g.*, *Handel v. Long Trs.*, 757 S.W.2d 848, 854-55 (Tex. App.—Texarkana 1988, no writ) (80-year-old settlor of gas-exploration trusts, who had severe deficit in recent memory, was capable of observing intelligently at time of events giving rise to suit, could recall and narrate those events at time of trial, was capable of understanding obligation of oath, and thus was competent to testify).
16. Refer to note 13 *supra* and accompanying text.
17. *See, e.g.*, *Thompson v. State*, 691 S.W.2d 627, 634 (Tex. Crim. App. 1984) (witness who took methadone two hours before testifying and was a narcotics user at the time of the events in question was competent to testify); *see also United States v. Jackson*, 576 F.2d 46, 48 (5th Cir. 1978) (no abuse of discretion when trial judge denied motion to examine drug users to determine competency before testifying).

he is unable to observe, recall, or relate the events in question.[18] In such a case, the witness's testimony of the event might be excluded under Rule 602[19] or Rule 403,[20] rather than under Rule 601, which would prevent him from taking the witness stand in the presence of the jury. If the potential witness is so affected by intoxicants that he is incoherent when called to the witness stand, the judge should defer the testimony to a later time rather than declare the witness incompetent to testify.[21]

The trial judge sees the witnesses, observes their demeanor, and notices their apparent level of intelligence and understanding of truth and falsity; thus, great discretion is given to a judge's determination of witness competency.[22] Because these competency questions are resolved under Rule 104(a), the judge is not bound by the Rules of Evidence (except those on privilege) and may determine competency by any reliable means.[23] The party challenging the witness's competency must raise and prove the issue of testimonial incapacity.[24] In close cases, the judge should resolve the issue in favor of the witness's competency and permit the jury to make its own determination of the worth and weight of the witness's testimony.[25]

Rule 601 speaks only to the witness's general inherent capacity to perceive, recall, and recount accurately.[26] It does not deal with the sufficiency of the specific informa-

---

18. *See **Herrera v. State***, 462 S.W.2d 597, 599 (Tex. Crim. App. 1971) (habitual use of drugs or alcohol does not render a witness incompetent unless his mental capacity is so impaired that he cannot be a qualified witness); 1 RAY, *supra* note 4, §276, at 302 (witness's testimony should be rejected if he is so inebriated that he cannot give intelligent answers).

19. *See* TEX. R. EVID. 602 (need for personal knowledge).

20. *See* TEX. R. EVID. 403 (general balancing test of probative value against prejudicial counterfactors).

21. *See* 27 CHARLES A. WRIGHT & VICTOR J. GOLD, FEDERAL PRACTICE AND PROCEDURE §6005, at 53-54 (1990) (credibility of an intoxicated witness is a jury issue, while judge must determine whether to give instructions on credibility or to order physical examinations to assist in assessing credibility); *see, e.g.*, ***United States v. Van Meerbeke***, 548 F.2d 415, 417-18 (2d Cir. 1976) (witness who consumed opium while testifying was not necessarily incompetent to continue testifying). In ***United States v. Hyson***, the court allowed a witness to be recalled and start his testimony over. 721 F.2d 856, 863-64 (1st Cir. 1983). The witness had trouble speaking and appeared to be under the influence of drugs. *Id.* The trial court recommended a medical examination, and the doctor found the witness to be under the influence of a drug whose effects would clear in 24 hours. *Id.* The court then explained the situation to the jury, struck the earlier testimony, and allowed the witness to be recalled. *Id.* at 864.

22. The standard of review for competency decisions is abuse of discretion. ***Villarreal v. State***, 576 S.W.2d 51, 57 (Tex. Crim. App. 1978); ***Clark v. State***, 558 S.W.2d 887, 890 (Tex. Crim. App. 1977); ***Fields v. State***, 500 S.W.2d 500, 502 (Tex. Crim. App. 1973); ***In re Commitment of Edwards***, 443 S.W.3d 520, 528 (Tex. App.—Beaumont 2014, pet. denied).

23. *See* TEX. R. EVID. 104(a); ***Gilley v. State***, 418 S.W.3d 114, 121 (Tex. Crim. App. 2014); ***Kipp v. State***, 876 S.W.2d 330, 334 (Tex. Crim. App. 1994). Refer to *Article I: General Provisions, supra* p. 86.

24. ***Gilley***, 418 S.W.3d at 120; ***Foster v. State***, 142 Tex. Crim. 615, 618, 155 S.W.2d 938, 940 (1941); ***Baldit v. State***, 522 S.W.3d 753, ___ (Tex. App.—Houston [1st Dist.] 2017, no pet.); 1 STEVEN GOODE ET AL., TEXAS PRACTICE: GUIDE TO THE TEXAS RULES OF EVIDENCE: CIVIL AND CRIMINAL §601.2, at 508 (2d ed. 1993); 1 RAY, *supra* note 4, §253, at 291. Refer to note 15 *supra* and accompanying text.

25. 1 RAY, *supra* note 4, §277, at 303; *see **United States v. Odom***, 736 F.2d 104, 112 (4th Cir. 1984) (modern trend is to view all witnesses as competent); 27 WRIGHT & GOLD, *supra* note 21, §6005, at 42-43 (drafters of the Federal Rules recognized that witness competency "should not be made to depend on variable and unreliable judicial efforts at amateur psychiatry" and thus judges are not permitted to conduct threshold competency evaluations).

26. *See **Rodriguez v. State***, 772 S.W.2d 167, 170 (Tex. App.—Houston [14th Dist.] 1989, pet. ref'd); *see, e.g.*, ***Kokes v. College***, 148 S.W.3d 384, 390 (Tex. App.—Beaumont 2004, no pet.) (per curiam) (witness's testimony did not cast doubt on his "ability to perceive, recollect, and recount the events at issue here").

tion about which the witness proposes to testify, although some cases have implied that the basis for the witness's testimony might be assessed under Rule 601.[27] The informational foundation for the witness's testimony is addressed in Rules 602 (need for personal knowledge), 701 (general rule on lay testimony), 702 (general rule on expert testimony), and 703 (rule on basis for expert testimony), not Rule 601.

Under Rule 601, the fact that a witness is mentally disabled will not necessarily disqualify him from testifying.[28] Even when a witness has previously been found criminally insane or incompetent, he is not necessarily incompetent to testify in the present case.[29] A convicted felon may be a competent witness, as may a person who is held under civil contempt or for whom there is an outstanding arrest warrant.[30] The issues are not the witness's criminal status and standing; rather, they are whether the witness had the capacity to observe and remember the event and whether the witness presently has the capacity to recall and accurately narrate facts related to that event.[31] Thus, mere

---

27. *See Fairow v. State*, 943 S.W.2d 895, 902 (Tex. Crim. App. 1997) (Baird & Overstreet, JJ., concurring) (competency under Rule 601 requires personal knowledge of a matter); *see, e.g.*, *Fletcher v. State*, 960 S.W.2d 694, 697-98 (Tex. App.—Tyler 1997, no pet.) (under Rule 601, witness did not lack the "specificity as to content and identity necessary to make such testimony competent").

28. *See Watson v. State*, 596 S.W.2d 867, 870-71 (Tex. Crim. App. [Panel Op.] 1980) ("If a person afflicted with a physical or mental disability possesses sufficient intelligence to receive correct impressions of events he sees, retains clear recollection of them and *is able to communicate them through some means* there is no reason for rejecting his testimony."); *Kokes*, 148 S.W.3d at 390 ("If a witness meets the requirements of competency, though the issue may be close, the factfinder should be allowed to hear the testimony and make the determination of how much weight is to be given to the testimony in light of a mental infirmity."); *see, e.g.*, *In re Commitment of Edwards*, 443 S.W.3d 520, 528-29 (Tex. App.—Beaumont 2014, pet. denied) (although witness made some delusional statements, he testified "clearly and coherently" about his name, date of birth, Texas Department of Criminal Justice numbers, and offenses he had committed); *Rodriguez*, 772 S.W.2d at 170 (witness who suffered a nervous breakdown and had Alzheimer's disease was competent to testify; "her testimony was sufficiently coherent and intelligible concerning the incident in question that it deserved to be heard"); *Handel v. Long Trs.*, 757 S.W.2d 848, 855 (Tex. App.—Texarkana 1988, no writ) (witness who had severe memory loss due to multiple strokes was competent to testify; "testimony ... corroborates that [witness] was in a position to know the facts about which he testified. Therefore, the evidence does not show that [witness] was incapable of observing intelligently at the time the events in question occurred.").

29. *See Ebers v. State*, 129 Tex. Crim. 287, 293, 86 S.W.2d 761, 764 (1935) (previous judgment of insanity will not by itself render the witness incompetent); *Downing v. State*, 113 Tex. Crim. 235, 238, 20 S.W.2d 202, 203-04 (1929) (same; court should consider witness's conduct and actions); *see, e.g.*, *Jackson v. State*, 403 S.W.2d 145, 147-48 (Tex. Crim. App. 1966) (although witness had been declared mentally handicapped and had been appointed a guardian, trial judge who had observed witness and engaged him in conversation did not err in concluding that witness was competent); *cf. United States v. Lightly*, 677 F.2d 1027, 1028 (4th Cir. 1982) (trial court erred in ruling that witness was incompetent solely because he had been declared criminally insane and incompetent to stand trial when a doctor had testified that the witness possessed a sufficient memory, could understand the oath, and could communicate what he had seen); *United States v. McRary*, 616 F.2d 181, 183 (5th Cir. 1980) (defendant should have been permitted to show that his wife, who had been found incompetent to stand trial, was competent to testify on his behalf).

30. *See Great Glob. Assur. Co. v. Keltex Props., Inc.*, 904 S.W.2d 771, 774 (Tex. App.—Corpus Christi 1995, no writ) ("The Rules of Civil Evidence do not say that a person is incompetent to testify as a witness because a court has held that person in civil contempt and has issued a civil arrest warrant for that person."); *Parrish v. Brooks*, 856 S.W.2d 522, 528 (Tex. App.—Texarkana 1993, writ denied) (convicted felon is a competent witness).

31. *See, e.g.*, *Watson*, 596 S.W.2d at 870-73 (trial court erred in admitting testimony of stroke victim who could only respond to questions with "uh-huh" and whose answers were then interpreted by a woman who had been caring for the witness). In *Villarreal v. State*, the court allowed a deaf-mute person to testify. 576 S.W.2d 51, 57 (Tex. Crim. App. 1978). The witness could only testify in very simple terms and relied heavily on photographic exhibits.

difficulty in articulating answers or in speaking English is not sufficient to render a witness incompetent.[32]

Rule 601(a)(2) does not specify an age below which a child is, as a matter of law, incompetent to testify.[33] Children as young as four[34] or five[35] may possess sufficient intellect to relate events competently. Texas courts, like those in other jurisdictions, almost always hold that even very young children have sufficient intellectual capacity to take the witness stand.[36] Rule 601(a) does not require the judge to conduct an examination of all children to determine their competency before testifying.[37] Only when a question of the child's testimonial capacity arises and a party requests a competency examination should the judge conduct such an examination.[38] There is no requirement

Id. The court, however, found her competent to testify because she had been taught to tell the truth and was adequately able to relate her experiences. *Id.*; *see also Rodriguez*, 772 S.W.2d at 170 (80-year-old witness who had previously suffered a nervous breakdown and had Alzheimer's disease was sufficiently coherent and intelligible to testify).

32. *See, e.g., Hernandez v. State*, 643 S.W.2d 397, 400 (Tex. Crim. App. 1982) (witness who had difficulty speaking English was allowed to testify).

33. *See Fields v. State*, 500 S.W.2d 500, 502 (Tex. Crim. App. 1973); *Baldit v. State*, 522 S.W.3d 753, ___ (Tex. App.—Houston [1st Dist.] 2017, no pet.); *Pipkin v. Kroger Tex., L.P.*, 383 S.W.3d 655, 668 (Tex. App.—Houston [14th Dist.] 2012, pet. denied); *Escamilla v. State*, 334 S.W.3d 263, 265 (Tex. App.—San Antonio 2010, pet. ref'd).

34. *See Dufrene v. State*, 853 S.W.2d 86, 88 (Tex. App.—Houston [14th Dist.] 1993, pet. ref'd) (four-year-old child is considered competent to testify unless it appears to the court that he does not possess sufficient intellect to relate the transaction about which he will testify); *see, e.g., Hollinger v. State*, 911 S.W.2d 35, 38-39 (Tex. App.—Tyler 1995, pet. ref'd) (four-year-old child witness, who was three at the time of the alleged incident, was competent to testify even though he "was really not very old to have an independent recollection of what happened"); *Long v. State*, 770 S.W.2d 27, 29 (Tex. App.—Houston [14th Dist.] 1989) (four-year-old was competent to testify), *rev'd on other grounds*, 800 S.W.2d 545 (Tex. Crim. App. 1990); *Kirchner v. State*, 739 S.W.2d 85, 88 (Tex. App.—San Antonio 1987, no pet.) (same).

35. *See Macias v. State*, 776 S.W.2d 255, 256-57 (Tex. App.—San Antonio 1989, pet. ref'd).

36. *See* Robin W. Morey, Comment, *The Competency Requirement for the Child Victim of Sexual Abuse: Must We Abandon It?*, 40 U. MIAMI L. REV. 245, 281 n.178 (1985). Texas Code of Criminal Procedure article 38.074 sets out procedures for the testimony of child witnesses in criminal prosecutions. The court must first "administer an oath to [the] child in a manner that allows the child to fully understand the child's duty to tell the truth." TEX. CODE CRIM. PROC. art. 38.074, §3(a)(1). In addition, the court must (1) ensure that the questions are stated in language appropriate to the child's age, (2) explain to the child that he has the right to notify the court if he cannot understand a question and to have the question restated in language he can understand, (3) ensure that the child testifies at a time of day when he is best able to understand the questions and to participate in the proceedings without being traumatized, and (4) prevent any party from intimidating or harassing the child. *Id.* §3(a)(2)-(a)(5). To prevent intimidation or harassment, the court can "rephrase as appropriate any question asked of the child." *Id.* §3(a)(5).

37. *Grayson v. State*, 786 S.W.2d 504, 505 (Tex. App.—Dallas 1990, no pet.); *see Morgan v. State*, 403 S.W.2d 150, 152 (Tex. Crim. App. 1966) (under former TEX. CODE CRIM. PROC. art. 38.06).

38. *See McGinn v. State*, 961 S.W.2d 161, 165 (Tex. Crim. App. 1998) ("Rule 601 does not expressly impose upon the trial court the duty to conduct [a child-competency] inquiry on its own motion."); *Baldit*, 522 S.W.3d at ___ ("trial court does not have a duty to conduct a sua sponte preliminary competency examination of a child witness"; once party raises competency issue, trial court must make an independent ruling on competency); *see also* 18 U.S.C. §3509(c)(2) ("A child is presumed to be competent."), *id.* §3509(c)(4) ("A competency examination regarding a child may be conducted only if the court determines, on the record, that compelling reasons exist. A child's age alone is not a compelling reason."). The trial court can allow the parties to participate in the examination and ask questions, as long as the court itself rules on the child's competency. *Gilley v. State*, 418 S.W.3d 114, 121 (Tex. Crim. App. 2014). The language of the rule does not, however, require the court to allow party participation. *Gilley*, 418 S.W.3d at 121. Failure to object to a child's competency in the trial court and to object to the lack of a competency hearing by the trial court waives the issue for appellate review. *Baldit*, 522 S.W.3d at ___.

that such an examination be conducted outside the presence of the jury,[39] even though outside examinations are preferable. Although a trial judge may conduct an examination of the child, Texas courts have held that the trial judge does not have the authority to require a child to undergo psychological testing to determine witness competency.[40]

When originally promulgated, Civil Rule 601(a) included a provision that children "who do not understand the obligation of an oath" were incompetent to testify.[41] This phrase was deleted in 1988[42] because children who did not understand the phrase "obligation of an oath" might be otherwise perfectly competent to testify.[43] Although the inability to distinguish between truth and falsehood may be implied in the criterion of "sufficient intellect," no separate showing of an understanding of the obligation of an oath is required under current Rule 601(a).[44] Because young children are unlikely to understand the meaning of a legal oath or affirmation, a child does not have to take the formal witness's oath.[45]

---

39. *Reyna v. State*, 797 S.W.2d 189, 192 (Tex. App.—Corpus Christi 1990, no pet.).

40. *See Broussard v. State*, 910 S.W.2d 952, 960 (Tex. Crim. App. 1995); *State ex rel. Holmes v. Lanford*, 764 S.W.2d 593, 594 (Tex. App.—Houston [14th Dist.] 1989, orig. proceeding); *see also* 18 U.S.C. §3509(c)(9) ("Psychological and psychiatric examinations to assess the competency of a child witness shall not be ordered without a showing of compelling need."). Federal courts have found that court-ordered psychological examinations to determine a witness's competency might constitute an infringement on the witness's privacy, could serve as a tool of harassment, and could deter witnesses from coming forward. *United States v. Raineri*, 670 F.2d 702, 709 (7th Cir. 1982); *United States v. Jackson*, 576 F.2d 46, 49 (5th Cir. 1978); *see also United States v. Fountain*, 840 F.2d 509, 517 (7th Cir. 1988) (courts have broad discretion in deciding whether to compel mental examinations; trial court was justified in declining to order psychiatric examination of witness). Federal decisions acknowledge the trial court's inherent power to order mental examinations; however, to protect witness privacy, the proponent of the examination must prove it is necessary. *See generally* 27 WRIGHT & GOLD, *supra* note 21, §6010, at 108-13 (discussing criteria that court should consider before ordering psychological testing of witness).

41. *Re: New Rules of Evidence*, 641-642 S.W.2d (Tex. Cases) LI (1983). This language originally came from former Texas Code of Criminal Procedure art. 38.06 (Code of Criminal Procedure, 59th Leg., R.S., ch. 722, art. 38.06, vol. 2, 1965 Tex. Gen. Laws 317, 466 (former Texas Code of Criminal Procedure art. 38.06 deemed repealed as to criminal proceedings effective 1986)).

42. *See Order Adopting and Amending Texas Rules of Civil Evidence*, 733-734 S.W.2d (Tex. Cases) XCV (1987) (amendments to rule effective Jan. 1, 1988).

43. *See Fields v. State*, 500 S.W.2d 500, 502 (Tex. Crim. App. 1973) ("[I]t is well established that even though a child states he does not know the meaning of an oath or what it means to swear, he may nevertheless be a competent witness if he knows it is wrong to lie and that he will be punished if he does so."); *Torres v. State*, 424 S.W.3d 245, 254 (Tex. App.—Houston [14th Dist.] 2014, pet. ref'd) (child need not understand "obligation of the oath," but trial court must impress child with duty to be truthful); *Upton v. State*, 894 S.W.2d 426, 429 (Tex. App.—Amarillo 1995, pet. ref'd) (whether child can define such terms as "truth" or "lie" is unimportant if he otherwise understands the need to be truthful); *Long v. State*, 770 S.W.2d 27, 29 (Tex. App.—Houston [14th Dist.] 1989) (Rule 601(a), unlike the prior statute, does not require a finding that the child "understands the obligations of the oath"), *rev'd on other grounds*, 800 S.W.2d 545 (Tex. Crim. App. 1990); *see, e.g.*, *Berotte v. State*, 992 S.W.2d 13, 17-18 (Tex. App.—Houston [1st Dist.] 1997, pet. ref'd) (even though four-year-old child was not able to articulate the difference between the truth and a lie, or between being good and bad, when judge asked her if she would "promise she would answer the questions asked of her, tell the truth, and do good so she wouldn't get a whipping," she said yes; court did not abuse discretion in permitting her to testify); *Macias v. State*, 776 S.W.2d 255, 256-57 (Tex. App.—San Antonio 1989, pet. ref'd) (five-year-old witness's answers to prosecutor's questioning demonstrated that she could distinguish between truth and a lie).

44. *Long*, 770 S.W.2d at 29. The rule does not require the court to question a child on the child's understanding of the punishment for lying. *Davis v. State*, 268 S.W.3d 683, 699 (Tex. App.—Fort Worth 2008, pet. ref'd).

45. *See, e.g.*, *Hollinger v. State*, 911 S.W.2d 35, 39 (Tex. App.—Tyler 1995, pet. ref'd) (four-year-old did not have to take oath when questions were designed to impress upon him the duty to be truthful); *Gonzales v. State*, 748 S.W.2d

Although a young child's answers may, at times, be somewhat conflicting and confusing, this fact does not render the witness legally incompetent to testify; rather, it speaks to the child's credibility.[46] After all, the testimony of many adult witnesses is conflicting and confusing. These issues normally go to the weight and credibility of the testimony, not to the witness's competency.

B. Rule 601(b): The "Dead Man's Rule"

Rule 601(b), also known as the Dead Man's Rule,[47] generally prohibits a party from testifying against another party about (1) "an oral statement by the testator, intestate, or ward" in civil cases by or against an executor, administrator, or guardian acting in that capacity, or (2) "an oral statement by [a] decedent" in civil cases by or against a decedent's heirs or legal representatives when the case is based at least in part on the decedent's oral statement.[48] This rule is considerably narrower than its predecessor, former Texas Revised Civil Statutes article 3716,[49] which extended the Dead Man's Rule "to any transaction with or statement by the testator."[50] The phrase "any transaction with" obviously included more than uncorroborated oral statements of a deceased or incompetent person. The phrase also "include[d] every method by which one person can derive impressions or information from the conduct, condition, or language of another."[51]

The purpose of the Dead Man's Rule was to prevent one party from testifying to conversations with the deceased, who was no longer available to refute the existence or truth of those conversations.[52] Once one of the parties to a conversation died, the opportunity and incentive to invent false claims against that party's estate increased dramatically.[53]

510, 512 (Tex. App.—Houston [1st Dist.] 1988, pet. ref'd) (9- and 11-year-old witnesses' responses to questions were sufficient to determine that the minors understood their duty to be truthful and that a formal oath was not necessary). Texas Code of Criminal Procedure article 38.074, which sets out procedures for the testimony of child witnesses in criminal prosecutions, requires an oath. Refer to note 36 *supra*.

46. *Berotte*, 992 S.W.2d at 17; *Upton*, 894 S.W.2d at 429; *see Dufrene v. State*, 853 S.W.2d 86, 89 (Tex. App.—Houston [14th Dist.] 1993, pet. ref'd); *Macias*, 776 S.W.2d at 257.

47. Act approved May 19, 1871, 12th Leg., R.S., ch. 104, §2, 1871 Tex. Gen. Laws 108, *reprinted in* 6 H.P.N. Gammel, The Laws of Texas 1882-1897, at 1010 (Austin, Gammel Book Co. 1898) (former Texas Revised Civil Statutes art. 3716 deemed repealed as to civil proceedings effective 1983 and as to criminal proceedings effective 1986).

48. *See* Tex. R. Evid. 601(b)(1)-(b)(3).

49. Article 3716 provided as follows:

In actions by or against executors, administrators, or guardians, in which judgment may be rendered for or against them, neither party shall be allowed to testify against the other as to any transaction with or statement by the testator, intestate or ward, unless called to testify thereto by the opposite party, or required to testify thereto by the court.

Act approved May 19, 1871, 12th Leg., R.S., ch. 104, §2, 1871 Tex. Gen. Laws 108, *reprinted in* 6 H.P.N. Gammel, The Laws of Texas 1882-1897, at 1010 (Austin, Gammel Book Co. 1898) (former Texas Revised Civil Statutes art. 3716 deemed repealed as to civil proceedings effective 1983 and as to criminal proceedings effective 1986).

50. *Id.*

51. *Dominguez v. Garcia*, 36 S.W.2d 299, 299 (Tex. Civ. App.—Austin 1931), *aff'd*, 53 S.W.2d 459 (Tex. Comm'n App. 1932, holding approved).

52. *In re Estate of Watson*, 720 S.W.2d 806, 807 (Tex. 1986).

53. *See* 2 Wigmore, *supra* note 4, §578, at 820.

The doctrine has been criticized by every modern authority as reflecting a cynicism inconsistent with the underlying assumption of modern evidence codes.[54] The Model Code of Evidence, the Uniform Rules of Evidence, and several other states have eliminated or omitted the doctrine.[55] Nonetheless, the supreme court promulgated a truncated version of the Dead Man's Rule for use in civil actions. By deleting transactions with the decedent from the category of prohibited testimony, the scope of the doctrine has been narrowed considerably.[56] For example, before the promulgation of Rule 601(b), the doctrine had been applied to bar an interested party's testimony about his deceased mother's adverse possession of land;[57] a physician's testimony on the medical services rendered to a deceased person;[58] an injured guest's description of a deceased driver's speed, intoxication, and abusive conduct;[59] and a widow's testimony about her deceased husband's mental competency.[60] Testimony of this type is permitted under Rule 601(b).[61]

Rule 601(b) bars only the uncorroborated testimony of a party to a particular oral communication.[62] The corroboration requirement may be satisfied by evidence from any other competent witness or document,[63] and it must only "tend to confirm and strengthen the testimony of the witness and show the probability of its truth."[64] An

---

54. *See id.* §578, at 821 (criticizing Dead Man's Statutes); Mason Ladd, *A Modern Code of Evidence*, 27 Iowa L. Rev. 213, 220 (1942) (criticizing Dead Man's Statutes; model code of evidence should presuppose "a society in which honest people outnumber the degraded, the deceitful, and the false-swearing").

55. *See* Ark. R. Evid. 601; Me. R. Evid. 601 & note (1976); Minn. R. Evid. 617 & cmt.; N.D. R. Ev. 601 & note; Okla. Stat. Ann. tit. 12, §2601; Model Code of Evid. R. 101 cmt. (1942); Unif. R. Evid. 601 cmt. (1974); *see also* McCormick on Evidence, *supra* note 2, §65, at 159-60 (courts and lawmakers are making liberal changes to Dead Man's Statutes). The Federal Rules of Evidence also do not include the Dead Man's Rule. *See* Fed. R. Evid. 601.

56. *See, e.g., Jordan v. Shields*, 674 S.W.2d 464, 468 (Tex. App.—Beaumont 1984, no writ) (in wrongful-death action, court allowed widower's testimony about contents of deceased wife's car trunk and daughter's testimony that she expected her mother to pick her up at school).

57. *See Dominguez v. Garcia*, 36 S.W.2d 299, 299 (Tex. Civ. App.—Austin 1931), *aff'd*, 53 S.W.2d 459 (Tex. Comm'n App. 1932, holding approved).

58. *See Wilkinson v. Clark*, 558 S.W.2d 490, 492 (Tex. Civ. App.—Waco 1977, writ ref'd n.r.e.); *Anderson v. Caulk*, 5 S.W.2d 816, 822 (Tex. Civ. App.—El Paso 1928), *aff'd*, 120 Tex. 253, 37 S.W.2d 1008 (1931).

59. *See Grant v. Griffin*, 390 S.W.2d 746, 749 (Tex. 1965).

60. *See Logsdon v. Segler*, 225 S.W.2d 435, 437 (Tex. Civ. App.—San Antonio 1949, writ ref'd).

61. Because Rule 601(b) is a rule of exclusion, the admissibility of any testimony that is permitted under the rule will be determined by other applicable rules of evidence. Tex. R. Evid. 601 cmt.

62. *See* Tex. R. Evid. 601(b)(2), (b)(3)(A).

63. *See* Tex. R. Evid. 601(b)(3)(A); *Fraga v. Drake*, 276 S.W.3d 55, 61 (Tex. App.—El Paso 2008, no pet.); *see, e.g., Donaldson v. Taylor*, 713 S.W.2d 716, 717 (Tex. App.—Beaumont 1986, no writ) (decedent's oral statements were admissible because they were corroborated by a newspaper advertisement and the admission of decedent's son that decedent advertised a lifetime guarantee); *see also Quitta v. Fossati*, 808 S.W.2d 636, 641 (Tex. App.—Corpus Christi 1991, writ denied) (dicta; corroborating evidence is sufficient if it shows decedent's conduct to be consistent with testimony about decedent's statements).

64. *Fraga*, 276 S.W.3d at 61; *Escamilla v. Estate of Escamilla*, 921 S.W.2d 723, 726-27 (Tex. App.—Corpus Christi 1996, writ denied); *e.g., Eckels v. Davis*, 111 S.W.3d 687, 698 (Tex. App.—Fort Worth 2003, pet. denied) (testimony by trust settlor's attorney about deceased settlor's intent to divide trust assets between wife and children did not violate Dead Man's Statute because that testimony was corroborated by disinterested witness and decedent's written statements); *Powers v. McDaniel*, 785 S.W.2d 915, 920 (Tex. App.—San Antonio 1990, writ denied) (cor-

uncorroborated oral statement is inadmissible under the rule.[65] Of course, if the opposing party calls the party to testify at trial about the oral statement, the rule does not bar the evidence.[66] Similarly, in accordance with the general rule on contemporaneous objections, the evidence is not barred if a party does not object to testimony offered in violation of Rule 601(b).[67]

Rule 601(b) does not deal with the admissibility of evidence of the event itself.[68] For example, letters written by the decedent to the proponent of a will were held admissible under Rule 601(b) when offered to show the parties' attitudes and the affection between them.[69] On the other hand, testimony about nonverbal assertions, which are meaningful only when accompanied by contemporaneous oral statements, are covered by the rule.[70]

Texas courts construe Rule 601(b) very narrowly.[71] The rule never applies in a criminal proceeding[72] but instead applies only in a civil action when the party is suing or being sued in his capacity as an executor, administrator, or guardian.[73] Thus, Rule 601(b) would apply in will contests, probate cases, suits to recover a debt owed to or by an estate, actions against an estate for injuries caused by the decedent, or suits to recover

---

roboration requirement was satisfied by evidence of decedent's later actions in carrying out terms of his oral statement); *Parham v. Wilbon*, 746 S.W.2d 347, 350 (Tex. App.—Fort Worth 1988, no writ) (further testimonial evidence by the same interested witness was not sufficient corroboration).

65. *See Parham*, 746 S.W.2d at 350; *Defoeldvar v. Defoeldvar*, 666 S.W.2d 668, 671 (Tex. App.—Fort Worth 1984, no writ), *overruled on other grounds*, *Spiers v. Maples*, 970 S.W.2d 166 (Tex. App.—Fort Worth 1998, no pet.). *See generally* Linda Addison, *Night of the Living Dead Man's Statute*, 49 Tex. B.J. 628 (1986) (discussing Texas courts' earliest interpretation of the new Dead Man's Statute).

66. *See* Tex. R. Evid. 601(b)(3)(B). Refer to notes 79-81 *infra* and accompanying text.

67. *Tuttle v. Simpson*, 735 S.W.2d 539, 542 (Tex. App.—Texarkana 1987, no writ); *see* Tex. R. Evid. 103(a)(1).

68. *In re Estate of Watson*, 720 S.W.2d 806, 807 (Tex. 1986).

69. *Id.*

70. *See, e.g.*, *Tuttle*, 735 S.W.2d at 542 (testimony about decedent's action of pointing out the intended boundary of land, though not an oral statement itself, was meaningless without the admission of oral statements accompanying the gestures; thus, the entire testimony was inadmissible under Rule 601(b)).

71. *Fraga v. Drake*, 276 S.W.3d 55, 61 (Tex. App.—El Paso 2008, no pet.); *Quitta v. Fossati*, 808 S.W.2d 636, 641 (Tex. App.—Corpus Christi 1991, writ denied); *see also* *Lewis v. Foster*, 621 S.W.2d 400, 404 (Tex. 1981) (setting forth the pre-Rules construction).

72. *E.g.*, *Godsey v. State*, 989 S.W.2d 482, 497 (Tex. App.—Waco 1999, pet. ref'd) (Rule 601(b) did not apply to statement made by assault victim before her death; rule applies only to civil actions concerning a decedent's estate); *see* Tex. R. Evid. 601(b)(1).

73. Tex. R. Evid. 601(b)(1)(A). For example, in *Tramel v. Estate of Billings*, the San Antonio court held that Civil Rule 601(b) did not apply in an interpleader action to determine whether the wife or the estate was entitled to proceeds of life-insurance policies. 699 S.W.2d 259, 263-64 (Tex. App.—San Antonio 1985, no writ). The court held that the determining factor was the capacity in which the parties were sued. *Id.* at 263. Because the parties were not sued in the capacity of administrator or executor but instead sought the proceeds only in their own right, the rule did not apply. *Id.* Conversely, in *Seymour v. American Engine & Grinding Co.*, a suit for insurance proceeds brought by the decedent's wife in her capacity as executor of her husband's estate, Civil Rule 601(b) did bar the admission of an uncorroborated statement by the decedent. 956 S.W.2d 49, 56 (Tex. App.—Houston [14th Dist.] 1996, writ denied).

workers' compensation benefits due to the decedent before his death.[74] The rule also extends to the decedent's heirs or other legal representatives.[75]

However, the rule does not apply when the party is suing or being sued in its own capacity,[76] such as in a wrongful-death action.[77] When a single lawsuit contains claims brought both individually and as a representative of the decedent, Rule 601(b) applies unless the claims are severable.[78]

On the other hand, the Dead Man's Rule permits a party to testify to an oral statement when called to testify at the trial by a party whose actual interest on that issue is adverse, regardless of the formal party alignment.[79] Under earlier law, the rule's operation did not depend on whether the prospective witness was a named party but instead looked to whether the witness had "a direct and substantial interest in the issue to which the testimony relates" and would be bound by any judgment entered.[80] The purpose of the rule is to prevent those with a financial interest in the outcome of the litigation from testifying about statements made by a person who cannot refute those statements. Thus, logic supports a continuation of this limited application of the Dead Man's Rule

---

74. *See* 1 GOODE ET AL., *supra* note 24, §601.3, at 514-15 (discussing when Rule 601(b) applies); 1 RAY, *supra* note 4, §325, at 316-17 (3d ed. 1980), at 102 (Supp. 1991) (listing actions to which the Dead Man's Rule has been held to apply).

75. *See* TEX. R. EVID. 601(b)(1)(B); ***Powers v. McDaniel***, 785 S.W.2d 915, 920 (Tex. App.—San Antonio 1990, writ denied); ***Tramel***, 699 S.W.2d at 263. However, devisees and legatees were not considered heirs or legal representatives under the former statute. *See* ***Pugh v. Turner***, 145 Tex. 292, 298, 197 S.W.2d 822, 825 (1946). Their testimony continues to be unaffected by Rule 601(b). *See* ***Tramel***, 699 S.W.2d at 263 (admitting applicable testimony against legatees).

76. *See* TEX. R. EVID. 601(b)(1)(A); *see, e.g.*, ***Quitta***, 808 S.W.2d at 641 (Rule 601(b) did not apply when landlord-plaintiffs were neither heirs nor legal representatives of deceased landlord but brought their action for rental payments as co-owners of leased property); ***Cain v. Whitlock***, 741 S.W.2d 528, 530 (Tex. App.—Houston [14th Dist.] 1987, no writ) (proceeding for appointment of an administrator is not an action by or against executors; thus, Dead Man's Rule does not apply); ***Tramel***, 699 S.W.2d at 263 (administrator of estate was not being sued in that capacity when insurance company sought declaration of the legal beneficiary of insurance proceeds).

77. *See* ***Jordan v. Shields***, 674 S.W.2d 464, 468 (Tex. App.—Beaumont 1984, no writ).

78. 1 RAY, *supra* note 4, §325, at 320-21; *see, e.g.*, ***Ford v. Roberts***, 478 S.W.2d 129, 131-32 (Tex. Civ. App.—Dallas 1972, writ ref'd n.r.e) (when defendant was sued both as executor of decedent's estate and in her individual capacity, provisions of the former Dead Man's Rule applied).

79. *See* TEX. R. EVID. 601(b)(3)(B); ***Tuttle v. Simpson***, 735 S.W.2d 539, 542-43 (Tex. App.—Texarkana 1987, no writ). In ***Tuttle***, a stepson and a widow, although nominally adverse parties, shared a common interest in the location of a boundary marker for 20 acres of land willed to a neighbor. *Id.* at 542. Thus, the widow could not complain when the stepson testified about the decedent's oral statement about the location of the boundary because the testimony was not against an "opposite party." *Id.* at 542-43.
While the original rule did not include the phrase "at the trial," this phrase was added in 1984 to ensure that pretrial discovery inquiries in depositions or interrogatories did not act as a waiver of the protections of the Dead Man's Rule. *See In re: Adopted, Amended and Promulgated Rules of Evidence*, 669-670 S.W.2d (Tex. Cases) XXXVII (1984, amended 1998); 1 GOODE ET AL., *supra* note 24, §601.3, at 518; 1 RAY, *supra* note 4, §334, at 105 (Supp. 1991). Judicial decisions under the former statute held that an adverse party's deposition inquiring into transactions or communications with the decedent waived the protections of the statute. 1 GOODE ET AL., *supra* note 24, §601.3, at 517; 1 RAY, *supra* note 4, §334, at 352-53; *see, e.g.*, ***Fulmer v. Rider***, 635 S.W.2d 875, 878-79 (Tex. App.—Tyler 1982, writ ref'd n.r.e.) (waiver of Dead Man's Rule was allowed because inquiry initiated the specific testimony).

80. ***Chandler v. Welborn***, 156 Tex. 312, 322, 294 S.W.2d 801, 809 (1956).

to those named or unnamed parties to the litigation who, at the time of their testimony, have an interest in the outcome of the lawsuit.[81]

Rule 601(b)(4) requires the trial judge to instruct the jury on the existence and applicability of the rule in a proper case.[82] This instruction is intended to prevent the favored party from using the protections of the Dead Man's Rule during closing arguments by suggesting that if the decedent had made any statements to the opposing party, the jury would have heard about them.

The final form of Rule 601(b) represents a retreat from the version recommended by the Liaison Committee, which had eliminated the Dead Man's Rule.[83] A majority of the committee said they believed the Dead Man's Rule was an idea whose time had passed.[84] The rule had been defended as preventing the successful assertion of fraudulent claims against an estate,[85] but this justification was based on a distrust of the jury system—a fear that jurors would not understand that a witness testifying in support of his own claim against an estate could lie without fear of contradiction.

RULE 602

NEED FOR PERSONAL KNOWLEDGE

A witness may testify to a matter only if evidence is introduced sufficient to support a finding that the witness has personal knowledge of the matter. Evidence to prove personal knowledge may consist of the witness's own testimony. This rule does not apply to a witness's expert testimony under Rule 703.

COMMENTARY ON RULE 602

Rule 602 follows long-standing Texas law[86] and is identical to Federal Rule 602. Without some evidence to show that a lay witness has personal knowledge of the subject matter of his testimony, the jury cannot be helped by listening to him.[87] This re-

---

81. Rule 601(b) prohibits only a party from testifying. Tex. R. Evid. 601 cmt. The Texas Supreme Court explained that "courts have indicated that the rule (or its statutory predecessor) may be applicable to a witness who is not nominally a party and inapplicable to a witness who is only nominally a party. But these decisions are based on an interpretation of the meaning of 'party.' Therefore, limiting the court's instruction under … Rule 601(b)(4) to 'a party' does not change Texas practice." Tex. R. Evid. 601 cmt.

82. The instruction was added to the former civil rule in 1987. *See Order Adopting and Amending Texas Rules of Civil Evidence*, 733-734 S.W.2d (Tex. Cases) xcv (1987, amended 1998). Although the text of the former civil rule and its statutory predecessor prohibited only a "party" from testifying about a decedent's statements, the last sentence of former Rule 601(b) required the court to instruct the jury when the rule "prohibits an interested party or witness" from testifying. *See* Tex. R. Evid. 601 cmt. The instruction now conforms to the language of the rest of the rule; that is, only a party is prohibited from testifying. *See* Tex. R. Evid. 601(b)(4) & cmt. This rewording does not change Texas practice. Tex. R. Evid. 601 cmt.

83. Tex. R. Evid. 601(b) (1982 Liaison Committee proposal), *reprinted infra* p. 1086.

84. Interim Study IV, *supra* note 10, at 250 (Mar. 19-20, 1982).

85. McCormick on Evidence, *supra* note 2, §65, at 159-60.

86. *See Tex. & Pac. Ry. Co. v. Reed*, 88 Tex. 439, 449-50, 31 S.W. 1058, 1061 (1895).

87. *See Marks v. St. Luke's Episcopal Hosp.*, 319 S.W.3d 658, 666 (Tex. 2010) ("Affidavits … must be based on personal knowledge, not supposition. An affidavit not based on personal knowledge is legally insufficient."); *In re*

quirement is closely related to the concept of relevance under Rule 401.[88] Unless the witness perceived an event or fact, his testimony will have no relevance to the material issues in dispute. The rule explicitly states that the foundation of personal knowledge may be shown by the witness's own testimony, and this foundation may also be shown by circumstantial evidence.[89]

While the law demands personal knowledge, it does not require certainty of memory or perfect attention to the observation.[90] Thus, a witness's testimony is not rejected merely because he cannot be positive about what he saw or remembered. He may testify to the best of his recollection, and his testimony should not be excluded because he uses such phrases as "it is my impression," "I think," or "I believe"—especially if his uncertainty is based on faulty attention or the vagaries of memory rather than on sheer speculation, conjecture, or hearsay.[91]

Rule 602's requirement of personal knowledge is frequently confused with the rule against hearsay.[92] However, Rule 602 clearly deals with witness testimony about a specific fact that is purportedly the result of personal observation but was actually the re-

---

Christus Spohn Hosp. Kleberg, 222 S.W.3d 434, 440 (Tex. 2007) ("[L]ay witnesses may only testify regarding matters of which they have personal knowledge ...."); *Strickland Transp. Co. v. Ingram*, 403 S.W.2d 192, 195 (Tex. Civ. App.—Texarkana 1966, writ dism'd) ("Perception of fact by the senses of the witness, that is, firsthand knowledge, is a fundamental qualification of testimonial competency.").

88. Refer to *Article IV: Relevance & Its Limits*, supra p. 193.

89. *See* Tex. R. Evid. 602; *see, e.g.*, *Minn. Life Ins. v. Vasquez*, 133 S.W.3d 320, 325-26 (Tex. App.—Corpus Christi 2004) (decedent's widow had personal knowledge of her own diabetic condition and offered sufficient circumstantial facts of a link between her changed circumstances and her changed blood-sugar level and diabetic condition for jury to conclude that stress of her husband's death was the cause of the health change), *rev'd on other grounds*, 192 S.W.3d 774 (Tex. 2006); *Celotex Corp. v. Tate*, 797 S.W.2d 197, 206 (Tex. App.—Corpus Christi 1990, writ dism'd) (although no evidence was introduced to show exact source of witness's knowledge, trial court could properly infer that witness had personal knowledge based on his occupation and observations); *Contreras v. State*, 745 S.W.2d 59, 62 (Tex. App.—San Antonio 1987, no pet.) (court rejected defendant's argument that because victim was shot in the back, victim could not have had personal knowledge of who shot him); *cf. United States v. Quezada*, 754 F.2d 1190, 1195-96 (5th Cir. 1985) (circumstantial evidence of personal knowledge was sufficient when witness, who admitted that he had never personally observed the execution of a deportation warrant, stated that he was familiar with "the normal rule of things and the normal processes of deportation").

90. McCormick on Evidence, supra note 2, §10, at 24-25. For example, in *In re J.P.O.*, during a juvenile transfer hearing, the victim-witness first stated that he had no present recollection of the events of the night of the burglary; after he was shown his earlier testimony, he then recalled those events and what he had seen and done. 904 S.W.2d 695, 699 (Tex. App.—Corpus Christi 1995, writ denied). Thus, the trial court did not abuse its discretion in permitting him to testify, as it appeared that he had only temporarily lost his memory and did not lack personal knowledge of the events. *Id.*

91. *See In re J.P.O.*, 904 S.W.2d at 699; *see, e.g.*, *Riggs v. Sentry Ins.*, 821 S.W.2d 701, 709 (Tex. App.—Houston [14th Dist.] 1991, writ denied) (trial court properly sustained objection to question asking witness to testify about what someone else allegedly thought; such questioning calls for speculation and "does not ask for testimony satisfying the Rule 602 requirement of testimony about matters within a witness' personal knowledge"); *Middlebrook v. State*, 803 S.W.2d 355, 358-59 (Tex. App.—Fort Worth 1990, pet. ref'd) (police officer who qualified his testimony of what defendant said to him with "I can't give you an exact quote, but he said something to the effect ... It's just what I feel he said ..." had personal knowledge of the event; "it would be impractical to require a witness to recall verbatim a conversation between himself and another").

92. *See, e.g.*, *Quezada*, 754 F.2d at 1195 (defendant's hearsay objection to witness's testimony that his knowledge of deportation-warrant procedures was based "on what he had been told" and "the normal rule of things" was "more appropriately understood as implicating the personal knowledge requirement of F. R. Evid. 602" rather than hearsay); *Elizarraras v. Bank of El Paso*, 631 F.2d 366, 373-74 (5th Cir. 1980) (although hearsay objection was techni-

sult of another person's communication or actions (e.g., a witness testifies that a car was speeding, and it is later discovered that the witness did not personally see the car speeding but is merely relating what another person told him). In contrast, Rule 802—the rule against hearsay—applies when the witness's statement indicates on its face that the witness is repeating what another has told him (e.g., the witness testifies that another person told him that the car was speeding). Practitioners should separate objections based on lack of personal knowledge from those involving hearsay.[93]

Sometimes a witness may base his testimony on both personal knowledge and information received from others. A classic example of this situation involves the question: "When were you born?" The witness was obviously present at the occasion but has no personal memory of it. Yet for many years, he has relied on the accuracy of his birth certificate, his parents' celebration of his birthday, and his personal knowledge of the attendant circumstances of that anniversary.[94] If this dual bias exists, the trial court has the discretion to admit or exclude the evidence, depending on the probable reliability of the information.[95] If the witness's knowledge is based primarily on hearsay, the evidence should be excluded.[96] If the testimony is "substantially" based on personal knowledge, it should be admitted.[97]

---

cally incorrect, court would not draw "such a fine line" between hearsay and personal knowledge). For a discussion of the hearsay rule and its exceptions, refer to *Article VIII: Hearsay, infra* p. 864.

93. For example, in ***Higgins v. State***, the defendant objected under Rule 602 to one witness's testimony on the grounds that it was speculative. 924 S.W.2d 739, 745 (Tex. App.—Texarkana 1996, pet. ref'd). The witness testified that she had seen the victim with injuries on previous occasions when "her lip was busted. She had a black eye, and she had a hand print around her neck where she had been choked ... and she was bald-headed, where [the defendant] had pulled a bunch of her hair out." *Id.* The court held that the witness's testimony was admissible under Rule 602 because it was based on her own personal observations of the victim. *Id.* What could have been objectionable as hearsay was the witness's testimony that the victim was bald where the defendant had pulled her hair out. *Id.* However, the defendant did not object, so the complaint was waived. *Id.*

94. *See, e.g.,* ***Antelope v. United States***, 185 F.2d 174, 175 (10th Cir. 1950) (statutory-rape victim could testify to her own age and date of birth); *see also* 27 WRIGHT & GOLD, *supra* note 21, §6026, at 226 (discussing whether a witness has knowledge about his age).

95. MCCORMICK ON EVIDENCE, *supra* note 2, §10, at 25; *see* ***State v. Brainard***, 968 S.W.2d 403, 412 (Tex. App.—Amarillo 1998) (witness's opinion testimony, based on both hearsay and personal knowledge, was admissible), *rev'd in part on other grounds*, 12 S.W.3d 6 (Tex. 1999); ***Skruck v. State***, 740 S.W.2d 819, 821 (Tex. App.—Houston [1st Dist.] 1987, pet. ref'd) (witness can assert the existence of fact if his knowledge comes from personal observation and related reasonable inferences).

96. *See* TEX. R. EVID. 802.

97. *See, e.g.,* ***Southwick v. State***, 701 S.W.2d 927, 930 (Tex. App.—Houston [1st Dist.] 1985, no pet.) (police officers could testify to the purpose and use of obscene devices based partly on their own personal observations and partly on having read certain magazine advertisements); *see also* ***United States v. Mandel***, 591 F.2d 1347, 1369-70 (4th Cir. 1979) (testimony that is a combination of hearsay and personal observation should not be allowed). In *Mandel*, the Governor of Maryland was charged with racketeering and mail fraud. 591 F.2d at 1352. Several state senators had testified to the governor's position on a veto override but had based their testimony partly on hearsay and partly on statements made by the governor and his authorized agents. *Id.* at 1369. The court noted that a difficult problem arises when the witness's belief is based on both admissible and inadmissible testimony:

> If the belief is primarily based on hearsay, it is inadmissible. But, if the belief is substantially based on admissible evidence, such as direct statements or acts by one of Governor Mandel's agents, then it should be admitted. The basis for the belief should be explored in each instance and a ruling on admissibility made when those facts are before the trial court.

Id. at 1370.

Rule 602 also works in tandem with Rule 701, which limits the admission of a lay witness's opinions to those that are "rationally based on the witness's perception."[98] Rule 701 should be invoked when testimony purports to give the witness's lay opinion without a predicate showing that the facts forming the basis of that opinion are the result of personal knowledge. This situation occurs, for example, when the witness gives his opinion that the car was speeding, but no testimony is offered to show that the witness was watching the car.[99] On the other hand, Rule 602 does not bar testimony by an expert witness under Rule 703 because an expert witness may rely on information outside his personal knowledge.[100]

The determination of whether a witness has sufficient personal knowledge of the events about which he testifies is a question of relevance that depends on a fact, to be decided under Rule 104(b).[101] If the judge finds that the proponent of the evidence has produced sufficient admissible evidence to support a finding by a reasonable jury that the witness has personal knowledge of the events, the testimony must be admitted. This low threshold permits the witness to testify based on a minimal foundation of personal knowledge and leaves to the jury the assessment of the evidence's potentially slight probative value and how much weight, if any, it should be given.[102]

---

98. TEX. R. EVID. 701(a); *see Fairow v. State*, 943 S.W.2d 895, 898 (Tex. Crim. App. 1997) (Rule 701's perception requirement "is consistent with the personal knowledge requirement of Rule 602"; personal knowledge may come directly from the witness's senses or personal experience); *see, e.g.*, *Viscaino v. State*, 513 S.W.3d 802, 812 (Tex. App.—El Paso 2017, no pet.) (as lay witness in theft case, police officer did not meet perception and personal-knowledge requirements when he had no personal knowledge of transaction at issue in case); *Wilson v. State*, No. 05-15-01407-CR (Tex. App.—Dallas 2017, no pet.) (memo op.; 1-5-17) (trial court could have reasonably concluded that assistant detective on case, who had previously worked as 911 dispatcher, had sufficient personal knowledge and experience to say whether person seeking to establish alibi would "set up" 911 call). Refer to *Article VII: Opinions & Expert Testimony*, infra p. 685.

99. *See, e.g.*, *Rabon v. Great Sw. Fire Ins.*, 818 F.2d 306, 309 (4th Cir. 1987) (evidence that plaintiff, suing to collect under a fire-insurance policy, was not prosecuted for arson was inadmissible under Rules 602 and 701 because prosecutor's opinion on whether the insured started the fire was not based on personal knowledge).

100. *See* TEX. R. EVID. 602; *Aguilar v. State*, 887 S.W.2d 27, 29 n.7 (Tex. Crim. App. 1994). Refer to *Article VII: Opinions & Expert Testimony*, infra p. 742.

101. Refer to *Article I: General Provisions*, supra p. 91.

102. *See* EDMUND M. MORGAN, BASIC PROBLEMS OF EVIDENCE 59-60 (1961) (court may reject testimony only when no rational trier of fact could believe that the witness perceived what he claims); 2 STEPHEN A. SALTZBURG ET AL., FEDERAL RULES OF EVIDENCE MANUAL 873 (7th ed. 1998) (as long as some evidence shows that a witness has personal knowledge, trial judge must let jury decide if witness is really knowledgeable); *see also United States v. Davis*, 792 F.2d 1299, 1304-05 (5th Cir. 1986) (trial court has discretion in evaluating an initial showing of personal knowledge by a witness on the subject of his testimony). It is generally not an abuse of discretion to accept as provisionally adequate the witness's own assertion of personal knowledge, particularly when nothing suggests otherwise, and the probable absence of personal knowledge could be shown by the opposing party. *See Davis*, 792 F.2d at 1304-05. The Austin Court of Appeals noted that when

> there is some reason to doubt whether the witness possesses the requisite personal knowledge, it may be appropriate for the court to afford the opposing party a chance to take the witness on voir dire. But it is neither reasonable nor practical to permit such voir dire when there is no apparent reason for doubting that the witness is testifying from personal knowledge.

Shugars v. State, 814 S.W.2d 897, 898 (Tex. App.—Austin 1991, no pet.) (per curiam) (no abuse of discretion in overruling a request to voir dire a witness when defendant neither objected that witness lacked personal knowledge nor stated any basis for doubting that witness had personal knowledge).

However, Rule 602 does not apply to statements made by the opposing party under Rule 801(e)(2).[103] An adverse party's statements are admissible even when he lacks personal knowledge of the event or circumstance described in his testimony.[104] The rationale for this exception is the notion that a party who makes a statement must have believed that it was true at the time it was made. In an attempt to exclude the statement at trial, the speaker is very likely to make a self-serving claim that he lacked personal knowledge when he made the earlier statement. The statement is admissible, but the party will be permitted to explain why he made it.

RULE 603

OATH OR AFFIRMATION TO TESTIFY TRUTHFULLY

Before testifying, a witness must give an oath or affirmation to testify truthfully. It must be in a form designed to impress that duty on the witness's conscience.

COMMENTARY ON RULE 603

Rule 603 is identical to Federal Rule 603. The requirement of an oath is designed to ensure that the witness will speak accurately and truthfully. The Texas Constitution states that "all oaths or affirmations shall be administered in the mode most binding upon the conscience, and shall be taken subject to the pains and penalties of perjury."[105] Regardless of whether the potential threats of divine retribution and perjury charges act as realistic deterrents to false testimony, the taking of the oath or affirmation has more than symbolic value in the judicial system.

At common law, the belief in a divine being who punishes false swearing was a prerequisite to witness competency.[106] An atheist or agnostic could not testify in a court of law.[107] The inclusion of the term "affirmation" in Rule 603 eases whatever difficulties might arise from witnesses who do not believe in a divine being or whose religious beliefs prohibit them from taking an oath.[108] The Advisory Committee's note to Federal Rule 603 states that an "[a]ffirmation is simply a solemn undertaking to tell the truth; no special verbal formula is required."[109] The requirement of an oath is not a

---

103. *See* Tex. R. Evid. 801(e)(2); ***Honea v. State***, 585 S.W.2d 681, 686 (Tex. Crim. App. [Panel Op.] 1979), *overruled on other grounds*, ***Thompson v. State***, 236 S.W.3d 787 (Tex. Crim. App. 2007); Fed. R. Evid. 801 advisory committee's note, subdiv. (d)(2). Refer to *Article VIII: Hearsay, infra* p. 845.

104. *See* Tex. R. Evid. 801(e)(2); ***Honea***, 585 S.W.2d at 686; Fed. R. Evid. 801 advisory committee's note, subdiv. (d)(2).

105. Tex. Const. art. I, §5.

106. McCormick on Evidence, *supra* note 2, §63, at 157.

107. *Id.*

108. *See* ***Gordon v. Idaho***, 778 F.2d 1397, 1400 (9th Cir. 1985) (First Amendment and Federal Rule 603 encourage flexibility in the form of the oath or affirmation to accommodate religious objections).

109. Fed. R. Evid. 603 advisory committee's note. In one Texas case, the defendant was permitted to take his oath on a tribal icon, but outside the presence of the jury. ***Faghemi v. State***, 778 S.W.2d 119, 120 (Tex. App.—Texarkana

matter of witness competency but one of moral stimulus.[110] The rule allows maximum flexibility for courts to use whatever form is meaningful to the witness and is likely to appeal to his conscience.[111] For example, any statement showing that a child witness will testify truthfully and accurately is sufficient to satisfy the rule.[112] As noted in the discussion of Rule 601, a child witness does not need to take a formal oath to be a competent witness.[113] In one case, the court of appeals stated that the criminal defendant did not need to sign an indigency affidavit because any sort of oath or affirmation conflicted with his religious beliefs.[114] The court stated that "[t]o require a witness to affirmatively state that he is testifying 'under penalty of perjury' when such a statement is contrary to his religious beliefs would violate the Free Exercise Clause just as much as a requirement that the witness testify under 'oath' or 'affirmation.'"[115] While courts do not need to discuss the semantic difference between "oath" and "affirmation," the witness must, in whatever form is appropriate to impress on his conscience, state that he will tell the truth and that he recognizes that he may be prosecuted for perjury if he lies.[116]

1989, pet. ref'd). The defendant objected that he was not permitted to take that oath in the presence of the jury. *Id.* The court noted that the purpose of the oath, to encourage the witness to be truthful, can be achieved without the jury being present. *Id.* at 121. The court of appeals concluded that "[t]he taking of the oath should not become a contest between witnesses to try to convince the jury that one oath was more binding than another oath." *Id.*

110. *See* 4 MICHAEL H. GRAHAM, HANDBOOK OF FEDERAL EVIDENCE §603:1, at 56 (7th ed. 2012) ("Neither [Federal] Rule 603 nor Rule 601 imposes any requirement of moral capacity in the sense of requiring that the witness actually possess a sense of responsibility to speak the truth."); 3 JACK B. WEINSTEIN & MARGARET A. BERGER, WEINSTEIN'S EVIDENCE ¶603[01], at 603-06 (1995) (Federal Rule 603 rejected the standard of moral qualification as a rule of competency); 6 JOHN H. WIGMORE, EVIDENCE IN TRIALS AT COMMON LAW §1827, at 413-14 (Chadbourn rev. 1976) (true purpose of oath "is not to exclude any competent witness, but merely to add a stimulus to truthfulness wherever such a stimulus is feasible").

111. For example, in ***Bisby v. State***, the witness refused to take a standard oath on religious grounds. 907 S.W.2d 949, 953 (Tex. App.—Fort Worth 1995, pet. ref'd). He did agree that he would "accurately and truthfully answer under penalty of perjury" all questions. *Id.* In holding that this was an acceptable affirmation, the court quoted the Advisory Committee's note to Federal Rule 603, which explains that an "[a]ffirmation is simply a solemn undertaking to tell the truth; no special verbal formula is required." ***Bisby***, 907 S.W.2d at 954. Furthermore, the court held that trial judges faced with a witness who refuses to take an oath on religious grounds "should take reasonable steps to accommodate the witness's beliefs" and "strive to devise, in consultation with the witness if necessary, some alternative form of 'serious public commitment to answer truthfully that does not transgress the prospect's sincerely held beliefs.'" *Id.* at 954-55 (quoting 1 GOODE ET AL., *supra* note 24, §603.1, at 524).

112. Simple questioning such as, "You must tell us the truth. Don't tell us anything you made up or what somebody else told you. Will you do that?" should suffice. *See* ***Gonzales v. State***, 748 S.W.2d 510, 511-12 (Tex. App.—Houston [1st Dist.] 1988, pet. ref'd) (questions to child witnesses were sufficient to "impress" the children with their duty to testify truthfully).

113. Refer to notes 42-45 *supra* and accompanying text.

114. ***Scott v. State***, 80 S.W.3d 184, 194-95 (Tex. App.—Waco 2002, pet. ref'd). In ***Scott***, the defendant was excused from "strict adherence" to the rule requiring that indigence be "'sworn to before an officer authorized to administer oaths'" because he stated that his religion forbade him from making any oaths or affirmations. *Id.* at 195 (quoting TEX. GOV'T CODE §312.011(1)).

115. ***Scott***, 80 S.W.3d at 196.

116. *See* TEX. CONST. art. I, §5; *see, e.g.*, ***Scott***, 80 S.W.3d at 197 (defendant's declaration that "I vow to my heavenly Creator that I will tell the truth and that I will do so under any penalties that are equivalent to the penalties for perjury for those who swear or affirm oaths" was sufficient under Rule 603 to qualify witness to testify).

The Rule 603 requirement that every witness take an oath or affirmation is waived if the opponent does not make a timely objection to unsworn testimony.[117] If the problem is noticed during the trial while the witness is still available, he may be recalled and either swear that the testimony previously given was truthful[118] or be sworn in and repeat his original testimony.[119] The latter is a clumsy technique, but it more correctly complies with the express language of the rule, which requires the taking of an oath before testifying.[120]

RULE 604

INTERPRETER

An interpreter must be qualified and must give an oath or affirmation to make a true translation.

COMMENTARY ON RULE 604

Rule 604 is identical to Federal Rule 604. The policy underlying the rule is the determination of the truth through accurate and reliable testimony. The witness's testimony must be given in a form that makes sense to the jury and can be used by them. When interpreters are necessary, Rule 604 requires that they be experts and that they affirm the accuracy of their translations; these requirements are clearly supported by the Texas statutes and rules of civil and criminal procedure regulating the use of interpreters.[121]

---

117. *E.g.*, ***Banda v. Garcia***, 955 S.W.2d 270, 272 (Tex. 1997) (per curiam) (although an attorney's statements must normally be under oath to be considered evidence, opposing party did not object to such statements, so they could be considered as evidence); *see* ***Thomas Trammell & Co. v. Mount***, 68 Tex. 210, 215, 4 S.W. 377, 379 (1887); ***Castillo v. State***, 739 S.W.2d 280, 297-98 (Tex. Crim. App. 1987); ***Beck v. State***, 719 S.W.2d 205, 211-12 (Tex. Crim. App. 1986); ***De La Garza v. Salazar***, 851 S.W.2d 380, 383 (Tex. App.—San Antonio 1993, no writ).

118. *See* ***Beck***, 719 S.W.2d at 213 n.5.

119. *See id.* at 213. A rather bizarre situation arose in ***Butler v. State***. 890 S.W.2d 951 (Tex. App.—Waco 1995, pet. ref'd). The defendant had not been sworn in before testifying, and when this omission was discovered by his own counsel, the court then administered the oath and asked the defendant whether his testimony would be the same as it had been when he was not sworn in. *Id.* at 956. The defendant replied that he would not have admitted under oath that he had been previously convicted of a felony for sexual abuse because it was more than ten years old and thus inadmissible. *Id.* He then refused to testify again. *Id.* Faced with this peculiarity, the trial court informed the jury that it must disregard all of the defendant's testimony because he had never been sworn in. *Id.* But because the jury had already been improperly informed of the defendant's prior conviction for sexual assault, his conviction was reversed because "[a]sking jurors to forget that [the defendant] is a convicted child molester simply asks too much of fallible human beings." *Id.*

120. *See* TEX. R. EVID. 603. In ***Torres v. State***, the court of criminal appeals held that the failure to admonish a child or place her under oath before she gave her videotaped statement under Texas Code of Criminal Procedure article 38.071, §5(a)(10) was not cured by asking the child witness at the end of the interview whether she had been telling the truth. 33 S.W.3d 252, 257 (Tex. Crim. App. 2000). Although the admission of the videotape was not directly controlled by Rule 603, the situation is analogous; thus, if a party objects to unsworn testimony, the witness should be sworn in and the testimony repeated.

121. *See* TEX. CIV. PRAC. & REM. CODE §21.002; TEX. CODE CRIM. PROC. arts. 38.30, 38.31; TEX. GOV'T CODE §57.002; TEX. R. CIV. P. 183.

Interpreters are generally of two distinct types: witness interpreters and party interpreters.[122] A witness interpreter translates for a witness whose testimony would not otherwise be comprehensible to the parties, judge, or jury.[123] A party interpreter translates the entire trial proceeding for a party who could not otherwise understand the testimony, trial judge, or even his own attorney.[124] Rule 604 speaks only to witness interpreters, although it has been invoked occasionally when discussing the constitutional necessity of appointing an interpreter for a criminal defendant.[125]

---

122. *See* **United States v. Dempsey**, 830 F.2d 1084, 1088 (10th Cir. 1987) (interpreters act for a party or a witness).

123. *See id.* (discussing when witnesses require interpreters to testify); *see also* **Balderas v. State**, 517 S.W.3d 756, 777 (Tex. Crim. App. 2016) (when trial court appoints interpreter, there is no requirement for record to establish that witness's English skills are so poor that defendant would be deprived of effective cross-examination without interpreter's assistance; trial judges have wide discretion in determining need for interpretive services), *cert. denied*, 137 S. Ct. 1207 (2017).

124. *See* **Dempsey**, 830 F.2d at 1088 (defining parties who may require an interpreter, including criminal defendants).

125. *See* **Linton v. State**, 275 S.W.3d 493, 508 (Tex. Crim. App. 2009) (due process does not require "the best" interpretive service "unless the defendant also shows that, without it, he was unable to understand the nature and objective of the proceedings against him and to assist in his own defense"); **Baltierra v. State**, 586 S.W.2d 553, 559 (Tex. Crim. App. 1979) (court's failure to provide interpreter for defendant who does not understand the trial proceedings violates defendant's right of confrontation); *see also* **Balderas**, 517 S.W.3d at 777 (courts have regarded use of interpreter for material witness who has difficulty communicating in English as something Confrontation Clause requires rather than prohibits because use of interpreter allows defendant to conduct meaningful cross-examination); **Adams v. State**, 749 S.W.2d 635, 639 (Tex. App.—Houston [1st Dist.] 1988, pet. ref'd) (under Code of Criminal Procedure 38.31(a), failure to provide a deaf defendant with some means to understand the trial proceedings violates his right of confrontation); *cf.* **Jackson v. Garcia**, 665 F.2d 395, 396 (1st Cir. 1981) (in Puerto Rico, where Spanish is the official language, a non-Spanish-speaking defendant has a constitutionally protected right to an interpreter). For a discussion of the constitutional right of confrontation, refer to *Article VIII: Hearsay, infra* p. 787.

In **Mendiola v. State**, the defendant complained during trial about the court's bailiff acting as a translator and asked for a different translator because he was not getting a "word-by-word" translation. 924 S.W.2d 157, 161-62 (Tex. App.—Corpus Christi 1995, pet. ref'd). The trial court overruled that request, finding that the bailiff was sufficiently competent to serve the defendant's needs. *Id.* at 161. This fact was verified by defense counsel, who stated that the bailiff was generally competent but was not translating word-for-word. *Id.* Because the defendant did not complain about any specific errors or omissions in the translation, did not ask the testifying witnesses to slow down for the bailiff's translation, and did not request an opportunity to reexamine a witness because the defendant could not follow the testimony, the appellate court held that he had not preserved any error. *Id.* at 162-63. Justice Yañez, in dissent, argued that the defendant repeatedly objected to the translator's inadequacy, and thus it was incumbent on the court to make a determination of the translator's competency. *Id.* at 166 (Yañez, J., dissenting). The dissent stated that giving a witness's testimony "in its 'essence'" is not the same as translating it word-for-word. *Id.* at 167; *see* 75 AM. JUR. 2d *Trial* §234 (1991) (an interpreter should not merely render a "summary" of what the primary witness has stated but, as far as possible, should translate word-for-word exactly what the primary witness has said).

The El Paso Court of Appeals has discussed whether an English transcript of a defendant's videotaped confession given in Spanish was sufficient under Code of Criminal Procedure 38.30. **Flores v. State**, 299 S.W.3d 843, 854-56 (Tex. App.—El Paso 2009, pet. ref'd). In **Flores**, the defendant requested a contemporaneous translation of the videotape by a live interpreter. *Id.* at 854. Because the jurors who did not speak Spanish would have only a written translation, the defendant argued, they would be "unable to correlate the English translation with [the defendant's] statements and the context in which they were made." *Id.* The court rejected this argument, noting that the interpretive services needed only to be "constitutionally adequate such that the defendant could understand and participate in the proceedings." *Id.* at 855. In holding that a contemporaneous translation was not necessary, the court observed:

> It is as if the non-English language was never spoken before the jury and the interpreter stands in place of the witness. There is in fact no requirement or means available at trial to preserve the original foreign language spoken in court. It is the translation presented by the interpreter that creates the record and that ultimately serves as the basis for any potential appeal.

The fact that a party may be more fluent in a language other than English does not mean that the appointment of an interpreter is necessary. An interpreter is required only when a party speaks and understands little or no English.[126]

Although no statute establishes the qualifications of such interpreters, Rule 604 requires an interpreter to be qualified as an expert under Rule 702 by means of special "knowledge, skill, experience, training, or education."[127] If the interpreter is not sufficiently skilled, his translation could further hinder the accuracy of the proceedings, instead of helping to discover the truth.

Accordingly, the interpreter acts solely as a conduit for the words of the testifying witness and may not add any explanation or summary.[128] In questioning a witness through an interpreter, practitioners should direct their questions to the witness as if no interpreter were present.[129] The interpreter must then "translate the question and answer in a literal manner."[130] Attorneys should not begin their questions with a phrase such as "ask him if ...," and interpreters should not initiate their responses with a phrase such as "he says ...."[131]

Additionally, although Rule 604 requires the witness interpreter to take an oath or affirmation, that requirement is waived by the failure to make a timely objection to its absence.[132]

Id. at 855-56. The written translation satisfied the requirements of Code of Criminal Procedure article 38.30. *Flores*, 299 S.W.3d at 856.

126. *See, e.g.*, *Flores v. State*, 509 S.W.2d 580, 581 (Tex. Crim. App. 1974) (defendant's motion for interpreter was denied because he was proficient in English); *Vasquez v. State*, 819 S.W.2d 932, 937-38 (Tex. App.—Corpus Christi 1991, pet. ref'd) (trial court did not need to appoint an interpreter for defendant sua sponte without a showing that he could not understand English, even though the State stipulated that he did not speak English). Although Texas Code of Criminal Procedure article 38.30 requires the appointment of an interpreter only for a defendant or witness who does not understand or speak English, the statute does not prohibit interpreters in other situations. *E.g.*, *Balderas*, 517 S.W.3d at 773-74 (trial court's appointment of witness interpreter was not improper even though defendant claimed witness could speak "perfect English").

127. TEX. R. EVID. 702; *see Leal v. State*, 782 S.W.2d 844, 849 (Tex. Crim. App. 1989) (interpreter must "'possess adequate interpreting skills for the particular situation'" and must be "'familiar with the use of slang'" (quoting TEX. CODE CRIM. PROC. art. 38.30)). In *Leal*, the court also found error in admitting written translations when "there was no positive identification of who made the translation, there was no evidence they were qualified to make the translation, and there was no record that they were officially sworn to make the translation." 782 S.W.2d at 849-50; *see also Watson v. State*, 596 S.W.2d 867, 872-73 (Tex. Crim. App. [Panel Op.] 1980) (error to permit stroke victim's caretaker to interpret his "uh-huh" responses with no showing that she was able to translate accurately).

128. *See United States v. Anguloa*, 598 F.2d 1182, 1186 n.5 (9th Cir. 1979) (interpreter is not a participant in trial but rather "only acts as a transmission belt or telephone").

129. *See Guzmon v. State*, 697 S.W.2d 404, 407 n.1 (Tex. Crim. App. 1985).

130. *See id.*

131. *See id.*

132. *See Castillo v. State*, 807 S.W.2d 8, 9 (Tex. App.—Corpus Christi 1991, pet. ref'd); *Lara v. State*, 761 S.W.2d 481, 482 (Tex. App.—Eastland 1988, no pet.); *Solis v. State*, 647 S.W.2d 95, 98 (Tex. App.—San Antonio 1983, no pet.). *But see Leal*, 782 S.W.2d at 847-49 (defendant's objection to errors and omissions in the English transcription of a tape recording of a conversation in Spanish was sufficient to preserve error in the failure to interpret the tape through a sworn translator).

RULE 605

JUDGE'S COMPETENCY
AS A WITNESS

The presiding judge may not testify as a witness at the trial. A party need not object to preserve the issue.

COMMENTARY ON RULE 605

Rule 605, like the identical Federal Rule 605, renders the presiding trial judge incompetent to testify as a witness.[133] Unlike the general common-law assumption that some categories of potential witnesses were inherently untrustworthy, judicial testimony was seen as a reverse problem: jurors would be overly persuaded by the judge's position and hence uncritical of his statements.

There are few federal or state cases discussing Rule 605 because a case in which the presiding judge testifies is usually decided on due-process grounds.[134] These cases generally conclude that a judge who testifies as a witness "violates due process rights by creating a constitutionally intolerable appearance of partiality."[135]

Rule 605 applies not only to members of the judiciary but also to any person performing judicial functions that would conflict with the role of a witness.[136] For example, aldermen presiding over a quo warranto removal trial of a mayor would violate this rule by testifying against the mayor at the trial.[137]

---

133. Rule 605 is contrary to a former provision of the Texas Code of Criminal Procedure, which expressly made the presiding judge a competent witness. *See* Act approved June 18, 1965, 59th Leg., ch. 722, 1965 Tex. Gen. Laws 467 (former Code of Criminal Procedure art. 38.13 deemed repealed as to criminal proceedings effective 1986); *see, e.g.*, *Kemp v. State*, 382 S.W.2d 933, 934 (Tex. Crim. App. 1964) (county judge could testify); *Howell v. State*, 146 Tex. Crim. 454, 455, 176 S.W.2d 186, 187 (1943) (judge may testify as a witness as long as he is sworn in); *Young v. State*, 629 S.W.2d 247, 249-50 (Tex. App.—Fort Worth 1982) (trial judge can testify that defendant was the same person who was alleged to have prior felony convictions), *appeal dismissed*, 465 U.S. 1016 (1984). Additionally, Rule 605 may have changed Texas civil law; one pre-Rules Texas appellate court had remarked, in dicta: "That the judge of a court may testify in a cause being tried before him is not now an open question." *Conyer v. Burckhalter*, 275 S.W. 606, 613 (Tex. Civ. App.—Dallas 1925), *rev'd on other grounds*, 9 S.W.2d 1029 (Tex. Comm'n App. 1928, judgm't adopted); *see also* *Great Liberty Life Ins. v. Flint*, 336 S.W.2d 434, 436 (Tex. Civ. App.—Fort Worth 1960, no writ) (judges can testify if all the required procedures that apply to other witnesses are met).

134. *Bradley v. State ex rel. White*, 990 S.W.2d 245, 248 (Tex. 1999).

135. *Id.*; *see also* *Brown v. Lynaugh*, 843 F.2d 849, 850 (5th Cir. 1988) ("It is difficult to see how the neutral role of the court could be more compromised, or more blurred with the prosecutor's role, than when the judge serves as a witness for the state.").

136. *Bradley*, 990 S.W.2d at 249; *Fears v. State*, 479 S.W.3d 315, 335 n.10 (Tex. App.—Corpus Christi 2015, pet. ref'd). Rule 605 also applies to members of the court's staff. *See* *O'Quinn v. Hall*, 77 S.W.3d 438, 447-48 (Tex. App.—Corpus Christi 2002, no pet.) (because the trial court's staff is an "agent" of the court, trial judge cannot properly state on the record that he is relying on a contested fact conveyed by his staff; such action "created the appearance of bias which rule 605 seeks to prevent"). It is also improper for the judge's law clerk to testify as a witness. *See* *Kennedy v. Great Atl. & Pac. Tea Co.*, 551 F.2d 593, 597-99 (5th Cir. 1977); *see also* *Price Bros. v. Phila. Gear Corp.*, 629 F.2d 444, 446 (6th Cir. 1980) (sending law clerk to get evidence destroys judge's appearance of impartiality).

137. *See* *Bradley*, 990 S.W.2d at 249-50. The *Bradley* court noted that, although aldermen "are not members of the judiciary, they assumed judicial roles in the removal trial, ... which conflicted with their roles as witnesses. ... Their testimony created the appearance of bias that Rule 605 seeks to prevent and such a potential for prejudice ... that inquiry into actual prejudice is fruitless." *Id.* at 249.

At least one federal court has held that the word "testify" should be construed so broadly as to include viewing any evidence outside the context of a judicial proceeding.[138] The court of criminal appeals, however, has used the term "testify" in Rule 605 very narrowly.[139]

Rule 605 does not prohibit a judge from testifying in a trial over which some other judge is presiding. However, even when a judge is not presiding over the proceeding in question, his testimony may be problematic.[140] Canon 2 of the Texas Code of Judicial Conduct states that "[a] judge shall not testify voluntarily as a character witness."[141] Nonetheless, Canon 2 is one of professional behavior, not a rule of evidence, and thus does not dictate whether relevant testimony is admissible. As noted by Jack Weinstein, "a party should not be denied the benefit of character witnesses merely because his friends happen to be judges."[142] Similarly, a judge could testify in a collateral proceeding about the conduct of a trial in which he was the judge.[143] Rule 605 is not violated when a party offers into evidence a signed jury charge from a related trial.[144] However, the Texas Supreme Court has held that a trial judge should not admit into evidence his own written findings of fact from a previous hearing, even if the admission does not technically violate Rule 605.[145]

138. *See, e.g.*, ***Lillie v. United States***, 953 F.2d 1188, 1191 (10th Cir. 1992) (in bench trial, court erred under Rule 605 in viewing accident scene without providing counsel an opportunity to attend; "[w]hen a judge engages in off-the-record fact gathering, he essentially has become a witness in the case"); *see also* ***O'Quinn***, 77 S.W.3d at 447-48 (trial court abused its discretion in relying on information relayed by its court staff that party had been informed on a specific date of trial court's ruling; this was not information that could be judicially noticed, and it gave the appearance of bias by a member of the court's staff as an unsworn witness at the hearing).

139. *See, e.g.*, ***Hammond v. State***, 799 S.W.2d 741, 746-47 (Tex. Crim. App. 1990) (in capital-murder case, trial judge did not err by constructively testifying when he asked court clerk to telephone jurors and tell them that defendant had escaped; although the calls "did inform jurors of a relevant fact not yet in evidence pertaining to the issue of future dangerousness," they were aimed at ensuring jurors' safety and were unrelated to the presentation of evidence at trial); ***In re E.L.W.***, No. 11-16-00010-CV (Tex. App.—Eastland 2017, no pet.) (memo op.; 1-26-17) (under Rule 605, "the question is whether the judge's statement is the functional equivalent of witness testimony"; judge's comments during bench trial, which were made based on personal recollection of events involving party's boyfriend, were not functional equivalent of witness testimony because they did not reveal factual information not already in evidence).

140. *See* ***Great Liberty Life Ins. v. Flint***, 336 S.W.2d 434, 436 (Tex. Civ. App.—Fort Worth 1960, no writ) (prestige, dignity, and authority may be imparted to the prosecution's case by judge's appearance on its behalf).

141. TEX. CODE JUD. CONDUCT, Canon 2(B).

142. 3 WEINSTEIN & BERGER, *supra* note 110, ¶605[01], at 605-08 n.12.

143. *See, e.g.*, ***Castaneda v. Partida***, 430 U.S. 482, 490 (1977) (state judge testified in federal habeas corpus hearing about whether judge's method of instruction and selection of grand-jury commissioners resulted in denial of due process and equal protection); ***Ex parte Bruce***, 112 S.W.3d 635, 638 & n.1 (Tex. App.—Fort Worth 2003, pet. dism'd, untimely filed) (trial judge who had declared mistrial was not barred by Rule 605 from testifying at later hearing on defendant's claim of double jeopardy when a different judge presided over that hearing and the testifying trial judge later recused himself from underlying prosecution); *see also* 2 SALTZBURG ET AL., *supra* note 102, at 893-95 (discussing judicial testimony).

144. *See, e.g.*, ***In re M.E.C.***, 66 S.W.3d 449, 457-58 (Tex. App.—Waco 2001, no pet.) (trial judge's signature on jury charge from mother's trial for termination of parental rights did not violate Rule 605 or constitute "testimony" or "convey factual information not in evidence" in father's trial for termination of parental rights).

145. *See* ***In re M.S.***, 115 S.W.3d 534, 538 (Tex. 2003) ("[O]rders submitted into evidence, containing findings based on pretrial evidence by the very judge presiding over the termination proceeding, could be, like a judicial comment on the weight of the evidence, a form of judicial influence no less proscribed than judicial testimony."); *see, e.g.*, ***In***

The Texas Supreme Court has expanded the scope of Canon 2 to include other judicial testimony, especially expert testimony. In **Joachim v. Chambers**, the supreme court suggested that "the principles of Canon 2 have been treated not only as ethical precepts but as guidelines for determining whether judges should be permitted to testify in specific cases."[146] In this legal-malpractice proceeding, the defendants attempted to use a recently retired district-court judge as their expert witness.[147] The trial court denied the plaintiff's motion to strike the retired judge's deposition testimony, but the supreme court granted the relator-plaintiff's motion for a writ of mandamus and held that Canon 2 prohibits the defendants from calling the retired judge as an expert witness or using his deposition testimony.[148] The court noted that Canon 2 does not prohibit a judge from ever testifying in court,[149] but judicial testimony is only appropriate in an unusual situation.[150] The supreme court explained that testimony given by a judge for either party "confers his very considerable prestige as a judicial officer in support of" that party's position.[151] Further, cross-examination of the judge by the nonsponsoring attorney would likely taint future dealings between that attorney and the judge.[152]

The court of criminal appeals, on the other hand, has held that Rule 605 does not bar a judge who presided over the defendant's criminal trial from testifying in a contested retrospective competency hearing presided over by another judge.[153] The court noted that Rule 605 is unambiguous in addressing only the specific situation in which the judge is presiding at trial: he may not "step down from the bench" and take the witness stand.[154] The court suggested that this very narrow interpretation of Rule 605 fulfills its purpose to preserve the judge's role as a neutral arbiter and his posture of impartiality before the parties and the jury.[155] Whether a judge speaks from the witness

---

re T.T., 39 S.W.3d 355, 359 (Tex. App.—Houston [1st Dist.] 2001, no pet.) (trial judge erred in admitting copy of temporary order he had previously signed in case; "[t]he effect of admitting the judge's written statements in the order was the same as if the judge had violated Rule 605 by testifying to those statements"); *cf. In re S.G.S.*, 130 S.W.3d 223, 242-43 (Tex. App.—Beaumont 2004, no pet.) (harmless error to admit written factual findings signed by one judge in jury trial presided over by another judge).

146. 815 S.W.2d 234, 239 (Tex. 1991).

147. *Id.* at 236.

148. *Id.* at 240; *see also* **Orion Enters., Inc. v. Pope**, 927 S.W.2d 654, 660-61 (Tex. App.—San Antonio 1996, orig. proceeding) (although judge who had previously presided over case was competent under Civil Rule 605 to swear to an affidavit in the reconsideration-of-venue motion before second judge, affidavit was improper under Code of Judicial Conduct; mandamus granted).

149. **Joachim**, 815 S.W.2d at 239. For example, "a judge must, like anyone else, testify to relevant facts within his personal knowledge when summoned to do so." *Id.* The supreme court even opened the door to a judge testifying as an expert in some circumstances (e.g., if he does not reveal that he is a judicial officer). *Id.*

150. *Id.*

151. *Id.* In essence, the judge will have appeared to align himself and his prestige with one side of the litigation, to the obvious detriment of the other party. *See id.* at 239-40.

152. *Id.* at 239-40.

153. **Hensarling v. State**, 829 S.W.2d 168, 170-71 (Tex. Crim. App. 1992).

154. *Id.* at 170.

155. *Id.* at 171.

stand or the bench, however, a jury will likely value his words much more than those of any witness.[156]

Unlike other witness-competency rules, error is not waived by the failure to object to a presiding judge's testimony.[157] Thus, practitioners are spared the Hobson's choice of either objecting and incurring the wrath of the trial judge, who is "likely to feel that his integrity had been attacked," or waiving error by failing to object.[158] However, a party cannot offer the former testimony or written orders of a judge into evidence at a trial over which the judge is presiding and then claim error on appeal.[159]

RULE 606
JUROR'S COMPETENCY AS A WITNESS

(a) At the Trial. A juror may not testify as a witness before the other jurors at the trial. If a juror is called to testify, the court must give a party an opportunity to object outside the jury's presence.

(b) During an Inquiry into the Validity of a Verdict or Indictment.

(1) *Prohibited Testimony or Other Evidence.* During an inquiry into the validity of a verdict or indictment, a juror may not testify about any statement made or incident that occurred during the jury's deliberations; the effect of anything on that juror's or another juror's vote; or any juror's mental processes concerning the verdict or indictment. The court may not receive a juror's affidavit or evidence of a juror's statement on these matters.

(2) *Exceptions.* A juror may testify:

(A) about whether an outside influence was improperly brought to bear on any juror; or

(B) to rebut a claim that the juror was not qualified to serve.

COMMENTARY ON RULE 606

A. Rule 606(a): At the Trial

Under Rule 606(a), which is identical to Federal Rule 606(a), a juror cannot testify as a witness at trial. Common sense prohibits a sitting juror from testifying as a witness in the trial. First, any juror who has sufficient personal knowledge of the facts of

---

156. *See id.* at 173-74 (Maloney, Baird, Overstreet, JJ., dissenting) (judge who testified to his opinion of defendant's competency at the time of the original trial was not an impartial observer, and his testimony in a contested retrospective competency hearing denied the defendant due process).

157. FED. R. EVID. 605; TEX. R. EVID. 605.

158. FED. R. EVID. 605 advisory committee's note.

159. *See, e.g., Franks v. State*, 90 S.W.3d 771, 781 (Tex. App.—Fort Worth 2002, no pet.) (although trial judge's testimony from recusal hearing in case on the merits was improperly admitted under Rule 605, defendant affirmatively offered this evidence and could not complain about it on appeal); *In re M.E.C.*, 66 S.W.3d 449, 455-56 (Tex. App.—Waco 2001, no pet.) (party could not offer evidence of trial judge's signature on prior temporary orders and then complain on appeal that his own exhibit was a judicial comment on the evidence).

the case is automatically disqualified to act as an impartial, unbiased juror.[160] Second, other jurors might give his testimony greater or lesser weight depending on their assessment of him from conversations and conduct in the jury room.[161] Third, the opposing party might be hesitant in cross-examining a juror-witness for fear of antagonizing him or his fellow jurors.[162]

Strangely, even though the impropriety of calling a sitting juror to testify is obvious, the "automatic" objection under Rule 605 does not apply.[163] The opponent must object to preserve error, but the objection may be made outside the presence of the jurors.[164]

The rule applies only to testimony before the jury;[165] thus, jurors may be called out individually from the jury room during trial to testify to whether they have read any newspaper articles, overheard any improper conversations, or been subjected to any other outside influence.[166]

B. Rule 606(b): During an Inquiry into the Validity of a Verdict or Indictment

1. History of the rule. Under early common law, litigants in civil cases were relatively free to "try the jury" at the end of a trial on the merits.[167] This practice was terminated by Lord Mansfield, who, consistent with his philosophy that no official should testify about his own shortcomings, excluded all testimony of jurors describing jury misconduct.[168] Mansfield's common-law rule was followed in Texas until 1905,[169] when

---

160. 27 WRIGHT & GOLD, *supra* note 21, §6072, at 387; *see Gregory v. St. Louis Sw. Ry. Co.*, 377 S.W.2d 847, 852-54 (Tex. Civ. App.—Texarkana 1964) (misconduct for juror to seek out personal knowledge of the case; jurors are not allowed to testify), *rev'd on other grounds*, 387 S.W.2d 27 (Tex. 1965); 1 GOODE ET AL., *supra* note 24, §606.1, at 386 (juror would not be able to weigh his own testimony).

161. *See* 1 GOODE ET AL., *supra* note 24, §606.1, at 534 (other jurors might give undue weight to the testimony of a juror-witness); 27 WRIGHT & GOLD, *supra* note 21, §6072, at 387 (discussing the potential impact of juror testimony on the rest of the jury).

162. 1 GOODE ET AL., *supra* note 24, §606.1, at 534.

163. Rule 605 specifies that no objection is necessary to preserve the point when a presiding judge testifies. TEX. R. EVID. 605. Rule 606 does not have a similar provision.

164. *See* TEX. R. EVID. 606(a).

165. 1 GOODE ET AL., *supra* note 24, §606.1, at 534.

166. Cases interpreting Federal Rule 606(a) hold that juror testimony is not prohibited at a hearing about outside influences on the jury and their effects. *See United States v. Day*, 830 F.2d 1099, 1104-05 (10th Cir. 1987) (jurors can testify in a hearing on publicity and extent of contact with outsiders); *United States v. Robinson*, 645 F.2d 616, 618 (8th Cir. 1981) (jurors can testify in a hearing on such issues as publicity or tampering with jurors).

167. *See Colyer v. State*, 428 S.W.3d 117, 122-23 (Tex. Crim. App. 2014) ("[A]fter the jury trial, the jury was tried."); 1 RAY, *supra* note 4, §393, at 380 (juror testimony and affidavits were always admissible under the common law); 8 JOHN H. WIGMORE, EVIDENCE IN TRIALS AT COMMON LAW §2352, at 696 (McNaughton rev. 1961) (same); David E. Keltner, *Jury Misconduct in Texas: Trying the Trier of Fact*, 34 Sw. L.J. 1131, 1131 (1981) (Lord Mansfield's 1785 decision that excluded juror testimony was a radical departure from early common law).

168. *See Peña-Rodriguez v. Colorado*, ___ U.S. ___, 137 S. Ct. 855, 863 (2017); *Vaise v. Delaval*, 99 Eng. Rep. 944, 944 (K.B. 1785). The rule was viewed as promoting the finality of verdicts and protecting jurors from outside influences. *Warger v. Shauers*, ___ U.S. ___, 135 S. Ct. 521, 526 (2014).

169. *See Golden Eagle Archery, Inc. v. Jackson*, 24 S.W.3d 362, 367 (Tex. 2000); *St. Louis Sw. Ry. Co. v. Ricketts*, 96 Tex. 68, 71, 70 S.W. 315, 317 (1902).

the Legislature passed a statute[170] that evolved into Texas Rule of Civil Procedure 327. Texas courts interpreted this rule as permitting juror testimony about jury misconduct, including events or statements occurring during jury deliberations, as long as the jurors did not discuss their own mental processes.[171]

Civil Rule 606(b), after which the unified Rule 606(b) was modeled, changed the evidentiary rules fostered by Texas Rule of Civil Procedure 327 and its corresponding case law by changing the subject matter of the affidavit and testimony admissible under Rule of Civil Procedure 327. Under Civil Rule 606(b), a juror's testimony was restricted solely to the question of whether any outside influence was improperly brought to bear on any juror.[172] Thus, a juror could not testify about events or statements occurring during jury deliberations.[173] The rule expressly continued the former rule that disallowed testimony about the effect of such statements or events on a juror's mind or mental processes.[174] It also continued the rule that forbade jurors from testifying that the jury's verdict was contrary to the findings of some, but not all, of the jurors.[175]

RULE 606

---

170. Act of Feb. 24, 1905, 29th Leg., R.S., ch. 18, 1905 Tex. Gen. Laws 21 (juror testimony permitted on issues of jury misconduct at hearing on motion for new trial) (current version at TEX. R. CIV. P. 327). The history of Texas statutory and common law on the admissibility of evidence of jury misconduct and the problems encountered in applying the former Texas rule is fully treated by other authorities. *See generally* 1 RAY, *supra* note 4, §§393-394, at 380-85 (discussing the history of the common law (§393) and Texas law (§394) on the issue of juror testimony regarding jury misconduct); Keltner, *supra* note 167 (discussing the evolution and application of the former Texas rule); Jack Pope, *The Mental Operations of Jurors*, 40 TEX. L. REV. 849, 853-66 (1962) (using the distinction between mental processes and overt acts as a guideline in discussing the history of Texas law on the admissibility of evidence of jury misconduct).

171. *See Strange v. Treasure City*, 608 S.W.2d 604, 606 (Tex. 1980) (although overt acts may be considered, testimony on the mental processes of the jury must be disregarded); *Trousdale v. Tex. & N.O. R. Co.*, 264 S.W.2d 489, 492-93 (Tex. Civ. App.—San Antonio 1953) (rule includes statements made during deliberations but excludes testimony on juror's mental processes), *aff'd*, 154 Tex. 231, 276 S.W.2d 242 (1955); Pope, *supra* note 170, at 850 (under the 1905 Texas rule, jurors could testify about overt conduct during deliberations but not about their mental processes); *see, e.g., Flores v. Dosher*, 622 S.W.2d 573, 575 (Tex. 1981) (juror testimony of statement made during deliberations was allowed, but evidence of jury's mental processes was excluded from consideration in determining misconduct).

172. *See* Linda L. Addison, *Conduct Unbecoming a Jury: Rule 606(b)*, 50 TEX. B.J. 872, 872 (1987) (unless outside influence can be shown, court can refuse to permit testimony on juror misconduct); M. Joseph Copeland, Comment, *The Room Without a View: Inquiries into Jury Misconduct After the Adoption of Texas Rule of Evidence 606(b)*, 38 BAYLOR L. REV. 965, 965-66 (1986) (under Rule 606(b), jurors may not testify about events or statements occurring during deliberations).

173. Allowing testimony on outside influence is the sole exception to Rule 606(b)'s general prohibition against juror testimony relating "to any matter or statement occurring during the course of the jury's deliberations." *See Robinson Elec. Supply Co. v. Cadillac Cable Corp.*, 706 S.W.2d 130, 132 (Tex. App.—Houston [14th Dist.] 1986, writ ref'd n.r.e.) (noting the change from earlier law, which permitted a juror to testify to matters, statements, and overt acts occurring during deliberations, and which insulated only jurors' mental processes).

174. *See Strange*, 608 S.W.2d at 606 (juror testimony about mental processes of jurors must be disregarded); *see also* 1 RAY, *supra* note 4, §396, at 387 (policy of certainty and finality of the verdict underlies Rule 606(b)).

175. *See H.E. Butt Grocery Co. v. Pais*, 955 S.W.2d 384, 387-88 (Tex. App.—San Antonio 1997, no pet.) (only if there is a unanimous mistake in the nature of a clerical error may a jury's verdict be undermined or impeached; jurors may not testify to their mistakes resulting from confusion, misunderstanding, or misinterpretation of the instructions or of the evidence); *Branham v. Brown*, 925 S.W.2d 365, 368 (Tex. App.—Houston [1st Dist.] 1996, no writ) ("A juror's doubts and misgivings, uncertainty, hesitancy, and mental reservations about the verdict do not destroy a verdict.").

The change that Civil Rule 606(b) made in Texas law generated controversy[176] because it theoretically insulated serious jury misconduct from exposure.[177] However, the former rule was difficult to administer because of the vague line between admissible evidence of overt acts and inadmissible evidence of mental processes.[178] Additionally, most lawyers and judges recognized that encouraging losing parties in jury trials to initiate wholesale review of jury deliberations was undesirable.[179]

For example, in *Tanner v. United States*, the U.S. Supreme Court held that denial of a post-verdict evidentiary hearing after the defendant's conviction for mail fraud was not error despite affidavits from several jurors stating that during the trial, numerous jurors drank alcohol at noon recess, several smoked marijuana regularly, at least two ingested cocaine, and one juror sold a quarter pound of marijuana to another juror.[180]

---

176. For example, Rule 606(b) was opposed at the public hearing held at the State Bar meeting in June 1982. Interim Study IV, *supra* note 10, at 22-23 (June 29, 1982) (testimony of Mr. Dave Kruger, Officer, Texas Association of Defense Counsel). *See generally* **Robinson Elec. Supply**, 706 S.W.2d at 134-35 (Draughn, J., concurring) (discussing the inequities of Rule 606(b)); Susan Crump, *Jury Misconduct, Jury Interviews, and the Federal Rules of Evidence: Is the Broad Exclusionary Principle of Rule 606(b) Justified?*, 66 N.C. L. Rev. 509, 520-25 (1988) (Rule 606(b) does not serve desired policy objectives); Copeland, *supra* note 172, at 972-75 (Rule 606(b) insulates jury misconduct from review).

177. Many forms of serious misconduct can occur during jury deliberations. *See* **Strange**, 608 S.W.2d at 606-09 (discussing a number of objectionable statements made during deliberations). For instance, a juror might make a statement about a party's economic status. *See, e.g.*, **Scoggins v. Curtiss & Taylor**, 148 Tex. 15, 19, 219 S.W.2d 451, 453 (1949) (juror stated during deliberations that plaintiff did not need any consideration in the suit because he was "not a poor man").

178. *See generally* 1 Ray, *supra* note 4, §§394-396, at 381-89 (collecting circumstances held to constitute overt acts and inquiry into juror mental processes); Pope, *supra* note 170, at 864-65 (discussing the difficulties inherent in applying the distinction).

179. *See* **Soliz v. Saenz**, 779 S.W.2d 929, 935 (Tex. App.—Corpus Christi 1989, writ denied) (insulating jury deliberations from review prevents the delay, expense, and uncertainty associated with frivolous attacks on jury verdicts). *See generally* 1 Goode et al., *supra* note 24, §606.2, at 535-36 (listing policy considerations against allowing unlimited attack on jury verdicts); 27 Wright & Gold, *supra* note 21, §6072, at 389-404 (discussing complex policy considerations underlying Rule 606(b)). Cases after the 1998 unification of the Rules have also suggested the following public-policy reasons for prohibiting testimony about statements made during jury deliberations: "(1) keeping jury deliberations private to encourage candid discussion of a case, (2) protecting jurors from post-trial harassment or tampering, (3) preventing a disgruntled juror whose view did not prevail from overturning the verdict, and (4) protecting the need for finality." **Ford Motor Co. v. Castillo**, 279 S.W.3d 656, 666 (Tex. 2009); *see* **Golden Eagle Archery, Inc. v. Jackson**, 24 S.W.3d 362, 367 (Tex. 2000); **Colyer v. State**, 428 S.W.3d 117, 123-24 (Tex. Crim. App. 2014). The *Castillo* court noted that "[d]iscovery involving jurors will not be appropriate in most cases, but in this case there was more than just a suspicion that something suspect occurred—there was some circumstantial evidence that it did." 279 S.W.3d at 666.

The Advisory Committee's note to Federal Rule 606(b) reads as follows: "The mental operations and emotional reactions of jurors in arriving at a given result would, if allowed as a subject of inquiry, place every verdict at the mercy of jurors and invite tampering and harassment." Fed. R. Evid. 606 advisory committee's note, subdiv. (b). It is improper for the parties to impeach a verdict based on what jurors tell them about their deliberations, and it is equally improper for a trial court to grant a new trial based on its ex parte conversation with jurors. *See* **Peterson v. Wilson**, 141 F.3d 573, 577-78 (5th Cir. 1998) (impeachment of jury verdict on the basis of information obtained by a trial judge who met privately with jurors after their verdict constitutes abuse of discretion per se). In *Peterson*, the trial court granted the defendant a new trial with the cryptic statement that it had concluded, based on juror comments, that "the jury completely disregarded the Court's instructions [and] considered improper factors in reaching its verdict." *Id.* at 575.

180. 483 U.S. 107, 115-16, 127 (1987). Excluding these affidavits did not violate the defendant's Sixth Amendment right to a trial by an impartial jury. *Id.* at 126-27; *see* **Warger v. Shauers**, ___ U.S. ___, 135 S. Ct. 521, 529 (2014). For a discussion of *Warger*, refer to notes 255-259 *infra* and accompanying text.

One juror's affidavit stated that he "'felt like ... the jury was on one big party.'"[181] The Court noted that "[t]here is little doubt that postverdict investigation into juror misconduct would in some instances lead to the invalidation of verdicts reached after irresponsible or improper juror behavior. It is not at all clear, however, that the jury system could survive such efforts to perfect it."[182] Allowing jury verdicts to be attacked on the basis of juror misconduct undermines the finality of judgments,[183] threatens the privacy of the deliberation process,[184] and encourages jury tampering.[185] The Texas Supreme Court and Texas Court of Criminal Appeals have discussed the balance between "the goal of a trial by a jury free from bias or misconduct" and the policy reasons that losing parties should not be permitted to "try the jury" after its verdict.[186] Those courts, like the U.S. Supreme Court, have struck the balance in favor of the privacy of juror deliberations.[187]

While the Texas Supreme Court narrowed the scope of inquiry into jury deliberations by adopting Civil Rule 606(b) in 1983, the Texas Court of Criminal Appeals expanded that scope in adopting its peculiar version of Rule 606(b) in the Criminal Rules of Evidence in 1986. Although the civil and criminal versions began with the same language, which generally barred post-trial juror testimony, the last phrase of the lengthy first sentence of the Criminal Rule seemingly contradicted the first part of the rule when

RULE 606

181. *Tanner*, 483 U.S. at 115.

182. *Id.* at 120; *see Colyer*, 428 S.W.3d at 124 (juror-misconduct rule "protects a good system that cannot be made perfect"). In 2017, the U.S. Supreme Court acknowledged the impracticality of attempting to address all juror misconduct but determined that the Sixth Amendment requires an exception to the no-impeachment rule in certain criminal cases. *See Peña-Rodriguez v. Colorado*, ___ U.S. ___, 137 S. Ct. 855, 868-69 (2017). The no-impeachment rule must give way when a juror makes a clear statement indicating he relied on racial stereotypes or racial animus in convicting the defendant. *Id.* at ___, 137 S. Ct. at 869. Refer to notes 208-214 *infra* and accompanying text.

183. *Tanner*, 483 U.S. at 120; *see Sims' Crane Serv., Inc. v. Ideal Steel Prods., Inc.*, 800 F.2d 1553, 1556 n.9 (11th Cir. 1986) (Rule 606(b) places greater weight on finality by eliminating continual attacks on verdicts); *United States v. Moten*, 582 F.2d 654, 664 (2d Cir. 1978) (allowing unlimited attack on jury verdicts undermines public interest in finality and casts judges as "Penelopes, forever engaged in unravelling the webs they wove").

184. *See McDonald v. Pless*, 238 U.S. 264, 267-68 (1915) (effect of allowing a post-trial attack on the verdict is to invade the privacy of the deliberation process, which threatens juror candor and freedom of discussion); *Robinson Elec. Supply Co. v. Cadillac Cable Corp.*, 706 S.W.2d 130, 132 (Tex. App.—Houston [14th Dist.] 1986, writ ref'd n.r.e.) (Rule 606(b) is designed to insulate the majority of the deliberation process from review to promote full discussion during deliberations and reduce juror harassment).

185. *See McDonald*, 238 U.S. at 267-68 (permitting jurors to attack their verdict in post-trial proceedings encourages juror harassment by the defeated party in an effort to secure evidence that will establish jury misconduct); *Mattox v. United States*, 146 U.S. 140, 148-49 (1892) (allowing post-trial attacks gives a single juror the power to overturn the verdict and thus encourages jury tampering); *United States v. Eagle*, 539 F.2d 1166, 1170 (8th Cir. 1976) (same); *Robinson Elec. Supply*, 706 S.W.2d at 132 (Rule 606(b) is designed in part to reduce juror harassment).

186. *Golden Eagle Archery, Inc. v. Jackson*, 24 S.W.3d 362, 366-67 (Tex. 2000); *Colyer*, 428 S.W.3d at 124.

187. *See Golden Eagle*, 24 S.W.3d at 367; *Colyer*, 428 S.W.3d at 124; *see also Davis v. State*, 119 S.W.3d 359, 365 (Tex. App.—Waco 2003, pet. ref'd) (limiting a juror's testimony about jury deliberations under Rule 606(b) is not unconstitutional in criminal cases); *Thomas v. State*, 84 S.W.3d 370, 371-72 (Tex. App.—Beaumont 2002, pet. ref'd) (per curiam) (trial court did not abuse its discretion in denying defendant's motion for new trial based on juror misconduct under Rule 606(b); juror's affidavit and testimony that she had been "assaulted" by other jurors during deliberations was not evidence of improper influence); *Chavarria v. Valley Transit Co.*, 75 S.W.3d 107, 111 (Tex. App.—San Antonio 2002, no pet.) (under Rule 606(b), court could not consider juror affidavits claiming that one juror told others that she had visited the accident scene on "breaks" during initial deliberations; once deliberations had begun, even "breaks" taken during that process fall under the protection of Rule 606(b)).

---

it stated: "except that a juror may testify as to any matter relevant to the validity of the verdict or indictment."[188] This exception swallowed the general rule prohibiting jurors from testifying to their mental processes and conduct during deliberations. The rule was called "deceptively worded,"[189] "internally self-contradictory,"[190] and "rather convoluted."[191] As a result, most Texas courts simply interpreted Criminal Rule 606(b) as a continuation of the law as it developed under the former statute, Texas Code of Criminal Procedure article 40.03.[192] In *Buentello v. State*, the court of criminal appeals addressed the meaning and significance of the exception in former Criminal Rule 606(b).[193] It noted that while the Texas Rules generally follow the Federal Rules and the federal courts' interpretation of those rules, the court of criminal appeals had in

---

188. Former Criminal Rule 606(b) read as follows:

(b) Inquiry Into Validity of Verdict or Indictment. Upon an inquiry into the validity of a verdict or indictment, a juror may not testify as to any matter or statement occurring during the course of the jury's deliberations or to the effect of anything upon his or any other juror's mind or emotions as influencing him to assent to or dissent from the verdict or indictment or concerning his mental processes in connection therewith, except that a juror may testify as to any matter relevant to the validity of the verdict or indictment. Nor may his affidavit or evidence of any statement by him concerning a matter about which he would be precluded from testifying be received for these purposes.

TEX. R. CRIM. EVID. 606(b), 701-702 S.W.2d (Tex. Cases) XLVII (1986, amended 1998).

189. 1 GOODE ET AL., *supra* note 24, §606.3, at 545.

190. *Rose v. State*, 752 S.W.2d 529, 544 (Tex. Crim. App. 1987) (Teague, J., concurring in part and dissenting in part).

191. *Buentello v. State*, 770 S.W.2d 917, 918 (Tex. App.—Amarillo 1989), *rev'd on other grounds*, 826 S.W.2d 610 (Tex. Crim. App. 1992).

192. Act approved June 18, 1965, 59th Leg., R.S., ch. 722, 1965 Tex. Gen. Laws 476, *amended by* Act approved June 14, 1973, 63rd Leg., R.S., ch. 399, §2(A), 1973 Tex. Gen. Laws 973, *amended by* Act approved June 14, 1973, 63rd Leg., R.S., ch. 426, art. 3, §5, 1973 Tex. Gen. Laws 1127 (former Code of Criminal Procedure art. 40.03 deemed repealed as to criminal proceedings effective 1986) [now codified as TEX. R. APP. P. 21.3]; *see Brown v. State*, 804 S.W.2d 566, 569 (Tex. App.—Houston [14th Dist.] 1991, pet. ref'd) ("A matter is relevant to the validity of the verdict or indictment if it concerns an overt act which constitutes jury misconduct under [former TEX. R. APP. P. 30(b), now TEX. R. APP. P. 21.3] and its predecessor TEX. CODE CRIM. PROC. art. 40.03."); *Hernandez v. State*, 774 S.W.2d 319, 325 (Tex. App.—Dallas 1989, pet. ref'd) ("[T]he law in the area of jury misconduct is not changed by [Criminal R]ule 606(b)."). *But see Reese v. State*, 772 S.W.2d 288, 291 (Tex. App.—Waco 1989, pet. ref'd) (per curiam) (plain language of Criminal Rule 606(b) indicates that jurors are not completely immune from testifying at hearing on motion for new trial).
In criminal cases, jurors were incompetent to impeach their verdicts by affidavit or testimony about their deliberations except to show an overt act of jury misconduct such as the discussion of parole law, the receipt of evidence that was not introduced at trial, or the discussion of a defendant's failure to testify. *See, e.g.*, *Sneed v. State*, 670 S.W.2d 262, 266 (Tex. Crim. App. 1984) (to demonstrate reversible error, a defendant must establish "(1) a misstatement of the law; (2) asserted as a fact; (3) by one professing to know the law; (4) which is relied upon by other jurors; (5) who for that reason changed their vote to a harsher punishment"); *Hunt v. State*, 603 S.W.2d 865, 868-69 (Tex. Crim. App. [Panel Op.] 1980) (if new evidence detrimental to the defendant is received by the jury, the case should be remanded); *Barnett v. State*, 847 S.W.2d 678, 679 n.3 (Tex. App.—Texarkana 1993, no pet.) (juror's testimony about discussions of a defendant's failure to testify was assumed to be competent evidence under Criminal Rule 606(b)). At least one Texas court put a strange twist on traditional case law on juror misconduct by stating that "a juror *may testify* to the fact that the impermissible conduct occurred, but *may not testify* to the actual content of the statement or statements constituting the impermissible conduct." *Hernandez*, 774 S.W.2d at 325. This interpretation would leave courts in the anomalous position of admitting a juror's conclusion that an overt act of misconduct occurred in the jury room but excluding any account of precisely what that conduct was.

193. 826 S.W.2d 610, 612-14 (Tex. Crim. App. 1992). The court admitted that the rule "does not lend itself to easy application due to the clear internal contradiction between the first and second part of the rule." *Id.* at 612.

tentionally drafted Criminal Rule 606(b) "to allow for impeachment of the verdict through all relevant testimony as to both internal and external influences."[194] The court of criminal appeals expressly rejected the intermediate courts' attempts to draw a line between jurors' "overt acts" and their mental processes when ruling on jury misconduct and held that the sole test for admission of juror testimony is whether the testimony is deemed relevant by the trial judge.[195]

Thus, under former Criminal Rule 606(b), jurors who had served in a Texas criminal proceeding could later be called to testify to "any matter" at all as long as it was "relevant to the validity of the verdict." The right to unlock the jury deliberation room was limited only by the trial court's discretion.[196] The result and reasoning in **Buentello** was harshly criticized as destructive of the secrecy of jury deliberations and as a rule that would likely result in the harassment of jurors.[197] The 1998 version of Rule 606(b) rejected the **Buentello** line of cases.[198] Under the unified Rule 606(b), the same rule that

---

194. *Id.* at 613; *see also* **Garrett v. State**, 946 S.W.2d 338, 341 (Tex. Crim. App. 1997) (Overstreet & Baird, JJ., dissenting from dismissal of petition for discretionary review) ("The drafters of Texas Rule 606(b) determined that the federal rule was too narrow and this Court adopted a broad exception that allowed for the impeachment of the verdict through all relevant testimony as to both internal and external influences.").

195. **Buentello**, 826 S.W.2d at 614. "What is considered 'relevant' will be determined on a case-by-case basis, taking into account the court's experiences and observations, the grounds for a new trial set forth in [former TEX. R. APP. P. 30(b), now TEX. R. APP. P. 21.3], and the caselaw which was developed under the predecessor to 30(b), Art. 40.03, V.A.C.C.P." *Id.*; *see Lewis v. State*, 911 S.W.2d 1, 11 (Tex. Crim. App. 1995) (trial judge has broad discretion in deciding what is "relevant" under this standard). In **Buentello**, affidavits and testimony stating that jurors had discussed the applicability of early release on parole when assessing the defendant's sentence were relevant and admissible at the hearing on the defendant's motion for new trial. 826 S.W.2d at 615-16; *see also* **Valdez v. State**, 893 S.W.2d 721, 724 (Tex. App.—Austin 1995, pet. ref'd) (trial judge did not abuse his discretion in permitting jurors' testimony on discussion of parole law during jury deliberations). Although the court of criminal appeals did not define the outer boundaries of what was relevant to the validity of the verdict, at a minimum Criminal Rule 606(b) carried forward earlier Texas law. Thus, jurors were competent to testify either in person or by affidavit in post-trial hearings when (1) the verdict had been decided by lot or in any other manner than by a fair expression of opinion by the jurors, (2) a juror had received a bribe to convict or had been guilty of any other corrupt conduct, (3) the jury received other evidence after retiring to deliberate, (4) a juror had conversed with any other person in regard to the case, (5) a juror became so intoxicated that his verdict was likely influenced, or (6) the court found that the jury had engaged in such misconduct that the accused had not received a fair and impartial trial. TEX. R. APP. P. 21.3(c), (d), (f), (g); *see, e.g.,* **Buentello**, 826 S.W.2d at 615-16 (jury's discussion of parole law was jury misconduct and so detrimental that defendant was deprived of a fair and impartial trial); **Bearden v. State**, 648 S.W.2d 688, 692-93 (Tex. Crim. App. 1983) (new trial granted when a juror added outside testimony); **Duncan v. State**, 138 Tex. Crim. 172, 178, 135 S.W.2d 111, 114 (1939) (case remanded for new trial after jurors used secret ballots to reach guilty verdict).

196. **Buentello**, 826 S.W.2d at 613.

197. *See* **Dunkins v. State**, 838 S.W.2d 898, 900-01 (Tex. App.—Texarkana 1992, pet. ref'd). In **Dunkins**, the Texarkana Court of Appeals minced no words in arguing that the court of criminal appeals had destroyed the protection of the jurors' private decision-making process "because the **Buentello** opinion encourages losing defense counsel in future cases to make inquiries of all the jurors about everything that occurred in the jury room, including their mental processes." **Dunkins**, 838 S.W.2d at 900.

198. **Hicks v. State**, 15 S.W.3d 626, 630 (Tex. App.—Houston [14th Dist.] 2000, pet. ref'd); **Hines v. State**, 3 S.W.3d 618, 621 (Tex. App.—Texarkana 1999, pet. ref'd). In **Hines**, the Texarkana Court of Appeals held that amended Rule 606(b) does not conflict with Texas Rule of Appellate Procedure 21.3, which requires a trial judge to grant a new trial for various acts of jury misconduct. 3 S.W.3d at 621-22. The court stated that

> Texas Rule of Evidence 606(b) now defines jury misconduct as only outside influence that was improperly brought to bear upon any juror, whereas TEX. R. APP. P. 21.3(g) only states that a new trial

had applied to offering the testimony or affidavits of jurors in Texas civil cases[199] also applies to criminal cases.

2. Current Rule 606(b).

(1) Rule 606(b)(1): Prohibited testimony or other evidence. Rule 606(b)(1) prohibits juror testimony about "any statement made or incident that occurred during the jury's deliberations; the effect of anything on that juror's or another juror's vote; or any juror's mental processes concerning the verdict or indictment."[200] This principle is generally referred to as the no-impeachment rule.[201] As before the adoption of Rule 606(b), jurors are still forbidden to testify about their recollection of the evidence introduced[202] or their reservations about the verdict.[203] Jurors also cannot testify that they decided the verdict by lot,[204] that they decided the case based on another juror's incorrect statement of applicable law,[205] that they read or did not read the jury charge aloud in the jury room as instructed by the trial court,[206] or that the jury discussed the defendant's failure to testify and used that failure as a basis for conviction.[207]

---

should be granted where jury misconduct deprived the defendant of a fair and impartial trial. We conclude that Tex. R. Evid. 606(b) is more specific and thus is the controlling statute.
Hines, 3 S.W.3d at 622. Rule 606(b), however, does not attempt to define what constitutes jury misconduct; it simply states that the only time evidence of jury misconduct is admissible through a juror's testimony or affidavit is when that misconduct was the result of an outside influence. *See* ***White v. State***, 225 S.W.3d 571, 574-75 (Tex. Crim. App. 2007) ("Rule 606(b) does not prevent appellant from demonstrating such 'significant harm' by use of non-juror evidence."); ***Sanders v. State***, 1 S.W.3d 885, 887 (Tex. App.—Austin 1999, no pet.) ("[T]he rule does not preclude proof of jury misconduct by other means, such as through the testimony of a nonjuror with personal knowledge of the misconduct.").

199. Refer to notes 172-179 *supra* and accompanying text.

200. Tex. R. Evid. 606(b)(1). Rule 606(b)(1) is identical to Federal Rule 606(b)(1). The federal rule has been held to bar juror testimony on four topics: (1) the method of deliberation or the arguments of the jurors, (2) the effect of any particular thing on an outcome in the deliberations, (3) the mindset or emotions of any juror during deliberations, and (4) the testifying juror's own mental processes during deliberations. ***Pyles v. Johnson***, 136 F.3d 986, 991 (5th Cir. 1998). The Texas rule applies only to jurors, not to bailiffs. *E.g.*, ***Hayes v. State***, 484 S.W.3d 554, 557 & n.1 (Tex. App.—Amarillo 2016, pet. ref'd) (Rule 606(b) did not prohibit bailiff's testimony about his comment to jurors that parties were discussing plea bargain; several jurors also testified about what bailiff said, but State did not object to that aspect of their testimony).

201. ***Peña-Rodriguez v. Colorado***, ___ U.S. ___, 137 S. Ct. 855, 861 (2017).

202. *See, e.g.*, ***Speer v. State***, 890 S.W.2d 87, 91-92 (Tex. App.—Houston [1st Dist.] 1994, pet. ref'd) (affidavits setting out jurors' understanding and recollection of evidence at trial could not be considered under Criminal Rule 606(b) in deciding whether there was sufficient evidence of remuneration or promise of remuneration as element of capital murder).

203. *See* Tex. R. Evid. 606(b)(1); *see, e.g.*, ***Tompkins v. State***, 869 S.W.2d 637, 641 (Tex. App.—Eastland 1994) (juror's private reservations about her verdict did not demonstrate jury misconduct, and thus trial court did not err in striking post-verdict juror affidavits), *pet. dism'd, improvidently granted*, 888 S.W.2d 825 (Tex. Crim. App. 1994).

204. *See* Tex. R. Evid. 606(b)(1).

205. In ***Salazar v. State***, the court of criminal appeals left open the question of whether a Rule 606(b) objection would preclude a defendant from proving that the jury relied on a misstatement of parole law in reaching a harsher punishment. 38 S.W.3d 141, 147-48 (Tex. Crim. App. 2001). In that case, both the State and the defendant withdrew their Rule 606(b) objections, so the court could not decide the issue. *Salazar*, 38 S.W.3d at 147.

206. *See* ***Casanova v. State***, 383 S.W.3d 530, 543-44 (Tex. Crim. App. 2012). Generally, there is a presumption that "jurors follow the trial court's explicit instructions to the letter." *Id.* at 543; *see* ***Thrift v. State***, 176 S.W.3d 221, 224 (Tex. Crim. App. 2005). The court of criminal appeals has not determined, however, to what extent Rule 606(b) might restrict a party's ability to overcome this presumption. *See* ***Casanova***, 383 S.W.3d at 544 & n.57 (court did not de-

In 2017, the U.S. Supreme Court held that the no-impeachment rule must give way when a juror makes a clear statement indicating he relied on racial stereotypes or racial animus in convicting a criminal defendant.[208] Allowing the no-impeachment rule to prevent consideration of evidence of such a statement violates a defendant's Sixth Amendment trial right.[209] The Court distinguished racial bias from the juror misconduct in cases such as **Tanner v. United States**[210] by explaining that racial bias is "a familiar and recurring evil that, if left unaddressed, would risk systemic injury to the administration of justice."[211] The Court found that the safeguards of voir dire, juror reports before the verdict, and nonjuror evidence after the trial may be less effective at uncovering racial bias than they are at uncovering other forms of juror misconduct.[212] Under the Court's holding in **Peña-Rodriguez v. Colorado**, inquiry into a juror's racial bias may proceed if there is a showing that "one or more jurors made statements exhibiting overt racial bias that cast serious doubt on the fairness and impartiality of the jury's deliberations and resulting verdict."[213] The statement must tend to demonstrate that the juror's racial bias was a "significant motivating factor" in the juror's vote to convict the defendant.[214]

---

cide issue because "[n]either the State nor the [defendant] has offered affidavits or testimony from any juror to show whether or not the jury actually did read the jury charge aloud in the jury room, as instructed").

207. *See* TEX. R. EVID. 606(b)(1); *cf.* **United States v. Rutherford**, 371 F.3d 634, 639-40 (9th Cir. 2004) (Federal Rule 606(b) bars consideration of juror affidavits or testimony stating that jurors discussed a defendant's failure to testify during deliberations because that discussion does not concern extraneous facts or outside influence).

208. **Peña-Rodriguez v. Colorado**, ___ U.S. ___, 137 S. Ct. 855, 869 (2017).

209. *See id.*

210. 483 U.S. 107 (1987).

211. **Peña-Rodriguez**, ___ U.S. at ___, 137 S. Ct. at 868. In **Peña-Rodriguez v. Colorado**, the Court explained that cases such as **McDonald v. Pless**, 238 U.S. 264, 267-68 (1915), **Tanner**, and **Warger v. Shauers**, ___ U.S. ___, 135 S. Ct. 521, 529-30 (2014), involved "anomalous behavior from a single jury—or juror—gone off course." **Peña-Rodriguez**, ___ U.S. at ___, 137 S. Ct. at 868. In **McDonald**, the jury allegedly calculated a damages award by averaging the jurors' submissions. 238 U.S. at 265-66. In **Warger**, a juror allegedly lied about her pro-defendant bias during voir dire but was nevertheless seated on the jury and selected as foreperson. ___ U.S. at ___, 135 S. Ct. at 524. The **Peña-Rodriguez** Court observed that "neither history nor common experience show that the jury system is rife with mischief of these or similar kinds." ___ U.S. at ___, 137 S. Ct. at 868. The Court in **Warger**, however, warned of "juror bias so extreme that, almost by definition, the jury trial right has been abridged. If and when such a case arises, the Court can consider whether the usual safeguards are or are not sufficient to protect the integrity of the process." ___ U.S. at ___, 135 S. Ct. at 529 n.3. For a discussion of **Tanner**, refer to notes 180-185 *supra* and accompanying text; for a discussion of **Warger**, refer to notes 255-259 *infra* and accompanying text.

212. **Peña-Rodriguez**, ___ U.S. at ___, 137 S. Ct. at 868-69.

213. *E.g., id.* at ___, 137 S. Ct. at 869-70 (on motion for new trial, court should have considered evidence from two jurors that another juror made statements expressing anti-Hispanic bias toward defendant and one of defendant's witnesses).

214. *Id.* at ___, 137 S. Ct. at 869. The trial court has substantial discretion to determine whether the threshold showing is satisfied. *Id.* The Supreme Court did not address "what procedures a trial court must follow when confronted with a motion for new trial based on juror testimony of racial bias" or decide the appropriate standard for determining when a new trial must be granted on these grounds. *Id.* at ___, 137 S. Ct. at 870.

(2) Exceptions under Rule 606(b).

(a) Rule 606(b)(2)(A): Outside influence.

[1] Under the Texas rule. Texas Rule 606(b) allows a juror to testify about whether "outside influence" was improperly brought to bear.[215] The term "outside influence" is not defined in the rule, but courts have interpreted it to refer to only that information that emanates from outside the courtroom, the jury room, and the formal deliberative process.[216] The Texas Court of Criminal Appeals has clarified that information does not have to be communicated by someone other than a juror to be considered an outside influence, noting that "such a definition [requiring communication from a nonjuror] is far more narrow than the plain meaning of the rule requires."[217] This broader view marks a shift from the interpretation used by the courts of appeals.[218] Under the former interpretation, information gathered by one of the jurors, such as a visit to the scene of the event,[219] or derived from specialized expertise that was not introduced into

---

215. Tex. R. Evid. 606(b)(2)(A); *see* ***Ford Motor Co. v. Castillo***, 279 S.W.3d 656, 666 (Tex. 2009); *see also* ***Ocon v. State***, 284 S.W.3d 880, 886 (Tex. Crim. App. 2009) (party moving for mistrial on grounds of juror misconduct has the burden to request that jurors be questioned about outside influence). In ***Castillo***, the supreme court applied Rule 606(b) and Texas Rule of Civil Procedure 327(b) to a case that settled before a verdict was rendered because "the policies inherent in those rules are implicated by this record and the positions of the parties." 279 S.W.3d at 666.

216. *See* ***Golden Eagle Archery, Inc. v. Jackson***, 24 S.W.3d 362, 370 (Tex. 2000) (outside influence must originate "from sources other than the jurors themselves"); ***McQuarrie v. State***, 380 S.W.3d 145, 151 (Tex. Crim. App. 2012) (plain language of Rule 606(b) suggests that outside influence is something outside of both jury room and juror); ***White v. State***, 225 S.W.3d 571, 574 (Tex. Crim. App. 2007) (same); ***Editorial Caballero, S.A. de C.V. v. Playboy Enters., Inc.***, 359 S.W.3d 318, 324 (Tex. App.—Corpus Christi 2012, pet. denied) (outside influence must come from a source outside the jury and its deliberations); ***Perry v. Safeco Ins.***, 821 S.W.2d 279, 281 (Tex. App.—Houston [1st Dist.] 1991, writ denied) (Texas Rules of Evidence and Texas Rules of Civil Procedure do not define "outside influence," but case law defines term narrowly); *see also* ***Tanner v. United States***, 483 U.S. 107, 117-18 (1987) (rigid distinction based only on whether information is introduced inside or outside the jury room is unhelpful).

217. ***McQuarrie***, 380 S.W.3d at 151. The court examined the history of Rule 606(b), including the interplay with Federal Rule 606(b). *See* ***McQuarrie***, 380 S.W.3d at 151-52. Ultimately, the court determined that "we do not believe that the history of Rule 606(b) dictates that we adopt a more narrow construction of the rule than the plain language suggests." ***McQuarrie***, 380 S.W.3d at 152. For a comparison of the Texas and federal rules, refer to notes 247-268 *infra* and accompanying text.

218. *See* ***Wooten v. S. Pac. Transp. Co.***, 928 S.W.2d 76, 79 (Tex. App.—Houston [14th Dist.] 1995, no writ) ("[I]t is well-established that, to constitute outside influence, information must come from outside the jury, *i.e.*, from a non-juror who introduces information to affect the verdict ...."); ***Durbin v. Dal-Briar Corp.***, 871 S.W.2d 263, 272 (Tex. App.—El Paso 1994, writ denied) (under Civil Rule 606(b), the only evidence of jury misconduct that trial court may consider is that of information not in evidence that comes from a nonjuror; "[i]nformation introduced into deliberations by a member of the jury, even if submitted with the intention of influencing and prejudicing a verdict, is not outside influence"), *disapproved on other grounds*, ***Golden Eagle Archery, Inc. v. Jackson***, 24 S.W.3d 362 (Tex. 2000); ***McQuarrie***, 380 S.W.3d at 157-58 (Keller, P.J., Cochran, J., dissenting) (four courts of appeals have held that outside influence must emanate from outside the jury and its deliberations, "and these courts have expressed a narrow view of what emanated from outside the jury"). For further discussion of the dissents in ***McQuarrie***, refer to note 252 *infra*.

219. *See, e.g.*, ***Chavarria v. Valley Transit Co.***, 75 S.W.3d 107, 110-11 (Tex. App.—San Antonio 2002, no pet.) (under Rule 606(b), court could not consider juror affidavit claiming that one juror told others that she had visited the accident scene on "breaks" during deliberations; once deliberations had begun, even "breaks" taken during that process fall under the protection of Rule 606(b)); ***Wooten***, 928 S.W.2d at 78-79 (juror's statement that, based on his past experiences and observations, he thought the intersection where accident occurred was safe was not an "outside influence"). In ***Soliz v. Saenz***, one juror asked if other jurors had been to the bar where the defendant, according to his testimony, became intoxicated before crashing into the plaintiff's car. 779 S.W.2d 929, 932 (Tex. App.—Corpus

evidence[220] would not constitute an outside influence; however, that same information conveyed to the jurors by a bailiff or other unauthorized person would.[221] The court of criminal appeals in *McQuarrie* criticized this narrow reading of the rule, saying that "[t]he potential for absurd results is clear."[222] In that case, the court held that a juror's Internet research constituted an outside influence because it (1) occurred outside of the jury room and outside of deliberations and (2) originated from a source other than the jurors themselves.[223]

The court of criminal appeals in *McQuarrie v. State* clarified that, although it was adopting a broader definition of "outside influence" than the one used by the courts of appeals, inquiries into deliberations are still prohibited.[224] Trial courts can question jurors about outside influence without delving into deliberations by "limiting the questions asked of the jurors to the nature of the unauthorized information or communication and then conducting an objective analysis to determine whether there is a reasonable possibility that it had a prejudicial effect on the 'hypothetical average juror.'"[225]

Christi 1989, writ denied). At least five other jurors stated that they had been to the bar and agreed that the noise level was high. *Id.* This information reduced the persuasiveness of the defendant's argument that the establishment should have known he was drunk by the level of his voice. *Id.* The court held that such information amounted to a juror's injection of personal experience but did not amount to an outside influence. *Id.*

220. *See, e.g., Kendall v. Whataburger, Inc.*, 759 S.W.2d 751, 755-56 (Tex. App.—Houston [1st Dist.] 1988, no writ) (paralegal-juror's statements about negligence and proximate-cause issues did not amount to an "outside influence" under Civil Rule 606(b) and were not admissible on the issue of jury misconduct); *Baker v. Wal-Mart Stores, Inc.*, 727 S.W.2d 53, 54-55 (Tex. App.—Beaumont 1987, no writ) (per curiam) (nurse-juror's statement that medication plaintiff was taking could cause drowsiness or dizziness and could cause her to fall from the ladder was not an "outside influence" under Civil Rule 606(b)).

221. *Soliz*, 779 S.W.2d at 932. Texas Code of Criminal Procedure article 36.22 specifically prohibits unauthorized communication with jurors about the trial. The purpose of this provision is to "insulate jurors from outside influence." *Ocon v. State*, 284 S.W.3d 880, 884 (Tex. Crim. App. 2009); *see Chambliss v. State*, 647 S.W.2d 257, 266 (Tex. Crim. App. 1983) (purpose of article 36.22 "is to prevent *an outsider* from saying anything that might influence a juror").

222. 380 S.W.3d at 151. The court continued:

> To illustrate, under the narrow definition, if a juror in a DWI trial sneaks out to the defendant's car during the lunch break and sees a bottle of whiskey on the passenger seat, that is not an outside influence. But if a third party tells the juror about the whiskey bottle, that would be an outside influence.

Id.

223. *Id.* at 154; *see also Ryser v. State*, 453 S.W.3d 17, 41 (Tex. App.—Houston [1st Dist.] 2014, pet. ref'd) (juror obtained dictionary definition of term that was not defined in statute or jury charge and shared this information during deliberations; definition was outside influence). It is unclear if the holding in *McQuarrie* will affect civil cases, particularly those involving Internet research. *See, e.g., Editorial Caballero, S.A. de C.V. v. Playboy Enters., Inc.*, 359 S.W.3d 318, 325-26 (Tex. App.—Corpus Christi 2012, pet. denied) (no outside influence when juror conducted Internet research and read appellate decision from first trial of case); *In re Atun*, No. 09-16-00334-CV (Tex. App.—Beaumont 2016, orig. proceeding) (memo op.; 12-15-16) (jurors' testimony about a fellow juror's Internet search during jury deliberations was improper and violated Rule 606 and Texas Rule of Civil Procedure 327(b)).

224. *See McQuarrie*, 380 S.W.3d at 154.

225. *Id.*; *see, e.g., Balderas v. State*, 517 S.W.3d 756, 782-83, 785-86 (Tex. Crim. App. 2016) (trial court and defense counsel asked jurors about conduct of defendant's brother that constituted alleged outside influence and how that conduct was likely to affect jurors' ability to serve in case), *cert. denied*, 137 S. Ct. 1207 (2017). Trial courts often instruct juries that they must consider only the testimony and exhibits admitted into evidence, and the jury instructions in the Texas Rules of Civil Procedure address the problem of jurors conducting their own online research. *See* Tex. R. Civ. P. 226a, 284; John G. Browning, *Social Media in the Jury Box*, 34th Annual Advanced Civil Trial

Coercive influence by one juror over the other jurors is not an "outside influence,"[226] nor is the discussion of a juror's own personal experiences or knowledge.[227] Even the presence of an "absolutely disqualified" juror—for example, one with a prior conviction for theft—who participates in jury deliberations is not an "outside influence" under Rule 606(b).[228] The *McQuarrie* court explained that "[a] Rule 606(b) inquiry is limited to that which occurs outside of the jury room and outside of the juror's personal knowledge and experience."[229] In *Colyer v. State*, the court of criminal appeals further clarified the scope of the "outside influence" exception: "[N]ot everything that comes from outside the jury room qualifies as an outside influence for purposes of the rule. The 'outside influence' exception in Rule 606(b) does not include influences or information that are unrelated to the trial issues."[230] The court explained that an outside influence must "*improperly* affect[] a juror's verdict in a particular

---

Course, State Bar of Texas CLE, ch. 6, p. 5 (2011). See *O'Connor's Texas Rules * Civil Trials* (2017), "Juror Communication," ch. 8-A, §9, p. 785. The following is a proposed jury instruction, which would do more to educate jurors about why they must not conduct any outside research:

> In our daily lives we may be used to routinely looking for information online, on Google, or on social media. In a trial it can be very tempting for jurors to do their own research or to look up a definition of a term to make sure they are making the correct decision. You must resist that temptation for our system of justice to work as it should. The information you find may be inaccurate, out-of-date, or incomplete, or it may not apply to the case for another reason. The parties are entitled to have a trial based on evidence and information that they know about, and it is only fair that the parties have the opportunity to refute, explain, or correct any evidence that you consider. For these reasons, I specifically instruct that you must decide the case only on the evidence received here in court and on the law that I give you.

Emily Johnson-Liu, McQuarrie *Jurors: "Who Needs Sworn Testimony when We've Got Google?"*, THE PROSECUTOR, Jan.-Feb. 2013, vol. 43, no. 1, www.tdcaa.com/print/10802.

226. *Colyer v. State*, 428 S.W.3d 117, 125 (Tex. Crim. App. 2014); *Mitchell v. S. Pac. Transp. Co.*, 955 S.W.2d 300, 322 (Tex. App.—San Antonio 1997, no writ), *disapproved on other grounds*, *Golden Eagle Archery, Inc. v. Jackson*, 24 S.W.3d 362 (Tex. 2000); *see, e.g.*, *Romero v. State*, 396 S.W.3d 136, 152-53 (Tex. App.—Houston [14th Dist.] 2013, pet. ref'd) (juror testimony sought by defendant about intimidation and harassment by other jurors was not permissible under Rule 606(b) because it concerned matters and statements occurring during jury deliberations); *Thomas v. State*, 84 S.W.3d 370, 371-72 (Tex. App.—Beaumont 2002, pet. ref'd) (per curiam) (juror's affidavit and testimony that she had been "assaulted" by other jurors during deliberations was not evidence of improper influence under Rule 606(b)).

227. *Colyer*, 428 S.W.3d at 125; *McQuarrie*, 380 S.W.3d at 153; *Mitchell*, 955 S.W.2d at 322; *see, e.g.*, *Ex parte Parra*, 420 S.W.3d 821, 826-27 (Tex. Crim. App. 2013) (in trial for aggravated sexual assault of a child, defendant argued ineffective assistance of counsel based on attorney's failure to question juror about whether she had been a victim of sexual assault as a child; because juror's personal experiences are not an outside influence under Rule 606(b), court of criminal appeals refused to consider affidavit from another juror contending that challenged juror claimed during deliberations that she had been sexually abused as a child).

228. *See White v. State*, 225 S.W.3d 571, 574 (Tex. Crim. App. 2007).

229. 380 S.W.3d at 153.

230. 428 S.W.3d at 127. In that case, the defendant moved for a new trial based on juror misconduct and offered the testimony of the jury foreman as his only evidence. *Id.* at 120. The foreman testified that several "outside influences" affected his verdict, citing the time of day the verdict was reached, the distance to the parking lot, impending bad weather, and a desire to get home quickly to his sick daughter. *Id.* at 120-21. The trial court denied the motion for new trial, and the court of appeals reversed. *Id.* at 121. The court of criminal appeals reversed the judgment of the court of appeals and affirmed the judgment of the trial court because the factors cited by the foreman were unrelated to the trial issues and thus were not "outside influences" under Rule 606(b). *Colyer*, 428 S.W.3d at 127-29.

manner—for or against a particular party."[231] Outside influences do not, however, result in automatic reversals.[232]

The Texas Supreme Court has held that premature juror discussions about the merits of the lawsuit that occur before the jury is properly charged with the case do not constitute "deliberations" for purposes of Rule 606(b).[233] Thus, Rule 606(b) does not bar a party from (1) offering post-verdict juror affidavits or testimony that one or more jurors discussed the merits of the case before the jury charge, (2) setting out the content of those conversations, and (3) seeking a new trial because of that juror misconduct.[234] Two of the justices, however, suggested that the rule should be amended to apply not just to formal jury deliberations but also to "the course of deliberations" and all actions and statements (excluding outside influences) that occur once the jury is impaneled.[235]

[2] Under the federal rule. As with Texas Rule 606(b), Federal Rule 606(b) allows a juror to testify about whether outside influence was improperly brought to bear.[236] The term "outside influence" is not defined under Federal Rule 606(b), but it could be interpreted to include "any private communication, contact, or tampering, directly or indirectly, with a juror during a trial about the matter pending before the jury ...."[237] The appropriate inquiry in this situation is "whether the unauthorized conduct or contact is potentially prejudicial, not whether the parties alleged to have tampered with the jury did so intentionally."[238] Juror testimony and affidavits are admissible under Federal

---

231. *Id.* at 129. The pressures in this case may have influenced the jury to reach a verdict more quickly, but they did not favor one party over the other. *Id.* As the court concluded, "[e]xternal events or information, unrelated to the trial, which happen to cause jurors to feel personal pressure to hasten (or end) deliberations are not 'outside influences' because those pressures are caused by a juror's personal and emotional reaction to information that is irrelevant to the trial issues." *Id.* at 125.

232. *E.g.*, ***Ryser v. State***, 453 S.W.3d 17, 42-43 (Tex. App.—Houston [1st Dist.] 2014, pet. ref'd) (juror's use of dictionary to define term that was not defined in statute or jury charge was outside influence, but definition was compatible with word's common meaning and did not conflict with jury charge; outside influence was harmless error); *see Colyer*, 428 S.W.3d at 129.

233. ***Golden Eagle Archery, Inc. v. Jackson***, 24 S.W.3d 362, 371-72 (Tex. 2000) (rejecting reasoning of cases that had held that improper juror discussions before jury was formally charged were "deliberations" for purposes of Rule 606(b)). *But see id.* at 377 (Abbott, J., concurring) (disagreeing with court's "narrow interpretation" of the word "deliberations" and arguing that juror comments to each other during the course of trial "are part of the deliberative process and should be cloaked with the protection [of Rule 606(b)]").

234. *See id.* at 372 ("Juror testimony is still permitted on the issues of juror misconduct, communications to the jury, and erroneous answers on voir dire, provided such testimony does not require delving into deliberations."); *see also **Noland v. State***, 264 S.W.3d 144, 152-54 (Tex. App.—Houston [1st Dist.] 2007, pet. ref'd) (affidavit alleged that jurors discussed evidence during breaks before all evidence had been heard, but there was no showing that any alleged juror misconduct influenced the jury's verdict, that the jurors discussed evidence with nonjurors, or that they discussed inadmissible or outside evidence; trial court properly denied motion for new trial); ***Pena v. State***, 102 S.W.3d 450, 455 (Tex. App.—Eastland 2003, no pet.) (Rule 606(b) would not bar consideration of discharged juror's affidavit or testimony about her conversations with other jurors before her discharge because she was excused before formal jury deliberations began).

235. ***Golden Eagle***, 24 S.W.3d at 375 (Hecht & Owen, JJ., concurring).

236. *See* FED. R. EVID. 606(b)(2)(B). Texas Rule 606(b)(2)(A) is identical to Federal Rule 606(b)(2)(B).

237. ***Remmer v. United States***, 347 U.S. 227, 229 (1954) (predating the Federal Rules of Evidence).

238. ***United States v. Rutherford***, 371 F.3d 634, 641-42 (9th Cir. 2004).

Rule 606(b) to demonstrate both the existence of such conduct and the effect of that conduct on a juror's state of mind (e.g., his general fear and anxiety) but not on whether the conduct actually influenced his vote or deliberations.[239] However, it is "not the mere fact of [jury] infiltration ... but the nature of what has been infiltrated and the probability of prejudice" that is at issue in the "outside influence" inquiry.[240] Jurors may testify to the occurrence of an outside influence, as well as the nature and content of that outside influence, but they may not testify about how that occurrence may have affected their vote.[241] The trial judge must resolve the issue of whether jury misconduct has resulted in prejudice to one of the parties by drawing reasonable inferences about the probable effect of the misconduct on a hypothetical average juror.[242]

(b) Rule 606(b)(2)(B): Juror not qualified to serve. A provision in Texas Rule 606(b) explicitly permits a juror to testify (or submit an affidavit) to rebut a claim that he was not qualified to serve as a juror.[243] It does not, however, expressly permit him to testify that he was, in fact, disqualified to serve as a juror.[244] Rule 606(b) protects only the sanctity of the jury deliberation room; it does not insulate the persons who went into the jury room from scrutiny of their fitness to serve.

(3) No equal-protection violation. Texas courts have held that neither Rule 606(b) nor Texas Rule of Civil Procedure 327 violates a party's equal-protection rights because these rules are rationally related to the legitimate state interests in promoting full and open discussions during jury deliberation and in reducing juror harassment.[245] Similarly, the rules do not violate due process or the right to a fair and impartial trial

---

239. *See* Fed. R. Evid. 606(b)(1); *Rutherford*, 371 F.3d at 644-45.

240. *United States ex rel. Owen v. McMann*, 435 F.2d 813, 818 (2d Cir. 1970); *see Manley v. Ambase Corp.*, 337 F.3d 237, 251-52 (2d Cir. 2003) (although court clerk's communication with juror was improper, it was harmless).

241. *See Pyles v. Johnson*, 136 F.3d 986, 991 (5th Cir. 1998) ("'Post-verdict inquiries into the existence of impermissible influences on a jury's deliberations are allowed under appropriate circumstances so that a jury-man may testify to any facts bearing upon the question of the *existence* of any extraneous influence, although not as to how far that influence operated upon his mind.'" (quoting *Llewellyn v. Stynchcombe*, 609 F.2d 194, 196 (5th Cir. 1980))); *McMann*, 435 F.2d at 819-20 (jurors may testify to facts contributing extraneous influence but not to the effect of those facts); *see also Bayramoglu v. Estelle*, 806 F.2d 880, 887 (9th Cir. 1986) (listing factors that courts should consider when deciding complaints that extrinsic material was injected into jury deliberations).

242. *See United States v. Howard*, 506 F.2d 865, 869 (5th Cir. 1975) ("[T]he district court is precluded from investigating the subjective effects of any breach on any jurors, whether such effects might be shown to affirm or negate the conclusion of actual prejudice."); *see also Haley v. Blue Ridge Transfer Co.*, 802 F.2d 1532, 1537 & n.9 (4th Cir. 1986) (if there is competent evidence of extraneous communication, presumption of prejudice arises; prevailing party must prove no reasonable possibility of improper influence).

243. *See* Tex. R. Evid. 606(b)(2)(B). Texas Government Code §62.102 sets out the minimum threshold requirements for juror qualification in either civil or criminal proceedings, and §62.105 states the general disqualifications for jury service in a particular case. See *O'Connor's Texas Rules * Civil Trials* (2017), "Qualifications & Exemptions of Jurors," ch. 8-A, §3, p. 769. Code of Criminal Procedure articles 35.16 and 35.19 set out additional matters that affect the qualifications of a juror in a criminal case.

244. *See White v. State*, 225 S.W.3d 571, 574-75 (Tex. Crim. App. 2007) (trial court properly prohibited statutorily disqualified jurors from testifying about potential harm to defendant caused by their presence on jury; mere presence of disqualified juror is not "outside influence" under Rule 606(b)).

245. *See Soliz v. Saenz*, 779 S.W.2d 929, 934 (Tex. App.—Corpus Christi 1989, writ denied).

---

because they serve the legitimate state interest in avoiding unjustifiable expense and delay by preventing parties from arbitrarily attacking the validity of the verdict.[246]

(4) Differences between federal and Texas rules. Texas Rule 606(b)(1) and Federal Rule 606(b)(1) are identical;[247] however, Federal Rule 606(b)(2) has two exceptions in addition to the ones in Texas Rule 606(b)(2).[248] The federal rule allows jurors to testify about mistakes in entering the verdict onto the verdict form.[249] It also permits testimony about whether "extraneous prejudicial information was improperly brought to the jury's attention."[250] The Texas Supreme Court deleted this phrase from the rule proposed by the Liaison Committee.[251] The extent of the difference between the rules generally depends on how the phrase "extraneous prejudicial information" is defined.[252] One interpretation is that the term refers to any matter that is not properly in evidence

---

246. *Id.* at 934-35; *see* **Glover v. State**, 110 S.W.3d 549, 551-52 (Tex. App.—Waco 2003, pet. ref'd); **Sanders v. State**, 1 S.W.3d 885, 888 (Tex. App.—Austin 1999, no pet.). Several Texas appellate courts have also rejected the argument that Rule 606(b) is unconstitutional. *See* **Davis v. State**, 119 S.W.3d 359, 365-66 (Tex. App.—Waco 2003, pet. ref'd) (Rule 606(b) is not unconstitutional in criminal cases); **Hines v. State**, 3 S.W.3d 618, 622 (Tex. App.—Texarkana 1999, pet. ref'd) (Rule 606(b) presumed to be constitutional); **Sanders**, 1 S.W.3d at 888 (both federal and state courts have upheld constitutionality of Rule 606(b) and its prohibition against jurors testifying to jury misconduct).

247. Refer to note 200 *supra.*

248. Federal Rule 606(b)(2) also does not have an exception for rebutting a claim that a juror was not qualified to serve. *See* TEX. R. EVID. 606(b)(2)(B). Refer to notes 243-244 *supra* and accompanying text.

249. FED. R. EVID. 606(b)(2)(C). This change responds to the divergence in case law that had established a narrow and a broad exception for the use of juror testimony: (1) to prove clerical errors in entering the verdict and (2) to prove jurors misunderstood the consequences of the result on which they had agreed. *See* FED. R. EVID. 606 advisory committee's note to 2006 amendments. The amendment rejects the broader exception permitting juror testimony to prove that jurors misunderstood the consequences of the result on which they agreed because an inquiry into such matters goes to the jurors' mental processes underlying the verdict, rather than the accuracy of the verdict based on the jurors' agreement. *Id.*; *see* **Robles v. Exxon Corp.**, 862 F.2d 1201, 1208 (5th Cir. 1989) (error to consider juror testimony that goes to the "substance of what the jury was asked to decide, necessarily implicating the jury's mental processes insofar as it questions the jury's understanding of the court's instructions and application of those instructions to the facts of the case"). The exception encompassed by the amendment is limited to cases such as "'where the jury foreperson wrote down, in response to an interrogatory, a number different from that agreed upon by the jury, or mistakenly stated that the defendant was 'guilty' when the jury had actually agreed that the defendant was not guilty.'" FED. R. EVID. 606 advisory committee's note to 2006 amendments, subdiv. (b) (quoting **Robles**, 862 F.2d at 1208); *see* **Plummer v. Springfield Terminal Ry. Co.**, 5 F.3d 1, 3 (1st Cir. 1993) ("[J]uror testimony regarding an alleged clerical error, such as announcing a verdict different than that agreed upon, does not challenge the validity of the verdict or the deliberation or mental processes, and therefore is not subject to Rule 606(b)."). At least one Texas court of appeals has referred to the same exception. *See* **H.E. Butt Grocery Co. v. Pais**, 955 S.W.2d 384, 387-88 (Tex. App.—San Antonio 1997, no pet.) (jurors can testify about unanimous clerical mistake).

250. FED. R. EVID. 606(b)(2)(A).

251. *See* TEX. R. EVID. 606(b) (1982 Liaison Committee proposal), *reprinted infra* p. 1087 (including the phrase); *Re: New Rules of Evidence*, 641-642 S.W.2d (Tex. Cases) LII (1983, amended 1998) (deleting the phrase). The Liaison Committee eliminated the phrase "or indictment" in Rule 606(b) because criminal indictments are irrelevant to civil proceedings. Nonetheless, the phrase found its way back into the rule as promulgated. *See Re: New Rules of Evidence*, 641-642 S.W.2d (Tex. Cases) LII (1983, amended 1998).

252. The Texas Supreme Court "did not explain the significance of its decision to reject an exception for extraneous prejudicial information, leaving scholars to speculate whether the Texas rules are more restrictive than the federal rule." **Golden Eagle Archery, Inc. v. Jackson**, 24 S.W.3d 362, 368 (Tex. 2000); *see* **Salazar v. Dretke**, 419 F.3d 384, 402 n.30 (5th Cir. 2005) (practical effect of difference in language between Texas Rule 606(b) and Federal Rule 606(b) is not easily understood); **McQuarrie v. State**, 380 S.W.3d 145, 152 (Tex. Crim. App. 2012) ("Debate exists as to the significance of the omission of the 'extraneous prejudicial information' exception in Texas Rule of Evidence 606(b)."). Based on this uncertainty and after examining the history of Texas Rule 606(b), the **McQuarrie**

but is considered by the jury.[253] This definition would allow a juror in federal court to testify that matters not in evidence, such as insurance, the plaintiff's bad character, or a juror's personal knowledge of the facts of the case, were discussed during jury deliberations. Such a definition, however, is inconsistent with Rule 606(b)'s general prohibition against juror testimony about "any statement made or incident that occurred during the jury's deliberations."[254] In essence, all statements made in the jury room are "not properly in evidence." Defining "extraneous prejudicial information" in such terms results in an exception that is broader than the underlying general rule.[255] This position is obviously insupportable. Indeed, jurors are encouraged to consider generalized knowledge or facts of common knowledge that have not been introduced into evidence.[256] Discussion of this "general knowledge" by jurors is not only proper but also frequently the subject of judicial instruction.[257]

court decided to adopt a broader view of the term "outside influence" in Rule 606(b) than previous courts had. *See McQuarrie*, 380 S.W.3d at 152. Refer to notes 217-223 *supra* and accompanying text. But the dissents in *McQuarrie* concluded that such a broad interpretation should be restricted to the federal rule and should not be applied to the Texas rule. *See McQuarrie*, 380 S.W.3d at 160-61 (Keller, P.J., Cochran, J., dissenting) ("[W]hatever dispute or uncertainty there is or may have been among scholars or the federal courts about the meaning of the Texas rule, our own courts of appeals seem to be in agreement: the term 'outside influence' does not encompass information gathering by a juror that does not involve communicating with other people. ... Given the more restrictive nature of the Texas rule, we should conclude ... that internet research [although covered by the federal rule] does not constitute an outside influence [under the Texas rule] so long as the juror does not receive a communication from a person outside the jury."); *id.* at 166-67 (Cochran, Keller, Price, Womack, JJ., dissenting) ("[T]he Texas Supreme Court intentionally deleted the extraneous prejudicial information exception. Although it offered no explanation for its action, the most plausible explanation is that the Court was consciously trying to curtail the widespread, and widely criticized, practice of trying the jury. ... Having adopted the Supreme Court's version of the rule, we ought not change its meaning and content without first (1) consulting that court, and (2) changing the wording of the rule to explicitly incorporate the federal exception for extraneous prejudicial information.") (internal quotes omitted).

253. *See* 1 GOODE ET AL., *supra* note 24, §606.2, at 538-39 ("extraneous" is defined in terms of extra record material); 27 WRIGHT & GOLD, *supra* note 21, §6075, at 444-45 ("extraneous" implies facts or data not received in open court).

254. FED. R. EVID. 606(b)(1); TEX. R. EVID. 606(b)(1).

255. *See Warger v. Shauers*, ___ U.S. ___, 135 S. Ct. 521, 530 (2014) ("We cannot agree that whenever a juror should have been excluded from the jury, anything that juror says is necessarily 'extraneous' within the meaning of [Federal] Rule 606(b)(2)(A). [Under this interpretation,] all evidence of what that juror said during deliberations would be admissible. The 'extraneous' information exception would swallow much of the rest of Rule 606(b)."). In *Warger*, the Court held that Rule 606(b) does not allow a party to use a juror's affidavit about what another juror said in deliberations to show that juror's dishonesty during voir dire. ___ U.S. at ___, 135 S. Ct. at 524. That is, the fact that a juror might have been struck for incompetence or bias during voir dire does not make evidence about that juror's statements during deliberations admissible. *Id.* at ___, 135 S. Ct. at 530.

256. *See Gov't of V.I. v. Gereau*, 523 F.2d 140, 151 (3d Cir. 1975) (jurors do not need to be "totally ignorant about a case"; jurors may have generalized knowledge about the parties and events of the lawsuit); *see, e.g., Warger*, ___ U.S. at ___, 135 S. Ct. at 529 (juror's statements about daughter's car accident were not extraneous prejudicial information; "[juror's] daughter's accident may well have informed her general views about negligence liability for car crashes, but it did not provide either her or the rest of the jury with any specific knowledge" about crash at issue in case); *Womble v. J.C. Penney Co.*, 431 F.2d 985, 989 (6th Cir. 1970) (juror comments about their personal experiences were generalized background information and not impermissible extraneous material). In *Fields v. Brown*, the jury foreman made notes "for" and "against" imposition of the death penalty, which included Biblical quotes and references. 503 F.3d 755, 777 (9th Cir. 2007). He brought these notes to the deliberations the next day and shared them with the other jurors. *Id.* at 777-78. The Ninth Circuit suggested the notes were not extraneous prejudicial information, calling the Bible verses "notions of general currency." *Id.* at 780; *see Robinson v. Polk*, 438 F.3d 350, 364 (4th Cir. 2006) ("[R]eading the Bible is analogous to the situation where a juror quotes the Bible from memory, which assuredly would not be considered an improper influence."); *see also Lucero v. State*, 246 S.W.3d 86, 95 n.10 (Tex.

Another interpretation of "extraneous prejudicial information" suggests that the term refers to information that is external to the jury rather than information that is outside the record.[258] The Supreme Court explained in *Warger* that "'[e]xternal' matters include publicity and information related specifically to the case the jurors are meant to decide, while 'internal' matters include the general body of experiences that jurors are understood to bring with them to the jury room."[259] Some commentators, however, suggest that the word "extraneous" describes information that is outside the scope of the admissible evidence revealed in open court rather than external to the jurors themselves. The Advisory Committee's note to Federal Rule 606(b) is less than helpful in distinguishing between the two interpretations:

> Under the federal decisions the central focus has been upon insulation of the manner in which the jury reached its verdict, and this protection extends to each of the components of deliberation, including arguments, statements, discussions, mental and emotional reactions, votes, and any other feature of the process. ... The policy does not, however, foreclose testimony by jurors as to prejudicial extraneous information or influences injected into or brought to bear upon the deliberative process.[260]

There is little point to using two distinct phrases, "extraneous prejudicial information" and "outside influence," if they cover the same ground. Thus, those courts and commentators that have read the phrase "extraneous prejudicial information" as including irregular behavior on the part of the jurors themselves have the better theoretical argument. Under this interpretation, Federal Rule 606(b) permits jurors to testify to their consideration of information derived from books and newspapers brought into the jury room by a juror,[261] objects not admitted into evidence,[262] and experiments in

---

Crim. App. 2008) (discussing *Fields*). *But see* ***Oliver v. Quarterman***, 541 F.3d 329, 340 (5th Cir. 2008) (jurors' consultation of Bible passages and comparison of facts of case to passage about appropriateness of capital punishment was improper external influence on jury deliberations; harmless error because defendant offered no evidence to rebut state court's finding that Bible did not prejudice jury's decision); ***Williams v. Kelley***, 858 F.3d 464, 477 (8th Cir. 2017) (Kelly, J., concurring in part and dissenting in part) ("The jury's group reliance on the Bible ... indicates that the jury relied on extraneous information in sentencing [defendant] to death."), *cert. denied*, 137 S. Ct. 1842 (2017).

257. *See, e.g.*, ***In re Beverly Hills Fire Litig.***, 695 F.2d 207, 214 & n.7 (6th Cir. 1982) (jury instructed to use judgment and common sense).

258. *See* 27 WRIGHT & GOLD, *supra* note 21, §6075, at 445 n.12. *But see* 1 GOODE ET AL., *supra* note 24, §606.2, at 538-39 (best interpretation is not to read the exclusion so narrowly).

259. *Warger*, ___ U.S. at ___, 135 S. Ct. at 529. Refer to note 255 *supra* and accompanying text.

260. FED. R. EVID. 606 advisory committee's note, subdiv. (b) (citations omitted).

261. *See, e.g.*, ***Mattox v. United States***, 146 U.S. 140, 147-49 (1892) (newspaper); ***United States v. Calbas***, 821 F.2d 887, 895-96 (2d Cir. 1987) (telephone directory).

262. *See, e.g.*, ***Farese v. United States***, 428 F.2d 178, 179-80 (5th Cir. 1970) (defendant's shirt was properly admitted as evidence, but neither prosecution nor defense had discovered large amount of cash in shirt pocket; jury discovered the money, which had not been introduced or admitted as evidence, after retiring for deliberations and improperly considered it in reaching verdict).

the jury room[263] or elsewhere whose results are reported to other jurors,[264] as well as specialized information that one juror communicates to others.[265]

Texas Rule 606(b), which permits jurors in both civil and criminal cases to testify post-verdict only to any "outside influence," appears to preserve the finality of verdicts and the sanctity of the jury room even more than Federal Rule 606(b), which permits juror testimony on "extraneous prejudicial information" as well.[266] The Texas Supreme Court's conscious deletion of that phrase is some indication that it wanted to curtail the practice of relitigating a jury's verdict in post-trial proceedings.[267] Despite the potential for improper jury conduct during the deliberative process, Texas Rule 606(b) favors the finality of jury verdicts.[268]

RULE 607
WHO MAY IMPEACH A WITNESS

Any party, including the party that called the witness, may attack the witness's credibility.

COMMENTARY ON RULE 607

Adoption of Rule 607, which might be described as wide-open impeachment, marked an important change in Texas law. The traditional view had been that a party

---

263. *See, e.g.,* **Simon v. Kuhlman**, 488 F. Supp. 59, 67-68 (S.D.N.Y. 1979) (habeas corpus petitioner was entitled to a hearing on whether an experiment conducted by jurors that involved placing a stocking over one juror's face violated petitioner's constitutional rights; Federal Rule 606(b) permits juror testimony on how the experiment came about, who was involved, any discussion of the results, and at what point in the deliberations the experiment took place).

264. *See, e.g.,* **In re Beverly Hills Fire Litig.**, 695 F.2d 207, 214-15 (6th Cir. 1982) (new trial was required when juror conducted experiment at home and reported results to other jurors).

265. *See generally* 3 DAVID W. LOUISELL & CHRISTOPHER B. MUELLER, FEDERAL EVIDENCE §288, at 133-42 (1979) (discussing the scope of "extraneous" information); 3 JACK B. WEINSTEIN & MARGARET A. BERGER, WEINSTEIN'S EVIDENCE, STUDENT EDITION, ¶606[04], at 606-14 to 606-16 (2005), at 18-19 (Supp. 2005) (discussing the scope of "extraneous" information in state and federal courts).

266. *See* FED. R. EVID. 606(b)(2)(A); TEX. R. EVID. 606(b)(2)(A). But the court of criminal appeals in **McQuarrie v. State** seemed to find that the difference between the "outside influence" exception and the "extraneous prejudicial information" exception was not so great. *See* Johnson-Liu, *supra* note 225. Refer to notes 217-225, 252 *supra* and accompanying text.

267. *See* **Kirby Forest Indus., Inc. v. Kirkland**, 772 S.W.2d 226, 234 (Tex. App.—Houston [14th Dist.] 1989, writ denied) (amended Civil Rule 606(b) adopts a stringent "outside influence" test that excludes most of the deliberation process from scrutiny); **Robinson Elec. Supply Co. v. Cadillac Cable Corp.**, 706 S.W.2d 130, 132-33 (Tex. App.—Houston [14th Dist.] 1986, writ ref'd n.r.e.) (supreme court expressly rejected the more liberal federal rule); 1 GOODE ET AL., *supra* note 24, §606.2, at 540 (supreme court deleted the "extraneous prejudicial information" language in a conscious attempt to curtail the widespread practice of relitigating the jury's verdict).

268. *See* **Casanova v. State**, 383 S.W.3d 530, 544 (Tex. Crim. App. 2012) (defendant's inability to offer testimony about whether jury read charge aloud is "just another one of the unavoidable systemic costs imposed by the policy of jury insulation that Rule 606(b) favors"). Wright and Gold suggest a more effective way of analyzing the tension between finality and reliability of the result than Federal Rule 606(b) creates. They argue that the balance should be struck by considering whether the "extra-record" information that the jury evaluates could be properly done without the assistance of the adversary process. *See* 27 WRIGHT & GOLD, *supra* note 21, §6075, at 452 (if information is general and most jurors would be expected to know it, deliberation process may be sufficient to eliminate unreliability, but if information is complex, deliberation process might be insufficient).

"vouched" for its witnesses[269] and could not impeach them unless the witness's testimony had caused surprise and injury.[270] The policy behind the traditional rule had been severely criticized by evidence scholars.[271] The Advisory Committee's note to Federal Rule 607, which is identical to the Texas rule, indicated that

> [t]he traditional rule against impeaching one's own witnesses is abandoned as based on false premises. A party does not hold out his witnesses as worthy of belief, since he rarely has a free choice in selecting them. Denial of the right leaves the party at the mercy of the witness and the adversary.[272]

In response to this criticism, Texas Rule 607 allows impeachment by any party, including the party that calls the witness, without requiring a showing of surprise or injury.[273] The reasons for this change come mainly from criminal-law situations in which both sides, particularly the prosecution, frequently face turncoat witnesses.[274]

A. No "Strawman" Witnesses

While a party may impeach its own witnesses under Rule 607, it may not call a "strawman" witness who it knows will testify adversely solely to introduce that person's prior inconsistent statement, which is hearsay and otherwise inadmissible.[275] For ex-

---

269. *See Palafox v. State*, 608 S.W.2d 177, 182-83 (Tex. Crim. App. 1979) (State must disprove exculpatory statements contained in defendant's confession).

270. *See Sweeney v. State*, 704 S.W.2d 33, 34 (Tex. Crim. App. 1985) (attorney may impeach his own witness only if the testimony has surprised him and injured his cause); *Puckett v. State*, 640 S.W.2d 284, 287 (Tex. Crim. App. [Panel Op.] 1982) (State cannot impeach its own witness when no surprise is shown); *Lewis v. State*, 593 S.W.2d 704, 706 (Tex. Crim. App. [Panel Op.] 1980) (both surprise and injury must be shown); *see also Phlegm v. Pac. Emp'rs Ins.*, 453 S.W.2d 320, 321-22 (Tex. Civ. App.—Houston [14th Dist.] 1970, no writ) (attorney cannot impeach his own witness merely because he is disappointed in the testimony).

271. 1 RAY, *supra* note 4, §631, at 561-62.

272. FED. R. EVID. 607 advisory committee's note.

273. *See Hughes v. State*, 4 S.W.3d 1, 5 (Tex. Crim. App. 1999) (Criminal Rule 607 abandons the common-law voucher rule and does not require showing of surprise or injury); *Russeau v. State*, 785 S.W.2d 387, 390 (Tex. Crim. App. 1990) (enactment of Criminal Rule 607 rejected voucher rule). Rule 607 does not apply to those who are merely potential witnesses; it applies only to those who actually testify or whose testimony is actually offered at trial. *See, e.g., McDuffie v. State*, 854 S.W.2d 195, 220-21 (Tex. App.—Beaumont 1993, pet. ref'd) (trial court did not err in refusing to order production of personnel files for possible impeachment material of potential witness in murder trial when that witness did not testify; "[a] witness must testify to some fact before he can be impeached"); *cf. United States v. Stephens*, 365 F.3d 967, 975 (11th Cir. 2004) ("[T]he term 'witness' appears to refer solely to someone whose testimony is actually offered as evidence at trial, and not merely someone with extensive knowledge of or involvement in the events at issue."). In *Stephens*, the court noted that there are at least two circumstances in which a person who did not actually testify at trial could be considered a witness for purposes of Federal Rule 607: (1) when the parties stipulate to the content of the person's testimony or (2) when the person's former testimony is offered into evidence. 365 F.3d at 976.

274. *See, e.g., United States v. Bileck*, 776 F.2d 195, 197-98 (7th Cir. 1985) (government had no choice in whom defendant chose as his compatriots, and thus should not be required to vouch for their credibility); *United States v. Black*, 525 F.2d 668, 669 (6th Cir. 1975) (government's witness gave testimony exculpating defendant). *See generally* 3 WEINSTEIN & BERGER, *supra* note 110, ¶607[01], at 607-13 to 607-14 (quoting *Chambers v. Mississippi*, 410 U.S. 284, 296-98 (1973), which noted that parties do not always freely pick their witnesses but must rely on those who observed the incident).

275. *E.g., Hughes*, 4 S.W.3d at 6-7 (trial court abused its discretion in allowing State to call wife of sexual-abuse defendant, knowing that she would not testify favorably; State's primary purpose was to impeach her with a prior inconsistent statement); *see United States v. Johnson*, 802 F.2d 1459, 1466 (D.C. Cir. 1986) (prosecutor cannot call

ample, in ***Pruitt v. State***, an aggravated-robbery case, the prosecutor called the defendant's stepfather knowing that the witness would testify that he had driven two unknown black males to a shopping center, the scene of the offense.[276] The court held that the State's sole purpose in calling this witness was to introduce his former statement, made to investigating police officers, that he had driven his stepson and a codefendant to the shopping center.[277] Because the statement to the police officers was hearsay, it could be used only as impeachment evidence, not as substantive evidence to prove that the witness drove the defendant and his cohort to the scene of the crime.[278] Citing federal precedent in support of its conclusion, the court held that such a subterfuge is impermissible.[279] Similarly, in ***Truco Properties, Inc. v. Charlton***, a court of appeals addressed the same issue in a negligence action and held that an adverse witness may not be called "solely for the purpose of later impeachment by the use of otherwise inadmissible hearsay."[280]

Further, a witness associated with the defendant may not be called solely to be impeached with evidence of the witness's own prior convictions in the hope that the jury will infer that the defendant is guilty because of his association with a convicted criminal.[281]

Of course, when a witness is called with the expectation that he will testify to both favorable and unfavorable matters, the situation is different. A trial judge may properly permit impeachment with a prior inconsistent statement to take the sting away from

---

a witness for the purpose of introducing inadmissible hearsay evidence); ***United States v. Hogan***, 763 F.2d 697, 702 (5th Cir. 1985) (government may not use prior inconsistent statements under the guise of impeachment when the primary purpose is to place otherwise inadmissible evidence before the jury), *modified on other grounds*, 771 F.2d 82 (5th Cir. 1985); 1 GOODE ET AL., *supra* note 24, §607.2, at 551-52 (noting the danger that a party could call a witness knowing that he will testify unfavorably, impeach him with a prior inconsistent statement, and hope that the jury will misuse the prior statement for substantive purposes); 1 RAY, *supra* note 4, §632, at 235 (Supp. 1991) (party may not use Rule 607 as "a mere subterfuge" for placing hearsay evidence before the jury); *see also* ***Montoya v. State***, 65 S.W.3d 111, 114-15 (Tex. App.—Amarillo 2000, no pet.) (defendant in drug-delivery prosecution could not call confidential informant as adverse witness to "impeach" him with fact that his own drug charges were dismissed in exchange for acting as an undercover operative; this evidence did not impeach witness's credibility, the witness did not testify unfavorably about defendant, and evidence of the disposition of the witness's charges was not relevant in defendant's trial).

276. 770 S.W.2d 909, 910 (Tex. App.—Fort Worth 1989, pet. ref'd).

277. *Id.* at 910-11.

278. *Id.* at 911.

279. *Id.*; *see* ***Brasher v. State***, 139 S.W.3d 369, 371-72 (Tex. App.—San Antonio 2004, pet. ref'd); ***Zule v. State***, 802 S.W.2d 28, 34 (Tex. App.—Corpus Christi 1990, pet. ref'd); *see, e.g.*, ***Ramirez v. State***, 987 S.W.2d 938, 944 (Tex. App.—Austin 1999, no pet.) (reversible error in permitting State to call defendant's wife, knowing she was hostile, primarily for purpose of impeaching her with a prior inconsistent statement); ***Armstead v. State***, 977 S.W.2d 791, 795-96 (Tex. App.—Fort Worth 1998, pet. ref'd) (harmless error in permitting State to call witness "knowing that he would feign a memory loss only to introduce facts into evidence by asking leading questions"; State knew from voir dire outside jury's presence that witness claimed to have the "don't remembers").

280. 749 S.W.2d 893, 896 (Tex. App.—Texarkana 1988, writ denied).

281. *See* ***United States v. West***, 22 F.3d 586, 593-94 (5th Cir. 1994) (trial court did not err in permitting government to impeach its own witness with prior convictions when it called witness primarily to produce substantive evidence against defendant, not solely to impeach witness with convictions and show him as defendant's confederate).

the unfavorable testimony.[282] In this instance, the problem is properly addressed by balancing under Rule 403 the testimony's probative value against resulting unfair prejudice.[283] Similarly, if the sponsoring party did not know and could not have been expected to know before calling the witness that his testimony would be unfavorable, the "strawman" theory is inapplicable, and the witness may be impeached with his prior inconsistent statements.[284]

---

282. *See **United States v. Webster***, 734 F.2d 1191, 1193 (7th Cir. 1984) (party should be allowed to impeach its own witness; otherwise, a witness who will give helpful and harmful evidence would have to be kept off the stand because the harmful testimony could not be discredited). *See generally* 1 GOODE ET AL., *supra* note 24, §607.2, at 553-54 (harmful testimony may be neutralized by a prior inconsistent statement).

283. *See **Miranda v. State***, 813 S.W.2d 724, 734-35 (Tex. App.—San Antonio 1991, pet. ref'd) (although Criminal Rule 607 dispenses with the common-law "surprise and injury" predicate requirements for impeachment of one's own witness, these concerns are important factors in a Criminal Rule 403 balancing test); *see, e.g., **Hughes v. State**,* 4 S.W.3d 1, 7 (Tex. Crim. App. 1999) (because State did not explain why it expected witness to testify differently when she had not testified favorably before and because State had little legitimate purpose in offering prior inconsistent statement, probative value of impeachment evidence was substantially outweighed by unfair prejudice of inadmissible hearsay). "A Rule 403 balancing approach would require that 'impeachment by prior inconsistent statement may not be permitted where employed as a mere subterfuge to get before the jury evidence not otherwise admissible.'" *Miranda*, 813 S.W.2d at 735 (quoting ***Whitehurst v. Wright***, 592 F.2d 834, 839 (5th Cir. 1979)); *cf. **United States v. Buffalo***, 358 F.3d 519, 523-24 (8th Cir. 2004) (disavowing any rule that would require trial courts to inquire into calling party's subjective state of mind; proper inquiry is whether, viewed objectively, the probative value of a statement for impeaching the credibility of a witness is "substantially outweighed" by any Rule 403 counterfactors); ***United States v. Ince***, 21 F.3d 576, 581 (4th Cir. 1994) (trial court erred in permitting prosecution to impeach its own witness with prior inconsistent statement that defendant admitted firing gun when defendant was on trial for assault with a dangerous weapon; probative value of evidence for impeachment purposes was low while prejudicial effect was high because that evidence contained defendant's admission of guilt; "trial judge should rarely, if ever, permit the Government to 'impeach' its own witness by presenting what would otherwise be inadmissible hearsay if that hearsay contains an alleged confession to the crime for which the defendant is being tried"). Refer to *Article IV: Relevance & Its Limits, supra* p. 211.

284. In ***Barley v. State***, the court of criminal appeals distinguished the "strawman" cases from acceptable impeachment under Criminal Rule 607:

> [I]n each of [the strawman] cases, the witness had *already* recanted his or her statement in prior sworn testimony at a previous trial or hearing. Therefore the State could be charged with "knowing" that the witness would do the same in their case and thus having the subjective *primary* intent of placing otherwise inadmissible substantive evidence before the jury. Whereas, in the present case, no showing is made of this knowledge on the part of State and thus, there is no evidence of the State's primary intent.

906 S.W.2d 27, 37 n.11 (Tex. Crim. App. 1995). Although it may be going too far to suggest that the witness must have repudiated the prior inconsistent statement in a previous official hearing or trial before the State is on notice that the witness will not testify favorably, most Texas and federal cases have held that this impeachment is permissible when there is no clear indication that the sponsoring party was aware of the recantation. *See, e.g., **United States v. Patterson***, 23 F.3d 1239, 1245 (7th Cir. 1994) (when there was no evidence to show that government knew its witness would lie to protect the defendant, his cousin, court did not err in permitting impeachment with otherwise inadmissible prior inconsistent statement); ***Kelly v. State***, 60 S.W.2d 299, 302 (Tex. App.—Dallas 2001, no pet.) (State did not know witness would testify unfavorably, although it "suspected" as much; because this witness's testimony was crucial to show defendant's connection to murder scene, trial court did not err in allowing impeachment with prior inconsistent statement made to police on day of shooting); ***Braggs v. State***, 951 S.W.2d 877, 883 (Tex. App.—Texarkana 1997, pet. ref'd) (although it was arguable that State's sole purpose in calling witness was to introduce his earlier hearsay statement because there was no indication of "surprise" by State when witness testified unfavorably, there was no clear showing that State should have known witness had recanted his statement before trial; impeachment permissible under Rule 607).

B. Methods of Impeachment

While Rule 607 does not specify how a witness may be impeached, five general methods of attack are permitted. The first, and arguably most effective, is to prove that the witness has made an inconsistent or contradictory statement in the past.[285] The foundation requirement for this type of impeachment is covered by Rule 613(a).[286] The second method of attack is to show that the witness is biased for or against a party or has a pecuniary interest in the case.[287] Under the Texas Rules, the impeaching party must lay a foundation for impeachment by proof of bias.[288] The third method is to attack the character of the witness by proving that he is generally unworthy of belief.[289] This attack may be accomplished by impeachment with prior convictions offered in accord with Rule 609[290] or with character witnesses offered in accord with Rule 405.[291] The fourth method involves an attack on the witness's ability to perceive, remember, or recount accurately.[292] The final form of impeachment is that of specific contradiction, which entails bringing another witness to disprove the facts related by the first witness.[293] Here, courts are concerned with whether the evidence to be contradicted is "collateral" to the material issues. Texas courts have traditionally held that facts that

---

285. *See* Tex. R. Evid. 613(a). Refer to notes 582-635 *infra* and accompanying text.

286. The foundation requirement was changed slightly in the 2015 amendments to the rule. Refer to notes 613-618 *infra* and accompanying text.

287. *See* **United States v. Abel**, 469 U.S. 45, 49-51 (1984) (impeachment through bias is a permissible mode of attack under Rule 607 even though it is not explicitly mentioned in the rule); **United States v. Smith**, 550 F.2d 277, 282 (5th Cir. 1977) (witness's testimony was admissible as rebuttal testimony to establish bias of two other witnesses); McCormick on Evidence, *supra* note 2, §40, at 85 (while the Rules do not explicitly "refer to attacking the witness by showing bias, prejudice, or corruption, they clearly contemplate the use of the above-mentioned grounds of impeachment"); 1 Ray, *supra* note 4, §670, at 606 (witness may be impeached "by a showing of interest, bias, prejudice or other motive which tends to affect his credibility").

288. Tex. R. Evid. 613(b). The foundation requirement was changed slightly in the 2015 amendments to the rule. Refer to notes 671-676 *infra* and accompanying text. For a complete discussion of Rule 613(b), refer to notes 636-682 *infra* and accompanying text.

289. *See, e.g.*, **Quiroz v. State**, 764 S.W.2d 395, 399 (Tex. App.—Fort Worth 1989, pet. ref'd) (by taking the stand, defendant put his character and reputation for veracity in issue; thus, his testimony was subject to impeachment).

290. *See, e.g.*, **Simpson v. State**, 886 S.W.2d 449, 451-53 (Tex. App.—Houston [1st Dist.] 1994, pet. ref'd) (prior convictions for robbery and aggravated robbery were admissible in narcotics prosecution under Criminal Rule 609); *see also* **Theus v. State**, 845 S.W.2d 874, 879 (Tex. Crim. App. 1992) (prior arson conviction is admissible under Criminal Rule 609 if evidence's probative value outweighs its prejudicial effect). Refer to notes 374-474 *infra* and accompanying text.

291. Refer to *Article IV: Relevance & Its Limits, supra* p. 242.

292. *See* Tex. R. Evid. 601(a); *see, e.g.*, **Virts v. State**, 739 S.W.2d 25, 28-29 (Tex. Crim. App. 1987) (error to prohibit defendant from cross-examining codefendant about her mental illness near the time of the offense); **Perry v. State**, 236 S.W.3d 859, 867 (Tex. App.—Texarkana 2007, no pet.) (defendant should have been permitted to cross-examine codefendant about his hallucinations and mental-health history); **Sandow v. State**, 787 S.W.2d 588, 598 (Tex. App.—Austin 1990, pet. ref'd) (whether appellant regularly consumed alcohol was relevant evidence for impeachment); **Sidney v. State**, 753 S.W.2d 410, 413 (Tex. App.—Houston [14th Dist.] 1986, pet. ref'd) (defendant should have been permitted to cross-examine State's witness on extent, duration, and treatment of his mental condition). *See generally* McCormick on Evidence, *supra* note 2, §45, at 104-09 (any deficiency of a witness's senses may be used to attack the credibility of the witness). Refer to notes 1-46 *supra* and accompanying text.

293. *See generally* McCormick on Evidence, *supra* note 2, §47, at 109-13 (discussing the uses of contradiction to impeach a witness's testimony).

are independently provable in the case are not collateral for purposes of impeachment by contradiction.[294] The difficulty in deciding which facts are collateral and which are not continues to mystify courts, commentators, and practitioners.[295]

C. Impeachment Evidence as Substantive Evidence

When a party impeaches a witness—whether its own or that of the opposing party—with a prior inconsistent statement, that prior statement cannot be considered substantive evidence unless it meets the requirements of Rule 801(e)(1)(A) or 801(e)(3).[296] Impeachment is aimed at attacking the credibility of the witness, and testimony admitted solely for impeachment purposes is without probative value and thus is not substantive evidence to prove a material fact in the case.[297] Some evidence may both impeach the credibility of a witness and have independent relevance to the material issues; in that case, the evidence is admissible for its substantive value.[298]

D. Limits on Impeachment

While Rule 607 greatly liberalizes the opportunities for witness impeachment, it should not be read as carte blanche permission for unlimited attacks on witnesses. The rule does not require the admission of all possible impeachment evidence.[299] The trial judge continues to have considerable discretion to limit impeachment evidence under other rules, particularly Rules 403[300] and 611(a),[301] when the evidence is unduly harass-

---

294. *Gutierrez v. State*, 764 S.W.2d 796, 798 (Tex. Crim. App. 1989); *see Ramirez v. State*, 802 S.W.2d 674, 675 (Tex. Crim. App. 1990) (test for whether fact is collateral is whether cross-examining party would be entitled to prove fact as part of its case); *Bates v. State*, 587 S.W.2d 121, 133 (Tex. Crim. App. 1979) (same); *Celeste v. State*, 805 S.W.2d 579, 580-81 (Tex. App.—Tyler 1991, no pet.) (evidence of extraneous acts between third party and defendant is barred unless admitted to prove a relevant contested issue). Refer to note 590 *infra* and accompanying text.

295. *Compare* 3A JOHN H. WIGMORE, EVIDENCE IN TRIALS AT COMMON LAW §1003, at 961 (Chadbourn rev. 1970) (traditional standard), *with* 1 GOODE ET AL., *supra* note 24, §607.3, at 560 (Wigmore standard is inadequate), McCORMICK ON EVIDENCE, *supra* note 2, §47, at 111-12 (contradiction of a collateral fact on which witness would not be mistaken had he actually been there should be permitted), *and* 3 WEINSTEIN & BERGER, *supra* note 110, ¶607[05], at 607-84 to 607-87 ("collateral matter" rule should be recast as one of discretion under Rule 403).

296. For a discussion of Rule 801(e)(1)(A), refer to *Article VIII: Hearsay, infra* p. 835. For a discussion of Rule 801(e)(3), refer to *Article VIII: Hearsay, infra* p. 863.

297. *See, e.g.*, *Adams v. State*, 862 S.W.2d 139, 147-48 (Tex. App.—San Antonio 1993, pet. ref'd) (trial court properly instructed jury to consider prior inconsistent statement only for impeachment purposes and not as substantive evidence); *cf. In re K.W.*, 666 S.E.2d 490, 494 (N.C. Ct. App. 2008) (in child-abuse case, evidence from complainant's MySpace page was admissible for impeachment purposes as a prior inconsistent statement related to complainant's testimony about her sexual history; that evidence was not admissible as substantive evidence that someone else caused the trauma found by examining physician).

298. *See, e.g.*, *Dotson v. State*, 28 S.W.3d 53, 57 (Tex. App.—Texarkana 2000, pet. ref'd) (evidence that bank teller had embezzled half the money that she testified bank robber had stolen not only impeached her credibility but was substantive evidence that went "directly to one of the elements of the case"); *see also* *United States v. Buffalo*, 358 F.3d 519, 525-27 (8th Cir. 2004) (error to exclude evidence that defendant's own witness made prior out-of-court confession to third persons and that other physical evidence potentially corroborated that confession). In practice, attorneys rarely attempt to limit the use or purpose of the impeachment evidence, and the jury is rarely notified of how the evidence should be considered.

299. *See* TEX. R. EVID. 607.

300. Refer to *Article IV: Relevance & Its Limits, supra* p. 211.

301. Refer to notes 483-501 *infra* and accompanying text.

ing, unfair, collateral, or cumulative.[302] The appellate courts must be able to determine from reading the "cold record" that the trial judge has exercised his discretion by considering and balancing the various countervailing interests. Practitioners and judges are thus well advised to ensure that the reasons for limiting impeachment evidence are clearly articulated in the record.

E. Rehabilitation of Impeached Witnesses

When a witness's credibility has been attacked in one of the five methods discussed above,[303] the sponsoring party may rehabilitate the witness only in direct response to the impeachment attack.[304] If the witness is impeached with a prior inconsistent statement or evidence of bias, rehabilitation is permitted only in accord with Rule 613.[305] If the witness's character for truthfulness is attacked, he may be rehabilitated only in accord with Rule 608.[306] There are no specific rules on rehabilitation evidence for the other two methods of impeachment—specific contradiction and defect of capacity. Trial courts nonetheless retain discretion to admit or exclude rehabilitation evidence under general principles of relevance.[307] Here, the judge should exercise his discretion in light of such factors as the importance of the witness's testimony, the effect of the impeachment evidence, the time needed to provide the rehabilitative evidence, and the likelihood that such evidence will detract from the main issues.

RULE 608
A WITNESS'S CHARACTER FOR TRUTHFULNESS OR UNTRUTHFULNESS

(a) Reputation or Opinion Evidence. A witness's credibility may be attacked or supported by testimony about the witness's reputation for having a character for truthfulness or untruthfulness, or by testimony in the form of an opin-

---

302. *See Adams*, 862 S.W.2d at 146 n.4 ("The right to impeach one's own witness, however, is subject to the trial court's authority under [Criminal] Rules 403 and 610 … to protect against abuse."); *see, e.g.*, *Keene Corp. v. Gardner*, 837 S.W.2d 224, 230 (Tex. App.—Dallas 1992, writ denied) (no error to prohibit cross-examination of expert witness with criticism of research he conducted on a separate matter not related to his testimony; impeachment evidence was irrelevant and collateral).

303. Refer to notes 285-295 *supra* and accompanying text.

304. *See* McCormick on Evidence, *supra* note 2, §49, at 116 (stating that "[t]he wall, attacked at one point, may not be fortified at another and distinct point"). A witness who has not been impeached may not be "bolstered" with extrinsic evidence to support his credibility or add luster to his testimony. *See Rousseau v. State*, 855 S.W.2d 666, 681 (Tex. Crim. App. 1993) (bolstering occurs when one item of evidence is improperly used by a party to add credence or weight to some earlier uncontested piece of evidence offered by the same party); *State v. Balderas*, 915 S.W.2d 913, 919 (Tex. App.—Houston [1st Dist.] 1996, pet. ref'd) (same); *see, e.g.*, *Washington v. State*, 771 S.W.2d 537, 545 (Tex. Crim. App. 1989) (although State improperly bolstered witness's testimony, evidence was harmless error); *Norris v. State*, 788 S.W.2d 65, 69 (Tex. App.—Dallas 1990, pet. ref'd) (although State improperly bolstered witness's testimony, the later impeachment of the witness's testimony cured the error). Refer to *Article VIII: Hearsay*, *infra* p. 841.

305. Refer to notes 616-625 *infra* and accompanying text.

306. Refer to notes 329-343 *infra* and accompanying text.

307. Refer to *Article IV: Relevance & Its Limits*, *supra* p. 191.

ion about that character. But evidence of truthful character is admissible only after the witness's character for truthfulness has been attacked.

(b) Specific Instances of Conduct. Except for a criminal conviction under Rule 609, a party may not inquire into or offer extrinsic evidence to prove specific instances of the witness's conduct in order to attack or support the witness's character for truthfulness.

COMMENTARY ON RULE 608

A. Rule 608(a): Reputation or Opinion Evidence

An important mode of impeachment is to present evidence that the witness does not have a truthful character. If the witness is generally untruthful, the jury is less likely to believe that he is telling the truth about the present event. The Rules generally prohibit evidence of bad character offered to prove conforming conduct on the present occasion,[308] but Rule 404(a)(4) specifically excepts evidence of a witness's character trait for truthfulness from the general ban when the evidence is offered under Rules 607, 608, and 609.[309] This credibility evidence is crucial to the accuracy and reliability of the trial process.

Specifically, Rule 608 permits a party to call a witness to attack the credibility of some other witness, usually a fact witness, by attacking that witness's character for truthfulness. Thus, when witness X testifies that "the light was green," the opposing party may call Y to testify to X's bad character for truthfulness. However, Rule 608 permits only the witness's character for truthfulness to be impeached.[310] Thus, while a lay witness may give opinion or reputation testimony about the other witness's general character for truthfulness, he may not give an opinion on the other witness's truthfulness about the particular allegations at issue.[311] The inquiry under this rule also may not extend to the witness's general moral character[312] or to allied character traits, such as "honesty"[313] or "peacefulness."[314]

Rule 608(b), unlike Federal Rule 608(b), forbids the cross-examiner from attacking the witness's character with evidence of specific instances of prior conduct exem-

---

308. Tex. R. Evid. 404.

309. Refer to *Article IV: Relevance & Its Limits, supra* p. 266.

310. Tex. R. Evid. 608(a).

311. *Salinas v. State*, 368 S.W.3d 550, 555 (Tex. App.—Houston [14th Dist.] 2011), *aff'd*, 369 S.W.3d 176 (Tex. Crim. App. 2012).

312. *Shannon v. State*, 567 S.W.2d 510, 515 (Tex. Crim. App. [Panel Op.] 1978); *Hartford Acc. & Indem. Co. v. Williams*, 516 S.W.2d 425, 428 (Tex. Civ. App.—Amarillo 1974, writ ref'd n.r.e.).

313. *See, e.g., Wiggins v. State*, 778 S.W.2d 877, 887-94 (Tex. App.—Dallas 1989, pet. ref'd) (after defendant testified, his mother was called as a character witness to support defendant's truthfulness and testified that he was "an honest person" when asked whether defendant was a "truth teller"; trait of being an "honest person" and trait of being a "truth teller" are not synonymous; harmless error to permit the State to impeach witness with specific instances of dishonest conduct).

314. *See, e.g., United States v. Fountain*, 768 F.2d 790, 795 (7th Cir. 1985) (prosecutor improperly asked if defendant was a peaceable man), *amended on other grounds*, 777 F.2d 345 (7th Cir. 1985).

plifying untruthfulness.[315] However, both Federal Rule 608(a) and Texas Rule 608(a) allow a witness's character to be impeached or supported with opinion as well as reputation testimony.[316] Texas Rule 608(a) expands earlier Texas law, which confined character impeachment to reputation testimony.[317] The expansion is merited because a witness who testifies about another witness's general reputation for veracity is actually expressing his personal opinion of the witness, and the jury takes it as such.[318] Under Rule 608(a), a witness may be asked to state an opinion of the fact witness's character for truthfulness, and the witness may answer: "In my opinion, X is a liar," or "In my opinion, X is a truthful person."

On the other hand, opinion testimony about character is not always obtained from those who know as much as humanly possible about the character of the witness. Such testimony can also come from one who knows just enough to express an opinion but does not know enough for the opinion to be of significant value.[319] This problem occurs primarily in criminal cases when police officers offer their opinions of a witness's character for truth and veracity after a very brief and usually unpleasant encounter.[320] Such problems are solved by the proper administration of Rules 403, 405, and 701.

Because opinion testimony is admissible to attack a witness's truthfulness, the question arises of whether expert testimony may be offered to prove that character trait. For example, suppose X testifies as an eyewitness to a car collision at First and Main. He states that "the light was green." May the opposing party then call a psychiatrist to testify that, based on a psychiatric evaluation, X does not have a truthful character? This issue did not exist under former Texas law because only reputation evidence was admissible to attack credibility. Further, under common-law principles, the court of criminal appeals had specifically rejected the proposition that psychiatric evidence was suf-

---

315. Refer to notes 344-373 *infra* and accompanying text.

316. FED. R. EVID. 608(a); TEX. R. EVID. 608(a); *see* TEX. R. EVID. 405 (when admissible, opinion or reputation testimony may prove character); *see, e.g.*, **United States v. Melton**, 739 F.2d 576, 579 (11th Cir. 1984) (no error in permitting prosecution to call five witnesses to state that they would not believe defendant under oath after he had testified). Texas Rule 608(a) is identical to Federal Rule 608(a).

317. *See* **Compton v. Jay**, 389 S.W.2d 639, 640 (Tex. 1965) (credibility can be attacked only by showing a witness's general reputation for veracity); **Commonwealth Lloyd's Ins. v. Thomas**, 678 S.W.2d 278, 295 (Tex. App.—Fort Worth 1984, writ ref'd n.r.e.) (personal opinion of witness's character is inadmissible); **Garza v. Garza**, 109 S.W.2d 1079, 1081 (Tex. Civ. App.—San Antonio 1937, writ dism'd) (rule confining impeachment of witness's veracity to general reputation evidence has been the rule since "an early day").

318. **Scott v. State**, 222 S.W.3d 820, 825 (Tex. App.—Houston [14th Dist.] 2007, no pet.); *see also* 1 RAY, *supra* note 4, §652, at 577 ("It seems a queer turn in the law of evidence that excludes persons who know as much as humanly possible about the character of another and yet admits second-hand guesses as to reputation."); *cf.* FED. R. EVID. 608 advisory committee's note, subdiv. (a) ("[W]itnesses who testify to reputation seem in fact often to be giving their opinions, disguised somewhat misleadingly as reputation.").

319. For example, in **United States v. Dotson**, several police officers testified that, in their opinions, the defendant and his witnesses did not have truthful characters. 799 F.2d 189, 190-91 (5th Cir. 1986). However, the only basis for their opinions was that they had previously conducted a criminal investigation of the defendant. *Id.* at 193. No testimony was offered to demonstrate how long the officers had known the defendant or the basis on which the officers acted to form their opinions of his truthfulness. *Id.* The court found that these opinions were nothing more than "bare assertions" without adequate factual basis. *Id.*

320. *See* **Wright v. State**, 609 S.W.2d 801, 806-07 (Tex. Crim. App. [Panel Op.] 1980) (Roberts, J., concurring).

ficiently reliable to support an expert opinion on credibility.[321] One facet of this issue involves the distinction between the moral (character) and nonmoral (witness capacity) aspects of "truthfulness."[322] In a lengthy court of criminal appeals decision, *Schutz v. State*,[323] the admissibility of expert and lay testimony to attack or support a fact witness's credibility was thoroughly analyzed. While the court in *Schutz* did not reject the notion of expert testimony that indirectly supports or attacks a witness's credibility by expressing an opinion that the witness has trouble distinguishing between fantasy and reality or by testifying to the symptoms or traits of a person who is fantasizing or being manipulated, the court held that Rule 608 does not permit an expert to testify to his opinion that this witness is or is not lying.[324] Admission of such testimony was reversible error.[325] Even before the *Schutz* decision, at least two other Texas courts had concluded that the exclusion of such expert testimony was not error.[326] Thus, an ex-

---

321. In *Hopkins v. State*, the court of criminal appeals stated:

> The state of psychiatry is such that it is more an art than a science. ... Also, being of the nature that it is, psychiatric opinion is not only often divergent, but is often inexact. In view of this nature, the benefit to be gained by the jury would quite probably be slight. Often the jury would be subjected to conflicting witnesses and inexact opinions, the value of which would be minimal in enabling the jury to decide the issue of credibility.

480 S.W.2d 212, 221 (Tex. Crim. App. 1972).

322. The drafters of the Federal Rules recognized the difficulty of distinguishing between these two aspects of character but decided to treat them both in the same manner:

> Traditionally character has been regarded primarily in moral overtones of good and bad: chaste, peaceable, truthful, honest. Nevertheless, on occasion nonmoral considerations crop up, as in the case of the incompetent driver, and this is bound to happen increasingly. If character is defined as the kind of person one is, then account must be taken of varying ways of arriving at the estimate. These may range from the opinion of the employer who has found the man honest to the opinion of a psychiatrist based upon examination and testing. No effective dividing line exists between character and mental capacity, and the latter traditionally has been provable by opinion.

FED. R. EVID. 405 advisory committee's note. Other commentators have noted that most courts exclude expert testimony on witnesses' capacity for truthfulness and also on their moral character for truthfulness:

> Occasionally courts try to distinguish between expert testimony relating to capacity and expert testimony relating to disposition, but usually they ignore the distinction. Apparently the reason is that trying to make the distinction raises unanswerable questions about human nature and does not coincide with lines drawn by experts. Deciding when expert testimony goes to capacity (credibility generally) and/or character (veracity in particular) promises difficulty similar to that involved in defining and applying concepts of *mens rea* and the defense of insanity. And the arguments for excluding expert testimony (it threatens the jury's role, is not scientifically sound, and may cause more confusion than it's worth) operate regardless which category applies.

3 CHRISTOPHER B. MUELLER & LAIRD C. KIRKPATRICK, FEDERAL EVIDENCE §312, at 422-23 (2d ed. 1994) (footnotes omitted).

323. 957 S.W.2d 52 (Tex. Crim. App. 1997).

324. *Id.* at 68-69. The Fourteenth Court of Appeals has held that therapy records indicating a witness's inability to distinguish between fantasy and reality would have been admissible at the guilt-innocence stage of a trial if they had been offered. *See State v. Moreno*, 297 S.W.3d 512, 523-24 (Tex. App.—Houston [14th Dist.] 2009, pet. ref'd).

325. *Schutz*, 957 S.W.2d at 74.

326. *See Virts v. State*, 739 S.W.2d 25, 27 n.1 (Tex. Crim. App. 1987) (trial court did not err in excluding a doctor's testimony about mental state of prosecution witness); *Munoz v. State*, 763 S.W.2d 30, 33 (Tex. App.—Corpus Christi 1988, pet. ref'd) (psychiatric evidence of witness's mental state is not per se inadmissible, but trial court has "great latitude" in limiting such collateral evidence based on its relative probative value and potential for abuse). Federal courts generally reach the same result. *See, e.g.*, *United States v. Beasley*, 72 F.3d 1518, 1528 (11th Cir. 1996) (defense expert's opinion that witness was a psychopath who had no concept of the truth was inadmissible; "[a]b-

pert is generally forbidden from testifying not only to the fact witness's general character for truthfulness but also to his opinion of whether the witness is testifying truthfully in this instance.[327] This determination follows the principle that the jury is the only lie detector in the courtroom.[328]

Evidence of the fact witness's good character for truthfulness may be introduced only after his character has been attacked.[329] Rule 608(a) thus provides a specific application of the general prohibition against bolstering the testimony of an unimpeached witness[330] because a person's character is assumed to be good unless there is evidence to indicate otherwise.[331]

Texas precedent held that impeachment with prior inconsistent statements amounted to an attack on credibility, and thus courts could admit character evidence of truth and veracity to rehabilitate a witness.[332] However, not all impeachment with prior inconsistent statements amounts to an attack on credibility; such impeachment

---

sent unusual circumstances, expert medical testimony concerning the truthfulness or credibility of a witness is inadmissible"); *Westcott v. Crinklaw*, 68 F.3d 1073, 1076-77 (8th Cir. 1995) (expert testimony that officer suffered from posttraumatic stress syndrome, which often causes "incomplete, inaccurate or in some cases even total memory lapses," was improper testimony directed at the reliability of officer's statements and provided a psychological label or diagnosis to excuse or justify them); *United States v. Cecil*, 836 F.2d 1431, 1441 (4th Cir. 1988) (psychiatrist could not testify to the credibility of a fact witness); *United States v. Thomas*, 768 F.2d 611, 618 (5th Cir. 1985) (no error to exclude polygraph examiner's testimony that defendant was a truthful person, which was intended to bolster credibility; defendant's character had not been attacked); *United States v. Riley*, 657 F.2d 1377, 1387 (8th Cir. 1981) (court properly rejected defendant's expert psychiatric testimony on prosecution witness's "mental condition" and "capacity for telling the truth," which was based on in-court observation and hypothetical questions).

327. *See Miller v. State*, 757 S.W.2d 880, 883 (Tex. App.—Dallas 1988, pet. ref'd) ("[A] witness may not give an opinion concerning the truth or falsity of another witness's testimony.").

328. *United States v. Barnard*, 490 F.2d 907, 912-13 (9th Cir. 1973).

329. Tex. R. Evid. 608(a); *Rivas v. State*, 275 S.W.3d 880, 886 (Tex. Crim. App. 2009); *Flores v. State*, 513 S.W.3d 146, 161 (Tex. App.—Houston [14th Dist.] 2016, pet. ref'd); *Kirven v. State*, 751 S.W.2d 212, 215-16 (Tex. App.—Dallas 1988, no pet.); *Rose v. Intercontinental Bank*, 705 S.W.2d 752, 757 (Tex. App.—Houston [1st Dist.] 1986, writ ref'd n.r.e.). In *Rose*, the court incorrectly used pre-Rules precedent in stating that "[a] witness' personal opinion of a party's character is inadmissible." 705 S.W.2d at 757. Although such an opinion was inadmissible under Texas common law, Rule 608 expressly permits either opinion or reputation evidence to attack or support a witness's credibility. The *Rose* court relied on *Commonwealth Lloyd's Ins. v. Thomas*, 678 S.W.2d 278, 295 (Tex. App.—Fort Worth 1984, writ ref'd n.r.e.), which expressly limited its discussion to "the rules of evidence then in effect" (i.e., before Civil Rule 608 had been promulgated) when stating that a witness's personal opinion of a party's character is inadmissible. *Rose*, 705 S.W.2d at 757.

330. *See Livingston v. State*, 739 S.W.2d 311, 332 (Tex. Crim. App. 1987) (bolstering occurs when evidence is used by a party to add weight to some earlier unimpeached evidence offered by the same party); *Stewart v. State*, 587 S.W.2d 148, 154-55 (Tex. Crim. App. [Panel Op.] 1979) (when witness has not been impeached and the only evidence is contradictory evidence, "it is not permissible to bolster the testimony of the witness by proof of his good reputation for truth and veracity"; otherwise, every defendant would bolster his defense simply by disagreeing with opponent's case); *Flores*, 513 S.W.3d at 161 (bolstering occurs if sole purpose of evidence is to convince fact-finder that witness is worthy of credit); *see also Rivas*, 275 S.W.3d at 886 (Rule 608(a) is encompassed by a generic "bolstering" objection). Refer to *Article VIII: Hearsay, infra* p. 841.

331. *Boon v. Weathered's Adm'r*, 23 Tex. 675, 681 (1859); McCormick on Evidence, *supra* note 2, §49, at 115 n.1; *see* 1A Ray, *supra* note 4, §1325, at 501 (claiming that the "absence of unfavorable comment is a sufficient basis for an inference that the general opinion is favorable").

332. *See* 1 Ray, *supra* note 4, §772, at 650; *see, e.g.*, *O'Bryan v. State*, 591 S.W.2d 464, 476 (Tex. Crim. App. 1979) (evidence of witness's good reputation for veracity was admissible after witness was impeached with prior inconsistent statements); *Adams v. State*, 514 S.W.2d 262, 264 (Tex. Crim. App. 1974) (State could rehabilitate rape victim's testimony after she was impeached with prior inconsistent statement).

"is normally just an attack on the witness's accuracy, not his character for truthfulness."[333] The question should be "whether the overall tone and tenor of the cross-examination implied that the witness is a liar."[334] Thus, rehabilitative evidence is permitted if a reasonable juror would believe the witness's character for truthfulness has been attacked.[335]

Although a criminal defendant may always introduce evidence of a pertinent character trait during the defense's case-in-chief as circumstantial proof that he did not commit the offense charged,[336] his character for truthfulness is not automatically a pertinent character trait merely because he testifies as a witness at trial.[337] Thus, he may not offer opinion or reputation evidence of his good character for truthfulness as a witness unless the State first impeaches his general credibility on cross-examination.[338] Of course, if the criminal charge itself involves the character trait of untruthfulness, he may offer opinion or reputation evidence of his good character for truthfulness regardless of whether he testifies and regardless of whether the State impeaches his credibility as a witness.[339]

Sometimes the opposing party may indirectly attack a witness's general character for truthfulness by calling into question the witness's moral character for truthfulness. When the plaintiff in a federal civil-rights lawsuit argued in her opening statement that the defendant-police officer was corrupt and performed his official duties improperly to help out a fellow officer, the defendant was entitled to present evidence of his good character for truthfulness, regardless of the extent or type of impeachment used to discredit his testimony.[340]

---

333. *Michael v. State*, 235 S.W.3d 723, 726 (Tex. Crim. App. 2007); *cf.* FED. R. EVID. 608 advisory committee's note, subdiv. (a) ("Whether evidence in the form of contradiction is an attack upon the character of the witness must depend in part upon the circumstances.").

334. *Michael*, 235 S.W.3d at 727.

335. *Id.* at 728.

336. *See* TEX. R. EVID. 404(a)(2)(A).

337. *See, e.g.*, *Stitt v. State*, 102 S.W.3d 845, 848-49 (Tex. App.—Texarkana 2003, pet. ref'd) (defendant was not entitled to introduce evidence of his character trait for truthfulness to show he was a "believable" witness when State had not impeached his general credibility).

338. *See id.*; *see, e.g.*, *Moore v. State*, 143 S.W.3d 305, 315 (Tex. App.—Waco 2004, pet. ref'd) (trial court did not abuse its discretion in excluding defendant's "truthful character" witnesses when State's "vigorous" cross-examination did not directly implicate defendant's general character for truthfulness).

Normally, impeachment with a prior inconsistent statement or bias is not considered an attack on general credibility. *Renda v. King*, 347 F.3d 550, 554 (3d Cir. 2003). Evidence of bias relates only to the witness's motive to be untruthful in the particular case, not to the witness's general character for untruthfulness. *Id.* Similarly, there may be many reasons why a witness has made a prior inconsistent statement, including a defect in capacity, a specific bias, or a general lack of truthfulness. *Id.* Refer to notes 582-635 *infra* and accompanying text.

339. *See Stitt*, 102 S.W.3d at 849.

340. *Renda*, 347 F.3d at 553-56. During the opening statement to the jury, the plaintiff's attorney argued that the defendant, "during the course of a police investigation, ... maliciously harassed her; ... attempted to coerce her into making false confessions; and ... filed false charges against her." *Id.* at 555. The Third Circuit stated that arguing that the officer would "lie and engage in illegal police investigative techniques[]" went far beyond an allegation that the defendant was biased; instead, it alleged corruption. *Id.* A charge of corruption allows counterproof of a good character for truthfulness. *Id.* at 556.

General opinion or reputation evidence supporting the witness's truthful character under Rule 608(a) should be liberally employed to respond to attacks on truthful character; thus, there needs to be only a "loose" fit between the rebuttal evidence and the predicate attack.[341] However, merely asking questions designed to cast doubt on the witness's general character for truthfulness does not open the door to rehabilitation with another person's opinion about the truthfulness of the specific allegations or testimony of the fact witness.[342] For example, in a trial for sexual assault of a child, the defense might cross-examine the child complainant about "fantasizing" the offense or being manipulated by others to believe or pretend that the event had occurred. That cross-examination indirectly attacks the child witness's capacity or character for truthfulness and permits the prosecution to rehabilitate the witness with opinion or reputation evidence that the child has the general capacity for distinguishing truth from falsehood or that the child is a truthful person. The cross-examination does not, however, permit the prosecution to offer either lay- or expert-opinion testimony that the child is telling the truth about this offense or event.[343]

B. Rule 608(b): Specific Instances of Conduct

Rule 608(b) excludes for general impeachment purposes all evidence of the witness's specific conduct other than criminal convictions, which are governed by Rule 609.[344] The court of criminal appeals has explained this prohibition as follows:

> For example, the defense may not ask the witness: Didn't you cheat on your income tax last year? Didn't you lie on Tuesday about having an affair with your boss? Didn't you steal five dollars from the church collection plate last week and then lie to the priest about it? While all of those questions attack the witness's general character for truthfulness, that mode of impeachment is specifically barred by Rule 608(b). Our state evidentiary rules frown on unnecessary character assassination.[345]

---

341. *Schutz v. State*, 957 S.W.2d 52, 72 (Tex. Crim. App. 1997).

342. *Id.*

343. *See id.* at 73; *see, e.g.*, *Sandoval v. State*, 409 S.W.3d 259, 292-93 (Tex. App.—Austin 2013, no pet.) (trial court erred in permitting police officer to testify that because child complainant's statements were consistent, he believed she was not fabricating allegations of sexual assault).

344. *See, e.g.*, *TXI Transp. Co. v. Hughes*, 306 S.W.3d 230, 242 (Tex. 2010) (admission of statements about defendant's immigration status and his alleged misrepresentation of that status was harmful error because immigration status was not admissible under Rule 608(b) and did not meet the criteria of Rule 609; "[s]uch appeals to racial and ethnic prejudices, whether 'explicit and brazen' or 'veiled and subtle,' cannot be tolerated because they undermine the very basis of our judicial process" (quoting *Tex. Employers' Ins. v. Guerrero*, 800 S.W.2d 859, 864 (Tex. App.—San Antonio 1990, writ denied))); *Lovelace v. Sabine Consol., Inc.*, 733 S.W.2d 648, 654 (Tex. App.—Houston [14th Dist.] 1987, writ denied) (trial court properly refused to permit impeachment of witness with negligent acts in other, unrelated construction projects); *Nix v. H.R. Mgmt. Co.*, 733 S.W.2d 573, 575-76 (Tex. App.—San Antonio 1987, writ ref'd n.r.e.) (evidence that plaintiff-tenant lied in an unrelated collateral matter was inadmissible in suit against apartment complex for injuries stemming from two alleged rapes). Refer to notes 374-474 *infra* and accompanying text.

345. *Hammer v. State*, 296 S.W.3d 555, 563 (Tex. Crim. App. 2009); *see* McCormick on Evidence, *supra* note 2, §42, at 90-91 (noting dangers of prejudice, distraction, and confusion, as well as possible abuse by asking unfounded questions).

The rule contains no explicit exceptions.[346] For example, a witness's general character for truthfulness[347] may not be impeached with evidence of prior drug use,[348] acts of violence,[349] specific instances of lying,[350] sexual behavior,[351] or unsavory associations.[352]

RULE 608

346. *See Ramirez v. State*, 802 S.W.2d 674, 676 (Tex. Crim. App. 1990); *see, e.g., Tanner v. Karnavas*, 86 S.W.3d 737, 742-43 (Tex. App.—Dallas 2002, pet. denied) (evidence of defendant's sworn application for hardship driver's license purportedly containing falsehoods was properly excluded under Rule 608(b) when offered to impeach defendant's general credibility); *Simpson v. State*, 975 S.W.2d 364, 367-69 (Tex. App.—Waco 1998, no pet.) (evidence that assault victim had previously choked defendant and pushed her in front of car was barred under Rule 608(b) and was not made admissible under optional-completeness doctrine to explain victim's relationship with defendant). Beginning with the 1859 case *Boon v. Weathered's Administrator*, Texas civil courts have consistently rejected evidence of specific instances of conduct for impeachment purposes, no matter how probative of truthfulness. 23 Tex. 675, 678 (1859); *e.g., Christie v. Brewer*, 374 S.W.2d 908, 913-14 (Tex. Civ. App.—Austin 1964, writ ref'd n.r.e.) (evidence relating to why plaintiff left his job was a collateral matter and thus inadmissible in an action to rescind a stock purchase). The Liaison Committee chose to follow this clear-cut approach.

In *Lopez v. State*, the court of appeals held that Rule 608(b)'s prohibition against using specific instances of prior conduct to prove a general lack of credibility "impermissibly conflicted with" the defendant's constitutional right of confrontation. 989 S.W.2d 402, 404 (Tex. App.—San Antonio 1999), *rev'd*, 18 S.W.3d 220 (Tex. Crim. App. 2000). In this case, the defendant, charged with aggravated sexual assault of a child, wanted to cross-examine the learning-disabled child victim with evidence that he had falsely accused his mother of hitting him and throwing him against a "steel washer." *Lopez*, 989 S.W.2d at 404. The court of appeals held that "[t]o the extent Rule 608(b) would prevent the appellant from confronting his accuser [with evidence of a prior false accusation], the Rule must bow to the Constitution." *Lopez*, 989 S.W.2d at 408. However, the court of criminal appeals reversed the appellate court and declined to create a per se exception to Rule 608(b) for sexual offenses. *See Lopez v. State*, 18 S.W.3d 220, 225 (Tex. Crim. App. 2000) ("[T]he rationale of the out-of-state cases creating a universal sexual offense exception is unpersuasive ...."); *see also Hammer*, 296 S.W.3d at 564-65 (sexual-assault complainant "is not a volunteer for an exercise in character assassination"; prior false accusation of sexual activity may be admissible, however, for some purpose other than to prove propensity). Although refusing to create this special exception to Rule 608(b), the *Lopez* court acknowledged that in some instances, the Confrontation Clause may require admissibility of evidence that the Rules of Evidence would exclude. 18 S.W.3d at 225; *see Billodeau v. State*, 277 S.W.3d 34, 40 (Tex. Crim. App. 2009) ("[T]his Court has acknowledged that the Confrontation Clause of the Sixth Amendment may require admission of evidence that Rule 608(b) would otherwise bar."). But the Confrontation Clause does not create a right to impeach a witness's general credibility through otherwise prohibited cross-examination methods. *E.g., Tollett v. State*, 422 S.W.3d 886, 893 (Tex. App.—Houston [14th Dist.] 2014, pet. ref'd) (defendant could not cross-examine police officer about officer's intentional withholding of evidence at a hearing six years earlier on an unrelated matter; evidence would not have proved officer was lying about defendant's reckless driving and would have been general character assassination prohibited by Rule 608(b)); *see Hammer*, 296 S.W.3d at 562.

347. Refer to note 353 *infra*.

348. *See Lagrone v. State*, 942 S.W.2d 602, 612-13 (Tex. Crim. App. 1997) (Criminal Rule 608(b) "expressly prohibits the utilization of specific instances of conduct—such as drug addiction evidence—for impeachment except to expose bias, correct any affirmative misrepresentations made on direct examination, or demonstrate lack of capacity"; witness is subject to attack on cross-examination only when his perceptual capacity was physically impaired by alcohol or drugs at time of event); *Minns v. Piotrowski*, 904 S.W.2d 161, 172 (Tex. App.—Waco 1995) (cross-examination about specific instances of prior illegal drug use was not permitted under Civil Rule 608(b)), *writ denied*, 917 S.W.2d 796 (Tex. 1996); *see, e.g., Ramirez*, 802 S.W.2d at 676 (when child victim's mother testified for defendant charged with aggravated assault of the child, State could not question mother about her prior heroin use to show her untruthfulness); *Commerce & Indus. Ins. v. Ferguson-Stewart*, 339 S.W.3d 744, 747 (Tex. App.—Houston [1st Dist.] 2011, no pet.) (decedent's use of prescription pain medication was inadmissible as a possible motive to falsify his workers' compensation claim; "Texas courts have consistently upheld the exclusion of evidence of a witness's prior drug use for general impeachment purposes").

349. *See, e.g., Booker v. State*, 929 S.W.2d 57, 66 (Tex. App.—Beaumont 1996, pet. ref'd) (extraneous offense of attempted murder that was collateral to the present offense of attempted murder was not admissible under Criminal Rule 608 or any other theory); *Ray v. State*, 764 S.W.2d 406, 413 (Tex. App.—Houston [14th Dist.] 1988, pet. ref'd) (evidence of prior specific violent acts by the State's witness was inadmissible in murder trial).

350. *See, e.g., Clay v. State*, 390 S.W.3d 1, 12-13 (Tex. App.—Texarkana 2012, pet. ref'd) (in sexual-assault case, defendant could not offer impeachment evidence that complainant had lied to her parents about where she was go-

Federal Rule 608(b), unlike Texas Rule 608(b), gives the trial judge discretion to admit evidence of specific instances of a witness's conduct to be used for impeachment of his general character for truthfulness.[353] Specific instances, other than criminal convictions, cannot be proved by extrinsic evidence[354] but can be investigated on cross-examination, provided they are probative of truthfulness.[355] The rationale behind the

ing that night; evidence was presented only for general attack on credibility and was not relevant as proof of bias, prejudice, or ulterior motive for her to accuse defendant of sexually assaulting her); *Hiatt v. State*, 319 S.W.3d 115, 127 (Tex. App.—San Antonio 2010, pet. ref'd) (defendant was properly prohibited from attacking witness's credibility with evidence of misrepresentations on a credit application); *West v. State*, 121 S.W.3d 95, 101-02 (Tex. App.—Fort Worth 2003, pet. ref'd) (specific entry in victim's diary in which she admitted lying about defendant was not admissible under Rule 608(b) to show that her character for truth-telling was poor because evidence "involved a specific instance of conduct, i.e., writing false things in a diary"); *Felan v. State*, 44 S.W.3d 249, 254-55 (Tex. App.—Fort Worth 2001, pet. ref'd) (defendant was not entitled to impeach statutory-rape victim's testimony with prior statement that she purportedly lied about a rival's sexual conduct with defendant); *Tinlin v. State*, 983 S.W.2d 65, 69 (Tex. App.—Fort Worth 1998, pet. ref'd) (Rule 608(b) prohibited impeachment of defendant's stepdaughter with purportedly false accusation of sexual molestation by another person to show her general lack of credibility; even if such evidence could establish bias, defendant did not demonstrate that prior accusation was false); *Ruiz v. State*, 891 S.W.2d 302, 306 (Tex. App.—San Antonio 1994, pet. ref'd) (Criminal Rule 608(b) forbade cross-examination of witness on whether she had a false birth certificate and fictitious name); *Serv. Lloyds Ins. v. Martin*, 855 S.W.2d 816, 823 (Tex. App.—Dallas 1993, no writ) (Civil Rule 608(b) prohibited admission of plaintiff's false answer on job application in workers' compensation action because attempt to impeach claimant with this evidence violated rule providing that credibility of witness may not be attacked by offering evidence of specific instances of conduct); *Nix v. H.R. Mgmt. Co.*, 733 S.W.2d 573, 576 (Tex. App.—San Antonio 1987, writ ref'd n.r.e.) (evidence that tenant lied in an unrelated matter was not admissible in the tenant's action against apartment complex).

351. *See, e.g.*, *Arriola v. State*, 969 S.W.2d 42, 43 (Tex. App.—Beaumont 1998, pet. ref'd) (evidence of sexual-assault victim's prior sexual behavior with others was barred by Rule 608(b) and was not admissible to show any motive to lie about defendant).

352. *See, e.g.*, *West v. State*, 790 S.W.2d 3, 4 (Tex. App.—San Antonio 1989, pet. ref'd) (in prosecution for manufacture of a controlled substance, error to ask defendant if he was the Grand Dragon of the Ku Klux Klan in Texas in the 1970s; conviction was affirmed because defendant did not make a specific objection).

353. *See* FED. R. EVID. 608(b). Federal Rule 608(b) was amended in 2003 "to clarify that the absolute prohibition on extrinsic evidence applies only when the sole reason for proffering that evidence is to attack or support the witness' character for truthfulness." FED. R. EVID. 608 advisory committee's note to 2003 amendments. The phrase "character for truthfulness" was substituted for the word "credibility" in the last sentence of Rule 608(b). The Advisory Committee noted that the word "credibility" had sometimes been read too broadly as barring extrinsic evidence for bias, competency, and contradiction impeachment. *Id.* Use of the phrase "character for truthfulness" is thus intended to clarify that extrinsic evidence is barred only if the evidence is offered to prove the witness's general character for veracity. *Id.* Texas Rule 608(b) also now uses "character for truthfulness" instead of "credibility."

The Advisory Committee also noted that Federal Rule 608(b) bars

any reference to the consequences that a witness might have suffered as a result of an alleged bad act. For example, Rule 608(b) prohibits counsel from mentioning that a witness was suspended or disciplined for the conduct that is the subject of impeachment, when that conduct is offered only to prove the character of the witness.

FED. R. EVID. 608 advisory committee's note to 2003 amendments. That questioning technique would improperly attempt to evade both Rule 608(b)'s bar against extrinsic evidence and the rule against hearsay. *Id.*

354. Thus, the questioner must accept the witness's answer on this collateral issue. *See, e.g.*, *United States v. Reed*, 700 F.2d 638, 643-44 (11th Cir. 1983) (defendant's conviction was reversed because prosecutor improperly questioned defendant about the possession of a marijuana cigarette at the time of arrest and then offered extrinsic evidence to contradict his answers).

355. *See* FED. R. EVID. 608(b); *see, e.g.*, *United States v. Umawa Oke Imo*, 739 F.3d 226, 238-39 (5th Cir. 2014) (under Rule 608(b)(1), government could cross-examine defendant on fraudulent acts because they were indicative of her character for truthfulness; Rule 404(b) did not apply because evidence was offered to discredit defendant, not to prove an issue in the case such as identity or intent); *United States v. Redditt*, 381 F.3d 597, 601-02 (7th Cir. 2004) (under Rule 608(b), government could impeach witness with fact that she did not list a prior conviction on an ear-

federal rule is complicated, and the rule is frequently difficult to apply. Factors that federal courts consider in exercising this discretion include: whether the character of the witness himself is at issue or whether the witness is testifying about the character of another person; the extent to which the evidence is probative of an untruthful character; the extent to which the evidence is also probative of other relevant matters; whether the circumstances surrounding the specific instances of conduct are similar to those surrounding the witness's present testimony; the remoteness of the prior conduct; the likelihood that the prior conduct actually occurred; the extent to which the prior conduct is cumulative or unnecessary in light of other evidence showing the witness's character for truthfulness or lack thereof; and whether the evidence is necessary to rebut other evidence of character for truthfulness.[356]

Texas Rule 608(b) is not a complete bar to the admission of impeachment evidence of prior specific conduct; it simply prohibits evidence of prior specific conduct offered to attack the witness's general character for truthfulness. For example, when a witness affirmatively creates a false impression about some aspect of his character, other rules may permit the opponent to use prior specific instances of conduct to rebut that false impression.[357] But courts construe the false-impression exception narrowly.[358] The

---

lier employment application; error to admit document itself, but error was waived because opposing counsel affirmatively stated that he had no objections to admission of exhibit); **United States v. Parker**, 133 F.3d 322, 326-27 (5th Cir. 1998) (Rule 608(b) did not permit defendant to cross-examine witness about pending state charge of murder to impeach her general credibility; violent crimes are irrelevant to witness's character for truthfulness); **United States v. Howard**, 774 F.2d 838, 844-45 (7th Cir. 1985) (prosecutor could question defendant about lying on an employment application nine years earlier); **United States v. Zandi**, 769 F.2d 229, 236 (4th Cir. 1985) (witness was properly impeached with questioning about prior false statements on bank-loan applications and tax returns); **Simmons, Inc. v. Pinkerton's, Inc.**, 762 F.2d 591, 605 (7th Cir. 1985) (under Civil Rule 608(b), permissible to cross-examine witness with the fact that he had lied about passing a lie-detector test because it was a specific instance of conduct probative of his truthfulness), *overruled on other grounds*, **Hedgpeth v. Pulido**, 555 U.S. 57 (2008).

The types of dishonest or untruthful conduct that may be admitted under Federal Rule 608(b) include the following: bribery, fraud, and embezzlement, **United States v. Tomblin**, 46 F.3d 1369, 1389 (5th Cir. 1995); soliciting a bribe and income-tax violations, **United States v. Bustamante**, 45 F.3d 933, 946 (5th Cir. 1995); bank fraud, **United States v. Chevalier**, 1 F.3d 581, 583 (7th Cir. 1993); using a false identification card to cash stolen checks, **United States v. Williams**, 986 F.2d 86, 89 (4th Cir. 1993); and forgery, **United States v. Waldrip**, 981 F.2d 799, 803 (5th Cir. 1993).

356. *See* 28 WRIGHT & GOLD, *supra* note 21, §6118, at 94-97 (1993).

357. *See, e.g.,* **King v. State**, 773 S.W.2d 302, 303 (Tex. Crim. App. 1989) (State could impeach defendant with evidence that he had delivered drugs to a police officer two days after committing the charged offense after defendant testified that he had never been convicted of a misdemeanor and that he would not engage in any future criminal acts). In **Pyles v. State**, the capital-murder defendant testified and created the impression that he was a nonviolent person interested in committing only property crimes. 755 S.W.2d 98, 115 (Tex. Crim. App. 1988). This testimony opened the door for the State to impeach the defendant by showing that the defendant had a predisposition for violence against law-enforcement personnel. *Id.* Thus, the court held that it was not error to admit photographs of the defendant's jail-cell wall, on which he had written "Kill, kill, Judge, D.A." and "Kill all white pig police." *Id.* at 112. The court characterized this evidence as impeachment by prior inconsistent statements rather than proof of prior specific acts. *Id.* at 115; *see also* **Grant v. State**, 247 S.W.3d 360, 366-67 (Tex. App.—Austin 2008, pet. ref'd) (defendant's remote prior conviction for assault was admissible to correct affirmative misrepresentations made when he denied ever having behaved violently); **Paita v. State**, 125 S.W.3d 708, 712-13 (Tex. App.—Houston [1st Dist.] 2003, pet. ref'd) (even though conviction was inadmissible under Rule 609, State could impeach testifying defendant with prior conviction for interference with duties of a public servant because defendant left false impression with jury by his nonresponsive testimony that he "acted out of respect for police"); **Lewis v. State**, 933 S.W.2d 172, 179 (Tex. App.—Corpus Christi 1996, pet. ref'd) (defendant's statement that he "will not" drink and drive does not amount

cross-examiner may not rely on artful questioning to "open the door" for the witness and then attempt to offer evidence that is otherwise inadmissible under Rule 608(b) to correct a false impression that he helped to create.[359]

Further, Rule 608 does not affect the admissibility of prior specific acts offered to show the witness's bias or motive to testify.[360] Courts have sometimes confused this

---

to an assertion, or even an implication, that he had never driven while intoxicated; it neither invoked the past nor implied that he had never committed a crime; therefore, his statement did not open the door to impeachment with prior DWI conviction); *House v. State*, 909 S.W.2d 214, 216-17 (Tex. App.—Houston [14th Dist.] 1995) (State could cross-examine defendant on the reason an acquaintance would want to burn down defendant's business when defendant had gratuitously testified that he did not know why that person would want to destroy his business), *aff'd*, 947 S.W.2d 251 (Tex. Crim. App. 1997); *Hernandez v. State*, 897 S.W.2d 488, 494 (Tex. App.—Tyler 1995, no pet.) (defense counsel's question, "Have you ever had any other type of problems with the law?" and defendant's answer of "No," opened the door to the fact that defendant was wanted for murder in Mexico); *Cunningham v. State*, 815 S.W.2d 313, 319 (Tex. App.—Dallas 1991, no pet.) ("[W]hen the accused testifies gratuitously about some matter that is irrelevant or collateral to the proceeding, as with any other witness, the State may impeach him by a showing that he has lied or is in error regarding that matter."). For federal cases to the same effect, see *United States v. Cusmano*, 729 F.2d 380, 383 (6th Cir. 1984) (when defendant in Hobbs Act prosecution denied threatening anyone, including any drivers, the government could cross-examine him on a specific prior assault on one of his truck drivers), and *United States v. Billups*, 692 F.2d 320, 329 (4th Cir. 1982) (when defendant-labor official testified that he had never accepted "anything" from waterfront employers, evidence that he had received gratuities over the course of several years was admissible).

358. *James v. State*, 102 S.W.3d 162, 181 (Tex. App.—Fort Worth 2003, pet. ref'd); *e.g.*, *Clay v. State*, 390 S.W.3d 1, 13-14 (Tex. App.—Texarkana 2012, pet. ref'd) (in sexual-assault case, defendant could not offer extrinsic evidence of complainant's drug use to correct alleged false impression left by her statement of good character about unfamiliarity with cocaine; because the matter was collateral to the charged offense, any false impression should have been addressed in cross-examination).

359. *See, e.g.*, *Crenshaw v. State*, 125 S.W.3d 651, 655-56 (Tex. App.—Houston [1st Dist.] 2003, pet. ref'd) (cross-examiner could not use leading questions to elicit witness's response that he had never committed robbery and then offer evidence that witness had been involved in an unrelated robbery one week before charged offense); *see also Arebalo v. State*, 143 S.W.3d 402, 407-08 (Tex. App.—Austin 2004, pet. ref'd) (trial court erred in allowing State to impeach testifying defendant with details of a prior conviction for aggravated assault with a pistol; defendant's statement during direct examination that he had previously seen somebody get shot did not open the door to past criminal history); *James*, 102 S.W.3d at 180-81 (defendant's testimony that she did not know the smell of cocaine or what it would do to her did not "open the door" to impeachment with her prior probation for possession of cocaine with intent to deliver that was otherwise inadmissible under Rule 609).

360. *Hammer v. State*, 296 S.W.3d 555, 563 (Tex. Crim. App. 2009); *see* TEX. R. EVID. 613(b). "Furthermore, Rule 404(b) explicitly permits the defense, as well as the prosecution, to offer evidence of other acts of misconduct to establish a person's motive for performing some act—such as making a false allegation against the defendant." *Hammer*, 296 S.W.3d at 563. Refer to *Article IV: Relevance & Its Limits*, *supra* p. 282.

In *Moody v. State*, the court of criminal appeals drew a distinction between evidence that attacks or supports a witness's character for truthfulness and evidence that tends to show a witness's motive to lie or bias the defendant that would affect his testimony. 827 S.W.2d 875, 891 (Tex. Crim. App. 1992). The court concluded that if the evidence would show bias or motive by the witness against the defendant, the evidence should be admitted as part of constitutionally protected cross-examination. *Id.*; *see also Shelby v. State*, 819 S.W.2d 544, 549-51 (Tex. Crim. App. 1991) (in case for aggravated sexual assault, harmful error when trial court refused to allow defendant to cross-examine complainant's mother about her civil lawsuit against apartment complex where assault took place; evidence showed possible bias by a crucial witness); *Fox v. State*, 115 S.W.3d 550, 566-69 (Tex. App.—Houston [14th Dist.] 2002, pet. ref'd) (harmful error to prevent defendant from cross-examining his wife about her purported extramarital affair, which was offered to show her motive for testifying against him and to support claim that she had "plant[ed] the notion of sexual abuse in her young daughters' minds because she wanted a divorce and custody of her children"); *Driggers v. State*, 940 S.W.2d 699, 705-06 (Tex. App.—Texarkana 1996, pet. ref'd) (harmless error to exclude testimony about extramarital relationships during cross-examination of minor-complainant's mother, which was offered to demonstrate witness's motive in prosecution of complainant's father for aggravated sexual assault); *Adams v. Petrade Int'l, Inc.*, 754 S.W.2d 696, 711-12 (Tex. App.—Houston [1st Dist.] 1988, writ de-

distinction. For example, in **Dixon v. State**,[361] the court of criminal appeals originally held that Rule 608(b), forbidding impeachment with specific instances of conduct to show a general lack of truthfulness, is a more "specific" provision than Rule 613,[362] which permits impeachment with specific instances of conduct to show bias, interest, or motive in the particular case.[363] Thus, it concluded that Rule 608(b) bars the admission of impeachment evidence that would be permitted under Rule 613.[364] As the court noted in the opinion on rehearing, however, Rules 608(b) and 613 deal with two entirely different types of impeachment; thus, they are not inconsistent and neither trumps the other.[365] As explained on rehearing, there are various means of impeachment. "One of those means is by demonstrating that the witness, *as a general proposition* ..., is not a truth teller."[366] One way of demonstrating the witness's general lack of credibility is to show he has a bad character for truthfulness by offering opinion or reputation testimony of that trait under Rule 608(a).[367] Another mode is to offer evidence that on specific prior occasions the witness has acted or spoken in an untruthful way (e.g., he lied to his boss, cheated on his income taxes, stole pens from the office).[368] This mode of impeachment, presenting evidence of specific examples of behavior inconsistent with the character trait of truthfulness to show a general lack of truthfulness, is what Rule 608(b) forbids.[369] However, those very same examples of specific instances of conduct may be admissible under Rule 613 if they are offered to show a witness's specific bias, interest, or motive in the particular case. The theory underlying Rule 613 is that, although the witness may generally be a person with an excellent character for truthfulness, "for some unique, special reason, he might have a particular reason to slant his testimony, unconsciously or consciously, for or against one party."[370] Rule 608(b) deals with impeaching a witness who, it is asserted, is generally lacking in truthfulness and should never be believed under oath. Rule 613 deals with a specific reason why a witness might slant or shade the truth in the particular case.[371]

---

nied) (permissible to impeach witness with corporate opportunities that led to personal gain because questioning was directed to witness's bias, interest, and motive in denying partnership's existence). For a discussion of Rule 613, refer to notes 578-688 *infra* and accompanying text.

361. 2 S.W.3d 263 (Tex. Crim. App. 1998).

362. At the time of the defendant's trial, what is now Rule 613 was Criminal Rule 612. *See Dixon*, 2 S.W.3d at 266 n.4. For the sake of simplicity, all references to former Criminal Rule 612 in *Dixon* are referred to in this discussion as Rule 613.

363. *See Dixon*, 2 S.W.3d at 267 (orig. op.).

364. *Id.*

365. *Id.* at 270-73 (op. on reh'g).

366. *Id.* at 272.

367. *Id.*

368. *Id.*

369. *Id.*

370. *Id.* at 272-73.

371. *Id.* at 273; *see also* **Lopez v. State**, 989 S.W.2d 402, 409 (Tex. App.—San Antonio 1999) (Angelini, J., dissenting) (discussing which method of impeachment applies to facts of case), *rev'd on other grounds*, 18 S.W.3d 220 (Tex. Crim. App. 2000).

RULE 608

Finally, Rule 608(b) does not bar the admission of evidence that is independently relevant to the issues at trial, regardless of whether it might also affect a witness's credibility.[372] The rule bars evidence of specific conduct only when a party's *sole* purpose in offering it is to impeach the witness's general character for truthfulness. If the evidence is being offered for a reason other than character impeachment, Rule 608(b) is not implicated and should not affect admissibility.[373]

RULE 609

IMPEACHMENT BY EVIDENCE OF A CRIMINAL CONVICTION

(a) In General. Evidence of a criminal conviction offered to attack a witness's character for truthfulness must be admitted if:

(1) the crime was a felony or involved moral turpitude, regardless of punishment;

(2) the probative value of the evidence outweighs its prejudicial effect to a party; and

(3) it is elicited from the witness or established by public record.

(b) Limit on Using the Evidence After 10 Years. This subdivision (b) applies if more than 10 years have passed since the witness's conviction or release from confinement for it, whichever is later. Evidence of the conviction is admissible only if its probative value, supported by specific facts and circumstances, substantially outweighs its prejudicial effect.

(c) Effect of a Pardon, Annulment, or Certificate of Rehabilitation. Evidence of a conviction is not admissible if:

(1) the conviction has been the subject of a pardon, annulment, certificate of rehabilitation, or other equivalent procedure based on a finding that the person has been rehabilitated, and the person has not been convicted of a later crime that was classified as a felony or involved moral turpitude, regardless of punishment;

---

372. *See, e.g.*, *State v. One Super Cherry Master Video 8-Liner Mach.*, 55 S.W.3d 51, 57-58 (Tex. App.—Austin 2001) (Rule 608(b) did not bar defendant's testimony that, after officers seized 8-liner machines and other materials under search warrant, $25,000 cash inheritance from his mother was missing; although this evidence might affect the credibility of the testifying officers, it was offered to show that a significant portion of the money officers seized was his inheritance, not gambling proceeds), *rev'd on other grounds*, 102 S.W.3d 132 (Tex. 2003).

373. *See, e.g.*, *Hudson v. State*, 112 S.W.3d 794, 799-802 (Tex. App.—Houston [14th Dist.] 2003, pet. ref'd) (in trial for domestic-violence aggravated assault, State could cross-examine defendant about his use of a knife in previous assaults on his wife; evidence was not offered to impeach his general character for truthfulness but rather to rebut defense that defendant was delusional when he set her on fire and threatened to stab her; evidence showed that in earlier assaults he had used a knife, demonstrating that he was not delusional or acting unusually on day of offense); *cf. Stovall v. Horizon Offshore Contractors, Inc.*, 349 F. Supp. 2d 1021, 1023-24 (E.D. La. 2004) ("although Rule 608 prohibits admission of extrinsic evidence to attack a witness's character for truthfulness, it does not apply to evidence introduced to disprove a specific fact material to a party's claim"; in personal-injury suit, defendant argued that plaintiff's postaccident conviction for assaulting girlfriend was admissible to contradict claim that plaintiff was physically impaired as a result of worksite injury, not to impeach his general character).

> (2) probation has been satisfactorily completed for the conviction, and the person has not been convicted of a later crime that was classified as a felony or involved moral turpitude, regardless of punishment; or
>
> (3) the conviction has been the subject of a pardon, annulment, or other equivalent procedure based on a finding of innocence.
>
> **(d) Juvenile Adjudications.** Evidence of a juvenile adjudication is admissible under this rule only if:
>
> (1) the witness is a party in a proceeding conducted under title 3 of the Texas Family Code; or
>
> (2) the United States or Texas Constitution requires that it be admitted.
>
> **(e) Pendency of an Appeal.** A conviction for which an appeal is pending is not admissible under this rule.
>
> **(f) Notice.** Evidence of a witness's conviction is not admissible under this rule if, after receiving from the adverse party a timely written request specifying the witness, the proponent of the conviction fails to provide sufficient written notice of intent to use the conviction. Notice is sufficient if it provides a fair opportunity to contest the use of such evidence.

COMMENTARY ON RULE 609

A. Rule 609(a): In General

Rule 609 governs the use of prior criminal convictions offered to impeach a testifying witness's character for truthfulness.[374] The traditional rationale for permitting

---

374. *See **Murray v. Tex. Dep't of Family & Prot. Servs.**, 294 S.W.3d 360, 369 (Tex. App.—Austin 2009, no pet.) ("[R]ule 609 is not a categorical limitation on the introduction of convictions for any purpose. Rather, it applies only to convictions offered for purposes of impeachment.").

Rule 609(a) formerly referred to a witness's credibility rather than a witness's character for truthfulness. Both Texas Rule 609(a) and Federal Rule 609(a) now refer to the witness's character for truthfulness. *See* FED. R. EVID. 609(a); TEX. R. EVID. 609(a). Neither the Texas rule nor the federal rule imposes a limitation on the use of prior convictions for other purposes such as to demonstrate a basis for a witness's bias or to contradict testimony that a witness has never been convicted of a crime. *See **Delk v. State**, 855 S.W.2d 700, 704 (Tex. Crim. App. 1993) ("[A]n exception to Rule 609 applies when a witness makes statements concerning his past conduct that suggest he has never been arrested, charged, or convicted of any offense."), *overruled on other grounds*, **Ex parte Moreno**, 245 S.W.3d 419 (Tex. Crim. App. 2008); FED. R. EVID. 609 advisory committee's note to 2006 amendments ("The amendment also substitutes the term 'character for truthfulness' for the term 'credibility' in the first sentence of the Rule. The limitations of Rule 609 are not applicable if a conviction is admitted for a purpose other than to prove the witness's character for untruthfulness."); *see, e.g.*, **United States v. Norton**, 26 F.3d 240, 243-44 (1st Cir. 1994) (Rule 609 did not apply when conviction for possession of a firearm was used to contradict testimony that defendant had never possessed a gun).

For many years, Texas civil courts refused to allow evidence of a criminal conviction to impeach a witness. This rule was set out in **Boon v. Weathered's Adm'r**, 23 Tex. 675, 678 (1859). Refer to note 346 *supra* and accompanying text. However, most of the cases that referred to this rule actually involved indictments or arrests on criminal charges that had not matured into convictions. *See, e.g.*, **Mo., Kan. & Tex. Ry. Co. of Tex. v. Creason**, 101 Tex. 335, 336-37, 107 S.W. 527, 527-28 (1908) (in personal-injury suit, whether witness had been indicted for arson was irrelevant to the issue of his credibility); **Kruger v. Spachek**, 22 Tex. Civ. App. 307, 308, 54 S.W. 295, 296 (Austin 1899,

such impeachment is the belief that a person who has committed certain types of crimes will be more willing than most to lie under oath.[375] A conviction for a felony or a minor offense involving moral turpitude is generally probative of a defect in character that arguably bears a logical relationship to the witness's character for truthfulness.[376] Prior convictions go to the weight of the witness's testimony, not to the admissibility of the testimony.[377]

1. Differences between Texas & Federal Rule 609(a). Rule 609(a) differs in three ways from Federal Rule 609(a). First, the Texas rule permits impeachment with any conviction for a felony or crime of "moral turpitude,"[378] while the federal rule is confined to felonies[379] and those crimes involving dishonesty or false statement.[380] Federal courts have occasionally struggled with the question of which crimes involve dishonesty or

---

no writ) (objection to question of whether witness had been indicted for theft should have been sustained). In 1928, the Texas Commission of Appeals made the distinction and ruled that evidence of a conviction could be used for impeachment purposes. *See **Kennedy v. Int'l-Great N. R.R.**,* 1 S.W.2d 581, 583 (Tex. Comm'n App. 1928, judgm't adopted).

375. *See **United States v. Lipscomb**,* 702 F.2d 1049, 1054 (D.C. Cir. 1983) (defense witness's recent conviction for robbery was admissible to impeach; trial court stated that "the desperate person who would commit an armed robbery would also lie under oath"); FED. R. EVID. 609 advisory committee's note, 46 F.R.D. 161, 297 (1969 preliminary draft) ("A demonstrated instance of willingness to engage in conduct in disregard of accepted patterns is translatable into willingness to give false testimony."). *See generally* 3 WEINSTEIN & BERGER, *supra* note 110, ¶609[02], at 609-27 to 609-32 (discussing the theory that convictions are relevant to credibility); 3A WIGMORE, *supra* note 295, §982, at 839-40 (reviewing the limitations of relevance for impeachment with prior convictions).

376. *See* 3A WIGMORE, *supra* note 295, §982, at 839. *See generally* Robert F. Holland, *It's About Time: The Need for a Uniform Approach to Using a Prior Conviction to Impeach a Witness,* 40 ST. MARY'S L.J. 455 (2008) (analyzing Rule 609 and the Texas courts' inconsistent application of the rule).

377. *See **Brown v. State**,* 270 S.W.3d 564, 568 (Tex. Crim. App. 2008) ("The fact that the [witness's] testimony may have been subject to impeachment as coming from an admitted perjurer and drug user goes to the weight of the evidence and not to its admissibility.").

378. TEX. R. EVID. 609(a)(1).

379. *See* FED. R. EVID. 609(a)(1). Federal Rule 609(a) discusses crimes punishable by death or by imprisonment for more than one year, rather than using the term "felony," because jurisdictions differ in their groupings of "infamous" or serious crimes and misdemeanors. *See* McCORMICK ON EVIDENCE, *supra* note 2, §43, at 93-94. The federal drafters intended this language to encompass all convictions for felony-grade offenses. *See* FED. R. EVID. 609 advisory committee's note, subdiv. (a).

380. *See* FED. R. EVID. 609(a)(2); ***United States v. Hayes**,* 553 F.2d 824, 826-27 (2d Cir. 1977); *see, e.g.,* ***United States v. Mahone**,* 328 F. Supp. 2d 77, 82-84 (D. Me. 2004) (forgery is a crime of dishonesty, but robbery charge that was reduced to aggravated assault is not; court declined to decide whether theft by receiving is crime of dishonesty), *aff'd,* 453 F.3d 68 (1st Cir. 2006). Crimes involving "dishonesty or false statement" do not include armed robbery, assault, or crimes of stealth such as burglary, while others, such as perjury, false statement, criminal fraud, embezzlement, or false pretenses, are clearly within that category. *Hayes,* 553 F.2d at 827; *see **United States v. Givens**,* 767 F.2d 574, 579 n.1 (9th Cir. 1985) ("[C]rimes of violence, theft crimes, and crimes of stealth do not involve dishonesty or false statement within the meaning of Rule 609(a)(2)."). Other offenses may leave room for doubt, and the prosecutor in those cases must demonstrate "'that a particular prior conviction rested on facts warranting the dishonesty or false statement description.'" *Hayes,* 553 F.2d at 827 (quoting ***United States v. Smith**,* 551 F.2d 348, 364 n.28 (D.C. Cir. 1976)); *see, e.g.,* ***United States v. Mehrmanesh**,* 689 F.2d 822, 833-34 (9th Cir. 1982) (prior conviction for smuggling hashish was not automatically admissible to impeach testifying defendant). The ***Mehrmanesh*** court noted that "[c]onvictions for such surreptitious activity, not necessarily involving misrepresentations or falsification, do not bear *directly* on the likelihood that the defendant will testify truthfully." 689 F.2d at 833. *But see* Edward W. Cleary, *Preliminary Notes on Reading the Rules of Evidence,* 57 NEB. L. REV. 908, 919 (1978) (sarcastically noting displeasure with courts that would hold that attempted burglary involves neither dishonesty nor false statement).

false statement. This issue, however, was addressed by the 2006 amendment to Federal Rule 609(a)(2).[381] The use of the amorphous phrase "moral turpitude" in the Texas rule has been called a "serpent of uncertainty."[382] Frequently, crimes that involve moral turpitude do not bear any direct or necessary relationship to the character trait of truthfulness. Prostitution, for example, is a crime of moral turpitude,[383] yet it bears little logical relationship to the lack of truthfulness. Nonetheless, Rule 609 carries forward the traditional Texas practice in criminal proceedings of permitting impeachment with prior convictions for felonies and crimes of "moral turpitude."[384]

---

381. The rule's focus is on whether the conviction offered for impeachment purposes required proof of an act of dishonesty or false statement, such as in crimes of perjury, subornation of perjury, false statement, embezzlement, or any other offense "the commission of which involves some element of deceit, untruthfulness, or falsification bearing on the [witness's] propensity to testify truthfully." FED. R. EVID. 609 advisory committee's note to 2006 amendments. It does not matter whether the witness actually exhibited dishonesty or made a false statement during the commission of a crime. *Id.* Thus, evidence that a witness was convicted of a violent crime such as murder is not admissible under Federal Rule 609(a)(2), even if the witness acted dishonestly during the commission of the crime. *Id.*

382. McCORMICK ON EVIDENCE, *supra* note 2, §43, at 93 n.5 (detailed catalog of crimes involving "moral turpitude" is a waste of judicial energy and misses the real issue, which is whether the conviction is one probative of credibility); *see also* 1 GOODE ET AL., *supra* note 24, §609.2, at 589 (comparing crimes that have been held to involve moral turpitude to those that have not; categorization "fails to inspire confidence that principled lines have been drawn in the past").

As an example of the peculiar result this distinction causes, see *Patterson v. State*, 783 S.W.2d 268 (Tex. App.—Houston [14th Dist.] 1989, pet. ref'd). In *Patterson*, the defendant, on trial for aggravated robbery, attempted to impeach a State's witness with a prior misdemeanor conviction for reckless conduct. 783 S.W.2d at 271. If the assaultive conduct involved in that conviction had been committed on a female, that conviction, under traditional Texas law, would have constituted a crime of moral turpitude. However, because the witness testified that he assaulted two males who were in a car with their two daughters, the offense was not one involving moral turpitude and thus not admissible to impeach. *Id.* at 271-72. On the other hand, in *Hardeman v. State*, the defendant's prior misdemeanor conviction for assault by a man against a woman was admissible under Criminal Rule 609 as a crime involving moral turpitude. 868 S.W.2d 404, 407 (Tex. App.—Austin 1993), *pet. dism'd, improvidently granted*, 891 S.W.2d 960 (Tex. Crim. App. 1995). The court stated that moral turpitude has been defined as "[t]he quality of a crime involving grave infringement of the moral sentiment of the community as distinguished from statutory mala prohibita." *Id.* at 405. Under that definition, the chivalrous court held that assaulting a woman meets the test of gravely infringing the moral sentiment of the community. *Id.* at 407.

A more logical line of cases follows the reasoning in *Robertson v. State*, in which the court held that "[t]here can be no question that a crime involving false statement and dishonesty is relevant to the credibility of a witness." 685 S.W.2d 488, 492 (Tex. App.—Fort Worth 1985, no pet.); *see also Lape v. State*, 893 S.W.2d 949, 958 (Tex. App.—Houston [14th Dist.] 1994, pet. ref'd) (offense of making a false report is a misdemeanor involving moral turpitude, regardless of whether it is done for personal gain, because it involves dishonesty; conviction admissible under Criminal Rule 609).

383. *Holgin v. State*, 480 S.W.2d 405, 408 (Tex. Crim. App. 1972); *Taylor v. State*, 470 S.W.2d 663, 664 (Tex. Crim. App. 1971); *Johnson v. State*, 453 S.W.2d 828, 830 (Tex. Crim. App. 1970).

384. *See* 1 RAY, *supra* note 4, §§659-660, at 592-99 (outlining the history of impeachment by prior conviction in criminal and civil cases).

The court of criminal appeals has considered various situations in determining whether a given offense involves moral turpitude. *See, e.g., Bell v. State*, 620 S.W.2d 116, 121 (Tex. Crim. App. [Panel Op.] 1980) (misdemeanor possession of marijuana does not involve moral turpitude); *Milligan v. State*, 554 S.W.2d 192, 196 (Tex. Crim. App. 1977) (theft involves moral turpitude); *Trippell v. State*, 535 S.W.2d 178, 180 (Tex. Crim. App. 1976) (unlawfully carrying a pistol does not involve moral turpitude); *Garza v. State*, 532 S.W.2d 624, 625 (Tex. Crim. App. 1976) (disturbing the peace does not involve moral turpitude); *Holgin*, 480 S.W.2d at 408 (prostitution involves moral turpitude); *Crisp v. State*, 470 S.W.2d 58, 59-60 (Tex. Crim. App. 1971) (receiving stolen property involves moral turpitude); *Stephens v. State*, 417 S.W.2d 286, 287 n.1 (Tex. Crim. App. 1967) (DWI does not involve moral turpitude); *Sherman v. State*, 124 Tex. Crim. 273, 280, 62 S.W.2d 146, 150 (1933) (swindling involves moral turpitude);

Texas courts have defined moral turpitude as: "(1) the quality of a crime involving grave infringement of the moral sentiment of the community as distinguished from statutory *mala prohibita*; (2) conduct that is base, vile, or depraved; and (3) something that is inherently immoral or dishonest."[385] While Texas courts have permitted impeachment with misdemeanors involving moral turpitude, the approach is not supported by logic or ease of administration.[386]

When out-of-state convictions are offered under Rule 609, they are classified as crimes of moral turpitude according to Texas law rather than the convicting jurisdiction's categorization.[387] In contrast, when classifying an offense as a felony or misdemeanor, Texas courts look to the other jurisdiction's categorization of the crime.[388]

Garrison v. State, 94 Tex. Crim. 541, 542, 252 S.W. 511, 512 (1923) (drunkenness in a public place does not involve moral turpitude); *Miller v. State*, 67 Tex. Crim. 654, 657, 150 S.W. 635, 636 (1912) (gambling does not involve moral turpitude); *Kemper v. State*, 63 Tex. Crim. 1, 7, 138 S.W. 1025, 1028 (1911) (assault does not involve moral turpitude).

    This peculiar analysis of the term "moral turpitude" for purposes of impeachment for general truthfulness continues even under the Rules. *See, e.g., Davis v. State*, ___ S.W.3d ___ (Tex. App.—Corpus Christi 2017, pet. filed 8-7-17) (No. 13-15-00355-CR; 6-1-17) (misdemeanor assault is not crime of moral turpitude unless it is committed by man against woman or victim is child; witness's misdemeanor assault convictions would not have been admissible to impeach him under Rule 609 when no evidence showed sex or age of any victim); *Urtado v. State*, 333 S.W.3d 418, 428-29 (Tex. App.—Austin 2011, pet. ref'd) (interference with an emergency call does not involve moral turpitude because it does not require an act of violence or deception); *Lopez v. State*, 990 S.W.2d 770, 779 (Tex. App.—Austin 1999, no pet.) (misdemeanor bail jumping was admissible as offense of moral turpitude as it involves deceit and deception); *Hardeman*, 868 S.W.2d at 407 (misdemeanor assault by man against woman was admissible as offense of moral turpitude); *Polk v. State*, 865 S.W.2d 627, 630 (Tex. App.—Fort Worth 1993, pet. ref'd) (misdemeanor conviction for indecent exposure was admissible as offense of moral turpitude; moral turpitude includes "acts which are base, vile or depraved"); *see also In re Humphreys*, 880 S.W.2d 402, 408-09 (Tex. 1994) (in disbarment proceeding, Texas Supreme Court held that income-tax evasion is crime of moral turpitude and that Texas Rules of Disciplinary Procedure compelled disbarment of attorney convicted of that crime).

  385. *E.g., Arnold v. State*, 36 S.W.3d 542, 546-47 (Tex. App.—Tyler 2000, pet. ref'd) (criminally negligent homicide is not a crime of moral turpitude); *Ludwig v. State*, 969 S.W.2d 22, 28-29 (Tex. App.—Fort Worth 1998, pet. ref'd) (conviction for violation of protective order is a crime of moral turpitude when underlying offense involves family violence).

  386. Before the adoption of Rule 609, prior convictions were admissible to impeach a testifying witness in civil cases only when the conviction involved moral turpitude. *See Jackson v. Granite State Ins.*, 685 S.W.2d 16, 17 (Tex. 1985) (felony conviction for dispensing nonnarcotic drugs "not in the usual course of professional practice" was inadmissible because crime did not involve moral turpitude); *Compton v. Jay*, 389 S.W.2d 639, 641-42 (Tex. 1965) (impeachment should be limited to convictions for crimes of moral turpitude; error to admit evidence of prior convictions for DWI); *Harris Cty. v. Jenkins*, 678 S.W.2d 639, 641 (Tex. App.—Houston [14th Dist.] 1984, writ ref'd n.r.e.) ("[C]onvictions for crimes involving moral turpitude are admissible in civil cases for the purpose of impeaching a witness."). In criminal proceedings, any felony conviction was admissible to impeach credibility, as were misdemeanors that involved moral turpitude. *See Taylor v. State*, 612 S.W.2d 566, 572 (Tex. Crim. App. [Panel Op.] 1981); *Dillard v. State*, 153 Tex. Crim. 134, 137, 218 S.W.2d 476, 477 (1949).

  387. *See, e.g., Davis v. State*, 645 S.W.2d 288, 291-92 (Tex. Crim. App. 1983) (while probation might be a "final conviction" for federal purposes, Texas courts look to state law to determine the admissibility of impeachment evidence); *see also* 3 WEINSTEIN & BERGER, *supra* note 110, ¶609[04], at 609-49 (under Federal Rule 609, characterization of an offense is a federal matter and not a state matter, but the State's definition of the offense—rather than the underlying details of how the crime was committed—governs). For example, because prostitution is a misdemeanor punishable by imprisonment for one year or less under Illinois law, the Eighth Circuit found that evidence of a conviction for prostitution would not be admissible to impeach a witness under Rule 609. *See United States v. Wright*, 564 F.2d 785, 791 (8th Cir. 1977). The conviction would be inadmissible under Rule 609 because subsection (a)(1) admits only convictions punishable by death or imprisonment in excess of one year and subsection (a)(2) admits convictions involving dishonesty or false statement. *Id.; see* 4 GRAHAM, *supra* note 110, §609:4, at 515 (prostitution does not involve dishonesty or false statement). In contrast, under Texas Rule 609(a), a foreign conviction

A second difference between the Texas rule and the federal rule concerns the trial court's obligation to balance the probative value of admitting the evidence against its prejudicial effect. The Texas rule is broadly phrased and requires that in every instance the trial court balance the probative value of the conviction against its prejudicial effect in determining whether to permit impeachment under Rule 609.[389]

In contrast, Federal Rule 609(a)(1) refers to Rule 403, which favors admitting relevant evidence unless the probative value of that evidence is substantially outweighed by unfair prejudice.[390] Thus, the federal rule slants heavily toward the admissibility of prior felony-grade convictions for the impeachment of all witnesses in civil or criminal trials except for the testifying defendant in a criminal case.[391] When determining the admissibility of prior felony convictions to impeach the testifying defendant, the federal rule and the Texas rule are the same—the probative value of the conviction must outweigh its prejudicial effect.[392] Federal Rule 609(a)(2) states, however, that any conviction for a crime with elements that require proof or admission of an act of dishonesty or false statement, regardless of the punishment, is always admissible. In these situations, the trial court has no discretion to weigh probative value against unfair preju-

---

for prostitution would be admitted as a crime involving moral turpitude even though the other jurisdiction may not classify it as such. *See* 1 GOODE ET AL., *supra* note 24, §609.2, at 589.

388. *See* 1 GOODE ET AL., *supra* note 24, §609.2, at 591. For example, if Illinois categorized reckless conduct as a felony offense, it would be admissible under Rule 609 even if Texas categorized reckless conduct as a Class B misdemeanor.

389. *See* TEX. R. EVID. 609(a)(2) (evidence of criminal conviction offered to attack witness's character for truthfulness must be admitted if, among other things, probative value outweighs its prejudicial effect to a party); ***Engelman Irrigation Dist. v. Shields Bros.***, 960 S.W.2d 343, 355 (Tex. App.—Corpus Christi 1997) (before admitting a prior conviction into evidence, trial court must determine that the probative value of the evidence outweighs the prejudicial effect to the party against whom the evidence is offered; complaining party must demonstrate that the trial court abused its discretion in admitting or excluding evidence of the witness's conviction), *pet. denied*, 989 S.W.2d 360 (Tex. 1998); ***Borden, Inc. v. Rios***, 850 S.W.2d 821, 833-34 (Tex. App.—Corpus Christi 1993) (trial court has discretion to admit or exclude prior convictions), *writ granted w.r.m.*, 859 S.W.2d 70 (Tex. 1993).

390. *See* FED. R. EVID. 609(a)(1)(A). Refer to *Article IV: Relevance & Its Limits*, *supra* p. 209.

391. Under Federal Rule 609(a)(1), trial courts should be more willing to allow impeachment with prior convictions of any witness in either a civil or criminal trial other than the defendant. *See generally **United States v. Tse***, 375 F.3d 148, 159-64 (1st Cir. 2004) (analyzing operation of Federal Rule 609(a) for both testifying criminal defendants and government witnesses). The First Circuit summarized the import of the rule:

> With respect to the use of prior convictions for impeachment, Rule 609 distinguishes between the accused and mere witnesses. A court may admit a conviction of the accused only if the probative value "outweighs its prejudicial effect to the accused." By contrast, a court shall admit a conviction of a government witness unless that conviction should be excluded under Rule 403. The burden under Rule 403 is on the party opposing admission, who must show that the probative value "is *substantially outweighed* by the danger of *unfair prejudice.*"

Id. at 164 (quoting FED. R. EVID. 403 & 609). In *Tse*, the trial court appeared to have used the same standard in deciding whether similar prior convictions should be admissible to impeach either the defendant or a government witness. If so, said the First Circuit, that was "an error of law." 375 F.3d at 164. However, any error was harmless. *Id.*

392. *See* FED. R. EVID. 609(a)(1)(B); TEX. R. EVID. 609(a)(2); ***Theus v. State***, 845 S.W.2d 874, 879-80 (Tex. Crim. App. 1992).

dicial effect.[393] The Texas rule, on the other hand, always requires the trial judge to balance probative value against prejudicial effect in determining the admissibility of any prior conviction, including those involving dishonesty or false statement.[394]

Third, the Texas rule specifically requires that the conviction be elicited from the witness or established by public record.[395] The federal rule does not have this specification.

2. The operation of Texas Rule 609(a). The proponent of the prior conviction must demonstrate its admissibility under the rule.[396] A trial judge may refuse to permit the impeachment if the proponent does not introduce sufficient evidence to link the convictions to the witness.[397] While a party may offer a prior conviction to impeach a witness's character for truthfulness, the party may not offer the details of those offenses or the circumstances of the conviction for the jury's consideration.[398] Similarly, evidence should not be admitted to show that the witness was indicted for a crime greater than the conviction.[399]

On the other hand, if a witness affirmatively gives the jury a false impression of his previous experiences with the criminal-justice system, Rule 609 does not bar impeachment of that witness with prior arrests or acts of misconduct that are otherwise inad-

---

393. *See* FED. R. EVID. 609(a)(2). The Conference Report to Federal Rule 609 states the following:

> The admission of prior convictions involving dishonesty and false statement is not within the discretion of the Court. Such convictions are particularly probative of credibility and, under this rule, are always to be admitted. Thus, judicial discretion granted with respect to the admissibility of other prior convictions is not applicable to those involving dishonesty or false statement.

JOINT EXPLANATORY STATEMENT OF THE COMMITTEE OF CONF. REP. NO. 93-1597, at 9 (1974), *reprinted in* 1974 U.S.C.C.A.N. 7098, 7102.

394. *See* TEX. R. EVID. 609(a)(2).

395. TEX. R. EVID. 609(a)(3). Refer to notes 407-412 *infra* and accompanying text.

396. *Theus*, 845 S.W.2d at 880; *Butler v. State*, 890 S.W.2d 951, 954-55 (Tex. App.—Waco 1995, pet. ref'd).

397. *See Davis v. State*, 791 S.W.2d 308, 310 (Tex. App.—Corpus Christi 1990, pet. ref'd); *see, e.g.*, *Moore v. State*, 826 S.W.2d 775, 778 (Tex. App.—Houston [14th Dist.] 1992, pet. ref'd) (trial court erred in denying defendant's motion for new trial when he was impeached with a murder conviction and evidence showed that he was not the person who had been convicted).

398. *See Stevens v. State*, 671 S.W.2d 517, 522 (Tex. Crim. App. 1984) (when a prior conviction is admitted against the accused, the State may not inquire into details of the offense); *Murphy v. State*, 587 S.W.2d 718, 722 (Tex. Crim. App. [Panel Op.] 1979) ("[A]n issue regarding the general credibility of a witness in a criminal trial is not a material issue in the sense that it will justify the admission of inherently prejudicial evidence of details of an extraneous offense committed by the witness."); *Jabari v. State*, 273 S.W.3d 745, 753 (Tex. App.—Houston [1st Dist.] 2008, no pet.) (details of conviction are generally inadmissible under Rule 609); McCORMICK ON EVIDENCE, *supra* note 2, §43, at 98 (cross-examiner may touch on facts included in judgment and sentence, including the punishment assessed, but not the victim's name or the aggravating circumstances); *see, e.g.*, *Mays v. State*, 726 S.W.2d 937, 952-53 (Tex. Crim. App. 1986) (disallowing cross-examination of State's witness about the number and type of prior felony convictions); *Andrews v. State*, 429 S.W.3d 849, 858-59 (Tex. App.—Texarkana 2014, pet. ref'd) (trial court did not err in preventing cross-examination of witness about his parole status at time of shooting; defendant did not show nexus between witness's testimony and his parole status or any bias in favor of testifying for State); *Rogers v. State*, 756 S.W.2d 332, 342-43 (Tex. App.—Houston [14th Dist.] 1988, pet. ref'd) (allowing defendant's conviction to stand because prosecution gained no information from improper questions to defendant's wife about the details of her prior felony conviction).

399. *Yates v. State*, 917 S.W.2d 915, 920 (Tex. App.—Corpus Christi 1996, pet. ref'd); *Damian v. State*, 881 S.W.2d 102, 113 (Tex. App.—Houston [1st Dist.] 1994, pet. ref'd).

missible under this rule.[400] The rebuttal evidence, however, may not exceed the scope of the question asked and answered by the witness.[401]

Under Rule 609, only a true "conviction"[402] for a crime is admissible to impeach a witness. A person currently on probation has been convicted and has had punishment assessed; the sentence has simply been probated. Thus, a person may be impeached under Rule 609 with evidence of a current probated conviction if it otherwise fits the requirements of the rule. However, if the witness was placed on probation and has successfully terminated the probation, the probated conviction is not admissible under the rule.[403] The fact that the witness is presently or was once on deferred adjudication is

RULE 609

---

400. *See* ***Delk v. State***, 855 S.W.2d 700, 704 (Tex. Crim. App. 1993) ("[A]n exception to Rule 609 applies when a witness makes statements concerning his past conduct that suggest he has never been arrested, charged, or convicted of any offense. Where the witness creates a false impression of law abiding behavior, he 'opens the door' on his otherwise irrelevant past criminal history and opposing counsel may expose the falsehood."); ***Ochoa v. State***, 481 S.W.2d 847, 850 (Tex. Crim. App. 1972) (exception to the rule occurs when "the witness makes blanket statements concerning his exemplary conduct such as having never been arrested, charged, or convicted of any offense, or having never been 'in trouble,' or purports to detail his convictions leaving the impression there are no others"); *see, e.g.,* ***Prescott v. State***, 744 S.W.2d 128, 131 (Tex. Crim. App. 1988) (defendant did not open the door to impeachment with prior felony offense by stating that "this is the first time of going through this" in reference to the procedure of taking witnesses' affidavits); ***Reese v. State***, 531 S.W.2d 638, 641 (Tex. Crim. App. 1976) (when defendant selectively detailed his troubles with the law, failure to relate other instances left a false impression and he could be impeached with other comparable incidents); ***Rowshan v. State***, 445 S.W.3d 294, 299-301 (Tex. App.—Houston [1st Dist.] 2013, pet. ref'd) (State could impeach defendant with evidence of conviction for prostitution, revocation of deferred adjudication for theft conviction, and information charging defendant with "terroristic threatening" when he denied those matters on direct examination); ***U.S.A. Precision Machining Co. v. Marshall***, 95 S.W.3d 407, 410-11 (Tex. App.—Houston [1st Dist.] 2002, pet. denied) (plaintiff's testimony that he had worked and lived with his parents "pretty much" continuously before being employed by defendant did not open the door to impeachment with prior murder conviction that was dismissed after trial court granted motion for new trial, during which time defendant had been incarcerated); ***Nunez v. State***, 27 S.W.3d 210, 215-16 (Tex. App.—El Paso 2000, no pet.) (defendant-attorney's testimony that he had been acquitted on forgery charge opened the door to State's cross-examination to establish reason for acquittal); ***Veteto v. State***, 8 S.W.3d 805, 815 (Tex. App.—Waco 2000, pet. ref'd) (sexual-assault defendant's agreement with prosecutor that it was not the first time he "had endured these accusations" did not leave false impression or open the door to impeachment with other accusations of sexual misconduct); ***Turner v. State***, 4 S.W.3d 74, 79-80 (Tex. App.—Waco 1999, no pet.) (when defendant offered self-flattering remarks about his good relations with police, State could impeach him using violent confrontation he had with police several weeks after DWI arrest); ***Otero v. State***, 988 S.W.2d 457, 458-59 (Tex. App.—Houston [1st Dist.] 1999, pet. ref'd) (DWI defendant did not open the door to impeachment with her offer of medical records containing a box marked "no" for prior DWI when defense counsel attempted to withdraw this page before jury could see or hear of it); ***Patterson v. State***, 783 S.W.2d 268, 272 (Tex. App.—Houston [14th Dist.] 1989, pet. ref'd) (prosecutor did not open the door to impeachment with prior convictions when he asked State's witness if he had ever testified in court before); ***Hinojosa v. State***, 780 S.W.2d 299, 302 (Tex. App.—Beaumont 1989, pet. ref'd) (trial court erred in excluding cross-examination about a prior conviction and completed probation when State's direct examination of its witness gave false impression that witness had never been convicted of an offense); ***Kendrick v. State***, 729 S.W.2d 392, 396 (Tex. App.—Fort Worth 1987, pet. ref'd) (when defense witness's testimony gave the false impression of disposition of a criminal conviction, State was entitled to cross-examine witness on the facts of the offense to correct that impression). Refer to notes 357-359 *supra* and accompanying text.

401. ***Feldman v. State***, 71 S.W.3d 738, 755-56 (Tex. Crim. App. 2002); ***Schutz v. State***, 957 S.W.2d 52, 71 (Tex. Crim. App. 1997).

402. With a true conviction, "there must ordinarily be a judgment of guilt for the crime in question." ***Lopez v. State***, 253 S.W.3d 680, 685 (Tex. Crim. App. 2008); *see* BLACK'S LAW DICTIONARY 408 (10th ed. 2014).

403. *Ex parte Menchaca*, 854 S.W.2d 128, 130-31 (Tex. Crim. App. 1993) (expiration of probationary terms equals "satisfactory conclusion of probation" under rule; prior probation is not admissible to impeach unless there has been an intervening conviction). However, to render the conviction inadmissible, the party sponsoring the witness

not admissible under the rule. A person on deferred adjudication has not been finally convicted of the crime of which he is accused; thus, a deferred adjudication is not a conviction for purposes of Rule 609.[404] And, of course, a pending charge is not a conviction; thus, Rule 609 does not permit impeachment of the witness's character for truthfulness with the fact that the witness is under indictment for a criminal offense, although that evidence might be admissible to establish bias or motive under Rule 613.[405]

Convictions that are based on a plea of nolo contendere are admissible under Rule 609 despite the apparent prohibition of Rule 410. Under Rule 410, evidence of the plea is inadmissible, but the fact of conviction is admissible when offered to impeach a testifying witness's character for truthfulness.[406]

The witness may be asked, on either direct[407] or cross-examination, about his prior convictions. The good faith of the person asking the questions is a sufficient basis for the impeachment attempt.[408] The initial question has generally been phrased "Have you been convicted of a felony or crime of moral turpitude in this state or any other state or jurisdiction within the past ten years?" If the response is affirmative, the questioner could continue with "Were you convicted of the felony offense of perjury on May 31, 2005, in the 461st District Court of Harris County, Texas?" If the witness answers yes, the impeachment is complete. If the witness denies the conviction, the questioner may

---

must establish that the witness has satisfactorily completed probation. *E.g.*, **Jackson v. State**, 888 S.W.2d 912, 916 (Tex. App.—Houston [1st Dist.] 1994, no pet.) (because defendant never challenged finality of his prior conviction for which he was placed on probation, trial court erred in allowing State to question defendant about probation revocation, but error was harmless).

404. *See* **Lopez**, 253 S.W.3d at 685 ("Although deferred adjudication clearly involves a recognition of the defendant's guilt by the trial judge, no actual pronouncement of judgment of guilt occurs."); **Moreno v. State**, 22 S.W.3d 482, 485 (Tex. Crim. App. 1999) (evidence of unadjudicated crimes cannot be used to show bad character for truthfulness under Rule 609).

405. *See* TEX. R. EVID. 609, 613(b); *see, e.g.*, **Carpenter v. State**, 979 S.W.2d 633, 635 & n.7 (Tex. Crim. App. 1998) (witness could not be impeached with evidence of pending federal charges; no final conviction and no demonstration that pending charge showed any bias or motive for witness to testify favorably for State); *see also* **Moreno**, 22 S.W.3d at 488-89 (under Rule 403, testifying DWI defendant should not have been impeached with the fact that he was on felony deferred adjudication because the probative value of that evidence in showing his possible motive to testify untruthfully was slight, but the jury was likely to misuse the evidence as proof of the defendant's general character as a criminal). Refer to notes 636-682 *infra* and accompanying text.

406. *See* **United States v. Williams**, 642 F.2d 136, 139-40 & n.3 (5th Cir. 1981) ("[C]ommentators uniformly support the position that a nolo conviction is admissible under Rule 609."); *see, e.g.*, **Cedillo v. Paloff**, 792 S.W.2d 830, 833 (Tex. App.—Fort Worth 1990, writ denied) (evidence of a nolo contendere plea for DWI was admissible to impeach defendant, who claimed sobriety). Refer to *Article IV: Relevance & Its Limits*, *supra* p. 338.

407. Until the 1990 amendments, Federal Rule 609 seemed to permit impeachment with prior convictions only on cross-examination. This limitation was usually ignored by federal courts because it is both logical and common practice to elicit such convictions on direct examination to "remove the sting" of the impeachment. FED. R. EVID. 609 advisory committee's note to 1990 amendments.

408. *See* **Davis v. State**, 645 S.W.2d 288, 291 n.3 (Tex. Crim. App. 1983) (while a cross-examiner is not required to have documentation in hand before questioning a witness about a prior conviction, having extrinsic proof of the facts is preferable because a denial or objection will require the cross-examiner to make a prima facie showing of the question's propriety); *see, e.g.*, **Aleman v. State**, 795 S.W.2d 332, 334 (Tex. App.—Amarillo 1990, no pet.) (defendant should have been permitted to question State's witness in front of jury about a prior conviction despite the fact that witness denied any knowledge of the conviction on voir dire).

then introduce a copy of the judgment of conviction.[409] In fact, under Rule 609(a), the witness does not need to ever be asked about the prior conviction. After the witness has departed the stand, the cross-examiner may impeach him by offering the judgment into evidence.[410] However, the rule explicitly restricts proof of prior convictions to the witness's admission or to the extrinsic evidence of a copy of the public record of conviction.[411] Another witness may not be called to testify to personal knowledge of the witness's conviction.[412]

A criminal defendant may not raise or preserve for review a claim that the trial court erroneously ruled that his prior conviction would be admissible to impeach his testimony unless the defendant actually takes the witness stand, testifies, and is impeached with those prior convictions.[413] In addressing this issue, the U.S. Supreme Court has held that the defendant must testify because, in order to weigh the probative value of the prior conviction against its prejudicial effect, the reviewing court must know the precise nature of the defendant's testimony.[414]

Additionally, if the defense preemptively introduces evidence of the defendant's prior conviction to take the sting out of that testimony on cross-examination, the defense has waived any right to appeal the trial court's ruling admitting the conviction under Rule 609.[415] The rationale for waiver in this context is the same as it is generally: a party cannot complain on appeal that evidence he introduced himself was erroneously admitted.[416]

409. *See Poore v. State*, 524 S.W.2d 294, 297 (Tex. Crim. App. 1975) (for impeachment purposes, proof of prior conviction may come from a copy of the judgment or the witness's own admission of the conviction); *Aleman*, 795 S.W.2d at 334 (once a witness denies a prior conviction, the party may introduce proof of the conviction for purposes of impeachment).

410. *See Simmons v. State*, 456 S.W.2d 66, 71 (Tex. Crim. App. 1970) (witness can be compelled to answer questions about prior convictions, or the record of conviction can be introduced to attack credibility).

411. *See* TEX. R. EVID. 609(a)(3); *see, e.g.*, *Allied Chem. Co. v. DeHaven*, 824 S.W.2d 257, 265-66 (Tex. App.—Houston [14th Dist.] 1992, no writ) (witness could not be impeached with a written agreement stating that he would cooperate with an investigating judicial agency and would enter a guilty plea at some future date because this document was not evidence of a conviction under the requirements of Criminal Rule 609).

412. The careful practitioner will have available a certified copy of the prior conviction; otherwise, if the witness denies the conviction, the cross-examiner must accept his answer. *See* 1 GOODE ET AL., *supra* note 24, §609.4, at 603 & n.17 (Rule 609(a) requires proof of a prior conviction by witness testimony or public record).

413. *See Luce v. United States*, 469 U.S. 38, 43 (1984); *Marett v. State*, 415 S.W.3d 514, 516 (Tex. App.—Houston [1st Dist.] 2013, no pet.); *see, e.g.*, *United States v. Fallon*, 348 F.3d 248, 254 (7th Cir. 2003) (defendant waived any argument about trial court's ruling on admissibility of prior remote conviction when he declined to testify at trial); *Long v. State*, 245 S.W.3d 563, 572-73 (Tex. App.—Houston [1st Dist.] 2007, no pet.) (defendant waived error on claim of improper impeachment by prior convictions when he did not testify at trial and did not tell trial court that he was not testifying because of court's ruling that would have allowed impeachment by prior convictions if he had testified).

414. *Luce*, 469 U.S. at 42-43.

415. *Ohler v. United States*, 529 U.S. 753, 760 (2000); *Ford v. State*, 313 S.W.3d 434, 437 (Tex. App.—Waco 2010), *rev'd on other grounds*, 334 S.W.3d 230 (Tex. Crim. App. 2011); *see Johnson v. State*, 981 S.W.2d 759, 760-61 (Tex. App.—Houston [1st Dist.] 1998, pet. ref'd); *Gaffney v. State*, 940 S.W.2d 682, 687 (Tex. App.—Texarkana 1997, pet. ref'd) (op. on reh'g).

416. *Ohler*, 529 U.S. at 755.

RULE 609

B. Rule 609(b): Limit on Using the Evidence After 10 Years

Texas common law permitted a witness to be impeached with evidence of a prior conviction only if the conviction was not too remote to be probative of the witness's present credibility. Although ten years was a convenient measure of remoteness, there was considerable judicial discretion about the standard.[417] Federal Rule 609(b) is more specific than this common-law remoteness standard.[418] Texas Rule 609(b) follows the federal rule and allows the use of a conviction for impeachment purposes if a period of less than ten years has elapsed between the date of the witness's testimony and the later of the date the witness was convicted or the date the witness was released from the confinement imposed for that conviction,[419] with judicial discretion to admit older convictions only if the court finds that the prior conviction's probative value, supported by specific facts and circumstances, substantially outweighs its prejudicial effect.[420]

---

417. *See, e.g.,* **Landry v. Travelers Ins.**, 458 S.W.2d 649, 650-51 (Tex. 1970) (trial court's exclusion of five-year-old conviction was a valid exercise of discretion); **Crisp v. State**, 470 S.W.2d 58, 59-60 (Tex. Crim. App. 1971) (admission of several prior convictions was proper, even though the oldest conviction occurred 14 years before trial, because the short time between offenses showed a lack of reform); **Gill v. State**, 147 Tex. Crim. 392, 394, 181 S.W.2d 276, 277 (1944) (conviction of a State witness 18 years before trial was not too remote, given evidence of the conviction of two other felonies within seven years before trial); **Harris Cty. v. Jenkins**, 678 S.W.2d 639, 642 (Tex. App.—Houston [14th Dist.] 1984, writ ref'd n.r.e.) (nine-year-old conviction was sufficiently remote for the trial judge to properly refuse admission into evidence); **Guerra v. State**, 648 S.W.2d 715, 717-18 (Tex. App.—Corpus Christi 1982, pet. ref'd) (conviction older than ten years was admissible because the major cause of remoteness was defendant's failure to appear for trial).

418. *See* Fed. R. Evid. 609(b) ("This subdivision (b) applies if more than 10 years have passed since the witness's conviction or release from confinement for it, whichever is later."); **United States v. Redditt**, 381 F.3d 597, 601 (7th Cir. 2004) (Rule 609 ensures "that 'convictions over ten years old will be admitted very rarely and only in exceptional circumstances'"; district court's decision to admit such evidence will be upheld "as long as the record shows that the district court thoughtfully analyzed the facts and properly weighed the probative value of the evidence against its prejudicial effect"); *see, e.g.,* **United States v. Portillo**, 633 F.2d 1313, 1323 (9th Cir. 1980) (when trial court did not make specific findings of fact indicating that probative value of remote conviction substantially outweighed its prejudicial effect, remote prior conviction was presumptively inadmissible).

419. *See* Tex. R. Evid. 609(b); **Leyba v. State**, 416 S.W.3d 563, 567 (Tex. App.—Houston [14th Dist.] 2013, pet. ref'd); *see, e.g.,* **Butler v. State**, 890 S.W.2d 951, 954-55 (Tex. App.—Waco 1995, pet. ref'd) (reversible error to impeach defendant with prior conviction that was more than ten years old when State did not establish that defendant had been released from confinement for the prior offense less than ten years prior to his current trial); **Brown v. State**, 880 S.W.2d 249, 252-53 (Tex. App.—El Paso 1994, no pet.) (admission of defendant's 15-year-old rape conviction was reversible error when he was on trial for sexual assault of child; crimes were similar, and prior rape conviction was not probative of credibility); **Sinegal v. State**, 789 S.W.2d 383, 388 (Tex. App.—Houston [1st Dist.] 1990, pet. ref'd) (trial court erred in admitting defendant's prior convictions when he had been released 10½ years before trial, was between 16 and 19 years old when those offenses were committed, his longest sentence was five years, and none of the convictions involved narcotics offenses, for which he was currently on trial).

420. *See* Tex. R. Evid. 609(b); **Kizart v. State**, 811 S.W.2d 137, 141 (Tex. App.—Dallas 1991, no pet.); *see also* **Husting v. State**, 790 S.W.2d 121, 126 (Tex. App.—San Antonio 1990, no pet.) (Texas common-law "revitalization doctrine still appears alive and well"; 14-year-old conviction for prostitution was rendered admissible for impeachment by an intervening federal conviction). *See generally* **Sinegal**, 789 S.W.2d at 387 (listing factors that trial judge should consider in determining whether prior conviction is too remote).
     In **Butler**, the court used the five **Theus** factors—which are used to balance probative value versus unfair prejudice in determining the admissibility of a more recent conviction offered to impeach—to decide the admissibility of a remote conviction. 890 S.W.2d at 954-55. Refer to notes 434-439 *infra* and accompanying text for delineation of the five **Theus** factors. The issue of remoteness, however, is distinct from, and must be considered in addition to, the general probative/prejudicial question. The focus in assessing the probative value of an "old" prior conviction is whether the conviction is still sufficiently relevant in determining the witness's present character for

Remote convictions are inadmissible because the law presumes that a person is capable of rehabilitation and that his character for truthfulness has reformed after a suitable period of law-abiding conduct.[421] Earlier Texas law had routinely permitted the "tacking" of intervening criminal convictions to resurrect otherwise remote convictions.[422] The theory underlying this "revitalization" doctrine is that an intervening felony conviction or other evidence showing a lack of character reformation rebuts the normal presumption of rehabilitation.[423] Some Texas courts had carried the tacking doctrine forward under Rule 609(b) as being the type of "specific facts and circumstances" that demonstrate the high probative value of convictions older than ten years.[424] However, the Texas Court of Criminal Appeals has held that "the unambiguous plain language of [Rule 609] supplants the tacking doctrine."[425]

The relevant time span for purposes of the remoteness rule is from the later of (1) the date of conviction or (2) the date of release from confinement from the conviction[426] until the date the witness testifies at trial.[427] If, however, the trial has been de-

RULE 609

---

truthfulness. The fact that a 17-year-old was convicted of shoplifting may have very little probative value for this purpose if the witness is now 56 and the president of a bank. Conversely, if the 17-year-old went on to become a convicted embezzler, the theft conviction may indicate a lifelong pattern of theft and deception.

421. *See Transp. Ins. v. Cossaboon*, 291 S.W.2d 746, 749 (Tex. Civ. App.—El Paso 1956, writ ref'd n.r.e.).

422. *See, e.g.*, *Williams v. State*, 449 S.W.2d 264, 265-66 (Tex. Crim. App. 1970) (intervening convictions between the defendant's first conviction in 1943 and the present conviction showed failure to reform); *Walker v. State*, 166 Tex. Crim. 297, 299-300, 312 S.W.2d 666, 668 (1958) (pattern of convictions showed failure to reform).

423. *See, e.g.*, *Husting*, 790 S.W.2d at 126 (defense witness could be impeached with 14-year-old conviction for prostitution because intervening felony drug conviction showed lack of reformation); *Allen v. State*, 740 S.W.2d 81, 83 (Tex. App.—Dallas 1987, pet. ref'd) (two 17-year-old convictions were not too remote for impeachment given intervening convictions, one of which was for the same type of offense).

424. *See, e.g.*, *Morris v. State*, 67 S.W.3d 257, 263-64 (Tex. App.—Houston [1st Dist.] 2001, pet. ref'd) (defendant's otherwise remote convictions for burglary of a motor vehicle, theft by receiving, and engaging in organized criminal activity were admissible because the "tacking" of intervening theft and burglary convictions within ten years rendered older convictions no longer remote; "intervening convictions for felonies or crimes of moral turpitude demonstrate a lack of reformation, attenuating the possible prejudice interposed by a distant conviction"); *Jackson v. State*, 50 S.W.3d 579, 591-92 (Tex. App.—Fort Worth 2001, pet. ref'd) (defendant's remote convictions for robbery were revitalized by later convictions for deadly conduct, theft, escape, and assault on a female); *Rodriguez v. State*, 31 S.W.3d 359, 363 (Tex. App.—San Antonio 2000, pet. ref'd) (defendant's remote DWI convictions were rendered not remote under former Penal Code §49.09(e) by "tacking" a third, more recent conviction).

425. *Meadows v. State*, 455 S.W.3d 166, 169 (Tex. Crim. App. 2015). The tacking doctrine contradicts the express language of Rule 609. *Meadows*, 455 S.W.3d at 169; *see Leyba v. State*, 416 S.W.3d 563, 569 (Tex. App.—Houston [14th Dist.] 2013, pet. ref'd) ("In the more than twenty-six years since the rules of evidence were adopted for use in criminal cases, the Court of Criminal Appeals has not applied the tacking doctrine in a single reported case. We agree with the Austin court of appeals that Rule 609 has supplanted the common-law exception and that under the rule's plain meaning, tacking is no longer permitted."); *Hankins v. State*, 180 S.W.3d 177, 180 (Tex. App.—Austin 2005, pet. ref'd) ("[W]e do not find ... that the tacking doctrine was intended to survive the creation of the rules."); Holland, *supra* note 376, at 498-99 (Texas Court of Criminal Appeals should reject the tacking doctrine as inconsistent with Rule 609(b)). The rule creates a carefully crafted distinction between convictions that are more than ten years old and those that are less than ten years old. *See* TEX. R. EVID. 609(b); *Meadows*, 455 S.W.3d at 170. The tacking doctrine effectively created a third category of convictions not included in the rule—convictions that are more than ten years old but have an intervening conviction.

426. TEX. R. EVID. 609(b); *Taylor v. State*, 612 S.W.2d 566, 572 (Tex. Crim. App. [Panel Op.] 1981). Release from confinement relates to the latest confinement for probation or parole violations. *See, e.g.*, *United States v. McClintock*, 748 F.2d 1278, 1288 (9th Cir. 1984) (probation violation that resulted in revocation and imprisonment in 1972 and parole in 1973 was not too remote even though the defendant was originally convicted in 1967 and the trial was

layed because of the witness's own dilatory tactics, the trial court may consider that fact as a circumstance that would extend the ten-year limit.[428]

In some instances, a trial court could admit a remote prior conviction into evidence while excluding a more recent one that, though useful to prove lack of rehabilitation, was insufficiently probative of character for truthfulness or was unfairly prejudicial.[429]

C. Rules 609(a) & 609(b): Judicial Discretion

Texas Rules 609(a) and 609(b) follow Federal Rules 609(a) and 609(b) in giving the trial court discretion in assessing the balance of prejudice against probative value to decide whether to admit or exclude evidence of convictions offered for impeachment purposes. Accordingly, the court may exclude convictions that are otherwise admissible under Rule 609(a), and it may admit convictions that are otherwise inadmissible under the ten-year time limit of Rule 609(b). Rule 609(a) requires that the probative value of a prior criminal conviction outweigh its prejudicial effect to a party before it can be admitted.[430] This balancing test is different from the Rule 403 test, under which evidence will be admitted unless the unfair prejudice substantially outweighs the probative value.[431]

When exercising discretion in making Rule 609 rulings, the trial judge should ensure that the record adequately reflects the factors balanced and the weight given to each factor.[432] According to the Texas Court of Criminal Appeals, the "better prac-

---

held in 1982, as long as the probation violation directly tracked the original crime). *See generally* **Davis v. State**, 259 S.W.3d 778 (Tex. App.—Houston [1st Dist.] 2007, pet. ref'd) (analyzing remoteness of convictions with release dates from confinement).

427. **Buffington v. State**, 801 S.W.2d 151, 154 (Tex. App.—San Antonio 1990, pet. ref'd). In **Buffington**, the defendant argued that he should have been permitted to impeach the State's witness with a remote prior conviction because this proceeding was a retrial of an earlier one that was reversed on appeal for error committed by the State. *Id.* The defendant asserted that the relevant date should have been that of the witness's testimony at the first trial, not the date of his testimony at the second trial. *Id.* The court of appeals rejected this argument, stating that the trial court had not abused its discretion in finding that the 18-year-old convictions were too remote to shed any light on the witness's testimony before the jury. *Id.* at 155.

428. *See, e.g.*, **Guerra v. State**, 648 S.W.2d 715, 718 (Tex. App.—Corpus Christi 1982, pet. ref'd) (trial court did not err in admitting evidence of conviction for impeachment purposes because defendant's failure to appear for trial was a major reason for rendering the prior conviction remote); *see also* **United States v. Mullins**, 562 F.2d 999, 1000 (5th Cir. 1977) (defendant's flight from prosecution tolled the ten-year limit).

429. *Cf.* **Weaver v. State**, 87 S.W.3d 557, 561-62 (Tex. Crim. App. 2002) (State was allowed to allege and prove before jury remote prior DWI convictions for enhancement purposes when it proved, outside jury's presence, existence of more recent DWI conviction).

430. TEX. R. EVID. 609(a)(2). For a discussion of the differences between Texas Rule 609(a) and Federal Rule 609(a), refer to notes 378-395 *supra* and accompanying text.

431. Refer to *Article IV: Relevance & Its Limits*, *supra* p. 211. This inherent danger of prejudice is, of course, more pronounced in criminal trials when the accused is a witness. *See* **State v. Santiago**, 492 P.2d 657, 661 (Haw. 1971). This situation prompted the **Santiago** court to hold that a rule allowing impeachment by prior conviction is unconstitutional. *Id.*

432. *See* **Theus v. State**, 845 S.W.2d 874, 880 n.6 (Tex. Crim. App. 1992); *see also* **United States v. Fountain**, 642 F.2d 1083, 1090 (7th Cir. 1981) (trial judges should explicitly articulate their balancing process on the record); **United States v. Mahler**, 579 F.2d 730, 734 (2d Cir. 1978) (when a party seeks to introduce convictions more than ten years old, the trial court must make an on-the-record finding of admissibility). *But see* **United States v. Grandmont**, 680 F.2d 867, 872 (1st Cir. 1982) (on-the-record balancing is not required); **Gov't of V.I. v. Bedford**, 671 F.2d

tice" is for the trial judge "to make specific findings of fact and conclusions of law in weighing probative value and prejudicial effect."[433]

In *Theus v. State*, the court of criminal appeals delineated a nonexclusive list of factors that the trial court should consider in the balancing process:[434]

(1) the impeachment value of the crime,[435]

(2) the temporal proximity of the past crime to the charged offense and the witness's subsequent criminal history,[436]

758, 761 n.3 (3d Cir. 1982) (Rule 609(a)(1) balancing does not need to be explicit); *Medina v. State*, 367 S.W.3d 470, 475 (Tex. App.—Texarkana 2012, no pet.) (court of appeals "presume[d] that the trial court conducted the necessary balancing test; the court's reasoning does not need to be announced for the record").

433. *Theus*, 845 S.W.2d at 880 n.6.

434. 845 S.W.2d at 880; *see, e.g.*, *Davis v. State*, 259 S.W.3d 778, 780-84 (Tex. App.—Houston [1st Dist.] 2007, pet. ref'd) (trial court properly admitted prior convictions for theft and robbery; probative value of convictions substantially outweighed prejudicial effect); *Moore v. State*, 143 S.W.3d 305, 312-13 (Tex. App.—Waco 2004, pet. ref'd) (trial court properly excluded prior theft and DWI convictions more than ten years old that were offered to impeach State's witness in retaliation trial because danger of unfair prejudice outweighed probative value); *Rodriguez v. State*, 129 S.W.3d 551, 559-60 (Tex. App.—Houston [1st Dist.] 2003, pet. ref'd) (prior theft convictions were admissible to impeach, and convictions for promoting prostitution and robbery might have been admissible; therefore, trial counsel was not ineffective in questioning defendant about robbery conviction or in failing to object to State's cross-examination); *Deleon v. State*, 126 S.W.3d 210, 214-16 (Tex. App.—Houston [1st Dist.] 2003, pet. dism'd, untimely filed) (defendant's two prior convictions for murder were not admissible to impeach his credibility; probative value of murder convictions was "slight" in showing his general character for truthfulness, while prejudicial effect was great; error was harmless); *Butler v. State*, 890 S.W.2d 951, 954-55 (Tex. App.—Waco 1995, pet. ref'd) (although defendant's credibility and the value of his testimony were crucial, defendant's 13-year-old prior conviction for sexual abuse of a child should have been excluded because prior conviction was not for a crime of deceit, was remote, and was very similar to charged offense and thus highly prejudicial).

435. *Theus*, 845 S.W.2d at 880. This factor relates to how strongly the crime bears on the witness's character for truthfulness. Crimes involving deception or moral turpitude have greater impeachment value than violent crimes. *Id.* at 881; *Huerta v. State*, 359 S.W.3d 887, 892 (Tex. App.—Houston [14th Dist.] 2012, no pet.); *Thomas v. State*, 312 S.W.3d 732, 739 (Tex. App.—Houston [1st Dist.] 2009, pet. ref'd); *see United States v. Hayes*, 553 F.2d 824, 827-28 (2d Cir. 1977) (conviction for smuggling cocaine is more closely related to veracity than is a crime of violence or possession of narcotics); *Vasquez v. State*, 417 S.W.3d 728, 732 (Tex. App.—Houston [14th Dist.] 2013, pet. ref'd) (crime of failing to register as sex offender bears on defendant's character for truthfulness); *Tristan v. State*, 393 S.W.3d 806, 812 (Tex. App.—Houston [1st Dist.] 2012, no pet.) (question is whether crime is the type that bears on defendant's character for truthfulness, not whether conviction may lead jury to speculate about underlying offense); *Cuba v. State*, 905 S.W.2d 729, 734 (Tex. App.—Texarkana 1995, no pet.) (aggravated assault is not an offense that usually involves untruthfulness or deception and thus would not ordinarily bear heavily against a witness's veracity; moreover, aggravated assault on a peace officer might be especially prejudicial to a jury and thus might outweigh its probative value for impeachment); *see, e.g.*, *Pierre v. State*, 2 S.W.3d 439, 442 (Tex. App.—Houston [1st Dist.] 1999, pet. ref'd) (trial court erred in permitting State to impeach sexual-assault defendant with prior misdemeanor assaults of women because these were violent offenses, not offenses showing deceit or deception). The 2006 amendments to Federal Rule 609(a)(2) reflect this same type of analysis for offenses relating directly to truthfulness or dishonesty. Refer to note 381 *supra* and accompanying text.

The name of the statutory offense, however, is not determinative. Courts retain the discretion to elicit the facts underlying the conviction in deciding whether the offense tends to reflect on the character trait of truthfulness. *See United States v. Lipscomb*, 702 F.2d 1049, 1064 (D.C. Cir. 1983) (district court may inquire into the background circumstances surrounding the offense but is not required to do so); *United States v. Smith*, 551 F.2d 348, 364 n.28 (D.C. Cir. 1976) (when the formal title of an offense leaves room for doubt about whether the offense involves dishonesty or false statement, the prosecution must supply facts warranting that description).

436. *Theus*, 845 S.W.2d at 880. The temporal proximity of a past crime and a witness's subsequent history will favor admission if the past crime was recently committed and if the witness has demonstrated a propensity for breaking the law. *Thomas*, 312 S.W.3d at 739-40. Conversely, a remote conviction loses its probative value of the witness's present character for truthfulness because the lack of a recent conviction reflects the likelihood of rehabilitation.

(3) the similarity of the crime charged to the previous conviction,[437]

(4) the importance of the defendant's testimony,[438] and

(5) the importance of the credibility issue.[439]

See **Lucas v. State**, 791 S.W.2d 35, 51 (Tex. Crim. App. 1989) (remote convictions may be admissible when there is evidence of later convictions or lack of reformation), *vacated on other grounds*, 509 U.S. 918 (1993). In **Dillard v. State**, the court of criminal appeals described the factors that Texas courts consider in determining whether a prior conviction is too remote, including "the age of the accused, his conduct as reflecting nonreformation on his part, the nature of the accusation and attendant facts for which he is on trial, and the length and severity of the penalty inflicted." 153 Tex. Crim. 134, 137-38, 218 S.W.2d 476, 478 (1949). The same factors apply to both a testifying defendant and a nondefendant-witness. *Lucas*, 791 S.W.2d at 51.

437. **Theus**, 845 S.W.2d at 880. The similarity of the charged crime to the prior conviction militates against admissibility because jurors might "convict on the perception of a past pattern of conduct, instead of on the facts of the charged offense." *Id.* at 881; *accord* **Thomas**, 312 S.W.3d at 740. The more similar the crimes, the greater the probable prejudice that the jury will misuse the conviction as propensity evidence. *See, e.g.*, **United States v. De Angelis**, 490 F.2d 1004, 1009 (2d Cir. 1974) (prior conviction was not so similar to the offense charged that "the jury was likely to slip into the belief that the crime alleged was merely a repetition of one previously proven"); **Pierre**, 2 S.W.3d at 443 (trial court erred in permitting State to impeach sexual-assault defendant with prior misdemeanor assaults of women because prior offenses were so similar to charged offense and did not involve deceit or deception); **Edwards v. State**, 883 S.W.2d 692, 694-95 (Tex. App.—Texarkana 1994, pet. ref'd) (defendant's prior convictions for unauthorized use and burglary of automobile were admissible as impeachment evidence in prosecution for unauthorized use of automobile; because defendant also had seven ordinary felony theft convictions unrelated to automobiles, overall effect of his prior convictions bore on his credibility generally and would not have influenced jury to convict on the basis of past similar crimes).

438. **Theus**, 845 S.W.2d at 881. A defendant who fears impeachment with prior convictions may be dissuaded from testifying and thus be unable to present any meaningful defense. *See, e.g.*, **United States v. Ortiz**, 553 F.2d 782, 788 (2d Cir. 1977) (Mansfield, J., dissenting) (when crucial portion of government's case in prosecution for distribution of cocaine rested on testimony of paid informer with ten prior convictions, it was important for the jury to hear defendant's version but also reasonable to assume that he was deterred from testifying because a prior conviction for the sale of narcotics would be admissible to impeach his credibility). *See generally* 3 WEINSTEIN & BERGER, *supra* note 110, ¶609[03], at 609-33 to 609-41 (discussing effect of impeachment by prior convictions on defendant's decision to testify).

439. **Theus**, 845 S.W.2d at 881. When a case involves the testimony of only the defendant and the State's witnesses, the importance of the defendant's testimony and thus his credibility (now discussed in terms of character for truthfulness) escalates; so does the State's need for an opportunity to impeach the defendant's character for truthfulness. *See id.*; *see, e.g.*, **Tristan**, 393 S.W.3d at 813 (defendant was the only witness on his behalf and contradicted testimony of complainant, who was the only other witness with direct knowledge of incident; State had great need to impeach defendant's credibility). Here, the focus is on whether the defendant is a "star" witness on his own behalf—in which case, his character for truthfulness or lack thereof is crucial—or whether there are other defense witnesses. *See* **Gaffney v. State**, 937 S.W.2d 540, 543 (Tex. App.—Texarkana 1996, pet. ref'd) (when alibi defense depends primarily on testimony of other witnesses, defendant's credibility is not likely crucial, but when defense turns largely on defendant's testimony, importance of defendant's credibility escalates, and so does the need to allow the State an opportunity to impeach defendant's credibility); *see, e.g.*, **Norris v. State**, 902 S.W.2d 428, 441 (Tex. Crim. App. 1995) (when State's evidence on defendant's intent was entirely circumstantial, his version and his credibility was crucial; prior murder conviction was admissible as impeachment), *overruled on other grounds*, **Roberts v. State**, 273 S.W.3d 322 (Tex. Crim. App. 2008); **Johnson v. State**, 271 S.W.3d 756, 764 (Tex. App.—Waco 2008, pet. ref'd) (prior aggravated-assault conviction was admissible as impeachment evidence when defendant's testimony contradicted the testimony of all of the State's witnesses on the only disputed issue in the case; defendant's testimony and credibility were important); **Sinegal v. State**, 789 S.W.2d 383, 386 (Tex. App.—Houston [1st Dist.] 1990, pet. ref'd) (prior convictions were so remote that they had little bearing on defendant's present credibility, even though prosecution argued that they should be admitted to impeach testifying defendant because his version of the events conflicted with the prosecution witness's version); *see also* **United States v. Fountain**, 642 F.2d 1083, 1089-90 (7th Cir. 1981) (prior convictions for premeditated murder and robbery were admissible; credibility was a central issue because six correctional officers were testifying to one version and the defendant and his five witnesses were testifying to different version).

The trial court's decision to admit or exclude prior convictions to impeach under Rule 609 is reviewed for clear abuse of discretion,[440] but the careful trial judge should expressly articulate the balance of the *Theus* factors on the record.[441]

A recent prior conviction will be admissible only if its probative value outweighs the prejudicial effect.[442] If the prior conviction is more than ten years old, its probative value must *substantially* outweigh its prejudicial effect.[443] Rules 609(a) and 609(b) alter the normal balancing process under Rule 403, which is tilted toward admitting probative evidence unless its unfair prejudicial effect substantially outweighs that probative value. Thus, Rule 609(a) is slightly exclusionary, Rule 609(b) is very exclusionary, and Rule 403 is very inclusionary.[444]

D. Rules 609(c) & 609(d): Effect of a Pardon, Annulment, or Certificate of Rehabilitation; Juvenile Adjudications

Rule 609(c) changed Texas law[445] by eliminating the use of most convictions that are the subject of a pardon, annulment, certificate of rehabilitation, or satisfactory completion of probation.[446] Under earlier Texas law, any final conviction was admissible to impeach: a pardon, annulment, or certificate of rehabilitation had no effect on

---

440. *Theus*, 845 S.W.2d at 881. In *Arroyo v. State*, the court of appeals stated that when the defendant did not present to the trial court any evidence or argument about the *Theus* factors, the trial court did not err in excluding defendant's offer of prior convictions to impeach the nontestifying complainant whose hearsay statements were admissible. 123 S.W.3d 517, 520 (Tex. App.—San Antonio 2003, pet. ref'd). The proponent of the evidence must demonstrate that prior convictions are admissible to impeach a witness. *Id.*

441. *See Theus*, 845 S.W.2d at 880 n.6; *cf. Grant v. State*, 247 S.W.3d 360, 367 (Tex. App.—Austin 2008, pet. ref'd) (even though trial court did not specify grounds for admitting evidence of remote prior conviction, admission was proper because defendant opened the door to impeachment under exceptions to Rules 608 and 609). Refer to notes 432-433 *supra* and accompanying text.

442. TEX. R. EVID. 609(a)(2); *see, e.g.*, *Theus*, 845 S.W.2d at 880 (low probative value of defendant's prior conviction for arson did not outweigh its prejudicial effect); *Enriquez v. State*, 56 S.W.3d 596, 601 (Tex. App.—Corpus Christi 2001, pet. ref'd) (nontestifying defendant could not be impeached with prior drug-related convictions merely because testifying officer stated that defendant, while in the hospital, told him three different versions of how accident occurred; prior convictions were not probative of whether defendant's story was believable).

443. TEX. R. EVID. 609(b); *Meadows v. State*, 455 S.W.3d 166, 170 (Tex. Crim. App. 2015); *e.g.*, *Moore v. State*, 143 S.W.3d 305, 312-13 (Tex. App.—Waco 2004, pet. ref'd) (trial court did not err in excluding two remote prior misdemeanor convictions for theft; probative value of convictions was substantially outweighed by danger of unfair prejudice); *Woodall v. State*, 77 S.W.3d 388, 394-97 (Tex. App.—Fort Worth 2002, pet. ref'd) (trial court did not abuse its discretion in excluding remote convictions offered to impeach testifying eyewitness; five out of six *Theus* factors showed that probative value of convictions was substantially outweighed by danger of unfair prejudice); *Morris v. State*, 67 S.W.3d 257, 263-65 (Tex. App.—Houston [1st Dist.] 2001, pet. ref'd) (trial court did not abuse its discretion in admitting remote convictions to impeach defendant's credibility; while several *Theus* factors weighed against admission of convictions, danger of unfair prejudice did not substantially outweigh probative value).

444. *Cf. United States v. Tse*, 375 F.3d 148, 161-64 (1st Cir. 2004) (distinguishing balancing test in Federal Rule 403, applicable when prior convictions are offered to impeach government witnesses, from that in Federal Rule 609(a) when prior convictions are offered to impeach a criminal defendant). Refer to note 391 *supra* and accompanying text.

445. *E.g.*, *Sipanek v. State*, 100 Tex. Crim. 489, 492, 272 S.W. 141, 142 (1925) (witness could be impeached with conviction despite having been pardoned); *Bernard's, Inc. v. Austin*, 300 S.W. 256, 258 (Tex. Civ. App.—Dallas 1927, writ ref'd) (same).

446. *See* TEX. R. EVID. 609(c). Texas Rule 609(c) excludes a somewhat wider range of prior convictions that have been subject to pardon, annulment, or rehabilitation than Federal Rule 609(c) does. *See* FED. R. EVID. 609(c); TEX. R. EVID. 609(c).

admissibility.[447] While Rule 609(c) changed earlier law by limiting the admissibility of pardoned prior convictions, it also broadened the admissibility of probated prior convictions if the person is later convicted of another felony or crime of moral turpitude.[448] Earlier law had held that a successfully served probation was never admissible to impeach.[449]

A witness who is on probation at the time he testifies at trial may be impeached with the conviction underlying that probated sentence.[450] Although successful completion of probation may be considered a final conviction under the laws of another jurisdiction, evidence of that jurisdiction's conviction will not be admissible under Texas Rule 609(c).[451] Conversely, a conviction that might be considered absolved under the laws of another jurisdiction would nonetheless be admissible under Rule 609(c) unless it met the specific criteria set out in the rule.[452]

In accordance with previous Texas law, Rule 609(d) prohibits the use of juvenile adjudications unless the witness is a party in a juvenile-court proceeding under Title 3 of the Texas Family Code or the admission of the juvenile adjudication is constitutionally required.[453] Title 3 of the Texas Family Code permits the use of prior adjudica-

---

447. *See Taylor v. State*, 612 S.W.2d 566, 571-72 (Tex. Crim. App. [Panel Op.] 1981). *But see Watkins v. State*, 572 S.W.2d 339, 341-42 (Tex. Crim. App. 1978) (although a pardon may forgive the penalty, it does not affect the status of the conviction; issue of admissibility is reserved if the pardon is based on a finding of innocence).

448. *See* TEX. R. EVID. 609(c)(1), (c)(2); *see, e.g., Polk v. State*, 865 S.W.2d 627, 630 (Tex. App.—Fort Worth 1993, pet. ref'd) (defendant's later conviction for aggravated robbery made his prior conviction for murder without malice admissible under Criminal Rule 609(c), even though defendant had completed probation for murder conviction).

449. *Adams v. State*, 685 S.W.2d 661, 669-70 (Tex. Crim. App. 1985); *Wintters v. State*, 616 S.W.2d 197, 200-01 (Tex. Crim. App. 1981).

450. *See* TEX. R. EVID. 609(c)(2); *Mead v. State*, 759 S.W.2d 437, 443 (Tex. App.—Fort Worth 1988), *rev'd on other grounds*, 819 S.W.2d 869 (Tex. Crim. App. 1991). Some courts of appeals have distinguished regular probation from deferred adjudication. *See, e.g., Hernandez v. State*, 897 S.W.2d 488, 492-93 (Tex. App.—Tyler 1995, no pet.) (error, though harmless, to impeach witness with evidence that he was serving probation for a deferred adjudication and had never been convicted of any crime); *Soliz v. State*, 809 S.W.2d 257, 258 (Tex. App.—San Antonio 1991, pet. ref'd) (witness could not be impeached with the fact that he was presently on deferred adjudication under Criminal Rule 609 because deferred adjudication does not constitute a "conviction" under Texas law).

451. *See Davis v. State*, 645 S.W.2d 288, 291-92 (Tex. Crim. App. 1983) (former Texas Code of Criminal Procedure art. 38.29, forerunner of Criminal Rule 609, requires the application of state law, so the fact that federal authorities might characterize successfully completed federal probation as a final conviction does not control the use of that evidence under Texas law).

452. *Cf. U.S. Xpress Enters., Inc. v. J.B. Hunt Transp., Inc.*, 320 F.3d 809, 816 (8th Cir. 2003) (how conviction obtained in Canada is viewed under Canadian law was not determinative; "the issue is whether the absolved conviction meets the requirements of Fed. R. Evid. 609(c)(1), and we do not find that it does").

453. *See* TEX. R. EVID. 609(d); *see, e.g., Warren v. State*, 514 S.W.2d 458, 465 (Tex. Crim. App. 1974) (defendant was properly prohibited from introducing evidence of witness's juvenile record for purposes of general impeachment; no showing of probationary status, unlike in *Davis v. Alaska*, 415 U.S. 308 (1974)). Rule 609 applies only to the impeachment of a witness for lack of character for truthfulness; thus, the general prohibition against the use of juvenile convictions applies only in this context. *See* TEX. R. EVID. 609(a). Juvenile felony convictions are explicitly admissible in the sentencing stage of a criminal trial under Texas Code of Criminal Procedure article 37.07, §3(a)(1).

The federal rule is perhaps broader. It permits impeachment of a nondefendant witness with evidence of a juvenile adjudication if "admitting the evidence is necessary to fairly determine guilt or innocence." FED. R. EVID. 609(d)(4). While the wording of the federal rule may seem broader than the Texas rule, it is unlikely to result in any practical differences in the admission or exclusion of juvenile adjudications.

tions only in later Family Code proceedings in which the child is a party, for the purposes of sentencing under either the Family Code or the Code of Criminal Procedure, or as part of civil-commitment proceedings under Health & Safety Code chapter 841.[454] In a criminal case,[455] however, such evidence will be admitted "if the United States or Texas Constitution requires that it be admitted."[456] This phrase in the rule refers to the U.S. Supreme Court's decision in *Davis v. Alaska*,[457] but *Davis* does not broadly require the trial court to permit impeachment of character for truthfulness with prior convictions. In that case, the admission of a juvenile's prior conviction and probation for burglary was constitutionally required because he was the State's main witness and the evidence was necessary to impeach him by showing his bias and motive to shift the blame for the crime to another.[458] The Texas Court of Criminal Appeals offered the following discussion of the *Davis* rule:

> *Davis v. Alaska* is not a blunderbuss that decimates all other evidentiary statutes, rules, and relevance requirements in matters of witness impeachment. It is a rapier that targets only a specific mode of impeachment—bias and motive—when the cross-examiner can show a logical connection between the evidence suggesting bias or motive and the witness's testimony. We therefore reject [the] position that "[a] probationer, particularly a probationer whose guilt has not yet been adjudicated, is always in a vulnerable relationship with the State" and that mere status is always automatically relevant to show a witness's possible bias and motive to testify favorably for the State ....[459]

---

454. TEX. FAM. CODE §51.13(b); *see Gilmore v. State*, 871 S.W.2d 848, 850-51 (Tex. App.—Houston [14th Dist.] 1994, no pet.) (no error to exclude any cross-examination by defendant about complaining witness's prior juvenile record).

455. "The trial court has no discretion to admit such evidence in a civil proceeding." *Powell v. Levit*, 640 F.2d 239, 241 (9th Cir. 1981).

456. TEX. R. EVID. 609(d)(2).

457. 415 U.S. 308 (1974).

458. *Id.* at 319; *see also United States v. Decker*, 543 F.2d 1102, 1105 (5th Cir. 1976) (distinguishing *Davis* as a case involving bias and not one allowing a constitutional right to impeach a witness's general credibility with juvenile adjudications); *United States v. Lind*, 542 F.2d 598, 599 (2d Cir. 1976) (trial court did not abuse its discretion in preventing defendant from impeaching kidnapping victim with her juvenile record because those adjudications were both remote and irrelevant to defendant's theory).

In *Gilmore v. State*, the court rejected the defendant's argument that the complaining witness's prior juvenile adjudications should have been admitted under *Davis* because, in the present case, the complaining witness was the victim of the crime and thus could not have been trying to shift the suspicion away from himself. *Gilmore*, 871 S.W.2d at 850-51. Furthermore, because the complainant was not on probation at the time, the element of fear of probation revocation was absent. *Id.* Finally, the complainant was not a crucial witness to the offense, and testing his credibility was not essential because two other witnesses were present and also testified to the defendant's conduct. *Id.*

459. *Irby v. State*, 327 S.W.3d 138, 152 (Tex. Crim. App. 2010); *see, e.g., Beltran v. State*, 517 S.W.3d 243, 251-52 (Tex. App.—San Antonio 2017, no pet.) (in prosecution for sexual assault of child, trial court did not err in limiting cross-examination of complainant about pending theft charges against her when there was no evidence that her testimony was given in exchange for plea agreement on pending charges or that she believed there was such an agreement; without causal connection between pending charges and complainant's testimony, pending charges were not relevant to show bias or motive).

If a jury convicts a person but the trial court grants his motion for new trial and the case is ultimately dismissed, the earlier jury verdict cannot be used to impeach.[460]

E. Rule 609(e): Pendency of an Appeal

Rule 609(e) requires that a conviction be final before it can be used for impeachment. Thus, a conviction pending on appeal is not admissible.[461] The Texas rule differs from the federal rule, which admits convictions that are pending on appeal but allows the opponent to prove the pendency of the appeal.[462]

Rule 609(e) conforms to earlier Texas law.[463] It eliminates the slight possibility of unjustly impeaching a witness with a conviction that is later reversed and avoids burdening the jury with assessing the impeachment value of an appealed conviction. Commentators, however, justifiably criticize this provision—in the vast majority of cases, it inappropriately prevents the jury from considering probative evidence.[464] In view of the extraordinarily high percentage of convictions that are affirmed,[465] the federal rule is more realistic, particularly in civil cases.

F. Rule 609(f): Notice

To admit a conviction that is more than ten years old, Federal Rule 609(b) requires written notice sufficient to enable the adverse party to contest its use.[466] Texas Rule 609(f) applies a notice provision to all convictions sought to be used for impeachment (regardless of their remoteness) and requires a timely written request for such notice by the adverse party.[467] Under the notice provision, any party planning to use a witness either known or suspected to have been convicted in the past can determine before trial whether the conviction might be used for impeachment by filing a request for

---

460. *See, e.g.,* **U.S.A. Precision Machining Co. v. Marshall**, 95 S.W.3d 407, 409-10 (Tex. App.—Houston [1st Dist.] 2002, pet. denied) (when plaintiff's murder conviction was vacated by grant of new trial and dismissal of charges, murder conviction was not a "final conviction" and could not be used to impeach party in civil suit).

461. Tex. R. Evid. 609(e).

462. Fed. R. Evid. 609(e); *see* Fed. R. Evid. 609 advisory committee's note, subdiv. (e) (witness can explain pendency of appeal as a "qualifying circumstance"). The Advisory Committee states that "[t]he presumption of correctness which ought to attend judicial proceedings supports the position that pendency of an appeal does not preclude use of a conviction for impeachment." Fed. R. Evid. 609 advisory committee's note, subdiv. (e).

463. *E.g.,* **Ringer v. State**, 137 Tex. Crim. 242, 246-47, 129 S.W.2d 654, 656 (1939) (op. on motion to reinstate appeal) (conviction that is being appealed cannot be used to impeach).

464. *See* 1 Goode et al., *supra* note 24, §609.3, at 600 (rule ignores the presumptive validity of a trial court's verdict, and only a small percentage of criminal appeals result in reversal); Wendorf et al., *supra* note 13, at VI-58 to VI-59 (contrary federal rule recognizes the presumption of correctness accompanying convictions); Rhonda M. Harmon, Comment, *Bringing Light to the Non-Capital Felony Punishment Phase: Article 37.07, Section 3a and Evidence of Unadjudicated Extraneous Offenses*, 44 Baylor L. Rev. 101, 128 n.168 (1992) (Criminal Rule 609(e) should not be interpreted to exclude evidence of nonfinal convictions from a jury during sentencing deliberations).

465. *See* 1 Goode et al., *supra* note 24, §609.3, at 600 n.12 (Texas courts of appeals had a rate of ten affirmances for each reversal during 1991).

466. Fed. R. Evid. 609(b)(2).

467. Tex. R. Evid. 609(f).

notice of intent.[468] The purpose of the notice requirement is to prevent an "ambush" on the opposing party's witness.[469]

The rule does not define how much advance notice is sufficient to provide the party sponsoring the witness a fair opportunity to contest the use of a prior conviction for impeachment.[470] In one case, the Dallas Court of Appeals held that there was sufficient notice to give the defense counsel a "fair opportunity" to contest the use of prior convictions when the defendant had filed his request more than two weeks before trial, the State responded on the day trial started, and the witness testified two days later, after an evidentiary hearing on the prior convictions.[471] In another case, the Texarkana Court of Appeals held that the State's failure to notify the defendant of its intent to use one of his prior convictions until the morning of trial was insufficient notice, and it thus was error to admit evidence of the prior conviction.[472] And the Tyler Court of Appeals held that the State's official notice, given well into the trial and on the morning that the defendant was to testify, was timely because the defendant clearly was not "ambushed"

468. *See id.* Although this provision was originally intended for use in criminal cases, it may prove useful in some civil proceedings. However, the problems with this sort of impeachment are particularly acute for criminal defendants. *See* 3 WEINSTEIN & BERGER, *supra* note 110, ¶609[02], at 609-29 (criminal defendants run the risk of having the jury punish them for their prior bad conduct regardless of their present guilt).

469. *Johnson v. State*, 885 S.W.2d 578, 581 (Tex. App.—Dallas 1994, no pet.), *overruled on other grounds*, *Pierce v. State*, 32 S.W.3d 247 (Tex. Crim. App. 2000); *see Cream v. State*, 768 S.W.2d 323, 325-26 (Tex. App.—Houston [14th Dist.] 1989, no pet.). In *Cream*, the prosecutor responded to the defendant's request for notice of intent to use prior convictions by stating that the State had no knowledge of any impeachable convictions. *Id.* at 325. At trial, the defendant requested that the judge order the prosecutor to abstain from making any inquiry into the defendant's criminal history, but the trial court agreed that the State should not be precluded from asking the defendant if he had been convicted. *Id.* The court of appeals held that the defendant could not be "ambushed" in this situation because the only convictions that the defendant had to consider before taking the stand were those already known to him. *Id.* at 326; *see also Geuder v. State*, 142 S.W.3d 372, 374-75 (Tex. App.—Houston [14th Dist.] 2004, pet. ref'd) (court noted that *Cream* had been criticized but did not revisit that case's reasoning and result because any error in failure to give defendant notice of his prior convictions was harmless in present case). *But see Brown v. State*, 880 S.W.2d 249, 251-52 (Tex. App.—El Paso 1994, no pet.) ("If we were to read [Criminal] Rule 609(f) as did the *Cream* Court, the notice requirement would never apply unless a witness could show complete unawareness of his or her own prior convictions. Such an interpretation would render Rule 609(f) meaningless."). The *Brown* court stated the following:

> [T]he State appears to have ambushed Brown by allowing him to take the stand and then bringing up the issue of his prior conviction only after he had given his direct testimony. Not only were the State's "ambush tactics" unfair, they presented a clear case of discovery abuse since the State ignored both the defense counsel's request for notice of extraneous offenses and convictions, and the trial court's discovery order requiring the State to advise the defense of all prior felony convictions and misdemeanor convictions involving moral turpitude that would be used to impeach Brown.

880 S.W.2d at 252. However, because the defendant did not object to the lack of notice at trial, he waived any error under Criminal Rule 609(f). *Id.*

470. *See* TEX. R. EVID. 609(f).

471. *Johnson*, 885 S.W.2d at 581.

472. *Bryant v. State*, 997 S.W.2d 673, 676-77 (Tex. App.—Texarkana 1999, no pet.); *see also Harper v. State*, 930 S.W.2d 625, 630-31 (Tex. App.—Houston [1st Dist.] 1996, no pet.) (harmless error for State to give notice of intent to use prior conviction after defendant had taken witness stand and testified on direct).

by the tardiness of the notice.[473] The failure to provide adequate notice is subject to harmless-error review.[474]

RULE 610

RELIGIOUS BELIEFS
OR OPINIONS

Evidence of a witness's religious beliefs or opinions is not admissible to attack or support the witness's credibility.

Notes and Comments

Comment to 1998 change: This is prior Rule of Criminal Evidence 615.

COMMENTARY ON RULE 610

Both the Texas Constitution and statutory law have long prohibited the disqualification of a witness on the basis of his religious beliefs or lack thereof.[475] Those provisions, however, did not deal with whether a witness's credibility could be attacked on the basis of his religion. Nonetheless, Texas cases had generally prohibited impeachment or support of a witness's credibility with evidence of his religious beliefs or opinions.[476] Rule 610 codified these common-law holdings.[477] The rule, however, does not affect the admissibility of religious beliefs or tenets if offered on some theory of relevance other than general credibility.[478] As the comment to the former civil rule ex-

---

473. *Green v. State*, 55 S.W.3d 633, 645 (Tex. App.—Tyler 2001, pet. ref'd).

474. *See Geuder*, 142 S.W.3d at 376 ("Texas courts of appeals have taken various approaches to analyzing harm when the State has failed to respond to a requested notice of its intent to use evidence" of prior convictions).

475. *See* Tex. Const. art. I, §5 ("No person shall be disqualified to give evidence in any of the Courts of this State on account of his religious opinions or for the want of any religious belief ...."); Tex. Code Crim. Proc. art. 38.12 (witness cannot be deemed incompetent on the basis of his religious belief).

476. *See, e.g., Brundige v. State*, 49 Tex. Crim. 596, 599, 95 S.W. 527, 528 (1906) (impermissible impeachment for defendant to show that prosecution witness stated he did not believe there was any heaven, hell, or God).

477. When the Civil Rules were first promulgated in 1983, the supreme court deleted the Liaison Committee's recommended Rule 610; the court later amended the Civil Rules to include Civil Rule 610, which tracked the analogous federal rule. *See* Fed. R. Evid. 610; *Order Adopting and Amending Texas Rules of Civil Evidence*, 733-734 S.W.2d (Tex. Cases) LXXXVIII (1987, amended 1998). The probable rationale for the court's deletion of this rule is that religious-cult participation is frequently an issue in child-custody proceedings. Texas Revised Civil Statutes article 3717, which did not allow inquiries into religious belief for impeachment purposes, was still in effect at that time. *See* Act approved March 4, 1925, 39th Leg., ch. 28, §1, 1925 Tex. Gen. Laws 146 (repealed 1985).

When adding Civil Rule 610, the supreme court renumbered the remainder of Article VI to conform with the federal numbering. The Criminal Rules were promulgated in 1986 and included a rule prohibiting impeachment with evidence of religious beliefs that was modeled on the federal rule. To maintain comparable numbering with the Texas Civil Rules, however, the criminal rule was placed at the end of Article VI. Thus, the same rule was in different sections of the Civil and Criminal Rules. At least one set of commentators called for a renumbering of the Criminal Rules to conform to the analogous civil and federal versions. 1 Goode et al., *supra* note 24, §610.1, at 607. Because the rule is so rarely invoked in either civil or criminal proceedings, its placement was not a major concern; however, the remainder of the civil and criminal rule numbers in Article VI were misaligned. The 1998 unification of the Civil and Criminal Rules of Evidence corrected this misalignment problem by eliminating the former Criminal Rule 615 and following the numbering system of the civil and federal rules. Rule 610 is identical to Federal Rule 610.

478. *See, e.g., Nassouri v. State*, 503 S.W.3d 416, 419-20 (Tex. App.—San Antonio 2016, no pet.) (State's question about whether, under witness's "belief system," it would be wrong to lie was not improper bolstering when de-

plained,[479] evidence of religious affiliation or church membership might be admissible to show a specific bias or motive for the witness's testimony if the church were involved in the litigation.[480]

RULE 611
MODE & ORDER OF EXAMINING WITNESSES & PRESENTING EVIDENCE

(a) Control by the Court; Purposes. The court should exercise reasonable control over the mode and order of examining witnesses and presenting evidence so as to:

(1) make those procedures effective for determining the truth;

(2) avoid wasting time; and

(3) protect witnesses from harassment or undue embarrassment.

(b) Scope of Cross-Examination. A witness may be cross-examined on any relevant matter, including credibility.

(c) Leading Questions. Leading questions should not be used on direct examination except as necessary to develop the witness's testimony. Ordinarily, the court should allow leading questions:

(1) on cross-examination; and

(2) when a party calls a hostile witness, an adverse party, or a witness identified with an adverse party.

---

fense counsel opened the door to witness's religious beliefs and directly attacked her credibility); *Fort Worth & Denver City Ry. Co. v. Travis*, 45 Tex. Civ. App. 117, 117-18, 99 S.W. 1141, 1142 (Fort Worth 1907, no writ) (proper to cross-examine personal-injury plaintiff about her beliefs as a Christian Scientist when offered to show the degree of suffering and whether her faith caused her to refuse to take the prescribed medicine).

479. When Civil Rule 610 was promulgated in 1988, it contained the following comment:

Comment: This is a new rule, thus causing renumbering of former Rule 610 to 611.

While the rule forecloses inquiry into the religious beliefs or opinions of a witness for the purpose of showing that his character for truthfulness is affected by their nature, an inquiry for the purpose of showing interest or bias because of them is not within the prohibition. Thus disclosure of affiliation with a church which is a party to the litigation would be allowable under the rule.

TEX. R. CIV. EVID. 610 cmt., 733-734 S.W.2d (Tex. Cases) LXXXVIII (1987, amended 1998). The official comment was deleted in the 1998 unification of the Rules because the principle is well established in Texas.

480. *See, e.g., Malek v. Fed. Ins.*, 994 F.2d 49, 54-55 (2d Cir. 1993) (trial court erred in permitting defendant-insurance company to cross-examine witness about fact that both witness and plaintiff were Hasidic Jews because defense was attempting to show that witness's general character for truthfulness was affected by his religion); *United States v. Teicher*, 987 F.2d 112, 118 (2d Cir. 1993) (Federal Rule 610 does not prohibit inquiry into religious beliefs for the purpose of showing interest or bias because of those beliefs, but trial court did not err in excluding evidence that witness had entertained messianic thoughts when there was no evidence that witness was biased against Jewish defendants as a result of those beliefs). *But see Malek*, 994 F.2d at 59 (McLaughlin, J., dissenting) (Rule 610 does not bar admission of evidence of witness's religious beliefs when offered to impeach for bias).

COMMENTARY ON RULE 611

Under the 1998 unification of the Civil and Criminal rules, former Criminal Rule 610 was renumbered as Rule 611. No substantive changes were made to either the civil or criminal provision.[481] The 2015 restyling of the Texas Rules of Evidence brought the language of Rule 611 more in line with Federal Rule 611.[482]

A. Rule 611(a): Control by the Court; Purposes

Rule 611(a) carries forward the trial judge's traditional role: to exercise reasonable control over how the proceedings are conducted.[483] The judge has the responsibility to ensure that both sides receive a fair opportunity to present their cases in a search for the truth and to prevent the injection of prejudicial or confusing extraneous material.[484] The judge has great, although somewhat channeled, discretion in controlling the order of proof at trial to accommodate the legitimate interests of the parties, prevent harassment or embarrassment of witnesses, and ensure that the evidence is presented in a way that minimizes confusion and avoids wasting time.[485] When the judge's

---

481. The 1988 comment to former Civil Rule 611 was deleted because it merely restated well-established Texas legal practice. It read as follows:

> Comment: This is former Rule 610; the number has been changed and the rule amended to permit leading questions in order to develop the testimony of the witness.
>
> The purpose of the amendment is to permit, in the court's discretion, the use of leading questions on preliminary or introductory matters, refreshing memory, questions to ignorant or illiterate persons or children, all as permitted by prior Texas practice and the common law.
>
> The rule also conforms to tradition in making the use of leading questions on cross-examination a matter of right. The purpose of the qualification "ordinarily" is to furnish a basis for denying the use of leading questions when the cross-examination is cross-examination in form only and not in fact, as for example the "cross-examination" of a party by his own counsel after being called by the opponent (savoring more of re-direct) or of an insured defendant who proves to be friendly to the plaintiff.

TEX. R. CIV. EVID. 611 cmt., 733-734 S.W.2d (Tex. Cases) LXXXIX (1987, amended 1998).

482. *See* FED. R. EVID. 611. Texas Rule 611 is identical to Federal Rule 611 except in subsection (b). Refer to notes 502-514 *infra* and accompanying text.

483. *See Laws v. State*, 549 S.W.2d 738, 741 (Tex. Crim. App. 1977) (trial judge has discretion to control the introduction of evidence).

484. *See* TEX. R. EVID. 611(a)(1) (court should exercise reasonable control over examination of witnesses and presentation of evidence to "make those procedures effective for determining the truth"); *Alexander v. State*, 282 S.W.3d 143, 146 (Tex. App.—Texarkana 2009, pet. ref'd) (trial court's power under Rule 611(a) "includes restricting conduct or displays that might detract from an orderly, impartial trial focused on the issues to be tried and the legitimate evidence"); *Metzger v. Sebek*, 892 S.W.2d 20, 38 (Tex. App.—Houston [1st Dist.] 1994, writ denied) (trial court has "'inherent power' to control the disposition of the cases on its docket 'with economy of time and effort for itself, for counsel, and for litigants'"; judge should not make unnecessary comments or remarks that may result in prejudice to litigants (quoting *Landis v. N. Am. Co.*, 299 U.S. 248, 254 (1936))); *Uhlir v. Golden Triangle Dev. Corp.*, 763 S.W.2d 512, 517 (Tex. App.—Fort Worth 1988, writ denied) ("The trial judge should liberally exercise that discretion to permit both sides to fully develop their cases."); *Turner v. Lone Star Indus.*, 733 S.W.2d 242, 245 (Tex. App.—Houston [1st Dist.] 1987, writ ref'd n.r.e.) (trial judge should use discretion to ensure that both sides fully present their cases).

485. *See* TEX. R. EVID. 611(a)(2) & (a)(3) (court should exercise reasonable control over examination of witnesses and presentation of evidence to avoid wasting time and to prevent witnesses from being harassed or embarrassed); *Dow Chem. Co. v. Francis*, 46 S.W.3d 237, 241 (Tex. 2001) ("[A] trial court may properly intervene to maintain control in the courtroom, to expedite the trial, and to prevent what it considers to be a waste of time."); *State v. Gaylor Inv. Tr. P'ship*, 322 S.W.3d 814, 819 (Tex. App.—Houston [14th Dist.] 2010, no pet.) (court's inherent power, along

ruling prevents one of the parties from adequately presenting its case, the judge's discretion may be deemed unreasonable and reversible.[486] But the trial court may place reasonable time limits on the parties to limit the length of the trial.[487]

Rule 611 is rarely cited in appellate decisions, but it is among the workhorses of the trial. It authorizes the trial judge to permit or disallow witnesses to testify out of order,[488] to offer rebuttal evidence, to recall a witness,[489] to reopen a party's case,[490] and to make a myriad of other housekeeping decisions.[491] It also authorizes the trial judge

---

with rules of procedure and evidence, gives court "broad, but not unfettered, discretion in handling trials"); *see, e.g.*, *Thomas v. State*, No. 07-11-00081-CR (Tex. App.—Amarillo 2012, pet. ref'd) (memo op.; 1-31-12) (trial court acted within scope of Rule 611 by asking witness to repeat or clarify what he had said; testimony was confusing, and judge's questions made testimony more effective and avoided needless consumption of time).

486. *See Prezelski v. Christiansen*, 775 S.W.2d 764, 766 & n.2 (Tex. App.—San Antonio 1989), *rev'd on other grounds*, 782 S.W.2d 842 (Tex. 1990). In *Prezelski*, the medical-malpractice defendant was in the middle of his testimony when he requested permission to interrupt his testimony and call two out-of-town experts. *Id.* The plaintiffs agreed to that arrangement but requested 30 minutes to cross-examine the defendant first. *Id.* The court refused this request, permitted the experts to testify, and then excused them. *Id.* After the experts had testified to the defendant's reasonable reliance on certain critical X-rays, the defendant then changed his testimony and admitted that he had never taken these X-rays. *Id.* at 767. It was apparent that the experts' testimony about the propriety of the surgical procedure performed by the defendant would probably have been affected if they had known that the crucial X-rays were never ordered. *See id.* The appellate court, in reversing, noted that "[t]his case illustrates why a trial court must be very cautious before permitting experts, whose testimony is so dependent on the testimony of a party, to testify out of order prior to terminating the testimony of the party upon whose testimony their testimonies depend." *Id.* at 766 n.2.

487. *See, e.g.*, *Gaylor Inv.*, 322 S.W.3d at 819 (court had discretion to limit both sides to one expert witness each); *Jones v. Lurie*, 32 S.W.3d 737, 744 (Tex. App.—Houston [14th Dist.] 2000, no pet.) (trial court did not abuse its discretion under Rule 611 in limiting trial to two weeks, which also limited cross-examination of defendant's witnesses, because defendant did not show how ruling harmed his case); *Walton v. Canon, Short & Gaston*, 23 S.W.3d 143, 154 (Tex. App.—El Paso 2000, no pet.) (trial court did not abuse its discretion under rule in limiting each side to 90 minutes to present case).

488. *See Wal-Mart Stores, Inc. v. Cordova*, 856 S.W.2d 768, 773 (Tex. App.—El Paso 1993, writ denied) (decision to allow expert to testify out of order is usually a discretionary matter for the trial court); *Travelers Ins. v. Hurst*, 358 S.W.2d 883, 886 (Tex. Civ. App.—Texarkana 1962, writ ref'd n.r.e.) ("[I]t is largely discretionary for the trial court to permit the introduction of testimony out of order.").

489. *See Johnson v. State*, 773 S.W.2d 721, 727 (Tex. App.—Houston [1st Dist.] 1989, pet. ref'd) (error to refuse defendant's request to recall State's witness when later testimony raises an issue not addressed in witness's earlier testimony).

490. *See Peek v. State*, 106 S.W.3d 72, 79 (Tex. Crim. App. 2003) ("due administration of justice" requires a trial court to reopen "if the evidence would materially change the case in the proponent's favor"); *Cain v. State*, 666 S.W.2d 109, 111 (Tex. Crim. App. 1984) (while trial court retains some discretion in permitting a party to reopen the case for additional testimony if the evidence is both admissible and offered before the reading of the jury charge, error to refuse request unless it appears that additional evidence would impede the trial or interfere with the orderly administration of justice); *cf. In re Perry*, 345 F.3d 303, 310 (5th Cir. 2003) (under Federal Rule 611(a), trial court has authority to reopen a hearing for further testimony on its own motion).

491. *See, e.g.*, *In re D.S.*, 333 S.W.3d 379, 388 (Tex. App.—Amarillo 2011, no pet.) (trial court had discretion under Rule 611 to conduct termination hearing with father appearing by telephone); *Owens-Corning Fiberglas Corp. v. Malone*, 916 S.W.2d 551, 556 (Tex. App.—Houston [1st Dist.] 1996) (trial court did not err in requiring that an objection by one defendant would be considered as having been made by all defendants; under Civil Rule 611, trial court has authority to exercise reasonable control over presentation of evidence to avoid needless consumption of time), *aff'd*, 972 S.W.2d 35 (Tex. 1998).

to permit out-of-court jury views,[492] in-court experiments, the use of charts and summaries,[493] computer-generated exhibits,[494] and other unorthodox forms of proof.[495] Furthermore, under Rule 611(a), a judge can provide guidance and manage the presentation of evidence while remaining neutral.[496]

These rules must be read in conjunction with the applicable civil[497] and criminal[498] statutes that govern the order of trials, but they do permit the judge to alter the order of proceedings[499] or use discretion in deviating from the rules when necessary for the fair administration of justice.

During cross-examination especially, the trial judge has the power and the duty to protect witnesses from improper harassment, unfair prejudice, and confusion of the issues and to ensure the witnesses' safety.[500] The judge may even interrupt or sua sponte end cross-examination that is immaterial or improper.[501]

---

492. *See Mauricio v. State*, 153 S.W.3d 389, 393 (Tex. Crim. App. 2005) (trial court has discretion to grant jury views and may consider the following: timing of the request, difficulty and expense of arranging jury view, importance of information to be gained, whether the information has been or can be attained from a more convenient source, and extent to which the place or object to be viewed may have changed).

493. *Cf. United States v. Janati*, 374 F.3d 263, 272-73 (4th Cir. 2004) (government could use pedagogical charts and exhibits to summarize thousands of transactions over seven-year period); *United States v. Buck*, 324 F.3d 786, 790-91 (5th Cir. 2003) (Federal Rule 611(a) permits trial judge to allow use of pedagogical summary charts and diagrams as demonstrative aids, but such charts are not admissible in evidence); *United States v. Posada-Rios*, 158 F.3d 832, 869 (5th Cir. 1998) (under Federal Rule 611(a), trial court had discretion to permit government's use of pedagogical summary and organizational charts when accompanied by court's limiting instructions).

494. *See, e.g., Verizon Directories Corp. v. Yellow Book USA, Inc.*, 331 F. Supp. 2d 136, 144 (E.D.N.Y. 2004) (computer-created pedagogical exhibits were admissible in evidence).

495. *See* MCCORMICK ON EVIDENCE, *supra* note 2, §212, at 665 (inclusion or exclusion of demonstrative evidence is generally within the court's discretion). Although Criminal Rule 610 had been cited to support a trial court's authority to permit the jury to submit written questions for the witnesses, the court of criminal appeals has since held that such jury questioning is not permitted under the present rules or statutory authority. *See Buchanan v. State*, 846 S.W.2d 853, 853 (Tex. Crim. App. 1993); *Morrison v. State*, 845 S.W.2d 882, 888-89 (Tex. Crim. App. 1992). Allowing juror questioning of witnesses in the criminal setting is, therefore, impermissible, and any excursion into this area is error and, under former rules of appellate procedure, not subject to a harm analysis. *Allen v. State*, 845 S.W.2d 907, 907 (Tex. Crim. App. 1993).

496. *E.g., Strong v. State*, 138 S.W.3d 546, 552-53 (Tex. App.—Corpus Christi 2004, no pet.) (trial court did not err in instructing defendant, outside presence of jury, to retake witness stand to permit State to confront him with prior inconsistent statement before State's rebuttal witness offered contradicting evidence; "trial judge can make comments regarding whether or not testimony can be allowed"); *see, e.g., In re State ex rel. Skurka*, 512 S.W.3d 444, 456 (Tex. App.—Corpus Christi 2016, orig. proceeding) (trial court's order directing State to identify which of the more than 1,000 recorded jail telephone calls it intended to use was within court's discretion under Rule 611(a)); *Thomas v. Robert*, No. 13-02-504-CV (Tex. App.—Corpus Christi 2007, pet. denied) (memo op.; 2-15-07) (in family-law case, trial court acted within scope of Rule 611 by requesting that defense attorney wrap up an extensive line of cross-examination questions and ask witness about child custody).

497. *See* TEX. R. CIV. P. 265 (for good cause stated in the record, the court may direct a change in the order of proceedings).

498. *See* TEX. CODE CRIM. PROC. art. 36.01 (order of proceedings).

499. *See Ochoa v. Winerich Motor Sales Co.*, 127 Tex. 542, 551, 94 S.W.2d 416, 420-21 (1936) (trial court has discretion to control order of evidence's presentation).

500. *Lopez v. State*, 18 S.W.3d 220, 222 (Tex. Crim. App. 2000); *Virts v. State*, 739 S.W.2d 25, 28 (Tex. Crim. App. 1987); *see Castle v. State*, 748 S.W.2d 230, 233 (Tex. Crim. App. 1988) (trial court may utilize its control over cross-examination to prevent harm to witness); *Nguyen v. State*, 506 S.W.3d 69, 85 (Tex. App.—Texarkana 2016, pet. ref'd) (trial court may limit scope of cross-examination to prevent harassment, prejudice, confusion of issues, and repetitive or marginally relevant interrogation); *see, e.g., Cook v. State*, 738 S.W.2d 339, 339-42 (Tex. App.—

B. Rule 611(b): Scope of Cross-Examination

Rule 611(b) allows wide-open cross-examination of witnesses, following traditional Texas practice.[502] Federal Rule 611(b) limits cross-examination to the subject matter of direct examination and matters related to the witness's credibility.[503] The federal trial court also has discretion to allow cross-examination on "additional matters."[504] In practice, the trial court's discretion under this rule allows federal judges to permit wide-open cross-examination.

While trial courts have wide discretion in controlling the form and manner of cross-examination, their discretion is considerably more limited when it comes to the scope of cross-examination, particularly in criminal cases. Cross-examination is frequently extolled as the single best mechanism for discovering the truth;[505] any limitations on its legitimate scope are strictly reviewed. Three main functions of wide-open cross-

---

Houston [1st Dist.] 1987, pet. ref'd) (trial court did not err in restricting cross-examination of State's witnesses on their home addresses when one witness had been threatened and defendant was not otherwise denied thorough and effective cross-examination); *see also* ***Walker v. State***, 300 S.W.3d 836, 845 (Tex. App.—Fort Worth 2009, pet. ref'd) ("Unless the inquiry on cross-examination is addressing an issue that relates to the charged offense or the credibility of the witness, 'allowing a party to delve into the issue beyond the limits of cross-examination wastes time and confuses the issue.'" (quoting ***Hayden v. State***, 296 S.W.3d 549, 554 (Tex. Crim. App. 2009))).

501. *See, e.g.,* ***Stam v. Mack***, 984 S.W.2d 747, 752 (Tex. App.—Texarkana 1999, no pet.) (trial court could sua sponte interrupt cross-examination of expert on immaterial and improper topics to maintain control and expedite trial); ***Thomas***, No. 13-02-504-CV (memo op.) (Rule 611 permitted trial judge to interrupt extensive line of cross-examination questions and ask for questions on a different topic).

502. *See* ***Wentworth v. Crawford***, 11 Tex. 127, 133 (1853) ("We believe that it is regular to ask a witness, on a cross-examination, any question that may be pertinent to the questions to be decided by the jury ....."); ***Lopresti v. Wells***, 515 S.W.2d 933, 938 (Tex. Civ. App.—Fort Worth 1974, no writ) (defendant is to be given the greatest latitude in cross-examining plaintiff); ***Morris v. State***, 16 S.W. 757, 757 (Tex. Ct. App. 1891) (Texas does not have a rule confining cross-examination to questions asked on direct examination).

Before the adoption of the Criminal Rules, the courts recognized two exceptions to wide-open cross-examination in criminal proceedings. First, a spouse testifying for a spouse could not be cross-examined beyond the scope of direct. ***Mitchell v. State***, 517 S.W.2d 282, 287 (Tex. Crim. App. 1974). Second, an accused testifying in a preliminary hearing on the propriety of a confession could not be cross-examined beyond that subject. ***Myre v. State***, 545 S.W.2d 820, 825 (Tex. Crim. App. 1977); ***Lopez v. State***, 384 S.W.2d 345, 348 (Tex. Crim. App. 1964). The former of these restrictions was expressly deleted, and Rule 504(b)(1) was further amended to clarify that a spouse testifying either for or against a defendant spouse may be cross-examined in the same manner and to the same extent as any other witness. *See* TEX. R. EVID. 504(b)(1) & cmt. (2015). For a discussion of this amendment, refer to *Article V: Privileges, supra* p. 454. The latter limitation continues to apply in pretrial suppression hearings. TEX. R. EVID. 104(d); *see* 1 RAY, *supra* note 4, §602, at 230 (Supp. 1991) (Criminal Rule 104(d) codifies common-law right that defendant, by testifying out of the hearing of the jury about the admissibility of evidence, does not thus subject himself to cross-examination on other issues in case). Refer to *Article I: General Provisions, supra* p. 95.

503. FED. R. EVID. 611(b).

504. *Id.*

505. ***Degelos v. Fid. & Cas. Co.***, 313 F.2d 809, 814 (5th Cir. 1963) (cross-examination is "a tool of advocacy which our long judicial heritage marks as one of the most effective in the quest of truth"); 5 JOHN H. WIGMORE, EVIDENCE IN TRIALS AT COMMON LAW, §1367, at 32 (Chadbourn rev. 1974) (cross-examination is "the greatest legal engine ever invented for the discovery of truth"); *see* ***Davidson v. Great Nat'l Life Ins.***, 737 S.W.2d 312, 314 (Tex. 1987) ("Cross-examination is a safeguard essential to a fair trial and a cornerstone in the quest for truth."); *see also* ***Brookhart v. Janis***, 384 U.S. 1, 3 (1966) ("[D]enial of cross-examination ... would be constitutional error of the first magnitude and no amount of showing of want of prejudice would cure it."); ***Skillern v. State***, 890 S.W.2d 849, 866-67 (Tex. App.—Austin 1994, pet. ref'd) (Criminal Rule 610 "'recognizes the centrality of cross-examination in the adversary system, sanctioning the use of leading questions and attacks upon credibility'" (quoting 1 GOODE ET AL., *supra* note 24, §611.4, at 621)).

examination are evident: (1) eliciting any facts relevant to a material issue in the case, (2) eliciting any further facts that would shed light on the evidence presented during the direct examination, and (3) presenting any evidence that bears on the witness's credibility or direct testimony.[506]

In Texas, "[a] witness may be cross-examined on any relevant matter, including credibility."[507] Trial judges must permit the cross-examiner a wide latitude in developing the facts that would affect credibility, particularly when the questioning is directed at the witness's possible bias and motive.[508] However, trial judges do retain considerable latitude in limiting the form and extent of cross-examination to prevent harassment or embarrassment of the witness,[509] to provide for the safety of the witness or others,[510] and to prevent repetitious, speculative, or marginally relevant evidence.[511] Generally, if the primary purposes of cross-examination have already been achieved,

---

506. McCORMICK ON EVIDENCE, *supra* note 2, §29, at 63; *see, e.g.*, *JLG Trucking, LLC v. Garza*, 466 S.W.3d 157, 163 (Tex. 2015) (in personal-injury case, trial court's exclusion of evidence about second accident limited defense's ability to cross-examine expert witness on credibility of his methods for determining cause of plaintiff's injuries; defense could not adequately cross-examine witness on methods without discussing improperly excluded evidence).

507. TEX. R. EVID. 611(b); *see JLG Trucking*, 466 S.W.3d at 163. In addressing whether a witness's mental-health history is relevant to credibility, Texas courts have considered several factors on a case-by-case basis. *See Virts v. State*, 739 S.W.2d 25, 28 (Tex. Crim. App. 1987); *Torres v. Danny's Serv. Co.*, 266 S.W.3d 485, 487-88 (Tex. App.—Eastland 2008, pet. denied). The factors include how recent a mental illness was, how the illness manifested itself, and how important the witness's testimony is. *Torres*, 266 S.W.3d at 488; *see Virts*, 739 S.W.2d at 30. The mere fact that the witness has suffered from a mental illness does not make evidence of that illness admissible for impeachment. *Virts*, 739 S.W.2d at 30; *Torres*, 266 S.W.3d at 488.

508. *See Carroll v. State*, 916 S.W.2d 494, 497 (Tex. Crim. App. 1996) ("The scope of appropriate cross-examination is necessarily broad. A defendant is entitled to pursue all avenues of cross-examination reasonably calculated to expose a motive, bias or interest for the witness to testify."); *Hurd v. State*, 725 S.W.2d 249, 252 (Tex. Crim. App. 1987) (trial court does not have discretion to prohibit defendant from engaging in "'otherwise appropriate cross-examination designed to show a prototypical form of bias on the part of the witness'" (quoting *Delaware v. Van Arsdall*, 475 U.S. 673, 680 (1986))); *see, e.g.*, *Cantu v. State*, 939 S.W.2d 627, 635 (Tex. Crim. App. 1997) (under Criminal Rule 610, now Rule 611, trial court has discretion in the extent of cross-examination of a witness on credibility or bias, and its decision is not subject to reversal on appeal without a clear abuse of discretion; State could cross-examine defense witness with letter she wrote to jailed defendant); *Nguyen v. State*, 506 S.W.3d 69, 85-86 (Tex. App.—Texarkana 2016, pet. ref'd) (trial court erred in preventing defendant from cross-examining witness about witness's civil suit against defendant for damages arising from same incident; civil suit may have been economic motive for witness to "shade his testimony" in criminal trial); *Walker v. State*, 300 S.W.3d 836, 845-46 (Tex. App.—Fort Worth 2009, pet. ref'd) (defendant was able to cross-examine witness about potential bias or improper motive and could emphasize the difference in testimony between witnesses).

509. TEX. R. EVID. 611(a)(3); *see Delaware v. Van Arsdall*, 475 U.S. 673, 679 (1986) (trial courts have latitude to impose reasonable restrictions on cross-examination based on concerns such as harassment, prejudice, and confusion of the issues); *Carrillo v. State*, 591 S.W.2d 876, 886-87 (Tex. Crim. App. 1979) (extent of cross-examination to show bias of witness rests within trial court's discretion to consider the potential risks, such as "the possibility of undue prejudice, embarrassment, or harassment to either a witness or a party"); *Cloud v. State*, 567 S.W.2d 801, 802-03 (Tex. Crim. App. [Panel Op.] 1978) (risks of unlimited cross-examination include undue prejudice, harassment, confusing or misleading the jury, and undue delay).

510. *See Van Arsdall*, 475 U.S. at 679; *see also Salinas v. State*, 773 S.W.2d 779, 781 (Tex. App.—San Antonio 1989, pet. ref'd) (defendant could not cross-examine police officer about precise location from which the police had conducted surveillance because although witness's security was not a concern, revealing the location would jeopardize ongoing investigation).

511. *See* TEX. R. EVID. 611(a)(2); *Van Arsdall*, 475 U.S. at 679; *Nguyen*, 506 S.W.3d at 85; *Walker*, 300 S.W.3d at 845-46; *see, e.g.*, *Johnson v. State*, 433 S.W.3d 546, 556-57 (Tex. Crim. App. 2014) (trial court properly limited questioning of witnesses about potential bias in favor of the State to whether pending charges were misdemeanors or

the trial judge can properly limit further questions whose probative value are substantially outweighed by Rule 403 counterfactors.[512]

The rule does not make any reference to redirect or recross-examination, but the trial judge has discretion to permit such examination, even though he generally retains the authority to prevent inquiry into new matters during redirect and recross-examination.[513] However, at least one case has held that it is reversible error under Rule 611 to prohibit redirect examination when that redirect is intended to give the witness an opportunity to explain answers given on cross-examination.[514]

C. Rule 611(c): Leading Questions

Rule 611(c) codifies well-understood Texas common law that ordinarily prohibits leading witnesses on direct examination[515] but allows it on both cross-examination[516] and direct examination of an adverse witness, which is essentially cross-examination.[517] The rationale for the general prohibition on leading questions during direct examination is to prevent an attorney from testifying and then merely asking for agreement from the witness.[518] But the use of leading questions, even on direct examination, is rarely reversible error.[519]

---

felonies; punishment ranges for these crimes were only marginally probative of allegation of bias); ***Easterling v. State***, 710 S.W.2d 569, 579 (Tex. Crim. App. 1986) (proper to restrict a cross-examination that called for pure speculation and was redundant).

512. *See, e.g.,* ***Ahlschlager v. Remington Arms Co.***, 750 S.W.2d 832, 836 (Tex. App.—Houston [14th Dist.] 1988, writ denied) (trial court did not abuse its discretion in limiting further questions when it found every consideration in Rule 403 present).

513. *See* ***Long v. State***, 742 S.W.2d 302, 322 n.21 (Tex. Crim. App. 1987) ("Allowing *new* evidence to be introduced as rebuttal … is discretionary with the court and is permissible consistent with the administration of justice."), *overruled on other grounds*, ***Briggs v. State***, 789 S.W.2d 918 (Tex. Crim. App. 1990); ***Brooks v. State***, 642 S.W.2d 791, 795 (Tex. Crim. App. [Panel Op.] 1982) (proper to restrict redirect examination on purely repetitious matters); ***Jarvis v. K&E Re One, LLC***, 390 S.W.3d 631, 644 (Tex. App.—Dallas 2012, no pet.) (trial court may give examining counsel "nearly complete freedom" to bring out new material on redirect examination, subject to recross-examination); *see, e.g.,* ***Tex. Emp'rs Ins. v. Hitt***, 125 S.W.2d 323, 329 (Tex. Civ. App.—Galveston 1939, no writ) (trial court did not abuse its discretion in refusing to allow inquiry during second redirect into matters not elicited on cross-examination).

514. ***Sims v. Brackett***, 885 S.W.2d 450, 455 (Tex. App.—Corpus Christi 1994, writ denied). In this case, the trial judge declared on day two of the trial that, in the interest of speed of presentation of the case, he would prohibit redirect and recross of the witnesses except with leave of court. *Id.* Here, the trial judge overstepped the bounds of reasonable control and denied the medical-malpractice plaintiff his right to redirect examination. *Id.* The error was not harmless. *Id.* at 456.

515. *See* ***St. John v. Moorman***, 272 S.W. 223, 223 (Tex. Civ. App.—El Paso 1925, no writ) (departure from established rule authorized only with unwilling or unintelligent witnesses).

516. Tex. R. Evid. 611(c)(1); ***Jones v. Travelers Ins.***, 374 S.W.2d 779, 782 (Tex. Civ. App.—Beaumont 1964, writ ref'd n.r.e.).

517. *See* Tex. R. Evid. 611(c)(2); ***Holbert v. State***, 457 S.W.2d 286, 289 (Tex. Crim. App. 1970).

518. Commentators have offered several explanations for why leading questions may be harmful in developing a witness's direct testimony: (1) they may prompt a "false memory" of events, (2) they may induce the witness to agree with the examiner's version of events because the courtroom is an unfamiliar and intimidating place, because the witness is normally involved in social discourse (in which imprecision is acceptable and goes unchallenged), because the witness does not fully understand the consequences of his testimony, or because the witness hopes to "speed the process along" by agreeing, and (3) they distract the witness from important details in favor of the limited version desired by the questioner. 4 GRAHAM, *supra* note 110, §611:8, at 656 n.4.

519. *See* ***United States v. Grassrope***, 342 F.3d 866, 869 (8th Cir. 2003) (reviewing court will ordinarily "defer to the trial court in determining when leading questions are necessary, and review for abuse of discretion"); Dabney

Leading questions are those that obviously suggest the correct answer.[520] Questions that contain a phrase such as "didn't he," "isn't it true that," "would you agree," or "correct," are obviously and invariably leading. Nevertheless, questions may be phrased much more subtly and still suggest the desired answer. The mere addition of a word such as "whether" does not make a request, as in "tell the jury whether the masked robber frightened you when he held his knife up against your throat," any less suggestive. Although questions that begin with the open-ended queries of "who," "what," "where," "when," "why," or "how many" are generally not leading,[521] such phrases are not talismans of nonleading questions. Even verbal tone and inflections or nonverbal body language can convert an ostensibly neutral question into a leading one.[522] If everyone in the courtroom knows what the "right" answer is before the witness responds, the question is likely leading.[523]

Leading questions can be used on direct examination "as necessary to develop the witness's testimony."[524] For example, leading questions to establish the witness's background have long been acceptable as an expedient method of permitting the jury to learn a little bit about the witness and better judge his credibility without unduly prolonging the trial.[525] Sometimes a child witness or a witness who has a mental disability or who speaks little English will be unable to communicate the relevant information without the use of some leading questions.[526] Leading questions may also be permit-

---

Bassel & Connie Hall, *Almost Fifty Shades of Grey: Leading Questions on Direct Examination*, STATE BAR LITIG. SECTION NEWS FOR THE BAR, Fall 2015, at 16, 17 (burden to demonstrate harmful error of leading questions is "probably insurmountable"); John B. Stevens, Jr., *Please Tell the Jury in My Own Words*, 79 TEX. B.J. 282, 284 (2016) ("There is an almost universal unwillingness by appellate courts to reverse trial verdicts over misuse of leading questions.").

520. *See **Tinlin v. State***, 983 S.W.2d 65, 70 (Tex. App.—Fort Worth 1998, pet. ref'd) ("Leading questions are questions that suggest the desired answer, instruct the witness how to answer, or put words into the witness's mouth to be echoed back."); ***Implement Dealers Mut. Ins. v. Castleberry***, 368 S.W.2d 249, 253 (Tex. Civ. App.—Beaumont 1963, writ ref'd n.r.e.) ("'[T]he essential element necessary to render the question improper is that it suggest the specific answer desired.'" (quoting 1 CHARLES T. MCCORMICK & ROY R. RAY, TEXAS PRACTICE, TEXAS LAW OF EVIDENCE CIVIL AND CRIMINAL §571, at 451 (2d ed. 1956))); MCCORMICK ON EVIDENCE, *supra* note 2, §6, at 11 (leading question "is one that suggests to the witness the answer desired by the examiner"). *See generally* 3 WIGMORE, *supra* note 295, §§769-772 (discussing questions that assume controverted facts or call for a "yes" or "no" answer).

521. *See* Bassel & Hall, *supra* note 519, at 17; *see, e.g.*, ***Myers v. State***, 781 S.W.2d 730, 733 (Tex. App.—Fort Worth 1989, pet. ref'd) (prosecutor's direct questions asking who was in charge of the premises and who was responsible for the care, custody, control, and management over the premises were not leading because the State did not suggest who the witness was supposed to identify).

522. 1 GOODE ET AL., *supra* note 24, §611.2, at 615; Fred A. Simpson & Deborah J. Selden, *Objection: Leading Question!*, 61 TEX. B.J. 1123, 1124 (1998); Stevens, *supra* note 519, at 283.

523. 1 GOODE ET AL., *supra* note 24, §611.2, at 615.

524. TEX. R. EVID. 611(c); *see* MCCORMICK ON EVIDENCE, *supra* note 2, §6, at 13 (rather than abandoning all efforts to bring out witness's testimony, judge may exercise discretion in allowing leading questions); 3 WIGMORE, *supra* note 295, §770, at 161-62, §773, at 166 (suggesting guidelines for trial court's discretionary rulings but stating that "where the reason [for permitting leading questions] ceases, the rule ceases also"). Leading questions are permitted, for example, to establish an evidentiary foundation.

525. *See* 1 RAY, *supra* note 4, §576, at 533.

526. *See **Uhl v. State***, 479 S.W.2d 55, 57 (Tex. Crim. App. 1972) ("The asking of leading questions is seldom a ground for reversal (especially where a child is testifying)."); ***Clark v. State***, 952 S.W.2d 882, 886 (Tex. App.—

ted to clarify the witness's previous testimony[527] or to jog the memory of a witness whose recollection has been exhausted.[528]

Some pre-Rules Texas authority advocated limiting the use of leading questions on direct to those asked of an actual adverse party.[529] To this extent, Rule 611 expands former Texas law by allowing leading questions on direct of "a hostile witness, an adverse party, or a witness identified with an adverse party."[530] Obviously, the trial judge may use his discretion in determining when witnesses are actually adverse despite what their formal alignment is or which party called them.[531] Thus, when a plaintiff calls the defendant or the defendant's expert as an adverse witness, the defendant's attorney should not be permitted to "cross-examine" his own client or witness through leading questions.[532] Similarly, as the comment to the former civil rule points out, an insured defendant who is aligned with the plaintiff is not an adverse witness for purposes of the rule.[533] The investigating police officer who has been called by the criminal defendant for impeachment purposes is also not considered adverse to the government under the rule.[534] These witnesses are "friendly" to the cross-examiner even though the

---

Beaumont 1997, no pet.) ("In cases dealing with child witnesses, the rule against leading questions is somewhat relaxed."); *see, e.g.*, ***Hernandez v. State***, 643 S.W.2d 397, 400 (Tex. Crim. App. 1982) (leading questions were permitted when witness had difficulty understanding English); ***Padilla v. State***, 278 S.W.3d 98, 106 (Tex. App.—Texarkana 2009, pet. ref'd) (child witness had to be reminded to speak louder, was reluctant to testify, could not remember events that occurred over a year before trial, and was overcome with emotion during direct examination; no evidence that leading questions supplied her with a false memory); ***Trevino v. State***, 783 S.W.2d 731, 733 (Tex. App.—San Antonio 1989, no pet.) (prosecutor could ask leading questions of 15-year-old victim who attended special education classes). *See generally* MCCORMICK ON EVIDENCE, *supra* note 2, §6, at 12-13 (identifying situations in which leading questions are permitted during direct examination).

527. *See* ***Myers v. State***, 781 S.W.2d 730, 733 (Tex. App.—Fort Worth 1989, pet. ref'd) (witness who gives an unresponsive answer may be asked a more specific question to clarify his testimony); Stevens, *supra* note 519, at 283 (leading questions allowed if witnesses are "uncooperative, biased, evasive, or reluctant").

528. *See* MCCORMICK ON EVIDENCE, *supra* note 2, §6, at 13; Stevens, *supra* note 519, at 283; *see also* ***Holbert v. State***, 457 S.W.2d 286, 289 (Tex. Crim. App. 1970) (judge can permit leading questions "to a hostile witness or to refresh a witness's memory").

529. *See, e.g.*, ***Zamora v. Romero***, 581 S.W.2d 742, 746-47 (Tex. Civ. App.—Corpus Christi 1979, writ ref'd n.r.e.) (error, but harmless, for plaintiff to call defendant's son and ask leading questions because son was not adverse party); ***Coronado v. Emps. Nat'l Ins.***, 577 S.W.2d 525, 531 (Tex. Civ. App.—El Paso 1979) (error, but harmless, when trial court permitted defendant-insurer's counsel to ask leading questions of an individual codefendant), *aff'd*, 596 S.W.2d 502 (Tex. 1979).

530. TEX. R. EVID. 611(c)(2).

531. *See* ***Scurlock Oil Co. v. Smithwick***, 724 S.W.2d 1, 10 (Tex. 1986) (Spears & Gonzalez, JJ., concurring) (trial judge should determine alignment of parties in deciding whether to allow plaintiff to lead an ostensibly adverse witness on cross-examination).

532. *E.g.*, ***GAB Bus. Servs., Inc. v. Moore***, 829 S.W.2d 345, 351 (Tex. App.—Texarkana 1992, no writ) (defendant's former employee "could still be characterized as a friendly witness" for purposes of Civil Rule 611(c), and trial court did not err in excluding excerpts of her deposition testimony that contained leading questions); *see* ***Coronado***, 577 S.W.2d at 531; ***Deal v. Madison***, 576 S.W.2d 409, 424 (Tex. Civ. App.—Dallas 1978, writ ref'd n.r.e.), *overruled on other grounds*, ***Cypress Creek Util. Serv. Co. v. Muller***, 640 S.W.2d 860 (Tex. 1982).

533. TEX. R. CIV. EVID. 611 cmt., 733-734 S.W.2d (Tex. Cases) LXXXIX (1987, amended 1998).

534. *See, e.g.*, ***United States v. Bryant***, 461 F.2d 912, 918-19 (6th Cir. 1972) (defendant could ask leading questions of government informer because the rationale for the prohibition was not present when questioning witness closely identified with opposing party's interest).

other side has called them to the witness stand.[535] Thus, the "cross-examination" of a friendly witness should generally proceed in accord with the rules of direct examination.[536] Similarly, in a hearing on a motion for new trial, testifying jurors are not aligned with either party, and thus neither side may ask leading questions.[537]

RULE 612

WRITING USED TO REFRESH A WITNESS'S MEMORY

(a) **Scope.** This rule gives an adverse party certain options when a witness uses a writing to refresh memory:

(1) while testifying;

(2) before testifying, in civil cases, if the court decides that justice requires the party to have those options; or

(3) before testifying, in criminal cases.

(b) **Adverse Party's Options; Deleting Unrelated Matter.** An adverse party is entitled to have the writing produced at the hearing, to inspect it, to cross-examine the witness about it, and to introduce in evidence any portion that relates to the witness's testimony. If the producing party claims that the writing includes unrelated matter, the court must examine the writing in camera, delete any unrelated portion, and order that the rest be delivered to the adverse party. Any portion deleted over objection must be preserved for the record.

(c) **Failure to Produce or Deliver the Writing.** If a writing is not produced or is not delivered as ordered, the court may issue any appropriate order. But if the prosecution does not comply in a criminal case, the court must strike the witness's testimony or—if justice so requires—declare a mistrial.

---

535. Michael Graham suggests that in determining the "hostility" of a witness, "often the most important single factor is whether the calling party has been able to prepare the witness to testify at trial." 4 GRAHAM, *supra* note 110, §611:8, at 664 n.23. *See generally* Michael H. Graham, *Examination of a Party's Own Witness Under the Federal Rules of Evidence: A Promise Unfulfilled*, 54 TEX. L. REV. 917, 922-59 (1976) (analyzing changes from earlier federal practice, brought about by the adoption of the Federal Rules, when a party calls his own witness).

536. *See Cecil v. T.M.E. Invs., Inc.*, 893 S.W.2d 38, 47-48 (Tex. App.—Corpus Christi 1994, no writ) (although trial court erred in allowing defense attorney to ask leading questions during friendly cross-examination of his own party who had been called to testify by opposing party, error was harmless).

537. *See Ausley v. Johnston*, 450 S.W.2d 351, 356 (Tex. Civ. App.—El Paso 1970, writ ref'd n.r.e.).

COMMENTARY ON RULE 612

The use of a writing[538] to refresh a witness's memory was well established in Texas common law,[539] and Rule 612 did not introduce any major change to the process. The Texas rule is patterned after Federal Rule 612.[540] The 1998 unification of former Criminal Rule 611[541] and Civil Rule 612 did not substantively change either provision, though the rule operates somewhat differently in criminal and civil proceedings.

A. Practical Considerations

Witnesses at trial may forget some fact about the event that is the subject of the litigation. The stress and confusion of testifying has even rendered some witnesses unable to remember their own names or addresses. When the witness temporarily forgets some aspect of his anticipated testimony, counsel may refresh his recollection at trial by handing the witness a writing.[542] Similarly, the witness may review his anticipated testimony before trial, either with or without the aid of counsel, and he may at that time use some writing or document as an aid to refresh his memory of past events relevant to the trial. Rule 612 deals with those written materials that the witness uses either on the witness stand or before trial.[543] The two main problems in practice have been (1) ensuring that the writing is merely refreshing the witness's memory so that the witness's

---

538. Traditionally, refreshing a witness's memory has not been confined to writings; even a song can bring back memories. ***Jewett v. United States***, 15 F.2d 955, 956 (9th Cir. 1926); *see also* ***Baker v. State***, 371 A.2d 699, 704-05 (Md. Ct. Spec. App. 1977) (anything may refresh memory, including "a line from Kipling or the dolorous refrain of 'The Tennessee Waltz'; a whiff of hickory smoke; the running of the fingers across a swatch of corduroy; the sweet carbonation of a chocolate soda; [or] the sight of a faded snapshot in a long-neglected album").

539. *See, e.g.*, ***Putnam v. Pannell***, 507 S.W.2d 811, 813 (Tex. Civ. App.—Waco 1974, no writ) (plaintiff could use a piece of paper to refresh her recollection); ***Paul v. Johnson***, 314 S.W.2d 338, 342 (Tex. Civ. App.—Houston 1958, writ dism'd) (witness could refer to an exhibit already entered into evidence).

540. Rule 612 is substantively identical to Federal Rule 612 except in subsections (a)(2) and (a)(3) and the opening phrase in subsection (b). Refer to notes 549-550 *infra* and accompanying text.

541. Judicial decisions rendered before March 1998 refer to Texas Rule of Criminal Evidence 611 when discussing writings used to refresh memory.

542. *See, e.g.*, ***Arthur J. Gallagher & Co. v. Dieterich***, 270 S.W.3d 695, 706-07 (Tex. App.—Dallas 2008, no pet.) (trial court did not abuse its discretion in allowing witness to refresh his recollection with a document that he had prepared but that was not provided in discovery; witness did not testify about any matters contained in the document other than the total amount of attorney fees); ***McCoy v. State***, 877 S.W.2d 844, 845 (Tex. App.—Eastland 1994, no pet.) (police officers could read their offense reports to refresh their memories and then testify to their present recollections); ***Williams v. State***, 760 S.W.2d 292, 297 (Tex. App.—Texarkana 1988, pet. ref'd) (police officer could refresh his memory from a written report because he lacked independent recall of the suspect's clothing).

To refresh the witness's memory, counsel may simply show the written material to the witness and ask him to read it silently. Neither the witness nor counsel should read any of the material aloud in the presence of the jury. If the witness testifies that his memory is now refreshed, he may continue to testify without reference to the written material. If the witness's memory is not refreshed, the witness cannot testify about the matter in question. The written material is not admissible under Rule 612 as a substitute for the witness's testimony. It may sometimes qualify for admission under Rule 803(5), recorded recollection, in which case it does substitute for the witness's testimony on that point. Refer to *Article VIII: Hearsay, infra* p. 895.

543. *See* Tex. R. Evid. 612(a). It is true that anything, such as a painting, a face, or even a cup of tea may produce a remembrance of things past, but the rule is wisely confined to the production of written materials and documents. *See* ***Jewett***, 15 F.2d at 956; ***Baker***, 371 A.2d at 705.

recollection, and not the writing, is the basis of the final testimony,[544] and (2) giving the opponent a fair opportunity to inspect the writing, to examine the witness about it, and to bring to the jury's attention any inconsistencies between the writing and the testimony.[545]

Rule 612 does not entirely resolve the first problem.[546] However, by expressly stating that the adverse party may "introduce in evidence any portion that relates to the witness's testimony,"[547] the rule implies that the proponent may not introduce the writing. Rather, the proponent, in accordance with tradition, must rely solely on the witness's testimony.[548] This practice at least mitigates the potential harm from a writing that does more than refresh a witness's memory.

The rule is more successful in handling the second problem: it allows an adverse party to have the writing produced for inspection at the hearing, whether it is used before or during the testimony.[549] In civil cases, the rule contemplates that before a writing used out of court is required to be produced, the court must determine that justice requires such production.[550] This requirement prevents a wholesale fishing expedition

---

544. If a writing is substituted for the witness's testimony because of lost memory, this recorded recollection must qualify as an exception to the hearsay rule. *See* TEX. R. EVID. 803(5).

545. *See* **Winters v. Winters**, 282 S.W.2d 749, 751-53 (Tex. Civ. App.—Amarillo 1955, no writ).

546. The rule assumes that any party may refresh the witness's recollection with any written statement regardless of the author or source of that statement. *See, e.g.,* **Callahan v. State**, 937 S.W.2d 553, 559 (Tex. App.—Texarkana 1996, no pet.) (when a witness is shown to have had personal knowledge at some time in the past that he cannot now remember, counsel may produce a writing for his review in an attempt to refresh his present recollection; in this case, no showing was made that witness was unable to answer questions about his school records before the attempt to refresh his memory; trial court properly refused to allow witness to consult those records and excluded them from evidence).

547. TEX. R. EVID. 612(b).

548. *See, e.g.,* **Md. Cas. Co. v. Hearks**, 188 S.W.2d 262, 266-67 (Tex. Civ. App.—Beaumont 1945) (in workers' compensation case, trial court properly excluded doctor's written report when doctor testified and used the report only to refresh his memory; no question of report's authenticity), *aff'd*, 144 Tex. 317, 190 S.W.2d 62 (1945).

549. *See* TEX. R. EVID. 612(a), (b). Federal Rule 612(b) is identical to Texas Rule 612(b) except the federal rule qualifies the adverse party's right to have the writing produced at the hearing if "18 U.S.C. §3500 provides otherwise in a criminal case." *See* FED. R. EVID. 612(b).
In **Powell v. State**, the defendant requested a copy of the witness's offense report, which he used to refresh his memory during the cross-examination by a codefendant. 5 S.W.3d 369, 379 (Tex. App.—Texarkana 1999, pet. ref'd). The State argued that because the defendant had already cross-examined the witness before the codefendant, it was harmless error to deny that request. *Id.* at 380. The Texarkana court disagreed, noting that the defendant conducted only a short recross-examination of the witness. *Id.* Indeed, had the defendant had a copy of the offense report, he might have conducted a much lengthier cross-examination. The error was harmless, however, because the report was entirely consistent with the witness's testimony. *Id.* at 382.
The **Powell** court also stated that former Criminal Rule 611 (now Rule 612) requires production of material used to refresh the witness's memory during *any* hearing, not merely during a trial or in front of the jury. *Id.* at 380.

550. TEX. R. EVID. 612(a)(2); *cf. Sporck v. Peil*, 759 F.2d 312, 317 (3d Cir. 1985) ("By its very language, [Federal] Rule 612 requires that a party meet three conditions before it may obtain documents used by a witness prior to testifying: 1) the witness must use the writing to refresh his memory; 2) the witness must use the writing for the purpose of testifying; and 3) the court must determine that production is necessary in the interests of justice."). The corresponding federal rule gives the trial court this discretion in both civil and criminal cases. *See* FED. R. EVID. 612(a)(2).

into everything that witnesses read in the weeks before testifying.[551] It also supports the notion that attorneys should be allowed some degree of privacy when preparing their witnesses to testify.[552]

The rule for criminal cases, on the other hand, requires that any and all writings used by witnesses to refresh their memories before trial be produced for inspection.[553] Earlier Texas law had held that the criminal defendant was entitled to the production of any earlier writing authored by a testifying witness for inspection and use during cross-examination.[554] However, the defendant did not have the right to inspect or use statements authored by another person that were used only to refresh the witness's recollection.[555] Thus, the rule for criminal cases is much broader than earlier common-law rules governing the admissibility of documents used or relied on by witnesses in refreshing their memories.[556] If the witness denies having reviewed a particular document before testifying, the cross-examiner is not entitled to its production.[557]

Suppose that the witness is called by the opposing party or that the witness is unfriendly to the sponsoring party. In the likely scenario that the unwilling witness does

---

551. *See Portland Sav. & Loan Ass'n v. Bernstein*, 716 S.W.2d 532, 541 (Tex. App.—Corpus Christi 1985, writ ref'd n.r.e.) (trial court has discretion to require production of document used to refresh witness's memory), *overruled on other grounds*, *Dawson-Austin v. Austin*, 968 S.W.2d 319 (Tex. 1998).

552. *See* 2 SALTZBURG ET AL., *supra* note 102, at 1119 (judge will likely prevent discovery of statements used to refresh so that lawyers are not inhibited in preparing witnesses to testify).

553. TEX. R. EVID. 612(a)(3); *e.g.*, *Young v. State*, 830 S.W.2d 122, 124 (Tex. Crim. App. 1992) (under former Criminal Rule 611, defendant was absolutely entitled to have produced for his inspection and use during cross-examination all records reviewed by State's witness before her testimony; irrelevant that the State did not have records in its possession or that the witness did not bring the documents to court with her); *see Marsh v. State*, 749 S.W.2d 646, 648 (Tex. App.—Amarillo 1988, pet. ref'd) (wording of former Criminal Rule 611 is "unambiguous and unequivocal" that once a witness uses a writing to refresh his memory for the purposes of testifying, an adverse party is entitled to immediate production of that writing for use on cross-examination).

554. *Gaskin v. State*, 172 Tex. Crim. 7, 9, 353 S.W.2d 467, 469 (1961).

555. *Kemner v. State*, 589 S.W.2d 403, 408-09 (Tex. Crim. App. [Panel Op.] 1979); *Artell v. State*, 372 S.W.2d 944, 945 (Tex. Crim. App. 1963); *Epperson v. State*, 650 S.W.2d 110, 112 (Tex. App.—Tyler 1983, no pet.).

556. *Robertson v. State*, 871 S.W.2d 701, 709 n.9 (Tex. Crim. App. 1993). Earlier law had also held that it did not matter who authored a statement in the "use before the jury" rule if the witness used the statement while testifying in such a manner that its contents became an issue. Once the witness used the statement before the jury, the opposing party was entitled to inspect and use the written statement during cross-examination. *See White v. State*, 478 S.W.2d 506, 511-12 (Tex. Crim. App. 1972) (when the contents of a document become an issue before the jury, the document must be produced for opposing counsel). Shortly before the adoption of the Rules, the court of criminal appeals brought together both of the above doctrines in *Ballew v. State* and held that the prosecution was entitled to inspect a defense psychiatrist's notes, under the reasoning that the witness's recent referral to the writings to refresh his memory was the "functional equivalent" of their use before the jury. 640 S.W.2d 237, 244 (Tex. Crim. App. [Panel Op.] 1982) (op. on reh'g). Thus, civil practice differed from criminal practice even before adoption of the Rules.

557. *See, e.g.*, *Saldivar v. State*, 980 S.W.2d 475, 497 (Tex. App.—Houston [14th Dist.] 1998, pet. ref'd) (disclosure of documents unnecessary when there was no evidence that witness had actually reviewed particular business records to refresh his memory before testifying); *see also Thomas v. State*, 336 S.W.3d 703, 711 (Tex. App.—Houston [1st Dist.] 2010, pet. ref'd) (witness testified that although he had document with him while testifying, he did not use it to refresh his memory; trial court did not abuse its discretion in refusing to admit document under Rule 612).

not recall fully the events about which he is questioned, the sponsoring party may refresh his memory with whatever written material is appropriate.[558]

The practical difference between Rules 612(a)(2) and 612(a)(3) is significant. For example, in a criminal trial, if a state social worker has reviewed the department's case file on a particular complainant before testifying in court, the defendant is automatically entitled to have that entire file produced for inspection and to use it during cross-examination.[559] In civil proceedings, however, if the file was reviewed before trial but not used or referred to by the witness during direct examination, the adverse party must convince the trial judge that justice requires that the adverse party be allowed to review the file's contents.[560] The wording of the provision gives the trial judge broad discretion to refuse production in civil cases. The writing is still admissible solely for impeachment purposes. Because it is hearsay, it will not constitute substantive evidence unless it falls within some exception to the hearsay rule.[561]

In either civil or criminal proceedings, the rule allows the opponent to introduce relevant portions of the writing into evidence, subject to the court's deletion of any unrelated portion.[562] If the sponsoring party asserts that the writing includes unrelated matter, the trial court must inspect the entire document in camera.[563] The court may then

---

558. *See* ***State v. Williams***, 846 S.W.2d 408, 411 (Tex. App.—Houston [14th Dist.] 1992, pet. ref'd). In ***Williams***, the defendant called the arresting officer to testify during a pretrial motion-to-suppress hearing. *Id.* at 409. The officer's memory failed him, and the defendant requested a copy of his offense report from the State to show the officer in the hope of refreshing his memory. The State refused and claimed that the defense had no right to discover the report. *Id.* The trial judge then granted the defendant's motion to suppress the officer's testimony because the officer was unable to testify to his actions. The State appealed, claiming that the trial judge erred in requiring the State to produce the offense report on pain of having the motion to suppress granted. The court of appeals agreed with the trial judge and stated the following:

> While Rule 611 [now Rule 612] technically does not apply because appellee had called the officer as a witness on direct examination, we find that the provisions of the rule apply equally in a case where a party has called an adverse witness who is unable to recall the requested information without refreshing his recollection. Allowing the officer not to answer appellee's questions because he could not recall, and then to prohibit the officer from refreshing his memory with his offense report defeats the interests of justice.

Id. at 411.

559. ***Marsh v. State***, 749 S.W.2d 646, 647-49 (Tex. App.—Amarillo 1988, pet. ref'd).

560. *See* TEX. R. EVID. 612(a)(2), (b).

561. *See* ***Robertson***, 871 S.W.2d at 709 ("A document admitted under Rule 611 [now Rule 612] is not admitted for the truth of the matter asserted, but rather it is admitted for purposes of testing the credibility of the testifying witness."); ***Garza v. State***, 18 S.W.3d 813, 823 (Tex. App.—Fort Worth 2000, pet. ref'd) (document introduced under Rule 612 was "not offered for the truth of its content, but rather for the jury's use in comparing the document to the witness' testimony"); *see also* 3 WEINSTEIN & BERGER, *supra* note 110, ¶612[01], at 612-18 (such writings must satisfy the requirements of Federal Rule 801(d)(1)(A), which deals with prior inconsistent statements).

562. TEX. R. EVID. 612(b).

563. *Id.* It is error to withhold any portion of the written materials that the witness has reviewed from the trial court's in camera inspection. *E.g.*, ***Yates v. State***, 941 S.W.2d 357, 362-63 (Tex. App.—Waco 1997, pet. ref'd) (when officer testified that he had "browsed" through the entire police case file in preparation for pretrial hearing, trial judge erred in not requiring witness to produce entire file for in camera inspection; harmless error because nothing in file contradicted witness's testimony).

delete any unrelated portion and order that the rest be delivered to the opposing party.[564] Any portion of the writing that is deleted over objection must be preserved for the record.[565]

B. Sanctions for Not Producing Document

If, in a civil case, the party who has called the witness refuses to produce the writing with which the witness has refreshed his memory, and if the court has ordered disclosure, the trial judge has wide discretion in fashioning a suitable sanction.[566] The rule simply states that "the court may issue any appropriate order."[567] Appropriate sanctions might include striking the testimony, contempt, a continuance for the opponent, or even dismissal of the pertinent claim or defense.[568]

In a criminal case, if the prosecutor does not on request produce any writing that the witness has used to refresh his memory, the judge is required to strike that witness's testimony unless the more severe measure of declaring a mistrial is necessary.[569] If a defendant refuses to produce a writing under the rule, the remedy is the same as in civil proceedings, except, of course, that a defendant's defensive claim cannot constitutionally be dismissed.

C. Privilege Concerns

A problem arises when the document that the witness has used to refresh his memory is otherwise privileged material or subject to a valid claim of work-product protection. Certainly, the work-product doctrine would give way when the witness uses the document to refresh his memory on the witness stand.[570] Less certain, at least in civil cases, is whether a valid evidentiary privilege or the work-product doctrine would

---

564. TEX. R. EVID. 612(b). Although the rule speaks in terms of the cross-examiner's entitlement to introduce relevant portions of the document, the court of criminal appeals has held that the trial court's refusal to admit those portions is subject to a harmless-error analysis. *See, e.g., Robertson*, 871 S.W.2d at 709 (trial court's erroneous refusal to admit psychological evaluation relied on by testifying expert to refresh his memory for trial was harmless because report did not contradict testimony and thus had no impeachment value); *see also de la Rosa v. State*, 961 S.W.2d 495, 498-500 (Tex. App.—San Antonio 1997, no pet.) (harmless error under TEX. R. APP. P. 44.2(a) and (b) to exclude witness's written statement to police, which contradicted his trial testimony, because contradictory portions of that statement were read aloud to the jury). In *Robertson*, the court of criminal appeals reiterated that the rule cannot be used to discover or introduce all written materials in a witness's possession:

> While [Rule] 611 [now Rule 612] is not a *carte blanche* rule allowing admission into evidence of all the documents in an opposing witness's files, the rule does allow for the discovery of the documents used to refresh a witness's memory prior to or during testimony, and admission of portions of the documents which relate to the witness's testimony.

871 S.W.2d at 708.

565. TEX. R. EVID. 612(b).

566. *See* TEX. R. EVID. 612(c).

567. *Id.*

568. *See* 1 GOODE ET AL., *supra* note 24, §612.3, at 634.

569. TEX. R. EVID. 612(c).

570. *See City of Denison v. Grisham*, 716 S.W.2d 121, 123 (Tex. App.—Dallas 1986, orig. proceeding) (use of writing to refresh witness's memory while he is testifying waives both attorney-client privilege and work-product protection); *see, e.g., Wheeling-Pittsburgh Steel Corp. v. Underwriters Labs., Inc.*, 81 F.R.D. 8, 9 (N.D. Ill. 1978) (plaintiff waived attorney-client privilege by using documents to refresh his memory before deposition). *See generally* 3

override the requirements of production under Rule 612 when a witness has used work-product materials to refresh his memory before trial. The decisions under the federal rule have generally required the production of the material in such an instance.[571] Nonetheless, the trial judge should have discretion to consider the extent to which (1) the documents contain relevant material similar to the witness's testimony, (2) the witness reviewed the materials, and (3) the attorney's own thoughts and strategy are contained within the materials.[572]

In Texas criminal cases, the evidentiary rule apparently reigns supreme.[573] There are no work-product exceptions or privilege exemptions.[574] If the witness has reviewed, either before the trial or on the witness stand, any writing to refresh his memory for the purpose of testifying, that document must be produced either for the trial judge to review in camera or for the opponent's use on cross-examination.[575]

This issue has arisen several times in the context of *Batson*[576] hearings on the discriminatory use of peremptory challenges. If the attorney overtly uses his voir dire notes to refresh his memory in explaining his nondiscriminatory reasons for peremptory challenges, then those notes must be produced for the opposing attorney's use in cross-examination. If, however, the attorney took notes but did not refer to them in the *Batson* hearing, they remain protected work product and are not subject to production.[577]

WEINSTEIN & BERGER, *supra* note 110, ¶612[04], at 612-37 to 612-49 (discussing application of Rule 612 to privileges and work-product doctrine and suggesting a balancing approach in deciding whether materials are subject to production on demand).

571. *See Leybold-Heraeus Techs., Inc. v. Midwest Instr. Co.*, 118 F.R.D. 609, 614-15 (E.D. Wis. 1987) (company "cannot allow their witnesses to review such [privileged] documents to refresh their recollections for the purpose of testifying, without allowing [an adversary] to inspect the documents prior to trial"); *James Julian, Inc. v. Raytheon Co.*, 93 F.R.D. 138, 145 (D. Del. 1982) ("Those courts which have considered the issue have generally agreed that the use of protected documents to refresh a witness' memory prior to testifying constitutes a waiver of the protection."); 2 SALTZBURG ET AL., *supra* note 102, at 1119 (courts usually rule for disclosure).

572. *See* 2 SALTZBURG ET AL., *supra* note 102, at 1119-20.

573. *See Marsh v. State*, 749 S.W.2d 646, 649 (Tex. App.—Amarillo 1988, pet. ref'd) (under Criminal Rule 611, "any writing, regardless of authorship, may be discovered if the witness uses it to refresh his memory").

574. *See Goldberg v. United States*, 425 U.S. 94, 106 (1976) (Federal Jencks Act provides no work-product exception, but the "[p]roper application of the Act will not compel disclosure of a Government lawyer's recordation of mental impressions, personal beliefs, trial strategy [or] legal conclusions"); *Mayfield v. State*, 758 S.W.2d 371, 375 (Tex. App.—Amarillo 1988, no pet.) ("[A]ttorney-client privilege and the work product rule cannot be asserted to prevent discovery under [Criminal] Rule 614(a), formerly the *Gaskin* rule.").

575. *See* TEX. R. EVID. 612(a)(1), (a)(3), (b).

576. *Batson v. Kentucky*, 476 U.S. 79 (1986).

577. *See Pondexter v. State*, 942 S.W.2d 577, 582 (Tex. Crim. App. 1996) (in *Batson* hearing, opposing attorney is entitled to attorney's voir dire notes only if they were actually used to refresh attorney's memory during or before testimony); *Salazar v. State*, 795 S.W.2d 187, 193 (Tex. Crim. App. 1990) (production of a prosecutor's juror-information notes is both "necessary and proper" when the prosecutor refreshes his memory about the exercise of peremptory challenges by reviewing those notes before the *Batson* hearing); *cf. Goode v. Shoukfeh*, 943 S.W.2d 441, 449 (Tex. 1997) ("We hold that an *Edmonson* [*v. Leesville Concrete Co.*, 500 U.S. 614 (1991),] movant has the right to examine the voir dire notes of the opponent's attorney when the attorney relies upon these notes while giving sworn or unsworn testimony in the *Edmonson* hearing. Absent such reliance, the voir dire notes are privileged work product, and the movant may not examine them.").

RULE 613
WITNESS'S PRIOR STATEMENT & BIAS OR INTEREST

(a) Witness's Prior Inconsistent Statement.

(1) *Foundation Requirement.* When examining a witness about the witness's prior inconsistent statement—whether oral or written—a party must first tell the witness:

(A) the contents of the statement;

(B) the time and place of the statement; and

(C) the person to whom the witness made the statement.

(2) *Need Not Show Written Statement.* If the witness's prior inconsistent statement is written, a party need not show it to the witness before inquiring about it, but must, upon request, show it to opposing counsel.

(3) *Opportunity to Explain or Deny.* A witness must be given the opportunity to explain or deny the prior inconsistent statement.

(4) *Extrinsic Evidence.* Extrinsic evidence of a witness's prior inconsistent statement is not admissible unless the witness is first examined about the statement and fails to unequivocally admit making the statement.

(5) *Opposing Party's Statement.* This subdivision (a) does not apply to an opposing party's statement under Rule 801(e)(2).

(b) Witness's Bias or Interest.

(1) *Foundation Requirement.* When examining a witness about the witness's bias or interest, a party must first tell the witness the circumstances or statements that tend to show the witness's bias or interest. If examining a witness about a statement—whether oral or written—to prove the witness's bias or interest, a party must tell the witness:

(A) the contents of the statement;

(B) the time and place of the statement; and

(C) the person to whom the statement was made.

(2) *Need Not Show Written Statement.* If a party uses a written statement to prove the witness's bias or interest, a party need not show the statement to the witness before inquiring about it, but must, upon request, show it to opposing counsel.

(3) *Opportunity to Explain or Deny.* A witness must be given the opportunity to explain or deny the circumstances or statements that tend to show the witness's bias or interest. And the witness's proponent may present evidence to rebut the charge of bias or interest.

(4) *Extrinsic Evidence.* Extrinsic evidence of a witness's bias or interest is not admissible unless the witness is first examined about the bias or interest and fails to unequivocally admit it.

(c) Witness's Prior Consistent Statement. Unless Rule 801(e)(1)(B) provides otherwise, a witness's prior consistent statement is not admissible if offered solely to enhance the witness's credibility.

Notes and Comments

Comment to 2015 restyling: The amended rule retains the requirement that a witness be given an opportunity to explain or deny (a) a prior inconsistent statement or (b) the circumstances or a statement showing the witness's bias or interest, but this requirement is not imposed on the examining attorney. A witness may have to wait until redirect examination to explain a prior inconsistent statement or the circumstances or a statement that shows bias. But the impeaching attorney still is not permitted to introduce extrinsic evidence of the witness's prior inconsistent statement or bias unless the witness has first been examined about the statement or bias and has failed to unequivocally admit it. All other changes to the rule are intended to be stylistic only.

COMMENTARY ON RULE 613

Rule 613 governs two distinct forms of impeachment: impeachment with proof of a witness's prior inconsistent statements under Rule 613(a) and impeachment with proof of a witness's bias or interest under Rule 613(b). Rule 613(c) deals with possible rehabilitation of the impeached witness with prior consistent statements. The rule differs from the analogous federal rule in its foundational requirements for use of inconsistent statements.[578] Additionally, the Texas rule, unlike the federal provision, contains explicit foundational requirements for impeachment by proof of bias or interest.[579] The 1998 unification of the Civil and Criminal Rules simply renumbered former Criminal Rule 612 as Rule 613. No substantive changes were made.

Rule 613 carries forward earlier Texas law on the use of prior inconsistent statements and clarifies that the same foundation that applies to inconsistent statements also applies to proof of bias or interest.[580] In 2015, this foundation requirement in Rule 613 was amended to be more in line with actual practice in Texas courts.[581]

A. Rule 613(a): Witness's Prior Inconsistent Statement

A witness may be examined for impeachment purposes about a prior statement that is inconsistent with his present testimony. This form of impeachment is universally rec-

---

578. *See* FED. R. EVID. 613(b). Refer to notes 606-613 *infra* and accompanying text.

579. Refer to notes 665-667 *infra* and accompanying text.

580. *See* 1 RAY, *supra* note 4, §680, at 261 (Supp. 1991) (rule requires "that a foundation be laid").

581. *See* Tex. Sup. Ct. Order, Misc. Docket No. 15-9048, §2 (eff. Apr. 1, 2015). Refer to notes 613-618, 672-676 *infra* and accompanying text.

ognized[582] and routinely allowed in Texas.[583] The rationale for permitting such impeachment is to show that the witness's testimony is unreliable.[584] The prior statement is not used to prove any substantive fact at issue in the trial[585] but solely to demonstrate self-contradiction by the witness. The rule admitting prior inconsistent statements should be liberally construed; thus, the trial judge has the discretion to admit any evidence that gives promise of exposing a falsehood.[586] The jury may consider the statement only as it affects the witness's credibility,[587] and the adversely affected party is entitled to an instruction to this effect on timely request.[588] Rule 613(a) presupposes that the witness was not called as a "strawman." That is, the sponsoring party may not

---

582. *See generally* MCCORMICK ON EVIDENCE, *supra* note 2, §§34-38, at 73-85 (discussing impeachment by prior inconsistent testimony); 3A WIGMORE, *supra* note 295, §1017, at 993 (same).

583. *See **Birch v. Howard**,* 435 S.W.2d 945, 949-50 (Tex. Civ. App.—Tyler 1968, writ ref'd n.r.e.) (testimony elicited to impeach witness was "clearly admissible"); *see also **Guerra v. State**,* No. 01-15-00650-CR (Tex. App.—Houston [1st Dist.] 2016, no pet.) (memo op.; 10-25-16) (although impeachment is permissible, "decision not to raise inconsistent testimony or impeach a witness may constitute sound trial strategy because the attempt to impeach may be more harmful than beneficial").

584. *See **Cirilo v. Cook Paint & Varnish Co.**,* 476 S.W.2d 742, 748 (Tex. Civ. App.—Houston [1st Dist.] 1972, writ ref'd n.r.e.) (theory behind impeaching a witness by prior inconsistent statements "is to show that he has a capacity for making errors"; if previous statement and present testimony are contradictory, at least one must be erroneous); MCCORMICK ON EVIDENCE, *supra* note 2, §34, at 74 (explaining that "[t]he theory of attack by prior inconsistent statements is not based on the assumption that the present testimony is false and the former statement true but rather upon the notion that talking one way on the stand and another way previously is blowing hot and cold, and raises a doubt as to the truthfulness of both statements"); 1 RAY, *supra* note 4, §687, at 625 (general theory is "to show that the witness has a capacity for making errors"; error on one point may imply error on other matters). As such, the prior inconsistent statement must have been made by the testifying witness to be admissible against him. *E.g.,* ***Abdygapparova v. State**,* 243 S.W.3d 191, 204 (Tex. App.—San Antonio 2007, pet. ref'd) (letter written by third party to defendant-witness is not a prior inconsistent statement).

585. The statement is hearsay unless it was made in compliance with the terms set forth in Rule 801(e)(1)(A) or falls within some hearsay exception. For a discussion of Rule 801(e)(1)(A), refer to *Article VIII: Hearsay, infra* p. 835. For a discussion of hearsay exceptions under Rules 803 and 804, refer to *Article VIII: Hearsay, infra* p. 871, and *Article VIII: Hearsay, infra* p. 942.

586. ***Aranda v. State**,* 736 S.W.2d 702, 707 (Tex. Crim. App. 1987); ***Smith v. State**,* 520 S.W.2d 383, 386 (Tex. Crim. App. 1975); *see, e.g., **Lopez v. State**,* 86 S.W.3d 228, 230-31 (Tex. Crim. App. 2002) (child complainant could not be impeached with evidence that he had previously accused his mother of throwing him against a washer when child testified that he had told lies about little things but not big things; because defendant did not show that accusation against mother was false, trial court did not err in prohibiting impeachment).

587. *See **Lawhon v. State**,* 284 S.W.2d 730, 730 (Tex. Crim. App. 1955) (prior inconsistent statement used to impeach witness cannot be used as primary evidence against criminal defendant); ***Pope v. Stephenson**,* 774 S.W.2d 743, 745 (Tex. App.—El Paso 1989) (An "inconsistent statement can only be considered for the purpose of impeachment, and not as substantive evidence of the truth of the matters stated."), *writ denied,* 787 S.W.2d 953 (Tex. 1990); *cf. **In re K.W.**,* 666 S.E.2d 490, 494 (N.C. Ct. App. 2008) (in child-abuse case, evidence from complainant's MySpace page was admissible for impeachment purposes as a prior inconsistent statement related to complainant's testimony about her sexual history; that evidence was not admissible as substantive evidence that someone else caused the trauma found by the examining physician).

588. *See **Goodman v. State**,* 665 S.W.2d 788, 792 (Tex. Crim. App. 1984) (jury should be instructed to consider testimony only for impeachment purposes); ***Contreras v. State**,* 766 S.W.2d 891, 892-93 (Tex. App.—San Antonio 1989, no pet.) (trial court's failure to give limiting instruction on use of prior inconsistent statements is reversible error when reliance on statements was harmful); *see, e.g., **Adams v. State**,* 862 S.W.2d 139, 146-48 (Tex. App.—San Antonio 1993, pet. ref'd) (trial court properly instructed jury to consider prior inconsistent statement only for impeachment purposes and not as substantive evidence).

knowingly call a witness whose testimony will be unfavorable solely for the purpose of impeaching him with a prior inconsistent statement.[589]

When impeaching the witness with his prior statements, the cross-examiner may not resort to statements about immaterial or collateral matters.[590] The attacker may impeach only with a prior inconsistency on a relevant, material point. Trial courts should not waste time with trivial inconsistencies.

To fulfill the necessary requirement of inconsistency, the witness's statements do not need to be directly and explicitly contradictory (e.g., "the light was red" versus "the light was green").[591] Inconsistency may be found in evasive answers, feigned inability to remember,[592] silence,[593] or changes in position.[594] The testifying witness may even be impeached with prior statements that are inconsistent with the "impression" created by the witness's testimony.[595] Inconsistency may also be shown when the witness testi-

---

589. Refer to notes 275-284 *supra* and accompanying text.

590. ***Young v. James Green Mgmt., Inc.***, 327 F.3d 616, 627 (7th Cir. 2003); ***United States v. Senn***, 129 F.3d 886, 893-94 (7th Cir. 1997); ***United States v. Roulette***, 75 F.3d 418, 423 (8th Cir. 1996); *see **United States v. Bolzer***, 367 F.2d 1032, 1038-39 (8th Cir. 2004) (subject matter of the prior inconsistent statement must be material to trial and "[t]he relevant issue under [Federal] Rule 613(b) is not whether there is some material issue that would be affected in some way by the admission of the prior inconsistent testimony, but rather whether the *precise subject* of the prior inconsistent testimony is material"). The test for whether a fact is collateral is whether the cross-examining party would be entitled to prove the fact as part of its case. ***Ramirez v. State***, 802 S.W.2d 674, 675 (Tex. Crim. App. 1990); ***Bates v. State***, 587 S.W.2d 121, 133 (Tex. Crim. App. 1979). In other words, any statement or fact that would have been admissible in evidence for any purpose other than contradiction may be used to impeach the witness. *See **Young***, 327 F.3d at 627.

591. *See* 1 McCORMICK ON EVIDENCE, §34, at 127 (John W. Strong ed., 5th ed. 1999) (test is whether the jury could "reasonably find that a witness who believed the truth of the facts testified to would have been unlikely to make a prior statement of this tenor"); 1 RAY, *supra* note 4, §697, at 644 (test is whether statements, when compared, "have a tendency to repel" each other).

592. If the witness truly does not remember at trial the event about which he has made statements at some previous time, there is nothing to impeach. A present lack of memory is not inconsistent with the act of having made statements when the witness did have a recollection of the events. If the court concludes that the present memory loss is feigned, however, prior inconsistent statements may be used to impeach the witness. *See **United States v. Bigham***, 812 F.2d 943, 946-47 (5th Cir. 1987) (court properly admitted prior testimony to impeach a witness because the witness's memory loss may have been feigned); ***United States v. Shoupe***, 548 F.2d 636, 643 (6th Cir. 1977) (when witness's memory loss is "so selective as to be incredible," impeachment with prior inconsistent statements is proper). If the witness does not recall a prior statement but asserts that it is not possible that he could have made the statement, he may be impeached. *See, e.g., **Jackson v. State***, 756 S.W.2d 82, 83-84 (Tex. App.—San Antonio 1988) (police officer who testified that he could not have told anyone that defendant was not intoxicated when he stopped him for DWI could be impeached with defendant's testimony that officer commented that defendant did not appear to be drunk), *rev'd in part on other grounds*, 772 S.W.2d 117 (Tex. Crim. App. 1989); *see also* Michael H. Graham, *The Confrontation Clause, the Hearsay Rule, and the Forgetful Witness*, 56 TEX. L. REV. 151, 201-03 (1978) (professed lack of recollection at trial will affect substantive admissibility of witness's prior statements).

593. "Silence" means that the witness testifies to his recollection of a past event when he had previously remained silent or stated that he had no knowledge or memory of that event. *See **Cisneros v. State***, 692 S.W.2d 78, 83 (Tex. Crim. App. 1985) ("[T]he prior silence of a witness as to a fact to which he has testified, where such silence occurred under circumstances in which he would be expected to speak out, may be used to impeach ...."); *see, e.g., **Turner v. State***, 719 S.W.2d 190, 193 (Tex. Crim. App. 1986) (defendant who offered alibi at trial could be impeached with his pre-arrest silence when officers first arrived at crime scene).

594. ***United States v. McCrady***, 774 F.2d 868, 873 (8th Cir. 1985).

595. *See, e.g., **Pyles v. State***, 755 S.W.2d 98, 115 (Tex. Crim. App. 1988) (when capital-murder defendant stated that he was a nonviolent thief, the State could impeach him with exhibits showing "Kill all white pig police" and "Kill, Kill, Judge, D.A." written on his jail-cell wall).

fies at trial to significant details that would not likely have been omitted but were not contained in a prior statement.[596] However, if the witness refuses to testify, he cannot be impeached with prior statements.[597]

Problems have arisen in determining the proper manner of confronting a witness with inconsistent statements because the procedure involves at least three interests. The first problem involves the interest of the witness and, incidentally, of the party placing him on the stand.[598] The witness wants the statement presented in a manner that not only avoids surprise but also allows for denial or explanation in a convenient manner.[599] Therefore, the witness must be confronted with the statement on cross-examination.

The adverse party's interest is virtually the opposite of the witness's interest. The adverse party wants to pin down the witness to a definite position while on the stand and then dramatically reveal the inconsistent statement after the witness has completed his testimony and left the courtroom.[600] In most instances, this technique would be the most effective manner of impeaching a witness by prior inconsistent statements.[601]

Somewhere in between is the interest of the court and the jury in an effective judicial process.[602] Both the court and the jury want impeachment to be handled in an efficient manner consistent with justice and fairness. Their interest is probably more aligned with the witness than with his opponent because it is normally inefficient to excuse the witness, impeach his testimony with a prior inconsistent statement, and then, if necessary, bring him back to explain or deny the statement. Nor is it efficient to take up time by independently presenting an inconsistent statement that the witness would

---

596. *See, e.g.*, ***Ayers v. State***, 606 S.W.2d 936, 939 (Tex. Crim. App. 1980) (defendant who claimed self-defense at trial and claimed to have blacked out could be impeached with his pre-arrest statements that did not mention either self-defense or blacking out). *But see **Whiting v. State***, 755 S.W.2d 936, 941 (Tex. App.—San Antonio 1988) (when police officer testified about defendant's actions in resisting arrest, defendant could not offer offense report, which did not contain a description of those actions, to impeach witness with inconsistent statement; "[i]f a statement simply is not there it cannot form the basis of inconsistency with later testimony"), *rev'd on other grounds*, 797 S.W.2d 45 (Tex. Crim. App. 1990).

597. *See **Davis v. State***, 773 S.W.2d 592, 593 (Tex. App.—Eastland 1989, pet. ref'd) (prior testimony is not inconsistent with refusal to testify).

598. *See* McCormick on Evidence, *supra* note 2, §37, at 79 (avoidance of surprise and provision of fairness to a witness are two reasons for the rule).

599. *See, e.g.*, ***State v. Smith***, 671 S.W.2d 32, 35-36 (Tex. 1984) (defendant was entitled to introduce any portions of a prior inconsistent statement that would explain inconsistency); ***Williams v. State***, 604 S.W.2d 146, 149 (Tex. Crim. App. 1980) (witness who was impeached by prior inconsistent statement could explain contradiction).

600. *See, e.g.*, ***Girndt v. State***, 623 S.W.2d 930, 931-32 (Tex. Crim. App. [Panel Op.] 1981) (State could call witness to impeach defendant once defendant testified).

601. *See* McCormick on Evidence, *supra* note 2, §28, at 61 (pinning down a witness to contradictory testimony and then springing the prior inconsistent statement, when compared to traditional foundation, has the effect "of atomic energy against a firecracker" (quoting Louis Nizer, *The Art of the Jury Trial*, 32 Cornell L.Q. 59, 68 (1946))).

602. *See* 3 Weinstein & Berger, *supra* note 110, ¶613[02], at 613-11 (federal rule on which Texas rule was modeled "seeks to promote accuracy of testimony").

readily have admitted or could easily have explained if confronted with it on the stand.[603]

The traditional common-law view favors the interests of the witness and the court by requiring that a foundation for inconsistent statements be laid on cross-examination of the witness.[604] This tradition is deeply embedded in Texas practice.[605]

On the other hand, Federal Rule 613 abolished the foundation requirement. The federal rule allows a witness to be cross-examined without being shown a written statement or given details of an oral one;[606] it also allows independent presentation of such statements as long as the witness is given an opportunity to explain them or deny them at some point in the trial.[607] This rule favors the impeaching party. Although the rule requires that a written statement be shown to counsel to prevent false insinuations that a statement has been made,[608] and further allows a witness to return later to the stand to explain or deny the statement,[609] these provisions represent the minimum requirements of fairness rather than any attempt at balancing the various interests. Some federal courts, however, have held that the trial judge retains discretion to exclude testimony about a witness's prior inconsistent statement if that witness was not first given an opportunity to be confronted with the statement.[610]

After considerable debate, the Liaison Committee chose to keep the traditional foundation requirement.[611] This decision was sound because the requirement has not

---

603. *See* RICHARD O. LEMPERT & STEPHEN A. SALTZBURG, A MODERN APPROACH TO EVIDENCE 306-08 (2d ed. 1982).

604. *See **Queen Caroline's Case***, 129 Eng. Rep. 976, 977-78 (1820) (advisory opinion for the House of Lords) (letter used for cross-examination must be read into evidence before witness may be questioned about the letter).

605. *See **Moore v. State***, 652 S.W.2d 411, 413 (Tex. Crim. App. 1983) (before witness may be impeached by evidence of prior inconsistent statement, proper predicate must be laid); ***Trussell v. State***, 585 S.W.2d 736, 738-39 (Tex. Crim. App. [Panel Op.] 1979) (same); ***Huff v. State***, 576 S.W.2d 645, 647 (Tex. Crim. App. 1979) (proper predicate for impeaching witness includes interrogating witness about the inconsistent statement); ***Citadel Constr. Co. v. Smith***, 483 S.W.2d 283, 286 (Tex. Civ. App.—Austin 1972, writ ref'd n.r.e.) (proper predicate must be laid before a witness can be impeached using prior inconsistent statements); ***Garcia v. Sky Climber, Inc.***, 470 S.W.2d 261, 266 (Tex. Civ. App.—Houston [1st Dist.] 1971, writ ref'd n.r.e.) (witness must be confronted with alleged contradictory statement before statement is admissible into evidence).

606. *See* FED. R. EVID. 613(a).

607. *See* FED. R. EVID. 613(b); ***United States v. Bibbs***, 564 F.2d 1165, 1169 (5th Cir. 1977). In ***Bibbs***, the court also addressed the issue of impeachment with an inconsistent statement made by the witness after testifying. 564 F.2d at 1169. The Fifth Circuit held that such statements are not covered by Rule 613(b) and thus were not subject to any foundation requirement during the cross-examination of the witness. ***Bibbs***, 564 F.2d at 1169. The burden fell on the party who called the witness to recall her during rebuttal if he wished to give her an opportunity to explain or deny the subsequent inconsistent statement. *Id.*

608. FED. R. EVID. 613 advisory committee's note, subdiv. (a).

609. *See* FED. R. EVID. 613 advisory committee's note, subdiv. (b).

610. *See, e.g.,* ***United States v. Schnapp***, 322 F.3d 564, 570-72 (8th Cir. 2003) (trial court had discretion to exclude impeachment testimony about government investigator's inconsistent statement when investigator was not given opportunity to explain or deny that statement during cross-examination even though witness was still available to be recalled); ***United States v. Sutton***, 41 F.3d 1257, 1260 (8th Cir. 1994) (trial judge properly excluded testimony of inconsistent statements by prosecution witness when witness had not been given an opportunity during defense's cross-examination to explain or deny the prior statement); *see also* ***United States v. Marks***, 816 F.2d 1207, 1211 (7th Cir. 1987) (trial judge may, despite language of Rule 613(a), "conclude that in particular circumstances the older approach should be used in order to avoid confusing witnesses and jurors").

611. *See* Blake Tartt, *Federal Rules—Proposed Texas Code Overlay; Part I*, 45 TEX. B.J. 579, 592-93 (1982).

caused any serious impediment to efficient impeachment, and the Liaison Committee was unpersuaded by the reasons given for abolishing the requirement in the Federal Rules.[612] In 2015, however, the foundation requirement in Rule 613 was amended to be closer, in certain aspects, to the approach under the federal rule and to be more in line with actual practice in Texas courts.[613]

Before a witness may be impeached with a prior inconsistent statement in Texas, his attention must be drawn to the circumstances under which that statement, either oral or written, was made.[614] The witness must be told of the contents of the statement, the time and place of the statement, and the person to whom the witness made the statement.[615] At some point during the proceeding, the witness must be given an opportunity to deny making the statement or to explain its content or significance.[616] Before the 2015 amendments to Rule 613, the examining attorney had to first give the witness this opportunity as part of the foundation requirement for impeachment evidence before further examination of the witness could continue. The attorney is no longer required to interrupt the examination of the witness for this purpose.[617] The witness must still be given an opportunity to explain or deny the statement but may have to wait until redirect to do so.[618]

Extrinsic evidence of the prior statement may not be offered if the witness unequivocally admits making the prior inconsistent statement.[619] Such evidence is unnec-

---

612. For example, the Advisory Committee was concerned with the problem of "several collusive witnesses" who have made "a joint prior inconsistent statement." FED. R. EVID. 613 advisory committee's note, subdiv. (b). Guarding against this remote circumstance seems to be an inadequate justification for abandoning a traditional procedure and an otherwise satisfactory rule. *See* Letter from Edward W. Cleary, *in Supplement to Hearings Before the Subcomm. on Criminal Justice of the House Comm. on the Judiciary*, 93rd Cong., 1st Sess. 74-75 (1973) (setting forth rationale for modification of common-law foundation requirements).

613. Refer to notes 581, 606-610 *supra* and accompanying text.

614. TEX. R. EVID. 613(a)(1); *see* 1 RAY, *supra* note 4, §696, at 640 (form of inconsistent statement is immaterial; either oral or written is acceptable). If the statement is in writing, the party does not need to show it to the witness before asking about it, but the party must show it to opposing counsel on request. TEX. R. EVID. 613(a)(2).

615. TEX. R. EVID. 613(a)(1); *see **Irizarry v. State**,* 916 S.W.2d 612, 616 (Tex. App.—San Antonio 1996, pet. ref'd). The foundation is normally laid by the cross-examiner, but if the witness has been asked on direct examination about the earlier occasion, that may satisfy the predicate for directing the witness's attention to the time, place, and person to whom the statement was made. *See **Sandow v. State**,* 787 S.W.2d 588, 593-94 (Tex. App.—Austin 1990, pet. ref'd).

616. *See* TEX. R. EVID. 613(a)(3) & cmt.; *see, e.g.,* ***Williams v. State***, 604 S.W.2d 146, 149-50 (Tex. Crim. App. 1980) (at trial, eyewitness to murder could explain that he made his prior statement denying that defendant committed the murder because his grandmother told him not to do anything to hurt defendant).

617. *See* TEX. R. EVID. 613 cmt.

618. *See* TEX. R. EVID. 613(a)(3) & cmt.

619. TEX. R. EVID. 613(a)(4) & cmt.; ***McGary v. State***, 750 S.W.2d 782, 786 (Tex. Crim. App. 1988); ***Scott v. State***, 940 S.W.2d 353, 358 (Tex. App.—Dallas 1997, pet. ref'd); ***Downen v. Tex. Gulf Shrimp Co.***, 846 S.W.2d 506, 512-13 (Tex. App.—Corpus Christi 1993, writ denied). When the admission is qualified, partial, or equivocal, the statement may be offered into evidence. *See **McGary***, 750 S.W.2d at 786 n.3; ***Wyatt v. State***, 38 Tex. Crim. 256, 260, 42 S.W. 598, 598-99 (1897); *see, e.g.,* ***Staley v. State***, 888 S.W.2d 45, 49 (Tex. App.—Tyler 1994, no pet.) (when witnesses did not unequivocally admit to contents of prior inconsistent statements, videotape of those statements was admissible).

essary because the witness impeaches himself.[620] The witness, however, may be asked to explain specific phrases or sentences contained within the prior statement.[621] If the witness admits making the prior statement but denies portions of it, the cross-examiner may introduce only those portions that the witness denies.[622] He may not introduce the entirety of the statement.[623] However, a witness may not be called as a strawman solely for the purpose of introducing a prior inconsistent statement in the hope that the jury will misuse that statement as substantive evidence.[624]

Generally, the witness may not be rehabilitated by showing that he has made prior statements that are consistent with his present testimony because "mere repetition" does not imply veracity. If he concedes the inconsistency, the witness cannot simply dismiss it, even if he has told the other story innumerable times.[625]

Rule 613(a) does not apply to an opposing party's statement under Rule 801(e)(2), which is independent, primary evidence[626] and, as such, is not considered hearsay and is admissible as substantive evidence.[627] The rule does not apply to impeachment by specific contradiction of the facts testified to by a witness, even though this aspect of the rule is sometimes confused by the courts.[628] Finally, the rule does not require the pro-

---

620. *See* ***Wood v. State***, 511 S.W.2d 37, 43 n.1 (Tex. Crim. App. 1974) ("[U]nder such circumstances the witness has performed the act of impeachment upon himself or herself."); ***Walker v. State***, 17 Tex. Ct. App. 16, 31 (1884) ("When the contradictions are confessed, evidently there is no use or purpose for the impeaching testimony; for this work he performs upon himself."); *see also* 1 RAY, *supra* note 4, §695, at 640 (proof by the witness's own admission of inconsistency is adequate, and further proof by another witness is wasteful).

621. ***McGary***, 750 S.W.2d at 787.

622. *Id.*

623. *See* ***Ellingsworth v. State***, 487 S.W.2d 108, 112 (Tex. Crim. App. 1972) (only portion of statement that contradicts witness is admissible); *see, e.g.*, ***McGary***, 750 S.W.2d at 788 (reversible error to admit into evidence entire prior statement that included matters not specifically asked about and immaterial matters). *But see* ***Ramsey v. Lucky Stores, Inc.***, 853 S.W.2d 623, 637 (Tex. App.—Houston [1st Dist.] 1993, writ denied) (when witness admitted having given prior recorded statements but denied some statements and did not remember making other specific statements, there was no error in admitting evidence of the statements).

624. *See, e.g.*, ***Sills v. State***, 846 S.W.2d 392, 396-97 (Tex. App.—Houston [14th Dist.] 1992, pet. ref'd) (trial court erred in allowing prosecutor to use witness's prior statement to police to impeach witness who repeatedly refused to testify; State was attempting to use witness as a strawman to present jury otherwise inadmissible hearsay evidence). Refer to notes 275-284 *supra* and accompanying text.

625. 4 JOHN H. WIGMORE, EVIDENCE IN TRIALS AT COMMON LAW, §1126, at 259 (Chadbourn rev. 1972).

626. *See* ***Strong v. State***, 138 S.W.3d 546, 553-54 (Tex. App.—Corpus Christi 2004, no pet.) (when prior inconsistent statements are made by a party rather than a witness, Rule 613 does not apply; such prior out-of-court statements are fully admissible under Rule 801(e)(2)(A) and no foundation is required); ***Westchester Fire Ins. v. Lowe***, 888 S.W.2d 243, 252 (Tex. App.—Beaumont 1994, no writ) (party's former pleadings, if inconsistent with party's present position, are admissible into evidence as party's admission).

627. *See* TEX. R. EVID. 613(a)(5), 801(e)(2). Refer to *Article VIII: Hearsay*, *infra* p. 845.

628. *See* ***Jacobini v. Hall***, 719 S.W.2d 396, 402 (Tex. App.—Fort Worth 1986, writ ref'd n.r.e.). In ***Jacobini***, the defendant in a negligent-entrustment action was asked on cross-examination whether he had previously been accused of negligent entrustment. *Id.* When the defendant denied the allegation, the plaintiff attempted to offer petitions and lawsuits demonstrating that the defendant was alleged to have been the owner of vehicles driven by employees or independent contractors involved in several other accidents. *Id.* The trial court refused to permit impeachment with these documents. The appellate court held that the material constituted a contradiction and was admissible to impeach the witness, but the court cited Civil Rule 612. ***Jacobini***, 719 S.W.2d at 402. Civil Rule 612 was not applicable because the impeachment documents were not prior statements of the witness. They were independent docu-

duction of a recording of a prior inconsistent statement contained in an interview that the party asserts is protected work product if the party never refers to that recording and does not use it before the jury.[629]

The rule does not cover whether the trial court has discretion to waive the foundation requirement when, through no fault of the impeaching party, evidence of a witness's inconsistent statement (or bias or interest) was not discovered before completion of the witness's testimony, and the witness is thereafter unavailable.[630] This situation will occur infrequently,[631] but if and when it does, fairness demands waiver of the foundation requirement.[632] Presumably, the absence of an express provision will not deter any trial judge confronted with the situation from finding such a provision to be implied.

In criminal proceedings, a voluntary statement by the defendant taken in violation of the constitutionally required *Miranda*[633] warnings or the defendant's Sixth Amendment right to counsel is nonetheless admissible as a prior inconsistent statement if the defendant testifies in contradiction to that statement.[634] Even when a criminal defen-

ments, composed by others, which specifically contradicted the witness's testimony. *See id.* No foundation is necessary when the witness is impeached by specific contradiction.

629. *See Washington v. State*, 856 S.W.2d 184, 190 (Tex. Crim. App. 1993). In *Washington*, the defendant cross-examined a witness of the State about his prior conversation with a defense investigator. The State then claimed that the defendant had waived any work-product protection in the investigator's report by this line of questioning and asked that the defense produce the tape-recorded interview. *Id.* at 189. The trial court agreed and required the defendant to give the State the tape-recorded interview. This was error because the defendant never made testimonial use of the recording. He did not indicate that the interview had been recorded, did not offer the tape to refresh the witness's memory, and did not offer it into evidence as extrinsic evidence of the witness's prior inconsistent statement. *Id.* at 190. Although the court did not mention it, the recording also would not have been subject to production under former Criminal Rule 614, now Rule 615, because the defendant was not the sponsor of the witness and Rule 615 applies only to the production of prior witness statements in the possession of the sponsoring party. *See* Tex. R. Evid. 615.

630. *Hirschberg v. State*, 117 Tex. Crim. 504, 507-08, 35 S.W.2d 430, 431 (1930).

631. *Id. Hirschberg* appears to be the only such case reported in Texas. The court of criminal appeals admitted evidence of a prior inconsistent statement discovered after the witness had died. *Id.*

632. *See* 3A Wigmore, *supra* note 295, §1027, at 1022-23, §1030, at 1032-33.

633. *Miranda v. Arizona*, 384 U.S. 436, 478-79 (1966).

634. *See Kansas v. Ventris*, 556 U.S. 586, 593 (2009) (interests safeguarded by excluding tainted evidence for impeachment purposes are outweighed by interest in preserving the integrity of a trial and preventing perjury; "[o]nce the defendant testifies in a way that contradicts prior statements, denying the prosecution use of 'the traditional truth-testing devices of the adversary process' ... is a high price to pay for vindication of the right to counsel at the prior stage" (quoting *Harris v. New York*, 401 U.S. 222, 225 (1971)); *Harris v. New York*, 401 U.S. 222, 226 (1971) ("The shield provided by *Miranda* cannot be perverted into a license to use perjury by way of a defense, free from the risk of confrontation with prior inconsistent utterances."); *see, e.g., Huffman v. State*, 746 S.W.2d 212, 220 (Tex. Crim. App. 1988) (failure to comply with *Miranda* did not prevent use of prior inconsistent statements to impeach defendant); *Brownlee v. State*, 944 S.W.2d 463, 467 (Tex. App.—Houston [14th Dist.] 1997, pet. ref'd) (defendant's voluntary statement to police was admissible to impeach him on cross-examination). *See generally* Tex. Code Crim. Proc. art. 38.22, §5 (codification of holding in *Harris*).

In *Ventris*, an informant planted in the defendant's holding cell overheard the defendant admit to the murder and aggravated robbery that, at trial, he blamed on someone else. 556 U.S. at 589. The State sought to impeach the defendant's credibility with the informant's testimony on the inconsistent statement, even conceding that the defendant's Sixth Amendment right to counsel was probably violated when the defendant made the statement to the informant. *Id.* The Supreme Court held that the informant's testimony was admissible despite the Sixth Amendment violation, noting that "[w]e have held in every other context that tainted evidence—evidence whose very in-

RULE 613

dant's prior statement includes evidence of an extraneous offense, it is admissible to impeach the defendant if he has testified in contradiction to that prior statement.[635]

B. Rule 613(b): Witness's Bias or Interest

A witness may always be impeached by showing bias or interest.[636] Perhaps because the right to impeach a witness on these bases is so obvious, Rule 613(b) sets out the procedure for such impeachment without explicitly stating that a party has the right to impeach on these grounds.[637] Texas courts allow litigants great latitude in showing any fact that demonstrates "'ill-feeling, bias, motive and animus'" on the part of a witness.[638]

While the use of prior convictions and character testimony are generalized modes of impeachment that attack the witness's character for truthfulness across the board, impeachment with prior inconsistent statements and bias or interest attack the witness's veracity or reliability only in the specific lawsuit or toward the particular parties.[639] When using evidence of bias or interest, the attacker is attempting to show that the witness is not a neutral observer for reasons unrelated to the merits of the lawsuit.[640] Rule 613(b) clearly permits inquiry into the specific "circumstances or statements" showing a witness's bias or interest; thus, the rule is distinct from the rationale

---

troduction does not constitute the constitutional violation, but whose obtaining was constitutionally invalid—is admissible for impeachment. We see no distinction that would alter the balance here." *Id.* at 594.

635. *See, e.g.*, ***Bryant v. State***, 775 S.W.2d 48, 49-50 (Tex. App.—Houston [14th Dist.] 1989, pet. ref'd) (defendant, who had testified that he loved a witness who testified against him, was trying to get her to give up drugs, and had never threatened her with violence, could be impeached with letters in which he threatened to kill her).

636. *See* McCormick on Evidence, *supra* note 2, §40, at 85 (witness's credibility may be impeached by proving "[p]artiality, or any acts, relationships or motives reasonably likely to produce it"); 3A Wigmore, *supra* note 295, §940, at 775 (partiality is "always relevant as discrediting the witness and affecting the weight of his testimony"). The term "bias" is generally used to refer to any prejudice, emotional favor or disfavor, or hostility toward one or the other of the parties, while "interest" usually refers to a financial or personal stake in the outcome of the case. *See* 3A Wigmore, *supra* note 295, §945, at 782. The terms are broad enough to cover any form of coercion, duress, promise, or threat that might impel a witness to slant his testimony toward or against a party.

637. *See* ***Hammer v. State***, 296 S.W.3d 555, 563 (Tex. Crim. App. 2009).

638. ***Koehler v. State***, 679 S.W.2d 6, 9 (Tex. Crim. App. 1984) (quoting ***Blair v. State***, 511 S.W.2d 277, 279 (Tex. Crim. App. 1974)); *see* ***Billodeau v. State***, 277 S.W.3d 34, 42-43 (Tex. Crim. App. 2009) (defendant, subject to reasonable restrictions, can "show any relevant fact that might tend to establish ill feeling, bias, motive, interest, or animus on the part of any witness testifying against him"); ***Gonzales v. State***, 929 S.W.2d 546, 549 (Tex. App.—Austin 1996, pet. ref'd) ("The rules of evidence grant a party greater latitude to prove a witness's bias than to prove a witness's untruthful character. ... Rule 612 [now Rule 613] places no limits on the sort of evidence that may be adduced to show a witness's bias or interest."); ***Hinojosa v. State***, 788 S.W.2d 594, 600 (Tex. App.—Corpus Christi 1990, pet. ref'd) ("All facts going or tending to show mental bias, interests, prejudice, or any other motive, or mental state, or status of the witness, which, fairly considered and construed, might even remotely tend to affect his credibility, should be admitted."); ***Adams v. Petrade Int'l, Inc.***, 754 S.W.2d 696, 711 (Tex. App.—Houston [1st Dist.] 1988, writ denied) (allowing latitude because jury is entitled to know any relevant facts that might influence witness's testimony).

639. ***Dixon v. State***, 2 S.W.3d 263, 271 (Tex. Crim. App. 1999) (op. on reh'g); *e.g.*, ***Alford v. State***, 495 S.W.3d 63, 67-68 (Tex. App.—Houston [14th Dist.] 2016, pet. ref'd) (trial court did not err in excluding questions and answers about unrelated instances of alleged sexual abuse; evidence was not probative of witness's animus toward defendant or her bias, motive, or interest to testify in a particular way in case at issue).

640. *See* 3 Weinstein & Berger, *supra* note 110, ¶607[03], at 607-25 (showing bias reveals an impartiality that would cause a witness to shade his testimony).

of Rule 608(b), which prohibits proof of specific instances of conduct when offered to attack or support the witness's character for truthfulness.[641]

The possible reasons for a witness's bias or interest in the outcome of a particular lawsuit are as numerous and varied as the infinite range of human emotions and motives. Some common forms of impeachment to show bias include racial prejudice,[642] family relationship,[643] employment,[644] personal friendship or hatred,[645] prior business dealings,[646] prior "bad blood,"[647] threats,[648] and many others.[649] A witness's bias may be directed toward a particular person, or the witness may harbor a general bias against a group or class of which the opposing party is a member.[650] Interests in the lawsuit include Mary Carter agreements,[651] the fact that a crime victim has filed a

641. *See* TEX. R. EVID. 608(b), 613(b); *Dixon*, 2 S.W.3d at 271-72. Refer to notes 344-373 *supra* and accompanying text.

642. *See Hurd v. State*, 725 S.W.2d 249, 253 (Tex. Crim. App. 1987) (racial prejudice is "prototypical" bias).

643. *See, e.g., Lindley v. Transam. Ins.*, 437 S.W.2d 371, 375 (Tex. Civ. App.—Fort Worth 1969, no writ) (jury could have considered the fact that a witness was the brother of one of the parties when deciding his credibility). *See generally* 1 RAY, *supra* note 4, §676, at 610-11 (relationship by blood or marriage is frequently invoked to indicate bias).

644. *See G. & H. Equip. Co. v. Alexander*, 533 S.W.2d 872, 875 (Tex. Civ. App.—Fort Worth 1976, no writ) ("The fact that a witness is an employee of a party to the suit can be considered on the question of interest or partiality of the witness."); *Hammond v. Stricklen*, 498 S.W.2d 356, 361-62 (Tex. Civ. App.—Tyler 1973, writ ref'd n.r.e.) (employment as investigator for defendant's insurance company may affect witness's credibility).

645. *See, e.g., Wood v. State*, 486 S.W.2d 359, 361-62 (Tex. Crim. App. 1972) (error to exclude evidence of witness's ill-feeling toward defendant); *Davis v. State*, 121 Tex. Crim. 164, 166-67, 51 S.W.2d 705, 707 (1932) (question about witness's love and affection for defendant's father was relevant and provable in determining witness's credibility); *Felan v. State*, 44 S.W.3d 249, 254-55 (Tex. App.—Fort Worth 2001, pet. ref'd) (child complainant's statements about her friend's alleged relationship with defendant may have shown bias against friend but did not show bias against defendant; thus, they were not admissible to impeach her testimony by demonstrating bias against defendant); *see also Jacquet v. State*, No. 02-15-00377-CR (Tex. App.—Fort Worth 2017, pet. ref'd) (memo op.; 2-2-17) (evidence that witness was defendant's codefendant in prior conviction tended to show that witness may shade his testimony).

646. *See, e.g., City of Longview v. Boucher*, 523 S.W.2d 274, 278-79 (Tex. Civ. App.—Tyler 1975, writ ref'd n.r.e.) (proper to permit the impeachment of appraiser by showing that he had made other appraisals for the city and that the city had granted him a zoning variance).

647. *See, e.g., Koehler v. State*, 679 S.W.2d 6, 10 (Tex. Crim. App. 1984) (error to prevent evidence that State's witness had previously attacked defendant in public, had thrown drinks at him, and had attacked women who had been in defendant's company when evidence was offered to show malice, bias, and ill-feeling).

648. *See, e.g., Rodgers v. State*, 486 S.W.2d 794, 796 (Tex. Crim. App. 1972) (permissible to show that defendant's mother made threats against prosecutor); *Kamanga v. State*, 502 S.W.3d 871, 877-78 (Tex. App.—Fort Worth 2016, pet. ref'd) (error, though harmless, to exclude evidence of complainant's prior threat against defendant; evidence showed possible bias or motive to fabricate charges and was therefore admissible); *see also Carter v. State*, 668 S.W.2d 851, 853 (Tex. App.—San Antonio 1984, pet. ref'd) (prosecutor could ask defendant's mother if she was ever afraid of defendant).

649. *See generally* 3 WEINSTEIN & BERGER, *supra* note 110, ¶607[03], at 607-25 to 607-56 (noting common forms of bias in federal cases); 3A WIGMORE, *supra* note 295, §§948-950, at 783-96 (categorizing common circumstances demonstrating bias).

650. *See Chipman v. Mercer*, 628 F.2d 528, 532 (9th Cir. 1980) ("Bias of a general or pervasive sort is not, at least necessarily, less dangerous to objectivity than hostility to one individual.").

651. *See Scurlock Oil Co. v. Smithwick*, 724 S.W.2d 1, 4 (Tex. 1986) (evidence of "Mary Carter" agreements may be brought to the jury's attention to show bias, prejudice, or interest); *Gen. Motors Corp. v. Simmons*, 558 S.W.2d 855, 857 (Tex. 1977) ("The financial interest of parties and witnesses in the success of a party is a proper subject of disclosure by direct evidence or cross-examination."). Because Mary Carter agreements are no longer permitted in

civil lawsuit against the defendant or another person as a result of the alleged of-fense,[652] a business relationship with one of the parties,[653] heirship,[654] bribes,[655] or the fact that an expert witness is hired by the party.[656]

In criminal cases, a prosecution witness might be hoping for a lighter sentence in return for testifying against the defendant.[657] The witness might also testify in an at-tempt to divert suspicion from himself.[658] A witness may be impeached for motive and bias by demonstrating that he has made similar false accusations in the past.[659] Evi-

Texas, this mode of impeachment is presumably of minor importance. Refer to *Article IV: Relevance & Its Limits*, *supra* p. 330.

652. *See, e.g.*, *Cox v. State*, 523 S.W.2d 695, 700 (Tex. Crim. App. 1975) (witness's pending civil suit against de-fendant was admissible to show bias and interest); *Zuniga v. State*, 664 S.W.2d 366, 369-70 (Tex. App.—Corpus Christi 1983, no pet.) (evidence that victim-witness had filed a claim against the city as a result of the incident was admissible in a police officer's trial).

653. *See, e.g.*, *Aetna Ins. v. Paddock*, 301 F.2d 807, 812 (5th Cir. 1962) (error to exclude evidence that key witness for plaintiff had borrowed money from plaintiff to start his own business); *Barton Plumbing Co. v. Johnson*, 285 S.W.2d 780, 781-82 (Tex. Civ. App.—Galveston 1955, writ ref'd) (fact that witness owned an interest in defendant's company was admissible to show bias).

654. *See, e.g.*, *Allday v. Cage*, 148 S.W. 838, 840 (Tex. Civ. App.—Fort Worth 1912, no writ) (testimony that wit-ness would receive benefits if will were not entered into probate was admissible).

655. *See, e.g.*, *Campbell v. State*, 167 Tex. Crim. 321, 322-23, 320 S.W.2d 361, 362 (1959) (evidence that party of-fered witness money to testify favorably was admissible).

656. *See Collins v. Wayne Corp.*, 621 F.2d 777, 784 (5th Cir. 1980) (questioning expert witness about fees received in prior cases is proper); *Olinger v. Curry*, 926 S.W.2d 832, 834 (Tex. App.—Fort Worth 1996, orig. proceeding) (ex-perts may be impeached by questioning them about the number of times they have testified in lawsuits, payments for such testimony, and related issues); *see, e.g.*, *Sparks v. State*, 943 S.W.2d 513, 515-16 (Tex. App.—Fort Worth 1997, pet. ref'd) (State could impeach credibility of defendant's Intoxilyzer expert with prior consistent testimony from another trial to show his bias and interest as a paid professional). Although an expert witness may be cross-examined about payments from a party, a court may deny a request for all of a witness's accounting and fi-nancial records solely for impeachment purposes. *In re Weir*, 166 S.W.3d 861, 864 (Tex. App.—Beaumont 2005, orig. proceeding). The court must weigh the cross-examining party's interest in obtaining discovery for impeachment pur-poses against the witness's interest in protecting unrelated financial information. *Id.* at 865.

657. *See Miller v. State*, 741 S.W.2d 382, 389 (Tex. Crim. App. 1987) (defendant may question a prosecution wit-ness about pending criminal charges against that witness); *Carmona v. State*, 698 S.W.2d 100, 102 (Tex. Crim. App. 1985) (same); *Spain v. State*, 585 S.W.2d 705, 710 (Tex. Crim. App. 1979) (defendant may question witness about probated sentence to show bias); *see, e.g.*, *Alford v. United States*, 282 U.S. 687, 693 (1931) (defendant was entitled to ask prosecution witness where he was residing to establish that the witness might expect some leniency in return for his testimony because he was in federal custody).

658. *See, e.g.*, *Davis v. Alaska*, 415 U.S. 308, 311 (1974) (witness might have tried to shift suspicion away from him-self by identifying defendant as the robber); *Steve v. State*, 614 S.W.2d 137, 139-40 (Tex. Crim. App. 1981) (defen-dant could impeach witness with the fact that she was being investigated for child abuse during defendant's trial for indecency with a child).

659. *See, e.g.*, *Billodeau v. State*, 277 S.W.3d 34, 40 (Tex. Crim. App. 2009) (false accusations of sexual molesta-tion by neighbors made by child victim after accusing defendant of molestation were admissible to show possible motive for making false accusations against defendant; "[r]elevant facts that occurred before the witness testifies at trial are admissible if permitted by the Rules of Evidence or the Confrontation Clause. A witness's credibility does not escape scrutiny because he can be shown to have displayed the unprincipled qualities of his character only af-ter the date of the charged offense."); *Lopez v. State*, 18 S.W.3d 220, 225-26 (Tex. Crim. App. 2000) (Confrontation Clause did not require admission of prior accusation when purportedly false allegations were not similar to facts of case and prior accusation was never shown to be false); *see also Palmer v. State*, 222 S.W.3d 92, 95 (Tex. App.—Houston [14th Dist.] 2006, pet. ref'd) ("A defendant seeking to impeach a witness with evidence of a previous false accusation against a third party must, as a threshold evidentiary matter, produce evidence showing the prior accu-sation is actually false.").

dence that criminal charges against the witness have been dropped[660] or that the witness has been granted immunity in return for his testimony[661] are admissible to show possible bias.[662] Defense witnesses can also be, and frequently are, impeached for bias or interest.[663]

While the possible motives that might cause a witness to be biased or have an interest in the litigation are infinite, trial courts have discretion to limit the scope and extent of cross-examination on bias and interest based on concerns such as "harassment, prejudice, confusion of the issues, the witness' safety, or interrogation that is repetitive or only marginally relevant."[664]

The Federal Rules do not expressly allow impeachment for bias and interest, apparently reflecting a belief that the practice is so fundamental that no explicit rule is required.[665] However, the Federal Rules are also silent on the manner of impeachment for bias,[666] and this silence raises problems.[667]

---

660. *See, e.g., **Parker v. State**,* 657 S.W.2d 137, 138-39 (Tex. Crim. App. 1983) (error to prevent cross-examination of accomplice-witness to show that the State dismissed a robbery charge against the witness before his testimony and agreed to a plea bargain with him).

661. *See, e.g., **United States v. Ackal**,* 706 F.2d 523, 532 (5th Cir. 1983) (judge informed jury that prosecution witness had been granted immunity; no reversible error); ***United States v. Dickens**,* 417 F.2d 958, 960-61 (8th Cir. 1969) (trial court prevented the questioning of a government witness about the promise of immunity; reversible error).

662. *See generally* 3 WEINSTEIN & BERGER, *supra* note 110, ¶607[03], at 607-44 to 607-46 (witness's legal status—or treatment received or expected to be received—may manifest bias in a criminal case).

663. *See, e.g., **United States v. Abel**,* 469 U.S. 45, 52 (1984) (prosecution could introduce evidence that defendant and defense witness were both members of prison gang; evidence "supported the inference that [witness's] testimony was slanted or perhaps fabricated in [defendant's] favor"); ***Rodgers v. State**,* 486 S.W.2d 794, 796 (Tex. Crim. App. 1972) (State could ask defendant's mother on cross-examination whether she had made threats against prosecutor; evidence showed witness's bias or interest toward defendant and against State). Refer to notes 642-656 *supra* and accompanying text.

664. ***Delaware v. Van Arsdall**,* 475 U.S. 673, 679 (1986); *see **Janecka v. State**,* 739 S.W.2d 813, 830-31 (Tex. Crim. App. 1987) ("It has long been the rule that great latitude should be allowed the accused in showing a witness' possible bias, prejudice, or motive to falsify his testimony. Equally axiomatic is the trial court's wide discretion in determining how and when bias may be proven and whether purported evidence of bias is material."); *see, e.g., **Johnson v. State**,* 490 S.W.3d 895, 910-11 (Tex. Crim. App. 2016) (trial court erred in prohibiting defendant from cross-examining complainant about complainant's sexual abuse of his sister; testimony was offered as evidence of complainant's bias or motive to accuse defendant of sexual abuse, and record did not indicate that trial court excluded this evidence because it was concerned about ***Van Arsdall*** factors).
    Rule 403 is an exclusionary backstop to evidence offered under Rule 613. The trial court must always weigh the probative value of the evidence offered to show the witness's possible motive, interest, or bias against the risk of unfair prejudice, confusion of the issues, or misleading the jury. In ***Moreno v. State**,* the court of criminal appeals held that the trial court erred in permitting the State to impeach a testifying DWI defendant with the fact that he was currently on felony deferred adjudication. 22 S.W.3d 482, 488-89 (Tex. Crim. App. 1999). The court held that although the fact that his probationary status could be revoked as a result of conviction for another offense had slight probative value in showing a motive to slant his testimony, the risk that the jury would misuse that evidence to convict him for generally being a criminal significantly outweighed that probative value under Rule 403. *Id.*

665. *See **Abel**,* 469 U.S. at 51 ("[I]t is permissible to impeach a witness by showing his bias under the Federal Rules of Evidence just as it was permissible to do so before their adoption.").

666. *See* FED. R. EVID. 601 advisory committee's note (an interest in the outcome of the litigation requires no special treatment to be offered into evidence).

667. *See* 3A WIGMORE, *supra* note 295, §953, at 800-01 (raising the issue of whether a witness should have an opportunity to explain or deny a prior statement indicating bias and whether a witness must first be asked if he made the prior statement before proving the statement against him in order to avoid surprise).

The traditional procedure in Texas required a proper predicate before showing bias or interest, similar to the predicate required for inconsistent statements.[668] A significant minority on the Liaison Committee, however, wanted to echo the silence of the Federal Rules.[669] Bias and interest, it was argued, represent such basic and obvious areas of impeachment that they should be left unrestricted by any rule.[670] This view, although not without persuasive force, did not prevail, and Rule 613(b) codified the traditional foundation requirement for impeachment for bias and interest. The most persuasive argument supporting the rule was that it favors judicial economy over trial strategy. There is no good reason to take up the time of the court and jury by offering independent evidence of a bias that the witness could admit on the stand or by recalling a witness solely to explain or deny an alleged bias.

To lay the predicate for impeachment with evidence of bias or interest, the examining attorney must advise the witness of the conduct, circumstances, or situations that support a claim of bias or interest or advise him of the contents of any statement he has made indicating bias or interest, as is done with prior inconsistent statements.[671]

As with Rule 613(a), the foundation requirement for Rule 613(b) was amended in 2015.[672] At some point during the proceeding, the attorney must permit the witness to explain or deny the impeachment material.[673] Before the amendments, the examining attorney had to first give the witness this opportunity as part of the foundation requirement for impeachment evidence before further examination of the witness could continue. The attorney is no longer required to interrupt the examination of the witness for this purpose.[674] The witness must still be given an opportunity to explain the circumstances or to explain or deny the statement but may have to wait until redirect

668. *See Green v. State*, 566 S.W.2d 578, 587 (Tex. Crim. App. 1978) (impeachment for bias or interest requires asking witness about the agreement or conspiracy that shows bias before independent evidence to prove the conspiracy is admissible); *Williams v. State*, 649 S.W.2d 693, 696 (Tex. App.—Amarillo 1983, no pet.) (independent evidence of prior statements offered to show bias is not admissible unless a foundation is laid on cross-examination by asking witness about the statements); *S. Truck Leasing Co. v. Manieri*, 325 S.W.2d 912, 916 (Tex. Civ. App.—Houston 1959, writ ref'd n.r.e.) (witness must be interrogated about any bias or interest before the witness may be impeached for bias); *Good v. Tex. & Pac. Ry. Co.*, 166 S.W. 670, 672 (Tex. Civ. App.—El Paso 1914, writ ref'd) (witness must be interrogated about any bias or interest before the witness may be impeached for bias).

669. *See* Interim Study IV, *supra* note 10, at 72-73 (Mar. 19-20, 1982).

670. 3A WIGMORE *supra* note 295, §949, at 784 (stating that "[e]xact concrete rules are almost impossible to formulate, and where possible are usually undesirable").

671. *See* TEX. R. EVID. 613(b)(1)(A). The attorney must also tell the witness the time and place of the statement and the person to whom it was made. TEX. R. EVID. 613(b)(1)(B), (b)(1)(C). If the statement is in writing, the party does not need to show it to the witness before asking about it, but the party must show it to opposing counsel on request. TEX. R. EVID. 613(b)(2).

672. Refer to notes 613-618 *supra* and accompanying text.

673. TEX. R. EVID. 613(b)(3); *see* 3 WEINSTEIN & BERGER, *supra* note 110, at 607-55 (Rule 613 allows the witness an opportunity to explain or deny the bias situation).

674. TEX. R. EVID. 613 cmt.

to do so.[675] The witness's proponent, however, can present evidence to rebut the charge of bias or interest.[676]

If the witness unequivocally admits to either the bias or the impeaching material, the cross-examiner must stop that line of questioning.[677] If the witness does not unequivocally admit to the bias or to the impeaching material after being examined, the attorney may introduce extrinsic evidence of the bias or interest.[678] Bias and interest are never collateral or irrelevant;[679] extrinsic evidence is always admissible to prove bias once it has been denied.[680] Impeachment for bias and interest are so basic to effective cross-examination that an improper limitation on cross-examination for bias and interest violates a criminal defendant's constitutional right of confrontation.[681] It is, however, subject to a harmless-error analysis.[682]

C. Rule 613(c): Witness's Prior Consistent Statement

Rule 613(c) is probably an unnecessary provision because it simply shifts the problem of prior consistent statements to Rule 801(e)(1)(B). In Texas, the use of prior consistent statements to support a witness was traditionally limited to two situations. First, when the witness was accused of bias or interest, a consistent statement made before the existence of the alleged bias or interest was admissible to rebut the accusation.[683] This idea is embodied in Rule 801(e)(1)(B), which allows consistent statements to be used when the witness is accused of "improper influence or motive."[684] Second, the witness could testify to a prior consistent statement to rebut an accusation of recent fabrication.[685] This idea also falls under Rule 801(e)(1)(B).[686] Unless the prior consis-

---

675. *Id.*

676. Tex. R. Evid. 613(b)(3).

677. *See* Tex. R. Evid. 613(b)(4). This same principle applies under Rule 613(a). Refer to notes 619-624 *supra* and accompanying text.

678. Tex. R. Evid. 613(b)(4) & cmt.

679. *Billodeau v. State*, 277 S.W.3d 34, 42-43 (Tex. Crim. App. 2009); *see Steve v. State*, 614 S.W.2d 137, 140 (Tex. Crim. App. 1981) ("The motives which operate on the mind of a witness while he testifies should never be regarded as immaterial or irrelevant."). Refer to note 590 *supra* and accompanying text.

680. *See Dick v. Watonwan Cty.*, 562 F. Supp. 1083, 1106 (D. Minn. 1983) ("While [Criminal] Rule 608(b) bars the use of extrinsic evidence to prove specific instances of conduct bearing on character for truthfulness or untruthfulness, it does not bar the use of extrinsic evidence for other purposes such as impeachment by contradiction and proof of bias."), *rev'd on other grounds*, 738 F.2d 939 (8th Cir. 1984).

681. *Delaware v. Van Arsdall*, 475 U.S. 673, 679 (1986); *Hurd v. State*, 725 S.W.2d 249, 252-53 (Tex. Crim. App. 1987); *see Johnson v. State*, 490 S.W.3d 895, 910-11 (Tex. Crim. App. 2016).

682. *See Van Arsdall*, 475 U.S. at 684 (appropriate inquiry is whether the damaging potential of cross-examination was fully realized, and factors to consider include the importance of witness's testimony, the presence or absence of evidence corroborating or contradicting the testimony, the extent of cross-examination otherwise permitted, and the overall strength of the prosecution's case).

683. *Aetna Ins. v. Eastman*, 95 Tex. 34, 37-38, 64 S.W. 863, 863-64 (1901).

684. Tex. R. Evid. 801(e)(1)(B). Refer to *Article VIII: Hearsay*, *infra* p. 838.

685. *Skillern & Sons, Inc. v. Rosen*, 359 S.W.2d 298, 301-02 (Tex. 1962); *Barmore v. Safety Cas. Co.*, 363 S.W.2d 355, 358 (Tex. Civ. App.—Beaumont 1962, writ ref'd n.r.e.).

686. Refer to *Article VIII: Hearsay*, *infra* p. 838.

tent statement conforms with these requirements of Rule 801(e)(1)(B), it is not admissible to rehabilitate the witness's credibility.[687]

If the charge of recent fabrication or improper motive is not made explicit by the cross-examiner, the trial judge must determine whether the cross-examination as a whole has raised an implicit charge.[688]

RULE 614
EXCLUDING WITNESSES

At a party's request, the court must order witnesses excluded so that they cannot hear other witnesses' testimony. Or the court may do so on its own. But this rule does not authorize excluding:

(a) a party who is a natural person and, in civil cases, that person's spouse;

(b) after being designated as the party's representative by its attorney:

(1) in a civil case, an officer or employee of a party that is not a natural person; or

(2) in a criminal case, a defendant that is not a natural person;

(c) a person whose presence a party shows to be essential to presenting the party's claim or defense; or

(d) the victim in a criminal case, unless the court determines that the victim's testimony would be materially affected by hearing other testimony at the trial.

---

687. *See* TEX. R. EVID. 613(c); ***Rivas v. State***, 275 S.W.3d 880, 886-87 (Tex. Crim. App. 2009); *see, e.g.*, ***Haughton v. State***, 805 S.W.2d 405, 407-08 (Tex. Crim. App. 1990) (pretrial videotape of interview with child victim was inadmissible as a prior consistent statement because the alleged motive for fabrication arose before the making of the videotaped statement); ***Campbell v. State***, 718 S.W.2d 712, 715 (Tex. Crim. App. 1986) (prior consistent statement made after the motive to fabricate arose was inadmissible under the Rules).

In ***Bee v. State***, the trial court admitted, under Rules 613(c) and 801(e)(1)(B), a prior consistent statement by a witness who had testified at a former trial of the case but who was unavailable at the second trial. 974 S.W.2d 184, 189-90 (Tex. App.—San Antonio 1998, no pet.). The witness's former testimony was admissible under Rule 804, and at that trial the witness was impeached on cross-examination and rehabilitated with his prior consistent statement under Rule 801(e)(1)(B). ***Bee***, 974 S.W.2d at 189. However, neither Rule 613(c) nor Rule 801(e)(1)(B) expressly provides for the admissibility of a prior consistent statement for rehabilitation purposes when the witness is unavailable. ***Bee***, 974 S.W.2d at 189-90. Nonetheless, the trial court reached the correct result because Rule 806 states that when hearsay evidence has been introduced (here, the witness's former testimony), that testimony may be impeached or supported by any other evidence that would be admissible for those purposes if the witness had actually testified. ***Bee***, 974 S.W.2d at 190. Thus, under Rule 806, the prior consistent statement was admissible, but solely to rehabilitate and support the credibility of the unavailable witness. This is one instance in which a prior consistent statement is admissible to support the credibility of the declarant but not for its substantive value. Refer to *Article VIII: Hearsay*, *infra* p. 959.

688. *See* ***Ray v. State***, 764 S.W.2d 406, 411 (Tex. App.—Houston [14th Dist.] 1988, pet. ref'd).

COMMENTARY ON RULE 614

Sequestration of witnesses has long been a part of Texas law. Its jurisprudential roots are traced back to the biblical story of Susanna and the Elders.[689] "The Rule" is intended to prevent one witness from being influenced, either consciously or unconsciously, by the testimony of another.[690] As a result, the jury is able to hear and weigh any inconsistencies or contradictions in the testimony of the various witnesses.[691] The Rule provides that either party or the court on its own motion may order all witnesses excluded from the courtroom so that none may hear the testimony of any other witness.[692] Once the Rule is invoked by either party, if none of the exemptions apply, the court has no discretion; all witnesses must be excluded.[693] Before the promulgation of Civil Rule 614 and Criminal Rule 613, Texas law gave the trial court discretion to permit witnesses to remain in the courtroom.[694]

Rule 614 contains four express exemptions and is subject to exemptions specifically provided for by statute.[695] First, for obvious reasons, any party to the litigation who is a natural person is exempt from the operation of the Rule.[696] The constitutional rights of criminal defendants and civil litigants would be violated if those parties were banned

---

689. *Carlile v. State*, 451 S.W.2d 511, 512 (Tex. Crim. App. 1970).

690. *Russell v. State*, 155 S.W.3d 176, 179 (Tex. Crim. App. 2005); *Webb v. State*, 766 S.W.2d 236, 239 (Tex. Crim. App. 1989); *see Jimenez v. State*, 307 S.W.3d 325, 334 (Tex. App.—San Antonio 2009, pet. ref'd) ("The purpose of the Rule is to prevent corroboration, contradiction, and the influencing of witnesses."); *Franklin v. State*, 733 S.W.2d 537, 540 (Tex. App.—Tyler 1985, pet. ref'd) ("The premise underlying the rule is that the truth is more likely to be reached by presenting the jury each witness' unalloyed, independent version of an occurrence uncolored by previous testimony in the trial. Even the most righteous truthteller may be unconsciously influenced.").

691. Thus, the Rule "serves two purposes: (1) it prevents witnesses from tailoring, consciously or unconsciously, their testimony to fit that of other witnesses; and (2) in the case of witnesses testifying for the same side, it enhances the jury's ability to detect falsehood by exposing inconsistencies in their testimony." *Tell v. State*, 908 S.W.2d 535, 540 (Tex. App.—Fort Worth 1995, no pet.).

692. Tex. R. Evid. 614. The same exclusion is allowed under the federal rules, but some of the exemptions differ. *See* Fed. R. Evid. 615.

693. *Kelley v. State*, 817 S.W.2d 168, 171 (Tex. App.—Austin 1991, pet. ref'd); *see Bryant v. State*, 282 S.W.3d 156, 161 (Tex. App.—Texarkana 2009, pet. ref'd).

694. *See Moore v. State*, 882 S.W.2d 844, 848 (Tex. Crim. App. 1994); *Elbar, Inc. v. Claussen*, 774 S.W.2d 45, 51 (Tex. App.—Dallas 1989, writ dism'd). The 1998 unification of the Rules of Evidence simply melded the provisions in Civil Rule 614 and Criminal Rule 613 into a single rule. Rule 614 makes distinctions between civil and criminal trials when necessary.

695. Courts interpret these exemptions narrowly. For example, court employees are not exempt from the Rule. *See, e.g., In re H.M.S.*, 349 S.W.3d 250, 253 (Tex. App.—Dallas 2011, pet. denied) (officers of the court are not exempt from Rule 614; trial court "erred in refusing to exclude witnesses on the basis that they were court employees"). For a discussion of exemptions by statute, refer to notes 711-712 *infra* and accompanying text.

696. Tex. R. Evid. 614(a). The person does not need to be a named party in the lawsuit. Any person who has a "real interest" in the outcome of the litigation is a party for purposes of the Rule. *See, e.g., Bishop v. Wollyung*, 705 S.W.2d 312, 313-14 (Tex. App.—San Antonio 1986, writ ref'd n.r.e.) (because land in a suit for trespass to try title was community property, wife who was not a named party could not be excluded from the courtroom); *Martin v. Burcham*, 203 S.W.2d 807, 811 (Tex. Civ. App.—Fort Worth 1947, no writ) (because wife had a community interest in the judgment, she could not be excluded); *Sanders v. Lowrimore*, 73 S.W.2d 148, 150 (Tex. Civ. App.—Eastland 1934) (wife could not be excluded from the courtroom in a suit brought by her husband for her injuries), *rev'd on other grounds*, 129 Tex. 563, 103 S.W.2d 739 (1937) (op. on reh'g).

from the courtroom.[697] The spouse of any party in a civil case is also exempt from the operation of the Rule.[698]

Second, in civil cases, an officer or employee of a party that is not a natural person is exempt from Rule 614 if the officer or employee has been designated by the party's attorney as its representative.[699] In criminal cases, this exemption applies only to the defendant-corporation or association; it does not apply to the State.[700] Thus, the prosecution cannot designate an investigator or law-enforcement officer as its representative under the Rule.[701]

Third, any person whose presence is "essential" to the party's presentation may be exempted from Rule 614.[702] Here, the party claiming the exemption must show that the witness's presence in the courtroom is necessary, and the trial judge has wide discretion in determining if the party has met its burden.[703] A mere conclusory explanation

697. *See* FED. R. EVID. 615 advisory committee's note ("Exclusion of persons who are parties would raise serious problems of confrontation and due process."); *see also* **Geders v. United States**, 425 U.S. 80, 91 (1976) (trial court violated defendant's Sixth Amendment right to assistance of counsel by sequestering him and preventing him from discussing his testimony with his attorney during a 17-hour overnight recess between direct and cross-examination); **Potashnick v. Port City Constr. Co.**, 609 F.2d 1101, 1118-19 (5th Cir. 1980) (trial court violated due process by not allowing defendant to communicate with his attorney during breaks and recesses in defendant's testimony).

698. TEX. R. EVID. 614(a); *see* **Bishop**, 705 S.W.2d at 313-14; **Martin**, 203 S.W.2d at 811; **Sanders**, 73 S.W.2d at 150. Federal Rule 615(a) does not have an exception for the spouse of a party. *See* FED. R. EVID. 615(a).

699. TEX. R. EVID. 614(b)(1); *see also* **In re M-I L.L.C.**, 505 S.W.3d 569, 578 (Tex. 2016) (orig. proceeding) (exemption for designated representatives under Texas Rule of Civil Procedure 267(b), which is substantively identical to Rule 614(b)(1), does not apply to in camera hearings under Texas Uniform Trade Secrets Act). Only one such representative may be designated. *See, e.g.*, **Century 21 Real Estate Corp. v. Hometown Real Estate Co.**, 890 S.W.2d 118, 129-30 (Tex. App.—Texarkana 1994, writ denied) (trial court erred by not requiring party to designate one representative and by not excluding other officers and shareholders from courtroom under Civil Rule 614; harmless error in this instance).

700. *See* TEX. R. EVID. 614(b)(2).

701. *See id.* Federal Rule 615, however, permits the government to designate a law-enforcement officer as its representative even when that officer will testify. *See* FED. R. EVID. 615(b); *see, e.g.*, **United States v. Jones**, 687 F.2d 1265, 1267-68 (8th Cir. 1982) (government's designation of local police officer as a "case agent" exempt from sequestration was upheld); **In re United States**, 584 F.2d 666, 667 (5th Cir. 1978) (trial judge erred in excluding from the courtroom a government agent designated as the government's representative under Federal Rule 615(2), now Rule 615(b)). *See generally* 3 WEINSTEIN & BERGER, *supra* note 110, ¶615[02], at 615-10 to 615-22 (discussing designated representatives under Federal Rule 615). The Texas drafters of former Criminal Rule 613 simply changed the wording of the federal rule from "party" to "defendant."

This difference between the federal rule and the Texas rule was addressed in **Russell v. State**, 155 S.W.3d 176 (Tex. Crim. App. 2005). The prosecutor in **Russell** asked to have a homicide detective exempted from Rule 614, arguing he was a "case agent" because he was the primary homicide investigator in the case. 155 S.W.3d at 180. The defense attorney objected, commenting, "I thought that was a federal rule. I didn't think it applied to state court." *Id.* The trial court allowed the detective to sit at counsel's table as a "case agent" but admonished him that he was still "under the Rule" and could not discuss his testimony with the other witnesses. *Id.* at 181. The court of criminal appeals acknowledged that the Federal Rules include a "case agent" exception but noted that the exception was purposefully omitted from the Texas rule: "This Court deliberately chose to make our rule different when we adopted Rule 614(2) [now Rule 614(b)]. Neither the State nor a defendant who is a natural person may take away the court's authority to exclude one of its witnesses by simply designating the witness." *Id.* Thus, allowing the investigator to sit at counsel's table was error. *Id.*

702. TEX. R. EVID. 614(c). Federal Rule 615(c) is identical. *See* FED. R. EVID. 615(c).

703. *See* TEX. R. EVID. 614(c); **Aguilar v. State**, 739 S.W.2d 357, 358 (Tex. Crim. App. 1987). In **Aguilar**, the court of criminal appeals outlined the recommended procedure:

by the party requesting the exemption is not an adequate showing under the Rule.[704] This third exemption is usually invoked for experts who base their expert opinions on facts testified to by other witnesses[705] or who may offer critical technical assistance to the attorney during the trial.[706] But a witness is not exempt from the Rule merely because he has been designated as an expert.[707] Although the prosecution may not designate a law-enforcement agent as its party representative under Rule 614, the prosecution might be able to claim an exemption under Rule 614(c) if that witness's presence is essential to the development of the State's case.[708]

> When a trial court must decide if an exemption from the rule is justified, it should first exclude all of the witnesses. Then the trial court should hear the parties' requests for exemptions from the rule for certain witnesses. It is within the trial court's discretion to decide if a requested exemption from the rule is justified.

739 S.W.2d at 358; *see also **Kelley v. State***, 817 S.W.2d 168, 171-72 (Tex. App.—Austin 1991, pet. ref'd) (trial court did not abuse its discretion in exempting witness from the Rule when prosecutor established under oath that witness's presence in the courtroom was essential to prosecution's case, and defendant agreed that witness might be excused from the Rule during presentation of physical evidence and expert witnesses). In ***Oliver B. Cannon & Son v. Fidelity & Casualty Co.***, the court set forth the following test for discretionary exemption under Federal Rule 615(3), now Rule 615(c):

> What must be shown is that a witness has such specialized expertise or intimate knowledge of the facts of the case that a party's attorney could not effectively function without the presence and aid of the witness or that the witness would be unable to present essential testimony without hearing the trial testimony of other witnesses.

519 F. Supp. 668, 678 (D. Del. 1981); *see **Miller v. Univ'l City Studios, Inc.***, 650 F.2d 1365, 1374 (5th Cir. 1981).

704. *See, e.g.*, ***Aguilar***, 739 S.W.2d at 358-59 (error to exempt rape victim from Criminal Rule 613 when State made no showing that she was needed to advise and confer with the prosecutor during trial or that she did so); ***Hernandez v. State***, 791 S.W.2d 301, 306 (Tex. App.—Corpus Christi 1990, pet. ref'd) (prosecutor's conclusory statement to court that it would be "necessary and essential" for prosecutor to confer with deputy during testimony was insufficient to show necessity under Criminal Rule 613); ***Barnhill v. State***, 779 S.W.2d 890, 892-93 (Tex. App.—Corpus Christi 1989, no pet.) (prosecutor's statement that "we are entitled to have a case worker" exempted under Criminal Rule 613 was insufficient to show that witness's presence was essential).

705. *See **Moore v. State***, 493 S.W.2d 844, 845 (Tex. Crim. App. 1973) (under common law, expert witnesses, witnesses who are attorneys in the case, and reputation witnesses are ordinarily exempt from the Rule); ***Elbar, Inc. v. Claussen***, 774 S.W.2d 45, 51-52 (Tex. App.—Dallas 1989, writ dism'd) (expert witnesses are exempt from the Rule); *see, e.g.*, ***Lewis v. State***, 486 S.W.2d 104, 106 (Tex. Crim. App. 1972) (expert could remain in the courtroom to hear a witness's testimony and watch a witness's demonstration of the force used to strike the decedent and properly based his opinion on such testimony).

706. *See **Tell v. State***, 908 S.W.2d 535, 542 (Tex. App.—Fort Worth 1995, no pet.); 3 WEINSTEIN & BERGER, *supra* note 110, ¶615[02], at 615-15 to 615-18.

707. *See **Drilex Sys., Inc. v. Flores***, 1 S.W.3d 112, 118-19 (Tex. 1999) (although experts are frequently exempted from the Rule, they are not automatically exempt; sponsoring party must explain the necessity of the exemption); *see, e.g.*, ***Allen v. State***, 436 S.W.3d 815, 823 (Tex. App.—Texarkana 2014, pet. ref'd) (error to allow witness to remain in courtroom based on State's argument that she was testifying as expert witness; because witness's testimony was fact-based and not based on her expert qualifications, State did not show that her presence in courtroom was essential to its case).

708. *See, e.g.*, ***Bath v. State***, 951 S.W.2d 11, 23 (Tex. App.—Corpus Christi 1997, pet. ref'd) (State made sufficient showing that lead investigator who helped coordinate investigation with law-enforcement agencies, who assisted in preparing case for trial, and whose assistance and expertise would be needed with the evidence should be exempt from the Rule under Criminal Rule 613(3)); ***Hullaby v. State***, 911 S.W.2d 921, 928-29 (Tex. App.—Fort Worth 1995, pet. ref'd) (in attempted-murder trial arising from gang-related drive-by shooting, trial court did not abuse its discretion in concluding that police officer was essential to presentation of the State's case; officer's presence was needed to interpret gang slang and symbolic gestures); ***Kelley***, 817 S.W.2d at 172 (trial court did not abuse its discretion, under the particular circumstances of the case, in exempting a Texas Ranger from the Rule under Criminal Rule 613(3)); *see also **Moore v. State***, 882 S.W.2d 844, 847-48 (Tex. Crim. App. 1994) (trial court abused its discretion in

A fourth exemption in criminal cases was added in 1990.[709] The victim of a crime is exempt from the operation of Rule 614 unless the court determines that the victim's testimony would be materially affected by remaining in the courtroom to hear other witnesses' testimony.[710] The opposing party must demonstrate the likelihood not only that the victim's testimony would be affected by hearing other testimony but also that it would be *materially* affected. Thus, the opponent apparently has an almost impossible burden—one that must be met before any evidence has been presented. However, if the victim testifies at the beginning of the case, it seems most improbable that his testimony could be affected by any other witness. Thus, the change is unlikely to raise serious concerns.

Finally, although it is not set out in Rule 614, if a statute specifically provides that a particular witness (such as a guardian ad litem)[711] is entitled to be present during the trial, then the provisions of that statute trump Rule 614 as required by Rule 101.[712]

The party seeking an exemption from Rule 614 must prove that one of the exemptions applies to a particular witness.[713] A witness exempt from the Rule is, unlike other witnesses, permitted to discuss the case and facts with others.[714]

Rule 614 does not speak explicitly to remedies for a violation of the Rule, but the traditional power of the judge to exclude the testimony of a witness who has violated the Rule is an implicit part of Rule 614.[715] When the Rule is violated, the trial court

---

exempting State's expert from the Rule based on "expediency" alone; however, if a party shows that an expert's presence is necessary to aid counsel during testimony of another expert because his expertise is required to fully understand the testifying witness, that expert may be exempted from the Rule); *cf. United States v. Agnes*, 753 F.2d 293, 306-07 (3d Cir. 1985) (trial court did not err in denying defense request to have investigator exempted from the Rule because investigator was defendant's girlfriend and would be able to modify her testimony to comport with that of other witnesses); ***Gov't of V.I. v. Edinborough***, 625 F.2d 472, 475 (3d Cir. 1980) (parents of a young victim were exempt from the Rule when child was testifying); ***United States v. Phillips***, 515 F. Supp. 758, 761 (E.D. Ky. 1981) (psychiatric hypnosis expert was entitled to remain in the courtroom and aid the prosecutor during defense expert's testimony).

709. *See Amendments to Texas Rules of Criminal Evidence*, 789-790 S.W.2d (Tex. Cases) XXXII (1990, amended 1998).

710. TEX. R. EVID. 614(d). The federal rule does not contain a similar exemption. *See* FED. R. EVID. 615.

711. *See* TEX. FAM. CODE §§107.002(c)(4), (e).

712. *See* TEX. R. EVID. 101(d); *see, e.g.*, ***In re K.C.P.***, 142 S.W.3d 574, 585 (Tex. App.—Texarkana 2004, no pet.) (guardian ad litem could not be excluded from trial under Rule 614). Refer to *Article I: General Provisions*, *supra* p. 49. Federal Rule 615 provides an exemption for a person to be present if authorized by statute. FED. R. EVID. 615(d).

713. ***Russell v. State***, 155 S.W.3d 176, 180 (Tex. Crim. App. 2005); ***Parks v. State***, 463 S.W.3d 166, 174 (Tex. App.—Houston [14th Dist.] 2015, no pet.); *e.g.*, ***Moore***, 882 S.W.2d at 848 (error to permit expert witnesses to remain in courtroom during trial without proof that an exception applied); ***Tell v. State***, 908 S.W.2d 535, 541-42 (Tex. App.—Fort Worth 1995, no pet.) (under the facts presented, witness who was called but not sequestered could testify because attorney did not foresee calling that witness until after the State's case; otherwise, party could have been sanctioned and witness could have been disqualified).

714. ***Drilex Sys., Inc. v. Flores***, 1 S.W.3d 112, 119 (Tex. 1999).

715. *See* ***Madrigal Rodriguez v. State***, 749 S.W.2d 576, 579 (Tex. App.—Corpus Christi 1988, pet. ref'd) (trial courts continue to have their traditional power to disqualify witnesses under Criminal Rule 613); ***Cook v. State***, 30 Tex. Ct. App. 607, 612, 18 S.W. 412, 412 (1892) ("The admissibility of witnesses who have violated the rule, or who have not been placed under the rule, is within the sound discretion of the trial court, and such discretion will be presumed to be correctly exercised until the contrary appears."); *see, e.g.*, ***Sw. Bell Tel. Co. v. Johnson***, 389 S.W.2d 645, 647-48

may, considering all the circumstances, (1) allow the testimony of the offending witness, (2) disallow the testimony, or (3) hold the violator in contempt.[716] However, a trial court's decision to allow the testimony of a witness who has been present in the courtroom while others have testified does not make that witness exempt under Rule 614—the witness may not then discuss the case with others.[717]

It has long been held that a violation of the Rule is not in itself reversible error but becomes so only when the objected-to testimony is admitted and the opposing party is harmed as a result.[718] It would be difficult to show harm if the violation occurred after the witness completed his testimony.[719] Relevant criteria for determining injury are whether the witness actually heard the testimony of either (1) a witness for the other side whom he then contradicts or (2) a witness for the same side whom he later corroborates on a material fact.[720] Texas courts have held that if the witness's testimony

(Tex. 1965) (trial court did not abuse its discretion in excluding the testimony of a witness who was in the courtroom during the testimony of other witnesses even though the witness himself had never been placed under the Rule).

716. *Drilex Sys.*, 1 S.W.3d at 117; *Jimenez v. State*, 307 S.W.3d 325, 334 (Tex. App.—San Antonio 2009, pet. ref'd); *see Bell v. State*, 938 S.W.2d 35, 50 (Tex. Crim. App. 1996). Factors that the trial court should consider in exercising its discretionary authority to permit the witness to testify include the following: whether the party calling the witness was at fault in causing or allowing the violation; whether the witness's testimony is crucial or cumulative; and whether the witness is a fact witness. *Drilex Sys.*, 1 S.W.3d at 117 n.3.

717. *See Drilex Sys.*, 1 S.W.3d at 118 ("[A] decision to allow a witness to testify despite his presence in the courtroom is not the same as a finding that the witness is exempt from the Rule.").

718. *See Bell*, 938 S.W.2d at 50 (in deciding whether trial court abused its discretion in allowing a witness who violated the Rule to testify, court looks to whether defendant was harmed or prejudiced by witness's violation); *Guerra v. State*, 771 S.W.2d 453, 475 (Tex. Crim. App. 1988) (objectionable witness must produce harm); *Archer v. State*, 703 S.W.2d 664, 666 (Tex. Crim. App. 1986) (harm must result from the testimony); *Haas v. State*, 498 S.W.2d 206, 210 (Tex. Crim. App. 1973) (injury must occur for the error to be reversible); *Parks*, 463 S.W.3d at 174 (violation of evidentiary rule is nonconstitutional error and will be disregarded unless it affected defendant's substantial rights); *see also United States v. Posada-Rios*, 158 F.3d 832, 871-72 (5th Cir. 1998) (in determining whether trial court abused its discretion in permitting testimony of a witness who violated sequestration order, "'the focus is upon whether the witness's out-of-court conversation concerned substantive aspects of the trial and whether the court allowed the [opposing party] to fully explore the conversation during cross-examination'" (quoting *United States v. Wylie*, 919 F.2d 969, 976 (5th Cir. 1990))).

719. *See, e.g., Beets v. State*, 767 S.W.2d 711, 746-47 (Tex. Crim. App. 1988) (op. on reh'g) (when defendant's children, both prosecution witnesses, had conversed together in courtroom hallway after testifying, trial court did not err in refusing to grant a mistrial because defendant did not show how this violation "thwarted the purpose for the rule or how [defendant] was harmed thereby"); *State v. Saylor*, 319 S.W.3d 704, 710 (Tex. App.—Dallas 2009, pet. ref'd) (trial court abused its discretion in granting motion for new trial after alleged violation of the Rule; although witness was present while prosecutor talked with another witness about case, she had already testified and could not have been influenced by conversation).

720. *See Guerra*, 771 S.W.2d at 475 (relevant criteria are whether witness heard the testimony and whether witness contradicted the testimony); *Haas*, 498 S.W.2d at 210 (same); *see, e.g., Bryant v. State*, 282 S.W.3d 156, 162-63 (Tex. App.—Texarkana 2009, pet. ref'd) (when defendant had no direct, affirmative evidence that witness was present in the courtroom and heard testimony by other witnesses, objection under Rule 614 was invalid); *Marx v. State*, 953 S.W.2d 321, 338 (Tex. App.—Austin 1997) (trial court did not abuse its discretion in allowing testimony from witness who was requested to leave courtroom as soon as prosecution became aware that he would testify and witness's testimony was limited to rebutting defendant's impeachment evidence), *aff'd*, 987 S.W.2d 577 (Tex. Crim. App. 1999); *Rodriguez v. State*, 772 S.W.2d 167, 168-69 (Tex. App.—Houston [14th Dist.] 1989, pet. ref'd) (trial court did not abuse its discretion in permitting two police officers to testify even though they had met with prosecutor together after the Rule was invoked because they testified on completely different aspects of the case; "[i]n order to violate

could not have been affected in any way by hearing the testimony of others, the purpose of the Rule has not been violated.[721] Thus, if the witnesses testify about entirely separate issues or occurrences, the fact that one witness may have heard the testimony of others could not affect his testimony, and the court does not err in permitting the witness to testify.[722]

Texas courts have generally held that trial courts do not abuse their discretion when they permit a party to call a rebuttal witness who had been present in the court and heard the testimony of other witnesses if the sponsoring party could not reasonably have anticipated the need to call that person as a witness when the Rule was invoked.[723] Similarly, if an anticipated witness violates the Rule but is never actually called to testify during the trial, there is no error.[724] It has also been held that there will seldom be

---

the rule, it is necessary that two (or more) witnesses confer on an issue bearing on the guilt or innocence of the accused *and about which they later testify*"); ***English v. State***, No. 04-02-00107-CR (Tex. App.—San Antonio 2003, pet. ref'd) (memo op.; 8-29-03) (trial court did not abuse its discretion in permitting two witnesses to testify after one witness translated for the other and then altered his testimony to corroborate the other witness's testimony; change in testimony did not directly affect issue of defendant's guilt or innocence).

721. *E.g.*, ***Parrack v. State***, 753 S.W.2d 467, 468 (Tex. App.—Eastland 1988, pet. ref'd) (bailiff's testimony, identifying a picture of defendant, who left in the middle of the trial, complied with the Rule because the testimony of other witnesses could not have affected his perfunctory testimony); ***Collazo v. State***, No. 04-12-00004-CR (Tex. App.—San Antonio 2013, no pet.) (memo op.; 6-26-13) (trial court did not abuse its discretion in admitting testimony of two custodians of records after prosecutor spoke with both of them in hallway about procedure of testifying; given the nature of their testimony, they could not have been influenced by conversation).

722. *See, e.g.*, ***In re C.J.B.***, 137 S.W.3d 814, 825 (Tex. App.—Waco 2004, no pet.) (trial court could have reasonably believed that witness did not discuss her testimony with a second witness but "only relayed her emotional response" to second witness when recalling the event she had witnessed; trial court did not abuse its discretion in allowing second witness to testify); ***Minor v. State***, 91 S.W.3d 824, 830 (Tex. App.—Fort Worth 2002, pet. ref'd) (when "the witness has no connection with either the State's or the defendant's case-in-chief and was not likely to be called as a witness because of a lack of personal knowledge regarding the offense, the trial court does not abuse its discretion in allowing the testimony"; victim's sister was properly permitted to testify in rebuttal that her deceased brother was left-handed after murder defendant testified that victim was hiding a weapon behind his back with his right hand); ***Mestiza v. State***, 923 S.W.2d 720, 725-26 (Tex. App.—Corpus Christi 1996, no pet.) (when testimony of two identification witnesses had nothing in common, purpose of the Rule was not violated).

723. *See, e.g.*, ***Valdez v. State***, 776 S.W.2d 162, 170 (Tex. Crim. App. 1989) (trial court did not abuse its discretion in permitting State's witness, who had been in the courtroom and heard other witnesses testify, to take the stand when State was unaware of that person's potential as a witness because the person "became a necessary witness due to events during trial"); ***Harris v. State***, 122 S.W.3d 871, 882-83 (Tex. App.—Fort Worth 2003, pet. ref'd) (admission of DA investigator's testimony in rebuttal to impeach defense witness's testimony on material point was upheld; investigator had no personal knowledge of the offense and State had no reason to believe he would be a witness when the Rule was invoked); ***Holloman v. State***, 942 S.W.2d 773, 775-76 (Tex. App.—Beaumont 1997, no pet.) (complainant's husband was allowed to testify on rebuttal although he had heard his wife and two other witnesses testify; prosecutor had originally anticipated that he would be a witness and had sworn him in but later changed his mind and allowed him in courtroom; he then called him during rebuttal on a different issue); ***Coots v. State***, 826 S.W.2d 955, 960-61 (Tex. App.—Houston [1st Dist.] 1992, no pet.) (harmful error to permit bailiff, who had not been excluded under the Rule, to testify in rebuttal when it should have been obvious to the State before trial that testimony rebutting defendant's alibi would be needed); ***Sallings v. State***, 789 S.W.2d 408, 416 (Tex. App.—Dallas 1990, pet. ref'd) (witness who had heard others' testimony was allowed to testify when it had not been anticipated that this person would be a witness).

724. *E.g.*, ***Harrison v. State***, 929 S.W.2d 80, 84 (Tex. App.—Eastland 1996, pet. ref'd) (although prosecutor had been expected to testify, no error in fact that he sat as "second chair" during trial because he was never called as a witness); *see* ***Karnes v. State***, 873 S.W.2d 92, 99 (Tex. App.—Dallas 1994, no pet.).

harmful error when a witness who has violated the Rule by listening to testimony during the guilt stage of a criminal trial testifies only during the punishment stage.[725]

Exclusion of testimony when a criminal defendant's witness violates the Rule raises the issue of the defendant's constitutional right to the compulsory attendance of witnesses.[726] Thus, under Texas precedent, a defense witness may not be disqualified under the Rule if "neither the defendant nor his counsel have consented, procured, connived or have knowledge of a witness or potential witness who is in violation of the sequestration rule, and the testimony of the witness is crucial to the defense."[727] In determining whether to disqualify a particular defense witness under the Rule, the trial court must balance the interests of the State and the accused, consider alternative sanctions, and consider the benefit and detriment arising from a disqualification in light of the nature and weight of the testimony to be offered.[728]

While Rule 614 speaks only to exclusion of the witnesses from the courtroom, the Rules of Civil[729] and Criminal[730] Procedure require the court to instruct witnesses who

---

725. *See* **Upton v. State**, 894 S.W.2d 426, 428 (Tex. App.—Amarillo 1995, pet. ref'd) ("[T]he admission of testimony related to something other than guilt or innocence is unlikely to result in the violation of [the Rule].").

726. *See* **Holder v. United States**, 150 U.S. 91, 92 (1893). In noting the constitutional problem, the Supreme Court stated the following:

> If a witness disobeys the order of withdrawal, while he may be proceeded against for contempt and his testimony is open to comment to the jury by reason of his conduct, he is not thereby disqualified, and the weight of authority is that he cannot be excluded on that ground merely, although the right to exclude under particular circumstances may be supported as within the sound discretion of the trial court.

Id.; *see* **Davis v. State**, 872 S.W.2d 743, 745 (Tex. Crim. App. 1994) (generally, a defense witness cannot be excluded solely for violation of the Criminal Rule, although the right to exclude under "particular circumstances" is within the sound discretion of the trial court).

727. **Webb v. State**, 766 S.W.2d 236, 244 (Tex. Crim. App. 1989). In **Webb**, the trial court abused its discretion in excluding the testimony of a defense witness rebutting the testimony of an accomplice-witness because nothing indicated that the defendant or his counsel knew of the witness's presence in the courtroom or knew that her testimony would become crucial to the defense. *Id.* at 244-46; *accord* **Delapaz v. State**, 229 S.W.3d 795, 801-02 (Tex. App.—Eastland 2007) (trial court did not abuse its discretion in excluding testimony of witness who had been in courtroom because her testimony would have been cumulative and was not crucial to the defense), *rev'd on other grounds sub nom.* **De La Paz v. State**, 273 S.W.3d 671 (Tex. Crim. App. 2008); **Chavez v. State**, 794 S.W.2d 910, 914-15 (Tex. App.—Houston [1st Dist.] 1990, pet. ref'd) (trial court did not abuse its discretion in excluding defense witnesses' testimony when defense attorney was negligent in permitting the witnesses to remain in the courtroom during trial); **Coons v. State**, 758 S.W.2d 330, 335-36 (Tex. App.—Houston [14th Dist.] 1988, pet. ref'd) (trial court did not abuse its discretion in excluding defense witness's testimony when witness had violated the Rule and the evidence was not crucial).

728. **Webb**, 766 S.W.2d at 244; *e.g.*, **Tell v. State**, 908 S.W.2d 535, 541-43 (Tex. App.—Fort Worth 1995, no pet.) (harmless error for court to allow defense investigator who had heard witnesses' testimony to testify because his testimony was not crucial).

729. TEX. R. CIV. P. 267.

730. TEX. CODE CRIM. PROC. art. 36.06.

have been placed under the Rule that they are not to converse with each other or any other person[731] about the case, except with the court's permission.

RULE 615
PRODUCING A WITNESS'S STATEMENT IN CRIMINAL CASES

(a) Motion to Produce. After a witness other than the defendant testifies on direct examination, the court, on motion of a party who did not call the witness, must order an attorney for the state or the defendant and the defendant's attorney to produce, for the examination and use of the moving party, any statement of the witness that:

(1) is in their possession;

(2) relates to the subject matter of the witness's testimony; and

(3) has not previously been produced.

(b) Producing the Entire Statement. If the entire statement relates to the subject matter of the witness's testimony, the court must order that the statement be delivered to the moving party.

(c) Producing a Redacted Statement. If the party who called the witness claims that the statement contains information that does not relate to the subject matter of the witness's testimony, the court must inspect the statement in camera. After excising any unrelated portions, the court must order delivery of the redacted statement to the moving party. If a party objects to an excision, the court must preserve the entire statement with the excised portion indicated, under seal, as part of the record.

(d) Recess to Examine a Statement. If the court orders production of a witness's statement, the court, on request, must recess the proceedings to allow the moving party time to examine the statement and prepare for its use.

(e) Sanction for Failure to Produce or Deliver a Statement. If the party who called the witness disobeys an order to produce or deliver a statement, the court

---

731. The Civil Rule explicitly permits the witnesses to talk to the attorneys. *See* TEX. R. CIV. P. 267(d). The Criminal Rule does not specifically exempt conversations with the attorneys but does imply such an exemption. *See* TEX. CODE CRIM. PROC. art. 36.06; *Archer v. State*, 703 S.W.2d 664, 666 n.1 (Tex. Crim. App. 1986).

In *Drilex Systems, Inc. v. Flores*, the court held that the trial judge did not abuse his discretion in striking an expert witness who had not only stayed in the courtroom after the Rule had been invoked, but had "freely converse[d] with the parties and other witnesses regarding the case." 961 S.W.2d 209, 212 (Tex. App.—San Antonio 1996), *aff'd as modified*, 1 S.W.3d 112 (Tex. 1999). In this case, the expert's sponsor had made no effort to have the trial court exempt the expert from the Rule when it was invoked. *Drilex Sys.*, 961 S.W.2d at 212. In fact, the expert himself testified that hearing the testimony of other witnesses was not necessary for him to form his opinions. *Id.* Further, the record demonstrated that the witness discussed the case with the party's representative and another expert witness. *Id.* Because the witness violated the sequestration rule and his violation went to the very rationale for the Rule—preventing witnesses from collaborating about their testimony during trial—the trial court properly struck the witness's testimony.

must strike the witness's testimony from the record. If an attorney for the state disobeys the order, the court must declare a mistrial if justice so requires.

(f) "Statement" Defined. As used in this rule, a witness's "statement" means:

(1) a written statement that the witness makes and signs, or otherwise adopts or approves;

(2) a substantially verbatim, contemporaneously recorded recital of the witness's oral statement that is contained in any recording or any transcription of a recording; or

(3) the witness's statement to a grand jury, however taken or recorded, or a transcription of such a statement.

Notes and Comments

Comment to 2016 change: The Michael Morton Act, codified at Texas Code of Criminal Procedure art. 39.14, affords defendants substantial pre-trial discovery, requiring the state, upon request from the defendant, to produce and permit the defendant to inspect and copy various items, including witness statements. In many instances, therefore, art. 39.14 eliminates the need, after the witness testifies on direct examination, for a defendant to request, and the court to order, production of a witness's statement.

But art. 39.14 does not entirely eliminate the need for in-trial discovery of witness statements. Art. 39.14 does not extend equivalent discovery rights to the prosecution, and so prosecutors will still need to use Rule 615 to obtain witness statements of defense witnesses. Moreover, some defendants may fail to exercise their discovery rights under art. 39.14 and so may wish to obtain a witness statement under Rule 615. In addition, the Michael Morton Act applies only to the prosecution of offenses committed after December 31, 2013. Defendants on trial for offenses committed before then have no right to pre-trial discovery of the witness statements of prosecution witnesses.

Consequently, Rule 615(a) has been amended to account for the changed pre-trial discovery regime introduced by the Michael Morton Act. If a party's adversary has already produced a witness's statement—whether through formal discovery under art. 39.14 or through more informal means—Rule 615(a) no longer gives a party the right to obtain, after the witness testifies on direct examination, a court order for production of the witness's statement. But if a party's adversary has not already produced a witness's statement, the party may still use Rule 615(a) to request and obtain a court order requiring production of the witness's statement after the witness finishes testifying on direct examination.

Comment to 1998 change: This is prior Rule of Criminal Evidence 614.

COMMENTARY ON RULE 615

Rule 615, applicable only in criminal cases, is an expanded codification of the *Gaskin* rule as adopted into Texas law in a 1962 court of criminal appeals decision, *Gaskin v. State*.[732] The rule requires the party sponsoring the witness to produce for inspection and use on cross-examination any prior statements related to the subject matter of the testimony that the witness has ever made that are in the sponsoring party's possession and have not previously been produced.[733] The *Gaskin* rule and Criminal Rule 615 were modeled after Rule 26.2 of the Federal Rules of Criminal Procedure; thus, most of the terms and definitions found in Rule 615 are the same as those in the federal rule. Criminal Rule 615 had no equivalent in the Civil Rules. In the 1998 unification of the Rules, former Criminal Rule 614 was simply renumbered as Rule 615, and gender-neutral phrases were substituted for the word "him" in appropriate places.

Adoption of what is now Rule 615 changed Texas practice in three important ways. First, Rule 615 applies to the defense as well as to the State.[734] Once a defense witness testifies, the prosecution is entitled to the production of any prior statement made by that witness that is in the possession of the defense, relates to the subject matter of the witness's testimony, and has not previously been produced.[735] An exception is made for the testifying defendant.[736] His prior statements are protected by the attorney-client privilege and are not discoverable. Second, the rule explicitly covers recordings as well as writings,[737] whereas the *Gaskin* rule had generally been limited to prior written statements.[738] Third, the rule makes all prior grand-jury testimony by the witness

---

732. 172 Tex. Crim. 7, 353 S.W.2d 467 (1961).

733. *See* Tex. R. Evid. 615(a); *see, e.g.*, *Balderas v. State*, 517 S.W.3d 756, 781-82 (Tex. Crim. App. 2016) (exclusion of audio recording of witness's statement to police did not violate *Gaskin* rule because defendant acknowledged, and record reflected, that he already had copy of statement), *cert. denied*, 137 S. Ct. 1207 (2017). Rule 615(a) was amended effective January 1, 2016, to account for the expanded pretrial discovery afforded by the 2013 amendments to Texas Code of Criminal Procedure article 39.14. *See* Tex. R. Evid. 615 cmt. (2016). Specifically, a party can use Rule 615(a) to require production of a witness statement only if the statement has not already been produced; if a witness statement has already been produced, either under article 39.14 or informally, the party no longer has a right under Rule 615(a) to obtain a court order for the statement's production. Tex. R. Evid. 615 cmt. (2016); *see* Tex. R. Evid. 615(a)(3). The prosecution, any defendants who do not exercise their discovery rights under article 39.14, or any defendants on trial for offenses committed before December 31, 2013, will still need to use Rule 615 to obtain witness statements during trial. Tex. R. Evid. 615 cmt. (2016). For a discussion of article 39.14, refer to *Article V: Privileges*, *supra* p. 431.

734. *See* Tex. R. Evid. 615(a) & cmt. (2016).

735. *See* Tex. R. Evid. 615(a); *see also* *Ballew v. State*, 640 S.W.2d 237, 242 (Tex. Crim. App. [Panel Op.] 1982) (op. on reh'g) (in pre-Rules case, prosecutor could not obtain defense expert's notes under the *Gaskin* rule because witness was called by defendant). In *Ballew*, the court of criminal appeals set the stage for application of Criminal Rule 614 to defense witnesses, however, when it held that the defense expert's notes were subject to production because he testified that he had referred to those notes before testifying. 640 S.W.2d at 244.

736. *See* Tex. R. Evid. 615(a).

737. Tex. R. Evid. 615(f)(1), (f)(2).

738. *See* *Cullen v. State*, 719 S.W.2d 195, 198 (Tex. Crim. App. 1986) ("[I]t would be grossly unfair ... to make a blanket holding that a tape-recorded statement of a witness will never be discoverable under *Gaskin* .... Thus we now hold that the *Gaskin* rule is not limited to *written* statements but may also encompass tape-recorded statements and transcripts made therefrom."); *see also* *Johnson v. State*, 650 S.W.2d 784, 790 (Tex. Crim. App. 1983) (surreptitious tape recording and transcript of that recording of defendant soliciting undercover agent to commit capital

discoverable.[739] Former Texas law had permitted the discovery of secret grand-jury testimony only when the defendant showed a "particularized need" for it.[740]

The rule applies to any written or recorded statement the witness has ever made; however, if the statement is written, he must have, at some time,[741] made, signed, or otherwise adopted or approved the statement.[742] But he need not have used the statement to refresh his memory either before the trial or while on the witness stand.[743] The rule does not apply to secondhand statements (e.g., the notes of a prosecutor, police officer, or law-enforcement investigator, unless those notes are a "substantially verbatim, contemporaneously recorded recital" of a witness's words).[744] Such notes constitute attorney work product and are therefore protected, unless discoverable under Rule 612 or another rule. On the other hand, it is unlikely that either the attorney-client privilege or the work-product doctrine would prevent production of statements that are otherwise discoverable under Rule 615.[745] A victim-impact statement is one example of a witness's prior statement that is discoverable if the victim testifies at trial.[746]

If the prior statement consists of a recorded interview of the witness, the discoverability and use of that recording depends on whether it is more like a witness reciting a narrative of his observations and recollections or more like a witness-preparation session conducted by the attorney in which the attorney's comments, ideas, and strategy

---

murder was not discoverable under the **Gaskin** rule because agent did not testify; court did not reach issue of whether recording would have been discoverable if agent had testified).

739. *See* Tex. R. Evid. 615(f)(3).

740. *See* **Bynum v. State**, 767 S.W.2d 769, 781 (Tex. Crim. App. 1989) ("[T]o circumvent the traditional policy of grand jury secrecy the accused must show that either a special reason or particularized need exists before an inspection of the grand jury proceedings will be allowed.").

741. Contemporaneity between time of statement and of approval is not required. *See* **Clancy v. United States**, 365 U.S. 312, 314-15 (1961) (contemporaneity requirement applies only to verbatim recitation of an oral statement).

742. Tex. R. Evid. 615(f). This requirement ensures that it is the witness's own words, not some other person's rendition of the witness's words. *See* **Artell v. State**, 372 S.W.2d 944, 945 (Tex. Crim. App. 1963) ("'It is clear that Congress was concerned that only those statements which could properly be called the witness' own words should be made available to the defense for purposes of impeachment.'" (quoting **Palermo v. United States**, 360 U.S. 343, 352 (1959))); **Williams v. State**, 940 S.W.2d 802, 807 (Tex. App.—Fort Worth 1997, pet. ref'd) (for purposes of rule, statement must be (1) personally prepared by the witness and (2) signed or otherwise adopted or approved by the witness to be producible). To the extent that **Williams** stands for the proposition that the witness himself must "prepare" the statement, the opinion is probably too narrow a construction. A witness statement may always be—and usually is—physically prepared or written down by another person. The crucial aspects are twofold: (1) is the statement a substantially verbatim rendition of what the witness stated, and (2) did the witness sign, adopt, or approve that statement, either when it was made or at trial? A prosecutor's handwritten version of a witness's statement may be subject to production under Rule 615, but only if it is a substantially verbatim rendition, not mere excerpts or a summary of what the witness said. *See* **Williams**, 940 S.W.2d at 807.

743. **Epperson v. State**, 650 S.W.2d 110, 112 (Tex. App.—Tyler 1983, no pet.).

744. *See* Tex. R. Evid. 615(f)(2); *see, e.g.*, **Newsome v. State**, 829 S.W.2d 260, 263-64 (Tex. App.—Dallas 1992, no pet.) (prosecutor's handwritten notes made in preparation for a retrospective **Batson** hearing did not constitute a "statement" under Criminal Rule 614, now Rule 615).

745. *See* **Mayfield v. State**, 758 S.W.2d 371, 375 (Tex. App.—Amarillo 1988, no pet.) (neither attorney-client privilege nor work-product exemption prevents discovery under former Criminal Rule 614, now Rule 615).

746. *See, e.g.*, **Johnson v. State**, 919 S.W.2d 473, 479 (Tex. App.—Fort Worth 1996, pet. ref'd) (statement was written by victim's stepson with information supplied by victim; statement was thus discoverable under Criminal Rule 614, now Rule 615, as a statement adopted or approved by the witness).

predominate.[747] The trial judge must review the recording in camera and determine whether the material is discoverable.[748] If the judge determines that the recording is not discoverable, it must be sealed and held for the appellate court.[749]

When the witness's statement is written or recorded by another person or by electronic means, the recording must be made contemporaneously with the witness's oral statement.[750] That is, a police officer cannot listen to the witness's recital, return to the police station, and write down or record what he remembers the witness saying. The risk of inaccuracy or editorial comment removes these writings and recordings from the rule.[751]

Under the rule, only witness statements in the sponsoring party's possession must be produced.[752] A prosecutor must produce those statements "possessed by the prosecutorial arm of the government."[753] In one case, the court of criminal appeals interpreted this assertion as meaning that production is required only if a statement is literally possessed by the prosecutor himself.[754] Such an interpretation would render the rule useless because either the prosecutor or defense attorney could simply decline to accept possession of statements from a witness and then decline to have the witness produce them under the rule. Instead, the rule is interpreted in the federal system as applying to any statements in the actual or constructive possession of the government, which includes any statement actually possessed by any law-enforcement officer actively participating in the investigation of the particular case.[755] Of course, if the prior

---

747. **Cullen v. State**, 719 S.W.2d 195, 198 (Tex. Crim. App. 1986).

748. *Id.*

749. *Id.*

750. *See* Tex. R. Evid. 615(f)(2).

751. *Cf.* **United States v. Hodges**, 556 F.2d 366, 368 (5th Cir. 1977) (investigator's notes of witness interview were not a substantially verbatim recital, even though some phrases and sentences were verbatim excerpts); **United States v. Gross**, 766 F. Supp. 302, 311-12 (E.D. Pa. 1991) (individual lines in which attorney "accurately recorded isolated sentences or phrases" spoken by witness could not be compelled under the rule), *aff'd*, 961 F.2d 1097 (3d Cir. 1992).

752. *See* Tex. R. Evid. 615(a).

753. *See, e.g.*, **Jenkins v. State**, 912 S.W.2d 793, 819 (Tex. Crim. App. 1995) (op. on reh'g) (because record did not reflect that reports made by State's witness—a narcotics investigator for the prison system—were in the prosecutor's possession, trial court did not err in denying defendant's request to produce them).

754. *Id.*

755. *See* **Augenblick v. United States**, 377 F.2d 586, 597-98 (Ct. Cl. 1967) ("statement" under Jencks Act "need not be within the physical control of the prosecution" to be in its possession), *rev'd on other grounds*, 393 U.S. 348 (1969); *see, e.g.*, **United States v. Durham**, 941 F.2d 858, 861 & n.3 (9th Cir. 1991) (when federal authorities did not participate in a joint effort with local authorities, prosecutor did not have "possession" of statements taken by local authorities); **United States v. Heath**, 580 F.2d 1011, 1018-19 & n.1 (10th Cir. 1978) (when there was close cooperation between local police and federal prosecutor, prosecutor cannot "stand on technicality and say that he does not have actual possession" of the statement held by local authorities). In **Mayfield v. State**, the court avoided the issue of whether witnesses' prior statements made in contemplation of civil litigation, which were in the possession of a city attorney, not a prosecutor, must be produced for the defendant's use during cross-examination. 758 S.W.2d 371, 374-75 (Tex. App.—Amarillo 1988, no pet.). Instead, the court held that any possible error was harmless because the sealed record showed that the prior statements were consistent with the witnesses' trial testimony. *Id.* at 375.

The same definition applies under the rule set forth in **Brady v. Maryland**, 373 U.S. 83, 87 (1963), which requires the State to disclose exculpatory or impeaching reports and witness statements. *See* **Kyles v. Whitley**, 514 U.S.

statement has been lost or destroyed, the sponsoring party cannot produce it; thus, if the prior statement's nonculpable loss or destruction is adequately explained, the sponsoring party should not be sanctioned.[756] The sanction provision of Rule 615(e) applies only when a party "disobeys an order to produce or deliver a statement."[757]

As with Rule 612, Rule 615 trumps the work-product doctrine.[758] If, however, the prior writing or recording could be characterized wholly as work product, then it does not constitute a "statement" of the witness within the meaning of Rule 615 because it is the attorney's words, thoughts, and strategies that are memorialized, not those of the witness.[759] Conversely, if the writing or recording is composed wholly of the words of the witness himself, then the entire writing or recording is subject to production as a "statement" under the rule. The more difficult cases fall somewhere in between, such as an interview between the witness and the attorney or his representative. In those instances, the entire writing or recording should be submitted to the trial court for an in camera inspection, and only those specific portions that are the words of the witness should be produced for the impeaching party's use.[760]

RULE 615

419, 437-38 (1995) (individual prosecutor is held accountable for **Brady** evidence known only to police investigators); **Ex parte Mitchell**, 853 S.W.2d 1, 4 (Tex. Crim. App. 1993) (all members of law-enforcement team involved in any aspect of investigation or prosecution of a person are "agents of the State" for purposes of **Brady** and discovery material); **Ex parte Adams**, 768 S.W.2d 281, 291-92 (Tex. Crim. App. 1989) (federal precedent does not distinguish between different agencies under same government; "prosecution team" includes both investigative and prosecutorial personnel).

756. *See, e.g.*, **Villarreal v. State**, 504 S.W.3d 494, 520-21 (Tex. App.—Corpus Christi 2016, pet. ref'd) (trial court properly denied defendant's motion for production and for sanctions when prosecutor represented that witness's video statement to previous district attorneys was lost); **Cross v. State**, 877 S.W.2d 25, 27 (Tex. App.—Houston [1st Dist.] 1994, pet. ref'd) (although officer had made a prior "statement" by filling out an automobile inventory form, trial court did not err in declining to impose any sanctions when prosecution presented uncontroverted evidence showing that these forms were routinely destroyed one year after they were made).

757. Tex. R. Evid. 615(e); *e.g.*, **Villarreal**, 504 S.W.3d at 520-21 (trial court did not order production of witness's video statement because video was lost and no longer in State's possession; because State did not fail to comply with an order to deliver statement, sanctions were not appropriate); *see also* **Jenkins**, 912 S.W.2d at 804 (orig. op.) (party contesting production must show why the statement cannot or should not be produced under the rule). Refer to notes 768-769 *infra* and accompanying text.

758. *See* **Jordan v. State**, 897 S.W.2d 909, 913-16 (Tex. App.—Fort Worth 1995, no pet.) (Criminal Rule 614, now Rule 615, does not exempt otherwise producible statements from production because they constitute work product). Refer to notes 570-575 *supra* and accompanying text.

759. **Jordan**, 897 S.W.2d at 916.

760. *Id.* at 918. The **Jordan** court quoted and followed the reasoning of the Supreme Court in analyzing the discoverability of prior witness statements under the Jencks Act, the federal equivalent of Texas Rule 615:

> Proper application of the Act will not compel disclosure of a Government's lawyer's recordation of mental impressions, personal beliefs, trial strategy, legal conclusions, or anything else that "could not fairly be said to be the witness' own" statement. "If a government attorney has recorded only his own thoughts in his interview notes, the notes would seem both to come within the work product immunity and to fall without the statutory definition of a 'statement.'" Furthermore, if a witness has for some reason "adopted or approved" a writing containing trial strategy or similar matter, such matter would be excised under §3500(c) as not relating to the subject matter of the witness' testimony or direct examination. Thus, the primary policy underlying the work-product doctrine—*i.e.*, protection of the privacy of an attorney's mental processes—is adequately safeguarded by the Jencks Act itself.

Jordan, 897 S.W.2d at 917 (quoting **Goldberg v. United States**, 425 U.S. 94, 106 (1976)).

Procedurally, the rule authorizes the opposing party to request production of the witness's statement at the beginning of cross-examination.[761] The rule is not automatic because the cross-examiner must request the statement.[762] If the court orders production of the statement, the cross-examiner—after a proper request—is then entitled to a recess to examine the statement outside the presence of the jury.[763] Because some witnesses' statements may be quite lengthy and thus require a protracted recess, the sponsoring party may choose to produce the statement earlier.[764] If the entire statement relates to the subject matter of the witness's testimony, the cross-examiner is entitled to the entire statement.[765] On the other hand, if the statement contains irrelevant or privileged material, the trial judge must review the entire statement in camera, order disclosure of pertinent parts, and order the sponsoring party to provide the opponent with a redacted copy of the statement.[766] If a party objects to any deleted parts, the original, complete copy of the statement must then be sealed and made available to the appellate court in the event of an appeal.[767] If any party refuses to produce the witness's statement, the judge must strike the witness's testimony on direct examination.[768] The rule is not discretionary. If the State refuses to produce the witness's statement, the court must take the further step of declaring a mistrial if the interest of justice so requires.[769]

If the trial court declines to order the production of the prior statement to the defendant, the appellate court will reverse the trial judge's ruling only if the defendant demonstrates harmful error.[770]

---

761. *See Davis v. State*, 780 S.W.2d 945, 949 (Tex. App.—Fort Worth 1989, pet. ref'd) (under Criminal Rule 614, now Rule 615, a defendant is entitled to inspect a police officer's offense report only after the officer has testified on direct examination). In *Davis*, the prosecutor agreed to give a copy of the statement to defense counsel before direct examination began, and the court so ordered. *Id.* at 950. The court rejected the defendant's claim that the prosecutor's demand for the return of the report during an overnight recess while the officer was still on direct examination was prosecutorial misconduct when the failure to comply would lead to a "closed-file" policy in the future. *Id.*

762. *See* Tex. R. Evid. 615(a).

763. *See* Tex. R. Evid. 615(d).

764. *See, e.g., Davis*, 780 S.W.2d at 950 (prosecutor could agree to production of witness's statement before witness took the stand).

765. Tex. R. Evid. 615(b).

766. Tex. R. Evid. 615(c).

767. *Id.* If the party requesting production does not ensure that the statements are included in the appellate record, the failure to disclose will be held harmless. *See Guerra v. State*, 760 S.W.2d 681, 694 (Tex. App.—Corpus Christi 1988, pet. ref'd) (decided on common-law grounds).

768. Tex. R. Evid. 615(e); *see, e.g., Oldham v. State*, 743 S.W.2d 734, 735 (Tex. App.—Fort Worth 1987, pet. ref'd) (when State was unable to produce a copy of witness's statement during hearing on motion to revoke bond, court appropriately struck witness's testimony pursuant to the rule).

769. Tex. R. Evid. 615(e).

770. *See Fears v. State*, 479 S.W.3d 315, 326 (Tex. App.—Corpus Christi 2015, pet. ref'd); *see, e.g., Keith v. State*, 916 S.W.2d 602, 606 (Tex. App.—Amarillo 1996, no pet.) (when sealed report was consistent with witness's trial testimony and virtually all of the information in it had been developed at trial, nonproduction was harmless error; defendant was not deprived of effective cross-examination or possible impeachment); *Mayfield v. State*, 758 S.W.2d 371, 375 (Tex. App.—Amarillo 1988, no pet.) (any error from denial of defendant's request for production of po-

FEDERAL RULE 614:
COURT'S CALLING OR EXAMINING A WITNESS

Federal Rule 614 allows the court to call witnesses and to interrogate witnesses called by itself or by any party.[771] The Liaison Committee decided not to recommend—and the supreme court did not adopt—a similar provision for Texas. The consensus was that well-entrenched policies encouraging the trial judge to maintain an impartial posture in the trial[772] should not be eroded by a rule specifically allowing the court to participate in calling and interrogating witnesses.[773]

There is little Texas authority in this area. Presumably, the little authority that allows the judge to call and examine witnesses would still apply, and in appropriate situations, the trial judge may cautiously interrogate witnesses. In such questioning, the judge "should not indicate by words or manner" that he does not believe a witness's testimony.[774]

RULE 615

---

lice offense reports was harmless because the reports were consistent with trial testimony and with reports already in defendant's possession). For a discussion of harmful error, refer to *Article I: General Provisions, supra* p. 61.

771. *See **United States v. Modjewski***, 783 F.3d 645, 650 (7th Cir. 2015) (judge may examine witness but abuses that authority by acting as advocate; questioning by judge has less potential for prejudice in nonjury trials than in jury trials), *cert. denied*, 136 S. Ct. 183 (2015).

772. *See **Dall. Joint Stock Land Bank v. Britton***, 134 Tex. 529, 539, 135 S.W.2d 981, 986-87 (1940) (disapproving judicial comments on the evidence); ***Hargrove v. Fort Worth Elevator Co.***, 276 S.W. 426, 428 (Tex. Comm'n App. 1925, holding approved) (disapproving of judge's attempt to discredit witness).

773. *See **Morrison v. State***, 845 S.W.2d 882, 888 n.18 (Tex. Crim. App. 1992). In rejecting a trial court's discretion to permit jurors to pose questions for witnesses, the court of criminal appeals noted the following:

> We note that Texas' staunch loyalty to adversarial principles has been demonstrated in its stated disapproval of the nonadversarial practice of trial judges' examination of witnesses and in its rejection of Federal Rule of Evidence 614 which authorizes trial judges to call and interrogate witnesses. As recognized by Judge Benavides in his dissenting opinion, every state which has enacted a state version of the federal rules of evidence has adopted some version of Rule 614 with the exception of Oregon and Texas. Neither has Texas chosen to enact a rule authorizing the interrogation of witnesses by jury members. This absence indicates that the rule making authorities did not intend to endorse or authorize questioning of witnesses by judges or jurors.

Id.

774. ***Hargrove***, 276 S.W. at 428; *see **Rodrigues v. State***, 110 Tex. Crim. 267, 269, 8 S.W.2d 149, 150 (1928) (generally, court should refrain from active participation in examining witnesses to avoid reversal when injury is shown); ***Harrell v. State***, 39 Tex. Crim. 204, 225, 45 S.W. 581, 586 (1898) (it is not "any part of the duty of a judge to take in hand the examination or cross-examination of witnesses").

ARTICLE VII: OPINIONS & EXPERT TESTIMONY

Many common-law rules of evidence required a high level of specificity and were designed to promote the predictability and impartiality of trials.[1] Some commentators believe, however, that such specificity is based on a distrust of jurors' abilities and willingness to weigh properly the evidence placed before them.[2] Most of the modifications to these evidentiary rules[3] made by the Federal and Texas Rules of Evidence indicate an increased confidence in the jury system and the role of adversarial cross-examination.[4] The relaxed standards for admitting opinion testimony in federal courts reflect

---

1. Specific and detailed rules of evidence help make trials more efficient, uniform, and orderly by saving time and guarding against the eccentricity, bias, or thoughtlessness of a particular judge. *Cf.* PAUL E. ROTHSTEIN, EVIDENCE IN A NUTSHELL: STATE AND FEDERAL RULES 68-69 (2d ed. 1981) (focusing on the concern of some trial lawyers about the philosophical move apparent in the Federal Rules of Evidence toward the broader admissibility of relevant evidence and broader judicial discretion in evidentiary rulings). Paul Rothstein noted the following:

> These twin themes of admissibility and discretion have certain implications in addition to those already mentioned. Broad discretion means that even under the codification there will still be considerable diversity from circuit to circuit, district to district, judge to judge, which rules and codes are meant to eliminate. Discretion and broad phrases engender differences of opinion as to meaning and as to how discretion should be exercised.
>
> ....
>
> The ability of lawyers to plan, predict and advise—to proportion expenses to a case in advance, to give a reading of what it will cost and of the probabilities of outcome—is impaired under a code that gives broad discretion, because discretion means uncertainty. Can one precisely plan a case or give intelligent estimates of probability of outcome when he doesn't know what evidence is going to be admissible because admissibility hinges on the discretion of the judge? Can the attorney advise the client as to whether or not to go into litigation, how much to spend, how much it will cost, and the likelihood of success?

Id.

2. *See id.* at 6. Rothstein suggests that many, if not most, of the exclusionary rules and guidelines, whether mandatory or discretionary, exclude relevant evidence as unfairly prejudicial because jurors would otherwise allow the evidence, perhaps because of its emotional impact, to be more persuasive or influential than is warranted. *Id.* Jurors, it is reasoned, cannot be trusted to give the evidence its logical, rational weight or to perceive that it has none. *Id.* This view was frequently rejected by commentators even before the adoption of the original inclusionary Federal Rules of Evidence, on which the Texas Rules were built. *See* MCCORMICK'S HANDBOOK OF THE LAW OF EVIDENCE §62, at 140 (Edward W. Cleary ed., 2d ed. 1972) [hereinafter MCCORMICK'S HANDBOOK] (criticizing the Rules' ban on jurors hearing testimony from children or mentally incapacitated persons as "manifestly inappropriate").

3. *See, e.g.*, 2 JOHN H. WIGMORE, EVIDENCE IN TRIALS AT COMMON LAW §501, at 709 (Chadbourn rev. 1979) (noting the decline of the "mental derangement" exclusion), §515, at 721-22 ("moral depravity" is generally no longer a valid basis for exclusion); Edward J. Imwinkelried, *Federal Rule of Evidence 402: The Second Revolution*, 6 REV. LITIG. 129, 129-30, 174 (1987) (Federal rules have dramatically liberalized the admissibility of evidence, and Rule 402 is the centerpiece of the rules because it implicitly nullifies uncodified common-law rules of evidence).

4. During the 1980s, the U.S. Supreme Court was extraordinarily predisposed toward the admission of all relevant opinion evidence and relied on the adversary system of cross-examination to expose the possible unreliability of that evidence rather than advocating per se rules of exclusion. For example, in ***Barefoot v. Estelle***, the Supreme Court upheld the admission of expert testimony predicting that the capital-murder defendant would likely commit further acts of violence and thus represented a continuing threat to society, despite the American Psychiatric Association's view that psychiatrists and psychologists are wrong two out of three times when predicting violent behavior. 463 U.S. 880, 896-901 & n.7 (1983). The defendant's "entire argument ... is founded on the premise that a jury will not be able to separate the wheat from the chaff. We do not share in this low evaluation of the adversary process." *Id.* at 901 n.7; *see also* ***Rock v. Arkansas***, 483 U.S. 44, 61 (1987) (state evidentiary rule prohibiting admission of a defendant's hypnotically refreshed testimony without regard to the reliability of the evidence violated defendant's right to testify on his own behalf); ***Delaware v. Fensterer***, 474 U.S. 15, 16-17 (1985) (expert witness in a murder trial who could not remember which of three possible scientific methods he used to determine that hair found on the murder weapon had been forcibly removed from the murder victim could nonetheless give his opinion; witness's un-

this trend.[5] Texas's adoption of the original federal approach,[6] to the extent that it changed Texas law, was a similar expression of increased confidence in jurors' abilities.[7] Federal courts, however, had expressed concern about "junk science" in the courtroom. To guard against the admission of unreliable or irrelevant opinions offered by either lay or expert witnesses, the U.S. Supreme Court imposed a requirement that the trial judge act as a "gatekeeper" under Rules 702 and 104(a) to ensure the reliability of scientific evidence.[8] For the most part, Texas practitioners find that the Texas Rules of Evidence more readily admit opinion evidence than the common-law rules did and give considerably greater discretion to the trial judge in deciding whether a specific opinion is "helpful" to the fact-finder in a particular case.

RULE 701
OPINION TESTIMONY BY LAY WITNESSES

If a witness is not testifying as an expert, testimony in the form of an opinion is limited to one that is:

(a) rationally based on the witness's perception; and

(b) helpful to clearly understanding the witness's testimony or to determining a fact in issue.

Notes and Comments

Comment to 2015 restyling: All references to an "inference" have been deleted because this makes the Rule flow better and easier to read, and because any "inference" is covered by the broader term "opinion." Courts have not made

---

certainty about the scientific method used went to the weight of the evidence, not its admissibility). This view of the jury's ability to sort out reliable, firmly based opinions from those of dubious reliability had completely reversed itself by the 1990s in most federal and state courts.

5.   As noted by one commentator:

Article VII reflects the general philosophy of the Federal Rules, which favor admissibility of relevant evidence and leave attorneys to test the weight and persuasiveness of the evidence by free-wheeling cross-examination and effective summation. The opinion rules place much reliance, then, on the attorney and her abilities as an advocate. In the vast majority of cases, the natural dynamics of the adversary system operate effectively to determine truth and to produce fair, just, and sensible decisions.

George C. Pratt, *A Judicial Perspective on Opinion Evidence Under the Federal Rules*, 39 WASH. & LEE L. REV. 313, 331 (1982). In 2000, the U.S. Supreme Court transmitted to Congress significant amendments to Federal Rules 701 through 703 to reflect judicial limitations on the admission of opinion testimony by lay and expert witnesses. *See* Transmittal Letter, *Amendments to the Federal Rules of Evidence*, 192 F.R.D. 398, 400 (2000).

6.   Texas Rules 701 through 703 were originally almost identical to and had the same meaning as their federal counterparts.

7.   *See, e.g.*, **Montgomery v. State**, 810 S.W.2d 372, 375 (Tex. Crim. App. 1990) (orig. op.) (court rejected defendant's "invocation of the common-law's mechanistic rules which tended to favor exclusion of evidence"; Rules favor the admission of all logically relevant evidence for the jury's consideration); *see also* 2 STEVEN GOODE ET AL., TEXAS PRACTICE: GUIDE TO THE TEXAS RULES OF EVIDENCE: CIVIL AND CRIMINAL §701.1, at 3 (2d ed. 1993) (Texas rules on lay and expert testimony, like their federal counterparts, seek to reduce obstacles to the admissibility of relevant evidence).

8.   *See* **Daubert v. Merrell Dow Pharm., Inc.**, 509 U.S. 579, 597 (1993). Refer to notes 174-201 *infra* and accompanying text.

substantive decisions on the basis of any distinction between an opinion and an inference. No change in current practice is intended.

COMMENTARY ON RULE 701

Lay witnesses[9] traditionally were required to confine their testimony to facts they had perceived.[10] Rule 701 broadens the scope of lay-witness testimony, allowing a lay witness to offer opinions that are (1) rationally based on the witness's perception, and (2) helpful either to clearly understanding the witness's testimony or to determining a fact in issue.[11] Rule 701 does not substantively change earlier Texas law in either criminal or civil trials. It does, however, change how the witness testifies. Rather than asking whether the witness can testify more specifically and concretely, Rule 701 asks whether the witness's opinion is based on his own personal observations and is helpful to the fact-finder.

Federal Rule 701 was amended in 2000 to add another requirement that the opinion be "not based on scientific, technical, or other specialized knowledge within the scope of Rule 702."[12] The additional language was intended to prevent attempts to evade the reliability requirements of Federal Rule 702 for expert testimony by "proffering an expert in lay witness clothing."[13] When a witness in a federal case relies on

---

9.   The Rules classify witnesses as either "lay" or "expert," but the terms are not defined. This distinction, while traditional, is unfortunate. *See generally* Annotation, *Construction and Application of Rule 701 of Federal Rules of Evidence, Providing for Opinion Testimony by Lay Witnesses Under Certain Circumstances*, 44 A.L.R. FED. 919, 921-24 (1979) (summarizing the construction and application of testimony by lay witnesses under Federal Rule 701).

10.   Refer to notes 26-28 *infra* and accompanying text.

11.   *See* TEX. R. EVID. 701. Rule 701 was identical to the original version of Federal Rule 701. *See* Act of Jan. 2, 1975, Pub. L. No. 93-595, §1, 88 Stat. 1926, *reprinted in* 1974 U.S.C.C.A.N. 2215; 641-642 S.W.2d (Tex. Cases) LV (1983, amended 1998). Both rules were later amended to make the language gender-neutral. *See* FED. R. EVID. 701 advisory committee's note to 1987 amendments; 960 S.W.2d (Tex. Cases) LIX (1998).

Federal Rule 701 was restyled in 2011 to delete all references to "inference"; however, no substantive change was intended. FED. R. EVID. 701 advisory committee's note to 2011 amendments. The Advisory Committee explained that the restyling deleted all references to "inference" in the rule "on the grounds that the deletion made the Rule flow better and easier to read, and because any 'inference' is covered by the broader term 'opinion.' Courts have not made substantive decisions on the basis of any distinction between an opinion and an inference." *Id.* In the 2015 restyling of the Texas Rules, the Texas Supreme Court made the same change to Rule 701 based on the same reasoning. *See* TEX. R. EVID. 701 cmt. Texas Rule 701 is now identical to Federal Rule 701(a) and (b). *See* FED. R. EVID. 701.

12.   *See* FED. R. EVID. 701(c); FED. R. EVID. 701 advisory committee's note to 2000 amendments.

13.   FED. R. EVID. 701 advisory committee's note to 2000 amendments. The Committee noted, however, that "Rule 701 does not prohibit lay witness testimony on matters of common knowledge that traditionally have been the subject of lay opinions." 192 F.R.D. 405, 406 (2000) (report by Advisory Committee accompanying transmittal of proposed amendments to Federal Rules of Evidence to Congress). The Advisory Committee's notes seem to suggest that law-enforcement officers may testify to their opinions on the meaning or interpretation of their perceptions only as expert witnesses. *See* FED. R. EVID. 701 advisory committee's note to 2000 amendments (Committee cited *United States v. Figueroa-Lopez*, 125 F.3d 1241, 1246 (9th Cir. 1997), which held that law-enforcement agents could not testify under Federal Rule 701 that defendant's conduct was consistent with that of a drug trafficker); *see, e.g.*, *United States v. Garcia*, 291 F.3d 127, 140-41 (2d Cir. 2002) (participant in telephone conversation could testify to his use of drug code words during call but could not testify to defendant's use of code words or what those words meant to witness because no foundation was laid; witness offered no explanation for how defendant "could know

scientific, technical, or other specialized knowledge to formulate an opinion, the opinion must satisfy the stricter reliability requirements of Federal Rule 702 for expert testimony. Although the rationale for the federal rule's amendment is laudable, the amendment has sometimes led to technical debates over how much training and experience is enough to transform a witness's opinion from a layperson's into an expert's and whether a witness's opinions must be based *only* on personal perceptions or may be informed by general experience.[14]

Texas Rule 701, which has not been similarly amended, minimizes the importance of the distinction between lay and expert testimony.[15] Thus, Rule 701 is intended to prevent quarrels over whether a specific person is a lay witness or an expert.[16] Either kind

---

that they were speaking in code" or "that the code he used was a common one" or that defendant and he "had a prior agreement to speak in code or that they had discussed this possibility"); *cf. United States v. Novaton*, 271 F.3d 968, 1008-09 (11th Cir. 2001) (no abuse of discretion under former version of Rule 701 when trial court permitted police officers involved in investigation of drug conspiracy to give lay-opinion testimony, based on their perceptions and experience, about meaning of code words used by defendants in telephone conversations).

14.   *See, e.g., United States v. Haines*, 803 F.3d 713, 729-30 (5th Cir. 2015) (district court erred in not carefully distinguishing between lay and expert testimony offered by DEA agent), *cert. denied*, 137 S. Ct. 2107 (2017); *Bank of China v. NBM LLC*, 359 F.3d 171, 180-82 (2d Cir. 2004) (to the extent senior bank employee's opinions were based on his investigation of defendant's scheme, they were admissible as lay testimony, but to the extent the opinions "reflected specialized knowledge" based on employee's "extensive experience in international banking," they were not admissible as lay testimony); *Chen v. Mayflower Transit, Inc.*, 224 F.R.D. 415, 420 (N.D. Ill. 2004) (2000 amendments to Federal Rule 701 continue to permit "an officer of a business to testify about damages based on his personal knowledge and day-to-day experience with the business, without having to qualify as an expert"; court prohibited a witness who was not such an employee from testifying as a lay witness).

The difficulties of drawing a clear line between amended Federal Rules 701 and 702 were set out by Judge Gregory in *King v. Rumsfeld*:

> Although the contours of Rule 701 might upon first inspection appear straight-forward, considerable subtlety is often required to avoid the mischaracterization of competent lay opinion. Accordingly, courts have admitted lay opinion testimony under Rule 701 that goes well beyond the classic confines of physical perception, and which requires the exercise of judgment solidly grounded in personal knowledge. What we may derive from these cases is that the opinion testimony is not admitted due to the "specialized knowledge," which should be reserved for experts under Rule 702, but because of the particularized knowledge of a witness by virtue of his personal experience in a field (legal or not).

328 F.3d 145, 158 (4th Cir. 2003) (Gregory, J., concurring in part and dissenting in part) (citations omitted).

15.   *See* 3 JACK B. WEINSTEIN & MARGARET A. BERGER, WEINSTEIN'S EVIDENCE ¶701[02], at 701-32 (1995); *see, e.g., Lundy v. Allstate Ins.*, 774 S.W.2d 352, 357 (Tex. App.—Beaumont 1989, no writ) (in suit for recovery of insurance proceeds, fire technologist who testified that he had examined the fire site, expressed an opinion that the fire was intentionally set, and testified to various reasons why people deliberately set fires was qualified to testify as either an expert witness under Civil Rule 702 or a lay witness under Civil Rule 701); *cf. Teen-Ed, Inc. v. Kimball Int'l, Inc.*, 620 F.2d 399, 403-04 (3d Cir. 1980) (trial court abused its discretion in excluding lay opinion testimony from plaintiff's accountant about lost profits; it was immaterial that the accountant might also have been qualified as an expert because lay witnesses can give conclusions or opinion testimony based on personal experience with documentary or physical materials in a specific case). Refer to notes 140-141 *infra* and accompanying text.

16.   In *Osbourn v. State*, the court of criminal appeals explained the blurring between Rules 701 and 702:

> [E]xpert testimony serves the purpose of allowing certain types of relevant, helpful testimony by a witness who does not possess personal knowledge of the events about which he or she is testifying.
>
> When a witness who is capable of being qualified as an expert testifies regarding events which he or she personally perceived, the evidence may be admissible as both Rule 701 opinion testimony and Rule 702 expert testimony. A person with specialized knowledge may testify about his or her own observations under Rule 701 and may also testify about the theories, facts and data used in his or her area

of witness may give an opinion if it is based on personal knowledge and is helpful to the jury.[17] For example, courts routinely permit police officers, under either Rule 701 or 702, to interpret "street slang" that might otherwise have little or no meaning to the average juror.[18]

---

of expertise under Rule 702. … Thus, although police officers have training and experience, they are not precluded from offering lay testimony regarding events which they have personally observed.

. . . .

A distinct line cannot be drawn between lay opinion and expert testimony because all perceptions are evaluated based on experiences. However, as a general rule, observations which do not require significant expertise to interpret and which are not based on a scientific theory can be admitted as lay opinions if the requirements of Rule 701 are met. This is true even when the witness has experience or training. Additionally, even events not normally encountered by most people in everyday life do not necessarily require the testimony of an expert. The personal experience and knowledge of a lay witness may establish that he or she is capable, without qualification as an expert, of expressing an opinion on a subject outside the realm of common knowledge.

92 S.W.3d 531, 535-37 (Tex. Crim. App. 2002); *see, e.g.*, *Ellison v. State*, 201 S.W.3d 714, 723 (Tex. Crim. App. 2006) (probation officer could testify to her opinion of defendant's probation because "the probation officer not only based her testimony on her general professional knowledge and experience but also on her personal knowledge and perceptions of [defendant] and the complainant during their interviews"); *Williams v. State*, 191 S.W.3d 242, 253-54 (Tex. App.—Austin 2006, no pet.) (patrol officer trained as "mental health officer" could testify under Rule 701 that he did not see any indication that defendant suffered from mental illness; observations did not require significant expertise); *King v. State*, 129 S.W.3d 680, 683-84 (Tex. App.—Waco 2004, pet. ref'd) (police officer with ten years' experience who had many encounters with drug dealers and users could testify under Rule 701 that burn marks on lips and fingers are typical of crack-cocaine smokers; absence of such marks on defendant implied that he possessed cocaine for delivery, not personal use); *Salazar v. State*, 127 S.W.3d 355, 361-62 (Tex. App.—Houston [14th Dist.] 2004, pet. ref'd) (testimony by counselors of sexually abused children was admissible under Rule 701 during punishment stage because that testimony concerned factual accounts of counseling sessions and consisted primarily of observations, not expert opinions; because defense did not object that witnesses were offering expert opinions, any error in admission of testimony was waived). *But see King*, 129 S.W.3d at 684-85 (Gray, C.J., concurring) (police officer's testimony about burn marks or amount of cocaine generally held for personal use was not admissible as lay-opinion testimony but was admissible as expert testimony under Rule 702; lay witness "can give an opinion regarding things that are within the type that the average person would form based upon first hand observations"). Refer to notes 105-136 *infra* and accompanying text.

17. *See Osbourn*, 92 S.W.3d at 536; *see, e.g.*, *Davis v. State*, 313 S.W.3d 317, 349-50 (Tex. Crim. App. 2010) (police detective's testimony about wounds inflicted on murder victim's cat was properly admitted under Rule 701 because detective personally observed wounds and his observations did not require significant expertise to interpret; trial court would not have abused its discretion if it had admitted testimony under Rule 702); *Brown v. State*, 303 S.W.3d 310, 320-21 (Tex. App.—Tyler 2009, pet. ref'd) (police officers could testify as lay witnesses to what they observed at accident scene); *McRae v. State*, 152 S.W.3d 739, 745-46 (Tex. App.—Houston [1st Dist.] 2004, pet. ref'd) (police officer could testify as a lay witness about his observations of a DWI suspect's performance on the one-leg-stand test because it "is grounded in the common knowledge that excessive alcohol consumption can cause problems with coordination, balance, and mental agility"); *Robbins v. Reliance Ins.*, 102 S.W.3d 739, 748-49 (Tex. App.—Corpus Christi 2001, no pet.) (opinion of insurer's corporate representative that "an individual certificate controlled over the master certificate as to the benefits to which an insured was entitled," as a species of legal opinion by one experienced in this area, was admissible under either Rule 701 or 702); *Taylor Foundry Co. v. Wichita Falls Grain Co.*, 51 S.W.3d 766, 773-74 (Tex. App.—Fort Worth 2001, no pet.) (plaintiff's vice-president could give his lay and expert opinions in suit for damages resulting from defendant's interference with railway easement because his opinions were based on personal perception and business experience); *Harnett v. State*, 38 S.W.3d 650, 659 (Tex. App.—Austin 2000, pet. ref'd) (social worker who counseled sexual-assault defendant and victim could testify to her opinions under either Rule 701 or 702 based on her perceptions during counseling sessions and her years of training and experience); *Amunson v. State*, 928 S.W.2d 601, 606 (Tex. App.—San Antonio 1996, pet. ref'd) (under Criminal Rules 701 and 702, sheriff's deputy could give her opinion about the lividity—the pooling of blood causing skin discoloration—of murder victim's body based on her personal perception and experiences); *Ventroy v. State*, 917 S.W.2d 419, 422 (Tex. App.—San Antonio 1996, pet. ref'd) (officer's opinion about circumstances of car accident was admissible under both Rules 701 and 702 when officer personally investigated accident and had sig-

RULE 701

A. Rule 701(a): Testimony Rationally Based on Witness's Perception

The first requirement of Rule 701 is that the opinions about which a lay witness testifies must be rationally based on the witness's perceptions.[19] This requirement is two-pronged. "First, the witness must establish personal knowledge of the events from

nificant accident-investigation experience); *Thomas v. State*, 916 S.W.2d 578, 581 (Tex. App.—San Antonio 1996, no pet.) (police officer's opinion testimony on how "drug house" operations are run was admissible under both Criminal Rules 701 and 702); *McCray v. State*, 873 S.W.2d 126, 128 (Tex. App.—Beaumont 1994, no pet.) (officer's testimony that victim had been "trapped" behind door based on his analysis of blood-spatter evidence was admissible under either Criminal Rule 701 or 702 when officer had investigated homicide scene and had significant experience and formal training in crime-scene investigations); *Carter v. Steere Tank Lines, Inc.*, 835 S.W.2d 176, 182 (Tex. App.—Amarillo 1992, writ denied) (police officer may offer an opinion as a lay or expert witness; trial court improperly excluded a DPS trooper's opinion on the proper method of turning left because that testimony was based on his own personal observations and experiences as a police officer); *see also Loper v. Andrews*, 404 S.W.2d 300, 305 (Tex. 1966) (in Texas, opinion testimony that is not based on personal knowledge is not permitted unless given by an expert who is qualified in that subject matter).

Sometimes, however, Texas courts still attempt to rigidly categorize a witness's opinion as "lay" or "expert" determined by whether the opinion is based on "personal perception" or "personal perception, training, and experience." *See Tex. Dep't of Pub. Safety v. Struve*, 79 S.W.3d 796, 803 (Tex. App.—Corpus Christi 2002, pet. denied) (police officer may express his lay opinion, based on personal observation, that defendant is intoxicated, but if he "bases his opinion not only on observations, but also on his training and experience, then his qualification must be established under Rule 702"); *Riley v. State*, 988 S.W.2d 895, 898-99 (Tex. App.—Houston [14th Dist.] 1999, no pet.) (trial court erred in admitting officer's opinion that defendant was intoxicated based on his personal perception, training, and experience when witness had not been qualified as an expert). Generally speaking, "[a]n expert must possess some additional knowledge or expertise beyond that possessed by the average person, but the gap need not necessarily be monumental." *Davis*, 313 S.W.3d at 350.

18.   *See, e.g., Johnson v. State*, 975 S.W.2d 644, 654 (Tex. App.—El Paso 1998, pet. ref'd) (officer could testify that when defendant told him at murder scene that she was tired of victim trying to "talk to" another woman, she meant victim was flirting with another woman); *Austin v. State*, 794 S.W.2d 408, 409-11 (Tex. App.—Austin 1990, pet. ref'd) (vice officer could testify under either Rule 701 or 702 that advertisement in massage parlor for "Swedish Deep Muscle Rub" was a catchphrase for prostitution); *Revada v. State*, 761 S.W.2d 426, 431-32 (Tex. App.—Houston [14th Dist.] 1988, no pet.) (narcotics officer could testify that "set man" meant dealer in pentazocine); *cf. United States v. Parsee*, 178 F.3d 374, 379-80 (5th Cir. 1999) (in drug trial, witness could testify as lay witness to use of word "pants" in phone conversation as a code for drugs because she was a participant in those conversations).

19.   TEX. R. EVID. 701(a); *see Reid Rd. Mun. Util. Dist. No. 2 v. Speedy Stop Food Stores, Ltd.*, 337 S.W.3d 846, 850 (Tex. 2011) ("[N]ot all witnesses who are experts necessarily testify as experts. A witness may have special knowledge, skill, experience, training, or education in a particular subject, but testify only to matters based on personal perception and opinions."); *cf. United States v. Conn*, 297 F.3d 548, 554 (7th Cir. 2002) ("Lay opinion testimony most often takes the form of a summary of first-hand sensory observations."). The 2015 restyling deleted all references to "inference" in the rule; however, no substantive change was intended. Refer to note 11 *supra*.

In *Asplundh Mfg. Div. v. Benton Harbor Eng'g*, the court stated:

The prototypical example of the type of evidence contemplated by the adoption of Rule 701 relates to the appearance of persons or things, identity, the manner of conduct, competency of a person, degrees of light or darkness, sound, size, weight, distance, and an endless number of items that cannot be described factually in words apart from inferences. ... Other examples of this type of quintessential Rule 701 opinion testimony include identification of an individual, the speed of a vehicle, the mental state or responsibility of another, whether another was healthy, the value of one's property, and other situations in which the differences between fact and opinion blur and it is difficult or cumbersome for the examiner to elicit an answer from the witness that will not be expressed in the form of an opinion.

57 F.3d 1190, 1196-98 (3d Cir. 1995) (footnotes omitted).

"Perceptions refer to a witness's interpretation of information acquired through his or her own senses or experiences at the time of the event (i.e., things the witness saw, heard, smelled, touched, felt, or tasted)." *Osbourn*, 92 S.W.3d at 535. A witness's perception or opportunity to observe does not need to be extensive for the testimony to be relevant and admissible. *See, e.g., United States v. Mooney*, 417 F.2d 936, 939 (8th Cir. 1969) (15-second look was sufficient to identify defendant).

which his opinion is drawn and, second, the opinion drawn must be rationally based on that knowledge."[20] A witness's opinion about a personal perception must logically flow from his personal knowledge and experience to be "rationally" based.[21] Thus, opinion testimony cannot be excluded under Rule 701 merely because the witness was not certain of his observation or recollection.[22] Certainty is not required of a witness, and qualifications such as "I believe," "I think," "in my opinion," or "it was my impression" are not grounds for exclusion[23] unless it is apparent to the judge that the witness is merely speculating, guessing, or relying wholly on hearsay to form his opinion.[24] If the proponent does not establish personal perception and knowledge, the trial court must exclude the lay witness's opinion.[25]

The common-law rule prohibited lay opinions, requiring witnesses to testify to specific facts perceived rather than in terms of opinions drawn from those perceptions.[26]

20.   *Fairow v. State*, 943 S.W.2d 895, 898 (Tex. Crim. App. 1997); *see, e.g.*, *Yancy v. United Surgical Partners Int'l, Inc.*, 236 S.W.3d 778, 782 (Tex. 2007) (registered nurse was competent to testify about her personal observations of patient). The perception requirement is an extension of the requirement of firsthand knowledge established by Rule 602. *See* Tex. R. Evid. 602 ("A witness may testify to a matter only if evidence is introduced sufficient to support a finding that the witness has personal knowledge of the matter."). Refer to *Article VI: Witnesses, supra* p. 567.

21.   *See Fairow*, 943 S.W.2d at 900 ("An opinion is rationally based on perception if it is an opinion that a reasonable person could draw under the circumstances."); *see, e.g.*, *United States v. Diaz*, 637 F.3d 592, 600 (5th Cir. 2011) (DEA agent could testify that defendant was acting as a lookout based on agent's perception of defendant's behavior: "standing near a drug transaction, looking side to side, and observing potential street traffic"); *United States v. Perkins*, 470 F.3d 150, 156 (4th Cir. 2006) (in excessive-force trial, police officers could testify to the use of force they observed; other officers who had not observed the event were improperly allowed to testify to whether the use of force was appropriate; responses to hypothetical questions required specialized knowledge and thus were not admissible under Federal Rule 701); *United States v. Cox*, 633 F.2d 871, 875-76 (9th Cir. 1980) (lay witness's opinion on conversations with defendant about defendant's involvement in a car bombing was not rationally related to her personal perception and knowledge); *Merrill v. Sprint Waste Servs. LP*, ___ S.W.3d ___ & n.6 (Tex. App.—Houston [14th Dist.] 2017, n.p.h.) (No. 14-16-00006-CV; 8-15-17) (in personal-injury lawsuit involving vehicle collision, trial court abused its discretion in excluding eyewitness testimony that described traffic violations committed by both drivers and offering opinion on fault; reasonable person could conclude, based solely on perception of collision, that both drivers were equally at fault); *James v. State*, 335 S.W.3d 719, 723-24 (Tex. App.—Fort Worth 2011, no pet.) (in domestic-assault case, police officer could give lay opinion that complainant "had just had the crap beat out of her" based on officer's perceptions of the scene when she responded to disturbance calls).

22.   3 Weinstein & Berger, *supra* note 15, ¶701[02], at 701-29 (even though a witness's testimony is not absolutely certain, such testimony is not barred by Rule 701 when it is based on personal knowledge); 2 Wigmore, *supra* note 3, §658, at 894-96 (judges will allow opinion testimony when the witness is personally acquainted with the material).

23.   *See* Michael H. Graham, Federal Rules of Evidence in a Nutshell 370 (8th ed. 2011).

24.   This approach is consistent with earlier Texas practice. *See Cirilo v. Cook Paint & Varnish Co.*, 476 S.W.2d 742, 751 (Tex. Civ. App.—Houston [1st Dist.] 1972, writ ref'd n.r.e.) (the phrase "in my opinion" does not prohibit admission of otherwise admissible evidence); *Gibson v. Avery*, 463 S.W.2d 277, 281 (Tex. Civ. App.—Fort Worth 1970, writ ref'd n.r.e.) (the phrase "I guess" is not grounds for exclusion).

25.   *See Bigby v. State*, 892 S.W.2d 864, 889 (Tex. Crim. App. 1994) (lay witness may not give an opinion of a person's mental competency when that opinion is based on the observations and opinions of others); *McMillan v. State*, 754 S.W.2d 422, 425 (Tex. App.—Eastland 1988, pet. ref'd) (lay-witness opinion based on hearsay is inadmissible).

26.   There are two difficulties with this restriction. First, people normally communicate by using opinions and conclusions (such as the weather is "clear" or the woman is "angry"). Forcing a witness to avoid normal conversation patterns often results in disjointed, affected, and unconvincing testimony. *See, e.g.*, *United States v. Petrone*, 185 F.3d 334, 336 (2d Cir. 1950) ("To require [the witness] to unravel that nexus [of perceptions underlying an opinion] will, unless he is much practised in self scrutiny, generally make him substitute an utterly unreal—though honest—set of constituents, or will altogether paralyze his powers of expression."); *Nichols v. Seale*, 493 S.W.2d

RULE 701

Because the rule against opinion testimony stifled witnesses and created confusion rather than clarity, judges and commentators had long criticized it.[27] Further, strict enforcement of the prohibition on lay-opinion testimony was not only unworkable but also unhelpful to the courts.[28] The more flexible approach of Federal Rule 701 and Texas Rule 701 treats the opinion rule as a rule of preference that allows the witness to communicate firsthand knowledge as effectively as possible, without forcing a stilted

589, 593 (Tex. Civ. App.—Dallas 1973) (in the interest of judicial economy, witness may testify on the time of day without first disclosing the basis for that opinion), *rev'd on other grounds*, 505 S.W.2d 251 (Tex. 1974). Second, there is no distinct line between statements of facts perceived and statements of opinion. *See Beech Aircraft Corp. v. Rainey*, 488 U.S. 153, 168 (1988) (difficult to distinguish bright line between "fact" and "opinion," which ultimately becomes a matter of the degree of concreteness or specificity); *Lubbock Feed Lots, Inc. v. Iowa Beef Processors, Inc.*, 630 F.2d 250, 263 (5th Cir. 1980) (difference between "fact" and "opinion" is a difference in the degree of an expression's concreteness); *see, e.g., Woods v. State*, 13 S.W.3d 100, 104 n.9 (Tex. App.—Texarkana 2000, pet. ref'd) ("[T]he difference between what is fact testimony and what is opinion testimony becomes fuzzy. In the present case, when the witnesses are asked to compare a man in a picture on a videotape to a man present in court to determine if the person in court is the same as the person in the film, this would call for opinions or conclusions based on a comparative observation."). Even under the common law, Texas courts recognized that all testimony involves opinions. *See Gen. Motors Corp. v. Bryant*, 582 S.W.2d 521, 525 (Tex. Civ. App.—Houston [1st Dist.] 1979, writ ref'd n.r.e.); *Nichols*, 493 S.W.2d at 593. Further, opinions are often the best and sometimes the only way to bring facts to the jury. *See Colls v. Price's Creameries, Inc.*, 244 S.W.2d 900, 909 (Tex. Civ. App.—El Paso 1951, writ ref'd n.r.e.) (when there are numerous or complicated facts, the "best way" may be to give an opinion); *see, e.g., Mo. Pac. Ry. Co. v. Jarrard*, 65 Tex. 560, 566 (1886) (witness's opinion was the best way to recreate the scene).

Many common-law Texas cases recognized that a lay witness could testify in opinion form as a "shorthand rendition of facts" when giving a clear picture of the witness's impressions would otherwise be impossible. *See Fairow*, 943 S.W.2d at 900; *see, e.g., City of Fort Worth v. Lee*, 143 Tex. 551, 562, 186 S.W.2d 954, 960 (1945) (because it was apparently impossible for witness to describe her overall perceptions of an event on a fact-by-fact, perception-by-perception basis, it was not improper to allow her to testify to her mental impressions of the event produced by her perception of the facts); *Coxson v. Atlanta Life Ins.*, 142 Tex. 544, 548-49, 179 S.W.2d 943, 944-45 (1944) (lay witness could testify to another person's apparent good health and continuation of usual work manner); *H.E. Butt Grocery Co. v. Heaton*, 547 S.W.2d 75, 76 (Tex. Civ. App.—Waco 1977, no writ) (in slip-and-fall case, testimony was admitted that grapes looked as if they had been on the floor for a great length of time because pertinent fact based on witness's observations could not be adequately described). Post-Rules decisions have continued to admit opinion testimony as a "shorthand rendition of the facts." *See Jackson v. State*, 822 S.W.2d 18, 30 & n.7 (Tex. Crim. App. 1990); *Wilson v. State*, 854 S.W.2d 270, 276 (Tex. App.—Amarillo 1993, pet. ref'd); *Austin v. State*, 794 S.W.2d 408, 410 (Tex. App.—Austin 1990, pet. ref'd).

27. *See* GRAHAM, *supra* note 23, at 370 ("A clear line between fact and opinion is impossible to draw. In a sense all testimony to matters of fact is the conclusion of the witness formed from observed phenomena and mental impressions."); 3 DAVID W. LOUISELL & CHRISTOPHER B. MUELLER, FEDERAL EVIDENCE §375, at 614 (1979) (framers recognized that no satisfactory line divides "fact" and "opinion"); 7 JOHN H. WIGMORE, EVIDENCE IN TRIALS AT COMMON LAW §1929, at 39 (Chadbourn rev. 1978) (common-law opinion rule "has done more than any one rule of procedure to reduce our litigation towards a state of legalized gambling"). In *Central R.R. Co. v. Monahan*, Judge Learned Hand stated the following:

> The line between opinion and fact is at best only one of degree, and ought to depend solely upon practical considerations, as, for example, the saving of time and the mentality of the witness. It is hardly ever reversible error to admit such evidence; its foundation may generally be as conveniently left to cross-examination. Every judge of experience in the trial of causes has again and again seen the whole story garbled, because of insistence upon a form with which the witness cannot comply, since, like most men, he is unaware of the extent to which inference enters into his perceptions. He is telling the "facts" in the only way that he knows how, and the result of nagging and checking him is often to choke him altogether, which is, indeed, usually its purpose.

11 F.2d 212, 214 (2d Cir. 1926).

28. *See* EDMUND M. MORGAN, BASIC PROBLEMS OF EVIDENCE 220 (1962) (common-law opinion rule led to "many foolish reversals and still more foolish appeals"); 3 WEINSTEIN & BERGER, *supra* note 15, ¶701[01], at 701-07 (inconsistent delineation in rulings on opinion testimony has historically resulted in many reversals).

or unnatural form.[29] The witness should normally testify at the level of greatest specificity that is familiar to him and that also makes sense to the jury.[30]

B. Rule 701(b): Helpfulness of Witness's Testimony

The second requirement of Rule 701 is that the opinions about which a lay witness testifies must be "helpful to clearly understanding the witness's testimony or to determining a fact in issue."[31] Before the rule, Texas courts tended to base the admissibility of opinion evidence on whether a more specific statement was possible.[32] Under Rule 701, courtroom arguments focus more directly on whether the opinion is helpful, rather than whether a more specific statement of fact can possibly be made.[33] The helpfulness

---

29. *See United States v. Yazzie*, 976 F.2d 1252, 1255 (9th Cir. 1992) (lay-opinion testimony based on witness's observations is helpful in presenting information to the jury when the facts are complex or difficult to explain); *Petrone*, 185 F.2d at 336 (trial judge has discretion to allow conclusory lay-opinion testimony; foundation for opinions can be brought out on cross-examination). In some instances, the questioning may be phrased in a manner that only implicitly asks for an opinion. For example, in *Turro v. State*, the prosecutor asked the police-officer witness whether he had ever seen a drowning in which the victim entered the water fully clothed but was later found nude. 950 S.W.2d 390, 406 (Tex. App.—Fort Worth 1997, pet. ref'd). Because the officer was not explicitly asked for his opinion on whether those circumstances were reasonable or common, the testimony was not an opinion at all. *Id.*

30. Consider, for example, the following eyewitness testimony: "Mrs. Jones slapped her baby. The blow was very hard. That was what made the baby cry." The first sentence is factual, and the second includes both fact and opinion. Although the third sentence is opinion testimony, it still conveys factual information: that the baby had not been crying until Mrs. Jones hit him and that, except for the slap, there were no other apparent reasons for the baby to cry. Under the common law, a trial judge normally would have disallowed the third sentence and perhaps even the second. The witness would have had to explain laboriously that the baby did not appear to be hungry, thirsty, cold, or hot, and the jury would have had to infer from the individual facts that the baby cried because his mother slapped him. Under Rule 701, the judge has discretion to permit the witness to express an opinion even when the witness could explain all of his sensory perceptions and relate only the perceived facts. Refer to notes 70-76 *infra* and accompanying text. Thus, one trial judge might require the witness to testify to all the circumstances that he observed—the lack of a wet diaper, the comfort level of the room temperature, the empty formula bottle—and exclude the ultimate opinion that the baby cried because he was slapped. Another judge might exercise his discretion by deciding that the cause-and-effect relationship could, if disputed, be further explored on cross-examination and allow the opinion without further factual predicate. A third judge might allow the opinion to be offered, but if the other party objects, the judge might permit an immediate voir dire examination to test the witness's personal knowledge and basis for that opinion.

31. TEX. R. EVID. 701(b). The 2015 restyling deleted all references to "inference" in the rule; however, no substantive change was intended. Refer to note 11 *supra*.

32. *See* 2 ROY R. RAY, TEXAS PRACTICE: TEXAS LAW OF EVIDENCE CIVIL AND CRIMINAL §1398, at 17 (3d ed. 1980) (theory for receiving opinions of lay witnesses "contemplates that the opinion shall be an automatic reflection of facts incapable of adequate description to the jury").

Despite focusing primarily on the degree of testimonial specificity in deciding whether to admit opinion evidence, Texas courts often applied a common-law version of Rule 701(b)'s helpfulness test. *See Nichols v. Seale*, 493 S.W.2d 589, 596 (Tex. Civ. App.—Dallas 1973) (discretion to admit conclusory testimony "may properly be exercised to give the jury the benefit of specific data"), *rev'd on other grounds*, 505 S.W.2d 251 (Tex. 1974); *Found. Reserve Ins. v. Starnes*, 479 S.W.2d 330, 334 (Tex. Civ. App.—Fort Worth 1972, no writ) (nonexpert's opinion, conclusion, or inference will be received "only when it appears that it will be of assistance to the jury").

33. Some sensory experiences cannot be fully or accurately conveyed by giving a factual description of the witness's perceptions, and the witness must give an opinion. For example, if a witness testifies that an odor perceived on some earlier occasion "smelled like vinegar," the testimony is an opinion—the witness is comparing the odor to another odor. But if the witness were not allowed to express this opinion, it would be impossible to describe the odor so that the trier of fact would understand the witness's perception. In situations like this, opinion testimony is much more helpful to the judge or juror than any factual description the witness might give. *See* 4 JACK B. WEINSTEIN & MARGARET A. BERGER, WEINSTEIN'S FEDERAL EVIDENCE §701.02, at 701-4 (Joseph M. McLaughlin ed., 2d ed. 2010).

requirement is really an embellishment of the relevance requirement of Rule 403, which implicitly authorizes the exclusion of any testimony when its probative value is substantially outweighed by countervailing dangers of unfair prejudice, confusing the issues, or misleading the jury.[34] Rule 701 directs a court's attention to the potential benefit of some opinions and trusts the jury's ability to properly evaluate that type of testimony.[35]

Witnesses should not be allowed to give personal opinions on a subject when the jury possesses the same information as the witness, fully understands the matter, and can draw the proper conclusions.[36] On the other hand, if the jury cannot fully understand the matter or draw the proper conclusions, the witness's opinion testimony may be helpful under Rule 701.[37] Opinion testimony that amounts to little more than choosing which witnesses should be believed[38] or which party to the lawsuit should prevail is not admissible under Rule 701.[39] Thus, under Rule 701, neither a lay witness[40] nor

---

34. *See **Holloway v. State***, 613 S.W.2d 497, 502 (Tex. Crim. App. 1981) ("[E]xpert opinion evidence must be tested and limited by the same considerations as other evidence in determining its admissibility: whether its probative value outweighs its prejudicial potential."); Pratt, *supra* note 5, at 315 (helpfulness limitation "is nothing more than a special adaptation of Rule 403, which permits exclusion of relevant evidence on grounds of prejudice, confusion, or waste of time"); *see also **United States v. Scavo***, 593 F.2d 837, 844 (8th Cir. 1979) (expert testimony may be excluded under Federal Rules 702 and 403); ***Am. Bearing Co. v. Litton Indus., Inc.***, 540 F. Supp. 1163, 1170 (E.D. Pa. 1982) (admissibility of economist's testimony is subject to Federal Rule 403), *aff'd*, 729 F.2d 943 (3d Cir. 1984).

35. *See, e.g.*, ***Ruffin v. State***, 270 S.W.3d 586, 588, 595 (Tex. Crim. App. 2008) (both lay and expert witnesses can testify to "a mental disease or defect that directly rebuts the particular *mens rea* necessary for the charged offense"; jurors are "sufficiently sophisticated" to evaluate that testimony).

36. ***Roberts v. State***, 743 S.W.2d 708, 711 (Tex. App.—Houston [14th Dist.] 1987, pet. ref'd); *see, e.g.*, ***Woods v. State***, 13 S.W.3d 100, 103-04 (Tex. App.—Texarkana 2000, pet. ref'd) (opinions of witnesses about identity of robber based solely on viewing surveillance videotape were not helpful to jury and were inadmissible because jury had the same facts and could make the same comparison as those witnesses; however, opinions of witnesses who knew defendant or had personally seen robber could be helpful to jury and were admissible).

One common-law test required opinions to be "necessary" to the resolution of issues. *See* McCormick on Evidence §11, at 27 (Edward W. Cleary ed., 3d ed. 1984). However, "necessity as a standard for permitting opinions and conclusions has proved too elusive and too unadaptable to particular situations for purposes of satisfactory judicial administration." Fed. R. Evid. 701 advisory committee's note.

The helpfulness requirement of Rule 701 returns the opinion rule to its original basis. According to Roy Ray:
[T]he true theory of the Opinion rule is that of the exclusion of superfluous evidence. The witness may be competent and the sources of his information sufficient but his testimony is not needed. The principle rests entirely upon policy. It may be broadly stated thus: Whenever the tribunal is in possession of the same information as the witness and the latter can add nothing to that information his further testimony is unnecessary and in fact merely cumbers the proceedings.
2 Ray, *supra* note 32, §1393, at 4.

37. *See **Merrill v. Sprint Waste Servs. LP***, ___ S.W.3d ___ (Tex. App.—Houston [14th Dist.] 2017, n.p.h.) (No. 14-16-00006-CV; 8-15-17) (eyewitness opinion testimony can be helpful if it assists jury in making factual determinations or clarifies witness's perceptions); *see, e.g.*, ***Thomas v. State***, 774 S.W.2d 26, 29 (Tex. App.—Beaumont 1989, no pet.) (police officer could give opinion testimony interpreting defendant's actions as "stalking"); ***Byrum v. State***, 762 S.W.2d 685, 689-90 (Tex. App.—Houston [14th Dist.] 1988, no pet.) (police officer could testify about defendant's intent because officer's opinion was rationally related to his perception of defendant's actions and helped the jury understand the entirety of witness's testimony).

38. *See, e.g.*, ***Arzaga v. State***, 86 S.W.3d 767, 775-76 (Tex. App.—El Paso 2002, no pet.) (officer's opinion, based on having responded to 25 domestic-violence calls and offered under Rule 701, that victim and witnesses were telling the truth about assault was improper bolstering of those witnesses' credibility).

39. *See **Fairow v. State***, 943 S.W.2d 895, 899 (Tex. Crim. App. 1997) ("[I]f the witness's lack of personal knowledge yields testimony that amounts to 'choosing up sides' or an opinion of guilt or innocence, his opinion should

an expert witness[41] may express an opinion on the proper punishment for a criminal defendant. Also, a lay witness in a civil trial cannot give an opinion on how much a plaintiff should recover for pain and suffering because the amount of these damages is speculative and "peculiarly within the province of the jury."[42]

C. Permissible Subjects for Lay-Opinion Testimony

Rule 701 broadened the class of witnesses competent to express a lay opinion on a given subject.[43] For example, opinion testimony on the value of property or damages was frequently limited under the common law,[44] but under Rule 701 any witness who has personal knowledge of the property and an adequate basis for his opinion may give an opinion on the value of the property.[45] Thus, the owner of property can give lay-

---

be excluded."); *Viscaino v. State*, 513 S.W.3d 802, 812 (Tex. App.—El Paso 2017, no pet.) ("[N]o witness is competent to opine as to guilt or innocence, which is a conclusion to be reached by the jury ...."); MCCORMICK'S HANDBOOK, *supra* note 2, §12, at 26-29 (courts may exclude opinion testimony about how a case should be decided). This kind of testimony was also inadmissible under the common law. *See Gross v. State*, 730 S.W.2d 104, 106 & n.2 (Tex. App.—Texarkana 1987, no pet.) (Rule 701 "essentially codified the prior law on this subject").

40. *E.g.*, *Hughes v. State*, 787 S.W.2d 193, 196 (Tex. App.—Corpus Christi 1990, pet. ref'd) (opinion testimony by victim of aggravated robbery was not relevant to the jury's assessment of proper punishment because victim had no more expertise in assessing proper punishment than any juror); *Gross*, 730 S.W.2d at 105-06 (victim's opinion testimony that defendant should be given a lenient sentence was not admissible because victim was "in no better position to form an opinion than the jury itself, and the allowance of such an opinion in evidence would constitute merely an appeal to sympathy or prejudice, and would tend to suggest that the jurors may shift their responsibility to the witnesses").

41. *See Sattiewhite v. State*, 786 S.W.2d 271, 290-91 (Tex. Crim. App. 1989) (psychologist's expert opinion on whether the death penalty or life imprisonment was more appropriate for a capital-murder defendant would not assist jury in assessing proper punishment).

42. *Clark v. McFerrin*, 760 S.W.2d 822, 828 (Tex. App.—Corpus Christi 1988, writ denied). This type of opinion testimony is not helpful to the jury, which is in the same position as the witness and is capable of making its own determination on these issues.

43. The rule also broadened the kind of personal observations and experience on which a lay opinion can be based. For example, in *J.C. v. State*, the court held that a sexual-assault victim's stepfather could give his lay-opinion testimony about the age of bruises on the victim's legs and buttocks because he had seen victim's bruises and had previously had bruises himself. 892 S.W.2d 87, 89 (Tex. App.—El Paso 1995, no pet.).

44. *See* 2 RAY, *supra* note 32, §1422, at 63-64 (common law required a witness testifying about value to have knowledge of the market value, if one existed, knowledge of values in the vicinity, and knowledge based on personal observation rather than solely on hearsay).

45. *See Nat. Gas Pipeline Co. of Am. v. Justiss*, 397 S.W.3d 150, 155 (Tex. 2012) (property owner may testify to value of his property if testimony is based on market value and not on intrinsic or some other speculative value of property); *Dall. Cty. v. Crestview Corners Car Wash*, 370 S.W.3d 25, 41 (Tex. App.—Dallas 2012, pet. denied) (same); *see, e.g.*, *Coker v. Burghardt*, 833 S.W.2d 306, 309-11 (Tex. App.—Dallas 1992, writ denied) (automobile owner who went to various repair shops to determine the cost of restoring his car should be permitted to testify to the reasonable cost of repair despite his reliance on hearsay in forming his opinion); *Hochheim Prairie Farm Mut. Ins. v. Burnett*, 698 S.W.2d 271, 276 (Tex. App.—Fort Worth 1985, no writ) (witness with experience repairing fire-damaged houses who had viewed a house before and after a fire and who had been hired to make repair estimates was qualified to express a lay opinion about market value before and after the fire; court "could have found that his testimony was helpful to the jury").

The "Property Owner Rule" establishes that an owner is qualified to testify to the property's value, but the testimony must meet the same requirements as other opinion evidence. *Nat. Gas Pipeline*, 397 S.W.3d at 156. As with expert testimony, an owner's conclusory or speculative testimony will not support a judgment. *Id.*; *see Coastal Transp. Co. v. Crown Cent. Pet. Corp.*, 136 S.W.3d 227, 233 (Tex. 2004); *see, e.g.*, *Royce Homes, L.P. v. Humphrey*, 244 S.W.3d 570, 579-80 (Tex. App.—Beaumont 2008, pet. denied) (property owner who testified to value of his property but conceded he had pulled that figure "out of the air" gave speculative testimony that provided no evidence of damages); *Lefton v. Griffith*, 136 S.W.3d 271, 277 (Tex. App.—San Antonio 2004, no pet.) (homeowner's testimony that

RULE 701

opinion testimony on the value of that property even if he would not qualify to testify about the value of someone else's property.[46] Similarly, a business organization can also offer testimony through its employees on the market value of its property.[47] An employee of a company can also testify as a lay witness to his opinion of the company's operations.[48] Business owners and corporate officers are regularly allowed to testify as lay witnesses about profits reasonably anticipated from business activities that were lost because of another party's breach.[49]

---

she lost $60,000 on the sale of her home was conclusory because she did not provide any explanation or support for how she calculated that value). The Texas Supreme Court has held that a property owner's lay-opinion testimony about the value of the owner's property is "the functional equivalent of expert testimony"; thus, "property valuations may not be based solely on a property owner's *ipse dixit*. ... Evidence of price paid, nearby sales, tax valuations, appraisals, online resources, and any other relevant factors may be offered to support the claim. But the valuation must be substantiated; a naked assertion of 'market value' is not enough." *Nat. Gas Pipeline*, 397 S.W.3d at 159; *see DZM, Inc. v. Garren*, 467 S.W.3d 700, 703-04 (Tex. App.—Houston [14th Dist.] 2015, no pet.) (past purchase price alone is not sufficient to support finding of market value at later date); *see, e.g.*, *Zhu v. Lam*, 426 S.W.3d 333, 341 (Tex. App.—Houston [14th Dist.] 2014, no pet.) (witness's general familiarity with market value of homes in neighborhood was not sufficient to explain how he determined fair market value of particular home; trial court properly sustained objection that testimony was conclusory); *Oncor Elec. Delivery Co. v. El Halcon Invs. LLC*, No. 11-14-00164-CV (Tex. App.—Eastland 2016, pet. denied) (memo op.; 7-29-16) (although comparable-sales method was not available to determine ranch value, property owner could rely on knowledge from 15 years in ranch-real-estate market); *see also Sanchez v. State*, 521 S.W.3d 817, ___ & n.1 (Tex. App.—Houston [1st Dist.] 2017, pet. ref'd) (owner of stolen car testified about purchase price but did not specify when she bought it or how long she had it before it was stolen; without temporal context, testimony was insufficient to establish value of car at time of theft).

The Property Owner Rule is an exception to the requirement that a witness must establish certain qualifications to express an opinion on property values. *Nat. Gas Pipeline*, 397 S.W.3d at 157. However, not all people with personal knowledge of real property can necessarily testify to the property's market value as a lay witness under Rule 701. *See Reid Rd. Mun. Util. Dist. No. 2 v. Speedy Stop Food Stores, Ltd.*, 337 S.W.3d 846, 852 (Tex. 2011). If the witness's opinion is substantively based on specialized knowledge and training, not on personal familiarity with the property in question, the witness must be designated as an expert and be subject to discovery. *E.g.*, *id.* (witness's affidavit detailed his experience, knowledge, and expertise in real estate and did not demonstrate personal familiarity with the property; "[a]s such, and because he was not timely disclosed as an expert," trial court did not abuse its discretion in excluding his opinion under Rule 701); *see* Tex. R. Civ. P. 195.1-195.4; Tex. R. Evid. 702. See *O'Connor's Texas Rules * Civil Trials* (2017), "Securing Discovery from Experts," ch. 6-D, p. 579.

46. *Porras v. Craig*, 675 S.W.2d 503, 504 (Tex. 1984); *see Redman Homes, Inc. v. Ivy*, 920 S.W.2d 664, 669 (Tex. 1996); *Red Sea Gaming, Inc. v. Block Invs. (Nev.) Co.*, 338 S.W.3d 562, 572 (Tex. App.—El Paso 2010, pet. denied); *see also Holz v. State*, 320 S.W.3d 344, 350 (Tex. Crim. App. 2010) (in criminal-mischief case, unsupported lay opinion on property damage is insufficient to prove cost of repair, but expert testimony on cost of repair is not required under Penal Code §28.06(b)). This sort of lay-opinion testimony was also admissible under the common law. *See, e.g.*, *Std. Nat'l Ins. v. Bayless*, 338 S.W.2d 313, 320 (Tex. Civ. App.—Beaumont 1960, writ ref'd n.r.e.) (housewife with many years of experience as a shopper could give opinion on value of her property when the relevant measure of damages was value to the owner).

47. *See Reid Rd.*, 337 S.W.3d at 853. In *Reid Road*, the Texas Supreme Court held that business organizations, like individual property owners, are familiar with the value of their property; thus, certain employees can "com[e] within the Property Owner Rule and its presumption that a property owner is [qualified to testify to] the property's value." *Id.* The court further held that only "an officer in a management position with duties that at least in some part relate to the property at issue, or an employee of the entity in a substantially equivalent position," can give this testimony. *Id.* at 854-55.

48. *See, e.g.*, *Anthony Equip. Corp. v. Irwin Steel Erectors, Inc.*, 115 S.W.3d 191, 206-07 (Tex. App.—Dallas 2003, pet. dism'd) (owner of company could not testify under Rule 701 to the estimated cost to repair company crane with used parts when his only basis for knowledge was rejected dealer's bid using new parts); *Laprade v. Laprade*, 784 S.W.2d 490, 492-93 (Tex. App.—Fort Worth 1990, writ denied) (in divorce action, wife could testify as lay witness under Rule 701 to value of husband's trucking company because she had run the business for five years, knew what was paid for each of the trucks, and knew value of other similar businesses for sale); *cf. Lifewise Master Funding v.*

Although expert testimony is necessary to establish causation for medical conditions outside jurors' common knowledge and experience,[50] the Texas Supreme Court has held that "causation findings linking events and physical conditions could, under certain circumstances, be sufficiently supported by non-expert evidence."[51] Expert testimony is not necessary to prove causation when laypeople can reasonably use general experience and common sense to determine the causal relationship at issue.[52]

Both lay and expert witnesses may testify that a particular substance is marijuana[53] or that a person is intoxicated.[54] Long before the Rules were promulgated, the Texas Court of Criminal Appeals noted that "[i]n this State, the opinions of lay witnesses,

---

Telebank, 374 F.3d 917, 929-30 (10th Cir. 2004) ("In one group of cases, the courts found business owners' testimony admissible under [Federal] Rule 701 because the owners had sufficient personal knowledge of their respective businesses *and* of the factors on which they relied to estimate lost profits. In other cases, the owners offered valuations based on straightforward, common sense calculations."); *Tex. A&M Research Found. v. Magna Transp., Inc.*, 338 F.3d 394, 402-03 (5th Cir. 2003) (witness's affidavit testimony, based on particularized knowledge and experience, was admissible; Federal Rule 701 "does not preclude testimony by business owners or officers on matters that relate to their business affairs. Indeed, an officer or employee of a corporation may testify to industry practices and pricing without qualifying as an expert").

49. *Am. Heritage, Inc. v. Nev. Gold & Casino, Inc.*, 259 S.W.3d 816, 827 (Tex. App.—Houston [1st Dist.] 2008, no pet.); *see Ishin Speed Sport, Inc. v. Rutherford*, 933 S.W.2d 343, 352 (Tex. App.—Fort Worth 1996, no writ).

50. Refer to note 156 *infra* and accompanying text.

51. *Guevara v. Ferrer*, 247 S.W.3d 662, 665-66 (Tex. 2007).

52. *Id.* at 666; *Morgan v. Compugraphic Corp.*, 675 S.W.2d 729, 733 (Tex. 1984). In *Guevara*, the supreme court offered the following example:

> [I]f [decedent] had been pulled from a damaged automobile with overt injuries such as broken bones or lacerations, and undisputed evidence which reasonable jurors could not disbelieve showed that he did not have such injuries before the accident, then the physical conditions and causal relationship between the accident and the conditions would ordinarily be within the general experience and common knowledge of laypersons.

247 S.W.3d at 667.

53. *See, e.g.*, *Osbourn v. State*, 92 S.W.3d 531, 538-39 (Tex. Crim. App. 2002) (police officer could testify as lay witness that substance was marijuana; witness who can qualify as an expert may still offer a lay opinion under Rule 701 "about something she personally perceived"); *$7,058.84 v. State*, 30 S.W.3d 580, 584 (Tex. App.—Texarkana 2000, no pet.) (police officer could offer lay-opinion testimony under Rule 701 that "a green leafy substance" was marijuana even though he also qualified as an expert under Rule 702, but he could not offer expert testimony because he had not been designated as an expert before trial).

Under common-law precedent, a police officer could testify about the presence of marijuana but not about the presence of other controlled substances. *See Jordan v. State*, 486 S.W.2d 784, 785 (Tex. Crim. App. 1972); *Boothe v. State*, 474 S.W.2d 219, 220-21 (Tex. Crim. App. 1971); *see, e.g.*, *Curtis v. State*, 548 S.W.2d 57, 59 (Tex. Crim. App. 1977) (police officer could not look at a white or brown powdered substance and testify that it was heroin). Under Rule 701, however, an officer with personal knowledge of the distinctive appearance, smell, taste, or feel of a specific substance can testify that the exhibit is that substance (even though he is not a chemist or other expert) because his opinion would be helpful to the trier of fact. *Cf. Bender v. State*, 739 S.W.2d 409, 413 (Tex. App.—Houston [14th Dist.] 1987) (officer could testify about a substance based on sight and smell in accordance with the stipulation of facts signed by defendant in plea of no contest), *pet. ref'd*, 761 S.W.2d 378 (Tex. Crim. App. 1988). Further, under Rule 701, police officers may testify (based on their training, experience, and personal observations) that a defendant's actions are consistent with selling drugs, and they may give their lay opinion that a person was selling drugs. *See Reece v. State*, 878 S.W.2d 320, 325 (Tex. App.—Houston [1st Dist.] 1994, no pet.). Indeed, drug users may testify based on personal observations that a substance was an illicit drug. *See, e.g.*, *Roberts v. State*, 9 S.W.3d 460, 462-63 (Tex. App.—Austin 1999, no pet.) (girls who said they were familiar with appearance of marijuana, admitted they had smoked it, and knew its effects could testify that the substance they used was marijuana).

54. *See McCown v. State*, 192 S.W.3d 158, 164 (Tex. App.—Fort Worth 2006, pet. ref'd) ("A witness does not have to be an expert to testify that a person he observes is intoxicated by alcohol ...."); *see, e.g.*, *Webster v. State*, 26 S.W.3d 717, 724-25 (Tex. App.—Waco 2000, pet. ref'd) (defendant's ex-wife could testify that defendant was intoxi-

RULE 701

when competent, are admissible concerning sanity, insanity, value, handwriting, intoxication, physical condition—health and disease, estimates of age, size, weight, quantity, time, distance, speed, identity of persons and things."[55] Further, Texas courts have traditionally allowed lay witnesses to testify to a wide range of emotional states based on another person's appearance.[56]

Courts have admitted opinions about another person's state of mind (e.g., intent, knowledge) under Rule 701 that would have been excluded under the common law. Traditionally, Texas courts did not permit either lay or expert testimony about another person's state of mind, holding that such testimony violated the rule against opinions.[57] However, several Texas[58] and federal[59] courts have accepted testimony under Rule 701 about another person's unspoken state of mind.[60]

---

cated because of combination of alcohol and medication; "[c]onsidering the nature of the testimony and [witness's] relationship with [defendant], we conclude that her opinion was rationally based on her prior observations").

55. **Denham v. State**, 574 S.W.2d 129, 131 (Tex. Crim. App. 1978); see, e.g., **Bell v. State**, 163 Tex. Crim. 427, 428-29, 293 S.W.2d 771, 772 (1956) (though not a medical expert, police officer who examined wounds on victim's body could describe those wounds in terms of what kind of instrument caused them and which of two knives inflicted a specific wound); **Kindle v. State**, 162 Tex. Crim. 395, 397-98, 285 S.W.2d 740, 742 (1955) (sheriff who observed murder defendant while he was a prisoner before trial could give lay opinion of defendant's sanity); **Inness v. State**, 106 Tex. Crim. 524, 527-28, 293 S.W. 821, 822 (1926) (op. on reh'g) (lay witness who observed the facts on which he based his opinion could testify to another person's sobriety or lack thereof); **Gerland's Food Fair, Inc. v. Hare**, 611 S.W.2d 113, 119 (Tex. Civ. App.—Houston [1st Dist.] 1980, writ ref'd n.r.e.) (plaintiff could testify to her own physical health, but she could not testify that her seizures, headaches, poor vision, and motor impairment were caused by brain damage that she suffered in a fall).

56. See 2 RAY, supra note 32, §1429, at 89-90 ("[H]e may state that the person was boisterous or quiet, peaceable or threatening, respectful or insolent, friendly or hostile. He may also testify as to the existence or absence of emotions such as grief, anxiety, nervousness, joy, fear, anger, and surprise."); see, e.g., **Carmichael v. Harrison**, 165 S.W.2d 510, 511-12 (Tex. Civ. App.—Eastland 1942, no writ) (plaintiffs should have been allowed to offer witness testimony that defendant appeared scared or excited at the time of the accident).

57. See, e.g., **Winegarner v. State**, 505 S.W.2d 303, 305 (Tex. Crim. App. 1974) (upholding the exclusion of opinion testimony from a psychiatrist, who had examined defendant, about defendant's intent at the time of the murder). Refer to notes 26-28 supra and accompanying text.

The common law's general prohibition against a witness giving an opinion about another person's state of mind was roundly criticized by John Wigmore:

> The argument has been made that, because we cannot directly see, hear, or feel the state of another person's mind, therefore testimony to another person's state of mind is based on merely conjectural and therefore inadequate data. This argument is finical enough; and it proves too much, for if valid it would forbid the jury to find a verdict upon the supposed state of a person's mind. If they are required and allowed to find such a fact, it is not too much to hear such testimony from a witness who has observed the person exhibiting in his conduct the operations of his mind.

2 WIGMORE, supra note 3, §661, at 902.

58. See, e.g., **Turro v. State**, 950 S.W.2d 390, 402-03 (Tex. App.—Fort Worth 1997, pet. ref'd) (murder victim's sister could testify that victim had an "angry" telephone conversation with another person and could testify to her interpretation and opinions of the conversation because she heard the conversation, could perceive the inflections of the speakers' voices, and was familiar with both speakers); **Ethicon, Inc. v. Martinez**, 835 S.W.2d 826, 830-32 (Tex. App.—Austin 1992, writ denied) (trial court did not err in admitting lay-opinion testimony that the workers' compensation settlement award influenced employer's decision to disqualify employee; "Texas courts have consistently held that opinion or inference testimony about another's state of mind, rationally based on the witness's perception, is admissible under Rule 701"); **Campbell v. Groves**, 774 S.W.2d 717, 719 (Tex. App.—El Paso 1989, writ denied) (statements in witness's affidavit that the deceased "'would refer to various instances of someone persecuting him which did not happen'" and that "'he referred to the facts in the halucinating [sic] events, as if they were real,'" were not probative evidence of deceased's mental state because they were conclusory, but they could be considered "to the extent that they are what the witness based his perception on under Tex.R.Civ.Evid. 701 in deter-

In *Fairow v. State*,[61] the court of criminal appeals held that a lay witness may, under certain circumstances, testify to his opinion of another person's mental state. In *Fairow*, the defendant was charged with the capital murder of a robbery victim, and the defense attempted to introduce the testimony of the defendant's accomplice that another accomplice shot the victim "accidentally."[62] The court noted that applying the personal-knowledge requirement to testimony about another person's culpable mental state presents unique problems because "[i]t is impossible for a witness to possess personal knowledge of what someone else is thinking. The individual is the only one who knows for certain the mental state with which he is acting."[63] On the other hand, a lay

---

mining the testator was not of sound mind"); ***Chase Commercial Corp. v. Datapoint Corp.***, 774 S.W.2d 359, 368 (Tex. App.—Dallas 1989, no writ) (lay witness, defendant's employee who had worked closely with plaintiff, should have been permitted to express his opinion that if the witness had known that defendant's customer was in bankruptcy, he would not have assigned the lease to plaintiff; opinion was based on his personal knowledge and the working relationship between plaintiff and defendant; opinion would have been "helpful" to the determination of a fact in issue); ***Anguiano v. State***, 774 S.W.2d 344, 346 (Tex. App.—Houston [14th Dist.] 1989, no pet.) (police officer could testify in prostitution case to whether he believed the dialogue with defendant meant that "she was offering or agreeing to engage" in sex because the question asked officer's opinion of defendant's demeanor during their conversation and was therefore based on his perception); ***Byrum v. State***, 762 S.W.2d 685, 689-90 (Tex. App.—Houston [14th Dist.] 1988, no pet.) (police officer could testify to topless dancer's unspoken state of mind at dancer's public-lewdness trial because officer's testimony was rationally related to his perception of defendant's actions and helpful to understanding officer's testimony); ***Texaco, Inc. v. Pennzoil, Co.***, 729 S.W.2d 768, 838 (Tex. App.—Houston [1st Dist.] 1987, writ ref'd n.r.e.) (CEO of Pennzoil was properly permitted to testify on what certain parts of notes taken by another person during contract negotiations meant to him in forming an opinion that there was a binding contractual agreement between Pennzoil and Getty Oil).

59.   *See, e.g.*, ***United States v. Graham***, 856 F.2d 756, 759 (6th Cir. 1988) ("A government agent may, like any other witness, testify in the form of an opinion as to his understanding of a defendant's statement."); ***United States v. Davis***, 787 F.2d 1501, 1505 (11th Cir. 1986) (trial court did not commit reversible error in permitting witness in drug-conspiracy trial to tell the jury what he thought defendant meant by a certain statement); ***Bohannon v. Pegelow***, 652 F.2d 729, 731-32 (7th Cir. 1981) (trial court properly permitted witness in civil-rights action alleging wrongful arrest to testify that arrest was racially motivated because opinion was based on seeing the event occur); ***United States v. Smith***, 550 F.2d 277, 281 (5th Cir. 1977) (trial judge properly permitted government witness to testify that defendant knew and understood the requirements of a particular statute because witness had firsthand knowledge of that fact); *see also* ***United States v. Dicker***, 853 F.2d 1103, 1108 (3d Cir. 1988) (trial court erred in permitting witness to testify about meaning of conversation that did not use "code-like" language; interpretation of clear statements does not meet "helpfulness" test of Federal Rule 701).

60.   2 RAY, *supra* note 32, §1393, at 2 (Supp. 1991); *see, e.g.*, ***Rodriguez v. State***, 697 S.W.2d 463, 468-69 (Tex. App.—San Antonio 1985, no pet.) (trial court erred in permitting witness to testify to whether deceased thought he was going to die).

61.   943 S.W.2d 895 (Tex. Crim. App. 1997).

62.   *Id.* at 897.

63.   *Id.* at 899; *see also* ***Arnold v. State***, 853 S.W.2d 543, 546-47 (Tex. Crim. App. 1993) (opinion testimony about relevant campus conditions leading up to sit-in protest, offered to assist jury in deciding whether defendants acted willfully, was properly excluded because only defendants could testify to their state of mind at the time).

> As Judge Meyers reasoned in his concurring opinion in *Fairow*, however, this argument proves too much: *Arnold* reasons that an opinion about another's mental state should not be permitted because it is based on conjecture and can never be known for certain. This reasoning is at odds with what an "opinion" is. An opinion is one's *view* of something that cannot be known for certain, based on facts that can be known. …
>
> An opinion is simply the beliefs of the witness or inferences he has drawn; for this reason, it is important to ensure that the opinion is *based upon* identifiable facts within the personal knowledge of the witness.

943 S.W.2d at 904-05 (Meyers & Mansfield, JJ., concurring); *see also* ***Hall v. State***, 124 S.W.3d 246, 250 (Tex. App.—San Antonio 2003, pet. ref'd) (trial court did not err in prohibiting defense from cross-examining police of-

witness may express his own opinion or interpretation of the events he has perceived.[64] Thus, the witness may not testify, "A accidentally shot B." However, he may testify, "From all that I saw and heard, I concluded that A shot B accidentally." The court of criminal appeals noted, however, that sometimes a witness's opinion about another person's culpable mental state may not be helpful because the terms that describe such a mental state—"intentional," "knowing," "reckless," and "negligent"—have legal definitions that may differ from their common usage by the witness or the jury.[65] Therefore, the trial judge should consider any such differences in definition when deciding whether an opinion will help or confuse the jury.[66] In *Fairow*, the court of criminal appeals concluded that the trial court did not abuse its discretion in excluding the accomplice's opinion testimony.[67]

Under Rule 701, lay-opinion testimony on another person's sanity is admissible and may be sufficient to prove that issue.[68] Lay-opinion testimony may also be sufficient

---

ficer about what defendant was thinking when he first saw officer in parking lot; "lay witness cannot testify as to what a person is thinking because the actual subjective mental state of an actor can never be based on personal knowledge").

64. *Fairow*, 943 S.W.2d at 898-99. In reaching this conclusion, the court of criminal appeals discussed another opinion, *Doyle v. State*, 875 S.W.2d 21, 22-23 (Tex. App.—Tyler 1994, no pet.), in which the court of appeals discussed the distinction between a witness's testimony about another person's mental state and testimony about an event the witness has personally perceived. In *Doyle*, two prison guards witnessed a prisoner strike another guard and later testified that the blows were "intentional." 875 S.W.2d at 22. Although the guards did not, and could not, have personal knowledge of the mental state with which the defendant struck the blow, they did "possess personal knowledge of facts from which an opinion regarding mental state may be drawn." *Fairow*, 943 S.W.2d at 899; *see, e.g.*, *Ex parte White*, 160 S.W.3d 46, 53 (Tex. Crim. App. 2004) (lay witness's testimony that defendant "intentionally ran over the victims with his truck" was admissible under Rule 701); *Solomon v. State*, 49 S.W.3d 356, 364 (Tex. Crim. App. 2001) (car passenger's testimony that defendant was the person in the car who was responsible for robbery of pedestrian victim was based on personal knowledge and was admissible under Rule 701); *Roberson v. State*, 100 S.W.3d 36, 38-39 (Tex. App.—Waco 2002, pet. ref'd) (police officer could testify under Rule 701 that, based on his personal knowledge and experience, it was common for sexual-assault victims to "reveal progressively more" about abuse as they become more comfortable talking with law enforcement); *McKinney v. State*, 59 S.W.3d 304, 312-13 (Tex. App.—Fort Worth 2001, pet. ref'd) (harmless error to exclude child victim's testimony that he did not think his father—the defendant—meant to hurt him when defendant put victim in hot bath water; child's opinion about defendant's intent was rationally based on child's perception of event); *Aleman v. State*, 49 S.W.3d 92, 95 (Tex. App.—Beaumont 2001, no pet.) (child witness's testimony that another child reacted with an "ooh," which meant "nasty," on viewing pornographic videotape was admissible under rule because his opinion of what "ooh" meant was based on his own perception of another child's reaction).

65. *Fairow*, 943 S.W.2d at 900. This problem is addressed under Rule 704. Refer to notes 329-355 *infra* and accompanying text.

66. *E.g.*, *Fairow*, 943 S.W.2d at 900-01 (witness's testimony about whether defendant behaved "intentionally" was properly excluded when witness was never given the legal definition of "intentional").

67. *Id.* at 901 (trial judge could have excluded testimony because (1) the jury was in a position to form its own opinion, based on admissible facts, (2) the accomplice was never given the legal definition of "intentional," or (3) the opinion was based on inadmissible hearsay, not the witness's actual perception).

68. *See Ruffin v. State*, 270 S.W.3d 586, 588 (Tex. Crim. App. 2008) (both lay and expert witnesses can testify to "a mental disease or defect that directly rebuts the particular *mens rea* necessary for the charged offense"); *Bigby v. State*, 892 S.W.2d 864, 888 (Tex. Crim. App. 1994) ("[A] lay witness may testify as to his opinion that an individual is legally insane."); *Pacheco v. State*, 757 S.W.2d 729, 733 (Tex. Crim. App. 1988) ("Properly admitted opinion testimony of lay witnesses is sufficient to support a finding of insanity."); *see, e.g.*, *Williams v. State*, 191 S.W.3d 242, 253-54 (Tex. App.—Austin 2006, no pet.) (testimony of patrol officer that defendant "did not exhibit any signs characteristic of someone having a mental health issue" was admissible under Rule 701; officer's testimony "was not of

to prove other elements of a party's claim or defense (such as causation) whenever a layperson can determine that legal element with reasonable probability using general experience and common sense.[69]

D. Judicial Discretion Under Rule 701

The helpfulness standard of Rule 701(b) leaves the admissibility decision largely to the trial judge.[70] The judge is able to most accurately gauge the need for the opinion,[71] the centrality of the opinion to the material issues,[72] the adequacy of the factual basis for the opinion, and the witness's ability on direct or cross-examination to further specify and clarify his perceptions.[73] The emphasis is on what the witness knows, not on his ability to communicate with linguistic precision. Thus, Rule 701 gives greater discretion to the trial judge to assess whether the witness's opinion offers any help to the fact-finder and shifts the focus to the content of the witness's communication. Because different judges would undoubtedly assess these factors differently, and because the cold record never adequately conveys the nonverbal context of the trial, the trial court's de-

---

a scientific or technical nature, but was a patrol officer's opinions or inferences based on impressions and conclusions derived from perceptions of what he saw, heard, and observed during his encounter" with defendant).

69. *See, e.g.*, **Whalen v. Condo. Consulting & Mgmt. Servs., Inc.**, 13 S.W.3d 444, 448 (Tex. App.—Corpus Christi 2000, pet. denied) (lay witness's testimony that boardwalk wood had been split "for quite some time" was both admissible under Rule 701 and sufficient to prove causation in premises-liability case).

70. *Cf.* **United States v. Jackson**, 688 F.2d 1121, 1123-24 (7th Cir. 1982) ("The decision of whether or not to admit certain testimony under [Federal] Rule 701 is committed to the sound discretion of the district court .... [I]n order to conclude that such [opinion] testimony is admissible, the court must find that the witness' testimony is based upon his or her personal observation and recollection of concrete facts and that those facts cannot be described in sufficient detail to adequately convey to the jury the substance of the testimony."). Under this approach, the trial judge has great latitude in making a preliminary determination, in light of the specific circumstances, whether an opinion will be helpful to the jury in deciding a particular issue. Rule 104(a) details the procedure used to make preliminary determinations of admissibility. Refer to *Article I: General Provisions, supra* p. 86.

71. Generally, the greater the necessity for admitting a lay opinion, the more likely it will be helpful to the trier of fact. *See, e.g.*, **Nichols v. Seale**, 493 S.W.2d 589, 595 (Tex. Civ. App.—Dallas 1973) (the statement "I signed the promissory note ... in the capacity of officer of such corporation and in behalf of such corporation and not in my personal capacity" was an admissible "factual inference" because it was the only evidence on a decisive issue), *rev'd on other grounds*, 505 S.W.2d 251 (Tex. 1974).

72. The more central to the contested issues the opinion, the greater the need to testify to concrete factual data rather than generalized conclusions. *See* 2 GOODE ET AL., *supra* note 7, §701.2, at 9; 3 WEINSTEIN & BERGER, *supra* note 15, ¶701[02], at 701-25; *see also* **Traders & Gen. Ins. v. Smith**, 369 S.W.2d 847, 849 (Tex. Civ. App.—Texarkana 1963, no writ) (father's testimony in venue case that his son was defendant's employee was excluded as an opinion when the fact of his son's employment was crucial issue in the lawsuit).

However, if the witness has a particularly well-founded opinion on a crucial issue, it may be reversible error for the judge to exclude it. Consider the result in **Lape v. State**, 893 S.W.2d 949 (Tex. App.—Houston [14th Dist.] 1994, pet. ref'd). In **Lape**, the defendant was on trial for the aggravated sexual assault of his stepdaughter. 893 S.W.2d at 952. The victim testified that she had screamed for help many times during the attack. *Id.* at 962. The trial court excluded the opinion testimony of the defendant's mother (based on an anecdotal experiment she had conducted) that sound traveled well within her townhouse and that she had not heard any such screams. *Id.* at 961-62. The court of appeals held that excluding this testimony was error because the witness's "testimony was based on her own perception of sound in her home and her testimony would have helped the jury in determining whether [the victim's] testimony was credible, a very important issue in the case." *Id.* at 962.

73. *See* 3 WEINSTEIN & BERGER, *supra* note 15, ¶701[02], at 701-31 to 701-32 (Rule 701 leaves the determination of whether correctness, abstraction, or a combination of both is called for in a particular case to the discretion of trial judge).

RULE 701

cision to admit or exclude lay-opinion testimony under Rule 701 is subject to review only for abuse of discretion.[74]

Normally, the direct examination of the lay witness will elicit the underlying perceived facts that gave rise to the witness's opinion. If the jury is aware of the specific facts that led to the witness's opinion, it will more likely give greater weight to that opinion. Further, under Rule 611(a), the trial judge may require the witness to relate his specific observations and perceptions before allowing him to give an opinion.[75] Thus, if the judge concludes that the witness's opinion is neither rationally based on the witness's perceptions[76] nor helpful to the jury, the judge may prevent the proponent from eliciting the witness's ultimate opinion while admitting the underlying factual data. Appellate courts rarely reverse a judgment because the trial judge admitted an unnecessary opinion; normally, only time is lost and there is no prejudice to the parties.

RULE 702

TESTIMONY BY EXPERT WITNESSES

A witness who is qualified as an expert by knowledge, skill, experience, training, or education may testify in the form of an opinion or otherwise if the expert's scientific, technical, or other specialized knowledge will help the trier of fact to understand the evidence or to determine a fact in issue.

COMMENTARY ON RULE 702

Rule 702 is substantively identical to the original version of Federal Rule 702[77] and is now identical to Federal Rule 702(a). After three U.S. Supreme Court opinions interpreted Federal Rule 702 to impose trustworthiness and reliability requirements for the admission of expert testimony,[78] Federal Rule 702 was amended in 2000 to explic-

---

74. *Cf. **Hansard v. Pepsi-Cola Metro. Bottling Co.**, 865 F.2d 1461, 1466-67 (5th Cir. 1989) (trial court did not abuse its discretion in admitting lay opinion; the "decisive factor ... is that the district court is best suited to determine whether FED. R. EVID. 701 has been satisfied"); **United States v. Hoffner**, 777 F.2d 1423, 1425 (10th Cir. 1985) (under Federal Rule 701, the "admission of lay opinion testimony is within the sound discretion of the trial court and will not be overturned on appeal absent a clear abuse of discretion").

75. Refer to *Article VI: Witnesses, supra* p. 636.

76. *See, e.g.,* ***In re Estate of Cornes***, 175 S.W.3d 491, 496-97 (Tex. App.—Beaumont 2005, no pet.) (two witnesses gave clear, direct, and positive evidence that holographic will was all in decedent's handwriting; contradictory evidence was not clear, positive, or direct, and there was no proof that contradicting witness was familiar with decedent's handwriting); ***In re Estate of Price***, No. 04-05-00438-CV (Tex. App.—San Antonio 2006, pet. denied) (memo op.; 12-20-06) (niece who claimed the signature on her aunt's will was forged did not establish her familiarity with her aunt's signature and therefore offered no basis for her perception; evidence was not sufficient to raise a fact issue about the signature's validity).

77. *See* Act of Jan. 2, 1975, Pub. L. No. 93-595, §1, 88 Stat. 1926, *reprinted in* 1974 U.S.C.C.A.N. 2215; 641-642 S.W.2d (Tex. Cases) LV (1983, amended 1998).

78. *See **Kumho Tire Co. v. Carmichael***, 526 U.S. 137 (1999); ***Gen. Elec. Co. v. Joiner***, 522 U.S. 136 (1997); ***Daubert v. Merrell Dow Pharm., Inc.***, 509 U.S. 579 (1993).

itly incorporate the requirements imposed by case law.[79] Texas case law has also imposed trustworthiness and reliability requirements for the admission of expert testimony, but the supreme court has not chosen to amend Texas Rule 702.[80]

While expert witnesses have long been a staple of the Anglo-American courtroom,[81] expert-opinion testimony is now one of the most important types of evidence offered in federal and state trials.[82] Although the original Federal Rule 702 "represent[ed] no clear departure from prior practice, ... the door to expert testimony has been opened far wider than before."[83] Under common-law principles, the question was whether the subject matter of the expert testimony was "beyond the ken of lay persons."[84] Under Rule 702, however, the emphasis is on whether the expert can help the trier of fact either to understand the evidence or to determine a fact in issue.[85] Thus,

---

79. *See* FED. R. EVID. 702 advisory committee's note to 2000 amendments. These cases gave trial judges the responsibility to act as gatekeepers (to exclude all unreliable expert testimony) and "provide[d] some general standards that the trial court must use to assess the reliability and helpfulness of proffered expert testimony." *Id.*

80. Refer to notes 165-242 *infra* and accompanying text.

81. *See* 2 GOODE ET AL., *supra* note 7, §702.2, at 14 (Texas courts traditionally "received expert opinion on a wide range of subjects, including proper medical practice, foreign law, earning capacity, peanut farming, accident reconstruction, and airplane flying, to name but a few").

82. Paul C. Giannelli noted the following:

> In the past decade courts have faced the difficult task of ruling on the admissibility of evidence derived from a wide range of newly ascertained or applied scientific principles. Neutron activation analysis, sound spectrometry (voiceprints), psycholinguistics, atomic absorption, remote electromagnetic sensing, and bitemark comparisons are but a sample of the kinds of scientific evidence inundating the courts.

Paul C. Giannelli, *The Admissibility of Novel Scientific Evidence: Frye v. United States, a Half-Century Later*, 80 COLUM. L. REV. 1197, 1198 (1980); *see* ***Everitt v. State***, 407 S.W.3d 259, 263 (Tex. Crim. App. 2013) ("Scientific evidence and expert testimony are typically admitted together."); ***Kelly v. State***, 824 S.W.2d 568, 572 n.9 (Tex. Crim. App. 1992) ("Because of its nature, scientific evidence will almost always be offered through the testimony of experts."); *see also* William H. Donaher et al., *The Technological Expert in Products Liability Litigation*, 52 TEX. L. REV. 1303, 1310-12 (1974) (discussing role of technological experts in products-liability suits); Wayne Fisher, *Use of an Economist to Prove Future Economic Losses*, 18 S. TEX. L.J. 403, 403 (1977) (noting increased use and utility of presenting an economist as an expert witness to determine losses in personal-injury litigation).

83. 3 LOUISELL & MUELLER, *supra* note 27, §380, at 633.

84. *Id.*; *see* 2 RAY, *supra* note 32, §1400, at 23-24 (to justify using expert testimony, the subject must be "beyond the knowledge of average laymen"); 3 WEINSTEIN & BERGER, *supra* note 15, ¶702[02], at 702-10 (before enactment of Federal Rules, "courts frequently asserted that there was no need for expert testimony unless the issue to which the testimony would be directed is 'not within the common knowledge of the average layman'"). Under strict common-law standards of admissibility, expert testimony was frequently excluded because it was not beyond the jury's understanding. For example, in ***Dunnington v. State***, the court of appeals held that the trial court abused its discretion in permitting a Department of Human Resources caseworker to testify about various explanations for a child's belated outcry of sexual abuse because they "are not such complicated motivations as necessitate expert explanation." 740 S.W.2d 896, 897-99 (Tex. App.—El Paso 1987, pet. ref'd). The court further reasoned that the admissibility of expert testimony is "restricted to those situations in which the expert's knowledge and experience on a relevant issue are beyond that of the average juror." *Id.* at 898. It is difficult to understand the ***Dunnington*** reversal of the conviction because the trial court permitted the jurors to hear evidence with which, according to the appellate court, they were already familiar.

85. TEX. R. EVID. 702; *cf. **In re Japanese Elec. Prods. Antitrust Litig.**,* 723 F.2d 238, 279 (3d Cir. 1983) (whether "an opinion will be helpful to the jury involves discretion, but that discretion must be exercised consistent with the presumption that expert testimony will be helpful"; "requirement for admissibility that expert testimony be 'beyond

a court does not need to exclude expert testimony when the average juror can comprehend the subject matter, as long as the witness has some specialized knowledge on the same issue that would be helpful.[86] The expert "may add precision and depth to the ability of the trier of fact to reach conclusions about subjects which lie well within common experience."[87] If, however, the jury is equally competent to form an opinion on an ultimate fact issue, an expert's opinion on that issue may be excluded.[88] The Texas Supreme Court has broadly stated that "[w]here ... the issue involves only general knowledge and experience rather than expertise, it is within the province of the jury to decide, and admission of expert testimony on the issue is error."[89] Under Rule 702, however, experts may testify whenever their opinions or other testimony may help the jury.

---

the jury's sphere of knowledge'" was rejected by drafters of Federal Rule 702), *rev'd on other grounds sub nom. Matsushita Elec. Indus. Co. v. Zenith Radio Corp.*, 475 U.S. 574 (1986). While an expert may help the trier of fact, the jury must independently analyze the issues before it. *See In re Christus Spohn Hosp. Kleberg*, 222 S.W.3d 434, 440 (Tex. 2007) (orig. proceeding) ("[T]he expert is generally held out to be, and is seen by the jury as, an objective authority figure more knowledgeable and credible than the typical lay witness. For this reason, juries are prone to rely on experts to tell them how to decide complex issues without independently analyzing underlying factors."); *Gerron v. State*, ___ S.W.3d ___ (Tex. App.—Waco 2016, pet. ref'd) (No. 10-14-00121-CR; 10-26-16) ("The purpose of expert testimony is to assist the jury, and an expert's opinion is not determinative of an ultimate fact question. The jury is free to accept or reject some or all of the testimony of an expert witness.").

86. The court of criminal appeals has expressed this test as follows:

Where specialized knowledge will assist the jury to understand the evidence or will assist them to determine a fact in issue, an expert may be allowed to provide the jury with the benefit of that knowledge. Two themes are prevalent within the language of the rule. First, the jury must not be qualified to intelligently and to the best possible degree determine the particular issue without benefit of the expert witness's specialized knowledge. Second, the clear meaning of the rule must be observed. ... The use of expert testimony must be limited to situations in which the expert's knowledge and experience on a relevant issue are beyond that of an average juror.

Duckett v. State, 797 S.W.2d 906, 914 (Tex. Crim. App. 1990) (citation omitted), *disapproved on other grounds*, *Cohn v. State*, 849 S.W.2d 817 (Tex. Crim. App. 1993); *see also* *Glasscock v. Income Prop. Servs., Inc.*, 888 S.W.2d 176, 180-81 (Tex. App.—Houston [1st Dist.] 1994, writ dism'd) (trial court erred in excluding expert testimony on issue of adequate security for commercial enterprise); 3 WEINSTEIN & BERGER, *supra* note 15, ¶702[02], at 702-20 (to exclude expert testimony when the subject is comprehensible by the average juror "is incompatible with the standard of helpfulness expressed in Rule 702"). An expert's testimony does not meet the Rule 702 standard only when it offers the jury no appreciable aid. *See, e.g.*, *Pierce v. State*, 777 S.W.2d 399, 414 (Tex. Crim. App. 1989) (trial court did not err in excluding an architect's perspective drawings of a lineup that he did not personally observe; witness's testimony that "when an object is placed near a large object, the object will be perceived to be smaller than its actual size and vice-versa" represented no specialized knowledge).

87. 3 LOUISELL & MUELLER, *supra* note 27, §382, at 640. For example, numerous federal cases have allowed expert testimony on photographic comparisons even though jurors can make such comparisons themselves. *See, e.g.*, *United States v. Alexander*, 816 F.2d 164, 169 (5th Cir. 1987) (trial court improperly excluded defense expert's testimony, which would have indicated by comparison study that defendant was not the person in photograph); *United States v. Snow*, 552 F.2d 165, 167-68 (6th Cir. 1977) (expert witness could compare bank surveillance film with known photographs of defendants).

88. *GTE Sw., Inc. v. Bruce*, 956 S.W.2d 636, 640 (Tex. App.—Texarkana 1997), *aff'd*, 998 S.W.2d 605 (Tex. 1999); *Story Servs., Inc. v. Ramirez*, 863 S.W.2d 491, 499 (Tex. App.—El Paso 1993, writ denied); *see, e.g.*, *Speer v. State*, 890 S.W.2d 87, 96-97 (Tex. App.—Houston [1st Dist.] 1994, pet. ref'd) (trial court did not abuse its discretion in excluding expert psychological testimony because it was not outside the range of layperson's knowledge that teenagers commonly are insecure, are easily influenced by others, and act against their better judgment by following influential peers).

89. *GTE Sw., Inc. v. Bruce*, 998 S.W.2d 605, 620 (Tex. 1999); *see Story Servs.*, 863 S.W.2d at 499.

A. Classification of Witnesses

As discussed above, Rule 701 requires that a lay opinion be "helpful to clearly understanding the witness's testimony or to determining a fact in issue."[90] Rule 702 imposes a similar, if not identical, prerequisite that an expert's opinion help the trier of fact.[91] Both tests are probably an expansion of the concept of relevance.[92] But a witness's classification under the Rules of Evidence as a lay witness or an expert can have significant consequences. Experts, when giving opinions within their fields of expertise, have much more testimonial latitude than laypersons.

The primary advantages of using an expert are outlined in Rule 703, which relaxes the firsthand-knowledge requirement for experts, and Rule 705, which suspends the common-law requirement that the factual basis for an opinion be disclosed before the opinion is rendered.[93] Despite the advantages given to experts under Article VII, the lay/expert dichotomy is blurred and confusing.[94] The distinction between a layperson

---

90. TEX. R. EVID. 701(b).

91. TEX. R. EVID. 702; *see* 3 WEINSTEIN & BERGER, *supra* note 15, ¶702[01], at 702-07 to 702-08. Under both the Rules and the common law, Texas courts have recognized the test of helpfulness or assistance to the trier of fact in the expert-witness context. *See Holloway v. State*, 613 S.W.2d 497, 501 (Tex. Crim. App. 1981) (prerequisite for expert-opinion testimony is a showing of expert's qualifications and the helpfulness of the testimony to the jury); *see, e.g., K-Mart Corp. v. Honeycutt*, 24 S.W.3d 357, 360-61 (Tex. 2000) (per curiam) (testimony by expert on human factors and safety was properly excluded because jurors did not need assistance in determining whether employee knew how to properly push shopping carts); *see also Bounds v. Caudle*, 549 S.W.2d 438, 445 (Tex. Civ. App.—Corpus Christi 1977) (opinion testimony must go beyond the average understanding of laymen, and witness must have special expertise), *rev'd in part on other grounds*, 560 S.W.2d 925 (Tex. 1977).

92. *See Vela v. State*, 209 S.W.3d 128, 131 (Tex. Crim. App. 2006). Refer to notes 31-42 *supra* and accompanying text, notes 97-104 *infra* and accompanying text.

93. Refer to notes 257-328, 356-431 *infra* and accompanying text.

94. *See Reid Rd. Mun. Util. Dist. No. 2 v. Speedy Stop Food Stores, Ltd.*, 337 S.W.3d 846, 851 (Tex. 2011) ("The line between who is a Rule 702 expert witness and who is a Rule 701 witness is not always bright. But when the main substance of the witness's testimony is based on application of the witness's specialized knowledge, skill, experience, training, or education to his familiarity with the property, then the testimony will generally be expert testimony within the scope of Rule 702."). Refer to notes 15-18 *supra* and accompanying text. This confusion stems in part from the characteristics that both types of witnesses have. Generally, to testify on a particular matter, a witness must have the ability and opportunity to observe and the ability to understand, remember, and communicate the observation. *Cf.* MODEL CODE OF EVID. R. 101 (1942) (witness is qualified unless the judge decides that the witness is incapable of either "expressing himself concerning the matter so as to be understood by the judge and jury" or "understanding the duty of a witness to tell the truth"). Refer to *Article VI: Witnesses, supra* p. 556. Rule 702 focuses on the ability to understand observations, which Wigmore calls "experiential capacity." 2 WIGMORE, *supra* note 3, §555, at 749-50. Wigmore states the following:

> That sort of capacity which involves, not the organic powers, moral and mental, requisite for all testimony, nor yet the emotional power of unbiased observation and statement, but the skill to acquire accurate conceptions, may be termed experiential capacity.
>
> ....
>
> [T]he rules of evidence ... must see to it that the testimonial statements offered as representing knowledge are not offered by persons who are not fitted to acquire knowledge on the subject at hand. Such fitness or skill to acquire accurate impressions comes from circumstances which may broadly be summed up in the term "experience." If, at the one extreme, be imagined the babe in arms, practically lacking in any such skill or fitness, and, at the other extreme, the trained professional student of a

and an expert under the Rules is not and cannot be rigid because witnesses' abilities to understand what is perceived—their experiential capacities—span a broad spectrum.[95] This experiential capacity varies according to the particular witness's prior experience, training, and education, without regard to whether the witness is categorized as a layperson or an expert.[96]

B. Requirements for Admission of Expert Testimony

Rule 702 contains three basic prerequisites for the admission of any expert testimony: (1) the witness must be qualified, (2) the proposed testimony must be grounded in scientific, technical, or other specialized knowledge, and (3) the testimony must help the trier of fact to understand the evidence admitted at trial or to determine a fact in issue.[97] The requirements are distinct, and an objection to one of them does not preserve error for another.[98] To meet the second and third prerequisites, the proponent of

---

> department of science, in whom the fitness exists in the highest degree, it is seen that this attribution of the source of the fitness to "experience" is sufficiently accurate for purposes of nomenclature.
>
> In experience, then, are included all the processes—the continual use of the faculties, the habit and practice of an occupation, special study, professional training, and the rest—which contribute to produce a fitness to acquire accurate knowledge upon a given subject.

Id.

95. However, Federal Rule 701 attempts to more rigidly categorize testimony as either lay opinion or expert opinion depending on whether the witness who perceived an event or condition has training or experience. *See, e.g.,* **United States v. Williams**, 212 F.3d 1305, 1309-10 (D.C. Cir. 2000) (in trial for felon in possession of firearm, police officer who had made fewer than a dozen arrests involving possession of a firearm should not have been allowed to testify that it is common for people who use or sell drugs to carry weapons for protection; this limited experience was insufficient to qualify him as an expert; witness's opinions were not rationally based on personal perception, and thus did not qualify as lay-opinion testimony). Refer to notes 12-14 *supra* and accompanying text.

96. Refer to notes 15-18 *supra* and accompanying text, notes 140-145 *infra* and accompanying text.

97. TEX. R. EVID. 702; *E.I. du Pont de Nemours & Co. v. Robinson*, 923 S.W.2d 549, 556 (Tex. 1995); *Ex parte Lane*, 303 S.W.3d 702, 716 (Tex. Crim. App. 2009); *Rodgers v. State*, 205 S.W.3d 525, 527 (Tex. Crim. App. 2006); *Alvarado v. State*, 912 S.W.2d 199, 215-16 (Tex. Crim. App. 1995); *see Harnett v. State*, 38 S.W.3d 650, 659 (Tex. App.—Austin 2000, pet. ref'd) ("Unlike the common-law requirement, a trial court under Rule 702 may admit an expert's testimony on a matter within most jurors' understanding if the testimony concerns some type of technical or specialized knowledge and would assist the jurors in their fact-finding function."). The third prerequisite—whether the expert's testimony helps the jury understand or determine a material fact in issue in this case—is particularly important when courts attempt to keep "junk science" out of the courtroom. *See Tillman v. State*, 354 S.W.3d 425, 435 (Tex. Crim. App. 2011) (focus of reliability analysis is to keep "junk science" out of courtroom); *see, e.g.,* *S.V. v. R.V.*, 933 S.W.2d 1, 27-28 (Tex. 1996) (Gonzalez, J., concurring) (expert testimony about repressed memory is the type of "junk science" that should be kept out of the courtroom).

> In *Sattiewhite v. State*, the court of criminal appeals gave the following criteria for expert-opinion testimony: Before an expert witness can offer opinion testimony the following three criteria must be shown:
>
> (1) the witness must be competent and qualified to testify;
>
> (2) the subject must be one upon which the aid of an expert's opinion will be of assistance to the jury;
>
> (3) his testimony may not state a legal conclusion.

786 S.W.2d 271, 291 (Tex. Crim. App. 1989); *see also Hopkins v. State*, 480 S.W.2d 212, 218 (Tex. Crim. App. 1972) (articulating identical common-law standard). The third criterion is not so much a predicate to the admissibility of expert testimony as a limitation on any witness's testimony and is now covered by Rule 704. Refer to notes 330-354 *infra* and accompanying text.

98. *Salinas v. State*, 426 S.W.3d 318, 323 (Tex. App.—Houston [14th Dist.] 2014), *rev'd on other grounds*, 464 S.W.3d 363 (Tex. Crim. App. 2015).

the expert testimony must establish that the testimony is reliable and relevant.[99] Rule 702 then sets a minimal standard of helpfulness[100] and adopts Wigmore's threshold question: "On *this subject* can a jury receive from *this person* appreciable help?"[101] This standard is fairly generous and follows the Federal Rules' general framework, which favors the admissibility of all relevant evidence.[102] The proponent of the expert testimony must satisfy each of these requirements by a preponderance of evidence under Rule 104(a).[103] After an expert has met the qualification requirements and the testimony has been shown to be reliable and relevant, the expert's opinion must then meet the general balancing test of Rule 403.[104]

1. Qualifications of expert witnesses. Rule 702 and the cases interpreting the rule set out the requirements for qualifying as an expert witness and the permissible forms of expert testimony.

(1) Requirements for qualification. Rule 702 requires that a witness testifying as an expert must be "qualified as an expert by knowledge, skill, experience, training, or

---

99.   ***Robinson***, 923 S.W.2d at 556; ***Everitt v. State***, 407 S.W.3d 259, 263 (Tex. Crim. App. 2013); ***Ex parte Lane***, 303 S.W.3d at 716; *see* ***Ortiz v. State***, 834 S.W.2d 343, 347 (Tex. Crim. App. 1992) (Rules favor admission of relevant expert testimony). Refer to notes 165-250 *infra* and accompanying text. Much of the case law interpreting Texas Rule 702 and Federal Rule 702 has focused on the reliability of expert testimony. Texas and federal courts have issued a series of parallel opinions designed to ensure that any expert opinions presented are reliable. While there are differences in phrasing and sometimes in substance, the Texas and federal courts generally agree on what is required for the admissibility of expert opinions.

100.   Federal Rule 702 explicitly limits the admissibility of expert testimony to that which has been determined to be based on reliable principles, methodology, and data. *See* FED. R. EVID. 702(b)-(d). Refer to notes 4, 8 *supra* and accompanying text. The Advisory Committee's note to the original Federal Rule 702 provides the following:

Whether the situation is a proper one for the use of expert testimony is to be determined on the basis of assisting the trier. "There is no more certain test for determining when experts may be used than the common sense inquiry whether the untrained layman would be qualified to determine intelligently and to the best possible degree the particular issue without enlightenment from those having a specialized understanding of the subject involved in the dispute." When opinions are excluded, it is because they are unhelpful and therefore superfluous and a waste of time.

FED. R. EVID. 702 advisory committee's note (citations omitted). The phrase "to the best possible degree" is the key to appreciating the helpfulness standard of Rule 702. An expert might help even a trier of fact who already has considerable knowledge in a particular area if the expert's testimony adds a new dimension to or greater insight into that knowledge.

101.   7 WIGMORE, *supra* note 27, §1923, at 29. Refer to notes 243-250 *infra* and accompanying text.

102.   *See* ***United States v. Downing***, 753 F.2d 1224, 1229-30 (3d Cir. 1985) ("Rule 702 standard usually favors admissibility" and thus expert testimony on the perception of eyewitnesses may meet the helpfulness standard of Rule 702); ***United States v. Barker***, 553 F.2d 1013, 1024 (6th Cir. 1977) (noting change from common-law requirement that expert testimony be admitted only when factual issues could not be determined without technical assistance to liberal admissibility under Federal Rule 702).

103.   *See* ***Amis v. State***, 910 S.W.2d 511, 517 (Tex. App.—Tyler 1995, pet. ref'd); ***Kelly v. State***, 792 S.W.2d 579, 585 (Tex. App.—Fort Worth 1990), *aff'd*, 824 S.W.2d 568 (Tex. Crim. App. 1992). However, in ***Kelly v. State***, the court of criminal appeals held that the proponent of novel scientific evidence must prove the scientific reliability of the expert's theory and methodology by clear and convincing evidence. 824 S.W.2d 568, 573 (Tex. Crim. App. 1992); *see, e.g.*, ***Mata v. State***, 46 S.W.3d 902, 917 (Tex. Crim. App. 2001) (State did not prove by clear and convincing evidence that expert's testimony about retrograde extrapolations was reliable). For a discussion of Rule 104(a), refer to *Article I: General Provisions, supra* p. 86.

104.   Refer to notes 251-256 *infra* and accompanying text and *Article IV: Relevance & Its Limits, supra* p. 211.

RULE 702

education."[105] The proponent of the expert testimony has the burden of establishing that the witness's qualifications satisfy Rule 702.[106] Whether the expert possesses the necessary qualifications is a preliminary question for the court under Rule 104(a).[107] Because the possible spectrum of education, skill, and training is so wide, a trial court has great discretion in determining whether a particular witness has sufficient qualifications to help the jury as an expert in a specific area.[108] The trial court's ruling on the witness's qualifications is reviewed for abuse of discretion.[109]

The Texas Court of Criminal Appeals has laid out a three-part test to determine whether a trial court has abused its discretion in evaluating a witness's qualifications as an expert: (1) whether the field of expertise is complex, (2) how conclusive the witness's opinion is, and (3) how central the area of expertise is to the resolution of the lawsuit.[110] These three factors should also govern the trial court's initial determination

105. TEX. R. EVID. 702.

106. *Gammill v. Jack Williams Chevrolet, Inc.*, 972 S.W.2d 713, 718 (Tex. 1998); *United Blood Servs. v. Longoria*, 938 S.W.2d 29, 31 (Tex. 1997); *Davis v. State*, 329 S.W.3d 798, 813 (Tex. Crim. App. 2010); *Vela v. State*, 209 S.W.3d 128, 132 (Tex. Crim. App. 2006). If the opponent of the expert testimony stipulates that the expert is qualified, the appellate court does not need to review that finding. *Harris Cty. Appr. Dist. v. Hous. 8th Wonder Prop., L.P.*, 395 S.W.3d 245, 254 (Tex. App.—Houston [1st Dist.] 2012, pet. denied) (op. on reh'g).

107. *Gammill*, 972 S.W.2d at 718; *Schronk v. Laerdal Med. Corp.*, 440 S.W.3d 250, 261 (Tex. App.—Waco 2013, pet. denied); *see Penry v. State*, 903 S.W.2d 715, 762 (Tex. Crim. App. 1995). Refer to *Article I: General Provisions*, *supra* p. 86. See *O'Connor's Texas Rules * Civil Trials* (2017), "Qualifications test," ch. 5-N, §2.1, p. 475. A trial court's recognition of a witness as an expert, even in the jury's presence, is not an impermissible comment on the weight of the expert's testimony. *See Kihega v. State*, 392 S.W.3d 828, 834 (Tex. App.—Texarkana 2013, no pet.).

108. *Rodgers v. State*, 205 S.W.3d 525, 527-28 (Tex. Crim. App. 2006); *see, e.g.*, *Layton v. State*, 280 S.W.3d 235, 242 (Tex. Crim. App. 2009) (trial court erred in admitting video of traffic stop in which police officer made statements about defendant's prescription-drug use; "[t]here was no testimony indicating that [officer] had any medical knowledge regarding the uses of Xanax and Valium, or about the effect of combining the medications with alcohol"). In some areas of expertise, such as accident reconstruction, it is difficult to reconcile the seemingly inconsistent judicial holdings. *Compare Rhomer v. State*, 522 S.W.3d 13, ___ (Tex. App.—San Antonio 2017, pet. filed 6-9-17) (police officer with accident-reconstruction training was qualified to testify about point of impact between vehicle and motorcycle even though training did not involve motorcycles), *Wooten v. State*, 267 S.W.3d 289, 303-04 (Tex. App.—Houston [14th Dist.] 2008, pet. ref'd) (police officer educated and trained in accident reconstruction was qualified to testify as expert about speed of vehicle based on use of drag sled), *Ter-Vartanyan v. R&R Freight, Inc.*, 111 S.W.3d 779, 781 (Tex. App.—Dallas 2003, pet. denied) (police officer certified as accident investigator was qualified to testify as expert on cause of auto accident), *Chavers v. State*, 991 S.W.2d 457, 460-61 (Tex. App.—Houston [1st Dist.] 1999, pet. ref'd) (state trooper trained in accident reconstruction and certified by Texas Department of Public Safety on use of device commonly used in accident reconstruction was qualified to give expert opinion on speed of vehicle based on "yaw marks" at scene), *and Trailways, Inc. v. Clark*, 794 S.W.2d 479, 483 (Tex. App.—Corpus Christi 1990, writ denied) (police officer was qualified to testify about speed of bus and its contribution to cause of accident), *with Pilgrim's Pride Corp. v. Smoak*, 134 S.W.3d 880, 892 (Tex. App.—Texarkana 2004, pet. denied) (police officer was not qualified to testify about cause of accident because he was not an accident reconstructionist), *Lopez v. S. Pac. Transp. Co.*, 847 S.W.2d 330, 334-35 (Tex. App.—El Paso 1993, no writ) (police officer was not qualified to testify about cause of accident when there was no showing of specialized knowledge in accident reconstruction), *and Bounds v. Scurlock Oil Co.*, 730 S.W.2d 68, 71 (Tex. App.—Corpus Christi 1987, writ ref'd n.r.e.) (police officer was not qualified to testify about cause of accident because he was not an accident analyst or reconstruction expert). This inconsistency may depend, at least in part, on the specific testimony by police officers about (1) their credentials and experience, (2) the depth and breadth of their training for accident investigation, and (3) the complexity of the accident reconstructions in the particular cases.

109. *Gammill*, 972 S.W.2d at 718-19. Refer to notes 123-128 *infra* and accompanying text.

110. *Vela*, 209 S.W.3d at 131.

of the expert's qualifications. The qualification requirement is independent of the issues of reliability and relevance and should be considered separately.[111] The court of criminal appeals further explained:

> [T]he mere fact that a witness "'possesse[s] knowledge and skill not possessed by people generally …' does not in and of itself mean that such expertise will assist the trier of fact regarding the issue before the court." And because a witness will not always qualify as an expert merely by virtue of a general background, qualification is a two-step inquiry. A witness must first have a sufficient background in a particular field, but a trial judge must then determine whether that background "goes to the very matter on which [the witness] is to give an opinion."[112]

Courts look at whether the witness's expertise "goes to the very matter on which he or she is to give an opinion."[113] Put another way, the focus is on the "fit" between

---

111. *Id.*

112. *Id.* (footnotes omitted) (quoting ***Broders v. Heise***, 924 S.W.2d 148, 153 (Tex. 1996)); *see **Gammill***, 972 S.W.2d at 719 ("Just as not every physician is qualified to testify as an expert in every medical malpractice case, not every mechanical engineer is qualified to testify as an expert in every products liability case."); ***Cura-Cruz v. CenterPoint Energy Hous. Elec., LLC***, 522 S.W.3d 565, ___ (Tex. App.—Houston [14th Dist.] 2017, pet. filed 7-3-17) (general experience in specialized field is insufficient; offering party must show that expert has knowledge, skill, experience, training, or education related to specific issue); *see, e.g.*, ***Roise v. State***, 7 S.W.3d 225, 237 (Tex. App.—Austin 1999, pet. ref'd) (expert psychologist was not qualified to testify to health or mental problems likely to be suffered by child-pornography models; "[d]egrees, experience, and training do not qualify an expert to answer every conceivable question about psychology").

113. ***Broders v. Heise***, 924 S.W.2d 148, 153 (Tex. 1996); *see **Gammill***, 972 S.W.2d at 718; ***Cura-Cruz***, 522 S.W.3d at ___; *see, e.g.*, ***Helena Chem. Co. v. Wilkins***, 47 S.W.3d 486, 499-500 (Tex. 2001) (witness, though not a plant pathologist, was qualified to testify as expert on suitability of specific grain seed for dry-land farming based on his experience in conducting crop-variety testing, his study of other independent testing, his education and experience as plant consultant, and his personal observations of seed's suitability); ***Hospadales v. McCoy***, 513 S.W.3d 724, 736 (Tex. App.—Houston [1st Dist.] 2017, no pet.) (orthopedic surgeon who had spine subspecialty but general orthopedic practice was qualified to testify about cause of knee injury); ***Livingston v. Montgomery***, 279 S.W.3d 868, 875-77 (Tex. App.—Dallas 2009, no pet.) (labor-and-delivery expert was qualified to testify about the cause of newborn's neurological injuries); ***Mosely v. Mundine***, 249 S.W.3d 775, 779 (Tex. App.—Dallas 2008, no pet.) (internist who was also emergency-room physician was qualified to give an opinion about detection of abnormal mass on routine chest X-ray, even though he was not an oncologist); ***Loram Maint. of Way, Inc. v. Ianni***, 141 S.W.3d 722, 730 (Tex. App.—El Paso 2004) (psychiatrist was qualified to testify as an expert on amphetamine use and its effect even though .04% of his practice dealt with amphetamine abuse; he stated that he sees patients with such abuse at least once a month), *rev'd on other grounds*, 210 S.W.3d 593 (Tex. 2006); ***Schindler Elevator Corp. v. Anderson***, 78 S.W.3d 392, 401-02 (Tex. App.—Houston [14th Dist.] 2001, pet. granted, judgm't vacated w.r.m.) (witness with extensive experience in field of escalators and escalator safety was qualified to give an expert opinion on cause of accident, even though he was not an engineer, did not design or test his own safety device, had never personally maintained escalator, and was not trained in accident reconstruction), *disapproved on other grounds*, ***Roberts v. Williamson***, 111 S.W.3d 113 (Tex. 2003); ***Keeton v. Carrasco***, 53 S.W.3d 13, 25-26 (Tex. App.—San Antonio 2001, pet. denied) (doctor was qualified to give opinion on standards applicable to care of patients who have had spinal-cord stimulators implanted even though his specialty was physical medicine and rehabilitation, not orthopedic medicine; expert's particular field of medicine is not the focus of the analysis, but rather "the condition underlying the claim and the standard of care that the defendant doctor is required to exercise with regard to that condition"); *cf.* ***Tuf Racing Prods., Inc. v. Am. Suzuki Motor Corp.***, 223 F.3d 585, 591 (7th Cir. 2000) (accountant was qualified to testify about damages based on financial information given to him; dismissing as "radically unsound" the idea that ***Daubert*** requires "particular credentials" for experts; anyone with relevant expertise may testify as expert); ***United States v. Chang***,

the subject matter at issue and the expert's familiarity with that specific matter.[114] As the court of criminal appeals explained:

> "[F]it" is not just a component of reliability and relevance—it is also a component of the qualification inquiry. Just as the subject matter of an expert's testimony should be tailored to the facts of a case, the expert's background must be tailored to the specific area of expertise in which the expert desires to testify.[115]

Courts might consider several factors in assessing the expert's qualifications. Formal education without any experience in the field may be a sufficient qualification,[116] as may experience without formal education.[117] "The special knowledge which quali-

---

207 F.3d 1169, 1171-73 (9th Cir. 2000) (testimony in bank-fraud trial by professor of clinical marketing about genuineness of purported "Certificate of Payback Balance" was excluded because witness "had no experience in identifying counterfeit foreign securities").

114. *Hayes v. Carroll*, 314 S.W.3d 494, 504 (Tex. App.—Austin 2010, no pet.); *Gregory v. State*, 56 S.W.3d 164, 180 (Tex. App.—Houston [14th Dist.] 2001, pet. dism'd); *e.g.*, *Perez v. State*, 113 S.W.3d 819, 832 (Tex. App.—Austin 2003, pet. ref'd) (psychologist's expertise in child-sexual-abuse cases "fit" his proposed testimony on characteristics of sexually abused children), *overruled on other grounds*, *Taylor v. State*, 268 S.W.3d 571 (Tex. Crim. App. 2008); *see Broders*, 924 S.W.2d at 153; *Jordan v. State*, 928 S.W.2d 550, 555 (Tex. Crim. App. 1996); *see, e.g.*, *PNS Stores, Inc. v. Munguia*, 484 S.W.3d 503, 512-13 (Tex. App.—Houston [14th Dist.] 2016, no pet.) (in personal-injury case involving fallen merchandise, trial court did not abuse discretion in excluding testimony of "merchandise safety expert" whose education and experience showed expertise in marketing but not in safety; witness was unaware of specific industry guidelines for stocking products safely, had not reviewed store's policies, procedures, or training manuals, and had no information about incident other than what store's counsel told her); *Pack v. Crossroads, Inc.*, 53 S.W.3d 492, 506-07 (Tex. App.—Fort Worth 2001, pet. denied) (nurse who had doctorate degree and many years of experience and had written published articles was nonetheless unqualified to express opinion on standard of care for nursing home because her expertise did not "fit" the proposed opinion).

115. *Vela*, 209 S.W.3d at 133.

116. *See, e.g.*, *United States v. Gilliss*, 645 F.2d 1269, 1277-78 (8th Cir. 1981) (psychologist who had not yet obtained a diploma and had no clinical experience when he examined defendant was nonetheless qualified to testify as an expert on the classification of pathological gambling disorder as a mental disorder); *Gardner v. Gen. Motors Corp.*, 507 F.2d 525, 528 (10th Cir. 1974) (several professors of mechanical engineering were qualified to give opinions on the design of a truck's exhaust system despite the lack of actual experience in design or manufacture of such systems); *Ford Motor Co. v. Aguiniga*, 9 S.W.3d 252, 265 (Tex. App.—San Antonio 1999, pet. denied) (metallurgist and engineer who had no experience in automobile industry were qualified to testify based on their extensive training in research and design of relay systems).

117. *See United States v. Valle*, 72 F.3d 210, 214 n.4 (1st Cir. 1995) ("[S]treet savvy and practical experience can qualify a witness as an expert as surely as 'a string of academic degrees or multiple memberships in learned societies.'" (quoting *United States v. Hoffman*, 832 F.2d 1299, 1310 (1st Cir. 1987))); *Rogers v. Raymark Indus., Inc.*, 922 F.2d 1426, 1429 (9th Cir. 1991) (witness can qualify as an expert through practical experience in a particular field, not just through academic training); *Circle J Dairy, Inc. v. A.O. Smith Harvestore Prods., Inc.*, 790 F.2d 694, 700 (8th Cir. 1986) ("Rule 702 ... does not rank academic training over demonstrated practical experience, and we credit a jury, when evaluating the evidence in a case, with the ability also to consider the background and credentials of the expert witnesses who testified before it."); *Vela*, 209 S.W.3d at 135 ("To qualify a witness as an expert by practical experience alone, a trial judge must fully explore that witness's experience in the particular field in which the witness intends to give an expert opinion. A cursory reference to the witness's credentials is insufficient to support expert status."); *Holloway v. State*, 613 S.W.2d 497, 501 (Tex. Crim. App. 1981) (expert witness is qualified by specialized education, practical experience, or a combination of both; his answers must indicate he possesses knowledge that will assist the jurors in making inferences more effectively than they could if unaided); *see, e.g.*, *United States v. Haines*, 803 F.3d 713, 727-28 (5th Cir. 2015) (DEA agent who worked as drug investigator for 11 years and listened to more than 100,000 wiretapped telephone calls could testify as expert witness about drug code language; formal education opportunities not common in field), *cert. denied*, 137 S. Ct. 2107 (2017); *United States v. Abrego*, 141 F.3d 142, 173 (5th Cir. 1998) (although doctor did not say he was an "expert" on Valium habituation or depen-

fies a witness to give an expert opinion may be derived from specialized education, practical experience, a study of technical works, or a varying combination of these things."[118] As a general proposition, the degree of experience, education, skill, or training that a witness should have before he can qualify as an expert in a field is directly related to the complexity of that field.[119] Thus, the expert's qualifications are more important when the evidence is well outside the jury's own experiences than when the evi-

---

dency, it was not an abuse of discretion for trial court to allow his testimony on subject because he had sufficient practical experience); *United States v. Christophe*, 833 F.2d 1296, 1300 (9th Cir. 1987) (FBI agent with seven years' experience and who had investigated 800-1,000 robberies qualified as a "skilled" expert to testify why "latent fingerprints are obtained in only ten percent of the bank robbery cases"); *Roberts v. Williamson*, 111 S.W.3d 113, 121-22 (Tex. 2003) (although board-certified pediatrician was not a neurologist, he had sufficient education and experience to testify about the specific causes and effects of infant's neurological injuries); *In re Marriage of Bivins*, 393 S.W.3d 893, 900-01 (Tex. App.—Waco 2012, pet. denied) (building contractors with 10 and 15 years' experience were qualified to testify about repairs; formal education was not required); *Dixon v. State*, 244 S.W.3d 472, 479 (Tex. App.—Houston [14th Dist.] 2007, pet. ref'd) (police officer who had worked for 23 years and had received training on family-violence cases was qualified to testify about behavior of family-violence victims; officer's lack of college education did not make him unqualified); *Huckaby v. A.G. Perry & Son, Inc.*, 20 S.W.3d 194, 208 (Tex. App.—Texarkana 2000, pet. denied) (highway patrol officer who had assisted in more than 3,800 accidents in 16 years and whose job responsibilities included perceiving and reporting flaws in highway design was qualified to testify as an expert about highway design); *Hardin v. State*, 20 S.W.3d 84, 92 (Tex. App.—Texarkana 2000, pet. ref'd) (witness with 20 years' experience in investigating and supervising sex offenders was qualified to testify on the issue of whether a convicted sex offender poses a continuing threat to society); *Burleson v. State*, 802 S.W.2d 429, 440 (Tex. App.—Fort Worth 1991, pet. ref'd) (senior programmer/analyst with 15 years' experience was qualified as an expert because he was familiar with the computer system at issue, was familiar with the way records were stored in the system, routinely commanded the computer to bring up the file at issue in the case, tested the system, and was the person at the company most experienced with the system).

118. *Penry v. State*, 903 S.W.2d 715, 762 (Tex. Crim. App. 1995); *accord Wyatt v. State*, 23 S.W.3d 18, 27 (Tex. Crim. App. 2000); *Dixon*, 244 S.W.3d at 479; *see, e.g.*, *Wolfe v. State*, 509 S.W.3d 325, 337-38 (Tex. Crim. App. 2017) (physicians with training in pediatric medicine and experience as treating physicians were qualified to testify about nature and cause of child's abusive head trauma); *Washington v. State*, 485 S.W.3d 633, 639 (Tex. App.—Houston [1st Dist.] 2016, no pet.) (police officer could testify about identity of gang members based on his training and experience in area of Houston gangs); *Fleming v. Kinney ex rel. Shelton*, 395 S.W.3d 917, 927-28 (Tex. App.—Houston [14th Dist.] 2013, pet. denied) (trial court did not abuse its discretion in concluding that attorney-witness was qualified by her background and experience to testify as expert about attorneys' fiduciary duties to clients); *Von Hohn v. Von Hohn*, 260 S.W.3d 631, 636-37 (Tex. App.—Tyler 2008, no pet.) (witness with specialized knowledge and experience in valuing a partner's interest in a law firm was qualified to testify as an expert, even though he had never before used information from a patent case to perform such a valuation); *Holmes v. State*, 135 S.W.3d 178, 182-84 (Tex. App.—Waco 2004, no pet.) (police officer with more than six years' experience in special crimes unit and Level 1 training in blood-spatter analysis was qualified to testify as expert in that field); *Am. W. Airlines, Inc. v. Tope*, 935 S.W.2d 908, 918 (Tex. App.—El Paso 1996, no writ) (clinical psychologist with 20 years' experience, two graduate degrees, membership to numerous professional societies and who was licensed to practice in two states was qualified to testify as an expert even though she did not have an M.D. or a Ph.D.); *Thomas v. State*, 915 S.W.2d 597, 600-01 (Tex. App.—Houston [14th Dist.] 1996, pet. ref'd) (crime-prevention officer was qualified to explain how defendant's role was consistent with that of a con artist in a "pigeon drop" scheme); *Agbogun v. State*, 756 S.W.2d 1, 4 (Tex. App.—Houston [1st Dist.] 1988, pet. ref'd) (licensed pharmacist with 36 years' experience was qualified to testify as an expert about procedures commonly followed within the pharmacy profession); *see also Davis v. State*, 313 S.W.3d 317, 349-50 (Tex. Crim. App. 2010) (police detective's testimony about murder victim's wounds was admitted under Rule 701 because detective personally observed wounds and his observations did not require significant expertise to interpret; trial court would not have abused its discretion if it had admitted the testimony under Rule 702 because officer's training and expertise would have qualified him as an expert).

119. *Rodgers v. State*, 205 S.W.3d 525, 528 (Tex. Crim. App. 2006); *see, e.g.*, *Harnett v. State*, 38 S.W.3d 650, 658-59 (Tex. App.—Austin 2000, pet. ref'd) (experienced social worker without professional license was qualified to give expert opinion derived from her perceptions based on eight counseling sessions with defendant; "[t]he expertise must be measured against the particular opinion the expert is offering").

dence is close to the jury's common understanding.[120] The expert's qualifications are also more important when his opinion is more conclusive.[121] Finally, the expert's qualifications are more important when his area of expertise is central to the resolution of the lawsuit.[122]

Appellate courts will not disturb the trial court's determination about whether a specific witness is qualified to testify as an expert unless there was a clear abuse of discretion.[123] Only occasionally has the trial judge been reversed for abuse of discretion in assessing a proposed expert's qualifications—usually when the expert's opinion has been excluded.[124] While the expert must be qualified to testify regarding the spe-

---

120. **Rodgers**, 205 S.W.3d at 528; *see* **Blasdell v. State**, 420 S.W.3d 406, 410 (Tex. App.—Beaumont 2014) ("[W]hether a gun is a distraction during a brief encounter does not appear to be a question far removed from what the jury would likely expect based on their common experience; thus, the focus on the witness's qualifications with respect to this topic [is] less important than whether the testimony is reliable."), *aff'd*, 470 S.W.3d 59 (Tex. Crim. App. 2015).

121. **Rodgers**, 205 S.W.3d at 528.

122. *Id.*

123. *E.g.*, **United Blood Servs. v. Longoria**, 938 S.W.2d 29, 30-31 (Tex. 1997) (trial court did not abuse its discretion in excluding expert testimony in summary-judgment proceeding because expert was not qualified to testify to the relevant standard of care in a particular case); **Broders v. Heise**, 924 S.W.2d 148, 151 (Tex. 1996) (trial court did not abuse its discretion in holding that witness was not qualified as an expert in medical-malpractice case); **Balderama v. State**, 421 S.W.3d 247, 251-52 (Tex. App.—San Antonio 2013, no pet.) (trial court did not abuse its discretion in refusing to allow retired breath-test technical adviser to testify as an expert; witness testified he had not kept up with literature and studies in the field and no longer felt comfortable testifying as an expert on the subject); **Fox v. State**, 115 S.W.3d 550, 565-66 (Tex. App.—Houston [14th Dist.] 2002, pet. ref'd) (trial court did not abuse its discretion in excluding social worker's expert testimony on child sexual abuse when expert did not concentrate solely on children and "had never conducted independent scientific studies on sexually abused children ... or the [proper] protocols for interviewing abused children"); **Morton Int'l v. Gillespie**, 39 S.W.3d 651, 655-56 (Tex. App.—Texarkana 2001, pet. denied) (trial court did not abuse its discretion in qualifying witness as an expert, even though witness admitted his training, education, and experience relating to airbags and their components was "significantly lacking"; he had a doctorate in mechanical engineering, was a member of various professional engineering societies, was a professor of vehicular dynamics, and was familiar with different types of sensors used in airbag electronic triggering device systems, and expertise fit his testimony); **1st Coppell Bank v. Smith**, 742 S.W.2d 454, 458 (Tex. App.—Dallas 1987, no writ) (trial court did not abuse its discretion in permitting a witness to testify as an expert when he was trained in the analysis of questioned documents, even though training had taken place ten years earlier and he had worked primarily in a different field); **Cortijo v. State**, 739 S.W.2d 486, 488 (Tex. App.—Corpus Christi 1987, pet. ref'd) (trial court properly determined that a forensic chemist who had been applying his knowledge and training in the field of bloodstain interpretation for ten years was qualified as an expert); **Burlington N. R.R. v. Harvey**, 717 S.W.2d 371, 377-78 (Tex. App.—Houston [14th Dist.] 1986, writ ref'd n.r.e.) (trial court could determine that expert in anesthesiology had skills and knowledge necessary to give expert testimony about urology); *see* 3 LOUISELL & MUELLER, *supra* note 27, §381, at 638 (question of expert qualification is for trial judge's discretion).

124. *See, e.g.*, **Exum v. Gen. Elec. Co.**, 819 F.2d 1158, 1163-64 (D.C. Cir. 1987) (error to exclude expert opinion when engineer had considerable experience with issues of industrial safety and product design); **Hall v. Huff**, 957 S.W.2d 90, 100-01 (Tex. App.—Texarkana 1997, pet. denied) (doctor was sufficiently qualified to give an opinion on the standard of care for appropriate diagnosis and treatment of patients with renal failure; trial court abused its discretion in refusing to consider doctor's summary-judgment affidavit because he was unfamiliar with nursing standards in Texas; focus is not on a specific locale, but on similar conditions of practice); **Southland Lloyd's Ins. v. Tomberlain**, 919 S.W.2d 822, 827-28 (Tex. App.—Texarkana 1996, writ denied) (reversible error to exclude testimony of state-approved insurance instructor; expert does not need to be licensed in pertinent area to be qualified to testify; "[t]he rule is meant to insure that if specialized knowledge will help the trier of fact examine the evidence, a person who has acquired such knowledge through any one of a number of methods may testify based on that knowledge"); **Negrini v. State**, 853 S.W.2d 128, 130-31 (Tex. App.—Corpus Christi 1993, no pet.) (reversible error to exclude expert testimony on alcohol burn-off rate offered by instructor who taught course about the effects of alco-

cific area of expertise involved in the lawsuit,[125] there is no "best-expert rule."[126] Normally, the focus is simply on the "fit" between the subject matter at issue and the proposed expert's familiarity with that topic, not on degrees, licenses, titles, or length of resumes.[127] There are, however, some exceptions to this general rule. For example, the

hol on the body and on driving skills); *Moore v. State*, 836 S.W.2d 255, 259 (Tex. App.—Texarkana 1992, pet. ref'd) (reversible error to exclude testimony by physician who had sufficient expertise to testify that defendant's "drunken tantrum" may have been caused by physical ailments instead of alcohol); *Fultz v. State*, 770 S.W.2d 595, 598 (Tex. App.—Houston [14th Dist.] 1989, pet. ref'd) (reversible error to exclude expert testimony by former Department of Public Safety technical supervisor because witness was not qualified; lack of documentation on reliability of Intoxilyzer tests would affect weight of opinion, not qualifications of witness).

125. *See Broders*, 924 S.W.2d at 152-53 (disagreeing with the contention that "every medical doctor is qualified to testify as an expert on all medical matters in a suit against a medical doctor because they are of 'the same school of practice'"; instead, issue is "whether the expert's expertise goes to the very matter on which he or she is to give an opinion"); *Nethery v. State*, 692 S.W.2d 686, 708 (Tex. Crim. App. 1985) ("Special knowledge of the specific matter upon which the expert is to testify must be shown."); *see, e.g.*, *United States v. Lopez*, 543 F.2d 1156, 1157-58 (5th Cir. 1976) (trial court properly excluded expert testimony by a "professor and scholar" that the defendant suffered sensory-deprivation psychosis because the expert was not a clinical psychologist and had never been licensed to practice clinical psychology); *MCI Sales & Serv., Inc. v. Hinton*, 272 S.W.3d 17, 30-31 (Tex. App.—Waco 2008) (trial court did not abuse its discretion in qualifying structural engineer with a master's degree in applied mechanics as an expert on the issue of how a motor coach could have been retrofitted with seat belts), *aff'd*, 329 S.W.3d 475 (Tex. 2010); *Olveda v. Sepulveda*, 141 S.W.3d 679, 682-83 (Tex. App.—San Antonio 2004) (obstetric anesthesiologist was not qualified to testify that urologist provided substandard medical care even though plaintiff claimed that urologist "deviated from a standard of care common to all physicians"), *pet. denied*, 189 S.W.3d 740 (Tex. 2006); *Cortijo*, 739 S.W.2d at 488 (forensic chemist with bachelor's and master's degrees in chemistry who had worked in a crime lab for ten years was qualified as an expert to testify to his interpretation of bloodstain patterns); *U.S. Fire Ins. v. Bishop*, 613 S.W.2d 52, 54 (Tex. Civ. App.—Fort Worth 1981, writ ref'd n.r.e.) (trial judge properly excluded testimony of a vocational expert who was asked to interpret the medical records of a patient he had never seen or examined; although the witness had a Ph.D., it was not established that he had any medical training that would qualify him to interpret these records).

126. *See Huss v. Gayden*, 571 F.3d 442, 452 (5th Cir. 2009) ("[Federal] Rule 702 does not mandate that an expert be highly qualified in order to testify about a given issue. Differences in expertise bear chiefly on the weight to be assigned to the testimony by the trier of fact, not its admissibility.").

127. *See Christopherson v. Allied-Signal Corp.*, 939 F.2d 1106, 1112-13 (5th Cir. 1991) (medical degree alone does not qualify a witness to give an opinion on every conceivable medical problem); *In re Commitment of Bohannan*, 388 S.W.3d 296, 304 (Tex. 2012) ("Credentials are important, but credentials alone do not qualify an expert to testify."); *Hayes v. Carroll*, 314 S.W.3d 494, 504 (Tex. App.—Austin 2010, no pet.) (in health-care-liability claim, "[t]he focus is on the 'fit' between the subject matter at issue and the expert's familiarity with the subject matter, and not on a comparison of the expert's specialty or experience with that of the defendant"); *Collini v. Pustejovsky*, 280 S.W.3d 456, 464 (Tex. App.—Fort Worth 2009, no pet.) (proper question in assessing physician's qualifications to submit an expert report "is not his area of practice, but his familiarity with the issues involved in the claim before the court"); *see, e.g.*, *Huss*, 571 F.3d at 453-55 (internist who had knowledge of cardiac conditions and toxicology was qualified to give his opinion that a drug did not cause a pregnant patient's cardiomyopathy; internist was not required to be board-certified in cardiology or toxicology to testify); *ExxonMobil Corp. v. Pagayon*, 467 S.W.3d 36, 52-53 (Tex. App.—Houston [14th Dist.] 2015) (physician from one specialty may testify about negligence of physician from different specialty as long as standard of care for task at issue is the same across specialties; physician who did not specialize in emergency-room medicine could testify about negligence of emergency-room physician in reading chest X-ray), *rev'd on other grounds*, ___ S.W.3d ___ (Tex. 2017) (No. 15-0642; 6-23-17); *Shelton v. Sargent*, 144 S.W.3d 113, 123 (Tex. App.—Fort Worth 2004, pet. denied) (trial court did not err in excluding expert's affidavit on standard of care in diagnosing cancer when sponsoring party did not establish that expert had sufficient knowledge and experience in that field).

RULE 702

Texas Legislature has set out minimum qualification standards for experts in a medical-malpractice lawsuit that are significantly more stringent than the general expert qualifications under Rule 702.[128]

The Texas Supreme Court's treatment of expert qualifications in ***Birchfield v. Texarkana Memorial Hospital***[129] and ***Louder v. De Leon***[130] has been criticized by evidence scholars.[131] In both cases, the supreme court apparently sanctioned the use of expert testimony on mixed questions of law and fact, such as questions of "negligence," "gross negligence," or "proximate cause."[132] A witness who is an expert in medicine, for ex-

---

128. *See* Tex. Civ. Prac. & Rem. Code §74.401(a) (to qualify as an expert witness on whether a physician departed from accepted standards of medical care, witness must have training and experience and must be a currently practicing physician who has knowledge of accepted standards of medical care for diagnosis, care, or treatment of the particular illness, injury, or condition involved in the lawsuit); ***Larson v. Downing***, 197 S.W.3d 303, 305 (Tex. 2006) (per curiam) ("'[G]iven the increasingly specialized and technical nature of medicine, there is no validity ... to the notion that every licensed medical doctor should be automatically qualified to testify as an expert on every medical question.'" (quoting ***Broders v. Heise***, 924 S.W.2d 148, 152 (Tex. 1996)); ***Estorque v. Schafer***, 302 S.W.3d 19, 25-26 (Tex. App.—Fort Worth 2009, no pet.) ("A physician does not need to be a practitioner in the same specialty as the defendant to qualify as an expert. The proper inquiry in assessing a doctor's qualifications to submit an expert report is not his area of expertise but his familiarity with the issues involved in the claim before the court."); *see, e.g.*, ***Johnson v. Harris***, ___ S.W.3d ___ (Tex. App.—El Paso 2017, no pet.) (No. 08-15-00149-CV; 4-19-17) (doctor was not qualified to give procedure-specific opinion when his knowledge of that procedure was outdated); ***Costello v. Christus Santa Rosa Health Care Corp.***, 141 S.W.3d 245, 248 (Tex. App.—San Antonio 2004, no pet.) (registered nurse did not qualify as an expert on patient's cause of death in medical-malpractice suit because she was statutorily precluded from rendering a medical diagnosis); *see also* ***Salais v. Tex. Dep't of Aging & Disability Servs.***, 323 S.W.3d 527, 536 (Tex. App.—Waco 2010, pet. denied) (expert's qualifications must appear in report and cannot be inferred). See *O'Connor's Texas Causes of Action* (2017), "Expert's qualifications," ch. 20-A, §8.3, p. 655.

129. 747 S.W.2d 361 (Tex. 1987).

130. 754 S.W.2d 148 (Tex. 1988).

131. *See* 2 Goode et al., *supra* note 7, §702.3, at 28 (expert testimony should be limited to expert's field of specialization); 2 Ray, *supra* note 32, §1401, at 9-10 (Supp. 1991) (questioning an expert's ability to give opinions on legal issues outside the scope of the expert's experiences).

132. In ***Birchfield***, the plaintiff's expert witness testified that a defendant-hospital's conduct constituted "negligence," "gross negligence," and "heedless and reckless conduct." 747 S.W.2d at 365. The court stated that "[f]airness and efficiency dictate that an expert may state an opinion on a mixed question of law and fact as long as the opinion is confined to the relevant issues and is based on proper legal concepts." *Id.* In ***Louder***, the supreme court held that the trial court properly permitted a state trooper to testify that the plaintiff's "failure to yield the right-of-way was a proximate cause of the accident." 754 S.W.2d at 148-49. The court relied on ***Birchfield*** and elaborated that "[j]urors realize that they are the final triers to decide the issues. They may accept or reject an expert's view. Thus there is little danger in an expert's answer to an all-embracing question on a mixed question of law and fact." ***Louder***, 754 S.W.2d at 149.

Texas courts historically held that opinions based on legal definitions or involving questions of law were improper. *See, e.g.*, ***Snow v. Bond***, 438 S.W.2d 549, 550 (Tex. 1969) (because negligence is a mixed question of law and fact, medical expert was not competent to express an opinion on negligence); ***Carr v. Radkey***, 393 S.W.2d 806, 813 (Tex. 1965) (in will-contest cases, evidence of "mental condition and mental ability or lack of it which does not involve legal definitions, legal tests, or pure questions of law should be admitted"); ***Lindley v. Lindley***, 384 S.W.2d 676, 682 (Tex. 1964) (legal capacity is not a proper subject for expert- or nonexpert-opinion testimony because it involves the application of a legal definition); ***Speck v. Speck***, 588 S.W.2d 853, 854 (Tex. Civ. App.—Houston [14th Dist.] 1979, no writ) (no error in a question asking whether the testatrix was "rational" in a case involving the capacity to make a will); ***Burks v. Meredith***, 546 S.W.2d 366, 370 (Tex. Civ. App.—Waco 1976, writ ref'd n.r.e.) (refusing to allow medical expert to testify about negligence or malpractice of defendant doctor). For a more complete discussion of the concerns about expert testimony on mixed questions of law and fact, see 2 Goode et al., *supra* note 7, §702.3, at 28.

ample, is not necessarily qualified to give an opinion on whether certain medical actions constitute legal negligence.[133] The expert witnesses in *Birchfield* and *Louder*, however, were qualified to testify about the specific issues in those cases. In *Birchfield*, a medical-malpractice action, the applicable legal standard was based on conduct in compliance with the accepted practices of the medical profession.[134] Thus, a doctor is fully qualified to express an opinion on whether another doctor's conduct is "negligent" in relation to that standard. In *Louder*, a personal-injury suit arising from a traffic accident, the experienced officer was well qualified to testify as an expert on the factual cause of the accident, a major component of legal proximate cause.[135] Nonetheless, practitioners should not use legal terminology such as "probable cause," "gross negligence," and "proximate cause" when questioning an expert and should instead use phrases that match the expert's field, asking for factual opinions that will lead the trier of fact to reach the desired legal conclusion.[136]

---

133. *Cf. Hendricks v. Todora*, 722 S.W.2d 458, 464-65 (Tex. App.—Dallas 1986, writ ref'd n.r.e.) (engineer's affidavit, which recited that a parking lot where an accident took place was "unreasonably dangerous" and that the accident "might reasonably have been anticipated," had no probative value because the court could not determine what standard the engineer employed in his conclusions; while "the affiant may be an expert in the field of engineering, the question of dangerousness and foreseeability in this case is not a matter of engineering, but of law"). This distinction between expertise in the law and expertise in another specific field led a court of appeals to distinguish *Birchfield* and hold that a management expert's opinion that it was "foreseeable" that an employee would be assaultive was not helpful and thus was superfluous. *Dieter v. Baker Serv. Tools*, 776 S.W.2d 781, 784 (Tex. App.—Corpus Christi 1989, writ denied). In *Dieter*, the plaintiff sued the defendant for the negligent hiring and supervision of two employees who assaulted the plaintiff. *Id.* at 782. The court of appeals rejected the testimony of an expert in the field of personnel and management who stated that a reasonable employer should have foreseen these employees' violent tendencies and should not have hired them. *Id.* at 783-84. This testimony was not probative because this was a question of legal "foreseeability" and the witness was qualified in personnel and management. *Id.* at 784. Thus, the witness was in no better position to draw these conclusions than anyone else. *Id.*

134. *See Birchfield*, 747 S.W.2d at 364-65.

135. *See Louder*, 754 S.W.2d at 148-49.

136. *See* Tex. R. Evid. 704; *see, e.g., Greenberg Traurig of N.Y., P.C. v. Moody*, 161 S.W.3d 56, 94-95 (Tex. App.—Houston [14th Dist.] 2004, no pet.) (in trial for fraud and conspiracy, trial court erred in allowing law professor and former justice to testify about fiduciary duties, to explain the applicable law, and to interpret disciplinary rules of professional conduct; "[i]t is not the role of the expert witness to define the particular legal principles applicable to a case"). Refer to notes 329-355 *infra* and accompanying text.
In several lower-court opinions following *Birchfield* and *Louder*, the proper predicate for eliciting an opinion on a legal term of art appears to have been laid. *See, e.g., Rodgers v. Comm'n for Lawyer Discipline*, 151 S.W.3d 602, 617 (Tex. App.—Fort Worth 2004, pet. denied) (trial court did not abuse discretion in allowing lawyer to give her expert opinion that attorney's advertisement violated the disciplinary rules of professional conduct); *Royal Maccabees Life Ins. v. James*, 146 S.W.3d 340, 354 (Tex. App.—Dallas 2004, pet. denied) (op. on reh'g) (insurance claims adjuster could testify as expert about his interpretation of insurance policy and state his opinion on mixed questions of fact and law of whether insurer's conduct "constituted bad faith, unfair dealing and fraud" or was a violation of Insurance Code provisions); *Pittsburgh Corning Corp. v. Walters*, 1 S.W.3d 759, 777 (Tex. App.—Corpus Christi 1999, pet. denied) (expert could state opinion on defendant's negligence and gross negligence because he was provided the proper legal standard as a predicate); *Lyondell Pet. Co. v. Fluor Daniel, Inc.*, 888 S.W.2d 547, 554-56 (Tex. App.—Houston [1st Dist.] 1994, writ denied) (expert's opinion that contractor violated OSHA regulations was admissible; even though language of regulation was straightforward, its application to particular facts was not, and expert was helpful in correlating factual compliance with legal requirements of regulations; reversible error to exclude his opinion); *Transp. Ins. v. Faircloth*, 861 S.W.2d 926, 937-39 (Tex. App.—Beaumont 1993) (former Texas Supreme Court Justice could testify as expert on procedures required by law), *rev'd on other grounds*, 898 S.W.2d 269 (Tex. 1995). *But cf. Puente v. A.S.I. Signs*, 821 S.W.2d 400, 402 (Tex. App.—Corpus Christi 1991, writ denied)

(2) Forms of expert testimony. A witness who qualifies as an expert may testify in three different ways: the witness may testify under Rule 701 based on personal knowledge of the facts in issue;[137] the witness may provide the fact-finder with general background information under Rule 702 about the theory and principles relative to the witness's field of expertise;[138] and the witness may give opinions under Rule 702 about specific disputed data and facts based on the witness's experience in a particular specialized field.[139]

A witness with specialized training or experience is not limited to giving opinion testimony as a Rule 702 "expert." If an opinion rests on firsthand knowledge—that is, if it is rationally based on the witness's own perceptions—then testimony under Rule 701 is also permissible.[140] The greater a witness's experiential capacity, the more likely the testimony will help the trier of fact under either Rule 701 or Rule 702.[141] The degree of experience or training a witness should have before being allowed to render an opinion depends on the testimony. A witness testifying to facts normally encountered in everyday life (whether because the facts themselves are relevant or because they illustrate the significance of other facts) does not need a particularly high degree of experience or special training. Lay witnesses perform these functions routinely without any demonstration of superior knowledge or ability. Courts assume without advance

---

(under Civil Rule 704, an expert who articulates the underlying factual basis for his conclusion could give an opinion that a duty of care exists in a particular situation, but an expert could not give his "naked legal conclusion" that such a duty exists).

137. Refer to notes 140-145 *infra* and accompanying text.

138. *See* FED. R. EVID. 702 advisory committee's note (Rule 702 recognizes that an expert may give a dissertation or exposition of scientific principles relevant to the case, leaving the trier of fact to apply them to the relevant issues). Refer to notes 146-152 *infra* and accompanying text.

139. Refer to notes 153-155 *infra* and accompanying text.

140. *Austin v. State*, 794 S.W.2d 408, 410 (Tex. App.—Austin 1990, pet. ref'd). Refer to notes 15-18 *supra* and accompanying text.

141. For example, the plaintiff in *Teen-Ed, Inc. v. Kimball Int'l, Inc.* offered his tax accountant's testimony on lost profits. 620 F.2d 399, 402 (3d Cir. 1980). The trial court, proceeding under the erroneous assumption that only an expert could offer opinion testimony, excluded the evidence because the plaintiff had not designated the accountant as an expert before trial. *Id.* at 402-03. The Third Circuit vacated the decision, stressing that the proffered opinion was based entirely on the witness's firsthand knowledge of Teen-Ed's books. *Id.* at 403-04. He was thus eligible under Rule 701 to give an opinion on lost profits based on the inferences drawn from that knowledge. *Teen-Ed*, 620 F.2d at 403-04. The court held that the accountant's potential qualifications as an expert did not prevent him from testifying within the narrower confines of Rule 701. *Teen-Ed*, 620 F.2d at 403-04. To the extent the defendant in *Teen-Ed* was able to cross-examine and rebut the accountant's opinion adequately, the decision is sound. However, if a trial court determines that the failure to designate a witness as an expert unfairly prejudices an opponent's ability to cross-examine and rebut the witness, the court may exclude the proffered testimony under Rule 403. Rule 403 provides for exclusion of otherwise relevant evidence on the grounds of unfair prejudice. TEX. R. EVID. 403; *see also* FED. R. CIV. P. 26(a)(2) (party may require an opponent to disclose the names and the subject matter of the testimony of testifying experts, and, in some cases, nontestifying experts); TEX. R. CIV. P. 192.3(e) (party must disclose, on request, the names of all testifying experts, the subject matter of the testimony, and the mental impressions and all facts known to the experts; in some instances, disclosure is also required for nontestifying experts).

The reasoning and result of *Teen-Ed* would be abrogated in federal proceedings by the 2000 amendments to Federal Rule 701, which prohibit a witness whose experience and training would qualify him to testify as an expert from giving a lay opinion. *See* FED. R. EVID. 701 advisory committee's note to 2000 amendments. Refer to notes 12-14 *supra* and accompanying text.

proof that a witness has enough experience to provide a reliable account of facts encountered in ordinary, everyday life.[142] Parties can explore any deficiencies in this assumption on cross-examination.[143]

Commonly, courts distinguished a lay witness from an expert on the basis that a lay witness testifies to mere facts perceived, while an expert witness serves as an evaluator. An arbitrary and artificial distinction between lay and expert witnesses should not prompt exclusion of relevant, helpful information from witnesses who have adequate experiential qualifications and personal knowledge of the disputed facts.[144] A person must evaluate what he perceives in light of his experiences. Courts should not classify a witness as an expert witness merely because he perceived a situation or event not normally encountered by most people in everyday life. Rather, courts should allow a witness to testify as a lay witness under Rule 701 if he has the experiential capacity to understand the situation or event he perceived.[145]

While an expert witness can testify to his own observations, experiments, and data pertinent to the specific facts of a case under Rule 701, he can also testify to the general principles and theories of his area of expertise under Rule 702. Expert testimony helps the jury "to understand the evidence" and is helpful in an educational sense.[146] The expert witness may teach the fact-finder about an area of science, technology, or other specialized knowledge of which the fact-finder may either lack a complete and

RULE 702

---

142. 2 WIGMORE, *supra* note 3, §556, at 751.

143. *Id.*; *see* **Safeway Stores, Inc. v. Combs**, 273 F.2d 295, 296 (5th Cir. 1960) (expert witness is subject to broad cross-examination about the basis for his inferences); **Tex. Elec. Serv. Co. v. Wheeler**, 551 S.W.2d 341, 342-43 (Tex. 1977) (per curiam) (lack of supportive data for an expert's opinion goes to its weight, not its admissibility, because an expert's competency can be challenged by critical cross-examination).

144. *See, e.g.*, **W. Indus., Inc. v. Newcor Can. Ltd.**, 739 F.2d 1198, 1202-03 (7th Cir. 1984) (executives experienced in the trade of welding machines were qualified to testify on trade custom in that industry under either Federal Rule 701 or 702); **Farner v. Paccar, Inc.**, 562 F.2d 518, 528-29 (8th Cir. 1977) (witness with almost 30 years' trucking experience should be allowed to testify about the simple use of safety chains on trucks with air-leaf suspension systems under either Federal Rule 701 or 702). Texas Rule 701 is intended to minimize this distinction. Refer to notes 15-18 *supra* and accompanying text.

In **Randolph v. Collectramatic, Inc.**, however, the court did not allow a restaurant owner with five years of experience to testify that he knew how pressure cookers were manufactured and how they operated. 590 F.2d 844, 847-48 (10th Cir. 1979). The court held that Federal Rule 701 "does not permit a lay witness to express an opinion as to matters which are beyond the realm of common experience and which require the special skill and knowledge of an expert witness." **Randolph**, 590 F.2d at 846. Apparently turning to Federal Rule 702, the court also said that "there was no evidence admitted concerning [the restaurant owner's] formal or informal training, other than his four to five years in the restaurant business, which qualified him to comment on the design of an admittedly technical and complex machine" and that the "trial court was most liberal in allowing [him] to testify as to the manner in which the Collectramatic pressure cooker is operated." **Randolph**, 590 F.2d at 848. The court concluded that only a qualified engineering expert could comment on product design. *Id.*

145. Therefore, the tax accountant in **Teen-Ed** could testify as a lay witness to his personal knowledge about lost profits. 620 F.2d at 403; *see also* **DIJO, Inc. v. Hilton Hotels Corp.**, 351 F.3d 679, 685-86 (5th Cir. 2003) (distinguishing **Teen-Ed**; lender-representative lay witness who had no personal knowledge of developer's operations could not testify to lost profits); **Miss. Chem. Corp. v. Dresser-Rand Co.**, 287 F.3d 359, 373-74 (5th Cir. 2002) (following **Teen-Ed**; witness who had personal knowledge and familiarity with calculating lost profits could give lay opinion under Rule 701). Refer to note 141 *supra*. Similarly, a witness to a shooting can testify as a lay witness that a revolver was a Colt .38 if he has the experiential capacity to recognize that fact.

146. *See* TEX. R. EVID. 702.

thorough understanding[147] or have some misconceptions.[148] Here, the witness acts "as an advisor to the jury, much like a consultant might advise a business ...."[149] Thus, the expert witness does not need to be familiar with the facts of the particular case or express any opinion relative to those facts.[150] In criminal cases particularly, this aspect

147. Rule 702 permits the use of expert testimony whenever the expert would shed further light on a subject that may in some respects be quite familiar to jurors. *See* 3 LOUISELL & MUELLER, *supra* note 27, §382, at 640 (helpfulness requirement "may also be satisfied where specialized knowledge or skill may add precision or depth to the ability of the trier of fact to reach conclusions about subjects which lie well within common experience"). The question under Rule 702 is not whether the jurors know something about the field, but whether the expert can expand the jurors' understanding in any way that is relevant to the disputed issues. *Coble v. State*, 330 S.W.3d 253, 288 (Tex. Crim. App. 2010); *e.g.*, *Tillman v. State*, 354 S.W.3d 425, 442 (Tex. Crim. App. 2011) ("[W]hile jurors might have their own notions about the reliability of eyewitness identification, that does not mean they would not be aided by the studies and findings of a trained psychologist on the issue. Additional explanation of eyewitness-identification theories may help guide the jury in its understanding of the standards in the area."); *see, e.g.*, *Fielder v. State*, 756 S.W.2d 309, 321 (Tex. Crim. App. 1988) (defense expert psychologist in murder trial should have been permitted to offer her opinion on why a woman who was being physically and sexually abused would continue to stay with her abusive husband because the "average lay person has no basis for understanding the conduct of a woman who endures an abusive relationship"); *Loera v. Fuentes*, 511 S.W.3d 761, 774-75 (Tex. App.—El Paso 2016, n.p.h.) (expert testimony was required to support opinion that already frail person in frontal collision would suffer no serious injuries if wearing seat belt; proposition was outside jury's common knowledge); *Hill v. State*, 392 S.W.3d 850, 855 (Tex. App.—Amarillo 2013, pet. ref'd) (licensed counselor could testify that it is common for victims of domestic violence to stay with their abusers and "not uncommon" for them to file affidavits of nonprosecution); *Lundy v. Allstate Ins.*, 774 S.W.2d 352, 356-57 (Tex. App.—Beaumont 1989, no writ) (expert fire investigator could testify about the general motives of people who deliberately set fires); *March v. Victoria Lloyds Ins.*, 773 S.W.2d 785, 789 (Tex. App.—Fort Worth 1989, writ denied) (although an expert's testimony would have enhanced the jury's understanding of a blood-alcohol report, it was not necessary to their understanding of the test results); *Kirkpatrick v. State*, 747 S.W.2d 833, 835-36 (Tex. App.—Dallas 1987, pet. ref'd) (expert could testify to show general behavior characteristics of child sexual-abuse victims to assist jury in assessing the child witness's credibility); *Brown v. State*, 689 S.W.2d 219, 222-23 (Tex. Crim. App. 1985) (Teague, J., dissenting from denial of motion for rehearing on petition for discretionary review) (because jurors overvalue eyewitness testimony, per se rules excluding expert witnesses on reliability of eyewitness identification should be abandoned when an "eyewitness expert is simply presenting testimony about the factors that affect the reliability of an eyewitness's account").

148. Here, the expert frequently has a "myth-reducing" function. Jurors may believe they have a good understanding of a particular area of knowledge, but that understanding could be inaccurate or based on misperception. *See State v. Jensen*, 432 N.W.2d 913, 918 (Wis. 1988) (behavior of child sexual-assault victim often does not conform to commonly held expectations of how a victim reacts to sexual assault, and courts thus admit expert-opinion testimony to help avoid verdicts based on misconceptions of victims' behavior).

149. 2 STEPHEN A. SALTZBURG ET AL., FEDERAL RULES OF EVIDENCE MANUAL 1250 (7th ed. 1998); *see, e.g.*, *United States v. Masson*, 582 F.2d 961, 963-64 (5th Cir. 1978) (FBI agent could testify as expert about bookmaking operations and terminology); *Fund of Funds, Ltd. v. Arthur Andersen & Co.*, 545 F. Supp. 1314, 1372 (S.D.N.Y. 1982) (accountants could testify as experts to the ordinary practices of a profession "to enable the jury to evaluate the conduct of the parties against the standards of ordinary practice in the industry"); *Stanley v. S. Pac. Co.*, 466 S.W.2d 548, 551 (Tex. 1971) (witness who was a fireman and an engineer could testify as expert about the customs of firemen); *Wood v. State*, 573 S.W.2d 207, 211 (Tex. Crim. App. 1978) (police sergeant could testify as expert to explain coded client lists and index cards used in prostitution enterprises).

150. *See, e.g.*, *Scugoza v. State*, 949 S.W.2d 360, 363 (Tex. App.—San Antonio 1997, no pet.) (expert witness who had no knowledge of parties in particular trial could testify about the emotional and behavioral patterns typical of spousal abuse, describe the cycle of abuse in family-violence situations, and explain why some victims of spousal abuse eventually recant their accusations of abuse). In *Sattiewhite v. State*, a defense psychologist testified during the punishment stage of a capital-murder trial about various factors that affect the difficulty of predicting the potential for future dangerousness. 786 S.W.2d 271, 290 (Tex. Crim. App. 1989). The trial court allowed the witness to educate the jury in his particular area of psychological inquiry but properly refused to allow his opinion on which punishment was appropriate for the defendant—his opinion was of no help to the jury because the witness was neither competent nor qualified to give an opinion on proper punishment. *Id.* at 290-91; *see also Lucero v. State*, 246 S.W.3d 86, 96-97 (Tex. Crim. App. 2008) (testimony, given by chief investigator for Special Prosecution Unit, that

of Rule 702 has permitted the admission of a wide range of "educational expertise" on the operation of illegal enterprises because the modus operandi of such industries are not normally within the average juror's experience.[151] The proposed expert testimony must, however, "fit" the specific facts or situation of the particular case to be relevant.[152]

An expert may also help the fact-finder by evaluating the specific facts in issue.[153] Unlike lay witnesses, qualified experts may explain their view of the significance of facts. It is in this third form of testimony that the qualifications of the expert must be shown to be so superior that his evaluation of facts in evidence will help the fact-finder, as required by Rule 702.[154] Increasingly, expert witnesses also serve as fact-finders because they may give opinions based in whole or in part on inadmissible evidence that is not before the jury.[155]

---

inmate violence can occur under current prison conditions could aid jury in determining defendant's future dangerousness); *In re Commitment of Dodson*, 311 S.W.3d 194, 201-02 (Tex. App.—Beaumont 2010, pet. denied) (witness licensed as counselor and sex-offender-treatment provider was qualified to give an opinion on the risk that defendant would commit future acts of sexual violence; lack of medical degree goes to weight of evidence, not admissibility).

151. *See, e.g.*, *United States v. Buchanan*, 70 F.3d 818, 832 (5th Cir. 1996) (narcotics agent could testify to the significance of conduct or modus operandi of drug-distribution business); *United States v. Dunn*, 846 F.2d 761, 762-63 (D.C. Cir. 1988) (police detective could testify that "the quantities of drugs, drug-packaging material, drug paraphernalia and weapons located in the townhouse where defendants were arrested indicated the presence of a retail drug operation"); *United States v. Daly*, 842 F.2d 1380, 1388 (2d Cir. 1988) (FBI agent could testify about nature and structure of organized-crime families that operated in New York area and discuss rules of conduct, the code of silence, and specialized jargon); *United States v. Ginsberg*, 758 F.2d 823, 830 (2d Cir. 1985) (police detective could testify about narcotics dealers' use of beepers and codes; such specialized knowledge was based on information given to him by other arrested narcotics dealers); *United States v. Maher*, 645 F.2d 780, 783-84 (9th Cir. 1981) (DEA agent qualified as an expert on modus operandi of persons conducting countersurveillance while transporting drugs); *United States v. Sellaro*, 514 F.2d 114, 118-19 (8th Cir. 1973) (FBI agent qualified as an expert on modus operandi of bookmakers and could define the meaning of various bookmaker terms, even though he had never placed a bet with a bookmaker).

Several Texas cases have followed the federal lead in permitting expert "educational" testimony about illegal business operations. *See, e.g.*, *Taylor v. State*, 106 S.W.3d 827, 832-33 (Tex. App.—Dallas 2003, no pet.) (police officer could testify as expert about whether seized cocaine was intended for personal use or for distribution purposes); *Fields v. State*, 932 S.W.2d 97, 107-08 (Tex. App.—Tyler 1996, pet. ref'd) (DPS lieutenant in narcotics service could testify to characteristics and patterns common to "people who would be traveling with quantities" of controlled substances, especially cocaine); *Foster v. State*, 909 S.W.2d 86, 88-89 (Tex. App.—Houston [14th Dist.] 1995, pet. ref'd) (experienced police officer could offer expert testimony on modus operandi of "juggings"— well-organized robberies involving "complicated maneuvers of the co-actors with various automobiles and license plates"); *Miller v. State*, 874 S.W.2d 908, 914 (Tex. App.—Houston [1st Dist.] 1994, pet. ref'd) (in gambling prosecution, expert assisted jury by testifying about the rules of craps, whether there was an economic benefit other than personal winnings, and whether the risks of losing and chances of winning were the same for all participants).

152. Refer to notes 243-250 *infra* and accompanying text.

153. *See Birchfield v. Texarkana Mem'l Hosp.*, 747 S.W.2d 361, 365 (Tex. 1987) (Civil Rule 704 allows an expert to testify to a mixed question of fact and law as long as the testimony is relevant and based on proper legal concepts); *Fleming v. Kinney ex rel. Shelton*, 395 S.W.3d 917, 928 (Tex. App.—Houston [14th Dist.] 2013, pet. denied) (to give testimony that assists jury, expert "must have some leeway to reference the controlling 'legal terms' and related concepts while testifying"); *Herrera v. FMC Corp.*, 672 S.W.2d 5, 7 (Tex. App.—Houston [14th Dist.] 1984, writ ref'd n.r.e.) (expert may testify on an ultimate issue of fact, but trial court has broad discretion to determine admissibility if, for example, jury is as competent as expert to form an opinion on an ultimate fact issue).

154. When determining the admissibility of evidence as required by Rule 104, the judge has discretion under Rule 104(c) to conduct a hearing outside the jury's presence and to permit voir dire examination by opposing counsel. Refer to *Article I: General Provisions*, *supra* p. 94. Under Rule 705(b), the opposing attorney is explicitly entitled to

RULE 702

Without expert assistance, the jury would have extreme difficulty evaluating factual evidence in cases involving complicated skills or standards, such as medical-malpractice cases.[156] However, even when a jury cannot make an intelligent finding of fact without

---

conduct a voir dire examination outside the jury's hearing to examine the facts or data on which the expert is basing his opinion. Refer to notes 389-395 *infra* and accompanying text. The 1998 comment to this rule, however, includes the caveat that this provision does not preclude the opposing attorney from conducting a preliminary voir dire examination to test the expert's qualifications to testify under Rule 702. TEX. R. EVID. 705 cmt. (1998). Because a witness's experience or special knowledge affects the weight of his testimony, the jury is entitled to hear the witness's experiential qualifications. The opponent cannot curtail this right by stipulating that the witness is qualified. *See Murphy v. Nat'l R.R. Passenger Corp.*, 547 F.2d 816, 817 (4th Cir. 1977) ("[A] jury can better assess the weight to be accorded an expert's opinion if the witness is permitted to explain his qualifications.").

Some cases state that the admissibility of expert evidence depends on whether the knowledge and skill involved is beyond that of the average juror. *See Agbogun v. State*, 756 S.W.2d 1, 4 (Tex. App.—Houston [1st Dist.] 1988, pet. ref'd) (special knowledge of the subject matter may qualify a witness to give an expert opinion); *Adams v. Smith*, 479 S.W.2d 390, 396 (Tex. Civ. App.—Amarillo 1972, no writ) (allowing testimony from an expert witness who "should have more skill and knowledge in this area of inquiry than the jury"); 2 RAY, *supra* note 32, §1400, at 23-24 (expert must possess knowledge of the subject exceeding that possessed by the average juror). This test, while relevant to whether the evidence will help the jury, is confusing when used to justify the admission of factual evaluations by a witness who may know more than the average juror but whose experiential capacity is minimal. The jurors' knowledge is important in determining how helpful the expert's opinion will be. Thus, when the opinion conveys nothing that the jurors do not already know, courts should exclude it. *See* 7 WIGMORE, *supra* note 27, §1918, at 11 (opinion evidence on subjects within the realm of common knowledge should be excluded); *see, e.g., Powers v. State*, 757 S.W.2d 88, 93-94 (Tex. App.—Houston [14th Dist.] 1988, pet. ref'd) (in murder trial, police officer could not testify on whether shooting was intentional or accidental because no showing was made that officer was a homicide expert; "when the jury is in possession of the same information as the witness, and the jury can fully understand the matter and draw the proper inferences and conclusions, the witness's opinion testimony is unnecessary and inadmissible").

155. *See* TEX. R. EVID. 703. Refer to notes 257-328 *infra* and accompanying text.

156. *See Guevara v. Ferrer*, 247 S.W.3d 662, 665 (Tex. 2007) ("The general rule has long been that expert testimony is necessary to establish causation as to medical conditions outside the common knowledge and experience of jurors."); *Roark v. Allen*, 633 S.W.2d 804, 809 (Tex. 1982) (most medical-malpractice cases require expert testimony to establish a reasonable standard of care); *see, e.g., Hood v. Phillips*, 554 S.W.2d 160, 165-66 (Tex. 1977) (medical treatment at issue was not a matter of common knowledge and thus required expert testimony to satisfy the burden of proof); *see also Bioderm Skin Care, LLC v. Sok*, 426 S.W.3d 753, 756 (Tex. 2014) (allegedly improper laser hair removal was health-care-liability claim, and expert testimony was necessary to prove or refute plaintiff's claim; laser is a medical instrument that requires extensive training and experience, and its proper use is not in layperson's common knowledge); *In re McAllen Med. Ctr., Inc.*, 275 S.W.3d 458, 462 (Tex. 2008) (claims of negligent hiring, retention, and supervision of physicians are health-care-liability claims and must be "supported within 180 days of filing by an expert report signed by a person with knowledge, training, or experience concerning the applicable standard of care"); *cf. Elizondo v. Krist*, 415 S.W.3d 259, 270 (Tex. 2013) (in legal-malpractice cases, proof of negligence requires expert testimony "because establishing such negligence requires knowledge beyond that of most laypersons[;] [t]he same is true of proof of damages under a theory that a settlement was inadequate"); *Reed v. State*, 59 S.W.3d 278, 282-83 (Tex. App.—Fort Worth 2001, pet. ref'd) (in murder trial, trial court did not err in excluding copies of highly technical mental-health medical records offered without expert testimony; without any explanation, records could have misled jury and confused issues). In medical-malpractice cases, the expert must, to a reasonable degree of medical probability, explain how and why the defendant's negligence caused the plaintiff's injury. *Jelinek v. Casas*, 328 S.W.3d 526, 536 (Tex. 2010); *see Bustamante v. Ponte*, ___ S.W.3d ___ (Tex. 2017) (No. 15-0509; 9-29-17); *Columbia Valley Healthcare Sys., L.P. v. Zamarripa*, ___ S.W.3d ___ (Tex. 2017) (No. 15-0909; 6-9-17); *Van Ness v. ETMC First Physicians*, 461 S.W.3d 140, 142 (Tex. 2015). Expert opinions must be "grounded in a sound evidentiary basis." *Jelinek*, 328 S.W.3d at 536; *see Columbia Valley Healthcare Sys.*, ___ S.W.3d at ___ ("An expert's simple *ipse dixit* is insufficient to establish a matter; rather, the expert must explain the basis of his statements to link his conclusions to the facts." (quoting *Earle v. Ratliff*, 998 S.W.2d 882, 890 (Tex. 1999)); *Van Ness*, 461 S.W.3d at 142 (bare expert opinion that breach of standard of care caused injury is not sufficient). Thus,

> [w]hen the only evidence of a vital fact is circumstantial, the expert cannot merely draw possible inferences from the evidence and state that "in medical probability" the injury was caused by the de-

expert-witness assistance, the expert's testimony can be excluded if it is unreliable, cumulative, superfluous, or otherwise irrelevant.[157]

Considerable confusion has resulted when the expert's testimony directly or indirectly touches on another witness's credibility. Traditionally, Texas common law broadly excluded all expert psychological evidence that was offered solely for impeachment purposes.[158] Because the jury is the "lie detector in the courtroom,"[159] only the jury can assess the credibility of witnesses.[160] An expert cannot testify that a particular witness is or is not telling the truth about an event,[161] but expert testimony is not inadmissible simply because it could make a witness's testimony more or less believable.[162]

---

fendant's negligence. The expert must explain why the inferences drawn are medically preferable to competing inferences that are equally consistent with the known facts.
Jelinek, 328 S.W.3d at 536; *see Bustamante*, ___ S.W.3d at ___. See *O'Connor's Texas Causes of Action* (2017), "Injury & causation," ch. 20-A, §8.1.2, p. 654. Even when expert testimony is desirable, it is not always essential to sustain a judgment. In *March v. Victoria Lloyds Ins.*, the plaintiff unsuccessfully argued that a blood-alcohol-concentration lab report was not evidence of the deceased's intoxication without expert testimony to support its meaning. 773 S.W.2d 785, 789 (Tex. App.—Fort Worth 1989, writ denied). The court responded to the plaintiff's argument by stating that "[w]hile the jury's comprehension of the significance of the test results would have been enhanced by expert testimony, they did not need an expert's interpretation of the results to understand that it was evidence that there was alcohol in [deceased's] bloodstream at the time of the accident." *Id.*

157. *See* 2 CHARLES T. MCCORMICK & ROY R. RAY, TEXAS PRACTICE: TEXAS LAW OF EVIDENCE §1393, at 217-18 (2d ed. 1956) ("The true theory of the Opinion rule is that of the exclusion of superfluous evidence. ... Whenever the tribunal is in possession of the same information as the witness and the latter can add nothing to that information his further testimony is unnecessary and in fact merely cumbers the proceedings."); *see also Chesebrough-Pond's, Inc. v. Faberge, Inc.*, 666 F.2d 393, 397-98 (9th Cir. 1982) (expert evidence on the similarity of trademarks "Macho" and "Match" in trademark-infringement litigation would not likely assist the trier of fact within the meaning of Federal Rule 702).

158. *See, e.g., Hopkins v. State*, 480 S.W.2d 212, 220-21 (Tex. Crim. App. 1972) (expert psychological evidence offered to impeach another witness's credibility was inadmissible because it was likely to lead to a battle of experts in a field that is more inexact art than precise science); *see also Brown v. State*, 689 S.W.2d 219, 221-23 (Tex. Crim. App. 1985) (Teague, J., dissenting from denial of motion for rehearing on petition for discretionary review) (expert cannot be called solely to testify that another witness is not believable, but expert testimony on the inherent unreliability of eyewitness identifications does not go solely to credibility of an identification witness; because expert witness provides jury with factors that affect the reliability of an eyewitness account and describes scientific studies, witness puts jury in a better position to evaluate evidence). In *Pierce v. State*, the court of criminal appeals disavowed the broad language in *Hopkins* but upheld the trial court's exclusion of expert testimony on the inherent unreliability of eyewitness identifications. 777 S.W.2d 399, 414-16 (Tex. Crim. App. 1989). The *Pierce* court ruled that a "jury is amply qualified to make a determination on the credibility of eyewitnesses, aided by cross-examination and common knowledge of memory and its effects upon perception" when, as in this case, the expert, whose testimony was excluded, admitted that he had no specific knowledge about the testimony of the witnesses in the present trial. *Id.* at 415-16. Nonetheless, the court noted that it was not holding that all expert testimony on eyewitness identification is inadmissible or that it would be an abuse of discretion to admit it. *Id.* at 416 n.5. For a discussion of the treatment under Rule 702 of expert psychological evidence about eyewitness identification, refer to notes 220-221 *infra* and accompanying text.

159. *United States v. Barnard*, 490 F.2d 907, 912 (9th Cir. 1973).

160. *See Thota v. Young*, 366 S.W.3d 678, 695 (Tex. 2012); *cf. Perry v. New Hampshire*, 565 U.S. 228, 245 (2012) ("The fallibility of eyewitness evidence does not, without the taint of improper state conduct, warrant a due process rule requiring a trial court to screen such evidence for reliability before allowing the jury to assess its creditworthiness.").

161. *See Schutz v. State*, 957 S.W.2d 52, 59 (Tex. Crim. App. 1997) (expert testimony does not assist jury if it is "direct opinion on the truthfulness" of a witness or criminal allegation; expert may not testify that a child sexual-assault victim is or is not fantasizing events or being manipulated); *Yount v. State*, 872 S.W.2d 706, 711 (Tex. Crim.

As with lay opinions, absolute certainty is not a prerequisite to the admission of an expert's opinion.[163] A qualified opinion may nonetheless help the jury. Thus, the degree of the expert's certainty normally goes to the weight of the evidence, not to its admissibility.[164]

App. 1993) (expert testimony that a particular witness is truthful is inadmissible under Rule 702; "[a]n expert who testifies that a class of persons to which the victim belongs is truthful is essentially telling the jury that they can believe the victim in the instant case as well. This is not 'expert' testimony of the kind which will assist the jury under Rule 702."); **Salinas v. State**, 368 S.W.3d 550, 555 (Tex. App.—Houston [14th Dist.] 2011) ("Texas Rule of Evidence 702 prohibits expert witnesses from directly testifying that a particular witness is truthful."), *aff'd*, 369 S.W.3d 176 (Tex. Crim. App. 2012); *see, e.g.*, **Arrington v. State**, 451 S.W.3d 834, 842 (Tex. Crim. App. 2015) (in case involving sexual assault of child, school counselor should not have been allowed to testify that complainant was truthful in her accusations against defendant; because defendant did not object and evidence was admitted for all purposes, jury could still consider it); **Flores v. State**, 513 S.W.3d 146, 164-65 (Tex. App.—Houston [14th Dist.] 2016, pet. ref'd) (pediatrician's testimony that consistency was most important indicator of credibility and that child victim's outcry statements were consistent was inadmissible because it attested to truthfulness of child's statement); **Sandoval v. State**, 409 S.W.3d 259, 293-94 (Tex. App.—Austin 2013, no pet.) (police officer testified that he believed complainant's account of sexual assault because her statements were consistent; trial court erred in allowing testimony, although error was harmless); **Chavez v. State**, 324 S.W.3d 785, 788-89 (Tex. App.—Eastland 2010, no pet.) (expert could not give opinion on child complainant's truthfulness or testify that a class of persons, such as child sexual-abuse victims, should be believed; however, testimony about behavioral characteristics of children whose mothers do not support their outcries of abuse was admissible to assist the jury in understanding complainant's behavior); **Wilson v. State**, 90 S.W.3d 391, 393-94 (Tex. App.—Dallas 2002, no pet.) (harmless error to admit expert's testimony that, according to studies, only 2 to 8% of children lie about being sexually assaulted; this testimony was an indirect comment on child victim's credibility and supplanted jury's role in determining credibility); **Shaw v. State**, 764 S.W.2d 815, 820-21 (Tex. App.—Fort Worth 1988, pet. ref'd) (trial court should have prevented counselor at rape-crisis center from suggesting in testimony that complainant had been raped or that defendant was the rapist; error was harmless because jury was continually reminded that the expert could not testify to those facts); *see also* **Ex parte Miles**, 359 S.W.3d 647, 662 & n.14 (Tex. Crim. App. 2012) (in habeas corpus proceeding, court of criminal appeals did not consider polygraph results as evidence of defendant's innocence "[b]ecause polygraph exams are not admissible evidence"); **Perkins v. State**, 902 S.W.2d 88, 93 (Tex. App.—El Paso 1995, pet. ref'd) ("polygraph evidence offered to show that the defendant is truthful is inadmissible under Rule 702" because that type of expertise impermissibly decides the issue of credibility for jury); **Kirkpatrick v. State**, 747 S.W.2d 833, 837 & n.5 (Tex. App.—Dallas 1987, pet. ref'd) ("An expert who gives his opinion as to the credibility of a witness is, by any available measure, the human equivalent of a polygraph machine. The overwhelming majority of American jurisdictions reject polygraph results as evidence. Expert testimony of truthfulness should be excluded on the same grounds.").

162. *See* **Cohn v. State**, 849 S.W.2d 817, 819-20 (Tex. Crim. App. 1993) (otherwise admissible expert testimony is not excludable merely because it corroborates another witness's testimony or enhances the inferences that may be drawn from other evidence); **Duckett v. State**, 797 S.W.2d 906, 915 (Tex. Crim. App. 1990) ("'[T]here is a significant distinction between presenting a witness, such as a polygraph operator, to testify that a person is telling the truth, and presenting a witness who can state that the behavior of a witness falls within a common pattern.'" (quoting **Rodriquez v. State**, 741 P.2d 1200, 1204 (Alaska Ct. App. 1987))), *disapproved on other grounds*, **Cohn v. State**, 849 S.W.2d 817 (Tex. Crim. App. 1993); *see, e.g.*, **Gonzales v. State**, 4 S.W.3d 406, 417-18 (Tex. App.—Waco 1999, no pet.) (expert's testimony about propensity of child sexual-abuse victims to recant their testimony and her response to hypothetical question, which indicated that a child in victim's position would be under pressure to recant, was admissible explanation of why child victim might recant her prior accusation, not evidence of victim's credibility); **Vasquez v. State**, 975 S.W.2d 415, 418-19 (Tex. App.—Austin 1998, pet. ref'd) (psychologist's testimony that "statement validity assessment" of victim's outcry statements indicated victim's statement had characteristics commonly found in descriptions of actual events was admissible, not a direct comment on victim's credibility); **Turro v. State**, 950 S.W.2d 390, 399-400 (Tex. App.—Fort Worth 1997, pet. ref'd) (medical examiner could give his expert opinion that assertions in defendant's statement to police that murder victim was screaming and struggling in water were not consistent with medical examiner's findings; testimony was not an improper direct expert opinion on witness's credibility).

163. *See* **Duff v. Yelin**, 751 S.W.2d 175, 176 (Tex. 1988) (while experts do not need to recite their opinions in terms of reasonable probability, testimony must establish the issue beyond mere speculation or conjecture); *see, e.g.*,

2. Reliability & relevance of expert testimony. After an expert witness has met the qualification requirements, the proponent of the expert's testimony must show that (1) there is a body of scientific, technical, or other specialized knowledge that is pertinent to the facts at issue (i.e., the testimony is based on a reliable foundation),[165] and (2) the testimony is relevant (i.e., the witness's particular field of specialized knowledge must encompass the facts evaluated).[166]

Under Texas case law, the trial judge serves as gatekeeper in assessing the reliability of expert testimony.[167] "[E]xpert testimony based on an unreliable foundation or flawed methodology is unreliable and does not satisfy Rule 702's relevancy requirement."[168] But the facts on which an expert's opinion is based do not need to be undisputed.[169] The proponent of expert testimony has the burden of establishing that the testimony is sufficiently relevant and reliable to help the jury in determining a fact in

---

DaSilva v. Am. Brands, Inc., 845 F.2d 356, 361 (1st Cir. 1988) (physician could testify to his "beliefs" on how plaintiff's injuries occurred because he expressed "his conclusions in terms of reasonable probabilities"); *United States v. Fleishman*, 684 F.2d 1329, 1336-37 (9th Cir. 1982) (police officer qualified as an expert in handwriting analysis and could testify that there were "definite indications" that the defendant wrote a particular note, even though "he could not provide a definite conclusion"). Refer to notes 22-24 *supra* and accompanying text.

164. *See* 3 LOUISELL & MUELLER, *supra* note 27, §382, at 472 (Supp. 1993) (expert's inability to be definitive "should not stand in the way of receiving his testimony," and jury should be able to "reach its own conclusions" on the weight of the expert's testimony).

165. Refer to notes 172-242 *infra* and accompanying text.

166. Refer to notes 243-250 *infra* and accompanying text.

167. *TXI Transp. Co. v. Hughes*, 306 S.W.3d 230, 235 (Tex. 2010); *see Mack Trucks, Inc. v. Tamez*, 206 S.W.3d 572, 579 (Tex. 2006) ("A significant part of the trial court's gatekeeper function is to evaluate the expert's qualifications, listen to the testimony, view the evidence, and determine which factors and evaluation methodology are most appropriate to apply."); *Gammill v. Jack Williams Chevrolet, Inc.*, 972 S.W.2d 713, 726 (Tex. 1998) ("The court in discharging its duty as gatekeeper must determine how the reliability of particular testimony is to be assessed."); *Wolfe v. State*, 509 S.W.3d 325, 336 (Tex. Crim. App. 2017) (trial judges serve as gatekeepers to keep out evidence that is unreliable because it is based on untested or invalid theories); *Layton v. State*, 280 S.W.3d 235, 241 (Tex. Crim. App. 2009) ("[T]he trial judge [is] in the role of a 'gatekeeper,' whose responsibility it is to weed out inadmissible evidence based on a lack of reliability."). The trial court has discretion to conduct a pretrial evidentiary hearing when an expert's testimony has been challenged. *State v. Petropoulos*, 346 S.W.3d 525, 529 n.1 (Tex. 2011). In making a preliminary determination on the admissibility of the expert's testimony at the hearing, the trial court is not bound by the Rules of Evidence, except those related to privileges. *Id.*; *see* TEX. R. EVID. 104(a). Refer to *Article I: General Provisions*, *supra* p. 86.

168. *TXI Transp.*, 306 S.W.3d at 234; *see Seger v. Yorkshire Ins.*, 503 S.W.3d 388, 410 n.23 (Tex. 2016) ("An expert's opinion that relies on flawed methodology is unreliable, even if the underlying data is sound."); *Helena Chem. Co. v. Wilkins*, 47 S.W.3d 486, 499 (Tex. 2001) ("If an expert relies upon unreliable foundational data, any opinion drawn from that data is likewise unreliable."); *Merrell Dow Pharm., Inc. v. Havner*, 953 S.W.2d 706, 714 (Tex. 1997) ("If the foundational data underlying opinion testimony are unreliable, an expert will not be permitted to base an opinion on that data because any opinion drawn from that data is likewise unreliable. Further, an expert's testimony is unreliable even when the underlying data are sound if the expert draws conclusions from that data based on flawed methodology.").

169. *Sw. Energy Prod. Co. v. Berry-Helfand*, 491 S.W.3d 699, 718 (Tex. 2016); *Caffe Ribs, Inc. v. State*, 487 S.W.3d 137, 144 (Tex. 2016); *Hous. Unlimited, Inc. Metal Processing v. Mel Acres Ranch*, 443 S.W.3d 820, 833 (Tex. 2014). An expert's opinion is unreliable if it is contrary to actual, undisputed facts. *Caffe Ribs*, 487 S.W.3d at 144; *see also Hous. Unlimited*, 443 S.W.3d at 832-33 ("If an expert's opinion is unreliable because it is 'based on assumed facts that vary from the actual facts,' the opinion 'is not probative evidence.'" (quoting *Whirlpool Corp. v. Camacho*, 298 S.W.3d 631, 637 (Tex. 2009))).

issue.[170] This burden is separate from the task of disproving an opponent's expert testimony.[171]

(1) Reliability. To be admissible under Rule 702, an expert's testimony must be reliable. If the expert's field of knowledge does not have a scientific, technical, or otherwise specialized base, courts should exclude the expert's testimony because the expert's opinions would be more likely to prejudice or confuse than to help the trier of fact.[172] The difficulty lies in determining when knowledge is baseless or scientifically unreliable.

When the expert is the source of evidence on the specific facts at issue in the trial, the expert's testimony may be highly probative, but it also carries the potential for causing unfair prejudice. If the expert's knowledge is incomplete or inaccurate, the facts on which the jury is deciding the case may be unreliable, which increases the risk of an improper verdict.[173] However, a court should not exclude testimony based on innovative techniques and developing bodies of specialized knowledge merely because of a lack of general acceptance.

---

170. **Layton**, 280 S.W.3d at 241. See **O'Connor's Texas Rules * Civil Trials** (2017), "Helpfulness test," ch. 5-N, §2.3, p. 476.

171. See **Whirlpool Corp. v. Camacho**, 298 S.W.3d 631, 639 (Tex. 2009) ("The proponent must satisfy its burden regardless of the quality or quantity of the opposing party's evidence on the issue and regardless of whether the opposing party attempts to conclusively prove the expert testimony is wrong."). To preserve error, a party must object to the reliability of scientific evidence either before trial or when the evidence is offered so that the proponent has an opportunity to cure the defect. **City of San Antonio v. Pollock**, 284 S.W.3d 809, 817 (Tex. 2009); **Mar. Overseas Corp. v. Ellis**, 971 S.W.2d 402, 409 (Tex. 1998). If there is no objection, expert testimony may be considered probative evidence regardless of whether the basis for the opinion is reliable. **Sw. Energy Prod. Co.**, 491 S.W.3d at 717; **Hous. Unlimited**, 443 S.W.3d at 829; see **City of San Antonio**, 284 S.W.3d at 818. "But if no basis for the opinion is offered, or the basis offered provides no support, the opinion is merely a conclusory statement and cannot be considered probative evidence, regardless of whether there is no objection." **City of San Antonio**, 284 S.W.3d at 818; accord **Sw. Energy Prod. Co.**, 491 S.W.3d at 717; see also **Rogers v. Zanetti**, 518 S.W.3d 394, 406-07 (Tex. 2017) ("[R]elaying the opinion of another witness without providing any basis for the borrowed conclusion is itself no evidence. Said differently, repeating another's ipse dixit does not make it any less of an ipse dixit."). Refer to notes 236-238, 246 infra and accompanying text.

172. See, e.g., **Kelly v. State**, 824 S.W.2d 568, 574 (Tex. Crim. App. 1992) (expert properly relied on scientific technique of DNA fingerprinting as basis for his opinion; opinion was properly admitted under Rule 403); **Pierce v. State**, 777 S.W.2d 399, 414 (Tex. Crim. App. 1989) (architect's knowledge of drafting and the use of perspective did not represent specialized knowledge and was properly excluded); **Thompson v. Mayes**, 707 S.W.2d 951, 956-57 (Tex. App.—Eastland 1986, writ ref'd n.r.e.) (psychologist's "psychological autopsy" was not based on existing scientific, technical, or other specialized knowledge; because there was no showing that the expert's principles were sufficiently reliable for testimony to be of assistance, trial court did not abuse its discretion in excluding expert's opinion); **Warren v. Hartnett**, 561 S.W.2d 860, 863 (Tex. Civ. App.—Dallas 1977, writ ref'd n.r.e.) (no probative effect of handwriting expert's testimony that, based on a handwriting comparison, testatrix had been of unsound mind because of alcoholism; "we are aware of no recognized field of scientific inquiry which permits divination of mental capacity by persons whose expertise is limited to handwriting analysis"); cf. **United States v. Amaral**, 488 F.2d 1148, 1152 (9th Cir. 1973) ("Scientific or expert testimony [presents] the … danger [of causing undue prejudice or confusing and misleading the jury] because of its aura of special reliability and trustworthiness."). Refer to notes 251-256 infra and accompanying text.

173. See **United States v. Downing**, 753 F.2d 1224, 1241 (3d Cir. 1985) (admissibility of expert evidence is favored under Federal Rule 702, although "some caution is appropriate, especially in the criminal context, whenever proffered novel scientific evidence, if unreliable or likely to mislead, will increase the likelihood of an erroneous verdict"). The original **Frye** test of "general scientific acceptance" was created to address this concern. See **Frye v. United**

The U.S. Supreme Court, in **Daubert v. Merrell Dow Pharmaceuticals, Inc.**, stated that Article VII of the Federal Rules of Evidence had superseded the **Frye** test, which had stood for 70 years.[174] Although the Supreme Court in **Daubert** jettisoned the old **Frye** test, it did impose a requirement that the trial judge must act as a "gatekeeper" under Rules 702 and 104(a) to ensure the reliability of scientific evidence.[175] Thus in **Daubert**, the Supreme Court held that when the subject of the expert's testimony is "scientific knowledge," the basis for the testimony must be grounded in accepted scientific methods and procedures.[176] The Court explained:

> [T]o qualify as "scientific knowledge," an inference or assertion must be derived by the scientific method. Proposed testimony must be supported by appropriate validation—*i.e.*, "good grounds," based on what is known. In short, the requirement that an expert's testimony pertain to "scientific knowledge" establishes a standard of evidentiary reliability.[177]

The Court listed, as "general observations," the following four nonexclusive factors for trial judges to use in determining scientific reliability of the underlying theory and methodology: (1) the testability of the proffered theory,[178] (2) its submission to peer review and publication,[179] (3) the error rate of its application,[180] and (4) its level of general acceptance within the relevant scientific community.[181] The Court emphasized that

---

States, 293 F. 1013, 1014 (D.C. Cir. 1923). The **Frye** court articulated the test as follows: "[W]hile courts will go a long way in admitting expert testimony deduced from a well-recognized scientific principle or discovery, the thing from which the deduction is made must be sufficiently established to have gained general acceptance in the particular field in which it belongs." *Id.*

174. 509 U.S. 579, 587-89 (1993).

175. *See id.* at 597. The Supreme Court later extended its reasoning and result in **Daubert** to *all* expert testimony, not merely scientific expertise. *See* **Kumho Tire Co. v. Carmichael**, 526 U.S. 137, 147 (1999) ("gatekeeping" role assigned to trial judges under **Daubert** applies same reliability standard to all "scientific," "technical," or "other specialized" matters within scope of Rule 702).

176. **Daubert**, 509 U.S. at 589-90.

177. *Id.* at 590.

178. Thus, trial judges should determine whether the theory and technique can be and have been tested. The Court explained that "[s]cientific methodology today is based on generating hypotheses and testing them to see if they can be falsified; indeed, this methodology is what distinguishes science from other fields of human inquiry." *Id.* at 593.

179. The Court noted that "[t]he fact of publication (or lack thereof) in a peer-reviewed journal ... will be a relevant, though not dispositive, consideration in assessing the scientific validity of a particular technique or methodology on which an opinion is premised." *Id.*; *see, e.g.*, **United States v. Metzger**, 778 F.2d 1195, 1203-04 (6th Cir. 1985) (opinion testimony from witness who had coauthored article in specialized field was allowed; "[a]rticles in professional journals are also of great value in that the basis of the article is subjected to close scrutiny by other experts in the field").

180. **Daubert**, 509 U.S. at 594. This factor relates to both the frequency and the type of errors generated by a scientific technique. *See* **United States v. Williams**, 583 F.2d 1194, 1198 (2d Cir. 1978) (discussing admissibility of voice-spectrography test and noting that one indicator of evidentiary reliability is the potential rate of error); *see, e.g.*, **Murdock v. Murdock**, 811 S.W.2d 557, 558-59 (Tex. 1991) (blood tests to establish nonpaternity were admitted when expert testified that there was zero probability of error in the tests because duplicate tests were performed).

181. The Court noted that "'general acceptance' can yet have a bearing on the inquiry. ... Widespread acceptance can be an important factor in ruling particular evidence admissible, and 'a known technique which has been able to attract only minimal support within the community,' may properly be viewed with skepticism." **Daubert**, 509 U.S. at 594 (quoting **United States v. Downing**, 753 F.2d 1224, 1238 (3d Cir. 1985)).

the "gatekeeping" inquiry is flexible and focuses on "the scientific validity—and thus the evidentiary relevance and reliability—of the principles" and methodology of the particular expertise offered.[182] The trial judge scrutinizes only the scientific theory and methodology;[183] the validity of the expert's specific conclusions is for the jury to assess, aided by cross-examination.[184]

Even before the **Daubert** decision, the Texas Court of Criminal Appeals had announced and implemented a similar gatekeeping role for trial judges in evaluating the reliability of scientific expertise offered in criminal cases. In **Kelly v. State**,[185] a case involving the admissibility of DNA "genetic fingerprinting" evidence, the court explic-

---

As noted by the Advisory Committee on the Federal Rules, federal courts, both before and after **Daubert**, have used additional or different factors to determine whether expert testimony is sufficiently reliable to be admissible, including:

(1) Whether experts are "proposing to testify about matters growing naturally and directly out of research they have conducted independent of the litigation, or whether they have developed their opinions expressly for purposes of testifying." **Daubert v. Merrell Dow Pharmaceuticals, Inc.**, 43 F.3d 1311, 1317 (9th Cir. 1995).

(2) Whether the expert has unjustifiably extrapolated from an accepted premise to an unfounded conclusion. See **General Elec. Co. v. Joiner**, 522 U.S. 136, 146, (1997) (noting that in some cases a trial court "may conclude that there is simply too great an analytical gap between the data and the opinion proffered").

(3) Whether the expert has adequately accounted for obvious alternative explanations. See **Claar v. Burlington N.R.R.**, 29 F.3d 499 (9th Cir. 1994) (testimony excluded where the expert failed to consider other obvious causes for the plaintiff's condition). Compare **Ambrosini v. Labarraque**, 101 F.3d 129 (D.C. Cir. 1996) (the possibility of some uneliminated causes presents a question of weight, so long as the most obvious causes have been considered and reasonably ruled out by the expert).

(4) Whether the expert "is being as careful as he would be in his regular professional work outside his paid litigation consulting." **Sheehan v. Daily Racing Form, Inc.**, 104 F.3d 940, 942 (7th Cir. 1997); accord **Kumho Tire Co. v. Carmichael**, 119 S. Ct. 1167, 1176 (1999) (**Daubert** requires the trial court to assure itself that the expert "employs in the courtroom the same level of intellectual rigor that characterizes the practice of an expert in the relevant field").

(5) Whether the expert's field of expertise is known to reach reliable results for the type of opinion the expert would give. See **Kumho Tire Co. v. Carmichael**, 119 S.Ct. 1167, 1175 (1999) (**Daubert**'s general acceptance factor does not "help show that an expert's testimony is reliable where the discipline itself lacks reliability, as, for example, do theories grounded in any so-called generally accepted principles of astrology or necromancy."); **Moore v. Ashland Chemical, Inc.**, 151 F.3d 269 (5th Cir. 1998) (en banc) (clinical doctor precluded from testifying to the toxicological cause of the plaintiff's respiratory problem when the opinion was not sufficiently grounded in scientific methodology); **Sterling v. Velsicol Chem. Corp.**, 855 F.2d 1188 (6th Cir.1988) (rejecting testimony based on "clinical ecology" as unfounded and unreliable).

FED. R. EVID. 702 advisory committee's note to 2000 amendments.

182. **Daubert**, 509 U.S. at 594-95.

183. See **TXI Transp. Co. v. Hughes**, 306 S.W.3d 230, 239 (Tex. 2010); **Mack Trucks, Inc. v. Tamez**, 206 S.W.3d 572, 578 (Tex. 2006); **Exxon Pipeline Co. v. Zwahr**, 88 S.W.3d 623, 629 (Tex. 2002); **Southland Lloyds Ins. v. Cantu**, 399 S.W.3d 558, 563 (Tex. App.—San Antonio 2011, pet. denied).

184. **Daubert**, 509 U.S. at 596; see **TXI Transp.**, 306 S.W.3d at 239; **Southland Lloyds**, 399 S.W.3d at 563; see also **State v. Smith**, 335 S.W.3d 706, 714 (Tex. App.—Houston [14th Dist.] 2011, pet. ref'd) ("Issues of credibility and reliability are not the same. A jury should evaluate a witness's credibility, but unreliable evidence should never reach the jury."); **Waring v. Wommack**, 945 S.W.2d 889, 893 (Tex. App.—Austin 1997, no writ) (objection to accident-reconstruction expert's testimony was directed primarily at his conclusions, not the reliability of his theory or methodology; accuracy of conclusions "reached by an expert whose theory and methodology are reliable may be challenged by cross-examination").

185. 824 S.W.2d 568 (Tex. Crim. App. 1992).

itly rejected the *Frye* test[186] and held that the admissibility of novel scientific evidence is governed by Rules 702 and 403.[187] To prevent the admission of "junk science" in the courtroom,[188] however, the court adopted several procedural and substantive limitations. Under *Kelly*, a trial judge must first determine whether scientific evidence is sufficiently reliable[189] and relevant[190] to help the jury in reaching an accurate result, and then decide whether that expert testimony might nonetheless be unhelpful or distracting for other reasons.[191] To be considered reliable, evidence from a scientific theory must satisfy three criteria: "(a) the underlying scientific theory must be valid; (b) the technique applying the theory must be valid; and (c) the technique must have been properly applied on the occasion in question."[192] Because jurors may have difficulty in criti-

---

186. In rejecting *Frye*, the *Kelly* court stated the following: "[f]irst, there is no textual basis in [Criminal] Rule 702 for a special admissibility standard for novel scientific evidence. Second, as should be fairly obvious, scientific evidence may be shown reliable even though not yet generally accepted in the relevant scientific community." *Kelly*, 824 S.W.2d at 572.

187. *Id.* at 571-72. The reasoning and result in *Kelly* were reaffirmed in *Bethune v. State*, 828 S.W.2d 14, 14 (Tex. Crim. App. 1992), *Trimboli v. State*, 826 S.W.2d 953, 954 (Tex. Crim. App. 1992), and *Glover v. State*, 825 S.W.2d 127, 128 (Tex. Crim. App. 1992).

188. *See Kelly*, 824 S.W.2d at 576 (Clinton, Baird, Overstreet, JJ., concurring) (advantage of *Frye* test is "that it essentially leaves the question of the validity of novel theories and techniques to those whose vocation it is to view the world from the perspective of the scientific method, viz: the scientists").

189. Refer to note 192 *infra* and accompanying text.

190. *See Bekendam v. State*, 441 S.W.3d 295, 301 (Tex. Crim. App. 2014) (both relevance and reliability are components of trial court's ruling on admissibility); *Everitt v. State*, 407 S.W.3d 259, 263 (Tex. Crim. App. 2013) (same). In a post-*Kelly* decision dealing with the admissibility of expert testimony on eyewitness reliability, *Jordan v. State*, the court discussed "relevance" in the Criminal Rule 702 gatekeeping analysis as the closeness of the "fit" between the scientific evidence and the fact to which it is offered. 928 S.W.2d 550, 553 n.4 (Tex. Crim. App. 1996). The court noted that "[r]elevance is by nature a looser notion than reliability. Whether evidence 'will assist the trier of fact' and is sufficiently tied to the facts of the case is a simpler, more straight-forward matter to establish than whether the evidence is sufficiently grounded in science to be reliable." *Id.* at 555. In *Jordan*, the court further held that expert testimony on eyewitness reliability could be relevant even though the expert "did not testify as to *every conceivable factor* that might affect the reliability of eyewitness identification present in [the] case ...." *Id.* at 556. The court then remanded the case to the court of appeals to determine whether the expert testimony, which was relevant, was also scientifically reliable. *Id.* On remand, the court of appeals held that it was not reliable. *Jordan v. State*, 950 S.W.2d 210, 212 (Tex. App.—Fort Worth 1997, pet. ref'd); *see also Tillman v. State*, 354 S.W.3d 425, 442 (Tex. Crim. App. 2011) (trial court abused its discretion in excluding reliable, relevant evidence that would have increased jurors' awareness of biasing factors in eyewitness identification). Refer to notes 243-250 *infra* and accompanying text.

191. *Kelly*, 824 S.W.2d at 572.

192. *Id.* at 573; *see, e.g., Bekendam*, 441 S.W.3d at 302-03 (trial court did not abuse its discretion in allowing expert testimony on blood tests that did not strictly follow DPS policy; court conducted hearing in which expert testified to her qualifications, to the utilization of tests, and to the general acceptance of the tests in both the scientific and judicial communities).

The court of criminal appeals set out its own list of nonexclusive factors that could affect a trial court's determination of reliability: (1) the extent to which the underlying scientific theory and technique are accepted as valid by the relevant scientific community (i.e., the old *Frye* "general acceptance" test), (2) the qualifications of the testifying experts, (3) the existence of literature supporting or rejecting the underlying scientific theory and technique, (4) the potential error rate, (5) the availability of other experts to test and evaluate the technique, (6) the clarity with which the underlying scientific theory and technique can be explained to the court, and (7) the experience and skill of the persons who applied the technique. *Kelly*, 824 S.W.2d at 573. Numerous Texas cases have followed *Kelly* and applied these criteria to the admission of scientific evidence in criminal cases. *See, e.g., Wolfe v. State*, 509 S.W.3d 325, 336 (Tex. Crim. App. 2017) (applying *Kelly* factors, court of criminal appeals held that experts could testify on nature of abusive head trauma and fact that child's injuries were result of intentionally inflicted impact); *Reynolds*

RULE 702

cally assessing the reliability of scientific evidence, the proponent must establish the reliability of the evidence by "clear and convincing" evidence[193] in a preliminary hearing held outside the presence of the jury.[194] If the trial court is persuaded that the evidence is both reliable and relevant, it is admissible under Rule 402 unless its probative value is substantially outweighed by the Rule 403 counterfactors.[195]

---

v. State, 204 S.W.3d 386, 390-91 (Tex. Crim. App. 2006) (to comply with ***Kelly*** in the context of breath alcohol tests, Legislature has already established that the underlying science is valid; thus, trial court simply must "determine whether the technique was properly applied in accordance with the [department's] rules ... on the particular occasion in question"); ***Hernandez v. State***, 116 S.W.3d 26, 29-31 (Tex. Crim. App. 2003) (court of appeals did not err in reversing admission of urinalysis evidence); ***Sexton v. State***, 93 S.W.3d 96, 100-01 (Tex. Crim. App. 2002) (trial court abused its discretion in admitting expert's testimony about "magazine mark" comparison on two sets of shell casings; toolmark examination may be a generally reliable theory, but expert in this case did not have the weapon used or the magazine from which bullets were fired and thus could not make a reliable comparison); ***Haley v. State***, 396 S.W.3d 756, 765-66 (Tex. App.—Houston [14th Dist.] 2013, no pet.) (expert could testify that defendant's level of intoxication from methamphetamine was so high that his coordination and driving ability must have been affected; limited and specific scope of opinion lessened importance of lack of assignment of error rate to studies' findings); ***Wooten v. State***, 267 S.W.3d 289, 301 (Tex. App.—Houston [14th Dist.] 2008, pet. ref'd) (trial court did not abuse discretion in admitting testimony about blood-alcohol results from the Dimension RXL, which detects alcohol using photomatic absorbents and blood serum instead of the more customary gas chromatography); ***Croft v. State***, 148 S.W.3d 533, 542-44 (Tex. App.—Houston [14th Dist.] 2004, no pet.) (in trial for aggravated sexual assault of a child, expert's opinion about bleeding during a female's first sexual intercourse was both reliable and relevant, as was his testimony on doctor's ability to detect semen on clothing and skin); ***Presswood v. State***, 124 S.W.3d 837, 843-44 (Tex. App.—Eastland 2003, pet. ref'd) (excluding physician's testimony on naturopathic medicine under ***Daubert/Kelly*** because witness could not identify names or locations of tests conducted using naturopathic medicine, and he never saw or interviewed the victim); ***Perales v. State***, 117 S.W.3d 434, 441-42 (Tex. App.—Corpus Christi 2003, pet. ref'd) (upholding admission of radar evidence); ***Moore v. State***, 109 S.W.3d 537, 542 (Tex. App.—Tyler 2001, pet. ref'd) (upholding admission of fingerprint evidence); ***Hurrelbrink v. State***, 46 S.W.3d 350, 352-56 (Tex. App.—Amarillo 2001, pet. ref'd) (testimony by two anthropologists that footprint at murder scene closely matched defendant's footprint was admissible; although defendant's expert witness said he would not make positive identification, all three experts agreed that footprint analysis was valid science and described same technique used to make comparisons); ***Hines v. State***, 38 S.W.3d 805, 808-09 (Tex. App.—Houston [14th Dist.] 2001, no pet.) (upholding admission of DNA evidence); ***Ochoa v. State***, 994 S.W.2d 283, 285 (Tex. App.—El Paso 1999, no pet.) (testimony on use of radar gun was inadmissible when witness could not explain theory behind its operation); ***Godsey v. State***, 989 S.W.2d 482, 491 (Tex. App.—Waco 1999, pet. ref'd) (testimony on standard of care for patients with Alzheimer's disease and dementia was admissible); ***Durham v. State***, 956 S.W.2d 62, 66 (Tex. App.—Tyler 1997, pet. ref'd) (upholding admission of expert testimony on the time and degree of impairment caused by marijuana ingestion based on the level of cannabinoids found in a blood sample).

193. ***In re M.P.A.***, 364 S.W.3d 277, 285-86 & n.10 (Tex. 2012); ***Wolfe***, 509 S.W.3d at 335; ***Blasdell v. State***, 470 S.W.3d 59, 62 (Tex. Crim. App. 2015); ***Tillman***, 354 S.W.3d at 435; ***Kelly***, 824 S.W.2d at 573. *But see* ***State v. Medrano***, 127 S.W.3d 781, 789-92 (Tex. Crim. App. 2004) (Cochran, Keller, Holcomb, JJ., concurring) (admissibility of expert testimony should be determined by "preponderance of proof" standard in Rule 104(a) as it is under ***Daubert***, under Federal Rule 702, and under other Texas rules of evidence).

194. ***Kelly***, 824 S.W.2d at 573.

195. *Id.*; *see* ***Tillman***, 354 S.W.3d at 435 ("[T]he proponent [of expert testimony] must prove two prongs: (1) the testimony is based on a reliable scientific foundation, and (2) it is relevant to the issues in the case."); *see, e.g.*, ***Franco v. State***, 25 S.W.3d 26, 29-30 (Tex. App.—El Paso 2000, pet. ref'd) (expert testimony on blood-spatter evidence was "dangerously misleading" and should have been excluded under Rule 403; "[w]e find nothing in the blood spatter analysis from which any 'expert' could draw an opinion as to who was (or who was not) the initial aggressor, an opinion repeatedly made and emphasized in this case"); ***Fitts v. State***, 982 S.W.2d 175, 181-84 (Tex. App.—Houston [1st Dist.] 1998, pet. ref'd) (hydrocarbon-sniffing dog alerts were admissible; training theory and methods were valid, technique was properly applied, and "there is nothing in the record to suggest that the probative value of the dog-sniffing evidence was outweighed by any of the rule 403 factors favoring inadmissibility"). Refer to notes 251-256 *infra* and accompanying text.

The Texas Supreme Court, in *E.I. du Pont de Nemours & Co. v. Robinson*, adopted the same type of analysis as set out in both *Daubert* and *Kelly* and emphasized that trial judges must "scrutinize proffered evidence for scientific reliability when it is based upon novel scientific theories, sometimes referred to as 'junk science.'"[196] The *Robinson* opinion gave its own list of nonexclusive factors that trial courts should consider in assessing the validity or reliability[197] of a particular scientific theory or methodology.[198] The

---

196. 923 S.W.2d 549, 554 (Tex. 1995).

197. Although courts tend to use the terms "validity" and "reliability" interchangeably, scientists use the word "validity" to refer to the ability of a scientific test to measure what it purports to measure, while "reliability" refers to the ability of a scientific test to obtain consistent results. Giannelli, *supra* note 82, at 1201 n.20. For example, a valid breathalyzer test accurately measures alcohol content in the body. A reliable breathalyzer test does so consistently. Thus, a breathalyzer that tests multiple breath samples increases the reliability of the specific device, but it does not reveal anything about the testing instrument's validity. Validity can be checked by measuring the body's alcohol content through a blood test. If the blood alcohol level measured by a previously established reliable test procedure is the same as the result obtained by the new procedure, there is at least some evidence that the new procedure can and does obtain valid results.

198. The specific factors set out in *Robinson* are the following:
    (1) the extent to which the theory has been or can be tested,
    (2) the extent to which the technique relies on a subjective interpretation by the expert,
    (3) whether the theory or technique has been subjected to peer review or publication,
    (4) the technique's potential error rate,
    (5) the general acceptance of the theory or technique in the relevant scientific community, and
    (6) the nonjudicial uses to which the theory or technique has been put.
923 S.W.2d at 557. In addition, "trial courts may consider other factors which are helpful to determining the reliability of scientific evidence." *Id.* Related to these factors is whether the expert considered alternative causes of the incident in question. *See Transcon. Ins. v. Crump*, 330 S.W.3d 211, 217-18 (Tex. 2010). An expert's opinion that does not rule out alternative causes of the damage may be unreliable. *TXI Transp. Co. v. Hughes*, 306 S.W.3d 230, 237 (Tex. 2010); *see Bustamante v. Ponte*, ___ S.W.3d ___ (Tex. 2017) (No. 15-0509; 9-29-17) (expert must exclude other plausible causes but need not exclude all other potential causes); *Transcon. Ins.*, 330 S.W.3d at 218 ("[A] medical causation expert need not 'disprov[e] or discredit[] every possible cause other than the one espoused by him.' Few expert opinions would be reliable if the rule were otherwise. Still, if evidence presents 'other plausible causes of the injury or condition that *could* be negated, the [proponent of the testimony] *must* offer evidence excluding those causes with reasonable certainty.'"); *see, e.g., Robinson*, 923 S.W.2d at 558-59 (trial court properly excluded expert testimony that did not rule out other possible causes of damage to orchard; expert did not conduct any testing to exclude other possible causes, even though he admitted in deposition that symptoms could have been caused by something other than contaminated fungicide); *see also JLG Trucking, LLC v. Garza*, 466 S.W.3d 157, 162-63 (Tex. 2015) (in personal-injury case, defendant sought to introduce evidence of second accident that occurred three months after accident at issue as alternative cause of plaintiff's injuries; trial court improperly excluded evidence as irrelevant).

    Cases following *Robinson* and upholding the admissibility of expert testimony under the factors outlined in that case include the following: *Lincoln v. Clark Freight Lines, Inc.*, 285 S.W.3d 79, 87-88 (Tex. App.—Houston [1st Dist.] 2009, no pet.) (trial court did not abuse its discretion in allowing testimony by accident-reconstruction expert; expert used generally accepted methods and conducted the tests on high-performance tires with the same consistency as those in the accident), *Loram Maint. of Way, Inc. v. Ianni*, 141 S.W.3d 722, 730-32 (Tex. App.—El Paso 2004) (psychiatrist's testimony about employee's amphetamine use and its effect was sufficiently reliable to be admissible; expert explained that psychiatrists frequently rely on observations by family, friends, and coworkers; his technique of analyzing data was the standard clinical practice taught in general residency programs, and any ordinary psychiatrist would have arrived at same opinion), *rev'd on other grounds*, 210 S.W.3d 593 (Tex. 2006), *Tex. Workers' Comp. Ins. Fund v. Lopez*, 21 S.W.3d 358, 364-66 (Tex. App.—San Antonio 2000, pet. denied) (expert testimony about cause of worker's chronic obstructive pulmonary disease was admissible), and *Pittsburgh Corning Corp. v. Walters*, 1 S.W.3d 759, 775-76 (Tex. App.—Corpus Christi 1999, pet. denied) (expert testimony that asbestos exposure caused mesothelioma was admissible). Cases that have excluded the expert's testimony under *Robinson* include the following: *DaimlerChrysler Corp. v. Hillhouse*, 161 S.W.3d 541, 554-55 (Tex. App.—San Antonio 2004, pet. granted, judgm't vacated w.r.m.) (expert's opinion on whether depowered air bag would have prevented child's injuries was unreliable and based on conjecture under *Robinson* when the only test he performed, using a similar vehicle and plaintiff's sister as a "surrogate," was based on speculation), *Wiggs v. All Saints Health Sys.*, 124 S.W.3d

RULE 702

supreme court has reiterated that the **Kelly** and **Robinson** tests are functionally the same: "Reliable evidence should be admitted in both the civil and criminal context, and unreliable evidence or 'junk science' should be kept out of court in either context."[199]

The supreme court has also held that the **Robinson** test for the admissibility of scientific expertise also applied to a "no evidence" sufficiency review.[200] The same rigor-

---

407, 410-12 (Tex. App.—Fort Worth 2003, pet. denied) (exclusion of expert testimony about cause of plaintiff's ischemic optic neuropathy was proper under **Robinson** because expert's theory was controversial, insufficiently tested, required subjective interpretation, and had not been subjected to sufficient peer review), **Wolfson v. BIC Corp.**, 95 S.W.3d 527, 533-34 (Tex. App.—Houston [1st Dist.] 2002, pet. denied) (trial court did not err in excluding expert's testimony on cause of decedent's burns by defective lighter because expert: (1) "has not observed, performed, or attempted to perform any test which may duplicate or verify" his theory of lighter's explosion, (2) "relies heavily on his own subjective assumptions that debris entering the lighter caused it to explode," (3) "has neither published a work on the theory of failure to extinguish, nor is he aware of any such publication," (4) "did not provide any evidence relating to the potential rate of error," (5) "offered no evidence whether the failure to extinguish theory has been generally accepted as valid by the relevant scientific community," and (6) "has not demonstrated the non-judicial uses which have been made of the theory"), **Neal v. Dow Agrosciences LLC**, 74 S.W.3d 468, 474 (Tex. App.—Dallas 2002, no pet.) (trial court did not abuse discretion in excluding expert testimony in toxic-tort case to show that deceased child's brain tumor was caused by pesticide exposure because expert in scientific literature did not show a statistically significant association between pesticide exposure and brain tumor), **State Farm Lloyds v. Mireles**, 63 S.W.3d 491, 499-500 (Tex. App.—San Antonio 2001, no pet.) (engineer's opinion that plumbing leak in bathroom caused heave in foundation approximately six to eight feet away from the leak was scientifically unreliable and inadmissible when expert did not show basis for his opinion, did not rule out other causes, and made unsupportable assumptions), **Weiss v. Mech. Associated Servs., Inc.**, 989 S.W.2d 120, 124-25 (Tex. App.—San Antonio 1999, pet. denied) (trial court properly excluded expert testimony that claimant's health problems were caused by her alleged exposure to X-ray chemicals from neighboring office), **Minn. Mining & Mfg. Co. v. Atterbury**, 978 S.W.2d 183, 201 (Tex. App.—Texarkana 1998, pet. denied) (error to admit expert testimony that silicone-gel breast implants caused injury or illness), and **Purina Mills, Inc. v. Odell**, 948 S.W.2d 927, 933-34 (Tex. App.—Texarkana 1997, pet. denied) (error to admit expert testimony that Purina's feed caused "hardware disease" in some of plaintiff's dairy cows; expert had not conducted tests to exclude other potential causes or to determine how much of feed was contaminated with metal or to what degree; opinion was prepared solely for litigation purposes; no evidence that expert's technique was an appropriate and reliable method to determine chemical contamination or what potential rate of error was).

199. **In re M.P.A.**, 364 S.W.3d 277, 286 n.10 (Tex. 2012); see **Blasdell v. State**, 470 S.W.3d 59, 62 (Tex. Crim. App. 2015) ("The purpose of the reliability inquiry is to 'separate the wheat from the chaff.'").

200. E.g., **Bostic v. Ga.-Pac. Corp.**, 439 S.W.3d 332, 358-60 (Tex. 2014) (in mesothelioma case, expert testimony about decedent's exposure to asbestos was legally insufficient to support verdict when testimony was based on theory that both supreme court and other scientific evidence had rejected; testimony purported to rely on studies that did not confirm experts' theory of causation and on other sources that were not scientific studies and thus were unreliable); **Merrell Dow Pharm., Inc. v. Havner**, 953 S.W.2d 706, 713-14 (Tex. 1997) ("[i]f the expert's scientific testimony is not reliable, it is not evidence," and thus evidence was legally insufficient to establish that child's birth defect was caused by exposure to drug; trial court jury verdict and judgment reversed); see **Whirlpool Corp. v. Camacho**, 298 S.W.3d 631, 638 (Tex. 2009) ("Unlike review of a trial court's ruling as to admissibility of evidence where the ruling is reviewed for abuse of discretion, in a no-evidence review we independently consider whether the evidence at trial would enable reasonable and fair-minded jurors to reach the verdict. Further, a no-evidence review encompasses the entire record, including contrary evidence tending to show the expert opinion is incompetent or unreliable."); see, e.g., **Tex. Mut. Ins. v. Lerma**, 143 S.W.3d 172, 177-78 (Tex. App.—San Antonio 2004, pet. denied) (defendant's "no evidence" challenge to opinion of plaintiff's medical expert was reviewed under de novo standard; trial court erred in admitting doctor's testimony that tetanus caused death when expert could not exclude other potential causes with certainty and relied on scientific evidence that 10% of tetanus cases can incubate for more than 14 days; symptoms in this case did not appear for 60 days); **Daniels v. Lyondell-Citgo Ref. Co.**, 99 S.W.3d 722, 729-30 (Tex. App.—Houston [1st Dist.] 2003, no pet.) (trial court did not err in granting no-evidence summary-judgment motion when plaintiff did not present scientifically reliable evidence that deceased's lung cancer was caused by occupational exposure to benzene); **Praytor v. Ford Motor Co.**, 97 S.W.3d 237, 246 (Tex. App.—Houston [14th Dist.] 2002, no pet.) (expert's causation testimony was scientifically unreliable and could not defeat no-evidence summary-judgment motion); **Weingarten Realty Inv'rs v. Harris Cty. Appr. Dist.**, 93 S.W.3d 280, 284-86 (Tex.

ous Rule 702 gatekeeping analysis applies to evidence offered in rebuttal by the party that does not have the burden of proof on a particular issue.[201]

After ***Robinson***, some Texas appellate courts have applied "an almost de novo-like review" in determining whether expert testimony is reliable.[202] This standard, however, runs counter to the U.S. Supreme Court's statement that courts of appeals should apply an abuse-of-discretion standard when reviewing a district court's reliability determination.[203] "[T]he deference that is the hallmark of abuse-of-discretion review" requires an appellate court to uphold the trial court's evidentiary decision, including the reliability of proffered expert testimony, "'unless the ruling is manifestly erroneous.'"[204] The Texas Supreme Court applies this abuse-of-discretion standard to reliability rulings under Rule 702.[205]

App.—Houston [14th Dist.] 2002, no pet.) (trial court's no-evidence take-nothing judgment was upheld when plaintiff's scientific evidence was excluded as scientifically unreliable); ***Manasco v. Ins. Co. of Pa.***, 89 S.W.3d 239, 244-45 (Tex. App.—Texarkana 2002, no pet.) (summary judgment was proper when workers' compensation claimant's expert did not demonstrate scientific relationship between worker's head injury and the brain tumor that ultimately resulted in his death; scientific articles that expert relied on were those seeking to "rule out" head trauma as causative of brain tumors; medical literature reflected that no causal link had yet been established); ***Coastal Tankships, U.S.A., Inc. v. Anderson***, 87 S.W.3d 591, 610-11 (Tex. App.—Houston [1st Dist.] 2002, pet. denied) (judgment was reversed because evidence of toxic-tort causation was unreliable and thus was "no evidence" of causation); ***Mireles***, 63 S.W.3d at 499-500 (evidence was legally insufficient because opinion evidence of plaintiff's expert witness was scientifically unreliable).

201. *E.g.*, ***Brownsville Pediatric Ass'n v. Reyes***, 68 S.W.3d 184, 195 (Tex. App.—Corpus Christi 2002, no pet.) (defense expert witness was subject to same scrutiny under Rule 702 as plaintiff's experts, even though defense did not have the burden of proof on the issue of causation).

202. *See* ***Gross v. Burt***, 149 S.W.3d 213, 237 (Tex. App.—Fort Worth 2004, pet. denied) (quoting ***Austin v. Kerr-McGee Ref. Corp.***, 25 S.W.3d 280, 285 (Tex. App.—Texarkana 2000, no pet.)). In *Gross*, the court of appeals concluded that the opinion testimony of a pediatric ophthalmologist was scientifically unreliable because it lacked a sufficient foundation. 149 S.W.3d at 241. Although the physician had considerable personal clinical experience, there were no scientific epidemiological studies supporting his theory that the infant's retinopathy of prematurity could have been successfully treated outside of the 72-hour period recommended by published studies. *Id.* at 240. The inability to cite epidemiological studies in areas in which scientific "testing" on human beings would be professionally unethical has resulted in the exclusion of expert testimony in Texas medical-malpractice cases. *See, e.g.*, ***Couch v. Simmons***, 108 S.W.3d 338, 341-43 (Tex. App.—Amarillo 2003, no pet.) (expert's testimony that earlier administration of IV fluids would have prevented patient's stroke was properly excluded as unreliable and inadmissible; expert's own affidavit stated that theory had not been tested because no physician would intentionally withhold IV fluids to test theory and two peer-reviewed articles that expert relied on indicated there is no "specific beneficial relationship" between administration of IV fluids and stroke outcome); ***Helm v. Swan***, 61 S.W.3d 493, 497-98 (Tex. App.—San Antonio 2001, pet. denied) (expert testimony that earlier IV-fluid therapy would have improved patient's chances of recovery from severe necrotizing pancreatitis was unreliable because no medical literature supported the opinion; such support was unavailable because "no medical professional would intentionally delay" the therapy).

203. *See* ***Kumho Tire Co. v. Carmichael***, 526 U.S. 137, 142 (1999). *But see* Christopher B. Mueller, Daubert *Asks the Right Questions: Now Appellate Courts Should Help Find the Right Answers*, 33 SETON HALL L. REV. 987, 1019-22 (2003) (appellate courts should abandon abuse-of-discretion standard when reviewing admissibility of scientific evidence and apply a more stringent standard with more analysis).

204. ***Gen. Elec. Co. v. Joiner***, 522 U.S. 136, 142-43 (1997) (quoting ***Spring Co. v. Edgar***, 99 U.S. 645, 658 (1879)); *see* ***United States v. Frazier***, 387 F.3d 1244, 1259 (11th Cir. 2004) (abuse-of-discretion standard "recognizes a range of possible conclusions that the trial judge may reach").

205. *See* ***Gharda USA, Inc. v. Control Sols., Inc.***, 464 S.W.3d 338, 347 (Tex. 2015); ***Whirlpool Corp.***, 298 S.W.3d at 638; ***Gammill v. Jack Williams Chevrolet, Inc.***, 972 S.W.2d 713, 727 (Tex. 1998); ***E.I. du Pont de Nemours & Co. v. Robinson***, 923 S.W.2d 549, 558 (Tex. 1995).

The court of criminal appeals next extended the ***Daubert/Kelly/Robinson*** reliability analysis and criteria to all scientific evidence, not merely "novel" or experimental scientific theories.[206] Of course, many scientific theories and techniques are so well established that trial and appellate courts (or even the Legislature) can take judicial notice of their validity,[207] and the trial court must consider only whether the technique has been properly applied in the particular case.[208] For example, it would be a waste of time and resources to require the prosecutor in a murder trial to introduce independent evidence that every procedure and test that the medical examiner conducted as a part of a routine autopsy is scientifically valid and reliable.[209]

Texas courts have also considered whether the ***Daubert/Kelly/Robinson*** criteria, or some other form of judicial gatekeeping role, applied to all expert testimony and not merely to scientific evidence. In ***Nenno v. State***, the court of criminal appeals held that, although the specific factors set out in the ***Daubert/Kelly/Robinson*** line may not apply to a particular field of specialized knowledge, the trial judge is a gatekeeper for all ex-

---

206. ***Reynolds v. State***, 204 S.W.3d 386, 389-90 (Tex. Crim. App. 2006); ***Jackson v. State***, 17 S.W.3d 664, 670 (Tex. Crim. App. 2000); *see In re M.P.A.*, 364 S.W.3d 277, 286 n.9 (Tex. 2012) ("***Kelly*** applies to all scientific evidence, regardless of whether or not it is novel."); *see, e.g.*, ***Hartman v. State***, 946 S.W.2d 60, 62-63 (Tex. Crim. App. 1997) (scientific evidence involved Intoxilyzer tests to measure breath alcohol content). This extension of the ***Daubert/Kelly/Robinson*** gatekeeping role of the trial judge to the admissibility of all scientific evidence, has caused considerable anxiety for trial judges who may themselves have little or no scientific training. *See generally* Joëlle Anne Moreno, *Beyond the Polemic Against Junk Science: Navigating the Oceans That Divide Science and Law with Justice Breyer at the Helm*, 81 B.U. L. REV. 1033 (2001) (discussing difficulties inherent in merging law and science); Mueller, *supra* note 203 (same).

207. ***Hartman***, 946 S.W.2d at 63-64 (Keller & McCormick, JJ., concurring in part and dissenting in part); *see United States v. Downing*, 753 F.2d 1224, 1234 (3d Cir. 1985) (once novel scientific evidence is judicially recognized, no special foundational requirements will be needed); MCCORMICK ON EVIDENCE §330, at 554 (John W. Strong et al. eds., 4th ed. 1992) ("[C]ourts have taken judicial notice of the scientific principles which, while verifiable but not likely commonly known, justify the evidentiary use of radar, blood tests for intoxication and non-paternity, handwriting and typewriter identification, and ballistics."); *see, e.g.*, ***Emerson v. State***, 880 S.W.2d 759, 764 (Tex. Crim. App. 1994) (taking judicial notice on appeal of the scientific theory and technique supporting HGN test for intoxication); ***Moore v. State***, 109 S.W.3d 537, 542 (Tex. App.—Tyler 2001, pet. ref'd) (taking judicial notice of scientific validity of fingerprint-comparison theory and methodology).

208. *See Kelly v. State*, 824 S.W.2d 568, 573 (Tex. Crim. App. 1992). Even when the scientific reliability of a particular theory and methodology is well established, the proponent of the expert testimony must always demonstrate that the method was properly applied in the particular case. *See Enbridge Pipelines (E. Tex.) L.P. v. Avinger Timber, LLC*, 386 S.W.3d 256, 262 (Tex. 2012); ***Emerson***, 880 S.W.2d at 769; *see, e.g.*, ***Mata v. State***, 46 S.W.3d 902, 910, 917 (Tex. Crim. App. 2001) (taking judicial notice of scientific research not presented by either party at trial or on appeal in deciding that, although the underlying scientific theory of DWI retrograde analysis was reliable and its methodology may be reliable, expert did not explain and apply it properly); ***Smith v. State***, 65 S.W.3d 332, 347-48 (Tex. App.—Waco 2001, no pet.) (police officer could testify to results of HGN test, but he improperly expressed mathematical correlation between test results and probability of intoxication; trial court also erred in allowing witness to testify to mathematical correlation between one-leg-stand and walk-and-turn tests and intoxication); ***Kerr v. State***, 921 S.W.2d 498, 502 (Tex. App.—Fort Worth 1996, no pet.) (HGN test was properly applied by qualified officer and was admissible).

209. In some instances, expert testimony that had been traditionally admissible in Texas trial courts if the expert was qualified is now being subjected to a full ***Daubert/Kelly/Robinson*** analysis. *See, e.g.*, ***Waring v. Wommack***, 945 S.W.2d 889, 892-93 (Tex. App.—Austin 1997, no writ) (Texas "has a long history of allowing qualified accident reconstruction experts to testify regarding the way in which an accident occurred"; reviewing and applying ***Daubert*** criteria before upholding admission of expert testimony).

---

pert testimony, not merely for scientific expertise.[210] The court stated that the reliability of expert testimony should be evaluated with reference to standards "depending upon the [particular] field of expertise."[211] When determining the reliability of non-scientific expertise, trial courts should focus on three questions: "(1) whether the field of expertise is a legitimate one, (2) whether the subject matter of the expert's testimony is within the scope of that field, and (3) whether the expert's testimony properly relies upon and/or utilizes the principles involved in the field."[212] This standard for admission applies to expert evidence in the "soft sciences" as well as all nonscientific expertise.[213] However, evidence that may otherwise be considered "soft sciences" but has been subject to peer review and testing should be reviewed using the ***Daubert/Kelly/Robinson*** criteria.[214]

---

210. 970 S.W.2d 549, 560-61 (Tex. Crim. App. 1998), *overruled on other grounds*, **State v. Terrazas**, 4 S.W.3d 720 (Tex. Crim. App. 1999); *see* **Morris v. State**, 361 S.W.3d 649, 654 (Tex. Crim. App. 2011) ("[E]xpert testimony does not have to be based upon science at all; by its terms, Rule 702, by applying to 'technical or other specialized knowledge,' permits even nonscientific expert testimony.").

211. **Nenno**, 970 S.W.2d at 561.

212. *Id.*

213. *See* **Tillman v. State**, 354 S.W.3d 425, 435-36 (Tex. Crim. App. 2011); **Russeau v. State**, 171 S.W.3d 871, 883 (Tex. Crim. App. 2005); **State v. Medrano**, 127 S.W.3d 781, 785 (Tex. Crim. App. 2004); *see, e.g.*, **Morris**, 361 S.W.3d at 667-68 (police officer's testimony on "grooming" behavior by people who sexually victimize children was admissible under **Nenno** as a subject matter within a legitimate field of expertise); **Davis v. State**, 329 S.W.3d 798, 815 (Tex. Crim. App. 2010) (trial court did not abuse its discretion in admitting expert testimony under **Nenno** about Satanism; expert "had conferred with other experts on the subject in various cases, and had spent years teaching the subject to college students and law-enforcement personnel," was considered an expert by others, and had read numerous books and articles on the subject); **Gallo v. State**, 239 S.W.3d 757, 765-67 (Tex. Crim. App. 2007) (trial court properly analyzed and rejected expert testimony under **Nenno** standards because witness testified that research in the study of filicide—parents killing their children—was not extensive enough); **Weatherred v. State**, 975 S.W.2d 323, 323-24 (Tex. Crim. App. 1998) (admissibility of expert testimony on eyewitness identification was determined under **Nenno** standards for "soft sciences"); **Rhomer v. State**, 522 S.W.3d 13, ___ (Tex. App.—San Antonio 2017, pet. filed 6-9-17) (police officer's testimony on point of impact in vehicle collision was evaluated using **Nenno** factors because accident reconstruction was based on officer's experience and training rather than scientific inquiry); **In re J.R.**, 501 S.W.3d 738, 747-49 (Tex. App.—Waco 2016, pet. denied) (in case terminating parental rights, court applied **Nenno** factors and determined that psychologist's testimony on parental and psychological assessments was admissible); **Washington v. State**, 485 S.W.3d 633, 639 (Tex. App.—Houston [1st Dist.] 2016, no pet.) (gang membership is legitimate field of expertise, police officer's testimony that defendant was current or former gang member was within scope of that field, and testimony relied on self-admission and gang tattoos, which are factors frequently relied on by law enforcement to identify gang members); **Brewer v. State**, 370 S.W.3d 471, 474 (Tex. App.—Amarillo 2012, no pet.) (in aggravated-assault case, expert could testify about "cycle of violence" to assist jury in understanding victim's delay in calling police; trial court properly asked expert in voir dire whether her testimony would be "standard in the industry"); **Hamal v. State**, 352 S.W.3d 835, 841-43 (Tex. App.—Fort Worth 2011) (police officer's testimony on handling drug-detection dog was reliable under **Nenno**), *rev'd on other grounds*, 390 S.W.3d 302 (Tex. Crim. App. 2012); **State v. Smith**, 335 S.W.3d 706, 712 (Tex. App.—Houston [14th Dist.] 2011, pet. ref'd) (proponent of expert testimony on dog-scent lineup did not show that expert's opinion was reliable; expert's testimony that his dogs were reliable and accurate in identifying scents, without any evidence to support those claims, was not sufficient to show reliability); **Salazar v. State**, 127 S.W.3d 355, 359-60 (Tex. App.—Houston [14th Dist.] 2004, pet. ref'd) (upholding exclusion under **Nenno** of defense expert's testimony on "content-based criteria analysis" to evaluate interviewing techniques used with sexually abused children; method was not generally accepted, study of technique was still ongoing, and potential for error was great); **Roise v. State**, 7 S.W.3d 225, 236-37 (Tex. App.—Austin 1999, pet. ref'd) (testimony of psychologist that photographs would promote sexual impulses and sexual fantasies and that children in photographs would have been developmentally harmed was not relevant or reliable under **Nenno** standards for "soft sciences"); *see also* **Winfrey v. State**, 323 S.W.3d 875, 885 (Tex. Crim. App. 2010)

In *Gammill v. Jack Williams Chevrolet, Inc.*, the Texas Supreme Court followed similar reasoning in concluding that nonscientific expert testimony based on a witness's individual skill, experience, or training must still meet relevance and reliability standards, though the specific factors set out in *Robinson* did not necessarily apply.[215] In deciding whether the trial court in *Gammill* abused its discretion, the supreme court added a more general analysis, similar to that in *Nenno*, of whether "'there is simply too great an analytical gap between the data and opinion proffered.'"[216]

In *Kumho Tire Co. v. Carmichael*, the U.S. Supreme Court held that the general principles of *Daubert* apply to all expert testimony offered under Federal Rule 702, including testimony involving only technical or experiential expertise.[217] The trial court's re-

---

(Cochran, Womack, Johnson, Holcomb, JJ., concurring) (because defendant did not object to testimony about dog-scent lineup, neither court of appeals nor court of criminal appeals reviewed the admissibility of the testimony under either *Kelly* or *Nenno*).

214. *See, e.g.*, *In re M.P.A.*, 364 S.W.3d 277, 288 (Tex. 2012) (in case of sexual assault of a child, court used *Kelly* criteria to analyze evidence of sexual assessment test—used to predict person's interest in particular sexes and age groups—that had been subject to peer review and testing of its accuracy rate; case was unlike *Nenno*, in which expert "did not contend that he had a particular methodology" (quoting *Nenno*, 970 S.W.2d at 562)). Refer to notes 178-181, 189, 198 *supra* and accompanying text.

215. 972 S.W.2d 713, 726 (Tex. 1998); *see Hous. Unlimited, Inc. Metal Processing v. Mel Acres Ranch*, 443 S.W.3d 820, 829 (Tex. 2014) ("Expert appraisal witnesses are subject to the same relevance and reliability standards that apply to all expert witnesses."); *see, e.g.*, *Mack Trucks, Inc. v. Tamez*, 206 S.W.3d 572, 581 (Tex. 2006) (trial court did not abuse its discretion under *Gammill* in excluding as unreliable an expert's testimony on cause of fire because witness did not testify to methodology by which he reached his conclusions); *Cooper Tire & Rubber Co. v. Mendez*, 204 S.W.3d 797, 805 (Tex. 2006) (in manufacturing-defect products-liability case, "wax contamination theory" for tire failure was "a naked hypothesis untested and unconfirmed by the methods of science and was legally insufficient to establish a manufacturing defect that caused the failure"); *Guadalupe-Blanco River Auth. v. Kraft*, 77 S.W.3d 805, 808-09 (Tex. 2002) (trial court erred in admitting expert's "sales comparison method" of valuing land when independent review of his underlying data showed that he did not apply that methodology correctly to the specific land involved); *Helena Chem. Co. v. Wilkins*, 47 S.W.3d 486, 500-01 (Tex. 2001) (admission of expert testimony on suitability of particular grain seed for dryland farming was upheld; expert's "experience, coupled with his thorough testimony about the methodology he employed, demonstrate that the opinions he drew from the underlying data are reliable"); *Five Star Int'l Holdings Inc. v. Thomson, Inc.*, 324 S.W.3d 160, 168-69 (Tex. App.—El Paso 2010, pet. denied) (testimony of property manager about overcharging for common-area expenses was properly analyzed under *Gammill*; trial court did not abuse its discretion by admitting testimony); *Goodyear Tire & Rubber Co. v. Rios*, 143 S.W.3d 107, 113-15 (Tex. App.—San Antonio 2004, pet. denied) (tire expert's opinion not reliable under *Robinson/Gammill/Kumho* criteria); *In re Estate of Robinson*, 140 S.W.3d 782, 791-92 (Tex. App.—Corpus Christi 2004, pet. denied) (psychiatrist's opinion testimony that deceased lacked testamentary and mental capacity when contested will was signed was sufficiently reliable under *Gammill*'s analytic-gap analysis); *Taylor v. Am. Fabritech, Inc.*, 132 S.W.3d 613, 619-21 (Tex. App.—Houston [14th Dist.] 2004, pet. denied) (admission of plaintiff's expert witness's testimony on construction safety was upheld; analysis was based on established principles of safety engineering and management, and his technique was widely accepted in the field); *Burns v. Baylor Health Care Sys.*, 125 S.W.3d 589, 596-97 (Tex. App.—El Paso 2003, no pet.) (trial court abused its discretion in excluding plaintiff's safety-engineering expert's summary-judgment affidavit on human visual process and its effect in determining whether paint on parking-garage curb created unsafe optical illusion).

216. *Gammill*, 972 S.W.2d at 726 (quoting *Gen. Elec. Co. v. Joiner*, 522 U.S. 136, 146 (1997)); *accord TXI Transp. Co. v. Hughes*, 306 S.W.3d 230, 239 (Tex. 2010); *Volkswagen of Am., Inc. v. Ramirez*, 159 S.W.3d 897, 904-05 (Tex. 2004); *see Gharda USA, Inc. v. Control Sols., Inc.*, 464 S.W.3d 338, 349 (Tex. 2015) ("Whether an analytical gap exists is largely determined by comparing the facts the expert relied on, the facts in the record, and the expert's ultimate opinion."). Ultimately, the trial court is the gatekeeper in determining the reliability of all expert testimony offered at trial. *Gammill*, 972 S.W.2d at 728. Refer to notes 231-234 *infra* and accompanying text.

217. *See Kumho Tire Co. v. Carmichael*, 526 U.S. 137, 147-49 (1999). Many federal circuit opinions have discussed the application of the *Daubert* reliability principles, though not necessarily the specific factors suggested in that case, to nonscientific expertise. *See, e.g.*, *United States v. Romero*, 189 F.3d 576, 584-85 (7th Cir. 1999) (applying *Kumho*

sponsibility "is to make certain that an expert, whether basing testimony upon professional studies or personal experience, employs in the courtroom the same level of intellectual rigor that characterizes the practice of an expert in the relevant field."[218] The reliability of the proffered opinion must be judged on the particular facts and circumstances of each case, and although the **Daubert** factors may be useful in some instances, courts should use a flexible approach depending on the particular expertise involved and its centrality to the case.

Expansion of the **Daubert/Kelly/Robinson** analysis poses a dilemma for courts evaluating nonscientific expertise:

> Scientific evidence is only part of the larger domain of expert testimony. In addition to listing scientific testimony, Rule 702 expressly refers to "technical, or other specialized knowledge." There are numerous examples of technical but nonscientific experts whose credentials normally include substantial formal instruction in the techniques of a discipline. Attorneys, historians, and musicians fall into this category. There are also many nonscientific experts who have informally acquired specialized knowledge through practical experience. This category includes auctioneers, bankers, railroad brakemen, businesspersons, carpenters, farmers, security guards, and trapshooters.[219]

Decisions following the **Daubert/Kelly/Robinson** line have frequently found, particularly with psychological testimony, that the proffered nonscientific expertise was insuf-

---

to expert testimony on the characteristics of "preferential" child molesters); *United States v. Kayne*, 90 F.3d 7, 11-12 (1st Cir. 1996) (in mail-fraud case, examining the reliability of opinions of coin-evaluation experts); *United States v. 14.38 Acres of Land*, 80 F.3d 1074, 1078-79 (5th Cir. 1996) (vacating lower court decision, which had excluded expert testimony by civil engineer and real-estate appraiser in eminent-domain action; both experts relied on types of information normally used by experts in their respective fields and used acceptable methodology); *Den Norske Bank AS v. First Nat'l Bank of Bos.*, 75 F.3d 49, 57 (1st Cir. 1996) (examining reliability of expert evidence on banking-industry practices by analyzing how expert reached his conclusion regarding "usage of trade"); *Pedraza v. Jones*, 71 F.3d 194, 197 (5th Cir. 1995) (affirming exclusion of affidavit by long-term drug addict describing effects of heroin withdrawal; insufficient indicia of reliability); *Gier v. Educ. Serv. Unit No. 16*, 66 F.3d 940, 943-44 (8th Cir. 1995) (affirming trial court's severe limitation of the testimony of three psychiatric experts who had evaluated mentally retarded students; testimony was unreliable under *Daubert* factors); *United States v. Velasquez*, 64 F.3d 844, 850-51 (3d Cir. 1995) (*Daubert* factors are helpful to the court in determining admissibility of expert testimony on handwriting analysis; methodology used by expert was reliable); *Marcel v. Placid Oil Co.*, 11 F.3d 563, 567-68 (5th Cir. 1994) (upholding inadmissibility of expert economist's testimony; analysis on which it was based lacked important underlying data); *Joy v. Bell Helicopter Textron, Inc.*, 999 F.2d 549, 568-70 (D.C. Cir. 1993) (examining methods and assumptions underlying economist's expert testimony and concluding that his opinion was "based solely on guesswork, speculation, and conjecture" and therefore was inadmissible; under *Daubert*, the word "knowledge" in Federal Rule 702 "connotes more than subjective belief or unsupported speculation"). For articles discussing the possible impact of *Daubert* on nonscientific evidence, see Sofia Adrogue & Alan Ratliff, *Kicking the Tires After* Kumho: *The Bottom Line on Admitting Financial Expert Testimony*, 37 HOUS. L. REV. 431 (2000), Robert J. Goodwin, *The Hidden Significance of* Kumho Tire Co. v. Carmichael: *A Compass for Problems of Definition and Procedure Created by* Daubert v. Merrell Dow Pharmaceuticals, Inc., 52 BAYLOR L. REV. 603 (2000), and Kimberly S. Keller, *Bridging the Analytical Gap: The* Gammill *Alternative to Overcoming* Robinson & Havner *Challenges to Expert Testimony*, 33 ST. MARY'S L.J. 277 (2002).

218. *Kumho*, 526 U.S. at 152.

219. Edward J. Imwinkelried, *The Next Step After* Daubert: *Developing a Similarly Epistemological Approach to Ensuring the Reliability of Nonscientific Expert Testimony*, 15 CARDOZO L. REV. 2271, 2278 (1994) (footnotes omitted); *accord S.V. v. R.V.*, 933 S.W.2d 1, 41 (Tex. 1996) (Cornyn, J., concurring).

ficiently reliable to help the jury.[220] However, the court of criminal appeals has held that the study of the reliability of eyewitness identification is a legitimate field in the area of psychology.[221]

In *Daubert*, the U.S. Supreme Court embraced the concept of "Newtonian science," in which a scientist forms a hypothesis and then conducts experiments, tests, or observations to validate or refute the theory. According to the Supreme Court, experimental methodology is "'what distinguishes science from other fields of human inquiry.'"[222] Thus, a theory derives its scientific status from "its falsifiability, or refutability, or testability."[223] If a theory cannot be empirically tested, it is not scientific under these standards. The various factors set out in *Daubert*, *Kelly*, and *Robinson* are designed to assess the validity of scientific theories that undergo extensive experimental testing, peer review, and publication. However, the Texas Supreme Court has cautioned that

> in very few cases will the evidence be such that the trial court's reliability determination can properly be based only on the experience of a qualified ex-

220. *See, e.g.*, ***United States v. White Horse***, 316 F.3d 769, 774-75 (8th Cir. 2003) (testimony by psychologist about "sexual interest assessment" did not satisfy ***Daubert***; assessment had not been sufficiently tested using statistically significant sample of Native American subjects and did not use pictures of Native American adults or children, and incest cases were excluded from the published study); ***United States v. Langan***, 263 F.3d 613, 621-23 (6th Cir. 2001) (exclusion of psychologist's testimony on reliability of eyewitness identification was upheld under ***Daubert***); ***Coble v. State***, 330 S.W.3d 253, 277-80 (Tex. Crim. App. 2010) (trial court abused its discretion in admitting psychologist's testimony on capital-murder defendant's future dangerousness; witness did not cite any sources to substantiate his methodology, and prosecution thus did not show by clear and convincing evidence that witness's methodology was reliable); ***Jordan v. State***, 950 S.W.2d 210, 212 (Tex. App.—Fort Worth 1997, pet. ref'd) (insufficient showing of scientific validity of the theories and methodology for psychological expertise on eyewitness reliability); ***Am. W. Airlines, Inc. v. Tope***, 935 S.W.2d 908, 918-19 (Tex. App.—El Paso 1996, no writ) (mental-health worker's testimony about former employee's mental anguish was not scientifically reliable; although the methodology was generally accepted in the psychology community and was used for nonjudicial purposes, diagnosis was subjective and based on claimant's statements, which could only be tested by re-interviewing claimant; peer review of expert's method was limited, and she offered no examples of publications; potential error rate was unexamined); *see also* ***S.V.***, 933 S.W.2d at 17-20 (no "discovery rule" tolling of limitations period based on claim of "repressed memory"; scientific "literature on repression and recovered memory syndrome establishes that fundamental theoretical and practical issues remain to be resolved"; thus, opinions in that area cannot meet "objective verifiability" required under ***Robinson***). *But see* ***Muhammad v. State***, 46 S.W.3d 493, 506 (Tex. App.—El Paso 2001, no pet.) (reversible error to exclude defense expert psychologist's testimony explaining defendant's calm, apparently unremorseful demeanor after murder; expert administered and relied on results of well-recognized psychological tests with established potential error rates as reliable techniques to assess personality, and testimony was within scope of expert's field).

221. ***Blasdell v. State***, 470 S.W.3d 59, 63 (Tex. Crim. App. 2015); ***Tillman v. State***, 354 S.W.3d 425, 436 (Tex. Crim. App. 2011). In ***Tillman***, the defendant offered the testimony of a psychology professor who was an expert on eyewitness identifications to discuss how the lineup and photo spread were used in that particular investigation. 354 S.W.3d at 429. The expert referenced over 30 studies involving the use of a photo spread in which no suspect was identified, followed by a live lineup in which the target suspect was identified; in these studies, only the target suspect was included in both the photo spread and the lineup. *See id.* at 437-38. The expert testified that such a procedure is suggestive, detailing the psychological explanations for that conclusion and discussing various hypothetical scenarios during his testimony. *Id.* at 438. The court found that the expert's testimony was reliable under the ***Nenno*** analysis for "soft sciences." *Id.* at 435-38. Refer to notes 210-213 *supra* and accompanying text.

222. ***Daubert v. Merrell Dow Pharm., Inc.***, 509 U.S. 579, 593 (1993) (quoting Michael D. Green, *Expert Witnesses and Sufficiency of Evidence in Toxic Substances Litigation: The Legacy of Agent Orange and Bendectin Litigation*, 86 Nw. U. L. Rev. 643, 645 (1992)).

223. *See id.*

pert to the exclusion of factors such as those set out in **Robinson**, or, on the other hand, properly be based only on factors such as those set out in **Robinson** to the exclusion of considerations based on a qualified expert's experience.[224]

The Texas Supreme Court's assessment applies to reliability determinations for both scientific and nonscientific testimony. Thus, the admissibility of any expert testimony, at least when it aims to advance a theoretical model and then explain specific facts or data in accord with that model,[225] should be determined by considering both the witness's experience under the **Gammill** analysis and the **Daubert/Kelly/Robinson** factors or some variation of them.[226]

Technical expertise or other areas of specialized knowledge, such as handwriting analysis,[227] police-officer testimony about the modus operandi of drug traffickers,[228] the use of anatomically correct dolls to help a child witness demonstrate testimony,[229] or other practical arts and skills, may be of great assistance to a jury even though the topics and opinions of such experts have never been and could never be systematically tested and thus have no known "error rate."[230] Courts have traditionally focused on the

---

224. **Whirlpool Corp. v. Camacho**, 298 S.W.3d 631, 638 (Tex. 2009).

225. This kind of evidence might include testimony by psychologists, psychiatrists, sociologists, economists, or social-science experts in areas such as memory, the reliability of eyewitness identification, child abuse, rape trauma, and hypnotic refreshment. On the whole, their work is guided by the Newtonian scientific methodology of "proposing and refining theoretical explanations about the world." **Daubert**, 509 U.S. at 590. Thus, the admissibility of their testimony has generally been determined by considering the **Daubert/Kelly/Robinson** factors. *See, e.g.*, **Jordan v. State**, 928 S.W.2d 550, 555-56 (Tex. Crim. App. 1996) (expert testimony on eyewitness misidentification should have been evaluated under **Daubert/Kelly** principles); **Perez v. State**, 25 S.W.3d 830, 837-38 (Tex. App.—Houston [1st Dist.] 2000, no pet.) (psychiatric testimony on "child abuse accommodation syndrome" was inadmissible under **Kelly** factors); *see also* **Tillman**, 354 S.W.3d at 437 (expert testimony on reliability of eyewitness identification should have been admitted under **Nenno**; expert properly used and relied on principles of relevant field of psychology); **Hernandez v. State**, 53 S.W.3d 742, 750-51 (Tex. App.—Houston [1st Dist.] 2001, pet. ref'd) (admission of expert's opinions on characteristics and dynamics of sexually abused children was upheld under **Nenno** standards; expert had extensive experience with child sexual-assault victims, knew the characteristics and dynamics of sexually abused children, outlined Child Abuse Accommodation Syndrome, and, on voir dire, established that her data and opinions were recognized in fields of psychology and psychiatry).

226. *See* **Transcon. Ins. v. Crump**, 330 S.W.3d 211, 215-16 (Tex. 2010); **Whirlpool Corp.**, 298 S.W.3d at 639-40; *see also* **TXI Transp. Co. v. Hughes**, 306 S.W.3d 230, 235 (Tex. 2010) ("[The **Robinson** factors] are particularly difficult to apply in vehicular accident cases involving accident reconstruction testimony. ... Rather than focus entirely on the reliability of the underlying technique used to generate the challenged opinion, as in **Robinson**, we have found it appropriate ... to analyze whether the expert's opinion actually fits the facts of the case. In other words, we determine whether there are any significant analytical gaps in the expert's opinion that undermine its reliability."). See **O'Connor's Texas Rules * Civil Trials** (2017), "Reliability of opinion," ch. 5-N, §2.3.1, p. 477. For a discussion of the court's reliability determination based on the expert's experience under **Gammill**, refer to notes 215-216 *supra* and accompanying text, notes 231-234 *infra* and accompanying text.

227. *See, e.g.*, **United States v. Jones**, 107 F.3d 1147, 1158 (6th Cir. 1997) (admissibility of expert testimony on handwriting analysis was not governed by **Daubert** factors). *But see* **Sosa v. State**, 841 S.W.2d 912, 917 (Tex. App.—Houston [1st Dist.] 1992, no pet.) (defense expertise on graphoanalysis was rejected under **Kelly** analysis).

228. Refer to note 151 *supra* and accompanying text.

229. *See* **Perez v. State**, 925 S.W.2d 324, 326 (Tex. App.—Corpus Christi 1996, no pet.) (use of anatomically correct dolls is not scientific evidence that must be shown to be scientifically reliable under **Daubert/Kelly**).

230. *See* **Whirlpool Corp.**, 298 S.W.3d at 639 ("We have recognized, and do recognize, that some subjects do not lend themselves to scientific testing and scientific methodology.").

technical expert's qualifications and the helpfulness of the testimony without specific inquiry into the reliability of the testimony in determining the admissibility of non-scientific expertise.

After *Daubert*, *Kumho*, *Kelly*, and *Robinson*, however, Texas courts must analyze the admissibility of technical or practical expertise to ensure that it is sufficiently reliable to help the jury. In making a threshold determination of reliability for the practical expert's testimony,[231] courts might focus on the expert's methodology or reasoning and the type of data or information he has relied on, as well as the "fit" between that data and the expert's conclusions.[232] In other words, courts must ensure that there is no "analytical gap" between the data and the opinions proffered.[233] The "analytical gap" examination is presumably similar to the methodology set out by the Advisory Committee on the Federal Rules:

---

231. The trial court's role is not to determine whether an expert's conclusions are correct, but only whether the analysis used to reach those conclusions is reliable. *Kerr-McGee Corp. v. Helton*, 133 S.W.3d 245, 254 (Tex. 2004); *Exxon Pipeline Co. v. Zwahr*, 88 S.W.3d 623, 629 (Tex. 2002); *Gammill v. Jack Williams Chevrolet, Inc.*, 972 S.W.2d 713, 728 (Tex. 1998). The same analysis applies to appellate courts in their reliability review. *See Gharda USA, Inc. v. Control Sols., Inc.*, 464 S.W.3d 338, 349 (Tex. 2015).

232. *See Hous. Unlimited, Inc. Metal Processing v. Mel Acres Ranch*, 443 S.W.3d 820, 835-37 (Tex. 2014); *Whirlpool Corp.*, 298 S.W.3d at 642; *see, e.g.*, *Seatrax, Inc. v. Sonbeck Int'l, Inc.*, 200 F.3d 358, 371-72 (5th Cir. 2000) (trial court properly excluded expert's testimony on gross profits under *Kumho* because witness had no formal or professional training in accounting and did not conduct any independent examination of gross sales figures); *Muñoz v. Orr*, 200 F.3d 291, 301-02 (5th Cir. 2000) (trial court properly refused to consider expert's summary-judgment opinion under *Kumho* because he made miscalculations, assumed discrimination, did not consider other variables, and relied solely on plaintiff's data); *Black v. Food Lion, Inc.*, 171 F.3d 308, 313-14 (5th Cir. 1999) (trial court abused its discretion in admitting expert's opinion because doctor's testimony on cause of contributing factors to fibromyalgia was unsupported by a specific reliable methodology and was "contradicted by the general level of current medical knowledge").

233. *Gen. Elec. Co. v. Joiner*, 522 U.S. 136, 146 (1997); *TXI Transp. Co. v. Hughes*, 306 S.W.3d 230, 235 (Tex. 2010); *Gammill*, 972 S.W.2d at 726-27; *see, e.g.*, *Hous. Unlimited*, 443 S.W.3d at 836-37 (in case involving land contamination, expert appraiser's failure to account for differences between properties at issue, differences between nature of contamination and remediation of the properties, and contamination not attributable to defendant created analytical gaps; once questioned on them, expert should have better explained why she did not need to consider those factors); *Kia Motors Corp. v. Ruiz*, 432 S.W.3d 865, 876-78 (Tex. 2014) (in products-liability case against vehicle manufacturer, expert's testimony on structural deficiencies in air-bag system was specific enough that there was no analytical gap between data and opinion that these defects prevented air bag from deploying); *Elizondo v. Krist*, 415 S.W.3d 259, 264 (Tex. 2013) (in legal-malpractice case, "an attorney-expert, however well qualified, cannot defeat summary judgment if there are fatal gaps in his analysis that leave the court to take his word that the settlement was inadequate"); *Transcon. Ins. v. Crump*, 330 S.W.3d 211, 219-20 (Tex. 2010) (in workers' compensation case, physician who treated or directly oversaw treatment of patient's work-related injury could give expert opinion on cause of death; "[a]t this point, any 'gaps' that remain between the data and the conclusion drawn from it go to the weight of [physician's] testimony—not its reliability"); *Volkswagen of Am., Inc. v. Ramirez*, 159 S.W.3d 897, 905-06 (Tex. 2004) (accident-reconstruction expert's theory of causation was unreliable because the expert cited no other studies, publications, or peer review to support his opinion; expert's theory "is not supported by objective scientific evidence and is based solely upon his subjective interpretation of the facts"); *McMahon v. Zimmerman*, 433 S.W.3d 680, 688 (Tex. App.—Houston [1st Dist.] 2014, no pet.) (in legal-malpractice case arising from divorce representation, too great an analytical gap between expert's opinion on expected judicial division of community debt and data that ostensibly supported opinion); *Davis v. Aetrex Worldwide, Inc.*, 392 S.W.3d 213, 217 (Tex. App.—Amarillo 2012, no pet.) (too great an analytical gap in podiatrist's testimony that plaintiff's black shoes caused blisters on his feet because black shoes absorb more heat than white shoes; without any details about conditions in which injury occurred, testimony was unreliable and speculative); *Page v. State Farm Lloyds*, 259 S.W.3d 257, 267-68 (Tex.

If the witness is relying solely or primarily on experience, then the witness must explain how that experience leads to the conclusion reached, why that experience is a sufficient basis for the opinion, and how that experience is reliably applied to the facts. The trial court's gatekeeping function requires more than simply "taking the expert's word for it."[234]

The level of judicial scrutiny of the practical expert's methodology and the type of data relied on might be related to the complexity of the subject matter and the corresponding likelihood of an erroneous conclusion by jury members who are presumably not sufficiently familiar with the subject matter or the appropriate methodology. The supreme court, however, has cautioned against accepting the expert's experience as a substitute for proof that the opinions are reliable, encouraging courts to evaluate the **Daubert/Kelly/Robinson** factors in addition to the "analytical gap" test.[235]

The data underlying an expert's opinion must be independently evaluated by the trial judge in a "gatekeeping" hearing to determine if the opinion itself is reliable.[236] An expert's mere assertion that his methodology is "generally accepted" in the relevant

App.—Waco 2008) (no analytical gap between insurance adjuster's testimony on estimates for repairs and the basis for that testimony; expert's opinions were based on knowledge, training, and experience in assessing property damage, his own inspection of property, and information produced by software program frequently used in insurance and construction industries), *rev'd in part on other grounds*, 315 S.W.3d 525 (Tex. 2010); ***Ruckman v. State***, 109 S.W.3d 524, 530 (Tex. App.—Tyler 2000, pet. ref'd) (not error to exclude defense expert's testimony on "false confessions" when expert did not tie his testimony to any particular study or article and did not rely on any of the scientific articles in the record); ***In re D.S.***, 19 S.W.3d 525, 529-30 (Tex. App.—Fort Worth 2000, no pet.) (no analytical gap between doctor's opinion that child suffered an immersion burn and the basis on which his opinion was founded; medical opinion on cause of child's burns was not the type of evidence that could be tested under ***Daubert/Robinson***); ***Roise v. State***, 7 S.W.3d 225, 236-37 (Tex. App.—Austin 1999, pet. ref'd) (too great an analytical gap between data that expert relied on and his testimony that nude photographs of children would promote sexual fantasies in viewers and that child models would be developmentally harmed by their participation in child pornography); ***Kroger Co. v. Betancourt***, 996 S.W.2d 353, 362-63 (Tex. App.—Houston [14th Dist.] 1999, pet. denied) (even though expert had no experience with allegedly defective equipment, his testimony was admissible under ***Kumho*** and ***Gammill*** because he had reviewed numerous depositions and the operator's manual and had inspected equipment after accident); *see also* ***Vega v. Fulcrum Energy, LLC***, 415 S.W.3d 481, 492-93 (Tex. App.—Houston [1st Dist.] 2013, pet. denied) (in partnership dispute, expert who testified about value of partnership did not include goodwill in his valuation; although decision not to use generally accepted guidelines in reaching his conclusion was not automatically a dispositive analytical gap, court held expert's opinion was unreliable because he did not demonstrate a reliable basis for his contradictory conclusion). See ***O'Connor's Texas Rules * Civil Trials*** (2017), "***Gammill*** 'analytical gap' analysis," ch. 5-N, §2.3.1(2), p. 478.

234. FED. R. EVID. 702 advisory committee's note to 2000 amendments. Refer to note 238 *infra* and accompanying text.

235. *See* ***Whirlpool Corp.***, 298 S.W.3d at 639 ("If courts merely accept 'experience' as a substitute for proof that an expert's opinions are reliable and then only examine the testimony for analytical gaps in the expert's logic and opinions, an expert can effectively insulate his or her conclusions from meaningful review by filling gaps in the testimony with almost any type of data or subjective opinions."). Refer to notes 224-226 *supra* and accompanying text.

236. ***Merrell Dow Pharm., Inc. v. Havner***, 953 S.W.2d 706, 713 (Tex. 1997); *see* ***Merck & Co. v. Garza***, 347 S.W.3d 256, 262 (Tex. 2011); *see also* ***In re Paoli R.R. Yard PCB Litig.***, 35 F.3d 717, 747-48 (3d Cir. 1994) (Third Circuit overruled its holding in ***DeLuca v. Merrell Dow Pharm., Inc.***, 911 F.2d 941, 952 (3d Cir. 1990), that an expert's own statement that his testimony is based on the type of data on which other experts in his field reasonably rely is generally enough to satisfy a Federal Rule 703 inquiry). Refer to note 167 *supra* and accompanying text.

field does not suffice.[237] Further, an expert's unsubstantiated assertion that his conclusions are true (i.e., the expert's "ipse dixit") does not make the evidence reliable.[238]

Of course, not every trial court must conduct a **Daubert/Kelly/Robinson** gatekeeping hearing whenever expert testimony is offered.[239] Once the reliability of a particular scientific theory and methodology has been adequately explored through evidentiary hearings in one or more trial courts, other courts may take judicial notice of the adequacy of those hearings as establishing the reliability (or unreliability) of that area of expertise.[240] As the court of criminal appeals has noted:

> Trial courts are not required to re-invent the scientific wheel in every trial. However, some trial court must actually examine and assess the reliability of the particular scientific wheel before other courts may ride along behind. Some court, somewhere, has to conduct an adversarial gatekeeping hearing to determine the reliability of the given scientific theory and its methodology.[241]

237. *See, e.g.*, **E.I. du Pont de Nemours & Co. v. Robinson**, 923 S.W.2d 549, 559 (Tex. 1995) (expert's "self-serving statements that his methodology was generally accepted and reasonably relied on by other experts in the field are not sufficient to establish the reliability of the technique"); **Blasdell v. State**, 470 S.W.3d 59, 65-66 & n.13 (Tex. Crim. App. 2015) (trial court did not err in excluding expert testimony about "weapon focus effect" when expert generally described topic but did not describe principles that applied to it or methodology by which he would apply those principles).

238. *See Joiner*, 522 U.S. at 146 ("[C]onclusions and methodology are not entirely distinct from one another. Trained experts commonly extrapolate from existing data. But nothing in either **Daubert** or the Federal Rules of Evidence requires a district court to admit opinion evidence that is connected to existing data only by the *ipse dixit* of the expert."); **Rogers v. Zanetti**, 518 S.W.3d 394, 409 (Tex. 2017) ("An *ipse dixit* is still an *ipse dixit* even if offered by the most trustworthy of sources. An expert's familiarity with the facts is not alone a satisfactory basis for his or her opinion."); **Gharda USA, Inc. v. Control Sols., Inc.**, 464 S.W.3d 338, 351 (Tex. 2015) (testimony connected to existing data only by expert's "*ipse dixit*" is unreliable and not evidence); **Hous. Unlimited**, 443 S.W.3d at 829 ("[T]he evidentiary value of expert testimony is derived from its basis, not from the mere fact that the expert has said it."); *see, e.g.*, **Moore v. Ashland Chem. Inc.**, 151 F.3d 269, 277-79 (5th Cir. 1998) (trial court did not err in excluding treating physician's opinion testimony in toxic-tort case that exposure to fumes led to reactive-airways-dysfunction syndrome; physician "could cite no scientific support for his conclusion that exposure to any irritant at unknown levels triggers this asthmatic-type condition"); **Gen. Motors Corp. v. Iracheta**, 161 S.W.3d 462, 471 (Tex. 2005) ("[Expert's] testimony was rather clearly unreliable. It had no basis outside his own assertions, which were irreconcilably self-conflicting. A fair view of his testimony is that he was willing to say almost anything, directly contradicting himself."); **Loera v. Fuentes**, 511 S.W.3d 761, 775-76 (Tex. App.—El Paso 2016, n.p.h.) (trial court abused its discretion in admitting physicians' expert opinions that general principles of seat-belt effectiveness applied to double amputee as they would to a person with her feet on floor and that had double amputee been properly wearing seat belt, she would have suffered no serious injuries; opinions were unreliable because experts offered their own theories with no published or peer-reviewed study for support); *see also* **Starwood Mgmt., LLC v. Swaim**, ___ S.W.3d ___ (Tex. 2017) (No. 16-0431; 9-29-17) (per curiam) (whether expert's affidavit is an *ipse dixit* depends on inferences required to bridge gap between underlying data and expert's conclusion; if analytical gap is too great, testimony is conclusory).

239. *See Saenz v. State*, 421 S.W.3d 725, 759 (Tex. App.—San Antonio 2014), *rev'd on other grounds*, 451 S.W.3d 388 (Tex. Crim. App. 2014); *Piro v. Sarofim*, 80 S.W.3d 717, 720 (Tex. App.—Houston [1st Dist.] 2002, no pet.).

240. *See Blasdell*, 470 S.W.3d at 66 n.13 ("[W]e cannot take judicial notice of a scientific theory or hypothesis without evidence of a sufficient number of adversarial hearings at which the reliability of [the] scientific principle was examined, assessed, and approved."). Courts can take judicial notice in the context of both hard and soft sciences. *Id.* at 63 n.6.

241. **Hernandez v. State**, 116 S.W.3d 26, 29 (Tex. Crim. App. 2003); *see Blasdell*, 470 S.W.3d at 63. Refer to note 207 *supra* and accompanying text.

Once the reliability of the underlying theory and methodology of an area of expertise has been satisfactorily established in a number of cases, the proponent needs to demonstrate only that the theory and methodology have been applied correctly on this occasion and that the ultimate result is reliable.[242]

(2) Relevance. To be admissible under Rule 702, an expert's testimony must be relevant.[243] That is, the witness's particular field of specialized knowledge must encompass the facts evaluated; both the expert's background and the proposed testimony must "fit" a fact of consequence.[244] Otherwise, the expert's opinion would not help the jury. "Conclusory or speculative opinion testimony is not relevant evidence because it does not tend to make the existence of material facts more probable or less probable."[245] Fur-

---

242. *See, e.g.*, *State v. Petropoulos*, 346 S.W.3d 525, 529 (Tex. 2011) (in partial-taking condemnation proceeding, expert used "comparable sales approach" to determine property's pre-taking value; because supreme court has recognized that this method is a traditional way to determine land value and expert applied the method correctly, trial court did not abuse its discretion in admitting testimony); *Coronado v. State*, 384 S.W.3d 919, 927-28 (Tex. App.— Dallas 2012, no pet.) (trial court did not abuse its discretion in admitting expert testimony on using forensic odontology to exclude suspects in closed population, a purpose for which that science has been deemed reliable; deficiencies and limitations of scientific evidence go to weight of evidence, not admissibility).

243. *See Daubert v. Merrell Dow Pharm., Inc.*, 509 U.S. 579, 589 (1993).

244. *See Everitt v. State*, 407 S.W.3d 259, 263 (Tex. Crim. App. 2013) ("Reliability refers to the scientific basis for the expert testimony, while relevance refers to the 'fit' of the scientific principles to the evidence at hand."); *see, e.g.*, *Petropoulos*, 346 S.W.3d at 529 (expert's testimony on property's pre-taking value was relevant to calculation of partial-taking damages); *Blasdell v. State*, 384 S.W.3d 824, 830-31 (Tex. Crim. App. 2012) (testimony of eyewitness-identification expert is relevant if witness states "that a particular identification procedure, or the facts or circumstances attending a particular eyewitness event, has been empirically demonstrated to be fraught with the *potential* to cause a mistaken identification"; court of appeals erred in excluding expert testimony on "weapons focus effect" on eyewitnesses because "even the 'possibility' of distorted perception under the circumstances was sufficient to establish a 'fit' with the facts of the case, and hence, the relevance of [witness's] expert testimony"); *Tillman v. State*, 354 S.W.3d 425, 441 (Tex. Crim. App. 2011) (expert's testimony fit relevant facts when he applied scientific theories and principles to detailed hypotheticals that mirrored facts of case); *Jordan v. State*, 928 S.W.2d 550, 555-56 (Tex. Crim. App. 1996) (expert on eyewitness reliability had established the relevance of his proposed testimony on the factors that affect the reliability of eyewitness testimony by correlating those studies with the specific identification facts in the case; for expert testimony to be relevant under Rule 702, expert "must make an effort to tie pertinent facts of the case to the scientific principles which are the subject of his testimony"); *Williams v. State*, 895 S.W.2d 363, 366-67 (Tex. Crim. App. 1994) (expert did not connect generic testimony about the psychological profile of a typical "offender who makes harassing telephone calls of a sexual nature" to the facts of the case; psychologist testified only that defendant's psychological-test results indicated he was an overachiever and extremely moralistic); *Pierce v. State*, 777 S.W.2d 399, 414-16 (Tex. Crim. App. 1989) (trial court did not err in excluding testimony of expert on eyewitness reliability when expert did not "fit" his testimony to the evidence at trial); *Werner v. State*, 711 S.W.2d 639, 644-45 (Tex. Crim. App. 1986) (defense expert who would have testified to "Holocaust Syndrome" was excluded because such testimony was not relevant to any contested fact or issue).

245. *Whirlpool Corp. v. Camacho*, 298 S.W.3d 631, 637 (Tex. 2009); *see, e.g.*, *Bostic v. Ga.-Pac. Corp.*, 439 S.W.3d 332, 359-60 (Tex. 2014) (expert's testimony was legally insufficient to prove that decedent's mesothelioma was caused by exposure to asbestos while employed by defendant because expert stated that decedent's exposure at another job was minimal compared to exposure from construction for defendant but did not base this testimony on any scientific studies or any attempt to scientifically measure relative exposures); *Wal-Mart Stores, Inc. v. Merrell*, 313 S.W.3d 837, 840 (Tex. 2010) (per curiam) (expert's testimony was legally insufficient to support a finding of causation because testimony did not establish how the lamp in question caused the fire at issue in the case; "[a]n expert's failure to explain or adequately disprove alternative theories of causation makes his or her own theory speculative and conclusory"); *see also* *Nat. Gas Pipeline Co. of Am. v. Justiss*, 397 S.W.3d 150, 159 (Tex. 2012) (lay-opinion testimony offered under Property Owner Rule is the "functional equivalent of expert testimony"; thus, property owner's conclusory or speculative testimony will not support a judgment). For a further discussion of the Property Owner Rule, refer to notes 45-46 *supra* and accompanying text.

thermore, "a party may complain that conclusory opinions are legally insufficient evidence to support a judgment even if the party did not object to the admission of the testimony."[246]

Sometimes, courts must make subtle distinctions when a proponent seeks to elicit opinion testimony near the fringes of an expert's field. Again, the helpfulness of the opinion, in light of the witness's experiential capacity, should be determinative.[247] Considerations such as the expense to the respective parties[248] and the Rule 403 balancing factors are also relevant in the determination of an expert opinion's helpfulness.[249] These countervailing factors, as well as variations in experiential capacity, help reconcile apparently conflicting holdings in Texas case law.[250]

3. Rule 403 balancing test. After an expert has met the qualification requirements and his testimony has been shown to be reliable and relevant, the expert's opinion must meet the general balancing test of Rule 403.[251] The factors to consider are whether the

246. *City of San Antonio v. Pollock*, 284 S.W.3d 809, 816 (Tex. 2009); *see Coastal Transp. Co. v. Crown Cent. Pet. Corp.*, 136 S.W.3d 227, 233 (Tex. 2004).

247. *See, e.g., Payton v. Abbott Labs*, 780 F.2d 147, 155-56 (1st Cir. 1985) (two physicians could testify about injuries resulting from the use of a prescription drug during pregnancy, even though neither was a research scientist or a specialist in the field); *In re Related Asbestos Cases*, 543 F. Supp. 1142, 1149-50 (N.D. Cal. 1982) (testimony of environmental consultant would not help trier of fact understand the reaction of the medical community to certain technical medical articles); *Texaco, Inc. v. Pennzoil, Co.*, 729 S.W.2d 768, 837-38 (Tex. App.—Houston [1st Dist.] 1987, writ ref'd n.r.e.) (witness did not give an improper legal opinion when he testified that "[b]ased on the evidence that I have seen and only as an experienced executive who served on boards, I would come to the conclusion that the Getty board had reached an agreement with Pennzoil"); *Texaco, Inc. v. Romine*, 536 S.W.2d 253, 256-57 (Tex. Civ. App.—El Paso 1976, writ ref'd n.r.e.) (testimony of witness with Ph.D. in management statistics about plaintiff's ability to perform manual work was not within witness's field of expertise). *See generally* 2 WIGMORE, *supra* note 3, §555, at 749-50 (discussing how expertness is relative to both the particular topic and the testimony's potential helpfulness to the jury). For a discussion of experiential capacity, refer to note 94 *supra*.

248. *See* TEX. R. EVID. 102 (Rules should be construed to eliminate unjustifiable expense).

249. *See* TEX. R. EVID. 403. Refer to notes 251-256 *infra* and accompanying text.

250. Cases involving the testimony of accident investigators are illustrative. Courts have admitted these opinions in many situations. *See, e.g., Waring v. Wommack*, 945 S.W.2d 889, 892-93 (Tex. App.—Austin 1997, no writ) (expert testimony by accident-reconstruction engineer on the avoidability of an accident based on tests at collision scene and other physical evidence from accident); *O'Kelly v. Jackson*, 516 S.W.2d 748, 752 (Tex. Civ. App.—Corpus Christi 1974, no writ) (opinion testimony on the avoidability of an accident based on photographs, inspection of the vehicles, and measurements of skid marks); *Bates v. Barclay*, 484 S.W.2d 955, 957-58 (Tex. Civ. App.—Beaumont 1972, writ ref'd n.r.e.) (opinion testimony, from both patrolman with 10 years' experience and special training and consulting engineer with Ph.D. and 20 years' experience, on the speed of a vehicle involved in an accident).

On the other hand, courts have sometimes excluded similar, but perhaps weaker, testimony. *See, e.g., King v. Skelly*, 452 S.W.2d 691, 695-96 (Tex. 1970) (highway patrolman qualified as an expert, but his opinion testimony on vehicle positioning was not admissible); *Hailes v. Gentry*, 520 S.W.2d 555, 558 (Tex. Civ. App.—El Paso 1975, no writ) (police officer's opinion on speed should have been excluded because no qualifications were shown other than his accident-investigating experience); *Std. Motor Co. v. Blood*, 380 S.W.2d 651, 653 (Tex. Civ. App.—Houston [14th Dist.] 1964, writ dism'd) (trial court's rejection of expert testimony was affirmed when expert witness did not have technical or scientific basis for testimony); *Jenkins v. Hennigan*, 298 S.W.2d 905, 909 (Tex. Civ. App.—Beaumont 1957, writ ref'd n.r.e.) (police officer's opinion on the position of vehicle at impact, based on direction of skid marks, was excluded).

251. *See Schutz v. State*, 957 S.W.2d 52, 70 (Tex. Crim. App. 1997) (expert testimony may be excluded under Rule 403 if the probative value of the evidence is substantially outweighed by the danger of unfair prejudice or other Rule 403 counterfactors); *Ortiz v. State*, 834 S.W.2d 343, 347 (Tex. Crim. App. 1992) (determinations under Rules 702 and 403 must be done on case-by-case basis); *cf. United States v. Downing*, 753 F.2d 1224, 1242-43 (3d Cir. 1985)

probative value of the expert's testimony is substantially outweighed by the danger of unfair prejudice,[252] confusing the issues, misleading the jury,[253] undue delay, or the needless presentation of cumulative evidence.[254] Given the generally liberal attitude of the Federal and Texas Rules toward the admission of relevant evidence, however, courts should resolve any doubts about whether an expert's testimony will sufficiently help the jury in favor of admitting the evidence and should then allow vigorous cross-examination to expose potential weaknesses in the evidence.[255] The determination of whether an expert's testimony will help the trier of fact and whether this level of assistance is substantially outweighed by Rule 403 counterfactors is subject to the trial judge's discretion and will not be disturbed except for an abuse of that discretion.[256]

("[E]ven if the proffered evidence satisfies [Federal] Rule 702, the district court may decide nonetheless to invoke Rule 403 to exclude the evidence if the court finds its probative value to be substantially outweighed by other dangers ...."). *See generally* 2 GOODE ET AL., *supra* note 7, §702.5, at 36 (discussing Texas Rule 403); 3 LOUISELL & MUELLER, *supra* note 27, §382, at 642-43 (discussing Federal Rule 403); 3 WEINSTEIN & BERGER, *supra* note 15, ¶702[02], at 702-23 to 702-29 (Federal Rule 403 helps in determining the admissibility of expert testimony; courts may be more concerned with unfair prejudice as an exclusion factor in criminal trials than in civil trials).

252. *See, e.g.*, **United States v. Solomon**, 753 F.2d 1522, 1525-26 (9th Cir. 1985) (prejudicial effect of narcoanalysis, which an expert admitted did not reliably induce truthful statements, outweighed its slight probative value); **Nenno v. State**, 970 S.W.2d 549, 562 (Tex. Crim. App. 1998) (expert's testimony on future dangerousness of capital-murder defendant was reliable and relevant, and its probative value was not substantially outweighed by the danger of unfair prejudice), *overruled on other grounds*, **State v. Terrazas**, 4 S.W.3d 720 (Tex. Crim. App. 1999); **Kos v. State**, 15 S.W.3d 633, 641-42 (Tex. App.—Dallas 2000, pet. ref'd) (probative value of expert testimony that defendant met criteria of seduction-type child sex offender was not substantially outweighed by danger of unfair prejudice in punishment stage of trial for sexual assault of children).

253. *See, e.g.*, **Sattiewhite v. State**, 786 S.W.2d 271, 290-91 (Tex. Crim. App. 1989) (without reference to Criminal Rule 403, psychologist's testimony that defendant should receive a life sentence and not the death penalty was properly excluded because it would "only tend to confuse the jury" and lead to a battle of experts).

254. *See* TEX. R. EVID. 403. For a general discussion of the Rule 403 balancing test, refer to *Article IV: Relevance & Its Limits*, *supra* p. 211.

255. 3 WEINSTEIN & BERGER, *supra* note 15, ¶702[02], at 702-36 to 702-38; *see, e.g.*, **Ruffin v. State**, 270 S.W.3d 586, 595-96 (Tex. Crim. App. 2008) (judges and jurors are "sufficiently sophisticated" to evaluate expert testimony about a defendant's mental disease intended to rebut proof of mens rea; evidence may be excluded under other evidentiary rules); **Fields v. State**, 932 S.W.2d 97, 109 (Tex. App.—Tyler 1996, pet. ref'd) (probative value of DPS officer's testimony about characteristics of and various factors common among persons transporting drugs by car was not substantially outweighed by any Criminal Rule 403 counterfactor).

256. *See, e.g.*, **JBS Carriers, Inc. v. Washington**, 513 S.W.3d 703, 714-15 (Tex. App.—San Antonio 2017, pet. filed 4-27-17) (no abuse of discretion in excluding doctor's testimony that decedent was bipolar schizophrenic drug addict when testimony was based only on medical records made two months before incident; probative value was substantially outweighed by risk of unfair prejudice); **Gregg Cty. Appr. Dist. v. Laidlaw Waste Sys., Inc.**, 907 S.W.2d 12, 19-20 (Tex. App.—Tyler 1995, writ denied) (no abuse of discretion in excluding expert appraisal testimony and reports that commingled value of business and real property when probative value was substantially outweighed by potential for confusion of issues); **Wade v. State**, 769 S.W.2d 633, 635-36 (Tex. App.—Dallas 1989, no pet.) (no abuse of discretion for trial court to admit expert evidence on possible benefits and detriments to victim from imprisoning defendant); **Dorsett v. State**, 761 S.W.2d 432, 433 (Tex. App.—Houston [14th Dist.] 1988, pet. ref'd) (trial judge in case of indecency with a child did not abuse his discretion in excluding expert psychological testimony on defendant's personality profile). This approach is in accord with earlier Texas practice. *See* **Steve v. State**, 614 S.W.2d 137, 139 (Tex. Crim. App. 1981) (appellate review of trial court's decision to admit expert evidence is limited to whether trial court abused its discretion); **Storm Assocs., Inc. v. Texaco, Inc.**, 645 S.W.2d 579, 589 (Tex. App.—San Antonio 1982) ("The trial court has broad discretion in determining whether to allow expert testimony, and the exercise of that discretion will not be overturned absent an abuse."), *aff'd sub nom.* **Freidman v. Texaco, Inc.**, 691 S.W.2d 586 (Tex. 1985).

RULE 702

RULE 703
BASES OF AN EXPERT'S OPINION TESTIMONY

An expert may base an opinion on facts or data in the case that the expert has been made aware of, reviewed, or personally observed. If experts in the particular field would reasonably rely on those kinds of facts or data in forming an opinion on the subject, they need not be admissible for the opinion to be admitted.

Notes and Comments

Comment to 2015 restyling: All references to an "inference" have been deleted because this makes the Rule flow better and easier to read, and because any "inference" is covered by the broader term "opinion." Courts have not made substantive decisions on the basis of any distinction between an opinion and an inference. No change in current practice is intended.

Comment to 1998 change: The former Civil Rule referred to facts or data "perceived by or reviewed by" the expert. The former Criminal Rule referred to facts or data "perceived by or made known to" the expert. The terminology is now conformed, but no change in meaning is intended.

COMMENTARY ON RULE 703

Rule 703 describes the type of information on which an expert may base an opinion. Rule 703 is substantively identical to the original version of Federal Rule 703.[257] The federal rule was amended in 2000 to "emphasize that when an expert reasonably relies on inadmissible information to form an opinion or inference, the underlying information is not admissible simply because the opinion or inference is admitted."[258] Texas Rule 705(d) similarly restricts the jury's ability to consider inadmissible facts or data underlying an expert's opinion.[259] Texas Rule 703 allows an expert to base opinions on

---

257. *See* Act of Jan. 2, 1975, Pub. L. No. 93-595, §1, 88 Stat. 1926, *reprinted in* 1974 U.S.C.C.A.N. 2215; 641-642 S.W.2d (Tex. Cases) LV (1983, amended 1998).

258. FED. R. EVID. 703 advisory committee's note to 2000 amendments. Federal Rule 703 was restyled in 2011 to delete all references to "inference"; however, no substantive change was intended. FED. R. EVID. 703 advisory committee's note to 2011 amendments. The Advisory Committee explained that the restyling deleted all references to "inference" in the rule "on the grounds that the deletion made the Rule flow better and easier to read, and because any 'inference' is covered by the broader term 'opinion.' Courts have not made substantive decisions on the basis of any distinction between an opinion and an inference." *Id.* In the 2015 restyling of the Texas Rules, the Texas Supreme Court made the same change to Rule 703 based on the same reasoning. *See* TEX. R. EVID. 703 cmt. (2015).

259. *See* TEX. R. EVID. 705(d) ("If the underlying facts or data would otherwise be inadmissible, the proponent of the opinion may not disclose them to the jury if their probative value in helping the jury evaluate the opinion is outweighed by their prejudicial effect. If the court allows the proponent to disclose those facts or data the court must, upon timely request, restrict the evidence to its proper scope and instruct the jury accordingly."). Refer to notes 407-418 *infra* and accompanying text.

facts or data "reviewed" by the expert;[260] the federal rule does not include this language, but it allows the expert to consider "facts or data in the case that the expert has been made aware of or personally observed."[261]

A. Bases of Opinion Testimony

An expert's opinion can be based on (1) facts the expert has personally observed, (2) facts reviewed by the expert, (3) facts the expert has been made aware of, (4) facts presented to the expert at a trial or hearing in the form of hypothetical questions, and (5) facts that are inadmissible as evidence.

1. Facts personally observed by expert. An expert may base an opinion on facts personally observed and experienced firsthand.[262] These bases for an expert opinion have always been permissible[263] and are arguably the most persuasive.[264] When giving this type of testimony, the expert is similar to a lay witness because the opinion is based on firsthand knowledge of the underlying data. The Texas Court of Criminal Appeals has recognized that "[w]hen a witness who is capable of being qualified as an expert testifies regarding events which he or she personally perceived, the evidence may be admissible as both Rule 701 opinion testimony and Rule 702 expert testimony."[265] Frequently, an expert personally observes, examines, or tests the place, object, or person that is the subject of the testimony.[266] For example, a physician may routinely examine an injured plaintiff and then testify at trial to the medical diagnosis and prognosis.[267] Similarly, a fingerprint expert may testify that he has compared the defendant's prints with another

---

260. The inclusion of "reviewed" in Rule 703 tracks the language of Texas Rule of Civil Procedure 192.3(e)(6) and was not intended to change the scope of Rule 703. *See* TEX. R. CIV. P. 192.3(e)(6). Refer to notes 272-274 *infra* and accompanying text.

261. FED. R. EVID. 703.

262. *See* TEX. R. EVID. 703.

263. *See, e.g.*, *A. Cohen & Co. v. Rittimann*, 139 S.W. 59, 62 (Tex. Civ. App.—San Antonio 1911, writ dism'd) (expert could testify about the health effects of decaying meat because expert had actual knowledge of facts in the case); *St. Louis & S.F. R.R. v. Kiser*, 136 S.W. 852, 856 (Tex. Civ. App.—Dallas 1911, writ ref'd) (doctor could testify about probable cause of injury because he had conducted an examination on the injured).

264. *See* 3 LOUISELL & MUELLER, *supra* note 27, §389, at 657 (an "expert with firsthand knowledge is obviously better informed than one without it, and may offer more effective support to the calling party's cause, becoming at once more valuable to the forum and more attractive from a tactical standpoint"); 3 WEINSTEIN & BERGER, *supra* note 15, ¶703[01], at 703-07 (testimony of expert "with firsthand knowledge is likely to be credible and convincing").

265. *Osbourn v. State*, 92 S.W.3d 531, 536 (Tex. Crim. App. 2002); *accord Scott v. State*, 222 S.W.3d 820, 827-28 (Tex. App.—Houston [14th Dist.] 2007, no pet.). Refer to note 17 *supra* and accompanying text.

266. 3 LOUISELL & MUELLER, *supra* note 27, §388, at 654 (distinguishing firsthand observation or "personal knowledge" from secondhand or indirect information, such as reports or test results from others).

267. *See Reserve Life Ins. v. Ross*, 356 S.W.2d 393, 395 (Tex. Civ. App.—Amarillo 1962, no writ) ("[Q]ualified physicians and surgeons ... may testify as to the nature of disease or injury, whether temporary or permanent and as to the extent of incapacity or disability, whether total or partial, caused by the disease or injury."); *see, e.g., Hart v. Van Zandt*, 399 S.W.2d 791, 798 (Tex. 1965) (in medical-malpractice suit, doctor should have been allowed to give opinion on cause of patient's condition based on personal examination, patient's history, and correspondence with other doctors); *Nat'l Life & Acc. Ins. v. Morris*, 402 S.W.2d 297, 299-303 (Tex. Civ. App.—Austin 1966, writ ref'd n.r.e.) (doctor who had seen and treated plaintiff at the emergency room could testify that plaintiff died of blunt blow to forehead, received in car collision).

set of fingerprints and that they are the same in both instances.[268] When an expert's testimony is based on personal knowledge and investigation or on other evidence already admitted at trial, there is no additional requirement that the facts and data used be "of a type reasonably relied upon by experts in the particular field."[269] That phrase applies only to otherwise inadmissible data that an expert relies on.[270]

2. Facts reviewed by expert. An expert may base an opinion on facts and data reviewed by the expert.[271] This method is the most common basis for an expert's opinion other than personal observations. Experts base their opinions on many sources—deposition transcripts, witness interviews, scientific reports and studies, medical records, technical publications, business records, and even reports prepared by opposing experts.[272] The facts and data that form the basis for an expert's opinion do not need to be introduced into evidence.[273] Generally, most attorneys will choose to offer the underlying facts and data for admission into evidence because the evidence is more persuasive and may be probative of an element of the cause of action, crime, or defense.

When an expert witness gives an opinion based in part on facts and data that have not been introduced into evidence, the opinion itself (rather than the underlying facts

---

268. *See **United States v. Llera Plaza***, 188 F. Supp. 2d 549, 571-72 (E.D. Pa. 2002). In a pretrial hearing for this case, the federal district court had originally excluded expert evidence of fingerprint comparisons under ***Daubert***, based on scientific testimony taken in a different case. *See **Llera Plaza***, 188 F. Supp. 2d at 552-53. On the government's motion for reconsideration, the trial court heard considerable additional testimony about the standards used by fingerprint experts to compare latent prints with known prints and reversed its ruling. *See id.* at 571-72. Originally, one of the court's major concerns was the lack of any established "rate of error" for fingerprint comparisons, but on rehearing, it determined that "in the absence of actual data on rate of error, proficiency test scores of those who would be expert witnesses should be taken as a surrogate form of proof." *Id.* at 565. After an exhaustive discussion of the history of forensic fingerprinting, the court held that this evidence should be assessed under the standards set out in ***Kumho*** for the admission of "technical" expertise rather than those in ***Daubert*** relating to "scientific" expertise. ***Llera Plaza***, 188 F. Supp. 2d at 551-52, 571-72; *see, e.g.*, ***United States v. Janis***, 387 F.3d 682, 690 (8th Cir. 2004) (expert's fingerprint comparison evidence was admitted as sufficiently reliable under ***Daubert/Kumho*** standards); ***United States v. Mitchell***, 365 F.3d 215, 250-51 (3d Cir. 2004) (same); ***United States v. Crisp***, 324 F.3d 261, 266-68 (4th Cir. 2003) (same).

269. *See **E.I. du Pont de Nemours & Co. v. Robinson***, 923 S.W.2d 549, 563 (Tex. 1995) (Cornyn, Hightower, Gammage, Spector, JJ., dissenting) ("If an expert bases an opinion on admitted evidence, that is, evidence already before the jury, 'sufficient guarantees of trustworthiness are ordinarily present to assure the reasonableness of the expert's reliance in the particular case.'" (quoting 2 GOODE ET AL., *supra* note 7, §703.3, at 51)).

270. Refer to notes 293-319 *infra* and accompanying text.

271. TEX. R. EVID. 703.

272. *See* 2 RAY, *supra* note 32, §1404, at 43 (medical experts base their opinions on many sources, including "medical studies, experience in other cases, medical books, reports of doctors and nurses and statements of the patient").

273. *See, e.g.*, ***Southland Lloyds Ins. v. Cantu***, 399 S.W.3d 558, 567-68 (Tex. App.—San Antonio 2011, pet. denied) (expert could offer testimony on insurance adjusting that was based on report prepared by another adjuster; witness was experienced adjuster who had used the same methods, and he independently inspected and verified damage to house). Even before the adoption of the Rules, Texas judges could permit an expert witness to express an opinion based in part on facts that were admissible but never introduced. *See **John Hancock Mut. Life Ins. v. Stanley***, 215 S.W.2d 416, 421 (Tex. Civ. App.—Fort Worth 1948, writ ref'd n.r.e.) (hypothetical questions may include facts that counsel proposes to prove later, and trial court has duty to protect parties' rights if such facts are not later offered); *see also **Geochem. Surveys v. Dietz***, 340 S.W.2d 114, 120 (Tex. Civ. App.—Austin 1960, writ ref'd n.r.e.) (trial court did not abuse its discretion in allowing counsel to present hypothetical questions with hearsay facts, but issue was not ruled on because opponent's objection was too general).

and data) is the primary evidence. The jury can evaluate the opinion only on the basis of the expert's credentials and the usual credibility factors.[274]

3. Facts expert has been made aware of. An expert may base an opinion on facts and data the expert has not personally observed but has been made aware of.[275] If the expert is made aware of facts or data through another witness's testimony, the expert must testify that the trial testimony on which the expert's opinion is based is assumed to be true for purposes of forming the opinion.[276]

Rule 614, which provides for the exclusion of witnesses from the courtroom, does not automatically exempt all expert witnesses from an exclusion order.[277] The Rule does exempt "a person whose presence a party shows to be essential to presenting the party's claim or defense."[278] This exception "is often relied on to allow expert witnesses to be exempt from the Rule."[279]

4. Facts presented to expert through hypothetical questions. An expert may base an opinion on facts presented through hypothetical questions.[280] To be proper under Rule 703, the hypothetical questions must be based on "facts in evidence, facts within the personal knowledge of the witness, or facts assumed from common or judicial knowledge."[281] The rule does not require that the expert have personal knowledge of the facts contained in the hypothetical question.[282] Further, the questions can assume facts in accordance with the questioner's theory of the case, as long as the assumed facts can be inferred from facts in evidence.[283] The questions do not need to assume all of the facts presented in evidence; the questioner can limit the facts the expert should con-

RULE 703

---

274. Refer to notes 105-136 *supra* and accompanying text.

275. Tex. R. Evid. 703; *see Williams v. Illinois*, 567 U.S. 50, 67 (2012) (plurality op.) ("It has long been accepted that an expert witness may voice an opinion based on facts concerning the events at issue in a particular case even if the expert lacks first-hand knowledge of those facts."); *Duckett v. State*, 797 S.W.2d 906, 920 n.17 (Tex. Crim. App. 1990) ("Rule 703 provides that the facts or information upon which an expert witness bases an opinion or inference includes that which he or she perceives or is made known to the expert at or before the hearing. The rule foresees the witness' presence in the courtroom and does not prohibit his testimony simply because he did not examine the particular person at issue. Examination, or lack thereof, would go to the weight of the testimony, not its admissibility."), *disapproved on other grounds*, *Cohn v. State*, 849 S.W.2d 817 (Tex. Crim. App. 1993).

276. An expert cannot give an opinion on a witness's credibility. Refer to notes 158-162 *supra* and accompanying text.

277. *See Drilex Sys., Inc. v. Flores*, 1 S.W.3d 112, 118 (Tex. 1999).

278. Tex. R. Evid. 614(c).

279. *See, e.g., Drilex Sys.*, 1 S.W.3d at 118-19 & n.6 (expert witness was excluded from courtroom under Rule 614; party did not present evidence that expert needed to be present during other witnesses' testimony to form opinions "based on more accurate factual assumptions"). Refer to *Article VI: Witnesses, supra* p. 668.

280. *Gonzales v. State*, 4 S.W.3d 406, 417 (Tex. App.—Waco 1999, no pet.). For an additional discussion of hypothetical questions, refer to notes 368-388 *infra* and accompanying text.

281. *Gonzales*, 4 S.W.3d at 417-18.

282. *See Matson v. State*, 819 S.W.2d 839, 852 (Tex. Crim. App. 1991); *Moore v. State*, 836 S.W.2d 255, 259 (Tex. App.—Texarkana 1992, pet. ref'd).

283. *See Barefoot v. State*, 596 S.W.2d 875, 887-88 (Tex. Crim. App. 1980); *Held v. State*, 948 S.W.2d 45, 53 (Tex. App.—Houston [14th Dist.] 1997, pet. ref'd). Refer to note 378 *infra* and accompanying text.

sider on direct examination, anticipating that the opposing party will vary the hypothetical on cross-examination.[284] If the omission makes the question misleading, however, the question is improper.[285]

Hypothetical questions can include facts not yet admitted into evidence, as long as the proponent of the expert testimony eventually introduces the facts.[286] If testimony supporting the hypothetical facts is never offered, the court has discretion to make "such ruling before finishing the trial as seems necessary to take care of the rights of the parties."[287] Usually, the trial judge will, on request, strike the expert's opinion and instruct the jury not to consider the testimony in its deliberations. If an instruction to the jury appears insufficient to cure the harm, the trial judge may declare a mistrial.

An expert who answers hypothetical questions aids the jury by evaluating the significance of the evidentiary facts before the court.[288] Under Texas common law, the hypothetical question, which is based on facts that either have been proved or are assumed, was the traditional method used to obtain an expert's opinion when the expert had no firsthand knowledge of the facts of the case.[289] Lawyers, judges, juries, and experts themselves have criticized the use of the hypothetical question and characterized it as clumsy, artificial, time-consuming, and likely to misfire.[290] Although the hypotheti-

---

284. *See Barefoot*, 596 S.W.2d at 887-88; *see, e.g.*, *Commercial Std. Ins. v. Washington*, 399 S.W.2d 155, 161 (Tex. Civ. App.—Austin 1966, writ ref'd n.r.e.) (because defendant's expert medical witness testified on direct examination that the plaintiff was not totally and permanently disabled, plaintiff's attorney, on cross-examination, could ask if plaintiff would be considered incapacitated if he were required, as part of a job, to lift more than 50 pounds above the waist or 10 pounds above the head).

285. *Cf. United States v. Alden*, 476 F.2d 378, 384 (7th Cir. 1973) ("[I]f the question does not omit facts of such significance as to cause the answer to be misleading and if it includes enough that the expert can give an opinion, it is not necessary that all material facts be included."); *Harris v. Smith*, 372 F.2d 806, 812 (8th Cir. 1967) ("Although a hypothetical question need not embrace all facts having any relationship to the issue before the court, fairness requires that it embody all plain substantial facts in evidence and be supported by evidence that is relevant and material, for otherwise the jury is given an unfair picture upon which to base its determination."); *Kale v. Douthitt*, 274 F.2d 476, 482 (4th Cir. 1960) ("The facts upon which the expert bases his opinion or conclusion must permit reasonably accurate conclusions as distinguished from mere guess or conjecture.").

286. Refer to note 377 *infra* and accompanying text.

287. *John Hancock Mut. Life Ins. v. Stanley*, 215 S.W.2d 416, 421 (Tex. Civ. App.—Fort Worth 1948, writ ref'd n.r.e.).

288. *See* 2 RAY, *supra* note 32, §1395, at 8 (opinions in response to hypothetical questions "are receivable whenever they are likely to be of appreciable aid to the jury in arriving at correct conclusions").

289. *See Moore v. Grantham*, 599 S.W.2d 287, 290 n.4 (Tex. 1980) (expert opinion in response to a hypothetical question is a long-standing tradition in Texas); *Holloway v. State*, 613 S.W.2d 497, 502 n.14 (Tex. Crim. App. 1981) ("'[W]here the expert speaks from personal knowledge or observation he may give his opinion without an advance hypothetical statement. But if the witness cannot supply the facts upon which his expert inference is to be founded they must be presented hypothetically.'" (quoting 2 RAY, *supra* note 32, §1402, at 35-36)); *Barefoot*, 596 S.W.2d at 887 ("The use of hypothetical questions in the examination of expert witnesses is a well established practice."). Refer to note 369 *infra* and accompanying text.

290. There are two major drawbacks to using hypothetical questions. First, these questions are generally very long, awkwardly phrased, and difficult for everyone to understand. While the expert's ultimate conclusion may be easy to comprehend, the bases for that conclusion are frequently obscure. Second, hypotheticals frequently distort the expert's actual opinion because an advocate presents a wholly one-sided factual basis, leaving out those facts that

cal question is permissible under Rule 703 and is occasionally used,[291] modern evidentiary rules have lessened the need for hypothetical questions.[292]

5. Facts inadmissible as evidence. An expert may base an opinion on facts and data that are inadmissible as evidence, as long as "experts in the particular field would reasonably rely on those kinds of facts or data in forming an opinion on the subject."[293]

---

do not favor his own theory of the case. *See* Mason Ladd, *Expert Testimony*, 5 VAND. L. REV. 414, 427 (1952). Wigmore, the most influential critic of the common-law reliance on the hypothetical question, stated as follows:

> The hypothetical question, misused by the clumsy and abused by the clever, has in practice led to intolerable obstruction of truth. In the first place, it has artificially clamped the mouth of the expert witness, so that his answer for a complex question may not express his actual opinion on the actual case. This is because the question may be so built up and contrived by counsel as to represent only a partisan conclusion. In the second place, it has tended to mislead the jury as to the purport of actual expert opinion.

2 WIGMORE, *supra* note 3, §686, at 962. Additionally, Charles McCormick criticized the hypothetical question as

> a failure in practice and an obstruction to the administration of justice. If we require that it recite all the relevant facts, it becomes intolerably wordy. If we allow, as most courts do, the interrogating counsel to select such of the material facts as he sees fit, we tempt him to shape a one-sided hypothesis.

MCCORMICK'S HANDBOOK, *supra* note 2, §16, at 36 (footnotes omitted); *see also* **Smith v. Ford Motor Co.**, 626 F.2d 784, 791-92 (10th Cir. 1980) (recognizing problems inherent in hypothetical questions); 3 LOUISELL & MUELLER, *supra* note 27, §389, at 658 (hypothetical questions are "subject to mishandling, abuse, [and] confusion"); James W. McElhaney, *Expert Witnesses and the Federal Rules of Evidence*, 28 MERCER L. REV. 463, 472-73 (1977) (discussing the awkwardness of required hypothetical questions).

291. *See* **McBride v. State**, 862 S.W.2d 600, 609-10 & n.20 (Tex. Crim. App. 1993) (under Rule 703, the hypothetical question is one permissible form of admitting psychological testimony on capital-murder defendant's future dangerousness; there is no requirement that hypothetical facts be proved beyond a reasonable doubt, and counsel may "assume the facts in accordance with his theory of the case"); **Moore v. State**, 836 S.W.2d 255, 259 (Tex. App.—Texarkana 1992, pet. ref'd) (experts can testify solely on the basis of a hypothetical question even if the facts on which they base their opinions are not admissible); *see, e.g.*, **Amos v. State**, 819 S.W.2d 156, 164 (Tex. Crim. App. 1991) (experienced psychiatrist could testify on the basis of hypothetical questions about sanity and deliberateness); **Perez v. State**, 113 S.W.3d 819, 834-35 (Tex. App.—Austin 2003, pet. ref'd) (expert could testify in response to hypothetical question, based on facts in case, concerning symptoms and behaviors commonly seen in child sexual-abuse victims), *overruled on other grounds*, **Taylor v. State**, 268 S.W.3d 571 (Tex. Crim. App. 2008); **Taylor v. State**, 106 S.W.3d 827, 832-33 (Tex. App.—Dallas 2003, no pet.) (police officer testified in response to hypothetical question, that a person would be possessing cocaine with the intent to deliver it rather than for personal use, based on specific circumstances that matched those proved at trial; testimony was admissible); **Gonzales v. State**, 4 S.W.3d 406, 417-18 (Tex. App.—Waco 1999, no pet.) (expert witness properly testified to hypothetical questions about Child Sexual Abuse Accommodation Syndrome); **Held v. State**, 948 S.W.2d 45, 53-54 (Tex. App.—Houston [14th Dist.] 1997, pet. ref'd) (testimony about Intoxilyzer test was allowed when expert was asked to assume defendant had consumed his last drink 15 minutes before he was stopped by police even though that fact was not in evidence; hypothetical question may include assumptions based on facts within witness's personal knowledge, assumed from common or judicial knowledge, or assumed as facts in accordance with party's theory of the case); **SPT Fed. Credit Union v. Big H Auto Auction, Inc.**, 761 S.W.2d 800, 802-03 (Tex. App.—Houston [1st Dist.] 1988, no writ) (court should have permitted expert marine surveyor to give his opinion on value of boat through the use of a hypothetical question even though he had no personal observation of the boat); **Tex. Employers' Ins. v. Jackson**, 719 S.W.2d 245, 248-49 (Tex. App.—El Paso 1986, writ ref'd n.r.e.) (court should have permitted expert to give his medical opinion in answering hypothetical questions based on statements and other medical reports introduced into evidence).

292. *See* **Williams v. Illinois**, 567 U.S. 50, 69 (2012) (plurality op.) ("Modern rules of evidence continue to permit experts to express opinions based on facts about which they lack personal knowledge, but these rules dispense with the need for hypothetical questions. [A]n expert may base an opinion on facts that are 'made known to the expert at or before the hearing,' but such reliance does not constitute admissible evidence of this underlying information.").

293. TEX. R. EVID. 703; *see* **Martinez v. State**, 22 S.W.3d 504, 508 (Tex. Crim. App. 2000); **Ramirez v. State**, 815 S.W.2d 636, 651 (Tex. Crim. App. 1991); **Wood v. State**, 299 S.W.3d 200, 212 (Tex. App.—Austin 2009, pet. ref'd); **Blaylock v. State**, 259 S.W.3d 202, 206-07 (Tex. App.—Texarkana 2008, pet. ref'd); **In re A.J.L.**, 136 S.W.3d 293, 301 (Tex. App.—Fort Worth 2004, no pet.); *see, e.g.*, **Seaside Indus., Inc. v. Cooper**, 766 S.W.2d 566, 571 (Tex.

Thus, "[i]f the methodology or data underlying an expert's opinion would not survive the scrutiny of a Rule 702 reliability analysis, Rule 703 does not render the opinion admissible."[294] Many professionals necessarily rely on hearsay and other inadmissible data on a daily basis. Physicians, for example, base their diagnoses not only on objective findings from tests performed on a given patient but also on their medical studies, personal experiences in other cases, medical treatises, discussions with their peers, findings and tests compiled by other medical personnel, and the patient's statements.[295] The physician is unlikely to be able to disentangle the parts that each piece of information played in the formation of his ultimate opinion. If these sources of information are reliable enough for the physician to make "life and death" medical decisions, they are presumably reliable enough to form at least a partial basis for his testimony.[296] Rule 703

App.—Dallas 1989, no writ) (although certain business records were inadmissible hearsay, expert's opinion on business's net worth and defendant's ability to pay judgment was admissible even though predicated on the inadmissible records).

The breadth of this provision is a significant departure from earlier Texas law. Under Texas common law, an expert could give an opinion based in part on inadmissible hearsay. *See, e.g.*, *Slaughter v. Abilene State Sch.*, 561 S.W.2d 789, 791 (Tex. 1977) (doctor's opinion testimony about patient's diagnosis and prognosis was allowed because "it was clearly not based wholly upon hearsay"); *Lewis v. Southmore Sav. Ass'n*, 480 S.W.2d 180, 186 (Tex. 1972) (expert-opinion testimony about new savings-and-loan office's probable effects on the business community was admitted when opinion was based on personal knowledge as well as hearsay data); *Royal Indem. Co. v. Little Joe's Catfish Inn, Inc.*, 636 S.W.2d 530, 533-34 (Tex. App.—San Antonio 1982, no writ) (insurance adjuster's expert-opinion testimony was admissible because an expert of this type must in part utilize hearsay in forming an opinion); *Ralph v. Mr. Paul's Shoes, Inc.*, 572 S.W.2d 812, 814-15 (Tex. Civ. App.—Corpus Christi 1978, writ ref'd n.r.e.) (fire inspector's opinion testimony on cause of fire was admissible even though partially based on conjecture because it was also based on information obtained in his inspection of the property). The common law did not allow expert opinions based entirely on inadmissible hearsay. *See Moore*, 599 S.W.2d at 289 ("It has long been the law of this state that an expert's opinion may not be based solely on the statements or reports of third persons, unless those statements are properly in evidence and the opinion is sought through hypothetical questions."); *see, e.g.*, *Holloway*, 613 S.W.2d at 502-03 (capital-murder conviction was reversed because expert psychological testimony on defendant's future dangerousness, based solely on inadmissible ex parte statements of third persons, was improperly admitted). Rule 703 rejects this limitation. *See Aguilar v. State*, 887 S.W.2d 27, 29 & n.8 (Tex. Crim. App. 1994) (Rule 703 abrogated former case law, which held that an expert opinion was not admissible if based entirely on hearsay); *State v. Resolution Tr. Corp.*, 827 S.W.2d 106, 108 (Tex. App.—Austin 1992, writ denied) ("It is clear that Rule 703 ... overturned the common-law rule, previously followed in Texas, that opinions based solely on inadmissible evidence are themselves inadmissible."); *cf.* FED. R. EVID. 703 advisory committee's note (Federal Rule 703 was designed to broaden the admissibility standard for expert-opinion testimony and to include evidence based entirely on inadmissible data).

294. *See, e.g.*, *Leonard v. State*, 385 S.W.3d 570, 582-83 (Tex. Crim. App. 2012) (op. on reh'g) (although psychotherapist stated "that those in his field [of sex-offender psychotherapy] reasonably rely on polygraph results, the sole basis of his opinion was the results of a [polygraph] test that we have held inadmissible *because it is not reliable*"; trial court abused its discretion in admitting psychotherapist's testimony under Rule 703). Refer to notes 165-250 *supra* and accompanying text.

295. 2 RAY, *supra* note 32, §1404, at 43. Requiring that every basis for an expert's opinion be admissible into evidence would greatly prolong trials—the testimony of several witnesses would be necessary to establish the admissibility of that evidence. For example, an expert could not testify to an injured patient's prognosis until the jury had heard the testimony of every doctor, nurse, and technician who had observed the patient.

296. FED. R. EVID. 703 advisory committee's note; 4 WEINSTEIN & BERGER, *supra* note 33, §703.05[1], at 703-25; *see Jenkins v. United States*, 307 F.2d 637, 641 (D.C. Cir. 1962) (en banc) (to eliminate all reliance on hearsay in a doctor's expert testimony, court would be forced to ignore a source of information that is needed to do justice between the parties and is generally relied on).

does not, however, provide a basis for admitting otherwise inadmissible materials simply because an expert has relied on them in forming an opinion.[297]

Any deficiencies in the inadmissible information that forms the basis for the expert's opinion can be attacked on cross-examination.[298] Even if the underlying facts and data are inadmissible, the trial judge must perform the proper gatekeeping function to ensure that the expert's opinions are trustworthy.[299] Similarly, the proponent of the expert testimony must establish the relevance and reliability of the opinions.[300] The opposing party is entitled to a limiting instruction under Rule 105(a),[301] and the inadmissible data on which the expert's opinion is based cannot be argued to the jury as primary evidence or used to support a verdict.[302] The trial court may prevent the expert from testifying to this data if its admission, even for a limited purpose, is unfairly prejudicial to the opposing party.[303]

---

297. *See, e.g.,* ***Huff v. Harrell***, 941 S.W.2d 230, 240 (Tex. App.—Corpus Christi 1996, writ denied) (unauthenticated schedule of assets and liabilities was not admissible under Civil Rule 703 when it was admitted only at deposition and not at trial and was reviewed by the expert in preparation for his testimony); *see also* ***Cole v. State***, 839 S.W.2d 798, 806 (Tex. Crim. App. 1990) (laboratory reports written by chemist employed by law-enforcement agency were inadmissible hearsay, not exempt from hearsay rule as public records or reports under Rule 803(8)(B), now Rule 803(8)(A)(ii)). For further discussion of ***Cole***, refer to *Article VIII: Hearsay, infra* p. 913.

298. *See, e.g.,* ***Penry v. State***, 903 S.W.2d 715, 761 (Tex. Crim. App. 1995) (State could cross-examine defense expert about hearsay statements, contained in medical reports, of defendant's past homosexual conduct and arson-related activities because expert had relied on those reports in forming his opinion); ***In re Commitment of Polk***, 187 S.W.3d 550, 555 (Tex. App.—Beaumont 2006, no pet.) (State could cross-examine defendant's mental-health expert about hearsay statements contained in records packet because expert relied on those records in forming his opinion).

299. Refer to notes 167-171, 173-184 *supra* and accompanying text.

300. Refer to notes 165-250 *supra* and accompanying text.

301. *Cf.* FED. R. EVID. 703 advisory committee's note to 2000 amendments ("If the otherwise inadmissible information is admitted under this balancing test, the trial judge must give a limiting instruction upon request, informing the jury that the underlying information must not be used for substantive purposes."). Refer to *Article I: General Provisions, supra* p. 97.

302. When otherwise inadmissible data that forms the basis for an expert opinion is elicited on direct or cross-examination, this evidence is admissible only for the limited purpose of showing the foundation of the expert's opinion. *See* ***United States v. Sims***, 514 F.2d 147, 149-50 (9th Cir. 1975) ("Upon admission of such evidence, it then, of course, becomes necessary for the court to instruct the jury that the hearsay evidence is to be considered solely as a basis for the expert opinion and not as substantive evidence."); ***Lewis v. Southmore Sav. Ass'n***, 480 S.W.2d 180, 187 (Tex. 1972) (hearsay evidence bears only on the expert's credibility). For example, a doctor might reasonably rely on a paramedic's statement that the injured plaintiff was struck by the defendant's car in forming the opinion that the patient's injuries were caused by blunt trauma. *Cf.* ***Depena v. State***, 148 S.W.3d 461, 470 (Tex. App.—Corpus Christi 2004, no pet.) (trial court did not err in permitting doctor to testify that nurse told him she did a standard drug-test screening; statement was offered merely to show facts on which he based his opinion). However, the jury could not use the paramedic's hearsay statement to hold the defendant liable in the lawsuit.

If the opposing party does not object to the substantive use of this inadmissible evidence or request a limiting instruction, courts may consider the evidence in deciding the sufficiency of other evidence. *See, e.g.,* ***Gen. Elec. Co. v. Kunze***, 747 S.W.2d 826, 831-32 (Tex. App.—Waco 1987, writ denied) (economist's expert testimony was sufficient to support the amount of damages, even though expert based his calculations on the assumption that plaintiff had received a cost-of-living raise when no evidence was admitted to support that assumption; because defendant did not object or impeach expert, evidence could be considered in determining the sufficiency of evidence to uphold the verdict).

303. *See* ***Stam v. Mack***, 984 S.W.2d 747, 750 (Tex. App.—Texarkana 1999, no pet.); ***Boswell v. Brazos Elec. Power Coop., Inc.***, 910 S.W.2d 593, 602 (Tex. App.—Fort Worth 1995, writ denied); ***First Sw. Lloyds Ins. v. MacDowell***, 769 S.W.2d 954, 957-58 (Tex. App.—Texarkana 1989, writ denied); *cf.* ***United States v. Mest***, 789 F.2d 1069, 1073

Allowing expert testimony to be based solely on inadmissible evidence has been the subject of considerable controversy.[304] To the extent that an expert's opinion is based on data that is not before the jury, the witness no longer merely helps the jury evaluate evidence but acts as a fact-finder.[305] The jury can evaluate this evidence only indirectly by judging the expert's credibility.[306] One court characterized the admission of an opinion premised entirely on hearsay that was not in evidence as allowing an expert to synthesize inadmissible evidence into admissible form.[307] Federal Rule 703 was amended in 2000 to ensure that the trial court adequately performs its gatekeeping function in assessing the reliability of the expert's theory and methodology.[308] Texas Rule 705(d)

(4th Cir. 1986) (trial court did not err in excluding a videotaped hypnotic session of defendant, which formed part of the basis for expert's opinion, because taped session was an attempt to offer defendant's version of the facts without subjecting him to cross-examination); *United States v. McCollum*, 732 F.2d 1419, 1422-23 (9th Cir. 1984) (in trial for attempted bank robbery, trial court properly excluded portion of videotaped interview of defendant purportedly under hypnosis, on which expert based opinion that defendant was under hypnosis when he entered the bank, because the tape was an attempt to put defendant's testimony before the jury without subjecting him to cross-examination and impeachment); *Rose Hall, Ltd. v. Chase Manhattan Overseas Banking Corp.*, 576 F. Supp. 107, 158 & n.70 (D. Del. 1983) (although "expert witness may base his opinion on [hearsay] evidence, this does not magically render the hearsay evidence admissible"; trial court did not err in refusing to permit an expert to testify to a hearsay telephone conversation), *aff'd*, 740 F.2d 958 (3d Cir. 1984) (table case). For a more detailed discussion of the *First Southwest Lloyds* case, refer to notes 410-413 *infra* and accompanying text.

    Many commentators agree with the rulings admitting the opinion but excluding the prejudicial hearsay. *See* 3 LOUISELL & MUELLER, *supra* note 27, §389, at 520 (Supp. 1993) (trial judge has "considerable discretion under Rules 403 and 611 to limit or even disallow [inadmissible material underlying an expert's opinion] if the danger looms large that the jury will be unable to resist making impermissible and damaging use of such material"); 2 SALTZBURG ET AL., *supra* note 149, at 1371 (trial court "can, and should, exercise its authority under Rule 403 to limit the presentation of inadmissible evidence used as the basis of an expert's opinion"); Ronald L. Carlson, *Collision Course in Expert Testimony: Limitations on Affirmative Introduction of Underlying Data*, 36 U. FLA. L. REV. 234, 242-43 & nn.35-36 (1984) (judicial controversy continues over whether hearsay data relied on by an expert might be admissible by a proponent to substantiate his opinion; raising the question whether such an admission would create a new and "giant" exception to the hearsay rule).

    304. For a discussion of the problems with basing expert-opinion testimony on inadmissible evidence, see Ronald L. Carlson, *Policing the Bases of Modern Expert Testimony*, 39 VAND. L. REV. 577 (1986).

    305. *See* MCCORMICK'S HANDBOOK, *supra* note 2, §15, at 34 (by giving opinion testimony, an expert indirectly incorporates facts that the jury has no way to validate).

    306. *See* 3 WEINSTEIN & BERGER, *supra* note 15, ¶703[03], at 703-38 (jury will often discount testimony too much when judging an expert).

    307. In *Sims*, the court explained the theory behind permitting an expert to base opinions on otherwise inadmissible hearsay:

> The rationale … is that the expert is fully capable of judging for himself what is, or is not, a reliable basis for his opinion. This relates directly to one of the functions of the expert witness, namely to lend his special expertise to the issue before him. … In a sense, the expert synthesizes the primary source material—be it hearsay or not—into properly admissible evidence in opinion form. The trier of fact is then capable of judging the credibility of the witness as it would that of anyone else giving expert testimony. This rule respects the functions and abilities of both the expert witness and the trier of fact, while assuring that the requirement of witness confrontation is fulfilled.

514 F.2d at 149.

    308. The Advisory Committee gave the following explanation about the amendment:

> When information is reasonably relied upon by an expert and yet is admissible only for the purpose of assisting the jury in evaluating an expert's opinion, a trial court applying this Rule must consider the information's probative value in assisting the jury to weigh the expert's opinion on the one hand, and the risk of prejudice resulting from the jury's potential misuse of the information for substantive purposes on the other. The information may be disclosed to the jury, upon objection, only if the trial court finds that the probative value of the information in assisting the jury to evaluate the ex-

sets out a very similar limitation on the disclosure of otherwise inadmissible data reasonably relied on by the expert.[309] The only substantive difference between Federal Rule 703 and Texas Rule 705(d) is that the inadmissible data may not be disclosed under the federal rule unless the court finds that the data's probative value *substantially* outweighs the prejudicial effect.[310] Thus, the federal rule presumes nondisclosure of the inadmissible underlying data. Under Texas Rule 705(d), "the proponent of the opinion may not disclose [the underlying facts or data] to the jury if their probative value in helping the jury evaluate the opinion is outweighed by their prejudicial effect"; the evidence does not need to be substantially more probative than prejudicial to be admitted.[311]

Under Texas Rule 703, an expert is able to base an opinion on inadmissible facts or data only if "experts in the particular field would reasonably rely on those kinds of facts or data."[312] Although the rule does not explicitly say so, an expert may reasonably rely on another expert's opinions as well as his own factual findings.[313] But "interrelated expert testimony cannot be used to 'form a hybrid for which no [single] expert can offer support.'"[314] Whether experts in the field rely on such data or opinions and are reasonable in doing so is a matter for preliminary determination by the trial judge under Rules 104(a) and 702.[315] Thus, as part of the judicial gatekeeping role, the

pert's opinion substantially outweighs its prejudicial effect. If the otherwise inadmissible information is admitted under this balancing test, the trial judge must give a limiting instruction upon request, informing the jury that the underlying information must not be used for substantive purposes.

FED. R. EVID. 703 advisory committee's note to 2000 amendments.

309. *See* TEX. R. EVID. 705(d). Refer to notes 407-418 *infra* and accompanying text.

310. *See* FED. R. EVID. 703; TEX. R. EVID. 705(d).

311. *See* TEX. R. EVID. 705(d).

312. TEX. R. EVID. 703. Federal Rule 703 uses the same language. *See* FED. R. EVID. 703 advisory committee's note (this phrase addresses the fear that a broader scope of admissible data would swallow the exclusionary rule); *see, e.g.,* **United States v. Scrima**, 819 F.2d 996, 1002 (11th Cir. 1987) (trial judge properly excluded expert accountant's testimony that was based largely on hearsay statement of defense witness that he had a larger amount of money because no showing was made that accountants reasonably rely on such statements; conviction for income-tax evasion was affirmed); **Ricciardi v. Children's Hosp. Med. Ctr.**, 811 F.2d 18, 25 (1st Cir. 1987) (trial judge properly excluded expert-opinion testimony based on a doctor's "bizarre" handwritten note stating that aortic cannula had accidentally fallen out of a patient during an operation; doctor, unable to recall the source of the information, had no personal knowledge of that fact, and no evidence showed that doctors in the field would reasonably rely on such unattributed material).

313. *See* **Gharda USA, Inc. v. Control Sols., Inc.**, 464 S.W.3d 338, 352 (Tex. 2015) ("No rule prohibits experts from using other experts' opinions to formulate new opinions based on their own expertise."); 2 GOODE ET AL., *supra* note 7, §703.3, at 57-58 (in their daily practice, experts often rely on opinions expressed by other experts, and as "long as the opinion of another is of the type that would reasonably be relied upon by experts in the field in forming opinions on the subject, it should be considered a proper basis for an expert's testimony"). In some contexts, even a lay witness's opinion might be of the sort that experts in a particular field would reasonably rely on. For example, pediatricians reasonably rely on a parent's recitation of a child's symptoms, condition, and behavior in forming a medical diagnosis.

314. **Gharda USA**, 464 S.W.3d at 352 (quoting **Gen. Motors Corp. v. Iracheta**, 161 S.W.3d 462, 472 (Tex. 2005)). In **Gharda USA**, the plaintiffs offered the testimony of two chemists and two investigators to prove the cause of a fire. 464 S.W.3d at 352. The Texas Supreme Court held that the trial court did not abuse its discretion in disregarding the testimony of the investigators, who relied on the chemists' opinions, because the chemists' expert testimony was unreliable. *Id.*

315. **Moore v. Polish Power, Inc.**, 720 S.W.2d 183, 192 (Tex. App.—Dallas 1986, writ ref'd n.r.e.) (citing John F. Sutton, Jr., *Article VII: Opinions and Expert Testimony*, 20 HOUS. L. REV. 445, 465 (1983 Tex. R. Evid. Handbook));

trial court must determine that the facts or data the expert relies on are reliable and that the expert's reliance on this data is reasonable.[316] In making this determination, the judge must make an independent evaluation of the reasonableness of the expert's reliance.[317] The judge may also consider the testifying expert's own testimony[318] and

---

see Souris v. Robinson, 725 S.W.2d 339, 341-42 (Tex. App.—Houston [14th Dist.] 1987, no writ) (whether experts in the field reasonably rely on specific data is a matter for preliminary determination under Rule 104(a) and "will not be reversed unless the trial court is clearly wrong"); *see, e.g., Mannino v. Int'l Mfg. Co.*, 650 F.2d 846, 853 (6th Cir. 1981) (trial court erred in excluding testimony because expert had adequate basis for his opinion); *Am. Bearing Co. v. Litton Indus., Inc.*, 540 F. Supp. 1163, 1169 (E.D. Pa. 1982) (court granted new trial because expert testimony partially based on inadmissible hearsay was not customarily relied on by experts in the field), *aff'd*, 729 F.2d 943 (3d Cir. 1984). Refer to *Article I: General Provisions, supra* p. 86.

　　The trial court, under Rule 104(a), determines whether experts in the field would reasonably rely on the inadmissible data that is the basis for an expert's opinion. The court generally cannot make this determination, however, unless the opponent of the opinion raises the issue. Rule 705(a) permits an expert to testify to an opinion "without first testifying to the underlying facts or data" unless the court requires otherwise. Refer to notes 366-388 *infra* and accompanying text. If the proponent of an expert opinion chooses to have the expert testify to the opinion without first disclosing the underlying facts or data, the court will be unaware of the basis for the opinion unless (1) the court on its own motion requires the disclosure of the underlying facts or data, (2) the opponent of the opinion brings a pretrial motion challenging the underlying facts or data, (3) the opponent requests at trial that the court require the expert to disclose the facts or data before giving the opinion, (4) the court permits the opponent to voir dire the expert on the underlying facts or data before the expert gives the opinion, or (5) the underlying facts or data are revealed on cross-examination and the opponent moves to strike the expert's opinion on the basis of the cross-examination. In *Trailways, Inc. v. Mendoza*, the defendant complained on appeal that it was error to allow the plaintiff's doctor to testify about X-rays of the plaintiff's spine and give his opinion based on a review of those X-rays because they were not introduced into evidence and no testimony was offered to prove that such X-rays were reasonably relied on by other doctors in forming a medical diagnosis. 745 S.W.2d 63, 66 (Tex. App.—San Antonio 1987, no writ). Because the defendant did not argue that the X-rays were inadmissible, Rule 703 did not apply. *Trailways*, 745 S.W.2d at 66. Instead, on cross-examination, the defendant should have requested that the doctor produce the X-rays under Rule 705. *Trailways*, 745 S.W.2d at 66-67.

　　In one Texas post-Rules decision, an appellate court took judicial notice that an attorney's discussions with counsel and his perusal of pertinent time sheets was hearsay "of a type relied upon by the attorney expert in forming an opinion upon the subject of reasonable attorney's fees." *Liptak v. Pensabene*, 736 S.W.2d 953, 957-58 (Tex. App.—Tyler 1987, no writ). The result seems proper because the trial judge had discretion under Rule 104(a) to find that this information was the type relied on by other attorneys in evaluating reasonable attorney fees. *See Liptak*, 736 S.W.2d at 957-58; *see also Rio Grande Valley Gas Co. v. City of Edinburg*, 59 S.W.3d 199, 222-23 (Tex. App.—Corpus Christi 2000) (expert on attorney fees could rely on summaries of attorneys' time, prepared by others, as basis for his testimony when that evidence was of a type reasonably relied on by experts in the particular field, even though the underlying records were not made contemporaneously), *rev'd in part on other grounds sub nom. Southern Union Co. v. City of Edinburg*, 129 S.W.3d 74 (Tex. 2003).

　　316. *See Cooper Tire & Rubber Co. v. Mendez*, 204 S.W.3d 797, 800-01 (Tex. 2006); *see, e.g., Collini v. Pustejovsky*, 280 S.W.3d 456, 466 (Tex. App.—Fort Worth 2009, no pet.) (expert witness's report, which briefly stated the conclusions of the physicians who examined plaintiff but did not provide any background on those physicians' experience or training, did not establish that expert's reliance on the data was reasonable); *Peters v. State*, 31 S.W.3d 704, 712 (Tex. App.—Houston [1st Dist.] 2000, pet. ref'd) (expert's reliance on study contained in professional corrections journal showing recidivism rates for treated incest offenders was the type of information on which an expert in corrections could reasonably rely); *Tex. Workers' Comp. Comm'n v. Garcia*, 862 S.W.2d 61, 105 (Tex. App.—San Antonio 1993) (trial court did not abuse its discretion in excluding expert's testimony about actuarial study when study itself stated that information available was incomplete and that preparers relied on outdated information), *rev'd on other grounds*, 893 S.W.2d 504 (Tex. 1995).

　　317. *See In re Paoli R.R. Yard PCB Litig.*, 35 F.3d 717, 748 (3d Cir. 1994) ("We now make clear that it is the judge who makes the determination of reasonable reliance, and … the judge must conduct an independent evaluation into reasonableness.").

　　318. *See Baumholser v. Amax Coal Co.*, 630 F.2d 550, 551 (7th Cir. 1980). The court will usually follow the expert's advice in this regard. *See* 3 WEINSTEIN & BERGER, *supra* note 15, ¶703[01], at 703-08 (experts are in a better position to judge the validity of relevant facts). In *United States v. Williams*, the court explained that "[t]he rationale

---

rely on other evidence, such as the testimony of different experts, learned treatises, and expert opinions admitted or rejected in other trials.[319]

B. Rule 703 & the Confrontation Clause

Rule 703 allows expert witnesses to base opinions on inadmissible facts, but rules of evidence do not trump constitutional provisions.[320] Thus, Confrontation Clause issues[321] can arise in criminal cases when an expert witness relies on hearsay information in forming an opinion. There is no Confrontation Clause problem if the expert is available for cross-examination and the underlying information is not used to prove the truth of the matter asserted but instead is used only to explain the basis for the expert's opinion.[322] But if the expert witness conveys the substance of the testimonial out-of-court hearsay statements to the jury, the defendant has not had an opportunity to cross-examine the person who made the statements, and the proponent of the expert testi-

for this exception to the rule against hearsay is that the expert, because of his professional knowledge and ability, is competent to judge for himself the reliability of the records and statements on which he bases his expert opinion." 447 F.2d 1285, 1290 (5th Cir. 1971) (en banc). The trial judge may also base the determination on other evidence in the record or even take judicial notice of the reasonableness of the reliance. *See, e.g.*, *United States v. Arias*, 678 F.2d 1202, 1206 (4th Cir. 1982) (testimony was based on reasonable hearsay considering the circumstantial evidence in the record); *United States v. Lawson*, 653 F.2d 299, 302 & n.7 (7th Cir. 1981) (taking judicial notice that expert's testimony was based on information customarily relied on by similar experts in that field); *Bauman v. Centex Corp.*, 611 F.2d 1115, 1120 (5th Cir. 1980) (evidence was admissible because expert testimony was customary to those in the profession with similar training and experience).

319. *See, e.g.*, *Lynch v. Merrell-Nat'l Labs.*, 830 F.2d 1190, 1194-97 (1st Cir. 1987) (summary judgment for drug manufacturer was affirmed in suit alleging that drug caused birth defect; scientific studies of the drug conducted on animals and studies of "analogous" chemicals were not a sufficient basis to confirm expert opinion that the drug caused birth defects in humans because there was no confirmatory epidemiological evidence); *In re "Agent Orange" Prod. Liab. Litig.*, 611 F. Supp. 1267, 1280-83 (E.D.N.Y. 1985) (expert's opinion was inadmissible because data relied on were not the kind reasonably relied on by experts in his field; (1) personal recollections of the deceased's widow were not a reliable type of information on which doctors base an expert opinion, (2) other experts disputed that expert's reliance on deceased's medical records was reasonable, (3) expert did not consider relevant epidemiological studies, and (4) scientific commentators and treatises disputed expert's conclusion), *aff'd*, 818 F.2d 187 (2d Cir. 1987); *In re Swine Flu Immunization Prods. Liab. Litig.*, 508 F. Supp. 897, 903-04 (D. Colo. 1981) (expert's opinion was excluded when other medical experts testified that they would not rely on the rudimentary data used by plaintiff's expert), *aff'd sub nom. Lima v. United States*, 708 F.2d 502 (10th Cir. 1983). *See generally* 2 GOODE ET AL., *supra* note 7, §703.3, at 46-48 (reiterating the accepted policy and noting several other case examples).

320. *See Crawford v. Washington*, 541 U.S. 36, 61 (2004) ("[W]e do not think the Framers meant to leave the Sixth Amendment's protection to the vagaries of the rules of evidence ...."); *Wood v. State*, 299 S.W.3d 200, 212 (Tex. App.—Austin 2009, pet. ref'd) ("[E]vidence rules cannot trump the Sixth Amendment.").

321. Refer to *Article VIII: Hearsay, infra* p. 787.

322. *See Barrett v. Acevedo*, 169 F.3d 1155, 1162 n.7 (8th Cir. 1999) ("Rule 703 evidence is not generally regarded as hearsay" because it is offered "simply to show a basis for an expert's opinion."); *Martinez v. State*, 311 S.W.3d 104, 112 (Tex. App.—Amarillo 2010, pet. ref'd) (Confrontation Clause is not violated merely because an expert bases an opinion on inadmissible testimonial hearsay; testifying expert's opinion is not hearsay, and testifying expert is available for cross-examination); *Wood*, 299 S.W.3d at 213 (same); FED. R. EVID. 703 advisory committee's note to 2000 amendments ("If the otherwise inadmissible information is admitted under this balancing test, the trial judge must give a limiting instruction upon request, informing the jury that the underlying information must not be used for substantive purposes."); *see, e.g.*, *Williams v. Illinois*, 567 U.S. 50, 78-79 (2012) (plurality op.) (expert witness referred to laboratory report that was offered as evidence "not to prove the truth of the matter asserted in the report, *i.e.*, that the report contained an accurate profile of the perpetrator's DNA, but only to establish that the report contained a DNA profile that matched the DNA profile deduced from [defendant's] blood"; under Federal Rule 703, basis evidence that is not admissible for its truth may be disclosed under appropriate circumstances).

mony does not establish the declarant's unavailability, the defendant's right of confrontation has been violated.[323] Out-of-court testimonial statements cannot be communicated to the jury "in the guise of an expert opinion."[324]

Testimonial statements do not have to be spoken communications, and further Confrontation Clause issues arise when the testifying expert does not have personal knowledge of the information that forms the basis for the expert's opinion. In ***Melendez-Diaz v. Massachusetts***, the U.S. Supreme Court held that "certificates of analysis"— affidavits by chemists declaring that evidence seized was cocaine—were testimonial statements under ***Crawford***.[325] Admission of the certificates without the chemists' testimony violated the defendant's right of confrontation because the certificates were "functionally identical to live, in-court testimony" and there was no showing "that the analysts were unavailable to testify at trial *and* that [the defendant] had a prior opportunity to cross-examine them."[326] This decision significantly restricts the ability of expert witnesses to disclose the contents of inadmissible evidence on which their opinions are based.[327] However, when an expert bases an opinion on inadmissible evidence but does not reveal the contents of that evidence—that is, the evidence is not offered

323. *See **Crawford***, 541 U.S. at 68 ("Where testimonial evidence is at issue, ... the Sixth Amendment demands ... unavailability and a prior opportunity for cross-examination."); *see, e.g.*, ***United States v. Steed***, 548 F.3d 961, 975-76 (11th Cir. 2008) (no Confrontation Clause problem with expert's testimony because it was based on expert's personal training and experience, not on out-of-court statements); ***United States v. Mejia***, 545 F.3d 179, 198-99 (2d Cir. 2008) ("[Expert's] reliance on and repetition of out-of-court testimonial statements made by individuals during the course of custodial interrogations violated [defendant's] rights under the Confrontation Clause of the Sixth Amendment.").

324. ***United States v. Lombardozzi***, 491 F.3d 61, 72 (2d Cir. 2007); *see **United States v. Flores-de-Jesús***, 569 F.3d 8, 19-20 (1st Cir. 2009) ("[O]verview testimony may have serious ***Crawford***/Confrontation Clause implications. ... Overview testimony frequently reflects reliance on the statements of non-testifying informants, who implicate the defendants in criminal activity. The problematic nature of such testimony is self-evident."). This conduct sometimes occurs in drug-conspiracy prosecutions, when the government offers the testimony of a witness who gives an overview of the case or summarizes the evidence presented. Confrontation Clause issues arise if some part of the witness's summary is based on interviews with and information obtained from nontestifying informants. *See **Flores-de-Jesús***, 569 F.3d at 19-20. In that situation, the "overview" witness essentially serves as a conduit for presenting hearsay evidence to the jury in violation of the Confrontation Clause. *See **United States v. Lawson***, 653 F.2d 299, 301-03 (7th Cir. 1981) (while Federal Rule 703 might authorize testimony "based entirely on hearsay reports," such testimony "would nevertheless violate a defendant's constitutional right to confront adverse witnesses" if the government "simply produce[s] a witness who [does] nothing but summarize out-of-court statements made by others"; trial court's admission of expert opinion affirmed because defense had "sufficient access" to underlying information and "had an adequate opportunity to prepare his cross-examination"). In contrast, courts have often permitted experts to testify on the structure and operation of a typical drug conspiracy. ***Flores-de-Jesús***, 569 F.3d at 20; *see **Steed***, 548 F.3d at 975-76. The Confrontation Clause problems that arise with overview witnesses can be avoided if the informants who provide the basis for the overview witness's testimony later testify at trial. *See **Flores-de-Jesús***, 569 F.3d at 20.

325. 557 U.S. 305, 310-11 (2009).

326. *Id.*

327. *See, e.g.*, ***Martinez***, 311 S.W.3d at 112 (expert disclosed testimonial statements in autopsy report, prepared by another medical examiner, to explain and support expert's opinion; however, because those statements supported expert's opinion only if they were deemed true, they were offered for the truth of the matter asserted in violation of the Confrontation Clause); ***Wood***, 299 S.W.3d at 213 (same).

for the truth of the matter asserted—there is generally no violation of the Confrontation Clause.[328]

RULE 704

OPINION ON AN ULTIMATE ISSUE

An opinion is not objectionable just because it embraces an ultimate issue.

COMMENTARY ON RULE 704

Rule 704 allows witnesses to express opinions on ultimate issues to be decided by the trier of fact.[329] Under traditional common-law principles, no witness—lay or expert—could testify to an ultimate issue in the trial for fear that the witness might "invad[e] the province of the jury."[330] The common-law rule was based on the concern that certain testimony might persuade the jury to abandon its own responsibility to weigh the evidence and, instead, determine facts by uncritically adopting whatever a witness might say.[331] Rule 704 rejected the common-law rule by stating that a witness's opinion, whether lay or expert, "is not objectionable just because it embraces an ultimate

---

328. *See* ***Williams v. Illinois***, 567 U.S. 50, 78-79 (2012) (plurality op.); *see also* ***Wood***, 299 S.W.3d at 213 ("[T]he Confrontation Clause is not violated merely because an expert bases an opinion on inadmissible testimonial hearsay. The testifying expert's opinion is not hearsay, and the testifying expert is available for cross-examination regarding his opinion. The Confrontation Clause does not prohibit *any* use of testimonial hearsay; it only prohibits the use of testimonial hearsay to prove the truth of the matter asserted. When an expert bases an opinion on testimonial hearsay but does not disclose the testimonial hearsay on which that opinion is based, the jury hears only the expert's direct, in-court testimony."). Refer to notes 321-322 *supra* and accompanying text. For further discussion of the effect of ***Williams v. Illinois***, refer to *Article VIII: Hearsay, infra* p. 809.

329. *See* TEX. R. EVID. 704; *see also* BLACK'S LAW DICTIONARY 960 (10th ed. 2014) (defining "ultimate issue" as "[a] not-yet-decided point that is sufficient either in itself or in connection with other points to resolve the entire case"). The 2015 restyling of Rule 704 deleted the phrase "to be decided by the trier of fact." No substantive change was intended. *See* Tex. Sup. Ct. Order, Misc. Docket No. 15-9048, §2 (eff. Apr. 1, 2015).

330. *See* M.C. Slough, *Testamentary Capacity: Evidentiary Aspects*, 36 TEX. L. REV. 1, 13 (1957); *cf.* ***United States v. Brown***, 540 F.2d 1048, 1054 (10th Cir. 1976) (expert testimony of eyewitness identification was excluded because it would "usurp the function of the jury"); ***United States v. Fosher***, 449 F. Supp. 76, 77 (D. Mass. 1978) (testimony on the reliability of eyewitness accounts invaded the province of the jury). In its most extreme form, the rule held that no witness could express "[a]ny opinion which would even tend to be decisive of an issue." Slough, *supra*, at 12; *see* 2 RAY, *supra* note 32, §1395, at 6 (if the ultimate-issue rule had been strictly applied, nearly all opinion testimony would have disappeared from the courtroom). For more background information on the origins and implications of the phrase "province of the jury," see James R. Norvell, *Invasion of the Province of the Jury*, 31 TEX. L. REV. 731 (1953).

331. 3 LOUISELL & MUELLER, *supra* note 27, §394, at 692. The rule was widely criticized by major commentators. *See id.* §394, at 690-91 (ultimate-issue objection is usually advanced as a "makeweight" for opinions and testimony that are inadmissible for other reasons); MCCORMICK ON EVIDENCE, *supra* note 36, §12, at 31 (rule is unduly restrictive). Wigmore announced that "[w]hen all is said, it remains simply one of those impracticable and misconceived utterances which lack any justification in principle." 7 WIGMORE, *supra* note 27, §1921, at 22.

The distinction between "ultimate" or "decisive" facts, which were improper subjects for opinion testimony, and "evidentiary" facts, which were suitable for opinion testimony, was never easy to explain. For instance, courts historically permitted a medical examiner to give an opinion on cause of death. If courts had strictly followed the opinion rule, they should have disallowed this testimony when cause of death was one of the ultimate issues.

A second problem with the common-law prohibition was that it was frequently impossible for the witness to testify in any way except as to the ultimate fact. For example, a police officer may, from personal observations, form the opinion that a driver is intoxicated. At the DWI trial, the officer can testify to each of the observations—the driver's slurred speech, staggering, and bloodshot eyes, and the smell of alcohol. The opinion, however, will be that

issue."[332] The rule focuses on whether an opinion is otherwise admissible or is objectionable under another evidentiary rule.[333]

Rule 704 is substantively identical to the original version of Federal Rule 704[334] and is now identical to Federal Rule 704(a). The federal rule was later amended to add subdivision (b), which prohibits expert witnesses in criminal cases from giving an opinion about the defendant's mental state when a particular mental state or condition is an element of the crime charged or of a defense.[335]

Both lay witnesses[336] and experts[337] can give an opinion about an ultimate fact or issue under Rule 704 as long as the lay opinion is helpful under Rule 701 or the expert's

---

the driver was intoxicated, an ultimate fact frequently held to be essential to sustain a verdict. *See Mays v. State*, 563 S.W.2d 260, 263 (Tex. Crim. App. 1978) ("Opinion testimony is required to prove intoxication.").

    A third objection to the ultimate-issue rule was that it simply did not make sense. The jury has always been free to accept or reject an opinion, just as it has always been free to reject any testimony. *See* 3 WEINSTEIN & BERGER, *supra* note 15, ¶704[01], at 704-07.

332. TEX. R. EVID. 704; *see Ex parte Nailor*, 149 S.W.3d 125, 134-35 (Tex. Crim. App. 2004); *Ortiz v. State*, 834 S.W.2d 343, 348 (Tex. Crim. App. 1992); *Merrill v. Sprint Waste Servs. LP*, ___ S.W.3d ___ (Tex. App.—Houston [14th Dist.] 2017, n.p.h.) (No. 14-16-00006-CV; 8-15-17). Before the promulgation of Rule 704, the Texas Supreme Court had rejected the common-law rule. *See Carr v. Radkey*, 393 S.W.2d 806, 812 (Tex. 1965) ("The province of the jury is to believe or disbelieve, weigh evidence, and to evaluate it. The witness could not invade that province if he wanted to."). The court also pointed out that questions posed to experts involving ultimate facts are often necessary and that their admission is supported by the weight of authority. *Id.*; *see also Fed. Underwriters Exch. v. Cost*, 132 Tex. 299, 305-06, 123 S.W.2d 332, 335-36 (1938) (expert testimony on plaintiff's physical condition was allowed, even though ultimate issue involved plaintiff's degree of incapacity). In 1972, the Texas Court of Criminal Appeals adopted the holding of *Carr*. *See Hopkins v. State*, 480 S.W.2d 212, 218 (Tex. Crim. App. 1972) ("We perceive no reason why certain expert opinion evidence should be excluded merely because the opinion covers some ultimate fact issue."). Rule 704 codifies the holdings of *Carr*, *Hopkins*, and their progeny.

333. The 2015 restyling of Rule 704 deleted the phrase "otherwise admissible." However, because no substantive changes were intended, the rule necessarily implies and still requires that such an opinion must be otherwise admissible. *See* Tex. Sup. Ct. Order, Misc. Docket No. 15-9048, §2 (eff. Apr. 1, 2015).

334. *See* Act of Jan. 2, 1975, Pub. L. No. 93-595, §1, 88 Stat. 1926, *reprinted in* 1974 U.S.C.C.A.N. 2215; 641-642 S.W.2d (Tex. Cases) LV (1983, amended 1998).

335. FED. R. EVID. 704(b). This exclusion creates a heavier burden of persuasion for criminal defendants raising an insanity defense. *See* 2 SALTZBURG ET AL., *supra* note 149, at 1405.

    In 1984, Congress amended Federal Rule 704 to add subdivision (b) as part of its extensive reform of federal criminal law and procedure. *See* Comprehensive Crime Control Act of 1984, Pub. L. No. 98-473, 98 Stat. 2067-68 (1984) (defendant's mental state is a matter for the trier of fact alone). The amendment was made in the wake of John Hinckley's acquittal for the attempted assassination of President Reagan. *See* 2 SALTZBURG ET AL., *supra* note 149, at 1405 (Hinckley's acquittal helped lead to higher burden of proof for criminal defendants asserting insanity defense).

336. *See, e.g.*, *United States v. Smith*, 550 F.2d 277, 281 (5th Cir. 1977) (lay witness could give her opinion, based on personal observation, that defendant understood government regulations; knowledge of the meaning of government regulations was an ultimate issue, but testimony was not barred because Federal Rule 704 applied and the opinion was helpful); *Cass v. State*, 676 S.W.2d 589, 590-92 (Tex. Crim. App. 1984) (lay witnesses who had known defendant all of his life were competent to give their opinions in capital-murder trial that defendant was unlikely to commit violent acts in the future); *Reid v. State*, 749 S.W.2d 903, 906-07 (Tex. App.—Dallas 1988, pet. ref'd) (testimony was admitted that police officer did not dust evidence he had collected for fingerprints because he felt no need to do so; testimony was not barred by Rule 704 and was "helpful" under Rule 701).

337. *See, e.g.*, *Richardson v. State*, 83 S.W.3d 332, 350-51 (Tex. App.—Corpus Christi 2002, pet. ref'd) (rejecting defendant's contention that psychiatrist's testimony on "whether this offense resulted from sudden passion arising from an adequate cause" improperly decided an ultimate issue instead of properly "embracing" it); *Hernandez v. State*, 772 S.W.2d 274, 275 (Tex. App.—Corpus Christi 1989, no pet.) (in murder trial, medical examiner could give his expert opinion that knife wounds were deliberate and not accidental).

RULE 704

opinion will help the trier of fact under Rule 702.[338] When the jury is as qualified to form an opinion from the facts as a witness, the witness's opinion will not be helpful to the jury under either Rule 701 or Rule 702.[339] Similarly, when an expert witness gives an opinion outside his area of expertise, the witness is not qualified to testify under Rule 702; thus, the testimony will not help the jury.[340] Further, opinions that do no more than tell the jury what verdict to return,[341] whether a criminal defendant is guilty or inno-

---

338. *See* ***Helena Chem. Co. v. Wilkins***, 47 S.W.3d 486, 499 (Tex. 2001) (otherwise admissible opinion testimony is not objectionable because it embraces an ultimate issue of fact); *see, e.g.*, ***Blumenstetter v. State***, 135 S.W.3d 234, 248-49 (Tex. App.—Texarkana 2004, no pet.) (expert's testimony that defendant was intoxicated based on his breath-test results and retrograde extrapolation should have been excluded as a scientifically unreliable opinion on an ultimate issue under Rule 704); ***Gonzales v. State***, 4 S.W.3d 406, 417-18 (Tex. App.—Waco 1999, no pet.) (expert testimony about Child Sexual Abuse Accommodation Syndrome and typical behavior patterns of victims aided jury and did not decide ultimate fact issue); ***Russell v. Ramirez***, 949 S.W.2d 480, 489 (Tex. App.—Houston [14th Dist.] 1997, no writ) (under Civil Rule 704, accident reconstructionist could testify that defendant-driver's failure to drive at legal speed limit was a "cause in fact" of passenger's death); ***Thornhill v. Ronnie's I-45 Truck Stop, Inc.***, 944 S.W.2d 780, 793 (Tex. App.—Beaumont 1997, writ dism'd) (expert could properly testify that defendant was "possessor" of motel and thus had a responsibility to correct fire hazards even though one ultimate issue at trial was question of who had legal right to possess and control premises); ***Parra Gonzales v. State***, 756 S.W.2d 413, 417 (Tex. App.—El Paso 1988, pet. ref'd) (experts may offer opinions on ultimate issues under Criminal Rule 704, but defendant's private preliminary sentencing investigation was not admissible because factual information was gained solely through defendant and his family; expert's conclusion that defendant was "worthy" of probation "moves in the direction of supplanting the jury, and is well down the road to the 'battle of experts'"), *overruled on other grounds*, ***Mock v. State***, 848 S.W.2d 215 (Tex. App.—El Paso 1992, pet. ref'd).

339. *See* ***K-Mart Corp. v. Honeycutt***, 24 S.W.3d 357, 360 (Tex. 2000) (per curiam) ("Expert testimony assists the trier-of-fact when the expert's knowledge and experience on a relevant issue are beyond that of the average juror and the testimony helps the trier-of-fact understand the evidence or determine a fact issue. When the jury is equally competent to form an opinion about the ultimate fact issues or the expert's testimony is within the common knowledge of the jury, the trial court should exclude the expert's testimony."); ***Duckett v. State***, 797 S.W.2d 906, 914 (Tex. Crim. App. 1990) ("The use of expert testimony must be limited to situations in which the expert's knowledge and experience on a relevant issue are beyond that of an average juror."), *disapproved on other grounds*, ***Cohn v. State***, 849 S.W.2d 817 (Tex. Crim. App. 1993); ***Pierce v. State***, 777 S.W.2d 399, 414 (Tex. Crim. App. 1989) (test for admission of expert testimony is whether the untrained juror would be able to intelligently decide an issue without the expert testimony); ***Hopkins v. State***, 480 S.W.2d 212, 218 (Tex. Crim. App. 1972) ("[A] lay witness, or non-expert witness usually will not be permitted to state an opinion, because he is in no better position to form an opinion, based on the facts which he possesses, than is the jury. Both are equally well qualified. His opinion testimony adds nothing to the case. It is entirely superfluous."); *see, e.g.*, ***Dietz v. Hill Country Rests., Inc.***, 398 S.W.3d 761, 765-66 (Tex. App.—San Antonio 2011, no pet.) (trial court did not abuse its discretion in excluding expert testimony about cause of falls on restaurant walkway; jury would have been able to form its own conclusion about whether walkway posed unreasonable risk of harm by looking at photographs and hearing testimony about other falls). Refer to notes 36-37, 85-89, 165-256 *supra* and accompanying text.

340. *See* ***Hopkins***, 480 S.W.2d at 219; *cf.* ***Leitch v. Hornsby***, 935 S.W.2d 114, 119 (Tex. 1996) (plaintiff's coworker, who was not offered as an expert witness, nevertheless expressed his opinion that a lift belt would have prevented plaintiff's injury; testimony "has no probative worth and is not proper evidence of causation because [witness's] testimony amounts to mere conjecture, and because [witness] was not qualified to testify about what type of lifting devices might have prevented [plaintiff's] injuries"). Refer to notes 105-136 *supra* and accompanying text.

341. ***Owen v. Kerr-McGee Corp.***, 698 F.2d 236, 240 (5th Cir. 1983); *see, e.g.*, ***United States v. Valverde***, 846 F.2d 513, 517 (8th Cir. 1988) (in a trial for conspiring to escape while in federal custody, trial court properly prohibited defense expert from testifying that tape-recorded statements were consistent with casual conversations between guards and inmates; defendant "essentially wanted to ask the expert to tell the jury whether his conversations with the guards were in fact bribery attempts. This was precisely the issue before the jury"); ***Matthews v. Ashland Chem., Inc.***, 770 F.2d 1303, 1310 (5th Cir. 1985) (all-inclusive hypothetical question posed to expert was rejected because it requested that expert tell jury what result to reach); *see also* FED. R. EVID. 704 advisory committee's note (Rules 701, 702, and 403 "afford ample assurances against the admission of opinions which would merely tell the jury what result to reach, somewhat in the manner of the oath-helpers of an earlier day").

cent,[342] what punishment to assess,[343] or which witness to believe[344] are mere personal conclusions and are not helpful to the jury.[345]

A witness cannot give an opinion on a pure question of law[346] "because such a question is exclusively for the court to decide and is not an ultimate issue for the trier of fact."[347] An expert may not intrude on the trial judge's function, which is to instruct the jury on the requirements of the law that apply to the case. Thus, an expert witness cannot express an opinion on the meaning or content of the law in the jurisdiction.[348]

---

342. *See Fairow v. State*, 943 S.W.2d 895, 899 (Tex. Crim. App. 1997); *Viscaino v. State*, 513 S.W.3d 802, 812 (Tex. App.—El Paso 2017, no pet.); *Sandoval v. State*, 409 S.W.3d 259, 292-93 (Tex. App.—Austin 2013, no pet.); *Mowbray v. State*, 788 S.W.2d 658, 668 (Tex. App.—Corpus Christi 1990, pet. ref'd).

343. *See, e.g., Brown v. State*, 741 S.W.2d 453, 454-55 (Tex. Crim. App. 1987) (probation officer's testimony on operation of probation department and the rules and regulations for a probationer's conduct was properly excluded as "a recitation of the law applicable to probation"); *Schulz v. State*, 446 S.W.2d 872, 874 (Tex. Crim. App. 1969) (court did not err in excluding expert testimony that it would be better for defendant to be placed on probation than sentenced to confinement); *Peters v. State*, 31 S.W.3d 704, 720-22 (Tex. App.—Houston [1st Dist.] 2000, pet. ref'd) (psychiatrist's expert testimony on recidivism rates for treated incest offenders should have been admitted as relevant and probative punishment evidence because testimony did not tell jury what punishment to assess; "trial judge's broad discretion should perhaps be exercised with a view toward the law's broad, consistent, and longstanding trend to admit more and more evidence—for both sides—at the punishment stage"); *Gross v. State*, 730 S.W.2d 104, 105-06 (Tex. App.—Texarkana 1987, no pet.) (in trial for indecency with a child, trial judge did not err in excluding the minor victim's opinion that defendant should receive "a lenient sentence"; such an opinion "would constitute merely an appeal to sympathy or prejudice, and would tend to suggest that the jurors may shift their responsibility to the witnesses"); *see also Hall v. State*, 935 S.W.2d 852, 856 (Tex. App.—San Antonio 1996, no pet.) (error, but harmless, to admit testimony by victim's aunt that involuntary-manslaughter defendant "should have ten years in the penitentiary"); *Wade v. State*, 769 S.W.2d 633, 635-36 (Tex. App.—Dallas 1989, no pet.) (no error in permitting expert's opinion that sending a sex offender to prison frequently benefits the victim); *Brown*, 741 S.W.2d at 456-57 (Clinton & Miller, JJ., dissenting) (probation officer's testimony on terms and conditions of probation did not include an opinion on whether defendant should be placed on probation or confined and should have been admitted as neutral and informative in nature).

344. *See Fairow*, 943 S.W.2d at 899 ("[I]f the witness's lack of personal knowledge yields testimony that amounts to 'choosing up sides' ..., his opinion should be excluded."); *Mowbray*, 788 S.W.2d at 668 ("Opinions of nonexpert witnesses are not admissible if they ... amount to little more than the witness' choosing sides on the case outcome."); *Kirkpatrick v. State*, 747 S.W.2d 833, 836 (Tex. App.—Dallas 1987, pet. ref'd) (while Rule 704 authorizes opinion testimony on an ultimate issue, the opinion "must be 'otherwise admissible,' and the opinion of one witness as to the veracity of another's testimony is not 'otherwise admissible'"); *see, e.g., Taylor v. State*, 774 S.W.2d 31, 34 (Tex. App.—Houston [14th Dist.] 1989, pet. ref'd) (error to permit police officer to testify that defendant's statement to him was not credible; witness could not give an opinion about the truth or falsity of other testimony, but error was harmless because the "jury could not logically have reached a different conclusion"); *see also Ayala v. State*, 171 Tex. Crim. 687, 688-89, 352 S.W.2d 955, 956 (1962) (counsel cannot ask a witness's opinion on whether another witness's testimony was true or false, but defendant was not harmed when State cross-examined him on whether police officers were incorrect in their testimony about his intoxicated demeanor); *Smith v. State*, 737 S.W.2d 910, 915-16 (Tex. App.—Fort Worth 1987, pet. ref'd) (defendant could not ask a doctor his opinion about whether a child "had been raped or not" because the response would have amounted to an impermissible comment on the child's credibility).

345. *Lum v. State*, 903 S.W.2d 365, 370 (Tex. App.—Texarkana 1995, pet. ref'd). Refer to notes 38-42 *supra* and accompanying text.

346. *Fleming v. Kinney ex rel. Shelton*, 395 S.W.3d 917, 928 (Tex. App.—Houston [14th Dist.] 2013, pet. denied); *Great W. Drilling, Ltd. v. Alexander*, 305 S.W.3d 688, 696 (Tex. App.—Eastland 2009, no pet.); *Anderson v. State*, 193 S.W.3d 34, 38 (Tex. App.—Houston [1st Dist.] 2006, pet. ref'd).

347. *Nat'l Convenience Stores, Inc. v. Matherne*, 987 S.W.2d 145, 149 (Tex. App.—Houston [14th Dist.] 1999, no pet.).

348. *See Burkhart v. Wash. Metro. Area Transit Auth.*, 112 F.3d 1207, 1213 (D.C. Cir. 1997) (only judge can instruct jury on relevant legal standards); *United States v. Milton*, 555 F.2d 1198, 1203 (5th Cir. 1977) ("[A]n expert

In cases involving foreign laws, when judges likely are not familiar with the subject matter of the foreign laws, experts may help the trial judge determine the content and applicability of those laws.[349] Because the content and applicability of a foreign law is a question of pure law and not fact, however, the matter is decided solely by the judge, who then instructs the jury on the applicable foreign law.[350]

Texas courts have permitted expert witnesses to offer opinions on mixed questions of law and fact in which "a standard or measure has been fixed by law and the question is whether the person or conduct measures up to that standard."[351] Rule 704 does

witness may not substitute for the court in charging the jury regarding the applicable law."); *see, e.g.*, ***Askanase v. Fatjo***, 130 F.3d 657, 672-73 (5th Cir. 1997) (court properly excluded expert's opinion on "'[w]hether [company's] officers and directors fulfilled their fiduciary duties to the Company, its creditors, and shareholders. If not, how and to what extent did [they] breach their fiduciary duties'"; this testimony was pure legal opinion); ***Specht v. Jensen***, 853 F.2d 805, 808-09 (10th Cir. 1988) (in civil-rights suit alleging unlawful search of home and office, trial judge erred in permitting attorney to testify as an expert for plaintiff that a search had taken place, that the search was illegal per se, and that there was no consent); ***Anderson***, 193 S.W.3d at 38 (trial court properly excluded officers' testimony on the difference between assault and terroristic threat because that distinction is a matter of statutory interpretation, which is a question of law); ***Dickerson v. DeBarbieris***, 964 S.W.2d 680, 690 (Tex. App.—Houston [14th Dist.] 1998, no pet.) (expert could not interpret the legal effect of a document authorizing a condominium association to conduct a nonjudicial foreclosure because such an interpretation is purely a legal question for the trial judge).

349. *See* ***Alosio v. Iranian Shipping Lines***, 426 F. Supp. 687, 689 (S.D.N.Y. 1976) ("In deciding questions of foreign law, the court may look to the testimony of expert witnesses as well as the underlying statutes."), *aff'd*, 573 F.2d 1287 (2d Cir. 1977) (table case); *see, e.g.*, ***State v. Valmont Plantations***, 346 S.W.2d 853, 865 (Tex. Civ. App.—San Antonio 1961) (expert could testify on Mexican law), *aff'd*, 163 Tex. 381, 355 S.W.2d 502 (1962). *See generally* 3 LOUISELL & MUELLER, *supra* note 27, §382, at 645-46 (trial court may be aided on questions of foreign law by any source, including expert testimony); 2 RAY, *supra* note 32, §1424, at 74-75 (court may resort to opinions of skilled persons on questions of the existence, construction, or application of foreign law); 2 WIGMORE, *supra* note 3, §564, at 776-78 (discussing the history of the rule allowing witnesses to testify on questions involving foreign law).

350. *See* ***Reading & Bates Constr. Co. v. Baker Energy Res. Corp.***, 976 S.W.2d 702, 707-08 (Tex. App.—Houston [1st Dist.] 1998, pet. denied) ("The Texas courts of appeals that have considered rule 203 have tended to label it as a 'hybrid rule' or one involving 'mixed questions of law and fact.' To the extent these opinions imply that the determination of foreign country law is in any way a 'factual' determination, we disagree with them. The court's ruling on the content of foreign country law is a ruling on a question of law."); *see, e.g.*, ***Chavez v. Carranza***, 559 F.3d 486, 498 (6th Cir. 2009) (expert's testimony on how Salvadoran Amnesty Law would apply to defendant was a legal question and was properly excluded; because district court did not grant comity to foreign law, testimony was not relevant). *See generally* TEX. R. EVID. 203 (procedure for determining laws of foreign countries). Refer to *Article II: Judicial Notice, supra* p. 147.

351. ***Blumenstetter v. State***, 135 S.W.3d 234, 248 (Tex. App.—Texarkana 2004, no pet.); ***Mega Child Care, Inc. v. Tex. Dep't of Prot. & Regulatory Servs.***, 29 S.W.3d 303, 309 (Tex. App.—Houston [14th Dist.] 2000, no pet.); *accord* ***Great W. Drilling***, 305 S.W.3d at 696.

Whether an action constitutes negligence is a classic example of a mixed question of law and fact. ***Blumenstetter***, 135 S.W.3d at 248; *see also* ***Royal Maccabees Life Ins. v. James***, 146 S.W.3d 340, 354 (Tex. App.—Dallas 2004, pet. denied) (expert gave opinion that insurance company's actions constituted bad faith, unfair dealing, and fraud and violated Deceptive Trade Practices Act). Refer to notes 129-136 *supra* and accompanying text. Some mixed questions of law and fact are within the jurors' ability to decide without expert testimony. *See, e.g.*, ***GTE Sw., Inc. v. Bruce***, 998 S.W.2d 605, 619-20 (Tex. 1999) (in case for intentional infliction of emotional distress, jury could decide without expert testimony whether defendant's conduct was extreme and outrageous); ***Blumenstetter***, 135 S.W.3d at 248-49 (expert testimony about whether an issue had been proved beyond a reasonable doubt should not have been allowed because the jury was as competent as the witness to decide). Refer to note 338 *supra* and accompanying text.

Federal courts, on the other hand, prohibit any expert testimony that encompasses legal conclusions. *See* ***Chavez***, 559 F.3d at 498 ("An expert opinion on a question of law is inadmissible."). Expert testimony on this type of question is problematic because it "convey[s] the witness' unexpressed, and perhaps erroneous, legal standards to the jury." ***Torres v. Cty. of Oakland***, 758 F.2d 147, 150 (6th Cir. 1985). The Fourth Circuit has explained how to determine if an opinion is a legal conclusion:

not permit any witness, lay or expert, to testify that a particular legal standard has or has not been met when that standard is expressed as a legal term of art that would be unclear to those outside the legal profession. Thus, for the opinion to be admissible, there must be a showing that the witness knows the proper legal definition in the question.[352] If the legal term carries an ordinary meaning that is understood by or can be made clear to the witness, Rule 704 does not bar opinion testimony on that matter.[353] On the other hand, if the term is one that the witness does not normally use or that does not carry its ordinary meaning, the witness may not use that term in testimony unless the term has been defined or clarified by the judge.[354]

Finally, an opinion should be excluded under Rule 403 if its probative value is substantially outweighed by the counterfactors of "unfair prejudice, confusing the issues, misleading the jury, undue delay, or needlessly presenting cumulative evidence."[355]

The best way to determine whether opinion testimony contains legal conclusions, "is to determine whether the terms used by the witness have a separate, distinct and specialized meaning in the law different from that present in the vernacular." To determine when a question posed to an expert witness calls for an improper legal conclusion, the district court should consider first whether the question tracks the language of the legal principle at issue or of the applicable statute, and second, whether any terms employed have specialized legal meaning. *United States v. Barile*, 286 F.3d 749, 760 (4th Cir. 2002) (quoting *Torres*, 758 F.2d at 151). The Fourth Circuit observed, however, that opinion testimony encompassing legal conclusions may be otherwise admissible because it is helpful to the jury. *Barile*, 286 F.3d at 760 n.7; *see, e.g., Peckham v. Cont'l Cas. Ins.*, 895 F.2d 830, 837 (1st Cir. 1990) (expert-opinion testimony on proximate cause was properly admitted in insurance case because "[i]nsurance is a complicated subject .... Defendant's proffered experts could reasonably be expected to shed some light in a shadowy domain."); *see also Burkhart*, 112 F.3d at 1212 ("[T]he line between an inadmissible legal conclusion and admissible assistance to the trier of fact in understanding the evidence or in determining a fact in issue is not always bright."). The Advisory Committee has noted that "opinions phrased in terms of inadequately explored legal criteria" should be excluded. FED. R. EVID. 704 advisory committee's note. "Thus the question, 'Did T have capacity to make a will?' would be excluded, while the question, 'Did T have sufficient mental capacity to know the nature and extent of his property and the natural objects of his bounty and to formulate a rational scheme of distribution?' would be allowed." *Id.* Presumably, Texas courts would permit both questions.

352. *Lawrence v. City of Wichita Falls*, 122 S.W.3d 322, 328 (Tex. App.—Fort Worth 2003, pet. denied); *see, e.g., Isern v. Watson*, 942 S.W.2d 186, 193 (Tex. App.—Beaumont 1997, pet. denied) (doctor's testimony that defendant-doctor was "negligent and/or grossly negligent" was admissible because expert was provided with proper legal definition of that term); *Metot v. Danielson*, 780 S.W.2d 283, 288 (Tex. App.—Tyler 1989, writ denied) (trial court erred in excluding expert's testimony when expert was asked in his deposition to assume the legally correct definitions of negligence and proximate cause and then express his opinion on whether medical-malpractice defendant's conduct was negligent and a proximate cause of plaintiff's injuries); *see also* McCORMICK'S HANDBOOK, *supra* note 2, §12, at 28 (questions "phrased in terms of a legal criterion" must be adequately defined "so as to be correctly understood by laymen"). For further discussion of these issues, refer to notes 129-136 *supra* and accompanying text.

353. 3 LOUISELL & MUELLER, *supra* note 27, §395, at 696; Pratt, *supra* note 5, at 320 (witness may give an opinion when "facts must be applied in light of a fairly well established legal standard"). For example, a police officer who is familiar with the usual meaning of the word "intoxicated" as it applies under the DWI law can give an opinion on whether a person was intoxicated when arrested. *See* TEX. PENAL CODE §49.01(2) (defining the term "intoxicated"); TEX. TRANSP. CODE §724.001(9) ("intoxicated" has meaning assigned by TEX. PENAL CODE §49.01); *see, e.g., Garza v. State*, 442 S.W.2d 693, 695 (Tex. Crim. App. 1969) (police officer could express his opinion that the defendant was drunk based on officer's personal experience of having observed and arrested intoxicated people before). Although "intoxicated" is a legal term and an ultimate issue for the jury to decide, the jury and the witness are familiar with its meaning. Refer to notes 53-56 *supra* and accompanying text.

354. Refer to note 352 *supra* and accompanying text.

355. *See* TEX. R. EVID. 403. Refer to *Article IV: Relevance & Its Limits*, *supra* p. 211.

RULE 705
DISCLOSING THE UNDERLYING FACTS OR DATA & EXAMINING AN EXPERT ABOUT THEM

(a) Stating an Opinion Without Disclosing the Underlying Facts or Data. Unless the court orders otherwise, an expert may state an opinion—and give the reasons for it—without first testifying to the underlying facts or data. But the expert may be required to disclose those facts or data on cross-examination.

(b) Voir Dire Examination of an Expert About the Underlying Facts or Data. Before an expert states an opinion or discloses the underlying facts or data, an adverse party in a civil case may—or in a criminal case must—be permitted to examine the expert about the underlying facts or data. This examination must take place outside the jury's hearing.

(c) Admissibility of Opinion. An expert's opinion is inadmissible if the underlying facts or data do not provide a sufficient basis for the opinion.

(d) When Otherwise Inadmissible Underlying Facts or Data May Be Disclosed; Instructing the Jury. If the underlying facts or data would otherwise be inadmissible, the proponent of the opinion may not disclose them to the jury if their probative value in helping the jury evaluate the opinion is outweighed by their prejudicial effect. If the court allows the proponent to disclose those facts or data the court must, upon timely request, restrict the evidence to its proper scope and instruct the jury accordingly.

Notes and Comments

Comment to 2015 restyling: All references to an "inference" have been deleted because this makes the Rule flow better and easier to read, and because any "inference" is covered by the broader term "opinion." Courts have not made substantive decisions on the basis of any distinction between an opinion and an inference. No change in current practice is intended.

Comment to 1998 change: Paragraphs (b), (c), and (d) are based on the former Criminal Rule and are made applicable to civil cases. This rule does not preclude a party in any case from conducting a *voir dire* examination into the qualifications of an expert.

COMMENTARY ON RULE 705

The elaborate procedural provisions of Rule 705 serve three purposes: (1) to ensure that the judge and opposing party have an opportunity to discover whether the proffered expertise is based on sufficiently reliable underlying facts or data to be admissible, (2) to ensure that inadmissible facts or data reasonably relied on by an expert and disclosed to the jury are not misused as substantive evidence by the fact-finder, and (3) to provide the trial judge with the discretion to prevent disclosure of inadmissible facts

RULE 705

or data that, although supportive of the expert's opinion, are unfairly prejudicial.[356] Rule 705 permits a broader range of expert-witness testimony than the common law did and allows greater flexibility in how an expert may testify.

Rule 705(a) permits an expert to give an opinion without first testifying to the underlying facts or data.[357] Rule 705(b), as it applies in criminal cases, requires the trial judge to give the opposing party an opportunity, if the party so requests, to voir dire the expert outside the jury's presence on the facts and data underlying his opinion.[358] In civil cases, this voir dire opportunity is discretionary rather than mandatory.[359] Rule 705(c) makes the expert's opinion inadmissible if the court finds that the expert does not have a sufficient basis for his opinion.[360] This provision is in accord with earlier Texas criminal[361] and civil[362] law as well as with federal cases.[363] Rule 705(d) provides

---

356. As a part of the 1998 unification of the Civil and Criminal Rules, the lengthy former Criminal Rule 705 was modified slightly and made explicitly applicable to civil proceedings as well. Although the present rule on its face appears to change Texas civil law, the provisions in sections (b) through (d) had been applied to civil cases even before formal adoption of the rule. Thus, the 1998 version of Rule 705 does not significantly change Texas civil practice.

    The more elaborate framework of the original Criminal Rule 705 reflected three concerns that are particularly acute in criminal trials: (1) that jurors may overvalue expert opinion, particularly when that opinion is based on hearsay, inadmissible facts, or unreliable scientific data, (2) that the opponent of the opinion may not be fully aware of the content or basis for the opinion before the jury hears it because there is very little pretrial discovery in criminal trials, and (3) that the jury will be influenced by an opinion that is later struck because of an inadequate basis. The first and third of these concerns apply equally in civil proceedings, especially after the *Daubert/ Kelly/Robinson* line of cases elaborated on the trial judge's gatekeeping role in assessing the reliability and relevance of scientific evidence. Thus, in both criminal and civil trials, the trial judge should be satisfied that the expert's opinion is adequately based on reliable sources before the jury hears it. 2 GOODE ET AL., *supra* note 7, §705.2, at 71. For a discussion of the reliability and relevance of expert testimony under Rule 702, refer to notes 165-250 *supra* and accompanying text.

357. Refer to notes 366-388 *infra* and accompanying text.

358. Refer to notes 389-396 *infra* and accompanying text.

359. Even before the 1998 amendment to Rule 705, both the Texas civil rule and Federal Rule 705 had been construed to permit the opponent of the opinion to conduct a preliminary voir dire of the witness to test the adequacy of the basis for his opinion. *See* 2 GOODE ET AL., *supra* note 7, §705.2, at 71 (stating that "civil courts have permitted opposing counsel to conduct voir dire examinations of experts identical to those mandated by Criminal Rule 705(b)"); 3 LOUISELL & MUELLER, *supra* note 27, §400, at 710 (the rule "does not stand in the way" of preliminary voir dire, but voir dire should generally not be permitted because it negates the purpose of Federal Rule 705, which is "to-the-point" expert testimony); *see, e.g., Vallot v. Cent. Gulf Lines*, 641 F.2d 347, 350-51 (5th Cir. 1981) (trial court properly excluded expert medical testimony when witness testified on voir dire that he formed his opinion based on facts related to him by plaintiff's attorney before he examined plaintiff); *Coastal Indus. Water Auth. v. Trinity Portland Cement Div.*, 523 S.W.2d 462, 471 (Tex. Civ. App.—Houston [1st Dist.] 1975, writ ref'd n.r.e.) (trial court did not abuse its discretion in declining to permit voir dire examination of witness outside presence of jury). Refer to note 390 *infra* and accompanying text.

360. Refer to notes 397-406 *infra* and accompanying text.

361. *See, e.g., St. Pe v. State*, 495 S.W.2d 224, 225-26 (Tex. Crim. App. 1973) (no error in excluding expert-opinion testimony when facts were insufficient to form a basis for opinion; psychiatrist testified that "there are many factors to be considered in determining what effect drugs may have on an individual," had no knowledge of the facts in the present case, and "was unable to express an opinion").

362. *See* 2 GOODE ET AL., *supra* note 7, §705.2, at 71 (while the civil rule does not explicitly state that a court may disallow expert testimony that does not have a sufficient basis for the opinion, "the authority of the trial court to exclude an unsupported opinion has never been questioned"); *see, e.g., Brown v. Tex. Employers' Ins.*, 635 S.W.2d 415, 415-17 (Tex. 1982) (in workers' compensation case, "take nothing" judgment was affirmed when plaintiff's experts had insufficient facts to support opinion on deceased's cause of death); *see also 1st Coppell Bank v. Smith*, 742 S.W.2d 454, 459 (Tex. App.—Dallas 1987, no writ) ("Opinion evidence based upon speculation or conjecture lacks probative value ....").

that if the probative value of the inadmissible facts or data on which the expert is reasonably relying in helping the jury evaluate the opinion is outweighed by their prejudicial effect, courts must exclude these underlying facts or data.[364] Thus, Rule 705(d) is slanted more toward exclusion of testimony than is Rule 403, in which probative value must be "substantially" outweighed by a counterfactor before relevant evidence may be excluded.[365]

A. Rule 705(a): Stating an Opinion Without Disclosing the Underlying Facts or Data

Rule 705(a) permits the expert to give an opinion at the outset of the explanatory testimony without first testifying to the underlying facts or data.[366] In fact, the rule permits the witness to be qualified as an expert and then give a one-sentence opinion on direct examination.[367]

363. *See, e.g.,* ***J.B. Hunt Transp., Inc. v. Gen. Motors Corp.***, 243 F.3d 441, 444 (8th Cir. 2001) (testimony by accident-reconstruction expert was excluded because he had insufficient evidence to completely reconstruct the accident as he theorized; testimony of "foamology" expert was not allowed because testimony was highly doubtful and was linked to rejected testimony of reconstruction expert); ***Blue Dane Simmental Corp. v. Am. Simmental Ass'n***, 178 F.3d 1035, 1041 (8th Cir. 1999) (proposed expert economist could not testify because no "other economists use before-and-after modeling to support conclusions of causes of market fluctuation"); ***Jaurequi v. Carter Mfg. Co.***, 173 F.3d 1076, 1084 (8th Cir. 1999) (proposed expert testimony on alternative design was excluded because expert did not provide basis for belief that opinion was anything more than speculation); ***Viterbo v. Dow Chem. Co.***, 826 F.2d 420, 423-24 (5th Cir. 1987) (physician's unsupported personal opinion of causation was inadmissible); *see also* ***Calhoun v. Honda Motor Co.***, 738 F.2d 126, 132 (6th Cir. 1984) (expert testimony must be based on the evidence so as to be removed from "'realm of guesswork and speculation'" (quoting ***Polk v. Ford Motor Co.***, 529 F.2d 259, 271 (8th Cir. 1976))).

364. *See* ***Joiner v. State***, 825 S.W.2d 701, 708 (Tex. Crim. App. 1992) (court must determine whether disclosure of data would be "more prejudicial than probative"); ***Kramer v. State***, 818 S.W.2d 923, 925 (Tex. App.—Houston [14th Dist.] 1991, pet. ref'd) (evidence may be admitted if "the probative value outweighs the probability that it will be improperly used by the jury"); ***Speering v. State***, 763 S.W.2d 801, 807 (Tex. App.—Texarkana 1988) (court must not permit disclosure of underlying evidence to the jury if evidence's value in supporting expert's opinion is outweighed by the danger that it will be used for an improper purpose), *reformed on other grounds*, 797 S.W.2d 36 (Tex. Crim. App. 1990); 2 GOODE ET AL., *supra* note 7, §705.3, at 75 (court must balance probative value of underlying facts to determine whether they are outweighed by any possible improper use). Refer to notes 407-418 *infra* and accompanying text.

365. Refer to *Article IV: Relevance & Its Limits, supra* p. 211.

366. Rule 705(a) is identical to Federal Rule 705. Federal Rule 705 was restyled in 2011 to delete all references to "inference"; however, no substantive change was intended. FED. R. EVID. 705 advisory committee's note to 2011 amendments. The Advisory Committee explained that the restyling deleted all references to "inference" in the rule "on the grounds that the deletion made the Rule flow better and easier to read, and because any 'inference' is covered by the broader term 'opinion.' Courts have not made substantive decisions on the basis of any distinction between an opinion and an inference." *Id.* In the 2015 restyling of the Texas Rules, the Texas Supreme Court made the same change to Rule 705 based on the same reasoning. *See* TEX. R. EVID. 705 cmt. (2015).

367. Rule 705(a) formerly permitted this disclosure on direct examination explicitly: "The expert may ... disclose on direct examination, or be required to disclose on cross-examination, the underlying facts or data." The rule no longer includes this reference to disclosure on direct examination. Federal Rule 705 also implicitly permits the sponsoring party to have the expert give the factual bases for his opinion on direct examination. *See* FED. R. EVID. 705; 3 LOUISELL & MUELLER, *supra* note 27, §400, at 576-77 (Supp. 1993); *see also* MCCORMICK ON EVIDENCE, *supra* note 36, §324.2, at 910 (expert must be allowed to disclose the factual basis for his opinion or his "opinion is left unsupported in midair with little if any means for evaluating its correctness"). Louisell and Mueller discuss the pitfalls of asking for nothing more than a "bare bones" opinion on direct examination, relying on the cross-examiner to bring out the extensive bases for that opinion. 3 LOUISELL & MUELLER, *supra* note 27, §400, at 576-77 (Supp. 1993). The cross-examiner may avoid all cross-examination and later present his own expert who does lay out, in full detail, the facts and rationale for his differing opinion. *Id.* The proponent cannot expect his opponent to fall into strategic

A primary goal of Rule 705 was to eliminate the need for the often-criticized and cumbersome hypothetical question[368] that had historically been the only mode for an expert with no personal knowledge of the facts to express an opinion.[369] While Rule 705 permits hypothetical questions, it does not require them.[370] By eliminating the requirement that hypothetical questions be used in eliciting expert opinions, Rule 705 actually enhances the use of hypothetical questions by allowing them to be short and to the point.[371] Nonetheless, the trial judge retains discretion to require advance disclosure of the facts and data the expert used in forming the opinion.[372]

Traditionally, hypothetical questions were of two types: (1) those that called for an opinion based on facts to which some other witness had testified, but that were not repeated in posing the hypothetical for the expert,[373] and (2) those that asked for a reci-

---

traps, and should thus ask his expert to set forth at least some basis for his opinion on direct examination. *Id.*; *see also* **City of San Antonio v. Pollock**, 284 S.W.3d 809, 818 (Tex. 2009) ("[I]f no basis for the opinion is offered, or the basis offered provides no support, the opinion is merely a conclusory statement and cannot be considered probative evidence, regardless of whether there is no objection."). Refer to notes 236-237, 246 *supra* and accompanying text.

368. Refer to notes 289-292 *supra* and accompanying text.

369. *See* FED. R. EVID. 705 advisory committee's note; *see also* McElhaney, *supra* note 290, at 471-72 (under common-law rule, expert who explains meaning of other witnesses' testimony must answer hypothetical questions to avoid giving impression that he believes facts on which his opinion is based). Historically, there were three rationales for hypothetical questions: (1) to supply the expert witness, who was unfamiliar with the facts of the lawsuit, with the data needed to form an opinion, (2) to inform the jury of the facts underlying the expert's opinion, and (3) to restrict the use of data underlying the expert's opinion to matters that had been introduced into evidence. *See* 2 WIGMORE, *supra* note 3, §§672-680, at 934-42 (hypothetical questions help give the jury a premise on which to base the inferences or conclusions they might draw from an expert's testimony); *see, e.g.*, **Classified Parking Sys. v. Kirby**, 507 S.W.2d 586, 588-89 (Tex. Civ. App.—Houston [14th Dist.] 1974, no writ) (property owner could testify about value of the property through hypothetical question to inform the jury of necessary facts); **Topletz v. Thompson**, 342 S.W.2d 151, 159-60 (Tex. Civ. App.—Dallas 1960, no writ) (expert would have been allowed to give his opinion of a property's value if a proper hypothetical question had described the condition of the property). *See generally* 2 RAY, *supra* note 32, §1403, at 36-41 (analyzing the value of hypothetical questions in presenting the bases of an expert's opinion to aid the jury). The first two justifications remain valid under the Rules and may prompt optional use of hypotheticals by proponents of expert testimony. The third justification, however, is largely made unnecessary by Rule 703, which relaxes the standards for allowable data underlying expert opinions. *See* TEX. R. EVID. 703. Refer to notes 257-328 *supra* and accompanying text.

370. *See* **Gonzales v. State**, 4 S.W.3d 406, 417-18 (Tex. App.—Waco 1999, no pet.) (discussing use of hypothetical questions under Rule 703); *see also* **Jordan v. State**, 928 S.W.2d 550, 556 n.8 (Tex. Crim. App. 1996) (Rule 703 specifically permits an expert to base his opinion on facts or data made known to him during trial). For further discussion of hypothetical questions, refer to notes 280-292 *supra* and accompanying text.

371. *See* McElhaney, *supra* note 290, at 487 (Rule 705 calls for a relaxation in the detail required in hypothetical questions). For one example of the long-winded, clumsy hypotheticals required under the common law, see **Pyles v. State**, 755 S.W.2d 98, 119-22 (Tex. Crim. App. 1988).

372. *See* 2 RAY, *supra* note 32, §1402, at 12 (Supp. 1991). Note, however, that the rule does not permit the trial judge to circumscribe the expert's role as a fact-finder by limiting the types of data on which the opinion may be based.

373. For example, the expert may have been sitting in the courtroom listening to the testimony of fact witnesses A and B. When called to the stand, the questioner could ask the expert: "Assuming that the facts that A and B have just testified to are undisputed and true, and taking into account your experience, training, and research in this field, do you have any opinion ...?" However, if the testimony of A and B was disputed or a different version of the facts was developed on cross-examination, the questioner could not have used this simplified form of posing the hypothetical but instead must have given the specific facts he wanted the expert to rely on. *See* 2 RAY, *supra* note 32, §1403, at 37. The testimony from the fact witnesses should be reasonably short and simple and should be quickly followed by the expert's testimony; otherwise, the jury, expert, and attorneys are likely to have difficulty recalling it. *See*

tation of all the facts on which the expert was to rely in forming the opinion.[374] The question could include prior opinion testimony, if experts in the field reasonably rely on such opinions,[375] and reasonable inferences from prior facts.[376] Further, the hypothetical could include facts not yet admitted into evidence, as long as the proponent eventually introduces them,[377] or could "assume the facts in accordance with [the proponent's] theory of the case," as long as those assumed facts are consistent with facts that have been proved.[378] Texas cases allow trial judges "considerable latitude" in these matters,[379] and the cases under the Federal Rules are in accord.[380]

Because an expert who has no personal knowledge of the specific facts in the trial is not limited under Rule 703 to giving an opinion in response to a hypothetical question, he can base an opinion solely on inadmissible and unadmitted evidence.[381] Rule 705 also dispenses with the need to inform the jury, before the expert gives the opinion, of all the facts and data taken into account in forming that opinion.[382] Testimony

Frankel v. Lull Eng'g Co., 334 F. Supp. 913, 927 (E.D. Pa. 1971) (hypothetical questions that assume the testimony of witnesses as facts "are generally proper where the testimony of specific witnesses is asked to be assumed and the court determines that the question will be intelligible to the jury"), *aff'd*, 470 F.2d 995 (3d Cir. 1973).

374. Eliminating the requirement of laboriously outlining all of the facts that the expert was to assume in forming his opinion is the only way Rule 705 significantly affected the procedure of posing a hypothetical question. *See* 2 GOODE ET AL., *supra* note 7, §705.4, at 79.

375. *See* **Royal Indem. Co. v. Little Joe's Catfish Inn, Inc.**, 636 S.W.2d 530, 533 (Tex. App.—San Antonio 1982, no writ) (expert is allowed to express an opinion based on personal experience and the opinion of another expert). *See generally* 2 WIGMORE, *supra* note 3, §682(d), at 956-57 (discussing the lack of difference between data observed and data inferred as the basis for an expert's opinion).

376. *See* **Burns v. Bridge Eng'g Corp.**, 465 S.W.2d 427, 432 (Tex. Civ. App.—Houston [14th Dist.] 1971, writ ref'd n.r.e.) (hypothetical may include inferences reasonably drawn from facts consistent with the questioner's theory).

377. *See, e.g.,* **Home Ins. v. Banda**, 736 S.W.2d 812, 815 (Tex. App.—San Antonio 1987, writ denied) (trial court did not err in permitting expert to give opinion based on hypothetical that assumed facts not yet in evidence because they were later offered); **Burke v. State**, 642 S.W.2d 197, 199 (Tex. App.—Houston [14th Dist.] 1982, no pet.) (because hypothetical assumed that complaining witness had seen defendant, but no evidence was ever offered to this effect, trial court properly excluded defendant's proffered expert opinion on misidentification). Refer to notes 286-287 *supra* and accompanying text.

378. *See, e.g.,* **McBride v. State**, 862 S.W.2d 600, 609-10 & n.20 (Tex. Crim. App. 1993) (under Criminal Rule 703, the hypothetical question is one permissible form to admit psychological testimony on capital-murder defendant's future dangerousness; no requirement that hypothetical facts be proved beyond a reasonable doubt, and questioner may "assume the facts in accordance with his theory of the case"); **Held v. State**, 948 S.W.2d 45, 53 (Tex. App.—Houston [14th Dist.] 1997, pet. ref'd) (State's Intoxilyzer expert could give his opinion about intoxication based on the assumption that the subject had consumed his last drink 15 minutes before he was stopped by police, even though that fact was not in evidence; hypothetical questions may include assumptions based on facts within the personal knowledge of the witness, assumed from common or judicial knowledge, or assumed as facts in accordance with party's theory of the case).

379. *See* **J. Weingarten, Inc. v. Tripplett**, 530 S.W.2d 653, 655 (Tex. Civ. App.—Beaumont 1975, writ ref'd n.r.e.) (form and wording of hypothetical is mainly subject to trial court's discretion); **Mobil Oil Co. v. Dodd**, 528 S.W.2d 297, 304 (Tex. Civ. App.—Corpus Christi 1975, writ ref'd n.r.e.) (same); **Burns**, 465 S.W.2d at 431-32 (trial court has discretion to determine whether hypothetical question is based on a "fair assumption of facts").

380. *See* **Smith v. Ford Motor Co.**, 626 F.2d 784, 793 (10th Cir. 1980) (Federal Rule 705, in conjunction with Federal Rule 703, allows an expert to testify to his opinion); **Iconco v. Jensen Constr. Co.**, 622 F.2d 1291, 1301 (8th Cir. 1980) (form of hypothetical is left largely to discretion of trial court).

381. Refer to notes 293-319 *supra* and accompanying text.

382. *See* TEX. R. EVID. 705(a) (expert can state opinion and give reasons for it without first testifying to underlying facts or data); **Bryan v. John Bean Div. of FMC Corp.**, 566 F.2d 541, 544-47 (5th Cir. 1978) ("Rule 705 ... removes the need for the expert to make elaborate disclosure of the bases of his opinion. Rather, the onus of eliciting

about the witness's familiarity with specific types of data and professional sources may sometimes be necessary to establish his expert qualifications under Rule 702. Nonetheless, it is possible, for example, to qualify a medical expert in his given field and then abruptly ask him the following:

Attorney: Doctor, do you have an opinion based on a reasonable degree of medical certainty as to the deceased's cause of death?

Witness: Yes, I do.

Attorney: What is that opinion?

Witness: The deceased died from a self-inflicted overdose of heroin.

Attorney: Thank you, doctor. Pass the witness.

This abbreviated presentation is not likely to be persuasive to the jury but would be allowed if the expert's sponsor decided that a shortened qualification would be most effective and that a complete explanation of the underlying data would confuse the jury or waste time.[383] Under the rule, the trial judge still has discretion to require the expert to testify to the bases for an opinion before giving it.[384] However, courts should require this foundation testimony only when there is a special concern, such as the possibility that the opinion may be based on impermissible or unreliable data.[385]

The facts and data on which the opinion is based should ordinarily be disclosed when the opponent requests disclosure.[386] That is, both the direct examiner and cross-examiner normally have great discretion to explore the factual basis for the expert's

the bases of the opinion is placed on the cross-examiner."); *Joiner v. State*, 825 S.W.2d 701, 707-08 (Tex. Crim. App. 1992) (experts can base their opinions partially on inadmissible facts; trial court will examine the factual basis for the opinion and determine whether disclosure of those facts would be more prejudicial than probative); *Ramirez v. State*, 815 S.W.2d 636, 651 (Tex. Crim. App. 1991) (Criminal Rule 705 allows expert to testify to his opinion without prior disclosure of underlying facts unless the court requires otherwise); *see, e.g.*, *Trailways, Inc. v. Mendoza*, 745 S.W.2d 63, 66-67 (Tex. App.—San Antonio 1987, no writ) (expert medical-opinion testimony was admissible under Civil Rule 705 even though it was based partially on X-rays that were not introduced into evidence; defendant on cross-examination could have, but did not, attempt to have the doctor produce the X-rays).

383. *See* 2 SALTZBURG ET AL., *supra* note 149, at 1437-38.

384. *See* TEX. R. EVID. 705(a) (expert can give opinion without first testifying to underlying facts or data unless court orders otherwise); *Arkoma Basin Expl. Co. v. FMF Assocs. 1990-A, Ltd.*, 249 S.W.3d 380, 389-90 (Tex. 2008) ("[E]xperts are not required to introduce ... foundational data at trial unless the opposing party or the court insists."); 2 GOODE ET AL., *supra* note 7, §705.2, at 72 (discussing when a court should require an expert to testify to the underlying facts of his opinion).

385. *See, e.g.*, *Tabatchnick v. G.D. Searle & Co.*, 67 F.R.D. 49, 55 (D.N.J. 1975) (plaintiff's expert was not allowed to testify because voir dire examination and deposition demonstrated that he could express only a "bare conclusion" and the basis for the conclusion was factually incorrect); *see also* 3 LOUISELL & MUELLER, *supra* note 27, §400, at 707 (discussing when a court should require an expert to testify to the underlying facts of his opinion).

386. *See* TEX. R. EVID. 705(a) (expert may be required to disclose underlying facts and data on cross-examination); *Arkoma Basin Expl. Co.*, 249 S.W.3d at 389-90 (expert is not required to disclose underlying data "unless the opposing party or the court insists"); *see, e.g.*, *Nenno v. State*, 970 S.W.2d 549, 564 (Tex. Crim. App. 1998) (State could cross-examine capital-murder defendant's expert witness about contents of report made by expert's colleague who had interviewed defendant about crime because expert relied on that report in forming his opinion), *overruled on other grounds*, *State v. Terrazas*, 4 S.W.3d 720 (Tex. Crim. App. 1999); *Moranza v. State*, 913 S.W.2d 718, 727-28 (Tex. App.—Waco 1995, pet. ref'd) (trial court did not err in allowing State to impeach expert witness with hearsay statements included in another expert's report because witness relied on a summary of the report to form his opinions).

opinion.[387] However, the problem with permitting the expert an unfettered right to disclose to the jury otherwise inadmissible facts he reasonably relied on to form his opinion is that the jury might improperly use those facts as substantive evidence, a matter addressed by Rule 705(d).[388]

B. Rule 705(b): Voir Dire Examination of an Expert About the Underlying Facts or Data

In criminal cases, Rule 705(b) requires a voir dire examination outside the jury's presence to determine the underlying facts or data of the expert's opinion whenever the opponent of the expert testimony requests one.[389] This procedure is discretionary in civil cases.[390] Because there is so little formal pretrial discovery in Texas criminal pro-

---

387. *See* 2 SALTZBURG ET AL., *supra* note 149, at 1438 (subject to limitation under Rules 403 and 611(a), the cross-examiner has a right to inquire into the details of an expert's opinion); *see, e.g.*, ***Skinner v. State***, 956 S.W.2d 532, 540 (Tex. Crim. App. 1997) (document prepared by capital-murder defendant's toxicology expert that reflected expert's thoughts, questions, comments, and mental impressions about the strengths and weaknesses of the defensive theory was not subject to production under Rule 705 during State's cross-examination; document did not constitute "facts or data" on which expert based his opinion). For a discussion of disclosure of underlying facts and data on direct examination, refer to note 367 *supra* and accompanying text.

388. *See, e.g.*, ***United States v. Wright***, 783 F.2d 1091, 1100-01 (D.C. Cir. 1986) (while expert psychiatrist might reasonably rely on codefendant's statements that defendant would "do anything for money," Federal Rule 705 does not pave the way for a jury to use such hearsay as substantive evidence against a defendant; trial court did not err in permitting hearsay testimony because codefendant testified and was cross-examined, so defendant's right of confrontation was not violated); ***Love v. State***, 909 S.W.2d 930, 949 (Tex. App.—El Paso 1995, pet. ref'd) (court did not abuse its discretion in allowing mental-health expert to relate hearsay to the jury when much of what expert related to the jury had already been testified to by two witnesses and formed the basis for expert's diagnosis). For a discussion of Rule 705(d), refer to notes 407-418 *infra* and accompanying text.

389. TEX. R. EVID. 705(b). In ***Vasquez v. State***, the court took a narrower view of the purpose of a voir dire examination under Criminal Rule 705(b) and announced the following:

> Rule 705 addresses the situation when the expert is testifying as to an opinion that is directly related to an issue at trial. … When an expert gives only general opinions not based on an analysis of the specific facts at issue, the voir dire allowed by Rule 705(b) is not implicated.

819 S.W.2d 932, 935 (Tex. App.—Corpus Christi 1991, pet. ref'd). The court of appeals stated that the voir dire process contemplated under Criminal Rule 705(b) "should be used sparingly as its overuse would undermine the purpose of the rule: to quickly and efficiently elicit helpful expert opinions which aid the jury in its fact finding task." *Id.*

Rule 705(b), however, is intended to guard against the admission of expert opinions—whether focused on the specific facts of the particular trial or a general area of educational expertise—that do not have a sufficient or a reliable factual basis. *See* ***Goss v. State***, 826 S.W.2d 162, 168 (Tex. Crim. App. 1992); ***Shaw v. State***, 329 S.W.3d 645, 655 (Tex. App.—Houston [14th Dist.] 2010, pet. ref'd). Rule 703 allows a party to quickly and efficiently elicit an expert opinion in front of the jury once an adequate and reliable factual basis for the opinion has been established outside the presence of the jury. Refer to notes 293-319 *supra* and accompanying text.

Unlike Texas Rule 705(b), Federal Rule 705 does not expressly permit a voir dire examination to determine the admissibility of the expert's testimony. However, the Advisory Committee states that

> [i]f a serious question is raised under Rule 702 or 703 as to the admissibility of expert testimony, disclosure of the underlying facts or data on which opinions are based may, of course, be needed by the court before deciding whether, and to what extent, the person should be allowed to testify. This rule does not preclude such an inquiry.

FED. R. EVID. 705 advisory committee's note to 1993 amendments.

390. TEX. R. EVID. 705(b). The provision is discretionary in civil cases because extensive pretrial discovery is conducted in most civil cases. *See* TEX. R. CIV. P. 192.3(e) (party is entitled to (1) the names, addresses, and telephone numbers of discoverable expert witnesses, (2) the subject matter of their testimony, (3) their mental impressions and opinions, and (4) any expert reports, tangible objects, compilations of data, or other documents prepared by or for the expert). Generally, a party can secure information about experts through a request for disclosure, an expert report, or a deposition. *See* TEX. R. CIV. P. 194.2(f), 195.1, 205.1; *see, e.g.*, ***In re Nat'l Lloyds Ins.***, ___ S.W.3d ___ (Tex.

ceedings, there is a much greater need for an opportunity to discover the basis for the expert's opinion during a midtrial voir dire outside the jury's presence.[391] Otherwise, the opponent of the expert testimony would risk not knowing what the expert's answers will be on cross-examination.

The purpose of Rule 705(b) is to prevent the jury from hearing underlying facts and data that might ultimately be ruled inadmissible.[392] The voir dire requirement applies only to an expert who appears in court and testifies within the context of Rule 705. The provision cannot be used to exclude written documents that are self-authenticating and admissible without an expert's testimonial sponsorship.[393] As the comment to the 1998 amendment to Rule 705 states, Rule 705(b) deals only with the voir dire of the expert about the facts and data underlying his opinion.[394] The opponent's right to voir dire the witness about his expert qualifications is left undisturbed.[395]

2017) (No. 15-0591; 6-9-17) (orig. proceeding) (because plaintiffs sought discovery from experts using interrogatories and requests for production, which are not permitted under Texas Rule of Civil Procedure 195.1, trial court erred in relying on Rule 192.3(e) to determine scope of discovery). *But see **In re Nat'l Lloyds Ins.**,* ___ S.W.3d at ___ (Johnson, Lehrmann, Boyd, JJ., dissenting) (disagreeing with majority's conclusion because defendant did not object to method of discovery, and witness could have been considered both fact witness and expert witness for discovery purposes). See ***O'Connor's Texas Rules * Civil Trials*** (2017), "Testifying experts," ch. 6-D, §3.1, p. 582. Thus, civil litigants who have conducted appropriate pretrial discovery into the facts and data supporting an expert's opinion usually do not need to invoke Rule 705(b).

    Because of the trial judge's gatekeeping role in assuring that any scientific expertise offered at trial is sufficiently reliable and relevant to the litigated issues, Rule 705(b) may be used in civil trials, especially in the context of pretrial hearings, to exclude the expert's testimony under ***Daubert/Robinson***. The purpose of requiring a voir dire outside the jury's presence under Rule 705(b) is to ensure that the jury does not hear otherwise inadmissible facts or data that underlie the expert's opinion before the trial judge has made a final determination of whether that expert's opinion is admissible. Knowing before trial precisely what facts the expert used in reaching his opinions allows the civil litigant to request a pretrial ruling (1) excluding the expert's opinion if those facts and data are insufficient to support the opinion or (2) admitting the opinion but excluding any mention of the inadmissible facts and data as being unfairly prejudicial. Of course, if the trial judge permits a midtrial voir dire on the underlying facts supporting the expert's opinion, that voir dire must take place outside the jury's presence as specified by Rule 705(b).

    391. *See* 2 GOODE ET AL., *supra* note 7, §705.2, at 70 (meaningful pretrial discovery is lacking in Texas criminal cases).

    392. *See, e.g.,* ***Jenkins v. State***, 912 S.W.2d 793, 814 (Tex. Crim. App. 1995) (op. on reh'g) (harmless error to deny Rule 705(b) hearing outside jury's presence because defendant already had a copy of psychologist witness's report setting out facts and data and expert did not testify to damaging inadmissible material); ***Harris v. State***, 133 S.W.3d 760, 773-75 (Tex. App.—Texarkana 2004, pet. ref'd) (harmless error for trial court to not allow defendant to voir dire expert on domestic violence outside presence of jury before discussing "the cycle of violence"; expert testimony on that concept prefaced a discussion of "patterns of response she had seen in victims' behavior" and was not offered to show that defendant physically abused complainant).

    393. *See* ***Luxton v. State***, 941 S.W.2d 339, 342 (Tex. App.—Fort Worth 1997, no pet.) ("The language of [Criminal] Rule 705 contains no inference or even a suggestion that its provisions override the admissibility of a physician's observations, diagnoses, or opinions, that are recorded in a business record qualified and admitted into evidence under [Criminal] Rule 803(6)."). For a discussion of self-authenticated business records, refer to *Article IX: Authentication & Identification, infra* p. 1027.

    394. *See* TEX. R. EVID. 705 cmt. (1998); *see, e.g.,* ***Daniel v. State***, 485 S.W.3d 24, 35 (Tex. Crim. App. 2016) (trial court permitted voir dire about underlying facts or data of expert's opinion but did not permit defense counsel to question expert about her findings because she had not yet testified to any findings; defendant did not preserve complaint that trial court improperly limited voir dire of expert when defendant continued to question expert on basis of opinion without further objection).

    395. TEX. R. EVID. 705 cmt. (1998); *see Jenkins*, 912 S.W.2d at 814 (op. on reh'g) (objection to expert's qualifications is not a request for a Rule 705(b) hearing, which explores only the underlying facts or data of an expert's opinion); *see, e.g.,* ***Daniel***, 485 S.W.3d at 34 (before expert witness testified, defense counsel asked "to do a qualification

In ***Kerr-McGee Corp. v. Helton***, the Texas Supreme Court held that an objection and motion to strike the expert's opinion testimony was timely even though it was made after cross-examination of that witness because cross-examination was the only time that the opponent had a full opportunity to explore the factual basis for the opinion.[396] However, such an objection may come too late to sufficiently repair the damage of the jury's having heard and digested all of the expert's opinion testimony if the opponent's only remedy is a motion to strike that testimony and continue the trial.

C. Rule 705(c): Admissibility of Opinion

Rule 705(c) makes the expert's opinion inadmissible if the trial court finds that the expert does not have a sufficient factual basis for the opinion.[397] While the inquiry under the ***Daubert/Kelly/Robinson*** line of cases focuses on the reliability and relevance of an expert's scientific theory and methodology without regard for the conclusions, Rule 705(c) focuses on the specific factual data that supports the expert's conclusions. The issue here is not whether experts can reach reliable results on a certain issue but whether the facts that the expert in the present case relied on were adequate to support a conclusion.[398]

For example, suppose an expert proposes to testify that a DNA test has excluded the defendant as the possible perpetrator of a rape. The basic scientific theory of DNA testing is now so widely accepted as scientifically reliable that a ***Daubert/Kelly/Robinson*** inquiry would not be necessary, given the scientific community's general acceptance of the theories and techniques used.[399] The court must still act as a gatekeeper for the application of DNA technology in each case—has the testing laboratory properly applied the accepted scientific techniques in analyzing the forensic

RULE 705

---

hearing … outside the presence of the jury"). The right to voir dire an expert on his qualifications is determined under common-law principles subject to the judge's discretion under Rule 611.

396. 133 S.W.3d 245, 252 (Tex. 2004).

397. TEX. R. EVID. 705(c). This provision is consistent with earlier Texas law. *See, e.g.*, ***St. Pe v. State***, 495 S.W.2d 224, 225-26 (Tex. Crim. App. 1973) (no error in excluding expert-opinion testimony when facts were insufficient to form basis for opinion; psychiatrist had testified that "there are many factors to be considered in determining what effect drugs may have on an individual"; because doctor had no knowledge of facts in present case, "he was unable to express any opinion"). Rule 705(c) has no explicit counterpart in the Federal Rules.

398. *See **Hous. Unlimited, Inc. Metal Processing v. Mel Acres Ranch***, 443 S.W.3d 820, 832-33 & n.11 (Tex. 2014); ***Wolfe v. State***, 509 S.W.3d 325, 335 (Tex. Crim. App. 2017); ***Alaniz v. Rebello Food & Bev., L.L.C.***, 165 S.W.3d 7, 19-20 (Tex. App.—Houston [14th Dist.] 2005, no pet.). In ***Alaniz***, a Dram Shop Act suit, the court of appeals upheld the exclusion of the plaintiff's expert's testimony about the intoxication of the driver (who was a bar patron) because the expert relied on inaccurate assumptions about the driver's alcohol consumption and admitted that without any known blood alcohol level, he could not extrapolate a blood alcohol level at the time the driver drank at the bar, making his opinion, in his own words, "less reliable." 165 S.W.3d at 19-20.

399. *See **Kelly v. State***, 824 S.W.2d 568, 573-74 (Tex. Crim. App. 1992). *See generally* William C. Thompson, *Evaluating the Admissibility of New Genetic Identification Tests: Lessons from the "DNA War,"* 84 J. CRIM. L. & CRIMINOLOGY 22 (1993) (discussion of general history of the advent of DNA evidence, early methods used for DNA testing, issues raised by methods of DNA analysis, and application of those methods in individual cases). For more recent information about testing methods, see William C. Thompson et al., *Part 1: Evaluating Forensic DNA Evidence: Essential Elements of a Competent Defense Review*, 27 CHAMPION 16, 17 (Apr. 2003), and Charlotte J. Word, *The Future of DNA Testing and Law Enforcement*, 67 BROOK. L. REV. 249, 249-51 (2001). Refer to notes 207-209, 239-242 *supra* and accompanying text.

samples in that case?[400] Thus, to prevent the misuse of DNA-expert testimony and the admission of unreliable results, courts should allow parties to ask about the specific methodologies employed in each case and the application of those methods to the available data. Under Rule 705(c), the opponent can attack the admissibility of the DNA expert's testimony on the basis that the specific factual data supporting the expert's opinion is based on speculation or assumptions and is thus so inadequate that no reasonable expert could base an opinion on them.[401]

Factual data supporting DNA analysis might be inadequate for a number of reasons. For example, testimony may indicate that the laboratory did not comply with appropriate standards and controls, and evidence could thus be contaminated or misinterpreted.[402] The court may find that the testifying expert has no information or insufficient information about the laboratory's error rate.[403] Any doubts about the performance of DNA testing in a specific case should be decided as an issue of the evidence's admissibility rather than its weight,[404] in accordance with *Kelly*'s reliability test.[405]

---

400. *See Kelly*, 824 S.W.2d at 573; *cf.* *In re "Agent Orange" Prod. Liab. Litig.*, 611 F. Supp. 1223, 1245 (E.D.N.Y. 1985) ("[T]he court may not abdicate its independent responsibilities to decide if the bases [of the expert's opinion] meet minimum standards of reliability as a condition of admissibility. If the underlying data are so lacking in probative force and reliability that no reasonable expert could base an opinion on them, an opinion which rests entirely upon them must be excluded."), *aff'd*, 818 F.2d 187 (2d Cir. 1987). In *People v. Castro*, New York was one of the first jurisdictions to require that the DNA-analysis technique must have been properly applied on the occasion in question. 545 N.Y.S.2d 985, 987 (N.Y. Sup. Ct. 1989). This would become a criterion of reliability for scientific evidence under *Kelly*. *See Kelly*, 824 S.W.2d at 573. In *Castro*, testimony showed that the testing laboratory did not properly perform the necessary and accepted scientific tests on the forensic samples in that case, so the DNA analysis was inadmissible. 545 N.Y.S.2d at 997-98. Some jurisdictions have simply taken judicial notice of previous appellate rulings on a challenged technique or method. *See, e.g.*, *State v. Bible*, 858 P.2d 1152, 1185 (Ariz. 1993) (based on other appellate decisions, court held that DNA-match criteria were generally accepted in scientific community and complied with *Frye* requirements). *See generally* Garrett E. Land, *Judicial Assessment or Judicial Notice? An Evaluation of the Admissibility Standards for DNA Evidence and Proposed Solutions to Repress the Current Efforts to Expand Forensic DNA Capabilities*, 9 J. MED. & L. 95, 121-26 (2005) (discussing current problems in admission of DNA evidence). For analysis of the *Daubert/Kelly/Robinson* test, refer to notes 174-201 *supra* and accompanying text.

401. *Cf. Vadala v. Teledyne Indus., Inc.*, 44 F.3d 36, 38-39 (1st Cir. 1995) (expert's testimony was properly excluded when he admitted that he had no idea what temperature would be required to alter the appearance of the aircraft parts that he had concluded must have been damaged during flight rather than during fire on the ground; exclusion was proper "not because of any flawed scientific principle—heat admittedly can cause in-flight polymerization—but because there was no substantial basis for concluding that it had done so here"); *Mac Sales, Inc. v. E.I. du Pont de Nemours & Co.*, 24 F.3d 747, 752-53 (5th Cir. 1994) (trial court "may exclude expert testimony that lacks an adequate foundation"; expert admitted he had analyzed only the domestic market, and he thus lacked sufficient foundation to testify about the foreign market at issue).

402. *See, e.g.*, *State v. Schwartz*, 447 N.W.2d 422, 428 (Minn. 1989) (DNA tests were inadmissible because laboratory did not prove it followed appropriate controls and standards).

403. *See* Land, *supra* note 400, at 134-35.

404. The gatekeeping role of judges is particularly important in cases involving DNA evidence, as judges may be better qualified by experience to evaluate complex, technical explanations about DNA testing than juries are. As the court of criminal appeals has pointed out, "DNA profiling is scientifically complex; latent-print comparison ... is not." *Rodgers v. State*, 205 S.W.3d 525, 528 (Tex. Crim. App. 2006). A juror can quickly and easily grasp testimony about a visual comparison of fingerprints. The presentation of DNA evidence, however, can be extremely lengthy and detailed, especially when opponents question the examiner about controls, protocols, reagents, and other features of the analysis. *See* Bert Black et al., *Science and the Law in the Wake of* Daubert: *A New Search for Scien-*

The science of DNA testing and comparison continues to advance. Experts in the field of population genetics are still debating key questions about the statistics used to estimate how frequently a DNA profile occurs within segments of the population.[406] Juries are frequently given a statistic purporting to express the likelihood of finding another person with the same profile as the suspect. These statistics are usually impressively large numbers that would lead any jury to believe it is nearly impossible for a DNA match to be mistaken, but these probability statistics are only as good as our current understanding of population genetics. As science develops in this area, courts should take care to exercise their gatekeeping function to avoid admitting misleading or outdated testimony.

D. Rule 705(d): When Otherwise Admissible Underlying Facts or Data May Be Disclosed; Instructing the Jury

Rule 705(d) provides that the inadmissible facts or data on which the expert is reasonably relying will be excluded if their probative value in helping the jury evaluate the opinion is outweighed by their prejudicial effect.[407] The balance is between the probative value of the inadmissible data to help the jury evaluate the reasonableness of the expert's opinion and either (1) the unfairly prejudicial effect of this inadmissible material on the opposing party or (2) the likelihood that the jury may use this inadmissible data as substantive evidence or for some other purpose.[408] If the otherwise inadmissible facts and data supporting the expert's opinion are disclosed to the jury, the opponent, on a timely request, is entitled to an instruction restricting the jury's consideration of that inadmissible data solely to its permissible explanatory purpose.[409]

tific Knowledge, 72 TEX. L. REV. 715, 787-88 (1994) (both judges and juries are capable of deciding disputes over scientific evidence, but over time, judges develop some scientific understanding beyond that of a juror; other issues in the case could be overwhelmed by a detailed presentation of scientific evidence to the jury).

405. For the *Kelly* factors that affect a trial court's determination of reliability, refer to note 192 *supra* and accompanying text.

406. *See People v. Wilson*, 136 P.3d 864, 868-69 (Cal. 2006); *People v. Pizarro*, 3 Cal. Rptr. 3d 21, 58-60 (Cal. Ct. App. 2003), *disapproved on other grounds*, *People v. Wilson*, 136 P.3d 864 (Cal. 2006). *See generally* D.H. Kaye, *Logical Relevance: Problems with the Reference Population and DNA Mixtures in* People v. Pizarro, 3 LAW, PROBABILITY & RISK 211 (2004) (analyzing *Pizarro* court's treatment of DNA evidence); Richard Lempert, *The Suspect Population and DNA Identification*, 34 JURIMETRICS J. 1 (1993) (discussing probative value and probabilities of DNA matching).

407. *See* TEX. R. EVID. 705(d). Under Rule 705(d), mere equality between probative value and unfair prejudicial effect is sufficient to exclude testimony of the underlying inadmissible data.

A provision that is very similar to Rule 705(d) was adopted in Federal Rule 703. Under Federal Rule 703, there is a presumption against the disclosure of otherwise inadmissible data underlying an expert's opinion unless the probative value of that data *substantially* outweighs its prejudicial effect. FED. R. EVID. 703 advisory committee's note to 2000 amendments. Refer to notes 308-319 *supra* and accompanying text.

408. *See Stam v. Mack*, 984 S.W.2d 747, 749-50 (Tex. App.—Texarkana 1999, no pet.) (Rule 705 "now allow[s] a testifying expert to relate on direct examination the reasonably reliable facts and data on which he relied in forming his opinion, subject to an objection under TEX. R. EVID. 403 that the probative value of such facts and data is outweighed by the risk of undue prejudice").

409. *See* TEX. R. EVID. 705(d). In *Depena v. State*, the court of appeals set out the following model limiting instruction:

An expert may testify in terms of opinion .... The expert may disclose the underlying facts or data relied upon to formulate that opinion .... When the underlying facts or data are disclosed, they may

In both civil and criminal cases decided under Rule 705, trial courts have occasionally permitted experts to give opinions but not to testify to all of the inadmissible facts that led to their conclusions. In one civil case, ***First Southwest Lloyds Insurance Co. v. MacDowell***, the court of appeals held that Rule 705 "does not indicate an absolute right of the expert to disclose *all* of the facts and underlying data under all circumstances."[410] The court of appeals explained:

> If the expert were held to be entitled to detail every statement made to him that contributed to his conclusion, then the expert could be effectively used to present an infinite amount of evidentiary matters to the jury. The rules do not necessarily allow the expert to recount the entire basis of any opinion which may be admissible. Although some courts have allowed the direct admission of all data upon which an expert relies to form an opinion, a much better argument can be made against the admission on direct examination of unauthenticated underlying data.[411]

---

be considered by you to aid you in determining (if it does so) the weight, if any, to be given the testimony of the expert at trial and his credibility; but such underlying facts or data, if any, shall not be considered as tending to establish the alleged guilt of the defendant in this case.

148 S.W.3d 461, 470 n.10 (Tex. App.—Corpus Christi 2004, no pet.); *see also* ***Plante v. State***, 692 S.W.2d 487, 493 (Tex. Crim. App. 1985) (discussing the request for a limiting instruction); 2 GOODE ET AL., *supra* note 7, §705.3, at 75 (discussing the effect and purpose of limiting instructions). This instruction would apply only when the underlying facts and data were otherwise inadmissible. The right to a limiting instruction had been implicit in the former civil rule. *See* TEX. R. CIV. EVID. 705, 641-642 S.W.2d (Tex. Cases) LV (1983, amended 1998) ("The expert may testify in terms of opinion or inference and [give] his reasons therefor without prior disclosure of the underlying facts or data, unless the court requires otherwise. The expert may in any event be required to disclose the underlying facts or data on cross-examination."). For a general discussion of limiting instructions, refer to *Article I: General Provisions, supra* p. 97.

410. 769 S.W.2d 954, 958 (Tex. App.—Texarkana 1989, writ denied); *see also* ***Kramer v. Lewisville Mem'l Hosp.***, 831 S.W.2d 46, 49 (Tex. App.—Fort Worth 1992) (use of the permissive "may" under Civil Rule 705 does not indicate an absolute right for an expert to disclose all the facts and data he relied on, but decision is within trial court's sound discretion; "[w]hile such supporting evidence is not automatically excludable because it *is* supporting data to an expert's opinion, neither is it automatically excludable simply because it is hearsay"), *aff'd*, 858 S.W.2d 397 (Tex. 1993); ***Beavers v. Northrop Worldwide Aircraft Servs., Inc.***, 821 S.W.2d 669, 674 (Tex. App.—Amarillo 1991, writ denied) (courts should not admit otherwise inadmissible facts "merely because such matters happen to be underlying data upon which an expert relies").

In ***First Southwest Lloyds***, MacDowell sued First Southwest Lloyds to recover on a fire-insurance policy after the insurance company had alleged arson and refused to pay his claim. 769 S.W.2d at 956. The city fire marshal, as an expert for First Southwest Lloyds, testified that the fire was incendiary in origin. *Id.* at 957. His opinion was based partially on a report by an eyewitness who told the fire marshal that he had seen the fire begin from a nightclub across the street and then saw a white male run from the front of the store and speed away in a car. *Id.* The trial court prevented the fire marshal from testifying to this hearsay report, although he had reasonably relied on it. *Id.* If the proper foundation had been laid, the eyewitness account might have been admissible under the Rule 803(2) excited-utterance exception to the hearsay rule. The eyewitness account then would have been independently admissible and the court would have had less discretion in prohibiting the fire marshal from testifying to his reliance on that account. *See* ***First Sw. Lloyds***, 769 S.W.2d at 959.

411. ***First Sw. Lloyds***, 769 S.W.2d at 958. The supreme court expressed a similar rationale in ***Birchfield v. Texarkana Memorial Hospital***. 747 S.W.2d 361, 365 (Tex. 1987). The court stated that it was error for an expert to testify to a hearsay conversation with another expert, but held that the error was harmless because the testimony was cumulative of other evidence. *Id.* This reasoning has not been without its critics. In ***Decker v. Hatfield***, the court noted that ***Birchfield*** had been criticized and stated the following:

Thus, the court of appeals ruled that the trial judge has discretion to limit the admission of such underlying inadmissible data under Rule 403 if it is unduly prejudicial, confusing, or misleading.[412] The rationale in *First Southwest Lloyds* appears sound and in accord with the general framework of the Rules, which gives the trial judge great discretion to restrict the evidence to its proper scope under Rule 105(a) and to exclude otherwise relevant evidence under Rule 403 when its probative value is substantially outweighed by its prejudicial effect or other counterfactors listed in the rule.[413]

This language [in *Birchfield*], contained in dictum and made without reference to Rules 703 and 705, is ill-considered and overbroad. The design of these rules was to allow experts to testify in a way consistent with the manner in which they conduct their professional activities. *If an expert has relied upon hearsay in forming an opinion, and the hearsay is of a type reasonably relied upon by such experts, the jury should ordinarily be permitted to hear it.* Exclusion is proper only when the court finds that the danger that the jury will improperly use the hearsay outweighs its probative value ....

798 S.W.2d 637, 638 (Tex. App.—Eastland 1990, writ dism'd). In *Sosa v. Koshy*, the court held that the defendants' accident-reconstruction expert was properly allowed to demonstrate the basis for his opinion by testifying about hearsay statements made to him by eyewitnesses. 961 S.W.2d 420, 426-27 (Tex. App.—Houston [1st Dist.] 1997, pet. denied). The court distinguished its decision from the reasoning in *Birchfield* on the grounds that the *Birchfield* opinion was based on the old Civil Rule 705. *Sosa*, 961 S.W.2d at 427. The court reasoned that the new Civil Rule 705 was broader than its predecessor because it specifically allowed an expert on direct examination to give the underlying facts and data on which his opinion is based. *Sosa*, 961 S.W.2d at 427. Under the old Civil Rule 705, the expert was explicitly allowed to disclose the information only on cross-examination. Refer to note 367 *supra* and accompanying text.

Indeed, under Rules 703 and 705, an expert normally is allowed to rely on hearsay evidence in reaching his conclusions and can testify about the inadmissible data that supports his opinion, but that general rule is subject to the limitations set out in Rule 705(d). *See, e.g.*, **Tex. Workers' Comp. Comm'n v. Wausau Underwriters Ins.**, 127 S.W.3d 50, 56-57 (Tex. App.—Houston [1st Dist.] 2003, pet. denied) (under Rule 705, probative value of hearsay data underlying assistant medical examiner's opinion—that security guard's death was suicide because guard jumped from a height—outweighed its risk of prejudicial harm, especially because both witnesses whose reports formed basis for expert opinion testified at trial); **Morris v. State**, 123 S.W.3d 425, 428-29 (Tex. App.—San Antonio 2003, pet. ref'd) (trial court did not abuse its discretion in allowing State to cross-examine defense expert on witness's statement to police about three prior incidents of violence that allegedly occurred between victim and defendant because expert testified on direct examination that he could find no motive for defendant to have committed the crime; under Rule 705, State was entitled to explore whether expert's opinions were valid in light of witness's statement because expert relied on that statement in forming part of his opinion).

412. **First Sw. Lloyds**, 769 S.W.2d at 958; *see* **Boswell v. Brazos Elec. Power Coop., Inc.**, 910 S.W.2d 593, 602 (Tex. App.—Fort Worth 1995, writ denied) (use of the word "may" in Civil Rule 705 gives trial judge discretion to exclude any reference to inadmissible underlying facts or data supporting expert's opinion); *see, e.g.*, **Resendiz v. State**, 112 S.W.3d 541, 544-45 (Tex. Crim. App. 2003) (in capital-murder trial, upholding trial court's exclusion of gruesome photographs of other crimes committed by defendant that were relied on by defense expert to support his opinion that defendant was insane at time of charged offense); **Valle v. State**, 109 S.W.3d 500, 505-06 (Tex. Crim. App. 2003) (trial court did not abuse its discretion under Rule 705 in excluding otherwise inadmissible videotaped interview of capital-murder defendant's mother that formed part of basis for defense expert's opinion; jury might have considered mother's hearsay statements as substantive evidence); **In re Commitment of Talley**, 522 S.W.3d 742, ___ (Tex. App.—Houston [1st Dist.] 2017, no pet.) (in civil-commitment case, evidence of previous sexual assaults was admissible to help jury understand expert's opinion that person being committed had behavioral abnormality, the truth of which was placed at issue during trial; trial court reasonably could have concluded that probative value outweighed risk of unfair prejudice); **N. Am. Refractory Co. v. Easter**, 988 S.W.2d 904, 916 (Tex. App.—Corpus Christi 1999, pet. denied) (trial court did not err in prohibiting expert from discussing pathologist's hearsay report, even though she had relied on it in forming her opinion).

413. *See* 2 GOODE ET AL., *supra* note 7, §705.3, at 75-76 (under former civil rules, trial court has discretion under Rules 105(a) and 403 to exclude underlying inadmissible data on which the testifying expert has relied, but only when the court finds that "the danger that the jury will improperly use the hearsay outweighs its probative value for explanatory purposes"); 3 WEINSTEIN & BERGER, *supra* note 15, ¶705[01], at 705-10 (under Rule 403, court can "exclude foundational evidence if it finds that its probative value is substantially outweighed by the dangers of prejudice,

RULE 705

This discretion is now explicit under Rule 705(d), which states that the proponent of the opinion may not disclose underlying facts or data that would otherwise be inadmissible for any purpose if their probative value in helping the jury evaluate the expert's opinion is outweighed by their prejudicial effect.[414] This balancing test does not need to be conducted on the record.[415] Unlike Rule 403, the unfairly prejudicial effect does not need to "substantially" outweigh probative value before the underlying facts or data can be excluded; a preponderance is enough.[416] The provision is also mandatory; thus, the trial judge must, on a timely request, exclude any references to the inadmissible material if he determines that the prejudicial effect outweighs its probative value.[417]

---

confusion, or waste of time"). For a general discussion of limiting instructions, refer to *Article I: General Provisions, supra* p. 97; for a discussion of the Rule 403 counterfactors, refer to *Article IV: Relevance & Its Limits, supra* p. 211.

414. *See* Tex. R. Evid. 705(d). Similarly, an expert witness cannot be used as a conduit to put the party's self-serving hearsay version of an event before the jury. *See, e.g.*, **Davis v. State**, 268 S.W.3d 683, 701-02 (Tex. App.—Fort Worth 2008, pet. ref'd) (trial court properly prohibited defendant from asking detective, as an expert witness, about statements that defendant had made to detective; defendant "admits that the value of the statements was not as an 'explanation or support' for [detective's] opinion, but rather as substantive evidence to advance his own self-defense claim—a purpose rule 705(d) aims to *prevent*"); **Walck v. State**, 943 S.W.2d 544, 545 (Tex. App.—Eastland 1997, pet. ref'd) (trial court did not err in barring defendant's expert from relating on direct examination the content of interview between defendant and expert). In **Walck**, the defendant claimed that under Rule 803(4), his expert could relate inadmissible hearsay on the defendant's state of mind at the time of the offense because it was imperative to the expert's opinion. 943 S.W.2d at 544. The trial and appellate courts disagreed, concluding that the evidence was not admissible under Rule 803(4) because the expert did not examine the defendant for purposes of medical diagnosis or treatment, but instead to formulate an opinion about "sudden passion." **Walck**, 943 S.W.2d at 545. The appellate court reasoned that the trial judge had the discretion to exclude the defendant's self-serving out-of-court statements under Rule 705(d) because the danger that they would be used for an improper purpose outweighed any probative value they might have had in explaining the expert's opinion. **Walck**, 943 S.W.2d at 545-46.

415. **Davis**, 268 S.W.3d at 701.

416. *See* Tex. R. Evid. 705(d).

417. *See id.*; **Davis**, 268 S.W.3d at 701. For example, the trial judge in **Speering v. State** used Rule 705(d) to exclude an expert's testimony on blood-spatter evidence from an unrelated criminal case. 763 S.W.2d 801, 807 (Tex. App.—Texarkana 1988), *reformed on other grounds*, 797 S.W.2d 36 (Tex. Crim. App. 1990). A defense expert in **Speering** wanted to introduce evidence from a different crime to support his contention that the blood spatters found on the stabbing victim could have occurred when the knife was withdrawn. 763 S.W.2d at 807. The trial court ruled that the expert could express his opinion on the cause of the blood spatters in this case but excluded photographs and testimony about evidence from the other criminal case as irrelevant and confusing to the jury. *Id.* The appellate court, relying on Rule 705(d), held that the trial court did not abuse its discretion in excluding this evidence. **Speering**, 763 S.W.2d at 807. The rationale and result in **Speering** are both in accord with the purpose of the rule. *See* 2 Goode et al., *supra* note 7, §705.3, at 75 (Rule 705(d) allows the court to prohibit "any mention whatsoever of the otherwise inadmissible underlying facts" supporting the expert's opinion, but such a circumstance will be rare and a limiting instruction to the jury will usually suffice); 2 Ray, *supra* note 32, §1402, at 14 (Supp. 1991) (under Criminal Rule 705(d), a trial judge may exclude underlying evidence if he concludes that the danger that it will be used for an "improper" purpose outweighs its value as support for the expert's opinion and that "disclosure of such otherwise inadmissible facts and data may not be used by the offering party as a subterfuge to get the jury to consider them as substantive evidence").

The mandatory nature of Rule 705(d) could lead a trial court to admit an expert's opinion but exclude all of the data the expert used to form that opinion. In such a situation, jurors cannot evaluate the expert's opinion because they have no knowledge of the underlying facts he used to reach his conclusions. The jurors are forced to evaluate the expert's demeanor and qualifications alone and accept or reject his opinion at face value. To avoid this problem, some jurisdictions have allowed an expert to identify the inadmissible factual information or data he relied on without giving any specific details. *See* **People v. Campos**, 38 Cal. Rptr. 2d 113, 114-15 (Cal. Ct. App. 1995). In criminal cases, expert opinions based on inadmissible hearsay may implicate the Confrontation Clause. *See, e.g.*, **Mar-**

Whenever an expert is allowed to disclose the inadmissible facts that support his opinion, the opponent of the expert testimony is entitled to a limiting instruction stating that the jury must not consider the inadmissible data as substantive evidence.[418]

E. Conclusion

Overall, Rule 705 places a premium on adequate cross-examination of the expert,[419] which requires adequate pretrial discovery of anticipated expert testimony.[420] The Advisory Committee's note to Federal Rule 705 assumes that pretrial discovery will be extensive enough for effective cross-examination.[421] For this reason, Texas civil discovery rules provide that a court may prohibit an expert from testifying if his name and the basic content of his testimony have not been provided to the opposing party.[422] Part of the rationale for the more elaborate trial procedures originally adopted for criminal cases was the relative lack of pretrial discovery in those cases and the resulting need

---

tinez v. State, 311 S.W.3d 104, 112 (Tex. App.—Amarillo 2010, pet. ref'd) (medical examiner, in support of his opinions, disclosed to jury some testimonial statements contained in autopsy report; because testimonial statements supported expert's opinions only if they were deemed true, their disclosure violated Confrontation Clause). Refer to notes 320-328 *supra* and accompanying text. For a discussion of the Confrontation Clause and its application to the admissibility of hearsay statements, refer to *Article VIII: Hearsay, infra* p. 787.

418. Refer to notes 301-319 *supra* and accompanying text. Some courts and commentators have taken a dim view of asking a jury to evaluate otherwise inadmissible evidence for the sole purpose of understanding the basis for an expert's opinion. *See* **Gong v. Hirsch**, 913 F.2d 1269, 1273 n.4 (7th Cir. 1990); Edward J. Imwinkelried, *The 'Bases' of Expert Witness Testimony: The Syllogistic Structure of Scientific Testimony*, 67 N.C. L. REV. 1, 12 (1988).

419. *See* 3 LOUISELL & MUELLER, *supra* note 27, §399, at 703 (stating that "[i]t is a faith in the skill of trial counsel, the power of the process of cross-examination, and the skepticism, common sense, and critical faculties of judges and juries, which justify the conclusion that the exposure of weakness or fatal deficiencies in expert testimony may be left to the calling party's opponent").

420. In **Smith v. Ford Motor Co.**, the appellate court reversed a judgment for the plaintiff in a products-liability action because the plaintiff had materially misled the defendant about the subject matter of his expert's medical testimony. 626 F.2d 784, 800 (10th Cir. 1980). The court noted that the plaintiff had indicated in his pretrial submission that his physician would testify about the medical treatment he had provided and the plaintiff's prognosis but had not mentioned testimony about causation. *Id.* at 797-98. The appellate court emphasized the importance of pretrial discovery in preparing for expert testimony under Federal Rules 703 and 705 as a means for adequate cross-examination at trial. **Smith**, 626 F.2d at 793-94. Because the defendant could not conduct effective discovery due to plaintiff's failure to disclose, the defense was prejudiced in its presentation of its case. *Id.* at 798-99.

421. The Advisory Committee's note to Federal Rule 705 states the following:

If the objection is made that leaving it to the cross-examiner to bring out the supporting data is essentially unfair, the answer is that he is under no compulsion to bring out any facts or data except those unfavorable to the opinion. The answer assumes that the cross-examiner has the advance knowledge which is essential for effective cross-examination. This advance knowledge has been afforded, though imperfectly, by the traditional foundation requirement. Rule 26(b)(4) of the Rules of Civil Procedure, as revised, provides for substantial discovery in this area, obviating in large measure the obstacles which have been raised in some instances to discovery of findings, underlying data, and even the identity of the experts.

FED. R. EVID. 705 advisory committee's note; *see also* 3 WEINSTEIN & BERGER, *supra* note 15, ¶705[01], at 705-10 to 705-11 (the need to prepare for effective cross-examination is "compelling" when expert testimony is involved; failure to abide by discovery provisions on expert testimony may lead to the exclusion of an expert's testimony).

422. *See* TEX. R. CIV. P. 192.3(e); *see, e.g.*, *Tinkle v. Henderson*, 777 S.W.2d 537, 539 (Tex. App.—Tyler 1989, writ denied) (harmful error to admit deposition testimony from two expert witnesses not named on expert-witness list); *Williams v. Union Carbide Corp.*, 734 S.W.2d 699, 700-01 (Tex. App.—Houston [1st Dist.] 1987, writ ref'd n.r.e.) (trial court should have disallowed expert's testimony for failure to abide by former TEX. R. CIV. P. 166b(6), now TEX. R. CIV. P. 193.5, because defendant had not shown "good cause").

for an opportunity to discover the basis for the expert's opinion during a voir dire examination of the witness outside the presence of the jury.[423]

On the other hand, the cross-examiner cannot use Rule 705 to introduce otherwise inadmissible facts and data through an expert who did not know of or rely on the data in forming his opinion.[424] However, if the expert was aware of certain information but chose not to rely on it, the cross-examiner can ask why the expert did not take that data into account in forming his opinion.[425]

A party may also submit an expert opinion through affidavits in a summary-judgment motion under Texas Rule of Civil Procedure 166a.[426] Because Rule 705 does not require disclosure of the specific facts underlying the expert's opinion, an affidavit submitted under Rule 166a should state a factual basis for the expert opinion (e.g., personal knowledge, discussion with other experts, review of reports), but it does not need to outline all of the factual details and reasoning that led to the opinion.[427]

The relative simplicity of the standards for the admission of opinion evidence, once the trial judge has determined that it has a reliable basis, further illustrates the Rules' policy of trusting jurors' abilities. Because opposing counsel can ask about the bases for the opinion on cross-examination if they are not disclosed on direct examination, the danger of misleading the jury is substantially reduced. Moreover, the jury can evaluate the expert's trustworthiness based on other indicia of credibility, such as creden-

---

423. Refer to notes 389-391 *supra* and accompanying text.

424. *See* ***Ramirez v. State***, 815 S.W.2d 636, 651 (Tex. Crim. App. 1991) (under Rule 705, it is improper to disclose the results of studies through leading questions when those studies have not been established as forming the basis for the expert's opinion); *see, e.g.*, ***United Serv. Auto. Ass'n v. Gordon***, 103 S.W.3d 436, 441-42 (Tex. App.—San Antonio 2002, no pet.) (error, but harmless, to admit report written by another person under Rule 705 when testifying expert stated that he did not rely on report in forming his opinion and his opinion was contrary to that expressed in otherwise inadmissible report); *see also* ***Bryan v. John Bean Div. of FMC Corp.***, 566 F.2d 541, 545-46 (5th Cir. 1978) (trial court should have excluded evidence not relied on by the expert because it lacked independent trustworthiness).

425. *See* ***Wheeler v. State***, 67 S.W.3d 879, 884-85 (Tex. Crim. App. 2002); *see also* ***Moranza v. State***, 913 S.W.2d 718, 727-28 (Tex. App.—Waco 1995, pet. ref'd) (State could use hearsay statements in full psychiatric report to impeach defense expert when State was challenging basis for expert's conclusion that defendant was insane at time of offense, which had been based on abbreviated version of the report).

426. *See* Tex. R. Civ. P. 166a(f) ("Supporting and opposing affidavits shall be made on personal knowledge, shall set forth such facts as would be admissible in evidence, and shall show affirmatively that the affiant is competent to testify to the matters stated therein."); ***Giao v. Smith & Lamm, P.C.***, 714 S.W.2d 144, 148 (Tex. App.—Houston [1st Dist.] 1986, no writ) (opinion of interested expert witness is competent summary-judgment proof).

427. *See, e.g.*, ***Denny's, Inc. v. Rainbo Baking Co.***, 776 S.W.2d 246, 248-49 (Tex. App.—Houston [1st Dist.] 1989, writ denied) (in personal-injury suit brought by restaurant patron who ingested lead-coated wire allegedly contained in hamburger bun, expert-witness affidavit was insufficient basis for granting summary judgment for third-party-defendant bakery; affidavit did not show that expert had ever been in third-party defendant's plant or had any personal knowledge of how plant was run or the purity of ingredients used, and it did not prove as a matter of law that wire did not get into hamburger bun at bakery's plant); ***Marek v. Tomoco Equip. Co.***, 738 S.W.2d 710, 714 (Tex. App.—Houston [14th Dist.] 1987, no writ) (unnecessary for nonexpert affiant to state how he gained knowledge, as long as he asserts that the statements are based on personal knowledge); *cf.* ***Bulthuis v. Rexall Corp.***, 789 F.2d 1315, 1318 (9th Cir. 1985) (in suit against drug manufacturer, trial court erred in excluding expert-witness affidavits offered by plaintiff to oppose defendant's summary-judgment motion because affidavits were sufficient to raise an issue of fact; in affidavits, doctors stated that they observed changes in plaintiff's vaginal tissues, which they believed to be common in women exposed to the drug in utero).

tials, demeanor, apparent honesty, and ability to withstand cross-examination.[428] However, the shift under Rule 705 from the mandatory use of hypothetical questions[429] to reliance on effective cross-examination magnifies the importance of extensive discovery and careful trial preparation so that opposing counsel can adequately test the expert's credibility during cross-examination.[430] This focus on trial preparation is especially critical when, as permitted under Rule 703, the expert's opinion is based on inadmissible and arguably unreliable data.[431]

RULE 706

AUDIT IN CIVIL CASES

Notwithstanding any other evidence rule, the court must admit an auditor's verified report prepared under Rule of Civil Procedure 172 and offered by a party. If a party files exceptions to the report, a party may offer evidence supporting the exceptions to contradict the report.

COMMENTARY ON RULE 706

Rule 706 applies only to civil proceedings. It was not among the original rules promulgated by the Texas Supreme Court in 1983, and it does not have any federal analogue. The Texas Supreme Court adopted the rule in 1987[432] as the result of an amendment to Rule 172 of the Texas Rules of Civil Procedure.[433] Traditionally, Rule 172 permitted a trial judge to appoint an independent auditor to prepare and submit a report settling accounts between parties.[434] The 1987 amendments did not purport to change the earlier law but merely placed evidentiary issues in the Rules of Evidence and kept the procedural aspects of verified auditor accounts in the Rules of Civil Procedure.[435] Rule 172 authorizes the trial court to appoint an auditor "[w]hen an investigation of accounts or examination of vouchers appears necessary for the purpose of justice between the parties to any suit ...."[436] Appointing an auditor is within the

---

428. *See **Bormaster v. Henderson***, 624 S.W.2d 655, 659 (Tex. App.—Houston [14th Dist.] 1981, no writ) (even uncontroverted expert-opinion testimony is generally not binding on the trier of fact).

429. Refer to notes 368-372 *supra* and accompanying text.

430. *See **Smith v. Ford Motor Co.***, 626 F.2d 784, 793 (10th Cir. 1980) (Federal Rule 705 places the burden of extensive pretrial discovery on opposing counsel as cross-examiner); Pratt, *supra* note 5, at 331 (much reliance is placed on the attorney to effectively test evidence through cross-examination).

431. *See **Smith***, 626 F.2d at 793-94; *see, e.g.*, ***United States v. Williams***, 447 F.2d 1285, 1291-92 (5th Cir. 1971) (trial court did not err in admitting expert's testimony because his opinion was based on the type of information customarily relied on by such experts and was not challenged on cross-examination); ***Lewis v. Southmore Sav. Ass'n***, 480 S.W.2d 180, 187 (Tex. 1972) (trial court properly admitted expert testimony based on hearsay because publications containing hearsay were easily obtainable through discovery); *see also* Pratt, *supra* note 5, at 331 (acknowledging the importance of the adversarial process in relation to the opinion rules of Article VII).

432. *Order Adopting and Amending Texas Rules of Civil Evidence*, 733-734 S.W.2d (Tex. Cases) XCVII (1987, amended 1998) (amendments to rule effective Jan. 1, 1998).

433. *Order Adopting and Amending Texas Rules of Civil Procedure*, 733-734 S.W.2d (Tex. Cases) LVI (1987).

434. 2 GOODE ET AL., *supra* note 7, §706.1, at 81.

435. *Id.*

436. TEX. R. CIV. P. 172.

trial judge's discretion,[437] but if the auditor files a verified report and a party offers it into evidence, that report is admissible "[n]otwithstanding any other evidence rule."[438]

Either side may contest the auditor's findings if an exception to the report has been filed within 30 days after the auditor submitted the report.[439] This procedure changes earlier law; under the former Rule 172, parties could file exceptions any time before trial.[440] The filing of exceptions by either or both of the parties does not make the verified report of the auditor inadmissible; it merely permits either side to introduce evidence in opposition to that report.[441] The fact-finder must then weigh the conflicting evidence. Under earlier law, if neither side contested the accuracy of the report by filing a pretrial exception, the report's findings were conclusive for the parties in the specific lawsuit.[442] The language of Rule 706 does not indicate any change in that result.[443]

FEDERAL RULE 706

Federal Rule 706 authorizes the trial court to appoint independent experts and outlines the procedures for appointing and compensating them.[444] Texas has not incorporated any corresponding rule for independent experts. While trial judges have traditionally had the inherent power to call lay or expert witnesses,[445] Texas law has always been structured so that the trial judge acts as a neutral referee between the litigants and not as a participant in the lawsuit.[446] The drafting committees for the original Civil and Criminal Rules chose not to include any provision for court-appointed experts.[447] A draft of a proposed rule permitting the trial judge to appoint an independent expert was

---

437. *See Padon v. Padon*, 670 S.W.2d 354, 360 (Tex. App.—San Antonio 1984, no writ) (trial court's decision about whether to appoint auditor is reversible only for gross abuse of discretion).

438. TEX. R. EVID. 706. Under Texas Rule of Civil Procedure 172, the auditor must swear that "he has carefully examined the state of the account between the parties, and that his report contains a true statement thereof, so far as the same has come within his knowledge."

439. *See* TEX. R. CIV. P. 172 ("Exceptions to such report or of any item thereof must be filed within 30 days of the filing of such report.").

440. *See Daniels v. U.S. Rubber Co.*, 199 S.W.2d 533, 534 (Tex. Civ. App.—Waco 1946, writ ref'd n.r.e.).

441. *See* TEX. R. EVID. 706.

442. *See Villiers v. Republic Fin. Servs., Inc.*, 602 S.W.2d 566, 570 (Tex. Civ. App.—Texarkana 1980, writ ref'd n.r.e.).

443. *See* 2 GOODE ET AL., *supra* note 7, §706.1, at 82.

444. *See* FED. R. EVID. 706.

445. *See* 3 LOUISELL & MUELLER, *supra* note 27, §405, at 726 (before Federal Rule 706, judicial authority indicated that courts had "inherent authority to appoint expert witnesses"); 2 RAY, *supra* note 32, §1405, at 47 (this inherent power is widely recognized and declared by statute in many states); 3 WEINSTEIN & BERGER, *supra* note 15, ¶706[01], at 706-8 (judge's right to appoint expert witnesses as part of the power to call witnesses under Federal Rule 614 "is an inherent power which he would have even in the absence of [Federal] Rule 706"); Judge Harvey Brown, *Procedural Issues Under* Daubert, 36 HOUS. L. REV. 1133, 1168 (1999) (while Texas does not have a counterpoint to FED. R. EVID. 706, appointment of an independent expert "is probably part of a court's inherent authority"). *See generally* R.E. Barber, Annotation, *Trial Court's Appointment, in Civil Case, of Expert Witness*, 95 A.L.R.2d 390, 392-94 (1964) (discussing how various jurisdictions view a judge's inherent power to call witnesses).

446. *See Morrison v. State*, 845 S.W.2d 882, 885 & n.10 (Tex. Crim. App. 1992) (Texas is "second to none" in its disapproval of the practice of trial judges examining witnesses and is virtually alone in rejecting adoption of Federal Rule of Evidence 614, which authorizes trial judges to call and interrogate witnesses).

447. *See* Texas Senate Interim Study on Rules of Evidence, Pt. IV, at 289 (Mar. 19-20, 1982) [hereinafter Interim Study IV]. A Texas rule on court-appointed experts was considered by the Liaison Committee when the Civil Rules

submitted during the 1998 unification process, but the proposed rule was roundly rejected by the Administration of the Rules of Evidence Committee and was not adopted by the supreme court or court of criminal appeals.

Many commentators have long favored the use of independent expert witnesses, particularly in emerging scientific fields.[448] Nonetheless, there are serious potential drawbacks associated with the use of independent experts. The litigants themselves frequently oppose having the court appoint experts because it takes control of the lawsuit away from the parties and gives it to the trial judge. Second, such experts may "acquire an aura of infallibility to which they are not entitled"[449] because they may not be truly neutral and unbiased.[450] Third, as assistants to the judge, independent experts may be perceived as weakening the adversarial system of justice.[451]

While the Texas Rules of Evidence do not provide for the judicial appointment of independent experts, Texas statutes authorize the trial judge to appoint experts in specific instances. These include court appointment of an expert to examine a criminal defendant, write a report, and testify to the defendant's sanity or competency to stand trial;[452] court appointment of an expert to examine a person whose civil commitment is sought;[453] and court appointment of surveyors,[454] auditors,[455] and appraisers[456] in various situations. Thus, while the Rules do not contain a general authorization for trial courts to appoint experts, earlier laws providing for court-appointed experts in specific instances are carried forward.[457]

POSTSCRIPT ON EXPERT-WITNESS PRIVILEGES

Some jurisdictions have allowed for certain expert-witness privileges that affect the adverse party's ability to compel the testimony of the proponent's expert. First, some

---

were being drafted, but it was not among the final rules proposed to the Texas Supreme Court. *See* Interim Study IV, *supra*, at 88-100 (Feb. 26-27, 1982).

448. *See* 3 LOUISELL & MUELLER, *supra* note 27, §404, at 720 (three rationales support the appointment of independent experts: (1) obtaining information needed for the decision, (2) assisting in resolving conflicts in the testimony of party-sponsored experts on complex subjects, and (3) minimizing the temptation of litigants and their experts to exaggerate their position); 2 RAY, *supra* note 32, §1405, at 46 ("Under our adversary system experts have come to be regarded as witnesses of the party and in effect have now assumed the role of expert advocates. Today shocking exhibitions of partisanship are common in personal injury suits, will contests and criminal prosecutions."); 3 WEINSTEIN & BERGER, *supra* note 15, ¶706[01], at 706-10 (legal writers and revisers have long favored implementing and expanding a trial judge's power to call experts).

449. FED. R. EVID. 706 advisory committee's note.

450. *See* 3 LOUISELL & MUELLER, *supra* note 27, §404, at 721.

451. The Ninth Circuit has clarified that although Rule 706 experts may act as advisers on complex, scientific, or technical matters, they should not act in an adjudicative capacity, and that all recommendations made by the expert are subject to review by the district court. *See **Armstrong v. Brown**, 768 F.3d 975, 987 (9th Cir. 2014).

452. TEX. CODE CRIM. PROC. arts. 46B.021(a), 46C.101(a).

453. *See* TEX. HEALTH & SAFETY CODE §574.009(b).

454. TEX. R. CIV. P. 796.

455. TEX. R. CIV. P. 172. Refer to notes 436-438 *supra* and accompanying text.

456. TEX. BUS. ORGS. CODE §10.361(e)(2) (appointment of appraiser when dissenting shareholders seek valuation of their shares in a corporation); TEX. EST. CODE §309.001 (appointment of appraiser for property of estate).

457. *See* 2 GOODE ET AL., *supra* note 7, §702.7, at 41.

courts have held that the party who retained an expert can claim work-product protection and can object to its witness being called to testify by its opponent.[458] Texas has declined to recognize any privilege in this situation,[459] and one Texas court noted that such a privilege would amount to a "judicial smothering of the search for truth" that conceivably could allow one party to monopolize all the qualified experts in a particular community.[460]

Second, courts in other jurisdictions have allowed an expert to refuse to testify when subpoenaed.[461] In *Kaufman v. Edelstein*, the Second Circuit acknowledged the potential for abuse of the subpoena power but refused to grant experts a privilege against testifying.[462] The fact that an expert has no privilege for refusing to testify does not mean that the trial court must always grant a motion to compel testimony when the expert or the opposing party objects to such a subpoena. In deciding whether to compel

---

458. *See Gugliano v. Levi*, 262 N.Y.S.2d 372, 374 (N.Y. App. Div. 1965) (party who calls expert retained by its opponent indirectly contravenes prohibition against use of adversary's attorney work product). *But see Carrasquillo v. Rothschild*, 443 N.Y.S.2d 113, 115 (N.Y. Sup. Ct. 1981) (retained expert can testify for opposing party if opposing party is willing to pay appropriate fees; "[t]he testimony of a witness, particularly an expert, should be totally unaffected by the question of which party to the litigation retains that expert"). *See generally* Herbert B. Chermside, Jr., Annotation, *Right in Eminent Domain Proceeding to Call as Witness Expert Engaged but Not Called as Witness by Opposing Party*, 71 A.L.R.3d 1119, 1123-49 (1976) (discussing factors and opinions to be balanced in deciding whether the opposing party is allowed to call the expert witness on direct examination or whether that action violates the attorney-client privilege or the work-product doctrine).

459. *See Boyles v. Hous. Lighting & Power Co.*, 464 S.W.2d 359, 361 (Tex. 1971); *State v. Biggers*, 360 S.W.2d 516, 517 (Tex. 1962); *see also State v. Ashworth*, 484 S.W.2d 565, 566-67 (Tex. 1972) (holding in *Boyles* and *Biggers* is narrow; applied to eminent-domain proceedings).

460. *City of Hous. v. Autrey*, 351 S.W.2d 948, 949 (Tex. Civ. App.—Waco 1961, writ ref'd n.r.e.). *See generally* Stephen D. Easton, *"Red Rover, Red Rover, Send that Expert Right Over": Clearing the Way for Parties to Introduce the Testimony of Their Opponents' Expert Witnesses*, 55 SMU L. Rev. 1427 (2002) (discussing the use of an opposing party's expert witnesses).

461. *See Evans v. Otis Elevator Co.*, 168 A.2d 573, 580 (Pa. 1961) (expert who has already been called to testify by one party has the right to refuse to testify when called for direct examination by adverse party); *Sousa v. Chaset*, 519 A.2d 1132, 1136 (R.I. 1987) ("An expert who has not been engaged, but only subpoenaed, cannot be compelled to give opinion testimony against his or her will."), *overruled on other grounds*, *Cruz v. DaimlerChrysler Motors Corp.*, 66 A.3d 446 (R.I. 2013); *Carney-Hayes v. Nw. Wis. Home Care, Inc.*, 699 N.W.2d 524, 535-36 (Wis. 2005) ("[U]nless the circumstances are exceptional, a medical witness who is unwilling to testify as an expert should not be required to give her opinion on the standard of care applicable to another person or be asked to second-guess another person's performance."); *see, e.g.*, *People ex rel. Kraushaar Bros. & Co. v. Thorpe*, 72 N.E.2d 165, 165 (N.Y. 1947) (witness "had a right to refuse to answer any question connected with his experience and judgment as a real estate expert and not as an ordinary lay witness"). The expert is at least entitled to reasonable compensation when forced to disclose his opinions. *See Carney-Hayes*, 699 N.W.2d at 534 ("To compel an expert to testify involuntarily, a party must … present a plan of reasonable compensation."); *cf.* Fed. R. Civ. P. 26(b)(4)(E) (party seeking discovery must pay expert reasonable fee for time spent in responding to discovery under Rule 26(b)(4)(A) or (b)(4)(D) and must pay opposing party "fair portion of the fees and expenses it reasonably incurred in obtaining the expert's facts and opinions"). For a complete discussion on subpoenaing a witness to testify, see *O'Connor's Texas Rules * Civil Trials* (2017), "Subpoenas," ch. 1-L, p. 105.

462. *See Kaufman v. Edelstein*, 539 F.2d 811, 819-21 (2d Cir. 1976) (government could subpoena expert witnesses against their will to explain their prior services and advice to clients but not to conduct examinations or studies or to compile new material; "[t]o clothe all such expert testimony with privilege solely on the basis that the expert 'owns' his knowledge free of any testimonial easement would be to seal off too much evidence important to the just determination of disputes").

expert testimony from an expert after the expert or opposing party objects to the subpoena, the trial court should consider various factors, such as

> the degree to which the expert is being called because of his knowledge of facts relevant to the case rather than in order to give opinion testimony; the difference between testifying to a previously formed or expressed opinion and forming a new one; the possibility that, for other reasons, the witness is a unique expert; the extent to which the calling party is able to show the unlikelihood that any comparable witness will willingly testify; [and] the degree to which the witness is able to show that he has been oppressed by having continually to testify ....[463]

The refusal of Texas courts to recognize a privilege for the expert to decline to testify when called by a party is consistent with Texas Rules 701 through 705, which offer no express support for such a privilege. Further, Rule 501 limits the privileges that Texas courts may recognize under the Texas Rules of Evidence.[464]

CONCLUSION

Article VII demonstrates a policy more favorable to the admission of opinion evidence than had been the prevailing practice under common law. Under the Rules, debate over whether a lay opinion is sufficiently specific has waned because courts now permit any witness to use the opinion form of testimony whenever it is helpful to the jury's understanding. In addition, the distinction between lay and expert witnesses is less important. In effect, the only concern is whether the witness has the background, knowledge, and experience that make it helpful for the jury to hear his opinion.

The use of complicated, awkward hypothetical questions is no longer necessary and has fortunately declined. More and more, specialized witnesses serve as fact-finders working with data not in evidence, and they aid the jury by providing their own skilled evaluations of those outside facts. To prevent the admission of opinion testimony that has no theoretically or factually reliable basis, trial courts serve as evidentiary "gatekeepers." A trial court's preliminary assessment of the theoretical and methodological soundness of proffered expertise helps keep "junk science" and unsupported speculation out of the judicial system. Article VII's increased permissiveness in the admission of opinion evidence functions well only if all lawyers involved engage in extensive discovery and, forewarned and prepared by that discovery, use cross-examination effectively so that the jury can determine the trustworthiness of the various opinions and expert explanations found in most lawsuits.

---

463. *Id.* at 822; *see, e.g.*, **Zander v. Craig Hosp.**, No. 09-CV-02121-REB-BNB (D. Colo. 2010) (order; 9-22-10) (treating physician has no privilege to refuse to testify as fact witness, even when examination by adverse party will implicate his expertise as doctor, but court should balance **Kaufman** factors); *see also* **Young v. United States**, 181 F.R.D. 344, 348 (W.D. Tex. 1997) (Federal Rule of Civil Procedure 45(c), now Rule 45(d), "adequately protects government witnesses from being called to testify as expert witnesses against their will"; identifying factors that courts should consider in deciding whether to quash a subpoena for an unretained expert, based on **Kaufman**).

464. *See* TEX. R. EVID. 501. Refer to *Article V: Privileges*, *supra* p. 378.

RULE 706

ARTICLE VIII: HEARSAY

INTRODUCTION

The hearsay provisions of the Texas Rules of Evidence, although modeled after the Federal Rules of Evidence, depart from the Federal Rules in several respects. Some of these variations were designed to preserve aspects of earlier Texas law that the Texas drafters preferred over corresponding federal provisions. In other places, however, Texas modified the federal rules simply to improve on both the federal approach and earlier Texas law. The drafters of the Texas hearsay provisions, responding to criticism from scholars and practitioners, did not hesitate to change the law in an effort to improve it.

Before examining the provisions in detail, it is useful to review the basic purposes and concepts that underlie the hearsay rule and its exceptions. All hearsay doctrines, including those in the Federal Rules, the Texas common law, and the Texas Rules, derive from a single set of essential values and objectives related to the trustworthiness of hearsay statements. To thoroughly understand any version of the hearsay rule, practitioners must comprehend these fundamentals.

The Hearsay Problem & the Hearsay Rule

A hearsay problem arises when a person's belief in a matter is communicated to the trier of fact by a method other than that person's present sworn testimony, which must be subject to cross-examination.[1] This type of communication is inherently susceptible to certain defects, which fall into four categories traditionally called the "hearsay dangers."[2] First, a person's perception of another's belief may be incorrect because it results from a false impression of objective reality—a defect in perception—that is a common product of our imperfect physical and psychological faculties.[3] Second, even a true perception may later yield a false belief because of the tricks of human memory: the unconscious scrambling and regrouping of elements drawn from disparate experiences and fantasies.[4] Third, even an accurate account of a person's belief may be misleading, when used as evidence by another, if it is communicated imperfectly.[5] However carefully focused, our instruments of verbal and nonverbal communication may be clouded by ambiguity and misinterpretation. Fourth, a valid memory may be falsified intentionally.[6]

---

1. *See* Judson F. Falknor, *Silence as Hearsay*, 89 U. PA. L. REV. 192, 192 (1940); Edmund M. Morgan, *Hearsay Dangers and the Application of the Hearsay Concept*, 62 HARV. L. REV. 177, 177 (1948); John S. Strahorn, Jr., *A Reconsideration of the Hearsay Rule and Admissions*, 85 U. PA. L. REV. 484, 486 (1937); Laurence H. Tribe, *Triangulating Hearsay*, 87 HARV. L. REV. 957, 958 (1974); Jack B. Weinstein, *Probative Force of Hearsay*, 46 IOWA L. REV. 331, 331 (1961); Olin G. Wellborn III, *The Definition of Hearsay in the Federal Rules of Evidence*, 61 TEX. L. REV. 49, 52 (1982).

2. *See, e.g.*, Morgan, *supra* note 1, at 185-88; Tribe, *supra* note 1, at 958-61; Wellborn, *supra* note 1, at 52-53.

3. Wellborn, *supra* note 1, at 53.

4. *Id.*

5. *Id.*

6. *Id.*

The hearsay dangers—faulty perception, faulty memory, accidental miscommunication,[7] and insincerity—can be minimized or exposed to the trier of fact by controlling the use of beliefs as evidence. The modern[8] Anglo-American trial at common law represents an attempt to provide controlled conditions designed to minimize or expose defects in belief evidence. Most commonly noted in this regard are the oath, the physical presence of the witness, and cross-examination.[9] Other protections can be added to these, such as the sequestering of witnesses[10] and limitations on the use of leading questions[11] in eliciting testimony.[12]

With certain qualifications and exceptions, the hearsay doctrine excludes from the trier of fact's consideration all belief evidence not presented under these controlled conditions. One important qualification deals with out-of-court statements offered against the party who made them. Although such statements have the appearance of hearsay, the hearsay rule does not apply to them.[13] Parties cannot claim that their own remarks are untrustworthy because they were not made under ideal testimonial conditions.

The numerous exceptions to the hearsay rule are based on the idea that hearsay statements can have independent, circumstantial guarantees of trustworthiness. The general idea is that the circumstances of some hearsay statements, occasionally including a statement's contents, may reduce the likelihood of one or more of the four hearsay defects. These circumstantial guarantees of trustworthiness are considered adequate substitutes for the ideal testimonial conditions of oath, presence at trial, and cross-examination.[14] For many of the exceptions, the circumstantial factors make the state-

---

7.   Authorities have used a number of terms to describe this danger. *See, e.g.*, McCORMICK'S HANDBOOK OF THE LAW OF EVIDENCE §245, at 581 (Edward W. Cleary et al. eds., 2d ed. 1972) [hereinafter McCORMICK'S HANDBOOK II] ("narration"); Morgan, *supra* note 1, at 185 ("misuse of language"); Strahorn, *supra* note 1, at 485 ("narration"); Tribe, *supra* note 1, at 959 ("ambiguity"). None of these terms is sufficiently comprehensive. *See* Wellborn, *supra* note 1, at 53 n.24, 62-63.

8.   The approach of early forms of trial in England was radically different. Many modern restrictions on the sources of information used by the jury (or its ancestor, the Norman Inquest), including the hearsay rule, were not established until the 18th century. *See* EDMUND M. MORGAN, SOME PROBLEMS OF PROOF UNDER THE ANGLO-AMERICAN SYSTEM OF LITIGATION 115-16 (1956).

9.   *See California v. Green*, 399 U.S. 149, 158 (1970); FED. R. EVID. art. VIII advisory committee's introductory note; McCORMICK'S HANDBOOK II, *supra* note 7, §245, at 581; 1A ROY R. RAY, TEXAS PRACTICE: TEXAS LAW OF EVIDENCE CIVIL AND CRIMINAL §782, at 5 (3d ed. 1980).

10.   *See* FED. R. EVID. 615; TEX. R. EVID. 614. Refer to *Article VI: Witnesses, supra* p. 667.

11.   *See* FED. R. EVID. 611(c); TEX. R. EVID. 611(c). Refer to *Article VI: Witnesses, supra* p. 641.

12.   *See* Wellborn, *supra* note 1, at 53 & n.28.

13.   *See* TEX. R. EVID. 801(e)(2). Refer to notes 344-445 *infra* and accompanying text.

14.   According to John Wigmore, Thomas Starkie was the first writer to clearly state the philosophy of the hearsay exceptions. 5 JOHN H. WIGMORE, EVIDENCE IN TRIALS AT COMMON LAW §1420, at 252 n.1 (Chadbourn rev. 1974); *see* THOMAS STARKIE, A PRACTICAL TREATISE OF THE LAW OF EVIDENCE 44-65 (8th Am. ed. Philadelphia 1860). Wigmore authoritatively elaborated the philosophy of circumstantial guarantees of trustworthiness. *See* 5 WIGMORE, *supra*, §§1420-1423, at 251-55. But some later writers have remained skeptical. *See, e.g.*, MODEL CODE OF EVID. ch. VI introductory note, at 223 (1942) (hearsay doctrine is a conglomeration of inconsistencies as developed by conflicting theories); James H. Chadbourn, *Bentham and the Hearsay Rule—A Benthamic View of Rule 63(4)(c) of the*

ment admissible even if the declarant is available to testify in person.[15] These exceptions demonstrate the relative equality of the hearsay statement and testimony, perhaps even showing a preference for hearsay.[16] Other exceptions, however, reveal a clear preference for testimony by admitting the hearsay only if the declarant is unavailable to testify. The unavailability requirement indicates that, although the particular circumstantial guarantees in these exceptions are regarded as inferior to the testimonial conditions, receiving the declarant's evidence in hearsay form is better than losing it completely.[17]

Criticism of the common-law hearsay doctrine has mostly been directed at the methods developed by courts to implement the system rather than at the system's fundamental purposes or values. The perennial complaint has been that the system is too formal[18] and that the numerous exceptions should be abandoned in favor of a more informal approach.[19] The critics' proposals for reform have varied considerably, with some proposing to replace the exclusionary rule with a flexible standard in all instances,[20] some proposing to admit all hearsay of unavailable declarants,[21] and some proposing to admit all hearsay of available declarants.[22]

History of the Federal & Texas Responses to the Hearsay Rule

A. Federal Response

When the Advisory Committee on the Federal Rules addressed the hearsay problem, it responded to this criticism by rejecting the more radical proposals—those that would wholly or substantially abolish the exclusionary rule—and choosing instead a middle ground between revolution and the status quo.[23] In its 1969 draft, the commit-

---

Uniform Rules of Evidence, 75 HARV. L. REV. 932, 944-45 (1962) (drafters of the code found the guarantee of trustworthiness, supposedly an adequate substitute for cross-examination in several hearsay exceptions, to be "imperceptible").

15. *See* TEX. R. EVID. 803. Refer to notes 463-862 *infra* and accompanying text.

16. Practitioners often prefer to introduce the out-of-court statement through a neutral, third-party listener rather than through the speaker himself, who may have some bias or interest in the lawsuit by the time of trial.

17. *See* TEX. R. EVID. 804. Refer to notes 863-957 *infra* and accompanying text.

18. *E.g.*, Mason Ladd, *The Hearsay We Admit*, 5 OKLA. L. REV. 271, 286-288 (1952) [hereinafter Ladd, *The Hearsay We Admit*]; Mason Ladd, *The Relationship of the Principles of Exclusionary Rules of Evidence to the Problem of Proof*, 18 MINN. L. REV. 506, 515-16 (1934) [hereinafter Ladd, *The Relationship*]; Charles T. McCormick, *Tomorrow's Law of Evidence*, 24 A.B.A. J. 507, 512 (1938); Morgan, *supra* note 1, at 218-19; Edmund M. Morgan & John M. Maguire, *Looking Backward and Forward at Evidence*, 50 HARV. L. REV. 909, 921-22 (1937); Epaphroditus Peck, *The Rigidity of the Rule Against Hearsay*, 21 YALE L.J. 257, 259 (1912); Talbot Smith, *The Hearsay Rule and the Docket Crisis: The Futile Search for Paradise*, 54 A.B.A. J. 231, 235-37 (1968); Ezra R. Thayer, *Observations on the Law of Evidence*, 13 MICH. L. REV. 355, 360-61 (1915); Tribe, *supra* note 1, at 957, 973-74; Weinstein, *supra* note 1, at 342-46.

19. McCormick, *supra* note 18, at 512, 580-81.

20. *Id.* at 512; Smith, *supra* note 18, at 237; Thayer, *supra* note 18, at 361-63; Weinstein, *supra* note 1, at 353-55.

21. *E.g.*, MODEL CODE OF EVID. R. 503(a) (1942); Chadbourn, *supra* note 14, at 949-50.

22. *E.g.*, UNIF. R. EVID. 803 (1986); Lawrence E. Taylor, *The Case for Secondary Evidence*, CASE & COMMENT, Jan.-Feb. 1976, at 46.

23. *See* FED. R. EVID. art. VIII advisory committee's introductory note.

tee substituted two informal exceptions[24] for the myriad of common-law exceptions. Both were codified "[b]y way of illustration only and not by way of limitation."[25] In the version actually promulgated by the Supreme Court in 1972, however, the common-law system of formal exceptions was retained;[26] informal exceptions merely supplemented the formal exceptions.[27]

Congress's response, when it revised the Court's rules,[28] was even more conservative. The House Committee on the Judiciary proposed to delete the informal exceptions and enact a system structured exactly like that under the common law.[29] The Senate Committee, on the other hand, was more receptive to the Court's proposal.[30] Ultimately, Congress enacted modified informal exceptions.[31] Apart from these "residual exceptions," the structure of the federal hearsay rule does not differ substantially from that of the common-law hearsay doctrine.

B. Texas Response

In Texas, the State Bar Liaison Committee on Rules of Evidence recommended a version of Article VIII that differed only slightly from the Federal Rules.[32] The Committee's draft contained versions of the residual exceptions for civil cases that were similar to those promulgated by the U.S. Supreme Court in 1972 before congressional modification.[33] The Texas Supreme Court, however, eliminated the residual exceptions

---

24. FED. R. EVID. 803(a) (1969 preliminary draft), 46 F.R.D. 161, 345 (1969) ("A statement is not excluded by the hearsay rule if its nature and the special circumstances under which it was made offer assurances of accuracy not likely to be enhanced by calling the declarant as a witness, even though he is available."); FED. R. EVID. 804(a) (1969 preliminary draft), 46 F.R.D. at 377 ("A statement is not excluded by the hearsay rule if its nature and the special circumstances under which it was made offer strong assurances of accuracy and the declarant is unavailable as a witness.").

25. FED. R. EVID. 803(b) (1969 preliminary draft), 46 F.R.D. at 345-50; FED. R. EVID. 804(b) (1969 preliminary draft), 46 F.R.D. at 377-78.

26. FED. R. EVID. 803 (1972 proposed final draft), 56 F.R.D. 183, 300-03 (1973); FED. R. EVID. 804 (1972 proposed final draft), 56 F.R.D. at 320-22.

27. FED. R. EVID. 803(24) (1972 proposed final draft), 56 F.R.D. at 303 ("A statement not specifically covered by any of the foregoing exceptions but having comparable circumstantial guarantees of trustworthiness."); FED. R. EVID. 804(b)(6) (1972 proposed final draft), 56 F.R.D. at 322 (identical to proposed Federal Rule 803(24)).

28. Act of Jan. 2, 1975, Pub. L. No. 93-595, 88 Stat. 1926, *reprinted in* 1974 U.S.C.C.A.N. 2215. The Supreme Court had promulgated its version of the Rules in 1972 pursuant to the Rules Enabling Act of 1934, 28 U.S.C. §2072. The proposed final draft was published in 56 F.R.D. 183 (1972). In its Act of Mar. 30, 1973, Pub. L. No. 93-12, 87 Stat. 9, Congress suspended the effective operation of the Rules in order to review them in detail. The congressional history of the Federal Rules is recounted in 21 CHARLES A. WRIGHT & KENNETH W. GRAHAM, FEDERAL PRACTICE AND PROCEDURE §5006, at 92-109 (1977).

29. *See* H.R. REP. NO. 93-650, at 5-6 (1974), *reprinted in* 1974 U.S.C.C.A.N. 7075, 7079.

30. *See* S. REP. NO. 93-1277, at 18-20 (1974), *reprinted in* 1974 U.S.C.C.A.N. 7051, 7065-66.

31. FED. R. EVID. 807; *see* H.R. CONF. REP. NO. 93-1597, at 11-12 (1974), *reprinted in* 1974 U.S.C.C.A.N. 7098, 7106. These informal exceptions, formerly Federal Rules 803(24) and 804(b)(5), were transferred to Rule 807 in 2000. Refer to note 848 *infra*.

32. *See* 2 STEVEN GOODE ET AL., TEXAS PRACTICE: GUIDE TO THE TEXAS RULES OF EVIDENCE: CIVIL AND CRIMINAL §801.1, at 129 (2d ed. 1993).

33. Compare TEX. R. EVID. 803(25) (1982 Liaison Committee proposal), which read as follows:
    a. In civil proceedings. A statement not specifically covered by any of the foregoing exceptions but having substantial guarantees of trustworthiness.

altogether when it promulgated the Civil Rules. Similarly, when the Criminal Rules were promulgated in 1986, they did not contain the federal residual exception. The unified Rules of Evidence also have no residual exception. As a result, although the Rules of Evidence significantly alter Texas common law for some doctrines, they do not depart from the basic structure of the common-law hearsay rule: a defined rule of exclusion qualified by formal exemptions and exceptions.

The Texas Hearsay Rules

The basic definition of hearsay is set out in Rule 801(a) through (d). Rule 801(e) exempts from the hearsay category certain classes of statements that would, in form, fit the hearsay definition but do not by their nature invoke all the policies behind the hearsay rule. Certain prior statements by witnesses who actually testify at the trial, an opposing party's statements, and (in civil proceedings only) depositions are exempted from the hearsay rule. Rule 802 states the hearsay rule itself—that hearsay, as defined in Rule 801, is ordinarily inadmissible. Rules 803 and 804 contain the numerous exceptions based on circumstantial guarantees of trustworthiness. Rule 805 deals with evidence containing multiple levels of hearsay. Rule 806 authorizes impeachment and rehabilitation of declarants whose hearsay statements have been admitted into evidence under the other rules.

INTERSECTION OF THE HEARSAY RULE & THE CONFRONTATION CLAUSE IN CRIMINAL CASES

In criminal proceedings, the hearsay rule is not the only potential bar to the admission of out-of-court statements. The Confrontation Clause, contained in the Sixth Amendment to the U.S. Constitution, acts as the primary barrier against the admission of out-of-court statements offered against an accused.[34] The historical principle

---

b. In criminal proceedings. A statement not specifically covered by any of the foregoing exceptions but having equivalent circumstantial guarantees of trustworthiness, if the court determines that (A) the statement is offered as evidence of a material fact; (B) the statement is more probative on the point for which it is offered than any other evidence which the proponent can procure through reasonable efforts; and (C) the general purposes of these rules and the interests of justice will best be served by admission of the statement into evidence. However, a statement may not be admitted under this exception unless the proponent of it makes known to the adverse party sufficiently in advance of the trial or hearing to provide the adverse party with a fair opportunity to prepare to meet it, his intention to offer the statement and the particulars of it, including the name and address of declarant.

and Tex. R. Evid. 804(b)(4) (1982 Liaison Committee proposal), which read the same as proposed Civil Rule 803(25) (above), with Fed. R. Evid. 803(24) (1972 proposed final draft), 56 F.R.D. 183, 303 (1973), and Fed. R. Evid. 804(b)(6) (1972 proposed final draft), 56 F.R.D. at 322. The Texas proposals differed from the federal proposals only in using "substantial guarantees" in place of "comparable circumstantial guarantees."

34.   The text of the Confrontation Clause reads: "In all criminal prosecutions, the accused shall enjoy the right … to be confronted with the witnesses against him …." U.S. Const. amend. VI; *see* Tex. Const. art. I, §10. The right of confrontation applies to criminal cases in both federal and state courts. ***Pointer v. Texas***, 380 U.S. 400, 406 (1965); ***Woodall v. State***, 336 S.W.3d 634, 641 (Tex. Crim. App. 2011); *see* U.S. Const. amends. VI, XIV; ***Ohio v. Clark***, ___ U.S. ___, 135 S. Ct. 2173, 2179 (2015). It does not apply to civil proceedings. ***In re S.A.G.***, 403 S.W.3d 907, 912 (Tex. App.—Texarkana 2013, pet. denied); ***Shren-Yee Cheng v. Wang***, 315 S.W.3d 668, 671 (Tex. App.—Dallas 2010, no pet.).

ARTICLE VIII

behind the Confrontation Clause is that a witness's testimony may not be used to convict a person of a crime unless it was given under oath, made in the presence of the accused, and subject to cross-examination.[35]

A. History of Confrontation Clause Jurisprudence: *Ohio v. Roberts*

During the last 50 years, the Supreme Court has very broadly construed the scope of the Confrontation Clause but has simultaneously created numerous ad hoc exceptions to its application. The Court's construction, as first set out in ***Ohio v. Roberts***,[36] resulted in the doctrine that any hearsay statement made by an out-of-court declarant was presumptively excluded by the Confrontation Clause.[37] However, an out-of-court hearsay statement could be admitted against an accused if it were sufficiently reliable.[38] A statement was deemed to be reliable if it fell "'within a firmly rooted hearsay exception'" or "contain[ed] 'particularized guarantees of trustworthiness' such that adversarial testing would be expected to add little, if anything, to the [statement's] reliability."[39] This reliability doctrine, while useful in practice, found no support in the Confrontation Clause itself, which contains no hint of a reliability test and no exceptions.[40] Furthermore, the reliability test "is an amorphous, if not entirely subjec-

---

35. *See **United States v. Diaz***, 637 F.3d 592, 597 (5th Cir. 2011) ("The Confrontation Clause guarantees a defendant's right to cross-examine his accusers. The right is not unlimited. What is required is that defense counsel be 'permitted to expose to the jury the facts from which jurors, as the sole triers of fact and credibility, could appropriately draw inferences relating to the reliability of the witness.'" (quoting ***United States v. Hitt***, 473 F.3d 146, 156 (5th Cir. 2006))); ***Johnson v. State***, 433 S.W.3d 546, 557 (Tex. Crim. App. 2014) ("[A] 'less than optimal' opportunity for cross-examination does not, of itself, violate the Sixth Amendment. Only when the trial court's limitation on cross-examination sweeps so broadly as to render the examination wholly ineffective can it be said that the trial court commits an error of constitutional dimension."); ***Lopez v. State***, 18 S.W.3d 220, 222 (Tex. Crim. App. 2000) ("Confrontation means more than being allowed to confront the witness physically. A primary interest secured by the Confrontation Clause is the right of cross-examination."); *see, e.g.*, ***United States v. Richardson***, 781 F.3d 237, 243-45 (5th Cir. 2015) (because witness was adequately cross-examined in first trial, admission of his testimony did not violate Confrontation Clause even though he had been murdered and was thus unavailable for cross-examination in second trial; "while excessive limitations on the scope of cross-examination may violate a defendant's Sixth Amendment right of confrontation, the Clause requires only an adequate *opportunity* for cross-examination"), *cert. denied*, 136 S. Ct. 159 (2015); ***Holder v. State***, ___ S.W.3d ___ (Tex. App.—Dallas 2016, pet. granted 6-7-17) (No. 05-15-00818-CR; 8-19-16) (testimony of hospitalized witness, given over telephone, preserved "salutary effects" of confrontation; witness had previously appeared in person in courtroom and defendant had opportunity to cross-examine her, telephonic testimony was under oath and included cross-examination, and witness's face was visible on large video screen during testimony). *See generally **Crawford v. Washington***, 541 U.S. 36, 42-50 (2004) (discussing history of Confrontation Clause); Richard D. Friedman & Bridget McCormack, *Dial-In Testimony*, 150 U. PA. L. REV. 1171, 1202-09 (2002) (discussing historical development of the right of confrontation).

36. 448 U.S. 56 (1980).

37. *See id.* at 66.

38. *Id.* As originally set out in ***Roberts***, the Confrontation Clause doctrine also generally barred the admission of hearsay unless the declarant was unavailable to testify at trial. *Id.* The unavailability doctrine continued to apply to former testimony, as in ***Roberts*** itself, but unavailability was not required for (1) coconspirator statements or (2) excited utterances and statements made for medical purposes. *See **White v. Illinois***, 502 U.S. 346, 355-57 (1992) (discussing #2); ***United States v. Inadi***, 475 U.S. 387, 394-95 (1986) (discussing #1). It was unclear to what extent the Confrontation Clause required unavailability of the declarant as a prerequisite to the admission of otherwise reliable out-of-court statements.

39. ***Lilly v. Virginia***, 527 U.S. 116, 124-25 (1999) (plurality op.) (quoting ***Roberts***, 448 U.S. at 66).

40. ***Crawford***, 541 U.S. at 60-62. While the terms of the Confrontation Clause are absolute, the U.S. Supreme Court has recognized two exceptions to the confrontation requirements: dying declarations and forfeiture by inten-

ARTICLE VIII

tive, concept."[41] It was, in fact, a constitutional doctrine that was unpredictable in its reach and relied on ad hoc decisions by individual trial courts for its implementation.[42] As a result, it was subject to considerable scholarly criticism.[43]

B. "Expectations" Test for Testimonial Statements: *Crawford v. Washington*

In *Crawford v. Washington*,[44] the U.S. Supreme Court dramatically changed its interpretation of the Confrontation Clause as it applies to the admissibility of out-of-court statements. It held that a witness's out-of-court testimonial statement to law-enforcement officials is barred by the Confrontation Clause—even if the trial judge found that it had particularized guarantees of trustworthiness—unless the defendant had a prior opportunity to cross-examine the witness and the witness is unavailable to testify at trial.[45] In *Crawford*, the defendant was charged with assault but claimed self-defense.[46] The police interrogated both Crawford and his wife, Sylvia. Sylvia's tape-recorded statement, though generally consistent with Crawford's own statements, undermined his self-defense claim.[47] Sylvia did not testify at trial because her husband invoked the state spousal testimonial privilege.[48] The prosecutor then offered her tape-recorded statement to police as a statement against her penal interest.[49] Crawford objected on Confrontation Clause grounds, but the trial court found the statement trustworthy and admissible under *Ohio v. Roberts*.[50]

After examining the historical origins of the clause, the Supreme Court rejected its *Roberts* framework of "open-ended balancing tests" in favor of a "categorical" rule that requires "unavailability and a prior opportunity for cross-examination" for "core testimonial statements that the Confrontation Clause plainly meant to exclude."[51] The Su-

---

tionally causing a witness to be unavailable to testify. *See Giles v. California*, 554 U.S. 353, 357-59 (2008) ("[T]he Confrontation Clause requires that a defendant have the opportunity to confront the witnesses who give testimony against him, except in cases where an exception to the confrontation right was recognized at the time of the founding."). Refer to notes 132-133, 163-171 *infra* and accompanying text.

41. *Crawford*, 541 U.S. at 63.

42. *See id.* at 62-63 ("The legacy of *Roberts* in other courts vindicates the Framers' wisdom in rejecting a general reliability exception. The framework is so unpredictable that it fails to provide meaningful protection from even core confrontation violations.").

43. *See* Brief Amicus Curiae of Law Professors at 4, *Crawford v. Washington*, 541 U.S. 36 (2004) (No. 02-9410) (Supreme Court had "never offered a clear set of criteria for determining what makes an exception 'firmly rooted'"; framework is "unpredictable and over-complicated").

44. 541 U.S. 36 (2004).

45. *Id.* at 68-69; *see Melendez-Diaz v. Massachusetts*, 557 U.S. 305, 319 n.6 (2009) (witnesses who made testimonial statements must be made available even if they "possessed ... the veracity of Mother Teresa").

46. 541 U.S. at 40.

47. *See id.* at 39-40.

48. *Id.* at 40. Refer to *Article V: Privileges, supra* p. 453.

49. *Crawford*, 541 U.S. at 40.

50. *Id.* The Supreme Court noted that the trial court offered several reasons why Sylvia's tape-recorded statements were reliable: "Sylvia was not shifting blame but rather corroborating her husband's story that he acted in self-defense or 'justified reprisal'; she had direct knowledge as an eyewitness; she was describing recent events; and she was being questioned by a 'neutral' law enforcement officer." *Id.*

51. *Id.* at 63, 67-68. In his concurring opinion, Chief Justice Rehnquist stated that "the Court of course overrules *Ohio v. Roberts*." *Id.* at 75 (Rehnquist, C.J., O'Connor, J., concurring). While the majority did not explicitly

preme Court declined to "spell out a comprehensive definition of 'testimonial,'"[52] but it did not leave lower courts entirely without guidance, stating that "the principal evil at which the Confrontation Clause was directed was the civil-law mode of criminal procedure, and particularly its use of *ex parte* examinations as evidence against the accused."[53]

The Supreme Court then set forth three potential tests for determining whether a particular statement comes within that "core class of 'testimonial' statements":[54]

(1) "'*ex parte* in-court testimony or its functional equivalent—that is, material such as affidavits, custodial examinations, prior testimony that the defendant was unable to cross-examine, or similar pretrial statements that declarants would reasonably expect to be used prosecutorially'";[55]

(2) "'extrajudicial statements … contained in formalized testimonial materials, such as affidavits, depositions, prior testimony, or confessions'";[56] and

(3) "'statements that were made under circumstances which would lead an objective witness reasonably to believe that the statement would be available for use at a later trial.'"[57]

Although the Supreme Court left open the exact contours of a "testimonial" statement, the term "applies at a minimum to prior testimony at a preliminary hearing, before a grand jury, or at a former trial; and to police interrogations."[58] A

---

overrule *Roberts*, it implicitly did so. In *Davis v. Washington*, the Supreme Court was even more emphatic about the demise of *Roberts*, stating, "We overruled *Roberts* in *Crawford* by restoring the unavailability and cross-examination requirements." 547 U.S. 813, 825 n.4 (2006); *see Whorton v. Bockting*, 549 U.S. 406, 413 (2007) ("While this appeal was pending, we issued our opinion in *Crawford*, in which we overruled *Roberts* ...."). To establish a witness's unavailability for purposes of the Confrontation Clause, the prosecution must show a good-faith effort to obtain the witness's presence at trial. *E.g.*, *United States v. Tirado-Tirado*, 563 F.3d 117, 123-24 (5th Cir. 2009) (prosecution did not establish witness's unavailability because it did not make good-faith or reasonable efforts to secure witness's presence at trial; witness did not receive written notice of trial, and attempts to arrange attendance were not made until eight days before trial); *Reed v. State*, 312 S.W.3d 682, 685-86 (Tex. App.—Houston [1st Dist.] 2009, pet. ref'd) (State established witness's unavailability by showing good-faith efforts to secure witness's presence at trial; investigator made repeated efforts to locate witness and "exhausted his contacts among [witness's] family and friends"). A witness who dies after his testimony in an earlier proceeding is "unavailable" under *Crawford*. *Martinez v. State*, 327 S.W.3d 727, 738 (Tex. Crim. App. 2010).

52. *Crawford*, 541 U.S. at 68.
53. *Id.* at 50.
54. *Id.* at 51.
55. *Id.* (quoting Brief for Petitioner).
56. *Crawford*, 541 U.S. at 51-52 (quoting *White v. Illinois*, 502 U.S. 346, 365 (1992) (Thomas & Scalia, JJ., concurring in part and concurring in judgment)).
57. *Crawford*, 541 U.S. at 52 (quoting Brief for National Association of Criminal Defense Lawyers et al. as Amici Curiae).
58. *Crawford*, 541 U.S. at 68; *see Paul v. State*, 419 S.W.3d 446, 455 (Tex. App.—Tyler 2012, pet. ref'd) ("If the person obtaining the statement is a governmental employee or police officer carrying out an investigation or prosecutorial functions, the statement is 'testimonial.'"); *see, e.g.*, *Martinez v. State*, 327 S.W.3d 727, 738 (Tex. Crim. App. 2010) (former testimony of witness who testified at defendant's first trial and died before punishment hearing was admissible under *Crawford* because testimony was given as a witness at another trial or hearing and witness was shown to be unavailable).

practical rule is that if the out-of-court statement was made casually or without anticipation of any potential legal consequences—that is, by a person simply "living his life"—the statement would normally be nontestimonial.[59] Conversely, a

Although the term "testimonial" applies to statements made at a preliminary hearing, courts determine on a case-by-case basis whether the particular hearing allows the defendant an adequate opportunity for cross-examination. *See Kentucky v. Stincer*, 482 U.S. 730, 739 (1987) (Confrontation Clause guarantees opportunity for effective cross-examination but does not guarantee that cross-examination will be as effective as the defendant wishes: "[t]his limitation is consistent with the concept that the right to confrontation is a functional one for the purpose of promoting reliability in a criminal trial"); *see, e.g., Gilley v. State*, 383 S.W.3d 301, 308 (Tex. App.— Fort Worth 2012) (defendant's exclusion from competency hearing for child witness did not interfere with his opportunity to confront the witness through cross-examination; "the questions the trial court asked at the competency examination [generally] did not relate to the crime itself but only to the child's general capacity to recall facts and distinguish between truth and falsehood. Many of these background questions asked in chambers were repeated at trial, the complainant was subject to 'full and complete' cross-examination at trial, and the judge's preliminary ruling at the in-chambers examination was subject to reconsideration in light of the complainant's testimony at trial."), *aff'd*, 418 S.W.3d 114 (Tex. Crim. App. 2014). In *Sanchez v. State*, the court of criminal appeals held that a pretrial hearing under Texas Code of Criminal Procedure article 38.072 does not provide an adequate opportunity for cross-examination to satisfy the Confrontation Clause. 354 S.W.3d 476, 489 (Tex. Crim. App. 2011). Article 38.072 applies to certain sex crimes or assault charges committed against a child younger than 14 or a person with a disability. *See* TEX. CODE CRIM. PROC. art. 38.072, §1. It allows for the admission of out-of-court outcry statements made by the complainant, as long as the statement describes the offense and is offered through the testimony of the first adult (the outcry witness) the complainant told about the offense. *Id.* §2(a); *Sanchez*, 354 S.W.3d at 484; *see also Allen v. State*, 436 S.W.3d 815, 820-22 (Tex. App.—Texarkana 2014, pet. ref'd) (representative of children's advocacy center was not proper outcry witness because complainant's aunt was first person told about assault and statements to aunt were more than general allusion to sexual abuse; error in permitting representative to testify as outcry witness was harmless, however, because complainant testified at trial to same facts as contained in statements to aunt and testimony from representative and because complainant was subject to cross-examination). The Texas Court of Criminal Appeals has clarified that this hearsay exception in the outcry statute is limited to live testimony of the outcry witness; a child's videotaped statement is not admissible under this exception. *Bays v. State*, 396 S.W.3d 580, 591-92 (Tex. Crim. App. 2013). The only relevant question at a hearing under article 38.072 is "whether, based on the time, content, and circumstances of the outcry, the outcry is reliable." *Sanchez*, 354 S.W.3d at 487. Because the hearing provides the defendant an inadequate opportunity to cross-examine an outcry witness's credibility, a defendant's Sixth Amendment right of confrontation is violated when a court admits testimony from an article 38.072 hearing at a trial when the witness is unavailable. *Sanchez*, 354 S.W.3d at 489.

59. *See Crawford*, 541 U.S. at 51 ("An accuser who makes a formal statement to government officers bears testimony in a sense that a person who makes a casual remark to an acquaintance does not."); *Paul*, 419 S.W.3d at 455 (casual remarks to acquaintances are generally not testimonial); *Davis v. State*, 268 S.W.3d 683, 709 (Tex. App.— Fort Worth 2008, pet. ref'd) (same); *see, e.g., Brown v. Epps*, 686 F.3d 281, 288 (5th Cir. 2012) (recorded conversations between drug dealers and confidential informant were nontestimonial; casual exchange setting up drug deal was made to further criminal enterprise, not in anticipation of trial, and participants were unaware conversations were being recorded); *Ramirez v. Dretke*, 398 F.3d 691, 695 & n.3 (5th Cir. 2005) (accomplice's out-of-court statements that defendant had hired him to kill a fireman and his description of the murder to a friend were not "testimonial evidence" under *Crawford*; "[t]here is nothing in *Crawford* to suggest that 'testimonial evidence' includes spontaneous out-of-court statements made outside any arguably judicial or investigatory context"); *United States v. Morgan*, 385 F.3d 196, 209 & n.8 (2d Cir. 2004) (codefendant's letter to boyfriend that indicated both defendants were expecting a suspiciously large payment for their willingness to go to Europe as couriers was nontestimonial and not subject to the rule in *Crawford*); *United States v. Manfre*, 368 F.3d 832, 838 n.1 (8th Cir. 2004) (*Crawford* had no effect on accomplice's "I'm not gonna tell" street-corner statements "made to loved ones or acquaintances [because they] are not the kind of memorialized, judicial-process-created evidence of which *Crawford* speaks"); *Woods v. State*, 152 S.W.3d 105, 112-14 (Tex. Crim. App. 2004) (codefendant's statements to two other people— that "he had a job to do" for defendant that night and that he did not want to do it, that he and defendant had used victim's credit card to make an online purchase of tickets, and that they had attempted to make a third person appear responsible for the murders by buying the tickets in his name and having them sent to his house—did not fall within the categories of testimonial evidence described in *Crawford* because they were casual remarks made spontaneously to acquaintances); *Walker v. State*, 406 S.W.3d 590, 597 (Tex. App.—Eastland 2013, pet. ref'd) (statements made to confidential informant by her common-law husband, who was a potential codefendant, about drugs

"structured" police interview, even in a casual setting such as a hospital, will normally result in a testimonial statement.[60]

---

that police had not discovered were not testimonial; potential codefendant initiated conversation, statements were not formal or official, and circumstances of conversation would not have objectively led him to believe they would be available in later trial); *Orona v. State*, 341 S.W.3d 452, 463-64 (Tex. App.—Fort Worth 2011, pet. ref'd) (coconspirator's statement that he and defendant "'beat on [murder victim]' was a spontaneous, volunteered statement made in front of acquaintances" and was not testimonial); *Mims v. State*, 238 S.W.3d 867, 872 (Tex. App.—Houston [1st Dist.] 2007, no pet.) (murder victim's statements telling witness that he parked his car behind a church and that defendant was chasing him, and asking witness not to tell defendant where victim was were nontestimonial under *Crawford* because victim would not have reasonably expected the statements to be used at a later trial); *Campos v. State*, 186 S.W.3d 93, 97 (Tex. App.—Houston [1st Dist.] 2005, no pet.) (robbery victim's statements asking her neighbor for help and detailing the attack, made immediately after crime, were nontestimonial under *Crawford*); *Flores v. State*, 170 S.W.3d 722, 723-25 (Tex. App.—Amarillo 2005, pet. ref'd) (statements made by mother of dead child to her future sister-in-law—defendant's sister—were nontestimonial under *Crawford* because they were made in casual conversation within hours of child's death; they were not made in consideration of future prosecution); *Wilson v. State*, 151 S.W.3d 694, 698 (Tex. App.—Fort Worth 2004, pet. ref'd) (statements of vehicle owner, defendant's girlfriend, to responding police officer were not testimonial under *Crawford* because when declarant approached officer at the scene of the car wreck, she appeared nervous and visibly upset and was inquiring about her car and its missing occupants).

60. *See, e.g.*, *United States v. Saner*, 313 F. Supp. 2d 896, 901-02 (S.D. Ind. 2004) (statements made in response to questioning at codefendant's home by DOJ prosecutor were testimonial and inadmissible at joint trial when codefendant would not testify; "[t]he most obvious distinguishing factor between the circumstances in *Crawford* and the present circumstances is that [codefendant] was not in custody when he made the statements to the prosecutor. However, this does not appear to be a meaningful distinction under *Crawford*. When the Court concluded that interrogation by law enforcement officers constituted testimonial hearsay, it was careful to note that it was using the term 'interrogation' in the colloquial sense, not in the narrow, legal sense ...."); *People v. Pirwani*, 14 Cal. Rptr. 3d 673, 685 (Cal. Ct. App. 2004) (admission of videotaped statement made by dependent-adult to police and a Justice Department Medi-Cal Fraud and Elder Abuse Bureau investigator two days before she died, in which she disclosed that she had entrusted the management of her finances to defendant, violated *Crawford*); *Wall v. State*, 184 S.W.3d 730, 744-45 (Tex. Crim. App. 2006) (assault victim's statement to police officer at hospital during investigation of crime was testimonial under *Crawford*); *Samarron v. State*, 150 S.W.3d 701, 705-07 (Tex. App.—San Antonio 2004, pet. ref'd) (eyewitness's written statement made to officer at police station recounting murder was testimonial and was inadmissible under *Crawford*; rejecting State's argument that statement was an excited utterance); *Lee v. State*, 143 S.W.3d 565, 569-70 (Tex. App.—Dallas 2004, pet. ref'd) ("the out-of-court statement [that the cash in the purple bag was from the sale of ecstasy], made in response to the questions of the officer during the roadside stop after appellant had been arrested, is ... testimonial"; rejecting State's argument that the setting lacked the formality of the testimonial statements described in *Crawford*: "[T]he officers' questioning was recorded on the audio-video equipment of the patrol car. Although the statement in question was not audible on the recording, that does not alter the formality of the setting that was intended to record testimony for the prosecution of the case being investigated.").

Even statements made by children, if made in a formal interview with law-enforcement or allied personnel, may be testimonial. *See, e.g.*, *People v. Sisavath*, 13 Cal. Rptr. 3d 753, 758 (Cal. Ct. App. 2004) (child's statements in interview at facility designed to interview abused children were testimonial because an objective observer would reasonably expect the statement to be available for use in a prosecution: "[the child's] interview took place after a prosecution was initiated, was attended by the prosecutor and the prosecutor's investigator, and was conducted by a person trained in forensic interviewing"); *People v. Vigil*, 104 P.3d 258, 262-63 (Colo. App. 2004) (videotaped statement given by child to police officer was testimonial under *Crawford* even though seven-year-old child would not reasonably expect his statements to be used prosecutorially), *rev'd in part on other grounds*, 127 P.3d 916 (Colo. 2006); *People v. Geno*, 683 N.W.2d 687, 692 (Mich. Ct. App. 2004) (child's statement was "made to the executive director of the Children's Assessment Center, not to a government employee, and the child's answer to the question whether she had an 'owie' was not a statement in the nature of 'ex parte in-court testimony or its functional equivalent'"; statement was nontestimonial), *appeal denied*, 688 N.W.2d 829 (Mich. 2004); *State v. Courtney*, 682 N.W.2d 185, 196 (Minn. Ct. App. 2004) (circumstances of interview show that child was questioned to develop case against defendant, and "[a]t one point, the interview was stopped by the police officer when he directed the child-protection worker to ask [child] to draw the guns she saw [defendant] allegedly use to threaten" another; statement was testimonial), *rev'd on other grounds*, 696 N.W.2d 73 (Minn. 2005); *see also* Brief Amicus Curiae of Law Professors at 22

In ***Crawford***, the Supreme Court observed that "when the declarant appears for cross-examination at trial, the Confrontation Clause places no constraints at all on the use of his prior testimonial statements."[61] It is the "literal right to 'confront' the witness at the time of trial that forms the core of the values furthered by the Confrontation Clause."[62] Thus, once the declarant personally appears at the trial, takes the oath, and is subject to cross-examination, his out-of-court statements (if otherwise admissible under the hearsay rule) are not affected by the rule in ***Crawford***.[63] Even if a witness cannot remember his prior out-of-court statements, and thus cannot be effectively cross-examined on their accuracy, the Confrontation Clause is nonetheless satisfied if the accused has the opportunity to cross-examine the witness.[64]

Several courts have held that ***Crawford*** does not bar a testifying expert witness from reviewing or relying on out-of-court hearsay statements in forming an opinion.[65] Further, there is no Confrontation Clause issue if the evidence is offered for a nonhearsay purpose.[66]

---

n.12, ***Crawford v. Washington***, 541 U.S. 36 (2004) (No. 02-9410) (young children's statements "will present some of the closest issues under the testimonial approach"). In ***Ohio v. Clark***, however, a case in which the child's statements were made to preschool teachers rather than the police, the Supreme Court observed that "[s]tatements by very young children will rarely, if ever, implicate the Confrontation Clause. Few preschool students understand the details of our criminal justice system." ___ U.S. ___, 135 S. Ct. 2173, 2182 (2015). Refer to notes 122-126 *infra* and accompanying text.

61.   541 U.S. at 59 n.9.

62.   ***California v. Green***, 399 U.S. 149, 157 (1970).

63.   *See* ***Mumphrey v. State***, 155 S.W.3d 651, 657 n.1 (Tex. App.—Texarkana 2005, pet. ref'd) (if witness testifies at trial, concerns raised by ***Crawford*** are not relevant); ***Carter v. State***, 150 S.W.3d 230, 241 n.13 (Tex. App.—Texarkana 2004, no pet.) (same).

64.   *See* ***Woodall v. State***, 336 S.W.3d 634, 644 (Tex. Crim. App. 2011) ("[M]emory loss does not render a witness 'absent' for Confrontation Clause purposes if she is present in court and testifying."); *see, e.g.*, ***People v. Candelaria***, 107 P.3d 1080, 1087 (Colo. App. 2004) (witness's inability to recall prior statements at trial did not change fact that defendant had opportunity, in accordance with ***Crawford*** requirements, to cross-examine witness about her statement), *rev'd in part on other grounds*, 148 P.3d 178 (Colo. 2006); ***People v. Bueno***, 829 N.E.2d 402, 411-12 (Ill. App. Ct. 2005) (witness answered all questions asked of him by defense counsel; therefore, despite claimed loss of memory, witness had appeared for cross-examination under ***Crawford***), *appeal denied*, 839 N.E.2d 1028 (Ill. 2005) (table case); ***State v. Gorman***, 854 A.2d 1164, 1177-78 (Me. 2004) (rejecting defendant's contention that witness was effectively unavailable because of her lack of memory of statements she made to grand jury and because she was under influence of psychiatric medications and had a history of delusional thought; "the Confrontation Clause was satisfied when [defendant] was given the opportunity to examine and cross-examine [witness] before the jury regarding what she did and did not recall and the reasons for her failure of recollection").

65.   *See* ***Martinez v. State***, 311 S.W.3d 104, 112 (Tex. App.—Amarillo 2010, pet. ref'd) ("The Confrontation Clause is not violated merely because an expert bases an opinion on inadmissible testimonial hearsay. This is so because the testifying expert's opinion is not hearsay and the testifying expert is available for cross-examination regarding his opinion."); *see, e.g.*, ***United States v. Stone***, 222 F.R.D. 334, 339 (E.D. Tenn. 2004) (***Crawford*** did not prevent IRS expert from considering the substance of witness-interview statements in forming expert opinion because "the purpose of the out-of-court statements would not be for hearsay purposes but rather would be for evaluating the merit of the opinions [the expert] offered on direct examination").

66.   *See* ***Crawford***, 541 U.S. at 59 n.9 ("The [Confrontation] Clause ... does not bar the use of testimonial statements for purposes other than establishing the truth of the matter asserted."); ***Langham v. State***, 305 S.W.3d 568, 576 (Tex. Crim. App. 2010) ("[A]n out-of-court statement ... is not objectionable under the Confrontation Clause to the extent that it is offered for some evidentiary purpose other than the truth of the matter asserted. When the relevance of an out-of-court statement derives solely from the fact that it was made, and not from the content of the assertion it contains, there is no constitutional imperative that the accused be permitted to confront the declarant."). Refer to *Article VII: Opinions & Expert Testimony*, *supra* p. 753.

The Texas Court of Criminal Appeals has held that the *Crawford* rule does not apply when a presentence investigation report is used in a noncapital case in which the judge determined sentencing.[67] The *Crawford* rule does apply, however, during the punishment phase in a capital case in which the jury determined sentencing.[68]

Several federal and state courts have also held that the *Crawford* rule does not apply to proceedings revoking parole, probation, or supervised release because those are not "criminal proceedings" to which the Sixth Amendment applies.[69] A defendant's limited right to confront witnesses at a revocation hearing stems from the Due Process Clause of the Fourteenth Amendment.[70] "Unlike the confrontation clause, due process demands that evidence be reliable in substance, not that its reliability be evaluated in 'a particular manner.'"[71]

C. "Purpose" Test for Testimonial Statements: *Davis v. Washington*

Two years after the *Crawford* decision, the Supreme Court provided additional guidance on the meaning of the term "testimonial" in the context of the Confrontation Clause. In *Davis v. Washington*, the Court addressed the question of "when statements made to law enforcement personnel during a 911 call or at a crime scene are 'testimonial.'"[72] The case actually involved two separate prosecutions and resulted in two different conclusions.

---

67. *Stringer v. State*, 309 S.W.3d 42, 48 (Tex. Crim. App. 2010); *see Sell v. State*, 488 S.W.3d 397, 399 (Tex. App.—Fort Worth 2016, pet. ref'd). Whether the *Crawford* rule applies when a jury determines a sentence in a noncapital case has not been determined. *Stringer*, 309 S.W.3d at 48.

68. *See Stringer*, 309 S.W.3d at 45-46; *Russeau v. State*, 171 S.W.3d 871, 880-81 (Tex. Crim. App. 2005).

69. *See, e.g.*, *Ash v. Reilly*, 431 F.3d 826, 829-30 (D.C. Cir. 2005) (parole); *United States v. Hall*, 419 F.3d 980, 985-86 (9th Cir. 2005) (supervised release); *United States v. Kirby*, 418 F.3d 621, 627-28 (6th Cir. 2005) (supervised release); *United States v. Aspinall*, 389 F.3d 332, 342-43 (2d Cir. 2004) (probation); *United States v. Martin*, 382 F.3d 840, 844 & n.4 (8th Cir. 2004) (supervised release); *People v. Johnson*, 18 Cal. Rptr. 3d 230, 232 (Cal. Ct. App. 2004) (probation); *State v. Abd-Rahmaan*, 111 P.3d 1157, 1161 (Wash. 2005) (parole). The Ninth Circuit noted that "[p]arole, probation, and supervised release revocation hearings are constitutionally indistinguishable and are analyzed in the same manner." *Hall*, 419 F.3d at 985 n.4.

Although not in the context of the Confrontation Clause, the court of criminal appeals has held that Texas community-supervision proceedings are not administrative hearings but rather judicial proceedings, "to be governed by the rules established to govern judicial proceedings." *Ex parte Doan*, 369 S.W.3d 205, 212 (Tex. Crim. App. 2012). Thus, the *Crawford* rule would seem to apply to these proceedings in Texas. *See Blackman v. State*, No. 01-12-00525-CR (Tex. App.—Houston [1st Dist.] 2014, pet. ref'd) (memo op.; 1-7-14) (assuming without deciding that defendant can raise Confrontation Clause objection in proceeding to revoke community supervision).

70. *Johnson*, 18 Cal. Rptr. 3d at 232; *see Black v. Romano*, 471 U.S. 606, 610 (1985); *Ash*, 431 F.3d at 829; *Hall*, 419 F.3d at 985; *Abd-Rahmaan*, 111 P.3d at 1161. In *Johnson*, the court upheld as "routine documentary evidence" the admission of a laboratory report analyzing rock cocaine. 18 Cal. Rptr. 3d at 233. The court reasoned that "the witness's demeanor is not a significant factor in evaluating foundational testimony relating to the admission of evidence such as laboratory reports, invoices, or receipts, where often the purpose of this testimony simply is to authenticate the documentary material." *Id.*

71. *Commonwealth v. Given*, 808 N.E.2d 788, 794 n.9 (Mass. 2004) ("That the focus on reliability may not accommodate a simple, predictable, bright-line rule, does not alter the fact that reliability, not cross-examination, is the 'due process touchstone.'"); *cf. In re Commitment of G.G.N.*, 855 A.2d 569, 579 (N.J. 2004) (court did not find any case that extended *Crawford* to civil-commitment proceeding, in which burden of proof is less than beyond a reasonable doubt).

72. 547 U.S. 813, 817 (2006).

In *Davis*, the State's only witnesses were two police officers who responded to a 911 call originally made by Michelle McCottry. Ms. McCottry called 911 but hung up without saying anything. After the 911 dispatcher reversed the call, Ms. McCottry picked it up and, when asked by the dispatcher "What's going on?," said, "He's here jumpin' on me again."[73] Then she said, "He's usin' his fists."[74] The operator asked who it was, and McCottry said that it was Adrian Davis. As the call continued, the dispatcher learned that Davis had "just [run] out the door," and that he was leaving in a car with someone else.[75] The police arrived within four minutes of the 911 call and saw Mc-Cottry's "shaken state, the 'fresh injuries on her forearm and her face,' and her 'frantic efforts to gather her belongings and her children so that they could leave the residence.'"[76]

In the second case, *Hammon v. Indiana*, police responded to a domestic-disturbance call and found Amy Hammon alone on the front porch, appearing "somewhat frightened."[77] She told the officers that nothing was the matter but gave them permission to enter her home, where the officers saw a broken heating unit with glass strewn around it.[78] Her husband, Hershel, was in the kitchen, and he told the officers that the couple had quarreled earlier, but everything was fine now.[79] When Amy came inside, one officer took her into the living room; the other officer stayed with Hershel, who made several attempts to come into the living room and join in Amy's conversation.[80] Amy told the officer what had happened and then handwrote a statement for him: "Broke our Furnace & shoved me down on the floor into the broken glass. Hit me in the chest and threw me down. Broke our lamps & phone. Tore up my van where I couldn't leave the house. Attacked my daughter."[81]

In both cases, the women did not testify at trial; instead, the State offered their out-of-court statements into evidence as excited utterances. Both defendants objected on Confrontation Clause grounds. The Supreme Court upheld the admission of much of the 911 recording in *Davis* but reversed the decision in *Hammon* that had admitted both the officer's testimony about what Amy told him and Amy's written statement. The Court compared the two situations and explained the distinction:

> Statements are nontestimonial when made in the course of police interrogation under circumstances objectively indicating that the primary purpose of the interrogation is to enable police assistance to meet an ongoing emergency.

---

73. *Id.*
74. *Id.*
75. *Id.* at 818.
76. *Id.*
77. *Id.* at 819.
78. *Id.*
79. *Id.*
80. *Id.* at 819-20.
81. *Id.* at 820.

They are testimonial when the circumstances objectively indicate that there is no such ongoing emergency, and that the primary purpose of the interrogation is to establish or prove past events potentially relevant to later criminal prosecution.[82]

The Court stated that Ms. McCottry was speaking about "events *as they were actually happening*, rather than 'describ[ing] past events,'"[83] during the 911 call. Her statements were (1) a call for help, (2) to resolve an ongoing emergency, (3) while she was frantic and in an environment that was neither tranquil nor safe.[84] The primary purpose of the 911 dispatcher's interrogation "was to enable police assistance to meet an ongoing emergency."[85] Amy Hammon, however, was speaking of past events, not ongoing conduct, and the officer was questioning her about "what happened," not "what is happening."[86] Further, (1) Amy was not, at the time she spoke to the officer, making a "call for help," (2) there was no ongoing emergency, and (3) she was, at that time, in

---

82.   *Id.* at 822; *see **Stancil v. United States**,* 866 A.2d 799, 812 (D.C. 2005) (because "police who respond to emergency calls for help and ask preliminary questions to ascertain whether the victim, other civilians, or the police themselves are in danger, are not obtaining information for the purpose of making a case against a suspect," statements made to officers at this initial stage of the encounter are not testimonial; however, "where police officers engage in structured questioning of victims or witnesses to a crime after the emergency has passed …, the resulting statements are more like the 'formal statements to government officers' of concern in *Crawford*"); *Coronado v. State*, 351 S.W.3d 315, 324 (Tex. Crim. App. 2011) ("If the objective purpose of the interview is to question a person about past events and that person's statements about those past events would likely be relevant to a future criminal proceeding, then they are testimonial."); *see, e.g.*, **United States v. Duron-Caldera**, 737 F.3d 988, 993-94 (5th Cir. 2013) (government did not meet its burden to prove that affidavit by defendant's grandmother about his immigration status was nontestimonial because it was created for the primary purpose of providing evidence for immigration proceedings and not criminal proceedings; government conceded that affidavit was taken as part of document-fraud investigation that resulted in criminal charges, and affidavit exculpated grandmother and inculpated four other people in fraud). Factors a court should consider in determining whether there was an ongoing emergency include whether the situation was still in progress, whether the questions were aimed at what was presently happening, whether the primary purpose of the questioning was to render aid rather than memorialize a possible crime, whether the questioning took place in a separate room away from the alleged attacker, and whether the declarant recounted the events deliberately and step by step. **Vinson v. State**, 252 S.W.3d 336, 339 (Tex. Crim. App. 2008).

83.   **Davis v. Washington**, 547 U.S. 813, 827 (2006).

84.   *Id.*

85.   *Id.* at 828; *see also **Hereford v. State**,* 444 S.W.3d 346, 352-53 (Tex. App.—Amarillo 2014, no pet.) (police officer's testimony about anonymous 911 call violated defendant's right of confrontation; statements were testimonial because their primary purpose was to aid in investigation of a crime, and prosecution did not show that caller was unavailable or that defendant had prior opportunity for cross-examination); **Amador v. State**, 376 S.W.3d 339, 343 (Tex. App.—Houston [14th Dist.] 2012, pet. ref'd) (statements made to police officer as he was responding to report of armed robbery, at crime scene and shortly after crime had occurred, were nontestimonial; primary purpose of obtaining statements was to respond to ongoing emergency); **Reyes v. State**, 314 S.W.3d 74, 79 (Tex. App.—San Antonio 2010, no pet.) (911 call was nontestimonial when "[t]he questions by the 911 operator clearly indicate their primary purpose was to determine the extent of the emergency rather than memorializing information for later use in a criminal prosecution"). In **Vinson v. State**, the assault victim's initial statements to the responding police officer, identifying her boyfriend—who was in the room when he was identified—as the assailant when the officer asked her what had happened, were nontestimonial. 252 S.W.3d at 337 & n.2. When she answered the door, she "appeared to be bleeding and in pain from recently inflicted injuries," and the officer was merely attempting to assess whether the victim needed assistance. *See id.* at 337. At this time, an emergency situation was still ongoing. *See id.* at 339-40. However, once the defendant was taken out of the room and secured in the police car, the emergency situation ceased; thus, the victim's detailed description of the assault was testimonial and inadmissible under *Crawford*. *Vinson*, 252 S.W.3d at 341-42.

86.   *Davis*, 547 U.S. at 830.

a safe environment, away from her husband.[87] Her statements were therefore made during an official interrogation and were "an obvious substitute for live testimony, because they do precisely *what a witness does* on direct examination"—that is, describe past events.[88]

In sum, Ms. McCottry was "seeking aid, not telling a story about the past. McCottry's present-tense statements showed immediacy; Amy's narrative of past events was delivered at some remove in time from the danger she described."[89] The Supreme Court, therefore, affirmed Davis's conviction for violation of a protective order but reversed Hammon's conviction for domestic battery. It remanded that case to the state court to address the potential issue of whether Hammon had forfeited his right to confront Amy because his own act of wrongdoing led to her absence from the trial.[90] The Supreme Court also reiterated its statement from *Crawford* that the "forfeiture by wrongdoing" doctrine applies to the Confrontation Clause.[91]

Even before *Davis*, 911 calls had sometimes been held to be nontestimonial under the *Crawford* framework because they resembled an "electronically augmented equivalent of a loud cry for help ... made while an assault or homicide is still in progress" or "in the *immediate* aftermath of the crime."[92] Other courts had found that a 911 call was testimonial because it was made to report a crime and supply information about its commission; thus, its purpose was for investigation, prosecution, and potential use at a judicial proceeding.[93] This distinction between a 911 call for help and one providing

---

87. *See id.* at 829-30.

88. *Id.* at 830.

89. *Id.* at 831-32.

90. *Id.* at 834.

91. *Id.* at 833. Refer to notes 163-171 *infra* and accompanying text.

92. *People v. Moscat*, 777 N.Y.S.2d 875, 880 (N.Y. Crim. Ct. 2004). In *Moscat*, the court explained that the domestic-violence victim's 911 call was not testimonial because (1) the call was initiated by the victim, not police, (2) the call was made not to provide evidence, but to be rescued from imminent peril, (3) the call could be seen as part of the criminal event itself because it was made while the assault was still in progress, and (4) there was no time for the caller-victim to contemplate her words. *Id.* at 878-80; *see, e.g.*, *Leavitt v. Arave*, 383 F.3d 809, 830 & n.22 (9th Cir. 2004) (murder victim's 911 call the night before her death was admissible under *Crawford* because victim was seeking help from police to end a frightening intrusion into her home; statements naming defendant as probable prowler were admissible as excited utterances); *People v. Corella*, 18 Cal. Rptr. 3d 770, 776 (Cal. Ct. App. 2004) (911 statements were not equivalent to those made in a police interrogation "because they were not 'knowingly given in response to structured police questioning,' and bear no indicia common to the official and formal quality of the various statements deemed testimonial by *Crawford*"; victim is only "making a 911 call in need of assistance, [and] the 911 operator is determining the appropriate response[,] not conducting a police interrogation in contemplation of a future prosecution"); *People v. Conyers*, 824 N.Y.S.2d 301, 302 (N.Y. App. Div. 2006) (911 calls made by defendant's sister after defendant stabbed complainant were nontestimonial under *Crawford*; calls were made to obtain police assistance and request ambulance, and "statements did not result from questioning designed to establish or prove a past fact"), *appeal denied*, 862 N.E.2d 795 (N.Y. 2007) (table case); *see also* ***Dixon v. State***, 244 S.W.3d 472, 484-85 (Tex. App.—Houston [14th Dist.] 2007, pet. ref'd) (assault victim's 911 call was a cry for help and thus was admissible under *Davis*; operator's questions and victim's responses were to determine whether she needed medical assistance and was still in danger).

93. *See, e.g.*, *People v. Dobbin*, 791 N.Y.S.2d 897, 900 (N.Y. Sup. Ct. 2004, appeal denied) (911 call "contains a solemn declaration for the purpose of establishing the fact that the defendant is committing a robbery. ... The caller was officially reporting a crime to the government agency entrusted with this very serious and important function"; statement was testimonial under *Crawford*); *People v. Cortes*, 781 N.Y.S.2d 401, 415-16 (N.Y. Sup. Ct. 2004) (911

information to police was explored in a pre-*Crawford* law-review article that accurately predicted the dichotomy in the *Davis* and *Hammon* cases.[94]

D. Contours of "Testimonial" After *Crawford & Davis*

Davis raises many questions about what is required for the declarant's statements to be deemed "testimonial" under the Confrontation Clause. The Court stated in *Davis* that it was not presenting a comprehensive definition of "testimonial."[95] Nonetheless, it offered a test that focuses on the primary purpose of the police interrogation.[96] In *Crawford*, the Court claimed to be leaving a comprehensive definition of "testimonial" for another day,[97] but described several situations in which a declarant's statements would be considered testimonial.[98]

Although the opinions in *Davis* and *Crawford* were both written by Justice Scalia, the discussion of the "primary purpose" test in *Davis*[99] does not refer to the "expectations" test contained in *Crawford*.[100] It has been unclear whether the lower courts should infer from this silence that the *Davis* Court effectively overruled the expecta-

---

call "was for the purpose of invoking police action and the prosecutorial process"; 911 caller reporting an attempted murder was never identified and yelled, "He's killing him, he's killing him, he's shooting him again," and hung up with the comment, "I gotta hang up because people, people are gonna think I'm out calling the cops"; statement was testimonial under *Crawford*); *State v. Powers*, 99 P.3d 1262, 1266 (Wash. Ct. App. 2004) (domestic-violence victim's 911 call was to report defendant's violation of protective order and to describe him to assist in his apprehension and prosecution, rather than to protect herself and her child from his return; statement was testimonial under *Crawford*).

94. *See* Friedman & McCormack, *supra* note 35, at 1242-43 (911 caller's statements may "serve either or both of two primary objectives—to gain immediate official assistance in ending or relieving an exigent, perhaps dangerous, situation, and to provide information to aid investigation and possible prosecution related to that situation"). Courts still make this distinction when determining whether a 911 call was testimonial. *See, e.g.*, *Hernandez v. State*, ___ S.W.3d ___ (Tex. App.—Houston [1st Dist.] 2017, n.p.h.) (No. 01-16-00755-CR; 8-10-17) (trial court did not err in admitting recording of 911 call because statements on recording described events in immediate past and were necessary to determine nature of emergency, defendant was still in immediate vicinity, complainant's voice was shaking, and she was breathing heavily; statements were nontestimonial); *Gutierrez v. State*, 516 S.W.3d 593, 598-99 (Tex. App.—Houston [1st Dist.] 2017, pet. ref'd) (trial court erred in admitting recording of 911 call and testimony about interview with police officer that focused on past events, included details that were not immediately necessary, and occurred without any concern that alleged attacker would come back; evidence was testimonial). Some courts have held that part of a 911 call was testimonial and part was not. *See, e.g.*, *People v. West*, 823 N.E.2d 82, 91-92 (Ill. App. Ct. 2005) (victim's statements to 911 dispatcher about attack and victim's medical needs, age, and location were not testimonial; statements describing victim's vehicle, the direction in which her assailants fled, and items of personal property they took were testimonial because they were made in response to dispatcher's questions for the stated purpose of involving the police), *appeal denied*, 871 N.E.2d 61 (Ill. 2007) (table case).

95. 547 U.S. 813, 822 (2006).

96. Refer to note 82 *supra* and accompanying text. The Texas Court of Criminal Appeals has discussed what the *Davis* Court meant by the "primary" purpose of an interrogation. *See* *Langham v. State*, 305 S.W.3d 568, 579 (Tex. Crim. App. 2010). The court of criminal appeals rejected the interpretation advanced in the court of appeals, which was to define "primary" purpose as a police officer's "first-in-time" purpose. *Id.* at 578-79. The court of criminal appeals offered a different reading: "[i]t is far more likely that, by 'primary purpose,' the Supreme Court meant to convey the purpose that is 'first' among all potentially competing purposes 'in rank or importance.'" *Id.* at 579.

97. *Crawford v. Washington*, 541 U.S. 36, 68 (2004).

98. Refer to notes 54-60 *supra* and accompanying text.

99. Refer to note 82 *supra* and accompanying text.

100. Refer to notes 54-60 *supra* and accompanying text. Further confusing the issue is footnote 1 in *Davis*, which states that the focus of the Confrontation Clause inquiry should be on the declarant's statements, not the interro-

tions test contained in *Crawford* or intended for the two tests to coexist.[101] If the *Davis* Court intended for the expectations and primary-purpose tests to coexist, the circumstances under which each of the tests should be applied are also unclear.[102]

In *Michigan v. Bryant*, however, the Court expanded on the primary-purpose test, further distancing itself from the expectations test of *Crawford*.[103] The Court reiterated that determining the primary purpose of an interrogation requires an objective inquiry.[104] As part of this objective standard, "*Davis* requires a combined inquiry that accounts for both the declarant and the interrogator."[105] The *Bryant* Court acknowl-

---

gator's questioning. 547 U.S. at 822 n.1. The footnote does not explain what that focus should include. But the Court in *Michigan v. Bryant* addressed this footnote from *Davis* and explained its meaning. Refer to notes 106-108 *infra* and accompanying text.

101. *Compare United States v. Udeozor*, 515 F.3d 260, 268-69 (4th Cir. 2008) (applying expectations test), *and United States v. Townley*, 472 F.3d 1267, 1272-73 (10th Cir. 2007) (same), *with De La Paz v. State*, 273 S.W.3d 671, 680 (Tex. Crim. App. 2008) (primary focus in determining whether statement is "testimonial" is on objective purpose of interview or interrogation, not on declarant's expectations), *and Paul v. State*, 419 S.W.3d 446, 454-55 (Tex. App.—Tyler 2012, pet. ref'd) (same). See Tom Lininger, *Reconceptualizing Confrontation After* Davis, 85 TEX. L. REV. 271, 280 (2006), for a discussion of this issue.

102. Regardless of the test used, whether an out-of-court statement is testimonial is a question of law. *De La Paz*, 273 S.W.3d at 680; *Hereford v. State*, 444 S.W.3d 346, 350 (Tex. App.—Amarillo 2014, no pet.); *Wood v. State*, 299 S.W.3d 200, 207 (Tex. App.—Austin 2009, pet. ref'd); *see Wall v. State*, 184 S.W.3d 730, 742-43 (Tex. Crim. App. 2006).

103. *See Michigan v. Bryant*, 562 U.S. 344, 359 (2011) ("[W]e confront for the first time circumstances in which the 'ongoing emergency' discussed in *Davis* extends beyond an initial victim to a potential threat to the responding police and the public at large. This new context requires us to provide additional clarification with regard to what *Davis* meant by 'the primary purpose of the interrogation is to enable police assistance to meet an ongoing emergency.'"); *see also Bullcoming v. New Mexico*, 564 U.S. 647, 671-72 (2011) (Sotomayor, J., concurring) (discussing primary-purpose test in determining that lab report was testimonial).

104. *Bryant*, 562 U.S. at 359. The Court continued:

An objective analysis of the circumstances of an encounter and the statements and actions of the parties to it provides the most accurate assessment of the "primary purpose of the interrogation." The circumstances in which an encounter occurs—*e.g.*, at or near the scene of the crime versus at a police station, during an ongoing emergency or afterwards—are clearly matters of objective fact. The statements and actions of the parties must also be objectively evaluated. That is, the relevant inquiry is not the subjective or actual purpose of the individuals involved in a particular encounter, but rather the purpose that reasonable participants would have had, as ascertained from the individuals' statements and actions and the circumstances in which the encounter occurred.

Id. at 360; *see, e.g.*, *Cazares v. State*, ___ S.W.3d ___ (Tex. App.—El Paso 2017, n.p.h.) (No. 08-15-00266-CR; 8-16-17) (error, though harmless, to admit recording of conversation between nontestifying codefendant and his aunt, who was acting as agent of police; even if defendant did not know contents of conversation would be used against him or his codefendant, statements were testimonial because objective circumstances indicated that conversation's primary purpose was to record past event and that defendant knew he was implicating himself and his codefendant in circumstances that would likely lead to prosecution); *Hernandez v. State*, ___ S.W.3d ___ & n.3 (Tex. App.—Houston [1st Dist.] 2017, n.p.h.) (No. 01-16-00755-CR; 8-10-17) (although defendant was not present when complainant called 911, reasonable listener would conclude there was ongoing emergency because complainant's voice was shaking and she was breathing heavily; even if complainant's subjective motivation for calling was to prevent defendant from eluding police, relevant inquiry is what purpose reasonable participants would have had).

105. *Bryant*, 562 U.S. at 367. *But see id.* at 381 (Scalia, J., dissenting) ("*Crawford* and *Davis* did not address whose perspective matters—the declarant's, the interrogator's, or both—when assessing 'the primary purpose of [an] interrogation.' In those cases the statements were testimonial from any perspective. I think the same is true here, but because the Court picks a perspective so will I: The declarant's intent is what counts."). The Court summarized that "[o]bjectively ascertaining the primary purpose of the interrogation by examining the statements and actions of all participants is … consistent with our past holdings." *Id.* at 370 (majority op.).

edged, however, that "[s]ome portions of *Davis* ... have caused confusion about whether the inquiry prescribes examination of one participant to the exclusion of the other."[106] The *Bryant* Court interpreted footnote 1 in *Davis* as "merely acknowledg[ing]" that the Confrontation Clause applies only to statements offered for the truth of the matter asserted.[107] As the Court explained:

> An interrogator's questions, unlike a declarant's answers, do not assert the truth of any matter. The language in the footnote was not meant to determine *how* the courts are to assess the nature of the declarant's purpose, but merely to remind readers that it is the statements, and not the questions, that must be evaluated under the Sixth Amendment.[108]

In determining the primary purpose of the interrogation, the Court in *Bryant* focused primarily on the "ongoing emergency" at the time of the encounter between the victim in the case and the police.[109] First, the Court acknowledged that "whether an emergency exists and is ongoing is a highly context-dependent inquiry."[110] Because both the *Davis* and *Hammon* cases involved domestic violence, *Bryant* was the first case in which the Court had to consider the ongoing-emergency circumstance in a different context. In *Bryant*, the mortally wounded victim told police officers that he "fled [defendant's] back porch, indicating that he perceived an ongoing threat. The police did not know, and [victim] did not tell them, whether the threat was limited to him."[111] Thus, a threat to public safety, such as the situation in *Bryant*, may be ongoing for a longer period of time than a domestic-violence emergency.[112]

---

106. *Id.* at 367 n.11. *Davis* indicated that whether a statement was testimonial was determined by the primary purpose of the interrogation; however, footnote 1 of *Davis* states that the focus of the Confrontation Clause analysis is on the declarant's statements. *Bryant*, 562 U.S. at 367 n.11.

107. *Id.*

108. *Id.* Thus, the defendant's reliance on footnote 1 in *Davis* "to argue that the primary purpose inquiry must be conducted solely from the perspective of the declarant" was misplaced. *See Bryant*, 562 U.S. at 367 n.11.

109. *See id.* at 361.

110. *Id.* at 363. The Court explained that *Davis* did not define "ongoing emergency" and "did not even define the extent of the emergency in that case." *Bryant*, 562 U.S. at 363.

111. *Id.* at 373.

112. *See id.* at 363 ("Domestic violence cases like *Davis* and *Hammon* often have a narrower zone of potential victims than cases involving threats to public safety. An assessment of whether an emergency that threatens the police and public is ongoing cannot narrowly focus on whether the threat solely to the first victim has been neutralized because the threat to the first responders and public may continue."). In his dissent, Justice Scalia argued that:

> None—absolutely none—of [the officers'] actions indicated that they perceived an imminent threat. They did not draw their weapons, and indeed did not immediately search the gas station for potential shooters. To the contrary, all five testified that they questioned [victim] *before conducting any investigation at the scene*. Would this have made any sense if they feared the presence of a shooter? Most tellingly, none of the officers started his interrogation by asking what would have been the obvious first question if any hint of such a fear existed: Where is the shooter?

Id. at 386-87 (Scalia, J., dissenting). Justice Scalia concluded that "[t]he Court's distorted view creates an expansive exception to the Confrontation Clause for violent crimes. Because [defendant] posed a continuing threat to public safety in the Court's imagination, the emergency persisted for confrontation purposes at least until the police learned his 'motive for and location after the shooting.'" *Id.* at 388.

The *Bryant* majority recognized, as the Court did in *Davis*, that an interrogation can begin with the primary purpose of determining the need for emergency assistance and later evolve into testimonial statements. *Bryant*, 562

Second, the Court explained that "the duration and scope of an emergency may depend in part on the type of weapon employed."[113] Because the defendants in **Davis** and **Hammon** used their fists, physical separation from the victims was considered sufficient to end the emergency.[114] The defendant in **Bryant**, however, used a gun, and "[a]n emergency does not last only for the time between when the assailant pulls the trigger and the bullet hits the victim."[115] Finally, the Court stated that the victim's medical condition is relevant to determining whether there is an ongoing emergency.[116]

The Court also examined the formality of the interrogation as a factor in determining the primary purpose of the questioning.[117] The questioning in **Bryant** was disorganized and occurred in a public area before emergency services had arrived; these facts distinguished the case from the formal station-house interrogation in **Crawford**.[118] The Court cautioned, however, that

> [f]ormality is not the sole touchstone of our primary purpose inquiry because, although formality suggests the absence of an emergency and therefore an increased likelihood that the purpose of the interrogation is to 'establish or prove past events potentially relevant to later criminal prosecution,' ...

U.S. at 365 (majority op.). For example, the declarant may provide information indicating that the emergency no longer exists or that the perceived public threat is actually a private dispute. *Id.*

113. *Id.* at 364.

114. *See **Bryant***, 562 U.S. at 364.

115. *Id.* at 373. In this case, the Court declined to decide when the emergency ended: "[w]e need not decide precisely when the emergency ended because [victim's] encounter with the police and all of the statements he made during that interaction occurred within the first few minutes of the police officers' arrival." *Id.* at 374.

116. *Id.* at 364-65. As the Court explained, the victim's medical condition "is important to the primary purpose inquiry to the extent that it sheds light on the ability of the victim to have any purpose at all in responding to police questions and on the likelihood that any purpose formed would necessarily be a testimonial one." *Id.* In **Bryant**, the victim's statements were made while he "was lying in a gas station parking lot bleeding from a mortal gunshot wound to his abdomen. His answers to the police officers' questions were punctuated with questions about when emergency medical services would arrive." *Id.* at 375. Thus, he did not have a "'primary purpose' 'to establish or prove past events potentially relevant to later criminal prosecution.'" *Id.* The victim's medical condition is also important in helping first responders assess any continuing threat to the victim or to the public at large. *Id.* at 365.

117. *See id.* at 377 ("[T]he situation was fluid and somewhat confused: the officers arrived at different times; apparently each, upon arrival, asked [declarant] 'what happened?'; and ... they did not conduct a structured interrogation. The informality suggests that the interrogators' primary purpose was simply to address what they perceived to be an ongoing emergency, and the circumstances lacked any formality that would have alerted [declarant] to or focused him on the possible future prosecutorial use of his statements."); *see, e.g.*, ***United States v. De-Leon***, 678 F.3d 317, 324-25 (4th Cir. 2012) (child-abuse victim's statements to social worker were not testimonial when social worker was not employed as forensic investigator, but rather was questioning child to develop treatment plan, and did not tell child his statements would be reported to authorities; no evidence indicated child believed otherwise), *vacated on other grounds*, ___ U.S. ___, 133 S. Ct. 2850 (2013); ***Bobadilla v. Carlson***, 575 F.3d 785, 793 (8th Cir. 2009) (child-abuse victim's statements to social worker were testimonial when police officer initiated interview and structured questioning to confirm prior allegations of abuse; social worker functioned as agent of police).

118. ***Bryant***, 562 U.S. at 366; *see also **Bullcoming v. New Mexico***, 564 U.S. 647, 671-72 & n.3 (2011) (Sotomayor, J., concurring) (certification of forensic lab report was "a formal statement, despite the absence of notarization. The formality derives from the fact that the analyst is asked to sign his name and 'certify' to both the result and the statements on the form"; report's primary purpose was to substitute for trial testimony and thus was testimonial).

ARTICLE VIII

informality does not necessarily indicate the presence of an emergency or the lack of testimonial intent.[119]

After the **Bryant** Court's objective examination of the victim's and police officers' statements and the circumstances of their encounter, the Court concluded that "the 'primary purpose of the interrogation' was 'to enable police assistance to meet an ongoing emergency.'"[120] Thus, the victim's statements were not testimonial and did not violate the defendant's rights under the Confrontation Clause.[121]

In **Ohio v. Clark**, the Court delved into a question that it had declined to address in previous opinions under the Confrontation Clause: whether out-of-court statements made to someone other than law-enforcement personnel are subject to the Confrontation Clause.[122] In **Clark**, a three-year-old child answered questions from his teachers about bruises and marks on his body when the teachers suspected he was being abused.[123] The Court accepted the child's statements as nontestimonial, in part because they were made to preschool teachers rather than the police.[124] In determining that the statements were not testimonial, the Court reasoned that the primary purpose of the conversation, like the one in **Michigan v. Bryant**, was to meet an ongoing emergency rather than to gather evidence against the father.[125] The Court refused to adopt a cat-

---

119. **Bryant**, 562 U.S. at 366 (citations omitted).

120. *See id.* at 377-78.

121. *Id.* at 378. The Court also explained:

When, as in **Davis**, the primary purpose of an interrogation is to respond to an 'ongoing emergency,' its purpose is not to create a record for trial and thus is not within the scope of the Clause. But there may be *other* circumstances, aside from ongoing emergencies, when a statement is not procured with a primary purpose of creating an out-of-court substitute for trial testimony. In making the primary purpose determination, standard rules of hearsay, designed to identify some statements as reliable, will be relevant. Where no such primary purpose exists, the admissibility of a statement is the concern of state and federal rules of evidence, not the Confrontation Clause.

Id. at 358-59. In his **Bryant** dissent, Justice Scalia questioned whether the Court's discussion of reliability would bring back the reliability framework from **Ohio v. Roberts**, which the Court overruled in **Crawford**. *See id.* at 391 (Scalia, J., dissenting) ("The Court announces that in future cases it will look to 'standard rules of hearsay, designed to identify some statements as reliable,' when deciding whether a statement is testimonial. **Ohio v. Roberts** ... said something remarkably similar .... We tried that approach to the Confrontation Clause for nearly 25 years before **Crawford** *rejected* it as an unworkable standard unmoored from the text and the historical roots of the Confrontation Clause."). He also criticized the majority for "reced[ing] from **Crawford** [by] requir[ing] judges to conduct 'open-ended balancing tests' and 'amorphous, if not entirely subjective,' inquiries into the totality of the circumstances bearing upon reliability." *Id.* at 393. Refer to notes 36-71 *supra* and accompanying text.

122. ___ U.S. ___, 135 S. Ct. 2173, 2181 (2015); *see* **Davis v. Washington**, 547 U.S. 813, 823 n.2 (2006).

123. *See* **Clark**, ___ U.S. at ___, 135 S. Ct. at 2178. In response to questions about how he got the bruises, the child identified "Dee" as the person responsible. *Id.* "Dee" was his father's nickname. *Id.* at ___, 135 S. Ct. at 2177.

124. *See id.* at ___, 135 S. Ct. at 2183.

125. **Clark**, ___ U.S. at ___, 135 S. Ct. at 2181. The Court treated the situation in **Clark** as an ongoing emergency because the teachers, after noticing the child's injuries, became concerned about releasing him at the end of the day if he was the victim of serious violence. *Id.* Thus, because they were unsure of exactly who had abused the child, whether he was safe, and whether there were other children at risk, the teachers' questions and the child's answers were aimed at protecting the child and identifying and ending the threat. *Id.* Further, "[a]t no point did the teachers inform [the child] that his answers would be used to arrest or punish his abuser[, and the child] never hinted that he intended his statements to be used by the police or prosecutors." *Id.* The conversation also took place in the preschool lunchroom in an informal setting and occurred immediately after the child's injuries were discovered. *Id.*

egorical rule that all out-of-court statements to individuals other than law-enforcement officers are nontestimonial, but "[s]tatements made to someone who is not principally charged with uncovering and prosecuting criminal behavior are significantly less likely to be testimonial than statements given to law enforcement officers."[126]

The following is a discussion about whether other statements, either spoken or contained in business records, are testimonial.

1. Statements made during custodial & noncustodial interrogations are testimonial. When the police are detecting crime, investigating crime, and gathering evidence for criminal prosecution, they may conduct both custodial and noncustodial interrogations. Statements obtained during such interrogations are testimonial as a matter of law.[127] Redacting an accomplice's testimonial statements to eliminate any reference to the defendant does not make the rest of the statement nontestimonial.[128] "Forensic" interviews by persons allied with law enforcement—for example, child-abuse workers, domestic-violence-center personnel, even doctors or nurses when they are acting in concert with law enforcement—generally result in testimonial statements.[129]

---

126. *Id.* at ___, 135 S. Ct. at 2182; *see, e.g.*, ***United States v. Barker***, 820 F.3d 167, 171-72 (5th Cir. 2016) (four-year-old's statements to certified sexual-assault nurse examiner were nontestimonial; primary purpose was to medically evaluate and treat child during ongoing emergency, child lacked understanding of criminal-justice system and did not intend for her comments to be a substitute for trial testimony, and questioning took place in hospital emergency room with no police present), *cert. denied*, 137 S. Ct. 209 (2016); ***Cazares v. State***, ___ S.W.3d ___ (Tex. App.—El Paso 2017, n.p.h.) (No. 08-15-00266-CR; 8-16-17) (error, though harmless, to admit recording of conversation between nontestifying codefendant and his aunt, who was acting as agent of police; despite informal setting, she asked him pointed questions about past events that could lead to prosecution and did not ask those questions to address ongoing emergency).

127. *See* ***Brooks v. State***, 132 S.W.3d 702, 707 (Tex. App.—Dallas 2004, pet. ref'd). In ***Wall v. State***, the court of criminal appeals held that an excited-utterance statement made by an assault victim to investigating police officers at the hospital one hour after the assault was testimonial because the officers were conducting an investigation into the past event and the victim knew it (they were taking notes and photographing his injuries as they interviewed him). 184 S.W.3d 730, 744-45 (Tex. Crim. App. 2006). The court noted that "generally statements made to police while the declarant (or another person) is still in personal danger are not made with consideration of their legal ramifications because the declarant usually speaks out of urgency and a desire to obtain a prompt response; thus, those statements will not normally be deemed testimonial." *Id.* at 742. Conversely, "after the immediate danger has dissipated, a person who speaks while still under the stress of a startling event is more likely to comprehend the larger significance of his words." *Id.* These latter, backward-looking statements are testimonial.

128. *See, e.g.*, ***United States v. Jones***, 371 F.3d 363, 368-69 (7th Cir. 2004) (admission of redacted version of conspirator's confession that implicated defendant in illegal resale of a firearm was error under ***Crawford*** because defendant never had the opportunity to cross-examine conspirator, who had become a fugitive); ***Scott v. State***, 165 S.W.3d 27, 46-48 (Tex. App.—Austin 2005) (rejecting State's argument that because accomplice's custodial statement had been redacted to omit any reference to defendant, it was not "accusatory" and its introduction in evidence did not make accomplice a witness against defendant within the meaning of the Sixth Amendment), *rev'd on other grounds*, 227 S.W.3d 670 (Tex. Crim. App. 2007) (erroneous admission of accomplice's testimonial statement to police was not harmless beyond a reasonable doubt); ***Hale v. State***, 139 S.W.3d 418, 420-22 & n.1 (Tex. App.—Fort Worth 2004, no pet.) (reversing conviction based on admission of written statement from unavailable accomplice made during police interrogation; although that statement had been redacted, "[t]he redacted statement simply replaces Hale's name with generic pronouns such as 'he' or 'him,' but does not delete references to conduct attributed to Hale").

129. *See* ***Coronado v. State***, 351 S.W.3d 315, 324 & n.52 (Tex. Crim. App. 2011) ("Virtually all courts that have reviewed the admissibility of forensic child-interview statements or videotapes after the ***Davis*** decision have found them to be 'testimonial' and inadmissible unless the child testifies at trial or the defendant had a prior opportunity for cross-examination."). The question in ***Coronado*** was whether the defendant had a prior opportunity to cross-

It seems clear that *Crawford* does not apply to coconspirator statements admissible under Rule 801(e)(2)(E),[130] as those are not testimonial statements made to law enforcement.[131]

2. Dying declarations are nontestimonial: *Giles v. California*. The U.S. Supreme Court in *Giles v. California* explicitly recognized dying declarations as an exception to the requirements of the Confrontation Clause.[132] The Court reasoned that dying declarations were admissible under the common law and are therefore admissible today under the Confrontation Clause.[133]

---

examine the child victim under *Crawford*. *Id.* at 325. The court of appeals had held that written interrogatories given more than a year after the child victim's initial videotaped interview were a sufficient substitute for cross-examination. *Id.* at 329. In reversing the court of appeals, the court of criminal appeals found no "post-*Crawford* precedent from any jurisdiction that states, or even suggests, that a list of written interrogatories, posed by a forensic examiner to a child in an *ex parte* interview, is a constitutional substitute for live cross-examination and confrontation." *Id.* The *Coronado* court observed:

> [t]he content of the constitutional rights to confrontation and cross-examination do not depend upon the type of crime charged or the fragility of the witnesses; all accused citizens are entitled to the full protection of the constitution.
>
> … There is no "balancing" the defendant's constitutional right of confrontation and cross-examination against other social policies, even compelling ones.

Id. at 328-29. In dissent, Presiding Judge Keller concluded that the interrogatories procedure did not violate the Confrontation Clause because there was expert testimony that the child victim would be traumatized and unable to testify either at trial or in a closed-circuit setting and because defense counsel decided to delegate follow-up questions to the forensic interviewer rather than compose them himself. *Id.* at 331 (Keller, P.J., dissenting).

130. Refer to note 430 *infra* and accompanying text.

131. *See Crawford v. Washington*, 541 U.S. 36, 74 (2004) (Rehnquist, C.J., O'Connor, J., concurring) (discussing the rationale supporting admission of coconspirator statements regardless of their hearsay nature; "[b]ecause the statements are made while the declarant and the accused are partners in an illegal enterprise, the statements are unlikely to be false and their admission actually furthers the Confrontation Clause's very mission which is to advance the accuracy of the truth-determining process in criminal trials"); *United States v. Lee*, 374 F.3d 637, 644 (8th Cir. 2004) (coconspirator statements are nontestimonial under *Crawford*); *Orona v. State*, 341 S.W.3d 452, 463 (Tex. App.—Fort Worth 2011, pet. ref'd) ("[A] co-conspirator's statements made in furtherance of the conspiracy are nontestimonial."); *see, e.g.*, *United States v. Smalls*, 605 F.3d 765, 779-80 (10th Cir. 2010) (coconspirator's statements to confidential informant were nontestimonial under *Crawford* and *Davis*; coconspirator "in no sense intended to bear testimony against [defendant or] sought to establish facts for use in a criminal investigation or prosecution"); *United States v. Saget*, 377 F.3d 223, 228-30 (2d Cir. 2004) (coconspirator's statements to confidential informant were not testimonial under *Crawford*; declarant made statements to someone he thought was an ally or friend and defendant had no motive to shift blame or diminish responsibility). The Court in *Giles v. California* adopted Chief Justice Rehnquist's position that admitting a coconspirator's statements does not violate the Confrontation Clause, but did not adopt his reasoning. *See Giles v. California*, 554 U.S. 353, 374 n.6 (2008). Instead, the *Giles* court reasoned that such statements "would probably never be … testimonial" and therefore not subject to the Confrontation Clause. *Id.*

132. 554 U.S. at 358; *see also Gardner v. State*, 306 S.W.3d 274, 288 n.20 (Tex. Crim. App. 2009) (exemption of dying declarations from Sixth Amendment requirements was not explicitly addressed in *Crawford* or *Davis*, but the point "seems well taken"). Even before *Giles*, dying declarations (otherwise admissible under Rule 804(b)(2) and now referred to in the rule as statements under the belief of imminent death) appeared to be unaffected by *Crawford* for two reasons. First, these statements are generally not made in response to any structured questioning, and the declarant would usually not have any expectation that his dying words would later be used at a trial. *See State v. Nix*, No. C-030696 (Ohio Ct. App. 2004) (no pub.; 10-15-04). Second, a footnote in *Crawford* seems to exclude dying declarations from the scope of the Confrontation Clause. *See Crawford*, 541 U.S. at 56 n.6 (dying-declaration hearsay exception is sui generis as a "general rule of criminal hearsay law" and, according to one cited authority, is the "*only* recognized criminal hearsay exception at common law"; Court did not decide "whether the Sixth Amendment incorporates an exception for testimonial dying declarations"). For a discussion of statements under the belief of imminent death, refer to notes 932-951 *infra* and accompanying text.

3. Business records may be testimonial. Traditional business records—the kind kept in the ordinary course of business and not compiled for any law-enforcement purposes or for potential litigation—are not testimonial.[134] In *Crawford*, the Supreme Court explicitly noted that, at the time of the Bill of Rights, "[m]ost of the hearsay exceptions covered statements that by their nature were not testimonial—for example, business records or statements in furtherance of a conspiracy."[135] The ordinary business record, though it may contain multiple levels of hearsay, is at the far end of the nontestimonial spectrum. However, business records are also kept by government agencies, law-enforcement agencies, and adjuncts of government agencies. Some of these business records—or at least certain entries within them—may be testimonial under *Crawford*.

As a general rule, business records of a government or law-enforcement agency that are compiled for routine, nonadversarial, or public-record-keeping purposes are nontestimonial.[136] As the Court in *Melendez-Diaz v. Massachusetts* explained, "[b]usiness and public records are generally admissible absent confrontation not because they qualify under an exception to the hearsay rules, but because—having been created for the administration of an entity's affairs and not for the purpose of establishing or proving some fact at trial—they are not testimonial."[137] Records created for a particular criminal investigation or potential prosecution, however, are testimonial.[138] In

---

The *Giles* Court also suggested in dicta that a domestic-violence victim's statements made to "friends and neighbors about abuse and intimidation and statements to physicians in the course of receiving treatment" are nontestimonial and therefore are not governed by the Confrontation Clause. *See Giles*, 554 U.S. at 376. However, the Court would likely find such statements testimonial if, for instance, the statements were made to a physician at the request of law enforcement.

133. *Giles*, 554 U.S. at 358.

134. *See Melendez-Diaz v. Massachusetts*, 557 U.S. 305, 324 (2009).

135. 541 U.S. at 56.

136. *See Melendez-Diaz*, 557 U.S. at 324. Hospital laboratory tests are usually considered nontestimonial. *See, e.g.*, *State v. Musser*, 721 N.W.2d 734, 753-54 (Iowa 2006) (HIV-test report was "clearly nontestimonial"; "[a]lthough lab personnel possibly realized the report could be used in a later prosecution for criminal transmission of HIV, that use would be rare and certainly collateral to the primary purpose of providing the defendant and his medical providers with the information they needed to make informed treatment decisions"); *Commonwealth v. Lampron*, 839 N.E.2d 870, 875 (Mass. App. Ct. 2005) (hospital records containing drug- and alcohol-test results were nontestimonial), *appeal denied*, 843 N.E.2d 638 (Mass. 2006) (table case); *see also Sullivan v. State*, 248 S.W.3d 746, 750 (Tex. App.—Houston [1st Dist.] 2008, no pet.) (substance-abuse counselor's notes on defendant's drinking history were nontestimonial business records of hospital).

137. *Melendez-Diaz*, 557 U.S. at 324; *see, e.g.*, *Infante v. State*, 404 S.W.3d 656, 664 (Tex. App.—Houston [1st Dist.] 2012, no pet.) (in theft case involving theft of police radio, business records from radio shop containing radio's serial number were nontestimonial; primary purpose for obtaining serial number was not to generate evidence against defendant).

138. *See Bullcoming v. New Mexico*, 564 U.S. 647, 658-59 (2011); *Melendez-Diaz*, 557 U.S. at 310-11; *United States v. Martinez-Rios*, 595 F.3d 581, 586 (5th Cir. 2010); *Burch v. State*, 401 S.W.3d 634, 636-37 (Tex. Crim. App. 2013); *see, e.g.*, *United States v. Norwood*, 603 F.3d 1063, 1068-69 (9th Cir. 2010) (in drug prosecution, government offered records officer's affidavit that defendant did not report any wages for a three-year period as circumstantial evidence that defendant had no legal source for large amounts of cash found in his possession; admission of affidavit, without requiring officer to testify, was constitutional error under *Crawford* and *Melendez-Diaz* but harmless beyond a reasonable doubt because affidavit was cumulative). Although prison business records themselves may be nontestimonial, disciplinary reports and statements contained within those reports are generally considered testimonial and thus inadmissible under *Crawford* absent confrontation. *See, e.g.*, *Smith v. State*, 297 S.W.3d 260, 277 (Tex. Crim. App. 2009) (prison disciplinary reports describing defendant's offenses contained testimonial statements that were

Melendez-Diaz, the U.S. Supreme Court held that "certificates of analysis"—affidavits by chemists declaring that evidence seized was cocaine—were testimonial statements under *Crawford*.[139] Admission of the certificates without the chemists' testimony violated the defendant's right of confrontation because the certificates were "functionally identical to live, in-court testimony" and there was no showing "that the analysts were unavailable to testify at trial *and* that [the defendant] had a prior opportunity to cross-examine them."[140] Following *Melendez-Diaz*, some Texas courts of appeals have held that autopsy reports are testimonial when they are prepared as part of a criminal investigation.[141]

---

inadmissible under the Confrontation Clause because defendant did not have an opportunity to cross-examine the declarants; admission of reports was harmless error because the reports were read aloud to the jury but never emphasized again by the State); *Russeau v. State*, 171 S.W.3d 871, 880-81 (Tex. Crim. App. 2005) (prison disciplinary reports describing defendant's numerous incidents of fighting, verbal abuse, and possession of contraband while in custody, although contained within prison's business records, were testimonial and inadmissible without an opportunity to confront those who made out-of-court statements); *see also* **Grant v. State**, 218 S.W.3d 225, 232 (Tex. App.—Houston [14th Dist.] 2007, pet. ref'd) (school records containing specific descriptions of defendant's "behavior and quotations of language he used are not intended merely to establish that [he] committed a disciplinary infraction, but to establish that he violated school rules by engaging in the specific behavior described"; those statements were testimonial and inadmissible over Confrontation Clause objection). However, standard boilerplate language that does not contain a factual description of specific observations or events is nontestimonial and admissible. *See Smith*, 297 S.W.3d at 276; *see, e.g.*, **Segundo v. State**, 270 S.W.3d 79, 106-07 (Tex. Crim. App. 2008) (op. on reh'g) (preprinted boilerplate statements on official certificates revoking parole were not testimonial and were admissible as business records and public records).

139. *Melendez-Diaz*, 557 U.S. at 310-11.

140. *Id.*; *see also* **Martinez-Rios**, 595 F.3d at 586-87 (in case involving illegal reentry after deportation, defendant's Sixth Amendment rights were violated by prosecution's reliance on a Certificate of Nonexistence of Record (CNR) without providing the testimony of the records analyst who prepared the certificate; introduction of CNR in violation of Sixth Amendment was harmless error); **Cuadros-Fernandez v. State**, 316 S.W.3d 645, 657-58 (Tex. App.—Dallas 2009, no pet.) (admission of DNA reports without analyst's testimony violated defendant's right of confrontation; analyst believed that report would be available for use at a later trial, and State used report as a substitute for in-person testimony; introduction of DNA reports in violation of Sixth Amendment was harmful error). The *Melendez-Diaz* Court noted, however, that its holding was limited:

> [W]e do not hold, and it is not the case, that anyone whose testimony may be relevant in establishing the chain of custody, authenticity of the sample, or accuracy of the testing device, must appear in person as part of the prosecution's case. ... It is up to the prosecution to decide what steps in the chain of custody are so crucial as to require evidence; but what testimony *is* introduced must (if the defendant objects) be introduced live. Additionally, documents prepared in the regular course of equipment maintenance may well qualify as nontestimonial records.

557 U.S. at 311 n.1; *see* **Paredes v. State**, 462 S.W.3d 510, 515 (Tex. Crim. App. 2015), *cert. denied*, 136 S. Ct. 483 (2015); *see, e.g.*, **Mayer v. State**, 494 S.W.3d 844, 852 (Tex. App.—Houston [14th Dist.] 2016, pet. ref'd) (defendant's right of confrontation was not violated when she cross-examined analyst who performed DNA test and analyst who signed it; defendant was not entitled to cross-examine former employee who allegedly had tampered with other samples). Some courts have used this caveat in *Melendez-Diaz* to hold that records prepared by technical analysts who calibrate or maintain equipment are nontestimonial. *See, e.g.*, **Trigo v. State**, 485 S.W.3d 603, 610 (Tex. App.—Houston [1st Dist.] 2016, pet. ref'd) (technical supervisor who was custodian of records for Intoxilyzer at time of trial properly testified to test results; defendant's right of confrontation was not violated because records were nontestimonial and because he had opportunity to cross-examine police officer who administered field sobriety test and evidence technician who administered breathalyzer test); **Lara v. State**, 487 S.W.3d 244, 253 (Tex. App.—El Paso 2015, pet. ref'd) (on-duty technical supervisor's statements about Intoxilyzer's maintenance and condition were nontestimonial under **Settlemire v. State**; because no higher court addresses which aspects of breathalyzer use and maintenance produce testimonial statements, **Settlemire** controls); **Boutang v. State**, 402 S.W.3d 782, 789-90 (Tex. App.—San Antonio 2013, pet. ref'd) (technical supervisor in charge of Intoxilyzer at time of trial, but not when defendant received Intoxilyzer test, properly testified to test results and maintenance records; defendant's right of

In *Bullcoming v. New Mexico*, the Court expanded on what is required under the Confrontation Clause and *Melendez-Diaz* to admit lab reports that contain testimonial statements.[142] The U.S. Supreme Court held that the Confrontation Clause prohibited the in-court testimony of a forensic analyst who did not sign the certified forensic lab report at issue and did not perform or observe the blood-alcohol test reported in the certification.[143] Because the analyst who performed the test did more than report a machine-generated number—he certified the condition of the defendant's blood sample, confirmed that the number on the forensic report corresponded with the number on the sample, and performed a particular test on the sample—the Court concluded that "[t]hese representations, relating to past events and human actions not revealed in

confrontation was not violated because records were nontestimonial); *Settlemire v. State*, 323 S.W.3d 520, 522 (Tex. App.—Fort Worth 2010, pet. ref'd) (same); *see also Infante*, 404 S.W.3d at 666-67 (technician's recording of stolen radio's serial number was not testimonial; "he performed no analysis, made no representations as to his own personal observations or opinion, and did not attest to the accuracy of the number produced by the radio or the means by which it was obtained"). *But see Boutang*, 402 S.W.3d at 795-96 (Martinez, J., dissenting from denial of reh'g en banc) (majority's reliance on *Melendez-Diaz* and *Settlemire* is misplaced; footnote 1 from *Melendez-Diaz* is dicta, and both cases predate U.S. Supreme Court's decision in *Bullcoming v. New Mexico*).

The *Melendez-Diaz* Court also noted that several states have notice-and-demand statutes that require the prosecution to notify the defendant of its intent to use an analyst's report as evidence at trial; the statutes then give the defendant an opportunity to object to the admission of that evidence if the analyst is not going to testify at trial. 557 U.S. at 325-26; *see* TEX. CODE CRIM. PROC. art. 38.41, §4. This procedure permits the defendant "to assert (or forfeit by silence) his Confrontation Clause right after receiving notice of the prosecution's intent to use a forensic analyst's report." *Melendez-Diaz*, 557 U.S. at 326. Federal Rule 803(10) has been amended to include this notice-and-demand procedure. Refer to notes 737-738 *infra* and accompanying text.

141. *E.g.*, *Lee v. State*, 418 S.W.3d 892, 896 (Tex. App.—Houston [14th Dist.] 2013, pet. ref'd) ("While we need not decide whether autopsy reports will always be testimonial, … in this case, an objective medical examiner would reasonably believe that her report would be used in a later prosecution."); *Martinez v. State*, 311 S.W.3d 104, 111 (Tex. App.—Amarillo 2010, pet. ref'd) ("[T]he circumstances surrounding [victim's] death warranted the police to suspect that [victim] had been killed, an officer attended the autopsy and took photographs of the body, and it was reasonable for [medical examiner] to have assumed that his autopsy report would be used prosecutorially. Since the statutory basis giving rise to [medical examiner's] duty to perform the autopsy was that the circumstances surrounding [victim's] death warranted the suspicion that the death was caused by unlawful means, … we hold that [medical examiner's] autopsy report was a testimonial statement and that [medical examiner] was a witness within the meaning of the Confrontation Clause …."); *Wood v. State*, 299 S.W.3d 200, 209-10 (Tex. App.—Austin 2009, pet. ref'd) ("We do not hold that all autopsy reports are categorically testimonial. In this case, however, the circumstances surrounding [victim's] death warranted the police in the suspicion that his death was a homicide, and there is evidence that this is exactly what the police did suspect. The homicide detective who was the lead investigator in this case and a police evidence specialist attended the autopsy of [victim's] body. Under these circumstances, it is reasonable to assume that [medical examiner] understood that the report containing her findings and opinions would be used prosecutorially. We hold that [medical examiner's] autopsy report was a testimonial statement and that [medical examiner] was a witness within the meaning of the Confrontation Clause."); *see Williams v. State*, 513 S.W.3d 619, 637 (Tex. App.—Fort Worth 2016, pet. ref'd) (autopsy report is testimonial when objective medical examiner would believe report would be used in later prosecution, but expert may disclose facts from report conducted by someone else if expert relied on those facts to form his own conclusions). Some courts have held that, unlike autopsy reports, autopsy photographs are not statements and thus are not testimonial. *See Williams*, 513 S.W.3d at 637; *Herrera v. State*, 367 S.W.3d 762, 773 (Tex. App.—Houston [14th Dist.] 2012, no pet.); *Wood*, 299 S.W.3d at 214-15.

142. As in *Melendez-Diaz*, the lab report at issue contained testimonial statements. The laboratory was required by state law to assist in police investigations, and a law-enforcement officer provided seized evidence so the forensic analysts could perform the blood-alcohol test. *Bullcoming*, 564 U.S. at 664-65.

143. *Id.* at 657-58. The New Mexico Supreme Court erroneously held that a testifying analyst could rely on the results of a blood-alcohol test performed by another analyst because the analyst who performed the test was a "mere scrivener" who transcribed the results from the machine. *See id.* at 657.

raw, machine-produced data," were subject to cross-examination under the Confrontation Clause.[144] The prosecution also never asserted that the analyst who performed the test was unavailable, and the defendant did not have an opportunity to cross-examine him.[145] The Court concluded its analysis by stating that the Confrontation Clause "does not tolerate dispensing with confrontation simply because the court believes that questioning one witness about another's testimonial statements provides a fair enough opportunity for cross-examination."[146]

---

144. *Id.* at 659-60.

145. *E.g.*, *id.* at 657 (testimonial statement "may not be introduced against the accused at trial unless the witness who made the statement is unavailable and the accused has had a prior opportunity to confront that witness"; surrogate testimony could not convey what forensic analyst who performed blood-alcohol test observed). The analyst who performed the test had been placed on unpaid leave but was not designated as "unavailable." *Id.* at 662. The testifying analyst did not know why the analyst who performed the test had been placed on unpaid leave; "[w]ith [analyst who performed the test] on the stand, [defendant's] counsel could have asked questions designed to reveal whether incompetence, evasiveness, or dishonesty accounted for [analyst's] removal from his work station." *Id.* Further, the prosecution did not assert that the testifying analyst had an independent opinion about the results of the blood-alcohol test. *Id.*

146. *Id.*; *see Burch v. State*, 401 S.W.3d 634, 637-38 (Tex. Crim. App. 2013) ("Without having the testimony of the analyst who actually performed the tests, or at least one who observed their execution, the defendant has no way to explore the types of corruption and missteps the Confrontation Clause was designed to protect against. ... Rather, the witness being called needs to have personal knowledge of the facts in issue—the specific tests and their execution."); *see, e.g.*, *Kou v. State*, ___ S.W.3d ___ (Tex. App.—San Antonio 2017, n.p.h.) (No. 04-16-00346-CR; 8-16-17) (in prosecution for continuous sexual abuse of child, testimony of sexual-assault nurse examiner and child-abuse pediatrician violated Confrontation Clause; both witnesses based their testimony on results of tests conducted by analyst who was not called to testify, and witnesses offered no independent opinions or conclusions). In *Burch*, the testing analyst and the reviewing analyst signed a lab report that the State offered into evidence, but only the reviewer was called to testify at trial. *See Burch*, 401 S.W.3d at 635. The reviewer testified that she "basically double-checked everything that was done," but she did not explain her statement further, and there was no indication that she observed any tests being performed or that she conducted any herself. *Id.* at 635-36. In following *Bullcoming*, the court of criminal appeals held that the reviewer's testimony violated the Confrontation Clause because she had no personal knowledge that the tests were performed correctly or that the results had not been fabricated. *See Burch*, 401 S.W.3d at 637. As Justice Sotomayor explained in her *Bullcoming* concurrence:

> [T]his is not a case in which the person testifying is a supervisor, reviewer, or someone else with a personal, albeit limited, connection to the scientific test at issue. ... It would be a different case if, for example, a supervisor who observed an analyst conducting a test testified about the results or a report about such results.

564 U.S. at 672-73 (Sotomayor, J., concurring); *see, e.g.*, *Grim v. Fisher*, 816 F.3d 296, 308-09 (5th Cir. 2016) (no Confrontation Clause violation in admitting testimony from technical supervisor who examined report and all data, ensured that proper tests were conducted and that analyst's interpretations were correct, ensured that the results coincided with conclusion, agreed with reasonable degree of scientific certainty with analyst's examinations and results, and signed report; defendant was not entitled to habeas corpus relief on Confrontation Clause grounds because *Bullcoming* did not clearly establish degree of involvement required for witness who did not perform forensic testing), *cert. denied*, 137 S. Ct. 211 (2016); *Paredes v. State*, 462 S.W.3d 510, 517-18 (Tex. Crim. App. 2015) (opinion of supervising DNA analyst, based on analysis she performed using raw computer-generated data that was not admitted into evidence, did not violate Confrontation Clause; analyst had personal knowledge of tests used, performed crucial analysis herself, testified to her own conclusions, and was available for cross-examination), *cert. denied*, 136 S. Ct. 483 (2015); *Whitfield v. State*, ___ S.W.3d ___ (Tex. App.—Houston [14th Dist.] 2017, pet. ref'd) (No. 14-15-00820-CR; 3-9-17) (testimony of DNA analyst supervisor, who interpreted raw data to perform comparisons and form opinion that DNA sample matched defendant, did not violate Confrontation Clause; although supervisor did not observe testing, she performed her own analysis, was trained in every step of process, and had to review and confirm each technician's work); *Ellison v. State*, 494 S.W.3d 316, 325 (Tex. App.—Eastland 2015, pet. ref'd) (opinion of ballistics analyst, although he was not supervisor at time of crime, did not violate Confrontation Clause; analyst conducted his own independent comparison between test bullets and

In *Williams v. Illinois*, the Supreme Court addressed a question left unanswered by *Melendez-Diaz* and *Bullcoming*: "does *Crawford* bar an expert from expressing an opinion based on facts about a case that have been made known to the expert but about which the expert is not competent to testify?"[147] A plurality of the justices[148] took up the issue posed by Justice Sotomayor in her *Bullcoming* concurrence, which was "the constitutionality of allowing an expert witness to disclose others' testimonial statements if the testimonial statements themselves were not admitted as evidence."[149] The *Williams* case involved the testimony of a forensic DNA analyst who relied on the tests performed by another laboratory to form her opinion that the samples in this case matched the defendant's DNA.[150] A majority of the Court held that the disclosure of the laboratory's out-of-court statements through the expert witness did not violate the Confrontation Clause.[151] The plurality explained that the truth of the expert's statements did not depend on the predicate facts in the report; thus, the information in the report was not offered for the truth of the matter asserted.[152] The report formed the basis for the expert's opinion, and she could include those facts in her testimony under both the Illinois and Federal Rules of Evidence.[153] Further, the limitation that the expert may disclose inadmissible facts or data "only if their probative value in helping

---

evidence bullets, testified to those comparisons, and was available for cross-examination); *see also* ***Boutang v. State***, 402 S.W.3d 782, 788 (Tex. App.—San Antonio 2013, pet. ref'd) (expert on Intoxilyzer machines could offer testimony about maintenance of machine and interpret report by explaining significance of numbers in report; no Confrontation Clause violation because "[s]he did not testify she prepared or created a report that was actually created by another analyst, nor was she certifying such a report based on the machine's results [but instead] was interpreting the results from the machine's own print-out"). In ***Paredes***, the computer-generated DNA profiles—unlike the certificates in ***Melendez-Diaz***—were not the functional equivalent of live, in-court testimony because they came from a computer rather than from a witness who could be cross-examined. *See* ***Paredes***, 462 S.W.3d at 519. Refer to notes 139-140 *supra* and accompanying text.

147. 567 U.S. 50, 56 (2012) (plurality op.).

148. The plurality opinion was written by Justice Alito and joined by Chief Justice Roberts, Justice Kennedy, and Justice Breyer. These four justices were the dissenters in ***Melendez-Diaz*** and ***Bullcoming***.

149. ***Williams***, 567 U.S. at 67; *see* ***Bullcoming***, 564 U.S. at 673 (Sotomayor, J., concurring).

150. ***Williams***, 567 U.S. at 60-62.

151. *See id.* at 58. Justice Thomas concurred in the judgment because the laboratory's out-of-court statements "lacked the requisite 'formality and solemnity' to be considered 'testimonial' for purposes of the Confrontation Clause." *Id.* at 104 (Thomas, J., concurring in judgment). Justice Thomas concluded that the report "lack[ed] the solemnity of an affidavit or deposition, for it [was] neither a sworn nor a certified declaration of fact. Nowhere [did] the report attest that its statements accurately reflect[ed] the DNA testing processes used or the results obtained." *Id.* at 111.

152. *See id.* at 77 (plurality op.). The expert witness referred to the report "not to prove … that the report contained an accurate profile of the perpetrator's DNA, but only to establish that the report contained a DNA profile that matched the DNA profile deduced from [defendant's] blood." *Id.* at 79. Refer to note 66 *supra* and accompanying text.

153. *Id.* at 69; *see* FED. R. EVID. 703; ILL. R. EVID. 703. The plurality explained that under Federal Rule 703, "basis evidence" that is not admissible for its truth may be disclosed even in a jury trial under appropriate circumstances. The purpose for allowing this disclosure is that it may "assis[t] the jury to evaluate the expert's opinion." The Rule 703 approach … is based on the idea that the disclosure of basis evidence can help the factfinder understand the expert's thought process and determine what weight to give to the expert's opinion.
Williams, 567 U.S. at 78. Refer to *Article VII: Opinions & Expert Testimony, supra* p. 747.

the jury evaluate the opinion substantially outweighs their prejudicial effect"[154] does not apply in bench trials.[155] The plurality concluded that the laboratory's report would have been admissible as evidence, even if it had been offered for its truth, because it was not a testimonial statement.[156] The primary purpose of the laboratory's report was not to accuse the defendant or prepare evidence for trial, but rather to "catch a dangerous rapist who was still at large."[157]

The dissent's rationale was based on the comparability of the facts of *Williams* to those in *Bullcoming*. According to Justices Kagan, Scalia, Ginsburg, and Sotomayor,[158] the reports at issue in the two cases served the same purpose,[159] and the testimony that the expert witness offered in *Williams* was "functionally identical" to that offered in *Bullcoming*.[160] Because the plurality reached a different result on similar facts, the dissent signaled the end of the "clear" rule that had developed through the previous line of cases: "Before today's decision, a prosecutor wishing to admit the results of forensic testing had to produce the technician responsible for the analysis. That was the result of not one, but two decisions this Court issued in the last three years. But that clear rule is clear no longer."[161] The decision in *Williams* is likely to cause "significant confusion"[162] for courts going forward in determining whether laboratory reports are admissible under the Confrontation Clause and which laboratory personnel are required to testify.

---

154. FED. R. EVID. 703. Refer to *Article VII: Opinions & Expert Testimony, supra* p. 750.

155. *See Williams*, 567 U.S. at 69 ("When the judge sits as the trier of fact, it is presumed that the judge will understand the limited reason for the disclosure of the underlying inadmissible information and will not rely on that information for any improper purpose."); *Harris v. Rivera*, 454 U.S. 339, 346 (1981) ("In bench trials, judges routinely hear inadmissible evidence that they are presumed to ignore when making decisions."). *But see Williams*, 567 U.S. at 130 (Kagan, Scalia, Ginsburg, Sotomayor, JJ., dissenting) ("[T]he presence of a judge does not transform the constitutional question. In applying the Confrontation Clause, we have never before considered relevant the decisionmaker's identity.").

156. *See Williams*, 567 U.S. at 81-82 (plurality op.).

157. *Id.* at 84. The plurality described the test as determining whether "out-of-court statements hav[e] the primary purpose of accusing a targeted individual of engaging in criminal conduct." *See id.* at 82. Justice Thomas, in his concurrence, criticized the "new primary purpose test" and stated that it "lacks any grounding in constitutional text, in history, or in logic." *Id.* at 114 (Thomas, J., concurring in judgment); *see also id.* at 135 (Kagan, Scalia, Ginsburg, Sotomayor, JJ., dissenting) ("We have previously asked whether a statement was made for the primary purpose of establishing 'past events potentially relevant to later criminal prosecution'—in other words, for the purpose of providing evidence. None of our cases has ever suggested that, in addition, the statement must be meant to accuse a previously identified individual ...."). For a discussion of how the primary-purpose test has evolved, refer to notes 95-126 *supra* and accompanying text.

158. While Justice Thomas concurred in the judgment, he noted that he "share[d] the dissent's view of the plurality's flawed analysis." *Id.* at 104 (Thomas, J., concurring in judgment).

159. *See id.* at 123 (Kagan, Scalia, Ginsburg, Sotomayor, JJ., dissenting) (report was identical to one in *Bullcoming* in "all material respects"; it discussed results of forensic testing on evidence gathered by police and was made to establish facts in criminal proceeding).

160. *Id.* at 124 (Kagan, Scalia, Ginsburg, Sotomayor, JJ., dissenting).

161. *Id.* at 140-41 (Kagan, Scalia, Ginsburg, Sotomayor, JJ., dissenting).

162. *Id.* at 141; *see Paredes v. State*, 462 S.W.3d 510, 516 (Tex. Crim. App. 2015) (*Williams* has limited precedential value; "because each of the *Williams* opinions applies a different rationale to determining whether the use of forensic evidence violates the Confrontation Clause, and because five members of the Supreme Court disagreed with

E. Forfeiture by Wrongdoing: *Giles v. California*

In both ***Crawford*** and ***Davis***, the Supreme Court reiterated that the "forfeiture by wrongdoing" doctrine applies to the Confrontation Clause.[163] If the witness cannot appear at trial because the defendant has prevented that appearance by a wrongful act—for example, murder, bribery, or intimidation—the defendant forfeits the right to insist on face-to-face confrontation.[164] The doctrine does not, however, apply to every act by a defendant that prevents a witness from testifying at trial. The Court held in ***Giles v. California*** that the rule applies only if the defendant's actions were *designed* to prevent the witness from testifying.[165] For example, the doctrine does not apply if the defendant murders a witness for reasons other than preventing the witness from testifying at trial.[166] But if the reason for the murder was to prevent the witness from testifying, the rule applies and the witness's out-of-court statements can be admitted without violating the Confrontation Clause.[167] To determine the defendant's motives for causing the witness's unavailability, the trial judge must closely examine the

the plurality's rationale, there is no narrow rule that this Court can apply from ***Williams***), *cert. denied*, 136 S. Ct. 483 (2015); ***Burch v. State***, 401 S.W.3d 634, 638 (Tex. Crim. App. 2013) ("***Williams*** was a splintered decision in which only an outcome, and not an opinion, received a majority vote. This made its full impact hard to discern."); ***Lee v. State***, 418 S.W.3d 892, 898 (Tex. App.—Houston [14th Dist.] 2013, pet. ref'd) (***Williams*** "raises as many questions as it answers").

163. ***Davis v. Washington***, 547 U.S. 813, 833 (2006) ("[W]hen defendants seek to undermine the judicial process by procuring or coercing silence from witnesses and victims, the Sixth Amendment does not require courts to acquiesce. While defendants have no duty to assist the State in proving their guilt, they *do* have the duty to refrain from acting in ways that destroy the integrity of the criminal-trial system."); ***Crawford v. Washington***, 541 U.S. 36, 62 (2004) ("[T]he rule of forfeiture by wrongdoing ... extinguishes confrontation claims on essentially equitable grounds ....").

164. *See, e.g.*, ***People v. Moore***, 117 P.3d 1, 5 (Colo. App. 2004) (300-pound defendant who sat on his wife's chest until she died of asphyxiation forfeited his right to claim a Confrontation Clause violation in connection with the admission of her out-of-court statement implicating him in a previous instance of domestic violence); ***Gonzalez v. State***, 195 S.W.3d 114, 114-15 (Tex. Crim. App. 2006) ("[A]ppellant forfeited, by his own misconduct of fatally shooting [murder victim] during a robbery or the burglary of her home, his right to confront [victim] in court about hearsay statements she made before she died.").

165. *See* ***Giles v. California***, 554 U.S. 353, 368 (2008).

166. *See, e.g.*, ***Render v. State***, 347 S.W.3d 905, 918 (Tex. App.—Eastland 2011, pet. ref'd) (doctrine of forfeiture by wrongdoing did not apply because victim died from injuries that did not appear to be life-threatening and defendant did not intend to kill victim); ***Davis v. State***, 268 S.W.3d 683, 706 (Tex. App.—Fort Worth 2008, pet. ref'd) (because there was no evidence that defendant murdered victim to prevent her from testifying, defendant did not forfeit his right to confront her; trial court erred under ***Giles*** in allowing police officer's hearsay testimony on victim's statements to him about defendant).

167. In ***Giles***, the defendant was convicted in California state court of murdering his ex-girlfriend, Brenda Avie. *See* ***Giles***, 554 U.S. at 356-57. California law permits the admission at trial of out-of-court statements describing the infliction or threat of physical injury on a declarant when the declarant is unavailable to testify and the prior statements are deemed trustworthy. CAL. EVID. CODE §1370; ***Giles***, 554 U.S. at 357. Over the defendant's objection, the trial court admitted statements made by Avie about three weeks before the murder to a police officer who responded to a domestic-violence report. ***Giles***, 554 U.S. at 356-57. The defendant was convicted of first-degree murder. *Id.* at 357. On appeal, the California Court of Appeal held that admission of the statements did not violate the Confrontation Clause because the statements were admissible under the doctrine of forfeiture by wrongdoing. *Id.* The Court of Appeal held that the defendant forfeited his right to confront Avie when he murdered her, and the California Supreme Court affirmed the conviction on the same ground. *Id.* The United States Supreme Court vacated the judgment of the California Supreme Court and remanded the case for further proceedings. *Id.* at 377.

evidence.[168] The *Giles* Court concluded that at common law the rule imposed a purpose-based definition of forfeiture: forfeiture occurs only when the defendant intended and designed to prevent a witness from testifying; mere wrongdoing without the required intent is not enough to permit the admission of unconfronted testimony.[169] The Court refused to expand the forfeiture rule beyond its scope at common law.[170]

The defendant may also forfeit the right to face-to-face confrontation even if the witness is present in the courtroom; "physical unavailability is not the only way to find forfeiture by wrongdoing."[171]

F. Waiver; Standard of Review

A party waives any potential Confrontation Clause error by not objecting on this specific basis.[172] A hearsay objection does not preserve error on Confrontation Clause grounds.[173] And a defendant who uses the declarant's testimonial statement waives any Confrontation Clause objection.[174] However, the defendant has no obligation to call an out-of-court declarant even if that declarant is available; the defendant does not waive his right to confront the declarant by not calling him as a witness.[175] The right

---

168. *See Giles*, 554 U.S. at 377. The Court illustrated the kind of analysis a trial court must perform to determine whether forfeiture by wrongdoing has occurred:

> Acts of domestic violence often are intended to dissuade a victim from resorting to outside help, and include conduct designed to prevent testimony to police officers or cooperation in criminal prosecutions. Where such an abusive relationship culminates in murder, the evidence may support a finding that the crime expressed the intent to isolate the victim and to stop her from reporting abuse to the authorities or cooperating with a criminal prosecution—rendering her prior statements admissible under the forfeiture doctrine. Earlier abuse, or threats of abuse, intended to dissuade the victim from resorting to outside help would be highly relevant to this inquiry, as would evidence of ongoing criminal proceedings at which the victim would have been expected to testify.

Id.

169. *See id.* at 367-68.

170. *Id.* at 377.

171. *Sohail v. State*, 264 S.W.3d 251, 259 (Tex. App.—Houston [1st Dist.] 2008, pet. ref'd). In *Sohail*, the defendant's repeated physical violence against the complainant and threats to kill her were sufficient to support a finding that defendant's intimidation caused the complainant to refuse to testify. *Id.* at 260. Although the complainant was present in court, the trial court did not abuse its discretion by finding her "unavailable" because of the defendant's deliberate wrongdoing. *Id.* at 259-60.

172. *Davis v. State*, 313 S.W.3d 317, 347 (Tex. Crim. App. 2010); *Beham v. State*, 476 S.W.3d 724, 732 (Tex. App.—Texarkana 2015, no pet.); *see Paredes v. State*, 129 S.W.3d 530, 535 (Tex. Crim. App. 2004); *Wright v. State*, 28 S.W.3d 526, 536 (Tex. Crim. App. 2000); *see, e.g., United States v. Rashid*, 383 F.3d 769, 776 (8th Cir. 2004) (although admission of accomplice's testimonial statements—taken by FBI agents in the course of interrogations—violated defendant's Confrontation Clause rights, he did not preserve this error for appellate review), *vacated on other grounds sub nom. Abu Nahia v. United States*, 546 U.S. 803 (2005); *Lee v. State*, 418 S.W.3d 892, 897-98 (Tex. App.—Houston [14th Dist.] 2013, pet. ref'd) (court of appeals could not consider defendant's Confrontation Clause argument that autopsy photos were testimonial; by objecting at trial on Rule 403 grounds to some photos and stating he didn't have "any objection" to other photos admitted, defendant waived Confrontation Clause objection).

173. *Reyna v. State*, 168 S.W.3d 173, 179 (Tex. Crim. App. 2005); *Dreyer v. State*, 309 S.W.3d 751, 755 (Tex. App.—Houston [14th Dist.] 2010, no pet.).

174. *See, e.g., State v. Harris*, 871 A.2d 341, 346 (R.I. 2005) ("Having chosen to use [declarant's] statement in his cross-examination of both [officers], defendant waived any right that he arguably may have had under the Confrontation Clause with respect to that statement.").

175. *See, e.g., State v. Cox*, 876 So. 2d 932, 938-39 (La. Ct. App. 2004) (rejecting State's contention that defendant waived his right to object to the introduction of conspirator's statement because court had offered him the right

to confront an out-of-court declarant is also not waived by stipulating to that witness's incompetency or unavailability.[176]

Out-of-court statements admitted in violation of the Confrontation Clause are subject to a harmless-error analysis under ***Chapman v. California***.[177] The Texas Court of Criminal Appeals has listed the following as factors to be considered when performing a harmless-error analysis on such hearsay evidence: (1) the importance of the hearsay evidence to the State's case, (2) whether the hearsay evidence was cumulative of other evidence, (3) the presence or absence of other evidence corroborating or contradicting the hearsay evidence on material points, and (4) the overall strength of the State's case.[178] The reviewing court may also consider any other factor that "may shed light on the probable impact of the trial court's error on the minds of average jurors."[179] The court of criminal appeals has emphasized that "when evidence is erroneously admitted in violation of ***Crawford***, the question for the reviewing court is not whether the jury verdict was supported by the evidence, even discounting the erroneously admitted evidence."[180] Rather than "conduct such a truncated harm analysis," the court must consider the factors listed above.[181]

---

to subpoena her as a witness; "Defendant should not be required to call [conspirator] as a witness simply to facilitate the State's introduction of evidence against the Defendant. Moreover, there could be a whole host of reasons why Defendant would not want to call [conspirator] as a witness. Simply stated, if the State needed to have [conspirator's] testimony to enable the State to introduce the statement into evidence, the State could have called [her] as a witness."); ***Bratton v. State***, 156 S.W.3d 689, 694 (Tex. App.—Dallas 2005, pet. ref'd.) (rejecting State's argument that because defendant chose not to call witnesses, he could not complain he was denied his right to confront them; "[W]e find nothing in ***Crawford*** or elsewhere suggesting that a defendant waives his right to confront a witness whose testimonial statement was admitted into evidence by failing to call him as a witness at trial. … In fact, as the party seeking to admit [witnesses'] statements, it was the State's burden to show their statements were admissible, that is, that [witnesses] were *unavailable* and that [defendant] had been afforded a prior opportunity to cross-examine them.").

176. *See, e.g.*, ***People ex rel. R.A.S.***, 111 P.3d 487, 490 (Colo. Ct. App. 2004) ("The People argue that the juvenile waived his confrontation claim by stipulating that the victim was incompetent to testify as a witness. We do not agree. The stipulation merely established the unavailability of the witness; it was consistent with that stipulation for the juvenile to assert, as he did in the trial court, that the hearsay statement otherwise violated his right of confrontation.").

177. *See* ***Chapman v. California***, 386 U.S. 18, 24 (1967); ***Rubio v. State***, 241 S.W.3d 1, 3 (Tex. Crim. App. 2007); *see, e.g.*, ***United States v. Norwood***, 603 F.3d 1063, 1068-69 (9th Cir. 2010) (admission of records officer's affidavit, without requiring officer to testify, was constitutional error under ***Crawford*** but harmless beyond a reasonable doubt; other evidence established defendant's guilt, and affidavit was merely cumulative); ***United States v. Alvarado-Valdez***, 521 F.3d 337, 342-43 (5th Cir. 2008) (police officer's testimony about interrogation of defendant's coconspirator, who had fled the country, was constitutional error under ***Crawford*** and not harmless beyond a reasonable doubt; government relied heavily on improper testimony during closing argument); ***Smith v. State***, 436 S.W.3d 353, 371-72 (Tex. App.—Houston [14th Dist.] 2014, pet. ref'd) (admission of testimony of DNA lab supervisor without forensic report prepared by another analyst may have violated Confrontation Clause, but any error was harmless beyond a reasonable doubt; State's case did not hinge on the testimony, the testimony was corroborated by and cumulative of other evidence, and State's case was strong without the testimony); ***Ray v. State***, 176 S.W.3d 544, 551-52 (Tex. App.—Houston [1st Dist.] 2004, pet. ref'd) (admission of codefendant's custodial statement to police was constitutional error under ***Crawford*** but harmless beyond a reasonable doubt).

178. ***Langham v. State***, 305 S.W.3d 568, 582 (Tex. Crim. App. 2010); ***Clay v. State***, 240 S.W.3d 895, 904 (Tex. Crim. App. 2007); ***Davis v. State***, 203 S.W.3d 845, 852 (Tex. Crim. App. 2006).

179. ***Clay***, 240 S.W.3d at 904; *see* ***Davis***, 203 S.W.3d at 852.

180. ***Langham***, 305 S.W.3d at 582.

181. *See id.* at 583.

RULE 801

DEFINITIONS THAT APPLY TO THIS ARTICLE; EXCLUSIONS FROM HEARSAY

(a) Statement. "Statement" means a person's oral or written verbal expression, or nonverbal conduct that a person intended as a substitute for verbal expression.

(b) Declarant. "Declarant" means the person who made the statement.

(c) Matter Asserted. "Matter asserted" means:

(1) any matter a declarant explicitly asserts; and

(2) any matter implied by a statement, if the probative value of the statement as offered flows from the declarant's belief about the matter.

(d) Hearsay. "Hearsay" means a statement that:

(1) the declarant does not make while testifying at the current trial or hearing; and

(2) a party offers in evidence to prove the truth of the matter asserted in the statement.

(e) Statements That Are Not Hearsay. A statement that meets the following conditions is not hearsay:

(1) *A Declarant-Witness's Prior Statement.* The declarant testifies and is subject to cross-examination about a prior statement, and the statement:

(A) is inconsistent with the declarant's testimony and:

(i) when offered in a civil case, was given under penalty of perjury at a trial, hearing, or other proceeding or in a deposition; or

(ii) when offered in a criminal case, was given under penalty of perjury at a trial, hearing, or other proceeding—except a grand jury proceeding—or in a deposition;

(B) is consistent with the declarant's testimony and is offered to rebut an express or implied charge that the declarant recently fabricated it or acted from a recent improper influence or motive in so testifying; or

(C) identifies a person as someone the declarant perceived earlier.

(2) *An Opposing Party's Statement.* The statement is offered against an opposing party and:

(A) was made by the party in an individual or representative capacity;

(B) is one the party manifested that it adopted or believed to be true;

(C) was made by a person whom the party authorized to make a statement on the subject;

(D) was made by the party's agent or employee on a matter within the scope of that relationship and while it existed; or

(E) was made by the party's coconspirator during and in furtherance of the conspiracy.

(3) *A Deponent's Statement.* In a civil case, the statement was made in a deposition taken in the same proceeding. "Same proceeding" is defined in Rule of Civil Procedure 203.6(b). The deponent's unavailability as a witness is not a requirement for admissibility.

Notes and Comments

Comment to 2015 restyling: Statements falling under the hearsay exclusion provided by Rule 801(e)(2) are no longer referred to as "admissions" in the title to the subdivision. The term "admissions" is confusing because not all statements covered by the exclusion are admissions in the colloquial sense—a statement can be within the exclusion even if it "admitted" nothing and was not against the party's interest when made. The term "admissions" also raises confusion in comparison with the Rule 803(24) exception for declarations against interest. No change in application of the exclusion is intended.

The deletion of former Rule 801(e)(1)(D), which cross-references Code of Criminal Procedure art. 38.071, is not intended as a substantive change. Including this cross-reference made sense when the Texas Rules of Criminal Evidence were first promulgated, but with subsequent changes to the statutory provision, its inclusion is no longer appropriate. The version of article 38.071 that was initially cross-referenced in the Rules of Criminal Evidence required the declarant-victim to be available to testify at the trial. That requirement has since been deleted from the statute, and the statute no longer requires either the availability or testimony of the declarant-victim. Thus, cross-referencing the statute in Rule 801(e)(1), which applies only when the declarant testifies at trial about the prior statement, no longer makes sense. Moreover, article 38.071 is but one of a number of statutes that mandate the admission of certain hearsay statements in particular circumstances. *See, e.g.*, Code of Criminal Procedure art. 38.072; Family Code §§54.031, 104.002, 104.006. These statutory provisions take precedence over the general rule excluding hearsay, see Rules 101(c) and 802, and there is no apparent justification for cross-referencing article 38.071 and not all other such provisions.

RULE 801

COMMENTARY ON RULE 801

Rule 801 does four different things. First, it defines hearsay.[182] The formal definition of hearsay is in Rule 801(d), but that section depends on the definitions of "statement," "declarant," and, most importantly, "matter asserted," in Rule 801(a) through (c). Second, Rule 801(e)(1) exempts from the hearsay definition several specific types of out-of-court statements by a witness who testifies at trial and is subject to cross-examination about those statements.[183] Any other out-of-court statement made by the testifying witness and offered for its truth is hearsay.[184] Third, Rule 801(e)(2) removes from the definition of hearsay all statements by an opposing party—personal statements, statements made in a representative capacity, statements made by the opposing party's agent or employee, and statements made by a coconspirator.[185] Fourth, it exempts from the definition of hearsay civil depositions taken and offered in the same civil proceeding.[186]

The original comment to Rule 801 was deleted as unnecessary in the 1998 unification of the Texas Rules,[187] but the comment helpfully set out and distinguished the types of statements that the rule defines as hearsay. Rule 801 still covers the same types of statements.

---

182. *See* Tex. R. Evid. 801(a)-(d).

183. *See* Tex. R. Evid. 801(e)(1). Three types of out-of-court statements by the testifying witness—prior inconsistent statements, certain prior consistent statements, and prior identifications—are exempted from the hearsay definition. Refer to notes 282-343 *infra* and accompanying text.

184. *See* 1A Ray, *supra* note 9, §785, at 12 (hearsay rule applies even to evidence of previous statements made by witness). The rationale "is that a deferred opportunity to cross-examine is thought to be distinctly inferior to contemporaneous cross-examination." *Coronado v. State*, 351 S.W.3d 315, 327 (Tex. Crim. App. 2011). Dean Wigmore had once advocated this position but "on further reflection" rejected it. *See* 2 John H. Wigmore, A Treatise on the System of Evidence in Trials at Common Law §1018 (2d ed. 1923) (if witness is present and subject to cross-examination, "[t]here is ample opportunity to test him as to the basis for his former statement"); *see also* Laurie R. Rockett, Comment, *Substantive Use of Extrajudicial Statements of Witnesses Under the Proposed Federal Rules of Evidence*, 4 U. Rich. L. Rev. 110, 117-18 (1969) (excluding extrajudicial statements on the basis of the "hearsay dangers" criteria alone is "inconsistent with a practical definition of hearsay"). A more practical reason for excluding a testifying witness's former statements as hearsay is to deter the zealous advocate from encouraging witnesses to write down self-serving accounts and then using those written statements as substantive evidence at trial. *See* Fed. R. Evid. 801 advisory committee's note, subdiv. (d)(1) ("The position taken by the Advisory Committee in formulating this part of the rule is founded upon an unwillingness to countenance the general use of prior prepared statements as substantive evidence ....").

Further, the presently testifying witness may not rely on or recite the contents of hearsay documents offered for their truth. *See, e.g.*, **Marshall v. Telecomms. Specialists, Inc.**, 806 S.W.2d 904, 906 (Tex. App.—Houston [1st Dist.] 1991, no writ) (error to permit the plaintiff's witness to testify to the present value of unpaid rentals of telecommunication equipment by referring to a document that she had not prepared, that was not admitted into evidence, and that contained hearsay based on hearsay).

185. *See* Tex. R. Evid. 801(e)(2). Refer to notes 344-445 *infra* and accompanying text. Rule 801(e)(2) no longer uses the term "admissions." Refer to note 345 *infra*.

186. *See* Tex. R. Evid. 801(e)(3). Refer to notes 446-450 *infra* and accompanying text.

187. The original comment to both Civil and Criminal Rule 801 read:

Comment: The definitions in 801(a), (b), (c) and (d) combined bring within the hearsay rule four categories of conduct. These are described and illustrated below.

(1) A verbal (oral or written) explicit assertion. Illustration. Witness testifies that declarant said "A shot B." Declarant's conduct is a statement because it is an oral expression. Because it is an explicit

A. Rule 801(a)-(d): Definition of Hearsay

Defining hearsay is not a simple matter, and many definitions have been advanced.[188] In considering any of them, keep in mind that in hearsay situations, "[t]oo much should not be expected of a definition."[189] Rule 801 defines hearsay as a statement[190] that the declarant[191] made other than while testifying at the current trial or hearing and that a party is offering into evidence to prove the truth of the matter asserted.[192]

---

assertion, the matter asserted is that A shot B. Finally, the statement is hearsay because it was not made while testifying at the trial and is offered to prove the truth of the matter asserted.

(2) A verbal (oral or written) explicit assertion, not offered to prove the matter explicitly asserted, but offered for the truth of a matter implied by the statement, the probative value of the statement flowing from declarant's belief as to the matter. Illustration. The only known remedy for X disease is medicine Y and the only known use of medicine Y is to cure X disease. To prove that Oglethorpe had X disease, witness testifies that declarant, a doctor, stated, "The best medicine for Oglethorpe is Y." The testimony is to a statement because it was a verbal expression. The matter asserted was that Oglethorpe had X disease because that matter is implied from the statement, the probative value of the statement as offered flowing from declarant's belief as to the matter. Finally, the statement is hearsay because it was not made while testifying at the trial and is offered to prove the truth of the matter asserted.

(3) Non-assertive verbal conduct offered for the truth of a matter implied by the statement, the probative value of the statement flowing from declarant's belief as to the matter. Illustration. In a rape prosecution to prove that Richard, the defendant, was in the room at the time of the rape, W testifies that declarant knocked on the door to the room and shouted, "Open the door, Richard." The testimony is to a statement because it was a verbal expression. The matter asserted was that Richard was in the room because that matter is implied from the statement, the probative value of the statement as offered flowing from declarant's belief as to the matter. Finally, the statement is hearsay because it was not made while testifying at the trial and is offered to prove the truth of the matter asserted.

(4) Nonverbal assertive conduct not intended as a substitute for verbal expression. Illustration. W testifies that A asked declarant "Which way did X go?" and declarant pointed north. This nonverbal conduct of declarant was intended by him as a substitute for verbal expression and so is a statement. The matter asserted is that X went north because that is implied from the statement and the probative value of the statement as offered flows from declarant's belief that X went north. Finally, the statement is hearsay because it was not made at trial and is offered to prove the truth of the matter asserted. TEX. R. CIV. EVID. 801 cmt., 641-642 S.W.2d (Tex. Cases) LVI (1983, amended 1998); TEX. R. CRIM. EVID. 801 cmt., 701-702 S.W.2d (Tex. Cases) LIII (1986, amended 1998). Refer to notes 207-211 *infra* and accompanying text.

188. *See* RICHARD O. LEMPERT & STEPHEN A. SALTZBURG, A MODERN APPROACH TO EVIDENCE 338 (1977) (literally hundreds of different hearsay definitions can be found in the case law); Roger C. Park, *McCormick on Evidence and the Concept of Hearsay: A Critical Analysis Followed by Suggestions to Law Teachers*, 65 MINN. L. REV. 423, 424 (1981) (detailing complex definitions of hearsay; most are either assertion-oriented or declarant-oriented); Carl C. Wheaton, *What Is Hearsay?*, 46 IOWA L. REV. 210, 210 (1961) (there is no generally accepted definition of hearsay).

189. MCCORMICK'S HANDBOOK II, *supra* note 7, §246, at 584. Charles McCormick adds that a definition cannot furnish answers to all the complex problems of an extensive field (such as hearsay) in a sentence. The most it can accomplish is to furnish a helpful starting point for discussion of the problems, and a memory aid in recalling some of the solutions. But if the definition is to remain brief and understandable, it will necessarily distort some parts of the picture. Simplification has a measure of falsification.
Id.

190. A statement is "a person's oral or written verbal expression, or nonverbal conduct that a person intended as a substitute for verbal expression." TEX. R. EVID. 801(a). Refer to notes 207-211 *infra* and accompanying text.

191. The declarant is the person who made the statement. TEX. R. EVID. 801(b).

192. TEX. R. EVID. 801(d); *see also* **Los Fresnos Consol. Indep. Sch. Dist. v. Vazquez**, 481 S.W.3d 742, 745 (Tex. App.—Austin 2015, pet. denied) ("The current Texas Rules of Evidence contemplate that hearsay *is* evidence but

RULE 801

1. Differences between federal & Texas definitions. The definition in Rule 801 differs significantly in its breadth from the corresponding federal provision. Federal Rule 801 narrowly limits the common-law scope of hearsay, with consequences that some oppose in both principle and practice.[193] The Texas rule avoids these problems and establishes a definition that is nearly, if not exactly, consistent with the Texas common-law concept of hearsay.

Rule 801 has incorporated a hybrid of the common-law definition of hearsay and the approach taken by the Federal Rules. Rule 801(a) through (d) are virtually identical to Federal Rule 801(a) through (c). The rules contain two significant differences. First, Texas Rule 801(a)'s definition of "statement" uses the term "verbal expression," while the federal definition uses the narrower term "assertion."[194] Second, Texas Rule 801(c) defines "matter asserted" to include not only explicit assertions but also "any matter implied by a statement" if the statement's probative value depends on the declarant's belief about the matter.[195] The federal rule does not define "matter asserted."

The two primary definitions of hearsay are the "declarant-based" definition and the "assertion-based" definition. Texas has adopted a modified version of the declarant-based definition, and the Federal Rules use the assertion-based definition.

Under the declarant-based definition, evidence is hearsay when the probative value of the evidence requires the fact-finder to believe not only the witness providing the evidence in court but also some person out of court.[196] For example, the testimony of wit-

---

reflect the policy that hearsay is generally not reliable enough to be *admitted* as evidence in proceedings to which the Rules apply."). For the definition of "matter asserted," refer to note 195 *infra* and accompanying text.

193. *See* Wellborn, *supra* note 1, at 50-52 (examining the deficiencies of Federal Rule 801(a)-(c)).

194. Neither the rule nor the Advisory Committee's note defines "assertion." Assertions are usually thought of as declarative statements that are either true or false. Thus, other expressions, such as imperative commands ("Give the gun to my brother."), questions ("Do you have my dime bag ready to deliver?"), and exclamations ("Murder! Murder!") are sometimes thought to be outside the federal definition. *See Holland v. State*, 713 A.2d 364, 369-70 (Md. Ct. Spec. App. 1998) ("For an out-of-court utterance to qualify as an assertion, it generally must be in the indicative or declarative mood, rather than in the interrogative mood, the imperative mood, or the subjunctive mood."). However, it is not the grammatical form of the words that is important under the rule. Commands, questions, and exclamations may be assertions if the declarant intends to assert a fact. *See United States v. Parker*, 142 F. App'x 19, 23 (3d Cir. 2005) (the real issue in addressing whether questions are assertions is whether the speaker intended his questions as assertions); *Stoddard v. State*, 887 A.2d 564, 581 (Md. 2005) ("Our definition of hearsay leads to the conclusion that the particular form of an utterance is not determinative of whether an utterance is an 'assertion' and hence potential hearsay. An out-of-court question may be probative because, by asking it, the declarant potentially communicated a given factual proposition."). On the other hand, if the question is a neutral request for information, and it appears that the speaker did not intend to express a fact, opinion, or condition, the utterance is not an assertion. *See, e.g., Inmin v. State*, 654 So. 2d 86, 90 (Ala. Crim. App. 1994) (testimony in theft trial that defendant's wife asked victim's former daughter-in-law whether she knew if the victim kept money was not an assertion and not hearsay).

195. TEX. R. EVID. 801(c).

196. The common law generally followed the declarant-based definition of hearsay: "[B]y 'hearsay' is meant that kind of evidence which does not derive its value solely from the credit to be attached to the witness himself, but rests also in part on the veracity and competency of some other person from whom the witness has received this information." 2 JONES ON EVIDENCE, CIVIL AND CRIMINAL §8.1, at 159 (Spencer A. Gard ed., 6th ed. 1972). More simply stated, under a declarant-oriented definition, evidence is excluded as hearsay "because the value of the evidence

ness W would be hearsay under this definition if W testified that X had told W it was raining on Friday and the testimony was being offered to prove that it rained that day. To find that it was raining on Friday, the fact-finder would have to determine not only that W's testimony was credible but also that X was credible when she told W it was raining.

The assertion-based definition, in contrast, looks to the statement itself and what it is being offered to prove. This definition is often converted into a two-prong test: hearsay is (1) an out-of-court statement that is (2) being offered to prove the truth of the matter asserted in that statement. If both prongs of the test are met, a statement is hearsay under the Federal Rules. Using the above example with the assertion-based definition, X's statement that it was raining on Friday is (1) an out-of-court statement and (2) being offered to prove the truth of the matter asserted in that statement, i.e., that it was raining on Friday. Thus, the statement is also hearsay under the assertion-based definition.

The answer to whether a statement is hearsay will normally be the same under either the declarant-based definition or the assertion-based definition. The two definitions may yield different outcomes, however, when an out-of-court statement is being offered to prove an implied assertion—that is, any matter that the fact-finder is being asked to infer from the out-of-court statement.[197] Implied assertions are not hearsay under the assertion-based definition of Federal Rule 801.[198]

---

depends upon the credibility of the out-of-court declarant." Glen Weissenberger, *Unintended Implications of Speech and the Definition of Hearsay*, 65 TEMP. L. REV. 857, 858 (1992).

197. The issue of whether an implied assertion should be treated as hearsay was discussed in **United States v. Zenni**, a prosecution for illegal bookmaking. *See* **United States v. Zenni**, 492 F. Supp. 464, 467-69 (E.D. Ky. 1980). A federal agent answered the defendant's telephone several times while conducting a search of the premises. *Id.* at 465. The unknown callers gave instructions for placing bets on sporting events; this evidence was offered to show that the callers believed the defendant was operating an illegal betting operation, which tended to prove that fact. *Id.* Applying the assertion-based definition of Federal Rule 801(c), the court reasoned that the callers' statements were not hearsay because they were not being offered to prove the truth of the matter asserted in those statements. *Zenni*, 492 F. Supp. at 469. The callers' statements were made out of court, satisfying the first prong of the assertion-based definition. The statements, however, were not intended to be assertions that the defendant was operating an illegal betting operation; thus, the calls did not meet the definition of "statement" in Federal Rule 801(a). *See Zenni*, 492 F. Supp. at 469. The statements would be hearsay under the Texas Rules' declarant-based definition, however, because the probative value of the out-of-court statements depends not only on the testifying witness's credibility but also on the out-of-court declarant's credibility. *Cf.* **United States v. Reynolds**, 715 F.2d 99, 103-04 (3d Cir. 1983) (codefendant's statements were hearsay under Federal Rule 801(c) because implied meaning related to defendant's guilt and codefendant was not available for cross-examination).

198. The Advisory Committee's Note to Federal Rule 801 is explicit that out-of-court statements offered to prove an implied assertion are excluded from the rule's definition of hearsay: "The effect of the definition of 'statement' is to exclude from the operation of the hearsay rule all evidence of conduct, verbal or nonverbal, not intended as an assertion. The key to the definition is that nothing is an assertion unless intended to be one." FED. R. EVID. 801 advisory committee's note, subdiv. (a); *see also* Paul R. Rice, *Should Unintended Implications of Speech Be Considered Nonhearsay? The Assertive/Nonassertive Distinction Under Rule 801(a) of the Federal Rules of Evidence*, 65 TEMP. L. REV. 529, 533-35 (1992) (discussing trustworthiness of intended and unintended implications of speech as they relate to federal hearsay definition); Weissenberger, *supra* note 196, at 860-62 (same). Federal circuit courts disagree on whether questions or commands are assertions and thus can be hearsay. *Compare* **United States v. Love**, 706 F.3d 832, 840 (7th Cir. 2013) (questions are not "statements" and thus are not hearsay), **United States v. Rodriguez-Lopez**, 565 F.3d 312, 314 (6th Cir. 2009) (questions and commands are not assertions and thus cannot

The Advisory Committee on the Federal Rules of Evidence recognized that defining implied assertions as nonhearsay raised all of the hearsay dangers associated with assertive verbal conduct but thought that these concerns did not justify excluding implied assertions as hearsay.[199] The drafters of the Texas Rules of Evidence, particularly Olin Wellborn, were more concerned with the hearsay dangers of implied assertions. Wellborn was not persuaded by the Advisory Committee's reasoning on implied assertions and nonassertive verbal conduct and argued the following:

> An analysis of the hearsay dangers yields no basis for exempting all verbal expressions that are not direct assertions from the hearsay rule. Obviously, that the declarant's belief is expressed by implication [implied assertions] could have no bearing on the reliability of his antecedent perception or memory. Moreover, the danger of accidental miscommunication due to ambiguity and misinterpretation is in general much greater, not less, in the cases of nonassertive verbal conduct and assertions used inferentially than it is in the case of direct assertions. As for the risk of insincerity, an assertion used inferentially is nonetheless an assertion and therefore is as likely as any other to be insincere.

> One must conclude, therefore, that the case for nonhearsay treatment on grounds of reduced hearsay risks, weak and unpersuasive as it is when advanced regarding nonassertive nonverbal conduct, is even weaker for nonassertive verbal conduct and assertions used inferentially. Indeed, it is fair to say that no basis at all exists for distinguishing these categories from direct assertions in terms of the hearsay dangers presented.[200]

To address these concerns, the drafters of the Texas Rules included Rule 801(c), which classified implied assertions as hearsay.[201]

---

be hearsay); ***United States v. Thomas***, 451 F.3d 543, 548 (8th Cir. 2006) (same); ***Lexington Ins. v. W. Pa. Hosp.***, 423 F.3d 318, 330 (3d Cir. 2005) (same); ***United States v. Long***, 905 F.2d 1572, 1579-80 (D.C. Cir. 1990) (questions and other implied assertions are not hearsay), *and **United States v. Lewis***, 902 F.2d 1176, 1179 (5th Cir. 1990) (same), *with **United States v. Torres***, 794 F.3d 1053, 1061 (9th Cir. 2015) (questions may be implied assertions and thus may be hearsay), *cert. denied*, 136 S. Ct. 2005 (2016), ***United States v. Summers***, 414 F.3d 1287, 1299-1300 (10th Cir. 2005) (same), *and **Lyle v. Koehler***, 720 F.2d 426, 432-33 & n.11 (6th Cir. 1983) (implicit assertions in letters were hearsay).

199. As the Advisory Committee explained:
> Admittedly evidence of this character is untested with respect to the perception, memory, and narration (or their equivalents) of the actor, but the Advisory Committee is of the view that these dangers are minimal in the absence of an intent to assert and do not justify the loss of the evidence on hearsay grounds. No class of evidence is free of the possibility of fabrication, but the likelihood is less with nonverbal than with assertive verbal conduct. The situations giving rise to the nonverbal conduct are such as virtually to eliminate questions of sincerity. Motivation, the nature of the conduct, and the presence or absence of reliance will bear heavily upon the weight to be given the evidence. *Similar considerations govern nonassertive verbal conduct and verbal conduct which is assertive but offered as a basis for inferring something other than the matter asserted, also excluded from the definition of hearsay by the language of subdivision (c).*

FED. R. EVID. 801 advisory committee's note, subdiv. (a) (citations omitted, emphasis added).

200. Wellborn, *supra* note 1, at 66-67 (footnotes omitted).

201. *See* TEX. R. EVID. 801(c)(2).

Both the Texas and federal approaches depart from the common-law definition of hearsay as it relates to nonassertive conduct. The common law extended the definition of hearsay to actions when the probative value of those actions ultimately rests on the credibility of the person taking them. The most famous illustration of the common-law position is the English case of **Wright v. Tatham**,[202] in which Baron Parke posed a hypothetical question involving a sea captain who inspected a ship and then left on the ship with his family, never to be seen again: Should the captain's inspection and departure on the ship with his family be admissible to establish the fact that the ship was seaworthy at the time of sailing? Baron Parke gave the following answer:

> [P]roof of a particular fact, which is not of itself a matter in issue, but which is relevant only as implying a statement or opinion of a third person on the matter in issue, is inadmissible in all cases where such a statement or opinion not on oath would be of itself inadmissible ....[203]

Because actions are not "statements" under either Texas Rule 801(a) or Federal Rule 801(a) unless those actions are intended as assertions, the captain's actions in **Wright** would not be hearsay under either the Texas Rules or the Federal Rules.

The Texas rule's definition is generally consistent with earlier Texas case law.[204] The Texas definition departs from the former Texas position only with regard to nonassertive nonverbal conduct, which was hearsay under the common law but is not hearsay under the Texas Rules.[205] On the other hand, many Texas cases treating as hearsay verbal conduct that is not a direct assertion clearly indicate that Texas Rule 801 remains consistent with the common-law approach to implied assertions, unlike Federal Rule 801.[206]

In summary, four types of evidence have caused hearsay concerns, and are treated as follows under the Texas and Federal Rules of Evidence:

(1) Verbal assertions. A verbal assertion[207] is a statement, often in declaratory form, being offered in evidence to prove a fact contained in the statement. For example, a

---

202. 112 Eng. Rep. 488 (Ex. 1837).

203. *Id.* at 516-17.

204. *See* 1A RAY, *supra* note 9, §784, at 7-11.

205. Roy Ray characterizes the Texas decisions as following Baron Parke's dicta in **Wright v. Tatham** and as holding "that evidence of either [assertive or nonassertive] conduct is inadmissible to show the belief or opinion of the actor *where offered to show that the belief is true*, i.e., that the facts are in accordance with the belief." 1A RAY, *supra* note 9, §784, at 8; *see* **Johnson v. State**, 987 S.W.2d 79, 90 (Tex. App.—Houston [14th Dist.] 1999, pet. ref'd) (op. on reh'g) (hearsay rule does not apply to conduct that is not intended as a substitute for verbal expression; victim's testimony, when asked at punishment stage about impact of crime on her family, that "[m]y dad was in counseling for over a year" was not hearsay because there was no evidence that victim's father "intended to communicate anything by his act of seeking medical assistance"). Refer to notes 212-215 *infra* and accompanying text.

206. Federal case law before Federal Rule 801 also classified verbal expression in this category as hearsay. *See, e.g.,* **Krulewitch v. United States**, 336 U.S. 440, 443-44 (1949) (nonassertive statement of conspirator implying defendant's involvement in the conspiracy was inadmissible); **United States v. Pacelli**, 491 F.2d 1108, 1115-16 (2d Cir. 1974) (third party's extrajudicial statements, which clearly implied knowledge of the ultimate fact issue, were inadmissible); *see also* Wellborn, *supra* note 1, at 68-71, 85-88 (analyzing federal-court holdings).

207. Refer to note 194 *supra* and accompanying text.

statement by an out-of-court witness that "the light was red for the westbound traffic at the time of the accident," offered to prove that the light was red for westbound traffic, is a verbal assertion. In other words, the statement has probative value only if it is true. Verbal assertions are hearsay under the Texas and Federal Rules of Evidence.[208]

(2) Nonverbal conduct intended as an assertion. Nonverbal conduct intended as an assertion is conduct by the out-of-court declarant that is intended to make a statement and is being offered to prove some fact contained in the intended statement. When a patient is asked where it hurts and he points to his chest, the patient's gesture is nonverbal conduct intended to assert that the pain is in his chest. This action is the equivalent of a verbal assertion. Nonverbal conduct intended as an assertion is hearsay under the Federal[209] and Texas Rules of Evidence.[210]

---

208. Written and oral out-of-court statements are hearsay if offered for the truth of their contents. *See, e.g., Farley v. Farley*, 731 S.W.2d 733, 736 (Tex. App.—Dallas 1987, no writ) (husband's IRS forms and "earnings and production report" were "clearly hearsay" when offered to show the amount of his earnings to justify a modification of child-support payments); *Tempo Tamers, Inc. v. Crow-Houston Four, Ltd.*, 715 S.W.2d 658, 661-62 (Tex. App.—Dallas 1986, writ ref'd n.r.e.) (invoices stating the cost of reinstalling and rewiring air-conditioning units were inadmissible hearsay when offered to prove cost of repairs). *See generally* 1A RAY, *supra* note 9, §790, at 20 (the same hearsay rule applies to both out-of-court writings and out-of-court oral statements).

209. *See, e.g., White Indus., Inc. v. Cessna Aircraft Co.*, 611 F. Supp. 1049, 1075-76 (W.D. Mo. 1985) (in an action under the Robinson-Patman Act, witness could not testify to the secretary's action of segregating files that related to "direct" or "pass through" sales because the conduct was in direct response to her supervisor's request and was intended by her as an assertion that the segregated files were the correct ones). *See generally* 4 JACK B. WEINSTEIN & MARGARET A. BERGER, WEINSTEIN'S EVIDENCE ¶801(a)[01], at 801-56 to 801-57 (1995) (assertive nonverbal conduct is covered as hearsay under the federal rule).

210. *See, e.g., Graham v. State*, 643 S.W.2d 920, 926-27 (Tex. Crim. App. 1983) (op. on reh'g) (police officer's testimony that shooting victim, when shown a photograph of defendant, "made a shooting motion, cocking her thumb with her finger pointed out" was inadmissible hearsay because the testimony was significant only to indicate her belief that defendant was the individual who shot her); *Clabon v. State*, 111 S.W.3d 805, 807-08 (Tex. App.—Houston [1st Dist.] 2003, no pet.) (officers' testimony in capital-murder trial about stabbing hand motions that nontestifying witness had made while describing defendant's visit to her home after murder was hearsay; witness's acts were assertions and conveyed that defendant had knowledge of murders, manner in which they were committed, and location of victims' wounds); *see also Mega Child Care, Inc. v. Tex. Dep't of Prot. & Regulatory Servs.*, 29 S.W.3d 303, 310-11 (Tex. App.—Houston [14th Dist.] 2000, no pet.) (gestures by employee of child-care facility toward infant room and file cabinet in response to questions about whether there were additional children at facility and whether there was paperwork on them was not hearsay because neither gesture was offered to prove truth of matter asserted, namely, that other children were in direction of infant room or that paperwork was in a particular place; instead, testimony was elicited to show that child-care facility was open and caring for children); *Burleson v. State*, 802 S.W.2d 429, 439-40 (Tex. App.—Fort Worth 1991, pet. ref'd) (expert's testimony describing how he initiated a computer-generated display that indirectly showed the conduct of several persons was not assertive nonverbal conduct and thus was not hearsay). *But see Foster v. State*, 779 S.W.2d 845, 862-63 (Tex. Crim. App. 1989) (police officer's testimony that defendant's girlfriend led officers to a pond and "made a throwing gesture" toward the pond—whereupon the police retrieved from the pond a sawed-off shotgun that had been used in a capital murder—was nonassertive nonverbal conduct and thus not hearsay). The *Foster* rationale appears faulty under both the federal and Texas definitions of hearsay. The court of criminal appeals in *Foster* stated that the assertive conduct of the nontestifying witness "was only an explanation of the circumstances which led to the recovery of the shotgun," not an assertion that she or the defendant had put the shotgun in the pond. 779 S.W.2d at 862. Clearly, however, the only reason that the officers searched the pond for the shotgun was because the witness told them, through the nonverbal assertion of pointing and making a throwing motion, that the shotgun had been disposed of there. The court distinguished *Graham* by stating: "This was not a substitute for verbal expression where a declarant is asked a specific question and responds assertively to that question in a non-verbal manner." *Foster*, 779 S.W.2d at 862.

(3) Implied verbal assertions. Implied verbal assertions are statements in which the fact-finder is being asked to infer facts not contained in the out-of-court statement. Implied assertions are classified as hearsay under the Texas Rules of Evidence but are not hearsay under the Federal Rules.[211]

(4) Nonassertive nonverbal conduct. Nonassertive nonverbal conduct is conduct by an out-of-court person that is not intended to make a statement or an assertion. Evidence of the conduct is being offered to prove the person's belief in a fact, which in turn is evidence of that fact's existence. An example of nonassertive nonverbal conduct is evidence that a child cringed whenever his father came into the room, offered to prove that the child feared his father. The common law[212] and earlier Texas law[213] treated nonassertive nonverbal conduct as hearsay, but this evidence is not hearsay under the Texas[214] or Federal Rules of Evidence.[215]

2. Computer data as hearsay. Several Texas cases have addressed the applicability of the hearsay rule to two categories of computer data: computer output and computer operations.[216] "Computer output" refers to data storage and retrieval, for which the computer is simply a memory machine that depends on human input. Computer data

---

211. Refer to notes 197-201 *supra* and accompanying text.

212. Refer to notes 202-203 *supra* and accompanying text.

213. *See, e.g.*, ***Vines v. State***, 479 S.W.2d 322, 324 (Tex. Crim. App. 1972) (improper admission of hearsay when witness in DWI case testified that a jailer detained defendant after talking with him; because evidence was offered to show defendant's intoxication, testimony of jailer's actions was inadmissible to show truth of jailer's belief). The definition of hearsay in Rule 801 has changed the ***Vines*** reasoning and result. If the actor does not intend to communicate any message by his nonverbal actions, testimony about those actions is not hearsay even if the testimony is being offered to show the actor's underlying belief system (e.g., the jailer in ***Vines*** would not have acted as he did unless he believed that the defendant was intoxicated).

214. *See, e.g.*, ***Foster***, 779 S.W.2d at 862 ("throwing gesture" by witness was nonassertive nonverbal conduct because it was not "an assertive substitution for verbal expression"); *see also* ***Burnett v. State***, 754 S.W.2d 437, 445-46 (Tex. App.—San Antonio 1988, pet. ref'd) (accused did not intend to communicate anything by staring at an area that officers later realized was murder victim's gravesite; conduct was not hearsay under Criminal Rule 801).

215. *See* 4 WEINSTEIN & BERGER, *supra* note 209, ¶801(a)[01], at 801-60 to 801-62. The rationale for removing nonassertive nonverbal conduct from the classic definition of hearsay is twofold. First, the out-of-court declarant's sincerity is not in question. He is not attempting to communicate; thus, "the trustworthiness of evidence of this conduct is the same whether he is an egregious liar or a paragon of veracity." Judson F. Falknor, *The "Hear-Say" Rule as a "See-Do" Rule: Evidence of Conduct*, 33 ROCKY MTN. L. REV. 133, 136 (1961). Second, the trustworthiness of the actor's conduct is self-verifying because he has based his own actions on the correctness of his belief—his actions speak louder than his words. *See id.* at 137 ("[T]he absence of the danger of misrepresentation does work strongly in favor of by-passing the hearsay objection, at least where the evidence of conduct is cogently probative. And it will be, where the action taken was important to the individual in his own affairs ....").

216. *See, e.g.*, ***Taylor v. State***, 93 S.W.3d 487, 507-08 (Tex. App.—Texarkana 2002, pet. ref'd) (investigator's testimony that he knew he had made an identical copy of defendant's computer hard drive because of "acquisition" and "verification" hash marks on computer screen was not hearsay because these marks were the result of a computer program analyzing data); ***Stevenson v. State***, 920 S.W.2d 342, 343 (Tex. App.—Dallas 1996, no pet.) (Intoxilyzer printout is computer-generated information and was not barred by hearsay rule); ***Ly v. State***, 908 S.W.2d 598, 600 (Tex. App.—Houston [1st Dist.] 1995, no pet.) (computer-generated printout of electronic monitoring process was not hearsay); ***Murray v. State***, 804 S.W.2d 279, 283 (Tex. App.—Fort Worth 1991, pet. ref'd) (computer-generated printout of electronic door lock was not hearsay); ***Burleson v. State***, 802 S.W.2d 429, 439 (Tex. App.—Fort Worth 1991, pet. ref'd) (computer-generated display showing the number of records missing from payroll-commission file was not hearsay); *see also* David Schlueter, *Hearsay—When Machines Talk*, 53 TEX. B.J. 1135, 1135 (1990) (discussing difference between computer storage of data and computer generation of data).

RULE 801

that is a compilation of information entered by a person is hearsay.[217] The reliability of the information depends on the reliability of the person entering and manipulating the information, and thus, the traditional hearsay concerns about perception, memory, narration, and credibility are implicated.

"Computer operations" refers to computer data that does not represent information entered by a person but instead reflects the internal operation of the computer itself. This type of data is not hearsay.[218] For example, an automatic recording device, such as an electronic door lock,[219] an electronic monitoring device,[220] a telephone caller-ID box, or an Intoxilyzer,[221] is a machine-created information source. Nonetheless, such computer-generated data is still subject to the requirement of a proper foundation demonstrating that the particular computer or machine that generated the data operates reliably and generates accurate information.[222]

3. Silence as hearsay. Before the adoption of Rule 801, courts had reached inconsistent results on the question of whether silence or a lack of action constituted hearsay.[223] Under both the federal and Texas rules, such nonverbal conduct is excluded from the definition of hearsay unless the silence or failure to act was intended as an assertion.[224]

4. Statements not offered for truth of the matter asserted. Under Rule 801, as under any other definition of hearsay, an out-of-court statement is not hearsay if it has relevance apart from the truth of the matter that it asserts or implies.[225] In other words, a

---

217. *See* ***Murray***, 804 S.W.2d at 284 (computer printout is often simply "the feeding back of data placed into the computer by a person; although the data may be in a different form than it was when it was fed into the computer, it retains its status as the statement or statements made by a person" and thus fits the definition of hearsay).

218. *Id.*

219. *Id.*

220. ***Ly***, 908 S.W.2d at 600.

221. ***Stevenson***, 920 S.W.2d at 343.

222. *See, e.g.,* ***Miller v. State***, 208 S.W.3d 554, 563 (Tex. App.—Austin 2006, pet. ref'd) (because State did not present testimony that cell-phone bill was printout of computer-generated data, its admissibility was not established); ***Murray***, 804 S.W.2d at 284-85 (State presented testimony about operations of hotel's door-locking computer system, adequately proving reliability of the computer printout); ***Burleson v. State***, 802 S.W.2d 429, 441 (Tex. App.—Fort Worth 1991, pet. ref'd) (State presented "ample evidence for the court to conclude by a preponderance of the evidence that the computer technology behind the computer-generated display was trustworthy, reliable, and standard to the computer industry").

223. *See* McCORMICK ON EVIDENCE §250, at 742-43 (Edward W. Cleary et al. eds., 3d ed. 1984) (while courts infrequently recognize or mention instances of silence as a hearsay problem, those that do tend to admit the evidence as nonhearsay). *Compare* ***Trussell v. State***, 585 S.W.2d 736, 739 (Tex. Crim. App. [Panel Op.] 1979) (witness's failure to identify defendant in out-of-court lineup constituted inadmissible implied hearsay that defendant was not one of the men the witness saw getting out of the robbery vehicle), *with* ***St. Louis Sw. Ry. Co. v. Ark. & Tex. Grain Co.***, 42 Tex. Civ. App. 125, 132, 95 S.W. 656, 660 (Dallas 1906, writ dism'd) (in conversion suit, evidence that consignor sold corn as No. 2 corn and received no complaints from purchasers was not hearsay).

224. *See* FED. R. EVID. 801(a); TEX. R. EVID. 801(a); *see, e.g.,* ***Rodriguez v. State***, 903 S.W.2d 405, 411 (Tex. App.—Texarkana 1995, pet. ref'd) (witness's failure to state that police had arrested the wrong person could not be assumed to be intended as a substitute for verbal expression). Refer to notes 209-210, 212-215 *supra* and accompanying text.

225. *See* ***Bell v. State***, 877 S.W.2d 21, 24 (Tex. App.—Dallas 1994, pet. ref'd) ("If the out-of-court statement is relevant only if the trier of fact believes that the statement was both truthful and accurate, then the statement is

statement is not hearsay if it is being offered for some purpose other than proving the truth of the matter asserted in the statement.[226] However, a party cannot turn hearsay into nonhearsay merely by asserting that the out-of-court statement is being offered only to show that it was made.[227] The proponent must articulate a legitimate nonhearsay purpose for offering the statement and demonstrate that the statement is relevant apart from the truth of its content.[228] Such statements generally fall into one of the following categories: (1) verbal acts, (2) verbal parts of acts, (3) impeachment, (4) effect on the listener or reader, (5) identifying characteristics, such as verbal objects and markers, (6) circumstantial evidence of state of mind, and (7) circumstantial evidence of memory or belief.[229]

(1) Verbal acts. If the making of the statement is itself legally relevant, evidence that the statement was made is not barred by the hearsay rule.[230] In these instances, the statement is sometimes said to be a "verbal act" or an "operative fact," or to have "independent legal significance."[231] An out-of-court "operative fact" statement may be ad-

---

hearsay. If the relevancy of the statement does not hinge on the truthfulness of the statement, it is not hearsay."); *see, e.g., Ellis v. State*, 517 S.W.3d 922, 930 (Tex. App.—Fort Worth 2017, no pet.) (text messages sent from murder victim's phone to witness were not hearsay because they were not offered to prove the messages were true; relevance hinged on fact that they were sent after victim's body had been discovered and that phone was in defendant's possession when apprehended); *Peaster Indep. Sch. Dist. v. Glodfelty*, 63 S.W.3d 1, 9 (Tex. App.—Fort Worth 2001, no pet.) (at hearing for nonrenewal of teacher's contract, superintendent's testimony that a former student allegedly had consensual sexual relationships with two of his high school teachers, and that such allegations received widespread publicity in the community, was not offered as "hearsay" to prove those allegations, but rather to prove that allegations received widespread publicity).

226. *See Dinkins v. State*, 894 S.W.2d 330, 347 (Tex. Crim. App. 1995); *Johnson v. State*, 425 S.W.3d 344, 346 (Tex. App.—Houston [1st Dist.] 2011, pet. ref'd). On the other hand, it is not error to admit hearsay evidence when it clarifies other hearsay evidence elicited by the opposing party. *See, e.g., Livingston v. State*, 739 S.W.2d 311, 331 (Tex. Crim. App. 1987) (prosecution witness's prior statement giving a description of a gunman was admissible under the rule of optional completeness when defendant had cross-examined the witness from portions of that hearsay statement; alternatively, the statement was admissible to provide a context in which a particular statement was made and not for the truth of matter asserted); *Martinez v. State*, 749 S.W.2d 556, 559-60 (Tex. App.—San Antonio 1988, no pet.) (when the defense elicited hearsay evidence to create an impression that a third party was solely responsible for heroin dealings, Criminal Rule 107 entitled the prosecution to offer hearsay evidence to clarify that defendant was involved with the third party).

227. *See DuBose v. State*, 774 S.W.2d 328, 329 (Tex. App.—Beaumont 1989, pet. ref'd).

228. Courts all too frequently hold that when the questioner cleverly avoids asking the witness to repeat the precise words of an out-of-court conversation, instead relating the more generalized "I heard X and Y discussing how they were going to rob the pizza deliveryman," this summary of the out-of-court conversation is not hearsay either because the witness did not repeat a "statement" verbatim or because the summary purportedly was not offered for the truth of the matter asserted. *See, e.g., Alexander v. State*, 820 S.W.2d 821, 823 (Tex. App.—Waco 1991, pet. ref'd) (testimony of discussions about robbing pizza deliveryman was not hearsay because witness did not relate a specific statement by a third-party declarant that was offered for the truth of the matter asserted); *see also Fletcher v. State*, 960 S.W.2d 694, 699 (Tex. App.—Tyler 1997, no pet.) (discussion between defendants about "getting a car and going to Gladewater" was not offered for the truth of the matters asserted, "but rather that [defendant] was part of a conspiracy to commit an illegal act"). Refer to notes 265-268 *infra* and accompanying text.

229. *See* CHRISTOPHER B. MUELLER & LAIRD C. KIRKPATRICK, EVIDENCE §§8.16-8.21 (3d ed. 2003); 4 WEINSTEIN & BERGER, *supra* note 209, ¶801(c)[01], at 801-69 to 801-106.

230. *See* 1A RAY, *supra* note 9, §795, at 39-43 (question involved in suit is "[W]ere these words *used*? To answer this question the evidence is offered, and the question, Were they true? does not arise.").

231. McCORMICK'S HANDBOOK II, *supra* note 7, §249, at 588; 1A RAY, *supra* note 9, §795, at 39; *see Royal Globe Ins. v. Bar Consultants, Inc.*, 566 S.W.2d 724, 727 (Tex. Civ. App.—Austin 1978), *aff'd*, 577 S.W.2d 688 (Tex. 1979).

RULE 801

missible nonhearsay in countless situations. Examples include (1) words that constitute the offer, acceptance, or terms of a contract,[232] (2) words that operate as a conveyance,[233] (3) words of a principal that create authority in an agent,[234] (4) a defamatory utterance,[235] (5) newspaper articles as evidence of a person's poor reputation,[236] (6) checks,[237] (7) threats,[238] (8) solicitation of perjury,[239] (9) evidence that shows an attempt to give notice or to contact someone when such attempts are relevant,[240] (10) notification of breach as an element of a warranty claim,[241] (11) proof of loss as required

---

232. ***Thomas C. Cook, Inc. v. Rowhanian***, 774 S.W.2d 679, 685 (Tex. App.—El Paso 1989, writ denied); *see, e.g.*, ***Boyd v. Diversified Fin. Sys.***, 1 S.W.3d 888, 891 (Tex. App.—Dallas 1999, no pet.) (hearsay rule did not apply to admission of promissory note that formed basis of claim); ***Cherokee Water Co. v. Forderhause***, 727 S.W.2d 605, 614 (Tex. App.—Texarkana 1987) (in action to reform an option clause in a deed, testimony was admissible to show operative acts constituting mutual mistake; statements were not offered to prove the truth of the matter stated "because the gist of the statements was to the effect that the written document did not cover mineral leases. ... This was essentially a part of the offer and acceptance of the contract which constitutes operative facts and not hearsay."), *rev'd on other grounds*, 741 S.W.2d 377 (Tex. 1987); ***Okon v. Levy***, 612 S.W.2d 938, 942 (Tex. Civ. App.—Dallas 1981, writ ref'd n.r.e.) (depreciation schedule of railroad track and building was admissible to show that they were carried on the books at depreciated value, which the parties had agreed on as the proper measure; "[t]his evidence was proof of what the contract of the parties was and thus, was a necessary part of the cause of action"); ***Irving Lumber Co. v. Alltex Mortg. Co.***, 446 S.W.2d 64, 71 (Tex. Civ. App.—Dallas 1969) (out-of-court statements were admissible to show offer or acceptance in contract suits), *aff'd*, 468 S.W.2d 341 (Tex. 1971); ***Cunningham v. R.W. McPherson & Assocs., Inc.***, 392 S.W.2d 145, 146 (Tex. Civ. App.—Waco 1965, writ ref'd n.r.e.) (pricing quotes were admissible as evidence of parties' agreement to establish an alleged contract).

233. *See, e.g.*, ***Hanover Ins. v. Hoch***, 469 S.W.2d 717, 724 (Tex. Civ. App.—Corpus Christi 1971, writ ref'd n.r.e.) (testimony about conversations offered to show whether money paid on a home was a gift or a loan was not hearsay).

234. *See, e.g.*, ***Black v. State***, 46 Tex. Crim. 590, 596-97, 81 S.W. 302, 304 (1904) (agent's testimony that his principal directed him to deputize certain persons was not hearsay).

235. *See* McCORMICK'S HANDBOOK II, *supra* note 7, §249, at 588-89 (statements constituting slander are admissible as having independent legal significance); *see, e.g.*, ***Scotchcraft Bldg. Materials, Inc. v. Parker***, 618 S.W.2d 835, 836-37 (Tex. Civ. App.—Houston [1st Dist.] 1981, writ ref'd n.r.e.) (court erred in excluding slanderous statements).

236. *See* ***Swate v. Schiffers***, 975 S.W.2d 70, 77-78 (Tex. App.—San Antonio 1998, pet. denied); *see also* ***City of Austin v. Hous. Lighting & Power Co.***, 844 S.W.2d 773, 791 (Tex. App.—Dallas 1992, writ denied) (although newspaper articles are generally treated as hearsay, they are not hearsay if offered to prove notice of matters and not for truth of matters asserted).

237. ***United States v. Pang***, 362 F.3d 1187, 1192 (9th Cir. 2004); *see* ***Spurlock v. Comm'r***, 85 T.C.M. (CCH) 1236, 1240 (2003) ("A check is a negotiable instrument, a legally operative document, and falls within the category of 'verbal acts' which are excludable from the hearsay rule."); ***United States v. Dababneh***, 28 M.J. 929, 935 (N.M.C.M.R. 1989) ("[C]hecks themselves, together with the tellers' markings and routing stamps, ... are commercial events which create legal rights and obligations, and therefore no exception to hearsay need be found [to admit checks into evidence].").

238. *See* ***Dorchy v. Jones***, 320 F. Supp. 2d 564, 578 (E.D. Mich. 2004) (threats are normally considered nonhearsay verbal acts not admitted for the truth of the matter asserted), *aff'd*, 398 F.3d 783 (6th Cir. 2005); *see, e.g.*, ***Tompkins v. Cyr***, 202 F.3d 770, 779 n.3 (5th Cir. 2000) (in physician's suit against abortion protesters, testimony about threats and threatening letters was not hearsay; threats were not factual statements, the truth of which was in question, but were verbal acts not offered as truthful facts and thus nonhearsay).

239. *See* ***United States v. Smith***, 354 F.3d 390, 396 n.6 (5th Cir. 2003) (solicitation of perjury is a verbal act, not hearsay).

240. *See, e.g.*, ***Wheat v. State***, 165 S.W.3d 802, 804 (Tex. App.—Texarkana 2005, pet. dism'd, untimely filed) (admission of returned, unopened letters sent by probation department to defendant that could not be forwarded were admitted for nonhearsay purpose of proving efforts taken to contact defendant).

241. *See, e.g.*, ***Krueger v. Gol***, 787 S.W.2d 138, 141 (Tex. App.—Houston [14th Dist.] 1990, writ denied) (statements in plaintiff's affidavit in opposition to a summary-judgment motion were admissible to show the date that plaintiff was put on notice of possible malpractice action); ***McGinty v. Motor Truck Equip. Corp.***, 397 S.W.2d 263,

by an insurance policy,[242] (12) notice that affects the operation of the statute of limitations,[243] (13) a written or oral statement that is allegedly perjurious,[244] (14) statements that form the basis of a fraud claim,[245] (15) statements that show discrimination in a lawsuit alleging discrimination,[246] (16) letters of complaint when the mere incidence of complaints, regardless of their truth, has legal significance,[247] (17) a person's consent to a search,[248] and (18) arrest reports as evidence of arrests made but ultimately dismissed or not prosecuted.[249]

(2) Verbal parts of acts. Verbal parts of acts are another category of nonhearsay out-of-court statements. When conduct, viewed in isolation, is ambiguous in nature, contemporaneous statements clarifying that ambiguity may be exempt from the hearsay rule.[250] For example, if A walks up to B and hands him an envelope filled with $100 bills, the words spoken by A and B at the time of that occurrence impart meaning to the ambiguous act. Thus, if the litigation involves the making of a contract for the delivery of widgets, the fact that A said to B "here is the first installment for the widget delivery" signifies and clarifies that there was a contract between them. Similarly, if the

---

266 (Tex. Civ. App.—Dallas 1965, no writ) (manufacturer's document was admissible to show breach of warranty and that manufacturer had notice of product's dangerous condition).

242. *See, e.g.,* **Guar. Cty. Mut. Ins. v. Williams**, 732 S.W.2d 57, 59-60 (Tex. App.—Amarillo 1987, no writ) (third party's out-of-court estimates were admissible to show compliance with a proof-of-loss clause in an insurance policy).

243. *See, e.g.,* **Merrell Dow Pharm., Inc. v. Havner**, 907 S.W.2d 535, 563 (Tex. App.—Corpus Christi 1995) (op. on reh'g) (plaintiff could testify to having seen television program on effects of Bendectin because defendant had pleaded statute of limitations; date when plaintiffs first suspected that Bendectin caused their child's birth defects may have been at issue), *rev'd on other grounds*, 953 S.W.2d 706 (Tex. 1997); **Krueger**, 787 S.W.2d at 141 (in medical-malpractice case, summary-judgment affidavit in which plaintiff stated she did not know surgery was unnecessary until doctor told her she had multiple sclerosis was nonhearsay; statement was not offered to prove multiple sclerosis but to prove when plaintiff was put on notice of a possible legal claim).

244. *See, e.g.,* **Tamayo v. State**, 924 S.W.2d 213, 215 (Tex. App.—Beaumont 1996, no pet.) (typewritten statement, signed and sworn to by defendant, was not hearsay because it constituted the act of perjury itself).

245. *See, e.g.,* **Busse v. Pac. Cattle Feeding Fund No. 1, Ltd.**, 896 S.W.2d 807, 816 (Tex. App.—Texarkana 1995, writ denied) (out-of-court statements made by defendant's employees were admissible as operative facts to prove elements of plaintiff's fraud claim).

246. *E.g.,* **Wal-Mart Stores, Inc. v. McKenzie**, 979 S.W.2d 364, 368 (Tex. App.—Eastland 1998) (coworker's statement that "we finally got rid of that nigger" was nonhearsay admitted as operative fact in employment-discrimination suit), *rev'd on other grounds*, 997 S.W.2d 278 (Tex. 1999).

247. *E.g.,* **O'Connor v. Nat'l Motor Club of Tex., Inc.**, 385 S.W.2d 558, 560-61 (Tex. Civ. App.—Houston 1964, no writ) (complaint letters were admissible for limited purpose of showing they were received but not to prove merits of complaints).

248. *See* **United States v. Moreno**, 233 F.3d 937, 940 (7th Cir. 2000) (like statements of offer and acceptance in forming a contract, a consent to search is a verbal act because "statements that grant or withhold permission to the authorities to conduct a search carry legal significance independent of the assertive content of the words used").

249. **Gaitan v. State**, 905 S.W.2d 703, 708 (Tex. App.—Houston [14th Dist.] 1995, pet. ref'd). In **Gaitan**, the defendant, an investigator with a district attorney's office, was charged with theft by a public servant for dismissing DWI charges in return for a fee. *Id.* at 705. The State offered 29 offense reports as evidence of arrests that had been made but were ultimately dismissed or not prosecuted in return for payments made to the defendant. *Id.* at 708. The **Gaitan** court held that these reports were not offered to prove the truth of the matters asserted (i.e., that the arrestees were driving while intoxicated) but rather as evidence of arrests that were dismissed in connection with payments made to the defendant. *Id.*

250. 4 DAVID W. LOUISELL & CHRISTOPHER B. MUELLER, FEDERAL EVIDENCE §417, at 107 (1980).

RULE 801

lawsuit is a prosecution for delivery of cocaine, the statement from A to B "here is the money for the five kilos of cocaine" is nonhearsay because it gives meaning to the physical act and is relevant in proving a material fact.[251]

(3) Impeachment. When a witness is impeached with a prior inconsistent statement, the statement is generally being offered not for its truth but to show that the witness lacks credibility. Under Rule 801(e)(1)(A)(i), a prior inconsistent statement "given under penalty of perjury at a trial, hearing, or other proceeding, or in a deposition" may be offered in a civil case for the truth of the matter asserted in that statement if the declarant testifies at the trial or hearing and is subject to cross-examination about the statement.[252] A prior inconsistent statement that does not meet those criteria can still be used to impeach the witness's credibility; this type of use does not violate the hearsay rule.[253]

(4) Effect on the listener or reader. Out-of-court statements may be offered to show that the making of the statement had some effect on the person who made, heard, or read the statement if that person's state of mind is relevant to the lawsuit.[254] For example, knowledge of a fact may be the critical issue in the lawsuit, as in prosecutions for the knowing receipt of stolen property. Thus, evidence of what A told the accused pawn-shop owner when A brought in a diamond ring to sell would tend to shed light on whether the accused knew that the diamond ring had been taken in a burglary and

---

251. *See, e.g.*, **United States v. Jackson**, 588 F.2d 1046, 1049 n.4 (5th Cir. 1979) (witness in a narcotics prosecution could testify that she was approached by an unidentified woman who handed her a bag and told her to pack it up with the things she was taking on her trip; because the statements related to and threw light on a contemporaneous act, they were not barred by the hearsay doctrine); **Perez v. State**, 653 S.W.2d 878, 881 (Tex. App.—Corpus Christi 1983, pet. ref'd) (rape victim's recounting of defendant's threatening statements was admissible for the limited purpose of describing the relevant details of her abduction).

252. Tex. R. Evid. 801(e)(1)(A)(i). The rule for criminal cases is identical except that it excludes statements made in a grand-jury proceeding. *See* Tex. R. Evid. 801(e)(1)(A)(ii). Refer to notes 284-307 *infra* and accompanying text.

253. Refer to note 298 *infra* and accompanying text.

254. *See* McCormick's Handbook II, *supra* note 7, §249, at 589-90 (evidence to show the probable effect of a statement on the hearer is not subject to attack as hearsay); 1A Ray, *supra* note 9, §799, at 53-54 (3d ed. 1980), at 21 (Supp. 1991) (hearsay rule is inapplicable when a statement is offered to show its effect on the hearer); 6 John H. Wigmore, Evidence in Trials at Common Law §1789, at 314 (Chadbourne rev. 1976) (statements made to show the effect of an utterance on the mind of another who heard it are admissible); *see, e.g.*, **United States v. Kohan**, 806 F.2d 18, 21-22 (2d Cir. 1986) (in bank-fraud prosecution, statements made to defendant were admissible to show defendant's state of mind and lack of specific intent); **United States v. Herrera**, 600 F.2d 502, 504 (5th Cir. 1979) (threatening statements made to defendant were admissible as nonhearsay to show defendant's coerced state of mind in support of her duress defense); **McAfee v. Travis Gas Corp.**, 137 Tex. 314, 323-24, 153 S.W.2d 442, 448 (1941) (plaintiff in personal-injury case should have been permitted to testify that, immediately before a gas-pipe explosion, a stranger approached, identified himself as an employee of the pipeline company, and asked plaintiff to show him where the gas leaks were; because plaintiff acted on this information, it was admissible to show a nonnegligent frame of mind); **Cooke v. Dykstra**, 800 S.W.2d 556, 562 (Tex. App.—Houston [14th Dist.] 1990, no writ) (trial court properly admitted bank memo for limited purpose of showing that plaintiff believed he did not have access to partnership line of credit; "[u]nder Texas Rule of Civil Evidence 801, an out-of-court statement is not hearsay if it has relevancy apart from the truth of the matter that it asserts or implies. If the making of the statement is in itself relevant, evidence that the statement was made is not barred by the hearsay rule."); **Howard v. State**, 713 S.W.2d 414, 417 (Tex. App.—Fort Worth 1986) (officer's testimony on what accomplice told him about defendant's earlier drug sales was admissible to show knowledge or intent because those issues were material), *pet. ref'd*, 789 S.W.2d 280 (Tex. Crim. App. 1988).

thus would not constitute hearsay. Harassing statements are admissible to show that the speaker intended to harass the listener and that the words had that effect on him.[255] Also admissible as nonhearsay are out-of-court statements that explain why a person performed or neglected to perform a particular act, regardless of the truth or falsity of the statement.[256]

(5) Identifying characteristics—verbal objects & markers. Words can be identifying characteristics and used as nonhearsay. For example, the letters and numbers on a license plate, when used to identify a car as having been at the scene of an accident, are not being offered for the truth of the matter asserted in those written letters and numbers. Instead, they are "verbal objects" used to identify the car and thus are not hearsay.[257] Oral words, when used in the same way, are called "verbal markers." Verbal objects and verbal markers are part of a physical description.

(6) Circumstantial evidence of state of mind. Statements about a declarant's state of mind are usually hearsay,[258] but they may be nonhearsay when used as circumstantial evidence of another fact.[259] For example, the statement "I am the richest man in the world," made by a poverty-stricken declarant, would be hearsay if offered to prove the declarant is wealthy. But the statement would not be hearsay if offered as circumstantial evidence that the man suffers from mental instability.[260] Similarly, when fraud or "good faith" is in issue, statements are relevant apart from their truth to show the presence or absence of good faith or fraudulent intent.[261]

---

255. *See, e.g.*, **Barrera v. State**, 978 S.W.2d 665, 668 (Tex. App.—Corpus Christi 1998, pet. ref'd) (evidence that defendant made telephone calls saying "I love you" and "I want to be with you" were admissible regardless of truth; they were offered to show that defendant intended to harass victim).

256. In **Stewart v. State**, the defendant's ex-wife testified that before her divorce, but after charges had been filed against her husband, she had a conference with her husband's attorney who told her that she had a marital privilege not to testify against the defendant. 767 S.W.2d 455, 457 (Tex. App.—Dallas 1988, pet. ref'd). This evidence was offered to explain why the ex-wife had delayed in coming forward with her testimony—because of the privilege not to testify—not for the truth of the matter asserted. *Id.* Thus, it was admissible as an explanation for her conduct. *Id.* The court noted, in dicta, that "'[a]n out-of-court statement offered for the purpose of *showing what was said* rather than the truth of the matter stated therein does not … constitute hearsay.'" *Id.* (quoting **Livingston v. State**, 739 S.W.2d 311, 331 (Tex. Crim. App. 1987)). But the court did not explain that the fact that the statement was made must be independently relevant to a material issue in the lawsuit.

257. *See, e.g.*, **Huff v. State**, 560 S.W.2d 652, 653 (Tex. Crim. App. 1978) (license-plate number written on back of check was admissible to describe the relevant details of the transaction, not to prove whether declaration about license-plate number was true); *see also* **Utsey v. State**, 921 S.W.2d 451, 454-55 (Tex. App.—Texarkana 1996, pet. ref'd) (bus tickets with defendant's name on them, found in accomplice's possession, were admissible to show "the circumstantial relationship of the parties to the scene, the contraband, or other parties"; bus tickets were not admissible to show the truth of the matter on the tickets, that is, the defendant's name). The **Huff** court used the phrase "verbal act" to describe the license-plate number, but it was a verbal object. *See* **Huff**, 560 S.W.2d at 653.

258. MUELLER & KIRKPATRICK, *supra* note 229, §8.20, at 736.

259. *See, e.g.*, **Lagaite v. State**, 995 S.W.2d 860, 863 (Tex. App.—Houston [1st Dist.] 1999, pet. ref'd) (defendant's statement, "I wish the guy were dead," made the morning after murder, offered by defense as circumstantial evidence that defendant did not know victim was already dead, was admissible for nonhearsay purpose).

260. MUELLER & KIRKPATRICK, *supra* note 229, §8.20, at 738.

261. *See, e.g.*, **Butler v. Hide-A-Way Lake Club, Inc.**, 730 S.W.2d 405, 411 (Tex. App.—Eastland 1987, writ ref'd n.r.e.) (board member's affidavits recounting factors board considered when deciding to relocate an airstrip and including copies of their meeting minutes were not hearsay because they were offered to establish the directors' good faith).

RULE 801

(7) Circumstantial evidence of memory or belief. Out-of-court statements can be used as circumstantial evidence of memory or belief. For example, in **Bridges v. State**, the defendant was accused of taking a child to his room and molesting her.[262] The child later gave police an out-of-court description of the room where the assault occurred, and the description matched the defendant's room.[263] The statement was offered at trial to prove that the defendant molested the child. On appeal, the court held that the statement was not hearsay because it was not being offered to prove the appearance of the defendant's room, but rather that the child had been in the defendant's room. The statement was circumstantial evidence of her memory or belief and thus was not hearsay.[264]

5. Hearsay by implication. Another area of recurring concern is "hearsay by implication" or "indirect hearsay": the attempt to dodge an explicit recitation of the out-of-court declarant's statement by artful questioning.[265] In **Schaffer v. State**, the Texas Court of Criminal Appeals held that when a piece of evidence is being offered to prove the truth of statements made outside the courtroom, a party cannot artfully circumvent the rule against hearsay by an indirect or oblique narrative.[266] Thus, testimony such as "based on our interrogation of X about the robbery committed by him and another, we arrested the defendant" is properly treated as hearsay.[267] However, testimony by a

---

262. 19 N.W.2d 529, 530-31 (Wis. 1945).

263. *Id.* at 531-32.

264. *Id.* at 536.

265. Courts do not always catch these clever stratagems. For example, in **Alexander v. State**, a prosecution for attempted capital murder involving the robbery-shooting of a pizza deliveryman, the court of appeals held that the prosecutor did not improperly elicit hearsay when he asked the question: "[W]hen the Pizza Man walked up toward the apartment there, was there any discussion in the group from anyone about robbing him?" 820 S.W.2d 821, 822-23 (Tex. App.—Waco 1991, pet. ref'd). The court held that because the witness did not relate a "statement" by a third party, but merely agreed that "discussions" about robbing the victim took place, this testimony was not hearsay. *Id.* at 823. This reasoning entirely overlooked the problem of indirect hearsay.

266. 777 S.W.2d 111, 114 (Tex. Crim. App. 1989). In this prosecution for possession of peyote, the defendant testified that he was a police informer who worked for Officer Jimmie Seals. *Id.* at 112. In rebuttal, the State did not call Officer Seals, but rather Officer Segovia, who testified that he had just called Officer Seals and that based on that telephone call he, Officer Segovia, would not ask the State to drop charges against the defendant. *Id.* at 113. This line of testimony was intended to convey to the jury that Officer Seals told Officer Segovia that the defendant was not a police informant. *Id.* at 114. As the court correctly noted, a jury is not likely to make any distinction between the outright hearsay narrative—"[Officer] Seals told me that [the defendant] is not an informant"—and the oblique hearsay narrative—"Without telling us what [Officer Seals] told you ... would you ask the State to drop the charges." *Id.* Either one is inadmissible hearsay. *See id.* at 113-14; *see also* **Coots v. State**, 826 S.W.2d 955, 959 (Tex. App.—Houston [1st Dist.] 1992, no pet.) (trial court improperly permitted a deputy to imply that (1) an out-of-court witness had named defendant as a possible robbery suspect, and (2) the witness had told him that defendant had used the same phone number as the robber); *cf.* **Gurka v. State**, 82 S.W.3d 416, 425 (Tex. App.—Austin 2002, pet. ref'd) (testimony was not "backdoor hearsay" because prosecutor's "sole intent" in having witness testify was not merely to prove contents of out-of-court statement); **McCullough v. State**, 116 S.W.3d 86, 87-88 & n.2 (Tex. App.—Houston [14th Dist.] 2001, pet. ref'd) (plurality op.) (police officer's statement that "[t]he [Crime Stoppers] tip that we got gave us the name of Kenneth McCullough that was responsible for robbing this hotel" was not indirect hearsay because it was offered to explain why officer put defendant's photograph in photo spread, not for its truth).

267. *See, e.g.,* **United States v. Brown**, 767 F.2d 1078, 1083-84 (4th Cir. 1985) (while government was entitled to offer evidence of what occurred after the offense as background, hearsay evidence of charged offense was not admissible as background); **United States v. Hernandez**, 750 F.2d 1256, 1257-58 (5th Cir. 1985) (because DEA agent's state of mind was not at issue in defendant's trial for possession and distribution of cocaine, government was not

witness that he went to a certain place or performed a certain act in response to gener-alized "information received" is normally not considered hearsay because the witness should be allowed to give some explanation of his behavior.[268] The line between non-hearsay and hearsay is drawn between testimony reflecting that the witness received some unspecified information and statements revealing or implying the content of that information.[269] Courts should, but do not always, discriminate between situations in which hearsay information is admissible to explain a person's conduct and those in

---

entitled to elicit a hearsay statement that agent "received a referral by the U.S. Customs [that defendant was] a drug smuggler" to prove a motivation for, or "background" to, the investigation); ***Deary v. State***, 681 S.W.2d 784, 788 (Tex. App.—Houston [14th Dist.] 1984, pet. ref'd) (when officer testified that he asked one shoplifter for names of two other persons involved with him and, as a result of that conversation, a photograph was located that led to the identification of defendant, statement was inadmissible hearsay by inference); *see also* McCORMICK ON EVIDENCE, *supra* note 223, §249, at 735 (evidence "as to the purport of 'information received' by the witness, or testimony of the results of investigations made by other persons, offered as proof of the facts asserted out of court, are properly classed as hearsay"). *But see **Miller v. State***, 755 S.W.2d 211, 214-15 (Tex. App.—Dallas 1988) (in kidnapping pros-ecution, when police officer testified that he took a physical description of the kidnapper from multiple witnesses, combined them into one description in his report, and disseminated the description to other officers, the statement was not hearsay because it was admitted for the purpose of showing what description was disseminated), *rev'd on other grounds*, 815 S.W.2d 582 (Tex. Crim. App. 1991). *See generally* Judson F. Falknor, *Indirect Hearsay*, 31 TUL. L. REV. 3 (1956) (collecting cases of "obscured" hearsay in which statements of witnesses were in effect statements of what out-of-court declarants had told testifying witnesses).

268. *See, e.g.*, ***Black v. State***, 503 S.W.2d 554, 557 (Tex. Crim. App. 1974) (police officer could testify that defen-dant was arrested as a result of a general broadcast over police radio); ***Johnson v. State***, 379 S.W.2d 329, 333 (Tex. Crim. App. 1964) (police officer could testify that he received a radio dispatch about a robbery and an automobile description, without relating the dispatch's content); ***Davis v. State***, 169 S.W.3d 673, 676-77 (Tex. App.—Fort Worth 2005, no pet.) (officer's testimony about anonymous tips he received about defendant was not hearsay be-cause it was offered to show how the investigation focused on defendant and why officer put together photo spread that included his photograph); ***Sparks v. State***, 935 S.W.2d 462, 467 (Tex. App.—Tyler 1996, no pet.) (officer's tes-timony that he was looking for suspicious activity in a specific area because he had received a report of some bur-glaries taking place was not hearsay because it was offered to show why officer was in area); ***Ulloa v. State***, 901 S.W.2d 507, 516 (Tex. App.—El Paso 1995, pet. ref'd) (officer's testimony explaining that he photographed certain items because he thought they had evidentiary value based on victim's statements was not hearsay); ***Salazar v. State***, 716 S.W.2d 733, 735-36 (Tex. App.—Corpus Christi 1986, pet. ref'd) (officer's testimony that, based on an informant's tip, he placed defendant's photograph in the lineup was not hearsay; officer did not divulge the contents of the tip, but rather how he acted as a result of receiving the information); ***Earls v. State***, 715 S.W.2d 731, 732-33 (Tex. App.—San Antonio 1986, pet. ref'd) (officer could testify that he went to New Orleans, had a conversation with two named people, returned to San Antonio, and issued an arrest warrant for defendant; these statements were not hearsay by implication because officer did not relate the contents of the conversation); *see also* McCORMICK ON EVI-DENCE, *supra* note 223, §249, at 734 ("arresting or investigating officer should not be put in the false position of seem-ing just to have happened upon the scene; he should be allowed some explanation of his presence and conduct"; there is the possibility of abuse if officers are permitted to divulge the content of the information received).

Texas courts have occasionally used a related practice of admitting out-of-court statements when they are offered to explain another person's conduct, but the rationale for doing so is poorly developed. For example, in ***Lewis v. State***, the court of appeals held that the defendant's wife could testify that she had been told that two weap-ons belonging to the defendant were illegal because that testimony explained why she had brought the weapons to the attention of the police. 759 S.W.2d 773, 774 (Tex. App.—Beaumont 1988, no pet.). The court, however, did not discuss how her conduct was relevant to the prosecution of the defendant for possession of a prohibited weapon, other than to prove that the weapon he possessed was indeed illegal. If otherwise inadmissible hearsay were always admissible to explain why someone acted in a certain manner, the rule against hearsay would collapse entirely. On the other hand, out-of-court statements admitted to shed light on otherwise ambiguous conduct are admissible as the verbal part of an act. Refer to notes 250-251 *supra* and accompanying text.

269. *See, e.g.*, ***Shuffield v. State***, 189 S.W.3d 782, 790 (Tex. Crim. App. 2006) (witness testified that accomplice's statement was "consistent" with defendant's; court assumed without deciding that testimony was indirect hearsay because it implied the content of accomplice's statement).

which such hearsay information is inadmissible based on the degree to which the witness's conduct has been challenged as inexplicable, inappropriate, or unlawful.[270] Otherwise, claiming a need to explain the witness's presence or conduct would become a thinly disguised method for "back-dooring" inadmissible hearsay evidence.

As the court of criminal appeals stated in *Schaffer*:

> The police officer … should not be permitted to relate historical aspects of the case, replete with hearsay statements in the form of complaints and reports on grounds that she was entitled to tell the jury the information upon which she acted.[271]

Thus, hearsay details of the information received from some other person or source are generally not admissible.[272] In Texas cases, this rule has been more frequently broken than observed.[273] Of course, if the issue to be determined is whether an officer had

---

270. *See, e.g.*, ***Morin v. State***, 960 S.W.2d 132, 138-39 (Tex. App.—Corpus Christi 1997, no pet.) (State had no obligation to explain investigator's actions because they were never challenged by defendant; reversible error to admit informant's hearsay statement).

271. 777 S.W.2d at 114-15; *see, e.g.*, ***Burks v. State***, 876 S.W.2d 877, 898 (Tex. Crim. App. 1994) (officer's testimony that—after he had talked to informants—he "went looking for" a black male, small build, approximately 5'6" to 5'7", having in his possession a black ski mask or toboggan-type cap was indirect hearsay inadmissible under *Schaffer*, but error was harmless).

272. *See* ***Smith v. State***, 574 S.W.2d 555, 557 (Tex. Crim. App. 1978).

273. *Compare* ***Dinkins v. State***, 894 S.W.2d 330, 347 (Tex. Crim. App. 1995) (admission of appointment book and patient-application form containing name of defendant was proper as nonhearsay to demonstrate how defendant became a suspect in murder investigation), ***Mendoza v. State***, 69 S.W.3d 628, 633 (Tex. App.—Corpus Christi 2002, pet. ref'd) (arresting officer could testify that he was informed of the assailant's identity over police radio because the testimony was not offered to prove that defendant was the assailant, but rather to show why officer arrested defendant), ***In re J.S.***, 35 S.W.3d 287, 294 (Tex. App.—Fort Worth 2001, no pet.) (upholding admission of testimony that police officer suspected a juvenile because of information received by child-abuse interviewer with district attorney's office in a separate investigation; testimony was offered to show how juvenile became a suspect), ***Gomez v. State***, 9 S.W.3d 189, 192 (Tex. App.—San Antonio 1999, no pet.) (officer's testimony that 14-year-old victim told him defendant abused her was what "led to his investigation" of case and thus was not hearsay), ***Cano v. State***, 3 S.W.3d 99, 110 (Tex. App.—Corpus Christi 1999, pet. ref'd) (officer's testimony that he had received information that "drugs were being dealt" from defendants' residence was not offered to prove they were, but merely to show why investigation focused on defendants), ***Cormier v. State***, 955 S.W.2d 161, 162 (Tex. App.—Austin 1997, no pet.) (officer's testimony was admissible as nonhearsay because statements "were not offered to prove that [defendant] was a drug dealer but to explain why the drug task force chose to investigate him"), ***Schneider v. State***, 951 S.W.2d 856, 864 (Tex. App.—Texarkana 1997, pet. ref'd) (officer's testimony was "arguably" admissible to show circumstances leading up to drug-transaction meeting or to explain why officer obtained an arrest warrant), ***Rosales v. State***, 932 S.W.2d 530, 536 (Tex. App.—Tyler 1995, pet. ref'd) (confidential informant's report of child neglect was not hearsay because it was offered to explain the response of police dispatcher and officers), ***Russell v. State***, 904 S.W.2d 191, 200-01 (Tex. App.—Amarillo 1995, pet. ref'd) (sheriff's testimony that New Mexico narcotics unit had informed him defendant planned to move a quantity of marijuana through sheriff's jurisdiction was nonhearsay because it was offered to show probable cause and why sheriff acted as he did), ***Oberg v. State***, 890 S.W.2d 539, 542 (Tex. App.—El Paso 1994, pet. ref'd) (officer's statement about information that defendant was going to engage in drug sale was not hearsay because it was offered to establish the circumstances leading to officer's search), *and* ***Jackson v. State***, 889 S.W.2d 615, 616 (Tex. App.—Houston [14th Dist.] 1994, pet. ref'd) (sexual-assault complainant's statement to her father that she was afraid to tell him about sexual assault because defendants would kill him was admissible to show why victim delayed in speaking about offense), *with* ***Sandoval v. State***, 409 S.W.3d 259, 283-84 (Tex. App.—Austin 2013, no pet.) (in prosecution for sexual assault of a child, police officer's testimony was not generalized information describing how defendant became a suspect, but rather provided specific details of assault and defendant's involvement in it; trial court erred in admitting testimony), ***Thompson v. State***, 981 S.W.2d 319,

probable cause to arrest or search a person, then the reasonableness of the officer's conduct is called into question and the hearsay details of information that he received are admissible.[274]

The issue of whether the proffered testimony is indirect hearsay depends primarily on "how strongly the content of the out-of-court statement can be inferred from the context."[275] When the substance of the out-of-court statement is "an inescapable conclusion" drawn from the in-court witness's testimony, that evidence is clearly hearsay by implication.[276] Trial courts have great discretion in determining, from all surrounding circumstances, including the witness's and questioner's tone, demeanor, and emphasis, whether the jury is likely to infer the content of the out-of-court statement from the testimony given.[277]

Even when the proponent of the out-of-court statement identifies a relevant nonhearsay rationale for admitting that evidence, the mere identification of a nonhearsay

---

322-24 (Tex. App.—Houston [14th Dist.] 1998) (reversible error for admitting "backdoor" hearsay when officer's testimony "left the jurors with the clear impression" that the nontestifying identification witnesses had identified defendant in photo spread), *rev'd on other grounds*, 9 S.W.3d 808 (Tex. Crim. App. 1999), *Morin*, 960 S.W.2d at 138-39 (testimony that officer had obtained defendant's name from informant, which was offered to explain officer's actions in focusing on defendant as a suspect, was reversible error because defendant never challenged officer's conduct or investigative methods), *Judd v. State*, 923 S.W.2d 135, 139 (Tex. App.—Fort Worth 1996, pet. ref'd) (testimony offered for the limited purpose of illustrating investigator's state of mind was inadmissible hearsay because statement's only real value was as explanation for why victim's body was never recovered), *and Hill v. State*, 817 S.W.2d 816, 818 (Tex. App.—Eastland 1991, pet. ref'd) (hearsay explaining why officer focused on defendant was not admissible because probable cause and appropriateness of officer's actions were not at issue).

The reasoning in some of these cases permitting a description of the out-of-court conversation should be reexamined after *Head v. State*, 4 S.W.3d 258, 261-62 (Tex. Crim. App. 1999). Refer to notes 275-277 *infra* and accompanying text. After *Head*, the appropriate inquiry should focus on whether the "information received" testimony is a *general* description of possible criminality or a *specific* description of the defendant's purported involvement or link to that activity. For example, "I received information of possible drugs being sold at 5th and Main" is an admissible general description of why an officer investigated the situation. *See, e.g.*, *Short v. State*, 995 S.W.2d 948, 954 (Tex. App.—Fort Worth 1999, pet. ref'd) (officer's testimony that he received information that "controlled substances were being brought into the jail by staff personnel" was not indirect hearsay). More specific statements that point to the defendant, such as "I received information that drugs were being sold from the defendant's house," clearly convey the content of the out-of-court statement and are inadmissible indirect hearsay under *Head*.

274. *See, e.g.*, *Benford v. State*, 895 S.W.2d 716, 718 (Tex. App.—Houston [14th Dist.] 1994, no pet.) ("Statements made by a third party to an officer, who uses these statements to determine probable cause, are not hearsay ...."); *Parks v. State*, 858 S.W.2d 623, 632 (Tex. App.—Fort Worth 1993, pet. ref'd) ("An officer's actions ... may be made an issue [requiring] the officer to testify not only about how he happened upon the scene, but also regarding the specific information received so that the jury may resolve any issues regarding an officer's actions.").

275. *E.g.*, *Head*, 4 S.W.3d at 261-62 (detective's testimony that statements by outcry witness and victim's mother were "consistent with the facts related" by child victim were not indirect hearsay and "did not lead to any inescapable conclusions as to the substance of the out-of-court statements"); *see also Thornton v. State*, 994 S.W.2d 845, 853-54 (Tex. App.—Fort Worth 1999, pet. ref'd) (testimony that officer spoke with numerous other people, including relatives of child complainant, before filing charges was not "back door" hearsay; testimony merely described officer's investigation); *cf. United States v. Check*, 582 F.2d 668, 678 (2d Cir. 1978) (detective's testimony that he arrested defendant after interviewing witnesses was "a transparent conduit for the introduction of inadmissible hearsay information").

276. *See Head*, 4 S.W.3d at 261-62 & n.3 (the phrase "inescapable conclusion" is not a talisman, but merely a shortcut in focusing inquiry on whether the testimony is being offered to prove the content of the out-of-court statement).

277. *See id.* at 262-63; *see also id.* at 264 (Womack, J., concurring) ("inescapable conclusion" forms no part of the bar against indirect hearsay; the proper issue is whether the proponent is, in fact, offering the testimony as indirect proof of the out-of-court statement).

RULE 801

use may be insufficient to justify admission if the jury is likely to consider the statement for the truth of its contents and that misuse would result in significant, unfair prejudice to the opposing party.[278]

Thus, testimony containing hearsay may be admissible not for its truth but as background information or explanation only if (1) its nonhearsay purpose is relevant, and (2) under Rule 403, the probative value of the evidence for its nonhearsay purpose is not substantially outweighed by any risk of unfair prejudice resulting from an impermissible hearsay use of the declarant's statement.[279] Two common scenarios in which the admission of such testimony as background evidence may be appropriate are when the testimony (1) clarifies noncontroversial matters and (2) is used as rebuttal to the opponent's initiatives or selective portrayal of events.[280]

B. Rule 801(e): Statements that Are Not Hearsay

Each of the three subparagraphs of Rule 801(e) exempts a category of statements from the hearsay rule. Even though these statements fit the hearsay definition in form, they are not hearsay because they do not invoke all the policies behind the hearsay rule. Nonhearsay statements, however, must still meet all other evidentiary requirements for admissibility.[281]

---

278. *See United States v. Reyes*, 18 F.3d 65, 70-71 (2d Cir. 1994). In this case, the Second Circuit discussed at length the problems that arise when the government offers evidence from investigating officers, not for the truth of the matter, but as a "background" to explain the investigation or to show an agent's state of mind so that the jury will understand the reasons for the agent's actions. *Id.* at 70. The court noted:

> [t]he proffer of such evidence generally raises two questions: first, whether the non-hearsay purpose by which the evidence is sought to be justified is relevant, *i.e.*, whether it supports or diminishes the likelihood of any fact 'that is of consequence to the determination of the action,' and second, whether the probative value of this evidence for its non-hearsay purpose is outweighed by the danger of unfair prejudice resulting from the impermissible hearsay use of the declarant's statement.

Id. (citation omitted). The court then set out a series of questions involved in the determination of the relevance and importance of this evidence and in the assessment of potential prejudice. *Id.* at 70-71; *see also **Ryan v. Miller**,* 303 F.3d 231, 248-49 (2d Cir. 2002) (collecting cases condemning artful questioning of a witness about what he *learned* from an out-of-court witness as an attempt to avoid asking directly what the witness *said*, which would invoke explicit hearsay response; "[s]uch hearsay testimony containing implicit accusations violates the Confrontation Clause"). The Eighth Circuit has concluded that

> to hold the government to its stated non-hearsay purpose and to prevent undue prejudice, the trial court should instruct the prosecution to avoid hearsay statements whenever possible in presenting its background evidence, and should instruct the jury as to the limited purpose of any hearsay statements that cannot be avoided.

United States v. Alonzo, 991 F.2d 1422, 1427 (8th Cir. 1993); *see also **United States v. Sallins**,* 993 F.2d 344, 346-47 (3d Cir. 1993) (although government contended that radio dispatch message was offered to explain officers' actions, testimony was inadmissible hearsay because details of radio call were actually offered for their truth value).

279. *See Reyes*, 18 F.3d at 70. Refer to *Article IV: Relevance & Its Limits, supra* p. 211.

280. *See Reyes*, 18 F.3d at 70; *see also **United States v. Forrester**,* 60 F.3d 52, 60-61 (2d Cir. 1995) (party may introduce otherwise inadmissible evidence when (1) the opposing party has already introduced inadmissible evidence on the same issue and (2) the evidence is needed to rebut a false impression that the opposing party's evidence may have created).

281. *See **TXI Transp. Co. v. Hughes**,* 306 S.W.3d 230, 241 (Tex. 2010); ***Willover v. State**,* 70 S.W.3d 841, 846 n.9 (Tex. Crim. App. 2002).

1. Rule 801(e)(1): A declarant-witness's prior statement. Rule 801(e)(1) contains three types of out-of-court statements[282] that would have been considered hearsay at common law in Texas and elsewhere[283] but have been defined by the rule as nonhearsay. Because the statements are nonhearsay, they can be offered for the truth of the matter asserted in the statements or for any other permissible purpose. A statement is considered nonhearsay under Rule 801(e)(1) if (1) the statement falls into one of the rule's three categories and (2) the declarant testifies at the trial or hearing and is subject to cross-examination about the statement.

(1) Rule 801(e)(1)(A): Prior inconsistent testimony. At common law, a prior inconsistent statement used for impeachment purposes could not be considered for the truth of any matter asserted in the statement.[284] Rule 801(e)(1)(A), in a radical change from

---

282. Before the 2015 restyling of the Texas Rules, the rule contained a fourth type of statement. Former Rule 801(e)(1)(D) exempted filmed or videotaped statements, taken under the provisions of article 38.071 of the Texas Code of Criminal Procedure, that were made by a child age 13 or younger who was the alleged victim of certain specified offenses. Because the statute no longer requires the declarant to be available to testify at trial, "its inclusion [in the text of Rule 801(e)(1)] is no longer appropriate." TEX. R. EVID. 801 cmt. The comment to the 2015 restyling also observed that "article 38.071 is but one of a number of statutes that mandate the admission of certain hearsay statements in particular circumstances." TEX. R. EVID. 801 cmt. Because Rule 801(e)(1) does not mention any of the other statutes, its reference to article 38.071 made little sense. *See* TEX. R. EVID. 801 cmt. The deletion of former Rule 801(e)(1)(D) is not intended as a substantive change. TEX. R. EVID. 801 cmt.

283. *See* MCCORMICK'S HANDBOOK II, *supra* note 7, §§34, 39, 49, 251; 1 RAY, *supra* note 9, §688, at 626, §§773-774, at 652-56; 1A RAY, *supra* note 9, §785 & n.30, at 12; 3A JOHN H. WIGMORE, EVIDENCE IN TRIALS AT COMMON LAW §1018, at 996 (Chadbourn rev. 1970); Charles T. McCormick, *The Turncoat Witness: Previous Statements as Substantive Evidence*, 25 TEX. L. REV. 573, 574-75 (1947). If the prior statement was inconsistent with the witness's testimony in court, it was admissible under certain conditions only for the limited purpose of discrediting the testimony, not as "substantive evidence." *See* MCCORMICK'S HANDBOOK II, *supra* note 7, §§34-39, 251; 1 RAY, *supra* note 9, §§687-698, at 625-47. A prior consistent statement, under certain conditions, was admissible only for the limited purpose of counteracting some types of impeachment. *See* MCCORMICK'S HANDBOOK II, *supra* note 7, §§49, 251; 1 RAY, *supra* note 9, §§773-774, at 652-56 (3d ed. 1980), §775, at 273 (Supp. 1991).

284. The traditional position that prior inconsistent statements are hearsay and not admissible as substantive evidence has been severely criticized by eminent judges and scholars for many years. *See* **United States v. De Sisto**, 329 F.2d 929, 932-34 (2d Cir. 1964) (rule defies the dictates of common sense); **Di Carlo v. United States**, 6 F.2d 364, 367-68 (2d Cir. 1925) (nothing requires jury to decide case in accordance with testimony in court alone); 3A WIGMORE, *supra* note 283, §1018, at 996 (rule should not apply to prior inconsistent testimony because the witness is available for cross-examination and the rationale for the hearsay rule has therefore been satisfied); McCormick, *supra* note 283, at 575-77 (admission of prior inconsistent statements provides opportunity to test veracity of witnesses through cross-examination); Morgan, *supra* note 1, at 192-96 (when declarant is also a witness, no substantial degree of risk justifies excluding prior declarations as hearsay); *see also* MCCORMICK'S HANDBOOK II, *supra* note 7, §251, at 602 (earlier statements are more trustworthy because memory fades with time); 1 RAY, *supra* note 9, §688, at 627 (summarizing arguments against the rule). Critics have argued that the safeguards of delayed cross-examination and opportunity for the trier of fact to observe the demeanor of the declarant-witness, plus the inherent attractiveness of the prior statement's relative proximity in time to the subject matter, justify full admissibility. They have also maintained that any limiting instruction attempting to restrict the jury's use of the prior statement is unrealistic because it prescribes a distinction that jurors are unlikely to understand and follow.

The history of Federal Rule 801(d)(1)(A) demonstrates that the issue remains controversial. The Supreme Court's version of the rule would have made all prior inconsistent statements of a testifying witness admissible as substantive evidence. *See* FED. R. EVID. 801(d)(1)(A) (1972 proposed final draft), 56 F.R.D. 183, 293 (1973); *see also* **California v. Green**, 399 U.S. 149, 164 (1970) (upholding constitutionality of CAL. EVID. CODE §1235). The House of Representatives would have accorded nonhearsay status only to inconsistent statements given under oath and "subject to cross-examination at a trail [sic] or hearing or in a deposition." H.R. REP. NO. 93-650, *supra* note 29, at 13, *reprinted in* 1974 U.S.C.C.A.N. 7075, 7087. The Senate preferred the Court's version. *See* S. REP. NO. 93-1277, *su-*

RULE 801

the common law, defines prior inconsistent statements as nonhearsay and thus permits their use as substantive evidence (i.e., to prove the truth of the matter asserted in the statements). The prior inconsistent statements can be used as substantive evidence if, in addition to the declarant's testifying at the trial or hearing and being subject to cross-examination, three other conditions are met: (1) the statement is inconsistent with the declarant's testimony, (2) the statement was given under penalty of perjury, and (3) the statement was given at a trial, hearing, or other proceeding (other than a grand-jury proceeding in a criminal case)[285] or in a deposition.[286]

The prior statement must be inconsistent with the witness's testimony at the trial or hearing.[287] The inconsistency requirement does not mean that the prior inconsistent statement must flatly contradict the present testimony—if the prior statement differs in any significant way from the declarant's trial testimony, in either omissions or positive statements, it meets the requirement of Rule 801(e)(1)(A).[288] Similarly, a selective or feigned lack of memory may be sufficient inconsistency to admit the prior statement.[289] However, a flat refusal to testify at trial has been held not to be an inconsistent statement.[290]

The prior inconsistent statement must have been given under penalty of perjury.[291] This straightforward requirement has not generated any significant controversy.[292]

pra note 30, at 16-17, reprinted in 1974 U.S.C.C.A.N. 7051, 7063. Ultimately, Congress compromised and enacted a rule that did not include the requirement of cross-examination from the House amendment. Thus, the rule allows for the substantive use of inconsistent statements that are made before a grand jury. See H.R. CONF. REP. NO. 93-1597, supra note 31, at 10, reprinted in 1974 U.S.C.C.A.N. 7098, 7104. The 1983 Texas civil rule embraced the same compromise and adopted the enacted federal version verbatim in Rule 801(e)(1)(A). The Texas criminal rule, originally promulgated in 1986, followed the rationale of the House of Representatives by specifically excluding statements made in a grand-jury proceeding and requiring the opportunity for contemporaneous cross-examination. Thus, Texas Rule 801(e)(1)(A) is substantively identical to Federal Rule 801(d)(1)(A) for civil proceedings but is slightly different for criminal proceedings—in criminal trials, the Texas rule treats prior inconsistent testimony before a grand jury as hearsay. See TEX. R. EVID. 801(e)(1)(A)(ii). Because the great majority of prior inconsistent statements do not satisfy the requirements of Rule 801(e)(1)(A), the exception under Rule 801(e)(1)(A) is far closer to the common law than to the original Supreme Court version. See Contreras v. State, 766 S.W.2d 891, 892 (Tex. App.—San Antonio 1989, no pet.) (affidavit sworn to before a notary does not meet Rule 801(e)(1)(A) requirements and does not make the prior inconsistent statement nonhearsay).

285. Rule 801(e)(1)(A)(ii) does not, however, preclude the admission of grand-jury testimony that is otherwise admissible under a hearsay exception. Priester v. State, 478 S.W.3d 826, 835 n.7 (Tex. App.—El Paso 2015, no pet.); see, e.g., Brown v. State, 333 S.W.2d 606, 613 (Tex. App.—Dallas 2009, no pet.) (grand-jury testimony admissible as recorded recollection under Rule 803(5)).

286. TEX. R. EVID. 801(e)(1)(A).

287. Id.

288. See United States v. Williams, 737 F.2d 594, 608 (7th Cir. 1984) (inconsistency may be found in evasive answers, silence, or changes in positions).

289. See United States v. Bigham, 812 F.2d 943, 946-47 & n.2 (5th Cir. 1987) (the policy of the rule is to protect against "turncoat witnesses"; trial court could have determined that witness's memory loss was feigned); United States v. DiCaro, 772 F.2d 1314, 1317, 1322 (7th Cir. 1985) (professed memory lapse must often be treated as inconsistent testimony).

290. E.g., Davis v. State, 773 S.W.2d 592, 593 (Tex. App.—Eastland 1989, pet. ref'd) (prior testimony was inadmissible under Criminal Rule 801(e)(1) because "refusal to testify is not an inconsistent statement").

291. TEX. R. EVID. 801(e)(1)(A).

292. See Owens v. State, 916 S.W.2d 713, 717 (Tex. App.—Waco 1996, no pet.).

Most prior inconsistent statements offered in criminal cases were not given "under penalty of perjury at a trial, hearing, or other proceeding—except a grand jury proceeding—or in a deposition."[293] Thus, they are rarely admissible as substantive evidence to prove an element of the offense or defense. Generally, these prior inconsistent statements are offered solely to impeach the testifying witness's present in-court statements and must be accompanied by a limiting instruction if requested.

For civil cases, the prior inconsistent statement must have been given "at a trial, hearing, or other proceeding or in a deposition."[294] The rule for criminal cases excludes statements from grand-jury proceedings.[295] The term "other proceeding" has been construed broadly in Texas. In a significant ruling, the court in *American Maintenance & Rentals, Inc. v. Estrada* held that interrogatory answers satisfied this requirement.[296] The court stated:

> We believe that term ["proceeding"] as used here is meant to denote steps and events in the process of litigation besides a trial or hearing (hence the word "other" before the word "proceeding"). Our reading of rule 801(e)(1)(A) convinces us that the term was meant to have a comprehensive definition, encompassing the various stages of the progress of a lawsuit, such as answering interrogatories.[297]

Prior inconsistent statements that do not satisfy the requirements of Rule 801(e)(1)(A) are hearsay and can be used only to impeach a witness's credibility, not to prove the truth of any matter asserted in the statements.[298] Whenever a prior inconsistent statement that does not satisfy these requirements is admitted to impeach the witness, the jury must, on request, be given a limiting instruction.[299] Impeachment with a prior inconsistent statement cannot be used simply to present otherwise inadmissible hearsay evidence before the jury.[300] The failure to inform the

293. *See* TEX. R. EVID. 801(e)(1)(A)(ii).

294. TEX. R. EVID. 801(e)(1)(A)(i).

295. TEX. R. EVID. 801(e)(1)(A)(ii). Federal Rule 801(d)(1)(A), on the other hand, does not classify statements from grand-jury proceedings as hearsay. *See* FED. R. EVID. 801(d)(1)(A).

296. 896 S.W.2d 212, 218 (Tex. App.—Houston [1st Dist.] 1995, writ dism'd by agr.).

297. *Id.*; *see also* BLACK'S LAW DICTIONARY 1398 (10th ed. 2014) (defining "proceeding" as "[t]he regular and orderly progression of a lawsuit, including all acts and events between the time of commencement and the entry of judgment"); *cf.* *United States v. Castro-Ayon*, 537 F.2d 1055, 1057 (9th Cir. 1976) (immigration interrogation qualified as "other proceeding" under Federal Rule 801(d)(1)).

298. *See Smith v. State*, 520 S.W.2d 383, 386 (Tex. Crim. App. 1975) (prior inconsistent statements are admissible to impeach witnesses); *Baldree v. State*, 248 S.W.2d 224, 231 (Tex. App.—Houston [1st Dist.] 2007, pet. ref'd) (same); *Flores v. State*, 48 S.W.3d 397, 404 (Tex. App.—Waco 2001, pet. ref'd) (inconsistent statement can be used to impeach a witness's credibility but cannot be used as primary evidence of the defendant's guilt); *Ramirez v. State*, 987 S.W.2d 938, 944 (Tex. App.—Austin 1999, no pet.) (same); *see, e.g.*, *Halstead v. State*, 891 S.W.2d 11, 12-13 & n.1 (Tex. App.—Austin 1994, no pet.) (per curiam) (letter written by sexual-assault complainant did not satisfy requirements of Criminal Rule 801(e)(1) and was inadmissible to prove the truth of the matter asserted in the letter).

299. *See Miranda v. State*, 813 S.W.2d 724, 735 (Tex. App.—San Antonio 1991, pet. ref'd).

300. *Hughes v. State*, 4 S.W.3d 1, 5 & n.9 (Tex. Crim. App. 1999); *Brasher v. State*, 139 S.W.3d 369, 371 (Tex. App.—San Antonio 2004, pet. ref'd). Refer to *Article VI: Witnesses*, *supra* p. 597.

jurors that they can consider the prior inconsistent statement solely for impeachment purposes and not as substantive evidence is error.[301]

The U.S. Supreme Court, in ***California v. Green***, rejected the argument that a criminal defendant's right of confrontation is necessarily violated by the admission of prior inconsistent statements offered as substantive evidence.[302] The Court went on to suggest that the Confrontation Clause is not violated by the admission of a declarant's out-of-court statements as long as he testifies at trial and is subject to cross-examination.[303] In ***Green***, Melvin Porter, a 16-year-old prosecution witness, told a police officer shortly after his original arrest that the defendant had supplied him with drugs.[304] At trial, however, he claimed to be unable to recall how he had obtained the drugs.[305] Porter had also testified at a preliminary hearing, where he was subject to cross-examination, that the defendant had supplied him with drugs.[306] This prior statement was not automatically barred by the Confrontation Clause, even though the "forgetful" witness could not be cross-examined about the content of the prior inconsistent statement.[307]

(2) Rule 801(e)(1)(B): Prior consistent statements. Rule 801(e)(1)(B) gives substantive, nonhearsay status to a witness's prior consistent statements "offered to rebut an express or implied charge that the declarant recently fabricated [testimony] or acted from a recent improper influence or motive in so testifying."[308] Such statements may be used not only to rehabilitate a witness's credibility, but also to prove the truth of any matter asserted in the statement.[309] Rule 613(c), however, makes prior consistent state-

301. *See **Contreras v. State***, 766 S.W.2d 891, 892-93 (Tex. App.—San Antonio 1989, no pet.). This reasoning is in accord with earlier Texas law. *See **Goodman v. State***, 665 S.W.2d 788, 792 & n.2 (Tex. Crim. App. 1984); ***Key v. State***, 492 S.W.2d 514, 516 (Tex. Crim. App. 1973).

302. 399 U.S. 149, 165-68 (1970).

303. *Id.* at 158. ***Green*** left open the question of whether the Confrontation Clause would be violated by the use of a witness's prior out-of-court statement when the witness, now on the witness stand, could not remember the content of that statement or even having made it. *See id.* at 168-69. In *United States v. Owens*, the Supreme Court answered that question, holding that the Confrontation Clause was not violated as long as the declarant took the witness stand and was subject to cross-examination, even if he could not be examined on the prior statement itself. 484 U.S. 554, 559 (1988); 4 LOUISELL & MUELLER, *supra* note 250, §419, at 179-80. Refer to note 340 *infra* and accompanying text. For a discussion of the development of Confrontation Clause jurisprudence, refer to notes 36-162 *supra* and accompanying text.

304. 399 U.S. at 151.

305. *Id.* at 151-52.

306. *Id.* at 151.

307. *See id.* at 166-68. The Court did not specifically hold that the prior inconsistent statement was admissible because due-process concerns that were not raised on certiorari could have barred its use. *Id.* at 168-70 & n.18; *see, e.g.*, ***Delaware v. Fensterer***, 474 U.S. 15, 20-22 (1985) (Confrontation Clause did not bar the admission of the witness's opinion even though he could no longer recall the basis for that opinion; Confrontation Clause "guarantees an *opportunity* for effective cross-examination, not cross-examination that is effective in whatever way, and to whatever extent, the defense might wish"). Refer to note 35 *supra* and accompanying text.

308. TEX. R. EVID. 801(e)(1)(B). Rule 801(e)(1)(B) is not the only possible avenue for the admission of prior consistent statements. They might also be admissible under the doctrine of completeness when "one party has made use of a portion of a document, such that misunderstanding or distortion can be averted only through presentation of another portion ...." ***Beech Aircraft Corp. v. Rainey***, 488 U.S. 153, 172 (1988).

309. The rule is in accord with earlier Texas law and does not alter the Texas doctrine that a prior consistent statement is admissible only in the particular circumstances described. *See **McInnes v. Yamaha Motor Corp., U.S.A.***, 673

ments inadmissible for any other purpose.[310] Mere impeachment of a witness by a prior inconsistent statement, without the suggestion of recent fabrication or recent improper influence or motive, does not justify rehabilitation by the use of a prior consistent statement.[311]

The prior consistent statement does not have to be proved by the declarant but rather can be established through other witnesses. The declarant must nonetheless be available for the opponent to cross-examine on the statement.[312]

Rule 801(e)(1)(B) is identical to Federal Rule 801(d)(1)(B)(i),[313] and the Texas Court of Criminal Appeals has explicitly stated that federal decisions can be looked to in interpreting the Texas rule.[314] The leading case interpreting the federal rule is **Tome v. United States**, which held that prior consistent statements are admissible under Federal Rule 801(d)(1)(B) only if they are made before the charged recent fabrication or recent improper influence or motive arose.[315] Thus, in addition to the declarant's testifying at the trial or hearing and being subject to cross-examination, there are three other requirements for the admission of prior consistent statements: the statement must (1) be consistent with the declarant's testimony, (2) be offered to rebut an express or implied charge against the declarant of recent fabrication or improper influence or motive, and (3) have been made before the supposed fabrication or improper influence or motive arose.[316] The trial court retains discretion, however,

---

S.W.2d 185, 189 (Tex. 1984) (Texas Supreme Court had previously recognized, as an exception to the hearsay rule, the admissibility of prior consistent statements to support a witness who had been charged with recent fabrication of his testimony); *Campbell v. State*, 718 S.W.2d 712, 715 (Tex. Crim. App. 1986) (Criminal Rule 801(e)(1) is merely a codification of Texas case law); 1 RAY, *supra* note 9, §§773-774, at 272 (Supp. 1991) (prior consistent statement that satisfies the recent-fabrication or improper-motive requirements of Rule 801(e)(1)(B) is not hearsay).

310. *See* TEX. R. EVID. 613(c) ("Unless Rule 801(e)(1)(B) provides otherwise, a witness's prior consistent statement is not admissible if offered solely to enhance the witness's credibility."). Refer to *Article VI: Witnesses, supra* p. 665.

311. *See* TEX. R. EVID. 613(c), 801(e)(1)(B); *Aetna Ins. v. Eastman*, 95 Tex. 34, 37-38, 64 S.W. 863, 863-64 (1901).

312. *See, e.g.*, **Mo. Pac. R.R. v. Vlach**, 687 S.W.2d 414, 417-18 (Tex. App.—Houston [14th Dist.] 1985, writ ref'd n.r.e.) (trial court properly excluded evidence of prior consistent statements given by person who heard the prior statements because declarants had already been excused from courtroom and opponent did not have an opportunity to cross-examine declarants about these statements); *cf.* **United States v. Green**, 258 F.3d 683, 692 (7th Cir. 2001) (prior consistent statement can be introduced through testimony of someone other than declarant, as long as declarant is available for cross-examination). Obviously, then, a party who wants to introduce a prior consistent statement through a nondeclarant must ensure that the declarant is still available to testify and to be cross-examined about the statement.

313. Under Federal Rule 801(d)(1)(B)(ii), prior consistent statements that are offered to rehabilitate the declarant's credibility as a witness when attacked on other grounds—such as inconsistency or faulty memory—are also admissible as substantive evidence. *See* FED. R. EVID. 801(d)(1)(B)(ii); FED. R. EVID. 801 advisory committee's note to 2014 amendments.

314. *See* **Campbell**, 718 S.W.2d at 716-17.

315. 513 U.S. 150, 156 (1995). The Supreme Court observed that this requirement was carried over from the common law. *Id.* The rule retains this requirement. FED. R. EVID. 801 advisory committee's note to 2014 amendments.

316. *See* TEX. R. EVID. 801(e)(1)(B); **Tome**, 513 U.S. at 156; **Hammons v. State**, 239 S.W.3d 798, 804 (Tex. Crim. App. 2007). The opponent of a prior consistent statement must alert the trial court to any elements of Rule 801(e)(1)(B) that would require exclusion of the statement. *See* **Klein v. State**, 273 S.W.3d 297, 312 (Tex. Crim. App. 2008). Otherwise, error is not properly preserved. *See id.*

to exclude the prior consistent statement under Rule 403 if its probative value is significantly outweighed by countervailing factors.[317]

(a) Consistent with the declarant's testimony. A prior statement must be consistent with the declarant's testimony to be admissible under Rule 801(e)(1)(B).[318] But it is admissible only if it is limited to the point on which the witness has been impeached; otherwise, the prior statement is inadmissible, even if it is consistent with the witness's testimony.[319]

(b) Offered to rebut express or implied charge of recent fabrication or recent improper influence or motive. A prior consistent statement is admissible only if it is offered to rebut an express or implied charge of recent fabrication or recent improper influence or motive.[320] Prior consistent statements are most often used to rebut suggestions that a witness is biased, but a witness can also be impeached with accusations of corruption or interest on the witness's part. The trial court has substantial discretion to admit a prior consistent statement when there has been "'only a suggestion' of conscious alteration or fabrication."[321] On the other hand, "the rule cannot be construed to permit the admission of what would otherwise be hearsay any time a witness's credibility or memory is challenged."[322] "There is no bright line between a general challenge to memory or credibility and a suggestion of conscious fabrication, but the trial court should determine whether the cross-examiner's questions or the tenor of that questioning would reasonably imply an intent by the witness to fabricate."[323] The trial court's determination is reviewed for abuse of discretion.[324] The charge of recent fabrication or recent improper influence or motive can be express or implied from the nature of

---

317. *Cf. Christmas v. Sanders*, 759 F.2d 1284, 1288-89 (7th Cir. 1985) (trial court properly excluded police reports offered by defendant-police officer as a prior consistent statement after she had been "minimally" impeached; if trial judge were required to admit prior statements in such a situation, he "would have to admit unnecessary cumulative evidence that would only confuse the jury and lead to unlimited bolstering of witness' credibility"); *United States v. Crosby*, 713 F.2d 1066, 1071-72 (5th Cir. 1983) (prior consistent statement was excluded under Federal Rule 403).

318. TEX. R. EVID. 801(e)(1)(B).

319. If the prior statement does not address the same specific incident as the trial testimony, it does not satisfy this requirement. *See Kipp v. State*, 876 S.W.2d 330, 338 (Tex. Crim. App. 1994). In *Kipp*, the prior statement offered by the prosecution pertained to an incident involving indecency with the child victim that occurred approximately one year before the charged offense. *Id.* In finding the testimony inadmissible, the court of criminal appeals held that a "prior consistent statement for purposes of Rule 801(e)(1)(B) must relate to the same matter or incident testified to by the declarant at trial." *Id.*

320. TEX. R. EVID. 801(e)(1)(B). The language of the rule requires a charge of recent fabrication *or* recent improper influence or motive, not that the recent fabrication was made for an improper reason. *Klein*, 273 S.W.3d at 315.

321. *Hammons*, 239 S.W.3d at 804-05 (quoting *United States v. Frazier*, 469 F.3d 85, 88 (3d Cir. 2006)).

322. *Hammons*, 239 S.W.3d at 805; *Linney v. State*, 401 S.W.3d 764, 781 (Tex. App.—Houston [14th Dist.] 2013, pet. ref'd); *see* 1 MCCORMICK ON EVIDENCE §47, at 223-24 (Kenneth S. Broun ed., 6th ed. 2006) (judge should consider in each case "whether a particular impeachment for inconsistency or a conflict in testimony amounts in effect to an attack on general character for truthfulness").

323. *Hammons*, 239 S.W.3d at 805.

324. *Id.* at 806; *see Lawton v. State*, 913 S.W.2d 542, 561 (Tex. Crim. App. 1995).

the questions asked.[325] A court can also consider the questions asked in voir dire, counsel's opening statement, and the cross-examination of other witnesses to determine whether the opposing party intends to suggest fabrication by the witness.[326] Use of a prior consistent statement is proper to rehabilitate a witness even when the offering party first suggested the possible motive for fabrication on direct examination, as long as the witness has been impeached with an express or implied accusation of recent fabrication.[327]

(c) Made before fabrication or improper influence or motive arose. A prior consistent statement can be offered to rebut a charge of recent fabrication only if the statement was made before the alleged recent fabrication or recent improper influence or motive arose.[328] In practice, it is often difficult to pinpoint exactly when the recent fabrication or recent improper influence or motive arose. The prior consistent statement

---

325. *See **Hammons**,* 239 S.W.3d at 804; ***Lawton**,* 913 S.W.2d at 561; *see, e.g., **Klein**,* 273 S.W.3d at 313 (sexual-assault complainant testified on cross-examination that defendant did not sexually abuse her and that she lied when she initially accused defendant; trial court could have reasonably found that cross-examination implicitly charged that complainant's direct-examination testimony that defendant did abuse her was a recent fabrication); *see also **United States v. Baron**,* 602 F.2d 1248, 1253 (7th Cir. 1979) (defense counsel's attack on a witness need not have been intended to imply recent fabrication as long as the jury might infer the charge from the manner of questioning); Michael H. Graham, *Prior Consistent Statements: Rule 801(d)(1)(B) of the Federal Rules of Evidence, Critique and Proposal,* 30 HASTINGS L.J. 575, 586, 607 (1979) (the query "Didn't you talk with plaintiff's counsel shortly before testifying here today?" is sufficient to raise an implied charge of fabrication, and the query "You are the mother of the defendant, aren't you?" implies a charge of "partiality" that could be a sufficient predicate for a prior consistent statement).

326. *See **Hammons**,* 239 S.W.3d at 808; *see, e.g., **McInnes v. Yamaha Motor Corp., U.S.A.**,* 673 S.W.2d 185, 189-90 (Tex. 1984) (court examined defendant's voir dire questions, opening statement, and cross-examination to determine that defendant charged plaintiff with recent fabrication; error to exclude testimony offered to rebut that charge); ***Dowthitt v. State**,* 931 S.W.2d 244, 263-64 (Tex. Crim. App. 1996) (cross-examination raised implied charge that accomplice fabricated his testimony because of plea bargain; prior consistent statement made before plea bargain was admissible to rebut charge of fabrication).

327. *See **Hammons**,* 239 S.W.3d at 806 ("[T]he fact that the State might 'bring out its own uglies' on direct examination in anticipation of an attack on a witness's credibility does not preclude the introduction of a witness's prior consistent statement as rebuttal evidence after a witness has, in fact, been impeached on cross-examination with an express or implied accusation of recent fabrication."); ***Bolden v. State**,* 967 S.W.2d 895, 898-99 (Tex. App.—Fort Worth 1998, pet. ref'd) ("The fact that the State framed its direct of [witness] to defuse [defendant's] anticipated attempt to impugn [witness's] motives did not deprive the State of the right to rehabilitate [witness] with the prior consistent statement."); *see also **Klein**,* 273 S.W.3d at 315-16 (allegation of improper influence or motive is generally made during cross-examination, but that is not required; predicate for admissibility of prior consistent statements may be satisfied atypically, such as by the complainant himself on direct examination). The court in ***Klein*** noted:

> The trial court would not have abused its discretion to find that the complainant claimed on direct examination that her testimony that [defendant] sexually abused her was improperly influenced by the State's trickery in questioning her with this being vociferously repeated by the defense during the admissibility hearing and during closing jury arguments. [T]he trial court did not abuse its discretion to decide that Rule 801(e)(1)(B) permitted the State to show that the complainant had said the same thing to [investigators] without being "seduced" into doing so with "trick" questions from the State.

273 S.W.3d at 316-17.

328. *See* TEX. R. EVID. 801(e)(1)(B); ***Hammons**,* 239 S.W.3d at 804; ***Haughton v. State**,* 805 S.W.2d 405, 408 (Tex. Crim. App. 1990); ***Campbell v. State**,* 718 S.W.2d 712, 716-17 (Tex. Crim. App. 1986); *see, e.g., **Dowthitt**,* 931 S.W.2d at 263-64 (accomplice's statement that defendant killed victim was made before plea bargain and thus was admissible to rebut implied charge that accomplice fabricated his testimony because of the plea bargain); ***Perez v. State**,* 994 S.W.2d 233, 236 (Tex. App.—Waco 1999, no pet.) (when defendant challenged witness's truthfulness about earlier family violence and implied motive to lie by questioning her about recent friendship with victim's widow, prior consistent statement was admissible under rule); ***Alvarado v. State**,* 816 S.W.2d 792, 797 (Tex. App.—Corpus

RULE 801

does not have to predate all motives to lie, only those suggested by the charge.[329] Of course, if the witness is not impeached, the prior consistent statement is inadmissible hearsay and would be considered improper bolstering.[330] But when the prior statement has merely bolstered a witness's credibility by repeating testimony already in evidence—"'an extra helping of what the jury had heard before'"—the error in admitting the statement may well be harmless.[331]

   (3) Rule 801(e)(1)(C): Prior statements of identification. Rule 801(e)(1)(C), which is identical to Federal Rule 801(d)(1)(C) and makes prior statements of identification by a witness admissible, is generally used in criminal trials but could apply in the civil context as well.[332] In a normal case, the declarant has seen a person commit some act—

Christi 1991) (although an accomplice-witness's prior consistent statement was made to the police after his arrest, it was nonetheless admissible because it was made before the alleged improper motive arose, based on defendant's claim that the improper motive was collusion with the prosecutor, not the police), *aff'd as reformed*, 840 S.W.2d 442 (Tex. Crim. App. 1992); *cf. Tome v. United States*, 513 U.S. 150, 156 (1995) (prior consistent statements are admissible under Federal Rule 801(d)(1) only if they are made before the charged recent fabrication or improper influence or motive arose); *United States v. Trujillo*, 376 F.3d 593, 611 (6th Cir. 2004) (prior consistent statements by testifying conspirators after their arrest with 50 kilos of marijuana in their car were inadmissible because statements were made after they had motive to lie to receive lenient treatment); *United States v. Esparza*, 291 F.3d 1052, 1054-55 (8th Cir. 2002) (trial court properly excluded defendant's statement, made when he was arrested, that he did not know drugs were in his trailer; statement was not a prior consistent statement because defendant had the same motive to lie at time of statement as at trial); *United States v. Prieto*, 232 F.3d 816, 820-21 (11th Cir. 2000) (trial court did not err in admitting prior consistent statement made after arrest but before any "deal" negotiations commenced; motive to fabricate does not necessarily attach on arrest, but "whether a statement is tinged with a motive to lie is a question of fact to be determined by the trial court according to the particular circumstances of each case").

   For example, assume a witness testifies on direct examination that a traffic light was red for westbound traffic. On cross-examination, it is suggested that the witness was bribed ten days before the trial to give that testimony. Under these facts, a prior consistent statement made 15 days before the trial is admissible because it occurred before the improper influence or motive (i.e., the bribe) arose. But if the prior consistent statement had been made after the alleged bribe, it could not be used to rebut a charge of recent fabrication or recent improper influence or motive because both the testimony on direct examination and the prior consistent statement could have resulted from the bribe.

   329. *Dowthitt*, 931 S.W.2d at 263-64; *cf. United States v. Wilson*, 355 F.3d 358, 361 (5th Cir. 2003) ("A prior consistent statement need not rebut all motives to fabricate, but only the specific motive alleged at trial.").

   330. *See, e.g., Perez v. San Antonio Transit Co.*, 342 S.W.2d 802, 803-04 (Tex. Civ. App.—Eastland 1961, writ ref'd) (admission of bolstering prior consistent statement was erroneous but, under the facts of the case, not reversible error); *Wylie v. State*, 908 S.W.2d 307, 310 (Tex. App.—San Antonio 1995, pet. ref'd) (prior consistent statement was not bolstering because witness had been extensively cross-examined to raise doubts about fabrication and improper influence); *cf. United States v. Navarro-Varelas*, 541 F.2d 1331, 1334 (9th Cir. 1976) (prior consistent statement is not admissible under Federal Rule 801(d)(1)(B), now Rule 801(d)(1)(B)(i), unless opposing party has attacked witness's in-court testimony as a recent fabrication).

   331. *United States v. Ramos-Caraballo*, 375 F.3d 797, 803-04 (8th Cir. 2004) (quoting *United States v. Simonelli*, 237 F.3d 19, 29 (1st Cir. 2001)).

   332. *See, e.g., In re S.C.V.*, 750 S.W.2d 762, 765 (Tex. 1988) (wife's statement identifying her husband when a laboratory drew blood was admissible in a paternity suit). While Rule 801(e)(1)(C) is generally consistent with pre-Rules Texas case law, common-law precedent did not permit a third party to testify to the prior identification unless the identifying witness was impeached on the identification. *See Sledge v. State*, 686 S.W.2d 127, 129 (Tex. Crim. App. 1984) ("Before third party accounts of a complainant's extrajudicial identification become admissible, it should be determined by a careful analysis of the facts of the particular case that such evidence will serve to rehabilitate the complainant on the specific point upon which he has been impeached or attacked."); *Lyons v. State*, 388 S.W.2d 950, 950-51 (Tex. Crim. App. 1965) ("[W]hile a witness who has identified her assailant at the trial may testify that she also identified him while he was in custody of the police, others may not bolster her unimpeached testimony by corroborating the fact that she did identify him."); *see, e.g., Sharp v. State*, 707 S.W.2d 611, 617-18 (Tex. Crim. App. 1986) (although third-party witness's testimony about prior identification was erroneously permitted before pri-

usually a criminal offense. At some later time, the declarant sees that person again and makes a statement that it is the same person the witness saw commit the act on the earlier occasion. The rationale for exempting these prior identifications from the hearsay rule is that such pretrial identifications are generally more reliable than those made under the suggestive conditions at trial.[333] Because corporeal lineups or photographic "showups" are made relatively soon after the offense, while the incident is still fresh in the witness's mind, these identifications are more likely to be accurate than later in-court identifications.[334] Further, they are sometimes necessary when the witness's memory fades or fails because of delays in arrest, indictment, or trial.[335]

This provision is especially interesting in three respects. First, its scope is exceedingly wide. The prior identification does not need to have been made while under oath or in a judicial proceeding.[336] The rule encompasses any and all prior statements of identification, regardless of (1) whether the identification was made at a chance encounter or a carefully staged police lineup, (2) whether the identification was in person, by photograph, or even by sketch, voice, or affidavit,[337] (3) whether the identification took place shortly after the event or long after it, or (4) whether the witness perceived the actor through sight or some other sense. Second, it provides that the admissibility of the prior identification does not depend on the impeachment process.[338] The prior identification is admissible when the witness is able to make an in-court iden-

mary witness was impeached, error was cured when primary witness was later attacked on the identification); *Turner v. State*, 486 S.W.2d 797, 800-01 (Tex. Crim. App. 1972) (admission of a pretrial identification was harmless error when defendant attempted to impeach witness at trial); *see also* *Wilhoit v. State*, 638 S.W.2d 489, 495 (Tex. Crim. App. 1982) (defendant cannot invoke the *Lyons* rule if he has merely attempted to impeach the witness). Rule 801(e)(1)(C) rejects this limitation. *See Solomon v. State*, 854 S.W.2d 265, 268-69 (Tex. App.—Fort Worth 1993, no pet.) (introducing substantive evidence admissible under Criminal Rule 801(e)(1)(C) is not objectionable under Criminal Rule 612(c) as bolstering); *Smith v. State*, 830 S.W.2d 328, 329 (Tex. App.—Houston [14th Dist.] 1992, no pet.) (bolstering a witness's identification of a defendant had historically been disallowed because that testimony was hearsay, but Criminal Rule 801(e)(1)(C) changed the law, and bolstering is no longer a valid objection).

333. FED. R. EVID. 801 advisory committee's note, subdiv. (d)(1)(C); *see United States v. Elemy*, 656 F.2d 507, 508 (9th Cir. 1981) (availability of declarant for cross-examination eliminates the risks of hearsay testimony).

334. *See* H.R. REP. No. 94-355, at 3 (1975), *reprinted in* 1975 U.S.C.C.A.N. 1092, 1094.

335. *Id.*

336. Rule 801(e)(1)(C) excludes statements from the hearsay rule if (1) the declarant testifies at the trial or hearing, (2) the declarant is subject to cross-examination, and (3) the statement is one that identifies a person as someone the declarant perceived earlier. TEX. R. EVID. 801(e)(1)(C).

337. *See, e.g.*, *United States v. Ramirez*, 45 F.3d 1096, 1101 (7th Cir. 1995) (transcript entry identifying defendant's voice was admissible under Federal Rule 801(d)(1)(C) because it reflected witness's in-court attribution of the statement to defendant); *United States v. Marchand*, 564 F.2d 983, 996 (2d Cir. 1977) (witness's photographic identification of defendant and sketch made by witness, which bore a "remarkable resemblance" to photograph he later selected, were admissible under Federal Rule 801(d)(1)(C) because the rule is not limited to in-person identifications); *Bodmer v. State*, 161 S.W.3d 9, 11 (Tex. App.—Houston [14th Dist.] 2004, no pet.) (memo op.) (witness's affidavit identifying defendant was admissible under Rule 801(e)(1)(C) when witness testified at trial and was cross-examined about the affidavit).

338. Before the adoption of the Federal Rules of Evidence, the Supreme Court in *Gilbert v. California* noted that:
[u]nlike other testimony that cannot be corroborated by proof of prior consistent statements unless it is first impeached ... evidence of an extrajudicial identification is admitted regardless of whether the testimonial identification is impeached, because the earlier identification has greater probativevalue than an identification made in the courtroom after the suggestions of others and the circumstances of the trial may have intervened to create a fancied recognition in the witness' mind.

RULE 801

tification,[339] is unable to recall the actor or the prior identification,[340] or identifies a different person at trial.[341] Third, it permits a third party, as well as the identifier-declarant, to testify to the prior statement of identification as long as the declarant is a witness at the trial and is subject to cross-examination on the statement.[342] Frequently, the identifying witness can no longer recall the person he previously picked out of the lineup, but the police officer who was present during the lineup can recall the identification. Under the rule, the officer may testify that the witness identified the specific person in a previous lineup.[343]

---

388 U.S. 263, 272 n.3 (1967) (quoting *People v. Gould*, 354 P.2d 865, 867 (Cal. 1960), *overruled on other grounds*, *People v. Cuevas*, 906 P.2d 1290 (Cal. 1995)).

339. *See, e.g.*, *Chaney v. State*, No. 01-08-00204-CR (Tex. App.—Houston [1st Dist.] 2009, no pet.) (memo op.; 4-23-09) (police officer's testimony about declarant's prior identification of defendant was not hearsay; declarant testified about prior identification, made an in-court identification, and was cross-examined); *Millican v. State*, No. 12-03-00230-CR (Tex. App.—Tyler 2004, no pet.) (memo op.; 12-22-04) (same).

340. In *United States v. Owens*, the Supreme Court held that the Confrontation Clause did not bar admission of a prior statement of identification even though the witness could no longer recall having previously identified the defendant as the man who assaulted him. 484 U.S. 554, 559-64 (1988). The defendant was on trial for attacking and beating a corrections officer with a metal pipe. *Id.* at 556. More than three weeks after the attack, an FBI agent visited the officer in the hospital and asked him who had beaten him. *Id.* The officer told the agent that it was the defendant and identified him from a photo array. *Id.* The assault left the officer with severe head injuries that severely impaired his memory. *Id.* At trial, the officer was unable to remember the assault and "could not remember seeing his assailant." *Id.* Nonetheless, the earlier identification was admissible under Federal Rule 801(d)(1)(C) because the officer was a witness at trial and could be cross-examined, even though he could not be effectively cross-examined on the offense itself or on his prior identification. *Id.* at 557-64.

341. *See United States v. O'Malley*, 796 F.2d 891, 899 (7th Cir. 1986) ("Nothing in this rule prohibits the introduction of out-of-court statements identifying the defendant made by the declarant who at trial admitted that he made the prior identification but now denies that the defendant was the same involved in the crime.").

342. *See Delacerda v. State*, 425 S.W.3d 367, 390 (Tex. App.—Houston [1st Dist.] 2011, pet. ref'd) (rule requires only that declarant testify at trial and be subject to cross-examination, not that declarant actually be cross-examined about identification; *Smith v. State*, 830 S.W.2d 328, 329 (Tex. App.—Houston [14th Dist.] 1992, no pet.) (under Criminal Rule 801(e)(1)(C), third-party witnesses may testify to the declarant's prior identification as long as the declarant also testifies and is subject to cross-examination; although the third-party witnesses testified before the identification witness, the common-law bolstering rule did not apply); *Rogers v. State*, 756 S.W.2d 332, 339-40 (Tex. App.—Houston [14th Dist.] 1988, pet. ref'd) (raising, but declining to decide, the question of the admissibility of third-party testimony of prior identifications under the Texas rule); *see, e.g.*, *Sanders v. State*, ___ S.W.3d ___ (Tex. App.—Beaumont 2017, no pet.) (No. 09-16-00004-CR; 6-21-17) (witness's testimony about her prior identification of defendant from photo array was admissible under Rule 801(e)(1)(C) because she could have been cross-examined on this testimony); *Hill v. State*, 392 S.W.3d 850, 858 (Tex. App.—Amarillo 2013, pet. ref'd) (detective could testify under Rule 801(e)(1)(C) to interview with victim, in which she identified defendant; victim testified at trial and was subject to cross-examination on her statement to detective); *Thomas v. State*, 811 S.W.2d 201, 208 (Tex. App.—Houston [1st Dist.] 1991, pet. ref'd) (police officer's testimony that witness identified defendant at lineup was neither hearsay nor bolstering when the identification witness testified and was subject to cross-examination); *cf. United States v. Jarrad*, 754 F.2d 1451, 1456 (9th Cir. 1985) (Federal Rule 801(d)(1)(C) permits a witness to testify about an identification made by another witness); *United States v. Cueto*, 611 F.2d 1056, 1063 (5th Cir. 1980) (testimony by FBI agent that witness picked out defendant's photograph was admissible under Federal Rule 801(d)(1)(C)).

During congressional debates on the adoption of Federal Rule 801(d)(1)(C), two problems were noted as the rationale for why the primary witness does not need to testify to the identification before it is admissible through a third party. First, the witness's memory may no longer permit a current identification; second, the witness may, out of fear, refuse to acknowledge his prior identification in court. *See* 121 CONG. REC. 31866-67 (1975) (statements of Congressmen Hungate and Wiggins).

343. *See, e.g.*, *Rodriguez v. State*, 975 S.W.2d 667, 682-83 (Tex. App.—Texarkana 1998, pet. ref'd) (officer's testimony about eyewitness's out-of-court identification was not hearsay even though eyewitness did not make in-court identification and was never specifically cross-examined as to whether he made prior identification).

2. Rule 801(e)(2): An opposing party's statement. Rule 801(e)(2), which is identical to Federal Rule 801(d)(2) other than the last paragraph of the federal rule,[344] covers the very important subject of statements of an opposing party.[345]

The rationale behind admitting party statements differs from that underlying hearsay exceptions based on circumstantial guarantees of trustworthiness. Party statements fall outside the hearsay rule because the policies of the rule do not logically apply to them. They are admissible not because of any guarantees of trustworthiness, but because the party against whom they are offered, being the author of the statements, is estopped from complaining of any untrustworthiness of the statements. When a party's own out-of-court statement is offered against him, it would be incongruous to permit him to object to the statement by claiming that it is untrustworthy and should not be received because it was not given under oath, in the presence of the trier of fact, and subject to cross-examination.[346] The estoppel that justifies allowing a party's own state-

---

344. Refer to note 438 *infra*.

345. *See* FED. R. EVID. 801(d)(2); TEX. R. EVID. 801(e)(2). Texas Rule 801(e)(2) was restyled in 2015 to no longer refer to statements under the rule as "admissions." TEX. R. EVID. 801 cmt. The term was deemed confusing because "a statement can be within the exclusion even if it 'admitted' nothing and was not against the party's interest when made." *Id.* Further, the term "admissions" can be confusing when compared with declarations against interest under Rule 803(24). TEX. R. EVID. 801 cmt. The change is not intended to affect the application of the Rule 801(e)(2) exclusion. TEX. R. EVID. 801 cmt. The change follows the 2011 restyling of Federal Rule 801(d)(2) and was made for the same reason. *See* FED. R. EVID. 801 advisory committee's note to 2011 amendments.

Rule 801(e)(2) has treated only the subject of "evidentiary admissions." *See, e.g.*, *Herring v. State*, 202 S.W.3d 764, 766 (Tex. Crim. App. 2006) (defendant's threat to robbery victim that he had a knife and would kill the victim qualified as an admission under Rule 801(e)(2); thus, it was not hearsay and was admissible as substantive evidence). As the name suggests, evidentiary admissions are merely admissible, not conclusive. *See Cleveland Reg'l Med. Ctr., L.P. v. Celtic Props., L.C.*, 323 S.W.3d 322, 338 (Tex. App.—Beaumont 2010, pet. denied); MCCORMICK'S HANDBOOK II, *supra* note 7, §262, at 630; 1A RAY, *supra* note 9, §1128, at 282-83. The subject of "judicial admissions," which are conclusive, is governed not by evidence law but by the law of procedure. *See* MCCORMICK'S HANDBOOK II, *supra* note 7, §262, at 630; 1A RAY, *supra* note 9, §1127, at 282. Consequently, earlier Texas law determining what acts or statements by a party constitute judicial admissions is undisturbed by the rule. *See Mendoza v. Fid. & Guar. Ins. Underwriters, Inc.*, 606 S.W.2d 692, 694 (Tex. 1980) (judicial admissions are formal waivers of proof in pleadings or stipulations); *Rangel v. Hartford Acc. & Indem. Co.*, 821 S.W.2d 196, 201 (Tex. App.—Dallas 1991, writ denied) (Stewart, Baker, Thomas, Maloney, Chapman, JJ., dissenting) (discussing five requirements for a judicial admission, which dispense with the production of evidence); *see, e.g.*, *Davidson v. State*, 737 S.W.2d 942, 948 (Tex. App.—Amarillo 1987, pet. ref'd) (defense attorney's statement, made in open court, that "someone shot [victim], that he is dead, and he is dead from these gunshot wounds" was judicial admission of the cause of death because it remained unretracted and had to be taken as true); *see also* 1A RAY, *supra* note 9, §1127, at 282 (discussing the distinction between formal judicial admissions, which do not come under the evidentiary rules, and extrajudicial admissions, which do).

Under earlier Texas law, statements by a person in privity of interest with a party were frequently held to be admissible against that party. *See generally* 1A RAY, *supra* note 9, §§1165-1179, at 327-44 (describing various kinds of privies in interest). Neither the Federal Rules nor the Texas Rules recognize "privity admissions." *See Butler v. De La Cruz*, 812 S.W.2d 422, 425-26 (Tex. App.—San Antonio 1991, writ denied). However, because nearly all statements admitted under this theory were against the interest of the declarant when made, and because Texas Rule 803(24) abolished the requirement of the declarant's unavailability for the declaration-against-interest hearsay exception, the outcomes of cases are the same under the Rules—only the theory of admissibility is different. Federal Rule 804(b)(3), on which Texas Rule 803(24) is based, requires the declarant's unavailability. *See* FED. R. EVID. 804(b)(3). Refer to notes 811-847 *infra* and accompanying text.

346. *See Shavers v. State*, 985 S.W.2d 284, 290 (Tex. App.—Beaumont 1999, pet. ref'd) (theory of admitting party-opponent admissions is the "notion that a party should not be allowed to exclude his own statement on the ground that what he said was untrustworthy"); *Peoples v. State*, 928 S.W.2d 112, 117-18 (Tex. App.—Houston [1st Dist.] 1996, pet. ref'd) ("[W]hen dealing with admissions, the concern is not about the reliability and trustworthi-

RULE 801

ments to be used against him (Rule 801(e)(2)(A)) extends to statements of others that the party has adopted or ratified in some way (Rule 801(e)(2)(B)), statements of a representative that he has authorized to speak on his behalf (Rule 801(e)(2)(C)), statements of his chosen agent or employee about the subject matter of the employment (Rule 801(e)(2)(D)), and statements of his coconspirator made in furtherance of the conspiracy (Rule 801(e)(2)(E)).[347]

Of course, a party cannot offer his *own* out-of-court statement under the rule. Rule 801(e)(2) applies only to out-of-court statements made by the opposing party, not the offering party.[348] A party seeking to offer his own statement must look to the hearsay exemptions under Rule 801(e)(1) and the exceptions under Rules 803 and 804 for admissibility grounds.

The exemption from the hearsay rule for an opposing party's statement should not be confused with the hearsay exception for declarations against interest, covered by Texas Rule 803(24).[349] A statement by an opposing party qualifies under Rule 801(e)(2) even if it was not made against the interest of the party-declarant.[350] Also, the common-

---

ness of an out-of-court statement. Admissions are admitted because a party should not be allowed to exclude his own statement on the ground that what he said was untrustworthy.").

347. The estoppel rationale may be somewhat attenuated in the last two categories, but it remains plausible. *See, e.g.*, ***Mathes v. State***, 765 S.W.2d 853, 856-57 (Tex. App.—Beaumont 1989, pet. ref'd) (murder defendant who made a full noncustodial confession to a testifying witness could not complain that his own statements were hearsay).

348. ***Williams v. State***, 402 S.W.3d 425, 438 (Tex. App.—Houston [14th Dist.] 2013, pet. ref'd); *see, e.g.*, ***Ripstra v. State***, 514 S.W.3d 305, 315 (Tex. App.—Houston [14th Dist.] 2016, pet. ref'd) (statements made by defendant on Facebook and offered into evidence by prosecution were admissible under Rule 801(e)(2)); *see also* ***Lagaite v. State***, 995 S.W.2d 860, 863 (Tex. App.—Houston [1st Dist.] 1999, pet. ref'd) (defendant's statement, "I wish the guy were dead," made the morning after murder, was not offered by defendant to prove the truth of the statement—that he did wish the victim were dead—but rather as circumstantial evidence that defendant did not know that victim was already dead; thus, statement was admissible as nonhearsay).

349. *See* ***Bingham v. State***, 987 S.W.2d 54, 56-57 (Tex. Crim. App. 1999) (while some courts have confused the requirements of a statement against interest with admissions by a party-opponent, the provisions are distinct; "[w]hile statements against interest are admissible due to their reliability, admissions by party-opponents are admissible precisely because they are being admitted against the party alleged to have made those statements"). As the court of criminal appeals noted:

> If allowed to stand, the holding by the Court of Appeals that statements against interest are not admissible unless the defendant is the declarant of the statements would make 803(24) largely redundant, since any declaration against interest in which the defendant is the declarant of the statement would virtually always be admissible under 801(e)(2), as an admission by a party-opponent.

Id. at 57. Refer to notes 811-847 *infra* and accompanying text. This confusion was one of the rationales for the wording change in Rule 801(e)(2) in the 2015 restyling. *See* TEX. R. EVID. 801 cmt. Refer to note 345 *supra*.

350. *See* ***Marquis Theatre Corp. v. Condado Mini Cinema***, 846 F.2d 86, 90 n.3 (1st Cir. 1988) (statement must be against interest only when introduced under Federal Rule 804(b)(3), not when offered as an admission under Federal Rule 801(d)(2)); ***Hartford Acc. & Indem. Co. v. McCardell***, 369 S.W.2d 331, 337 (Tex. 1963) (party's admissions are true exceptions to the hearsay rule because they prove the truth of the facts admitted); ***Bell v. State***, 877 S.W.2d 21, 24 n.2 (Tex. App.—Dallas 1994, pet. ref'd) (an admission by party-opponent under Rule 801(e)(2)(A) need not be against interest when made, while a statement offered under Rule 803(24) must be against interest when it was made); ***Waldon v. City of Longview***, 855 S.W.2d 875, 878 (Tex. App.—Tyler 1993, no writ) (Rule 801(e)(2) does not contain an inconsistency requirement for admitting party's prior statement as an admission); ***Cunningham v. State***, 846 S.W.2d 147, 151 (Tex. App.—Austin 1993) (admission by party-opponent under Rule 801(e)(2) is not subject to requirements of Rule 803(24)), *aff'd*, 877 S.W.2d 310 (Tex. Crim. App. 1994); *see also* 1A RAY, *supra* note 9, §1122, at 271 (with "declarations against interest the guaranty of correctness is found in the disserving quality of the fact

RULE 801

law requirement of unavailability of the declarant for declarations against interest,[351] abolished in the Rules,[352] obviously never applied to party admissions. Thus, the former testimony of an opposing party is excluded from the hearsay rule and is admissible under Rule 801(e)(2) regardless of the declarant's unavailability.[353]

One area of controversy in earlier Texas law had been whether the common-law rule against opinions applied to out-of-court statements, such as admissions, that were not banned by the hearsay rule. The courts had been divided on the issue, but many of them applied the opinion rule to out-of-court statements.[354] Evidence scholars criticized these cases:

> The opinion-rule is a rule designed to regulate the examination of witnesses on the stand, so as to receive from them as far as practicable concrete descriptions, rather than opinions which describe less definitely the facts inquired about. Obviously this policy can have no application to the question of admitting statements made out of court, for such statements may be of great value as evidence, whether or not they happen to be what would be called in the courthouse, "facts," meaning the most concrete description of the situation, or "opinion," meaning a less concrete statement.[355]

The Rules put this issue to rest.[356] Rule 801(e)(2) places no restrictions on the admissibility of an opposing party's out-of-court statements based on any fact-opinion distinction, and Rule 701, the opinion rule, clearly applies only to "testimony."

In addition to the opinion rule, another restriction on testimony does not apply to an opposing party's statements: the personal-knowledge requirement. Under the Rules,

---

stated" but "an admission need have no warrant of truth"). *But see* **Reynolds v. State**, 744 S.W.2d 156, 160-61 (Tex. App.—Amarillo 1987, pet. ref'd) (trial court incorrectly analyzed defendant's admission as a statement against penal interest subject to the corroboration requirements of Rule 803(24)).

351. *See* **Big Mack Trucking Co. v. Dickerson**, 497 S.W.2d 283, 290 (Tex. 1973) (requiring proof that the declarant is unavailable to testify before admitting a declaration against interest); 1A RAY, *supra* note 9, §1003, at 250 (noting the circumstances that suffice to show unavailability so that a declarant's statement against interest is admissible).

352. TEX. R. EVID. 803(24).

353. **Tryco Enters., Inc. v. Robinson**, 390 S.W.3d 497, 506 (Tex. App.—Houston [1st Dist.] 2012, pet. dism'd); *see, e.g.,* **Oyster Creek Fin. Corp. v. Richwood Invs. II, Inc.**, 176 S.W.3d 307, 317 (Tex. App.—Houston [1st Dist.] 2004, pet. denied) (in retrial of lawsuit, party's testimony from first trial was an admission by a party-opponent; trial court did not need to find party "unavailable" under Rule 804(b) before admitting former testimony under Rule 801(e)(2)(A)).

354. *See* 1A RAY, *supra* note 9, §1126, at 275 (party's admissions are "in no way" limited by the opinion rule); William T. Catterton, Note, *The Admissibility of Admissions in Opinion Form*, 28 BAYLOR L. REV. 752, 759 (1976) ("The view expressed in some cases—that if the agent's admission takes the form of an opinion it should not be admissible—seems unsound."). *But see* **In re L.G.**, 728 S.W.2d 939, 942 (Tex. App.—Austin 1987, writ ref'd n.r.e.) (accomplice's testimony that defendant told her that the accused possessed a controlled substance was direct evidence of such possession; "the witness is not testifying in the form of an opinion, but rather he is testifying to a statement of fact within his knowledge").

355. 1A RAY, *supra* note 9, §1126, at 276.

356. *See* **State v. Buckner Constr. Co.**, 704 S.W.2d 837, 846 (Tex. App.—Houston [14th Dist.] 1985, writ ref'd n.r.e.) (Rule 801(e)(2) "places no restrictions on opinions that are admissions by party opponents").

RULE 801

as under the common law,[357] if a party or the party's agent makes a statement as a matter of fact, it is admissible even if the declarant's knowledge is based entirely on hearsay. The personal-knowledge rule, Rule 602, like the opinion rule, applies only to testimony, and Rule 801(e)(2) contains no personal-knowledge requirement.[358] Of course, the witness testifying to the opposing party's statement must have personal knowledge of the statement.[359] If not, any testimony by that witness about the statement would be hearsay.[360]

Furthermore, Rule 613(a)—which requires that a witness being impeached with a prior inconsistent statement must first be told of the statement's content and, at some point during the proceeding, be given an opportunity to explain or deny the making of the statement—does not apply to an opposing party's statements.[361] An opposing party's statements are admissible under Rule 801(e)(2) regardless of their inconsistency with the party's present testimony and are not subject to the foundation requirement in Rule 613(a).

Finally, the prior deposition of an opposing party is not hearsay under Rule 801(e)(2), and therefore it is admissible without regard to the foundation requirements of Rule 804(b)(1).[362]

---

357. *See* **Fant v. Howell**, 410 S.W.2d 294, 298 (Tex. Civ. App.—Austin 1966, writ dism'd) (averments in a pleading are admissible in a later proceeding against the party making them, even though the averments were based only on information and belief); *see, e.g.*, **McNeely v. Sw. Settlement & Dev. Corp.**, 284 S.W.2d 167, 167-68 (Tex. Civ. App.—Beaumont 1955, no writ) (approving an admission by a party even though the party lacked personal knowledge); *see also* 1A RAY, *supra* note 9, §1125, at 274-75 (reviewing the general rule that admissions do not require personal knowledge).

358. *See* FED. R. EVID. 801 advisory committee's note, subdiv. (d)(2).

359. *See, e.g.*, **Jacobs v. State**, 951 S.W.2d 900, 901 (Tex. App.—Texarkana 1997, pet. ref'd) (an admission "may be allowed in evidence by the testimony of the person to whom the admission is made"; letter that defendant wrote to his wife admitting offense and requesting wife to fabricate an alibi was admissible under the rule and did not need to be signed because it was otherwise proved to have been written by defendant). Even if a witness has personal knowledge, the witness's previously recorded out-of-court statements about a party's out-of-court statements are not admissible under Rule 801(e)(2); in such a case, the witness must testify in open court about the party's out-of-court statements. *See, e.g.*, **Billings v. State**, 399 S.W.3d 581, 589 (Tex. App.—Eastland 2013, no pet.) (excerpt of news broadcast in which reporter talked about his interview with defendant after defendant's arrest was not admissible under Rule 801(e)(2); reporter could have testified in open court about defendant's out-of-court statements, but recording of reporter's own out-of-court statements did not qualify as admission by party-opponent).

360. *See* **Hughes v. State**, 4 S.W.3d 1, 6 (Tex. Crim. App. 1999) ("[T]he witness testifying to the party admission must have firsthand knowledge of the party's admission; otherwise any testimony regarding the admission is hearsay."); *see, e.g.*, **Braggs v. State**, 951 S.W.2d 877, 882 (Tex. App.—Texarkana 1997, pet. ref'd) (officer's testimony that informant told him that defendant admitted committing the robbery was "once removed from actual contact with the statement" by defendant, and thus was not admissible under Rule 801(e)(2)).

361. TEX. R. EVID. 613(a)(5); *see, e.g.*, **Strong v. State**, 138 S.W.3d 546, 553-54 (Tex. App.—Corpus Christi 2004, no pet.) (predicate for admission of prior inconsistent statements set out in Rule 613 does not apply to party-opponent admissions; defendant's out-of-court statement to a coworker that he picked up a girl the night before and had "rough sex" with her in his car was admissible under Rule 801(e)(2)(A) without first inquiring of defendant whether he had made the statement or giving him an opportunity to explain its content or context). Refer to *Article VI: Witnesses*, *supra* p. 652.

362. *E.g.*, **Kemmerer v. State**, 113 S.W.3d 513, 517-18 (Tex. App.—Houston [1st Dist.] 2003, pet. ref'd) (felony-murder defendant's civil deposition was not hearsay when offered by State; therefore, admissibility of de-

The fact that an out-of-court statement qualifies as an opposing party's statement does not automatically ensure that it will be admissible. Rule 801(e)(2) deals only with hearsay issues. Such statements may still be excluded on constitutional grounds,[363] statutory grounds,[364] or some other exclusionary provision of the Rules.[365]

(1) Rule 801(e)(2)(A): Statements made in an individual or representative capacity. Rule 801(e)(2)(A) covers a party's statement made "in an individual or representative capacity."[366] According to the Advisory Committee's note to Federal Rule 801(d)(2)(A), "[i]f he has a representative capacity and the statement is offered against him in that capacity, no inquiry whether he was acting in the representative capacity in making the statement is required; the statement need only be relevant to represent affairs."[367]

The rule applies to all such statements, whether oral or written,[368] without regard to the circumstances under which they were made[369] or whether the party denies that he made them.[370] Nonverbal assertions may also constitute an opposing party's statement.[371]

---

position did not depend on compliance with Code of Criminal Procedure rules governing the taking of depositions in criminal cases). Rule 801(e)(3) makes depositions in civil cases admissible as nonhearsay in the same proceeding. Refer to notes 446-450 *infra* and accompanying text.

363. Statements may be excluded as violating the federal or state constitution, such as when a custodial statement is obtained without informing the arrestee of his rights, a statement is obtained after an illegal arrest, a custodial statement is obtained in the absence of counsel, a confession is involuntary or coerced, or a confession is the product of illegal electronic surveillance. *See, e.g.*, **McCarthy v. State**, 65 S.W.3d 47, 49 (Tex. Crim. App. 2001) (custodial statement was inadmissible when police questioned defendant without her attorney present after she invoked right to counsel).

364. *See, e.g.*, TEX. CODE CRIM. PROC. art. 38.22 (Texas confession statute).

365. For example, Rules 404-411, the Rule 403 balancing test, and the Article V privilege rules contain exclusionary provisions.

366. TEX. R. EVID. 801(e)(2)(A).

367. FED. R. EVID. 801 advisory committee's note, subdiv. (d)(2)(A). To the extent that Texas courts agree with this construction, the rule changes previous Texas law, which required that the statement be made in the representative capacity. *See* **Phillips v. Herndon**, 78 Tex. 378, 383, 14 S.W. 857, 859 (1890) (objection should have been sustained because the speakers were not authorized to make the statements); *see also* 1A RAY, *supra* note 9, §1161, at 315-16 (discussing the previous rule that barred representative admissions unless made by the declarant acting in his representative capacity and within the scope of his duties). In two cases, Texas courts apparently doubted whether a statement by a representative would be admissible against a principal even if made in a representative capacity. *See, e.g.*, **Gilbert v. Odum**, 69 Tex. 670, 672-73, 7 S.W. 510, 511 (1888) (statement by administrator of estate was not admissible unless the evidence was competent and pertinent to the issue); **Williams v. Fuerstenberg**, 12 S.W.2d 812, 815 (Tex. Civ. App.—Amarillo 1928) (dicta; same), *rev'd on other grounds*, 23 S.W.2d 305 (Tex. Comm'n App. 1930, judgm't adopted).

Clear authority in Texas indicates that statements by a guardian ad litem do not constitute admissions of the ward ad litem. *See* **Gersdorff v. Torres**, 293 S.W. 560, 562 (Tex. Comm'n App. 1927, judgm't adopted). This doctrine, perhaps drawn from the substantive law on guardianship ad litem, probably survived the adoption of Rule 801(e)(2)(A).

368. *See, e.g.*, **Roy v. State**, 997 S.W.2d 863, 866 (Tex. App.—Fort Worth 1999, pet. ref'd) (defendant's oral statement to officer that he was a gang member was admissible as admission by party-opponent); **Kan. City S. Ry. Co. v. Carter**, 778 S.W.2d 911, 914 (Tex. App.—Texarkana 1989, writ denied) (stipulation from another lawsuit was admissible as an admission by a party-opponent); **Kamani v. Port of Hous. Auth.**, 725 S.W.2d 336, 339 (Tex. App.—Houston [14th Dist.] 1987, no writ) (transcript of statement made by injured worker to insurance adjuster, recorded with worker's permission, was admissible as an admission against the injured worker in a personal-injury suit); **Hall v. Birchfield**, 718 S.W.2d 313, 323-24 (Tex. App.—Texarkana 1986) (statements taken from written transcript of a conference of pediatricians in an attorney's office in connection with another pending lawsuit were admissions of a

However, when two plaintiffs or defendants are joined together, a statement by one of them is not automatically admissible against the other without a showing that the coparty is a representative of or is legally liable for the words or conduct of the

---

party), *rev'd on other grounds sub nom.* ***Birchfield v. Texarkana Mem'l Hosp.***, 747 S.W.2d 361 (Tex. 1987); ***Port Neches Indep. Sch. Dist. v. Soignier***, 702 S.W.2d 756, 757 (Tex. App.—Beaumont 1986, writ ref'd n.r.e.) (letter authorizing medical expenses for injured plaintiff-employee was a statement of admission by employer); *see also* ***Lorraine v. Markel Am. Ins.***, 241 F.R.D. 534, 568 (D. Md. 2007) ("Given the near universal use of electronic means of communication, it is not surprising that statements contained in electronically made or stored evidence often have been found to qualify as admissions by a party opponent if offered against that party."); *cf.* ***United States v. Siddiqui***, 235 F.3d 1318, 1323 (11th Cir. 2000) (properly authenticated e-mails sent by defendant were admissible as nonhearsay admissions of party-opponent under Federal Rule 801(d)(2)(A)).

369. *See* ***Trevino v. State***, 991 S.W.2d 849, 853 (Tex. Crim. App. 1999) (defendant's own statements are admissible and not hearsay when offered by State "on the logic that a party is estopped from challenging the fundamental reliability or trustworthiness of his own statements"); *see, e.g.*, ***Keith v. State***, 384 S.W.3d 452, 458-59 (Tex. App.—Eastland 2012, pet. ref'd) (burglary defendant's statement to witness, who was related to accomplice, that he would harm her family "if any of [them] had said anything, snitched him out" was admissible under Rule 801(e)(2)(A)); ***Church & Dwight Co. v. Huey***, 961 S.W.2d 560, 571 (Tex. App.—San Antonio 1997, pet. denied) (DTPA defendant's patent applications and descriptions of problems with prior art were admissible as party admissions); ***Short v. Black & Decker, Inc.***, 728 S.W.2d 832, 840 (Tex. App.—Beaumont 1987, no writ) (personal-injury plaintiff's statement to his employer that he was capable of repairing an impact wrench was admissible because the statement was inconsistent with his position at trial); ***Fontenot v. State***, 708 S.W.2d 555, 558 (Tex. App.—Houston [1st Dist.] 1986, pet. dism'd) (therapist for defendant in prosecution for aggravated sexual abuse could testify to defendant's admission that he pulled down "his" pants to teach "him" a lesson; although the testimony was equivocal on whether it was defendant's or victim's pants that were pulled down, the statement was an admission from which guilt could be inferred); ***Davis v. State***, 692 S.W.2d 185, 188 (Tex. App.—Houston [1st Dist.] 1985, no pet.) (prosecutor could testify to defendant's admission before the grand jury that tended to prove defendant was attempting to fabricate, conceal, or suppress testimony of the only other witness to the shooting; such a statement was not hearsay because it qualified as an admission under Rule 801(e)(2)).

370. *See* ***United States v. Velarde***, 528 F.2d 387, 389 (9th Cir. 1975).

371. *See* TEX. R. EVID. 801(a) (defining "statement" to include nonverbal conduct intended as substitute for verbal expression); *see, e.g.*, ***Legate v. State***, 52 S.W.3d 797, 802 (Tex. App.—San Antonio 2001, pet. ref'd) ("[a]doption of statements may be manifested in actions, responses, or acquiescence"; defendant's statement that he was working for nightclub owner and would "watch [owner's] back," coupled with evidence that defendant acquired a weapon was sufficient to establish that defendant adopted owner's statements that he needed "protection" from victim); ***Nguyen v. State***, 811 S.W.2d 165, 168 (Tex. App.—Houston [1st Dist.] 1991, pet. ref'd) (when defendant, store's cashier, sold bottle of Thunderbird from store's cooler for wine, defendant represented the product to be wine; this nonverbal conduct was intended as a substitute for verbal expression and was admissible against defendant as a nonhearsay admission); ***Hendrick v. State***, 731 S.W.2d 147, 149 (Tex. App.—Houston [1st Dist.] 1987, pet. ref'd) (defendant's act of handing requested bank records to the city secretary constituted a nonverbal admission that those were his true records of a police-run narcotics operation).

For an interesting case discussing the theory and applicability of nonverbal assertions in this context, see ***American Maintenance & Rentals, Inc. v. Estrada***, 896 S.W.2d 212 (Tex. App.—Houston [1st Dist.] 1995, writ dism'd by agr.). In *Estrada*, the plaintiff, a badly burned laborer, attempted to prove that the oxygen cylinder that exploded as he was attempting to open it belonged to the defendant. 896 S.W.2d at 223. Before trial, one codefendant made statements admitting that the cylinder came from the defendant's storage yard, but by the time of trial, he denied that fact. *Id.* at 216. Evidence that the CEO of the defendant-company had paid the codefendant money and forgiven him loans after the latter had made the pretrial statements, conduct that the jury could infer was an attempt to change the codefendant's testimony, constituted an "admission by conduct." *Id.* at 225. The original statement and the change in the codefendant's position were admissible because "[a] party's improper suppression or alteration of future testimony or other evidence constitutes an 'admission by conduct,' and is evidence that the party is conscious that its case is weak or unfounded." *Id.* at 224; *see also* ***McQueeney v. Wilmington Tr. Co.***, 779 F.2d 916, 922 (3d Cir. 1985) (describing "admission by conduct" as a party's case-related wrongdoing that amounts to an obstruction of justice and that may compel the fact-finder to believe the wrongdoer considers its case "'weak and not to be won by fair means'" (quoting MCCORMICK'S HANDBOOK II, *supra* note 7, §273, at 660)).

other.[372] In civil trials, a limiting instruction under Rule 105(a) may be sufficient to preserve the coparty's rights.[373] In criminal trials, however, the U.S. Supreme Court has held that admissions by a codefendant are not admissible in a joint trial unless (1) the statement can be redacted to delete any reference to the first defendant,[374] or (2) the declarant-defendant takes the witness stand and is subject to cross-examination.[375] The applicability of party statements in criminal cases is further limited in that Rule 801(e)(2)(A) only applies to the State as a "party" and not to, for example, a complaining witness, a crime victim, or a police officer.[376]

(2) Rule 801(e)(2)(B): Statements adopted or believed to be true. An opposing party may make a statement under Rule 801(e)(2)(B) by adopting another person's statement.[377] The adoption can occur in many ways, including expressly agreeing with another's statement,[378] reading and signing another's written statement,[379] complying

---

372. *See, e.g.*, *Estrada*, 896 S.W.2d at 218-19 (interrogatory answers made by declarant were not admissible against codefendant because declarant was not agent of codefendant); *Freestone Cty. Title & Abstract Co. v. Johnson*, 594 S.W.2d 817, 820 (Tex. Civ. App.—Dallas 1980, no writ) (no relationship was proved establishing that declarant had a joint interest with third-party defendant when admissions were made).

373. 4 LOUISELL & MUELLER, *supra* note 250, §423, at 259. Refer to *Article I: General Provisions, supra* p. 97.

374. *Richardson v. Marsh*, 481 U.S. 200, 211 (1987) ("[T]he Confrontation Clause is not violated by the admission of a nontestifying codefendant's confession … when, as here, the confession is redacted to eliminate not only the defendant's name, but any reference to his or her existence.").

375. *Bruton v. United States*, 391 U.S. 123, 127-28 (1968); *see also Cruz v. New York*, 481 U.S. 186, 193 (1987) (Confrontation Clause bars admission at joint trial of nontestifying codefendant's confession incriminating defendant even when jury is given limiting instruction and defendant's own corroborating confession is admitted).

376. *See Willover v. State*, 70 S.W.3d 841, 847 n.10 (Tex. Crim. App. 2002) (some courts of appeals in Texas and the majority of other jurisdictions hold that admission by party-opponent does not include that of the complaining witness); *Davis v. State*, 177 S.W.3d 355, 362 (Tex. App.—Houston [1st Dist.] 2005, no pet.) (complainant in criminal prosecution is not a party within the meaning of Rule 801(e)(2); "[a] complaining witness is a crime victim who has no control over what charges the State brings against an accused, who the State charges, and when the State brings the charges. Perhaps more importantly, the complainant has no authority over the disposition of the offense, whether charges are dismissed or pursued, or what sentence a defendant ultimately receives."); *Logan v. State*, 71 S.W.3d 865, 869 (Tex. App.—Fort Worth 2002, pet. ref'd) (the State, not a complainant or witness, is the party opposing a defendant in criminal cases; thus, family-violence complainant's affidavit of nonprosecution was not admissible as admission by party-opponent); *Owens v. State*, 916 S.W.2d 713, 717 (Tex. App.—Waco 1996, no pet.) (rejecting State's contention that alleged victim of assault became a party-opponent when she recanted her former statement against defendant); *Halstead v. State*, 891 S.W.2d 11, 12 n.1 (Tex. App.—Austin 1994, no pet.) ("[W]e conclude that the complainant in a criminal prosecution is not a party within the meaning of Rule 801(e)(2) and that we erred by holding to the contrary in *Cuyler* [*v. State*, 841 S.W.2d 933, 935 (Tex. App.—Austin 1992, no pet.)].").

377. The rule covers statements "the party manifested that it adopted or believed to be true." TEX. R. EVID. 801(e)(2)(B).

378. *See, e.g.*, *United States v. Young*, 814 F.2d 392, 395-96 (7th Cir. 1987) (under Federal Rule 801(d)(2)(B), judge properly admitted testimony in bank-robbery trial that a fellow robber told defendant "that they had a fingerprint on a newspaper," and "it wasn't [the fellow robber's] because he wasn't standing up there" and that defendant responded, "Yeah, I guess it must be mine").

379. *Cf. United States v. Johnson*, 529 F.2d 581, 584 (8th Cir. 1976) (under Federal Rule 801(d)(2)(A) and (d)(2)(B), statement signed by defendant in a prosecution for possession of stolen Treasury checks was properly admitted; statement that "is reduced to writing by one other than the accused is generally admissible where the accused reads it over and signs it"); *Guidry v. State*, 121 S.W.3d 849, 852 (Tex. App.—Beaumont 2003, no pet.) (fax containing defendant's real name as the sender constituted party admission of assertion in fax about insurance coverage for motorcycle; fax was admissible as a false-identity document used in commission of crime).

RULE 801

with another's statement, repeating another's statement,[380] or, under appropriate circumstances, remaining silent or acquiescing in response to another's statement.[381] Eliciting the testimony of a witness in another trial may be considered adopting the statement, depending on the circumstances.[382] Similarly, calling a witness and offering his testimony or affidavit into evidence at a trial may serve as a party's adoption of the contents of the testimony or affidavit.[383] Using the statements of others in support of a request for action can also make those statements admissible under Rule 801(e)(2)(B).[384] Some federal courts have held that the possession and use of a document in a manner that shows the person's adoption of its accuracy makes the document admissible under Federal Rule 801(d)(2)(B).[385]

---

380. *See, e.g.*, ***United States v. Weaver***, 565 F.2d 129, 135 (8th Cir. 1977) (when government witness testified to statements that coconspirator had made in defendant's presence and then "stated that [defendant] himself had told her everything about which she had just testified," the statements made by coconspirator qualified as adoptive admissions); ***United States v. Safavian***, 435 F. Supp. 2d 36, 43 (D.D.C. 2006) (e-mails were admissible under Federal Rule 801(d)(2)(B) because forwarding was analogous to repeating others' statements; "[t]he context and content of certain e-mails demonstrate clearly that [defendant] 'manifested an adoption or belief' in the truth of the statements of other people as he forwarded their e-mails").

381. *See* FED. R. EVID. 801 advisory committee's note, subdiv. (d)(2)(B); *cf.* ***Fox v. Taylor Diving & Salvage Co.***, 694 F.2d 1349, 1354-56 (5th Cir. 1983) (in Jones Act case, expert's statement that he based his testimony about lost wages on the assumption that plaintiff was not a Jones Act seaman was binding as adverse admission against plaintiff because plaintiff's attorney did not object to the testimony or question expert on assumption). Rule 801(e)(2)(B) is consistent with earlier Texas law. *See generally* 1A RAY, *supra* note 9, §§1149-1153, at 303-13 (describing various methods of adopting admissions).

382. *See* MUELLER & KIRKPATRICK, *supra* note 229, §8.29, at 775-76.

383. *See, e.g.*, ***Reid Rd. Mun. Util. Dist. No. 2 v. Speedy Stop Food Stores, Ltd.***, 337 S.W.3d 846, 856-57 (Tex. 2011) (expert witness's property appraisal was admissible against municipal utility district as adoptive admission when district called witness to testify and offered his written appraisal into evidence to support the testimony).

384. *See* MUELLER & KIRKPATRICK, *supra* note 229, §8.29, at 776.

385. *See* ***United States v. Ospina***, 739 F.2d 448, 451 (9th Cir. 1984) ("Other courts have held that possession of a written statement becomes an adoption of its contents, and that when a person acts on written instructions, and the instructions are found in his possession, the instructions are admissible as adopted admissions under [Federal] Rule 801."); *see, e.g.*, ***United States v. Paulino***, 13 F.3d 20, 22-24 (1st Cir. 1994) (receipt for money order bearing defendant's name and address was admissible to prove that defendant had paid rent for the apartment used as a drug-distribution center; "so long as the surrounding circumstances tie the possessor and the document together in some meaningful way, the possessor may be found to have adopted the writing and embraced its contents"); ***United States v. Marino***, 658 F.2d 1120, 1124-25 (6th Cir. 1981) (possession of airline tickets was an adoptive admission). *But see* ***United States v. Jefferson***, 925 F.2d 1242, 1253 & n.13 (10th Cir. 1991) (pager bill was inadmissible by adoption because "[c]ommon every day experience teaches us that disputes with creditors based upon inaccuracies contained in their bills is not a rarity"). In ***Menchaca v. State***, the El Paso Court of Appeals could have analyzed the introduction of a letter found in the glove compartment of the defendant's car as an adoptive admission because the contents of the letter corroborated the defendant's statements about who he planned to meet and where. 901 S.W.2d 640, 650 & n.8 (Tex. App.—El Paso 1995, pet. ref'd). Rather, the court held:

> [w]hether or not the author's statements were truthful, their very existence elucidates [defendant's] state of mind, and therefore the closely related issue of whether he knowingly or intentionally possessed the contraband, because independent evidence, the ultimate source of which was [defendant's] mouth, showed he planned to go to the very place the letter's author said he would wait.

Id. at 650. Although the court insisted that the content of the letter was significant for its existence, apart from its veracity, the relevance of the statements in the letter depended on the defendant's belief that they were accurate. *See id.* Because the defendant's conduct was in accord with the instructions in the letter, he had manifested his adoption of their accuracy, and thus, the letter could have been offered and admitted under Criminal Rule 801(e)(2)(B).

The prevailing rule in Texas is that the prosecution does not adopt the statements of a complainant in a criminal case.[386] The Texas Court of Criminal Appeals has yet to decide the issue but has indicated that it is likely to hold the same.[387]

Silence in response to another's statement may qualify as an opposing party's statement under Rule 801(e)(2)(B) when (1) the statement is made in the party's presence, (2) the party understood the statement, (3) the statement called for a response if the party did not agree with it, and (4) the party was not under arrest.[388]

Some courts have erroneously held that any statement made in a party's presence is automatically admissible against him unless he shows his disagreement. A mere listening presence, however, begins the inquiry, rather than ends it.[389] Some indication

---

386. *See Davis v. State*, 177 S.W.3d 355, 362 (Tex. App.—Houston [1st Dist.] 2005, no pet.); *Logan v. State*, 71 S.W.3d 865, 869 (Tex. App.—Fort Worth 2002, pet. ref'd). Refer to note 376 *supra* and accompanying text.

387. *See Willover v. State*, 70 S.W.2d 841, 847 n.10 (Tex. Crim. App. 2002).

388. *Crestfield v. State*, 471 S.W.2d 50, 53 (Tex. Crim. App. 1971); *see, e.g., Paredes v. State*, 129 S.W.3d 530, 534-35 (Tex. Crim. App. 2004) (witness's testimony on content of codefendant's out-of-court statements describing victims' murders was admissible as adoptive admission when defendant was present during conversation and stated that witness "should have been there" because he "would have had some fun"; rejecting defendant's contention that because declarant was "the boss" of the gang and intimidating, he felt unable to disagree when statements were made). The *Crestfield* doctrine was carried forward and codified as Criminal Rule 801(e)(2)(B). *Tucker v. State*, 771 S.W.2d 523, 535 n.5 (Tex. Crim. App. 1988); *see, e.g., Cantu v. State*, 939 S.W.2d 627, 634-35 (Tex. Crim. App. 1997) (statements made by capital-murder defendant's cohorts, in which they described raping and killing two girls, were admissible against defendant under Criminal Rule 801(e)(2)(B); defendant was present when statements were made and by his actions and words signified agreement with them); *Alvarado v. State*, 912 S.W.2d 199, 214-15 (Tex. Crim. App. 1995) (statement by codefendant that he and defendant had "taken somebody out" was admissible as adoptive admission because statement clearly called for a response if untrue and defendant acquiesced by his silence to statement); *Wilkerson v. State*, 933 S.W.2d 276, 279 (Tex. App.—Houston [1st Dist.] 1996, pet. ref'd) (codefendant's statement, made while pointing at defendant, "I'm his partner. Give me the money. I'll take the $20. I'll take it." was admissible as adoptive admission when defendant handed rock of cocaine to informant after payment to codefendant; defendant's cooperation with codefendant in drug transaction "manifested his adoption of [her] statement"); *Gilliland v. State*, 786 S.W.2d 385, 386 (Tex. App.—Beaumont 1990, no pet.) (court properly admitted testimony that witness engaged in conversation in which one participant stated that a fellow participant had shot victim and that the fellow participant was in a position to hear this conversation and never denied the statement). Adoptive admissions have been upheld by federal courts under Federal Rule 801(d)(2)(B) as nonhearsay and nonviolative of the Confrontation Clause. *See, e.g., United States v. Kenny*, 645 F.2d 1323, 1340 (9th Cir. 1981) (defendant adopted statements by government informer on tape-recorded telephone conversation); *United States v. Lemonakis*, 485 F.2d 941, 948-49 (D.C. Cir. 1973) (when "reciprocal and integrated utterance[s]" between two parties were adopted by defendant, their admission did not violate the Confrontation Clause).

389. In *United States v. Flecha*, the defendant and four codefendants were arrested on a freighter after they were seen dragging four bales of marijuana along an unlighted deck. 539 F.2d 874, 876 (2d Cir. 1976). When the five arrestees were standing in line, one of them turned toward the defendant and said in Spanish, "Why so much excitement? If we are caught, we are caught." *Id.* While the trial judge instructed the jury that the codefendant's statement was "not binding" on the other three codefendants, he refused such an instruction on behalf of the defendant. *Id.* Though holding any error was harmless, the Second Circuit declared that the statement was not an adoptive admission under Federal Rule 801(d)(2)(B). *See id.* at 877-78. As Judge Friendly noted:

> [T]he judge fell into the error ... of jumping from the correct proposition that hearing the statement of a third person is a necessary condition for adoption by silence ... to the incorrect conclusion that it is a sufficient one. After quoting the maxim "silence gives consent," Wigmore explains "that the inference of assent may safely be made only when no other explanation is equally consistent with silence; and there is always another possible explanation—namely, ignorance or dissent—*unless the circumstances are such that a dissent would in ordinary experience have been expressed if the communication had not been correct.*"

....

RULE 801

must be given that, under the particular circumstances, the party probably would have denied the other person's statement if the assertion had been false.[390]

(3) Rule 801(e)(2)(C): Statements authorized by the opposing party. A party may authorize almost anyone to speak for him—an attorney, real-estate broker, employer, employee, friend, spouse, parent—even a coconspirator.[391] When the person authorized to speak does so, any statements made are admissible as nonhearsay against the opposing party under Rule 801(e)(2)(C).[392] The Texas Court of Criminal Appeals has held that when an interpreter "is translating the out-of-court statement of a *party* who has either *authorized* the interpreter to speak for him or adopted the interpreter as his *agent* for purposes of the specific translation,"[393] the translation is admissible under Rule 801(e)(2)(C) or 801(e)(2)(D).[394]

> We find it hard to think of a case where response would have been less expectable than this one. [Defendant] was under arrest, and although the Government emphasizes that he was not being questioned by the agents, and had not been given *Miranda* warnings, it is clear that many arrested persons know, without benefit of warnings, that silence is usually golden. Beyond that, what was [defendant] to say? If the Spanish verb used by [codefendant] has the same vagueness as "caught," it would have been somewhat risible for [defendant], surrounded by customs agents, to have denied that he had been. Of course, [defendant] could have said "Speak for yourself" or something like it, but it was far more natural to say nothing.

Id. at 876-77 (quoting 4 JOHN H. WIGMORE, EVIDENCE IN TRIALS AT COMMON LAW §1071, at 102 (Chadbourn rev. 1972)).

390. *See* 4 LOUISELL & MUELLER, *supra* note 250, §424, at 265-69; *see, e.g.*, **Fletcher v. State**, 960 S.W.2d 694, 698 (Tex. App.—Tyler 1997, no pet.) (doctrine of adoptive admission by silence did not apply when there was no evidence describing defendant's position in room, his demeanor during conversation, any specific comment he might have made, or whether he was listening to cohort's statement). In **Martinez v. State**, the court held that the declarant's statement to a witness that the defendant owed a debt and "if he did not pay it, he would be in trouble," qualified as an adoptive admission, even though there was no indication that the defendant "adopted" or otherwise agreed with this statement. 131 S.W.3d 22, 37 (Tex. App.—San Antonio 2003, no pet.). The court noted that the witness testified that the defendant was present in the room at the time the declarant spoke, and therefore he thought the defendant heard the statement but did not reply. *Id.* A party's mere failure to react or respond to another person's statement about owing money generally does not suffice to show that party's adoption of the accuracy of the statement unless there are additional circumstances to indicate that the person probably would have denied it had it been false. Thus, this holding seems overly broad at best.

391. *See, e.g.*, **Mitchell v. State**, 780 S.W.2d 862, 864 (Tex. App.—Houston [14th Dist.] 1989, no pet.) (defendant authorized informant to discuss drug purchase with undercover police officer).

392. Earlier Texas law recognized that a statement of an agent authorized to speak on a subject was admissible against the principal but enforced the limitation that an agent's authorized report to the principal (i.e., "in-house" statement), as opposed to a statement made with authority to a third person, did not qualify as an authorized admission. *See* **Big Mack Trucking Co. v. Dickerson**, 497 S.W.2d 283, 287 (Tex. 1973); 1A RAY, *supra* note 9, §1164, at 321-23. This limitation was harshly criticized. *See* Frank W. Elliott, *Annual Survey of Texas Law: Evidence*, 28 SW. L.J. 158, 161-63 (1974); John R. Heard, Note, *Evidence—Vicarious Admissions*, 52 TEX. L. REV. 593, 597-98 (1974); Richard A. Stanford, Note, *Admissibility Against Employer of Hearsay Evidence of Employee's Negligence*, 11 HOUS. L. REV. 481, 490 (1974). Rule 801(e)(2)(C) abolished it. *Cf.* FED. R. EVID. 801 advisory committee's note, subdiv. (d)(2)(C) ("No authority is required for the general proposition that a statement authorized by a party to be made should have the status of an admission by the party. However, the question arises whether only statements to third persons should be so regarded, to the exclusion of statements by the agent to the principal. The rule is phrased broadly so as to encompass both.").

393. **Saavedra v. State**, 297 S.W.3d 342, 346 (Tex. Crim. App. 2009).

394. *Id.* at 349; *see, e.g.*, **Gomez v. State**, 49 S.W.3d 456, 459 (Tex. App.—Houston [1st Dist.] 2001, pet. ref'd) (officer's testimony that defendant had admitted, through interpreter, that he had drunk two or three beers and had been driving was not hearsay; translated statement was attributable to defendant himself). The interpreter "serves as an agent of, or a language conduit for, the declarant." **Gomez**, 49 S.W.3d at 459. The Ninth Circuit Court of Appeals has further held that the use of a translator does not implicate the Confrontation Clause as long as the translator

RULE 801

Normally, the pleadings, answers to interrogatories, and responses to requests for admissions filed by a party or his attorney in a civil suit qualify under Rule 801(e)(2)(C) as statements authorized by the opposing party. They are binding on a party even if they have been amended or superseded.[395] Furthermore, an authorized agent's deposition testimony taken in an unrelated lawsuit may be admissible under this rule in a second lawsuit.[396]

The existence and extent of authority to speak on behalf of the principal should be determined under the substantive law of agency[397] by examining the conduct of the party and the declarant under the circumstances.[398] The proponent of the statement has the burden of proving, by a preponderance of the evidence, the existence and extent of the agent's authority.[399] The court will determine under Rule 104(a) whether the proponent has met this burden, and the decision will be reviewed only for an abuse of discretion.[400] Several Texas cases construing Rule 801(e)(2)(E) have held that a cocon-

---

acts only as a language conduit. *See United States v. Ye*, 808 F.3d 395, 401 (9th Cir. 2015), *cert. denied*, 136 S. Ct. 2462 (2016). For a discussion of the Confrontation Clause, refer to notes 34-181 *supra* and accompanying text.

395. *See Bay Area Healthcare Grp., Ltd. v. McShane*, 239 S.W.3d 231, 235 (Tex. 2007); *Sw. Energy Prod. Co. v. Berry-Helfand*, 411 S.W.3d 581, 604 (Tex. App.—Tyler 2013), *rev'd on other grounds*, 491 S.W.3d 699 (Tex. 2016); *Quick v. Plastic Sols. of Tex., Inc.*, 270 S.W.3d 173, 185 (Tex. App.—El Paso 2008, no pet.). The Rules of Evidence do not require inconsistency between superseded pleadings and a party's position at trial for the supersed pleadings to be admissible, which marks a change from earlier Texas law. *Bay Area Healthcare Grp.*, 239 S.W.3d at 235; *see Sw. Energy Prod.*, 411 S.W.3d at 604. The information in the superseded pleadings must still be relevant and comply with the other rules of admissibility. *E.g., Sw. Energy Prod.*, 411 S.W.3d at 604-05 (trial court did not abuse its discretion in excluding superseded pleadings with slight probative value that were unfairly prejudicial to plaintiff; their admission "would have served to suggest that [plaintiff] was suspicious, litigious, and generally undeserving").

396. *E.g., Shanklin v. Norfolk S. Ry. Co.*, 369 F.3d 978, 990-91 (6th Cir. 2004) (in wrongful-death suit, videotaped deposition testimony of railroad's CEO about a grade-crossing accident was admissible either as an admission by an authorized agent under Rule 801 or as former testimony under Rule 804; CEO was authorized to make statements on behalf of railroad, and his deposition addressed the same general problems of railroad-crossing safety that were at issue in pending litigation).

397. *See Staniewicz v. Beecham, Inc.*, 687 F.2d 526, 529-30 (1st Cir. 1982) (discussing the admissibility of an article authored by the company's agent on the age of employees in a discrimination case).

398. *See* 4 LOUISELL & MUELLER, *supra* note 250, §425, at 297. Federal Rule 801(d)(2), the equivalent of Texas Rule 801(e)(2), was amended in 1997 to resolve an issue that was not decided by the Supreme Court in *Bourjaily v. United States*, 483 U.S. 171 (1987):

> [Amended Federal Rule 801(d)(2)] provides that the contents of the declarant's statement do not alone suffice to establish a conspiracy in which the declarant and the defendant participated. The court must consider in addition the circumstances surrounding the statement, such as the identity of the speaker, the context in which the statement was made, or evidence corroborating the contents of the statement in making its determination as to each preliminary question. This amendment is in accordance with existing practice. Every court of appeals that has resolved this issue requires some evidence in addition to the contents of the statement.

FED. R. EVID. 801(d)(2) advisory committee's note to 1997 amendments. Refer to note 438 *infra* and accompanying text.

399. *See Am. Maint. & Rentals, Inc. v. Estrada*, 896 S.W.2d 212, 219 n.4 (Tex. App.—Houston [1st Dist.] 1995, writ dism'd by agr.) (fact of agency must be clearly established before declarations of an agent or employee are admitted against the principal or employer); *see also Buchoz v. Klein*, 143 Tex. 284, 286, 184 S.W.2d 271, 271 (1944) (requiring proof of agency by preponderance of the evidence under the common law); *cf. Meador v. State*, 812 S.W.2d 330, 333 (Tex. Crim. App. 1991) (requiring proof by preponderance of the evidence before statements are admissible under Rule 801(e)(2)(E)).

400. *See Norton v. Martin*, 703 S.W.2d 267, 272 (Tex. App.—San Antonio 1985, writ ref'd n.r.e.) ("Whether the relationship of principal and agent exists under established facts is a question of law for the court."); *cf. United States*

spirator's statements may be considered in determining whether the State has proved the existence of a conspiracy but are not alone sufficient to establish that fact.[401] Although the courts were discussing coconspirators, the same reasoning should apply to statements offered under Rule 801(e)(2)(C)—some independent evidence of the agency relationship must be introduced beyond the out-of-court statement that is being offered,[402] even though the statement could presumably be considered as part of that proof.

(4) **Rule 801(e)(2)(D): Statements made by opposing party's agent or employee.** Under Rule 801(e)(2)(D), a statement made by an agent or employee is admissible against a party if (1) the statement is made by the party's agent or employee, (2) the statement concerns a matter within the scope of the agency or employment, and (3) the statement is made during the existence of the relationship.[403] The statements are admissible against the principal even if the agent or employee had no authority to speak for the principal.[404] Thus, when the company truck driver jumps out of the truck after an ac-

---

v. Flores, 679 F.2d 173, 178 (9th Cir. 1982) (trial judge "decides the preliminary question of whether agency existed" under Federal Rule 104(a); court analogized the situation to that of coconspirator statements in requiring "substantial independent evidence" of agency). Refer to *Article I: General Provisions, supra* p. 86.

401. *See Rodriguez v. State*, 896 S.W.2d 203, 205 (Tex. App.—Corpus Christi 1994, no pet.); *Crawford v. State*, 863 S.W.2d 152, 164 (Tex. App.—Houston [1st Dist.] 1993), *rev'd on other grounds*, 892 S.W.2d 1 (Tex. Crim. App. 1994); *cf.* FED. R. EVID. 801(d)(2) (statement must be considered but is not alone sufficient to establish fact of agency under rule). Before the adoption of the Rules, coconspirators' statements could not be considered in determining the existence of the conspiracy. *See, e.g., White v. State*, 451 S.W.2d 497, 502 (Tex. Crim. App. 1969) (op. on reh'g) (coconspirator's statements were inadmissible because there was no proof of existence of a conspiracy). Refer to note 438 *infra* and accompanying text.

402. *See Lubbock Feed Lots, Inc. v. Iowa Beef Processors, Inc.*, 630 F.2d 250, 262 (5th Cir. 1980) (generally, "out-of-court declarations of an alleged agent are not competent proof of the existence of the agency relationship"); *cf. GXG, Inc. v. Texacal Oil & Gas*, 977 S.W.2d 403, 420 (Tex. App.—Corpus Christi 1998, pet. denied) (agency must be established before a declaration can be admitted under Rule 801(e)(2)(D)).

403. TEX. R. EVID. 801(e)(2)(D); *Walker & Assocs. Surveying, Inc. v. Roberts*, 306 S.W.3d 839, 855 (Tex. App.—Texarkana 2010, no pet.); *see, e.g., Tex. Dep't of Pub. Safety v. Bonilla*, 481 S.W.3d 646, 650-51 (Tex. App.—El Paso 2014) (report by accident-reconstruction team was admissible against DPS under Rule 801(e)(2)(D); team members were DPS employees and report was made according to routine DPS practice of investigating accidents involving DPS troopers), *rev'd on other grounds*, 481 S.W.3d 640 (Tex. 2015) (per curiam). The inclusion of Rule 801(e)(2)(D) overturned the much-criticized holding of *Big Mack Trucking Co. v. Dickerson* that an agent's or servant's statements were admissible against the principal or master only if the statements were within the scope of the agent's authority to speak on the principal's behalf. 497 S.W.2d 283, 287 (Tex. 1973).

If the proponent of the evidence does not affirmatively show that the statement related to a matter within the scope of the declarant's agency or employment, the statement is not admissible under Rule 801(e)(2)(D). *See Handel v. Long Trs.*, 757 S.W.2d 848, 851 (Tex. App.—Texarkana 1988, no writ) (per curiam). However, the statement may be admissible as nonhearsay under a different subsection of Rule 801(e). *E.g., Reid Rd. Mun. Util. Dist. No. 2 v. Speedy Stop Food Stores, Ltd.*, 337 S.W.3d 846, 856 (Tex. 2011) (there was no evidence that appraiser was employee of municipal utility district, "[b]ut even assuming there was no evidence of an agency relationship either, Rule 801(e)(2)(B) allows for admissions by a party-opponent when the party-opponent has manifested an adoption or belief in the statement's truth"). Refer to notes 377-390 *supra* and accompanying text.

404. *Cleveland Reg'l Med. Ctr., L.P. v. Celtic Props., L.C.*, 323 S.W.3d 322, 337 (Tex. App.—Beaumont 2010, pet. denied); *City of Stephenville v. Tex. Parks & Wildlife Dep't*, 940 S.W.2d 667, 677 (Tex. App.—Austin 1996, writ denied); *State v. Buckner Constr. Co.*, 704 S.W.2d 837, 846 (Tex. App.—Houston [14th Dist.] 1985, writ ref'd n.r.e.) (citing Olin G. Wellborn, *Article VIII: Hearsay*, 20 HOUS. L. REV. 477, 502 (1983 Tex. R. Evid. Handbook)); *see, e.g., City of San Antonio v. Rodriguez*, 934 S.W.2d 699, 704-05 (Tex. App.—San Antonio 1995) (work order signed by city employee who had supervisory authority at recreation center was a party admission under Civil Rule

cident and declares that the accident was his fault because he was in such a hurry to deliver his employer's merchandise, his statement is admissible against both the company and the driver himself. He is authorized to drive a truck, not to speak, but once he has spoken, his words become those of his employer. Further, the setting of the statement is immaterial if it otherwise qualifies under the rule. Thus, even an agent's casual conversation on the golf course may be admissible under Rule 801(e)(2)(D).[405]

Statements and letters, as well as official court documents such as pleadings or discovery responses made by a party's attorney, may qualify as an opposing party's statement under either Rule 801(e)(2)(C) or Rule 801(e)(2)(D). Rule 801(e)(2)(C) relates to those statements that the client has explicitly or implicitly authorized his attorney to make on his behalf;[406] Rule 801(e)(2)(D) relates to any statements that the attorney may make as his client's agent during the existence of the attorney-client relationship that concern a matter within the scope of the attorney's agency.[407] The court of criminal appeals has applied these subsections to a party's statements that have been translated by an interpreter.[408] Under Rule 801(e)(2)(C), the declarant must be specifically authorized by the party to speak on the subject. Under Rule 801(e)(2)(D), the declarant must be the party's agent or employee who is authorized to act, not necessarily to speak on behalf of the party; however, if the agent does speak about a matter within the scope of the agency or employment, he speaks for the party.[409]

801(e)(2)(D)), *rev'd on other grounds*, 931 S.W.2d 535 (Tex. 1996); ***Herzing v. Metro. Life Ins.***, 907 S.W.2d 574, 580 (Tex. App.—Corpus Christi 1995, writ denied) (rejecting life-insurance company's contention that telephone conversation by its agent was hearsay under Civil Rule 801(e)(2)(D) because "an insurance company is generally liable for any misconduct by an agent that is within the actual or apparent scope of the agent's authority"); ***Cherokee Water Co. v. Forderhause***, 727 S.W.2d 605, 614 (Tex. App.—Texarkana 1987) (principals' subagent's statements made during negotiations about the conveyance of property were not hearsay because the matter was within the scope of subagent's employment), *rev'd on other grounds*, 741 S.W.2d 377 (Tex. 1987). On occasion, however, courts may go too far in admitting unattributed statements to the opposing party. For example, in ***McAlister v. Medina Electric Cooperative***, a breach-of-contract case for termination of an employee, the court of appeals held that the plaintiff's summary-judgment affidavit was not hearsay. 830 S.W.2d 659, 663-64 (Tex. App.—San Antonio 1992, writ denied). The affidavit stated: "I was told the employee manual contained statements of the Cooperative's obligation to me and my employment obligations to them." *Id.* at 663. Although the plaintiff also named her hiring supervisor in her affidavit, the affidavit apparently did not state that her supervisor told her about the employee manual. *Id.* at 663-64. For a statement to be admissible under Rule 801(e)(2)(D), there must be some showing that the statement was actually made by an agent, not an outsider.

405. ***Tucker's Beverages, Inc. v. Fopay***, 145 S.W.3d 765, 768 (Tex. App.—Texarkana 2004, no pet.); *see, e.g.*, ***Fojtik v. First Nat'l Bank***, 752 S.W.2d 669, 671-72 (Tex. App.—Corpus Christi 1988) (statements made by a member of a bank's board of directors at a golf tournament were admissible against the bank as a vicarious admission), *writ denied*, 775 S.W.2d 632 (Tex. 1989).

406. Refer to notes 395-396 *supra* and accompanying text.

407. *See, e.g.*, ***Edwards v. Tex. Emp't Comm'n***, 936 S.W.2d 462, 466-67 (Tex. App.—Fort Worth 1996, no writ) (letter written by attorney for unemployment-compensation claimant appealing adverse decision was admissible under Civil Rule 801(e)(2)(D)); ***L.M.W. v. State***, 891 S.W.2d 754, 765 (Tex. App.—Fort Worth 1994, pet. ref'd) (offer made by attorney to influence criminal proceedings in return for concessions in divorce case constituted a party admission under Criminal Rule 801(e)(2)(D)), *overruled on other grounds*, ***Logan v. State***, 71 S.W.3d 865 (Tex. App.—Fort Worth 2002, pet. ref'd).

408. Refer to notes 393-394 *supra* and accompanying text.

409. *See, e.g.*, ***Herzing***, 907 S.W.2d at 579-80 (court considered agent's statement that he had authority to broker loan as proof of scope of agency).

RULE 801

Statements by a party's independent contractors generally do not come within the rule.[410] Because the agency relationship must have existed when the statement was made, statements by a former agent are also not covered by the rule.[411] Some courts have suggested that a law-enforcement officer's statements might be admissible against the government in a criminal prosecution,[412] and one court has even held that an informant could be considered an agent of the government.[413] The wording of Rule 801(e)(2)(D) supports the argument that law-enforcement officers should be treated as agents of the prosecution.[414]

The statement made by the agent or employee must, of course, be about a matter within the scope of the declarant's agency or employment.[415] But it is not necessary that the agent or employee be performing the duties of the agency or employment when the statements are made.[416] The declarant does not need to be identified by name if there is sufficient evidence to establish that there was an agency or employment relationship and that the statement concerned a matter within the scope of that relationship.[417] Fail-

---

410. *Cf. Dora Homes, Inc. v. Epperson*, 344 F. Supp. 2d 875, 885 (E.D.N.Y. 2004) (summary-judgment affidavit containing out-of-court statements by nonparty contractor and subcontractor did not qualify as nonhearsay statements by an agent under Federal Rule 801(d)(2)(D); both were independent contractors, not party's agents).

411. *Hartman v. Trio Transp., Inc.*, 937 S.W.2d 575, 579-80 (Tex. App.—Texarkana 1996, writ denied); *Patterson v. Mobiloil Fed. Credit Union*, 890 S.W.2d 551, 555 (Tex. App.—Beaumont 1994, no writ); *see, e.g.*, *Trencor, Inc. v. Cornech Mach. Co.*, 115 S.W.3d 145, 151-52 (Tex. App.—Fort Worth 2003, pet. denied) (service reports made by defendant while it was acting as authorized agent for plaintiff were admissible under Rule 801(e)(2)(D) even though parties were adverse by the time of litigation).

412. *See, e.g.*, *United States v. Doe*, 655 F.2d 920, 924 & n.7 (9th Cir. 1980) (harmless error when court excluded defendant's brother's testimony that a DEA agent had said "they were recommending a reduced sentence" for defendant); *Rodela v. State*, 829 S.W.2d 845, 849 (Tex. App.—Houston [1st Dist.] 1992, pet. ref'd) (statement made by police officer about the force he allegedly used against defendant while in his official capacity was an admission by a party-opponent); *see also United States v. Kattar*, 840 F.2d 118, 130-31 (1st Cir. 1988) (government is a party-opponent of defendants in criminal cases; thus, sentencing memoranda filed by the Justice Department in other cases were admissible for the defense in the present case, but their exclusion was harmless error); *Hoptowit v. Ray*, 682 F.2d 1237, 1262 (9th Cir. 1982) (report prepared by employees of State Attorney General's office was non-hearsay because it was a statement that related to a matter within the scope of the employees' agency). *See generally* 4 LOUISELL & MUELLER, *supra* note 250, §426, at 326-30 (criticizing the traditional rule that held that the admissions doctrine was not applicable against the government).

413. *See, e.g.*, *United States v. Morgan*, 581 F.2d 933, 937-38 & n.15 (D.C. Cir. 1978) (statements by a government informant contained in a police officer's sworn search-warrant affidavit were admissible as adoptive admissions under Federal Rule 801(d)(2)(B); as with Rule 801(d)(2)(B), "there is no indication in the history of the Rules that the draftsmen meant to except the government from operation of Rule 801(d)(2)(D) in criminal cases"). *But see United States v. Yildiz*, 355 F.3d 80, 82 (2d Cir. 2004) (out-of-court statements of government informant are not admissible in criminal trial under Rule 801(d)(2)(D)).

414. *See* MUELLER & KIRKPATRICK, *supra* note 229, §8.32, at 795.

415. *See, e.g.*, *Ash v. Hack Branch Distrib. Co.*, 54 S.W.3d 401, 411 (Tex. App.—Waco 2001, pet. denied) (in antitrust case, testimony of beer distributor's sales manager about distributor's owner instructing him not to sell beer to plaintiff restaurant owner was admissible as nonhearsay under Rule 801(e)(2)(D) because it was within scope of employment); *McEwen v. Wal-Mart Stores, Inc.*, 975 S.W.2d 25, 28 (Tex. App.—San Antonio 1998, pet. denied) (statement by Wal-Mart employee, "[t]his is not the first time this has happened," was admissible under rule when evidence showed employee made statement at work, on employer's premises, and at a time when it appeared she was working, and statement concerned events that occurred at the Wal-Mart store).

416. *Tucker's Beverages, Inc. v. Fopay*, 145 S.W.3d 765, 768 (Tex. App.—Texarkana 2004, no pet.).

417. *See Yellow Freight Sys., Inc. v. N. Am. Cabinet Corp.*, 670 S.W.2d 387, 390 (Tex. App.—Texarkana 1984, no writ).

ure to identify the declarant by name goes only to the weight of the statement, not its admissibility.[418] Finally, the language of the rule is broad enough to include statements by the agent to the principal.[419]

As with authorized statements under Rule 801(e)(2)(C), a party seeking to introduce evidence under Rule 801(e)(2)(D) must establish the existence of the agency or employment relationship by a preponderance of the evidence.[420] The court will determine as a matter of law whether the statements are admissible under Rule 801(e)(2)(D).[421] The court must consider the circumstances under which the statements were made to determine whether the principal and agent or employee had conflicting interests.[422] If there is no conflict, the statements are admissible under the rule.[423] As with authorized statements, the statement can be considered in determining whether there is an agency or employment relationship, but the statement alone is not sufficient to establish that relationship.[424] The rule does not require that the evidence of the agency relationship be corroborated.[425]

(5) Rule 801(e)(2)(E): Coconspirator statements. Rule 801(e)(2)(E) makes out-of-court statements by a coconspirator admissible as nonhearsay against other members of the conspiracy.[426] Once a conspiracy is established, the declarations of any conspirator are admissible against all others, even if the statements were made before some of the members joined the conspiracy.[427]

---

418. *Id.*

419. *Cf.* FED. R. EVID. 801 advisory committee's note, subdiv. (d)(2)(C) ("[T]he question arises whether only statements to third persons should be so regarded, to the exclusion of statements by the agent to the principal. The rule is phrased broadly so as to encompass both.").

420. *See Tryco Enters., Inc. v. Robinson*, 390 S.W.3d 497, 506 (Tex. App.—Houston [1st Dist.] 2012, pet. dism'd) (party must establish existence of agency or employment relationship, but rule does not require independent corroborating evidence); *Trencor, Inc. v. Cornech Mach. Co.*, 115 S.W.3d 145, 151 (Tex. App.—Fort Worth 2003, pet. denied) (fact of agency must be established before evidence can be admitted under Rule 801(e)(2)(D)); *see, e.g., Norton v. Martin*, 703 S.W.2d 267, 271-72 (Tex. App.—San Antonio 1985, writ ref'd n.r.e.) (trial court properly excluded evidence from nonparty-witness's deposition containing statement made by an unknown declarant when deponent merely "thought" the unknown declarant was a fellow employee and agent of defendant); *see also Tex. Gen. Indem. Co. v. Scott*, 152 Tex. 1, 8, 253 S.W.2d 651, 655-56 (1952) ("Not only must the fact of agency be established before the declarations can be admitted, but it must also be established that the declaration was one of fact as distinguished from a mere expression of an opinion."); *Buchoz v. Klein*, 143 Tex. 284, 286, 184 S.W.2d 271, 271 (1944) (under common law, agency is not presumed; proponent of evidence must prove agency by preponderance of the evidence). Refer to note 399 *supra* and accompanying text.

421. *See* TEX. R. EVID. 104(a). Refer to note 400 *supra* and accompanying text.

422. *See Trencor*, 115 S.W.3d at 151.

423. *E.g., id.* at 151-52 (when plaintiff-corporation prepared the reports at issue, it was acting as defendant's agent and parties did not have adverse interests; trial court did not abuse its discretion in admitting the reports as party-opponent admissions against defendant).

424. *See Edwards v. Tex. Emp't Comm'n*, 936 S.W.2d 462, 467 (Tex. App.—Fort Worth 1996, no writ) ("To show an item is an admission by a party-opponent, the agency relationship must be established by some independent evidence."). Refer to notes 401-402 *supra* and accompanying text.

425. *Tucker's Beverages, Inc. v. Fopay*, 145 S.W.3d 765, 768 (Tex. App.—Texarkana 2004, no pet.).

426. This provision is consistent with earlier Texas law.

427. *United States v. U.S. Gypsum Co.*, 333 U.S. 364, 393 (1948); *see Peoples v. State*, 928 S.W.2d 112, 117 (Tex. App.—Houston [1st Dist.] 1996, pet. ref'd) ("It is not necessary for the defendant to have joined or have been a part of the conspiracy at the time the statements were made by the co-conspirator as long as the statements were made

RULE 801

Although coconspirator statements are usually offered in criminal cases, Texas courts have recognized their admissibility in civil cases as well.[428] The coconspirator rule applies regardless of the type of lawsuit; it is not restricted to lawsuits alleging a conspiracy.[429] The coconspirator exemption to the hearsay rule does not violate the Confrontation Clause[430] and does not require that the declarant be unavailable to testify before admitting the statement through a third-party witness.[431]

The coconspirator rule has four basic requirements: (1) a conspiracy must exist,[432] (2) the declarant and the party against whom the statement is being offered must both be participants in the conspiracy,[433] (3) the statement must be made during the course

---

in furtherance of the conspiracy."); *see, e.g., United States v. Handlin*, 366 F.3d 584, 590-91 (7th Cir. 2004) (rejecting defendant's claim that coconspirator's statements about specific arsons were inadmissible under rule because defendant claimed not to be member of those specific arson conspiracies; arson was part of the overarching conspiracy, and thus "it is irrelevant when the defendant joined the conspiracy, so long as he joined it at some point").

428. *See, e.g., Walter E. Heller & Co. v. Barnes*, 412 S.W.2d 747, 757 (Tex. Civ. App.—El Paso 1967, writ ref'd n.r.e.) (conduct and statements of one conspirator were admissible against all of the conspirators in fraud case); *Harang v. Aetna Life Ins.*, 400 S.W.2d 810, 818 (Tex. Civ. App.—Houston 1966, writ ref'd n.r.e.) (tort of one conspirator made during and in furtherance of the conspiracy was admissible against his coconspirators).

429. *Meador v. State*, 812 S.W.2d 330, 332 (Tex. Crim. App. 1991); *Roy v. State*, 608 S.W.2d 645, 651 (Tex. Crim. App. 1980).

430. *United States v. Inadi*, 475 U.S. 387, 400 (1986); *Figueroa v. State*, 740 S.W.2d 537, 539-40 (Tex. App.—Houston [1st Dist.] 1987, pet. ref'd); *see Crawford v. Washington*, 541 U.S. 36, 56 (2004) (statements to conspirator in furtherance of conspiracy are not testimonial and therefore not barred by the Confrontation Clause).

431. In *Inadi*, the court addressed the reliability of coconspirator statements:

> Because they are made while the conspiracy is in progress, such statements provide evidence of the conspiracy's context that cannot be replicated, even if the declarant testifies to the same matters in court. … Conspirators are likely to speak differently when talking to each other in furtherance of their illegal aims than when testifying on the witness stand. Even when the declarant takes the stand, his in-court testimony seldom will reproduce a significant portion of the evidentiary value of his statements during the course of the conspiracy.
>
> In addition, the relative positions of the parties will have changed substantially between the time of the statements and the trial. The declarant and the defendant will have changed from partners in an illegal conspiracy to suspects or defendants in a criminal trial, each with information potentially damaging to the other.

475 U.S. at 395.

432. *Guidry v. State*, 9 S.W.3d 133, 148 (Tex. Crim. App. 1999); *see P. McGregor Enters., Inc. v. Hicks Constr. Grp., LLC*, 420 S.W.3d 45, 54 (Tex. App.—Amarillo 2012, no pet.) ("[T]here must be evidence to establish a prima facie case of conspiracy separate and apart from the otherwise hearsay statements."). Nothing requires that the conspiracy or agreement be illegal in its nature; it may be a joint venture. *United States v. Saimiento-Rozo*, 676 F.2d 146, 149 (5th Cir. 1982); *United States v. Postal*, 589 F.2d 862, 886 n.41 (5th Cir. 1979). In *Garza v. State*, the defendant argued on appeal that the trial judge improperly took judicial notice that the defendant and codefendant were conspirators when referring to testimony at the codefendant's trial. 996 S.W.2d 276, 279 (Tex. App.—Dallas 1999, pet. ref'd). The court of appeals held that "assertions made by an individual, even under oath, are not the type of facts that are capable of accurate and ready determination by a source whose accuracy cannot reasonably be questioned." *Id.* at 279-80. There must be actual evidence of a conspiracy in which the defendant participated; if such evidence is not offered and admitted at the defendant's trial, a codefendant's testimony cannot properly be admitted under Rule 801(e)(2)(E). In *Garza*, however, there was other evidence of a conspiracy and the defendant's participation in that conspiracy. 996 S.W.2d at 280. Thus, the trial judge reached the right result, though he gave the wrong reason for it. *Id.*

433. *Bourjaily v. United States*, 483 U.S. 171, 175 (1987); *Armentrout v. State*, 645 S.W.2d 298, 301 (Tex. Crim. App. 1983); *Fletcher v. State*, 960 S.W.2d 694, 698 (Tex. App.—Tyler 1997, no pet.); *Sorce v. State*, 736 S.W.2d 851, 860 (Tex. App.—Houston [14th Dist.] 1987, pet. ref'd). The rule does not, however, require that the person to whom

of the conspiracy,[434] and (4) the statement must be made in furtherance of the conspiracy, not merely "related to" the conspiracy.[435]

the statement is made be a member of the conspiracy. *United States v. Gupta*, 747 F.3d 111, 125 (2d Cir. 2014). As a matter of law, there can be no conspiracy solely between a defendant and a government agent. *United States v. Castellini*, 392 F.3d 35, 51 n.11 (1st Cir. 2004).

434. *See United States v. Rashid*, 383 F.3d 769, 777 (8th Cir. 2004) ("Statements or admissions made by a co-conspirator after apprehension, to law enforcement officials, are not 'in furtherance' of the conspiracy."), *vacated on other grounds sub nom. Abu Nahia v. United States*, 546 U.S. 803 (2005); *United States v. Manzella*, 782 F.2d 533, 545 (5th Cir. 1986) (once members of a conspiracy begin to cooperate with the government in its investigation, their statements are not made in the course of the conspiracy or in its furtherance); *Deeb v. State*, 815 S.W.2d 692, 696-97 (Tex. Crim. App. 1991) (when a conspiracy had been terminated by failure, statements made thereafter by conspirator in jail were not admissible under the rule); *see, e.g., United States v. Reed*, 726 F.2d 570, 580 (9th Cir. 1984) (statements made after termination of a conspiracy were not admissible under Federal Rule 801(d)(2)(E)); *Ward v. State*, 657 S.W.2d 133, 137 (Tex. Crim. App. 1983) (statements were inadmissible because even assuming the existence of a conspiracy, the evidence showed that the statements were made after completion of the conspiracy); *Am. Maint. & Rentals, Inc. v. Estrada*, 896 S.W.2d 212, 226 (Tex. App.—Houston [1st Dist.] 1995, writ dism'd by agr.) (statements made before any conspiracy was formed were not admissible under rule); *Bass v. State*, 830 S.W.2d 142, 147 (Tex. App.—Houston [14th Dist.] 1992, pet. ref'd) (codefendants' statements to a police officer who had stopped defendants on the highway were admissible under the rule when the conspiracy was to transport and possess marijuana across state lines and the conspiracy had not yet either succeeded or failed); *Burnett v. State*, 754 S.W.2d 437, 446 (Tex. App.—San Antonio 1988, pet. ref'd) (even though two victims had already been killed, statements by conspirator were admissible because the entire conspiracy—which entailed plans to kill three victims and to create an alibi to cover the conspirators' participation—was not finally terminated).

435. *Guidry*, 9 S.W.3d at 148; *Williams v. State*, 790 S.W.2d 643, 645 (Tex. Crim. App. 1990); *Orona v. State*, 341 S.W.3d 452, 464 (Tex. App.—Fort Worth 2011, pet. ref'd); *Guevara v. State*, 297 S.W.3d 350, 361 (Tex. App.—San Antonio 2009, pet. ref'd); *see Meador v. State*, 812 S.W.2d 330, 333-34 (Tex. Crim. App. 1991) (when conspirator's statements are made "to *frustrate* rather than further the common objectives of the conspiracy," they are inadmissible under Criminal Rule 801(e)(2)(E)); *see, e.g., Jones v. State*, 466 S.W.3d 252, 266 (Tex. App.—Houston [1st Dist.] 2015, pet. ref'd) (text messages between defendant and coconspirators with details about depositing large amounts of money in different bank accounts, consistent with drug-dealing operation, were admissible against defendant under Rule 801(e)(2)(E)), *cert. denied*, 136 S. Ct. 2519 (2016); *Maynard v. State*, 166 S.W.3d 403, 411-12 (Tex. App.—Austin 2005, pet. ref'd) (trial court did not abuse discretion in holding that coconspirator's statement to witness that he needed her to drive him to his girlfriend's house because he had to borrow car to use in killing intended murder victim was made in furtherance of conspiracy); *Deeb*, 815 S.W.2d at 697-98 (statements made in jail by a conspirator about a past murder were not admissible under the rule because they did not serve to further the conspiracy to murder for remuneration).

A statement furthers a conspiracy if it advances the conspiracy's cause or facilitates the conspiracy. *Guidry*, 9 S.W.3d at 148; *Brown v. State*, 334 S.W.3d 789, 805 (Tex. App.—Tyler 2010, pet. ref'd). The *Brown* court noted that

> [s]tatements that are made in furtherance of a conspiracy include those made (1) with intent to induce another to deal with co-conspirators or in any other way to cooperate with or assist co-conspirators, (2) with intent to induce another to join the conspiracy, (3) in formulating future strategies of concealment to benefit the conspiracy, (4) with intent to induce continued involvement in the conspiracy, or (5) for the purpose of identifying the role of one conspirator to another.

334 S.W.3d at 805; *accord Fairow v. State*, 920 S.W.2d 357, 362 (Tex. App.—Houston [1st Dist.] 1996), *aff'd*, 943 S.W.2d 895 (Tex. Crim. App. 1997); *see, e.g., Crum v. State*, 946 S.W.2d 349, 363 (Tex. App.—Houston [14th Dist.] 1997, pet. ref'd) (codefendant's statement that he thought defendant was a "crook" who was selling goods that did not exist was not made in furtherance of conspiracy and thus was not admissible under Rule 801(e)(2)(E)); *Blondett v. State*, 921 S.W.2d 469, 473 (Tex. App.—Houston [14th Dist.] 1996, pet. ref'd) (statement by conspirator to third person that he and defendant "were planning to do a 'drive-by'" was admissible because conspirator was trying to encourage third person to join conspiracy); *Vasquez v. State*, 902 S.W.2d 627, 636 (Tex. App.—El Paso 1995) (conspirator's statements about hiding weapons were in furtherance of conspiracy because "criminals generally wish to conceal their crimes, and ... conspiring by its very nature occurs out of the public light"), *rev'd on other grounds*, 919 S.W.2d 433 (Tex. Crim. App. 1996); *Speer v. State*, 890 S.W.2d 87, 95 (Tex. App.—Houston [1st Dist.] 1994, pet. ref'd) (conspirator's statement was "mere conversation" and did not meet the furtherance test).

The admissibility of a coconspirator's statement must be established by a preponderance of the evidence.[436] The court will determine under Rule 104(a) whether the proponent has met this burden.[437] The Supreme Court has held that the conspirator's statement may be considered in determining whether the State has proved the existence of a conspiracy, but it has expressly declined to hold that the statement alone is sufficient to prove the necessary predicate.[438]

The court of criminal appeals set out the rationale for the coconspirator exemption as based on agency principles, "'the underlying concept being that a conspiracy is a common undertaking where the conspirators are all agents of each other and where the acts and statements of one can be attributed to all.'"[439] This agency rationale is "'not based primarily upon any particular guarantees of reliability or trustworthiness that [are] intended to ensure the truthfulness of the admitted statement.'"[440] Although the rule contains no specific "trustworthiness" requirement, the "course and in furtherance of" requirements "provide some limited guarantees of trustworthiness under the rationale that active conspirators have 'no incentive to misdescribe the actions of their fellow members.'"[441]

The requirement that the statement be made in furtherance of the conspiracy is often the most difficult to satisfy because many, if not most, of the statements offered under this exception do not actually advance the objectives of the conspiracy.[442]

---

436. *Meador*, 812 S.W.2d at 333.

437. *See Casillas v. State*, 733 S.W.2d 158, 168 (Tex. Crim. App. 1986). Refer to note 400 *supra* and accompanying text.

438. *Bourjaily*, 483 U.S. at 180-81. Later cases suggest that some independent evidence is still required to prove the existence and membership of a conspiracy. *See United States v. Crespo de Llano*, 838 F.2d 1006, 1017 (9th Cir. 1987) ("Before admitting a statement of a coconspirator into evidence against a defendant, the government must establish by a preponderance of the evidence the existence of the conspiracy and of the defendant's connection to it ...."); *United States v. Martinez*, 825 F.2d 1451, 1452-53 (10th Cir. 1987) (under *Bourjaily*, court properly considered conspirator's statement in determining whether defendant was linked to the conspiracy); *see, e.g., Howard v. State*, 962 S.W.2d 119, 123 (Tex. App.—Houston [1st Dist.] 1997, pet. ref'd) (additional evidence from a witness who was not a conspirator also showed that a conspiracy existed); *Wilkerson v. State*, 933 S.W.2d 276, 280 (Tex. App.—Houston [1st Dist.] 1996, pet. ref'd) (proof that defendant and coconspirator were selling drugs together was sufficient proof of conspiracy); *Rodriguez v. State*, 896 S.W.2d 203, 205-06 (Tex. App.—Corpus Christi 1994, no pet.) (when defendant arrived with cocaine and pointed to it, after coconspirator stated that cocaine was "just a phone call away" and placed a call, defendant's actions demonstrated that he was member of conspiracy).

In 1997, Federal Rule of Evidence 801(d)(2)(E) was amended to codify the holding in *Bourjaily* and ensure that statements offered under the coconspirator exception (as well as those offered as authorized statements under Rule 801(d)(2)(C) or statements by an employee or agent under Rule 801(d)(2)(D)) can be used as partial proof of the predicate facts or foundation for admission of those statements. The offered statement alone, however, is not sufficient foundation for admission; thus, some evidence other than the offered statement itself must be produced as foundation for the exception. Of course, under either the federal or Texas rule, the conspiracy and the party's participation could be proved solely by his own out-of-court statement because that statement would qualify as nonhearsay. *See* FED. R. EVID. 801(d)(2)(A); TEX. R. EVID. 801(e)(2)(A).

439. *Byrd v. State*, 187 S.W.3d 436, 440 (Tex. Crim. App. 2005) (quoting *Bourjaily*, 483 U.S. at 188 (Blackmun, Brennan, Marshall, JJ., dissenting)).

440. *Byrd*, 187 S.W.3d at 440 (quoting *Bourjaily*, 483 U.S. at 189 (Blackmun, Brennan, Marshall, JJ., dissenting)).

441. *Byrd*, 187 S.W.3d at 440 (quoting *Bourjaily*, 483 U.S. at 191 (Blackmun, Brennan, Marshall, JJ., dissenting)).

442. *See, e.g., Byrd*, 187 S.W.3d at 442-43 (conspirator's out-of-court statement, rhetorically asking why defendant had to hit victim, did not advance the objective of the conspiracy to hinder defendant's apprehension); *Guidry*

Statements made by a conspirator that are retrospective, made during idle conversation, or made under circumstances that do not permit an inference that they are intended to further the objectives of the conspiracy are inadmissible.[443] Statements made to recruit new members into the conspiracy, however, are made "in furtherance" of its aims.[444]

Sometimes there is a question about whether multiple conspiracies exist and which conspiracy or conspiracies the particular statement was intended to further. In determining whether there was a single conspiracy or multiple conspiracies, courts should consider whether the conspirators shared a common goal or objective, the degree of interdependence inherent in the conspiracy objectives, and the overlap of participation by the conspirators in the different conspiracy objectives.[445]

3. Rule 801(e)(3): Depositions in a civil case. Rule 801(e)(3) makes clear that the Texas Rules of Evidence do not disturb the provisions of the Texas Rules of Civil Procedure that allow depositions to be used in lieu of testimony without any requirement that the deponent be unavailable to testify at trial.[446] The Federal Rules of Evidence do not contain an equivalent provision because the Federal Rules of Civil Procedure require the unavailability of the deponent before a witness's deposition may be introduced.[447]

---

v. State, 9 S.W.3d 133, 148 (Tex. Crim. App. 1999) (conspirator's statements were inadmissible because they merely described what was occurring in the murder conspiracy; they "did nothing to advance the cause of or facilitate the conspiracy [and] were not made in an effort to enlist [listener's] assistance or cooperation, elicit information that could be used in the conspiracy, or do anything other than report the status of the conspiracy"); *Lee v. State*, 21 S.W.3d 532, 538 (Tex. App.—Tyler 2000, pet. ref'd) (mother's statement to witness that her child hurt himself did not facilitate any conspiracy between mother and defendant charged with failing to seek medical treatment for child's injuries).

443. *See United States v. Means*, 695 F.2d 811, 818 (5th Cir. 1983); *see, e.g.*, *United States v. Cornett*, 195 F.3d 776, 784-85 (5th Cir. 1999) (lengthy recorded conversation by conspirator to informant at bowling alley was "mere idle chatter"; although it included reference to certain drug transactions, it was not an effort to further goals of conspiracy); *Fletcher v. State*, 960 S.W.2d 694, 698-99 (Tex. App.—Tyler 1997, no pet.) (when State did not offer any evidence that purpose of conspirators' discussion was to advance the object of the conspiracy, statements amounted to no more than "mere conversation" and a "casual admission of culpability" to nonconspirators, and were inadmissible under rule). But the concept of "furthering" the conspiracy should not be applied too strictly or it will defeat the purpose of the rule. *See United States v. Green*, 180 F.3d 216, 223 (5th Cir. 1999) (listing various types of conspiratorial statements that have been found to further goals of conspiracy); *see, e.g.*, *United States v. Miller*, 664 F.2d 94, 98 (5th Cir. 1981) ("puffing, boasts, and other conversation" was admissible when used by the declarant to obtain the confidence of the other conspirators).

444. *United States v. Lee*, 374 F.3d 637, 644 (8th Cir. 2004); *see also United States v. Gupta*, 747 F.3d 111, 125 (2d Cir. 2014) (statements designed to induce listener's assistance with conspiracy's goals are in furtherance of conspiracy).

445. *See Cox v. State*, 843 S.W.2d 750, 753-54 (Tex. App.—El Paso 1992, pet. ref'd) (in determining the existence of a single or multiple conspiracies, the most important factor is whether the conspirators shared a common goal or objective); *see, e.g.*, *Peoples v. State*, 928 S.W.2d 112, 117 (Tex. App.—Houston [1st Dist.] 1996, pet. ref'd) (evidence established a single conspiracy by two men to kill their spouses: both parties used the same intermediary to find a "hitman," one party provided the gun and bullets for both killings, the second murder was contingent on the success of the first, and the two men and the intermediary planned both murders).

446. *See* TEX. R. CIV. P. 203.6; *In re J.A.M.*, 945 S.W.2d 320, 323 (Tex. App.—San Antonio 1997, no pet.).

447. *See* FED. R. CIV. P. 32(a)(4).

Only depositions that are admissible under Texas Rule of Civil Procedure 203.6 are admissible under Rule 801(e)(3).[448] Rule 203.6 allows any party to use any part of any deposition taken in the same proceeding.[449] It permits a deposition to be used against a party that joined the lawsuit after the deposition was taken if (1) the deposition is admissible as former testimony under Rule of Evidence 804(b)(1), or (2) the newly joined party had an opportunity to redepose the witness and did not do so.[450]

RULE 802

THE RULE AGAINST HEARSAY

Hearsay is not admissible unless any of the following provides otherwise:

- a statute;
- these rules; or
- other rules prescribed under statutory authority.

Inadmissible hearsay admitted without objection may not be denied probative value merely because it is hearsay.

COMMENTARY ON RULE 802

Rule 802 states the basic principle that hearsay statements are generally inadmissible. Although practitioners and courts frequently cite Rule 801 as "the hearsay rule," it is not. Rule 801 merely defines hearsay. It is Rule 802 that bars the admission of hearsay statements. Thus, a hearsay objection should be made under Rule 802 and, if there is some question about whether testimony meets the definition of hearsay, also under Rule 801.[451] The sponsoring party may then show that the proffered evidence does not meet the definition of hearsay under Rule 801, or the

---

448. Depositions taken in a civil case are not admissible in a criminal trial under this provision. *See* Tex. R. Evid. 801(e)(3). However, depositions taken in a civil case and offered as an opposing party's statement under Rule 801(e)(2) are not barred by this provision. *See **Kemmerer v. State**,* 113 S.W.3d 513, 516-18 (Tex. App.—Houston [1st Dist.] 2003, pet. ref'd) (felony-murder defendant's civil deposition was not hearsay when offered by State under Rule 801(e)(2)(A); therefore, admissibility of deposition did not depend on compliance with Code of Criminal Procedure rules governing the taking of depositions in criminal cases).

449. Tex. R. Civ. P. 203.6(b). The rule defines "same proceeding" to include "a proceeding in a different court but involving the same subject matter and the same parties or their representatives or successors in interest." *Id.*

450. *Id.* Refer to notes 903-931 *infra* and accompanying text.

451. *See, e.g.,* ***Dolcefino v. Randolph***, 19 S.W.3d 906, 930 (Tex. App.—Houston [14th Dist.] 2000, pet. denied) (defamation plaintiff's affidavit relating conversation mayor had with plaintiff about defendant-reporter's investigation of plaintiff was offered for truth of matter asserted by mayor and was therefore inadmissible hearsay).

If the Rules of Evidence generally do not apply to a particular proceeding under Rule 101, then the hearsay rule does not apply either. For example, hearsay statements contained within a preliminary-sentencing-investigation report (PSI report) may be considered by a trial judge in determining an appropriate punishment. *See **Fryer v. State**,* 68 S.W.3d 628, 631 (Tex. Crim. App. 2002); *see, e.g.,* ***Champion v. State***, 126 S.W.3d 686, 699 (Tex. App.—Amarillo 2004, pet. ref'd) (rules of evidence do not apply to judicial use of PSI reports; thus, hearsay rule did not bar consideration of extraneous-offense information contained within report).

party may rely on some exception to the rule under Rule 803, Rule 804, or "other rules prescribed under statutory authority."[452]

The first sentence of Rule 802 has the same essential meaning as its federal counterpart.[453] The second sentence of Rule 802 overturned the long-standing Texas doctrine that inadmissible hearsay admitted because of failure to object was deemed to have no probative value and could not in any way support a finding of fact or a verdict.[454] In addition to being unsound in principle,[455] the doctrine had pernicious practical consequences. The doctrine permitted a party without the burden of proof to deceive a party with the burden of proof into believing that he had adduced sufficient evidence on all necessary elements of his case by choosing not to object to hearsay when offered. The party without the burden of proof would then argue on appeal that the verdict or judgment was not supported by evidence. Rule 802 represents the sounder approach.[456]

When no objection has been made to hearsay evidence,[457] the jury may consider it for whatever value it may have.[458] That is, such evidence should be given its natural probative force as if it were, in fact, admissible.[459] On the other hand, evidence may

---

452. TEX. R. EVID. 802; **Sanchez v. State**, 354 S.W.3d 476, 484 (Tex. Crim. App. 2011); *see* **Guidry v. State**, 9 S.W.3d 133, 147 (Tex. Crim. App. 1999) (example of proper mode of objection, response, and resolution of hearsay objections); **Martinez v. State**, 993 S.W.2d 751, 758 (Tex. App.—El Paso 1999) (proponent of testimony has burden to show that statement fell under an exception to hearsay rule), *rev'd on other grounds*, 22 S.W.3d 504 (Tex. Crim. App. 2000); *see, e.g.*, **Couchman v. State**, 3 S.W.3d 155, 158-59 (Tex. App.—Fort Worth 1999, pet. ref'd) (child victim's statements to her aunt about sexual molestation were admissible as an excited utterance under Rule 803(2)).

453. Federal Rule 802 refers to a federal statute, the other Federal Rules of Evidence, and rules prescribed by the U.S. Supreme Court.

454. *E.g.*, **Aetna Ins. v. Klein**, 160 Tex. 61, 68, 325 S.W.2d 376, 381 (1959) (inadmissible hearsay may not be given probative value, even if admitted without objection and used only as secondary evidence of the terms of a written instrument); **Tex. Co. v. Lee**, 138 Tex. 167, 171-72, 157 S.W.2d 628, 631 (1941) (incompetent hearsay evidence cannot form the basis of a finding of fact or the judgment of a court); **Lumpkin v. State**, 524 S.W.2d 302, 305 (Tex. Crim. App. 1975) (hearsay is without probative value, even when admitted without objection); **City of Keller v. Wilson**, 168 S.W.3d 802, 812 & n.29 (Tex. 2005); 1 RAY, *supra* note 9, §31, at 43. This view is still followed in Georgia. *See* **In re Burton**, 521 S.E.2d 568, 571 (Ga. 1999); **Jones v. O'Day**, 692 S.E.2d 774, 778 (Ga. Ct. App. 2010).

455. *See* 1 RAY, *supra* note 9, §31, at 43; *see also* Thomas Black, *Hearsay Admitted Without Objection—A Defense of Its Probative Value*, 17 S. TEX. L.J. 69, 71 (1975) (hearsay "dangers" revolve around lack of confrontation and cross-examination to determine a witness's perception, memory, narration, and sincerity, not lack of probative value).

456. Even before the promulgation of the Rules, the Texas Court of Criminal Appeals had held that unobjected-to hearsay evidence had probative value and could be considered. *See* **Chambers v. State**, 711 S.W.2d 240, 247 (Tex. Crim. App. 1986); **Lalande v. State**, 676 S.W.2d 115, 118 (Tex. Crim. App. 1984); **Ex parte Martinez**, 530 S.W.2d 578, 580-82 (Tex. Crim. App. 1975); **Frazier v. State**, 600 S.W.2d 271, 274 (Tex. Crim. App. 1979) (Odom, J., dissenting).

457. Hearsay evidence will support a default judgment even if the opposing party is not present at the trial and could not object to its admission. *See, e.g.*, **Tex. Commerce Bank v. New**, 3 S.W.3d 515, 517 (Tex. 1999) (trial court properly considered affidavits in rendering default judgment; unobjected-to hearsay is probative evidence, and "[n]othing in rule 802 limits its application to contested hearings"); **Wilemon v. Wilemon**, 930 S.W.2d 290, 294-95 (Tex. App.—Waco 1996, no writ) (when father did not appear at modification hearing and object to evidence, inadmissible hearsay could nonetheless support default judgment modifying child-support payments).

458. *See* TEX. R. EVID. 802.

459. *See* **Poindexter v. State**, 153 S.W.3d 402, 408-09 (Tex. Crim. App. 2005) (unobjected-to hearsay may be considered for its inherent probative value and may be sufficient proof, by itself, of element of crime), *overruled on other grounds*, **Robinson v. State**, 466 S.W.3d 166 (Tex. Crim. App. 2015); **Harris v. State**, 727 S.W.2d 537, 541 (Tex. Crim.

be excluded as hearsay even when the opposing party does not object specifically on hearsay grounds.[460]

Thus, a particular hearsay statement may have sufficient probative value by itself to support a finding of a particular fact,[461] or it may be wholly without probative value.[462]

App. 1987) (reviewing court will consider unobjected-to hearsay in determining the sufficiency of evidence to sustain a conviction); *In re W.C.*, 56 S.W.3d 863, 870 (Tex. App.—Houston [14th Dist.] 2001, no pet.) ("Even under the heavier beyond-a-reasonable-doubt burden in criminal cases, unobjected-to inadmissible hearsay may still support a conviction."), *overruled on other grounds*, *In re C.H.*, 89 S.W.3d 17 (Tex. 2002); *Campbell v. Salazar*, 960 S.W.2d 719, 723 n.1 (Tex. App.—El Paso 1997, pet. denied) (setting out rationale for allowing unobjected-to hearsay to have probative value under Civil Rule 802); *Taylor v. State*, 921 S.W.2d 740, 747 (Tex. App.—El Paso 1996, no pet.) (appeals court must consider unobjected-to hearsay in determining sufficiency of evidence); *see, e.g.*, *Peters v. State*, 997 S.W.2d 377, 382-83 (Tex. App.—Beaumont 1999, no pet.) (unobjected-to hearsay testimony was "direct" evidence of criminal conduct and sufficient to support verdict); *Doyle v. State*, 779 S.W.2d 492, 497 (Tex. App.—Houston [1st Dist.] 1989, no pet.) (evidence was sufficient to uphold defendant's conviction for possession of contraband based on unobjected-to hearsay statements by informer); *Irlbeck v. John Deere Co.*, 714 S.W.2d 54, 57-58 (Tex. App.—Amarillo 1986, writ ref'd n.r.e.) (affidavit supporting the amount due on a written instrument was sufficient to support an award for that amount even though affidavit, admitted without objection, contained inadmissible hearsay); *Aatco Transmission Co. v. Hollins*, 682 S.W.2d 682, 685 (Tex. App.—Houston [1st Dist.] 1984, no writ) (unobjected-to testimony by car owner that unidentified car-repair-shop manager told him that the car keys had been left in the ignition on the night the car was stolen from the shop was sufficient proof of that fact and of shop's negligence).

460. *See Jefferson v. State*, 900 S.W.2d 97, 100 (Tex. App.—Houston [14th Dist.] 1995, no pet.) (trial court did not err in sustaining State's general and imprecise objection because evidence was inadmissible hearsay; party does not have a right to have inadmissible hearsay admitted simply because opponent does not object specifically on hearsay grounds). The provision of former Criminal Rule 802 stating that "'inadmissible hearsay admitted without objection shall not be denied probative value' ... applies only to hearsay which is inadvertently admitted despite its defined inadmissibility." *Jefferson*, 900 S.W.2d at 100 (quoting former TEX. R. CRIM. EVID. 802). Thus, if the opposing party makes a general objection to hearsay evidence that is sustained, then the excluded evidence has no probative force at all.

461. Refer to note 459 *supra* and accompanying text.

462. *See Lee v. Dykes*, 312 S.W.3d 191, 198 (Tex. App.—Houston [14th Dist.] 2010, no pet.) ("We recognize that inadmissible evidence does not necessarily lose its probative value if admitted without objection. However, it does not follow that inadmissible evidence is necessarily probative if it is admitted without objection or is uncontroverted."); *see also Porras v. Craig*, 675 S.W.2d 503, 505 (Tex. 1984) (not a hearsay case; "[i]rrelevant evidence, even when admitted without objection, will not support a judgment"). In *Machado v. State*, the court noted:

> However, unobjected to hearsay may be denied probative value for reasons other than its hearsay nature. In this case, Sofos' testimony that Williams was one of the men who told him that appellant had started the fire was without probative value because Williams testified that he did not see the fire start, nor did he know at what point appellant had exited the storage room. Therefore, he could not have known from personal knowledge that appellant started the fire. The remaining evidence that could potentially link appellant with the fire is Sofos' testimony that the other man with Williams, a man named "Candy," told him that appellant started the fire. Although this evidence may tend to prove that appellant was the person who started the fire, and so has "probative" value, we are unable to conclude that a rational trier of fact could have found that this evidence, even combined with the evidence of appellant's opportunity to start the fire, was sufficient to exclude every other reasonable hypothesis except that of the guilt of appellant.

753 S.W.2d 252, 254 (Tex. App.—Houston [1st Dist.] 1988), *pet. ref'd*, 767 S.W.2d 809 (Tex. Crim. App. 1989). The result in this case is open to question because it is normally the trier of fact who determines whether the out-of-court version or in-court version that a witness tells is the truth. Credibility is solely a jury question. *See Forrest v. State*, 805 S.W.2d 462, 463-64 (Tex. Crim. App. 1991) (reversing a lower-court holding that "out-of-court, unsworn, unsupported hearsay repudiated in court by the declarant cannot, standing alone, prove guilt by a preponderance of the evidence" in a probation-revocation proceeding); *Chambers v. State*, 805 S.W.2d 459, 461 (Tex. Crim. App. 1991) (jury is entitled to disbelieve a witness when he recants a prior hearsay statement).

RULE 803

EXCEPTIONS TO THE RULE AGAINST HEARSAY—REGARDLESS OF WHETHER THE DECLARANT IS AVAILABLE AS A WITNESS

The following are not excluded by the rule against hearsay, regardless of whether the declarant is available as a witness:

(1) *Present Sense Impression.* A statement describing or explaining an event or condition, made while or immediately after the declarant perceived it.

(2) *Excited Utterance.* A statement relating to a startling event or condition, made while the declarant was under the stress of excitement that it caused.

(3) *Then-Existing Mental, Emotional, or Physical Condition.* A statement of the declarant's then-existing state of mind (such as motive, intent, or plan) or emotional, sensory, or physical condition (such as mental feeling, pain, or bodily health), but not including a statement of memory or belief to prove the fact remembered or believed unless it relates to the validity or terms of the declarant's will.

(4) *Statement Made for Medical Diagnosis or Treatment.* A statement that:

(A) is made for—and is reasonably pertinent to—medical diagnosis or treatment; and

(B) describes medical history; past or present symptoms or sensations; their inception; or their general cause.

(5) *Recorded Recollection.* A record that:

(A) is on a matter the witness once knew about but now cannot recall well enough to testify fully and accurately;

(B) was made or adopted by the witness when the matter was fresh in the witness's memory; and

(C) accurately reflects the witness's knowledge, unless the circumstances of the record's preparation cast doubt on its trustworthiness.

If admitted, the record may be read into evidence but may be received as an exhibit only if offered by an adverse party.

(6) *Records of a Regularly Conducted Activity.* A record of an act, event, condition, opinion, or diagnosis if:

(A) the record was made at or near the time by—or from information transmitted by—someone with knowledge;

RULE 803

(B) the record was kept in the course of a regularly conducted business activity;

(C) making the record was a regular practice of that activity;

(D) all these conditions are shown by the testimony of the custodian or another qualified witness, or by an affidavit or unsworn declaration that complies with Rule 902(10); and

(E) the opponent fails to demonstrate that the source of information or the method or circumstances of preparation indicate a lack of trustworthiness.

"Business" as used in this paragraph includes every kind of regular organized activity whether conducted for profit or not.

(7) *Absence of a Record of a Regularly Conducted Activity.* Evidence that a matter is not included in a record described in paragraph (6) if:

(A) the evidence is admitted to prove that the matter did not occur or exist;

(B) a record was regularly kept for a matter of that kind; and

(C) the opponent fails to show that the possible source of the information or other circumstances indicate a lack of trustworthiness.

(8) *Public Records.* A record or statement of a public office if:

(A) it sets out:

(i) the office's activities;

(ii) a matter observed while under a legal duty to report, but not including, in a criminal case, a matter observed by law-enforcement personnel; or

(iii) in a civil case or against the government in a criminal case, factual findings from a legally authorized investigation; and

(B) the opponent fails to demonstrate that the source of information or other circumstances indicate a lack of trustworthiness.

(9) *Public Records of Vital Statistics.* A record of a birth, death, or marriage, if reported to a public office in accordance with a legal duty.

(10) *Absence of a Public Record.* Testimony—or a certification under Rule 902—that a diligent search failed to disclose a public record or statement if the testimony or certification is admitted to prove that:

(A) the record or statement does not exist; or

(B) a matter did not occur or exist, if a public office regularly kept a record or statement for a matter of that kind.

RULE 803

(11) *Records of Religious Organizations Concerning Personal or Family History.* A statement of birth, legitimacy, ancestry, marriage, divorce, death, relationship by blood or marriage, or similar facts of personal or family history, contained in a regularly kept record of a religious organization.

(12) *Certificates of Marriage, Baptism, and Similar Ceremonies.* A statement of fact contained in a certificate:

(A) made by a person who is authorized by a religious organization or by law to perform the act certified;

(B) attesting that the person performed a marriage or similar ceremony or administered a sacrament; and

(C) purporting to have been issued at the time of the act or within a reasonable time after it.

(13) *Family Records.* A statement of fact about personal or family history contained in a family record, such as a Bible, genealogy, chart, engraving on a ring, inscription on a portrait, or engraving on an urn or burial marker.

(14) *Records of Documents That Affect an Interest in Property.* The record of a document that purports to establish or affect an interest in property if:

(A) the record is admitted to prove the content of the original recorded document, along with its signing and its delivery by each person who purports to have signed it;

(B) the record is kept in a public office; and

(C) a statute authorizes recording documents of that kind in that office.

(15) *Statements in Documents That Affect an Interest in Property.* A statement contained in a document that purports to establish or affect an interest in property if the matter stated was relevant to the document's purpose—unless later dealings with the property are inconsistent with the truth of the statement or the purport of the document.

(16) *Statements in Ancient Documents.* A statement in a document that is at least 20 years old and whose authenticity is established.

(17) *Market Reports and Similar Commercial Publications.* Market quotations, lists, directories, or other compilations that are generally relied on by the public or by persons in particular occupations.

RULE 803

(18) ***Statements in Learned Treatises, Periodicals, or Pamphlets.*** A statement contained in a treatise, periodical, or pamphlet if:

(A) the statement is called to the attention of an expert witness on cross-examination or relied on by the expert on direct examination; and

(B) the publication is established as a reliable authority by the expert's admission or testimony, by another expert's testimony, or by judicial notice.

If admitted, the statement may be read into evidence but not received as an exhibit.

(19) ***Reputation Concerning Personal or Family History.*** A reputation among a person's family by blood, adoption, or marriage—or among a person's associates or in the community—concerning the person's birth, adoption, legitimacy, ancestry, marriage, divorce, death, relationship by blood, adoption, or marriage, or similar facts of personal or family history.

(20) ***Reputation Concerning Boundaries or General History.*** A reputation in a community—arising before the controversy—concerning boundaries of land in the community or customs that affect the land, or concerning general historical events important to that community, state, or nation.

(21) ***Reputation Concerning Character.*** A reputation among a person's associates or in the community concerning the person's character.

(22) ***Judgment of a Previous Conviction.*** Evidence of a final judgment of conviction if:

(A) it is offered in a civil case and:

(i) the judgment was entered after a trial or guilty plea, but not a nolo contendere plea;

(ii) the conviction was for a felony;

(iii) the evidence is admitted to prove any fact essential to the judgment; and

(iv) an appeal of the conviction is not pending; or

(B) it is offered in a criminal case and:

(i) the judgment was entered after a trial or a guilty or nolo contendere plea;

(ii) the conviction was for a criminal offense;

(iii) the evidence is admitted to prove any fact essential to the judgment;

(iv) when offered by the prosecutor for a purpose other than impeachment, the judgment was against the defendant; and

(v) an appeal of the conviction is not pending.

(23) *Judgments Involving Personal, Family, or General History or a Boundary.* A judgment that is admitted to prove a matter of personal, family, or general history, or boundaries, if the matter:

(A) was essential to the judgment; and

(B) could be proved by evidence of reputation.

(24) *Statement Against Interest.* A statement that:

(A) a reasonable person in the declarant's position would have made only if the person believed it to be true because, when made, it was so contrary to the declarant's proprietary or pecuniary interest or had so great a tendency to invalidate the declarant's claim against someone else or to expose the declarant to civil or criminal liability or to make the declarant an object of hatred, ridicule, or disgrace; and

(B) is supported by corroborating circumstances that clearly indicate its trustworthiness, if it is offered in a criminal case as one that tends to expose the declarant to criminal liability.

COMMENTARY ON RULE 803

Rule 803 lists 24 exceptions to the hearsay rule; all but one of them may be invoked regardless of whether the declarant is available to testify.[463] In only three sections does the operation of the rule differ depending on whether the case is civil or criminal: 803(8), 803(22), and 803(24). Other than in the following instances, Texas has adopted the corresponding federal provisions without substantive changes. Texas Rule 803(5) departs slightly from its federal model.[464] In Texas Rule 803(6), the definition of "business" is different from that in the federal version,[465] as is the terminology in Rule 803(6)(D).[466] Texas Rule 803(10) does not include a notice requirement for criminal cases, as Federal Rule 803(10) does.[467] Texas Rule 803(22) reflects minor substantive changes from the federal rule,[468] and Texas Rule 803(24) differs in location and slightly in substance from its counterpart, Federal Rule 804(b)(3).[469] Finally, the Texas Rules

---

463. Rule 803(5) requires that the declarant be present and testify. *See* TEX. R. EVID. 803(5). Refer to notes 585-590 *infra* and accompanying text.

464. Refer to notes 589-590 *infra* and accompanying text.

465. Refer to note 637 *infra*.

466. Refer to note 655 *infra*.

467. Refer to notes 737-738 *infra* and accompanying text.

468. Refer to notes 798-804 *infra* and accompanying text.

469. Refer to notes 812-814 *infra* and accompanying text.

RULE 803

do not contain in any form the "residual" exception codified as Federal Rule 807.[470] The following survey of the particular provisions of Rule 803 will note and discuss these differences. When no difference is mentioned, the Texas provisions are substantively identical to the corresponding federal rules.

The hearsay exceptions under Rule 803 may be roughly categorized into unreflective statements, reliable documents, and reputation evidence.[471] "The rationale for all of the exceptions is that, over time, experience has shown that these types of statements are generally reliable and trustworthy."[472] The first category, unreflective statements, are "'street corner' utterances made by ordinary people before any thoughts of litigation have crystallized" (i.e., the speaker was not thinking about the legal consequences of his statements).[473] "In most instances, the speaker was not thinking at all; the statement was made without any reflection, thought process, or motive to fabricate or exaggerate."[474] The second set of hearsay exceptions, reliable documents, involve written materials normally accepted as accurate and on which reasonable people generally rely in their everyday affairs. If documents of this nature are reliable enough to be trusted for business decisions, courts normally find them reliable enough for admission in a lawsuit. The third category, reputation, is based on the uncertain notion that community gossip about one of its members is likely to be reliable.

A. Unreflective Statements

1. Rule 803(1): Present sense impression. A hearsay statement is admissible under Rule 803(1), the present-sense-impression exception, if the statement (1) describes or explains an event or condition and (2) was made while or immediately after the declarant perceived it.[475] The rationale for the present-sense-impression exception is that when the statement occurs at the same time as the event it describes, the dangers of faulty memory and insincerity are eliminated.[476]

---

470. Refer to notes 848-862 *infra* and accompanying text.

471. *Walter v. State*, 267 S.W.3d 883, 889 (Tex. Crim. App. 2008); *Fischer v. State*, 252 S.W.3d 375, 379 (Tex. Crim. App. 2008).

472. *Fischer*, 252 S.W.3d at 379.

473. *Id.*

474. *Id.*

475. TEX. R. EVID. 803(1). Implicit in the requirement that the statement be made while or immediately after the declarant perceived the event or condition is that the declarant have personal knowledge of the facts contained in the statement. *See* 5 JACK B. WEINSTEIN & MARGARET A. BERGER, WEINSTEIN'S FEDERAL EVIDENCE §803.03[2], at 803-15 (Joseph M. McLaughlin ed., 2d ed. 2009). This requirement is also independently imposed by Rule 602. Refer to *Article VI: Witnesses, supra* p. 567.

476. *Fischer*, 252 S.W.3d at 380; *Fields v. State*, 515 S.W.3d 47, 55 (Tex. App.—San Antonio 2016, no pet.); FED. R. EVID. 803(1) advisory committee's note; *see Hous. Oxygen Co. v. Davis*, 139 Tex. 1, 6, 161 S.W.2d 474, 476-77 (1942) (spontaneity saves the evidence from suspicion of being manufactured or calculated).

The court of criminal appeals explained the rationale as follows:

If a person observes some situation or happening which is not at all startling or shocking in its nature, nor actually producing excitement in the observer, the observer may yet have occasion to comment on what he sees (or learns from other senses) *at the very time that he is receiving the impression.* Such a comment, as to a situation then before the declarant, does not have the safeguard of impulse,

(1) Statement describes or explains event or condition. Rule 803(1) encompasses only statements that describe or explain an event or condition. Opinions, inferences, or conclusions about that event or condition are not admissible.[477] For example, the declarant's statement of "Look! There's Jimmy hitting John," is an admissible statement describing an event, while the further sentence, "I always knew this would happen because Jimmy hates John," is the witness's opinion about the event and is not admissible.

Similarly, the present-sense-impression exception cannot be used to circumvent the prohibition against the admission of a police officer's report setting out "matter[s] observed by law-enforcement personnel" under Rule 803(8)(A)(ii), by an officer contemporaneously videotaping his observations, impressions, and opinions of a DWI suspect he has stopped.[478] Present sense impressions are admissible "precisely because they are non-narrative, off-hand comments made without any thought of potential litigation by a neutral and detached observer without any motive to fabricate, falsify, or otherwise exaggerate his observations."[479] But police officers investigating crime and collecting evidence against a suspect are not neutral and detached observers.[480] The contemporaneous recording of a police officer's observations and impressions does not

---

emotion, or excitement, but there are other safeguards. In the first place, the report at the moment of the thing then seen, heard, etc., is safe from any error from defect of *memory* of the declarant. Secondly, there is little or no *time* for calculated misstatement, and thirdly, the statement will usually be made to another (the witness who reports it) who would have equal opportunities to observe and hence to check a misstatement. Consequently, it is believed that such comments, strictly limited to reports of *present* sense-impressions, have such exceptional reliability as to warrant their inclusion within the hearsay exception for Spontaneous Declarations. *Rabbani v. State*, 847 S.W.2d 555, 560 (Tex. Crim. App. 1992) (quoting 1A RAY, *supra* note 9, §916, at 158-59); *accord Fischer*, 252 S.W.3d at 380; *see Russo v. State*, 228 S.W.3d 779, 808-09 (Tex. App.—Austin 2007, pet. ref'd); *Anderson v. State*, 15 S.W.3d 177, 183 (Tex. App.—Texarkana 2000, no pet.).

Texas was the first jurisdiction to recognize this exception by name, and its leading case, *Houston Oxygen Co. v. Davis*, is cited in the Advisory Committee's note to the federal rule. *Fischer*, 252 S.W.3d at 380; *see* FED. R. EVID. 803(1) advisory committee's note; 1A RAY, *supra* note 9, §916, at 159-60. For a history of the exception to the hearsay rule for present sense impressions, see Jon R. Waltz, *The Present Sense Impression Exception to the Rule Against Hearsay: Origins and Attributes*, 66 IOWA L. REV. 869 (1981) (tracing history of present-sense-impression exception to show how corroboration requirement developed).

477. *See Linney v. State*, 401 S.W.3d 764, 779 (Tex. App.—Houston [14th Dist.] 2013, pet. ref'd) (Rule 803(1) "relates to statements about something external to the declarant, whereas [Rule 803(3)] pertains to something internal"); *Anderson*, 15 S.W.3d at 184 ("'We do not believe that a statement of *opinion* about a condition or event, as opposed to a statement of description or explanation about something observed or otherwise sensed, qualifies as a present sense impression.'" (quoting *Beauchamp v. State*, 870 S.W.2d 649, 652 (Tex. App.—El Paso 1994, pet. ref'd))).

478. *See Fischer*, 252 S.W.3d at 385 (parties cannot use Rule 803(1) as a "back door" to admit evidence that is inadmissible under Rule 803(8)(B), now Rule 803(8)(A)(ii)).

479. *Id.* at 383.

480. *See id.* at 384 ("[O]n-the-scene observations and narrations of a police officer conducting a roadside investigation into a suspected DWI offense are fraught with the thought of a future prosecution …. [T]he officer is gathering evidence, he is not making an off-hand, non-reflective observation about the world as it passes by."); *see, e.g.*, *Eggert v. State*, 395 S.W.3d 240, 244 (Tex. App.—San Antonio 2012, no pet.) (officer's recorded commentary as he searched and inventoried DWI defendant's vehicle was not admissible under Rule 803(1); comments were made for purpose of gathering evidence against defendant and were thus "testimonial statements that cannot be considered the 'non-narrative, off-hand comments' the present sense impression exception is designed to allow").

decrease the cause of their potential unreliability; the unreliability stems from the in-herently adversarial relationship between law-enforcement personnel and those under observation.[481]

(2) Statement made while or immediately after declarant perceived event or condition. The rule requires that the declaration, if not made simultaneously with the event, be made "immediately" afterward.[482] Obviously, what constitutes "immediately" requires judicial discretion, but Texas courts have both admitted and excluded declarations made 30 minutes after the event.[483] A functional test is applied to determine admissibility—that is, "whether the proximity in time is sufficient to reduce the hear-say danger of faulty memory and insincerity."[484]

On the other hand, if the declarant has had time to reflect on the event and the con-ditions he observed or has learned further facts after the event, lack of contempora-neity diminishes the reliability of the statements and makes them inadmissible under

---

481. *See, e.g., Fischer*, 252 S.W.3d at 386 ("[M]ost of the statements made by [the officer] on the videotape con-stituted a calculated narrative in an adversarial, investigative setting. These particular statements may be entirely reliable ones, but the setting is one that human experience and the law recognizes is brimming with the potential for exaggeration or misstatement.").

482. TEX. R. EVID. 803(1); *Russo v. State*, 228 S.W.3d 779, 809 (Tex. App.—Austin 2007, pet. ref'd); *see, e.g., Brooks v. State*, 990 S.W.2d 278, 287 (Tex. Crim. App. 1999) (when time lapse between declarant's perception of event and his description of it was "minimal," testimony was admissible under exception); *Cardenas v. State*, 115 S.W.3d 54, 62-63 (Tex. App.—San Antonio 2003, no pet.) (murder victim's statement to her neighbors that "[defendant] is in my apartment" was admissible as present sense impression; evidence suggested that victim's walk to neighbor's apartment took less than one minute); *Barber v. State*, 989 S.W.2d 822, 836-37 (Tex. App.—Fort Worth 1999, pet. ref'd) (when declarant made statement describing an event he overheard—defendant hitting witness—"only a few minutes" after event, testimony was admissible under the rule); *1.70 Acres v. State*, 935 S.W.2d 480, 489 (Tex. App.—Beaumont 1996, no writ) (when State contended that there was only a ten-minute lapse between drug trans-action and declarant's statement of where and from whom she had bought marijuana, but offered no evidence of that contention, immediacy requirement of hearsay exception was not met); *Green v. State*, 876 S.W.2d 226, 228 (Tex. App.—Beaumont 1994, no pet.) (officer's testimony that two witnesses shouted "The man in the brown trench coat was shooting" as they were running from direction in which shots were fired was admissible under rule; declarants were describing an event they had seen almost immediately before encountering officer).

483. *Compare Harris v. State*, 736 S.W.2d 166, 167 (Tex. App.—Houston [14th Dist.] 1987, no pet.) (admitting a statement under Criminal Rule 803(1) despite a lapse of approximately 30 minutes between the event and the state-ment), *with Moore v. Drummet*, 478 S.W.2d 177, 182 (Tex. Civ. App.—Houston [14th Dist.] 1972, no writ) (exclud-ing a statement made approximately 30 minutes after the event).

484. *Beauchamp v. State*, 870 S.W.2d 649, 653 (Tex. App.—El Paso 1994, pet. ref'd); *see, e.g., Kubin v. State*, 868 S.W.2d 394, 396-97 (Tex. App.—Houston [1st Dist.] 1993, pet. ref'd) (statement made four to six minutes after event was sufficiently contemporaneous to provide little opportunity for declarant to make a calculated misstatement of the events he witnessed); *cf. United States v. Peacock*, 654 F.2d 339, 350 (5th Cir. 1981) (allowing testimony under Federal Rule 803(1) when the declarant described a conversation to his wife "immediately following a telephone conversation" because there was "no time" for the declarant to "consciously manipulate the truth"), *vacated in part on other grounds*, 686 F.2d 356 (5th Cir. 1982).

In *Franklin v. State*, the court of appeals held that a witness's testimony that when she called the murder vic-tim on the morning of the murder, she came to believe that the defendant was in the house was admissible as a present sense impression. 858 S.W.2d 537, 544 (Tex. App.—Beaumont 1993, pet. ref'd). The court noted that the witness "could have personally heard" the defendant's voice through the telephone receiver or the victim could have told her that the defendant had just entered the room. *Id.* The former is not hearsay at all, and the latter is admissible as the victim's present sense impression. *Id.* However, there was no indication in the record as to what basis, if any, the witness had for her belief. The evidentiary requirements for admission of a present sense impression were not met. In this instance, the defendant could have also objected on grounds of a lack of personal knowledge under Rule 602 or a lack of personal perception for lay-opinion testimony under Rule 701(a).

the rule.[485] Thus, it has been held that statements made during the reenactment of an earlier event cannot be considered a "present sense impression" of that earlier event.[486]

(3) Proof. The proponent of present-sense-impression evidence has the burden of establishing, by a preponderance of the evidence, that the evidence is admissible.[487] The requirements for a present sense impression may be met by circumstantial evidence, including the hearsay statement itself.[488]

One of the frequent justifications for the present-sense-impression exception to the hearsay rule is that "the statement will usually be made to another (the witness who reports it) who would have equal opportunities to observe and hence to check a misstatement."[489] While this reasoning bolsters the rationale for the exception, it is not a requirement of Rule 803(1).[490] Contemporaneity of the event and the declaration alone are sufficient guarantees for admissibility. Rule 803(1) does not require that the witness have had an opportunity to observe and verify the declarant's statements.[491]

Nor does it matter whether the statement was made over the telephone or in the presence of the person testifying about the statement.[492] Even if the declarant's iden-

---

485. *Fischer*, 252 S.W.3d at 381; *see, e.g.*, *Fields v. State*, 515 S.W.3d 47, 55-56 (Tex. App.—San Antonio 2016, no pet.) (error, though harmless, to admit note written by defendant's girlfriend under Rule 803(1); wording of note and girlfriend's testimony indicated she formulated and carried out plan to leave note); *Ferguson v. State*, 97 S.W.3d 293, 297-98 (Tex. App.—Houston [14th Dist.] 2003, pet. ref'd) (officer's testimony that witness identified defendant in a photo spread as a participant in earlier raid was inadmissible under rule; identification occurred long after raid itself); *Chambers v. State*, 905 S.W.2d 328, 330 (Tex. App.—Fort Worth 1995, no pet.) (defendant's written statement to police describing the shooting with which he was charged, made more than a month after the event, was not contemporaneous with event and thus was not admissible as a present sense impression); *Beauchamp*, 870 S.W.2d at 653-54 (police officer's statement to witness that he did not believe defendant was intoxicated, made 10 to 20 minutes after his last observation of defendant, was not made contemporaneously and was a reflective opinion about condition, not a description of a condition or event, and thus was not admissible).

486. *Kipp v. State*, 876 S.W.2d 330, 338 n.13 (Tex. Crim. App. 1994).

487. *Cf. Bemis v. Edwards*, 45 F.3d 1369, 1373 (9th Cir. 1995) (proponent has burden of establishing personal perception by preponderance of the evidence); 5 WEINSTEIN & BERGER, *supra* note 475, §803.03[2], at 803-16 ("The burden of establishing personal perception rests with the proponent of the evidence. This burden may be met by circumstantial evidence of firsthand knowledge.").

488. *See, e.g.*, *Russo v. State*, 228 S.W.3d 779, 809 (Tex. App.—Austin 2007, pet. ref'd) (statement that "this guy just left" was contemporaneous with the event it described and thus was admissible under Rule 803(1)).

489. *Hous. Oxygen Co. v. Davis*, 139 Tex. 1, 6, 161 S.W.2d 474, 476-77 (1942); 1A RAY, *supra* note 9, §916, at 159; *see* FED. R. EVID. 803(1) advisory committee's note.

490. *See Rabbani v. State*, 847 S.W.2d 555, 560 n.9 (Tex. Crim. App. 1992) (Rule 803(1) contains no requirement that the witness have an opportunity to check the veracity of the declarant's statement).

491. *See* 7 MICHAEL H. GRAHAM, HANDBOOK OF FEDERAL EVIDENCE §803:1, at 19 (7th ed. 2012) (nothing in Rule 803(1) "actually requires that the in court witness … have personal knowledge of the underlying event"); McCORMICK'S HANDBOOK II, *supra* note 7, §298, at 710 (third person "will usually have an opportunity to observe the situation himself"; actual observation is not required); 4 WEINSTEIN & BERGER, *supra* note 209, ¶803(1)[01], at 803-94 (statement is usually made to a person with an equal opportunity to observe and check any misstatements; direct observation is not necessary).

492. *See Russo*, 228 S.W.3d at 809; *see, e.g.*, *Reyes v. State*, 314 S.W.3d 74, 78 (Tex. App.—San Antonio 2010, no pet.) (statements on 911 recording that victim was "limping" and "needs" an ambulance indicated that caller was describing events as they were happening; statements were admissible as a present sense impression); *see also State v. Damper*, 225 P.3d 1148, 1152 (Ariz. Ct. App. 2010) (text message that said "Can you come over? Me and Marcus are fighting and I have no gas." constituted a present sense impression; message described argument between victim and her boyfriend before he shot her).

RULE 803

tity is unknown, that fact alone should not preclude admission of the evidence; instead, it goes to the proof of whether the declarant had personal knowledge of the facts contained in the statement.[493]

2. Rule 803(2): Excited utterance. Texas courts have always recognized the hearsay exception for excited utterances or spontaneous declarations.[494] A statement is admissible under Rule 803(2), the excited-utterance exception, if it relates to a startling event or condition and was made while the declarant was under the stress of excitement that it caused.[495]

According to the federal drafters, "[t]he theory of [paragraph] (2) is simply that circumstances may produce a condition of excitement which temporarily stills the capacity of reflection and produces utterances free of conscious fabrication."[496] The same rationale has been adopted by Texas courts.[497]

---

493. *See* 5 WEINSTEIN & BERGER, *supra* note 475, §803.03[2], at 803-16.

494. *See generally* 1A RAY, *supra* note 9, §§911-927 (citing cases indicating the long history of the hearsay doctrine's use in Texas). In Texas, as in many jurisdictions, use of the phrase "res gestae" (which has no particular meaning) has created confusion about this hearsay exception and other, distinct doctrines. EDWARD W. CLEARY, ET AL., EVIDENCE 770 (4th ed. 1988); *see* 1A RAY, *supra* note 9, §911, at 144-45 (use of res gestae creates confusion); G.T. Banks, Comment, *Res Gestae in the Texas Court of Criminal Appeals: A Method to Their Madness?*, 50 TEX. L. REV. 119, 119 (1971) (most American courts "use the term to some extent, but the Texas Court of Criminal Appeals seems to have gone the furthest in distilling chaos from simplicity"); Michael E. Bornhouser, Comment, *Res Gestae: A Synonym for Confusion*, 20 BAYLOR L. REV. 229, 229 (1968) (res gestae "has been used to mean so many things that it is impossible to know exactly what it does mean"). For a discussion of how the Texas Court of Criminal Appeals has clarified the doctrine of res gestae, refer to *Article IV: Relevance & Its Limits, supra* p. 287. Under both the Texas and Federal Rules of Evidence, reference to res gestae should be avoided. *See* ***City of Dall. v. Donovan***, 768 S.W.2d 905, 906-07 (Tex. App.—Dallas 1989, no writ); 7 GRAHAM, *supra* note 491, §803:2, at 57-58.

495. TEX. R. EVID. 803(2); *see* ***Sellers v. State***, 588 S.W.2d 915, 918 (Tex. Crim. App. 1979) (courts should not examine each requirement independently but rather should focus on whether the combined effect shows the reliability of the statement); ***In re A.W.B.***, 419 S.W.3d 351, 356 (Tex. App.—Amarillo 2010, no pet.) (same). In determining whether the excited-utterance exception applies, the court may consider (1) the length of time elapsed between the event and the statement, (2) the declarant's nature and condition (e.g., his age and demeanor at the time of the statement), (3) whether the statement was made in response to a question, and (4) whether the statement was self-serving. *See* ***Apolinar v. State***, 155 S.W.3d 184, 187 (Tex. Crim. App. 2005).

496. FED. R. EVID. 803(2) advisory committee's note. As Louisell and Mueller note, other factors contribute to the continued vitality of the spontaneous-utterance exception to the hearsay doctrine:

> Often the startling occurrence is itself at the heart of a litigated dispute, and often it is so fleeting that the need of the trier of fact is for more rather than less information in order to make an informed determination of exactly what happened; particularly in light of the nature of startling occurrences, the fresh statement of the observer is likely to be at least as reliable as his later reconstruction of events; finally, the startling occurrence is often an accident or violent crime which ultimately claims the life of the declarant and which he was better able to observe than any available witness, which means that excluding his statement would often result in doing without the best available evidence, and in the unattractive consequence of ignoring the cries of the victim.

4 LOUISELL & MUELLER, *supra* note 250, §439, at 493-94; *see also* ***Bondurant v. State***, 956 S.W.2d 762, 765 (Tex. App.—Fort Worth 1997, pet. ref'd) ("The excited utterance exception to the hearsay rule is founded on the belief that statements made as a result of a startling or exciting event are involuntary and do not allow the declarant an adequate opportunity to fabricate, thereby ensuring enough trustworthiness to fall outside the hearsay exception.").

The rationale for the exception has been questioned because the same excitement that enhances sincerity is apt to diminish the faculties of perception and communication. *See* 4 LOUISELL & MUELLER, *supra* note 250, §439, at 493-94; *see also* Robert M. Hutchins & Donald Slesinger, *Some Observations on the Law of Evidence*, 28 COLUM. L. REV. 432, 438 (1928) (participants and bystanders have perceptions clouded by intense emotion); M.C. Slough,

(1) Statement relating to startling event or condition. The purpose of requiring that the statement be related to a startling event or condition is to ensure that the statement is truly spontaneous and not the result of reflection, which could inject such factors as self-interest, anger, or vindictiveness into the utterance. That purpose is not fulfilled if the statement is not related to the startling event. Therefore, the declarant's statement must be more than just the result of, or caused by, the startling event.

Opinions contained in the excited utterance are generally admissible to the same extent as facts, as long as there is a basis for the opinions.[498]

(2) Statement made while declarant was under stress of excitement that event or condition caused. Unlike present sense impressions, there is no temporal requirement for excited utterances. Instead, an excited utterance can be made anytime after the startling event or condition, as long as the declarant remains under the stress of excitement the event or condition caused.[499] The time lapse between the startling event and the statement is not dispositive, but it can be a factor in determining

---

Res Gestae, 2 KAN. L. REV. 246, 249 (1954) (words "bubbling in the froth of panic will oftentimes relate impressions that are far removed from sober reality"). As an example:

> [e]xcitement is not a guarantee against lying, especially since the courts often hold that excitement may endure many minutes and even hours beyond the event. More important, excitement exaggerates, sometimes grossly, distortion in perception and memory especially when the observer is a witness to a nonroutine, episodic event such as occurs in automobile collision cases and crimes. The likelihood of inaccurate perception, the drawing of inferences to fill in memory gaps, and the reporting of nonfacts is high.

I. Daniel Stewart, Jr., *Perception, Memory, and Hearsay: A Criticism of Present Law and the Proposed Federal Rules of Evidence*, 1970 UTAH L. REV. 1, 28 (citations omitted). But the theory is so ingrained in the judiciary that any criticism has no practical effect. *See* 1A RAY, *supra* note 9, §913 n.21, at 153.

497. *See Apolinar*, 155 S.W.3d at 186; *Edmondson v. State*, 399 S.W.3d 607, 612-13 (Tex. App.—Eastland 2013, no pet.); *Harvey v. State*, 123 S.W.3d 623, 630 (Tex. App.—Texarkana 2003, pet. ref'd).

498. *See, e.g.*, *King v. State*, 953 S.W.2d 266, 269-70 (Tex. Crim. App. 1997) (declarant's statement that she believed defendant possibly killed victim was an introduction to events she had personally observed the night before the murder; trial court could have properly found that witness had a basis for her opinion).

499. *Zuliani v. State*, 97 S.W.3d 589, 596 (Tex. Crim. App. 2003) (court must determine whether statement was made "'under such circumstances as would reasonably show that it resulted from impulse rather than reason and reflection.'" (quoting *Fowler v. State*, 379 S.W.2d 345, 347 (Tex. Crim. App. 1964))); *see, e.g.*, *King*, 953 S.W.2d at 269 (upholding admissibility of excited utterance made to police 30 minutes after officers arrived at murder scene; declarant was "crying profusely and in an extreme emotional state"); *Lawton v. State*, 913 S.W.2d 542, 553-54 (Tex. Crim. App. 1995) (when officer testified that declarant-eyewitness to murder was still "excited and upset" an hour after "the rapid sequence of staggering events culminating in the victim's death," statement he made to officer was admissible); *McFarland v. State*, 845 S.W.2d 824, 846 (Tex. Crim. App. 1992) (though the time frame between the startling event—an assault in which declarant received 43 stab wounds—and the statement was not conclusively established, "it is apparent to this Court that the declarant was still under the emotional and physical stress of the assault" when the statement was made); *Dixon v. State*, 358 S.W.3d 250, 260-61 (Tex. App.—Houston [1st Dist.] 2011, pet. ref'd) (statement of witness, who was "very visibly shaken, very upset, scared, excited, and crying" when describing event, was admissible as excited utterance under Rule 803(2) even though statement occurred one hour after event); *Drew v. State*, 76 S.W.3d 436, 457-59 (Tex. App.—Houston [14th Dist.] 2002, pet. ref'd) (felony-murder victim's statement, "Please don't rape me," made in hospital one to three hours after assault was admissible under the rule despite time lapse; testimony showed victim was unresponsive to questions and her behavior demonstrated that she was still dominated by the emotion, excitement, fear, and pain of the events); *Moyer v. State*, 948 S.W.2d 525, 529 (Tex. App.—Fort Worth 1997, pet. ref'd) (when victim was found bruised, battered, and nude while struggling with defendant's wife in the front yard of a house that was on fire, trial court could have reasonably concluded

whether the declarant is under the stress of the event.[500] The most critical factor is the lack of opportunity to reflect or fabricate details.[501]

The startling event or condition need not be the crime itself,[502] and the state of excitement must be continuous from the startling event or condition to the time of the

---

that her statements to paramedic were admissible under Criminal Rule 803(2)); *Wigiert v. State*, 948 S.W.2d 54, 57-58 (Tex. App.—Fort Worth 1997, no pet.) (false-imprisonment victim's statements to police officer were admissible when officer testified that victim ran to his car, was very upset and crying, knocked on his window, was out of breath, and had difficulty speaking); *Adams v. State*, 936 S.W.2d 313, 315-16 (Tex. App.—Tyler 1996, pet. ref'd) (child victim's statement to her older sister about defendant molesting her on airplane, made within five minutes after walking away from plane, when she was crying and visibly upset, was admissible under rule).

It is not essential that the witness personally perceive every aspect of the startling event. It is enough that the witness observed some aspect of the startling event and became excited as a result. *See, e.g.*, *King*, 953 S.W.2d at 269 (declarant's excited-utterance statement that defendant might have killed victim was based on having seen victim and defendant go into motel room where victim was murdered; admissible even though witness did not personally observe the killing); *Woodall v. State*, 77 S.W.3d 388, 398-99 (Tex. App.—Fort Worth 2002, pet. ref'd) (witness's statement to officer that her husband "might have shot" victim was based on her personal observations of events that occurred before the startling event, even though she did not observe the shooting).

500. *See Apolinar*, 155 S.W.3d at 186-87; *Zuliani*, 97 S.W.3d at 596. Refer to note 495 *supra* and accompanying text, notes 504-505 *infra* and accompanying text.

501. *See Zuliani*, 97 S.W.3d at 595 ("[T]he statement is trustworthy because it represents an event speaking through the person rather than the person speaking about the event."); *Wells v. State*, 319 S.W.3d 82, 90-91 (Tex. App.—San Antonio 2010, pet. ref'd) (same); *see, e.g.*, *Sandoval v. State*, 409 S.W.3d 259, 286 (Tex. App.—Austin 2013, no pet.) (assault complainant's disclosure of assault was improperly admitted as excited utterance because it was narrative and she had time and capacity to reflect on assault; she waited three or four months to disclose assault, was reluctant to tell, and expressed concern about her family's reaction); *Harris v. State*, 133 S.W.3d 760, 772 (Tex. App.—Texarkana 2004, pet. ref'd) (murder victim's statement to assistant DA during interview seeking a protective order against defendant was not admissible under rule even though victim appeared very upset and was crying during interview; victim had taken the initiative to seek a protective order, thus showing that she had given the matter some reflection and thought). In *Zuliani*, the court of criminal appeals explained that both the elapsed time and whether the statement was made in response to a question are factors to be considered in determining whether the statement is truly spontaneous. 97 S.W.3d at 595. "However, it is not dispositive that the statement is an answer to a question or that it was separated by a period of time from the startling event; these are simply factors to consider in determining whether the statement is admissible under the excited utterance hearsay exception." *Id.* at 596. The court held that the domestic-violence-assault victim's statements qualified as excited utterances when the evidence showed that she was scared and tired, though not "excited"; her statements were in response to questions and were made about 20 hours after the original assault, but she had an untreated injury and had not been separated from her assailant since the assault. *Id.* Numerous cases following *Zuliani* have upheld the admission of statements made in response to questioning or made a considerable time after the occurrence of the exciting event if the evidence clearly demonstrated that the declarant was still under the stress of the event. *See, e.g.*, *Wilson v. State*, 151 S.W.3d 694, 699 (Tex. App.—Fort Worth 2004, pet. ref'd) (in robbery trial, declarant's statements to police were admissible under Rule 803(2) when she made statements shortly after seeing her abandoned and wrecked car and seemed "upset, nervous, … and about to cry"); *Carter v. State*, 150 S.W.3d 230, 243 (Tex. App.—Texarkana 2004, no pet.) (assault victim's statements to police minutes after assault were admissible under rule when evidence showed that victim was "extremely upset and was still crying" as a result of attack); *Jaggers v. State*, 125 S.W.3d 661, 671 (Tex. App.—Houston [1st Dist.] 2003, pet. ref'd) (upholding witness's testimony that murder victim told witness that she thought defendant was going to kill her; record indicated that defendant had assaulted victim within 16 hours of victim's making statement and that victim "broke down" and was crying when witness asked her "What happened?" after seeing victim's injuries).

502. *E.g.*, *McCarty v. State*, 257 S.W.3d 238, 239 & n.3 (Tex. Crim. App. 2008) (child declarant's statement that she did not like being tickled by "boys and men" because defendant, her stepfather, had "pulled up [her] blouse and was tickling [her] ribs and touched [her]" was properly admitted even though startling event or condition was not the indecency or assault with which defendant was charged); *Pickron v. State*, 515 S.W.3d 462, 465-66 (Tex. App.—Houston [14th Dist.] 2017, pet. ref'd) (murder victim's statements to her sister that she was afraid to be alone with

statement.[503] Periods of the declarant's unconsciousness between the event and the statement is another factor for the courts to consider when determining whether the statement is admissible as an excited utterance.[504] The periods of unconsciousness do

---

defendant and that defendant was "trashing" her house at the time were admissible as excited utterance even though they occurred before crime); *Edmondson*, 399 S.W.3d at 613-14 (in drug-possession case, statements by defendant's roommate were admissible as excited utterance even though startling event or condition was her arrest and the search of her home; declarant was crying and talking in a high-pitched voice when she told detective that defendant was a drug dealer and described transactions); *Bondurant v. State*, 956 S.W.2d 762, 766 (Tex. App.—Fort Worth 1997, pet. ref'd) (declarant's statements about murder, made days after murder itself, were admissible under Rule 803(2) even though they were not triggered solely by murder itself; startling series of events relating to murder, including escape attempts and death threats, caused declarant's excited condition).

In *Hunt v. State*, the court addressed the admissibility of an excited utterance about a child sexual-assault victim's fear of being pregnant after watching a television news story. 904 S.W.2d 813, 815-17 (Tex. App.—Fort Worth 1995, pet. ref'd). The startling event triggering the excited utterance was a news story detailing the stabbing death of a child by the man who had raped and impregnated her. *Id.* at 816. The child testified that when she saw the news story, she began to wonder if she was pregnant because, at that time, she did not know how women became pregnant. *Id.* She fell to the floor crying and was very emotionally upset when she made the statements. *Id.* The court noted that the startling event does not need to be the crime itself. *Id.* As long as the statement relates to the startling event and is made without opportunity to reflect or fabricate, the statement may be relevant to prove some entirely different occurrence. *See id.* at 816-17. *Compare Couchman v. State*, 3 S.W.3d 155, 159-60 (Tex. App.—Fort Worth 1999, pet. ref'd) (child's statements of pain in her genital area, made while she was crying and upset, qualified under rule, even though they were made long after the alleged sexual abuse), *with Hughes v. State*, 128 S.W.3d 247, 252-55 (Tex. App.—Tyler 2003, pet. ref'd) (15-year-old child's narrative statements about past sexual abuse to officer during two-hour-long interview at police station were not unreflective, spontaneous utterances; "[w]e decline to further expand the excited utterance exception to include a summary distilled from a protracted interrogation"), *and Glover v. State*, 102 S.W.3d 754, 763-66 (Tex. App.—Texarkana 2002, pet. ref'd) (mother's probing questions to daughter about her activities the previous night were intended "to elicit details of past events of which the questioner was presumed to be already aware"; circumstances suggested "reflective consideration and ... an opportunity for conscious fabrication").

503. *See, e.g., Ricketts v. State*, 89 S.W.3d 312, 319-20 (Tex. App.—Fort Worth 2002, pet. ref'd) (testimony about murder witness's statements, made to third person while declarant was dominated by the emotion, fear, pain, and excitement of witnessing shooting, was admissible under rule despite passage of time and second visit to crime scene); *Aguilera v. State*, 75 S.W.3d 60, 67-68 (Tex. App.—San Antonio 2002, pet. ref'd) (reversible error to admit statements made by alleged child victim that defendant had sexually abused her nearly one year earlier because child was not still under the stress or excitement caused by the event); *Gay v. State*, 981 S.W.2d 864, 867 (Tex. App.—Houston [1st Dist.] 1998, pet. ref'd) (child victim who made statement to witness ten days after last alleged molestation had opportunity to reflect or deliberate about offense; thus, statement was inadmissible); *Mosley v. State*, 960 S.W.2d 200, 204 (Tex. App.—Corpus Christi 1997, no pet.) (when evidence showed an interval of several days between time child was molested and her statement relating to that event, requirements of rule were not fulfilled even though child was distressed and agitated when she made the statement); *Guerra v. State*, 942 S.W.2d 28, 32 (Tex. App.—Corpus Christi 1996, pet. ref'd) (defendant's repeated statements to pastors shortly after shooting his wife that it was an accident qualified as excited utterances because he was still in the grip of emotion from that shooting); *Snellen v. State*, 923 S.W.2d 238, 243 (Tex. App.—Texarkana 1996, pet. ref'd) (child-abuse victim was still under stress of emotion from event 12 to 13 hours later when she told CPS worker of event), *overruled on other grounds*, *Howland v. State*, 990 S.W.2d 274 (Tex. Crim. App. 1999).

504. *Apolinar*, 155 S.W.3d at 189. As the court in *Apolinar* explained:

Each case that involves a period of unconsciousness between the time of the startling event and the statement must be reviewed in light of the facts and circumstances of the case. Rather than say that unconsciousness is a substitute for continuity of the stress of the event, we conclude that the declarant's state of consciousness is a factor to consider in the analysis. Trial courts and reviewing courts should address this fact within the factors for a traditional analysis to determine whether a hearsay statement falls within the excited utterance exception.

Id.

not need to be continuous, "so long as the record supports the reasonable conclusion that the declarant did not have a meaningful opportunity to reflect."[505]

Likewise, statements made in response to questions can still be excited utterances as long as the declarant is "'still dominated by the emotions, excitement, fear, or pain of the event' or condition at the time of the statement."[506]

(3) Personal knowledge. Although there is no language in Rule 803(2) requiring that the declarant have personal knowledge of the facts contained in the statement, this requirement is implicit in the language that the declarant's excitement be caused by the startling event or condition.[507] Cases interpreting Federal Rule 803(2) have included a personal-knowledge requirement for excited utterances.[508] The declarant does not need to have participated in the event or condition; he may have been a bystander or observer.

(4) Proof. The proponent of an excited utterance has the burden of establishing the excited-utterance requirements.[509] The burden of proof is by a preponderance of the

505. *Id.* at 189-90.

506. *Zuliani*, 97 S.W.3d at 596 (quoting *McFarland v. State*, 845 S.W.2d 824, 846 (Tex. Crim. App. 1992)); *Neal v. State*, 186 S.W.3d 690, 693 (Tex. App.—Dallas 2006, no pet.); *see, e.g.*, *Salazar v. State*, 38 S.W.3d 141, 153-55 (Tex. Crim. App. 2001) (trial court did not err in admitting statement by two-year-old victim, made three months before charged murder, that defendant "did it" when neighbor asked who had caused injury to her shoulder; child was upset and in pain at time she answered question); *Tienda v. State*, 479 S.W.3d 863, 877-78 (Tex. App.—Eastland 2015, no pet.) (trial court erred in admitting statements made by complainant in interview with detective as excited utterances; answers in first part of interview were quick, direct, and calm, and answers in second part were preceded by long pauses that could indicate time to fabricate answers); *Arzaga v. State*, 86 S.W.3d 767, 775 (Tex. App.—El Paso 2002, no pet.) (domestic-assault victim's answers to police officer's questions were admissible under rule when testimony showed declarant was still dominated by fear or pain of assault; officer testified he arrived at scene only 10 to 15 minutes after assault, declarant answered questions shortly after officer arrived, and officer described victim as crying, very distraught, and stuttering as she described assault); *Tejeda v. State*, 905 S.W.2d 313, 316 (Tex. App.—San Antonio 1995, pet. ref'd) (victim's statement to officer was admissible under rule; officer testified that she was very upset when he first approached her, she volunteered that her husband had hit her, and she continued to show excitement when officer questioned her about where and how she had been hit); *Jones v. State*, 772 S.W.2d 551, 554-55 (Tex. App.—Dallas 1989, pet. ref'd) (police officer could testify about statements made in response to his specific questioning of an eyewitness to a shooting); *see also Woodard v. State*, 696 S.W.2d 622, 626 (Tex. App.—Dallas 1985, no pet.) (burned child's responses to social worker's questions soon after hospital admission were admissible under the "spontaneous exclamation" exception because the questions were neither leading nor suggestive, and circumstances showed improbability that the child was falsifying answers); 1A RAY, *supra* note 9, §914, at 154-55 (answers to questions have to be considered with other circumstances to determine spontaneity).

507. *See* TEX. R. EVID. 803(2). Rule 803(1) also has an implicit requirement of personal knowledge. Refer to note 475 *supra*.

508. *See United States v. Mitchell*, 145 F.3d 572, 576 (3d Cir. 1998) (declarant must have personally perceived event or condition about which statement is made); *Bemis v. Edwards*, 45 F.3d 1369, 1373 & n.2 (9th Cir. 1995) (witness testifying only to the fact that the declarant made a statement needs personal knowledge that the declarant made the statement but not of the events described in the statement).

509. *See Volkswagen of Am., Inc. v. Ramirez*, 159 S.W.3d 897, 908 n.5 (Tex. 2004) (proponent of hearsay evidence has the burden of showing that evidence satisfies a hearsay exception); *Martinez v. State*, 178 S.W.3d 806, 815 (Tex. Crim. App. 2005) (same); *see, e.g.*, *Rosendorf v. Blackmon*, 800 S.W.2d 377, 380 (Tex. App.—Corpus Christi 1990, orig. proceeding) (child's statements to his mother in response to her questioning him about his father's sexual abuse several weeks after the alleged events were not admissible); *Urquhart v. Antrum*, 776 S.W.2d 595, 597 (Tex. App.—Houston [14th Dist.] 1988, no writ) (statement was inadmissible when the proponent did not show that (1) the declarant's excitement "was spontaneous or in response to the accident," and (2) the statement was not made in response to questioning).

evidence.[510] The statement itself can be proof of the startling event or condition. Courts will generally look at the statement along with the declarant's appearance, behavior, and condition in determining whether the startling event or condition occurred and in evaluating the declarant's perception of it.[511]

The rule does not require that the spontaneous utterance be made by a "named" or known declarant,[512] but the lack of identity could go to whether the declarant had personal knowledge of the facts contained in the statement.[513]

An excited utterance may be admissible even if the declarant is incompetent to testify because he is extremely young or no longer remembers having made the

---

510. *Cf. Meador v. State*, 812 S.W.2d 330, 333 (Tex. Crim. App. 1991) (requiring a preponderance of the evidence under Rule 801(e)(2)(E)); *Gant v. State*, 153 S.W.3d 294, 299 (Tex. App.—Beaumont 2004, pet. ref'd) (requiring a preponderance of the evidence under Rule 801(e)(2)(B)).

511. *Ross v. State*, 154 S.W.3d 804, 809 (Tex. App.—Houston [14th Dist.] 2004, pet. ref'd). Because the circumstantial guarantee of trustworthiness under this exception is the declarant's emotional excitement, it could be argued that the statement itself is not sufficient evidence of the event or condition. Logically, some independent evidence should be required to prove that a startling event or condition occurred, so that the hearsay statement is not permitted "to lift itself by its own bootstraps" into the exception. *Travelers Ins. v. Smith*, 448 S.W.2d 541, 544 (Tex. Civ. App.—El Paso 1969, writ ref'd n.r.e.). However, such a requirement led to undesirable results in some common-law Texas workers' compensation cases, in which courts excluded utterances of deceased workers indicating that their fatal injuries or illnesses occurred during employment. *See Hartford Acc. & Indem. Co. v. Hale*, 400 S.W.2d 310, 311 (Tex. 1966) (deceased worker's statement must have been a spontaneous reaction to an exciting event to be admissible; statement itself cannot be used to prove the exciting event); *see, e.g., Truck Ins. Exch. v. Michling*, 364 S.W.2d 172, 174 (Tex. 1963) (excluding a hearsay statement that was the only evidence that the decedent suffered an injury while working); *Smith*, 448 S.W.2d at 544-45 (same). *But see Smith*, 448 S.W.2d at 546 (Preslar, J., dissenting) ("Is [a worker] more to be believed when seeking money benefits or when, as here, he is seeking to stay alive?"). These cases were criticized on the ground that the worker's injury or illness was an exciting event of which the statement was not the only evidence. *See* Frank W. Elliott, *Annual Survey of Texas Law: Evidence*, 25 Sw. L.J. 135, 141-45 (1971) [hereinafter *1971 Survey*] (evidence of the injury itself is also admissible); Frank W. Elliott, *Annual Survey of Texas Law: Evidence*, 27 Sw. L.J. 158, 160-61 (1973) [hereinafter *1973 Survey*] (Texas Supreme Court should retreat from this harsh position); Jerry L. Beane, Note, *Evidence-Hearsay-Res Gestae*, 18 BAYLOR L. REV. 658 (1966) (discussing the requirement that independent evidence of the act must be admitted). Most other jurisdictions have taken the latter view, and Texas Rule 803(2) corrects earlier Texas case law on this point. *See* FED. R. EVID. 803(2) advisory committee's note ("Whether proof of the startling event may be made by the statement itself is largely an academic question, since in most cases there is present at least circumstantial evidence that something of a startling nature must have occurred. ... Nevertheless, on occasion the only evidence may be the content of the statement itself, and rulings that it may be sufficient are described as 'increasing' ... and as the 'prevailing practice' ...."); McCORMICK'S HANDBOOK II, *supra* note 7, §297, at 705 (under generally prevailing practice, the declaration is taken as proof that an exciting event has occurred); Slough, *supra* note 496, at 255 (trend is toward decisions in which the only direct evidence of an exciting event is the declaration itself). *But see Kelt v. Kelt*, 67 S.W.3d 364, 367 (Tex. App.—Waco 2001, no pet.) ("[T]here must be independent proof of the occurrence to which the statements relate; the statements themselves cannot be used to prove the exciting event."); *Rodriguez v. State*, 802 S.W.2d 716, 722 (Tex. App.—San Antonio 1990) (although Rule 803(2) does not require independent proof when declarant's injury or shock shows that exciting event occurred, mother could not testify about child's alleged excited utterance when medical evidence did not show that sexual assault occurred, child's statements and nods refuted occurrence of offense, and mother used her own terms to describe offense that child never used), *aff'd as reformed*, 819 S.W.2d 871 (Tex. Crim. App. 1991).

512. *See, e.g., Liggens v. State*, 50 S.W.3d 657, 662 (Tex. App.—Fort Worth 2001, pet. ref'd) (although excited utterances were made by unidentified employee-declarants who had witnessed robbers' getaway, their statements were made immediately after robbery and otherwise qualified for admission under Rule 803(2); no error to admit).

513. *See* 5 WEINSTEIN & BERGER, *supra* note 475, §803.04[1], at 803-21. Refer to notes 507-508 *supra* and accompanying text.

RULE 803

statement.[514] Similarly, an excited utterance is not rendered inadmissible simply because the declarant may have been intoxicated at the time of the startling event or statement.[515]

(5) Confrontation Clause issues. Although it had formerly been the rule that the excited-utterance exception is so firmly rooted that the reliability of such statements surmounted both the hearsay bar and any Confrontation Clause objection,[516] the Supreme Court decisions in ***Crawford v. Washington***[517] and ***Davis v. Washington***[518] have dramatically changed the analysis of confrontation issues. Under ***Crawford*** and ***Davis***, "testimonial" excited utterances are inadmissible unless the declarant testifies at trial or the defendant has had a prior opportunity to cross-examine a declarant who is unavailable at trial.[519]

(6) Comparison with Rule 803(1). Rule 803(2) is used more often in litigation than Rule 803(1), the present-sense-impression exception, because most people are more likely to remark on unusual and exciting events rather than ordinary ones. The excited-utterance exception is favored because (1) it permits any statement "relating to" the startling event, whereas the present sense impression must describe or explain the event, and (2) the statement will be admissible under Rule 803(2) as long as the declarant is still under the stress of the excitement—a time frame considerably longer than the occurrence of the event itself or its immediate aftermath as required under Rule 803(1).[520] Under that language, courts have permitted statements triggered by a startling event that relate to "a *much earlier* incident."[521]

---

514. *See, e.g.,* ***Morgan v. Foretich***, 846 F.2d 941, 946-47 (4th Cir. 1988) (in civil suit by child and mother against child's father, child's excited utterances made on her return from visits with her father were admissible even though child was incompetent to testify); ***Scugoza v. State***, 949 S.W.2d 360, 362-63 (Tex. App.—San Antonio 1997, no pet.) (wife's excited utterance to officer about being beaten by her husband was admissible under rule and was sufficient evidence to prove offense, even though she testified that she no longer remembered what she told officer and that the reported assault had occurred only in her mind).

515. *See* ***Hudson v. State***, 179 S.W.3d 731, 737 (Tex. App.—Houston [14th Dist.] 2005, no pet.) ("[Defendant] does not cite, nor have we found, any authority to support [his] contention that [complainant's] intoxication would make her statement more likely a product of reason and reflection than a product of an exciting event.").

516. ***White v. Illinois***, 502 U.S. 346, 355 n.8 (1992); *see* ***Penry v. State***, 903 S.W.2d 715, 751 (Tex. Crim. App. 1995); ***Woodall v. State***, 77 S.W.3d 388, 399 (Tex. App.—Fort Worth 2002, pet. ref'd); *see, e.g.,* ***Ricketts v. State***, 89 S.W.3d 312, 324 (Tex. App.—Fort Worth 2002, pet. ref'd) (statements made by codefendant to his fiancée naming defendant as shooter were admissible over Confrontation Clause objection because excited-utterance exception is "firmly rooted" and these particular statements were made under reliable circumstances to a friend, not under custodial questioning by law-enforcement officers); *see also* ***Bernal v. State***, 13 S.W.3d 852, 853-54 (Tex. App.—Austin 2000, pet. ref'd) ("[T]he circumstances under which a statement is made may adequately substitute for the ideal testimonial conditions of oath, presence at trial, and cross-examination. ... The excited utterance exception is firmly rooted.").

517. 541 U.S. 36 (2004).

518. 547 U.S. 813 (2006).

519. Refer to the discussion of the intersection of the hearsay rule and the Confrontation Clause in criminal cases, notes 34-181 *supra* and accompanying text.

520. *See* 1A RAY, *supra* note 9, §917, at 39 (Supp. 1991); *see also* ***Kubin v. State***, 868 S.W.2d 394, 396 (Tex. App.—Houston [1st Dist.] 1993, pet. ref'd) (distinguishing Criminal Rules 803(1) and (2); "the contemporaneous requirement is much more important in the present sense impression"); ***Jones v. State***, 772 S.W.2d 551, 554-55 (Tex. App.—Dallas 1989, pet. ref'd) (statements made "while the witness is in the grip of emotion, excitement, fear, or

3. Rule 803(3): Then-existing mental, emotional, or physical condition. Rule 803(3) provides a hearsay exception for statements expressing a declarant's then-existing (1) state of mind or emotional or sensory condition[522] in issue in the case, (2) physical condition, (3) state of mind—usually motive, intent, or plan—offered as circumstantial evidence of future conduct, or (4) memory or belief relating to the validity or terms of the declarant's will.[523] In short, anything the declarant was thinking or feeling at the time of the statement may be admitted as an exception to the hearsay rule.

The hearsay dangers associated with Rule 803(3) are minimal. Statements of present thoughts and feelings carry little danger of faulty perception or memory and are usually made in situations involving little likelihood of deception. Such out-of-court statements made at the time of the thoughts and feelings often have greater truthfulness than later recollection in court.

An important limitation on the exception is that the statements must concern current, then-existing, or contemporaneous thoughts and feelings.[524] The exception does not extend to statements of past thoughts and feelings unless they involve the validity or terms of the declarant's will.[525] Thus, the statement "My tooth hurts" is admissible

---

pain, [which] relate to the exciting event ... are admissible even after an appreciable time has elapsed between the exciting event and the making of the statement"). Continued emotional or physical shock, loss of consciousness, or unabated fear may prolong the impact of the stressful event for hours or even days after the occurrence of the event, thus permitting statements made during this period to be admissible under Criminal Rule 803(2). *Cf. United States v. Napier*, 518 F.2d 316, 317-18 (9th Cir. 1975) (victim's exclamation "He killed me, he killed me" was admissible under Federal Rule 803(2) when victim had been hospitalized with serious head injuries and immediately became upset and distressed when, a week after being released from the hospital, he was shown a photograph of defendant, because statement was made under stress of seeing photograph that related to earlier assault).

521. *McCarty v. State*, 257 S.W.3d 238, 240 (Tex. Crim. App. 2008); *see* 1A RAY, *supra* note 9, §918, at 171-72 (declarations about incidents occurring before the event, which explain the cause of that event, are admissible).
For example, in *City of Dallas v. Donovan*, a personal-injury case, a witness testified that shortly after the accident, a woman drove up, became excited or upset at the scene, and "volunteered the statement that days prior to the accident she had reported to the city that the stop sign was down." 768 S.W.2d 905, 906 (Tex. App.—Dallas 1989, no writ). The city objected that the statement had no relationship to the events immediately preceding the accident, the accident itself, or the resulting injuries; the court held, however, that "excited utterances are not confined to statements describing or explaining the startling event itself." *Id.* at 906-07; *see, e.g.*, *King v. State*, 953 S.W.2d 266, 269 (Tex. Crim. App. 1997) (discovery that murder victim was dead prompted declarant's statement about who might have committed the murder; trial court did not abuse its discretion in admitting statement as excited utterance); *Wilkerson v. State*, 933 S.W.2d 276, 278-79 (Tex. App.—Houston [1st Dist.] 1996, pet. ref'd) (in drug prosecution, codefendant's statement "flush the dope, flush the dope" was admissible as excited utterance; statement did not describe the startling event—the arrest team's approach and entering the house—but was related to that event). Nor did it matter that the incident being referred to (the reporting of the stop sign being down) was remote in time from the exciting event or condition (the accident). *See Donovan*, 768 S.W.2d at 908 ("We conclude that the only requirement concerning time with respect to admission of excited utterances is the necessity that the statement be made while in a state of excitement caused by the startling event.").

522. Emotional or sensory condition refers to issues such as mental feeling or pain. TEX. R. EVID. 803(3).

523. *Id.*

524. *E.g.*, *Linney v. State*, 401 S.W.3d 764, 779 (Tex. App.—Houston [14th Dist.] 2013, pet. ref'd) (declarant's statement that she was uncomfortable about contact with defendant was not admissible under Rule 803(3) because she did not make the statement while she was feeling uncomfortable).

525. *See* 1A RAY, *supra* note 9, §843, at 89. Refer to notes 566-569 *infra* and accompanying text. Such statements might, however, qualify for admission under Rule 803(4) if they are made for medical diagnosis or treatment. Refer to notes 570-584 *infra* and accompanying text.

RULE 803

while the statement "Yesterday, my tooth hurt" is not. Similarly, the exception does not extend to statements about why the declarant held the particular state of mind or what he believes induced that state of mind.[526]

(1) State of mind or emotional or sensory condition in issue in the case. Out-of-court statements about a declarant's state of mind or emotional or sensory condition are admissible under the rule only if the declarant's state of mind or emotional or sensory condition is in issue in the case.[527] The rationale and corresponding limitations for this category of statements are parallel to those for statements of present physical condition.[528] Statements about a declarant's state of mind or emotional or sensory condition have been offered to prove intent[529] (including fraudulent[530] or domiciliary[531] intent), motive,[532] malice,[533] presence or absence of affection,[534] reliance,[535] mental suffering,[536] and bias or prejudice on the part of a witness.[537]

---

526. *Delapaz v. State*, 228 S.W.3d 183, 209 (Tex. App.—Dallas 2007, pet. ref'd).

527. *See, e.g.*, *Judd v. State*, 923 S.W.2d 135, 139 (Tex. App.—Fort Worth 1996, pet. ref'd) (investigator's state of mind was "wholly immaterial to any issue in the case"; thus, sewer-line operator's statement to him was inadmissible hearsay); *cf. United States v. Makhlouta*, 790 F.2d 1400, 1402 (9th Cir. 1986) (FBI agent's testimony relating to what another had told him tended to prove his state of mind at a relevant time, but agent's state of mind was not relevant to defendant's guilt or defensive issue of entrapment).

528. *See* 1A RAY, *supra* note 9, §861, at 95. Refer to notes 544-547 *infra* and accompanying text.

529. *See, e.g.*, *Sec. Ins. v. Nasser*, 755 S.W.2d 186, 193-94 (Tex. App.—Houston [14th Dist.] 1988, no writ) (when restaurant manager was assaulted by customer's boyfriend, customer could testify to what her boyfriend had told her about his hallucinations because those statements were relevant to the issue of his mental condition and ability to form a rational intent).

530. *See* 1A RAY, *supra* note 9, §869, at 108-09.

531. *See id.* §868, at 104.

532. *See, e.g.*, *Lopez v. State*, 846 S.W.2d 90, 94 (Tex. App.—Corpus Christi 1992, pet. ref'd) (in barratry prosecution, witness could testify that attorney told her he was interested only in the money he could get from the case, not in her daughter's legal claim, because attorney's statement showed his motive for obtaining daughter as a client; statement of his then-existing state of mind was admissible under Criminal Rule 803(3)).

533. *See* 1A RAY, *supra* note 9, §866, at 98. In *Whitmire v. State*, the murder victim's ex-wife was permitted to testify that the victim had told her "that he had gotten himself into a predicament that he couldn't get out of." 789 S.W.2d 366, 371 (Tex. App.—Beaumont 1990, pet. ref'd). The State offered this statement to rebut the defense's contention that the victim had threatened to kill the defendant if she tried to leave him. *Id.* The court held that the statement was "clearly offered not to prove that the victim was in some sort of predicament from which he could not escape, [but] to show the victim's state of mind that *he*, not the appellant, was the trapped partner in the marriage," and was therefore admissible. *Id.*

534. *See* 1A RAY, *supra* note 9, §865, at 97.

535. *See, e.g.*, *Payne v. Edmonson*, 712 S.W.2d 793, 797 (Tex. App.—Houston [1st Dist.] 1986, writ ref'd n.r.e.) (admitting evidence that the owner of an allegedly dominant estate and the owner of servient estate engaged in lease negotiations in order to show dominant-estate owner's reliance on statements made by servient-estate owner).

536. *See* 1A RAY, *supra* note 9, §867, at 103; *see, e.g.*, *Chance v. Chance*, 911 S.W.2d 40, 55 (Tex. App.—Beaumont 1995, writ denied) (in divorce and child-custody suit, statements by child that "Daddy hits Matthew," "Daddy put him in the fire," and "Daddy puts his tee-tee in my mouth" were held admissible to show mental and emotional condition of the two- or three-year-old child under Rule 803(3)). The holding in this case seems dubious because the statements were clearly a narrative of past acts by the father, not a direct statement of the child's state of mind.

537. *See, e.g.*, *Lape v. State*, 893 S.W.2d 949, 960 (Tex. App.—Houston [14th Dist.] 1994, pet. ref'd) (reversible error to exclude defendant's offered testimony about threats made by the child complainant's mother "to do whatever she had to do in order to regain custody of" child; statements showed that witness had a motive to lie about defendant and were admissible under Criminal Rule 803(3)).

On the other hand, statements of belief about another person's state of mind or emotional or sensory condition do not satisfy the exception. For example, a murder victim's written statement that "I believe X may be contemplating murdering me for my $100,000 insurance policy," is not a statement of the declarant's state of mind.[538] It is a statement of his belief and concerns about another person's purported state of mind. If the statement, on its face, expresses or exemplifies the declarant's state of mind or emotional or sensory condition—for example, fear, hate, love, pain—then it is the type of statement contemplated by the rule.[539] If, however, the declarant's state of mind or emotional or sensory condition can only be inferred from the statement—he would not have said this unless he was afraid, in pain, or in love—then it is not the type of statement contemplated by the rule.[540]

---

538. ***Barnum v. State***, 7 S.W.3d 782, 789-90 (Tex. App.—Amarillo 1999, pet. ref'd); *see, e.g.*, ***Rogers v. State***, 183 S.W.3d 853, 857-60 (Tex. App.—Tyler 2005, no pet.) (murder victim's unsigned, unnotarized draft affidavits found in her office drawer after her death were statements of past domestic-violence events and beliefs, inadmissible under Rule 803(3)); ***Glover v. State***, 102 S.W.3d 754, 762 (Tex. App.—Texarkana 2002, pet. ref'd) (error to admit child's statement to mother that she had sex with defendant the night before; "[e]vidence that seeks to establish a purported fact remembered and related in the utterance is specifically excluded from the state of mind exception"); ***Power v. Kelley***, 70 S.W.3d 137, 140-41 (Tex. App.—San Antonio 2001, pet. denied) (affiant's statement that "I heard [deceased] say in person prior to her death that, had she known of the existence of the lung cancer that ultimately took her life ... she would not have had those procedures performed" was not admissible under Rule 803(3) because it was a "statement relating to a past external fact," not one of present state of mind); ***Easley v. State***, 986 S.W.2d 264, 268-69 (Tex. App.—San Antonio 1998, no pet.) (evidence that murder victim told witness that her sister had threatened to have victim's children removed from home if victim did not end her relationship with defendant was not admissible under Rule 803(3) because it did not relate to victim's state of mind but rather her understanding of her sister's disapproval).

539. *See* Tex. R. Evid. 803(3); *see, e.g.*, ***Martinez v. State***, 17 S.W.3d 677, 688-89 (Tex. Crim. App. 2000) (in capital-murder case, upholding admission of victim-declarant's statement that she was afraid of man with same first name as appellant); ***Garcia v. State***, 246 S.W.3d 121, 132 (Tex. App.—San Antonio 2007, pet. ref'd) (murder victim's statements to her coworkers and close friends about being afraid of defendant were admissible as evidence of her then-existing state of mind); ***Martinez v. State***, 186 S.W.3d 59, 67 (Tex. App.—Houston [1st Dist.] 2005, pet. ref'd) (witness's testimony about victim's statement to him on night of her murder that she wanted to leave defendant and that she sounded scared as defendant approached was admissible as evidence of her then-existing state of mind); ***Cardenas v. State***, 115 S.W.3d 54, 62-63 (Tex. App.—San Antonio 2003, no pet.) (murder victim's statements to neighbor that defendant was in her apartment and made her "uncomfortable" were admissible in murder trial; first statement was admissible as present sense impression, second statement was admissible as statement of then-existing emotional state); ***Shugart v. State***, 32 S.W.3d 355, 362-63 (Tex. App.—Waco 2000, pet. ref'd) (testimony by witness that defendant had written him stating that he, defendant, was afraid of victim was admissible under Rule 803(3) as present state of mind, but harmless error to exclude); ***Williams v. State***, 798 S.W.2d 368, 371 (Tex. App.—Beaumont 1990, no pet.) (testimony describing declarant's disturbed emotional state was admissible under rule because declarant explicitly expressed her fear of defendant when she said defendant was going to kill her and her children).

One court of appeals has held that sexual-abuse counselors may testify during the punishment phase that the child victims were emotionally disturbed by the crimes committed against them. *See, e.g.*, ***Salazar v. State***, 127 S.W.3d 355, 363 (Tex. App.—Houston [14th Dist.] 2004, pet. ref'd) (upholding admission of one counselor's testimony that victim stated "that she couldn't believe the incident happened and that she was afraid, angry, and sad" and another counselor's testimony that a different victim "stated that she was 'very, very frightened,' that she blamed herself, and that she was angry, sad, scared, and felt helpless and alone"). This seems to be an unwarranted extension of the hearsay exception to an area where the declarant's then-existing emotional state is not actually in issue.

540. *See, e.g.*, ***Barnes v. State***, 56 S.W.3d 221, 231-32 (Tex. App.—Fort Worth 2001, pet. ref'd) (witness's statement to police officer that he "wanted to help with everything, but he felt that his life would be in danger if he did,"

RULE 803

Statements recalling the declarant's previous state of mind or emotional or sensory condition are not admissible under this exception.[541] However, the declarant's statement of his present state of mind or emotional or sensory condition may be admissible even if it was not made exactly at the time in issue. Because mental states normally continue for some period, as long as the evidence meets the relevance test, it will be admissible.[542]

Frequently, the declarant's state of mind or emotional or sensory condition is not initially relevant to the litigation but may be placed in issue by the opposing party. If so, the declarant's statements of present state of mind or emotional or sensory condition will then become relevant. For example, the victim's state of mind is not at issue in an assault or murder prosecution. If, however, the defendant's theory is that the victim was the first aggressor, then any statements by the victim demonstrating either a bellicose and aggressive state of mind (offered by the defense) or, conversely, a peaceful, frightened, or timid state of mind (offered by the State) are admissible.[543]

---

was not admissible under Rule 803(3) because it was "one of belief offered to prove the truth of the matter asserted: that if he helped the detective's investigation, his life would be in danger").

541. *See, e.g.*, **Couchman v. State**, 3 S.W.3d 155, 158 (Tex. App.—Fort Worth 1999, pet. ref'd) (child victim's statement to witness that defendant "put his finger inside her genitals and hurt her" was inadmissible statement of memory offered to prove the fact remembered); **Minn. Mining & Mfg. Co. v. Nishika, Ltd.**, 885 S.W.2d 603, 631 (Tex. App.—Beaumont 1994) (complaint letters about film-processing delays were statements of memory or belief offered to prove fact remembered or believed and thus were not admissible under Civil Rule 803(3)), *rev'd on other grounds*, 953 S.W.2d 733 (Tex. 1997); *cf.* **United States v. Rodriguez-Pando**, 841 F.2d 1014, 1019 (10th Cir. 1988) (trial court properly excluded defendant's recorded statement made on the day he was arrested for possession of cocaine with intent to distribute; defendant offered statement to prove he was coerced into carrying the cocaine, but Federal Rule 803(3) did not apply because his post-arrest statement was one of memory or belief and his post-arrest state of mind was not equivalent to his state of mind at moment of arrest).

542. *See* 7 GRAHAM, *supra* note 491, §803:3, at 85-90; 4 WEINSTEIN & BERGER, *supra* note 209, ¶803(3)[03], at 803-125; *see, e.g.*, **Thompson v. Mayes**, 707 S.W.2d 951, 957 (Tex. App.—Eastland 1986, writ ref'd n.r.e.) (in will contest in which son was accused of intentionally causing his father's death two years before his own suicide, trial court properly refused to admit son's suicide tapes under Rule 803(3) because his state of mind when he recorded the tapes was not relevant); *see also* **Fain v. State**, 986 S.W.2d 666, 679-80 (Tex. App.—Austin 1998, pet. ref'd) (murder victim's statement to witness that she was frustrated with relationship with defendant but intended to continue relationship with him was admissible under Rule 803(3) to show victim's state of mind two weeks before her disappearance).

543. *See, e.g.*, **Anderson v. State**, 15 S.W.3d 177, 184-85 (Tex. App.—Texarkana 2000, no pet.) (victim's statements that she was afraid of defendant were admissible to prove her present state of mind and offered to show that defendant committed burglary and did not enter home with victim's consent); **Wilks v. State**, 983 S.W.2d 863, 865-66 (Tex. App.—Corpus Christi 1998, no pet.) (murder victim's statement that defendant would have to kill her before she signed change-of-beneficiary form was offered to prove her state of mind, not defendant's future conduct); **Williams v. State**, 927 S.W.2d 752, 764 (Tex. App.—El Paso 1996, pet. ref'd) (victim's statements about her fears of what defendant would do to her if witness confronted defendant about coming to victim's house were admissible under Criminal Rule 803(3) to rebut defense claim that victim was the aggressor and physically attacked defendant); **McDonald v. State**, 911 S.W.2d 798, 806 (Tex. App.—San Antonio 1995, pet. dism'd) (when defendant, on trial for murdering his wife, claimed self-defense, State was entitled to offer victim's statements to her daughter that she had changed the locks at her home to protect herself from defendant; victim's fear of defendant was a "mental feeling" admissible under Criminal Rule 803(3)); **Pena v. State**, 864 S.W.2d 147, 149-50 (Tex. App.—Waco 1993, no pet.) (testimony that murder victim said she wanted to leave defendant but felt economically trapped was offered to show her state of mind and was not offered to prove the truth of the victim's statement); **Whitmire v. State**, 789 S.W.2d 366, 371 (Tex. App.—Beaumont 1990, pet. ref'd) (murder victim's statement that he had "gotten himself into a predicament that he couldn't get out of" was properly admitted under state-of-mind hearsay exception; statement was offered not to prove the truth of the matter asserted, but to show victim's state of mind that he, and not defendant,

---

(2) Physical condition. Statements indicating a declarant's present physical condition are admissible under this rule, whether made to a physician[544] or to a layperson.[545] The rule does not permit the admission of statements offered to prove the cause of a physical ailment or condition.[546] If the declarant tells his wife, "My tooth hurts because Joe kicked me in the mouth," only the first phrase is admissible. Statements made to obtain a medical diagnosis or treatment may also be admissible under the broader provisions of Rule 803(4).[547]

(3) State of mind—motive, intent, or plan. A person's state of mind can be evidence of that person's future conduct. For example, if a person says that he is going to New

---

was "the trapped partner" in their marriage). *But see* **Chambers v. State**, 905 S.W.2d 328, 330 (Tex. App.—Fort Worth 1995, no pet.) (defendant's out-of-court statement to police that he believed victim may have had a weapon at the time of the assault, offered to prove that defendant was acting in self-defense, was not admissible under Criminal Rule 803(3) because it was a statement of memory or belief to prove the fact remembered or believed); **Navarro v. State**, 863 S.W.2d 191, 197-98 (Tex. App.—Austin 1993) (trial court's admission of deceased's statements that defendant had "put a gun to her head and threatened to kill her" was harmless error; these were statements of memory to prove the fact remembered, thus not admissible under Criminal Rule 803(3)), *pet. ref'd*, 891 S.W.2d 648 (Tex. Crim. App. 1994).

Although the courts are correct in holding that an assault or murder victim's state of mind may be relevant when the defendant claims self-defense, admissible out-of-court statements under Rule 803(3) are confined to those that, on their face, show the declarant's present state of mind (e.g., "I am so frightened of X," or "I fear that X may kill me"). Statements relating the defendant's earlier aggressive acts (e.g., "I am changing the locks because X beat me," or "X said that if I ever burned dinner again, he would kill me") might circumstantially demonstrate the speaker's fearful state of mind, but those are statements of past facts, memory, or belief, and are not admissible under the rule.

In **Vann v. State**, the Corpus Christi Court of Appeals discussed this distinction. 853 S.W.2d 243, 249-50 (Tex. App.—Corpus Christi 1993, pet. ref'd). In this case, the State appropriately elicited testimony from the witness that the deceased was not happy about his current marriage and wanted to find a way out. *Id.* at 250. However, the prosecution went on to inquire about the victim's specific statements explaining why he was unhappy. The witness testified that the victim said: "I wouldn't be surprised if [defendant, victim's wife] was waiting for me at home with a gun and shot me." *Id.* at 249. This was error because "the State attempted to go behind the victim's mental condition to uncover its cause. In other words, the State used the victim's mental condition to produce evidence of events …." *Id.* at 250. The court held that this is not permitted under Criminal Rule 803(3) and constituted reversible error. *Id.*; *see also* **Dorsey v. State**, 24 S.W.3d 921, 928 (Tex. App.—Beaumont 2000, no pet.) (witness's testimony that murder victim said she was thinking of leaving defendant, her husband, and wanted the name of a divorce attorney was admissible under Rule 803(3) because it showed her future intent to leave defendant, but testimony recounting victim's statement that if anything strange happened to her, like a car crash, it meant that defendant had killed her was a statement of belief and was not admissible under rule). All such statements of present mental state offered to show a future intention to act must be entirely forward-looking. Explanations of why the declarant intends to perform the future act are likely to be based on past events and the declarant's memory or belief about those past events. In the retrial of Mr. Dorsey, the admission of the murder victim's present-state-of-mind statements was again upheld. **Dorsey v. State**, 117 S.W.3d 332, 341 (Tex. App.—Beaumont 2003, pet. ref'd).

544. *See* **Miller Mut. Fire Ins. v. Ochoa**, 432 S.W.2d 118, 122 (Tex. Civ. App.—Corpus Christi 1968, writ ref'd n.r.e.) (admitting over hearsay objections psychiatrist's testimony about defendant's disabling psychiatric condition).

545. *See* **Cas. Ins. v. Salinas**, 160 Tex. 445, 456, 333 S.W.2d 109, 117 (1960) (statements by plaintiff indicating bodily condition do not need to be made to physician to be admissible); *see, e.g.*, **Pittsburgh Corning Corp. v. Walters**, 1 S.W.3d 759, 771-72 (Tex. App.—Corpus Christi 1999, pet. denied) (videotape of hospitalized cancer plaintiff four days before his death was admissible under state-of-mind exception in products-liability suit; declarant explained pain he was enduring, present difficulties he was having, and sensations he was feeling at the time of recording). Texas common law also made no distinction between statements made to a physician and those made to a layperson. *See* 1A RAY, *supra* note 9, §832, at 65-66.

546. 4 LOUISELL & MUELLER, *supra* note 250, §440, at 523.

547. Refer to notes 570-584 *infra* and accompanying text.

RULE 803

York tomorrow, the statement is circumstantial evidence that he traveled to New York the next day. The statement is one of future intent and is thus admissible under Rule 803(3).

The leading case on offering state-of-mind evidence as circumstantial evidence of future conduct is ***Mutual Life Insurance Co. v. Hillmon***.[548] The *Hillmon* doctrine—admitting statements of intent, plan, motive, or design to prove the performance of the act intended—has been widely accepted by courts, including those of Texas.[549] It was "left undisturbed"[550] by the drafters of the Federal Rules of Evidence, and the Texas drafters agreed.

The *Hillmon* doctrine has been limited by both case law and the Rules to statements indicating the declarant's future conduct.[551] Statements of "memory or belief to prove the fact remembered or believed"—except in will cases—are not admissible under the doctrine.[552] This results in the anomalous outcome that the statement "I am going to New York tomorrow" is admissible to show that the declarant went to New York the next day, but the statement "I went to New York yesterday" is not admissible to show that he went to New York the day before. Although the distinction between the two situations may appear to lack a logical basis,[553] it persists because, as Justice Cardozo said

---

548. 145 U.S. 285 (1892).

549. *See, e.g.*, ***Davis v. Argonaut Sw. Ins.***, 464 S.W.2d 102, 103-04 (Tex. 1971) (admitting evidence to show deceased's state of mind about his plans to make a weekend trip for business rather than personal reasons); ***Liberty Mut. Ins. v. Nelson***, 142 Tex. 370, 375, 178 S.W.2d 514, 515-17 (1944) (admitting testimony that the deceased, before making an automobile trip, stated that he was making the trip to pick up material for work); ***Lowe v. State***, 163 Tex. Crim. 578, 579-82, 294 S.W.2d 394, 396-98 (1956) (admitting evidence of defendant's threats made one year before committing burglary); *see also* 1A RAY, *supra* note 9, §870, 110-13 (Texas courts recognize an exception for a declaration of intent, plan, or design to prove it was enacted). The rationale of the *Hillmon* doctrine has been a favorite subject of debate among legal writers. *See, e.g.*, Edward W. Hinton, *States of Mind and the Hearsay Rule*, 1 U. CHI. L. REV. 394 (1934); Robert M. Hutchins & Donald Slesinger, *Some Observations on the Law of Evidence—State of Mind to Prove an Act*, 38 YALE L.J. 283 (1929); John M. Maguire, *The Hillmon Case—Thirty-Three Years After*, 38 HARV. L. REV. 709 (1925); James W. Payne, Jr., *The Hillmon Case—An Old Problem Revisited*, 41 VA. L. REV. 1011 (1955); Eustace Seligman, *An Exception to the Hearsay Rule*, 26 HARV. L. REV. 146, 155-60 (1912).

550. FED. R. EVID. 803(3) advisory committee's note.

551. *See, e.g.*, ***Blount v. Bordens, Inc.***, 892 S.W.2d 932, 937-39 (Tex. App.—Houston [1st Dist.] 1994) (declarant's statement to his father that he would make insurance payment on his car as soon as he returned from trip was admissible under the rule as showing son's then-existing intent to perform an act in the future; noting lack of precedent and discussing numerous out-of-state cases), *rev'd on other grounds*, 910 S.W.2d 931 (Tex. 1995).

552. When testimony about "state of mind" and "statements of belief" are intertwined, the proponent or court must disentangle the two and admit only the former. For example, in ***Saldivar v. State***, the murder victim told a witness, shortly before her death, that "[I'm] going to fire Yolanda [Saldivar] because [I think] she [is] embezzling from [my] company." 980 S.W.2d 475, 494 (Tex. App.—Houston [14th Dist.] 1998, pet. ref'd). The first clause, "I'm going to fire Yolanda," was admissible to show the victim's state of mind and her intent to perform that act, an act which was a possible motive for the defendant to commit the murder. *Id.* at 495. The second clause, "because I think she is embezzling from my company," was an inadmissible statement of belief. Although the second clause explained why the declarant had a particular state of mind and intended to perform a future act, it denoted the declarant's belief about the past and was explicitly barred by Rule 803(3). *Id.* The proponent should have offered only the first clause, not the second.

553. *See* 7 GRAHAM, *supra* note 491, §803:3, at 97; Payne, *supra* note 549, at 1011-18; Seligman, *supra* note 549, at 155-60. The distinctions become even more illogical when the declarant's statement refers to future action involving the declarant and another person. For example, the statement "I am going to New York tomorrow with John"

in the leading case marking this limitation, "[t]here would be an end, or nearly that, to the rule against hearsay if the distinction were ignored."[554]

The *Hillmon* case itself strongly suggests that such statements can be used to indicate joint conduct of the declarant and another person. In *Hillmon*, the Supreme Court characterized the declarant's letters "as evidence that … he had the intention of going, and of going with Hillmon, which made it more probable both that he did go and that he went with Hillmon."[555] The *Hillmon* opinion did not explore the soundness of using state-of-mind evidence in this manner, but some later opinions have been more penetrating. For example, *United States v. Pheaster*[556] presented a situation very similar to that of *Hillmon*. The Ninth Circuit ruled in favor of admissibility because "the authority in favor of such an application is impressive, beginning with the seminal *Hillmon* decision itself."[557] The *Pheaster* court acknowledged, however, that serious objections have been raised against the use of statements of intention in joint-conduct cases.[558]

Whether state-of-mind hearsay may properly be used to prove joint conduct under the Federal Rules of Evidence is not altogether clear. The Report of the House Committee on the Judiciary stated that "the Committee intends that … Rule [803(3)] be construed to limit the doctrine of [*Hillmon*] so as to render statements of intent by a declarant admissible only to prove his future conduct, not the future conduct of another

---

can be used as circumstantial evidence that the declarant went to New York the next day. But because the exception does not cover statements about another person's state of mind, the statement cannot be used as circumstantial evidence that John went to New York.

554. *Shepard v. United States*, 290 U.S. 96, 106 (1933); *see also Gibbs v. State*, 819 S.W.2d 821, 836-37 (Tex. Crim. App. 1991) (defendant's statement to witness after his arrest that "he was going to stop all questioning and they were absolutely going to charge him and get a lawyer or he was going home" was a statement of memory or belief, not a forward-looking statement of defendant's present state of mind).

555. *Mut. Life Ins. v. Hillmon*, 145 U.S. 285, 295-96 (1892).

556. 544 F.2d 353, 376-77 (9th Cir. 1976).

557. *Id.* at 377.

558. *See id.* at 376-77. The Ninth Circuit explained:

When hearsay evidence concerns the declarant's statement of his intention to do something with another person, the *Hillmon* doctrine requires that the trier of fact infer from the state of mind of the declarant the probability of a particular act not only by the declarant, but also by the other person. Several objections can be raised against a doctrine that would allow such an inference to be made. One such objection is based on the unreliability of the inference but is not, in our view, compelling. A much more significant and troubling objection is based on the inconsistency of such an inference with the state of mind exception. This problem is more easily perceived when one divides what is really a compound statement into its component parts. In the instant case, the statement by Larry Adell, "I am going to meet Angelo in the parking lot to get a pound of grass," is really two statements. The first is the obvious statement of Larry's intention. The second is an implicit statement of Angelo's intention. Surely, if the meeting is to take place in a location which Angelo does not habitually frequent, one must assume that Angelo intended to meet Larry there if one is to make the inference that Angelo was in the parking lot and the meeting occurred. The important point is that the second, implicit statement has nothing to do with Larry's state of mind. For example, if Larry's friends had testified that Larry had said, "Angelo is going to be in the parking lot of Sambo's North tonight with a pound of grass," no state of mind exception or any other exception to the hearsay rule would be available. Yet, this is in effect at least half of what the testimony did attribute to Larry.

Id.

RULE 803

person."[559] Neither the Senate Report[560] nor the Conference Report,[561] however, contains any mention of the matter, and the Federal Advisory Committee's note says only that the ***Hillmon*** rule "is of course, left undisturbed."[562] The federal cases since the enactment of the Rules have not definitively settled the question.[563] In Texas, there is common-law precedent for using state-of-mind hearsay to prove joint conduct,[564] and Rule 803(3) has been interpreted to permit that practice[565] despite the theoretical problems involved.

(4) Statements of a testator indicating his state of mind, offered on certain issues in will cases. Rule 803(3) excludes "a statement of memory or belief to prove the fact remembered or believed unless it relates to the validity or terms of the declarant's will."[566] In other words, statements of backward-looking memories and beliefs are hearsay and do not fit the exception unless they help explain the declarant's will.[567] It is important to note, however, that this special treatment applies only to a testator's statement that "relates to the validity or terms" of his will. It does not extend, for example, to a statement about the conduct of others that influenced the terms of the will.[568]

---

559. H.R. REP. No. 93-650, *supra* note 29, at 13-14, *reprinted in* 1974 U.S.C.C.A.N. at 7087.

560. S. REP. No. 93-1277, *supra* note 30, *reprinted in* 1974 U.S.C.C.A.N. at 7051-75.

561. H.R. CONF. REP. No. 93-1597, *supra* note 31, *reprinted in* 1974 U.S.C.C.A.N. at 7098-7107.

562. FED. R. EVID. 803(3) advisory committee's note.

563. *See **United States v. Sperling**,* 726 F.2d 69, 73-74 (2d Cir. 1984) (declining to join the debate on whether, under Federal Rule 803(3), the ***Hillmon*** doctrine can be extended to admit testimony to show the state of mind of the nondeclarant); ***United States v. Cicale**,* 691 F.2d 95, 104 (2d Cir. 1982) (refusing to discuss the merit and vitality of the ***Hillmon*** doctrine because defendant's participation was proved by independent evidence); *see also* 7 GRAHAM, *supra* note 491, §803:3, at 101 ("Courts faced with deciding whether a statement of intent is admissible as evidence of actions of another under the Federal Rules of Evidence have opted in favor of admissibility."); 4 WEINSTEIN & BERGER, *supra* note 209, ¶803(3)[04], at 803-126 (federal courts' "uneasiness in admitting statements of intent to prove a subsequent act is attributable in part to doubts about the existence of the requisite probative relationship"). *But see **United States v. Houlihan**,* 871 F. Supp. 1495, 1500 (D. Mass. 1994) ("[Federal] Rule 803(3) codifies ***Hillmon*** as written and does not disturb its conclusion or its reasoning.").

564. *See, e.g., **Parker v. State**,* 91 Tex. Crim. 68, 76, 238 S.W. 943, 947-48 (1921) (admitting hearsay to prove defendant's state of mind at time of homicide); ***Porter v. State**,* 86 Tex. Crim. 23, 47, 215 S.W. 201, 212-13 (1919) (op. on reh'g) (admitting hearsay on suspected murderer's state of mind).

565. *See **Green v. State**,* 839 S.W.2d 935, 942 (Tex. App.—Waco 1992, pet. ref'd) ("Texas precedent allows state-of-mind declarations to be admitted to prove the joint conduct of the declarant and another"; Rule 803(3) "should, therefore, be interpreted as permitting this practice"); *see, e.g., **Norton v. State**,* 771 S.W.2d 160, 165-66 (Tex. App.—Texarkana 1989, pet. ref'd) (murder victim's statement to his wife that he intended to go to defendant's shop was admitted for the limited purpose of showing that he intended to go to the shop to help defendant, but admission of wife's testimony that victim told her that he was going to the shop because defendant had called and asked him to come was overturned because that testimony "clearly states a fact remembered which is specifically excluded from the exception").

566. TEX. R. EVID. 803(3).

567. The peculiar feature of this category of state-of-mind statements, both at common law and under Rule 803(3), is that even statements of memory or belief—prohibited by all the other categories—are admissible. *See* McCORMICK'S HANDBOOK II, *supra* note 7, §296, at 702; 1A RAY, *supra* note 9, §§891-897, at 124-43.

568. In all these respects, the rule is consistent with Texas common law. *See, e.g., **Compton v. Dannenbauer**,* 120 Tex. 14, 18-21, 35 S.W.2d 682, 683-85 (1931) (declarations to show revocation were admissible); ***Scott v. Townsend**,* 106 Tex. 322, 332-33, 166 S.W. 1138, 1143 (1914) (declarations to show acts of undue influence were inadmissible); ***Self v. Thornton**,* 343 S.W.2d 485, 488 (Tex. Civ. App.—Texarkana 1960, writ ref'd n.r.e.) (same); ***Edwards v. Wil-***

Backward-looking statements of memory and belief about a declarant's will are permitted under the rule because the testator is deceased and cannot testify at trial about his frame of mind—an important issue in the case.[569] Thus, statements made both before and after making a will are the best, and frequently the only, available evidence of the testator's state of mind when the will was made.

4. Rule 803(4): Statements for medical diagnosis or treatment. A statement is admissible under Rule 803(4) if it (1) was "made for—and is reasonably pertinent to—medical diagnosis or treatment"[570] and (2) "describes medical history; past or present symptoms or sensations; their inception; or their general cause."[571]

The rationale behind this exception is that patients seeking medical help generally do not lie or exaggerate about their physical condition.[572] Because proper medical treatment depends on a reliable diagnosis, patients have a strong motivation to be truthful.

---

liams, 291 S.W.2d 783, 787 (Tex. Civ. App.—Eastland 1956, no writ) (same); *Miller v. Miller*, 285 S.W.2d 373, 376 (Tex. Civ. App.—Eastland 1955, no writ) (declarations to show identification or terms were admissible).

569. McCORMICK'S HANDBOOK II, *supra* note 7, §296, at 702 (in will cases, there is special need for the use of the testator's hearsay declarations to show his previous acts).

570. TEX. R. EVID. 803(4)(A).

571. TEX. R. EVID. 803(4)(B); *see Guzman v. State*, 253 S.W.3d 306, 308 (Tex. App.—Waco 2008, no pet.). This hearsay exception significantly changed Texas common law. Except for statements of present symptoms, Texas courts had never recognized an actual hearsay exception for statements for the purpose of medical diagnosis or treatment. Such statements were admissible in Texas only to show the basis for a physician's opinion, not for their truth. *See Travelers Ins. v. Smith*, 448 S.W.2d 541, 543-44 (Tex. Civ. App.—El Paso 1969, writ ref'd n.r.e.); Roy R. Ray, *Restrictions on Doctors' Testimony in Personal Injury Cases*, 14 Sw. L.J. 133, 146-48 (1960); *see, e.g.*, *Slaughter v. Abilene State Sch.*, 561 S.W.2d 789, 790-91 (Tex. 1977) (doctor saw patient once and prescribed no treatment; doctor could testify to his opinion on patient's condition); *Walker v. Great Atl. & Pac. Tea Co.*, 131 Tex. 57, 62, 112 S.W.2d 170, 172 (1938) (in food-poisoning case, doctor could testify to what plaintiff told him he and others ate for dinner; testimony was basis for doctor's opinion, not independent evidence of exposure). Before the Federal Rules, however, the great majority of other jurisdictions admitted statements in this category for their truth if they were made to a physician consulted for treatment. Such statements were not admissible if they were made to a physician consulted only to testify on the declarant's behalf. *See* McCORMICK'S HANDBOOK II, *supra* note 7, §§292-293, at 690-94. Most courts nonetheless permitted a nontreating physician to recite relevant statements made to him by the patient, not for their truth, but to show the basis for the physician's opinion. *See Slaughter*, 561 S.W.2d at 790-91; McCORMICK'S HANDBOOK II, *supra* note 7, §§292-293, at 690-94.

572. Of course, if a specific situation or statement does not fit the exception's rationale, a trial court may exclude the evidence if it lacks indicia of reliability. *See, e.g.*, *Sneed v. State*, 955 S.W.2d 451, 454 (Tex. App.—Houston [14th Dist.] 1997, pet. ref'd) (DWI defendant's post-arrest medical records containing his statements that he previously suffered a head injury and was presently on medication were properly excluded even though, on their face, they met the requirements of the rule; reliability of records significantly decreased because they contained self-serving statements and sufficient time had elapsed for defendant to reflect and fabricate an explanation).

One Texas court has expressed concern that the rationale behind the exception "seemingly breaks down when the patient is a very young child because younger children may not be able to understand the necessity for making truthful statements for the purposes of medical diagnosis or treatment." *Zinger v. State*, 899 S.W.2d 423, 431 (Tex. App.—Austin 1995), *rev'd on other grounds*, 932 S.W.2d 511 (Tex. Crim. App. 1996). The rule, however, is based on a recognition that patients generally have no motive to fabricate or falsify statements to their doctors. Thus, the opponent must show that the specific statement does not bear the general indicia of reliability. *See Zinger*, 899 S.W.2d at 429. The proponent of the evidence does not need to prove, as a preliminary matter, that the particular patient did, in fact, recognize the need to be truthful with the doctor or other medical personnel. *See Fahrni v. State*, 473 S.W.3d 486, 497-98 (Tex. App.—Texarkana 2015, pet. ref'd); *Estes v. State*, 487 S.W.3d 737, 755-56 (Tex. App.—Fort Worth 2016, pet. granted 9-14-16); *Zinger*, 899 S.W.2d at 431.

RULE 803

When considering whether statements made by children to mental-health professionals are admissible under Rule 803(4), the court of criminal appeals has observed that

> it is incumbent upon the proponent of the hearsay exception to make the record reflect both 1) that truth-telling was a vital component of the particular course of therapy or treatment involved, and 2) that it is readily apparent that the child-declarant was aware that this was the case. Otherwise, the justification for admitting the out-of-court statement over a valid hearsay objection is simply too tenuous.[573]

The record must show that the declarant was actually seeking a medical diagnosis or treatment; otherwise, statements made to medical personnel are not admissible under the rule.[574] The rule does not require, however, that the statement be made to a physician or even to medical personnel, as long as it is being made for medical diagnosis or treatment.[575] Thus, a statement by a child to a parent, which in turn is relayed to a

---

573. ***Taylor v. State***, 268 S.W.3d 571, 590 (Tex. Crim. App. 2008); *see, e.g.*, ***Munoz v. State***, 288 S.W.3d 55, 58-60 (Tex. App.—Houston [1st Dist.] 2009, no pet.) (child's statements to therapist about identity of abuser were admissible; State presented evidence that therapist emphasized to child the importance of telling the truth and that child was aware of the need to be truthful); ***Green v. State***, 191 S.W.3d 888, 895-96 (Tex. App.—Houston [14th Dist.] 2006, pet. ref'd) (child's statements to doctor about cause and source of abuse were admissible; even though there was no showing that child was aware that her statements were made for the purpose of medical diagnosis or treatment, there was a sufficient showing that she knew the importance of being truthful with the doctor).

In child-abuse cases, the Family Code allows for the admission of a child's hearsay statement describing the alleged abuse—regardless of whether the statement is otherwise inadmissible—if there are sufficient indications of the statement's reliability and the child testifies or is available to testify, or the court determines that using the statement instead of the child's testimony is necessary to protect the child's welfare. TEX. FAM. CODE §104.006.

574. *See* TEX. R. EVID. 803(4)(A); *see, e.g.*, ***Garcia v. State***, 126 S.W.3d 921, 927 (Tex. Crim. App. 2004) (in capital-murder trial, error to admit business records of women's shelter, which contained murder victim's hearsay statements that defendant had physically and psychologically abused her; no evidence that declarant went to shelter to seek medical assistance or that shelter provided such assistance to her).

575. *See* ***Taylor***, 268 S.W.3d at 587 ("A declarant's statement made to a non-medical professional under circumstances that show he expects or hopes it will be relayed to a medical professional as pertinent to the declarant's diagnosis or treatment would be admissible under the rule, even though the direct recipient of the statement is not a medical professional."); ***Bautista v. State***, 189 S.W.3d 365, 369 (Tex. App.—Fort Worth 2006, pet. ref'd) ("Texas courts have allowed non-physicians to testify under the medical diagnosis and treatment exception to hearsay"); statements to a nurse qualify for admission under the rule); *see, e.g.*, ***Horner v. State***, 129 S.W.3d 210, 219-20 (Tex. App.—Corpus Christi 2004, pet. ref'd) (nonphysicians can testify to statements of medical diagnosis or treatment made to them; statements made to medical social worker were admissible); ***Burns v. State***, 122 S.W.3d 434, 438-39 (Tex. App.—Houston [1st Dist.] 2003, pet. ref'd) (statements to psychologist were admissible under Rule 803(4) because knowledge of victim's emotional issues helped psychologist determine future course of treatment); ***Lane v. State***, 111 S.W.3d 203, 211 (Tex. App.—Eastland 2003) (assault victim's statements to paramedic were admissible under Rule 803(4) because they helped paramedic determine proper treatment), *aff'd*, 151 S.W.3d 188 (Tex. Crim. App. 2004); ***Gohring v. State***, 967 S.W.2d 459, 461-62 (Tex. App.—Beaumont 1998, no pet.) (statements to therapist were admissible under rule, but statements to CPS social worker were inadmissible because those were not made for any medical purpose).

The rule does not distinguish between statements to treating and nontreating physicians, as long as the statements were made for purposes of medical diagnosis or treatment. The Advisory Committee on the Federal Rules abandoned any discrimination between treating and nontreating physicians and made relevant patient statements fully admissible in either category. The committee members' rationale was apparently purely practical: they believed that the distinction between statements admitted for their truth and statements admitted to show the basis of an opinion "was one most unlikely to be made by juries." FED. R. EVID. 803(4) advisory committee's note.

physician, will be covered by the rule.[576] The declarant generally must be the person seeking the medical treatment; thus, statements by a physician to a patient are not covered by the rule.[577] The rule, however, does not require that the statement be made by the patient. For example, statements made by parents of small children to further the children's medical treatment have been admitted under Rule 803(4).[578]

Rule 803(4) permits the admission of statements about the causes of a patient's condition as long as they are "reasonably pertinent" to diagnosis or treatment.[579] As the Federal Advisory Committee's note explains, "[s]tatements as to fault would not ordinarily qualify under this latter language."[580] However, some courts have admitted testimony of blame or fault when medical personnel had used such information in their medical treatment.[581] Federal courts have been especially liberal in admitting such evidence in child-sexual-assault cases.[582] Texas cases, following the rationale

---

576. *See Taylor*, 268 S.W.3d at 587.

577. *See, e.g., Nw. Nat'l Ins. v. Garcia*, 729 S.W.2d 321, 325 (Tex. App.—El Paso 1987, writ ref'd n.r.e.) (letters written by doctor to patient containing diagnosis were not admissible under Civil Rule 803(4)).

578. *See, e.g., Burns*, 122 S.W.3d at 438-39 (statements to psychologist were admissible under Rule 803(4) regardless of whether victim or victim's mother made the statements); *cf. Miller v. Watts*, 436 S.W.2d 515, 521 (Ky. 1969) ("If an adult may relate history to his treating doctor, so as to make that doctor competent to testify, it seems plain that history related to a treating doctor by a parent, custodian, guardian, or nurse of an infant of tender years must also be admissible.").

579. Tex. R. Evid. 803(4)(A); *see, e.g., State v. Lasalle*, 135 S.W.3d 94, 97 (Tex. App.—Corpus Christi 2003, pet. ref'd) (trial court properly excluded statements by assault victim that her husband assaulted her; treatment would have been the same regardless of who committed the assault); *Reyes v. State*, 48 S.W.3d 917, 922 (Tex. App.—Fort Worth 2001, no pet.) (medical record containing family-violence victim's statement—"Says husband assaulted her [with] fists"—to treating physician was admissible). The *Reyes* dissent stated that because the victim did not seek medical treatment, her statement was not reasonably pertinent to medical diagnosis or treatment; thus, the medical records should not have been admitted. *See Reyes*, 48 S.W.3d at 927-28 (Dauphinot, J., dissenting).

580. Fed. R. Evid. 803(4) advisory committee's note. To further clarify the scope of the exception, the Advisory Committee noted that "a patient's statement that he was struck by an automobile would qualify but not his statement that the car was driven through a red light." *Id.*; *see also United States v. Iron Thunder*, 714 F.2d 765, 772-73 (8th Cir. 1983) (rape victim's statement to her doctor that she had been raped was admissible because she did not name the assailants and because her statement did not contain any facts irrelevant to her medical diagnosis or treatment).

581. *See, e.g., Syndex Corp. v. Dean*, 820 S.W.2d 869, 873 (Tex. App.—Austin 1991, writ denied) (testimony by certified social worker and psychotherapist about the identity and conduct of defendant who had sexually harassed plaintiff was admissible under Rule 803(4) because the cause of the injury was pertinent to physical and psychological treatment and diagnosis).

In *Cameron v. State*, the court of appeals held that the defendant's statements to a jail psychiatrist were admissible because they were given for the purpose of evaluating the defendant's competency and suicidal tendencies. 988 S.W.2d 835, 851-52 (Tex. App.—San Antonio 1999, pet. ref'd). When the psychiatrist asked how he felt about the fact that he was in jail, charged with a capital murder, the defendant responded with a smile, "Shit happens." *Id.* at 851. This is an instance in which the rationale for the rule does not apply. It is not necessarily true that a jailed suspect, undergoing a psychiatric evaluation, is highly motivated to tell the truth or interested in an accurate medical diagnosis or treatment. Certainly, this defendant's response was not reasonably related to either diagnosis or treatment.

582. *See, e.g., United States v. JDT*, 762 F.3d 984, 1004-05 (9th Cir. 2014) (victim's statements identifying sexual abuser were admissible under Federal Rule 803(4); social-services counselor was not interviewing child to notify authorities but rather to assess his needs); *United States v. Peneaux*, 432 F.3d 882, 894 (8th Cir. 2005) (child-sexual-assault victim's statement identifying abuser may be relevant to prevent future occurrences of abuse and to child's medical safety); *Danaipour v. McLarey*, 386 F.3d 289, 297 (1st Cir. 2004) ("Statements by young chil-

RULE 803

of federal cases, have permitted testimony about the identity of the person who allegedly committed a sexual assault on a child.[583]

---

dren amounting to disclosure to treating therapists that they have been abused by a member of their family are usually reasonably pertinent to treatment of the child.").

    The federal circuits differ on what is required to admit testimony on blame or fault in child-sexual-assault cases. The Eighth Circuit uses a two-part standard: (1) the declarant's motive in making the statement must be consistent with the purposes of obtaining treatment and (2) the content of the statement must be reasonably relied on by a physician in treatment or diagnosis. *E.g.*, **United States v. Turning Bear**, 357 F.3d 730, 738-39 (8th Cir. 2004) (error to admit 3½-year-old child's statements to forensic interviewer under rule; government did not show that child's frame of mind during interview was that of a patient seeking medical treatment, that she understood the medical significance of being truthful in discussing the details of the alleged abuse, or that she had the selfish subjective motive of receiving proper treatment); *see* **Peneaux**, 432 F.3d at 893; *see, e.g.*, **United States v. Gabe**, 237 F.3d 954, 957-58 (8th Cir. 2001) (error, though harmless, to admit doctor's testimony that 15-year-old complainant told him that defendant had abused her since first grade; doctor did not explain that identifying child's abuser was important to medical treatment, and identity of abuser was, in fact, not important to doctor's diagnosis or treatment); **United States v. Renville**, 779 F.2d 430, 438-39 (8th Cir. 1985) (admitting statements of a sexually abused child because they were of a type that physicians rely on in diagnosing a patient, but requiring foundation showing that "the physician makes clear to the victim that the inquiry into the identity of the abuser is important to diagnosis and treatment, and the victim manifests such an understanding"); *see also* **United States v. DeLeon**, 678 F.3d 317, 326-27 (4th Cir. 2012) (in case not involving sexual assault, trial court did not abuse its discretion in admitting statements made by child-abuse and murder victim to social worker accusing defendant of causing bruises to child's forehead; child's motive was consistent with purposes of treatment, and social worker relied on those statements to develop treatment plan), *vacated on other grounds*, ___ U.S. ___, 133 S. Ct. 2850 (2013). Other circuits have taken a less demanding view when determining whether this kind of testimony is admissible. *See* **United States v. Joe**, 8 F.3d 1488, 1494 n.5 (10th Cir. 1993) (Eighth Circuit test "is not contemplated by the rule and is not necessary to ensure that the rule's purpose is carried out"); *see, e.g.*, **United States v. Lukashov**, 694 F.3d 1107, 1115 (9th Cir. 2012) (no error to admit child's statements to social worker under Federal Rule 803(4); district court reasonably concluded that child understood evaluation was part of "a medical process, something that she was brought to participate in for purposes of determining her safety and to ensure that she would be protected and would be treated if she needed help"); **United States v. Kappell**, 418 F.3d 550, 556-57 (6th Cir. 2005) (upholding admission of statements by child-abuse victims to psychotherapist under Federal Rule 803(4); psychotherapist told children "'that it's important to tell the truth, [so] that if something happened, then you can get help for that'"); **United States v. Norman T.**, 129 F.3d 1099, 1105 (10th Cir. 1997) (Federal Rule 803(4) is "based on the longstanding assumption patients have an overriding interest in telling the truth when seeking medical treatment"; court rejected defendant's argument that the exception does not apply to young children); **United States v. George**, 960 F.2d 97, 100 (9th Cir. 1992) (for Federal Rule 803(4) to apply, court must determine only that statements were made for purposes of medical diagnosis or treatment and were reasonably pertinent to diagnosis and treatment; child's age and other personal factors should go to weight of evidence and not admissibility).

    This expansion of the hearsay exception has been criticized by some courts and commentators. *See* **State v. Hinnant**, 523 S.E.2d 663, 668-69 (N.C. 2000) (admission of hearsay statements made by children to doctors because doctors rely on them is "highly questionable"); 4 CHRISTOPHER B. MUELLER & LAIRD C. KIRKPATRICK, FEDERAL EVIDENCE §442, at 464 (2d ed. 1994) (this expansion of the exception is "troubling" because it "builds on the process of providing conventional medical care, which requires doctors to learn basic facts from patients, not on the process of providing larger social remedies aimed at detecting abuse, identifying and punishing abusers, and preventing further mistreatment, which involves skills and social intervention lying beyond the expertise of doctors").

    583. *See* **Estes v. State**, 487 S.W.3d 737, 756 (Tex. App.—Fort Worth 2016, pet. granted 9-14-16) (in cases involving sexual assault of child, identity of offender falls under Rule 803(4) because it can present safety issue that could frustrate diagnosis and treatment); **Bargas v. State**, 252 S.W.3d 876, 896 (Tex. App.—Houston [14th Dist.] 2008, no pet.) (because treatment of child abuse involves removing child from abusive setting, identity of abuser is pertinent to child's medical treatment); **Fleming v. State**, 819 S.W.2d 237, 247 (Tex. App.—Austin 1991, pet. ref'd) (same); **In re L.S.**, 748 S.W.2d 571, 577 (Tex. App.—Amarillo 1988, no writ) ("[I]n the case of a child abuse victim where the cause of the injury is pertinent to both physical and psychological treatment and diagnosis, the statements of the child as to the identity of the abuser are admissible as an exception to the hearsay rule."); *see, e.g.*, **Ponce v. State**,

Of course, if the person is not being examined for a medical diagnosis or treatment, the statements made to medical personnel are not admissible under the rule.[584]

B. Reliable Documents

1. Rule 803(5): Recorded recollection. Rule 803(5) creates a hearsay exception for records that contain a witness's recorded recollection about a matter in issue.[585] There are three prerequisites to admissibility under this exception: (1) the witness must once have known about the matter but now does not recall well enough to testify fully and accurately,[586] (2) the statement contained in the recorded recollection must have been either made or adopted by the witness when the matter was fresh in the witness's memory,[587] and (3) the recorded recollection must accurately reflect the witness's knowledge.[588] The exception does not apply, however, if "the circumstances of the

---

89 S.W.3d 110, 119-20 (Tex. App.—Corpus Christi 2002, no pet.) (statements made by child sexual-assault victim's mother to examining nurse as contained within hospital records about the details of defendant's relationship with the victim and the pattern of sexual assaults against her were admissible; object of exam was to determine if child had been sexually abused and if medical treatment was needed); *Mendoza v. State*, 69 S.W.3d 628, 634 (Tex. App.—Corpus Christi 2002, pet. ref'd) (child's statements to nurse about nature of her injuries and naming defendant as person who caused them were admissible); *Ware v. State*, 62 S.W.3d 344, 350-51 (Tex. App.—Fort Worth 2001, pet. ref'd) (statements made by grandmother of aggravated-sexual-assault victim to physician in which grandmother said that child was afraid of defendant were admissible; no evidence that grandmother had any motive to make such statement other than a desire to care for victim); *Sandoval v. State*, 52 S.W.3d 851, 856-57 (Tex. App.—Houston [1st Dist.] 2001, pet. ref'd) (in trial for aggravated sexual assault of a child, statements by child victim's mother contained in victim's medical records were admissible; mother gave the information for the purpose of seeking medical treatment for her child and the contents of the records were relied on by medical professionals); *Molina v. State*, 971 S.W.2d 676, 683-84 (Tex. App.—Houston [14th Dist.] 1998, pet. ref'd) (Rule 803(4) permitted doctor to testify that child-molestation victim told him that defendant had touched her genital area; doctor testified that taking "history" and giving physical were crucial in arriving at appropriate diagnosis); *Turner v. State*, 924 S.W.2d 180, 182 (Tex. App.—Eastland 1996, pet. ref'd) (under Rule 803(4), statements describing abusive acts are pertinent to medical diagnosis and treatment; trial court did not err in permitting doctor's testimony of victim's statement that her stepfather had penetrated her with his penis); *see also Syndex*, 820 S.W.2d at 873 (testimony by certified social worker and psychotherapist about the identity and conduct of defendant who had sexually harassed plaintiff was admissible under Rule 803(4) because the cause of the injury was pertinent to physical and psychological treatment and diagnosis).

584. *See* Tex. R. Evid. 803(4)(A); *see, e.g., Walck v. State*, 943 S.W.2d 544, 544-45 (Tex. App.—Eastland 1997, pet. ref'd) (psychologist interviewed defendant to assess his state of mind at time of murder, not to make a medical diagnosis or provide treatment; thus, defendant's statements to psychologist during interview were not admissible under Rule 803(4)).

585. Before the 2015 restyling of the Texas Rules, Rule 803(5) explicitly included both memoranda and records. *See* Tex. Sup. Ct. Order, Misc. Docket No. 15-9048 (eff. Apr. 1, 2015). Although the restyled rule refers only to records, the definition of "record" includes "a memorandum, report, or data compilation." Tex. R. Evid. 101(h)(4). The term also includes electronically stored information. *See* Tex. R. Evid. 101(h)(7) (reference to any kind of written material or other medium includes electronically stored information).

586. Tex. R. Evid. 803(5)(A). Interestingly, although Rule 803(5) is included in the rule titled "Exceptions to the Rule Against Hearsay—Regardless of Whether the Declarant Is Available as a Witness," this exception requires the declarant's testimony. Only the declarant can establish insufficient recollection of the facts contained in the document.

587. Tex. R. Evid. 803(5)(B).

588. Tex. R. Evid. 803(5)(C); *Johnson v. State*, 967 S.W.2d 410, 416 (Tex. Crim. App. 1998); *Smith v. State*, 420 S.W.3d 207, 215-16 (Tex. App.—Houston [1st Dist.] 2013, pet. ref'd); *Lund v. State*, 366 S.W.3d 848, 856 (Tex. App.—Texarkana 2012, pet. ref'd).

RULE 803

record's preparation cast doubt on its trustworthiness."[589] Except for that phrase in Rule 803(5)(C), Rule 803(5) is identical to Federal Rule 803(5).[590]

(1) Insufficient recollection. The witness must have known about the facts contained in the record when the record was created or adopted.[591] Rule 803(5) does not require a complete lack of recollection of those facts, only an inability to testify fully and accurately.[592] Thus, the sponsoring party must attempt to refresh the witness's recollection with the written statement. Only if the witness's memory is not fully refreshed should the document be read to the jury.

(2) Statement made or adopted by the witness when the matter was fresh in the witness's memory. The statement must have been either made or adopted by the witness.[593] A witness can adopt statements recorded in another person's words by signing and swearing to the document.[594] Further, the recollection must have been recorded when the matter was fresh in the witness's memory.[595] The language of the rule does not, however, explicitly require that the recollection have been recorded at or even near the time of the event.[596]

---

589. Tex. R. Evid. 803(5)(C); *see Phea v. State*, 767 S.W.2d 263, 267 (Tex. App.—Amarillo 1989, pet. ref'd) ("The language 'unless the circumstances of preparation cast doubt on the document's trustworthiness' ... does not require any 'indicia of reliability' over and above the other provisions of the rule."); *see also* Newell H. Blakely, *Past Recollection Recorded: Restrictions on Use as Exhibit and Proposals for Change*, 17 Hous. L. Rev. 411, 463-65 (1980) (explaining "trustworthiness" proviso).

590. The addition does not amount to any substantive difference between the Texas and federal rules.

591. *See* Tex. R. Evid. 803(5)(A), (5)(B); *Johnson*, 967 S.W.2d at 416; *see, e.g., Brown v. State*, 333 S.W.3d 606, 613 (Tex. App.—Dallas 2009, no pet.) (in animal-cruelty case, State established that witness had personal knowledge of facts contained in written statement when witness testified that he knew defendant and was present on the day the dog was burned; report was admissible under Rule 803(5)).

592. *See* Tex. R. Evid. 803(5)(A); *see, e.g., Priester v. State*, 478 S.W.3d 826, 838 (Tex. App.—El Paso 2015, no pet.) (State established that witness had insufficient recollection of events detailed in written statement when he repeatedly denied having any present recollection of events that were key to State's case); *Smith*, 420 S.W.3d at 216 (State established that witness had insufficient recollection of events detailed in written statement when he testified that he remembered the "important, big things that happened" but did not remember everything that he had told the law-enforcement officer because it had "been so long" since the shooting); *Brown*, 333 S.W.3d at 613 (State established that witness had insufficient recollection of events detailed in written statement when witness testified repeatedly that he did not remember the incident); *cf. United States v. Williams*, 571 F.2d 344, 349 (6th Cir. 1978) (when witness had clear recollection of conversation with defendant, but could not remember crucial details of what defendant told him about how certain checks came into his possession, trial court properly admitted a written statement under Federal Rule 803(5)); 4 Louisell & Mueller, *supra* note 250, §445, at 623 (insisting on "complete failure of memory as the precondition to the use of past recollection recorded would be perverse: The fact that the witness remembers in general terms the matter recorded should serve to increase confidence in the recorded recollection, not to decrease it").

593. Tex. R. Evid. 803(5)(B); *see Phea*, 767 S.W.2d at 267.

594. *Phea*, 767 S.W.2d at 267.

595. Tex. R. Evid. 803(5)(B); *see Johnson*, 967 S.W.2d at 416; *see, e.g., Brown*, 333 S.W.3d at 613 (written statement made less than two weeks after event and grand-jury testimony given one month after event were admissible under Rule 803(5)).

596. *See, e.g., Kuczaj v. State*, 848 S.W.2d 284, 288 (Tex. App.—Fort Worth 1993, no pet.) (foundation requirements of Criminal Rule 803(5) were met when witness could testify to serial number of VCR stolen from her home based on that number's inclusion in an insurance list she had prepared "the day after or within the week after" the burglary; witness testified that she had personal knowledge of all items listed, that it would be very difficult for her to remember the serial numbers of the items without the aid of that list, that she obtained the numbers on the list

(3) Recorded recollection accurately reflects the witness's knowledge. The recorded recollection must accurately reflect the witness's knowledge.[597] That is, the witness may have forgotten the details of the earlier event, but he does remember that he wrote those details down.[598] Or he may have forgotten both the details and the making of the specific prior statement but remembers that he followed a particular established habit or routine that was trustworthy.[599]

(4) Generally inadmissible as exhibit. The last sentence of Rule 803(5), which makes the record inadmissible as an exhibit and thus unavailable to the jury during deliberations unless offered by an adverse party,[600] apparently changed Texas law.[601] The purpose of prohibiting introduction of the record itself is that the jury might be overly impressed by a writing and give it more weight than they would the oral testimony.[602]

2. Rule 803(6): Records of a regularly conducted business activity. Rule 803(6) creates an exception to the hearsay rule for a record of "an act, event, condition, opinion, or diagnosis" if that record was made at or near the time of the event described and

---

from the manufacturer's cards she had, and that the numbers were in her own handwriting); *cf.* ***United States v. Sollars***, 979 F.2d 1294, 1298 (8th Cir. 1992) (recorded statement made two months after event was admissible); ***United States v. Lewis***, 954 F.2d 1386, 1393 (7th Cir. 1992) (Federal Rule 803(5) "does not have specific time constraints on the timing of the preparation and adoption of memoranda"); ***United States v. Patterson***, 678 F.2d 774, 778-80 (9th Cir. 1982) (grand-jury testimony describing a conversation between witness and defendant ten months earlier was admissible).

597. TEX. R. EVID. 803(5)(C); *see Johnson*, 967 S.W.2d at 416 (witness must vouch for accuracy of the statement); *see, e.g.,* ***Lund v. State***, 366 S.W.3d 848, 856 (Tex. App.—Texarkana 2012, pet. ref'd) (offering party did not meet predicate for admissibility because witness did not vouch for accuracy of statement; she "did not remember much of what was in the statement, and further claimed that portions of the statement were not in her handwriting"). The witness does not, however, need to testify explicitly that the statement was accurate when made. *See, e.g.,* ***Wigiert v. State***, 948 S.W.2d 54, 59 (Tex. App.—Fort Worth 1997, no pet.) (although witness did not specifically testify that statement was accurate when made, evidence showed that she wrote statement herself and signed it before a police officer just a few days after incident; "[a]bsent any showing that the statement is inaccurate, the general tenor of her testimony shows sufficient truthfulness to support a finding that the statement correctly reflects the knowledge [witness] had when she made it").

598. *Cf.* ***Greger v. Int'l Jensen, Inc.***, 820 F.2d 937, 943 (8th Cir. 1987) (allowing a witness to read her diary as a past recollection recorded under Federal Rule 803(5)).

599. At the extreme, such statements are admissible, at the court's discretion, when the witness recalls nothing more than the fact of his signature and testifies that he signs only what he has read and knows is accurate. *See Johnson*, 967 S.W.2d at 416; 3 JOHN H. WIGMORE, EVIDENCE IN TRIALS AT COMMON LAW §747, at 99 (Chadbourn rev. 1970). John Wigmore states as follows:

> Is it enough that the witness (as is usual with attesting witnesses to a document) merely recognizes his handwriting and knows that he would not have written or signed without believing the record to be correct? Here the witness is really calling to his aid, not his specific business custom, but his general moral attitude; but, as a rule, the indication should be and is treated as sufficient.

3 WIGMORE, *supra*, §747, at 99.

600. *See* ***Wood v. State***, 511 S.W.2d 37, 43 (Tex. Crim. App. 1974) (when a memorandum is used to refresh the present recollection of a witness, it does not become part of the evidence); ***Godsey v. State***, 989 S.W.2d 482, 496 (Tex. App.—Waco 1999, pet. ref'd) (under Rule 803(5), memorandum may be read into evidence but may not be received as an exhibit unless offered by adverse party).

601. *See* Blakely, *supra* note 589, at 472-76.

602. *See* 4 LOUISELL & MUELLER, *supra* note 250, §445, at 644 (purpose of rule is "to prevent the jury from according undue emphasis to the written word").

RULE 803

was made by a person with knowledge of the event (or from information transmitted by a person with such knowledge).[603] Further, the record must have been "kept in the course of a regularly conducted business activity,"[604] and making that record must have been a regular practice of that activity.[605] This information under Rules 803(6)(A) through 803(6)(C) can be proved at trial by the custodian of the records or another qualified witness, or by an affidavit or unsworn declaration that complies with Rule 902(10).[606]

The party offering business records has the burden of showing that they meet the requirements of Rule 803(6).[607] Business records that are admissible under Rule 803(6) can be admitted for the truth of the matters asserted in those records.[608] A business record may nonetheless be ruled inadmissible if the opponent of the evidence demonstrates that "the source of information or the method or circumstances of preparation indicate a lack of trustworthiness."[609]

Part of the rationale for the business-records exception is the high probability of trustworthiness that attaches to records that an organization regularly keeps and routinely relies on in conducting its own affairs.[610] Another part of the rationale is simple

---

603. TEX. R. EVID. 803(6)(A); *see Ortega v. CACH, LLC*, 396 S.W.3d 622, 629 (Tex. App.—Houston [14th Dist.] 2013, no pet.); **Martinez v. Midland Credit Mgmt., Inc.**, 250 S.W.3d 481, 484-85 (Tex. App.—El Paso 2008, no pet.); **Johnston v. State**, 959 S.W.2d 230, 238 (Tex. App.—Dallas 1997, no pet.).

604. TEX. R. EVID. 803(6)(B).

605. TEX. R. EVID. 803(6)(C); *see Ortega*, 396 S.W.3d at 629; **Martinez**, 250 S.W.3d at 484; **Johnston**, 959 S.W.2d at 238.

606. TEX. R. EVID. 803(6)(D). Refer to notes 655-658 *infra* and accompanying text. These foundation requirements carry over from the former Texas statute that included the business-records exception. *Compare* TEX. R. EVID. 803(6)(C) (regular practice of business activity to make record), *with* Act approved June 2, 1951, 52nd Leg., ch. 321, 1951 Tex. Gen. Laws 545 (former Texas Revised Civil Statutes art. 3737e, §§1, 2, 4, deemed repealed as to civil proceedings effective 1983 and as to criminal proceedings effective 1986) (regular course of business to make record). In addition, the affidavit-authentication provisions of the former statute have been retained with minor changes in Rule 902(10), which is based on the most general and comprehensive language of the former provisions. *See* TEX. R. EVID. 902(10); Act of May 27, 1969, 61st Leg., ch. 353, §1, 1969 Tex. Gen. Laws 1076, *amended by* Act approved May 18, 1973, 63rd Leg., ch. 128, §§1, 2, 1973 Tex. Gen. Laws 276 (former Texas Revised Civil Statutes art. 3737e, §§5-8, deemed repealed as to civil proceedings effective 1983 and as to criminal proceedings effective 1986). Refer to *Article IX: Authentication & Identification, infra* p. 1027.

607. *See, e.g.*, **Good v. Baker**, 339 S.W.3d 260, 273 (Tex. App.—Texarkana 2011, pet. denied) ("Although the trial court might be justified in assuming certain aspects of the … requirements necessary to establish the bills [for attorney fees] as business records, there must have been some testimony to establish the … requirements. Counsel admitted, 'I guess I'm really not sure on how to address that as I'm not sure what predicate is necessary ....' It was error to admit the bills.").

608. *See* **Overall v. Sw. Bell Yellow Pages, Inc.**, 869 S.W.2d 629, 633 (Tex. App.—Houston [14th Dist.] 1994, no writ) ("By authorizing admission of business records as a hearsay exception, the Rule intends such records to be admissible for the truth of the matter asserted.").

609. TEX. R. EVID. 803(6)(E); **Ortega**, 396 S.W.3d at 630. Refer to notes 659-664 *infra* and accompanying text.

610. **Ortega**, 396 S.W.3d at 629; *see* **Coulter v. State**, 494 S.W.2d 876, 883-84 (Tex. Crim. App. 1973) ("Even though the formal requirements for admissibility of such records may be shown, they are not to be admitted automatically; the indispensable fundamental trustworthiness of the proffered record must be evident."); *see, e.g.*, **New Orleans Cold Storage & Whs. Co. v. NLRB**, 201 F.3d 592, 601 n.9 (5th Cir. 2000) (defendant's warehouse receiving record was admissible when offered by plaintiff under rule because defendant itself had relied on these records both in ordinary business and as rationale for discharging plaintiff; party cannot argue that records are

necessity. Modern business activities are usually conducted by a wide variety of employees such that no single person is likely to know all of the facts surrounding even a simple transaction.[611] Moreover, the task of bringing all those who did have knowledge about the event to court would consume an inordinate amount of time and effort for both the court and the witnesses.

(1) Business record. The term "record" in Rule 803(6) is very broad—the definition of "record" includes a memorandum, report, or data compilation.[612] The term also includes electronically stored information.[613] Rule 803(6) applies to all business records, regardless of their form.[614]

Because the admissibility of computer records requires no special foundation, the jury does not need to hear how the computers operate, what programs are utilized, or other technical data.[615] If the computer record is itself made and kept as a business record, it is not a "summary" for purposes of Rule 1006;[616] thus, the underlying documents or sources of information need not be made available in court to the opposing party.[617] Similarly, other "summary records" may be created and maintained as independent business records, and they are also admissible under Rule 803(6) if it is part of the business's regular operations to keep that type of summary report.[618] Federal

---

reliable for one purpose but not another); *see also* 1A RAY, *supra* note 9, §1252, at 405 (business records are "unusually reliable," and there is an "exceptional need" to resort to them).

611. 4 LOUISELL & MUELLER, *supra* note 250, §446, at 646; *see* 1A RAY, *supra* note 9, §1252, at 405 (transactions are frequently reported and recorded by many employees).

612. TEX. R. EVID. 101(h)(4).

613. *See* TEX. R. EVID. 101(h)(7) (reference to any kind of written material or other medium includes electronically stored information).

614. *E.g.*, **Barnhart v. Morales**, 459 S.W.3d 733, 744 (Tex. App.—Houston [14th Dist.] 2015, no pet.) (handwritten notes on preprinted hospital forms were admissible under Rule 803(6)).

615. *See* **Longoria v. Greyhound Lines, Inc.**, 699 S.W.2d 298, 303 (Tex. App.—San Antonio 1985, no writ) (knowledge of the general procedures for collecting and maintaining data in electronic records is sufficient to lay the predicate necessary for admission); **McAllen State Bank v. Linbeck Constr. Corp.**, 695 S.W.2d 10, 17 (Tex. App.—Corpus Christi 1985, writ ref'd n.r.e.) (plaintiff was not required to prove additional predicate for admission of computer records); *see, e.g.*, **United States v. Vela**, 673 F.2d 86, 89-90 (5th Cir. 1982) (fact that Southwestern Bell's custodian of records could not identify the brand, type, or model of each computer or vouch for the working condition of specific equipment during billing periods did not betray any lack of trustworthiness of business records offered at trial); *see also* **McCarley v. State**, 763 S.W.2d 630, 632 (Tex. App.—San Antonio 1989, no pet.) (overruling appellant's general objection to the admission of a computer printout copy of a licensing history).

616. Refer to *Article X: Contents of Writings, Recordings, & Photographs, infra* p. 1060.

617. *See, e.g.*, **McAllen State Bank**, 695 S.W.2d at 16 (although each computer printout was a summary of underlying business records, the printouts themselves were kept as business records and thus were not a summary of business records for trial purposes); *see also* **Okon v. Levy**, 612 S.W.2d 938, 942 (Tex. Civ. App.—Dallas 1981, writ ref'd n.r.e.) (records, although summaries, were compiled by the business and kept as business records and are therefore primary evidence for the purposes of the best-evidence rule: "[m]erely because a writing summarizes a number of transactions does not make the writing inadmissible if it is identified as the writing by which the parties have agreed to be bound").

618. *See* **Perry v. State**, 957 S.W.2d 894, 900 (Tex. App.—Texarkana 1997, pet. ref'd) (although a calculation summary record of child-support payments is a summary of underlying records, it is itself a record of regularly conducted activity and is to be afforded the same deference that other records of regularly conducted business activities are afforded).

cases have also held that Internet postings may qualify as an exception to the hearsay rule under Federal Rule 803(6),[619] but e-mail messages do not.[620]

(2) Record of act, event, condition, opinion, or diagnosis. The single point on which Rule 803(6) changed earlier Texas law concerns records containing medical diagnoses or opinions. Under the former statute, diagnostic entries in medical or hospital records were often excluded. In *Loper v. Andrews*, the Texas Supreme Court held that such entries were admissible "only in those instances where it can be said that the diagnosis records a condition resting in reasonable medical certainty."[621] If, instead, "the facts and findings may be such that their meaning and the resulting medical opinion as to the patient's condition rests primarily in expert medical opinion, conjecture and speculation," the entry would be excluded.[622] The chief problem with this restriction was the distinction required to implement it. As Justice Pope pointed out in his concurring opinion: "When a doctor gives his expert opinion about medical causes lawyers and judges, who are not medical experts, are bold indeed to say that the evidence is mere conjecture or speculation."[623] The *Loper* doctrine was widely criticized,[624] and Rule 803(6) clearly rejects it. While the former statute covered records of "an act, event or condition,"[625] the current rule covers records of "an act, event, condition, opinion, or diagnosis."[626] The Advisory Committee's note to the federal rule makes it clear that the inclusion of the additional terms was intended to reject interpretations like *Loper*.[627] Adoption of the identical language in the Texas rule had the same effect.[628]

---

619. *See, e.g.*, ***United States v. Jackson***, 208 F.3d 633, 637-38 (7th Cir. 2000) (business-records exception includes data compilations and may apply to web postings claiming responsibility for hate mail; evidence was excluded because no proper foundation was established for authenticity of postings).

620. *See, e.g.*, ***Monotype Corp. PLC v. Int'l Typeface Corp.***, 43 F.3d 443, 450 (9th Cir. 1994) (e-mail transmissions are "far less of a systematic business activity" than computerized inventory-recording system whose computer printouts did qualify under rule; former "ongoing electronic message and retrieval system" was not admissible under rule).

621. 404 S.W.2d 300, 305 (Tex. 1966).

622. *Id.*

623. *Id.* at 307 (Pope & Smith, JJ., concurring).

624. *See* 1A RAY, *supra* note 9, §1262, at 444 (judges are not medical experts capable of distinguishing between sound and speculative medical opinions); *1973 Survey*, *supra* note 511, at 158-60 (*Loper* doctrine created the problem of determining which party has the burden of persuasion on admissibility of evidence); Roy R. Ray, *Annual Survey of Texas Law: Evidence*, 21 Sw. L.J. 173, 176-78 (1967) (supporting Justice Pope's position); John West, Comment, *Opinion Entry Problems in Medical Records*, 19 BAYLOR L. REV. 122, 125-31 (1967) (Texas Supreme Court confused the issue).

625. Act approved June 2, 1951, 52nd Leg., ch. 321, 1951 Tex. Gen. Laws 545 (former Texas Revised Civil Statutes art. 3737e, §1, deemed repealed as to civil proceedings effective 1983 and as to criminal proceedings effective 1986).

626. TEX. R. EVID. 803(6); *see, e.g.*, ***Burroughs Wellcome Co. v. Crye***, 907 S.W.2d 497, 500 (Tex. 1995) (in products-liability case involving antibiotic spray, diagnoses in plaintiff's medical records were admissible under Civil Rule 803(6)); ***Sullivan v. State***, 248 S.W.3d 746, 751 (Tex. App.—Houston [1st Dist.] 2008, no pet.) (notes of substance-abuse counselor were admissible under Rule 803(6); "[t]he observations in the report memorialize [counselor's] impressions of [defendant's] medical condition at that time, and it was normal for hospital workers to memorialize their notes in this fashion").

627. *See* FED. R. EVID. 803(6) advisory committee's note.

628. In 1984, the Texas Supreme Court added a specific comment to Rule 803(6) to resolve any lingering doubt about the validity of the *Loper* doctrine. TEX. R. CIV. EVID. 803(6), cmt., 669-670 S.W.2d (Tex. Cases) XXXVIII (1984,

(3) Record made at or near the time of the event recorded. Rule 803(6) requires that the record be made close in time to the event recorded, while the recorder's memory is still fresh.[629] This requirement is based not so much on the passage of time itself but on the likelihood that the recorder in the particular case will be accurate in the specific entry.[630]

(4) Record made by someone with knowledge or from information transmitted by someone with knowledge. The source of the information must be someone with personal knowledge of the recorded act, event, condition, opinion, or diagnosis.[631] The person making the business record does not need to have personal knowledge of all the facts in the record.[632] The information can be transmitted to the person making the record as long as each person in the chain of reporting has a duty to report.[633] The duty

---

amended 1998) (this provision "rejects the doctrine of *Loper v. Andrews*"); Tex. R. Crim. Evid. 803(6), cmt., 701-702 S.W.2d (Tex. Cases) lv (1986, amended 1998) (same). In the 1998 unification of the Civil and Criminal Rules, this comment was deleted as unnecessary because the proposition was by then well established under the rule.

629. *See* Tex. R. Evid. 803(6)(A).

630. *See* 1A Ray, *supra* note 9, §1256, at 421 (entries should be admitted if businesspersons would consider them current); *see, e.g.,* **Curran v. Unis**, 711 S.W.2d 290, 295-96 (Tex. App.—Dallas 1986, no writ) (admitting annual tax returns prepared from contemporaneous ledger cards and spreadsheets); **Carr Well Serv., Inc. v. Liberty Mut. Ins.**, 587 S.W.2d 62, 63 (Tex. Civ. App.—El Paso 1979, no writ) (excluding a statement of account prepared in 1975 about conditions or events that occurred in 1972 and 1973 under former Texas Revised Civil Statutes art. 3737e, now codified at Tex. R. Evid. 803(6), because the memorandum was not prepared at or near the time of the acts).

631. Tex. R. Evid. 803(6)(A); *see, e.g.,* **Granbury Marina Hotel, L.P. v. Berkel & Co. Contractors, Inc.**, 473 S.W.3d 834, 842 (Tex. App.—El Paso 2015, no pet.) (trial court abused its discretion in admitting exhibits under Rule 803(6) when predicate witness never testified that they were made by knowledgeable person with duty to make them); **Valdez v. Hollenbeck**, 410 S.W.3d 1, 13 (Tex. App.—San Antonio 2013) (accountant who prepared tax return and was custodian of records could attest to accuracy of return's content), *rev'd on other grounds*, 465 S.W.3d 217 (Tex. 2015); **Venable v. State**, 113 S.W.3d 797, 800-01 (Tex. App.—Beaumont 2003, pet. ref'd) (error to admit business record when "certification" document lacked both notarial seal and statement that person who made business entry had personal knowledge of the information entered).

632. *See, e.g.,* **Harris v. State**, 846 S.W.2d 960, 963-64 (Tex. App.—Houston [1st Dist.] 1993, pet. ref'd) (vehicle manufacturer's "certificate of origin" was admissible as business record of car dealership to prove stolen car's Vehicle Identification Number; test of trustworthiness was met because both manufacturers and dealerships have great interest in accuracy of records).

633. In **Lucas v. State**, a pre-Rules decision, the court of criminal appeals held that the trial court improperly admitted certain shipping documents when the State did not prove that any employee of the custodian of business records had personal knowledge of the contents of those documents. 721 S.W.2d 315, 318 (Tex. Crim. App. 1986). The testimony at trial indicated that the broker who prepared the shipping documents did not have any personal knowledge of the cargo's value but was relying on a bill of lading prepared by a shipper in Italy. *Id.* The same result would have been reached under Rule 803(6) because the person who prepared the business record did not have personal knowledge of the cargo's value and no testimony was given that the Italian shipper who transmitted the information had either personal knowledge of the value or a duty to report the value accurately. *See id.; see also* **Stapleton v. State**, 868 S.W.2d 781, 784 (Tex. Crim. App. 1993) (tape recording of call to police department was a business record, but citizen who placed call had no "business duty" to make report; thus, record contained hearsay within hearsay and was not admissible for truth of its contents); **Cheek v. State**, 119 S.W.3d 475, 478-79 (Tex. App.—El Paso 2003, no pet.) (trial court did not err in excluding videotaped interview of child offered by defendant; child witness did not have a business duty to make report; thus, her statements within an otherwise admissible business record were not admissible because defendant did not demonstrate applicability of any other hearsay exception for the hearsay within hearsay). *But see* **King v. State**, 953 S.W.2d 266, 270-71 (Tex. Crim. App. 1997) (overruling defendant's contention that motel registration card bearing his name should have been excluded because State did not demonstrate that form was made by someone with personal knowledge, such as a motel employee or representative).

to report helps ensure the accuracy and trustworthiness of the business records because making a poor or inaccurate record could result in termination of employment. Thus, if a police officer has a duty to report traffic accidents, their location, the names of the drivers, the weather conditions, and so forth in an accident report, those portions of the report are admissible under Rule 803(6). But statements from the drivers involved in the accident that are included in the accident report are not admissible because the drivers had no "business" duty to make these statements.[634] Similarly,

> [s]tatements contained in a medical record as to how an accident happened or where it happened, age, medical history, etc. are not admissible as a business-record exception to the hearsay rule, because the party making the entry in the record does not have personal knowledge as to these matters, and the statements do not become trustworthy just because it is hospital routine to record them.[635]

Because the guarantee of accuracy in business records rests on a business duty to make an accurate record, all persons who participate in providing the information contained in the report must have a duty to furnish and record that information. Thus, the guest-identification information contained in such records as hotel registration cards is generally not admissible under Rule 803(6) because the guest who is registering at a hotel or motel is under no business duty to report accurately. However, if the business entity has adequate verification measures in place or otherwise validates the accuracy of information supplied by an outsider, then the record may be admitted under the rule. *See **United States v. Mitchell***, 49 F.3d 769, 778 (D.C. Cir. 1995) ("If the records contain information obtained from a customer, thus constituting hearsay within hearsay, the information will come within the business records exception only 'if it is shown that [the business's] standard practice was to verify the information provided by [the] customer.'"); ***United States v. McIntyre***, 997 F.2d 687, 700 (10th Cir. 1993) (if business employee is able to verify information provided, as with a driver's license, credit card, or other form of identification, or if the interests of the business itself are such that there is a heightened self-interest in the accuracy of the record, then these circumstantial guarantees of accuracy may be sufficient under the business-records exception); *see, e.g.*, ***Kuczaj v. State***, 848 S.W.2d 284, 288-89 (Tex. App.—Fort Worth 1993, no pet.) (sufficient foundation for admission of pawn slip under Rule 803(6) when pawn-shop employee testified that pawn-shop slips were prepared as a part of regular course of business for each and every pawn; he personally took items from defendant and prepared the pawn slip; he compared serial numbers on VCR and TV with numbers he wrote on pawn slip; and he verified defendant's identity from his driver's license).

In one civil case, ***Trinity Universal Insurance Co. v. Bleeker***, the court held that a letter written by the DWI defendant's attorney to his insurance company was admissible as a business record of the insurance company. 944 S.W.2d 672, 676-77 (Tex. App.—Corpus Christi 1997), *rev'd in part on other grounds*, 966 S.W.2d 489 (Tex. 1998). It is unclear whether the criminal defense attorney had a "business duty" to report accurately to the insurance company. Litigation-oriented documents generally do not have sufficient indicia of reliability to be admitted under Rule 803(6).

634. *See **Ramrattan v. Burger King Corp.***, 656 F. Supp. 522, 529 (D. Md. 1987) (exception does not apply if the person who supplies the record is not acting in the regular course of business); *see, e.g.*, ***Logan v. Grady***, 482 S.W.2d 313, 317 (Tex. Civ. App.—Fort Worth 1972, no writ) (statement in accident report written by motorist who allegedly witnessed an accident was not admissible as a business record under former Texas Revised Civil Statutes article 3737e, now codified at Tex. R. Evid. 803(6), because motorist was not an employee of the highway department who had a duty to report); *see also **Crane v. State***, 786 S.W.2d 338, 353-54 & n.5 (Tex. Crim. App. 1990) (sheriff's department's tape recordings of defendant's telephone calls from jail to family members did not qualify for admission under Criminal Rule 803(6) because recording telephone calls was not a regularly conducted business activity, defendant had no duty to make the statements, and recorded statements were "self-serving hearsay" that lacked "fundamental trustworthiness").

635. ***Cornelison v. Aggregate Haulers, Inc.***, 777 S.W.2d 542, 545 (Tex. App.—Fort Worth 1989, writ denied).

(5) Record kept in the course of a regularly conducted business activity. The record must have been made and kept in the course of a regularly conducted business activity.[636] The term "business activity" is broad enough to encompass any regularly conducted business actions, whether for-profit, nonprofit, or even personal business.[637] All that is necessary is that the record-keeping entail some degree of formality and be performed for business reasons.[638] The records of one entity may even become the business records of another entity if a sponsoring witness is qualified to testify about the other entity's record-keeping.[639] That is, a record may be "made" by the business offering it even though "it was initially authored by a different business."[640] A witness is qualified to testify about the other entity's record-keeping "if it can be established the documents were kept in the ordinary course of business and the documents formed the basis for the ongoing transactions."[641] Specifically, the witness must establish the following: "(a) the document is incorporated and kept in the course of the testifying wit-

---

636. TEX. R. EVID. 803(6)(B).

637. *See* TEX. R. EVID. 803(6) ("business" defined as "every kind of regular organized activity whether conducted for profit or not"); *see, e.g.,* ***Leach v. State***, 80 Tex. Crim. 376, 379-80, 189 S.W. 733, 734-35 (1916) (reversible error to exclude a Sunday-school attendance record offered by defendant as a regularly kept record in support of defendant's alibi); *cf.* ***Keogh v. Comm'r***, 713 F.2d 496, 499-500 (9th Cir. 1983) (casino employee's personal diary of wages and tips was admitted under business-records rule); ***United States v. Foster***, 711 F.2d 871, 882 n.6 (9th Cir. 1983) (in narcotics-conspiracy case, ledger containing records of drug transactions was allowed under Federal Rule 803(6) because running accounts of illegal operations are business records and are therefore subject to the usual requirements for admissibility of writings); ***United States v. Hedman***, 630 F.2d 1184, 1197-98 (7th Cir. 1980) (small diary kept by an employee of a lumber company was admitted under Federal Rule 803(6), even though diary was not used or relied on by other employees and was not required to be kept as part of employee's job).

The rule's definition of "business" was taken from the old Texas statute, rather than from Federal Rule 803(6). ***Ortega v. CACH, LLC***, 396 S.W.3d 622, 630 n.4 (Tex. App.—Houston [14th Dist.] 2013, no pet.); *see* Act approved June 2, 1951, 52nd Leg., ch. 321, 1951 Tex. Gen. Laws 545 (former Texas Revised Civil Statutes art. 3737e, §4, deemed repealed as to civil proceedings effective 1983 and as to criminal proceedings effective 1986). The Texas definition of "business" was preferred because it has been recognized as the broadest, most comprehensive possible description of the category of enterprises whose records are admissible under the exception. ***Ortega***, 396 S.W.3d at 630 n.4; *see* 1A RAY, *supra* note 9, §1260, at 432-33 (definition allows records of noncommercial enterprises and government agencies to be admitted); *see also* Thomas R. Needham, Note, *Art. 3737e—What Is a "Business"?*, 26 BAYLOR L. REV. 700, 705 (1974) (discussing the Legislature's adoption of the definition). Federal Rule 803(6)(B) is similarly broad and requires that the record be "kept in the course of a regularly conducted activity of a business, organization, occupation, or calling, whether or not for profit." *See* FED. R. EVID. 803(6)(B).

638. Individual household shopping lists, diaries, and statements for personal checking accounts do not qualify, while ledgers for business-expense accounts probably do. *See* 4 LOUISELL & MUELLER, *supra* note 250, §446, at 652-54.

639. ***Dodeka, L.L.C. v. Campos***, 377 S.W.3d 726, 732 (Tex. App.—San Antonio 2012, no pet.); ***Martinez v. Midland Credit Mgmt., Inc.***, 250 S.W.3d 481, 485 (Tex. App.—El Paso 2008, no pet.); *see* ***Nat'l Health Res. Corp. v. TBF Fin., LLC***, 429 S.W.3d 125, 130 (Tex. App.—Dallas 2014, no pet.). For a discussion of the foundation that must be laid by the custodian of records or another qualified witness, refer to notes 648-654 *infra* and accompanying text.

640. ***Simien v. Unifund CCR Partners***, 321 S.W.3d 235, 244 (Tex. App.—Houston [1st Dist.] 2010, no pet.) (op. on reh'g).

641. ***Dodeka, L.L.C.***, 377 S.W.3d at 732; *see, e.g.,* ***Martinez***, 250 S.W.3d at 485 (although business records that were created by one entity but have become another entity's primary record of the transaction may be admissible, error to admit business record when attached affidavit did not provide information indicating affiant was qualified to testify; affiant did not identify the predecessor, state how record was acquired, or provide any information about predecessor's record-keeping policies or the record's trustworthiness); ***Powell v. Vavro, McDonald & Assocs., L.L.C.***, 136 S.W.3d 762, 765 (Tex. App.—Dallas 2004, no pet.) (custodian of records for travel agency could not provide foundation for admission of business records from credit-card company because he was not qualified to testify about another entity's record-keeping).

ness's business; (b) that business typically relies upon the accuracy of the contents of the document; and (c) the circumstances otherwise indicate the trustworthiness of the document."[642]

(6) Made as regular practice of business activity. The record must be among those that are made as part of the regular practice of that particular business activity.[643] Thus, an unusual type of record would not qualify even if it were kept as part of regularly conducted business.[644] For example, if the business record was prepared for specific litigation purposes, it might lack sufficient indicia of reliability.[645] Similarly, if the record

---

642. ***Rogers v. RREF II CB Acquisitions, LLC***, ___ S.W.3d ___ (Tex. App.—Corpus Christi 2016, no pet.) (No. 13-15-00321-CV; 11-17-16); ***Dodeka, L.L.C.***, 377 S.W.3d at 732; ***Simien***, 321 S.W.3d at 240-41 (op. on reh'g); *see also **Duncan Dev., Inc. v. Haney***, 634 S.W.2d 811, 813-14 (Tex. 1982) (under former Texas Revised Civil Statutes art. 3737e, now Rule 803(6), invoices that originated with subcontractors were admissible as business records of contractor when contractor confirmed invoices' accuracy through site supervisors who had personal knowledge of activities at construction sites). Some courts of appeals have held that personal knowledge of the procedures used in creating the original documents is not required if these three elements are shown. *See **Dodeka, L.L.C.***, 377 S.W.3d at 732; ***Simien***, 321 S.W.3d at 244-45.

643. Tex. R. Evid. 803(6)(C); *see, e.g., **Granbury Marina Hotel, L.P. v. Berkel & Co. Contractors, Inc.***, 473 S.W.3d 834, 842 (Tex. App.—El Paso 2015, no pet.) (trial court abused its discretion in admitting exhibits under Rule 803(6) when predicate witness did not testify that it was company's regular practice to make exhibits); ***West v. State***, 124 S.W.3d 732, 735-36 (Tex. App.—Houston [1st Dist.] 2003, pet. ref'd) (error to admit defendant's bank records when bank custodian did not testify that records were kept as part of a regularly conducted activity or that the bank's regular practice was to make such records); ***Travelers Constr., Inc. v. Warren Bros.***, 613 S.W.2d 782, 786 (Tex. Civ. App.—Houston [14th Dist.] 1981, no writ) (affidavit attached to business record was insufficient when affiant did not swear that records were made in regular course of business or that it was affiant's regular duty to make such records).

644. *See, e.g., **Crane v. State***, 786 S.W.2d 338, 353-54 (Tex. Crim. App. 1990) (recordings of telephone conversations between incarcerated defendant and defendant's family were inadmissible because they were discretionary rather than conducted in the regular course of business); ***In re K.C.P.***, 142 S.W.3d 574, 579-80 (Tex. App.—Texarkana 2004, no pet.) (in case for termination of parental rights, error to admit drug-test results as business record; record lacked indicia of reliability because State did not offer any evidence showing qualifications of person administering drug test, type of drug test used, whether it was properly administered, and whether it was a standard drug test); ***Tex. Employer's Ins. v. Sauceda***, 636 S.W.2d 494, 499 (Tex. App.—San Antonio 1982, no writ) (doctor's letter to insurance carrier was not part of a routine entry in the regular course of the doctor's business, nor was it maintained as a part of normal business procedure); *cf. **Redken Labs., Inc. v. Levin***, 843 F.2d 226, 229 (6th Cir. 1988) (sales slips offered under Federal Rule 803(6) were properly excluded because "defendants admitted that these slips were not all of the slips because 'they don't save them all'"); ***Paddack v. Dave Christensen, Inc.***, 745 F.2d 1254, 1258 (9th Cir. 1984) (excluding audit reports that were not part of a regular routine, particularly because they were prepared in anticipation of litigation).

645. *See, e.g., **Sessums v. State***, 129 S.W.3d 242, 249 (Tex. App.—Texarkana 2004, pet. ref'd) (doctor's letter to prosecutor summarizing treatment of child-abuse victim was written in preparation for litigation and thus did not qualify as business record under rule); ***Hardy v. State***, 71 S.W.3d 535, 537 (Tex. App.—Amarillo 2002, no pet.) (faxed letter from South African representative of pump manufacturer, stating that pump submitted to him for examination belonged to particular distributor, was erroneously admitted as proof that defendant had offered to sell pumps stolen from distributor; letter did not qualify as business record because there was evidence that it was prepared for use in criminal trial at prosecutor's request); ***Freeman v. Am. Motorists Ins.***, 53 S.W.3d 710, 714-15 (Tex. App.—Houston [1st Dist.] 2001, no pet.) (physician's letter to plaintiff's attorney relating to claim that statute of limitations was tolled based on plaintiff's disability was not admissible under Rule 803(6) because it was sent more than ten years after the cause of action accrued and ten days before the summary-judgment hearing, it appeared to be in response to attorney's request, and it was not a routine entry in the doctor's records, but instead was prepared for litigation purposes); *see also **United States v. Frazier***, 53 F.3d 1105, 1110 (10th Cir. 1995) (regulatory-compliance-audit report was admissible under rule despite contention that it was prepared for litigation; its preparation had business significance apart from its use in prosecution); *cf. **United States v. Blackburn***, 992 F.2d 666, 670 (7th Cir. 1993) (report prepared specifically at FBI's request was not admissible under rule; "when a document is created for

is generated by the business as part of an internal investigation into a possible crime, it is not a regularly maintained business record and is not admissible under the rule.[646] On the other hand, handwritten notes routinely made on the particular business records would be admissible.[647]

(7) Testimony by custodian of records or another qualified witness. Rule 803(6) requires that the foundation be laid by the custodian of the record or by "another qualified witness,"[648] but the rule does not require the witness through whom the record is introduced to have been a part of the business activity at the time the record was made.[649] Nor does it require that the sponsoring witness (1) have personal knowledge of the events,[650] (2) be the creator of the records,[651] or (3) attest to the accuracy or trust-

---

a particular use that lies outside the business's usual operations—especially when that use involves litigation—neither of [Federal Rule 803(6)'s] justifications for admission holds. [W]e adhere to the well-established rule that documents made in anticipation of litigation are inadmissible under the business records exception").

646. *See, e.g.,* ***Campos v. State***, 317 S.W.3d 768, 778-79 (Tex. App.—Houston [1st Dist.] 2010, pet. ref'd) (record of items missing from warehouse and their values was not admissible under Rule 803(6) because it was "created for purposes of recovery, with knowledge that theft had taken place in the warehouse"); ***Dixon v. State***, 940 S.W.2d 192, 195 (Tex. App.—San Antonio 1996, no pet.) (list of missing items from business inventory, created specifically to investigate the loss, was not the type of document regularly produced in the course of business activities and was not admissible under Criminal Rule 803(6)).

647. *See, e.g.,* ***United States v. Robinson***, 700 F.2d 205, 209-10 (5th Cir. 1983) (excluding handwritten notes that one member of Board of Supervisors regularly made at meetings for his own use because they were not a part of official duties); ***United States v. Sheppard***, 688 F.2d 952, 953 (5th Cir. 1982) (regular practice of freight company to draw up freight bills with handwritten notations; bills on which notations were made stating that several items in shipment were missing were admissible); ***Barnhart v. Morales***, 459 S.W.3d 733, 744 (Tex. App.—Houston [14th Dist.] 2015, no pet.) (trial court did not abuse its discretion in admitting emergency-room records without redacting handwritten notes; notes were made by hospital staff in treating patient, and there was no showing of untrustworthiness).

648. Tex. R. Evid. 803(6)(D). A "qualified witness" may be "anyone who is familiar with the manner in which the record was prepared." 4 LOUISELL & MUELLER, *supra* note 250, §446, at 663; *see* ***Martinez v. Midland Credit Mgmt., Inc.***, 250 S.W.3d 481, 485 (Tex. App.—El Paso 2008, no pet.).

649. *See, e.g.,* ***Hayden v. State***, 753 S.W.2d 461, 463 (Tex. App.—Beaumont 1988, no pet.) (although a supervising chemist was not supervising when the lab test was made, sufficient indicia of reliability of the results remained to comport with the defendant's rights of confrontation and cross-examination); ***Armijo v. State***, 751 S.W.2d 950, 952-53 (Tex. App.—Amarillo 1988, no pet.) (affirming trial court's decision that supervising DPS chemist could testify about the contents of a lab report made by another technician because adequate indicia of trustworthiness were established when the testimony showed that the substance was received in a sealed bag and handled in accord with regularly established procedures and that these were standard tests, results of which were recorded in the usual course of business).

650. ***Ortega v. CACH, LLC***, 396 S.W.3d 622, 629 (Tex. App.—Houston [14th Dist.] 2013, no pet.); ***Infante v. State***, 404 S.W.3d 656, 663 (Tex. App.—Houston [1st Dist.] 2012, no pet.); *e.g.,* ***Shaw v. State***, 826 S.W.2d 763, 765 (Tex. App.—Fort Worth 1992, pet. ref'd) (qualified witness under Criminal Rule 803(6) does not need to be the creator of the records or even an employee of the same company; rejecting defendant's argument that transactions at an ATM cannot be admitted as business records because testifying witness needs personal knowledge of the mode of preparation, and no one has personal knowledge of these automated activities); *see* ***Martinez***, 250 S.W.3d at 485 ("Although rule 803(6) does not require the predicate witness to ... have personal knowledge of the content of the record, the witness must have personal knowledge of the manner in which the records were prepared."); ***Huff v. State***, 897 S.W.2d 829, 839 (Tex. App.—Dallas 1995, pet. ref'd) ("A qualified witness need not have personal knowledge of the record's contents; he need only have personal knowledge of the mode of preparing the record."); *see, e.g.,* ***Texmarc Conveyor Co. v. Arts***, 857 S.W.2d 743, 748-49 (Tex. App.—Houston [14th Dist.] 1993, writ denied) (when witness testified that he had personal knowledge of each individual item he testified about that was contained within business record, there was sufficient foundation to admit specific portion of records under Civil Rule 803(6),

worthiness of the report.[652] The witness does not even need to be an employee of the business creating the records.[653] The rule requires only that the witness currently be familiar with the record-keeping process as it existed when the entry was made.[654]

(8) Affidavit or unsworn declaration complying with Rule 902(10). Rule 803(6) also allows a business record to be introduced by an affidavit or unsworn declaration rather than by live testimony of the custodian of records.[655] Because the records are self-authenticating under Rule 902(10), a sponsoring witness's testimony is not necessary.[656] Rule 902(10) contains a form affidavit for authenticating business

---

even though witness did not have personal knowledge of ledger entry); ***Strickland v. State***, 784 S.W.2d 549, 553 (Tex. App.—Texarkana 1990, pet. ref'd) (chemical-analysis record was properly introduced into evidence through lab supervisor, even though chemist who actually performed the test did not testify because his supervisor testified that standard procedures were followed in analyzing the substance, and the report was made by a person with personal knowledge of report's contents).

651. ***Ortega***, 396 S.W.3d at 629; ***Infante***, 404 S.W.3d at 663; *see* ***Desselles v. State***, 934 S.W.2d 874, 876 (Tex. App.—Waco 1996, no pet.) (Criminal Rule 803(6) does not require custodian to create the documents, be the head of the pertinent business department, or have personal knowledge of the information recorded therein); ***Huff***, 897 S.W.2d at 839 ("Rule 803(6) does not require a witness laying the predicate for introduction of a business record to be the creator of the document ...."); *see, e.g.,* ***Hous. Shell & Concrete Co. v. Kingsley Constructors, Inc.***, 987 S.W.2d 184, 186 (Tex. App.—Houston [14th Dist.] 1999, no pet.) (test-core results of concrete provided by subcontractor were admissible under Rule 803(6) when president of general contractor explained testing process and testified that he and his employees personally watched samples being taken and noted the results of the tests when they were performed).

652. *See* ***March v. Victoria Lloyds Ins.***, 773 S.W.2d 785, 788-89 (Tex. App.—Fort Worth 1989, writ denied) (sponsoring witness does not need to attest to the trustworthiness of the report; "[t]he witness or affiant is to set forth the facts upon which an assessment of trustworthiness can be made by the court"). However, when the witness states that he has not seen the documents in the business-records files and cannot testify that they are true and accurate copies of documents contained within the business records, the records are inadmissible. *See* ***Ronk v. Parking Concepts, Inc.***, 711 S.W.2d 409, 416 (Tex. App.—Fort Worth 1986, writ ref'd n.r.e.).

653. ***Haq v. State***, 445 S.W.3d 330, 334 (Tex. App.—Houston [1st Dist.] 2013, pet. ref'd); ***Huff***, 897 S.W.2d at 839; *e.g.,* ***Apple v. State***, 744 S.W.2d 256, 257 (Tex. App.—Texarkana 1987, no pet.) (upholding admission of traveler's checks through check-company official, even though the individual who sold the checks was a supermarket employee).

654. *See* ***Haq***, 445 S.W.3d at 334; ***Martinez***, 250 S.W.3d at 485; *see, e.g.,* ***Thawer v. Comm'n for Lawyer Discipline***, 523 S.W.3d 177, ___ (Tex. App.—Dallas 2017, no pet.) (witness who worked as receptionist and then as legal assistant for attorney could serve as sponsoring witness for chart showing fees paid to attorney even though witness was not custodian of records; witness testified that she entered the information on the logs and that it accurately reflected attorney's consultation fees). In ***Clark v. Walker-Kurth Lumber Co.***, the court found that a sufficient predicate is established

> if it is demonstrated that the documents are records that are generated pursuant to a course of regularly conducted business activity and that the records are, as a practical matter, always created by or from information transmitted by a person with knowledge, at or near the time of the event. The trial judge shall determine from all the evidence offered whether the personal knowledge required by rule 803(6) is present.

689 S.W.2d 275, 281 (Tex. App.—Houston [1st Dist.] 1985, writ ref'd n.r.e.). For a discussion of the procedure for offering third-party business records under Rule 803(6), refer to notes 639-642 *supra* and accompanying text.

655. TEX. R. EVID. 803(6)(D); *see* ***Hernandez v. State***, 939 S.W.2d 665, 667 (Tex. App.—El Paso 1996, pet. ref'd) (business records offered under Rule 803(6) may be admitted either through in-court testimony of qualified witness or by self-authenticating affidavit under Rule 902(10)). Federal Rule 803(6)(D) allows for the introduction of business records by a certification that complies with Federal Rule 902(11) (domestic records), Federal Rule 902(12) (foreign records), or a statute that permits certification.

656. The original Civil Rule 803(6) did not contain any reference to a self-authenticating affidavit. *See* 641-642 S.W.2d (Tex. Cases) LVIII (1983, amended 1998). When the Criminal Rules were promulgated in 1986, Criminal Rule 803(6) made explicit reference to affidavits that complied with Rule 902(10), *see* 701-702 S.W.2d (Tex. Cases) LV (1986,

records.[657] The form affidavit refers to the "custodian of records" or "an employee or owner" of the business as someone who could establish the record's foundation under Rule 803(6).[658]

(9) Reasons to exclude business records. Even if the components of Rule 803(6)'s evidentiary foundation have been established, business records (or certain statements within those records) may still be excluded for the following reasons.

(a) Lack of trustworthiness. Rule 803(6) states that a business record may be ruled inadmissible if "the source of information or the method or circumstances of preparation indicate a lack of trustworthiness."[659] The party opposing the admission of the business records has the burden to show a lack of trustworthiness.[660] But if the proponent of the evidence does not establish all the components of Rule 803(6)'s foundation requirement, the party opposing the admission does not need to establish lack of trustworthiness.[661] If a party opposes the admission of business records based on a lack of trustworthiness, the party must raise the issue when the evidence is offered or else the error is waived.[662]

---

amended 1998), so the Texas Supreme Court amended the civil rule in 1988 to conform with the criminal version and clarify that a self-authenticated business record may be admitted without a sponsoring witness. *See* 733-734 S.W.2d (Tex. Cases) xc (1987, amended 1998). Refer to *Article IX: Authentication & Identification, infra* p. 1027.

657. Tex. R. Evid. 902(10)(B).

658. *See id.*

659. Tex. R. Evid. 803(6)(E); *see, e.g.,* **Crane v. State**, 786 S.W.2d 338, 353-54 (Tex. Crim. App. 1990) (transcript of telephone conversation recorded by sheriff's department, which was made between jailed defendant and others, was not sufficiently trustworthy to be admitted under Rule 803(6); statements were self-serving hearsay when offered by defendant-declarant); **Philpot v. State**, 897 S.W.2d 848, 852 (Tex. App.—Dallas 1995, pet. ref'd) (sponsoring witness, a parole officer, provided proper foundation for admission of report but did not establish the trustworthiness of defendant's urinalysis test results).

In **Philpot**, the court relied on a pre-Rules decision of the court of criminal appeals, **Porter v. State**, 578 S.W.2d 742, 746 (Tex. Crim. App. 1979), for the holding that even when certain evidence falls within a recognized exception to the hearsay rule, that evidence is not admissible if it does not have the indicia of reliability sufficient to ensure the integrity of the fact-finding process. **Philpot**, 897 S.W.2d at 852. With regard to the letters, reports, and documents that the trial judge admitted from the defendant's federal parole file, the court of criminal appeals in **Porter** stated as follows:

> These letters contain hearsay upon hearsay, as well as opinions regarding [defendant's] mental and physical condition and his amenability to rehabilitation. The sources of these opinions are in most cases unnamed, and in no case are the authors or the unnamed sources shown to be competent to make the statements attributed to them. It defies reason to suggest that these letters, merely because they were collected in a file in a government office, have the indicia of reliability sufficient to insure the integrity of the fact finding process commensurate with the constitutional rights of confrontation and cross-examination.

578 S.W.2d at 746; *see also* **Trevino v. State**, 815 S.W.2d 592, 597-98 (Tex. Crim. App. 1991) (admissibility of Texas Youth Council files), *rev'd on other grounds*, 503 U.S. 562 (1992).

660. Tex. R. Evid. 803(6)(E). The same is true under Federal Rule 803(6)(E). *See* Fed. R. Evid. 803 advisory committee's note to 2014 amendments (rule amendment clarifies that opponent has burden to show lack of trustworthiness).

661. *See* **Granbury Marina Hotel, L.P. v. Berkel & Co. Contractors, Inc.**, 473 S.W.3d 834, 844 (Tex. App.—El Paso 2015, no pet.).

662. *See* Tex. R. App. P. 33.1(a)(1)(A); **Calvillo v. Carrington Mortg. Servs.**, 487 S.W.3d 626, 633 (Tex. App.—El Paso 2015, pet. denied).

Lack of trustworthiness is most frequently found when the record was prepared in anticipation of litigation.[663] When a party anticipates that a record will be used in later litigation, there are strong motives to slant or shape the record to present the party in the best possible light. As a result, courts routinely exclude these documents.[664]

(b) Hearsay within hearsay. Frequently, a business record that, in itself, may be admissible under Rule 803(6) contains information that is also hearsay. For example, a medical record may contain statements made by the patient, or an accident report filled out by a police officer may contain eyewitness accounts of the accident. This is "hearsay within hearsay."[665] Unless the hearsay statements within the otherwise admissible business record fit some other exception to the hearsay rule—for example, a statement for purposes of medical diagnosis or treatment,[666] an excited utterance, or an opposing party's statement—those hearsay statements are not admissible simply because they are contained within a business record.[667] As Rule 805 points out, if each level of hearsay "conforms with an exception to the [hearsay] rule,"[668] the entire business record will be admissible; otherwise, the second level of hearsay—the out-of-court statements within the business record—must be redacted before the business record can be admitted.[669]

---

663. *Ortega v. CACH, LLC*, 396 S.W.3d 622, 630 (Tex. App.—Houston [14th Dist.] 2013, no pet.).

664. Refer to note 645 *supra* and accompanying text. In *Fischer v. State*, the court of criminal appeals discussed why Rule 803(1) cannot be used to admit police reports, which are inadmissible under Rule 803(8)(B) (now Rule 803(8)(A)(ii)), in criminal cases. 252 S.W.3d 375, 382-84 (Tex. Crim. App. 2008). Refer to notes 478-481 *supra* and accompanying text, notes 704-713 *infra* and accompanying text. The rationale is the same for excluding business records prepared in anticipation of litigation. For Confrontation Clause issues associated with the admission of business records, refer to notes 134-162 *supra* and accompanying text.

665. *See, e.g.*, *Garcia v. State*, 126 S.W.3d 921, 926-27 (Tex. Crim. App. 2004) (statements made by murder victim contained in women's shelter's business records were hearsay within hearsay; although State laid a proper foundation for admission of the shelter's business records, murder victim was outside shelter's business and she had no business duty to report accurately to shelter; no independent hearsay exception applied to declarant's out-of-court statements); *see also* *Russeau v. State*, 171 S.W.3d 871, 880-81 (Tex. Crim. App. 2005) (corrections officers' written jail and prison disciplinary reports that relied on the observations of others at the jail who were not shown to be unavailable and whom defendant did not have opportunity to cross-examine were inadmissible under the Confrontation Clause).

666. *See, e.g.*, *Moyer v. State*, 948 S.W.2d 525, 528 (Tex. App.—Fort Worth 1997, pet. ref'd) (paramedic's report was admissible under Rule 803(6); victim's statements within that report were separately admissible under Rule 803(4)).

667. *See Perry v. State*, 957 S.W.2d 894, 899-900 (Tex. App.—Texarkana 1997, pet. ref'd) ("If a report contains some hearsay statement, the hearsay statement must fall under some hearsay exception of its own because neither the public records and reports exception nor the records of regularly conducted activities exception protects hearsay within hearsay."). *See generally* 4 MUELLER & KIRKPATRICK, *supra* note 582, §449, at 526-32 (discussing information from sources outside business and its admissibility under Federal Rule 803(6); "[i]f both the source and recorder act in regular course, and everyone in the chain of transmission does likewise, the message of FRE 803(6) is that the fact of layered hearsay does not matter .... If the people in the chain of transmission are not acting in normal course, the exception does not apply and the record is likely to be excluded. If the source of information is an outsider to the business, the exception alone is not enough and the record can be admitted only if what the source said is itself within an exception.").

668. TEX. R. EVID. 805. Refer to notes 958-965 *infra* and accompanying text.

669. *See Jones v. State*, 843 S.W.2d 487, 492 (Tex. Crim. App. 1992) ("Inadmissible hearsay testimony does not become admissible simply because it is contained within an admissible document or transcript."), *overruled on other*

(c) Record does not meet requirements of Rule 803(8)(A)(ii) & (8)(A)(iii). In a criminal proceeding, evidence that is admissible under Rule 803(6) must still be excluded if it is a public record or report and does not meet the requirements of Rule 803(8)(A)(ii) and (8)(A)(iii).[670] Otherwise, the business-records exception would allow a party to circumvent the express limitations on the admissibility of public records and reports in Rule 803(8)(A)(ii) and (8)(A)(iii) by "back-dooring" the evidence through Rule 803(6).[671] Thus, the court of criminal appeals has held that reports compiled by law-enforcement officers—which are expressly barred under Rule 803(8)(A)(ii)—may not qualify as an exception under Rule 803(6), even though they might otherwise fit all of the requirements of the business-records exception.[672] This limitation does not apply in civil cases.[673]

On the other hand, the defendant in a criminal trial may offer public reports compiled by law-enforcement officers, such as police offense reports, into evidence under either Rule 803(6) or Rule 803(8)(A)(ii) or (8)(A)(iii) unless those particular reports are untrustworthy or contain inadmissible hearsay.[674]

3. Rule 803(7): Absence of a record of a regularly conducted activity. Rule 803(7) allows parties to offer the absence of a matter in a business record as proof that an event did not occur or a matter did not exist.[675] The effect of this provision is identical to that of the corresponding provision of the former Texas statute.[676] The probative value of this "negative evidence" flows from the same factors that ensure the reliability of "posi-

---

grounds, **Maxwell v. State**, 48 S.W.3d 196 (Tex. Crim. App. 2001); *see also* **Willis v. State**, 2 S.W.3d 397, 401 (Tex. App.—Austin 1999, no pet.) (narrative report in probation file about details of theft that defendant purportedly committed was inadmissible as hearsay within hearsay).

670. Refer to notes 697-731 *infra* and accompanying text.

671. *See* **Perry**, 957 S.W.2d at 897.

672. *See, e.g.*, **Cole v. State**, 839 S.W.2d 798, 805-06 (Tex. Crim. App. 1990) (orig. op.) (reversible error to admit DPS lab report under Criminal Rule 803(6) after determining that such a report would be barred under Criminal Rule 803(8)(B), now Rule 803(8)(A)(ii)); **Cruz v. State**, 827 S.W.2d 83, 86 (Tex. App.—Corpus Christi 1992, no pet.) (medical examiner's autopsy report was not admissible under Criminal Rule 803(6) after it was found inadmissible under Criminal Rule 803(8)(B), now Rule 803(8)(A)(ii), but harmless error in the particular case); *see also* **State v. Reyna**, 89 S.W.3d 128, 131 (Tex. App.—Corpus Christi 2002, no pet.) (Dorsey, J., dissenting) (police offense reports are inadmissible under Rules 803(6) and 803(8)(B), now Rule 803(8)(A)(ii), in criminal proceedings except when they are not offered for the truth of their contents); *cf.* **Cook v. State**, 832 S.W.2d 62, 68 (Tex. App.—Dallas 1992, no pet.) (parole-violation warrant was admissible under Criminal Rule 803(6) because it was issued by the Board of Pardons and Paroles and thus was not a matter observed by law-enforcement personnel); **Ponce v. State**, 828 S.W.2d 50, 51-52 (Tex. App.—Houston [1st Dist.] 1991, pet. ref'd) (reports indicating that an Intoxilyzer machine is working properly are admissible under Criminal Rule 803(6) because these reports are made routinely and are not for use in any specific litigation).

673. *See, e.g.*, **Sciarrilla v. Osborne**, 946 S.W.2d 919, 923-24 (Tex. App.—Beaumont 1997, pet. denied) (DPS trooper's accident report was admissible in civil lawsuit under Civil Rules 803(6) and 803(8)).

674. *See* **Jefferson v. State**, 900 S.W.2d 97, 101-02 (Tex. App.—Houston [14th Dist.] 1995, no pet.) (error, but harmless, to exclude defendant's offer of police offense report as an exception to hearsay rule under Rule 803(6)).

675. *See* TEX. R. EVID. 803(7)(A). For the definition of "record," refer to notes 612-613 *supra* and accompanying text.

676. Act of May 14, 1951, 52nd Leg., R.S., ch. 321, 1951 Tex. Gen. Laws 545 (former Texas Revised Civil Statutes art. 3737e, §3, deemed repealed as to civil proceedings effective 1983 and as to criminal proceedings effective 1986).

tive evidence" under the business-records exception.[677] The foundational requirements under Rule 803(7) are similar to those under Rule 803(6),[678] but in addition to showing that the record was regularly kept,[679] the proponent should show that the matter not mentioned in any business record would have been so mentioned had it occurred or existed.[680] While evidence admitted under Rule 803(6) is generally the document itself, evidence offered under Rule 803(7) will be testimony that a search of the pertinent records revealed that no such record exists.[681] Evidence offered under Rule 803(7) will be excluded if the opponent of the evidence demonstrates that "the possible source of the information or other circumstances indicate a lack of trustworthiness."[682]

4. Rule 803(8): Public records. Rule 803(8) provides a hearsay exception for a "record or statement of a public office."[683] The Texas provision, which carries forward the ex-

677. In ***United States v. De Georgia***, the Ninth Circuit noted the following:

Regularly-maintained business records are admissible in evidence as an exception to the hearsay rule because the circumstance that they are regularly-maintained records upon which the company relies in conducting its business assures accuracy not likely to be enhanced by introducing into evidence the original documents upon which the records are based.

In our view, this same circumstance offers a like assurance that if a business record designed to note every transaction of a particular kind contains no notation of such a transaction between specified dates, no such transaction occurred between those dates.

420 F.2d 889, 893 (9th Cir. 1969).

678. "The initial foundational predicate of [R]ule 803(7) is that the records that would include the matter, if it were not absent from those records, are kept in accordance with the provisions of [R]ule 803(6)." ***Coleman v. United Sav. Ass'n***, 846 S.W.2d 128, 131 (Tex. App.—Fort Worth 1993, no writ). If the proponent of the "negative" evidence under Rule 803(7) does not lay the proper business-records foundation under Rule 803(6), the testimony of the business-records witness is not admissible. *Id.*

679. *See* Tex. R. Evid. 803(7)(B).

680. *See* Tex. R. Evid. 803(7)(A).

681. *See, e.g.*, *De Georgia*, 420 F.2d at 891-93 (in case involving stolen rental car, testimony of security manager was offered to show no rental or lease activity after date of last recorded return); ***Young v. State***, 891 S.W.2d 945, 950 (Tex. Crim. App. 1994) (McCormick, P.J., White & Meyers, JJ., dissenting) (setting out testimony to establish absence of entry in business records and dissenting from reversal of conviction for failure to produce all business records that witness reviewed before this testimony). In the original ***Young*** opinion, a majority of the court had held that the business custodian was required to produce all of the company's business records that she had reviewed to enable the witness to testify under this hearsay exception. ***Young v. State***, 830 S.W.2d 122, 124 (Tex. Crim. App. 1992). The court maintained that these records were required by Criminal Rule 611 as documents used to refresh the witness's memory before testifying. *Id.* In its later decision, a majority held that this error was not harmless. ***Young***, 891 S.W.2d at 949. The majority of the court apparently misunderstood the purpose of Rule 803(7). The rule was intended precisely to avoid the requirement of carting in all of a business's regular records for the attorneys and jury to pore through looking for a nonexistent entry. *See* 4 John H. Wigmore, Evidence in Trials at Common Law §1230, at 546 (Chadbourn rev. 1972) ("testimony, by one who has examined records, that *no record* of a specific tenor is there contained is receivable instead of producing the entire mass for perusal in the courtroom").

682. Tex. R. Evid. 803(7)(C).

683. Tex. R. Evid. 803(8). Before the 2015 restyling of the Texas Rules, Rule 803(8) explicitly included "records, reports, statements, or data compilations, in any form, of public offices and agencies." *See* Tex. Sup. Ct. Order, Misc. Docket No. 15-9048 (eff. Apr. 1, 2015). Although the restyled rule refers only to a record or statement of a public office, the definition of "record" includes "a memorandum, report, or data compilation." Tex. R. Evid. 101(h)(4). The term also includes electronically stored information. *See* Tex. R. Evid. 101(h)(7) (reference to any kind of written material or other medium includes electronically stored information). Further, the definition of "public office" includes a public agency. Tex. R. Evid. 101(h)(3).

ception from earlier law,[684] is basically identical to Federal Rule 803(8).[685] The public records admissible under this exception contain three categories of information: (1) the activities of the office that prepared the records,[686] (2) "matter[s] observed while under a legal duty to report,"[687] and (3) "factual findings from a legally authorized investigation."[688] Records under Rule 803(8) do not have to be sworn to be admissible.[689] They will be excluded, however, if "the source of information or other circumstances indicate a lack of trustworthiness."[690] The party opposing the admission of the records has the burden to show that the evidence is untrustworthy.[691] Al-

---

684. The common law recognized the public-records exception. *See* McCormick's Handbook II, *supra* note 7, §315 (discussing the development of the exception, from the common-law rule to statutory law); 1A Ray, *supra* note 9, §1271, at 451 (exception is largely for convenience; if public officials were required to attend, public business would be disrupted). The admissibility of public records and reports has also been addressed in "statutes without number" across the United States. Fed. R. Evid. 803(8) advisory committee's note.

Texas enacted a comprehensive official-records statute in 1951. Act of May 29, 1951, 52nd Leg., R.S., ch. 471, 1951 Tex. Gen. Laws 830, *amended by* Act of May 22, 1953, 53rd Leg., R.S., ch. 304, §1, 1953 Tex. Gen. Laws 756, 756, *amended by* Act of May 27, 1961, 57th Leg., R.S., ch. 321, §1, 1961 Tex. Gen. Laws 685, 685-86, *amended by* Act of May 15, 1975, 64th Leg., R.S., ch. 280, §1, 1975 Tex. Gen. Laws 666, 666-67 (former Texas Revised Civil Statutes art. 3731a deemed repealed as to civil proceedings effective 1983 and as to criminal proceedings effective 1986). While the former Texas statute contained a notice requirement, Rule 803(8) does not. *See id.* Further, the relevant authentication provisions of the Texas Rules are considerably more convenient than those of the former statute. *Compare* Act of May 15, 1975, 64th Leg., R.S., ch. 280, §1, sec. 4, 1975 Tex. Gen. Laws 666, 667 (former Texas Revised Civil Statutes art. 3731a required writings to be evidenced by an official publication or certificate from the attesting officer with legal custody of the writing), *with* Tex. R. Evid. 901(b)(7) (authentication of public record is satisfied by evidence that document is authorized to be filed in a public office or is from the public office where items of that kind are kept), *and* Tex. R. Evid. 902(1)-(5) (extrinsic evidence of authenticity is not required).

685. The only wording difference, which is nonsubstantive, is in Rule 803(8)(B). *Compare* Tex. R. Evid. 803(8)(B) ("the opponent fails to demonstrate that the source of information or other circumstances indicate a lack of trustworthiness"), *with* Fed. R. Evid. 803(8)(B) ("the opponent does not show that the source of information or other circumstances indicate a lack of trustworthiness").

686. Tex. R. Evid. 803(8)(A)(i).

687. Tex. R. Evid. 803(8)(A)(ii). This subsection explicitly excludes reports detailing "matter[s] observed by law-enforcement personnel" from the hearsay exception in criminal cases. *Id.*

688. Tex. R. Evid. 803(8)(A)(iii). This subsection applies against any party in civil proceedings and against the State in criminal proceedings. *See id.*

689. *Tex. Dep't of Pub. Safety v. Caruana*, 363 S.W.3d 558, 561 (Tex. 2012).

690. Tex. R. Evid. 803(8)(B). In determining the admissibility of any public record under Rule 803(8), the trial court may exclude any document that otherwise meets the foundation requirements of the rule if the court finds that the document lacks sufficient indicia of reliability. *See Caruana*, 363 S.W.3d at 564; *see, e.g., Zhu v. Lam*, 426 S.W.3d 333, 342-43 (Tex. App.—Houston [14th Dist.] 2014, no pet.) (trial court did not abuse its discretion in excluding printouts from Harris County Appraisal District's website because the printouts contradicted each other and proponent did not establish any reason for the discrepancy, which indicated lack of trustworthiness under Rule 803(8)); *Camp v. Harris Methodist Fort Worth Hosp.*, 983 S.W.2d 876, 882 (Tex. App.—Fort Worth 1998, no pet.) (trial court did not abuse its discretion in excluding DHHS records showing that hospital violated duty to stabilize patient; although DHHS records could have qualified for admission under rule, these particular findings were not made by a physician as required by statute, and thus they lacked indicia of reliability); *Horvath v. Baylor Univ. Med. Ctr.*, 704 S.W.2d 866, 870 (Tex. App.—Dallas 1985, no writ) (Department of Health, Education, and Welfare publication containing recommended guidelines for phenylketonuria screening programs excluded because it "lack[ed] the indicia of reliability displayed by public records of factual events"). *See generally* Judge Harvey Brown, Daubert *Objections to Public Records: Who Bears the Burden of Proof?*, 39 Hous. L. Rev. 413, 428-36 (2002) (*Daubert* issues regarding the reliability of expert opinions apply to those opinions contained within public records that are otherwise admissible under Rule 803(8)).

691. Tex. R. Evid. 803(8)(B); *Lozano v. State*, 359 S.W.3d 790, 818 (Tex. App.—Fort Worth 2012, pet. ref'd); *Corrales v. Dep't of Family & Prot. Servs.*, 155 S.W.3d 478, 486 (Tex. App.—El Paso 2004, no pet.); *Beavers v. Northrop*

though Rule 803(8) presumes admissibility, the presumption "does not exempt the offered document from satisfying other requirements of the rules."[692]

There are three rationales for this hearsay exception: (1) public records are inherently reliable because public officials are presumed to perform their duties in accordance with the law, (2) public officers lack a motive to make or keep false records, and (3) public inspection of these records ensures that any inaccuracies will be noticed and corrected.[693] The rule's internal limitation on the admissibility of public records that lack such indicia of trustworthiness applies both to categories of documents that do not meet the public-policy rationale and to those specific documents that on their face, in their contents, or under the circumstances of their preparation do not meet the traditional criteria.

(1) Rule 803(8)(A)(i): Office's activities. Rule 803(8)(A)(i) refers to the records that a public office[694] keeps of its own activities. Examples include the office's disbursement records or records of receipt, internal policy guidelines, court-ordered judgments and sentences kept in the court's files, documents that are required to be filed with the office offered to show when and where they were so filed, and copies of licenses issued by the public office.[695] The rationale behind this exception is that the simple factual nature of such records, which focus on the office's internal operation, diminish the risk of inaccurate reporting.[696]

(2) Rule 803(8)(A)(ii): Matters observed while under a legal duty to report. Rule 803(8)(A)(ii) refers to factual reports prepared by a public office as required by law and made by a person with personal knowledge who has a legal duty both to observe and to report.[697] The reports may deal with subject matter beyond the internal activities of the agency, but the reports should be of a factual, concrete nature.[698] Here, there is no motive to exaggerate or color the information; rather, the person is presumed to have mechanically recorded specific factual material.[699] The rule reaches a variety of docu-

---

Worldwide Aircraft Servs., Inc., 821 S.W.2d 669, 675 (Tex. App.—Amarillo 1991, writ denied). The same is true under Federal Rule 803(8)(B). *See* FED. R. EVID. 803 advisory committee's note to 2014 amendments (rule amendment clarifies that opponent has burden to show lack of trustworthiness).

692. *Benefield v. State*, 266 S.W.3d 25, 34 (Tex. App.—Houston [1st Dist.] 2008, no pet.).

693. *Perry v. State*, 957 S.W.2d 894, 897 (Tex. App.—Texarkana 1997, pet. ref'd). Another reason for admitting such records is to spare the public official time-consuming and inconvenient court appearances to testify to the information contained in his records. *Id.*; *see* McCORMICK'S HANDBOOK II, *supra* note 7, §315, at 736.

694. The definition of "public office" includes a public agency. TEX. R. EVID. 101(h)(3).

695. *See, e.g., Brown v. State*, 391 S.W.2d 425, 428 (Tex. Crim. App. 1965) (under former TEX. REV. CIV. STAT. art. 3731a, admitting copies of licenses issued by the Texas Liquor Control Board); *Watson v. State*, 917 S.W.2d 65, 67-68 (Tex. App.—Fort Worth 1996, pet. ref'd) ("criminal person case list" printed from district attorney's computer and indicating that venireman had a pending theft-by-check case was a public record under Criminal Rule 803(8)(A), now Rule 803(8)(A)(i)).

696. 4 LOUISELL & MUELLER, *supra* note 250, §455, at 726.

697. *See id.* §455, at 727.

698. *See id.* §455, at 728.

699. *See United States v. Quezada*, 754 F.2d 1190, 1193-94 (5th Cir. 1985) (affirming a decision to admit a deportation warrant).

ments, including police accident reports on matters the investigator actually observes in a civil case,[700] weather-bureau records,[701] safety investigations,[702] and building-inspection reports on a building's particular condition.[703]

The law-enforcement exception applicable in criminal cases[704] primarily reflects the possibility that observations[705] made by police officers during the investigation of a crime may be unreliable because of the adversarial nature of the enterprise.[706] How-

---

700. *See, e.g.,* ***Samuels-Wickham v. Dep't of Pub. Safety***, 121 S.W.3d 829, 831 (Tex. App.—Fort Worth 2003, no pet.) (DPS Form DIC-23—officer's sworn report—was admissible under Rule 803(8)); ***Tex. Alcoholic Bev. Comm'n v. Sanchez***, 96 S.W.3d 483, 488-89 (Tex. App.—Austin 2002, no pet.) (police reports, which included eyewitness accounts of officers investigating criminal activity, were admissible under Rule 803(8)(B), now Rule 803(8)(A)(ii), in civil action for obtaining wine-and-beer retailer's permit; reports indicated that TABC and police found pattern of criminal activity at motel sharing same location as permit applicant's business); ***Tex. Dep't of Pub. Safety v. Struve***, 79 S.W.3d 796, 803-04 (Tex. App.—Corpus Christi 2002, pet. denied) (in civil suspension-of-license hearing under Rule 803(8)(B) and 803(8)(C), now Rule 803(8)(A)(ii) and 803(8)(A)(iii), administrative-law judge properly admitted police officer's sworn affidavit that contained observations and factual findings resulting from the arresting officer's investigation; nothing indicated that the sources of the information lacked trustworthiness); ***McRae v. Echols***, 8 S.W.3d 797, 799-800 (Tex. App.—Waco 2000, pet. denied) (accident reports were admissible under Rule 803(8) because there was no evidence showing a lack of trustworthiness; narrative opinion of investigating officer within report was also admissible because it was based on his factual investigation); ***Leyva v. Soltero***, 966 S.W.2d 765, 768-69 (Tex. App.—El Paso 1998, no pet.) (accident report and investigating officer's statement were admissible under Rule 803(8)(B), now Rule 803(8)(A)(ii), in personal-injury case); ***Porter v. Tex. Dep't of Pub. Safety***, 712 S.W.2d 263, 264-65 (Tex. App.—San Antonio 1986, no writ) (police officer's affidavit stating that he arrested the driver and requested that driver take a breathalyzer test was admissible under Rule 803(8)(B), now Rule 803(8)(A)(ii)). *But see* ***McRae***, 8 S.W.3d at 802-03 (Gray, J., dissenting) (officer's opinions and conclusions contained within accident report should not be admitted under Rule 803(8) without expert-witness sponsor who is subject to cross-examination and can demonstrate reliability of expert opinions within report under ***Daubert/Robinson***).

701. *See, e.g.,* ***Minnehaha Cty. v. Kelley***, 150 F.2d 356, 361 (8th Cir. 1945) (weather-bureau records showing rainfall in South Dakota were admissible).

702. *See, e.g.,* ***Hyundai Motor Co. v. Alvarado***, 989 S.W.2d 32, 41 (Tex. App.—San Antonio 1998, pet. granted, judgm't vacated w.r.m.) (document prepared by National Highway Transportation Safety Administration after investigation of seat-belt safety in certain cars was admissible under rule even though report was based on customer complaints); ***Brewer v. Capital Cities/ABC, Inc.***, 986 S.W.2d 636, 644 (Tex. App.—Fort Worth 1998, no pet.) (Department of Human Services report, detailing nursing-home inspections and investigations, was admissible under rule in defamation case to prove truth of matter and also defendant's state of mind—lack of malice).

703. *See* ***Glens Falls Ins. v. Peters***, 379 S.W.2d 946, 948 (Tex. Civ. App.—Fort Worth 1964), *rev'd on other grounds*, 386 S.W.2d 529 (Tex. 1965).

704. The limitation does not apply in civil proceedings, even when those proceedings are related to a criminal offense. *See* ***Tex. Dep't of Pub. Safety v. Caruana***, 363 S.W.3d 558, 564 (Tex. 2012) (because administrative license-revocation proceedings are civil, not criminal, Rule 803(8)(B), now Rule 803(8)(A)(ii), does not apply and investigation reports by law enforcement are admissible); ***Tex. Dep't of Pub. Safety v. Duggin***, 962 S.W.2d 76, 80 (Tex. App.—Houston [1st Dist.] 1997, no pet.) (because administrative hearing to suspend driver's license for failure to take breath test is a civil proceeding, law-enforcement limitation of Criminal Rule 803(8)(B), now Rule 803(8)(A)(ii), does not apply and probable-cause affidavits are admissible); ***Tex. Dep't of Pub. Safety v. Edwards***, 941 S.W.2d 266, 266-67 (Tex. App.—Eastland 1996, no writ) (driver's-license-suspension proceeding is not a "quasi criminal" proceeding that requires exclusion of law-enforcement reports under Criminal Rule 803(8)(B), now Rule 803(8)(A)(ii)).

705. Although Rule 803(8)(A)(ii) uses the phrase "a matter *observed* while under a legal duty to report," the rule covers more than those specific events or acts that a public officer literally saw. ***Perry v. State***, 957 S.W.2d 894, 898 (Tex. App.—Texarkana 1997, pet. ref'd). For example, a person's driving record is covered by the rule, even though no public officer may have actually seen each infraction contained within that record. *See* ***Spaulding v. State***, 896 S.W.2d 587, 588-89 (Tex. App.—Houston [1st Dist.] 1995, no pet.); ***Smith v. State***, 895 S.W.2d 449, 455 (Tex. App.—Dallas 1995, pet. ref'd); ***Tanner v. State***, 875 S.W.2d 8, 9 (Tex. App.—Houston [1st Dist.] 1994, pet. ref'd).

706. ***Caruana***, 363 S.W.3d at 564; ***Fischer v. State***, 252 S.W.3d 375, 382-83 (Tex. Crim. App. 2008); *see* ***United States v. Quezada***, 754 F.2d 1190, 1193-94 (5th Cir. 1985) (exclusion is based on presumption that police officer's observa-

RULE 803

ever, this exception does not necessarily apply to law-enforcement reports that are prepared in a nonadversarial setting, that are unrelated to any specific litigation, and that record objective observations.[707] In *Cole v. State*, the court of criminal appeals held that a laboratory report made by a nontestifying chemist employed by the Department of Public Safety was not admissible under former Rule 803(8)(B), now Rule 803(8)(A)(ii), because such chemists are "law enforcement personnel" within the meaning of the rule.[708] The court specifically rejected the State's argument that such laboratory analyses are objective, ministerial reports and thus outside the rationale for the law-enforcement exception.[709]

In a later opinion, the court of criminal appeals applied the two-pronged standard established in *Cole* to hold that a medical examiner's reports were admissible because medical examiners are not "law enforcement personnel."[710] The court reiterated the two

---

tions at a crime scene may not be as reliable as observations by other public officials due to the adversarial nature of the confrontation between a criminal defendant and police); *Garcia v. State*, 868 S.W.2d 337, 342 (Tex. Crim. App. 1993) (medical examiner's office is generally not a "uniquely litigious and prosecution-oriented environment as to create an adversarial context").

707. *See, e.g.*, *United States v. Gilbert*, 774 F.2d 962, 964-65 (9th Cir. 1985) (criminologist's note on latent-fingerprint card indicating that prints were lifted from a statuette used in smuggling heroin were admissible under Federal Rule 803(8)(B), now Rule 803(8)(A)(ii), because the routine act of reporting a latent print is ministerial, not adversarial or evaluative); *United States v. Union Nacional de Trabajadores*, 576 F.2d 388, 390-91 (1st Cir. 1978) (under Federal Rule 803(8)(B), now Rule 803(8)(A)(ii), introduction of marshal's return of service to prove that certain persons had been served was admitted because adversarial circumstances were not present); *United States v. Grady*, 544 F.2d 598, 604 (2d Cir. 1976) (law-enforcement reports that related to routine functions were admissible); *Pondexter v. State*, 942 S.W.2d 577, 585 (Tex. Crim. App. 1996) (when police officer was performing his ordinary, routine duties of recording property that was taken in and out of the police property room, his observations and notation should be presumed reliable; matters observed or recorded by police officers are admissible under Criminal Rule 803(8)(B), now Rule 803(8)(A)(ii), if the observations are made and recorded in a ministerial manner); *Ponce v. State*, 828 S.W.2d 50, 52 (Tex. App.—Houston [1st Dist.] 1991, pet. ref'd) (operating reports on Intoxilyzer machine were admitted because reports were not made in an adversarial setting).

708. 839 S.W.2d 798, 803 (Tex. Crim. App. 1990) (orig. op.); *see also* *United States v. Sharpe*, 193 F.3d 852, 868 (5th Cir. 1999) (FBI lab reports were inadmissible under rule even when offered by defendant). *But see* *Durham v. State*, 956 S.W.2d 62, 65 (Tex. App.—Tyler 1997, pet. ref'd) (toxicologist with county forensic laboratory was not part of law-enforcement personnel for purposes of rule); *Caw v. State*, 851 S.W.2d 322, 324 (Tex. App.—El Paso 1993) (chemists working for Dallas County forensic laboratory were not law-enforcement personnel because county laboratory does not have the "inherently adversarial, litigious and prosecution-oriented environment characterized in *Cole*"), *pet. ref'd*, 864 S.W.2d 546 (Tex. Crim. App. 1993).

To avoid this problem, especially in the context of reports from a criminology lab where technician turnover is high and frequently the person who performed a lab test has left before trial begins, the court of criminal appeals held that a supervising chemist may rely on lab reports prepared by his subordinates in forming an opinion as an expert. *Aguilar v. State*, 887 S.W.2d 27, 29-30 (Tex. Crim. App. 1994).

709. *Cole*, 839 S.W.2d at 803-04 (orig. op.). *But see id.* at 816 (McCormick, P.J., White, J., dissenting) (op. on reh'g) (legislative history of exception in Federal Rule 803(8)(B), now Rule 803(8)(A)(ii), was specifically concerned with the prosecution offering the offense report of "the policeman on the beat" instead of live testimony that would be subject to confrontation and cross-examination). On rehearing, the court rejected or distinguished the 16 cases that the State relied on while acknowledging "the existence of considerable authority holding that chemical analyses and certain laboratory tests and reports are routine and objective in nature and therefore admissible." *Id.* at 808 & n.7 (op. on reh'g).

710. *See* *Garcia*, 868 S.W.2d at 341-42 (medical examiners' primary responsibility is to determine cause of death; thus, they are generally "disinterested third parties who do not have an *inherent* motive to distort the results of their reports"; litigation is not the focus of their duties); *see also* *Moreno Denoso v. State*, 156 S.W.3d 166, 180-81 (Tex. App.—Corpus Christi 2005, pet. ref'd) (following *Garcia* in upholding admission of autopsy report; "[e]ven though

parts of the test: (1) whether the reports consist of "objective, routine, scientific determinations of an unambiguous factual nature prepared by officials with no inherent motivation to distort the results on the issue" and (2) whether they were prepared in an adversarial context or for purposes independent of specific litigation.[711] Thus, if public reports are not made by someone engaged in the "competitive enterprise" of criminal investigation and are based on routine, objective evaluation, they qualify for admission under Rule 803(8)(A)(ii).[712] Certainly, individual public-office reports might lack sufficient indicia of reliability under Rule 803(8)(B), but that should be determined on a case-by-case basis. Only those reports that are compiled by true law-enforcement agents setting out matters they have observed are categorically barred by the rule. Even though such hearsay reports may not be admissible, they may form the basis of a testifying expert's opinion.[713]

Public records and reports that are not admissible under Rule 803(8)(A)(ii) because they are prepared by members of law enforcement may not be admitted as business records under Rule 803(6) because of the same reliability problems that make them inadmissible under the public-records exception.[714]

Public records created for purposes of a criminal prosecution will also be barred by the Confrontation Clause. The U.S. Supreme Court held that the trial court erred in admitting chemists' certificates, which were affidavits stating that evidence seized was

---

autopsy reports are partially subjective, they are generally prepared by officials with no motive to fabricate the results of the reports, and as a general rule, a medical examiner's office is not such a uniquely litigious and prosecution-oriented environment as to create an adversarial context"). However, some Texas courts of appeals, following ***Melendez-Diaz v. Massachusetts***, 557 U.S. 305 (2009), have held that autopsy reports prepared as part of a criminal investigation are testimonial and thus not admissible under the Confrontation Clause. Refer to note 141 *supra* and accompanying text.

711. ***Garcia***, 868 S.W.2d at 341-42; *see* ***Cole***, 839 S.W.2d at 808-09 (op. on reh'g).

712. *See, e.g.,* ***Greer v. State***, 999 S.W.2d 484, 489 (Tex. App.—Houston [14th Dist.] 1999, pet. ref'd) (probation officers are not members of law enforcement, and nature of probation is rehabilitative; probation file contained objective and routine information and was thus admissible under Rule 803(8)(B), now Rule 803(8)(A)(ii)); ***Johnston v. State***, 959 S.W.2d 230, 240-41 (Tex. App.—Dallas 1997, no pet.) (jail nurse's notes were admissible because she was not part of law-enforcement personnel for purposes of rule; if nurse were part of law enforcement, her observations would be of a routine, ministerial type); ***Perry v. State***, 957 S.W.2d 894, 899 (Tex. App.—Texarkana 1997, pet. ref'd) (child-support-enforcement officer who had created a summary of defendant's total arrearage of child-support payments was not a law-enforcement officer for purposes of Criminal Rule 803(8)(B), now Rule 803(8)(A)(ii)); ***Smith v. State***, 895 S.W.2d 449, 455 (Tex. App.—Dallas 1995, pet. ref'd) (DPS driving record and order of suspension were not prepared for litigation, but rather recorded routine, objective observations and thus were admissible under rule). Similarly, business records of a government or law-enforcement agency that are compiled for routine, nonadversarial, or public-record-keeping purposes are nontestimonial and do not violate the Confrontation Clause. *See* ***Melendez-Diaz***, 557 U.S. at 324. Refer to notes 134-162 *supra* and accompanying text.

713. *See, e.g.,* ***Martinez v. State***, 22 S.W.3d 504, 507-08 (Tex. Crim. App. 2000) (expert opinion of DPS laboratory supervisor who testified that certain substance was cocaine weighing .34 grams was not hearsay, even though supervisor did not conduct tests; expert relied on report prepared by subordinate who conducted tests, but neither report nor its contents were offered into evidence). Refer to *Article VII: Opinions & Expert Testimony, supra* p. 747.

    If the hearsay is testimonial, the testifying expert must be available for cross-examination and must not disclose the contents of the hearsay statements. *See* ***Martinez v. State***, 311 S.W.3d 104, 112 (Tex. App.—Amarillo 2010, pet. ref'd); ***Wood v. State***, 299 S.W.3d 200, 213 (Tex. App.—Austin 2009, pet. ref'd). Refer to *Article VII: Opinions & Expert Testimony, supra* p. 753.

714. *See* ***Cole***, 839 S.W.2d at 805-06 (orig. op.). Refer to notes 670-674 *supra* and accompanying text.

RULE 803

cocaine.[715] Because the certificates were created for use at trial, they were testimonial statements under ***Crawford v. Washington*** and admission of the certificates violated the defendant's Sixth Amendment right of confrontation.[716]

(3) Rule 803(8)(A)(iii): Factual findings from a legally authorized investigation.
Records that are admissible under Rule 803(8)(A)(iii) must relate to matters that the public office is authorized to investigate,[717] but the rule permits the introduction of records based on statements by outsiders to the public office.[718] Thus, the source of the information does not need to be an official with personal knowledge.[719] A primary example is the record of an investigative agency's administrative findings,[720] such as autopsy reports.[721] Reports that are admissible under this subsection are not limited to "factual findings," but may also contain opinions and conclusions.[722] Legal conclusions, however, are not permitted.[723]

---

715. ***Melendez-Diaz***, 557 U.S. at 310-11.

716. *Id.* Refer to notes 138-140 *supra* and accompanying text.

717. The proponent of the record must show that the public office is, in fact, authorized by law to conduct this type of investigation and that the report resulted from this authorized investigation. *See* ***Cowan v. State***, 840 S.W.2d 435, 438 n.11 (Tex. Crim. App. 1992) (under Criminal Rule 803(8)(C), now Rule 803(8)(A)(iii), investigation need only be authorized, not required by law).

718. *See, e.g.*, ***Corrales v. Dep't of Family & Prot. Servs.***, 155 S.W.3d 478, 486-87 (Tex. App.—El Paso 2004, no pet.) (police reports containing the results of police investigations, including statements by witnesses who were not present for trial and unavailable for cross-examination, were admissible under Rule 803(8)(C), now Rule 803(8)(A)(iii), in trial for termination of parental rights; opposing party did not carry its burden to show their lack of trustworthiness); ***Truck Ins. Exch. v. Smetak***, 102 S.W.3d 851, 857-58 (Tex. App.—Dallas 2003, no pet.) (because appeals-panel decision issued by Workers' Compensation Commission met requirements of Rule 803(8)(C), now Rule 803(8)(A)(iii), and opponent did not show any specific lack of trustworthiness in that decision, trial court did not err in admitting it).

719. *See, e.g.*, ***Robbins v. Whelan***, 653 F.2d 47, 52 (1st Cir. 1981) (performance-data report, prepared by public-agency officials "who personally neither produced the figures [nor] verified their accuracy," was admissible because the agency determined that "the information was sufficiently reliable to publish for the buying public to rely upon when comparing car safety performances").

720. *See, e.g.*, ***In re Plywood Antitrust Litig.***, 655 F.2d 627, 636-37 (5th Cir. 1981) (findings by an administrative-law judge that were adopted by the Federal Trade Commission in a department opinion were admissible when the opinion was redacted to eliminate the agency's conclusions and the outcome of the proceeding); ***Local Union No. 59 v. Namco Elec., Inc.***, 653 F.2d 143, 145 (5th Cir. 1981) (National Labor Relations Board findings were admissible). *But see* ***Gilchrist v. Jim Slemons Imps., Inc.***, 803 F.2d 1488, 1499-1500 (9th Cir. 1986) (no automatic rule of admissibility for public records dealing with administrative findings; prejudicial impact should be examined instead).

721. *See* ***Tex. Workers' Comp. Comm'n v. Wausau Underwriters Ins.***, 127 S.W.3d 50, 62 (Tex. App.—Houston [1st Dist.] 2003, pet. denied).

722. *See* ***Beech Aircraft Corp. v. Rainey***, 488 U.S. 153, 170 (1988) (investigatory reports may contain opinions or conclusions as long as they are based on a factual investigation and they satisfy the trustworthiness provisions of Federal Rule 803(8)); ***McRae v. Echols***, 8 S.W.3d 797, 800 (Tex. App.—Waco 2000, pet. denied) (following ***Rainey*** under Texas Rule 803(8)(C), now Rule 803(8)(A)(iii)); *see, e.g.*, ***Cowan***, 840 S.W.2d at 437-39 (Marine Corps Medical Board report of defendant's mental condition, containing both factual findings and opinions, was sufficiently reliable to be admissible under rule).

In ***Rainey***, Justice Brennan stated that neither the language of Federal Rule 803(8)(C) (now Rule 803(8)(A)(iii)) nor its legislative history called for a distinction between fact and opinion. 488 U.S. at 168. Thus, a broad reading of the rule is necessary because of the analytical difficulties of distinguishing between fact and opinion. *See id.* at 169. As long as the opinion or conclusion is based on a factual investigation and otherwise satisfies the trustworthiness requirement, it should be admissible. *Id.* at 170; *see also* ***McRae***, 8 S.W.3d at 800 (narrative-opinion section in DPS officer's accident report was admissible in personal-injury case). *But see* ***McRae***, 8 S.W.3d at 802-03 (Gray, J., dissenting) (officer's opinions and conclusions contained in accident report should not

Legislative reports are frequently not admissible under the rule because they deal "with documents produced by the Congress—a politically-motivated, partisan body."[724] Similarly, academic papers or journal articles based on studies conducted by public agencies do not fall within the rule,[725] nor do preliminary or interim reports.[726] The trial court has considerable discretion in excluding public records that might facially meet the foundation requirements of Rule 803(8)(A)(iii) but nonetheless indicate a lack of trustworthiness under Rule 803(8)(B).[727]

(4) Relationship between Rules 803(8) & 803(6). It is important to distinguish the particular features of the public-records exception from those of the business-records exception. Neither regularity nor contemporaneity is required to qualify a public record for admission, but both are essential elements of any record offered under Rule 803(6).[728] Consequently, the foundation requirements for a public record under Rule 803(8) are only that the document be authentic and that it contain one of the three types of matters specified in the rule.[729] The proponent of a public record does not need to show that the record or report was regularly prepared or made at or near the time of

---

be admitted under Rule 803(8) without expert-witness sponsor who is subject to cross-examination and can demonstrate reliability of expert opinions within report under **Daubert/Robinson**).

723. *Cf.* **Hines v. Brandon Steel Decks, Inc.**, 886 F.2d 299, 302-03 (11th Cir. 1989) (legal conclusions are not admissible under Federal Rule 803(8)(C), now Rule 803(8)(A)(iii), "because the jury would have no way of knowing whether the preparer of the report was cognizant of the requirements underlying the legal conclusion").

724. *E.g.*, **Pearce v. E.F. Hutton Grp., Inc.**, 653 F. Supp. 810, 813-14 (D.D.C. 1987) (draft report of congressional subcommittee that was neither based on an adjudicatory hearing nor offered to resolve a factual dispute was inadmissible in opposing defendant's summary-judgment motion in libel suit; report lacked trustworthiness because of the political nature of the investigating body); *see, e.g.*, **Anderson v. City of N.Y.**, 657 F. Supp. 1571, 1577-79 (S.D. N.Y. 1987) (report by a House of Representatives Subcommittee was inadmissible because the subcommittee lacked personal knowledge of the events under investigation "and heard, primarily, only one side of the story").

725. *See, e.g.*, **Robinson v. Warner-Lambert**, 998 S.W.2d 407, 412 (Tex. App.—Waco 1999, no pet.) (article based on study conducted by Bureau of Public Health and Centers for Disease Control and published in medical-association journal was not a report issued directly by public agency and therefore was not admissible under rule).

726. **Smith v. Isuzu Motors Ltd.**, 137 F.3d 859, 862 (5th Cir. 1998).

727. *See* **Rainey**, 488 U.S. at 167 ("[A] trial judge has the discretion, and indeed the obligation, to exclude an entire report or portions thereof—whether narrow 'factual' statements or broader 'conclusions'—that she determines to be untrustworthy."); *see, e.g.*, **Pilgrim's Pride Corp. v. Smoak**, 134 S.W.3d 880, 892 n.2 (Tex. App.—Texarkana 2004, pet. denied) (police officer's opinion on cause of accident contained in his public-records police report was inadmissible under Rule 803(8) in personal-injury case because officer was insufficiently qualified to give expert opinion on whose negligence caused the accident); **Ter-Vartanyan v. R&R Freight, Inc.**, 111 S.W.3d 779, 784 (Tex. App.—Dallas 2003, pet. denied) (police officer's written public-record accident report met "trustworthiness" requirement of Rule 803(8)(C), now Rule 803(8)(B), because officer was sufficiently qualified to express his expert opinion on cause of accident).

728. *See* TEX. R. EVID. 803(6)(A)-(6)(C). Refer to notes 603-674 *supra* and accompanying text.

729. *See* **Cowan v. State**, 840 S.W.2d 435, 437 n.7 (Tex. Crim. App. 1992) ("Once a document has been authenticated, no formal laying of a foundation is required for admission under Rule 803(8)(C) [now Rule 803(8)(A)(iii)]."). Documents that are prepared by an individual or a private group of people do not take on the status of public reports under any of the three subsections of Rule 803(8)(A) merely because those privately prepared documents are then filed with a public office. *See, e.g.*, **Fibreboard Corp. v. Pool**, 813 S.W.2d 658, 676 (Tex. App.—Texarkana 1991, writ denied) (chart prepared by union consultant and filed with OSHA was not an official document under the rule; document or exhibit itself must be prepared by a public officer or by an employee under the officer's supervision in the course of their official duties); **Wright v. Lewis**, 777 S.W.2d 520, 524 (Tex. App.—Corpus Christi 1989, writ de-

the event recorded.[730] Further, Rule 803(8)(A)(iii) is more liberal than the correlative business-records exception because it allows the admission of investigative reports that depend on outsiders unconnected with the record-keeping process. However, as with the business-records exception, hearsay statements in a public record or report are not admissible merely because they happen to be included in that public report.[731]

Records that are not admissible as business records under Rule 803(6) may nonetheless be admissible as public records of "a matter observed" under Rule 803(8).

5. Rule 803(9): Public records of vital statistics. Rule 803(9) provides a hearsay exception for a "record of a birth, death, or marriage, if reported to a public office in accordance with a legal duty."[732] The vital-statistics exception is based on considerations of trustworthiness and necessity.[733] A record such as a birth certificate is admissible to prove any fact contained within the certificate such as name, time and date of birth, place of birth, name and age of parents, and any other facts in that record. A death certificate qualifies for admission under this exception, as well as under Texas Health & Safety Code section 191.052.[734]

6. Rule 803(10): Absence of public record. As with Rule 803(7), dealing with the absence of business records, Rule 803(10) allows parties to offer the absence of a public record or statement as proof that the record or statement does not exist or that a matter did not occur or exist if a public office regularly kept a record or statement of that type of matter.[735] Testimony can be in the form of a certification under Rule 902.[736]

---

nied) (letter from Assistant U.S. Attorney contained within the public records of Texas State Board of Podiatry Examiners was not admissible under Rule 803(8) because it was "not a record, report, statement or data compilation of either the Podiatry Board or the U.S. Department of Justice").

730. *Porter v. Tex. Dep't of Pub. Safety*, 712 S.W.2d 263, 265 (Tex. App.—San Antonio 1986, no writ).

731. *See* TEX. R. EVID. 805; *see, e.g.*, *Kratz v. Exxon Corp.*, 890 S.W.2d 899, 905 (Tex. App.—El Paso 1994, no writ) (dicta; eyewitness statements contained in police accident report were not admissible under any subsection of Rule 803(8)); *Levelland Indep. Sch. Dist. v. Contreras*, 865 S.W.2d 474, 476 (Tex. App.—Amarillo 1993, writ denied) (public-records exception to hearsay rule did not permit admission of hearsay statements within Texas Employment Commission hearing record into evidence before reviewing court).

732. TEX. R. EVID. 803(9). For the definitions of "record" and "public office," refer to note 683 *supra*.

733. *See* 4 LOUISELL & MUELLER, *supra* note 250, §457, at 777-78. The vital-statistics exception is consistent with earlier Texas case law. *See, e.g.*, *Reserve Life Ins. v. Estate of Shacklett*, 412 S.W.2d 920, 922 (Tex. Civ. App.—Tyler 1967, writ ref'd n.r.e.) (death certificate was prima facie evidence of facts that it contained); *Neff v. Johnson*, 391 S.W.2d 760, 762-63 (Tex. Civ. App.—Houston 1965, no writ) (birth certificate was admitted to prove age). *See generally* 1A RAY, *supra* note 9, §1274, at 462-65 (discussing admissibility of marriage, birth, and death registers).

734. *E.g.*, *Tex. Workers' Comp. Comm'n v. Wausau Underwriters Ins.*, 127 S.W.3d 50, 61-62 (Tex. App.—Houston [1st Dist.] 2003, pet. denied) (death certificate itself is admissible under exception, but specific contents within that certificate are not necessarily admissible if certificate contains hearsay within hearsay; expert opinion by medical examiner that cause of death was suicide was admissible under Rule 705, thus, no error in admitting unredacted death certificate); *see* TEX. HEALTH & SAFETY CODE §191.052.

735. TEX. R. EVID. 803(10); *see, e.g.*, *Tex. Mun. Power Agency v. Johnston*, 405 S.W.3d 776, 783 & n.3 (Tex. App.—Houston [1st Dist.] 2013, no pet.) (certification from assistant secretary of agency's board of directors that minutes and records from board's meetings contained no records of any action by board requiring filing of condemnation proceeding against plaintiff-landowner was admissible under Rule 803(10)); *Mega Child Care, Inc. v. Tex. Dep't of Prot. & Regulatory Servs.*, 29 S.W.3d 303, 311-12 (Tex. App.—Houston [14th Dist.] 2000, no pet.) (witness's testimony that: "(1) child care facilities are required to submit the names of their employees to DPRS before they begin working; (2) DPRS maintains a record of all names of all employees submitted by child care facilities; (3) these

RULE 803

The federal counterpart to this rule, Federal Rule 803(10), includes a notice requirement for criminal cases.[737] This requirement was added in response to the U.S. Supreme Court's decision in *Melendez-Diaz v. Massachusetts*.[738]

7. Rule 803(11): Records of religious organizations. Rule 803(11) provides a hearsay exception for "[a] statement of birth, legitimacy, ancestry, marriage, divorce, death, relationship by blood or marriage, or similar facts of personal or family history, contained in a regularly kept record of a religious organization."[739] A "regularly kept record of a religious organization"[740] would qualify as a business record under Rule 803(6), but that provision does not permit the admission of records to prove facts reported by persons who do not have a business duty to report (i.e., all participants acting "in the regular course of business").[741] Conversely, Rule 803(11) allows records to prove matters where no member is acting "in the course of the activity."[742] The rationale for the special treatment of matters covered by this rule is "the unlikelihood that false information would be furnished on occasions of this kind ...."[743]

8. Rule 803(12): Certificates of marriage, baptism & similar ceremonies. Rule 803(12) provides a hearsay exception for statements of fact in a certificate (1) that is made by a person "authorized by a religious organization or by law to perform the act certified" and (2) "attesting that the person performed a marriage or similar ceremony or admin-

---

files are regularly compiled for the purpose of conducting criminal background checks; and (4) after searching DPRS files, she could find no record of the employee in question" was admissible under rule to show absence of a public record as proof that child-care center had not complied with DPRS regulations); *Towne Square Assocs. v. Angelina Cty. Appr. Dist.*, 709 S.W.2d 776, 777 (Tex. App.—Beaumont 1986, no writ) (court upheld trial court's grant of summary judgment based on affidavits stating that a diligent search of the relevant public records did not reveal a required notice of appeal of property-tax evaluation). Refer to notes 675-682 *supra* and accompanying text. The effect of this provision is identical to that of a section of the former official-records statute. Act of May 29, 1951, 52nd Leg., R.S., ch. 471, 1951 Tex. Gen. Laws 830, *amended by* Act of May 22, 1953, 53rd Leg., R.S., ch. 304, §1, 1953 Tex. Gen. Laws 756, 756, *amended by* Act of May 27, 1961, 57th Leg., R.S., ch. 321, §1, 1961 Tex. Gen. Laws 685, 685-86, *amended by* Act of May 15, 1975, 64th Leg., R.S., ch. 280, §1, 1975 Tex. Gen. Laws 666, 666-67 (former Texas Revised Civil Statutes art. 3731a deemed repealed as to civil proceedings effective 1983 and as to criminal proceedings effective 1986). For the definitions of "record" and "public office," refer to note 683 *supra*.

736. TEX. R. EVID. 803(10).

737. FED. R. EVID. 803(10)(B).

738. FED. R. EVID. 803 advisory committee's note to 2013 amendments. The Advisory Committee also noted that the amendment is based on Texas Code of Criminal Procedure article 38.41, which was cited by the *Melendez-Diaz* Court. *See* TEX. CODE CRIM. PROC. art. 38.41, §4; *Melendez-Diaz v. Massachusetts*, 557 U.S. 305, 326 (2009); FED. R. EVID. 803 advisory committee's note to 2013 amendments. For a discussion of *Melendez-Diaz*, refer to notes 136-141 *supra* and accompanying text.

739. TEX. R. EVID. 803(11). This exception has no direct common-law authority, and the same is true for Federal Rule 803(11). *See* FED. R. EVID. 803(11) advisory committee's note.

740. TEX. R. EVID. 803(11).

741. *See Skillern & Sons, Inc. v. Rosen*, 359 S.W.2d 298, 305 (Tex. 1962); FED. R. EVID. 803(6) advisory committee's note.

742. FED. R. EVID. 803(11) advisory committee's note.

743. *Id.* A document's admissibility under Rule 803(11) "does not depend on the personal views or religious beliefs of those making the records. Nor does Rule 803(11) depend on the popularity or acceptance of the religious organization in question or the character of the organization's leader." *Jessop v. State*, 368 S.W.3d 653, 684 (Tex. App.—Austin 2012, no pet.).

istered a sacrament."[744] The certificate must have been issued when the act occurred or within a reasonable time after.[745] The rule slightly extends the official-records concept to include certifications by persons who are not public officials but who act in that capacity on a particular occasion.[746]

9. Rule 803(13): Family records. Rule 803(13) creates a hearsay exception for statements of fact about personal or family history that are contained in family records.[747] According to Graham, "[t]he basis of the exception is that the family would not allow an untruthful entry or inscription to be made or to remain without protest."[748]

10. Rule 803(14): Records of documents that affect an interest in property. Rule 803(14), the reliable-records exception, makes a properly recorded document admissible to prove not only its contents, but also "its signing and its delivery by each person who purports to have signed it."[749] To meet the exception, the record must be one that is kept in a public office, and a statute must authorize that office to record those types of documents.[750] Thus, documents such as deeds, liens, mortgages, or easements that show on their face that they have been properly recorded may be admitted as an exception to the hearsay rule even when they are not offered as a public record. A homeowner may offer his own copy of a publicly recorded document; it does not need to come directly from the district clerk's office.

---

744. Tex. R. Evid. 803(12)(A), (12)(B).

745. Tex. R. Evid. 803(12)(C).

746. While there was no authority in earlier Texas cases for this doctrine, the former official-records act could have been interpreted to allow for such an exception. *See* 1A Ray, *supra* note 9, §1286, at 480-81 (clergy member's act of certifying a marriage should be read as official, even though the duty is performed only occasionally).

747. *Jessop*, 368 S.W.3d at 683. A family record can include items such as a Bible, genealogy, chart, inscription on a portrait, or engraving on a ring, urn, or burial marker. Tex. R. Evid. 803(13). Statements covered by Rule 803(13) were admissible under a hearsay exception at common law. But in Texas, as in other jurisdictions, the common-law version required that the declarant be unavailable, that the declarant be a member of the family with no motive to misrepresent, and that the declaration be made before the controversy arose. *See* 1A Ray, *supra* note 9, §§1342-1345; E.J. Ball, Comment, *Admissibility of Hearsay Evidence on Matters of Family History*, 5 Ark. L. Rev. 58, 59-61 (1951). The rule abolishes these restrictions, as the written-records exception describes. *See* Tex. R. Evid. 804(b)(3). For a discussion of the hearsay exception covering testimony about personal or family history, refer to notes 952-956 *infra* and accompanying text.

748. 7 Graham, *supra* note 491, §803:13, at 442.

749. Tex. R. Evid. 803(14)(A); *see, e.g.*, *Graff v. Whittle*, 947 S.W.2d 629, 640-41 (Tex. App.—Texarkana 1997, writ denied) (documents were admissible not to show an interest in property, but to establish location of road). Texas law had long provided that such an instrument "shall be admitted as evidence in any suit in this State without the necessity of proving its execution." Act approved May 13, 1846, 1st Leg., An Act to Regulate Proceedings in the District Courts: Evidence, §90, 1846 Tex. Gen. Laws 363, 387-88, *reprinted in* 2 H.P.N. Gammel, The Laws of Texas 1822-1897, at 1669, 1693-94 (Austin, Gammel Book Co. 1898), *amended by* Act approved April 23, 1907, 30th Leg., R.S., ch. 165 (CLXV), §1, 1907 Tex. Gen. Laws 308, 308, *amended by* Act approved June 7, 1927, 40th Leg., 1st C.S., ch. 73, §1, 1927 Tex. Gen. Laws 198, 198-99, *amended by* Act of May 16, 1939, 46th Leg., R.S., ch. 2, §1, 1939 Tex. Gen. Laws 325, 325-26, *amended by* Act of May 15, 1941, 47th Leg., R.S., ch. 299, §1, 1941 Tex. Gen. Laws 476, 476-77 (former Texas Revised Civil Statutes art. 3726 deemed repealed as to civil proceedings effective 1983 and as to criminal proceedings effective 1986). Rule 803(14) effectively abolished the advance-filing and notice requirements of the earlier statute, former Texas Revised Civil Statutes article 3726. *See id.*

750. Tex. R. Evid. 803(14)(B), (14)(C); *see also* Tex. R. Evid. 101(h)(3) (definition of "public office" includes public agency).

11. Rule 803(15): Statements in documents that affect an interest in property. Unlike Rule 803(14), which deals with recorded documents affecting an interest in property, Rule 803(15) authorizes the admission of statements contained in unrecorded documents purporting to affect an interest in property if the statement was relevant to the document's purpose.[751]

The rationale for the rule is that

> [t]he circumstances under which dispositive documents are executed and the requirement that the recital be germane to the purpose of the document are believed to be adequate guarantees of trustworthiness, particularly in view of the nonapplicability of the rule if dealings with the property have been inconsistent with the document.[752]

This exception allows for the admission of information such as an automobile's Vehicle Identification Number and the owner's name, contained in the manufacturer's certificate of origin.[753] In an unorthodox use of the rule, the court of criminal appeals held in ***Madden v. State*** that a murder victim's handwritten list of weapons and corresponding serial numbers, found by his widow in a box containing the deceased's "personal papers," constituted a statement in documents affecting an interest in property under Rule 803(15).[754] Reasoning that exceptions to the hearsay rule should be liberally construed, the court held that the handwritten document, although it was not a dispositive document such as a mortgage, deed, or lease, indicated the deceased's interest in the property.[755] Second, the document bore adequate indicia of reliability because the deceased's widow testified that it was written in her husband's handwriting.[756] Third,

---

751. TEX. R. EVID. 803(15); *see* 33 GOODE ET AL., *supra* note 32, §§803.19, 803.20 (Tex. Practice 1988); *see, e.g.,* ***Guidry v. State***, 9 S.W.3d 133, 146-47 (Tex. Crim. App. 1999) (inventory and appraisal list filed in divorce action were admissible to prove that codefendant in capital-murder case had a property interest in a Jeep; adequate indicia of reliability because document was sworn to by defendant and filed in court); *see also* ***McCraw v. Maris***, 828 S.W.2d 756, 757 (Tex. 1992) (duplicate beneficiary form in deceased's handwriting—although it had not been witnessed or filed—was admissible to prove its existence, not for truth of matter asserted).

    Rule 803(15), like Rule 803(14), broadens and liberalizes a doctrine that Texas statutes had previously recognized. The previous statutes allowed statements in recorded instruments only on the subjects of family history, heirship, marital status, and genealogy of a decedent. Moreover, such statements were admissible only if the instrument had been recorded for five years or more. Act of April 17, 1957, 55th Leg., R.S., ch. 125, §1, 1957 Tex. Gen. Laws 266, 266, *amended by* Act of May 20, 1965, 59th Leg., R.S., ch. 480, §1, 1965 Tex. Gen. Laws 994, 994 (former Texas Revised Civil Statutes art. 3726a deemed repealed as to civil proceedings effective 1983 and as to criminal proceedings effective 1986). In addition, one of the former statutes contained a notice requirement. *See id.* Rule 803(15) does not contain these restrictions and does not require that the instrument be recorded.

752. FED. R. EVID. 803(15) advisory committee's note. Under Texas Rule 803(15), statements can be excluded as hearsay if "later dealings with the property are inconsistent with the truth of the statement or the purport of the document." TEX. R. EVID. 803(15).

753. *See, e.g.,* ***Harris v. State***, 846 S.W.2d 960, 964-65 (Tex. App.—Houston [1st Dist.] 1993, pet. ref'd) (certificate of origin was admissible as statement affecting an interest in property under Rule 803(15)).

754. 799 S.W.2d 683, 697-98 (Tex. Crim. App. 1990).

755. *Id.*

756. *Id.*

RULE 803

the assumption that the deceased made this list for his own protection was reasonable (e.g., for insurance purposes in the event of theft or loss), and thus the "recitals therein [were] 'germane to the purpose of the document.'"[757]

12. Rule 803(16): Statements in ancient documents. Statements contained in documents that are at least 20 years old constitute an exception to the hearsay rule under Rule 803(16) if the document's authenticity is established.[758] Rule 803(16) must be read together with Rule 901(b)(8), which governs the authentication aspect.[759]

To qualify for admission under Rules 803(16) and 901(b)(8), the document must be (1) in a condition that creates no suspicion about its authenticity,[760] (2) in a place where it would likely be if it were authentic,[761] and (3) 20 or more years old when it is offered.[762]

13. Rule 803(17): Market reports & similar commercial publications. Rule 803(17) creates a hearsay exception for market reports and similar commercial publications.[763] To qualify as an exception to the hearsay rule, market reports and similar commercial publications must be properly authenticated. The foundation may be established by testimony of qualified experts or practitioners of "particular occupations" or by judicial

---

757. *Id.* (quoting FED. R. EVID. 803(15) advisory committee's note).

758. TEX. R. EVID. 803(16). The Judicial Conference Committee on Rules of Practice and Procedure has approved—and the U.S. Supreme Court has adopted—amendments to Federal Rule 803(16) that would limit the rule's application to documents that were prepared before January 1, 1998. *See* U.S. Supreme Court, *Miscellaneous Order, Rules of Evidence* (Apr. 27, 2017), www.supremecourt.gov/orders/courtorders/frev17_d186.pdf; *Report of the Judicial Conference: Committee on Rules of Practice & Procedure*, Agenda E-19, at Rules 31-33 & App. C (Sept. 2016), www.uscourts.gov/rules-policies/archives/committee-reports/reports-judicial-conference-september-2016. Because electronically stored information can be kept for more than 20 years, the Committee reasoned, the rule's 20-year limitation could have been "used as a vehicle to admit vast amounts of unreliable electronically stored information." FED. R. EVID. 803 advisory committee's note to 2017 amendments. If Congress does not take contrary action, the amendments will take effect December 1, 2017. For the final version of the amendments, go to www .uscourts.gov/rules-policies.

759. The two rules taken together embody Texas common law, except that they shorten the antiquity requirement from 30 years to 20. *See* 1A RAY, *supra* note 9, §§1371-1376, at 526-37 (discussing the problems associated with admitting statements in ancient documents); *see, e.g.*, *Kamel v. Kamel*, 760 S.W.2d 677, 678 (Tex. App.—Tyler 1988, writ denied) (23-year-old will was properly authenticated and admitted under Civil Rule 803(16)). Refer to *Article IX: Authentication & Identification*, *infra* p. 998.

760. TEX. R. EVID. 901(b)(8)(A).

761. TEX. R. EVID. 901(b)(8)(B).

762. TEX. R. EVID. 803(16), 901(b)(8)(C); *e.g.*, *Guthrie v. Suiter*, 934 S.W.2d 820, 825 (Tex. App.—Houston [1st Dist.] 1996, no writ) (letter from testatrix's mother to physician stating that testatrix had not been the same since her lobotomy was not admissible under Rule 803(16) because it had not been in existence for 20 years when it was offered at trial); *Fibreboard Corp. v. Pool*, 813 S.W.2d 658, 694 (Tex. App.—Texarkana 1991, writ denied) (no predicate was laid for where letter had been kept; thus, it was inadmissible under Rule 803(16)).

763. This exception was recognized by Texas common law in a variety of situations. *See, e.g.*, *Lewis v. Southmore Sav. Ass'n*, 480 S.W.2d 180, 186 (Tex. 1972) (offering publications of reliable market prices or statistical compilations as examples of this hearsay exception); *Am. Bankers Ins. v. Fish*, 412 S.W.2d 723, 726-27 (Tex. Civ. App.—Amarillo 1967, no writ) (admitting information in professional directories); *McMillen Feeds, Inc. v. Harlow*, 405 S.W.2d 123, 136 (Tex. Civ. App.—Austin 1966, writ ref'd n.r.e.) (allowing admission of magazine charts used in industry); *City Nat'l Bank v. Kiel*, 348 S.W.2d 260, 266 (Tex. Civ. App.—Fort Worth 1961, writ ref'd n.r.e.) (accepting published market reports as credible evidence); *see also* 1A RAY, *supra* note 9, §1378, at 539 (first explicit use of the exception was the admission of charts from the magazine *Turkey World* in *McMillen Feeds*).

notice.[764] In addition to laying a proper foundation, the proponent must show that the publication is "generally relied on by the public or by persons in particular occupations."[765]

Survey results may be admissible under this exception if the opposing party is given an opportunity to cross-examine the person who conducted the survey.[766] However, because this exception is limited to information that is readily ascertainable and about which there can be no real dispute, it does not include learned treatises or other scientific articles that are admissible only to a limited extent under Rule 803(18).[767]

The label on cold medicines and other drug containers may qualify for admission under this exception if the container is unopened, the label lists the contents, and the container appears to be from a reliable source.[768]

14. Rule 803(18): Statements in learned treatises, periodicals, or pamphlets. Rule 803(18) creates a hearsay exception for statements in treatises, periodicals, or pamphlets.[769] To introduce statements from a learned treatise under Rule 803(18), (1) the statement must be called to an expert witness's attention on cross-examination

---

764. *See* TEX. R. EVID. 803(17); *see, e.g., Curran v. Unis*, 711 S.W.2d 290, 296-97 (Tex. App.—Dallas 1986, no writ) (trial court erred in excluding excerpts from Dun & Bradstreet when a certified public accountant testified that Dun & Bradstreet is an accredited business-reporting service and is relied on by accountants and businessmen).

765. TEX. R. EVID. 803(17); *see Daimler-Benz A.G. v. Olson*, 21 S.W.3d 707, 716 (Tex. App.—Austin 2000, pet. dism'd) ("[P]ublications of market prices or statistical compilations that are proven to be generally recognized as reliable and regularly used in a trade or specialized activity by persons so engaged are admissible for the truth of the matter published."); *Curran*, 711 S.W.2d at 296-97 (same).

766. *See New Braunfels Factory Outlet Ctr., Inc. v. IHOP Realty Corp.*, 872 S.W.2d 303, 310 (Tex. App.—Austin 1994, no writ). In this case, the court held that an article that rated area restaurants was not admissible under the rule because the offering party did not use the results of the survey and did not make the person who conducted the survey available for cross-examination. *Id.*

767. *See Kahanek v. Rogers*, 12 S.W.3d 501, 504 (Tex. App.—San Antonio 1999, pet. denied) (Physician's Desk Reference may be used by an expert but is not independently admissible as a "commercial publication" under Rule 803(17); information within PDR goes beyond objective data "to items on which learned professionals could disagree").

768. *See Shaffer v. State*, 184 S.W.3d 353, 362 (Tex. App.—Fort Worth 2006, pet. ref'd) (cold-medication label from unopened container was admissible under Rule 803(17) because "[f]ederal regulations provide extensive requirements for the labeling of drugs, including the established name and quantity of the active ingredients, which suggests that the cold medication labels are accurate and trustworthy").

769. Adopting this reliable-document provision represented a significant change from Texas common law. Texas, like most jurisdictions, had never recognized a common-law hearsay exception for "learned treatises." *See* FED. R. EVID. 803(18) advisory committee's note; McCORMICK'S HANDBOOK II, *supra* note 7, §321, at 743. Professional or scientific literature was admissible, if at all, only on cross-examination of an expert witness for the limited purpose of testing his expertise and credibility. *E.g., Bowles v. Bourdon*, 148 Tex. 1, 6, 219 S.W.2d 779, 783 (1949) (excerpts from treatises could be read solely to discredit the witness and could not be entered as original evidence). Moreover, Texas formerly followed a highly restrictive rule on the use of published materials on cross-examination: only those publications that the witness admitted to be authoritative could be used. *See id.; Webb v. Jorns*, 530 S.W.2d 847, 856-57 (Tex. Civ. App.—Fort Worth 1975, writ ref'd n.r.e.) (witness must, in part, recognize the absent author of the publication as an authority in the particular field of expertise). The Texas position was criticized by commentators and was characterized by one Texas court as somewhat "harsh." *See Seeley v. Eaton*, 506 S.W.2d 719, 723 (Tex. Civ. App.—Houston [14th Dist.] 1974, writ ref'd n.r.e.); Frank W. Elliott, *Annual Survey of Texas Law: Evidence*, 29 Sw. L.J. 235, 242-43 (1975). The Texas position was also unrealistic—an expert witness is unlikely to espouse the authority of a work that he knows is about to be read as contradicting his own sworn testimony. *See* Elliott, *supra*, at 242-43.

or relied on by the expert on direct examination[770] and (2) the publication must be "established as a reliable authority by the expert's admission or testimony, by another expert's testimony, or by judicial notice."[771] If admitted, the statements may be read into evidence but may not be received as an exhibit.[772]

An expert witness may no longer "at the outset block cross-examination by refusing to concede reliance or authoritativeness."[773] If the expert refuses to admit that the material is a reliable authority, its authority may be established "by another expert's testimony[] or by judicial notice."[774] Consequently, opposing expert testimony would seem necessary in nearly all cases because courts would probably be hesitant to take judicial notice of a particular scientific or professional publication's authority if that authoritativeness is denied by the first expert.[775]

An important feature of Rule 803(18) is that, unlike the earlier Model Code[776] and Uniform Rules,[777] the federal and Texas provisions permit learned publications to be used only in conjunction with expert testimony, either on direct or cross-examination, even when the authority of the publication is otherwise established.[778] This limitation

---

770. Tex. R. Evid. 803(18)(A).

771. Tex. R. Evid. 803(18)(B). Before the 2015 restyling, the rule required that the publication be "on a subject of history, medicine, or other science or art." The phrase was deleted in the restyling, but no substantive change was intended. *See* Tex. Sup. Ct. Order, Misc. Docket No. 15-9048, §2 (eff. Apr. 1, 2015).

772. Tex. R. Evid. 803(18).

773. Fed. R. Evid. 803(18) advisory committee's note. *But see* ***Reynolds v. Warthan***, 896 S.W.2d 823, 827 (Tex. App.—Tyler 1995, no writ) ("An expert witness may properly be impeached by asking whether he or she agrees or disagrees with the statements contained in treatises and scientific materials; however, such cross-examination is limited to publications which the witness recognizes as authoritative or publications upon which the expert has relied."); ***Carter v. Steere Tank Lines, Inc.***, 835 S.W.2d 176, 182 (Tex. App.—Amarillo 1992, writ denied) (relying on pre-Rules precedent; cross-examination of an expert with a learned treatise "is limited to publications which the witness recognizes as authoritative or publications upon which the expert has relied"). The reasoning in ***Reynolds*** and ***Carter*** may be faulty under Rule 803(18), but the result is sound because the cross-examiner did not have an expert who could testify at some point during the trial that the publication was an authoritative one. *See, e.g.*, ***Reynolds***, 896 S.W.2d at 827 (no other expert testimony was offered to show that drug-company inserts accompanying medication were reliable authority).

774. *See* Tex. R. Evid. 803(18)(B).

775. *See* 7 Graham, *supra* note 491, §803:18, at 470 n.12; *see also* ***Robinson v. Warner-Lambert***, 998 S.W.2d 407, 412 (Tex. App.—Waco 1999, no pet.) (court could not take judicial notice that article published in medical-association journal was a learned treatise under rule; Rule 803(18) explicitly requires sponsoring expert witness).

776. Model Code of Evid. R. 529 (1942).

777. Unif. R. Evid. 803(18) (1986).

778. *See* Fed. R. Evid. 803(18)(A); Tex. R. Evid. 803(18)(A); *see, e.g.*, ***Loven v. State***, 831 S.W.2d 387, 395 (Tex. App.—Amarillo 1992, no pet.) (learned treatise is not inferior to live testimony; admitting videotape as learned treatise because expert was available for cross-examination about videotape). In ***Loven***, the trial court admitted a videotape produced by the Epilepsy Foundation of America on the subject of seizure disorders as a "contemporary variant of a published treatise, periodical or pamphlet." 831 S.W.2d at 397. The State used the videotape in conjunction with its expert's testimony to rebut the defendant's defense that she involuntarily killed her baby during a seizure. *Id.* at 391-92. The defendant claimed that use of the videotape would deny her the right to confront and cross-examine the narrator of the tape and argued that the learned treatise was not a firmly rooted exception that would permit introduction of hearsay unless the original declarant were shown to be unavailable. *See id.* at 392-93. The court of appeals was unaware of any case authority discussing whether the learned treatise was a firmly rooted

ensures that a jury will not receive arcane information without some guidance from a live witness.[779] Consequently, it is not proper under the rule for an attorney to read a publication into evidence, no matter how much the publication is authenticated and established as authoritative, except while examining an expert witness.[780] Tables and charts contained in a learned treatise may be read to and displayed for the jury during an expert's testimony, but the charts themselves should not be entered into evidence or given to the jury during their deliberations.[781] The fact that the treatise was not published until after the incident at issue occurred is not a proper basis for excluding that treatise.[782]

When statements in a publication are read on cross-examination, they become substantive evidence rather than merely impeachment evidence, although the publication may not be received as an exhibit.[783] Also, statements from a properly qualified publication may be read into evidence on direct examination by an expert.[784] Abolishing the distinction between substantive and impeachment use "avoids the unreality" of asking the jury to follow an instruction they are unlikely to understand.[785]

exception to the hearsay rule; however, the court noted that the "firmly rooted" concept does not depend on how long an exception has been accepted but on how solidly it is grounded on considerations of reliability. *Id.* at 396. According to the court, learned treatises are reliable because (1) they are "written primarily and impartially for professionals," (2) they are "subject to scrutiny and exposure for inaccuracy, with the reputation of the writer at stake," (3) the author is likely to have been motivated by a "strong desire to accurately state the full truth," and (4) the author "is impartial, disinterested and not awaiting a fee for testifying." *Id.* Because of the high indicia of reliability, the court of appeals held that the learned-treatise exception to the hearsay rule is firmly rooted and that its use, in conjunction with the testimony of an expert witness, does not violate the Confrontation Clause. *Id.*

779. 4 WEINSTEIN & BERGER, *supra* note 209, ¶803(18)[02], at 803-375.

780. *See, e.g., Zwack v. State*, 757 S.W.2d 66, 67-69 (Tex. App.—Houston [14th Dist.] 1988, pet. ref'd) (trial court properly prevented defense counsel from reading aloud from a learned treatise after experts had all been excused; though treatise had been properly authenticated, it could "be used only in conjunction with testimony by an expert witness, either on direct or cross-examination"). In *Dartez v. Fibreboard Corp.*, the Fifth Circuit stated that the rule's restrictions on the use of learned treatises avoids the possibility that the jury will misunderstand and misapply the technical language in such an article if they are allowed to consider the publication itself instead of receiving the information through the testimony of an expert in the field. 765 F.2d 456, 465 (5th Cir. 1985).

781. *See* TEX. R. EVID. 803(18); *Mauzey v. Sutliff*, 125 S.W.3d 71, 83-84 (Tex. App.—Austin 2003, pet. denied); *see, e.g., United States v. Mangan*, 575 F.2d 32, 48 (2d Cir. 1978) (attorney could use charts from learned treatise during cross-examination of State's expert, but jury could not have access to the charts during its deliberations).

782. *E.g., King v. Bauer*, 767 S.W.2d 197, 199-200 (Tex. App.—Corpus Christi 1989, writ denied) (trial court did not err in admitting into evidence a portion of a radiotherapy textbook published two years after plaintiff was given radiotherapy treatment).

783. *See* TEX. R. EVID. 803(18) (if admitted, statement may be read into evidence but not received as exhibit); *Godsey v. State*, 989 S.W.2d 482, 492 (Tex. App.—Waco 1999, pet. ref'd) (treatise itself is not admitted in evidence to prevent "'a jury from rifling through a learned treatise and drawing improper inferences from technical language it might not be able properly to understand without expert guidance'" (quoting *Loven*, 831 S.W.2d at 395)).

784. *See* TEX. R. EVID. 803(18)(A); *see, e.g., Mendoza v. State*, 787 S.W.2d 502, 503-04 (Tex. App.—Austin 1990, pet. ref'd) ("The fact that [witness] did not know the author or credentials of a particular article of the publication does not vitiate compliance with the rule"; witness is permitted to read into evidence portions of treatise if she is "an expert in the relevant area and establishes by her testimony that the publication is a reliable source in her field"); *cf. United States v. Sene X Eleemosynary Corp.*, 479 F. Supp. 970, 975 (S.D. Fla. 1979) (under Federal Rule 803(18), physicians could read into evidence excerpts of an article published in a trade journal).

785. FED. R. EVID. 803(18) advisory committee's note.

C. Reputation Evidence

1. Rule 803(19): Reputation concerning personal or family history. Rule 803(19) creates a hearsay exception for family or community reputation on certain matters of personal or family history.[786] Rule 803(19) permits testimony about reputation only, however, and does not extend to specific, out-of-court statements about a family. Those statements are governed by Rule 804(b)(3)(B), which requires the unavailability of the declarant.[787] If the statement is about a person other than the declarant, Rule 804(b)(3)(B) further requires that the declarant be "related to the person by blood, adoption, or marriage or … so intimately associated with the person's family that the declarant's information is likely to be accurate."[788] These restrictions do not apply to the admissibility of personal or family reputational history under Rule 803(19).

2. Rule 803(20): Reputation concerning boundaries or general history. Rule 803(20) creates a hearsay exception for reputational history about a community's boundaries, customs that affect land in the community, and "general historical events important to that community, state, or nation."[789] Several important restrictions apply to this ex-

---

786. Matters of personal or family history that are included in the rule are a person's "birth, adoption, legitimacy, ancestry, marriage, divorce, death, relationship by blood, adoption, or marriage," or other similar facts. TEX. R. EVID. 803(19).

   Rule 803(19) is consistent with Texas common law in permitting family or community reputation to prove certain matters of personal or family history. *See Akers v. Stevenson*, 54 S.W.3d 880, 885 (Tex. App.—Beaumont 2001, pet. denied) ("These exceptions arise from necessity and are founded on the general reliability of statements by family members about family affairs when the statements by deceased persons regarding family history were made at a time when no pecuniary interest or other biased reason for the statements were present."); *Johnson v. State*, 737 S.W.2d 901, 905-06 (Tex. App.—Beaumont 1987) (commentators on Texas evidence have described this rule "as one of the oldest exceptions to the hearsay rule" and have stated that its trustworthiness "lies in the strong 'probability that the natural effusions of those who talk over family affairs … are fairly trustworthy'" (quoting 1A RAY, *supra* note 9, §§1341-1350)), *aff'd as reformed*, 784 S.W.2d 47 (Tex. Crim. App. 1990); 1A RAY, *supra* note 9, §1323, at 497 (use of family or community reputation "to evidence certain facts of family history has long been sanctioned by many courts, including those of Texas"); *see also* Thomas Black, *The Texas Rules of Evidence—A Proposed Codification*, 31 Sw. L.J. 969, 1003 (1977) (Rule 803(19) allows proof "of marriage, age, and matters of pedigree").

   However, some early Texas cases indicated that only family reputation, not community reputation, could be used to prove matters of pedigree or relationship. *See, e.g.*, *Gibson v. Dickson*, 178 S.W. 44, 47 (Tex. Civ. App.—Dallas 1915, writ ref'd) (excluding a neighbor's testimony to establish maternity). This limitation may have resulted from confusion about the distinction between the use of reputation to prove these facts and the hearsay exception for particular declarations about another person's personal or family history, the latter of which ordinarily requires a familial relationship between the declarant and the subject. *See* TEX. R. EVID. 804(b)(3)(B); *see also* 1A RAY, *supra* note 9, §1323, at 499 (when hearsay is used to prove a relationship, it must be restricted to those persons related by blood or marriage). *But see Jones v. State*, 950 S.W.2d 386, 388-89 (Tex. App.—Fort Worth 1997, pet. ref'd, untimely filed) ("close family associate" who was not related but who had lived with the family for two or three years could testify to deceased child's age under either Rule 803(19) or Rule 804(b)(3)(A)). Refer to notes 953-956 *infra* and accompanying text. Whatever its source, the limitation was abolished by the broad language of Rule 803(19).

787. *See, e.g.*, *Lacy v. Lacy*, 922 S.W.2d 195, 198 (Tex. App.—Tyler 1995, writ denied) (investigator's report containing names of people known in community to have been decedent's heirs was not admissible under Rule 803(19) in proceeding to determine heirship when offered to prove the names of the heirs, not reputation in community about blood relationship). *But see Johnson*, 737 S.W.2d at 905-06 (approving admission of police officer's testimony "that Teresa Johnson had told him that the Appellant was her brother").

788. TEX. R. EVID. 804(b)(3)(B).

789. TEX. R. EVID. 803(20). The adoption of the federal rule slightly liberalizes a doctrine long recognized in Texas. Texas had allowed reputation arising before the dispute to prove land boundaries and customs but, unlike the fed-

ception: (1) the reputation evidence must be about the community where the land is located, (2) the reputation must have existed before the controversy about the boundaries or custom arose, and (3) if the reputation evidence is about general history, those events must be important to the community (although the community may be local or encompass the state or the entire nation).[790]

The rationale for this exception, like that for Rules 803(19) and 803(21), is that "the matter is of such general or public interest to the community that a prolonged and constant discussion will sift possible errors and give rise to a fairly trustworthy reputation."[791] Again, the exception permits testimony of reputation only; it does not allow proof of an individual family's specific assertion of some fact about boundaries or history.[792]

3. Rule 803(21): Reputation concerning character. Traditionally, a person's character or character trait may be proved by testimony of his reputation in the community.[793] Rule 803(21) simply ratifies that tradition.[794] It does not govern aspects of the character-evidence problem that have nothing to do with hearsay.[795] Other rules, such as Rules 404, 405, and 608, place restrictions on the use of character evidence.

---

eral rule, required antiquity as an element of this exception. *See **Clark v. Hills**,* 67 Tex. 141, 152-53, 2 S.W. 356, 362 (1886); ***Seaway Co. v. Atty. Gen.**,* 375 S.W.2d 923, 939-40 (Tex. Civ. App.—Houston 1964, writ ref'd n.r.e.); 1A RAY, *supra* note 9, §1322, at 494-97; *cf.* FED. R. EVID. 803(20) advisory committee's note ("The reputation is required to antedate the controversy, though not to be ancient."). As for "general historical events," there is no Texas common-law authority for proof of these by community reputation. Presumably, judicial notice sufficed to cover such cases when direct proof was lacking.

    The Texas common law also recognized a hearsay exception for individual declarations about boundaries when the declarant was dead at the time of trial and had no motive to misrepresent when the statement was made. *See **Tucker v. Smith**,* 68 Tex. 473, 478, 3 S.W. 671, 673 (1887); ***Brateman v. Upper Channel Site Co.**,* 378 S.W.2d 882, 888 (Tex. Civ. App.—Houston 1964, writ ref'd n.r.e.); 1A RAY, *supra* note 9, §§1361-1365, at 522-25. There is no equivalent specific exception in the present Texas Rules or the Federal Rules. However, many of the declarations received in the past appeared in writings that would qualify as ancient documents under Rules 803(16) and 901(b)(8). Refer to notes 758-762 *supra* and accompanying text and *Article IX: Authentication & Identification, infra* p. 998. An oral declaration that would have met the requirements of the former case law might also qualify as a declaration against proprietary interest under Rule 803(24). Refer to notes 811-847 *infra* and accompanying text.

790. *See* TEX. R. EVID. 803(20).

791. 1A RAY, *supra* note 9, §1322, at 495.

792. *See, e.g.,* ***Roberts v. Allison**,* 836 S.W.2d 185, 191 (Tex. App.—Tyler 1992, writ denied) (trial court properly excluded evidence of an alleged oral agreement to an easement when the evidence was based solely on an individual family's assertion and no showing was made of any community interest in or discussion of the easement). *But see **Akers v. Stevenson**,* 54 S.W.3d 880, 885-86 & n.8 (Tex. App.—Beaumont 2001, pet. denied) (original property owner's great-grandson, who had undertaken genealogical investigation of his family and property, could testify under Rules 803(19), 803(20), and 804(b)(3)(B) as to information "told to him by his own family members and people in the community" about land ownership history, right of access, roadway, and easements).

793. *See* MCCORMICK'S HANDBOOK II, *supra* note 7, §186, at 442-43 (analyzing the purpose and manner of proof as the important considerations for proving character); 1A RAY, *supra* note 9, §1324, at 500 (there is an important distinction between character and reputation, and reputation is simply the collective opinion of a person's inherent qualities).

794. *See **Siverand v. State**,* 89 S.W.3d 216, 220-21 (Tex. App.—Corpus Christi 2002, no pet.) (Rule 803(21) "specifically provides that reputation testimony of a person's character among associates or in the community is not excluded by the hearsay rule").

795. *See* FED. R. EVID. 803(21) advisory committee's note.

4. Rule 803(22): Judgment of previous conviction. Rule 803(22) creates a hearsay exception for judgments of prior convictions in certain circumstances to prove any facts essential to sustain the judgment or conviction.[796] The federal rule contains this same general exception;[797] however, Texas Rule 803(22) differs from the federal version in some details. First, the Texas rule excludes any conviction for which an appeal is pending.[798] Under Federal Rule 803(22), the pendency of an appeal affects the weight of the conviction, not its admissibility.[799] Second, the Texas rule for civil cases substitutes the term "felony" for the federal wording "crime punishable by death or by imprisonment for more than a year";[800] in criminal cases, the rule permits proof of a judgment of conviction for any criminal offense, not just a felony.[801] Third, the Texas rule admits a judgment of conviction based on a plea of nolo contendere in a later criminal case,[802] though not in a later civil case.[803] The federal rule, like the rule for Texas civil proceedings, prohibits the admission of judgments based on a nolo contendere plea.[804]

Rule 803(22) permits only felony criminal convictions to be used as evidence in civil cases.[805] Misdemeanor convictions and civil judgments are not admissible in civil suits

---

796. *See* TEX. R. EVID. 803(22)(A)(iii), (22)(B)(iii). The extent to which Rule 803(22) changed preexisting Texas law is not entirely clear. *See* ***McCormick v. Tex. Commerce Bank***, 751 S.W.2d 887, 889 (Tex. App.—Houston [14th Dist.] 1988, writ denied) (Civil Rule 803(22) "supplanted the Texas common law and need not be reconciled with prior case law"; conviction of a party who had been tried and convicted of a felony over his plea of not guilty was admissible as substantive evidence). Traditionally, Texas courts did not permit evidentiary use of judgments to prove issues of fact. *See* 1A RAY, *supra* note 9, §1279, at 472; Black, *supra* note 786, at 1004; *see, e.g.*, ***Fire Ass'n v. Coomer***, 158 S.W.2d 355, 357 (Tex. Civ. App.—Waco 1942, no writ) (in an action to collect fire-insurance proceeds, earlier conviction for causing fire was admissible to impeach insured but was not conclusive of whether insured had caused fire at issue); ***Stewart v. Profit***, 146 S.W. 563, 564 (Tex. Civ. App.—Galveston 1912, writ ref'd) (evidence of previous property owner's conviction for marrying a black man as a white woman was inadmissible to prove whether owner had a right to unilaterally transfer property at issue). This position, however, was criticized. *See* 1A RAY, *supra* note 9, §1279, at 473-74 (consistency and common sense favor admitting the evidence). In 1979, the Texas Supreme Court interpreted the former official-records statute to authorize the admission of a previous judgment to prove the facts underlying the judgment in a civil case. ***Estate of Wilson v. Wilson***, 587 S.W.2d 674, 674-75 (Tex. 1979). The holding in ***Wilson*** was much broader than Rule 803(22) because it did not limit the types of judgments that could be used as evidence. *See id.*

797. *See* FED. R. EVID. 803(22)(C). The Texas and federal rules also both create a hearsay exception for a judgment of a prior conviction when the judgment was against the defendant and it was offered by the prosecutor in a criminal case for a reason other than impeachment. FED. R. EVID. 803(22)(D); TEX. R. EVID. 803(22)(B)(iv).

798. *See* TEX. R. EVID. 803(22)(A)(iv) (evidence of final conviction is admissible in civil case only if appeal for conviction is not pending), TEX. R. EVID. 803(22)(B)(v) (same rule for criminal cases); ***Reese v. State***, 273 S.W.3d 344, 349 (Tex. App.—Texarkana 2008, no pet.) (final judgments of previous convictions are not excluded under Rule 803(22)).

799. *See* FED. R. EVID. 803(22) ("The pendency of an appeal may be shown but does not affect admissibility."); 4 LOUISELL & MUELLER, *supra* note 250, §470, at 894-95 (party against whom a judgment of conviction is offered may explain that the conviction is on appeal or that post-trial motions have been or could be made).

800. *See* FED. R. EVID. 803(22)(B); TEX. R. EVID. 803(22)(A)(ii).

801. TEX. R. EVID. 803(22)(B)(ii).

802. TEX. R. EVID. 803(22)(B)(i).

803. TEX. R. EVID. 803(22)(A)(i).

804. *See* FED. R. EVID. 803(22)(A). Although the nolo contendere plea itself is not admissible, the facts underlying the conviction to which the person pleaded are admissible. ***United States v. Wyatt***, 762 F.2d 908, 911 (11th Cir. 1985).

805. TEX. R. EVID. 803(22)(A)(ii). A jury verdict of guilty in a felony trial for conduct that later becomes an issue in a civil suit may act as offensive collateral estoppel in the civil suit. *See, e.g.*, ***Dover v. Baker, Brown, Sharman &***

under Rule 803(22). For example, a judgment of conviction for a misdemeanor traffic offense would not be admissible in a negligence action arising out of the same facts. As explained by the Advisory Committee on the Federal Rules: "Practical considerations require exclusion of convictions of minor offenses, not because the administration of justice in its lower echelons must be inferior, but because motivation to defend at this level is often minimal or nonexistent."[806]

Although Texas courts, at least before the supreme court decided *Wilson* in 1979,[807] did not allow the evidentiary use of a criminal judgment in later civil litigation, evidence that a civil party had entered a plea of guilty in a previous criminal case with the same fact issues was permitted on the theory that the guilty plea constituted an admission.[808]

5. Rule 803(23): Judgment involving personal, family, or general history or a boundary. Rule 803(23) permits proof by judgments of the same matters that are provable by reputation under Rules 803(19) and 803(20).[809] It extends beyond Rule 803(22) because the evidentiary judgment does not need to be a felony criminal conviction. The rule applies to any civil or criminal judgment that necessarily required a determination of a relevant fact in the designated categories. The matter to be proved must have been essential to the judgment and one that could be proved by reputation evidence.[810]

Parker, 859 S.W.2d 441, 449-50 (Tex. App.—Houston [1st Dist.] 1993, no writ) (under Civil Rule 803(22), an earlier federal criminal conviction for making a false statement to a federally insured bank acted as collateral estoppel in later civil proceeding); *Boozier v. Hambrick*, 846 S.W.2d 593, 597-98 (Tex. App.—Houston [1st Dist.] 1993, no writ) (airport superintendent's conviction for assaulting police officer collaterally estopped him from denying the assault in later civil proceeding); *McCormick v. Tex. Commerce Bank*, 751 S.W.2d 887, 889-90 (Tex. App.—Houston [14th Dist.] 1988, writ denied) (collateral estoppel prevented defendant sued by the bank for a "check kiting scheme" from relitigating or explaining a felony criminal conviction for identical conduct); *Britt v. Cambridge Mut. Fire Ins.*, 717 S.W.2d 476, 482 (Tex. App.—San Antonio 1986, writ ref'd n.r.e.) (insured's earlier judgment of felony conviction would not collaterally estop wrongful-death plaintiffs from attempting to enforce a later civil judgment that the insured negligently caused a death).

806. FED. R. EVID. 803(22) advisory committee's note.

807. Refer to note 796 *supra*.

808. *See, e.g.*, *Harville v. Siebenlist*, 582 S.W.2d 621, 623 (Tex. Civ. App.—Amarillo 1979) (defendant's guilty plea to complaint of driving in an unlawful manner was admissible in civil negligence action), *rev'd on other grounds*, 596 S.W.2d 113 (Tex. 1980); *Atkinson v. Rister*, 422 S.W.2d 821, 823-24 (Tex. Civ. App.—Eastland 1967, writ ref'd n.r.e.) (sheriff could testify in civil personal-injury suit that he heard defendant plead guilty to traffic charges); *Carrick v. Hedrick*, 351 S.W.2d 659, 662 (Tex. Civ. App.—Amarillo 1961, no writ) (evidence of guilty plea to traffic violation was admissible in civil personal-injury suit); *see also* 1A RAY, *supra* note 9, §1145, at 296-97 (plea of nolo contendere is not admissible).

809. Former Texas law permitted this type of proof, subject to the limitations of certain pertinent statutes. *Wood v. Paulus*, 524 S.W.2d 749, 759-60 (Tex. Civ. App.—Corpus Christi 1975, writ ref'd n.r.e.) (citing former Texas Revised Civil Statutes arts. 3726a and 3731a). The current rule abolishes those limitations. Former Texas Revised Civil Statutes art. 3726a was limited to family history, while art. 3731a required pretrial notice. Act of April 30, 1957, 55th Leg., ch. 125, §1, 1957 Tex. Gen. Laws 266, *amended by* Act approved June 16, 1965, 59th Leg., ch. 480, §1, 1965 Tex. Gen. Laws 994 (former Texas Revised Civil Statutes art. 3726a deemed repealed as to civil proceedings effective 1983 and as to criminal proceedings effective 1986); Act approved June 21, 1951, 52nd Leg., ch. 471, 1951 Tex. Gen. Laws 830, *amended by* Act of June 5, 1953, 53rd Leg., ch. 304, §1, 1953 Tex. Gen. Laws 756, *amended by* Act approved June 16, 1961, 57th Leg., ch. 321, §1, 1961 Tex. Gen. Laws 685, *amended by* Act approved May 20, 1975, 64th Leg., ch. 280, §1, 1975 Tex. Gen. Laws 666 (former Texas Revised Civil Statutes art. 3731a deemed repealed as to civil proceedings effective 1983 and as to criminal proceedings effective 1986).

810. TEX. R. EVID. 803(23).

D. Statements Against Interest: Rule 803(24)

Statements against interest, which do not fit neatly into any of the three categories of hearsay exceptions (unreflective statements, reliable documents, or reputation evidence), are exceptions to the hearsay rule to the extent that they are shown to be trustworthy and reliable under the particular circumstances.[811]

Rule 803(24) is based on Federal Rule 804(b)(3). The Texas rule differs from the federal model in two respects. First, and most importantly, the exception was moved from Rule 804 to Rule 803, thus eliminating the requirement of the declarant's unavailability. Second, the drafters of the Texas Rules restored language that was deleted by Congress[812] from the Supreme Court's version of the federal rule so that the exception covers a statement against social interest.[813] One important similarity between the Texas and federal rules is that they expressly require corroboration for all statements against penal interest offered by either party in a criminal proceeding, not merely those offered to exculpate the accused.[814]

---

811. Rule 803(24) changed Texas civil law in three respects. First, the former law required unavailability of the declarant. *E.g.*, ***Big Mack Trucking Co. v. Dickerson***, 497 S.W.2d 283, 290 (Tex. 1973) (exception did not apply when the record lacked proof of any attempt to establish that declarant was unavailable). Second, no Texas case had admitted a declaration against social interest under the exception. *See* David A. Furlow & Lisa H. Pennington, *Determining What Types of Hearsay Disparage a Declarant's "Social Interest": An Innovation for Texas Evidence Law*, 48 TEX. B.J. 1058, 1062 (1985). Third, no Texas civil case had admitted a declaration against penal interest. *See* ***Hill v. Robinson***, 592 S.W.2d 376, 382 (Tex. Civ. App.—Tyler 1979, writ ref'd n.r.e.). Declarations against penal interest had been allowed in criminal cases, subject to strict conditions. *See* ***Ramirez v. State***, 543 S.W.2d 631, 632-33 (Tex. Crim. App. 1976); ***Cameron v. State***, 153 Tex. Crim. 29, 31, 217 S.W.2d 23, 24 (1949); *see also* 1A RAY, *supra* note 9, §1006, at 255-56 (discussing the current rule in Texas that represents a compromise between cases excluding declarations against penal interest and decisions that treat them as any other statements against interest). Many scholars had argued against unavailability as a requirement for this exception. *See* MCCORMICK'S HANDBOOK II, *supra* note 7, §280, at 678; Edmund M. Morgan, *Declarations Against Interest*, 5 VAND. L. REV. 451, 475 (1952) [hereinafter Morgan, *Declarations*]. Coverage of declarations against social interest finds similar support. *See* CAL. EVID. CODE §1230; MODEL CODE OF EVID. R. 509(1) (1942); UNIF. R. EVID. 804(b)(3) (1986); MCCORMICK'S HANDBOOK II, *supra* note 7, §§253-257, at 608-22; Bernard S. Jefferson, *Declarations Against Interest: An Exception to the Hearsay Rule*, 58 HARV. L. REV. 1, 39 (1944); Morgan, *Declarations*, *supra*, at 475. Although Congress deleted coverage of social-interest declarations, many states' versions of the Rules (including Texas's) have restored it. *See* 4 WEINSTEIN & BERGER, *supra* note 209, ¶804(b)(3)[04], at 804-168 to 804-174. Evidence scholars have urged extension of the exception to declarations against penal interest. *See* 1A RAY, *supra* note 9, §1005, at 253; 5 WIGMORE, *supra* note 14, §§1476-1477, at 349-62; Jefferson, *supra*, at 39-40; Morgan, *Declarations*, *supra*, at 473-75; E. M. Morgan, *Declarations Against Interest in Texas*, 10 TEX. L. REV. 399, 413 (1932). This extension has also been the pattern of modern codifications. *See, e.g.*, CAL. EVID. CODE §1230; MODEL CODE OF EVID. R. 509(1) (1942); UNIF. R. EVID. 804(b)(3) (1986).

Further, Rule 803(24) changed Texas criminal law. In criminal cases, as in civil cases, the former law required unavailability of the declarant and had no hearsay exception for declarations against social interest. In addition, declarations against penal interest offered to exonerate the accused were admitted under the former law only when the prosecution's case was entirely circumstantial, the guilt of the declarant was inconsistent with the guilt of the defendant, and facts showed that the declarant could have committed the crime. *Ramirez*, 543 S.W.2d at 632-33; *Cameron*, 153 Tex. Crim. at 31, 217 S.W.2d at 24; *see also* 1A RAY, *supra* note 9, §1006, at 255-59 (courts will allow extrajudicial confessions only when the evidence against the accused is entirely circumstantial and circumstantial evidence pointing to declarant's guilt is also offered).

812. *See* H.R. REP. NO. 93-650, *supra* note 29, at 16, *reprinted in* 1974 U.S.C.C.A.N. at 7089.

813. *See* TEX. R. EVID. 803(24)(A). Refer to notes 836-840 *infra* and accompanying text.

814. *See* FED. R. EVID. 804(b)(3); TEX. R. EVID. 803(24)(B). Federal Rule 804(b)(3) was amended in 2010 to provide that the corroboration requirement "applies to all declarations against penal interest offered in criminal cases." FED. R. EVID. 804 advisory committee's note to 2010 amendments. Some federal courts, before the 2010 amend-

The rationale behind the exception for statements against interest is that "people ordinarily do not say things that are damaging to themselves unless they believe they are true."[815] If the statement was made by a party, the statement is admissible as non-hearsay *against* that party under Rule 801(e)(2),[816] though it is hearsay if offered *by* the declarant-party.[817] Rule 803(24) is reserved for out-of-court statements[818] made by a nonparty.[819]

1. Statements against penal interest. Whenever a statement is offered against a declarant's penal interest, the trial court must assess its admissibility under a two-part

---

ments, had interpreted the corroboration requirement to apply to all statements against interest in criminal trials, not just those offered to exculpate the accused. *See United States v. Shukri*, 207 F.3d 412, 416 (7th Cir. 2000) ("For the [Federal] Rule 804(b)(3) exception to apply, the proponent of an inculpatory hearsay statement must show that (1) the declarant is unavailable to testify at trial; (2) the statement was against the declarant's penal interest; and (3) corroborating circumstances bolster the statement's trustworthiness."); *United States v. Rasmussen*, 790 F.2d 55, 56 (8th Cir. 1986) (the proviso "'corroborating circumstances [must] clearly indicate the trustworthiness of the statement' ... has been read into [Federal] Rule 804(b)(3) to satisfy the Confrontation Clause rights of an accused whose penal interest is implicated by the declarant's out-of-court statement"); *United States v. Alvarez*, 584 F.2d 694, 701 (5th Cir. 1978) ("To bring [Federal] Rule 804(b)(3) within [the] mandate for reliability, we hold that the admissibility of *inculpatory* declarations against interest requires corroborating circumstances that 'clearly indicate the trustworthiness of the statement.'"). The amendment brought the rule in line with these decisions.

815. *Walter v. State*, 267 S.W.3d 883, 890 (Tex. Crim. App. 2008); *see* Tex. R. Evid. 803(24)(A) (declarant must have believed statement to be true because, when made, it was contrary to his proprietary or pecuniary interest or it most likely would invalidate his claim against someone, would expose him to civil or criminal liability, or would make him subject to hatred, ridicule, or disgrace); *cf. Williamson v. United States*, 512 U.S. 594, 599 (1994) (Federal Rule 804(b)(3), the federal counterpart to Texas Rule 803(24), "is founded on the common sense notion that reasonable people, even reasonable people who are not especially honest, tend not to make self-inculpatory statements unless they believe them to be true"); *United States v. Watson*, 525 F.3d 583, 586 (7th Cir. 2008) ("Most people would not say that they knocked over a bank, spit on a policeman, or shoved their mother if it wasn't true.").

816. When an opposing party's out-of-court statement is offered, neither of the requirements of Rule 803(24)—that the statement be "against interest" or corroborated—applies. *See Godwin v. State*, 899 S.W.2d 387, 390 (Tex. App.—Houston [14th Dist.] 1995, pet. ref'd).

817. *See Spivey v. State*, 748 S.W.2d 18, 19-20 (Tex. App.—Houston [1st Dist.] 1988, no pet.) (rule does not permit a defendant to offer his own out-of-court statement as a statement against interest); *see, e.g.*, *Davis v. State*, 970 S.W.2d 758, 760-61 (Tex. App.—Austin 1998, pet. ref'd) (defendant's statements, partially exculpatory and partially inculpatory, were not admissible when offered by him under Rule 803(24)).

818. Obviously, the rule does not apply when the declarant is on the witness stand. *See, e.g.*, *Nix v. State*, 750 S.W.2d 348, 353 (Tex. App.—Beaumont 1988, no pet.) (codefendant's in-court confession to participation in a murder was not subject to the corroboration requirement of Criminal Rule 803(24) because the right of cross-examination provided adequate protection).

819. *See, e.g.*, *Bingham v. State*, 987 S.W.2d 54, 56-57 (Tex. Crim. App. 1999) (lower court "was clearly in error in holding that a declarant's hearsay statements against interest are admissible in the criminal trial of that declarant only"; such an interpretation would make Rule 803(24) redundant because defendant's out-of-court statement is always admissible under Rule 801(e)(2)); *Ballard v. State*, 110 S.W.3d 538, 542 (Tex. App.—Eastland 2003, pet. dism'd) (defendant's out-of-court confession was admissible under Rule 801(e)(2)(A), and did not need to meet requirements of Rule 803(24); "[t]he hearsay exception for statements against a declarant's interest and the exclusion as non-hearsay for admissions by a party opponent are distinct"); *McNair v. State*, 75 S.W.3d 69, 72-73 (Tex. App.—San Antonio 2002, no pet.) (mentally ill defendant's statement that he killed his wife was admissible under Rule 801(e)(2)). *But see Reynolds v. State*, 744 S.W.2d 156, 160-61 (Tex. App.—Amarillo 1987, pet. ref'd) (orig. op.) (applying Criminal Rule 803(24) to a statement made by a DWI defendant who argued that corroborating circumstances were insufficient to prove the trustworthiness of his out-of-court statement to a police officer that he had been driving and almost had an accident). The court in *Bingham* noted that confusion between admissions by a party-opponent and the exception for statements against interest was "hardly uncommon," but reiterated their differences:

RULE 803

foundation test.[820] First, the court must determine whether the statement is truly against the declarant's interest for the crime being tried[821] and whether the declarant realized this when the statement was made.[822] Second, the court must determine whether there are sufficient corroborating circumstances that clearly indicate the trustworthiness of the statement, if the statement is offered in a criminal case as one that

---

> While statements against interest are admissible due to their reliability, admissions by party-opponents are admissible precisely because they are being admitted against the party alleged to have made those statements. Thus, that party cannot complain of an inability to cross-examine him/herself, and since s/he is their author, s/he is estopped from complaining of their untrustworthiness.

987 S.W.2d at 56-57.

820. *Walter*, 267 S.W.3d at 890; *Bingham*, 987 S.W.2d at 57; *Walker v. State*, 406 S.W.3d 590, 598 (Tex. App.—Eastland 2013, pet. ref'd).

821. *See Bingham*, 987 S.W.2d at 57 ("[T]he trial court must determine whether the statement in question tends to expose the declarant to criminal liability."); *Miles v. State*, 918 S.W.2d 511, 515 (Tex. Crim. App. 1996) (when declarant asserts that he was merely present during commission of offense, his statement does not subject him to criminal liability and thus is not admissible under Criminal Rule 803(24)); *see, e.g.*, *Simpson v. State*, 119 S.W.3d 262, 269 (Tex. Crim. App. 2003) (declarant "did not implicate herself at all except to suggest her presence" at the murder scene; statement was not against her penal interest); *Trevino v. State*, 218 S.W.3d 234, 240 (Tex. App.—Houston [14th Dist.] 2007, no pet.) (declarant's statement, which did not implicate himself but rather was an attempt to shift blame to defendant, was not admissible under Rule 803(24)); *Kennedy v. State*, 184 S.W.3d 309, 316-18 (Tex. App.—Texarkana 2005, pet. ref'd) (trial court did not err in excluding witness's testimony that complainant in prosecution for indecency with a child encouraged her friends to "get their stories straight"; statement was not against her penal interest because she was not under oath at that time and could not be prosecuted for perjury for making those out-of-court statements); *Hernandez v. State*, 171 S.W.3d 347, 355-56 (Tex. App.—Houston [14th Dist.] 2005, pet. ref'd) (in capital-murder trial, court properly excluded defendant's statement that he intended only to commit robbery when defense offered it as a statement against interest; "[a]ny inculpatory significance of the statement—i.e., admitting involvement in a robbery—is minor in comparison to the self-serving nature of appellant's statement that he did not plan or anticipate the shooting"); *In re U.G.*, 128 S.W.3d 797, 800-01 (Tex. App.—Corpus Christi 2004, pet. denied) (mother's statement to police did not satisfy *Bingham* test as being sufficiently against her own interest or exposing her to liability for the crime in question; her statement did mention other, unrelated acts involving drugs and "passing illegals" that might have triggered criminal liability if investigated, but her statements about crime in question were not self-inculpatory); *Ramirez v. State*, 987 S.W.2d 938, 943-44 (Tex. App.—Austin 1999, no pet.) (wife's statement to officer did not clearly tend to subject her to criminal liability because she did not admit that she knowingly failed to provide medical treatment to her daughters and nothing in her statement proved she knew that defendant posed a threat to children). When the statement is both self-serving and disserving, the court must determine if "the disserving nature of the proffered evidence outweighs the self-serving aspect." *Robinson v. Harkins & Co.*, 711 S.W.2d 619, 621 (Tex. 1986); *see, e.g.*, *Urquhart v. Antrum*, 776 S.W.2d 595, 596-97 (Tex. App.—Houston [14th Dist.] 1988, no writ) (statement by taxi driver that he hit plaintiff was inadmissible hearsay because overriding thrust of statement was exculpatory and tended to shift blame for the accident to another); *see also* Morgan, *Declarations*, *supra* note 811, at 471 (if a statement contains both self-serving and disserving matter, but is against interest by a preponderance of the evidence, "it should fall within the exception" when offered to prove a neutral matter also contained in the statement "unless that matter is so connected with or affected by the self-serving portion as to be an integral part of it"). Bernard Jefferson, however, has stated:

> [t]he basis of this exception is not that a declarant is in a general trustworthy frame of mind. The probability of trustworthiness comes from the facts asserted being disserving in character. Once those facts are left behind the probability of trustworthiness for other statements seems highly speculative and conjectural. It would seem, therefore, that the courts are not justified in admitting self-serving statements merely because they accompany disserving statements, and a neutral collateral statement should fare no better.

Jefferson, *supra* note 811, at 60.

822. *Walter*, 267 S.W.3d at 890-91; *see* Tex. R. Evid. 803(24)(A); *see, e.g.*, *United States v. Martino*, 648 F.2d 367, 391 (5th Cir. 1981) (statement that declarant "might" have been the one who started a fire was properly excluded under Federal Rule 804(b)(3) as not sufficiently subjecting declarant to liability), *vacated in part on other grounds sub nom.* *United States v. Holt*, 650 F.2d 651 (5th Cir. 1981).

tends to expose the declarant to criminal liability.[823] These requirements apply when either the State or the defendant offers a statement against interest.[824]

In a criminal case, the proponent of a statement against penal interest must offer corroborating circumstances clearly indicating the trustworthiness of the statement.[825] The "corroborating circumstances" requirement is intended to deter a criminal defendant from presenting a manufactured confession by another who is either unavailable or beyond the reach of the law[826] and to prevent the State from offering "blame-shifting" statements from criminal cohorts.[827] There is no definitive test for the sufficiency of the corroborating circumstances, but some of the factors that may be considered are (1) whether the guilt of the declarant is inconsistent with the guilt of the defendant,[828] (2) whether the declarant was so situated that he might have committed the crime,[829] (3) the timing of the declaration and its spontaneity,[830] (4) the relation-

---

823. Tex. R. Evid. 803(24)(B); *Walter*, 267 S.W.3d at 891; *Bingham*, 987 S.W.2d at 57; *Davis v. State*, 872 S.W.2d 743, 747-48 (Tex. Crim. App. 1994); *Walker*, 406 S.W.3d at 598; *see Lester v. State*, 120 S.W.3d 897, 901 (Tex. App.—Texarkana 2003, no pet.) ("The structure of the rule and its wording demonstrate the obvious suspicion with which the drafters of the rule regarded a statement exposing the declarant to criminal liability, but exculpating the accused. The requirement of corroboration is therefore construed in such a manner as to effectuate its purpose of circumventing fabrication."); *see, e.g., Morris v. State*, 214 S.W.3d 159, 183-85 (Tex. App.—Beaumont 2007) (trial court did not err in finding insufficient corroborating circumstances indicating that deceased declarant's statement against interest was trustworthy; trial court weighed evidence both in favor of and against a finding of trustworthiness, and ruling was within the zone of reasonable disagreement), *aff'd*, 301 S.W.3d 281 (Tex. Crim. App. 2009).

824. *See, e.g., Clark v. State*, 947 S.W.2d 650, 654 (Tex. App.—Fort Worth 1997, pet. ref'd) (excluding codefendant's videotaped statement to police to prove defendant did not intend to shoot store clerk was proper under Criminal Rule 803(24) because statement describing clerk's struggle for defendant's gun was not a statement against codefendant's interest).

825. Tex. R. Evid. 803(24)(B); *Davis*, 872 S.W.2d at 749; *Walker*, 406 S.W.3d at 598.

826. *See, e.g., Nauert v. State*, 838 S.W.2d 328, 330-31 (Tex. App.—Austin 1992, pet. ref'd) (per curiam) (trial court properly excluded defendant's testimony that rape victim's father, while in jail with defendant years earlier, had said that he had sexually assaulted his daughter because the statement against penal interest was not corroborated by other circumstances; corroboration requirement could not be avoided by labeling the statements as against social interest); *Williams v. State*, 800 S.W.2d 364, 367-68 (Tex. App.—Fort Worth 1990) (trial court properly excluded defense witness's testimony inculpating another for the robbery with which defendant was charged; court applied rule for corroboration of accomplice-witness testimony to statements against penal interest), *pet. ref'd*, 805 S.W.2d 474 (Tex. Crim. App. 1991); *Jennings v. State*, 748 S.W.2d 606, 608 (Tex. App.—Fort Worth 1988, pet. ref'd) (codefendant's cellmate could not testify that he overheard codefendant talking on the phone and saying "that [appellant] didn't want to do it, but that is the way it went down" when appellant did not establish corroborating circumstances to demonstrate the trustworthiness of the statement). *See generally Reynolds v. State*, 744 S.W.2d 156, 165 (Tex. App.—Amarillo 1988, pet. ref'd) (op. on reh'g) (discussing the amount of corroborating circumstances sufficient to indicate trustworthiness of a statement against interest).

827. Refer to notes 841-846 *infra* and accompanying text.

828. *Lester*, 120 S.W.3d at 901. This factor is directed toward the defendant offering the evidence, who must demonstrate that if the declarant is guilty, the defendant is not. For example, in *Lester*, only one person's footprints were found at the car dealership where cars were vandalized. *Id.* The out-of-court declarant's confession to his parents indicated that he, not the defendant or anyone else, was guilty of the offense. *See id.*; *see also James v. State*, 102 S.W.3d 162, 177 (Tex. App.—Fort Worth 2003, pet. ref'd) (first factor showed trustworthiness of statement offered by defendant when both declarant and defendant could have jointly committed crime).

829. *Lester*, 120 S.W.3d at 901. This factor also is directed toward the admission of a statement exculpating the defendant, who must show that the declarant physically could have committed the crime. *See id.* These first two factors logically do not apply when the State is attempting to offer a statement against interest to prove the defendant's guilt. *Woods v. State*, 152 S.W.3d 105, 113 (Tex. Crim. App. 2004).

RULE 803

ship between the declarant and the party to whom the declaration was made,[831] and (5) the existence of independent corroborating facts apart from the statement itself that tend either directly or circumstantially to establish the truth of the matter asserted by the statement.[832] Conversely, courts have found a lack of trustworthiness when the declarant has a strong motive to lie, will suffer little or no adversity by making the statement, or wants to gain favor with the listener.[833] In assessing the sufficiency of the corroborating facts, the trial court may consider evidence that undermines as well as supports the trustworthiness of the statement and the credibility of the declarant, although the court may not weigh or assess the credibility of the in-court witness.[834] That is the job of the jury if the testimony is admitted.[835]

---

830. *See, e.g.,* **Woods**, 152 S.W.3d at 113 (reliability of statement against interest shown, in part, by the fact that it was a "street corner" statement made by codefendant to two acquaintances without any motive to shift blame to another or minimize his own involvement in capital murder; timing and spontaneity showed statement's reliability).

831. *See id.; see, e.g.,* **Mason v. State**, 416 S.W.3d 720, 733-34 (Tex. App.—Houston [14th Dist.] 2013, pet. ref'd) (witness's statement about murder to fellow inmate was not admissible as statement against interest under Rule 803(24); although it was made after his plea bargain, when he had no motive to minimize his involvement, he may have had a motive to bolster his reputation with other inmates). In **Lester**, the court of appeals relied heavily on the fact that the declarant confessed to his mother, to whom he talked "about everything." 120 S.W.3d at 901-02; *see also* **Gongora v. State**, 214 S.W.3d 58, 64-65 (Tex. App.—Fort Worth 2006, pet. ref'd) (finding sufficient corroborating circumstances, especially the fact that accomplice's statement against penal interest was made to a friend as they "hung out" together several days before police had developed any leads or questioned accomplice and when accomplice had no motive to shift blame).

832. *See* **Dewberry v. State**, 4 S.W.3d 735, 751-52 (Tex. Crim. App. 1999); **Bingham v. State**, 987 S.W.2d 54, 58 (Tex. Crim. App. 1999); **Cunningham v. State**, 877 S.W.2d 310, 312-14 (Tex. Crim. App. 1994); **Davis v. State**, 872 S.W.2d 743, 749 (Tex. Crim. App. 1994); **James**, 102 S.W.3d at 177-79; *see, e.g.,* **Cofield v. State**, 891 S.W.2d 952, 955-56 (Tex. Crim. App. 1994) (statement by passenger to arresting officer, admitting that both passenger and defendant had smoked cocaine immediately before arrest, was not admissible against defendant; statement exposed both passenger and defendant to criminal liability and may have been made to curry favor with police); **Mason**, 416 S.W.3d at 734-35 (witness's statement to other inmate that he was the shooter was not corroborated by evidence at trial; other witnesses identified someone else as shooter and indicated that witness served as lookout); **Howard v. State**, 945 S.W.2d 303, 306-07 (Tex. App.—Amarillo 1997, no pet.) (accomplice's tearful statement to his mother, shortly after capital murder of grocery-store owner, in which accomplice admitted to participating in robbery and stated that defendant had shot victim, qualified under rule and was admissible against defendant; statement was clearly against accomplice's penal interest, as it implicated him in murder and exposed him to possible death sentence, and statement was corroborated by defendant's own admissions and discussion of details of robbery); **Tidrow v. State**, 916 S.W.2d 623, 627-28 (Tex. App.—Fort Worth 1996, no pet.) (out-of-court written statements by codefendants were admissible under rule because they were consistent with defendant's confession, were clearly self-inculpatory, and did not attempt to exonerate declarants); **Fonseca v. State**, 908 S.W.2d 519, 521-22 (Tex. App.—San Antonio 1995, no pet.) (reversible error to exclude defense witness's testimony offered under Criminal Rule 803(24) when witness testified that declarant told him shortly before murder that he and companion were going to "rock 'n roll" at victim's house and that declarant told him, day after murder, that he and companion had in fact killed victim; this testimony was corroborated by two other witnesses' testimony that same declarant told them that he and companion murdered victim and by a third witness's testimony that declarant's companion told him that declarant shot victim); **Auston v. State**, 892 S.W.2d 141, 143-44 (Tex. App.—Houston [14th Dist.] 1994, no pet.) (trial court did not abuse discretion in excluding defendant's proffered statement against interest because he did not demonstrate corroborating circumstances clearly indicating the trustworthiness of the statement as required under rule).

833. **Burks v. State**, 876 S.W.2d 877, 904-05 (Tex. Crim. App. 1994).

834. **Davis**, 872 S.W.2d at 749; **Lester**, 120 S.W.3d at 901; **James**, 102 S.W.3d at 177 & n.10. In 2017, the Texas Legislature added a subsection to Texas Code of Criminal Procedure article 39.14 that requires the State, if it intends to offer the testimony of a witness to whom the defendant made a statement against the defendant's interest while they were imprisoned in the same correctional facility, to disclose to the defendant any information in the State's possession or control that is relevant to the witness's credibility. TEX. CODE CRIM. PROC. art. 39.14(h-1). This infor-

2. Statements against social interest. Texas has adopted a hearsay exception for a statement against social interest, which is a statement that tends "to make the declarant an object of hatred, ridicule, or disgrace."[836] However, statements by one person accusing another of committing a crime do not qualify merely because the person accused might attempt to retaliate and would presumably hate the declarant for making such a statement.[837] As one Texas court explained:

> Logically, it can be argued that any statement made by a declarant against another will subject the declarant to hatred and retaliation by the person or persons the statement implicates. … If the State's broad argument was accepted then virtually every statement a declarant made against another would be admissible.[838]

In one case, the court of appeals held that a statement that would expose the child declarant to disgrace in the eyes of her mother qualified as a statement against interest.[839] Usually, however, a statement against social interest is the type that the de-

---

mation includes the witness's criminal history, including any plea bargains, any grants or offers of leniency given in exchange for the witness's testimony in the present case, and information on any other cases in which the witness has given similar testimony. *Id.* The subsection applies to prosecutions of offenses committed on or after September 1, 2017. H.B. 34, §14, 85th Leg., R.S., eff. Sept. 1, 2017.

835. *See, e.g.*, ***Lester***, 120 S.W.3d at 902 (reversible error to exclude nondefendant-declarant's confession to his mother even though declarant now denied making the statement; "whether [declarant or testifying witness] is to be believed is ultimately for the jury").

836. Tex. R. Evid. 803(24)(A); *see, e.g.*, ***Robinson v. Harkins & Co.***, 711 S.W.2d 619, 621 (Tex. 1986) (husband's statement that he was responsible for automobile accident in which his wife became a paraplegic qualified as statement against social interest and was admissible under Rule 803(24)); ***Purtell v. State***, 761 S.W.2d 360, 369 (Tex. Crim. App. 1988) (confession of homosexual conduct is a statement that "would tend to bring ridicule and disgrace upon a small-town minister" and thus qualifies as statement against social interest under Rule 803(24)); ***Franklin v. State***, 992 S.W.2d 698, 706 (Tex. App.—Texarkana 1999, pet. ref'd) ("it is arguable" that Rule 803(24) would permit admission of CPS worker's testimony that defendant, defendant's wife, and molestation victim were HIV-positive as a statement against social interest).

837. *See, e.g.*, ***Miles v. State***, 918 S.W.2d 511, 516 (Tex. Crim. App. 1996) (deceased declarant's hearsay statement about defendant's role in homicide was not admissible as a statement against social interest; "[e]ven if a declarant may be the subject of retaliation because of an accusatory statement, it does not necessarily follow that it makes him a subject of hatred, ridicule, or disgrace as envisioned by the rule of evidence"); ***Owens v. State***, 916 S.W.2d 713, 718 (Tex. App.—Waco 1996, no pet.) (victim's hearsay statement giving the details of a "savage beating" she received was not a statement against her interest, even though she may have been embarrassed to give the statement; to hold otherwise would make all victims "disgraceful" and declare that it is against one's social interest to admit to being a crime victim); ***Sills v. State***, 846 S.W.2d 392, 396-97 (Tex. App.—Houston [14th Dist.] 1992, pet. ref'd) (declarant's out-of-court written statement detailing commission of murder by defendant and stating that defendant had threatened to kill declarant and his family if he told anyone of the event was inadmissible as a statement against social interest when declarant refused to testify at trial).

838. *Sills*, 846 S.W.2d at 397.

839. *Glover v. State*, 102 S.W.3d 754, 766 (Tex. App.—Texarkana 2002, pet. ref'd). In this case, the declarant was a 14-year-old girl who admitted to her mother, under extensive questioning, that she had had sexual relations with a 26-year-old man. *Id.* The court of appeals reasoned:

> Examining the circumstances, a reasonable person in A.H.'s position would have known that her statements would subject her to disgrace in the eyes of her mother. That A.H. recognized and understood this is illustrated by the fact that she took pains to hide her conduct from her parents by sneaking out of her father's house and by keeping her liaison a secret. She made the statements reluctantly, and only when confronted by the possibility that her mother already knew the "secret." The audience was A.H.'s mother. A.H. was fourteen and still lived with her mother, so A.H. was still subject to her moth-

RULE 803

clarant would consider as exposing him to "hatred, ridicule, or disgrace" by a significant segment of society, not by one specific individual, even the person to whom the declarant is speaking.[840]

3. Collateral statements. Frequently, the question arises whether collateral statements—those that are exculpatory or neutral—accompanying a statement against interest should be admissible under the rule. For example, a masked man holding a bag full of money might be arrested outside a bank and tell officers, "I robbed the bank." This statement is wholly against interest. If he says, "Joe and I robbed the bank," this statement is against the declarant's interest, but it also inculpates Joe as an equal participant. If the declarant says, "Joe robbed the bank; I was the lookout man," the statement, while somewhat inculpatory, largely shifts blame to another.[841] The U.S. Supreme Court, interpreting the federal counterpart to Rule 803(24), has held that "the most faithful reading of [Federal] Rule 804(b)(3) is that it does not allow admission of non-self-inculpatory statements, even if they are made within a broader narrative that is generally self-inculpatory."[842]

According to the Supreme Court, "[t]he fact that a person is making a broadly self-inculpatory confession does not make more credible the confession's non-self-inculpatory parts."[843] The concern is that the declarant may be attempting to shift blame to another or gain favor with the authorities by lessening his own culpability and increasing someone else's.[844] For that reason, the Supreme Court held that only those statements that are wholly self-inculpatory are trustworthy enough to be admissible under the exception. The Supreme Court left unresolved whether "equal blame" statements, such as "Joe and I robbed the bank," are admissible under the federal rule. The Texas Court of Criminal Appeals has resolved this issue for Texas courts: "Both statements that are directly against the declarant's interest and collateral 'blame-sharing' statements may be admissible under Rule 803(24), if corroborating circumstances clearly indicate their trustworthiness. 'Blame-shifting' statements that minimize the

---

er's authority and control. The risk to A.H. of being untruthful was that certain punishment would be compounded, because she was told that her mother already "knew everything." Considering all of the circumstances, we conclude that the statements of which Glover complains fall within the scope of Rule 803(24), in that they would so far tend to subject the declarant to disgrace that a reasonable person in her position would not have made these statements unless believing them to be true.

Id. Although the reasoning and result in this particular case seem appropriate, an extension of the rationale for the "against social interest" exception to include any statement that might anger the specific listener is beyond the scope of the rule as drafted.

840. *See* Tex. R. Evid. 803(24)(A).

841. *See* ***Walter v. State***, 267 S.W.3d 883, 891 (Tex. Crim. App. 2008) (discussing different types of statements against penal interest).

842. ***Williamson v. United States***, 512 U.S. 594, 600-01 (1994). For a discussion of ***Williamson*** and its application in Texas courts, see ***Walter***, 267 S.W.3d at 892-97.

843. ***Williamson***, 512 U.S. at 599.

844. *See id.* at 603; ***Lilly v. Virginia***, 527 U.S. 116, 131 (1999) (plurality op.); *see, e.g.*, ***Zarychta v. State***, 961 S.W.2d 455, 458-59 (Tex. App.—Houston [1st Dist.] 1997, pet. ref'd) (accomplice's statement that defendant told him to shoot victim was inadmissible under Criminal Rule 803(24) because it was an attempt to shift blame to defendant and minimize declarant's own role).

speaker's culpability are not, absent extraordinary circumstances, admissible under the rule."[845] The court went on to hold that "the trial judge is obligated to parse a generally self-inculpatory narrative and weed out those specific factual statements that are self-exculpatory or shift blame to another."[846]

4. Confrontation Clause. Lastly, the rule permits the State to offer a statement against penal interest to inculpate the defendant if (1) the declarant testifies at trial or (2) the statement is not "testimonial" and therefore not barred by the Confrontation Clause.[847]

E. Proposed Rule 803(25): Residual Exception

In addition to the foregoing specific exceptions, the State Bar Committee recommended that the Texas Supreme Court include a "residual" exception in the Civil Rules; no such exception was proposed or adopted for the Criminal Rules. The Texas Supreme Court deleted the residual provision, which would have made admissible in a civil case any "statement not specifically covered by any of the foregoing exceptions but having substantial guarantees of trustworthiness."[848] Montana also deleted the congressional additions when it enacted a version of the Federal Rules in 1977.[849] Montana's drafters explained as follows:

---

845. *Walter*, 267 S.W.3d at 896; *see Cofield v. State*, 891 S.W.2d 952, 956 (Tex. Crim. App. 1994); *see, e.g.*, *Guidry v. State*, 9 S.W.3d 133, 148-49 (Tex. Crim. App. 1999) (conspirator's statements, although they included term "we" on occasion, inculpated defendant alone as the triggerman in murder prosecution and described how defendant killed victim; inadmissible under Criminal Rule 803(24)); *Dewberry v. State*, 4 S.W.3d 735, 751-52 (Tex. Crim. App. 1999) (codefendant's statements incriminating himself and defendant equally were admissible under Criminal Rule 803(24)); *Orona v. State*, 341 S.W.3d 452, 465 (Tex. App.—Fort Worth 2011, pet. ref'd) (coconspirator's statement that he and defendant "beat on" murder victim exposed both himself and defendant to criminal responsibility and was corroborated by other testimony; statement was admissible under Rule 803(24)).

846. *Walter*, 267 S.W.3d at 897.

847. *See Crawford v. Washington*, 541 U.S. 36, 51-54 (2004); *see, e.g.*, *Woods v. State*, 152 S.W.3d 105, 113-14 (Tex. Crim. App. 2004) (discussing impact of *Crawford* on admissibility of statements offered under Rule 803(24); "street corner" casual remarks against interest made by codefendant to acquaintances were not "testimonial" statements under *Crawford*, and thus not barred by Confrontation Clause); *Orona*, 341 S.W.3d at 463-64 (coconspirator's statement that he and defendant "'beat on [murder victim]' was a spontaneous, volunteered statement made in front of acquaintances" and was not testimonial); *Gutierrez v. State*, 150 S.W.3d 827, 829-30 (Tex. App.—Houston [14th Dist.] 2004, no pet.) (accomplice's videotaped confession to police, which implicated defendant, violated defendant's right of confrontation because he had no opportunity to cross-examine accomplice either before or during trial); *Jahanian v. State*, 145 S.W.3d 346, 350 (Tex. App.—Houston [14th Dist.] 2004, no pet.) (written statement against interest given to police by cohort allegedly involved in organized criminal activity with defendant violated defendant's right to confront witnesses under *Crawford*; cohort's statement was "testimonial" because it was given during a criminal investigation after cohort had become a suspect and cohort did not testify at trial); *Brooks v. State*, 132 S.W.3d 702, 707 (Tex. App.—Dallas 2004, pet. ref'd) (admission of nontestifying accomplice's out-of-court written statement about circumstances of robbery given to police during interrogation violated Confrontation Clause under *Crawford*; statements were "testimonial," and defendant had no opportunity to cross-examine accomplice either before or during trial); *Springsteen v. State*, No. AP-74,223 (Tex. Crim. App. 2006) (no pub.; 5-24-06) (although accomplice's custodial confession statement "may well have been admissible under the exception in Rule ... 803(24) for hearsay statements that subject a person to criminal liability and the trustworthiness of which are clearly indicated by corroborating circumstances," it was inadmissible under the Confrontation Clause because it was a testimonial statement "'taken by police officers in the course of interrogations'" (quoting *Crawford*, 541 U.S. at 52)); *cf. United States v. Rodriguez-Marrero*, 390 F.3d 1, 17 (1st Cir. 2004) (murdered conspirator's signed confession, presented under oath to the prosecutor, was testimonial hearsay barred by the Con-

The Commission believed this exception should allow "room for growth and development of the law of evidence in the area of hearsay" and that the amendments by Congress are too restrictive and contrary to the purpose of the provision. These amendments can be criticized as follows: the requirement that the statement be offered as evidence of a "material" fact is redundant in requiring relevance as defined in Rule 401 and uses outmoded language .... The requirement that the evidence be more probative on the point for which it is offered restricts the use of these types of exceptions by imposing a requirement similar to that of unavailability under Rule 804; this restriction would have the effect of severely limiting the instances in which the exception would be used and be impractical in the sense that a party would generally offer the strongest evidence available regardless of the existence of this requirement. The requirement that the general purposes of these rules and interests of justice will be served is unnecessarily repetitive in view of Rule 102. Finally, the notice requirement is unnecessary because of discovery procedures and the discretion of the court in allowing advance rulings on the admissibility of evidence.[850]

The Texas drafters were moved by the same considerations. Furthermore, the federal experience has shown that the notice requirement in this context is unnecessary, impractical, and unrealistic.[851]

Besides omitting the congressional additions, the Texas Committee's proposal included the phrase "substantial guarantees of trustworthiness" instead of "equivalent circumstantial guarantees of trustworthiness."[852] The elimination of the word "circum-

---

frontation Clause, even if it had been otherwise admissible under the forfeiture-by-wrongdoing doctrine in Federal Rule 804(b)(6)). Refer to notes 34-181 *supra* and accompanying text.

848. TEX. R. EVID. 803(25)(a) (1982 Liaison Committee proposal), *reprinted infra* p. 1094. In 2000, the residual exceptions in Federal Rules 803(24) and 804(b)(5) were deleted and replaced with a single rule, Rule 807. That rule has the same effect as the former rules and applies to hearsay statements not specifically covered by either Rule 803 or Rule 804. *See* FED. R. EVID. 807(a). Reasonable notice of the intent to use the statement is required under Rule 807(b).

849. *See* MONT. CODE ANN., tit. 26, ch. 10, Rule of Evid. 803(24) & cmt.

850. *Id.* cmt. (citation omitted).

851. Federal courts have been lenient in enforcing the pretrial-notice requirements of the residual exception. *See* 7 GRAHAM, *supra* note 491, §807:1, at 828-29 (although courts generally enforce the notice requirement, some courts interpret the requirement with flexibility and dispense of it when no prejudice to the opponent is apparent); 4 WEINSTEIN & BERGER, *supra* note 209, ¶803(24)[01], at 803-440 n.30 (citing a case in which federal courts have been lenient in interpreting the notice requirement). *But see United States v. Ruffin*, 575 F.2d 346, 358 (2d Cir. 1978) (FBI agent's testimony about the contents of various documents in the county clerk's land records was inadmissible under former Federal Rule 803(24), now Rule 807, because government did not notify defendant before trial that the government intended to rely on the testimony); *United States v. Davis*, 571 F.2d 1354, 1360 n.11 (5th Cir. 1978) (documents were inadmissible under former Federal Rule 803(24), now Rule 807, because government did not give defense the required advance notice of the hearsay evidence); *United States v. Oates*, 560 F.2d 45, 72 n.30 (2d Cir. 1977) ("There is absolutely no doubt that Congress intended that the requirement of advance notice be rigidly enforced."). The flexible approach is mandated not by the provisions themselves but by "trial realities." 4 WEINSTEIN & BERGER, *supra* note 209, ¶803(24)[01], at 803-441 (criticizing courts that have interpreted the notice requirement with absolute and unwarranted rigidity, unmindful of trial realities).

852. TEX. R. EVID. 803(25)(a) (1982 Liaison Committee proposal), *reprinted infra* p. 1094.

stantial" was probably not significant because the word seems redundant in context; any guarantee of trustworthiness would be circumstantial. The substitution of "substantial" for "equivalent" was more meaningful. The term "equivalent" in Federal Rule 807 has been troublesome. First, "there is an enormous variation in the guarantee of trustworthiness" among the many specific exceptions.[853] To meet the "equivalent" test, must a statement offered under the federal residual exception possess apparent trustworthiness equivalent only to the "least trustworthy" of the specific exceptions? Or should its apparent trustworthiness be equal to that of the most nearly analogous specific exception? It would appear difficult to characterize such a statement as "equivalent" in guarantees of trustworthiness to a statement that fully meets the requirement of the specific exception, yet many of the reported federal cases admitting statements under the residual exceptions are of this nature. These include business records that did not meet the standards of Rule 803(6),[854] prior statements of witnesses that did not satisfy Rule 801(d)(1),[855] and former testimony that did not qualify under Rule 804(b)(1).[856] At the same time, similar offers have been rejected in other cases.[857] Of course, in applying any informal standard, perfect consistency cannot be expected. The Texas Committee's proposal, by directing the court to determine simply whether the indicia of a statement's trustworthiness were "substantial," would at least have avoided the problem of whether evidence not quite possessing the requisites of a specific exception could nevertheless be "equivalent" in indicia of trustworthiness.

Apart from their tendency to admit statements in the "near miss" category, federal cases reported under the residual exceptions do not seem to follow any pattern.[858] This result seems inevitable. The provisions were not designed to allow courts to develop new formal exceptions, but to allow for flexibility and judgment. Because the particular circumstances relating to both the declaration and the case in which it is offered are critical under this sort of provision, it is not surprising that precedent has not often been determinative or even helpful in resolving a particular case.

Determining the extent to which the residual exception would have changed Texas civil law had it been adopted by the Texas Supreme Court is impossible. No Texas case has explicitly stated that sufficiently trustworthy hearsay would be admitted even if it could not fit within a specific exception. On the other hand, no Texas case has suggested that the hearsay exceptions recognized by common law or by statute as of any

---

853. 4 WEINSTEIN & BERGER, *supra* note 209, ¶803(24)[01], at 803-430 to 803-431.

854. *E.g.*, **United States v. Pfeiffer**, 539 F.2d 668, 670-71 (8th Cir. 1976); **Keyes v. Sch. Dist. No. 1**, 439 F. Supp. 393, 411 (D. Colo. 1977).

855. *E.g.*, **United States v. Barnes**, 586 F.2d 1052, 1055-56 (5th Cir. 1978); **United States v. Leslie**, 542 F.2d 285, 289-91 (5th Cir. 1976); **United States v. Iaconetti**, 540 F.2d 574, 577-78 (2d Cir. 1976).

856. *E.g.*, **United States v. West**, 574 F.2d 1131, 1134-36 (4th Cir. 1978); **United States v. Carlson**, 547 F.2d 1346, 1352-55 (8th Cir. 1976).

857. *E.g.*, **United States v. Gonzalez**, 559 F.2d 1271, 1273-74 (5th Cir. 1977) (former testimony); **United States v. Palacios**, 556 F.2d 1359, 1362-63 & n.7 (5th Cir. 1977) (prior statement of witness).

858. *See* 7 GRAHAM, *supra* note 491, §807:1, at 831-33; 4 WEINSTEIN & BERGER, *supra* note 209, ¶¶803(24)[01], 804(b)(5)[01], at 803-433 to 803-437, 804-182 to 804-189.

particular time were to be regarded as exclusive. Presumably, one could always argue in a Texas court that a particular hearsay statement should be admitted, despite its failure to meet a specific exception, on the basis of the statement's peculiar guarantees of trustworthiness. Nevertheless, had the Rules expressly adopted the concept, courts would have undoubtedly admitted hearsay statements that would have been excluded in the past for want of a specific traditional or statutory exception.

Why did the Texas Supreme Court decide to delete the residual exception? As the federal experience has shown, the flexibility and growth that an informal residual exception is supposed to provide can only occur at some cost to predictability and uniformity. Presumably, the supreme court felt that predictability and uniformity outweighed the need for flexibility and growth. Several other states that have adopted versions of the Federal Rules of Evidence have likewise elected to omit the residual hearsay exception.[859] In Maine, the drafters explained this decision:

> The Court decided not to adopt any catch-all provision. It was impressed by the theoretical undesirability of foreclosing further development of the law of evidence on a case-by-case basis. It concluded, however, that despite the purported safeguards, there was a serious risk that trial judges would differ greatly in applying the elastic standard of equivalent trustworthiness. The result would be a lack of uniformity which would make preparation for trial difficult. Nor would it be likely that the Law Court on appeal could effectively apply corrective measures. There would indeed be doubt whether an affirmance of an admission of evidence under the catch-all provision amounted to the creation of a new exception with the force of precedent or merely a refusal to rule that the trial judge had abused his discretion.
>
> Flexibility in construction of the rules so as to promote growth and development of the law of evidence is called for by Rule 102. Under this mandate there will be room to construe an existing hearsay exception broadly in the interest of ascertaining truth, as distinguished from creating an entirely new exception based upon the trial judge's determination of equivalent trustworthiness, a guideline which the most conscientious of judges would find extremely difficult to follow.[860]

The reference to Rule 102 is noteworthy. That rule mandates: "These rules should be construed so as to … promote the development of evidence law, to the end of ascertaining truth and securing a just determination."[861] The Maine Supreme Court recognized that the excision of the residual hearsay exception may require Maine's courts "to construe an existing hearsay exception broadly in the interest of ascertaining

---

859. *See, e.g.*, FLA. STAT. §90.803.

860. ME. R. EVID. 803 advisory committee's note. The Maine Rules of Evidence were restyled in 2015. Maine Rule 803 maintains the substantive differences between the Maine Rules and the Federal Rules and still does not have a residual hearsay exception. ME. R. EVID. 803 advisory committee's note to 2015 restyling.

861. ME. R. EVID. 102. Maine Rule 102 is identical to Federal Rule 102. *See* FED. R. EVID. 102.

truth ...."[862] Perhaps the Texas Supreme Court, having made the same decision about the residual exception, will also foster broad constructions of the specific exceptions in the spirit of Rule 102.

RULE 804
EXCEPTIONS TO THE RULE AGAINST HEARSAY—WHEN THE DECLARANT IS UNAVAILABLE AS A WITNESS

(a) Criteria for Being Unavailable. A declarant is considered to be unavailable as a witness if the declarant:

(1) is exempted from testifying about the subject matter of the declarant's statement because the court rules that a privilege applies;

(2) refuses to testify about the subject matter despite a court order to do so;

(3) testifies to not remembering the subject matter;

(4) cannot be present or testify at the trial or hearing because of death or a then-existing infirmity, physical illness, or mental illness; or

(5) is absent from the trial or hearing and the statement's proponent has not been able, by process or other reasonable means, to procure the declarant's attendance or testimony.

But this subdivision (a) does not apply if the statement's proponent procured or wrongfully caused the declarant's unavailability as a witness in order to prevent the declarant from attending or testifying.

(b) The Exceptions. The following are not excluded by the rule against hearsay if the declarant is unavailable as a witness:

(1) *Former Testimony.* Testimony that:

(A) when offered in a civil case:

(i) was given as a witness at a trial or hearing of the current or a different proceeding or in a deposition in a different proceeding; and

(ii) is now offered against a party and the party—or a person with similar interest—had an opportunity and similar motive to develop the testimony by direct, cross-, or redirect examination.

(B) when offered in a criminal case:

(i) was given as a witness at a trial or hearing of the current or a different proceeding; and

---

862. Me. R. Evid. 803 advisory committee's note.

(ii) is now offered against a party who had an opportunity and similar motive to develop it by direct, cross-, or redirect examination; or

(iii) was taken in a deposition under—and is now offered in accordance with—chapter 39 of the Code of Criminal Procedure.

(2) *Statement Under the Belief of Imminent Death.* A statement that the declarant, while believing the declarant's death to be imminent, made about its cause or circumstances.

(3) *Statement of Personal or Family History.* A statement about:

(A) the declarant's own birth, adoption, legitimacy, ancestry, marriage, divorce, relationship by blood, adoption or marriage, or similar facts of personal or family history, even though the declarant had no way of acquiring personal knowledge about that fact; or

(B) another person concerning any of these facts, as well as death, if the declarant was related to the person by blood, adoption, or marriage or was so intimately associated with the person's family that the declarant's information is likely to be accurate.

COMMENTARY ON RULE 804

Like Rule 803, Rule 804 contains exceptions to the hearsay rule.[863] Its three exceptions, however, may be used only if the declarant is unavailable to testify at trial.[864] The requirement of unavailability in Rule 804 implicitly establishes a preference for live testimony, indicating that the particular indicia of trustworthiness in these exceptions are theoretically inferior to the testimonial conditions. These indicia, however, are deemed sufficient when the alternative to receiving the declarant's evidence in specified hearsay form is losing that evidence completely.[865] Nonetheless, little connection can be found between theory and application in this instance because "[i]t is apparent that history as well as a certain degree of arbitrariness determined whether an exception should be placed in Rule 803 or 804."[866]

Rule 804 differs from the federal rule in several respects. Substantive differences appear in the definition of "unavailability" in Rule 804(a)(5)[867] and in both the civil and criminal applications of the former-testimony exception (Rule 804(b)(1))[868] and the exception for statements made under the belief of imminent death, also known as dying

---

863. The 1998 unification of the Civil and Criminal Rules did not substantively alter Texas Rule 804. Gender-neutral language was substituted where appropriate, and the civil and criminal distinctions in the former-testimony exception were merged.

864. *See, e.g.*, *St. Paul Fire & Marine Ins. v. Confer*, 956 S.W.2d 825, 831 (Tex. App.—San Antonio 1997, pet. denied) (when proponent of former testimony did not prove unavailability of declarant, evidence was inadmissible hearsay).

865. *See* FED. R. EVID. 804 advisory committee's note, subdiv. (b).

866. 4 WEINSTEIN & BERGER, *supra* note 209, ¶804(a)[01], at 804-40.

867. Refer to notes 890-901 *infra* and accompanying text.

868. Refer to notes 903-931 *infra* and accompanying text.

declarations (Rule 804(b)(2)).[869] Federal Rule 804(b)(3), on declarations against interest, was the model for Texas Rule 803(24).[870] And the federal residual exception (former Rule 804(b)(5), now Rule 807) was not adopted in Texas in any form.[871]

A. Rule 804(a): Definition of Unavailability

Rule 804(a) names five separate grounds that make a witness unavailable to testify: (1) a claim of privilege,[872] (2) refusal to testify,[873] (3) loss of memory,[874] (4) death or physical or mental illness or infirmity,[875] and (5) absence from the trial or hearing and inability of the proponent, "by process or other reasonable means, to procure the declarant's attendance or testimony."[876] Rule 804(a) is consistent with earlier Texas case law even though the cases appear to limit the definition of unavailability to the last two grounds.[877] While authority for the first ground is scant[878] and for the second and third nonexistent, it is unlikely that a Texas court would have refused to accept them as satisfying the unavailability requirement if the need had arisen in a proper case.[879]

The last sentence of Rule 804(a) provides an important caveat: a declarant is not considered unavailable to testify if "the statement's proponent procured or wrongfully caused the declarant's unavailability as a witness in order to prevent the declarant from attending or testifying."[880] Thus, the proponent of the evidence cannot invoke the Rule 804(b) exceptions if he has, for example, exercised his own Fifth Amendment right not to testify;[881] bribed the witness into refusing to testify; threatened to kill the witness if

---

869. Refer to notes 932-951 *infra* and accompanying text.

870. Refer to notes 811-847 *supra* and accompanying text.

871. Refer to notes 848-862 *supra* and accompanying text.

872. Tex. R. Evid. 804(a)(1).

873. Tex. R. Evid. 804(a)(2); *see Davis v. State*, 773 S.W.2d 592, 593 (Tex. App.—Eastland 1989, pet. ref'd) (witness who refuses to testify even after being held in contempt falls within the definition of a declarant who is unavailable as a witness under Criminal Rule 804(a)(2)).

874. Tex. R. Evid. 804(a)(3); *see Marable v. State*, 840 S.W.2d 88, 92-93 (Tex. App.—Texarkana 1992, pet. ref'd) (State can introduce former testimony of witness at retrial of criminal case if witness can no longer remember the relevant matters to which he testified at the first trial).

875. Tex. R. Evid. 804(a)(4).

876. Tex. R. Evid. 804(a)(5).

877. *See Hall v. White*, 525 S.W.2d 860, 862 (Tex. 1975).

878. *See Liberty Mut. Ins. v. Heard & Jones Drug Stores, Inc.*, 446 S.W.2d 911, 912-13 (Tex. Civ. App.—Amarillo 1969, no writ).

879. *See* Black, *supra* note 786, at 1005.

880. Tex. R. Evid. 804(a).

881. *See, e.g., Davis v. State*, 961 S.W.2d 156, 156-57 (Tex. Crim. App. 1998) (defendant who testified at pretrial suppression hearing could not introduce that testimony at trial as former testimony when he invoked his Fifth Amendment privilege not to testify at the trial on the merits). As the court of criminal appeals explained:

> In the present case, appellant was exempt from testifying because he invoked his privilege against self-incrimination. By invoking his Fifth Amendment privilege, appellant procured this exemption for the purpose of preventing himself from testifying as a witness. And appellant was the proponent of his prior testimony. Therefore, under the plain language of the rule, appellant was not unavailable.

Id.; accord Dennis v. State, 961 S.W.2d 245, 247 (Tex. App.—Houston [1st Dist.] 1997, pet. ref'd); *Castro v. State*, 914 S.W.2d 159, 163 (Tex. App.—San Antonio 1995, pet. ref'd). Federal courts have reached the same conclusion under the analogous federal rule. *See United States v. Peterson*, 100 F.3d 7, 13-14 (2d Cir. 1996); *United States v. Kimball*, 15 F.3d 54, 55-56 & n.5 (5th Cir. 1994).

RULE 804

he does not testify to a complete lack of memory; killed or maimed the witness; or arranged for the witness to be out of the country during the trial. Essentially, the sponsor of the Rule 804 evidence cannot create the condition of unavailability and then benefit from it.[882]

1. Rule 804(a)(1): Privilege. A person who asserts a valid privilege not to testify is unavailable under Rule 804.[883] The witness himself must assert the privilege, and it must be ruled on by the court.[884] Of course, when a party to the lawsuit claims a privilege not to testify, he is not unavailable for purposes of Rule 804[885] and he cannot offer his own former testimony into evidence. On the other hand, when a party to a lawsuit invokes a privilege not to testify, the *opposing* party may always offer the invoking party's former testimony, not under this rule, but under Rule 801(e)(2), which makes several types of prior statements by an opposing party admissible.[886]

2. Rule 804(a)(2): Refusal to testify. If a witness persists in refusing to testify even after being ordered to do so by the trial court, he is unavailable under the rule.[887]

Of course, if the defendant invokes his privilege against self-incrimination at a second proceeding, he is unavailable to the State because the State did not "procure" his unavailability; the defendant's prior testimony would be admissible not only as an exemption to the hearsay rule under Rule 801(e)(2)(A) (opposing party's statement), but also as an exception under Rule 804(b)(1). *See, e.g., **Bryan v. State**,* 837 S.W.2d 637, 644 (Tex. Crim. App. 1992) (defendant's testimony at his first trial was admissible at second trial when he declined to testify in later proceeding; defendant was "unavailable" under Criminal Rule 804(a)(1)). The analysis in **Bryan** of Rule 804 was not necessary because a defendant's prior testimony is defined as a nonhearsay statement by an opposing party and thus is admissible under Rule 801(e)(2).

882. *E.g., **Kimball**,* 15 F.3d at 55-56 (defendant who invoked his Fifth Amendment privilege not to testify could not offer his own former testimony as an exception to the hearsay rule).

883. *See, e.g., **Jones v. State**,* 843 S.W.2d 487, 490 (Tex. Crim. App. 1992) (witness who asserted her privilege against self-incrimination was unavailable as a witness to defendant), *overruled on other grounds,* **Maxwell v. State**, 48 S.W.3d 196 (Tex. Crim. App. 2001); ***Clark v. State**,* 947 S.W.2d 650, 654 (Tex. App.—Fort Worth 1997, pet. ref'd) (indicted codefendant was "unavailable" under Criminal Rule 804(a) when he invoked his Fifth Amendment privilege not to testify at defendant's trial; trial court had discretion to exclude his prior videotaped and written confession to police under Criminal Rule 804; court did not note that codefendant's out-of-court confession did not qualify for admission under Criminal Rule 804 as former testimony); ***Reyes v. State**,* 845 S.W.2d 328, 332-33 (Tex. App.—El Paso 1992, no pet.) (witness was unavailable under Rule 804(a)(1) at defendant's second trial when witness claimed privilege against self-incrimination, and his testimony from defendant's first trial was thus admissible; witness's attorney testified in bill of exception that he would have advised his client not to testify in first trial if he had known that witness had been subpoenaed).

884. *See* TEX. R. EVID. 804(a)(1).

885. *See **Guidry v. State**,* 9 S.W.2d 133, 146 (Tex. Crim. App. 1999) (defendant who invokes his Fifth Amendment right not to testify is not unavailable for purposes of Rule 804 when he seeks to introduce his own prior testimony; declarant "'is not unavailable if his exemption from testifying is procured by the party offering the declarant's testimony'" (quoting **Davis**, 961 S.W.2d at 156)).

886. Refer to notes 344-445 *supra* and accompanying text.

887. TEX. R. EVID. 804(a)(2); *see, e.g., **Nat. Gas Pipeline Co. of Am. v. Pool**,* 30 S.W.3d 618, 631 (Tex. App.—Amarillo 2000) (witness's "refusal to testify on the advice of his counsel made the witness 'unavailable' for purposes of this trial"; his prior deposition in a federal trial on same matters was thus admissible), *rev'd on other grounds,* 124 S.W.3d 188 (Tex. 2003); **Ward v. State**, 910 S.W.2d 1, 3 & n.2 (Tex. App.—Tyler 1995, pet. ref'd) (when child victim of sexual assault first suggested that she could not remember events and then persisted in refusing to testify about event, she became unavailable; with an adult, trial court should "threaten a recalcitrant witness with sanctions, [but] we don't believe that the court is required to threaten a young child with contempt to satisfy the requirement of an order" under Criminal Rule 804(a)(2)).

3. Rule 804(a)(3): Loss of memory. If a witness testifies at trial that he is presently unable to recall the relevant events about which he is questioned, he is unavailable under the rule.[888]

4. Rule 804(a)(4): Death or infirmity. A witness who is dead, has become insane, or is too physically or mentally infirm to attend or to testify at trial is unavailable under the rule.[889]

5. Rule 804(a)(5): Absence from the trial or hearing. If a witness is absent from a trial or hearing and his attendance or testimony cannot be procured by service of process or other reasonable means, he is unavailable under the rule.[890] In **Hall v. White**, the Texas Supreme Court held that when absence from the trial or hearing is relied on as the ground of unavailability, the proponent of a hearsay statement must show that he was unable to take the declarant's testimony by deposition, not simply that the declarant is beyond the court's subpoena jurisdiction at the time of trial.[891] Rule 804(a)(5) continues this doctrine.

The original version of Federal Rule 804(a)(5) promulgated by the Supreme Court required only that the proponent be unable to procure the "attendance" of the declarant, with no separate reference to inability to procure his "testimony."[892] Congress amended the rule, adding the inability to procure the declarant's testimony as a distinct requirement.[893] According to the House Committee on the Judiciary, where the amendment originated, the amendment was "designed primarily to require that an attempt be made to depose a witness (as well as to seek his attendance) as a precondition to the witness being deemed unavailable."[894] Congress ultimately adopted the House amendment despite the Senate Committee's protest that "[n]one of these situations would seem to warrant this needless, impractical and highly restrictive complication."[895] In the federal rule, however, the requirement of an attempt to depose does not apply to the former-testimony exception, Rule 804(b)(1).[896]

---

888. TEX. R. EVID. 804(a)(3); *see, e.g.*, **Marable v. State**, 840 S.W.2d 88, 92-93 (Tex. App.—Texarkana 1992, pet. ref'd) (when witness testified at retrial that he had no substantive recollection of the relevant conversations and events recounted at the previous trial, he was unavailable under Rule 804(a), and his former testimony was admissible).

889. *See* TEX. R. EVID. 804(a)(4); *see, e.g.*, **Keene Corp. v. Rogers**, 863 S.W.2d 168, 177-78 (Tex. App.—Texarkana 1993, writ filed, bankruptcy stay granted 3-30-94) (proponent of former testimony did not prove that witness in his eighties was unavailable when only evidence offered was attorney's statements that witness had refused to attend previous trials due to ill health).

890. TEX. R. EVID. 804(a)(5).

891. 525 S.W.2d 860, 862 (Tex. 1975).

892. FED. R. EVID. 804(a)(5) (1972 proposed final draft), 56 F.R.D. 183, 320 (1973).

893. H.R. REP. NO. 93-650, *supra* note 29, at 15, *reprinted in* 1974 U.S.C.C.A.N. at 7088.

894. *Id.*

895. S. REP. NO. 93-1277, *supra* note 30, at 20, *reprinted in* 1974 U.S.C.C.A.N. at 7067.

896. *See* FED. R. EVID. 804(a)(5)(A).

RULE 804

The Texas version refers to the inability to procure the "attendance or testimony" of the declarant as a prerequisite for this category of unavailability, regardless of which exception is being used.[897] In light of ***Hall v. White***, a former-testimony case, the Texas version was designed to leave earlier Texas law intact. Cases decided under the Texas Rules of Evidence have relied on ***Hall v. White*** in holding that the party offering former testimony had not shown that the witness was unavailable in those instances for purposes of Rule 804.[898] Thus, when absence from the trial or hearing alone is relied on as constituting unavailability, the proponent in Texas civil litigation must show that he was unable "by process or other reasonable means" to obtain either the attendance of the declarant at the hearing or an opportunity to depose him beforehand.[899]

In criminal cases, it is not sufficient merely to show that the witness cannot be subpoenaed. To show unavailability under Rule 804(a)(5), a party must show further that "a good-faith effort was made prior to trial to locate and present the witness."[900] Furthermore, because depositions are so rarely used in Texas criminal trials, the requirement of an attempt to depose the witness is not a prerequisite to a showing of unavailability under Rule 804(a)(5) in criminal cases.[901]

---

897. *See* TEX. R. EVID. 804(a)(5). In the federal rule, the inability to procure the declarant's "attendance or testimony" applies only to the exceptions in Rule 804(b)(2)-(b)(4); the inability to procure the declarant's "attendance" applies to the exceptions in Rule 804(b)(1) and (b)(6). *See* FED. R. EVID. 804(a)(5).

898. *See, e.g.,* ***Fuller-Austin Insulation Co. v. Bilder***, 960 S.W.2d 914, 921 (Tex. App.—Beaumont 1998, pet. granted, judgm't vacated w.r.m.) (doctor, who was 92, uncooperative in attending trial, and residing well outside subpoena range, was not unavailable under the rule when proponent of former testimony did not establish that it was unable to take his deposition or otherwise procure his testimony); ***Owens-Corning Fiberglas Corp. v. Wasiak***, 917 S.W.2d 883, 888 (Tex. App.—Austin 1996) (proponent of former testimony did not establish unavailability of witness although witness lived beyond subpoena power of court and was vacationing in Europe; no evidence that party had attempted to depose him or otherwise secure his testimony), *aff'd sub nom.* ***Owens-Corning Fiberglas Corp. v. Malone***, 972 S.W.2d 35 (Tex. 1998); ***Victor M. Solis Underground Util. & Paving Co. v. Laredo***, 751 S.W.2d 532, 537 (Tex. App.—San Antonio 1988, writ denied) (trial court correctly excluded former testimony of a witness who lived within the court's jurisdictional boundaries when a subpoena was issued, but not served, three days before trial; proponent knew of the potential witness for two years and made no effort to take his deposition).

899. *See* TEX. R. EVID. 804(a)(5).

900. ***Reed v. State***, 312 S.W.3d 682, 685 (Tex. App.—Houston [1st Dist.] 2009, pet. ref'd); *see* ***Otero-Miranda v. State***, 746 S.W.2d 352, 354-55 (Tex. App.—Amarillo 1988, pet. ref'd, untimely filed) ("unavailability" claim must be proved not only by evidence that a witness lives in a foreign country but also that "other reasonable means" were pursued to obtain the witness's attendance); *see, e.g.,* ***Ledbetter v. State***, 49 S.W.3d 588, 594 (Tex. App.—Amarillo 2001, pet. ref'd) (State made sufficient efforts to secure presence of former sheriff at trial under Rule 804 even though it did not seek attachment; State showed that prosecutor told sheriff several weeks before trial that his testimony would be necessary, sheriff was served with subpoena more than three weeks before trial date, deputy sheriff testified that it was uncertain when sheriff would be back, if ever, and defendant offered no evidence that State knew that sheriff planned to leave county; former testimony was admissible under rule); ***Caldwell v. State***, 916 S.W.2d 674, 676 (Tex. App.—Texarkana 1996, no pet.) (State offered sufficient evidence that witness was unable to attend and made good-faith efforts to secure testimony of the witness in her late seventies who told the testifying officer that she could not make the two-hour drive and would not be able to attend trial because of knee-replacement surgery, physically manifested by a scar and her walking with extreme difficulty); ***Reyes v. State***, 845 S.W.2d 328, 330-31 (Tex. App.—El Paso 1992, no pet.) (State did not use "due diligence" to secure witness when subpoena was issued three days before trial and when State did not seek assistance of foreign officials to locate and extradite witness after investigator had learned witness may have been out of the country). The same showing of a good-faith effort must be made to satisfy the Confrontation Clause's unavailability requirement. Refer to note 51 *supra*.

901. Refer to notes 924-928 *infra* and accompanying text.

B. Rule 804(b): Hearsay Exceptions

Unavailability of the witness is a prerequisite to the admissibility of former testimony, a statement made under the belief of imminent death, or a statement of personal or family history. But unavailability does not by itself create a hearsay exception for the admissibility of a declarant's out-of-court statement.[902] Only after a court determines that the witness is presently unavailable might one of the exceptions under Rule 804(b) allow the admission of the proffered evidence.

1. Rule 804(b)(1): Former testimony. Rule 804(b)(1) differs from the federal rule in several respects: (1) the federal rule uses the word "lawful" before "deposition," but the Texas rule does not,[903] (2) Texas Rule 804(b)(1) does not govern the admissibility of a deposition taken in the same civil proceeding because such depositions are admissible under Rule 801(e)(3), which has no federal corollary,[904] and (3) the Texas rule, as it applies in civil cases, replaces the phrase "predecessor in interest" with the phrase "person with similar interest."[905]

The Advisory Committee on the Federal Rules believed that the common law's identity-or-privity requirement was unduly narrow. Therefore, its version of Rule 804(b)(1) would have permitted former testimony to be used if the court had afforded

---

902. One court of appeals held that a defendant's out-of-court statement was admissible under Criminal Rule 804(a)(1) when he invoked his Fifth Amendment privilege not to testify. *See* ***Appling v. State***, 904 S.W.2d 912, 916 (Tex. App.—Corpus Christi 1995, pet. ref'd). But Rule 804(a)(1)-(a)(5) does not set out exceptions to the hearsay rule. It merely lists those conditions under which a witness is unavailable for purposes of the exceptions listed in Rule 804(b)(1)-(b)(3).

903. *See* FED. R. EVID. 804(b)(1)(A); TEX. R. EVID. 804(b)(1)(A)(i).

904. *See* FED. R. EVID. 801(d); TEX. R. EVID. 801(e)(3), 804(b)(1)(A)(i). Refer to notes 446-450 *supra* and accompanying text. On the other hand, testimony that was given at a trial or hearing from the current proceeding or a different one is excluded from the rule against hearsay when offered in either a civil or criminal case. *See* TEX. R. EVID. 804(b)(1)(A)(i), (b)(1)(B)(i).

905. *See* FED. R. EVID. 804(b)(1)(B); TEX. R. EVID. 804(b)(1)(A)(ii). As adopted, the rule made some changes in Texas civil proceedings. The early common law required identity of parties on both sides in the former and later proceedings to admit the former testimony of a witness who was unavailable in the later proceeding. Later, the "mutuality" requirement was eliminated, so that only the party against whom the testimony was offered had to have been a party to the proceeding in which the testimony was taken. *See, e.g.,* ***Bryant v. Trinity Univ'l Ins.***, 411 S.W.2d 945, 949 (Tex. Civ. App.—Dallas 1967, writ ref'd n.r.e.) (former testimony of witness from previous arson prosecution was admitted because an issue from that case was the same as in a later civil action to recover the loss of building contents destroyed by the fire, and counter-defendant was a party to both suits with a full opportunity to cross-examine witness in the earlier trial); *see also* MCCORMICK'S HANDBOOK II, *supra* note 7, §255, at 616 (if another party had a similar motive to cross-examine the witness and was given an adequate opportunity to do so in an earlier trial, that testimony should be received against the present party). Furthermore, at least some courts allowed into evidence the former testimony of a person in privity with the party against whom the evidence was later offered. *See, e.g.,* ***Metro. St. Ry. Co. v. Gumby***, 99 F. 192, 198 (2d Cir. 1900) (testimony is admissible when parties are so privy in interest that same motive and need for cross-examination existed). As the Second Circuit explained:

> "The term 'privity' denotes mutual or successive relationships to the same rights of property, and privies are distributed into several classes, according to the manner of this relationship. Thus, there are privies in estate, as donor and donee, lessor and lessee, and joint tenants; privies in blood, as heir and ancestor, and co-parceners; privies in representation, as executor and testator, administrator and intestate; privies in law, where the law, without privity of blood or estate, casts the land upon another, as by escheat."

Id. (quoting 19 AMERICAN AND ENGLISH ENCYCLOPEDIA OF LAW 156 (1892)).

a party an opportunity to develop the testimony in the earlier proceeding and that party had "motive and interest similar to those of the party against whom [the testimony is] now offered."[906] Congress rejected this proposal, considering it "generally unfair to impose upon the party against whom the hearsay evidence is being offered responsibility for the manner in which the witness was previously handled by another party."[907] The current rule allows the exceptions for testimony that "is now offered against a party who had—or, in a civil case, whose predecessor in interest had—an opportunity and similar motive to develop it by direct, cross-, or redirect examination."[908] In context, the concept of "predecessor in interest" must have been intended to be identical to the existing common-law concept of privity.

Under Texas common law, the doctrine on this point was not altogether clear. The leading treatise observed that in Texas, "the person against whom the evidence is now offered must have been a party to the proceedings wherein the testimony was taken, or someone having the same interest in the subject matter and thus the same motive to cross-examine, must have been a party"; "privity in the strict sense" was not required.[909] Indeed, Texas authority allowed former testimony without a strict privity relationship.[910] On the other hand, it was by no means established in Texas that mere similarity of interest would suffice.

In any event, the adoption of Rule 804(b)(1) established that mere similarity of interest was enough in civil cases. Moreover, considering the history of the congressionally restricted federal rule in the federal courts, the Texas drafters seem to have been closer to present judicial attitudes on the matter than Congress was. Though the intent of the congressional amendment seems clear, the federal courts have so liberally construed the term "predecessor in interest" that it is hard to see how outcomes are any different from what they would have been under the original Supreme Court version.[911]

In addition to identity of parties, the common-law version of this exception also required identity (later relaxed to "substantial" identity) of issues between the two

---

906. FED. R. EVID. 804(b)(1) (1972 proposed final draft), 56 F.R.D. 183, 321 (1973); *see* FED. R. EVID. 804 advisory committee's note, subdiv. (b)(1).

907. H.R. REP. NO. 93-650, *supra* note 29, at 15, *reprinted in* 1974 U.S.C.C.A.N. at 7088.

908. FED. R. EVID. 804(b)(1)(B).

909. 1A RAY, *supra* note 9, §949, at 208 (footnote omitted).

910. *See, e.g.*, *Sec. Realty & Dev. Co. v. Bunch*, 143 S.W.2d 687, 692-94 (Tex. Civ. App.—Beaumont 1940, writ dism'd judgm't cor.) (testimony in suit involving a husband was admissible in later suit involving partition of his wife's separate property).

911. *See Lloyd v. Am. Exp. Lines, Inc.*, 580 F.2d 1179, 1185-87 (3d Cir. 1978) (Congress's failure to define "predecessor in interest" allows for a broad interpretation of the phrase); *In re Master Key Antitrust Litig.*, 72 F.R.D. 108, 109 (D. Conn. 1976) (courts have interpreted "predecessor in interest" beyond the privity requirement that Congress desired), *aff'd*, 551 F.2d 300 (2d Cir. 1976) (table case); 7 GRAHAM, *supra* note 491, §804:1, at 567-68 & n.20 (same); 4 WEINSTEIN & BERGER, *supra* note 209, ¶804(b)(1)[04], at 804-100 to 804-106 (1995 & Supp. 1996) (cases largely indicate judicial reluctance to narrowly interpret "predecessor in interest").

proceedings.[912] In both the federal and Texas versions of Rule 804(b)(1), this requirement is stated in terms of "similar motive to develop" the testimony[913] because "identity of issues is significant only in that it bears on motive and interest in developing fully the testimony of the witness."[914] Of course, "in determining when the motive to develop was 'similar', looking at the relationship of the issues in controversy will be of assistance."[915] For example, it has been held that testimony given at a juvenile's certification hearing may be admissible at the punishment stage of the criminal trial after the juvenile has been transferred into the adult system.[916]

---

912. *See* McCormick's Handbook II, *supra* note 7, §257 at 620 (there is no more need for the exact identity of the issues than need for the exact identity of the parties); 1A Ray, *supra* note 9, §950, at 210 (requirement of identical issues in the two suits is too strict).

913. Fed. R. Evid. 804(b)(1)(B); Tex. R. Evid. 804(b)(1)(A)(ii); *see* **Coffin v. State**, 885 S.W.2d 140, 147 (Tex. Crim. App. 1994) ("'[N]either the form of the proceeding, the theory of the case, nor the nature of the relief sought need be the same.' '[O]nly the particular issue as to which the testimony was first offered must be substantially similar to the issue upon which offered in the current action.'" (quoting Michael H. Graham, Federal Practice and Procedure: Evidence §6793, at 784 (Interim ed. 1992))).

914. Fed. R. Evid. 804 advisory committee's note, subdiv. (b)(1); *see* **Jones v. State**, 843 S.W.2d 487, 491 (Tex. Crim. App. 1992) (requiring similarity of motive protects the party against whom the former testimony was offered from the ill effects of not being able to examine in the present proceeding the witness who gave the testimony in the earlier proceeding), *overruled on other grounds*, **Maxwell v. State**, 48 S.W.3d 196 (Tex. Crim. App. 2001). This formulation is fully consistent with earlier Texas cases, which had interpreted the identity-of-issues requirement in light of its purposes. *See* **Trinity & B.V. Ry. Co. v. Geary**, 194 S.W. 458, 460 (Tex. Civ. App.—Galveston 1917, writ ref'd) (testimony at a previous trial between the same parties on substantially the same issues is admissible if a witness is unavailable at the later trial); *see, e.g.*, **Md. Cas. Co. v. Lee**, 165 S.W.2d 135, 137 (Tex. Civ. App.—Galveston 1942, writ ref'd) (admitting in a civil action statements made in a previous civil proceeding by a since-deceased witness because plaintiff was party in both suits and issue was substantially the same in both cases); **Bryant v. Trinity Univ'l Ins.**, 411 S.W.2d 945, 949 (Tex. Civ. App.—Dallas 1967, writ ref'd n.r.e.) (admitting in a civil action statements made in a previous criminal proceeding by a since-deceased witness because plaintiff was a party to both suits and issue was substantially the same in both cases).

915. 7 Graham, *supra* note 491, §804:1, at 586. In **Jones v. State**, the court of criminal appeals held that the grand-jury testimony of a witness who is unavailable to testify at trial may be offered by the defendant against the State as former testimony and that the State is estopped from complaining that it did not have a similar motive to develop the testimony at the grand jury that it has at trial. 843 S.W.2d at 491-92. In **Jones**, the witness asserted her right against self-incrimination at the trial. *Id.* at 490. The capital-murder defendant requested that the witness be granted immunity and ordered to testify; the State objected, and the trial court denied the request. *Id.* At that point, the witness became "unavailable" to the defendant, even though she would have been available to the State because it had the authority to grant her immunity. *Id.* at 490-91. The court of criminal appeals then held that "[b]ecause the State is the only party who may examine the witness during a grand jury proceeding" and because the State could, if it wished, offer the witness immunity and thus gain the right to cross-examine at trial, it cannot complain that it did not have a similar motive to develop the testimony at the grand jury. *See id.* at 491-92. In support of this argument, the Texas court incorrectly relied on the Second Circuit's decision in **United States v. Salerno**, 937 F.2d 797, 805 (2d Cir. 1991), *rev'd*, 505 U.S. 317 (1992), apparently not realizing that the Supreme Court had already rejected the position of the circuit court. *See* **Jones**, 843 S.W.2d at 491-92.

916. *See* **Coffin**, 885 S.W.2d at 147-49. In **Coffin**, the court agreed that "[t]he ultimate purpose of a juvenile certification hearing differs greatly, of course, from the purpose of a punishment proceeding following a guilty verdict in the trial of an adult offender." *Id.* at 147-48. Nonetheless, the juvenile's motives to cross-examine the State's psychologist, who testified that it would take a number of years to rehabilitate the juvenile, were substantially the same at the juvenile certification hearing as during the punishment phase of the criminal trial. *Id.* at 148. "Thus, each proceeding involved an issue of whether appellant might be exposed to the public at a time when he still posed a significant danger." *Id.*

In a later case, **Ward v. State**, the court of appeals relied on **Coffin**'s "similar motive" analysis in holding that a child sexual-assault victim's testimony at a pretrial bond hearing was admissible as former testimony. 910 S.W.2d

Rule 804(b)(1) is consistent with earlier Texas law on the nature of the "opportunity ... to develop the testimony" that must have been presented in the former proceeding. Only opportunity is required; actual examination of the witness by the party or person with a similar interest need not have taken place.[917] Moreover, it need not have been an opportunity for cross-examination; direct and redirect examination will suffice.[918] However, if the former hearing involved only a limited purpose, such as a suppression hearing in a criminal case, the parties may not have had the opportunity or motive to fully develop the witness's testimony or to conduct a wide-ranging cross-examination.[919] In that case, the prior testimony is not admissible under the rule.

Rule 804(b)(1) as it applies in criminal cases differs in two respects from the rule in civil cases. First, the phrase "or a person with a similar interest" was omitted from the criminal provision.[920] Thus, the former testimony of a witness who is now unavailable is admissible only if the opposing party was also a party at the proceeding in which the former testimony was taken and had, at that time, an opportunity and similar motive to develop the testimony.[921] Texas criminal law had recognized a common-law exception for testimony given in an earlier judicial proceeding when "(1) the witness who made such statement should be shown to be dead or unavailable and, (2) someone else claiming under the same right had an opportunity to cross-examine the witness on the

1, 3 (Tex. App.—Tyler 1995, pet. ref'd). The court concluded that the "central disputed factual issue, whether [defendant] in fact sexually assaulted the two complainants, was identical in both proceedings, with [defendant's] interest in each to rebut such allegations." *Id.* Thus, the defendant had both a similar motive and opportunity to develop the child's testimony at the bond hearing as he did at the trial on the merits. *Id.* This result seems questionable because the defendant's risk of flight and danger to the community is at issue in a pretrial bond hearing, not the act of committing the charged sexual assault.

917. *See **United States v. Salerno***, 505 U.S. 317, 329-30 (1992) (Stevens, J., dissenting) (having a similar motive and opportunity, but choosing not to act on it for tactical reasons, does not make former testimony inadmissible); *see, e.g., **O'Neill v. Brown***, 61 Tex. 34, 37-38 (1884) (deceased plaintiff testified in first trial and obtained judgment on his testimony; although defendant was not present and could not cross-examine in the first trial, testimony was properly admitted in second trial when defendant was present and could testify to rebut deceased plaintiff's testimony).

918. *See* TEX. R. EVID. 804(b)(1)(A)(ii), (b)(1)(B)(ii); ***Pratt v. State***, 53 Tex. Crim. 281, 286-88, 109 S.W. 138, 141 (1908); McCORMICK's HANDBOOK II, *supra* note 7, §255, at 616; 1A RAY, *supra* note 9, §949, at 209.

919. *See, e.g., **United States v. Powell***, 894 F.2d 895, 901 (7th Cir. 1990) (upholding trial court's exclusion of co-defendant's former testimony at a guilty-plea hearing that partially exonerated defendant; prosecution did not have an incentive at that hearing to cross-examine codefendant about defendant's involvement in the offense); ***Davis v. State***, 961 S.W.2d 156, 160-61 (Tex. Crim. App. 1998) (Baird, Overstreet, Meyers, JJ., concurring) (because the State did not have a full opportunity to cross-examine defendant at a pretrial hearing to suppress, which was limited solely to the issue of whether his confession was involuntary, trial court did not err in excluding defendant's pretrial testimony offered under Criminal Rule 804(b)(1) at trial); *see also **United States v. Taplin***, 954 F.2d 1256, 1259 (6th Cir. 1992) (trial court erred in permitting government to offer codefendant's testimony from a pretrial hearing on defendant's motion to suppress under Federal Rule 804(b)(1) because there was no "substantial identity of issues" between suppression hearing and trial itself).

920. *See* TEX. R. EVID. 804(b)(1)(A)(ii), (b)(1)(B)(ii).

921. TEX. R. EVID. 804(b)(1)(B)(ii); *see **Bryan v. State***, 837 S.W.2d 637, 644 (Tex. Crim. App. 1992) (when parties, charge, and issues to be litigated were the same in first and second trial, the proceedings are necessarily the same and former testimony is admissible); *see, e.g., **Davis v. State***, 773 S.W.2d 592, 593 (Tex. App.—Eastland 1989, pet. ref'd) (trial court erred in permitting State to introduce testimony of codefendant from his own trial as former testimony when he refused to testify at defendant's trial because defendant had no opportunity to cross-examine codefendant in the earlier trial).

same issue as that upon which the evidence is now offered."[922] Rule 804(b)(1) limits that common-law exception to situations in which the accused was a party to the judicial proceeding and the statement is now being offered against him.[923] Conversely, if the defendant is offering the former testimony, the same prosecuting jurisdiction must have been the party at the earlier judicial proceeding.

Second, Rule 804(b)(1) in criminal cases refers to depositions taken under Texas Code of Criminal Procedure chapter 39.[924] Under that chapter, judges rarely determine that "good reason exists for taking the deposition,"[925] and any depositions may be used at trial only under very limited circumstances.[926] Thus it has been held that a deposition taken in a civil proceeding by the criminal defendant cannot be offered by the State against that defendant in a future criminal case.[927] However, a deposition given by a defendant in a civil proceeding is admissible against him in a criminal trial as an opposing party's statement under Rule 801(e)(2).[928] Recourse to Rule 804 is unnecessary.

---

922. ***Boyd v. State***, 643 S.W.2d 708, 708 (Tex. Crim. App. 1982).

923. *See* TEX. R. EVID. 804(b)(1)(B)(ii); *see, e.g.*, ***Bryan***, 837 S.W.2d at 643-44 (at defendant's second trial, prosecution could introduce portions of his testimony from his first trial because he was "unavailable" under Rule 804(a)(1) at the second trial, claiming his Fifth Amendment right against self-incrimination, and because he voluntarily testified at his first trial with the opportunity, through counsel, to develop the testimony on direct and redirect).

924. *See* TEX. R. EVID. 804(b)(1)(B)(iii).

925. TEX. CODE CRIM. PROC. art. 39.02.

926. *See id.* art. 39.01 (depositions taken in an examining trial), art. 39.12 (predicate to reading a deposition during trial).

927. *See* ***State v. Roberts***, 909 S.W.2d 110, 112-13 (Tex. App.—Houston [14th Dist.] 1995), *vacated on other grounds*, 940 S.W.2d 655 (Tex. Crim. App. 1996). In ***Roberts***, the court of appeals held that for a deposition to be used in a criminal proceeding, it must comport with Code of Criminal Procedure chapter 39. 909 S.W.2d at 112. That chapter permits a deposition in only two instances: (1) if it is taken "before an examining trial or a jury of inquest ... or taken at any prior trial of the defendant for the same offense," or (2) if the defendant can show in an affidavit and hearing that "good reason" exists for taking the deposition. *See* TEX. CODE CRIM. PROC. arts. 39.01, 39.02. Thus, chapter 39 provides no basis for the State to use a civil deposition in a later criminal trial. *See* TEX. CODE CRIM. PROC. arts. 39.01, 39.02; *see also* ***United States v. Feldman***, 761 F.2d 380, 387 (7th Cir. 1985) (suggesting that strategies for civil and criminal trials differ greatly and concluding that civil deposition offered by government was not admissible against defendant in later criminal trial).

928. *E.g.*, ***Johnson v. State***, 208 S.W.3d 478, 507 (Tex. App.—Austin 2006, pet. ref'd) (although defendant's deposition in civil case was not taken in compliance with Code of Criminal Procedure chapter 39, and thus was not admissible under Rule 804(b)(1), it was a statement by a party-opponent and therefore not hearsay at all); ***Kemmerer v. State***, 113 S.W.3d 513, 517-18 (Tex. App.—Houston [1st Dist.] 2003, pet. ref'd) (defendant's civil deposition was not hearsay when offered by State; therefore, admissibility of deposition did not depend on compliance with Code of Criminal Procedure rules on the taking of depositions in criminal cases). In ***Kemmerer***, the court of appeals explained:

> Appellant appears to interpret rule 804(b)(1) to require that any civil deposition, including one that is not itself hearsay, must meet all of chapter 39's requirements before it can be used in a criminal proceeding. In contrast, the State interprets rule 804(b)(1) to require ... that depositions used in criminal cases meet chapter 39's requirements only within the context of the former-testimony exception to hearsay, that is, only when the deposition testimony is itself hearsay. We hold that chapter 39 did not apply to appellant's own civil-deposition testimony when used against her at her criminal trial because that testimony was not hearsay. A statement is not hearsay if it is offered against a party and is the party's own statement.

113 S.W.3d at 517.

Of course, if the declarant is available to testify in the present trial, his former testimony cannot be introduced under Rule 804.[929]

If former testimony is admissible under the rule, it generally must be introduced through an accurate and authenticated transcript of that testimony;[930] that testimony, however, can also be introduced by reading it aloud and "acting out" the part of the declarant.[931]

2. Rule 804(b)(2): Statements under the belief of imminent death. Under Rule 804(b)(2), a statement under the belief of imminent death[932] must meet three requirements: first, the declarant must be unavailable to testify; second, the declarant, when he made the statement, must have believed that his death was imminent; and third, the statement must be about the cause or circumstances of his potentially impending death.[933]

Rule 804(b)(2) is identical to the federal rule as it was promulgated by the Supreme Court.[934] The Texas version, however, omits language added by Congress that disallowed statements under the belief of imminent death in criminal cases other than homicide prosecutions.[935]

At common law, dying declarations were admissible only in prosecutions for the homicide of the declarant.[936] The Supreme Court's version of the exception, on the other

---

929. *See, e.g.*, **Sneed v. State**, 209 S.W.3d 782, 792 (Tex. App.—Texarkana 2006, pet. ref'd) (defendant's impeachment of child complainant with one portion of her testimony from first trial did not open the door to admission of all of that testimony, nor was it admissible under Rule 804(b)(1) because she was not "unavailable" for the second trial).

930. *E.g.*, **Escamilla v. Estate of Escamilla**, 921 S.W.2d 723, 726 (Tex. App.—Corpus Christi 1996, writ denied) (trial judge cannot take judicial notice of his recollection of former testimony from a previous proceeding).

931. *See* **Smith v. State**, 907 S.W.2d 522, 532 (Tex. Crim. App. 1995).

932. Before the 2015 restyling of the Texas Rules, a statement offered under Rule 804(b)(2) was referred to as a "dying declaration"; no substantive change was intended by the restyling. *See* Tex. Sup. Ct. Order, Misc. Docket No. 15-9048, §2 (eff. Apr. 1, 2015).

933. Tex. R. Evid. 804(b)(2); **Scott v. State**, 894 S.W.2d 810, 811 (Tex. App.—Tyler 1994, pet. ref'd) (per curiam); *e.g.*, **Martinez v. State**, 17 S.W.3d 677, 689 (Tex. Crim. App. 2000) (upholding admission of police officer's testimony that murder victim identified other victim's "ex-boyfriend" as shooter when statement was made after victim had been shot seven times and later died; evidence supported inference that victim believed his death was imminent); **Pritchett v. State**, 874 S.W.2d 168, 176-77 (Tex. App.—Houston [14th Dist.] 1994, pet. ref'd) (robbery accomplice's statement to officer that he robbed the pawn shop with "Junior," which he made after the proprietor shot him, met the requirements of a dying declaration; when accomplice made the statements, he believed death was imminent, and his statement concerned the cause of or circumstances surrounding his impending death), *overruled on other grounds*, **Sarmiento v. State**, 93 S.W.3d 566 (Tex. App.—Houston [14th Dist.] 2002, pet. ref'd). As the court of criminal appeals has explained:

> It is both (1) the solemnity of the occasion—the speaker peering over the abyss into the eternal—which substitutes for the witness oath, and (2) the necessity principle—since the witness had died, there was a necessity for taking his only available trustworthy statements—that provide the underpinning for the doctrine.

Gardner v. State, 306 S.W.3d 274, 290-91 (Tex. Crim. App. 2009) (footnotes omitted).

934. *See* Fed. R. Evid. 804(b)(3) (1972 proposed final draft), 56 F.R.D. 183, 321 (1973); Tex. R. Evid. 804(b)(2).

935. *See* Fed. R. Evid. 804(b)(2); H.R. Rep. No. 93-650, *supra* note 29, at 15-16, *reprinted in* 1974 U.S.C.C.A.N. at 7089.

936. *See* McCormick's Handbook II, *supra* note 7, §283, at 681-83; 1A Ray, *supra* note 9, §979, at 236.

hand, would have followed long-standing critical opinion[937] in making the exception available in any civil or criminal proceeding. Congress limited the federal exception to homicide and civil cases.[938] The Texas rule makes the exception applicable in any civil or criminal proceeding.[939]

Under Rule 804(b)(2), "the focus turned more to the severity of the injuries than the declarant's explicit words indicating knowledge of imminent death."[940] Further, it is not necessary to offer medical testimony that the declarant was, in fact, dying;[941] "[a]ll

---

937. *See* McCormick's Handbook II, *supra* note 7, §283, at 682; 1A Ray, *supra* note 9, §979, at 237; 5 Wigmore, *supra* note 14, §1436, at 285.

938. *See* Fed. R. Evid. 804(b)(2).

939. *See* Tex. R. Evid. 804(b)(2). Rule 804(b)(2) changed Texas law in several ways. First, because the dying-declaration exception had not been recognized in Texas civil cases, Civil Rule 804(b)(2) obviously represented a departure from earlier law. For criminal cases, the Texas Code of Criminal Procedure had codified the common-law doctrine of the dying declaration. *See* Tex. Code Crim. Proc. art. 38.20 (Act approved June 18, 1965, 59th Leg., ch. 722, 1965 Tex. Gen. Laws 317) (repealed as to criminal proceedings effective 1986). The former article read as follows:

> The dying declaration of a deceased person may be offered in evidence, either for or against a defendant charged with the homicide of such deceased person, under the restrictions hereafter provided. To render the declarations of the deceased competent evidence, it must be satisfactorily proved:
> **1.** That at the time of making such declaration he was conscious of approaching death, and believed there was no hope of recovery;
> **2.** That such declaration was voluntarily made, and not through the persuasion of any person;
> **3.** That such declaration was not made in answer to interrogatories calculated to lead the deceased to make any particular statement; and
> **4.** That he was of sane mind at the time of making the declaration.

Id.; **Graham v. State**, 643 S.W.2d 920, 928 (Tex. Crim. App. 1983) (op. on reh'g); *see* **Martinez v. State**, 533 S.W.2d 20, 22-23 (Tex. Crim. App. 1976).

Second, Rule 804(b)(2) abrogated the common-law requirement that the declarant must have believed that death was imminent and that "there was no hope of recovery." **Gardner v. State**, 306 S.W.3d 274, 290 (Tex. Crim. App. 2009); **Burks v. State**, 876 S.W.2d 877, 901 (Tex. Crim. App. 1994). Unlike under the old rule, the declarant is not required to die before the statement is admissible; unavailability is sufficient. Thus, if the declarant made a statement when he believed that his death was imminent but then made a miraculous recovery and left the country, and if all reasonable means have failed to make him return to the trial, Rule 804(b)(2) would not bar admission of the statement. Third, the common law required that the statement have been made spontaneously, not in response to any questioning. *See* **Lewis v. State**, 137 Tex. Crim. 197, 200-01, 128 S.W.2d 798, 800 (1939). Rule 804(b)(2) admits statements made as the result of questioning as long as the questioning is not designed to elicit a specific response. *See, e.g.*, **Magee v. State**, 994 S.W.2d 878, 886-87 (Tex. App.—Waco 1999, pet. ref'd) (when emergency-room doctor told burn victim she was dying and asked her how she had been burned, her statement that "her husband had thrown gasoline on her and ignited it" was admissible under rule); **Scott v. State**, 894 S.W.2d 810, 812 (Tex. App.—Tyler 1994, pet. ref'd) (per curiam) (declarant's reply to officer, though made after repeated questioning, and in response to query of "If you die do you want the person who did this to you to go free?" was admissible as a dying declaration); **Hayes v. State**, 740 S.W.2d 887, 889 (Tex. App.—Dallas 1987, no pet.) (statements were admissible as a dying declaration when conversation took place no more than five minutes after deceased was shot and deceased was obviously in pain, under stress, and in fear of imminent death).

940. **Gardner**, 306 S.W.3d at 290; *see, e.g.*, **Charles v. State**, 955 S.W.2d 400, 404 (Tex. App.—San Antonio 1997, no pet.) (although declarant did not die until 30 days after making her statements, evidence showed that she believed her death was imminent when she spoke; length of time "declarant lives after making the dying declaration is immaterial"); **Bisby v. State**, 907 S.W.2d 949, 956 (Tex. App.—Fort Worth 1995, pet. ref'd) (dying declaration was admissible because deceased's statements and the severity of his wound were sufficient to infer that he was aware of his approaching death; while declaration must be made under a sense of approaching death, declarant does not need to state in specific terms that he is conscious of impending death).

941. **Johnson v. State**, 770 S.W.2d 72, 76 (Tex. App.—Texarkana 1989), *aff'd*, 815 S.W.2d 707 (Tex. Crim. App. 1991).

RULE 804

that the rule requires is sufficient evidence, direct or circumstantial, that demonstrates that the declarant must have realized that he was at death's door at the time that he spoke."[942] In addition, under former Texas Code of Criminal Procedure article 38.20, the proponent was required to prove that the declarant was of sane mind at the time he spoke.[943] Under the Rules of Evidence, however, every person is presumed competent;[944] thus, the opponent of the statement must assert and prove that the declarant did not possess sufficient mental capacity to make a coherent statement.[945]

Rule 804(b)(2) also allows dying "opinions" as evidence.[946] While the court of criminal appeals sometimes excluded such offers on the ground that they violated the opinion rule,[947] Rule 701 does not exclude an otherwise admissible out-of-court statement, and the opinion rule applies only to testimony.[948]

To be admissible under Rule 804(b)(2), the declaration must be "made about [the] cause or circumstances" of what the declarant believed to be his imminent death.[949] A declaration on some other subject will not qualify under this rule.[950]

When a hearsay statement does not qualify as a statement under the belief of imminent death, the proponent is not without recourse. A possibility remains that a declaration that fails under Rule 804(b)(2)—either because of its subject matter or because it does not prove belief of imminent death—might nevertheless qualify for admission under some other exception, such as present sense impression under Rule 803(1) or excited utterance under Rule 803(2).[951]

3. Rule 804(b)(3): Statement of personal or family history. Rule 804(b)(3), which is identical to Federal Rule 804(b)(4), allows for two types of statements of personal or

---

942. *Gardner*, 306 S.W.3d at 290. Under former article 38.20, the jury, not the judge, determined disputed preliminary issues of fact, such as whether the declarant was conscious of approaching death. See *Crow v. State*, 147 Tex. Crim. 292, 298, 180 S.W.2d 354, 357 (1944) (op. on reh'g); 1A RAY, *supra* note 9, §975, at 228. Under Rule 104(a), the judge determines all preliminary questions of fact, including the admissibility of a statement under the belief of imminent death. See TEX. R. EVID. 104(a); *Gardner*, 306 S.W.3d at 291; *Contreras v. State*, 745 S.W.2d 59, 63 (Tex. App.—San Antonio 1987, no pet.). Refer to *Article I: General Provisions*, *supra* p. 86.

943. Refer to note 939 *supra*.

944. TEX. R. EVID. 601(a). Refer to *Article VI: Witnesses*, *supra* p. 556.

945. *Contreras*, 745 S.W.2d at 62.

946. *See* TEX. R. EVID. 804(b)(2).

947. *See* 1A RAY, *supra* note 9, §982, at 242.

948. *See* TEX. R. EVID. 701.

949. TEX. R. EVID. 804(b)(2). In **Wilks v. State**, the court held that the dying woman's statement to a witness at the hospital that "I always figured he would kill me, but I figured he would use a gun," implied that the defendant did, in fact, kill her as she had earlier suspected he would and was thus admissible as to the cause of her death. 983 S.W.2d 863, 866 (Tex. App.—Corpus Christi 1998, no pet.).

950. In **Thompson v. Mayes**, the plaintiff brought a suit to impose a constructive trust on assets that were willed to Donald Thompson by his father, whom Donald had killed two years before committing suicide himself. 707 S.W.2d 951, 953 (Tex. App.—Eastland 1986, writ ref'd n.r.e.). The defendant, Donald's mother and executor of his estate, attempted to introduce Donald's "alleged suicide tapes" as, among other things, a dying declaration. *Id.* at 957. The trial court properly excluded the tapes because, even if they technically concerned the cause or the circumstances of what the declarant believed to be his impending death, Donald's death was not relevant to the case—only the cause of his father's death was relevant. *Id.*

951. Refer to notes 475-521 *supra* and accompanying text.

family history. First, the rule allows for a statement about the declarant's "own birth, adoption, legitimacy, ancestry, marriage, divorce, relationship by blood, adoption or marriage, or similar facts of personal or family history," even if the declarant could not acquire personal knowledge of the fact.[952] Second, the rule allows for a statement about another person on any of these facts, if the declarant was related to the person or so closely associated with the person's family that the declarant's statement is most likely accurate.[953]

The rule is intended to apply to noncontroversial facts of a family's history, such as a person's birth date or place of birth.[954] It is not intended to permit the introduction of "facts" such as a person's child-rearing or disciplinary practices, the "fact" that a person would never commit child abuse,[955] or another person's childhood experiences and positive character.[956]

---

952. TEX. R. EVID. 804(b)(3)(A). The language in Rule 804(b)(3)(A) dispensing with any personal-knowledge requirement for statements about the declarant's own history, while not specifically supported by Texas common law, is an innocuous practical doctrine. As explained by the Advisory Committee on the Federal Rules: "In some instances [personal knowledge] is self-evident (marriage) and in others impossible and traditionally not required (date of birth)." FED. R. EVID. 804 advisory committee's note, subdiv. (b)(4); *cf.* 1A RAY, *supra* note 9, §1343, at 511 (general principles of competency "require that the declarant must have had a knowledge or opportunity of acquiring knowledge of the subject matter of the declaration. ... However, this does not mean that personal observation is necessary").

953. TEX. R. EVID. 804(b)(3)(B).

954. In nearly all respects, Rule 804(b)(3) is consistent with Texas common law, which always recognized this exception. *See* 1A RAY, *supra* note 9, §1341.5, at 174-75. (Supp. 1991). Like the rule, pre-Rules Texas cases approved statements about the declarant's own history and statements about the history of another person. *See, e.g.,* **Louder v. Schluter**, 78 Tex. 103, 105, 14 S.W. 205, 205 (1890) (declarant's own history); **Bowden v. Caldron**, 554 S.W.2d 25, 28 (Tex. Civ. App.—Texarkana 1977, writ ref'd n.r.e.) (history of another person); **Simpson v. Simpson**, 380 S.W.2d 855, 859 (Tex. Civ. App.—Dallas 1964, writ ref'd n.r.e.) (declarant's own history); **Smith v. Lynn**, 152 S.W.2d 838, 840 (Tex. Civ. App.—San Antonio 1941, no writ) (history of another person). Texas common law also admitted history of another person when the declarant was not part of the family but was personally familiar with it. *E.g.,* **Coffee v. William Marsh Rice Univ.**, 408 S.W.2d 269, 284 (Tex. Civ. App.—Houston 1966, writ ref'd n.r.e.). The rule makes only one change: it does not require, as did the common law, that the declaration have been made before the dispute arose. *See* **Nehring v. McMurrian**, 94 Tex. 45, 51-52, 57 S.W. 943, 945-46 (1900); *see also* 1A RAY, *supra* note 9, §1345, at 175 (Supp. 1991) (although there is no longer any requirement that the declaration have been made before the dispute arose, the fact that the declarant made the statement after the controversy arose is admissible as to the weight of the evidence). That requirement was "dropped, as bearing more appropriately on weight than admissibility." FED. R. EVID. 804 advisory committee's note, subdiv. (b)(4); *see, e.g.,* **Compton v. WWV Enters.**, 679 S.W.2d 668, 670 (Tex. App.—Eastland 1984, no writ) (affidavits of heirship prepared after lawsuit was filed would have been admissible under Civil Rule 804(b)(3) if the requisite showing of witnesses' unavailability had been made).

955. **Henderson v. State**, 77 S.W.3d 321, 326 (Tex. App.—Fort Worth 2002, no pet.). As the court explained in **Henderson**, this hearsay exception

> rests on the assumption that the type of declarant specified by the rule will not ... make a statement, such as a date of a marriage or the existence of a ceremony, unless it is trustworthy. Here, the declarant provided far different information than the matters set forth in the rule. Summarized, his statement concerned methods of child discipline practiced in the home and asserted the "fact" that his wife would not intentionally have caused the death of their son. Rule 804(b)(3) does not apply where the matter asserted by the declarant involves nontrustworthy "facts" such as state of mind.

Id. (citation omitted).

956. *See, e.g.,* **Valle v. State**, 109 S.W.3d 500, 505 (Tex. Crim. App. 2003) (court properly excluded videotaped interview of capital-murder defendant's mother, who testified about her own medical problems, defendant's legal difficulties in juvenile-corrections facilities and lack of legal difficulties in Cuba, defendant's desire to leave Cuba, and abuse of defendant by his stepfather; these subjects were not noncontroversial facts covered by Rule 804(b)(3)).

4. Proposed Rule 804(b)(4): Residual exception. The version of Civil Rule 804 that the State Bar Committee recommended to the Supreme Court of Texas contained a residual exception, Rule 804(b)(4), which was identical in language and purpose to the Committee's proposed Rule 803(25). Proposed Rule 803(25) is discussed above.[957] The Texas Rules, as adopted, contain no such provisions.

RULE 805
HEARSAY WITHIN HEARSAY

Hearsay within hearsay is not excluded by the rule against hearsay if each part of the combined statements conforms with an exception to the rule.

COMMENTARY ON RULE 805

Rule 805 is identical to Federal Rule 805. Rule 805 declares a principle long recognized at Texas common law: even what is often called "multiple hearsay" may be admissible if an exception properly applies to each "layer" of hearsay.[958] The most common instance of this situation is a business record containing a statement made by a person who was not speaking or writing in the regular course of the organization's business, but rather was recorded by the entrant in the regular course of the business.[959] The business-records exception covers only the last layer of hearsay and alone will not allow the statement to prove the truth of its contents.[960] However, the opponent must make an objection specific to the parts of the offered evidence that are inadmissible

---

957. Refer to notes 848-862 *supra* and accompanying text.

958. *E.g.*, ***Lopez v. State***, 200 S.W.3d 246, 254-55 (Tex. App.—Houston [14th Dist.] 2006, pet. ref'd) (mother's testimony that her parents told her that officers told them that defendant was a suspect in her child's murder was double hearsay, neither level of which was admissible under hearsay rules); *see* ***Philpot v. State***, 897 S.W.2d 848, 851 (Tex. App.—Dallas 1995, pet. ref'd) ("[T]o admit multiple-level hearsay statements, each statement must independently be admissible."); *see, e.g.*, ***Khoshayand v. State***, 179 S.W.3d 779, 784 (Tex. App.—Dallas 2005, no pet.) (investigator's notes taken during interview of child complainant were inadmissible under Rule 805 because they "memorialized out-of-court observations of a third party's interview" of child and were hearsay within hearsay). If any of the second-level-hearsay records contain "memoranda, letters, [or] reports based upon accounts of conversations with others," the documents are not admissible under Rule 805. *E.g.*, ***Knox v. Taylor***, 992 S.W.2d 40, 64 (Tex. App.—Houston [14th Dist.] 1999, no pet.) (business records containing hearsay material were not admissible because not all levels of hearsay satisfied an exception to hearsay rule).

959. Refer to notes 665-669 *supra* and accompanying text.

960. *See* ***Perry v. State***, 957 S.W.2d 894, 899-900 (Tex. App.—Texarkana 1997, pet. ref'd) ("A report under the public records exception or the records of regularly conducted activities exception to the hearsay rule may present a trial court with a double hearsay problem. If a report contains some hearsay statement, the hearsay statement must fall under some hearsay exception of its own because neither the public records and reports exception nor the records of regularly conducted activities exception protects hearsay within hearsay."); ***Mary Lee Found. v. Tex. Emp't Comm'n***, 817 S.W.2d 725, 728 (Tex. App.—Texarkana 1991, writ denied) ("[The] public records exception to the hearsay rule does not mean that *ex parte* statements, hearsay, conclusions, and opinions contained within such records are admissible."); *see, e.g.*, ***Crane v. State***, 786 S.W.2d 338, 353-54 (Tex. Crim. App. 1990) (even if transcript offered by defendant were a business record, the self-serving hearsay statements contained within that transcript did not fall within any hearsay exception); ***Urquhart v. Antrum***, 776 S.W.2d 595, 596-97 (Tex. App.—Houston [14th Dist.] 1988, no writ) (while police officer's deposition testimony was admissible in a personal-injury suit, statements contained in officer's accident report did not independently satisfy any exceptions to the hearsay rule).

hearsay; otherwise, the court can admit the entire document.[961] If the hearsay statement contained in the business record falls within another exception to the hearsay rule—or is otherwise exempted from the rule, such as an opposing party's statement under Rule 801(e)(2)—Rule 805 permits it to be received for its truth. Otherwise, the statement should be excluded.[962]

For example, in **Skillern & Sons, Inc. v. Rosen**,[963] a hospital record that contained a statement by the plaintiff was received, over the plaintiff's hearsay objection, for the truth of the matter stated. The Texas Supreme Court upheld the ruling with an analysis that reflects the same approach now mandated by Rule 805:

> Some employee or representative who either made the record or transmitted the information to another to record must have had *personal knowledge* of the act, event or condition in order for such record to be admissible under the business records exception to the hearsay rule. For example, a doctor's statement as to whether a patient had or had not lacerations of the face, as to his pulse rate or blood pressure, and as to things that happen within the hospital are within the doctor's or nurse's personal knowledge. However, statements as to how an accident happened or where it happened, age, medical history, etc., do not become particularly trustworthy just because it is hospital routine to record them and they should be excluded. The legislature has provided for their exclusion by the requirement of *personal knowledge* by an employee or representative of the "business" (e.g., hospital). ... However, some of such statements may be admissible on other grounds: as declarations against interest, spontaneous exclamations, dying declarations, and admissions of a party. The person in the hospital to whom such a statement is made may not have personal knowledge of the fact or facts contained in the statement, but if he has personal knowledge of the fact that the statement was made and if proper record thereof is made, the record would be admissible under the statute to prove that an admission of a party was made.[964]

---

961. *E.g.*, **Gen. Motors Corp. v. Harper**, 61 S.W.3d 118, 125-26 (Tex. App.—Eastland 2001, pet. denied) (although patents themselves were public records under Rule 803(8), some statements within those patents were hearsay; however, because opponent made only a general hearsay objection without specifying what information within patents was inadmissible hearsay, trial court did not err in admitting entire documents).

962. *See, e.g.*, **Garcia v. State**, 126 S.W.3d 921, 926-27 (Tex. Crim. App. 2004) (business records of women's shelter were admissible under Rule 803(6), but murder victim's hearsay statements contained in the records did not meet the requirements of any hearsay exception; trial court erred in admitting records because State did not prove victim made the statements for purpose of medical diagnosis or treatment); **Bryant v. State**, 282 S.W.3d 156, 164-65 (Tex. App.—Texarkana 2009, pet. ref'd) (sheriff's testimony about statements made by defendant's girlfriend was double hearsay and improperly admitted; defendant's statements to girlfriend were statements against interest under Rule 803(24), but her statements to sheriff did not meet the requirements of any hearsay exception). Refer to notes 665-669 *supra* and accompanying text.

963. 359 S.W.2d 298, 306 (Tex. 1962).

964. *Id.* at 305-06 (citations omitted).

Affidavits submitted as part of summary-judgment proof are not themselves considered hearsay documents for the purpose of assessing the summary-judgment evidence.[965]

RULE 806

ATTACKING & SUPPORTING THE DECLARANT'S CREDIBILITY

When a hearsay statement—or a statement described in Rule 801(e)(2)(C), (D), or (E), or, in a civil case, a statement described in Rule 801(e)(3)—has been admitted in evidence, the declarant's credibility may be attacked, and then supported, by any evidence that would be admissible for those purposes if the declarant had testified as a witness. The court may admit evidence of the declarant's statement or conduct, offered to impeach the declarant, regardless of when it occurred or whether the declarant had an opportunity to explain or deny it. If the party against whom the statement was admitted calls the declarant as a witness, the party may examine the declarant on the statement as if on cross-examination.

COMMENTARY ON RULE 806

Texas Rule 806 follows the federal rule with two minor changes. The cross-references have been renumbered to conform to the Texas numbers and to include a reference to depositions in civil proceedings under Rule 801(e)(3), for which there is no federal counterpart.[966] Additionally, in the sentence dispensing with the requirement of "opportunity to deny or explain," the Texas rule uses the phrase "offered to impeach the declarant" so that it is clear that the sentence covers impeachment by means other than inconsistent statements, such as evidence of bias or interest.[967] Evidence to impeach the declarant is admissible under Rule 806, but it can be used only for impeachment purposes.[968]

---

965. *See* **Washington v. McMillan**, 898 S.W.2d 392, 397 n.5 (Tex. App.—San Antonio 1995, no writ) (fact that out-of-court statement is contained within summary-judgment affidavit does not present double-hearsay issue because summary-judgment affidavits are not hearsay under TEX. R. CIV. P. 166a(f)), *overruled in part on other grounds*, **Carpenter v. Cimarron Hydrocarbons Corp.**, 98 S.W.3d 682 (Tex. 2002); *see also* TEX. R. CIV. P. 166a(f) ("Supporting and opposing affidavits shall be made on personal knowledge, shall set forth such facts as would be admissible in evidence, and shall show affirmatively that the affiant is competent to testify to the matters stated therein.").

966. *See* TEX. R. EVID. 801(e)(3) (exempting depositions from hearsay). The Texas rule applies to hearsay statements, statements under Rule 801(e)(2)(C), (e)(2)(D), or (e)(2)(E), and statements under Rule 801(e)(3). TEX. R. EVID. 806. Refer to notes 391-450 *supra* and accompanying text.

967. TEX. R. EVID. 806; *see* TEX. R. EVID. 613(b). Federal Rule 806 reads in relevant part: "The court may admit evidence of the declarant's inconsistent statement or conduct, regardless of when it occurred or whether the declarant had an opportunity to explain or deny it."

968. **Sohail v. State**, 264 S.W.3d 251, 262 (Tex. App.—Houston [1st Dist.] 2008, pet. ref'd); *see, e.g.*, **Del Carmen Hernandez v. State**, 273 S.W.3d 685, 688-89 (Tex. Crim. App. 2008) (codefendant's prior inconsistent statement was

The principle that a hearsay declarant may be impeached and, if impeached, rehabilitated as if he were a witness[969] seems a logical and practical necessity.[970] The second sentence of Rule 806, dispensing with any requirement that the declarant be afforded an opportunity to deny or explain the impeaching matter—which would be necessary if the declarant were a witness[971]—is no less a logical and practical necessity in this situation.[972]

In **Bee v. State**, the court of appeals noted an anomaly in the hearsay rules that permits the admission of the former testimony of an unavailable witness but does not expressly allow the admission of a written prior consistent statement that was offered to rehabilitate that witness at the former trial.[973] However, Rule 806 solves this problem by "permit[ting] impeachment and rehabilitation by any means that could be used if the declarant were a witness."[974] But the State may not impeach a nontestifying defendant with prior convictions solely because the defense offers evidence, for example, of another person's response to the defendant's conflicting statements.[975] In that case, the defendant's words to the third person are offered to explain why the third person acted as he did, not for the truth of the matter asserted.

---

admissible to impeach her credibility; trial judge properly gave jurors limiting instructions that they were to consider the evidence only for impeachment purposes); *see also* **Logan v. State**, 71 S.W.3d 865, 870 (Tex. App.—Fort Worth 2002, pet. ref'd) (hearsay statements that were not inconsistent with prior testimony could not be admitted for impeachment purposes under Rule 806).

969. *See, e.g.,* **Hall v. State**, 764 S.W.2d 19, 20-21 (Tex. App.—Amarillo 1988, no pet.) (under Rule 806, trial court erred in excluding a videotape offered by defendant to impeach nontestifying child declarant's excited utterances).

970. This principle was recognized in previous Texas cases. *See* **Mitchell v. State**, 87 Tex. Crim. 530, 533-34, 222 S.W. 983, 984-85 (1920); **Lyles v. State**, 64 Tex. Crim. 621, 624-25, 142 S.W. 592, 593-94 (1912); **Hamblin v. State**, 34 Tex. Crim. 368, 384-85, 30 S.W. 1075, 1075-76 (1895); Black, *supra* note 786, at 1008.

971. *See* TEX. R. EVID. 613; **Griffith v. State**, 983 S.W.2d 282, 290 (Tex. Crim. App. 1998).

972. *See, e.g.,* **Appling v. State**, 904 S.W.2d 912, 916-17 (Tex. App.—Corpus Christi 1995, pet. ref'd) (State was entitled to attack defendant's credibility by introducing his non-Mirandized custodial statement after defense witness testified to defendant's out-of-court exculpatory statement).

973. 974 S.W.2d 184, 188 (Tex. App.—San Antonio 1998, no pet.).

974. *E.g., id.* at 190-91 (if the witness had testified at the second trial, "his written statement would have been admissible under Rule 801(e)(1)(B) to rehabilitate any impeachment based on a charge of recent fabrication or improper motive to lie"; therefore, that same statement was admissible under Rule 806 for rehabilitative purposes only, not for the truth of the matter asserted).

975. *See* **Enriquez v. State**, 56 S.W.3d 596, 599-601 (Tex. App.—Corpus Christi 2001, pet. ref'd). In this case, defense counsel, in an intoxication-manslaughter trial, questioned the police officer investigating a fatal traffic accident about why he had returned to the car-impound lot a second time to examine the defendant's car. *Id.* at 599. The officer stated that he returned because when he had visited the defendant in the hospital, the defendant had told him several different stories about what caused the accident. *Id.* The officer then explained the three inconsistent versions that the defendant had given. *Id.* Based on the fact that the defendant had related these versions to the officer, the State cited Rule 806 as authority to permit it to impeach the nontestifying defendant with his earlier drug-related convictions. *Id.* at 600. The court of appeals concluded that "the statements were not offered to prove the truth of the matter asserted"; thus, those statements were not hearsay so the defendant could not be impeached as a hearsay declarant under Rule 806. *Id.* at 601. *But see id.* at 604 (Rodriguez, Valdez, Hinojosa, JJ., concurring in part and dissenting in part) (at trial, both the defense and State treated these statements as hearsay, offered for the truth of defendant's explanations of how the accident occurred; thus, the convictions were admissible to impeach his credibility).

RULE 806

The last sentence of the rule permits a party against whom a hearsay statement has been introduced to call the declarant as a hostile witness[976] so that it may ask leading questions and impeach him as if he had been called by the party who introduced his hearsay statement.[977]

CONCLUSION

Generations of legal writers who have criticized the common law of evidence and proposed its reform have focused much of their attention on hearsay doctrines.[978] Article VIII of the Rules altered Texas common law in many respects. In most instances, these changes were among the reforms urged by critics. Almost all of the changes sought to expand admissibility. Such changes were accomplished by creating or recognizing new exceptions,[979] liberalizing the substantive requirements of an existing exception,[980] or relaxing formal or procedural prerequisites.[981] Codifying common-law doctrines into black-and-white rules facilitates continual reexamination and improvement, and the codified hearsay provisions are an effort to further aid the pursuit of justice.

---

976. Of course, the State may not call the defendant-declarant in a criminal trial. Under Rule 806, the State may only call another witness to impeach the defendant-declarant's statements. *See Moranza v. State*, 913 S.W.2d 718, 729 (Tex. App.—Waco 1995, pet. ref'd).

977. This sensible doctrine was not always applied in pre-Rules Texas cases, at least for depositions. *See Indus. Fabricating Co. v. Christopher*, 220 S.W.2d 281, 287-88 (Tex. Civ. App.—Galveston 1949, writ ref'd n.r.e.); 3 ROY W. McDONALD, TEXAS CIVIL PRACTICE §13.22, at 267 (1992); John E. Banks, Note, *Depositions: Two Suggested Procedural Reforms*, 6 Sw. L.J. 237, 242-44 (1952); *see also Gen. Acc. Fire & Life Assur. Corp. v. Reina*, 597 S.W.2d 10, 13 (Tex. Civ. App.—Dallas 1980) (test of whether a witness may be cross-examined is whether the witness was initially presented in support of the opposing party's case), *rev'd on other grounds*, 611 S.W.2d 415 (Tex. 1981). To the extent that the last sentence of Rule 806 changed Texas law, the change was a sound one.

978. For a compilation of articles on proposed reforms to the hearsay rule, see Hearsay Reform Conference, 76 MINN. L. REV. 363 (1992).

979. *E.g.*, TEX. R. EVID. 803(4). Refer to notes 570-584 *supra* and accompanying text.

980. *E.g.*, TEX. R. EVID. 803(24). Refer to notes 811-847 *supra* and accompanying text.

981. *E.g.*, TEX. R. EVID. 803(8). Refer to notes 683-731 *supra* and accompanying text.

ARTICLE IX: AUTHENTICATION & IDENTIFICATION

Exhibits and certain other forms of evidence must be authenticated before they can be admitted for the fact-finder to consider. The authentication requirement stems from common-law skepticism—a sense that courts should not blindly assume that an offered piece of evidence is what it appears to be or what the proponent claims it is.[1] Rather, the sponsoring party should offer some formal proof of the evidence's identity.[2]

The rules for authentication and identification address three related concerns: (1) preventing a fraud on the court, (2) preventing innocent mistakes, and (3) guarding against "jury credulity," the natural tendency to take matters at face value.[3] For example, before a gun may be admitted at a murder trial, some evidence must indicate that the gun is the actual murder weapon. Before a bag of cocaine may be introduced at a drug-possession trial, evidence must indicate that the bag contains cocaine and was taken from the defendant. Before an aerosol can is admitted as evidence in a personal-injury suit, some evidence must show that the can is the one that blew up in the injured person's face. If an object is not the same one that is involved in the litigation, it is irrelevant and cannot be admitted as evidence. The object may, however, be offered for demonstrative purposes only.[4]

Authentication and identification "represent a special aspect of relevancy."[5] The issues of identification and authenticity arise whenever the relevance of particular testimony or an item of evidence[6] depends on its identity, source, or connection to a specific person, place, thing, or event that is at issue in the case.[7] Because authentication is an issue of relevance conditioned on facts, the trial judge determines the sufficiency of the foundation under Rule 104(b).[8] Under Rule 104(b), the evidence that the trial judge uses to decide the authenticity of the offered material must be admissible.[9] Here, the trial judge serves only a screening function and must let the jury consider the ques-

---

1. 5 CHRISTOPHER B. MUELLER & LAIRD C. KIRKPATRICK, FEDERAL EVIDENCE §9:2, at 325-26 (3d ed. 2007).

2. *Id.* §9:2, at 326. Authentication issues most commonly arise in criminal cases; in civil cases, authentication objections are rarely heard at pretrial conferences or during trial. Civil litigants seem to take authenticity for granted.

3. *Id.* §9:2, at 327-28.

4. Refer to notes 104-105 *infra* and accompanying text.

5. FED. R. EVID. 901 advisory committee's note, subdiv. (a).

6. Every document introduced into evidence must be individually authenticated, even if multiple documents are part of the same exhibit. *See, e.g.,* **Campbell v. C.D. Payne & Geldermann Sec., Inc.**, 894 S.W.2d 411, 421 (Tex. App.—Amarillo 1995, writ denied) (when exhibit containing different documents was offered as a whole, each document within exhibit should have been authenticated; trial court did not err in excluding entire exhibit that contained some unauthenticated documents).

7. **Kephart v. State**, 875 S.W.2d 319, 321 (Tex. Crim. App. 1994), *overruled on other grounds,* **Angleton v. State**, 971 S.W.2d 65 (Tex. Crim. App. 1998); **Campbell v. State**, 382 S.W.3d 545, 548-49 (Tex. App.—Austin 2012, no pet.); *see* **Peña v. State**, 467 S.W.3d 71, 74 (Tex. App.—San Antonio 2015, no pet.); 2 STEVEN GOODE ET AL., TEXAS PRACTICE: GUIDE TO THE TEXAS RULES OF EVIDENCE §901.1, at 274 (3d ed. 2002).

8. Refer to *Article I: General Provisions, supra* p. 91.

9. **In re Japanese Elec. Prods. Antitrust Litig.**, 723 F.2d 238, 285 (3d Cir. 1983), *rev'd on other grounds sub nom.* **Matsushita Elec. Indus. Co. v. Zenith Radio Corp.**, 475 U.S. 574 (1986).

tion, as long as there is enough evidence to support a jury finding of authenticity.[10] The opponent is then free to offer rebutting evidence to persuade the jury that the item is not authentic.[11] The trial judge's determination of authenticity is reviewable only for abuse of discretion.[12] The trial court does not abuse its discretion in admitting evidence under Article IX if it concludes that a reasonable juror could find that the evidence has been authenticated or identified.[13] Once evidence has been authenticated and admitted, the jury must determine its reliability.[14]

The authentication and identification requirements of Article IX are based on ordinary, logical connections between objects, people, and events and are considerably more liberal than the common-law requirements. The rules expand the categories of matters that can be self-authenticated under Rule 902, allow some evidence to be authenticated under Rule 901 merely by its appearance and content, and provide a low-threshold burden for establishing authenticity.[15] Rule 901 "'does not erect a particularly high hurdle,' and that hurdle may be cleared by 'circumstantial evidence.'"[16] The proponent of the evidence does not need "'to rule out all possibilities inconsistent with authenticity, or to prove beyond any doubt that the evidence is what it purports to be.'"[17]

---

10. *See Butler v. State*, 459 S.W.3d 595, 600 (Tex. Crim. App. 2015); *Tienda v. State*, 358 S.W.3d 633, 638 (Tex. Crim. App. 2012). The Federal Advisory Committee's note explains why Rule 104(b) limits the judge's role in deciding authenticity issues:

> If preliminary questions of conditional relevancy were determined solely by the judge, ... the functioning of the jury as a trier of fact would be greatly restricted and in some cases virtually destroyed. These are appropriate questions for juries. Accepted treatment, as provided in the rule, is consistent with that given fact questions generally. The judge makes a preliminary determination whether the foundation evidence is sufficient to support a finding of fulfillment of the condition. If so, the item is admitted. If after all the evidence on the issue is in, pro and con, the jury could reasonably conclude that fulfillment of the condition is not established, the issue is for them. If the evidence is not such as to allow a finding, the judge withdraws the matter from their consideration.

Fed. R. Evid. 104 advisory committee's note, subdiv. (b).

11. *See In re Japanese Elec. Prods.*, 723 F.2d at 285 (prima facie showing of genuineness sufficiently authenticates materials against all parties, subject to any party's right to offer evidence disputing authenticity).

12. *Butler*, 459 S.W.3d at 600; *Tienda*, 358 S.W.3d at 638; *see Wood v. State*, 18 S.W.3d 642, 647 (Tex. Crim. App. 2000) (reviewing trial court's admission of authentication testimony under abuse-of-discretion standard); *Rezaie v. State*, 259 S.W.3d 811, 814 (Tex. App.—Houston [1st Dist.] 2007, pet. ref'd) ("As long as the trial court's evidentiary ruling is within the zone of reasonable disagreement, an appellate court may not disturb it. A trial court goes beyond the zone of reasonable disagreement in evidentiary rulings only when it 'act[s] without reference to *any* guiding rules and principles.'" (quoting *Montgomery v. State*, 810 S.W.2d 372, 380 (Tex. Crim. App. 1990))).

13. *Mendoza v. State*, 69 S.W.3d 628, 631 (Tex. App.—Corpus Christi 2002, pet. ref'd); *cf. United States v. Rembert*, 863 F.2d 1023, 1027 (D.C. Cir. 1988) (ultimate test for authentication is whether proponent of evidence has made a showing "sufficient to permit a reasonable juror to find that the evidence is what its proponent claims").

14. *See United States v. Tropeano*, 252 F.3d 653, 661 (2d Cir. 2001).

15. Evidence may be authenticated under either Rule 901 or Rule 902 and need not be authenticated under both rules. *Reed v. State*, 811 S.W.2d 582, 586 (Tex. Crim. App. 1991); *Haas v. State*, 494 S.W.3d 819, 823 (Tex. App.—Houston [14th Dist.] 2016, no pet.); *Hull v. State*, 172 S.W.3d 186, 189 (Tex. App.—Dallas 2005, pet. ref'd).

16. *United States v. Tin Yat Chin*, 371 F.3d 31, 37 (2d Cir. 2004) (quoting *United States v. Dhinsa*, 243 F.3d 635, 658-59 (2d Cir. 2001)); *Campbell v. State*, 382 S.W.3d 545, 549 (Tex. App.—Austin 2012, no pet.).

17. *Tin Yat Chin*, 371 F.3d at 37 (quoting *United States v. Pluta*, 176 F.3d 43, 49 (2d Cir. 1999)); *Campbell*, 382 S.W.3d at 549.

✦

However, the authentication foundation is somewhat more stringent for physical exhibits than for oral testimony such as voice identification.[18] These greater safeguards are necessary because exhibits cannot be cross-examined. Furthermore, exhibits frequently are more vivid and memorable than similar oral testimony.[19] Thus, jurors might give these exhibits special emphasis during deliberation.[20]

Rule 902, which treats a variety of documents as self-authenticating, has eliminated much of the need for authentication and identification witnesses at the trial level. Pretrial procedures such as written requests for admission of genuineness,[21] verified pleas,[22] and stipulations[23] also frequently make extrinsic evidence of authenticity unnecessary.[24] Authentication by extrinsic evidence at trial may be avoided if the court is willing to take judicial notice of the genuineness of an item.[25] Fulfilling the authentication or identification requirements of Rule 901(a) does not, however, guarantee admissibility. The authentication requirements must be considered along with the rules for relevance, competency, hearsay, and privileges, as well as any other rule that may preclude the admission of an item.[26]

---

18. *See, e.g., Gardner v. State*, 306 S.W.3d 274, 293 (Tex. Crim. App. 2009) (robe worn by murder victim was properly authenticated by responding paramedic's testimony about blood stains and cuts made with trauma shears); *Shea v. State*, 167 S.W.3d 98, 104-05 (Tex. App.—Waco 2005, pet. ref'd) (e-mails were properly authenticated using witness testimony and distinctive characteristics of messages). *But see United States v. Patterson*, 277 F.3d 709, 713 (4th Cir. 2002) (applying liberal standard of authentication to fingerprint images; "[t]o meet the threshold established by [Federal] Rule 901(a), the party seeking to introduce physical evidence must provide 'a basis for the jury to resolve the authenticity question in favor of' that party" (quoting *United States v. Capers*, 61 F.3d 1100, 1106 (4th Cir. 1995))).

19. *See* 2 McCORMICK ON EVIDENCE §212, at 7 (Kenneth S. Broun ed., 6th ed. 2006).

20. *See United States v. Ruggiero*, 928 F.2d 1289, 1303 (2d Cir. 1991) (recorded evidence is likely to have strong effect on jury).

21. TEX. R. CIV. P. 198.1.

22. TEX. R. CIV. P. 93; *Zodiac Corp. v. Gen. Elec. Credit Corp.*, 566 S.W.2d 341, 346 (Tex. Civ. App.—Tyler 1978, no writ).

23. *See In re Estate of Watson*, 720 S.W.2d 806, 807-08 (Tex. 1986) (in will contest, party opposing will could not dispute authenticity of decedent's letters after stipulation that decedent sent them to her sister; Dead Man's Statute did not bar identification of decedent's signature or handwriting).

24. Under Texas's statutory journalist's privilege, a party can introduce a recording "that purports to be a broadcast by a radio or television station that holds a license issued by the Federal Communications Commission at the time of the recording" without providing extrinsic evidence of the recording's authenticity. TEX. CIV. PRAC. & REM. CODE §22.027; TEX. CODE CRIM. PROC. art. 38.111. For a discussion of the statutory journalist's privilege, refer to *Article V: Privileges, supra* p. 380. For a more detailed discussion of the authenticity and admissibility of recordings, refer to notes 141-151 *infra* and accompanying text and *Article X: Contents of Writings, Recordings, & Photographs, infra* p. 1042.

25. *See Threlkeld-Covington, Inc. v. Baker Drywall Co.*, 837 S.W.2d 840, 843 n.2 (Tex. App.—Eastland 1992, no writ) (taking judicial notice of previous judgment in favor of plaintiffs); *see also* TEX. CIV. PRAC. & REM. CODE §22.027 (court may take judicial notice of radio or television station's recording license); TEX. CODE CRIM. PROC. art. 38.111 (same). Refer to *Article II: Judicial Notice, supra* p. 111.

26. TEX. R. CIV. P. 193.7 cmt. 7; *see Maldonado v. State*, 998 S.W.2d 239, 244 (Tex. Crim. App. 1999) (authentication rules do not permit proponent of evidence to bypass statutory requirements for admissibility of statement); *Ortega v. CACH, LLC*, 396 S.W.3d 622, 630 (Tex. App.—Houston [14th Dist.] 2013, no pet.) ("[W]hen an ex parte affidavit presents evidence beyond the simple authentication requirements of rule 902, the extraneous portions of the affidavit constitute inadmissible hearsay."); 5 JACK B. WEINSTEIN & MARGARET A. BERGER, WEINSTEIN'S FEDERAL EVIDENCE §901.02[1], at 901-11 (Joseph M. McLaughlin ed., 2d ed. 2010) ("An exhibit is not admissible simply be-

The Texas version of Article IX follows the corresponding federal provisions almost verbatim. The only substantive difference between Texas Rule 901 and Federal Rule 901 is in Rule 901(b)(3). The federal version permits the comparison of a disputed object with another object that has been authenticated by either the fact-finder or an expert witness.[27] Thus, the fact-finder may compare one disputed object with a second disputed object, as long as there is sufficient evidence to support a finding that the second object is authentic. Under the Texas version, however, the trial court must first find the proposed sample to be authentic before the jury can compare it to the disputed object. Thus, the sample in Texas may not be open to dispute about its authenticity, but under the federal rule, it may be.[28] There are also minor substantive differences between the two versions of Rule 902. For example, Texas Rule 902(3)(C)'s discussion of authentication requirements under specific international treaties does not appear in Federal Rule 902(3), even though such treaty conventions apply in both federal and state courts.[29] Additionally, Texas Rule 902(10), which permits self-authentication of business records by affidavit, has certain requirements that are different from Federal Rules 902(11) and 902(12), which provide some similar authentication procedures for domestic and foreign business records.[30]

RULE 901

AUTHENTICATING OR IDENTIFYING EVIDENCE

(a) In General. To satisfy the requirement of authenticating or identifying an item of evidence, the proponent must produce evidence sufficient to support a finding that the item is what the proponent claims it is.

(b) Examples. The following are examples only—not a complete list—of evidence that satisfies the requirement:

---

cause it has been authenticated. The proponent must still clear the other hurdles to admissibility."); *see, e.g.,* ***Stapleton v. State***, 868 S.W.2d 781, 784 (Tex. Crim. App. 1993) (tape recording of 911 call was sufficiently authenticated under Criminal Rule 901 but was nonetheless inadmissible hearsay); ***In re Estate of Vackar***, 345 S.W.3d 588, 593-94 (Tex. App.—San Antonio 2011, no pet.) (production of medical records during discovery authenticated the records but did not make them admissible; court abused its discretion in admitting records under Rule 803(6) when party did not lay predicate for admission as business records).

27.   FED. R. EVID. 901(b)(3).

28.   Refer to notes 119-123 *infra* and accompanying text.

29.   *See* 2 GOODE ET AL., *supra* note 7, §902.4, at 297. *See generally* 5 WEINSTEIN & BERGER, *supra* note 26, §902.05, at 902-18 to 902-22 (discussing foreign public documents under Federal Rule 902(3)). Refer to notes 334-338 *infra* and accompanying text.

30.   Refer to notes 411-420 *infra* and accompanying text. The Judicial Conference Committee on Rules of Practice and Procedure has approved—and the U.S. Supreme Court has adopted—amendments to Federal Rule 902 that would add two new subdivisions to the rule. *See* U.S. Supreme Court, Miscellaneous Order, *Rules of Evidence* (Apr. 27, 2017), www.supremecourt.gov/orders/courtorders/frev17_d186.pdf; *Report of the Judicial Conference: Committee on Rules of Practice & Procedure*, Agenda E-19, at Rules 31-33 & App. C (Sept. 2016), www.uscourts.gov/rules-policies/archives/committee-reports/reports-judicial-conference-september-2016. If Congress does not take contrary action, the amendments will take effect December 1, 2017. Refer to note 412 *infra*.

(1) *Testimony of a Witness with Knowledge.* Testimony that an item is what it is claimed to be.

(2) *Nonexpert Opinion About Handwriting.* A nonexpert's opinion that handwriting is genuine, based on a familiarity with it that was not acquired for the current litigation.

(3) *Comparison by an Expert Witness or the Trier of Fact.* A comparison by an expert witness or the trier of fact with a specimen that the court has found is genuine.

(4) *Distinctive Characteristics and the Like.* The appearance, contents, substance, internal patterns, or other distinctive characteristics of the item, taken together with all the circumstances.

(5) *Opinion About a Voice.* An opinion identifying a person's voice—whether heard firsthand or through mechanical or electronic transmission or recording—based on hearing the voice at any time under circumstances that connect it with the alleged speaker.

(6) *Evidence About a Telephone Conversation.* For a telephone conversation, evidence that a call was made to the number assigned at the time to:

(A) a particular person, if circumstances, including self-identification, show that the person answering was the one called; or

(B) a particular business, if the call was made to a business and the call related to business reasonably transacted over the telephone.

(7) *Evidence About Public Records.* Evidence that:

(A) a document was recorded or filed in a public office as authorized by law; or

(B) a purported public record or statement is from the office where items of this kind are kept.

(8) *Evidence About Ancient Documents or Data Compilations.* For a document or data compilation, evidence that it:

(A) is in a condition that creates no suspicion about its authenticity;

(B) was in a place where, if authentic, it would likely be; and

(C) is at least 20 years old when offered.

(9) *Evidence About a Process or System.* Evidence describing a process or system and showing that it produces an accurate result.

RULE 901

> **(10)** *Methods Provided by a Statute or Rule.* Any method of authentication or identification allowed by a statute or other rule prescribed under statutory authority.

COMMENTARY ON RULE 901

A. Rule 901(a): In General

Texas Rule 901(a) codifies the well-established Texas common-law principle that requires, as a condition precedent to admissibility, the authentication of documents and the identification of other types of real and testimonial evidence.[31] Federal Rule 901(a), which the Texas rule follows, is intended to simplify and liberalize the authentication process.[32] The rule provides that to authenticate an item of evidence, "the proponent must produce evidence sufficient to support a finding that the item is what the proponent claims it is."[33] Thus, once the party offering the evidence makes a prima facie case, the fact-finder decides the question of authenticity.[34] The proponent does not need to convince the court that the matter is genuine;[35] the proponent must only produce sufficient evidence that a reasonable jury could properly find genuineness.[36] Authenticity may be established by circumstantial evidence alone.[37]

---

31.   *See Vahlsing, Inc. v. Mo. Pac. R.R.*, 563 S.W.2d 669, 672 (Tex. Civ. App.—Corpus Christi 1978, no writ); *Morris v. Ratliff*, 291 S.W.2d 418, 422 (Tex. Civ. App.—Dallas 1956, writ ref'd n.r.e.).

32.   *See* 5 STEPHEN A. SALTZBURG ET AL., FEDERAL RULES OF EVIDENCE MANUAL §901.02[1], at 901-6 (9th ed. 2006).

33.   TEX. R. EVID. 901(a); *see Gunville v. Gonzales*, 508 S.W.3d 547, 559 (Tex. App.—El Paso 2016, no pet.); *Benefield v. State*, 266 S.W.3d 25, 34 (Tex. App.—Houston [1st Dist.] 2008, no pet.); *see, e.g., Fowler v. State*, 517 S.W.3d 167, 174 (Tex. App.—Texarkana 2017, pet. filed 4-19-17) (trial court abused its discretion in admitting copy of store surveillance video; although police officer adequately demonstrated that video was duplicate of relevant part of original surveillance recording, there was no evidence that surveillance system was working properly on day in question, that video's clock was correct, or that original recording accurately portrayed events that allegedly occurred at time and date shown in recording). As explained by one commentator: "Authentication signifies only that the proponent of the evidence has done enough to identify or to explain the evidence for the trier to be justified in finding that the evidence is what the proponent claims. After the item is admitted an opposing party can offer evidence attacking its authenticity and the factfinder may accept that as true." 5 SALTZBURG ET AL., *supra* note 32, §902.02[1], at 902-5.

34.   Texas common-law cases also allowed the jury to decide authenticity once the offering party made a prima facie case. *See Barrera v. Duval Cty. Ranch Co.*, 135 S.W.2d 518, 520 (Tex. Civ. App.—San Antonio 1939, writ ref'd) (once a reasonable probability of authenticity is established, issue goes to jury); *Porter v. Rogers*, 293 S.W. 577, 579 (Tex. Civ. App.—Waco 1927, writ ref'd) (same); *see, e.g., Prichard v. Bickley*, 175 S.W.2d 614, 617-18 (Tex. Civ. App.—Eastland 1943, writ ref'd w.o.m.) (trial court properly submitted issue of execution of promissory note to jury).

35.   *Tienda v. State*, 358 S.W.3d 633, 638 (Tex. Crim. App. 2012); *Barfield v. State*, 416 S.W.3d 743, 749 (Tex. App.—Houston [14th Dist.] 2013, no pet.); *see also* 1 GOODE ET AL., *supra* note 7, §104.2, at 40 (authentication requires only evidence sufficient to support jury finding of genuineness; judge merely determines whether proponent has presented prima facie case). In *United States v. Tin Yat Chin*, the Second Circuit stated that Federal Rule 901 sets out only a minimal standard of authentication. 371 F.3d 31, 37 (2d Cir. 2004). There may be questions about the ultimate *reliability* of the exhibits or evidence offered, but, under Rule 901, "[t]he proponent is not required 'to rule out all possibilities inconsistent with authenticity, or to prove beyond any doubt that the evidence is what it purports to be.'" *Id.* (quoting *United States v. Pluta*, 176 F.3d 43, 49 (2d Cir. 1999)). Once the minimal foundation requirements are met, the persuasive force of that evidence is a matter for the jury to decide. *See Tin Yat Chin*, 371 F.3d at 37-38.

36.   *Butler v. State*, 459 S.W.3d 595, 600 (Tex. Crim. App. 2015); *Tienda*, 358 S.W.3d at 638; *Washington v. State*, 485 S.W.3d 633, 640 (Tex. App.—Houston [1st Dist.] 2016, no pet.); *Barfield*, 416 S.W.3d at 749; *Llamas v. State*,

The liberal standard of admissibility under Rule 901(a)[38] is also consistent with earlier Texas law, which had traditionally recognized a relaxed standard for the quality and quantity of extrinsic proof needed to authenticate an item.[39] Courts have said that as long as there is a "reasonable probability" that the item is what the proponent claims, the jury can decide the question of authenticity.[40] The trial judge must admit the proffered evidence even if the preliminary proof raises a fact issue about the item's genuineness.[41] Further, Rule 901 does not require that the sponsoring witness be certain that the item is authentic.[42] An item's authenticity relates to its admissibility, which is a question for the judge under Rule 104(a);[43] the issue of its reliability relates to its weight, which is a question for the jury.[44] At least one court has held that if the exhib-

---

270 S.W.3d 274, 281 (Tex. App.—Amarillo 2008, no pet.). As Jack Weinstein notes: "This rule does not ignore or repudiate the policy justifications for the authentication requirement. It simply recognizes that where the question is one of probative force or credibility—as it necessarily always is with questions of authenticity and identity—the jury is as competent as the court." 5 JACK B. WEINSTEIN & MARGARET A. BERGER, WEINSTEIN'S EVIDENCE ¶901(a)[02], at 901-27 (Joseph M. McLaughlin ed., 1996).

37. *Gunville*, 508 S.W.3d at 559; *Nicholas v. Envtl. Sys. (Int'l) Ltd.*, 499 S.W.3d 888, 900 (Tex. App.—Houston [14th Dist.] 2016, pet. denied); *see Lexington Ins. v. W. Pa. Hosp.*, 423 F.3d 318, 328-29 (3d Cir. 2005) (burden of proof for authentication is slight and not on par with more technical rules of evidence; circumstantial proof of authenticity may be sufficient when a party produces a document pursuant to discovery requests); *see, e.g., United States v. Garcia*, 452 F.3d 36, 40 (1st Cir. 2006) (circumstantial evidence is sufficient to authenticate affidavit as that signed by defendant; its contents, circumstances surrounding its creation, and its location provide sufficient indicia of authenticity); *United States v. Lauder*, 409 F.3d 1254, 1265 (10th Cir. 2005) (authenticity of fingerprint cards may be inferred from wholly circumstantial proof); *Soria v. State*, 933 S.W.2d 46, 60 (Tex. Crim. App. 1996) (originator of drawing need not be shown by signature, but can be shown circumstantially; evidence that drawing was found in capital-murder defendant's jail cell was sufficient connection to admit drawing for jury's consideration); *Thierry v. State*, 288 S.W.3d 80, 88-89 (Tex. App.—Houston [1st Dist.] 2009, pet. ref'd) (copy of security-camera footage was authenticated through testimony of loss-prevention officer, even though he was not present during the incident); *Llamas*, 270 S.W.3d at 282 (DVD copy of security-camera footage was authenticated through testimony about how the data was captured and then transferred from CD-ROM to DVD).

38. *Butler*, 459 S.W.3d at 600.

39. *See Wallace v. State*, 782 S.W.2d 854, 856-57 & n.6 (Tex. Crim. App. 1989) (authentication requirement of Criminal Rule 901 is "satisfied by evidence to support a finding that the matter in question is what its proponent claims"; neither result nor analysis was different before adoption of Rules); Thomas Black, *The Texas Rules of Evidence—A Proposed Codification*, 31 Sw. L.J. 969, 1009 (1978) (while evidence "must be connected to the person or object from which it purports to emanate," Texas courts are "relatively relaxed about the quality and quantity of proof needed").

40. *Barrera v. Duval Cty. Ranch Co.*, 135 S.W.2d 518, 520 (Tex. Civ. App.—San Antonio 1939, writ ref'd); *City of Corsicana v. Herod*, 768 S.W.2d 805, 815 (Tex. App.—Waco 1989, no writ); *Jackson v. Nona Mills Co.*, 61 Tex. Civ. App. 141, 147, 128 S.W. 928, 930 (Galveston 1910, no writ).

41. *See Herod*, 768 S.W.2d at 814. In *Herod*, the trial court in a condemnation suit properly admitted a document from an engineer's business files even though the engineer who designed a structure for the city could not recall having read the document, did not believe his office had produced it, and denied it was in his file at the relevant time. *Id.* The trial judge did not have to blindly accept the engineer's testimony because circumstantial evidence raised the fact issue of the document's authenticity. *Id.* at 815.

42. *See, e.g., United States v. Whittington*, 783 F.2d 1210, 1215 (5th Cir. 1986) (although authenticating witness was not familiar with every page of document, identification foundation was sufficient—but subject to cross-examination—when witness identified signature page of lease); *United States v. Johnson*, 637 F.2d 1224, 1247-48 (9th Cir. 1980) (assault victim's testimony that he was "pretty sure" that exhibit was the ax used against him sufficiently authenticated the weapon).

43. Refer to *Article I: General Provisions, supra* p. 86.

44. *See Herod*, 768 S.W.2d at 814-15; *see also United States v. Tropeano*, 252 F.3d 653, 661 (2d Cir. 2001) (distinguishing between authentication and reliability of tape recordings; "[a]uthentication of course merely renders the

its have been properly identified and authenticated through testimony, it is not error to offer and admit those exhibits after the sponsoring witness has left the witness stand.[45] However, if the sponsoring witness is no longer available, it may be difficult to deal with later hurdles to admissibility.[46]

B. Rule 901(b): Examples

Rule 901(b) provides ten examples of how to satisfy the general authentication requirements of Rule 901(a). Some of the examples are general illustrations of sufficient showings of genuineness, and others are Texas statutory rules listing the authentication requirements for certain documents.[47] As the examples indicate, a proponent of physical evidence may prove the item's genuineness by either direct or circumstantial evidence, which may involve matters that are either intrinsic or extrinsic to the document or thing involved.[48] The text of Rule 901(b) unequivocally states, however, that the examples are not a complete list of permissible methods of proof.[49] Thus, the rule has left room for further developments in the law and for unanticipated and unique methods of demonstrating authenticity.[50] The last example in Rule 901(b) is a catchall provision validating any other method of authentication that is provided by a statute or other rule promulgated under statutory authority.[51] Some items may be authenticated by any of several different methods.[52]

---

tapes admissible, leaving the issue of their ultimate reliability to the jury. [Defendant] was free to challenge the tapes' reliability by, for example, cross-examination of the [witnesses] concerning their familiarity with [defendant's] voice and the tape recording system").

45. *Ordonez v. State*, 806 S.W.2d 895, 898 (Tex. App.—Corpus Christi 1991, pet. ref'd).

46. Refer to note 26 *supra* and accompanying text.

47. *See* FED. R. EVID. 901 advisory committee's note, subdiv. (b) (source of illustrations is the experience embodied in the common law and statutes).

48. *See Butler v. State*, 459 S.W.3d 595, 602 (Tex. Crim. App. 2015). Texas courts have always accepted proof of genuineness by indirect or circumstantial evidence. *See Abeel v. Weil*, 115 Tex. 490, 504, 283 S.W. 769, 775 (1926); *Borak v. Bridge*, 524 S.W.2d 773, 777 (Tex. Civ. App.—Corpus Christi 1975, writ ref'd n.r.e.); *Groesbeck v. Wiest*, 157 S.W. 258, 259 (Tex. Civ. App.—San Antonio 1913, no writ); *Int'l Harvester Co. v. Campbell*, 43 Tex. Civ. App. 421, 426, 96 S.W. 93, 95 (San Antonio 1906, no writ); *see also Wallace v. State*, 782 S.W.2d 854, 856-57 (Tex. Crim. App. 1989) (circumstantial evidence does not need to be distinguished from direct evidence). Refer to note 37 *supra* and accompanying text.

49. TEX. R. EVID. 901(b); *see Stapleton v. State*, 868 S.W.2d 781, 785 (Tex. Crim. App. 1993) (Rule 901 does not indicate when or how evidence must be authenticated, but it provides some examples); *In re B.J.*, 100 S.W.3d 448, 450 (Tex. App.—Texarkana 2003, no pet.) (examples in Rule 901(b) "were not intended to exclude other methods"); *Montoya v. State*, 43 S.W.3d 568, 570 (Tex. App.—Waco 2001, no pet.) (Rule 901(b) provides examples of how electronic recordings may be authenticated); *Mega Child Care, Inc. v. Tex. Dep't of Prot. & Regulatory Servs.*, 29 S.W.3d 303, 308 (Tex. App.—Houston [14th Dist.] 2000, no pet.) (authentication under Rule 901(a) "may be accomplished by various means"); *Mutz v. State*, 862 S.W.2d 24, 29 (Tex. App.—Beaumont 1993, pet. ref'd) (illustrations under Criminal Rule 901 are not to be given "talismanic power"); *see, e.g.*, *Hislop v. State*, 64 S.W.3d 544, 546 (Tex. App.—Texarkana 2001, no pet.) (although document was not authenticated in any of the ways listed in Rule 901, combination of factors provided sufficient authentication).

50. *See* Craig Spangenberg, *The Federal Rules of Evidence—An Attempt at Uniformity in Federal Courts*, 15 WAYNE L. REV. 1061, 1072 (1969) ("A short set of general principles is a much more workable tool than a voluminous compilation of specifics.").

51. TEX. R. EVID. 901(b)(10). Refer to notes 257-263 *infra* and accompanying text.

52. *See Ballard v. State*, 23 S.W.3d 178, 182 (Tex. App.—Waco 2000, no pet.) (audio-video recordings may be authenticated under Rule 901(b)(1), (b)(4), and (b)(5)); *see, e.g.*, *Butler*, 459 S.W.3d at 600-01 (text messages were authenticated under Rule 901(b)(1) and (b)(4)).

1. Rule 901(b)(1): Testimony of a witness with knowledge. Rule 901(b)(1) codifies Texas common law by stating that both documentary and physical evidence may be authenticated or identified by the testimony of a witness with knowledge that the item is what it is claimed to be.[53] This rule is one of the workhorses of the Rules because it provides the simplest and most common method for authenticating evidence. Examples of authenticating evidence by this method include testimony by a party who executed and signed a document,[54] testimony by a witness who was present when an instrument was executed,[55] testimony establishing a chain of custody linking contraband to a defendant,[56] and testimony by a witness who was present at and participated in an event that was photographed or recorded.[57] In short, people who participate in or witness an event, condition, or transaction can testify to factual knowledge derived from their observations.[58] Sometimes a mere opinion may be enough to authenticate a

---

53. *See* Tex. R. Evid. 901(b)(1); *see, e.g.*, ***Kmart Stores of Tex., L.L.C. v. Ramirez***, 510 S.W.3d 559, 567-68 (Tex. App.—El Paso 2016, pet. denied) (screenshot allegedly showing that plaintiff-employee received and acknowledged arbitration agreement was sufficiently authenticated by affidavit of defendant-employer's compliance programs manager, who testified that she was familiar with the software that created the screenshot and that the screenshot was true and correct); ***Ballard***, 23 S.W.3d at 182 (when confidential informant and officers who videotaped undercover drug transaction all testified about accuracy of original video and duplicate, authentication was sufficient under Rule 901); ***Crivello v. State***, 4 S.W.3d 792, 802 (Tex. App.—Texarkana 1999, no pet.) (DWI videotape could be authenticated by officer's testimony that videotape was what proponent claimed, was made on night of arrest, was reviewed by officer on date of trial, and had not been altered; jury could determine if voices on tape were those of defendant and officer); ***Johnson v. State***, 970 S.W.2d 716, 719 (Tex. App.—Beaumont 1998, no pet.) (insufficient authentication when child witness was asked if tape recording was accurate and she replied "not everything," then said she did not remember it all; error was harmless); ***Hanover Fire Ins. v. Slaughter***, 111 S.W.2d 362, 365-66 (Tex. Civ. App.—Amarillo 1937, no writ) (insurance agent could identify insurance policy); *see also* ***Angleton v. State***, 971 S.W.2d 65, 67 (Tex. Crim. App. 1998) (discussing sufficiency of foundation for tape recordings).

54. *See, e.g.*, ***Stephenson v. State***, 138 Tex. Crim. 384, 388, 135 S.W.2d 1005, 1007 (1939) (witness's testimony that he executed contract was sufficient authentication); ***Garza v. Guerrero***, 993 S.W.2d 137, 142 (Tex. App.—San Antonio 1999, no pet.) (doctor's deposition testimony that exhibit was a correct copy of letter he had written and original was in patient's medical file was sufficient authentication of letter under Rule 901(b)(1)); ***W. Fed. Sav. & Loan Ass'n v. Atkinson Fin. Corp.***, 747 S.W.2d 456, 464 (Tex. App.—Fort Worth 1988, no writ) (affidavit of letter's author established letter's authenticity).

55. *See, e.g.*, ***Zodiac Corp. v. Gen. Elec. Credit Corp.***, 566 S.W.2d 341, 346 (Tex. Civ. App.—Tyler 1978, no writ); ***Abrigo v. State***, 29 Tex. Ct. App. 143, 149, 15 S.W. 408, 411 (1890).

56. *See, e.g.*, ***Luna v. State***, 493 S.W.2d 854, 856 (Tex. Crim. App. 1973); ***Cartwright v. State***, 807 S.W.2d 654, 656 (Tex. App.—Beaumont 1991), *aff'd*, 833 S.W.2d 134 (Tex. Crim. App. 1992). Refer to notes 88-98 *infra* and accompanying text.

57. *See* ***Kelley v. State***, 22 S.W.3d 642, 644 (Tex. App.—Waco 2000, pet. ref'd); *see, e.g.*, ***Brooks v. State***, 921 S.W.2d 875, 880 (Tex. App.—Houston [14th Dist.] 1996) (officer's firsthand knowledge of the recorded events and his identification of defendant's voice was sufficient authentication under Rule 901(b)(1)), *aff'd*, 957 S.W.2d 30 (Tex. Crim. App. 1997); ***Chatham v. State***, 889 S.W.2d 345, 348 (Tex. App.—Houston [14th Dist.] 1994, pet. ref'd) (defendant's identification of his voice and his girlfriend's voice on recording was sufficient authentication).

58. 5 Weinstein & Berger, *supra* note 26, §901.03[2], at 901-22; *see, e.g.*, ***Nicholas v. Envtl. Sys. (Int'l) Ltd.***, 499 S.W.3d 888, 901 (Tex. App.—Houston [14th Dist.] 2016, pet. denied) (trial court did not abuse its discretion in finding that certified copy of Canadian judgment was sufficiently authenticated by testimony of Canadian attorney who explained how he obtained certified copy from court registry); ***Good v. Baker***, 339 S.W.3d 260, 273 (Tex. App.—Texarkana 2011, pet. denied) (attorney's testimony about bills for attorney fees, which were on the attorney's letterhead, was sufficient to prove the bills were genuine); *see also* ***Baker v. City of Robinson***, 305 S.W.3d 783, 792 (Tex. App.—Waco 2009, pet. denied) (copy of ordinance was sufficiently authenticated by affidavit stating that witness was somewhat familiar with city's zoning laws and that attached ordinance was a true and correct copy).

document.[59] However, a bare assertion that a particular document is a specifically described item is insufficient authentication.[60]

Rule 901(b)(1) does not require the trial court to find that the witness is "necessarily worthy of belief."[61] A sponsoring witness can testify under Rule 901(b)(1) even if the witness's credibility has been questioned.[62]

Electronic communications such as e-mails can be authenticated under Rule 901(b)(1).[63] A participant in an e-mail conversation can testify that a printed copy of a particular message fairly represents the content of that message.[64] Likewise, text messages can be authenticated through the testimony of a witness with knowledge about the communications.[65] Instant messages and chat-room conversations can also be authenticated in this way; however, this testimony is often difficult to obtain because the participants are usually identified only by screen names.[66] Thus, circumstantial evidence, generally shown by distinctive information about the electronic message or communication, is often necessary for proper authentication.[67]

When a piece of physical evidence is unique or has distinctive characteristics, its authentication is sufficient if a witness can testify that he has previously seen the object,

---

59. *See, e.g.*, ***Jordan-Maier v. State***, 792 S.W.2d 188, 191-92 (Tex. App.—Houston [1st Dist.] 1990, pet. ref'd) (sufficient authentication was made by West German vice-consul in consulate's legal department who, when asked if certain German criminal-conviction papers were a fraud, exclaimed "[c]ertainly not"). *But see* ***Wirtz v. Mass. Mut. Life Ins.***, 898 S.W.2d 414, 423 (Tex. App.—Amarillo 1995, no writ) (when witness did not identify unsigned financial statements as being correct but merely "assumed" that they were plaintiff's business records and stated that they looked "familiar" and were, "to the best of [his] knowledge," prepared by plaintiff's accounting firm, document was not authenticated under rule).

60. *E.g.*, ***Mega Child Care, Inc. v. Tex. Dep't of Prot. & Regulatory Servs.***, 29 S.W.3d 303, 308 (Tex. App.—Houston [14th Dist.] 2000, no pet.) (witness's testimony that exhibit was a copy of administrative judge's opinion and order was insufficient authentication because "she was not the author of the opinion and order; neither did she purport to have any personal knowledge of the opinion and order by which she could confidently authenticate a copy"; harmless error because opponent did not allege or suggest that document was not what proponent claimed).

61. ***Butler v. State***, 459 S.W.3d 595, 605 (Tex. Crim. App. 2015).

62. *E.g.*, *id.* at 605 & n.13 (witness could testify about exchanging text messages with defendant to authenticate messages under Rule 901(b)(1) even though her credibility was impeached through inconsistent statements about assault).

63. *See* Steven Goode, *The Admissibility of Electronic Evidence*, 29 REV. LITIG. 1, 10 (2009) ("This additional proof [of authorship of an e-mail message] can be provided by the testimony of a witness with personal knowledge, and numerous examples exist in which e-mails have been so authenticated.").

64. *See, e.g.*, ***United States v. Gagliardi***, 506 F.3d 140, 151 (2d Cir. 2007) (FBI agent testified that exhibit was accurate record of e-mail exchange she had with defendant while agent posed as 13-year-old girl; court did not abuse its discretion in admitting documents based on this authentication testimony); ***Talada v. City of Martinez***, 656 F. Supp. 2d 1147, 1158 (N.D. Cal. 2009) (declaration that e-mails were a true and correct copy of the e-mails received was sufficient to authenticate e-mails); ***Ussery v. State***, No. 03-07-00116-CR (Tex. App.—Austin 2008, pet. ref'd) (memo op.; 1-30-08) (witness's testimony that exhibits were "fair and accurate copies" of messages she had exchanged with defendant was sufficient to authenticate e-mails).

65. ***Butler***, 459 S.W.3d at 600-01; *see, e.g.*, ***Peña v. State***, 467 S.W.3d 71, 75 (Tex. App.—San Antonio 2015, no pet.) (text messages were sufficiently authenticated under Rule 901(b)(1) by witness who testified about text-message conversation between herself and defendant, including identifying photographs sent to her by defendant).

66. Goode, *supra* note 63, at 18.

67. *See* John G. Browning, *Digging for the Digital Dirt: Discovery and Use of Evidence from Social Media Sites*, 14 SMU SCI. & TECH. L. REV. 465, 479 (2011) ("Authentication of digital information can be accomplished by

noticed its distinctive characteristics, and presently recalls them.[68] Rule 901(b)(4) expressly permits identification by "distinctive characteristics of the item."[69] Photographs and recordings are types of evidence that are usually authenticated under this provision. A photograph or recording generally has sufficient distinctive characteristics to be easily identifiable by someone familiar with the facts or events it portrays.[70] The admissibility of a photograph or recording is conditioned on its identification by a witness as an accurate depiction of the person, place, thing, or event—even if the witness did not take the photograph or make the recording—and its verification by a person who knows that the photograph or recording is a correct representation of those facts.[71]

Digital images are "photographs" for purposes of Rule 1001(c). The rule defines a photograph as "a photographic image or its equivalent stored in any form."[72] Thus, digital photographs are subject to the same authentication and admissibility criteria

direct proof, circumstantial evidence, or a combination of both."); Goode, *supra* note 63, at 29 ("[T]he cryptography that is sometimes used in the transmission of an e-mail message may provide a means of authenticating an e-mail, as may an encrypted digital signature to an otherwise unencrypted message."). Refer to notes 157-172 *infra* and accompanying text.

68.　*See* EDWARD J. IMWINKELRIED, EVIDENTIARY FOUNDATIONS §4.08[1], [2], at 133-35 (7th ed. 2008); *see, e.g.*, ***Gardner v. State***, 306 S.W.3d 274, 293 (Tex. Crim. App. 2009) (robe worn by murder victim was properly authenticated by responding paramedic's testimony about blood stains and cuts made with trauma shears); ***Hughes v. State***, 878 S.W.2d 142, 154-55 (Tex. Crim. App. 1992) (autopsy photograph of deceased's wounds was sufficiently authenticated under Rule 901 by assistant medical examiner; "[a] witness who verifies a photograph need not have been the actual photographer, nor even have been present when the photograph was taken"); ***Hartsfield v. State***, 200 S.W.3d 813, 818-19 (Tex. App.—Texarkana 2006, pet. ref'd) (box with distinctive blood-spatter marking was properly authenticated by testimony of witness who had seen it at crime scene); ***Mendoza v. State***, 69 S.W.3d 628, 631 (Tex. App.—Corpus Christi 2002, pet. ref'd) (authentication was sufficient when sexual-assault victim's mother identified a hammer as the one she kept in a certain place in her house, victim testified she recognized it as the one defendant used to hit her, and officer testified it was the hammer he recovered from crime scene); ***Jackson v. State***, 968 S.W.2d 495, 500 (Tex. App.—Texarkana 1998, pet. ref'd) (defendant's bloodstained jeans were sufficiently authenticated by wife's testimony that she recognized them as the jeans he was wearing on night of assault); ***Conway v. State***, 740 S.W.2d 559, 562-63 (Tex. App.—Beaumont 1987, pet. ref'd) (photograph of defendant's thumbprint on telephone receiver was sufficiently authenticated when latent-fingerprint examiner testified that "[t]his is the photograph of the print that was on the brown phone").

69.　TEX. R. EVID. 901(b)(4). Refer to notes 129-181 *infra* and accompanying text.

70.　*See, e.g.*, ***Montoya v. State***, 43 S.W.3d 568, 570-71 (Tex. App.—Waco 2001, no pet.) (witness could authenticate 911 tape as an accurate copy of original telephone call because she had listened to original tape and was its custodian).

71.　*See* ***Peña v. State***, 467 S.W.3d 71, 75 (Tex. App.—San Antonio 2015, no pet.); ***Kelley v. State***, 22 S.W.3d 642, 644 (Tex. App.—Waco 2000, pet. ref'd); *see, e.g.*, ***Washington v. State***, 485 S.W.3d 633, 640-41 (Tex. App.—Houston [1st Dist.] 2016, no pet.) (testimony of patrol sergeant, who had worked in gang unit for ten years, about photographic images purportedly associated with gang was sufficient to authenticate images as fair and accurate depictions of what they purported to be, even though he did not know when or where photographs were made; proponent used exhibits for illustrative purposes and was not trying to link them to defendant); ***Kessler v. Fanning***, 953 S.W.2d 515, 522 (Tex. App.—Fort Worth 1997, no pet.) (admitting photographs and videotape on basis of personal familiarity with event; predicate does not need to be laid by photographer, person photographed, or even a person who was present when photograph or video was taken); ***S.D.G. v. State***, 936 S.W.2d 371, 382-83 (Tex. App.—Houston [14th Dist.] 1996, writ denied) (although officer was not present when photographs were taken, he could testify that pictures were fair and accurate depiction of defendants he had seen on day photos were taken; convenience-store clerk who was present during robbery could testify to accuracy of scene depicted in surveillance videotape).

72.　TEX. R. EVID. 1001(c). Refer to *Article X: Contents of Writings, Recordings, & Photographs, infra* p. 1049.

as any still photograph or motion picture.[73] The problem with authenticating digital photographs (and film, in some circumstances) is that they can be easily manipulated with software programs to modify the original images.[74] But even when such programs have been used to enhance[75] or "clean up" an image,[76] the authentication of the photographs is not compromised as long as (1) the computer program is used only to enhance the image and (2) the proponent supplies the original image and all enhanced images.[77]

---

73. *See Almond v. State*, 553 S.E.2d 803, 805 (Ga. 2001) ("[T]he [digital] pictures were introduced only after the prosecution properly authenticated them as fair and truthful representations of what they purported to depict. ... We are aware of no authority ... for the proposition that the procedure for admitting pictures should be any different when they were taken by a digital camera.").

74. *See* Goode, *supra* note 63, at 19 ("The advent of digital photography and the ease with which digital photographs can be manipulated with easy-to-use, off-the-shelf software has created a level of unease in the practicing bar.").

75. Courts will routinely admit some types of computer-enhanced images, such as CAT (computerized axial tomography) scans, which consist of a series of X-rays taken on different planes that are then subjected to various computer-imaging programs that produce three-dimensional images. *See* Andre M. Thapedi, Comment, *A.D.A.M.—The Computer Generated Cadaver: A New Development in Medical Malpractice and Personal Injury Litigation*, 13 J. MARSHALL J. COMPUTER & INFO. L. 313, 313-15 & n.7 (1995) (noting the use of CAT scans in medical-malpractice and personal-injury lawsuits). The technology of computer-enhanced imagery is well developed, but there is relatively little precedent directly discussing the admissibility of these images outside the medical context. *See, e.g., In re J.P.B.*, 180 S.W.3d 570, 575 (Tex. 2005) (per curiam) (no abuse of discretion in admitting X-rays printed from computer program that allowed alteration; radiologist testified that program could crop or adjust brightness and contrast but not otherwise alter X-ray); *Gilkey v. State*, No. 05-02-01820-CR (Tex. App.—Dallas 2003, no pet.) (memo op.; 11-21-03) (no abuse of discretion in admitting gas station's enhanced videotape; investigating officer testified that enhanced video accurately depicted events); *cf. Angleton v. State*, 971 S.W.2d 65, 68-69 (Tex. Crim. App. 1998) (enhanced audiotape was sufficiently authenticated by sergeant's testimony that enhanced tape only reduced background noise and was an accurate copy of original tape's relevant contents).

76. The basic theory of using computer programs to enhance photographic images is that computer software can reverse the degradation (blurring or graininess) of an image and enhance its clarity. The fundamental evidentiary issue is the reliability of the software program used to correct a blur, bring out detail in under- or overexposed areas of film, enlarge images without losing definition, and enhance an image's brightness, color, and definition so that the detail becomes more visible. *See generally* Robert F. Seltzer, *Digital Image Processing*, 3 TRIAL DIPLOMACY J. 57-61 (Winter 1980-81) (discussing early methods of digital-image processing and use of image enhancement for evidence).

77. *See, e.g., State v. Hayden*, 950 P.2d 1024, 1025 (Wash. Ct. App. 1998) (admitting digitally enhanced photographs of latent fingerprints). In *Hayden*, the court of appeals noted that the State had presented expert testimony on the digitally enhanced print process and had attached five scientific articles to its trial brief so that the trial judge would have the benefit of the most recent scientific research in the area. *Id.* at 1027. The State's expert explained the process of digital imaging in detail and noted that there is no subjectivity in the original digital-photography process. The original digital photographs are "enhanced using software that improves sharpness and image contrast. In addition, pattern and color isolation filters remove interfering colors and background patterns. This is a subtractive process in which elements are removed or reduced; nothing is added." *Id.* at 1028. Most importantly, the expert testified that the software he used "prevented him from adding to, changing, or destroying the original image. In contrast with 'image restoration,' a process in which things that are not there are added based on preconceived ideas about what the end result should look like, 'image enhancement' merely makes what is there more usable." *Id.* The appellate court was able to compare for itself the fabric from which the fingerprints were retrieved, the original digital photograph, and the enhanced image, and "[i]t is clear even to the untrained eye that the fabric contains a hand print and that nothing appears in the digitally enhanced photograph that was not present on the fabric." *Id.* The court agreed with the trial court's conclusions that (1) the expert's technique had a reliability factor of 100% and a zero-percent margin of error, (2) the results could be visually verifiable, and (3) those results could be easily duplicated by another expert using a digital camera and the appropriate software. *Id.*; *see also Nooner v. State*, 907 S.W.2d 677, 686 (Ark. 1995) (upholding admission of digitally enhanced still images taken by a surveillance video-

Websites, which can be authenticated by evidence of their distinctive characteristics under Rule 901(b)(4),[78] can also be authenticated through witness testimony under Rule 901(b)(1).[79] Because technology is constantly advancing, "there is no 'one size fits all' approach that can be taken when authenticating electronic evidence."[80] To introduce a printout from a website, a party must prove that the printout accurately reflects the website's contents and the image of the page on the computer that made the printout.[81] Although courts have moved away from a categorical distrust of websites,

---

tape; because jury had viewed a slowed-down version of original videotape before seeing enhanced stills, it was capable of identifying any distortion; "[r]eliability must be the watchword in determining the admissibility of enhanced videotape and photographs, whether by computer or otherwise"); *Dolan v. State*, 743 So. 2d 544, 546 (Fla. App. 1999) (upholding admission of computer-enhanced still images from surveillance tape; important to maintain unenhanced original for comparison purposes; key question is "whether the computer-enhanced still prints reflect distorted or altered images on the videotape; in essence, the same analysis which applies to photographic enlargements or blow-ups"); *English v. State*, 422 S.E.2d 924, 925 (Ga. App. 1992) (admitting enhanced still photograph taken from surveillance videotape; jury was shown both original and enhanced photos; technician who produced computer-enhanced photographic copy testified to that process and stated that the photo, as enhanced, was a fair and accurate representation of what appeared in the videotape; "the computer-enhanced photographic copy would be no less admissible ... than an enlargement of a photograph would be"); *State v. Hartman*, 754 N.E.2d 1150, 1165-66 (Ohio 2001) (digitally enhanced latent fingerprints were admissible under *Hayden* standard). The court in *Dolan* concluded that:

> Once the tape is authenticated and the forensic analyst explains the computer enhancement process and establishes that the images were not altered or edited, then the computer enhancements become admissible as a fair and accurate replicate of what is on the tape, provided the original tape is in evidence for comparison. The weight accorded to those computer-enhanced prints is determined by the jury. A jury possesses sufficient common sense to compare the images.

743 So. 2d at 546.

78. Refer to notes 173-181 *infra* and accompanying text.

79. When information from websites first started being offered as evidence, many courts considered it inherently unreliable. *See United States v. Jackson*, 208 F.3d 633, 637 (7th Cir. 2000) (any information from the Internet is "adequate for almost nothing" (quoting *St. Clair v. Johnny's Oyster & Shrimp, Inc.*, 76 F. Supp. 2d 773, 775 (S.D. Tex. 1999))); *Monotype Imaging, Inc. v. Bitstream, Inc.*, 376 F. Supp. 2d 877, 885 n.6 (N.D. Ill. 2005) ("[P]rintouts from websites should be closely scrutinized for reliability."). Since that time, however, courts have moved toward accepting this evidence, as long as it is properly authenticated. *See United States v. Cameron*, 762 F. Supp. 2d 152, 160 (D. Me. 2011) ("[I]n the decade since *Jackson*, the Internet has become more familiar and ubiquitous and its potential significance as a critical source for evidence in some cases has escalated. A conclusion that all Internet postings are so inherently unreliable that they are never admissible seems unwise."), *rev'd in part on other grounds*, 699 F.3d 621 (1st Cir. 2012); *Tienda v. State*, 358 S.W.3d 633, 638-39 (Tex. Crim. App. 2012) ("Courts and legal commentators have reached a virtual consensus that, although rapidly developing electronic communications technology often presents new and protean issues with respect to the admissibility of electronically generated, transmitted and/or stored information, including information found on social networking web sites, the rules of evidence already in place for determining authenticity are at least generally 'adequate to the task.'" (quoting Goode, *supra* note 63, at 7)).

80. *Lorraine v. Markel Am. Ins.*, 241 F.R.D. 534, 544 (D. Md. 2007); *see Cameron*, 762 F. Supp. 2d at 161 ("[T]his Court is less inclined to paint all websites with the same broad brush and exclude all Internet postings from the business records exception to the hearsay rule only because they are Web-based.").

81. Randy Wilson, *Admissibility of Web-Based Data*, THE ADVOCATE: STATE BAR LITIG. SECTION REPORT, Fall 2010, at 31, 32. Other suggestions for authenticating content from social-media sites include the following:

> To authenticate social-networking content, the party offering it must introduce sufficient evidence for a reasonable jury to conclude that the exhibit is what the sponsoring party claims it to be. At a minimum, one should proffer testimony from the person who performed the online research and printed the social media pages. Testimony should describe when and how the page was found, describe the circumstances of the search, and verify that the copy accurately reflects what was viewed online. The webpage itself and any page on the site reflecting its ownership should be printed out with the URL listed. Further, one should be prepared to offer evidence that the author of the posting or

they have demanded different amounts of supporting material before accepting a website as authenticated.[82] Some federal and Texas courts have accepted affidavits containing personal knowledge of the accuracy of website materials as sufficient to authenticate the materials under Rule 901(b)(1),[83] but others require further evidence of the materials' reliability.[84] Other courts have considered printouts from government-run websites to be self-authenticating "official publications" under Rule 902(5), as long as the printouts display the website URL and dates of access.[85]

Some cases may depend on a website's content as of a particular historical date, rather than the website's content at the time of litigation. This type of evidence, called the archived website, may be authenticated by the affidavit of an employee of a specialized Internet historical service.[86] The affidavit or testimony must establish not only

---

other social media content actually wrote it. This evidence can consist of an admission by the author, a stipulation entered into by the parties, the testimony of a witness who assisted in or observed the creation of the content or other indications or content from the profile itself that connects it to the author.
Browning, *supra* note 67, at 480.

82.   *See* Wilson, *supra* note 81, at 32; *see also* **Lorraine**, 241 F.R.D. at 543 ("[C]ourts increasingly are demanding that proponents of evidence obtained from electronically stored information pay more attention to the foundational requirements than has been customary for introducing evidence not produced from electronic sources.").

83.   *See* **In re Homestore.com, Inc. Sec. Litig.**, 347 F. Supp. 2d 769, 782-83 (C.D. Cal. 2004) ("Printouts from a web site do not bear the indicia of reliability demanded for other self-authenticating documents under Fed.R.Evid. 902. To be authenticated, some statement or affidavit from someone with knowledge is required; for example, [the] web master or someone else with personal knowledge would be sufficient."), *clarified on other grounds*, 347 F. Supp. 2d 811 (C.D. Cal. 2004); *see, e.g.*, **Perfect 10, Inc. v. Cybernet Ventures, Inc.**, 213 F. Supp. 2d 1146, 1153-54 (C.D. Cal. 2002) (plaintiff's exhibits printed off the Internet were sufficiently authenticated by declaration that exhibits were a true and correct copy of the originals); **Daimler-Benz A.G. v. Olson**, 21 S.W.3d 707, 717 (Tex. App.—Austin 2000, pet. dism'd) (affidavit of plaintiff's attorney that attachments containing information from defendant's website were within his personal knowledge and were accurate copies of original was sufficient to authenticate material); *see also* **TIP Sys., LLC v. SBC Opers., Inc.**, 536 F. Supp. 2d 745, 756 n.5 (S.D. Tex. 2008) (in summary-judgment proceeding, declaration from plaintiff's attorney was sufficient to authenticate excerpts from website); **Lorraine**, 241 F.R.D. at 545 ("Although [Federal] Rule 901(b)(1) certainly is met by the testimony of a witness that actually drafted the exhibit, it is not required that the authenticating witness have personal knowledge of the making of a particular exhibit if he or she has personal knowledge of how that type of exhibit is routinely made.").

84.   *See, e.g.*, **Jackson**, 208 F.3d at 638 (court excluded website postings because proponent did not show that website sponsor, not third party, authored the posts); **Jenkins v. NTE Aviation, Inc.**, No. 4:09-CV-117-A (N.D. Tex. 2010) (memo op.; 2-19-10) (footnote 3; court refused to consider materials from defendant's website because plaintiff's affidavit contained no support for reliability of materials and did not attempt to prove that defendant authored the materials); **Burnett Ranches, Ltd. v. Cano Pet., Inc.**, 289 S.W.3d 862, 871 (Tex. App.—Amarillo 2009, pet. denied) (affidavit from plaintiff's attorney that website printout was "true and correct copy" of defendant's corporate document was insufficient to authenticate printout because it did not establish that website from which he obtained document was defendant's).

85.   *See* **Williams v. Long**, 585 F. Supp. 2d 679, 685-89 (D. Md. 2008) (collecting cases that discuss requirements for a printout from government-run website to be self-authenticating under Federal Rule 902(5); advising litigants to include at least the "internet domain address" and "date on which it was printed"); *see, e.g.*, **Williams Farms Produce Sales, Inc. v. R&G Produce Co.**, 443 S.W.3d 250, 259 (Tex. App.—Corpus Christi 2014, no pet.) (docket sheet printed from uscourts.gov website that displayed date and time of printing was self-authenticating under Rule 902(5)). Refer to notes 348-357 *infra* and accompanying text.

86.   *See* Goode, *supra* note 63, at 14-16; *see, e.g.*, **Telewizja Polska USA, Inc. v. Echostar Satellite Corp.**, No. 02 C 3293 (N.D. Ill. 2004) (memo op.; 10-14-04) (affidavit from employee of archive company stating that company "retrieved copies of the website as it appeared on the dates in question from its electronic archives" was sufficient to meet the threshold requirement for admissibility of evidence of archived website).

RULE 901

that the printouts are accurate copies of the Internet archive's records, but also that the records are accurate representations of the archived website.[87]

If an object has no unique characteristics or is a fungible item (e.g., cash, a bag of cocaine, an aerosol can), it can be authenticated as the item that was involved in the litigated event through a "chain of custody."[88] Although Rule 901 does not specifically mention the chain of custody as a method of authentication,[89] both Texas and federal courts have long used it to prove that the item in the courtroom is the same item that is relevant to the lawsuit. To trace an item's chain of custody, the proponent offers the testimony of each person who had custody of the item from the time of its first connection with the litigated event until its production at trial[90] or its final connection with the litigated event.[91] When the proponent authenticates evidence by tracing a chain of custody, the mere possibility of a break in that chain does not render the item inadmissible but is an issue for the jury to consider in determining the sufficiency of the proof.[92] As long as a reasonable jury could find that

---

87. Goode, *supra* note 63, at 16; *see, e.g.*, **St. Luke's Cataract & Laser Inst., P.A. v. Sanderson**, No. 8:06-cv-223-T-MSS (M.D. Fla. 2006) (order; 5-12-06) (contents of archived website were not sufficiently authenticated by affidavit taken in an unrelated case and declarations from witnesses with no personal knowledge of archive).

88. *See* **Moore v. State**, 821 S.W.2d 429, 431 (Tex. App.—Waco 1991, no pet.) ("Prior to the rules of evidence, proof of a chain of custody was required to authenticate or identify an item properly when there was a possibility of commingling the item with items similar in appearance, when items not having distinctive characteristics had not been marked with distinctive markings by the sponsoring witness, and when necessary to refute a suggestion that the evidence had been tampered with or changed in some manner."). *See generally* Paul C. Gianelli, *Chain of Custody and the Handling of Real Evidence*, 20 AM. CRIM. L. REV. 527, 539-60 (1983) (describing the type of evidence required to show chain of custody for authentication).

89. *See* **Mendoza v. State**, 69 S.W.3d 628, 631 (Tex. App.—Corpus Christi 2002, pet. ref'd) (while rules do not specifically address chain of custody, authentication requirement is satisfied if the evidence is sufficient to support a finding that the matter in question is what the proponent claims).

90. A prima facie showing of a fungible item's authentication is often sufficient if the item was distinctively tagged or marked after its association with the event, when the potential for litigation became apparent. *See* **Stoker v. State**, 788 S.W.2d 1, 10 (Tex. Crim. App. 1989) (tagging of evidence at its seizure and then identifying it at trial based on tag is sufficient for admission if there was no tampering or alteration; conflicting testimony on type of container used to store evidence goes to weight of evidence, not admissibility).

91. The important links in the chain of custody in drug cases are those from the point of seizure to the laboratory test. *See, e.g.*, **Young v. State**, 183 S.W.3d 699, 704 (Tex. App.—Tyler 2005, pet. ref'd) ("This evidence shows a complete chain of custody from seizure to the laboratory. The record reveals no evidence of tampering and no gaps in the chain of custody. Therefore, we hold that the trial court did not abuse its discretion in overruling Appellant's chain of custody objection and admitting the cocaine into evidence."). Even if the item is later lost, destroyed, or altered, the authentication requirement has been met. *See, e.g.*, **Lake v. State**, 577 S.W.2d 245, 246 (Tex. Crim. App. 1979) (defendant's conviction for possession of heroin upheld even though drugs had been destroyed before trial by court order after previous trial; no error to convict without drugs' physical presence, as long as substance had been analyzed and chain of custody explained).

92. *See* **Lagrone v. State**, 942 S.W.2d 602, 617 (Tex. Crim. App. 1997) ("Without evidence of tampering, most questions concerning care and custody of a substance go to the weight attached, not the admissibility, of the evidence."); **Mendoza v. State**, 552 S.W.2d 444, 448-49 (Tex. Crim. App. 1977) (objections to chain of custody go to weight of evidence, not admissibility); **Llamas v. State**, 270 S.W.3d 274, 282 (Tex. App.—Amarillo 2008, no pet.) ("Proof of the beginning and end of the chain of custody will support admission of an object barring any evidence of tampering or alteration."); **Moore**, 821 S.W.2d at 431 ("'[M]inor theoretical breaches in the chain of custody' will not affect admissibility in absence of 'affirmative evidence of tampering or commingling.'" (quoting **Stone v. State**, 794 S.W.2d 868, 870 (Tex. App.—El Paso 1990, no pet.))); *see, e.g.*, **Kirby v. State**, 713 S.W.2d 221, 222 (Tex.

RULE 901

the item presented at trial is the same as the one involved in the event at issue and is in substantially the same condition now as it was then,[93] all other deficiencies in the chain of custody affect the weight of the evidence, not its admissibility.[94] The court must find only that, in reasonable probability, the item in question has not been altered in any significant respect.[95] Even when an object is not in the same condition as it was at the time of the litigated event, it is nonetheless admissible if the probative value of the altered item is not substantially outweighed by its unfair prejudicial effect.[96] Courts occasionally address chain-of-custody issues even when the evidence has been properly authenticated under some other method, such as through a witness's personal knowledge,[97] but this analysis is unnecessary.[98]

App.—El Paso 1986, no pet.) (although blood-sample vial did not have its original identifying number and security seal, law-enforcement personnel had no reason to tamper with evidence and dilute its alcohol content; minimal break in evidentiary chain was insufficient to justify exclusion of defendant's exhibit); *see also **Garner v. State**,* 848 S.W.2d 799, 803 (Tex. App.—Corpus Christi 1993, no pet.) (authentication was insufficient when identifying officer could not testify that syringe taken from defendant was same item brought to court and syringe was not immediately tagged at scene, had no identifiable markings on it, and was returned from lab in different packaging).

93. Gianelli, *supra* note 88, at 533. Affirmative proof of evidence tampering or a material change in the evidence's condition must be shown before a trial judge is authorized to exclude the item. *See **United States v. Mc-Cowan**,* 706 F.2d 863, 865 (8th Cir. 1983) ("Generally, a district court may assume that public officials who had custody of the evidence properly discharged their duty and did not tamper with the evidence. If the trial court is satisfied that in reasonable probability the article has not been changed in any important respect it may permit its introduction into evidence."); ***United States v. Coades**,* 549 F.2d 1303, 1306 (9th Cir. 1977) ("A mere showing that an opportunity existed for unlawful tampering with the evidence is insufficient to justify exclusion; affirmative evidence of bad faith or actual tampering is required.").

94. *See **Mitchell v. State**,* 419 S.W.3d 655, 660 (Tex. App.—San Antonio 2013, pet. ref'd) (unless there is evidence of fraud or tampering, any gaps in chain of custody affect weight of evidence, not its admissibility). In ***Wallace v. State**,* the fact that an officer put multiple drug packets in her purse and then put her purse in the refrigerator overnight did not affect the admissibility of the evidence because there was no allegation of tampering. 770 S.W.2d 874, 877 (Tex. App.—Dallas 1989, pet. ref'd). The fact that the officer who seized the evidence misdated the label on a drug-package exhibit went to the weight of the evidence, not its admissibility. *Id.* In addition, the fact that an undercover informant injected a portion of the seized drug before turning the drug over to the police officer did not affect the chain of custody. *Id.; see also **Haley v. State**,* 816 S.W.2d 789, 791 (Tex. App.—Houston [14th Dist.] 1991, pet. ref'd) (exhibit should not be rejected merely because it is not positively identified; any perceived conflict between one witness's unequivocal identification testimony and another witness's "understanding" of exhibit's origin goes to its weight and is issue for jury). In ***Ballou v. Henri Studios, Inc.**,* the Fifth Circuit held that the trial court committed reversible error in a personal-injury suit when it excluded blood tests indicating that the automobile driver was intoxicated at the time of the collision. 656 F.2d 1147, 1155-56 (5th Cir. 1981). As the court noted:

> [T]he question whether the proponent of evidence has proved an adequate chain of custody goes to the weight rather than the admissibility of the evidence, and is thus reserved for the jury. Likewise, the issue of alteration, contamination or adulteration of the evidence is a question for the jury once the proponent of the evidence makes a threshold showing that reasonable precautions were taken against the risk of alteration, contamination or adulteration.

Id. at 1154-55 (citations omitted).

95. ***United States v. Jones**,* 356 F.3d 529, 536 (4th Cir. 2004) (missing link in chain of custody does not prevent admission of real evidence, as long as there is sufficient proof that the evidence is what it purports to be and has not been altered); ***United States v. Albert**,* 595 F.2d 283, 290 (5th Cir. 1979) ("[A] trial judge may admit physical evidence if he is satisfied that in reasonable probability the article has not been changed in any important respect from its original condition.").

96. *See* 2 McCormick on Evidence, *supra* note 19, §213, at 11-12.

97. *See **Ennis v. State**,* 71 S.W.3d 804, 808 (Tex. App.—Texarkana 2002, no pet.) ("A chain of custody must be established when (1) there is a possibility of commingling the item with items similar in appearance, (2) the sponsoring witness has not marked with distinctive markings an item not having distinctive characteristics, or (3) there

Rule 901(b)(1) is identical to Federal Rule 901(b)(1), which has been liberally interpreted. For example, federal courts have permitted witnesses to testify to knowledge obtained through any of the five senses.[99] Under either Texas Rule 901(b)(1) or Federal Rule 901(b)(1), the witness does not need to be absolutely precise or certain in identifying a particular object or event.[100]

Both the Texas and federal rules allow either lay or expert testimony on the authenticity of evidence.[101] For example, the testimony of a firearms expert that the markings on a particular shotgun shell are consistent with having been fired from the shotgun in question may support an inference that the shell is authentic.[102] Similarly, the testimony of an eyewitness to a bank robbery that he picked up a shotgun shell from the bank floor two minutes after the robbery is a sufficient showing of authenticity and identification of the shell. A lay witness's testimony based on his personal knowledge can sometimes be sufficient to authenticate even something as technologically sophisticated as an X-ray.[103]

In many instances, the "real" object that is relevant to the lawsuit is not available, but a similar object may be used for demonstrative purposes.[104] In a criminal case, the

---

is a suggestion the evidence has been tampered with or changed in some manner."). Although the majority in *Ennis* cited a previous court of appeals case for this rule, the liberal construction of Rule 901 does not require such a rule. Normally, authentication by testimony of a chain of custody applies only to fungible items that have no distinctive characteristics.

98. *See Gardner v. State*, 306 S.W.3d 274, 292 n.35 (Tex. Crim. App. 2009) (not necessary to prove chain of custody if witness can authenticate evidence by other means); *Hartsfield v. State*, 200 S.W.3d 813, 817-18 (Tex. App.—Texarkana 2006, pet. ref'd) (not necessary to prove chain of custody if item has distinct characteristics); *Ennis*, 71 S.W.3d at 812 (Cornelius, C.J., concurring) (not necessary to prove chain of custody "unless the contraband in question is fungible so that it can lose its identity if it is commingled with another fungible substance"; witnesses' direct testimony identifying exhibits of broken pieces of mirrors as "similar to the weapons" used by the prison inmate was sufficient authentication without proof of any chain of custody).

99. *See Fox v. Order of United Commercial Travelers of Am.*, 192 F.2d 844, 846 (5th Cir. 1951) ("A witness may testify to what he hears, feels, tastes, and smells, as well as to what he sees, and regardless of whether he sees anything.").

100. *See, e.g.*, *United States v. Rodriguez*, 968 F.2d 130, 143 (2d Cir. 1992) (witness's testimony about identification card was properly admitted, even though witness could not exactly recall name on card); *Pass v. Firestone Tire & Rubber Co.*, 242 F.2d 914, 918 (5th Cir. 1957) (witness could testify that he thought mechanic put air in tire, even though witness was not positive); *Silva v. State*, 989 S.W.3d 64, 68 (Tex. App.—San Antonio 1998, pet. ref'd) (authentication was sufficient, even though chain-of-custody witness could not be "absolutely certain" that tinfoil packets taken from defendant were those offered at trial).

101. *See* FED. R. EVID. 901(b)(1); TEX. R. EVID. 901(b)(1).

102. The standard of knowledge that the expert must satisfy is determined by Rule 702. Refer to *Article VII: Opinions & Expert Testimony*, *supra* p. 705.

103. *See, e.g.*, *Jones v. State*, 111 S.W.3d 600, 607 (Tex. App.—Dallas 2003, pet. ref'd) (because witness "knew about her injuries and the treatment and because the plate and screws were clearly evident in the x-rays, we conclude she had the requisite personal knowledge to state the x-rays accurately represent her injuries and the medical treatment she received"; however, "a trial court could potentially abuse its discretion by admitting witnesses' x-rays through them, because lay witnesses, even if the x-rays are their own, may not have the requisite personal knowledge to state the x-rays accurately represent the scenes or events they purport to portray").

104. *See, e.g.*, *Torres v. State*, 116 S.W.3d 208, 214-15 (Tex. App.—El Paso 2003, no pet.) (trial court did not abuse its discretion in allowing physician to use chicken bone to demonstrate the difference between ordinary and spiral fracture). *See generally* IMWINKELRIED, *supra* note 68, §4.07, at 128-33 (demonstrative evidence also includes litigation-bound exhibits, such as diagrams and models). As long as the sponsoring witness testifies that (1) using

demonstrative exhibit should be obtained from a source other than the defendant to avoid any unfair prejudice that could result from a showing that the defendant owned such an item.[105]

2. Rule 901(b)(2): Nonexpert opinion about handwriting. The long-standing rule in Texas has been that a witness can testify to a signature's genuineness when he has established his familiarity with the handwriting of the individual whose signature is at issue, regardless of whether the witness is an expert in handwriting.[106] A witness can acquire the necessary familiarity in several ways, most commonly by watching the person write or sign some other document.[107] Rule 901(b)(2) also permits such testimony from nonexperts but imposes a significant limitation. Under the rule, a lay witness cannot testify if he has gained familiarity with the handwriting in question for the current litigation.[108] Only an expert witness is allowed to give opinion testimony based on knowledge of a person's handwriting when the knowledge has been acquired solely for the current litigation.

---

the exhibit will help illustrate his testimony, (2) the exhibit depicts a certain scene or area, (3) the witness is familiar with the scene, thing, or area, and (4) the exhibit is a true, accurate, or fair depiction of the scene, thing, or area, the visual aid may be offered into evidence for demonstrative purposes. *See id.* §4.07[2], at 129, §4.07[4], at 131. For further discussion of the relevance of real and demonstrative evidence, refer to *Article IV: Relevance & Its Limits, supra* p. 235.

In a criminal case, for example, the police may never find the gun that an alleged robber used in a bank robbery. When this occurs, the trial judge will normally permit the bank teller to use a similar gun to illustrate his oral testimony. In *Simmons v. State*, the court of criminal appeals noted that it has long been the law that:

> [v]isual, real, or demonstrative evidence, regardless of which term is applied, is admissible upon the trial of a criminal case if it tends to solve some issue in the case and is relevant to the cause—that is, if it has evidentiary value, i.e., if it sheds light on the subject at hand.

622 S.W.2d 111, 113 (Tex. Crim. App. 1981). However, if the demonstrative exhibit is not an exact replica of the original item, the judge must determine whether the differences between the two items are so great that it would be unfair to admit one as being "similar" to the other. *Id.* For example, a trial judge would have discretion under Rule 403 to exclude the offer of a 12-inch butcher knife as demonstrative evidence when the original 4-inch paring knife used in the robbery was never recovered if the judge determined that the butcher knife's unfair prejudicial effect substantially outweighed its limited illustrative value. *See id.* at 113-14.

105. *See United States v. Warledo*, 557 F.2d 721, 725 (10th Cir. 1977) ("The courts have quite uniformly condemned the introduction in evidence of testimony concerning dangerous weapons, even though found in the possession of the defendant, which have nothing to do with the crime charged."); *see also Miskis v. State*, 756 S.W.2d 350, 351-52 (Tex. App.—Houston [14th Dist.] 1988, pet. ref'd) (trial court committed harmless error in admitting, as demonstrative evidence, hammer that was found in defendant's car but was not the same one used in aggravated robbery; hammer probably could have been used for demonstrative purposes if jury had not heard that it was taken from defendant's car).

106. *See Janak v. Sec. Lumber Co.*, 513 S.W.2d 300, 302 (Tex. Civ. App.—Houston [1st Dist.] 1974, no writ); *Burton v. Lowry*, 77 S.W.2d 1059, 1059 (Tex. Civ. App.—Fort Worth 1934, writ dism'd).

107. *See, e.g.*, *S. Kan. Ry. Co. v. Barnes*, 173 S.W. 880, 882 (Tex. Civ. App.—Amarillo 1915, writ ref'd) (witness could testify about whether handwriting was his brother's because witness had seen his brother write before). A witness may also gain knowledge of the handwriting of the person in question by demonstrating that he has carried on a correspondence or other exchange of writing with the author. *See Sartor v. Bolinger*, 59 Tex. 411, 415 (1883). The author's identity must be proved if the witness is not personally acquainted with the author. *Id.* at 416.

108. Tex. R. Evid. 901(b)(2); *see Acosta v. State*, 752 S.W.2d 706, 709 (Tex. App.—Corpus Christi 1988, pet. ref'd) (when no evidence shows that witness acquired familiarity with handwriting for purposes of litigation, proponent of document has met authentication requirement under Rule 901(b)(2)); *see, e.g.*, *Hunter v. State*, 513 S.W.3d 638, 641 (Tex. App.—Houston [14th Dist.] 2016, no pet.) (letters were properly authenticated under Rule 901(b)(2) through testimony of lay witness who saw defendant's handwriting every day; witness testified that she recognized defendant's handwriting in each of three letters and noted that defendant's handwriting varied from time to time).

Rule 901(b)(2) is identical to Federal Rule 901(b)(2); both Texas and federal courts have been liberal in permitting the authentication of handwriting by nonexpert testimony. Under the federal rule, knowledge of a person's writing can be acquired by any means acceptable to the trial judge as long as it was not acquired for the current litigation.[109] In ***Rogers v. Ritter***,[110] the U.S. Supreme Court held that a witness who has not seen the person in question write and who has not personally communicated with that person may nevertheless testify about the genuineness of that person's handwriting if the witness demonstrates some familiarity with it:

> [I]n the varied affairs of life there are many modes in which one person can become acquainted with the handwriting of another, besides having seen him write or corresponded with him. There is no good reason for excluding any of these modes ... and if the court, on the preliminary examination of the witness, can see that he has that degree of knowledge of the party's handwriting which will enable him to judge of its genuineness, he should be permitted to give to the jury his opinion on the subject.[111]

Despite the broad language of Texas Rule 901(b)(2) and the liberal construction given by the federal courts, Rule 602's personal-knowledge requirement could exclude a witness's testimony if the court is not satisfied that the witness has sufficient familiarity with the writer's handwriting to make a reasonable identification.[112]

3. Rule 901(b)(3): Comparison by an expert witness or the trier of fact. Rule 901(b)(3) permits real and demonstrative evidence to be identified by comparison with previ-

---

The rationale for excluding such litigation-oriented identification is that "[s]uch one-shot comparisons made for purposes of the litigation lack the extent of familiarity contemplated by 901(b)(2)." ***United States v. Pitts***, 569 F.2d 343, 348 (5th Cir. 1978).

   Texas common law merely required that the lay witness demonstrate familiarity with a person's handwriting before the witness could give an opinion on whether that person wrote the item in question. ***Garner v. State***, 100 Tex. Crim. 626, 628-29, 272 S.W. 167, 169 (1925); *see* ***Bodiford v. State***, 630 S.W.2d 847, 852 (Tex. App.—Fort Worth 1982, pet. ref'd) (only necessary that witness have had "ample opportunity to view or observe the other's handwriting or that the witness be referred to papers containing the questioned handwriting"). Accordingly, a sufficiently qualified lay witness at common law presumably could have testified to the genuineness of handwriting attributed to an individual, even when the witness had gained his familiarity in preparation for litigation.

   The 2015 restyling of Rule 901(b)(2) changed the phrase "for purposes of the litigation" to "for the current litigation." *See* TEX. R. EVID. 901(b)(2). Under the former rule, a possible point of ambiguity was the use of the article "the" in the phrase "for purposes of the litigation." *See* David W. McMorrow, Comment, *Authentication and the Best Evidence Rule Under the Federal Rules of Evidence*, 16 WAYNE L. REV. 195, 200 (1969). Although it might have been argued that familiarity acquired for purposes of any legal proceedings other than the present litigation is acceptable, the purpose behind the rule seemed to indicate that knowledge acquired because of any litigation was unacceptable. *See id.* The restyled rule clearly indicates that a nonexpert's familiarity acquired only for the current litigation is unacceptable.

   109. *See* 5 WEINSTEIN & BERGER, *supra* note 26, §901.04[1], at 901-42 to 901-43; McMorrow, *supra* note 108, at 200; *see, e.g.,* ***Ryan v. United States***, 384 F.2d 379, 380 (1st Cir. 1967) (witness who asserted general familiarity with defendant's handwriting could testify that defendant signed a certain check).

   110. 79 U.S. 317 (1871).

   111. *Id.* at 322.

   112. Nicholas F. LaRocca, Jr., Comment, *Authentication, Identification, and the Best Evidence Rule*, 36 LA. L. REV. 185, 197 (1975). Refer to *Article VI: Witnesses, supra* p. 567.

ously authenticated evidence. Using this procedure of identification, tread marks can be compared to the tire that allegedly caused the marks and bullets can be compared to the weapon that purportedly fired them. The most common example is the identification of an individual's signature by comparing it to signatures found on various other documents alleged to have been executed by that person.[113]

Before the enactment of Rule 901(b)(3), a party's right to prove the genuineness of disputed handwriting by comparison to another handwriting specimen was controlled by Texas Revised Civil Statutes article 3737b.[114] The statute required the trial judge to rule on whether the handwriting specimen was genuine before it could be compared with the handwriting in dispute.[115] Once the trial judge determined that the specimen was authentic, it was introduced into evidence so the jury could compare it to the disputed signature.[116] Rule 901(b)(3) extends the article 3737b admissibility standard for a handwriting sample—a finding by the trial court that the specimen is genuine—to all types of physical evidence.[117] This rule reflects the liberal view that allows juries to make nondocumentary comparisons, a position consistent with the growing use of nondocumentary evidence.[118] Therefore, all specimens sought to be introduced under the rule must be established as genuine to the court's satisfaction before the jury or a witness can use them for comparison. The trier of fact can properly make the comparison when the similarity of the items is obvious to a person of ordinary understanding; otherwise, an expert should conduct the comparison.[119]

The standard for authentication remains the same even if the specimen that the witness claims to have seen has been lost or destroyed.[120] The loss of the document merely

---

113. *See* LaRocca, *supra* note 112, at 197 & n.82.

114. Act of May 2, 1933, 43rd Leg., R.S., ch. 106, 1933 Tex. Gen. Laws 234 (former Texas Revised Civil Statutes art. 3737b deemed repealed as to civil proceedings effective 1983 and as to criminal proceedings effective 1986). The statute provided as follows:

> In the trial of any civil case, it shall be competent to give evidence of handwriting by comparison, made by experts or by the jury. The standard of comparison offered in evidence must be proved to the satisfaction of the judge to be genuine before allowing same to be compared with the handwriting in dispute.

Id.

115. *Nass v. Nass*, 149 Tex. 41, 46, 228 S.W.2d 130, 132 (1950).

116. *Id.*; *Alexander v. State*, 115 S.W.2d 1122, 1125-26 (Tex. Civ. App.—Amarillo 1938, writ ref'd); *Askins, Inc. v. Sparks*, 56 S.W.2d 279, 281 (Tex. Civ. App.—Beaumont 1933, writ ref'd).

117. *See* TEX. R. EVID. 901(b)(3).

118. *See Cantu v. State*, 141 Tex. Crim. 99, 105-06, 135 S.W.2d 705, 708-09 (1939) (proposing to allow ballistics comparison by jury with aid of microscope). *See generally* E. LeFevre, Annotation, *Expert Evidence—Identification of Gun*, 26 A.L.R.2d 892 (1952) (discussing ballistics investigations by experts).

119. *See, e.g., Logan v. State*, 48 S.W.3d 296, 301 (Tex. App.—Texarkana 2001) (trial court properly admitted inventory forms that defendant had purportedly signed and submitted for insurance claims on lost or damaged personal property because "the authenticity of the forms could have been established by the jury's comparison of the signatures on the inventory forms with other exhibits containing [defendant's] signature which were also admitted into evidence without challenge to their authenticity"), *aff'd*, 89 S.W.3d 619 (Tex. Crim. App. 2002).

120. *Gibralter Colo. Life Co. v. Taylor*, 132 Tex. 328, 334, 123 S.W.2d 318, 320-21 (1939); *Miller v. Miller*, 202 S.W.2d 859, 861 (Tex. Civ. App.—San Antonio 1947, no writ).

affords a legal basis for secondary evidence; the proponent of the document must still prove that it was genuine.[121]

Rule 901(b)(3) differs from Federal Rule 901(b)(3) in one minor respect. As discussed above, the Texas rule requires the party tendering a comparative specimen to demonstrate the specimen's genuineness before the jury may compare it to the document or object the proponent seeks to authenticate.[122] The federal rule, however, merely subjects the specimen to the same scrutiny as the evidence intended to be proved, thus requiring sufficient evidence to permit a jury to find that the specimen is what the proponent claims.[123] According to the drafters of the federal rule, requiring the judge to decide the question of genuineness and imposing a higher burden of persuasion,[124] as found in Texas Rule 901(b)(3), is unnecessary in view of the federal relevance requirements.[125] Federal Rule 403, like its Texas counterpart, provides for the exclusion of otherwise relevant evidence because of prejudice, confusion, or waste of time.[126]

The traditional objection to the federal approach is that the issue of the sample's genuineness raises a collateral issue that may mislead and confuse the jury.[127] Under the Texas rule, for example, the jury needs to determine only one issue: the authenticity of the disputed item. But under Federal Rule 901(b)(3), the jury must determine two issues: the authenticity of the sample and the authenticity of the disputed item. According to John Wigmore, the only practical solution is to have the judge determine the genuineness of the sample.[128]

---

121. *Gibralter*, 132 Tex. at 334, 123 S.W.2d at 320-21; *Miller*, 202 S.W.2d at 861.

122. *See, e.g.*, *Anderson v. State*, 461 S.W.3d 674, 677 (Tex. App.—Texarkana 2015, pet. ref'd) (parties stipulated to surveillance video's genuineness when they stipulated to its admissibility; preliminary question for trial court was "whether the still photographs were similar enough to the video-recorded images to permit the jury to reasonably infer that the still photographs are authentic"). Refer to notes 117-118 *supra* and accompanying text.

123. *See* FED. R. EVID. 901 advisory committee's note, subdiv. (b)(3) (rule sets no higher standard for handwriting); 5 WEINSTEIN & BERGER, *supra* note 26, §901.03[7][b], at 901-37 ("The requirements for authenticating the specimen are no more rigid than they are for the authentication of any other exhibit. Nor does it matter what type of evidence the specimen consists of; the requirements for authenticating all types of specimens, whether handwriting or other physical exhibits, are the same: prima facie proof that they are what their proponent claims them to be.").

124. *See* 5 WEINSTEIN & BERGER, *supra* note 36, ¶901(b)(3)[02], at 901-44 (proof of genuineness must be by clear and convincing evidence).

125. FED. R. EVID. 901 advisory committee's note, subdiv. (b)(3) (Federal Rule 901(b)(3) does not set higher standard for handwriting). The Advisory Committee also justified this rule on the grounds that higher standards are not required for unwritten evidence such as ballistics. *Id.* Jack Weinstein criticizes the committee's analogy, however, because ballistics cases almost always involve known sources (e.g., one bullet from a body or a wall and the other fired by the expert from a known gun). "Such precision in source determination is often missing where documents are involved." 5 WEINSTEIN & BERGER, *supra* note 36, ¶901(b)(3)[02], at 901-44 n.3; *see also* **United States v. Arce**, 997 F.2d 1123, 1128 (5th Cir. 1993) (drug ledgers were sufficiently authenticated as those maintained by drug dealer from witness's testimony that he worked for drug dealer, particular ledgers resembled those used by dealer, and handwriting on ledgers was similar to that of drug dealer, and from officers' testimony that they found ledgers at dealer's home).

126. For a discussion of the relevance counterfactors under Texas Rule 403, refer to *Article IV: Relevance & Its Limits, supra* p. 211.

127. 7 JOHN H. WIGMORE, EVIDENCE IN TRIALS AT COMMON LAW §2000, at 271 (Chadbourn rev. 1978).

128. *Id.* §2000, at 272.

4. Rule 901(b)(4): Distinctive characteristics & the like. Rule 901(b)(4), which is identical to Federal Rule 901(b)(4), permits tendered items to be admitted into evidence based on distinctive qualities that identify or authenticate them. The rule is aimed at permitting items to be authenticated by distinctive circumstantial evidence,[129] which is a well-established concept in Texas common law.[130] Thus, a document may be authenticated by distinctive characteristics such as its contents,[131] appearance,[132] and location.[133]

---

129. *See, e.g.*, **Tienda v. State**, 358 S.W.3d 633, 638 (Tex. Crim. App. 2012) (photographs, comments, and music from MySpace pages were "ample" circumstantial evidence to support finding that defendant created and maintained pages); **Druery v. State**, 225 S.W.3d 491, 502-03 (Tex. Crim. App. 2007) (trial judge properly admitted letter and envelope purportedly written by capital-murder defendant based on several distinct internal characteristics that, viewed together, were sufficient to support a finding that defendant wrote it); *cf.* **United States v. Newton**, 891 F.2d 944, 947 (1st Cir. 1989) (government's offer of unsigned and undated typewritten document seized from participant in marijuana-importation conspiracy, containing lists of defendant's aliases, Swiss banking officers, and account information, was sufficiently authenticated by circumstantial evidence); **United States v. Whitworth**, 856 F.2d 1268, 1283 (9th Cir. 1988) (authenticating letters by linking dates of postmarks with defendant's location on the days letters were mailed).

130. *See* **Borak v. Bridge**, 524 S.W.2d 773, 777 (Tex. Civ. App.—Corpus Christi 1975, writ ref'd n.r.e.) (proof of execution may be circumstantial).

131. In **Hislop v. State**, the trial court admitted a letter containing a confession purportedly written and signed by the murder defendant even though "[t]here was no handwriting comparison either by an expert, the trier of fact, or by a non-expert witness, and there was no testimony by a witness with knowledge." 64 S.W.3d 544, 545-46 (Tex. App.—Texarkana 2001, no pet.). The letter's contents, its location next to the couch where the defendant was lying, and other evidence that corroborated the letter's contents were sufficient circumstantial evidence to support a finding that the defendant wrote the letter. *Id.* at 546. When the trial court admitted the letter, there was also evidence that the defendant called a neighbor stating that his mother was dead and that he had stabbed her, and that the letter contained what appeared to be the defendant's signature as well as his correct home address. *Id.*; *see also* **Wood v. United States**, 84 F.2d 749, 751 (5th Cir. 1936) (taken as a whole, telegrams giving specific details were authenticated by their contents); **Int'l Harvester Co. v. Campbell**, 43 Tex. Civ. App. 421, 426, 96 S.W. 93, 95-96 (San Antonio 1906, no writ) (language of letter and other facts can authenticate letter).

132. *See, e.g.*, **United States v. Holladay**, 566 F.2d 1018, 1020 (5th Cir. 1978) ("The notebooks themselves demonstrate that they are a part of a single entry bookkeeping system ...."); **Fed. Trade Comm'n v. Hughes**, 710 F. Supp. 1520, 1522-23 (N.D. Tex. 1989) (using a company logo to authenticate); **Gunville v. Gonzales**, 508 S.W.3d 547, 559-60 (Tex. App.—El Paso 2016, no pet.) (witness statement was authenticated under Rule 901(b)(4) when it was on form from county sheriff's office and bore office's emblem and when former attorney for objecting party had previously filed business-records affidavit proving up identical witness statement); **E.P. Oper. Co. v. Sonora Expl. Corp.**, 862 S.W.2d 149, 154 (Tex. App.—Houston [1st Dist.] 1993, writ denied) (record of plaintiff corporation's land-contracts department was sufficiently authenticated when it had department title, fit internal patterns, and contained signature of appropriate employee).

133. *See, e.g.*, **Johnson v. State**, 208 S.W.3d 478, 499 (Tex. App.—Austin 2006, pet. ref'd) (proof was sufficient to authenticate anonymous letter as being written by capital-murder defendant when a draft of it was found on her computer and the letter contained "numerous intimate details of [her] life, confirmed by other evidence, that collectively support an inference that she was the author"). In **City of Corsicana v. Herod**, a consulting engineer was cross-examined at trial with a document that had been found in his file when the file was produced at his deposition. 768 S.W.2d 805, 814 (Tex. App.—Waco 1989, no writ). Although the witness did not believe that his office had produced the document and denied that the document had been in his file at the time relevant to the disputed issue, the appellate court held that the trial judge was not required to accept this denial for the following reason:

> Circumstances surrounding the document and its production were unusual enough that the court could have reasonably questioned [the witness's] denial of any knowledge about its authorship or source. It was found in the file of the person who designed the project described in the document; its contents substantially matched the substance of [his] direct testimony describing the project; and the document had a distinctive characteristic which connected it to [him].

Rule 901(b)(4) is not limited to writings.[134] Telephone conversations, for example, may be shown to have involved a particular person if the conversation discloses information known only to that person.[135] Audio or video recordings may be authenticated by testimony on their distinctive characteristics, internal patterns, and other factors.[136] Evidence may also be authenticated by distinctive characteristics such as fingerprints,[137] shoe marks, and palm prints.[138] Two other authentication methods are analyzing language patterns (such as spelling) to prove authorship[139] and analyzing interrogation response patterns to establish the authorship of a written confession.[140]

The admission of recordings under Rule 901 is somewhat problematic. Civil cases frequently rely solely on the common-law predicate for admitting recordings without mentioning Article IX.[141] The common-law predicate under ***Seymour v. Gillespie*** and ***Edwards v. State*** required a showing that (1) the recording device was capable of taking testimony, (2) the operator of the device was competent, (3) the recording was authentic and correct, (4) no changes, additions, or deletions had been made, (5) the manner of preservation of the recording had been sufficient, (6) the speakers were identified,

---

Id. at 815. Thus, even when the sponsoring witness denies authorship of a document, circumstantial evidence may sufficiently authenticate the evidence, leaving to the jury any lingering questions of authorship. In ***Herod***, the court noted that proof of the authenticity of the document may be shown by either direct or circumstantial evidence. *Id.* at 814.

134. *See* Tex. R. Evid. 901(b)(4) (allowing authentication of other offered evidence by characteristics of evidence); *cf.* Fed. R. Evid. 901 advisory committee's note, subdiv. (b)(4) ("The characteristics of the offered item itself, considered in the light of circumstances, afford authentication techniques in great variety.").

135. ***Gleason v. Davis***, 155 Tex. 467, 473, 289 S.W.2d 228, 232 (1956); ***Earnhart v. State***, 582 S.W.2d 444, 448-49 (Tex. Crim. App. 1979); ***Moore v. State***, 666 S.W.2d 632, 634 (Tex. App.—Houston [1st Dist.] 1984, no pet.); ***Tidwell v. State***, 646 S.W.2d 474, 476 (Tex. App.—Tyler 1982), *pet. ref'd*, 645 S.W.2d 297 (Tex. Crim. App. 1983); ***City of Ingleside v. Stewart***, 554 S.W.2d 939, 944 (Tex. Civ. App.—Corpus Christi 1977, writ ref'd n.r.e.); *see* ***Tex. Candy & Nut Co. v. Horton***, 235 S.W.2d 518, 521 (Tex. Civ. App.—Dallas 1950, writ ref'd n.r.e.) (if telephone conversation gives facts revealing the speaker's identity, telephone call is admissible); *see also* Black, *supra* note 39, at 1009 (Texas utilizes distinctive-characteristics authentication method).

136. *See* ***Angleton v. State***, 971 S.W.2d 65, 68 (Tex. Crim. App. 1998); *see, e.g.,* ***Thornton v. State***, 994 S.W.2d 845, 855 (Tex. App.—Fort Worth 1999, pet. ref'd) (edited transcript of videotaped conversation was properly admitted when witnesses testified about their comparison of original recording to written transcript and videotape itself had been authenticated).

137. *See, e.g.,* ***United States v. Patterson***, 277 F.3d 709, 712-14 (4th Cir. 2002) (Tenprinter image of defendant's fingerprints was admissible under Rule 901(b)(4); adequate foundation was provided by testimony that one of the fingerprints recorded by the Tenprinter matched the fingerprint recovered from a bag containing cocaine base).

138. *See, e.g.,* ***Xanthull v. State***, 403 S.W.2d 807, 809-10 (Tex. Crim. App. 1966) (palm prints); ***Matula v. State***, 390 S.W.2d 263, 266 (Tex. Crim. App. 1965) (fingerprints); ***Martinez v. State***, 169 Tex. Crim. 229, 232-33, 333 S.W.2d 370, 373 (1960) (shoe marks).

139. *See* Fed. R. Evid. 901 advisory committee's note, subdiv. (b)(4); *see, e.g.,* ***Magnuson v. State***, 203 N.W. 749, 750 (Wis. 1925) (evidence indicated that spelling on disputed bomb wrapper was characteristic of Swedish language and that defendant was the only Swede in neighborhood).

140. *See generally* Richard Arens & Arnold Meadow, *Psycholinguistics and the Confession Dilemma*, 56 Colum. L. Rev. 19, 23-37 (1956) (describing analysis of responses to interrogation to determine whether admissions of guilt were freely and voluntarily made). *But cf.* ***Ruckman v. State***, 109 S.W.3d 524, 530 (Tex. App.—Tyler 2000, pet. ref'd) (excluding expert testimony on possibility of false confession because scientific reliability was not sufficiently established).

141. *See, e.g.,* ***Campbell v. Salazar***, 960 S.W.2d 719, 731-32 (Tex. App.—El Paso 1997, pet. denied) (upholding admissibility of tape recording under seven-pronged ***Seymour*** test; no mention of Civil Rule 901); ***In re Thoma***, 873 S.W.2d 477, 486-87 (Tex. Rev. Trib. 1994, no appeal) (same).

and (7) the testimony elicited was voluntarily made.[142] In ***Kephart v. State***, the court of criminal appeals held that the party offering a videotape must provide a sponsoring witness who could testify "that the evidence is what its proponent says it is."[143] Because the State's sponsoring witness, a police officer who had simply found the videotape in the codefendant's motel room, had no personal knowledge of where or when the tape had been made, he could not state "that the tape accurately represented the actual scene or event at the time it occurred."[144] Thus, the tape recording was inadmissible, and the defendant's conviction was reversed.[145] The reasoning in ***Kephart*** suggested that the proponent could never authenticate a recording without the testimony of a sponsoring witness who either made the recording or participated in the recorded event.

This construction appeared to be contrary to the plain wording of the rule. In ***Angleton v. State***, the court of criminal appeals recognized that its decision in ***Kephart*** was overly restrictive.[146] The court stated that "attempting to cling to the ***Edwards*** test

---

142. ***Seymour v. Gillespie***, 608 S.W.2d 897, 898 (Tex. 1980); ***Edwards v. State***, 551 S.W.2d 731, 733 (Tex. Crim. App. 1977).

143. 875 S.W.2d 319, 321 (Tex. Crim. App. 1994), *overruled*, ***Angleton v. State***, 971 S.W.2d 65 (Tex. Crim. App. 1998); *see* TEX. R. EVID. 901(a). Refer to notes 31-46 *supra* and accompanying text.

144. ***Kephart***, 875 S.W.2d at 322-23. The tape purportedly depicted the defendant, her husband, and her eight-year-old child in her home and showed various drug paraphernalia and a white powdery substance. *Id.* at 320. Although the defendant initially appeared sober on the tape, she became increasingly disoriented and appeared to be under the influence of drugs. *Id.*

145. *Id.* at 322-23. Cases following ***Kephart*** include ***Porter v. State***, 969 S.W.2d 60, 66 (Tex. App.—Austin 1998, pet. ref'd) (owner of answering machine could authenticate message on machine although it sometimes skipped or dragged voices); ***Hooker v. State***, 932 S.W.2d 712, 716 (Tex. App.—Beaumont 1996, no pet.) (because officer testified that he was present when videotape was made, "he had personal knowledge of when and where the tape had been made and that the tape accurately represented the actual events at the time they occurred"), and ***Chatham v. State***, 889 S.W.2d 345, 348 (Tex. App.—Houston [14th Dist.] 1994, pet. ref'd) (when defendant identified his voice and his girlfriend's voice, sufficient authentication was made under the rule, even though he denied their purported conversation contained on tape recording).

146. ***Angleton v. State***, 971 S.W.2d 65, 69 (Tex. Crim. App. 1998). In ***Angleton***, the defendant sought release on pretrial bail and argued that the State's pretrial proof of capital murder was not "evident" because the trial court had relied on an audiotape that had not been properly authenticated under ***Kephart***. ***Angleton***, 971 S.W.2d at 66. The audiotape was purportedly a conversation between the defendant and his brother planning a murder. *Id.* The tape was found in the brother's possession when he was arrested. *Id.* The sponsoring witness was a police officer who was familiar with the voices of both men and identified their voices on the tape recording but had not been present during the conversation. *Id.* The court of criminal appeals stated that although pre-Rules Texas cases and ***Kephart*** had held that authentication of a tape recording required the testimony of a witness with personal knowledge of the accuracy of the recording, Rule 901 does not contain any such requirement. ***Angleton***, 971 S.W.2d at 68-69. Under Rule 901, a tape recording may be authenticated solely through circumstantial evidence, and the proponent of the tape may use several different methods under Rule 901 to establish different parts of the authentication predicate. ***Angleton***, 971 S.W.2d at 67-68; *see, e.g.,* ***Thierry v. State***, 288 S.W.3d 80, 89-90 (Tex. App.—Houston [1st Dist.] 2009, pet. ref'd) (copy of security-camera footage was authenticated through testimony of loss-prevention officer, even though he was not present during the incident; witness testified to security-taping operation, his review of tape recording immediately after robbery, and further review immediately before trial); ***Fluellen v. State***, 104 S.W.3d 152, 162 (Tex. App.—Texarkana 2003, no pet.) (authentication was sufficient when one of the participants in undercover drug-purchase conversation testified that he had listened to tape recording made by surveillance officer and that it accurately recorded the conversation witness had with defendant; "[w]here a participant can testify that the final product accurately portrays the interview, then it may be inferred that the operator [of the recording device] was competent"); *cf.* ***United States v. O'Connell***, 841 F.2d 1408, 1419-22 (8th Cir. 1988) (tape seized by police during execution of search warrant was properly authenticated by circumstantial evidence). Refer to note 37 *supra* and accompanying text.

after the enactment of Rule 901 will result in unwarranted confusion for practitioners, trial courts, and appellate courts. Rule 901 is straightforward, containing clear language and understandable illustrations. *Kephart* is overruled."[147] Under Rule 901(b)(4) and *Angleton*, a video or audio recording may be authenticated with evidence of its "appearance, contents, substance, internal patterns, or other distinctive characteristics."[148] Under more recent cases, authentication may be sufficient even if (1) the person who made the recording does not testify, (2) there is no testimony about the specific recording device or procedures, and (3) not all voices on the recording are identified, as long as the unidentified voices are not significant to the conversation.[149] If the sponsoring party does not satisfy the authentication requirements for one of the nonexclusive methods in Rule 901(b), the evidence could still be authenticated by using a different method or combination of methods under the rule.[150] Video and sound recordings have become so routinely admitted that the court of criminal appeals has held that a witness could testify to the contents of a video surveillance tape that he had destroyed after viewing it.[151]

Another traditional method of authentication permitted by Rule 901(b)(4) is the common-law reply-letter doctrine.[152] This doctrine, which Texas courts have long accepted, states that a letter received in the due course of mail purportedly in answer to another letter is prima facie genuine and admissible without further proof of authenticity.[153] A reply letter needs no further authentication because it is unlikely that

---

147. *Angleton*, 971 S.W.2d at 69; *see Fowler v. State*, 517 S.W.3d 167, 173 n.12 (Tex. App.—Texarkana 2017, pet. filed 4-19-17) ("*Angleton* made clear that the Court of Criminal Appeals firmly believes Rule 901 speaks for itself when it states that the proponent of evidence must demonstrate that the evidence 'is what the proponent claims it is.' It is our belief that *Kephart* was overruled primarily because of its improper incorporation of caselaw in its analysis that existed prior to the adoption of the Rules.").

148. TEX. R. EVID. 901(b)(4); *see Angleton*, 971 S.W.2d at 68.

149. *See* TEX. R. EVID. 901(b)(5), (b)(9); *see, e.g., Jones v. State*, 80 S.W.3d 686, 688-89 (Tex. App.—Houston [1st Dist.] 2002, no pet.) (court was "unwilling to read into [Rule 901] a requirement that each person, no matter how irrelevant to the case, be identified by name"; authentication of recording sufficient when informer identified, on tape, his own voice, and that of defendant and "Kingpin"; although informant did not know name of black female whose voice appeared on tape, there was no evidence that she played any part in the recorded drug transaction). Refer to notes 182-191, 240-256 *infra* and accompanying text.

150. *See Angleton*, 971 S.W.2d at 68-69 (audiotape was authenticated circumstantially under Rule 901(b)(1), (b)(4), and (b)(5)). For example, recordings are sometimes authenticated by evidence about a process or system under Rule 901(b)(9). Refer to notes 240-256 *infra* and accompanying text.

151. *Wood v. State*, 18 S.W.3d 642, 647 (Tex. Crim. App. 2000). In this capital-murder case, the defendant's brother testified that the defendant returned home after robbing and killing a gas-station attendant and played a stolen video surveillance tape that showed the defendant and his codefendant committing the robbery-murder. *Id.* After the witness viewed the tape, he destroyed it with a blowtorch. *Id.* Because the witness was shown the video by his brother and he recognized both his brother and the codefendant on the tape, this testimony was sufficient to authenticate its contents. *Id.*

152. *See* 5 WEINSTEIN & BERGER, *supra* note 26, §901.04[3][c], at 901-51 to 901-52; Goode, *supra* note 63, at 27.

153. *Nat'l Mut. Acc. Ins. v. Davis*, 46 S.W.2d 351, 352 (Tex. Civ. App.—Amarillo 1932, no writ); *see W. Union Tel. Co. v. Sharp*, 5 S.W.2d 567, 568-69 (Tex. Civ. App.—Texarkana 1928, no writ); *cf. Consol. Grocery Co. v. Hammond*, 175 F. 641, 645 (5th Cir. 1910) (letter written in reply to previous letter can be treated as genuine if there is proof that the previous letter was written and mailed before reply letter); *Scofield v. Parlin & Orendorff Co.*, 61 F. 804, 806 (7th Cir. 1894) (letter received in due course by mail, especially in response to earlier letter, is presumptively the letter of person who signed it).

anyone other than the purported writer would know of and respond to the contents of the earlier letter addressed to him.[154] The reply-letter doctrine has also been applied to telegrams[155] and e-mails.[156]

E-mails and other types of electronic evidence such as instant messages, text messages, chat-room conversations, and websites are frequently authenticated under Rule 901(b)(4) by evidence of their distinctive characteristics.[157] They may be authenticated by "appearance, contents, substance, internal patterns, or other distinctive characteristics of the item, taken together with all the circumstances."[158]

(1) E-mails. To determine the authenticity of e-mails, courts should consider the following factors: (1) the return-address line, (2) the date and time of the correspondence, (3) the subject line, (4) the contents and context, (5) internal characteristics such as known spelling or grammatical usage, nicknames, or specialized terms, and (6) any other circumstances, such as conversations or events either before or after the e-mail that tend to make it more likely that the message came from a certain person.[159] The

154. 5 WEINSTEIN & BERGER, *supra* note 36, ¶901(b)(4)[05], at 901-76. However, the reply-letter doctrine may be limited to letters on letterhead or stationery. *See id.*

155. *See Menefee v. Bering Mfg. Co.*, 166 S.W. 365, 366 (Tex. Civ. App.—Fort Worth 1914, no writ). Other jurisdictions have argued that telegrams should not be subject to the reply-letter doctrine because telegraph-company employees are privy to the contents of the first telegram and because misdelivery of telegrams is more common than misdelivery of letters. *See Smith v. Easton*, 54 Md. 138, 145-46 (1880); *Howley v. Whipple*, 48 N.H. 487, 488 (1869). Charles McCormick agrees with the Texas view that the inference of authenticity of the reply telegram is substantial and sufficient. *See* 2 McCORMICK ON EVIDENCE, *supra* note 19, §224, at 66.

156. *Manuel v. State*, 357 S.W.3d 66, 75 (Tex. App.—Tyler 2011, pet. ref'd); 2 McCORMICK ON EVIDENCE, *supra* note 19, §224, at 66; *see Varkonyi v. State*, 276 S.W.3d 27, 35 (Tex. App.—El Paso 2008, pet. ref'd); Goode, *supra* note 63, at 26-27; *see, e.g., United States v. Siddiqui*, 235 F.3d 1318, 1322-23 (11th Cir. 2000) (authentication of e-mail was sufficient when it contained sender's e-mail address and when witness testified that he replied to sender at same address, that e-mail message contained information unique to sender, and that sender made the same requests over the telephone that he made in e-mail); *see also Fenje v. Feld*, 301 F. Supp. 2d 781, 809 (N.D. Ill. 2003) ("E-mail communications may be authenticated as being from the purported author based on an affidavit of the recipient; the e-mail address from which it originated; comparison of the content to other evidence; and/or statements or other communications from the purported author acknowledging the e-mail communication that is being authenticated."), *aff'd*, 398 F.3d 620 (7th Cir. 2005); *Slay v. Spell*, 882 So. 2d 254, 259 (Miss. Ct. App. 2004) (health department's field inspectors were required to submit weekly "kill reports" for each hog-packing plant they inspected; reports were prepared on-site and e-mailed to department's main headquarters; the unsigned e-mails were authenticated by custodian and were admissible as government records prepared in the regular course of business).

157. *See* Goode, *supra* note 63, at 25-33 (discussing various authentication requirements and procedures for electronic evidence under the Federal Rules of Evidence); Leah Voigt Romano, *Developments in the Law: Electronic Discovery: VI. Electronic Evidence and the Federal Rules*, 38 LOY. L.A. L. REV. 1745, 1748-69 (2005) (same).

158. TEX. R. EVID. 901(b)(4); *see Tienda v. State*, 358 S.W.3d 633, 641-42 (Tex. Crim. App. 2012) ("That an email on its face purports to come from a certain person's email address, that the respondent in an internet chat room dialogue purports to identify himself, or that a text message emanates from a cell phone number assigned to the purported author—none of these circumstances, without more, has typically been regarded as sufficient to support a finding of authenticity."); *Campbell v. State*, 382 S.W.3d 545, 549 (Tex. App.—Austin 2012, no pet.) (authentication issue that commonly arises with electronic communications is whether message is sufficiently linked to purported author); Jonathan J. Bates, *Social Media & Family Law*, THE ADVOCATE: STATE BAR LITIG. SECTION REPORT, Fall 2012, at 59, 61 ("In some instances, additional [authentication] evidence may be required, such as evidence regarding the Internet Protocol address (the unique address assigned at a given time to a computer connected to the Internet).").

159. *See Shea v. State*, 167 S.W.3d 98, 104-05 (Tex. App.—Waco 2005, pet. ref'd); *Massimo v. State*, 144 S.W.3d 210, 216 (Tex. App.—Fort Worth 2004, no pet.); *see, e.g., Commonwealth v. Purdy*, 945 N.E.2d 372, 381-82 (Mass.

testimony of a witness familiar with the transmission process may also be sufficient to authenticate an electronic message, as there are many ways to trace e-mail transmissions to their origin.[160]

(2) Instant messages & text messages. Instant messages and text messages can be authenticated like e-mails.[161] Instant messages may be sent over a computer, a cellular tele-

---

2011) (e-mails were sufficiently authenticated when defendant acknowledged using the account and owning the computer from which they were sent; at least one message contained an attached photograph of defendant); *Varkonyi*, 276 S.W.3d at 34-35 (in obscenity trial, defendant's e-mail was authenticated under Rule 901(b)(4) because it was sent in direct response to undercover officer's e-mail asking for the video "you showed us" and contained the video that defendant showed to officers at his home); *cf.* **United States v. Safavian**, 435 F. Supp. 2d 36, 39-41 (D.D.C. 2006) (e-mails could be authenticated by their distinctive characteristics, such as addresses, name of sender, and descriptive contents; other e-mails that did not contain the same address could be authenticated under Federal Rule 901(b)(3) by comparing the content of the known e-mails with the content of e-mails sent from an alternate address; the fact that some e-mails contained embedded or forwarded e-mails went to the weight of the testimony, not its admissibility). In *Shea*, the complainant testified that she was familiar with the defendant's e-mail address, having received the six e-mails in question from the defendant. 167 S.W.3d at 105. The complainant testified that the content of the e-mails was similar to telephone conversations she had had with the defendant. *Id.* Two of the e-mails referred to the defendant's occupation as a furniture maker. *Id.* Four of the e-mails were signed "Kev," and the defendant's first name was Kevin. *Id.* Although the complainant received the e-mails in question from two different e-mail addresses, she testified that the defendant would call to confirm that she had received the e-mails. *Id.* The complainant's testimony authenticated the e-mails under Rule 901(b)(1), and the content and substance of the e-mails also sufficiently authenticated them under Rule 901(b)(4). *Shea*, 167 S.W.3d at 105; *see* TEX. R. EVID. 901(b)(1), (b)(4).

Similarly, in **Massimo**, the defendant's e-mail was properly authenticated by showing that it was sent to the victim's e-mail address shortly after she and the defendant had a physical altercation and showing that the e-mail referenced this altercation. 144 S.W.3d at 216. The victim recognized the e-mail as coming from the defendant's usual address because she had received e-mails from the defendant before from this address, and the contents and style of the e-mails were consistent with how the defendant communicated. *Id.* The victim also testified that only the defendant and a few others knew about the subject matter discussed in the e-mail. *Id.* A witness testified that she saw the defendant send another life-threatening e-mail to the victim using the same vulgarities, although from a different e-mail address. *Id.* The defendant also told a second witness that she was sending the threatening e-mail because she and the victim did not like each other. *Id.*

160. *See* **Lorraine v. Markel Am. Ins.**, 241 F.R.D. 534, 555 (D. Md. 2007) ("The most frequent ways to authenticate e-mail evidence are [Federal Rule] 901(b)(1) (person with personal knowledge), 901(b)(3) (expert testimony or comparison with authenticated exemplar), 901(b)(4) (distinctive characteristics, including circumstantial evidence), 902(7) (trade inscriptions), and 902(11) (certified copies of business record)."); **Clement v. Cal. Dep't of Corr.**, 220 F. Supp. 2d 1098, 1111 (N.D. Cal. 2002) ("[M]ajor e-mail providers include a coded Internet Protocol address (IP address) in the header of every e-mail. The IP address allows the recipient of an e-mail to identify the sender by contacting the service provider."), *aff'd*, 364 F.3d 1148 (9th Cir. 2004); Goode, *supra* note 63, at 10 (major authentication issue with e-mails is establishing authorship; authorship is usually established through testimony of witness with personal knowledge).

161. *See* **Manuel**, 357 S.W.3d at 75; Goode, *supra* note 63, at 31; Pierre Grosdidier, *Authenticating: Can Cellphone Text Messages Stand Up in Court?*, 79 TEX. B.J. 278, 278 (2016); *see also* **In re F.P.**, 878 A.2d 91, 95 (Pa. Super. Ct. 2005) ("[A]ppellant would have us create a whole new body of law just to deal with e-mails or instant messages. ... We believe that e-mail messages and similar forms of electronic communication can be properly authenticated within the existing framework of Pa.R.E. 901 and Pennsylvania case law."). In **In re F.P.**, the recipient (Z.G.) printed the instant messages from his computer. 878 A.2d at 94. Z.G. testified that he believed that the other participant in the conversation was the appellant. *Id.* A friend of the two boys testified that the appellant was angry when a DVD he had rented "went missing," because he had to pay for it. *Id.* Throughout the instant messages, the appellant threatened Z.G. and accused him of stealing the DVD from him. *Id.* Z.G. went to school counselors, who "mediated" the dispute between the two boys over the messages. *Id.* During those sessions, the appellant did not deny sending the instant messages. *Id.* Shortly before Z.G. was assaulted, he received a new instant message from the same screen name again threatening to assault him. *Id.* at 94-95. The court held there was sufficient circumstantial evidence to show that the appellant sent the messages: (1) he referred to himself by his first name, (2) he repeatedly accused Z.G. of stealing from him, which mirrored testimony that the appellant was angry with Z.G., (3) the instant messages re-

RULE 901

phone, or another handheld communication device. Text messages are sent from the cellular telephone with the number identified on the messages and received on the telephone associated with the number to which they are sent.[162] Because cellular telephones are sometimes used by people other than the owners, establishing authorship is a difficulty that arises in authenticating instant messages and text messages.[163] Thus, authentication requires more than mere confirmation that a telephone number or an e-mail address belongs to a specific person; circumstantial evidence tending to corroborate the sender's identity is required.[164] Instant messages sometimes pose an additional authentication problem because one mode of preserving them is by copying and pasting the original messages into a word-processing program.[165] Such copying and pasting would permit the recipient to alter the instant messages without detection.[166] However, the testimony of a participant in an instant-message conversation can be sufficient to authenticate transcripts of the conversation.[167]

---

ferred to Z.G. approaching high school authorities about the dispute, and (4) the sender repeatedly threatened to beat up Z.G. *Id.* at 95. "All of this evidence, taken together, was clearly sufficient to authenticate the instant message transcripts as having originated from appellant." *Id.* With instant messages, as with e-mail, the authentication "foundation may consist of circumstantial evidence and may include factors relating to the contents of the writing and the events before and after the execution of the writing." *Id.*; *see* Goode, *supra* note 63, at 31-33.

162. ***Commonwealth v. Koch***, 39 A.3d 996, 1004-05 (Pa. Super. Ct. 2011), *aff'd by an equally divided court*, 106 A.3d 705 (Pa. 2014); *see **Butler v. State***, 459 S.W.3d 595, 600 (Tex. Crim. App. 2015).

163. *See **Commonwealth v. Koch***, 106 A.3d 705, 712-13 (Pa. 2014); ***Butler***, 459 S.W.3d at 601; Grosdidier, *supra* note 161, at 278.

164. *See **State v. Koch***, 334 P.3d 280, 288 (Idaho 2014) ("[E]stablishing the identity of the author of a text message ... through the use of corroborating evidence is critical to satisfying the authentication requirement for admissibility."); ***Tienda v. State***, 358 S.W.3d 633, 642 (Tex. Crim. App. 2012) ("[T]hat a text message emanates from a cell phone number assigned to the purported author ..., without more, has [not] typically been regarded as sufficient to support a finding of authenticity."); Grosdidier, *supra* note 161, at 278 ("Authenticating cellphone text message authorship ... requires something more than establishing originating cellphone authorship. But ... that 'something more' is not very demanding under Rule 901(b)(4)."); *see, e.g.*, ***People v. Chromik***, 946 N.E.2d 1039, 1056-57 (Ill. App. Ct. 2011) (trial court did not err in admitting transcript of text messages when defendant "acknowledged the accuracy of a number of the messages" and recipient of messages testified about their contents); ***Dickens v. State***, 927 A.2d 32, 36-37 (Md. Ct. Spec. App. 2007) (text messages from defendant were sufficiently authenticated because they contained details that few people besides defendant were likely to know and mentioned defendant's daughter with victim); ***State v. Taylor***, 632 S.E.2d 218, 230-31 (N.C. Ct. App. 2006) (text messages sent by murder victim were sufficiently authenticated because victim identified himself and mentioned the kind of car he drove); ***State v. Thompson***, 777 N.W.2d 617, 626 (N.D. 2010) (trial court did not err in allowing testimony about text messages that were sent by defendant and were sufficiently authenticated under N.D. R. EVID. 901(b)(1) and 901(b)(4); defendant's husband, the recipient of the text messages, testified that he was familiar with her cell-phone number and her message signature); ***Butler***, 459 S.W.3d at 604 (timing of phone call by defendant to witness, in between text messages, supported conclusion that defendant was author of text messages); *see also* ***Koch***, 106 A.3d at 713-14 (trial court did not abuse its discretion in determining that prosecution met its authentication burden for text messages sent from cell phone that defendant admitted she owned).

165. *See* Nicole Cohen, Note, *Using Instant Messages as Evidence to Convict Criminals in Light of National Security: Issues of Privacy and Authentication*, 32 NEW ENG. J. ON CRIM. & CIV. CONFINEMENT 313, 328 (2006). Instant messages are often "lost forever" once the dialog box is closed unless one of the users saves it to a disk or to a log on his computer. *Id.* at 317.

166. *Id.* at 328-29; *see also* Goode, *supra* note 63, at 7-8 (electronic evidence raises concerns about tampering, but heightened evidentiary standards would be counterproductive; these concerns should be addressed and investigated during discovery).

167. *E.g.*, ***United States v. Lanzon***, 639 F.3d 1293, 1300-01 (11th Cir. 2011) (police detective's testimony that he participated in instant-message conversations and that transcripts were accurate records of those conversations was

(3) Chat-room conversations. Internet chat-room conversations can be authenticated like e-mails and instant messages,[168] but the process becomes more complex because chat-room participants frequently use pseudonyms for screen names.[169] The primary authentication issue in this context is a prima facie showing of the chat-room participant's identity.[170] The connection between a particular posting and a specific person can be established if (1) the screen name can be traced to the identified person, who has previously used that screen name in chat-room conversations, (2) the identified person responded to a request for a meeting with the person using a specific screen name, (3) the person using the screen name identified himself, and other information such as a street address, e-mail address, job, or personal description supports that self-identification, (4) the identified person had information given to the chat-room participant using the screen name, or (5) a search of the identified person's hard drive shows that the user of that computer used the same screen name as the chat-room participant.[171] The testimony of a participant in a chat-room conversation can also be sufficient to authenticate transcripts of the conversation.[172]

---

sufficient to authenticate the transcripts); **People v. Pierre**, 838 N.Y.S.2d 546, 548-49 (N.Y. App. Div. 2007) (accomplice-witness testified to defendant's instant-messaging screen name, and witness testified that she sent a message to that screen name and received a reply, "the content of which made no sense unless it was sent by defendant").

168. *See* Goode, *supra* note 63, at 31-32.

169. *Lorraine v. Markel Am. Ins.*, 241 F.R.D. 534, 556 (D. Md. 2007).

170. *See* Goode, *supra* note 63, at 18, 31-33.

171. *See United States v. Tank*, 200 F.3d 627, 630-31 (9th Cir. 2000); *United States v. Simpson*, 152 F.3d 1241, 1249-50 (10th Cir. 1998). In *Tank*, the defendant was convicted of several crimes related to child pornography. 200 F.3d at 629. The evidence showed that he belonged to the "Orchid Club" chat-room group, in which members discussed, traded, and produced child pornography. *Id.* A search of a coconspirator's computer revealed text files of "recorded" chat-room discussions that took place among members of the Orchid Club and implicated the defendant. *Id.* The defendant objected that there was no foundation to admit the printouts of the chat-room log because (1) they were not complete and (2) the codefendant could have made undetectable "material alterations," such as changes in the substance of the chat-room logs or the names appearing in them. *Id.* at 630. The district court held that these objections went to the weight of the evidence, not its admissibility, and admitted the evidence. *Id.* Further, when arrested, the defendant possessed ZIP files containing pornographic images of children that he had distributed in the Orchid Club chat room. *Id.* at 629-30. The prosecution proved that the defendant participated in the chat room when the defendant and his coconspirator admitted that the defendant used the screen name "Cessna," which appeared in the chat-room printouts. *Id.* at 630. Finally, the codefendants testified that when they arranged a meeting with "Cessna," the defendant attended. *Id.* at 630-31. Likewise, in *Simpson*, the defendant was convicted of receiving child pornography based on image files obtained from his computer during a search. 152 F.3d at 1243-44. A computer printout of a chat-room discussion between the defendant and an undercover officer was properly authenticated:

> In the printout of the chat room discussion, the individual using the identity "Stavron" gave Detective Rehman his name as B. Simpson and his correct street address. The discussion and subsequent e-mail exchanges indicated an e-mail address which belonged to Simpson. And the pages found near the computer in Simpson's home and introduced as evidence ... contain a notation of the name, street address, e-mail address, and telephone number that Detective Rehman gave to the individual in the chat room.

Id. at 1249-50; *see* FED. R. EVID. 901(a).

172. *E.g.*, *United States v. Barlow*, 568 F.3d 215, 220 (5th Cir. 2009) (court did not err in admitting transcripts of chat-room conversations when witness testified that transcripts fairly and fully reproduced conversations between her and defendant); *Tank*, 200 F.3d at 630 (testimony by witness who created chat-room transcripts about how he created them and statement that printouts "appeared to be an accurate representation of the chat room conversations" was sufficient to authenticate transcripts); *Jackson v. State*, 320 S.W.3d 13, 18 (Ark. Ct. App. 2009) (trial court

(4) Websites. Websites, which can be authenticated under Rule 901(b)(1),[173] can also be authenticated by evidence of their distinctive characteristics.[174] The nature of the type and quality of evidence required to authenticate that the website and the information obtained from the website is what it purports to be varies with the nature of the website.[175] For example, information downloaded from an established website of a well-recognized business is likely to need less proof to meet authentication requirements than information downloaded from an obscure organization.[176] Furthermore, the nature of the website information and the purpose for which it is offered may affect its admissibility.[177]

For websites containing social-media profiles, authentication is often accomplished through photos, background information, commentary, and other distinctive characteristics of the user.[178] Thus, to authenticate the social-networking profile of a party or witness, the party offering the evidence must demonstrate the connection between the party or witness and the profile:

> For example, a distinctive nickname that doubles as an online pseudonym, photos depicting the user or witness, comments unique to the individual, and references in the profile to groups or causes with which the person is affiliated are all valid and effective ways of showing these [connections between the in-

---

did not abuse its discretion in admitting chat-room transcripts that were sufficiently authenticated by testimony of police detective who participated in conversation and by defendant's signature on portion of transcript); ***Ford v. State***, 617 S.E.2d 262, 265-66 (Ga. Ct. App. 2005) (trial court did not abuse its discretion in admitting chat-room transcripts that were sufficiently authenticated by testimony of police detective who was present while conversation was taking place).

173. Refer to notes 78-87 *supra* and accompanying text.

174. Goode, *supra* note 63, at 29; *see* ***Ciampi v. City of Palo Alto***, 790 F. Supp. 2d 1077, 1091-92 (N.D. Cal. 2011); ***Lorraine***, 241 F.R.D. at 555-56; Browning, *supra* note 67, at 479; *see, e.g.*, ***Perfect 10, Inc. v. Cybernet Ventures, Inc.***, 213 F. Supp. 2d 1146, 1153-54 (C.D. Cal. 2002) (plaintiff's exhibits printed off the Internet were sufficiently authenticated by declaration that exhibits were true and correct copies of the originals, "particularly in combination with circumstantial indicia of authenticity (such as the dates and web addresses)"); ***Madison One Holdings, LLC v. Punch Int'l***, No. 4:06-CV-3560 (S.D. Tex. 2009) (no pub.; 3-31-09) (presence of company's logo, web address, and date that website was accessed were "circumstantial factors" sufficient to authenticate printouts of press releases from company's website).

175. Goode, *supra* note 63, at 29.

176. *Id.* at 29-31; *see, e.g.*, ***Williams Farms Produce Sales, Inc. v. R&G Produce Co.***, 443 S.W.3d 250, 259 & n.7 (Tex. App.—Corpus Christi 2014, no pet.) (docket sheet printed from uscourts.gov website was self-authenticating under Rule 902(5) but could have been internally authenticated under Rule 901(b)(4)).

177. Goode, *supra* note 63, at 29. Thus, information offered for nonhearsay purposes will encounter fewer evidentiary hurdles than information offered for its truth. *Id.* at 29-30; *see* ***Perfect 10***, 213 F. Supp. 2d at 1155 ("[Defendant] objects to the printouts from third-party websites as a violation of the rule against hearsay. To the extent these images and text are being introduced to show the images and text found on the websites, they are not statements at all—and thus fall outside the ambit of the hearsay rule."); *see, e.g.*, ***Hall v. State***, 283 S.W.3d 137, 149 & n.13 (Tex. App.—Austin 2009, pet. ref'd) (State introduced evidence from defendant's Facebook page to advance theory that she "reveled in the role of the gangster's girlfriend and shared [her boyfriend's] dark traits" without authentication objections).

178. Browning, *supra* note 67, at 480-81; *see* ***Griffin v. State***, 19 A.3d 415, 424 (Md. 2011) ("The potential for abuse and manipulation of a social networking site by someone other than its purported creator and/or user leads to our conclusion that a printout of an image from such a site requires a greater degree of authentication than merely identifying the date of birth of the creator and her visage in a photograph on the site ....").

dividual and the evidence being offered]. More connections increase the likelihood that evidence offered will be authenticated.[179]

This evidence is necessary because anyone can establish a fictitious social-media profile under any name, and anyone who has access to a user's login information and password can send messages from that account.[180] Social-media profiles can also be revised at any time, which further complicates the authentication process for this type of evidence.[181]

5. Rule 901(b)(5): Opinion about a voice. Rule 901(b)(5) codifies the long-standing common-law principle that a voice can be identified by any person who is familiar with both the alleged speaker's voice and the voice to be identified.[182] Texas courts have liberally construed the familiarity requirement and have permitted voice-identification testimony upon proof of "any previous acquaintance" with the individual.[183] The witness can testify even if he heard the person's voice only once before the time in question,[184] and the witness's familiarity may be acquired by either a telephone conversation or personal contact.[185]

---

179. Browning, *supra* note 67, at 484; *see, e.g.,* **Tienda v. State**, 358 S.W.3d 633, 645 (Tex. Crim. App. 2012) (trial court did not abuse its discretion in admitting printouts from MySpace pages with sufficient distinctive characteristics to establish that defendant created them; pages contained photos of defendant, references to murder victim's death, details of shooting, mentions of defendant's gang, and references to defendant's widely known nickname); **Campbell v. State**, 382 S.W.3d 545, 551-52 (Tex. App.—Austin 2012, no pet.) (trial court did not err in admitting printouts of Facebook messages; recipient testified about messages' origin, and messages used defendant's unique speech pattern and referenced incidents that few people would have known about); **Rene v. State**, 376 S.W.3d 302, 307 (Tex. App.—Houston [14th Dist.] 2012, pet. ref'd) (trial court did not abuse its discretion in admitting printouts of photographs from MySpace pages; defendant appeared "in nearly every photograph posted on this profile" and displayed distinctive tattoos, and everything shown by photographs was also shown by other evidence admitted without objection).

180. **Campbell**, 382 S.W.3d at 550; *e.g.,* **Dering v. State**, 465 S.W.3d 668, 671-72 (Tex. App.—Eastland 2015, no pet.) (Facebook posts offered by defendant as offer of proof in motion to transfer venue were not sufficiently authenticated; because posts were not made or sent by defendant and original post was created by third party who did not testify, names and photos as shown on accounts were not sufficient to support finding of authenticity of ownership).

181. Lawrence Morales II, *Social Media Evidence: "What You Post or Tweet Can & Will Be Used Against You in a Court of Law,"* THE ADVOCATE: STATE BAR LITIG. SECTION REPORT, Fall 2012, at 32, 36.

182. *See* 7 WIGMORE, *supra* note 127, §2155.

183. **Locke v. State**, 453 S.W.2d 484, 485 (Tex. Crim. App. 1970); **Bishop v. State**, 160 Tex. Crim. 333, 337, 269 S.W.2d 372, 374 (1954); *see also* **Massey v. State**, 160 Tex. Crim. 49, 53-54, 266 S.W.2d 880, 883 (1954) (identification can be based on contact that occurred at any time).

184. **Locke**, 453 S.W.2d at 485; **Bishop**, 160 Tex. Crim. at 337, 269 S.W.2d at 374; *e.g.,* **Williams v. State**, 747 S.W.2d 812, 812-13 (Tex. App.—Dallas 1986, no pet.) (voice authentication was sufficient even though witness had heard defendant's voice only once before anonymous telephone call was made); *see, e.g.,* **Diamond v. State**, 496 S.W.3d 124, 141-42 (Tex. App.—Houston [14th Dist.] 2016, pet. ref'd) (police officer's testimony that he was familiar with defendant's voice and that voice in telephone calls belonged to defendant was sufficient to authenticate phone calls, even though familiarity was gained through one 22-minute interrogation). For an interesting article casting doubt on the reliability of voice identification by a witness who has limited knowledge of or exposure to the speaker's voice, see Lawrence M. Solan & Peter M. Tiersma, *Hearing Voices: Speaker Identification in Court*, 54 HASTINGS L.J. 373 (2002-03).

185. **Massey**, 160 Tex. Crim. at 53-54, 266 S.W.2d at 883. In one case, the witness was allowed to identify the screams of someone she knew. **France v. State**, 148 Tex. Crim. 341, 347, 187 S.W.2d 80, 83 (1945).

Rule 901(b)(5) is identical to Federal Rule 901(b)(5), which has been similarly interpreted. The Fifth Circuit has stated that only a "minimal showing" of familiarity with the voice is necessary for authentication.[186] The witness may even gain familiarity with the alleged speaker's voice solely for the purpose of litigation.[187] Furthermore, the rule requires only a minimal level of familiarity with the voice, not certainty; any objections based on the extent or "freshness" of that familiarity go to the weight of the testimony rather than its admissibility.[188]

The rule also provides that a voice heard indirectly through "mechanical or electronic transmission or recording" can be identified in the same way as a voice heard in person.[189] Accordingly, a witness who can establish sufficient prior familiarity with an individual's voice may identify that person from a recording.[190] The identity of a telephone caller can be authenticated by self-identification coupled with additional circumstances such as the content and timing of the call, the contents of the statement, and disclosure of facts known peculiarly to the speaker. A recording of people speaking, such as a telephone conversation, an undercover surveillance recording, or an informer's "wired" conversation, may be authenticated by voice identification under this provision without also having to prove a chain of custody for the recording.[191]

6. Rule 901(b)(6): Evidence about a telephone conversation. The identification of parties to telephone conversations under Rule 901(b)(6), which is identical to Federal Rule 901(b)(6), is closely related to the identification of voices under Rule 901(b)(5). Traditionally, Texas courts have admitted testimony about the content of telephone conversations once the proponent of the testimony has established the identity of the

---

186. ***United States v. Cuesta***, 597 F.2d 903, 915 (5th Cir. 1979); *see also **United States v. Verlin***, 466 F. Supp. 155, 160 (N.D. Tex. 1979) (witness who is familiar with defendant's voice can authenticate recording, even though witness did not participate in recorded conversation); FED. R. EVID. 901 advisory committee's note, subdiv. (b)(5) ("Since aural voice identification is not a subject of expert testimony, the requisite familiarity may be acquired either before or after the particular speaking which is the subject of the identification ....").

187. *See* TEX. R. EVID. 901(b)(5) (opinion "based on hearing the voice at any time"); *see, e.g., **Angleton v. State***, 971 S.W.2d 65, 68 (Tex. Crim. App. 1998) (police officer who investigated capital murder could authenticate audiotape of conversation between defendant and his brother). In contrast, a nonexpert opinion on handwriting must be based on familiarity that was not acquired for the current litigation. *See* TEX. R. EVID. 901(b)(2). Refer to notes 106-112 *supra* and accompanying text.

188. *See* TEX. R. EVID. 901(b)(5); ***Auerbach v. United States***, 136 F.2d 882, 885 (6th Cir. 1943); 5 WEINSTEIN & BERGER, *supra* note 26, §901.06[1], at 901-72.1.

189. TEX. R. EVID. 901(b)(5); *see **Mutz v. State***, 862 S.W.2d 24, 29 (Tex. App.—Beaumont 1993, pet. ref'd); ***Woodson v. State***, 777 S.W.2d 525, 531 (Tex. App.—Corpus Christi 1989, pet. ref'd).

190. *See, e.g., **Diamond v. State***, 496 S.W.3d 124, 142 (Tex. App.—Houston [14th Dist.] 2016, pet. ref'd) (police officer who had interviewed defendant could identify defendant's voice on recording of telephone calls); *cf. **Verlin***, 466 F. Supp. at 160 (voice identification through mechanical or electronic transmission is viable if based on circumstances connecting voice to speaker; defendant's ex-fiancée and his coworker were properly allowed to identify defendant's voice on fire-department dispatch recording, even though they were not parties to the conversation).

191. *See **United States v. Tropeano***, 252 F.3d 653, 661 (2d Cir. 2001); *see, e.g., **United States v. Capanelli***, 257 F. Supp. 2d 678, 679-81 (S.D.N.Y. 2003) (voice recordings made with a digital recording device and then transformed using computer programs into CDs or audiotapes were admissible under Rule 901(b)(5), even though original digital recordings had been destroyed).

person with whom the witness spoke.[192] The rule has also been applied to fax transmissions.[193]

(1) Rule 901(b)(6)(A): Personal telephone calls. Subsection (A) of Rule 901(b)(6) addresses how to authenticate personal telephone calls and is consistent with Texas common law. The rule preserves the most common method of authenticating a telephone conversation: a witness's recognition of the person's voice.[194]

Authenticating phone conversations is more difficult when the witness does not recognize the speaker's voice.[195] Texas courts have uniformly held that self-identification by the person calling, without other evidence, does not authenticate a conversation.[196] The conversation is not admissible unless there is additional proof of the speaker's identity.[197] When a witness places a call, the identity of the other party to the call will be sufficiently authenticated under the rule if that person identifies

---

192. *Gleason v. Davis*, 155 Tex. 467, 472-73, 289 S.W.2d 228, 232 (1956); *see City of Ingleside v. Stewart*, 554 S.W.2d 939, 944 (Tex. Civ. App.—Corpus Christi 1977, writ ref'd n.r.e.) (authentication could occur if communication reveals facts known to only one person). Rule 901(b)(6) is not the only way to authenticate a telephone call's contents. For example, in *In re B.J.*, the juvenile defendant claimed that the trial court erred in admitting a tape recording of a 911 call because the State did not authenticate it exactly as illustrated in Rule 901(b)(6). 100 S.W.3d 448, 450-51 (Tex. App.—Texarkana 2003, no pet.). The court of appeals rejected this claim because the State had demonstrated under Rule 901(a) that the recording was what the witness testified that it was: a tape recording of a bomb threat made to the 911 line of the sheriff's office on a certain date from a specific location. *In re B.J.*, 100 S.W.3d at 450-51.

193. *See, e.g., Tyson v. State*, 873 S.W.2d 53, 61-62 (Tex. App.—Tyler 1993, pet. ref'd) (front page of fax transmittal sheet containing statement that it was sent from Southwestern Bell Telephone Company was sufficient to show that document and its contents came from that source).

194. *See Colbert v. Dall. Joint Stock Land Bank*, 136 Tex. 268, 273-75, 150 S.W.2d 771, 774-75 (1941) (witness should assert that he recognized person's voice before court allows testimony about telephone conversation; whether witness actually recognized voice of person with whom he had allegedly spoken is question for jury); *Woodson*, 777 S.W.2d at 531 ("Identification of a voice through mechanical or electronic transmission by opinion based upon hearing the voice at any time under circumstances connecting it with the alleged speaker conforms to the requirement of authentication or identification as a condition precedent to admissibility."); *Tidwell v. State*, 646 S.W.2d 474, 476 (Tex. App.—Tyler 1982) (identity of person with whom witness had telephone conversation is established if witness identifies person's voice), *pet. ref'd*, 645 S.W.2d 297 (Tex. Crim. App. 1983). The Texas Rules seem to permit the authentication of a telephone conversation under either the "circumstances" provision of Rule 901(b)(6)(A) or the general "voice identification" provision of Rule 901(b)(5).

Under Texas common law, courts did not require the testifying witness to recognize the person's voice if a third party who was also listening to the conversation could identify the person. *See Schwartz v. State*, 158 Tex. Crim. 171, 176, 246 S.W.2d 174, 177-78 (1951) (quoting 22 C.J.S. *Telephone Conversations* §644), *aff'd*, 344 U.S. 199 (1952). The rule is broad enough to allow such third-party identifications.

195. *See, e.g., Herzing v. Metro. Life Ins.*, 907 S.W.2d 574, 580 (Tex. App.—Corpus Christi 1995, writ denied). In *Herzing*, evidence showed that an insurance agent told the plaintiff's president (the testifying witness) during a telephone call that his branch manager was on the phone. *Id.* at 578-79. That person, although unknown to the witness, identified himself as the branch manager and was familiar with the facts of the agent's loan proposal in discussing the matter with the witness. *Id.* at 579. That evidence, coupled with the witness's later identification of the branch manager's voice from his taped deposition, was sufficient authentication under Rule 901. *Herzing*, 907 S.W.2d at 580-81.

196. *See Tex. Candy & Nut Co. v. Horton*, 235 S.W.2d 518, 521 (Tex. Civ. App.—Dallas 1950, writ ref'd n.r.e.).

197. *Colbert*, 136 Tex. at 274, 150 S.W.2d at 775; 2 McCormick on Evidence, *supra* note 19, §228, at 78. Additional evidence that can prove the speaker's identity includes the context and timing of the phone call, the contents of the statements made during the call, and any internal patterns or distinct characteristics about the call. *Morris v. State*, 460 S.W.3d 190, 196 (Tex. App.—Houston [14th Dist.] 2015, no pet.); *Mosley v. State*, 355 S.W.3d 59, 69 (Tex. App.—Houston [1st Dist.] 2010, pet. ref'd).

himself and there is proof that the number called was assigned to that person by the telephone company.[198] Under the same rationale, it would seem that an incoming call to a witness could be authenticated using Caller ID and the caller's self-identification. According to Charles McCormick, the accuracy of the telephone system, the absence of a motive to falsify, and the lack of opportunity for premeditated fraud all tend to support the reliability of the speaker's self-identification.[199] Authenticity can also be established without voice recognition when the speaker acknowledges certain facts that only he is likely to know.[200] Events after a telephone call can also authenticate a conversation when the call produces results that would have been unlikely if the call had not been made.[201]

(2) Rule 901(b)(6)(B): Business telephone calls. Subsection (B) of Rule 901(b)(6) provides a two-step process for authenticating business telephone calls: the call must be made to a business and must relate to business reasonably transacted over the telephone. Texas courts have long recognized a business-telephone exception to the common-law rule requiring proof when identifying participants in a telephone conversation: "[I]f a call is made to a business office over a line maintained by it for business purposes, the conversation will be admitted if such person represents that he is the person called and is one authorized to take the message, in the absence of proof to the contrary."[202]

The rule eliminates the apparent Texas common-law requirement of proving that the person called was authorized to take that business call. The proponent must show only that the call was related to business, was placed to the business establishment, and

---

198. *See **Sorce v. State***, 736 S.W.2d 851, 859 (Tex. App.—Houston [14th Dist.] 1987, pet. ref'd) (telephone call over business line to person to whom number is assigned and who identifies himself will be admitted).

199. 2 McCormick on Evidence, *supra* note 19, §228, at 78.

200. ***Gleason v. Davis***, 155 Tex. 467, 472-73, 289 S.W.2d 228, 232 (1956); ***Sorce***, 736 S.W.2d at 859; *see, e.g.*, ***Morris***, 460 S.W.3d at 196 (evidence of telephone calls was sufficiently authenticated when documentation showed that number police officer dialed was same number defendant listed as his own and defendant gave police officer identifying information such as his Social Security number); ***Mosley***, 355 S.W.3d at 69 (evidence of telephone calls was sufficiently authenticated when witness testified that speaker identified herself and disclosed information specific to circumstances previously described by speaker and defendant).

201. In ***Dallas Gas Co. v. Bankers' & Shippers' Insurance Co.***, the plaintiff testified that his brother called the gas company to report a gas leak in his building. 53 S.W.2d 130, 132 (Tex. Civ. App.—Waco 1932, writ ref'd). According to the plaintiff, his brother dialed the number and said over the telephone, "We have a bad gas leak, please send someone out here. ... Thank you." *Id.* The plaintiff further testified that although he did not know who his brother called, some men from the gas company arrived later and were looking for a gas leak. *Id.* The court held that the events tended to confirm that the call had been placed to the gas company. *Id.*

In ***National Aid Life Ass'n v. Murphy***, a friend of the plaintiff agreed to pay the premium on the plaintiff's insurance policy. 78 S.W.2d 223, 225 (Tex. Civ. App.—Dallas 1934, writ dism'd). The plaintiff received a telephone call from a person claiming to be a representative of the insurance company, who stated that the plaintiff's friend was offering to pay the premium. *Id.* at 228. The speaker offered to give the friend a receipt, and the friend eventually brought the receipt to the plaintiff. *Id.* Although the plaintiff could not identify the person who called her, the court held that her testimony was admissible because "the circumstances sufficiently identify ... defendant's agent, as the person talking over the telephone." *Id.* at 229.

202. ***Gleason***, 155 Tex. at 473, 289 S.W.2d at 232; *see **Sanderlin v. Dransfield***, 523 S.W.2d 794, 796 (Tex. Civ. App.—Fort Worth 1975, no writ).

was answered by a person who appeared to have authority to act on the business's behalf.[203] The rationale for this change is that "[l]isting a business telephone number in a directory ... is assumed to be an invitation to the public to transact business with that company by calling that number without further identification."[204]

7. Rule 901(b)(7): Evidence about public records. The common-law practice of admitting into evidence documents from public custody is based on two premises: (1) an officer in custody of such records will carry out the public duty to record only genuine papers, and (2) it is difficult to falsify such papers.[205] Courts have presumed that public officers properly perform their duties and that records kept in a public office are generally what they appear to be.[206]

Rule 901(b)(7), which is identical to Federal Rule 901(b)(7), generally provides that documents or statements kept by an authorized public officer are admissible once the proponent shows that they are what they purport to be.[207] The rule applies to two categories of materials. The first category of documents includes those "recorded or filed in a public office as authorized by law."[208] A proponent seeking to authenticate a record

---

203. *See* TEX. R. EVID. 901(b)(6)(B); 5 WEINSTEIN & BERGER, *supra* note 26, §901.07[2], at 901-78.

204. 5 WEINSTEIN & BERGER, *supra* note 26, §901.07[2], at 901-78.

205. McMorrow, *supra* note 108, at 206.

206. *See* ***McGuire v. City of Dall.***, 141 Tex. 170, 178, 170 S.W.2d 722, 727 (1943) (public officials are presumed to have done their duty); ***Short v. W.T. Carter & Brother***, 133 Tex. 202, 219, 126 S.W.2d 953, 963 (1939) (same), *appeal dismissed*, 308 U.S. 513 (1939).

207. *See* TEX. R. EVID. 901(b)(7). Rule 901(b)(7) does not require original seals. ***Haas v. State***, 494 S.W.3d 819, 824 (Tex. App.—Houston [14th Dist.] 2016, no pet.).
  Although the rule codifies general common-law rules of authentication, it makes several changes to the Texas practice of admitting public documents, which was previously governed by former Texas Revised Civil Statutes article 3731a. Act approved June 21, 1951, 52nd Leg., R.S., ch. 471, 1951 Tex. Gen. Laws 830, *amended by* Act of June 5, 1953, 53rd Leg., R.S., ch. 304, §1, 1953 Tex. Gen. Laws 756, *amended by* Act approved June 16, 1961, 57th Leg., R.S., ch. 321, §1, 1961 Tex. Gen. Laws 685, *amended by* Act approved May 20, 1975, 64th Leg., R.S., ch. 280, §1, 1975 Tex. Gen. Laws 666 (former Texas Revised Civil Statutes art. 3731a deemed repealed as to civil proceedings effective 1983 and as to criminal proceedings effective 1986). Specifically, the rule eliminates two of article 3731a's prerequisites for proving the genuineness of public documents: notice and certified attestation of copies.
  Article 3731a, §3 specifically required parties tendering an official document to deliver a copy to the adverse party within a reasonable time before trial, unless the trial court determined that the adverse party had not been unfairly surprised by the failure to do so. Rule 901(b)(7) has no notice requirement. Article 3731a, §4 required copies of all documents to be either evidenced by an official publication or attested to by the legal custodian or his deputy. The attestation for out-of-state documents had to be accompanied by another certification that the attesting officer had legal custody of the records. *E.g.*, ***Aaron v. State***, 546 S.W.2d 277, 278 (Tex. Crim. App. 1976) (admitting records that official custodian attested to and that legal custodian certified); ***Hutchins v. Seifert***, 460 S.W.2d 955, 957 (Tex. Civ. App.—Houston [14th Dist.] 1970, writ ref'd n.r.e.) (requiring attestation by official custodian and certification that officer had custody). Rule 901(b)(7), on the other hand, gives a single standard of admissibility for all purported public records in any form—sufficient evidence to support a finding that the record is what its proponent claims it is. *See* TEX. R. EVID. 901(a), (b)(7). Thus, a document may be admitted as a public record if a public officer with knowledge testifies that the document is an accurate copy of a public record of the public entity. If, however, the proponent of the document does not want to call a sponsoring witness, the authentication requirements of Rule 902, including certification, must be met. *See, e.g.*, ***Klein Indep. Sch. Dist. v. Noack***, 830 S.W.2d 796, 797-98 (Tex. App.—Houston [14th Dist.] 1992, writ denied) (written decision of Texas Employment Commission was improperly admitted as public record because it was not authenticated; proponent "did not offer extrinsic evidence of authentication and the document was not properly certified, which would make it self-authenticating").

208. TEX. R. EVID. 901(b)(7)(A).

RULE 901

in this category should establish that the offered document (1) is of the sort that is filed or recorded, (2) is authorized by law to be filed or recorded in a particular public office, and (3) came from that office.[209]

The second category of documents is defined in terms of a "purported public record or statement."[210] Authenticating documents in this category requires proof that the document (1) appears on its face to be a public record, (2) is the sort of document that a public office is authorized to prepare and maintain, and (3) came from that public office.[211]

In **Reed v. State**,[212] the court of criminal appeals clarified an issue that had caused confusion about the admissibility of penitentiary packets containing copies of a convicted felon's prior judgment and sentence.[213] A pre-Rules case, **Dingler v. State**, held that copies of judgments of conviction contained in penitentiary packets and certified by the legal custodian of records for the Texas Department of Corrections were not admissible as self-authenticated when the judgments were not also certified by the convicting court's clerk.[214] In **Reed**, the court properly stated that this requirement from Texas Revised Civil Statutes article 3731a had not been carried forward under Rules

---

209. *See* **Benefield v. State**, 266 S.W.3d 25, 34 (Tex. App.—Houston [1st Dist.] 2008, no pet.). The hearsay exception for public records and reports is in Rule 803(8). Refer to *Article VIII: Hearsay, supra* p. 910.

210. Tex. R. Evid. 901(b)(7)(B). Before the 2015 restyling, the portion of Rule 901(b)(7) that is now Rule 901(b)(7)(B) referred to "a purported public record, report, statement, or data compilation, in any form." *See* Tex. Sup. Ct. Order, Misc. Docket No. 15-9048 (eff. Apr. 1, 2015). While Rule 901(b)(7)(B) now refers only to "a purported public record or statement," the definition of "record" in Rule 101(h) includes "a memorandum, report, or data compilation." *See* Tex. R. Evid. 101(h)(4); *see also* Tex. R. Evid. 101(h)(7) (reference to any kind of writing or any other medium includes electronically stored information).

211. *Cf.* **United States v. Locke**, 425 F.2d 313, 314-15 (5th Cir. 1970) (recognizing authentication when document was the kind that office normally kept and document came from office); Fed. R. Evid. 901 advisory committee's note, subdiv. (b)(7) ("Public records are regularly authenticated by proof of custody, without more."). Custody is commonly proved by presenting the exhibit record with an attached certification from its custodian stating that the record is a true and correct copy of a record maintained in the files of that public office. *See* Fed. R. Evid. 901(b)(7); Tex. R. Evid. 901(b)(7); **Hannum v. Gen. Life & Acc. Ins.**, 745 S.W.2d 500, 502 (Tex. App.—Corpus Christi 1988, no writ) (party could not "bootstrap" document into evidence by comparing it to similar document that was authenticated through public-records doctrine). An example of a simple but sufficient certification for a public record self-authenticated under Rules 901(b)(7), 902, and 1005 is found in **Texas Department of Public Safety v. Guajardo**, 970 S.W.2d 602, 608-09 (Tex. App.—Houston [14th Dist.] 1998, no pet.). Alternatively, a sponsoring witness may testify to the authenticity of a record kept in his custody at a public office. *See* **United States v. Estrada-Eliverio**, 583 F.3d 669, 672-73 (9th Cir. 2009); *Locke*, 425 F.2d at 315. The sponsoring witness does not need to be the custodian of records. *See, e.g.*, **United States v. Miller**, No. 09-4461 (4th Cir. 2010) (no pub.; 9-2-10) (Social Security Administration documents were properly authenticated by SSA acting district manager, who testified that he received them from another SSA office and that they were in the custody of the SSA office). The evidence, which may be circumstantial, must be sufficient to support a finding by a reasonable juror that the document came from a public office. Circumstantial evidence might include comparing the signature on a known public record with the signature on a purported public record, but sufficient, separate authentication of each exhibit would still be required. *See, e.g.*, *Hannum*, 745 S.W.2d at 502 (party could not "bootstrap" document into evidence by comparing it to similar document that was authenticated through public-records doctrine).

212. 811 S.W.2d 582 (Tex. Crim. App. 1991).

213. *See id.* at 584 n.6.

214. 768 S.W.2d 305, 306 (Tex. Crim. App. 1989), *overruled*, **Reed v. State**, 811 S.W.2d 582 (Tex. Crim. App. 1991).

901 and 902.[215] The holding in **Dingler** was inconsistent with the liberal admissibility of evidence under the Rules, the low prima facie showing of authenticity required under Rule 901, and the general deference given to trial judges to make admissibility decisions under Rule 104(a); thus, the **Reed** court overruled **Dingler**[216] and its progeny.[217] Under the Rules, the custodian of the original records does not need to certify their authenticity if the public-records custodian who presently maintains legal custody certifies that they are correct and authentic.[218] The holding in **Reed** follows earlier Texas cases[219] and federal precedent.[220] In criminal cases, prior convictions have most commonly been proved up through either certified copies of a trial court's judgment and sentence or authenticated copies of a defendant's prison record,[221] combined with ex-

215. 811 S.W.2d at 584; *see also* **Spaulding v. State**, 896 S.W.2d 587, 590 (Tex. App.—Houston [1st Dist.] 1995, no pet.) (copy of defendant's driver's license did not have to be individually certified before it was authenticated under Criminal Rule 901(b)(7) because it accompanied certified report of defendant's driving record; sufficient showing that driver's license was authenticated from official DPS records). In **Reed**, the court of criminal appeals held that the prison record clerk's certification of the penitentiary packet, which contained copies of a judgment and sentence, constitutes sufficient extrinsic evidence that the copies were authentic under Rule 901. *See* **Reed**, 811 S.W.2d at 586-87. The certificates made by the record clerk, the county judge, and the county clerk, as well as the judge's seal of office, provided sufficient self-authentication under Rule 902(4). *See* **Reed**, 811 S.W.2d at 586; *see also* **Taylor v. State**, 947 S.W.2d 698, 707 (Tex. App.—Fort Worth 1997, pet. ref'd) (certification of penitentiary packets in which deputy county clerk, not elected county clerk, signed attestation were sufficient under **Reed**). Refer to notes 340-347 *infra* and accompanying text. A trial judge nonetheless has discretion to exclude such exhibits if the records are suspicious on their face or in their contents. *See* 5 MUELLER & KIRKPATRICK, *supra* note 1, §9:31, at 562.

216. *See* **Reed**, 811 S.W.2d at 584.

217. *See* **Handspur v. State**, 792 S.W.2d 239, 240-41 (Tex. App.—Dallas 1990), *rev'd sub nom.* **State v. Handsbur**, 816 S.W.2d 749 (Tex. Crim. App. 1991); **Rodasti v. State**, 790 S.W.2d 379, 380-81 (Tex. App.—Houston [1st Dist.] 1990), *vacated*, 815 S.W.2d 591 (Tex. Crim. App. 1991); **Henderson v. State**, 788 S.W.2d 621, 624 (Tex. App.—Houston [14th Dist.] 1990), *rev'd*, 826 S.W.2d 156 (Tex. Crim. App. 1991); **Reed v. State**, 785 S.W.2d 412, 415 (Tex. App.—Dallas 1990), *rev'd*, 811 S.W.2d 582 (Tex. Crim. App. 1991).

218. *See* **Reed**, 811 S.W.2d at 587 & n.14 (because Texas Department of Criminal Justice, Institutional Division, is authorized to keep records of inmate's prior convictions and because it relies on these records as basis for admitting prisoner to its custody, records of correctional institutions may be held to be "public records" for purposes of Criminal Rule 901); *see, e.g.,* **Hull v. State**, 172 S.W.3d 186, 189-90 (Tex. App.—Dallas 2005, pet. ref'd) (juvenile-adjudication records were sufficiently self-authenticated; although one did not bear a certification, it bore the county clerk's seal and signature, and a later adjudication order was properly certified and referred to the earlier document).

219. *See, e.g.,* **Jones v. State**, 449 S.W.2d 277, 278 (Tex. Crim. App. 1970) (admitting prison records despite lack of certified judgment); **Kanaziz v. State**, 382 S.W.2d 485, 486 (Tex. Crim. App. 1964) (rejecting argument that sentence must be attested to by clerk of convicting court); **Evans v. State**, 677 S.W.2d 814, 820 (Tex. App.—Fort Worth 1984, no pet.) (because entire penitentiary packet was certified, each part of packet did not need to be certified).

220. *See* **United States v. Darveaux**, 830 F.2d 124, 126 (8th Cir. 1987) (under Texas law, Texas Department of Corrections Records Clerk is legal custodian; components of penitentiary packet were properly admitted as self-authenticating official records); *see, e.g.,* **United States v. Dancy**, 861 F.2d 77, 79 (5th Cir. 1988) (rejecting argument that under Federal Rule 902(4), penitentiary packet must be shown to have been recorded or filed in public office).

221. *See, e.g.,* **Haas v. State**, 494 S.W.3d 819, 823-24 (Tex. App.—Houston [14th Dist.] 2016, no pet.) (defendant's prior DWI conviction was proved up under Rule 901(b)(7) through certified copy of judgment, order, and bail bond; documents contained certified docket numbers and clerk's seal and thus were sufficiently authenticated). In one curious case, **Carlock v. State**, the court of appeals held that a defendant's former parole officer could not authenticate uncertified copies of judgments of the defendant's convictions because the parole officer was not the original custodian of the records. 99 S.W.3d 288, 294-95 (Tex. App.—Texarkana 2003, no pet.). The court of appeals stated that even though the parole officer was familiar with the defendant, his convictions, and his previous criminal record, "her testimony was not sufficient to authenticate the two judgments because she was unable to provide the necessary proof that those two judgments were from the public office responsible for maintaining those records." *Id.* Had

pert testimony identifying the fingerprint records as the defendant's.[222] As Rule 901 implies, however, there are numerous other ways to prove that a defendant has a prior conviction for a specific offense.[223]

8. Rule 901(b)(8): Evidence about ancient documents or data compilations. A party seeking to offer an ancient document into evidence faces two obstacles: the opponent's objection that the recitals in the document are hearsay and the objection that there is no direct proof of the document's execution. The first obstacle can be overcome by the hearsay exception in Rule 803(16);[224] the second problem requires an examination of Rule 901(b)(8). A long-standing rule of evidence in Texas has been that any instrument that is at least 30 years old is admissible without proof of execution if it comes from proper custody and is, on its face, free from suspicion.[225] Rule 901(b)(8) modifies earlier Texas law in two respects. First, the rule covers data compilations as well as traditional documents and instruments, so electronically stored records are included in the rule's scope.[226] Second, the age requirement was reduced from 30 years to 20.[227] The Advisory Committee on the Federal Rules, noting that any time limitation was neces-

---

the State attempted to introduce the prior judgments as self-proving business records under Rule 902(10) without a sponsoring witness, the court of appeals would have been correct to focus on the lack of certification. Rule 901(b)(7), however, does not require that a public record be certified as long as the sponsoring witness is a public official who, as a part of his official duty, maintains custody of documents originally filed with another public official. *See* TEX. R. EVID. 901(b)(7).

222. *See Elliott v. State*, 858 S.W.2d 478, 488 (Tex. Crim. App. 1993); *see, e.g., Littles v. State*, 726 S.W.2d 26, 32 (Tex. Crim. App. 1987) (op. on reh'g) (using fingerprints and photographs in defendant's penitentiary packet); *see also* TEX. CODE CRIM. PROC. art. 38.33, §1 (requiring defendant's thumbprint on judgment of conviction or docket sheet). In *Davila v. State*, the defendant complained that a penitentiary packet should not have been admitted because the accompanying fingerprint card was not physically attached to the packet. 930 S.W.2d 641, 652-53 (Tex. App.—El Paso 1996, pet. ref'd). The court rejected this argument because the defendant's name and prison ID number were on the fingerprint card, and the rest of the packet—including his photograph—corresponded exactly. *Id.* at 653. Any evidentiary deficiency went to the weight of the evidence, not to its admissibility. *Id.*

223. *See Henry v. State*, 509 S.W.3d 915, 918 (Tex. Crim. App. 2016); *Flowers v. State*, 220 S.W.3d 919, 921-22 (Tex. Crim. App. 2007). Such alternative methods include the defendant's admission or stipulation, testimony by a witness who was present and has personal knowledge of the prior conviction, and documentary proof containing sufficient information to establish the existence of the prior conviction and the defendant's identity. *Henry*, 509 S.W.3d at 918; *Flowers*, 220 S.W.3d at 921-22.

224. Refer to *Article VIII: Hearsay, supra* p. 922.

225. *City of Fort Worth v. Bewley*, 612 S.W.2d 257, 260 (Tex. Civ. App.—Eastland 1981, writ ref'd n.r.e.); *see also Beazley v. Beazley*, 273 S.W.2d 938, 942 (Tex. Civ. App.—Beaumont 1954, writ ref'd n.r.e.) (ancient affidavit is not inadmissible merely because affiant was still alive; helpful because of effect of long lapse of time on average human memory).

226. *See* TEX. R. EVID. 901(b)(8). Texas courts have applied the common-law rule to a wide variety of documents, such as deeds, wills, letters, and releases. *See Ochoa v. Miller*, 59 Tex. 460, 462 (1883) (wills); *Viersen v. Bucher*, 342 S.W.2d 203, 208 (Tex. Civ. App.—Amarillo 1960, no writ) (deeds); *Boucher v. Wallis*, 236 S.W.2d 519, 524 (Tex. Civ. App.—Eastland 1951, writ ref'd n.r.e.) (releases); *Woodward v. Keck*, 97 S.W. 852, 854-55 (Tex. Civ. App.—San Antonio 1906, no writ) (letters). The rule has also served to authenticate ancient lodge minutes, affidavits, and public survey orders. *See Howard v. Russell*, 75 Tex. 171, 176-77, 12 S.W. 525, 527 (1889) (lodge minutes); *Knowles v. Scofield*, 598 S.W.2d 854, 856 n.8 (Tex. Crim. App. 1980) (affidavits); *Sw. Settlement & Dev. Co. v. Vill. Mills Co.*, 245 S.W. 975, 978 (Tex. Civ. App.—Beaumont 1922, writ granted) (public survey orders), *agreed judgm't entered*, 265 S.W. 124 (Tex. Comm'n App. 1924). However, critics consider Rule 901(b)(8) to be too narrow. *See* 5 WEINSTEIN & BERGER, *supra* note 26, §901.11[1], at 901-94. It provides for authenticating nontraditional documents such as electronically stored data, but there is debate about whether it also covers items such as photographs, sound recordings, or X-ray films. Considering that Rule 901(b)(8) is merely illustrative, these types of items should be included

sarily arbitrary, also opted for the shorter period because a fraud is unlikely to be perpetrated for more than 20 years.[228] Texas Rule 901(b)(8) is identical to Federal Rule 901(b)(8).

One of the most common explanations for the ancient-documents rule is that there is a practical need to dispense with proof of execution—the parties and witnesses to the instrument probably are no longer alive or available.[229] In fact, after such a period of time, the law presumes that the subscribing witnesses are dead.[230] Another justification for the rule is that such documents carry a sufficient guarantee of genuineness because of their age, proper custody, and unsuspicious appearance.[231] However, there is no greater presumption of truth for the contents of ancient documents than for those of more recent documents. The admission of an ancient document indicates only that sufficient authenticity has been shown to let the jury consider the document.[232]

The age of a document offered under Rule 901(b)(8) may be proved by "any facts supporting the inference that the document or data compilation has been in existence for 20 years or more."[233] The court may consider the appearance of the instrument and any endorsements or attached certificates that indicate its age.[234] Moreover, to prove proper custody under the rule, the proponent must show that the document was where it would likely have been kept, if authentic.[235] As a general rule, however, no particular place of custody is considered absolutely essential.[236] Finally, for a document to be admissible under Rule 901(b)(8), it must be free from suspicion about its authenti-

---

if sufficient evidence indicates that a particular item is what its proponent claims and the proponent makes an appropriate showing of age, unsuspicious condition, and appropriate custody. Refer to notes 233-239 *infra* and accompanying text.

227. *See* TEX. R. EVID. 901(b)(8)(C).

228. FED. R. EVID. 901 advisory committee's note, subdiv. (b)(8). A number of other states have likewise reduced the age requirement from 30 years to 20. For a collection of statutes prescribing a period of less than 30 years, see 7 WIGMORE, *supra* note 127, §2143, at 739 n.5.

229. *West v. Hous. Oil Co.*, 56 Tex. Civ. App. 341, 344, 120 S.W. 228, 230 (San Antonio 1909, writ ref'd); *see* 1A ROY R. RAY, TEXAS PRACTICE: TEXAS LAW OF EVIDENCE CIVIL AND CRIMINAL §1372, at 529 (3d ed. 1980).

230. *Baldwin v. Goldfrank*, 9 Tex. Civ. App. 269, 275-76, 26 S.W. 155, 159 (San Antonio 1894), *aff'd*, 88 Tex. 249, 31 S.W. 1064 (1895).

231. *West*, 56 Tex. Civ. App. at 344, 120 S.W. at 230; *see* 1A RAY, *supra* note 229, §1372, at 529.

232. *West*, 56 Tex. Civ. App. at 344, 120 S.W. at 230.

233. *See* 5 WEINSTEIN & BERGER, *supra* note 26, §901.11[4][a], at 901-97 to 901-98 (discussing federal rule).

234. *See* *Bell v. Hutchings*, 41 S.W. 200, 200 (Tex. Civ. App.—Austin 1897, no writ). If, however, the document shows on its face that it was created less than 20 years before the trial, it is not subject to authentication under Rule 901(b)(8). *See, e.g.*, *Guthrie v. Suiter*, 934 S.W.2d 820, 825 (Tex. App.—Houston [1st Dist.] 1996, no writ) (letter dated less than 20 years before trial did not qualify as ancient document).

235. *See* TEX. R. EVID. 901(b)(8)(B); *see, e.g.*, *Fibreboard Corp. v. Pool*, 813 S.W.2d 658, 694 (Tex. App.—Texarkana 1991, writ denied) (letter was not admissible as ancient document under Civil Rule 901(b)(8) because no evidence was offered at trial to show where letter had been kept); *see also* *Stringfellow v. Brown*, 326 S.W.2d 1, 5 (Tex. Civ. App.—Fort Worth 1959, no writ) (if instrument comes from proper custody and is free from suspicion, it is not necessary to trace custody of document step by step from purported date of its execution); *Flores v. Hovel*, 125 S.W. 606, 609 (Tex. Civ. App.—San Antonio 1910, no writ) (if instrument comes from proper custody, no rule requires party to account for its possession during more than 100 years of its existence).

236. *Flores*, 125 S.W. at 609.

city.[237] "Erasures, discontinuity of handwriting, pagination, or the flow of its content, or any other indications of apparent changes in authorship that the proponent does not explain as being consistent with the document's authenticity may cause suspicion."[238] Generally, the party offering the document into evidence must explain such suspicious circumstances.[239]

9. Rule 901(b)(9): Evidence about a process or system. Rule 901(b)(9) is designed for situations in which the accuracy of a result depends on the process or system that produced it. The Advisory Committee's note to Federal Rule 901(b)(9), which is identical to the Texas rule, states that X-rays and computer printouts are two familiar examples but that the rule allows this principle to be extended to new areas.[240] The parameters of the "process or system" rule are limited only by Rule 901(a)'s requirement that the evidence of authentication be sufficient to allow a reasonable juror to find that the item (i.e., the result of the process or system) is what the proponent claims it is.[241]

Normally, evidence produced by a process or system is introduced through expert testimony. The expert first explains the scientific or technological basis for the process or system and how instruments, machinery, or technology have been developed to implement it. The expert then testifies to the specific operation of the process or system on the occasion in question to demonstrate that the process or system not only works in theory but also worked accurately in this instance.[242] After a process or system has been so well established in the courts that it is commonplace, a court often takes judicial notice of the validity of the principle and the technique, requiring the proponent to establish only that the process or system worked properly on the occasion in question.[243]

Texas law has long recognized the admissibility of results produced by various devices and processes when a sufficient showing of accuracy was made. These include ultraviolet and infrared spectrographic analyses,[244] chemical tests for intoxication,[245]

---

237. *See* Tex. R. Evid. 901(b)(8)(A); ***Stringfellow***, 326 S.W.2d at 5; ***Flores***, 125 S.W. at 609; *see, e.g.*, ***Roberts v. Waddell***, 94 S.W.2d 211, 212 (Tex. Civ. App.—Galveston 1936, no writ) (mutilated deed with "other indicia tending to cast suspicion upon it" was not admissible).

238. 5 Weinstein & Berger, *supra* note 26, §901.11[2], at 901-96.

239. ***Morgan v. Tutt***, 52 Tex. Civ. App. 301, 305, 113 S.W. 958, 960 (Dallas 1908, writ ref'd).

240. *See* Fed. R. Evid. 901(b)(9); Fed. R. Evid. 901 advisory committee's note, subdiv. (b)(9).

241. *See* Tex. R. Evid. 901(a).

242. For an example of using expert witnesses to lay the predicate for the admission of a novel process or system, see ***Kelly v. State***, 824 S.W.2d 568, 569-70 (Tex. Crim. App. 1992) (outlining expert testimony that was sufficient to demonstrate scientific reliability of DNA genetic-identification testing). Refer to *Article VII: Opinions & Expert Testimony, supra* p. 724.

243. *See* Fed. R. Evid. 901 advisory committee's note, subdiv. (b)(9) (provision does not foreclose taking judicial notice of the accuracy of the process or system). Refer to *Article II: Judicial Notice, supra* p. 124.

244. *See* ***Hernandez v. State***, 530 S.W.2d 563, 566-67 (Tex. Crim. App. 1975); *see, e.g.*, ***Bridges v. State***, 471 S.W.2d 827, 829-30 (Tex. Crim. App. 1971) (allowing expert testimony on testing of LSD by spectrography).

245. Tex. Transp. Code §724.063.

X-rays,[246] sound or video recordings,[247] blood-alcohol tests,[248] ultrasonic tests,[249] and gyroscopic directional surveys.[250]

Computer-generated data is frequently used at trial but seldom authenticated under the rule. Because today's litigants, courts, jurors, and businesses are familiar with and dependent on computer equipment, an elaborate authentication foundation is unnecessary.[251] As with "hard copy" business records, computer-generated data that is reliable enough for ordinary business transactions should be found reliable enough for admission at trial.[252] The output itself does not need to be prepared in the regular course of business and, in fact, may be generated solely for the purposes of the trial.[253]

Samples, polls, and other forms of scientific surveys may also be authenticated under Rule 901(b)(9). To authenticate a sample, the offeror must demonstrate that the sample was selected in a scientifically acceptable manner and that the conclusions are

---

246. Act approved May 27, 1969, 61st Leg., R.S., ch. 353, §1, 1969 Tex. Gen. Laws 1076, *amended by* Act approved May 18, 1973, 63rd Leg., R.S., ch. 128, §2, 1973 Tex. Gen. Laws 277 (former Texas Revised Civil Statutes art. 3737e, §6, deemed repealed as to civil proceedings effective 1983 and as to criminal proceedings effective 1986). Under Article IX, X-rays are not governed by special rules of authentication. Refer to note 412 *infra*. The authenticity of X-rays is seldom challenged in practice.

247. *See Seymour v. Gillespie*, 608 S.W.2d 897, 898 (Tex. 1980); *Edwards v. State*, 551 S.W.2d 731, 733 (Tex. Crim. App. 1977); *Cummings v. Jess Edwards, Inc.*, 445 S.W.2d 767, 772-73 (Tex. Civ. App.—Corpus Christi 1969, writ ref'd n.r.e.); *see, e.g.*, *Reavis v. State*, 84 S.W.3d 716, 719-20 (Tex. App.—Fort Worth 2002, no pet.) (following federal cases invoking "silent witness" authentication theory for admitting videos or photographs to "speak for themselves" if there is evidence that process or system that produced photo or video is reliable). For a discussion of other ways to authenticate sound and video recordings, refer to notes 141-151 *supra* and accompanying text.

248. *See Westchester Fire Ins. v. Wendeborn*, 559 S.W.2d 108, 109 (Tex. Civ. App.—Eastland 1977, writ ref'd n.r.e.).

249. *See Chem. Leaman Tank Lines, Inc. v. Trinity Indus., Inc.*, 478 S.W.2d 114, 116 (Tex. Civ. App.—Dallas 1972, writ ref'd n.r.e.).

250. *Harrington v. State*, 385 S.W.2d 411, 424 (Tex. Civ. App.—Austin 1964), *rev'd on other grounds*, 407 S.W.2d 467 (Tex. 1966).

251. Before computers became commonplace, commentators suggested the following foundation for computer-generated evidence:

> (1) the computer equipment is accepted in the field as standard and competent and was in good working order; (2) qualified computer operators were employed; (3) proper procedures were followed in connection with the input and output of information; (4) a reliable software program was utilized; (5) the equipment was programmed and operated properly; and (6) the exhibit is properly identified as the output in question.

5 MUELLER & KIRKPATRICK, *supra* note 1, §9:20, at 484; *see also United States v. Russo*, 480 F.2d 1228, 1239-40 (6th Cir. 1973) (medical insurer's computer printout of medical payments was admissible in mail-fraud case).

252. If a party does not lay the proper business-records predicate, however, computer-generated business records cannot be authenticated under Rule 901(b)(9). In *Miller v. State*, the court of appeals held that the State did not properly authenticate a cell-phone bill admitted to show that certain telephone calls, including one made by the capital-murder defendant after the crime, were made on the victim's cell phone. 208 S.W.3d 554, 563 (Tex. App.—Austin 2006, pet. ref'd). The State argued that it did not need to lay a business-records predicate to authenticate a cell-phone bill because it was a printout of computer self-generated data. *Id.* at 562-63. The court noted that a qualified witness must nonetheless describe "the computerized system by which the telephone billing record was generated and vouch[] for the reliability of that system." *Id.* at 563.

253. 5 WEINSTEIN & BERGER, *supra* note 36, ¶901(b)(9)[02], at 901-134; *see, e.g.*, *United States v. Meienberg*, 263 F.3d 1177, 1181 (10th Cir. 2001) (computer printouts were not result of "process or system used to produce a result" for purposes of authentication under Rule 901(b)(9); nonetheless, government offered circumstantial evidence that those printouts accurately depicted governmental agency's approval numbers assigned to defendant's firearms business).

statistically acceptable.[254] The proponent of the sample must also demonstrate that the sample was necessary (i.e., that not using the sample would cause great practical inconvenience).[255] Poll results are authenticated in much the same way as surveys. The party offering the results must show that the polls were conducted according to currently accepted polling methods and that the people polled were selected so the poll would accurately reflect the attitude of the entire target group.[256]

10. Rule 901(b)(10): Methods provided by a statute or rule. Rule 901(b)(10) is a catch-all provision stating that methods of authentication "allowed by a statute or other rule prescribed under statutory authority" continue to be valid as long as the particular statute or rule remains in effect.[257] The rule is substantively identical to Federal Rule 901(b)(10), and the Advisory Committee on the Federal Rules referred to examples such as provisions for the authentication of court proceedings by court reporters[258] and for the authentication of depositions.[259] Many Texas statutes dealing specifically with authentication requirements were repealed when the Rules were adopted. Others, including those dealing with breathalyzer test results,[260] outcry statements made by a child or a person with a disability,[261] audiovisual recordings of the testimony of a child who is the victim of an offense,[262] or a defendant's custodial statements,[263] are still in effect.

11. Admissibility of computer animations & computer simulations. Computers are a powerful evidentiary tool for presenting vast amounts of complex data in a comprehensible and coherent form, helping courts administer fair, efficient, and reliable trials. When used properly, computer-generated data, documents, and exhibits can provide great assistance to a jury. The key to the successful admission of computer-generated information in any form is presentation by an articulate, knowledgeable, and neutral expert witness who can use simple lay terminology and familiar analogies to explain complex technology, technical terms, and the steps in the process that ensure the out-

---

254. 5 WEINSTEIN & BERGER, *supra* note 26, §901.12[4], at 901-102.1; *see also **Bank of Utah v. Commercial Sec. Bank**,* 369 F.2d 19, 27 (10th Cir. 1966) (survey is inadmissible when sample is clearly not representative of universe that it is intended to reflect); *cf. **Bristol-Myers Co. v. Fed. Trade Comm'n**,* 185 F.2d 58, 60-61 (4th Cir. 1950) (questionnaire did not support advertisement claims and therefore misled general public).

255. ***United States v. Aluminum Co. of Am.**,* 35 F. Supp. 820, 823-24 (S.D.N.Y. 1940).

256. 5 WEINSTEIN & BERGER, *supra* note 36, ¶901(b)(9)[03], at 901-141 to 901-142; *see also* Allan H. McCoid, *The Admissibility of Sample Data into a Court of Law: Some Further Thoughts,* 4 UCLA L. REV. 233, 245 (1957) (testifying expert should explain to trier of fact which techniques were used by responsible and reputable statisticians and process by which universe was determined).

257. *See* TEX. R. EVID. 901(b)(10); *see, e.g.,* TEX. R. CIV. P. 193.7 (production of document in response to written discovery authenticates document for use against party unless producing party objects). See *O'Connor's Texas Rules * Civil Trials* (2017), "Using Requested Documents," ch. 6-I, §8, p. 658.

258. FED. R. EVID. 901 advisory committee's note, subdiv. (b)(10).

259. *Id.*

260. *See* TEX. TRANSP. CODE §724.063.

261. TEX. CODE CRIM. PROC. art. 38.072, §2.

262. *Id.* art. 38.071, §4.

263. *Id.* art. 38.22, §§2, 3.

put's reliability.[264] When offering technological evidence that is relatively new to the judicial system, the proponent should plan to provide ample scientific articles or treatise excerpts to the trial judge, which appellate courts may then refer to on appeal.[265]

(1) Animations. Computer-generated animations are pieces of high-tech demonstrative evidence that are used for illustrating or highlighting otherwise admissible information and testimony rather than for presenting conclusions about the evidence.[266] Computer-generated animations are not the same as computer-simulation evidence.[267] Unlike actual photographs of a person, scene, or event, however, they are not independently admissible. They are not substantive evidence, and they cannot be taken into the jury room during deliberations.[268] Demonstrative evidence, including computer animations, may be used before the jury if it fairly and accurately depicts the underlying testimony and assists the jury in understanding that testimony.[269] Because computer ani-

---

264. Refer to notes 251-253 *supra* and accompanying text.

265. *See **Hernandez v. State***, 116 S.W.3d 26, 29 n.6 (Tex. Crim. App. 2003) ("[T]he more extensive the gatekeeping hearing, the more noted and numerous the experts who testify, submit affidavits, or otherwise provide information, the more scientific material (both pro and con) that is consulted and discussed at a seminal gatekeeping hearing, the more likely it is that a reviewing court will declare that future trial courts may take judicial notice of the validity or invalidity of that extensively-litigated scientific proposition.").

266. *See **Hamilton v. State***, 399 S.W.3d 673, 682 (Tex. App.—Amarillo 2013, pet. ref'd) (quoting Goode, *supra* note 63, at 10); *see, e.g.*, ***People v. Cauley***, 32 P.3d 602, 606-07 (Colo. Ct. App. 2001) (upholding use of computer animation slides depicting shaken-baby syndrome as illustrative exhibit for expert to explain her testimony); ***State v. Sayles***, 662 N.W.2d 1, 7-11 (Iowa 2003) (same); ***Harris v. State***, 152 S.W.3d 786, 792-94 (Tex. App.—Houston [1st Dist.] 2004, pet. ref'd) (trial court did not abuse its discretion in excluding both a live videotaped reenactment of defendant running over her husband and a computer simulation of the same incident based on accident-reconstruction expert's mathematical data because there were considerable discrepancies between the actual event and the video reenactment and computer simulation).

267. *See **Cauley***, 32 P.3d at 606-07; ***Pierce v. State***, 718 So. 2d 806, 807-08 (Fla. Dist. Ct. App. 1997); ***State v. Farner***, 66 S.W.3d 188, 208 (Tenn. 2001). In ***Farner***, the court explained:

> Computer generated evidence is an increasingly common form of demonstrative evidence. If the purpose of the computer evidence is to illustrate and explain a witness's testimony, courts usually refer to the evidence as an animation. In contrast, a simulation is based on scientific or physical principles and data entered into a computer, which is programmed to analyze the data and draw a conclusion from it, and courts generally require proof to show the validity of the science before the simulation evidence is admitted.

66 S.W.3d at 208; *see* Fred Galves, *Where the Not-So-Wild Things Are: Computers in the Courtroom, the Federal Rules of Evidence, and the Need for Institutional Reform and More Judicial Acceptance*, 13 HARV. J.L. & TECH. 161, 256 (2000) (courts are not always consistent in distinguishing between computer animations and simulations); *see also* Gregory P. Joseph, *A Simplified Approach to Computer-Generated Evidence and Animations*, 43 N.Y.L. SCH. L. REV. 875, 875-78 (1999-2000) (identifying situations in which "ordinary evidence rules are sufficient to gauge admissibility without reference to the fact that the exhibits have in fact emanated from a computer"; normal computer foundation is unnecessary if the exhibit is simple demonstrative evidence, a business or public record, an admission, or a nonprejudicial illustration). *See generally* Kristin L. Fulcher, Comment, *The Jury as Witness: Forensic Computer Animation Transports Jurors to the Scene of a Crime or Automobile Accident*, 22 U. DAYTON L. REV. 55 (1996) (discussing the proper treatment of computer reconstruction evidence). Refer to notes 273-281 *infra* and accompanying text.

268. *See **Dunkle v. State***, 139 P.3d 228, 247 (Okla. Crim. App. 2006) ("[V]ideo and computer-generated reenactments 'are properly categorized as illustrative or demonstrative aids used to explain the expert's testimony' and ... should not be made available for the jury during deliberations, as they have 'no independent evidentiary value.'").

269. *See* Goode, *supra* note 63, at 23-24; *see, e.g.*, ***Farner***, 66 S.W.3d at 208-10 (in negligent-homicide trial, computer animation illustrating testimony of State's expert accident reconstructionist about "drag race" accident should have been excluded under Rule 901 for lack of authentication and under Rule 403 for being needlessly cumulative;

mations are more like charts and diagrams than scientific evidence, their use as demonstrative evidence does not require proof that the underlying scientific principles are valid.[270] Computer animations might be a computer graphic of a static object such as a computer model of a crime scene[271] or multiple images such as the depiction of a shooting.[272]

(2) Simulations. Computer-generated simulations are somewhat similar to an autopsy report—they have independent probative value for a material issue in the case. Simulations are generally computer-generated recreations of a past event or scenario based on scientific principles.[273] A computer program analyzes and draws conclusions from data based on the application of scientific principles.[274] Simulations involve the "projection of possible outcomes mathematically predicted by a computer pro-

---

animation was inconsistent with eyewitness and expert testimony, and State unnecessarily played animation at three different speeds from five different viewpoints); *State v. Drake*, No. E2004-00247-CCA-R3-CD (Tenn. Crim. App. 2005) (no pub.; 6-6-05) (trial court did not err in excluding defendant's three computer-animation reenactments of traffic accident because they were based on "pre-impact paths of travel" and other data not supported by trial testimony); *Mintun v. State*, 966 P.2d 954, 957-59 (Wyo. 1998) (computer-generated animation of automobile accident was admissible to illustrate State expert's opinion that defendant, who had no recollection of accident, was the driver, which rebutted sole eyewitness's testimony that he saw defendant ejected from passenger side of car; expert animation was intended to illustrate what expert believed would have been seen from eyewitness's vantage point, rather than what eyewitness claimed to have seen).

270. *See Ladeburg v. Ray*, 508 N.W.2d 694, 696 (Iowa 1993) (computer animations were "merely mechanical drawings" admissible with testimony of witness who created them); *People v. McHugh*, 476 N.Y.S.2d 721, 722 (N.Y. Sup. Ct. 1984) (computer animation is more similar to charts or diagrams than to scientific evidence).

271. *See, e.g.*, *State v. Harvey*, 649 So. 2d 783, 788-89 (La. Ct. App. 1995) (computer-drawn "still" animations of crime scene illustrating positions of murder victim and defendant and trajectory of bullet were admissible when used to illustrate coroner's opinion of how murder occurred).

272. *See, e.g.*, *People v. Hood*, 62 Cal. Rptr. 2d 137, 139-40 (Cal. Ct. App. 1997) (computer animation of shooting was admissible when based on eyewitness information, detective's measurements at the scene, reports and opinions of pathologist who performed autopsy on victim, and reports by ballistics and gunshot-residue experts; animation was used to illustrate witnesses' testimony, not as a scientific simulation of shooting); *Cornell v. State*, 463 S.E.2d 702, 703 (Ga. 1995) (felony-murder defendant's computer reenactment of crime scene was properly excluded for lack of proper foundation); *State v. Stewart*, 643 N.W.2d 281, 293-95 (Minn. 2002) (computer-animation reenactment of drive-by shooting was improperly admitted when much of the material was based on conjecture and the animation included passengers' facial expressions and movements that did not express or illustrate medical examiner's testimony); *State v. Clark*, 655 N.E.2d 795, 810-14 (Ohio Ct. App. 1995) (expert witness could reconstruct murder scene with aid of AutoCAD and data from police report); *Dunkle*, 139 P.3d at 250-51 ("crime scene reconstruction" testimony was based almost entirely on computer animator's analysis of the "consistency" of particular statements made by defendant with the State's evidence, not physical evidence or other data; "[b]ecause the animations were not fairly representative of the evidence in the case, they were not relevant"); *Harris v. State*, 13 P.3d 489, 495 (Okla. Crim. App. 2000) (videotaped computer animation showing trajectory of bullets into victim's body was admissible because (1) expert's testimony was consistent with animation scenes, (2) animation was a correct representation of scene portrayed, (3) animation was fair and accurate representation of the evidence, (4) expert explained animation as it progressed, and (5) expert stated that animation was designed to help him explain his conclusion); *Commonwealth v. Serge*, 896 A.2d 1170, 1182-83 (Pa. 2006) (three-dimensional computer animation reconstructing the fatal shooting was admissible because it "clearly, concisely, and accurately depicted the [prosecution's] theory of the case and aided the jury in the comprehension of the collective testimonies of the witnesses," and any inflammatory features that might have caused unfair prejudice were excluded); *Hamilton v. State*, 399 S.W.3d 673, 683-84 (Tex. App.—Amarillo 2013, pet. ref'd) (in murder trial, three-dimensional computer animation reconstructing events surrounding the shooting was improperly admitted; animation attempted to portray actions of at least four people and included details based on speculation).

273. *See* Goode, *supra* note 63, at 37.

274. *Id.*

gram."[275] Unlike animations, simulations are substantive evidence and may be considered by the jury during its deliberations.[276] Because the validity of conclusions reached by a computer-simulation program depends on the proper application of scientific principles, the admissibility of such evidence is treated like other scientific evidence, subject to Rules 702 through 705.[277] Computer-simulation evidence is a simple, visual way to present a large amount of complex data and numerous scientific assumptions. However, it is expensive to create this kind of evidence, there is no assurance that it will be admitted, and the simulation is frequently excluded because the scientific foundation is inadequate. At a minimum, the proponent must show through the testimony of either the computer expert who prepared the computer simulation or some other qualified witness that the simulation fairly and accurately depicts what it represents, and the opposing party must be given an opportunity for cross-examination.[278] The proponent may also be required to show that (1) the computer is functioning properly, (2) the input and underlying equations are sufficiently complete and accurate (and disclosed to the opposing party, who may challenge them), and (3) the program is generally accepted and relied on by the appropriate community of scientists or technicians.[279] Examples of computer-simulation evidence include the braking distance of a car, the flow of water or any other liquid, weather patterns, and weapon velocities.[280]

---

275. ANDRE MOENSSENS ET AL., SCIENTIFIC EVIDENCE IN CIVIL AND CRIMINAL CASES §2.19, at 180 (5th ed. 2007).

276. *See* Goode, *supra* note 63, at 37. Refer to notes 266-272 *supra* and accompanying text.

277. *See* Goode, *supra* note 63, at 39; *see, e.g.,* **Liquid Dynamics Corp. v. Vaughan Co.**, 449 F.3d 1209, 1220-21 (Fed. Cir. 2006) (expert's computer simulations were admissible even though their parameters were not precisely those of the known wastewater tanks because "they were based on reliable scientific methodology and subject to cross-examination and the proffering of further scientific evidence" by the opponent). Refer to *Article VII: Opinions & Expert Testimony, supra* p. 700.

278. This foundation should be presented to the trial court well in advance of trial to allow the proponent to plan its trial strategy and to reduce the burden on the judge during trial.

279. *See, e.g.,* **Commercial Union Ins. v. Bos. Edison Co.**, 591 N.E.2d 165, 167-70 (Mass. 1992) (computer simulation used to compute actual steam usage was admissible; it consisted of scientific formulas and algorithms that accounted for heat transfer, building materials, operating characteristics of various heating and air-handling equipment, and weather history, and the pertinent professional group had accepted it as scientifically reliable); **Kudlacek v. Fiat S.p.A.**, 509 N.W.2d 603, 617-18 (Neb. 1994) (expert's reconstruction of car accident using Engineering Dynamics Single Vehicle Simulator computer program was admissible given expert's step-by-step explanation of the theory, validation of data used, reliability and ubiquitous use of the program by reconstructionists, verification of results, and reasons why some data was not used); **State v. Sipin**, 123 P.3d 862, 871-72 (Wash. Ct. App. 2005) (prosecution's use of computer-simulation program to determine who was the driver in an accident and to predict multiple-occupant movement within vehicle during collision was reversible error because program had not been validated for those kinds of predictions). *See generally* Adam T. Berkoff, *Computer Simulations in Litigation: Are Television Generation Jurors Being Misled?*, 77 MARQ. L. REV. 829 (1994) (discussing history and admissibility standards of computer simulations; arguing for more caution by courts in admitting them because their effect on jurors might outweigh their basis in fact); Timothy W. Cerniglia, *Computer-Generated Exhibits—Demonstrative, Substantive or Pedagogical—Their Place in Evidence*, 18 AM. J. TRIAL ADVOC. 1 (1994) (discussing the different types of computer-generated evidence and how courts should deal with them); Betsy S. Fiedler, Note, *Are Your Eyes Deceiving You?: The Evidentiary Crisis Regarding the Admissibility of Computer Generated Evidence*, 48 N.Y.L. SCH. L. REV. 295 (2003) (discussing animations and simulations, including evidentiary standards for animations).

280. *See, e.g.,* **Liquid Dynamics Corp.**, 449 F.3d at 1221 (computer simulations of liquid flow in wastewater tanks were admissible because they were based on reliable scientific methodology); **Pino v. Gauthier**, 633 So. 2d 638, 652 (La. Ct. App. 1993) (computer-simulation videotape of car accident—which created four possible accident sce-

If computer-generated materials in a particular case do not fall neatly into either category (animations or simulations), the proponent is best served by following as closely as possible the foundation requirements for the admission of computer simulations.[281]

(3) Rule 403 safeguards. With either computer animations or simulations, the trial court has great discretion to admit or exclude the evidence under Rule 403. When balancing the probative value against the risk of unfair prejudicial effect, courts may consider whether the proponent disclosed the animation or simulation and the underlying data within a reasonable time before trial, thus giving the opposing party sufficient opportunity to analyze the exhibit and explain why the animation or simulation may not be a fair and accurate representation of the underlying event.[282] Other Rule 403 con-

---

narios by manipulating variables such as vehicle weight, speed, road conditions, and braking—was properly excluded as unduly prejudicial; opposing party could not change the variables to produce an alternate scenario); *Deffinbaugh v. Ohio Tpk. Comm'n*, 588 N.E.2d 189, 193-94 (Ohio Ct. App. 1990) (computer simulations that an accident-reconstruction expert used to prepare two reconstructions of a traffic accident were properly admitted because they offered an accurate depiction of the vehicle's motion and expert used known facts to generate them; simulations assisted the trier of fact in determining how the accident occurred, and opposing party knew through discovery that they would be offered at trial).

281. For example, in *State v. Tollardo*, the trial court admitted a computer representation of the possible trajectories of bullets that was created by an FBI expert on "reverse engineering of crime scenes." 77 P.3d 1023, 1026 (N.M. Ct. App. 2003). Reverse engineering of crime scenes involves using known information, such as the locations of objects at the scene or the trajectory of a bullet as described in an autopsy report, to determine unknown information. *Id.* The witness was also an expert in computer-aided design (CAD) programs, a program referred to as MAYA, and three-dimensional bullet-trajectory analysis in computer systems. *Id.* The State was attempting to prove that, given the physical evidence found at the scene, a shooter in a fixed location could quickly fire three shots that would create the wounds found in both victims. The State contended that the computer-generated depictions were simply animations to illustrate the expert's testimony. *Id.* at 1027. The trial court and court of appeals, however, concluded that the computer representation did more than simply illustrate the expert's testimony—the expert used the computer program to help form his opinions. *Id.* at 1028. The court of appeals explained that:

> [A]s we understand the testimony, [the expert] used the computer to help him form his opinions, not simply to illustrate opinions reached in another manner. On the other hand, the testimony also indicated that the computer did not "analyze" data fed into it; instead it created a visual image based on the same data that would have been used to create paper and pencil drafts on a drafting board. Thus, it does not fall squarely into either category espoused by those cases.

Id. Instead, the court focused on the following:

> [The central issue is] who (or what) is the source of the opinion. When the computer-generated evidence is used to illustrate an opinion that an expert has arrived at without using the computer, the fact that the visual aid was generated by a computer probably does not matter because the witness can be questioned and cross-examined concerning the perceptions or opinions to which the witness testifies. In that situation, the computer is no more or less than a drafting device. ... However, when an expert witness uses the computer to develop an opinion on the issue, the opinion is based in part on the computer-generated evidence. ... In that situation, the proponent of the evidence must be prepared to show that the computer-generated evidence was generated in a way that is scientifically valid.

Id. (citations omitted). The issue was whether the method used to generate computer images was a valid application of the principles of computer technology. *Id.* at 1029. In this case, the expert used two "off-the-shelf" software programs (CAD and MAYA) used by many members of the drafting professions and film industry. The programs were reliable, the expert explained their operation coherently, and he explained how the programs helped him form his opinion. Thus, the evidence was properly admitted. *Id.* at 1030.

282. *See Clark v. Cantrell*, 529 S.E.2d 528, 536-37 (S.C. 2000). In *Clark*, the South Carolina Supreme Court used a balancing test that is the opposite of Texas Rule 403, in which the evidence should be admitted unless its probative value is substantially outweighed by the danger of unfair prejudice:

siderations include whether the animation is overly dramatic or clinical in nature.[283] A final Rule 403 safeguard against the risk of unfair prejudice is the trial court's use of limiting instructions.[284]

RULE 902

EVIDENCE THAT IS

SELF-AUTHENTICATING

The following items of evidence are self-authenticating; they require no extrinsic evidence of authenticity in order to be admitted:

(1) *Domestic Public Documents That Are Sealed and Signed.* A document that bears:

(A) a seal purporting to be that of the United States; any state, district, commonwealth, territory, or insular possession of the United States; the former Panama Canal Zone; the Trust Territory of the Pacific Islands; a political subdivision of any of these entities; or a department, agency, or officer of any entity named above; and

(B) a signature purporting to be an execution or attestation.

(2) *Domestic Public Documents That Are Not Sealed But Are Signed and Certified.* A document that bears no seal if:

To ensure that the opposing party has sufficient time to analyze the animation, the trial court also should consider whether the proponent disclosed the animation and underlying data within a reasonable period of time before trial. Untimely disclosure should not, standing alone, necessarily result in exclusion of the animation. But late disclosure may prevent the opposing party from adequately attempting to explain why the animation is not a fair and accurate representation which, in turn, may prompt the court to conclude its probative value does not substantially outweigh the danger of unfair prejudice. *Id.*

283. *E.g.*, *People v. Hood*, 62 Cal. Rptr. 2d 137, 141 (Cal. Ct. App. 1997) (clinical and emotionless animation was properly admitted because it did not "prey on the emotions of the jury" and its probative value was not outweighed by any prejudicial impact); *Pierce v. State*, 718 So. 2d 806, 810 (Fla. Dist. Ct. App. 1997) (computer-generated animation of accident was properly admitted because no blood was shown, no sound was replicated, and mannequins used in demonstration had no facial expressions); *State v. Sayles*, 662 N.W.2d 1, 11 (Iowa 2003) (computer-generated slides illustrating shaken-baby syndrome were properly admitted because they were not overly dramatic and the computer-generated infant showed no facial expression and emitted no sound during the shaking); *Commonwealth v. Serge*, 896 A.2d 1170, 1183 (Pa. 2006) (computer-generated animation of murder scene was not inflammatory or unfairly prejudicial; animation emitted no sound and displayed no facial expressions, evocative movements, or evidence of injury, such as blood, but simply demonstrated how the bullets' trajectories were inconsistent with the location of victim's body, suggesting that defendant moved the body after the victim died in an attempt to stage a self-defense scene).

284. *See, e.g.*, *Kane v. Triborough Bridge & Tunnel Auth.*, 778 N.Y.S.2d 52, 55 (N.Y. App. Div. 2004) ("[T]he trial court erred in failing to instruct the jury that the computer-generated animation was being admitted for the limited purpose of illustrating the expert's opinion as to the cause of the accident and that it was not to consider the computer-generated animation itself in determining what actually caused the accident."); *Dunkle v. State*, 139 P.3d 228, 251-52 (Okla. Crim. App. 2006) (judicially promulgating a specifically worded limiting instruction that all courts must give when admitting "video, computer-based, or other comparable 'reenactment' evidence"); *Serge*, 896 A.2d at 1186-87 (recounting trial court's instruction to jury before computer animation was played). For a discussion of limiting instructions, refer to *Article I: General Provisions, supra* p. 97.

RULE 902

(A) it bears the signature of an officer or employee of an entity named in Rule 902(1)(A); and

(B) another public officer who has a seal and official duties within that same entity certifies under seal—or its equivalent—that the signer has the official capacity and that the signature is genuine.

(3) *Foreign Public Documents.* A document that purports to be signed or attested by a person who is authorized by a foreign country's law to do so.

(A) *In General.* The document must be accompanied by a final certification that certifies the genuineness of the signature and official position of the signer or attester—or of any foreign official whose certificate of genuineness relates to the signature or attestation or is in a chain of certificates of genuineness relating to the signature or attestation. The certification may be made by a secretary of a United States embassy or legation; by a consul general, vice consul, or consular agent of the United States; or by a diplomatic or consular official of the foreign country assigned or accredited to the United States.

(B) *If Parties Have Reasonable Opportunity to Investigate.* If all parties have been given a reasonable opportunity to investigate the document's authenticity and accuracy, the court may, for good cause, either:

(i) order that it be treated as presumptively authentic without final certification; or

(ii) allow it to be evidenced by an attested summary with or without final certification.

(C) *If a Treaty Abolishes or Displaces the Final Certification Requirement.* If the United States and the foreign country in which the official record is located are parties to a treaty or convention that abolishes or displaces the final certification requirement, the record and attestation must be certified under the terms of the treaty or convention.

(4) *Certified Copies of Public Records.* A copy of an official record—or a copy of a document that was recorded or filed in a public office as authorized by law—if the copy is certified as correct by:

(A) the custodian or another person authorized to make the certification; or

(B) a certificate that complies with Rule 902(1), (2), or (3), a statute, or a rule prescribed under statutory authority.

(5) *Official Publications.* A book, pamphlet, or other publication purporting to be issued by a public authority.

(6) *Newspapers and Periodicals.* Printed material purporting to be a newspaper or periodical.

(7) *Trade Inscriptions and the Like.* An inscription, sign, tag, or label purporting to have been affixed in the course of business and indicating origin, ownership, or control.

(8) *Acknowledged Documents.* A document accompanied by a certificate of acknowledgment that is lawfully executed by a notary public or another officer who is authorized to take acknowledgments.

(9) *Commercial Paper and Related Documents.* Commercial paper, a signature on it, and related documents, to the extent allowed by general commercial law.

(10) *Business Records Accompanied by Affidavit.* The original or a copy of a record that meets the requirements of Rule 803(6) or (7), if the record is accompanied by an affidavit that complies with subparagraph (B) of this rule and any other requirements of law, and the record and affidavit are served in accordance with subparagraph (A). For good cause shown, the court may order that a business record be treated as presumptively authentic even if the proponent fails to comply with subparagraph (A).

    (A) *Service Requirement.* The proponent of a record must serve the record and the accompanying affidavit on each other party to the case at least 14 days before trial. The record and affidavit may be served by any method permitted by Rule of Civil Procedure 21a.

    (B) *Form of Affidavit.* An affidavit is sufficient if it includes the following language, but this form is not exclusive. The proponent may use an unsworn declaration made under penalty of perjury in place of an affidavit.

        1. I am the custodian of records [*or* I am an employee or owner] of _____ and am familiar with the manner in which its records are created and maintained by virtue of my duties and responsibilities.

        2. Attached are _____ pages of records. These are the original records or exact duplicates of the original records.

        3. The records were made at or near the time of each act, event, condition, opinion, or diagnosis set forth. [*or* It is the regular practice of _____ to make this type of record at or near the time of each act, event, condition, opinion, or diagnosis set forth in the record.]

        4. The records were made by, or from information transmitted by, persons with knowledge of the matters set forth. [*or* It is the regular practice of _____ for this type of record to be made by, or from

information transmitted by, persons with knowledge of the matters set forth in them.]

    5. The records were kept in the course of regularly conducted business activity. [*or* It is the regular practice of _____ to keep this type of record in the course of regularly conducted business activity.]

    6. It is the regular practice of the business activity to make the records.

(11) ***Presumptions Under a Statute or Rule.*** A signature, document, or anything else that a statute or rule prescribed under statutory authority declares to be presumptively or prima facie genuine or authentic.

Notes and Comments

Comment to 2014 change: At the direction of the Legislature, the requirement that records be filed with the court before trial has been removed. *See* Act of May 17, 2013, 83rd Leg., R.S., ch. 560, §3, 2013 Tex. Gen. Laws 1509, 1510 (SB 679). The word "affidavit" in this rule includes an unsworn declaration made under penalty of perjury. TEX. CIV. PRAC. & REM. CODE §132.001. The reference to "any other requirements of law" incorporates the requirements of Sections 18.001 and 18.002 of the Civil Practice and Remedies Code for affidavits offered as prima facie proof of the cost or necessity of services or medical expenses. The form medical expenses affidavit that was added to this rule in 2013 has been removed as unnecessary. It can now be found in Section 18.002(b-1) of the Civil Practice and Remedies Code.

Comment to 2013 change: Rule 902(10)(c) is added to provide a form affidavit for proof of medical expenses. The affidavit is intended to comport with Section 41.0105 of the Civil Practice and Remedies Code, which allows evidence of only those medical expenses that have been paid or will be paid, after any required credits or adjustments. *See Haygood v. Escabedo*, 356 S.W.3d 390 (Tex. 2011). The records attached to the affidavit must also meet the admissibility standard of *Haygood*, 356 S.W.3d at 399-400 ("[O]nly evidence of recoverable medical expenses is admissible at trial.").

COMMENTARY ON RULE 902

Rule 902 is an exception to the general requirement that documents must be authenticated through a witness's testimony. It provides that certain documents are self-authenticating and may be admitted without preliminary proof of genuineness. The proponent of the document does not have to provide extrinsic evidence of authenticity as a condition precedent to admissibility.[285] To admit a self-authenticating docu-

---

285. *See* 2 MCCORMICK ON EVIDENCE, *supra* note 19, §229.1, at 81-82.

ment under Rule 902, the requirements of general authentication under Rule 901 must also be fulfilled. However, the foundation requirements of Rule 902 need not be met if the proponent has a sponsoring witness to authenticate the item under Rule 901.[286]

The theories underlying Rule 902 are that the vast majority of the documents listed in the rule are genuine,[287] that they generally show their origin on their face,[288] and that great inconvenience, "amounting sometimes to practical impossibility," would result from requiring the proponent to provide further evidence of authenticity.[289] Significantly, Rule 902, which is substantively identical to Federal Rule 902, does not provide a mere presumption of authenticity that shifts the burden of disproving authenticity to the opposing party.[290] Rather, a document is conclusively deemed genuine for admissibility purposes if it falls under one of the categories provided for by Rule 902. The determination of whether a given writing or other matter satisfies the self-authentication requirements of Rule 902 is a preliminary question for the judge under Rule 104(a).[291] Thus, the judge may use any reliable material or information, regardless of whether it is admissible, in making this decision.

Rule 902 makes no final determination on the worth or weight of the proffered evidence. The opponent can still object to admissibility on other grounds, such as relevance, hearsay, or unfair prejudicial effect, and can present evidence for the jury to consider in deciding how much weight should be given to the self-authenticated document.[292] The opponent is precluded only from disputing admissibility on the grounds of authentication.[293]

---

286. *See* **Reed v. State**, 811 S.W.2d 582, 586 (Tex. Crim. App. 1991); **Spaulding v. State**, 896 S.W.2d 587, 590 (Tex. App.—Houston [1st Dist.] 1995, no pet.); *see, e.g.*, **N.H. Ins. v. Magellan Reinsurance Co.**, No. 02-11-00334-CV (Tex. App.—Fort Worth 2013, pet. denied) (memo op.; 1-10-13) (party chose not to authenticate foreign-country judgment under Rule 902, but that was "not determinative of whether the judgments were properly authenticated because [party] could have properly authenticated the judgments in accordance with rule 901"; affidavits from party's attorneys stating that judgments were what they purported to be sufficiently authenticated them under Rule 901).

287. 5 WEINSTEIN & BERGER, *supra* note 26, §902.02[4], at 902-11; *see* FED. R. EVID. 902 advisory committee's note; 2 MCCORMICK ON EVIDENCE, *supra* note 19, §229.1, at 83.

288. *See* 5 WEINSTEIN & BERGER, *supra* note 26, §902.02[1], at 902-9.

289. 7 WIGMORE, *supra* note 127, §2161, at 782 (applying this principle to seals).

290. Federal Rule 902 was originally entitled "Presumption of Authenticity," and the opening phrase read: "The following are presumed to be authentic ...." 5 WEINSTEIN & BERGER, *supra* note 26, §902.02[3], at 902-11. The presumption terminology was eliminated because under Rule 301, a presumption is primarily concerned with the problems of shifting burdens and jury control, not with problems of admissibility. *See* FED. R. EVID. 301. Federal Rule 902 and Texas Rule 902 deal only with admissibility. *See* 5 WEINSTEIN & BERGER, *supra* note 26, §902.02[2], at 902-10.

291. 5 MUELLER & KIRKPATRICK, *supra* note 1, §9:29, at 543-44. Refer to *Article I: General Provisions*, *supra* p. 86.

292. *See* FED. R. EVID. 902 advisory committee's note. The opponent can also offer counter-evidence to show that the admitted evidence is not authentic.

293. *See* **Wright v. Lewis**, 777 S.W.2d 520, 524 (Tex. App.—Corpus Christi 1989, writ denied) (Rules 901 and 902 discuss only authentication and identification of evidence and in no way relate to admissibility of that evidence's contents); *see also* **United States v. Southard**, 700 F.2d 1, 22-23 (1st Cir. 1983) ("Self-authentication merely eliminates the requirement of testimony by a public official that a document is authentic. It does not eliminate the requirement of relevancy.").

A. Rule 902(1): Domestic Public Documents that Are Sealed & Signed

At common law, the genuineness of documents bearing official seals was proved merely by producing the document for inspection.[294] The justifications for treating the seal as sufficient evidence of genuineness included "the great inconvenience of furnishing further proof, the fact that forgery of a seal or signature was a crime, and the relative ease with which forgery could be detected."[295] One problem with the common-law practice, however, was determining where to draw the line in recognizing official seals. Although courts could be expected to take judicial notice of a state seal, they sometimes balked at presuming the genuineness of less prominent official seals.[296]

Texas never faced this problem because the authentication of public documents bearing official seals has been governed almost exclusively by statute. Former Texas Revised Civil Statutes article 3724, for example, provided that in suits by the State against any of its officers for failure to pay funds owed, a transcript from the Comptroller's Office of the true account between the State and such parties, "authenticated under the seal of said office, shall be admitted as prima facie evidence."[297] In an attempt to consolidate the veritable maze of legislative enactments that have governed the admissibility of various sealed documents in Texas, the Legislature enacted article 3731a, a comprehensive Official Records Act, in 1953.[298] The Act provided for the admissibility of most types of domestic, out-of-state, and foreign documents but did not grant any special status to documents under seal, which had to meet article 3731a's prerequisites of admissibility like any other type of official record or document.

In contrast to former article 3731a, Rule 902(1), which is identical to Federal Rule 902(1), gives preferential treatment to originally sealed documents.[299] Copies of public documents are not covered by the rule, regardless of whether the copies are

---

294. 7 WIGMORE, *supra* note 127, §2161, at 778; McMorrow, *supra* note 108, at 210 n.64.

295. McMorrow, *supra* note 108, at 210 n.64; *see* 7 WIGMORE, *supra* note 127, §2161, at 784 (seal may be sufficient evidence because forgery of seal or signature would be a crime that would easily and certainly be detected).

296. *See* 5 WEINSTEIN & BERGER, *supra* note 36, ¶902(1)[01], at 902-12 to 902-13 (not all seals of inferior officials were presumed genuine).

297. Act approved Feb. 8, 1861, 8th Leg., R.S., ch. XVI, §1, 1861 Tex. Gen. Laws 14, *reprinted in* 5 H.P.N. GAMMEL, THE LAWS OF TEXAS 1822-1897, at 350 (Austin, Gammel Book Co. 1898) (former Texas Revised Civil Statutes art. 3724 deemed repealed as to civil proceedings effective 1983 and as to criminal proceedings effective 1986); *see also* Act approved May 13, 1871, 1st Leg., R.S., An Act to Regulate Proceedings in the District Courts: Evidence, §92, 1846 Tex. Gen. Laws 388, *reprinted in* 2 H.P.N. GAMMEL, THE LAWS OF TEXAS 1822-1897, at 1694 (Austin, Gammel Book Co. 1898) (former Texas Revised Civil Statutes art. 3719 deemed repealed as to civil proceedings effective 1983 and as to criminal proceedings effective 1986) (certified copies of Secretary of State's papers under hand and seal are self-authenticating); Act approved May 13, 1871, 1st Leg., R.S., An Act to Regulate Proceedings in the District Courts: Evidence, §89, 1846 Tex. Gen. Laws 388, *reprinted in* 2 H.P.N. GAMMEL, THE LAWS OF TEXAS 1822-1897, at 1693 (Austin, Gammel Book Co. 1898) (former Texas Revised Civil Statutes art. 3720 deemed repealed as to civil proceedings effective 1983 and as to criminal proceedings effective 1986) (certain copies of state officers' documents are self-authenticating if accompanied by certificate under seal); *Moseby v. Burrow*, 52 Tex. 396, 405 (1880) (legislative acts of State could be authenticated by seal).

298. Refer to note 207 *supra*.

299. *See* 5 MUELLER & KIRKPATRICK, *supra* note 1, §9:30, at 550.

certified.[300] The rule presumes the authenticity of documents bearing both a signature purporting to be an execution or attestation[301] and a seal purporting to be that of the United States or any state, political subdivision, or department, agency, or officer thereof.[302] Thus, the proponent of an out-of-state sealed document no longer needs to obtain both an attestation and a properly phrased certificate as article 3731a required.[303] Under Rule 902(1), a prima facie showing of genuineness requires only a seal and a signature.[304] Additionally, Rule 902(1) rejects the common-law hesitation to recognize seals of lower-level government agencies.[305] The rationale for extending self-authentication to all sealed governmental documents is that tampering with or forging these documents is very unlikely given the stiff criminal penalties[306] and the ease of detecting such forgeries. If a public seal is attached, its faintness or lack of legibility does not affect its self-authentication.[307]

B. Rule 902(2): Domestic Public Documents that Are Not Sealed but Are Signed & Certified

Rule 902(2), which is identical to Federal Rule 902(2), governs the introduction of an original domestic public document signed by a public employee or officer whose office does not have its own seal. Under the rule, such a document will not be presumed genuine unless a public officer with a seal and official duties in the same political entity as the signer certifies under seal (or its equivalent) that the signer has the official capacity that he appears to have and that the signature is genuine.[308] This provision is

---

300. *See* ***Myer v. State***, 686 S.W.2d 735, 737 (Tex. App.—San Antonio 1985, pet. ref'd). *But cf.* ***Farley v. Farley***, 731 S.W.2d 733, 735 (Tex. App.—Dallas 1987, no writ) (certified copy of original judgment containing attestation and seal complied with Civil Rule 902(1) and was admissible under Civil Rule 902(4)).

301. Tex. R. Evid. 902(1)(B). The signature may be a facsimile from a stamp if the facsimile is intended to have the same effect as a written signature. *See* ***Paulus v. State***, 633 S.W.2d 827, 849-50 (Tex. Crim. App. 1982) (op. on reh'g); ***Benavides v. State***, 763 S.W.2d 587, 590 (Tex. App.—Corpus Christi 1988, pet. ref'd); 5 Mueller & Kirkpatrick, *supra* note 1, §9:30, at 552.

302. Tex. R. Evid. 902(1)(A). The seal may also be a facsimile or stamped impression. 5 Mueller & Kirkpatrick, *supra* note 1, §9:30, at 553-54. The rule specifically allows for a seal purporting to be that of any of the following: (1) the United States, (2) any state, district, commonwealth, territory, or insular possession of the United States, (3) the former Panama Canal Zone, (4) the Trust Territory of the Pacific Islands, (5) a political subdivision of any of these entities, or (6) a department, agency, or officer of any of these entities. Tex. R. Evid. 902(1)(A).

303. Refer to note 207 *supra*.

304. Unlike Rule 902(4), Rule 902(1) does not require certification. *See* ***Gutierrez v. State***, 745 S.W.2d 529, 530 (Tex. App.—Corpus Christi 1988, pet. ref'd). Refer to notes 340-347 *infra* and accompanying text.

305. *See* 5 Weinstein & Berger, *supra* note 36, ¶902(1)[01], at 902-12 to 902-13.

306. *See, e.g.*, 18 U.S.C. §494 (penalty for altering, forging, or counterfeiting public documents is fine or prison term up to ten years or both), *id.* §506(a) (penalty for forging, counterfeiting, mutilating, or altering seals is fine or prison term up to five years or both), *id.* §712 (penalty for misusing names, words, emblems, or insignia is fine or prison term up to one year or both); Tex. Penal Code §37.10(c) (penalty for tampering with government records is misdemeanor, state-jail felony, or third-degree felony).

307. ***Cuddy v. State***, 107 S.W.3d 92, 96 (Tex. App.—Texarkana 2003, no pet.); *see, e.g.*, ***F-Star Socorro, L.P. v. City of El Paso***, 281 S.W.3d 103, 106 (Tex. App.—El Paso 2008, no pet.) (certified tax statement was authenticated even though seal was too faint to appear on photocopies).

308. *See* Tex. R. Evid. 902(2)(B); *see, e.g.*, ***Carpenter v. State***, 781 S.W.2d 707, 707-10 (Tex. App.—Dallas 1989, pet. ref'd) (penitentiary packet containing neither signature nor seal of county clerk was not properly self-authenticating); ***Martinez v. State***, 754 S.W.2d 831, 833-34 (Tex. App.—Houston [1st Dist.] 1988, no pet.) (no

RULE 902

necessary because many public offices do not have their own seals. As is true under all subsections of Rule 902, the officer does not need to certify the document himself; his deputy may do so.[309]

When presented with properly attested documents under the seal of the second officer, a court must presume that the second officer has the official capacity to affix the seal to the document in question. Accordingly, "the document will be admitted without a preliminary showing that the officer signing the document had no seal."[310] Further, the certifier does not need to state that he has examined the contents of the public document or that he has knowledge of its accuracy. His sole duty is to certify the authenticity of the signature and the official capacity of the public officer who signed the document. The certifier does not need to be a supervisor of the signer.[311] A federal officer could even certify the authenticity of the signature of a county or state public official or vice versa.[312]

The second officer's certificate should state that (1) the person whose signature is on the public document has the authority to sign documents such as the one in question or is in an official position to know whether such documents are genuine, and (2) that the signature on the public document is, or at least is believed to be, genuine.[313] This rather convoluted "post-notary" certification procedure is similar to the process of authenticating out-of-state and foreign documents under former article 3731a.[314] The rationale behind the procedure appears to be the fear that forgery will become more prevalent if nothing more than a signature is required of an officer who lacks a seal. However, the procedure seems unnecessary in view of the seal's diminished importance and improved forgery-detection methods.[315]

Before the adoption of Rule 902(2), former article 3731a governed the Texas practice of authenticating domestic documents. As discussed earlier, that article drew no distinctions between sealed and unsealed documents. Rule 902(2) thus contains more stringent authentication requirements, at least for domestic records not under seal, than had previously existed under Texas law. Article 3731a permitted such records to be authenticated merely by the attestation of the officer having legal custody of the

---

self-authentication when mandate of affirmance was merely notarized by notary public as being true and correct copy of original mandate and did not show that notary was custodian of document or that it came from public office).

309. *See* Tex. Loc. Gov't Code §82.005(c); ***McCall v. State***, 750 S.W.2d 307, 308-09 (Tex. App.—Beaumont 1988, no pet.); ***Smith v. Smith***, 720 S.W.2d 586, 602 (Tex. App.—Houston [1st Dist.] 1986, no writ).

310. 5 Weinstein & Berger, *supra* note 26, §902.04[2], at 902-17.

311. 5 Mueller & Kirkpatrick, *supra* note 1, §9:31, at 560.

312. *Id.* §9:31, at 561.

313. *See* Tex. R. Evid. 902(2)(B); 5 Mueller & Kirkpatrick, *supra* note 1, §9:31, at 562. The certificate should also affirm the official capacity of the signer of the public document, but "the absence of such an affirmation should not be fatal if there are other circumstances from which official capacity may reasonably be inferred." 5 Mueller & Kirkpatrick, *supra* note 1, §9:31, at 561.

314. Refer to note 207 *supra*.

315. *See* McMorrow, *supra* note 108, at 212.

document. Rule 902(2), however, deals only with the admissibility of self-authenticating documents. Parties seeking to avoid the post-notary certification requirements of Rule 902(2) are free to introduce an unsealed document under the more flexible provisions found in Rule 901, specifically Rule 901(b)(7).[316] The difference is that official records introduced under Rule 901(b)(7) are not presumed to be genuine for purposes of admissibility; thus, an opponent is free to contest admissibility by presenting evidence controverting authenticity.

If the proffered public record is more than one page long, each page must be certified, or a single certification should specify how many pages are included in the certification.[317] Rubber stamps that produce a facsimile of a signature are acceptable.[318]

The court of criminal appeals has held that a fax transmission of a certified copy of a judgment and sentence from another county was admissible in lieu of an original certified copy under Rules 901(b)(7), 902, 1001(3), 1003, and 1005.[319] This decision is consistent with the liberal authentication rules of Article IX and may make it easier to provide authenticated documents at trial while minimizing the burden of production on public-office custodians. Obviously, if the opposing party contests the accuracy of the transmitted document or the original, the trial judge may require the proponent to provide an original certified copy or testimony from the custodian of the record.

Texas Code of Criminal Procedure article 42.09 sets out a separate method for self-authenticating judgments obtained from the convicting trial court.[320] In one case, the First Court of Appeals held that this statutory provision is an alternative mode for authenticating penitentiary packets, but it is not the exclusive mode.[321] The defendant had argued that under article 42.09, only the director of the Texas Department of Criminal Justice, and not any other designated agent, could certify penitentiary packets. The court of appeals rejected this claim, stating that "[i]n the absence of evidence suggesting that the records clerk of the Texas Department of Criminal Justice was not the designated officer, we note that there is a presumption of regularity of governmental affairs."[322] The court also found that such documents may be self-authenticated under

---

316. Refer to notes 205-223 *supra* and accompanying text.

317. *See, e.g.*, **Sanders v. State**, 787 S.W.2d 435, 438 (Tex. App.—Houston [1st Dist.] 1990, pet. ref'd) (because district clerk's certification identified only one page, other pages of court's minutes were not self-authenticating).

318. **Benavides v. State**, 763 S.W.2d 587, 590 (Tex. App.—Corpus Christi 1988, pet. ref'd); *see, e.g.*, **Manning v. State**, 864 S.W.2d 198, 204 (Tex. App.—Waco 1993, pet. ref'd) (certificate of authentication on penitentiary packet signed with county judge's signature stamp rather than his actual signature was sufficient under Criminal Rules 901 and 902(4)).

319. *See* **Englund v. State**, 946 S.W.2d 64, 71 (Tex. Crim. App. 1997) (potential for fraud is minimized because fax and certified copy have the same source).

320. *See* TEX. CODE CRIM. PROC. art. 42.09, §8(b). A document certified under this subsection is self-authenticated for purposes of Rules 901 and 902. *Id.*

321. **Hawkins v. State**, 89 S.W.3d 674, 678-79 (Tex. App.—Houston [1st Dist.] 2002, pet. ref'd).

322. *Id.*

Rule 902 without satisfying the certification requirements of article 42.09.[323] A document that is sufficiently reliable under one mode of authentication need not satisfy "all possible avenues of authentication."[324]

C. Rule 902(3): Foreign Public Documents

Rule 902(3) provides two distinct methods for authenticating foreign public documents, and neither requires a seal.[325] The first requires a post-notary certification executed by either an authorized foreign official[326] or a diplomatic official of the United States.[327] This method is sometimes called "chain certification" because it involves the original signer of the document, an attestation by a higher official affirming the signature and authority of the signer, a second attestation by an even higher official affirming the signature and authority of the first certifier, a third attestation by an even higher official, and so forth until a U.S. diplomatic or consular official can make a final certification to the signature and authority of someone in the chain.[328] This process can be very complicated.[329]

---

323. *Id.* at 679.

324. *Id.*

325. *See **Bruton v. State**,* 428 S.W.3d 865, 875 (Tex. Crim. App. 2014) (seal is not required but may be helpful in determining whether document purports to be foreign official document). The rule follows Federal Rule 902(3), which derives from Federal Rule of Civil Procedure 44(a)(2). *See* FED. R. EVID. 902 advisory committee's note, subdiv. (3).

Rule 902(3) made several changes to the practice of authenticating foreign documents under former Texas Revised Civil Statutes article 3731a. First, prior notice to the opposing party, by delivering copies of the documents to be introduced, is not a prerequisite to admissibility. Second, when custodial certification is required—that is, when the opposing party has not had a reasonable opportunity to investigate the document—Rule 902(3) requires only that the custodian certify the accuracy of the copy. *See* TEX. R. EVID. 902(3)(A). The former article 3731a requirement of a certificate of the custodian's authority was eliminated. Refer to note 207 *supra* (former Texas Revised Civil Statutes art. 3731a, §4, stated that "the attestation shall be accomplished with a certificate that the attesting officer has legal custody of such writings"). Third, unlike article 3731a, Rule 902(3) does not provide a specific method for proving that particular records or entries are not present in the records of the custodian's office. Refer to note 207 *supra* (former Texas Revised Civil Statutes art. 3731a, §5, provided that absence of records is admissible evidence if attested to in writing by custodian of legal records). Proving a lack of records, however, should be easy to do under Rule 901(b)(1) or Rule 901(b)(7). Rule 902(3) is not available because an absence-of-records certificate is not self-authenticating.

326. *See* TEX. R. EVID. 902(3)(A); *cf.* ***United States v. Koziy**,* 728 F.2d 1314, 1322 (11th Cir. 1984) (employment records used by Ukrainian police were self-authenticating under Federal Rule 902(3) because they were attested to by Russian official who was authorized to authenticate such documents).

327. *See* TEX. R. EVID. 902(3)(A); *cf.* ***United States v. Montemayor**,* 712 F.2d 104, 109 (5th Cir. 1983) (Mexican birth certificates certified by American consulate officials met self-authentication requirement of Federal Rule 902(3)).

328. *See* TEX. R. EVID. 902(3)(A); ***Bruton**,* 428 S.W.3d at 879. The final certification must vouch for the genuineness of the signature and position of the official who executes or attests to the document. *See **Bruton**,* 428 S.W.3d at 878. The rule says that a final certification "may be made" by one of the following listed officials: (1) a secretary of a U.S. embassy or legation, (2) a consul general, vice consul, or consular agent of the United States, or (3) a diplomatic or consular official of the foreign country assigned or accredited to the United States. TEX. R. EVID. 902(3)(A). The court of criminal appeals has clarified that in this context, "may" means that these officials are the only agents authorized to make the final certification. ***Bruton**,* 428 S.W.3d at 877-78; *see **Jordan-Maier v. State**,* 792 S.W.2d 188, 191 (Tex. App.—Houston [1st Dist.] 1990, pet. ref'd) (under Rule 902(3), final certification must be made by "a diplomatic or consular official").

329. *Cf. **N.Y. Life Ins. v. Aronson**,* 38 F. Supp. 687, 688 (W.D. Pa. 1941) (listing the series of certifications that made Polish birth certificates admissible under Federal Rule of Civil Procedure 44, former 28 U.S.C. §695(e), now 28 U.S.C.

RULE 902

The second method allows self-authentication of attested documents without final certification when good cause is shown and the parties have had a reasonable opportunity to investigate the foreign document's authenticity and accuracy.[330] The court also has discretion to admit attested summaries of foreign documents with or without final certification when good cause is shown and the parties have had a reasonable opportunity to investigate the summaries.[331] One possible point of confusion under the rule is determining what constitutes a "reasonable opportunity" to investigate.[332] Another question is how courts should measure good cause. The Texas Court of Criminal Appeals has held that this method requires the proponent of the evidence to show good cause for failing to obtain a final certification.[333]

Unlike Federal Rule 902(3), Texas Rule 902(3) includes a final subsection dealing with the authentication of documents from foreign countries that have a treaty or convention with the United States governing the authentication of public documents:

> If the United States and the foreign country in which the official record is located are parties to a treaty or convention that abolishes or displaces the final certification requirement, the record and attestation must be certified under the terms of the treaty or convention.[334]

Although the provision is probably unnecessary,[335] it calls attention to the Convention Abolishing the Requirement of Legalization for Foreign Public Documents, to which the United States became a signatory in 1979.[336] Under the convention, documents from participating countries are recognized in local courts if the documents contain a certificate or "apostille" executed by certain designated public

---

§1741, and common law). Indeed, such a requirement for intermediate "chain certificates" might be impossible to provide in some countries because their public offices do not use seals of office.

330. *See* Tex. R. Evid. 902(3)(B)(i); ***Bruton***, 428 S.W.3d at 879-80; ***Jordan-Maier***, 792 S.W.2d at 191.

331. *See* Tex. R. Evid. 902(3)(B)(ii); *see, e.g.*, ***Jordan-Maier***, 792 S.W.2d at 192 (foreign criminal record was admissible because State showed good cause and defendant was given time to authenticate document).

332. *See, e.g.*, ***Jordan-Maier***, 792 S.W.2d at 192 (record showed reasonable opportunity when defendant knew about State's document before it was offered and did not object on reasonable-opportunity grounds when document was offered); *cf.* ***Raphaely Int'l, Inc. v. Waterman S.S. Corp.***, 972 F.2d 498, 502 (2d Cir. 1992) (defendant had nine years before trial to investigate authenticity of certificates, which was a reasonable opportunity; trial court did not abuse its discretion in finding the certificates were authentic); ***United States v. De Jongh***, 937 F.2d 1, 4 (1st Cir. 1991) (no reasonable opportunity to investigate when defendant revealed certificate's existence to the prosecution at the start of her case and offered it into evidence the same day).

333. ***Bruton***, 428 S.W.3d at 880; *cf.* Fed. R. Civ. P. 44 advisory committee's note to 1966 amendments, subdiv. (a)(2) (final-certification requirement should be relaxed only when shown that party has not satisfied rule's requirements despite reasonable efforts). In ***Bruton***, no good cause was found when the State gave no reason for not obtaining a final certification and did not indicate it had contacted an appropriate official about authenticating the foreign public documents it sought to introduce. 428 S.W.3d at 881.

334. Tex. R. Evid. 902(3)(C); *see* Fed. R. Evid. 902(3).

335. *See* Tex. R. Evid. 902(11) (extrinsic evidence of authenticity is not required for any signature, document, or anything else that a statute or rule declares to be presumptively or prima facie genuine or authentic). Refer to notes 421-423 *infra* and accompanying text.

336. *See generally* 5 Weinstein & Berger, *supra* note 26, §902.05[4], at 902-21 to 902-22 (discussing history and application of Convention Abolishing the Requirement of Legalization for Foreign Public Documents).

officials.[337] Under the Supremacy Clause, the convention controls the authenticity of such documents in Texas.[338]

Frequently, foreign public documents are written in a foreign language and, on their face, are incomprehensible to a Texas judge or jury. Rule 1009 provides a relatively simple and effective method for providing an English translation of those documents.[339]

D. Rule 902(4): Certified Copies of Public Records

Rule 902(4) codifies the common-law rule that certified copies of public records,[340] given by a public officer who has a duty to keep the originals, are admissible without any further showing of authenticity.[341] The rule is necessary because most public offices will not permit the original of their reports or filed documents to be taken from that office. These public officials presumably have no incentive to falsify copies of their official records. Because making and obtaining certified copies is convenient, this method is the most common means of self-authentication.

The rule generally identifies the types of documents that qualify for this method of authentication and the officials authorized to execute the certificates.[342] Because

---

337. *Id.*; *see* 2 GOODE ET AL., *supra* note 7, §902.4, at 298.

338. 2 GOODE ET AL., *supra* note 7, §902.4, at 297.

339. Refer to *Article X: Contents of Writings, Recordings, & Photographs, infra* p. 1068.

340. Rule 902(4) is narrower than Rule 902(3) because only official records (not all public documents) qualify under Rule 902(4). *See **Bruton v. State***, 428 S.W.3d 865, 875 (Tex. Crim. App. 2014).

341. *See **Benefield v. State***, 266 S.W.3d 25, 34 (Tex. App.—Houston [1st Dist.] 2008, no pet.); *see, e.g.*, ***U.S. Fid. & Guar. Co. v. Goudeau***, 272 S.W.3d 603, 610 (Tex. 2008) (DPS accident report was properly authenticated by DPS custodian of records); ***Int'l Fid. Ins. v. State***, 65 S.W.3d 724, 727 & n.3 (Tex. App.—El Paso 2001, no pet.) (certified copy of bail bondsman's bond filed in principal's court file was self-authenticating under Rule 902(4)); ***Blankenbeker v. Tex. Dep't of Pub. Safety***, 990 S.W.2d 813, 816-17 (Tex. App.—Austin 1999, pet. denied) (printout of Intoxilyzer test results was self-authenticated under Rule 902(4) when copy of printout was stamped with DPS seal and signed with attestation that document came from DPS files); ***Tex. Dep't of Pub. Safety v. Guajardo***, 970 S.W.2d 602, 608-09 (Tex. App.—Houston [14th Dist.] 1998, no pet.) (certification by deputy custodian on back of exhibits was sufficient under Rule 902(4)). United States courts have long recognized that in the case of original public records that should not be frequently removed from custodial supervision, evidence should be permitted by offering "a copy given by a public officer whose duty it is to keep the original." ***United States v. Perchemen***, 32 U.S. (7 Pet.) 51, 85 (1833); *see* 5 WEINSTEIN & BERGER, *supra* note 26, §902.06[1], at 902-22 to 902-25. Rule 902(4) does not require a seal to authenticate foreign documents. ***Bruton***, 428 S.W.3d at 876.

342. *See* TEX. R. EVID. 902(4)(A). These public records can be either domestic or foreign. ***Bruton***, 428 S.W.3d at 875. Before the 2015 restyling of the Texas Rules, Rule 902(4) explicitly included "data compilations in any form certified as correct" in the scope of the rule. *See **Bruton***, 428 S.W.3d at 875; ***Haas v. State***, 494 S.W.3d 819, 823 (Tex. App.—Houston [14th Dist.] 2016, no pet.). The restyled rule, however, deleted the phrase because the definition of "record" includes data compilations. *See* TEX. R. EVID. 101(h)(4). Thus, "[a] computer-generated compilation of information setting out the specifics of a criminal conviction that is certified as correct by the county or district clerk of the court in which the conviction was obtained" is admissible under Rule 902(4). ***Flowers v. State***, 220 S.W.3d 919, 922-23 (Tex. Crim. App. 2007); ***Haas***, 494 S.W.3d at 823; *see* TEX. R. EVID. 101(h)(4), 902(4). The conviction must still be linked to the defendant; self-authentication of the record is not sufficient to prove that the prior conviction belonged to this defendant. *See **Flowers***, 220 S.W.3d at 921-22; *see, e.g.*, ***Benton v. State***, 336 S.W.3d 355, 358-59 (Tex. App.—Texarkana 2011, pet. ref'd) (prior convictions were self-authenticated and linked to defendant by his name, birth date, signature, and mother's name). The certification under Rule 902(4) is that the copy is a true and correct copy of the original; it does not need to attest to the truth of the matters in the record. ***Bruton***, 428 S.W.3d at 875.

these certificates are treated as original public documents and must comply with the rules governing the admissibility of the originals, Rule 902(4) generally must be used in conjunction with Rule 902(1), 902(2), or 902(3).[343] However, the rule further provides that certificates are also acceptable if they comply with any statute or other court rule prescribed under statutory authority.[344]

Rule 902(4) is substantively identical to Federal Rule 902(4);[345] according to the Advisory Committee's note, the certification procedure under the federal rule "extends only to public records, reports, and recorded documents, all including data compilations, and does not apply to public documents generally."[346] Thus, documents that may be admissible when tendered in original form under Rule 902(1), 902(2), or 902(3) might not be provable by certified copy under Rule 902(4). However, certified copies may be admitted under another statute or rule, such as Rule 902(8) or 902(10).[347]

E. Rule 902(5): Official Publications

Officially printed documents are presumed to be genuine without further proof of authenticity; the authentication of these documents has long been a matter of Texas statutory law.[348] Former Texas Revised Civil Statutes article 3718, for example, provided that statute books printed under the authority of Texas, sister states, the United States, and foreign countries were to be received as evidence of the acts and resolutions they contained.[349] The provision had limited practical application after the promulga-

---

343. **Bruton**, 428 S.W.3d at 876; *see* TEX. R. EVID. 902(4)(B); *see, e.g.*, **Reese v. State**, 273 S.W.3d 344, 349 (Tex. App.—Texarkana 2008, no pet.) (certified copy of judgment for DWI conviction, under seal, was self-authenticating under Rules 902(1) and (4)); **Price v. State**, 35 S.W.3d 136, 143 (Tex. App.—Waco 2000, pet. ref'd) (copies of defendant's prior Oregon convictions were self-authenticating under Rules 902(1) and (4) when certified by Oregon court clerk); **McLendon v. Tex. Dep't of Pub. Safety**, 985 S.W.2d 571, 574-75 (Tex. App.—Waco 1998) (certification of district clerk was sufficient self-authentication of abstract of judgment under Rules 902(1) and (4), even though judgment did not contain judge's signature), *rev'd on other grounds*, 35 S.W.3d 632 (Tex. 2000); **Mullins v. State**, 699 S.W.2d 346, 349-50 (Tex. App.—Corpus Christi 1985, no pet.) (federal criminal judgment bearing the seal of a federal district clerk's office was a certified copy of the original, and clerk's signature was sufficiently authenticated under Rule 901(b)(7), 902(1), or 902(4)).

344. *See* TEX. R. EVID. 902(4)(B).

345. There are minor wording differences in subsection (B) of the two rules. The federal rule discusses "a certificate that complies with Rule 902(1), (2), or (3), a federal statute, or a rule prescribed by the Supreme Court." FED. R. EVID. 902(4)(B). The corresponding Texas provision reads: "a certificate that complies with Rule 902(1), (2), or (3), a statute, or a rule prescribed under statutory authority." TEX. R. EVID. 902(4)(B).

346. FED. R. EVID. 902 advisory committee's note, subdiv. (4).

347. *See, e.g.*, **Fullick v. City of Baytown**, 820 S.W.2d 943, 945 (Tex. App.—Houston [1st Dist.] 1991, no writ) (tax statements were not admissible under Civil Rule 902(4) because they did not bear seal from public office, but they were self-authenticating under Civil Rule 902(10)).

348. *See* Act approved May 13, 1871, 1st Leg., R.S., An Act to Regulate Proceedings in the District Courts: Evidence, §92, 1846 Tex. Gen. Laws 388, *reprinted in* 2 H.P.N. GAMMEL, THE LAWS OF TEXAS 1822-1897, at 1694 (Austin, Gammel Book Co. 1898) (former Texas Revised Civil Statutes art. 3718 deemed repealed as to civil proceedings effective 1983 and as to criminal proceedings effective 1986); **Martin v. Payne**, 11 Tex. 292, 293-94 (1854); 5 JOHN H. WIGMORE, EVIDENCE IN TRIALS AT COMMON LAW, §1684, at 953 (Chadbourn rev. 1974).

349. Act approved May 13, 1871, 1st Leg., R.S., An Act to Regulate Proceedings in the District Courts: Evidence, §92, 1846 Tex. Gen. Laws 388, *reprinted in* 2 H.P.N. GAMMEL, THE LAWS OF TEXAS 1822-1897, at 1694 (Austin, Gammel Book Co. 1898) (former Texas Revised Civil Statutes art. 3718 deemed repealed as to civil proceedings effective 1983 and as to criminal proceedings effective 1986); *see, e.g.*, **Ex parte Cooper**, 308 S.W.2d 22, 22 (Tex. Crim. App. 1957) (Colorado laws would be recognized when evidence was introduced satisfying former TEX. REV. CIV.

RULE 902

tion of Texas Rule of Civil Procedure 184(a),[350] which provided that Texas courts would take judicial notice of the laws of Texas, the United States, and all states, territories, and jurisdictions of the United States.[351] Article 3718 was used in proving the law of foreign countries, however, because courts did not generally take judicial notice of foreign laws.[352]

Rule 902(5) expands the scope of self-authenticating official publications to include books, pamphlets, or other publications that appear to have been issued by public authority.[353] Forgery or misrepresentation of such material is unlikely, and official publications rarely contain serious substantive mistakes of official policy or procedures.

STAT. art. 3718); *Garza v. Greyhound Lines, Inc.*, 418 S.W.2d 595, 597 & n.3 (Tex. Civ. App.—San Antonio 1967, no writ) (admission of Mexican substantive law required introduction of statute book printed under authority of Mexican government); *Hunter v. West*, 293 S.W.2d 686, 687 (Tex. Civ. App.—San Antonio 1956, no writ) (Mexican statute was inadmissible because offering party did not show that it was published under Mexican authority); *see also* Act approved June 21, 1951, 52nd Leg., R.S., ch. 471, 1951 Tex. Gen. Laws 830, *amended by* Act of June 5, 1953, 53rd Leg., R.S., ch. 304, §1, 1953 Tex. Gen. Laws 756, *amended by* Act approved June 16, 1961, 57th Leg., R.S., ch. 321, §1, 1961 Tex. Gen. Laws 685, *amended by* Act approved May 20, 1975, 64th Leg., R.S., ch. 280, §1, 1975 Tex. Gen. Laws 666 (former Texas Revised Civil Statutes art. 3731a deemed repealed as to civil proceedings effective 1983 and as to criminal proceedings effective 1986) (permitting proof of foreign laws with properly executed attestations and certificates); Act approved May 13, 1871, 1st Leg., R.S., An Act to Regulate Proceedings in the District Courts: Evidence, §92, 1846 Tex. Gen. Laws 388, *reprinted in* 2 H.P.N. GAMMEL, THE LAWS OF TEXAS 1822-1897, at 1694 (Austin, Gammel Book Co. 1898) (former Texas Revised Civil Statutes art. 3719 deemed repealed as to civil proceedings effective 1983 and as to criminal proceedings effective 1986) (copies certified by Secretary of State of Texas of any act or resolution in statute books or of any law or bill deposited in his office must be received as evidence of that act, resolution, law, or bill).

350. In 1990, the Texas Supreme Court repealed Rule 184 (which had formerly been Rule 184a) of the Texas Rules of Civil Procedure because it was redundant with Civil Rule 202. *Amendments to the Texas Rules of Civil Procedure, Texas Rules of Appellate Procedure, and Texas Rules of Civil Evidence*, 785-786 S.W.2d (Tex. Cases) LX (1990, amended 1998).

351. *See Thomas v. Linder*, 231 S.W.2d 891, 894 (Tex. Civ. App.—Austin 1950, writ ref'd) (court was required to take judicial notice of Office of Price Administration regulation).

352. *Purvis v. Morehead*, 304 S.W.2d 221, 224 (Tex. Civ. App.—Waco 1957, no writ). Refer to *Article II: Judicial Notice, supra* p. 147. In one case, for example, the court would permit authentication of Mexican statutes contained in a volume only by a showing that the volume was a statute book printed under the authority of the Mexican government. *Garza*, 418 S.W.2d at 597.

353. *See* TEX. R. EVID. 902(5); *see, e.g., In re Doe*, 501 S.W.3d 313, 321 n.11 (Tex. App.—Houston [14th Dist.] 2016, n.p.h.) (booklet issued by Texas State Department of Health Services and posted on its website was self-authenticating under Rule 902(5)); *Bower v. Edwards Cty. Appr. Dist.*, 752 S.W.2d 629, 633 (Tex. App.—San Antonio 1988, writ denied) (copy of "Guidelines for the Valuation of Agricultural Land" promulgated by Texas State Property Tax Board was self-authenticated under Civil Rule 902(5)); *cf.* 5 MUELLER & KIRKPATRICK, *supra* note 1, §9:34, at 589 (Federal Rule 902(5) covers official maps, legislative reports, surveys conducted by public agencies, manuals, and other publications, as well as statute books and case reports). Some courts have considered printouts from government-run websites to be self-authenticating "official publications" under Rule 902(5), as long as the printouts contain the website URL and dates of access. *See, e.g., Williams Farms Produce Sales, Inc. v. R&G Produce Co.*, 443 S.W.3d 250, 259 (Tex. App.—Corpus Christi 2014, no pet.) (docket sheet printed from uscourts.gov website that displayed date and time of printing was self-authenticating under Rule 902(5)); *see also Gen. Motors Corp. v. Harper*, 61 S.W.3d 118, 125-26 (Tex. App.—Eastland 2001, pet. denied) (court implicitly accepted party's argument that patents downloaded from Internet were "self-authenticating, official government publications" but did not cite rule); *Kishor v. TXU Energy Retail Co.*, No. 05-10-01496-CV (Tex. App.—Dallas 2011, no pet.) (memo op.; 11-17-11) (trial court did not abuse its discretion in excluding exhibit that defendant attempted to introduce under Rule 902(5); document was not book or pamphlet, did not identify its source, and did not contain URL); *cf. Williams v. Long*, 585 F. Supp. 2d 679, 686-89 (D. Md. 2008) (printout from Maryland Judiciary Case Search website was self-authenticating official publication under FED. R. EVID. 902(5)); *Hispanic Broad. Corp. v. Educ. Media Found.*, No. CV-02-7134 (C.D. Cal. 2003) (order; 10-30-03) (footnote 5; records from FCC website were

Rule 902(5) is identical to Federal Rule 902(5).[354] Like its federal counterpart, Rule 902(5) is silent on what level of government must authorize the publication.[355] Rule 902(5) should be construed broadly to include as many different levels of government as provided for in Rules 902(1) and 902(3).[356] Finally, the rule does not make all official publications admissible; it merely provides a way to authenticate them.[357]

F. Rule 902(6): Newspapers & Periodicals

Printed materials from newspapers or periodicals are self-authenticating under Rule 902(6).[358] There are three reasons behind the rule. First, the realities of the publishing business make the chance of forgery highly unlikely.[359] Second, a party opposing the introduction of newspapers or periodicals is frequently in a good position to prove any forgery by producing a genuine copy of the publication.[360] Third, the facts that would prove or disprove the genuineness of the publication are often within the opponent's knowledge; thus, it is reasonable for the opponent to bear the burden of proving forgery.[361] Although no earlier Texas authority specifically interprets the authentication of newspapers or periodicals, Rule 902(6) changes the common-law practice of requiring extrinsic evidence, such as testimony of the printer, to authenticate printed materials.[362]

One question unanswered by the rule is whether the presumption of authenticity extends to the authorship of the various notices and ads found in a newspaper. Before the adoption of Federal Rule 902(6), which is identical to Texas Rule 902(6), the leading federal case on the subject, ***Mancari v. Frank P. Smith, Inc.***, held that the mere presence of printed materials in the name of a particular person was insufficient to raise a

---

self-authenticating official publications under FED. R. EVID. 902(5)); Goode, *supra* note 63, at 40 (Federal Rule 902(5) can be used to authenticate material downloaded from a government website).

354. Federal Rule 902(5) is based on Federal Rule of Civil Procedure 44(a). *See* FED. R. CIV. P. 44(a); FED. R. EVID. 902 advisory committee's note, subdiv. (5).

355. Article 3718 had been similarly interpreted, for example, to exclude published municipal ordinances. ***Int'l & Great N. R.R. v. Hall***, 35 Tex. Civ. App. 545, 547, 81 S.W. 82, 84 (1904) (interpreting former TEX. REV. CIV. STAT. art. 2304, later codified as art. 3718, but repealed when the Rules were promulgated), *writ dism'd*, 98 Tex. 100, 81 S.W. 520 (1904).

356. *See* 5 WEINSTEIN & BERGER, *supra* note 26, §902.07[1], at 902-29 to 902-30 (discussing application of Federal Rule 902(5)).

357. FED. R. EVID. 902 advisory committee's note, subdiv. (5).

358. TEX. R. EVID. 902(6); *see **Donaldson v. Taylor***, 713 S.W.2d 716, 717 (Tex. App.—Beaumont 1986, no writ) (copy of newspaper advertisement was self-authenticated); *cf. **Snyder v. Whittacker Corp.***, 839 F.2d 1085, 1089 (5th Cir. 1988) (magazine article was self-authenticated under Federal Rule 902(6)). Recordings of radio and television news broadcasts are also self-authenticating in both civil and criminal proceedings. TEX. CIV. PRAC. & REM. CODE §22.027; TEX. CODE CRIM. PROC. art. 38.111.

359. *See* 5 MUELLER & KIRKPATRICK, *supra* note 1, §9:35, at 591; H.D. Wendorf, *Should Texas Adopt the Federal Rules of Evidence?*, 28 BAYLOR L. REV. 249, 279 (1976).

360. *See* 5 MUELLER & KIRKPATRICK, *supra* note 1, §9:35, at 591.

361. *Id.*; see C.E. Royston, Note, *Evidence—Authentication of Documents—Proof of Publication*, 15 S. CAL. L. REV. 115, 117 (1941) (defendant-publisher should be required to prove that it was not responsible for publication when defendant is the only party in possession of evidence).

362. *See* 7 WIGMORE, *supra* note 127, §2150, at 749; *see, e.g., **Lochner v. Silver Sales Serv.***, 59 S.E.2d 218, 222-23 (N.C. 1950) (newspaper advertisement was not self-authenticating).

presumption of authorship.[363] Although neither Federal Rule 902(6) nor Texas Rule 902(6) specifically states that the person listed in the advertisement is presumed to be the author, this presumption would be logical.[364] Jack Weinstein argues that because publishers invariably look to the named advertisers for payment and because it is not customary in the business community to give free advertising, the presumption of authorship is the more sensible approach.[365] At least one commentator, however, has suggested that authorship of newspaper advertisements must still be proved by extrinsic evidence; the presumption in Federal Rule 902(6) only makes it unnecessary to offer extrinsic proof that the copy of the newspaper itself is genuine.[366] Weinstein's interpretation is consistent with both Federal Rule 902(7) and Texas Rule 902(7), which presume the authorship of labels and inscriptions affixed on products in the ordinary course of business.[367] This issue is perhaps best left to the discretion of the trial judge after viewing the particular printed material and determining the purpose for which the printed material is being offered.

G. Rule 902(7): Trade Inscriptions & the Like

Rule 902(7), which is identical to Federal Rule 902(7), extends the presumption of authenticity to inscriptions, signs, tags, or labels fixed in the course of business. Courts and legislatures outside Texas have traditionally presumed the authenticity of distinctive marks used to indicate control or ownership of chattel such as livestock.[368] Texas courts also have held that a company name or insignia on a truck raises a presumption of ownership of that truck.[369] In other jurisdictions, the principle has been applied to marks on logs and timber[370] and license plates on automobiles, railroad cars, and other vehicles.[371]

---

363. 114 F.2d 834, 836 (D.C. Cir. 1940); see A.M.S., Annotation, *Authorship or Authenticity of Written or Printed Matter as Inferable Without Extrinsic Proof from Name Used Therein or from Its Contents or Subject Matter*, 131 A.L.R. 301, 305 (1941) (without applicable statute, advertisements are not self-authenticating).

364. *Cf.* 39 U.S.C. §3005(b) ("The public advertisement by a person engaged in [lottery] activities …, that remittances may be made by mail to a person named in the advertisement, is prima facie evidence that the latter is the agent or representative of the advertiser …."). *But see* Royston, *supra* note 361, at 115 (discussing case in which court held that in national advertising, local retailer listed in advertisement does not necessarily have any control over advertisement's placement or responsibility for its authorship).

365. 5 WEINSTEIN & BERGER, *supra* note 36, ¶902(6)[01], at 902-42; see also 5 MUELLER & KIRKPATRICK, *supra* note 1, §9:35, at 591, 594 (suggesting that advertisements should be self-authenticating, but noting absence of judicial decisions on point).

366. McMorrow, *supra* note 108, at 213.

367. *See* FED. R. EVID. 902(7); TEX. R. EVID. 902(7); *see also* 5 WEINSTEIN & BERGER, *supra* note 26, §902.09[1], at 902-31 (because business operations require reliance on trademarks, they should be considered self-authenticating).

368. *See, e.g.*, MONT. CODE ANN. §81-3-105 (certificate of recorded mark or brand is prima facie evidence of ownership of animals bearing mark or brand, as specified in certificate); ***State v. Rines***, 269 A.2d 9, 14 (Me. 1970) (brand on livestock is evidence of ownership); *see also* FED. R. EVID. 902 advisory committee's note, subdiv. (7) (cattle brands have received acceptance as prima facie proof of ownership).

369. ***Strickland Transp. Co. v. Atkins***, 223 S.W.2d 675, 678 (Tex. Civ. App.—Dallas 1949, no writ).

370. *See* S.C. CODE ANN. §39-15-720.

371. *See* VA. CODE ANN. §46.2-213; *see also* FED. R. EVID. 902 advisory committee's note, subdiv. (7) ("Inscriptions on trains and vehicles are held to be prima facie evidence of ownership or control."); *cf.* 19 U.S.C. §1615(2) (marks, labels, brands, or stamps indicating foreign origin are prima facie evidence of foreign origin of merchandise in certain forfeiture proceedings).

Courts outside Texas have not been as quick to extend the presumption of authenticity to product labels or trademarks that indicate source or origin. In **Keegan v. Green Giant Co.**, for example, the court held that the existence of the Green Giant trademark on the label of a can of peas was not sufficient to create an inference that the Green Giant Company was the manufacturer.[372] In another case, a court refused to take judicial notice of the fact that "Campbell's Soup" was a well-recognized brand and held that the label alone, without extrinsic evidence to connect the defendant to the particular can of soup, was not proof that the manufacturer had produced the defective product.[373] In both cases, the courts insisted on extrinsic evidence connecting the manufacturer to the products.[374]

Texas courts had also been reluctant to treat trademarks and trade inscriptions as prima facie evidence of manufacturing source or origin. In **Coca-Cola Bottling Co. v. Fillmore**,[375] the plaintiff sued a local Coca-Cola bottler for damages resulting from the discovery of a cockroach in a bottle of Coke. Although the plaintiff introduced the bottle—which had the location of the defendant-bottler inscribed on the bottom—into evidence, the **Fillmore** court held that the plaintiff had not offered sufficient evidence that the defendant had actually bottled the cockroach-infested soda.[376] However, under Rule 902(7), the only evidence that the plaintiff must tender to connect the product to the manufacturer is the label or trademark itself, as long as that label or trademark was placed on the product "in the course of business."[377] The phrase "in the course of business" should be construed to include nonprofit organizations, such as private universities and social organizations, that use inscriptions on the products they distribute.[378]

The logical and practical considerations of the rule support the changes it made to Texas common law. First, trade inscriptions and trade names are ordinarily registered with federal and state agencies, making them heavily regulated and unlikely to be forged.[379] Second, when genuineness is contested, the trademark owner, not the party

---

372. 110 A.2d 599, 601 (Me. 1954).

373. *Murphy v. Campbell Soup Co.*, 62 F.2d 564, 565 (1st Cir. 1933).

374. *Id.*; *Keegan*, 110 A.2d at 601.

375. 453 S.W.2d 239 (Tex. Civ. App.—Amarillo 1970, no writ).

376. *Id.* at 241; *see also* 2 GOODE ET AL., *supra* note 7, §902.8, at 302 (result in *Fillmore* would be the same under Civil Rule 902(7), and plaintiff would still be required to offer extrinsic evidence to prove defendant-bottler had provided Coke-filled bottles to vending machine). In *Fillmore*, the inscription was "Greenville, Texas," not "Coca-Cola Bottling Company of Lubbock." 453 S.W.2d at 241. Given the facial ambiguity of the inscription, some evidence was required to show that the Coca-Cola Bottling Company of Lubbock used the inscription "Greenville, Texas" on their bottles. *Id.*; *see also* **Michelin Tire Co. v. Pendland**, 416 S.W.2d 586, 588-89 (Tex. Civ. App.—Beaumont 1967, no writ) (oral testimony about logo on allegedly defective tire was insufficient to establish that defendant's trademark or trade name was on tire).

377. TEX. R. EVID. 902(7); *see* 5 WEINSTEIN & BERGER, *supra* note 26, §902.09[1], at 902-31 (without "strong contrary proof, the court should assume that the mark was placed in the regular course of business if it is in a form that would ordinarily be used").

378. 5 WEINSTEIN & BERGER, *supra* note 26, §902.09[1], at 902-31.

379. *Cf.* LaRocca, *supra* note 112, at 192 (discussing Federal Rule 902(7), which allows trademarks and insignia to be self-authenticating).

offering the evidence, is generally in the best position to offer evidence of authenticity.[380] Finally, a presumption of authenticity should favor consumers because manufacturers frequently spend a great deal of money persuading the consumer to identify a particular logo or trademark with the company.[381]

H. Rule 902(8): Acknowledged Documents

Documents accompanied by a certificate of acknowledgment executed by a notary public or similar officer are self-authenticating under Rule 902(8).[382] The rule is identical to Federal Rule 902(8). It is also almost identical to Texas statutory and common law, which has long provided that properly acknowledged documents may be admitted into evidence without further proof of execution.[383] In Texas, such an acknowledgment is made by declaring before a qualified officer that a particular document was executed for the consideration and purposes indicated in the document.[384] The officer before whom the acknowledgment is made authenticates the acknowledgment in a certificate, which is attested by his signature and seal, and states that the named person is known to him and appeared before him.[385]

Notaries most commonly execute acknowledgments.[386] The rationale supporting self-authentication of acknowledged documents is that a notary public's duties require him to verify both the identity of the person who signs a document before him and the fact that the person swore to the document.[387] Forgery of a notary's signature and seal is difficult, and the penalties for misconduct by a notary[388] are sufficient to guard against misuse of the office.

Rule 902(8) states that the seal and certificate of acknowledgment may also come from "another officer who is authorized to take acknowledgments." The rule itself does

---

380. Kenneth S. Broun, *Authentication and Contents of Writings*, 1969 LAW SOC. ORDER 611, 629.

381. *See* 5 WEINSTEIN & BERGER, *supra* note 26, §902.09[1], at 902-31.

382. *See, e.g., Ortega v. CACH, LLC*, 396 S.W.3d 622, 630-31 (Tex. App.—Houston [14th Dist.] 2013, no pet.) (notarized affidavits were self-authenticating under Rule 902(8) but did not fall within business-records exception of Rule 803(6) because they did not indicate trustworthiness and were likely prepared in anticipation of litigation; trial court should have excluded affidavits as hearsay); *Rockwall Commons Assocs., Ltd. v. MRC Mortg. Grantor Tr. I*, 331 S.W.3d 500, 511 (Tex. App.—El Paso 2010, no pet.) (notarized construction loan and guaranty agreement were self-authenticating and admissible under Rule 902(8)).

383. *See, e.g., Jousan v. Presidio Corp.*, 590 S.W.2d 524, 525 (Tex. Civ. App.—Houston [1st Dist.] 1979, no writ) (note was considered self-authenticating because of proper notarization); *Hughes v. Dopson*, 135 S.W.2d 148, 150 (Tex. Civ. App.—Amarillo 1939, no writ) (notarized acknowledgment was self-authenticating despite contrary assertions by signer of document). Virtually every state deems acknowledged documents acceptable evidence without further authentication. *See* FED. R. EVID. 902 advisory committee's note, subdiv. (8).

384. *See* TEX. CIV. PRAC. & REM. CODE §§121.004-121.008 (establishing procedures for notarized acknowledgments); TEX. GOV'T CODE §§406.101-406.113 (establishing procedures for online notarization); *see also Punchard v. Masterson*, 100 Tex. 479, 481, 101 S.W. 204, 205 (1907) (stating requirements to make acknowledgment self-authenticating).

385. *See* TEX. CIV. PRAC. & REM. CODE §§121.004(a), (b), 121.005.

386. For a detailed history of the notary public in Texas, see Michael J. Vaughn, Comment, *The Notary Public*, 16 BAYLOR L. REV. 388, 388 (1964).

387. *See* 5 MUELLER & KIRKPATRICK, *supra* note 1, §9:37, at 607.

388. *See* TEX. GOV'T CODE §406.009; *see also* TEX. PENAL CODE §37.02 (perjury).

not authorize any particular officer to take acknowledgments; it speaks only to those officers who already have the power under Texas law. Therefore, clerks of the district and county courts and judges of the county courts in Texas may take self-authenticating acknowledgments under Rule 902(8).[389] When a document is acknowledged outside Texas, various other officers, including notaries, have the statutory power to take the acknowledgment.[390]

The rule is silent on the requirements for the certificate of acknowledgment, but the clear intent is to grant self-authenticating status only to those certificates that comply with Texas law.[391] Accordingly, an acknowledgment taken by a person who is financially or beneficially interested in a transaction is not admissible under Rule 902(8) because such individuals are disqualified from taking acknowledgments in Texas.[392] The same principle also makes acknowledgments taken by parties to an instrument or shareholders of parties to an instrument inadmissible under Rule 902(8).[393] Finally, although the rule does not indicate whether it applies to acknowledgments made in foreign countries, such acknowledgments should be treated as self-authenticating under the rule if the certificate meets the requirements of the Texas statute governing foreign acknowledgments.[394]

I. Rule 902(9): Commercial Paper & Related Documents

Rule 902(9) presumes that "[c]ommercial paper, a signature on it, and related documents" are admissible "to the extent allowed by general commercial law." As used in the rule, "general commercial law" refers to the Uniform Commercial Code (U.C.C.), which is codified in Texas as the Texas Business and Commerce Code.[395] Thus, Rule 902(9) made no change to Texas evidentiary law because commercial documents that are self-authenticating under the U.C.C. are treated similarly under the Rules.

---

389. *See* TEX. CIV. PRAC. & REM. CODE §121.001(a).

390. *See id.* §121.001(b)-(d); *see also* **McLeod v. State**, 56 S.W.3d 704, 709-10 (Tex. App.—Houston [14th Dist.] 2001, no pet.) (judgment of DWI conviction in Kansas was properly self-authenticated when it included certification form signed by Kansas deputy officer, which was then notarized by Kansas notary public).

391. *See* TEX. R. EVID. 902(8) (self-authenticating documents must be "lawfully executed").

392. **Phillips v. Brazosport Sav. & Loan Ass'n**, 366 S.W.2d 929, 931-32 (Tex. 1963), *appeal dismissed*, 375 U.S. 438 (1964); *see, e.g.*, **Gulf Prod. Co. v. Cont'l Oil Co.**, 139 Tex. 183, 195-96, 164 S.W.2d 488, 493-94 (1942) (notary public was disqualified from taking acknowledgment of assignment in partnership because notary public had interest in assignment; upholding assignment notwithstanding disqualification because assignment was valid between parties without acknowledgment).

393. *See* **Sharber v. Atlanta Nat'l Bank**, 130 Tex. 296, 298, 109 S.W.2d 1042, 1043 (1937) (corporate acknowledgment taken by stockholder is invalid); **Towery v. Plainview Bldg. & Loan Ass'n**, 72 S.W.2d 948, 950 (Tex. Civ. App.—Amarillo 1934, no writ) (same).

394. *See* TEX. CIV. PRAC. & REM. CODE §121.001 (discussing circumstances under which officers may take acknowledgments); *see also* TEX. R. EVID. 902(3) (concerning admissibility of certain foreign documents). Refer to notes 325-339 *supra* and accompanying text.

395. *See* TEX. BUS. & COM. CODE tit. 1. Even under Federal Rule 902(9), which is identical to the Texas provision, the normal practice has been to refer to the particular state's version of the Uniform Commercial Code (U.C.C.). *See* FED. R. EVID. 902(9); 5 WEINSTEIN & BERGER, *supra* note 26, §902.11[1], at 902-34 to 902-35.

RULE 902

The U.C.C. provides that three types of documents can be self-authenticating.[396] First, section 1.307 makes certain third-party documents, such as bills of lading, prima facie evidence of their own authenticity.[397] This presumption applies only to documents that are issued or prepared by third parties in actions arising from contracts that authorize the documents.[398]

Second, Texas Business & Commerce Code section 3.308 presumes the genuineness of signatures on negotiable instruments.[399] This section makes two important statements, which are incorporated into Rule 902(9): (1) each signature on an instrument is admitted unless specifically denied in the pleadings,[400] and (2) even when the signature's effectiveness is at issue, the party claiming the validity of the signature almost always enjoys a presumption of genuineness.[401] Frequently, a person receives a negotiable instrument that has already passed through several hands. Because the holder may have no knowledge about the instrument's execution, it would be difficult for him to obtain evidence on this issue; the presumption avoids this unfairness.[402] Under Rule 902(9), a document that is treated as presumptively genuine by the U.C.C. should be admitted if the document appears on its face to be what the proponent claims it is.[403] If the party challenging the document introduces sufficient evidence of its lack of genuineness and the court concludes that a reasonable person would find that the document is not genuine, the court should find for the opponent on the point.[404] Otherwise, evidence attacking the signature's authenticity goes only to the weight to be given by the jury, not to the admissibility of the document.

Finally, Texas Business & Commerce Code section 3.505 states that formal certificates of protest, stamps by a drawee (the person ordered in a draft to make a payment)[405] indicating that payment was refused, and bank records indicating dishonor

---

396. For a detailed discussion of the U.C.C. evidentiary provisions, see James A. Branch, III, Note, *The Law of Evidence in the Uniform Commercial Code*, 1 GA. L. REV. 44 (1966).

397. TEX. BUS. & COM. CODE §1.307; *see **Maurice Pincoffs Co. v. S. Stevedoring Co.***, 489 S.W.2d 277, 278 (Tex. 1972) (bill of lading is self-authenticating under former TEX. BUS. & COM. CODE §1.202, now §1.307).

398. *See* TEX. BUS. & COM. CODE §1.307, cmt. 2; *see, e.g.*, **Atchison, Topeka & Santa Fe Ry. Co. v. Lone Star Steel Co.**, 498 S.W.2d 512, 514 (Tex. Civ. App.—Texarkana 1973, no writ) (bill of lading tendered by plaintiff was not admissible under former TEX. BUS. & COM. CODE §1.202, now §1.307, because it was not issued or prepared by a third party). Preferred status given by the parties to documents authorized by a contract renders the documents particularly trustworthy. *See* 5 WEINSTEIN & BERGER, *supra* note 26, §902.11[2], at 902-36.

399. TEX. BUS. & COM. CODE §3.308(a).

400. *Id.* Although the comment to §3.308 states that the denial need not be under oath, Texas Rule of Civil Procedure 93 requires sworn denials of the execution or genuineness of certain documents.

401. TEX. BUS. & COM. CODE §3.308(a). The plaintiff is not required to prove that a presumptively authentic document is authentic until some evidence is introduced that would support a finding that the signature is forged. *Id.* §3.308 cmt. 1. There is no presumption of genuineness under §3.308 in an action to enforce the obligation of a purported signer who has died or become incompetent. *Id.* §3.308(a).

402. *See* W. Harold Bigham, *Presumptions, Burden of Proof and the Uniform Commercial Code*, 21 VAND. L. REV. 177, 192 (1968) (discussing burdens of proof under the U.C.C.).

403. 5 WEINSTEIN & BERGER, *supra* note 26, §902.11[6], at 902-38.

404. *See id.*

405. TEX. BUS. & COM. CODE §3.103(a)(4).

are all admissible and create a presumption of dishonor.[406] Formal certificates of protest were presumptively authentic at common law,[407] and this section merely expands the type of evidence admissible to prove dishonor. Bank records and a drawee's stamps are regarded as particularly trustworthy—bank records are unlikely to indicate a dishonor that did not exist, and a holder is unlikely to proceed on the basis of dishonor if he could obtain payment.[408]

Like Rule 803(6), the business-records exception to the hearsay rule,[409] the self-authentication provision of Rule 902(9) is based on the general reliability of commercial documents.[410] Courts may reasonably rely on the authenticity of these documents because people regularly rely on their facial validity when making important financial transactions.

J. Rule 902(10): Business Records Accompanied by Affidavit

Under Rule 902(10), business records accompanied by a properly phrased and executed affidavit or declaration[411] are self-authenticating.[412] The rule establishes the

---

406. *Id.* §3.505(a).

407. *See* Branch, *supra* note 396, at 73 (former TEX. BUS. & COM. CODE §3.510, now §3.505, "has not made any substantial change in authentication requirements").

408. *See* 5 WEINSTEIN & BERGER, *supra* note 26, §902.11[4], at 902-37.

409. Refer to *Article VIII: Hearsay*, *supra* p. 897.

410. *Cf.* Goode, *supra* note 63, at 51 ("[W]hen dealing with business records [under Federal Rule 803(6)], ... the routine nature of storing the information electronically and the business's reliance on it (as well as on computer-generated information) provide adequate assurance of trustworthiness in the run-of-the-mill case.").

411. The proponent of business records may use an unsworn declaration made under penalty of perjury. TEX. R. EVID. 902(10)(B) & cmt. (2014); *see* TEX. CIV. PRAC. & REM. CODE §132.001; *see, e.g.*, *Dominguez v. State*, 441 S.W.3d 652, 658-59 (Tex. App.—Houston [1st Dist.] 2014, no pet.) (telephone records were properly authenticated when accompanied by unsworn declaration by employee of phone company certifying under penalty of perjury that his statements were true and accurate to the best of his knowledge and belief). See *O'Connor's Texas Rules * Civil Trials* (2017), "Unsworn declaration," ch. 1-B, §3.2.18, p. 14.

412. *See, e.g.*, *Larson v. Family Violence & Sexual Assault Prevention Ctr.*, 64 S.W.3d 506, 511 (Tex. App.—Corpus Christi 2001, pet. denied) (business-records affidavits by custodians of records for two news stations met requirements of Rule 902(10); thus, videotapes of newscasts authenticated under Rule 901(a) were admissible as summary-judgment evidence without a sponsoring witness); *Fullick v. City of Baytown*, 820 S.W.2d 943, 945-46 (Tex. App.—Houston [1st Dist.] 1991, no writ) (tax statements from school districts were self-authenticated); *March v. Victoria Lloyds Ins.*, 773 S.W.2d 785, 789 (Tex. App.—Fort Worth 1989, writ denied) (blood-alcohol test was admissible as business record with affidavit).

Rule 902(10) restates the authentication-by-affidavit provisions of former article 3737e of the Texas Business Records Act, with one significant change: X-rays are no longer governed by special rules of authentication. Act of May 27, 1969, 61st Leg., R.S., ch. 353, §1, 1969 Tex. Gen. Laws 1076, *amended by* Act approved May 18, 1973, 63rd Leg., R.S., ch. 128, §1, 1973 Tex. Gen. Laws 276 (former Texas Revised Civil Statutes art. 3737e, §5, deemed repealed as to civil proceedings effective 1983 and as to criminal proceedings effective 1986); *see* TEX. R. CIV. EVID. 902 cmt., 641-642 S.W.2d (Tex. Cases) LXV (1983, amended 1998). Under article 3737e, a party seeking to introduce X-rays by affidavit had to meet certain prerequisites that were not required for business records in general. Specifically, the proponent had to show that the X-rays were taken in a U.S. hospital, in accordance with good radiological techniques, and by a person competent to take them. Act approved May 27, 1969, 61st Leg., R.S., ch. 353, §1, 1969 Tex. Gen. Laws 1076, *amended by* Act approved May 18, 1973, 63rd Leg., R.S., ch. 128, §2, 1973 Tex. Gen. Laws 277 (former Texas Revised Civil Statutes art. 3737e, §6, deemed repealed as to civil proceedings effective 1983 and as to criminal proceedings effective 1986). The proponent also had to show that the X-rays were made under the supervision of the head of the hospital radiology department, and the X-ray had to be accompanied by the affidavit of that person or one of his partners. *Id.* Rule 902(10) eliminated these requirements, under the theory that

predicate for the business-records exception to the hearsay rule[413] through the affidavit or declaration of the person who would otherwise testify to those facts. It is a simple, frequently used rule that saves considerable time for courts, parties, and businesses. Of course, business records may be introduced without a self-authenticating affidavit or declaration through the testimony of a custodian of records or another qualified person.[414] Rule 902(10) simply makes a sponsoring witness unnecessary if the business records are accompanied by that person's affidavit or declaration.

For an affidavit or declaration to be authenticated under Rule 902(10), certain prerequisites must be met. First, the records must meet the requirements of Rule 803(6) or 803(7).[415] Second, the affidavit accompanying the records must comply with Rule 902(10)(B)[416] and "any other requirements of law."[417] The reference to "any other re-

---

X-rays are no different from other regularly maintained records and should be treated accordingly. *See* TEX. R. CIV. EVID. 902 cmt., 641-642 S.W.2d (Tex. Cases) LXV (1983, amended 1998). Although the comment was deleted in the 1998 unification of the Civil and Criminal Rules as no longer necessary, it accurately states the current law.

The Federal Rules had no analogue to this rule until 2000. Federal Rules 902(11) and 902(12) address the self-authentication requirements for domestic and foreign business records. *See* FED. R. EVID. 902(11) (domestic), FED. R. EVID. 902(12) (foreign). The requirements in Federal Rule 902(11) have some similarities to those in Texas Rule 902(10), although the federal rule does not contain the specific service requirements or sample language that the Texas rule does. *See* FED. R. EVID. 902(11) (proponent of records must give adverse party reasonable notice of intent to offer records and must provide opportunity for inspection). Refer to notes 419-420 *infra* and accompanying text. In *DirecTV, Inc. v. Murray*, the trial court held that two business-records affidavits sufficiently authenticated e-mails contained in business records. 307 F. Supp. 2d 764, 770-73 (D.S.C. 2004). In that case, one person was the custodian of the business records for the business itself, but he then transferred those materials to another person; both people submitted affidavits that complied with the requirements of Federal Rule 902(11). *DirecTV*, 307 F. Supp. 2d at 772-73. The first custodian addressed the creation of the records, and the second provided evidence of their integrity. *Id.* Although the court stated that it was a close question, it noted that the opponent had received proper advance notice when the affidavits were filed and had not demonstrated that the affiants' foundation was "so weak as to fail to meet the minimal standards of authenticity established by Article 9." *Id.* at 773 n.4.

The Judicial Conference Committee on Rules of Practice and Procedure has approved—and the U.S. Supreme Court has adopted—amendments to Federal Rule 902. *See* U.S. Supreme Court, Miscellaneous Order, *Rules of Evidence* (Apr. 27, 2017), www.supremecourt.gov/orders/courtorders/frev17_d186.pdf; *Report of the Judicial Conference: Committee on Rules of Practice & Procedure*, Agenda E-19, at Rules 31-33 & App. C (Sept. 2016), www.uscourts.gov/rules-policies/archives/committee-reports/reports-judicial-conference-september-2016. New Rule 902(13) would allow a party to authenticate records generated by a process or system through certification of a qualified person and without the testimony of a foundation witness. New Rule 902(14) would provide the same self-authentication for data copied from an electronic device, storage medium, or file. Under both rules, the party must still comply with the certification requirements of Rule 902(11) or (12) and the notice requirements of Rule 902(11). If Congress does not take contrary action, the amendments will take effect December 1, 2017. For the final version of the amendments, go to www.uscourts.gov/rules-policies.

413. Refer to *Article VIII: Hearsay, supra* p. 897.

414. *See* **Brooks v. Hous. Auth.**, 926 S.W.2d 316, 322 (Tex. App.—El Paso 1996, no writ) ("In introducing business records, a party may proffer an affidavit from the custodian of records or call the custodian or other qualified person to testify in person concerning the business records."); *see, e.g.*, **U.S. Fid. & Guar. Co. v. Goudeau**, 272 S.W.3d 603, 610 (Tex. 2008) (underinsured-motorist policy was authenticated by custodian of records for insurance company).

415. TEX. R. EVID. 902(10). Refer to *Article VIII: Hearsay, supra* p. 897.

416. Rule 902(10)(B) is the form of the affidavit. While an affidavit is sufficient if it follows the language set out in Rule 902(10)(B), the form in the rule is not exclusive. TEX. R. EVID. 902(10)(B); *see also* TEX. CIV. PRAC. & REM. CODE §18.002(c) (form of affidavit under §18.002 is not exclusive). Before the 2014 amendments to Rule 902(10), an affidavit that "substantially complied" with the requirements of the rule was sufficient. *See* **Rockwall Commons Assocs., Ltd. v. MRC Mortg. Grantor Tr. I**, 331 S.W.3d 500, 509-10 (Tex. App.—El Paso 2010, no pet.); **Venable v. State**, 113 S.W.3d 797, 800 (Tex. App.—Beaumont 2003, pet. ref'd). Some courts had held that records were not

quirements of law" incorporates the requirements of Texas Civil Practice & Remedies Code sections 18.001 and 18.002 for affidavits offered as prima facie proof of the cost or necessity of services or medical expenses.[418] Third, the records and the affidavit must be served on each other party to the case at least 14 days before trial.[419] Even if the service requirements in Rule 902(10)(A) are not met, the court may order that a business record be treated as presumptively authentic if good cause is shown.[420]

K. Rule 902(11): Presumptions Under a Statute or Rule

Rule 902(11) provides that extrinsic evidence of authenticity is unnecessary for "[a] signature, document, or anything else that a statute or rule prescribed under statutory authority declares to be presumptively or prima facie genuine or authentic."[421] The rule is one of three in Article IX that prevent the Texas Rules from displacing other authen-

---

self-authenticating if the accompanying affidavit lacked a notarial seal or if the affidavit did not state that the affiant had personal knowledge. *See, e.g.*, ***Venable***, 113 S.W.3d at 799-801 (business-records affidavit by employee of cell-phone company did not substantially comply with Rule 902(10) because it lacked a statement of personal knowledge and a notarial seal; failure to exclude records was harmless error). Even when a business-records affidavit submitted under this rule is not completely accurate, such as when it misstates or omits the number of pages attached, the exhibit has been determined to be sufficiently self-authenticated for admission into evidence. *See, e.g.*, ***Spradlin v. State***, 100 S.W.3d 372, 382 (Tex. App.—Houston [1st Dist.] 2002, no pet.) (affidavit from custodian of business records substantially complied with requirements of Rule 902(10), even though the affidavit did not indicate the number of pages contained in the records); ***Adams v. State***, 985 S.W.2d 582, 584 (Tex. App.—Eastland 1998, pet. ref'd) (medical records were properly admitted under Criminal Rule 902(10), even though affidavit misstated number of pages in each exhibit). Such discrepancies go to the weight of the evidence, not its admissibility, unless there is specific evidence of the untrustworthiness of the affidavit or the underlying records. ***Adams***, 985 S.W.2d at 583-84.

417. Tex. R. Evid. 902(10).

418. Tex. R. Evid. 902 cmt. (2014). Specifically, those affidavits must (1) be made by the person who provided the service or the person in charge of records, (2) state that the services were necessary and were provided at a cost reasonable at the time and place of service, and (3) include an itemized statement of the services and charges. Tex. Civ. Prac. & Rem. Code §18.001(b), (c); *see id.* §18.002. The records attached to the medical-expenses affidavit (see Tex. Civ. Prac. & Rem. Code §18.002(b-1)) must also meet certain admissibility standards; that is, only evidence of recoverable medical expenses is admissible at trial. *See* Tex. Civ. Prac. & Rem. Code §18.002(b-2); ***Haygood v. De Escabedo***, 356 S.W.3d 390, 399 (Tex. 2011). For further discussion of the requirements under Texas Civil Practice & Remedies Code §§18.001 and 18.002, see ***O'Connor's Texas Rules * Civil Trials*** (2017), "Affidavit for past expenses," ch. 8-C, §8.4.4(2), p. 800.

419. Tex. R. Evid. 902(10)(A). See ***O'Connor's Texas Rules***, "Records & affidavit are served," ch. 8-C, §8.4.4(1)(c), p. 800. The records and affidavit can be served by any method permitted under Texas Rule of Civil Procedure 21a. Tex. R. Evid. 902(10)(A); *see* Tex. R. Civ. P. 21a. See ***O'Connor's Texas Rules***, "Methods of service," ch. 1-D, §4.2, p. 46.

A party is not required to file the records and affidavit with the court clerk. *See* Tex. R. Evid. 902 cmt. (2014); *see also* Tex. Sup. Ct. Order, Misc. Docket No. 14-9174 (eff. Sept. 1, 2014) (filing requirement eliminated for cases filed on or after Sept. 1, 2014). Rule 902(10) conforms with Texas Civil Practice & Remedies Code §18.001(d), which provides that the records attached to the affidavit to prove reasonable and necessary past expenses do not need to be filed with the court clerk before the trial begins, unless the Texas Rules of Evidence provide otherwise. *See* Tex. Civ. Prac. & Rem. Code §18.001(d).

420. Tex. R. Evid. 902(10). The rule does not establish what is necessary to show good cause. *See id. But cf.* ***Bruton v. State***, 428 S.W.3d 865, 880-81 (Tex. Crim. App. 2014) ("good cause" under Rule 902(3) means good cause for not obtaining a final certification, which is required by the rule, not good cause for believing a document is authentic despite the absence of the final certification; ignorance of rule's requirements is not a legitimate excuse).

421. Tex. R. Evid. 902(11). For example, a party's production of a document in response to written discovery authenticates the document for use against that party in any pretrial proceeding or at trial, unless the producing party timely objects to the document's authenticity. Tex. R. Civ. P. 193.7. Rule 902(11) is substantively the same as Federal Rule 902(10), even though the wording is slightly different. *See* Fed. R. Evid. 902(10).

tication rules. Rule 901(b)(10) accomplishes this objective for non-self-authenticating items by preserving any method of authentication provided for by statute or prescribed by courts under statutory authority.[422] Rule 902(4) also preserves the operative effect of statutes and rules on certified copies of public records.[423]

RULE 903

SUBSCRIBING WITNESS'S TESTIMONY

A subscribing witness's testimony is necessary to authenticate a writing only if required by the law of the jurisdiction that governs its validity.

COMMENTARY ON RULE 903

Under Texas common law, if an instrument was signed by one or more subscribing or attesting witnesses, its execution had to be proved by the testimony of at least one of the witnesses.[424] The logic behind the rule was that by selecting witnesses to attest to the instrument, the parties to that instrument agreed to depend on the witnesses' testimony to prove its execution.[425] Texas abandoned this rule for most cases in 1933, when the Legislature enacted Texas Revised Civil Statutes article 3734a.[426] That statute provided that when an attested writing was offered in evidence, and the writing was not required by law to be attested, the execution of the instrument could be proved in the same manner as if it were not attested.

Rule 903 is identical to Federal Rule 903 and almost identical to former article 3734a; the testimony of a subscribing witness is necessary to authenticate a writing only if specifically required by statute.[427] Thus, without contrary legislation, writings that frequently use a subscribing witness even though not required to do so by law (such as oil-and-gas division orders and releases) may be authenticated by the various methods illustrated in Rule 901.[428] In Texas, the most common example of a writing requiring subscribing witnesses is a will that is not entirely in the testator's handwriting.[429] But

---

422. Refer to notes 257-263 *supra* and accompanying text.

423. Refer to notes 340-347 *supra* and accompanying text.

424. *See* **Gainer v. Cotton**, 49 Tex. 101, 117 (1878); 2 McCORMICK ON EVIDENCE, *supra* note 19, §222, at 59; *see, e.g.,* **Hervey v. Edens**, 69 Tex. 420, 425, 6 S.W. 306, 308-09 (1887) (copy of deed was admissible when two of three signing witnesses acknowledged that it was copy of original). *See generally* H. Grady Chandler, Note, *Two New Rules of Evidence*, 11 TEX. L. REV. 501 (1933) (discussing the abrogation of a witness's testimony to authenticate a document).

425. 4 JOHN H. WIGMORE, A TREATISE ON THE ANGLO-AMERICAN SYSTEM OF EVIDENCE IN TRIALS AT COMMON LAW, §1288, at 697 (Chadbourn rev. 1972).

426. Act of May 6, 1933, 43rd Leg., R.S., ch. 109, 1933 Tex. Gen. Laws 279 (former Texas Revised Civil Statutes art. 3734a deemed repealed as to civil proceedings effective 1983 and as to criminal proceedings effective 1986).

427. *See* FED. R. EVID. 903; TEX. R. EVID. 903; Act of May 6, 1933, 43rd Leg., R.S., ch. 109, 1933 Tex. Gen. Laws 279 (former Texas Revised Civil Statutes art. 3734a deemed repealed as to civil proceedings effective 1983 and as to criminal proceedings effective 1986).

428. Black, *supra* note 39, at 1012.

429. *See* TEX. EST. CODE §§251.051, 251.052.

Texas statutes provide a self-proving procedure for these documents, making the testimony of subscribing witnesses unnecessary.[430] Thus, the final clause of Rule 903 would apply to wills that are not self-proving and to any other cases in which legislation requires the testimony of a subscribing witness.[431]

430. *See id.* §§251.101-251.107.
431. Black, *supra* note 39, at 1012.

ARTICLE X: CONTENTS OF WRITINGS, RECORDINGS, & PHOTOGRAPHS

Article X of the Texas Rules of Evidence codifies,[1] expands,[2] and liberalizes[3] the Texas common-law best-evidence doctrine.[4] The best-evidence rule provides that the original of a "writing, recording or photograph," or a reliable duplicate, is required when the content of that evidence is in dispute.[5] Article X of the Texas Rules is modeled after the provisions of Article X of the Federal Rules except for minor changes in language and the inclusion of Texas Rule 1009, which addresses the admissibility of translated foreign-language documents.[6]

The purpose of the best-evidence rule (also referred to as the "original document rule")[7] is to prevent inaccuracy and fraud.[8] The rule developed in the eighteenth century, when pretrial discovery was practically nonexistent and manual copying was the

---

1. *See* TEX. R. EVID. 1001-1009.

2. Under Article X, the best-evidence rule applies to writings, photographs, electronically stored information, and recordings. TEX. R. EVID. 1001. Under the common law, it applied only to the contents of writings. *See* ***Henriksen v. State***, 500 S.W.2d 491, 495 (Tex. Crim. App. 1973) (under Texas common law, best-evidence rule applies only to documents and not to photographs).

3. Rules 1001 and 1003 together liberalize the common-law doctrine by making "duplicates" of writings, recordings, electronically stored information, and photographs almost as admissible as "originals." *See* TEX. R. EVID. 1001, 1003.

4. ***Englund v. State***, 946 S.W.2d 64, 67 (Tex. Crim. App. 1997); ***Ballard v. State***, 23 S.W.3d 178, 181 (Tex. App.—Waco 2000, no pet.).

5. *See* TEX. R. EVID. 1002, 1003; ***Englund***, 946 S.W.2d at 67.

6. Olin G. Wellborn III, *The "Best Evidence" Article of the Texas Rules of Evidence*, 18 ST. MARY'S L.J. 99, 101-02 (1986); *see* TEX. R. EVID. 1009 & cmt. ("Comment to 1998 change: This is a new rule."). Refer to notes 208-238 *infra* and accompanying text.

7. *See* 2 MCCORMICK ON EVIDENCE §231, at 87 (Kenneth S. Broun ed., 6th ed. 2006). The best-evidence rule requires the production of an original document and not, as the name implies, the best evidence. Thus, many commentators refer to the rule as the "original document rule." ***Seiler v. Lucasfilm, Ltd.***, 808 F.2d 1316, 1318 (9th Cir. 1986).

8. The best-evidence rule developed because of the "central position which the written word occupies in the law." 2 MCCORMICK ON EVIDENCE, *supra* note 7, §232, at 88; *see **Seiler***, 808 F.2d at 1319. The historical rationale for the best-evidence rule has been explained as follows:

> The best evidence rule is designed to assist in the search for truth. The rule originated in the Middle Ages when the document itself was considered to be the right the party was attempting to assert, and was therefore strictly required. Exceptions developed as courts accepted secondary evidence to prove the contents of the writing, realizing the harsh consequences which sometimes resulted from loss of the original document. As technology has developed, diminishing the probability of error or fraud in the copying process, secondary evidence is judged to be more accurate and courts have developed a flexible approach to application of the best evidence rule.

In re Porras, 224 B.R. 367, 370 (Bankr. W.D. Tex. 1998); *see also* 4 JOHN H. WIGMORE, EVIDENCE IN TRIALS AT COMMON LAW §1180, at 418 (Chadbourn rev. 1972) (discussing reasons to produce original material and the law's dissatisfaction with secondary evidence). In *Englund v. State*, the court of criminal appeals set out four reasons for the common-law best-evidence rule: (1) the exact wording of a document is frequently important—particularly with operative or dispositive instruments, in which a slight variation in wording can mean a great difference in rights, (2) the rule enhances the accuracy of oral or written secondary evidence, which is susceptible to both human and mechanical error, (3) the rule promotes the prevention of fraud and misleading testimony about the documents—all parties can examine the documents for alterations, deletions, or additions, and the documents themselves will corroborate or refute testimony about their contents, and (4) the appearance of the original may supply information about its authenticity that a copy may lack. 946 S.W.2d at 67-68.

only means of reproducing documents.[9] The best-evidence rule is rarely litigated to-day because broad pretrial discovery has become routine, particularly in civil cases, and technological developments such as photocopiers and scanners reduce the risk of accidental errors.[10] The modern justification for the rule has expanded from prevention of fraud to the recognition that when the contents of a writing are at issue, oral testimony as to the terms of the writing is subject to a substantial risk of error.[11]

The best-evidence rule applies only when the contents of a writing, recording, or photograph are given legal significance by substantive law (for example, in contract litigation, libel suits, and obscenity cases) or when a party chooses to prove a fact in issue through the contents of a document.[12] It is not a general rule of evidentiary preference that would apply to nondocumentary evidence.[13] The rule does not apply to testimony

---

9. *See Seiler*, 808 F.2d at 1319; Fed. R. Evid. 1001 advisory committee's note, paragraph (1); *see also* 2 McCormick on Evidence, *supra* note 7, §232, at 88 ("The danger of mistransmitting critical facts which accompanies the use of written copies or recollection, but which is largely avoided when an original writing is presented to prove its terms, justifies the preference of original documents.").

10. *See Seiler*, 808 F.2d at 1318-19; Fed. R. Evid. 1001 advisory committee's note, paragraph (1).

11. *See Seiler*, 808 F.2d at 1319 ("The human memory is not often capable of reciting the precise terms of a writing ....").

12. *See* 5 Christopher B. Mueller & Laird C. Kirkpatrick, Federal Evidence §10:18, at 741-42 (3d ed. 2007). Although this observation pertains to the Federal Rules, it also applies to the Texas Rules. In *Overton v. State*, a litigant made a strategically unsound decision to prove a fact through the use of the contents of a document. 490 S.W.2d 556, 560 (Tex. Crim. App. 1973). The prosecutor attempted to prove ownership of a money bag stolen in a robbery through written records kept by Church's Fried Chicken. *Id.* Because the prosecutor's question was about the contents of the written records, the court stated that the defendant's best-evidence objection should have been sustained. *Id.* Nonetheless, the court held that the error was harmless because a witness had already testified that the money bag appeared to be the same one that was taken in the robbery. *Id.*

13. *See* 2 McCormick on Evidence, *supra* note 7, §230, at 86 ("While some modern opinions still refer to the 'best evidence' notion as if it were today a general governing legal principle, most would adopt the view of modern textwriters that there is no such general rule."); 2 Roy R. Ray, Texas Practice: Texas Law of Evidence Civil and Criminal §1561, at 254 & n.4 (3d ed. 1980) ("Apart from writings, there is no general requirement that the most satisfactory, persuasive or conclusive testimony must be produced."); *see, e.g., Henry v. State*, 509 S.W.3d 915, 918 (Tex. Crim. App. 2016) (taken together, judgments of conviction, testimony by defendant and another witness that defendant had been incarcerated for aggravated assault and aggravated robbery, and another witness's testimony about enhancement offenses were sufficient evidence to link defendant to enhancement offenses; "Texas does not have a 'best evidence' rule that requires that 'the fact of a prior conviction be proven with any document, much less any specific document'" (quoting *Flowers v. State*, 220 S.W.3d 919, 921 (Tex. Crim. App. 2007))); *Keaton v. State*, 755 S.W.2d 209, 210 (Tex. App.—Houston [1st Dist.] 1988, pet. ref'd) (production of copy of city ordinance was not required; police officer's testimony was sufficient because best-evidence rule did not apply); *Moreno v. State*, No. 13-15-00159-CR (Tex. App.—Corpus Christi 2016, pet. ref'd) (memo op.; 10-20-16) (best-evidence rule did not require State to introduce handgun itself instead of photograph of handgun). As summarized by Jack Weinstein and Margaret Berger:

> [T]he best evidence rule ... is designed to assist in the search for the truth. The rule is, however, only a minor tool. It is subject to many exceptions ... and should never be applied so rigidly as to interfere with good trial sense. Doubts should be resolved in favor of admissibility; there should almost never be a reversal for failing to exclude secondary evidence of content.
>
> ....
>
> [W]hen there is any doubt, secondary evidence can be admitted, [and] many courts will leave it to the [trier of fact] to determine its probative force discounted by the failure to produce an original. Reversals for admission will be rare since there is almost never real prejudice that the opponent of the evidence cannot overcome.

6 Jack B. Weinstein & Margaret A. Berger, Weinstein's Federal Evidence §1001.02, at 1001-7 to 1001-8, §1002.04[5][b], at 1002-14 to 1002-15 (Joseph M. McLaughlin ed., 2d ed. 2009).

about a writing, recording, or photograph if the testimony is not offered to prove the contents of that writing, recording, or photograph.[14] Thus, the rule does not apply when a witness (1) testifies about the existence, location, delivery, size, or execution of a document[15] or (2) uses a document to refresh his memory but does not introduce the document into evidence to prove its contents.[16] The rule also does not apply if a document concerns a collateral issue (i.e., one not closely related to a controlling issue), even when the contents of the document are to be proved.[17]

---

14. *See* TEX. R. EVID. 1002; *see, e.g.*, ***United States v. Rose***, 590 F.2d 232, 237 (7th Cir. 1978) (best-evidence doctrine did not apply when government sought to prove contents of conversation rather than contents of recording); ***Shugart v. State***, 32 S.W.3d 355, 363 (Tex. App.—Waco 2000, pet. ref'd) (best-evidence rule did not apply to letters purportedly written by defendant to friend, indicating defendant's fear of victim, and was not a proper basis for excluding friend's testimony).

15. *See, e.g.*, ***United States v. Levine***, 546 F.2d 658, 668-69 (5th Cir. 1977) (best-evidence rule did not apply to the witnesses' testimony about the existence and general nature of 16 obscene films that were not a part of the indictment for interstate shipment of obscene films); ***Reyna v. State***, 477 S.W.2d 564, 566 (Tex. Crim. App. 1972) (witness could testify that a beer license had been issued, without producing the license itself, to prove its existence); ***Osuna v. Quintana***, 993 S.W.2d 201, 206 (Tex. App.—Corpus Christi 1999, no pet.) (best-evidence rule did not require production of bank statements when testimony was offered to show the source of the money deposited, not the amount, because bank statement would not have shown that information); ***Jensen Constr. Co. v. Dall. Cty.***, 920 S.W.2d 761, 768 (Tex. App.—Dallas 1996, writ denied) (best-evidence rule did not apply to affidavit that was offered to explain the contract and its relationship to the damages complained of; affidavit was not offered to prove contract's contents), *disapproved on other grounds*, ***Travis Cty. v. Pelzel & Assocs.***, 77 S.W.3d 246 (Tex. 2002); ***Parkway/Lamar Partners, L.P. v. Tom Thumb Stores, Inc.***, 877 S.W.2d 848, 850 (Tex. App.—Fort Worth 1994, writ denied) (best-evidence rule did not apply to affidavits explaining accounting techniques, their relation to documents in record, and other accounting principles because they did not attempt to prove contents of any other documents); ***Cook v. State***, 832 S.W.2d 62, 67 (Tex. App.—Dallas 1992, no pet.) (best-evidence rule did not apply when State offered copy of parole-violation warrant solely to prove that an outstanding warrant existed; copy of warrant was admissible to determine warrant's sufficiency to justify arrest because defendant did not contest warrant's authenticity or the fairness of admitting a duplicate).

16. ***Green v. State***, 617 S.W.2d 253, 254 (Tex. Crim. App. [Panel Op.] 1981); *see also* ***In re J.C.K.***, 143 S.W.3d 131, 142 (Tex. App.—Waco 2004, no pet.) (Rule 1006 did not apply to witness's testimony about health-care expenses when witness used summary document to refresh her memory under Rule 612).

17. *See* TEX. R. EVID. 1004(e); *see, e.g.*, ***Ali v. State***, 26 S.W.3d 82, 88 (Tex. App.—Waco 2000, no pet.) (even assuming defense had made a best-evidence objection at trial, testimony about contents of car-rental agreement was admissible because that document and its contents were only collaterally related to the issues in case about counterfeit driver's license); ***White v. Bath***, 825 S.W.2d 227, 231 (Tex. App.—Houston [14th Dist.] 1992, writ denied) (when deposition's contents were only collaterally related to controlling issue of whether discovery abuse had occurred, best-evidence rule did not apply; counsel's statements about deposition's contents were sufficient); ***Keaton***, 755 S.W.2d at 210-11 (in case involving failure to maintain car insurance, issue of whether police officer stopped defendant within city limits was collateral; best-evidence rule did not apply to testimony about contents of city ordinance specifying incorporated areas); ***Prudential Ins. v. Black***, 572 S.W.2d 379, 380-81 (Tex. Civ. App.—Houston [14th Dist.] 1978, no writ) (ownership of property was only collaterally related to the breach-of-lease-contract issue; title evidence did not need to be produced). *See generally* 2 RAY, *supra* note 13, §1567 (discussing documents that are only collaterally involved). Refer to notes 142-147 *infra* and accompanying text.

In ***Mega Child Care, Inc. v. Texas Department of Protective & Regulatory Services***, the child-care facility raised a best-evidence objection to the testimony of a DPRS investigator who stated that when she asked an employee of the facility if there was any paperwork on certain children, the employee "pointed to ... an attachment to the file cabinet that had some files in it." 29 S.W.3d 303, 310 (Tex. App.—Houston [14th Dist.] 2000, no pet.). The court of appeals stated that the employee's gesture toward a file cabinet did not allude to the *contents* of any writing; thus, the best-evidence rule was inapplicable. *Id.* at 311. The child-care facility made the same objection to the investigator's reference to "a paperwork discrepancy." *Id.* at 310-11. While this testimony might allude to the contents of a writing, any factual dispute over a paperwork discrepancy was not "closely related to a controlling issue in the case"; thus, the production of the original paperwork was not required under Article X. *Id.* at 311.

Although the best-evidence rule requires the original or the most accurate rendition of a document (e.g., a photocopy or an electronic image), Rules 1004 to 1007 permit exceptions when the original (or a reliable duplicate) is unavailable,[18] when the document is a public record,[19] when production of the document would be unduly burdensome,[20] or when the contents of the document are proved by the testimony, deposition, or written statement of the party against whom the document is offered.[21]

RULE 1001

DEFINITIONS THAT APPLY TO THIS ARTICLE

In this article:

(a) A "writing" consists of letters, words, numbers, or their equivalent set down in any form.

(b) A "recording" consists of letters, words, numbers, or their equivalent recorded in any manner.

(c) A "photograph" means a photographic image or its equivalent stored in any form.

(d) An "original" of a writing or recording means the writing or recording itself or any counterpart intended to have the same effect by the person who executed or issued it. For electronically stored information, "original" means any printout—or other output readable by sight—if it accurately reflects the information. An "original" of a photograph includes the negative or a print from it.

(e) A "duplicate" means a counterpart produced by a mechanical, photographic, chemical, electronic, or other equivalent process or technique that accurately reproduces the original.

RULE 1002

REQUIREMENT OF THE ORIGINAL

An original writing, recording, or photograph is required in order to prove its content unless these rules or other law provides otherwise.

---

18. *See* TEX. R. EVID. 1004. Refer to notes 110-147 *infra* and accompanying text.
19. *See* TEX. R. EVID. 1005. Refer to notes 148-165 *infra* and accompanying text.
20. *See* TEX. R. EVID. 1006 (permitting summaries of voluminous records). Refer to notes 166-190 *infra* and accompanying text.
21. *See* TEX. R. EVID. 1007. Refer to notes 191-198 *infra* and accompanying text.

RULE 1003

ADMISSIBILITY OF DUPLICATES

A duplicate is admissible to the same extent as the original unless a question is raised about the original's authenticity or the circumstances make it unfair to admit the duplicate.

COMMENTARY ON RULES 1001-1003

The best-evidence doctrine provides that "[i]n proving the content of a writing, recording, or photograph, where the terms of the content are material to the case, the original document must be produced unless it is shown to be unavailable for some reason other than the serious fault of the proponent, or unless secondary evidence is otherwise permitted by rule or statute."[22] Rules 1001 and 1002 expand the doctrine to include recordings and photographs, and Rule 1001(a), (b), and (d) make the doctrine applicable to electronically stored information.[23] Thus, under Rule 1002, a party who chooses to prove the content of a writing, recording, or photograph must introduce the item itself unless its production is excused by statute or some other rule of evidence.[24] The broad definition of writings and recordings under the rule is consistent with the doctrine's policy of protecting against inaccuracy when minor variations can greatly affect a party's legal interests.[25]

This expansion of the best-evidence doctrine is offset by Rule 1003, which treats a duplicate like an original except when the opponent questions the original's authenticity or when admission of the duplicate would be unfair under the circumstances.[26] This liberalized version of the best-evidence doctrine appears to meet its two central purposes: prevention of error and protection against fraud.[27]

---

22. 2 McCORMICK ON EVIDENCE, *supra* note 7, §231, at 87; *see Gillum v. Temple*, 546 S.W.2d 361, 364 (Tex. Civ. App.—Corpus Christi 1976, writ ref'd n.r.e.); *Celanese Coating Co. v. Soliz*, 541 S.W.2d 243, 247-48 (Tex. Civ. App.—Corpus Christi 1976, writ ref'd n.r.e.); 2 RAY, *supra* note 13, §1561, at 254. Charles McCormick notes that, in the quotation above, "[t]he term 'document' ... refers to all three types of exhibits—writings, recordings, and photographs." 2 McCORMICK ON EVIDENCE, *supra* note 7, §231, at 87 n.1.

23. *See* TEX. R. EVID. 1001(a) (writing is letters, words, numbers, or equivalent "in any form"), TEX. R. EVID. 1001(b) (recording is letters, words, numbers, or equivalent "in any manner"), TEX. R. EVID. 1001(d) (defining "original" for electronically stored information); *see also* TEX. R. EVID. 101(h)(7) (reference to any kind of writing or any other medium includes electronically stored information). Refer to notes 77-95 *infra* and accompanying text. Rule 1001 is identical to Federal Rule 1001; Rule 1002 is substantively identical to Federal Rule 1002.

24. *See Jurek v. Couch-Jurek*, 296 S.W.3d 864, 871 (Tex. App.—El Paso 2009, no pet.) ("Tex. R. Evid. 1002 generally precludes admission of parol evidence to prove the contents of a document.").

25. Wellborn, *supra* note 6, at 102.

26. *See In re Estate of Jones*, 197 S.W.3d 894, 898 n.3 (Tex. App.—Beaumont 2006, pet. denied) (when trial court admits a duplicate, it implicitly rules that there is no genuine issue of the original's authenticity, that the copy is an accurate reproduction of the original, and that the circumstances do not make it unfair to admit the copy into evidence).

27. *See* 2 McCORMICK ON EVIDENCE, *supra* note 7, §232, at 87-89 (discussing mistake and fraud as rationales for the rule).

Article X is not an independent basis for the admission of evidence. Any evidence offered under Article X must be otherwise competent and admissible.[28]

A. Writings

Rules 1001 through 1004 apply the best-evidence doctrine to writings. Rule 1001(a) defines a writing as consisting of "letters, words, numbers, or their equivalent set down in any form." As used in both Texas Rule 1001(a) and Federal Rule 1001(a), a writing can be and has been construed to include drawings as the "equivalent" of letters, words, or numbers.[29]

The general circumstances under which writings are subject to the best-evidence doctrine are the same under Article X as they were under the common law.[30] For example, the doctrine still applies only when a proponent attempts to prove the contents of a writing.[31] Neither Texas common law nor Rules 1001(a) and 1002 subject ordinary physical objects (e.g., articles of clothing, flags, or guns) to the doctrine.[32] However, "inscribed chattel"—objects bearing a mark or inscription (e.g., tombstones)—could pose some problems under the wording of Rules 1001(a) and 1002,[33] even though they did

---

28. *See Halstead v. State*, 891 S.W.2d 11, 12 (Tex. App.—Austin 1994, no pet.) (per curiam) (proffered letter was an out-of-court statement offered to prove the truth of its contents and thus was hearsay; Rule 1002 did not offer an independent basis for its admission).

29. For example, in *Seiler v. Lucasfilm, Ltd.*, the court decided that drawings in a copyright dispute were writings under former Federal Rule 1001(1), now Rule 1001(a), and that to hold otherwise would frustrate the policies underlying the rule. 808 F.2d 1316, 1318-19 (9th Cir. 1986). Further, the court commented that for this reason, "blueprints, engineering drawings, [and] architectural designs" would also fall within the meaning of the rule. *Id.* at 1320.

30. *See Ramsey v. Jones Enters.*, 810 S.W.2d 902, 905 (Tex. App.—Beaumont 1991, writ denied) (reversing judgment for plaintiff in a trespass-to-try-title action because plaintiff's title evidence consisted solely of title examiner's expert testimony without any supporting documentary evidence of title to the real property). As the court explained, the best-evidence rule under Article X requires production of the original document, a duplicate, or a satisfactory explanation for nonproduction whenever the substantive law gives legal significance to the writing itself:

> Legal history as well as public policy requires that proof in trespass to try title actions be as certain as available documentary evidence will allow. Establishing legal or equitable interest or title to real property demands far more than a swearing match among witnesses, whether expert or otherwise. It demands strict proof based in records and documents.

Id.

31. TEX. R. EVID. 1002; *DeSoto Wildwood Dev., Inc. v. City of Lewisville*, 184 S.W.3d 814, 828 (Tex. App.—Fort Worth 2006, no pet.); *Double Diamond, Inc. v. Van Tyne*, 109 S.W.3d 848, 853 (Tex. App.—Dallas 2003, no pet.); 2 RAY, *supra* note 13, §1566, at 265.

32. *See Keeney v. Odom*, 534 S.W.2d 409, 412 (Tex. Civ. App.—Beaumont 1976, writ ref'd n.r.e.); *Moreno v. State*, No. 13-15-00159-CR (Tex. App.—Corpus Christi 2016, pet. ref'd) (memo op.; 10-20-16); 2 RAY, *supra* note 13, §1561, at 254.

33. 5 MUELLER & KIRKPATRICK, *supra* note 12, §10:2, at 659 ("An automobile license plate, a police officer's badge, an identification card or driver's license, a road sign, a brand containing alpha or numeric characters, and a sales receipt, are all 'writings' within FED. R. EVID. 1001(1) [now Rule 1001(a)], hence potentially covered by the Best Evidence Doctrine.").

Commentators have suggested that courts focus on several factors, including the following, when deciding whether to apply the best-evidence rule to inscribed chattel:

(1) the relative importance of the expressive or communicative content of the object;

(2) the simplicity or complexity of the content and consequent risk of error in admitting other evidence;

not under Texas common law. In ***Keeney v. Odom***,[34] a common-law case, the court seemingly followed Charles McCormick's suggestion that the trial judge has discretion whether to apply the best-evidence doctrine to inscribed chattel "in light of such factors as the need for precise information as to the exact inscription, the ease or difficulty of production, and the simplicity or complexity of the inscription."[35] The Texas court concluded that when the gross weight of a truck was a material fact and when such information was inscribed on a metal plate attached to the truck, the trial court properly exercised its discretion by admitting testimony about the plate.[36]

Rule 1001(d) defines an original writing as the writing itself "or any counterpart intended to have the same effect by the person who executed or issued it."[37] Sometimes, substantive law and litigated issues determine which of several documents is the original writing in a case. For example, when a defendant was charged with making a ma-

---

(3) the strength of the proffered evidence, taking into account corroborative witnesses or evidence and the presence or absence of bias or self-interest on the part of the witnesses;

(4) the breadth of the margin for error within which a mistake in any testimonial account or other proof would not undermine the point to be proved;

(5) the presence or absence of an actual dispute as to content;

(6) the ease or difficulty of producing the object itself; and

(7) the reasons why the proponent of other evidence or content does not have or offer the object itself.

5 MUELLER & KIRKPATRICK, *supra* note 12, §10:2, at 659-60; *see also* Wellborn, *supra* note 6, at 104 (Texas rule "should not apply to signs, buildings, vehicles, and tombstones, but it should apply, for example, to a profusely inscribed carton where the terms are material to the case, such as in a product liability case based upon inadequacy of warnings or instructions").

34. 534 S.W.2d at 412.

35. 2 McCORMICK ON EVIDENCE, *supra* note 7, §233, at 91.

36. *See, e.g.*, ***Keeney***, 534 S.W.2d at 412 (because the plate was a marking on a chattel, any testimony about the plate did not violate the best-evidence rule). In ***United States v. Yamin***, a prosecution for sales of counterfeit Rolex, Piaget, Gucci, and Cartier watches, the Fifth Circuit refused to require the government to offer the watches themselves as the best evidence of the counterfeit marks and stated that "[t]he viewing of a simple and recognized trademark is not likely to be inaccurately remembered." 868 F.2d 130, 134 (5th Cir. 1989). The court further stated that the trial judge has discretion to treat an inscribed object as chattel to which the best-evidence rule does not apply. *Id.*

37. TEX. R. EVID. 1001(d). This definition follows earlier Texas law, which ascribed the attributes of an original to multiple originals. ***Birdo v. State***, 476 S.W.2d 697, 697-98 (Tex. Crim. App. 1972); *see also* ***Cross v. Everybodys***, 357 S.W.2d 156, 159 (Tex. Civ. App.—Fort Worth 1962, writ ref'd n.r.e.) (a duplicate original will satisfy best-evidence rule), *disapproved on other grounds*, ***Dall. Mkt. Ctr. Dev. Co. v. Liedeker***, 958 S.W.2d 382 (Tex. 1997); ***Hughey v. Donovan***, 135 S.W.2d 265, 266 (Tex. Civ. App.—Galveston 1939, no writ) (duplicate of contract satisfies best-evidence rule); ***Killingsworth v. Gen. Motors Acceptance Corp.***, 37 S.W.2d 823, 825 (Tex. Civ. App.—Waco 1931, no writ) (each duplicate or counterpart of an original instrument or writing is "primary evidence").

Sometimes there are multiple original documents. *See, e.g.*, ***State v. Dotson***, 224 S.W.3d 199, 200 n.2 (Tex. Crim. App. 2007) (describing how a grand jury returns multiple "original" signed indictments; clerk's file stamp showed that one of the signed originals met the presentment requirement). For example, each signed counterpart of a carbon-copy document is sometimes considered an original. *See* ***Fistere, Inc. v. Helz***, 226 A.2d 578, 580 (D.C. App. 1967) (each part of a multiplicate form is deemed an original); *see, e.g.*, ***Greater Kan. City Laborers Pension Fund v. Thummel***, 738 F.2d 926, 928 (8th Cir. 1984) (fact that someone else had written over the carbon-copy signature of contracting party went to the weight of the exhibit, not its admissibility); ***Birdo***, 476 S.W.2d at 697-98 (carbon copy of sales receipt was an original). Occasionally, only the document with the original signature is sufficient for purposes of the rule. 5 MUELLER & KIRKPATRICK, *supra* note 12, §10:11, at 705 (rejection of carbon-copy duplicates "may be warranted under FED. R. EVID. 1003 if the adverse party makes a credible showing that risks of significant alteration are palpable in the particular case"). Carbon-copy documents, however, are now largely obsolete. *Id.* §10:11, at 704.

terial false statement on a loan application and had submitted photocopies of checks as part of the application, the photocopies were originals for purposes of the best-evidence rule.[38] Similarly, when a defendant had attached a photocopy of a credit-card sales slip to support his reimbursement request for travel expenses, the photocopy was the original for purposes of prosecuting the submission of false travel vouchers.[39]

Sometimes, an original business record is itself a copy. For example, banks routinely make electronic copies or scanned images of depositors' checks and maintain those copies, instead of the checks themselves, as their original business records. These copies qualify as originals when offered as the bank's business records.[40] Similarly, retained copies of business letters, receipts, or other records may frequently be viewed as originals. Every impression of published material (e.g., newspapers, magazines, and books) is an original because impressions are interchangeable and the publisher is responsible for the reproduction of every one.[41] The best-evidence rule is satisfied for a recorded property deed by a certified copy of the recorded instrument, regardless of who possesses the original deed or where it is located.[42]

Rules 1001(e) and 1003 confer "duplicate" status on copies produced by photocopiers or any other mechanical, photographic, chemical, electronic, or equivalent process or technique that accurately reproduces the original.[43] For example, a fax transmission qualifies as a "duplicate" under the Rules.[44] Second- and third-generation copies (cop-

---

38. **United States v. Gerhart**, 538 F.2d 807, 810 n.4 (8th Cir. 1976).

39. **United States v. Rangel**, 585 F.2d 344, 346 (8th Cir. 1978).

40. **Williams v. United States**, 404 F.2d 1372, 1373 (5th Cir. 1968); *see also* FED. R. EVID. 1001 advisory committee's note, paragraph (4) ("[A] bank's microfilm record of checks cleared is the original as a record. However, a print offered as a copy of a check whose contents are in controversy is a duplicate."). Before the adoption of the Rules, former Texas Revised Civil Statutes article 3731b governed the admissibility of routinely made reproductions of records that were regularly kept for any kind of organized activity. Act of June 6, 1957, 55th Leg., ch. 418, 1957 Tex. Gen. Laws 1257 (former Texas Revised Civil Statutes art. 3731b deemed repealed as to civil proceedings effective 1983 and as to criminal proceedings effective 1986). The statute expressly provided that the "existence or non-existence of the original shall not affect the admissibility of the reproduction." *Id.* Because the supreme court repealed the statute when it adopted the Rules, Rule 1003 governs the admissibility of these reproductions.

41. 5 MUELLER & KIRKPATRICK, *supra* note 12, §10:6, at 690-91.

42. *See* TEX. R. EVID. 1005. Refer to notes 148-165 *infra* and accompanying text.

43. *See* TEX. R. EVID. 1001(e); **Hood v. State**, 944 S.W.2d 743, 747 (Tex. App.—Amarillo 1997, no pet.); **Hickson v. Martinez**, 707 S.W.2d 919, 926 (Tex. App.—Dallas 1985), *writ ref'd n.r.e.*, 716 S.W.2d 499 (Tex. 1986); *see, e.g.*, **Cook v. State**, 832 S.W.2d 62, 67 (Tex. App.—Dallas 1992, no pet.) (duplicate of parole-violation warrant was as admissible as the original when defendant did not contest the warrant's authenticity or the fairness of admitting a duplicate).

44. *See* **Englund v. State**, 946 S.W.2d 64, 67 (Tex. Crim. App. 1997). In **Englund**, the State introduced a fax of the defendant's prior DWI conviction from Cameron County. *Id.* at 65. The fax included a "fax transmittal memo" showing that the document had been transmitted from the Cameron County Clerk's Office to the Brazoria County District Attorney's Office, and the attached judgment contained a seal and proper certification by the county clerk. *Id.* The court of criminal appeals noted that for public records, Criminal Rule 1005 supplanted Rules 1001 through 1004 and "create[d] a clear preference for certified or compared copies—thus departing from the general pattern of rejecting the concept of degrees of secondary evidence." **Englund**, 946 S.W.2d at 68 (quoting 5 JACK B. WEINSTEIN & MARGARET A. BERGER, WEINSTEIN'S EVIDENCE ¶1005[01], at 1005-3 (1995)). The court held that the proponent is not required to introduce the actual certified copy of a public record; a copy of that certified copy may be sufficient. **Englund**, 946 S.W.2d at 71. A fax is admissible as a duplicate of a certified copy of a public record unless a party objects to the authenticity of the original certified copy or the unfairness of admitting the duplicate. *See id.* at 71 &

ies of copies) may also qualify as duplicates.[45] Machine-made copies will almost always be given the same status as an original under Rule 1003, as long as the copy is complete and legible.[46] Handwritten copies, however, pose a higher risk of fraud or mistake.

Thus, under Rule 1003, a duplicate is as admissible as an original document unless the opponent raises a question about the authenticity of the original or shows that, because of specific circumstances, it would be unfair to admit the duplicate.[47] For example, if the authenticity of the signature on the original document is challenged, the original should be produced if possible so the document may be scrutinized for possible changes or forgery.[48] Alternatively, a document containing changes to the original is not "as good as" the original, even if those changes were agreed to by the signato-

---

n.13. But as the court noted, "[d]uplicates are not absolutely admissible in place of originals." *Id.* at 69. Two concerns may prevent the use of duplicates instead of the original: (1) possible inaccuracies in the reproduction process and (2) the possibility of fraud by altering the original during the reproduction process. *See id.* When circumstances make inaccuracy or alteration unlikely, duplicates are admissible. *Id.* The particular circumstances that a trial court may consider in such a situation include the source of the copy (here, the fax was from the same public entity that possessed the original and created the certified copy), the nature of the documents, and their apparent completeness or lack of completeness. *Id.* The dissent in *Englund* argued that a faxed copy is neither an original nor a duplicate of an original as contemplated under Article X and, thus, should not be admitted because it does not meet the strict requirements of Criminal Rule 1005. *Englund*, 946 S.W.2d at 72-73 (Mansfield, Baird, Overstreet, Meyers, JJ., dissenting).

45. The following is a rationale for treating copies of copies as duplicates under Federal Rules 1001 and 1003:
    If an original is machine-copied, and the first copy is itself then copied so as to produce what might be called a "second generation" copy two steps removed from the original, probably both copies qualify as "duplicates" of the original, and the same may be said of a third-generation copy produced from the second copy, and so on. Of course something may be lost with each further step away from the original, and the problem of demonstrating that second- and third-generation copies trace their lineage back to the original is greater than the problem of establishing the provenance of a copy made directly from the original, but "duplicate" status is warranted anyway. The same reasons to suppose that content is accurately reproduced in the first copy apply to the second and third copies. Only if the adversary can show that successive recopying may have so blurred the final product as to raise significant doubt on points of consequence should such "duplicates" be excluded, and the question of admissibility should be resolved under Fed. R. Evid. 1003.
5 MUELLER & KIRKPATRICK, *supra* note 12, §10:10, at 703-04 (footnotes omitted); *accord Englund*, 946 S.W.2d at 69-70; *see, e.g.*, *United States v. Gerhart*, 538 F.2d 807, 809-10 & n.4 (8th Cir. 1976) (photocopy of photocopy of check was admissible as duplicate because witnesses testified that proffered photocopy accurately reflected contents of original photocopy).

46. *Cf. Amoco Prod. Co. v. United States*, 619 F.2d 1383, 1391 (10th Cir. 1980) (trial judge properly excluded duplicate copy of deed under Federal Rule 1003 because the duplicate did not completely reproduce the most critical part of the original).

47. TEX. R. EVID. 1003; *see, e.g.*, *Coke v. Coke*, 802 S.W.2d 270, 275 (Tex. App.—Dallas 1990, writ denied) (uncertified duplicates of certified court orders were admissible because defendant did not question originals' authenticity or the fairness of admitting the duplicates); *Rodriguez v. Ed Hicks Imps.*, 767 S.W.2d 187, 191 (Tex. App.—Corpus Christi 1989, no writ) (copies of business records were admissible because no party objected to the authenticity of the original records); *Acosta v. State*, 752 S.W.2d 706, 709 (Tex. App.—Corpus Christi 1988, pet. ref'd) (duplicate of search warrant was admissible because defendant did not question original search warrant's authenticity and offered no argument or proof that, under the circumstances, it would be unfair to admit the duplicate). *See generally* Wellborn, *supra* note 6, at 113-17 (discussing the admissibility of duplicates). Federal Rule 1003 requires a "genuine" question about the original's admissibility. *See* FED. R. EVID. 1003.

48. *See Opals on Ice Lingerie v. Bodylines, Inc.*, 320 F.3d 362, 371 (2d Cir. 2003); *see also Gunda Corp. v. Yazhari*, No. 14-12-00263-CV (Tex. App.—Houston [14th Dist.] 2013, no pet.) (memo op.; 2-5-13) (when there was no concession that plaintiff's signature on arbitration agreement was forged, agreement was not automatically unenforceable under Rule 1003).

ries.[49] Similarly, if the opponent can demonstrate that the duplicate is not a faithful copy of the original, the duplicate is not admissible. For example, if there is evidence that the duplicate contains marks or material not found on the original or if portions of the original have been "whited out," the copy is not a true "duplicate" under Rule 1001(e) and is not admissible under Rule 1003.[50] Few federal or Texas cases have discussed circumstances under which it would be "unfair to admit the duplicate," but this language in Rule 1003 seems to address concerns about the duplicate's completeness and the opponent's inability to verify it.[51] A second possible concern is that the duplicate might contain prejudicial extraneous marks or additions that the original did not.[52] The burden of challenging the admissibility of a duplicate is on the party against whom the duplicate is offered.[53]

B. Recordings

Rules 1001 through 1004 apply the best-evidence doctrine to recordings. Rule 1001(b) defines a recording as consisting of "letters, words, numbers, or their equivalent recorded in any manner."[54] Courts have considered whether a recording of a con-

---

49. *See, e.g.*, ***Boswell v. Jasperson***, 266 F. Supp. 2d 1314, 1321 (D. Utah 2003) (deed containing "changes" that were purportedly agreed to by both signatories raised a genuine issue about the authenticity of the original), *aff'd*, 109 F. App'x 270 (10th Cir. 2004).

50. *Cf. **Opals on Ice Lingerie***, 320 F.3d at 371 (signatory of agreement stated in her affidavit that proponent's photocopy "whited out" a handwritten note below her signature on agreement that referred to separate addendum and made agreement subject to addendum, and opponent produced a copy of agreement that was materially different from proponent's copy; proponent's photocopy was inadmissible).

51. *See, e.g., id.* (proponent's copy of agreement, which purportedly had portions "whited out," was inadmissible under either prong of Rule 1003); ***United States v. Alexander***, 326 F.2d 736, 742-43 (4th Cir. 1964) (reversing a theft conviction because trial court had admitted an incomplete photocopy of an allegedly stolen check); ***Toho Bussan Kaisha, Ltd. v. Am. President Lines Ltd.***, 265 F.2d 418, 422-24 (2d Cir. 1959) (trial court properly excluded photocopies of original business records located in Japan because duplicates were made solely for litigation and opponent could not verify their completeness); ***Boswell***, 266 F. Supp. 2d at 1321 (unfair to admit duplicate of altered deed as either an original or a duplicate); ***Williams v. State***, 778 S.W.2d 155, 156 (Tex. App.—Texarkana 1989, no pet.) (when defendant objected to admission of duplicate videotape as unfair because he did not have an opportunity to compare it with the original, trial court properly overruled objection because the original had been taped over and was no longer available for viewing). *See generally* 5 MUELLER & KIRKPATRICK, *supra* note 12, §10:24, at 779-83 (discussing the unfair-circumstances provision of Federal Rule 1003 and its consequences). However, "[c]onduct by the proponent also seems unfair, and might justify excluding a duplicate, where the proponent refuses to produce an original during discovery. Such conduct can easily support a decision that a purported duplicate should be excluded." *Id.* §10:24, at 780.

52. *See, e.g.*, ***Owens-Corning Fiberglas Corp. v. Malone***, 916 S.W.2d 551, 558 (Tex. App.—Houston [1st Dist.] 1996) (markings on duplicates were not significant and did not affect document's meaning; trial court did not err in admitting duplicates), *aff'd*, 972 S.W.2d 35 (Tex. 1998); *cf. **United States v. Haddock***, 956 F.2d 1534, 1545-46 (10th Cir. 1992) (district court did not abuse its discretion in excluding photocopies that "bore markings and included statements that did not comport with similar documents prepared in the ordinary course of business"), *overruled on other grounds*, ***United States v. Wells***, 519 U.S. 482 (1997).

53. ***United States v. Garmany***, 762 F.2d 929, 938 (11th Cir. 1985); *see, e.g., **Jubert v. State***, 753 S.W.2d 458, 460 (Tex. App.—Texarkana 1988, no pet.) (trial court properly admitted duplicate of videotaped confession; appellant did not question original's authenticity or prove that duplicate tape did not accurately reproduce original); ***Acosta v. State***, 752 S.W.2d 706, 709 (Tex. App.—Corpus Christi 1988, pet. ref'd) (trial court properly overruled appellant's objection to original search warrant's authenticity because he offered no argument or proof that it would be unfair to admit duplicate warrant instead of original).

54. Rules 1001(b) and 1002 arguably do not apply in a suit alleging piracy of a recording of an instrumental musical performance. *Cf.* 5 MUELLER & KIRKPATRICK, *supra* note 12, §10:1, at 652-55 (although Congress considered

versation is the best evidence and thus must be produced in preference to live testimony about the conversation.[55] The best-evidence rule applies to tape recordings only when the content of the recording is in issue, not when the content of the conversation is in issue.[56] Courts interpreting the federal counterparts to these rules likewise hold that the best-evidence doctrine does not apply when the content of the conversation is in issue.[57]

When live testimony raises a dispute about the content of a conversation, the best-evidence doctrine does not prevent the introduction of a recording of the conversation to corroborate the live testimony.[58] However, if a party chooses to establish the content of a conversation by offering a recording, the best-evidence doctrine applies and Rule 1002 requires the introduction of the original recording unless its production is excused by another evidence rule or some other law.[59] Thus, the best evidence of an audio recording is the recording itself, not a written transcript made from the recording.[60]

In **Edwards v. State** and **Seymour v. Gillespie**, the Texas Court of Criminal Appeals and the Texas Supreme Court adopted a seven-step test for the authentication of an original recording. This test required a showing that (1) the recording device was capable of taking testimony, (2) the operator of the device was competent, (3) the recording was authentic and correct, (4) no changes, additions, or deletions were made, (5) the manner of preservation of the recording was sufficient, (6) the speakers were identi-

---

this problem in relation to computer output, it made no change in the federal rule). To suggest that musical sounds are the equivalent of letters, words, or numbers would be stretching the rule's application. Rule 1001(1) of the Uniform Rules of Evidence provides a solution to the problem. That rule adds the word "sounds" to a definition that is otherwise identical to the one in Federal Rule 1001(a) and (b) and in Texas Rule 1001(a) and (b). UNIF. R. EVID. 1001(1) (1974). Thus, amending Texas Rule 1001(b) to read "letters, words, sounds, numbers, or their equivalent" would bring musical recordings under the best-evidence doctrine. But such an amendment was not made in the 2015 restyling of the Texas Rules. *See* Tex. Sup. Ct. Order, Misc. Docket No. 15-9048 (eff. Apr. 1, 2015).

55.   *See* 5 MUELLER & KIRKPATRICK, *supra* note 12, §10:3, at 666 (best-evidence doctrine does not create a preference for live testimony or a recording; the rule does not "work backwards so as to disqualify a recording where live testimony is available"). Refer to notes 12-13 *supra* and accompanying text.

56.   *See* **Burdine v. State**, 719 S.W.2d 309, 318 n.5 (Tex. Crim. App. 1986). The court of criminal appeals noted that "[a]t issue here were the contents of the *conversation* on the recording, and not the recording itself. Since [witness] participated in the conversation, his testimony describing the interrogation was sufficient for best evidence purposes." *Id.* Further, the best-evidence rule in effect at the time of the defendant's trial was a common-law rule that applied only to proof of writings or documents, not to recordings or oral confessions. *Id.* at 318.

57.   *See* **United States v. Fagan**, 821 F.2d 1002, 1008 n.1 (5th Cir. 1987); *see also* **United States v. Rose**, 590 F.2d 232, 237 (7th Cir. 1978) (although Federal Rules expanded best-evidence doctrine to cover tape recordings, doctrine did not apply when government sought to prove contents of conversation rather than contents of recording); **United States v. Gonzales-Benitez**, 537 F.2d 1051, 1053 (9th Cir. 1976) (tapes would have been the best evidence if the inquiry had been to discover what sounds were embodied on the tapes in question).

58.   *See* **Seymour v. Gillespie**, 608 S.W.2d 897, 898-99 (Tex. 1980) (reversing lower court's exclusion of tape recording in case involving "sharply controverted" testimony).

59.   *See* FED. R. EVID. 1002; TEX. R. EVID. 1002; *cf.* **Reed v. State**, 811 S.W.2d 582, 589 (Tex. Crim. App. 1991) (Clinton, J., dissenting) (Texas Criminal Rules 1002 and 1005 require proof of public documents by presentation of the original except as otherwise provided by law or the Rules of Evidence).

60.   *See, e.g.*, **Wright v. Farmers Co-Op**, 681 F.2d 549, 553 & n.3 (8th Cir. 1982) (even though the written transcript of a previously recorded statement was neither an original nor a duplicate, it was admissible because the original recording had been destroyed).

fied, and (7) the testimony elicited was voluntarily made.[61] But in ***Angleton v. State***, the court of criminal appeals stated that "attempting to cling to the ***Edwards*** test after the enactment of Rule 901 will result in unwarranted confusion for trial courts, practitioners, and appellate courts. Rule 901 is straightforward, containing clear language and understandable illustrations."[62] Before a recording is admissible under the Rules, it must be authenticated under Rule 901,[63] must be offered under the terms of Rules 1001 through 1003, and must overcome any hearsay problems.

Rule 1003 makes a duplicate recording as admissible as an original unless an opponent questions the original's authenticity or otherwise shows that it would be unfair to admit the duplicate.[64] Under Rule 1001(e), a duplicate recording is any mechanical, electronic, or other equivalent process or technique that accurately reproduces the original.[65] Therefore, if a question arises about the original's authenticity, the party seeking to introduce a duplicate recording under Rule 1003 must establish the authenticity of both the original recording and the duplicate as predicates to the duplicate's admissibility.[66]

Authentication of a rerecording can require a different approach than authentication of an original recording because "[i]t is often possible to use the original as a master from which other recordings ... can be manipulated to cut background noise or amplify conversational tones with the result of enhancing critical content."[67] One commentator asserts that a rerecording should be authenticated as follows:

> The original recording should first be offered into evidence, together with testimony which clearly identifies it as the original. The technician who made the re-recording should then explain how he produced the re-recording. His testimony should include a statement that he made no additions or deletions and did not alter the original in any way except to improve its audibility or clarity. If the [opponent] wishes to challenge the admissibility of the re-recording, he should be given an opportunity, out of the hearing of the jury,

---

61. ***Seymour***, 608 S.W.2d at 898; ***Edwards v. State***, 551 S.W.2d 731, 733 (Tex. Crim. App. 1977). The courts pointed out that the trial court may infer some of these elements; the proponent does not need to show each element in detail. ***Seymour***, 608 S.W.2d at 898; ***Edwards***, 551 S.W.2d at 733; *see also* ***Wallace v. State***, 782 S.W.2d 854, 857-58 (Tex. Crim. App. 1989) (a party may meet the authentication requirements for admission of tape recordings through circumstantial evidence).

62. ***Angleton v. State***, 971 S.W.2d 65, 69 (Tex. Crim. App. 1998).

63. Refer to *Article IX: Authentication & Identification, supra* p. 983.

64. TEX. R. EVID. 1003; *e.g.*, ***Narvaiz v. State***, 840 S.W.2d 415, 431 (Tex. Crim. App. 1992) (enhanced rerecording of 911 call was admissible because defendant did not challenge reproduction's accuracy or original's authenticity); ***Ballard v. State***, 23 S.W.3d 178, 181 (Tex. App.—Waco 2000, no pet.) (duplicate video recording was admissible to same extent as original because defendant did not challenge authenticity of original); ***Jubert v. State***, 753 S.W.2d 458, 460 (Tex. App.—Texarkana 1988, no pet.) (copy of videotape was admissible because defendant did not question original's authenticity or copy's accuracy at trial). Refer to notes 47-53 *supra* and accompanying text.

65. TEX. R. EVID. 1001(e).

66. *See* FED. R. EVID. 1003 advisory committee's note (method of duplication must ensure accuracy and genuineness); *cf.* ***United States v. Devous***, 764 F.2d 1349, 1351-53 (10th Cir. 1985) (reel-to-reel copy of original cassette tape was properly admitted as a duplicate).

67. 5 MUELLER & KIRKPATRICK, *supra* note 12, §10:15, at 715.

to compare it to the original for accuracy and completeness. If the court concludes that the re-recording is an accurate reproduction of the original, the re-recording is then admitted into evidence and played at trial.[68]

A transcript made from a recording or rerecording is neither an "original" nor a "duplicate," as those terms are defined in Rule 1001(d) and (e). Thus, introducing a transcript as a substitute for an available recording would violate Rules 1002 and 1003.[69] However, many federal courts have held that Federal Rules 1002 and 1003 permit proponents to provide a transcript to the jury as a tool to assist them in listening to a recording.[70] The proponent must authenticate the transcript,[71] and the court must advise the jury that the transcripts are only an aid and that the recording itself is the substantive evidence.[72] The transcripts must not be taken into the jury room because

---

68. 2 CLIFFORD S. FISHMAN & ANNE T. MCKENNA, WIRETAPPING AND EAVESDROPPING §24:3, at 24-11 to 24-12 (2d ed. 1995) (footnotes omitted); *see Williams v. State*, 778 S.W.2d 155, 156 (Tex. App.—Texarkana 1989, no pet.) (copy of videotape is admissible when original is no longer available, original's authenticity is not questioned, and duplicate is the same as original); 5 MUELLER & KIRKPATRICK, *supra* note 12, §10:15, at 715 (proponent has threshold burden of authentication).

A rerecording can sometimes still be admissible even if it is not an exact duplicate of the original. For example, in one case, the Texas Court of Criminal Appeals (though not citing or relying on Rule 1003) held that a rerecording of original incoming calls to a police department was admissible even though the rerecording was not an exact duplicate of the original recording. *Webb v. State*, 760 S.W.2d 263, 276 (Tex. Crim. App. 1988). Trial testimony showed that the officer who made the rerecording had to sort through various channels recorded on the original tape and select only the conversations that were relevant to the particular incident. *Id.* Thus, while intentional changes and deletions were made to the original recording, they did not affect the reliability or accuracy of the relevant recording. *Id.* Although the original recording was not produced at trial, it should have been produced so the court or the opposing party could have made a comparison between the two versions and the opposing party could have discovered whether any relevant conversations had been omitted from the rerecording. In another case, the Texas Court of Criminal Appeals held that the rerecording of a capital-murder defendant's media interview was a "duplicate" admissible under Rule 1003 even though portions of the interview had been deleted and the order of other portions had been rearranged on the rerecording. *See, e.g., Hall v. State*, 67 S.W.3d 870, 876-77 (Tex. Crim. App. 2002) (television reporter testified "that she had watched the edited tape, and except for some portions of the interview being deleted and other portions being rearranged, it also accurately reflected the events of the interview"; court found no evidence that defendant's statements were taken out of context or substantially altered), *vacated on other grounds*, 537 U.S. 802 (2002).

69. *Cf.* FED. R. EVID. 1001 advisory committee's note, paragraph (4) (manually produced copies are not within definition of "duplicate"); 6 WEINSTEIN & BERGER, *supra* note 13, §1001.10, at 1001-47 ("A transcript of a recording is not admissible as a duplicate original because it is not made by mechanical or electronic means.").

70. *See, e.g., United States v. Reed*, 647 F.2d 678, 688 (6th Cir. 1981) (trial judge did not abuse discretion by instructing jury that tape transcript was a tool to assist them in listening to the tapes and that the tapes were the relevant evidence); *see also* 6 WEINSTEIN & BERGER, *supra* note 13, §1001.10, at 1001-47 to 1001-48 (typewritten transcripts of recordings are often introduced to aid the jury in understanding and following the recorded conversations, and courts should allow the use of such transcripts on a showing that the transcript is a true copy of the original recording).

71. *See United States v. Rochan*, 563 F.2d 1246, 1251 (5th Cir. 1977) (party proffering transcripts of tape recordings must prove that they are accurate reproductions of the words spoken and show that they accurately identify the recorded voices). The court in *United States v. Slade* held that the testimony of the person who prepared the written transcript satisfied these requirements. 627 F.2d 293, 303 (D.C. Cir. 1980). In addition, any person who has compared the written version to the original tape recording and has found it accurate can supply the necessary foundation. *Rochan*, 563 F.2d at 1252; *see also United States v. Vinson*, 606 F.2d 149, 155 (6th Cir. 1979) (without a stipulation about accuracy of transcripts, it was sufficient that judge reviewed tapes and transcripts, that opposing party had copies of transcripts before their use at trial, and that opposing counsel had opportunity to point out discrepancies between tapes and transcripts).

72. *See United States v. Bentley*, 706 F.2d 1498, 1508 (8th Cir. 1983); *Vinson*, 606 F.2d at 155.

they have not been admitted into evidence.[73] If the parties cannot agree on a stipulated transcript that meets the authentication requirements, each side may produce its own transcript or version of the disputed portions, and the trial court should then hold a hearing, in which the proponent must establish the transcript's accuracy by offering the testimony of the transcriber or a participant in the conversation.[74] Texas courts have not explicitly adopted the federal approach to transcripts of recordings.[75] When offering such transcripts, attorneys should emphasize that the transcripts are offered solely to help the fact-finder understand a recording while it is being played. The transcript is not an independent exhibit and must not be considered by the jury during its deliberations.[76]

C. Electronically Stored Information

The definitions of "writing" and "recording" in Rule 1001(a) and (b) implicitly include electronically stored information.[77] In addition, Rule 1001(d) expressly defines

---

73. *Vinson*, 606 F.2d at 155; *see United States v. Rinn*, 586 F.2d 113, 117-18 (9th Cir. 1978) (providing transcripts is appropriate only to facilitate listening); *see, e.g., Slade*, 627 F.2d at 303 (transcripts were not the real evidence to be considered). The court in *United States v. Tornabene* recognized "that as a general proposition, transcripts are appropriately used as an aid in listening to the tape recording itself, which constitutes actual evidence of the conversation." 687 F.2d 312, 317 (9th Cir. 1982). In *Tornabene*, the court held that admitting accurate transcripts was not erroneous even though the jury never listened to the actual tape. *Id.* The trial court instructed the jury that it could listen to the tape. *Id.*

74. *See United States v. Onori*, 535 F.2d 938, 948-49 (5th Cir. 1976) (outlining requirements for admission of transcripts when parties do not agree on a stipulated transcript).

75. *See In re Thoma*, 873 S.W.2d 477, 487-88 (Tex. Rev. Trib. 1994, no appeal) (court did not address issue of whether written transcript was admitted as substantive evidence of recording's contents or as aid to fact-finder in following and understanding words contained on tape recording); *Garrett v. State*, 639 S.W.2d 18, 20 (Tex. App.— Fort Worth 1982) ("The propriety of providing transcripts to the jury, *per se*, has never been specifically addressed in Texas."), *aff'd*, 658 S.W.2d 592 (Tex. Crim. App. 1983). *See generally Russell v. State*, 604 S.W.2d 914, 923-25 (Tex. Crim. App. [Panel Op.] 1980) (discussing authentication of a transcript of stenographer's tapes).

76. *See In re Thoma*, 873 S.W.2d at 487-88.

77. *See* TEX. R. EVID. 1001(a), (b); *see also* TEX. R. EVID. 101(h)(7) (any reference in the Rules to written material or any other medium includes electronically stored information). Electronically stored information includes the following: (1) databases, (2) data files, (3) program files, (4) image files (e.g., JPEG, TIFF), (5) e-mail messages and files, (6) voice-mail messages and files, (7) text messages, (8) temporary files, (9) system-history files, (10) deleted files, programs, or e-mails, (11) backup files and archival tapes, (12) website files, (13) website information stored in textual, graphical, or audio format, (14) cache files, and (15) cookies. *See Super Film of Am, Inc. v. UCB Films, Inc.*, 219 F.R.D. 649, 657 (D. Kan. 2004); *Thompson v. U.S. Dep't of Housing & Urban Dev.*, 219 F.R.D. 93, 96 (D. Md. 2003). Electronic information can be located in many places, including the following: (1) mainframe computers, (2) network servers, (3) Internet ("web") servers, (4) desktop and laptop computers, (5) hard drives, (6) flash drives, which include "thumb" drives, secure digital cards, and other flash memory cards, (7) e-mail servers, (8) handheld devices like personal digital assistants (PDAs) and personal media players (PMPs), (9) cell phones and smart phones (e.g., iPhones, BlackBerrys, Windows Mobile devices), (10) event recorders in cars, trucks, and trains, (11) medical devices, and (12) global positioning system (GPS) devices. *See In re Seroquel Prods. Liab. Litig.*, 244 F.R.D. 650, 654 (M.D. Fla. 2007). See *O'Connor's Federal Rules * Civil Trials* (2017), "What Is ESI," ch. 6-C, §2, p. 542; *O'Connor's Texas Rules * Civil Trials* (2017), "Understanding Electronic Discovery," ch. 6-C, §2, p. 561.

The Liaison Committee drafted the original definition for the Texas Rules broadly enough to encompass modern techniques for storing and retrieving data. The Advisory Committee's note to the federal rule similarly indicates that "considerations underlying the rule dictate its expansion to include computers." FED. R. EVID. 1001 advisory committee's note, subdiv. (1). The original Federal Rule 1001(1) was restyled as Federal Rule 1001(a) and (b) in 2011. The substance of the rule has not changed. FED. R. EVID. 1001 advisory committee's note to 2011 amendments.

the term "original" for electronically stored information to include "any printout—or other output readable by sight—if it accurately reflects the information."[78] This definition echoes Rule 901(b)(9), which requires authentication evidence "describing a process or system and showing that it produces an accurate result" as a condition precedent to admissibility.[79] Federal Rule 901(b)(9) is identical to its Texas counterpart, and the Advisory Committee's note to the federal rule states that the rule applies to computers.[80]

The important question is whether Texas Rules 1001(d) and 901(b)(9) together impose unique foundation requirements as a condition precedent to the admissibility of electronically stored information.[81] At least one commentator[82] and one circuit court of appeals[83] have concluded that the Federal Rules impose such requirements. The commentator suggests that in the case of computer output, the underlying method's validity can be proved by showing the following:

> (1) the computer equipment is accepted in the field as standard and competent and was in good working order; (2) qualified computer operators were employed; (3) proper procedures were followed in connection with the input and output of information; (4) a reliable software program was utilized; (5) the equipment was programmed and operated correctly; and (6) the exhibit is properly identified as the output in question.[84]

In **United States v. Scholle**, the Eighth Circuit held that a party seeking to introduce a printout of computerized business records must (1) show that the requirements of the

---

78. TEX. R. EVID. 1001(d); *see, e.g.*, **Burleson v. State**, 802 S.W.2d 429, 441 (Tex. App.—Fort Worth 1991, pet. ref'd) (computer-generated display was admissible under Criminal Rule 1001(3): "the display qualified as an original under the best evidence rule because it was output other than a printout, was readable by sight, and was shown to be an accurate reflection of the data").

79. TEX. R. EVID. 901(b)(9); *see also* 5 WEINSTEIN & BERGER, *supra* note 13, §901.12[1], at 901-99 to 901-100 ("The accuracy of the system or process may be shown by the testimony of lay witnesses who have personal knowledge of the system and its results or by the testimony of properly qualified expert witnesses. Alternatively, the trial court may take judicial notice of the accuracy of the process or system if the system or process is generally known to be accurate.").

80. *See* FED. R. EVID. 901(b)(9); TEX. R. EVID. 901(b)(9); FED. R. EVID. 901 advisory committee's note, subdiv. (b)(9). The Advisory Committee acknowledged that the computer is among the most recent developments to which Federal Rule 901(b)(9) applies. FED. R. EVID. 901 advisory committee's note, subdiv. (b)(9). One federal court has held that the best-evidence doctrine applies to Global Positioning System (GPS) display data when a proponent seeks to prove the contents of that data. In **United States v. Bennett**, the Ninth Circuit held that a customs officer's testimony about the contents of a GPS display he saw on the defendant's boat was inadmissible when offered to prove that the boat had traveled from Mexico, especially because the officer did not observe the boat's movements. 363 F.3d 947, 952-53 (9th Cir. 2004). In this situation, the best evidence was the data on the GPS display. The court also held that secondary evidence of the GPS data was not admissible under Federal Rule 1004 because the government had not shown that the original data had been lost or destroyed, or was otherwise unattainable. *Id.* at 954. Furthermore, the government did not offer any evidence that the GPS data would have been difficult to download or print. *Id.*

81. Refer to *Article IX: Authentication & Identification, supra* p. 1000.

82. *See* 5 MUELLER & KIRKPATRICK, *supra* note 12, §9:20, at 484-87.

83. *See* **United States v. Scholle**, 553 F.2d 1109, 1125 (8th Cir. 1977) (for computer evidence to be admissible, proponent must lay a comprehensive foundation to ensure evidence's trustworthiness).

84. 5 MUELLER & KIRKPATRICK, *supra* note 12, §9:20, at 484.

federal Business Records Act[85] (now incorporated in both Federal Rule 803(6) and Texas Rule 803(6)) have been satisfied, (2) explain the original source of the computer program, and (3) present the procedures for input control, including tests used to ensure the accuracy and reliability of the data.[86] In ***United States v. Vela***,[87] the Fifth Circuit specifically rejected ***Scholle***'s holding that special foundation evidence is a necessary predicate to the admissibility of computer output.[88] In ***United States v. Capanelli***, the federal district court admitted the government's recordings of conversations that took place during undercover surveillance even though the conversations had originally been recorded on memory chips that were later transferred to CDs and audiotapes using specially designed computer software, after which the original chips were destroyed.[89] The court concluded that the "duplicates" were admissible under Federal Rules 1001 through 1003 and that "[a]ny potential problems inherent in the software-assisted reproduction of the recordings may be fully explored by a defense expert witness, with the jury then asked to reject the recordings as technically unreliable."[90] Thus, a computer-created duplicate may be admissible under Article X even when both the original writing or recording and the software program used to create the duplicate are unavailable to the opponent.

In the Texas case of ***Broderick v. State***, a prosecution for aggravated sexual assault of a child, the defendant objected to the admission of a duplicate of his computer's hard drive, claiming that his original hard drive was the best evidence of the computer's programs, information, and images.[91] The court of appeals disagreed because the State's witness "testified that the copy made of the data encoded on the hard drive exactly duplicated the contents of that drive and explained the method used in its

---

85. *See* 28 U.S.C. §1732.

86. ***Scholle***, 553 F.2d at 1125.

87. 673 F.2d 86 (5th Cir. 1982).

88. *See id.* at 90 (no level of authentication beyond that normally practiced by the company is necessary to admit computer evidence); *see also* ***United States v. Young Bros.***, 728 F.2d 682, 693-94 (5th Cir. 1984) (regular business-records foundation applies to computer-generated business records).

   Pre-Rules Texas law is consistent with the Fifth Circuit's position. ***Wenk v. City Nat'l Bank***, 613 S.W.2d 345, 350 (Tex. Civ. App.—Tyler 1981, no writ); *see* ***Voss v. Sw. Bell Tel. Co.***, 610 S.W.2d 537, 538 (Tex. Civ. App.—Houston [1st Dist.] 1980, writ ref'd n.r.e.) (computer printouts are subject only to the admissibility requirements for business records). Refer to *Article IX: Authentication & Identification, supra* p. 1002, regarding authentication requirements for electronically stored information. In ***Wenk***, the defendant contended that the proponent of computerized business records must show, in addition to the requirements of the business-records exception, "(1) [that] the particular computing equipment is recognized as standard equipment and (2) that the records were prepared by persons who understood the operation of the equipment and whose regular duty was to operate it." 613 S.W.2d at 350. The court rejected the defendant's position and held, in effect, that once the proponent meets the requirements of the business-records exception, the computer printout is admissible. *Id.* An authenticating witness's lack of knowledge about the type of computer used, the computer's acceptability in the community, and the expertise of the operator all go to the weight of the evidence, not to its admissibility. ***Voss***, 610 S.W.2d at 539.

89. 257 F. Supp. 2d 678, 679-81 (S.D.N.Y. 2003).

90. *Id.* at 681.

91. 35 S.W.3d 67, 79 (Tex. App.—Texarkana 2000, pet. ref'd).

creation."[92] The parties and the reviewing court assumed that Article X applies to computer programs and data, but that duplicates of a computer's hard drive are admissible under Rule 1003.[93]

When a process, system, or device has become so well established that it is commonplace, testimonial description and endorsement of accuracy are unnecessary; the foundation can be assumed.[94] The Advisory Committee's note to Federal Rule 901(b)(9) says as much with its observation that the rule "does not, of course, foreclose taking judicial notice of the accuracy of the process or system."[95]

D. Photographs

1. Photographs. Rule 1001(c) defines a photograph as "a photographic image or its equivalent stored in any form." Rule 1001(d) defines an "original" of a photograph to include "the negative or a print from it." Although Rules 1002 through 1004 cover "photographs," the best-evidence doctrine usually will not apply to photographs offered into evidence because the doctrine does not set up a general order of preferred admissibility.[96] A photograph is usually not introduced as primary evidence offered to prove its contents, so the best-evidence rule does not apply.[97] Generally, a witness testifies that he knows the scene or object involved and that the photograph correctly represents that scene or object; the trial court then admits the photograph into evidence as a graphic illustration of the witness's testimony.[98]

On the other hand, the doctrine applies when the photograph's contents are a fact in issue (e.g., an obscenity prosecution involving a motion picture[99]) or when a photograph has independent probative value (e.g., an automatic surveillance camera's videotape of a bank robbery[100]). "The most commonly encountered [example] of this latter group is of course, the X-ray, with substantial authority calling for production of the original."[101]

---

92. *Id.*

93. For a further discussion of duplicates, refer to notes 43-53 *supra* and accompanying text.

94. The foundation can also be established by judicial notice. *See* **Burleson v. State**, 802 S.W.2d 429, 439 n.2 (Tex. App.—Fort Worth 1991, pet. ref'd) (computer science has led to the creation of many devices whose reliability is subject to judicial notice).

95. FED. R. EVID. 901 advisory committee's note, subdiv. (b)(9). Refer to *Article II: Judicial Notice, supra* p. 111.

96. Refer to notes 12-17 *supra* and accompanying text.

97. *See* **Garay v. State**, 954 S.W.2d 59, 67 (Tex. App.—San Antonio 1997, pet. ref'd) (best-evidence rule does not apply to enlarged photographs offered as a visual aid during testimony of expert witnesses); FED. R. EVID. 1002 advisory committee's note (testifying witness normally adopts the photograph as testimony or uses the picture to illustrate testimony).

98. *See* 2 RAY, *supra* note 13, §1466, at 149.

99. *See* **United States v. Levine**, 546 F.2d 658, 668 (5th Cir. 1977) (best-evidence rule applies to motion pictures; for purposes of best-evidence rule, the "work print or cut negative as well as the answer prints and release prints are regarded as originals of the film").

100. *See* **United States v. Taylor**, 530 F.2d 639, 641-42 (5th Cir. 1976) (photographs may be admissible as probative evidence, provided proffering party lays sufficient foundation to show circumstances under which photographs were taken and reliability of reproduction process); **United States v. Stephens**, 202 F. Supp. 2d 1361, 1368 (N.D. Ga. 2002) (recordings made by automatic surveillance camera may satisfy evidentiary requirements if witness tes-

2. X-rays & other medical images. Applying the best-evidence doctrine to X-rays or to other scientific or medical images, such as MRIs, presents two potential problems. First, because an X-ray has independent probative value, the literal application of Rule 1002 requires the production of the X-ray and bars testimonial evidence of its contents.[102] X-rays ordinarily require expert interpretation and explanation, however, if they are to be meaningful to the jury.[103] The ultimate answer to this dilemma is found in Rule 702, which provides: "A witness who is qualified as an expert ... may testify in the form of an opinion or otherwise if the expert's scientific, technical, or other specialized knowledge will help the trier of fact to understand the evidence ...."[104] Therefore, Rules 702 and 1002 together permit expert testimony on the significance of photographic depictions in admissible X-rays.

The second problem is somewhat more difficult. Rules 1001(c) and 1002 implicitly include X-rays in the best-evidence doctrine,[105] but a medical expert may nonetheless give expert testimony based on X-rays that are not offered or admitted into evidence. The Advisory Committee's note to Federal Rule 1002 states that because Federal Rule 703—which was originally virtually identical to Texas Rule 703—allows an expert to give an opinion based on matters not in evidence, the application of Rule 1002 is limited accordingly.[106] In *Trailways, Inc. v. Mendoza*, the San Antonio Court of Appeals held that a doctor could testify to medical observations and conclusions based on X-rays that were not produced in court or admitted into evidence.[107] This issue should

---

tifies to type of equipment used, its general reliability, quality of recording, process by which equipment was focused, or general reliability of system), *rev'd in part on other grounds*, 365 F.3d 967 (11th Cir. 2004).

101. FED. R. EVID. 1002 advisory committee's note. Before the 2015 restyling of the Texas Rules, the definition of "photographs" in Rule 1001(b) explicitly included X-rays. The restyled rule's language is broader, but no substantive change was intended. *See* Tex. Sup. Ct. Order, Misc. Docket No. 15-9048, §2 (eff. Apr. 1, 2015).

102. *Cf. Daniels v. Iowa City*, 183 N.W. 415, 416 (Iowa 1921) (because X-ray is a photograph, X-ray itself is the best evidence of what it portrays).

103. *See id.* at 417 (expert testimony is proper to aid in the interpretation of X-rays); *Patrick & Tillman v. Matkin*, 7 P.2d 414, 415 (Okla. 1932) (although an X-ray itself is the best evidence, an interpretation by an expert is usually necessary); 2 RAY, *supra* note 13, §1466, at 155 (X-rays require explanation by experts); *see also* **Cmty. Chapel Funeral Home v. Allen**, 499 S.W.2d 215, 216 (Tex. Civ. App.—Beaumont 1973, writ ref'd n.r.e.) (X-ray may not be the best evidence of what it reveals because it usually requires interpretation by an expert, though fairness requires its presence in court during its interpretation whenever possible); 5 MUELLER & KIRKPATRICK, *supra* note 12, §10:5, at 670-71 ("Medical images are always proved by means of expert testimony by a doctor, and the images are not usually the centerpiece of the testimony, but rather form one of many bases for a diagnostic opinion. It would make no sense to require production of such images while barring testimony interpreting content ....").

104. *See* TEX. R. EVID. 702. Refer to *Article VII: Opinions & Expert Testimony*, *supra* p. 700.

105. Refer to note 101 *supra*.

106. *See* FED. R. EVID. 1002 advisory committee's note ("Hospital records which may be admitted as business records under Rule 803(6) commonly contain reports interpreting X-rays by the staff radiologist, who qualifies as an expert, and these reports need not be excluded from the records by the instant rule."); *see, e.g.,* **United States v. Gavic**, 520 F.2d 1346, 1353 (8th Cir. 1975) (dicta; expert witness could testify about results of chemical test that used chromatographic plates without producing the plates).

107. 745 S.W.2d 63, 66-67 (Tex. App.—San Antonio 1987, no writ). Pre-Rules Texas law was split on this point. *See* **Avila v. U.S. Fid. & Guar. Co.**, 551 S.W.2d 453, 455-56 (Tex. Civ. App.—San Antonio 1977, writ ref'd n.r.e.) ("The Texas cases concerning whether an X-ray may be interpreted without its physical presence in court are divided. Some have permitted it and some have not, usually on the ground that the X-ray was the best evidence of what it revealed ...." (quoting **Cmty. Chapel Funeral Home**, 499 S.W.2d at 216)); 2 RAY, *supra* note 13, §1561, at 255-56 (3d

be a matter of discretion for the trial court. If an X-ray and its interpretation are central to a particular medical diagnosis, and if there is a genuine controversy about its interpretation and contents, the opponent of the X-ray should invoke Article X to require its production.[108] If the opponent does not seriously dispute the X-ray's interpretation and contents, the proponent does not need to produce it.[109]

RULE 1004
ADMISSIBILITY OF OTHER EVIDENCE OF CONTENT

An original is not required and other evidence of the content of a writing, recording, or photograph is admissible if:

(a) all the originals are lost or destroyed, unless the proponent lost or destroyed them in bad faith;

(b) an original cannot be obtained by any available judicial process;

(c) an original is not located in Texas;

(d) the party against whom the original would be offered had control of the original; was at that time put on notice, by pleadings or otherwise, that the original would be a subject of proof at the trial or hearing; and fails to produce it at the trial or hearing; or

(e) the writing, recording, or photograph is not closely related to a controlling issue.

COMMENTARY ON RULE 1004

Rule 1004 is substantively identical to Federal Rule 1004, except that the Texas rule excuses production of an original writing, recording, or photograph when "an original is not located in Texas."[110] Both rules excuse production of an original when it is

---

ed. 1980), at 74 (Supp. 1991) (acknowledging the discord among Texas cases). *Compare* **Hall v. State**, 153 Tex. Crim. 215, 219, 219 S.W.2d 475, 478-79 (1949) (doctor's expert testimony about X-rays was admissible), **Fed. Underwriters Exch. v. Ener**, 126 S.W.2d 769, 773 (Tex. Civ. App.—Beaumont 1939, writ dism'd judgm't cor.) (same), *and* **Md. Cas. Co. v. Dicken**, 80 S.W.2d 800, 804 (Tex. Civ. App.—Dallas 1935, writ dism'd) (X-rays are illustrations of the subject they represent and are "not the best evidence of the condition of the part of the body shown thereby"; expert testimony about what the X-ray film contains is the best evidence), *with* **Tex. Emp'rs Ins. v. Crow**, 218 S.W.2d 230, 232 (Tex. Civ. App.—Eastland 1949) ("It has been held that the opinion of experts as to what an X-ray picture shows is the best evidence thereof. However, the majority of the decisions and, in our opinion, the better reasoning are to the contrary."), *aff'd*, 148 Tex. 113, 221 S.W.2d 235 (1949), *and* **Am. Nat'l Ins. v. Points**, 81 S.W.2d 762, 766 (Tex. Civ. App.—El Paso 1935, writ dism'd) (X-rays themselves are the best evidence).

108. *See* 2 STEVEN GOODE ET AL., TEXAS PRACTICE SERIES: GUIDE TO THE TEXAS RULES OF EVIDENCE §1001.3, at 312 (3d ed. 2002); 5 MUELLER & KIRKPATRICK, *supra* note 12, §10:5, at 671-72.

109. *See generally* 2 RAY, *supra* note 13, §1561, at 74-75 (Supp. 1991) (best-evidence rule should apply if expert testifies about contents of X-ray, but not if a medical opinion is given based on X-ray); Wellborn, *supra* note 6, at 104-05 ("Rule 703 … allows an expert to give an opinion based on matters not in evidence, and the present rule must be read as being limited accordingly in its application." (quoting FED. R. EVID. 1002 advisory committee's note)).

110. TEX. R. EVID. 1004(c). Refer to notes 132-135 *infra* and accompanying text.

---

lost or destroyed in good faith or by accident,[111] when it is not obtainable by judicial process,[112] when it is in an opponent's possession,[113] or when it relates to a collateral matter (i.e., one not closely related to a controlling issue).[114]

Under Rule 1003, a proponent can introduce into evidence a "duplicate" (as defined in Rule 1001(e))[115] without satisfying any of Rule 1004's five excuses for failing to produce an original.[116] The opponent must invoke Rule 1003's limiting provision by raising a question about the original's authenticity or showing that it would be unfair to admit the duplicate.[117]

Once the court excuses the production of the original on one of the grounds set out in Rule 1004, a proponent can introduce any nonduplicate secondary evidence that meets the preponderance-of-the-evidence standard. For example, a proponent whose original handwritten note is destroyed through no fault of his own, and who has a typed copy of the note, can prove the contents of the note by introducing the copy or offering oral testimony.[118] In other words, "[t]he rule recognizes no 'degrees' of secondary evidence."[119] Introducing less convincing secondary evidence, however, allows an opponent to suggest that the fact-finder should draw an unfavorable inference from such

---

111. FED. R. EVID. 1004(a); TEX. R. EVID. 1004(a); *see* **Billings v. State**, 399 S.W.3d 581, 591 (Tex. App.—Eastland 2013, no pet.) ("When an original recording has been destroyed, other evidence of its contents is admissible if the proponent of the evidence did not destroy the original in bad faith."); **Jurek v. Couch-Jurek**, 296 S.W.3d 864, 871 (Tex. App.—El Paso 2009, no pet.) ("Tex. R. Evid. 1004 provides the exceptions for when an original document is not required, and permits other evidence of the contents of a writing if all originals are lost or have been destroyed, unless the proponent of the evidence lost or destroyed the evidence in bad faith."); *see, e.g.,* **Coleman v. State**, 760 S.W.2d 356, 360 (Tex. App.—Houston [1st Dist.] 1988, pet. ref'd) (when police officer testified that the original of a photospread was "misplaced" and officers were "attempting to locate it in the robbery division," trial court did not abuse its discretion in using an "unclear" copy to determine if the identification procedure was impermissibly suggestive; together, the unclear copy and the officer's testimony were enough to determine whether the characteristics of the individuals were sufficiently clear).

112. FED. R. EVID. 1004(b); TEX. R. EVID. 1004(b). Refer to notes 129-131 *infra* and accompanying text.

113. FED. R. EVID. 1004(c); TEX. R. EVID. 1004(d). Refer to notes 136-141 *infra* and accompanying text.

114. *See* FED. R. EVID. 1004(d); TEX. R. EVID. 1004(e). Refer to notes 142-147 *infra* and accompanying text.

115. Refer to notes 43-46 *supra* and accompanying text.

116. The five excuses listed in Rule 1004 for nonproduction of an original are the same ones that were recognized in Texas case law. *See* 2 RAY, *supra* note 13, §1567, at 272 (original relates to collateral matters), §§1569-1570, at 278-83 (original in possession of opponent), §1571, at 284-85 (originals lost or destroyed), §1574, at 291 (same), §1575, at 292 & n.19 (original outside the state), §1575, at 292-93 & n.20 (original unobtainable).

117. *See* TEX. R. EVID. 1003. Refer to notes 47-53 *supra* and accompanying text.

118. *Cf.* **United States v. Standing Soldier**, 538 F.2d 196, 203 (8th Cir. 1976) (oral testimony).

119. FED. R. EVID. 1004 advisory committee's note. According to the Advisory Committee, two rationales support this rule: first, the difficulty surrounding "the formulation of a hierarchy of preferences and a procedure for making it effective"; and second, the likelihood that the parties would themselves try to produce the most convincing evidence possible without being required to do so. *Id.*; *see* **United States v. Gerhart**, 538 F.2d 807, 809 (8th Cir. 1976) (when one of the conditions of Federal Rule 1004 is satisfied, "the proponent may prove the contents of a writing by any secondary evidence, subject to an attack by the opposing party not as to admissibility but to the weight to be given the evidence, with final determination left to the trier of fact").

a strategy.[120] Texas is among the majority of American jurisdictions that have chosen not to recognize degrees of secondary evidence under the best-evidence doctrine.[121]

A. Rule 1004(a): Original Lost or Destroyed

Rule 1004(a) excuses the production of an innocently lost or destroyed original.[122] Texas common law had long recognized accidental destruction or loss as an excuse for failing to produce the original of a document.[123] The rule requires only that the proponent did not lose or destroy the document "in bad faith."[124] Thus, the proponent must present evidence that he has undertaken a diligent but unsuccessful search for the document and that he has made a reasonable inquiry.[125] A "cavalier attitude" toward

---

120. *See* 2 McCormick on Evidence, *supra* note 7, §238, at 110.

121. *See id.* §238, at 109-10 & n.2. Most modern codes of evidence have adopted the "English" view, which rejects any degrees of secondary evidence. *Id.* §238, at 110. McCormick notes that the English position "has the virtues of simplicity and easiness of application." *Id.* Those states that do recognize degrees of secondary evidence justify the distinction on the ground "that there is some incongruity in pursuing the policy of accurately obtaining the terms of writings, recordings, and photographs by structuring a highly technical rule to that end, only to abandon the objective upon a showing of the original's unavailability." *Id.* Thus, Rule 1004 does not change Texas law in this regard, even though Rule 1004's federal counterpart apparently did change at least the theory of federal law. *See* 5 Mueller & Kirkpatrick, *supra* note 12, §10:25, at 784; *see also id.* §10:26, at 785-94 (analyzing Federal Rule 1004's recognition of no degrees of secondary evidence).

122. Tex. R. Evid. 1004(a); *see Billings v. State*, 399 S.W.3d 581, 591 (Tex. App.—Eastland 2013, no pet.); *Jurek v. Couch-Jurek*, 296 S.W.3d 864, 871 (Tex. App.—El Paso 2009, no pet.); *see, e.g., Johnson v. State*, 846 S.W.2d 373, 376 (Tex. App.—Houston [14th Dist.] 1992) (photocopy of ten-dollar bill used to make narcotics purchase was admissible under Rule 1004 when officer testified that original bill was unavailable because money is reused until it is either lost or returned to the city, and officer established that the loss of the original was not intentional and that photocopy was fair and accurate), *remanded in part on other grounds*, 853 S.W.2d 574 (Tex. Crim. App. 1993). It appears, however, that the best-evidence rule did not apply at all in this case because the purpose of offering the photocopy was not to prove the contents of the ten-dollar bill, but rather to show that a sum of money (any sum of money) changed hands to prove the essential element of the charge of delivery of a controlled substance. *See Johnson v. State*, 853 S.W.2d 574, 575 (Tex. Crim. App. 1993).

123. *See Utica Mut. Ins. v. Bennett*, 492 S.W.2d 659, 665 (Tex. Civ. App.—Houston [1st Dist.] 1973, writ dism'd); 2 Ray, *supra* note 13, §1571, at 284-85; *see, e.g., Cline v. State*, 685 S.W.2d 760, 762-63 (Tex. App.—Houston [1st Dist.] 1985, no pet.) (State could use secondary evidence in forgery prosecution after showing that insurance company lost original); *Edwards v. State*, 672 S.W.2d 10, 12 (Tex. App.—Houston [14th Dist.] 1984, no pet.) (when testimony showed that original sales receipt had been lost, copy was admissible; best-evidence rule "does not require that the exact location of an original document be pinpointed"). In *Edwards*, the court incorrectly stated that the best-evidence rule "requires production of the *best obtainable* evidence of the contents of a writing" when the original is lost. 672 S.W.2d at 12 (emphasis added). In the summary-judgment context, a nonmoving party's deposition testimony that he was "looking for" the contract in issue was sufficient to establish that the contract was lost; thus, the party could testify to its existence and contents. *Abraham v. Ryland Mortg. Co.*, 995 S.W.2d 890, 893 (Tex. App.—El Paso 1999, no pet.).

124. Tex. R. Evid. 1004(a). The federal rule includes the same requirement. Fed. R. Evid. 1004(a).

125. *See In re Estate of Berger*, 174 S.W.3d 845, 847 (Tex. App.—Waco 2005, no pet.); *see, e.g., Pinson v. State*, 733 S.W.2d 387, 389 (Tex. App.—El Paso 1987) (best-evidence objection was denied for admission of copies of affidavit and warrant because court was satisfied that proponent had met its burden of establishing that it had undertaken a reasonable but unsuccessful search for the original), *rev'd on other grounds*, 778 S.W.2d 91 (Tex. Crim. App. 1989); *cf. Seiler v. Lucasfilm, Ltd.*, 808 F.2d 1316, 1317 (9th Cir. 1986) (summary judgment was affirmed against graphic artist who alleged that George Lucas infringed his copyright by copying his drawings in the movie *The Empire Strikes Back* because the artist "could produce no originals of his Garthian Striders nor any documentary evidence that they existed" before the film's release in 1980); *Sylvania Elec. Prods., Inc. v. Flanagan*, 352 F.2d 1005, 1007-08 (1st Cir. 1965) (best-evidence objection to summaries based on data in tally sheets was upheld when proponent testified "that he knew he had some at home but was not sure whether he had them all"; testimony was insufficient proof that original tally sheets were unavailable or that a reasonable search had occurred).

RULE 1004

that search may be sufficient to sustain a finding of bad faith.[126] The negligent or intentional destruction of documents by another person or party does not preclude the admissibility of secondary evidence.[127] Although doubts are generally resolved in favor of admissibility, courts do not (and should not) hesitate to exclude secondary evidence when they are suspicious of the circumstances surrounding the "loss" of the original evidence.[128]

B. Rule 1004(b): Original Not Obtainable

Rule 1004(b) provides an excuse for nonproduction when the original is in the possession of a nonparty or otherwise cannot be obtained by any available judicial process.[129] Pre-Rules Texas law required that the proponent show only that reasonable efforts had been made to secure production of the original,[130] and Rule 1004(b) follows this standard.[131]

C. Rule 1004(c): Original Outside the State

Under Rule 1004(c), if the original document is located outside the state, the proponent does not need to produce it for best-evidence purposes.[132] If the original is located in Texas and is in the possession of a third party who has not voluntarily produced it, a civil litigant should issue a subpoena duces tecum in conjunction with a

---

126. 5 MUELLER & KIRKPATRICK, *supra* note 12, §10:27, at 794.

127. *Estate of Gryder v. Comm'r*, 705 F.2d 336, 338 (8th Cir. 1983). In *Gryder*, the court upheld the Tax Court's admission of portions of the transcript from an earlier criminal trial, which were offered to prove the contents of business records. *Id.* The IRS had "negligently"—but not in bad faith—destroyed the records after the criminal trial. *Id.*

In *Wood v. State*, the capital-murder defendant's brother testified that the defendant returned home after robbing and killing a gas-station attendant and played a stolen video surveillance tape that showed the defendant and his cohort committing the robbery and murder. 18 S.W.3d 642, 647 (Tex. Crim. App. 2000). After the witness viewed the tape, he destroyed it with a blowtorch. *Id.* Because the State, not the defendant, was the proponent of the secondary evidence, the brother's testimony on the contents of the destroyed tape was admissible under Rule 1004 because the original tape had not been destroyed "in bad faith" by the State. *Wood*, 18 S.W.3d at 647.

128. *See, e.g.*, *In re Porras*, 224 B.R. 367, 371 (Bankr. W.D. Tex. 1998) (copy of a crucial letter, purportedly written by trustor, that suddenly appeared in middle of bankruptcy proceeding with no explanation of the loss of original and was produced by parties whose "credibility [has] continually been challenged" was not admissible under Federal Rule 1003).

129. *See* TEX. R. EVID. 1004(b).

130. 2 RAY, *supra* note 13, §1575, at 293 & n.20.

131. *See* 5 MUELLER & KIRKPATRICK, *supra* note 12, §10:28, at 812 (when "compelled production of the original at trial would be difficult and perhaps impossible, the fact that a Herculean effort might have produced the original out of the custody of a distant holder for purposes of discovery should not foreclose a finding of practical unavailability, which is all that FED. R. EVID. 1004(2) [now Rule 1004(b)] should require"); *see, e.g.*, *Ellis v. State*, 517 S.W.3d 922, 931 (Tex. App.—Fort Worth 2017, no pet.) (trial court did not abuse discretion in admitting transcription of text messages when police sergeant could not directly download messages but instead transcribed them and had transcription reviewed for accuracy). Rule 1004(b) is identical to Federal Rule 1004(b).

132. TEX. R. EVID. 1004(c); *see, e.g.*, *Kerlin v. Arias*, 274 S.W.3d 666, 667-68 (Tex. 2008) (per curiam) (best-evidence rule did not apply to deed signed in Mexico; certified English translation filed in Texas was sufficient); *Vitiello v. State*, 848 S.W.2d 885, 887 (Tex. App.—Houston [14th Dist.] 1993, pet. ref'd) (because original check that formed basis of theft indictment was located in Pennsylvania, State could offer photocopy and was not required to produce the original under Rule 1004).

deposition hearing in the county where the third party resides or regularly does business.[133] Even though the third party does not need to relinquish possession of the original at such a deposition, the document would be available for photocopying, and the proponent could then produce an admissible duplicate at trial. Because a trial subpoena in civil cases reaches only 150 miles from the county where the suit is pending, the party should not wait until trial to issue a subpoena duces tecum.[134] In criminal cases, however, a subpoena duces tecum issued in conjunction with a trial subpoena operates anywhere in the state.[135] Thus, the failure of the subpoenaed person to appear at trial should excuse production of the original document in a criminal trial.

D. Rule 1004(d): Original in Possession of Opponent

Rule 1004(d), which is identical to Federal Rule 1004(c), codifies the long-standing common-law doctrine that an opponent who has possession of the original document cannot complain that secondary evidence of the document is inadmissible.[136] Instead, the opposing party should produce the original. This estoppel doctrine is based on the rationale that a party who has possession of the original document does not need the rule's protection; after proper notice, that party can prevent the use of secondary evidence by producing the original document.[137] The adequacy of the notice should be determined by practical standards, not technical requirements.[138] Oral or implied notice may be sufficient.[139] The notice procedure under Rule 1004(d) does not require compulsory process to produce the document. The other party must simply be put on notice that the document will play a role in the litigation.[140] The requirement of possession or control by the opposing party is satisfied by evidence of personal or constructive custody.[141] Thus, if the original is in the possession of a party's agent or employee, it is in the party's own possession for purposes of the rule.

---

133. *See* Tex. R. Civ. P. 176.2(b) (witness receiving a subpoena must "produce and permit inspection and copying of designated documents or tangible things in the possession, custody, or control of that person"), 199.2(b)(5) (notice of oral deposition may include request for witness to produce documents and tangible things at deposition).

134. *See* Tex. Civ. Prac. & Rem. Code §22.002 (trial subpoena and subpoena for production of documentary evidence may be served on witness who resides or may be found within 150 miles of the county where the suit is pending).

135. *See* Tex. Code Crim. Proc. arts. 24.01, 24.02, 24.16.

136. *See* Tex. R. Evid. 1004(d); ***Walters v. State***, 102 Tex. Crim. 243, 247, 277 S.W. 653, 656 (1925) (op. on reh'g); ***In re Estate of Jones***, 197 S.W.3d 894, 901 n.6 (Tex. App.—Beaumont 2006, pet. denied); 2 Goode et al., *supra* note 108, §1004.5, at 330.

137. *See* 2 Ray, *supra* note 13, §1569, at 278-79.

138. 2 Goode et al., *supra* note 108, §1004.5, at 330.

139. *See, e.g.*, ***McConnell Constr. Co. v. Ins. Co. of St. Louis***, 428 S.W.2d 659, 661-62 (Tex. 1968) (implied notice).

140. Tex. R. Evid. 1004(d); *see* Fed. R. Evid. 1004 advisory committee's note, paragraph (3); 5 Mueller & Kirkpatrick, *supra* note 12, §10:29, at 814.

141. *Cf.* ***Consol. Coal Co. v. Chubb***, 741 F.2d 968, 972 (7th Cir. 1984) (dicta; report that quoted reading of X-ray admitted in administrative hearing, in which rules of evidence do not apply, would have been admissible under Federal Rules because X-ray was under party's control).

E. Rule 1004(e): Collateral Matters

Rule 1004(e), which is identical to Federal Rule 1004(d), codifies a collateral-matters excuse, long recognized at common law both generally[142] and in Texas,[143] for the non-production of an original writing, recording, or photograph because it is not closely related to a controlling issue.[144] The collateral-matters doctrine is frequently applied in the context of ownership. For example, in an arson prosecution, the owner of the damaged or destroyed building may testify that he owns the property—he does not need to produce the original deed.[145] In a theft prosecution, the owner of a stolen Rolex does not need to produce a sales receipt—he may simply testify that he owns the watch. Suppose a witness to an oral confession identifies the date of the confession as the day after the crime because he read about the crime in the newspaper that day. Striking the testimonial reference to the newspaper and requiring production of the newspaper itself would serve no useful purpose because the newspaper's contents are not closely related to the real issue in the case—the confession and its date.[146] The newspaper is only collaterally relevant. Courts generally consider three factors in determining whether a writing is collateral: "the centrality of the document to the principal issues of the litigation; the complexity of the relevant features of the document; and the existence of genuine dispute as to its contents."[147] Under the Rules, the three factors apply to recordings and photographs as well as writings. The trial judge has considerable discretion in determining when evidence is so closely related to the controlling issues in the lawsuit that the production of the originals is required, and the judge's determination is reviewable only for abuse of that discretion.

RULE 1005

COPIES OF PUBLIC RECORDS TO PROVE CONTENT

The proponent may use a copy to prove the content of an official record—or of a document that was recorded or filed in a public office as authorized by law—if these conditions are met: the record or document is otherwise admis-

---

142. *See* 2 McCORMICK ON EVIDENCE, *supra* note 7, §239, at 111 & n.1; *see, e.g.*, *Farr v. Zoning Bd. of Appeals*, 95 A.2d 792, 794 (Conn. 1953) (in action appealing zoning board's grant of a variance, parol testimony was allowed to prove that plaintiffs were property owners because ownership was only a collateral issue); *Wilkins v. Hester*, 167 S.E.2d 167, 169 (Ga. Ct. App. 1969) (witness's testimony about his occupation was not an issue in a bailment-damages case; best-evidence rule was inapplicable); *Van Valkenberg v. Venters*, 197 P.2d 284, 285 (Okla. 1948) (in forcible-entry-and-detainer case, title to real property was a collateral issue; best-evidence rule was inapplicable).

143. *See Keeney v. Odom*, 534 S.W.2d 409, 412 (Tex. Civ. App.—Beaumont 1976, writ ref'd n.r.e.); *Freeman v. Commercial Union Assur. Co.*, 317 S.W.2d 563, 568 (Tex. Civ. App.—Texarkana 1958, writ ref'd n.r.e.); *Lawson v. Holloman*, 238 S.W.2d 987, 988 (Tex. Civ. App.—San Antonio 1951, writ ref'd n.r.e.); 2 RAY, *supra* note 13, §1567 (3d ed. 1980 & Supp. 1991).

144. *See* FED. R. EVID. 1004(d); TEX. R. EVID. 1004(e).

145. *See Drew v. State*, 147 Tex. Crim. 29, 31, 177 S.W.2d 787, 788-89 (1944).

146. 2 McCORMICK ON EVIDENCE, *supra* note 7, §239, at 111; *see* 5 MUELLER & KIRKPATRICK, *supra* note 12, §10:30, at 821 & n.6; 2 RAY, *supra* note 13, §1567, at 272.

147. 2 McCORMICK ON EVIDENCE, *supra* note 7, §239, at 112.

RULE 1005

> sible; and the copy is certified as correct in accordance with Rule 902(4) or is testified to be correct by a witness who has compared it with the original. If no such copy can be obtained by reasonable diligence, then the proponent may use other evidence to prove the content.

COMMENTARY ON RULE 1005

Before the promulgation of the Rules, public records were defined by statute to include official records and private documents that had been recorded or filed as authorized by law.[148] Rule 1005, which exempts public records from the best-evidence doctrine codified in Rules 1002, 1003, and 1004, follows this statutory definition. These records are treated differently because "[r]emoving [public records] from their usual place of keeping would be attended by serious inconvenience to the public and to the custodian."[149] Thus, Rule 1005 preempts Rules 1001 through 1004 and sets up an entirely different hierarchical system of best-evidence preference for public records.[150] Rule 1005 is identical to Federal Rule 1005.

A proponent can prove public records by introducing a copy certified as correct under Rule 902(4)[151] or by introducing the testimony of a witness who has compared a copy with the public record on file.[152] Other evidence of a public record's contents is

---

148. Act approved May 13, 1846, 1st Leg., R.S., An Act to Regulate Proceedings in the District Courts: Evidence, §90, 1846 Tex. Gen. Laws 387, *reprinted in* 2 H.P.N. GAMMEL, THE LAWS OF TEXAS 1822-1897, at 1693-94 (Austin, Gammel Book Co. 1898), *amended by* Act approved April 23, 1907, 30th Leg., R.S., ch. 165 (CLXV), §1, 1907 Tex. Gen. Laws 308, *reprinted in* 13 H.P.N. GAMMEL, at 308, *amended by* Act approved June 7, 1927, 40th Leg., C.S., ch. 73, §1, 1927 Tex. Gen. Laws 198, *amended by* Act of May 31, 1939, 46th Leg., ch. 2, §1, 1939 Tex. Gen. Laws 325, *amended by* Act approved May 20, 1941, 47th Leg., ch. 299, §1, 1941 Tex. Gen. Laws 476 (former Texas Revised Civil Statutes art. 3726 deemed repealed as to civil proceedings effective 1983 and as to criminal proceedings effective 1986). Texas Revised Civil Statutes article 3726 provided:
> [W]henever any party to a suit shall file among the papers of the cause an affidavit stating that any instrument or writing, recorded as aforesaid, has been lost, or that he cannot procure the original, a certified copy of the record of any such instrument shall be admitted in evidence in like manner as the original could be.
149. FED. R. EVID. 1005 advisory committee's note.
150. The Advisory Committee further notes that:
> no explanation need be given for failure to produce the original of a public record. This blanket dispensation from producing or accounting for the original [granted by Federal Rule 1005] would open the door to the introduction of every kind of secondary evidence of contents of public records were it not for the preference given certified or compared copies. Recognition of degrees of secondary evidence in this situation is an appropriate quid pro quo for not applying the requirement of producing the original.
Id. Refer to notes 118-121 *supra* and accompanying text.
151. *E.g.*, *Int'l Fid. Ins. v. State*, 65 S.W.3d 724, 727 (Tex. App.—El Paso 2001, no pet.) (certified copy of bail bond complied with best-evidence rule); *Guiles v. State*, No. 02-12-00086-CV (Tex. App.—Fort Worth 2013, no pet.) (memo op.; 1-24-13) (trial court did not abuse its discretion in admitting appearance bond that was stamped "Certified Copy" and contained signature and date handwritten by deputy district clerk). Refer to *Article IX: Authentication & Identification, supra* p. 1018.
152. *See, e.g.*, *Valdez v. Hollenbeck*, 410 S.W.3d 1, 14 (Tex. App.—San Antonio 2013) (copy of tax return was admissible under Rule 1005 when accountant who prepared return testified that copy was an exact duplicate of original submitted to IRS), *rev'd on other grounds*, 465 S.W.3d 217 (Tex. 2015); *Caldwell v. State*, 916 S.W.2d 674, 676 (Tex. App.—Texarkana 1996, no pet.) (copy of return of subpoena was admissible under Rule 1005 when witness

allowed only if the proponent cannot produce a certified or compared copy using reasonable diligence.[153] A certified copy of a public record that is itself a copy does not satisfy the best-evidence rule. But because the periodic destruction of original public records is permitted by statute,[154] photocopies of destroyed records would be admissible under Rule 1004(a).[155]

Certainly the easiest and probably the most frequently used means of proving the contents of a public record under Rule 1005 is with a copy certified as correct by the custodian or other authorized person under the self-authentication provisions of Rule 902(4). Rule 1005 makes it unnecessary to remove a public record from its usual place of keeping, and Rule 902(4) makes it unnecessary to subpoena a public officer to the courthouse to authenticate the records. The court of criminal appeals has held that a fax of a certified public record qualifies as a duplicate under Rule 1003 and is as admissible as an original certified copy under Rule 1005.[156]

Some courts and commentators have interpreted Federal Rule 1005 to allow other evidence of a record's contents to be admitted, even when a copy is available, if the original cannot be obtained. In *Amoco Production Co. v. United States*,[157] the issue was whether a particular deed reserved a one-half mineral interest to the lessors.[158] The plaintiffs-lessees of the mineral interest sued the defendants-lessors to quiet title.[159] Un-

---

testified that he had compared original with copy he had made and that it was a correct photocopy); *Guiles*, No. 02-12-00086-CV (memo op.) (deputy district clerk compared certified copy of bond offered as exhibit with bond in clerk's file and testified that document in file was what she copied when certifying exhibit). In *Hickson v. Martinez*, a witness testified that the offered document was a copy of a pertinent federal regulation for the standard of care that hospitals receiving Medicare and Medicaid must meet. 707 S.W.2d 919, 926 (Tex. App.—Dallas 1985), *writ ref'd n.r.e.*, 716 S.W.2d 499 (Tex. 1986). The court of appeals held that the copy was admissible under Rule 1005 because the witness testified that she had compared the copy to the original contained in a bound volume in the hospital library and had found it to be correct. *Id.* This use of the best-evidence rule seems peculiar because the rule is not usually applied to statutory documents or case authority. The trial judge probably should have taken judicial notice of the document because it was published in the Code of Federal Regulations. *See* 2 GOODE ET AL., *supra* note 108, §1005.1, at 335; *cf.* *ESIS, Inc., Servicing Contractor v. Johnson*, 908 S.W.2d 554, 561 (Tex. App.—Fort Worth 1995, writ denied) (trial court erred in admitting a copy of Workers' Compensation Commission Appeals panel opinion that was neither verified nor compared to the original, but error was harmless).

153. Refer to note 125 *supra* and accompanying text. Even this requirement arguably does not apply when the record involved is a publicly recorded private document. Thus, if the original of a publicly recorded private document is available but the recorded copy is not, Rule 1005 will permit the introduction of other evidence of the document's content. If both the original and the recorded copy are available, Rule 1005 will exclude other evidence.
Rule 1005 changed earlier Texas law in one respect. Under former Texas Revised Civil Statutes article 3726, certified copies of publicly recorded private documents were admissible as evidence only if the proponent made an adequate showing by affidavit that the original was lost or not procurable. Refer to note 148 *supra*. Rule 1005 allows the proponent to introduce certified copies without any such showing. Refer to notes 149-150 *supra* and accompanying text.

154. *See* TEX. LOC. GOV'T CODE §§203.044, 203.045.

155. *See* 2 RAY, *supra* note 13, §1576, at 85 (Supp. 1991).

156. Refer to note 44 *supra*, discussing *Englund v. State*, 946 S.W.2d 64 (Tex. Crim. App. 1997).

157. 619 F.2d 1383 (10th Cir. 1980).

158. *See id.* at 1386-87.

159. *Id.* at 1386.

der Federal Rule 1005, the plaintiffs introduced a certified copy of the deed, as recorded by the county recorder, which did not show any mineral reservation to the lessors.[160] Because the original and all copies of the deed had disappeared, defendants-lessors tried to reserve a one-half mineral interest by introducing secondary evidence of the original grantor's routine practice.[161] However, the trial court held that Federal Rule 1005 required the exclusion of all other evidence of content and granted summary judgment for the plaintiffs.[162]

The court of appeals reversed and remanded for a trial on the merits, holding that Federal Rule 1005 does not preclude the admission of other evidence of the contents of the missing original deed because, having been returned to its owner, the deed was not a public record and thus was outside the scope of Federal Rule 1005.[163] The appellate court explained that it could not

> embrace an interpretation of [Rule 1005] which would exclude all evidence of the original deed other than the recorded version when the very question in controversy [was] whether the original deed was correctly transcribed onto the recorded version. Rule 1004(1) [now Rule 1004(a)], which authorizes the admission of other evidence of the contents of a writing if [the original is] lost or destroyed, rather than Rule 1005, [was] applicable to the [original] deed.[164]

Texas Rule 1005 is not a rule of general admissibility; it involves only the best-evidence doctrine. Instead of requiring the production of original public records and documents, Rule 1005 permits the introduction of copies of the contents of public records if those contents are otherwise admissible. Thus, for example, documents introduced at trial to prove the truth of matters asserted would not be admissible under Rule 1005's provisions unless the documents fell under one of the hearsay exceptions in Rule 803 or Rule 804.[165]

---

160. *Id.* at 1389.

161. *Id.*

162. *See id.* at 1389-90.

163. *Id.* at 1390.

164. *Id.* The holding in **Amoco** has been well summarized:
> Where the proponent's purpose is to prove the content of an original private document, which happens also to have been filed or recorded in a public office, such as a deed or encumbrance upon real property, he may certainly do so by means of the public record. FED. R. EVID. 1005 does not compel him to do so, and he may offer the original document as proof of content and may resort to "other evidence" if nonproduction of the original is excused.

5 MUELLER & KIRKPATRICK, *supra* note 12, §10:32, at 830 (footnotes omitted).

165. *See, e.g.*, **Cole v. State**, 839 S.W.2d 798, 807-13 (Tex. Crim. App. 1992) (op. on reh'g) (written results of chemical tests performed by nontestifying DPS officer were not admissible when lab report was introduced through supervising chemist; Rules 803(6) and 803(8)(B), now Rules 803(6) and 803(8)(A)(ii), prohibit the admission in a criminal proceeding of any public or business records written by a nontestifying member of law enforcement); *cf.* **United States v. Ruffin**, 575 F.2d 346, 356 (2d Cir. 1978) (IRS computer printouts were inadmissible hearsay, but their admission was harmless error). Refer to *Article VIII: Hearsay, supra* p. 871.

RULE 1006
SUMMARIES TO PROVE CONTENT

The proponent may use a summary, chart, or calculation to prove the content of voluminous writings, recordings, or photographs that cannot be conveniently examined in court. The proponent must make the originals or duplicates available for examination or copying, or both, by other parties at a reasonable time and place. And the court may order the proponent to produce them in court.

COMMENTARY ON RULE 1006

Rule 1006 codifies and expands the voluminous-records exception to the best-evidence doctrine, as found in Texas case law[166] and in the common law generally,[167] to include recordings and photographs. The rule, which is identical to Federal Rule 1006, imposes two requirements before a summary of records may be admissible: the underlying records must be (1) voluminous and (2) made available to the opponent for inspection.[168]

Rule 1006 permits summary proof of large quantities of written, recorded, or photographic material only when such material is so voluminous that producing all of it for the jury is impractical.[169] To introduce summary material, the proponent does not need to show that examining the underlying material in court would be impossible;

---

166. *See **Duncan Dev., Inc. v. Haney**,* 634 S.W.2d 811, 812-13 (Tex. 1982).

167. *See* 4 WIGMORE, *supra* note 8, §1230, at 535 & n.1. Wigmore articulated the principle, which had long been recognized by common-law courts:

> Where a fact could be ascertained only by the inspection of a large number of documents made up of very *numerous detailed statements*—as, the net balance resulting from a year's vouchers of a treasurer or a year's accounts in a bank ledger—it is obvious that it would often be practically out of the question to apply the present principle by requiring the production of the entire mass of documents and entries to be perused by the jury or read aloud to them. The convenience of trials demands that other evidence be allowed to be offered, in the shape of the testimony of a competent witness who has perused the entire mass and will state summarily the net result. Such a practice is well established to be proper.

Id. §1230, at 535.

168. *See* TEX. R. EVID. 1006. Before the 2015 restyling, Texas Rule 1006 also explicitly required that the voluminous evidence be "otherwise admissible." *See **Duncan Dev.**,* 634 S.W.2d at 812-13 (supporting documents themselves must be admissible in evidence); ***Cooper Pet. Co. v. LaGloria Oil & Gas Co.**,* 436 S.W.2d 889, 891 (Tex. 1969) (court may admit summaries of voluminous records to expedite the trial and to aid the fact-finder if the source records themselves are admissible); ***Moroch v. Collins**,* 174 S.W.3d 849, 865 (Tex. App.—Dallas 2005, pet. denied) (Rule 1006 does not require that underlying documents be admitted, only that they be admissible). This requirement is now implicit in both Texas Rule 1006 and Federal Rule 1006; no substantive change was intended by the restyling. *See* Tex. Sup. Ct. Order, Misc. Docket No. 15-9048, §2 (eff. Apr. 1, 2015). Refer to notes 177-182 *infra* and accompanying text.

169. *See **Aquamarine Assocs. v. Burton Shipyard, Inc.**,* 659 S.W.2d 820, 821 (Tex. 1983); ***Black Lake Pipe Line Co. v. Union Constr. Co.**,* 538 S.W.2d 80, 92-93 (Tex. 1976); *see also **Dixon v. State**,* 940 S.W.2d 192, 194-95 (Tex. App.—San Antonio 1996, no pet.) ("The purpose of the summary rule is ease of handling the exhibits. It allows voluminous materials to be summarized and brought into court when the summary is accurate and will do the same job as the massive originals.").

however, a mere offer to shorten and simplify is not enough.[170] Texas cases recognize that trial courts have wide discretion in determining whether summaries are necessary to expedite a trial.[171] A summary must be authenticated as an accurate and fair presentation of the underlying voluminous material.[172] In ***United States v. Denton***, federal agents reduced a 20-day wiretap to a composite tape containing 39 telephone calls.[173] The court admitted the composite under Federal Rule 1006 after the agents who prepared it testified that they had neither augmented nor abridged the original tapes in ways that might create a false impression.[174]

The proponent must also make the underlying material available to the opponent for examination and copying at some reasonable time and place.[175]

> [T]he most promising way to satisfy [this requirement] involves advance written notice by the proponent ... indicating an intent to offer such proof and offering to make the underlying material available ....
>
> The notice should set out the gist or substance of the summary, so as to give ... some idea what to look for in the underlying material, and should identify the material ... with reasonable particularity. Notice given far enough in advance of trial insures that the opportunity to examine is real ....[176]

---

170. 5 MUELLER & KIRKPATRICK, *supra* note 12, §10:34, at 839. The central concern of Federal Rule 1006 is to establish an alternative method of presenting voluminous material that "cannot conveniently be examined in court." *See* FED. R. EVID. 1006; 5 MUELLER & KIRKPATRICK, *supra* note 12, §10:34, at 838. "Admitting summary evidence introduces a risk that important details may be overlooked because they are buried or perhaps hidden by accident or partisan zeal, and a risk that inadmissible evidence will creep in unnoticed, or that suggested conclusions will be accepted uncritically because the mass of underlying data [is] complex, and perhaps technical and forbidding." 5 MUELLER & KIRKPATRICK, *supra* note 12, §10:34, at 839.

171. ***Black Lake Pipe Line***, 538 S.W.2d at 93; *see **Aquamarine Assocs.***, 659 S.W.2d at 821 (trial court has discretion to relax best-evidence rule and admit summaries of voluminous records).

172. *See, e.g.*, ***Duncan Dev.***, 634 S.W.2d at 812-13 (summaries were properly admitted when offering party established that contractor's employees had personal knowledge of accounts on subcontractor's invoices and had duty of determining whether subcontractor had completed his work); ***Wilson v. State***, No. 05-15-01407-CR (Tex. App.—Dallas 2017, no pet.) (memo op.; 1-5-17) (trial court did not abuse its discretion in overruling defendant's objection to summary compiled from cell-phone records when underlying records were made available to defendant and admitted without objection and defendant questioned custodian of records about summary; trial court could have reasonably concluded that information omitted from summary but included in underlying records did not make summary inaccurate); ***Leander v. Fin & Feather Club***, No. 06-10-00135-CV (Tex. App.—Texarkana 2012, no pet.) (memo op.; 1-11-12) (witness who served as trustee of organization before and during the time summary document was created could testify to summary's accuracy); *cf.* ***United States v. Denton***, 556 F.2d 811, 816 (6th Cir. 1977) (composite tape of intercepted conversations was properly admitted because opposing counsel had reasonable opportunity to examine originals and proponent laid proper foundation for tape's accuracy and authenticity).

173. 556 F.2d at 814.

174. *Id.* at 815-16.

175. Rule 1006 does not require that the summary itself be produced in discovery or made available within a certain time before trial. ***Shaw v. Lemon***, 427 S.W.3d 536, 544-45 (Tex. App.—Dallas 2014, pet. denied).

176. 5 MUELLER & KIRKPATRICK, *supra* note 12, §10:35, at 849. Under some circumstances, producing the documents in court during trial may be sufficient notice. *See, e.g.*, ***Alarid v. State***, 762 S.W.2d 659, 661-62 (Tex. App.—Houston [14th Dist.] 1988, pet. ref'd) (prosecutor could introduce a chart showing 71 extraneous real-estate transactions to prove defendant's intent to defraud when "three stacks of certified documents" were available in court);

Although the admissibility requirement is no longer explicit in Rule 1006,[177] the rule does not provide an independent basis to admit otherwise inadmissible evidence.[178] However, when a summary is based on voluminous documents that may themselves be compiled from information contained in other materials, the underlying materials do not need to be produced for inspection. For example, in **State v. Buckner Construction Co.**, the court held that the plaintiff had complied with Rule 1006 when it used journals and ledgers to prepare its summary exhibit and then made those materials available to the defendant.[179] The defendant objected because the plaintiff had not produced the checks and invoices on which the original business-record journals and ledgers were based.[180] Because the journals and ledgers were the voluminous records from which the summary exhibit was prepared, nothing in Rule 1006 required the production of the underlying materials.[181] The **Buckner** case presents an issue frequently raised in Texas cases about the distinction between a summary prepared for litigation purposes under Rule 1006 and a summary of business entries or data, which is itself a business record kept by the company. Admissibility of the latter summaries is governed not by Rule 1006 but by Rule 803(6), the business-records exception to the hearsay rule.[182]

---

see also **White Indus., Inc. v. Cessna Aircraft Co.**, 611 F. Supp. 1049, 1070 & n.10 (W.D. Mo. 1985) (a "reasonable time" will generally occur at some point before trial, but "it would be within the trial court's discretion to permit the matter to be dealt with during trial").

177. Refer to note 168 *supra.*

178. *See, e.g.*, **Black Lake Pipe Line Co. v. Union Constr. Co.**, 538 S.W.2d 80, 95 (Tex. 1976) (underlying source records were inadmissible hearsay because they contained statements and opinions of plaintiff's employees; summaries of those documents were also inadmissible); **C.M. Asfahl Agency v. Tensor, Inc.**, 135 S.W.3d 768, 800 (Tex. App.—Houston [1st Dist.] 2004, no pet.) (because voluminous documents were business records of opposing party obtained through discovery, materials were admissible as nonhearsay admissions by party-opponent); **Rodriguez v. State**, 90 S.W.3d 340, 373-74 (Tex. App.—El Paso 2001, pet. ref'd) (summaries were admissible because underlying business records had already been admitted into evidence; "[t]he fact that certain characterizations were made to prepare the summaries did not bar their admission"); **Hanson Sw. Corp. v. Dal-Mac Constr. Co.**, 554 S.W.2d 712, 723 (Tex. Civ. App.—Dallas 1977, writ ref'd n.r.e.) (summary was inadmissible because proponent did not show that underlying source records were admissible).

In **Dixon v. State**, the defendant's theft conviction was reversed when the trial court had admitted a list of items that were missing from the corporation's inventory and their values. 940 S.W.2d 192, 195 (Tex. App.—San Antonio 1996, no pet.). The list was inadmissible as a summary of voluminous business records under Criminal Rule 1006 because the list was not otherwise admissible under the business-records exception to the hearsay rule. **Dixon**, 940 S.W.2d at 195. The list of missing items was compiled as part of the theft investigation and was not part of the routine business operation; thus, the list was not admissible under Rule 803(6). **Dixon**, 940 S.W.2d at 195; *see also* **Callahan v. State**, 937 S.W.2d 553, 559 (Tex. App.—Texarkana 1996, no pet.) (Rule 1006 does not apply to summary document offered as the basis of expert witness's medical opinion; because doctor's written report was hearsay, it was not otherwise admissible under the rule).

Similarly, in **City of Dallas v. GTE Southwest, Inc.**, the trial court properly excluded the city's exhibit that purportedly demonstrated its monetary damages from loss of telecommunication-franchise fees because that exhibit appeared to be a summary of other documents that were not produced for the court and that required expert testimony to explain their compilation, accuracy, and completeness. 980 S.W.2d 928, 934-35 (Tex. App.—Fort Worth 1998, pet. denied).

179. 704 S.W.2d 837, 843 (Tex. App.—Houston [14th Dist.] 1985, writ ref'd n.r.e.).

180. *Id.*

181. *Id.*; *see* 1A RAY, *supra* note 13, §1253, at 411 (3d ed. 1980 & Supp. 1991).

182. *See, e.g.*, **Longoria v. Greyhound Lines, Inc.**, 699 S.W.2d 298, 302 (Tex. App.—San Antonio 1985, no writ) (admissibility of computer-generated copy of an insurance policy was governed by the basic requirements for admissibility of business records); **McAllen State Bank v. Linbeck Constr. Corp.**, 695 S.W.2d 10, 16 (Tex. App.—

Rule 1006 is a rule of convenience. The rule permits a proponent to introduce a summary into evidence in place of admissible voluminous records or as an aid in understanding already-admitted voluminous records.[183] As was noted in *White Industries v. Cessna Aircraft Co.*,

> there is a distinction between a Rule 1006 summary and a so-called "pedagogical" summary. The former is admitted as substantive evidence without requiring that the underlying documents themselves be in evidence; the latter is simply a demonstrative aid which undertakes to summarize or organize other evidence already admitted.[184]

Demonstrative summaries are not independently admissible exhibits and probably should not be admitted into evidence,[185] but they frequently are.[186] Demonstrative summaries are used to clarify or amplify arguments based on other evidence already admitted, but that other evidence does not need to be voluminous records.[187] These pedagogical summaries are governed by Rules 403 and 611, not by Rule 1006.[188] Unfortunately, the distinction between the two types of summaries is nonexistent for most practical purposes.[189] Pedagogical summaries should not be sent to the jury room during deliberations, but any such error in allowing the jury to view them

---

Corpus Christi 1985, writ ref'd n.r.e.) (computer printouts, which were a business-accounting summary, were themselves business records and did not need to be made available for inspection). For a discussion of the business-records exception, refer to *Article VIII: Hearsay, supra* p. 897.

183. *See **Rizzuti v. Smith***, No. 09-14-00323-CV (Tex. App.—Beaumont 2016, no pet.) (memo op.; 3-10-16) (summaries of documents can be admitted as substantive evidence if proper foundation is established); *cf. **United States v. Strissel***, 920 F.2d 1162, 1164 (4th Cir. 1990) (charts summarizing voluminous evidence were admissible); ***United States v. Pinto***, 850 F.2d 927, 935 (2d Cir. 1988) (trial court did not err in permitting properly admitted summary charts into jury room); ***United States v. Campbell***, 845 F.2d 1374, 1381 (6th Cir. 1988) (chart summarizing voluminous medical files on 36 patients was properly admitted under Federal Rule 1006; individual files were also admitted and were available for the jury).

184. 611 F. Supp. 1049, 1069 (W.D. Mo. 1985); *see also **United States v. Buck***, 324 F.3d 786, 791 (5th Cir. 2003) (assumptions in pedagogical summaries are allowable if those assumptions are supported by evidence in the record).

185. *See **United States v. Posada-Rios***, 158 F.3d 832, 869 (5th Cir. 1998) (trial court had discretion to permit prosecution to use timeline and organizational summary charts in front of jury as "pedagogical devices" as long as they were not admitted into evidence and trial judge gave appropriate limiting instructions); ***Markey v. State***, 996 S.W.2d 226, 231-32 (Tex. App.—Houston [14th Dist.] 1999, no pet.) (harmless error to admit chart summarizing officer's testimony when chart simply reiterated evidence and did not itself constitute any proof).

186. *See **White Indus.***, 611 F. Supp. at 1069-70; *see, e.g.*, ***United States v. Gardner***, 611 F.2d 770, 776 (9th Cir. 1980) (no error in admitting chart that summarized facts and calculations already admitted into evidence and that was used only to clarify evidence for the jury); ***Uniroyal Goodrich Tire Co. v. Martinez***, 977 S.W.2d 328, 342 (Tex. 1998) (trial court did not abuse its discretion in admitting timeline prepared by witness to illustrate sequence of events he had testified to); ***Barnes v. State***, 797 S.W.2d 353, 357 (Tex. App.—Tyler 1990, no pet.) (dicta; chart summarizing admissible evidence may be admitted into evidence and used before the jury to aid them in their deliberations).

187. *See **Buck***, 324 F.3d at 790 (discussing distinction between Federal Rule 1006 summaries of voluminous material and pedagogical summaries used to clarify other evidence).

188. *Cf. id.* (discussing Federal Rules 403, 611, and 1006).

189. *See, e.g.*, ***United States v. Dorta***, 783 F.2d 1179, 1183 (4th Cir. 1986) (mistakenly relying on Federal Rule 1006 as authority for admitting chart that summarized evidence already admitted); ***Moore v. Johns-Manville Sales Corp.***, 781 F.2d 1061, 1066 (5th Cir. 1986) (mistakenly relying on Federal Rule 1006 as authority for admitting product-identification lists in an asbestos case as summary evidence).

has usually been held harmless because they are generally accurate summaries of evidence that is already before the jury.[190]

RULE 1007
TESTIMONY OR STATEMENT OF A PARTY TO PROVE CONTENT

The proponent may prove the content of a writing, recording, or photograph by the testimony, deposition, or written statement of the party against whom the evidence is offered. The proponent need not account for the original.

COMMENTARY ON RULE 1007

Rule 1007, which is identical to Federal Rule 1007, provides an exception to the best-evidence doctrine for an opposing party's statements[191] made in the course of giving testimony or in writing.[192] Texas case law has long recognized this exception.[193] However, there is a limitation to this exception when the testimony or statement is being offered to prove a document's execution. In **Sanders v. Lane**, the Texas Commission of Appeals recognized the exception for proof of contents but held that a document's execution could not be proved under the exception unless the record was shown to be lost

---

190. *See* **United States v. Possick**, 849 F.2d 332, 339-40 (8th Cir. 1988) (submission of purely demonstrative charts to the jury room is disfavored and a limiting instruction should be given, but the failure to give a limiting instruction is not reversible error); *see, e.g.*, **Buck**, 324 F.3d at 791-92 (admitting diagram was error of law and abuse of discretion, but "it was harmless, because the diagram accurately summarized testimony and other evidence that had been properly admitted and therefore was already before the jury"; any prejudice was diminished because opposing party had full opportunity to cross-examine summary witness); **United States v. Orlowski**, 808 F.2d 1283, 1289 (8th Cir. 1986) (trial court acted within its discretion when it sent summary exhibits to the jury because the summarized evidence had previously been admitted and the person giving the testimony had been subject to cross-examination).

191. Although no substantive change was intended by the 2015 restyling of Texas Rule 1007, the rule now refers to a party's "written statement" rather than "written admission." Rule 801(e)(2) was similarly changed to address an opposing party's "statement" rather than "admission." *See* TEX. R. EVID. 801(e)(2) & cmt. For a discussion of the change under Rule 801(e)(2), refer to *Article VIII: Hearsay, supra* p. 845.

192. Thus, Rule 1007 modifies the rule laid down in **Slatterie v. Pooley**, a leading English case followed in many American jurisdictions, which allowed proof of contents by evidence of an oral admission. 151 Eng. Rep. 579, 580-81 (Ex. 1840); *see* **Metro. Life Ins. v. Hogan**, 63 F.2d 654, 656 (7th Cir. 1933) ("The rule generally adopted is that oral admissions to the contents of a written instrument are competent evidence of its contents."); **Swing v. Cloquet Lumber Co.**, 141 N.W. 117, 118 (Minn. 1913) ("[A] written admission of the contents of a written document may be established against the party making the admission, without production of the document or accounting for its nonproduction."); **Aviation Enters., Inc. v. Cline**, 395 S.W.2d 306, 310 (Mo. Ct. App. 1965) (best-evidence rule does not apply when an adverse party admits the genuineness of a photostatic copy of the original); **Gardner v. City of Columbia Police Dep't**, 57 S.E.2d 308, 310 (S.C. 1950) (adverse party's testimonial admission is admissible to prove the contents of a document); *see, e.g.*, **Morrissey v. Powell**, 23 N.E.2d 411, 413 (Mass. 1939) (defendant's testimonial admission that he had previously confessed to drunken driving was admissible as proof of a confession's contents).

193. *See, e.g.*, **Hoefling v. Hambleton**, 84 Tex. 517, 519, 19 S.W. 689, 690 (1892) (adverse party's testimonial admission was admissible to prove the contents of a deed); **Mecaskey v. Bewley Mills**, 8 S.W.2d 688, 690 (Tex. Civ. App.—Fort Worth 1928, writ dism'd) (not necessary to produce an original document when an adverse party's verbal admission was introduced as proof of its contents).

or destroyed.[194] Because Rule 1007 expressly applies to contents only, this common-law limitation on proof of execution may be carried over under the Rules. However, the common-law doctrine seems peculiar because testimony or a statement about a document's contents would raise the problem of possible inaccuracy of recital, but testimony or a statement about the document's execution would not.

Rule 1007 is restricted to statements made during in-court testimony, during depositions, or in writing, while the common-law doctrine also applied to extrajudicial oral statements. Such statements would be admissible, however, to prove the contents of a document under Rule 1004 if the original could not be produced. For example, if A sues B for breach of contract and if A satisfies Rule 1004 by showing that the original of the contract was destroyed through no fault of his own, then he can offer into evidence B's oral statements about the contents of the contract.[195] Rule 1004 requires an accounting for the original while Rule 1007 does not.[196]

Rule 1007 logically applies to testimony or statements not only of the opposing party, but also of the party's representatives, employees, coconspirators, or other authorized agents. Thus, any testimony or statement that is exempt from the hearsay definition under Rule 801(e)(2) should qualify under Rule 1007.[197]

Whether the word "testimony" in Rule 1007 should include testimony taken before a grand jury is unclear. Some commentators suggest that any statement by the party against whom the statement is offered should qualify if the statement was taken under oath and recorded.[198]

RULE 1008

FUNCTIONS OF THE COURT & JURY

Ordinarily, the court determines whether the proponent has fulfilled the factual conditions for admitting other evidence of the content of a writing, record-

---

194. 227 S.W. 946, 947 (Tex. Comm'n App. 1921, judgm't adopted). The court stated:

> Declarations and admissions of the grantor against interest, as to the contents of an instrument, are receivable without producing it or accounting for its absence when no question arises as to its execution; but where its execution is directly involved, whether as proof of the precise question in issue or of some subordinate matter that tends to establish the ultimate fact upon which the case turns, the declarations by the grantor of its execution are inadmissible in the absence of proof of its execution or existence.

Id.; see also **Tarwater v. Donley Cty. State Bank**, 277 S.W. 176, 179 (Tex. Civ. App.—Amarillo 1925, no writ) ("Even though the purported statements of the father were against his interest, secondary proof that he had made them would not be admissible where the fact of the making of the statements was directly involved, since such fact was a material and not a collateral issue."); 4 WIGMORE, supra note 8, §1242, at 574, §1248, at 587 (facts about the physical document itself or its delivery or publication may be proved without production, but the terms of the document may not).

195. 5 STEPHEN A. SALTZBURG ET AL., FEDERAL RULES OF EVIDENCE MANUAL §1007.02[2], at 1007-2 (9th ed. 2006).

196. See TEX. R. EVID. 1004(a), 1007. Refer to notes 110-147 supra and accompanying text.

197. See 5 MUELLER & KIRKPATRICK, supra note 12, §10:37, at 859-60.

198. See id. §10:37, at 860-61; 5 SALTZBURG ET AL., supra note 195, §1007.02[4], at 1007-3.

> ing, or photograph under Rule 1004 or 1005. But in a jury trial, the jury determines—in accordance with Rule 104(b)—any issue about whether:
>
> **(a)** an asserted writing, recording, or photograph ever existed;
>
> **(b)** another one produced at the trial or hearing is the original; or
>
> **(c)** other evidence of content accurately reflects the content.

Commentary on Rule 1008

The trial judge decides preliminary questions of fact affecting the admissibility of evidence,[199] and the jury decides fact questions involving the merits of the controversy.[200] Rule 104 addresses the distinction between these two kinds of fact determinations, but the drafters added Rule 1008 to Article X as a special application of Rule 104 to the particular complexities of the best-evidence doctrine.[201] Thus, Rule 1008 does not alter the general allocation of duties between judge and jury outlined in Rule 104; it simply clarifies which best-evidence issues are questions of general admissibility for the judge and which are questions of conditional relevancy for the jury. Rule 1008 is identical to Federal Rule 1008.

The first sentence of Rule 1008 mandates that the trial judge determine whether (1) an item of evidence is an original, (2) an item of evidence qualifies as a duplicate and is thus presumptively admissible, (3) an original is authentic for purposes of Rule 1003, (4) admitting a duplicate instead of an original under Rule 1003 would be unfair, (5) an original is lost or destroyed and a diligent search has been conducted for it, (6) the proponent lost or destroyed evidence in bad faith, (7) an original can be obtained by any available judicial process, (8) an original is located in Texas, (9) an adverse party has possession of or control over the original and has received proper notice that the original's content would be a subject of proof at a hearing, and (10) evidence goes to a collateral matter or to a controlling issue.[202] For these questions, the trial judge follows the normal dictates of Rule 104(a). The trial judge can consider any reliable material (except privileged information), regardless of whether it is admissible, in making a determination[203] based on a preponderance of the evidence.[204]

The second sentence of Rule 1008 mandates that the jury decide such conditional-relevancy questions as whether (1) the asserted writing, recording, or photograph ever

---

199. Tex. R. Evid. 104(a); *see* 1 Ray, *supra* note 13, §2, at 3.

200. *See* 1 Ray, *supra* note 13, §3, at 6.

201. *See* 5 Mueller & Kirkpatrick, *supra* note 12, §10:38, at 862; 6 Weinstein & Berger, *supra* note 13, §1008.02[1], at 1008-5. For a discussion of Rules 104(a) and 104(b), refer to *Article I: General Provisions, supra* p. 86.

202. *See* Tex. R. Evid. 1001(d), (e), 1003, 1004, 1008; 5 Saltzburg et al., *supra* note 195, §1008.02[1], at 1008-2 to 1008-3; *cf. Seiler v. Lucasfilm, Ltd.*, 808 F.2d 1316, 1321 (9th Cir. 1986) (discussing the judge's role under Federal Rule 1008 in determining admissibility of duplicate evidence when the original evidence was lost or destroyed in bad faith).

203. Refer to *Article I: General Provisions, supra* p. 86.

204. *See* **United States v. Schipani**, 289 F. Supp. 43, 57 (E.D.N.Y. 1968) (summarizing common-law rule of burdens of proof necessary to admit evidence), *aff'd*, 414 F.2d 1262 (2d Cir. 1969).

existed, (2) another writing, recording, or photograph produced at the trial or a hearing is the original, and (3) other evidence of the contents accurately reflects the actual contents.[205] The Advisory Committee's note to Federal Rule 1008 gives an example of such a jury question. Assume the plaintiff in a breach-of-contract case offers secondary evidence of the contents of an alleged contract after introducing evidence of the original's loss. The defendant counters with evidence that no such contract was ever executed. At this point, the judge must allow the jury to decide each of the contested issues. If the judge were to decide, for example, that the contract was never executed, and the judge excluded the secondary evidence, he would improperly deny the jury an opportunity to rule on a central issue in the case.[206] These latter issues involve more than simply applying the best-evidence doctrine. They go to the heart of the litigation, and a decision on these issues is likely outcome-determinative. Further, because they are questions of pure fact, they are precisely the type of questions that jurors are qualified to answer in their deliberative process.[207]

RULE 1009
TRANSLATING A FOREIGN LANGUAGE DOCUMENT

(a) Submitting a Translation. A translation of a foreign language document is admissible if, at least 45 days before trial, the proponent serves on all parties:

(1) the translation and the underlying foreign language document; and

(2) a qualified translator's affidavit or unsworn declaration that sets forth the translator's qualifications and certifies that the translation is accurate.

(b) Objection. When objecting to a translation's accuracy, a party should specifically indicate its inaccuracies and offer an accurate translation. A party must serve the objection on all parties at least 15 days before trial.

(c) Effect of Failing to Object or Submit a Conflicting Translation. If the underlying foreign language document is otherwise admissible, the court must admit—and may not allow a party to attack the accuracy of—a translation submitted under subdivision (a) unless the party has:

---

205. TEX. R. EVID. 1008; *see* 5 MUELLER & KIRKPATRICK, *supra* note 12, §10:40, at 867-68; 5 SALTZBURG ET AL., *supra* note 195, §1008.02[2], at 1008-3.

206. FED. R. EVID. 1008 advisory committee's note (citing A. Leo Levin, *Authentication and Content of Writings*, 10 RUTGERS L. REV. 632, 644 (1956)); *see* Edmund M. Morgan, *The Law of Evidence, 1941-1945*, 59 HARV. L. REV. 481, 490-91 (1946); *see also* David W. McMorrow, Comment, *Authentication and the Best Evidence Rule Under the Federal Rules of Evidence*, 16 WAYNE L. REV. 195, 236 (1969) (while preliminary questions of fact are generally for the judge to decide, the court must modify the principle when such a question coincides with an ultimate issue, which lies within the province of the jury, such as the existence of an original writing or the authenticity of a writing offered as the original).

207. *See* John Kaplan, *Of Mabrus and Zorgs—An Essay in Honor of David Louisell*, 66 CALIF. L. REV. 987, 996 (1978) (conditional-relevancy questions under Federal Rule 1008 are left to the jury "simply because we safely can leave them to the jury").

(1) submitted a conflicting translation under subdivision (a); or

(2) objected to the translation under subdivision (b).

(d) Effect of Objecting or Submitting a Conflicting Translation. If conflicting translations are submitted under subdivision (a) or an objection is made under subdivision (b), the court must determine whether there is a genuine issue about the accuracy of a material part of the translation. If so, the trier of fact must resolve the issue.

(e) Qualified Translator May Testify. Except for subdivision (c), this rule does not preclude a party from offering the testimony of a qualified translator to translate a foreign language document.

(f) Time Limits. On a party's motion and for good cause, the court may alter this rule's time limits.

(g) Court-Appointed Translator. If necessary, the court may appoint a qualified translator. The reasonable value of the translator's services must be taxed as court costs.

Notes and Comments

Comment to 1998 change: This is a new rule.

COMMENTARY ON RULE 1009

Rule 1009, adopted as part of the 1998 Unified Rules of Evidence, is relatively new to Texas law and has no analogue in the Federal Rules of Evidence. It is a simplified procedure for providing English translations of foreign-language documents that are otherwise admissible in Texas civil and criminal proceedings.

As Texas has become more of an international business community, litigation in Texas courts has also become more international. Attorneys and courts are increasingly faced with the task of translating foreign-language documents and proving the accuracy of that translation at trial. Obtaining translations of foreign-language materials, which may be crucial to a lawsuit's outcome, is often expensive, difficult, and time-consuming. Rule 1009 provides an efficient, time-saving, and fair method of self-authenticating translations of foreign documents.[208]

Few Texas appellate decisions have addressed the issue of English translations of foreign documents, but when foreign-language documents have played a part in litigation, the proponent of the foreign-language document has frequently encountered difficulties. For example, in ***Gendebien v. Gendebien***, a divorce proceeding, the husband

---

208. Rule 1009 does not resolve all potential legal issues in cases involving foreign-language materials. For example, the rule does not prevent "ambush" translations in criminal cases. Refer to note 237 *infra* and accompanying text. Because pretrial discovery is limited, a defendant or the State might not even be aware before trial that the opponent intends to offer a foreign-language document or other material. Thus, an opponent may not be able to find a qualified translator in time to counter a proponent's translation that is offered only at trial through live testimony. Nonetheless, the rule is a cost-effective, time-saving procedure.

complained that, at the hearing on his motion for a new trial, the trial court erred in excluding a prenuptial agreement written entirely in French.[209] The court of appeals disagreed, noting that when a party seeks to introduce "a document written in a foreign language, it is the duty of the offering party, not the court, to have the document translated into English."[210] A trial court does not commit error when it excludes a document written in a foreign language and offered without an accompanying translation; the document is presumed to be incomprehensible to the trier of fact and, thus, incompetent evidence.[211] In ***International Commercial Bank of China v. Hall-Fuston Corp.***, the defendant-bank had offered two Chinese-language "certificates of negotiation," which were business records, but it did not offer a written English translation of the documents.[212] Instead, the bank offered to have its corporate representative qualify as an expert and give an oral translation. The trial court excluded the oral translation, but the court of appeals held that, under the circumstances, this ruling was reversible error.[213] Finally, in ***Leal v. State***, the court of criminal appeals reversed the defendants' murder convictions because the trial court admitted a Spanish-language tape recording, without a translation by a sworn interpreter,[214] and allowed the use of the State's unsworn (and hotly disputed) written translation to aid the jury.[215]

As these cases demonstrate, the failure to have proper English translations by qualified translators can significantly affect a lawsuit's outcome. In most instances, however, the translation of foreign documents into English is noncontroversial, and slight dif-

---

209. 668 S.W.2d 905, 908 (Tex. App.—Houston [14th Dist.] 1984, no writ).

210. *Id.*

211. *Id.*; *see, e.g.*, ***Arnell v. Arnell***, 416 S.W.3d 188, 200 (Tex. App.—Dallas 2013, no pet.) (trial court properly sustained objection to exhibit that had not been translated from French).

212. 767 S.W.2d 259, 261 (Tex. App.—Beaumont 1989, writ denied).

213. *Id.* The court reasoned as follows:

> We are unable to find a rule of evidence or case law addressing the issue either directly or by analogy. Although a Chinese document alone would completely lack probative value when offered to prove its contents and should be excluded, a Chinese document accompanied by an oral translation does not lack probative value. Admittedly, a written translation would have had greater probative value for the jury because the jury would have had access to a translation during its deliberations. However, the diminished value of the document without a written translation does not render it completely inadmissible. An oral translation would certainly have been adequate to lend meaning to the arabic numbers appearing on the "certificate," which were the relevant notations on the document since it was introduced solely to show [the bank] paid value for the draft.

Id.

214. 782 S.W.2d 844, 848 n.6 (Tex. Crim. App. 1989).

215. *Id.* at 849-50. The court stated the following:

> When the State offered the tapes into evidence, it had provided the trial court a verbatim and an English transcript of the tapes. Appellants objected to errors and critical omissions in the State's English transcript of the conversation. Appellants also objected to not being given enough time to prepare their own transcript. The trial court indicated it would play the tape and bring the official interpreter up from Brownsville to translate for the jury. The trial court then decided the tapes would be admitted into evidence, but that the State's English transcript would not be admitted. The trial court would only permit the jury to use the State's transcripts as an aid while listening to the tapes.

Id. at 848.

ferences in translation have little effect on the merits of the case.[216] Given the need for some standardized procedure for the translation of foreign-language documents, the supreme court and court of criminal appeals adopted Rule 1009, which applies to both civil and criminal proceedings. The rule establishes a procedure for proving up translations of foreign-language documents before trial, much like the procedure for offering evidence of foreign law under Rule 203[217] or the procedure for affidavits about costs and the necessity for services under the Civil Practice & Remedies Code.[218] The rule also attempts to resolve noncontroversial differences in translations before trial and thus eliminate or reduce the need for costly and time-consuming testimony by sworn translators. Compliance with Rule 1009 does not, however, guarantee the admissibility of the foreign-language document. The document must be otherwise admissible.[219] That is, it must not be barred by the hearsay rule, it must be authenticated under Article IX, and it must comply with the best-evidence rules in Article X. The document could also be excluded under Rule 403 if its probative value is substantially outweighed by any of that rule's counterfactors.[220]

A. Rule 1009(a): Submitting a Translation

Under Rule 1009(a), English translations of foreign-language documents[221] are admissible at trial if the foreign-language document itself and the written English translation are accompanied by the affidavit or unsworn declaration of a qualified translator setting forth his qualifications and certifying that the translation is fair and accurate.[222] These documents must be served on all parties at least 45 days before the date of trial.[223]

---

216. Sometimes, however, even slight differences in a translation may have an enormous impact on the case. For example, two New York cases reached opposite results on a crucial legal issue because of differing translations of the term "lesion corporelle." In *Rosman v. Trans World Airlines, Inc.*, the court of appeals held that this French term, contained in the Warsaw Convention, meant bodily injury only and did not include mental-anguish damages. 314 N.E.2d 848, 857 (N.Y. 1974). Conversely, in *Palagonia v. Trans World Airlines, Inc.*, a different New York court held that the same term had a broader meaning in French legal usage and did include mental-anguish damages. 442 N.Y.S.2d 670, 671 (N.Y. Sup. Ct. 1978).

In a more recent Texas case, *Arroyo Shrimp Farm, Inc. v. Hung Shrimp Farm, Inc.*, the English translation of one term of a Chinese letter of intent and contract was disputed at trial, with each side offering sworn testimony about the purportedly correct meaning of the term, which had a significant impact on the meaning of the contract. 927 S.W.2d 146, 152 n.3 (Tex. App.—Corpus Christi 1996, no writ).

217. *See* Tex. R. Evid. 203. Refer to *Article II: Judicial Notice, supra* p. 147.

218. *See* Tex. Civ. Prac. & Rem. Code §§18.001, 18.002. See *O'Connor's Texas Rules * Civil Trials* (2017), "Affidavit for past expenses," ch. 8-C, §8.4.4(2), p. 800.

219. *See* Tex. R. Evid. 1009(c). Refer to notes 229-231 *infra* and accompanying text.

220. Refer to *Article IV: Relevance & Its Limits, supra* p. 211.

221. Rule 1009(a) does not explicitly cover English translations of foreign-language audio or video recordings, but courts have used the rule for guidance on the admissibility of translations of foreign-language recordings. *See Peralta v. State*, 338 S.W.3d 598, 606 (Tex. App.—El Paso 2010, no pet.) ("The proponent of the [foreign-language] recording may rely on [Code of Criminal Procedure] Article 38.30 .... Alternatively, the proponent may comply with Rule 1009(a)."); *see, e.g., Castrejon v. State*, 428 S.W.3d 179, 186 (Tex. App.—Houston [1st Dist.] 2014, no pet.) (police officer translated portions of recording of her conversation with defendant; translation was admissible under Rule 1009(e)).

222. Tex. R. Evid. 1009(a); *see Peralta*, 338 S.W.3d at 606 ("Although not required by subsection (a), better practices dictate that the supporting affidavit should (1) establish the translator's identity; (2) itemize his or her creden-

Although foreign-language documents offered at trial are normally public reports and records or business records, they might also be personal notes or memoranda written in a foreign language. The rule does not require that the documents be filed with the clerk of the court where the case is pending, but that may be a useful procedure if there are any questions about receipt of service or objections to the translation. If a party follows the requirements of this section, the written translation will be admissible at trial without the testimony of a sponsoring witness.[224]

B. Rule 1009(b): Objection

Rule 1009(b) states that any party can object to the accuracy of the proponent's translation, but it must do so in writing and at least 15 days before the trial date.[225] The objecting party must specifically indicate inaccuracies in that translation and offer an accurate translation.[226] A blanket or global objection to the translation is not sufficient, and an objection to a specific portion of the translation is adequate only if the objecting party offers an alternative, accurate translation.[227]

Unlike the original translation offered under Rule 1009(a), the objecting party does not need to file the affidavit or unsworn declaration of a qualified translator or certify that the translation is fair and accurate.[228] While the proponent must go to the expense and effort of obtaining the services of a qualified translator, the objecting party can use informal means to provide an alternative translation.

C. Rule 1009(c): Effect of Failing to Object or Submit a Conflicting Translation

Rule 1009(c) states that if no party makes a timely objection to the proponent's translation, no party serves the other parties with a conflicting translation, and the underlying foreign-language document is otherwise admissible under the Rules of Evi-

---

tials in sufficient detail; (3) identify the document or recording being translated; (4) demonstrate that the translator has been administered an oath; and (5) certify that the translation is fair and accurate."); *see also* ***In re DC***, No. 01-11-00387-CV (Tex. App.—Houston [1st Dist.] 2012, pet. denied) (memo op.; 3-1-12) (Rule 1009(a) does not require translation of foreign-language returns of service into English; translation could be done in amended return under Texas Rule of Civil Procedure 118 while trial court still had plenary power). Rule 1009 does not require the translator to be certified or licensed. *E.g.*, ***Castrejon***, 428 S.W.3d at 188 (trial court did not abuse discretion in finding police officer qualified to translate Spanish portions of conversation; although she was not fluent in Spanish, she had taken Spanish classes and also had experience conversing with Spanish-speaking suspects, taking police reports in Spanish, and questioning witnesses in Spanish).

223. TEX. R. EVID. 1009(a). The 45-day notice requirement applies only to the admission of written translations offered under Rule 1009(a). *See* ***Castrejon***, 428 S.W.3d at 184-85. If neither party offers a written translation, materials can be translated through testimony under Rule 1009(e); the notice requirement does not apply to testimony given under that rule. ***Castrejon***, 428 S.W.3d at 184-85; *see* ***Peralta***, 338 S.W.3d at 606. Refer to note 236 *infra* and accompanying text.

224. Refer to notes 219-220 *supra* and accompanying text.

225. TEX. R. EVID. 1009(b).

226. *Id.*; *see* ***Castrejon***, 428 S.W.3d at 187; ***Peralta***, 338 S.W.3d at 605.

227. *See* TEX. R. EVID. 1009(b); *see, e.g.*, ***Doncaster v. Hernaiz***, 161 S.W.3d 594, 601-02 (Tex. App.—San Antonio 2005, no pet.) (trial court properly overruled defendant's objection to plaintiff's translation when defendant "did not point out any specific inaccuracy in the translation" and offered her own translation of the document that was substantially similar to plaintiff's translation).

228. *See* TEX. R. EVID. 1009(a)(2), (b).

dence, the trial court must admit the proponent's translation submitted under Rule 1009(a) at trial.[229] The rule is mandatory; the trial court does not have the discretion to exclude the translation. Furthermore, the opposing party cannot attack the accuracy of the translation at trial or provide a different translation.[230] Thus, the opposing party must make any complaints about the accuracy or completeness of the offered translation at least 15 days before the trial date.[231] Rule 1009 does not prevent the opponent from objecting to the admissibility of the foreign-language document on any other legal basis.

D. Rule 1009(d): Effect of Objecting or Submitting a Conflicting Translation

Rule 1009(d) states that if any party objects to the proponent's translation or provides a conflicting translation, the trial court must determine whether there is a genuine issue about the accuracy of any material part of the translation.[232] If the differences in the translation are on an immaterial or collateral point, the trial court may ignore those differences and admit the proponent's translation.[233] If, however, there are significant differences on a material point, the issue must be resolved by the trier of fact.[234]

The rule does not specify how these differences in translation should be submitted to or resolved by the trier of fact. Both parties presumably could submit their written translations and then offer sworn expert testimony about the accuracy of their own translation and the inaccuracy of the other party's.[235]

The rule does not permit the use of a special issue to resolve the accuracy of conflicting translations; it merely allows each side to offer evidence of the disputed factual accuracy of the translation.

E. Rule 1009(e): Qualified Translator May Testify

Under Rule 1009(e), if neither party offers a pretrial translation of a foreign document, or if a party offers a conflicting translation or objects to a translation, then either party can offer expert testimony to translate a foreign-language document.[236] Rule 1009

---

229. TEX. R. EVID. 1009(c); *cf. **San Pedro Impulsora de Inmuebles Especiales, S.A. de C.V. v. Villarreal**, 330 S.W.3d 27, 35 n.8 (Tex. App.—Corpus Christi 2010, no pet.) (at hearing on special appearance, both parties used foreign-language documents that were not translated for the record, and neither party objected to rough translations offered by counsel in argument at hearing).

230. *See* TEX. R. EVID. 1009(c).

231. TEX. R. EVID. 1009(b).

232. TEX. R. EVID. 1009(d).

233. *See id.*

234. *Id.*

235. *See, e.g.*, ***Arroyo Shrimp Farm, Inc. v. Hung Shrimp Farm, Inc.***, 927 S.W.2d 146, 152 n.3 (Tex. App.—Corpus Christi 1996, no writ) (both parties offered sworn expert testimony about the correct meaning of disputed terms in a Chinese letter of intent and contract).

236. *See* TEX. R. EVID. 1009(e); *see, e.g.*, ***Nois v. State***, No. 05-15-00203-CR (Tex. App.—Dallas 2016, no pet.) (memo op.; 3-9-16) (trial court did not abuse its discretion in allowing investigator to translate recordings of jail telephone calls for jury; investigator was bilingual, his first language was Spanish, he had lived in Mexico, he had minored in Spanish in college, and he had interpreted for Spanish speakers as a probation officer and peace officer).

is a discretionary provision; it permits, but does not require, pretrial resolution of the translation of foreign-language documents. Thus, if no party uses Rule 1009(a), all parties are free to translate foreign-language documents at trial through a qualified translator.

F. Rule 1009(f): Time Limits

Rule 1009(f) gives the trial judge the discretion to change the time limits, but only if the requesting party shows good cause.[237] This provision is especially important in criminal cases, which may be set for trial in less than 45 days. All too frequently, neither the defense nor the State has the time to thoroughly plan its case that far in advance. Constitutional considerations relating to the criminal defendant's right to present a defense might also require the adjustment of Rule 1009's time limits if their strict application would prevent the defendant from contesting a foreign-language translation crucial to his defense.

G. Rule 1009(g): Court-Appointed Translator

Rule 1009(g) permits the trial judge to appoint a qualified translator for the benefit of any party and to tax the translator's services as court costs.[238] This provision is primarily used in criminal proceedings, in which a defendant's constitutional rights are at issue, but it also applies in civil cases.

Before the 2015 restyling, Rule 1009(e) allowed for the translation "at trial either by live testimony or by deposition testimony …." *See **Castrejon v. State***, 428 S.W.3d 179, 184 (Tex. App.—Houston [1st Dist.] 2014, no pet.). The restyled rule deleted the phrase "at trial" and allows for the qualified translator to offer any "testimony." *See* Tex. R. Evid. 1009(e). Although no substantive change was intended by the restyling, the timing of the translator's testimony and the permissible type of testimony seem broader under the restyled rule. *See* Tex. Sup. Ct. Order, Misc. Docket No. 15-9048 (eff. Apr. 1, 2015).

237. Tex. R. Evid. 1009(f); *see, e.g.,* ***Doncaster v. Hernaiz***, 161 S.W.3d 594, 601 (Tex. App.—San Antonio 2005, no pet.) (plaintiff did not originally file translator's affidavit with translated document; after plaintiff supplemented motion for summary judgment with affidavit, trial court granted one-week continuance before conducting summary-judgment hearing).

238. Tex. R. Evid. 1009(g).

1982 PROPOSED TEXAS RULES OF EVIDENCE

TABLE OF CONTENTS

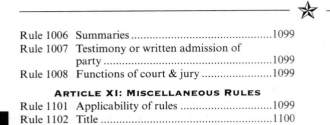

PROPOSED TEXAS RULES OF EVIDENCE*

ARTICLE I. GENERAL PROVISIONS

RULE 101. SCOPE

These rules govern proceedings in courts of Texas except where otherwise provided.

Comment. These rules are meant to apply in all civil and criminal proceedings unless otherwise provided by the Code of Criminal Procedure, Penal Code or Constitution of the United States or Texas, or court rule prescribed pursuant to statutory authority.

RULE 102. PURPOSE & CONSTRUCTION

These rules shall be construed to secure fairness in administration, elimination of unjustifiable expense and delay, and promotion of growth and development of the law of evidence to the end that the truth may be ascertained and proceedings justly determined.

RULE 103. RULINGS ON EVIDENCE

(a) Effect of erroneous ruling. Error may not be predicated upon a ruling which admits or excludes evidence unless a substantial right of the party is affected, and

(1) Objection. In case the ruling is one admitting evidence, a timely objection or motion to strike appears of record, stating the specific ground of objection, if the specific ground was not apparent from the context; or

(2) Offer of proof. In case the ruling is one excluding evidence, the substance of the evidence was made known to the court by offer or was apparent from the context within which questions were asked.

(b) Record of offer and ruling. The court may add any other or further statement which shows the character of the evidence, the form in which it was offered, the objection made, and the ruling thereon. It may, or at request of counsel shall, direct the making of an offer in question and answer form.

(c) Hearing of jury. In jury cases, proceedings shall be conducted, to the extent practicable, so as to prevent inadmissible evidence from being suggested to the jury by any means, such as mak-

ing statements or offers of proof or asking questions in the hearing of the jury.

(d) Fundamental error. Nothing in these rules precludes taking notice of fundamental errors affecting substantial rights although they were not brought to the attention of the court.

Comment. Adoption of this rule is not meant to change the Texas harmless error doctrine. In subsection (d) the federal rule refers to plain error. This has been changed to fundamental error which conforms to Texas practice. The Committee intends no change through 103(d) in present Texas law on the criminal side.

RULE 104. PRELIMINARY QUESTIONS

(a) Questions of admissibility generally. Preliminary questions concerning the qualification of a person to be a witness, the existence of a privilege, or the admissibility of evidence shall be determined by the court, subject to the provisions of subdivision (b). In making its determination it is not bound by the rules of evidence except those with respect to privileges.

(b) Relevancy conditioned on fact. When the relevancy of evidence depends upon the fulfillment of a condition of fact, the court shall admit it upon, or subject to, the introduction of evidence sufficient to support a finding of the fulfillment of the condition.

(c) Hearing of jury. Hearings on preliminary matters shall be conducted out of the hearing of the jury when the interests of justice so require.

(d) Testimony by accused out of the hearing of the jury. The accused does not, by testifying upon a preliminary matter out of the hearing of the jury, subject himself to cross-examination as to other issues in the case.

(e) Weight and credibility. This rule does not limit the right of a party to introduce before the jury evidence relevant to weight or credibility.

RULE 105. LIMITED ADMISSIBILITY

(a) When evidence which is admissible as to one party or for one purpose but not admissible as to another party or for another purpose is admitted, the court, upon request, shall restrict the evidence to its proper scope and instruct the jury accordingly; but, in the absence of such request the court's action in admitting such evidence without limitation shall not be a ground for complaint upon appeal.

---

* This is a reprint of the Texas Rules of Evidence Proposed Code, which was printed by the Senate Interim Study on Rules of Evidence and distributed at the 1982 Texas State Bar Convention. The final Rules, including all amendments since they were promulgated in 1998, are printed at the front of this book.

(b) When evidence referred to in paragraph (a) above is excluded, such exclusion shall not be a ground for complaint on appeal unless the proponent expressly offers the evidence for its limited, admissible purpose or limits its offer to the party against whom it is admissible.

RULE 106. RULE OF OPTIONAL COMPLETENESS

When a writing or recorded statement or part thereof is introduced by a party, an adverse party may at that time introduce any other part or any other writing or recorded statement which ought in fairness to be considered contemporaneously with it.

Comment. This rule is the federal rule with one modification. Under the federal rule, a party may require his opponent to introduce evidence contrary to the latter's own case. The Committee believes the better practice is to permit the party himself to introduce such evidence contemporaneously with the introduction of the incomplete evidence. This rule does not in any way circumscribe the right of a party to develop fully the matter on cross-examination or as part of his own case. Cf. Tex. C. Crim. P., art. 38.24. Nor does it alter the common law doctrine that the rule of optional completeness, as to writings, oral conversations, or other matters, may take precedence over exclusionary doctrines such as the hearsay or best evidence rule or the firsthand knowledge requirement.

ARTICLE II: JUDICIAL NOTICE

RULE 201. JUDICIAL NOTICE OF ADJUDICATIVE FACTS

(a) Scope of rule. This rule governs only judicial notice of adjudicative facts.

(b) Kinds of facts. A judicially noticed fact must be one not subject to reasonable dispute in that it is either (1) generally known within the territorial jurisdiction of the trial court or (2) capable of accurate and ready determination by resort to sources whose accuracy cannot reasonably be questioned.

(c) When discretionary. A court may take judicial notice, whether requested or not.

(d) When mandatory. A court shall take judicial notice if requested by a party and supplied with the necessary information.

(e) Opportunity to be heard. A party is entitled upon timely request to an opportunity to be heard as to the propriety of taking judicial notice and the tenor of the matter noticed. In the absence of prior notification, the request may be made after judicial notice has been taken.

(f) Time of taking notice. Judicial notice may be taken at any stage of the proceeding.

(g) Instructing jury. In a civil action or proceeding, the court shall instruct the jury to accept as conclusive any fact judicially noticed. In a criminal case, the court shall instruct the jury that it may, but is not required to, accept as conclusive any fact judicially noticed.

RULE 202. DETERMINATION OF FOREIGN LAW

A party who intends to raise an issue concerning the law of a foreign country shall give reasonable written notice. The court, in determining foreign law, may consider any relevant material or source, including testimony, whether or not submitted by a party or admissible under the Texas Rules of Evidence. The court's determination shall be treated as a ruling on a question of law.

ARTICLE III: PRESUMPTIONS IN CIVIL ACTIONS & PROCEEDINGS

RULE 301. PRESUMPTIONS IN CIVIL ACTIONS & PROCEEDINGS

Comment. Rule 301 of the Federal Rules of Evidence dealing with presumptions in civil cases has not been included. It deals with a very limited aspect of the overall subject of presumptions and may be inconsistent with Texas law in several respects. It was therefore considered advisable to leave this matter to the courts for further definition and development.

ARTICLE IV: RELEVANCY & ITS LIMITS

RULE 401. DEFINITION OF "RELEVANT EVIDENCE"

"Relevant evidence" means evidence having any tendency to make the existence of any fact that is of consequence to the determination of the action more probable or less probable than it would be without the evidence.

RULE 402. RELEVANT EVIDENCE GENERALLY ADMISSIBLE; IRRELEVANT EVIDENCE INADMISSIBLE

All relevant evidence is admissible, except as otherwise provided by constitutional law, Texas or Federal, by legislation, Texas or Federal, by these rules or by other rules prescribed pursuant to statutory authority. Evidence which is not relevant is inadmissible.

RULE 403. EXCLUSION OF RELEVANT EVIDENCE ON SPECIAL GROUNDS

Although relevant, evidence may be excluded if its probative value is substantially outweighed by the danger of unfair prejudice, confusion of the issues, or misleading the jury, or by considerations of undue delay, or needless presentation of cumulative evidence.

RULE 404. CHARACTER EVIDENCE NOT ADMISSIBLE TO PROVE CONDUCT; EXCEPTIONS; OTHER CRIMES

(a) Character evidence generally. Evidence of a person's character or a trait of his character is not admissible for the purpose of proving that he acted in conformity therewith on a particular occasion, except:

(1) Character of accused.

a. In criminal cases. Evidence of a pertinent trait of his character offered by an accused, or by the prosecution to rebut the same;

b. In civil cases. Evidence of a pertinent trait of his character offered by a party accused of conduct involving moral turpitude, or by the accusing party to rebut the same;

(2) Character of victim.

a. In criminal cases. Subject to Rule 412, evidence of a pertinent trait of character of the victim of the crime offered by an accused, or by the prosecution to rebut the same, or evidence of a character trait of peacefulness of the victim offered by the prosecution in a homicide case to rebut evidence that the victim was the first aggressor;

b. In civil cases. Evidence of character for violence of the victim of assaultive conduct offered on the issue of self-defense by a party accused of the assaultive conduct, or evidence of peaceable character to rebut the same;

(3) Character of witness. Evidence of the character of a witness, as provided in rules 607, 608 and 609.

(b) Other crimes, wrongs, or acts. Evidence of other crimes, wrongs, or acts is not admissible to prove the character of a person in order to show that he acted in conformity therewith. It may, however, be admissible for other purposes, such as proof of motive, opportunity, intent, preparation, plan, knowledge, identity, or absence of mistake or accident.

Comment. Since this rule only restricts the use of character evidence when it is offered for the purpose of proving conduct "on a particular occasion," it does not apply in the punishment phase of a criminal trial. Admissibility of character evidence concerning the defendant in the punishment phase is governed by Texas Code of Criminal Procedure, arts. 37.07, 37.071.

RULE 405. METHODS OF PROVING CHARACTER

(a) Reputation or opinion. In all cases in which evidence of character or trait of character of a person is admissible, proof may be made by testimony as to reputation or by testimony in the form of an opinion. On cross-examination, inquiry is allowable into relevant specific instances of conduct.

(b) Specific instances of conduct. In cases in which character or trait of character of a person is an essential element of a charge, claim, or defense, proof may also be made of specific instances of his conduct.

RULE 406. HABIT; ROUTINE PRACTICE

Evidence of the habit of a person or of the routine practice of an organization, whether corroborated or not and regardless of the presence of eyewitnesses, is relevant to prove that the conduct of the person or organization on a particular occasion was in conformity with the habit or routine practice.

RULE 407. SUBSEQUENT REMEDIAL MEASURES; NOTIFICATION OF DEFECT

(a) Subsequent remedial measures. When, after an event, measures are taken which, if taken previously, would have made the event less likely to occur, evidence of the subsequent measures is admissible.

(b) Notification of defect. A written notification by a manufacturer of any defect in a product produced by such manufacturer to purchasers thereof is admissible against the manufacturer on the issue of existence of the defect to the extent that it is relevant.

RULE 408. COMPROMISE & OFFERS TO COMPROMISE

Evidence of (1) furnishing or offering or promising to furnish, or (2) accepting or offering or promising to accept, a valuable consideration in compromising or attempting to compromise a claim which was disputed as to either validity or amount is not admissible to prove liability for or invalidity of the claim or its amount. Evidence of conduct or statements made in compromise negotiations is likewise not admissible. This rule does not require the exclusion of any evidence otherwise discoverable merely because it is presented in the course of compromise negotiations. This rule also does not require exclusion when the evidence is offered for another purpose, such as proving bias or prejudice or interest of a witness or a party, negativing a contention of undue delay, or proving an effort to obstruct a criminal investigation or prosecution.

RULE 409. PAYMENT OF MEDICAL & SIMILAR EXPENSES

In civil proceedings, evidence of furnishing or offering or promising to pay medical, hospital, or similar expenses occasioned by an injury is not admissible to prove liability for the injury.

RULE 410. INADMISSIBILITY OF PLEAS, PLEA DISCUSSIONS, & RELATED STATEMENTS

Except as otherwise provided in this rule, evidence of the following is not, in any civil or criminal proceeding, admissible against the defendant who made the plea or was a participant in the plea discussions:

(1) a plea of guilty which was later withdrawn;

(2) a plea of nolo contendere;

(3) any statement made in the course of any proceedings under Rule 11 of the Federal Rules of Criminal Procedure or comparable state procedure regarding either of the foregoing pleas; or

(4) any statement made in the course of plea discussions with an attorney for the prosecuting authority which do not result in a plea of guilty or which result in a plea of guilty later withdrawn.

However, such a statement is admissible (i) in any proceeding wherein another statement made in the course of the same plea or plea discussions had been introduced and the statement ought in fairness be considered contemporaneously with it, or (ii) in a criminal proceeding for perjury or false statement if the statement was made by the defendant under oath, on the record and in the presence of counsel.

RULE 411. LIABILITY INSURANCE

Evidence that a person was or was not insured against liability is not admissible upon the issue whether he acted negligently or otherwise wrongfully. This rule does not require the exclusion of evidence of insurance against liability when offered for another issue, such as proof of agency, ownership, or control, if disputed, or bias or prejudice of a witness.

RULE 412. EVIDENCE OF PREVIOUS SEXUAL CONDUCT

(a) Evidence of specific instances of the victim's sexual conduct, opinion evidence of the victim's sexual conduct, and reputation evidence of the victim's sexual conduct may be admitted in prosecutions under Sections 21.02 through 21.05 of the Texas Penal Code (rape, aggravated rape, sexual abuse, and aggravated sexual abuse), or an attempt to commit any of the foregoing, only if, and only to the extent that, the judge finds that the evidence is material to a fact at issue in the case and that its inflammatory or prejudicial nature does not outweigh its probative value.

(b) If the defendant proposes to ask any questions concerning specific instances, opinion evidence, or reputation evidence of the victim's sexual conduct, either by direct examination or cross-examination of any witness, the defendant must inform the court out of the hearing of the jury prior to asking any such question. After this notice, the court shall conduct an in camera hearing, recorded by the court reporter, to determine whether the proposed evidence is admissible under Subsection (a) of this section. The court shall determine what evidence is admissible and shall accordingly limit the questioning. The defendant shall not go outside these limits nor refer to any evidence ruled inadmissible in camera without prior approval of the court without the presence of the jury.

(c) The court shall seal the record of the in camera hearing required in Subsection (b) of this section for delivery to the appellate court in the event of an appeal.

(d) This section does not limit the right of the state or the accused to impeach credibility by showing prior felony conviction nor the right of the accused to produce evidence of promiscuous sexual conduct of a child 14 years old or older as a defense to rape of a child, sexual abuse of a child, or indecency with a child, or an attempt to commit any of the foregoing. If evidence of a previous felony conviction involving sexual conduct or evidence of promiscuous sexual conduct is admitted, the court shall instruct the jury as to the purpose of the evidence and as to its limited use.

ARTICLE V: PRIVILEGES
RULE 501. PRIVILEGES RECOGNIZED ONLY AS PROVIDED

Except as otherwise provided by Constitution, by statute, by these rules, or by other rules prescribed by the Supreme Court pursuant to statutory authority, no person has a privilege to:

(1) Refuse to be a witness; or

(2) Refuse to disclose any matter; or

(3) Refuse to produce any object or writing; or

(4) Prevent another from being a witness or disclosing any matter or producing any object or writing.

RULE 502. REQUIRED REPORTS PRIVILEGED BY STATUTE

A person, corporation, association, or other organization or entity, either public or private, making a return or report required by law to be made has a privilege to refuse to disclose and to prevent any other person from disclosing the return or report, if the law requiring it to be made so provides. A public officer or agency to whom a return or report is required by law to be made has a privilege to refuse to disclose the return or report if the law requiring it to be made so provides. No privilege exists under this rule in actions involving perjury, false statements, fraud in the return or report, or other failure to comply with the law in question.

RULE 503. LAWYER-CLIENT PRIVILEGE

(a) Definitions. As used in this rule:

(1) A "client" is a person, public officer, or corporation, association, or other organization or entity, either public or private, who is rendered professional legal services by a lawyer, or who consults a lawyer with a view to obtaining professional legal services from him.

(2) A representative of the client is one having authority to obtain professional legal services, or to act on advice rendered pursuant thereto, on behalf of the client.

(3) A "lawyer" is a person authorized, or reasonably believed by the client to be authorized, to engage in the practice of law in any state or nation.

(4) A "representative of the lawyer" is one employed by the lawyer to assist the lawyer in the rendition of professional legal services.

(5) A communication is "confidential" if not intended to be disclosed to third persons other than those to whom disclosure is made in furtherance of the rendition of professional legal services to the client or those reasonably necessary for the transmission of the communication.

(b) General rule of privilege. A client has a privilege to refuse to disclose and to prevent any other person from disclosing confidential communications made for the purpose of facilitating the rendition of professional legal services to the client (1) between himself or his representative and his lawyer or his lawyer's representative, (2) between his lawyer and the lawyer's representative, (3) by him or his representative or his lawyer or a representative of the lawyer to a lawyer, or a representative of a lawyer representing another party in a pending action and concerning a matter of common interest therein, (4) between representatives of the client or between the client and a representative of the client, or (5) among lawyers and their representatives representing the same client.

(c) Who may claim the privilege. The privilege may be claimed by the client, his guardian or conservator, the personal representative of a deceased client, or the successor, trustee, or similar representative of a corporation, association, or other organization, whether or not in existence. The person who was the lawyer or the lawyer's representative at the time of the communication is presumed to have authority to claim the privilege but only on behalf of the client.

(d) Exceptions. There is no privilege under this rule:

(1) Furtherance of crime or fraud. If the services of the lawyer were sought or obtained to enable or aid anyone to commit or plan to commit what the client knew or reasonably should have known to be a crime or fraud;

(2) Claimants through same deceased client. As to a communication relevant to an issue between parties who claim through the same deceased client, regardless of whether the claims are by testate or intestate succession or by inter vivos transaction;

(3) Breach of duty by a lawyer or client. As to a communication relevant to an issue of breach of duty by the lawyer to his client or by the client to his lawyer;

(4) Document attested by a lawyer. As to a communication relevant to an issue concerning an attested document to which the lawyer is an attesting witness;

(5) Joint clients. As to a communication relevant to a matter of common interest between or among two or more clients if the communication was made by any of them to a lawyer retained or consulted in common, when offered in an action between or among any of the clients.

Comment. This rule governs only the lawyer/client privilege. It does not restrict the scope of the work product doctrine, either in civil cases, see Tex. R. Civ. P. 186a, or in criminal cases. See Tex. C. Crim. P. 38.10.

RULE 504. PRIVILEGE NOT TO BE CALLED AS A WITNESS AGAINST SPOUSE IN A CRIMINAL CASE

(a) General rule of privilege. In a criminal case, the spouse of the accused has a privilege not to be called as a witness for the state. This rule does not prohibit the spouse from testifying voluntarily for the state, even over objection by the accused. A spouse who testifies on behalf of an accused is subject to cross-examination as provided in Rule 611(b). Failure by an accused to call his spouse as a witness, where other evidence indicates that the spouse could testify to relevant matters, is a proper subject of comment by counsel.

(b) Exceptions. There is no privilege under this rule (1) in a proceeding in which an accused is charged with a crime against the person of a minor child of either spouse or a minor child who is a member of the household of either spouse; or (2) as to matters occurring prior to the marriage.

RULE 505. COMMUNICATIONS TO CLERGYMEN

(a) Definitions. As used in this rule:

(1) A "clergyman" is a minister, priest, rabbi, accredited Christian Science Practitioner, or other similar functionary of a religious organization or an individual reasonably believed so to be by the person consulting him.

(2) A communication is "confidential" if made privately and not intended for further disclosure except to other persons present in furtherance of the purpose of the communication.

(b) General rule of privilege. A person has a privilege to refuse to disclose and to prevent another from disclosing a confidential communication by the person to a clergyman in his professional character as spiritual adviser.

(c) Who may claim the privilege. The privilege may be claimed by the person, by his guardian or conservator, or by his personal representative if he is deceased. The person who was the clergyman at the time of the communication is presumed to have authority to claim the privilege but only on behalf of the communicant.

RULE 506. POLITICAL VOTE

Every person has a privilege to refuse to disclose the tenor of his vote at a political election conducted by secret ballot unless the vote was cast illegally.

RULE 507. TRADE SECRETS

A person has a privilege, which may be claimed by him or his agent or employee, to refuse to disclose and to prevent other persons from disclosing a trade secret owned by him, if the allowance of the privilege will not tend to conceal fraud or otherwise work injustice. When disclosure is directed, the judge shall take such protective measure as the interests of the holder of the privilege and of the parties and the furtherance of justice may require.

RULE 508. IDENTITY OF INFORMER

(a) Rule of privilege. The United States or a state or subdivision thereof has a privilege to refuse to disclose the identity of a person who has furnished information relating to or assisting in an investigation of a possible violation of a law to a law enforcement officer or member of a legislative committee or its staff conducting an investigation.

(b) Who may claim. The privilege may be claimed by an appropriate representative of the public entity to which the information was furnished.

(c) Exceptions.

(1) Voluntary disclosure; informer a witness. No privilege exists under this rule if the identity of the informer or his interest in the subject matter of his communication has been disclosed to those who would have cause to resent the communication by a holder of the privilege or by the informers own action, or if the informer appears as witness for the public entity.

(2) Testimony on merits. If it appears from the evidence in the case or from other showing by a party that an informer may be able to give testimony necessary to a fair determination of the issue of guilt or innocence in a criminal case or of a material issue on the merits in a civil case to which the public entity is a party, and the public entity invokes the privilege, the judge shall give the public entity an opportunity to show in camera facts relevant to determining whether the informer can, in fact, supply that testimony. The showing will ordinarily be in the form of affidavits, but the judge may direct that testimony be taken if he finds that the matter cannot be resolved satisfactorily upon affidavit. If the judge finds that there is a reasonable probability that the informer can give the testimony, and the public entity elects not to disclose his identity, the judge on motion of the defendant in a criminal case shall dismiss the charges to which the testimony would relate, and the judge may do so on his own motion. In civil cases, he may make any order that justice requires. Evidence submitted to the judge shall be sealed and preserved to be made available to the appellate court in the event of an appeal, and the contents shall not otherwise be revealed without consent of the public entity. All counsel and parties shall be permitted to be present at every stage of proceedings under this

subdivision except a showing in camera, at which no counsel or party shall be permitted to be present.

(3) Legality of obtaining evidence. If information from an informer is relied upon to establish the legality of the means by which evidence was obtained and the judge is not satisfied that the information was received from an informer reasonably believed to be reliable or credible, he may require the identity of the informer to be disclosed. The judge shall, on request of the public entity, direct that the disclosure be made in camera. All counsel and parties concerned with the issue of legality shall be permitted to be present at every stage of proceedings under this subdivision except a disclosure in camera, at which no counsel or party shall be permitted to be present. If disclosure of the identity of the informer is made in camera, the record thereof shall be sealed and preserved to be made available to the appellate court in the event of an appeal, and the contents shall not otherwise be revealed without consent of the public entity.

RULE 509. PHYSICIAN/PATIENT PRIVILEGE

(a) Definitions. As used in this rule:

(1) a "patient" means any person who consults or is seen by a physician to receive medical care.

(2) a "physician" means a person licensed to practice medicine.

(3) a communication is "confidential" if not intended to be disclosed to third persons other than those present to further the interest of the patient in the consultation, examination, or interview, or persons reasonably necessary for the transmission of the communication, or persons who are participating in the diagnosis and treatment under the direction of the physician, including members of the patient's family.

(b) General rule of privilege.

(1) Confidential communications between a physician and a patient, relative to or in connection with any professional services rendered by a physician to the patient are privileged and may not be disclosed.

(2) Records of the identity, diagnosis, evaluation, or treatment of a patient by a physician that are created or maintained by a physician are confidential and privileged and may not be disclosed.

(3) The prohibitions of this section continue to apply to confidential communications or records concerning any patient irrespective of when the patient received the services of a physician.

(c) Who may claim the privilege.

(1) The privilege of confidentiality may be claimed by the patient or physician acting on the patient's behalf.

(2) The physician may claim the privilege of confidentiality, but only on behalf of the patient. The authority to do so is presumed in the absence of evidence to the contrary.

(d) Exceptions. Exceptions to confidentiality or privilege in court or administrative proceedings exist:

(1) when the proceedings are brought by the patient against a physician, including but not limited to malpractice proceedings, and in any license revocation proceeding in which the patient is a complaining witness and in which disclosure is relevant to the claims or defense of a physician;

(2) when the patient or someone authorized to act on his behalf submits a written consent to the release of any privileged information, as provided in paragraph (e);

(3) when the purpose of the proceedings is to substantiate and collect on a claim for medical services rendered to the patient;

(4) in any civil litigation or administrative proceeding, if relevant, brought by the patient or someone on his behalf if the patient is attempting to recover monetary damages for any physical or mental condition including death of the patient. Any information is discoverable in any court or administrative proceeding in this state if the court or administrative body has jurisdiction over the subject matter, pursuant to rules of procedure specified for the matters;

(5) in any disciplinary investigation or proceeding of a physician conducted under or pursuant to the Medical Practice Act, art. 4495b, Vernon's Texas Civil Statutes, provided that the board shall protect the identity of any patient whose medical records are examined, except for those patients covered under subparagraph (d)(1) or those patients who have submitted written consent to the release of their medical records as provided by paragraph (e);

(6) in any criminal investigation or proceeding;

(7) when the disclosure is relevant to an involuntary civil commitment or hospitalization proceeding under:

(A) the Texas Mental Health Code (Article 55471 et seq., Vernon's Texas Civil Statutes);

(B) the Mentally Retarded Persons Act of 1977 (Article 5547300, Vernon's Texas Civil Statutes);

(C) Section 9, Chapter 411, Acts of the 53rd Legislature, Regular Session, 1953 (Article 5561c, Vernon's Texas Civil Statutes);

(D) Section 2, Chapter 543, Acts of the 61st Legislature, Regular Session, 1969 (Article 5561c1, Vernon's Texas Civil Statutes);

(8) when the disclosure is relevant in any suit affecting the parent-child relationship.

(e) Consent.

(1) Consent for the release of privileged information must be in writing and signed by the patient, or a parent or legal guardian if the patient is a minor, or a legal guardian if the patient has been adjudicated incompetent to manage his personal affairs, or an attorney ad litem appointed for the patient, as authorized by the Texas Mental Health Code (Article 55471 et seq., Vernon's Texas Civil Statutes); the Mentally Retarded Persons Act of 1977 (Article 5547300, Vernon's Texas Civil Statutes); Section 9, Chapter 411, Acts of the 53rd Legislature, Regular Session, 1953 (Article 5561c, Vernon's Texas Civil Statutes); Section 2, Chapter 543, Acts of the 61st Legislature, Regular Session, 1969 (Article 5561c1, Vernon's Texas Civil Statutes); Chapter 5, Texas Probate Code; and Chapter 11, Family Code; or a personal representative if the patient is deceased, provided that the written consent specifies the following:

(A) the information or medical records to be covered by the release;

(B) the reasons or purposes for the release; and

(C) the person to whom the information is to be released.

(2) The patient, or other person authorized to consent, has the right to withdraw his consent to the release of any information. Withdrawal of consent does not affect any information disclosed prior to the written notice of the withdrawal.

(3) Any person who received information made privileged by this rule may disclose the information to others only to the extent consistent with the authorized purposes for which consent to release the information was obtained.

Comment. This rule only governs disclosures of patient-physician communications in judicial or administrative proceedings. Whether a physician may or must disclose such communications in other circumstances is governed by Tex. Rev. Civ. Stat. Ann. art. 4495b, Sec. 5.08.

RULE 510. CONFIDENTIALITY OF MENTAL HEALTH INFORMATION

(a) Definitions. As used in this rule:

(1) "Professional" means any person (A) authorized to practice medicine in any state or nation; or (B) licensed or certified by the State of Texas in the diagnosis, evaluation or treatment of any mental or emotional disorder; or (C) involved in the treatment or examination of drug abusers; or (D) reasonably believed by the patient/client to be included in any of the preceding categories.

(2) "Patient/client" means any person who (A) consults, or is interviewed by, a professional for purposes of diagnosis, evaluation, or treatment of any mental or emotional condition or disorder, including alcoholism and other drug addiction; or (B) is being treated voluntarily or being examined for admission to voluntary treatment for drug abuse.

(3) A representative of the patient/client is (A) any person bearing the written consent of the patient/client; or (B) a parent if the patient/client is a minor; or (C) a guardian if the patient/client has been adjudicated incompetent to manage his personal affairs; or (D) the patient/client's personal representative if the patient/client is deceased.

(4) A communication is "confidential" if not intended to be disclosed to third persons other than those present to further the interest of the patient/client in the diagnosis, examination, evaluation, or treatment, or persons reasonably necessary for the transmission of the communication, or persons who are participating in the diagnosis, examination, evaluation, or treatment under the direction of the professional, including members of the patient/client's family.

(b) General rule of privilege.

(1) Communication between a patient/client and a professional is confidential and shall not be disclosed.

(2) Records of the identity, diagnosis, evaluation, or treatment of a patient/client which are created or maintained by a professional are confidential and shall not be disclosed.

(3) Any person who receives information from confidential communications or records as defined herein, other than a representative of the patient/client acting on the patient/client's behalf, shall not disclose the information except to the extent that disclosure is consistent with the authorized purposes for which the information was first obtained.

(4) The prohibitions of this rule continue to apply to confidential communications or records concerning any patient/client irrespective of when the patient/client received services of a professional.

(c) Who may claim the privilege.

(1) The privilege of confidentiality may be claimed by the patient/client or by a representative of the patient/client acting on the patient/client's behalf.

(2) The professional may claim the privilege of confidentiality but only on behalf of the patient/client. The authority to do so is presumed in the absence of evidence to the contrary.

(d) Exceptions. Exceptions to the privilege in court proceedings exist:

(1) when the proceedings are brought by the patient/client against a professional, including but not limited to malpractice proceedings, and in any criminal or license revocation proceedings in which the patient/client is a complaining witness and in which disclosure is relevant to the claim or defense of a professional;

(2) when the patient/client waives his right in writing to the privilege of confidentiality of any information, or when a representative of the patient/client acting on the patient/client's behalf submits a written waiver to the confidentiality privilege;

(3) when the purpose of the proceeding is to substantiate and collect on a claim for mental or emotional health services rendered to the patient/client; or

(4) when the judge finds that the patient/client after having been previously informed that communications would not be privileged, has made communications to a professional in the course of a court-ordered examination relating to the patient/client's mental or emotional condition or disorder, providing that such communications shall not be privileged only with respect to issues involving the patient/client's mental or emotional health. On granting of the order, the court, in determining the extent to which any disclosure of all or any part of any communication is necessary, shall impose appropriate safeguards against unauthorized disclosure.

(5) in any civil litigation or administrative proceeding, if relevant, brought by the patient/client or someone on his behalf if the patient/client is attempting to recover monetary damages for any mental condition.

(6) when a defendant in a criminal case raises the defense of his insanity or incompetence.

Comment. This rule only governs disclosures of patient/client-professional communications in judicial or administrative proceedings. Whether a professional may or must disclose such communications in other circumstances is governed by Tex. Rev. Civ. Stat. Ann. art. 5561h.

RULE 511. WAIVER OF PRIVILEGE BY VOLUNTARY DISCLOSURE

A person upon whom these rules confer a privilege against disclosure waives the privilege if he or his predecessor while holder of the privilege voluntarily discloses or consents to disclosure of any significant part of the privilege matter. This rule does not apply if the disclosure itself is privileged.

RULE 512. PRIVILEGED MATTER DISCLOSED UNDER COMPULSION OR WITHOUT OPPORTUNITY TO CLAIM PRIVILEGE

A claim of privilege is not defeated by disclosure which was (1) compelled erroneously or (2) made without opportunity to claim the privilege.

RULE 513. COMMENT UPON OR INFERENCE FROM CLAIM OF PRIVILEGE; INSTRUCTION

(a) Comment or inference not permitted. Except as provided in Rule 504(a), the claim of a privilege, whether in the present proceeding or upon a prior occasion, is not a proper subject of comment by judge or counsel, and no inference may be drawn therefrom.

(b) Claiming privilege without knowledge of jury. In jury cases, proceedings shall be conducted, to the extent practicable, so as to facilitate the making of claims of privilege without the knowledge of the jury.

(c) Jury instruction. Upon request, any party against whom the jury might draw an adverse inference from a claim of privilege is entitled to an instruction that no inference may be drawn therefrom.

ARTICLE VI: WITNESSES
RULE 601. COMPETENCY & INCOMPETENCY OF WITNESSES

(a) Every person is competent to be a witness except as otherwise provided in these rules. The following witnesses shall be incompetent to testify in any proceeding subject to these rules:

(1) Insane persons. Insane persons who, in the opinion of the Court, are in an insane condition of mind at the time when they are offered as a witness, or who, in the opinion of the Court, were in that condition when the events happened of which they are called to testify.

(2) Children. Children or other persons who, after being examined by the Court, appear not to possess sufficient intellect to relate transactions with respect to which they are interrogated, or who do not understand the obligation of an oath.

(b) A witness is not precluded from giving evidence of or concerning any transaction with, any conversations with, any admissions of, or statement by, a deceased or insane party or person merely because the witness is a party to the action or a person interested in the event thereof.

RULE 602. LACK OF PERSONAL KNOWLEDGE

A witness may not testify to a matter unless evidence is introduced sufficient to support a finding that he has personal knowledge of the matter. Evidence to prove personal knowledge may, but need not, consist of the testimony of the witness himself. This rule is subject to the provisions of Rule 703, relating to opinion testimony by expert witnesses.

RULE 603. OATH OR AFFIRMATION

Before testifying, every witness shall be required to declare that he will testify truthfully, by oath or affirmation administered in a form calculated to awaken his conscience and impress his mind with his duty to do so.

RULE 604. INTERPRETERS

An interpreter is subject to the provisions of these rules relating to qualification as an expert and the administration of an oath or affirmation that he will make a true translation.

RULE 605. COMPETENCY OF JUDGE AS A WITNESS

The judge presiding at the trial may not testify in that trial as a witness. No objection need be made in order to preserve the point.

RULE 606. COMPETENCY OF JUROR AS A WITNESS

(a) At the trial. A member of the jury may not testify as a witness before that jury in the trial of the case in which he is sitting as a juror. If he is called so to testify, the opposing party shall be afforded an opportunity to object out of the presence of the jury.

(b) Inquiry into validity of verdict or indictment. Upon an inquiry into the validity of a verdict or indictment, a juror may not testify as to any matter or statement occurring during the course of the jury's deliberations or to the effect of anything upon his or any other juror's mind or emotions as influencing him to assent to or dissent from the verdict or indictment or concerning his mental processes in connection therewith, except that a juror may testify on the question whether extraneous prejudicial information was improperly brought to the jury's attention or whether any outside influence was improperly brought to bear upon any juror. Nor may his affidavit or evidence of any statement by him concerning a matter about which he would be precluded from testifying be received for these purposes.

RULE 607. WHO MAY IMPEACH

The credibility of a witness may be attacked by any party, including the party calling him.

RULE 608. EVIDENCE OF CHARACTER & CONDUCT OF WITNESS

(a) Opinion and reputation evidence of character. The credibility of a witness may be attacked or supported by evidence in the form of opinion or reputation, but subject to these limitations: (1) the evidence may refer only to character for truthfulness or untruthfulness, and (2) evidence of truthful character is admissible only after the character of the witness for truthfulness has been attacked by opinion or reputation evidence or otherwise.

(b) Specific instances of conduct. Specific instances of the conduct of a witness, for the purpose of attacking or supporting his credibility, other than conviction of crime as provided in Rule 609, may not be inquired into on cross-examination of the witness nor proved by extrinsic evidence.

The giving of testimony, whether by an accused or by any other witness, does not operate as a waiver of his privilege against self-incrimination when examined with respect to matters which relate only to credibility.

RULE 609. IMPEACH BY EVIDENCE OF CONVICTION OF CRIME

(a) General rule. For the purpose of attacking the credibility of a witness, evidence that he has been convicted of a crime shall be admitted if elicited from him or established by public record but only if the crime was a felony or involved moral turpitude, regardless of punishment, and the court determines that the probative value of admitting this evidence outweighs its prejudicial effect to a party.

(b) Time limit. Evidence of a conviction under this rule is not admissible if a period of more than ten (10) years has elapsed since the date of the conviction or of the release of the witness from the confinement imposed for that conviction, whichever is the later date, unless the court determines, in the interests of justice, that the probative value of the conviction supported by specific facts and circumstances substantially outweighs its prejudicial effect.

(c) Effect of pardon, annulment, or certificate of rehabilitation. Evidence of a conviction is not admissible under this rule if (1) based on the finding of the rehabilitation of the person convicted, the conviction has been the subject of a pardon, annulment, certificate of rehabilitation, or other equivalent procedure, and that person has not been convicted of a subsequent crime which was classified as a felony or involved moral turpitude, regardless of punishment, or (2) probation has been satisfactorily completed for the crime for which the person was convicted, and that person has not been convicted of a subsequent crime which was classified as a felony or involved moral turpitude, regardless of punishment, or (3) based on a finding of innocence, the conviction has been the subject of a pardon, annulment, or other equivalent procedure.

(d) Juvenile adjudications. Evidence of juvenile adjudications is not admissible under this rule unless required to be admitted by the Constitution of the United States or Texas.

(e) Pendency of appeal. Pendency of an appeal renders evidence of a conviction inadmissible.

(f) Notice. Evidence of a conviction is not admissible if after timely written request by the adverse party specifying the witness or witnesses, the proponent fails to give to the adverse party sufficient advance written notice of intent to use such evidence to provide the adverse party with a fair opportunity to contest the use of such evidence.

RULE 610. RELIGIOUS BELIEFS OR OPINIONS

Evidence of the beliefs or opinions of a witness on matters of religion is not admissible for the purpose of showing that by reason of their nature his credibility is impaired or enhanced.

RULE 611. MODE & ORDER OF INTERROGATION & PRESENTATION

(a) Control by court. The court shall exercise reasonable control over the mode and order of interrogating witnesses and presenting evidence so as to (1) make the interrogation and presentation effective for the ascertainment of the truth, (2) avoid needless consumption of time, and (3) protect witnesses from harassment or undue embarrassment.

(b) Scope of cross-examination. A witness may be cross-examined on any matter relevant to any issue in the case, including credibility.

(c) Leading questions. Leading questions should not be used on the direct examination of a witness except as may be necessary to develop his testimony. Ordinarily leading questions should be permitted on cross-examination. When a party calls a hostile witness, an adverse party, or a witness identified with an adverse party, interrogation may be by leading questions.

RULE 612. WRITING USED TO REFRESH MEMORY

If a witness uses a writing to refresh his memory for the purpose of testifying either—

(1) while testifying, or

(2) before testifying, if the court in its discretion determines it is necessary in the interests of justice,

an adverse party is entitled to have the writing produced at the hearing, to inspect it, to cross-examine the witness thereon, and to introduce in evidence those portions which relate to the testimony of the witness. If it is claimed that the writing contains matters not related to the subject matter of the testimony the court shall examine the writing in camera, excise any portion not so related, and order delivery of the remainder to the party entitled thereto. Any portion withheld over objections shall be preserved and made available to the appellate court in the event of an appeal. If a writing is not produced or delivered pursuant to order under this rule, the court shall make any order justice requires, except that in criminal cases when the prosecution elects not to comply, the order shall be one striking the testimony or, if the court in its discretion determines that the interests of justice so require, declaring a mistrial.

RULE 613. PRIOR STATEMENTS OF WITNESSES; IMPEACHMENT & SUPPORT

(a) Examining witness concerning prior inconsistent statement. In examining a witness concerning a prior inconsistent statement made by him, whether oral or written, and before further cross examination concerning, or extrinsic evidence of, such statement may be allowed, the witness must be told the contents of such statement and the time and place and the person to whom it was made, and must be afforded an opportunity to explain or deny such statement. If the witness unequivocally admits having made such statement, extrinsic evidence of same shall not be admitted. This provision does not apply to admissions of a party-opponent as defined in Rule 801(e)(2).

(b) Examining witness concerning bias or interest. In impeaching a witness by proof of circumstances or statements showing bias or interest, on the part of such witness, and before further cross examination concerning, or extrinsic evidence of, such bias or interest may be allowed, the circumstances supporting such claim or the details of such statement, including the contents and where, when and to whom made, must be made known to the witness, and the witness must be given an opportunity to explain or to deny such circumstances or statement. If the witness unequivocally admits such bias or interest, extrinsic evidence of same shall not be admitted. A party shall be permitted to present evidence rebutting any evidence impeaching one of said party's witnesses on grounds of bias or interest.

(c) Prior consistent statements of witnesses. A prior statement of a witness which is consistent with his testimony is inadmissible except as provided in 801(e)(1)(B).

RULE 614. PRODUCTION OF STATEMENTS OF WITNESSES IN CRIMINAL CASES

(a) Motion for production. In any criminal case, after a witness other than the defendant has testified on direct examination, the court, on motion of a party who did not call the witness, shall order the attorney for the government or the defendant and his attorney, as the case may be, to produce, for the examination and use of the moving party, any statement of the witness that is in their possession and that relates to the subject matter concerning which the witness has testified.

(b) Production of entire statement. If the entire contents of the statement relate to the subject matter concerning which the witness has testified, the court shall order that the statement be delivered to the moving party.

(c) Production of excised statement. If the other party claims that the statement contains matter that does not relate to the subject matter concerning which the witness has testified, the court shall order that it be delivered to the court in camera. Upon inspection, the court shall excise the portions of the statement that do not relate to the subject matter concerning which the witness has testified, and shall order that the statement, with such material excised, be delivered to the moving party. Any portion of the statement that is withheld from the defendant over his objection shall be preserved by the attorney for the government, and, in the event of a conviction and an appeal by the defendant, shall be made available to the appellate court for the purpose of determining the correctness of the decision to excise the portion of the statement.

(d) Recess for examination of statement. Upon delivery of the statement to the moving party, the court, upon application of that party, may recess proceedings in the trial for the examination of such statement and for preparation for its use in the trial.

(e) Sanction for failure to produce statement. If the other party elects not to comply with an order to deliver a statement to the moving party, the court shall order that the testimony of the witness be stricken from the record and that the trial proceed, or, if it is the attorney for the government who elects not to comply, shall declare a mistrial if required by the interest of justice.

(f) Definition. As used in this rule, a "statement" of a witness means:

(1) a written statement made by the witness that is signed or otherwise adopted or approved by him;

(2) a substantially verbatim recital of an oral statement made by the witness that is recorded contemporaneously with the making of the oral statement and that is contained in a stenographic, mechanical, electrical, or other recording or a transcription thereof; or

(3) a statement, however taken or recorded, or a transcription thereof, made by the witness to a grand jury.

RULE 615. EXCLUSION OF WITNESSES

At the request of a party the court shall order witnesses excluded so that they cannot hear the testimony of other witnesses, and it may make the order of its own motion. This rule does not authorize exclusion of (1) a party who is a natural person, or (2) an officer or employee of a party which is not a natural person designated as its representative by its attorney, or (3) a person whose presence is shown by a party to be essential to the presentation of his cause.

ARTICLE VII: OPINIONS & EXPERT TESTIMONY

RULE 701. OPINION TESTIMONY BY LAY WITNESSES

If the witness is not testifying as an expert, his testimony in the form of opinions of inferences is limited to those opinions or inferences which are (a) rationally based on the perception of the witness and (b) helpful to a clear understanding of his testimony or the determination of a fact in issue.

RULE 702. TESTIMONY BY EXPERTS

If scientific, technical, or other specialized knowledge will assist the trier of fact to understand the evidence or to determine a fact in issue, a witness qualified as an expert by knowledge, skill, experience, training, or education, may testify thereto in the form of an opinion or otherwise.

RULE 703. BASES OF OPINION TESTIMONY BY EXPERTS

(a) In civil cases, the facts or data in the particular case upon which an expert bases an opinion or inference may be those perceived by or made known to him at or before the hearing. If of a type reasonably relied upon by experts in the particular field in forming opinions or inferences upon the subject, the facts or data need not be admissible in evidence.

(b) In criminal cases, an expert may base an opinion upon (1) facts or data within his personal knowledge (2) facts or data within the personal knowledge of another expert upon which experts in the particular field as the witness usually rely (3) facts or data within the personal knowledge of nonexperts who acted at the direction of or under the supervision of an expert in obtaining the information where such information is usually relied upon by experts in the particular field (4) facts or data within the personal knowledge of a patient relating to a condition which the patient relates to aid an expert in diagnosing or treating the patient or (5) facts or data introduced in evidence.

RULE 704. OPINION ON ULTIMATE ISSUE

Testimony in the form of an opinion or inference otherwise admissible is not objectionable because it embraces an ultimate issue to be decided by the trier of fact.

RULE 705. DISCLOSURE OF FACTS OR DATA UNDERLYING EXPERT OPINION

(a) In civil cases, the expert may testify in terms of opinion or inference and give his reasons therefor without prior disclosure of the underlying facts or data, unless the court requires otherwise. The expert may in any event be required to disclose the underlying facts or data on cross-examination.

(b) In criminal cases, before an expert may state an opinion it must first be shown that the opinion is based on facts or data within the scope of Rule 703(b). The expert may testify in terms of opinion or inference and give his reasons therefor without prior disclosure of the underlying facts or data, unless the court requires otherwise. In any event, the expert shall, if requested, be required to disclose the underlying facts or data on cross-examination.

ARTICLE VIII: HEARSAY

RULE 801. DEFINITIONS

The following definitions apply under this article:

(a) Statement. A "statement" is (1) an oral or written verbal expression or (2) nonverbal conduct of a person, if it is intended by him as a substitute for verbal expression.

(b) Declarant. A "declarant" is a person who makes a statement.

(c) Matter asserted. "Matter asserted" includes any matter explicitly asserted, and any matter implied by a statement, if the probative value of the statement as offered flows from declarant's belief as to the matter.

(d) Hearsay. "Hearsay" is a statement, other than one made by the declarant while testifying at the trial or hearing, offered in evidence to prove the truth of the matter asserted.

(e) Statements which are not hearsay. A statement is not hearsay if—

(1) Prior statement by witness. The declarant testifies at the trial or hearing and is subject to cross-examination concerning the statement, and the statement is (A) inconsistent with his testimony, and was given under oath subject to the penalty of perjury at a trial, hearing, or other proceeding, or in a deposition, or (B) consistent with his testimony and is offered to rebut an express or implied charge against him of recent fabrication or improper influence or motive, or (C) one of identification of a person made after perceiving him; or

(2) Admission by party-opponent. The statement is offered against a party and is (A) his own statement in either his individual or representative capacity or (B) a statement of which he has manifested his adoption or belief in its truth, or (C) a statement by a person authorized by him to make a statement concerning the subject, or (D) a statement by his agent or servant concerning a matter within the scope of his agency or employment, made during the existence of the relationship, or (E) a statement by a coconspirator of a party during the course and in furtherance of the conspiracy.

(3) Depositions in civil proceedings. It is a deposition taken and offered in accordance with the Texas Rules of Civil Procedure.

Comment. The definitions in 801(a), (b), (c) and (d) combined bring within the hearsay rule four categories of conduct. These are described and illustrated below.

(1) A verbal (oral or written) explicit assertion. Illustration. Witness testifies that declarant said "A shot B." Declarant's conduct is a statement because it is an oral expression. Because it is an explicit assertion, the matter asserted is that A shot B. Finally, the statement is hearsay because it was not made while testifying at the trial and is offered to prove the truth of the matter asserted.

(2) A verbal (oral or written) explicit assertion, not offered to prove the matter explicitly asserted, but offered for the truth of a matter implied by the statement, the probative value of the statement flowing from declarant's belief as to the matter. Illustration. The only known remedy for X disease is medicine Y and the only known use of medicine Y is to cure X disease. To prove that Oglethorpe had X disease, witness testifies that declarant, a doctor, stated, "The best medicine for Oglethorpe is Y." The testimony is to a statement because it was a verbal expression. The matter asserted was that Oglethorpe had X disease because that matter is implied from the statement, the probative value of the statement as offered flowing from declarant's belief as to the matter. Finally, the statement is hearsay because it was not made while testifying at the trial and is offered to prove the truth of the matter asserted.

(3) Nonassertive verbal conduct offered for the truth of a matter implied by the statement, the probative value of the statement flowing from declarant's belief as to the matter. Illustration. In a rape prosecution to prove that Richard, the defendant, was in the room at the time of the rape, W testifies that declarant knocked on the door to the room and shouted, "Open the door, Richard." The testimony is to a statement because it was a verbal expression. The matter asserted was that Richard was in the room because that matter is implied from the statement, the probative value of the statement as offered flowing from declarant's belief as to the matter. Finally, the statement is hearsay because it was not made while testifying at the trial and is offered to prove the truth of the matter asserted.

(4) Nonverbal assertive conduct intended as a substitute for verbal expression. Illustration. W testifies that A asked declarant "Which way did X go?" and declarant pointed north. This nonverbal conduct of declarant was intended by him as a substitute for verbal expression and so is a statement. The matter asserted is that X went north because that is implied from the statement and the probative value of the statement as offered flows from declarant's belief that X went north. Finally, the statement is hearsay because it was not made at trial and is offered to prove the truth of the matter asserted.

RULE 802. HEARSAY RULE

Hearsay is not admissible except as provided by statute or these rules. Inadmissible hearsay admitted without objection shall not be denied probative value merely because it is hearsay.

RULE 803. HEARSAY EXCEPTIONS; AVAILABILITY OF DECLARANT IMMATERIAL

The following are not excluded by the hearsay rule, even though the declarant is available as a witness:

(1) Present sense impression. A statement describing or explaining an event or condition made while the declarant was perceiving the event or condition, or immediately thereafter.

(2) Excited utterance. A statement relating to a startling event or condition made while the declarant was under the stress of excitement caused by the event or condition.

(3) Then existing mental, emotional, or physical condition. A statement of the declarant's then existing state of mind, emotion, sensation, or physical condition (such as intent, plan, motive, design, mental feeling, pain, or bodily health), but not including a statement of memory or belief to prove the fact remembered or believed unless it relates to the execution, revocation, identification, or terms of declarant's will.

(4) Statements for purposes of medical diagnosis or treatment. Statements made for purposes of medical diagnosis or treatment and describing medical history, or past or present symptoms, pain, or sensations, or the inception or general character of the cause or external source thereof insofar as reasonably pertinent to diagnosis or treatment.

(5) Recorded recollection. A memorandum or record concerning a matter about which a witness once had personal knowledge but now has insufficient recollection to enable him to testify fully and accurately, shown to have been made or adopted by the witness when the matter was fresh in his memory and to reflect that knowledge correctly, unless the circumstances of preparation cast doubt on the document's trustworthiness. If admitted, the memorandum or record may be read into evidence but may not itself be received as an exhibit unless offered by an adverse party.

(6) Records of regularly conducted activity. A memorandum, report, record, or data compilation, in any form, of acts, events, conditions, opinions, or diagnoses, made at or near the time by, or from information transmitted by, a person with knowledge, if kept in the course of a regularly conducted business activity, and if it was the regular practice of that business activity to make the memorandum, report, record, or data compilation, all as shown by the testimony of the custodian or other qualified witness, unless the source of information or the method or circumstances of preparation indicate lack of trustworthiness. "Business" as used in this paragraph includes any and every kind of regular organized activity whether conducted for profit or not.

(7) Absence of entry in records kept in accordance with the provisions of paragraph (6). Evidence that a matter is not included in the memoranda reports, records, or data compilations, in any form, kept in accordance with the provisions of paragraph (6), to prove the nonoccurrence or nonexistence of the matter, if the matter was of a kind of which a memorandum, report, record, or data compilation was regularly made and preserved, unless the sources of information or other circumstances indicate lack of trustworthiness.

(8) Public records and reports. Records, reports, statements, or data compilations, in any form, of public offices or agencies setting forth (A) the activities of the office or agency, or (B) matters observed pursuant to duty imposed by law as to which matters there was a duty to report, excluding, however, in criminal cases matters observed by police officers and other law enforcement personnel, or (C) in civil actions and proceedings and against the Government in

PROPOSED RULE 801

criminal cases, factual findings resulting from an investigation made pursuant to authority granted by law, unless the sources of information or other circumstances indicate lack of trustworthiness.

(9) Records of vital statistics. Records or data compilations, in any form, of births, fetal deaths, deaths, or marriages, if the report thereof was made to a public office pursuant to requirements of law.

(10) Absence of public record or entry. To prove the absence of a record, report, statement, or data compilation, in any form, or the nonoccurrence or nonexistence of a matter of which a record, report, statement, or data compilation, in any form, was regularly made and preserved by a public office or agency, evidence in the form of a certification in accordance with Rule 902, or testimony, that diligent search failed to disclose the record, report, statement, or data compilation, or entry.

(11) Records of religious organizations. Statements of births, marriages, divorces, deaths, legitimacy, ancestry, relationship by blood or marriage, or other similar facts of personal or family history, contained in a regularly kept record of a religious organization.

(12) Marriage, baptismal, and similar certificates. Statements of fact contained in a certificate that the maker performed a marriage or other ceremony or administered a sacrament, made by a clergyman, public official, or other person authorized by the rules or practices of a religious organization or by law to perform the act certified, and purporting to have been issued at the time of the act or within a reasonable time thereafter.

(13) Family records. Statements of fact concerning personal or family history contained in family Bibles, genealogies, charts, engravings on rings, inscriptions on family portraits, engravings on urns, crypts, or tombstones, or the like.

(14) Records of documents affecting an interest in property. The record of a document purporting to establish or affect an interest in property, as proof of the content of the original recorded document and its execution and delivery by each person by whom it purports to have been executed, if the record is a record of a public office and an applicable statute authorizes the recording of documents of that kind in that office.

Comment. It is the intent of the Committee that 803(14) leaves undisturbed article 52 of the Texas Probate Code and articles 3726 and 3726a, Vernon's Texas Civil Statutes. To the extent that an offer of evidence is not covered by these statutes, 803(14) gives proponent an additional alternative.

(15) Statements in documents affecting an interest in property. A statement contained in a document purporting to establish or affect an interest in property if the matter stated was relevant to the purpose of the document, unless dealings with the property since the document was made have been inconsistent with the truth of the statement or the purport of the document.

(16) Statements in ancient documents. Statements in a document in existence twenty years or more the authenticity of which is established.

(17) Market reports, commercial publications. Market quotations, tabulations, lists, directories, or other published compilations, generally used and relied upon by the public or by persons in particular occupations.

(18) Learned treatises. To the extent called to the attention of an expert witness upon cross-examination or relied upon by him in direct examination, statements contained in published treatises, periodicals, or pamphlets on a subject of history, medicine, or other science or art, established as a reliable authority by the testimony or admission of the witness or by other expert testimony or by judicial notice. If admitted, the statements may be read into evidence but may not be received as exhibits.

(19) Reputation concerning personal or family history. Reputation among members of his family by blood, adoption, or marriage, or among his associates, or in the community, concerning a person's birth, adoption, marriage, divorce, death, legitimacy, relationship by blood, adoption, or marriage, ancestry, or other similar fact of his personal or family history.

(20) Reputation concerning boundaries or general history. Reputation in a community, arising before the controversy, as to boundaries of or customs affecting lands in the community, and

reputation as to events of general history important to the community or State or nation in which located.

(21) Reputation as to character. Reputation of a person's character among his associates or in the community.

(22) Judgment of previous conviction. Evidence of a judgment, entered after a trial or upon a plea of guilty (but not upon a plea of nolo contendere), adjudging a person guilty of a felony, to prove any fact essential to sustain the judgment of conviction, but not including, when offered by the State in a criminal prosecution for purposes other than impeachment, judgments against persons other than the accused. The pendency of an appeal renders such evidence inadmissible.

(23) Judgment as to personal, family, or general history, or boundaries. Judgments as proof of matters of personal, family or general history, or boundaries, essential to the judgment, if the same would be provable by evidence of reputation.

(24) Statement against interest. A statement which was at the time of its making so far contrary to the declarant's pecuniary or proprietary interest, or so far tended to subject him to civil or criminal liability, or to render invalid a claim by him against another, or to make him an object of hatred, ridicule, or disgrace, that a reasonable man in his position would not have made the statement unless he believed it to be true. A statement tending to expose the declarant to criminal liability and offered to exculpate the accused is not admissible unless corroborating circumstances clearly indicate the trustworthiness of the statement.

(25) Other exceptions.

a. In civil proceedings. A statement not specifically covered by any of the foregoing exceptions but having substantial guarantees of trustworthiness.

b. In criminal proceedings. A statement not specifically covered by any of the foregoing exceptions but having equivalent circumstantial guarantees of trustworthiness, if the court determines that (A) the statement is offered as evidence of a material fact; (B) the statement is

more probative on the point for which it is offered than any other evidence which the proponent can procure though reasonable efforts; and (C) the general purposes of these rules and the interests of justice will best be served by admission of the statement into evidence. However, a statement may not be admitted under this exception unless the proponent of it makes known to the adverse party sufficiently in advance of the trial or hearing to provide the adverse party with a fair opportunity to prepare to meet it, his intention to offer the statement and the particulars of it, including the name and address of declarant.

RULE 804. HEARSAY EXCEPTIONS; DECLARANT UNAVAILABLE

(a) Definition of unavailability. "Unavailability as a witness" includes situations in which the declarant—

(1) is exempted by ruling of the court on the ground of privilege from testifying concerning the subject matter of his statement; or

(2) persists in refusing to testify concerning the subject matter of his statement despite an order of the court to do so; or

(3) testifies to a lack of memory of the subject matter of his statement; or

(4) is unable to be present or to testify at the hearing because of death or then existing physical or mental illness or infirmity; or

(5) is absent from the hearing and the proponent of his statement has been unable to procure his attendance or testimony by process or other reasonable means.

A declarant is not unavailable as a witness if his exemption, refusal, claim or lack of memory, inability, or absence is due to the procurement or wrongdoing of the proponent of his statement for the purpose of preventing the witness from attending or testifying.

(b) Hearsay exceptions. The following are not excluded if the declarant is unavailable as a witness—

(1) Former testimony. Testimony given as a witness at another hearing of the same or a different proceeding, or in a deposition taken in the course of the same or another proceeding, if the party against whom the testimony is now offered, or in a civil action or proceeding, a person with a similar interest, had an opportunity and similar motive to develop the testimony by direct, cross, or redirect examination.

(2) Dying declarations. A statement made by a declarant while believing that his death was imminent, concerning the cause or circumstances of what he believed to be his impending death.

(3) Statement of personal or family history. (A) A statement concerning the declarant's own birth, adoption, marriage, divorce, legitimacy, relationship by blood, adoption, or marriage, ancestry, or other similar fact of personal or family history, even though declarant had no means of acquiring personal knowledge of the matter stated; or (B) a statement concerning the foregoing matters, and death also, of another person, if the declarant was related to the other by blood, adoption, or marriage or was so intimately associated with the other's family as to be likely to have accurate information concerning the matter declared.

(4) Other exceptions.

a. In civil proceedings. A statement not specifically covered by any of the foregoing exceptions but having substantial guarantees of trustworthiness.

b. In criminal proceedings. A statement not specifically covered by any of the foregoing exceptions but having equivalent circumstantial guarantees of trustworthiness, if the court determines that (A) the statement is offered as evidence of material fact; (B) the statement is more probative on the point for which it is offered than any other evidence which the proponent can procure through reasonable efforts; and (C) the general purposes of these rules and the interest of justice will best be served by admission of the statement into evidence. However, a statement may not be admitted under this exception unless the proponent of it makes known to the adverse party sufficiently in advance of the trial or hearing to provide the adverse party with a fair opportunity to prepare to meet it, his intention to offer the statement and the particulars of it, including the name and address of the declarant.

RULE 805. HEARSAY WITHIN HEARSAY

Hearsay included within hearsay is not excluded under the hearsay rule if each part of the combined statements conforms with an exception to the hearsay rule provided in these rules.

RULE 806. ATTACKING & SUPPORTING CREDIBILITY OF DECLARANT

When a hearsay statement, or a statement defined in Rule 801(e)(2), (C), (D), (E), or (3), has been admitted in evidence, the credibility of the declarant may be attacked, and if attacked may be supported, by any evidence which would be admissible for those purposes if declarant had testified as a witness. Evidence of a statement or conduct by the declarant at any time, offered to impeach the declarant, is not subject to any requirement that he may have been afforded an opportunity to deny or explain. If the party against whom a hearsay statement has been admitted calls the declarant as a witness, the party is entitled to examine him on the statement as if under cross-examination.

ARTICLE IX: AUTHENTICATION & IDENTIFICATION

RULE 901. REQUIREMENT OF AUTHENTICATION OR IDENTIFICATION

(a) General provision. The requirement of authentication or identification as a condition precedent to admissibility is satisfied by evidence sufficient to support a finding that the matter in question is what its proponent claims.

(b) Illustrations. By way of illustration only, and not by way of limitation, the following are examples of authentication or identification conforming with the requirements of this rule:

(1) Testimony of witness with knowledge. Testimony that a matter is what it is claimed to be.

(2) Nonexpert opinion on handwriting. Nonexpert opinion as to the genuineness of handwriting, based upon familiarity not acquired for purposes of the litigation.

(3) Comparison by trier or expert witness. Comparison by the trier of fact or by expert witness with specimens which have been found by the court to be genuine.

(4) Distinctive characteristics and the like. Appearance, contents, substance, internal patterns, or other distinctive characteristics, taken in conjunction with circumstances.

(5) Voice identification. Identification of a voice, whether heard firsthand or through mechanical or electronic transmission or recording by opinion based upon hearing the voice at any time under circumstances connecting it with the alleged speaker.

(6) Telephone conversations. Telephone conversations, by evidence that a call was made to the number assigned at the time by the telephone company to a particular person or business, if (A) in the case of a person, circumstances, including self-identification, show the person answering to be the one called, or (B) in the case of a business, the call was made to a place of business and the conversation related to business reasonably transacted over the telephone.

(7) Public records or reports. Evidence that a writing authorized by law to be recorded or filed and in fact recorded or filed in a public office, or a purported public record, report, statement, or data compilation, in any form, is from the public office where items of this nature are kept.

(8) Ancient documents or data compilation. Evidence that a document or data compilation, in any form, (A) is in such condition as to create no suspicion concerning its authenticity, (B) was in a place where it, if authentic, would likely be, and (C) has been in existence twenty years or more at the time it is offered.

(9) Process or system. Evidence describing a process or system used to produce a result and showing that the process or system produces an accurate result.

(10) Methods provided by statute or rule. Any method of authentication or identification provided by statute or by court rule prescribed pursuant to statutory authority.

RULE 902. SELF-AUTHENTICATION

Extrinsic evidence of authenticity as a condition precedent to admissibility is not required with respect to the following:

(1) Domestic public documents under seal. A document bearing a seal purporting to be that of the United States, or of any State, district, Commonwealth, territory, or insular possession thereof, or the Panama Canal Zone, or the Trust Territory of the Pacific Islands, or of a political subdivision, department, officer, or agency thereof, and a signature purporting to be an attestation or execution.

(2) Domestic public documents not under seal. A document purporting to bear the signature in his official capacity of an officer or employee of any entity included in paragraph (1) hereof, having no seal, if a public officer having a seal and having official duties in the district or political subdivision of the officer or employee certifies under seal that the signer has the official capacity and that the signature is genuine.

(3) Foreign public documents. A document purporting to be executed or attested in his official capacity by a person authorized by the laws of a foreign country to make the execution or attestation, and accompanied by a final certification as to the genuineness of the signature and official position (A) of the executing or attesting person, or (B) of any foreign official whose certificate of genuineness of signature and official position relates to the execution or attestation or is in a chain of certificates of genuineness of signature and official position relating to the execution or attestation. A final certification may be made by a secretary of embassy or legation, consul general, consul, vice consul, or consular agent of the United States, or a diplomatic or consular official of the foreign country assigned or accredited to the United States. If reasonable opportunity has been given to all parties to investigate the authenticity and accuracy of official documents, the court may, for good cause shown, order that they be treated as presumptively authentic without final certification or permit them to be evidenced by an attested summary with or without final certification. The final certification shall be dispensed with whenever both the United States and the foreign country in which the official record is located are parties to a treaty or convention that abolishes or displaces such requirement, in which case the record and the attestation shall be certified by the means provided in the treaty or convention.

(4) Certified copies of public records. A copy of an official record or report or entry therein, or of a document authorized by law to be recorded or filed and actually recorded or filed in a public office, including data compilations in any form, certified as correct by the custodian or other person authorized to make the certification, by certificate complying with paragraph (1), (2), or (3) of this rule or complying with any statute or court rule prescribed pursuant to statutory authority.

(5) Official publications. Books, pamphlets, or other publications purporting to be issued by public authority.

(6) Newspapers and periodicals. Printed materials purporting to be newspapers or periodicals.

(7) Trade inscriptions and the like. Inscriptions, signs, tags, or labels purporting to have been affixed in the course of business and indicating ownership, control, or origin.

(8) Acknowledged documents. Documents accompanied by a certificate of acknowledgement executed in the manner provided by law by a notary public or other officer authorized by law to take acknowledgements.

(9) Commercial paper and related documents. Commercial paper, signatures thereon, and documents relating thereto to the extent provided by general commercial law.

(10) Business records accompanied by affidavit.

a. Records or photocopies; admissibility; affidavit; filing. Any record or set of records or photographically reproduced copies of such records, which would be admissible under Rule 803(6) or (7) shall be admissible in evidence in any court in this state upon the affidavit of the person who would otherwise provide the prerequisites of Rule 803(6) or (7), that such records attached to such affidavit were in fact so kept as required by Rule 803(6) or (7), provided further, that such record or records along with such affidavit are filed with the clerk of the court for inclusion with the papers in the cause in which the record or records are sought to be used as evidence at least fourteen (14) days prior to the day upon which trial of said cause commences, and

provided the other parties to said cause are given prompt notice by the party filing same of the filing of such record or records and affidavit, which notice shall identify the name and employer, if any, of the person making the affidavit and such records shall be made available to the counsel for other parties to the action or litigation for inspection and copying. The expense for copying shall be borne by the party, parties or persons who desire copies and not by the party or parties who file the records and serve notice of said filing, in compliance with this rule. Notice shall be deemed to have been promptly given if it is served in the manner contemplated by Rule 21a, Texas Rules of Civil Procedure, fourteen (14) days prior to commencement of trial in said cause.

b. Form of affidavit. A form for the affidavit of such person as shall make such affidavit as is permitted in paragraph (a) above shall be sufficient if it follows this form, though this form shall not be exclusive, and an affidavit which substantially complies with the provisions of this rule shall suffice, to-wit:

No._____

John Doe	IN THE
	_____
(Name of Plaintiff)	
v.	COURT IN AND FOR
John Roe	
(Name of Defendant)	_____ COUNTY, TEXAS

AFFIDAVIT

Before me, the undersigned authority, personally appeared _____, who, being by me duly sworn, deposed as follows:

My name is _____, I am of sound mind, capable of making this affidavit, and personally acquainted with the facts herein stated:

I am the custodian of the records of _____. Attached hereto are ___ pages of records from _____. These said ___ pages of records are kept by _____ in the regular

★

course of business, and it was the regular course of business of _____ for an employee or representative of _____, with knowledge of the act, event, condition, opinion, or diagnosis, recorded to make the record or to transmit information thereof to be included in such record; and the record was made at or near the time or reasonably soon thereafter. The records attached hereto are the original or exact duplicates of the original.

_____
Affiant

SWORN TO AND SUBSCRIBED before me on the ____ day of _____, 19___.

_____
Notary Public in and for
_____ County, Texas.

(11) Presumptions under statute or court rule prescribed pursuant to statutory authority. Any signature, document, or other matter declared by court rule prescribed pursuant to statutory authority to be presumptively or prima facie genuine or authentic.

Comment. Paragraph (10) is based on portions of the affidavit authentication provisions of Tex. Rev. Civ. Stat. Ann. art. 3737e. The most general and comprehensive language from those provisions was chosen. It is intended that this method of authentication shall be available for any kind of regularly kept record that satisfies the requirements of rule 803(6) and (7), including X-rays, hospital records, or any other kind of regularly kept medical record.

RULE 903. SUBSCRIBING WITNESS' TESTIMONY UNNECESSARY

The testimony of a subscribing witness is not necessary to authenticate a writing unless required by the laws of the jurisdiction whose laws govern the validity of the writing.

ARTICLE X: CONTENTS OF WRITINGS, RECORDINGS, & PHOTOGRAPHS

RULE 1001. DEFINITIONS

For purposes of this article the following definitions are applicable:

(1) Writings and recordings. "Writings" and "recordings" consist of letters, words, or numbers, or their equivalent, set down by handwriting, typewriting, printing, photostating, photographing, magnetic impulse, mechanical or electronic recording, or other form of data compilation.

(2) Photographs. "Photographs" include still photographs, X-ray films, video tapes, and motion pictures.

(3) Original. An "original" of a writing or recording is the writing or recording itself or any counterpart intended to have the same effect by a person executing or issuing it. An "original" of a photograph includes the negative or any print therefrom. If data are stored in a computer or similar device, any printout or other output readable by sight, shown to reflect the data accurately, is an "original."

(4) Duplicate. A "duplicate" is a counterpart produced by the same impression as the original, or from the same matrix, or by means of photography, including enlargements and miniatures, or by mechanical or electronic rerecording, or by chemical reproduction, or by other equivalent techniques which accurately reproduce the original.

RULE 1002. REQUIREMENT OF ORIGINALS

To prove the content of a writing, recording, or photograph, the original writing, recording, or photograph is required except as otherwise provided in these rules or by statute.

RULE 1003. ADMISSIBILITY OF DUPLICATES

A duplicate is admissible to the same extent as an original unless (1) a genuine question is raised as to the authenticity of the original or (2) in the circumstances it would be unfair to admit the duplicate in lieu of the original.

RULE 1004. ADMISSIBILITY OF OTHER EVIDENCE OF CONTENTS

The original is not required, and other evidence of the contents of a writing, recording, or photograph is admissible if—

(1) Originals lost or destroyed. All originals are lost or have been destroyed, unless the proponent lost or destroyed them in bad faith; or

(2) Original not obtainable. No original can be obtained by any available judicial process or procedure; or

(3) Original outside the state. No original is located in Texas; or

(4) Original in possession of opponent. At a time when an original was under the control of the party against whom offered, he was put on notice, by the pleadings or otherwise, that the content would be a subject of proof at the hearing, and he does not produce the original at the hearing; or

(5) Collateral matters. The writing, recording, or photograph is not closely related to a controlling issue.

RULE 1005. PUBLIC RECORDS

The contents of an official record, or of a document authorized to be recorded or filed and actually recorded or filed, including data compilations in any form, if otherwise admissible, may be proved by copy, certified as correct in accordance with Rule 902 or testified to be correct by a witness who has compared it with the original. If a copy which complies with the foregoing cannot be obtained by the exercise of reasonable diligence, then other evidence of the contents may be given.

RULE 1006. SUMMARIES

The contents of voluminous writings, recordings, or photographs which cannot conveniently be examined in court may be presented in the form of a chart, summary, or calculation. The originals, or duplicates, shall be made available for examination or copying, or both, by other parties at reasonable time and place. The court may order that they be produced in court.

RULE 1007. TESTIMONY OR WRITTEN ADMISSION OF PARTY

Contents of writings, recordings, or photographs may be proved by the testimony or deposition of the party against whom offered or by his written admission, without accounting for the nonproduction of the original.

RULE 1008. FUNCTIONS OF COURT & JURY

When the admissibility of other evidence of contents of writings, recordings, or photographs under these rules depends upon the fulfillment of a condition of fact, the question whether the condition has been fulfilled is ordinarily for the court to determine in accordance with the provisions of Rule 104. However, when an issue is raised

(a) whether the asserted writing ever existed, or (b) whether another writing, recording, or photograph produced at the trial is the original, or (c) whether other evidence of contents correctly reflects the contents, the issue is for the trier of fact to determine as in the case of other issues of fact.

ARTICLE XI: MISCELLANEOUS RULES
RULE 1101. APPLICABILITY OF RULES

(a) These rules apply in civil and criminal proceedings in all Texas courts and in examining trials before magistrates.

(b) Rule of privilege. These rules with respect to privileges apply at all stages of all actions, cases and proceedings.

(c) Rules inapplicable. The rules (other than with respect to privileges) do not apply in the following situations:

(1) Preliminary questions of fact. The determination of questions of fact preliminary to admissibility of evidence when the issue is to be determined by the court under Rule 104;

(2) Grand jury. Proceedings before grand juries.

(3) Miscellaneous proceedings:

(A) Application for habeas corpus in extradition, rendition, or interstate detainer proceedings;

(B) A hearing under Texas Code of Criminal Procedure article 46.02, by the court out of the presence of a jury, to determine whether there is evidence to support a finding of incompetency to stand trial;

(C) Proceedings regarding bail except hearings to deny, revoke or increase bail;

(D) A hearing on justification for pretrial detention;

(E) A hearing in small claims court;

(F) Issuance of search or arrest warrant;

(G) Direct contempt determination;

(H) A hearing under the Texas Family Code section 54.02, Waiver of Jurisdiction and Discretionary Transfer to Criminal Court;

(I) Sentencing, or punishment assessment by Court.

(d) Rules applicable in part. In the following proceedings these rules apply to the extent matters of evidence are not provided for in the statutes which govern procedure therein or in another court rule prescribed pursuant to statutory authority:

(1) Punishment assessment by the jury;

(2) Probation revocation;

(3) A proceeding to revoke a deferred adjudication of guilt or a conditional discharge;

(4) Motions to suppress confessions, or to suppress illegally obtained evidence under Texas Code of Criminal Procedure article 38.23;

(5) Subject to subdivision (c)(3)(H) of this rule, proceedings under Titles 1, 2, 3, and 4 of the Family Code, with the civil Rules of Evidence governing under Titles 1, 2, and 4 and the criminal Rules of Evidence governing under Title 3; and,

(6) Proceedings governed by section 22 of the Texas Probate Code.

(e) In contested cases before state agencies as defined in section 3 of the Administrative Procedure and Texas Register Act, section 14 of the Act shall govern evidence.

(f) Evidence in hearings under the Texas Code of Military Justice, article 5788, shall be governed by that Code.

RULE 1102. TITLE

These rules shall be known and cited as the Texas Rules of Evidence.

CASE INDEX

CASE INDEX

Bodin v. State, 807 S.W.2d 313, **50, 191, 474, 475, 476, 477**

Bodmer v. State, 161 S.W.3d 9, **843**

Bogle v. McClure, 332 F.3d 1347, **406**

Bohannon v. Pegelow, 652 F.2d 729, **697**

Bolden v. State, 967 S.W.2d 895, **841**

Boles v. State, 598 S.W.2d 274, **455**

Bondurant v. State, 956 S.W.2d 762, **876, 879**

Bonham v. Baldeschwiler, 533 S.W.2d 144, **222, 227**

Bonner v. Mercantile Nat'l Bank, 203 S.W.2d 780, **231**

Booker v. State, 929 S.W.2d 57, **609**

Booker v. State, 103 S.W.3d 521, **276**

Boon v. Weathered's Adm'r, 23 Tex. 675, **606, 609, 615**

Boone v. State, 60 S.W.3d 231, **203, 215**

Boothe v. State, 474 S.W.2d 219, **695**

Boozier v. Hambrick, 846 S.W.2d 593, **929**

Borak v. Bridge, 524 S.W.2d 773, **968, 982**

Borawick v. Shay, 68 F.3d 597, **89**

Borden v. Hall, 255 S.W.2d 920, **167**

Borden, Inc. v. Rios, 850 S.W.2d 821, **619**

Borden, Inc. v. Valdez, 773 S.W.2d 718, **393, 409, 538**

Bordman v. State, 56 S.W.3d 63, **464**

Boren v. Texoma Med. Ctr., Inc., 258 S.W.3d 224, **525**

Boring & Tunneling Co. of Am., Inc. v. Salazar, 782 S.W.2d 284, **394, 428**

Bormaster v. Henderson, 624 S.W.2d 655, **777**

Borunda v. Richmond, 885 F.2d 1384, **98**

Bostic v. Ga.-Pac. Corp., 439 S.W.3d 332, **728, 739**

Boswell v. Brazos Elec. Power Coop., Inc., 910 S.W.2d 593, **89, 749, 773**

Boswell v. Jasperson, 266 F. Supp. 2d 1314, **1042**

Boucher v. Wallis, 236 S.W.2d 519, **998**

Bounds v. Caudle, 549 S.W.2d 438, **703**

Bounds v. Scurlock Oil Co., 730 S.W.2d 68, **706**

Bourjaily v. United States, 483 U.S. 171, **87, 89, 855, 860, 862**

Boutang v. State, 402 S.W.3d 782, **806, 807, 809**

Bowden v. Caldron, 554 S.W.2d 25, **955**

Bower v. Edwards Cty. Appr. Dist., 752 S.W.2d 629, **1020**

Bowie v. State, 135 S.W.3d 55, **343, 346**

Bowles v. Bourdon, 148 Tex. 1, 219 S.W.2d 779, **923**

Bowles v. United States, 439 F.2d 536, **550**

Bowley v. State, 310 S.W.3d 431, **350**

Boyd v. Diversified Fin. Sys., 1 S.W.3d 888, **826**

Boyd v. State, 643 S.W.2d 708, **951**

Boyer v. Scruggs, 806 S.W.2d 941, **72**

Boykin v. State, 818 S.W.2d 782, **114**

Boyle v. State, 820 S.W.2d 122, **364, 365, 366, 367**

Boyles v. Hous. Lighting & Power Co., 464 S.W.2d 359, **780**

Bracewell v. Bracewell, 31 S.W.3d 610, **58, 100**

Bradfield v. State, 524 S.W.2d 438, **227**

Bradford v. State, 608 S.W.2d 918, **239**

Bradford v. Vento, 997 S.W.2d 713, **188**

Bradley v. State ex rel. White, 990 S.W.2d 245, **576**

Bradshaw v. State, 65 S.W.3d 232, **278**

Bradshaw v. State, 466 S.W.3d 875, **375**

Brady v. Maryland, 373 U.S. 83, **678, 679**

Braggs v. State, 951 S.W.2d 877, **599, 848**

Brandley v. State, 691 S.W.2d 699, **271**

Branham v. Brown, 925 S.W.2d 365, **581**

Brasfield v. State, 600 S.W.2d 288, **410, 411**

Brasher v. State, 139 S.W.3d 369, **598, 837**

Bratcher v. State, 771 S.W.2d 175, **253, 255**

Brateman v. Upper Channel Site Co., 378 S.W.2d 882, **927**

Bratton v. State, 156 S.W.3d 689, **813**

Brazelton v. State, 947 S.W.2d 644, **248**

Brazosport Bank v. Oak Park Townhouses, 889 S.W.2d 676, **165**

Breeden v. State, 438 S.W.2d 105, **69**

Brem v. State, 571 S.W.2d 314, **432**

Brennan's, Inc. v. Brennan's Rests., Inc., 590 F.2d 168, **424**

Brentwood Fin. Corp. v. Lamprecht, 736 S.W.2d 836, **166**

Brewer v. Capital Cities/ABC, Inc., 986 S.W.2d 636, **913**

Brewer v. State, 370 S.W.3d 471, **731**

Briddle v. State, 742 S.W.2d 379, **540**

Bridges v. Bridges, 404 S.W.2d 48, **268**

Bridges v. City of Richardson, 163 Tex. 292, 354 S.W.2d 366, **69, 70**

Bridges v. State, 19 N.W.2d 529, **830**

Bridges v. State, 471 S.W.2d 827, **1000**

Bridges v. State, 909 S.W.2d 151, **476**

Brimage v. State, 918 S.W.2d 466, **200**

Brinkley v. Liberty Mut. Ins., 331 S.W.2d 423, **228**

Briones v. Levine's Dep't Store, Inc., 446 S.W.2d 7, **188**

Bristol-Myers Co. v. Fed. Trade Comm'n, 185 F.2d 58, **1002**

Bristol-Myers Co. v. Gonzales, 548 S.W.2d 416, **310**

Bristol-Myers Squibb Co. v. Hancock, 921 S.W.2d 917, **492**

Britt v. Cambridge Mut. Fire Ins., 717 S.W.2d 476, **929**

Broaddus v. Long, 135 Tex. 353, 138 S.W.2d 1057, **166**

Brock v. On Shore Quality Control Specialists, Inc., 811 F.2d 282, **472, 473**

Broderick v. State, 35 S.W.3d 67, **1048**

Broders v. Heise, 924 S.W.2d 148, **707, 708, 710, 711**

Brokenberry v. State, 788 S.W.2d 103, **248**

Brokenberry v. State, 853 S.W.2d 145, **475**

Brook v. Morriss, Morriss & Boatwright, 212 S.W.2d 257, **297**

Brookhart v. Janis, 384 U.S. 1, **639**

Brooks v. Hous. Auth., 926 S.W.2d 316, **1028**

Brooks v. State, 642 S.W.2d 791, **73, 641**

Brooks v. State, 686 S.W.2d 952, **441**

Brooks v. State, 921 S.W.2d 875, **969**

Brooks v. State, 990 S.W.2d 278, **874**

Brooks v. State, 132 S.W.3d 702, **803, 937**

Brooks v. State, 323 S.W.3d 893, **187**

Brookshire Bros. v. Lewis, 911 S.W.2d 791, **306, 307, 311**
Broussard v. State, 910 S.W.2d 952, **562**
Broussard v. State, 999 S.W.2d 477, **292**
Broussard v. State, 68 S.W.3d 197, **52**
Brown v. Epps, 686 F.3d 281, **791**
Brown v. Lynaugh, 843 F.2d 849, **576**
Brown v. State, 391 S.W.2d 425, **912**
Brown v. State, 477 S.W.2d 617, **255**
Brown v. State, 612 S.W.2d 83, **524**
Brown v. State, 632 S.W.2d 191, **264**
Brown v. State, 657 S.W.2d 117, **199**
Brown v. State, 689 S.W.2d 219, **716, 719**
Brown v. State, 741 S.W.2d 453, **758**
Brown v. State, 757 S.W.2d 739, **63, 196, 203, 205**
Brown v. State, 804 S.W.2d 566, **584**
Brown v. State, 880 S.W.2d 249, **624, 633**
Brown v. State, 122 S.W.3d 794, **175, 183**
Brown v. State, 270 S.W.3d 564, **616**
Brown v. State, 303 S.W.3d 310, **687**
Brown v. State, 333 S.W.3d 606, **836, 896**
Brown v. State, 334 S.W.3d 789, **861**
Brown v. Tex. Employers' Ins., 635 S.W.2d 415, **762**
Brown v. Walter, 62 F.2d 798, **351**
Brown & Root, Inc. v. Haddad, 142 Tex. 624, 180 S.W.2d 339, **69**
Brown & Root U.S.A., Inc. v. Moore, 731 S.W.2d 137, **404**
Brownlee v. State, 944 S.W.2d 463, **659**
Brownsville Pediatric Ass'n v. Reyes, 68 S.W.3d 184, **350, 729**
Brumit v. State, 206 S.W.3d 639, **85**
Brundige v. State, 49 Tex. Crim. 596, 95 S.W. 527, **634**
Brune v. Brown Forman Corp., 758 S.W.2d 827, **118**
Bruni v. State, 669 S.W.2d 829, **440**
Bruton v. State, 428 S.W.3d 865, **1016, 1017, 1018, 1019, 1029**
Bruton v. United States, 391 U.S. 123, **851**
Bryan v. John Bean Div. of FMC Corp., 566 F.2d 541, **765, 776**
Bryan v. State, 837 S.W.2d 637, **944, 950, 951**
Bryant v. State, 775 S.W.2d 48, **660**
Bryant v. State, 997 S.W.2d 673, **633**
Bryant v. State, 187 S.W.3d 397, **65**
Bryant v. State, 282 S.W.3d 156, **667, 671, 957**
Bryant v. Trinity Univ'l Ins., 411 S.W.2d 945, **947, 949**
Bryson v. State, 820 S.W.2d 197, **285**
Buchanan v. Byrd, 519 S.W.2d 841, **157**
Buchanan v. Mayfield, 925 S.W.2d 135, **488**
Buchanan v. State, 846 S.W.2d 853, **638**
Buchanan v. State, 911 S.W.2d 11, **294**
Buchoz v. Klein, 143 Tex. 284, 184 S.W.2d 271, **855, 859**
Buckaloo Trucking Co. v. Johnson, 409 S.W.2d 911, **130**
Buckley v. Gulf Ref. Co., 123 S.W.2d 970, **166**
Buckley v. Heckler, 739 F.2d 1047, **156**

Buentello v. State, 770 S.W.2d 917, **584, 585**
Buentello v. State, 826 S.W.2d 610, **584, 585**
Buffington v. State, 801 S.W.2d 151, **626**
Bullcoming v. New Mexico, 564 U.S. 647, **799, 801, 805, 807, 808, 809, 810**
Buls v. Fuselier, 55 S.W.3d 204, **234**
Bulthuis v. Rexall Corp., 789 F.2d 1315, **776**
Bunnett/Smallwood & Co. v. Helton Oil Co., 577 S.W.2d 291, **70**
Burch v. State, 401 S.W.3d 634, **805, 808, 811**
Burdine v. State, 719 S.W.2d 309, **1043**
Burke v. State, 642 S.W.2d 197, **765**
Burke v. State, 371 S.W.3d 252, **253**
Burkhart v. Wash. Metro. Area Transit Auth., 112 F.3d 1207, **758, 760**
Burks v. Meredith, 546 S.W.2d 366, **712**
Burks v. State, 876 S.W.2d 877, **832, 934, 953**
Burleson v. State, 802 S.W.2d 429, **709, 822, 823, 824, 1047, 1049**
Burlington N. R.R. v. Harvey, 717 S.W.2d 371, **710**
Burnett v. Rutledge, 284 S.W.2d 944, **307**
Burnett v. State, 642 S.W.2d 765, **402, 410, 536, 542, 545**
Burnett v. State, 754 S.W.2d 437, **823, 861**
Burnett v. State, 88 S.W.3d 633, **61**
Burnett Ranches, Ltd. v. Cano Pet., Inc., 289 S.W.3d 862, **974**
Burns v. Baylor Health Care Sys., 125 S.W.3d 589, **732**
Burns v. Bridge Eng'g Corp., 465 S.W.2d 427, **765**
Burns v. State, 556 S.W.2d 270, **454**
Burns v. State, 122 S.W.3d 434, **892, 893**
Burroughs Wellcome Co. v. Crye, 907 S.W.2d 497, **900**
Burrous v. Knotts, 482 S.W.2d 358, **356**
Burton v. Cravey, 759 S.W.2d 160, **393**
Burton v. Kirby, 775 S.W.2d 834, **268**
Burton v. Lowry, 77 S.W.2d 1059, **978**
Burton v. State, 471 S.W.2d 817, **360**
Burton v. State, 762 S.W.2d 724, **286**
Bush v. State, 697 S.W.2d 397, **63**
Bushell v. Dean, 781 S.W.2d 652, **225, 226**
Bushell v. Dean, 803 S.W.2d 711, **226**
Busse v. Pac. Cattle Feeding Fund No. 1, Ltd., 896 S.W.2d 807, **827**
Bustamante v. Ponte, ___ S.W.3d ___ (No. 15-0509; 9-29-17), **718, 719, 727**
Butler v. De La Cruz, 812 S.W.2d 422, **845**
Butler v. Hide-A-Way Lake Club, Inc., 730 S.W.2d 405, **829**
Butler v. State, 645 S.W.2d 820, **444, 449**
Butler v. State, 872 S.W.2d 227, **91**
Butler v. State, 890 S.W.2d 951, **573, 620, 624, 627**
Butler v. State, 936 S.W.2d 453, **291**
Butler v. State, 459 S.W.3d 595, **962, 966, 967, 968, 970, 988**
Buxton v. State, ___ S.W.3d ___ (No. 01-15-00857-CR; 7-6-17), **213, 218, 375**
Bynum v. State, 767 S.W.2d 769, **677**

CASE INDEX

CASE INDEX

CASE INDEX

Dorsett v. State, 761 S.W.2d 432, **57, 741**
Dorsey v. State, 24 S.W.3d 921, **887**
Dorsey v. State, 117 S.W.3d 332, **887**
Dotson v. State, 28 S.W.3d 53, **601**
Double Diamond, Inc. v. Van Tyne, 109 S.W.3d 848, **1038**
Douglas v. Am. Title Co., 196 S.W.3d 876, **125**
Dover v. Baker, Brown, Sharman & Parker, 859 S.W.2d 441, **928**
Dow Chem. Co. v. Francis, 46 S.W.3d 237, **636**
Dowling v. United States, 493 U.S. 342, **272**
Downen v. Tex. Gulf Shrimp Co., 846 S.W.2d 506, **657**
Downing v. State, 61 Tex. Crim. 519, 136 S.W. 471, **415**
Downing v. State, 113 Tex. Crim. 235, 20 S.W.2d 202, **560**
Dowthitt v. State, 931 S.W.2d 244, **841, 842**
Doyle v. State, 779 S.W.2d 492, **866**
Doyle v. State, 875 S.W.2d 21, **698**
Draheim v. State, 916 S.W.2d 593, **369**
Drake v. Holstead, 757 S.W.2d 909, **123, 130, 131**
Draper v. State, 596 S.W.2d 855, **539**
Drew v. State, 147 Tex. Crim. 29, 177 S.W.2d 787, **1056**
Drew v. State, 76 S.W.3d 436, **877**
Dreyer v. State, 309 S.W.3d 751, **812**
Driggers v. State, 940 S.W.2d 699, **81, 612**
Drilex Sys., Inc. v. Flores, 961 S.W.2d 209, **674**
Drilex Sys., Inc. v. Flores, 1 S.W.3d 112, **669, 670, 671, 745**
Druery v. State, 225 S.W.3d 491, **982**
DuBose v. State, 774 S.W.2d 328, **825**
Duckett v. State, 797 S.W.2d 906, **702, 720, 745, 757**
Duderstadt Surveyors Supply, Inc. v. Alamo Express, Inc., 686 S.W.2d 351, **131**
Dudley v. State, 730 S.W.2d 51, **489, 521**
Dudley v. Strain, 130 S.W. 778, **196**
Duff v. Yelin, 751 S.W.2d 175, **720**
Dufrene v. State, 853 S.W.2d 86, **561, 563**
Duhon v. State, 136 Tex. Crim. 404, 125 S.W.2d 550, **183**
Duke v. State, 365 S.W.3d 722, **554**
Duluth News-Tribune v. Mesabi Publ'g Co., 84 F.3d 1093, **134**
Duncan v. Bd. of Disciplinary Appeals, 898 S.W.2d 759, **392, 417**
Duncan v. State, 138 Tex. Crim. 172, 135 S.W.2d 111, **585**
Duncan v. State, 140 Tex. Crim. 606, 146 S.W.2d 749, **77**
Duncan v. State, 899 S.W.2d 279, **194**
Duncan Dev., Inc. v. Haney, 634 S.W.2d 811, **904, 1060, 1061**
Dunkins v. State, 838 S.W.2d 898, **585**
Dunkle v. State, 139 P.3d 228, **1003, 1004, 1007**
Dunn v. State, 979 S.W.2d 403, **283**
Dunnington v. State, 740 S.W.2d 896, **701**

Durbin v. Dal-Briar Corp., 871 S.W.2d 263, **221, 229, 588**
Durflinger v. Artiles, 727 F.2d 888, **430, 431**
Durham v. State, 956 S.W.2d 62, **726, 914**
Durst v. Hill Country Mem'l Hosp., 70 S.W.3d 233, **498**
Dutton v. Dutton, 18 S.W.3d 849, **132**
Duval Cty. Ranch Co. v. Alamo Lumber Co., 663 S.W.2d 627, **320, 391**
Dyer v. Metallic Bldg. Co., 410 S.W.2d 56, **174**
DZM, Inc. v. Garren, 467 S.W.3d 700, **694**

E

E. Tex. Theatres, Inc. v. Rutledge, 453 S.W.2d 466, **158**
Eagle Trucking Co. v. Tex. Bitulithic Co., 612 S.W.2d 503, **121, 122, 124, 137**
Earls v. State, 715 S.W.2d 731, **831**
Earnhart v. State, 582 S.W.2d 444, **983**
Earthman's, Inc. v. Earthman, 526 S.W.2d 192, **445, 450**
Easdon v. State, 552 S.W.2d 153, **182**
Easley v. State, 837 S.W.2d 854, **462**
Easley v. State, 986 S.W.2d 264, **885**
Easter v. McDonald, 903 S.W.2d 887, **527, 529**
Easterling v. State, 710 S.W.2d 569, **641**
Ebers v. State, 129 Tex. Crim. 287, 86 S.W.2d 761, **560**
Echols v. Wells, 510 S.W.2d 916, **74**
Eckels v. Davis, 111 S.W.3d 687, **564**
Eckman v. State, 600 S.W.2d 937, **182**
Eckmann v. Bd. of Educ., 106 F.R.D. 70, **460, 463**
Eckmann v. Des Rosiers, 940 S.W.2d 394, **152, 153**
Eddy v. Bosley, 34 Tex. Civ. App. 116, 78 S.W. 565, **445, 449**
Edgeworth v. Wilson, 113 S.W.3d 559, **108**
Editorial Caballero, S.A. de C.V. v. Playboy Enters., Inc., 359 S.W.3d 318, **588, 589**
Edmond v. State, 911 S.W.2d 487, **476**
Edmondson v. State, 399 S.W.3d 607, **877, 879**
Edwards v. State, 156 Tex. Crim. 146, 239 S.W.2d 618, **200**
Edwards v. State, 551 S.W.2d 731, **983, 984, 1001, 1043, 1044**
Edwards v. State, 672 S.W.2d 10, **1053**
Edwards v. State, 807 S.W.2d 338, **207**
Edwards v. State, 883 S.W.2d 692, **628**
Edwards v. Tex. Emp't Comm'n, 936 S.W.2d 462, **857, 859**
Edwards v. Williams, 291 S.W.2d 783, **890**
Eggert v. State, 395 S.W.3d 240, **873**
E.I. du Pont de Nemours & Co. v. Robinson, 923 S.W.2d 549, **88, 89, 113, 704, 705, 727, 728, 729, 730, 731, 732, 733, 734, 735, 736, 737, 738, 744, 762, 768, 769, 770, 913, 917**
El Chico Corp. v. Poole, 732 S.W.2d 306, **118**
Elbaor v. Smith, 845 S.W.2d 240, **331**
Elbar, Inc. v. Claussen, 774 S.W.2d 45, **667, 669**
Elizarraras v. Bank of El Paso, 631 F.2d 366, **568**
Elizondo v. Krist, 415 S.W.3d 259, **718, 736**
Ellingsworth v. State, 487 S.W.2d 108, **658**

Fairow v. State, 943 S.W.2d 895, **560, 570, 689, 690, 692, 697, 698, 758**
Faison v. State, 59 S.W.3d 230, **274**
Fant v. Howell, 410 S.W.2d 294, **848**
Farese v. United States, 428 F.2d 178, **595**
Farley v. Farley, 731 S.W.2d 733, **822, 1013**
Farm Servs., Inc. v. Gonzales, 756 S.W.2d 747, **68**
Farner v. Paccar, Inc., 562 F.2d 518, **308, 715**
Farnum v. Colbert, 293 A.2d 279, **323**
Farr v. Wright, 833 S.W.2d 597, **207**
Farr v. Zoning Bd. of Appeals, 95 A.2d 792, **1056**
Fasken v. Fasken, 113 Tex. 464, 260 S.W. 701, **439, 444, 446, 449**
Fearance v. State, 771 S.W.2d 486, **251**
Fears v. State, 479 S.W.3d 315, **576, 680**
Fed. Open Mkt. Comm. v. Merrill, 443 U.S. 340, **466**
Fed. Pac. Elec. Co. v. Woodend, 735 S.W.2d 887, **312**
Fed. Trade Comm'n v. Hughes, 710 F. Supp. 1520, **982**
Fed. Underwriters Exch. v. Cost, 132 Tex. 299, 123 S.W.2d 332, **756**
Fed. Underwriters Exch. v. Ener, 126 S.W.2d 769, **1051**
Federated Dep't Stores, Inc. v. Esser, 409 N.Y.S.2d 353, **445**
Felan v. State, 44 S.W.3d 249, **610, 661**
Feldman v. State, 71 S.W.3d 738, **621**
Felix v. Gonzalez, 87 S.W.3d 574, **302**
Felker v. Petrolon, Inc., 929 S.W.2d 460, **188**
Fenberg v. Rosenthal, 109 N.E.2d 402, **329**
Fender v. St. Louis Sw. Ry. Co., 513 S.W.2d 131, **111, 121, 122, 134**
Fenje v. Feld, 301 F. Supp. 2d 781, **986**
Ferguson v. State, 97 S.W.3d 293, **875**
Ferrell v. State, 429 S.W.2d 901, **454**
Ferrell v. State, 968 S.W.2d 471, **250**
Few v. Charter Oak Fire Ins., 463 S.W.2d 424, **207, 450**
Fibreboard Corp. v. Pool, 813 S.W.2d 658, **917, 922, 999**
Fid. Union Cas. Co. v. Koonce, 51 S.W.2d 777, **213**
Fielder v. State, 756 S.W.2d 309, **716**
Fields v. Brown, 503 F.3d 755, **594, 595**
Fields v. State, 500 S.W.2d 500, **559, 561, 562**
Fields v. State, 932 S.W.2d 97, **717, 741**
Fields v. State, 966 S.W.2d 736, **74**
Fields v. State, 515 S.W.3d 47, **214, 219, 238, 872, 875**
Fieve v. Emmeck, 78 N.W.2d 343, **331**
Figueroa v. State, 740 S.W.2d 537, **860**
Fina Oil & Chem. Co. v. Salinas, 750 S.W.2d 32, **533**
Finch v. Finch, 825 S.W.2d 218, **227**
Finck Cigar Co. v. Campbell, 134 Tex. 250, 133 S.W.2d 759, **351, 356**
Fire Ass'n v. Coomer, 158 S.W.2d 355, **928**
Firestone Tire & Rubber Co. v. Battle, 745 S.W.2d 909, **231**
Firo v. State, 654 S.W.2d 503, **455**
First Bank v. Hill, 151 S.W. 652, **445, 451**
First Nat'l Bank v. Thomas, 402 S.W.2d 890, **168**

First Nat'l Bank of Amarillo v. Jarnigan, 794 S.W.2d 54, **138**
First Sw. Lloyds Ins. v. MacDowell, 769 S.W.2d 954, **212, 278, 749, 750, 772, 773**
Fischer v. State, 252 S.W.3d 375, **872, 873, 874, 875, 908, 913**
Fischer v. State, 268 S.W.3d 552, **92, 93, 272**
Fish v. Ga.-Pac. Corp., 779 F.2d 836, **311, 312**
Fisher v. State, 511 S.W.2d 506, **455**
Fisher v. United States, 425 U.S. 391, **391, 410, 417**
Fisher v. Vassar Coll., 114 F.3d 1332, **156**
Fisk v. State, 510 S.W.3d 165, **375**
Fistere, Inc. v. Helz, 226 A.2d 578, **1039**
Fitts v. State, 982 S.W.2d 175, **726**
Fitzgerald v. Advanced Spine Fixation Sys., Inc., 996 S.W.2d 864, **114**
Fitzgerald v. A.L. Burbank & Co., 451 F.2d 670, **515**
Five Star Int'l Holdings Inc. v. Thomson, Inc., 324 S.W.3d 160, **732**
Flaminio v. Honda Motor Co., 733 F.2d 463, **309, 312**
Fleming v. Kinney ex rel. Shelton, 395 S.W.3d 917, **709, 717, 758**
Fleming v. State, 819 S.W.2d 237, **894**
Fletcher v. Minn. Mining & Mfg. Co., 57 S.W.3d 602, **59, 76, 78, 82**
Fletcher v. State, 852 S.W.2d 271, **194**
Fletcher v. State, 960 S.W.2d 694, **560, 825, 854, 860, 863**
Fletcher v. State, 214 S.W.3d 5, **125**
Fletcher v. Weir, 455 U.S. 603, **551**
Flora v. Hamilton, 81 F.R.D. 576, **505**
Flores v. Dosher, 622 S.W.2d 573, **581**
Flores v. Flores, 847 S.W.2d 648, **441**
Flores v. Fourth Ct. of Appeals, 777 S.W.2d 38, **428**
Flores v. Hovel, 125 S.W. 606, **999, 1000**
Flores v. State, 509 S.W.2d 580, **575**
Flores v. State, 920 S.W.2d 347, **77**
Flores v. State, 48 S.W.3d 397, **837**
Flores v. State, 170 S.W.3d 722, **792**
Flores v. State, 299 S.W.3d 843, **574, 575**
Flores v. State, 513 S.W.3d 146, **606, 720**
Flores v. State, No. 14-06-00813-CR (memo op.; 10-23-08), **128**
Flowers v. State, 220 S.W.3d 919, **998, 1018**
Fluellen v. State, 104 S.W.3d 152, **984**
Fojtik v. First Nat'l Bank, 752 S.W.2d 669, **857**
Fonseca v. State, 908 S.W.2d 519, **934**
Fontenot v. State, 708 S.W.2d 555, **850**
Forbes v. Lanzl, 9 S.W.3d 895, **264**
Ford v. Carpenter, 147 Tex. 447, 216 S.W.2d 558, **351**
Ford v. Roberts, 478 S.W.2d 129, **566**
Ford v. State, 617 S.E.2d 262, **990**
Ford v. State, 484 S.W.2d 727, **275**
Ford v. State, 919 S.W.2d 107, **72**
Ford v. State, 305 S.W.3d 530, **51, 87, 88, 89**
Ford v. State, 313 S.W.3d 434, **623**
Ford v. Wainwright, 477 U.S. 399, **115**

Ford Motor Co. v. Aguiniga, 9 S.W.3d 252, **708**
Ford Motor Co. v. Castillo, 279 S.W.3d 656, **582, 588**
Ford Motor Co. v. Leggat, 904 S.W.2d 643, **384, 385, 387, 397**
Ford Motor Co. v. Pool, 688 S.W.2d 879, **212**
Forrest v. State, 805 S.W.2d 462, **866**
Fort Worth & Denver City Ry. Co. v. Travis, 45 Tex. Civ. App. 117, 99 S.W. 1141, **635**
Fort Worth Belt Ry. v. Jones, 106 Tex. 345, 166 S.W. 1130, **186**
Fort Worth Hotel Co. v. Waggoman, 126 S.W.2d 578, **99**
Forte v. State, 935 S.W.2d 172, **116**
Foster v. Bailey, 691 S.W.2d 801, **74, 76**
Foster v. Buchele, 213 S.W.2d 738, **417**
Foster v. State, 142 Tex. Crim. 615, 155 S.W.2d 938, **559**
Foster v. State, 639 S.W.2d 691, **183**
Foster v. State, 779 S.W.2d 845, **106, 109, 822, 823**
Foster v. State, 909 S.W.2d 86, **717**
Found. Reserve Ins. v. Starnes, 479 S.W.2d 330, **691**
Fowler v. State, 171 Tex. Crim. 600, 352 S.W.2d 838, **70, 202**
Fowler v. State, 517 S.W.3d 167, **966, 985**
Fox v. Order of United Commercial Travelers of Am., 192 F.2d 844, **977**
Fox v. State, 115 S.W.3d 550, **75, 76, 199, 281, 612, 710**
Fox v. Taylor Diving & Salvage Co., 694 F.2d 1349, **852**
Fraga v. Drake, 276 S.W.3d 55, **564, 565**
France v. State, 148 Tex. Crim. 341, 187 S.W.2d 80, **991**
Francis v. Franklin, 471 U.S. 307, **175, 176, 177, 178**
Francis v. State, 445 S.W.3d 307, **295**
Franco v. State, 25 S.W.3d 26, **726**
Frank v. Cty. of Hudson, 924 F. Supp. 620, **372**
Frank v. State, 992 S.W.2d 756, **218**
Frankel v. Lull Eng'g Co., 334 F. Supp. 913, **765**
Franklin v. Smalldridge, 616 S.W.2d 655, **147**
Franklin v. State, 733 S.W.2d 537, **667**
Franklin v. State, 858 S.W.2d 537, **874**
Franklin v. State, 992 S.W.2d 698, **935**
Franks v. State, 90 S.W.3d 771, **579**
Frazier v. State, 600 S.W.2d 271, **865**
Fredericksburg Indus., Inc. v. Franklin Int'l, Inc., 911 S.W.2d 518, **223, 231**
Freedom Commc'ns, Inc. v. Coronado, 372 S.W.3d 621, **120, 126, 130**
Freeman v. Am. Motorists Ins., 53 S.W.3d 710, **904**
Freeman v. Bianchi, 820 S.W.2d 853, **418, 421, 533, 535, 540**
Freeman v. Commercial Union Assur. Co., 317 S.W.2d 563, **1056**
Freeman v. State, 786 S.W.2d 56, **440, 447, 448, 454**
Freeman v. State, 230 S.W.3d 392, **441**

Freestone Cty. Title & Abstract Co. v. Johnson, 594 S.W.2d 817, **851**
Freidus v. First Nat'l Bank of Council Bluffs, 928 F.2d 793, **326**
Freiermuth v. PPG Indus., Inc., 218 F.R.D. 694, **378, 406, 429**
Fry v. State, 915 S.W.2d 554, **260**
Frye v. United States, 293 F. 1013, **233, 234, 722, 723, 725, 770**
Fryer v. State, 68 S.W.3d 628, **49, 864**
F-Star Socorro, L.P. v. City of El Paso, 281 S.W.3d 103, **1013**
Fuentes v. State, 775 S.W.2d 64, **458**
Fulcher v. Young, 189 S.W.2d 28, **167**
Fuller v. Middleton, 453 S.W.2d 372, **166**
Fuller v. State, 829 S.W.2d 191, **91**
Fuller v. State, 835 S.W.2d 768, **534**
Fuller v. State, 30 S.W.3d 441, **125**
Fuller-Austin Insulation Co. v. Bilder, 960 S.W.2d 914, **946**
Fullick v. City of Baytown, 820 S.W.2d 943, **1019, 1027**
Fulmer v. Rider, 635 S.W.2d 875, **566**
Fultz v. State, 770 S.W.2d 595, **711**
Fund of Funds, Ltd. v. Arthur Andersen & Co., 545 F. Supp. 1314, **716**

G

G. & H. Equip. Co. v. Alexander, 533 S.W.2d 872, **661**
GAB Bus. Servs., Inc. v. Moore, 829 S.W.2d 345, **643**
Gaffney v. State, 937 S.W.2d 540, **628**
Gaffney v. State, 940 S.W.2d 682, **623**
Gainer v. Cotton, 49 Tex. 101, **1030**
Gaitan v. State, 905 S.W.2d 703, **827**
Gallo v. State, 239 S.W.3d 757, **69, 236, 731**
Galloway v. United States, 319 U.S. 372, **189**
Galvez v. State, 962 S.W.2d 203, **246**
Gamboa v. State, 296 S.W.3d 574, **273**
Gammill v. Jack Williams Chevrolet, Inc., 972 S.W.2d 713, **234, 706, 707, 721, 729, 732, 735, 736**
Gant v. State, 153 S.W.3d 294, **881**
Garay v. Cty. of Bexar, 810 S.W.2d 760, **488**
Garay v. State, 954 S.W.2d 59, **1049**
Garcia v. Peeples, 734 S.W.2d 343, **426, 466**
Garcia v. Sky Climber, Inc., 470 S.W.2d 261, **656**
Garcia v. State, 595 S.W.2d 538, **54**
Garcia v. State, 775 S.W.2d 879, **55**
Garcia v. State, 819 S.W.2d 667, **252**
Garcia v. State, 868 S.W.2d 337, **914, 915**
Garcia v. State, 887 S.W.2d 862, **101**
Garcia v. State, 126 S.W.3d 921, **892, 908, 957**
Garcia v. State, 201 S.W.3d 695, **290**
Garcia v. State, 246 S.W.3d 121, **885, 914**
Garden Ridge, L.P. v. Clear Lake, L.P., 504 S.W.3d 428, **74**
Gardner v. Best W. Int'l, Inc., 929 S.W.2d 474, **147**
Gardner v. City of Columbia Police Dep't, 57 S.E.2d 308, **1064**
Gardner v. Gen. Motors Corp., 507 F.2d 525, **708**

CASE INDEX

Handspur v. State, 792 S.W.2d 239, **997**

Handy v. State, 189 S.W.3d 296, **180**

Haney v. Purcell Co., 796 S.W.2d 782, **315**

Hankins v. State, 180 S.W.3d 177, **625**

Hanks v. Gulf, Colo. & Santa Fe Ry. Co., 159 Tex. 311, 320 S.W.2d 333, **227**

Hannum v. Gen. Life & Acc. Ins., 745 S.W.2d 500, **996**

Hanover Fire Ins. v. Slaughter, 111 S.W.2d 362, **969**

Hanover Ins. v. Hoch, 469 S.W.2d 717, **826**

Hansard v. Pepsi-Cola Metro. Bottling Co., 865 F.2d 1461, **700**

Hanson Sw. Corp. v. Dal-Mac Constr. Co., 554 S.W.2d 712, **1062**

Haq v. State, 445 S.W.3d 330, **906**

Harang v. Aetna Life Ins., 400 S.W.2d 810, **860**

Hardeman v. State, 552 S.W.2d 433, **472**

Hardeman v. State, 868 S.W.2d 404, **617, 618**

Hardesty v. State, 656 S.W.2d 73, **183**

Hardin v. State, 20 S.W.3d 84, **709**

Hardman v. State, 614 S.W.2d 123, **169**

Hardy v. Johns-Manville Sales Corp., 681 F.2d 334, **125**

Hardy v. State, 71 S.W.2d 535, **904**

Hargraves v. State, 738 S.W.2d 743, **278**

Hargrove v. Fort Worth Elevator Co., 276 S.W. 426, **681**

Hargrove v. State, 211 S.W.3d 379, **289, 290**

Harlandale Indep. Sch. Dist. v. Cornyn, 25 S.W.3d 328, **394, 403**

Harmon v. State, 889 S.W.2d 521, **294**

Harnett v. State, 38 S.W.3d 650, **88, 687, 704, 709**

Harnischfeger Corp. v. Stone, 814 S.W.2d 263, **431**

Harper v. Am. Motors Corp., 672 S.W.2d 44, **207**

Harper v. Highway Motor Freight Lines, 89 S.W.2d 448, **354**

Harper v. Killion, 345 S.W.2d 309, **121**

Harper v. Killion, 162 Tex. 481, 348 S.W.2d 521, **111, 119, 121, 122, 129, 132, 135, 137**

Harper v. State, 686 S.W.2d 738, **486**

Harper v. State, 930 S.W.2d 625, **293, 633**

Harper & Row Publ'rs, Inc. v. Decker, 423 F.2d 487, **396**

Harrell v. Atl. Ref. Co., 339 S.W.2d 548, **413**

Harrell v. State, 39 Tex. Crim. 204, 45 S.W. 581, **681**

Harrell v. State, 884 S.W.2d 154, **92, 93, 272**

Harrington v. State, 385 S.W.2d 411, **1001**

Harrington v. State, 547 S.W.2d 616, **103**

Harrington Mfg. Co. v. Powell Mfg. Co., 216 S.E.2d 379, **466**

Harris v. Borne, 933 S.W.2d 535, **123**

Harris v. New York, 401 U.S. 222, **96, 659**

Harris v. Rivera, 454 U.S. 339, **810**

Harris v. Smith, 372 F.2d 806, **746**

Harris v. State, 13 P.3d 489, **1004**

Harris v. State, 72 Tex. Crim. 117, 161 S.W. 125, **407, 447, 538**

Harris v. State, 727 S.W.2d 537, **865**

Harris v. State, 736 S.W.2d 166, **874**

Harris v. State, 738 S.W.2d 207, **128**

Harris v. State, 790 S.W.2d 568, **61, 273, 289**

Harris v. State, 846 S.W.2d 960, **901, 921**

Harris v. State, 122 S.W.3d 871, **672**

Harris v. State, 133 S.W.3d 760, **768, 878**

Harris v. State, 152 S.W.3d 786, **1003**

Harris v. State, 475 S.W.3d 395, **375**

Harris Cty. v. Jenkins, 678 S.W.2d 639, **618, 624**

Harris Cty. Appr. Dist. v. Hous. 8th Wonder Prop., L.P., 395 S.W.3d 245, **706**

Harrison v. State, 929 S.W.2d 80, **672**

Harrison v. State, 241 S.W.3d 23, **253, 255, 257**

Hart v. Gossum, 995 S.W.2d 958, **394**

Hart v. State, 152 Tex. Crim. 537, 215 S.W.2d 883, **187**

Hart v. Van Zandt, 399 S.W.2d 791, **743**

Hartford Acc. & Indem. Co. v. Hale, 400 S.W.2d 310, **881**

Hartford Acc. & Indem. Co. v. McCardell, 369 S.W.2d 331, **846**

Hartford Acc. & Indem. Co. v. Williams, 516 S.W.2d 425, **603**

Hartman v. State, 946 S.W.2d 60, **88, 89, 730**

Hartman v. Trio Transp., Inc., 937 S.W.2d 575, **858**

Hartsfield v. State, 200 S.W.3d 813, **971, 977**

Hartsfield v. State, 305 S.W.3d 859, **271**

Harvey v. State, 97 S.W.3d 162, **409**

Harvey v. State, 123 S.W.3d 623, **877**

Harville v. Siebenlist, 582 S.W.2d 621, **929**

Hathcock v. Hankook Tire Am. Corp., 330 S.W.3d 733, **311, 312**

Hatley v. State, 533 S.W.2d 27, **261**

Haughton v. State, 805 S.W.2d 405, **666, 841**

Havins v. First Nat'l Bank, 919 S.W.2d 177, **122**

Haw. Psychiatric Soc'y v. Ariyoshi, 481 F. Supp. 1028, **519, 520**

Hawkins v. State, 871 S.W.2d 539, **290**

Hawkins v. State, 89 S.W.3d 674, **1015**

Hawthorne v. Eckerson Co., 77 F.2d 844, **322**

Hayden v. State, 753 S.W.2d 461, **905**

Hayden v. State, 13 S.W.3d 69, **293**

Hayden v. State, 66 S.W.3d 269, **293, 295**

Hayden v. State, 155 S.W.3d 640, **128**

Hayden v. State, 296 S.W.3d 549, **203, 287, 291**

Hayes v. Carroll, 314 S.W.3d 494, **708, 711**

Hayes v. Coleman, 61 N.W.2d 634, **331**

Hayes v. Pennock, 192 S.W.2d 169, **408, 422**

Hayes v. State, 740 S.W.2d 887, **953**

Hayes v. State, 85 S.W.3d 809, **237**

Hayes v. State, 124 S.W.3d 781, **261**

Hayes v. State, 484 S.W.3d 554, **586**

Haygood v. De Escabedo, 356 S.W.3d 390, **1029**

H.E. Butt Grocery Co. v. Heaton, 547 S.W.2d 75, **690**

H.E. Butt Grocery Co. v. Pais, 955 S.W.2d 384, **581, 593**

Head v. State, 4 S.W.3d 258, **833**

Head v. State, 299 S.W.3d 414, **413, 416**

Heard v. State, 995 S.W.2d 317, **477**
Hedicke v. State, 779 S.W.2d 837, **249**
Hedrick v. State, 473 S.W.3d 824, **192, 199, 200, 267, 270**
Heidelberg v. State, 36 S.W.3d 668, **67**
Heidelberg v. State, 144 S.W.3d 535, **68, 69**
Heitman v. State, 815 S.W.2d 681, **206**
Held v. State, 948 S.W.2d 45, **745, 747, 765**
Helena Chem. Co. v. Wilkins, 47 S.W.3d 486, **707, 721, 732, 757**
Helm v. Swan, 61 S.W.3d 493, **729**
Helton v. State, 670 S.W.2d 644, **418**
Henderson v. State, 788 S.W.2d 621, **997**
Henderson v. State, 906 S.W.2d 589, **197, 201**
Henderson v. State, 962 S.W.2d 544, **416, 418, 419**
Henderson v. State, 77 S.W.3d 321, **955**
Hendrick v. State, 731 S.W.2d 147, **850**
Hendricks v. Todora, 722 S.W.2d 458, **713**
Henley v. State, 493 S.W.3d 77, **193, 194, 195, 201, 207, 208, 215, 270**
Henriksen v. State, 500 S.W.2d 491, **1033**
Henry v. Butts, 591 So. 2d 849, **120**
Henry v. Felici, 758 S.W.2d 836, **322**
Henry v. Mrs. Baird's Bakeries, 475 S.W.2d 288, **231**
Henry v. State, 509 S.W.3d 915, **998, 1034**
Hensarling v. State, 829 S.W.2d 168, **578**
Henson v. State, 794 S.W.2d 385, **339**
Hereford v. State, 444 S.W.3d 346, **796, 799**
Herfurth v. City of Dall., 410 S.W.2d 453, **204**
Heritage on the San Gabriel Homeowners Ass'n v. Tex. Comm'n on Envtl. Quality, 393 S.W.3d 417, **124, 153**
Hernandez v. Hous. Lighting & Power Co., 795 S.W.2d 775, **124, 130**
Hernandez v. State, 484 S.W.2d 754, **289**
Hernandez v. State, 530 S.W.2d 563, **1000**
Hernandez v. State, 643 S.W.2d 397, **561, 643**
Hernandez v. State, 772 S.W.2d 274, **756**
Hernandez v. State, 774 S.W.2d 319, **259, 263, 584**
Hernandez v. State, 791 S.W.2d 301, **669**
Hernandez v. State, 800 S.W.2d 523, **250, 251**
Hernandez v. State, 897 S.W.2d 488, **612, 630**
Hernandez v. State, 914 S.W.2d 226, **286, 295**
Hernandez v. State, 939 S.W.2d 665, **906**
Hernandez v. State, 956 S.W.2d 699, **474, 475**
Hernandez v. State, 53 S.W.3d 742, **70, 735**
Hernandez v. State, 116 S.W.3d 26, **87, 88, 116, 124, 726, 738, 1003**
Hernandez v. State, 171 S.W.3d 347, **291, 932**
Hernandez v. State, 203 S.W.3d 477, **277, 278**
Hernandez v. State, 205 S.W.3d 555, **458**
Hernandez v. State, 327 S.W.3d 200, **194**
Hernandez v. State, 351 S.W.3d 156, **253**
Hernandez v. State, 508 S.W.3d 752, **84**
Hernandez v. State, ___ S.W.3d ___ (No. 01-16-00755-CR; 8-10-17), **798, 799**
Hernandez v. State, No. 05-13-00202-CR (memo op.; 1-7-14), **248**

Herrera v. FMC Corp., 672 S.W.2d 5, **717**
Herrera v. State, 462 S.W.2d 597, **559**
Herrera v. State, 367 S.W.3d 762, **807**
Herring v. State, 202 S.W.3d 764, **845**
Herschensohn v. Weisman, 119 A. 705, **356**
Hervey v. Edens, 69 Tex. 420, 6 S.W. 306, **1030**
Herzing v. Metro. Life Ins., 907 S.W.2d 574, **857, 993**
Hess v. State, 20 P.3d 1121, **372**
Hiatt v. State, 319 S.W.3d 115, **610**
Hickman v. Taylor, 329 U.S. 495, **48, 424, 426, 429, 430**
Hicks v. State, 15 S.W.3d 626, **585**
Hickson v. Martinez, 707 S.W.2d 919, **1040, 1058**
Hiebert v. Weiss, 622 S.W.2d 150, **403, 404**
Higginbotham v. Gen. Life & Acc. Ins., 796 S.W.2d 695, **124**
Higginbotham v. State, 356 S.W.3d 584, **272**
Higgins v. Gen. Motors Corp., 465 S.W.2d 898, **313**
Higgins v. State, 924 S.W.2d 739, **569**
Hightower v. State, 629 S.W.2d 920, **441**
Hill v. Robinson, 592 S.W.2d 376, **930**
Hill v. Rolleri, 615 F.2d 886, **59**
Hill v. State, 748 S.W.2d 314, **260**
Hill v. State, 783 S.W.2d 257, **105, 109**
Hill v. State, 817 S.W.2d 816, **833**
Hill v. State, 392 S.W.3d 850, **145, 237, 716, 844**
Hilton v. State, 149 Tex. Crim. 22, 191 S.W.2d 875, **538**
Hinds v. State, 970 S.W.2d 33, **375**
Hines v. Brandon Steel Decks, Inc., 886 F.2d 299, **917**
Hines v. Nelson, 547 S.W.2d 378, **297**
Hines v. State, 3 S.W.3d 618, **585, 586, 593**
Hines v. State, 38 S.W.3d 805, **726**
Hinojosa v. State, 780 S.W.2d 299, **621**
Hinojosa v. State, 788 S.W.2d 594, **660**
Hirschberg v. State, 117 Tex. Crim. 504, 35 S.W.2d 430, **659**
Hislop v. State, 64 S.W.3d 544, **968, 982**
Hispanic Broad. Corp. v. Educ. Media Found., No. CV-02-7134 (order; 10-30-03), **1020**
Hitch v. Pima Cty. Super. Ct., 708 P.2d 72, **416**
Hitt v. State, 53 S.W.3d 697, **216**
Hobson v. Moore, 734 S.W.2d 340, **379, 472**
Hochheim Prairie Farm Mut. Ins. v. Burnett, 698 S.W.2d 271, **693**
Hodges, Grant & Kaufmann v. U.S. Gov't, 768 F.2d 719, **408**
Hoefling v. Hambleton, 84 Tex. 517, 19 S.W. 689, **1064**
Hogan v. State, 954 S.W.2d 875, **127**
Hogan v. State, 440 S.W.3d 211, **557**
Hogue v. Kroger Store No. 107, 875 S.W.2d 477, **498**
Hohn v. State, 951 S.W.2d 535, **295**
Holbert v. State, 457 S.W.2d 286, **641, 643**
Holden v. Capri Lighting, Inc., 960 S.W.2d 831, **145**
Holden v. State, 44 Tex. Crim. 382, 71 S.W. 600, **415**
Holder v. State, ___ S.W.3d ___ (No. 05-15-00818-CR; 8-19-16), **788**

Holder v. United States, 150 U.S. 91, **673**
Holgin v. State, 480 S.W.2d 405, **258, 617**
Holiday Inns, Inc. v. State, 931 S.W.2d 614, **226**
Holland v. State, 713 A.2d 364, **818**
Hollinger v. State, 911 S.W.2d 35, **561, 562**
Hollingsworth v. King, 810 S.W.2d 772, **153**
Holloman v. State, 942 S.W.2d 773, **672**
Holloway v. State, 148 Tex. Crim. 33, 184 S.W.2d 479, **103**
Holloway v. State, 613 S.W.2d 497, **86, 692, 703, 708, 746, 748**
Holloway v. State, 666 S.W.2d 104, **123, 125**
Holloway v. State, 751 S.W.2d 866, **360**
Holman v. Cayce, 873 F.2d 944, **472**
Holmes v. State, 135 S.W.3d 178, **124, 709**
Holmes v. State, 248 S.W.3d 194, **64, 79**
Holt v. State, 912 S.W.2d 294, **248**
Holt v. United States, 342 F.2d 163, **199**
Holz v. State, 320 S.W.3d 344, **694**
Home Ins. v. Balt. Whs. Co., 93 U.S. 527, **324**
Home Ins. v. Banda, 736 S.W.2d 812, **765**
Honea v. State, 585 S.W.2d 681, **571**
Hood v. Phillips, 554 S.W.2d 160, **484, 485, 718**
Hood v. State, 944 S.W.2d 743, **365, 366, 1040**
Hooker v. State, 932 S.W.2d 712, **984**
Hooper v. State, 214 S.W.3d 9, **187, 188, 189**
Hopfer v. Commercial Ins., 606 S.W.2d 354, **167**
Hopkins v. State, 480 S.W.2d 212, **605, 704, 719, 756, 757**
Hoptowit v. Ray, 682 F.2d 1237, **858**
Horizon/CMS Healthcare Corp. v. Auld, 34 S.W.3d 887, **99**
Horne v. State, 508 S.W.2d 643, **95**
Horner v. Rowan Cos., 153 F.R.D. 597, **498**
Horner v. State, 129 S.W.3d 210, **892**
Horning v. Dist. of Columbia, 254 U.S. 135, **141**
Horvath v. Baylor Univ. Med. Ctr., 704 S.W.2d 866, **911**
Hospadales v. McCoy, 513 S.W.3d 724, **707**
Hot Shot Messenger Serv., Inc. v. State, 798 S.W.2d 413, **299, 300**
Houghton v. Port Terminal R.R., 999 S.W.2d 39, **201**
Hous. & T.C. R.R. v. Burke, 55 Tex. 323, **166**
Hous. Chronicle Publ'g Co. v. City of Hous., 531 S.W.2d 177, **472**
Hous. Lighting & Power Co. v. Brooks, 319 S.W.2d 427, **311**
Hous. Lighting & Power Co. v. Taber, 221 S.W.2d 339, **310**
Hous. Oxygen Co. v. Davis, 139 Tex. 1, 161 S.W.2d 474, **872, 873, 875**
Hous. Shell & Concrete Co. v. Kingsley Constructors, Inc., 987 S.W.2d 184, **906**
Hous. Unlimited, Inc. Metal Processing v. Mel Acres Ranch, 443 S.W.3d 820, **721, 722, 732, 736, 738, 769**
House v. Combined Ins., 168 F.R.D. 236, **430**
House v. State, 909 S.W.2d 214, **250, 612**

Houston v. State, 208 S.W.3d 585, **291**
Howard v. Russell, 75 Tex. 171, 12 S.W. 525, **998**
Howard v. State, 599 S.W.2d 597, **63**
Howard v. State, 713 S.W.2d 414, **828**
Howard v. State, 945 S.W.2d 303, **934**
Howard v. State, 962 S.W.2d 119, **862**
Howell v. Burch, 616 S.W.2d 685, **209**
Howell v. State, 146 Tex. Crim. 454, 176 S.W.2d 186, **576**
Howeth v. State, 645 S.W.2d 787, **151**
Howley v. Whipple, 48 N.H. 487, **986**
Huckaby v. A.G. Perry & Son, Inc., 20 S.W.3d 194, **80, 232, 307, 709**
Huddleston v. State, 997 S.W.2d 319, **452**
Huddleston v. United States, 485 U.S. 681, **87, 89, 92, 93, 272, 372**
Hudetts v. McDaniel, No. 07-96-0353-CV (no pub.; 11-18-97), **215**
Hudson v. Aceves, 516 S.W.3d 529, **125**
Hudson v. Hightower, 394 S.W.2d 46, **301**
Hudson v. State, 112 S.W.3d 794, **215, 279, 614**
Hudson v. State, 179 S.W.3d 731, **882**
Huerta v. State, 359 S.W.3d 887, **627**
Huff v. Harrell, 941 S.W.2d 230, **749**
Huff v. State, 560 S.W.2d 652, **829**
Huff v. State, 576 S.W.2d 645, **656**
Huff v. State, 897 S.W.2d 829, **905, 906**
Huff Energy Fund, L.P. v. Longview Energy Co., 482 S.W.3d 184, **144, 146**
Huffman v. Caterpillar Tractor Co., 908 F.2d 1470, **308**
Huffman v. State, 450 S.W.2d 858, **90, 442**
Huffman v. State, 746 S.W.2d 212, **659**
Hughes v. Dopson, 135 S.W.2d 148, **1024**
Hughes v. Meade, 453 S.W.2d 538, **412**
Hughes v. State, 787 S.W.2d 193, **693**
Hughes v. State, 878 S.W.2d 142, **971**
Hughes v. State, 4 S.W.3d 1, **46, 104, 597, 599, 837, 848**
Hughes v. State, 128 S.W.3d 247, **879**
Hughey v. Donovan, 135 S.W.2d 265, **1039**
Huie v. DeShazo, 922 S.W.2d 920, **393, 395, 400, 405, 406, 413, 420, 424, 425, 427**
Huizar v. State, 12 S.W.3d 479, **272**
Hull v. State, 172 S.W.3d 186, **962, 997**
Hullaby v. State, 911 S.W.2d 921, **669**
Humphreys v. Caldwell, 881 S.W.2d 940, **468**
Humphreys v. Caldwell, 888 S.W.2d 469, **425**
Hundere v. Tracy & Cook, 494 S.W.2d 257, **318, 319**
Hunsucker v. Omega Indus., 659 S.W.2d 692, **156, 157**
Hunt v. State, 603 S.W.2d 865, **584**
Hunt v. State, 779 S.W.2d 926, **250**
Hunt v. State, 904 S.W.2d 813, **879**
Hunter v. State, 799 S.W.2d 356, **203**
Hunter v. State, 513 S.W.3d 638, **978**
Hunter v. West, 293 S.W.2d 686, **1020**
Huntley v. Snider, 86 F.2d 539, **326**

In re D.O., 338 S.W.3d 29, **210**
In re Doctors' Hosp. of Laredo, L.P., 2 S.W.3d 504, **431**
In re Doe, 501 S.W.3d 313, **126, 128, 152, 153, 1020**
In re Dolezal, 970 S.W.2d 650, **488, 495**
In re D.S., 19 S.W.3d 525, **737**
In re D.S., 333 S.W.3d 379, **637**
In re E.I. DuPont de Nemours & Co., 136 S.W.3d 218, **383, 384, 533**
In re E.L.W., No. 11-16-00010-CV (memo op.; 1-26-17), **577**
In re Essex Ins., 450 S.W.3d 524, **352**
In re Estate of Berger, 174 S.W.3d 845, **1053**
In re Estate of Cornes, 175 S.W.3d 491, **700**
In re Estate of Glover, 744 S.W.2d 197, **168**
In re Estate of Hardwick, 278 S.W.2d 258, **423**
In re Estate of Hemsley, 460 S.W.3d 629, **131**
In re Estate of Jones, 197 S.W.3d 894, **1037, 1055**
In re Estate of Miller, 243 S.W.3d 831, **59**
In re Estate of Price, No. 04-05-00438-CV (memo op.; 12-20-06), **700**
In re Estate of Robinson, 140 S.W.3d 782, **732**
In re Estate of Vackar, 345 S.W.3d 588, **964**
In re Estate of Watson, 720 S.W.2d 806, **563, 565, 963**
In re Estate of Weeks, 103 A.2d 43, **167**
In re Evansville TV, Inc., 286 F.2d 65, **324**
In re E.W., 494 S.W.3d 287, **127**
In re ExxonMobil Corp., 97 S.W.3d 353, **383, 384**
In re Fisher & Paykel Appliances, Inc., 420 S.W.3d 842, **541**
In re Ford Motor Co., 988 S.W.2d 714, **404, 413**
In re Ford Motor Co., 211 S.W.3d 295, **534, 537**
In re Foremost Ins., 966 S.W.2d 770, **357**
In re Fort Worth Children's Hosp., 100 S.W.3d 582, **492**
In re F.P., 878 A.2d 91, **987**
In re Gen. Motors Corp. Engine Interchange Litig., 594 F.2d 1106, **326**
In re George, 28 S.W.3d 511, **432**
In re G.K.H., 623 S.W.2d 447, **490, 516, 517, 518**
In re G.M.P., 909 S.W.2d 198, **258**
In re Goodyear Tire & Rubber Co., 392 S.W.3d 687, **468, 469**
In re Grand Jury Impaneled Jan. 21, 1975, 541 F.2d 373, **386**
In re Grand Jury Investigation, 599 F.2d 1224, **395, 397**
In re Grand Jury Investigation, 723 F.2d 447, **412**
In re Grand Jury Investigation, 842 F.2d 1223, **395**
In re Grand Jury Investigation, 918 F.2d 374, **460, 461, 463**
In re Grand Jury Investigation of Hugle (Hugle v. United States), 754 F.2d 863, **47**
In re Grand Jury Investigation of Ocean Transp., 604 F.2d 672, **538**
In re Grand Jury (Malfitano), 633 F.2d 276, **457**
In re Grand Jury Proceedings, 640 F. Supp. 988, **453**
In re Grand Jury Proceedings (85 Misc. 140), 791 F.2d 663, **411**

In re Grand Jury Proceedings (In re Pavlick), 680 F.2d 1026, **394, 412**
In re Grand Jury Proceedings (United States v. Jones), 517 F.2d 666, **412**
In re Grand Jury Proceedings (United States v. Lawson), 600 F.2d 215, **412**
In re Grand Jury Subpoena, 926 F.2d 1423, **411, 412, 510**
In re Grand Jury Subpoena, 204 F.3d 516, **411**
In re Grand Jury Subpoena 92-1(SJ), 31 F.3d 826, **421**
In re Grand Jury Subpoena of Santarelli, 740 F.2d 816, **443**
In re Grand Jury Subpoena United States, 755 F.2d 1022, **457**
In re Grand Jury Subpoenas Dated Mar. 19, 2002 & Aug. 2, 2002 (Mercator Corp. v. United States), 318 F.3d 379, **429**
In re Grand Jury Subpoenas (United States v. Anderson), 906 F.2d 1485, **412**
In re Guar. Ins. Servs., Inc., 343 S.W.3d 130, **171, 172**
In re Harris, 491 S.W.3d 332, **422**
In re Hicks, 252 S.W.3d 790, **413, 534**
In re Hinterlong, 109 S.W.3d 611, **379, 380**
In re H.M.S., 349 S.W.3d 250, **667**
In re Homestore.com, Inc. Sec. Litig., 347 F. Supp. 2d 769, **974**
In re Houseman, 66 S.W.3d 368, **402, 540**
In re Humphreys, 880 S.W.2d 402, **618**
In re J___ T___ H___, 630 S.W.2d 473, **323, 324**
In re J.A.M., 945 S.W.2d 320, **863**
In re Japanese Elec. Prods. Antitrust Litig., 723 F.2d 238, **49, 701, 961, 962**
In re J.C.K., 143 S.W.3d 131, **1035**
In re J.L., 163 S.W.3d 79, **125**
In re J.M.H., 414 S.W.3d 860, **124, 125**
In re Jobe Concrete Prods., Inc., 101 S.W.3d 122, **378**
In re John Doe Corp., 675 F.2d 482, **539**
In re John Doe, Inc., 13 F.3d 633, **88**
In re J.P.B., 180 S.W.3d 570, **972**
In re J.P.O., 904 S.W.2d 695, **568**
In re J.R., 501 S.W.3d 738, **731**
In re J.S., 35 S.W.3d 287, **832**
In re J.W.T., 872 S.W.2d 189, **163**
In re Kaiser Aluminum & Chem. Co., 214 F.3d 586, **378**
In re Kaplan, 168 N.E.2d 660, **412**
In re K.A.S., 131 S.W.3d 215, **66**
In re K.C.P., 142 S.W.3d 574, **670, 904**
In re K.F., 402 S.W.3d 497, **126**
In re Kinoy, 326 F. Supp. 400, **395**
In re Kozlov, 398 A.2d 882, **412**
In re K.W., 666 S.E.2d 490, **601, 653**
In re Learjet, Inc., 59 S.W.3d 842, **406**
In re Leviton Mfg. Co., 1 S.W.3d 898, **466, 468**
In re L.G., 728 S.W.2d 939, **847**
In re Lifschutz, 467 P.2d 557, **507, 526, 529**
In re Lipsky, 460 S.W.3d 579, **195**

CASE INDEX

John T. Lloyd Labs., Inc. v. Lloyd Bros. Pharmacists, 131 F.2d 703, **469**
Johnigan v. State, 482 S.W.2d 209, **454**
Johnson v. City of Hous., 928 S.W.2d 251, **302**
Johnson v. Cooper, 379 S.W.2d 396, **120, 122, 123, 129**
Johnson v. Elk Lake Sch. Dist., 283 F.3d 138, **371**
Johnson v. Harris, ___ S.W.3d ___ (No. 08-15-00149-CV; 4-19-17), **712**
Johnson v. J. Hiram Moore, Ltd., 763 S.W.2d 496, **268**
Johnson v. Norris, 537 F.3d 840, **506**
Johnson v. Reed, 464 S.W.2d 689, **356**
Johnson v. State, 76 Tex. Crim. 346, 174 S.W. 1047, **408**
Johnson v. State, 95 Tex. Crim. 483, 255 S.W. 416, **536, 540**
Johnson v. State, 379 S.W.2d 329, **831**
Johnson v. State, 453 S.W.2d 828, **617**
Johnson v. State, 509 S.W.2d 639, **293**
Johnson v. State, 583 S.W.2d 399, **199**
Johnson v. State, 633 S.W.2d 888, **361**
Johnson v. State, 650 S.W.2d 784, **676**
Johnson v. State, 698 S.W.2d 154, **204, 208**
Johnson v. State, 737 S.W.2d 901, **926**
Johnson v. State, 747 S.W.2d 451, **106**
Johnson v. State, 770 S.W.2d 72, **953**
Johnson v. State, 773 S.W.2d 721, **637**
Johnson v. State, 800 S.W.2d 563, **362**
Johnson v. State, 803 S.W.2d 272, **88, 455, 456, 457, 550**
Johnson v. State, 846 S.W.2d 373, **1053**
Johnson v. State, 853 S.W.2d 574, **1053**
Johnson v. State, 885 S.W.2d 578, **633**
Johnson v. State, 919 S.W.2d 473, **677**
Johnson v. State, 926 S.W.2d 334, **491, 492, 539**
Johnson v. State, 932 S.W.2d 296, **278, 291**
Johnson v. State, 967 S.W.2d 410, **895, 896, 897**
Johnson v. State, 970 S.W.2d 716, **969**
Johnson v. State, 975 S.W.2d 644, **688**
Johnson v. State, 977 S.W.2d 725, **68, 491**
Johnson v. State, 981 S.W.2d 759, **623**
Johnson v. State, 987 S.W.2d 79, **821**
Johnson v. State, 43 S.W.3d 1, **61**
Johnson v. State, 208 S.W.3d 478, **951, 982**
Johnson v. State, 271 S.W.3d 756, **628**
Johnson v. State, 425 S.W.3d 344, **825**
Johnson v. State, 433 S.W.3d 546, **640, 788**
Johnson v. State, 490 S.W.3d 895, **367, 369, 663, 665**
Johnson v. Woods, 315 S.W.2d 75, **342**
Johnson v. Zerbst, 304 U.S. 458, **535, 536, 547**
Johnston v. State, 959 S.W.2d 230, **898, 915**
Johnston v. State, 145 S.W.3d 215, **277, 286, 287**
Joiner v. State, 825 S.W.2d 701, **209, 763, 766**
Jones v. City of Stephenville, 896 S.W.2d 574, **124**
Jones v. Colley, 820 S.W.2d 863, **102, 104**
Jones v. Lurie, 32 S.W.3d 737, **637**
Jones v. O'Day, 692 S.E.2d 774, **865**
Jones v. Ray Ins. Agency, 59 S.W.3d 739, **74**

Jones v. S. Pac. R.R., 962 F.2d 447, **299**
Jones v. State, 449 S.W.2d 277, **997**
Jones v. State, 501 S.W.2d 308, **106**
Jones v. State, 544 S.W.2d 139, **264**
Jones v. State, 610 S.W.2d 535, **521**
Jones v. State, 613 S.W.2d 570, **523**
Jones v. State, 716 S.W.2d 142, **283**
Jones v. State, 751 S.W.2d 682, **280**
Jones v. State, 758 S.W.2d 356, **145**
Jones v. State, 772 S.W.2d 551, **880, 882**
Jones v. State, 843 S.W.2d 487, **62, 908, 944, 949**
Jones v. State, 944 S.W.2d 642, **102, 237**
Jones v. State, 950 S.W.2d 386, **926**
Jones v. State, 80 S.W.3d 686, **985**
Jones v. State, 111 S.W.3d 600, **977**
Jones v. State, 119 S.W.3d 412, **102**
Jones v. State, 338 S.W.3d 725, **479**
Jones v. State, 466 S.W.3d 252, **861**
Jones v. Travelers Ins., 374 S.W.2d 779, **641**
Joplin v. Meadows, 623 S.W.2d 442, **163**
Jordan v. Fourth Ct. of Appeals, 701 S.W.2d 644, **383, 407, 533, 534, 537, 539, 546, 547**
Jordan v. Jordan, 938 S.W.2d 177, **164**
Jordan v. Shields, 674 S.W.2d 464, **564, 566**
Jordan v. State, 486 S.W.2d 784, **695**
Jordan v. State, 897 S.W.2d 909, **679**
Jordan v. State, 928 S.W.2d 550, **708, 725, 735, 739, 764**
Jordan v. State, 950 S.W.2d 210, **725, 734**
Jordan-Maier v. State, 792 S.W.2d 188, **970, 1016, 1017**
Jordy v. State, 413 S.W.3d 227, **107**
Jousan v. Presidio Corp., 590 S.W.2d 524, **1024**
Joy v. Bell Helicopter Textron, Inc., 999 F.2d 549, **733**
Juarez v. State, No. 05-12-00125-CR (no pub.; 7-31-13), **255**
Jubert v. State, 753 S.W.2d 458, **1042, 1044**
Judd v. State, 923 S.W.2d 135, **833, 884**
Judwin Props., Inc. v. Griggs & Harrison, P.C., 981 S.W.2d 868, **422**
Judwin Props., Inc. v. Griggs & Harrison, P.C., 11 S.W.3d 188, **422**
Jurek v. Couch-Jurek, 296 S.W.3d 864, **1037, 1052, 1053**

K

Kaczmarek v. Allied Chem. Corp., 836 F.2d 1055, **306**
Kahanek v. Rogers, 12 S.W.3d 501, **923**
Ka-Hugh Enters., Inc. v. Fort Worth Pipe & Supply Co., 524 S.W.2d 418, **67**
Kainer v. Walker, 377 S.W.2d 613, **240**
Kale v. Douthitt, 274 F.2d 476, **746**
Kaman v. State, 923 S.W.2d 129, **133**
Kamanga v. State, 502 S.W.3d 871, **661**
Kamani v. Port of Hous. Auth., 725 S.W.2d 336, **849**
Kamel v. Kamel, 760 S.W.2d 677, **922**
Kan. City Life Ins. v. Fisher, 83 S.W.2d 1063, **168**

CASE INDEX

CASE INDEX

CASE INDEX

McClure v. Landis, 959 S.W.2d 679, **302**

McConnell Constr. Co. v. Ins. Co. of St. Louis, 428 S.W.2d 659, **1055**

McCormick v. Schtrenck, 59 Tex. Civ. App. 139, 130 S.W. 720, **265**

McCormick v. Tex. Commerce Bank, 751 S.W.2d 887, **342, 928, 929**

McCowan v. State, 739 S.W.2d 652, **125, 127**

McCown v. State, 192 S.W.3d 158, **695**

McCoy v. State, 877 S.W.2d 844, **645**

McCraw v. Maris, 828 S.W.2d 756, **921**

McCray v. Illinois, 386 U.S. 300, **479**

McCray v. State, 873 S.W.2d 126, **688**

McCulloch v. State, 740 S.W.2d 74, **135**

McCulloch v. State, 39 S.W.3d 678, **203**

McCullough v. State, 116 S.W.3d 86, **830**

McDaniel v. State, 46 Tex. Crim. 560, 81 S.W. 301, **447**

McDaniel v. State, 98 S.W.3d 704, **54**

McDonald v. Alamo Motor Lines, 222 S.W.2d 1013, **356**

McDonald v. Pless, 238 U.S. 264, **583, 587**

McDonald v. State, 911 S.W.2d 798, **886**

McDonald v. State, 179 S.W.3d 571, **293, 296**

McDonnell Douglas Corp. v. Green, 411 U.S. 792, **159**

McDuff v. State, 939 S.W.2d 607, **64**

McDuffie v. State, 854 S.W.2d 195, **441, 442, 550, 597**

McEwen v. Wal-Mart Stores, Inc., 975 S.W.2d 25, **858**

McFarland v. State, 845 S.W.2d 824, **877**

McGary v. State, 750 S.W.2d 782, **657, 658**

McGinn v. State, 961 S.W.2d 161, **561**

McGinty v. Motor Truck Equip. Corp., 397 S.W.2d 263, **826**

McGowan v. O'Neill, 750 S.W.2d 884, **493, 496**

McGrede v. Rembert Nat'l Bank, 147 S.W.2d 580, **394**

McGuire v. Brown, 580 S.W.2d 425, **170**

McGuire v. City of Dall., 141 Tex. 170, 170 S.W.2d 722, **995**

McGuire v. Commercial Union Ins., 431 S.W.2d 347, **321**

McHenry v. State, 823 S.W.2d 667, **192**

MCI Sales & Serv., Inc. v. Hinton, 272 S.W.3d 17, **711**

MCI Sales & Serv., Inc. v. Hinton, 329 S.W.3d 475, **126, 132**

McInnes v. Yamaha Motor Corp., U.S.A., 673 S.W.2d 185, **63, 838, 841**

McInnis v. State, 618 S.W.2d 389, **551**

McKee v. McNeir, 151 S.W.3d 268, **233**

McKinney v. State, 59 S.W.3d 304, **698**

McLean v. State, 312 S.W.3d 912, **85**

McLellan v. Benson, 877 S.W.2d 454, **215, 279**

McLendon v. Tex. Dep't of Pub. Safety, 985 S.W.2d 571, **1019**

McLeod v. State, 56 S.W.3d 704, **1025**

McMahon v. Zimmerman, 433 S.W.3d 680, **736**

McMillan v. State, 754 S.W.2d 422, **689**

McMillen Feeds, Inc. v. Harlow, 405 S.W.2d 123, **922**

McMillin v. State Farm Lloyds, 180 S.W.3d 183, **169**

McMullen v. Warren Motor Co., 25 P.2d 99, **159**

McNair v. State, 75 S.W.3d 69, **931**

McNeely v. Sw. Settlement & Dev. Corp., 284 S.W.2d 167, **848**

McNiel v. State, 757 S.W.2d 129, **101, 183, 185**

McQuarrie v. State, 380 S.W.2d 145, **588, 589, 590, 593, 594, 596**

McQueeney v. Wilmington Tr. Co., 779 F.2d 916, **850**

McRae v. Echols, 8 S.W.3d 797, **913, 916**

McRae v. State, 152 S.W.3d 739, **687**

Md. Am. Gen. Ins. v. Blackmon, 639 S.W.2d 455, **417**

Md. Cas. Co. v. Dicken, 80 S.W.2d 800, **1051**

Md. Cas. Co. v. Hearks, 188 S.W.2d 262, **646**

Md. Cas. Co. v. Lee, 165 S.W.2d 135, **949**

Mead v. State, 759 S.W.2d 437, **630**

Meador v. State, 812 S.W.2d 330, **89, 855, 860, 861, 862, 881**

Meadows v. State, 455 S.W.3d 166, **625, 629**

Mecaskey v. Bewley Mills, 8 S.W.2d 688, **1064**

Mediacomp, Inc. v. Capital Cities Commc'n, Inc., 698 S.W.2d 207, **299**

Medina v. State, 367 S.W.3d 470, **627**

Mega Child Care, Inc. v. Tex. Dep't of Prot. & Regulatory Servs., 29 S.W.3d 303, **759, 822, 918, 968, 970, 1035**

Melendez-Diaz v. Massachusetts, 557 U.S. 305, **754, 789, 805, 806, 807, 809, 915, 916, 919**

Meller v. Heil Co., 745 F.2d 1297, **308, 311**

Melody Home Mfg. Co. v. Barnes, 741 S.W.2d 349, **308**

Mem'l Hosp.-The Woodlands v. McCown, 927 S.W.2d 1, **545**

Mena v. State, 633 S.W.2d 564, **522**

Menchaca v. State, 901 S.W.2d 640, **197, 852**

Mendenhall v. Barber-Greene Co., 531 F. Supp. 951, **538**

Mendiola v. State, 924 S.W.2d 157, **574**

Mendiola v. State, 995 S.W.2d 175, **287**

Mendiola v. State, 21 S.W.3d 282, **197, 202**

Mendiola v. State, 61 S.W.3d 541, **107**

Mendoza v. Fid. & Guar. Ins. Underwriters, Inc., 606 S.W.2d 692, **845**

Mendoza v. State, 552 S.W.2d 444, **550, 975**

Mendoza v. State, 787 S.W.2d 502, **925**

Mendoza v. State, 69 S.W.3d 628, **832, 895, 962, 971, 975**

Mendoza v. Varon, 563 S.W.2d 646, **355**

Menefee v. Bering Mfg. Co., 166 S.W. 365, **986**

Menefee v. State, 928 S.W.2d 274, **290, 475**

Mentis v. Barnard, 870 S.W.2d 14, **62**

Menton v. Lattimore, 667 S.W.2d 335, **400**

Mercedes-Benz of N. Am., Inc. v. Dickenson, 720 S.W.2d 844, **320**

Merchants' Cotton Oil Co. v. Acme Gin Co., 284 S.W. 680, **319, 320, 321, 324**

Merck & Co. v. Garza, 347 S.W.3d 256, **737**

CASE INDEX

Myers v. State, 781 S.W.2d 730, **642, 643**
Myers v. Thomas, 143 Tex. 502, 186 S.W.2d 811, **351**
Myre v. State, 545 S.W.2d 820, **95, 639**

N

N. Am. Refractory Co. v. Easter, 988 S.W.2d 904, **773**
N. Am. Van Lines, Inc. v. Emmons, 50 S.W.3d 103, **231, 240**
Nabors Well Servs., Ltd. v. Romero, 456 S.W.3d 553, **94, 197**
Najar v. State, 74 S.W.3d 82, **202**
Nance v. State, 946 S.W.2d 490, **295**
Naranjo v. State, 217 S.W.3d 560, **184**
Narvaiz v. State, 840 S.W.2d 415, **1044**
Nass v. Nass, 149 Tex. 41, 228 S.W.2d 130, **980**
Nassouri v. State, 503 S.W.3d 416, **634**
Nat. Gas Pipeline Co. of Am. v. Justiss, 397 S.W.3d 150, **693, 694, 739**
Nat. Gas Pipeline Co. of Am. v. Pool, 30 S.W.3d 618, **208, 944**
Nat'l Acceptance Co. v. Bathalter, 705 F.2d 924, **552**
Nat'l Aid Life Ass'n v. Murphy, 78 S.W.2d 223, **994**
Nat'l Convenience Stores, Inc. v. Matherne, 987 S.W.2d 145, **758**
Nat'l Cty. Mut. Fire Ins. v. Hood, 693 S.W.2d 638, **137**
Nat'l Health Res. Corp. v. TBF Fin., LLC, 429 S.W.3d 125, **903**
Nat'l Life & Acc. Ins. v. Morris, 402 S.W.2d 297, **743**
Nat'l Med. Enters., Inc. v. Godbey, 924 S.W.2d 123, **171**
Nat'l Mut. Acc. Ins. v. Davis, 46 S.W.2d 351, **985**
Nat'l Tank Co. v. Brotherton, 851 S.W.2d 193, **396, 405, 425, 426, 428, 429**
Nat'l Union Fire Ins. v. Hoffman, 746 S.W.2d 305, **540**
Nat'l Union Fire Ins. v. Valdez, 863 S.W.2d 458, **425, 426, 540**
Nauert v. State, 838 S.W.2d 328, **933**
Navarro v. State, 863 S.W.2d 191, **887**
NCNB Tex. Nat'l Bank v. Coker, 765 S.W.2d 398, **171**
Neal v. Dow Agrosciences LLC, 74 S.W.3d 468, **728**
Neal v. State, 186 S.W.3d 690, **880**
Neder v. United States, 527 U.S. 1, **175**
Neff v. Johnson, 391 S.W.2d 760, **918**
Negociacion Agricola y Ganadera de San Enrique v. Love, 220 S.W. 224, **249**
Negrini v. State, 853 S.W.2d 128, **710**
Nehring v. McMurrian, 94 Tex. 45, 57 S.W. 943, **955**
Nehring v. Smith, 49 N.W.2d 831, **319, 321**
Nelson v. State, 765 S.W.2d 401, **95, 96**
Nelson v. State, 864 S.W.2d 496, **288**
Nelson v. State, 405 S.W.3d 113, **68**
Nenno v. State, 970 S.W.2d 549, **730, 731, 732, 734, 735, 741, 766**
Neosho Valley Inv. Co. v. Hannum, 66 P. 631, **206**
Nester v. Textron, Inc., No. A-13-CA-920-LY (no pub.; 3-9-15), **414**
Nethery v. State, 692 S.W.2d 686, **98, 711**
Neuman v. State, 951 S.W.2d 538, **295**

New Braunfels Factory Outlet Ctr., Inc. v. IHOP Realty Corp., 872 S.W.2d 303, **218, 223, 923**
New Orleans Cold Storage & Whs. Co. v. NLRB, 201 F.3d 592, **898**
Newberry v. Newberry, 351 S.W.3d 552, **164**
Newsome v. State, 829 S.W.2d 260, **677**
Newton v. State, 301 S.W.3d 315, **277**
Nguyen v. Excel Corp., 197 F.3d 200, **540**
Nguyen v. Myers, 442 S.W.3d 434, **356**
Nguyen v. State, 811 S.W.2d 165, **850**
Nguyen v. State, 21 S.W.3d 609, **91**
Nguyen v. State, 506 S.W.3d 69, **638, 640**
N.H. Ins. v. Magellan Reinsurance Co., No. 02-11-00334-CV (memo op.; 1-10-13), **1011**
Nicholas v. Envtl. Sys. (Int'l) Ltd., 499 S.W.3d 888, **967, 969**
Nichols v. Seale, 493 S.W.2d 589, **689, 690, 691, 699**
Nichols v. State, 138 Tex. Crim. 324, 136 S.W.2d 221, **93**
Nicholson v. Wittig, 832 S.W.2d 681, **460, 463**
Niemann v. State, 471 S.W.2d 124, **227**
Niles v. State, 104 Tex. Crim. 447, 284 S.W. 568, **451**
Nissan Motor Co. v. Armstrong, 145 S.W.3d 131, **232, 233**
Nix v. H.R. Mgmt. Co., 733 S.W.2d 573, **608, 610**
Nix v. State, 750 S.W.2d 348, **931**
Nixon v. State, 653 S.W.2d 443, **109**
Noble v. McClatchy Newspapers, 533 F.2d 1081, **307**
Nois v. State, No. 05-15-00203-CR (memo op.; 3-9-16), **1072**
Noland v. State, 264 S.W.3d 144, **591**
Nolen v. State, 872 S.W.2d 807, **284**
Nooner v. State, 907 S.W.2d 677, **972**
Norman v. State, 862 S.W.2d 621, **72**
Norris v. State, 788 S.W.2d 65, **602**
Norris v. State, 902 S.W.2d 428, **628**
Norton v. Martin, 703 S.W.2d 267, **855, 859**
Norton v. State, 771 S.W.2d 160, **74, 890**
Norwood v. State, 80 Tex. Crim. 552, 192 S.W. 248, **451**
Nubine v. State, 721 S.W.2d 430, **132, 145**
Nunez v. State, 27 S.W.3d 210, **108, 621**
Nw. Nat'l Ins. v. Garcia, 729 S.W.2d 321, **893**
N.Y. Life Ins. v. Aronson, 38 F. Supp. 687, **1016**

O

O. v. P., 560 S.W.2d 122, **80**
Oakwood Mobile Homes, Inc. v. Cabler, 73 S.W.3d 363, **230, 303**
Oberg v. State, 890 S.W.2d 539, **832**
Oberst v. Int'l Harvester Co., 640 F.2d 863, **309**
Oberwetter v. Hilliard, 639 F.3d 545, **134**
O'Bryan v. State, 591 S.W.2d 464, **249, 606**
Occidental Chem. Corp. v. Banales, 907 S.W.2d 488, **424, 426, 427**
Ochoa v. Miller, 59 Tex. 460, **998**
Ochoa v. State, 481 S.W.2d 847, **621**
Ochoa v. State, 994 S.W.2d 283, **726**

Porter v. Tex. Dep't of Pub. Safety, 712 S.W.2d 263, **913, 918**

Portland Sav. & Loan Ass'n v. Bernstein, 716 S.W.2d 532, **327, 379, 647**

Posey v. Hanson, 196 S.W. 731, **228, 229, 230, 268**

Posner v. Dall. Cty. Child Welfare Unit, 784 S.W.2d 585, **72, 75**

Potashnick v. Port City Constr. Co., 609 F.2d 1101, **668**

Potier v. State, 68 S.W.3d 657, **62**

Potter v. State, 74 S.W.3d 105, **238**

Pound v. Popular Dry Goods Co., 139 S.W.2d 341, **196, 231**

Powell v. Hocker, 516 S.W.3d 488, **432**

Powell v. Levit, 640 F.2d 239, **631, 646**

Powell v. State, 5 S.W.3d 369, **267, 646**

Powell v. State, 63 S.W.3d 435, **269, 285**

Powell v. State, 189 S.W.3d 285, **211, 215**

Powell v. Vavro, McDonald & Assocs., L.L.C., 136 S.W.3d 762, **903**

Power v. Kelley, 70 S.W.3d 137, **885**

Powers v. McDaniel, 785 S.W.2d 915, **564, 566**

Powers v. State, 757 S.W.2d 88, **718**

Pratt v. State, 53 Tex. Crim. 281, 109 S.W. 138, **950**

Pratt v. State, 748 S.W.2d 483, **109**

Praytor v. Ford Motor Co., 97 S.W.3d 237, **728**

Prentis v. Atl. Coast Line Co., 211 U.S. 210, **114**

Prentiss & Carlisle Co. v. Koehring-Waterous Div. of Timberjack, Inc., 972 F.2d 6, **309**

Prescott v. State, 744 S.W.2d 128, **621**

Prescott v. State, 123 S.W.3d 506, **101, 284**

Presswood v. State, 124 S.W.3d 837, **726**

Prestige Homes, Inc. v. Legouffe, 658 P.2d 850, **125**

Prezelski v. Christiansen, 775 S.W.2d 764, **637**

Prible v. State, 175 S.W.3d 724, **237, 238, 289**

Price v. State, 35 S.W.3d 136, **1019**

Price v. State, 351 S.W.3d 148, **276**

Price Bros. v. Phila. Gear Corp., 629 F.2d 444, **576**

Prichard v. Bickley, 175 S.W.2d 614, **966**

Priester v. State, 478 S.W.3d 826, **836, 896**

Prieto v. State, 879 S.W.2d 295, **278**

Prink v. Rockefeller Ctr., Inc., 398 N.E.2d 517, **526**

Pritchett v. State, 874 S.W.2d 168, **952**

Proenza v. State, 471 S.W.3d 35, **85**

Prudential Ins. v. Black, 572 S.W.2d 379, **1035**

Prudential Ins. v. Krayer, 366 S.W.2d 779, **167**

Prudential Sec. Inc. v. Marshall, 909 S.W.2d 896, **47**

Pruitt v. State, 770 S.W.2d 909, **598**

Prystash v. State, 3 S.W.3d 522, **64, 318**

Puckett v. State, 640 S.W.2d 284, **104, 597**

Puente v. A.S.I. Signs, 821 S.W.2d 400, **713**

Pugh v. Turner, 145 Tex. 292, 197 S.W.2d 822, **566**

Punchard v. Masterson, 100 Tex. 479, 101 S.W. 204, **1024**

Purcell v. Dist. Att'y for Suffolk Dist., 676 N.E.2d 436, **419**

Purina Mills, Inc. v. Odell, 948 S.W.2d 927, **728**

Purolator Armored, Inc. v. R.R. Comm'n, 662 S.W.2d 700, **207**

Purtell v. State, 761 S.W.2d 360, **935**

Purvis v. Morehead, 304 S.W.2d 221, **1020**

Putnam v. Pannell, 507 S.W.2d 811, **645**

Pyles v. Johnson, 136 F.3d 986, **586, 592**

Pyles v. State, 755 S.W.2d 98, **611, 654, 764**

Q

Queeman v. State, 520 S.W.3d 616, **188**

Queen Caroline's Case, 129 Eng. Rep. 976, **656**

Quick v. Plastic Sols. of Tex., Inc., 270 S.W.3d 173, **855**

Quinn v. United States, 349 U.S. 155, **49**

Quinones v. State, 592 S.W.2d 933, **432**

Quinonez-Saa v. State, 860 S.W.2d 704, **441, 477**

Quiroz v. Llamas-Soforo, 483 S.W.3d 710, **75**

Quiroz v. State, 764 S.W.2d 395, **253, 256, 600**

Quitta v. Fossati, 808 S.W.2d 636, **564, 565, 566**

R

Rabbani v. State, 847 S.W.2d 555, **873, 875**

Rabon v. Great Sw. Fire Ins., 818 F.2d 306, **570**

Rachlin v. United States, 723 F.2d 1373, **338**

RAD Servs., Inc. v. Aetna Cas. & Sur. Co., 808 F.2d 271, **553**

Ralph v. Mr. Paul's Shoes, Inc., 572 S.W.2d 812, **748**

Ramada Dev. Co. v. Rauch, 644 F.2d 1097, **325, 327, 333**

Ramirez v. Dretke, 398 F.3d 691, **791**

Ramirez v. State, 543 S.W.2d 631, **930**

Ramirez v. State, 802 S.W.2d 674, **601, 609, 654**

Ramirez v. State, 815 S.W.2d 636, **747, 766, 776**

Ramirez v. State, 987 S.W.2d 938, **598, 837, 932**

Ramirez-Memije v. State, 466 S.W.3d 894, **184, 185**

Ramos v. State, 124 S.W.3d 326, **489**

Ramrattan v. Burger King Corp., 656 F. Supp. 522, **902**

Ramsey v. Dunlop, 146 Tex. 196, 205 S.W.2d 979, **84**

Ramsey v. Jones Enters., 810 S.W.2d 902, **1038**

Ramsey v. Lucky Stores, Inc., 853 S.W.2d 623, **658**

Ramsey v. State, 473 S.W.3d 805, **188**

Randolph v. Collectramatic, Inc., 590 F.2d 844, **715**

Rangel v. Hartford Acc. & Indem. Co., 821 S.W.2d 196, **845**

Rankin v. Bell, 85 Tex. 28, 19 S.W. 874, **59, 100, 101**

Rankin v. State, 821 S.W.2d 230, **364**

Rankin v. State, 953 S.W.2d 740, **293**

Rankin v. State, 974 S.W.2d 707, **100, 101, 267, 270, 271**

Ransom v. State, 503 S.W.2d 810, **275**

Ransom v. State, 920 S.W.2d 288, **287**

Raphaely Int'l, Inc. v. Waterman S.S. Corp., 972 F.2d 498, **1017**

Rash v. Ross, 371 S.W.2d 109, **310**

Rathmell v. Morrison, 732 S.W.2d 6, **208**

Rawlins v. State, 521 S.W.3d 863, **92, 203**

Ray v. State, 764 S.W.2d 406, **609, 666**

Ray v. State, 176 S.W.3d 544, **813**

CASE INDEX

CASE INDEX

Strong v. State, 138 S.W.3d 546, **638, 658, 848**

Stuart v. Noble Ditch Co., 76 P. 255, **206**

Stuart v. State, 561 S.W.2d 181, **273**

Sturges v. Wal-Mart Stores, Inc., 39 S.W.3d 608, **228**

Suarez v. City of Tex. City, 465 S.W.3d 623, **188, 189**

Subia v. Tex. Dep't of Human Servs., 750 S.W.2d 827, **521, 522**

Suddarth v. Poor, 546 S.W.2d 138, **422**

Sudderth v. Grosshans, 581 S.W.2d 215, **121**

Sullivan v. Mo., Kan. & Tex. Ry. Co. of Tex., 110 Tex. 360, 220 S.W. 769, **316, 320**

Sullivan v. State, 248 S.W.3d 746, **805, 900**

Sumner v. Kinney, 136 S.W. 1192, **342**

Super Film of Am, Inc. v. UCB Films, Inc., 219 F.R.D. 649, **1046**

Sutkowski v. Univ'l Marion Corp., 281 N.E.2d 749, **308**

Sutton v. Bell, 77 A. 42, **351**

S.V. v. R.V., 933 S.W.2d 1, **704, 733, 734**

Sw. Bell Tel. Co. v. Johnson, 389 S.W.2d 645, **670**

Sw. Bell Tel. Co. v. Ramsey, 542 S.W.2d 466, **226**

Sw. Bell Tel. Co. v. Sims, 615 S.W.2d 858, **87**

Sw. Bell Tel., L.P. v. Chappell, No. 02-12-00071-CV (memo op.; 1-24-13), **117**

Sw. Country Enters., Inc. v. Lucky Lady Oil Co., 991 S.W.2d 490, **78**

Sw. Energy Prod. Co. v. Berry-Helfand, 411 S.W.3d 581, **855**

Sw. Energy Prod. Co. v. Berry-Helfand, 491 S.W.3d 699, **721, 722**

Sw. Settlement & Dev. Co. v. Vill. Mills Co., 245 S.W. 975, **998**

Swarb v. State, 125 S.W.3d 672, **288**

Swate v. Schiffers, 975 S.W.2d 70, **826**

Swearingen v. State, 101 S.W.3d 89, **405**

Sweeney v. State, 704 S.W.2d 33, **104, 597**

Sweeny v. State, 925 S.W.2d 268, **183**

Swidler & Berlin v. United States, 524 U.S. 399, **417, 510**

Swing v. Cloquet Lumber Co., 141 N.W. 117, **1064**

Sylvania Elec. Prods., Inc. v. Flanagan, 352 F.2d 1005, **1053**

Syndex Corp. v. Dean, 820 S.W.2d 869, **893, 895**

T

Tabatchnick v. G.D. Searle & Co., 67 F.R.D. 49, **766**

Tag Res., Inc. v. Pet. Well Servs., Inc., 791 S.W.2d 600, **319, 323**

Talada v. City of Martinez, 656 F. Supp. 2d 1147, **970**

Tamayo v. State, 924 S.W.2d 213, **827**

Tamez v. State, 11 S.W.3d 198, **80, 273**

Tanner v. Karnavas, 86 S.W.3d 737, **609**

Tanner v. State, 875 S.W.2d 8, **913**

Tanner v. United States, 483 U.S. 107, **582, 583, 587, 588**

Tarasoff v. Regents of the Univ. of Cal., 551 P.2d 334, **525**

Tarrant Cty. v. English, 989 S.W.2d 368, **327**

Tarrant Cty. Hosp. Dist. v. Hughes, 734 S.W.2d 675, **487**

Tarwater v. Donley Cty. State Bank, 277 S.W. 176, **249, 1065**

Tate v. State, 981 S.W.2d 189, **259, 260, 263**

Tate v. State, 500 S.W.3d 410, **187, 188**

Tatum v. Progressive Polymers, Inc., 881 S.W.2d 835, **320, 321**

Tatum v. State, 798 S.W.2d 569, **80, 81**

Tatum v. State, 919 S.W.2d 910, **491**

Taylor v. Am. Fabritech, Inc., 132 S.W.3d 613, **732**

Taylor v. Evans, 29 S.W. 172, **418**

Taylor v. Owen, 290 S.W.2d 771, **356**

Taylor v. State, 420 S.W.2d 601, **107**

Taylor v. State, 470 S.W.2d 663, **617**

Taylor v. State, 612 S.W.2d 566, **618, 625, 630**

Taylor v. State, 774 S.W.2d 31, **758**

Taylor v. State, 920 S.W.2d 319, **275, 293**

Taylor v. State, 921 S.W.2d 740, **866**

Taylor v. State, 945 S.W.2d 295, **181**

Taylor v. State, 947 S.W.2d 698, **997**

Taylor v. State, 93 S.W.3d 487, **823**

Taylor v. State, 106 S.W.3d 827, **717, 747**

Taylor v. State, 268 S.W.3d 571, **747, 892, 893**

Taylor v. State, 332 S.W.3d 483, **83**

Taylor v. Union Carbide Corp., 93 F.R.D. 1, **326**

Taylor, Bastrop & Hous. Ry. Co. v. Warner, 88 Tex. 642, 32 S.W. 868, **166**

Taylor Foundry Co. v. Wichita Falls Grain Co., 51 S.W.3d 766, **687**

TCA Bldg. Co. v. Nw. Res. Co., 922 S.W.2d 629, **315, 321, 327**

Team v. Tex. & Pac. Ry. Co., 199 S.W.2d 274, **231**

Teen-Ed, Inc. v. Kimball Int'l, Inc., 620 F.2d 399, **686, 714, 715**

Tejeda v. State, 905 S.W.2d 313, **880**

Telewizja Polska USA, Inc. v. Echostar Satellite Corp., No. 02 C 3293 (memo op.; 10-14-04), **974**

Tell v. State, 908 S.W.2d 535, **667, 669, 670, 673**

Tello v. Bank One, N.A., 218 S.W.3d 109, **125**

Temple Indep. Sch. Dist. v. English, 896 S.W.2d 167, **155**

Tempo Tamers, Inc. v. Crow-Houston Four, Ltd., 715 S.W.2d 658, **822**

Tennenbaum v. Deloitte & Touche, 77 F.3d 337, **541**

Terkel v. AT&T Corp., 441 F. Supp. 2d 899, **478**

Terrell State Hosp. v. Ashworth, 794 S.W.2d 937, **484, 540**

Ter-Vartanyan v. R&R Freight, Inc., 111 S.W.3d 779, **706, 917**

Tex. & N.O. R.R. v. Glass, 107 S.W.2d 924, **231**

Tex. & N.O. R.R. v. Grace, 144 Tex. 71, 188 S.W.2d 378, **187**

Tex. & Pac. Ry. Co. v. Empacadora de Ciudad Juarez, 309 S.W.2d 926, **166**

Tex. & Pac. Ry. Co. v. Reed, 88 Tex. 439, 31 S.W. 1058, **567**

Truck Ins. Exch. v. Michling, 364 S.W.2d 172, **881**
Truck Ins. Exch. v. Smetak, 102 S.W.3d 851, **916**
Truco Props., Inc. v. Charlton, 749 S.W.2d 893, **598**
Trujillo v. State, 809 S.W.2d 593, **124, 132**
Trussell v. State, 585 S.W.2d 736, **656, 824**
Tryco Enters., Inc. v. Robinson, 390 S.W.3d 497, **69, 72, 847, 859**
Tucker v. Smith, 68 Tex. 473, 3 S.W. 671, **927**
Tucker v. State, 771 S.W.2d 523, **853**
Tucker v. State, 456 S.W.3d 194, **269**
Tucker's Beverages, Inc. v. Fopay, 145 S.W.3d 765, **857, 858, 859**
Tuf Racing Prods., Inc. v. Am. Suzuki Motor Corp., 223 F.3d 585, **707**
Turbodyne Corp. v. Heard, 720 S.W.2d 802, **428**
Turner v. Lone Star Indus., 733 S.W.2d 242, **636**
Turner v. Peril, 50 S.W.3d 742, **76**
Turner v. State, 486 S.W.2d 797, **843**
Turner v. State, 715 S.W.2d 847, **282**
Turner v. State, 719 S.W.2d 190, **68, 72, 654**
Turner v. State, 733 S.W.2d 218, **125**
Turner v. State, 762 S.W.2d 705, **253, 254**
Turner v. State, 805 S.W.2d 423, **250**
Turner v. State, 924 S.W.2d 180, **895**
Turner v. State, 4 S.W.3d 74, **621**
Turner v. State, 413 S.W.3d 442, **248, 252**
Turner v. State, No. AP-76,580 (no pub.; 3-8-17), **54**
Turner v. United States, 396 U.S. 398, **115**
Turpin v. State, 606 S.W.2d 907, **155**
Turro v. State, 950 S.W.2d 390, **691, 696, 720**
Turton v. State Bar, 775 S.W.2d 712, **339**
Tuttle v. Simpson, 735 S.W.2d 539, **565, 566**
TXI Transp. Co. v. Hughes, 306 S.W.3d 230, **213, 608, 721, 724, 727, 732, 735, 736, 834**
Tyler Car & Truck Ctr. v. Empire Fire & Marine Ins., 2 S.W.3d 482, **169**
Tyson v. State, 873 S.W.2d 53, **993**
Tyson Foods, Inc. v. Guzman, 116 S.W.3d 233, **310**

U

U-Haul Int'l, Inc. v. Waldrip, 380 S.W.3d 118, **97, 232**
Uhl v. State, 479 S.W.2d 55, **642**
Uhlir v. Golden Triangle Dev. Corp., 763 S.W.2d 512, **636**
Ukwuachu v. State, 494 S.W.3d 733, **370**
Ulloa v. State, 901 S.W.2d 507, **831**
Underwriters Life Ins. v. Cobb, 746 S.W.2d 810, **224, 228**
Univ. of Hous. v. Barth, 403 S.W.3d 851, **123**
Univ. of Pa. v. EEOC, 493 U.S. 182, **377**
Univ. of Tex. v. Hinton, 822 S.W.2d 197, **239, 240, 357**
Uniroyal Goodrich Tire Co. v. Martinez, 977 S.W.2d 328, **231, 308, 1063**
United Blood Servs. v. Longoria, 938 S.W.2d 29, **706, 710**
United Cab Co. v. Mason, 775 S.W.2d 783, **358**
United Founders Life Ins. v. Carey, 347 S.W.2d 295, **170**

United Serv. Auto. Ass'n v. Gordon, 103 S.W.3d 436, **776**
United States v. 14.38 Acres of Land, 80 F.3d 1074, **733**
United States v. 320.0 Acres of Land, More or Less in the Cty. of Monroe, 605 F.2d 762, **320**
United States v. 33.90 Acres of Land, More or Less, Situated in Bexar Cty., 709 F.2d 1012, **226, 227**
United States v. 478.34 Acres of Land, Tract No. 400, 578 F.2d 156, **194**
United States v. 5.00 Acres of Land, More or Less, Situate in Orange Cty., 507 F. Supp. 589, **227**
United States v. Abel, 469 U.S. 45, **600, 663**
United States v. Aboumoussallem, 726 F.2d 906, **269**
United States v. Abrego, 141 F.3d 142, **708**
United States v. Ackal, 706 F.2d 523, **663**
United States v. Agnes, 753 F.2d 293, **670**
United States v. Akinrosotu, 637 F.3d 165, **134**
United States v. Albert, 595 F.2d 283, **976**
United States v. Alden, 476 F.2d 378, **746**
United States v. Alessi, 638 F.2d 466, **284**
United States v. Alexander, 326 F.2d 736, **1042**
United States v. Alexander, 816 F.2d 164, **702**
United States v. Alonzo, 991 F.2d 1422, **834**
United States v. Aluminum Co. of Am., 35 F. Supp. 820, **1002**
United States v. Alvarado, 519 F.2d 1133, **139**
United States v. Alvarado-Valdez, 521 F.3d 337, **813**
United States v. Alvarez, 519 F.2d 1036, **402**
United States v. Alvarez, 584 F.2d 694, **931**
United States v. Amado-Núñez, 357 F.3d 119, **118**
United States v. Amaral, 488 F.2d 1148, **722**
United States v. Anguloa, 598 F.2d 1182, **575**
United States v. Angwin, 271 F.3d 786, **300, 302**
United States v. Annoreno, 460 F.2d 1303, **100**
United States v. Apodaca, 522 F.2d 568, **458**
United States v. Arce, 997 F.2d 1123, **981**
United States v. Archer, 733 F.2d 354, **454**
United States v. Arias, 678 F.2d 1202, **753**
United States v. Arroyo-Angulo, 580 F.2d 1137, **341, 348**
United States v. Arthur Young & Co., 465 U.S. 805, **403**
United States v. Aspinall, 389 F.3d 332, **794**
United States v. Auster, 517 F.3d 312, **525**
United States v. Bad Wound, 203 F.3d 1072, **457**
United States v. Baker, 432 F.3d 1189, **107**
United States v. Ballard, 779 F.2d 287, **420**
United States v. Barile, 286 F.3d 749, **760**
United States v. Barker, 553 F.2d 1013, **705**
United States v. Barker, 820 F.3d 167, **803**
United States v. Barletta, 652 F.2d 218, **92**
United States v. Barlow, 568 F.3d 215, **989**
United States v. Barnard, 490 F.2d 907, **606, 719**
United States v. Barnes, 586 F.2d 1052, **939**
United States v. Baron, 602 F.2d 1248, **841**
United States v. Barrett, 539 F.2d 244, **283**

CASE INDEX

Velarde-Villarreal v. United States, 354 F.2d 9, **473**
Venable v. State, 113 S.W.3d 797, **901, 1028, 1029**
Ventroy v. State, 917 S.W.2d 419, **687**
Veracruz v. State, 713 S.W.2d 745, **456**
Verizon Directories Corp. v. Yellow Book USA, Inc., 331 F. Supp. 2d 136, **638**
Veteto v. State, 8 S.W.3d 805, **70, 621**
Vibbert v. PAR, Inc., 224 S.W.3d 317, **155**
Victaulic Co. v. Tieman, 499 F.3d 227, **129**
Victor M. Solis Underground Util. & Paving Co. v. Laredo, 751 S.W.2d 532, **946**
Viersen v. Bucher, 342 S.W.2d 203, **998**
Villa v. State, 514 S.W.3d 227, **187, 188**
Villanueva v. State, 768 S.W.2d 900, **198**
Villarreal v. State, 576 S.W.2d 51, **559, 560**
Villarreal v. State, 504 S.W.3d 494, **254, 255, 679**
Villiers v. Republic Fin. Servs., Inc., 602 S.W.2d 566, **778**
Vince Poscente Int'l, Inc. v. Compass Bank, 460 S.W.3d 211, **144**
Vines v. State, 479 S.W.2d 322, **823**
Vinson v. State, 252 S.W.3d 336, **89, 796**
Vinson Minerals, Ltd. v. XTO Energy, Inc., 335 S.W.3d 344, **315, 317**
Virts v. State, 739 S.W.2d 25, **600, 605, 638, 640**
Viscaino v. State, 513 S.W.3d 802, **570, 693, 758**
Viterbo v. Dow Chem. Co., 826 F.2d 420, **763**
Vitiello v. State, 848 S.W.2d 885, **1054**
Vockie v. Gen. Motors Corp., 66 F.R.D. 57, **312**
Volcanic Gardens Mgmt. Co. v. Paxson, 847 S.W.2d 343, **418**
Volkswagen of Am., Inc. v. Ramirez, 159 S.W.3d 897, **62, 732, 736, 880**
Vollbaum v. State, 833 S.W.2d 652, **239**
Volosen v. State, 227 S.W.3d 77, **151**
Von Hohn v. Von Hohn, 260 S.W.3d 631, **709**
Voss v. Sw. Bell Tel. Co., 610 S.W.2d 537, **1048**

W

W. Fed. Sav. & Loan Ass'n v. Atkinson Fin. Corp., 747 S.W.2d 456, **969**
W. Hills Harbor Owners Ass'n v. Baker, ___ S.W.3d ___ (No. 08-15-00060-CV; 3-22-17), **132**
W. Indus., Inc. v. Newcor Can. Ltd., 739 F.2d 1198, **715**
W. Tex. State Bank v. Tri-Serv. Drilling Co., 339 S.W.2d 249, **354**
W. Union Tel. Co. v. Sharp, 5 S.W.2d 567, **985**
Waddell v. State, 873 S.W.2d 130, **248, 298**
Wade v. Abdnor, 635 S.W.2d 937, **511**
Wade v. State, 769 S.W.2d 633, **741, 758**
Waggoman v. Fort Worth Well Mach. & Supply Co., 124 Tex. 325, 76 S.W.2d 1005, **257**
Wagner v. State, 687 S.W.2d 303, **250**
Wagner & Brown v. E.W. Moran Drilling Co., 702 S.W.2d 760, **123**
Walck v. State, 943 S.W.2d 544, **774, 895**
Walden v. Ga.-Pac. Corp., 126 F.3d 506, **78**

Waldon v. City of Longview, 855 S.W.2d 875, **299, 302, 846**
Waldrop v. State, 138 Tex. Crim. 166, 133 S.W.2d 969, **196**
Walker v. Citizens Nat'l Bank, 212 S.W.2d 203, **304**
Walker v. Great Atl. & Pac. Tea Co., 131 Tex. 57, 112 S.W.2d 170, **891**
Walker v. State, 64 Tex. Crim. 70, 141 S.W. 243, **447**
Walker v. State, 166 Tex. Crim. 297, 312 S.W.2d 666, **625**
Walker v. State, 300 S.W.3d 836, **97, 639, 640**
Walker v. State, 406 S.W.3d 590, **458, 791, 932, 933**
Walker v. State, 17 Tex. Ct. App. 16, **658**
Walker & Assocs. Surveying, Inc. v. Roberts, 306 S.W.3d 839, **856**
Wall v. State, 184 S.W.3d 730, **792, 799, 803**
Wallace v. State, 707 S.W.2d 928, **342**
Wallace v. State, 770 S.W.2d 874, **976**
Wallace v. State, 782 S.W.2d 854, **967, 968, 1044**
Waller v. Fin. Corp. of Am., 828 F.2d 579, **435**
Wal-Mart Stores, Inc. v. Cordova, 856 S.W.2d 768, **637**
Wal-Mart Stores, Inc. v. McKenzie, 979 S.W.2d 364, **827**
Wal-Mart Stores, Inc. v. Merrell, 313 S.W.3d 837, **739**
Wal-Mart Stores, Inc. v. Reece, 32 S.W.3d 339, **73**
Walsh v. Bos. Sand & Gravel Co., 175 F. Supp. 411, **336**
Walter v. State, 267 S.W.3d 883, **872, 931, 932, 933, 936, 937**
Walter E. Heller & Co. v. Barnes, 412 S.W.2d 747, **860**
Walters v. State, 102 Tex. Crim. 243, 277 S.W. 653, **1055**
Walters v. State, 247 S.W.3d 204, **59, 60, 62, 106, 107, 108, 109**
Walton v. Canon, Short & Gaston, 23 S.W.3d 143, **637**
Ward v. Hawkins, 418 S.W.3d 815, **144**
Ward v. State, 657 S.W.2d 133, **861, 949**
Ward v. State, 910 S.W.2d 1, **944, 949**
Ward v. State, 72 S.W.3d 413, **177**
Ware v. State, 62 S.W.3d 344, **895**
Warford v. Childers, 642 S.W.2d 63, **475**
Warger v. Shauers, ___ U.S. ___, 135 S. Ct. 521, **580, 582, 587, 594, 595**
Waring v. Wommack, 945 S.W.2d 889, **724, 730, 740**
Warner v. State, 969 S.W.2d 1, **74, 75**
Warrantech Corp. v. Comput. Adapters Servs., Inc., 134 S.W.3d 516, **418, 537**
Warren v. Hartnett, 561 S.W.2d 860, **722**
Warren v. State, 514 S.W.2d 458, **630**
Warriner v. Warriner, 394 S.W.3d 240, **164, 165**
Washburn v. State, 164 Tex. Crim. 448, 299 S.W.2d 706, **550**
Washington v. McMillan, 898 S.W.2d 392, **958**
Washington v. State, 771 S.W.2d 537, **602**
Washington v. State, 856 S.W.2d 184, **108, 432, 659**
Washington v. State, 902 S.W.2d 649, **476**
Washington v. State, 943 S.W.2d 501, **295**

Washington v. State, 485 S.W.3d 633, **709, 731, 966, 971**

Watchel v. Health Net, Inc., 482 F.3d 225, **391**

Watkins v. State, 572 S.W.2d 339, **630**

Watkins v. State, 245 S.W.3d 444, **131**

Watson v. State, 596 S.W.2d 867, **558, 560, 575**

Watson v. State, 917 S.W.2d 65, **912**

Watson v. State, 337 S.W.3d 347, **97**

Watson v. Todd, 322 S.W.2d 422, **164**

Watts v. Oliver, 396 S.W.3d 124, **75**

Watts v. State, 87 Tex. Crim. 442, 222 S.W. 558, **454**

Watts v. State, 99 S.W.3d 604, **117, 119, 145, 146**

Wayne v. State, 756 S.W.2d 724, **338, 339**

Wearly v. Fed. Trade Comm'n, 462 F. Supp. 589, **47**

Weatherred v. State, 975 S.W.2d 323, **731**

Weaver v. Benson, 152 Tex. 50, 254 S.W.2d 95, **231**

Weaver v. State, 855 S.W.2d 116, **441, 448**

Weaver v. State, 87 S.W.3d 557, **626**

Webb v. Jorns, 530 S.W.2d 847, **923**

Webb v. Maldonado, 331 S.W.3d 879, **553**

Webb v. State, 760 S.W.2d 263, **212, 216, 1045**

Webb v. State, 766 S.W.2d 236, **667, 673**

Webb v. State, 899 S.W.2d 814, **70**

Webb v. State, 991 S.W.2d 408, **204**

Webb v. State, 36 S.W.3d 164, **296**

Webber v. State, 29 S.W.3d 226, **184**

Webster v. State, 26 S.W.3d 717, **695**

Weingarten Realty Inv'rs v. Harris Cty. Appr. Dist., 93 S.W.3d 280, **728**

Weiss v. Mech. Associated Servs., Inc., 989 S.W.2d 120, **728**

Welch v. State, 908 S.W.2d 258, **441, 458**

Well Sols., Inc. v. Stafford, 32 S.W.3d 313, **74**

Wells v. Lewis, 108 S.W.2d 926, **257**

Wells v. State, 730 S.W.2d 782, **276**

Wells v. State, 319 S.W.3d 82, **878**

Welsh v. Welsh, 905 S.W.2d 615, **77**

Wendlandt v. Sommers Drug Stores Co., 551 S.W.2d 488, **303**

Wendlandt v. Wendlandt, 596 S.W.2d 323, **227**

Wenk v. City Nat'l Bank, 613 S.W.2d 345, **1048**

Wentworth v. Crawford, 11 Tex. 127, **639**

Werner v. Miller, 579 S.W.2d 455, **403**

Werner v. State, 711 S.W.2d 639, **89, 739**

Werner v. Upjohn Co., 628 F.2d 848, **309**

Wesbrook v. State, 29 S.W.3d 103, **101, 287, 288, 293, 418**

West v. First Baptist Church, 123 Tex. 388, 71 S.W.2d 1090, **197**

West v. Hous. Oil Co., 56 Tex. Civ. App. 341, 120 S.W. 228, **999**

West v. Solito, 563 S.W.2d 240, **390, 391, 416, 417, 422, 532, 538, 544**

West v. State, 790 S.W.2d 3, **610**

West v. State, 121 S.W.3d 95, **108, 610**

West v. State, 124 S.W.3d 732, **904**

Westchester Fire Ins. v. Lowe, 888 S.W.2d 243, **658**

Westchester Fire Ins. v. Wendeborn, 559 S.W.2d 108, **1001**

Westcott v. Crinklaw, 68 F.3d 1073, **606**

Westheimer v. Tennant, 831 S.W.2d 880, **417**

Westinghouse Elec. Corp. v. City of Burlington, 351 F.2d 762, **472, 473**

Westinghouse Elec. Corp. v. Republic of the Phil., 951 F.2d 1414, **434**

Whalen v. Condo. Consulting & Mgmt. Servs., Inc., 13 S.W.3d 444, **699**

Whalen v. Roe, 429 U.S. 589, **486**

Wheat v. State, 165 S.W.3d 802, **826**

Wheatfall v. State, 882 S.W.2d 829, **240**

Wheeler v. State, 67 S.W.3d 879, **213, 253, 254, 255, 285, 776**

Wheeler v. State, 79 S.W.3d 78, **369**

Wheeling-Pittsburgh Steel Corp. v. Underwriters Labs., Inc., 81 F.R.D. 8, **402, 649**

Whirlpool Corp. v. Camacho, 298 S.W.3d 631, **200, 722, 728, 729, 735, 736, 737, 739**

Whitaker v. State, 286 S.W.3d 355, **69, 350**

White v. Bath, 825 S.W.2d 227, **1035**

White v. Illinois, 502 U.S. 346, **788, 882**

White v. State, 329 S.W.2d 446, **340**

White v. State, 451 S.W.2d 497, **856**

White v. State, 478 S.W.2d 506, **647**

White v. State, 779 S.W.2d 809, **554**

White v. State, 784 S.W.2d 453, **71**

White v. State, 225 S.W.3d 571, **586, 588, 590, 592**

White Indus., Inc. v. Cessna Aircraft Co., 611 F. Supp. 1049, **822, 1062, 1063**

Whitfield v. State, ___ S.W.3d ___ (No. 14-15-00820-CR; 3-9-17), **808**

Whiting v. State, 755 S.W.2d 936, **655**

Whitmire v. State, 789 S.W.2d 366, **884, 886**

Whitmore v. State, 570 S.W.2d 889, **363**

Whittington v. Dep't of Pub. Safety, 342 S.W.2d 374, **303**

Whorton v. Bockting, 549 U.S. 406, **790**

Wiggins v. State, 778 S.W.2d 877, **248, 254, 278, 603**

Wiggins v. Tiller, 230 S.W. 253, **444, 445, 446, 448**

Wiggs v. All Saints Health Sys., 124 S.W.3d 407, **727**

Wigiert v. State, 948 S.W.2d 54, **878, 897**

Wilemon v. Wilemon, 930 S.W.2d 290, **865**

Wiley v. State, 74 S.W.3d 399, **62, 269**

Wiley v. Williams, 769 S.W.2d 715, **410**

Wilhoit v. State, 638 S.W.2d 489, **843**

Wilkens v. State, 847 S.W.2d 547, **539**

Wilkerson v. State, 927 S.W.2d 112, **183**

Wilkerson v. State, 933 S.W.2d 276, **853, 862, 883**

Wilkins v. Hester, 167 S.E.2d 167, **1056**

Wilkinson v. Clark, 558 S.W.2d 490, **564**

Wilks v. State, 983 S.W.2d 863, **886, 954**

Williams v. Chew, 19 S.W.2d 68, **133**

Williams v. Fuerstenberg, 12 S.W.2d 812, **849**

Williams v. Illinois, 567 U.S. 50, **745, 747, 753, 755, 809, 810**

TOPIC INDEX

TOPIC INDEX

TOPIC INDEX

TOPIC INDEX

NOTES

NOTES

NOTES

NOTES

NOTES

NOTES

NOTES

NOTES